Microsoft® Office 2003
VOLUME II

Microsoft®
Office 2003
VOLUME II

ROBERT T. GRAUER
UNIVERSITY OF MIAMI

MARYANN BARBER
UNIVERSITY OF MIAMI

PEARSON
Prentice Hall

**Upper Saddle River,
New Jersey 07458**

Library of Congress Cataloging-in-Publication Data

Grauer, Robert T.
  Microsoft Office 2003 / Robert T. Grauer, Maryann Barber.
    p. cm. -- (The exploring Office series)
  Includes index.
  ISBN 0-13-183852-0 (v. 1) -- ISBN 0-13-143442-X (v. 2)
  1. Microsoft Office. 2. Business--Computer programs.   I. Barber, Maryann M. II. Title.
  III. Series.
  HF5548.4.M525G77 2004
  005.5--dc22   2003068915

Executive Acquisitions Editor: Jodi McPherson
VP/ Publisher: Natalie E. Anderson
Senior Project Manager, Editorial: Eileen Clark
Editorial Assistants: Brian Hoehl, Alana Meyers, and Sandy Bernales
Media Project Manager: Cathleen Profitko
Marketing Manager: Emily Williams Knight
Marketing Assistant: Lisa Taylor
Project Manager, Production: Lynne Breitfeller
Production Editor: Greg Hubit
Associate Director, Manufacturing: Vincent Scelta
Manufacturing Buyer: Lynne Breitfeller
Design Manager: Maria Lange
Interior Design: Michael J. Fruhbeis
Cover Design: Michael J. Fruhbeis
Cover Printer: Phoenix Color
Composition and Project Management: The GTS Companies
Printer/ Binder: Banta Menasha

Microsoft and the Microsoft Office Specialist logo are trademarks or registered trademarks of Microsoft Corporation in the United States and/or other countries. Prentice Hall is independent from Microsoft Corporation, and not affiliated with Microsoft in any manner. This publication may be used in assisting students to prepare for a Microsoft Office Specialist Exam. Neither Microsoft Corporation, its designated review companies, nor Prentice Hall warrants that use of this publication will ensure passing the relevant Exam.

Use of the Microsoft Office Specialist Approved Courseware Logo on this product signifies that it has been independently reviewed and approved in complying with the following standards:
Acceptable coverage of all content related to the Specialist level Microsoft Office Exams entitled "Word 2003," "Excel 2003," "Access 2003," "PowerPoint 2003," and the Expert level exams entitled "Word 2003" and "Excel 2003," and sufficient performance-based exercises that relate closely to all required content based on sampling of text in conjunction with Volume I.

Copyright © 2004 by Pearson Education, Inc., Upper Saddle River, New Jersey, 07458. All rights reserved. Printed in the United States of America. This publication is protected by Copyright and permission should be obtained from the publisher prior to any prohibited reproduction, storage in a retrieval system, or transmission in any form or by any means, electronic, mechanical, photocopying, recording, or likewise. For information regarding permission(s), write to: Rights and Permissions Department.

10 9 8 7
ISBN 0-13-143442-X spiral
ISBN 0-13-145242-8 adhesive

To Marion —
my wife, my lover, and my best friend

Robert Grauer

To Frank —
I love you

To Holly —
for being my friend

Maryann Barber

What does this logo mean?

It means this courseware has been approved by the Microsoft® Office Specialist Program to be among the finest available for learning **Microsoft Word 2003, Microsoft Excel 2003, Microsoft Access 2003,** and **Microsoft PowerPoint 2003.** It also means that upon completion of this courseware, you may be prepared to take an exam for Microsoft Office Specialist qualification.

What is a Microsoft Office Specialist?

A Microsoft Office Specialist is an individual who has passed exams for certifying his or her skills in one or more of the Microsoft Office desktop applications such as Microsoft Word, Microsoft Excel, Microsoft PowerPoint, Microsoft Outlook, Microsoft Access, or Microsoft Project. The Microsoft Office Specialist Program typically offers certification exams at the "Specialist" and "Expert" skill levels.[*] The Microsoft Office Specialist Program is the only program approved by Microsoft for testing proficiency in Microsoft Office desktop applications and Microsoft Project. This testing program can be a valuable asset in any job search or career advancement.

More Information:

To learn more about becoming a Microsoft Office Specialist, visit
www.microsoft.com/officespecialist

To learn about other Microsoft Office Specialist approved courseware from Pearson Education visit www.prenhall.com

---

[*]The availability of Microsoft Office Specialist certification exams varies by application, application version, and language. Visit www.microsoft.com/officespecialist for exam availability.

Microsoft, the Microsoft Office Logo, PowerPoint, and Outlook are trademarks or registered trademarks of Microsoft Corporation in the United States and/or other countries, and the Microsoft Office Specialist Logo is used under license from owner.

Contents

Preface xv

MICROSOFT® OFFICE WORD 2003

five

Desktop Publishing: Creating a Newsletter and Other Documents — 1065

Objectives	1065
Case Study: New from the Wild Side	1065
Introduction to Desktop Publishing	1066
The Newsletter	1066
Typography	1068
The Columns Command	1069
HANDS-ON EXERCISE 1:	
NEWSPAPER COLUMNS	1070
Elements of Graphic Design	1078
The Grid	1078
Emphasis	1080
Clip Art	1080
The Drawing Toolbar	1082
HANDS-ON EXERCISE 2:	
COMPLETE THE NEWSLETTER	1083
Object Linking and Embedding	1093
HANDS-ON EXERCISE 3:	
OBJECT LINKING AND EMBEDDING	1095
Summary	1103
Key Terms	1103
Multiple Choice	1104
Practice with Word	1106
Mini Cases	1112

six

Introduction to HTML: Creating a Home Page and a Web Site — 1113

Objectives	1113
Case Study: Realtor of the Year	1113
Introduction to HTML	1114
Microsoft Word	1116
HANDS-ON EXERCISE 1:	
INTRODUCTION TO HTML	1117
A Commercial Home Page	1123
HANDS-ON EXERCISE 2:	
WORLD WIDE TRAVEL HOME PAGE	1124
Creating a Web Site	1130
HANDS-ON EXERCISE 3:	
CREATING A WEB SITE	1133
Summary	1139
Key Terms	1139
Multiple Choice	1140
Practice with Word	1142

seven

The Expert User: Workgroups, Forms, Master Documents, and Macros — 1151

Objectives	1151
Case Study: A Question of Ethics	1151
Workgroups and Collaboration	1152
The Versions of a Document	1152
Forms	1154
HANDS-ON EXERCISE 1:	
WORKGROUPS AND FORMS	**1155**
Table Math	1163
HANDS-ON EXERCISE 2:	
TABLE MATH	**1165**
Master Documents	1172
HANDS-ON EXERCISE 3:	
MASTER DOCUMENTS	**1174**
Introduction to Macros	1180
The Visual Basic Editor	1181
HANDS-ON EXERCISE 4:	
INTRODUCTION TO MACROS	**1183**
Summary	1193
Key Terms	1193
Multiple Choice	1194
Practice with Word	1196

Appendix A: Toolbars	1203

MICROSOFT® OFFICE EXCEL 2003

five

Consolidating Data: Worksheet References and File Linking — 1209

Objectives	1209
Case Study: Bandit's Pizza	1209
Consolidating Data	1210
The Three-Dimensional Workbook	1211
Copying Worksheets	1212
Multiple Workbooks	1213
HANDS-ON EXERCISE 1:	
COPYING WORKSHEETS	**1214**
Worksheet References	1219
3-D Reference	1220
Grouping Worksheets	1221
The AutoFormat Command	1221
HANDS-ON EXERCISE 2:	
WORKSHEET REFERENCES	**1222**
The Documentation Worksheet	1229
HANDS-ON EXERCISE 3:	
THE DOCUMENTATION WORKSHEET	**1230**
Linking Workbooks	1235
HANDS-ON EXERCISE 4:	
LINKING WORKBOOKS	**1236**
Summary	1242
Key Terms	1242
Multiple Choice	1243
Practice with Excel	1245
Mini Cases	1252

six

A Financial Forecast: Auditing, Protection, and Templates 1253

Objectives	1253
Case Study: Timely Signs	1253
A Financial Forecast	1254
Advanced Formatting	1256
Scenario Manager	1257
HANDS-ON EXERCISE 1:	
A FINANCIAL FORECAST	1258
Workgroups and Auditing	1269
Data Validation	1270
HANDS-ON EXERCISE 2:	
AUDITING AND WORKGROUPS	1272
Templates	1279
HANDS-ON EXERCISE 3:	
CREATING A TEMPLATE	1281
Summary	1286
Key Terms	1286
Multiple Choice	1287
Practice with Excel	1289
Mini Cases	1298

seven

List and Data Management: Converting Data to Information 1299

Objectives	1299
Case Study: The Spa Experts	1299
List and Data Management	1300
Implementation in Excel	1301
Data Form Command	1302
Sort Command	1303
The Text Import Wizard	1305
Excel and XML	1306
HANDS-ON EXERCISE 1:	
IMPORTING, CREATING, AND MAINTAINING A LIST	1307
Data versus Information	1314
AutoFilter Command	1316
Advanced Filter Command	1317
Criteria Range	1317
Database Functions	1319
Insert Name Command	1320
Subtotals	1321
HANDS-ON EXERCISE 2:	
DATA VERSUS INFORMATION	1322
Pivot Tables and Pivot Charts	1333
HANDS-ON EXERCISE 3:	
PIVOT TABLES AND PIVOT CHARTS	1336
Summary	1345
Key Terms	1345
Multiple Choice	1346
Practice with Excel	1348
Mini Cases	1358

eight

Automating Repetitive Tasks: Macros and Visual Basic for Applications 1359

Objectives	1359
Case Study: The Sleepy Showroom	1359
Introduction to Macros	1360
HANDS-ON EXERCISE 1:	
INTRODUCTION TO MACROS	1362
Relative versus Absolute References	1371
The Personal Macro Workbook	1372
HANDS-ON EXERCISE 2:	
THE PERSONAL MACRO WORKBOOK	1373
Data Management Macros	1380
HANDS-ON EXERCISE 3:	
DATA MANAGEMENT MACROS	1382
Visual Basic for Applications	1390
HANDS-ON EXERCISE 4:	
CREATING ADDITIONAL MACROS	1391
Loops and Decision Making	1402
If Statement	1402
Do Statement	1403
HANDS-ON EXERCISE 5:	
LOOPS AND DECISION MAKING	1404
Summary	1411
Key Terms	1411
Multiple Choice	1412
Practice with Excel	1414
Mini Cases	1422

nine

A Professional Application: VBA and Date Functions 1423

Objectives	1423
Case Study: Refinance Now	1423
Application Development	1424
The Amortization Workbook	1425
Date Functions	1428
HANDS-ON EXERCISE 1:	
THE AMORTIZATION WORKBOOK	1429
Exploring VBA Syntax	1436
Three Simple Procedures	1436
HANDS-ON EXERCISE 2:	
EXPLORING VBA SYNTAX	1438
Event Procedures	1447
User Forms	1449
HANDS-ON EXERCISE 3:	
EVENT PROCEDURES	1450
More Complex Procedures	1459
HANDS-ON EXERCISE 4:	
PERIODIC OPTIONAL PAYMENTS	1461
Summary	1468
Key Terms	1468
Multiple Choice	1469
Practice with Excel and VBA	1471
Mini Cases	1482

ten

Extending VBA: Processing Worksheets and Workbooks   1483

Objectives	1483	**HANDS-ON EXERCISE 3:**	
Case Study: End of the Month	1483	**CREATE THE SUMMARY WORKSHEET**	1505
The Expense Summary Application	1484	A Better Summary Workbook	1513
A Quick Review	1485	**HANDS-ON EXERCISE 4:**	
The Dir Function	1486	**A BETTER SUMMARY WORKBOOK**	1515
HANDS-ON EXERCISE 1:		Summary	1520
CREATE THE SUMMARY WORKBOOK	1487	Key Terms	1520
Displaying a Specific Worksheet	1493	Multiple Choice	1521
Error Trapping	1493	Practice with Excel and VBA	1523
HANDS-ON EXERCISE 2:		Mini Cases	1532
ERROR TRAPPING	1495		
Processing Worksheets in a Workbook	1501		
Adding Employees to the Summary Worksheet	1503		

Appendix A: Toolbars	1533	Appendix B: Solver	1543

MICROSOFT® OFFICE ACCESS 2003

five

One-to-many Relationships: Subforms and Multiple-table Queries   1561

Objectives	1561	**HANDS-ON EXERCISE 3:**	
Case Study: Evergreen Flying Club	1561	**QUERIES AND REPORTS**	1585
A Database for Consumer Loans	1562	Expanding the Database	1592
The AutoNumber Field Type	1565	Multiple Subforms	1594
Referential Integrity	1565	**HANDS-ON EXERCISE 4:**	
Implementation in Access	1565	**LINKED SUBFORMS**	1595
HANDS-ON EXERCISE 1:		Summary	1602
ONE-TO-MANY RELATIONSHIPS	1567	Key Terms	1602
Subforms	1572	Multiple Choice	1603
The Form Wizard	1574	Practice with Access	1605
HANDS-ON EXERCISE 2:		Mini Cases	1614
CREATING A SUBFORM	1575		
Multiple-table Queries	1583		

six

Many-to-many Relationships: A More Complex System 1615

Objectives	1615
Case Study: University Career Placement Center	1615
The Computer Superstore	1616
The AutoNumber Field Type	1619
The Relationships Window	1619
HANDS-ON EXERCISE 1: RELATIONSHIPS AND REFERENTIAL INTEGRITY	1621
Subforms, Queries, and AutoLookup	1626
HANDS-ON EXERCISE 2: SUBFORMS AND MULTIPLE-TABLE QUERIES	1628
Parameter Queries	1635
Total Queries	1635
Learning by Doing	1638
HANDS-ON EXERCISE 3: ADVANCED QUERIES	1639
Expanding the Database	1647
The Sales Commission Query	1649
HANDS-ON EXERCISE 4: EXPANDING THE DATABASE	1651
Summary	1659
Key Terms	1659
Multiple Choice	1660
Practice with Access	1662
Mini Cases	1671

seven

Building Applications: Macros and a Multilevel Switchboard 1673

Objectives	1673
Case Study: The Ecoadventures Cruise Line	1673
A Recreational Sports League	1674
The Switchboard Manager	1677
The Linked Tables Manager	1677
HANDS-ON EXERCISE 1: THE SWITCHBOARD MANAGER	1679
Introduction to Macros	1688
The Macro Window	1688
The AutoExec Macro	1689
Debugging	1689
Application Development	1690
HANDS-ON EXERCISE 2: MACROS AND PROTOTYPING	1692
The Player Draft	1699
Macro Groups	1700
HANDS-ON EXERCISE 3: THE PLAYER DRAFT	1701
Summary	1711
Key Terms	1711
Multiple Choice	1712
Practice with Access	1714
Mini Cases	1725

eight

Creating More Powerful Applications: Introduction to VBA   1727

Objectives	1727	**HANDS-ON EXERCISE 3:**	
Case Study: Back to Natalie's	1727	**ERROR TRAPPING**	**1753**
Introduction to VBA	1728	Data Validation	1760
A Better Student Form	1729	**HANDS-ON EXERCISE 4:**	
Modules and Procedures	1731	**DATA VALIDATION**	**1761**
HANDS-ON EXERCISE 1:		Summary	1768
CREATING A COMBO BOX AND		Key Terms	1768
ASSOCIATED VBA PROCEDURE	**1733**	Multiple Choice	1769
Facilitating Data Entry	1741	Practice with Access and VBA	1771
HANDS-ON EXERCISE 2:		Mini Cases	1776
FACILITATING DATA ENTRY	**1743**		
Error Trapping	1751		

Appendix A: Toolbars	1777	Appendix C: Mail Merge	1795
Appendix B: Designing a Relational Database	1785	Appendix D: A Project for the Semester	1805

MICROSOFT® OFFICE **POWERPOINT® 2003**

three

Animating a Presentation: Diagrams and Charts   1809

Objectives	1809	Custom Animation	1828
Case Study: The Kelso Performing Arts Center	1809	Animating a Chart	1829
		Animating an Organization Chart	1830
Animating a Presentation	1810	**HANDS-ON EXERCISE 3:**	
The Diagram Gallery	1810	**CUSTOM ANIMATION**	**1831**
HANDS-ON EXERCISE 1:		Summary	1840
DIAGRAMS AND ORGANIZATION CHARTS	**1812**	Key Terms	1840
Microsoft Graph	1819	Multiple Choice	1841
Stacked Column Charts	1819	Practice with PowerPoint	1843
HANDS-ON EXERCISE 2:		Mini Cases	1851
MICROSOFT GRAPH	**1822**		

four

Advanced Techniques: Slide Masters, Narration, and Web Pages 1853

Objectives	1853
Case Study: Get Up and Go	1853
A PowerPoint Quiz	1854
The Slide Master	1856
HANDS-ON EXERCISE 1:	
COLOR SCHEMES, SOUND,	
AND THE SLIDE MASTER	1857
Presentations on the Web	1866
Uploading a Presentation	1866
HANDS-ON EXERCISE 2:	
PRESENTATIONS ON THE WEB	1868
Narrating a Presentation	1876
Broadcasts and Online Meetings	1877
HANDS-ON EXERCISE 3:	
NARRATING A PRESENTATION	1878
Summary	1884
Key Terms	1884
Multiple Choice	1885
Practice with PowerPoint	1887
Mini Cases	1895

Appendix A: Toolbars 1897

GETTING STARTED WITH VBA

Getting Started with VBA: Extending Microsoft Office 2003 1905

Objectives	1905
Case Study: On-the-Job Training	1905
Introduction to VBA	1906
The MsgBox Statement	1907
The InputBox Function	1908
Declaring Variables	1909
The VBA Editor	1910
HANDS-ON EXERCISE 1:	
INTRODUCTION TO VBA	1911
If . . . Then . . . Else Statement	1920
Case Statement	1922
Custom Toolbars	1923
HANDS-ON EXERCISE 2:	
DECISION MAKING	1924
For . . . Next Statement	1932
Do Loops	1933
Debugging	1934
HANDS-ON EXERCISE 3:	
LOOPS AND DEBUGGING	1936
Putting VBA to Work (Microsoft Excel)	1945
HANDS-ON EXERCISE 4:	
EVENT-DRIVEN PROGRAMMING	
(MICROSOFT EXCEL)	1947
Putting VBA to Work (Microsoft Access)	1956
HANDS-ON EXERCISE 5:	
EVENT-DRIVEN PROGRAMMING	
(MICROSOFT ACCESS)	1958
Summary	1966
Key Terms	1966
Multiple Choice	1967

Index 1969

Preface

THE EXPLORING OFFICE SERIES FOR 2003

Continuing a tradition of excellence, Prentice Hall is proud to announce the new *Exploring Microsoft Office 2003* series by Robert T. Grauer and Maryann Barber. The hands-on approach and conceptual framework of this comprehensive series helps students master all aspects of the Microsoft Office 2003 software, while providing the background necessary to transfer and use these skills in their personal and professional lives.

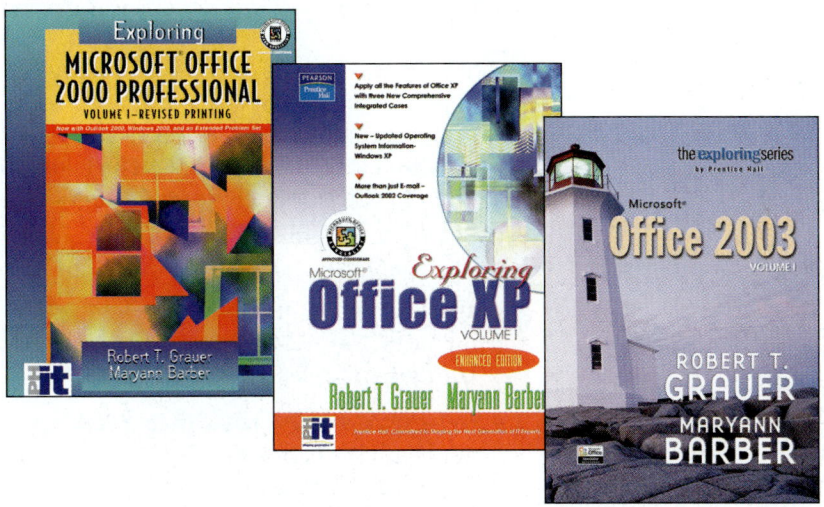

The entire series has been revised to include the new features found in the Office 2003 Suite, which contains Word 2003, Excel 2003, Access 2003, PowerPoint 2003, Publisher 2003, FrontPage 2003, and Outlook 2003.

In addition, this edition includes fully revised end-of-chapter material that provides an extensive review of concepts and techniques discussed in the chapter. Each chapter now begins with an *introductory case study* to provide an effective overview of what the reader will be able to accomplish, with additional *mini cases* at the end of each chapter for practice and review. The conceptual content within each chapter has been modified as appropriate and numerous end-of-chapter exercises have been added.

The new *visual design* introduces the concept of *perfect pages*, whereby every step in every hands-on exercise, as well as every end-of-chapter exercise, begins at the top of its own page and has its own screen shot. This clean design allows for easy navigation throughout the text.

Continuing the success of the website provided for previous editions of this series, Exploring Office 2003 offers expanded resources that include online, interactive study guides, data file downloads, technology updates, additional case studies and exercises, and other helpful information. Start out at **www.prenhall.com/grauer** to explore these resources!

Organization of the Exploring Office 2003 Series

The new Exploring Microsoft Office 2003 series includes five combined Office 2003 texts from which to choose:

- *Volume I* is Microsoft Office Specialist certified in each of the core applications in the Office suite (Word, Excel, Access, and PowerPoint). Five additional modules (*Essential Computing Concepts, Getting Started with Windows XP, The Internet and the World Wide Web, Getting Started with Outlook,* and *Integrated Case Studies*) are also included. **Volume I Enhanced Edition** adds 18 new chapter-opening case studies, two new integrated case studies, 30 additional end-of-chapter problems, and 20 new mini cases to the existing Volume I.

- *Volume II* picks up where Volume I leaves off, covering the advanced topics for the individual applications. A *Getting Started with VBA* module has been added.

- The *Plus Edition* extends the coverage of Access and Excel to six and seven chapters, respectively (as opposed to four chapters each in Volume I). It also maintains the same level of coverage for PowerPoint and Word as in Volume I so that both applications are Microsoft Office Specialist certified. The Plus Edition includes a new module on XML but does not contain the Essential Computing Concepts or Internet modules.

- The *Brief Microsoft Office 2003* edition provides less coverage of the core applications than Volume I (a total of 10 chapters as opposed to 18). It also includes the *Getting Started with Windows XP* and *Getting Started with Outlook* modules.

- *Getting Started with Office 2003* contains the first chapter from each application (Word, Excel, Access, and PowerPoint), plus three additional modules: *Getting Started with Windows XP, The Internet and the World Wide Web,* and *Essential Computing Concepts*.

Individual texts for Word 2003, Excel 2003, Access 2003, and PowerPoint 2003 provide complete coverage of the application and are Microsoft Office Specialist certified. For shorter courses, we have created brief versions of the Exploring texts that give students a four-chapter introduction to each application. Each of these volumes is Microsoft Office Specialist certified at the Specialist level.

This series has been approved by Microsoft to be used in preparation for Microsoft Office Specialist exams.

The Microsoft Office Specialist program is globally recognized as the standard for demonstrating desktop skills with the Microsoft Office suite of business productivity applications (Microsoft Word, Microsoft Excel, Microsoft PowerPoint, Microsoft Access, and Microsoft Outlook). With a Microsoft Office Specialist certification, thousands of people have demonstrated increased productivity and have proved their ability to utilize the advanced functionality of these Microsoft applications.

By encouraging individuals to develop advanced skills with Microsoft's leading business desktop software, the Microsoft Office Specialist program helps fill the demand for qualified, knowledgeable people in the modern workplace. At the same time, Microsoft Office Specialist helps satisfy an organization's need for a qualitative assessment of employee skills.

Instructor and Student Resources

The **Instructor's CD** that accompanies the Exploring Office series contains:
- Student data files
- Solutions to all exercises and problems
- PowerPoint lectures
- Instructor's manuals in Word format that enable the instructor to annotate portions of the instructor manuals for distribution to the class
- Instructors may also use our *test creation software,* TestGen and QuizMaster. TestGen is a test generator program that lets you view and easily edit test-bank questions, create tests, and print in a variety of formats suitable to your teaching situation. Exams can be easily uploaded into WebCT, BlackBoard, and CourseCompass. QuizMaster allows students to take the tests created with TestGen on a local area network.

Prentice Hall's Companion Website at www.prenhall.com/grauer offers expanded IT resources and downloadable supplements. This site also includes an online study guide for students containing true/false and multiple choice questions and practice projects.

WebCT www.prenhall.com/webct

Gold level customer support available exclusively to adopters of Prentice Hall courses is provided free-of-charge upon adoption and provides you with priority assistance, training discounts, and dedicated technical support.

Blackboard www.prenhall.com/blackboard

Prentice Hall's abundant online content, combined with Blackboard's popular tools and interface, result in robust Web-based courses that are easy to implement, manage, and use—taking your courses to new heights in student interaction and learning.

CourseCompass www.coursecompass.com

CourseCompass is a dynamic, interactive online course management tool powered by Blackboard. This exciting product allows you to teach with marketing-leading Pearson Education content in an easy-to-use, customizable format.

Training and Assessment www2.phgenit.com/support

Prentice Hall offers Performance Based Training and Assessment in one product, Train&Assess IT. The Training component offers computer-based training that a student can use to preview, learn, and review Microsoft Office application skills. Web or CD-ROM delivered, Train IT offers interactive multimedia, computer-based training to augment classroom learning. Built-in prescriptive testing suggests a study path based not only on student test results but also on the specific textbook chosen for the course.

The Assessment component offers computer-based testing that shares the same user interface as Train IT and is used to evaluate a student's knowledge about specific topics in Word, Excel, Access, PowerPoint, Windows, Outlook, and the Internet. It does this in a task-oriented, performance-based environment to demonstrate proficiency as well as comprehension on the topics by the students. More extensive than the testing in Train IT, Assess IT offers more administrative features for the instructor and additional questions for the student.

Assess IT also allows professors to test students out of a course, place students in appropriate courses, and evaluate skill sets.

OPENING CASE STUDY

New! Each chapter now begins with an introductory case study to provide an effective overview of what students will accomplish by completing the chapter.

CHAPTER 1: Getting Started with Microsoft® Windows® XP

OBJECTIVES

After reading this chapter you will:

1. Describe the Windows desktop.
2. Use the Help and Support Center to obtain information.
3. Describe the My Computer and My Documents folders.
4. Differentiate between a program file and a data file.
5. Download a file from the Exploring Office Web site.
6. Copy and/or move a file from one folder to another.
7. Delete a file, and then recover it from the Recycle Bin.
8. Create and arrange shortcuts on the desktop.
9. Use the Search Companion.
10. Use the My Pictures and My Music folders.
11. Use Windows Messenger for instant messaging.

hands-on exercises

1. WELCOME TO WINDOWS XP
   Input: None
   Output: None
2. DOWNLOAD PRACTICE FILES
   Input: Data files from the Web
   Output: Welcome to Windows XP (a Word document)
3. WINDOWS EXPLORER
   Input: Data files from exercise 2
   Output: Screen Capture within a Word document
4. INCREASING PRODUCTIVITY
   Input: Data files from exercise 3
   Output: None
5. FUN WITH WINDOWS XP
   Input: None
   Output: None

CASE STUDY: UNFORESEEN CIRCUMSTANCES

Steve and his wife Shelly have poured their life savings into the dream of owning their own business, a "nanny" service agency. They have spent the last two years building their business and have created a sophisticated database with numerous entries for both families and nannies. The database is the key to their operation. Now that it is up and running, Steve and Shelly are finally at a point where they could hire someone to manage the operation on a part-time basis so that they could take some time off together.

Unfortunately, their process for selecting a person they could trust with their business was not as thorough as it should have been. Nancy, their new employee, assured them that all was well, and the couple left for an extended weekend. The place was in shambles on their return. Nancy could not handle the responsibility, and when Steve gave her two weeks' notice, neither he nor his wife thought that the unimaginable would happen. On her last day in the office Nancy "lost" all of the names in the database—the data was completely gone!

Nancy claimed that a "virus" knocked out the database, but after spending nearly $1,500 with a computer consultant, Steve was told that it had been cleverly deleted from the hard drive and could not be recovered. Of course, the consultant asked Steve and Shelly about their backup strategy, which they sheepishly admitted did not exist. They had never experienced any problems in the past, and simply assumed that their data was safe. Fortunately, they do have hard copy of the data in the form of various reports that were printed throughout the time they were in business. They have no choice but to manually reenter the data.

Your assignment is to read the chapter, paying special attention to the information on file management. Think about how Steve and Shelly could have avoided the disaster if a backup strategy had been in place, then summarize your thoughts in a brief note to your instructor. Describe the elements of a basic backup strategy. Give several other examples of unforeseen circumstances that can cause data to be lost.

New! A listing of the input and output files for each hands-on exercise within the chapter. Students will stay on track with what is to be accomplished.

Perfect Pages

hands-on exercise
1 Welcome to Windows XP

Objective To log on to Windows XP and customize the desktop; to open the My Computer folder; to move and size a window; to format a floppy disk and access the Help and Support Center. Use Figure 7 as a guide.

Step 1: **Log On to Windows XP**

- Turn on the computer and all of the peripheral devices. The floppy drive should be empty prior to starting your machine.
- Windows XP will load automatically, and you should see a login screen similar to Figure 7a. (It does not matter which version of Windows XP you are using.) The number and names of the potential users and their associated icons will be different on your system.
- Click the icon for the user account you want to access. You may be prompted for a password, depending on the security options in effect.

> Each step in the hands-on exercises begins at the top of the page to ensure that students can easily navigate through the text.

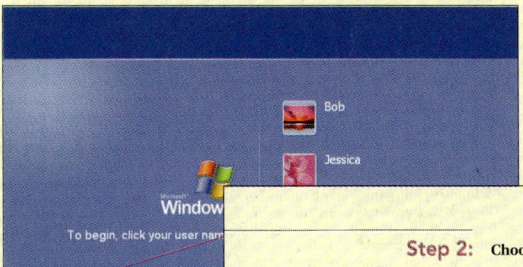

(a) Log On to Windows XP (step 1)
FIGURE 7 Hands-on Exercise 1

USER ACCOUNTS

The available user names are cr
Windows XP, but you can add or d
click Control Panel, switch to the Ca
the desired task, such as creating
then supply the necessary informati
user accounts in a school setting.

10 GETTING STARTED WITH MICROSOFT WINDOWS XP

Step 2: **Choose the Theme and Start Menu**

- Check with your instructor to see if you are able to modify the desktop and other settings at your school or university. If your network administrator has disabled these commands, skip this step and go to step 3.
- Point to a blank area on the desktop, click the **right mouse button** to display a context-sensitive menu, then click the **Properties command** to open the Display Properties dialog box. Click the **Themes tab** and select the **Windows XP theme** if it is not already selected. Click **OK**.
- We prefer to work without any wallpaper (background picture) on the desktop. **Right click** the desktop, click **Properties**, then click the **Desktop tab** in the Display Properties dialog box. Click **None** as shown in Figure 7b, then click **OK**. The background disappears.
- The Start menu is modified independently of the theme. **Right click** a blank area of the taskbar, click the **Properties command** to display the Taskbar and Start Menu Properties dialog box, then click the **Start Menu tab**.
- Click the **Start Menu option button**. Click **OK**.

> **New!** Larger screen shots with clear callouts.
>
> Boxed tips provide students with additional information.

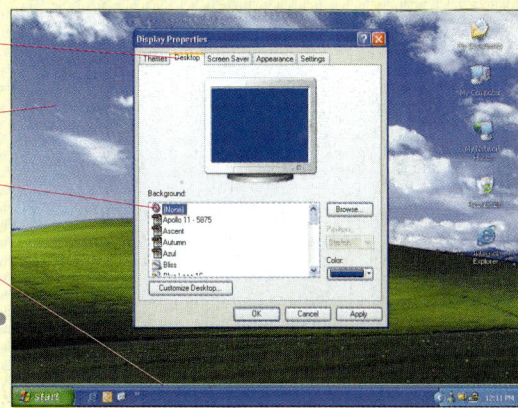

(b) Choose the Theme and Start Menu (step 2)
FIGURE 7 Hands-on Exercise 1 (*continued*)

IMPLEMENT A SCREEN SAVER

A screen saver is a delightful way to personalize your computer and a good way to practice with basic commands in Windows XP. Right click a blank area of the desktop, click the Properties command to open the Display Properties dialog box, then click the Screen Saver tab. Click the down arrow in the Screen Saver list box, choose the desired screen saver, then set the option to wait an appropriate amount of time before the screen saver appears. Click OK to accept the settings and close the dialog box.

GETTING STARTED WITH MICROSOFT WINDOWS XP 11

MINI CASES AND PRACTICE EXERCISES

MINI CASES

The Financial Consultant

A friend of yours is in the process of buying a home and has asked you to compare the payments and total interest on a 15- and 30-year loan at varying interest rates. You have decided to analyze the loans in Excel, and then incorporate the results into a memo written in Microsoft Word. As of now, the principal is $150,000, but it is very likely that your friend will change his mind several times, and so you want to use the linking and embedding capability within Windows to dynamically link the worksheet to the word processing document. Your memo should include a letterhead that takes advantage of the formatting capabilities within Word; a graphic logo would be a nice touch.

Fun with the If Statement

Open the *Chapter 4 Mini Case—Fun with the If Statement* workbook in the Exploring Excel folder, then follow the directions in the worksheet to view a hidden message. The message is displayed by various If statements scattered throughout the worksheet, but the worksheet is protected so that you cannot see these formulas. (Use help to see how to protect a worksheet.) We made it easy for you, however, because you can unprotect the worksheet since a password is not required. Once the worksheet is unprotected, pull down the Format menu, click the Cells command, click the Protection tab, and clear the Hidden check box. Prove to your professor that you have done this successfully, by changing the text of our message. Print the completed worksheet to show both displayed values and cell formulas.

The Lottery

Many states raise money through lotteries that advertise prizes of several million dollars. In reality, however, the actual value of the prize is considerably less than the advertised value, although the winners almost certainly do not care. One state, for example, recently offered a twenty million dollar prize that was to be distributed in twenty annual payments of one million dollars each. How much was the prize actually worth, assuming a long-term interest rate of five percent? Use the PV (Present Value) function to determine the answer. What is the effect on the answer if payments to the recipient are made at the beginning of each year, rather than at the end of each year?

A Penny a Day

What if you had a rich uncle who offered to double your salary each day for the next month...

The Rule of 72

Delaying your IRA for one year...

New!
We've added mini cases at the end of each chapter for expanded practice and review.

PRACTICE WITH EXCEL

1. **Theme Park Admissions:** A partially completed version of the worksheet in Figure 3.13 is available in the Exploring Excel folder as *Chapter 3 Practice 1*. Follow the directions in parts (a) and (b) to compute the totals and format the worksheet, then create each of the charts listed below.
   a. Use the AutoSum command to enter the formulas to compute the total number of admissions for each region and each quarter.
   b. Select the entire worksheet (cells A1 through F8), then use the AutoFormat command to format the worksheet. You do not have to accept the entire design, nor do you have to use the design we selected. You can also modify the design after it has been applied to the worksheet by changing the font size of selected cells and/or changing boldface and italics.
   c. Create a column chart showing the total number of admissions in each quarter as shown in Figure 3.13. Add the graphic shown in the figure for emphasis.
   d. Create a pie chart that shows the percentage of the total number of admissions in each region. Create this chart in its own chart sheet with an appropriate name.
   e. Create a stacked column chart that shows the total number of admissions for each region and the contribution of each quarter within each region. Create this chart in its own chart sheet with an appropriate name.
   f. Create a stacked column chart showing the total number of admissions for each quarter and the contribution of each region within each quarter. Create this chart in its own chart sheet with an appropriate name.
   g. Change the color of each of the worksheet tabs.
   h. Print the entire workbook, consisting of the worksheet in Figure 3.13 plus the three additional sheets that you create. Use portrait orientation for the Sales Data worksheet and landscape orientation for the other worksheets. Create a custom header for each worksheet that includes your name, your course, and your instructor's name. Create a custom footer for each worksheet that includes the name of the worksheet. Submit the completed assignment to your instructor.

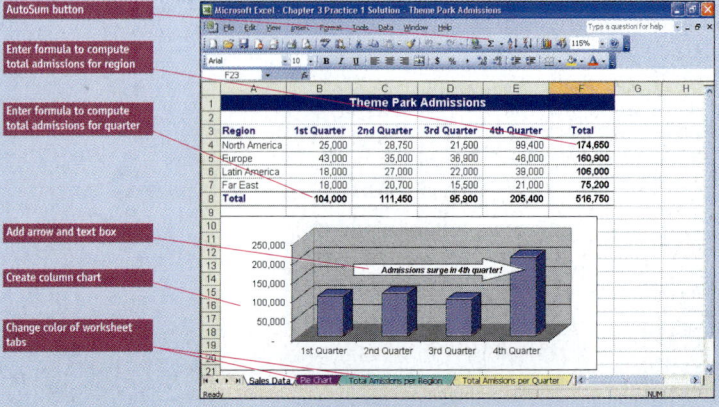

FIGURE 3.13 Theme Park Admissions (exercise 1)

New!
Each project in the end-of-chapter material begins at the top of a page—now students can easily see where their assignments begin and end.

Integrated Case Studies

New!
Each case study contains multiple exercises that use Microsoft Office applications in conjunction with one another.

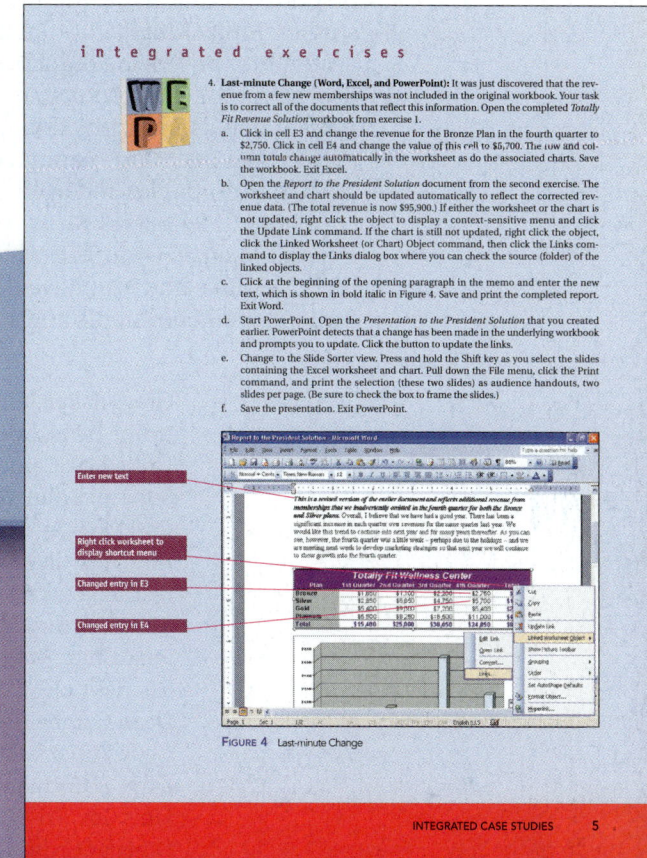

Companion Web site

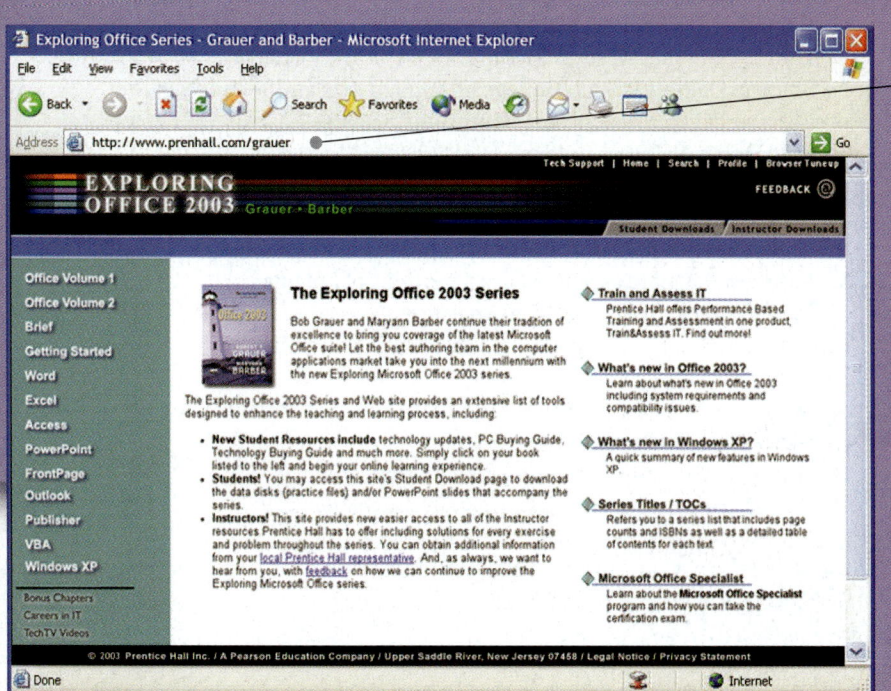

New!
Updated and enhanced Companion Web site. Find everything you need—student practice files, PowerPoint lectures, online study guides, and instructor support (solutions)!

www.prenhall.com/grauer

Acknowledgments

We want to thank the many individuals who have helped to bring this project to fruition. Jodi McPherson, executive acquisitions editor at Prentice Hall, has provided new leadership in extending the series to Office 2003. Cathi Profitko did an absolutely incredible job on our Web site. Shelly Martin was the creative force behind the chapter-opening case studies. Emily Knight coordinated the marketing and continues to inspire us with suggestions for improving the series. Greg Hubit has been masterful as the external production editor for every book in the series from its inception. Eileen Clark coordinated the myriad details of production and the certification process. Lynne Breitfeller was the project manager and manufacturing buyer. Lori Johnson was the project manager at The GTS Companies and in charge of composition. Chuck Cox did his usual fine work as copyeditor. Melissa Edwards was the supplements editor. Cindy Stevens, Tom McKenzie, and Michael Olmstead wrote the instructor manuals. Michael Fruhbeis developed the innovative and attractive design. We also want to acknowledge our reviewers who, through their comments and constructive criticism, greatly improved the series.

Gregg Asher, Minnesota State University
Lynne Band, Middlesex Community College
Don Belle, Central Piedmont Community College
Stuart P. Brian, Holy Family College
Carl M. Briggs, Indiana University School of Business
Kimberly Chambers, Scottsdale Community College
Jill Chapnick, Florida International University
Alok Charturvedi, Purdue University
Jerry Chin, Southwest Missouri State University
Charles Cole, East Stroudsburg University
Dean Combellick, Scottsdale Community College
Cody Copeland, Johnson County Community College
Larry S. Corman, Fort Lewis College
Janis Cox, Tri-County Technical College
Douglas Cross, Clackamas Community College
Martin Crossland, Southwest Missouri State University
Bill Daley, University of Oregon
Paul E. Daurelle, Western Piedmont Community College
Shawna DePlonty, Sault College of Applied Arts and Technology
Carolyn DiLeo, Westchester Community College
Judy Dolan, Palomar College
David Douglas, University of Arkansas
Carlotta Eaton, Radford University
Cheryl J. Fetterman, Cape Fear Community College
Judith M. Fitspatrick, Gulf Coast Community College
James Franck, College of St. Scholastica
Raymond Frost, Central Connecticut State University
Susan Fry, Boise State University
Midge Gerber, Southwestern Oklahoma State University
James Gips, Boston College
Vernon Griffin, Austin Community College
Ranette Halverson, Midwestern State University
Michael Hassett, Fort Hays State University
Mike Hearn, Community College of Philadelphia
Wanda D. Heller, Seminole Community College

Bonnie Homan, San Francisco State University
Ernie Ivey, Polk Community College
Walter Johnson, Community College of Philadelphia
Mike Kelly, Community College of Rhode Island
Jane King, Everett Community College
Rose M. Laird, Northern Virginia Community College
David Langley, University of Oregon
John Lesson, University of Central Florida
Maurie Lockley, University of North Carolina at Greensboro
Daniela Marghitu, Auburn University
David B. Meinert, Southwest Missouri State University
Alan Moltz, Naugatuck Valley Technical Community College
Kim Montney, Kellogg Community College
Bill Morse, DeVry Institute of Technology
Kevin Pauli, University of Nebraska
Mary McKenry Percival, University of Miami
Marguerite Nedreberg, Youngstown State University
Dr. Francisca Norales, Tennessee State University
Jim Pruitt, Central Washington University
Delores Pusins, Hillsborough Community College
Gale E. Rand, College Misericordia
Judith Rice, Santa Fe Community College
David Rinehard, Lansing Community College
Marilyn Salas, Scottsdale Community College
Herach Safarian, College of the Canyons
John Shepherd, Duquesne University
Barbara Sherman, Buffalo State College
Robert Spear, Prince George's Community College
Michael Stewardson, San Jacinto College—North
Helen Stoloff, Hudson Valley Community College
Margaret Thomas, Ohio University
Mike Thomas, Indiana University School of Business
Suzanne Tomlinson, Iowa State University
Karen Tracey, Central Connecticut State University
Antonio Vargas, El Paso Community College
Sally Visci, Lorain County Community College
David Weiner, University of San Francisco
Connie Wells, Georgia State University
Wallace John Whistance-Smith, Ryerson Polytechnic University
Jack Zeller, Kirkwood Community College

A final word of thanks to the unnamed students at the University of Miami who make it all worthwhile. Most of all, thanks to you, our readers, for choosing this book. Please feel free to contact us with any comments and suggestions.

Robert T. Grauer
rgrauer@miami.edu
www.prenhall.com/grauer

Maryann Barber
mbarber@miami.edu

CHAPTER 5

Desktop Publishing:
Creating a Newsletter and Other Documents

OBJECTIVES

After reading this chapter you will:

1. Distinguish between formatting at the paragraph level versus the section level.
2. Design and implement a multicolumn newsletter.
3. Define a pull quote and a reverse; implement these techniques in Microsoft Word.
4. Define typography; explain how styles can be used to facilitate changes in design.
5. Insert clip art into a document; use the Format Picture command to move and size a graphic.
6. Describe the importance of a grid in the design of a document.
7. Use the Drawing toolbar to add objects to a Word document.
8. Create a Word document with dynamic links to an Excel worksheet and an Excel chart.

hands-on exercises

1. NEWSPAPER COLUMNS
   Input: Text for Newsletter
   Output: Newsletter Solution

2. COMPLETE THE NEWSLETTER
   Input: Newsletter Solution (from exercise 1)
   Output: Newsletter Solution (additional modifications)

3. OBJECT LINKING AND EMBEDDING
   Input: Acme Software (Excel workbook)
   Output: Acme Software Financial Statement (Word document)

CASE STUDY
NEW FROM THE WILD SIDE

Wild n' Wooly is a theme park that combines education about animal life with fun-filled activities such as roller coasters, water slides, and other attractions. The most unique feature about Wild n' Wooly is that every ride is developed around a specific animal or group. Attractions such as "Lambs and Kittens" or "Where Are the Monkeys?" are aimed at younger children. Other rides such as "An Elephant's Life" or "Lions and Tigers" are for older children and adults. Wild n' Wooly prides itself on the detail and accuracy of all its exhibits.

This summer Wild n' Wooly is introducing a new ride called "The Mouth of the Python" that traverses the entire park and boasts a total ride time of 20 minutes. One enters the mouth of the reptile and is immediately exposed to its habitat, natural history, and feeding techniques. The rider sees many types of pythons as he or she speeds through, or creeps through. It is educational, playful, and engaging, and typical of the wonderful rides throughout the park. Indeed, Wild n' Wooly has just been honored with the first annual Wildlife Federation award for creativity in animal life exhibits. This is incredibly exciting news, and the owners want to share this information with their customers by sending out a newsletter that announces the new ride and their recent award.

Your assignment is to read the chapter, paying special attention on how to create an attractive and informative newsletter. You will then apply what you have learned to create a one-page newsletter for the park. The design and content are up to you, but we expect some creative writing to describe the new ride and the recent award. The owners of the park have requested that you include a dominant piece of clip art to add interest to the newsletter. The newsletter should also include the hours of operation as well as your name. Print the completed document for inclusion in a class contest—the winner earns a one-year pass to all attractions at the park.

INTRODUCTION TO DESKTOP PUBLISHING

Desktop publishing evolved through a combination of technologies, including faster computers, laser printers, and sophisticated page composition software to manipulate text and graphics. Desktop publishing was initially considered a separate application, but today's generation of word processors has matured to such a degree that it is difficult to tell where word processing ends and desktop publishing begins. Microsoft Word is, for all practical purposes, a desktop publishing program that can be used to create all types of documents.

The essence of *desktop publishing* is the merger of text with graphics to produce a professional-looking document without reliance on external services. Desktop publishing will save you time and money because you are doing the work yourself rather than sending it out as you did in traditional publishing. That is the good news. The bad news is that desktop publishing is not as easy as it sounds, precisely because you are doing work that was done previously by skilled professionals. Nevertheless, with a little practice, and a basic knowledge of graphic design, you will be able to create effective and attractive documents.

Our chapter begins with the development of a simple newsletter in which we create a multicolumn document, import clip art and other objects, and position those objects within a document. The newsletter also reviews material from earlier chapters on bullets and lists, borders and shading, and section formatting.

THE NEWSLETTER

The newsletter in Figure 5.1 demonstrates the basics of desktop publishing and provides an overview of the chapter. The material is presented conceptually, after which you implement the design in two hands-on exercises. We provide the text and you do the formatting. The first exercise creates a simple newsletter from copy that we provide. The second exercise uses more sophisticated formatting as described by the various techniques mentioned within the newsletter. Many of the terms are new, and we define them briefly in the next few paragraphs.

A *reverse* (light text on a dark background) is a favorite technique of desktop publishers to emphasize a specific element. It is used in the *masthead* (the identifying information) at the top of the newsletter and provides a distinctive look to the publication. The number of the newsletter and the date of publication also appear in the masthead in smaller letters.

A *pull quote* is a phrase or sentence taken from an article to emphasize a key point. It is typically set in larger type, often in a different typeface and/or italics, and may be offset with parallel lines at the top and bottom.

A *dropped-capital letter* is a large capital letter at the beginning of a paragraph. It, too, catches the reader's eye and calls attention to the associated text.

Clip art, used in moderation, will catch the reader's eye and enhance almost any newsletter. It is available from a variety of sources including the Microsoft Media Gallery, which is included in Office XP. Clip art can also be downloaded from the Web, but be sure you are allowed to reprint the image. The banner at the bottom of the newsletter is not a clip art image per se, but was created using various tools on the *Drawing toolbar*.

Borders and shading are effective individually, or in combination with one another, to emphasize important stories within the newsletter. Simple vertical and/or horizontal lines are also effective. The techniques are especially useful in the absence of clip art or other graphics and are a favorite of desktop publishers.

Lists, whether bulleted or numbered, help to organize information by emphasizing important topics. A *bulleted list* emphasizes (and separates) the items. A *numbered list* sequences (and prioritizes) the items and is automatically updated to accommodate additions or deletions.

Creating a Newsletter

Volume I, Number 1 — Fall 2003

Desktop publishing is easy, but there are several points to remember. This chapter will take you through the steps in creating a newsletter. The first hands-on exercise creates a simple newsletter with a masthead and three-column design. The second exercise creates a more attractive document by exploring different ways to emphasize the text.

Clip Art and Other Objects
Clip art is available from a variety of sources. You can also use other types of objects such as maps, charts, or organization charts, which are created by other applications, then brought into a document through the Insert Object command. A single dominant graphic is usually more appealing than multiple smaller graphics.

Techniques to Consider
Our finished newsletter contains one or more examples of each of the following desktop publishing techniques. Can you find where each technique is used, and further, explain, how to implement that technique in Microsoft Word?
1. Pull Quotes
2. Reverse
3. Drop Caps
4. Tables
5. Styles
6. Bullets and Numbering
7. Borders and Shading
8. The Drawing Toolbar

Newspaper-Style Columns
The essence of a newsletter is the implementation of columns in which text flows continuously from the bottom of one column to the top of the next. You specify the number of columns, and optionally, the space between columns. Microsoft Word does the rest. It will compute the width of each column based on the number of columns and the margins.

Beginners often specify margins that are too large and implement too much space between the columns. Another way to achieve a more sophisticated look is to avoid the standard two-column design. You can implement columns of varying width and/or insert vertical lines between the columns.

The number of columns will vary in different parts of a document. The masthead is typically a single column, but the body of the newsletter will have two or three. Remember, too, that columns are implemented at the section level and hence, section breaks are required throughout a document.

Typography
Typography is the process of selecting typefaces, type styles, and type sizes, and is a critical element in the success of any document. Type should reinforce the message and should be consistent with the information you want to convey. More is not better, especially in the case of too many typefaces and styles, which produce cluttered documents that impress no one. Try to limit yourself to a maximum of two typefaces per document, but choose multiple sizes and/or styles within those typefaces. Use boldface or italics for emphasis, but do so in moderation, because if you use too many different elements, the effect is lost.

A pull quote adds interest to a document while simultaneously emphasizing a key point. It is implemented by increasing the point size, changing to italics, centering the text, and displaying a top and bottom border on the paragraph.

Use Styles as Appropriate
Styles were covered in the previous chapter, but that does not mean you cannot use them in conjunction with a newsletter. A style stores character and/or paragraph formatting and can be applied to multiple occurrences of the same element within a document. Change the style and you automatically change all text defined by that style. You can also use styles from one edition of your newsletter to the next to insure consistency.

Borders and Shading
Borders and shading are effective individually or in combination with one another. Use a thin rule (one point or less) and light shading (five or ten percent) for best results. The techniques are especially useful in the absence of clip art or other graphics and are a favorite of desktop publishers.

All the News that Fits

FIGURE 5.1 The Newsletter

Typography

Typography is the process of selecting typefaces, type styles, and type sizes. It is a critical, often subtle, element in the success of a document, and its importance cannot be overstated. You would not, for example, use the same design to announce a year-end bonus and a plant closing. Indeed, good typography goes almost unnoticed, whereas poor typography calls attention to itself and detracts from a document. Our discussion reviews basic concepts and terminology that were presented in Chapter 2.

A ***typeface*** (or ***font***) is a complete set of characters (upper- and lowercase letters, numbers, punctuation marks, and special symbols). Typefaces are divided into two general categories, serif and sans serif. A ***serif typeface*** has tiny cross lines at the ends of the characters to help the eye connect one letter with the next. A ***sans serif typeface*** (sans from the French for *without*) does not have these lines. A commonly accepted practice is to use serif typefaces with large amounts of text and sans serif typefaces for smaller amounts. The newsletter in Figure 5.1, for example, uses **Times New Roman** (a serif typeface) for the text and **Arial** (a sans serif typeface) for the headings.

A second characteristic of a typeface is whether it is monospaced or proportional. A ***monospaced typeface*** (e.g., Courier New) uses the same amount of space for every character regardless of its width. A ***proportional typeface*** (e.g., Times New Roman or Arial) allocates space according to the width of the character. Monospaced fonts are used in tables and financial projections where items must be precisely lined up, one beneath the other. Proportional typefaces create a more professional appearance and are appropriate for most documents.

Any typeface can be set in different styles (such as bold or italic) to create *Times New Roman Italic*, **Arial bold**, or `Courier New Bold Italic`. Other effects are also possible, such as small caps, shadow, and outline, but these should be used with moderation.

Type size is a vertical measurement and is specified in points. One *point* is equal to $1/72$ of an inch. The text in most documents is set in 10 or 12 point type. (The book you are reading is set in 10 point.) Different elements in the same document are often set in different type sizes to provide suitable emphasis. A variation of at least two points, however, is necessary for the difference to be noticeable. The headings in the newsletter, for example, were set in 12 point type, whereas the text of the articles is in 10 point type.

The introduction of ***columns*** into a document poses another concern in that the type size should be consistent with the width of a column. Nine point type, for example, is appropriate in columns that are two inches wide, but much too small in a single-column term paper. In other words, longer lines or wider columns require larger type sizes.

There are no hard and fast rules for the selection of type, only guidelines and common sense. Your objective should be to create a document that is easy to read and visually appealing. You will find that the design that worked so well in one document may not work at all in a different document. Good typography is often the result of trial and error, and we encourage you to experiment freely. All of the techniques and definitions we have discussed can be implemented with commands you already know, as you will see in the hands-on exercise, which follows shortly.

USE MODERATION AND RESTRAINT

More is not better, especially in the case of too many typefaces and styles, which produce cluttered documents that impress no one. Try to limit yourself to a maximum of two typefaces per document, but choose multiple sizes and/or styles within those typefaces. Use boldface or italics for emphasis, but do so in moderation, because if you emphasize too many elements, the effect is lost. A simple design is often the best design.

The Columns Command

The columnar formatting in a newsletter is implemented through the **Columns command** as shown in Figure 5.2. Start by selecting one of the preset designs, and Microsoft Word takes care of everything else. It calculates the width of each column based on the number of columns, the left and right margins on the page, and the specified (default) space between columns.

Consider, for example, the dialog box in Figure 5.2, in which a design of three equal columns is selected with a spacing of ¼ inch between columns. The 2-inch width of each column is computed automatically based on left and right margins of 1 inch each and the ¼-inch spacing between columns. The width of each column is computed by subtracting the sum of the margins and the space between the columns (a total of 2½ inches in this example) from the page width of 8½ inches. The result of the subtraction is 6 inches, which is divided by 3, resulting in a column width of 2 inches.

You can change any of the settings in the Columns dialog box, and Word will automatically make the necessary adjustments. The newsletter in Figure 5.1, for example, uses a two-column layout with wide and narrow columns. We prefer this design to columns of uniform width, as we think it adds interest to our document. Note, too, that once columns have been defined, text will flow continuously from the bottom of one column to the top of the next.

Return for a minute to the newsletter in Figure 5.1, and notice that the number of columns varies from one part of the newsletter to another. The masthead is displayed over a single column at the top of the page, whereas the remainder of the newsletter is formatted in two columns of different widths. The number of columns is specified at the section level, and thus a **section break** is required whenever the column specification changes. A section break is also required at the end of the last column to balance the text within the columns.

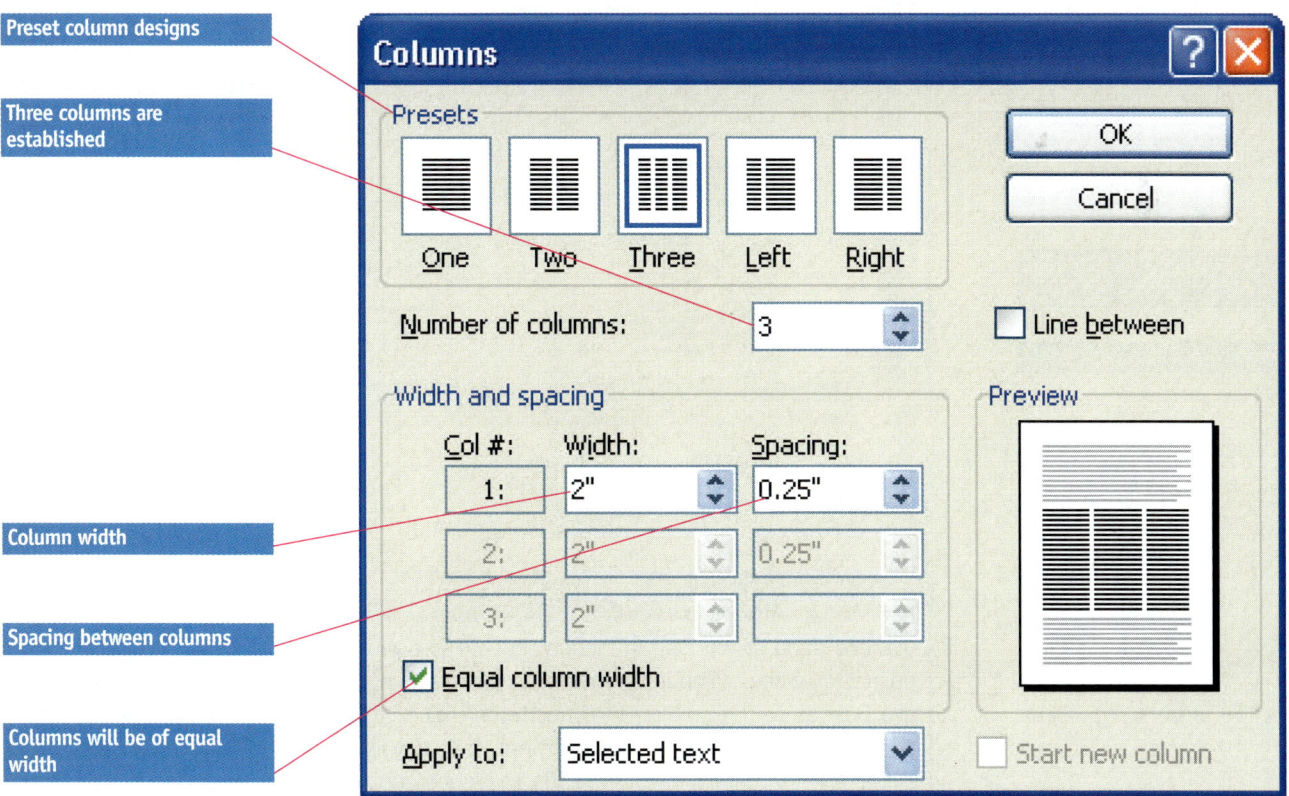

FIGURE 5.2 The Columns Command

hands-on exercise

1 Newspaper Columns

Objective To create a basic newsletter through the Format Columns command; to use section breaks to change the number of columns. Use Figure 5.3.

Step 1: **The Page Setup Command**

- Start Word. Open the **Text for Newsletter document** in the Exploring Word folder. Save the document as **Newsletter Solution**.
- Pull down the **File menu**. Click **Page Setup** to display the Page Setup dialog box as shown in Figure 5.3a.
- Click in the list box for the Top margin. Type **.75** and press the **Tab key** to move to the list box for the Bottom margin. Enter **.75** and press **Tab** again. Change the left and right margins in similar fashion. Click **OK** to accept these settings.
- Click the **Print Layout View button** above the status bar. Set the magnification (zoom) to **Page Width**.

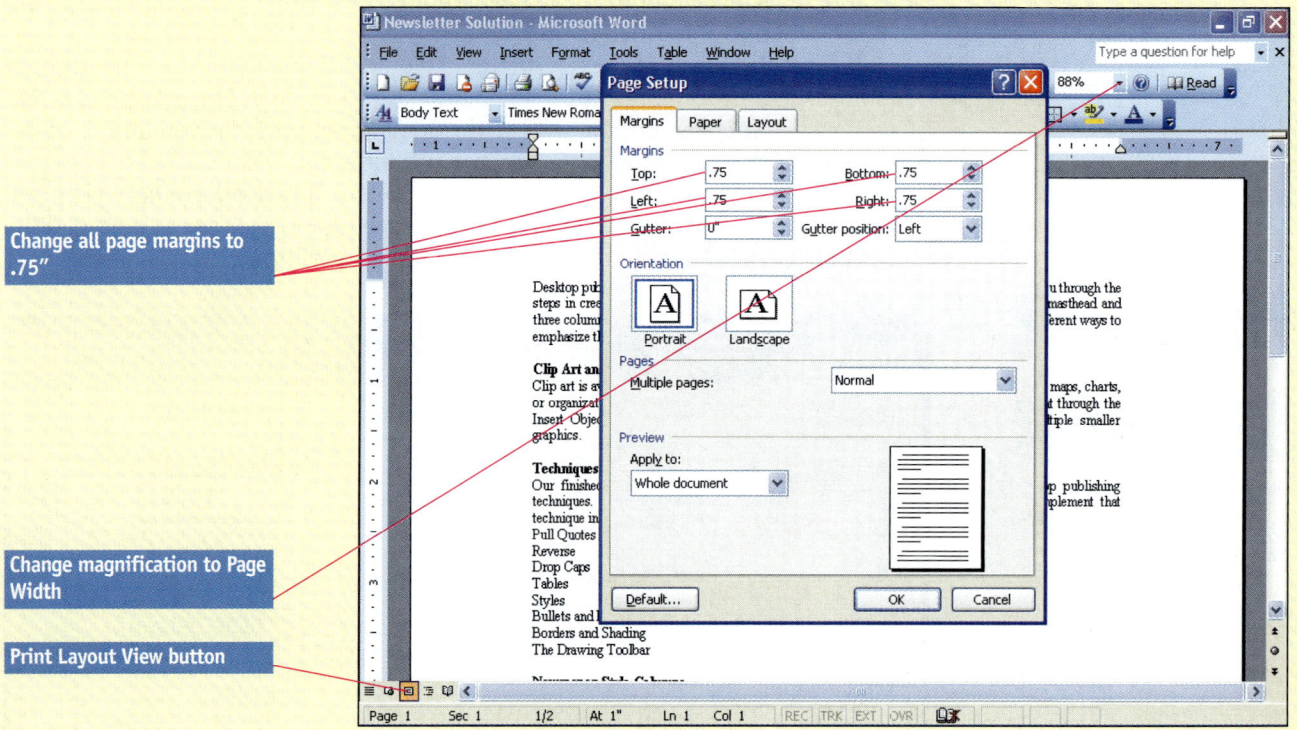

(a) The Page Setup Command (step 1)

FIGURE 5.3 Hands-on Exercise 1

CHANGE THE MEASUREMENT UNITS

We are used to working in inches, but what if you wanted to work in centimeters, points, or picas? (The latter two are common typographical measurements. There are 6 picas to the inch and 12 points in 1 pica. You are unlikely to use either measurement in an academic environment, but very likely to see the terms in a professional environment.) To change the measurement unit, pull down the Tools menu, click the Options command to display the Options dialog box, and click the General tab. Click the down arrow in the Measurement Unit list box to choose the desired unit, then click OK to accept the setting and close the dialog box.

Step 2: **Check the Document**

- Pull down the **Tools menu**, click **Options**, and click the **Spelling and Grammar tab**. Click the **drop-down arrow** on the Writing style list box and select **Grammar & Style**. Click **OK** to close the Options dialog box.

- Click the **Spelling and Grammar button** on the Standard toolbar to check the document for errors.

- The first error detected by the spelling and grammar check is the omitted hyphen between the words *three* and *column* as shown in Figure 5.3b. (This is a subtle mistake and emphasizes the need to check a document using the tools provided by Word.) Click **Change** to accept the indicated suggestion.

- Continue checking the document, accepting (or rejecting) the suggested corrections as you see fit.

- Save the document.

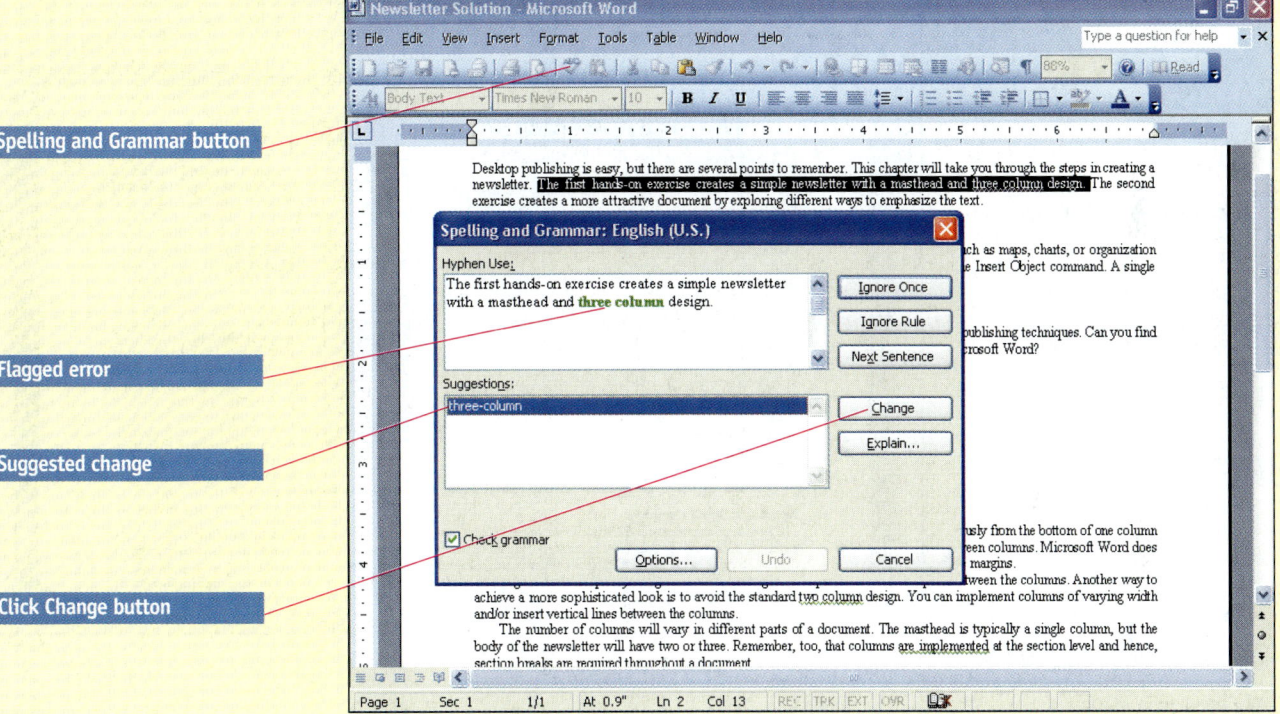

(b) Check the Document (step 2)

FIGURE 5.3   Hands-on Exercise 1 (*continued*)

USE THE SPELLING AND GRAMMAR CHECK

Our eyes are less discriminating than we would like to believe, allowing misspellings and simple typos to go unnoticed. To prove the point, count the number of times the letter f appears in this sentence, *"Finished files are the result of years of scientific study combined with the experience of years."* The correct answer is six, but most people find only four or five. Checking your document takes only a few minutes. Do it!

Step 3: **Implement Column Formatting**

- Pull down the **Format menu**. Click **Columns** to display the dialog box in Figure 5.3c. Click the **Presets icon** for **Two**. The column width for each column and the spacing between columns will be determined automatically from the existing margins.

- If necessary, clear the **Line between box**. Click **OK** to accept the settings and close the Columns dialog box.

- The text of the newsletter should be displayed in two columns. If you do not see the columns, it is probably because you are in the wrong view. Click the **Print Layout View button** above the status bar to change to this view.

- Save the document.

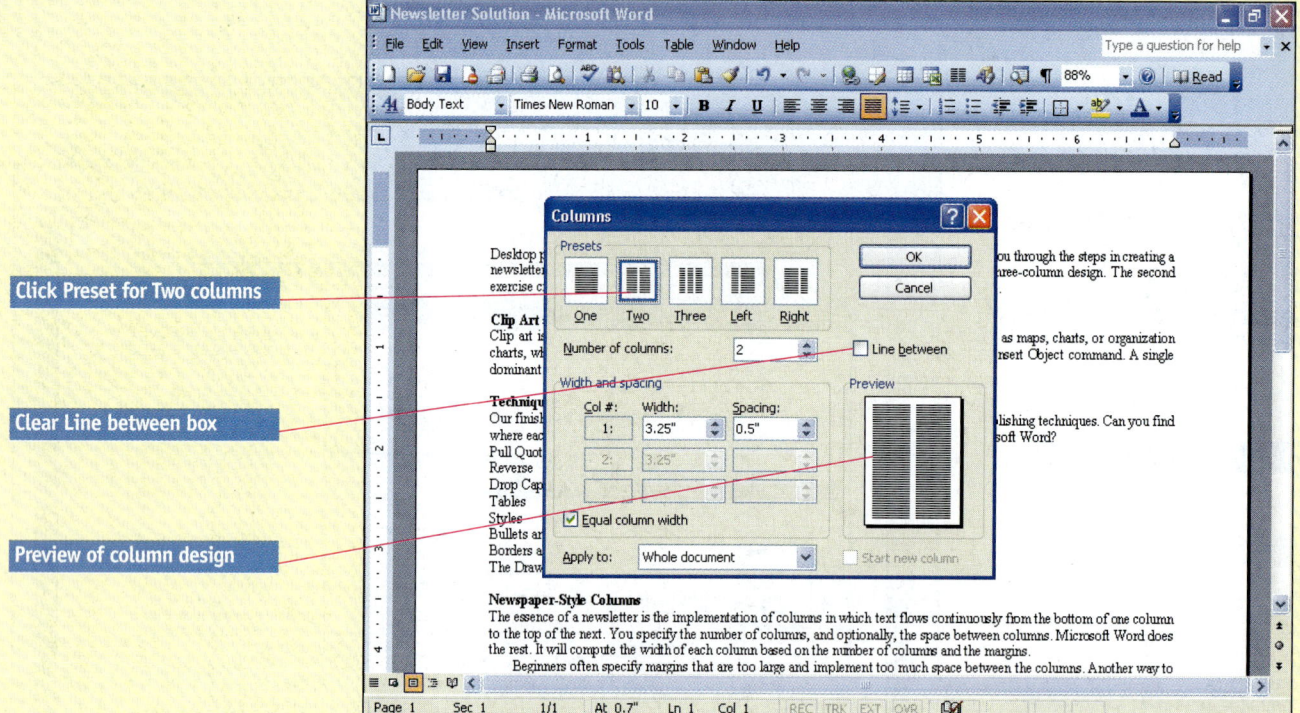

(c) Implement Column Formatting (step 3)

FIGURE 5.3 Hands-on Exercise 1 (*continued*)

PAGE BREAKS, COLUMN BREAKS, AND LINE BREAKS

Force Word to begin the next entry on a new page or column by inserting the proper type of break. Pull down the Insert menu, click the Break command to display the Break dialog box, then choose the option button for a page break or column break, respectively. It's easier, however, to use the appropriate shortcut, Ctrl+Enter or Shift+Ctrl+Enter, for a page or column break, respectively. You can also use Shift+Enter to force a line break, where the next word begins on a new line within the same paragraph. Click the Show/Hide button to display the hidden codes to see how the breaks are implemented.

Step 4: **Balance the Columns**

- Use the **Zoom box** on the Standard toolbar to zoom to **Whole Page** to see the entire newsletter as shown in Figure 5.3d. Do not be concerned if the columns are of different lengths.

- Press **Ctrl+End** to move the insertion point to the end of the document. Pull down the **Insert menu**. Click **Break** to display the Break dialog box in Figure 5.3d. Select the **Continuous option button** under Section breaks.

- Click **OK** to accept the settings and close the dialog box. The columns should be balanced, although one column may be one line longer than the other.

- Save the document.

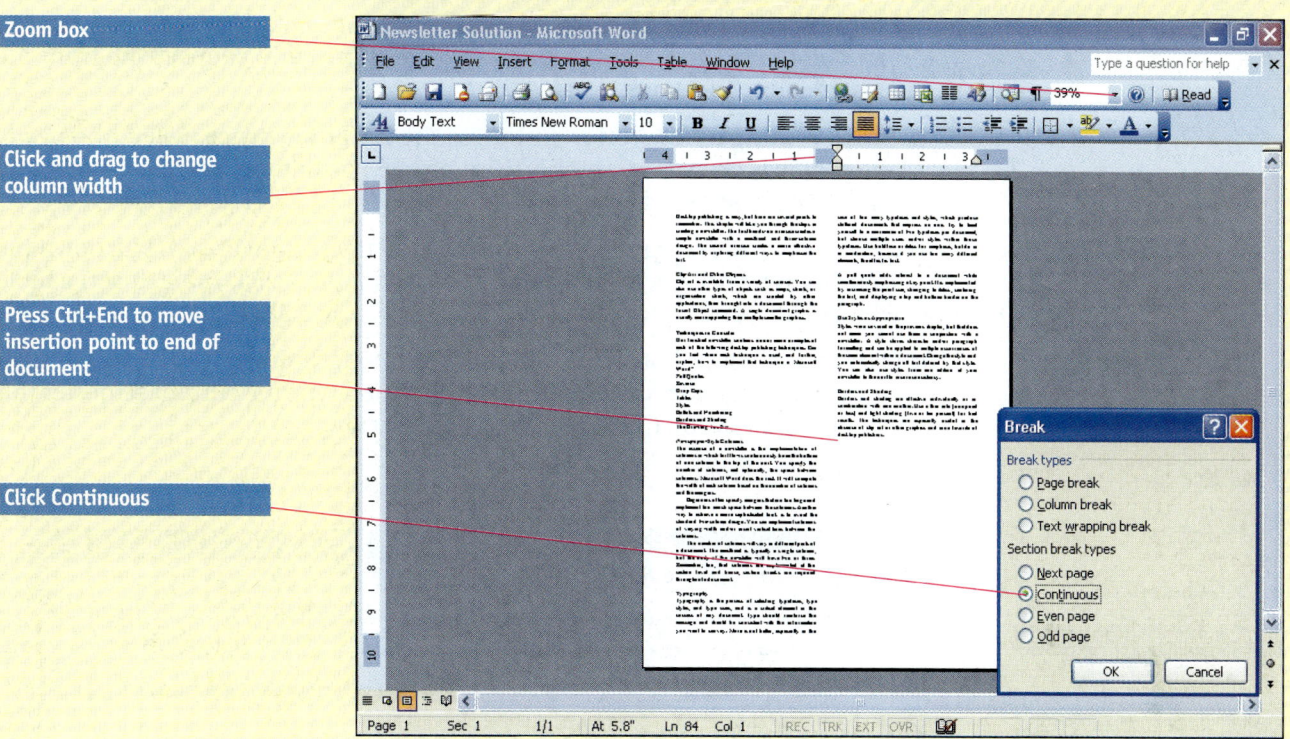

(d) Balance the Columns (step 4)

FIGURE 5.3 Hands-on Exercise 1 (*continued*)

USE THE RULER TO CHANGE COLUMN WIDTH

Click anywhere within the column whose width you want to change, then point to the ruler and click and drag the right column margin (the mouse pointer changes to a double arrow) to change the column width. Changing the width of one column in a document with equal-sized columns changes the width of all other columns so that they remain equal. Changing the width in a document with unequal columns changes only that column. You can also double click the margin area on the ruler to display the Page Setup dialog box, then click the Margins tab to change the left and right margins, which in turn will change the column width.

Step 5: **Create the Masthead**

- Use the **Zoom box** on the Standard toolbar to change to **Page Width**. Click the **Show/Hide ¶ button** to display the paragraph and section marks.

- Press **Ctrl+Home** to move the insertion point to the beginning of the document. Pull down the **Insert menu**, click **Break**, select the **Continuous option button**, and click **OK**. You should see a double dotted line indicating a section break as shown in Figure 5.3e.

- Click immediately to the left of the dotted line, which will place the insertion point to the left of the line. Check the status bar to be sure you are in section one.

- Change the format for this section to a single column by clicking the **Columns button** on the Standard toolbar and selecting one column. (Alternatively, you can pull down the **Format menu**, click **Columns**, and choose **One** from the Presets column formats.)

- Type **Creating a Newsletter** and press the **Enter key** twice. Select the newly entered text, click the **Center button** on the Formatting toolbar. Change the font to **48 point Arial Bold**.

- Click underneath the masthead (to the left of the section break). Pull down the **Table menu**, click **Insert** to display a submenu, then click **Table**. Insert a table with one row and two columns as shown in Figure 5.3e.

- Click in the left cell of the table. Type **Volume I, Number 1**. Click in the right cell (or press the **Tab key** to move to this cell and type the current semester (for example, **Fall 2003**). Click the **Align Right button**.

- Save the document.

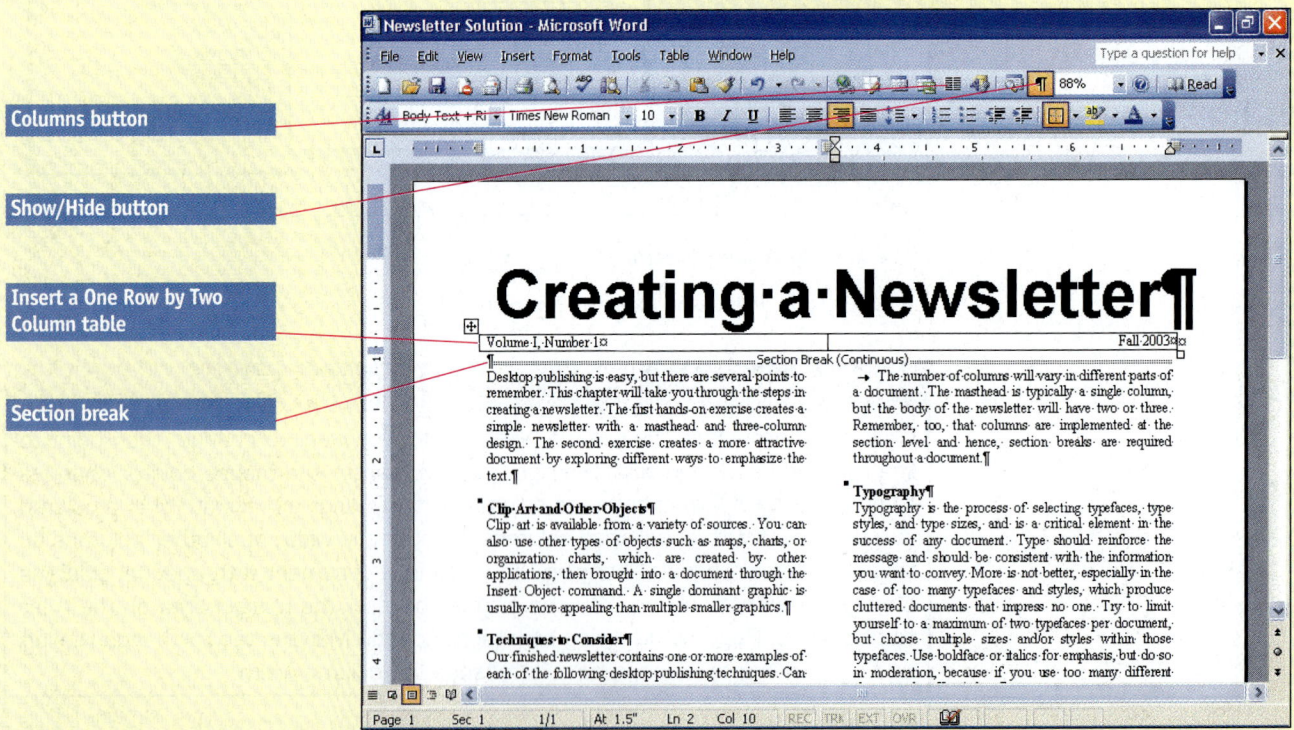

(e) Create the Masthead (step 5)

FIGURE 5.3 Hands-on Exercise 1 (*continued*)

Step 6: **Create a Reverse**

- Press **Ctrl+Home** to move the insertion point to the beginning of the newsletter. Click anywhere within the title of the newsletter.

- Pull down the **Format menu**, click **Borders and Shading** to display the Borders and Shading dialog box, then click the **Shading tab** in Figure 5.3f.

- Click the **drop-down arrow** in the Style list box (in the Patterns area) and select **Solid (100%)** shading. Click **OK** to accept the setting and close the dialog box. Click elsewhere in the document to see the results.

- The final step is to remove the default border that appears around the table. Click in the selection area to the left of the table to select the entire table.

- Pull down the **Format menu**, click **Borders and Shading**, and if necessary click the **Borders tab**. Click the **None icon** in the Presets area. Click **OK**. Click elsewhere in the document to see the result.

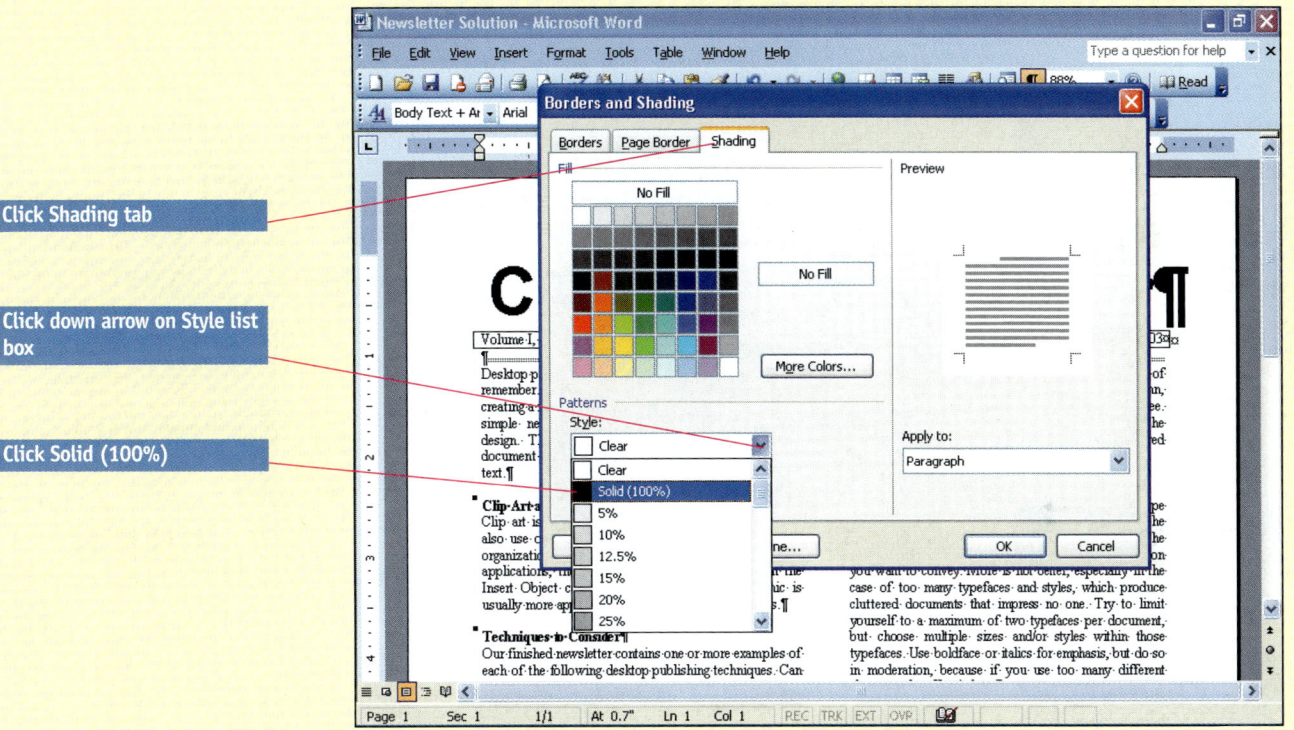

(f) Create a Reverse (step 6)

FIGURE 5.3 Hands-on Exercise 1 (*continued*)

LEFT ALIGNED	CENTERED	RIGHT ALIGNED

Many documents call for left-aligned, centered, and/or right-aligned text on the same line, an effect that is achieved through setting tabs, or more easily through a table. To achieve the effect shown at the top of this box, create a 1 × 3 table (one row and three columns), type the text in the cells, then use the buttons on the Formatting toolbar to left-align, center, and right-align the cells. Select the table, pull down the Format menu, click Borders and Shading, then specify None as the Border setting.

Step 7: **Modify the Heading Style**

- Two styles have been implemented for you in the newsletter. Click in any text paragraph, and you see the Body Text style name displayed in the Style box on the Formatting toolbar. Click in any heading, and you see the Heading 1 style.

- Pull down the **View menu** and click the **Task Pane command** to open the task pane. Click the **down arrow** within the task pane and choose **Styles and Formatting**.

- Point to the **Heading 1** style, click the **down arrow**, then click the **Modify command** to display the Modify Style dialog box shown in Figure 5.3g.

- Change the font to **Arial** and the font size to **12**. Click **OK** to accept the settings and close the dialog box. All of the headings in the document are changed automatically to reflect the changes in the Heading 1 style.

- Experiment with other styles as you see fit. (You can remove the formatting of existing text by clicking within a paragraph, then clicking **Clear Formatting** within the task pane.)

- Save the newsletter. Close the task pane.

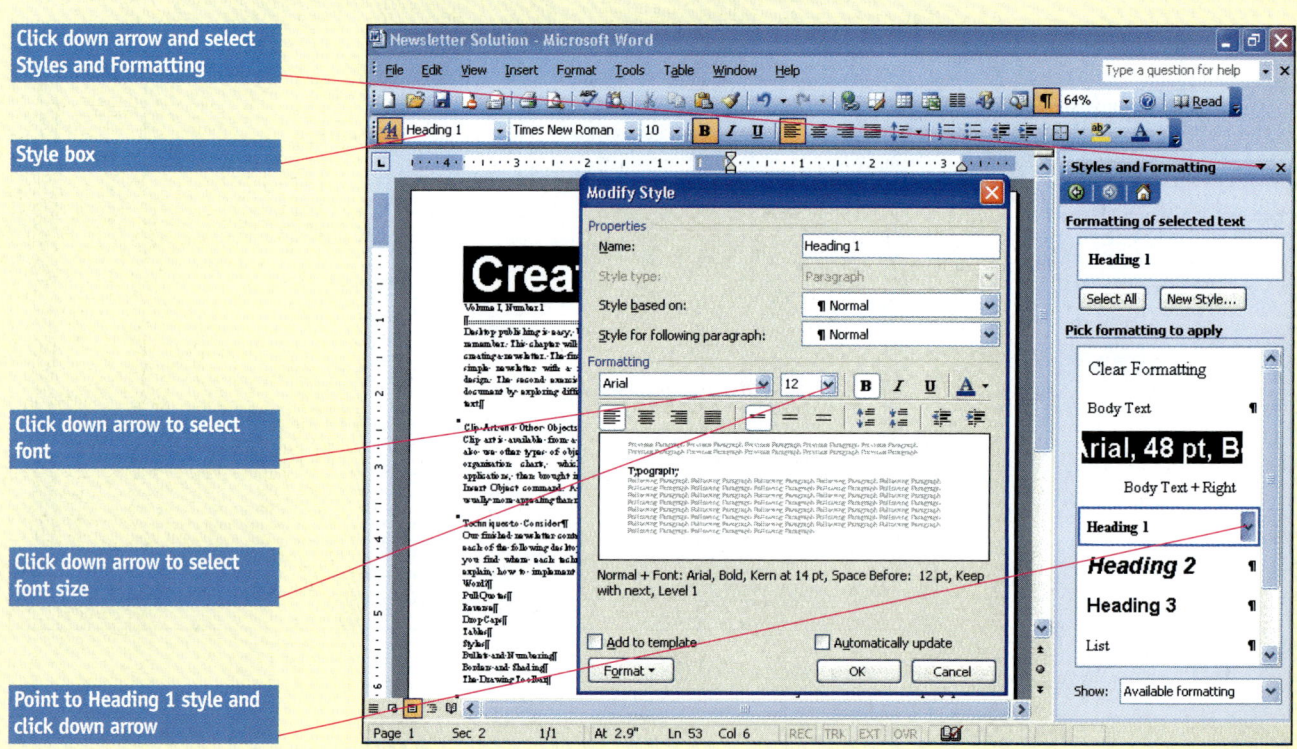

(g) Modify the Heading Style (step 7)

FIGURE 5.3 Hands-on Exercise 1 (*continued*)

USE STYLES AS APPROPRIATE

Styles were covered in the previous chapter, but that does not mean you cannot use them in conjunction with a newsletter. A style stores character and/or paragraph formatting and can be applied to multiple occurrences of the same element within a document. Change the style and you automatically change all text defined by that style. Use the same styles from one edition of your newsletter to the next to ensure consistency. Use styles in any document to promote uniformity and increase flexibility.

Step 8: **The Print Preview Command**

- Legend has it that the Print Preview command originated when a Microsoft programmer tired of walking down the hall to pick up a printout of his/her document only to be frustrated when the document did not appear as intended.

- Pull down the **File menu** and click **Print Preview** (or click the **Print Preview button** on the Standard toolbar) to view the newsletter as in Figure 5.3h. This is a basic two-column newsletter with the masthead appearing as a reverse and stretching over a single column.

- Click the **Print button** to print the newsletter at this stage so that you can compare this version with the finished newsletter at the end of the next exercise.

- Click the **Close button** on the Print Preview toolbar to close the Preview view and return to the Page Layout view.

- Save the document. Exit Word if you do not want to continue with the next exercise at this time.

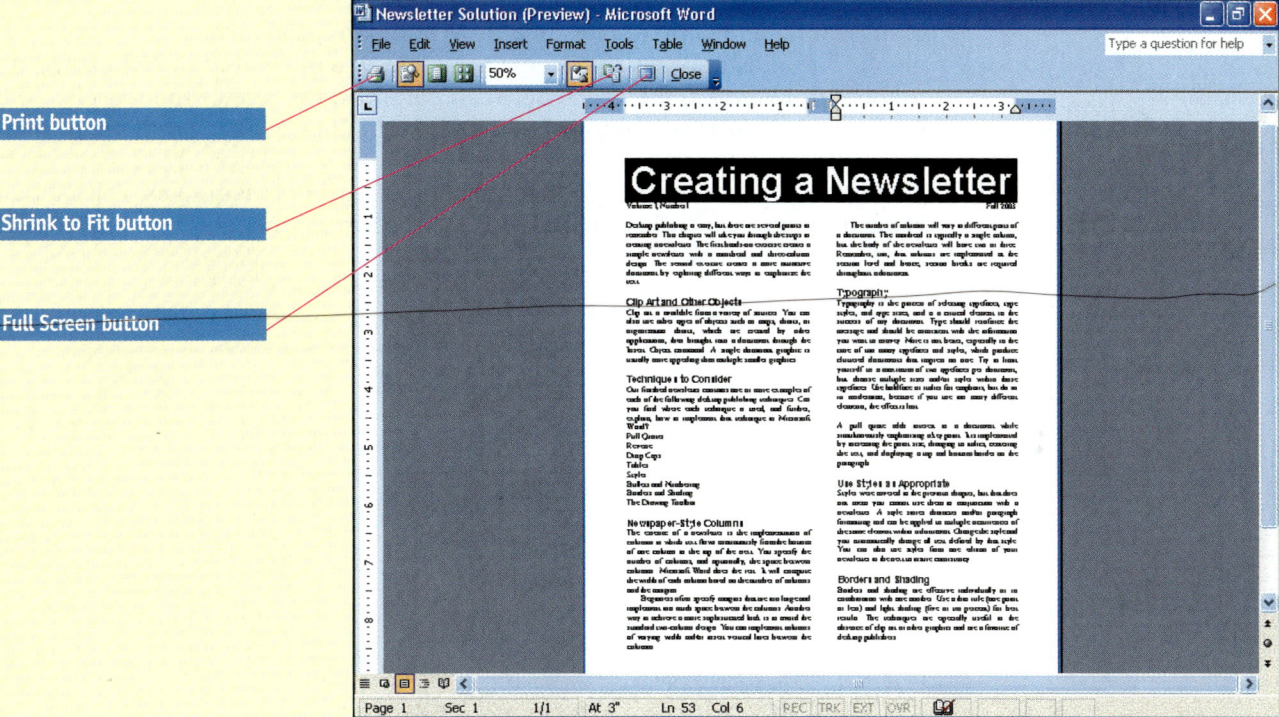

(h) The Print Preview Command (step 8)

FIGURE 5.3   Hands-on Exercise 1 (*continued*)

THE PRINT PREVIEW TOOLBAR

The Print Preview toolbar appears automatically when you switch to this view, and it contains several tools that are helpful prior to printing a document. The Shrink to Fit button is especially useful if a small portion of a document spills over to a second page—click this button, and it uniformly reduces the fonts throughout a document to eliminate the extra page. The down arrow on the Zoom box enables you to change the magnification to see more (less) of the page. The One Page/Multiple Page icons are useful with multipage documents. The View Ruler button toggles the display of the ruler on and off.

ELEMENTS OF GRAPHIC DESIGN

We trust you have completed the first hands-on exercise without difficulty and that you were able to duplicate the initial version of the newsletter. That, however, is the easy part of desktop publishing. The more difficult aspect is to develop the design in the first place because the mere availability of a desktop publishing program does not guarantee an effective document, any more than a word processor will turn its author into another Shakespeare. Other skills are necessary, and so we continue with a brief introduction to graphic design.

Much of what we say is subjective, and what works in one situation will not necessarily work in another. Your eye is the best judge of all, and you should follow your own instincts. Experiment freely and realize that successful design is the result of trial and error. Seek inspiration from others by collecting samples of real documents that you find attractive, then use those documents as the basis for your own designs.

The Grid

The design of a document is developed on a **grid**, an underlying, but *invisible*, set of horizontal and vertical lines that determine the placement of the major elements. A grid establishes the overall structure of a document by indicating the number of columns, the space between columns, the size of the margins, the placement of headlines, art, and so on. The grid does *not* appear in the printed document or on the screen.

Figure 5.4 shows the "same" document in three different designs. The left half of each design displays the underlying grid, whereas the right half displays the completed document.

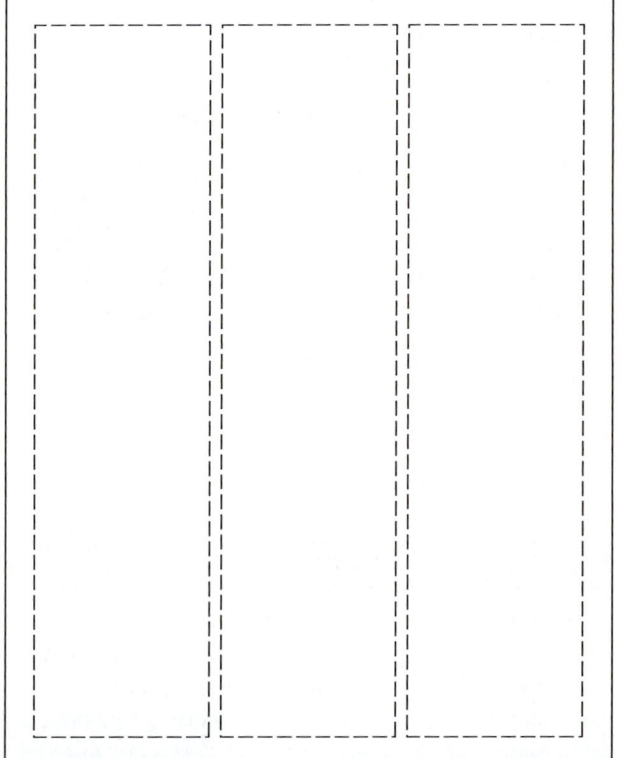

(a) Three-column Grid

FIGURE 5.4   The Grid System of Design

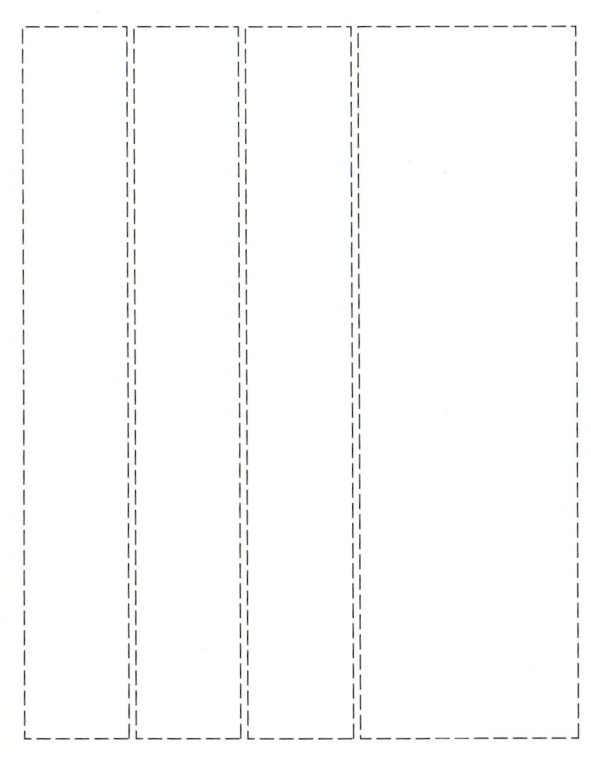

(b) Four-column Grid

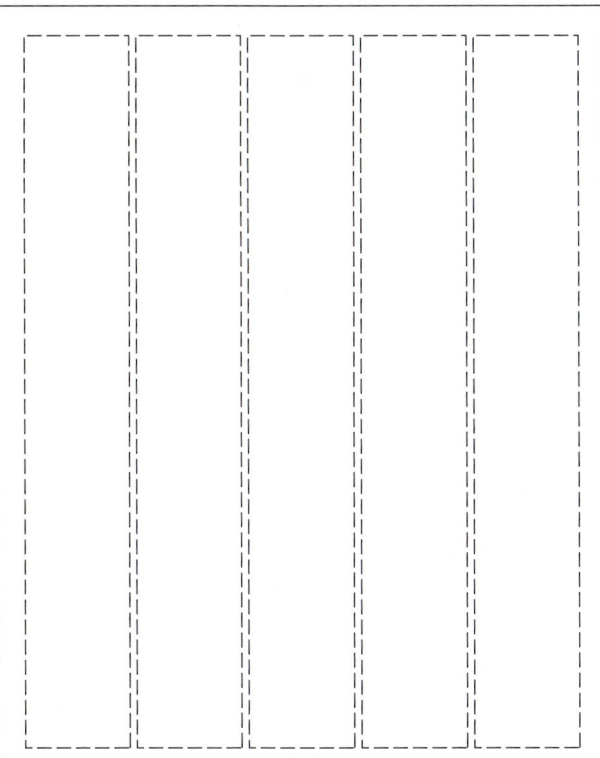

(c) Five-column Grid

FIGURE 5.4 The Grid System of Design (*continued*)

A grid may be simple or complex, but it is always distinguished by the number of columns it contains. The three-column grid of Figure 5.4a is one of the most common and utilitarian designs. Figure 5.4b shows a four-column design for the same document, with unequal column widths to provide interest. Figure 5.4c illustrates a five-column grid that is often used with large amounts of text. Many other designs are possible as well. A one-column grid is used for term papers and letters. A two-column, wide-and-narrow format is appropriate for textbooks and manuals. Two- and three-column formats are used for newsletters and magazines.

The simple concept of a grid should make the underlying design of any document obvious, which in turn gives you an immediate understanding of page composition. Moreover, the conscious use of a grid will help you organize your material and result in a more polished and professional-looking publication. It will also help you to achieve consistency from page to page within a document (or from issue to issue of a newsletter). Indeed, much of what goes wrong in desktop publishing stems from failing to follow or use the underlying grid.

Emphasis

Good design makes it easy for the reader to determine what is important. As indicated earlier, **emphasis** can be achieved in several ways, the easiest being variations in type size and/or type style. Headings should be set in type sizes (at least two points) larger than body copy. The use of **boldface** is effective as are *italics*, but both should be done in moderation. (UPPERCASE LETTERS and underlining are alternative techniques that we believe are less effective.)

Boxes and/or shading call attention to selected articles. Horizontal lines are effective to separate one topic from another or to call attention to a pull quote. A reverse can be striking for a small amount of text. Clip art, used in moderation, will catch the reader's eye and enhance almost any newsletter. (Color is also effective, but it is more costly.)

Clip Art

Clip art is available from a variety of sources including the Microsoft Clip Organizer and Microsoft Web site. The Clip Organizer can be accessed in a variety of ways, most easily by clicking the appropriate link at the bottom of the Clip Art task pane. Once clip art has been inserted into a document, it can be moved and sized just like any other Windows object, as will be illustrated in our next hands-on exercise.

The ***Format Picture command*** provides additional flexibility in the placement of clip art. The Text Wrapping tab, in the Advanced Layout dialog box, determines the way text is positioned around a picture. The Top and Bottom option (no wrapping) is selected in Figure 5.5a, and the resulting document is shown in Figure 5.5b. The sizing handles around the clip art indicate that it is currently selected, enabling you to move and/or resize the clip art using the mouse. (You can also use the Size and Position tabs in the Format Picture dialog box for more precision with either setting.) Changing the size or position of the object, however, does not affect the way in which text wraps around the clip art.

The document in Figure 5.5c illustrates a different wrapping selection in which text is wrapped on both sides. Figure 5.5c also uses an option on the Colors and Lines tab to draw a blue border around the clip art. The document in Figure 5.5d eliminates the border and chooses the tight wrapping style so that the text is positioned as closely as possible to the figure in a free-form design. Choosing among the various documents in Figure 5.5 is one of personal preference. Our point is simply that Word provides multiple options, and it is up to you, the desktop publisher, to choose the design that best suits your requirements.

Top and Bottom wrapping style

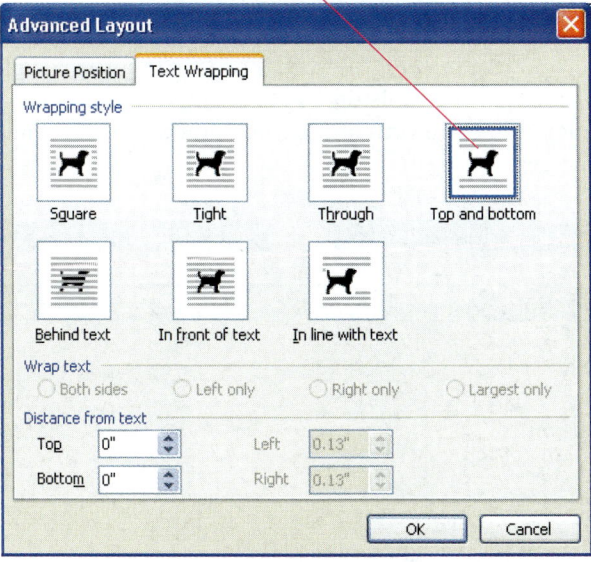

(a) Advanced Layout Dialog Box

(b) Top and Bottom Wrapping

(c) Square Wrapping (both sides)

(d) Tight Wrapping (both sides)

FIGURE 5.5 The Format Picture Command

THE DRAWING TOOLBAR

Did you ever stop to think how the images in the Clip Organizer were developed? Undoubtedly they were drawn by someone with artistic ability who used basic shapes, such as lines and curves in various combinations, to create the images. The Drawing toolbar in Figure 5.6a contains all of the tools necessary to create original clip art. Select the Line tool for example, then click and drag to create the line. Once the line has been created, you can select it, then change its properties (such as thickness, style, or color) by using other tools on the Drawing toolbar. Draw a second line, or a curve—then, depending on your ability, you have a piece of original clip art.

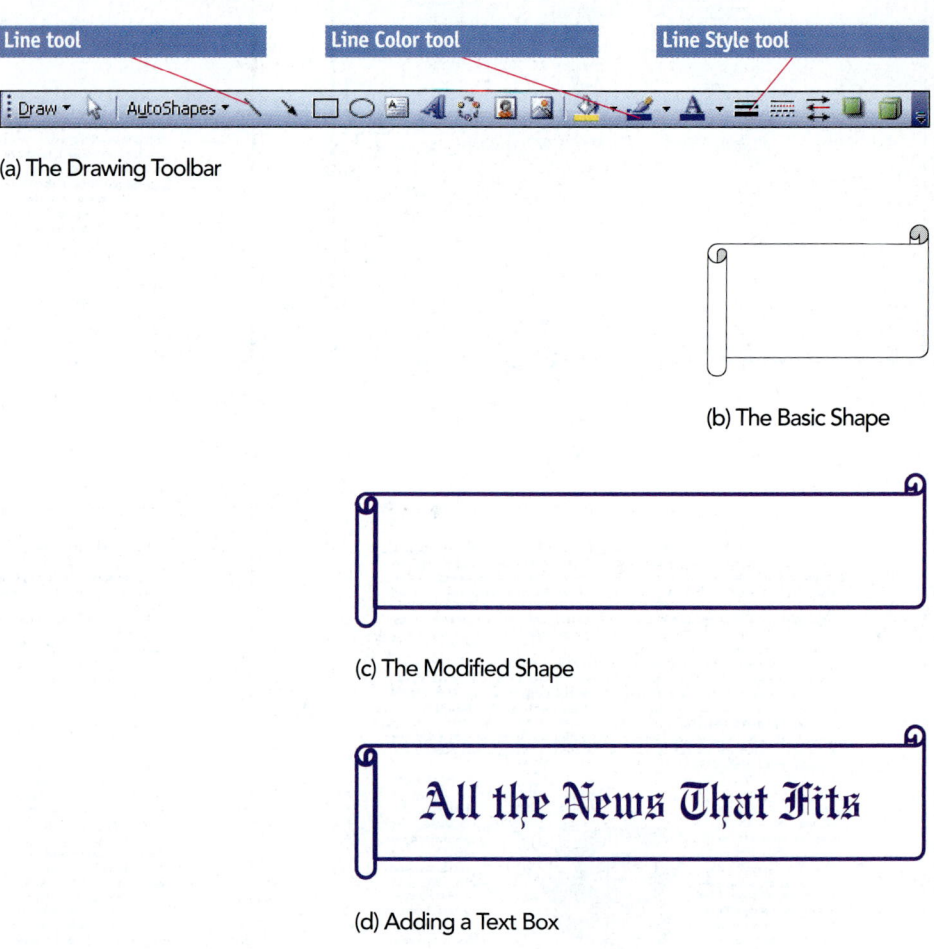

(a) The Drawing Toolbar

(b) The Basic Shape

(c) The Modified Shape

(d) Adding a Text Box

FIGURE 5.6 The Drawing Toolbar

We don't expect you to create clip art comparable to the images within the Clip Organizer. You can, however, use the tools on the Drawing toolbar to modify an existing image and/or create simple shapes of your own that can enhance any document. One tool that is especially useful is the AutoShapes button that displays a series of predesigned shapes. Choose a shape (the banner in Figure 5.6b), change its size and color (Figure 5.6c), then use the Textbox tool to add an appropriate message.

The Drawing toolbar is displayed through the Toolbars command in the View menu. The following exercise has you use the toolbar to create the banner and text in Figure 5.6d. It's fun, it's easy; just be flexible and willing to experiment. We think you will be pleased at what you will be able to do.

hands-on exercise

2 Complete the Newsletter

Objective To insert clip art into a newsletter; to format a newsletter using styles, borders and shading, pull quotes, and lists. Use Figure 5.7a as a guide in the exercise.

Step 1: Change the Column Layout

- Open the **Newsletter Solution** document from the previous exercise. Click in the masthead and change the number of this edition from 1 to **2**. Click the **Show/Hide button** to hide the nonprinting characters.

- Click anywhere in the body of the newsletter. The status bar should indicate that you are in the second section.

- Pull down the **Format menu**. Click **Columns** to display the dialog box in Figure 5.7a. Click the **Left Preset icon**.

- Change the width of the first column to **2.25** and the space between columns to **.25**. Check (click) the **Line Between box**. Click **OK**.

- Save the newsletter.

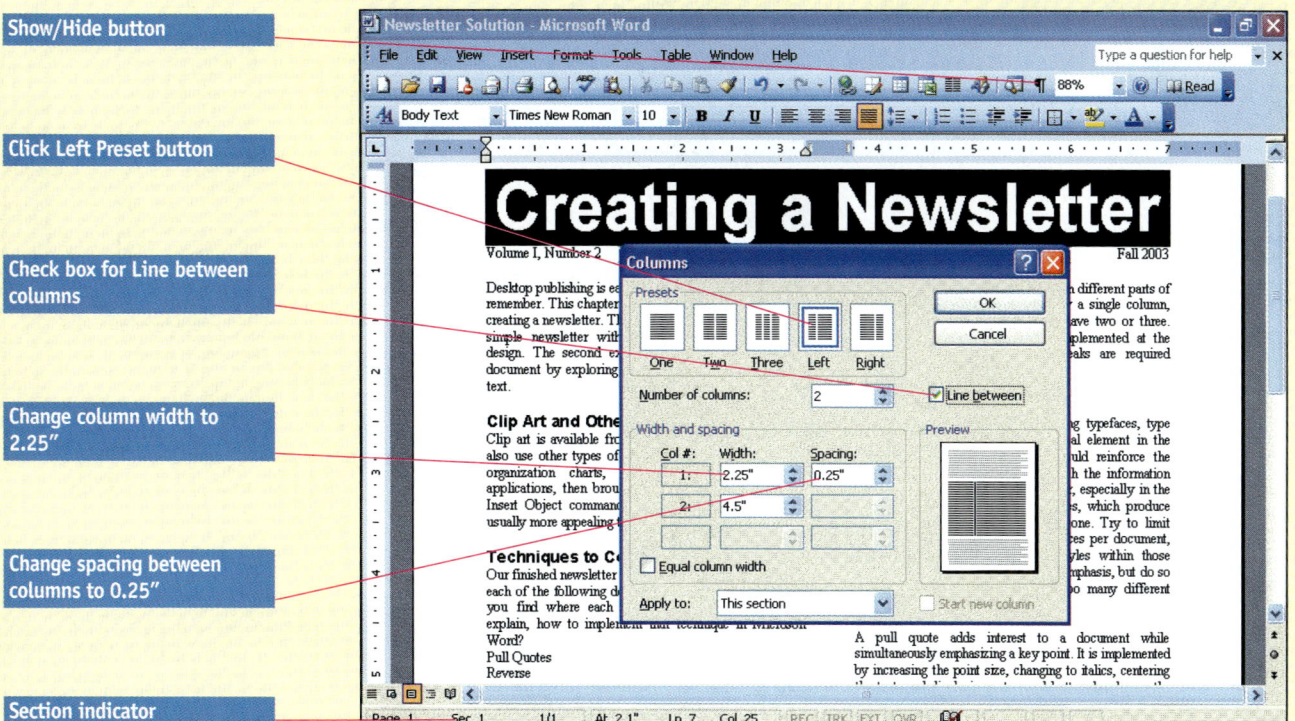

(a) Change the Column Layout (step 1)

FIGURE 5.7 Hands-on Exercise 2

EXPERIMENT WITH THE DESIGN

The number, width, and spacing of the columns in a newsletter is the most important element in its design. Experiment freely and try columns of varying width. Good design is often the result of trial and error. Use the Undo command as necessary to restore the document.

Step 2: **Bullets and Numbering**

- Scroll in the document until you come to the list within the **Techniques to Consider** paragraph. Select the entire list as shown in Figure 5.7b.

- Pull down the **Format menu** and click **Bullets and Numbering** to display the Bullets and Numbering dialog box.

- If necessary, click the **Numbered tab** and choose the numbering style with Arabic numbers followed by periods. Click **OK** to accept these settings and close the Bullets and Numbering dialog box.

- Click anywhere in the newsletter to deselect the text.

- Save the newsletter.

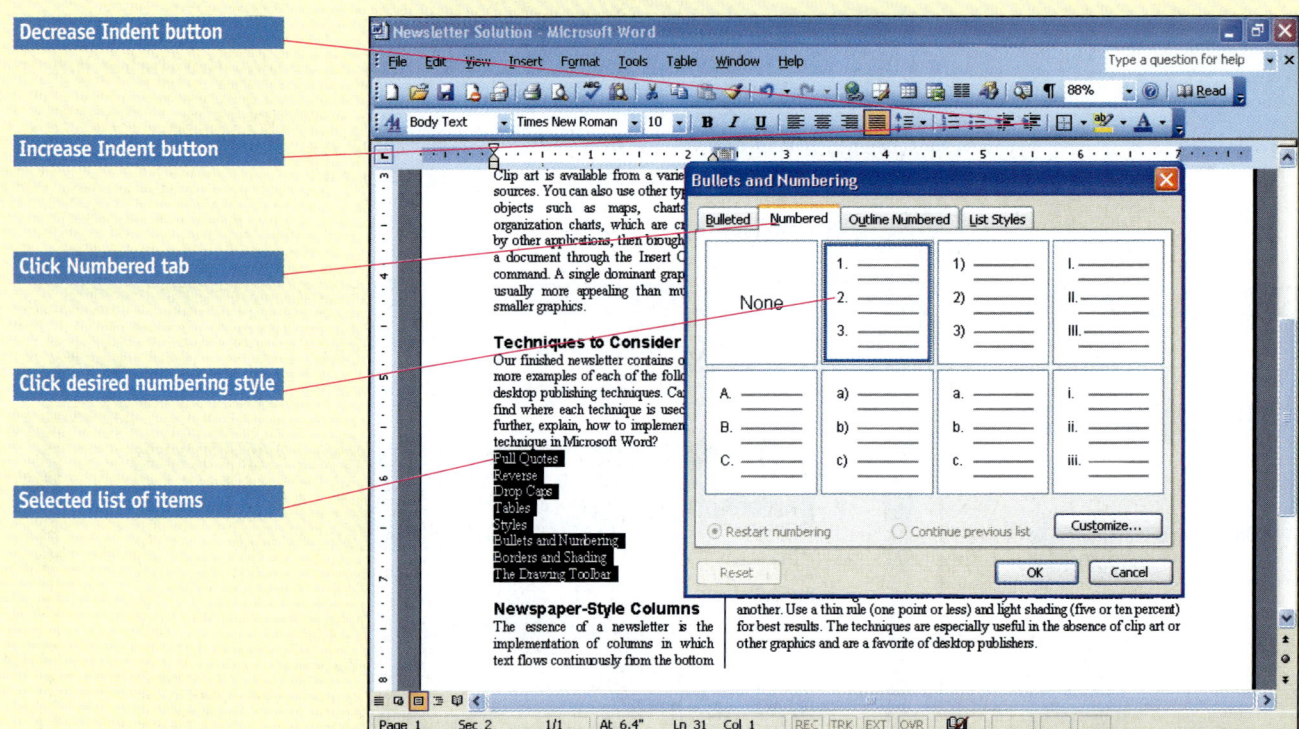

(b) Bullets and Numbering (step 2)

FIGURE 5.7 Hands-on Exercise 2 (*continued*)

LISTS AND THE FORMATTING TOOLBAR

The Formatting toolbar contains four buttons for use with bulleted and numbered lists. The Increase Indent and Decrease Indent buttons move the selected items one tab stop to the right and left, respectively. The Bullets button creates a bulleted list from unnumbered items or converts a numbered list to a bulleted list. The Numbering button creates a numbered list or converts a bulleted list to numbers. The Bullets and Numbering buttons also function as toggle switches; for example, clicking the Bullets button when a bulleted list is already in effect will remove the bullets.

Step 3: **Insert the Clip Art**

- Click immediately to the left of the article beginning **Clip Art and Other Objects**. Pull down the **Insert menu**, click **Picture**, then click **Clip Art** to display the Clip Art task pane.

- Click in the **Search for text box** and type **goals** to search for all pictures that have been catalogued to describe this attribute. Click the **Go button**. The search begins, and the various pictures appear individually within the task pane.

- Point to the image you want in your newsletter, click the **down arrow** that appears, then click **Insert** to insert the clip art.

- The picture should appear in the document, where it can be moved and sized as described in the next several steps. Click the **Close button** on the task pane.

- Save the document.

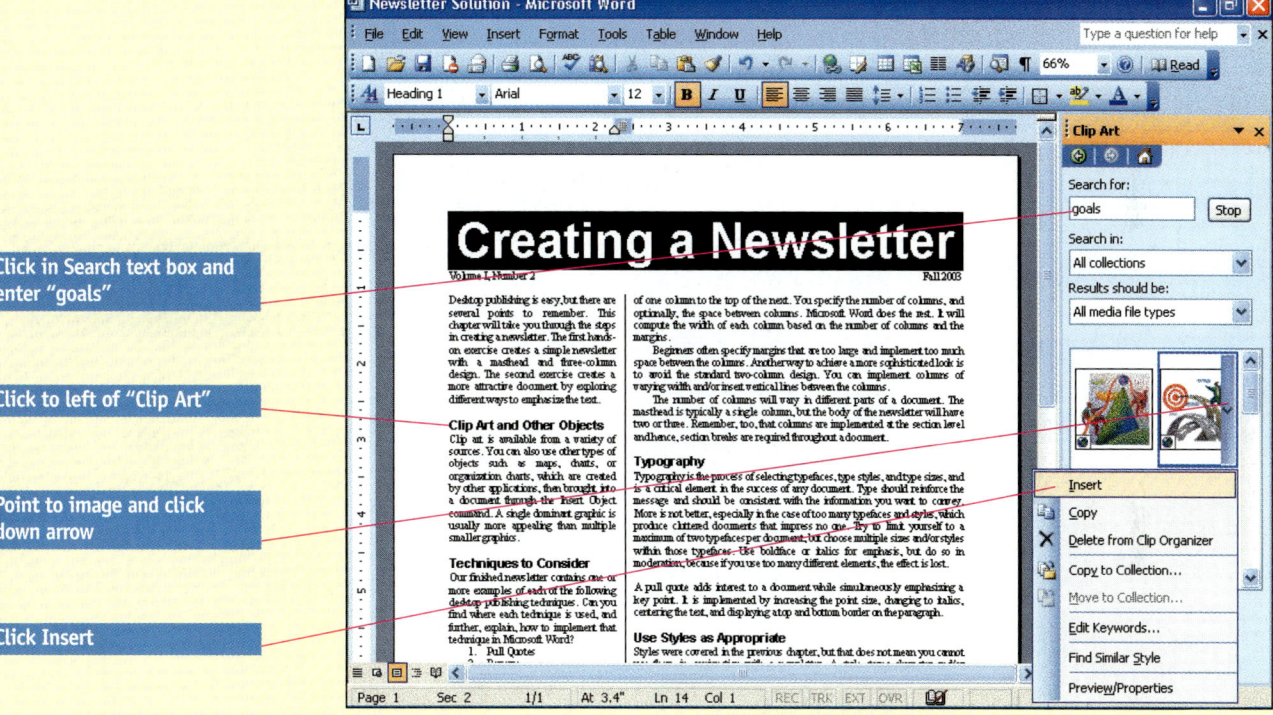

(c) Insert the Clip Art (step 3)

FIGURE 5.7 Hands-on Exercise 2 (*continued*)

CLIPS ONLINE

Why settle for the same old clip art when you can get new images from the Microsoft Web site? Pull down the Insert menu, click the Picture command, then choose Clip Art to open the task pane. Click the Clip Art on Office Online button to connect to the Microsoft site, where you have your choice of clip art, photographs, sounds, and motion clips in a variety of categories. Choose a category, then browse through the images. Click the box below an image to select it. Select as many images as you like and then click the Download link (on the left frame) when you are finished. The images will be imported into the Clip Organizer and stored in the associated folder.

Step 4: **Move and Size the Clip Art**

- Click the **drop-down arrow** on the Zoom list box and select **Whole Page**.

- Point to the picture, click the **right mouse button** to display a context-sensitive menu, then click the **Format Picture command** to display the Format Picture dialog box as shown in Figure 5.7d.

- Click the **Layout tab**, choose the **Square layout**, then click the option button for left or right alignment. Click **OK** to close the dialog box. You can now move and size the clip art just like any other Windows object.

- To size the clip art, click anywhere within the clip art to select it and display the sizing handles. Drag a corner handle (the mouse pointer changes to a double arrow) to change the length and width of the picture simultaneously and keep the object in proportion.

- To move the clip art, click the object to select it and display the sizing handles. Point to any part of the object except a sizing handle (the mouse pointer changes to a four-sided arrow), then click and drag to move the clip art.

- Save the document.

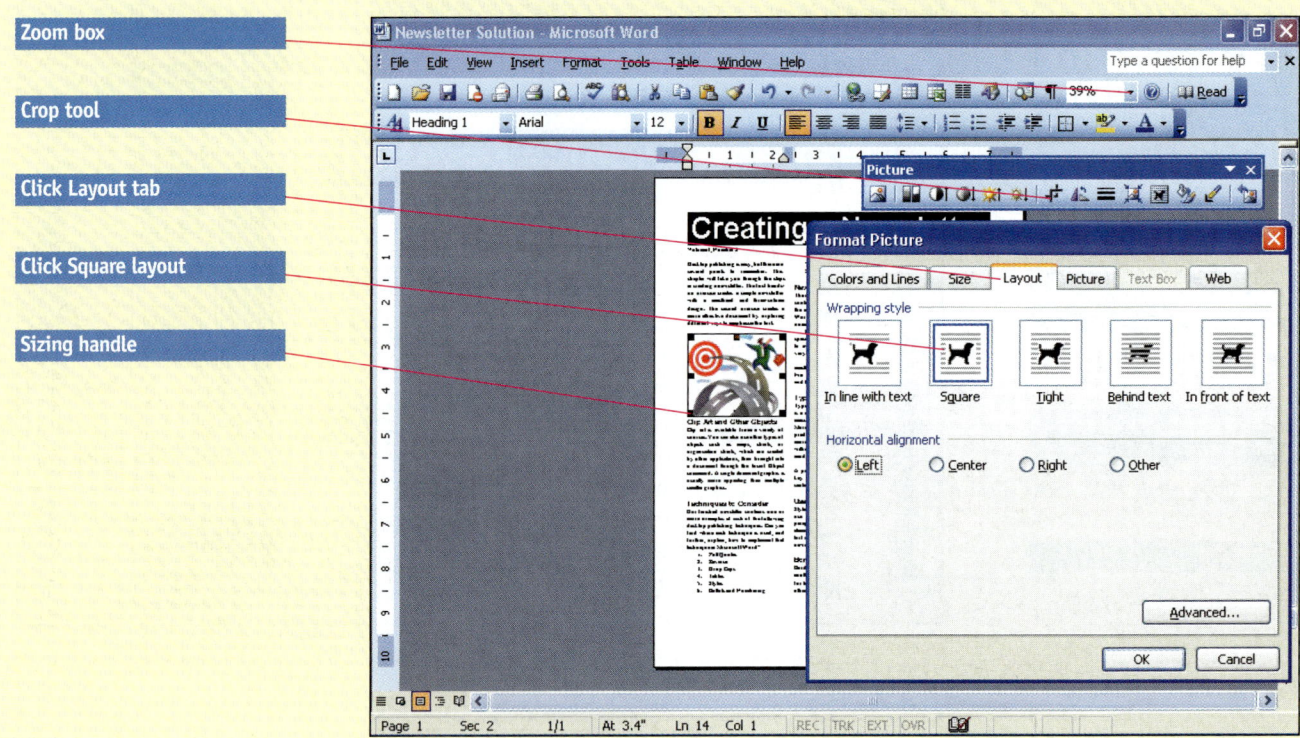

(d) Move and Size the Clip Art (step 4)

FIGURE 5.7 Hands-on Exercise 2 (*continued*)

CROPPING A PICTURE

Select a picture, and Word automatically displays the Picture toolbar, which enables you to modify the picture in subtle ways. The Crop tool enables you to eliminate (crop) part of a picture. Select the picture to display the Picture toolbar and display the sizing handles. Click the Crop tool (the ScreenTip will display the name of the tool), then click and drag a sizing handle to crop the part of the picture you want to eliminate.

Step 5: **Borders and Shading**

- Change to **Page Width** and click the **Show/Hide ¶ button** to display the paragraph marks. Press **Ctrl+End** to move to the end of the document, then select the heading and associated paragraph for Borders and Shading. (Do not select the ending paragraph mark.)

- Pull down the **Format menu**. Click **Borders and Shading**. If necessary, click the **Borders tab** to display the dialog box in Figure 5.4e. Click the **Box icon** in the Setting area. Click the **drop-down arrow** in the Width list box and select the **1 pt** line style.

- Click the **Shading tab**. Click the **drop-down arrow** in the Style list box (in the Patterns area) and select **5%** shading. Click **OK** to accept the setting.

- Click elsewhere in the document to see the results. The heading and paragraph should be enclosed in a border with light shading.

- Save the document.

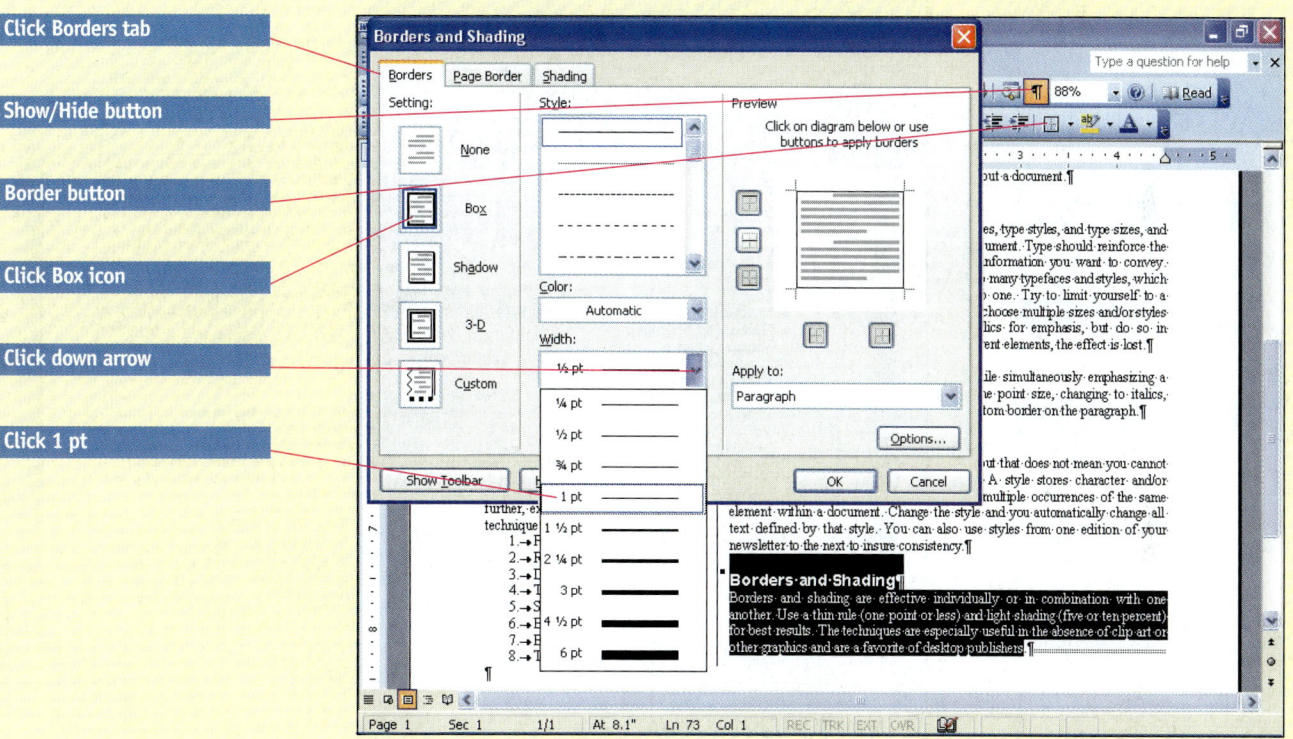

(e) Borders and Shading (step 5)

FIGURE 5.7 Hands-on Exercise 2 (*continued*)

USE THE TOOLBAR

The Border button on the Formatting toolbar changes the style of the border for the selected text. That tool is also accessible from the Tables and Borders toolbar, which contains additional tools to insert or merge cells and/or to change the line style, thickness, or shading within a table. If the toolbar is not visible, point to any visible toolbar, click the right mouse button to show the list of toolbars, then click the Tables and Borders toolbar to display it on your screen.

Step 6: **Create a Pull Quote**

- Scroll to the bottom of the document until you find the paragraph describing a pull quote. Select the entire paragraph and change the text to **14 point Arial italic**.

- Click in the paragraph to deselect the text, then click the **Center button** to center the paragraph.

- Click the **drop-down arrow** on the **Border button** to display the different border styles as shown in Figure 5.7f.

- Click the **Top Border button** to add a top border to the paragraph.

- Click the **Bottom border button** to create a bottom border and complete the pull quote.

- Save the document.

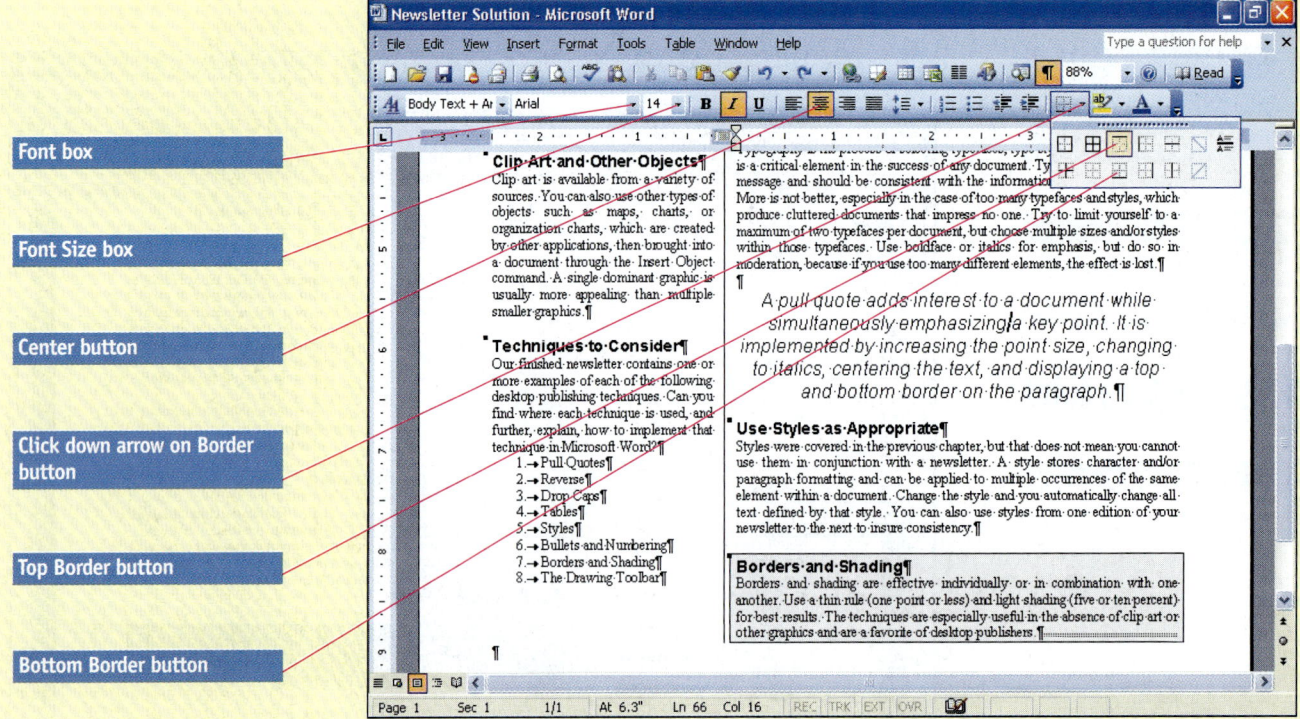

(f) Create a Pull Quote (step 6)

FIGURE 5.7 Hands-on Exercise 2 (*continued*)

EMPHASIZE WHAT'S IMPORTANT

Good design makes it easy for the reader to determine what is important. A pull quote (a phrase or sentence taken from an article) adds interest to a document while simultaneously emphasizing a key point. Boxes and shading are also effective in catching the reader's attention. A simple change in typography, such as increasing the point size, changing the typeface, and/or the use of boldface or italic, calls attention to a heading and visually separates it from the associated text.

Step 7: **Create a Drop Cap**

- Scroll to the beginning of the newsletter. Click immediately before the D in *Desktop publishing*.

- Pull down the **Format menu**. Click the **Drop Cap command** to display the dialog box in Figure 5.7g.

- Click the **Position icon** for **Dropped** as shown in the figure. We used the default settings, but you can change the font, size (lines to drop), or distance from the text by clicking the arrow on the appropriate list box.

- Click **OK** to create the Drop Cap dialog box. Click outside the frame around the drop cap.

- Save the newsletter.

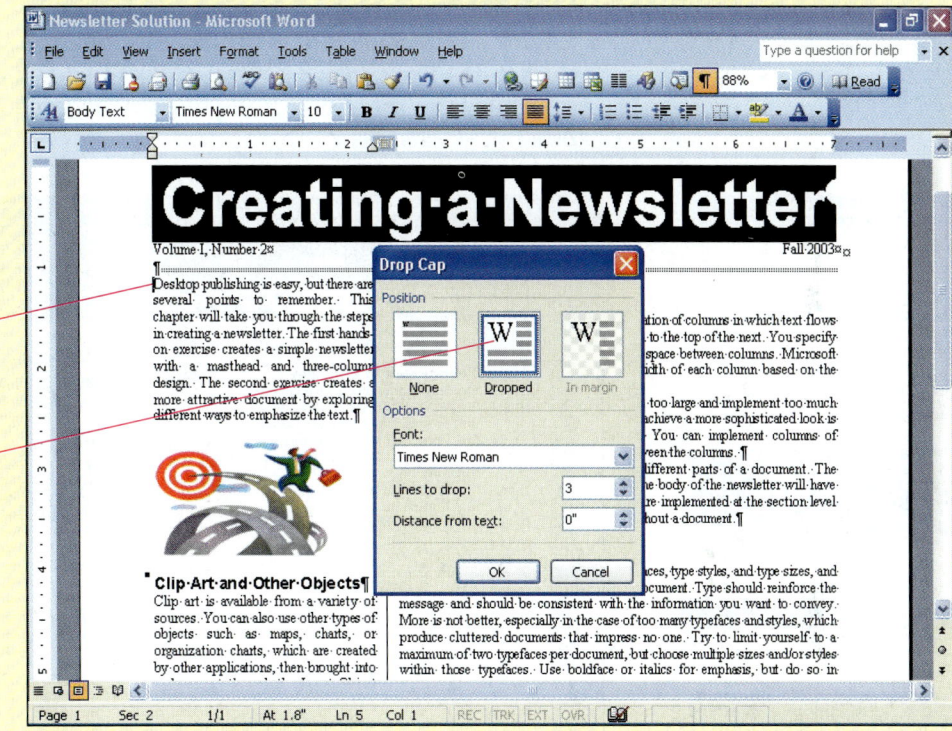

(g) Create a Drop Cap (step 7)

FIGURE 5.7 Hands-on Exercise 2 (*continued*)

> **MODIFYING A DROP CAP**
>
> Select (click) a dropped-capital letter to display a thatched border known as a frame, then click the border or frame to display its sizing handles. You can move and size a frame just as you can any other Windows object; for example, click and drag a corner sizing handle to change the size of the frame (and the drop cap it contains). Experiment with different fonts to increase the effectiveness of the dropped-capital letter, regardless of its size. To delete the frame (and remove the drop cap), press the delete key.

MICROSOFT OFFICE WORD 2003 **1089**

Step 8: **Create the AutoShape**

- Click the **Show/Hide button** to hide the nonprinting characters. Pull down the **View menu**, click (or point to) the **Toolbars command** to display the list of available toolbars, then click the **Drawing toolbar** to display this toolbar.

- Press **Ctrl+End** to move to the end of the document. Click the **down arrow** on the AutoShapes button to display the AutoShapes menu. Click the **Stars and Banners submenu** and select (click) the **Horizontal scroll**.

- Press **Esc** to remove the drawing canvas. The mouse pointer changes to a tiny crosshair. Click and drag the mouse at the bottom of the newsletter to create the scroll as shown in Figure 5.7h.

- Release the mouse. The scroll is still selected as can be seen by the sizing handles. (You can click and drag the yellow diamond to change the appearance of the scroll.)

- Click the **Line Style tool** to display this menu as shown in Figure 5.7h. Select a thicker line (we chose **3 points**). Click the **down arrow** on the **Line color tool** to display the list of colors (if you have access to a color printer. We selected **blue**).

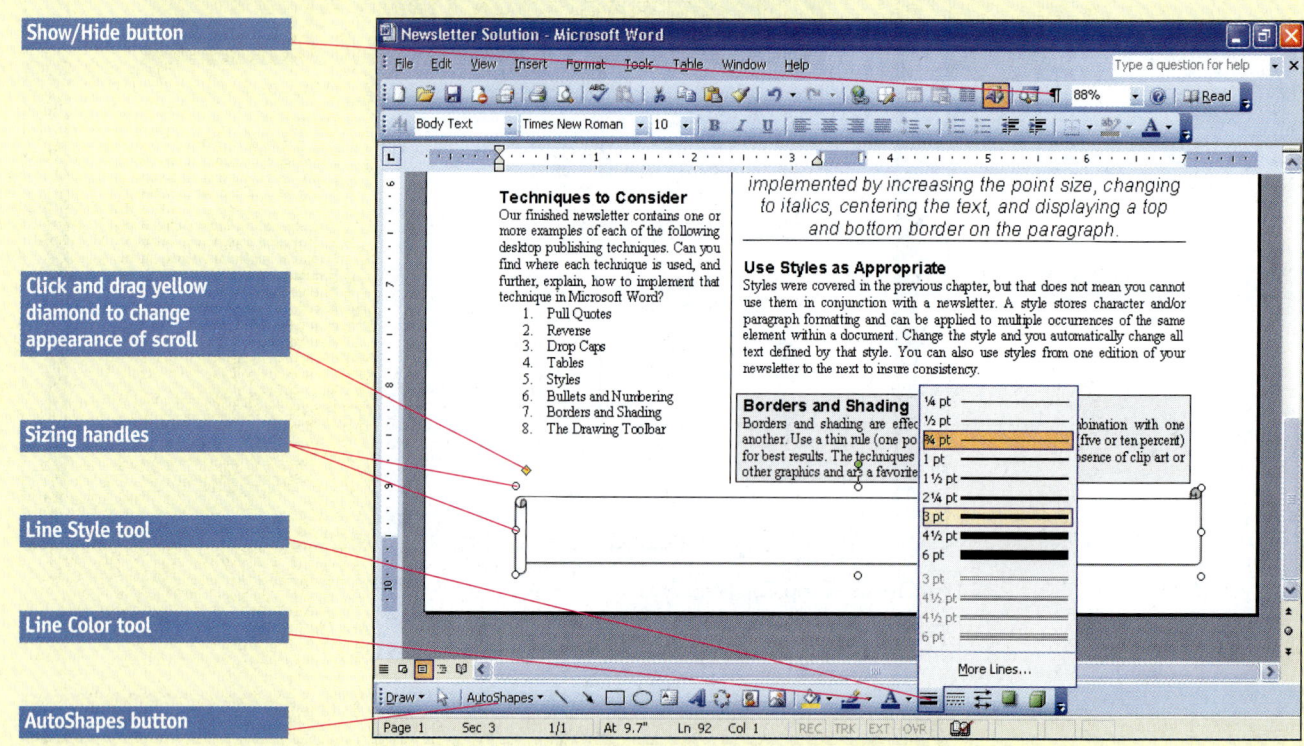

(h) Create the AutoShape (step 8)

FIGURE 5.7 Hands-on Exercise 2 (*continued*)

DISPLAY THE AUTOSHAPES TOOLBAR

Click the down arrow on the AutoShapes button on the Drawing toolbar to display a cascaded menu listing the various types of AutoShapes, then click and drag the move handle at the top of the menu to display the menu as a floating toolbar. Click any item on the AutoShapes toolbar (such as Stars and Banners), then click and drag its move handle to display the various buttons in their own floating toolbar.

Step 9: **Create the Text Box**

- Click the **Text Box tool**, then click and drag within the banner to create a text box as shown in Figure 5.7i. Type **All the News that Fits** as the text of the banner. Click the **Center button** on the Formatting toolbar.

- Click and drag to select the text, click the **down arrow** on the **Font Size list box**, and select a larger point size (22 or 24 points). If necessary, click and drag the bottom border of the text box, and/or the bottom border of the AutoShape, in order to see all of the text. Click the **down arrow** on the **Font list box** and choose a different font.

- Right click the text box to display a context-sensitive menu, then click the **Format Text Box command** to display the Format Text Box dialog box as shown in Figure 5.7i. Click the **Colors and Lines tab** (if necessary), click the **down arrow** next to Color in the Line section, click **No Line**, then click **OK** to accept the settings and close the dialog box.

- Click anywhere in the document to deselect the text box. Save the document.

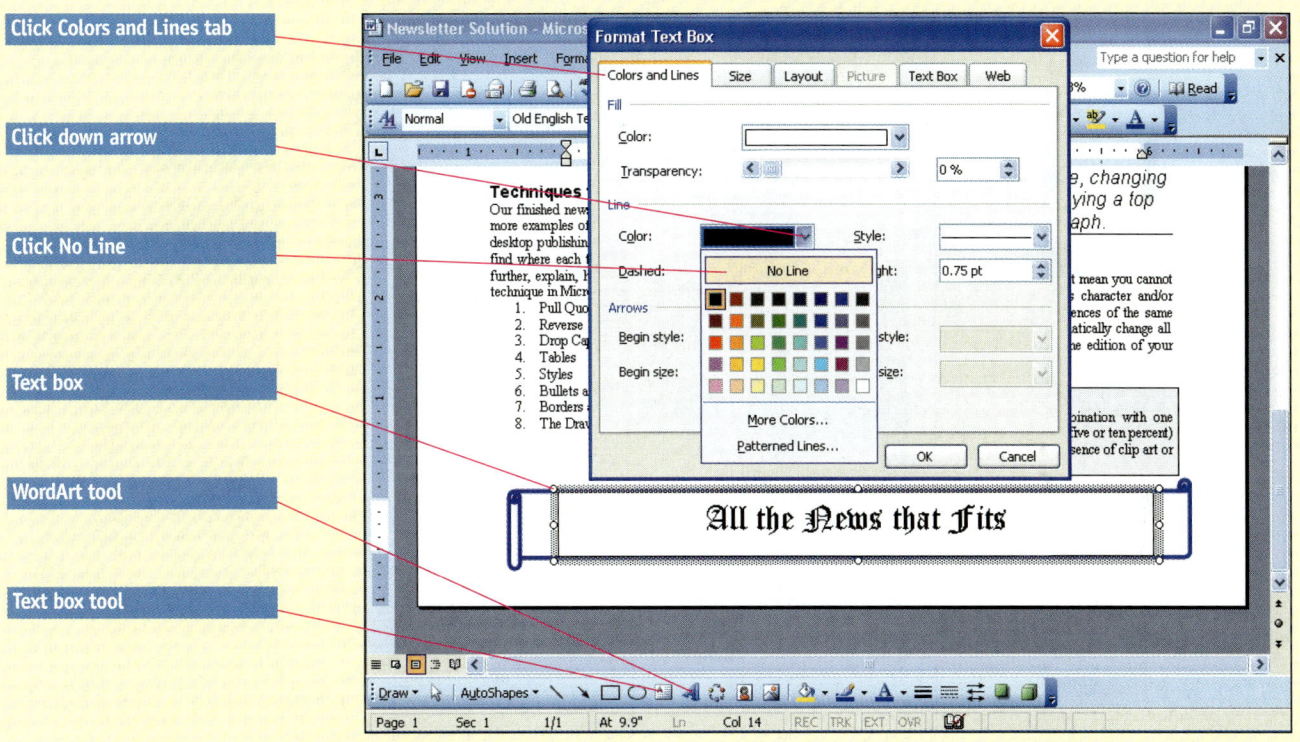

(i) Create the Text Box (step 9)

FIGURE 5.7   Hands-on Exercise 2 (*continued*)

DON'T FORGET WORDART

Microsoft WordArt is another way to create decorative text to add interest to a document. Pull down the Insert menu, click Picture, click WordArt, choose the WordArt style, and click OK. Enter the desired text, then click OK to create the WordArt object. You can click and drag the sizing handles to change the size or proportion of the text. Use any tool on the WordArt toolbar to further change the appearance of the object.

Step 10: **The Completed Newsletter**

- Zoom to **Whole Page** to view the completed newsletter as shown in Figure 5.7j.

- Select the clip art to display the Picture toolbar as shown in Figure 5.7j. Click the **Increase/Decrease Brightness tools** to see the effect on the clip art. Select the brightness level you like best.

- The newsletter should fit on a single page, but if not, there are several techniques that you can use:
    - Pull down the **File menu**, click the **Page Setup command**, click the **Margins tab**, then reduce the top and/or bottom margins to **.5** inch. Be sure to apply this change to the **Whole document** within the Page Setup dialog box.
    - Change the **Heading 1 style** to reduce the point size to **10 points** and/or the space before the heading to **6 points**.
    - Click the **Print Preview button** on the Standard toolbar, then click the **Shrink to Fit button** on the Print Preview toolbar.

- Save the document a final time. Print the completed newsletter and submit it to your instructor as proof you did this exercise.

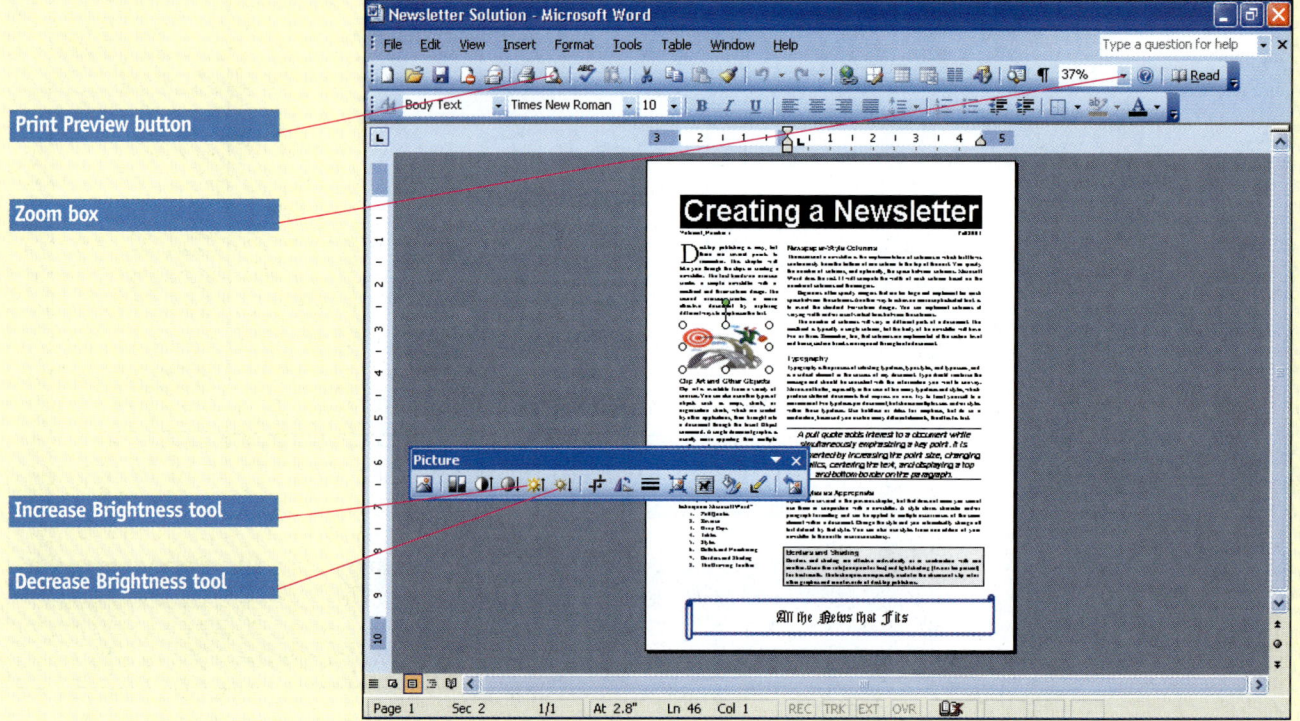

(j) The Completed Newsletter (step 10)

FIGURE 5.7 Hands-on Exercise 2 (*continued*)

A FINAL WORD OF ADVICE

Desktop publishing is not a carefree operation. It is time-consuming to implement, and you will be amazed at the effort required for even a simple document. Computers are supposed to save time, not waste it, and while desktop publishing is clearly justified for some documents, the extensive formatting is not necessary for most documents. And finally, remember that the content of a document is its most important element.

OBJECT LINKING AND EMBEDDING

Microsoft Office enables you to create documents that contain data (objects) from multiple applications. The document in Figure 5.8a, for example, was created in Microsoft Word, but it contains objects (a worksheet and a chart) that were developed in *Microsoft Excel. Object Linking and Embedding* (*OLE*, pronounced "oh-lay") is the means by which you create the document.

Every Excel chart is based on numerical data that is stored in a worksheet. Figures 5.8b and 5.8c enlarge the worksheet and chart that appear in the document of Figure 5.8a. The worksheet shows the quarterly sales for each of three regions, East, West, and North. There are 12 *data points* (four quarterly values for each of three regions). The data points are grouped into *data series* that appear as rows or columns in the worksheet. (The chart was created through the Chart Wizard that prompts you for information about the source data and the type of chart you want. Any chart can be subsequently modified by choosing appropriate commands from the Chart menu.)

The data in the chart is plotted by rows or by columns, depending on the message you want to convey. Our data is plotted by rows to emphasize the amount of sales in each quarter, as opposed to the sales in each region. Note that when the data is plotted by rows, the first row in the worksheet will appear on the X axis of the chart, and the first column will appear as the legend. Conversely, if you plot the data by columns, the first column appears on the X axis, and the first row appears as a legend.

Look closely at Figures 5.8b and 5.8c to see the correspondence between the worksheet and the chart. The data is plotted by rows. Thus there are three rows of data (three data series), corresponding to the values in the Eastern, Western, and Northern regions, respectively. The entries in the first row appear on the X axis. The entries in the first column appear as a legend to identify the value of each column in the chart. The chart is a *side-by-side column chart* that shows the value of each data point separately. You could also create a *stacked column chart* for each quarter that would put the columns one on top of another. And, as with the stacked-column chart, you have your choice of plotting the data in rows or columns.

After the chart has been created, it is brought into the Word document through Object Linking and Embedding. The essential difference between linking and embedding depends on where the object is stored. An embedded object is physically within the Word document. A *linked object*, however, is stored in its own file, which may in turn be tied to many documents. The same Excel chart, for example, can be linked to a Word document and a PowerPoint presentation or to multiple Word documents and/or to multiple presentations. Any changes to a linked object (the Excel chart) are automatically reflected in all of the documents to which it is linked. An *embedded object*, however, is stored within the Word document and it is no longer tied to its source. Thus, any changes made in the original object or in the embedded object are not reflected in one another.

EMPHASIZE YOUR MESSAGE

A graph exists to deliver a message, and you want that message to be as clear as possible. One way to help put your point across is to choose a title that leads the audience. A neutral title such as *Sales Data* does nothing and requires the audience to reach its own conclusion. A better title might be *Eastern Region Has Record 3rd Quarter* to emphasize the results in the individual sales offices. Conversely, *Western Region Has a Poor Year* conveys an entirely different message. This technique is so simple that we wonder why it isn't used more frequently.

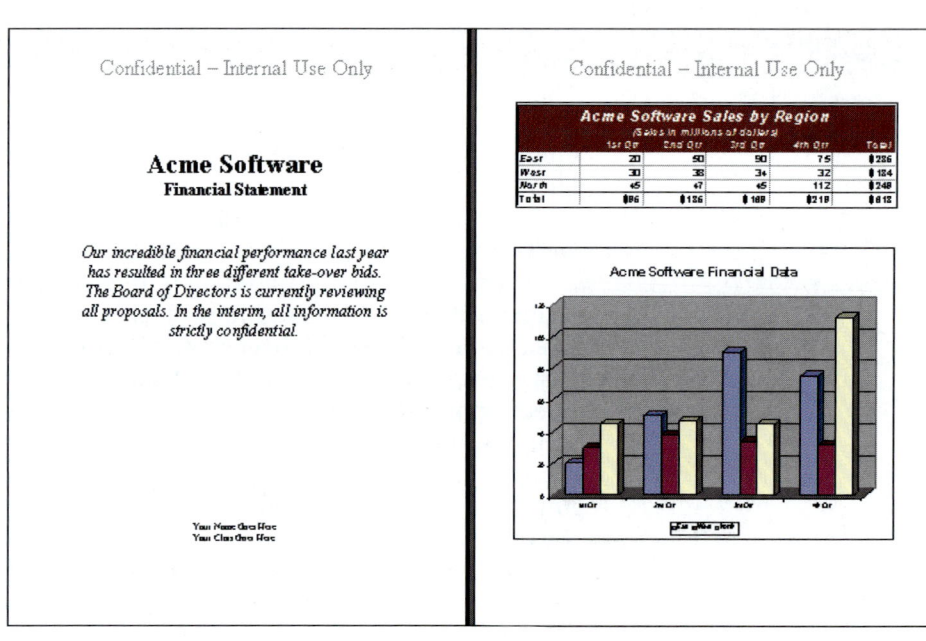

(a) The Word Document

Acme Software Sales by Region					
(Sales in millions of dollars)					
	1st Qtr	2nd Qtr	3rd Qtr	4th Qtr	Total
East	20	50	90	75	$235
West	30	38	34	32	$134
North	45	47	45	112	$249
Total	$95	$135	$169	$219	$618

(b) The Excel Worksheet

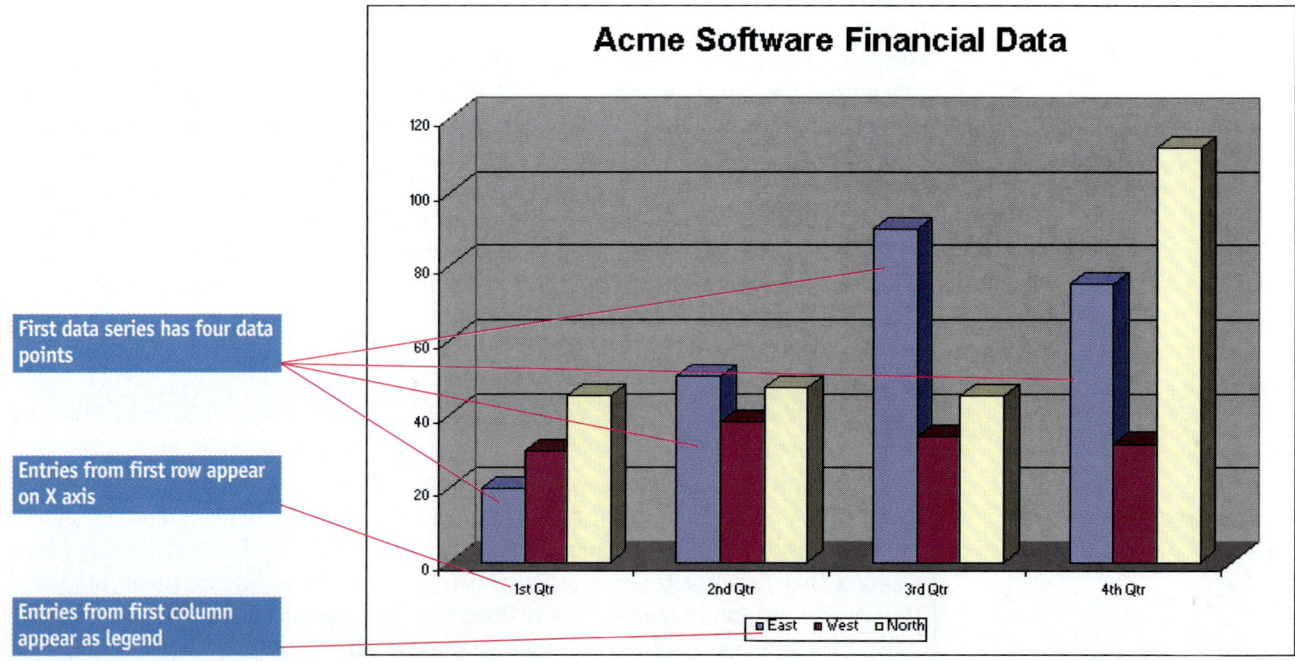

(c) Alternate Chart

FIGURE 5.8 Object Linking and Embedding

hands-on exercise

3 Object Linking and Embedding

Objective Use object linking to create a Word document that contains an Excel worksheet and an Excel chart. Use Figure 5.9 as a guide in the exercise.

Step 1: **Create the Title Page**

- Start Word. Close the task pane. If necessary, click the **New Blank Document button** on the Standard toolbar to open a new document.

- Press the **Enter key** 6 or 7 times, then enter the title of the document, **Acme Software Financial Statement**, **your name**, and the **course number** with appropriate formatting.

- Save the document as **Confidential Memo** as shown in Figure 5.9a.

- Click the **Print Layout View button** above the status bar, then click the **down arrow** on the Zoom list box and select **Two Pages**. Your document currently takes only a single page.

- Pull down the **View menu** and click the **Header and Footer command** to display the Header and Footer toolbar. The text in the document (its title, your name, and class) is dim since you are working in the header and footer area of the document.

- Click the **down arrow** on the Font Size box and change to **28 points**. Click inside the header and enter **Confidential - Internal Use Only**. Center the text.

- Click the **Close button** on the Header and Footer toolbar to close the toolbar. The header you just created is visible, but dim.

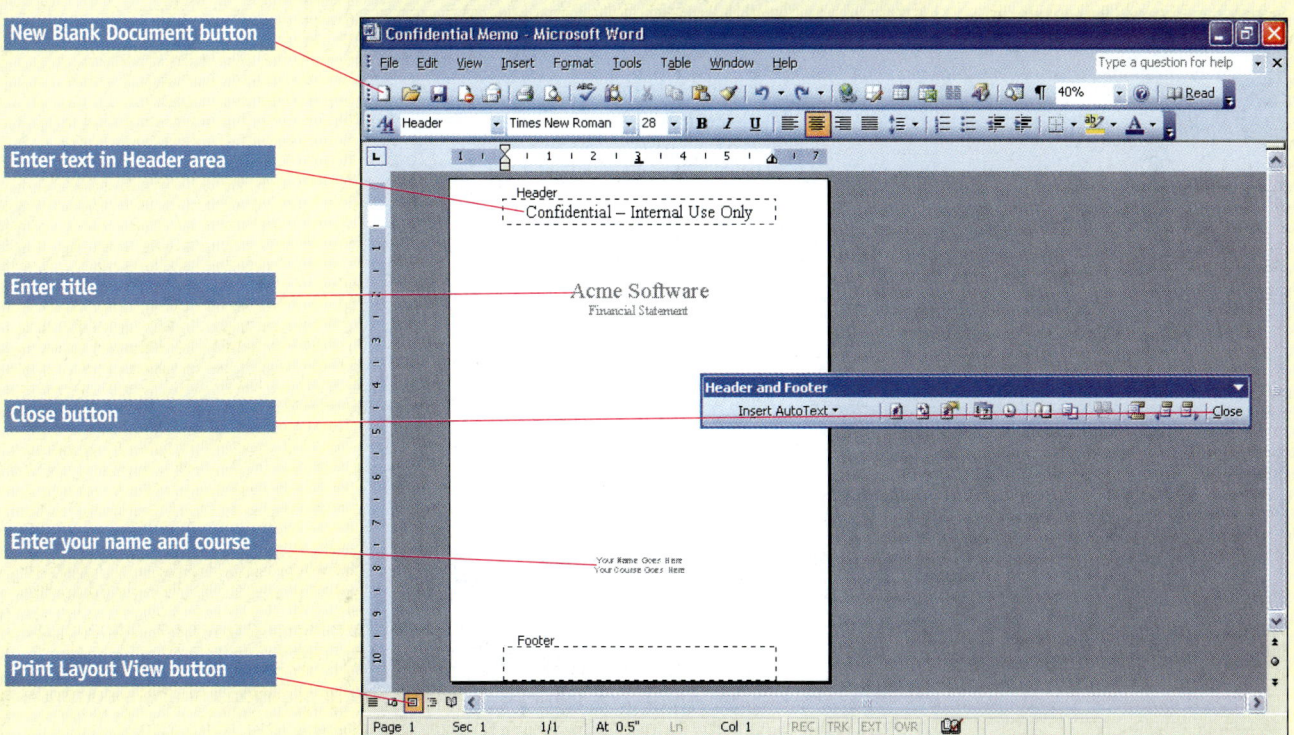

(a) Create the Title Page (step 1)

Figure 5.9 Hands-on Exercise 3

Step 2: **Copy the Worksheet**

- Click the **Start button**, click **All Programs**, click **Microsoft Office**, then click **Microsoft Office Excel 2003** to start Excel. The taskbar now contains buttons for both Word and Excel. Click either button to move back and forth between the open applications. End in Excel.

- Pull down the **File menu** and click the **Open command** (or click the **Open button** on the Standard toolbar) to display the Open dialog box.

- Click the **down arrow** on the Look in list box to select the Exploring Word folder that you have used throughout the text. Open the **Acme Software workbook**.

- Click the **Sales Data** worksheet tab. Click and drag to select **cells A1 through F7** as shown in Figure 5.9b.

- Pull down the **Edit menu** and click the **Copy command** (or click the **Copy button** on the Standard toolbar). A moving border appears around the entire worksheet, indicating that it has been copied to the clipboard.

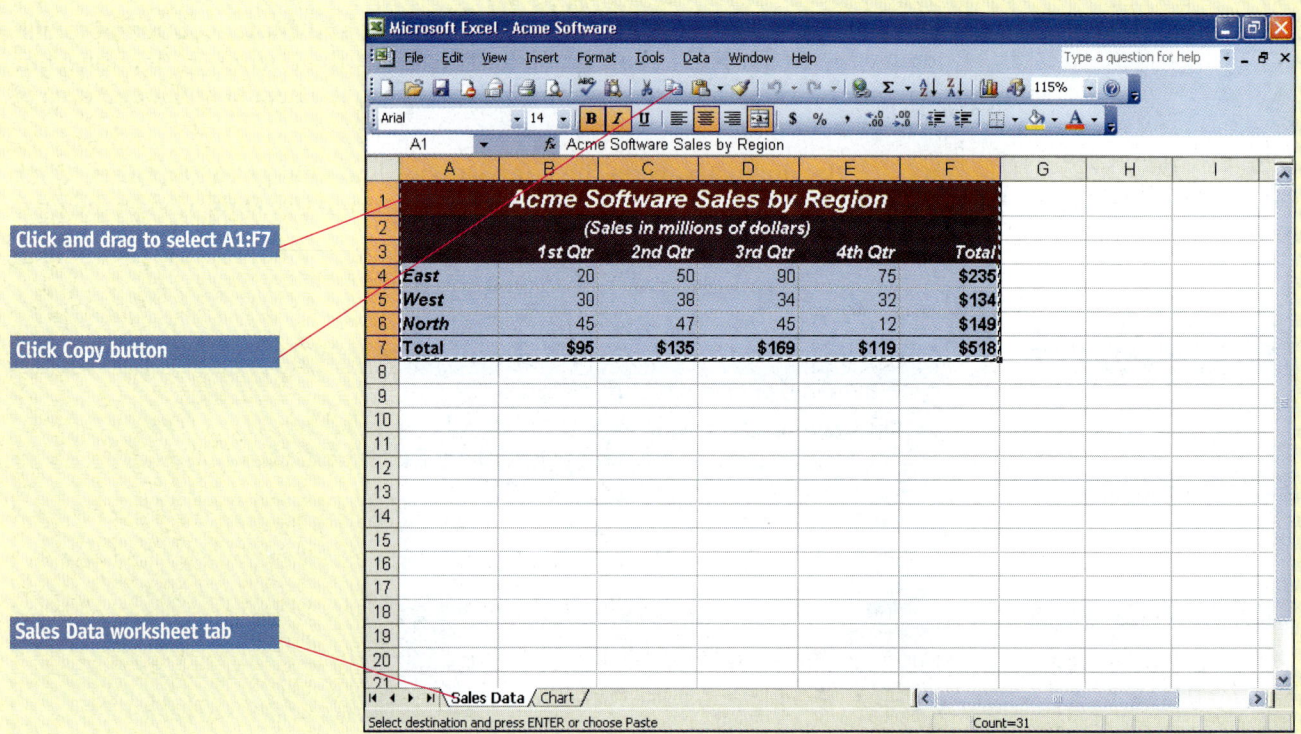

(b) Copy the Worksheet (step 2)

FIGURE 5.9 Hands-on Exercise 3 (*continued*)

THE COMMON USER INTERFACE

The common user interface provides a sense of familiarity from one Office application to the next. Even if you have never used Microsoft Excel, you will recognize many of the elements that are present in Word. The applications share a common menu structure with consistent ways to execute commands from those menus. The Standard and Formatting toolbars are present in both applications. Many keyboard shortcuts are also common; for example: Ctrl+X, Ctrl+C, and Ctrl+V to cut, copy, and paste, respectively.

Step 3: **Create the Link**

- Click the **Word button** on the taskbar to return to the document as shown in Figure 5.9c. Press **Ctrl+End** to move to the end of the document, which is where you will insert the Excel worksheet.

- Press **Ctrl+Enter** to create a page break, which adds a second page to the document. This page is blank except for the header, which appears automatically.

- Pull down the **Edit menu** and click **Paste Special** to display the dialog box in Figure 5.9c. Select **Microsoft Excel Worksheet Object**. Click the **Paste Link Option button**. Click **OK** to insert the worksheet into the document.

- Do not be concerned about the size or position of the worksheet at this time. Press the **Enter key** twice to create a blank line between the worksheet and the chart, which will be added later.

- Save the document.

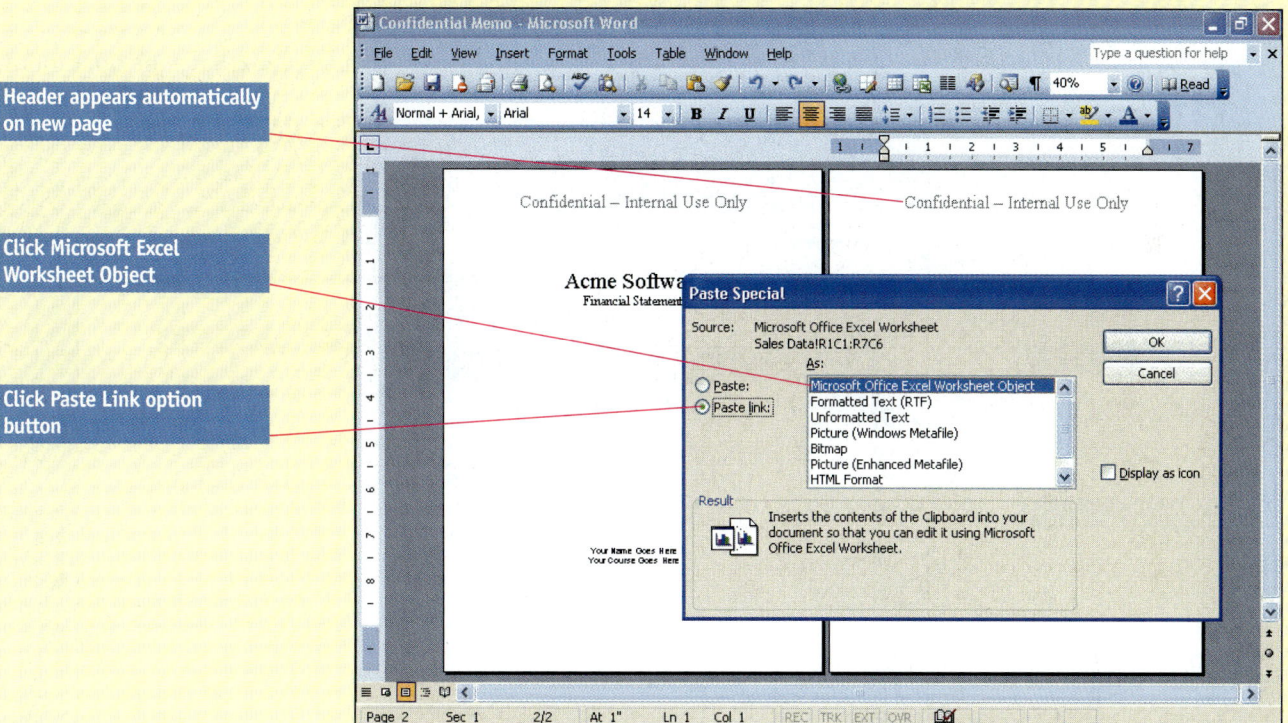

(c) Create the Link (step 3)

FIGURE 5.9 Hands-on Exercise 3 (*continued*)

THE WINDOWS TASKBAR

Multitasking, the ability to run multiple applications at the same time, is one of the primary advantages of the Windows environment. Each button on the taskbar appears automatically when its application or folder is opened and disappears upon closing. (The buttons are resized automatically according to the number of open windows.) You can customize the taskbar by right clicking an empty area to display a shortcut menu, then clicking the Properties command. You can resize the taskbar by pointing to the inside edge and then dragging when you see the double-headed arrow. You can also move the taskbar to the left or right edge, or to the top of the desktop, by dragging a blank area of the taskbar to the desired position.

Step 4: **Format the Object**

- Point to the newly inserted worksheet, click the **right mouse button** to display a context-sensitive menu, then click the **Format Object command** to display the dialog box in Figure 5.9d.

- Click the **Layout tab** and choose **Square**. Click the option button to **Center** the object. Click **OK**. You can now move and size the object.

- Select (click on) the worksheet to display its sizing handles. Click and drag a corner sizing handle to enlarge the worksheet, keeping it in its original proportions.

- Click and drag any element except a sizing handle to move the worksheet within the document.

- Right click the worksheet a second time and click the **Format Object command** to display the associated dialog box. Click the **Colors and Lines tab**, click the **drop-down arrow** next to color in the line area and choose **black**. Click the **Spin button** next to weight and choose **.25**.

- Click **OK** to accept these settings and close the dialog box. Save the document.

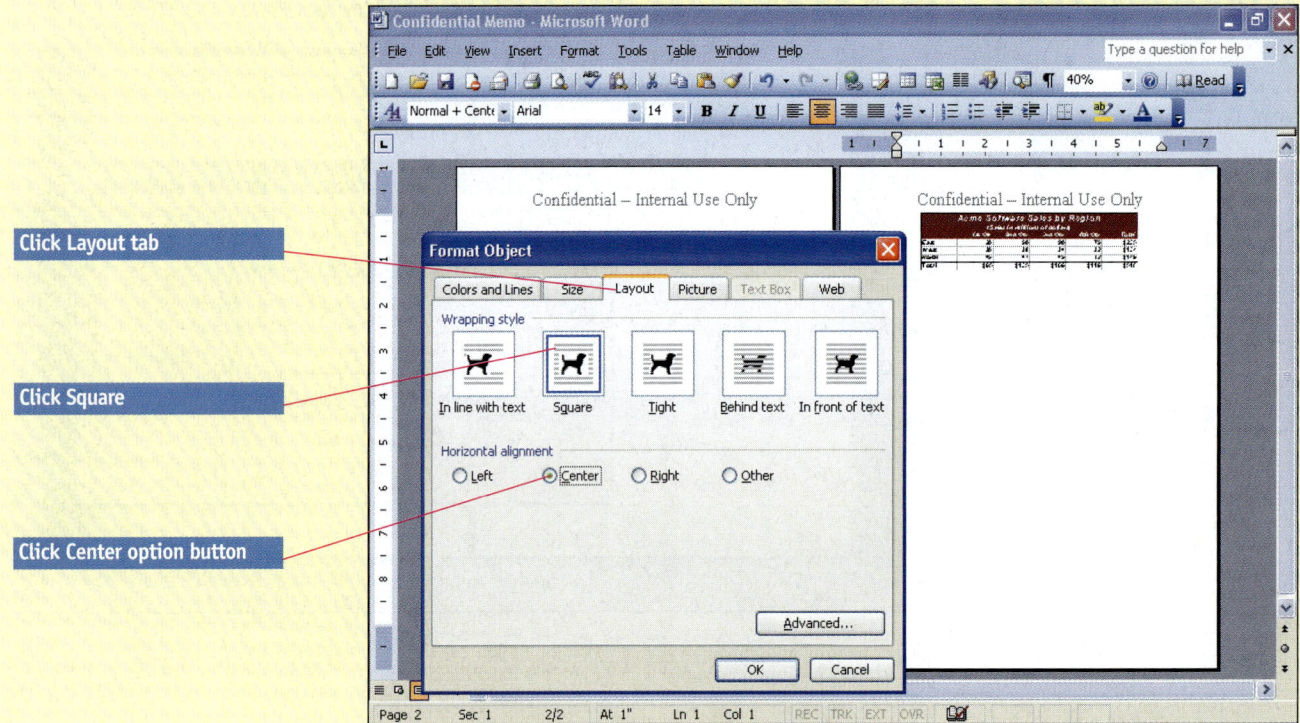

(d) Format the Object (step 4)

FIGURE 5.9 Hands-on Exercise 3 (*continued*)

TO CLICK OR DOUBLE CLICK

An Excel chart that is linked with or embedded into a Word document retains its connection to Microsoft Excel for easy editing. Click the chart to select it within the Word document, then move and size the chart just as any other object. (You can also press the Del key to delete the graph from a document.) Click outside the chart to deselect it, then double click the chart to restart Microsoft Excel (the chart is bordered by a hashed line), at which point you can edit the chart using the tools of the original application.

Step 5: **Copy the Chart**

- Click the **Excel button** on the taskbar to return to the worksheet. Click outside the selected area (cells A1 through F7) to deselect the cells.

- Click the **Chart tab** to select the chart sheet. Point just inside the white border of the chart, then click the left mouse button to select the chart. Be sure you have selected the entire chart as shown in Figure 5.9e.

- Pull down the **Edit menu** and click **Copy** (or click the **Copy button** on the Standard toolbar). Once again you see the moving border, indicating that the selected object (the chart in this example) has been copied to the clipboard.

- Click the **Word button** on the taskbar to return to the document.

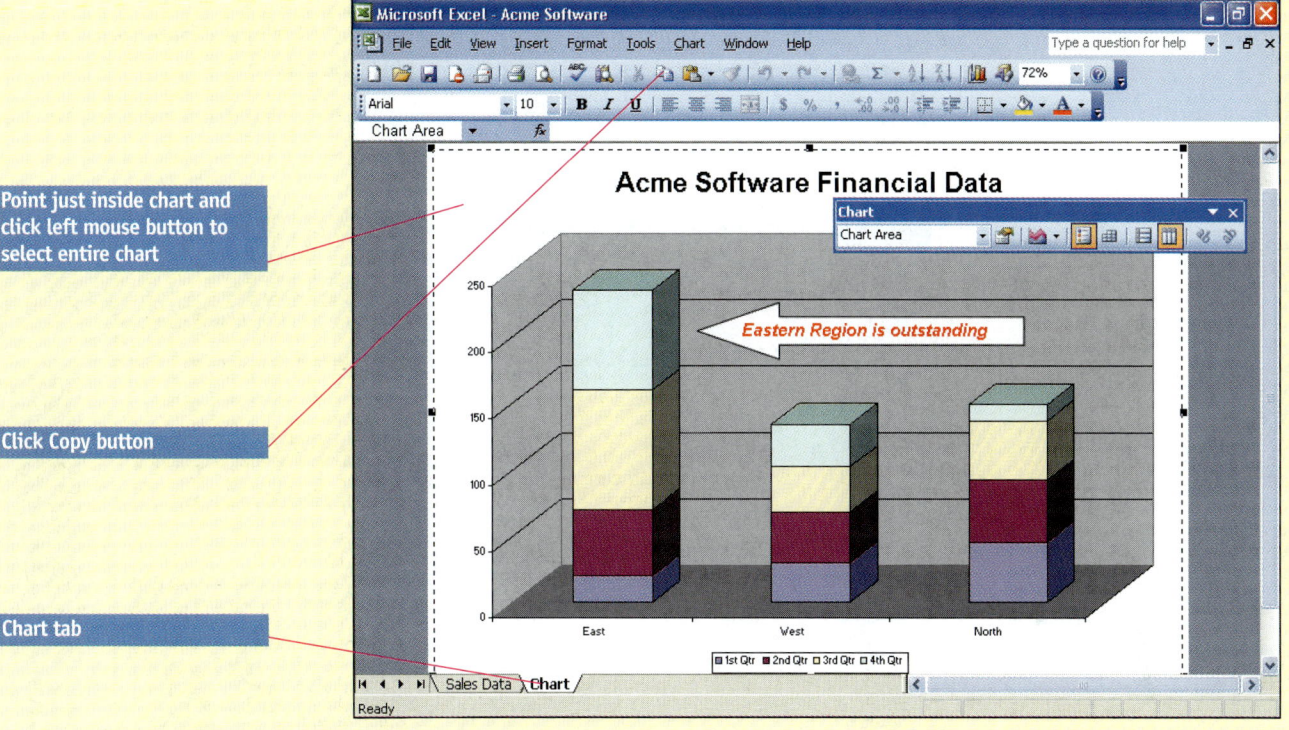

(e) Copy the Chart (step 5)

FIGURE 5.9   Hands-on Exercise 3 (*continued*)

KEEP IT SIMPLE

Microsoft Excel provides unlimited flexibility with respect to the charts it creates. You can, for example, right click any data series within a graph and click the Format Data Series command to change the color, fill pattern, or shape of a data series. There are other options, such as the 3-D View command that lets you fine-tune the graph by controlling the rotation, elevation, and other parameters. It's fun to experiment, but the best advice is to keep it simple and set a time limit, at which point the project is finished. Use the Undo command at any time to cancel your last action(s).

Step 6: Complete the Word Document

- You should be back in the Word document, where you may need to insert a few blank lines, so that the insertion point is beneath the spreadsheet. Press **Ctrl+End** to move to the end of the document, where you will insert the chart.

- Pull down the **Edit menu**, click the **Paste Special command**, and click the **Paste Link Option button**. If necessary, click **Microsoft Excel Chart Object**.

- Click **OK** to insert the chart into the document. (Do not be concerned if you do not see the entire chart.)

- Select the chart, pull down the **Format menu**, and click the **Object command**.

- Select the **Layout tab** and change the layout to **Square**. **Center** the chart. Click **OK**.

- Pull down the **Format menu** a second time and click the **Object command**. Select the **Color and Lines tab**, and add a **.25" black line**.

- Move and size the chart as shown in Figure 5.9f. Save the document. Print this version of the document for your instructor.

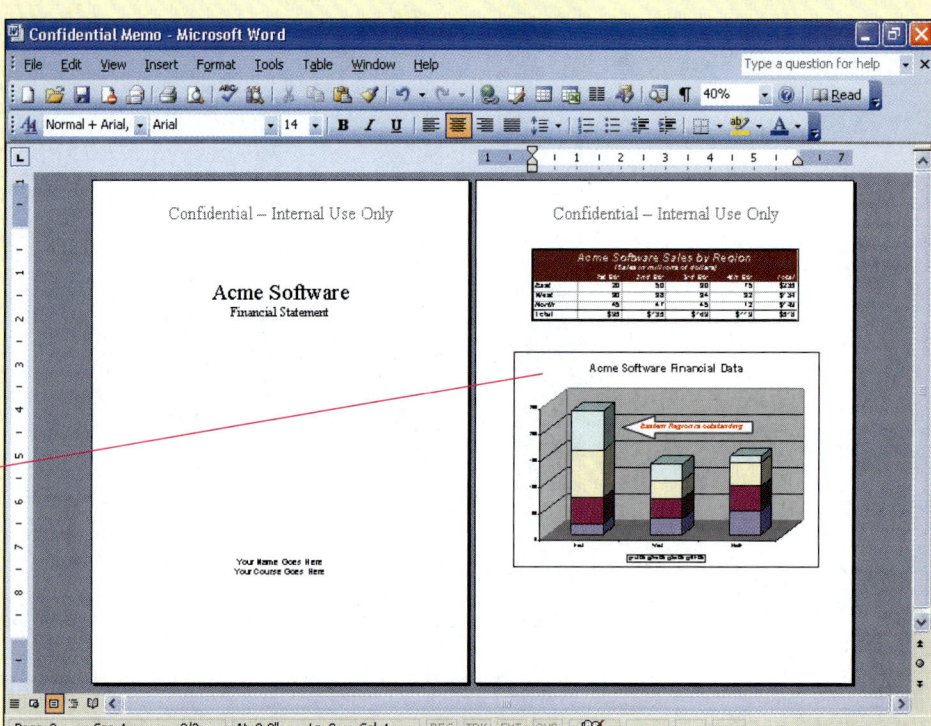

Move and size chart as shown

(f) Complete the Word Document (step 6)

FIGURE 5.9 Hands-on Exercise 3 (*continued*)

LINKING VERSUS EMBEDDING

The Paste Special command will link or embed an object, depending on whether the Paste Link or Paste Option button is checked. Linking stores a pointer to the file containing the object together with a reference to the server application, and changes to the object are automatically reflected in all documents that are linked to the object. Embedding stores a copy of the object with a reference to the server application, but changes to the object are not reflected in the document that originally contained the embedded (rather than linked) object.

Step 7: **Modify the Chart**

- Click the **Excel button** on the taskbar to return to Excel. Click the **Sales Data tab** to return to the worksheet.

- Click in **cell E6**, the cell containing the sales data for the Northern region in the fourth quarter. Type **112**, then press **Enter**. The sales totals for the region and quarter change to $249 and $219, respectively.

- Click the tab for the chart sheet. The chart has changed automatically to reflect the change in the underlying data. The columns for the Eastern and Northern regions are approximately the same size.

- Pull down the **Chart menu** and click the **Chart Type command** to display the Chart Type dialog box. Click the **Standard Types tab**. Select the **Clustered Column Chart with 3D Visual Effect** subtype (the first chart in the second row).

- Click **OK** to accept this chart type and close the dialog box. The chart type changes to side-by-side columns as shown in Figure 5.9g.

- Select the arrow on the chart. Press the **Del key** since the text is no longer applicable. Save the workbook.

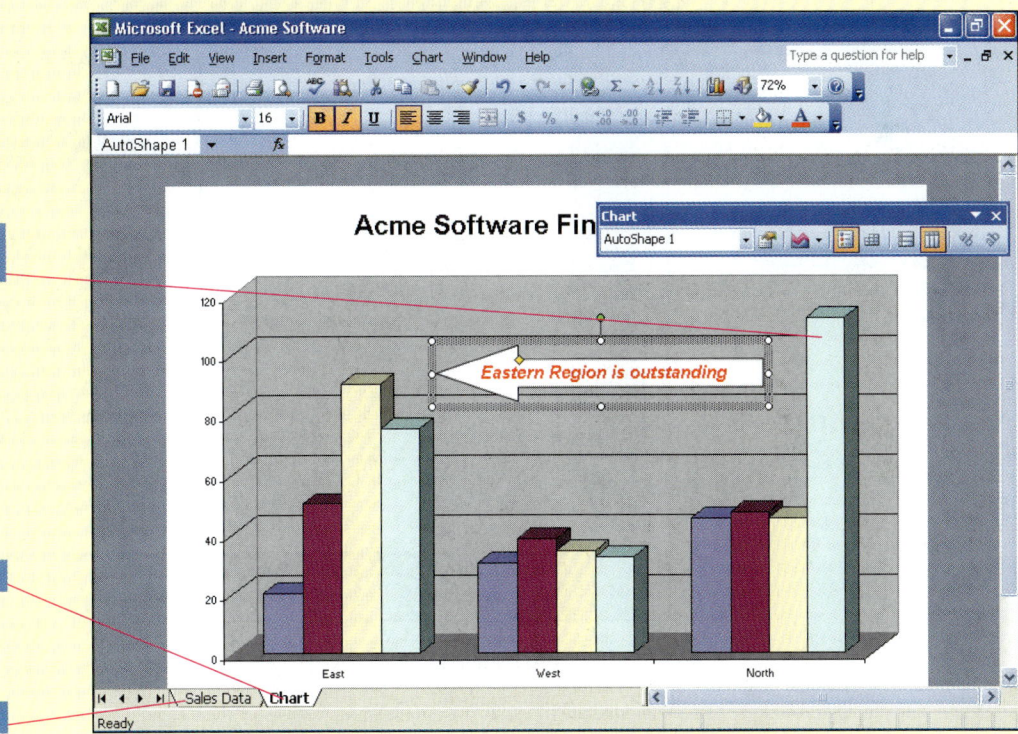

(g) Modify the Chart (step 7)

FIGURE 5.9 Hands-on Exercise 3 (*continued*)

THE DRAWING TOOLBAR

The Drawing toolbar is common to all applications in Microsoft Office. Click the down arrow next to the AutoShapes button to display the various shape menus, then click Block Arrows to display the arrows that are available. Select an arrow. The mouse pointer changes to a tiny crosshair that you click and drag to create the arrow within the document. Right click the arrow, then click the Add Text command to enter text within the arrow. Use the other buttons to change the color or other properties.

Step 8: **The Modified Document**

- Click the **Word button** on the taskbar to return to the Word document, which should automatically reflect the new chart and associated worksheet. (If this is not the case, right click the chart and click the **Update Link command**. Repeat the process to update the worksheet.)
- Move and/or resize the chart and spreadsheet within the Word document as necessary. Save the document.
- Complete the document by adding text as appropriate as shown in Figure 5.9h. You can use the text in our document that describes a confidential takeover, or make up your own.
- Save the document a final time. Click the **Print button** on the Standard toolbar to print the document for your instructor.
- Exit Word. Congratulations on a job well done.

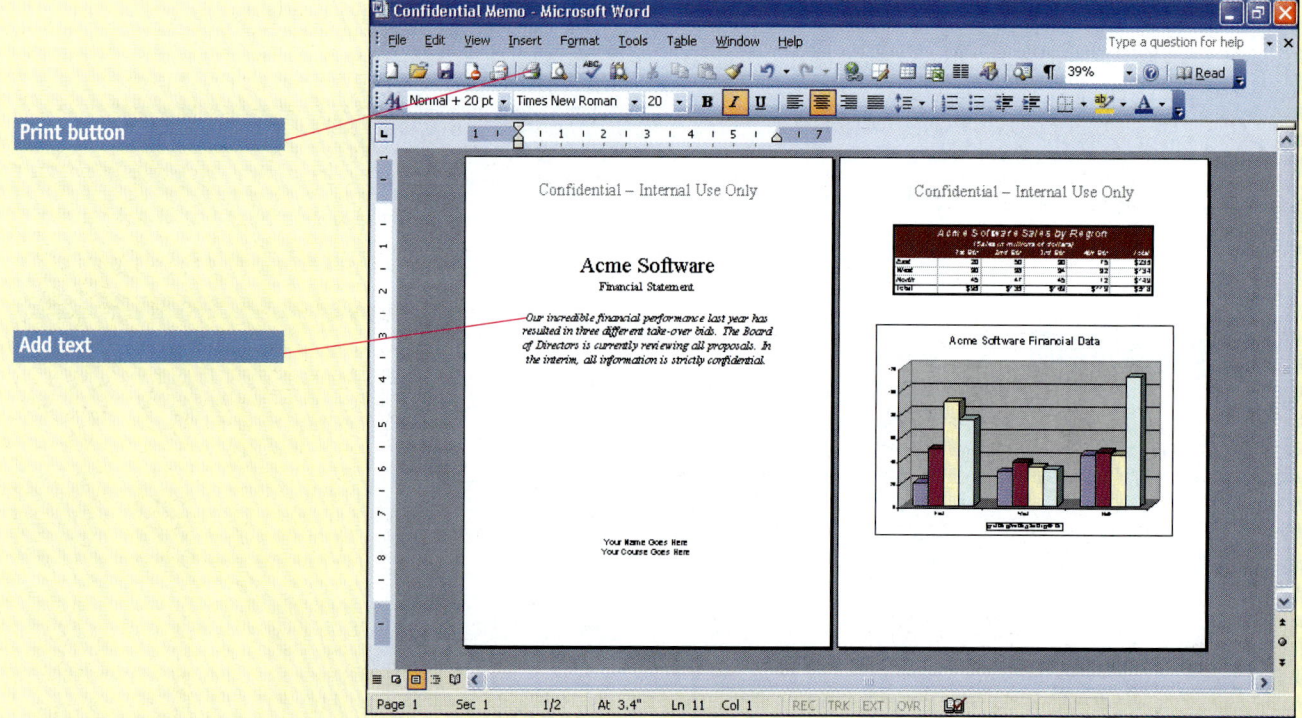

(h) The Modified Document (step 8)

FIGURE 5.9 Hands-on Exercise 3 (*continued*)

ALT+TAB STILL WORKS

Alt+Tab was a treasured shortcut in the original version of Windows that enabled users to switch back and forth between open applications. The shortcut also works in all subsequent versions of Windows. Press and hold the Alt key while you press and release the Tab key repeatedly to cycle through the open applications, whose icons are displayed in a small rectangular window in the middle of the screen. Release the Alt key when you have selected the icon for the application you want.

SUMMARY

The essence of desktop publishing is the merger of text with graphics to produce a professional-looking document. Proficiency in desktop publishing requires knowledge of the associated commands in Microsoft Word, as well as familiarity with the basics of graphic design.

Typography is the process of selecting typefaces, type styles, and type sizes. A typeface (or font) is a complete set of characters (upper- and lowercase letters, numbers, punctuation marks, and special symbols). Type size is a vertical measurement and is specified in points. One point is equal to $\frac{1}{72}$ of an inch.

The design of a document is developed on a grid, an underlying but invisible set of horizontal and vertical lines that determine the placement of the major elements. A newsletter can be divided into any number of newspaper-style columns in which text flows from the bottom of one column to the top of the next. Columns are implemented by clicking the Columns button on the Standard toolbar or by selecting the Columns command from the Format menu. Sections are required if different column arrangements are present in the same document. The Page Layout view is required to see the columns displayed side by side.

Emphasis can be achieved in several ways, the easiest being variations in type size and/or type style. Boxes and/or shading call attention to selected articles in a document. Horizontal lines are effective in separating one topic from another or calling attention to a pull quote (a phrase or sentence taken from an article to emphasize a key point). A reverse (light text on a solid background) is striking for a small amount of text.

Clip art is available from a variety of sources, including the Clip Art task pane, which is accessed through the Insert Picture command. Once clip art has been inserted into a document, it can be moved and sized just like any other Windows object. The Format Picture command provides additional flexibility and precision in the placement of an object. The Drawing toolbar contains various tools that are used to insert and/or modify objects into a Word document.

Graphic design does not have hard and fast rules, only guidelines and common sense. Creating an effective document is an iterative process and reflects the result of trial and error. We encourage you to experiment freely with different designs.

Object linking and embedding enables the creation of a document containing data (objects) from multiple applications. The essential difference between linking and embedding is whether the object is stored within the document (embedding) or stored within its own file (linking). The advantage of linking is that any changes to the linked object are automatically reflected in every document that is linked to that object.

KEY TERMS

Arial 1068	Font 1068	Reverse 1066
Borders and shading 1066	Format Picture command 1080	Sans serif typeface 1068
Bulleted list 1066	Grid 1078	Section break 1069
Clip art 1066	Linked object 1093	Serif typeface 1068
Columns command 1069	Masthead 1066	Side-by-side column chart 1093
Data points 1093	Microsoft Excel 1093	Stacked column chart 1093
Data series 1093	Monospaced typeface 1068	Times New Roman 1068
Desktop publishing 1066	Numbered list 1066	Type size 1068
Drawing toolbar 1066	Object Linking and	Typeface 1068
Dropped-capital letter 1066	Embedding (OLE) 1093	Typography 1068
Embedded object 1093	Proportional typeface 1068	
Emphasis 1080	Pull quote 1066	

MULTIPLE CHOICE

1. Which of the following is a commonly accepted guideline in typography?
   (a) Use a serif typeface for headings and a sans serif typeface for text
   (b) Use a sans serif typeface for headings and a serif typeface for text
   (c) Use a sans serif typeface for both headings and text
   (d) Use a serif typeface for both headings and text

2. According to the guidelines in the chapter, which of the following is most appropriate for the masthead of a newsletter?
   (a) A serif font at 45 points
   (b) A sans serif font at 45 points
   (c) A serif font in 12 point bold italics
   (d) A sans serif font in 12 point bold italics

3. What is the width of each column in a document with two uniform columns, given 1¼-inch margins and ½-inch spacing between the columns?
   (a) 2½ inches
   (b) 2¾ inches
   (c) 3 inches
   (d) Impossible to determine

4. What is the minimum number of sections in a three-column newsletter whose masthead extends across all three columns, with text *balanced* in all three columns?
   (a) One
   (b) Two
   (c) Three
   (d) Four

5. Which of the following describes the Arial and Times New Roman fonts?
   (a) Arial is a sans serif font, Times New Roman is a serif font
   (b) Arial is a serif font, Times New Roman is a sans serif font
   (c) Both are serif fonts
   (d) Both are sans serif fonts

6. How do you balance the columns in a newsletter so that each column contains the same amount of text?
   (a) Check the Balance Columns box in the Format Columns command
   (b) Visually determine where the break should go, then insert a column break at the appropriate place
   (c) Insert a continuous section break at the end of the last column
   (d) All of the above

7. What is the effect of dragging one of the four corner handles on a selected object?
   (a) The length of the object is changed but the width remains constant
   (b) The width of the object is changed but the length remains constant
   (c) The length and width of the object are changed in proportion to one another
   (d) Neither the length nor width of the object is changed

8. Which type size is the most reasonable for columns of text, such as those appearing in the newsletter created in the chapter?
   (a) 6 point
   (b) 10 point
   (c) 14 point
   (d) 18 point

9. A grid is applicable to the design of:
   (a) Documents with one, two, or three columns and moderate clip art
   (b) Documents with four or more columns and no clip art
   (c) Both (a) and (b)
   (d) Neither (a) nor (b)

10. Which of the following can be used to add emphasis to a document?
    (a) Borders and shading
    (b) Pull quotes and reverses
    (c) Both (a) and (b)
    (d) Neither (a) nor (b)

...continued

multiple choice

11. Which of the following is a recommended guideline in the design of a typical newsletter?
    - (a) Use at least three different clip art images in every newsletter
    - (b) Use at least three different typefaces in a document to maintain interest
    - (c) Use the same type size for the heading and text of an article
    - (d) None of the above

12. Which of the following is implemented at the section level?
    - (a) Columns
    - (b) Margins
    - (c) Both (a) and (b)
    - (d) Neither (a) nor (b)

13. How do you size an object so that it maintains the original proportion between height and width?
    - (a) Drag a sizing handle on the left or right side of the object to change its width, then drag a sizing handle on the top or bottom edge to change the height
    - (b) Drag a sizing handle on any of the corners
    - (c) Both (a) and (b)
    - (d) Neither (a) nor (b)

14. A reverse is implemented:
    - (a) By selecting 100% shading in the Borders and Shading command
    - (b) By changing the Font color to black
    - (c) Both (a) and (b)
    - (d) Neither (a) nor (b)

15. The Format Picture command enables you to:
    - (a) Change the way in which text is wrapped around a figure
    - (b) Change the size of a figure
    - (c) Place a border around a figure
    - (d) All of the above

16. Which of the following should be *avoided* according to the guidelines presented in the chapter?
    - (a) Large amounts of white space in the middle of a page
    - (b) A reverse (light text on a dark background) in the masthead of a newsletter
    - (c) A pull quote in the body of a newsletter
    - (d) Mixing a serif and a sans serif font in the same document

17. Which of the following techniques were used to create the pull quote developed in the chapter?
    - (a) Placing a horizontal line above and below the selected text
    - (b) Using a larger font than the surrounding paragraphs
    - (c) Setting the selected text in Italics
    - (d) All of the above

18. Which of the following is a recommended guideline in the design of a document?
    - (a) Use as many fonts as possible to make the page more interesting
    - (b) Use the same type size for the heading and text of an article
    - (c) Avoid borders and shading since both techniques tend to be distracting
    - (d) None of the above

ANSWERS

1. b
2. b
3. b
4. c
5. a
6. c
7. c
8. b
9. c
10. c
11. d
12. c
13. b
14. a
15. d
16. a
17. d
18. d

PRACTICE WITH WORD

1. **Study Tips:** Create a simple newsletter similar to the document in Figure 5.10. There is no requirement to write meaningful text, but the headings in the newsletter should follow the theme of the document. The intent of this problem is simply to provide practice in graphic design. Proceed as follows:

    a. Choose a topic for your newsletter, such as "Study Tips". Develop an overall design away from the computer; that is, with pencil and paper. Use a grid to indicate the placement of the articles, headings, clip art, and masthead. You may be surprised to find that it is easier to master commands in Word than it is to design the newsletter; do not, however, underestimate the importance of graphic design in the ultimate success of your document.

    b. Use meaningful headings that are consistent with the theme of your newsletter to give the document a sense of realism. The text under each heading can be a single sentence that repeats indefinitely to take up the allotted space. Your eye is the best judge of all, and you may need to decrease the default spacing between columns and/or change the type size to create an appealing document.

    c. Insert clip art to add interest to your document, then write one or two sentences in support of the clip art. Use the clip art within Microsoft Office or any other clip art you have available. You can also download pictures from the Web, but be sure to credit the source. The image you choose should be related to the theme. (A single dominant image is generally preferable to multiple pictures.)

    d. More is not better; that is, do not use too many fonts, styles, sizes, or clip art images just because they are available. Don't crowd the page, and remember white space is a very effective design element. There are no substitutes for simplicity and good taste.

    e. Submit the completed newsletter to your instructor for inclusion in a class contest. Your instructor may want to select the five best designs as semifinalists and let the class vote on the overall winner. You learn by observing good design.

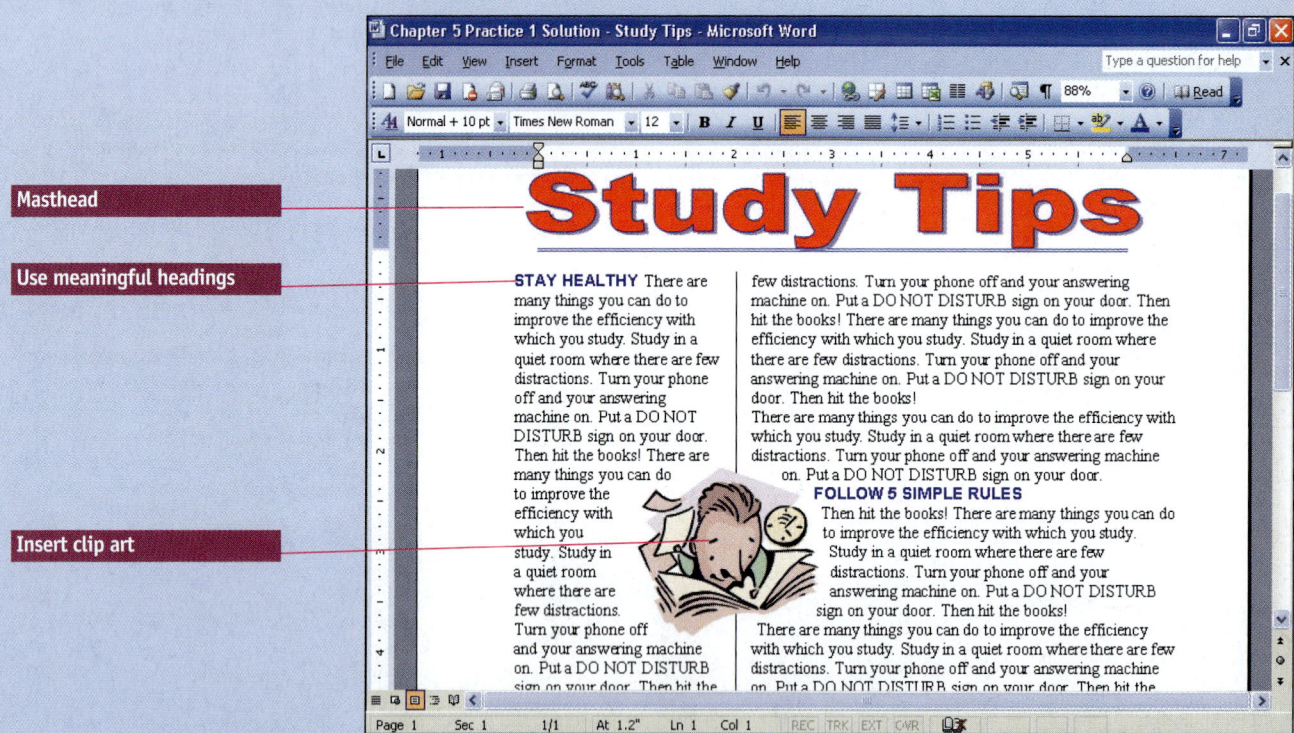

FIGURE 5.10 Study Tips (exercise 1)

practice exercises

2. **A Guide to Smart Shopping:** This problem is more challenging than the previous exercise in that you are asked to consider content as well as design. The objective is to develop a one- (or two-) page document with helpful tips to the novice on buying a computer, as shown in Figure 5.11. We have, however, written the copy for you. Your task is to create an attractive document from our text.

   a. Open and print the *Chapter 5 Practice 2* document in the Exploring Word folder, which takes approximately a page and a half as presently formatted.

   b. Read our text and determine the tips you want to retain and those you want to delete. Add other tips as you see fit. Did you learn anything about buying a computer? The two most important (and least known) tips are to use a major credit card to double the warranty and to insist on 30-day price protection.

   c. Examine the available clip art through the Insert Picture command. There is no requirement, however, to include a graphic; that is, you should use clip art only if you think it will enhance the document.

   d. Use an imaginary grid to develop a rough sketch of the document showing the masthead, the placement of the text, and clip art if any. Do this away from the computer.

   e. Implement your design in Microsoft Word. Try to create a balanced publication, which completely fills the space allotted; that is, your document should take exactly one or two pages (rather than the page and a half in the original document on the data disk). You can adjust the margins, space between columns, and/or type sizes to achieve this result. Inclusion (omission) of a pull quote is another way to change the amount of space that is required.

   f. Complete the final formatting of the document by experimenting with different fonts, styles, and/or point sizes. Set a time limit and stick to it!

   g. Use the AutoSummarize tool to create an executive summary for your document. Pull down the Tools menu and click the AutoSummarize command to display the associated dialog box. Choose the type of summary you want, such as Highlight Key Points, and then click OK. Use the AutoSummary toolbar to change the level of detail and/or use the Highlighting tool to fine-tune the summary. (Select 0% to remove all of the highlighting.)

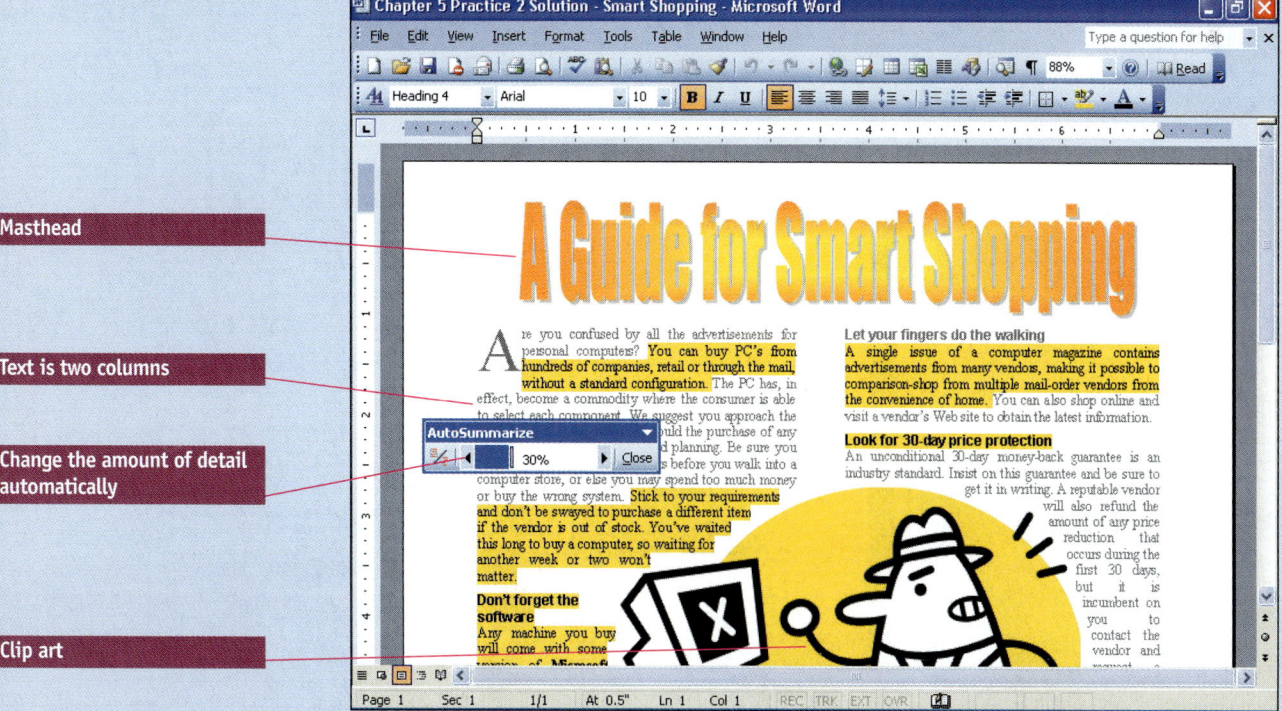

FIGURE 5.11 A Guide to Smart Shopping (exercise 2)

practice exercises

3. **The Equation Editor:** Microsoft Office includes several shared applications, each of which creates an object that can be inserted into a Word document. Microsoft WordArt and the Equation Editor are two such applications, and both are illustrated in Figure 5.12. Proceed as follows:

   a. Start a new document. Pull down the Insert menu, click the Picture command, then click the WordArt command to create the title for your document. Move and size the WordArt just as you would any other object, then use the WordArt toolbar to change its shape, fill color, and so on. Use the Format WordArt command to change the wrapping style to square.

   b. Click underneath the WordArt object and pull down the Insert menu. Click the Object command, click the Create New tab, select Microsoft Equation 3.0 as the object type, then click OK to start the Equation Editor. The Equation Editor will start and you will see the Drawing Canvas where you create the equation. It will be a trial-and-error process, but you can do it. Do not be intimidated by the Equation toolbar, even if you are not mathematically inclined. You can point to any symbol on the toolbar to see a ToolTip describing the symbol.

   c. Type the portion of the equation that does not require any special symbols ($x = -b$). Click the Operator Symbols icon to display a palette of available symbols, and then click the plus or minus sign to insert the symbol.

   d. Type the letter b, click the Subscript and Superscript tool, choose superscript, and enter 2 to display b^2. Click to the right of the superscripted 2, and then continue to develop the equation by typing $-4ac$. Select the expression $b^2 - 4ac$. Choose the Fraction and Radical templates tool to select the square root symbol.

   e. Complete the equation by selecting the entire entry, then select the Fraction and Radical templates tool once more to select the dividing symbol, then enter the denominator ($2a$). Click outside the drawing canvas to exit the Equation Editor and return to the Word document. The completed equation is a regular object that can be moved and sized within the document. You can also double click the equation to restart the Equation Editor to modify the equation.

   f. Add two or three sentences below the equation and submit the completed document.

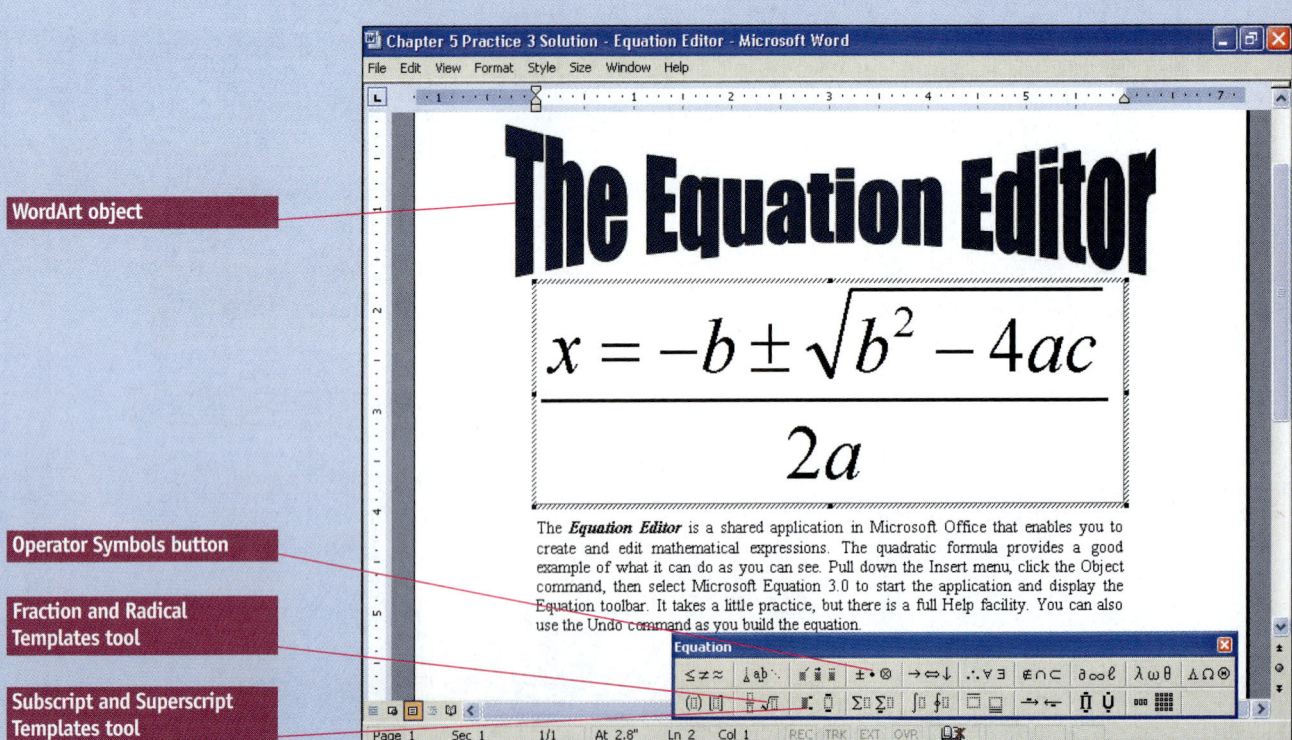

FIGURE 5.12 The Equation Editor (exercise 3)

practice exercises

4. **The Roth IRA:** Retirement is years away, but it is never too soon to start planning. Most corporations include some type of retirement contribution in their benefits package and/or you can supplement that money through an individual retirement account (IRA). The document in Figure 5.13 shows the results of careful planning and a conservative rate of return (starting at 4%). The key to successful saving is to begin as early as possible. Proceed as follows:

   a. Open the *Chapter 5 Practice 4* document that contains the text of the memo in Figure 5.13. Create an appropriate letterhead and substitute your name as the addressee. Apply basic formatting to the document. Insert an appropriate piece of clip art at the top of the document.

   b. Start Excel. Open the *Chapter 5 Practice 4* workbook that is found in the Exploring Word folder. Change the parameters that appear in the yellow cells at the bottom of the worksheet as you see fit. Experiment with different values, especially the number of years contributing. Our illustration goes out to 45 years, which enables an individual to begin saving at 20, assuming a retirement age of 65. Choose a conservative, but realistic, rate of interest. Anything over 8% should be considered as "irrational exuberance".

   c. Save the workbook. Select cells A1 through E11 and then link the worksheet to your Word document. Format the document appropriately. Add your name somewhere in the document and then print it for your instructor.

   d. Return to Excel and change one or more of the inputs to the worksheet. Save the modified worksheet, then return to the Word document, which should reflect these changes. Print this version of the document also.

   e. Use the PMT function in Excel to compute the monthly payment that is generated by your nest egg. What are the required parameters for the PMT function?

   f. Use your favorite search engine to learn more about a Roth IRA. How does this type of account different from an ordinary IRA (Individual Retirement Account)? How do both accounts differ from a 401K plan?

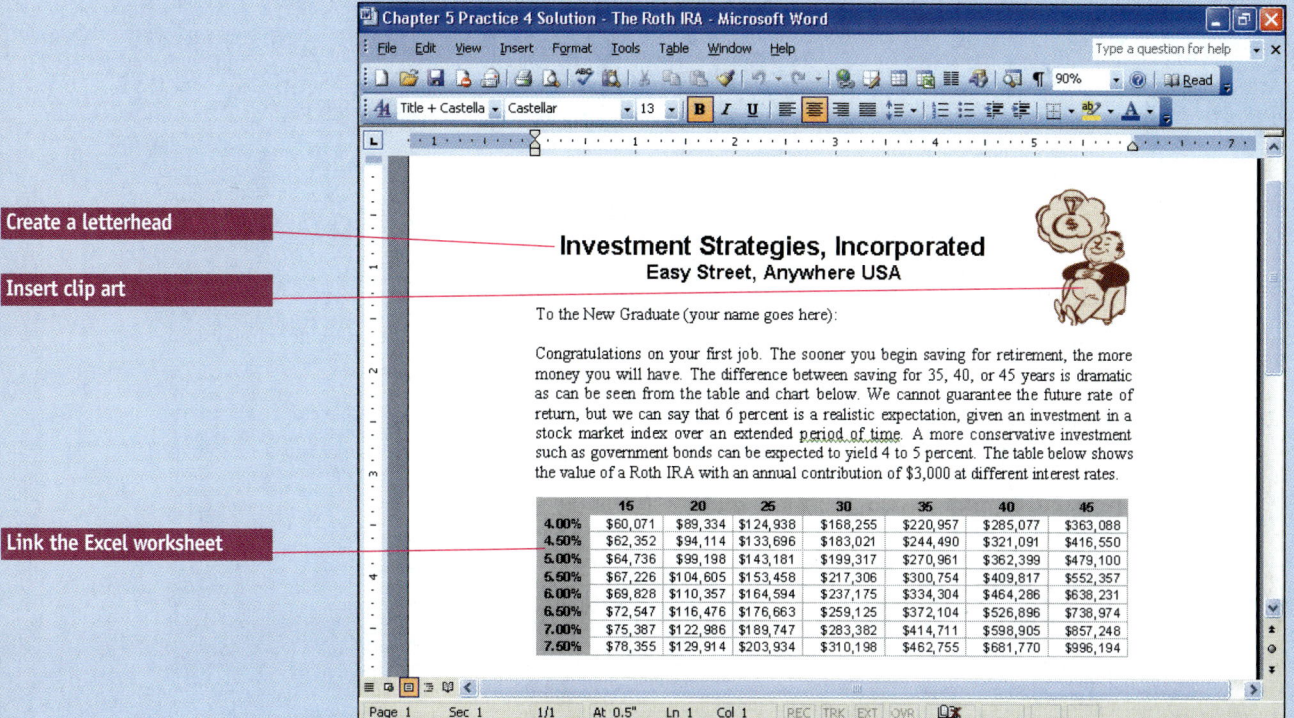

FIGURE 5.13   The Roth IRA (exercise 4)

practice exercises

5. **My Favorite Car:** The document in Figure 5.14 consists of descriptive text, a photograph, and an Excel worksheet to compute a car payment. We have created the spreadsheet for you, but you will have to obtain the other information. Proceed as follows:

   a. Choose any vehicle you like, then go to the Web to locate a picture of your vehicle together with descriptive material. *Be sure to credit your source in the completed document.* Start a new Word document. Enter a title for the document and the descriptive information. Do not worry about the precise formatting at this time.

   b. You can insert the photograph in conventional fashion, or you can set it in the background as a watermark. Pull down the Format menu, click Background, and then click Printed Watermark to display the associated dialog box. Select the option for Picture Watermark, click the Select Picture button, and insert the picture of your car as shown in Figure 5.14. (If necessary, pull down the View menu and click the Header and Footer command to change the size and/or position of the watermark.)

   c. Open the *Chapter 5 Practice 5* workbook that is found in the Exploring Word folder. Enter the information for your vehicle in cells B3, B4, B5, B7, and B8. (The amount to finance is computed automatically based on the price, rebate, and down payment.) The monthly payment will be computed automatically, based on the amount you are borrowing, the interest rate, and the term of your loan. Save the workbook.

   d. Click and drag to select cells A1:B9 within the worksheet, return to Word, and use object linking and embedding to link the worksheet to the document. Move and size the various objects as necessary to complete the document. (Right click the picture of the automobile to display a context-sensitive menu, click the Format Object command, click the Layout tab, and choose Square Layout as the wrapping style. Repeat this process for the worksheet.)

   e. Return to the Excel workbook, change one or more parameters for the car loan, then return to the Word document. If necessary, right click the worksheet, then click Update Link to see the new payment in the Word document.

   f. Add your name somewhere in the document and submit the completed document to your instructor.

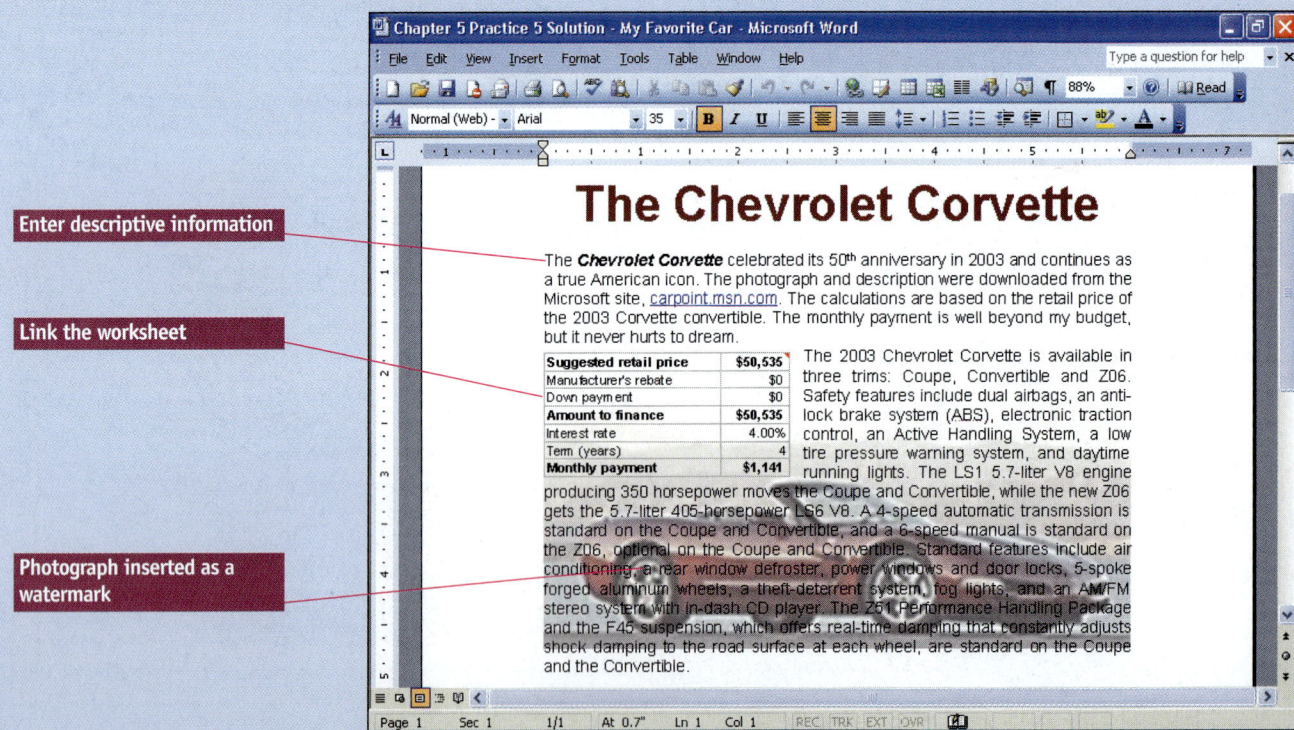

FIGURE 5.14 My Favorite Car (exercise 5)

practice exercises

6. **Exploring Templates:** This chapter described how to create a newsletter and other documents. You don't have to continually reinvent the wheel, however, but can take advantage of several templates that are provided by Microsoft. A template is a partially completed document that specifies the overall design of the document including formatting, but it does not contain specific text. The installation of Microsoft Office stores several templates locally, with additional templates available on the Microsoft Web site. Proceed as follows:

   a. Start Word and close any open document. Pull down the View menu, click the Task Pane command, and then click the down arrow in the task pane to select the New Document task pane. In the Templates section, click the link to On my computer to open the Templates dialog box as shown in Figure 5.15.

   b. Click the Publications tab and change to the Details view. (You may see a different set of templates from those in our figure.) Select the Manual template, and click OK. A new document is started that is based on the selected template. Print the document for your instructor.

   c. Save the document that you just created. What is the default name? How would you save the document under a different name? How many pages are in the document? Is the document easy to modify? Would you create a manual based on this template or would you prefer to create the document from scratch? Close the document.

   d. Repeat the procedure in part (b) to create a thesis or a brochure. Print either or both of these documents according to the requirements of your instructor. Do you think these templates would be useful in creating the actual documents?

   e. Click the link to the Templates on Office Online to see what is available. The contents of the Web site are continually changing, but our experience is that these templates are very useful, especially if you find a template that is similar to a document you need to create. Download at least one template from the Web site and create a document based on that template. Submit the completed document to your instructor. Add a cover sheet to complete the assignment.

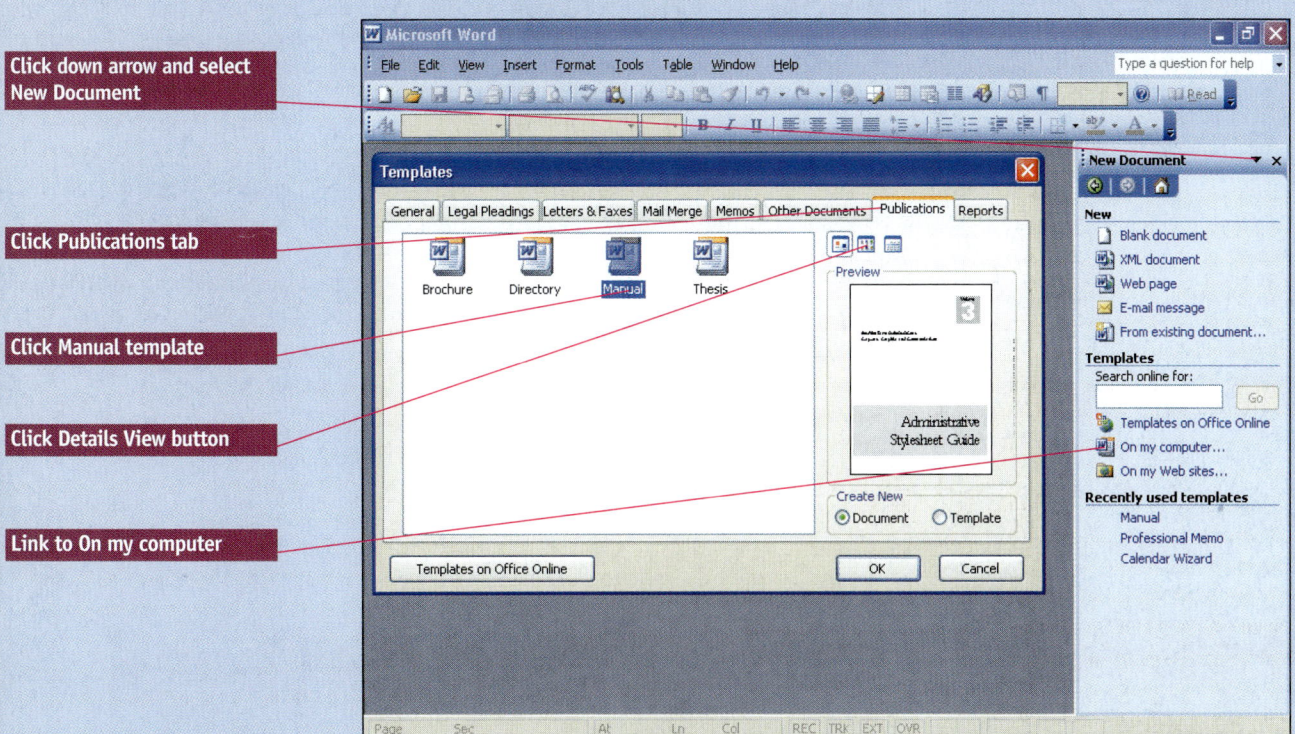

FIGURE 5.15 Exploring Templates (exercise 6)

MINI CASES

Study Session

It's the end of the semester and your instructor has asked you to publicize a review session for CIS100, the computer class you are currently taking. She has even given you the text of the flyer in the form of a poem that includes the place and time. Your assignment is to open the *Chapter 5 Mini Case—Study Session* document in the Exploring Word folder and create the flyer. Use WordArt and a photograph or clip art to complete the document.

Microsoft Office Publisher 2003

Microsoft Word enables you to create virtually any type of document, with full formatting, clip art, and photographs. Microsoft Publisher takes desktop publishing one step further by providing a wide selection of documents and templates from which to choose. It enables you to create a variety of professional-looking publications without reliance on graphic designers or other services. Publisher is ideal for any type of business communication, as it facilitates a uniform look across multiple publications through a series of templates or Master Design Sets. Each set contains the same design (logo and color scheme) for common publications such as newsletters, flyers, postcards, CD/DVD labels, and other publications. Locate a copy of Microsoft Publisher and use it to create two or three documents of different types—for example, a newsletter, brochure, and a flyer from within the same set. How do your results compare to the documents you created in this chapter? Which program do you prefer?

Before and After

The best way to learn about the dos and don'ts of desktop publishing is to study the work of others. Choose a particular type of document—for example, a newsletter, résumé, or advertising flyer—and then collect samples of that document. Choose one sample that is particularly bad and redesign the document. You need not enter the actual text, but you should keep all of the major headings so that the document retains its identity. Add or delete clip art as appropriate. Bring the before and after samples to class and hold a contest to determine the most radical improvement.

Subscribe to a Newsletter

There are literally thousands of regularly published newsletters that are distributed in printed and/or electronic form. Some charge a subscription fee, but many are available just for the asking. Use your favorite search engine to locate a free newsletter in an area of interest to you. Download an issue, then summarize the results of your research in a brief note to your instructor.

CHAPTER 6

Introduction to HTML: Creating a Home Page and a Web Site

OBJECTIVES

After reading this chapter you will:

1. Define HTML; explain how HTML codes control the appearance of a Web page.
2. Use Microsoft Word to create a Web page.
3. Explain the advantage of the Single File Web Page format in creating a Web page.
4. Distinguish between HTML and XML.
5. Use the Format Theme command to enhance a Web document.
6. Use the Insert Hyperlink command to insert a link to an e-mail address.
7. Insert a bookmark into a document.
8. Use the Insert Table command to facilitate the placement of clip art on a Web page.
9. Use the Frames toolbar to insert a horizontal and/or a vertical frame.
10. Explain how prototyping and an "under construction" page are used to create a Web site.

hands-on exercises

1. INTRODUCTION TO HTML
   Input: None
   Output: Index.mht (Single File Web Page Format)
2. WORLD WIDE TRAVEL HOME PAGE
   Input: None
   Output: World Wide Travel home page
3. CREATING A WEB SITE
   Input: World Wide Travel Home Page (from exercise 2)
   Output: Multiple Web Documents

CASE STUDY
REALTOR OF THE YEAR

Benjamin Lee, a successful realtor in South Florida, is seeking to expand his practice by establishing a Web presence to advertise his current listings and to attract new business. Ben is a dedicated professional and a born salesman. He has won the prestigious "Realtor of the Year Award" in South Florida, but is totally inept on the computer. Ben is a long-time family friend and has come to you for help. You agree to meet for a business lunch to learn more about his requirements.

Ben has several objectives for his site. He wants to describe his qualifications and the many services he provides for his clients. He wants to display his current listings and enable individuals who are looking for a home to fill out a form that describes their requirements. Ben also wants a place where individuals seeking to sell a home can describe their property. This information is changing continually as existing listings are sold and new properties become available. It is very important, therefore, that Ben be able to maintain the Web site after it has been created.

Your assignment is to read the chapter and focus on the third hands-on exercise that describes how to develop a Web site, as opposed to a single Web page. You will begin by creating a home page that describes Ben's credentials and basic services, and then expand that page into a Web site by adding navigation to other pages (such as Current Listings or Sell Your Home) through links on a vertical or horizontal frame.

The Web site will be developed incrementally, which requires you to create an "Under Construction" page as a placeholder for the various links. This enables Ben to experience the "look and feel" of the site before it is completed. Each page within the site should use the Single File Web Page command, and all of the pages for the site should be stored in a folder named "Realtor of the Year". An appealing and consistent visual design throughout the site is important. (You do not have to upload the finished site to a Web server.)

INTRODUCTION TO HTML

Sooner or later anyone who cruises the World Wide Web wants to create a home page and/or a Web site of their own. That, in turn, requires an appreciation for *HyperText Markup Language (HTML)*, the language in which all Web pages are written. A Web page consists of text and graphics, together with a set of codes (or tags) that describe how the document is to appear when viewed in a Web browser such as Internet Explorer.

In the early days of the Web, anyone creating a Web document (home page) had to learn each of these codes and enter it explicitly. Today, however, it's much easier as you can create a Web document within any application in Microsoft Office. In essence, you enter the text of a document, apply basic formatting such as boldface or italic, then simply save the file as a Web document. Microsoft Office also provides an FTP (File Transfer Protocol) capability that lets you upload your documents directly onto a Web server.

There are, of course, other commands that you will need to learn, but all commands are executed from within Word, through pull-down menus, toolbars, or keyboard shortcuts. You can create a single document (called a home page), or you can create multiple documents to build a simple Web site. Either way, the document(s) can be viewed locally within a Web browser such as Internet Explorer, and/or they can be placed on a Web server where they can be accessed by anyone with an Internet connection.

Figure 6.1 displays a simple Web page that is similar to the one you will create in the hands-on exercise that follows shortly. Our page has the look and feel of Web pages you see when you access the World Wide Web. It includes different types of formatting, a bulleted list, underlined links, and a heading displayed in a larger font. All of these elements are associated with specific HTML codes that identify the appearance and characteristics of the item. Figure 6.1a displays the document as it would appear when viewed in Internet Explorer. Figure 6.1b shows the underlying HTML codes *(tags)* that are necessary to format the page.

Fortunately, however, it is not necessary to memorize the HTML tags since you can usually determine their meaning from the codes themselves. Nor is it even necessary for you to enter the tags, as Word will create the HTML tags for you based on the formatting in the document. Nevertheless, we think it worthwhile for you to gain an appreciation for HTML by comparing the two views of the document.

HTML codes become less intimidating when you realize that they are enclosed in angle brackets and are used consistently from document to document. Most tags occur in pairs, at the beginning and end of the text to be formatted, with the ending code preceded by a slash, such as <p and </p> to indicate the beginning and end of a paragraph. Links to other pages (which are known as hyperlinks) are enclosed within a pair of anchor tags <a and </a> in which you specify the URL address of the document through the HREF parameter. There are additional codes for boldface, italic, font styles and sizes, and so on.

WHAT IS XML?

Extensible Markup Language, or XML for short, is an industry standard for structuring data. It is very different from HTML and serves an entirely different function. HTML describes how a document should look; for example, <B>John Doe</B> indicates that John Doe should appear in boldface, but it does not tell us anything more. You don't know that "John" is the first name or that "Doe" is the last name. XML on the other hand, is data about data, and it lets you define your own tags; for example, <name><first>John</first><last>Doe</last></name>. The XML codes can be read by any XML-compliant application and processed accordingly. See problem 9 at the end of the chapter.

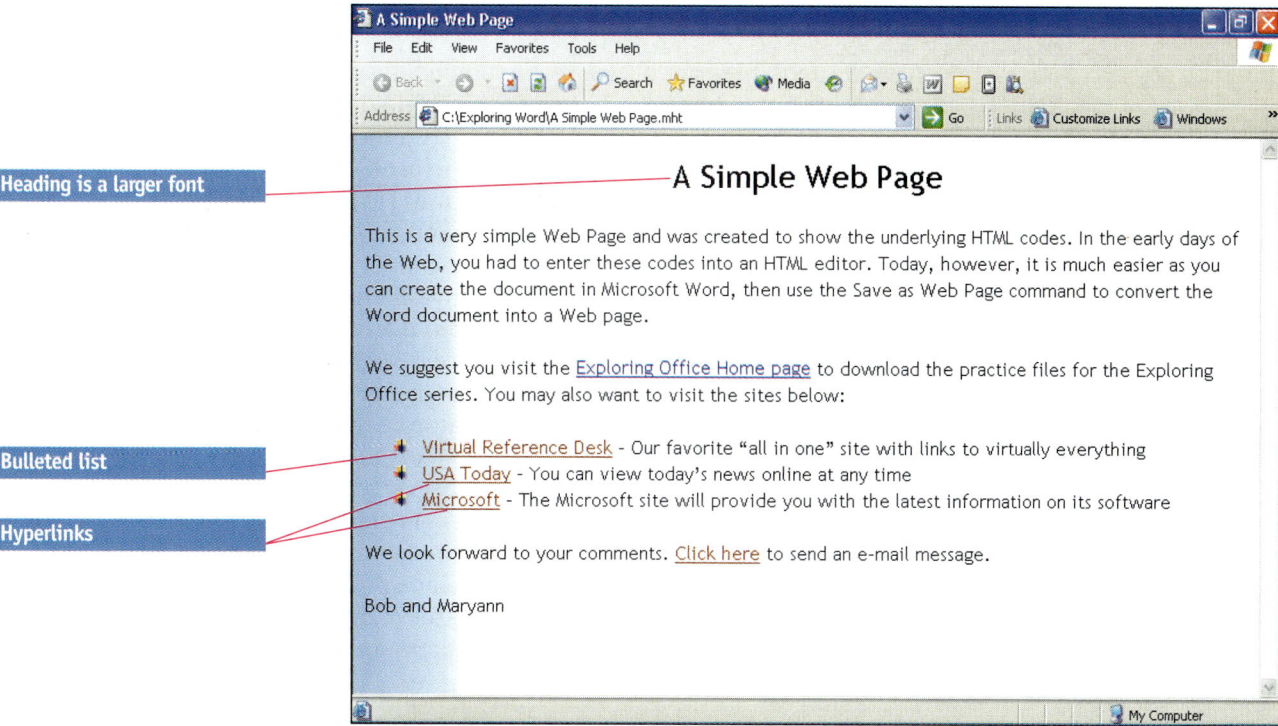

(a) Internet Explorer

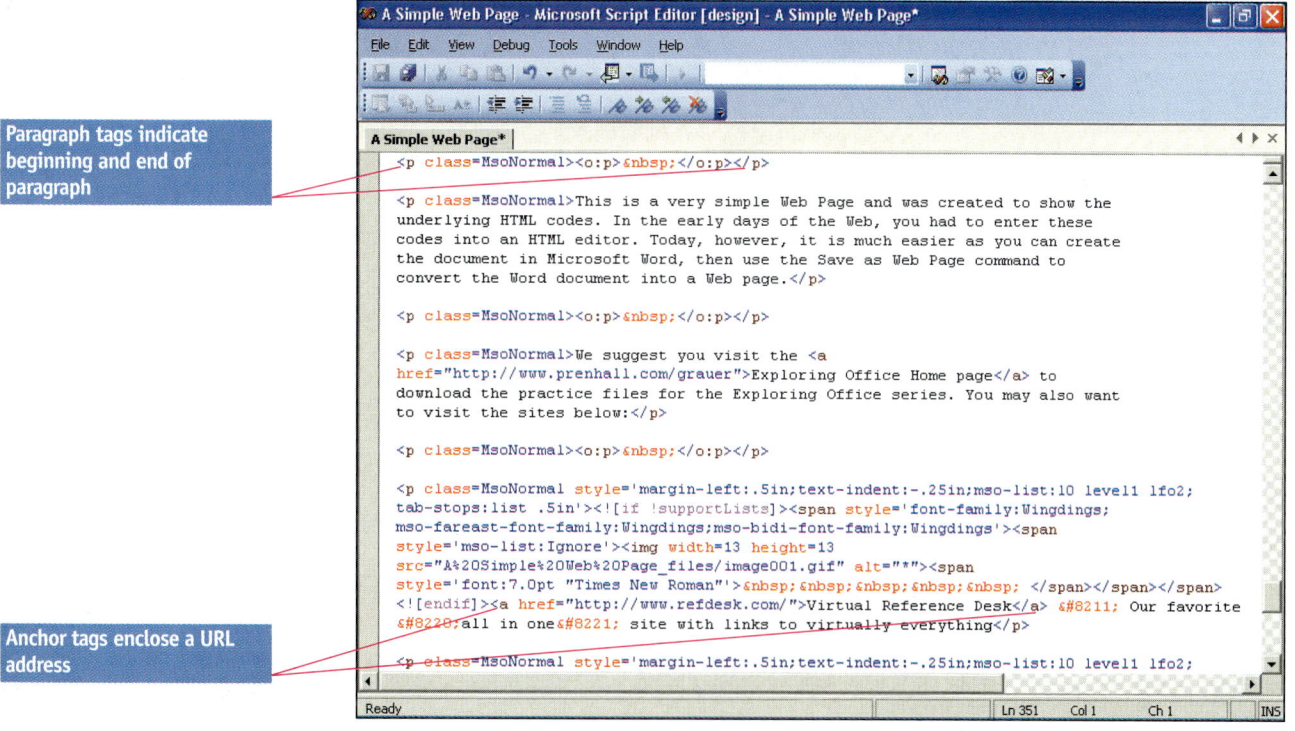

(b) HTML Source Code

FIGURE 6.1 Introduction to HTML

Microsoft Word

As indicated, there are different ways to create an HTML document. The original (and more difficult) method was to enter the codes explicitly in a text editor such as the Notepad accessory that is built into Windows. An easier way (and the only method you need to consider) is to use Microsoft Word to create the document for you, without having to enter or reference the HTML codes at all.

Figure 6.2 displays Jessica Benjamin's **home page** in Microsoft Word. You can create a similar page by entering the text and formatting just as you would enter the text of an ordinary document. The only difference is that instead of saving the document in the default format (as a Word document), you use the **Save As Web Page command** to specify the HTML format. Microsoft Word does the rest, generating the HTML codes needed to create the document. Microsoft Office 2003 introduces the **Single File Web Page** format that stores all of the elements that comprise a page (both text and graphics) in a single file.

Hyperlinks are added through the Insert Hyperlink button on the Standard toolbar or through the corresponding **Insert Hyperlink command** in the Insert menu. You can format the elements of the document (the heading, bullets, text, and so on) individually, or you can select a **theme** from those provided by Microsoft Word. A theme (or template) is a set of unified design elements and color schemes that will save you time, while making your document more attractive.

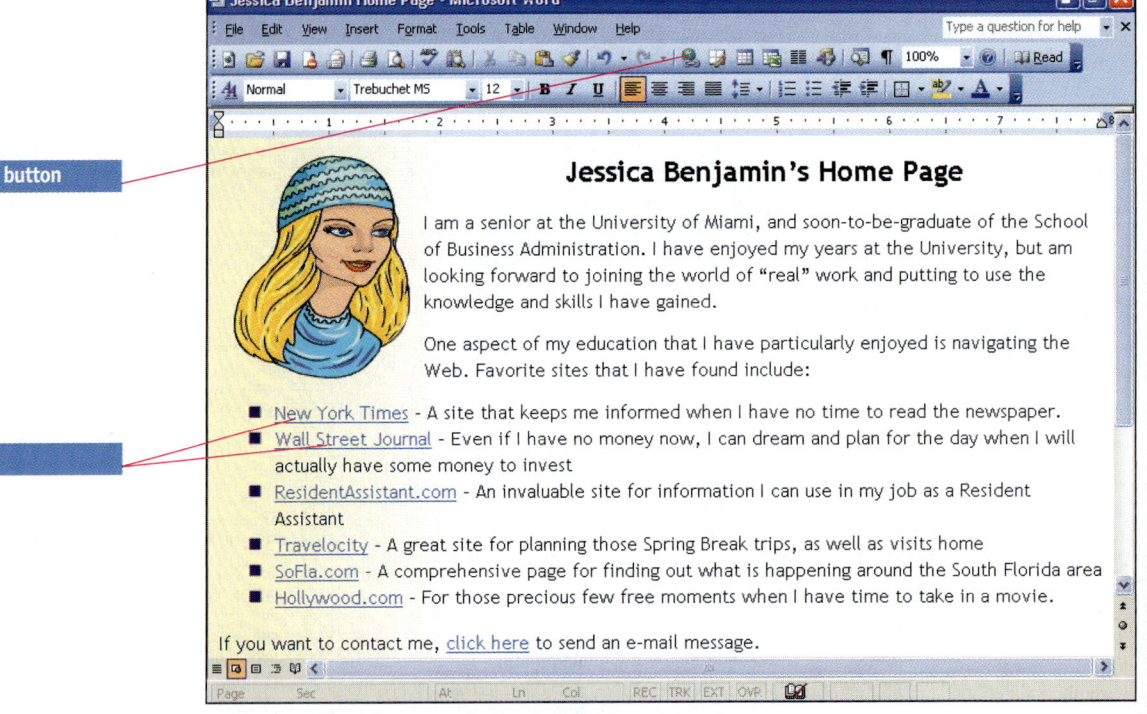

FIGURE 6.2 A Student's Home Page

ROUND-TRIP HTML

Each application in Microsoft Office lets you open a Web document in both Internet Explorer and the application that created the Web page initially. In other words, you can start with a Word document and use the Save As Web Page command to convert the document to a Web page, then view that page in a Web browser. You can then reopen the Web page in Word (the original Office application) with full access to all Word commands, should you want to modify the document.

hands-on exercise

1 Introduction to HTML

Objective To use Microsoft Word to create a simple home page with clip art and multiple hyperlinks; to format a Web page by selecting a theme. Use Figure 6.3 as a guide in the exercise.

Step 1: **Enter the Text**

- Start Microsoft Word. Close the task pane. Pull down the **View menu** and click the **Web Layout command**. Enter the text of your home page as shown in Figure 6.3a. Use any text you like and choose an appropriate font and type size. Center and enlarge the title for your page.

- Enter the text for our links (e.g., *New York Times* and the *Wall Street Journal* sites), or choose your own. You do not enter the URL addresses at this time.

- Click and drag to select all of your links, then click the **Bullets button** on the Formatting toolbar to precede each link with a bullet.

- Click the **Spelling and Grammar button** to check the document for spelling.

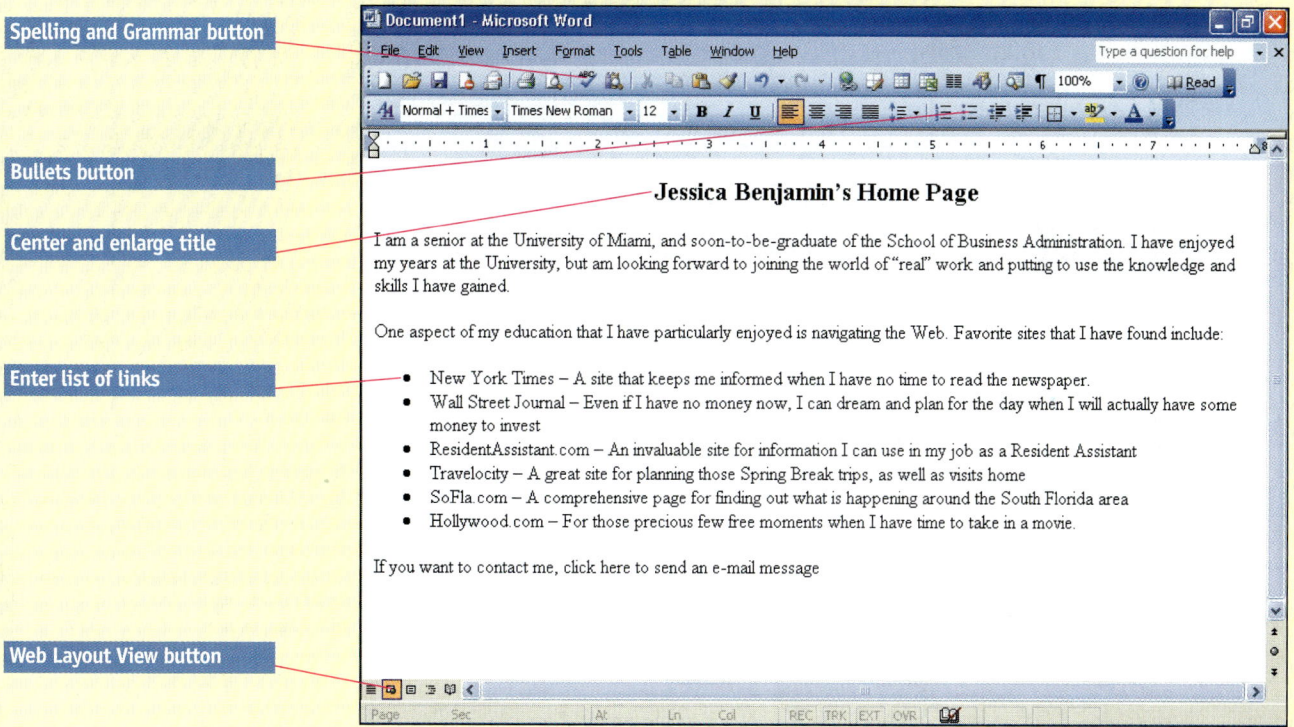

(a) Enter the Text (step 1)

FIGURE 6.3 Hands-on Exercise 1

FOREIGN LANGUAGE PROOFING TOOLS

The English version of Microsoft Word supports the spelling, grammar, and thesaurus features in more than 80 foreign languages. Support for Spanish and French is built in at no additional cost, whereas you will have to pay an additional fee for other languages. Pull down the Tools menu, click Language, and click the Set Language command to change to a different language. You can even check multiple languages within the same document.

MICROSOFT OFFICE WORD 2003 1117

Step 2: **Save the Document**

- Pull down the **File menu** and click the **Save as Web Page** command to display the Save As dialog box in Figure 6.3b.
- Click the **drop-down arrow** in the Save In list box to select the appropriate drive—drive C or drive A. Click to open the **Exploring Word folder** that contains the documents you have used throughout the text.
- Enter the file name, then be sure to select the **Single File Web Page** format as shown in Figure 6.3b. This enables you to save all of the elements for a Web page in one file.
- Click the **Change Title button** if you want to change the title of the Web page as it will appear in the Title bar of the Web browser. (The default title is the opening text in your document.)
- Click the **Save button**. The title bar reflects the name of the Web page, but the screen does not change in any other way.

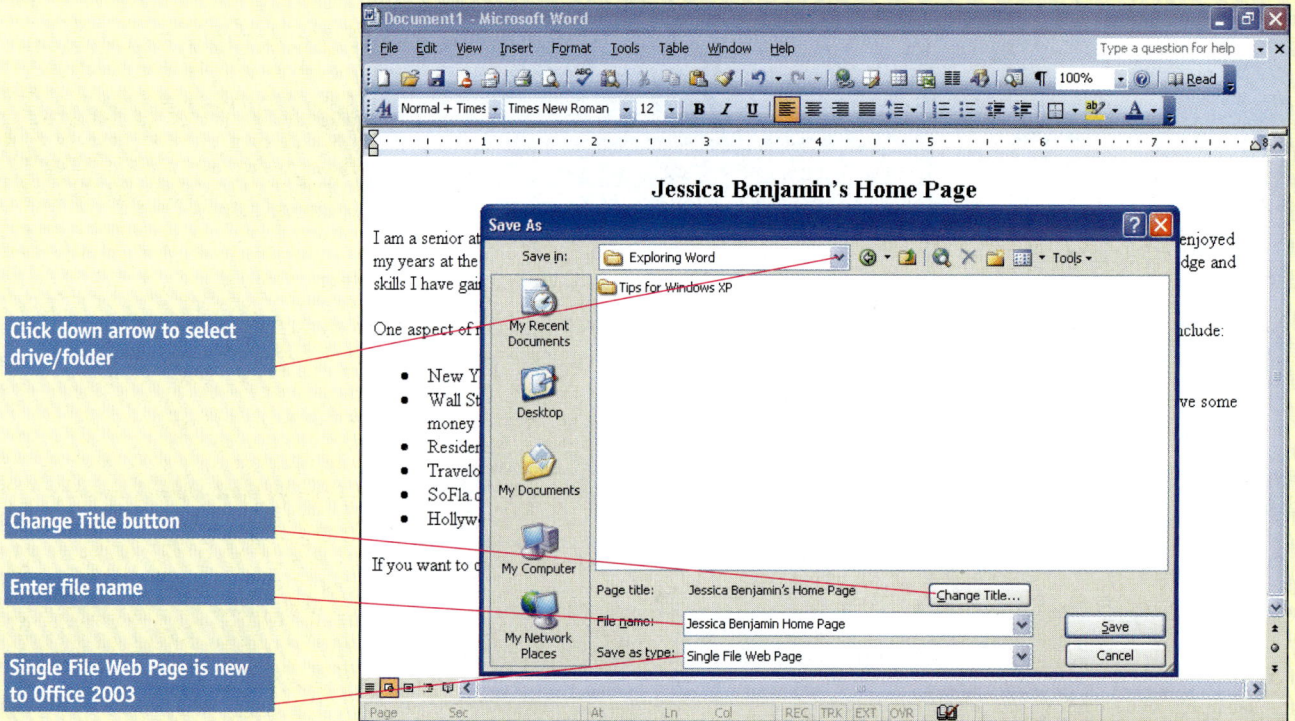

Click down arrow to select drive/folder

Change Title button

Enter file name

Single File Web Page is new to Office 2003

(b) Save the Document (step 2)

FIGURE 6.3 Hands-on Exercise 1 (*continued*)

WHAT'S IN A FILE NAME?

You can choose any meaningful file name for your home page. One common convention is to use "index" (with a lowercase "i") as the file name for the initial page on a Web site to take advantage of the convention of a Web browser, which automatically displays the index document if it exists. Start Internet Explorer, click in the address bar, enter a URL such as www.prenhall.com/grauer, and press Enter. You are taken to the home page of the Grauer Web site, but you do not see the document name; that is, the index.html document is displayed automatically and need not be shown in the URL within the address bar.

Step 3: **Insert the Clip Art**

- Click to the left of the first sentence in the document. Pull down the **Insert menu**, click (or point to) **Picture**, then click **Clip Art** to display the Insert Clip Art task pane in Figure 6.3c.

- Click in the **Search for** text box and type **woman** to search for all pictures that have been catalogued to describe this attribute. Click the **Go button**. The search begins and the various pictures appear individually within the task pane.

- Point to the image you want in your newsletter, click the **down arrow** that appears, then click **Insert** to insert the clip art.

- The picture should appear in the document. Close the task pane.

- Point to the picture and click the **right mouse button** to display the context-sensitive menu. Click the **Format Picture command** to display the Format Picture dialog box.

- Click the **Layout tab**, choose the **Square layout**, then click the option button for Left or Right alignment. Click **OK** to close the dialog box. Move and size the picture as appropriate. Save the document.

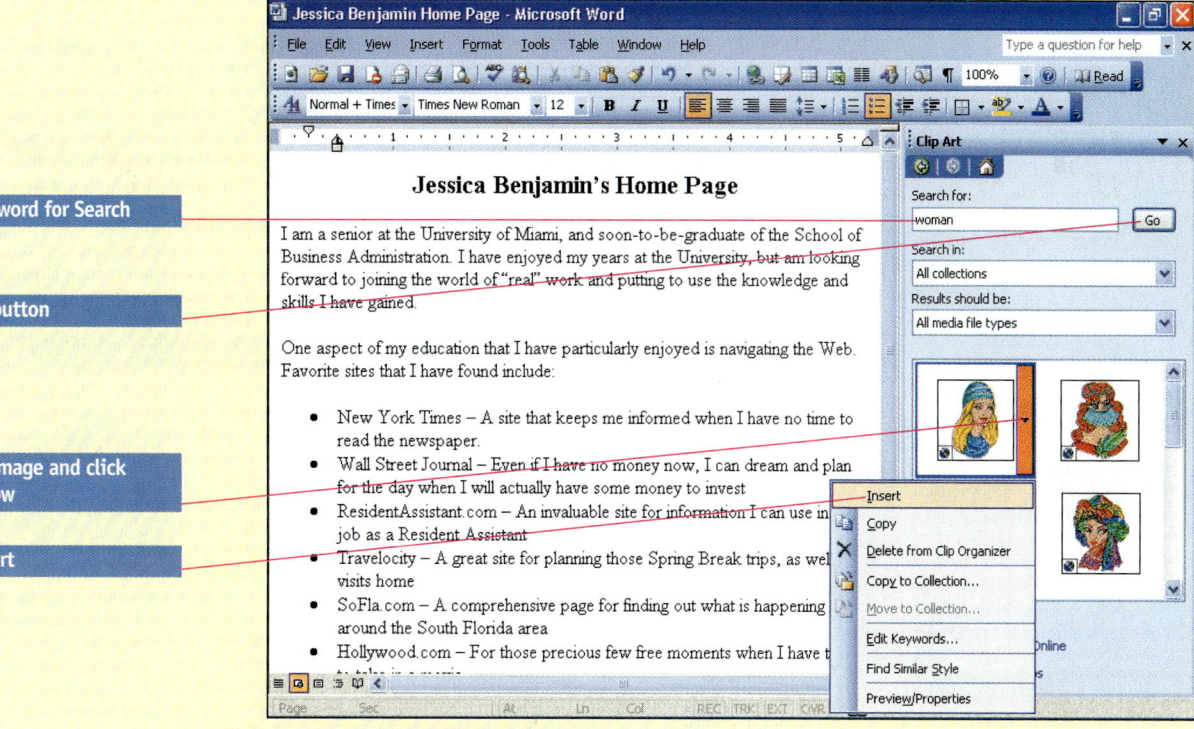

(c) Insert the Clip Art (step 3)

FIGURE 6.3 Hands-on Exercise 1 (*continued*)

SEARCH FOR THE APPROPRIATE CLIP ART OR PHOTOGRAPH

Pull down the Insert menu, click the Picture command, and click Clip Art to display the Clip Art task pane that enables you to enter search parameters for an appropriate media object. Click the down arrow in the Search in list box and select All collections. Click the down arrow in the Results should be list box and choose All media file types, then click the Go button to initiate the search. The search may take a little while as it includes the Web, but you should have a much larger selection of potential clips from which to choose. If necessary, use the drop-down arrow on either search box to limit the search as you see fit.

Step 4: **Add the Hyperlinks**

- Select **New York Times** (the text for the first hyperlink). Pull down the **Insert menu** and click **Hyperlink** (or click the **Insert Hyperlink button**) to display the Insert Hyperlink dialog box in Figure 6.3d.

- The text to display (New York Times) is already entered because the text was selected prior to executing the Insert Hyperlink command. If necessary, click the icon for **Existing File or Web Page**, then click **Browsed Pages**.

- Click in the second text box and enter the address **www.nytimes.com** (the http is assumed). Click **OK**.

- Add the additional links in similar fashion. The addresses we used in our document are: **www.wsj.com**, **www.residentassistant.com**, **www.travelocity.com**, **www.sofla.com**, and **www.hollywood.com**.

- Click and drag to select the words **click here**, then click the **Insert Hyperlink button** to display the Insert Hyperlink dialog box.

- Click the **E-mail Address icon**, then click in the E-mail Address text box and enter your e-mail address. Click **OK**.

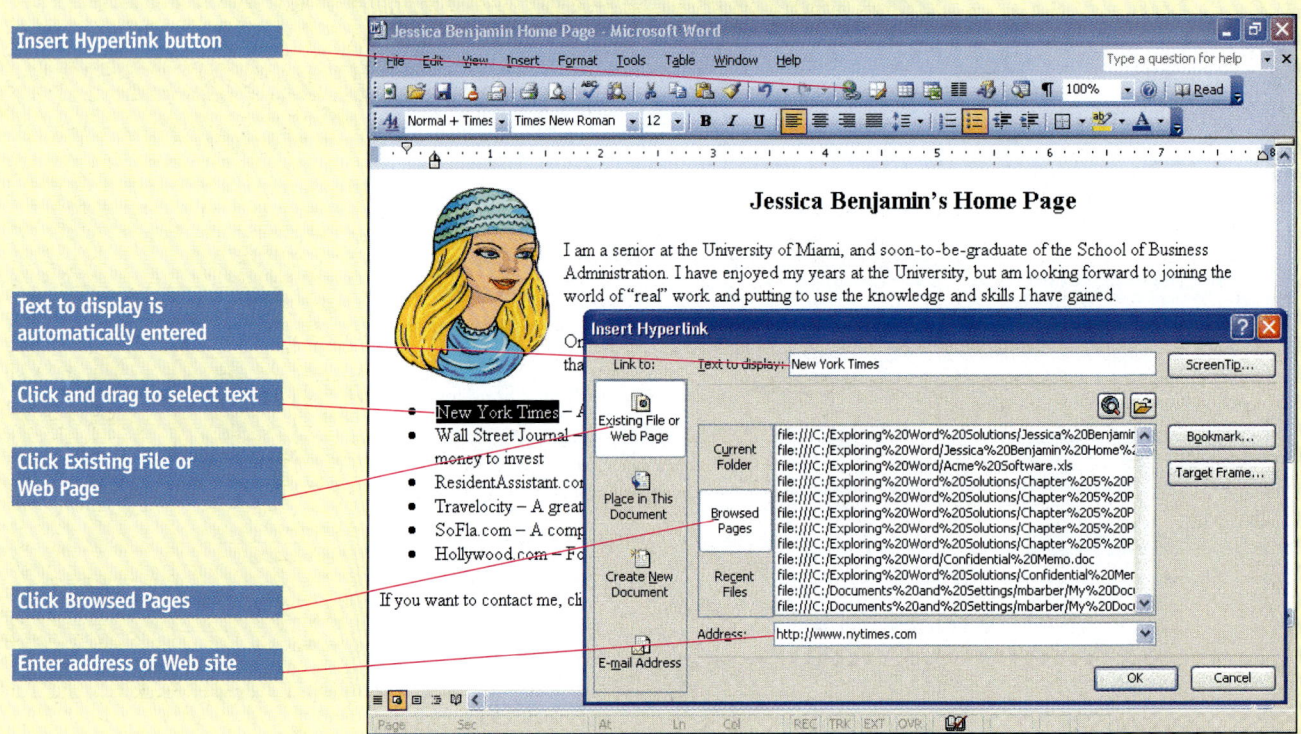

(d) Add the Hyperlinks (step 4)

FIGURE 6.3 Hands-on Exercise 1 (*continued*)

RIGHT CLICK TO SELECT, CTRL+CLICK TO FOLLOW

Point to a hyperlink within a Word document, and you see a ScreenTip that says to press and hold the Ctrl key (Ctrl+Click) to follow the link. This is different from what you usually do, because you typically just click a link to follow it. What if, however, you wanted to edit, copy, or remove the link? Clicking the link has no effect. Thus, you have to right click the link to display a context-sensitive menu from which you can make the appropriate choice—for example, to edit or remove the hyperlink.

Step 5: **Apply a Theme**

- You should see underlined hyperlinks in your document. Pull down the **Format menu** and click the **Theme command** to display the Theme dialog box in Figure 6.3e.

- Select (click) a theme from the list box on the left, and a sample of the design appears on the right. Only a limited number of the listed themes are installed by default, however, and thus you may be prompted for the Microsoft Office CD, depending on your selection. Click **OK**.

- You can go from one theme to the next by clicking the new theme. There are approximately 65 themes to choose from, and they are all visually appealing. Every theme offers a professionally designed set of formatting specifications for the various headings, horizontal lines, bullets, and links.

- Set a time limit, then make your decision as to which theme you will use when your time is up.

- Save the document.

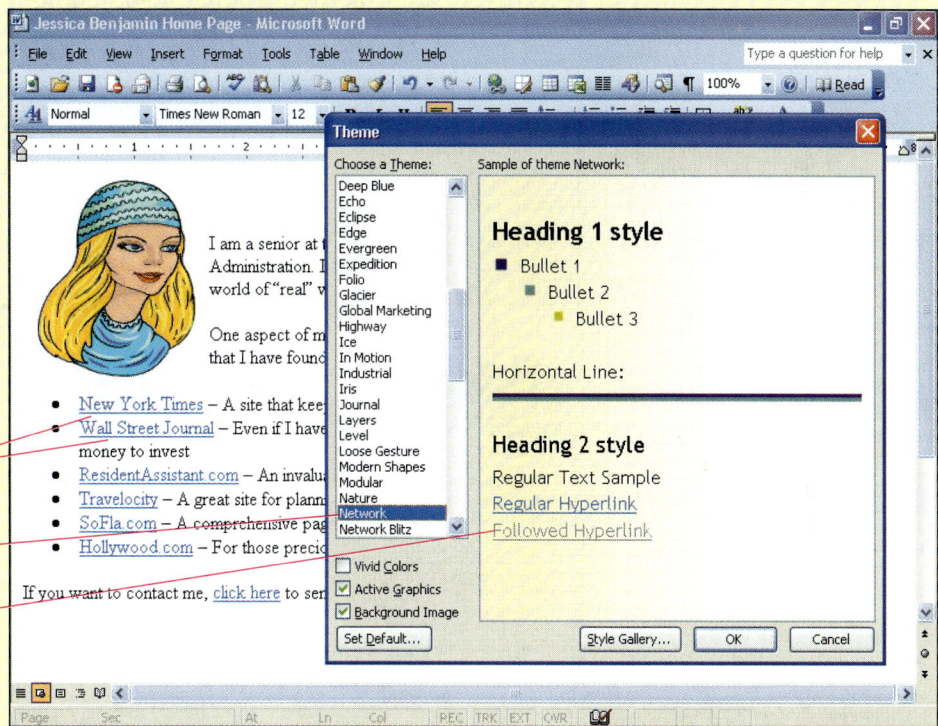

(e) Apply a Theme (step 5)

FIGURE 6.3 Hands-on Exercise 1 (*continued*)

KEEP IT SIMPLE

Too many would-be designers clutter a page unnecessarily by importing a complex background, which tends to obscure the text. The best design is a simple design—either no background or a very simple pattern. We also prefer light backgrounds with dark text (e.g., black or dark blue text on a white background), as opposed to the other way around. Design, however, is subjective, and there is no consensus as to what makes an attractive page. Variety is indeed the spice of life. Look at existing Web pages for inspiration.

Step 6: **View the Web Page**

- Start your Web browser. Pull down the **File menu** and click the **Open command** to display the Open dialog box in Figure 6.3f.
- Click the **Browse button**, then select the drive folder (e.g., Exploring Word on drive C) where you saved the Web page.
- Select (click) your home page, click **Open**, then click **OK** to open the document. You should see the Web page that was just created except that you are viewing it in your browser rather than in Microsoft Word.
- The Address bar shows the local address (C:\Exploring Word\Jessica Benjamin Home Page.mht) of the document. (You can also open the document from the Address bar, by clicking in the **Address bar**, then typing the address of the document—for example, **c:\Exploring word\Jessica Benjamin Home Page.mht**.)
- Click the **Print button** on the Internet Explorer toolbar to print this page for your instructor.
- Exit Word and Internet Explorer if you do not want to continue with the next exercise at this time.

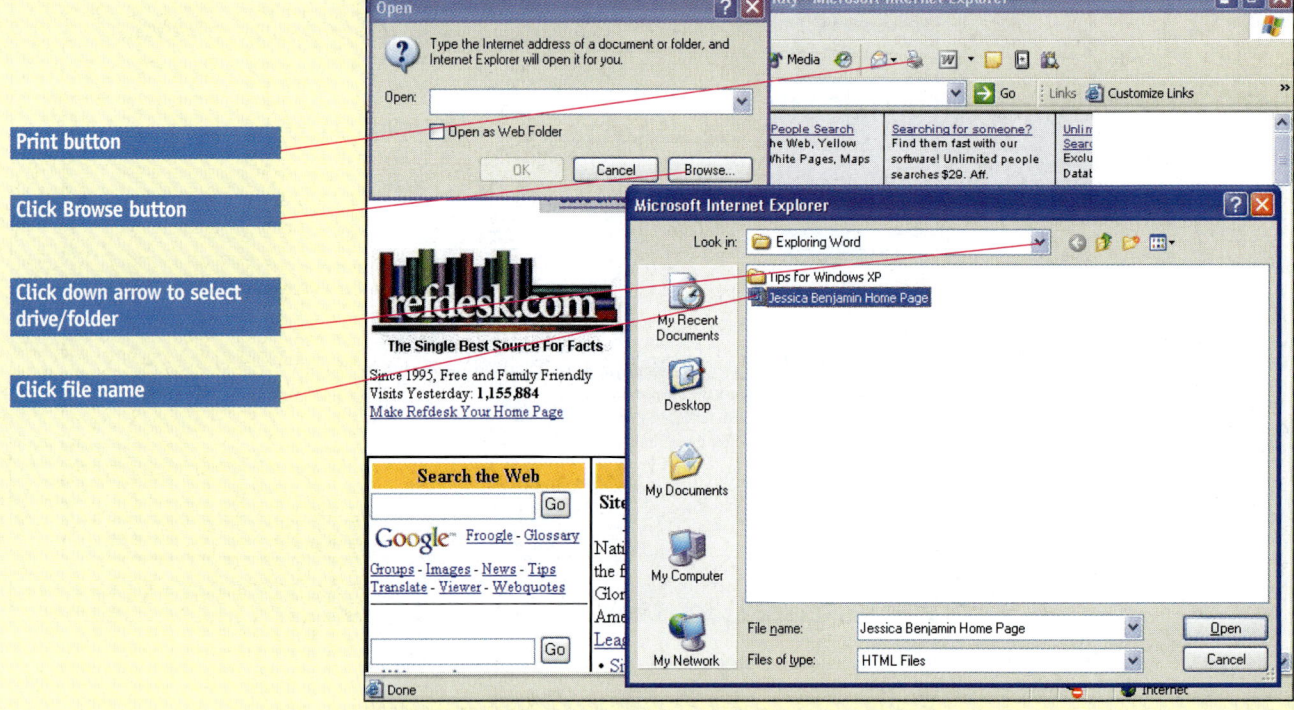

(f) View the Web Page (step 6)

FIGURE 6.3 Hands-on Exercise 1 (*continued*)

SINGLE FILE WEB PAGE

Microsoft Office 2003 introduces the Single File Web Page (MHTML) format that saves all of the elements of a Web page, including text and graphics, in a single file. The new format enables you to upload a single file to a Web server, as opposed to sending multiple files and folders. It also lets you send the entire page as a single e-mail attachment. The new file format is supported by Internet Explorer 4.0 and higher.

A COMMERCIAL HOME PAGE

Figure 6.4 displays the home page of a hypothetical travel agency. The Address bar displays the name of the document (World Wide Travel Home Page) and indicates that the document is stored in the World Wide Travel folder. (We created a separate folder to hold the home page because we will develop a Web site in the next exercise, and it is easiest to store all of the pages for the site in a single folder.) The extension in the file name (mht) indicates the Single File Web Page format.

The table at the top of the document facilitates the placement of text and/or graphical elements on the page. The cell on the left contains the name of the agency, a hyperlink, a telephone number, and an e-mail address. The latter is also a hyperlink that starts the default e-mail program to create a message to the travel agency. Note, too, that the first hyperlink, "Click here for travel agents", branches to a ***bookmark*** or place within the document, as opposed to a separate Web page. One or more bookmarks are helpful in long documents, as they enable you to move easily from one place to another (within a document) without having to manually scroll through the document. Creating a bookmark and branching to it is a two-step process. You use the Insert menu to create the bookmark, and then you insert a hyperlink to branch to the bookmark that you just created.

The second cell in the table contains the agency logo. You can center the clip art within the cell, and then you can center the table within the document. Microsoft Word is limited when compared to other Web editors, and thus a table makes it easier to position the graphics within a Web page.

Look once again at the Address bar and note that the page is stored on drive C, as opposed to a Web server. Creating the home page and viewing it locally is easy. Placing the page on the Web where it can be seen by anyone with an Internet connection is not as straightforward. You will need additional information from your instructor about how to obtain an account on a Web server (if that is available at your school), and further how to upload the Web page from your PC to the server. The latter is typically accomplished using ***File Transfer Protocol (FTP)***, a program that uploads files from a PC to a Web server.

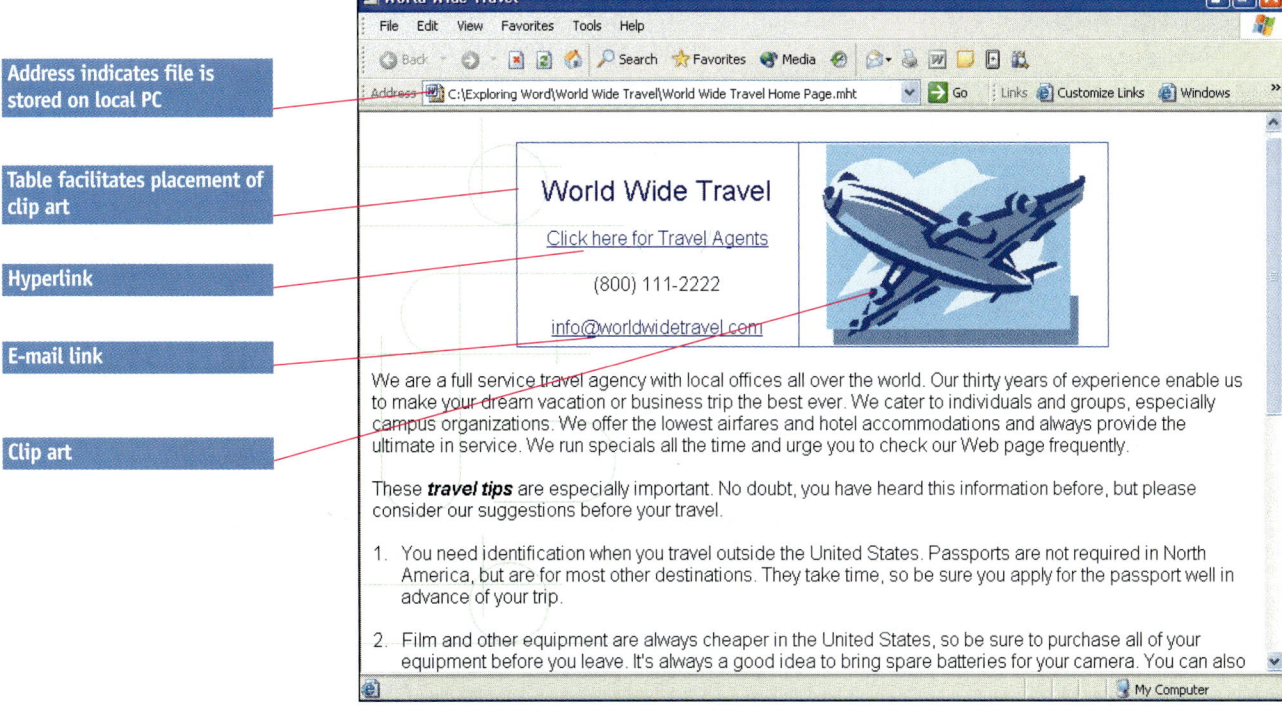

FIGURE 6.4 World Wide Travel Web Page

hands-on exercise

2 World Wide Travel Home Page

Objective To use a table to facilitate placement of clip art and other elements on a Web page; to insert a bookmark; to create hyperlinks to external Web pages, bookmarks, and e-mail addresses. Use Figure 6.5 as a guide.

Step 1: **Create the World Wide Travel Folder**

- Start Word. Open the **World Wide Travel Home Page document** in the **Exploring Word folder**.

- Pull down the **Format menu**, click the **Theme command**, select a theme (we chose **Capsules**), and click **OK**. The formatting changes as shown in Figure 6.5a.

- Pull down the **File menu** and click the **Save as Web page command** to display the Save as dialog box in Figure 6.5a. Click the **down arrow** in the Save in list box to select the **Exploring Word folder**.

- Click the **Create New Folder button** and enter **World Wide Travel** as the name of the folder. Click **OK** to close the New folder dialog box. Click the **Save button** to save the document. Close the Save As dialog box.

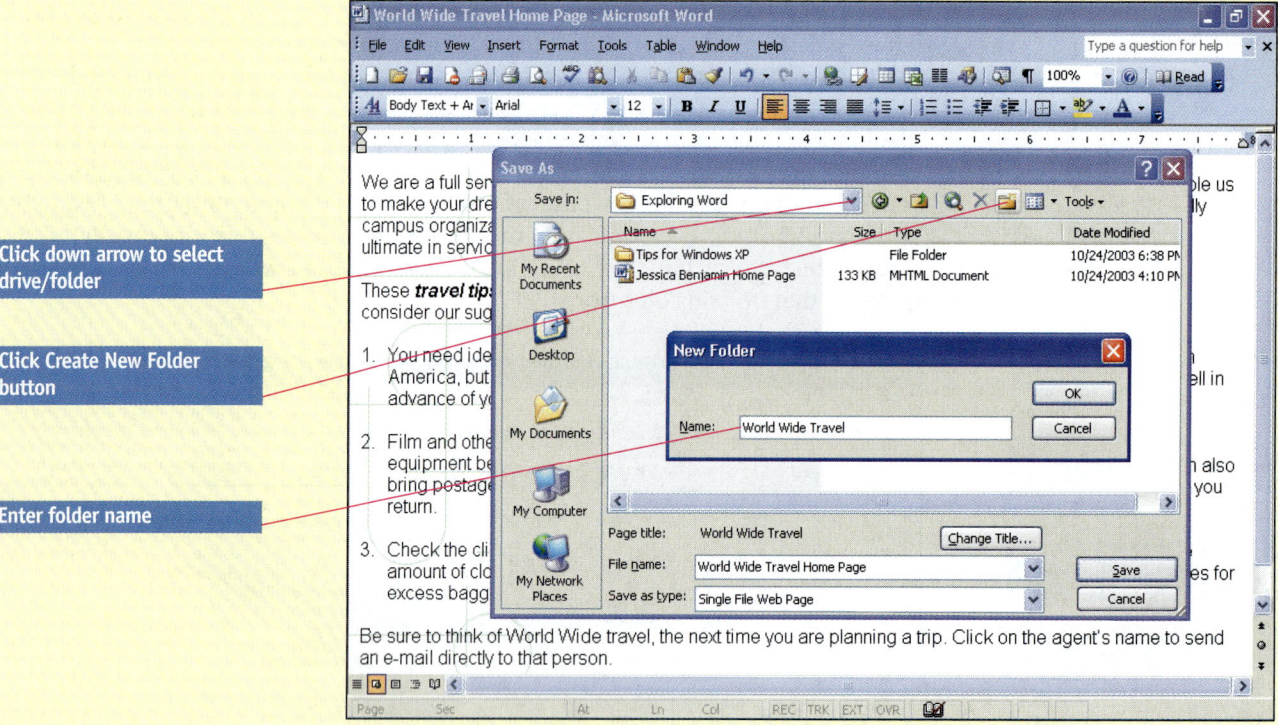

Click down arrow to select drive/folder

Click Create New Folder button

Enter folder name

(a) Create the World Wide Travel Folder (step 1)

FIGURE 6.5 Hands-on Exercise 2

MICROSOFT OFFICE FRONTPAGE 2003

Microsoft Word is an excellent way to begin creating Web documents. It is only a beginning, however, and there are many specialty programs that have significantly more capability. One such product is FrontPage, a product aimed at creating a Web site, as opposed to isolated documents. Search the Web for information on FrontPage, then summarize your findings in a short note to your instructor.

Step 2: **Insert the Clip Art**

- Press **Ctrl+Home** to move to the beginning of the document. Press **Enter** to add a blank line, then click the **Insert Table button** to display a table grid.

- Click and drag to select a **one-by-two grid** (one row and two columns). Release the mouse to create the table. Click in the left cell. Type **World Wide Travel**.

- Press the **Enter key** twice, type the sentence, **Click here for Travel Agents**, press the **Enter key** twice, and enter the agency's phone number, **(800) 111-2222**.

- Press **Enter** twice more, type **info@worldwidetravel.com** (or substitute your e-mail address instead), and press **Enter**. A hyperlink is created automatically. Click and drag to select the hyperlink to change the font to Arial.

- Click in the right pane. Pull down the **Insert menu**, click (or point to) **Picture**, then click **Clip Art** to display the Clip Art task pane in Figure 6.5b.

- Click in the Search for text box and type **airplane**. Click the **Go button**. Point to the image you want, click the **down arrow**, and then click **Insert** to insert the clip art into the document. Close the task pane.

- Click the picture to select it, then click and drag the sizing handle on the lower right to make the picture smaller. Click the **Center button** to center the picture.

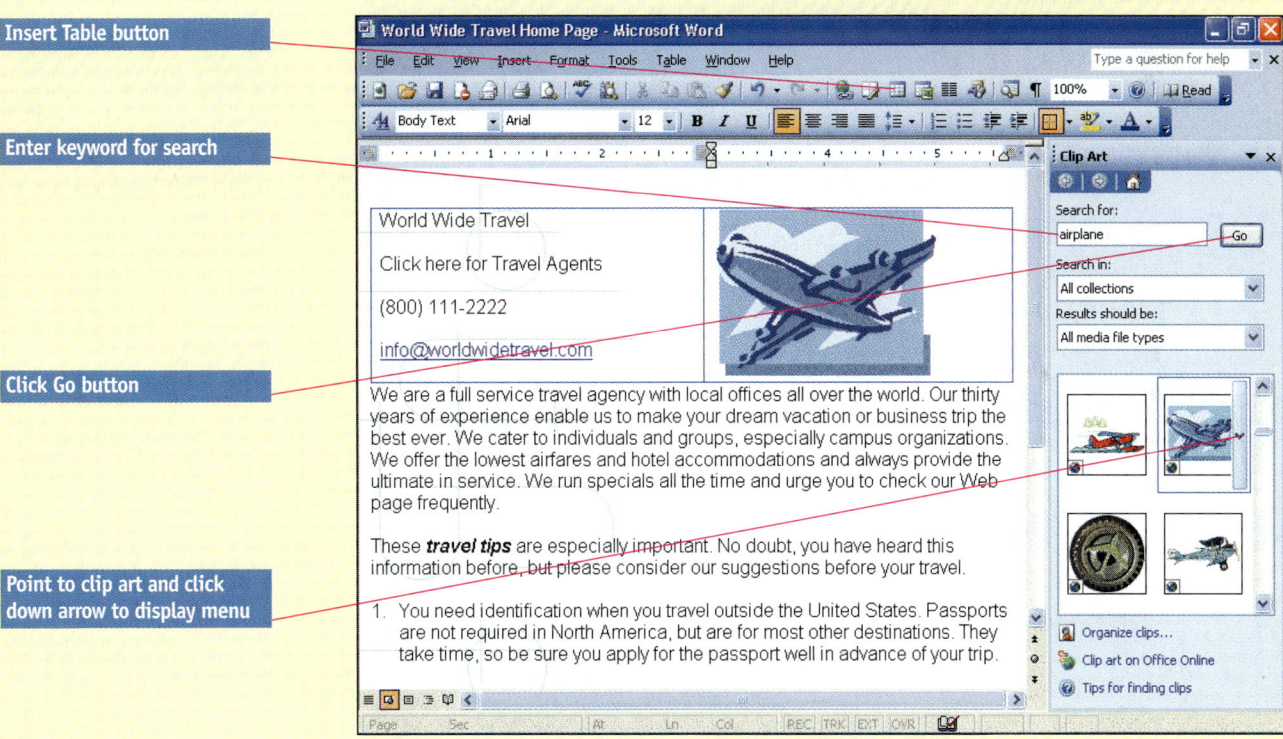

(b) Insert the Clip Art (step 2)

FIGURE 6.5 Hands-on Exercise 2 (*continued*)

WORKING WITH A TABLE—MENUS AND TOOLBARS

Click anywhere within a table and then pull down the Table menu to access the commands to modify the table. You can also display the Tables and Borders toolbar, which contains additional tools to change the line style, thickness, and/or shading within the table. Pull down the View menu, click the Toolbars command, and then click the Tables and Borders toolbar to toggle the toolbar on or off.

Step 3: **Insert Hyperlinks and a Bookmark**

- Press **Ctrl+End** to go to the end of the document. Click and drag to select the text **Click here for weather report**, then click the **Insert Hyperlink button** to display the Insert Hyperlink text box.

- Click the **Existing File or Web Page button**, then click the **Browsed Pages button**. Enter a Web address such as **http://www.intellicast.com** in the Address list box. Click **OK** to create the link and close the dialog box.

- Click at the end of the document, then enter the bulleted list with your name and your instructor's name as shown in Figure 6.5c. Enter the text **Return to the top of the document** after your instructor's name.

- Click and drag to select your name, then enter a hyperlink to your e-mail address. Enter a hyperlink to your instructor's e-mail address in similar fashion.

- Click at the beginning of the last paragraph. Pull down the **Insert menu** and click **Bookmark** to display the Bookmark dialog box.

- Enter **TravelAgents** (spaces are not allowed) as the name of the bookmark, then click the **Add button** to add the bookmark and close the dialog box.

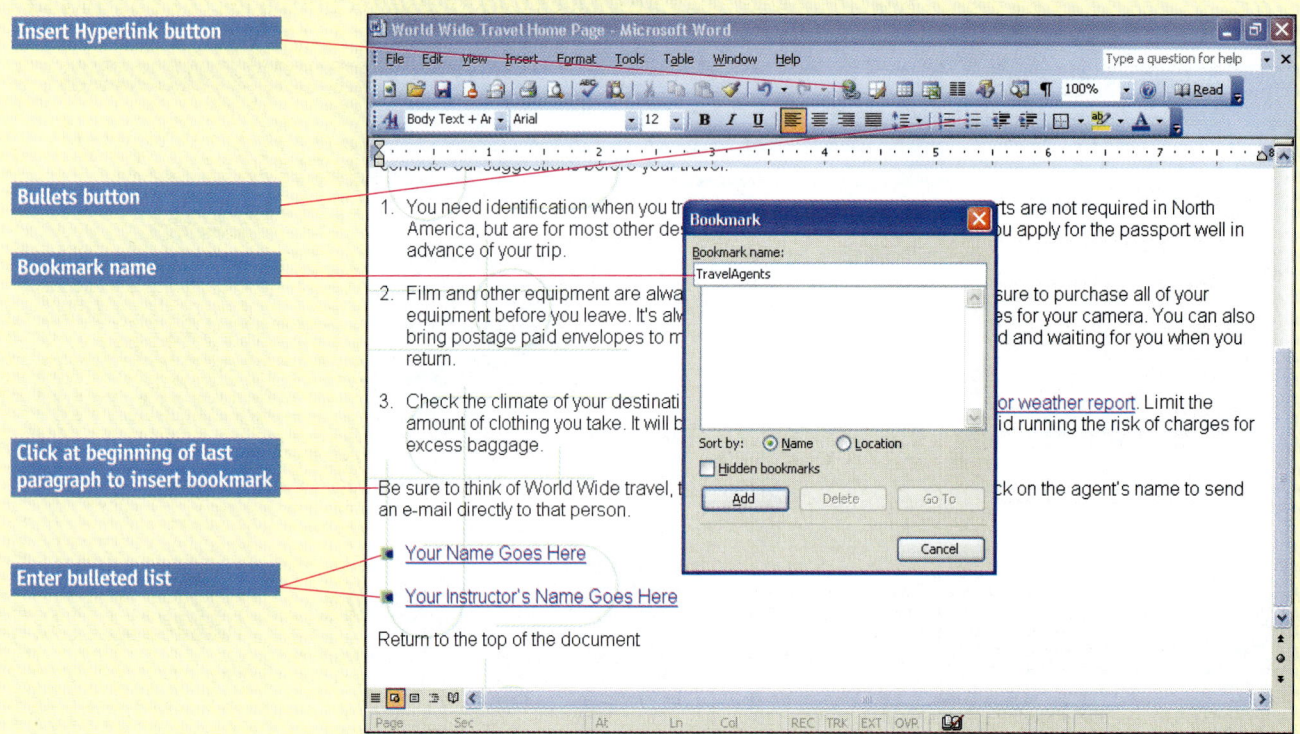

(c) Insert Hyperlinks and a Bookmark (step 3)

FIGURE 6.5 Hands-on Exercise 2 (*continued*)

AUTOMATIC CREATION OF HYPERLINKS

Type any Internet path or e-mail address, and Word will automatically convert the entry to a hyperlink. (If this does not work on your system, pull down the Tools menu, click AutoCorrect Options, then click the AutoFormat as you Type tab. Check the box in the Replace as you Type area for Internet and Network paths, and click OK.) To modify the hyperlink after it is created, right click the link to display a shortcut menu, then click the Edit Hyperlink command to display the associated dialog box in which to make the necessary changes.

Step 4: **Link to the Bookmark**

- Press **Ctrl+Home** to move to the beginning of the document. Click and drag to select the text **Click here for Travel Agents** as shown in Figure 6.5d. Click the **Insert Hyperlink button** to display the Insert Hyperlink dialog box.

- Click the icon for **Place in This Document**, click the **plus sign** next to Bookmarks to display the existing bookmarks, then click **TravelAgents**. Click **OK** to close the Insert Hyperlink dialog box.

- Click anywhere in the document to deselect the hyperlink you just created. The sentence, Click here for Travel Agents, should appear as underlined text to indicate that it is now a hyperlink.

- Point to the hyperlink, then press **Ctrl+click** to follow the link and position the insertion point at the bookmark you created in the previous step.

- Save the document.

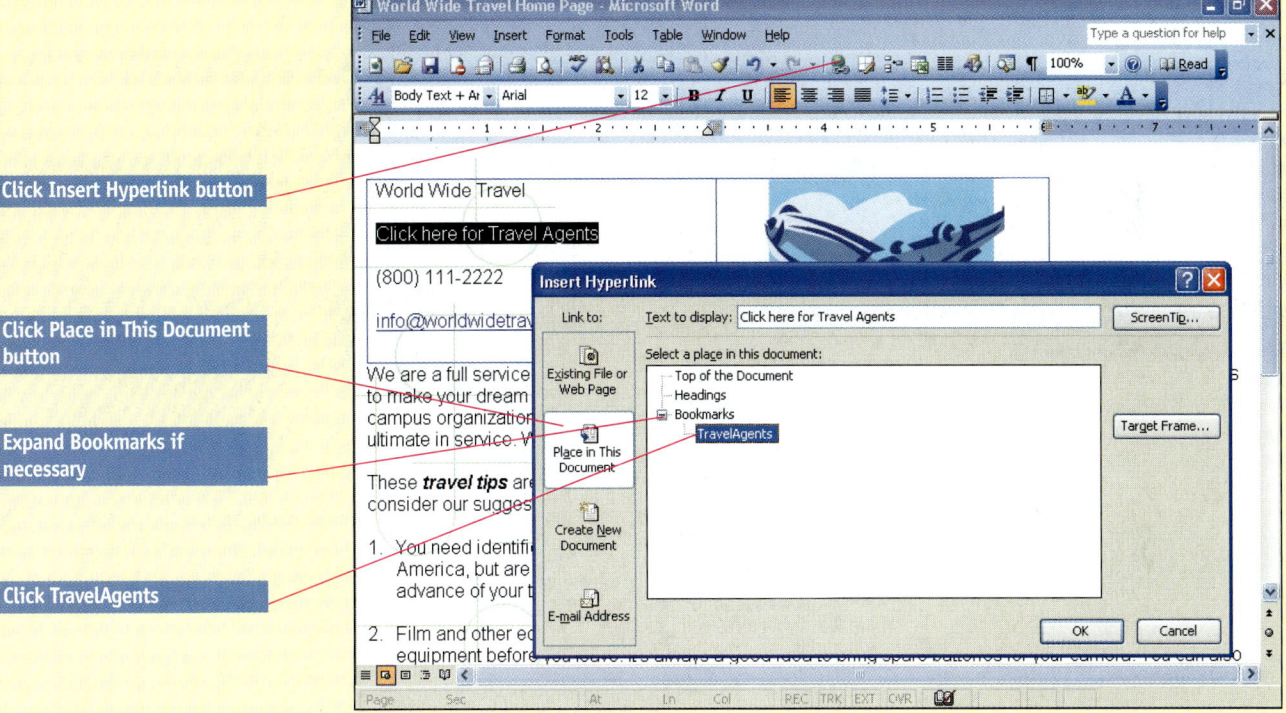

(d) Link to the Bookmark (step 4)

FIGURE 6.5 Hands-on Exercise 2 (*continued*)

THE TOP OF DOCUMENT BOOKMARK

Simplify the navigation within a long page with a link to the top of the document. Press Ctrl+End to move to the bottom of the document (one of several places where you can insert this link), then click the Insert Hyperlink button to display the Insert Hyperlink dialog box. Click the icon for Place in This Document, click Top of the Document from the list of bookmarks (Word creates this bookmark automatically), then click OK. You will see the underlined text, Top of Document, as a hyperlink. (Right click the link after it has been created, click Select Hyperlink, and press Ctrl+C to copy it. Move elsewhere in the document, then press Ctrl+V to paste the link to a second location.)

Step 5: **View the Web Page**

- Open the Web page that you just created in Internet Explorer. You can accomplish this in one of two ways:

- Start **Internet Explorer**. Pull down the **File menu**, click the **Open command**, click the **Browse button**, change to the **World Wide Travel folder** (within the **Exploring Word folder**), then open the **World Wide Travel Home Page**, *or*

- Start **Windows Explorer**. Click the **down arrow** in the Address bar, change to the **World Wide Travel folder** (within the **Exploring Word folder**), then double click the **World Wide Travel Home Page**.

- Either way you should see the home page for the World Wide Travel agency that you just created. The Address bar indicates that you are viewing the page locally, as opposed to viewing it on a Web server.

- Click the **Edit with Microsoft Word button** (or click the **Word button** on the Windows taskbar) to return to the document in Word to apply the finishing touches to your Web page.

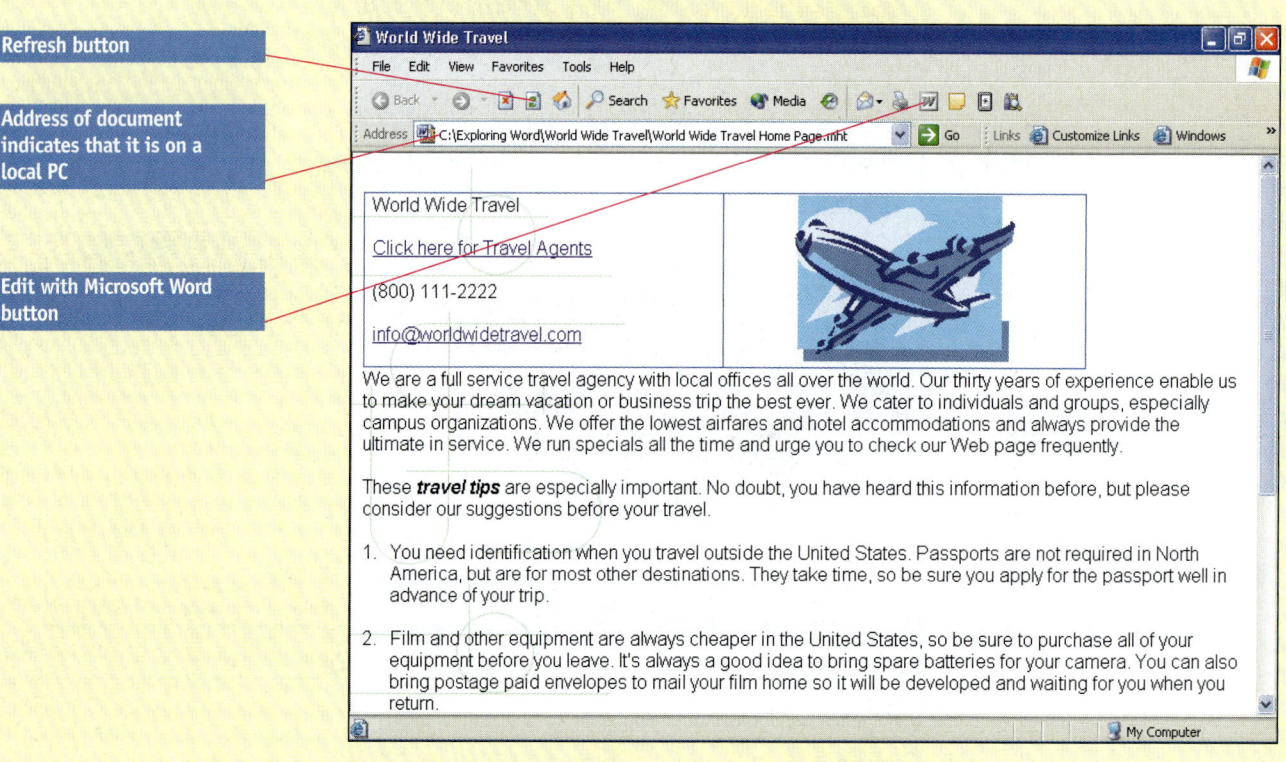

(e) View the Web Page (step 5)

FIGURE 6.5 Hands-on Exercise 2 (*continued*)

HYPERLINKS BEFORE AND AFTER (INTERNET EXPLORER)

Hyperlinks are displayed in different colors, depending on whether (or not) the associated page has been displayed. You can change the default colors, however, to suit your personal preference. Start Internet Explorer, pull down the Tools menu, click the Internet Options command to display the Internet Options dialog box, and click the General tab. Click the Colors button and then click the color box next to the Visited or Unvisited links to display a color palette. Select (click) the desired color, click OK to close the palette, click OK to close the Colors dialog box, then click OK to close the Internet Options dialog box.

Step 6: **The Finishing Touches**

- You should be back in Word where you can apply the final changes to the document.
- Click and drag to select the **World Wide Travel** in the left cell. Click the **Bold button**. Increase the font size and/or change the font color as appropriate.
- Click and drag to select the four lines of text in the left cell, then click the **Center button** on the Formatting toolbar to center each line within the cell.
- Point to the upper-left corner of the table to display a plus sign, then click the **plus sign** to select the entire table as shown in Figure 6.5f. Pull down the **Table menu**, click the **Table Properties command** to display the associated dialog box, and click the Table tab.
- Click the **Center icon** to center the table itself within the document. Click **OK** to accept the settings and close the dialog box. Click elsewhere in the document to deselect the table. Add and/or delete blank lines as needed.
- Save the document. Click the **Internet Explorer button** on the Windows taskbar to return to the Web browser, then click the **Refresh button** to view the revised version of the page. Return to Word to make additional changes as necessary.
- Close the Word document. Close Internet Explorer.

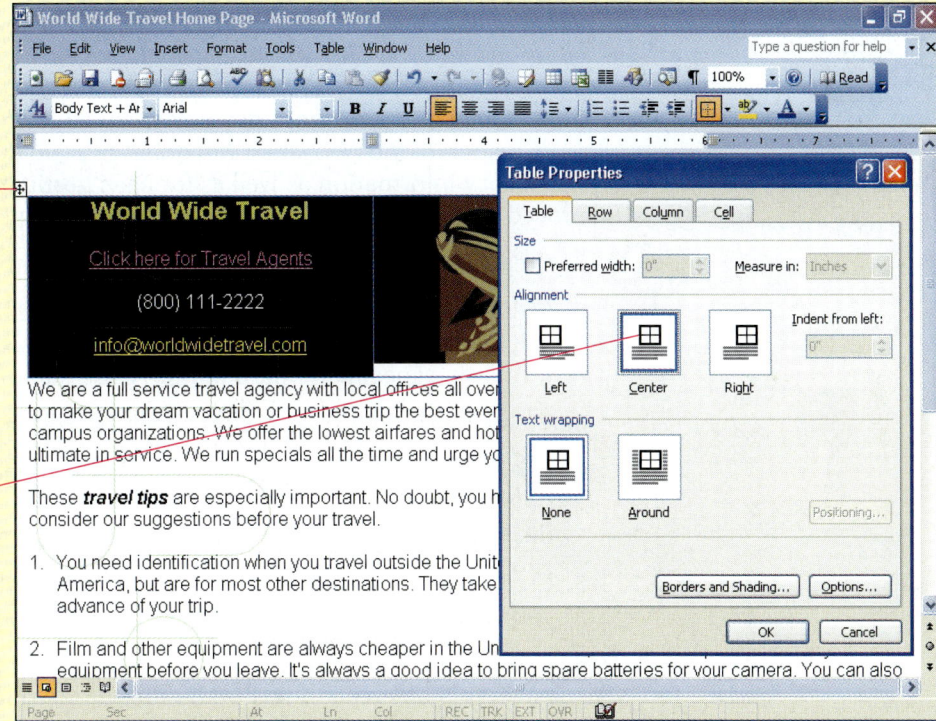

(f) The Finishing Touches (step 6)

FIGURE 6.5 Hands-on Exercise 2 (*continued*)

WHY REFRESH MAY NOT WORK

A Web browser cannot display an MHTML document directly, but must expand it to one or more temporary HTML documents. Thus, if you update a Word document that is saved in MHTML format, then click the Refresh button in Internet Explorer, the browser simply reloads the previous HTML documents. You have to close Internet Explorer, reopen Internet Explorer, and then open the updated MHTML file to create the updated set of HTML documents for the browser.

CREATING A WEB SITE

A **Web site** is composed of multiple pages, which include a home page, navigation page, and other pages as appropriate—for example, a New York Weekend and an Italian Holiday in the case of the travel agency. Two **frames** are typically visible—one displaying the navigation page and another displaying the detailed page (the latter is displayed by clicking the appropriate hyperlink within the navigation page). Vertical frames are the most common means of navigation, but you can also choose horizontal frames and/or open each document in a separate window. Figure 6.6 displays the Web site of our travel agency.

Figure 6.6a shows the home page as it existed at the end of the last exercise, whereas Figure 6.6b displays the home page within a Web site. Figure 6.6c displays a page within the site during development, whereas Figure 6.6d displays the same page after it has been completed. Vertical frames appear in Figures 6.6b, c, and d and divide the browser window in two. The left frame provides the overall navigation for the site via the hyperlinks that are associated with the other pages.

Click the Home Page link in the left pane, and you display information about the agency in the right frame as shown in Figure 6.6b. Click the link to the New York Weekend, however, and you display a page describing a trip to New York. Each frame can have its own vertical scroll bar, and the scroll bars function independently of one another. Thus, you can click the vertical scroll bar in the left pane to view additional links, and/or you can click the scroll bar in the right frame to view additional information on the displayed page. The address bar throughout Figure 6.6 indicates that the Web documents are stored in the World Wide Travel folder on drive C; that is, the site has not yet been uploaded to a Web server.

Creation of the Web site will require that you develop separate documents for the agency information as well as for each destination. It is helpful to outline the procedure for creating the Web site prior to attempting the exercise.

1. Create a new folder to hold all of the documents for the site.

2. Create the home page, and in so doing, establish the visual design that you will follow for every subsequent page. The design should include the font and formatting specifications, a theme (if any), and/or a logo.

3. Create an Under Construction page that follows the design of the home page.

4. Use the Save As command to duplicate the Under Construction page as many times as necessary to create the additional pages on the eventual site. Modify the title of each new Under Construction page to indicate its purpose.

5. Create the navigation page that contains hyperlinks to the various pages that you created. The navigation page should adhere to the visual design.

6. Use the **Frames toolbar** to insert a new frame to the right of the navigation page; this creates a new document with two frames that will eventually be saved as the Web site document. Designate the right frame as the **target frame** (the frame in which the documents will be displayed).

7. Set the home page as the default page when the Web site document is opened (the page that will be displayed in the right frame initially).

8. Save the Web site document.

A well-designed site simplifies the addition of new pages and/or the modification of existing pages. To add a new page, start Word, save the page in the folder that contains the other documents for the site, then modify the navigation page to include a hyperlink to the new page. It's even easier to modify an existing page—all you do is edit the page in Word and save it in the original folder. The navigation does not change.

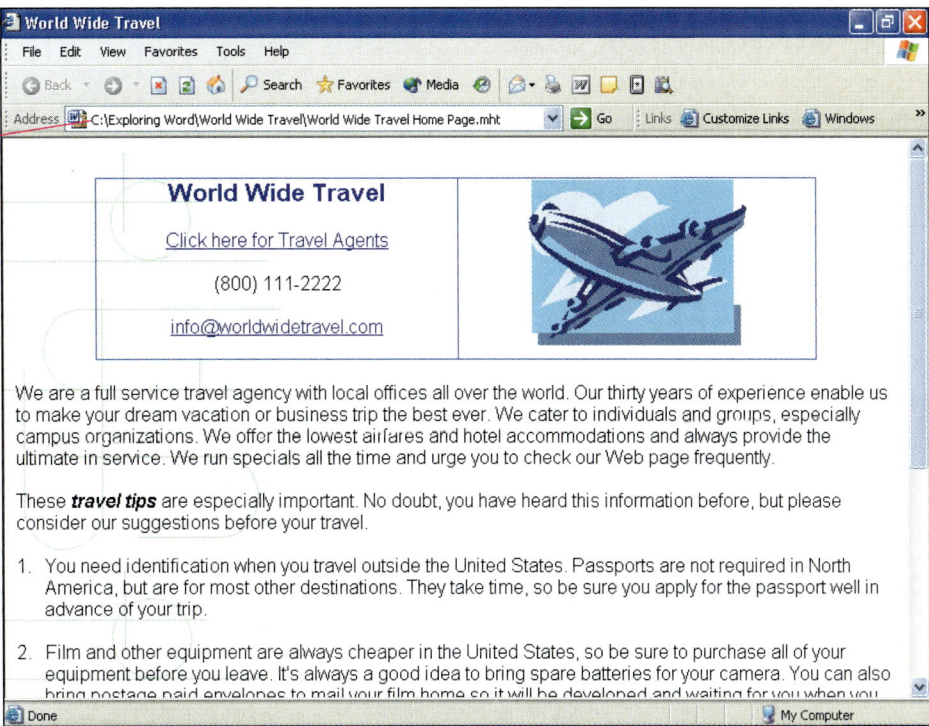

(a) Home Page

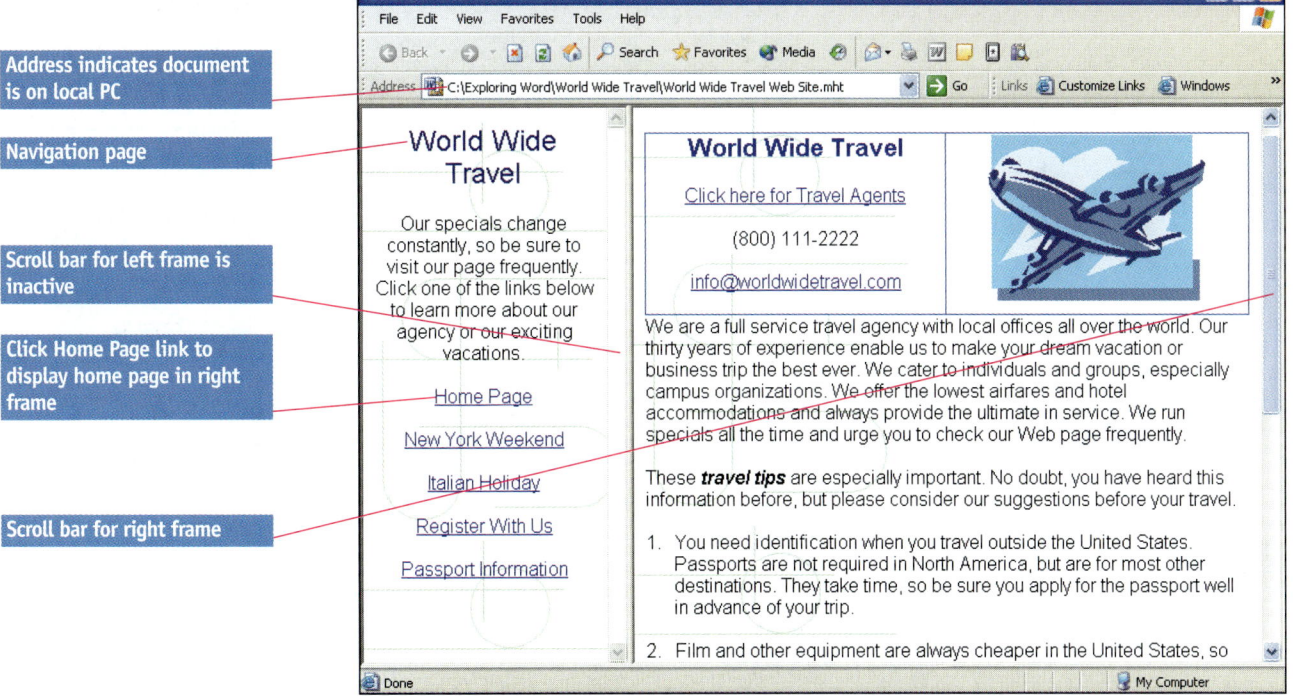

(b) Web Site

FIGURE 6.6 From a Home Page to a Web Site

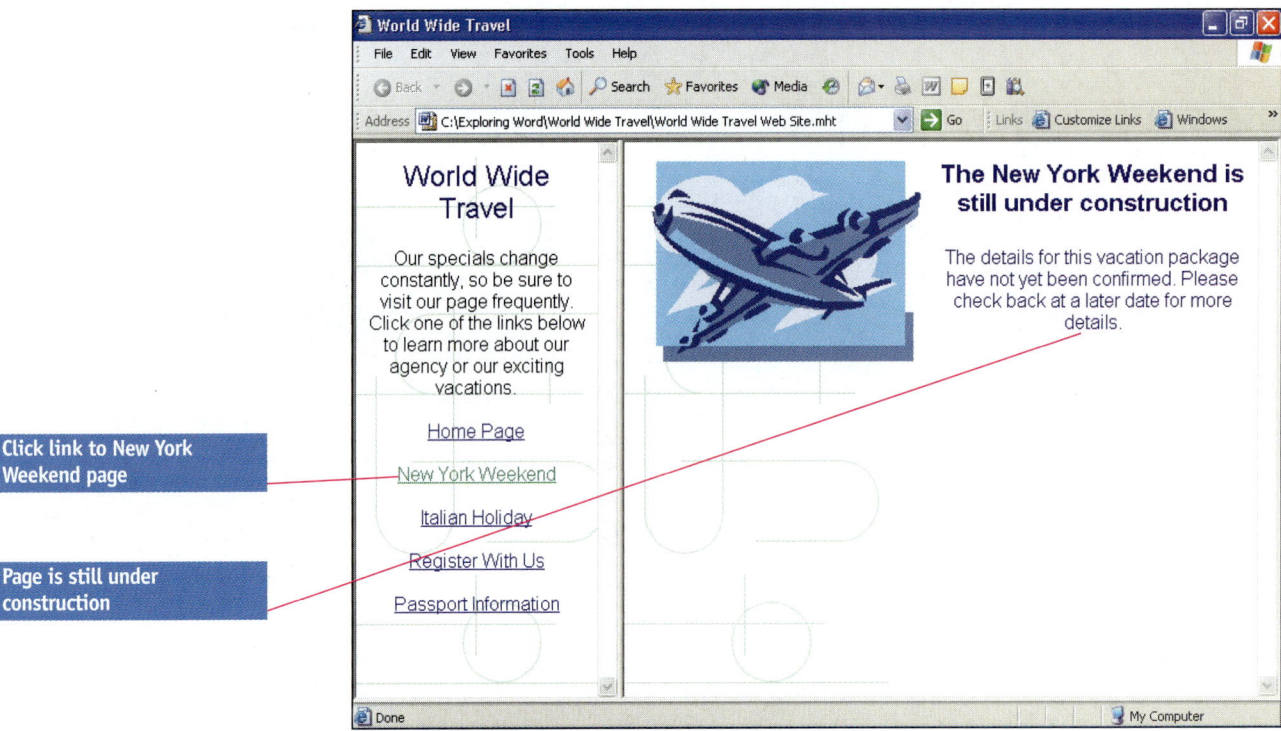

(c) Under Construction

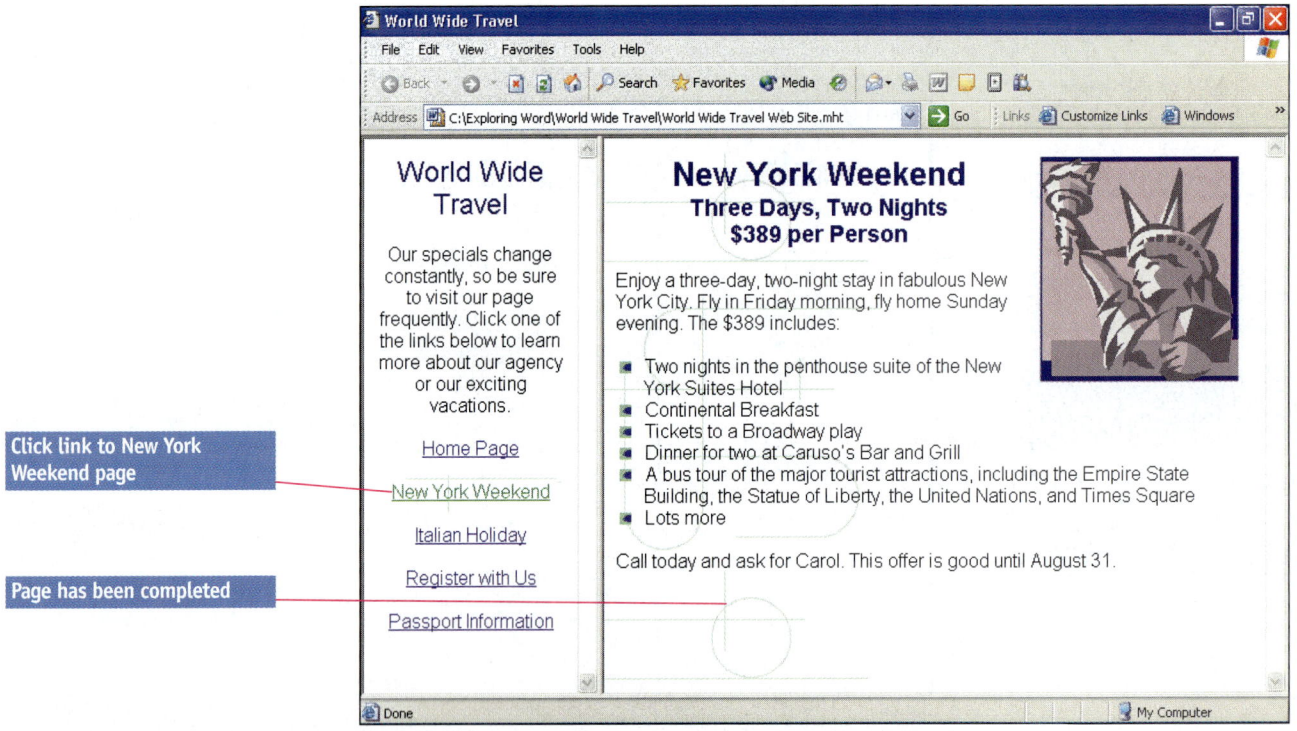

(d) New York Weekend

FIGURE 6.6   From a Home Page to a Web Site (continued)

hands-on exercise

3 Creating a Web Site

Objective To create a Web site consisting of multiple Web pages; to add a frame to an existing page. Use Figure 6.7 as a guide in the exercise.

Step 1: **Create the Under Construction Page**

- Start Word. Create a new document that is similar to the document in Figure 6.7a. Use the same clip art that you selected in the previous exercise.
- Pull down the **Format menu**, click the **Theme command**, and choose the same theme you used for the other pages. (We are using the **Capsules theme**.)
- Pull down the **File menu** and click the **Save as Web Page command**. Save the page as **Under Construction** in the **World Wide Travel folder** (within the Exploring Word folder). Specify **Single File Web Page** as the file format.
- Change the title to reflect the New York Weekend. Pull down the **File menu**, click the **Save As command** a second time, and enter **New York Weekend**. Change the title to reflect the Italian Holiday, then save the page one additional time as **Italian Holiday**. Close the Word document.

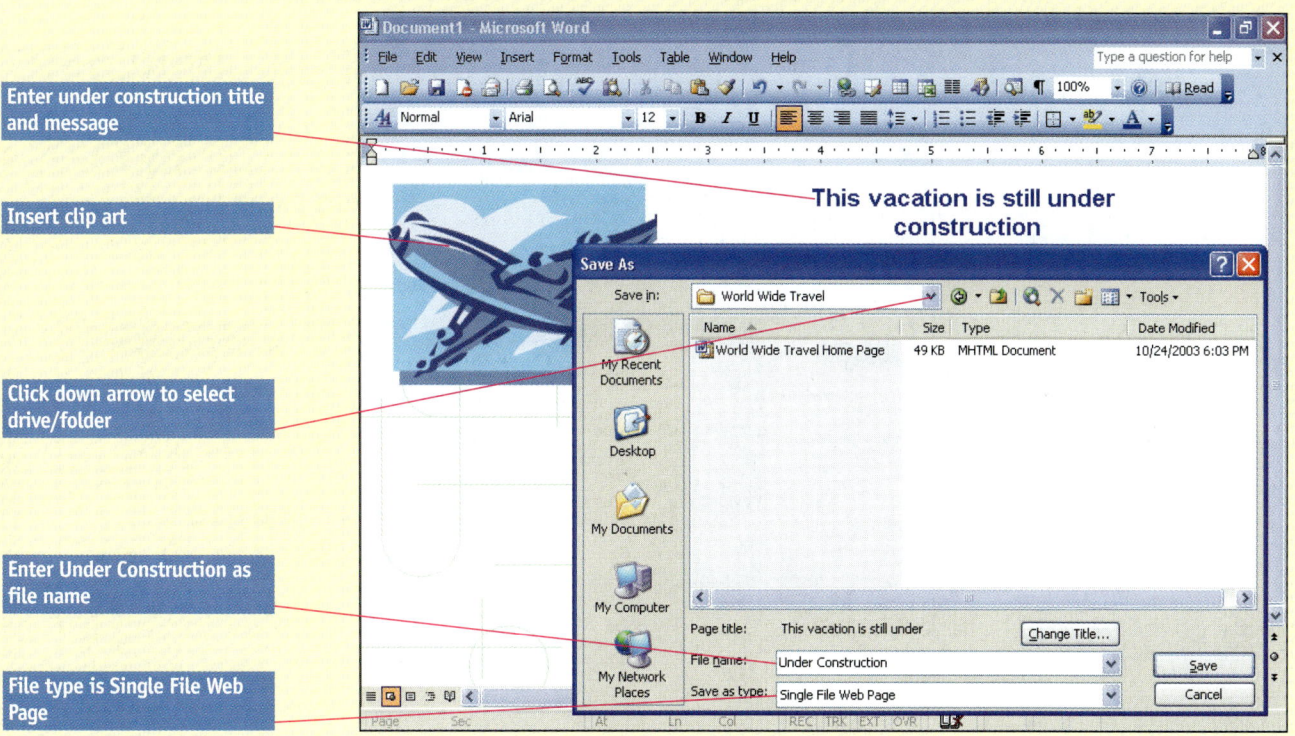

(a) Create the Under Construction Page (step 1)

FIGURE 6.7 Hands-on Exercise 3

UNDER CONSTRUCTION

Use prototyping to let the end user experience the "look and feel" of a site before the site has been finished. The user sees the opening document and a set of links to partially completed documents, which indicates how the eventual site will function. The site is "complete" but incomplete. The user can suggest improvements in the visual design, content, and/or navigation. The developer can then make the necessary adjustments before extensive work has been done.

MICROSOFT OFFICE WORD 2003   1133

Step 2: Create the Navigation Page

- Click the **New Blank document button** on the Standard toolbar to start a new Word document. Enter the text of the document as shown in Figure 6.7b.

- Pull down the **File menu** and click the **Save as Web Page command**. Save the page as **Navigation** in the **World Wide Travel folder** (within the Exploring Word folder). Be sure to specify **Single File Web Page** as the file format.

- Pull down the **Format menu**, click the **Theme command**, and choose the same theme you used for the other pages in this site. (We are using the **Capsules theme**.)

- Click and drag to select **Home Page** and then click the **Insert Hyperlink button** to display the associated dialog box. Click the **Existing File or Web Page button**, then click the **Current Folder button**.

- Click in the Look in list box and select the **World Wide Travel folder** as shown in Figure 6.7b. Select the **World Wide Travel Home Page** that you created earlier. Click **OK**.

- Add the hyperlinks for **New York Weekend** and **Italian Holiday** in similar fashion. Click and drag to select all of the text in the document, then click the Center button on the Standard toolbar. Click the **Save button** on the Standard toolbar.

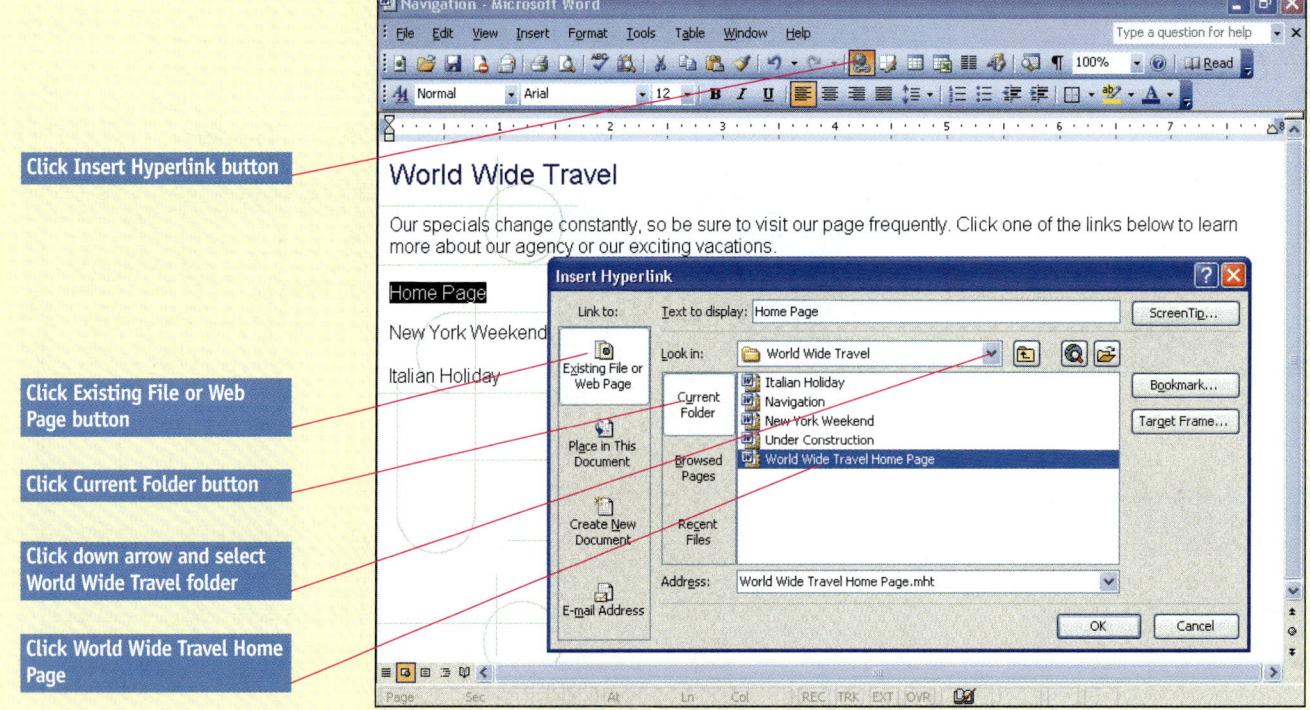

(b) Create the Navigation Page (step 2)

FIGURE 6.7 Hands-on Exercise 3 (*continued*)

THE WORLD WIDE TRAVEL FOLDER

A Web site is composed of multiple documents that are stored in a single folder. Each document is saved in the Single File Web Page (MHTML) format. Every site has a navigation page that contains links to the other documents within the site. The Under Construction page can be duplicated as necessary to create additional (temporary) documents that are used in testing and development.

Step 3: **Add a Second Frame**

- Pull down the **View menu**, click the **Toolbars command**, and then click the **Frames toolbar**. The command functions as a toggle switch; that is, execute the command a second time and the Frames toolbar is closed.

- Click the **New Frame Right button** to create a second frame to the right of the existing Navigation page as shown in Figure 6.7c. Click and drag the border of the left frame to make that frame narrower.

- Right click any hyperlink to display a context-sensitive menu, then click the **Edit Hyperlink command** to display the Edit Hyperlink dialog box. Click the **Target Frame button** to display the Set Target Frame dialog box.

- Click in the right frame within the dialog box. Frame2 appears in the list box that specifies where you want the page to appear.

- Check the box to **Set as default for all hyperlinks**, so that the associated page for every hyperlink in the left frame is displayed in the right frame.

- Click **OK** to close the Set Target Frame dialog box. Click **OK** to close the Edit Hyperlink dialog box.

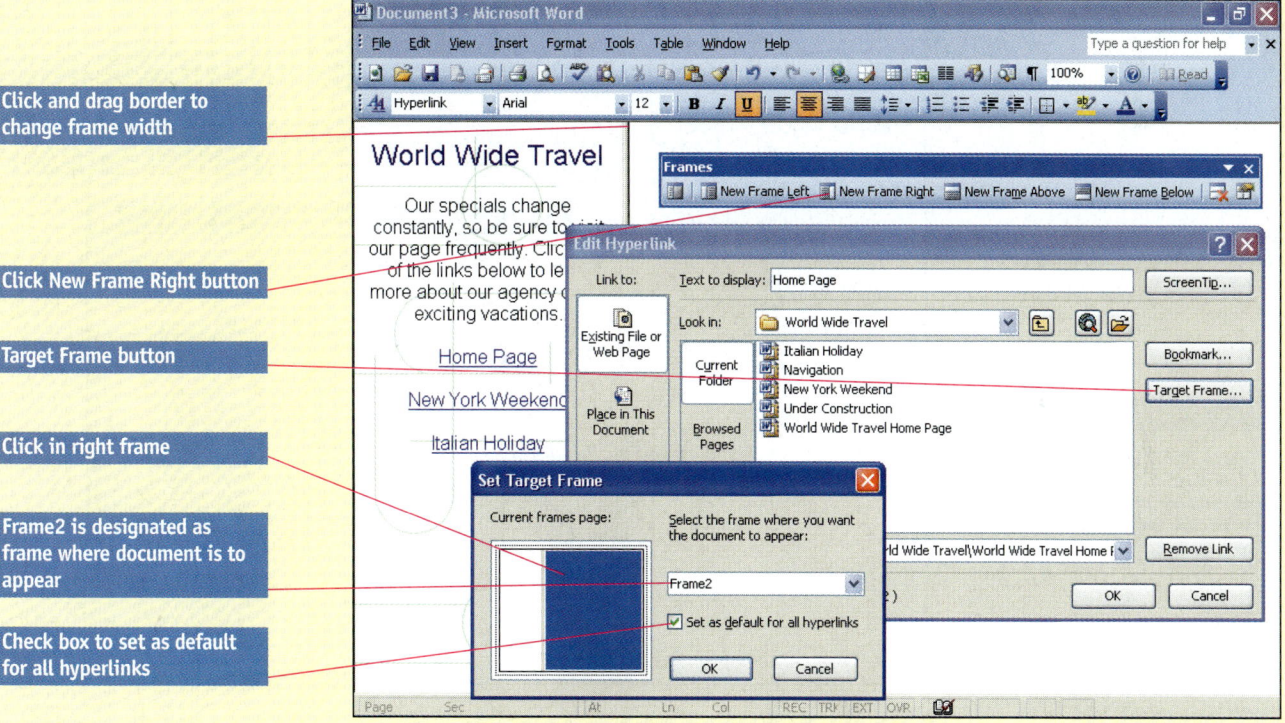

(c) Add a Second Frame (step 3)

FIGURE 6.7 Hands-on Exercise 3 (*continued*)

FIXED VERSUS FLOATING TOOLBARS

A toolbar is either fixed (docked) along an edge of a window or floating within the window. To move a docked toolbar, click and drag the move handle (the vertical dotted line that appears at the left of the toolbar) to a new position. To move a floating toolbar, click and drag its title bar—if you drag a floating toolbar to the edge of the window, it becomes a docked toolbar and vice versa. You can also change the shape of a floating toolbar by dragging any border in the direction you want to go.

Step 4: **Set the Default Frame**

- Click anywhere in the right frame, then click the **Frame Properties button** on the Frames toolbar to display the Frame Properties dialog box as shown in Figure 6.7d.

- Click in the initial page list box and then click the **Browse button**. Select the **World Wide Travel Home Page** that you created earlier.

- Click the **Borders tab** to view the options that are available. Select the option button to **Show all frame borders**. Set the list box to show scrollbars in browser if needed, and check the box to make the frame resizable in the browser.

- Use the **spin buttons** to experiment with the width of the border. Click the **down arrow** on the Border color list box to choose a different color.

- Click **OK** to accept your choices and close the Frame Properties dialog box. You should see the home page of the travel agency displayed in the right frame.

- Close the Frames toolbar.

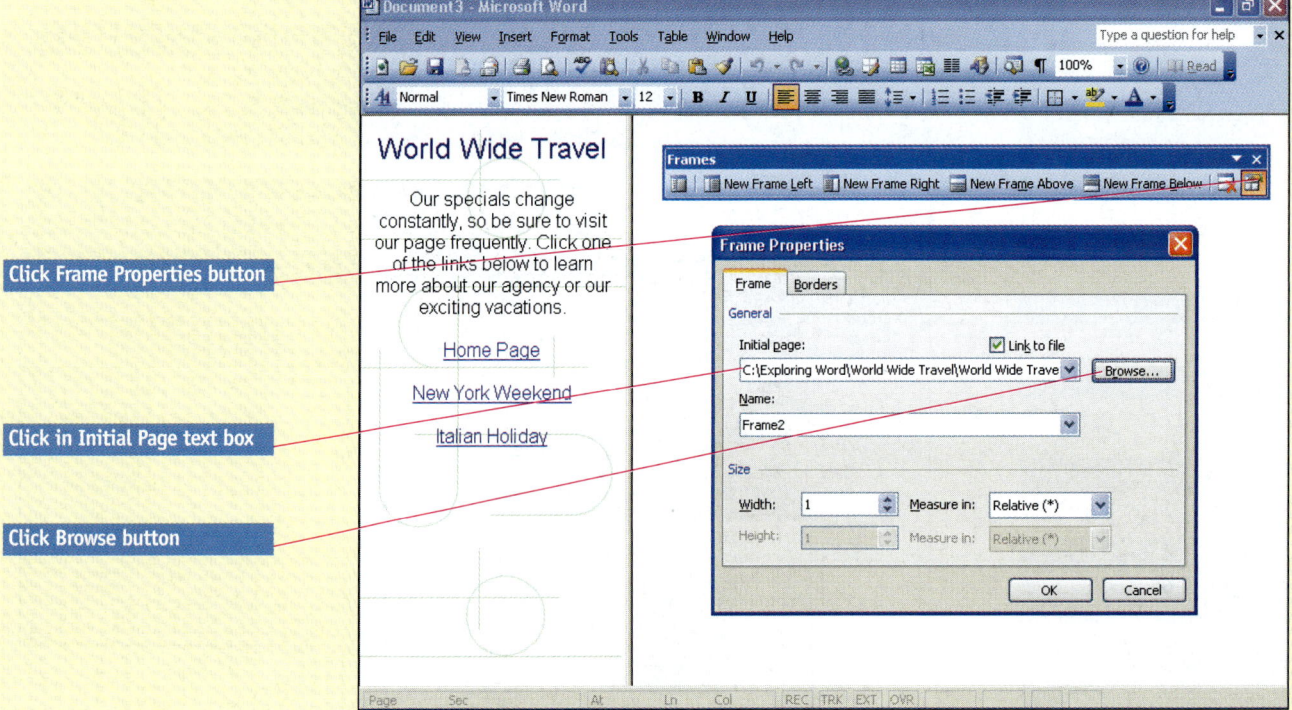

(d) Set the Default Frame (step 4)

FIGURE 6.7 Hands-on Exercise 3 (*continued*)

SET A TIME LIMIT

It's fun to experiment with the visual design of your Web page, but it can also be counterproductive. Try different settings for the width and color of the frame border, set a time limit, and stick to it when your time is up. The more important options are those that affect the *behavior* of the border. We recommend that you show all frame borders, show scrollbars if needed, and make the frame resizable in the browser.

Step 5: Test the Navigation

- Click on the **Navigation page**, then point to the New York Weekend. Press **Ctrl+Click** (press the **Ctrl key** while you click the mouse) to display this page in the right frame. Test the link to the Italian Holiday in similar fashion.

- Pull down the **File menu** and click the **Save button**, which in turn displays the Save As dialog box as shown in Figure 6.7e. You should be in the World Wide Travel folder with Single File Web Page selected as the file type. The following documents are already in the folder:
  - The Navigation document contains the hyperlinks in the left frame
  - The World Wide Travel Home Page, Italian Holiday, and New York Weekend are the specific pages that will be displayed in the right frame.
  - The Under Construction page can be used as the basis for additional pages.

- Enter **World Wide Travel Web Site** as the name of the current page. This is a small document that functions as a container to hold the left and right frames.

- Click the **Change Title button** to display the Set Page Title dialog box. Enter **World Wide Travel** as the title. Click **OK** to close this dialog box. Click the **Save button** to save the page. Exit Word.

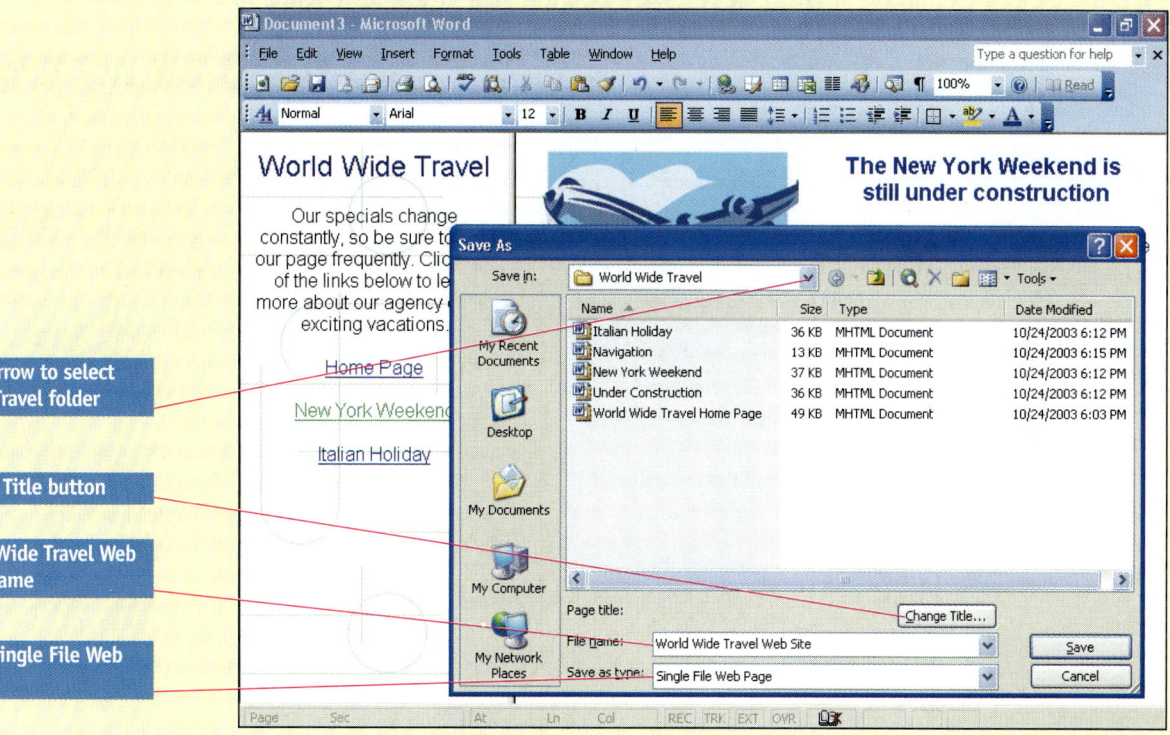

(e) Test the Navigation (step 5)

FIGURE 6.7 Hands-on Exercise 3 (*continued*)

THE WEB TOOLBAR

The Web toolbar appears automatically when you view Web pages within Microsoft Word as you develop a Web site. The buttons on the toolbar are similar to those on the Standard toolbar in Internet Explorer: the Back, Forward, and Favorites buttons, and the Address bar. You can display or hide the toolbar at any time by right clicking any visible toolbar to display the list of available toolbars, then clicking the Web toolbar to toggle the display on or off.

Step 6: **View the Completed Site**

- Start Internet Explorer. Pull down the **File menu** and click the **Open command** to display the Open dialog box. Click the **Browse button**, locate the **World Wide Travel folder**, then open the **World Wide Travel Web Site document**.

- You should see the Web site in Figure 6.7f. Look closely at the components of the URL in the address bar, reading from right to left:
  - You are viewing the **World Wide Travel Web Site.mht document** (mht is the extension to indicate the Single File Web Page format).
  - The document is in the **World Wide Travel folder** that is contained within the Exploring Word folder.
  - The document is on drive C; that is, you are viewing the site locally, as opposed to seeing it on the Web.

- Test the hyperlinks in the left frame to ensure that they are working correctly.

- Pull down the **File menu**, click the **Print Preview command**, then click the **down arrow** on the Print What list box to select **As laid out on screen**. Click the **Print button** in the Preview window to display the Print dialog box and print the page.

- Close Internet Explorer. Congratulations on a job well done.

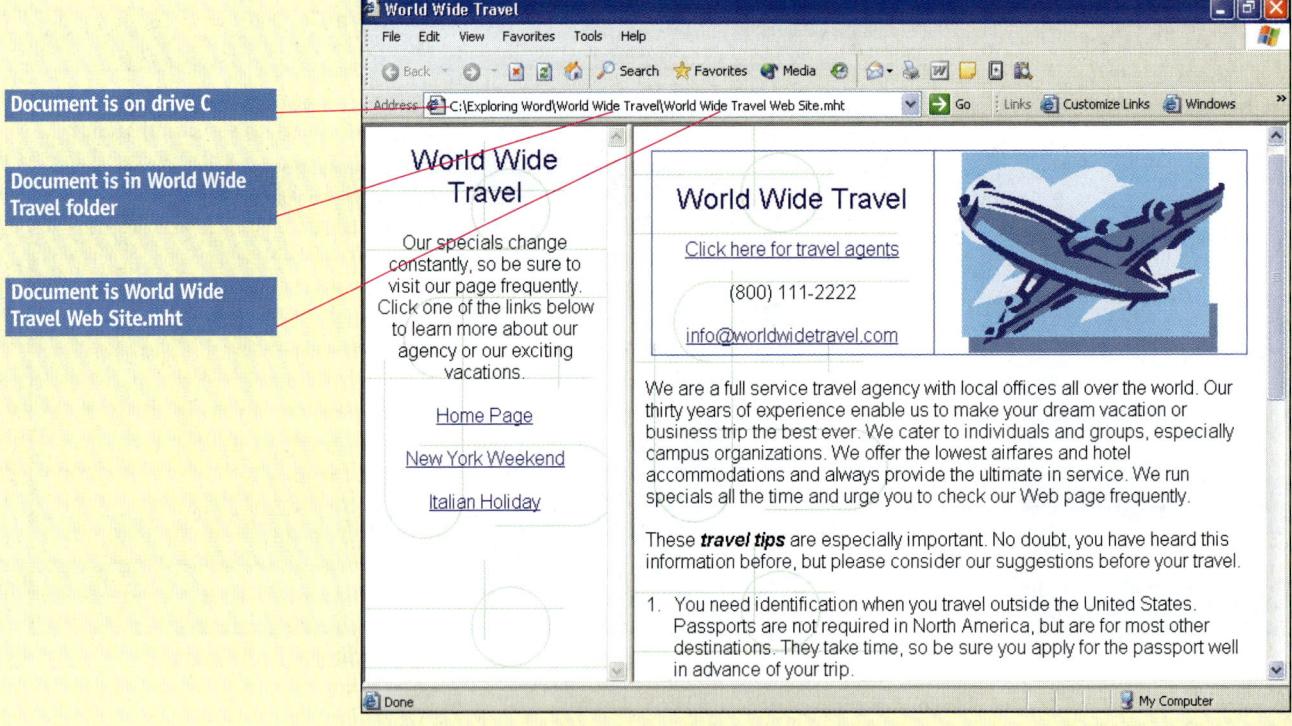

(f) View the Completed Site (step 6)

FIGURE 6.7 Hands-on Exercise 3 (*continued*)

EXPANDING THE SITE

You can expand the site at any time, by creating the additional Web pages, then adding the links to those pages to the navigation frame at the left. You can also add hyperlinks to external Web sites to the navigation frame and open those pages in the right frame within the Web site. See practice exercise 2 at the end of the chapter.

SUMMARY

All Web documents are written in HyperText Markup Language (HTML), a language that consists of codes (or tags) that format a document for display on the World Wide Web. The easiest way to create an HTML document is through Microsoft Word. You start Word in the usual fashion, enter the text of the document with basic formatting, then you use the Save as Web Page command to convert the Word document to its Web equivalent. Microsoft Word does the rest, generating the HTML tags that are needed to create the document. The new Single File Web Page format saves all of the elements of a Web site, including text and graphics, in a single file.

An existing Web page can be modified with respect to its content and/or appearance just like an ordinary Word document; that is, any Word command can be used to create and/or edit a Web page. The Insert Hyperlink command links a document to another page and/or to a bookmark on the same page. The Insert Picture command inserts clip art or a photograph. The Format Theme command applies a professional design to the document.

HTML is not to be confused with XML. HTML describes how a document should look; for example, it might specify that "John Doe" is to appear in bold when viewed in a browser. Extensible Markup Language (XML) is very different as it describes the structure of the data. It might specify that "John" and "Doe" represent an individual's first and last name, respectively, and it makes that information available to virtually any application.

A Web site is composed of multiple pages, which include a home page, navigation page, and other pages as appropriate. Two pages (frames) are typically visible—the navigation page and a detailed page that is displayed by clicking a hyperlink within the navigation page. Vertical frames are the most common means of navigation, but you can also choose horizontal frames and/or open each document in a separate window. All of the pages comprising the site should be stored in the same folder.

The development of a Web site starts with the creation of a home page to provide information about the site and establish the visual design. An Under Construction page is created and duplicated several times for use as the various pages that will comprise the site. A separate navigation page is also created that contains the hyperlinks to the individual pages. The navigation page is then expanded to include a (horizontal or vertical) frame, and the second frame is designated as the target frame. The next step is to specify the default page (the page that will be displayed in the right frame initially) when the Web site document is opened. And finally, you save the document that contains the two frames as the Web site document, the document that is opened to view the site.

After a Web document or Web site has been created, it can be placed on a server or local area network so that other people will be able to access it. This, in turn, requires you to check with your professor or system administrator to obtain the necessary username and password, after which you can use FTP (File Transfer Protocol) to upload your page. Even if your page is not placed on the Web, you can still view it locally on your PC through a Web browser.

KEY TERMS

Bookmark 1123	Hyperlink 1116	Save As Web Page command . . . 1116
File Transfer Protocol (FTP) 1123	Hypertext Markup Language	Single File Web Page 1116
Frame 1130	(HTML) 1114	Target frame 1130
Frames toolbar 1130	Insert Hyperlink command 1116	Theme 1116
Home page 1116	Prototyping 1133	Web site 1130
HTML tag 1114	Round-trip HTML 1116	XML 1114

MULTIPLE CHOICE

1. Which of the following requires you to enter HTML tags explicitly in order to create a Web document?
   (a) A text editor such as the Notepad accessory
   (b) Microsoft Word
   (c) Both (a) and (b)
   (d) Neither (a) nor (b)

2. What is the easiest way to switch back and forth between Word and Internet Explorer, given that both are open?
   (a) Click the appropriate button on the Windows taskbar
   (b) Click the Start button, click Programs, then choose the appropriate program
   (c) Minimize all applications to display the Windows desktop, then double click the icon for the appropriate application
   (d) All of the above are equally convenient

3. When should you click the Refresh button on the Internet Explorer toolbar?
   (a) Whenever you visit a new Web site
   (b) Whenever you return to a Web site within a session
   (c) Whenever you view a document on a corporate Intranet
   (d) Whenever you return to a document that has changed during the session

4. How do you view the HTML tags for a Web document from Internet Explorer?
   (a) Pull down the View menu and select the Source command
   (b) Pull down the File menu, click the Save As command, and specify HTML as the file type
   (c) Click the Web Page Preview button on the Standard toolbar
   (d) All of the above

5. Internet Explorer can display an HTML page that is stored on:
   (a) A local area network
   (b) A Web server
   (c) Drive A or drive C of a stand-alone PC
   (d) All of the above

6. How do you save a Word document as a Web page?
   (a) Pull down the Tools menu and click the Convert to Web Page command
   (b) Pull down the File menu and click the Save As Web Page command
   (c) Both (a) and (b)
   (d) Neither (a) nor (b)

7. Which program transfers files between a PC and a remote computer?
   (a) Telnet
   (b) FTP
   (c) Homer
   (d) PTF

8. Which of the following requires an Internet connection?
   (a) Using Internet Explorer to view a document that is stored locally
   (b) Using Internet Explorer to view the Microsoft home page
   (c) Both (a) and (b)
   (d) Neither (a) nor (b)

9. Which of the following requires an Internet connection?
   (a) The Save as Web Page command
   (b) The Single File Web Page format
   (c) Both (a) and (b)
   (d) Neither (a) nor (b)

10. Which file format is new to Office 2003?
    (a) HTML
    (b) XML
    (c) MHTML
    (d) All of the above

11. The Insert Hyperlink command can reference:
    (a) An e-mail address
    (b) A bookmark
    (c) A Web page
    (d) All of the above

... continued

multiple choice

12. The Format Theme command:
    (a) Is required in order to save a Word document as a Web page
    (b) Applies a uniform design to the links and other elements within a document
    (c) Both (a) and (b)
    (d) Neither (a) nor (b)

13. Which of the following features were introduced in Word 2003 to simplify the creation of a Web page?
    (a) The Save as Web Page command
    (b) The Format Theme command
    (c) The Single File Web Page format
    (d) All of the above

14. The Frames toolbar enables you to insert a frame:
    (a) To the left or right of the current frame
    (b) Above or below the current frame
    (c) Both (a) and (b)
    (d) Neither (a) nor (b)

15. Which of the following is true?
    (a) A Web page is saved as an HTTP document
    (b) All of the pages for an entire Web site are typically stored in a single document
    (c) Both (a) and (b)
    (d) Neither (a) nor (b)

16. How do you display the Frames toolbar?
    (a) Pull down the View menu, click the Toolbars command, and toggle the Frames toolbar on
    (b) Right click any visible toolbar, then toggle the Frames toolbar on
    (c) Both (a) and (b)
    (d) Neither (a) nor (b)

17. Which of the following best describes XML?
    (a) It is a replacement for HTML
    (b) It stores the documents for a Web site in a single file
    (c) It describes the structure of data, as opposed to the appearance of data
    (d) All of the above

18. You are viewing a Web page in Internet Explorer in which the hyperlinks are displayed in two different colors. What is the most likely explanation?
    (a) One or more errors must have occurred
    (b) One or more of the hyperlinks was previously accessed
    (c) Some of the hyperlinks are invalid and are shown in the second color
    (d) All of the above

ANSWERS

1. a	7. b	13. c
2. a	8. b	14. c
3. d	9. d	15. d
4. a	10. c	16. c
5. d	11. d	17. c
6. b	12. b	18. b

PRACTICE WITH WORD

1. **Milestones in Communications:** The document in Figure 6.8 describes various milestones in the history of communications and is truly informative. Hyperlinks to the various milestones are listed in a table near the top of the document. (Each hyperlink branches to a place within the document, as opposed to branching to an external document.) Proceed as follows:

   a. Open the *Chapter 6 Practice 1* document in the Exploring Word folder. Pull down the Format menu, click the AutoFormat command to display the AutoFormat dialog box, verify that the AutoFormat Now option is selected, and click OK. Modify the Body Text style and/or the Heading 1 style after the document has been formatted in any way that makes sense to you.

   b. Insert a three-by-three table at the top of the document that will contain the hyperlink to each milestone within the document. Enter the title of each milestone as shown in Figure 6.8. Format the text as desired, then create the hyperlinks to the associated text. (You do not have to create bookmarks to each milestone because the associated headings are automatically recognized as places within the document.) Click and drag to select the title—for example, The Pony Express—pull down the Insert menu, click the Hyperlink command, then click the Place in this Document button to select from the listed headings.

   c. You also need to insert a hyperlink at the end of the text for each milestone to return to the top of the document. Scroll down in the document to move to the end of a milestone and type "Top of Document". Click and drag to select this text, pull down the Insert menu, click the Hyperlink command, click the Place in This Document button, and select Top of the Document. Copy this hyperlink to the end of each milestone.

   d. Use the Format Theme command to complete the formatting. Save the document as a Web page in the Single File Web Page format. Exit Word.

   e. Start Windows Explorer, then go to the folder containing your Web page, and double click the file you just created. Internet Explorer will start automatically (because your document was saved as a Web page). Print the document for your instructor as proof you completed the assignment.

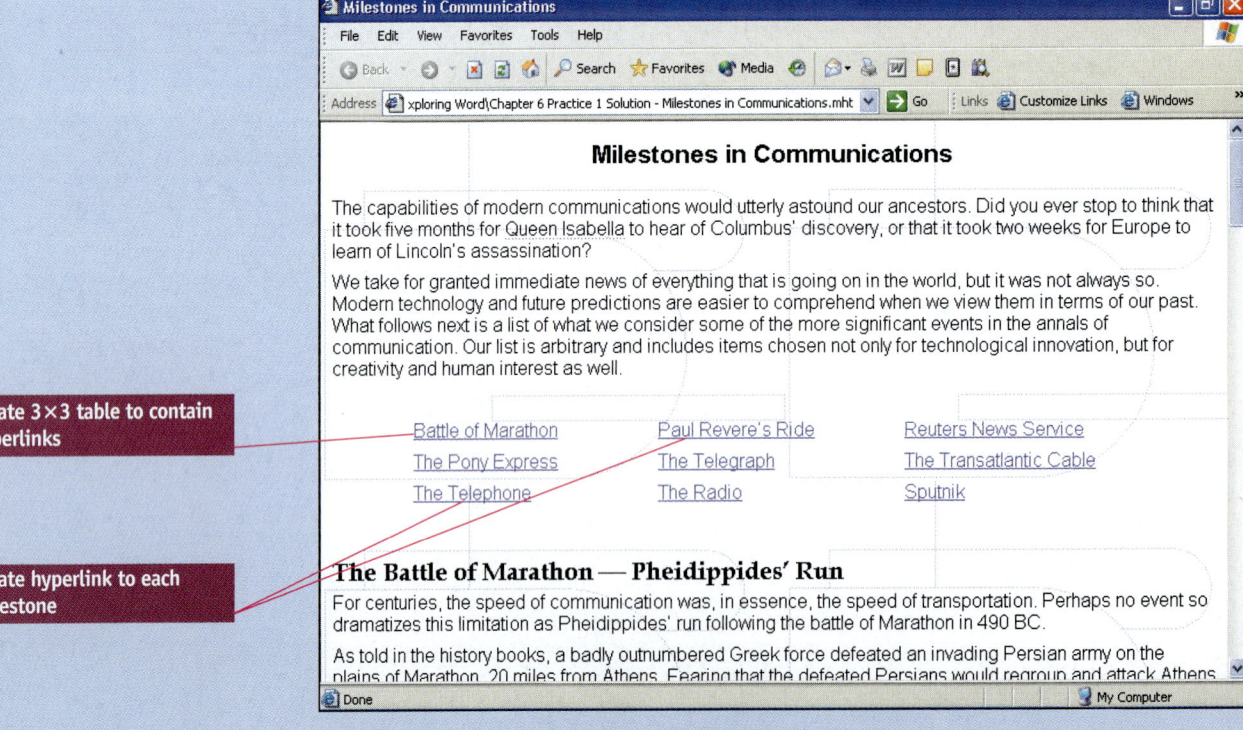

FIGURE 6.8 Milestones in Communications (exercise 1)

practice exercises

2. **Expanding the World Wide Web Site:** This assignment asks you to update the World Wide Travel Web site that was developed in the chapter as shown in Figure 6.9. Look closely and you will see that we added two links in the navigation pane. We have also expanded the content of the existing New York Weekend page. Proceed as follows:

   a. Start Word and open the existing New York Weekend Web document in the World Wide Travel folder. The page is currently under construction and does not contain any specific information. Your task is to create a page describing a weekend holiday similar to the page in Figure 6.9. You do not have to match our page exactly, but you are required to use clip art and a bulleted list. Save the completed page. Close the New York Weekend document.

   b. Start Internet Explorer and open the World Wide Travel Web Site document. Click the link to the New York Weekend, which should display the page that you just created. The modification was easy because the navigation already existed; that is, all you had to do to introduce the new vacation was modify the content of an existing page.

   c. Return to Word and open the existing Under Construction document. Pull down the File menu and click the Save as Web Page command to save the page as Register with Us in the Single File Web Page format. Close the document.

   d. Open the Navigation document that was created earlier. Press Ctrl+End to move to the end of the document, press Enter twice, and then insert a hyperlink to the Register with Us page that you just created. Save the document. Remain in the Navigation document and insert a second hyperlink to Passport Information. This time, however, you will link to an external page (http://travel.state.gov/passport_services), which is an official site of the U.S. government. Save the Navigation document. Exit Word.

   e. Return to Internet Explorer. Click in the Navigation pane and click the Refresh button to see the updated version of this page. (You may have to close Internet Explorer, then reopen it and reload the World Wide Travel Web site if the refresh button does not work.) Click the link to Register with Us to view the page you created previously. Now click the link to Passport Information to view the external site.

   f. Print all of the pages in the completed Web site for your instructor. Add a cover page to complete the assignment.

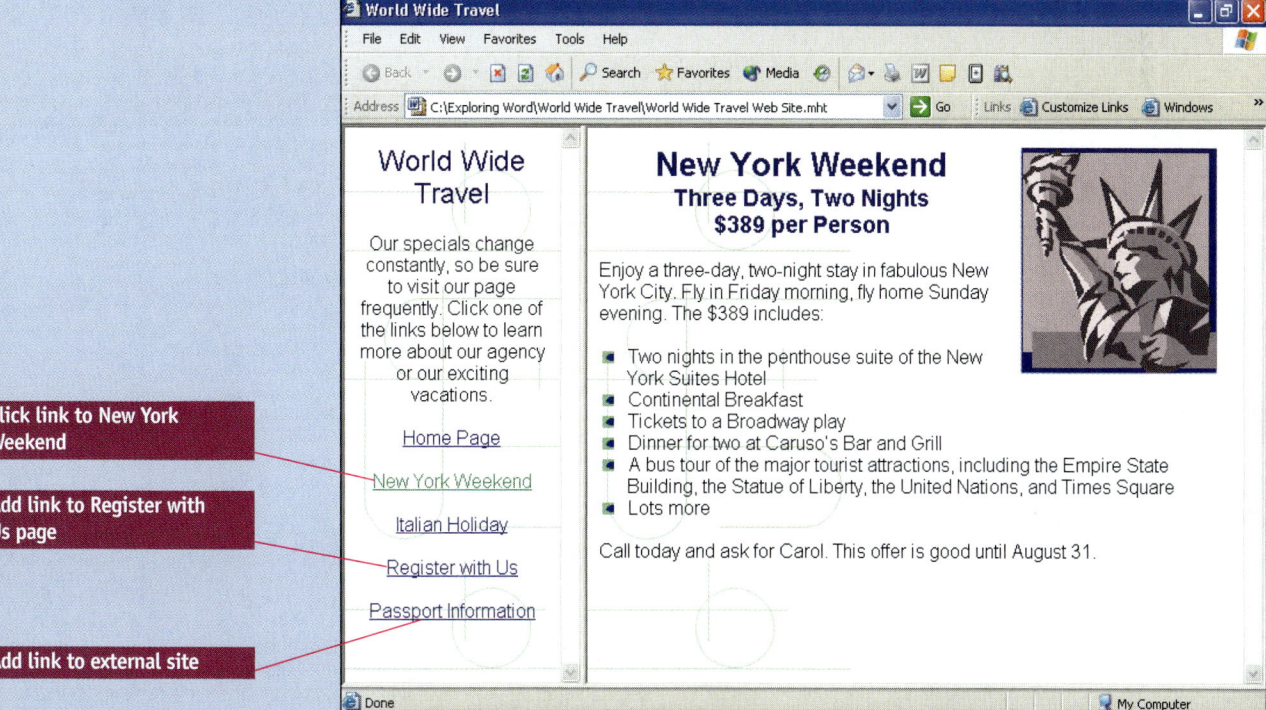

FIGURE 6.9 Expanding the World Wide Web Site (exercise 2)

practice exercises

3. **Realtor of the Year Home Page:** The home page in Figure 6.10 is appropriate for the Realtor of the Year Case study that was presented at the beginning of the chapter. You do not have to duplicate our page exactly, but you are asked to create an attractive page that contains clip art, one or more hyperlinks to an appropriate Web site, and a bulleted list. Proceed as follows:

   a. Start Word and create a new document. Use the Insert Table command to create a one-by-two table (one row and two columns) at the top of the document that contains clip art and the identifying information for the agency. Format the text within the table as appropriate.

   b. Enter the remaining text for your page. Pull down the Format menu, click the Themes command, and select a professionally chosen design. Make additional formatting changes as necessary.

   c. Use the Insert Hyperlink command to enter at least one hyperlink somewhere in the document. (Our link is to the *Miami Herald* at www.herald.com.)

   d. Pull down the File menu and click the Save as Web Page command to convert the Word document to a Web document. Save the document in a new folder (Realtor of the Year) within the Exploring Word folder. (The folder will be used in the next exercise as well, when we expand the page to include a Web site.) Choose an appropriate file name such as "Realtor Home Page" and use the Single File Web Page format. Use the Change Title command button to change the title of the page to reflect your name. Close Word.

   e. Start Windows Explorer, go to the folder containing your Web page, and double click the file you just created. Internet Explorer will start automatically (because your document was saved as a Web page). You should see your document within Internet Explorer as shown in Figure 6.10. Look carefully at the Address bar and note the local address on drive C, as opposed to a Web address. Print the document for your instructor as proof you completed the assignment.

   f. Creating the home page and viewing it locally is easy. Placing the page on the Web where it can be seen by anyone with an Internet connection is not as straightforward. You will need additional information from your instructor about how to obtain an account on a Web server (if that is available at your school), and further how to upload the Web page from your PC to the server.

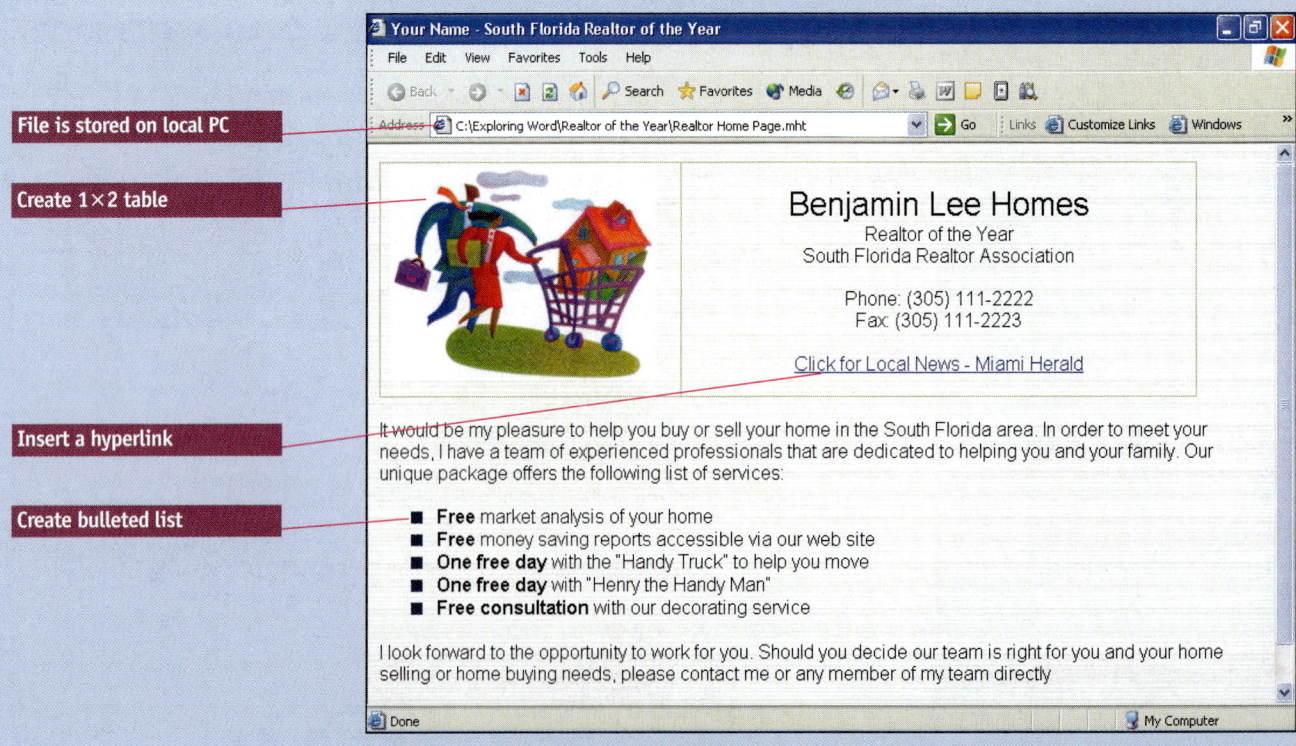

FIGURE 6.10 Realtor of the Year Home Page (exercise 3)

practice exercises

4. **Realtor of the Year Web Site:** This exercise expands the previous problem to create the Web site in Figure 6.11. You do not have to create all of the detailed pages, but you should complete at least one, such as the Current Listing page in Figure 6.11. An "Under Construction" page can be used for the remaining links. Proceed as follows:

   a. Create the Under Construction page. Save the document as a Single File Web Page in the Realtor of the Year folder from the previous exercise. The formatting and theme of your page should be consistent with the design of the Realtor of the Year home page.

   b. The Under Construction page should still be open. Change the text to reflect a new page (current listings). Pull down the File menu, click the Save as Web Page command, and save the page as Current Listings. Change the text and save the page a second time as Sell Your Current Home. Create additional pages corresponding to the links in Figure 6.11. Close all open documents.

   c. Open the Current Listings page that you just created. Complete the page by adding information similar to that in Figure 6.11. (The picture is optional.)

   d. Start a new document and create the navigation page that contains the hyperlinks to the various pages that you just created. Format the navigation page using the same theme as the other pages on your site. Save the page in the Realtor of the Year folder using the Single File Web Page format. Leave the document open.

   e. Display the Frames toolbar. Click the New Frame Right button to insert a frame to the right of the navigation page. Right click any hyperlink in the left frame; click the Edit Hyperlink command, then set the target frame as the frame on the right (frame 2). Click in the right frame, click the Frame Properties button, and set the initial page to the Realtor Home page.

   f. Save the current document as *Realtor of the Year Web Site* document in the Realtor of the Year folder. Change the title of the page.

   g. Start Internet Explorer and open the Realtor of the Year Web Site document that you just created. You should see the Web site in Figure 6.11. Pull down the File menu (from Internet Explorer), click the Print Preview command, then click the down arrow on the Print What list box to select As laid out on screen. Click the Print button from the Preview window to display the Print dialog box and print the page.

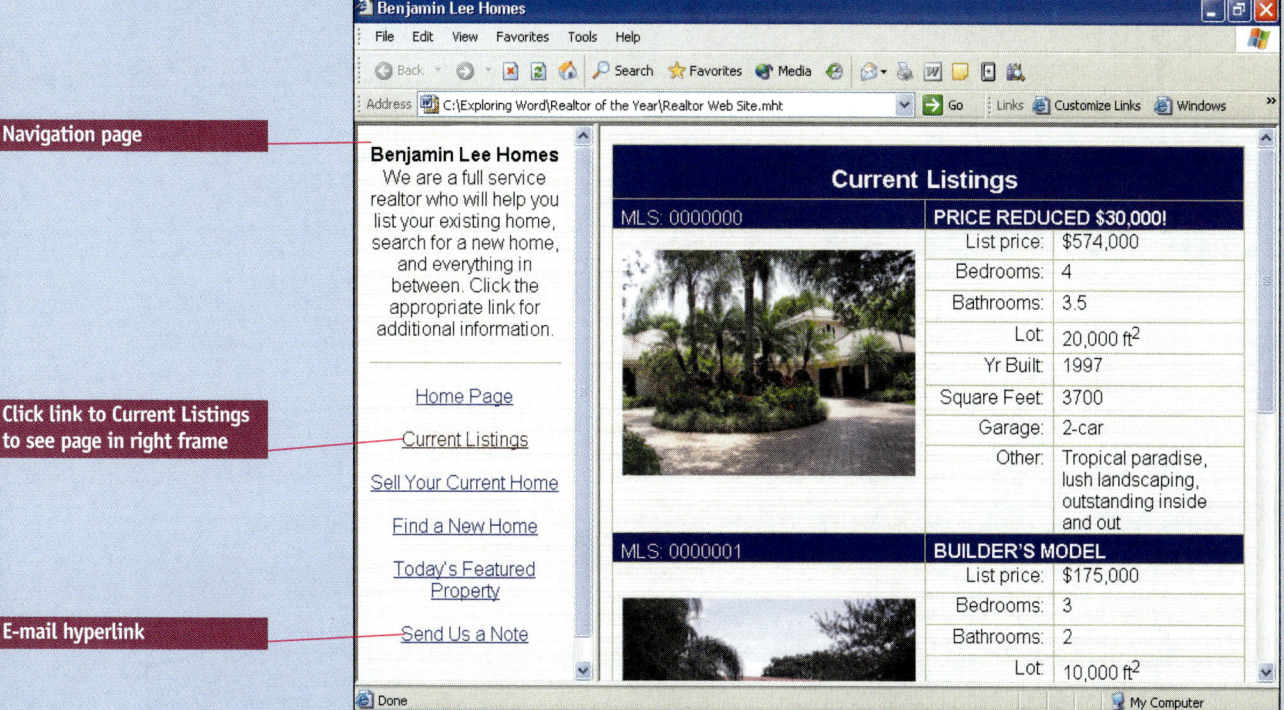

FIGURE 6.11 Realtor of the Year Web Site (exercise 4)

practice exercises

5. **Alternate Airways Home Page:** Open the *Chapter 6 Practice 5* document in the Exploring Word folder and use that document as the basis of the home page in Figure 6.12. Your first task will be to save the existing document as a Web page in its own folder. Proceed as follows:

   a. Pull down the File menu, click the Save as Web Page command, and create an Alternate Airways folder within the Exploring Word folder. Enter Alternate Airways Home Page as the file name and specify Single File Web Page as the file type. Use the Change Title button to change the title of the page to reflect the name of the Web site. Click Continue if a message appears that indicates pictures with text wrapping will become left or right justified.

   b. Review the document and make the basic formatting changes you deem appropriate. Use the Themes command in the Format menu to apply an overall design to the page. Use any theme you like, but the overall document formatting should be similar to the document in Figure 6.12.

   c. Format the title if you have not already done so. Select the text, "Click here to contact us" that appears toward the top of the document. Pull down the Insert menu and click the Hyperlink command (or click the Insert Hyperlink button on the Standard toolbar), click the E-mail Address button, and then enter your e-mail address.

   d. Go to the last paragraph and insert hyperlinks for the Boeing Company at www.boeing.com and FlyteComm at www.flytecomm.com. The latter Web site enables you to track a flight from takeoff to landing.

   e. Save the document a final time, then exit Word. Start Windows Explorer, then go to the folder containing your Web page, and double click the file you just created. Internet Explorer will start automatically (because your document was saved as a Web page). You should see your document within Internet Explorer as shown in Figure 6.12. Look carefully at the Address bar and note the local address on drive C, as opposed to a Web address.

   f. Print the document for your instructor as proof you completed the assignment. Add a cover sheet to complete the assignment.

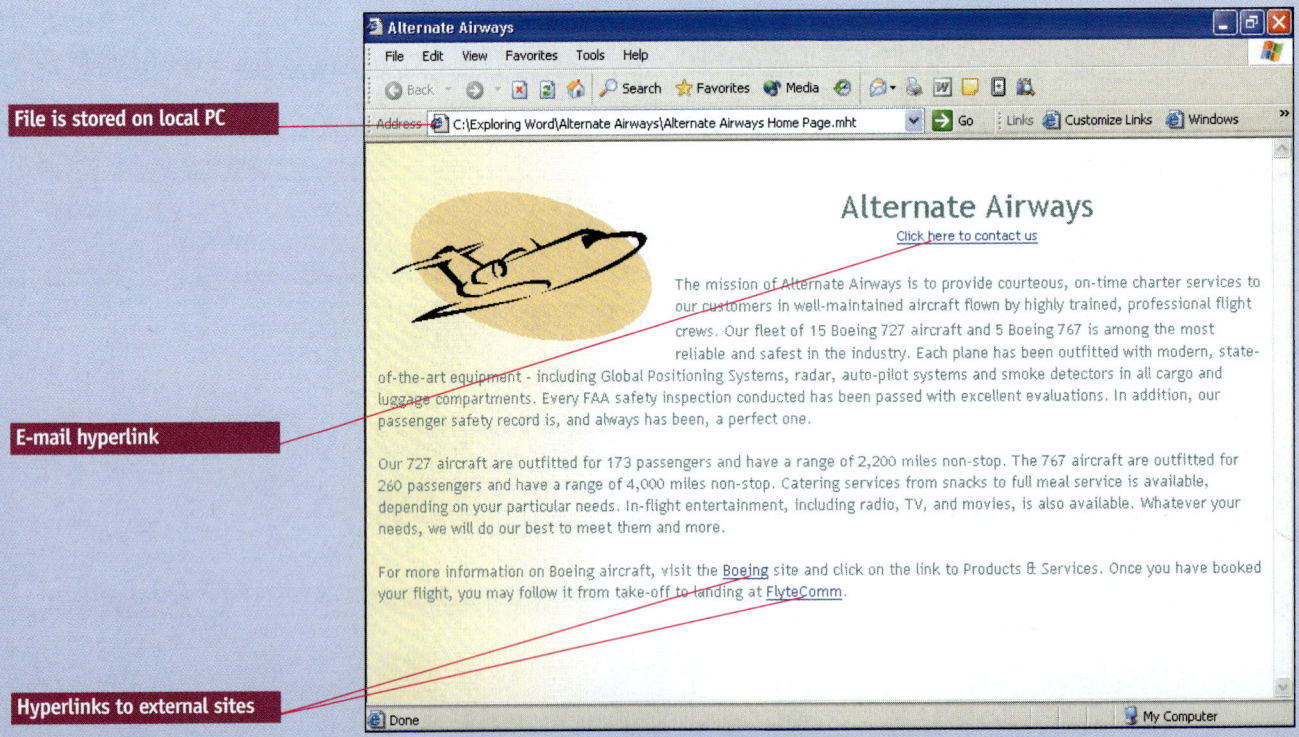

FIGURE 6.12   Alternate Airways Home Page (exercise 5)

1146   CHAPTER 6: INTRODUCTION TO HTML

practice exercises

6. **Alternate Airways Web Site:** This exercise expands the previous problem to create the Web site in Figure 6.13, as opposed to a single Web page. You do not have to create the detailed pages for Our Employees and Our Destinations, but you are required to complete the navigation for the site. Proceed as follows:

   a. Create the Under Construction page. Save the document as a Single File Web Page in the Alternate Airways folder from the previous exercise. You do not have to match our design exactly, but the formatting and theme of your page should be consistent with the design of the Alternate Airways home page.

   b. The Under Construction page should still be open. Change the text on the page to reflect Our Employees, pull down the File menu, click the Save As command, and save the page as Our Employees. Save the page a second time as Our Destinations. All three pages should be saved in the Alternate Airways folder. Close all open documents.

   c. Start a new document and create the navigation page that contains the hyperlinks to the various pages that you just created. Format the navigation page using the same theme as the other pages on your site. Save the page in the Alternate Airways folder using the Single File Web Page format.

   d. Display the Frames toolbar. Click the New Frame Right button to insert a frame to the right of the navigation page. Right click any hyperlink in the left frame; click the Edit Hyperlink command, then set the target frame as the frame on the right (frame 2). Click in the right frame, click the Frame Properties button, and set the initial page to the Alternate Airways home page.

   e. Save the current document as Alternate Airways Web Site in the Alternate Airways folder. Use the Change Title button to change the title of the page. Exit Word.

   f. Start Internet Explorer and open the Alternate Airways Web site that you just created. You should see the Web site in Figure 6.13. Test the navigation to be sure that the site is functioning correctly.

   g. Pull down the File menu (from Internet Explorer), click the Print Preview command, then click the down arrow on the Print What list box to select As laid out on screen. Click the Print button from the Preview window to display the Print dialog box and print the page.

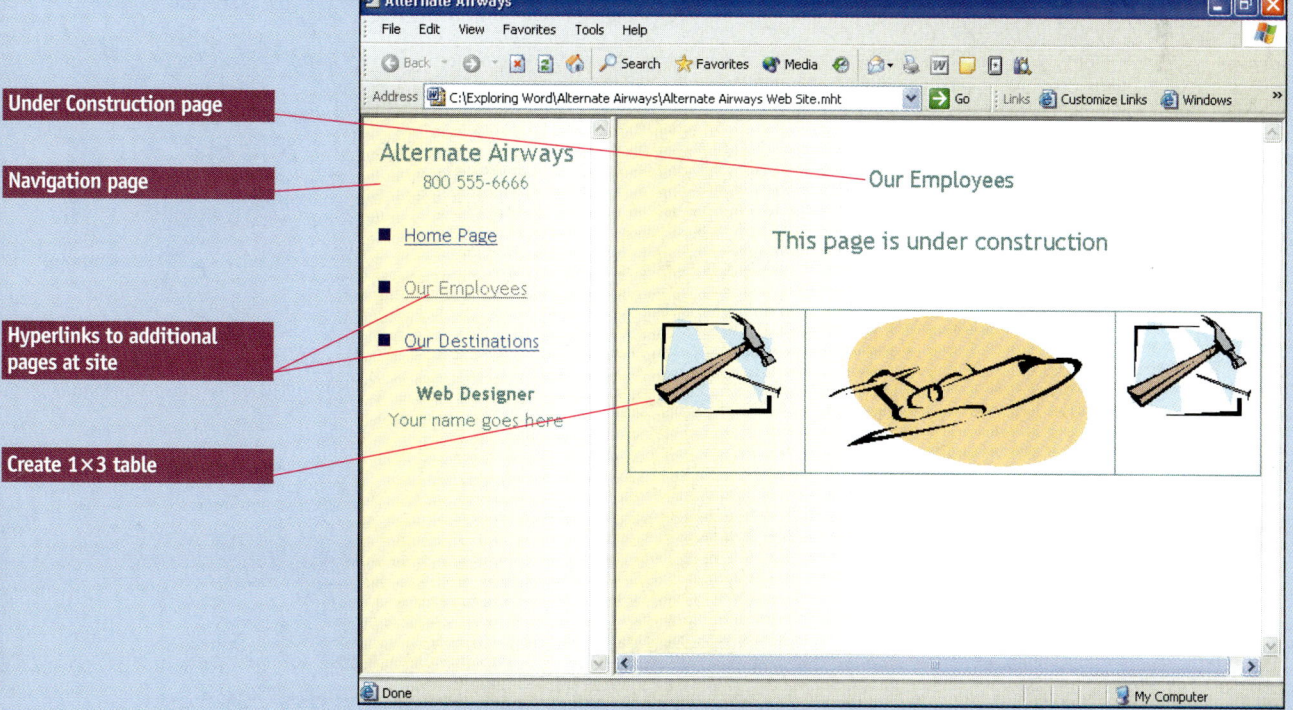

FIGURE 6.13 Alternate Airways Web Site (exercise 6)

practice exercises

7. **University Housing Web Site:** The Web site in Figure 6.14 uses horizontal (as opposed to vertical) navigation. We supply the text of the home page, which is displayed in the lower frame, but it is up to you to develop the site. (You can use an Under Construction page, as opposed to completing the detailed pages for Activities and Programs and Meal Plan.)

   a. Open the *Chapter 6 Practice 7* document in the Exploring Word folder. Review the document and insert bookmarks and associated links as appropriate—for example, to the visitation rules, rules and regulations, and payment options sections within the document. Format the document as you see fit. Use the Themes command in the Format menu to apply an overall design to the page.

   b. Pull down the File menu, click the Save as Web Page command, and create a University Housing folder within the Exploring Word folder. Enter University Housing Home Page as the file name and specify Single File Web Page as the file type.

   c. Start a new document and create the Under Construction page. Save the document as a Single File Web Page in the University Housing folder. The formatting of this page should be consistent with the home page. The Under Construction page should still be open. Change the text on the page to reflect Activities and Programs. Pull down the File menu, click the Save As command, and save the page as Activities and Programs. Save the page a second time as Meal Plan. All three pages should be saved in the University Housing folder. Close all open documents.

   d. Start a new document and create the navigation page that contains the hyperlinks to the various pages that you just created. Format the navigation page using the same theme as the other pages on your site. Use clip art to add interest to the page. Save the page in the University Housing folder.

   e. Display the Frames toolbar. Click the New Frame Below button to insert a frame below the navigation page. Right click any hyperlink in the left frame; click the Edit Hyperlink command, then set the target frame as the bottom frame. Click in the bottom frame and set the initial page to the home page. Save the current document as University Housing Web site in the University Housing folder. Exit Word.

   f. Start Internet Explorer and open the University Housing Web site as shown in Figure 6.14. Print the individual pages for your instructor.

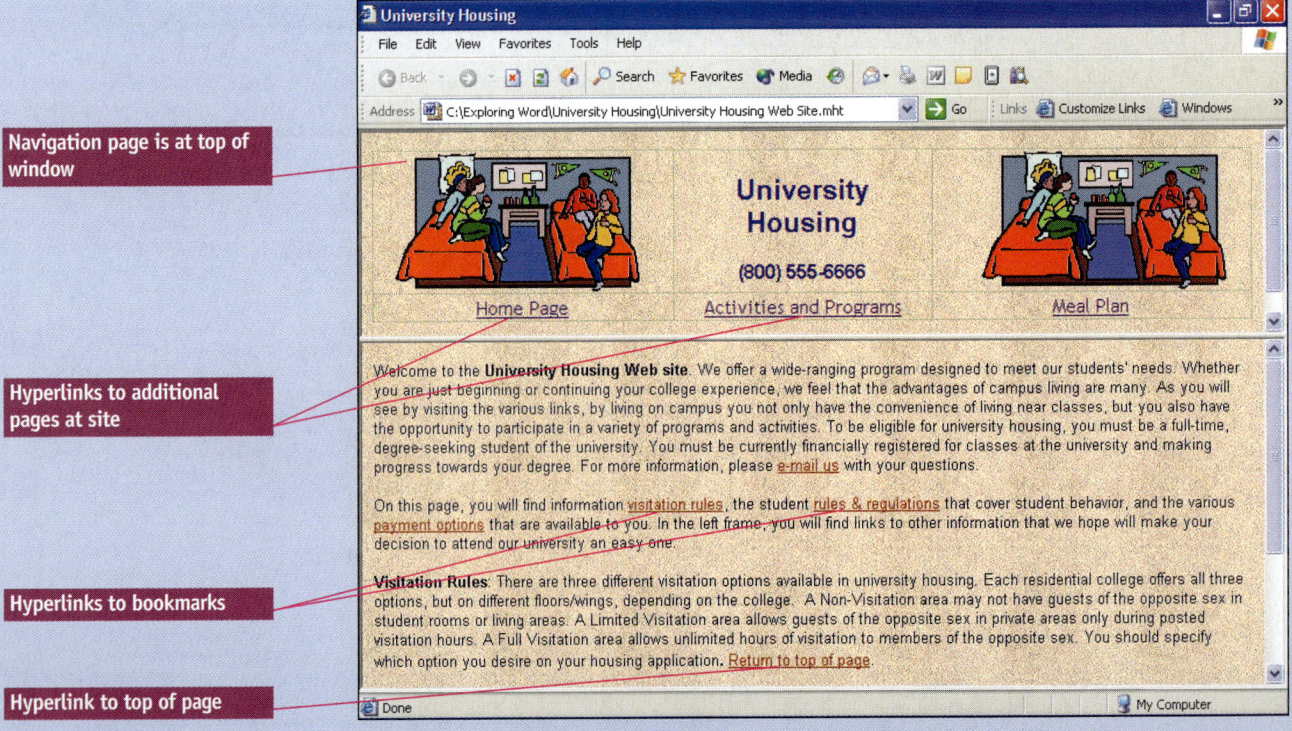

FIGURE 6.14 University Housing Web Site (exercise 7)

practice exercises

8. **Totally Fit Web Site:** The Web site in Figure 6.15 is for a hypothetical fitness center. We supply the text of the home page, which is displayed in the right frame, but it is up to you to develop the site. (You can use an Under Construction page, as opposed to completing the detailed pages for Exercise Tips and Enroll Now.) Proceed as follows:

   a. Open the *Chapter 6 Practice 8* document in the Exploring Word folder. Review the document and insert hyperlinks as appropriate, such as to the American Heart Association, which is referenced in the document. Format the document as you see fit. Use the Themes command in the Format menu to apply an overall design to the page.

   b. Pull down the File menu, click the Save as Web Page command, and create a Totally Fit folder within the Exploring Word folder. Enter Totally Fit Home Page as the file name and specify Single File Web Page as the file type. Close the document.

   c. Start a new document and create the Under Construction page. Save the document as a Single File Web Page in the Totally Fit folder. The formatting of this page should be consistent with the home page. The Under Construction page should still be open. Change the text on the page to reflect exercise tips. Pull down the File menu, click the Save As command, and save the page as Exercise Tips. Change the text on the page, then save the page a second time as Enroll Now. All three pages should be saved in the Totally Fit folder. Close all open documents.

   d. Start a new document and create the navigation page that contains the hyperlinks to the various pages that you just created. Add a (Contact Us) hyperlink to your e-mail address. Format the navigation page using the same theme as the other pages on your site. Save the page as a Web page in the Totally Fit folder.

   e. Display the Frames toolbar. Click the New Frame Right button to insert a frame to the right of the navigation page. Right click any hyperlink in the left frame, click the Edit Hyperlink command, then set the target frame as the frame on the right (frame 2). Click in the right frame, click the Frame Properties button, and set the initial page to the Totally Fit Home page. Save the current document as Totally Fit Web site in the Totally Fit folder. Exit Word.

   f. Start Internet Explorer and open the Totally Fit Web site as shown in Figure 6.15. Print the individual pages for your instructor.

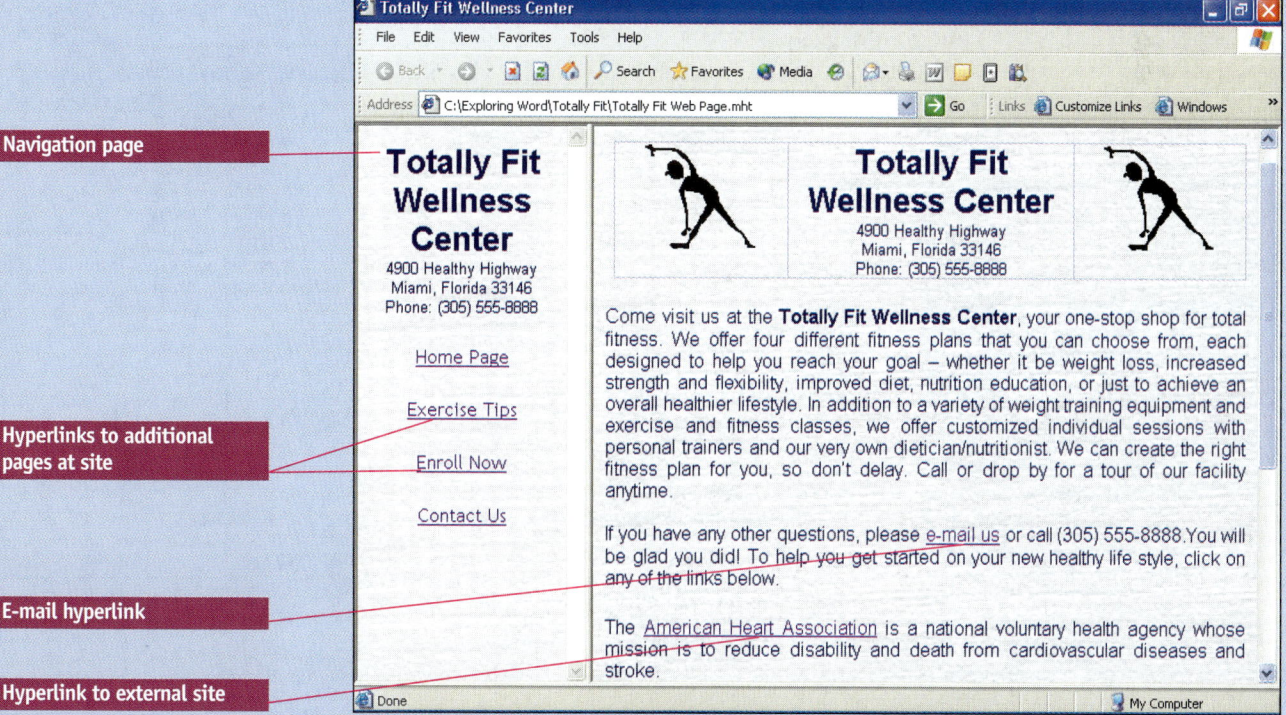

FIGURE 6.15 Totally Fit Web Site (exercise 8)

MICROSOFT OFFICE WORD 2003   1149

practice exercises

9. **Word and XML:** This exercise describes how to convert (map) the essential elements of a résumé to an XML document. You can use your own résumé or the sample we provide, but you will have to use the schema (XML definition) that is included on the data disk. Proceed as follows:

   a. Open the *Chapter 6 Practice 9* document that contains our sample résumé. Change the name and other information at the top of the document to reflect your name and e-mail address. Pull down the Tools menu, click Templates and Add-Ins to display the associated dialog box, and then click the XML Schema tab. Click the Add Schema button, then navigate to, then open, the Resume.XSD document in the Exploring Word folder. Type Resume as the Alias and clear the Changes affect current user only check box. Click OK. The résumé schema has been added to the Schema library.

   b. The Templates and Add-ins dialog box should still be open with the XML Schema tab selected. Be sure that the Resume schema is checked so that this schema is attached to the current document. Click OK. The XML Structure task pane opens automatically as shown in Figure 6.16.

   c. Select (click) the Resume element in the list of schema elements that appears in the lower portion of the task pane, then click Apply to Entire Document. XML tags for Resume will appear at the beginning and end of the document. You can now apply the various tags within the Resume schema to different portions of the document. Click and drag to select your name at the top of the résumé, and then apply the Name tag. Apply the FirstName and LastName tags in similar fashion.

   d. Map the other elements of your résumé in similar fashion, save the completed résumé, and then print it. The résumé prints as a regular Word document; i.e., you do not see the XML codes that you added.

   e. Save the document a second time, but specify XML document as the file type in the Exploring Word folder. Exit Word. Start Windows Explorer and locate the XML document that you just created. It is much smaller than the Word document (approximately 3K). Double click the XML document, which opens automatically in Internet Explorer. Print the XML document.

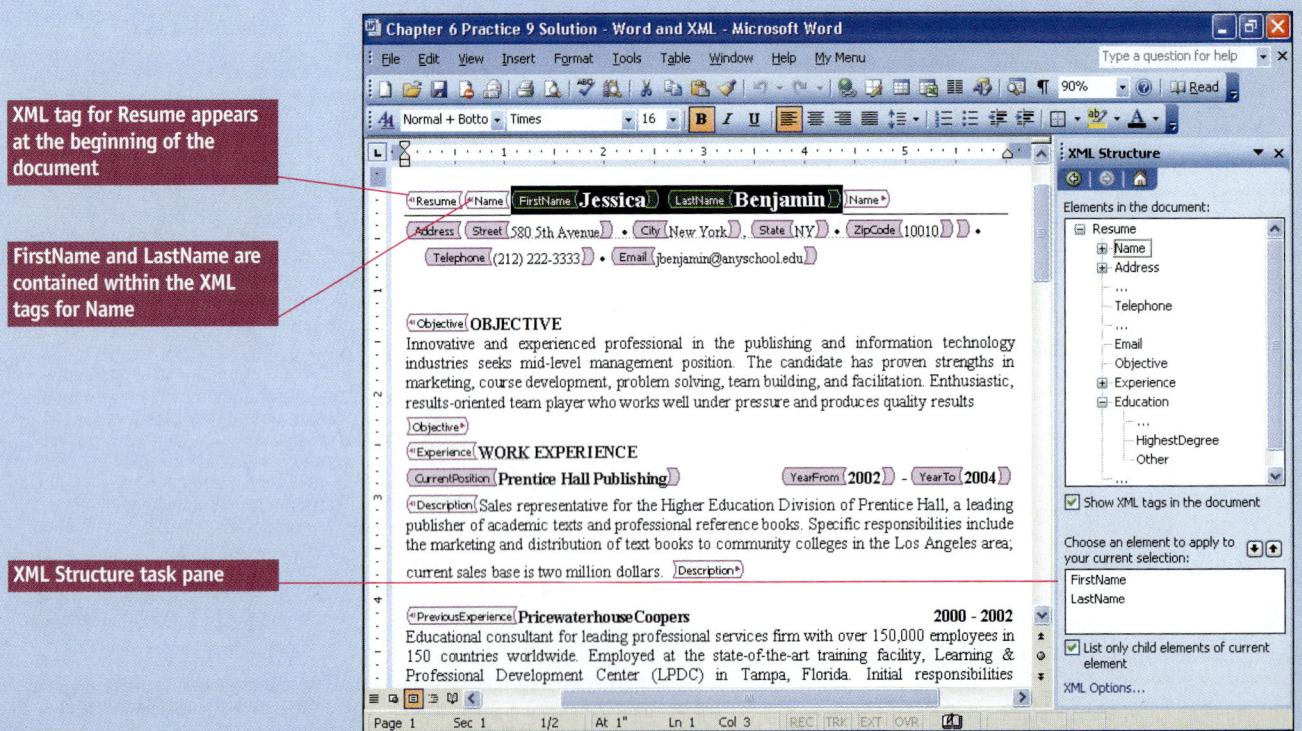

FIGURE 6.16 Word and XML (exercise 9)

CHAPTER 7

The Expert User: Workgroups, Forms, Master Documents, and Macros

OBJECTIVES

After reading this chapter you will:

1. Describe how to highlight editing changes and how to review, accept, or reject those changes.
2. Save multiple versions of a document; save a document with password protection.
3. Create and modify a form; use text fields, check boxes, and a drop-down list.
4. Perform calculations within a table.
5. Sort the rows in a table.
6. Create a master document; add and/or modify subdocuments.
7. Explain how macros facilitate the execution of repetitive tasks.
8. Record and run a macro; edit an existing macro.
9. Use the Copy and Paste commands to duplicate an existing macro, and then modify the copied macro.

hands-on exercises

1. WORKGROUPS AND FORMS
   Input: Contract
   Output: Contract Solution

2. TABLE MATH
   Input: Executed Contract
   Output: Executed Contract Solution

3. MASTER DOCUMENTS
   Input: None
   Output: About Acme Systems and multiple subdocuments

4. INTRODUCTION TO MACROS
   Input: Executed Contract (from Hands-on Exercise 2)
   Output: Executed Contract (additional modifications)

CASE STUDY
A QUESTION OF ETHICS

You would never walk into a music store, put a CD under your arm, and walk out without paying for it. What if, however, you could download the same CD from the Web for free? Are you hurting anyone? Or what if you gave a clerk a $5 bill, but received change for a $50? Would you return the extra money? Would you speak up if it was the person ahead of you on line who received change for the $50, when you clearly saw that they gave the clerk $5? Ethical conflicts occur all the time and result when one person or group benefits at the expense of another.

Your instructor has assigned a class project whereby students are divided into teams to consider questions of ethics and society. Each team is to submit a single document that represents the collective efforts of all the team members. The completed project is to include a brief discussion of ethical principles followed by five examples of ethical conflicts. Every member of the team will receive the same grade, regardless of their level of participation; indeed, this might be an ethical dilemma, in and of itself.

Your assignment is to read the chapter and focus on the Track Changes command whereby multiple individuals can enter changes electronically in the same document. You will then open the *Chapter 7 Case Study Ethics and Society* document in the Exploring Word folder and display the Reviewing toolbar if it is not already visible. Click the down arrow on the Display for Review list box and select Final Showing Markup to show the changes that have been entered, but not yet reviewed.

You will notice that several individuals have suggested changes, with each person's recommendations in a different color. Print the document in this format so that the suggested changes appear in the hard copy. Use the Show button on the Reviewing toolbar to match the reviewers with their suggested changes. Print the document in final form after all of the suggested changes have been accepted. Read the document carefully in preparation for a class discussion of the ethical decisions involved.

WORKGROUPS AND COLLABORATION

This chapter introduces several capabilities that will make you a true expert in Microsoft Word. The features go beyond the needs of the typical student and extend to capabilities that you will appreciate in the workplace, as you work with others on a collaborative project. We begin with a discussion of workgroup editing, whereby suggested revisions from one or more individuals can be stored electronically within a document. This enables the original author to review each suggestion individually before it is incorporated into the final version of the document, and further, allows multiple people to work on the same document in collaboration with one another.

The suggested revisions from the various reviewers are displayed in one of two ways, as the "Original Showing Markup" in Figure 7.1a or as the "Final Showing Markup" in Figure 7.1b. The difference is subtle and depends on personal preference with respect to displaying the insertions to, and deletions from, a document. (All revisions fall into one of these two categories: insertions or deletions. Even if you are simply substituting one word for another, you are deleting the original word, then inserting its replacement.)

The ***Original Showing Markup*** view in Figure 7.1a shows the deleted text within the body of the document (with a line through the deleted text) and displays the inserted text in a balloon to the right of the actual document. The ***Final Showing Markup*** view in Figure 7.1b is the opposite; that is, it displays the inserted text in the body of the document and shows the deleted text in a balloon. Both views display ***revision marks*** to the left of any line that has been changed. Comments are optional and are enclosed in balloons at the right of either document. The suggestions of multiple reviewers appear in different colors, with each reviewer assigned a different color.

The review process is straightforward. The initial document is sent for review to one or more individuals, who record their changes by executing the ***Track Changes command*** in the Tools menu (or by double clicking the TRK indicator in the status bar) to start (or stop) the recording process. The author of the original document receives the corrected document and then uses the ***Accept Change*** and ***Reject Change buttons*** on the ***Reviewing toolbar*** to review the document and implement the suggested changes.

The Versions of a Document

The Save command is one of the most basic in Microsoft Office. Each time you execute the command, the contents in memory are saved to disk under the designated file name, and the previous contents of the file are erased. What if, however, you wanted to retain the previous version of the file in addition to the current version that was just saved? You could use the Save As command to create a second file. It's easier to use the ***Versions command*** in the File menu because it lets you save multiple versions of a document in a single file.

The existence of multiple versions is transparent in that the latest version is opened automatically when you open the file at the start of a session. You can, however, review previous versions to see the changes that were made. Word displays the date and time each version was saved as well as the name of the person who saved each version.

Word provides two different levels of ***password protection*** in conjunction with saving a document. You can establish one password to open the document and a different password to modify it. A password can contain any combination of letters, numbers, and symbols, and can be 15 characters long. Passwords are case sensitive.

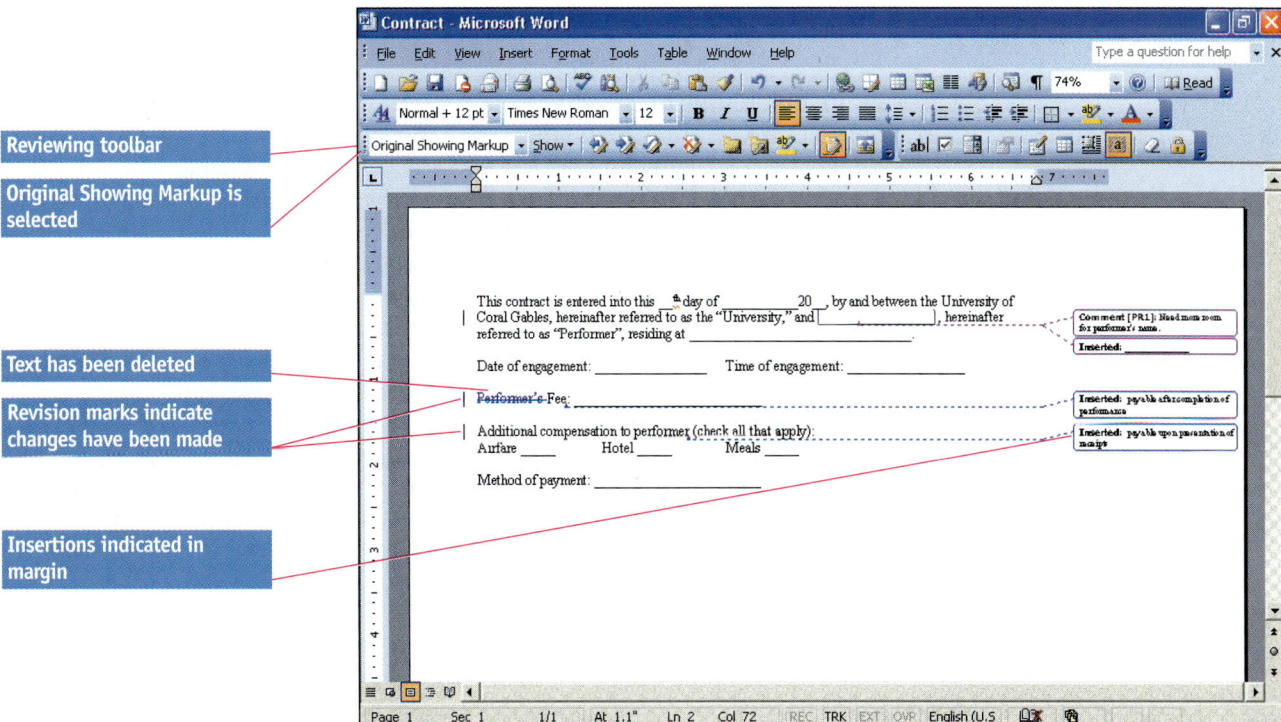

(a) Original Showing Markup

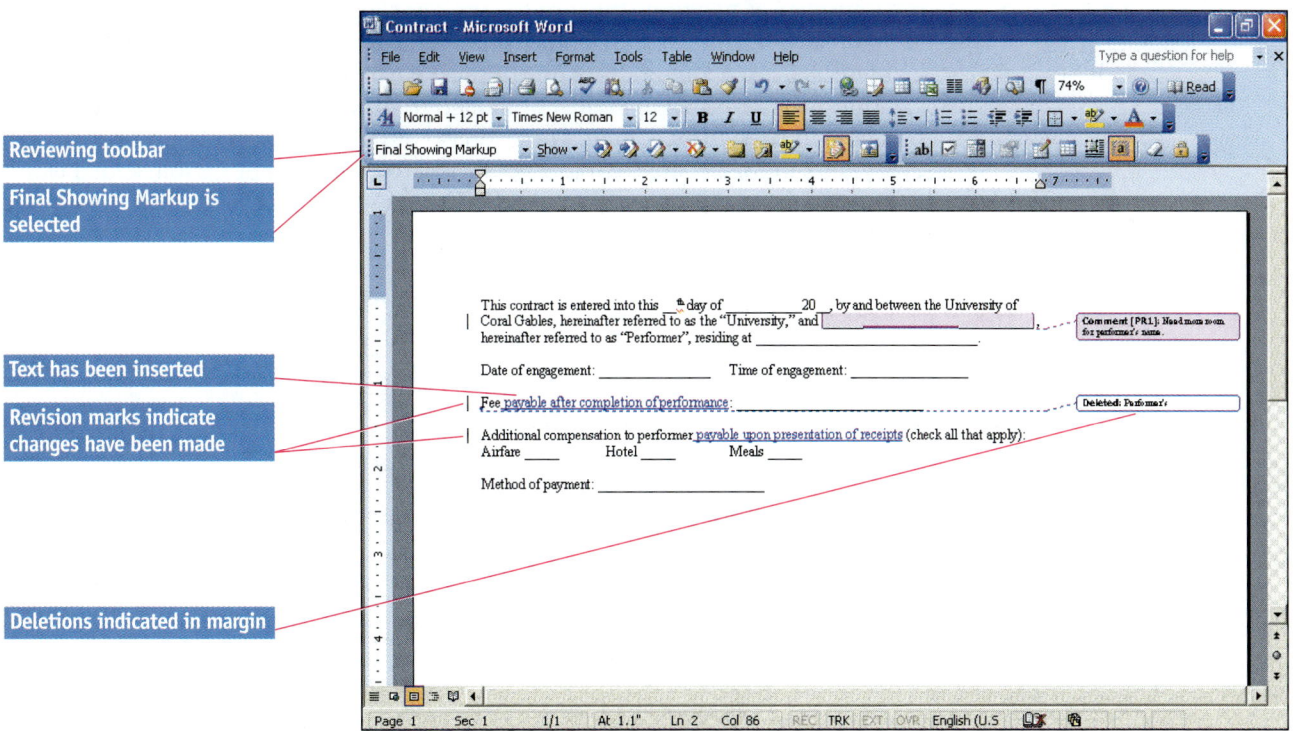

(b) Final Showing Markup

FIGURE 7.1 Workgroup Editing

MICROSOFT OFFICE WORD 2003

FORMS

Forms are ubiquitous in the workplace and our society. You complete a form, for example, when you apply for a job or open any type of account. The form may be electronic and completed online, or it may exist as a printed document. All forms, however, are designed for some type of data entry. Microsoft Word lets you create a special type of document called a *form*, which allows the user to enter data in specific places, but precludes editing the document in any other way. The process requires you to create the form and save it to disk, where it serves as a template for future documents. Then, when you need to enter data for a specific document, you open the original form, enter the data, and save the completed form as a new document.

Figure 7.2 displays a "forms" version of the document shown earlier in Figure 7.1. The form does not contain specific data, but it does contain the text of a document (a contract in this example) that is to be completed by the user. It also contains shaded entries, or *fields*, that represent the locations where the user enters data that is unique to the individual. To complete the form, the user presses the Tab key to go from one field to the next and enters data as appropriate. Then, when all fields have been entered, the form is printed to produce the finished document (a contract for a specific event). The data that was entered into the various fields appears as regular text.

The form is created as a regular document with the various fields added through tools on the **Forms toolbar**. Word enables you to create three types of fields—text boxes, check boxes, and drop-down list boxes. A ***text field*** is the most common and is used to enter any type of text. The length of a text field can be set exactly; for example, to two positions for the day in the first line of the document. The length can also be left unspecified, in which case the field will expand to the exact number of positions that are required as the data is entered. A ***check box***, as the name implies, consists of a box, which is checked or not. A ***drop-down list box*** enables the user to choose from one of several existing entries.

After the form is created, it is protected to prevent further modification other than data entry. Our next hands-on exercise has you open an existing document, review the multiple changes to that document as suggested by members of a workgroup, accept the changes as appropriate, then convert the revised document into a form for data entry.

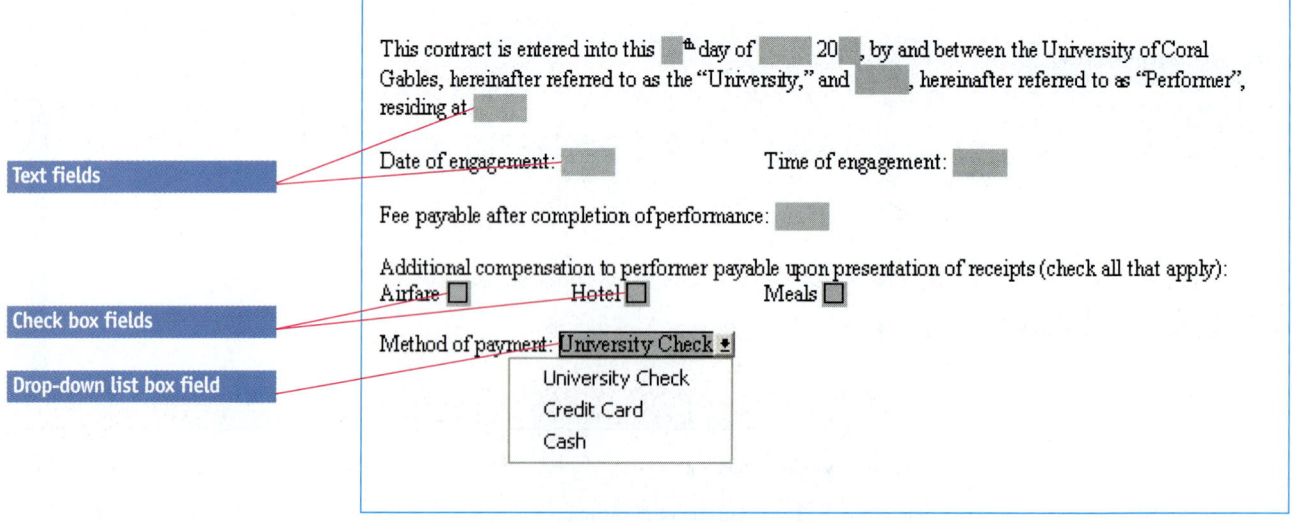

FIGURE 7.2 A Blank Form

hands-on exercise

1 Workgroups and Forms

Objective To review the editing comments within a document; to create a form containing text fields, check boxes, and a drop-down list.

Step 1: **Display the Forms and Reviewing Toolbars**

- Start Word. If Word is already open, pull down the **File menu** and click the **Close command** to close any open documents.

- Point to any visible toolbar, click the **right mouse button**, then click the **Customize command** to display the Customize dialog box as shown in Figure 7.3a.

- If necessary, click the **Toolbars tab** in the Customize dialog box. The boxes for the Standard and Formatting toolbars should be checked.

- Check the boxes to display the **Forms** and **Reviewing toolbars** as shown in Figure 7.3a. Click the **Close button** to close the Customize dialog box.

- Move the Forms toolbar so it is on the same row as the Reviewing toolbar.

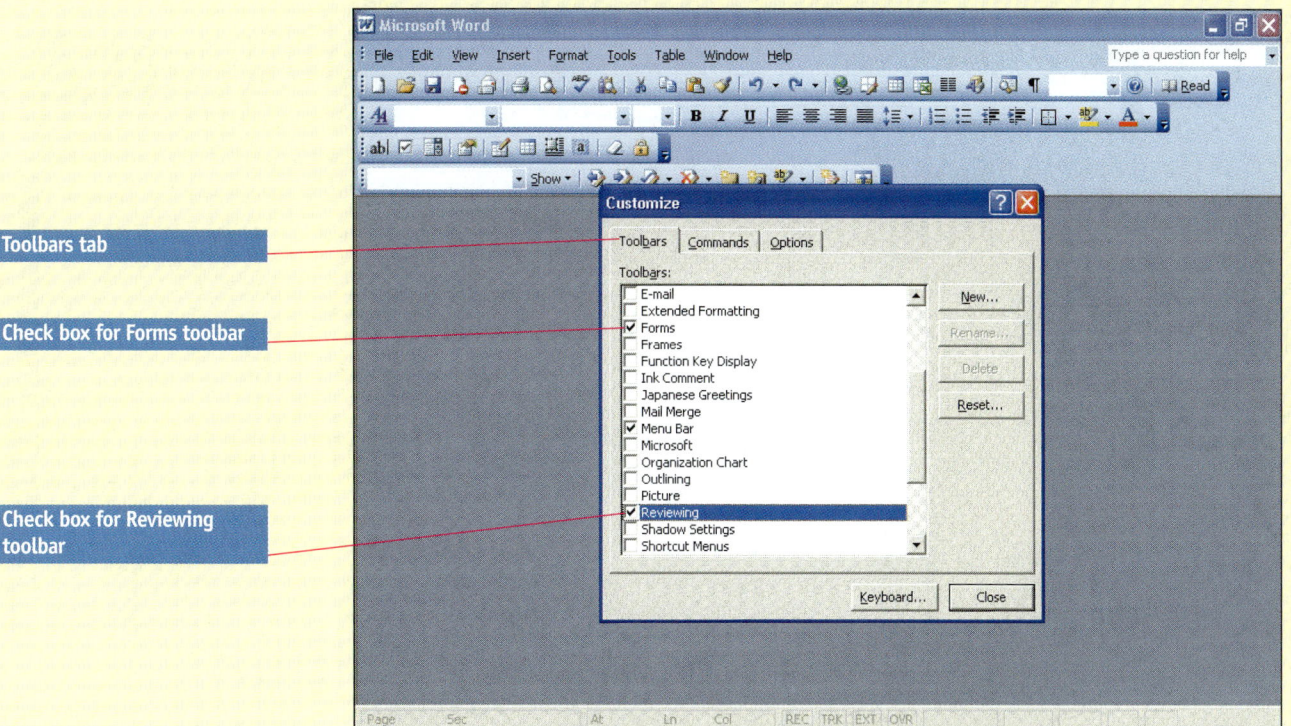

(a) Display the Forms and Reviewing Toolbars (step 1)

FIGURE 7.3 Hands-on Exercise 1

DOCKED VERSUS FLOATING TOOLBARS

A toolbar is either docked along an edge of a window or floating within the window. To move a docked toolbar, click and drag the move handle (the dotted vertical line that appears at the left of the toolbar) to a new position. To move a floating toolbar, click and drag its title bar—if you drag a floating toolbar to the edge of the window, it becomes a docked toolbar and vice versa. You can also change the shape of a floating toolbar by dragging any border in the direction you want to go.

Step 2: **Highlight the Changes**

- Open the document called **Contract** in the **Exploring Word folder** as shown in Figure 7.3b. Save the document as **Contract Solution**.

- The **Track Changes** command functions as a toggle switch; that is, execute the command, and the tracking is in effect. Execute the command a second time, and the tracking is off. You can track changes in one of three ways:
  - Pull down the **Tools menu** and click the **Track Changes command**.
  - Double click the **TRK indicator** on the status bar.
  - Click the **Track Changes button** on the Reviewing toolbar.

- Tracking is in effect if the TRK indicator is visible on the status bar.

- Press **Ctrl+Home** to move to the beginning of the document. Press the **Del key** four times to delete the word "The" and the blank space that follows. You will see an indication in the right margin that the text was deleted.

- Move to the end of the address (immediately after the zip code). Press the **space bar** three or four times, then enter the phone number **(305) 111-2222**. The new text is underlined.

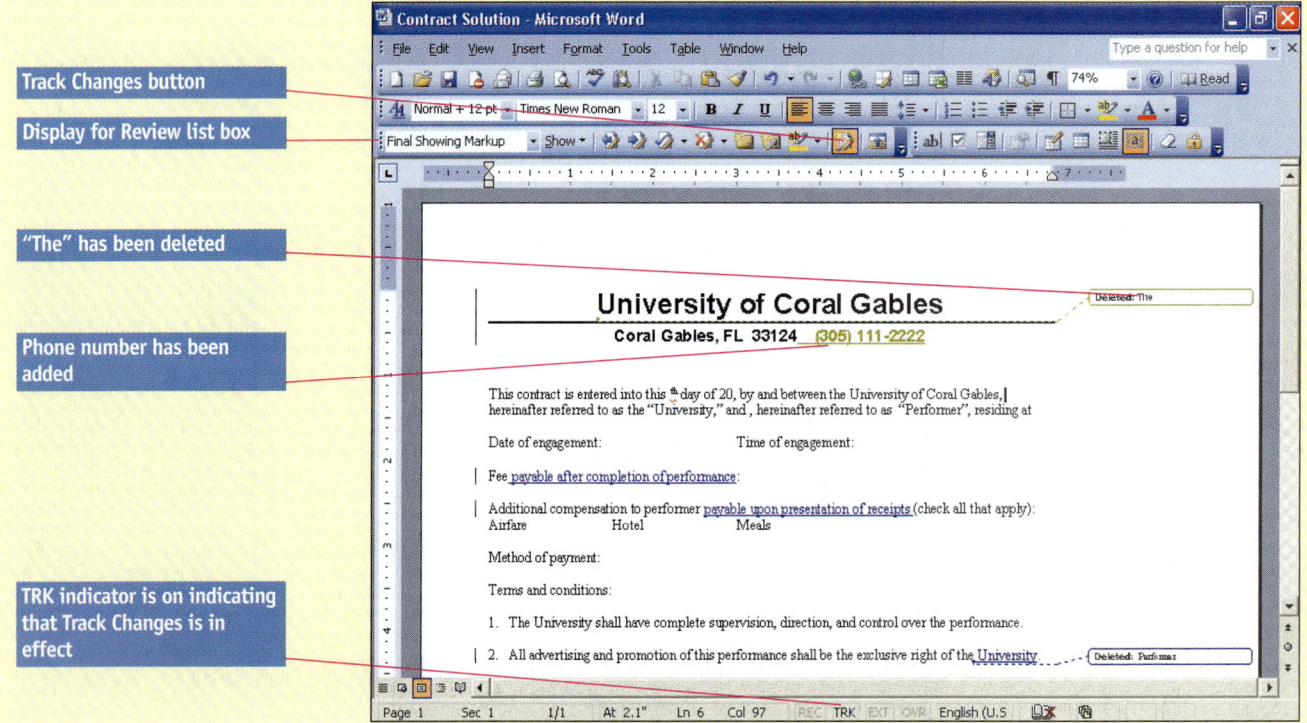

(b) Highlight the Changes (step 2)

FIGURE 7.3 Hands-on Exercise 1 (*continued*)

CHOOSE THE VIEW THAT YOU WANT

Click the down arrow on the Display for Review list box to choose the view you want. The Original Showing Markup view displays the deleted text within the body of the document (with a line through the deleted text) and shows the inserted text in a balloon to the right of the actual document. The Final Showing Markup view is the opposite; it displays the inserted text within the body of the document and displays the deleted text in a balloon at the right. Both views display revision marks to the left of any line that has been changed.

Step 3: **Accept or Reject Changes**

- Press **Ctrl+Home** to move to the beginning of the document, then click the **Next button** on the Reviewing toolbar to move to the first change, which is your deletion of the word "the".

- Click the **Accept Change button** to accept the change. Click the **Next button** to move to the next change, where you will review the next change.

- You can continue to review changes individually, or you can accept all of the changes as written. Click the **down arrow** on the Accept Change button and click **Accept All Changes in Document** as shown in Figure 7.3c.

- Save the document.

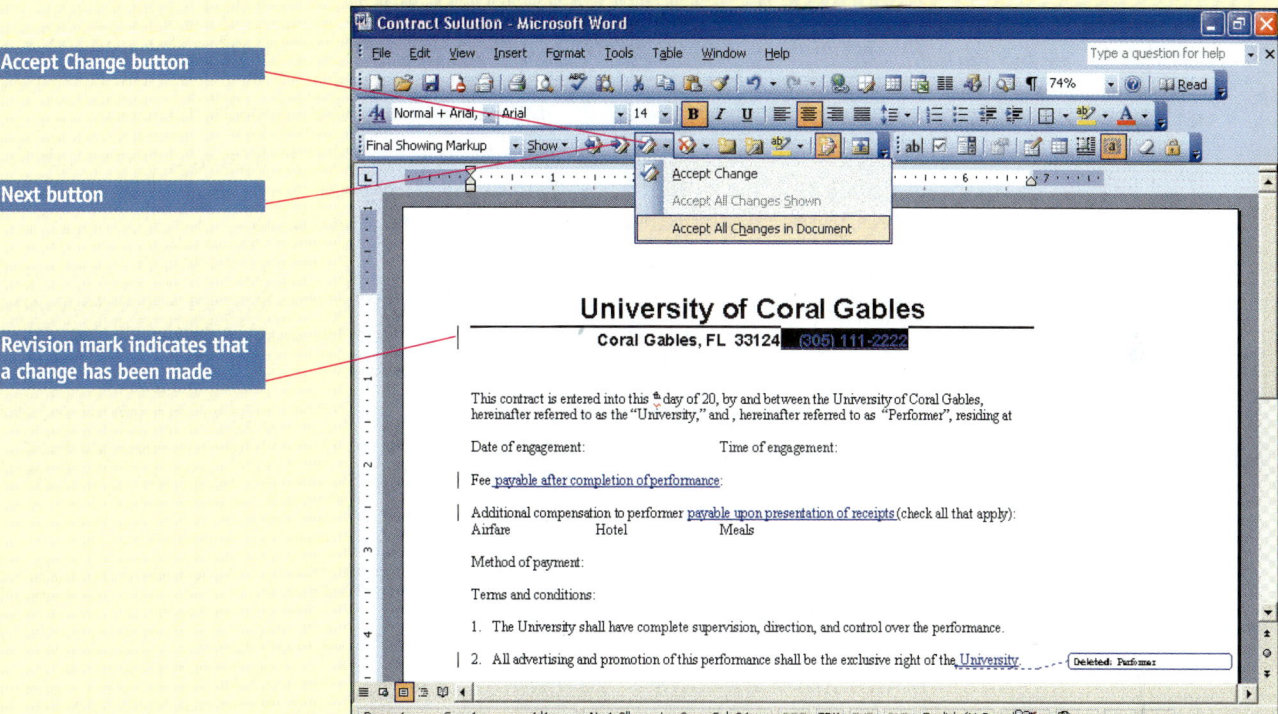

(c) Accept or Reject Changes (step 3)

FIGURE 7.3 Hands-on Exercise 1 (*continued*)

INSERT COMMENTS INTO A DOCUMENT

Add comments to a document to remind yourself (or a reviewer) of action that needs to be taken. Click in the document where you want the comment to appear, then pull down the Insert menu and click the Comment command (or click the Insert Comment button on the Reviewing toolbar) to open the Comments balloon. Enter the text of the comment and click outside the comment area. The word containing the insertion point is highlighted in the color assigned to the reviewer. To delete a comment, right click within the balloon, and then select the Delete Comment command.

Step 4: **Create the Text and Check Box Fields**

- Click the **Track Changes button** on the Reviewing toolbar to stop tracking changes, which removes the TRK indicator from the status bar. Click the button a second time and tracking is again in effect. (You can also double click the **TRK indicator** on the status bar to toggle tracking on or off.) End with tracking on.

- Move to the first line of text in the contract, then click to the right of the space following the second occurrence of the word "this".

- Click the **Text Form Field button** on the Forms toolbar to create a text field as shown in Figure 7.3d. The field should appear in the document as a shaded entry. Do not worry, however, about the length of this field as we adjust it shortly via the Text Form Field Options dialog box (which is not yet visible).

- Click after the space to the right of the word **of** on the same line and insert a second text field followed by a blank space. Insert the six additional text fields as shown in Figure 7.3d. Add blank spaces as needed before each field.

- Click immediately after the word **Airfare**. Add a blank space, then click the **Check Box Form Field** to create a check box as shown in the figure. Create additional check boxes after the words **Hotel** and **Meals**.

- Click in the first text field (after the word *this*), then click the **Form Field Options button** on the Forms toolbar to display the Text Form Field Options dialog box. Click the **down arrow** in the Type list box and choose **Number**. Enter **2** in the Maximum Length box.

- Click **OK** to accept these settings and close the dialog box. The length of the form field changes automatically to two positions. Change the options for the Year (Number, 2 positions) and Date of Engagement fields (Date, MMMM d, yyyy format) in similar fashion. Save the document.

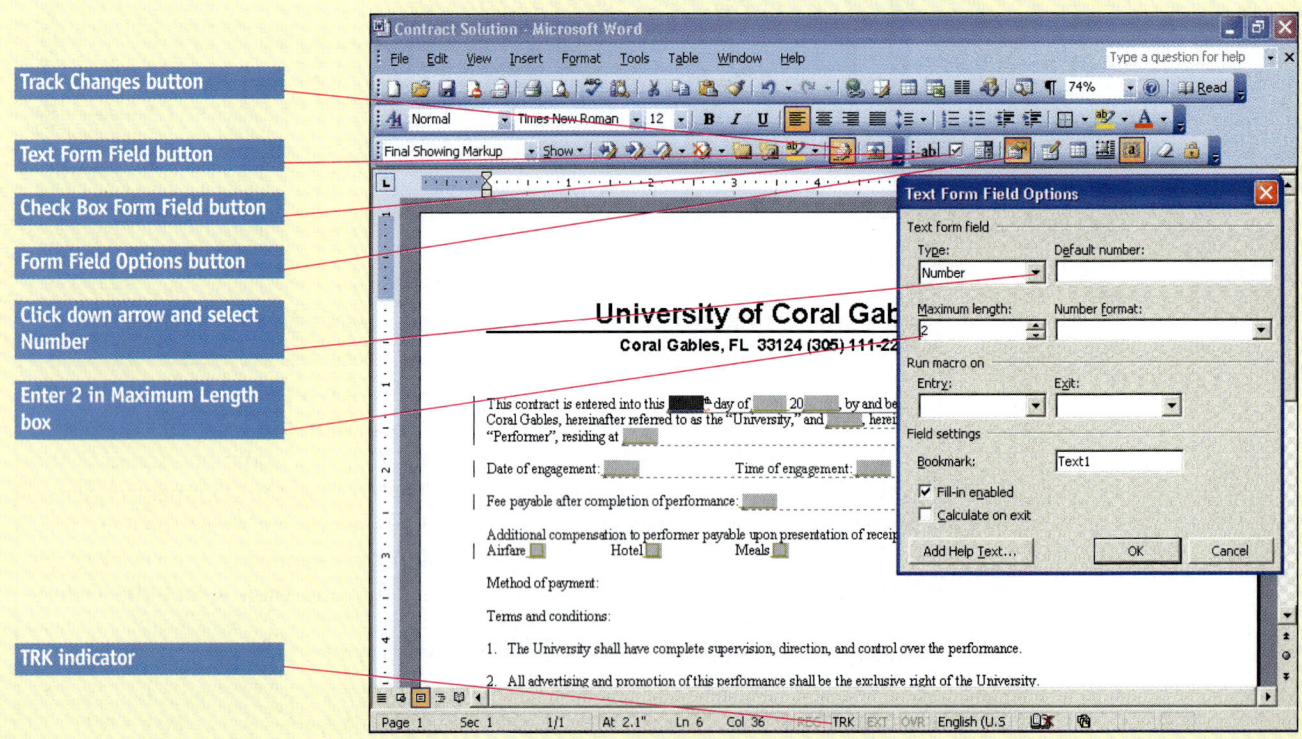

(d) Create the Text and Check Box Fields (step 4)

FIGURE 7.3 Hands-on Exercise 1 (*continued*)

Step 5: **Add the Drop-down List Box**

- Double click the **TRK indicator** on the status bar to stop tracking changes. (The indicator should be dim after double clicking.)
- Click the **down arrow** on the Accept Changes button on the Reviewing toolbar. Click **Accept All Changes in Document**.
- Click in the document after the words **Method of Payment**, then click the **Drop-down Form Field button** to create a drop-down list box. **Double click** the newly created field to display the dialog box in Figure 7.3e.
- Click in the Drop-down Item text box, type **University Check**, and click the **Add button** to move this entry to the Items in drop-down list box. Type **Credit Card** and click the **Add button**. Type **Cash**, then click the **Add button** to complete the entries for the drop-down list box.
- Click **OK** to accept the settings and close the dialog box.
- Save the document.

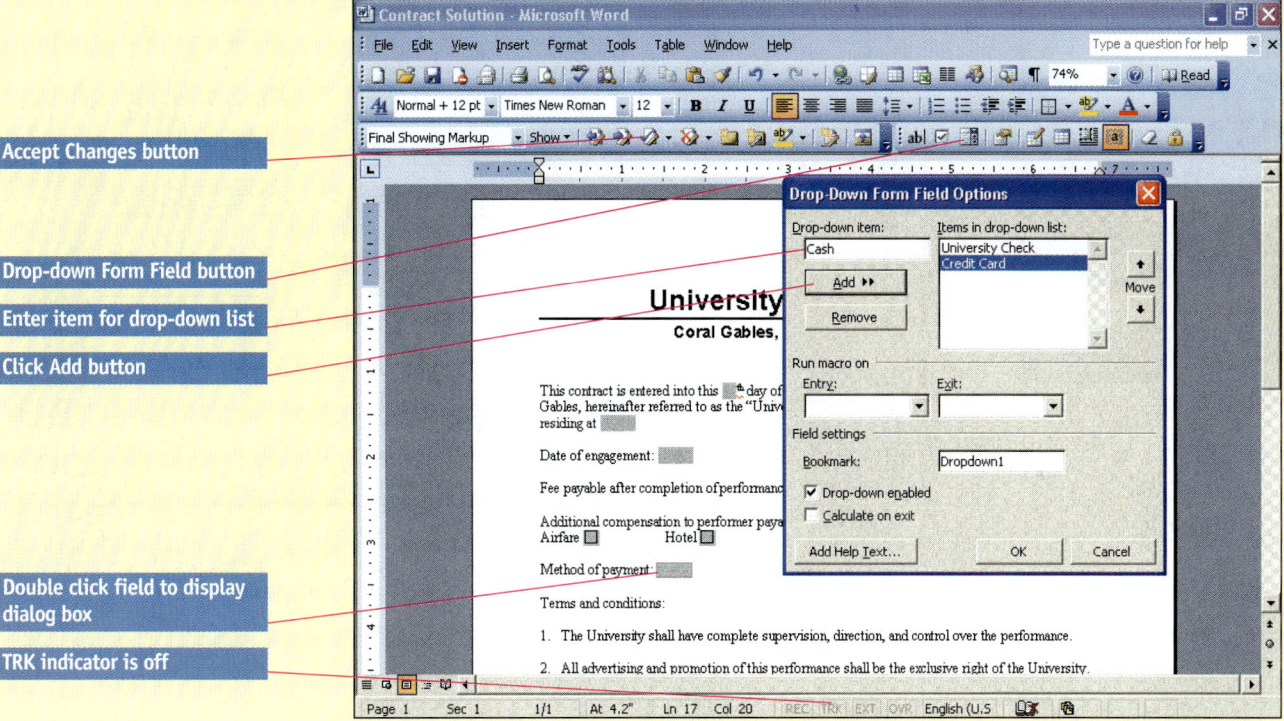

(e) Add the Drop-down List Box (step 5)

FIGURE 7.3 Hands-on Exercise 1 (*continued*)

FIELD CODES VERSUS FIELD RESULTS

All fields are displayed in a document in one of two formats, as a field code or as a field result. A field code appears in braces and indicates instructions to insert variable data when the document is printed; a field result displays the information as it will appear in the printed document. (The field results of a form field are blank until the data is entered into a form.) You can toggle the display between the field code and field result by selecting the field and pressing Shift+F9 during editing. To show (hide) field codes for all fields in the document, press Alt+F9.

Step 6: **Save a New Version**

- Proofread the document to be sure that it is correct. Once you are satisfied with the finished document, click the **Protect Form button** on the Forms toolbar to prevent further changes to the form. (You can still enter data into the fields on the form, as we will do in the next step.)

- Pull down the **File menu** and click the **Versions command** to display the Versions dialog box for this document. There is currently one previous version, the one created by Robert Grauer on May 5, 2003.

- Click the **Save Now button** to display the Save Version dialog box in Figure 7.3f. Enter the text of a comment you want to associate with this version.

- The author's name will be different on your screen and will reflect the person who registered the version of Microsoft Word you are using.

- Click **OK** to save the version and close the dialog box.

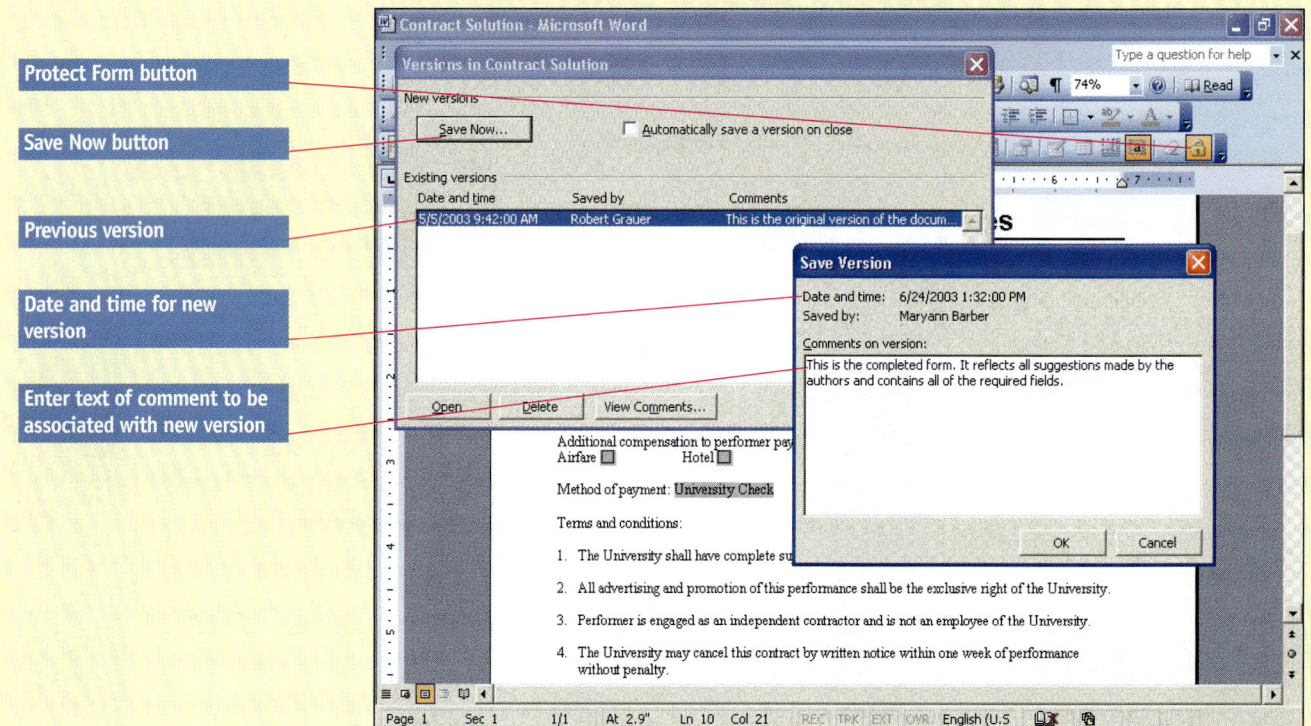

(f) Save a New Version (step 6)

FIGURE 7.3 Hands-on Exercise 1 (*continued*)

SET EDITING AND FORMATTING RESTRICTIONS

You can extend the protection associated with a document to impose a specific set of formatting and/or editing restrictions. Pull down the Tools menu and click the Protect Document command to display the associated task pane, and then implement the specific restrictions you want to impose. You can, for example, restrict the user to a limited number of formatting styles within a document. You can also make the entire document read-only and then select the parts of the document that are exempt (i.e., those parts of the document that can be modified). You can also restrict editing to specific users. See problem 3 at the end of the chapter.

Step 7: **Fill In the Form**

- Be sure that the form is protected; that is, that all buttons are dim on the Forms toolbar except for the Protect Form and Form Field Shading buttons. Press **Ctrl+Home** to move to the first field.

- Enter today's date, press the **Tab key** (to move to the next field), enter today's month, press the **Tab key**, and enter the year.

- Continue to press the **Tab key** to complete the form. Enter your name as the performer. Enter a fee of **$1,000**.

- Press the **space bar** on the keyboard to check or clear the various check boxes. Check the boxes for airfare, hotel, and meals.

- Click the **down arrow** on the Method of Payment list box and choose **University Check**.

- Your completed form should be similar to our form as shown in Figure 7.3g.

- You can make changes to the text of the contract by unprotecting the form. Do not, however, click the Protect Form button after data has been entered, or you will lose the data.

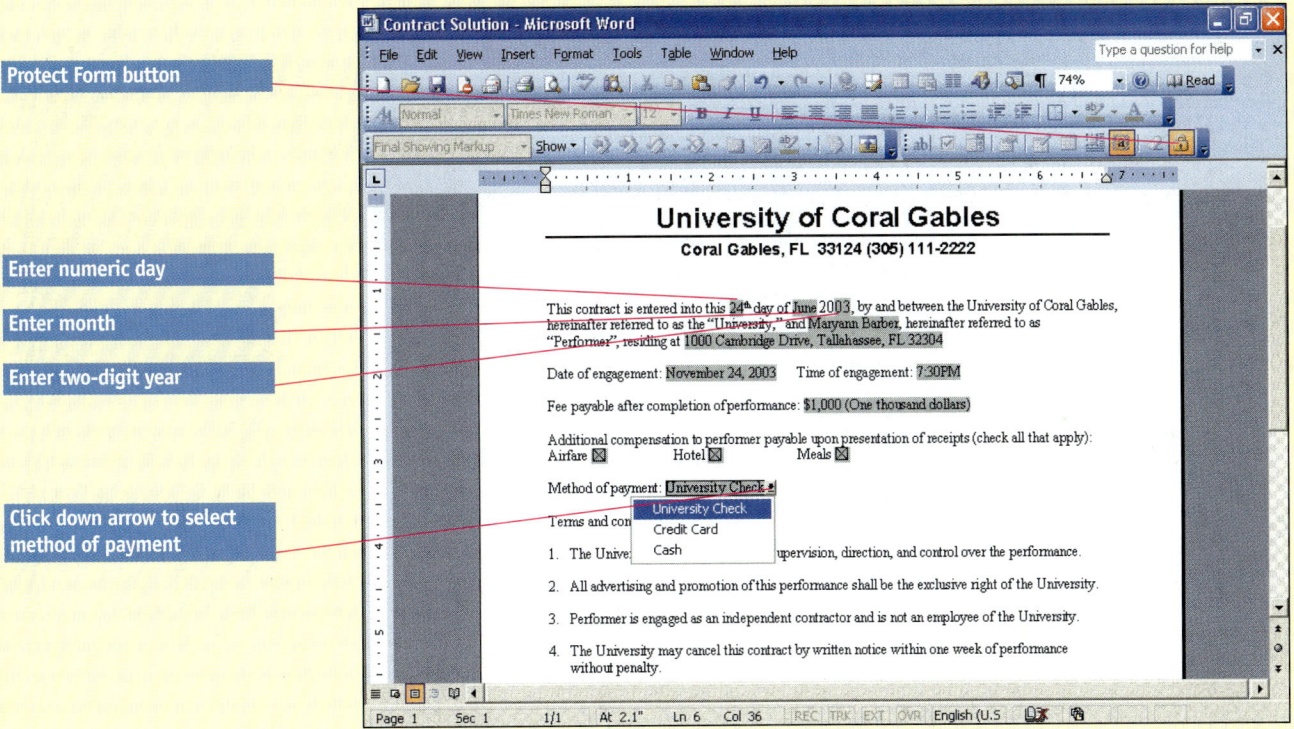

(g) Fill in the Form (step 7)

FIGURE 7.3 Hands-on Exercise 1 (*continued*)

PROTECTING AND UNPROTECTING A FORM

The Protect Form button toggles protection on and off. Click the button once, and the form is protected; data can be entered into the various fields, but the form itself cannot be modified. Click the button a second time, and the form is unprotected and can be fully modified. Be careful, however, about unprotecting a form once data has been entered. That action will not create a problem in and of itself, but protecting a form a second time (after the data was previously entered) will reset all of its fields.

Step 8: **Password Protect the Executed Contract**

- Pull down the **File menu**, click the **Save As command** to display the Save As dialog box, then type **Executed Contract** as the file name.

- Click the **drop-down arrow** next to the Tools button and click the **Security Options command** to display the Security dialog box in Figure 7.3h.

- Click in the **Password to open** text box and enter **password** (the password is case sensitive) as the password. Click **OK**.

- A Confirm Password dialog box will open, asking you to reenter the password and warning you not to forget the password; once a document is protected by a password, it cannot be opened without that password.

- Reenter the password and click **OK** to establish the password.

- Click **Save** to save the document and close the Save As dialog box. Exit Word if you do not want to continue with the next exercise at this time.

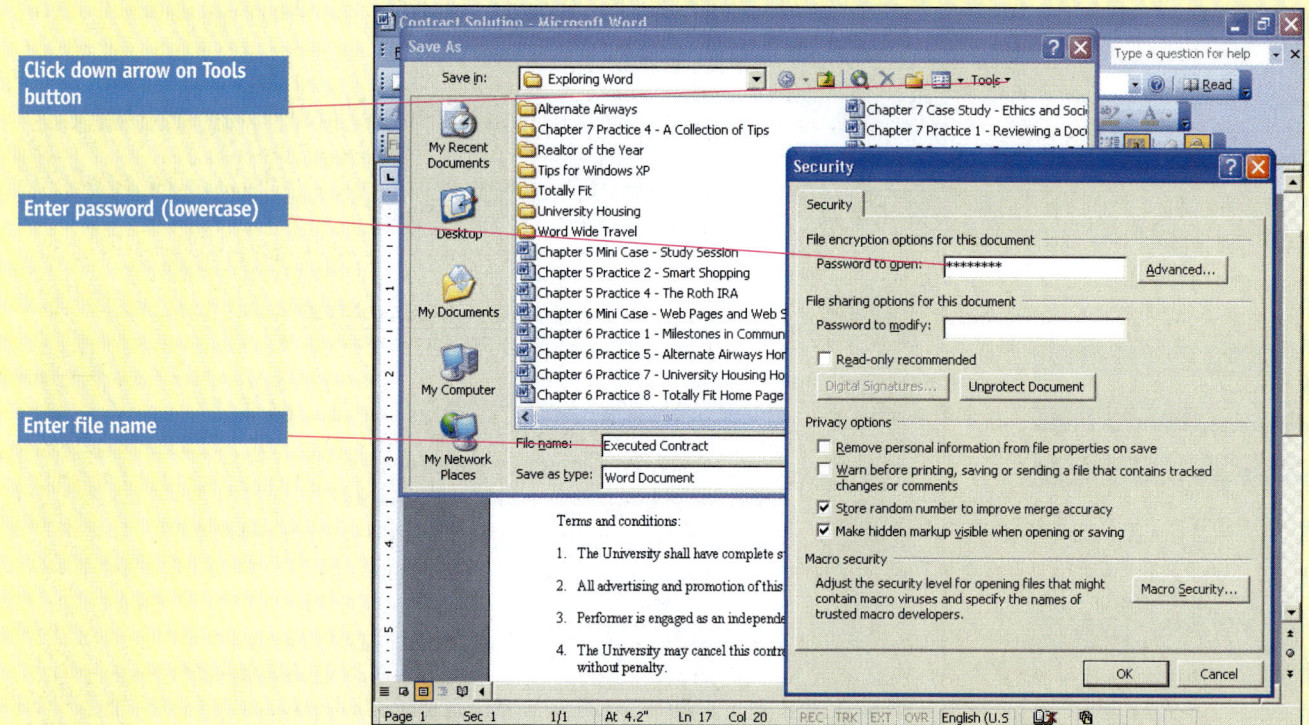

(h) Password Protect the Executed Contract (step 8)

FIGURE 7.3 Hands-on Exercise 1 (*continued*)

AUTHENTICATE YOUR DOCUMENTS

What if you sent a contract or other important document to a third party and the document was intercepted and altered en route? Or more likely, what if someone sent a forged document to a third party in your name? You can avoid both situations by using a digital signature to authenticate your correspondence. A digital signature is an electronic stamp of authenticity that confirms the origin and status of an e-mail attachment. You can obtain a digital signature from a variety of sources, then use Word to apply that signature to any document.

TABLE MATH

Tables were introduced in an earlier chapter and provide an easy way to arrange text, numbers, and/or graphics within a document. This section extends that discussion to include calculations within a table, giving a Word document the power of a simple spreadsheet. We also describe how to *sort* the rows within a table in a different sequence, according to the entries in a specific column of the table.

We begin by reviewing a few basic concepts. The rows and columns in a table intersect to form *cells*, each of which can contain text, numbers, and/or graphics. Text is entered into each cell individually, enabling you to add, delete, or format text in one cell without affecting the text in other cells. The rows within a table can be different heights, and each row may contain a different number of columns.

The commands in the *Tables menu* or the *Tables and Borders toolbar* operate on one or more cells. The Insert and Delete commands add new rows or columns, or delete existing rows or columns, respectively. Other commands shade and/or border selected cells or the entire table. You can also select multiple cells and merge them into a single cell. All of this was presented earlier, and should be familiar.

Figure 7.4 displays a table of expenses that is associated with the performer's contract. The table also illustrates two additional capabilities that are associated with a table. First, you can sort the rows in a table to display the data in different sequences as shown in Figures 7.4a and 7.4b. Both figures display the same 6×4 table (six rows and four columns). The first row in each figure is a header row and contains the field names for each column. The next four rows contain data for a specific expense, while the last row displays the total for all expenses

Figure 7.4a lists the expenses in alphabetical order—airfare, hotel, meals, and performance fee. Figure 7.4b, however, lists the expenses in *descending* (high to low) *sequence* according to the amount. Thus, the performance fee (the largest expense) is listed first, and the meals (the smallest expense) appear last. Note, too, that the sort has been done in such a way as to affect only the four middle rows; that is, the header and total rows have not moved. This is accomplished according to the select-then-do methodology that is used for many operations in Microsoft Word. You select the rows that are to be sorted, then you execute the command (the Sort command in the Tables menu in this example).

Figure 7.4c displays the same table as in Figure 7.4b, albeit in a different format that displays the field codes rather than the field results. The entries consist of formulas that were entered into the table to perform a calculation. The entries are similar to those in a spreadsheet. Thus, the rows in the table are numbered from one to six while the columns are labeled from A to D. The row and column labels do not appear in the table per se, but are used to enter the formulas.

The intersection of a row and column forms a cell. Cell D4, for example, contains the entry to compute the total hotel expense by multiplying the number of days (in cell B4) by the per diem amount (in cell C4). In similar fashion, the entry in cell D5 computes the total expense for meals by multiplying the values in cells B5 and C5, respectively. The formula is not entered (typed) into the cell explicitly, but is created through the Formula command in the Tables menu.

Figure 7.4d is a slight variation of Figure 7.4c in which the field codes for the hotel and meals have been toggled off to display the calculated values, as opposed to the field codes. The cells are shaded, however, to emphasize that these cells contain formulas (fields), as opposed to numerical values. (The shading is controlled by the Options command in the Tools menu. The *field codes* are toggled on and off by selecting the formula and pressing the Shift+F9 key or by right clicking the entry and selecting the Toggle Field Codes command.)

The formula in cell D6 has a different syntax and sums the value of all cells directly above it. You do not need to know the syntax since Word provides a dialog box that supplies the entry for you. It's easy, as you shall see in our next hands-on exercise.

Header row →

Expenses are in alphabetical order →

Expense	Number of Days	Per Diem Amount	Amount
Airfare			$349.00
Hotel	2	$129.99	$259.98
Meals	2	$75.00	$150.00
Performance Fee			$1000.00
Total			**$1758.98**

Total is displayed →

(a) Expenses (alphabetical order by expense)

Descending order by amount →

Expense	Number of Days	Per Diem Amount	Amount
Performance Fee			$1000.00
Airfare			$349.00
Hotel	2	$129.99	$259.98
Meals	2	$75.00	$150.00
Total			**$1758.98**

(b) Expenses (descending order by amount)

Column labels →
Row labels →
Field codes →

	A	B	C	D
1	Expense	Number of Days	Per Diem Amount	Amount
2	Performance Fee			$1000.00
3	Airfare			$349.00
4	Hotel	2	$129.99	{=b4*c4}
5	Meals	2	$75.00	{=b5*c5}
6	Total			{=SUM(ABOVE)}

(c) Field Codes

Shading indicates a cell formula →

	A	B	C	D
1	Expense	Number of Days	Per Diem Amount	Amount
2	Performance Fee			$1000.00
3	Airfare			$349.00
4	Hotel	2	$129.99	$259.98
5	Meals	2	$75.00	$150.00
6	Total			$1758.98

(d) Field Codes (toggles and shading)

FIGURE 7.4 Sorting and Table Math

hands-on exercise

2 Table Math

Objective To open a password-protected document and remove the password protection; to create a table containing various cell formulas. Use Figure 7.5.

Step 1: Open the Document

- Open the **Executed Contract** in the **Exploring Word folder** from the first exercise. You will be prompted for a password as shown in Figure 7.5a.

- Type **password** (in lowercase) since this was the password that was specified when you saved the document originally.

- Pull down the **File menu** and click the **Save As command** to display the Save As dialog box. Click the **Tools button**. Click **Security Options**.

- Click and drag to select the existing password (which appears as a string of eight asterisks). Press the **Del key** to remove the password. Click **OK** to close the Save dialog box.

- Click the **Save command button** to close the Save As dialog box. The document is no longer password protected.

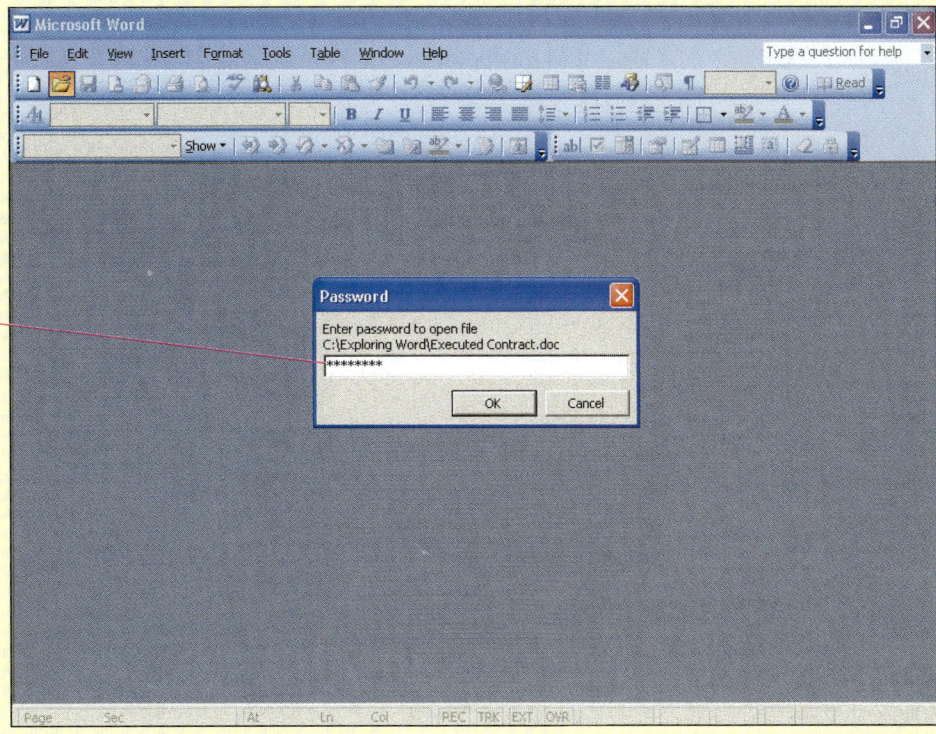

Enter password (lowercase)

(a) Open the Document (step 1)

FIGURE 7.5 Hands-on Exercise 2

CHANGE THE DEFAULT FOLDER

The default folder is the folder where Word saves and retrieves documents unless it is otherwise instructed. To change the default folder, pull down the Tools menu, click Options, click the File Locations tab, click Documents, and click the Modify command button to display the associated dialog box. Enter the name of the new folder (for example, C:\Exploring Word), click OK, then click the Close button.

Step 2: **Review the Contract**

- You should see the executed contract from the previous exercise. Click the **Protect Form button** on the Forms toolbar to unprotect the document so that its context can be modified.

- Do *not* click the Protect Form button a second time or else the data will disappear. (You can quit the document without saving the changes, as described in the boxed tip below.)

- Point to any toolbar, and click the **right mouse button** to display the list of toolbars shown in Figure 7.5b. Click the **Forms toolbar** to toggle the toolbar off (the check will disappear).

- Right click any visible toolbar a second time, and toggle the Reviewing toolbar off as well.

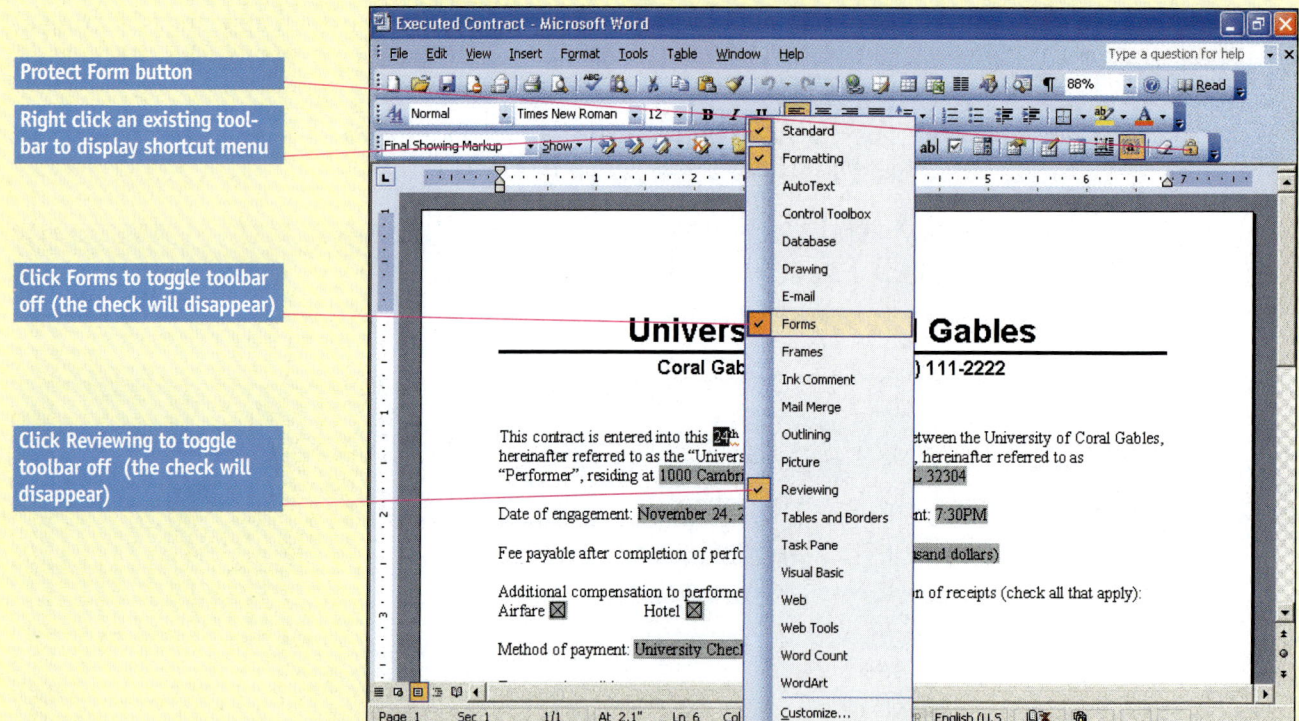

(b) Review the Contract (step 2)

FIGURE 7.5 Hands-on Exercise 2 (*continued*)

QUIT WITHOUT SAVING

There will be times when you do not want to save the changes to a document—for example, when you have edited it beyond recognition and wish you had never started. Pull down the File menu and click the Close command, then click No in response to the message asking whether you want to save the changes to the document. Pull down the File menu and reopen the document (it should appear as the first file in the list of most recently edited documents), then start over from the beginning.

Step 3: **Create the Table**

- Press **Ctrl+End** to move to the end of the contract, then press **Ctrl+Enter** to create a page break. You should be at the top of page two of the document.
- Press the **Enter key** three times and then enter **Summary of Expenses** in **24 point Arial bold** as shown in Figure 7.5c. Center the text. Press **Enter** twice to add a blank line under the heading.
- Change to **12 point Times New Roman**. Click the **Insert Table button** on the Standard toolbar to display a grid, then drag the mouse across and down the grid to create a 6 × 4 table (six rows and four columns). Release the mouse to create the table.
- Enter data into the table as shown in Figure 7.5c. You can format the entries by selecting multiple cells, then clicking the appropriate tools on the formatting toolbar.
- Save the document.

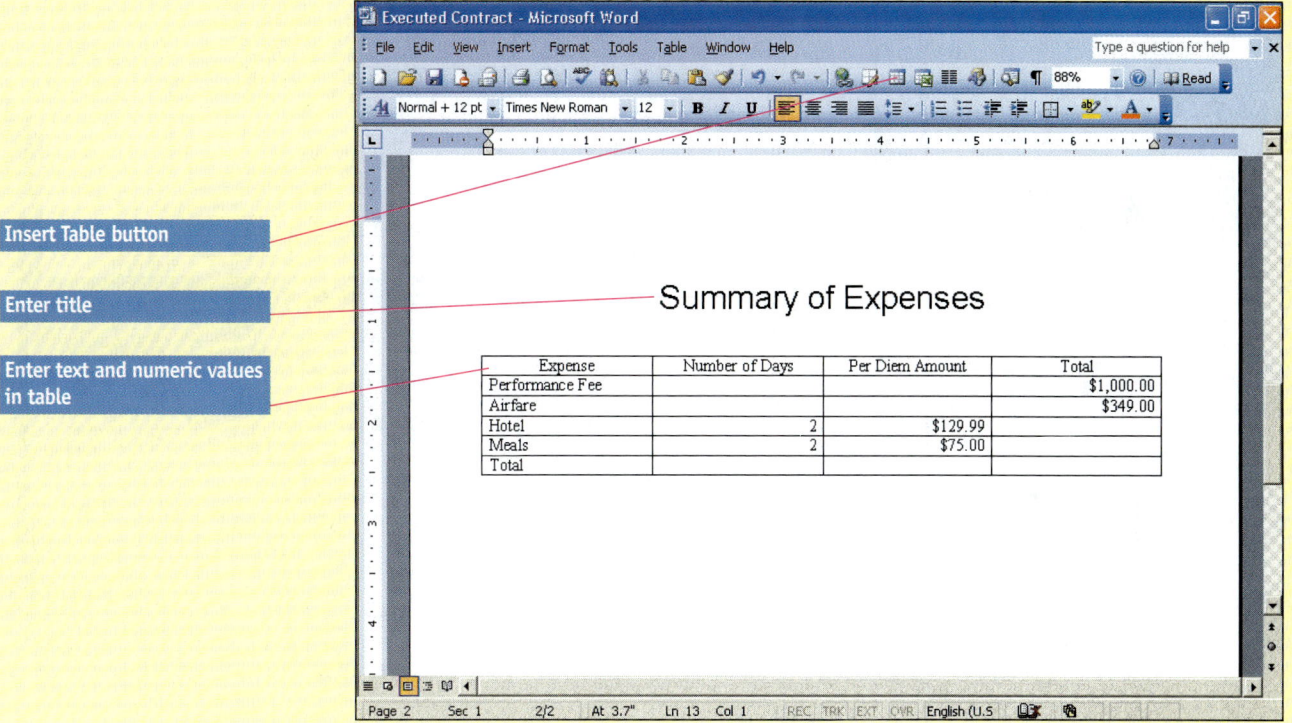

(c) Create the Table (step 3)

FIGURE 7.5 Hands-on Exercise 2 (*continued*)

TABS AND TABLES

The Tab key functions differently in a table than in a regular document. Press the Tab key to move to the next cell in the current row (or to the first cell in the next row if you are at the end of a row). Press Tab when you are in the last cell of a table to add a new blank row to the bottom of the table. Press Shift+Tab to move to the previous cell in the current row (or to the last cell in the previous row). You must press Ctrl+Tab to insert a regular tab character within a cell.

Step 4: **Sort the Table**

- Click and drag to select the entire table except for the last row. Pull down the **Table menu** and click the **Sort command** to display the Sort dialog box in Figure 7.5d.

- Click the **drop-down arrow** in the Sort by list box and select **Expense** (the column heading for the first column). The **Ascending option button** is selected by default.

- Verify that the option button to include a Header row is selected. Click **OK**. The entries in the table are rearranged alphabetically according to the entry in the Expenses column.

- The Total row remains at the bottom of the table since it was not included in the selected rows for the Sort command.

- Save the document.

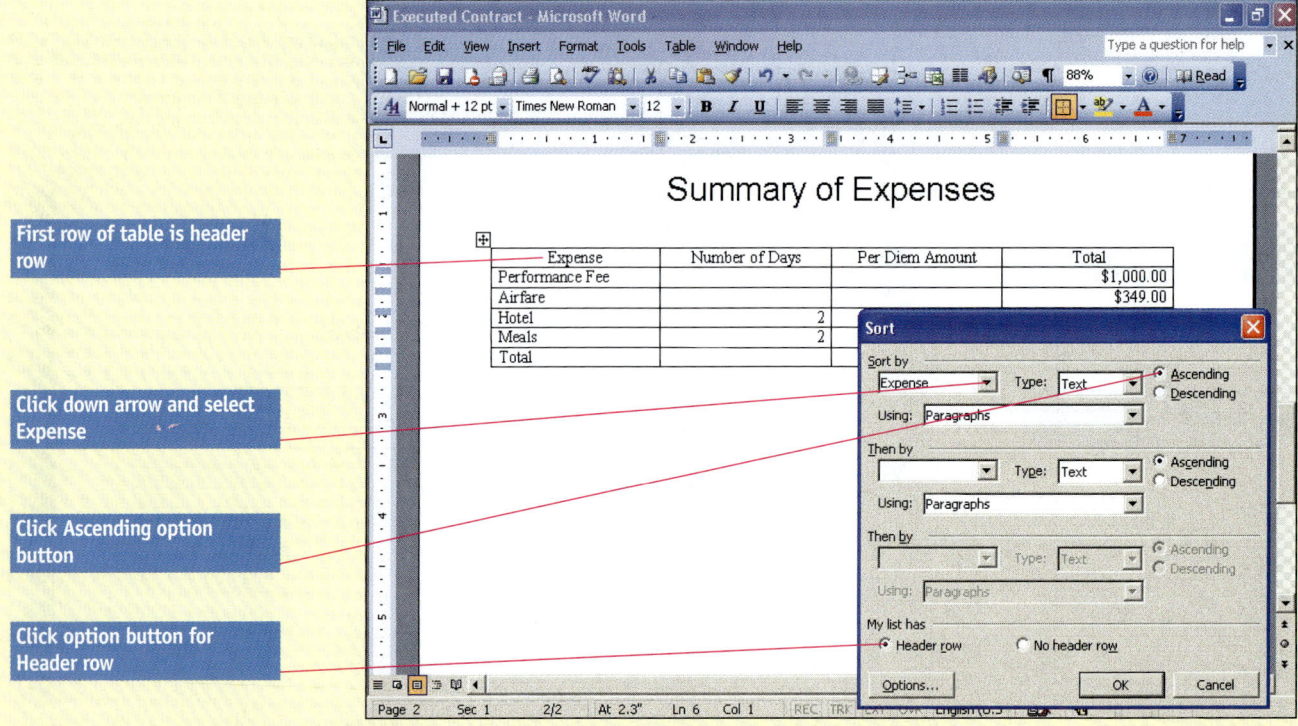

(d) Sort the Table (step 4)

FIGURE 7.5 Hands-on Exercise 2 (*continued*)

THE HEADER ROW

The first row in a table is known as the header row and contains the column names (headings) that describe the values in each column of the table. The header row is typically included in the range selected for the sort so that the Sort by list box displays the column names. The header row must remain at the top of the table, however, and thus it is important that the option button that indicates a header row be selected. In similar fashion, the last row typically contains the totals and should remain as the bottom row of the table. Hence it (the total row) is not included in the rows that are selected for sorting.

Step 5: **Enter the Formulas for Row Totals**

- Click in **cell D3** (the cell in the fourth column and third row). Pull down the **Table menu** and click the **Formula command** to display the Formula dialog box.

- Click and drag to select the =SUM(ABOVE) function, which is entered by default. Type **=b3*c3** as shown in Figure 7.5e to compute the total hotel expense. The total is computed by multiplying the number of days (in cell B3) by the per diem amount (in cell C3).

- Click **OK**. You should see $259.98 in cell D3.

- Click in **cell D4** and repeat the procedure to enter the formula **=b4*c4** to compute the total expense for meals. You should see $150.00 (two days at $75.00 per day).

- Save the document.

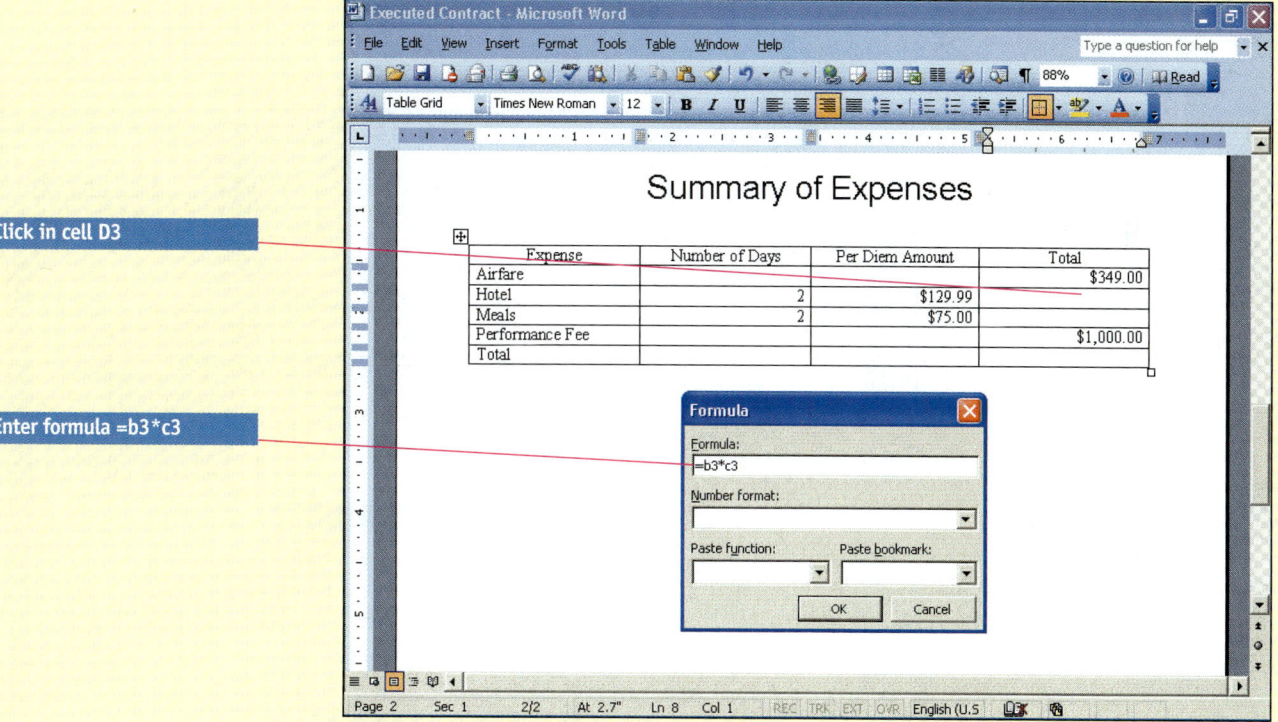

(e) Enter the Formulas for Row Totals (step 5)

FIGURE 7.5 Hands-on Exercise 2 (*continued*)

IT'S NOT EXCEL

Your opinion of table math within Microsoft Word depends on what you know about a spreadsheet. If you have never used Excel, then you will find table math to be very useful, especially when simple calculations are necessary within a Word document. If, on the other hand, you know Excel, you will find table math to be rather limited; for example, you cannot copy a formula from one cell to another, but must enter it explicitly in every cell. Nevertheless, the feature enables simple calculations to be performed entirely within Word, without having to link an Excel worksheet to a Word document.

Step 6: **Enter the SUM(ABOVE) Formula**

- Click in **cell D6** (the cell in row 6, column 4), which is to contain the total of all expenses. Pull down the **Table menu** and click the **Formula command** to display the Formula dialog box in Figure 7.5f.

- The =SUM(ABOVE) function is entered by default. Click **OK** to accept the formula and close the dialog box. You should see $1,758.98 (the sum of the cells in the last column) displayed in the selected cell.

- Select the formula and press **Shift+F9** to display the code {=SUM(ABOVE)}. Press **Shift+F9** a second time to display the field value ($1,758.98).

- Click in **cell D2** (the cell containing the airfare). Replace $349 with **$549.00** and press the **Tab key** to move out of the cell. The total expenses are *not* yet updated in cell D6.

- Point to **cell D6**, click the **right mouse button** to display a context-sensitive menu, and click the **Update Field command**. Cell D6 displays $1,958.98, the correct total for all expenses.

- Save the document.

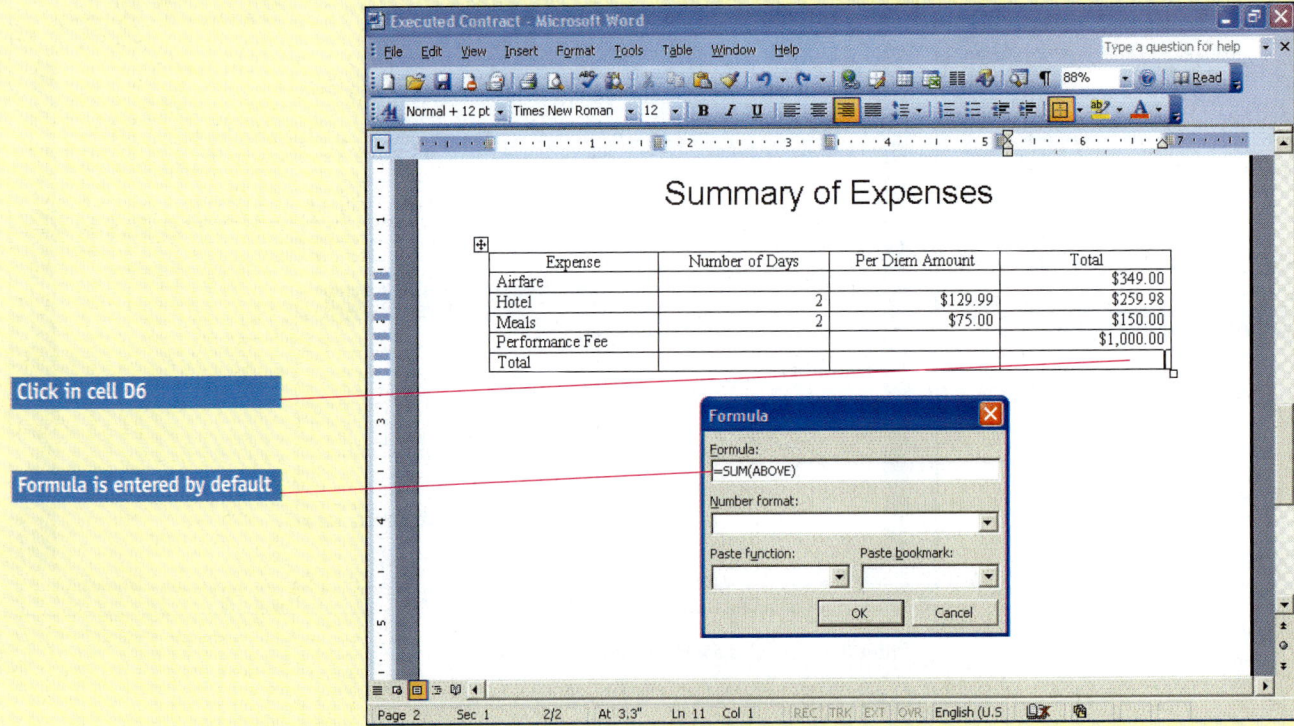

(f) Enter the SUM(ABOVE) Formula (step 6)

FIGURE 7.5 Hands-on Exercise 2 (*continued*)

FORMATTING A CALCULATED VALUE

Word does its best to format a calculation according to the way you want it. You can, however, change the default format while entering the formula by clicking the down arrow on the Number format list box and choosing a different format. You can also enter a format directly in the Number format text box. To display a dollar sign and comma without a decimal point, enter $#,##0 into the text box. You can use trial and error to experiment with other formats.

Step 7: **Print the Completed Contract**

- Zoom to two pages to preview the completed document. The first page contains the text of the executed contract that was completed in the previous exercise. The second page contains the table of expenses from this contract.

- Pull down the **File menu** and click the **Print command** to display the Print dialog box in Figure 7.5g. Click the **Options command button** to display the second Print dialog box.

- Check the box to include **Field codes** with the document. Click **OK** to close that dialog box, then click **OK** to print the document.

- Repeat the process to print the document a second time, but this time with field values, rather than field codes. Thus, pull down the **File menu**, click the **Print command** to display the Print dialog box, and click the **Options command button** to display a second Print dialog box.

- Clear the box to include **Field codes** with the document. Click **OK** to close that dialog box, then click **OK** to print the document.

- Exit Word if you do not want to continue with the next exercise at this time. Click **Yes** if asked to save the changes.

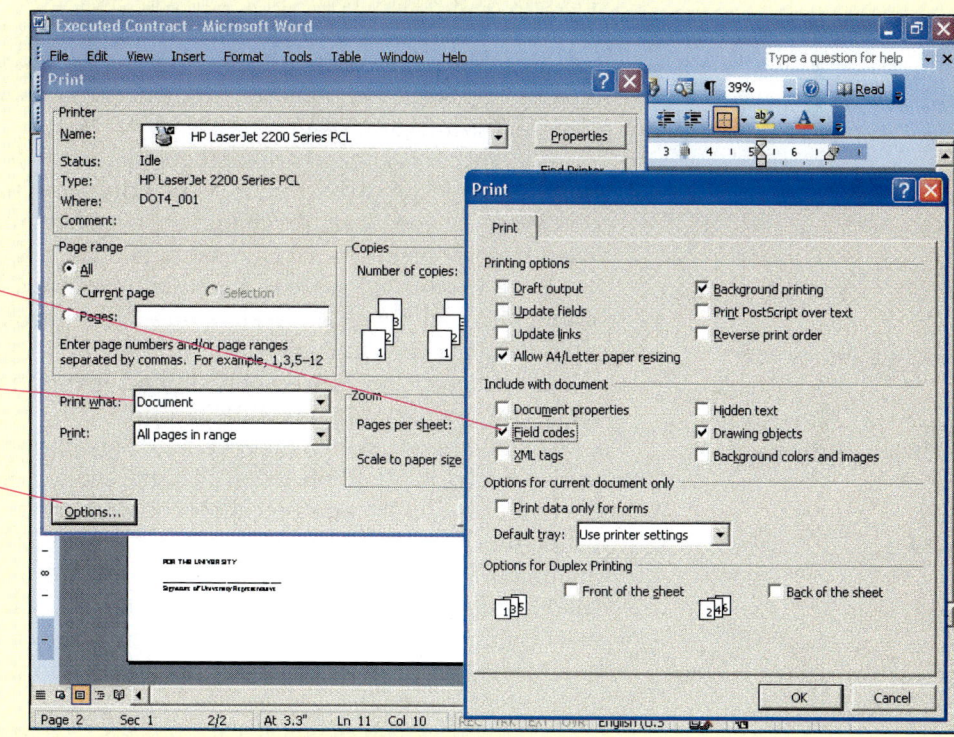

(g) Print the Completed Contract (step 7)

FIGURE 7.5 Hands-on Exercise 2 (*continued*)

DOCUMENT PROPERTIES

Prove to your instructor how hard you've worked by printing various statistics about your document, including the number of revisions and the total editing time. Pull down the File menu, click the Print command to display the Print dialog box, click the drop-down arrow in the Print What list box, select Document properties, then click OK.

MICROSOFT OFFICE WORD 2003 1171

MASTER DOCUMENTS

A ***master document*** is composed of multiple ***subdocuments***, each of which is stored as a separate file. The advantage of the master document is that you can work with several smaller documents, as opposed to a single large document. Thus, you edit the subdocuments individually and more efficiently than if they were all part of the same document. You can create a master document to hold the chapters of a book, where each chapter is stored as a subdocument. You can also use a master document to hold multiple documents created by others, such as a group project, where each member of the group is responsible for a section of the document.

Figure 7.6 displays a master document with five subdocuments. The subdocuments are collapsed in Figure 7.6a and expanded in Figure 7.6b. (The **Outlining toolbar** contains the Collapse and Expand Subdocuments buttons, as well as other tools associated with master documents.) The collapsed structure in Figure 7.6a enables you to see at a glance the subdocuments that comprise the master document. You can insert additional subdocuments and/or remove existing subdocuments from the master document. Deleting a subdocument from within a master document does *not* delete the subdocument from disk.

The expanded structure in Figure 7.6b enables you to view and/or edit the contents of the subdocuments. Look carefully, however, at the first two subdocuments in Figure 7.6b. A padlock appears to the left of the first line in the first subdocument, whereas it is absent from the second subdocument. These subdocuments are locked and unlocked, respectively. (All subdocuments are locked when collapsed as in Figure 7.6a.)

Changes to the master document can be made at any time. Changes to the subdocuments, however, can be made only when the subdocument is unlocked. Note, too, that you can make changes to a subdocument in one of two ways, either when the subdocument is expanded (and unlocked) within a master document as in Figure 7.6b or by opening the subdocument as an independent document within Microsoft Word. Both techniques work equally well, and we find ourselves alternating between the two.

Regardless of how you edit the subdocuments, the attraction of a master document is the ability to work with multiple subdocuments simultaneously. The subdocuments are created independently of one another, with each subdocument stored in its own file. Then, when all of the subdocuments are finished, the master document is created and the subdocuments are inserted into the master document, from where they are easily accessed. Inserting page numbers into the master document, for example, causes the numbers to run consecutively from one subdocument to the next. You can also create a table of contents or index for the master document that will reflect the entries in all of the subdocuments. And finally, you can print all of the subdocuments from within the master document with a single command.

Alternatively, you can reverse the process by starting with an empty master document and using it as the basis to create the subdocuments. This is ideal for organizing a group project in school or at work, the chapters in a book, or the sections in a report. Start with a new document, enter the topics assigned to each group member. Format each topic in a heading style within the master document, then use the ***Create Subdocument command*** to create subdocuments based on those headings. Saving the master document will automatically save each subdocument in its own file. This is the approach that we will follow in our next hands-on exercise.

The exercise also illustrates the ***Create New Folder command*** that lets you create a new folder on your hard drive (or floppy disk) from within Microsoft Word, as opposed to using Windows Explorer. The new folder can then be used to store the master document and all of its subdocuments in a single location apart from any other documents.

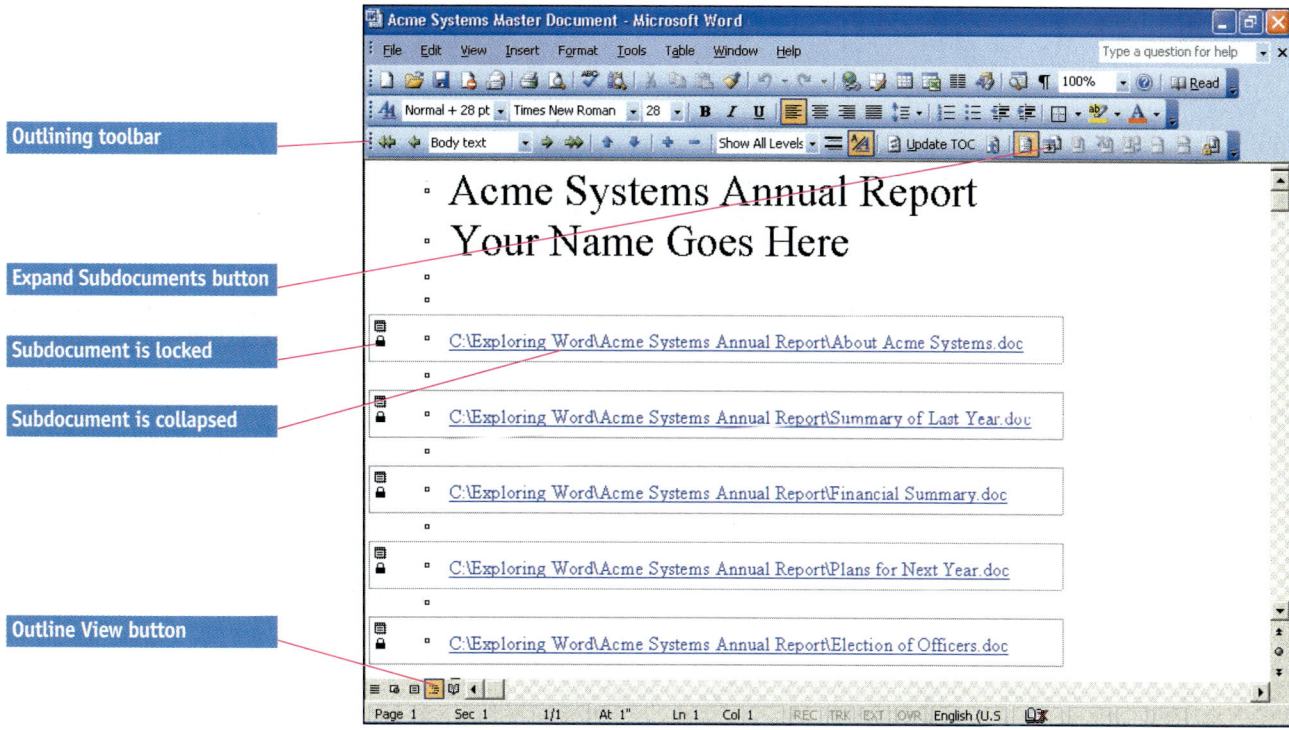

(a) Collapsed Subdocuments

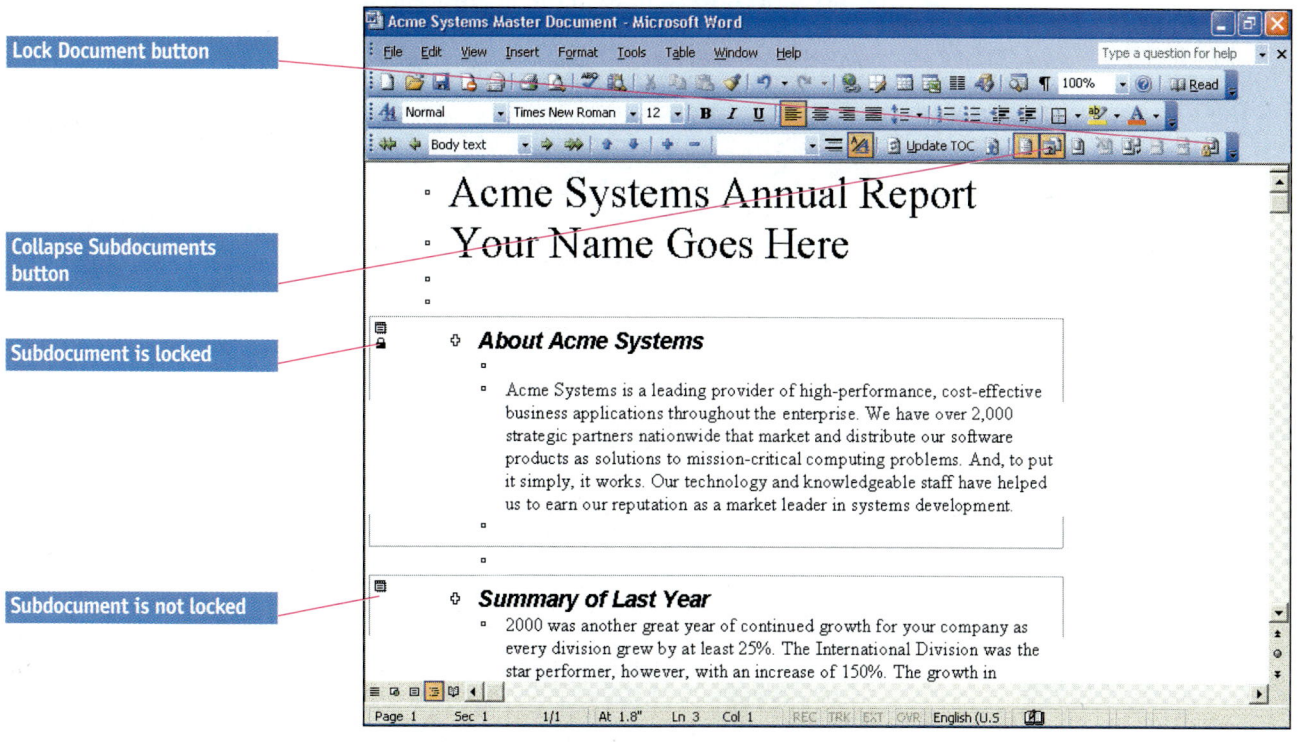

(b) Expanded Subdocuments

FIGURE 7.6 A Master Document

hands-on exercise

3 Master Documents

Objective To create a master document and various subdocuments; to create a new folder from within the Save As dialog box in Microsoft Word. Use Figure 7.7 as a guide in the exercise.

Step 1: **Create a New Folder**

- Start Word. If necessary, click the **New Blank Document button** on the Standard toolbar to begin a new document. Enter the text of the document in Figure 7.7a in **12 point Times New Roman**.

- Press **Ctrl+Home** to move to the beginning of the document. Pull down the **Style list box** on the Formatting toolbar, then select **Heading 2** as the style for the document title.

- Click the **Save button** to display the Save As dialog box. If necessary, click the **drop-down arrow** on the Save in list box to select the **Exploring Word folder** you have used throughout the text.

- Click the **Create New Folder button** to display the New Folder dialog box. Type **Acme Systems Annual Report** as the name of the new folder. Click **OK** to create the folder and close the New Folder dialog box.

- The Save in list box indicates that the Acme Systems Annual Report folder is the current folder. The name of the document, **About Acme Systems**, is entered by default (since this text appears at the beginning of the document).

- Click the **Save button** to save the document and close the Save As dialog box. The title bar changes to reflect the name of the document (About Acme Systems).

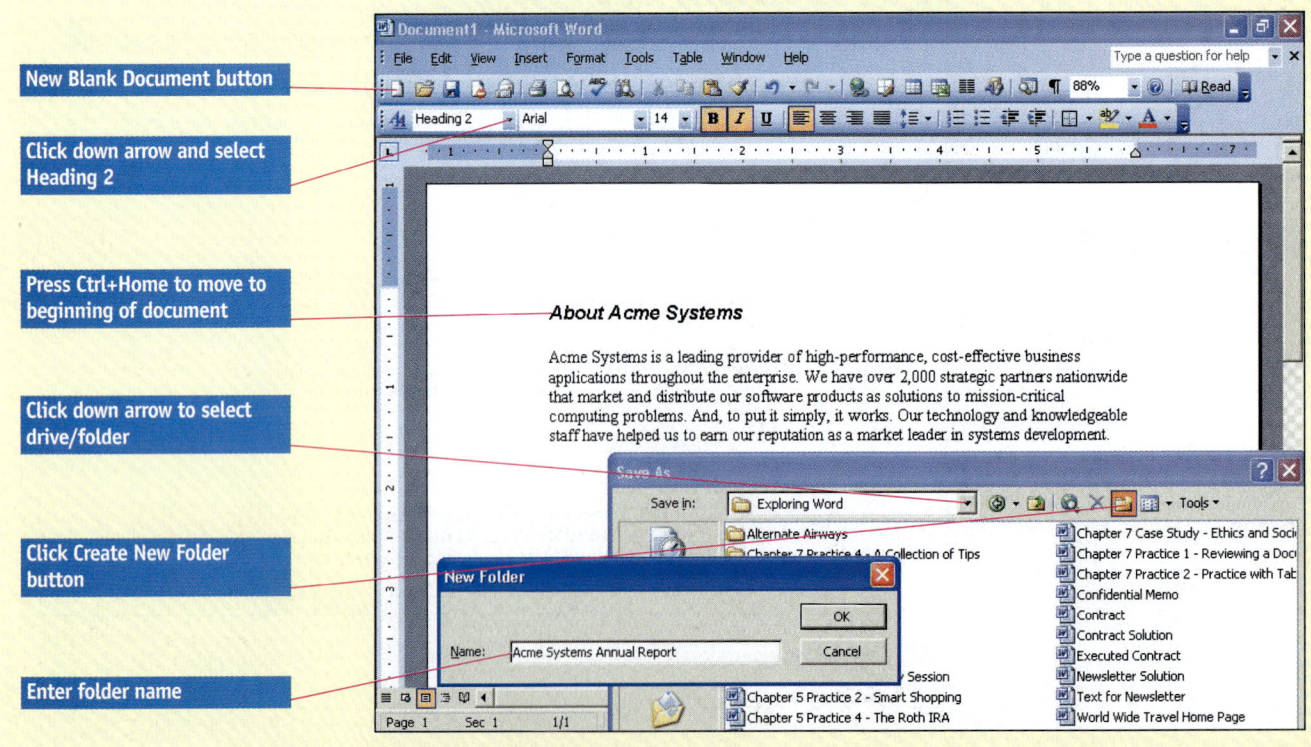

(a) Create a New Folder (step 1)

FIGURE 7.7 Hands-on Exercise 3

Step 2: **Create the Master Document**

- Click the **New Blank Document button** on the Standard toolbar. Enter **Acme Systems Annual Report** as the first line of the document. Enter your name under the title.

- Press the **Enter key** twice to leave a blank line after your name before the first subdocument. Type **Summary of Last Year** in the default typeface and size. Press **Enter**.

- Enter the remaining topics for the subdocuments, **Financial Summary**, **Plans for Next Year**, and **Election of Officers**.

- Change the format of the title and your name to **28 pt Times New Roman**.

- Pull down the **View menu** and click **Outline** to change to the Outline view. Click and drag to select the four headings as shown in Figure 7.7b. Click the **drop-down arrow** on the Style list box and select **Heading 2**.

- Be sure that all four headings are still selected. Click the **Create Subdocument button**. Each heading expands automatically into a subdocument.

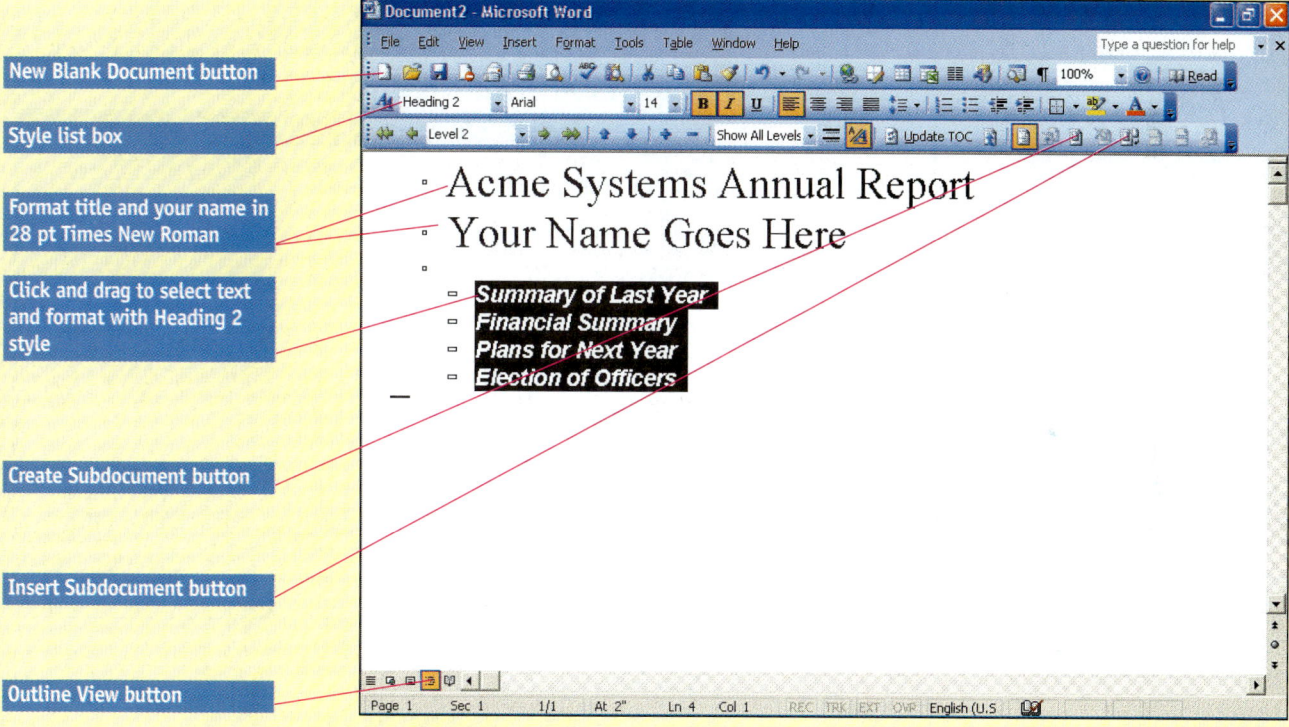

(b) Create the Master Document (step 2)

FIGURE 7.7 Hands-on Exercise 3 (*continued*)

THE CREATE SUBDOCUMENT BUTTON

You can enter subdocuments into a master document in one of two ways, through the Insert Subdocument button if the subdocuments already exist, or through the Create Subdocument button to create the subdocuments from within the master document. Start a new document, enter the title of each subdocument on a line by itself, format them in a heading style, then click the Create Subdocument button to create the subdocuments. Save the master document. The subdocuments are saved automatically as individual files in the same folder.

Step 3: **Save the Documents**

- Click the **Save button** to display the Save As dialog box in Figure 7.7c. If necessary, click the **drop-down arrow** on the Save in list box to select the **Acme Systems Annual Report folder** that was created in step 1. You should see the About Acme Systems document in this folder.

- Enter **Acme Systems Master Document** in the File name list box, then click the **Save button** within the Save As dialog box to save the master document (which automatically saves the subdocuments in the same folder).

- Press the **Collapse Subdocuments button** to collapse the subdocuments. You will see the name of each subdocument as it appears on disk, with the drive and folder information.

- Press the **Expand Subdocuments button**, and the subdocuments are reopened within the master document.

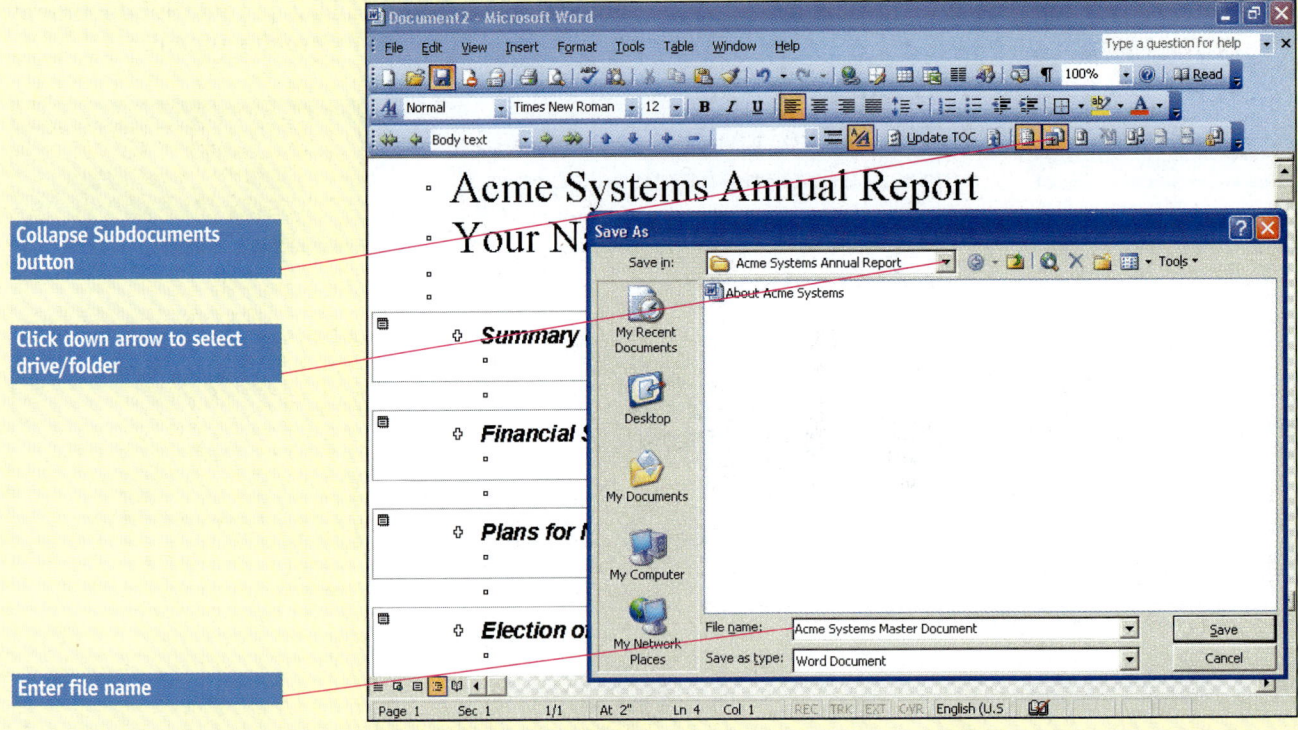

(c) Save the Documents (step 3)

FIGURE 7.7 Hands-on Exercise 3 (*continued*)

HELP WITH TOOLBAR BUTTONS

The Outlining toolbar is displayed automatically in the Outline view and suppressed otherwise. As with every toolbar you can point to any button to see a ToolTip with the name of the button. The Outlining toolbar contains buttons that pertain specifically to master documents such as buttons to expand and collapse subdocuments, or insert and remove subdocuments. The Outlining toolbar also contains buttons to promote and demote items, to display or suppress formatting, and/or to collapse and expand the outline.

Step 4: **Insert a Subdocument**

- Click below your name, but above the first subdocument. Click the **Insert Subdocument button** to display the Insert Subdocument dialog box in Figure 7.7d. If necessary, click the **drop-down arrow** on the Look in list box to change to the Acme Systems Annual Report folder.

- There are six documents, which include the About Acme Systems document from step 1, the Acme Systems Master document that you just saved, and the four subdocuments that were created automatically in conjunction with the master document.

- Select the **About Acme Systems** document, then click the **Open button** to insert this document into the master document.

- Save the master document.

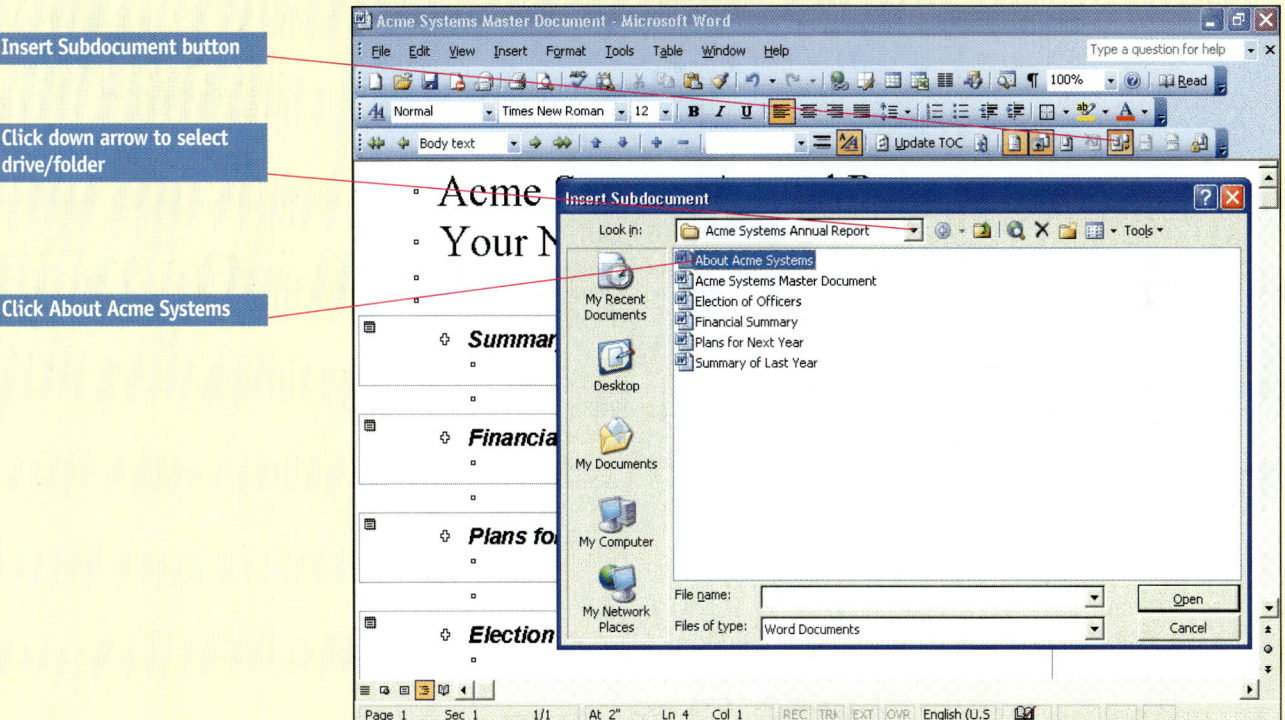

(d) Insert a Subdocument (step 4)

FIGURE 7.7 Hands-on Exercise 3 (*continued*)

CHANGE THE VIEW

The Outline view is used to create and/or modify a master document through insertion, repositioning, or deletion of its subdocuments. You can also modify the text of a subdocument within the Outline view (provided the document is unlocked) and/or implement formatting changes at the character level such as a change in font, type size, or style. More sophisticated formatting, however—such as changes in alignment, indentation, or line spacing—has to be implemented in the Normal or Print Layout views.

Step 5: **Modify a Subdocument**

- Click within the second subdocument, which will summarize the activities of last year. (The text of the document has not yet been entered.)
- Click the **Lock Document button** on the Outlining toolbar to display the padlock for this document. Click the **Lock Document button** a second time, which unlocks the document.
- Enter the text of the document as shown in Figure 7.7e, then click the **Save button** to save the changes to the master document.
- Be sure the subdocument is unlocked so that the changes you have made will be reflected in the subdocument file as well.

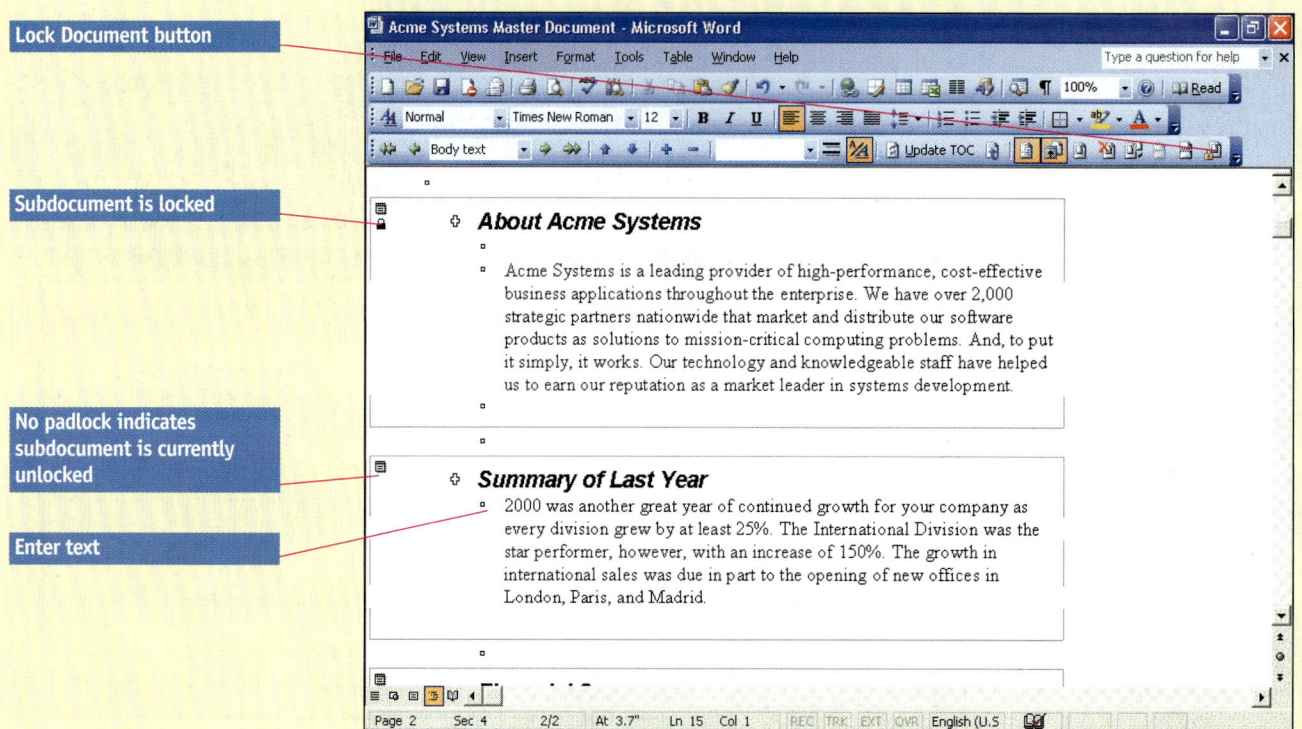

(e) Modify a Subdocument (step 5)

FIGURE 7.7 Hands-on Exercise 3 (*continued*)

OPEN THE SUBDOCUMENT

You can edit the text of a subdocument from within a master document, but it is often more convenient to open the subdocument when the editing is extensive. You can open a subdocument in one of two ways, by double clicking the document icon in the Outline view when the master document is expanded, or by following the hyperlink to the document when the Master Document is collapsed. Either way, the subdocument opens in its own window. Enter the changes into the subdocument, then save the subdocument and close its window to return to the master document, which now reflects the modified subdocument.

Step 6: Print the Completed Document

- Click the **Collapse Subdocuments button** to collapse the subdocuments as shown in Figure 7.7f. Click **OK** if asked to save the changes in the master document.

- Click the **Print button** on the Standard toolbar to print the document. Click **No** when asked whether to open the subdocuments before printing. The entire document appears on a single page. The text of the subdocuments is not printed, only the address of the documents.

- Click the **Print button** a second time, but click **Yes** when asked whether to open the subdocuments before printing.

- Submit both versions of the printed document to your instructor as proof that you did this exercise. Exit Word if you do not want to continue with the next exercise at this time.

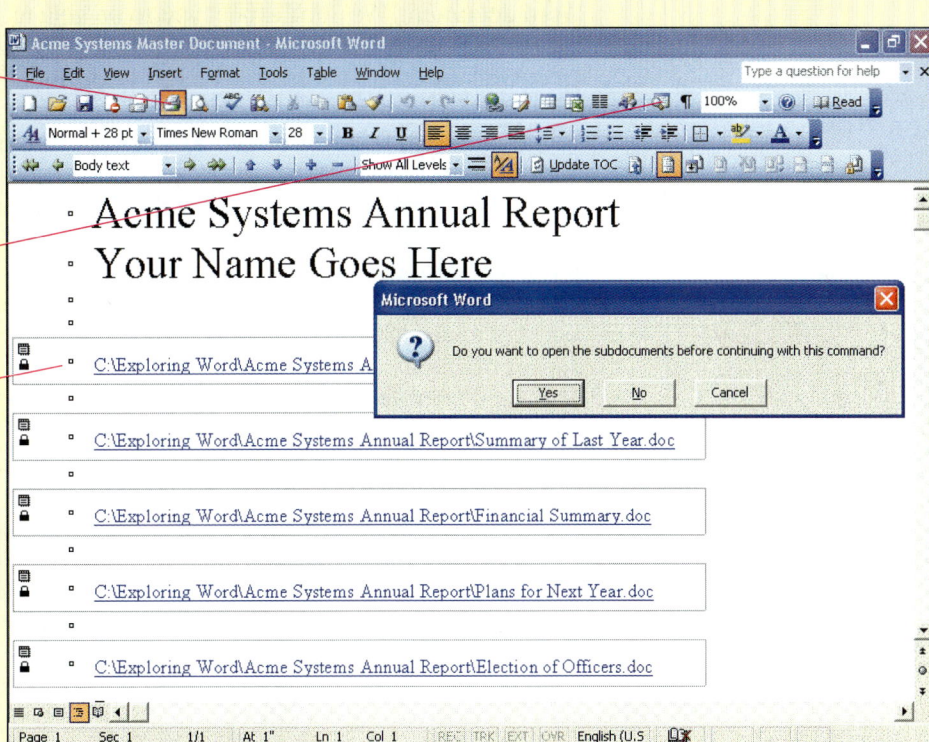

(f) Print the Completed Document (step 6)

FIGURE 7.7 Hands-on Exercise 3 (*continued*)

THE DOCUMENT MAP

The Document Map is one of our favorite features when working with large documents. Be sure that the master document is expanded to display the text of the subdocuments, then click the Document Map button on the Standard toolbar to divide the screen into two panes. The headings in a document are displayed in the left pane, and the text of the document is visible in the right pane. To go to a specific point in a document, click its heading in the left pane, and the insertion point is moved automatically to that point in the document, which is visible in the right pane. Click the Document Map button a second time to turn the feature off.

INTRODUCTION TO MACROS

Have you ever pulled down the same menus and clicked the same sequence of commands over and over? Easy as the commands may be to execute, it is still burdensome to continually repeat the same mouse clicks or keystrokes. If you can think of any task that you do repeatedly, whether in one document or in a series of documents, you are a perfect candidate to use macros.

A *macro* is a set of instructions (that is, a program) that executes a specific task. It is written in **Visual Basic for Applications (VBA)**, a programming language that is built into Microsoft Office. Fortunately, however, you don't have to be a programmer to use VBA. Instead, you use the *macro recorder* within Word to record your actions, which are then translated automatically into VBA. You get results that are immediately usable, and you can learn a good deal about VBA through observation.

Figure 7.8 illustrates a simple macro to enter your name, date, and class into a Word document. We don't expect you to be able to write the VBA code by yourself, but, as indicated, you don't have to. You just invoke the macro recorder and let it create the VBA statements for you. It is important, however, for you to understand the individual statements so that you can modify them as necessary. Do not be concerned with the precise syntax of every statement, but try instead to get an overall appreciation of what the statements do.

Every macro begins and ends with a Sub and End Sub statement, respectively. These statements identify the macro and convert it to a VBA *procedure*. The **Sub statement** contains the name of the macro, such as NameAndCourse in Figure 7.8. (Spaces are not allowed in a macro name.) The **End Sub statement** is always the last statement in a VBA procedure. Sub and End Sub are Visual Basic keywords and appear in blue.

The next several statements begin with an apostrophe, appear in green, and are known as *comments*. Comments provide information about the procedure, but do not affect its execution. The comments are inserted automatically by the macro recorder and include the name of the macro, the date it was recorded, and the author. Additional comments can be inserted at any time.

Every other statement in the procedure corresponds directly to a command that was executed in Microsoft Word. It doesn't matter how the commands were executed—whether from a pull-down menu, toolbar, or keyboard shortcut, because the end results, the VBA statements that are generated by the commands, are the same. In this example the user began by changing the font and font size,

Macro begins with Sub statement, which contains macro name

Comments are in green, begin with apostrophe, and do not affect execution

Macro ends with End Sub statement

```
Sub NameAndCourse()
'
' NameAndCourse Macro
' Macro recorded 6/25/2003 by John Doe
'
    With Selection.Font
        .Name = "Arial"
        .Size = 24
    End With
    Selection.TypeText Text:="John Doe"
    Selection.TypeParagraph
    Selection.TypeText Text:="June 25, 2003"
    Selection.TypeParagraph
    Selection.TypeText Text:="CIS120"
    Selection.TypeParagraph
End Sub
```

FIGURE 7.8   The NameAndCourse Macro

CHAPTER 7: THE EXPERT USER

and these commands were converted by the macro recorder to the VBA statements that specify Arial and 24 point, respectively. Next, the user entered his name and pressed the Enter key to begin a new paragraph. Again, the macro recorder converts these actions to the equivalent VBA statements. The user entered the date, pressed the Enter key, entered the class, and pressed the Enter key. Each of these actions resulted in an additional VBA statement.

You do not have to write VBA statements from scratch, but you should understand their function once they have been recorded. You can also edit the statements after they have been recorded. It's easy, for example, to change the procedure to include your name instead of John Doe. All changes to a macro are done through the Visual Basic Editor.

The Visual Basic Editor

Figure 7.9a displays the NameAndCourse macro as it appears within the ***Visual Basic Editor (VBE)***. The Visual Basic Editor is a separate application, and it is accessible from any application in Office XP. The left side of the VBE window displays the ***Project Explorer***, which is similar in concept and appearance to the Windows Explorer. Macros are stored by default in the Normal template, which is available to all Word documents. The VBA code is stored in the NewMacros module. (A *module* contains one or more procedures.)

The macros for the selected module (NewMacros in Figure 7.9) appear in the ***Code window*** in the right pane. (Additional macros, if any, are separated from one another by a horizontal line.) The VBA statements are identical to what we described earlier. The difference between Figure 7.8 and 7.9a is that the latter shows the macro within the Visual Basic Editor.

Figure 7.9b displays the TitlePage macro, which is built from the NameAndCourse macro. The new macro (a VBA procedure) is more complicated than its predecessor. "Complicated" is an intimidating word, however, and we prefer to use "powerful" instead. In essence, the TitlePage procedure moves the insertion point to the beginning of a Word document, inserts three blank lines at the beginning of the document, then enters three additional lines that center the student's name, date, and course in 24 point Arial. The last statement creates a page break within the document so that the title appears on a page by itself. The macro recorder created these statements for us, as we executed the corresponding actions from within Word.

Note, too, that the TitlePage macro changed the way in which the date is entered to make the macro more general. The NameAndCourse macro in Figure 7.9a specified a date (June 25, 2003). The TitlePage macro, however, uses the VBA InsertDateTime command to insert the current date. We did not know the syntax of this statement, but we didn't have to. Instead we pulled down the Insert menu from within Word, and chose the Date and Time command. The macro recorder kept track of our actions and created the appropriate VBA statement for us. In similar fashion, the macro recorder kept track of our actions when we moved to the beginning of the document and when we inserted a page break.

A SENSE OF FAMILIARITY

Visual Basic for Applications has the basic capabilities found in any other programming language. If you have programmed before, whether in Pascal, C, or even COBOL, you will find all of the logic structures you are used to. These include the Do While and Do Until statements, the If-Then-Else statement for decision making, nested If statements, a Case statement, and calls to subprograms. See the "Getting Started with VBA" module at the end of the text for additional information.

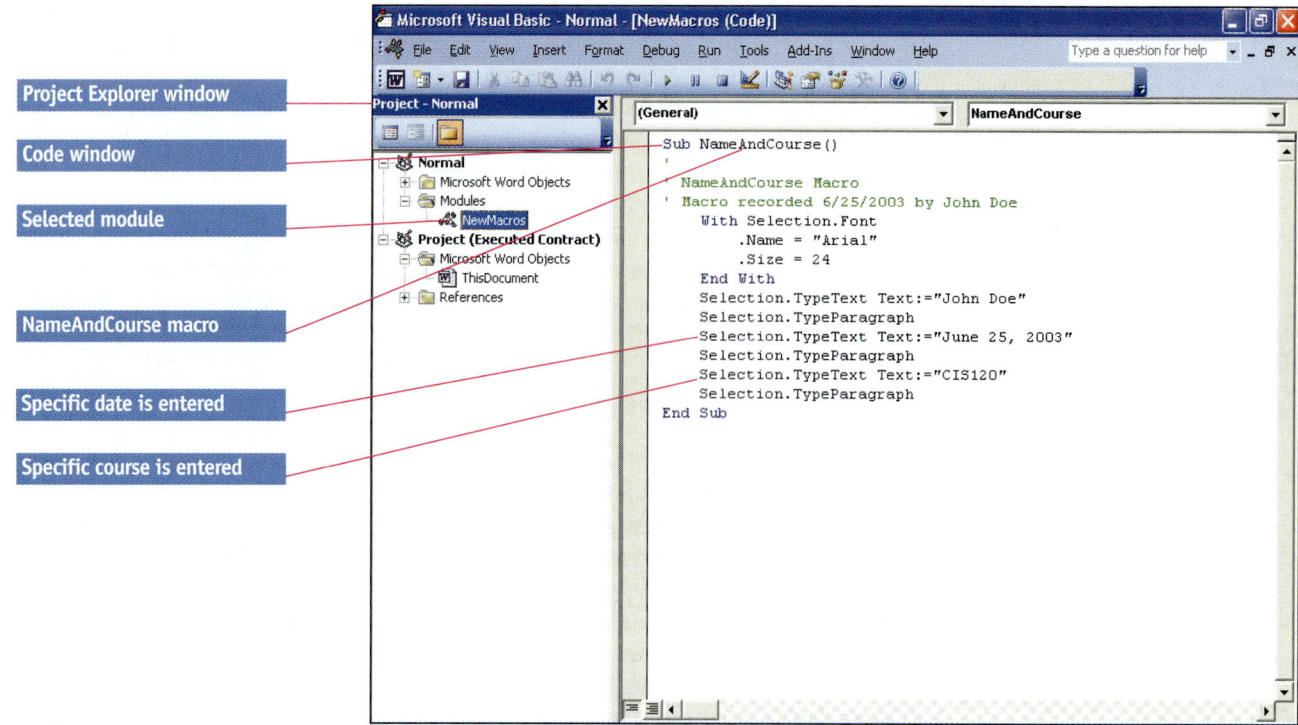

(a) NameAndCourse Macro

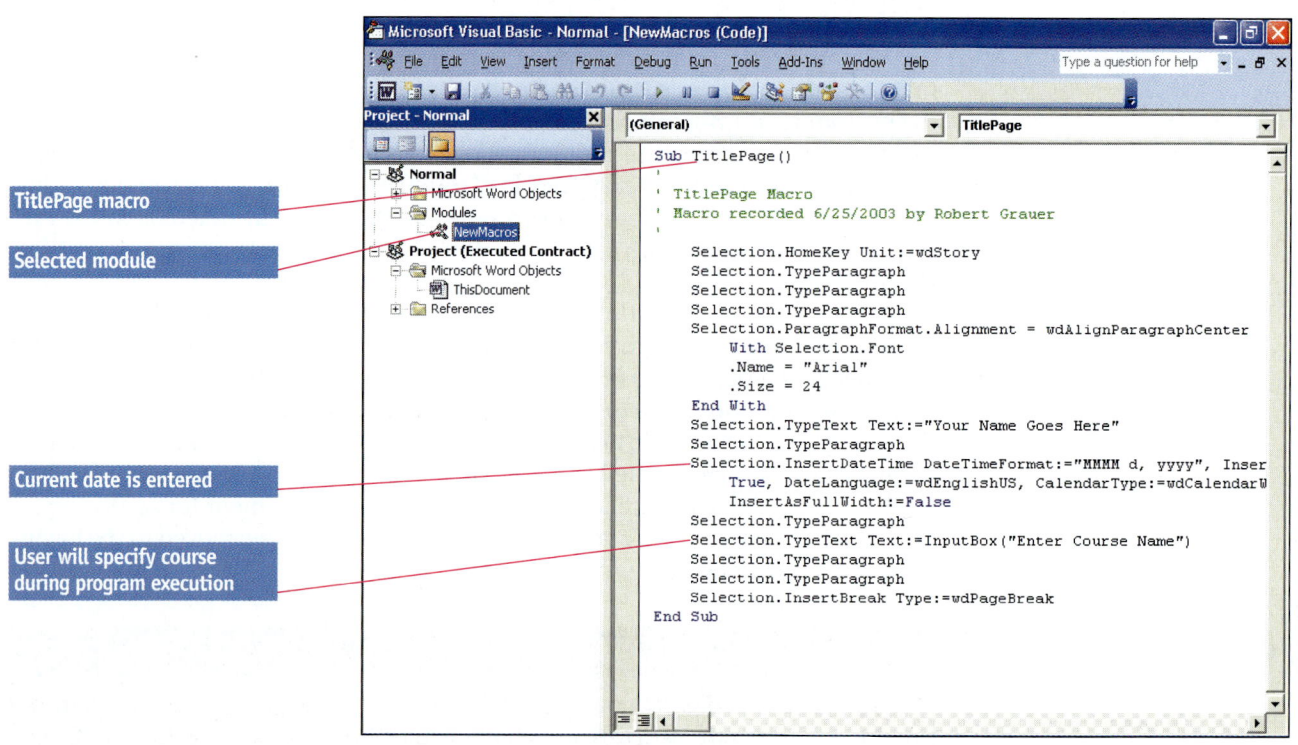

(b) TitlePage Macro

FIGURE 7.9 The Visual Basic Editor

1182 CHAPTER 7: THE EXPERT USER

hands-on exercise

4 Introduction to Macros

Objective To record, run, view, and edit simple macros; to run a macro from an existing Word document via a keyboard shortcut. Use Figure 7.10.

Step 1: **Create a Macro**

- Start Word. Open a new document if one is not already open.
- Pull down the **Tools menu**, click (or point to) the **Macro command**, then click **Record New Macro** to display the Record Macro dialog box in Figure 7.10a.
- Enter **NameAndCourse** as the name of the macro. (Do not leave any spaces.) If necessary, change the description to include your name. Click **OK**.
- Click **Yes** if asked whether you want to replace the existing macro. (The existing macro may have been created by another student or if you previously attempted the exercise. Either way, you want to replace the existing macro.)
- The mouse pointer changes to include a recording icon, and the Stop Recording toolbar is displayed.

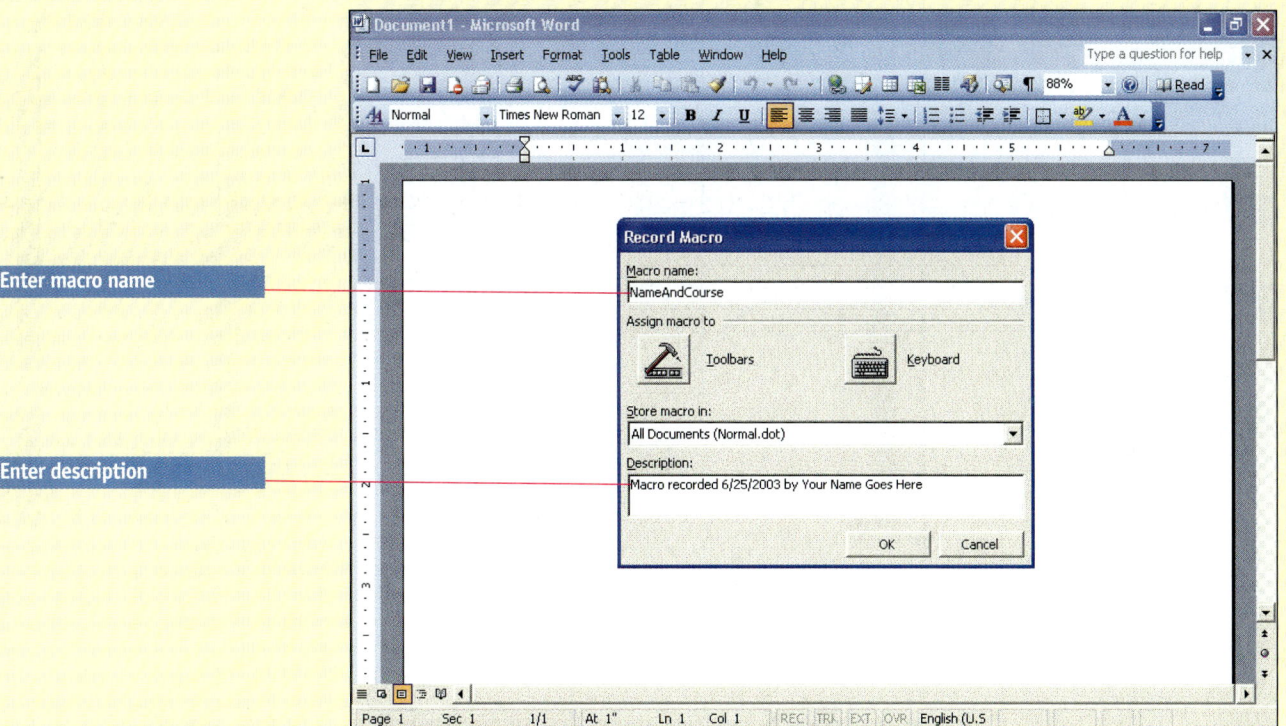

(a) Create a Macro (step 1)

FIGURE 7.10 Hands-on Exercise 4

MACRO NAMES

Macro names are not allowed to contain spaces or punctuation except for the underscore character. To create a macro name containing more than one word, capitalize the first letter of each word and/or use the underscore character—for example, NameAndCourse or Name_And_Course.

Step 2: **Record the Macro**

- The first task is to change the font. Pull down the **Format menu** and click the **Font command** to display the Font dialog box in Figure 7.10b. Select **14 point Arial**. Click **OK** to accept the setting and close the dialog box.

- Type your name. Press **Enter**.

- Pull down the **Insert menu** and click the **Date and Time command** to display the Date and Time dialog box. Choose the format of the date that you prefer. Check the box to **Update Automatically**, then click **OK** to accept the settings and close the dialog box.

- Press the **Enter key** to move to the next line.

- Enter the course you are taking this semester. Press the **Enter key** a final time.

- Click the **Stop Recording button** to end the macro.

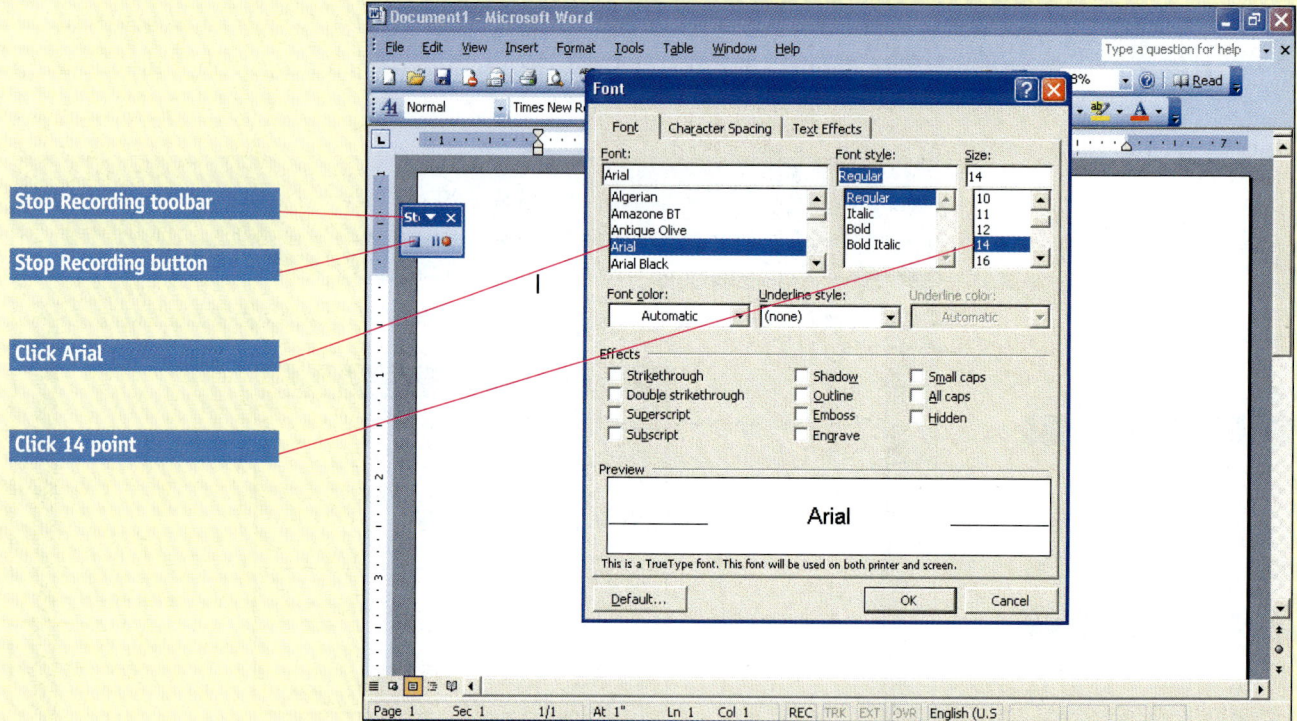

(b) Record the Macro (step 2)

FIGURE 7.10 Hands-on Exercise 4 (*continued*)

THE INSERT DATE COMMAND

A date is inserted into a document in one of two ways—as a field that is updated automatically to reflect the current date or as a specific value (the date and time on which the command is executed). The determination of which way the date is entered depends on whether the Update Automatically check box is checked or cleared, respectively. Be sure to choose the option that reflects your requirements.

Step 3: **Test the Macro**

- Click and drag to select your name, date, and class, then press the **Del key** to erase this information from the document.

- Pull down the **Tools menu**. Click **Macro**, then click the **Macros . . . command** to display the Macros dialog box in Figure 7.10c. Select **NameAndCourse** (the macro you just recorded) and click **Run**.

- Your name and class information should appear in the document. The typeface is 14 point Arial, which corresponds to your selection when you recorded the macro initially.

- Do not be dismayed if the macro did not work properly, as we show you how to correct it in the next several steps.

- Press the **Enter key** a few times. Press **Alt+F8** (a keyboard shortcut) to display the Macros dialog box.

- Double click the **NameAndCourse** macro to execute the macro. Your name and class information is entered a second time.

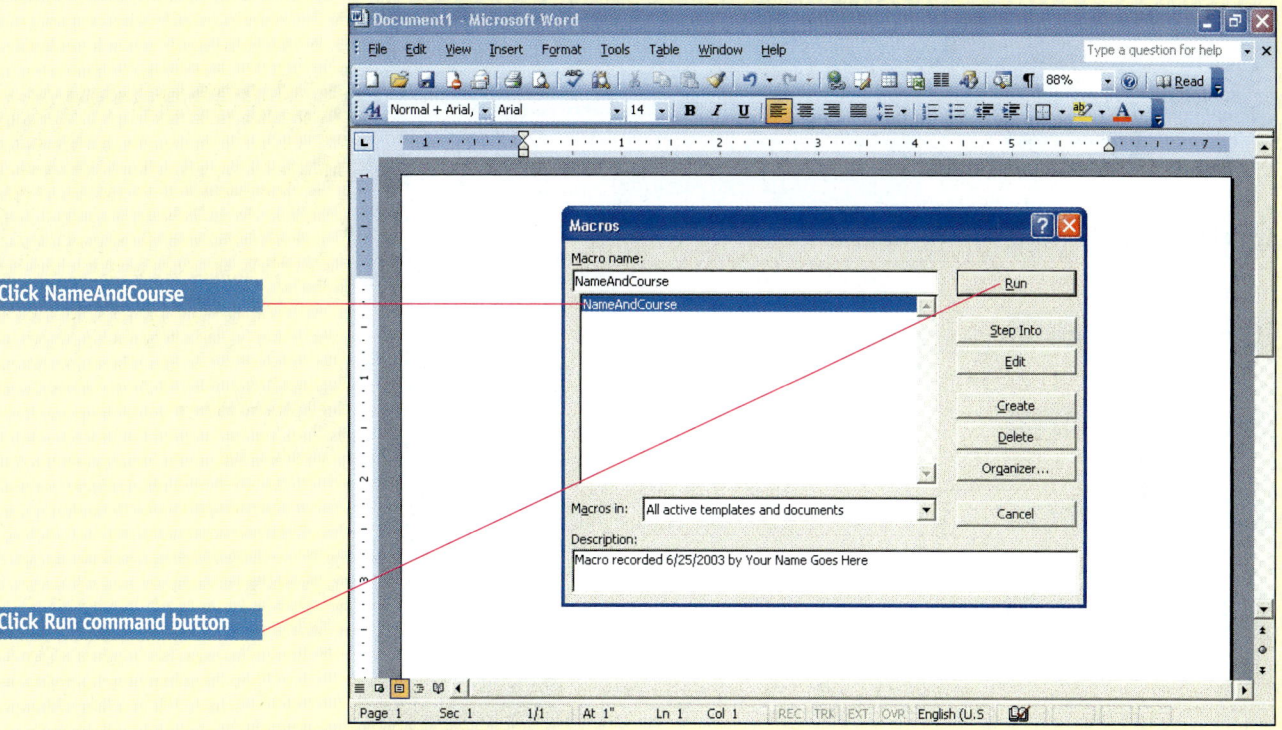

(c) Test the Macro (step 3)

FIGURE 7.10   Hands-on Exercise 4 (*continued*)

KEYBOARD SHORTCUTS

Take advantage of built-in shortcuts to facilitate the creation and testing of a macro. Press Alt+F11 to toggle between the VBA editor and the Word document. Use the Alt+F8 shortcut to display the Macros dialog box, then double click a macro to run it. You can also assign your own keyboard shortcut to a macro, as will be shown later in the exercise.

Step 4: **View the Macro**

- Pull down the **Tools menu**, click the **Macro command**, then click **Visual Basic Editor** (or press **Alt+F11**) to open the Visual Basic Editor. Maximize the VBE window. If necessary, pull down the **View menu** and click **Project Explorer** to open the Project window in the left pane. Close the Properties window if it is open.

- There is currently one project open, Document1, corresponding to the Word document on which you are working. Click the **plus sign** next to the Normal folder to expand that folder. Click the **plus sign** next to the **Modules folder** (within the Normal folder), then click **NewMacros**.

- Pull down the **View menu**, and click **Code** to open the Code window in the right pane. If necessary, click the **Maximize Button** in the Code window.

- Your screen should be similar to the one in Figure 7.10d except that it will reflect your name within the macro. The name in the comment statement may be different, however (especially if you are doing the exercise at school), as it corresponds to the person in whose name the program is registered.

- Select the statements as shown in Figure 7.10d. Press the **Del key** to delete the superfluous statements.

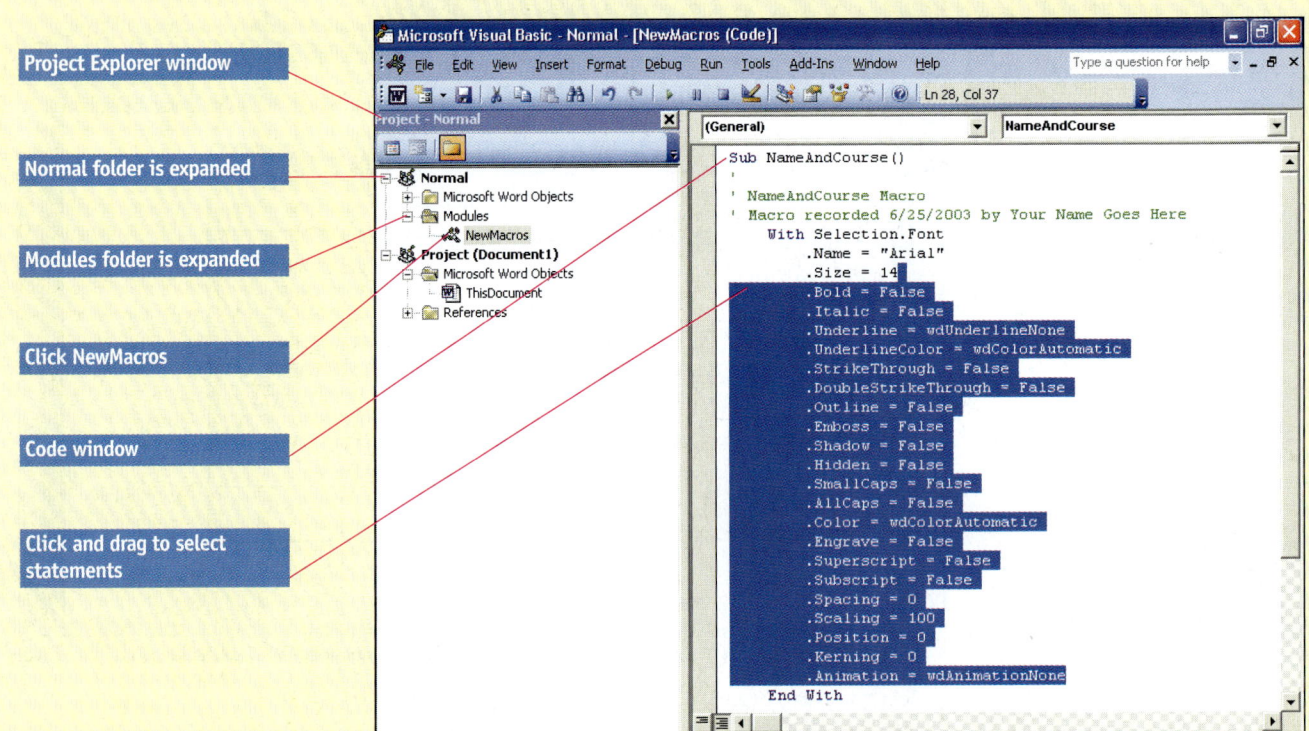

(d) View the Macro (step 4)

FIGURE 7.10 Hands-on Exercise 4 (*continued*)

RED, GREEN, AND BLUE

Visual Basic automatically assigns different colors to different types of statements (or a portion of those statements). Comments appear in green and are nonexecutable (i.e., they do not affect the outcome of a macro). Any statement containing a syntax error appears in red. Keywords such as Sub and End Sub, With and End With, and True and False, appear in blue.

Step 5: **Edit the Macro**

- If necessary, change the name in the comment statement to reflect your name. The macro will run identically regardless of the changes in the comments. Changes to the statements within the macro, however, affect its execution.

- Click and drag to select the existing font name, **Arial**, then enter **Times New Roman** as shown in Figure 7.10e. Be sure that the **Times New Roman** appears within quotation marks. Change the font size to **24**.

- Click and drag to select the name of the course, which is "CIS120" in our example. Type **InputBox("Enter Course Name")** to replace the selected text.

- Note that as you type the left parenthesis after the Visual Basic keyword InputBox, a prompt (containing the correct syntax) is displayed on the screen as shown in Figure 7.10e.

- Ignore the prompt and keep typing to complete the entry. Be sure you enter a closing parenthesis.

- Click the **Save button** to save the macro.

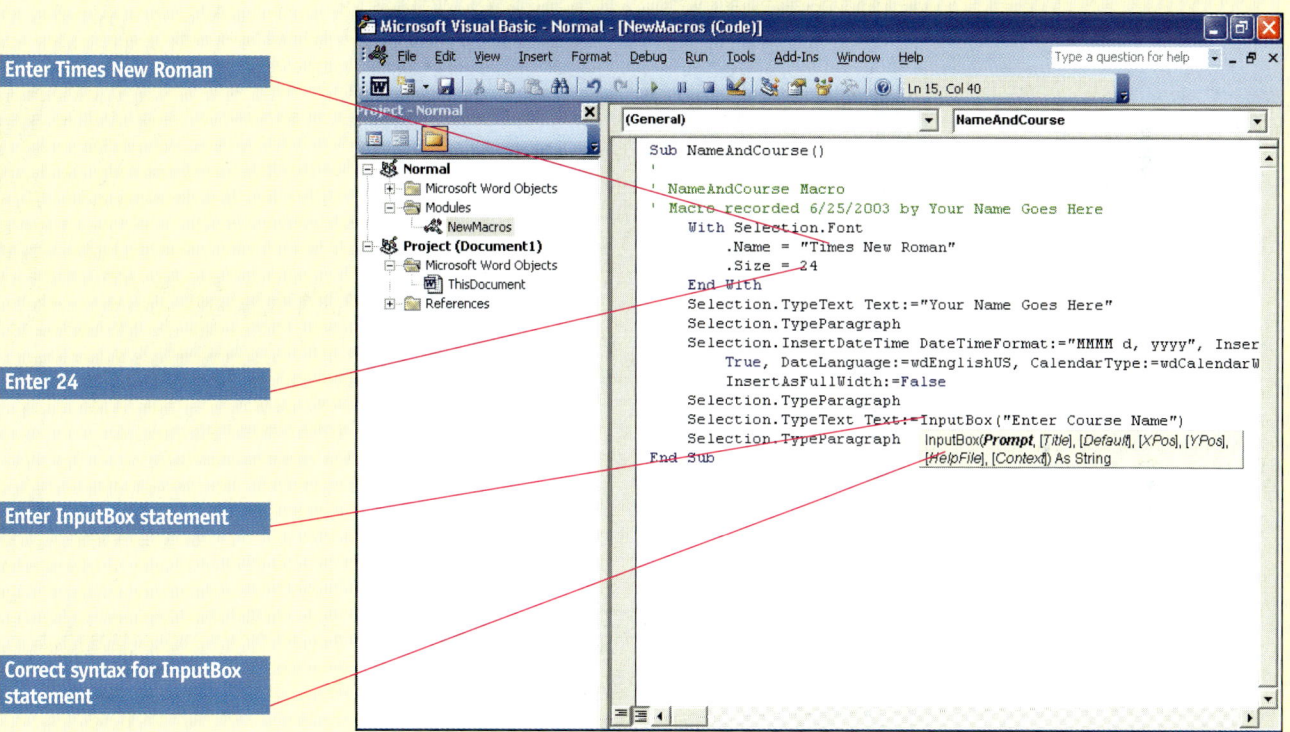

(e) Edit the Macro (step 5)

FIGURE 7.10 Hands-on Exercise 4 (*continued*)

COPY, RENAME, AND DELETE MACRO

You can copy a macro, change its name, then use the duplicate macro as the basis of a new macro. Click and drag to select the entire macro, click the Copy button, click after the End Sub statement, and click the Paste button to copy the macro. Click and drag to select the macro name in the Sub statement, type a new name, and you have a new (duplicate) macro. Make the necessary changes to the new macro. To delete a macro, click and drag to select the entire macro and press the Del key.

Step 6: **Test the Revised Macro**

- Press **Alt+F11** to toggle back to the Word document (or click the **Word button** on the taskbar). **Delete any text that is in the document**. If necessary, press **Ctrl+Home** to move to the beginning of the Word document.

- Press the **Alt+F8 key** to display the Macros dialog box, then double click the **NameAndCourse macro**. The macro enters your name and date, then displays the input dialog box shown in Figure 7.10f.

- Enter any appropriate course and click **OK** (or press the **Enter key**). You should see your name, today's date, and the course you entered in 24 point Times New Roman type.

- Press **Alt+F11** to return to the Visual Basic Editor if the macro does not work as intended. Correct your macro so that its statements match those in step 5 on the previous page.

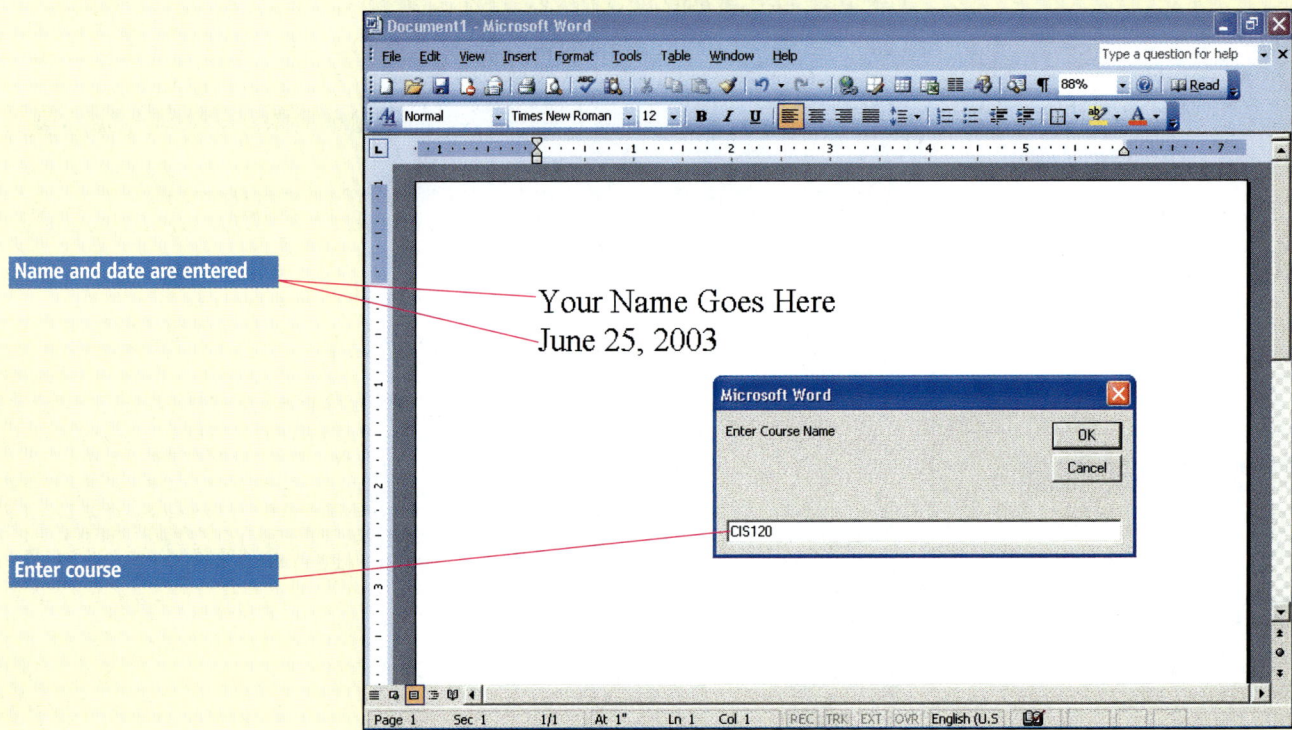

(f) Test the Revised Macro (step 6)

FIGURE 7.10 Hands-on Exercise 4 (*continued*)

HELP FOR VISUAL BASIC

Click within any Visual Basic keyword, then press the F1 key for context-sensitive help. You will see a help screen containing a description of the statement, its syntax, key elements, and several examples. You can print the help screen by clicking the Printer button. (If you do not see the help screens, ask your instructor to install Visual Basic Help.)

Step 7: **Record the TitlePage Macro**

- If necessary, return to Word and delete the existing text in the document. Pull down the **Tools menu**. Click the **Macro command**, then click **Record New Macro** from the cascaded menu. You will see the Record Macro dialog box as described earlier.

- Enter **TitlePage** as the name of the macro. Do not leave any spaces in the macro name. Click the **Keyboard button** in the Record Macro dialog box to display the Customize Keyboard dialog box in Figure 7.10g. The insertion point is positioned in the Press New Shortcut Key text box.

- Press **Ctrl+T** to enter this keystroke combination as the new shortcut; note, however, that this shortcut is currently assigned to the Hanging Indent command:
  - Click the **Assign button** if you do not use the Hanging Indent shortcut,
  - *Or*, choose a different shortcut for the macro (or omit the shortcut altogether) if you are already using Ctrl+T for the Hanging Indent command.

- Close the Customize Keyboard dialog box.

- You are back in your document and can begin recording your macro:
  - Press **Ctrl+Home** to move to the beginning of the document (even if you are already there).
  - Press the **Enter key** three times to insert three blank lines.
  - Click the **Center button** to center the text that will be subsequently typed.
  - Press the **Enter key** to create an additional blank line.
  - Press **Ctrl+Enter** to create a page break.

- Click the **Stop Recording button** to end the macro.

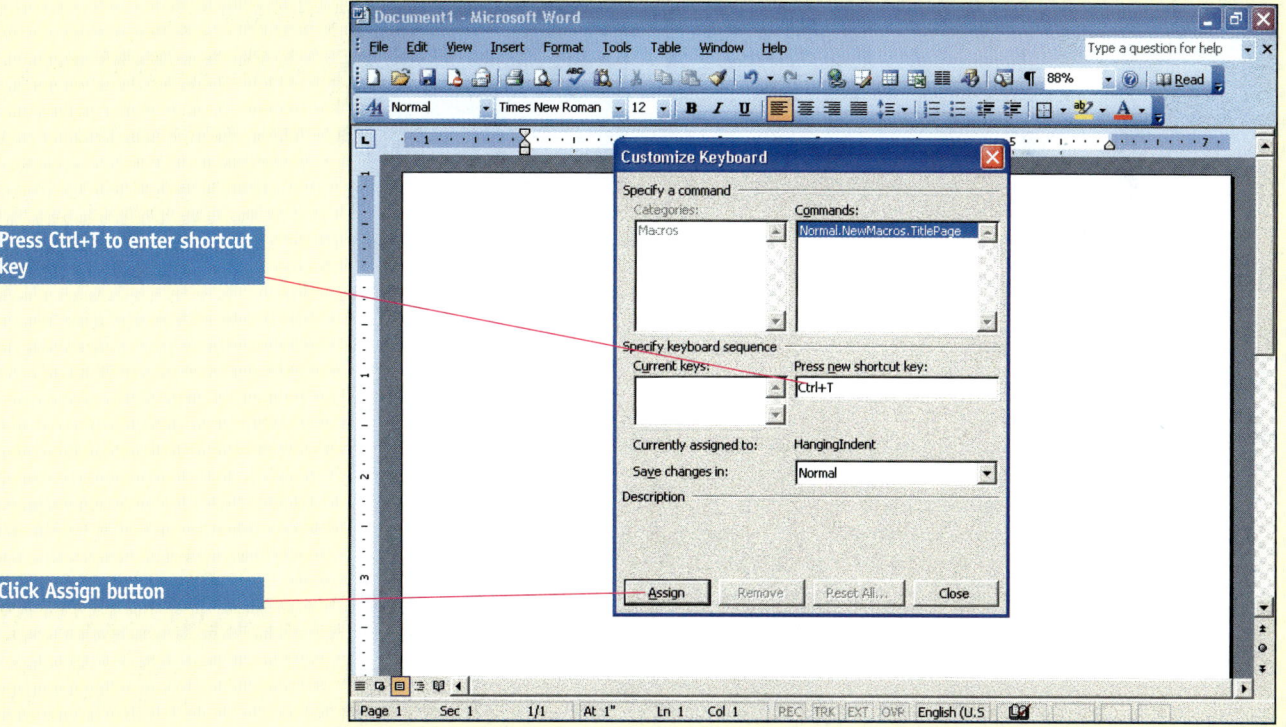

(g) Record the TitlePage Macro (step 7)

FIGURE 7.10 Hands-on Exercise 4 (*continued*)

Step 8: **Complete the TitlePage Macro**

- Press **Alt+F11** to return to the Visual Basic Editor. You should see two macros, NameAndCourse and TitlePage. Click and drag to select the statements in the **NameAndCourse macro** as shown in Figure 7.10h. Do not select the Sub or End Sub statements.

- Click the **Copy button** on the Standard toolbar (or use the **Ctrl+C** shortcut) to copy these statements to the clipboard.

- Move to the TitlePage macro and click at the end of the VBA statement to center a paragraph. Press **Enter** to start a new line. Click the **Paste button** on the Standard toolbar (or use the **Ctrl+V** shortcut) to paste the statements from the NameAndCourse macro into the TitlePage macro.

- You can see the completed macro by looking at Figure 7.10j, the screen in step 10. Click the **Save button** to save your macros.

- Press **Alt+F11** to return to Word. Pull down the File menu and click the **Close command** to close the document you were using to create the macros in this exercise. There is no need to save that document.

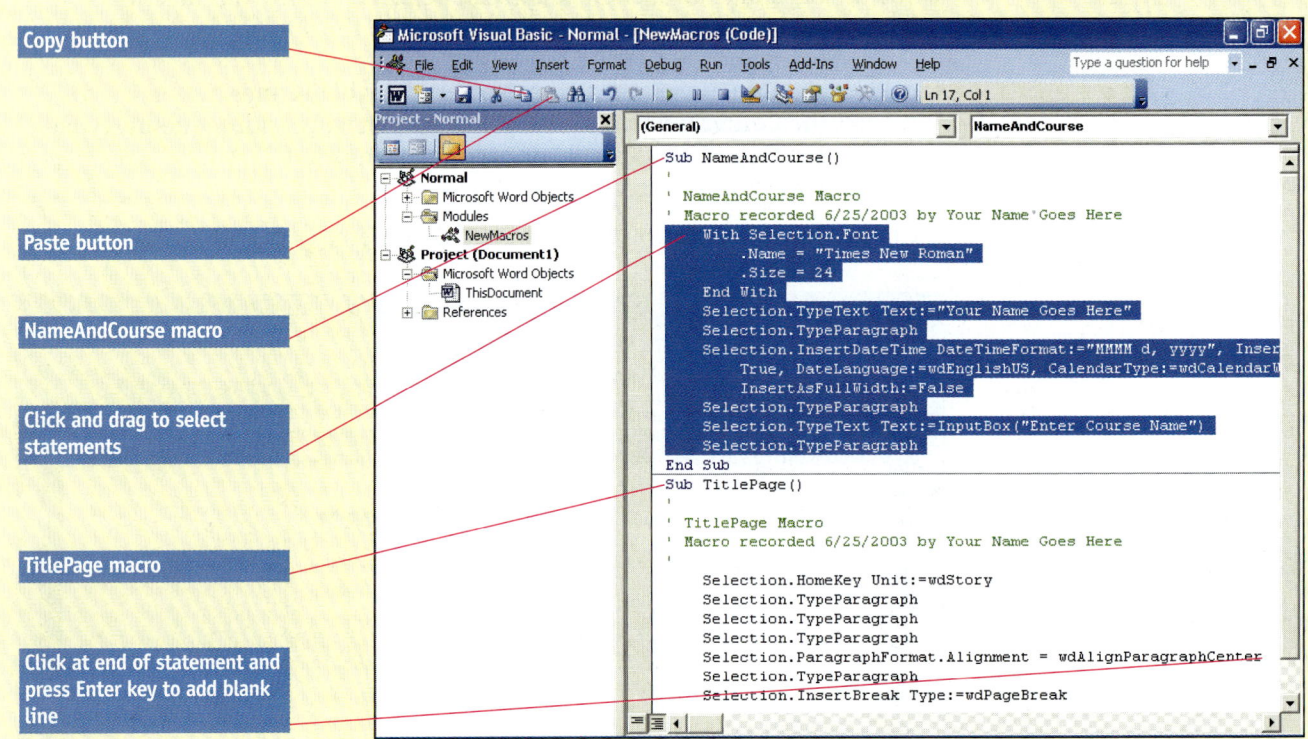

(h) Complete the TitlePage Macro (step 8)

FIGURE 7.10 Hands-on Exercise 4 (*continued*)

THE PAGE BORDER COMMAND

Add interest to a title page with a border. Click anywhere on the page, pull down the Format menu, click the Borders and Shading command, then click the Page Border tab in the Borders and Shading dialog box. You can choose a box, shadow, or 3-D style in similar fashion to placing a border around a paragraph. You can also click the drop-down arrow on the Art list box to create a border consisting of a repeating clip art image.

Step 9 **Test the TitlePage Macro**

- Open the completed Word document (Executed Contract) from the second hands-on exercise.

- Click anywhere in the document, then press **Ctrl+T** to execute the TitlePage macro.

- You will be prompted for your course. Enter the course you are taking, and the macro will create the title page.

- Pull down the **View menu** and change to the **Print Layout view**. Pull down the **View menu** a second time, click the **Zoom command**, click the option button for **Many Pages**, then click and drag the monitor icon to display three pages. Click **OK**.

- You should see the executed contract with a title page as shown in Figure 7.10i. Print this document for your instructor.

- Save the document.

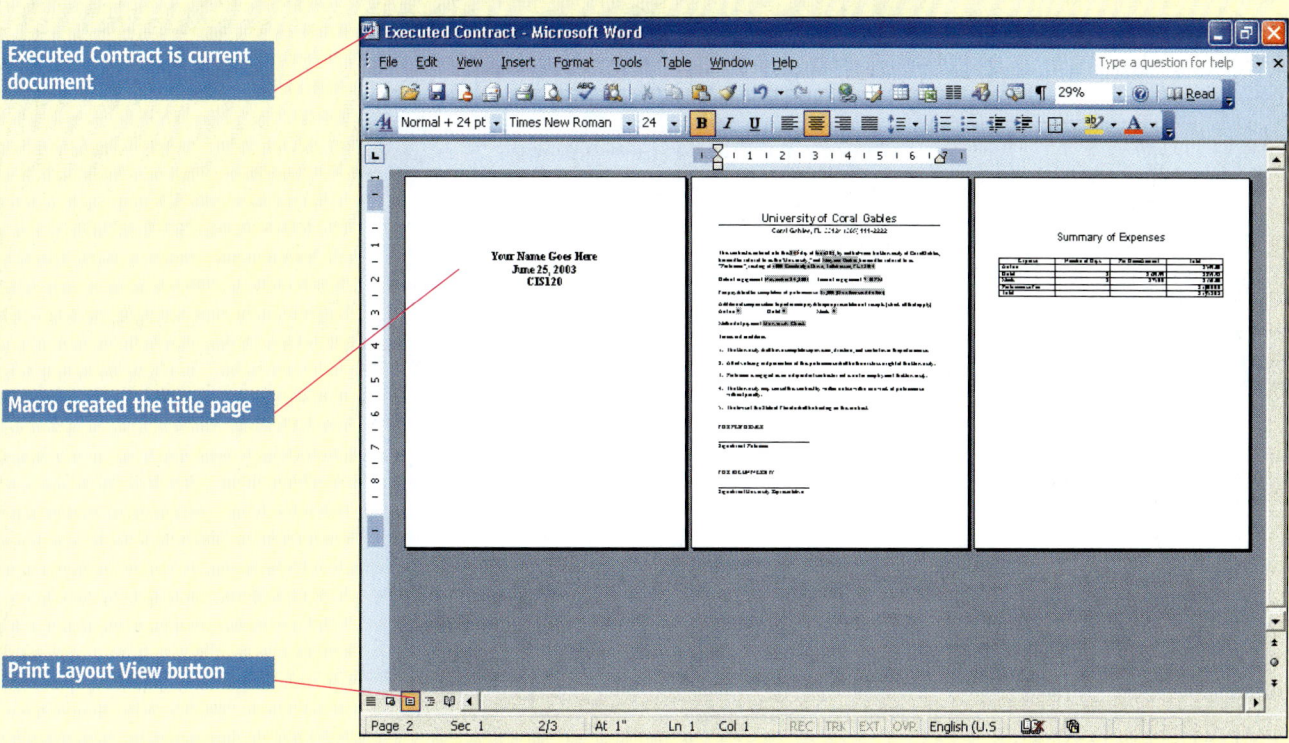

(i) Test the TitlePage Macro (step 9)

FIGURE 7.10 Hands-on Exercise 4 (*continued*)

TROUBLESHOOTING

If the shortcut keys do not work, it is probably because they were not defined properly. Pull down the View menu, click Toolbars, click Customize, click the Options tab, then click the Keyboard command button to display the Customize Keyboard dialog box. Drag the scroll box in the Categories list box until you can select the Macros category. Select (click) the macro that is to receive the shortcut and click in the Press New Shortcut Key text box. Enter the desired shortcut, click the Assign button to assign the shortcut, then click the Close button to close the dialog box.

Step 10: Print the Module

- Press **Alt+F11** to return to the Visual Basic Editor.

- Pull down the **File menu**. Click **Print** to display the Print dialog box in Figure 7.10j. Click the option button to print the current module. Click **OK**.

- Submit the listing of the current module, which contains the procedures for both macros, to your instructor as proof you did this exercise.

- Delete all of the macros you have created in this exercise if you are not working on your own machine. Pull down the **File menu**. Click the **Close and Return to Word command**.

- Exit Word. The Title Page macro will be waiting for you the next time you use Microsoft Word, provided you did the exercise on your own computer.

- Congratulations on a job well done.

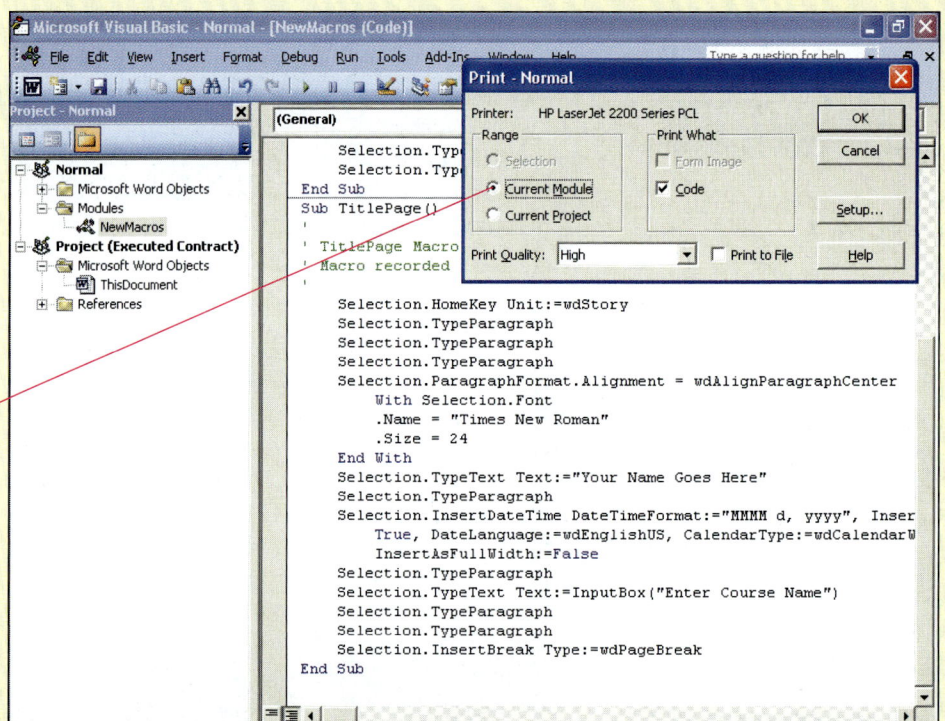

(j) Print the Module (step 10)

FIGURE 7.10 Hands-on Exercise 4 (*continued*)

INVEST IN MACROS

Creating a macro takes time, but that time can be viewed as an investment, because a well-designed macro will simplify the creation of subsequent documents. A macro is recorded once, tested and corrected as necessary, then run (executed) many times. It is stored by default in the Normal template, where it is available to every Word document. Yes, it takes time to create a meaningful macro, but once that's done, it is only a keystroke away.

SUMMARY

Multiple persons within a workgroup can review a document and have their revisions stored electronically within that document. The revisions are displayed in one of two ways, as "Original Showing Markup" or as "Final Showing Markup". The difference is subtle and depends on personal preference with respect to displaying the insertions to, and deletions from, a document. The Original Showing Markup view displays the deleted text within the body of the document (with a line through the deleted text) and shows the inserted text in a balloon to the right of the actual document. The Final Showing Markup view is the opposite; it displays the inserted text within the body of the document and displays the deleted text in a balloon at the right. Both views display revision marks to the left of any line that has been changed.

A form facilitates data entry when the document is made available to multiple individuals via a network. It is created as a regular document with the various fields added through tools on the Forms toolbar. Word enables you to create three types of fields—text boxes, check boxes, and drop-down list boxes. After the form is created, it is protected to prevent further modification other than data entry.

The rows in a table can be sorted to display the data in ascending or descending sequence, according to the values in one or more columns in the table. Sorting is accomplished by selecting the rows within the table that are to be sorted, then executing the Sort command in the Tables menu. Calculations can be performed within a table using the Formula command in the Tables menu.

A master document consists of multiple subdocuments, each of which is stored as a separate file. It is especially useful for very large documents such as a book or dissertation, which can be divided into smaller, more manageable documents. The attraction of a master document is that you can work with multiple subdocuments simultaneously. Changes to the master document can be made at any time. Changes to the subdocuments can be made in one of two ways—either when the subdocument is unlocked within a master document, or by opening the subdocument as an independent document within Microsoft Word.

A macro is a set of instructions that automates a repetitive task. It is, in essence, a program, and its instructions are written in Visual Basic for Applications (VBA), a programming language. A macro is created initially through the macro recorder in Microsoft Word, which records your commands and generates the corresponding VBA statements. Once a macro has been created, it can be edited manually by inserting, deleting, or changing its statements. A macro is run (executed) by the Run command in the Tools menu or more easily through a keyboard shortcut.

KEY TERMS

Accept Change button 1152
Cells 1163
Check box 1154
Code window 1181
Comment 1180
Create New Folder
    command 1172
Create Subdocument
    command 1172
Descending sequence 1163
Drop-down list box 1154
End Sub statement 1180
Field 1154
Field codes 1163

Final Showing Markup 1152
Form 1154
Forms toolbar 1154
Macro 1180
Macro recorder 1180
Master document 1172
Module 1181
Original Showing Markup 1152
Outlining toolbar 1172
Password protection 1152
Procedure 1180
Project Explorer 1181
Reject Change button 1152
Reviewing toolbar 1152

Revision mark 1152
Sort 1163
Sub statement 1180
Subdocument 1172
Tables and Borders toolbar 1163
Tables menu 1163
Text field 1154
Track Changes command 1152
Versions command 1152
Visual Basic for Applications
    (VBA) 1180
Visual Basic Editor (VBE) 1181
Workgroup 1152

MULTIPLE CHOICE

1. Which of the following is a true statement regarding password protection?

    (a) All documents are automatically saved with a default password
    (b) The password is case sensitive
    (c) A password cannot be changed once it has been implemented
    (d) All of the above

2. What happens if you double click the TRK indicator on the status bar?

    (a) Tracking changes is in effect
    (b) Tracking changes has been turned off
    (c) Tracking changes has been turned either on or off, depending on its current status
    (d) The situation is impossible; there is no TRK indicator on the status bar

3. Which of the following types of fields *cannot* be inserted into a form?

    (a) Check boxes
    (b) Text fields
    (c) A drop-down list
    (d) Radio buttons

4. Which of the following is true about a protected form?

    (a) Data can be entered into the form
    (b) The text of the form cannot be modified
    (c) Both (a) and (b)
    (d) Neither (a) nor (b)

5. Which of the following describes the function of the Form Field Shading button on the Forms toolbar?

    (a) Clicking the button shades every field in the form
    (b) Clicking the button shades every field in the form and prevents further modification to the form
    (c) Clicking the button removes the shading from every field
    (d) Clicking the button toggles the shading on or off

6. You have created a table containing numerical values and have entered the SUM(ABOVE) function at the bottom of a column. You then delete one of the rows included in the sum. Which of the following is true?

    (a) The row cannot be deleted because it contains a cell that is included in the sum function
    (b) The sum is updated automatically
    (c) The sum cannot be updated unless the Form Protect button is toggled off
    (d) The sum will be updated provided you right click the cell and select the Update field command

7. Which of the following is suitable for use as a master document?

    (a) An in-depth proposal that contains component documents
    (b) A lengthy newsletter with stories submitted by several people
    (c) A book
    (d) All of the above

8. Which of the following is a true statement regarding changes to a master document and its associated subdocuments?

    (a) The master document cannot be changed if subdocuments have been added to it
    (b) Changes can be made to any locked subdocument
    (c) Changes can be made to any unlocked subdocument
    (d) All of the above

9. What happens if you click inside a subdocument, then click the Lock button on the Outlining toolbar?

    (a) The subdocument is locked
    (b) The subdocument is unlocked
    (c) The subdocument is locked or unlocked depending on its status prior to clicking the button
    (d) All editing to the subdocument is disabled

... continued

multiple choice

10. Which of the following describes the storage of a master document and the associated subdocuments?
    (a) Each document is saved as a separate file
    (b) All of the subdocuments must be stored in the same folder
    (c) Both (a) and (b)
    (d) Neither (a) nor (b)

11. Which of the following best describes the recording and execution of a macro?
    (a) A macro is recorded once and executed once
    (b) A macro is recorded once and executed many times
    (c) A macro is recorded many times and executed once
    (d) A macro is recorded many times and executed many times

12. Which of the following is true regarding comments in Visual Basic?
    (a) A comment is not executable; that is, its inclusion or omission does not affect the outcome of a macro
    (b) A comment begins with an apostrophe
    (c) Both (a) and (b)
    (d) Neither (a) nor (b)

13. Which commands are used to copy an existing macro so that it can become the basis of a new macro?
    (a) Copy command
    (b) Paste command
    (c) Both (a) and (b)
    (d) Neither (a) nor (b)

14. What is the default location for a macro created in Microsoft Word?
    (a) In the Normal template, where it is available to every Word document
    (b) In the document in which it was created, where it is available only to that document
    (c) In the Macros folder on your hard drive
    (d) In the Office folder on your hard drive

15. Which of the following correctly matches the shortcut to the associated task?
    (a) Alt+F11 toggles between Word and the Visual Basic Editor
    (b) Alt+F8 displays the Macros dialog box
    (c) Both (a) and (b)
    (d) Neither (a) nor (b)

16. Which of the following is true regarding a document that has been sent for review to four different people on a project team?
    (a) The original author cannot begin to review changes until comments have been received from every reviewer
    (b) The revisions from each reviewer must be accepted or rejected collectively; that is, the changes cannot be reviewed individually
    (c) The document can be printed with or without the suggested changes
    (d) The suggested additions and deletions will appear in blue and red, respectively, for all reviewers

17. Which of the following is true about indented text in a VBA procedure?
    (a) The indented text is always executed first
    (b) The indented text is always executed last
    (c) The indented text is rendered a comment and is never executed
    (d) None of the above

18. Which of the following is *true* regarding VBA statements?
    (a) Comments appear in green, syntax errors appear in red
    (b) Comments appear in red, syntax errors appear in green
    (c) Comments appear in green, VBA keywords appear in red
    (d) Comments appear in blue, VBA keywords appear in green

ANSWERS

1. b
2. c
3. d
4. c
5. d
6. d
7. d
8. c
9. c
10. a
11. b
12. c
13. c
14. a
15. c
16. c
17. d
18. a

PRACTICE WITH WORD

1. **Reviewing a Document:** Figure 7.11 displays a document that has been reviewed by multiple individuals. Your assignment is to go through the document and accept or reject the various changes that have been suggested. Open the *Chapter 7 Practice 1* document in the Exploring Word folder and proceed as follows:

   a. Pull down the Tools menu, click the Options command, then click the Track Changes tab as shown in Figure 7.11. Examine the default options and experiment with the various settings—for example, change the width and/or location of the margin that contains the editing changes.

   b. Track Changes should be on as seen by the TRK indicator on the status bar. The indicator functions as a toggle switch; double click the indicator, and Track Changes is on. Double click the indicator a second time, and the feature is off. (You can also use the Track Changes button on the Reviewing toolbar to toggle Track Changes on and off.) Leave Track Changes on.

   c. Click the down arrow on the Show button and click the Reviewers command to see the names of the reviewers, each of which is displayed in a different color. The revisions in the document are also displayed in different colors, corresponding to the reviewers' names. Press Esc to close the menu.

   d. Click the down arrow on the Display for Review list box and select Final Showing Markup as shown in Figure 7.11. Pull down the File menu, click the Print command to display the Print dialog box, click Document Showing Markup in the Print What list box, then click OK to print the document in this format.

   e. Press Ctrl+Home to move the insertion point to the beginning of the document. Click the Next button to move to the first revision, then click the Accept Change button to accept this change. Click the Next button to move to the next change, then click the Accept Change button a second time. (It would be much easier if Word moved to the next revision automatically, but we could not make that happen.) Click the down arrow next to the Accept Change button, then click the command to Accept All Changes in Document.

   f. Insert a comment indicating that you have completed your review. Pull down the File menu, click the Print command to display the Print dialog box, click Document in the Print What list box, then click OK to print the final document.

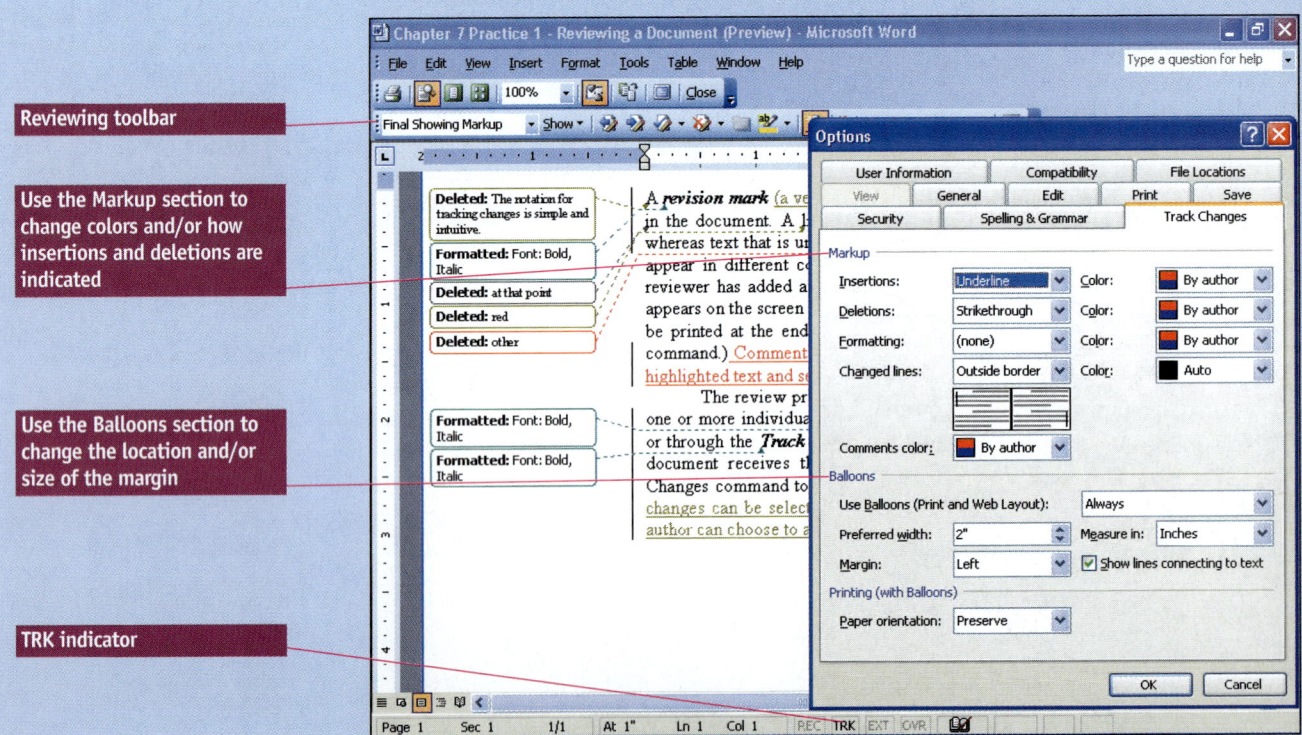

FIGURE 7.11 Reviewing a Document (exercise 1)

practice exercises

2. **Table Math:** The document in Figure 7.12 displays two versions of a table, the original table prior to any modification, and the completed table at the end of the exercise. Open the partially completed *Chapter 7 Practice 2* document in the Exploring Word folder. Select the existing table and copy it. Leave the original table in part (a) as it is, and apply all subsequent commands to the second table in part (b) of the document.

   a. Enter your last name in the indicated cell (replacing "Your Name Goes Here"). Click outside the table immediately to the left of the row containing your name to select that row. Pull down the Format menu, click the Borders and Shading command, click the Shading tab, select a color, and click OK.

   b. Click and drag to select the first five rows of the table (do not select the Total row). Pull down the Table menu, click the Sort command to display the Sort dialog box, sort by Sales Person, and click the option button to indicate a header row. Click OK to sort the table and display the sales persons in alphabetical order. The shading should travel with the sort.

   c. Click in the last column of the second row (the cell that will contain the first person's sales gain). Pull down the Table menu, click the formula command, click in the Formula text box, and replace the existing formula with =c2-b2. Click OK. You should see the result of the calculation.

   d. Enter parallel formulas to compute the sales gain for each sales person as well as the total sales gain. You have to enter each formula individually, adjusting the cell references as necessary; the Copy command will not adjust the formulas in each cell.

   e. Change Brown's sales for this year to 300, and note that the computed value does not change automatically. Select the computed value. Point to the selection and click the right mouse button, and then click the Update Field command to display the new result.

   f. Print the completed document for your instructor to show the displayed values.

   g. Print the document a second time to show the cell formulas. Pull down the File menu, click the Print command to display the Print dialog box, click the Options button to display a second Print dialog box, and check the box to print Field Codes. Click OK to close the Print Options dialog box, then click OK a second time to print the document showing the field codes.

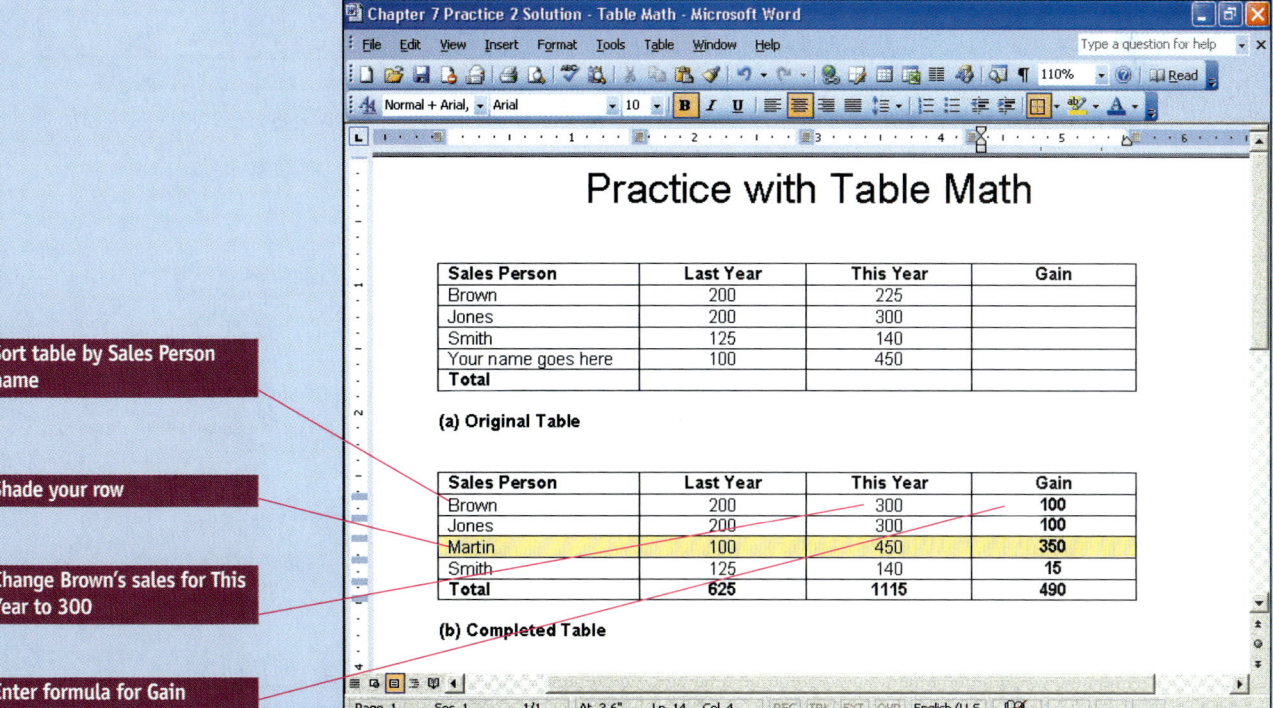

FIGURE 7.12 Table Math (exercise 2)

practice exercises

3. **Tips for Windows XP:** The master document in Figure 7.13 is composed of three subdocuments, each of which contains a series of tips for Windows XP. The documents were created by different individuals. Your assignment is to create the master document.

   a. Start Microsoft Word and create a new document. Pull down the View menu and change to the Outline view. The Outlining toolbar should be displayed automatically. (You cannot create a master document unless you are in the Outline view.)

   b. Enter the title of the document, Tips for Windows XP. Pull down the Insert menu, click the Symbol command, click the Symbols tab, and choose the Wingdings font. Scroll to the end of the displayed characters until you can click the Windows symbol. Insert the symbol. Close the Symbols dialog box. Change the title to 24-point Arial.

   c. Enter the additional text for the master document as shown in Figure 7.13. Format the text appropriately using 12 point Times New Roman for the first paragraph.

   d. Click the Master Document View button on the Outlining toolbar. Click the Insert Subdocument button, then insert the *Tips by Tom* Document from the Tips for Windows XP folder. Insert the two additional documents, *Tips by Dick*, and *Tips by Harry* that are stored in the same folder. (You may have to click the Expand Subdocuments button on the Outlining toolbar to insert a subdocument.)

   e. Protect the document by setting Formatting and/or Editing restrictions. Pull down the Tools menu and click the Protect Document command to display the task pane in Figure 7.13. Check the box to allow only the specified type of editing (no changes in our example), then check the box in the Exceptions area to designate sections of the document that can be edited; e.g., "Your Name Goes Here". Click the button to Start Enforcing Password Protection to display the associated dialog box. Click OK (you do not have to enter a password).

   f. Try to modify the document. You will not be able to change anything except the line containing your name. Enter your name in the indicated area.

   g. Click the Print Preview button, then click Yes if asked if you want to open the subdocuments before continuing with the command. The document will open in the Preview window. Click the Print button to print the completed document.

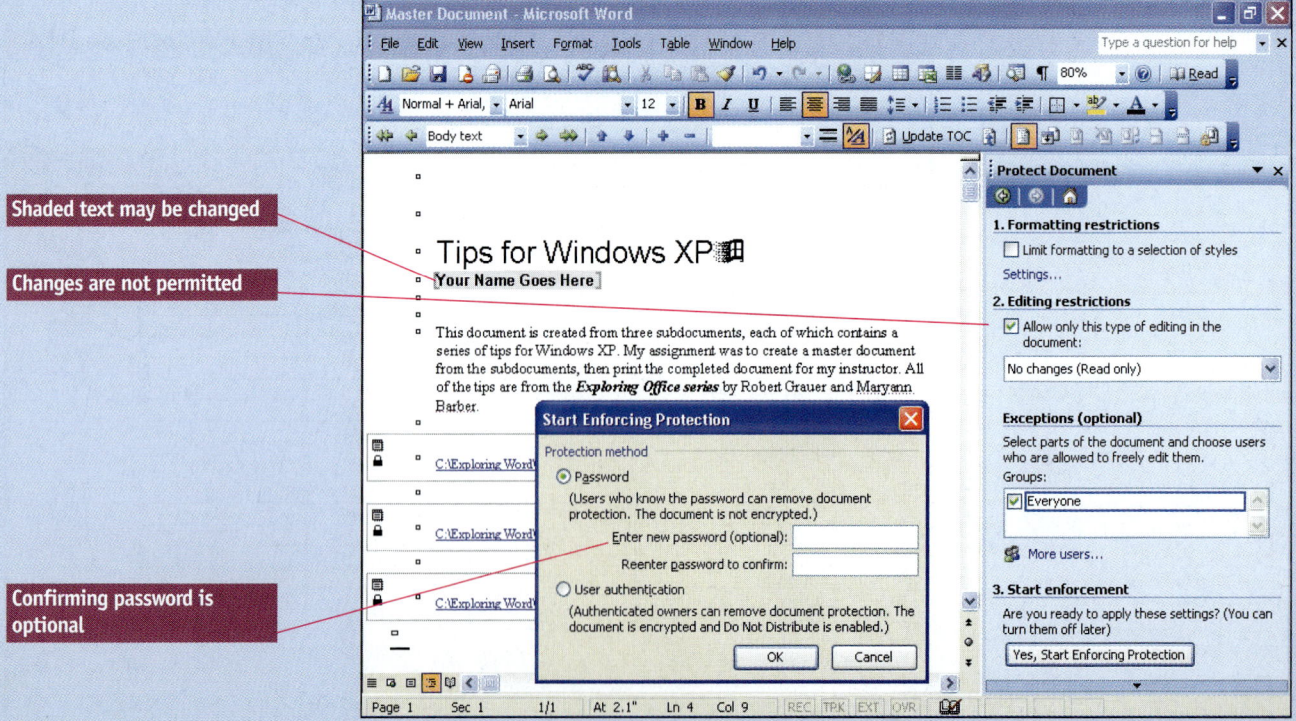

FIGURE 7.13 Tips for Windows XP (exercise 3)

practice exercises

4. **Debugging a Macro:** A "bug" is a mistake in a computer program and hence the term "debugging" refers to the process of finding and correcting programming errors. One of the best techniques for debugging is to execute the statements in a macro one at a time, so that you can see the effect of each statement. You can learn the technique with a working macro, and then apply the method if and when you need to debug another procedure. Complete Hands-on Exercise 4 if you have not already done so. Proceed as follows:

   a. Close all open applications. Start Word and open any document. Pull down the Tools menu, click the Macro command, and click the Visual Basic Editor command to start the editor. Click the Close button in the left pane to close the Project window within the Visual Basic Editor. The Code window expands to take the entire Visual Basic Editor window. Pull down the View menu, click the Toolbars command, and display the Debug toolbar.

   b. Point to an empty area on the Windows taskbar, then click the right mouse button to display a shortcut menu. Click the Tile Windows Vertically command to tile the open windows (Word and the Visual Basic Editor). Your desktop should be similar to Figure 7.14. It doesn't matter if the document is in the left or right window. If additional windows are open on the desktop, minimize the other windows, and then repeat the command to tile the open windows.

   c. Click in the Visual Basic Editor window, then click anywhere within the TitlePage macro. Click the Procedure View button. Click the Step Into button on the Debug toolbar (or press the F8 key) to enter the macro. The Sub statement is highlighted. Press the F8 key a second time to move to the first executable statement (the comments are skipped). The statement is selected (highlighted), but it has not yet been executed. Press the F8 key again to execute this statement and move to the next statement.

   d. Continue to press the F8 key to execute the statements in the macro one at a time. You can see the effect of each statement as it is executed in the Word window. Figure 7.14 displays the macro as the last statement (the statement to create a page break after the title has been entered) is about to be executed.

   e. Do you think this procedure is useful in finding any bugs that might exist? Summarize the steps in debugging a macro in a short note to your instructor.

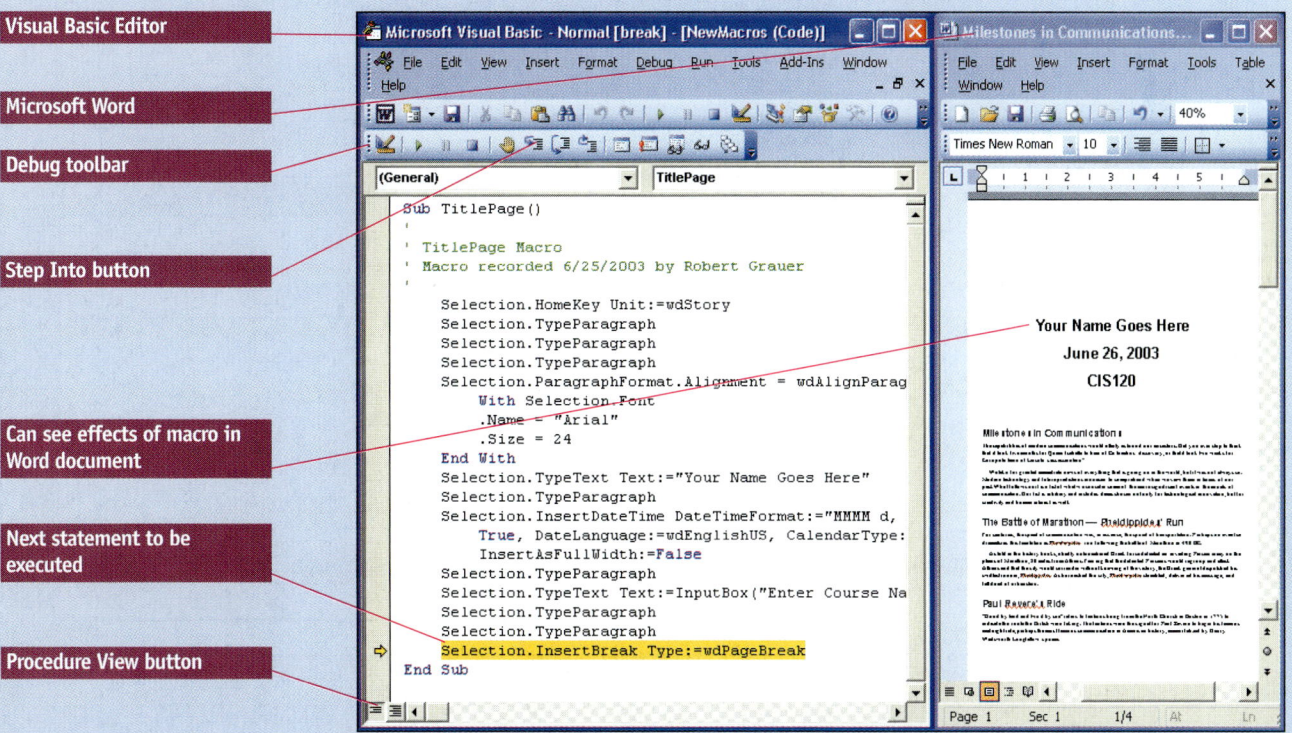

FIGURE 7.14 Debugging a Macro (exercise 4)

practice exercises

5. **Customizing a Toolbar:** The chapter illustrated different ways to execute a macro—from the Tools menu in Word, by pressing Alt+F8 to display the Macros dialog box, and via a keyboard shortcut. You can also add a customized button to a toolbar and/or add a new command to an existing menu. Proceed as follows:

   a. Complete the fourth hands-on exercise in the chapter, which creates the TitlePage macro. Start a new document and test the macro to be sure that it works properly. You should be prompted to enter the name of your course, after which the title page is created.

   b. Pull down the View menu, click Toolbars, click Customize to display the Customize dialog box, and then click the Commands tab. Click the down arrow in the Categories list box until you see the Macros category as shown in Figure 7.15.

   c. Click and drag the TitlePage macro from the Commands area to an existing toolbar (e.g., to the extreme left of the Formatting toolbar as shown in Figure 7.15), then release the mouse to drop the macro onto the toolbar. The icon on the mouse pointer will change from an "X" to a plus sign when you are able to drop the macro onto the toolbar. (You can delete the macro from the toolbar by dragging it off the toolbar.)

   d. You will see the name of the macro and/or a button icon (e.g., a smiley face), according to the options in effect. Click the macro button after it has been added to the toolbar, then click the Modify Selection button within the Customize dialog box. Select the desired option such as the default style (image only), text only, or image and text. (You can also choose the Change Button Image command to select a different button icon to diplay on the toolbar.) Close the Customize dialog box.

   e. Delete the title page from the existing document, then click the newly added toolbar button to test the button. Once again you are prompted for the course you are taking, after which the title page is created.

   f. Prove to your instructor that you have modified the toolbar successfully by capturing a screen similar to Figure 7.15. Press the Print Screen key to capture the screen to the clipboard, start a new Word document, then click the Paste button to paste the screen into your document. Print this document for your instructor.

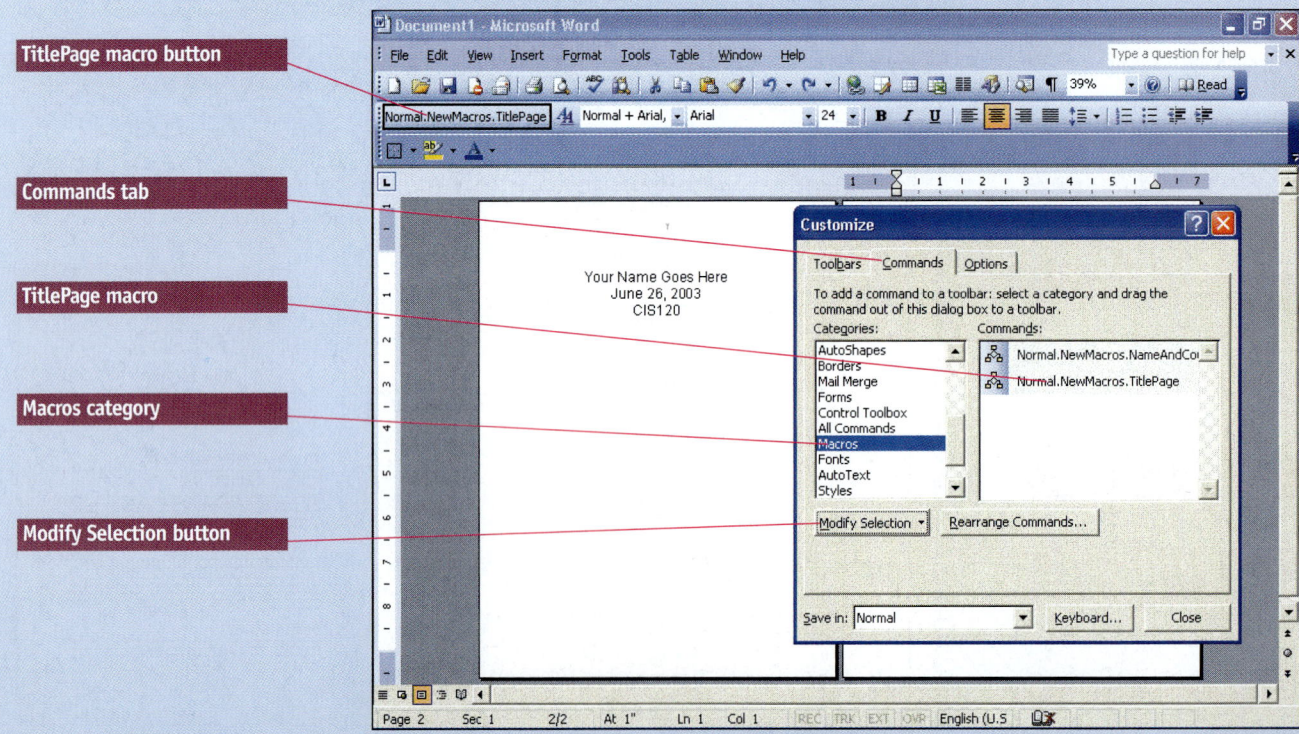

FIGURE 7.15 Customizing a Toolbar (exercise 5)

practice exercises

6. **Enhancing a Macro**: The macro recorder jump starts the creation of a macro (VBA procedure) by translating commands that are executed within Microsoft Word to the equivalent VBA statements. You can then open the VBA editor and edit the resulting code. Some changes are intuitive and do not require knowledge of VBA per se; for example, changing the font or point size. VBA is a language unto itself, however, that lets you enhance the functionality of any macro by adding statements as necessary as shown in Figure 7.16. Proceed as follows:

   a. Start Word and open a new document. Pull down the Tools menu, click the Macro command, click Record New Macro, and enter CreateTable as the name of the macro you are about to create. Click OK.

   b. Pull down the Table menu, click the Insert command, click Table, and then insert a two-by-five table (two rows and five columns) into the current document. Click the Stop Recording button.

   c. Open the VBA editor. Click the Full Module View button and display the macro you just created as shown in Figure 7.16. Note, however, that your procedure will contain additional statements (With . . . End With) that are not essential to the creation of the table. Delete these statements so that your procedure matches ours.

   d. Click and drag to select the entire CreateTable macro, including the Sub and End Sub statements. Click the Copy button, click beneath the End Sub statement, and then click the Paste button to duplicate the macro. Rename the duplicate procedure CreateBetterTable.

   e. Insert the indicated comments at the beginning of the CreateBetterTable procedure, then add the four VBA statements in Figure 7.16. The Dim statements define the variables intRows and intColumns, and the InputBox statements obtain these values from the user. Now replace the number 2 that appears in the ActiveDocument statement with the variable IntRows. Replace the number 5 with the variable IntColumns.

   f. Return to the original Word document and close the document without saving it. Start a new document. Pull down the Tools menu, click the Macro command, click Macros . . . and run the CreateBetterTable macro. You should be prompted for the number of rows and columns, respectively, after which the table should be created in your document.

   g. Return to the VBA editor and print the procedures you created in this exercise. Refer to the VBA primer at the end of the text for additional information on VBA.

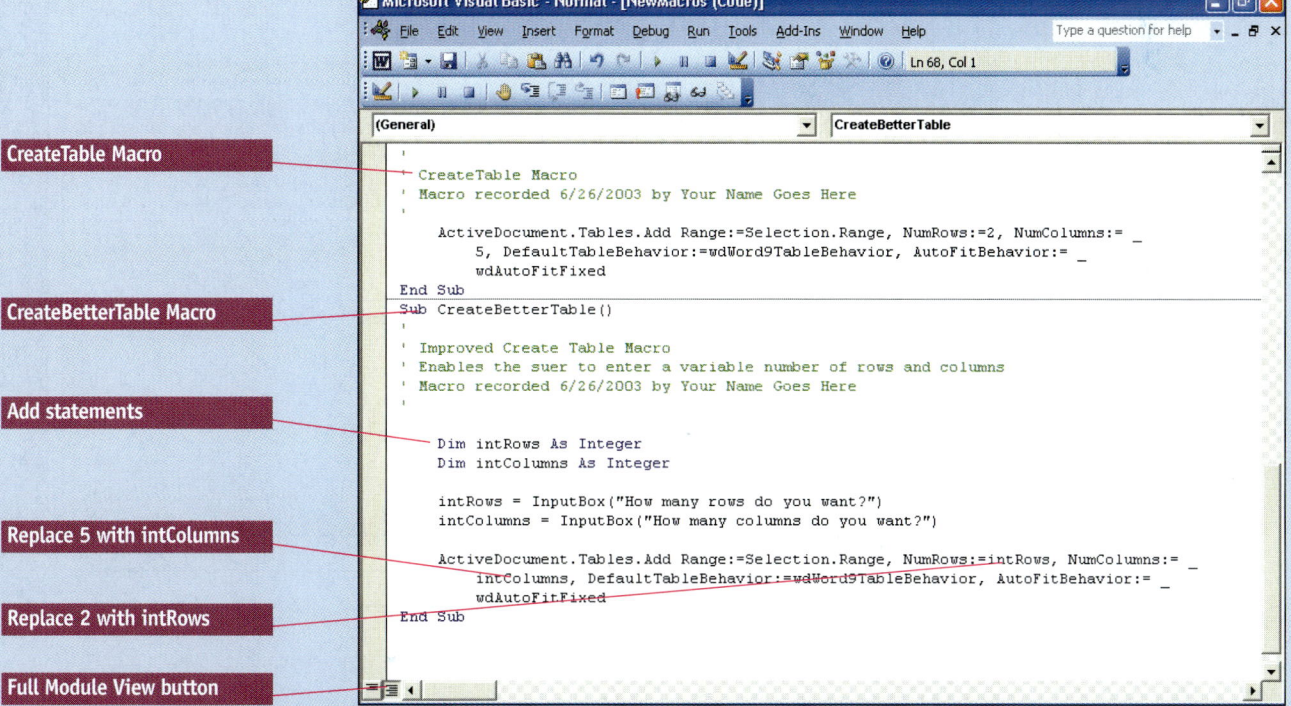

FIGURE 7.16 Enhancing a Macro (exercise 6)

practice exercises

7. **Create a Custom Menu:** You can create a custom menu that contains commands from any existing menu and/or additional commands corresponding to various macros that you have created. Proceed as follows:

   a. Pull down the View menu, click Toolbars, click Customize to display the Customize dialog box, click the Commands tab, and then scroll until you can select New menu from the Categories list box at the left. Click and drag the New menu command to the right of the menu bar, then release the mouse to create a new menu.

   b. Select the newly created menu on the menu bar, click the Modify Selection button in the Customize dialog box, then change the name of the menu to "&My Menu". The ampersand will not appear in the menu name, but the letter "M" will be underlined, enabling you to pull down the menu using the Alt+M keyboard shortcut. (This is the same shortcut used to pull down other menus; e.g., Alt+F and Alt+E pull down the File and Edit menus, respectively.)

   c. You are now ready to add commands to the menu. Select the Macros category in the Category area, and then drag an existing macro to the menu you just created. Repeat this process to add additional commands (corresponding to the macros you created in earlier exercises) to the menu. You can create a custom menu, even if you do not have any macros, by selecting commands from other categories. Test your menu to be sure that all of its commands work properly.

   d. Prove to your instructor that you have created the menu successfully by capturing the screen in Figure 7.17. Complete the menu as described above, pull down the menu to display the commands, and then press the Print Screen key to capture the screen to the Windows clipboard. Start a new Word document and press the enter key three times. Click the Paste button to paste the screen into your document. Press Ctrl+Home to return to the beginning of the document. Enter a title for the assignment followed by your name. Print the completed document to submit to your instructor.

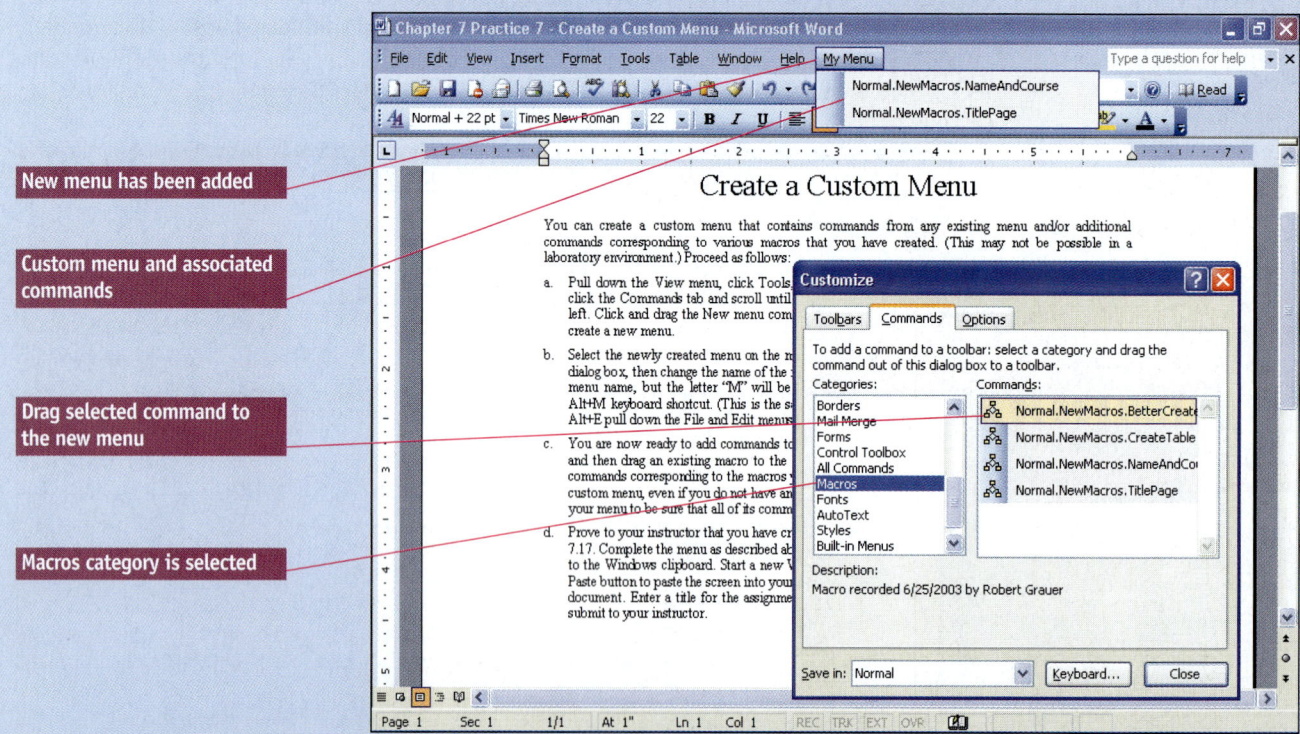

FIGURE 7.17 Create a Custom Menu (exercise 7)

Toolbars for Microsoft® Office Word 2003

TOOLBARS

- Standard
- Formatting
- 3-D Settings
- AutoText
- Control
- Database
- Diagram
- Drawing
- Drawing Canvas
- E-mail
- Extended Formatting
- Forms
- Frames
- Function Key Display
- Ink Comment
- Japanese Greeting
- Mail Merge
- Microsoft
- Organization Chart
- Outlining
- Picture
- Reviewing
- Shadow Settings
- Shortcut Menus
- Tables and Borders
- Visual Basic
- Web
- Web Tools
- Word Count
- WordArt

OVERVIEW

Microsoft Word has 30 predefined toolbars that provide access to commonly used commands. The toolbars are displayed in Figure A.1 and are listed here for convenience. They are: the Standard, Formatting, 3-D Settings, AutoText, Control, Database, Diagram, Drawing, Drawing Canvas, E-mail, Extended Formatting, Forms, Frames, Function Key Display, Ink Comment, Japanese Greeting, Mail Merge, Microsoft, Organization Chart, Outlining, Picture, Reviewing, Shadow Settings, Shortcut Menus, Tables and Borders, Visual Basic, Web, Web Tools, Word Count, and WordArt toolbars. The Standard and Formatting toolbars are displayed by default and appear on the same row immediately below the menu bar. The other predefined toolbars are automatically displayed (hidden) at the discretion of the user, and in some cases are displayed automatically when their corresponding features are in use (e.g., the Picture toolbar and the WordArt toolbar).

The buttons on the toolbars are intended to be indicative of their function. Clicking the Printer button, for example, (the sixth button from the left on the Standard toolbar) executes the Print command. If you are unsure of the purpose of any toolbar button, point to it, and a ScreenTip will appear that displays its name.

You can display multiple toolbars at one time, move them to new locations on the screen, customize their appearance, or suppress their display.

- To separate the Standard and Formatting toolbars and simultaneously display all of the buttons for each toolbar, pull down the Tools menu, click the Customize command, click the Options tab, then check the box to show the toolbars on two rows. Alternatively, the toolbars appear on the same row with only a limited number of buttons visible on each toolbar, and hence you may need to click the double arrow at the end of the toolbar to view additional buttons. Additional buttons will be added to either toolbar as you use the associated feature, and conversely, buttons will be removed from the toolbar if the feature is not used.

- To display or hide a toolbar, pull down the View menu and click the Toolbars command. Select (deselect) the toolbar that you want to display (hide). The selected toolbar will be displayed in the same position as when last displayed. You may also point to any toolbar and click with the right mouse button to bring up a shortcut menu, after which you can select the toolbar to be displayed (hidden). If the toolbar to be displayed is not listed, click the Customize command, click the Toolbars tab, check the box for the toolbar to be displayed, and then click the Close button.

- To change the size of the buttons, suppress the display of the ScreenTips, or display the associated shortcut key (if available), pull down the View menu, click Toolbars, and click Customize to display the Customize dialog box. If necessary, click the Options tab, then select (deselect) the appropriate check box. Alternatively, you can right click on any toolbar, click the Customize command from the context-sensitive menu, then select (deselect) the appropriate check box from within the Options tab in the Customize dialog box.

- Toolbars are either docked (along the edge of the window) or floating (in their own window). A toolbar moved to the edge of the window will dock along that edge. A toolbar moved anywhere else in the window will float in its own window. Docked toolbars are one tool wide (high), whereas floating toolbars can be resized by clicking and dragging a border or corner as you would with any window.
  - To move a docked toolbar, click anywhere in the background area and drag the toolbar to its new location. You can also click and drag the move handle (the single vertical line) at the left of the toolbar.
  - To move a floating toolbar, drag its title bar to its new location.

- To customize one or more toolbars, display the toolbar on the screen. Then pull down the View menu, click Toolbars, and click Customize to display the Customize dialog box. Alternatively, you can click on any toolbar with the right mouse button and select Customize from the shortcut menu.
  - To move a button, drag the button to its new location on that toolbar or any other displayed toolbar.
  - To copy a button, press the Ctrl key as you drag the button to its new location on that toolbar or any other displayed toolbar.
  - To delete a button, drag the button off the toolbar and release the mouse button.
  - To add a button, click the Commands tab in the Customize dialog box, select the category (from the Categories list box) that contains the button you want to add, then drag the button to the desired location on the toolbar.
  - To restore a predefined toolbar to its default appearance, pull down the View menu, click Toolbars, click Customize, click the Toolbars tab, select (highlight) the desired toolbar, and click the Reset command button.

- Buttons can also be moved, copied, or deleted without displaying the Customize dialog box.
  - To move a button, press the Alt key as you drag the button to the new location.
  - To copy a button, press the Alt and Ctrl keys as you drag the button to the new location.
  - To delete a button, press the Alt key as you drag the button off the toolbar.

- To create your own toolbar, pull down the View menu, click Toolbars, click Customize, click the Toolbars tab, then click the New command button. Alternatively, you can click on any toolbar with the right mouse button, select Customize from the shortcut menu, click the Toolbars tab, and then click the New command button.
  - Enter a name for the toolbar in the dialog box that follows. The name can be any length and can contain spaces.
  - The new toolbar will appear on the screen. Initially it will be big enough to hold only one button. Add, move, and delete buttons following the same procedures as outlined above. The toolbar will automatically size itself as new buttons are added and deleted.
  - To delete a custom toolbar, pull down the View menu, click Toolbars, click Customize, and click the Toolbars tab. *Verify that the custom toolbar to be deleted is the only one selected (highlighted).* Click the Delete command button. Click Yes to confirm the deletion. (Note that a predefined toolbar cannot be deleted.)

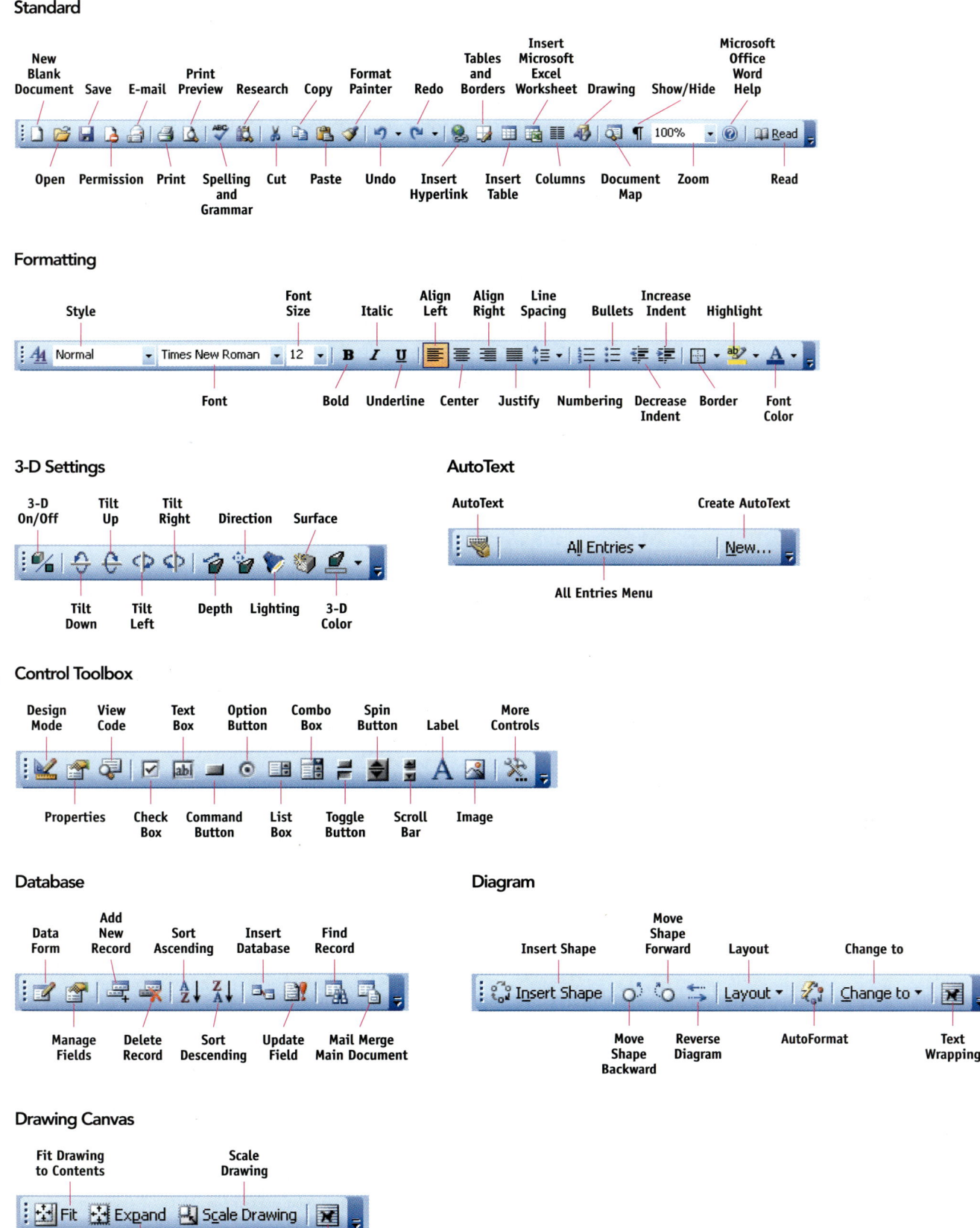

FIGURE A.1 Toolbars

MICROSOFT OFFICE WORD 2003

Drawing

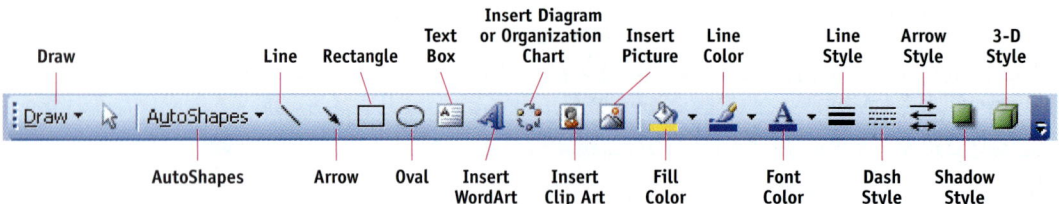

E-mail

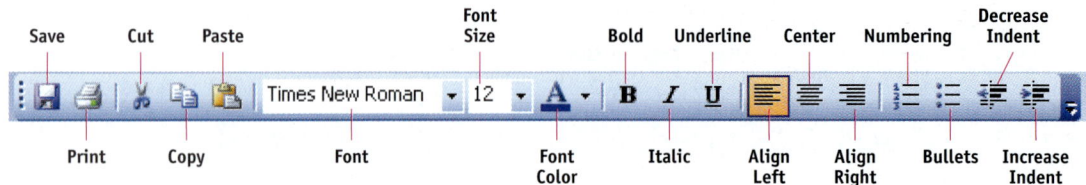

Extended Formatting

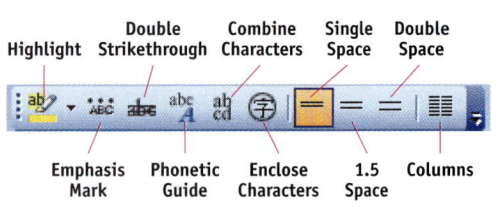

Forms

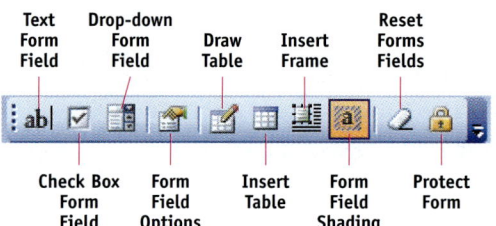

Frames

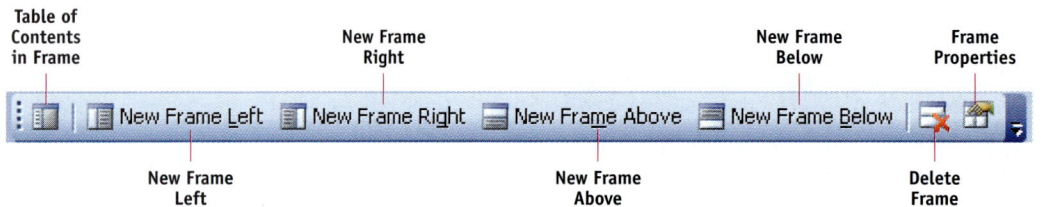

Function Key Display

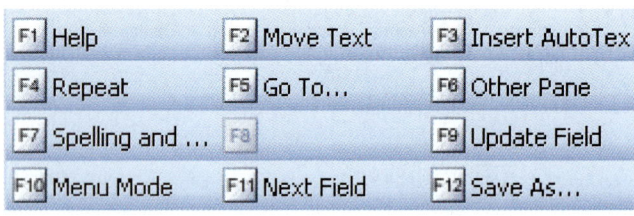

Japanese Greeting

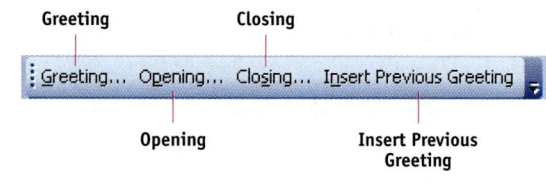

Mail Merge

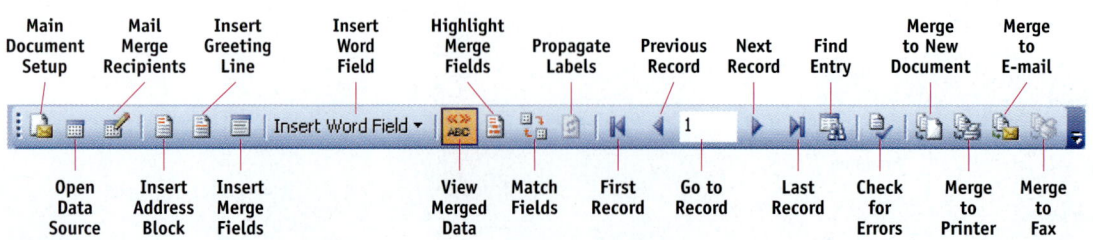

FIGURE A.1 Toolbars (*continued*)

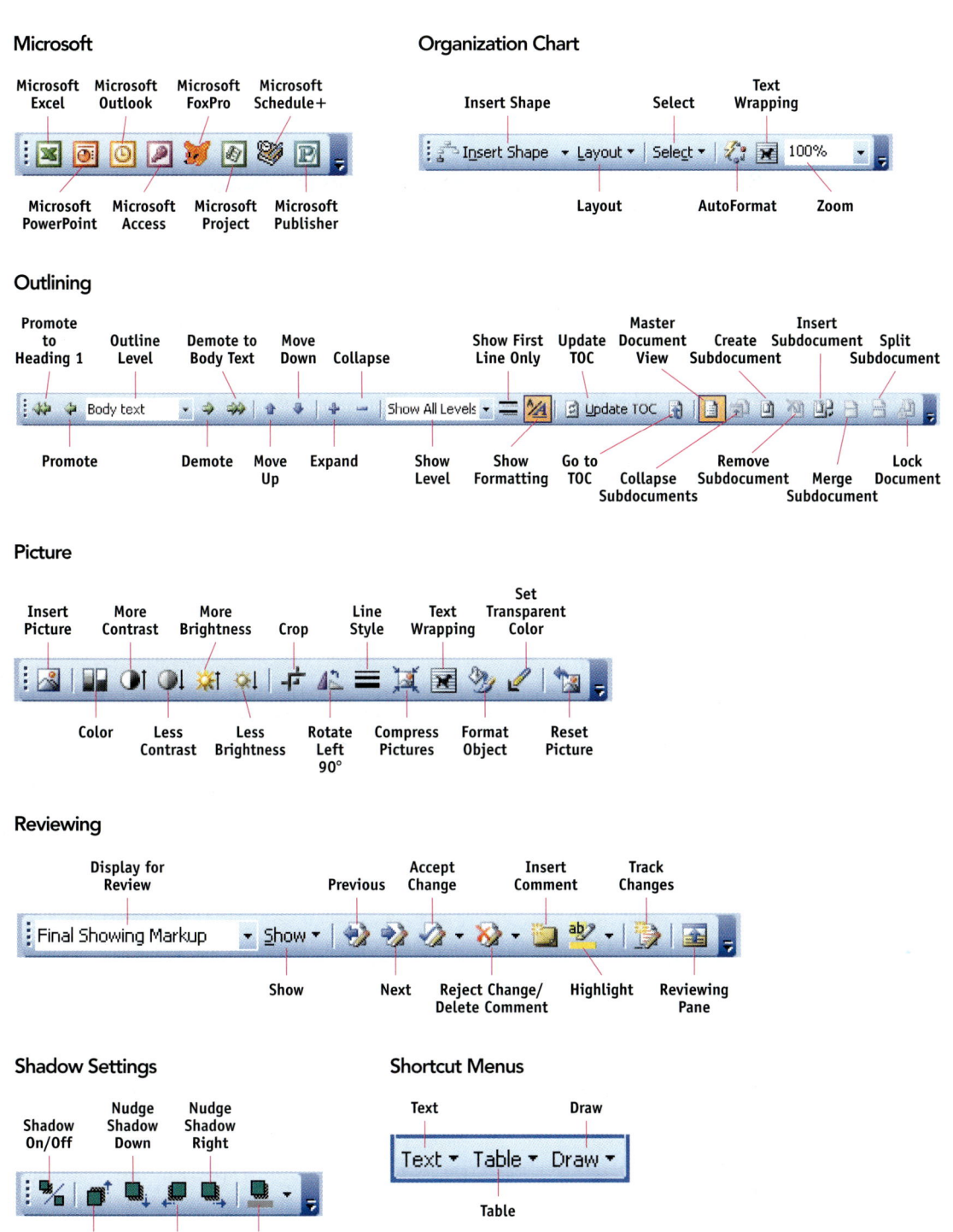

FIGURE A.1 Toolbars (continued)

Tables and Borders

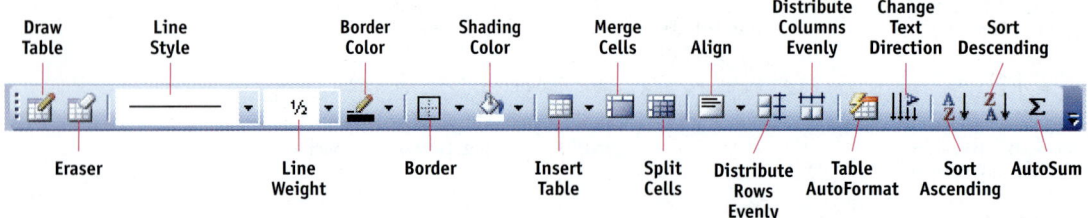

Visual Basic

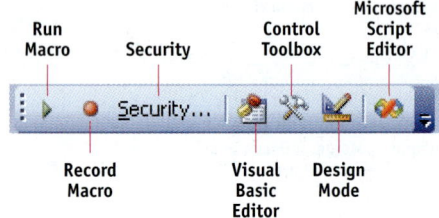

Web

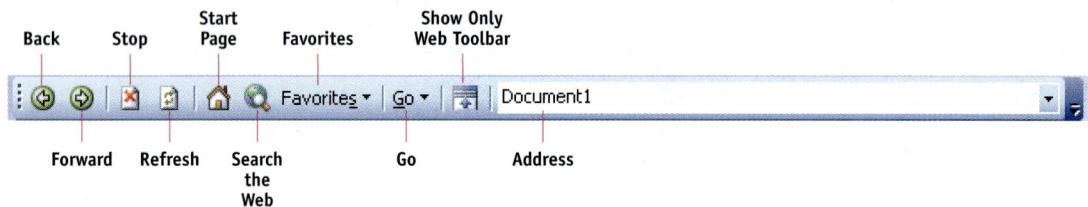

Web Tools

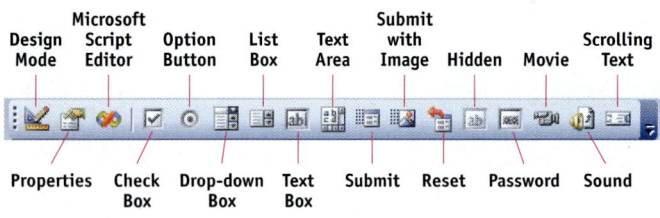

Word Count

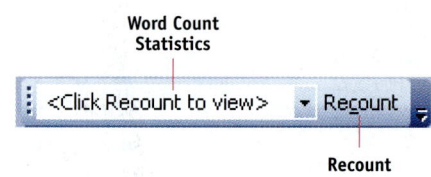

WordArt

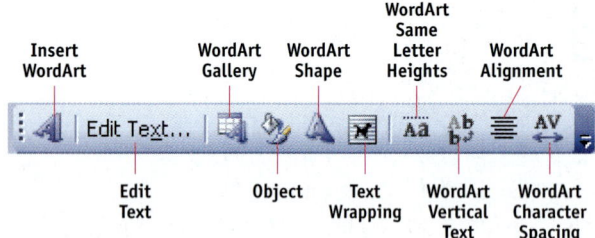

FIGURE A.1 Toolbars (*continued*)

CHAPTER 5

Consolidating Data: Worksheet References and File Linking

OBJECTIVES

After reading this chapter you will:

1. Describe two ways to consolidate data from multiple workbooks.
2. Distinguish between a cell reference and a worksheet reference.
3. Select multiple worksheets to enter common formulas and formatting.
4. Use the AutoFormat command.
5. Explain the advantage of using a function rather than a formula to consolidate data.
6. Create a documentation worksheet.
7. Use a workbook reference to link one workbook to another.

hands-on exercises

1. COPYING WORKSHEETS
   Input: Atlanta, Boston, and Chicago (three workbooks)
   Output: Corporate Sales

2. WORKSHEET REFERENCES
   Input: Corporate Sales workbook (from exercise 1)
   Output: Corporate Sales (with additional modifications)

3. THE DOCUMENTATION WORKSHEET
   Input: Corporate Sales workbook (from exercise 2)
   Output: Corporate Sales (with additional modifications)

4. LINKING WORKBOOKS
   Input: Atlanta, Boston, and Chicago (three workbooks)
   Output: Corporate Links

CASE STUDY
BANDIT'S PIZZA

Bandit's Pizza offers a tasty pizza at a "steal" of a price, with a strong appeal to the college and family crowds. Their pizzas are generously proportioned, made with a homemade spicy pizza sauce to create a unique zesty flavor, and their list of toppings includes some of the most off-the-wall selections around. This tried and true proven product offering, combined with great customer service, keep their pizzas flying out the door! Bandit's Pizza has expanded from its initial restaurant downtown to two additional sites elsewhere in the city.

The owner, Andreas Marquis, wants to evaluate the overall performance of the chain before expanding further. He is especially interested in the comparative results of three dining categories: dine-in, pick-up, and delivery. Andreas knows you are studying Excel at the local college and asked for your help in return for a small stipend and all the pizza you can eat. You have already prepared a template and distributed it to each restaurant manager, who has entered the sales data for last year. Your next task is to consolidate the data into a single workbook that shows the total sales for each quarter and each dining category. The information should be shown in tabular as well as graphical form.

Your assignment is to read the chapter, paying special attention to the two different ways in which to consolidate data. You can use either technique for the solution; that is, you can create a summary workbook with multiple worksheets, or you can create a summary workbook that links to the individual workbooks. In any event, start with the partially completed *Case Study Chapter 5—Bandit's Summary* workbook in the Exploring Excel folder. Data for the individual stores (Eastside, Westside, and Downtown) are found in three additional workbooks in the same folder. Print the completed summary workbook for your instructor to show both displayed values and cell formulas. Print the associated chart as well.

CONSOLIDATING DATA

Assume that you are the marketing manager for a national corporation with offices in several cities. Each branch manager reports to you on a quarterly basis, providing information about each product sold in his or her office. Your job is to consolidate the data into a single report. The situation is depicted graphically in Figure 5.1. Figures 5.1a, 5.1b, and 5.1c show reports for the Atlanta, Boston, and Chicago offices, respectively. Figure 5.1d shows the summary report for the corporation.

Atlanta Office

	Qtr 1	Qtr 2	Qtr 3	Qtr 4
Product 1	$10	$20	$30	$40
Product 2	$1,100	$1,200	$1,300	$1,400
Product 3	$200	$200	$300	$400

(a) Atlanta Data

Boston Office

	Qtr 1	Qtr 2	Qtr 3	Qtr 4
Product 1	$55	$25	$35	$45
Product 2	$150	$250	$350	$450
Product 3	$1,150	$1,250	$1,350	$1,400

(b) Boston Data

Chicago Office

	Qtr 1	Qtr 2	Qtr 3	Qtr 4
Product 1	$850	$950	$1,050	$1,150
Product 2	$100	$0	$300	$400
Product 3	$75	$150	$100	$200

(c) Chicago Data

Corporate Totals

	Qtr 1	Qtr 2	Qtr 3	Qtr 4
Product 1	$915	$995	$1,115	$1,235
Product 2	$1,350	$1,450	$1,950	$2,250
Product 3	$1,425	$1,600	$1,750	$2,000

(d) Corporate Summary

FIGURE 5.1 Consolidating Data

You should be able to reconcile the corporate totals for each product in each quarter with the detail amounts in the individual offices. Consider, for example, the sales of Product 1 in the first quarter. The Atlanta office has sold $10, the Boston office $55, and the Chicago office $850; thus, the corporation as a whole has sold $915 ($10+$55+$850). In similar fashion, the Atlanta, Boston, and Chicago offices have sold $1,100, $150, and $100, respectively, of Product 2 in the first quarter, for a corporate total of $1,350.

The chapter presents two approaches to computing the corporate totals in Figure 5.1. One approach is to use the three-dimensional capability within Excel, in which one workbook contains multiple worksheets. The workbook contains a separate worksheet for each of the three branch offices, and a fourth worksheet to hold the corporate data. An alternate technique is to keep the data for each branch office in its own workbook, then create a summary workbook that uses file linking to reference cells in the other workbooks.

There are advantages and disadvantages to each technique, as will be discussed in the chapter. As always, the hands-on exercises are essential to mastering the conceptual material.

THE THREE-DIMENSIONAL WORKBOOK

An Excel workbook is the electronic equivalent of the three-ring loose-leaf binder. It contains one or more worksheets, each of which is identified by a worksheet tab at the bottom of the document window. The workbook in Figure 5.2, for example, contains four worksheets. The title bar displays the name of the workbook (Corporate Sales). The tabs at the bottom of the workbook window display the names of the individual worksheets (Summary, Atlanta, Boston, and Chicago). The highlighted tab indicates the name of the active worksheet (Summary). To display a different worksheet, click on a different tab; for example, click the Atlanta tab to display the Atlanta worksheet.

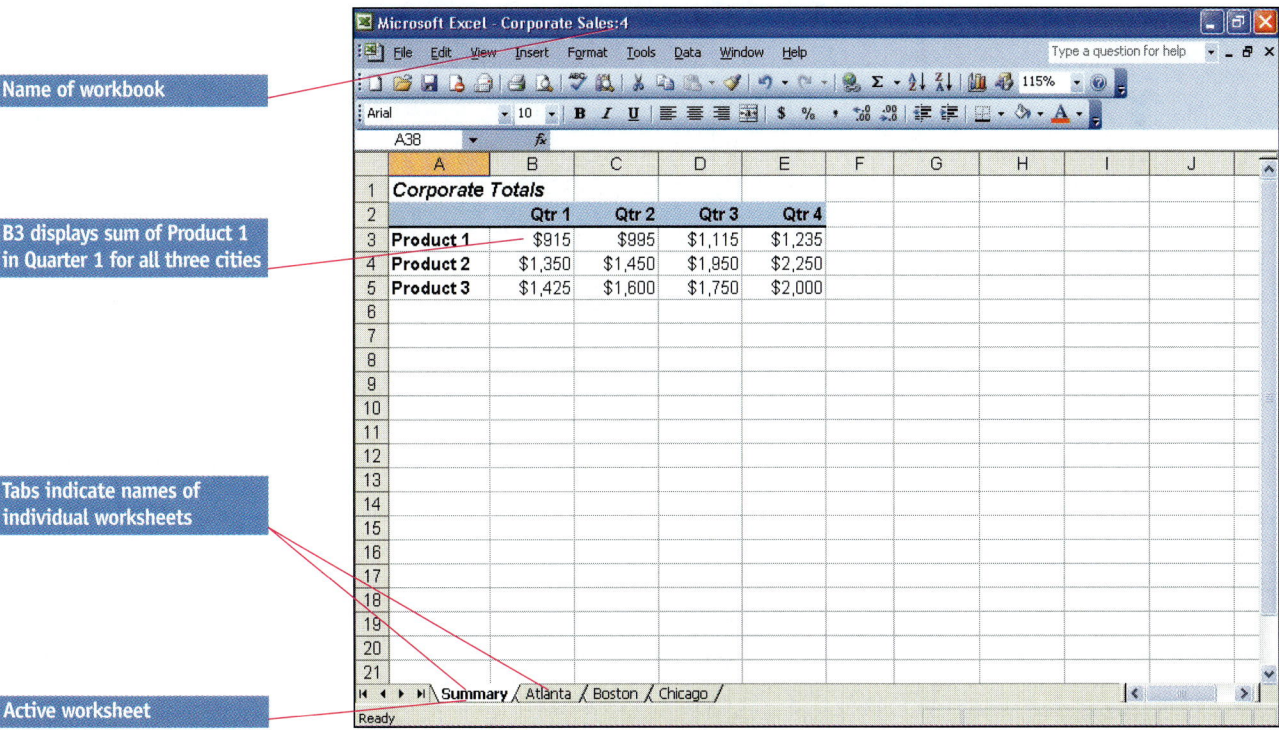

FIGURE 5.2 A Three-dimensional Workbook

The Summary worksheet shows the total amount for each product in each quarter. The data in the worksheet reflects the amounts shown earlier in Figure 5.1; that is, each entry in the Summary worksheet represents the sum of the corresponding entries in the worksheets for the individual cities. The amounts in the individual cities, however, are not visible in Figure 5.2. It is convenient, therefore, to open multiple windows to view the individual city worksheets at the same time you view the summary sheet.

Figure 5.3 displays the four worksheets in the Corporate Sales workbook, with a different sheet displayed in each window. The individual windows are smaller than the single view in Figure 5.2, but you can see at a glance how the Summary worksheet consolidates the data from the individual worksheets. The *New Window command* (in the Window menu) is used to open each additional window. Once the windows have been opened, the *Arrange command* (in the Window menu) is used to tile or cascade the open windows.

Only one window can be active at a time, and all commands apply to just the active window. In Figure 5.3, for example, the window in the upper left is active, as can be seen by the highlighted title bar. (To activate a different window, just click in that window.)

Copying Worksheets

The workbook in Figure 5.3 summarizes the data in the individual worksheets, but how was the data placed into the workbook? You could, of course, manually type in the entries, but there is an easier way, given that each branch manager sends you a workbook with the data for his or her office. All you have to do is copy the data from the individual workbooks into the appropriate worksheets in a new corporate workbook. (The specifics for how this is done are explained in detail in a hands-on exercise.)

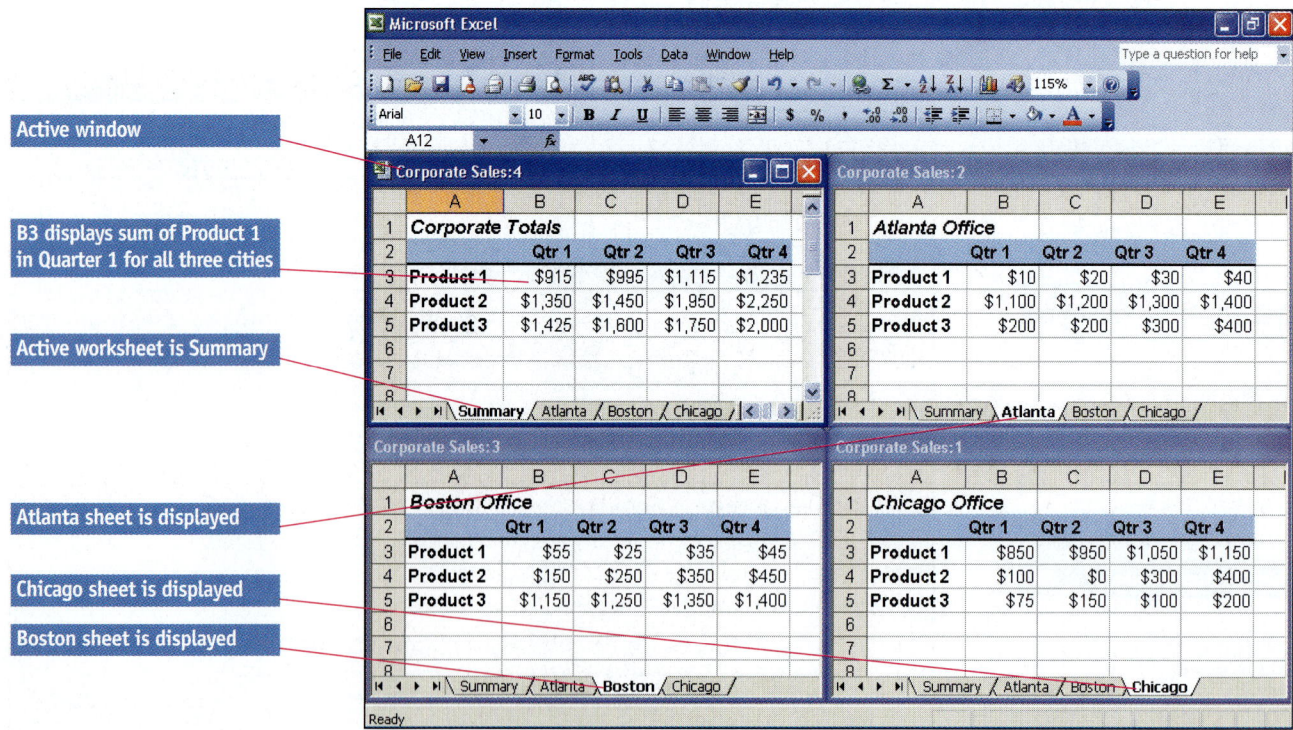

FIGURE 5.3 Multiple Worksheets

Multiple Workbooks

Consider now Figure 5.4, which at first glance appears to be almost identical to Figure 5.3. The two figures are very different, however. Figure 5.3 displayed four different worksheets from the same workbook. Figure 5.4, on the other hand, displays four different workbooks. There is one workbook for each city (Atlanta, Boston, and Chicago) and each of these workbooks contains only a single worksheet. The fourth workbook, Corporate Sales, contains four worksheets (Atlanta, Boston, Chicago, and Summary) and is the workbook displayed in Figure 5.3.

There are advantages and disadvantages to each technique. The single workbook in Figure 5.3 is easier for the manager in that he or she has all of the data in one file. The disadvantage is that the worksheets have to be maintained by multiple people (the manager in each city), and this can lead to confusion in that several individuals require access to the same workbook. The multiple workbooks of Figure 5.4 facilitate the maintenance of the data, but four separate files are required to produce the summary information. Both approaches are explored in detail within the chapter. The choice is up to you.

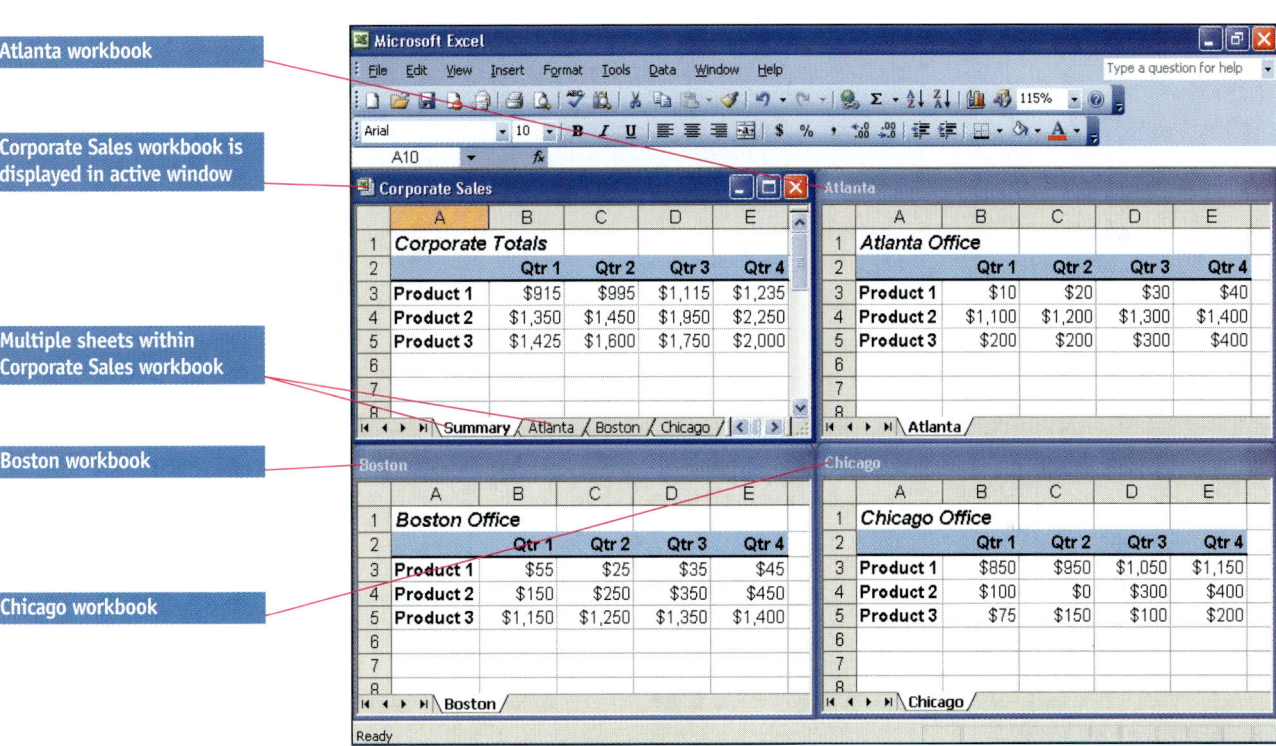

FIGURE 5.4 Multiple Workbooks

THE HORIZONTAL SCROLL BAR

The horizontal scroll bar contains four scrolling buttons to scroll through the worksheet tabs in a workbook. (The default workbook has three worksheets.) Click ◄ or ► to scroll one tab to the left or right. Click ◄◄ or ►► to scroll to the first or last tab in the workbook. Once the desired tab is visible, click the tab to select it. The number of tabs that are visible simultaneously depends on the setting of the horizontal scroll bar; that is, you can drag the tab split bar to change the number of tabs that can be seen at one time.

hands-on exercise 1

Copying Worksheets

Objective To open multiple workbooks; to use the Windows Arrange command to tile the open workbooks; to copy a worksheet from one workbook to another. Use Figure 5.5 as a guide in the exercise.

Step 1: **Open a New Workbook**

- Start Excel. Close the task pane if it is open. If necessary, click the **New button** on the Standard toolbar to open a new workbook as shown in Figure 5.5a.

- Delete all worksheets except for Sheet1:
  - Click the tab for **Sheet2**. Press the **Shift key** as you click the tab for **Sheet3**.
  - Point to the tab for **Sheet3** and click the **right mouse button** to display a shortcut menu. Click **Delete**.

- The workbook should contain only Sheet1 as shown in Figure 5.5a. Save the workbook as **Corporate Sales** in the **Exploring Excel folder**.

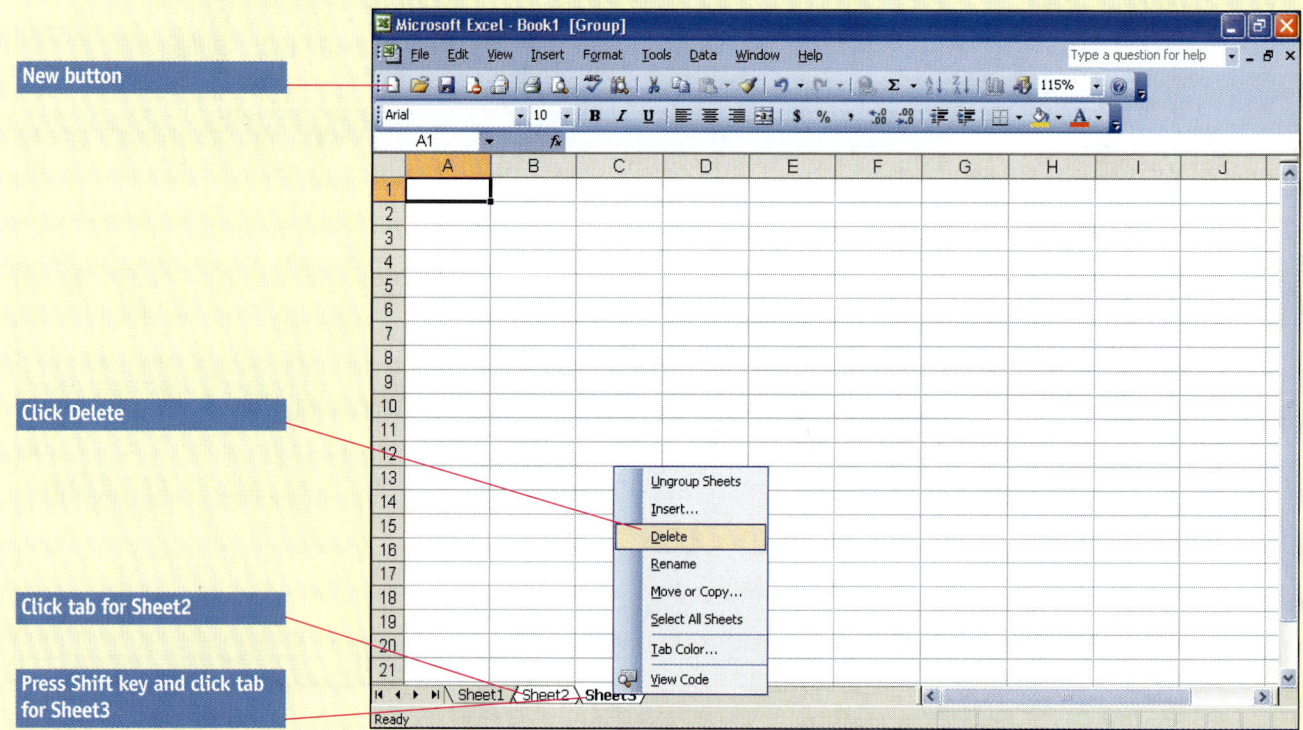

(a) Open a New Workbook (step 1)

FIGURE 5.5 Hands-on Exercise 1

THE RIGHT MOUSE BUTTON

Point to any object, then click the right mouse button to display a context-sensitive menu with commands appropriate to the item you are pointing to. Right clicking a cell, for example, displays a menu with selected commands from the Edit, Insert, and Format menus. Right clicking a toolbar displays a menu that lets you display (hide) additional toolbars. Right clicking a worksheet tab enables you to rename, move, copy, or delete a worksheet.

Step 2: **Open the Individual Workbooks**

- Pull down the **File menu**. Click **Open** to display the Open dialog box. (If necessary, open the Exploring Excel folder.)

- Click the **Atlanta workbook**, then press and hold the **Ctrl key** as you click the **Boston** and **Chicago workbooks** to select all three workbooks at the same time.

- Click **Open** to open the selected workbooks. The workbooks will be opened one after another with a brief message appearing on the status bar as each workbook is opened.

- Pull down the **Window menu**, which should indicate the four open workbooks at the bottom of the menu. Only one of the workbooks is visible at this time.

- Click **Arrange** to display the Arrange Windows dialog box. If necessary, select the **Tiled option**, then click **OK**. You should see four open workbooks as shown in Figure 5.5b. (Do not be concerned if your workbooks are arranged differently from ours.)

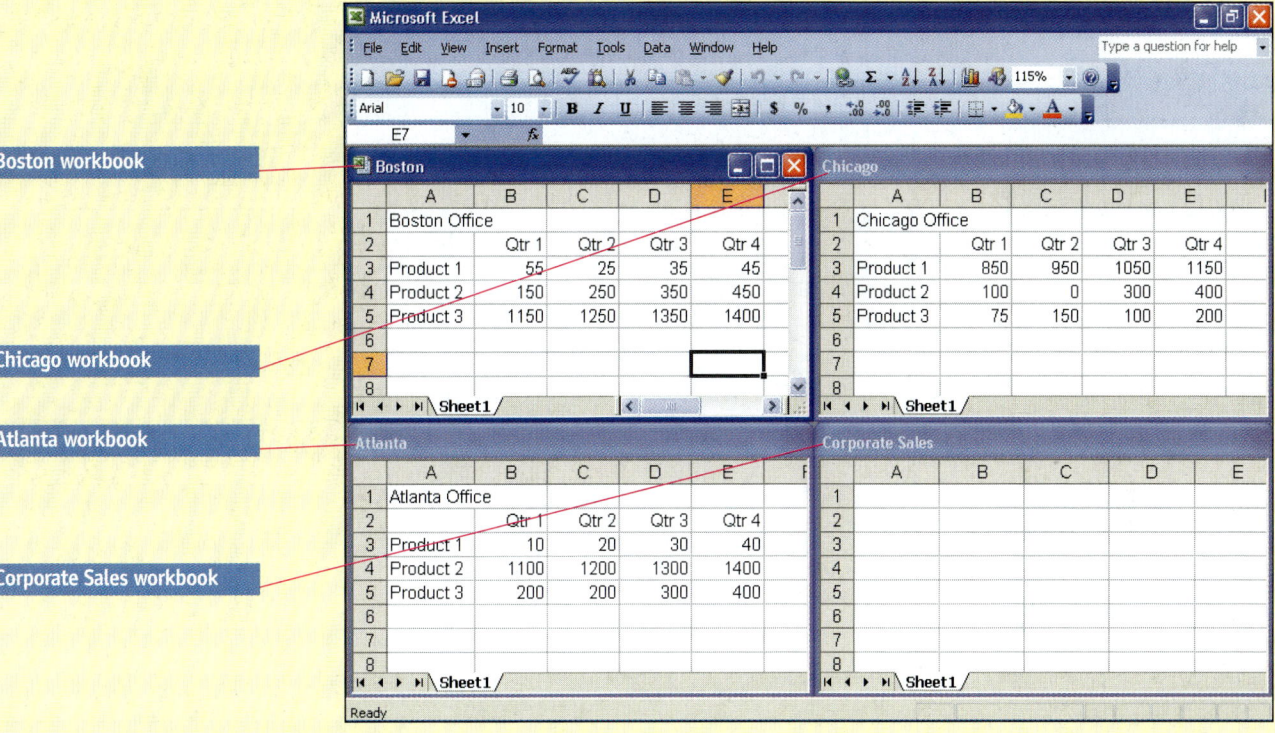

(b) Open the Individual Workbooks (step 2)

FIGURE 5.5 Hands-on Exercise 1 (*continued*)

DOWNLOAD THE PRACTICE FILES (DATA DISK)

The hands-on exercises in the text reference a series of practice files that are downloaded from our Web site. Go to www.prenhall.com/grauer, click the book icon for the series you want, and click the Student Download tab near the top of the window. Select the file you need according to the book you are using. Save the file to your desktop, then double click and follow the onscreen instructions. The installation procedure creates an Exploring Excel folder, which contains the files you need—for example, the Atlanta, Boston, and Chicago workbooks that are required for this exercise.

Step 3: Copy the Atlanta Data

- Click in the **Atlanta workbook** to make it the active workbook. Reduce the column widths (if necessary) so that you can see the entire worksheet.
- Click and drag to select **cells A1 through E5** as shown in Figure 5.5c. Pull down the **Edit menu** and click **Copy** (or click the **Copy button**).
- Click in **cell A1** of the **Corporate Sales workbook**.
- Click the **Paste button** on the Standard toolbar to copy the Atlanta data into this workbook. Press **Esc** to remove the moving border from the copy range.
- Point to the **Sheet1 tab** at the bottom of the Corporate Sales worksheet window, then click the **right mouse button** to produce a shortcut menu. Click **Rename**, which selects the worksheet name.
- Type **Atlanta** to replace the existing name and press **Enter**. The worksheet tab has been changed from Sheet1 to Atlanta. Reduce column widths as necessary.
- Click the **Save button** to save the active workbook (Corporate Sales).

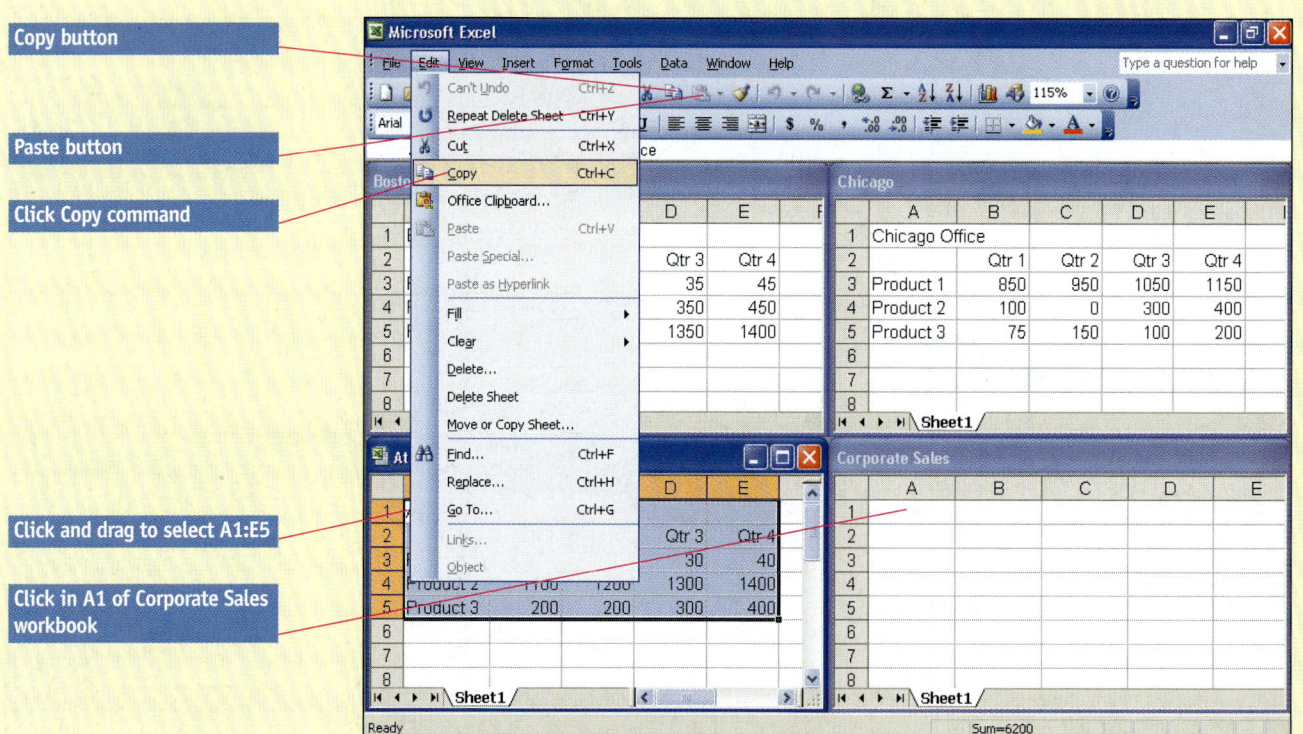

(c) Copy the Atlanta Data (step 3)

FIGURE 5.5 Hands-on Exercise 1 (*continued*)

CHANGE THE ZOOM SETTING

You can increase or decrease the size of a worksheet as it appears on the monitor by clicking the down arrow on the Zoom box and selecting an appropriate percentage. If you are working with a large spreadsheet and cannot see it at one time on the screen, choose a number less than 100%. Conversely, if you find yourself squinting because the numbers are too small, select a percentage larger than 100%. Changing the magnification on the screen does not affect printing; that is, worksheets are printed at 100% unless you change the scaling within the Page Setup command.

Step 4: **Copy the Boston and Chicago Data**

- Click in the **Boston workbook** to make it the active workbook as shown in Figure 5.5d.

- Click the **Sheet1 tab**, then press and hold the **Ctrl key** as you drag the tab to the right of the Atlanta tab in the Corporate Sales workbook. You will see a tiny spreadsheet with a plus sign as you drag the tab. The plus sign indicates that the worksheet is being copied; the ▼ symbol indicates where the worksheet will be placed.

- Release the mouse, then release the Ctrl key. The worksheet from the Boston workbook should have been copied to the Corporate Sales workbook and appears as Sheet1 in that workbook.

- The Boston workbook should still be open; if it isn't, it means that you did not press the Ctrl key as you were dragging the tab to copy the worksheet. If this is the case, pull down the **File menu**, reopen the Boston workbook, and if necessary, tile the open windows.

- Double click the **Sheet1 tab** in the Corporate Sales workbook to rename the tab. Type **Boston** as the new name, then press the **Enter key**.

- The Boston worksheet should appear to the right of the Atlanta worksheet; if the worksheet appears to the left of Atlanta, click and drag the tab to its desired position. (The ▼ symbol indicates where the worksheet will be placed.)

- Repeat the previous steps to copy the Chicago data to the Corporate Sales workbook, placing the new sheet to the right of the Boston sheet. Rename the copied worksheet **Chicago**.

- Save the Corporate Sales workbook. (The Summary worksheet will be built in the next exercise.)

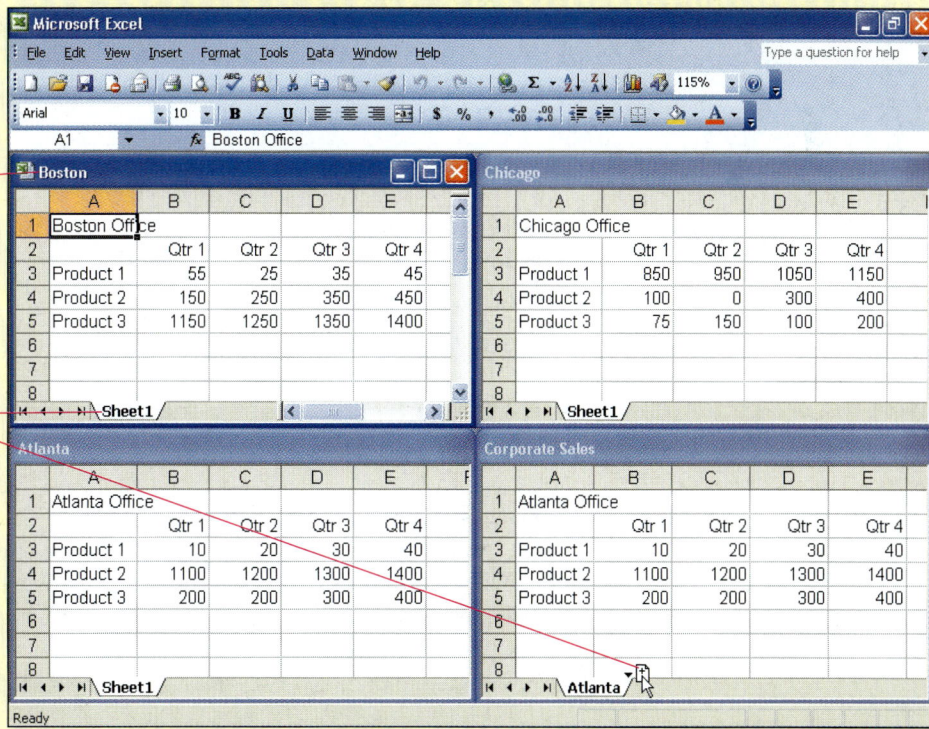

(d) Copy the Boston and Chicago Data (step 4)

FIGURE 5.5 Hands-on Exercise 1 (*continued*)

MICROSOFT OFFICE EXCEL 2003 1217

Step 5: **The Corporate Sales Workbook**

- Check that the Corporate Sales workbook is the active workbook. Click the **Maximize button** so that this workbook takes the entire screen.
- The Corporate Sales workbook contains three worksheets, one for each city, as can be seen in Figure 5.5e.
- Click the **Atlanta tab** to display the worksheet for Atlanta.
- Click the **Boston tab** to display the worksheet for Boston.
- Click the **Chicago tab** to display the worksheet for Chicago.
- Close all of the open workbooks, saving changes if requested to do so.
- Exit Excel if you do not want to continue with the next hands-on exercise at this time.

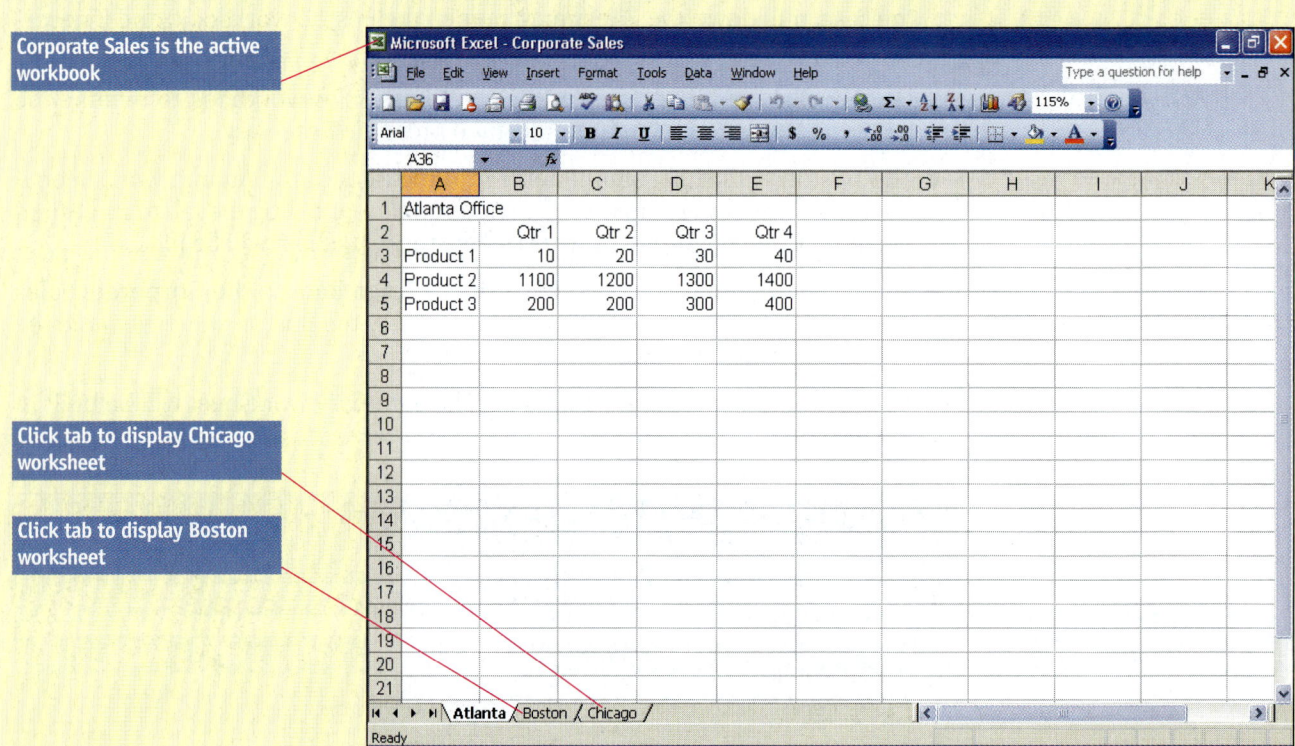

(e) The Corporate Sales Workbook (step 5)

FIGURE 5.5 Hands-on Exercise 1 (*continued*)

MOVING AND COPYING WORKSHEETS

You can move or copy a worksheet within a workbook by dragging its tab. To move a worksheet, click its tab, then drag the tab to the new location (a black triangle shows where the new sheet will go). To copy a worksheet, click its tab, then press and hold the Ctrl key as you drag the tab to its new location. The copied worksheet will have the same name as the original worksheet, followed by a number in parentheses indicating the copy number. Add color to your workbook by changing the color of a worksheet tab. Right click the worksheet tab, click the Tab Color command, select a new color, and click OK.

WORKSHEET REFERENCES

The presence of multiple worksheets in a workbook creates an additional requirement for cell references. You continue to use the same row and column convention when you reference a cell on the current worksheet; that is, cell A1 is still A1. What if, however, you want to reference a cell on another worksheet within the same workbook? It is no longer sufficient to refer to cell A1 because every worksheet has its own cell A1.

To reference a cell (or cell range) in a worksheet other than the current (active) worksheet, you need to preface the cell address with a ***worksheet reference***; for example, Atlanta!A1 references cell A1 in the Atlanta worksheet. A worksheet reference may also be used in conjunction with a cell range—for example, Summary!B2:E5 to reference cells B2 through E5 on the Summary worksheet. Omission of the worksheet reference in either example defaults to the cell reference in the active worksheet.

An exclamation point separates the worksheet reference from the cell reference. The worksheet reference is always an absolute reference. The cell reference can be either relative (e.g., Atlanta!A1 or Summary!B2:E5) or absolute (e.g., Atlanta!$A$1 or Summary!$B$2:$E$5).

Consider how worksheet references are used in the Summary worksheet in Figure 5.6. Each entry in the Summary worksheet computes the sum of the corresponding cells in the Atlanta, Boston, and Chicago worksheets. The cell formula in cell B3, for example, would be entered as follows:

=Atlanta!B3+Boston!B3+Chicago!B3

- Chicago is the worksheet reference
- Boston is the worksheet reference
- Atlanta is the worksheet reference

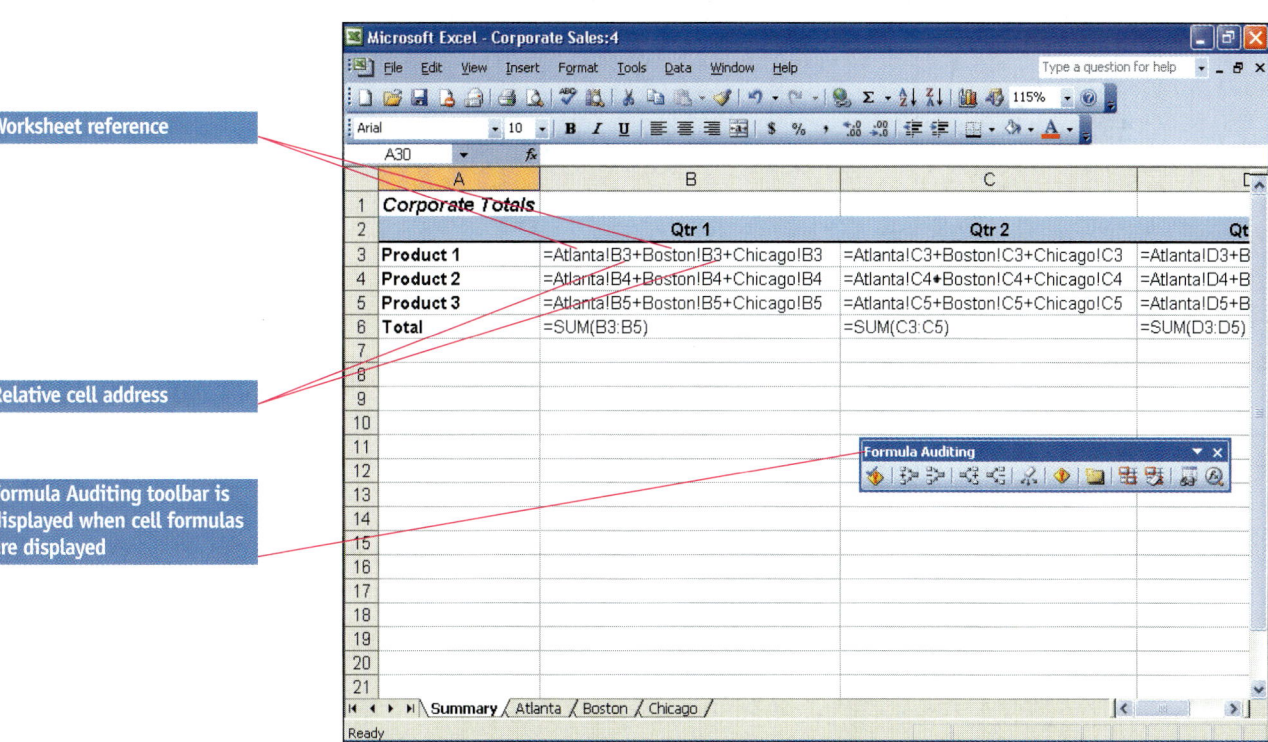

FIGURE 5.6 Worksheet References

The combination of relative cell references and constant worksheet references enables you to enter the formula once (into cell B3), then copy it to the remaining cells in the worksheet. In other words, you enter the formula into cell B3 to compute the total sales for Product 1 in Quarter 1, then you copy that formula to the other cells in row 3 (C3 through E3) to obtain the totals for Product 1 in Quarters 2, 3, and 4. You then copy the entire row (B3 through E3) to rows 4 and 5 (cells B4 through E5) to obtain the totals for Products 2 and 3 in all four quarters.

The proper use of relative and absolute references in the original formula in cell B3 is what makes it possible to copy the cell formulas. Consider, for example, the formula in cell C3 (which was copied from cell B3):

=Atlanta!C3+Boston!C3+Chicago!C3

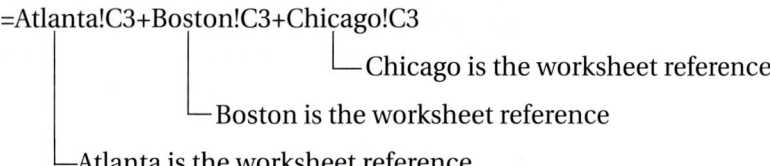

The worksheet references remain absolute (e.g., Atlanta!) while the cell references adjust for the new location of the formula (cell C3). Similar adjustments are made in all of the other copied formulas.

3-D Reference

A **3-D reference** is a range that spans two or more worksheets in a workbook—for example, =SUM(Atlanta:Chicago!B3) to sum cell B3 in the Atlanta, Boston, and Chicago worksheets. The sheet range is specified with a colon between the beginning and ending sheets. An exclamation point follows the ending sheet, followed by the cell reference. The worksheet references are constant and will not change if the formula is copied. The cell reference may be relative or absolute.

Three-dimensional references can be used in the Summary worksheet as an alternative way to compute the corporate total for each product–quarter combination. To compute the corporate sales for Product 1 in Quarter 1 (which appears in cell B3 of the Summary worksheet), you would use the following function:

=SUM(Atlanta:Chicago!B3)

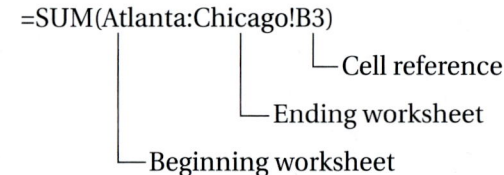

The 3-D reference includes all worksheets between the Atlanta and Chicago worksheets. (Only one additional worksheet, Boston, is present in the example, but the reference would automatically include any additional worksheets that were inserted between Atlanta and Chicago. In similar fashion, it would also adjust for the deletion of worksheets between Atlanta and Chicago.) Note, too, that the cell reference is relative and thus the formula can be copied from cell B3 in the Summary worksheet to the remaining cells in row 3 (C3 through E3). Those formulas can then be copied to the appropriate cells in rows 4 and 5.

A 3-D reference can be typed directly into a cell formula, but it is easier to enter the reference by pointing. Click in the cell that is to contain the 3-D reference, then enter an equal sign to begin the formula. To reference a cell in another worksheet, click the tab for the worksheet you want to reference, then click the cell or cell range you want to include in the formula. To reference a range from multiple worksheets, click in the cell in the first worksheet, press the Shift key as you click the tab for the last worksheet in the range, then click in the cell in the last worksheet.

Grouping Worksheets

The worksheets in a workbook are often similar to one another in terms of content and/or formatting. In Figure 5.3, for example, the formatting is identical in all four worksheets of the workbook. You can format the worksheets individually or more easily through grouping.

Excel provides the capability for *grouping worksheets* to enter or format data in multiple worksheets at the same time. Once the worksheets are grouped, anything you do in one of the worksheets is automatically done to the other sheets in the group. You could, for example, group all of the worksheets together when you enter row and column labels, when you format data, or when you enter formulas to compute row and column totals. You must, however, ungroup the worksheets when you enter data into a specific worksheet. Grouping and ungrouping is illustrated in the following hands-on exercise.

The AutoFormat Command

The formatting commands within Excel can be applied individually (as you have done throughout the text), or automatically and collectively by choosing a predefined set of formatting specifications. Excel provides several such designs as shown in Figure 5.7. You can apply any of these designs to your worksheet by selecting the range to be formatted, then executing the *AutoFormat command* from within the Format menu.

The AutoFormat command does not do anything that could not be done through the individual commands, but it does provide inspiration by suggesting several attractive designs. You can enter additional formatting commands after the AutoFormat command has been executed, as you will see in our next exercise.

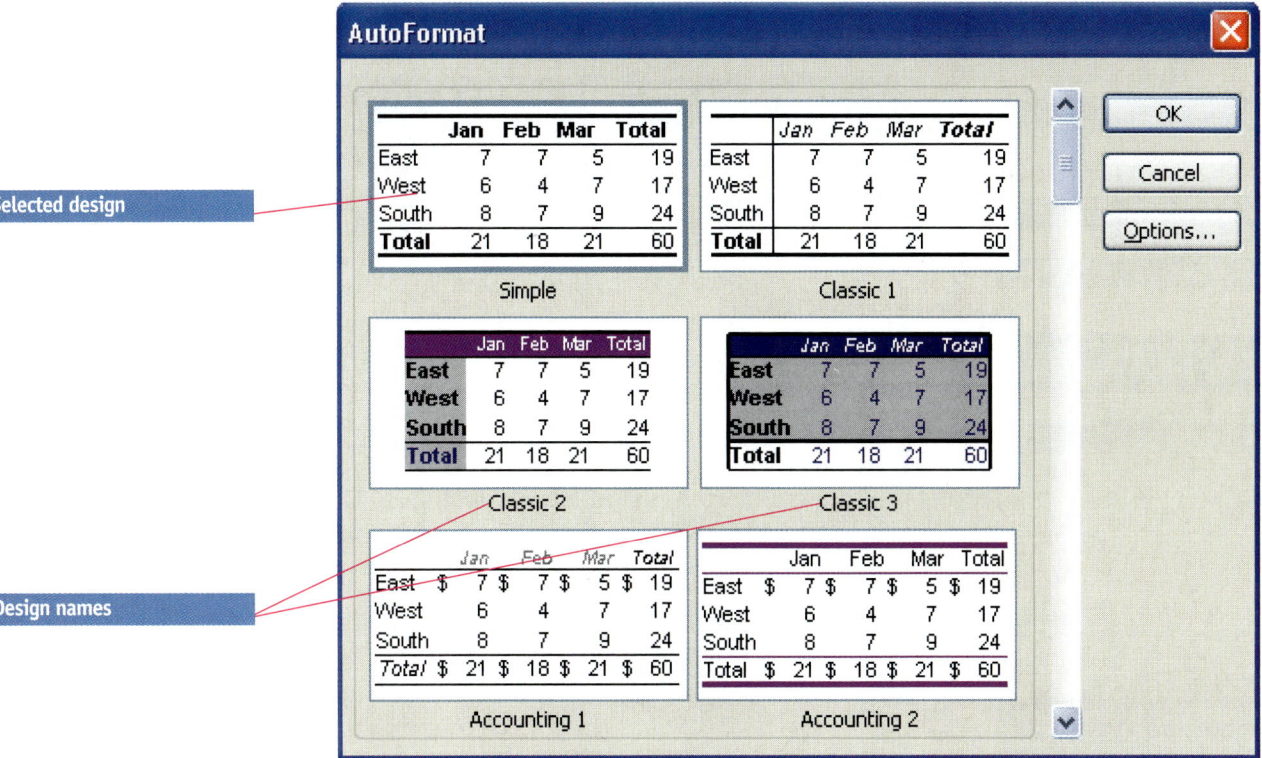

FIGURE 5.7 The AutoFormat Command

hands-on exercise 2

Worksheet References

Objective To use 3-D references to summarize data from multiple worksheets within a workbook; to group worksheets to enter common formatting and formulas; to open multiple windows to view several worksheets at the same time. Use Figure 5.8 as a guide in the exercise.

Step 1: Insert a Worksheet

- Start Excel. Open the **Corporate Sales workbook** created in the previous exercise. The workbook contains three worksheets.

- If necessary, click the ◀ to display all three tabs. Click the **Atlanta tab** to select this worksheet. Pull down the **Insert menu**, and click the **Worksheet command**. You should see a new worksheet, Sheet1.

- Double click the **tab** of the newly inserted worksheet to select the name. Type **Summary** and press **Enter**. The name of the new worksheet has been changed.

- Click in **cell A1** of the Summary worksheet. Type **Corporate Totals** as shown in Figure 5.8a.

- Click in **cell B2**. Enter **Qtr 1**. Click in **cell B2**, then point to the fill handle in cell B2. The mouse pointer changes to a thin crosshair.

- Click and drag the fill handle over **cells C2**, **D2**, and **E2**. A border appears to indicate the destination range. Release the mouse. Cells C2 through E2 contain the labels Qtr 2, Qtr 3, and Qtr 4, respectively. Right align the column labels.

- Click in **cell A3**. Enter **Product 1**. Use the AutoFill capability to enter the labels **Product 2** and **Product 3** in cells A4 and A5.

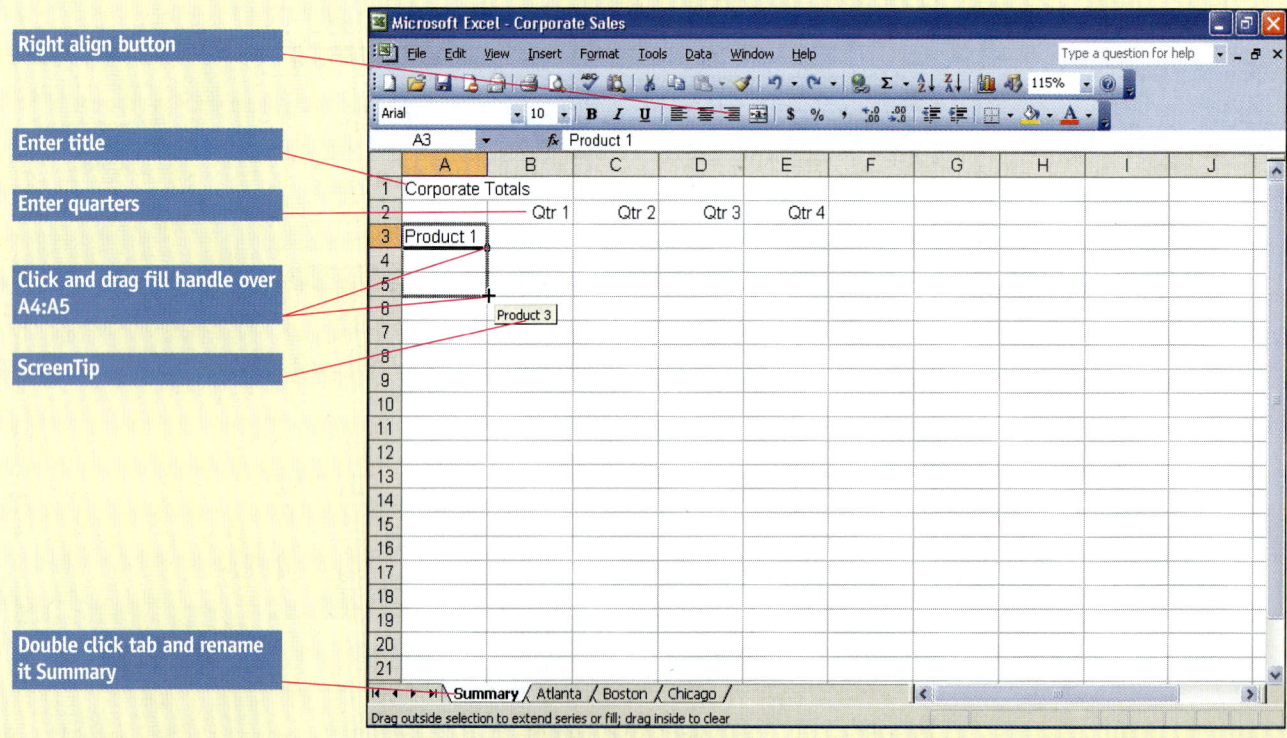

(a) Insert a Worksheet (step 1)

FIGURE 5.8 Hands-on Exercise 2

Step 2: **Sum the Worksheets**

- Click in **cell B3** of the Summary worksheet as shown in Figure 5.8b. Enter **=SUM(Atlanta:Chicago!B3)**, then press the **Enter key**. You should see 915 as the sum of the sales for Product 1 in Quarter 1 for the three cities (Atlanta, Boston, and Chicago).

- Click the **Undo button** on the Standard toolbar to erase the function so that you can reenter the function by using pointing.

- Check that you are in cell B3 of the Summary worksheet. Enter **=SUM(**.
  - Click the **Atlanta tab** to begin the pointing operation.
  - Press and hold the **Shift key**, click the **Chicago tab** (scrolling if necessary), then release the Shift key and click **cell B3**. The formula bar should now contain =SUM(Atlanta:Chicago!B3.
  - Press the **Enter key** to complete the function (which automatically enters the closing right parenthesis) and return to the Summary worksheet.

- You should see once again the displayed value of 915 in cell B3 of the Summary worksheet.

- If necessary, click in **cell B3**, then drag the fill handle over **cells C3 through E3** to copy this formula and obtain the total sales for Product 1 in all four quarters.

- Be sure that cells B3 through E3 are still selected, then drag the fill handle to **cell E5**. You should see the total sales for all products in all quarters.

- Click **cell E5** to examine the formula in this cell and note that the worksheet references are constant (i.e., they remained the same), whereas the cell references are relative (they were adjusted). Click in other cells to review their formulas in similar fashion.

- Save the workbook.

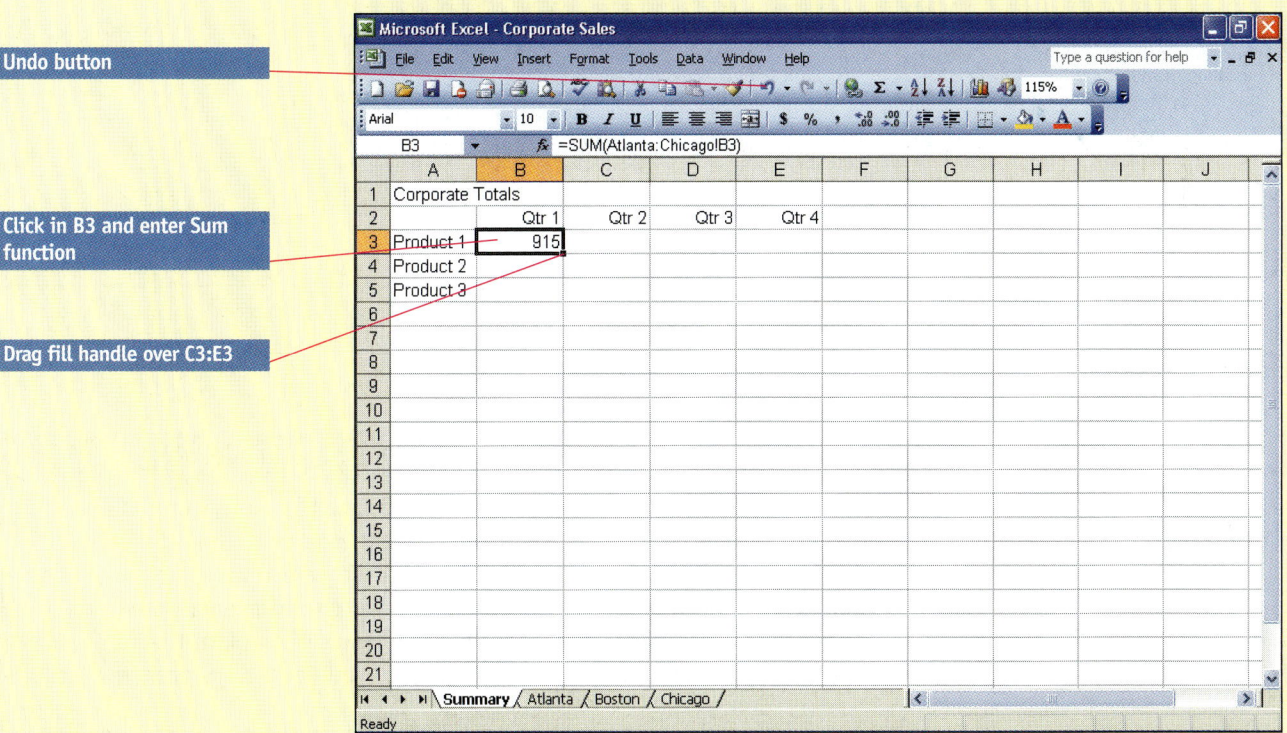

(b) Sum the Worksheets (step 2)

FIGURE 5.8 Hands-on Exercise 2 (*continued*)

Step 3: **The Arrange Windows Command**

- Pull down the **Window menu**, which displays the names of the open windows.
- The Corporate Sales workbook should be the only open workbook. Close any other open workbooks, including Book1.
- Pull down the **Window menu** a second time. Click **New Window** to open a second window. Note, however, that your display will not change at this time.
- Pull down the **Window menu** a third time. Click **New Window** to open a third window. Open a fourth window in similar fashion.
- Pull down the **Window menu** once again. You should see the names of the four open windows as shown in Figure 5.8c.
- Click **Arrange** to display the Arrange Windows dialog box. If necessary, select the **Tiled option**, then click **OK**. You should see four tiled windows.

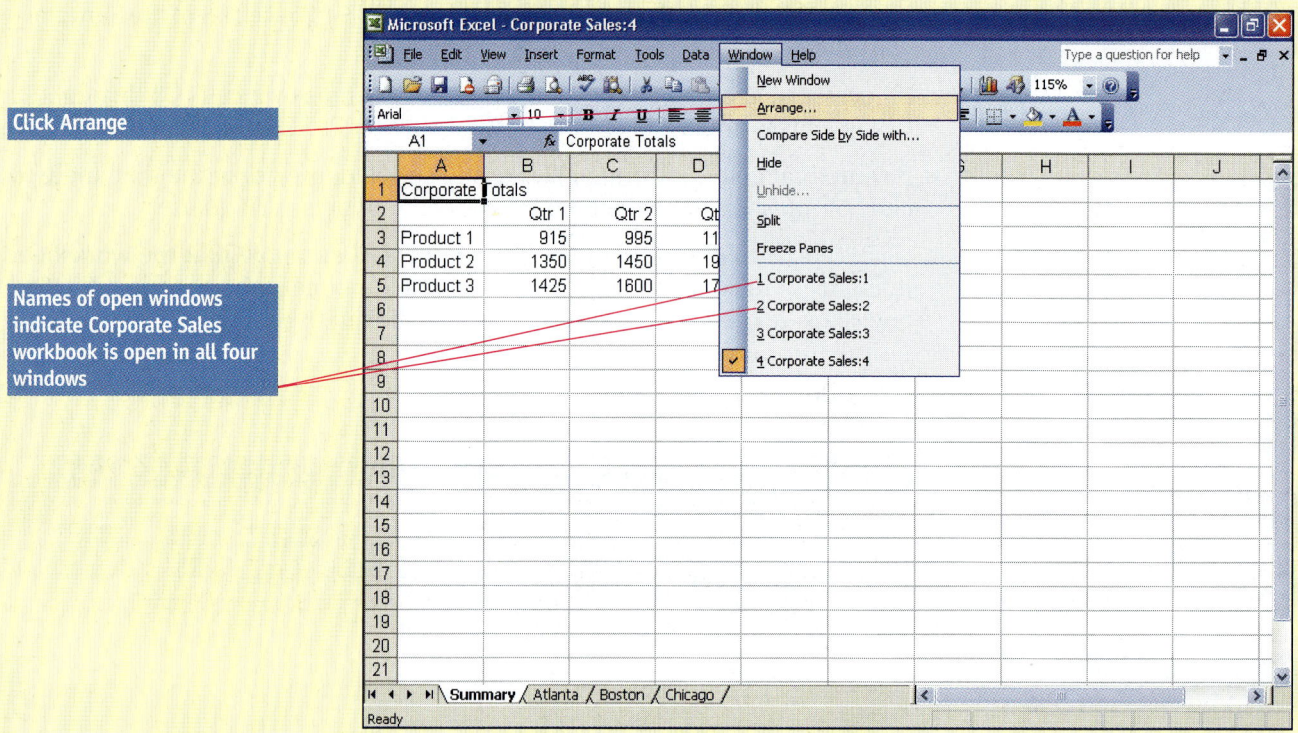

(c) The Arrange Windows Command (step 3)

FIGURE 5.8 Hands-on Exercise 2 (*continued*)

POINTING TO CELLS IN OTHER WORKSHEETS

A worksheet reference can be typed directly into a cell formula, but it is easier to enter the reference by pointing. Click in the cell that is to contain the reference, then enter an equal sign to begin the formula. To reference a cell in another worksheet, click the tab for the worksheet you want to reference, then click the cell or cell range you want to include in the formula. Complete the formula as usual, continuing to first click the tab whenever you want to reference a cell in another worksheet.

Step 4: **Changing Data**

- Click in the **upper-right window** in Figure 5.8d. Click the **Atlanta tab** to display the Atlanta worksheet in this window.

- Click the **lower-left window**. Click the **Boston tab** to display the Boston worksheet in this window.

- Click in the **lower-right window**. Click the **Tab scrolling button** until you can see the Chicago tab, then click the **Chicago tab**.

- Note that cell B3 in the Summary worksheet displays the value 915, which reflects the total sales for Product 1 in Quarter 1 for Atlanta, Boston, and Chicago (10, 55, and 850, respectively).

- Click in **cell B3** of the Chicago worksheet. Enter **250**. Press **Enter**. The value of cell B3 in the Summary worksheet changes to 315 to reflect the decreased sales in Chicago.

- Click the **Undo button** on the Standard toolbar. The sales for Chicago revert to 850 and the Corporate total is again 915.

- Save the workbook.

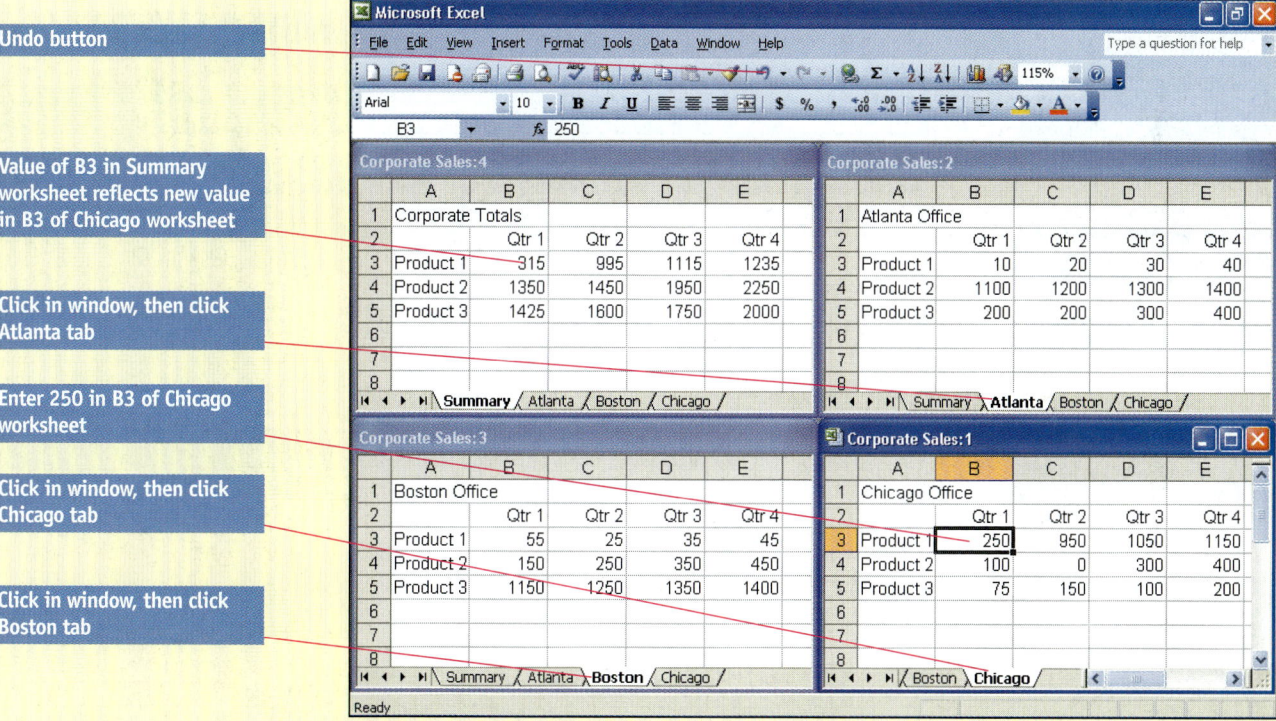

(d) Changing Data (step 4)

FIGURE 5.8 Hands-on Exercise 2 (*continued*)

CONTEXT-SENSITIVE MENUS

A context-sensitive menu provides an alternate (and generally faster) way to execute common commands. Point to a tab, then click the right mouse button to display a menu with commands to insert, delete, rename, move, copy, change color, or select all worksheets. Point to the desired command, then click the left mouse button to execute the command from the shortcut menu. Press the Esc key or click outside the menu to close the menu.

MICROSOFT OFFICE EXCEL 2003   1225

Step 5: **Group Editing**

- Click in the window where the Summary worksheet is active. Point to the split box separating the tab scrolling buttons from the horizontal scroll bar. (The pointer becomes a two-headed arrow.) Click and drag to the right until you can see all four tabs at the same time.

- If necessary, click the **Summary tab**. Press and hold the **Shift key** as you click the tab for the **Chicago worksheet**. All four tabs should be selected (and thus displayed in white) as shown in Figure 5.8e. You should also see [Group] in the title bar.

- Enter **Total** in **cell A6**. The text is centered in cell A6 of all four worksheets.

- Click in cell **B6** and enter the function **=SUM(B3:B5)**. Note that the formula is entered in all four sheets simultaneously because of group editing. Copy this formula to **cells C6 through E6**.

- Stay in the Summary worksheet and scroll until you can see column F. Enter **Total** in **cell F2**. Click in **cell F3** and enter the function **=SUM(B3:E3)**. Copy this formula to **cells F4 through F6**.

- Save the workbook.

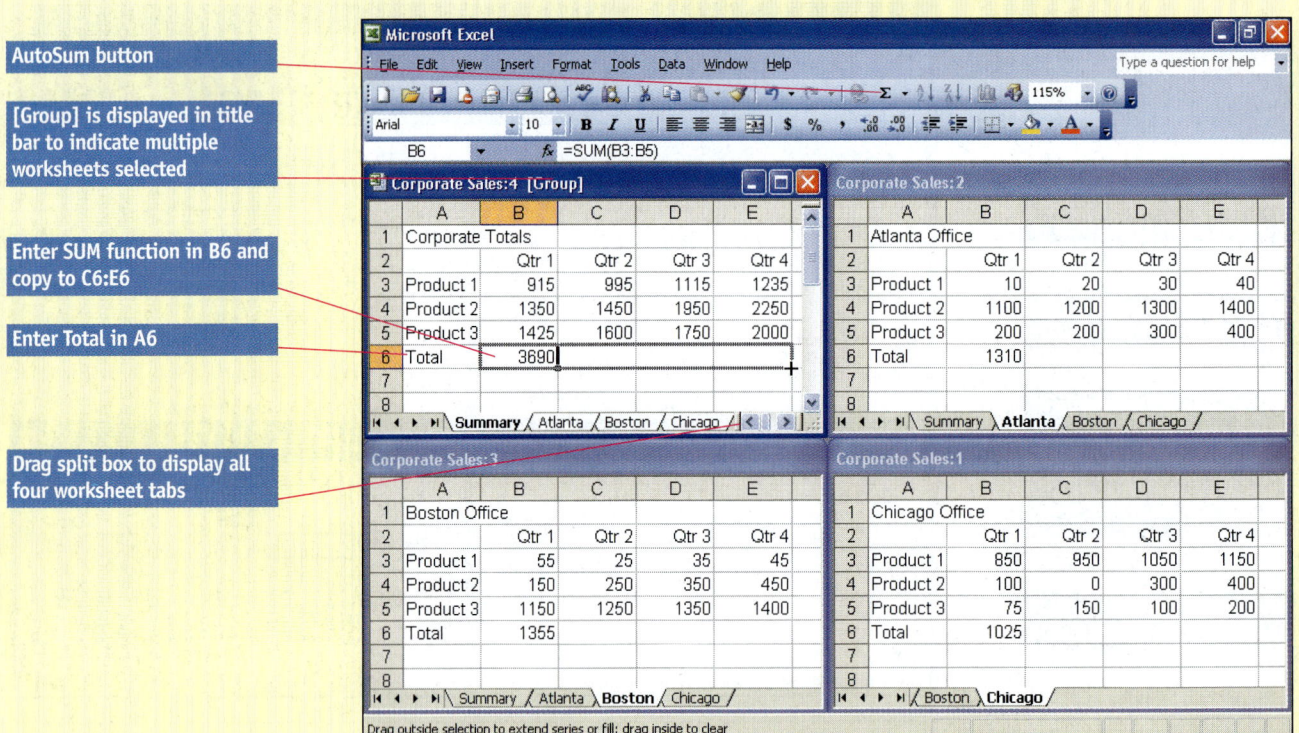

(e) Group Editing (step 5)

FIGURE 5.8 Hands-on Exercise 2 (*continued*)

THE AUTOSUM BUTTON

The AutoSum button on the Standard toolbar invokes the Sum function over a range of cells. To sum a single row or column, click in the blank cell at the end of the row or column, click the AutoSum button to see the suggested function, then click the button a second time to enter the function into the worksheet. To enter a sum function for multiple rows or columns, select the cell range prior to clicking the AutoSum button.

Step 6: **The AutoFormat Command**

- Be sure that all four tabs are still selected so that group editing is still in effect. Click and drag to select **cells A1 through F6** as shown in Figure 5.8f. (You may need to scroll in the worksheet to select all of the cells.)

- Pull down the **Format menu** and click the **AutoFormat command** to display the AutoFormat dialog box. Choose a format that appeals to you, then click the **Options button** to determine which parts of the format you want to apply.

- Experiment freely by selecting different designs and/or checking and unchecking the various check boxes within a design. Set a time limit, then make a decision. We chose the **Colorful 2** format and left all of the boxes checked. Click **OK**.

- The format is applied to all four selected sheets. You cannot see the effects in the summary worksheet, however, until you click elsewhere in the worksheet to deselect the cells.

- Save the workbook.

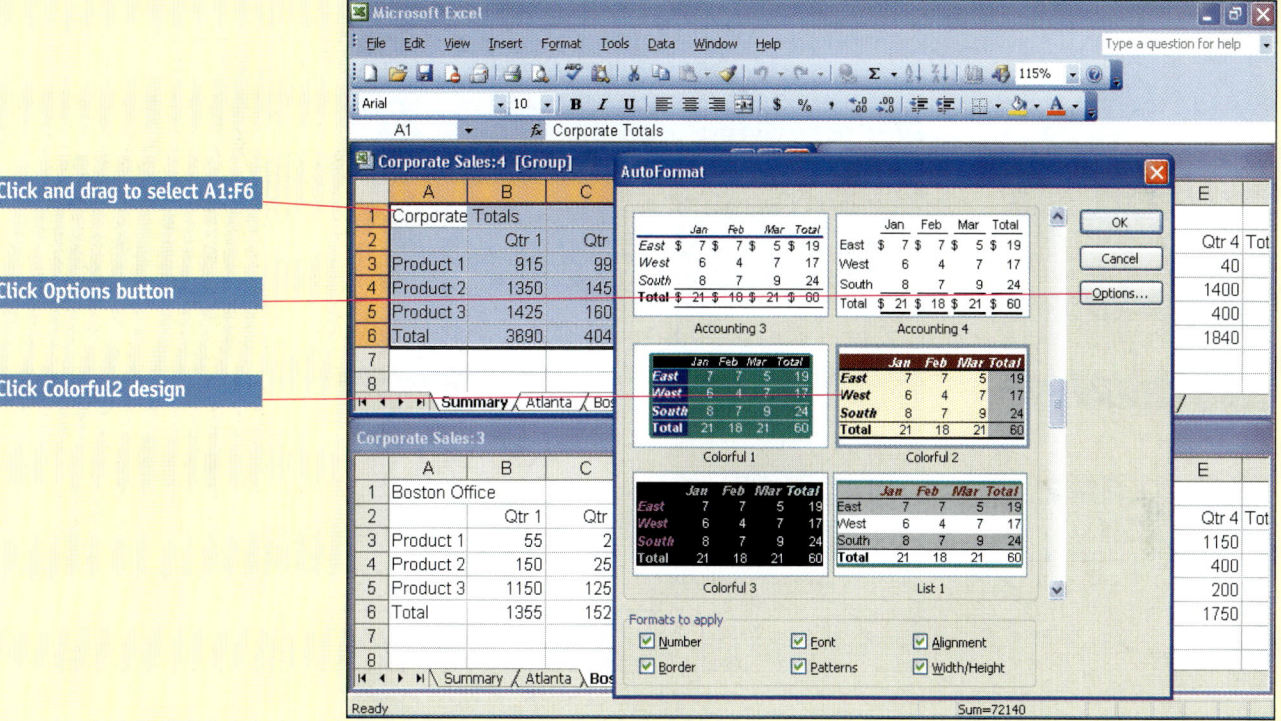

(f) The AutoFormat Command (step 6)

FIGURE 5.8 Hands-on Exercise 2 (*continued*)

SELECT MULTIPLE WORKSHEETS

You can group multiple worksheets simultaneously, then perform the same operation on the selected sheets at one time. To select adjacent worksheets, click the first sheet in the group, then press and hold the Shift key as you click the last sheet in the group. If the worksheets are not adjacent to one another, click the first tab, then press and hold the Ctrl key as you click the tab of each additional sheet. Excel indicates that grouping is in effect by appending [Group] to the workbook name in the title bar. Click any tab (other than the active sheet) to deselect the group.

Step 7: **The Finishing Touches**

- Click and drag to select **cells B3 through F6**, then pull down the **Format menu** and click the **Cells command** to display the Format Cells dialog box in Figure 5.8g. (You can also right click the selected cells, then select the **Format Cells command** from the context-sensitive menu.)

- Click the **Number tab**, click **Currency**, and set the number of decimal places to **zero**. Click **OK**.

- Change the width of columns B through F as necessary to accommodate the additional formatting. It's easiest to select all of the columns at the same time, then click and drag the border between any two of the selected columns to change the width of all selected columns.

- Click the **Atlanta tab** to ungroup the worksheets. Save the workbook. Close all four windows. Exit Excel if you do not want to continue with the next exercise at this time.

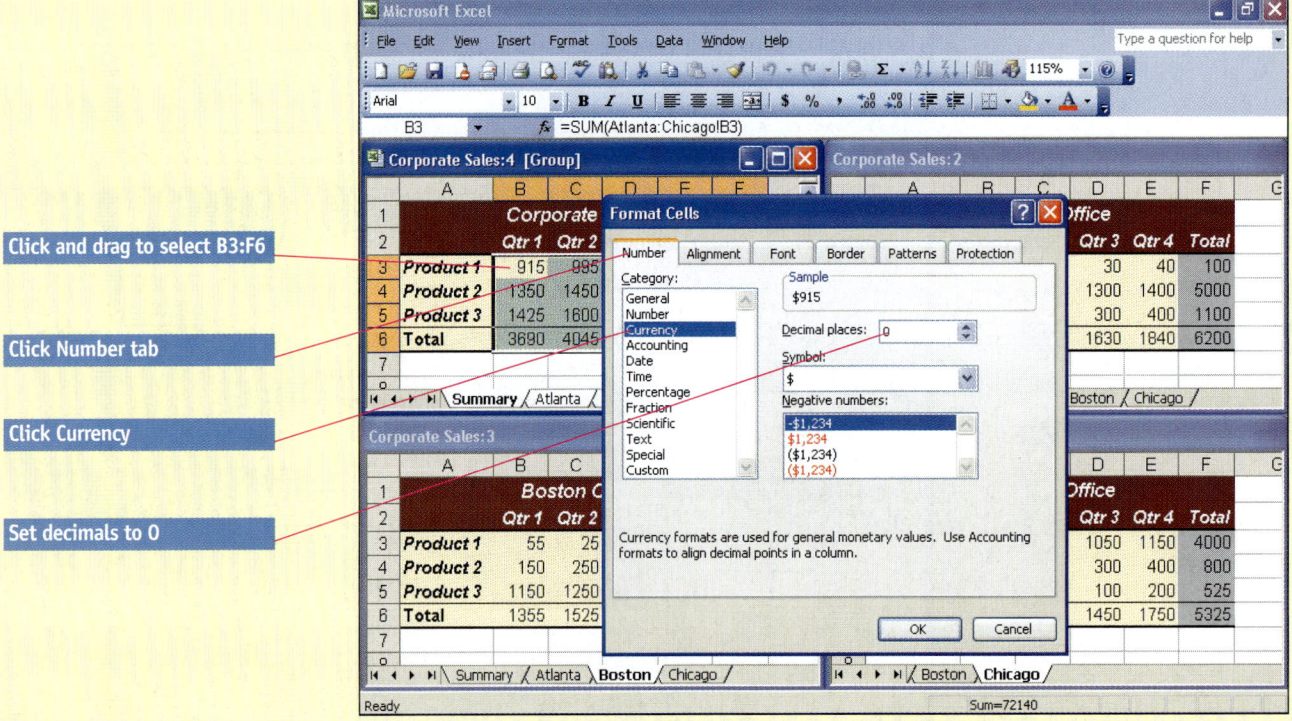

(g) The Finishing Touches (step 7)

FIGURE 5.8 Hands-on Exercise 2 (*continued*)

THE OPTIMAL (AUTOFIT) COLUMN WIDTH

The appearance of pound signs within a cell indicates that the cell width (column width) is insufficient to display the computed results in the selected format. Double click the right border of the column heading to change the column width to accommodate the widest entry in that column. For example, to increase the width of column B, double click the border between the column headings for columns B and C.

1228 CHAPTER 5: CONSOLIDATING DATA

THE DOCUMENTATION WORKSHEET

Throughout the text we have emphasized the importance of properly designing a worksheet and of isolating the assumptions and initial conditions on which the worksheet is based. A workbook can contain up to 255 worksheets, and it, too, should be well designed so that the purpose of every worksheet is evident. Documenting a workbook, and the various worksheets within it, is important because spreadsheets are frequently used by individuals other than the author. You are familiar with every aspect of your workbook because you created it. Your colleague down the hall (or across the country) is not, however, and that person needs to know at a glance the purpose of the workbook and its underlying structure. Even if you don't share your worksheet with others, you will appreciate the documentation six months from now, when you have forgotten some of the nuances you once knew so well.

One way of documenting a workbook is through the creation of a ***documentation worksheet*** that describes the contents of each worksheet within the workbook as shown in Figure 5.9. The worksheet in Figure 5.9 has been added to the Corporate Sales workbook that was created in the first two exercises. (The Insert menu contains the command to add a worksheet.)

The documentation worksheet shows the author and date the spreadsheet was last modified. It contains a description of the overall workbook, a list of all the sheets within the workbook, and the contents of each. The information in the documentation worksheet may seem obvious to you, but it will be greatly appreciated by someone seeing the workbook for the first time.

The documentation worksheet is attractively formatted and takes advantage of the ability to wrap text within a cell. The description in cell B6, for example, wraps over several lines (just as in a word processor). The worksheet also takes advantage of color and larger fonts to call attention to the title of the worksheet. The grid lines have been suppressed through the View tab in the Options command of the Tools menu. The documentation worksheet is an important addition to any workbook.

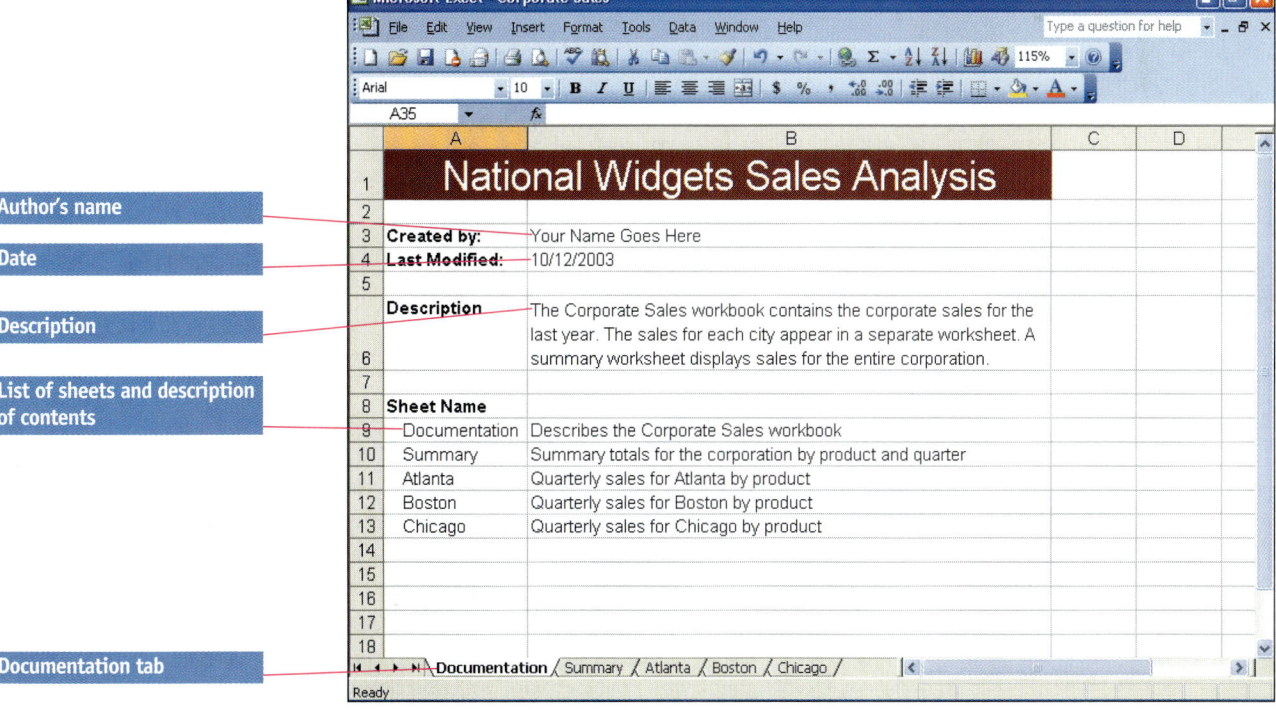

FIGURE 5.9 The Documentation Worksheet

MICROSOFT OFFICE EXCEL 2003   1229

hands-on exercise

3 The Documentation Worksheet

Objective To improve the design of a workbook through the inclusion of a documentation worksheet; to illustrate sophisticated formatting.

Step 1: **Add the Documentation Worksheet**

- Open the **Corporate Sales workbook** that was created in the previous exercise. Maximize the window. If necessary, click the **Atlanta tab** to turn off the group-editing feature. Click the **Summary tab** to select this worksheet.

- Pull down the **Insert menu** and click the **Worksheet command** to insert a new worksheet to the left of the Summary worksheet. Double click the **tab** of the new worksheet. Enter **Documentation** as the new name and press **Enter**.

- Enter the descriptive entries in column A as shown in Figure 5.10a. Enter your name in **cell B3**. Enter **=Today( )** in cell B4. Press **Enter**. Click the **Left Align button** to align the date as shown in the figure. Save the workbook.

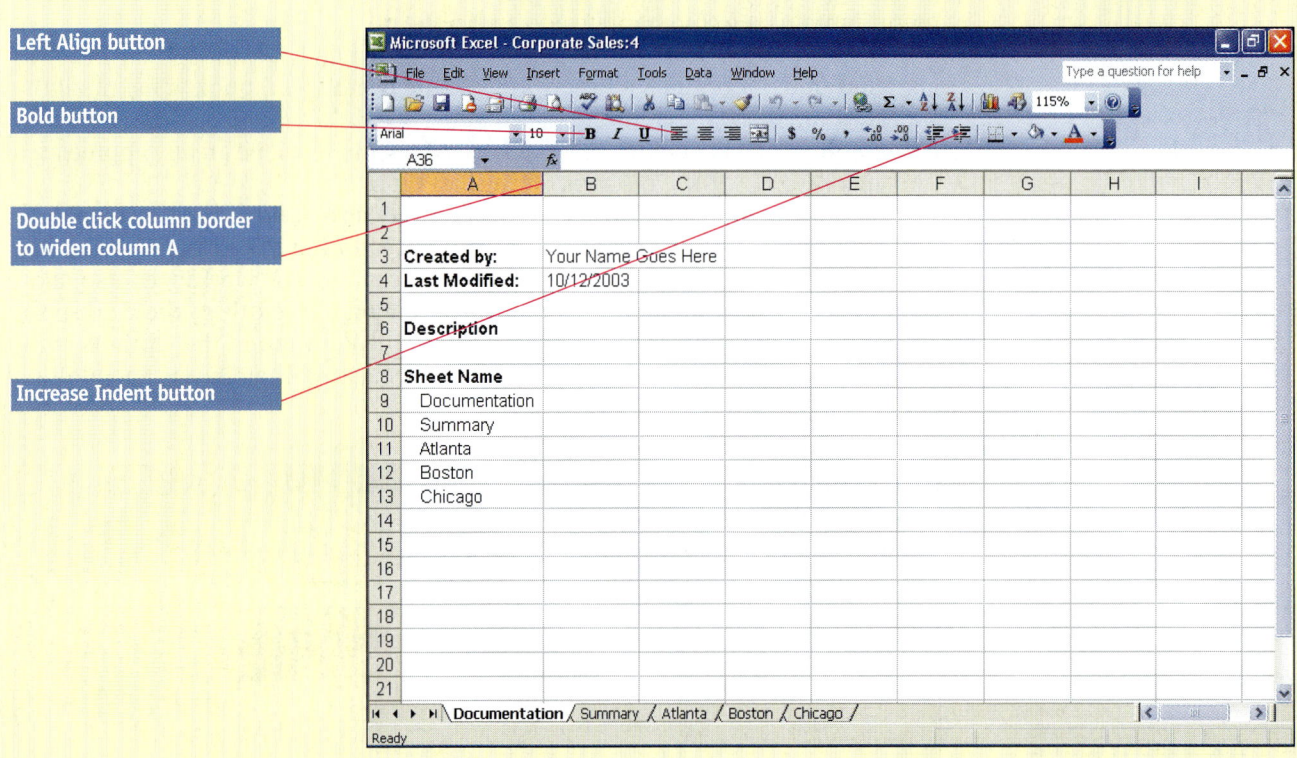

(a) Add the Documentation Worksheet (step 1)

FIGURE 5.10 Hands-on Exercise 3

WORKBOOK PROPERTIES

A documentation worksheet is one way to describe the author and other properties of a workbook. Excel also documents various properties automatically, but gives you the opportunity to modify that information. Pull down the File menu and click the Properties command to display the associated dialog box and explore the various tabs within the dialog box. Some properties are entered for you, such as the author in the Summary tab, the worksheet names in the Contents tab, and the date the worksheet was created and last modified in the Statistics tab. Other properties can be modified as necessary, especially in the Custom tab.

Step 2: **The Wrap Text Command**

- Increase the width of column B as shown in Figure 5.10b, then click in **cell B6** and enter the descriptive entry shown in the formula bar.

- Do not press the Enter key until you have completed the entire entry. Do not be concerned if the text in cell B6 appears to spill into the other cells in row six. Press the **Enter key** when you have completed the entry.

- Click in **cell B6**, then pull down the **Format menu** and click **Cells** (or right click **cell B6** and click the **Format Cells command**) to display the dialog box in Figure 5.10b.

- Click the **Alignment tab**, click the box to **Wrap Text** as shown in the figure, then click **OK**. The text in cell B6 wraps to the width of column B.

- Point to **cell A6**, then click the **right mouse button** to display a shortcut menu. Click **Format Cells** to display the Format Cells dialog box. If necessary, click the **Alignment tab**, click the **drop-down arrow** in the Vertical list box, and select **Top**. Click **OK**. Save the workbook.

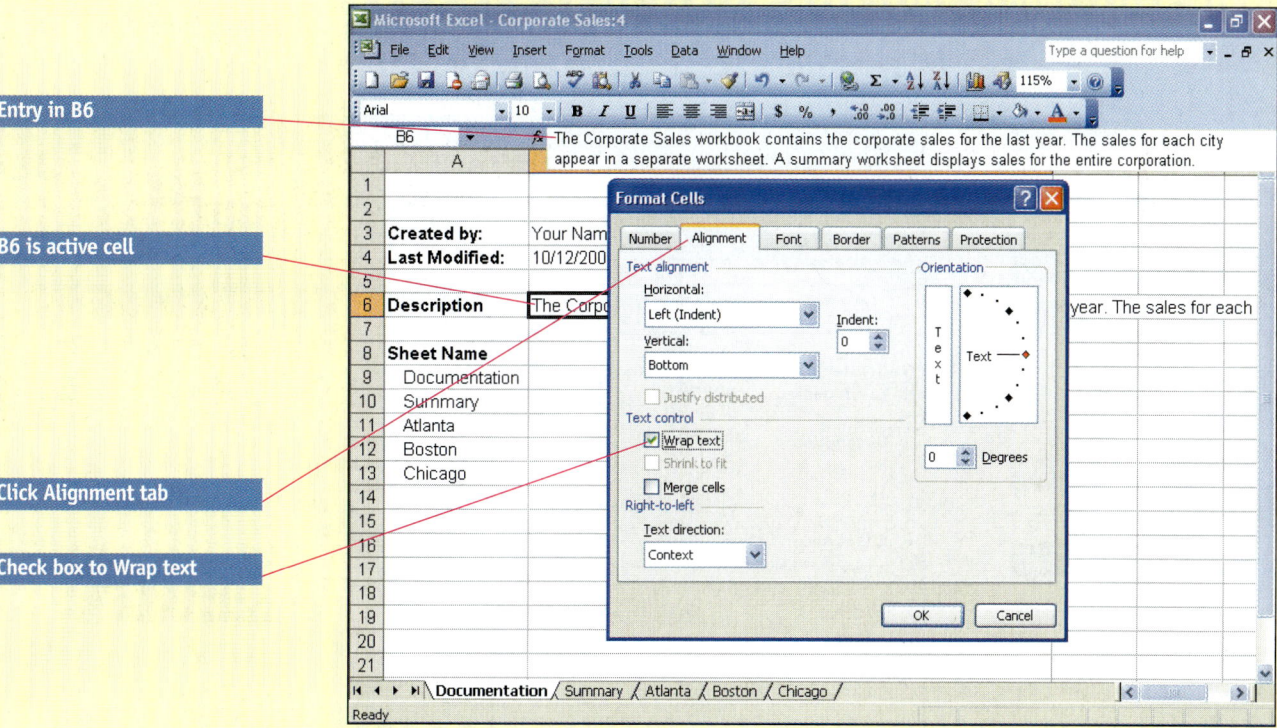

(b) The Wrap Text Command (step 2)

FIGURE 5.10 Hands-on Exercise 3 (*continued*)

EDIT WITHIN A CELL

Double click in the cell whose contents you want to change, then make the changes directly in the cell itself rather than on the formula bar. Use the mouse or arrow keys to position the insertion point at the point of correction. Press the Ins key to toggle between the insertion and overtype modes and/or use the Del key to delete a character. Press the Home and End keys to move to the first and last characters, respectively. If this feature does not work, pull down the Tools menu, click the Options command, click the Edit tab, then check the box to edit directly in a cell.

Step 3: **Add the Worksheet Title**

- Click in **cell A1**. Enter **National Widgets Sales Analysis**. Change the font size to **22**.

- Click and drag to select **cells A1 and B1**. Click the **Merge and Center button** to center the title across cells A1 and B1.

- Check that cells A1 and B1 are still selected. Pull down the **Format menu**. Click **Cells** to display the Format Cells dialog box as shown in Figure 5.10c.
  - Click the **Patterns tab**. Click the **Dark Red** color (to match the color used in the Colorful 2 AutoFormat that was applied in the previous exercise).
  - Click the **Font tab**. Click the drop-down arrow in the **Color list box**. Click the **White** color.
  - Click **OK** to accept the settings and close the Format Cells dialog box.

- Click outside the selected cells to see the effects of the formatting change. You should see white letters on a dark red background.

- Complete the text entries in **cells B9 through B13**. (Refer to Figure 5.9.) Add any additional documentation and formatting that you think is appropriate.

- Click in **cell A1**. Click the **Spelling button** to check the worksheet for spelling. Make corrections as necessary. Save the workbook.

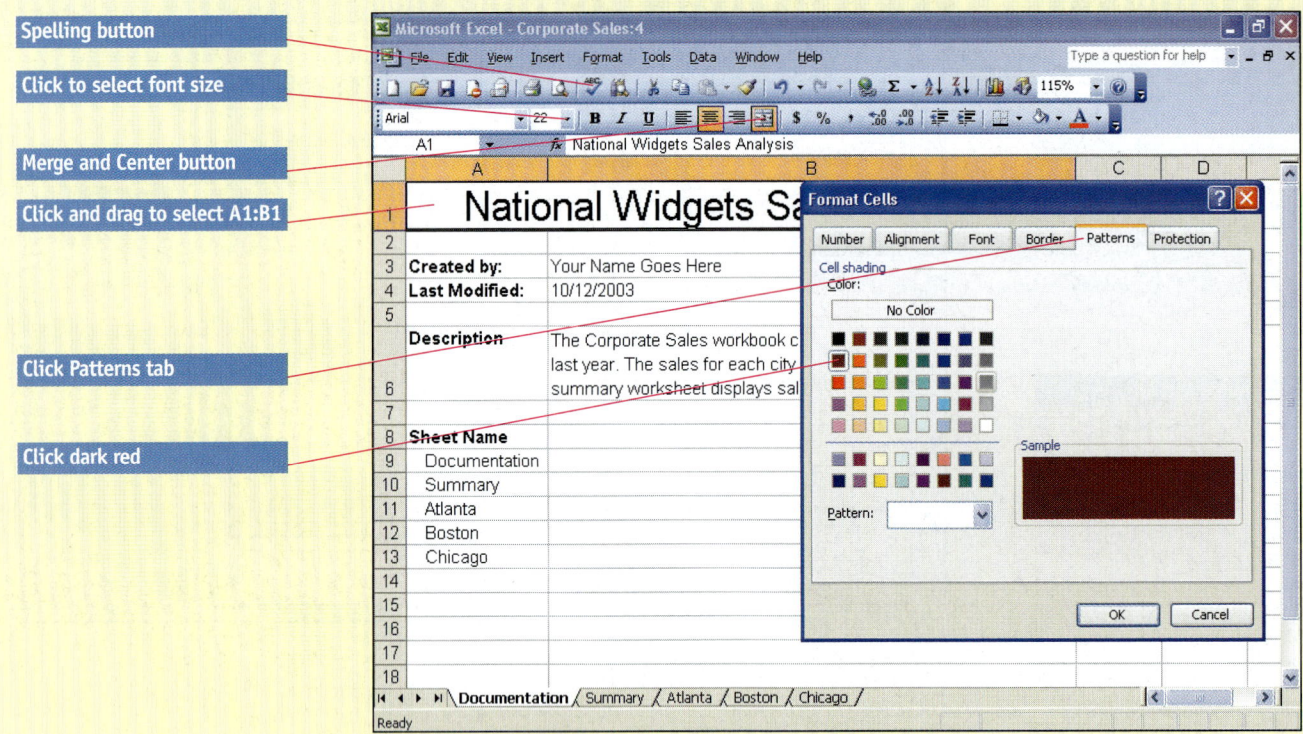

(c) Add the Worksheet Title (step 3)

FIGURE 5.10 Hands-on Exercise 3 (*continued*)

THE SPELL CHECK

Anyone familiar with a word processor takes the spell check for granted, but did you know the same capability exists within Excel? Click the Spelling button on the Standard toolbar to initiate the spell check, then implement corrections just as you do in Microsoft Word.

Step 4: **The Page Setup Command**

- If necessary, click the **Documentation tab** at the bottom of the window, then press and hold the **Shift key** as you click the tab for the **Chicago worksheet**. All five worksheet tabs should be selected, as shown in Figure 5.10d.

- Pull down the **File menu** and click the **Page Setup command** to display the Page Setup dialog box.
    - Click the **Header/Footer tab**. Click the **down arrow** on the Header list box and choose **Documentation** (the name of the worksheet). Click the **down arrow** on the Footer list box and choose **Corporate Sales** (the name of the workbook).
    - Click the **Margins tab**, then click the check box to center the worksheet horizontally. Change the top margin to **2 inches**.
    - Click the **Sheet tab**. Check the boxes to include row and column headings and gridlines. Click **OK** to exit the Page Setup dialog box.

- Save the workbook. Pull down the **File menu**. Click **Print** to display the Print dialog box. Click the option button to print the **Entire Workbook**. (Use the Preview command as necessary to ensure that the individual worksheets fit on a single page.) Click **OK**.

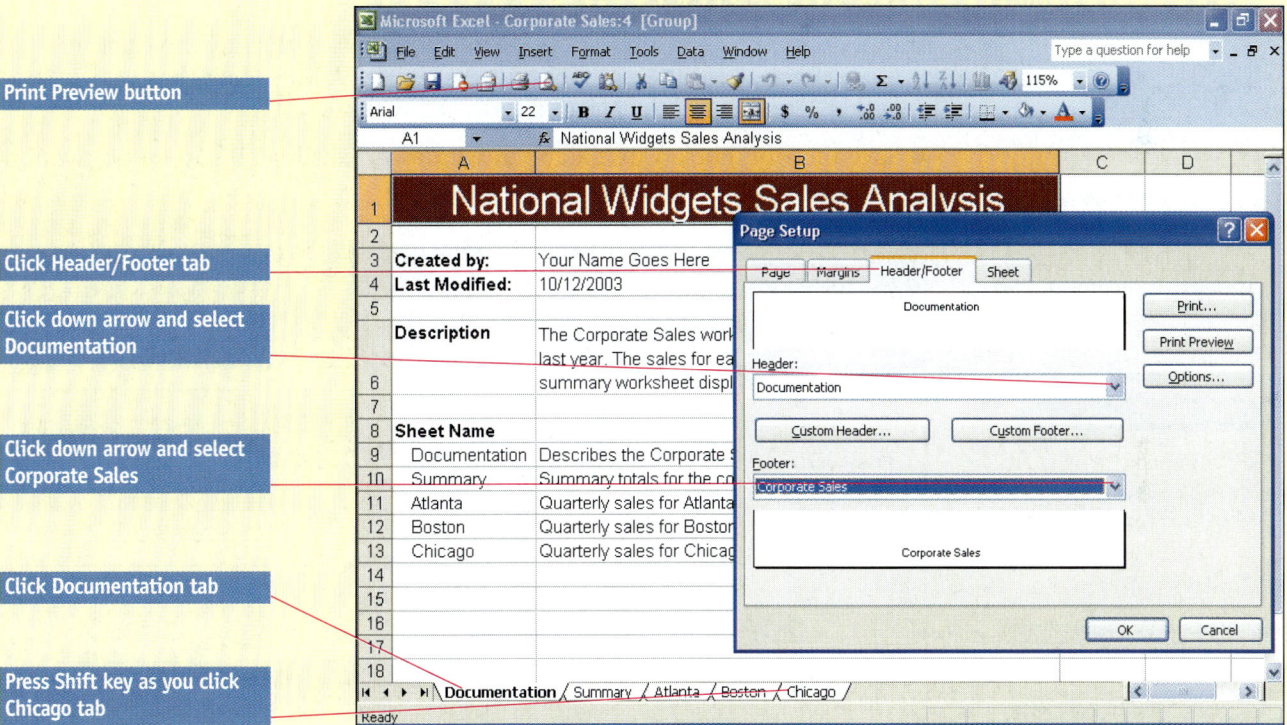

(d) The Page Setup Command (step 4)

FIGURE 5.10 Hands-on Exercise 3 (*continued*)

THE PRINT PREVIEW COMMAND

Use the Print Preview command to check the appearance of a worksheet to save time as well as paper. (Legend has it that the command was created by an unknown Microsoft programmer who tired of walking down the hall to pick up the printout.) You can execute the command by clicking the Print Preview button on the Standard toolbar or from the Print Preview command button within the Page Setup dialog box.

Step 5: **Print the Cell Formulas**

- Right click the **Summary tab** to display a context-sensitive menu, then click the **Ungroup Sheets command** to remove the group editing.

- Pull down the **View menu**, click **Custom Views** to display the Custom Views dialog box. Click the **Add button** to display the Add View dialog box.

- Enter **Displayed Values** as the name of the view (this is different from Figure 5.10e). Be sure that the Print Settings box is checked, and click **OK**.

- Press **Ctrl+`** to display the cell formulas. Double click the column borders between adjacent columns to increase the width of each column so that the cell formulas are completely visible.

- Pull down the **File menu** and click the **Page Setup command**. Click the **Page tab** and change to **Landscape orientation**. Click the option button to **Fit to 1 page**. Click **OK** to accept these settings and close the Page Setup dialog box. Click the **Print button** to print the summary worksheet.

- Pull down the **View menu**, click **Custom Views** to display the Custom View dialog box, then click the **Add button** to display the Add View dialog box. Enter **Cell Formulas** as shown in Figure 5.10f, verify that the Print Settings box is checked, and click **OK**.

- Pull down the **View menu**, click **Custom Views** to display the Custom View dialog box, then double click the **Displayed Values** view that was created earlier. You can switch back and forth at any time.

- Save the workbook. Close all open windows. Exit Excel if you do not want to continue with the next exercise at this time.

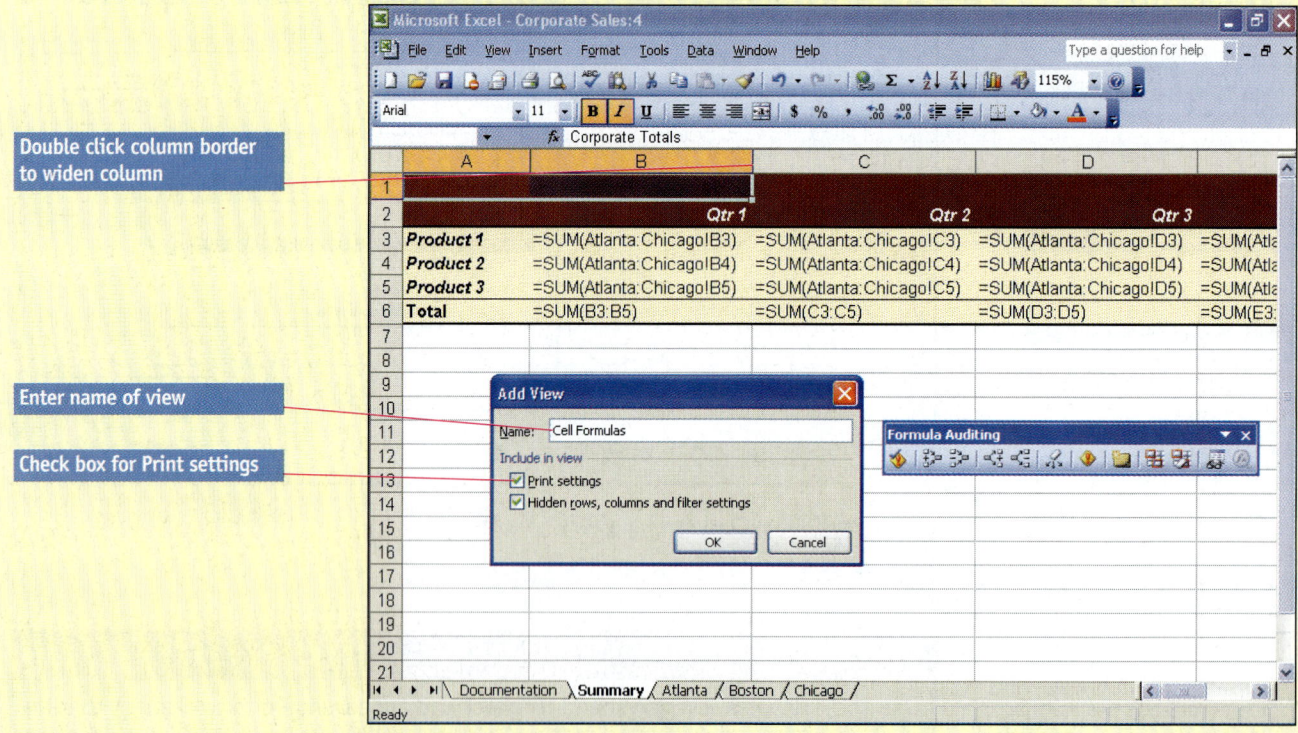

(e) Print the Cell Formulas (step 5)

FIGURE 5.10 Hands-on Exercise 3 (*continued*)

LINKING WORKBOOKS

There are two approaches to combining data from multiple sources. You can store all of the data on separate sheets in a single workbook, then create a summary worksheet within that workbook that references values in the other worksheets. Alternatively, you can retain the source data in separate workbooks, and create a summary workbook that references (links to) those workbooks.

Linking is established through the creation of ***external references*** that specify a cell (or range of cells) in another workbook. The ***dependent workbook*** (the Corporate Links workbook in our next example) contains the external references and thus reflects (is dependent on) data in the source workbook(s). The ***source workbooks*** (the Atlanta, Boston, and Chicago workbooks in our example) contain the data referenced by the dependent workbook.

Figure 5.11 illustrates the use of linking within the context of the example we have been using. Four different workbooks are open, each with one worksheet. The Corporate Links workbook is the dependent workbook and contains external references to obtain the summary totals. The Atlanta, Boston, and Chicago workbooks are the source workbooks.

Cell B3 is the active cell, and its contents are displayed in the formula bar. The corporate sales for Product 1 in the first quarter are calculated by summing the corresponding values in the source workbooks. Note how the workbook names are enclosed in square brackets to indicate the external references to the Atlanta, Boston, and Chicago workbooks.

The formulas to compute the corporate totals for Product 1 in the second, third, and fourth quarters contain external references similar to those shown in the formula bar. The ***workbook references*** and sheet references are absolute, whereas the cell reference may be relative (as in this example) or absolute. Once the formula has been entered into cell B3, it may be copied to the remaining cells in this row to compute the totals for Product 1 in the remaining quarters.

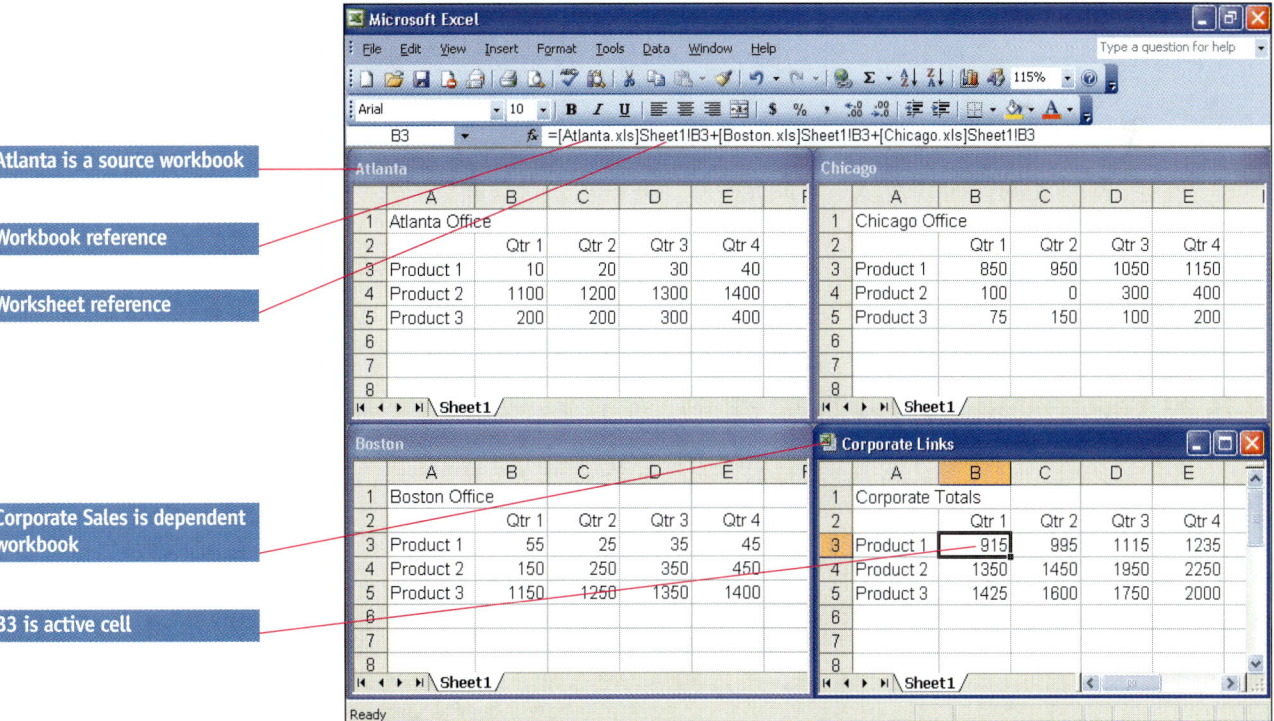

FIGURE 5.11 File Linking

hands-on exercise
4 Linking Workbooks

Objective To create a dependent workbook with external references to multiple source workbooks; to use pointing to create the external reference rather than entering the formula explicitly. Use Figure 5.12 as a guide in doing the exercise.

Step 1: **Open the Workbooks**

- Start Excel. If necessary, click the **New Workbook button** on the Standard toolbar to open a new workbook.

- Delete all worksheets except for Sheet1. Save the workbook as **Corporate Links** in the **Exploring Excel folder**.

- Pull down the **File menu**. Click **Open** to display the Open dialog box. Click the **Atlanta workbook**. Press and hold the **Ctrl key** as you click the **Boston** and **Chicago workbooks** to select all three workbooks at the same time as shown in Figure 5.12a.

- Click **Open** to open the selected workbooks. The workbooks will be opened one after another, with a brief message appearing on the status bar as each workbook is opened.

- Pull down the **Window menu**, which should indicate four open workbooks at the bottom of the menu. Click **Arrange** to display the Arrange Windows dialog box. If necessary, select the **Tiled option**, then click **OK**.

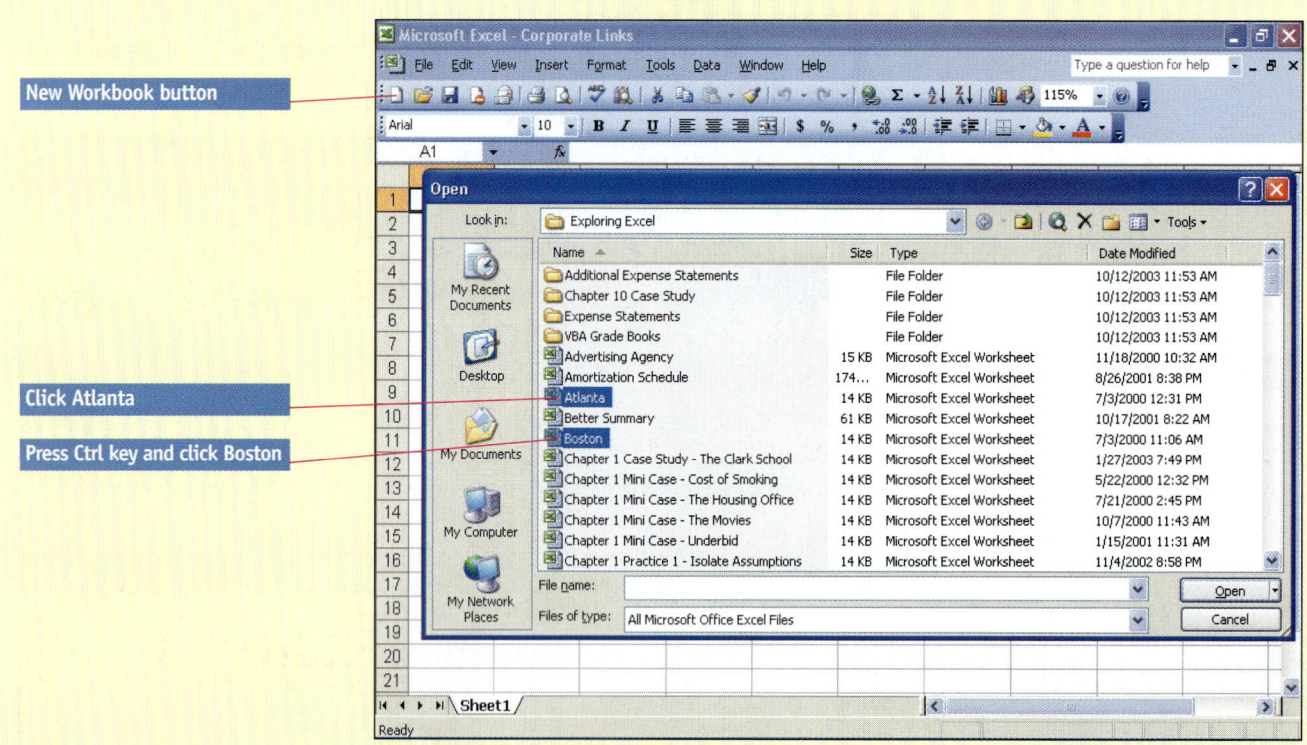

(a) Open the Workbooks (step 1)

FIGURE 5.12 Hands-on Exercise 4

1236 CHAPTER 5: CONSOLIDATING DATA

Step 2: **The AutoFill Command**

- You should see four open workbooks as shown in Figure 5.12b, although the row and column labels have not yet been entered in the Corporate Links workbook. (Do not be concerned if your workbooks are arranged differently.)

- Click in **cell A1** in the **Corporate Links workbook** to make this the active cell in the active workbook. Enter **Corporate Totals**.

- Click **cell B2**. Enter **Qtr 1**. Click in **cell B2**, then point to the fill handle in the lower-right corner. The mouse pointer changes to a thin crosshair.

- Drag the fill handle over **cells C2**, **D2, and E2**. A border appears, to indicate the destination range. Release the mouse. Cells C2 through E2 contain the labels Qtr 2, Qtr 3, and Qtr 4, respectively.

- Right-align the entries in **cells B2 through E2**, then reduce the column widths so that you can see the entire worksheet in the window.

- Click **cell A3**. Enter **Product 1**. Use the AutoFill capability to enter the labels **Product 2** and **Product 3** in cells A4 and A5.

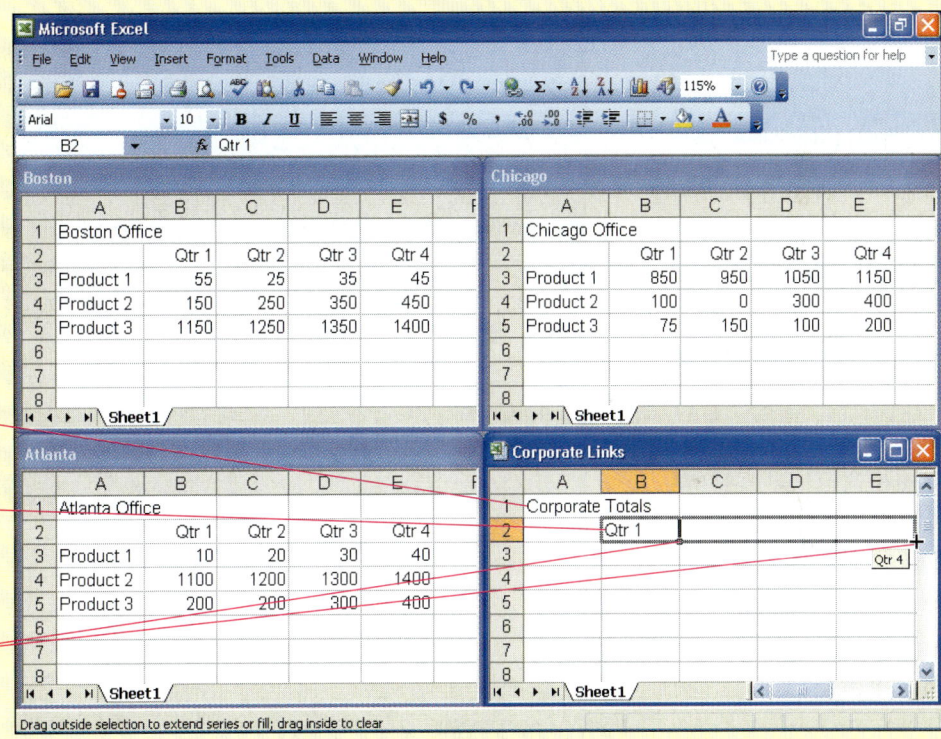

(b) The AutoFill Command (step 2)

FIGURE 5.12 Hands-on Exercise 4 (*continued*)

CREATE A CUSTOM SERIES

The AutoFill command is the fastest way to enter a series into adjacent cells. Type the first entry in the series (such as January, Monday, or Quarter 1), then click and drag the fill handle to adjacent cells to complete the series. You can also create your own series. Pull down the Tools menu, click Options, click the Custom Lists tab, and select New List. Enter the items in your series separated by commas (e.g., Tom, Dick, and Harry), click Add, and click OK. The next time you type Tom, Dick, or Harry in a cell you can use the fill handle to complete the series.

Step 3: **File Linking**

- Click **cell B3** of the **Corporate Links workbook**. Enter an **equal sign** so that you can create the formula by pointing.

- Click in the window for the **Atlanta workbook**. Click **cell B3**. The formula bar should display =[ATLANTA.XLS]Sheet1!$B$3. Press the **F4 key** continually until the cell reference changes to B3.

- Enter a **plus sign**. Click in the window for the **Boston workbook**. Click **cell B3**. The formula expands to include +[BOSTON.XLS]Sheet1!$B$3. Press the **F4 key** continually until the cell reference changes to B3.

- Enter a **plus sign**. Click in the window for the **Chicago workbook**. Click **cell B3**. The formula expands to include +[CHICAGO.XLS]Sheet1!$B$3. Press the **F4 key** continually until the cell reference changes to B3.

- Press **Enter**. The formula is complete, and you should see 915 in cell B3 of the Corporate Links workbook. Click in **cell B3**. The entry on the formula bar should match the entry in Figure 5.12c.

- Save the workbook.

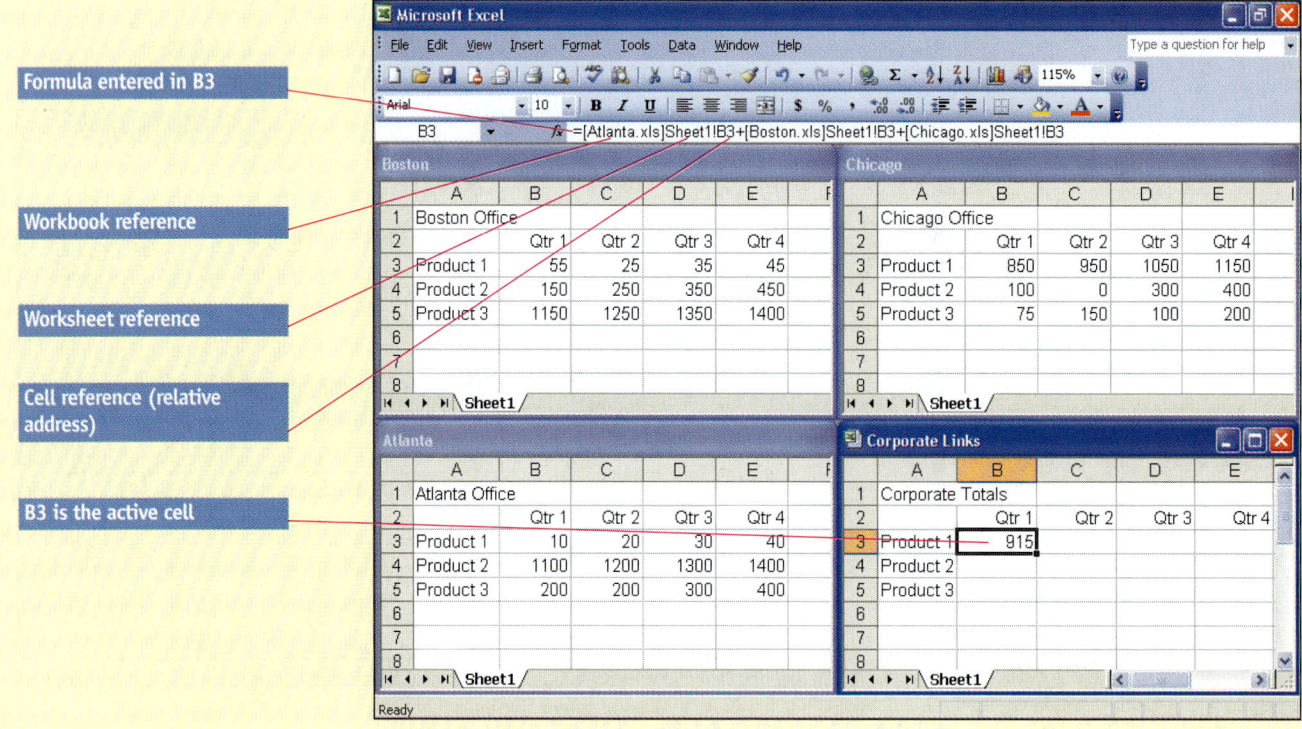

(c) File Linking (step 3)

FIGURE 5.12 Hands-on Exercise 4 (*continued*)

THE F4 KEY

The F4 key cycles through relative, absolute, and mixed addresses. Click on any reference within the formula bar; for example, click on A1 in the formula =A1+A2. Press the F4 key once, and it changes to an absolute reference, $A$1. Press the F4 key a second time, and it becomes a mixed reference, A$1; press it again, and it is a different mixed reference, $A1. Press the F4 key a fourth time, and it returns to the original relative address, A1.

Step 4: **Copy the Cell Formulas**

- If necessary, click **cell B3** in the **Corporate Links workbook**, then drag the fill handle over **cells C3 through E3** to copy this formula to the remaining cells in row 3.

- Be sure that cells B3 through E3 are still selected, then drag the fill handle to **cell E5**. You should see the total sales for all products in all quarters as shown in Figure 5.12d.

- Click **cell E5** to view the copied formula as shown in the figure. Note that the workbook and sheet references are the same but that the cell references have adjusted.

- Save the workbook.

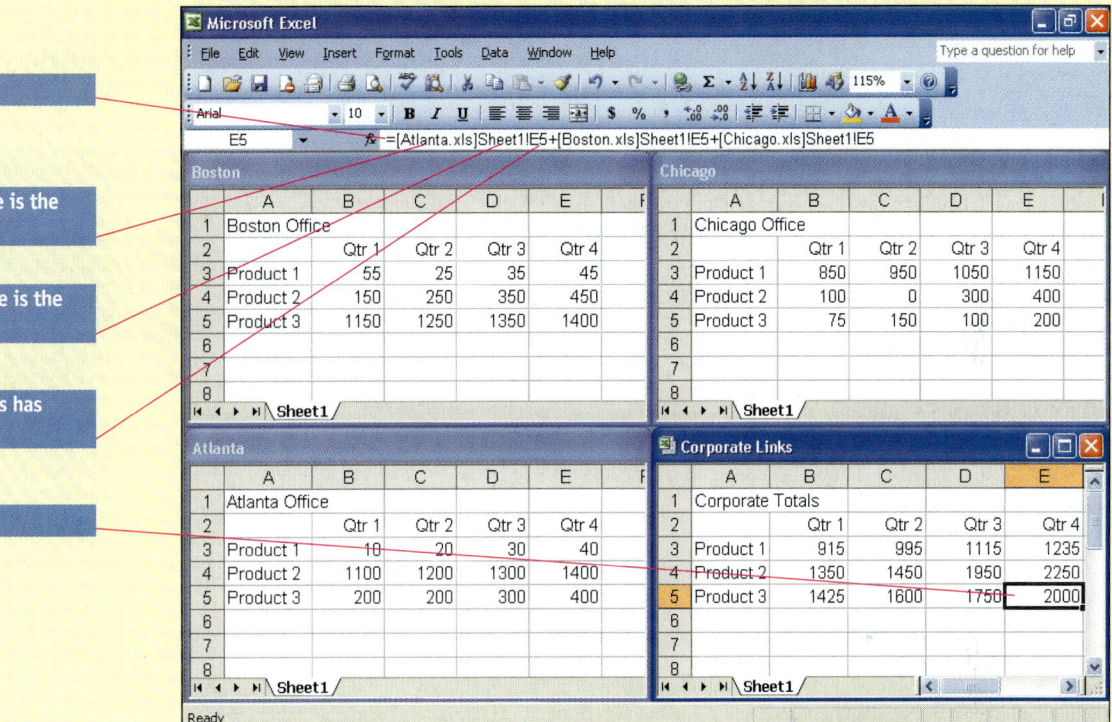

(d) Copy the Cell Formulas (step 4)

FIGURE 5.12 Hands-on Exercise 4 (*continued*)

DRIVE AND FOLDER REFERENCE

An external reference is updated regardless of whether or not the source workbook is open. The reference is displayed differently, depending on whether or not the source workbook is open. The references include the path (the drive and folder) if the source workbook is closed; the path is not shown if the source workbook is open. The external workbooks must be available to update the summary workbook. If the location of the workbooks changes (as may happen if you copy the workbooks to a different folder), pull down the Edit menu and click the Links command, then change the source of the external data.

Step 5: **Create a Workspace**

- Pull down the **File menu** and click the **Save Workspace command** to display the Save Workspace dialog box in Figure 5.12e.

- If necessary, click the **down arrow** in the Save in list box to select the **Exploring Excel folder**. Enter **Linked Workbooks** as the file name. Click the **Save button** in the dialog box to save the workspace. Click **Yes** if asked whether to save the changes to the Corporate Links workbook.

- The workspace is saved and you can continue to work as usual. The advantage of the workspace is that you can open all four workbooks with a single command.

- Click the **Close button** in each window to close all four workbooks. Pull down the **File menu**, click the **Open command**, then open the **Linked Workbooks** workspace that you just created.

- Click **Update** when asked whether you want to update the links within the Corporate Links workbook. All four workbooks are open as before.

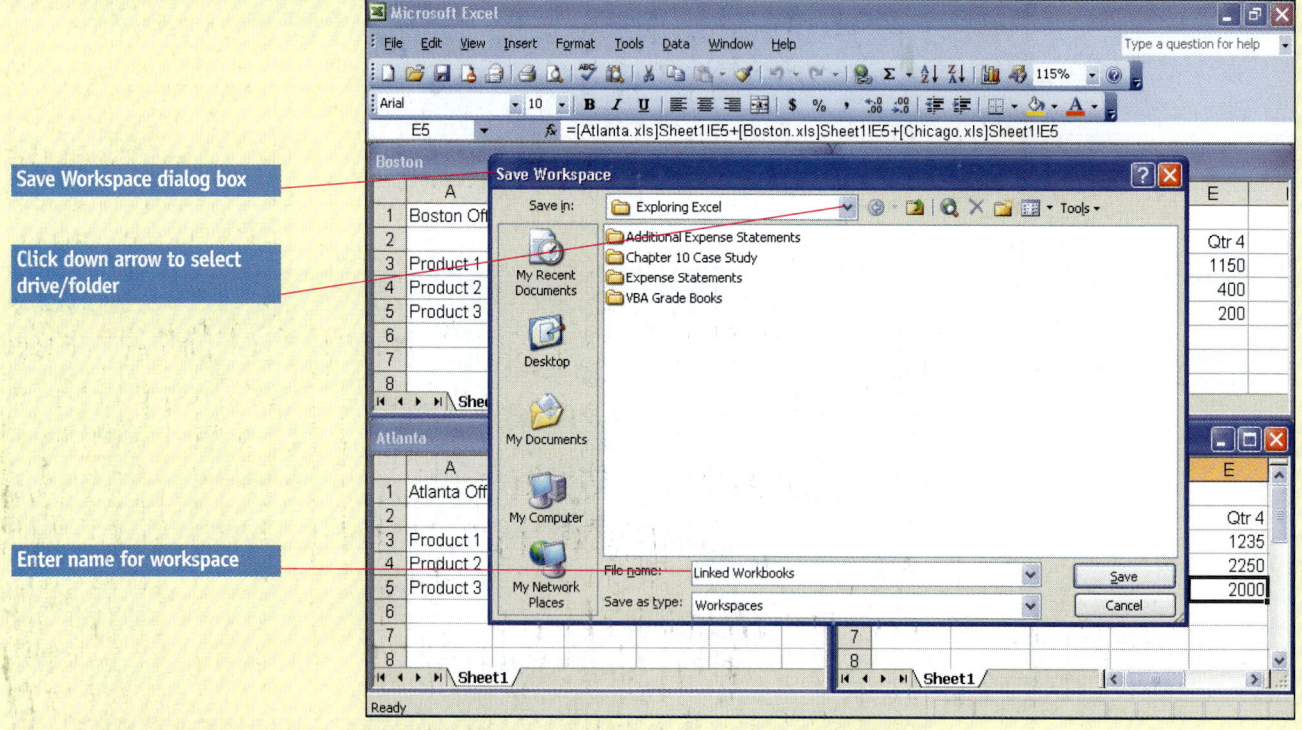

(e) Create a Workspace (step 5)

FIGURE 5.12 Hands-on Exercise 4 (*continued*)

THE WORKSPACE

A workspace enables you to open multiple workbooks in a single step, and further, will retain the arrangement of those workbooks within the Excel window. The workspace file does not contain the workbooks themselves, however, and thus you must continue to save changes you make to the individual workbooks.

Step 6: **Change the Data**

- Click **cell B3** in the **Corporate Links workbook** to make it the active cell. Note that the value displayed in the cell is 915.

- Pull down the **File menu**. Click **Close**. Answer **Yes** if asked whether to save the changes.

- Click in the window containing the **Chicago workbook**, click **cell B3**, enter **250**, and press **Enter**. Pull down the **File menu**. Click **Close**. Answer **Yes** if asked whether to save the changes. Only two workbooks, Atlanta and Boston, are now open.

- Pull down the **File menu** and open the **Corporate Links workbook**. You should see the dialog box in Figure 5.12f, asking whether to update the links. (Note that cell B3 still displays 915). Click **Update** to update the links.

- The value in cell B3 of the Corporate Links workbook changes to 315 to reflect the change in the Chicago workbook, even though the latter is closed.

- If necessary, click in **cell B3**. The formula bar displays the contents of this cell, which include the drive and folder reference for the Chicago workbook, because the workbook is closed.

- Close the Atlanta and Boston workbooks. Close the Corporate Links workbook. Click **Yes** if asked whether to save the changes.

- Saving the source workbook(s) before the dependent workbook ensures that the formulas in the source workbooks are calculated, and that all external references in the dependent workbook reflect current values.

- Exit Excel. Congratulations on a job well done.

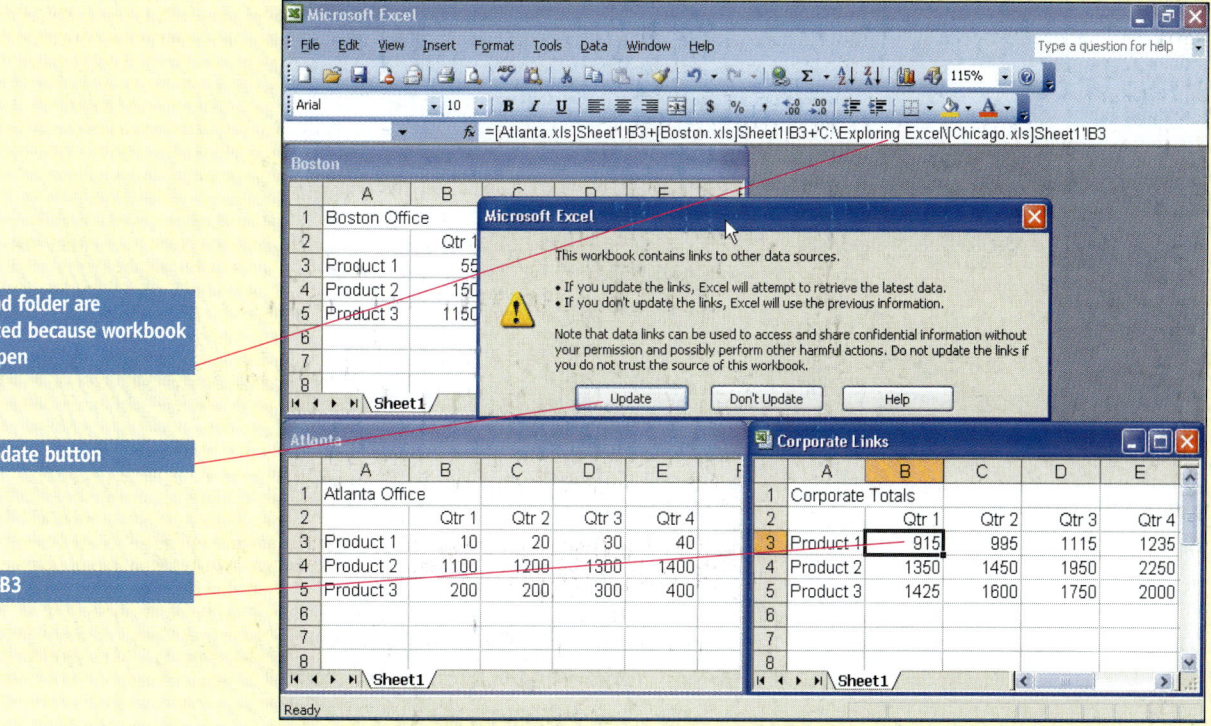

(f) Change the Data (step 6)

FIGURE 5.12 Hands-on Exercise 4 (*continued*)

SUMMARY

The chapter showed how to combine data from different sources into a summary report. The example is quite common and applicable to any business scenario requiring both detail and summary reports. One approach is to store all of the data in separate sheets of a single workbook, then summarize the data in a summary worksheet within that workbook. Alternatively, the source data can be kept in separate workbooks and consolidated through linking to a summary workbook. Both approaches are equally valid, and the choice depends on where you want to keep the source data.

An Excel workbook may contain up to 255 worksheets, each of which is identified by a tab at the bottom of the window. Worksheets may be added, deleted, moved, copied, or renamed through a shortcut menu. The color of the worksheet tab may also be changed. The highlighted tab indicates the active worksheet.

A worksheet reference is required to indicate a cell in another worksheet of the same workbook. An exclamation point separates the worksheet reference from the cell reference; e.g., =Atlanta!C3 references cell C3 in the Atlanta worksheet. The worksheet reference is absolute and remains the same when the formula is copied. The cell reference may be relative or absolute. A 3-D reference refers to a cell or range in another worksheet.

The best way to enter a reference to a cell in a different worksheet (or in a different workbook) is by pointing. Click in the cell that is to contain the formula, type an equal sign, click the worksheet tab that contains the external reference, then click in the appropriate cell. Use the F4 key as you select the cell to switch between relative, absolute, and mixed cell references.

Multiple worksheets may be selected (grouped) to execute the same commands on all of the selected worksheets simultaneously. You can, for example, insert formulas to sum a row or column and/or format the selected worksheets. The AutoFormat command provides access to a predefined set of formats that includes font size, color, boldface, alignment, and other attributes that can be applied automatically to a selected range.

A workbook should be clearly organized so that the purpose of every worksheet is evident. One way of documenting a workbook is through the creation of a documentation worksheet that describes the purpose of each worksheet within the workbook. Multiple worksheets (workbooks) can be displayed at one time, with each worksheet contained in its own window within the Excel application window. The Arrange command in the Window menu is used to tile or cascade the individual worksheets (workbooks).

A workbook may also be linked to cells in other workbooks through an external reference that specifies a cell (or range of cells) in a source workbook. The dependent workbook contains the external references and uses (is dependent on) the data in the source workbook(s). The external workbooks must be available to update the summary workbook. If the location of the workbooks changes (as may happen if you copy the workbooks to a different folder), pull down the Edit menu and click the Links command, then change the source of the external data.

KEY TERMS

3-D reference 1220	Dependent workbook 1235	New Window command 1212
Arrange command 1212	Documentation worksheet 1229	Source workbook 1235
AutoFormat command 1221	External reference 1235	Workbook properties 1230
AutoSum 1226	Grouping worksheets 1221	Workbook reference 1235
Custom view 1234	Linking 1235	Worksheet reference 1219

MULTIPLE CHOICE

1. Which of the following is true regarding workbooks and worksheets?
    (a) A workbook contains one or more worksheets
    (b) Only one worksheet can be selected at a time within a workbook
    (c) Every workbook contains the same number of worksheets
    (d) All of the above

2. Assume that a workbook contains three worksheets. How many cells are included in the function =SUM(Sheet1:Sheet3!A1)?
    (a) Three
    (b) Four
    (c) Twelve
    (d) Twenty-four

3. Assume that a workbook contains three worksheets. How many cells are included in the function =SUM(Sheet1:Sheet3!A1:B4)?
    (a) Three
    (b) Four
    (c) Twelve
    (d) Twenty-four

4. Which of the following is the preferred way to sum the value of cell A1 from three different worksheets?
    (a) =Sheet1!A1+Sheet2!A1+Sheet3!A1
    (b) =SUM(Sheet1:Sheet3!A1)
    (c) Both (a) and (b) are equally good
    (d) Neither (a) nor (b)

5. The reference CIS120!$A$2:
    (a) Is an absolute reference to cell A2 in the CIS120 workbook
    (b) Is a relative reference to cell A2 in the CIS120 workbook
    (c) Is an absolute reference to cell A2 in the CIS120 worksheet
    (d) Is a relative reference to cell A2 in the CIS120 worksheet

6. What does City! refer to in the reference City!A1:F9?
    (a) A cell range
    (b) An error in a formula
    (c) A workbook
    (d) A worksheet

7. Which of the following is true about the reference Sheet1:Sheet3!A1:B2?
    (a) The worksheet reference is relative, the cell reference is absolute
    (b) The worksheet reference is absolute, the cell reference is relative
    (c) The worksheet and cell references are absolute
    (d) The worksheet and cell references are relative

8. You are in the Ready mode and are positioned in cell B2 of Sheet1. You enter an equal sign, click the worksheet tab for Sheet2, click cell B1, and press Enter.
    (a) The content of cell B2 in Sheet1 is =Sheet2!B1
    (b) The content of cell B1 in Sheet2 is = Sheet1!B2
    (c) Both (a) and (b)
    (d) Neither (a) nor (b)

9. You are positioned in cell A10 of Sheet1. You enter an equal sign, click the worksheet tab for the worksheet called ThisYear, and click cell C10. You then enter a minus sign, click the worksheet tab for the worksheet called LastYear, click cell C10, and press Enter. What are the contents of cell A10?
    (a) =ThisYear:LastYear!C10
    (b) =(ThisYear–LastYear)!C10
    (c) =ThisYear!C10-LastYear!C10
    (d) =ThisYear:C10-LastYear:C10

10. Which of the following can be accessed from a shortcut menu?
    (a) Inserting or deleting a worksheet
    (b) Moving or copying a worksheet
    (c) Renaming a worksheet
    (d) All of the above

... continued

multiple choice

11. You are positioned in cell A1 of Sheet1 of Book1. You enter an equal sign, click in the open window for Book2, click the tab for Sheet1, click cell A1, then press the F4 key continually until you have a relative cell reference. What reference appears in the formula bar?

    (a) =[BOOK1.XLS]Sheet1!$A$1
    (b) =[BOOK1.XLS]Sheet1!A1
    (c) =[BOOK2.XLS]Sheet1!$A$1
    (d) =[BOOK2.XLS]Sheet1!A1

12. The Arrange Windows command can display:

    (a) Multiple worksheets from one workbook
    (b) One worksheet from multiple workbooks
    (c) Both (a) and (b)
    (d) Neither (a) nor (b)

13. Pointing can be used to reference a cell in:

    (a) A different worksheet
    (b) A different workbook
    (c) Both (a) and (b)
    (d) Neither (a) nor (b)

14. The appearance of [Group] within the title bar indicates that:

    (a) Multiple workbooks are open and are all active
    (b) Multiple worksheets are selected within the same workbook
    (c) Both (a) and (b)
    (d) Neither (a) nor (b)

15. Which of the following is true regarding the example on file linking that was developed in the chapter?

    (a) The Atlanta, Boston, and Chicago workbooks were dependent workbooks
    (b) The Linked workbook was a source workbook
    (c) Both (a) and (b)
    (d) Neither (a) nor (b)

16. The formula =Office1!A3+Office2!A3+Office3!A3

    (a) References the same cell in three different workbooks
    (b) References the same cell on three different worksheets in the same workbook
    (c) References the same cell on three different worksheets in three different workbooks
    (d) Impossible to determine

17. The formula =City1!$B$1+City2!$B$1+City3!$B$1 specifies that

    (a) The worksheet references are absolute and the cell references are relative
    (b) The worksheet references are relative and the cell references are absolute
    (c) Both the worksheet and the cell references are absolute
    (d) Both the worksheet and cell references are relative

18. Which of the following is a valid reference to an external workbook?

    (a) =Boston!B3
    (b) =Boston!Sheet2!B3
    (c) Both (a) and (b)
    (d) Neither (a) nor (b)

ANSWERS

1. a
2. a
3. d
4. b
5. c
6. d
7. b
8. a
9. c
10. d
11. d
12. c
13. c
14. b
15. d
16. b
17. c
18. d

PRACTICE WITH EXCEL

1. **Linking Worksheets:** The workbook in Figure 5.13 features a summary worksheet that displays exam results for multiple sections of an introductory computer course. It also contains an individual worksheet for each section of the course. Your assignment is to open the partially completed *Chapter 5 Practice 1* workbook in the Exploring Excel folder, compute the test averages for each section, and then create the summary worksheet.

    a. Select the worksheet for Section N. Press and hold the Shift key as you click the worksheet tab for Section S to group all of the worksheets. Click in cell B10 and enter the formula, =AVERAGE(B3:B8) to compute the average on the first test for the students in Section N. Copy this formula to cells C10 and D10. (The sections have different numbers of students, but the last student in every section appears in row 8 or before. The Average function ignores empty cells within the designated range and thus you can use the same function for all four worksheets.)

    b. Check that the worksheets are still grouped, and then apply the same formatting to each worksheet. You do not have to duplicate our formatting exactly, but you are to merge and center the name of the section in the first row, and use bold text and a colored background. Change the color of the worksheet tab to match the formatting in the worksheet. You will not see the color change until you ungroup the worksheets.

    c. Ungroup the worksheets, then insert a blank worksheet for the summary as shown in Figure 5.13. Enter the title and column headings as shown in rows 1 and 2. Click in cell A3 of the summary worksheet. Type an equal sign, click the Worksheet tab for Section N, click in cell A1 of this worksheet, then press Enter to display the section name in the summary worksheet. Enter the names of the other sections.

    d. Click in cell B3 of the summary worksheet. Type an equal sign, click the Worksheet tab for Section N, click in cell B10, then press Enter to obtain the class average for section N on test 1. Copy the formula in cell B1 to cells C1 and D1 of the summary worksheet. Enter the test grades for the other sections in similar fashion.

    e. Format the summary worksheet in a similar style to the detailed worksheets.

    f. Use the Page Setup command to create a custom footer for all worksheets that includes your name, the name on the worksheet tab, and today's date. Print the worksheet for section N and the summary worksheet for your instructor. Print both worksheets a second time to show the cell formulas rather than the displayed values.

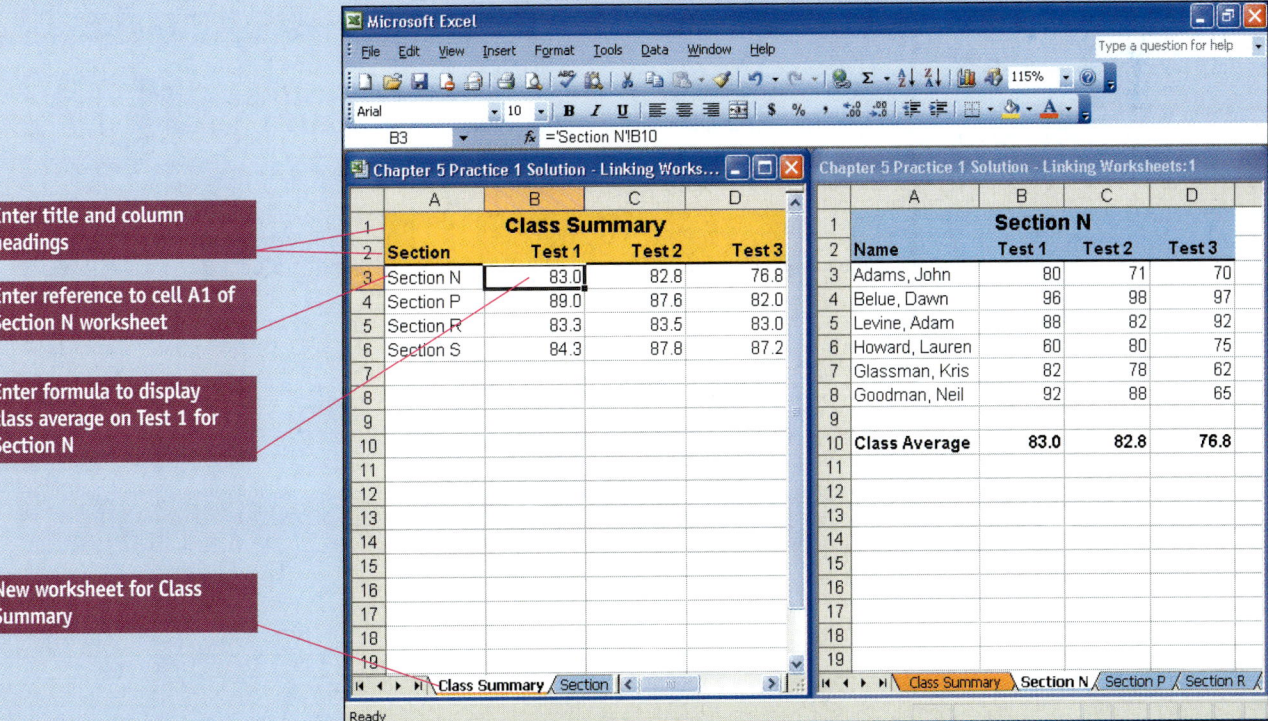

FIGURE 5.13 Linking Worksheets (exercise 1)

practice exercises

2. **Group Editing:** The workbook in Figure 5.14 contains a separate worksheet for each month of the year as well a summary worksheet for the entire year. Each monthly worksheet tallies the expenses for five divisions in each of four categories to compute a monthly total for each division. The summary worksheet is to display the total expense for each division. Thus far, however, only the months of January, February, and March are complete. Your assignment is to open the partially completed *Chapter 5 Practice 2* workbook in the Exploring Excel folder and proceed as follows:

   a. Insert a new worksheet for April to the right of the March worksheet and then enter the appropriate row and column headings. Assume that Division 1 spends $100 in each category, Division 2 spends $200 in each category, Division 3 spends $300 in each category, and so on. Change the worksheet tab to reflect April.

   b. Select the worksheet for January and then press and hold the Shift key as you click the worksheet tab for April. The title bar should reflect group editing. Click in cell F3 to compute the monthly total for Division 1, and then copy this formula to the remaining rows in this column. Compute the totals for each expense category in row eight.

   c. Format the worksheet in an attractive fashion. You do not have to match our formatting exactly, but you should include bold text, borders, and shaded cells as appropriate. Change the color of the worksheet tab. Right click any worksheet tab, click the Ungroup Worksheets command, then view the various monthly worksheets to verify that the formulas and formatting appear in each worksheet.

   d. Click the worksheet tab for the Summary worksheet. Insert a column for April to the right of the column for March. Click in cell B3, type an equal sign, click in the January worksheet, click in cell F3 (the cell that contains the January total for Division 1), and press Enter. Enter the formulas for the remaining months for Division 1 in similar fashion. Click in cell F3 and compute the year-to-date expenses for Division 1, then copy the formulas in cells B3 through F3 to the remaining rows in the Summary worksheet. Format the summary worksheet.

   e. Use the Page Setup command to create a custom footer for all worksheets that includes your name, the name on the worksheet tab, and today's date. Print the worksheet for April and the summary worksheet for your instructor. Print both worksheets a second time to show the cell formulas rather than the displayed values.

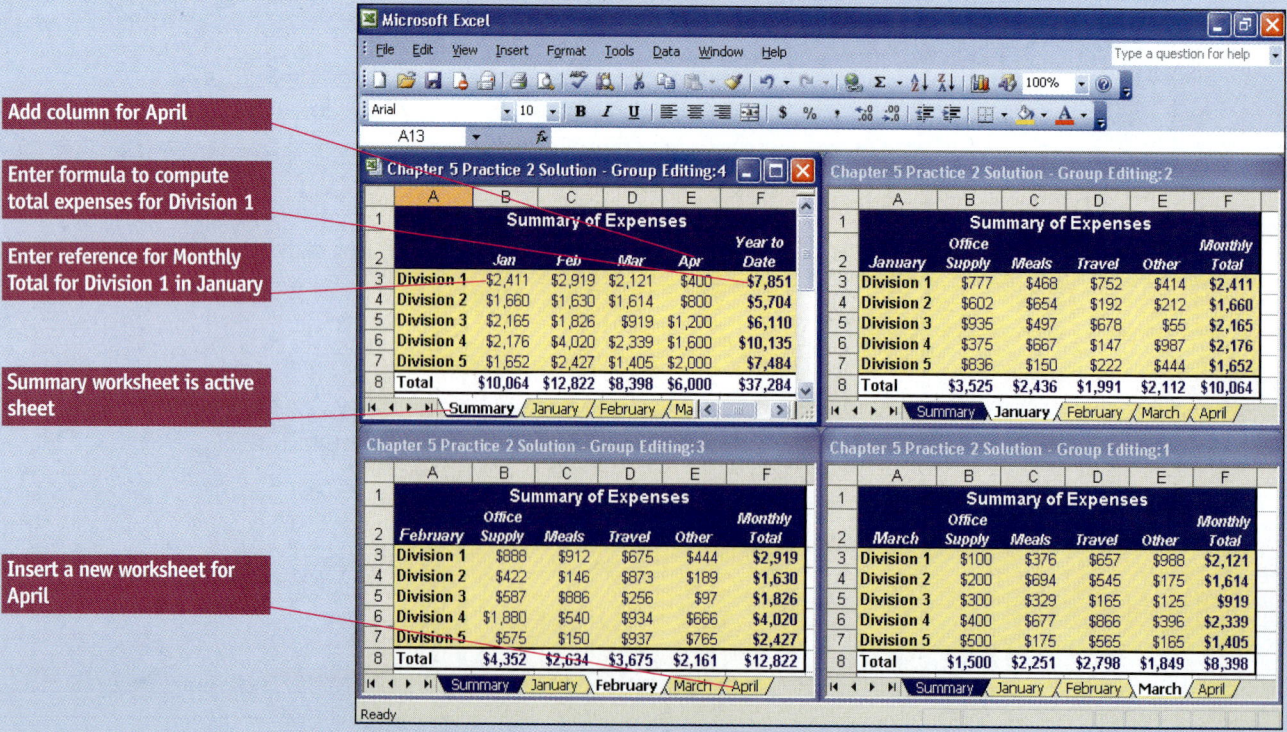

FIGURE 5.14 Group Editing (exercise 2)

practice exercises

3. **Object Linking and Embedding:** This exercise builds on the hands-on exercises within the chapter by creating a Word document that contains an Excel worksheet and associated chart. The chart is to be created in its own chart sheet within the Corporate Sales workbook and then incorporated into the memo. Proceed as follows:

   a. Start Word. Create a simple document that describes the corporate performance as shown in Figure 5.15. You do not have to match our document exactly, but you are required to create a letterhead and include your instructor's name and your name as indicated.

   b. Open the *Corporate Sales* workbook from the third hands-on exercise. Click the worksheet tab that contains the summary data, click and drag to select the completed worksheet, and then click the Copy button. Return to the Word document and click below the first paragraph. Pull down the Edit menu and click the Paste Special command to display the Paste Special dialog box. Select Microsoft Excel Worksheet Object in the displayed list, click the Paste Link button, and then click OK to insert the worksheet. Do not worry about the size or position at this time. Move the cursor so that it is below the worksheet. Add two or three blank lines.

   c. Return to the Excel workbook. Create a side-by-side column chart (in its own chart sheet) that plots the data in rows; that is, the X axis should display the four quarters, and the legend should display the product names. Use the same technique as in part (b) to link the side-by-side column chart to the Word document. Move and size the chart within the memo as necessary. You may find it convenient to change the zoom specification to "Whole Page" so that you can position the chart more easily.

   d. Save the completed document. Print the completed document for your instructor.

   e. Prove to yourself that Object Linking and Embedding really works by returning to the Atlanta worksheet *after* you have created the document in Figure 5.15. Change the sales for product 1 in Quarter 4 to $3,000. Switch back to the Word memo, and the chart should reflect the increase in the sales for product 1. Add a postscript to the memo indicating that the corrected chart reflects the last-minute sale of product 1 in Atlanta, and that you no longer want to discontinue the product. Print the revised memo and submit it to your instructor with the earlier version.

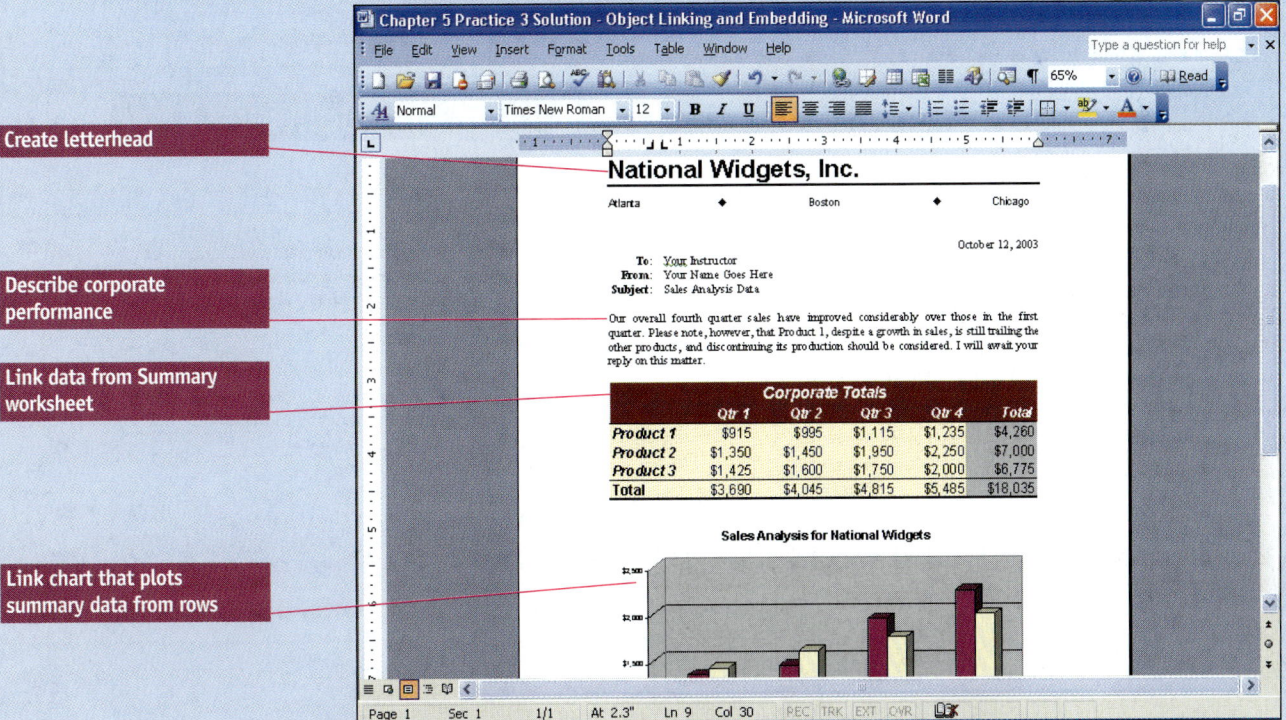

FIGURE 5.15 Object Linking and Embedding (exercise 3)

practice exercises

4. **National Computers:** You will find a partially completed version of the workbook in Figure 5.16 in the *Chapter 5 Practice 4* workbook in the Exploring Excel folder. That workbook has four partially completed worksheets, one for each city. Your assignment is to complete the workbook so that it parallels the Corporate Sales workbook that was used in the first three hands-on exercises in this chapter. Proceed as follows:

   a. Complete the individual worksheets by adding the appropriate formulas to compute the necessary row and column totals, then format these worksheets in attractive fashion. You can apply your own formatting, or you can use the AutoFormat command. You will find it easier, however, to use the group editing feature as you add the totals and apply the formatting, since all of the worksheets contain parallel data. Be sure to ungroup the worksheets after you have applied the formatting.

   b. Add a summary worksheet that provides corporate totals by product line. Apply the formatting from the individual worksheets to the summary worksheet.

   c. Create two side-by-side column charts, each in its own chart sheet, which display the summary information in graphical fashion. One chart should compare the sales revenue for each city by product, the other should compare the revenue for each product by city.

   d. Add a documentation worksheet similar to the worksheet in Figure 5.16. Change the color of the worksheet tabs as appropriate.

   e. Select the first worksheet, then press and hold the Shift key as you click the last worksheet tab to turn on the group editing feature. Use the Page Setup command to create a custom footer that includes your name, the name on the worksheet tab and today's date. Ungroup the worksheets, then change the orientation for the chart sheets to landscape.

   f. Print the entire workbook for your instructor. Print the Corporate (summary) worksheet a second time to show the cell formulas. (Change to landscape printing if necessary.)

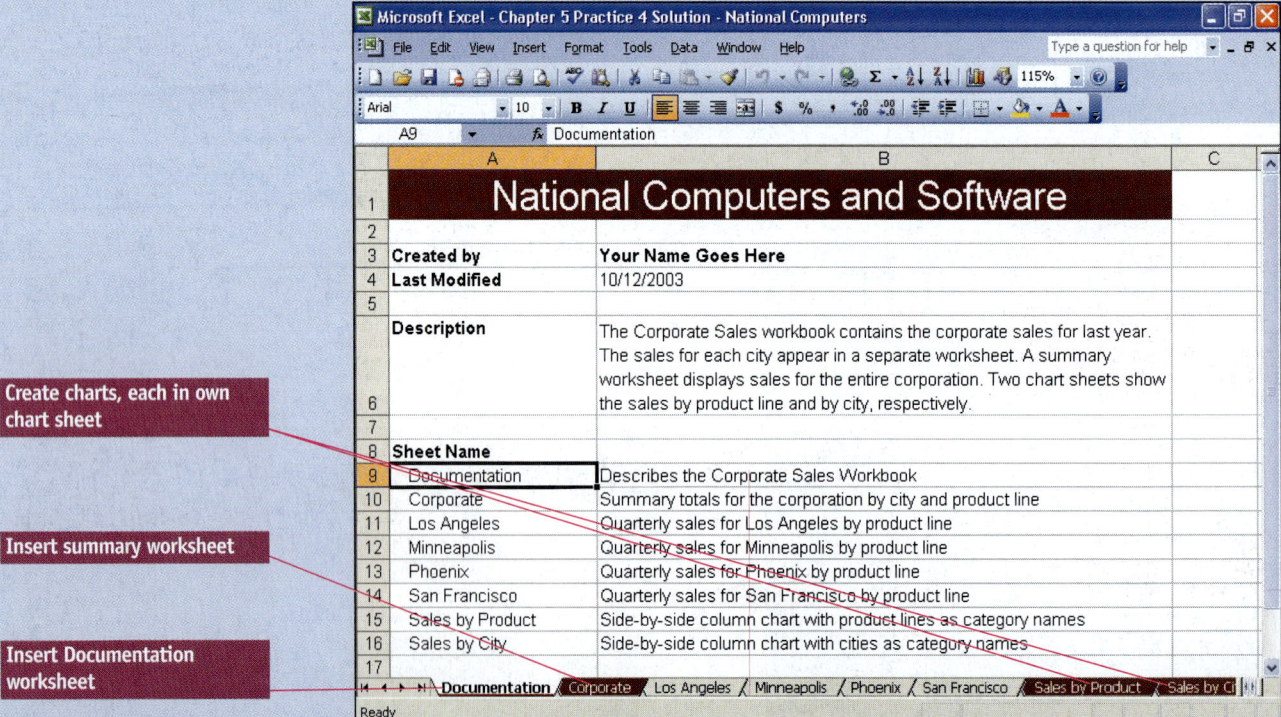

FIGURE 5.16 National Computers (exercise 4)

practice exercises

5. **The Stock Portfolio:** The workbook in Figure 5.17 uses Web queries (discussed in Chapter 2) to obtain current stock quotations from the Web, then uses those prices within an Excel workbook. The workbook contains five worksheets in all—a worksheet for each of three clients, Tom, Dick, and Harry; a worksheet containing stock prices as retrieved by the Web query; and a summary worksheet that shows the gain or loss for each client. Your assignment is to open the partially completed workbook in *Chapter 5 Practice 5*, and complete the workbook as follows.

   a. Complete the individual worksheets for Tom, Dick, and Harry by entering the appropriate formulas to obtain the current price of each company in the client's portfolio, then determining the value of that investment by multiplying the price times the number of shares. Tom, for example, has AOL in his portfolio, the current price of which is found in cell D11 of the Stock Prices worksheet. Compute the gain or loss for each investment, based on the difference between today's price and the purchase price.

   b. Update the current price of each client's portfolio by right clicking anywhere within the table of prices in the Stock Prices worksheet, then clicking the Refresh Data command. (The stock symbols that appear at the top of the Stock Prices worksheet were entered manually from the investments in the individual worksheets and are the basis of the Web query.)

   c. Enter the summary data for each client in the Summary worksheet using appropriate worksheet references. The total cost of Tom's portfolio, for example, is $9,260 and is found in cell E7 of Tom's worksheet. Thus, the corresponding entry in the summary worksheet would be =Tom!E7, indicating that the number is to come from this cell in Tom's worksheet.

   d. Add your name in row 9 of the summary worksheet as the investment adviser. Print the entire workbook for your instructor.

   e. Print the cell formulas for the summary worksheet. Add a cover sheet and submit the entire assignment to your instructor.

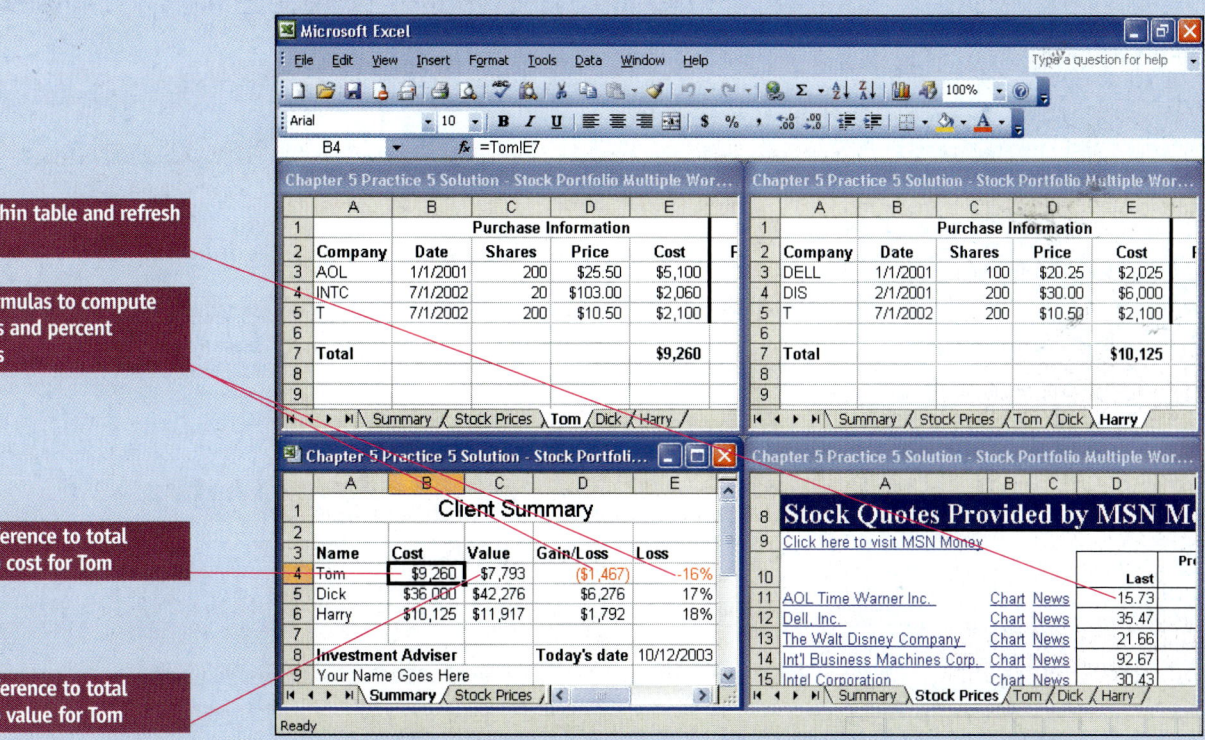

FIGURE 5.17 The Stock Portfolio (exercise 5)

practice exercises

6. **Weekly Sales:** The workbook in Figure 5.18 contains seven worksheets that provide detailed information on last week's sales for the Definitely Needlepoint boutique. The daily worksheets contain sales data for the indicated day of the week and are identical to one another except for the specific data. The summary worksheet displays the information for each day and computes the weekly total of all receipts in cell H13. In similar fashion, the total sales (across all categories of merchandise) are computed in cell H21, and the value should equal the value in cell H13. Open the *Chapter 5 Practice 6* workbook and complete the summary worksheet.

   a. Select the Monday worksheet. Press and hold the Shift key as you click the worksheet tab for Saturday, so that all six worksheets are selected and the Group editing formula is turned on. Enter the appropriate formulas and/or functions in the Monday worksheet to compute the totals in cells B6, B12, B13, and B21.

   b. Click the Weekly Summary worksheet tab (which also turns off the Group editing feature). Click in cell B4. Type an equal sign, click the worksheet tab for Monday, click in cell B4 of this worksheet, then press the Enter key. Enter the appropriate worksheet references for the remaining days of the week in similar fashion. Click in cell H4, then click the Sum button on the Standard toolbar to obtain the weekly total.

   c. Click and drag to select cells B4 through H4. Click the Copy button. Click and drag to select cells B5 through H21. Pull down the Edit menu, click the Paste Special command, then click the option button to paste the formulas. Delete the entries in cells B14 through H15 because these cells should not contain any formulas.

   d. Enter an IF function in cell A22 that compares the total payments in cell H13 to the total in cell H21. The numbers should be equal; if not, there is a potential accounting error somewhere in the worksheet. Use conditional formatting to display the text in blue or red, depending on whether the numbers check or are in error. (A similar IF function has been entered for you on the daily worksheets in cell A22.)

   e. Use the Page Setup command to create a custom footer for all worksheets that includes your name, the name on the worksheet tab, and today's date. Print the summary worksheet. (Use landscape orientation.) Print the summary worksheet a second time to show the cell formulas.

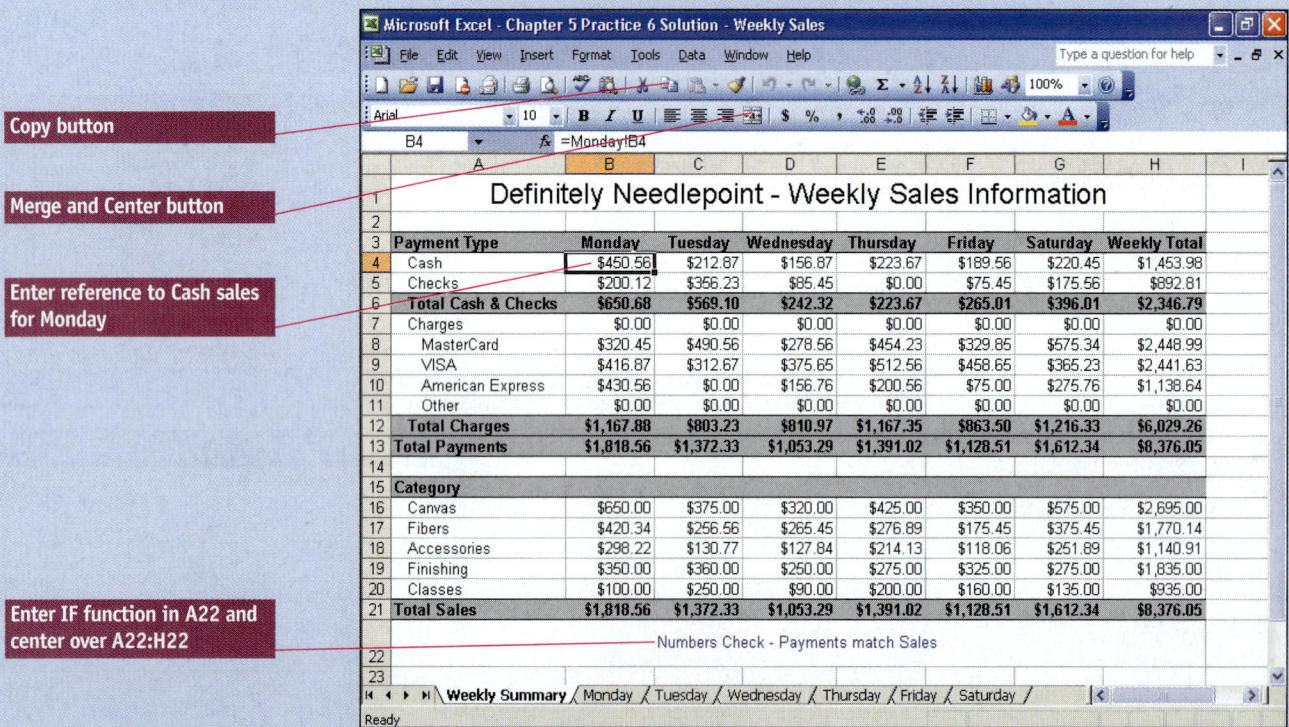

FIGURE 5.18 Weekly Sales (exercise 6)

practice exercises

7. **Pivot Tables:** A pivot table is an extremely flexible tool that enables you to manipulate the data in multiple worksheets to produce new reports as shown in Figure 5.19. (Pivot tables are covered in more detail in Chapter 7.) Complete the first three hands-on exercises, then follow the instructions below:

   a. Open the Corporate Sales workbook that was completed at the end of the third hands-on exercise. Pull down the Data menu and click the Pivot Table and PivotChart Report command. Click the option buttons to select Multiple Consolidation Ranges and to specify Pivot Table. Click Next.

   b. Click the option button that says I will create the page fields. Click Next.

   c. Specify the range in step 2b of the PivotTable Wizard through pointing. Click the Sheet tab for Atlanta, select cells A2 through E5, then click the Add command button. You should see Atlanta!A$2:$E$5 in the All Ranges list box. Repeat this step for the other two cities.

   d. Remain in step 2b of the PivotTable Wizard. Click the option button for 1 page field. Select (click) the Atlanta range within the All Ranges list box, then click in the Field One list box and type Atlanta. Do not press the Enter key. Select (click) the Boston range within the All ranges list box, then click in the Field One list box and type Boston. Repeat this step for Chicago.

   e. Click Next. Click the option button to create the pivot table on a New Worksheet. Click Finish.

   f. You have a pivot table, but it does not match our figure. Click in cell B3 (the entry in the cell is Column), then click the formula bar and type Quarter, replacing the previous entry. Change the entry in cell A4 from Row to Product. Change the entry in cell A1 from Page1 to City.

   g. Pivot the table to match the figure. Drag Quarter to the row position (cell A4), Product to the column position (cell C3), and City to the row position below Quarter (cell A5). Release the mouse, and the Quarter and City labels will move to the positions shown in the figure.

   h. Format the pivot table so that it matches Figure 5.19. Modify the description on the Documentation worksheet to include the pivot table, then print the pivot table (or the entire workbook if you haven't done so previously).

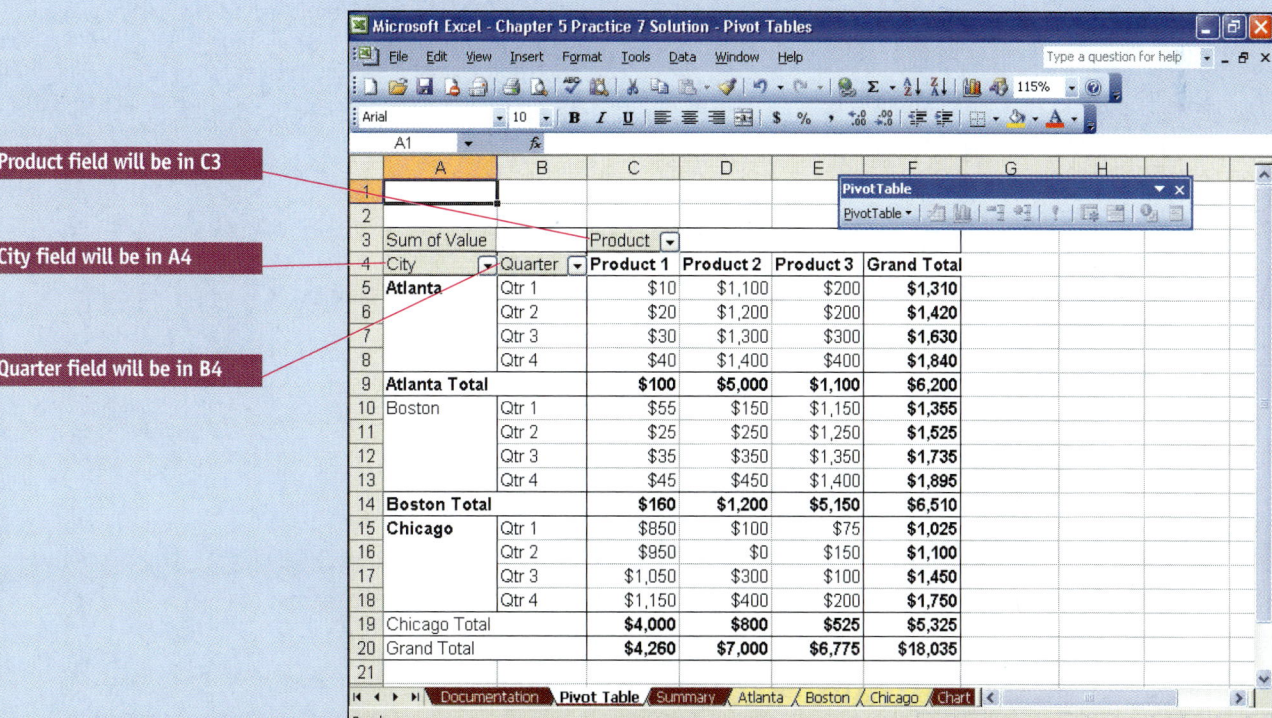

FIGURE 5.19 Pivot Tables (exercise 7)

MINI CASES

Babyland

The Babyland Toy Store has three branches, each of which operates independently. Your job is to consolidate the data in the *Chapter 5 Mini Case—Maplewood, Oakwood,* and *Ramblewood* workbooks, each of which is found in the Exploring Excel folder. You are to create a new workbook that contains a worksheet for each store, a summary worksheet that shows the corporate totals for each product in each quarter, and an appropriate chart reflecting the summary data. You are also asked to create a documentation worksheet with your name, date, and a list of all worksheets in the workbook. Print the completed workbook, along with the cell formulas from the summary worksheet, then submit the printout to your instructor as proof you did this exercise. Use the Page Setup command to display your name, today's date, and the name of the worksheet on the output.

Designs by Jessica

The *Chapter 5 Mini Case—Designs by Jessica* workbook in the Exploring Excel folder is only partially complete as it contains worksheets for individual stores, but does not as yet have a summary worksheet. Your job is to retrieve the workbook and create a summary worksheet that shows the corporate totals for each product in each quarter, and then use the summary worksheet as the basis of a three-dimensional column chart reflecting the sales for the past year. Add a documentation worksheet containing your name as financial analyst, then print the entire workbook and submit it to your instructor. Use the Page Setup command to display your name, today's date, and the name of the worksheet on the output.

External References

Each branch manager of Technology Associates creates an identically formatted workbook with the sales information for his or her branch office. Your job as marketing manager is to consolidate the information into a single workbook, and then graph the results appropriately. The branch data is to remain in the individual workbooks; that is, the formulas in your workbook are to contain external references to the *Chapter 5 Mini Case—Eastern, Western,* and *Foreign* workbooks in the Exploring Excel folder. Begin by opening the individual workbooks and entering the appropriate formulas to total the data for each product and each quarter. You can then create a summary workbook that reflects the quarterly totals for each branch through external references to the individual workbooks; that is, any change in the individual workbooks should be automatically reflected in the consolidated workbook.

CHAPTER 6

A Financial Forecast:
Auditing, Protection, and Templates

OBJECTIVES

After reading this chapter you will:

1. Develop a spreadsheet model for a financial forecast.
2. Use the Scenario Manager to facilitate decision making.
3. Differentiate between precedent and dependent cells.
4. Use the Formula Auditing toolbar.
5. Track the editing changes that are made to a spreadsheet.
6. Resolve editing conflicts among different users in a work group.
7. Use conditional formatting.
8. Create a template based on an existing workbook.

hands-on exercises

1. A FINANCIAL FORECAST
   Input: Financial Forecast
   Output: Financial Forecast Solution

2. AUDITING AND WORKGROUPS
   Input: Erroneous Financial Forecast
   Output: Erroneous Financial Forecast Solution

3. CREATING A TEMPLATE
   Input: Erroneous Financial Forecast Solution (from exercise 2)
   Output: Get Rich Quick (Excel template rather than a workbook)

CASE STUDY
TIMELY SIGNS

Gary and Tonya Smith are the sole proprietors of Timely Signs, a business that specializes in creating custom signs. The business lost $5,000 last year, and the Smiths are concerned about the future. They currently produce two types of signs—ink-jet signs and vinyl signs—and believe they need to continue to offer both types going forward. Greg Hubit, a family friend and successful entrepreneur, suggested that they create a simple spreadsheet to analyze income and expenses for the year just ended, and then project these numbers for a three- or four-year period.

The Smiths realize that they need to increase sales and/or to reduce costs if their business is to survive. Gary is in favor of focusing on the ink-jet signs. He wants to increase the marketing budget by 20% a year and reduce the selling price of the ink-jet signs by 10% a year. He believes that the aggressive advertising and reduced price will increase demand by 25% a year, and further that the higher volume will reduce the manufacturing cost for the ink-jet signs by 5% a year.

Tonya is in favor of moving their business to a smaller plant where the rent and utilities will decrease 20% a year for the next three years. She proposes to use the savings to increase the marketing budget by 20% a year, and projects a 5% increase in the number of units for each sign. Greg suggests that they focus on reducing costs and urges that they reduce the manufacturing unit cost of both types of signs by 10% a year. Greg would use the savings to increase the marketing budget by 15% a year, which in turn will boost the number of signs in each category by 10% a year.

Your assignment is to read the chapter, open the partially completed *Chapter 6 Case Study—Timely Signs* workbook, and complete the forecast by supplying the missing formulas. If you do the work correctly, you will see that the business should earn just under $3,000 in the fourth year according to the Status Quo scenario that exists within the worksheet. You will then create three new scenarios, one each for Gary (ink-jet focus), Tonya (move location), and Greg (control costs), then combine the results in a scenario summary which you will print for your instructor. Print the completed workbook showing the values for the best scenario.

A FINANCIAL FORECAST

Financial planning and budgeting are two of the most common business applications of a spreadsheet. We thought it appropriate, therefore, to use a financial forecast as the vehicle with which to illustrate several additional capabilities in Excel. We begin by developing the forecast itself, with emphasis on the importance of isolating the assumptions on which the spreadsheet is based. We introduce the Scenario Manager, which enables you to specify multiple sets of assumptions and input conditions (scenarios), then see the results at a glance. We also introduce the Formula Auditing toolbar and explain how its tools can help ensure the accuracy of a worksheet.

Figure 6.1 displays a financial forecast for Get Rich Quick Enterprises, which contains the projected income and expenses for the company over a five-year period. The spreadsheet enables management to vary any of the ***assumptions*** at the bottom of the spreadsheet to see the effects on the projected earnings. You don't have to be a business major to follow our forecast. All you have to realize is that the profit for any given year is determined by subtracting expenses from income.

The income is equal to the number of units sold times the unit price. The projected revenue in 2003, for example, is $300,000, based on selling 100,000 units at a price of $3.00 per unit. The variable costs for the same year are estimated at $150,000 (100,000 units times $1.50 per unit). The production facility costs $50,000, and administrative expenses add another $25,000. Subtracting the total expenses from the estimated income yields a net income before taxes of $75,000.

The income and expenses for each succeeding year are based on estimated percentage increases over the previous year, as shown at the bottom of the worksheet. It is absolutely critical to isolate the initial values and assumed rates of increase in this manner, and further, that all entries in the body of the spreadsheet are developed as formulas that reference these cells. The entry in cell C4, for example, is *not* the constant 100,000, but rather a reference to cell C18, which contains the value 100,000.

The distinction may seem trivial, but most assuredly it is not, as two important objectives are achieved. The user sees at a glance which factors affect the results of the spreadsheet (i.e., the cost and earnings projections) and, further, the user can easily change any of those values to see their effect on the overall forecast. Assume, for example, that the first-year forecast changes to 80,000 units sold and that this number will increase at 8% a year (rather than 10%). The only changes in the worksheet are to the entries in cells C18 and E18, because the projected gross revenue is calculated using the values in these cells.

Once you appreciate the necessity of isolating the assumptions and ***initial conditions***, you can design the actual spreadsheet. Ask yourself why you are building the spreadsheet in the first place and what you hope to accomplish. (The financial forecast in this example is intended to answer questions regarding projected rates of growth, and more importantly, how changes in the assumptions and initial conditions will affect the income, expenses, and earnings in later years.) This facilitates the creation of the spreadsheet, which is done in five general stages:

1. Enter the row and column headings, and the values for the initial conditions and the assumed rates of change.

2. Develop the formulas for the first year of the forecast based on the initial conditions at the bottom of the spreadsheet.

3. Develop the formulas for the second year based on the values in year one and the assumed rates of change.

4. Copy the formulas for year two to the remaining years of the forecast.

5. Format the spreadsheet, then print the completed forecast.

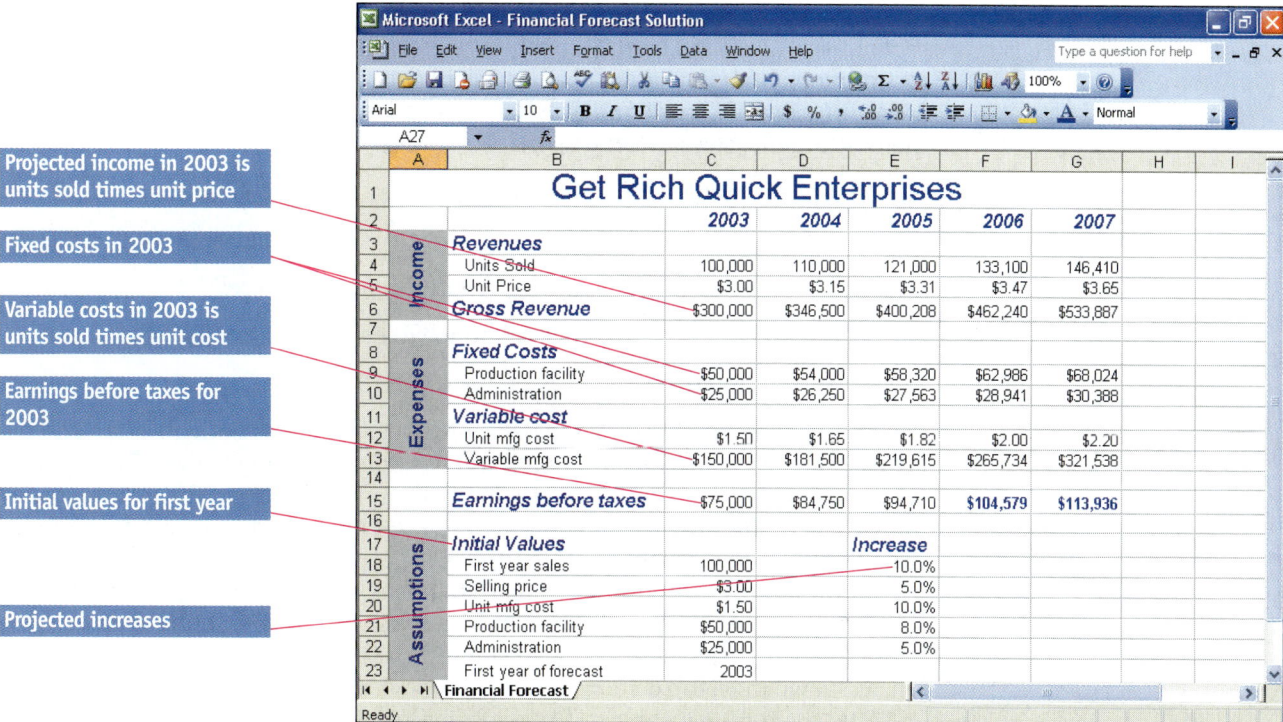

(a) Displayed Values

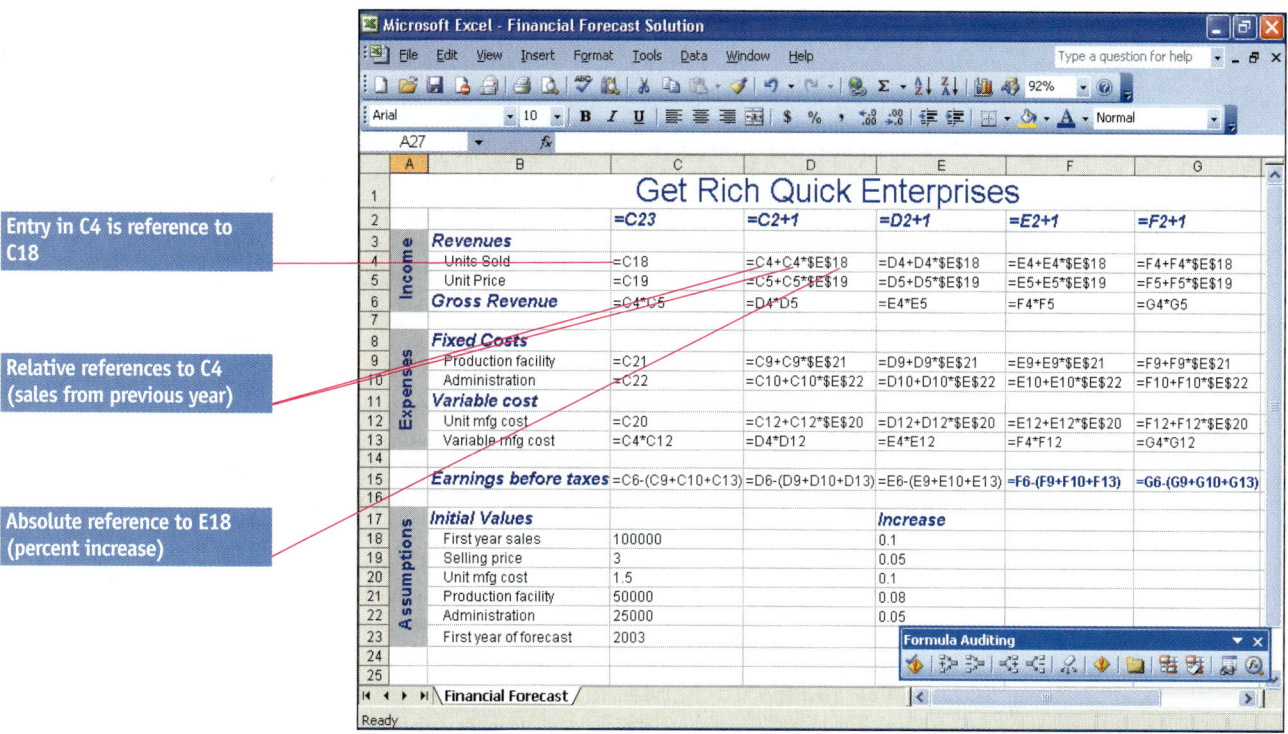

(b) Cell Formulas

FIGURE 6.1 Financial Forecast

Perhaps the most critical step is the development of the formulas for the second year (2004 in Figure 6.1), which are based on the results for 2003 and the assumption about how these results will change for the next year. The units sold in 2004, for example, are equal to the sales in 2003 (cell C4) plus the estimated increase in unit sales (C4*$E$18); that is,

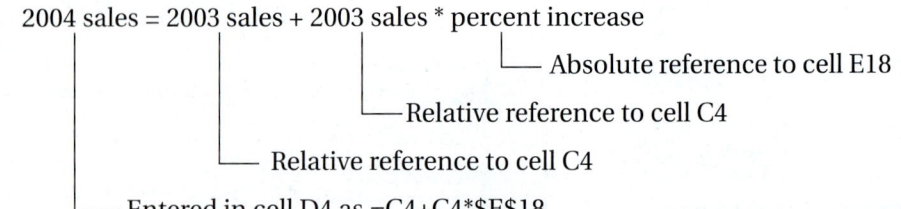

The formula to compute the sales for the year 2004 uses both absolute and relative references, which ensures that it will be copied properly to the other columns for the remaining years in the forecast. An absolute reference ($E$18) is necessary for the cell containing the percent increase in unit sales, because this reference should remain the same when the formula is copied. A relative reference (C4) is used for the sales from the previous year, because this reference should change when the formula is copied. Many of the other formulas in column D are also based on percentage increases from column C, and are developed in similar fashion, as shown in Figure 6.1b.

After the formulas for year two are completed in column D, the entire column is copied to columns E, F, and G to develop the remainder of the forecast. The worksheet is formatted and then printed to complete the exercise. It is now a simple matter to vary any of the assumptions or initial conditions at the bottom of the worksheet and see the result of those changes in the completed forecast.

Advanced Formatting

The spreadsheet in Figure 6.1 incorporates many of the formatting commands that have been used throughout the text. The spreadsheet also illustrates additional capabilities that will be implemented in the hands-on exercise that follows shortly. Some of these features are obvious, such as the ability to **rotate text** as seen in column A or the ability to **indent text** as was done in column B.

Other capabilities, such as **conditional formatting**, are more subtle. Look at the projected earnings, for example, and note that amounts over $100,000 are displayed in blue, whereas values under $100,000 are not. One could simply select the two cells and change the font color to blue, but as the earnings change, the cells would have to be reformatted. Accordingly, we implemented the color by selecting the entire row of projected earnings and specifying a conditional format to display the value in blue if it exceeds $100,000, display it in red if it is negative, and default to black otherwise. The use of conditional formatting lets you vary any of the assumptions or initial conditions, which in turn change the projected earnings, yet automatically display the projected earnings in the appropriate color.

The last formatting feature in Figure 6.1 is the imposition of a user-defined style (Main Heading) for various cells in the spreadsheet. A **style** (or **custom format**) is a set of formatting characteristics that is stored under a specific name. You've already used styles throughout the text that were predefined by Excel. Clicking the Comma, Currency, or Percent button on the Formatting toolbar, for example, automatically applies these styles to the selected cells. You can also define your own styles (e.g., Main Heading), as will be done in the hands-on exercise. The advantage of storing the formatting characteristics within a style, as opposed to applying the commands individually, is that you can change the definition of the style, which automatically changes the appearance of all cells defined by that style.

SCENARIO MANAGER

The **Scenario Manager** enables you to specify multiple sets of assumptions (**scenarios**), then see at a glance the results of any given scenario. Each scenario represents a different set of what-if conditions that you want to consider in assessing the outcome of a spreadsheet model. You could, for example, look at optimistic, pessimistic, and most likely (consensus) assumptions, as shown in Figure 6.2. The scenarios are saved with the workbook and are available whenever the workbook is opened.

Figure 6.2a displays the Scenario Manager dialog box that contains the various scenarios that have been created. Each scenario is stored under its own name and is composed of a set of cells whose values vary from scenario to scenario. Figure 6.2b, for example, shows the value of the **changing cells** for the consensus scenario. Figure 6.2c shows the values for the optimistic scenario. (The cells in the dialog box are identified by name, rather than cell reference through the **Define Name command** as will be shown in the next hands-on exercise. First_Year_Sales, for example, refers to cell C18 in the financial forecast. The use of a mnemonic name, as opposed to a cell reference, makes it much easier to understand precisely which values change from one scenario to the next.)

The **scenario summary** in Figure 6.2d compares the effects of the different scenarios to one another by showing the value of one or more **result cells**. We see, for example, that the consensus scenario yields earnings of $113,936 in the fifth year (the same value shown earlier), compared to significantly higher or lower values for the other two scenarios.

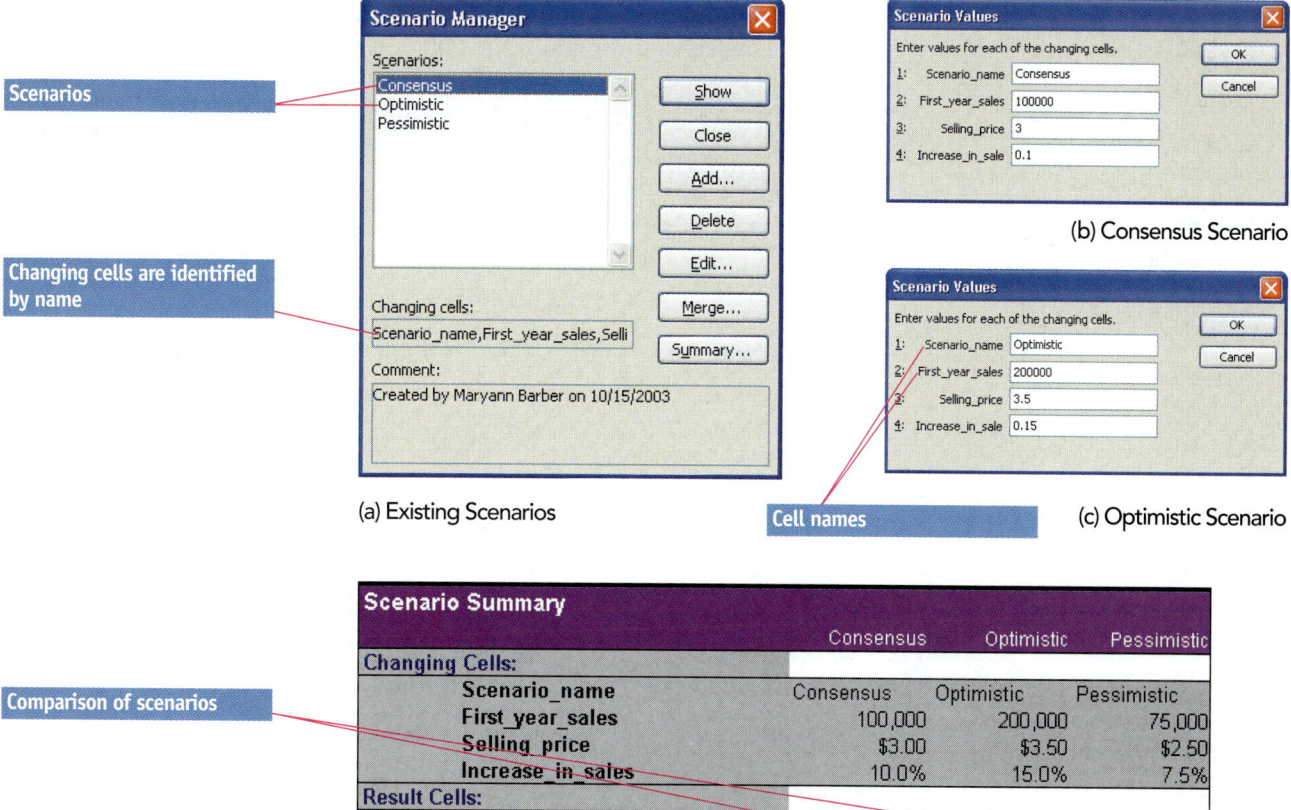

FIGURE 6.2 Scenario Manager

hands-on exercise
1   A Financial Forecast

Objective To develop a spreadsheet for a financial forecast that isolates the assumptions and initial values; to use conditional formatting, styles, indentation, and rotated text to format the spreadsheet. Use Figure 6.3 as a guide in the exercise.

Step 1:   **Enter the Formulas for Year One**

- Start Excel. Open the **Financial Forecast** workbook in the **Exploring Excel folder** to display the worksheet in Figure 6.3a. (Cells C4 through C15 are currently empty.)

- Click in **cell C2**. Type **=C23** and press **Enter**. Note that you are not entering the year explicitly, but rather a reference to the cell that contains the year, which is located in the assumptions area of the worksheet.

- Enter the remaining formulas for year one of the forecast:
  - Click in **cell C4**. Type **=C18**. Click in **cell C5**. Type **=C19**.
  - Click in **cell C6**. Type **=C4*C5**. Click in **cell C9**. Type **=C21**.
  - Click in **cell C10**. Type **=C22**. Click in **cell C12**. Type **=C20**.
  - Click in **cell C13**. Type **=C4*C12**.
  - Click in **cell C15**. Type **=C6-(C9+C10+C13)**.

- The cell contents for year one (2003 in this example) are complete. The displayed values in this column should match the numbers shown in Figure 6.3a.

- Save the workbook as **Financial Forecast Solution** in the **Exploring Excel Folder** you have used throughout the text.

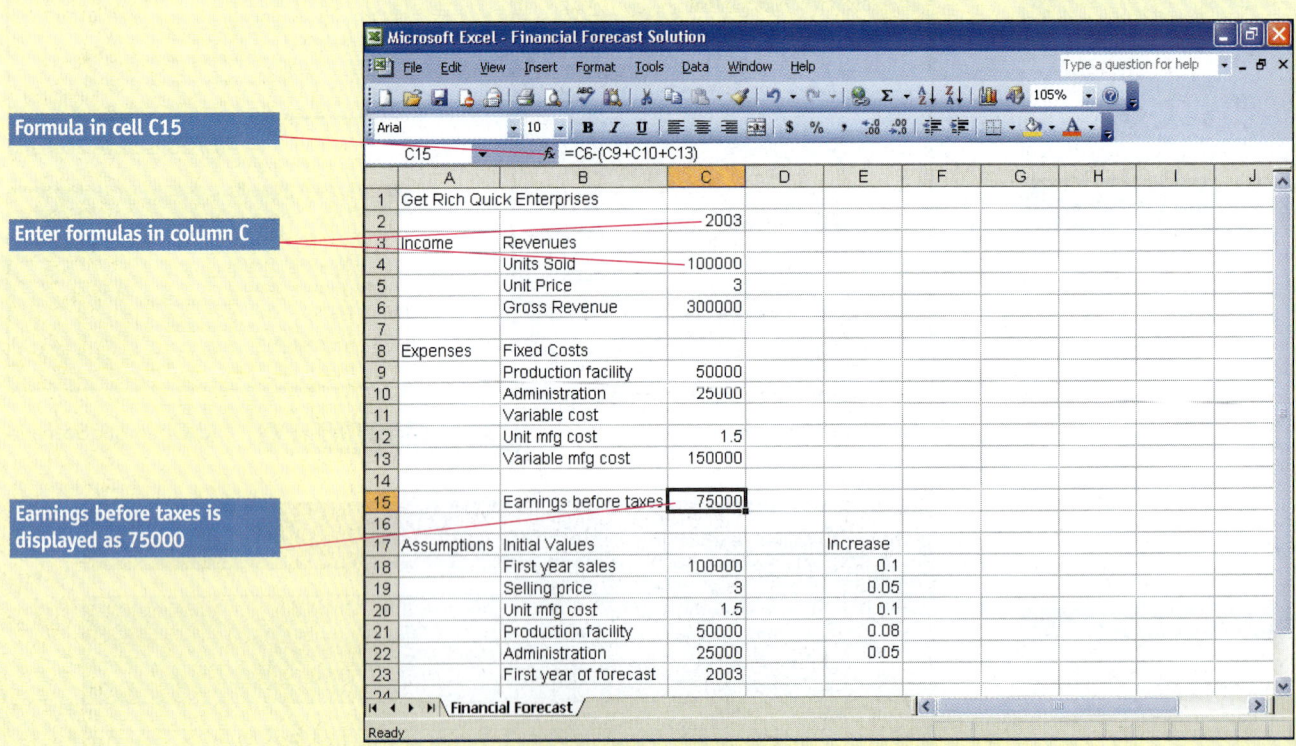

(a) Enter the Formulas for Year One (step 1)

FIGURE 6.3   Hands-on Exercise 1

Step 2: **Enter the Formulas for Year Two**

- Click in **cell D2**. Type **=C2+1** to determine the second year of the forecast.

- Click in **cell D4**. Type **=C4+C4*$E$18**. This formula computes the sales for year two as a function of the sales in year one and the rate of increase.

- Enter the remaining formulas for year two:
  - Click in **cell D5**. Type **=C5+C5*$E$19**. Copy the formula in cell C6 to D6.
  - Click in **cell D9**. Type **=C9+C9*$E$21**.
  - Click in **cell D10**. Type **=C10+C10*$E$22**.
  - Click in **cell D12**. Type **=C12+C12*$E$20**.
  - Copy the formulas in cells C13 and C15 to cells D13 and D15.

- The cell contents for the second year (2004) are complete. The displayed values should match the numbers shown in Figure 6.3b.

- Save the workbook.

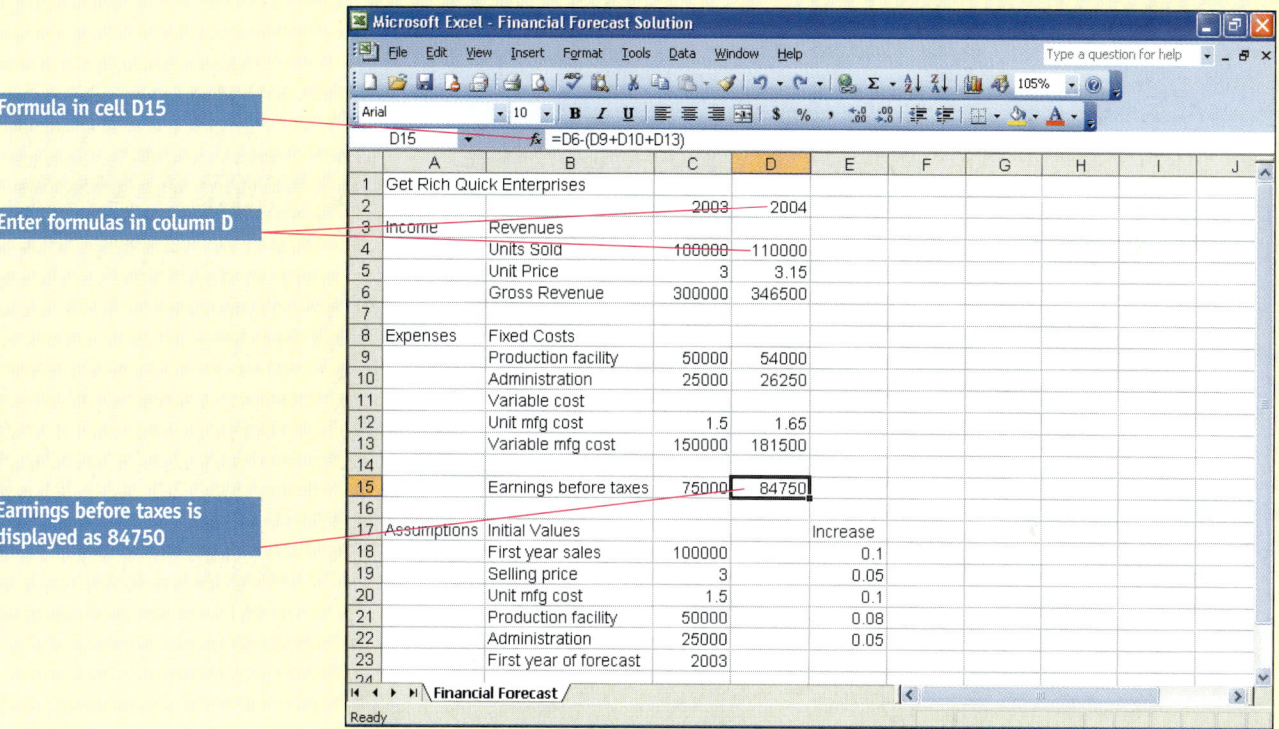

(b) Enter the Formulas for Year Two (step 2)

FIGURE 6.3 Hands-on Exercise 1 (*continued*)

USE POINTING TO ENTER CELL FORMULAS

A cell reference can be typed directly into a formula, or it can be entered more easily through pointing. The latter is also more accurate as you use the mouse or arrow keys to reference cells directly. To use pointing, select (click) the cell to contain the formula, type an equal sign to begin entering the formula, click (or move to) the cell containing the reference, then press the F4 key as necessary to change from relative to absolute references. Type any arithmetic operator to place the cell reference in the formula, then continue pointing to additional cells. Press the Enter key to complete the formula.

Step 3: **Copy the Formulas to the Remaining Years**

- Click and drag to select **cells D2 through D15** (the cells containing the formulas for year two). Click the **Copy button** on the Standard toolbar (or use the **Ctrl+C** keyboard shortcut).

- A moving border will surround these cells to indicate that their contents have been copied to the clipboard.

- Click and drag to select **cells E2 through G15** (the cells that will contain the formulas for years three to five). Point to the selection and click the **right mouse button** to display the context-sensitive menu in Figure 6.3c.

- Click **Paste** to paste the contents of the clipboard into the selected cells. The displayed values for the last three years of the forecast should be visible in the worksheet.

- You should see earnings before taxes of 113936 for the last year in the forecast. Press **Esc** to remove the moving border.

- Save the workbook.

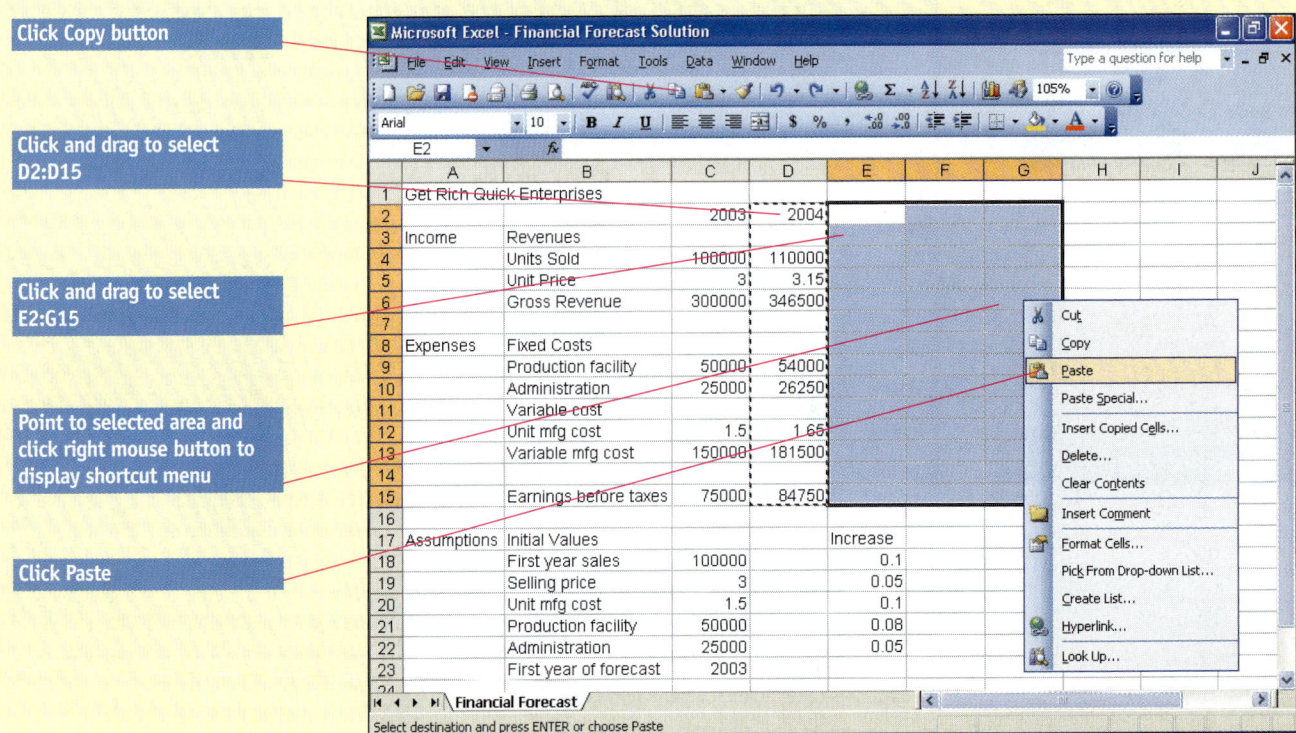

(c) Copy the Formulas to the Remaining Years (step 3)

FIGURE 6.3 Hands-on Exercise 1 (*continued*)

THE FILL HANDLE

There are several ways to copy a formula to cells in adjacent rows or columns. The easiest is the fill handle (the tiny black square) that appears in the lower-right corner of the selected cells. Select the cell (cells) to be copied, then click and drag the fill handle over the destination range. Release the mouse to complete the operation.

Step 4: **Create a Style**

- Point to any toolbar, click the **right mouse button** to display a context-sensitive menu, then click the **Customize command** to display the Customize dialog box. Click the **Commands tab**, then select (click) the **Format category**.

- Click and drag the **Style List box** from within the command section to the right of the font color button on the Formatting toolbar. (You must drag the tool inside the toolbar and will see a large I-beam as you do so.)

- Release the mouse when you position the tool where you want. Click **Close** to close the Custom dialog box.

- The Style list box now appears on the Formatting toolbar as shown in Figure 6.3d. (The Style dialog box is not yet visible.) Click in **cell C2** and note that the Style list box indicates the Normal style (the default style for all cells in a worksheet).

- Change the font in cell C2 to **12 point Arial bold italic**. Click the **down arrow** on the Font Color tool and click **blue**. Pull down the **Format menu** and click the **Style command** to display the Style dialog box.

- The Normal style is already selected. Type **Main Heading** to define a new style according to the characteristics of the selected cell. Click **OK** to create the style and close the dialog box.

- Click and drag to select **cells D2 through G2**. Click the down arrow on the Style list box and select the **Main Heading style** you just created to apply this style to the selected cells.

- Select **cell B3**. Press and hold the **Ctrl key** as you select **cells B6, B8, B11, B15, B17, and E17**, then apply the **Main Heading style** to these cells as well.

- Increase the width of column B so that you can see the text in cell B15. Save the workbook.

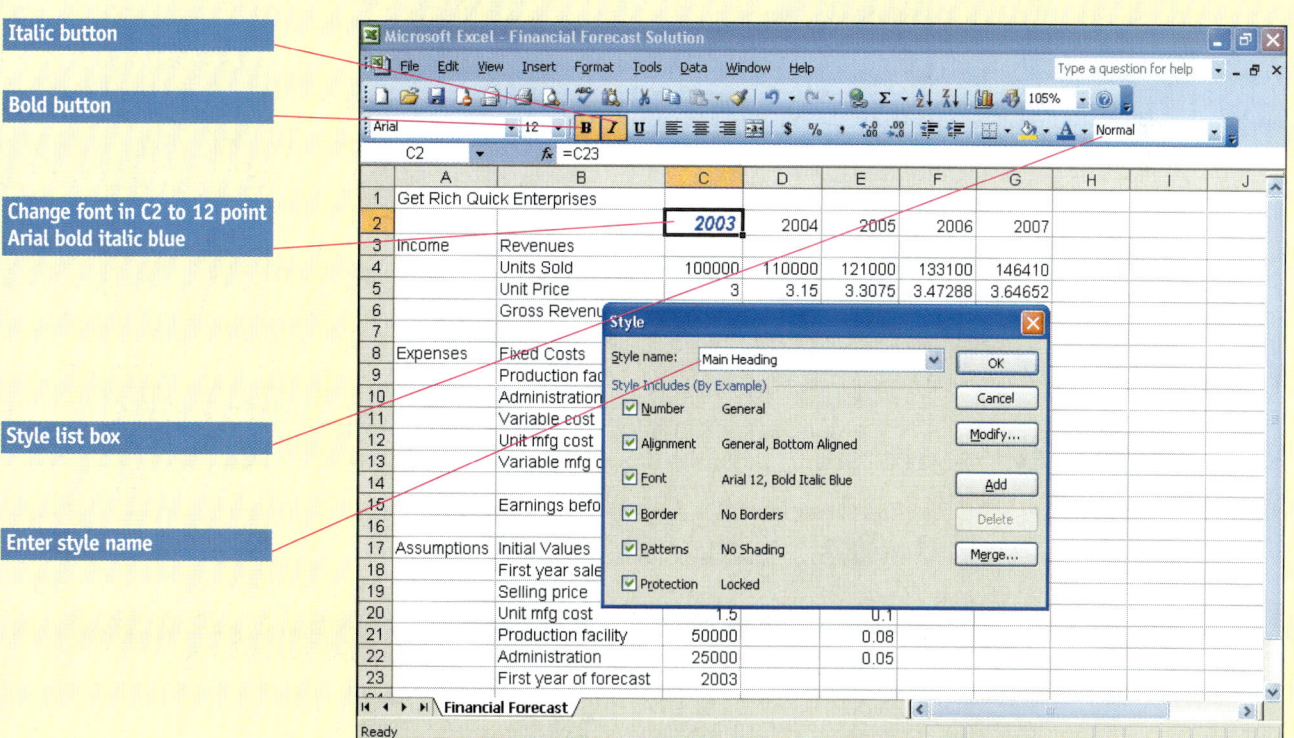

(d) Create a Style (step 4)

FIGURE 6.3 Hands-on Exercise 1 (*continued*)

Step 5: **Rotate and Indent Text**

- Click and drag to select **cell ranges A3:A6, A8:A13, and A17:A23** as shown in Figure 6.3e. Pull down the **Format menu** and click the **Cells command** to display the Format Cells dialog box shown in the figure.

- Click the **Alignment tab** and specify **center alignment** in both the horizontal and vertical list boxes. Check the box to **Merge cells**. Click in the **Degrees text box** and enter **90**.

- Click the **Font tab**, then change the font to **12 point Arial bold**. Change the font color to **blue**.

- Click the **Patterns tab** and choose **gray shading**.

- Click **OK** to accept these changes and close the Format Cells dialog box.

- Click and drag to select the labels in **cells B4 and B5**. Click the **Increase Indent button** on the Formatting toolbar to indent these labels.

- Press and hold the **Ctrl key** as you select **cells B9 and B10, B12 and B13**, and **B18 through B23**. Click the **Increase Indent button** to indent the labels that appear in these cells.

- Save the workbook.

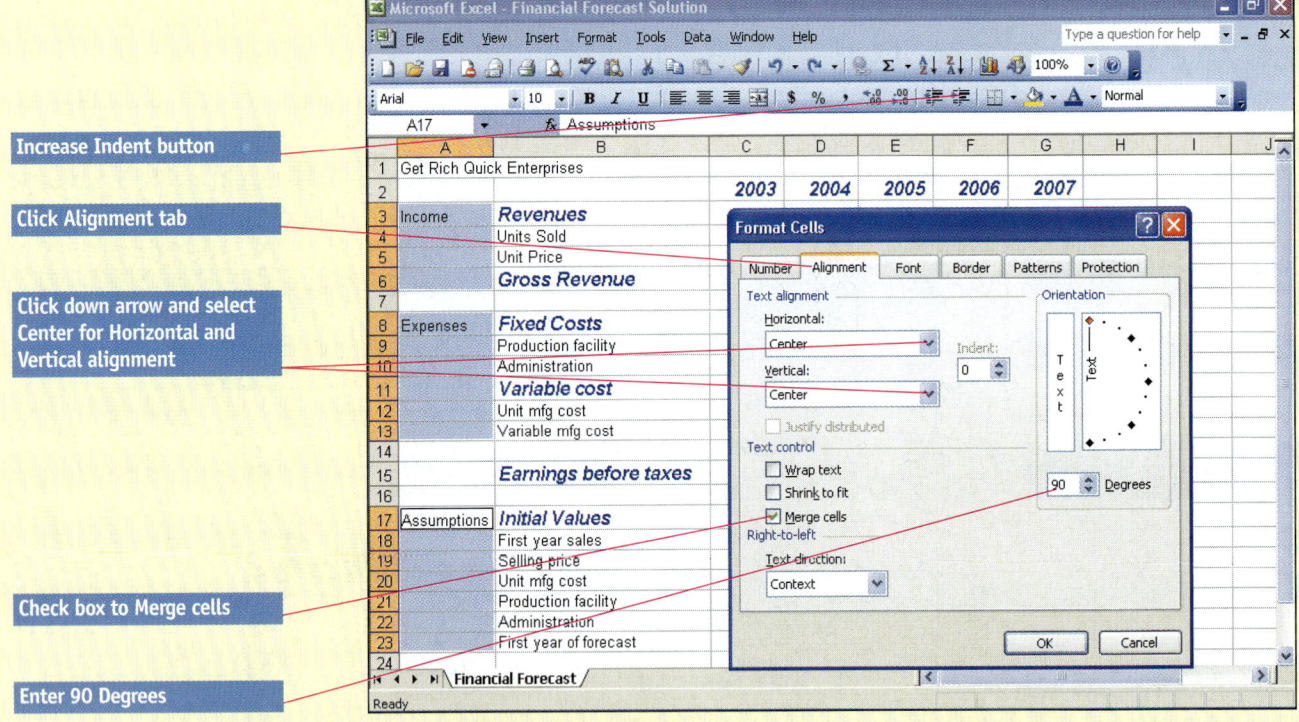

(e) Rotate and Indent Text (step 5)

FIGURE 6.3 Hands-on Exercise 1 (*continued*)

TOGGLE MERGE CELLS ON AND OFF

Click and drag to select multiple cells, then click the Merge and Center button on the Formatting toolbar to merge the cells into a single cell. Click in the merged cell, then click the Merge and Center button a second time and the cell is split. (This is different from Office 2000, where the only way to split cells was to clear the Merge cells check box within the Format Cells dialog box.)

Step 6: **Conditional Formatting**

- Click and drag to select **cells C15 through G15**. Pull down the **Format menu** and click the **Conditional Formatting command** to display the Conditional Formatting dialog box in Figure 6.3f.

- Set the relationships for condition 1 as shown in Figure 6.3f. Click the **Format button** to display the Format Cells dialog box and click the **Font tab**. Change the font style to **bold** and the font color to **blue**. Click **OK**.

- Click the **Add button** and enter the parameters for condition 2 as shown in Figure 6.3f. Click the **Format button**. Change the Font style to **bold** and the color to **red**. Click **OK**.

- Click **OK** to close the Conditional Formatting dialog box. Click any cell to deselect cells C15 to G15. The earnings before taxes for the last two years of the forecast are displayed in bold and in blue, since they exceed $100,000.

- Click in **cell C19**, change the selling price to **2.00**, and press the **Enter key**. The earnings before taxes are displayed in red since they are negative for every year. Click the **Undo button** to return the initial sales price to 3.00.

- Save the workbook.

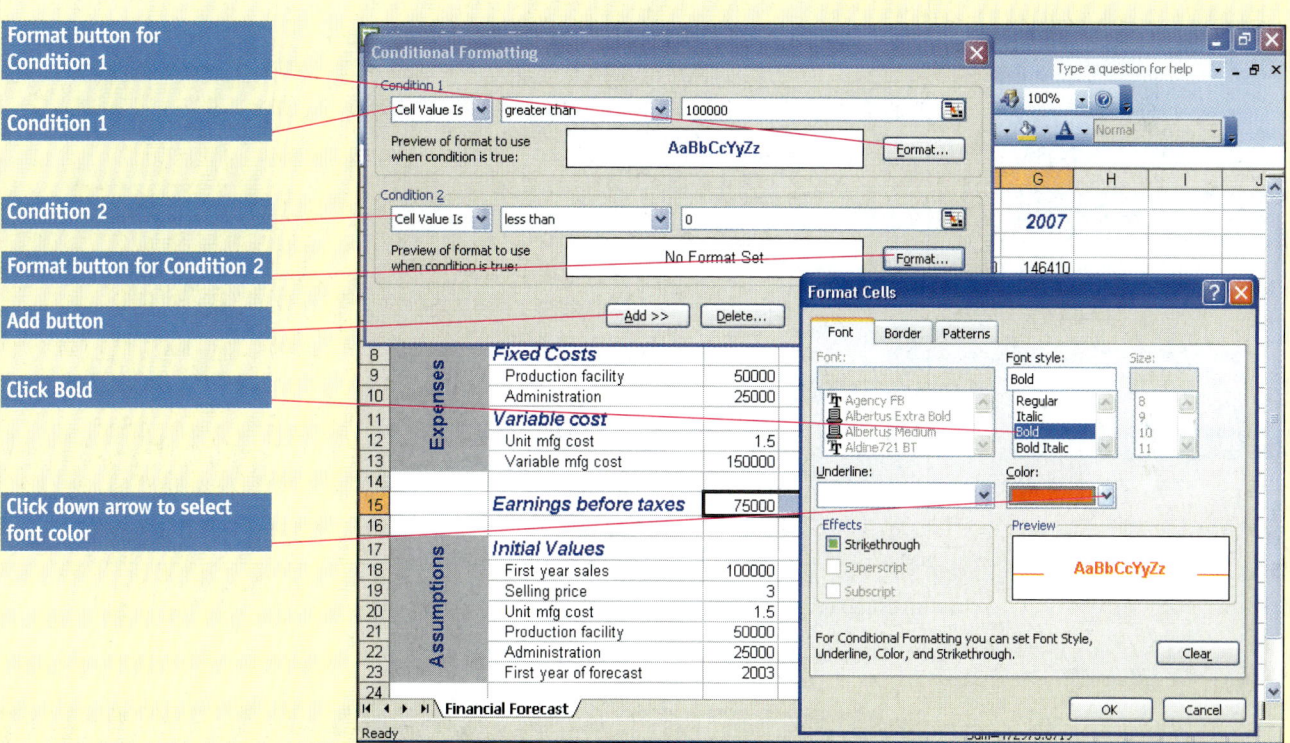

(f) Conditional Formatting (step 6)

FIGURE 6.3 Hands-on Exercise 1 (*continued*)

THE RIGHT MOUSE BUTTON

Point to a cell (or cell range), a worksheet tab, or a toolbar, then click the right mouse button to display a context-sensitive menu. Right clicking a cell, for example, displays a menu with selected commands from the Edit, Insert, and Format menus. Right clicking a toolbar displays a menu that lets you display or hide additional toolbars. Right clicking a worksheet tab enables you to rename, move, copy, or delete the worksheet.

Step 7: **Complete the Formatting**

- Click in **cell A1**. Change the font color to **blue**, and the font size to **22 points**. Click and drag to select **cells A1 through G1**, then click the **Merge and Center button** to center the entry.

- Use Figure 6.3g as a guide to implement the appropriate formatting for the remaining entries in the worksheet. Remember to press and hold the **Ctrl key** if you want to select noncontiguous cells prior to executing a command.

- Add your name in **cell A2**. Save the workbook.

- Print the spreadsheet twice, once to show the displayed values and once to show the cell formulas. Press **Ctrl+~** to toggle between cell formulas and displayed values.

- Submit both printouts to your instructor.

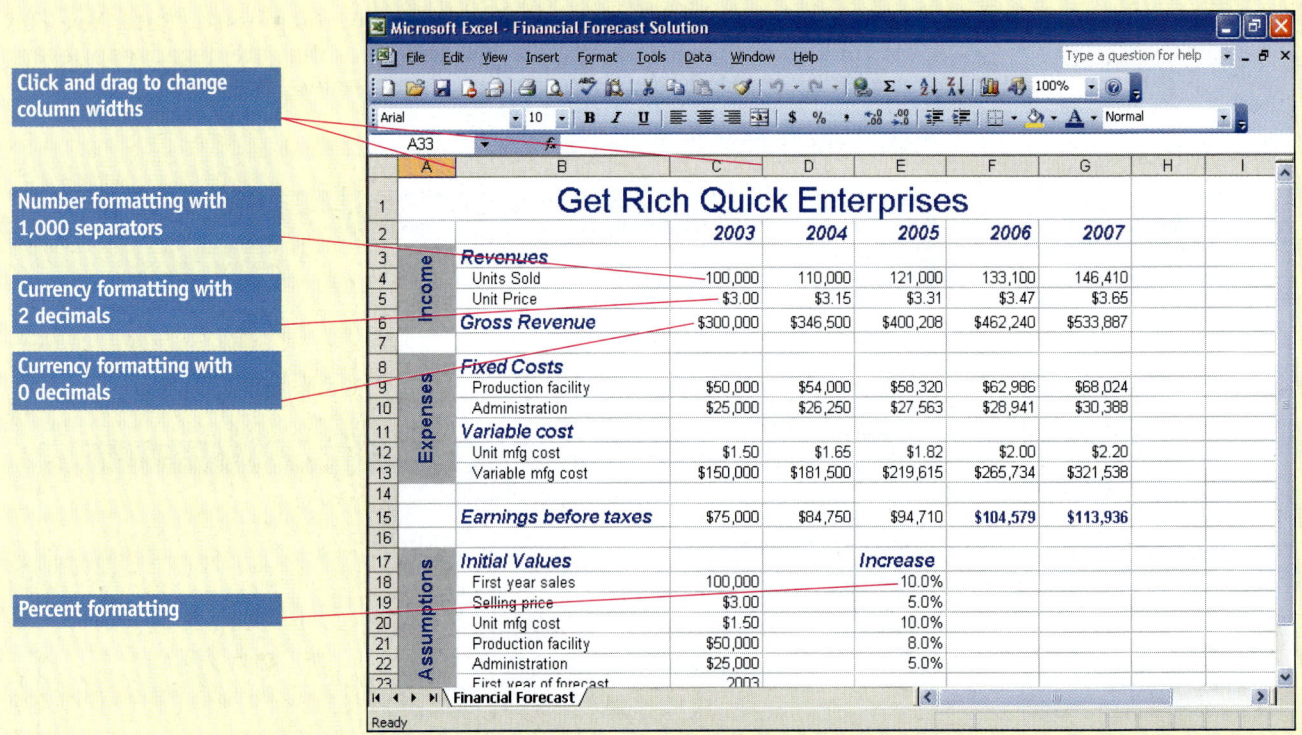

(g) Complete the Formatting (step 7)

FIGURE 6.3 Hands-on Exercise 1 (*continued*)

CREATE A CUSTOM VIEW

Format the spreadsheet to print the displayed values, then pull down the View menu and click Custom Views to display the Custom Views dialog box. Click the button to Add a view, enter the name (e.g., Displayed Values), and click OK. Press Ctrl+` to display the cell formulas, adjust the column widths as necessary, then pull down the View menu a second time to create a second custom view (e.g., Cell Formulas). You can switch to either view at any time by selecting the Custom Views command and selecting the appropriate view.

Step 8: The Insert Name Command

- Click in **cell C18**, pull down the **Insert menu**, select the **Name command**, then click **Define** to display the Define Name dialog box in Figure 6.3h.

- **First_year_sales** is already entered as the default name (because this text appears as a label in the cell immediately to the left of the active cell. Underscores were added between the words, however, because blanks are not permitted in a cell name.) Click **OK** to accept this name.

- Name the other cells that will be used in the various scenarios. Use **Selling_price** as the name for **cell C19**. Enter names of **Increase_in_sales** for **cell E18**, and **Scenario_name** for **cell E23**. (Do not be concerned that cell E23 is currently empty.)

- Save the workbook.

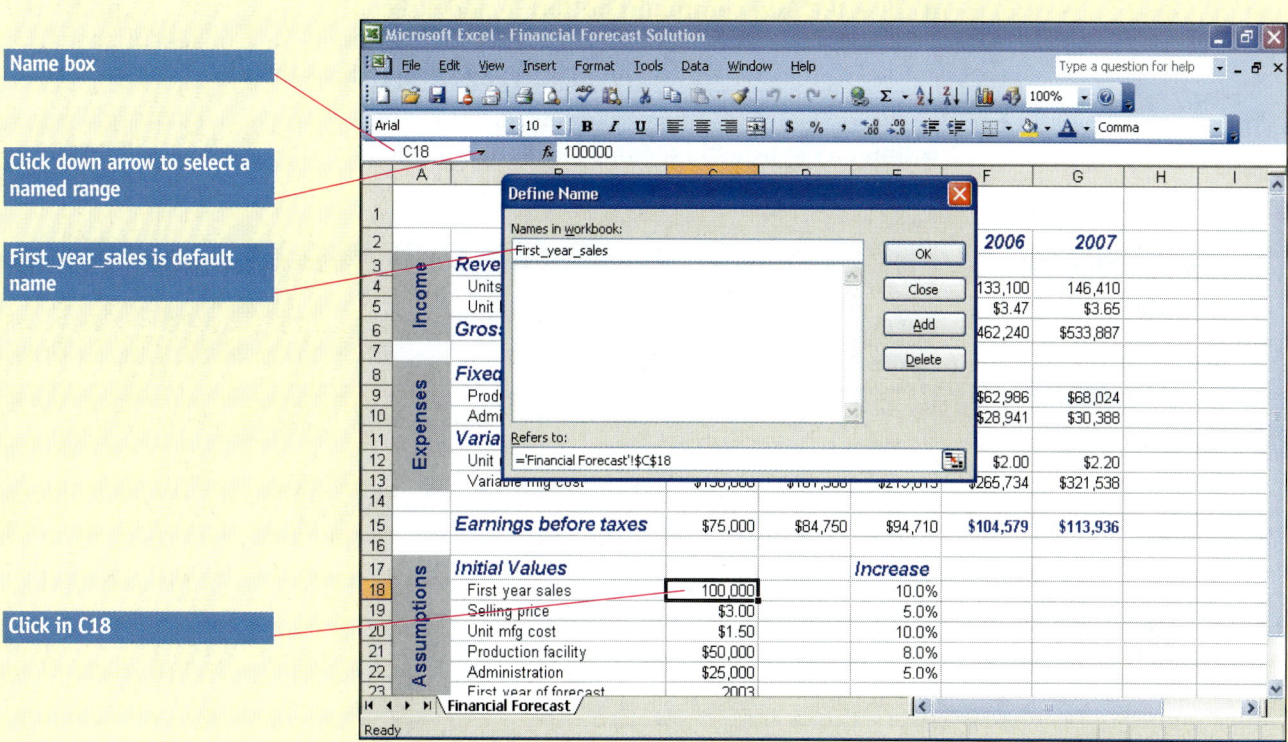

(h) The Insert Name Command (step 8)

FIGURE 6.3 Hands-on Exercise 1 (*continued*)

THE NAME BOX

Use the Name box on the formula bar to define a named range, by first selecting the cell in the worksheet to which the name is to apply, clicking in the Name box to enter the range name, and then pressing the Enter key. Once the name has been defined, you can use the Name box to select a named range by clicking in the box and then typing the appropriate cell reference or name or simply by clicking the drop-down arrow next to the Name box to select the name from a drop-down list. Named ranges make a scenario easier to read since we see mnemonic names as opposed to cell references such as C18.

Step 9: **Create the Scenarios**

- Click in **cell E23** and type the word **Consensus**. Click in **cell E17**, click the **Format Painter button** on the Formatting toolbar, then click in **cell E23** to copy the format from cell E17.

- Pull down the **Tools menu**. Click **Scenarios** to display the Scenario Manager dialog box. Click the **Add command button** to display the Add Scenario dialog box in Figure 6.3i. Type **Consensus** in the Scenario Name text box.

- Click in the **Changing Cells text box**. Cell E23 (the active cell) is already entered as the first cell in the scenario. Type a comma, then enter **C18, C19, and E18** as the remaining cells in the scenario. Click **OK**.

- You should see the Scenario Values dialog box with the values of this scenario already entered from the corresponding cells in the worksheet.

- Click the **Add command button** to add a second scenario called **Optimistic**. The changing cells are already entered and match the Consensus scenario. Click **OK**. Enter **Optimistic, 200000, 3.5**, and **.15**, as the values for the changing cells. Click **Add**.

- Enter a **Pessimistic scenario** in similar fashion, using **Pessimistic, 75000, 2.5**, and **.075**, for the changing cells. Click **OK**.

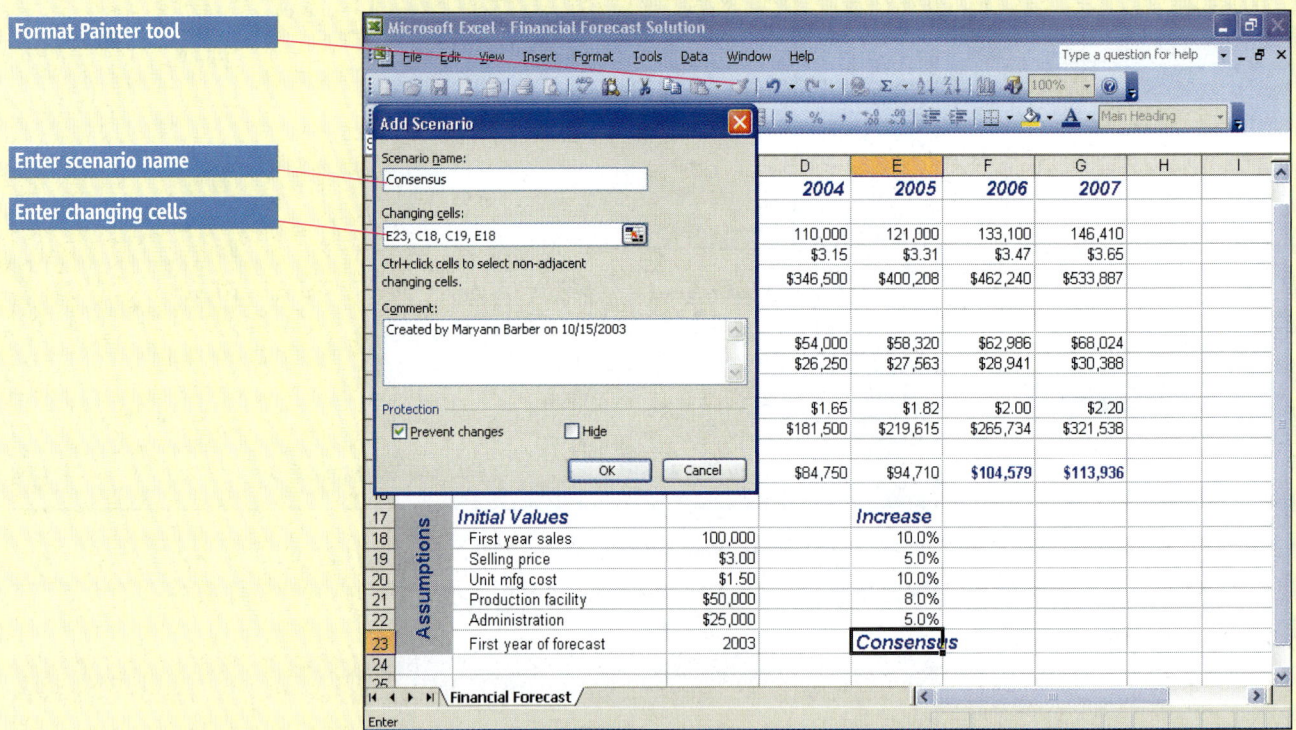

(i) Create the Scenarios (step 9)

FIGURE 6.3 Hands-on Exercise 1 (*continued*)

ISOLATE THE ASSUMPTIONS

The formulas in a worksheet should always be based on cell references that are clearly labeled, set apart from the rest of the worksheet. You can then vary the inputs (or assumptions) on which the worksheet is based to see the effect within the worksheet. You can change the values manually, or store sets of values within a specific scenario.

Step 10: **View the Scenarios**

- The Scenario Manager dialog box should still be open as shown in Figure 6.3j. If necessary, pull down the **Tools menu** and click the **Scenarios command** to reopen the Scenario Manager.

- There should be three scenarios listed—Consensus, Optimistic, and Pessimistic—corresponding to the scenarios that were just created.

- Select the **Optimistic scenario**, then click the **Show button** (or simply double click the scenario name) to display the financial forecast under the assumptions of this scenario.

- Double click the **Pessimistic scenario**, which changes the worksheet to show the forecast under these assumptions.

- Double click the **Consensus scenario** to return to this scenario. Do you see how easy it is to change multiple assumptions at one time by storing the values in a scenario?

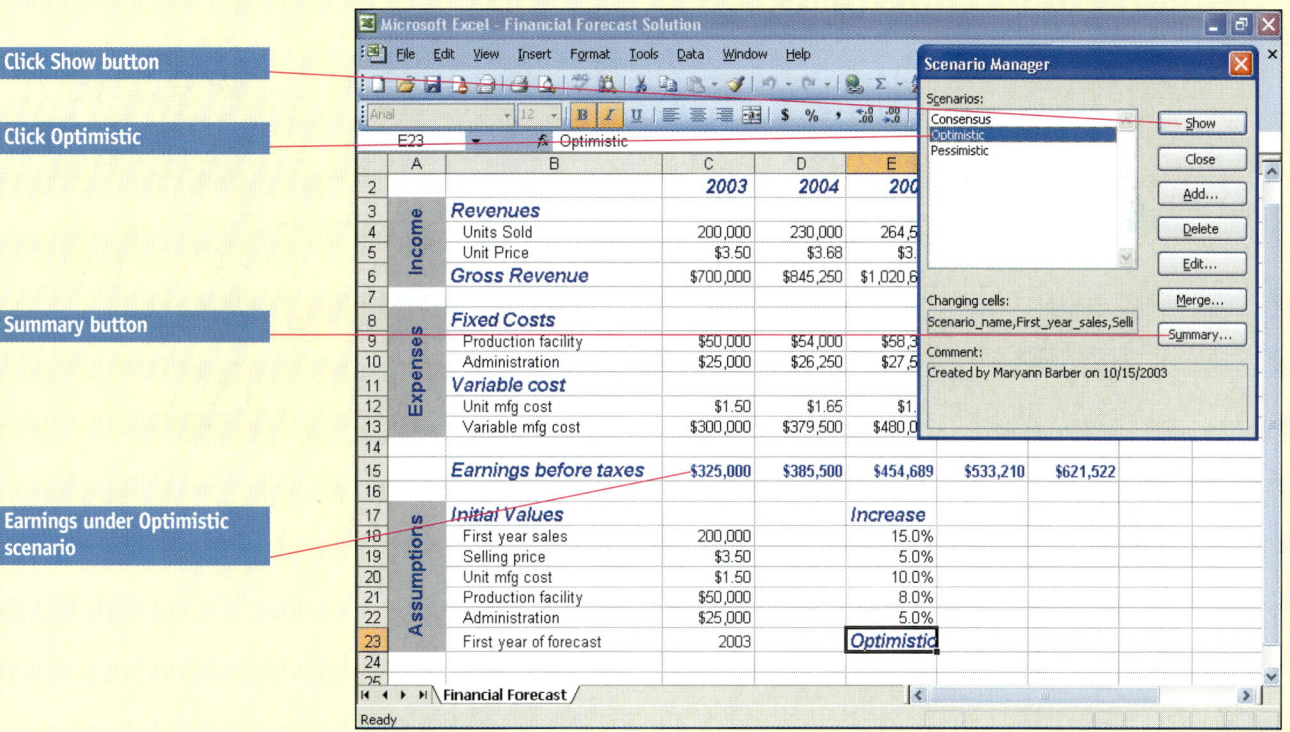

(j) View the Scenarios (step 10)

FIGURE 6.3 Hands-on Exercise 1 (*continued*)

THE SCENARIO MANAGER LIST BOX

The Scenario Manager list box lets you select a scenario directly from a toolbar. Point to any toolbar, click the right mouse button to display a shortcut menu, then click Customize to display the Customize dialog box. Click the Commands tab, select Tools in the Categories list box, then click and drag the Scenario list box to an empty space on the toolbar. Click Close to close the dialog box and return to the workbook. Click the down arrow on the Scenario list box, which now appears on the toolbar, to choose from the scenarios that have been defined within the current workbook. See exercise 6 at the end of the chapter.

Step 11: **The Scenario Summary**

- The Scenario Manager dialog box should still be open. Click the **Summary button** to display the Scenario Summary dialog box.

- If necessary, click the **Scenario Summary option button**. Click in the **Result Cells text box**, then click in **cell G15** (the cell that contains the earnings before taxes in the fifth year of the forecast). Click **OK**.

- You should see a Scenario Summary worksheet as shown in Figure 6.3k. Each scenario has its own column in the worksheet. The changing cells, identified by name rather than cell reference, are listed in column C.

- The Scenario Summary worksheet is an ordinary worksheet to the extent that it can be modified like any other worksheet. Click the header for **row 6**, then press and hold the **Ctrl key** as you click and drag **rows 12 to 14**. Right click the selected cells, then click the **Delete command** from the context-sensitive menu.

- Delete Column D in similar fashion. Add your name to the worksheet. Save the workbook, then print the summary worksheet for your instructor. Close the workbook.

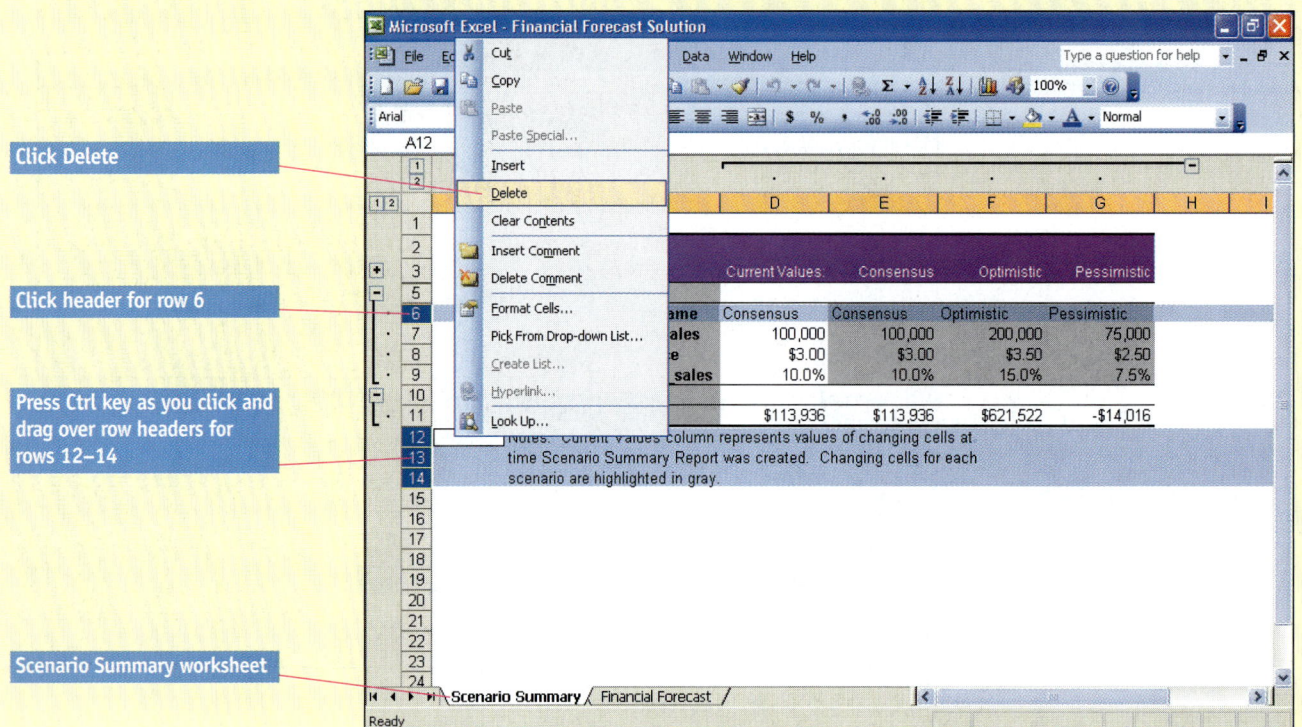

(k) The Scenario Summary (step 11)

FIGURE 6.3 Hands-on Exercise 1 (*continued*)

THE SCENARIO SUMMARY WORKSHEET

You can return to the Scenario Manager to add or modify an individual scenario, after which you can create a new scenario summary. You must, however, execute the command when the original worksheet is displayed on the screen. Note, too, that each time you click the Summary button within the Scenario Manager, you will create another summary worksheet called Scenario Summary 2, Scenario Summary 3, and so on. You can delete the extraneous worksheets by right clicking the worksheet tab, then clicking the Delete command.

WORKGROUPS AND AUDITING

The spreadsheet containing the financial forecast is a tool that will be used by management as the basis for decision making. Executives in the company will vary the assumptions on which the spreadsheet is based to see the effects on profitability, then implement changes in policy based on the results of the spreadsheet. But what if the spreadsheet is in error? Think, for a moment, how business has become totally dependent on the spreadsheet, and what the consequences might be of basing corporate policy on an erroneous spreadsheet.

It's one thing if the assumptions about the expected increases turn out to be wrong because the very nature of a forecast requires us to deal with uncertainty. It's inexcusable, however, if the formulas that use those assumptions are invalid. Thus, it's common for several people to collaborate on the same spreadsheet to minimize the chance for error. One person creates the initial version, then distributes copies to the ***work group*** (the persons working on a project). Each person enters his or her comments and/or proposed changes, then the various workbooks can be merged into a single workbook. It's also possible to create a ***shared workbook*** and place it on a network drive to give all reviewers access to a common file.

Consider, for example, Figure 6.4, which displays an *erroneous* version of the financial forecast. One of the first things you notice about Figure 6.4 is the comments by different people, Marion, Jodi, and Ben, who have reviewed the spreadsheet and suggested changes. Anyone with access to the shared workbook can change it using the tools on the ***Reviewing toolbar*** or through the ***Track Changes command***. The changes made by different people to cell formulas are even displayed in different colors. You, as the developer, can then review the collective changes and resolve any conflicts that might occur.

How can you, or any of the reviewers, know when a spreadsheet displays invalid results? One way is to "eyeball" the spreadsheet and try to approximate its results. Look for any calculations that are obviously incorrect. Look at the financial forecast, for example, and see whether all the values are growing at the projected rates

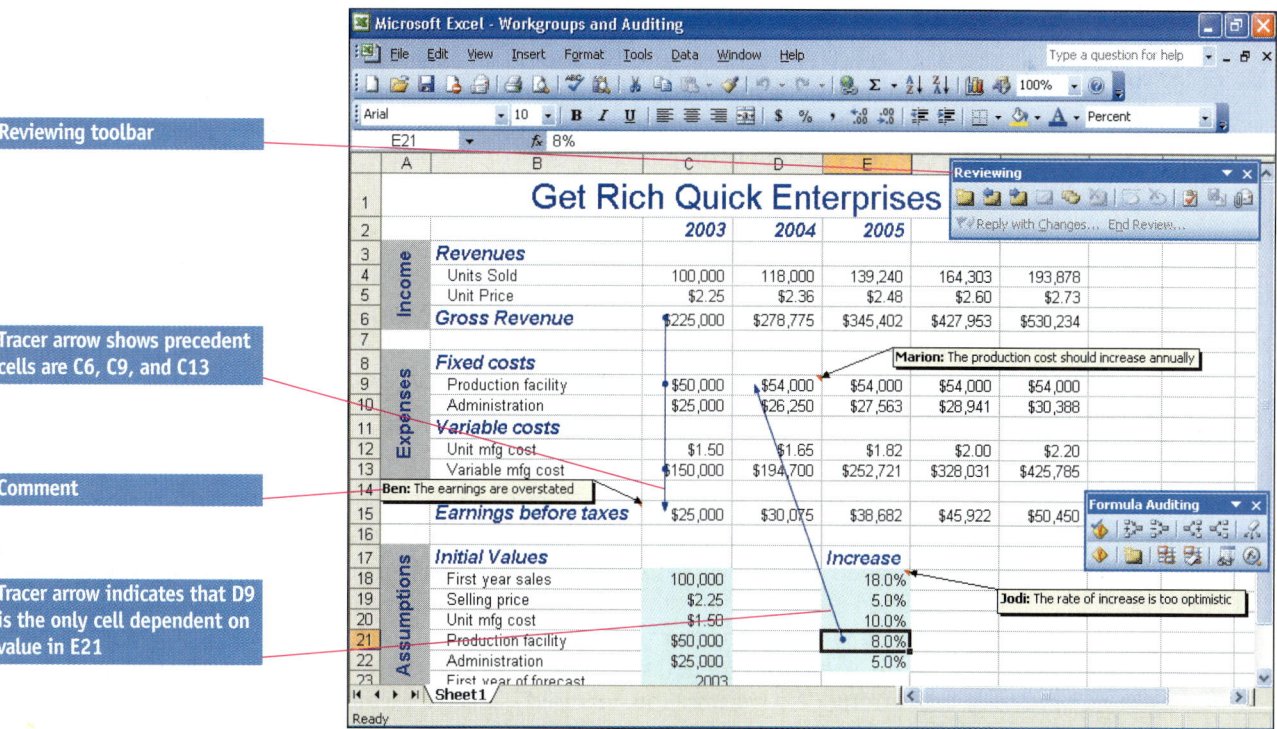

FIGURE 6.4 Workgroups and Auditing

of change. The number of units sold and the unit price increase every year as expected, but the cost of the production facility remains constant after 2004 (Marion's comment). This is an obvious error, because the production facility is supposed to increase at 8% annually, according to the assumptions at the bottom of the spreadsheet. The consequence of this error is that the production costs are too low and hence the projected earnings are too high. The error was easy to find, even without the use of a calculator.

A more subtle error occurs in the computation of the earnings before taxes. Look at the numbers for 2003. The gross revenue is $225,000. The total cost is also $225,000 ($50,000 for the production facility, $25,000 for administration, and $150,000 for the manufacturing cost). The projected earnings should be zero, but are shown incorrectly as $25,000 (Ben's comment), because the administration cost was not subtracted from the gross revenue in determining the profit.

You may be good enough to spot either of these errors just by looking at the spreadsheet. You can also use the **Formula Auditing toolbar** to display the relationships between the various cells in a worksheet. It enables you to trace the *precedents* for a formula and identify the cells in the worksheet that are referenced by that formula. It also enables you to trace the *dependents* of a cell and identify the formulas in the worksheet that reference that cell.

The identification of precedent and/or dependent cells is done graphically by displaying *tracers* on the worksheet. You simply click in the cell for which you want the information, then you click the appropriate button on the Formula Auditing toolbar. The blue lines (tracers) appear on the worksheet, and will remain on the worksheet until you click the appropriate removal button. The tracers always point forward, from the precedent cells to the dependent formula.

Look again at Figure 6.4 to see how the tracers are used. Cell C15 contains the formula to compute the earnings for the first year. There is a tracer (blue line) pointing to this cell, and it indicates the precedents for the cell. In other words, we can see that cells C6, C9, and C13 are used to compute the value of cell C15. Cell C10 is not a precedent, however, and therein lies the error.

The analysis of the cost of the production facility is equally telling. There is a single tracer pointing away from cell E21, indicating that there is only one other cell (cell D9) in the worksheet that depends on the value of cell E21. In actuality, however, cells E9, F9, and G9 should also depend on the value of cell E21. Hence the cost of the production facility does not increase as it is supposed to. Jodi's comment about the unrealistic rate of the sales increase is best addressed through the Data Validation command.

Data Validation

The results of the financial forecast depend on the accuracy of the spreadsheet as well as the underlying assumptions. One way to stop such errors from occurring is through the **Data Validation command**, which enables the developer to restrict the values that can be entered into a cell. If the cell is to contain a text entry, you can limit the values to those that appear in a list such as Atlanta, Boston, or Chicago. In similar fashion, you can specify a quantitative relationship for numeric values such as > 0 or < 100.

Figure 6.5a displays the Settings tab in the Data Validation dialog box in which the developer prevents the value in cell E18 (the annual sales increase) from exceeding 15%. Figure 6.5b shows the type of error alert (a Warning) and the associated message that is to appear if the user does not enter a valid value. Figure 6.5c displays the dialog box the user sees if the criteria are violated, together with the indicated choice of actions. "Yes" accepts the invalid data into the cell despite the warning, "No" returns the user to the cell for further editing, and "Cancel" restores the previous value to the cell. The Formula Auditing toolbar contains a tool to *circle invalid data* if the warning is disregarded. (See practice exercise 2 at the end of the chapter.)

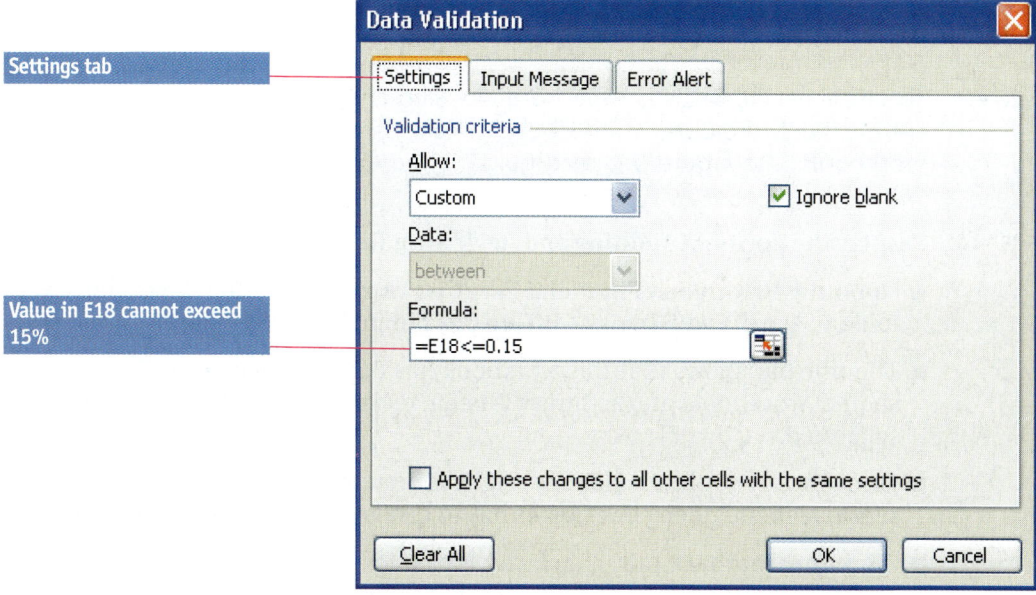

(a) Settings Tab

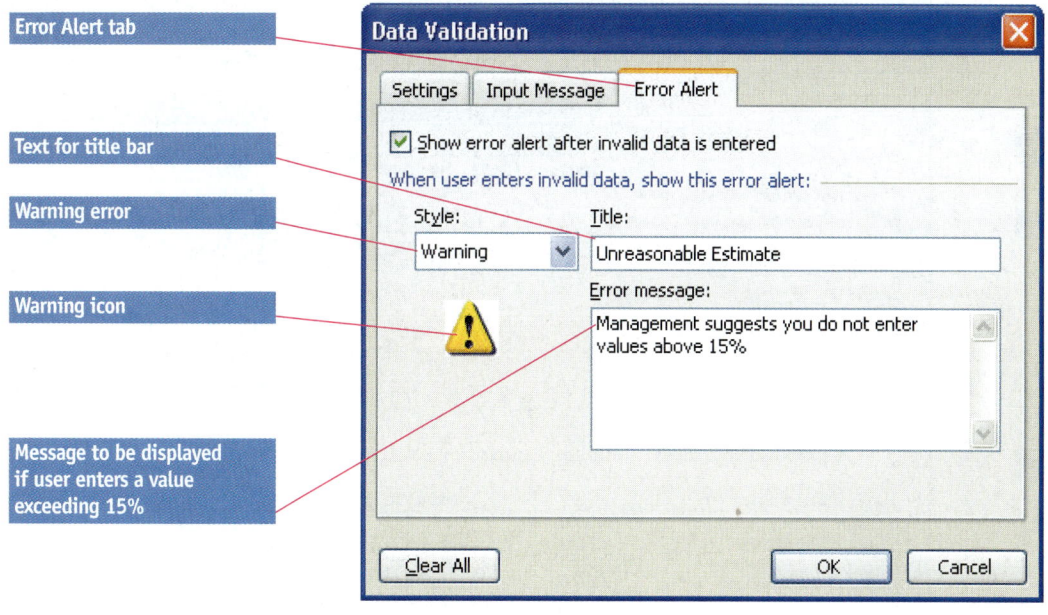

(b) Error Alert Tab

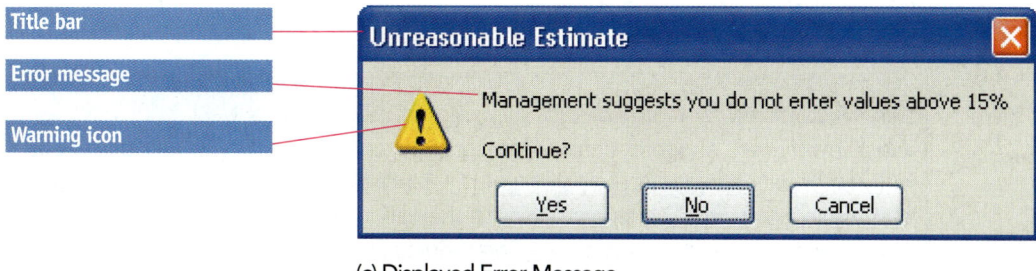

(c) Displayed Error Message

FIGURE 6.5 The Data Validation Command

hands-on exercise 2

Auditing and Workgroups

Objective To illustrate the tools on the Formula Auditing toolbar; to trace errors in spreadsheet formulas; to insert and delete comments; to track changes in a workbook. Use Figure 6.6 as a guide in the exercise.

Step 1: **Display the Formula Auditing and Reviewing Toolbars**

- Open the **Erroneous Financial Forecast workbook** in the **Exploring Excel folder**. Save the workbook as **Erroneous Financial Forecast Solution**.
- The title bar shows that this workbook has been previously established as a shared workbook. It has already been reviewed and changes have been suggested.
- Point to any toolbar, click the **right mouse button** to display a context-sensitive menu, then click **Customize** to display the Customize dialog box.
- Click the **Toolbars tab**, check the boxes for the **Reviewing** and **Formula Auditing toolbars**, then close the dialog box to display the toolbars as in Figure 6.6a.

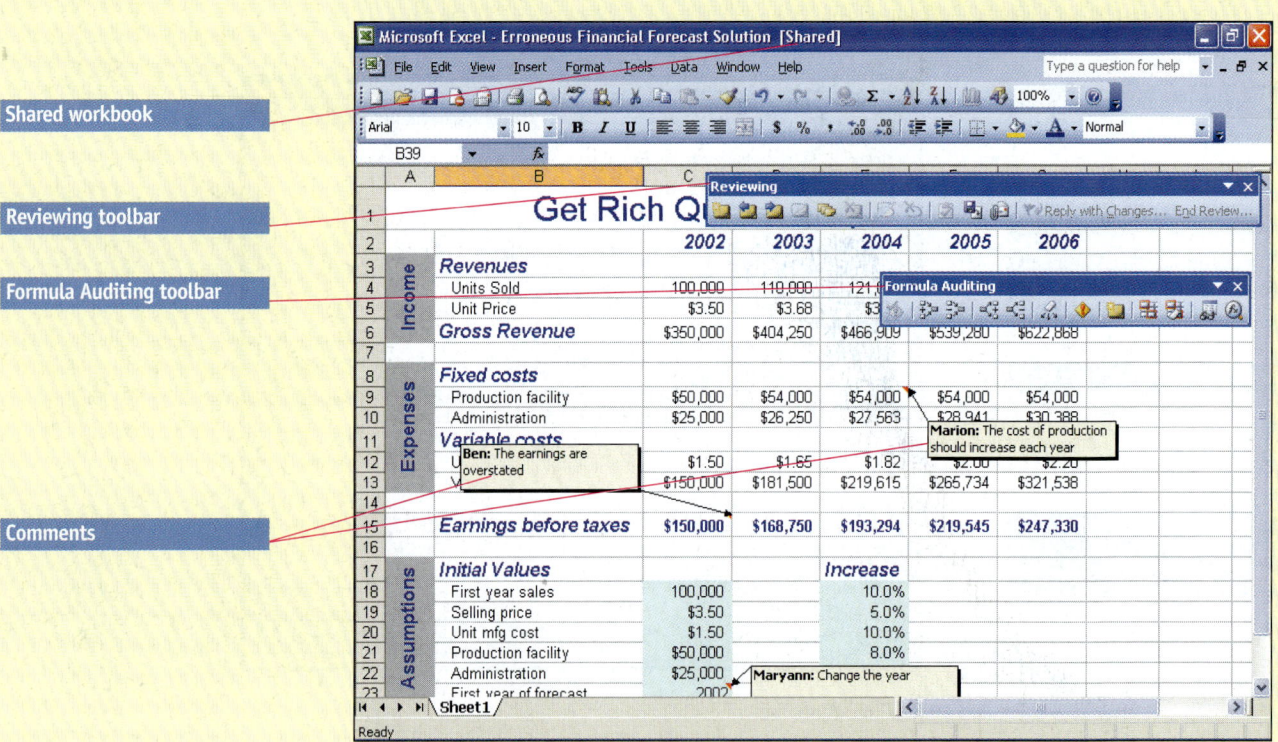

(a) Display the Formula Auditing and Reviewing Toolbars (step 1)

FIGURE 6.6 Hands-on Exercise 2

COMMENTS VERSUS CHANGES

A reviewer can suggest comments through the Insert Comment command and/or enter changes directly through the Track Changes command. Comments are visible immediately when you point to the cell, whereas changes are not visible until Track Changes is turned on. Comments display only the reviewer's name. Changes show the name, date, and time of the change.

Step 2: **Highlight Changes**

- Pull down the **Tools menu**, click (or point to) the **Track Changes command**, then click **Highlight Changes** to display the Highlight Changes dialog box. Set the various options to match our selections in Figure 6.6b. Click **OK**.

- You should see a border around cell C19 to indicate that a change has been made to the contents of that cell. Point to the cell and you will see a ScreenTip indicating that Robert Grauer changed the contents from $2.25 to $3.50.

- Click in **cell C23**. Type **2003** to modify the year (as suggested by Maryann) and press **Enter**. The years change automatically at the top of the forecast.

- Maryann's comment is now obsolete. Thus, right click in **cell C23** to display the context-sensitive menu, then click the **Delete Comment command**.

- The comment is removed from the cell and the red triangle disappears. The cell is still enclosed in a blue border and has a blue triangle to indicate that its value has changed. Point to **cell C23** to see the modification.

- Click the **Hide All Comments button** on the Reviewing toolbar. The comments are still in the worksheet, but are no longer visible.

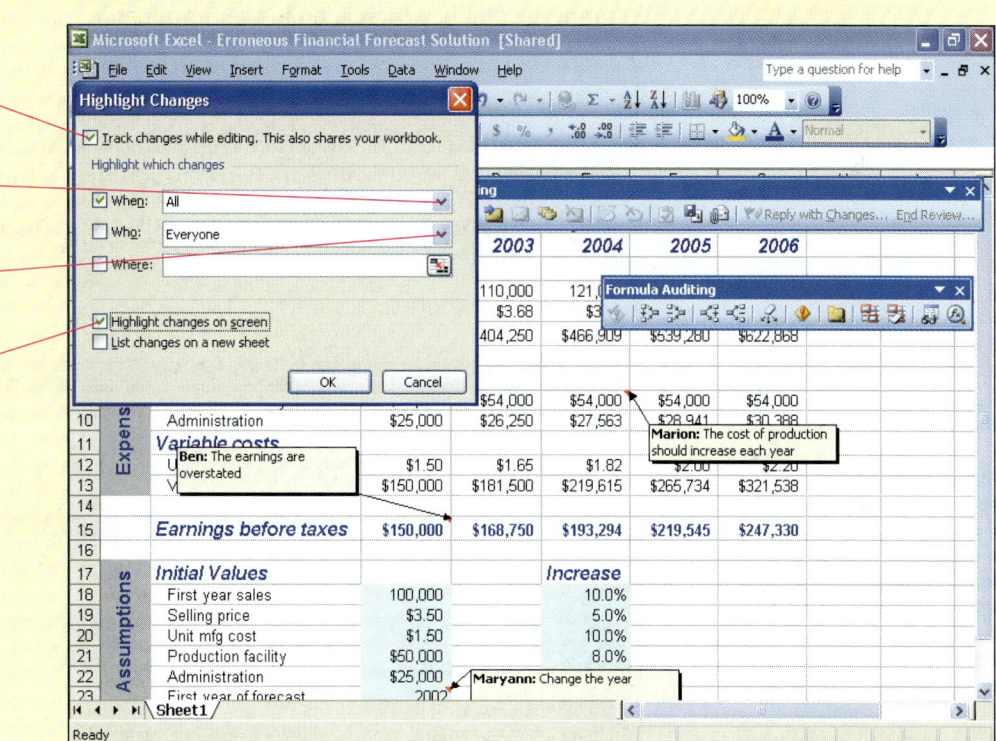

(b) Highlight Changes (step 2)

FIGURE 6.6 Hands-on Exercise 2 (*continued*)

CHANGE THE YEAR

A well-designed spreadsheet facilitates change by isolating the assumptions and initial conditions. 2002 has come and gone, but all you have to do to update the forecast is to click in cell C23, and enter 2003 as the initial year. The entries in cells C2 through G2 (containing years of the forecast) are changed automatically as they contain formulas (rather than specific values) that reference the value in cell C23.

Step 3: **Trace Dependents**

- Point to **cell E9** to display the comment, which indicates that the production costs do not increase after the second year. Click in **cell E21** (the cell containing the projected increase in the cost of the production facility).

- Click the **Trace Dependents button** on the Formula Auditing toolbar to display the dependent cells as shown in Figure 6.6c. Only one dependent cell (cell D9) is shown. This is clearly an error because cells E9 through G9 should also depend on cell E21.

- Click in **cell D9** to examine its formula. The production costs for the second year are based on the first-year costs (cell C9) and the rate of increase (cell E21). The latter, however, was entered as a relative rather than an absolute address.

- Change the formula in **cell D9** to include an absolute reference to cell E21 (i.e., the correct formula is =C9+C9*$E$21). The tracer arrow disappears due to the correction.

- Drag the fill handle in **cell D9** to copy the corrected formula to cells E9, F9, and G9. The displayed value for cell G9 should be $68,024. Delete Marion's comment in cell E9, which is no longer applicable.

- Cells D9 through G9 have a blue border and a blue triangle to indicate that changes were made to these cells.

- Click in **cell E21**. Click the **Trace Dependents button**, and this time it points to the production costs for years two through five in the forecast.

- Click the **Remove Dependent Arrows button** on the Formula Auditing toolbar to remove the arrows.

- Save the workbook.

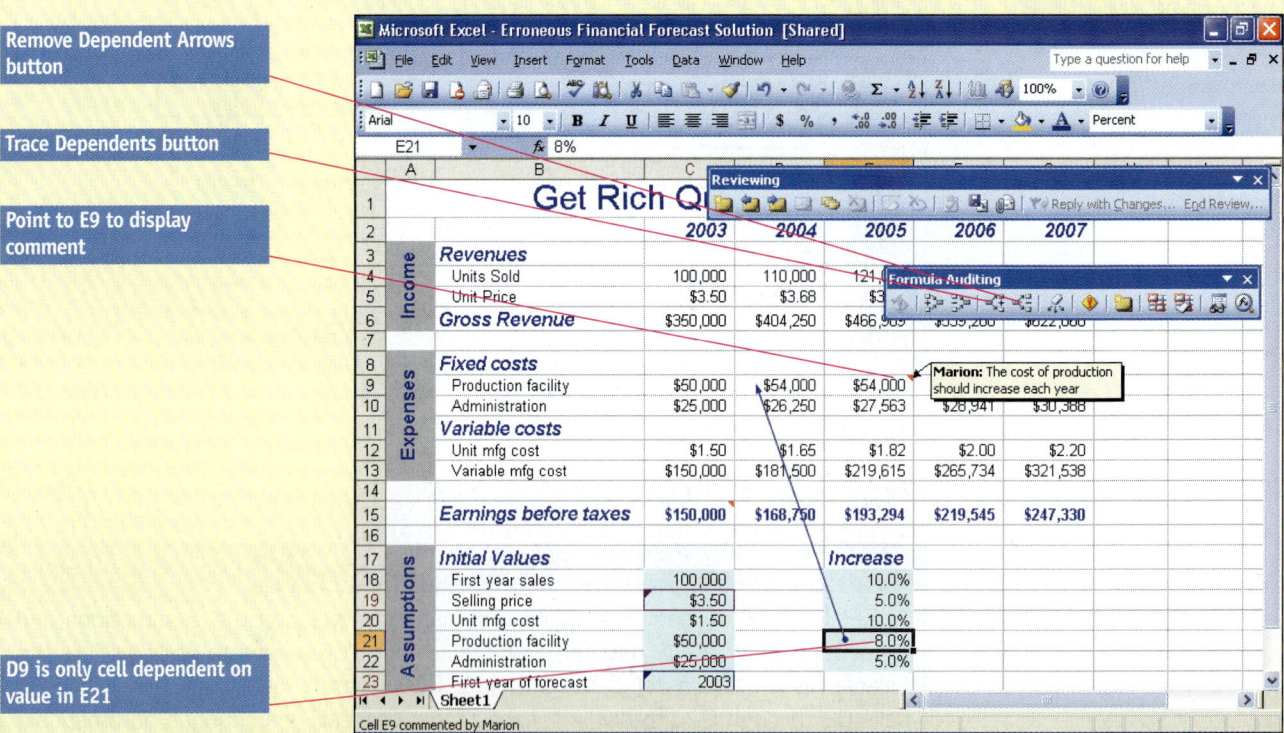

(c) Trace Dependents (step 3)

FIGURE 6.6 Hands-on Exercise 2 (*continued*)

Step 4: **Trace Precedents**

- Point to **cell C15** to display Ben's comment that questions the earnings before taxes. Now click in **cell C15** and click the **Trace Precedents button** to display the precedent cells as shown in Figure 6.6d.

- There is an error in the formula because the earnings do not account for the administration expense (cell C10).

- Change the formula in cell C15 to =**C6-(C9+C10+C13)**. The earnings change to $125,000 after the correction.

- Drag the fill handle in **cell C15** to copy the corrected formula to cells D15 through G15. (The latter displays a value of $202,918 after the correction.)

- Point to cell C15. You see both the change and the comment. Now right click in cell C15 and delete the comment, which is no longer applicable. Only the comment is deleted, not the ScreenTip associated with the change.

- Save the workbook.

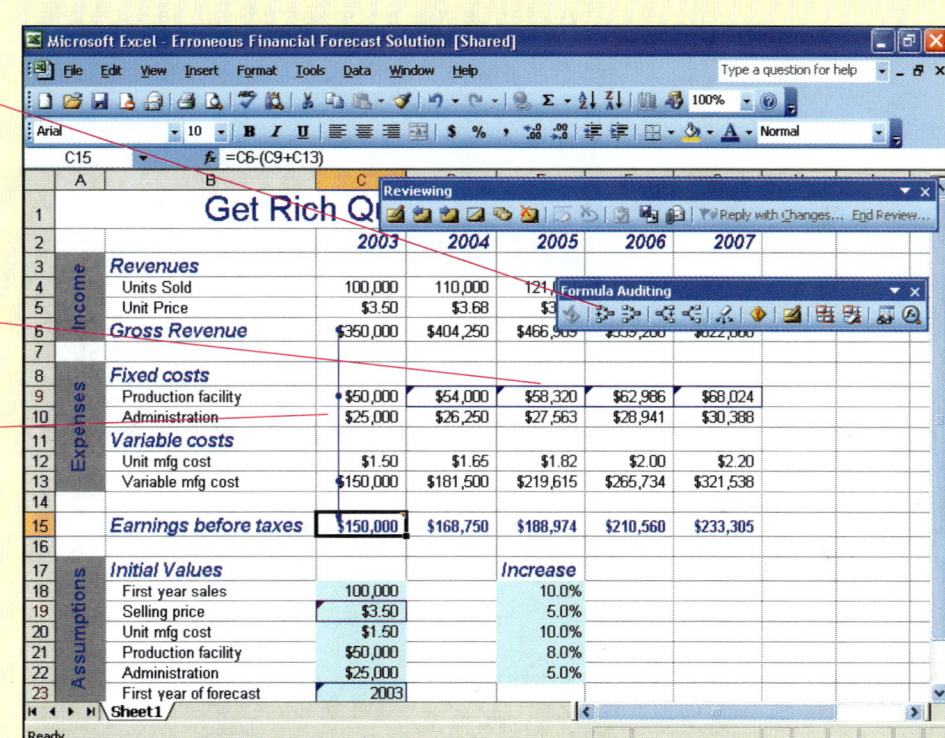

(d) Trace Precedents (step 4)

FIGURE 6.6 Hands-on Exercise 2 (*continued*)

THE FORMULAS ARE COLOR-CODED

The fastest way to change the contents of a cell is to double click in the cell, then make the changes directly in the cell rather than to change the entries on the formula bar. Note, too, that if the cell contains a formula (as opposed to a literal entry), Excel will display each cell reference in the formula in a different color, which corresponds to the border color of the referenced cells elsewhere in the worksheet. This makes it easy to see which cell or cell range is referenced by the formula. You can also click and drag the colored border to a different cell to change the cell formula.

Step 5: **Accept or Reject Changes (resolve conflicts)**

- Pull down the **Tools menu**, click the **Share Workbook command** to display the Share Workbook dialog box, then click the **Advanced tab**.

- Look for the Conflicting Changes Between Users section (toward the bottom of the dialog box), then if necessary, click the option button that says "Ask me which changes win". Click **OK**.

- Pull down the **Tools menu**, click (or point to) the **Track Changes command**, then click **Accept or Reject Changes**. You can accept the default selections in the Selection Changes dialog box. Click **OK**.

- You should see the Accept or Reject Changes dialog box in Figure 6.6e. You see Robert Grauer's change from $2.25 to $3.50. Click the **Reject button**. (The contents of cell C19 change in the worksheet to $2.25, which in turn affects several other values throughout the spreadsheet.)

- Click **Accept** (or press **Ctrl+A**) to accept the next change, which was the change you made earlier in the first year of the forecast. Press the **Accept button** as you are presented with each additional change.

- Save the workbook.

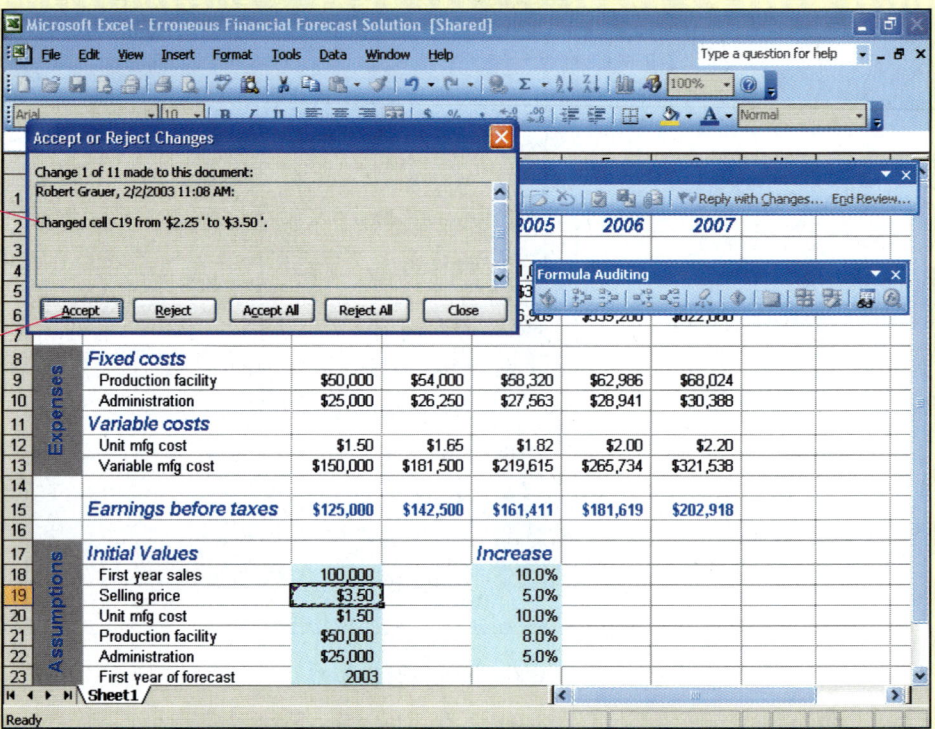

(e) Accept or Reject Changes (step 5)

FIGURE 6.6 Hands-on Exercise 2 (*continued*)

CIRCULAR REFERENCES

A circular reference occurs when a cell formula references itself, either directly or indirectly. Excel indicates the problem automatically and displays a circular reference toolbar which shows the interdependencies of the affected cells. Excel also gives you the option to remove the reference and/or to override the error and calculate the spreadsheet manually using multiple iterations to arrive at a steady state value. See practice exercise 8 at the end of the chapter.

Step 6: **Insert a Comment**

- Click in **cell C19** (the cell containing the selling price for the first year). Pull down the **Insert menu** and click the **Comment command** (or click the **New Comment button** on the Reviewing toolbar).

- A comment box opens, as shown in Figure 6.6f. Enter the text of your comment as shown in the figure, then click outside the comment when you are finished.

- The comment box closes, but a tiny red triangle appears in the upper-right corner of cell C19. (If you do not see the triangle, pull down the **Tools menu**, click **Options**, click the **View tab**, then click the option button in the Comments area to show **Comment Indicator only**.)

- Point to **cell C19** and the text of your comment appears. Point to a different cell and the comment disappears.

- Save the workbook.

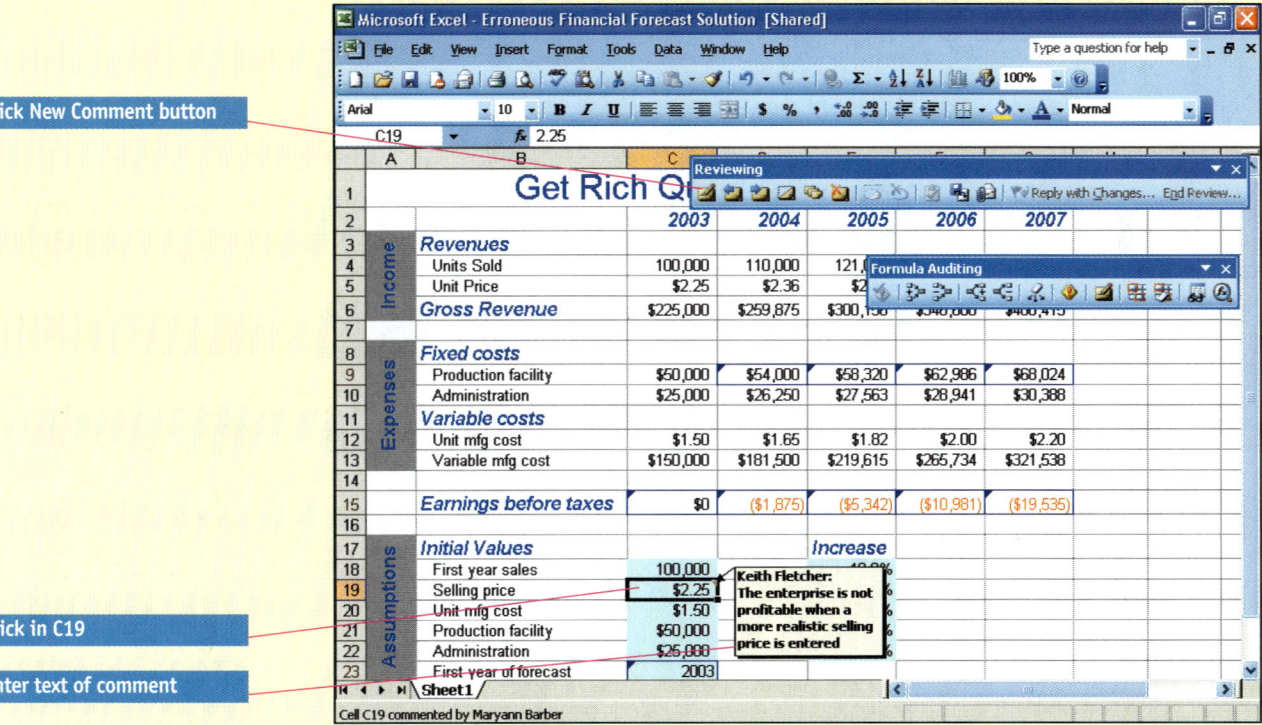

(f) Insert a Comment (step 6)

FIGURE 6.6 Hands-on Exercise 2 (*continued*)

EDITING OR DELETING COMMENTS

The easiest way to edit or delete an existing comment is to point to the cell containing the comment, then click the right mouse button to display a context-sensitive menu, in which you select the appropriate command. You can use the right mouse button to insert a comment by right clicking in the cell, then choosing the Insert Comment command. You can also insert or delete a comment by using the appropriate tool on the Reviewing toolbar.

Step 7: **Data Validation**

- Click in **cell E18**. Type **.18**. Excel displays the error message shown in Figure 6.6g. Press **Esc** to cancel and try another entry above 15%. No matter how many times you try, you will not be able to enter a value above .15 in cell E18 because the error type we previously defined was specified as "Stop" rather than a warning.

- Pull down the **Data menu**. The Validation command is dim and not currently accessible because the workbook is currently a shared workbook.

- Pull down the **Tools menu**, click (or point to) the **Track Changes command**, then click **Highlight Changes** to display the Highlight Changes dialog box. Clear the box to track changes while editing. Click **OK**.

- Click in **cell E18**. Pull down the **Data menu**. Click the **Validation command** (which is now accessible) to display the Data Validation dialog box, and if necessary, click the **Error Alert tab**.

- Click the **drop-down arrow** on the Style list box and click **Warning**. Change the text of the message to **Management frowns on values above 15%**. Click **OK** to accept the new settings and close the dialog box.

- Reenter .18 in **cell E18**. This time you see a Warning message, rather than a Stop message. Click **Yes** to accept the new value.

- Add your name somewhere in the workbook. Save the workbook, then print the completed workbook for your professor as proof that you completed the exercise.

- Close the Reviewing and Formula Auditing toolbars. Close the workbook. Exit Excel if you do not want to continue with the next exercise at this time.

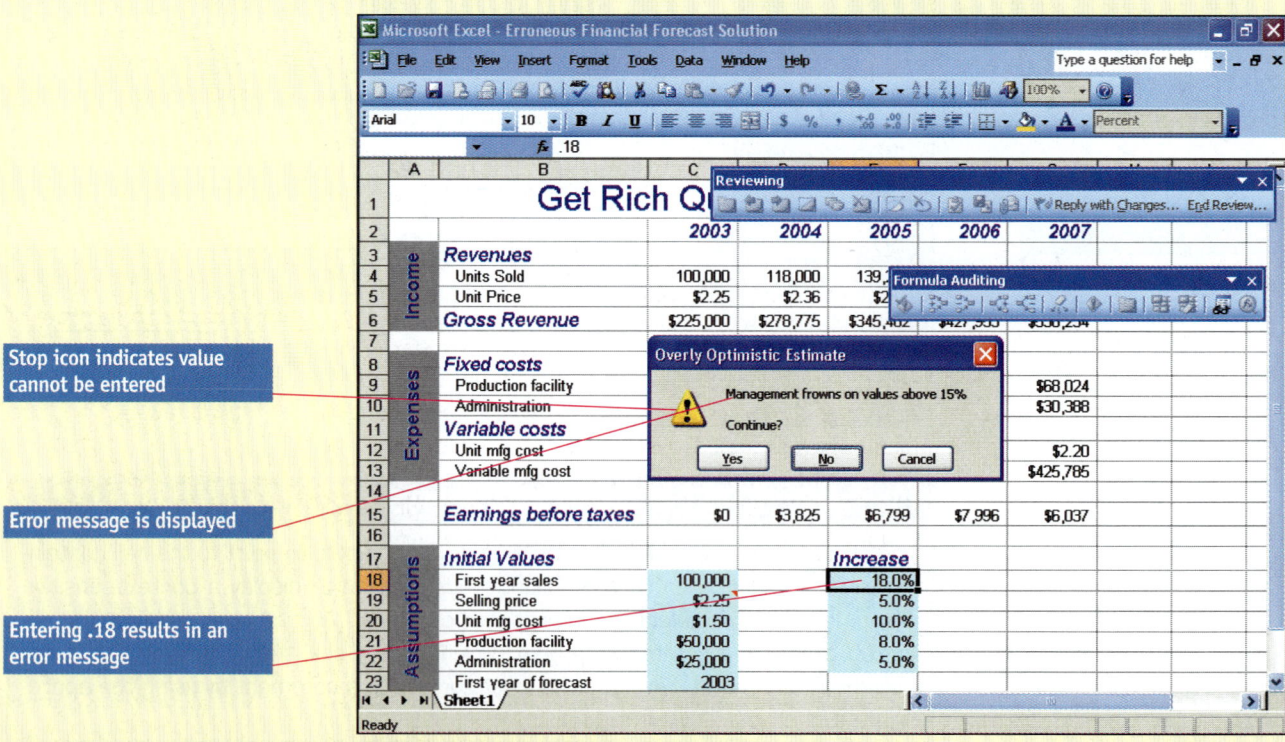

(g) Data Validation (step 7)

FIGURE 6.6 Hands-on Exercise 2 (*continued*)

1278 CHAPTER 6: A FINANCIAL FORECAST

TEMPLATES

The spreadsheet just completed is tailored to the needs of financial forecasting for Get Rich Quick Enterprises. It could also serve as the basis of a financial forecast for any organization, which leads in turn to the creation of a template. A **template** is a special type of workbook (it has its own file format) that is used as the basis for other workbooks. It contains text, formatting, formulas, and/or macros, but it does not contain data; the latter is entered by the end user as he or she uses the template to create a workbook.

Figure 6.7a contains the template you will create in the next hands-on exercise. It resembles the completed forecast from earlier in the chapter, except that the assumption area has been cleared of all values except the initial year of the forecast. Even the name of the company in cell A1 has been erased. Look at the active cell (cell C15), however, and note that its contents are visible in the Formula bar. Thus, you can see that the template contains the formulas from the worksheet, but without any data. (The results of the calculations within the body of the spreadsheet are uniformly zero, but the zeros are suppressed through an option set through the Tools menu.)

The template in Figure 6.7a is used to create specific forecasts such as the one in Figure 6.7b. Look closely at the entry in the title bar for that forecast, noting that it appears as Get Rich Quick1; that is, the number 1 has been appended to the name of the template. This is done automatically by Excel, which will add the next sequential number to the name of each additional forecast during a session. To create a specific forecast, just enter the desired values in the assumption area; then as each value is entered, the formulas in the body of the spreadsheet will automatically calculate the results.

Most templates are based on **protected worksheets** that enable the user to modify only a limited number of cells within the worksheet. The template for financial forecast, for example, enables the user to change the contents of any cell in the assumption area, but precludes changes elsewhere in the worksheet. This is very important, especially when templates are used throughout an organization. The protection prevents an individual who is not familiar with Excel from accidentally (or otherwise) changing a cell formula. Any attempt to do so produces a protected-cell message on the screen.

To create a template, you start with a finished workbook and check it for accuracy. Then you clear the assumption area and protect the worksheet. The latter is a two-step process. First, you **unlock** all of the cells that are subject to change, then you protect the worksheet. Once this is done, the user will be able to change the value of any cell that was unlocked, but will be unable to change the contents of any other cell. Finally, you save the template under its own name, but as a template rather than an ordinary workbook. Ideally, the template should be saved in a special **Templates folder** within the Microsoft Office folder so that it can be accessed automatically from the task pane. This is possible only if you have your own computer and/or if the network administrator puts the template in the folder for you. (You can, however, change the default folder when you save the template.)

Once created, a template can be accessed three different ways—through the File Open command, from the task pane, or by double clicking its icon from within Windows Explorer or My Computer. The File Open command opens the actual template, enabling you to modify the template if and when that becomes necessary. The task pane provides a link to General Templates that combines the function of the File Open command with that of the Save As command. It opens a template and automatically saves it as a workbook, assigning a name to the workbook by appending a number to the name of the template (e.g., Get Rich Quick1). Double clicking a file from within My Computer or Windows Explorer has the same effect as accessing the template from the task pane.

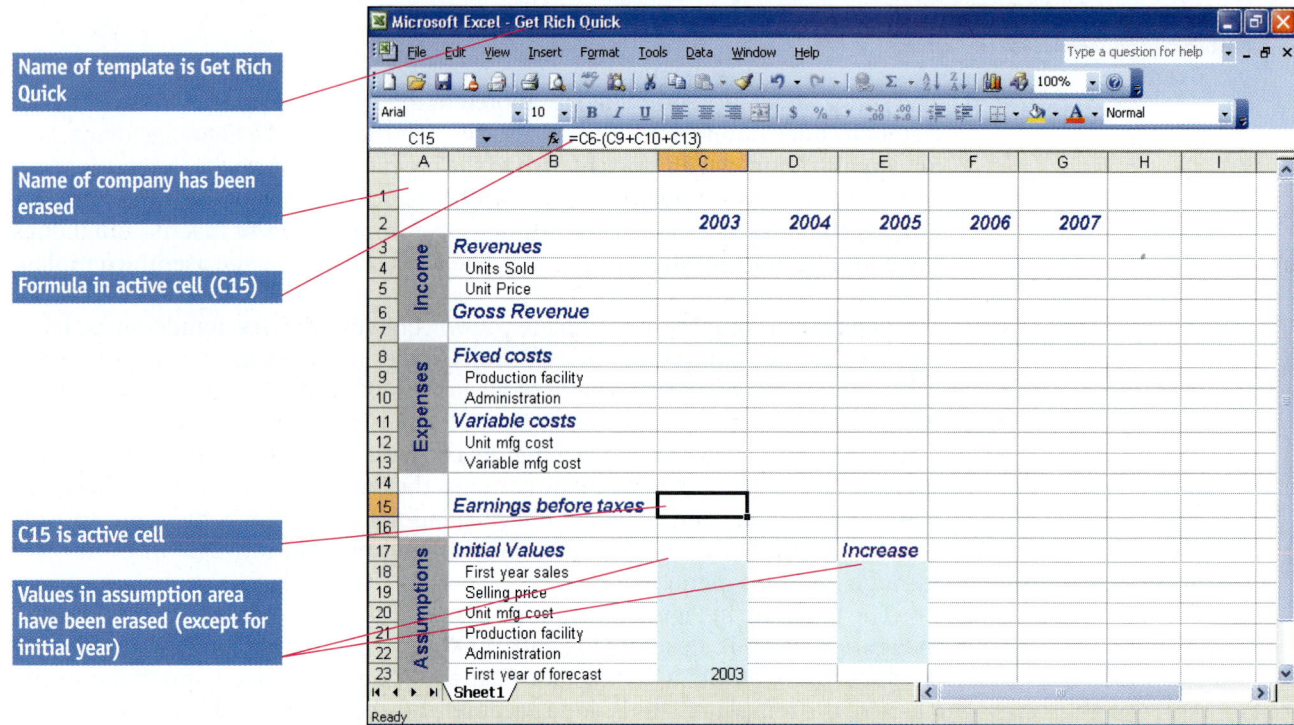

(a) Template

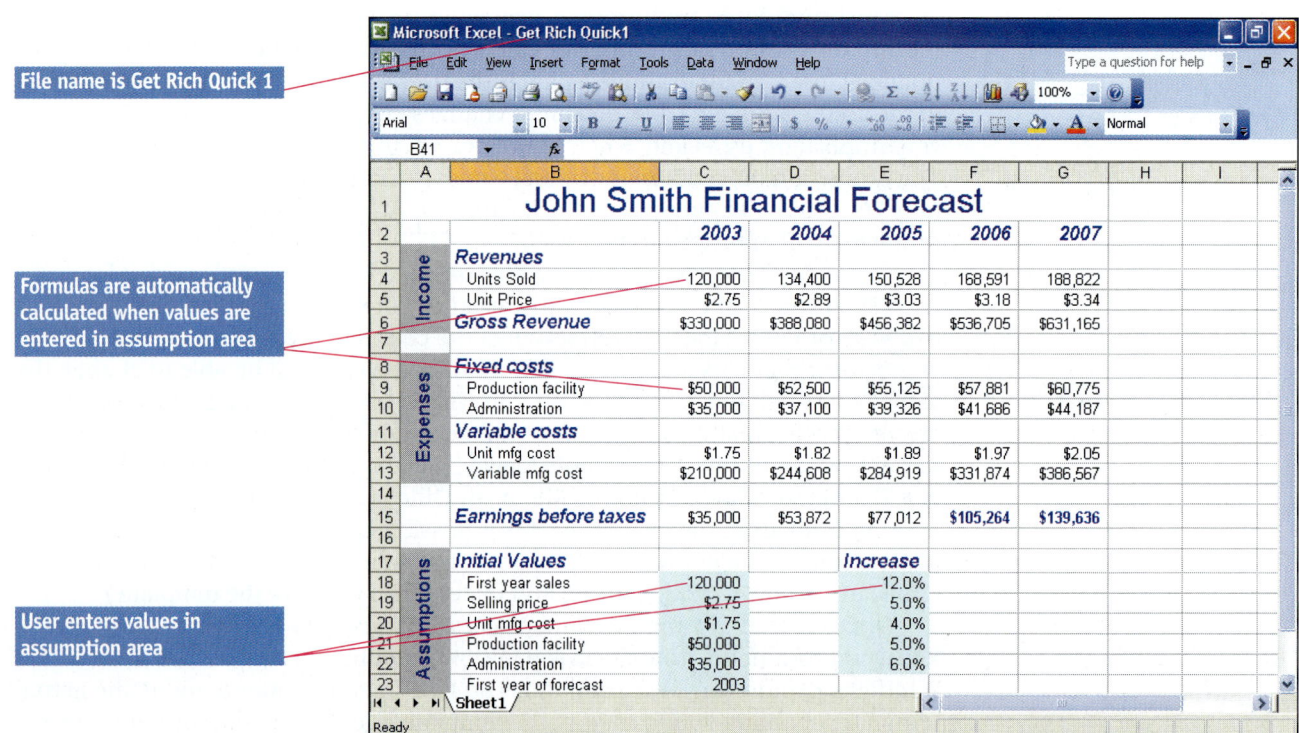

(b) Completed Worksheet

FIGURE 6.7 The Get Rich Quick Template

hands-on exercise

3 Creating a Template

Objective To unlock cells in a worksheet, then protect the worksheet; to create a template and then create a workbook from that template. Use Figure 6.8 as a guide in the exercise.

Step 1: **Clear the Assumption Area**

- Open the **Erroneous Financial Forecast Solution** from the previous exercise. Click in **cell A1**, then press and hold the **Ctrl key** as you click and drag to select **cells C18 through E23**.

- Pull down the **Edit menu**, click (or point to) the **Clear command**, then click **Contents** to delete the contents from the selected cells as shown in Figure 6.8a. The values in the body of the spreadsheet are all zero.

- Pull down the **Edit menu** a second time, click the **Clear command**, then click **Comments** to delete the comments from these cells as well.

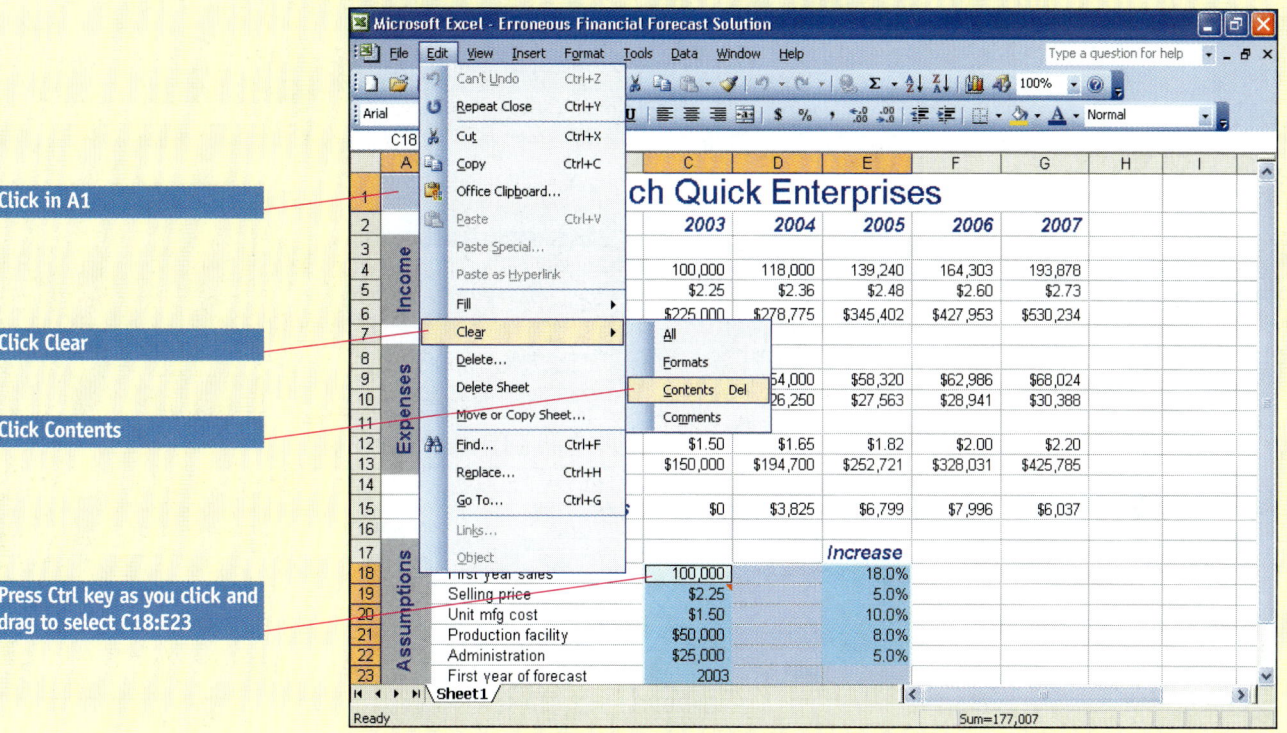

(a) Clear the Assumption Area (step 1)

FIGURE 6.8 Hands-on Exercise 3

WORKBOOK PROPERTIES

Do you know the original author of the workbook or other Office document that is currently open? When was the file created, modified, and last accessed? This and other information are stored within the workbook and can be viewed (or changed) by pulling down the File menu, clicking the Properties command, and clicking the Statistics tab.

Step 2: **Protect the Worksheet**

- Protecting a worksheet is a two-step process. First, you unlock the cells that you want to be able to change after the worksheet has been protected, then you protect the worksheet.

- Click in **cell A1**, then press and hold the **Ctrl key** as you click and drag to select **cells C18 through E23**. Pull down the **Format menu**, click the **Cells command** to display the Format Cells dialog box. Click the **Protection tab**, then clear the **Locked check box**. Click **OK**.

- Pull down the **Tools menu**, click **Protection**, then click the **Protect Sheet command** to display the Protect Sheet dialog box in Figure 6.8b. Be sure that your settings match those in the figure, then click **OK**. (A password is optional. If you do enter a password, be sure you remember it, or else you will not be able to modify the workbook.)

- Pull down the **Tools menu**, click the **Options command**, click the **View tab**, and clear the box to show zero values. Click **OK**. The zeros disappear.

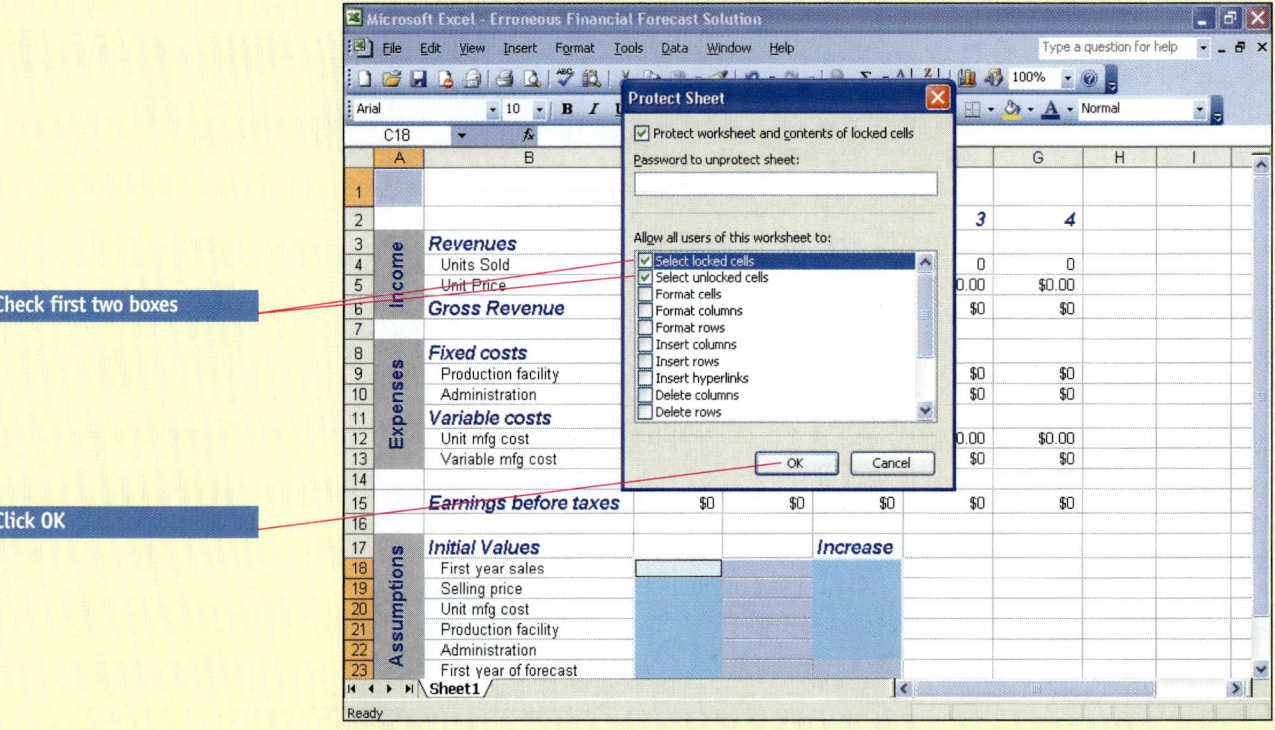

(b) Protect the Worksheet (step 2)

FIGURE 6.8 Hands-on Exercise 3 (*continued*)

THE OPTIONS MENU

Pull down the Tools menu and click the Options command to display the Options dialog box from where you can customize virtually every aspect of Excel. The General tab is especially useful as it enables you to change the default file location, the number of worksheets in a new workbook, the default font in a workbook, and/or the number of recently opened files that appear on the File menu. There is no need to memorize anything, just spend a few minutes exploring the options on the various tabs, then think of the Options command the next time you want to change an Excel feature.

Step 3: **Test the Template**

- Test the assumption area to be sure that you can change the contents of these cells. Click in **cell A1** and enter your name followed by the words **Financial Forecast**. The text will be centered automatically across the top of the worksheet.

- Click in **cell C23**, type **2003**, and press the **Enter key**. Excel should accept this value, and in addition, it should change the years as shown in Figure 6.8c. Enter the values **100000** and **.10** in **cells C18 and E18**, respectively. Excel should accept these values and build the spreadsheet accordingly.

- If you are prevented from entering a value in the assumption area, you need to unprotect the worksheet and unlock the cells.
  - Pull down the **Tools menu**, click **Protection**, then click the **Unprotect Sheet command**.
  - Select the cells in the assumption area, pull down the **Format menu**, click the **Cells command**, click the **Protection tab**, and clear the Locked box.
  - Repeat the steps to protect the worksheet.

- Test the protection feature by clicking in any cell in the body of the worksheet (e.g., cell C5) and entering a value. You should see the dialog box in Figure 6.8c indicating that the cell is protected. Click **OK**. If you do not see this message, undo the entry and then repeat the commands to protect the worksheet.

- Clear the contents from **cells A1, C18, E18, and C23**. You're ready to save the template.

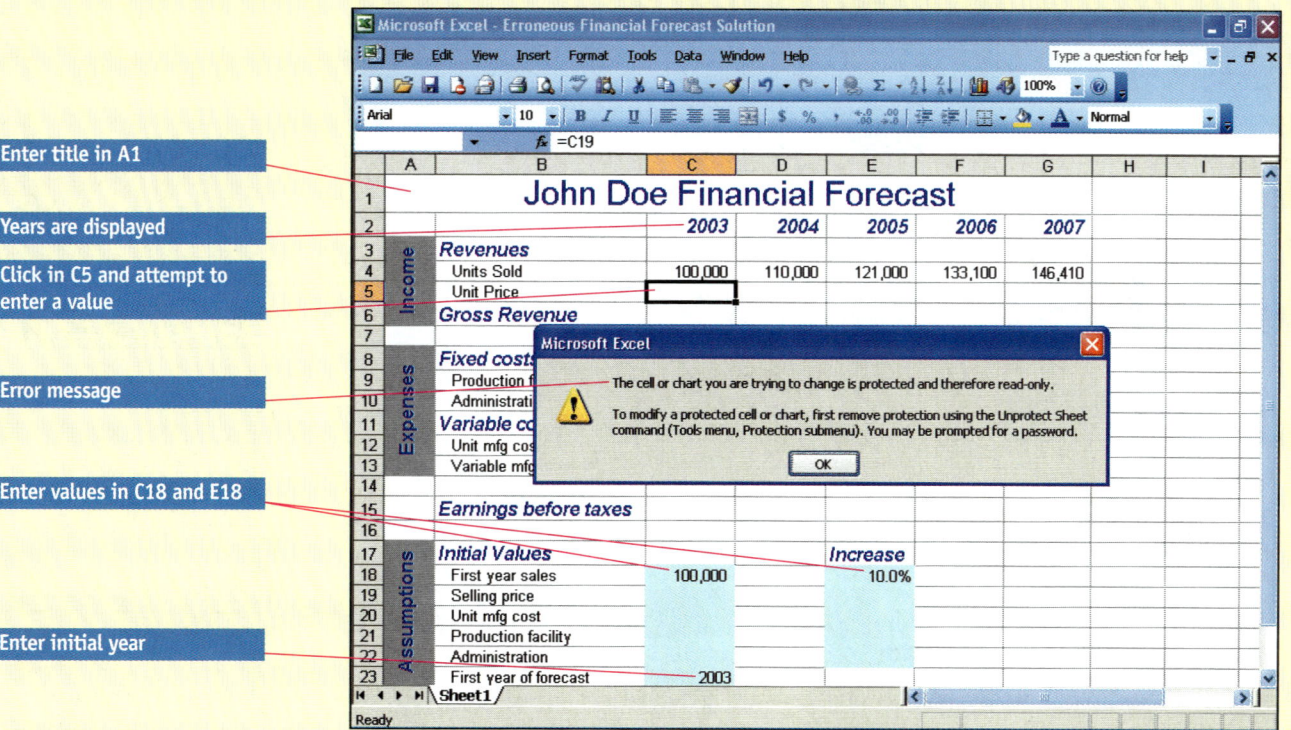

(c) Test the Template (step 3)

FIGURE 6.8 Hands-on Exercise 3 (*continued*)

Step 4: **Save the Template**

- Pull down the **File menu**, click the **Save As command** to display the Save As dialog box in Figure 6.8d. Enter **Get Rich Quick** as the name of the template.
- Click the **down arrow** in the Save as Type list box and choose **Template**. The folder where you will save the template depends on whether you have your own machine.
  - If you are working on your own computer and have access to all of its folders, save the template in the **Templates folder** (the default folder that is displayed automatically).
  - If you are working at school or otherwise sharing a computer, you should **change the default folder**. Click the down arrow in the Save in list box and save the template in the **Exploring Excel folder** that you have used throughout the text.
- Click the **Save button** to save the template.

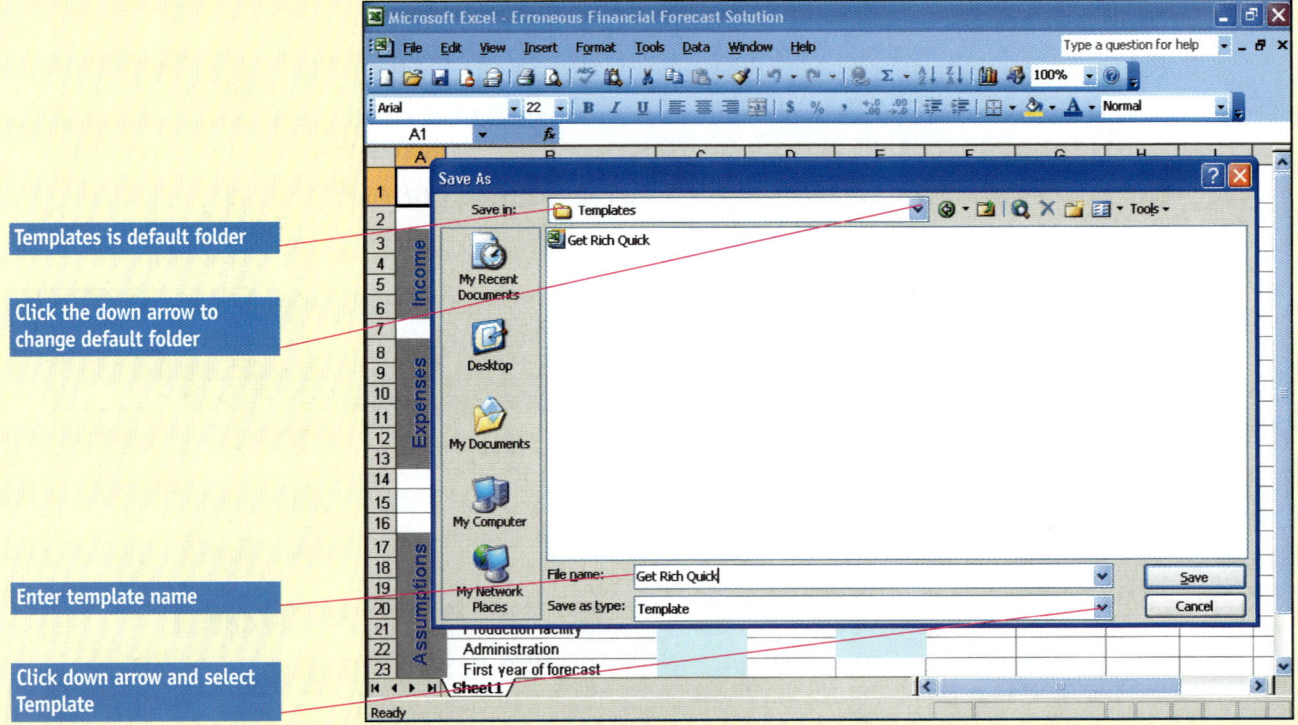

(d) Save the Template (step 4)

FIGURE 6.8 Hands-on Exercise 3 (*continued*)

PROTECT THE WORKBOOK

A template or workbook is not truly protected unless it is saved with a password, because a knowledgeable user can always pull down the Tools menu and access the Protect command to unprotect a worksheet. You can, however, use password protection to prevent this from happening. Pull down the File menu, click the Save As command to reveal the Save As dialog box, then click the Tools button and click General Options to display the Save Options dialog box. You can enter one or two passwords, one to open the file, and one to modify it. Be careful, however, because once you save a workbook or template with a password, you cannot open it if you forget the password.

Step 5: **Open the Template**

- Close Excel, then restart the program. The way in which you open the template depends on where you saved it in the previous step.
    - If you are working on your own computer, open the task pane, click the **down arrow** at the top of the task pane, and select **New workbook**. Click **On my computer** in the Templates section to display the dialog box in Figure 6.8e.
    - The Get Rich Quick template appears automatically because it was saved in the Templates folder. Double click the **Get Rich Quick template** to open it.
    - If you are working at school or otherwise sharing a computer, start Windows Explorer, change to the **Exploring Excel folder**, then double click the **Get Rich Quick template** to open it.
- You should see a blank workbook, named Get Rich Quick1. Excel automatically saves a copy of the template as a workbook and assigns it a name consisting of the template's name followed by a number.
- Complete and save the financial forecast. Print the completed workbook with displayed values and with the cell formulas. Exit Excel.

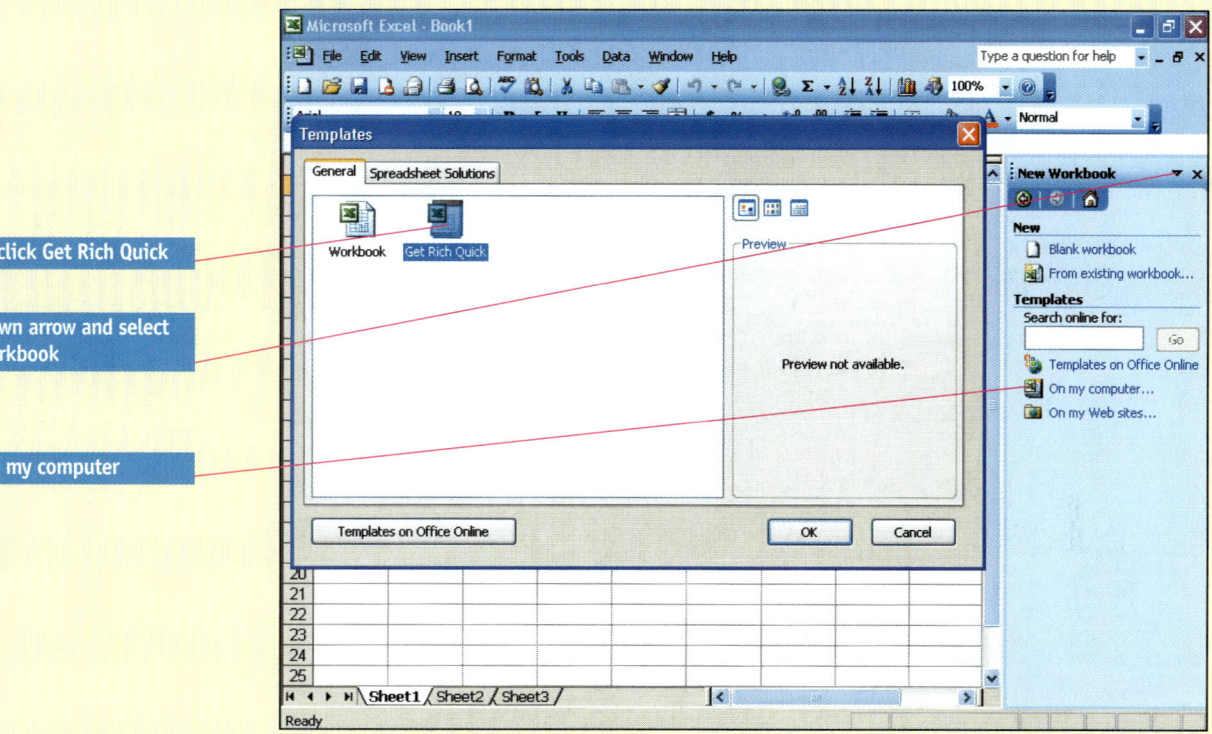

(e) Open the Template (step 5)

FIGURE 6.8 Hands-on Exercise 3 (*continued*)

CREATE A CHART AND ASSOCIATED TREND LINE

A chart adds impact to any type of numerical analysis. Use the template to create a financial forecast, and then plot the earnings before taxes against the associated year. A simple column chart is best. There is only one data series (the earnings before taxes) in cells C15 through G15. The category labels are in cells C2 through G2. Pull down the Chart menu after the chart has been created, then click the Add Trendline command to display the associated dialog box. Click the Type tab and choose a linear (straight-line) trend. Click OK to accept the setting and close the dialog box.

SUMMARY

A spreadsheet is used frequently as a tool in decision making, and as such, is the subject of continual what-if speculation. Thus, the initial conditions and assumptions on which the spreadsheet is based should be clearly visible so that they can be easily varied. In addition, the formulas in the body of the spreadsheet should be dependent on these cells.

A style is a set of formatting instructions that has been saved under a distinct name. Styles provide a consistent appearance to similar elements throughout a workbook. Existing styles can be modified to change the formatting of all cells that are defined by that style.

The Scenario Manager lets you specify multiple sets of assumptions (scenarios), then see the results at a glance within the associated worksheet. The scenario summary compares the effects of the different scenarios to one another by showing the value of one or more result cells in a summary table.

Conditional formatting may be implemented to change the appearance of a cell, based on its calculated value. The text in a cell may be rotated vertically to give the cell greater emphasis.

The Formula Auditing toolbar provides a graphical display for the relationships among the various cells in a worksheet. It enables you to trace the precedents for a formula and identify the cells in the worksheet that are referenced by that formula. It also enables you to trace the dependents of a cell and identify the formulas in the worksheet that reference that cell.

A shared workbook may be viewed and/or edited by multiple individuals simultaneously. The changes made by each user can be stored within the workbook, then subsequently reviewed by the developer, who has the ultimate authority to resolve any conflicts that might occur.

The Data Validation command enables you to restrict the values that will be accepted into a cell. You can limit the values to a list for cells containing text entries (e.g., Atlanta, Boston, or Chicago), or you can specify a quantitative relationship for cells that hold numeric values.

A template is a workbook that is used to create other workbooks. It contains text, formatting, formulas, and/or macros, but no specific data. A template that has been saved to the Templates or Spreadsheet Solutions folder is accessed automatically from the link to General Templates in the task pane.

A worksheet may be protected so that its contents cannot be altered or deleted. A protected worksheet may also contain various cells that are unlocked, enabling a user to vary the contents of these cells.

KEY TERMS

Assumptions 1254	Indent text 1256	Scenario summary 1257
Changing cells 1257	Initial conditions 1254	Shared workbook 1269
Circle invalid data 1270	Insert Comment command 1277	Style 1256
Circular reference 1276	Insert Name command 1265	Template 1279
Conditional formatting 1256	Precedent cells 1270	Templates folder 1279
Custom format 1256	Protected worksheet 1279	Tracers 1270
Custom view 1264	Result cells 1257	Track Changes command 1269
Data Validation command 1270	Reviewing toolbar 1269	Unlock cells 1279
Define Name command 1257	Rotate text 1256	Work group 1269
Dependent cells 1270	Scenario 1257	
Formula Auditing toolbar 1270	Scenario Manager 1257	

MULTIPLE CHOICE

1. Which of the following best describes the formula to compute the sales in the second year of the financial forecast?

    (a) It contains a relative reference to the assumed rate of increase and an absolute reference to the sales from the previous year
    (b) It contains an absolute reference to the assumed rate of increase and a relative reference to the sales from the previous year
    (c) It contains absolute references to both the assumed rate of increase and the sales from the previous year
    (d) It contains relative references to both the assumed rate of increase and the sales from the previous year

2. The estimated sales for the first year of a financial forecast are contained in cell B3. The sales for year two are assumed to be 10% higher than the first year, with the rate of increase (10%) stored in cell C23 at the bottom of the spreadsheet. Which of the following is the best way to enter the projected sales for year two, assuming that this formula is to be copied to the remaining years of the forecast?

    (a) =B3+B3*.10
    (b) =B3+B3*C23
    (c) =B3+B3*$C$23
    (d) All of the above are equivalent entries

3. Which of the following describes the placement of assumptions in a worksheet as required by Microsoft Excel?

    (a) The assumptions must appear in contiguous cells but can be placed anywhere within the worksheet
    (b) The assumptions must appear in contiguous cells and, further, must be placed below the main body of the worksheet
    (c) The assumptions are not required to appear in contiguous cells and, further, can be placed anywhere within the worksheet
    (d) None of the above

4. Given that cell D4 contains the formula =D1+D2:

    (a) Cells D1 and D2 are precedent cells for cell D4
    (b) Cell D4 is a dependent cell of cells D1 and D2
    (c) Both (a) and (b)
    (d) Neither (a) nor (b)

5. Which of the following is true, given that cell C23 is displayed with three blue tracers that point to cells E4, F4, and G4, respectively?

    (a) Cells E4, F4, and G4 are dependent cells for cell C23
    (b) Cell C23 is a precedent cell for cells E4, F4, and G4
    (c) Both (a) and (b)
    (d) Neither (a) nor (b)

6. How can you enter a comment into a cell?

    (a) Click the New Comment command on the Formula Auditing toolbar
    (b) Click the New Comment command on the Reviewing toolbar
    (c) Right click in the cell, then select the Insert Comment command
    (d) All of the above

7. Which of the following best describes how to protect a worksheet, but still enable the user to change the value of various cells within the worksheet?

    (a) Protect the entire worksheet, then unlock the cells that are to change
    (b) Protect the entire worksheet, then unprotect the cells that are to change
    (c) Lock the cells that are to change, then protect the entire worksheet
    (d) Unlock the cells that are to change, then protect the entire worksheet

8. Which of the following describes the protection associated with the financial forecast that was developed in the chapter?

    (a) The worksheet is protected and all cells are locked
    (b) The worksheet is protected and all cells are unlocked
    (c) The worksheet is protected and the assumption area is locked
    (d) The worksheet is protected and the assumption area is unlocked

9. Which of the following may be stored within a style?

    (a) The font, point size, and color
    (b) Borders and shading
    (c) Alignment and protection
    (d) All of the above

... continued

multiple choice

10. What is the easiest way to change the formatting of five cells that are scattered throughout a worksheet, each of which has the same style?
    (a) Select the cells individually, then click the appropriate buttons on the Formatting toolbar
    (b) Select the cells at the same time, then click the appropriate buttons on the Formatting toolbar
    (c) Change the format of the existing style
    (d) Reenter the data in each cell according to the new specifications

11. Each scenario in the Scenario Manager:
    (a) Is stored in a separate worksheet
    (b) Contains the value of a single assumption or input condition
    (c) Both (a) and (b)
    (d) Neither (a) nor (b)

12. The Formula Auditing and Reviewing toolbars are floating toolbars by default. Which of the following is (are) true about fixed (docked) and floating toolbars?
    (a) Floating toolbars can be changed to fixed toolbars, but the reverse is not true
    (b) Fixed toolbars can be changed into floating toolbars, but the reverse is not true
    (c) Fixed toolbars can be changed into floating toolbars and vice versa
    (d) Fixed toolbars can be displayed only at the top of the screen

13. You open a template called Expense Account but see Expense Account1 displayed on the title bar. What is the most likely explanation?
    (a) You are the first person to use this template
    (b) Some type of error must have occurred
    (c) All is in order since Excel has appended the number to differentiate the workbook from the template on which it is based
    (d) The situation is impossible

14. Two adjacent cells are enclosed in hairline borders of different colors. Each of these cells also contains a tiny shaded triangle in the upper-left part of the cell. Which of the following is the most likely explanation?
    (a) Conditional formatting is in effect
    (b) Data validation is in effect for the cells in question
    (c) A comment has been entered into each of the cells
    (d) The cells have been changed by different members of a workgroup

15. The value in cell A7 is to be displayed in blue if the computed value exceeds $100,000. To which cell(s) would you apply conditional formatting so that the color changes as requested? (Cell A7 contains the formula =A5*A6).
    (a) A5
    (b) A6
    (c) A7
    (d) A5, A6, and A7

16. Which command would you use to restrict the value that can be entered into a specific cell?
    (a) Protect Worksheet command
    (b) Lock Worksheet command
    (c) Data Validation command
    (d) Conditional Formatting command

17. What is the most common reason to protect selected cells in a worksheet?
    (a) To prevent the initial conditions and assumptions from ever being changed
    (b) To prevent formulas in the worksheet from being changed
    (c) To prevent additional scenarios from being added
    (d) To prevent the worksheet from review by outsiders

ANSWERS

1. b
2. c
3. c
4. c
5. c
6. d
7. d
8. d
9. d
10. c
11. d
12. c
13. c
14. d
15. c
16. c
17. b

PRACTICE WITH EXCEL

1. **Erroneous Payroll:** The worksheet in Figure 6.9 displays an *erroneous* version of a worksheet that computes the payroll for a fictitious company. The worksheet is nicely formatted, but several calculations are in error. Your assignment is to open the *Chapter 6 Practice 1* workbook in the Exploring Excel folder, find the errors, and correct the worksheet. Print the workbook as it exists initially, and then print the corrected workbook at the end of the exercise.

   You can "eyeball" the worksheet to find the mistakes, and/or you can use the Formula Auditing toolbar as shown in Figure 6.9. Note, too, that when you identify an error, such as the incorrect formula for gross pay in cell F4, you must first correct the error, then copy the corrected formula to the remaining cells in that column. The correct specifications are given below:

   a. The gross pay is the regular pay (hourly wage times regular hours) plus the overtime pay (hourly wage times the overtime hours times the overtime rate). The overtime rate is entered as an assumption within the worksheet; making it possible to change the overtime rate in a single place should that become necessary.

   b. The net pay is the gross pay minus the deductions (the withholding tax and the Social Security tax).

   c. The taxable income is the gross pay minus the deduction per dependent multiplied by the number of dependents.

   d. The withholding tax is based on the individual's taxable income. The Social Security tax is based on the individual's gross pay.

   e. Use the Page Setup command to include a custom footer with your name and today's date. Print the corrected worksheet with both displayed values and cell formulas. Add a cover sheet and submit the assignment to your instructor. Do you see the importance of checking a worksheet for accuracy?

   f. Describe the purpose of each tool on the Formula Auditing toolbar. Which tools were used in conjunction with the workbook displayed in Figure 6.9? Was the information useful in finding the errors within the worksheet?

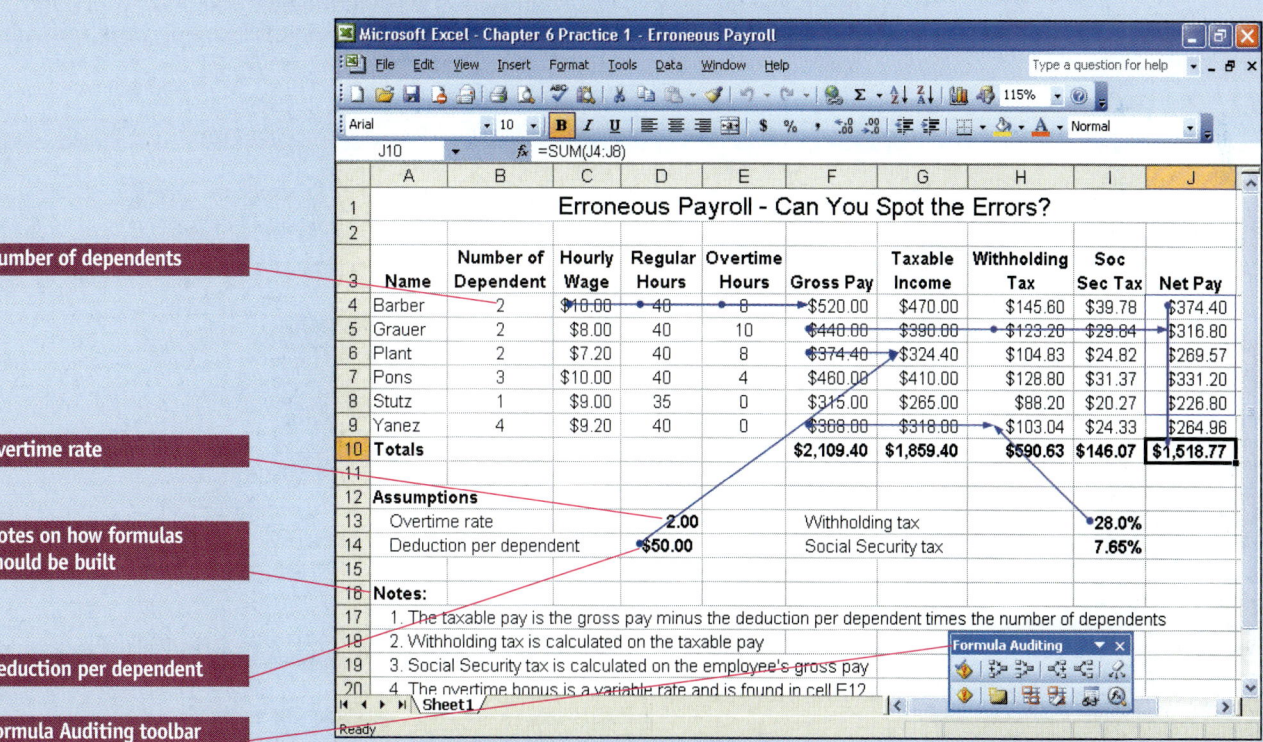

FIGURE 6.9 Erroneous Payroll (exercise 1)

practice exercises

2. **Protection and Validation:** The worksheet in Figure 6.10 will calculate the value of your retirement, based on a set of uniform annual contributions to a retirement account. In essence, you contribute a fixed amount of money each year ($3,000 in Figure 6.10), and the money accumulates at an estimated rate of return (7% in Figure 6.10). You indicate the age when you start to contribute, your projected retirement age, the number of years in retirement, and the rate of return you expect to earn on your money when you retire.

   a. The worksheet determines the total amount you will have contributed, the amount of money you will have accumulated, and the value of your monthly pension. The numbers are impressive, and the sooner you begin to save, the better. The calculations use the Future Value (FV) and Payment (Pmt) functions, respectively.

   b. You will find the completed worksheet in the *Chapter 6 Practice 2* workbook in the Exploring Excel folder. Your assignment is to implement data validation and password protection to ensure that the user does not enter unrealistic numbers nor alter the formulas within the worksheet.

   c. Three validity checks are required as indicated in the assumption area of the worksheet. The retirement age must be 59.5 or greater (as required by current law), the rate of return during the period you are investing money cannot exceed 8%, and the rate of return during retirement cannot exceed 7%. You are to display a warning message if the user violates any of these conditions. The warning will allow the user to override the assumptions.

   d. Enter the parameters that are displayed in Figure 6.10, including the *invalid* entry of .08 in cell B8 by overriding the warning message. Display the Formula Auditing toolbar, then click the button to circle invalid data to display the red circle.

   e. Unlock cells B2 through B8, where the user enters his or her name and assumptions. Protect the remainder of the worksheet. Use "password" as the password.

   f. Enter your name and your assumptions in the completed worksheet, then print the worksheet twice to show both displayed values and cell formulas for your instructor.

   g. A Roth IRA (Individual Retirement Account) is one of the best ways to save for retirement. The money that you contribute is taxed at the time you make your contribution, but the future withdrawals are tax free! In this example, the individual contributed a total of $135,000, which grew to more than $850,000.

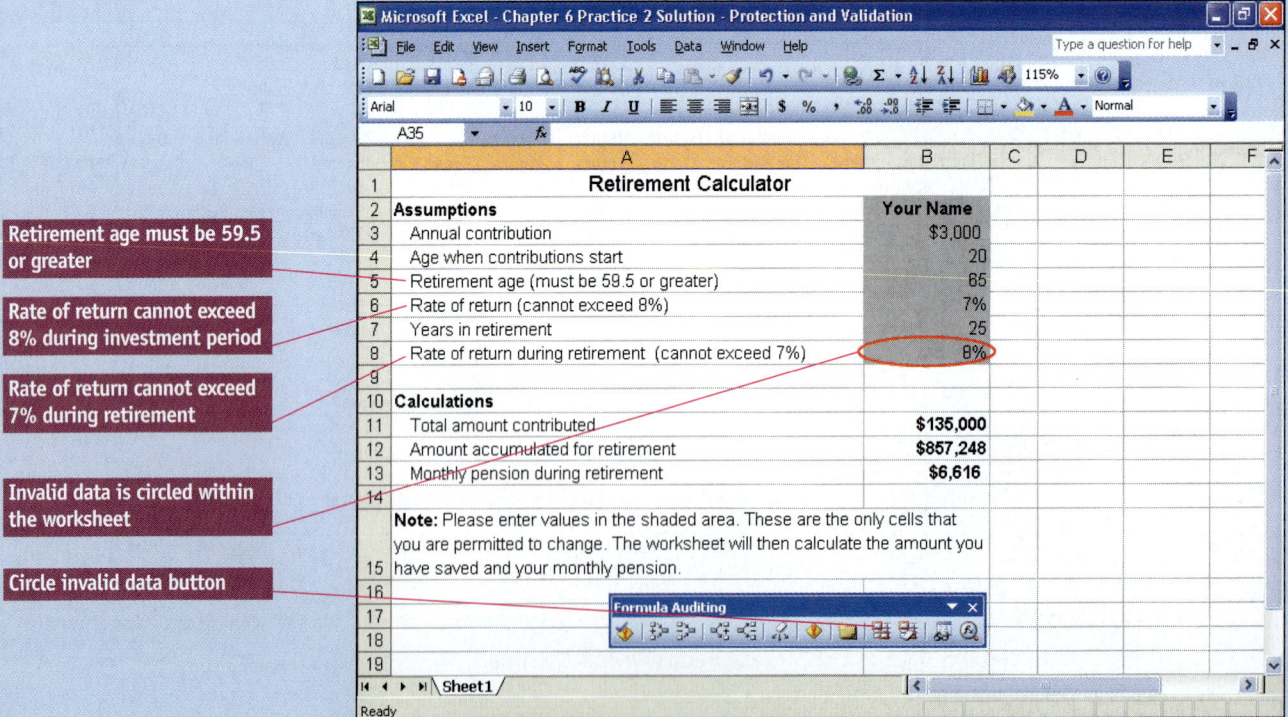

FIGURE 6.10 Protection and Validation (exercise 2)

practice exercises

3. **Retirement Scenarios:** The Social Security System has been in effect since 1935. An individual contributes a specified percentage of his or her pay check, which is matched by the employer. When the individual retires, he or she is paid a fixed amount as determined by law, with relatively little relation to the amount actually contributed. What if, however, Social Security were allowed to function as a private retirement plan, where the money was allowed to grow, and the monthly pension was a function of how much money had accumulated? This hypothetical plan is shown in Figure 6.11. Your assignment is to open the *Chapter 6 Practice 3* workbook in the Exploring Excel folder, create several scenarios, and then combine those scenarios in a scenario summary.

   a. The left side of the worksheet focuses on the accrual phase when money accumulates. The return on investment of 5% is conservative. The 45 years contributing to the plan matches the Social Security requirement, since a 22-year old entering the work force must reach age 67 before qualifying for the normal retirement benefit. The calculation is in constant dollars; that is, we did not build in an annual salary increase.

   b. The right side of the worksheet displays your monthly pension, which depends on a variety of factors, which include salary and the rates of return during both the accrual phase and the retirement phase. Note, however, that your income in retirement (approximately $6,500 per *month*) is almost 50% more than your income during your working life.

   c. Your assignment is to create several scenarios that vary these assumptions. Use the Define Name command prior to creating the scenarios so that the scenario summary is easily understood.

   d. It is interesting to compare the projected monthly pension in the worksheet of Figure 6.11 to the actual amounts provided by Social Security. Go to the Social Security Web site; locate the retirement calculator, then use the calculator to compute the projected benefit. (Choose a current salary of $35,000, $50,000, or $75,000 to match an existing scenario.) Press the Print Screen key to capture the Web page, and then paste the page into a new worksheet.

   e. Print the completed workbook for your instructor.

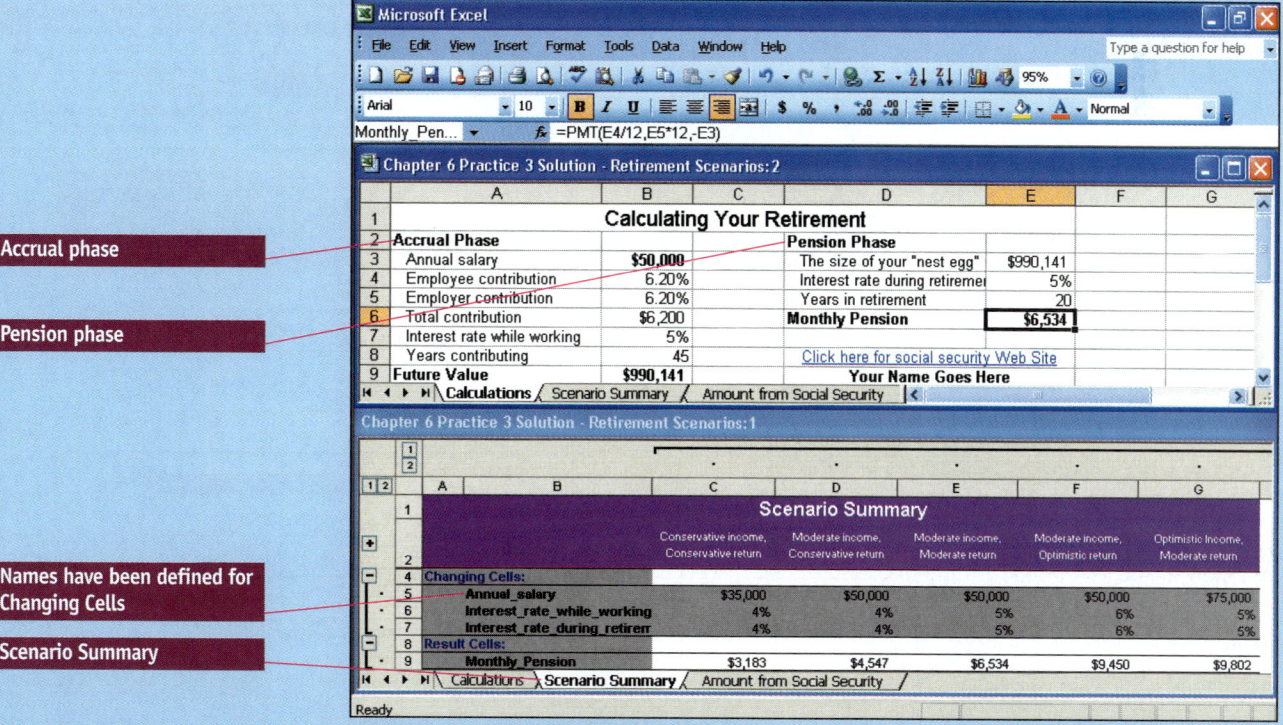

FIGURE 6.11 Retirement Scenarios (exercise 3)

practice exercises

4. **The Vacation Specialist:** The worksheet in Figure 6.12 computes the amount of vacation an employee has earned according to his or her years of service. An employee must complete the entire year to qualify for the next level; for example, an employee with 364 days of service has not worked a full year, and thus is not entitled to any vacation. Your assignment is to open the partially completed *Chapter 6 Practice 4* workbook, find and correct the errors that exist, and then complete the additional processing requirements. Note the following:
   a. Greg Hubit has reached five years of employment (January 31, 2002 has long since come and gone) and is now entitled to three weeks of vacation. Make the necessary correction, which will also change the amount of vacation for every employee.
   b. Click the Undo button to temporarily remove the correction from part (a) in order to address the next error. Note that Natalie Anderson, who was hired on February 4, 2001, has not yet earned any vacation (the date of the original spreadsheet was 1/31/02), yet she appears to have one year of service. Fix this error using the integer (Int) function to modify the appropriate formula, then copy the corrected formula to the remaining rows in the worksheet. Now restore the correction from part (a), which will increase everyone's vacation since today's date has been updated.
   c. Cathi Profitko has more than 25 years' service, but receives only four weeks of vacation. (The Show Precedents tool in the Auditing toolbar will help you to identify this error.) Fix the formula for Cathi, then copy the corrected formula to the other rows in the spreadsheet.
   d. Enter the appropriate formulas in cells F4 to F12 to compute the remaining days of vacation for each employee. (There are five days of vacation for every week of accrued vacation.) Enter the appropriate statistical functions in cells B15 through B18.
   e. Management is contemplating a new vacation plan, which will require less service than previously to earn the same amount of vacation; that is, an employee will need 1, 3, 5, 10, and 15 years of service to earn 2, 3, 4, 5, and 6 weeks of vacation, respectively. Create two scenarios that will allow management to quickly shift between existing and proposed plans.
   f. Print the completed worksheet to show the displayed values for each scenario. Print the worksheet again to show the cell formulas for the new plan.

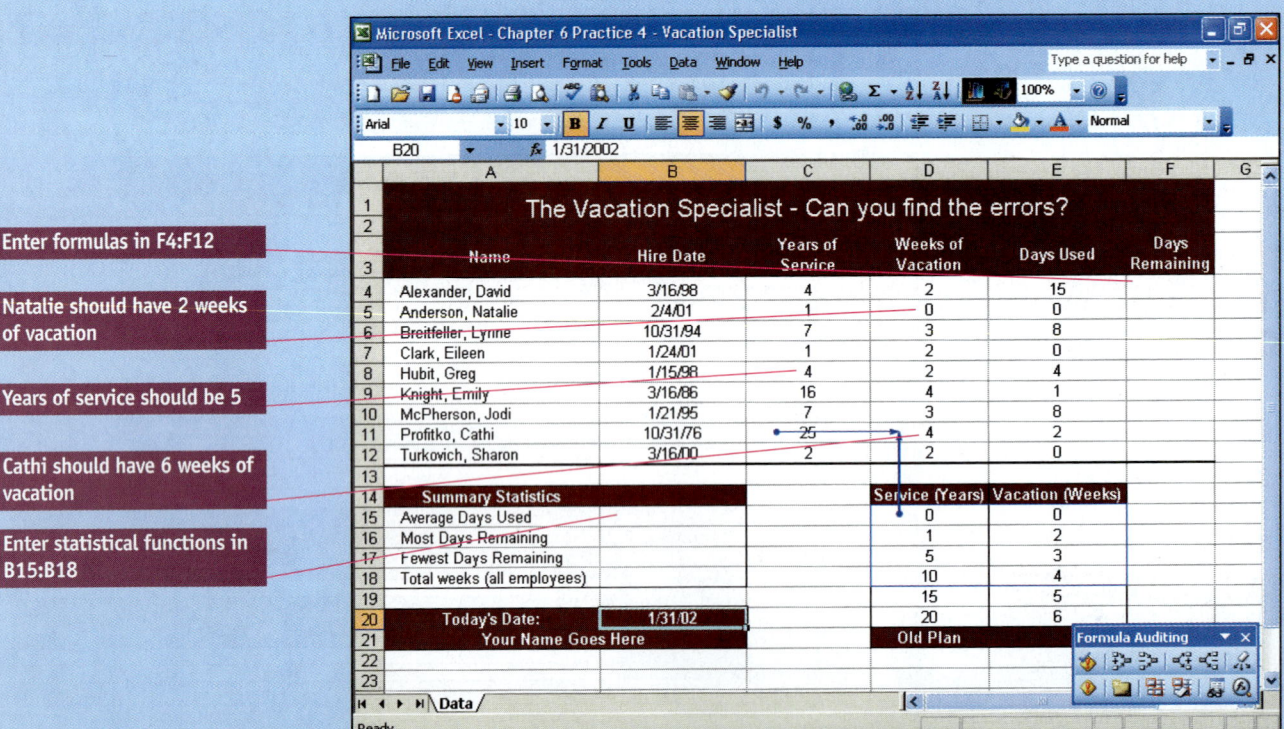

FIGURE 6.12 The Vacation Specialist (exercise 4)

practice exercises

5. **Erroneous Grade Book:** The worksheet in Figure 6.13 is intended to compute class grades. The worksheet is nicely formatted, but it contains some fundamental errors. Your assignment is to retrieve the *Chapter 6 Practice 5* workbook, correct the errors, and complete any additional processing requirements. Proceed as follows:

   a. Enter the appropriate VLOOKUP function in cell L3 to determine Alan's grade for the semester, based on the semester average in cell K3 and the table of numerical averages and associated grades at the bottom of the spreadsheet (cells G15 through H19). Copy the formula to the remaining cells in this column.

   b. Use the Formula Auditing toolbar to display the precedent cells for cell K3. Is the displayed value of 79.2 correct according to the indicated weights at the bottom of the spreadsheet? If not, fix the formula in this cell and then copy the corrected formula to the remaining rows in the column.

   c. Look closely at Charles' grades for the semester, especially the number of completed homework assignments. Did he really deserve a B, or should he have gotten an A? Display the precedent cells for cell J5, then correct the formula as necessary. Copy the corrected formula to all of the remaining students.

   d. What is the meaning of the green triangle that appears in cell H7 (the cell that contains the Quiz Average for Goodman)? How should the formula be corrected? Why does the green triangle remain after the formula has been corrected?

   e. Implement the necessary conditional formatting to display all grades of A and F (in column L) in blue and red, respectively.

   f. The professor has asked you to create two scenarios, with and without a curve. The changing cells are the same for each scenario, and consist of the name of the scenario (cell A14), the homework bonus (cell E15), and the minimum required semester average for each grade (cells G15 through G19). The values currently displayed in Figure 6.13 constitute one scenario. The new scenario includes a 3-point bonus for homework and breakpoints of 55, 67, 78, and 88, for grades of D, C, B, and A, respectively.

   g. Use the Page Setup command to create a custom footer with your name and today's date. Print the corrected worksheet to show the displayed values for each of the scenarios in part (f). Print the worksheet a third time to show the cell formulas for the new scenario.

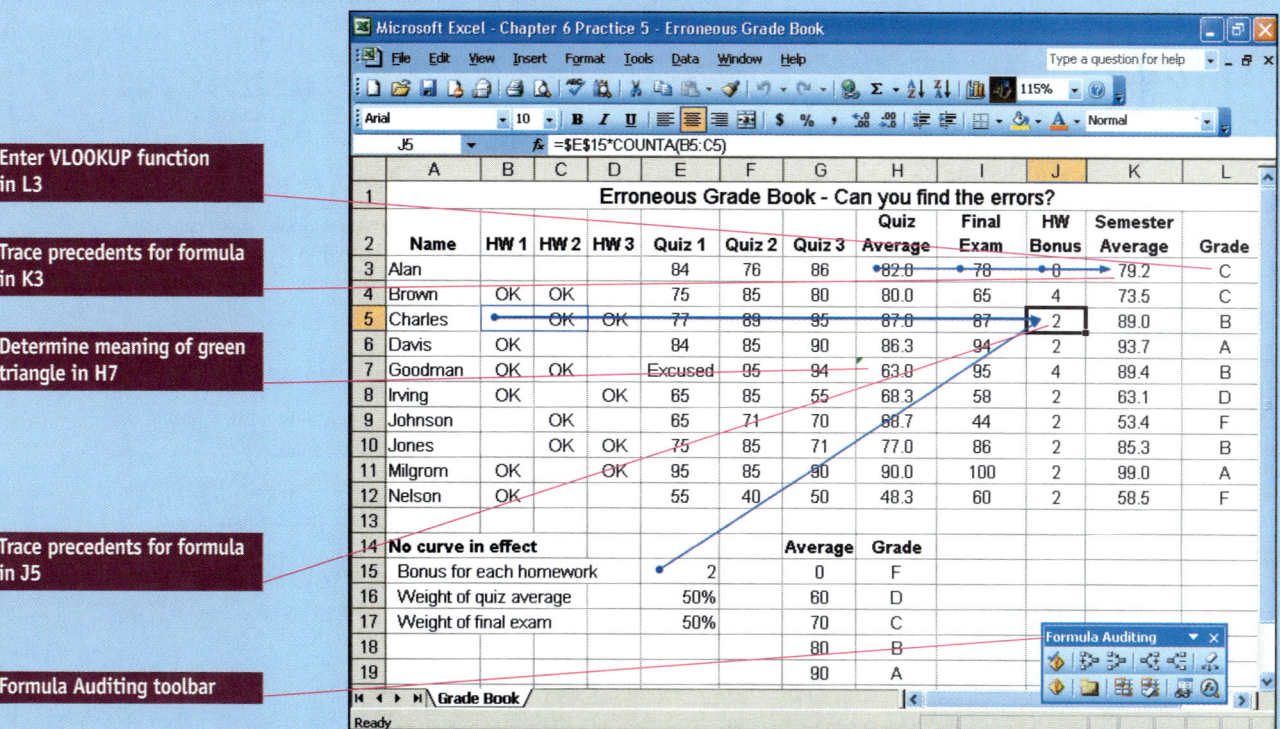

FIGURE 6.13 Erroneous Grade Book (exercise 5)

practice exercises

6. **The Scenario List Box:** Figure 6.14 displays a Word document that includes a screen capture of an Excel workbook. Look closely and note the presence of a scenario list box on the Formatting toolbar. This helpful list box lets you display a scenario (without going to the Tools menu) by clicking the down arrow and choosing the scenario from the displayed list. Proceed as follows:

   a. Choose any workbook that contains one or more scenarios (we used the Financial Forecast Solution workbook at the end of the first hands-on exercise). To display the list box, point to any toolbar, click the right mouse button to display a shortcut menu, then click Customize to display the Customize dialog box. Click the Commands tab, select Tools in the Categories list box, then click and drag the Scenario list box to an empty space on any toolbar. Click Close to close the dialog box and return to the workbook.

   b. The Scenario list box should appear on the toolbar. Click on the Financial Forecast tab and use the list box to view the various scenarios.

   c. Prove to your instructor that you have added the list box to your toolbar by capturing the Excel screen, then pasting it into a Word document. All you have to do is press the Print Screen key within Excel (after you display the scenario list box) to copy the screen to the Windows clipboard. Start Word, then click the Paste button to add the contents of the clipboard to the Word document. Word will ask if you want to compress the picture. Click Yes.

   d. You may find it useful to modify the position of the screen within the Word document. Thus, right click the figure from within Word to display a shortcut menu, click the Format Picture command to display the Format Picture dialog box, click the Layout tab, select Square wrapping, and click OK. You can now click and drag the picture anywhere within the document. You can also click and drag a sizing handle just as you can with any other Windows object.

   e. Complete the note in Figure 6.14, add your name somewhere in the document, then print the finished document for your instructor. Add a cover sheet to complete the assignment.

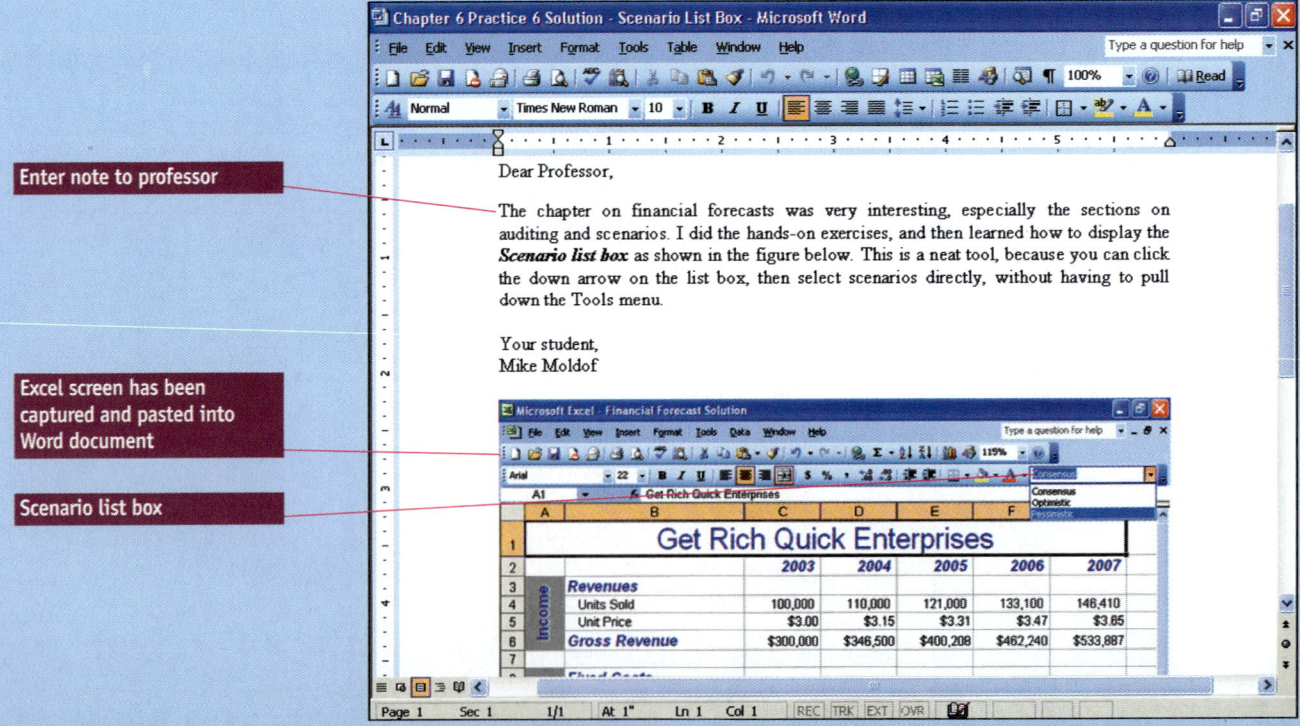

FIGURE 6.14 The Scenario List Box (exercise 6)

practice exercises

7. **The Mortgage Calculator:** The worksheet in Figure 6.15 is completely flexible in that it accepts the user's input in the shaded cells and then it computes the associated monthly payments in the body of the worksheet. It also introduces the Evaluate Formula tool on the Formula Auditing toolbar that lets you step through the calculation of any formula within a worksheet. Your assignment is to create the worksheet as shown in Figure 6.15. (You may want to review material on the PMT function and mixed references from Chapter 4.) Open the partially completed *Chapter 6 Practice 7* workbook, then proceed as follows:

   a. Click in cell B8 and enter the formula =E4; that is, the initial interest rate in the body of the spreadsheet is taken from the user's input in cell E4. Click in cell C8 and enter the formula, =B8+$E$5, then copy this formula to the remaining cells in this row. Enter parallel formulas in cells A9 to A19 to compute the various values for the principal amounts that will appear in the table. Check that your formulas are correct by changing the input parameters in rows 4 and 5. Any changes to the input parameters should be reflected in row 8 and/or column A.

   b. The "trick" to this assignment (if any) is to develop the PMT function with the correct mixed references in cell B9. The correct formula is =PMT(B$8/12,$B$6*12,-$A9) as can be seen by looking at the title bar in Figure 6.15. Enter this formula in cell B9 and copy it to the remaining rows and columns in the worksheet.

   c. Display the Formula Auditing toolbar. Click in Cell B9, then click the Evaluate Formula button to display the associated dialog box. You should see the complete formula for cell B9. Now click the Evaluate button, and the numeric value (.045) is substituted for the first argument, B$8. Continue to click the Evaluate button to see the numeric value of each cell reference until the computed value is shown. Do you see how this tool can help you to understand how a formula works?

   d. Enter your name in cell A1 and format the completed worksheet. You do not have to match our formatting exactly, but you are to shade the input parameters.

   e. Unlock cells B4 through B6 and cells E4 and E5, then protect the completed worksheet. Use "password" in lowercase letters as the password.

   f. Print the worksheet two ways, once with displayed values, and once with the cell formulas. Use landscape orientation.

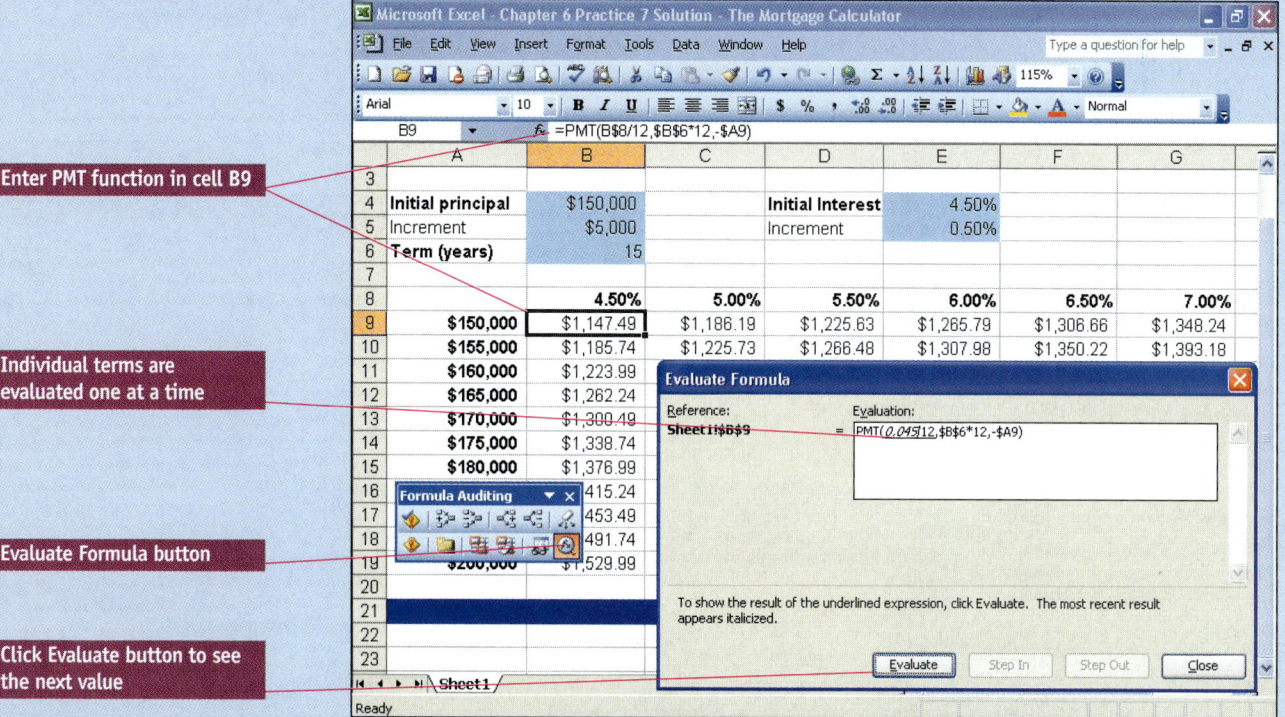

FIGURE 6.15 The Mortgage Calculator (exercise 7)

practice exercises

8. **Circular References:** A circular reference usually indicates a logic error, but there are instances when it can be valid. Figure 6.16 displays a hypothetical worksheet for an employee profit sharing plan, in which the company contributes 25% of its net income *after profit sharing is taken into account*, to profit sharing. The net income is determined by subtracting expenses from revenue, but one of those expenses is profit sharing, which in turn creates the circular reference. In other words, the formula in cell B7 depends on the formula in cell B6, which depends on the formula in cell B7. Open the partially completed spreadsheet in *Chapter 6 Practice 8* and proceed as follows:

   a. Click in cell B7 and enter the formula to compute the net income after profit sharing, =B4-B5-B6. Excel indicates that there is a circular reference. Click OK. Close the Help screen if it appears.

   b. The Circular Reference toolbar is displayed automatically, and the status bar shows a circular reference in cell B6. Pull down the View menu, click Toolbars, then click the Formula Auditing toolbar to display this toolbar as well. Click the Show Watch Window button and add cells B6 and B7.

   c. You can now recalculate the spreadsheet manually to see the effects of the circular reference. Pull down the Tools menu, click the Options command, then click the Calculation tab. Check the Iteration box and change the maximum number of iterations to one. Click the Manual option button in the Calculation area. Click OK to accept these settings and close the dialog box.

   d. Press the F9 (recalculate) key continually to see the spreadsheet go through multiple iterations, eventually settling on steady state values of $400,000 and $1,600,000 for the profit sharing and net income, respectively. Note that the profit sharing value of $400,000 is indeed 25% of the net income value of $1,600,000.

   e. Add your name to the worksheet, then print the completed worksheet for your professor. Close the Formula Auditing toolbar and Watch Window. Close the workbook.

   f. Open a blank workbook. Pull down the Tools menu, click the Options command, then click Calculation tab to restore the default settings. Click the option button for Automatic calculation and reset the maximum iterations to 100. Clear the iteration check box.

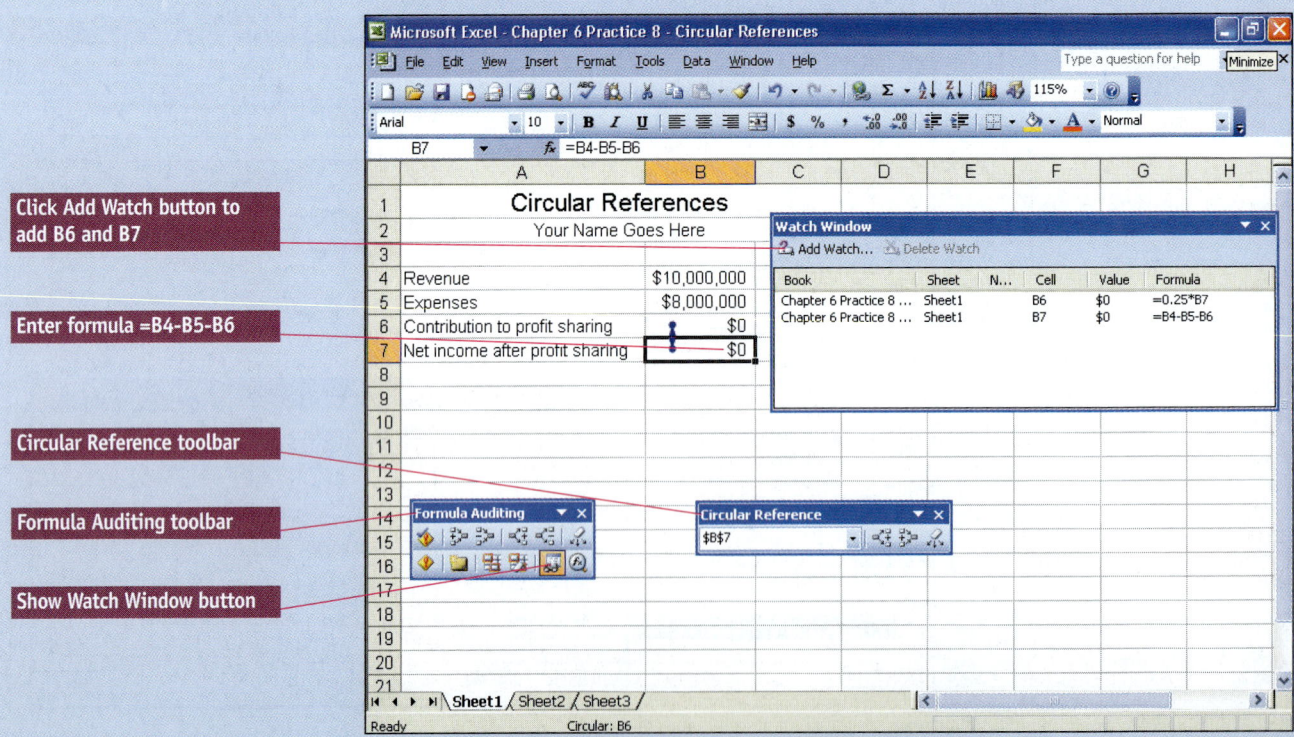

FIGURE 6.16 Circular References (exercise 8)

practice exercises

9. **Compare and Merge Workbooks:** The consensus workbook in Figure 6.17 is the result of merging three individual workbooks, provided by Tom, Dick, and Harry, each of whom added their comments to a shared workbook. Proceed as follows:

   a. Open the *Chapter 6 Practice 9* workbook that contains the original workbook sent out to each of the three reviewers.

   b. Pull down the Tools menu, click the Compare and Merge Workbooks command to display the associated dialog box, select the individual workbooks for Tom's Forecast, Dick's Forecast, and Harry's Forecast, then click OK. The workbooks will be opened individually, and any changes will be automatically merged into the consensus workbook. If there are conflicting changes (e.g., two individuals make different changes to the same cell), the changes are entered in the order that the workbooks are opened.

   c. Pull down the Tools menu, click Track Changes, and click the Highlight Changes command to display the Highlight Changes dialog box. Clear the Who, When, and Where check boxes so that you will see all of the changes made to the workbook. Check the box to list the changes on a new sheet. Click OK.

   d. A History worksheet is created automatically that shows all of the changes made to the shared workbook. Pull down the Window menu, click New window, then pull down the Window menu a second time, click Arrange, and tile the worksheets horizontally to match Figure 6.17. Click the Sales Data tab in one window and the History tab in the other.

   e. Look closely at the History worksheet and note that Harry and Tom changed the value of cell E4 to $90,000 and $125,000, respectively. The value that is shown in the consensus workbook ($125,000 in our figure) depends on the order in which the workbooks were merged. Tom was last in our example, so his change dominates. You can, however, use the Accept or Reject Changes command to go through all of the changes individually and accept (reject) the changes individually. If necessary, use this command to accept Tom's change ($125,000) rather than Harry's.

   f. Print the completed workbook, with both worksheets, for your instructor. Use the Page Setup command to include an appropriate footer that contains today's date and the name of the worksheet.

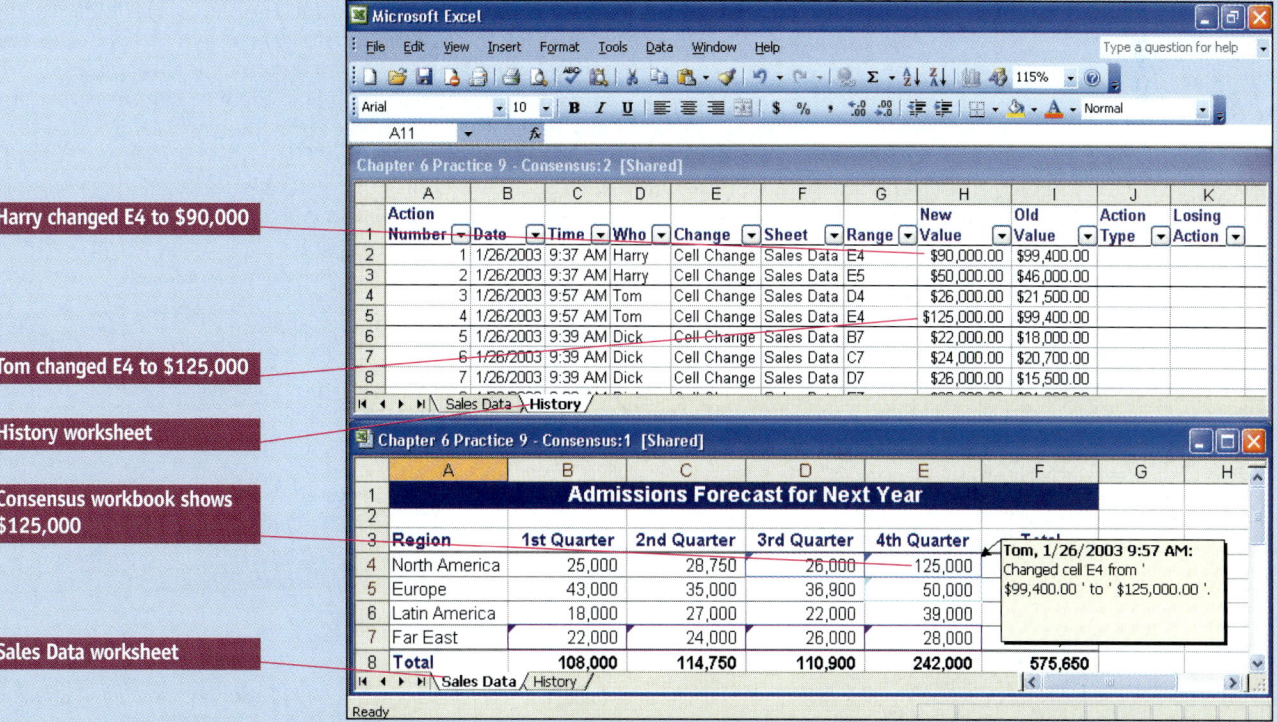

FIGURE 6.17 Compare and Merge Workbooks (exercise 9)

MINI CASES

The Entrepreneur

You have developed the perfect product and are seeking venture capital to go into immediate production. Your investors are asking for a projected income statement for the first four years of operation. The sales of your product are estimated at $350,000 the first year and are projected to grow at 10% annually. The cost of goods sold is 60% of the sales amount, and this percentage is expected to remain constant. You also have to pay a 10% sales commission, which is expected to remain constant.

Develop a financial forecast that will show the projected profits before and after taxes (assuming a tax rate of 36%). Your worksheet should be completely flexible and capable of accommodating a change in any of the initial conditions or projected rates of increase, *without* having to edit or recopy any of the formulas.

The worksheet should also be protected to the extent that users can make any changes they like in the assumption area, but are prevented from making changes in the body of the worksheet. Use "password" (in lowercase) as the password.

Error Checking—Good News and Bad

Microsoft Excel checks for certain errors automatically. If, for example, you are adding a column of numbers and you omit the top or bottom number, Excel will flag the formula to indicate a potential error. It will also flag an inconsistent formula within a row or column, and/or flag an unprotected cell if the cell contains a formula rather than a value. Potential errors are flagged with a green triangle, and the user is given the option to ignore or correct the error. Excel will even make the correction automatically for you.

This is a compelling feature, especially if you use Excel for financial calculations. Unfortunately, however, it falls short in one critical way. Your assignment is to open the *Chapter 6 Mini Case—Error Checking* workbook and correct all of the errors in the worksheet. Insert comments into the corrected cells to indicate which errors were detected by Excel, and which errors (if any) you had to correct manually.

Spreadsheet Solutions

Excel provides several templates locally with additional templates available on the Microsoft Web site. Start Excel, display the task pane, click the down arrow in the task pane to view the New Workbook task pane, then click the link to Other Templates on My Computer to open the Templates dialog box. Click the Spreadsheet Solutions tab, and then create at least one workbook based on the templates provided by Excel. Did the template contain formulas and/or protected cells? Was the formatting attractive? Was the template helpful, or would it have been just as easy to create the workbook from scratch? What additional templates are available on the Microsoft Web site?

CHAPTER 7

List and Data Management: Converting Data to Information

OBJECTIVES

After reading this chapter you will:

1. Add, edit, and/or delete records in a list within an Excel worksheet;
2. Use the Text Import Wizard to import data in character format.
3. Define XML; import XML data into an Excel workbook.
4. Describe the Today() function and its use in date arithmetic.
5. Use the Sort command; distinguish between an ascending and a descending sort.
6. Use DSUM, DAVERAGE, DMAX, DMIN, and DCOUNT functions.
7. Use the AutoFilter and Advanced Filter commands.
8. Use the Subtotals command.
9. Create a pivot table and corresponding pivot chart.
10. Save a pivot table as a Web page.

hands-on exercises

1. IMPORTING, CREATING, AND MAINTAINING A LIST
   Input: Employee List (text file)
   Output: Employee List Solution

2. DATA VERSUS INFORMATION
   Input: Employee List Solution (from exercise 1)
   Output: Employee List Solution (additional changes)

3. PIVOT TABLES AND PIVOT CHARTS
   Input: Advertising Agency
   Output: Advertising Agency Solution (Excel workbook and Web Page)

CASE STUDY
THE SPA EXPERTS

Dan and Tim like to relax. The two fraternity brothers went into business shortly after graduation selling spas and hot tubs. Business has been good, and their expansive showroom and wide selection appeal to a variety of customers. The partners maintain a large inventory to attract the impulse buyer and currently have agreements with three manufacturers: Serenity Spas, The Original Hot Tub, and Port-a-Spa. Each manufacturer offers spas and hot tubs that appeal to different segments of the market with prices ranging from affordable to exorbitant.

The business has grown rapidly, and there is a need to analyze the sales data in order to increase future profits—for example, which vendor generates the most sales? Who is the leading salesperson? Do most customers purchase their spa or finance it? Are sales promotions necessary to promote business, or will customers pay the full price? Dan has created a simple workbook that has sales data for the current month. Each transaction appears on a separate row and contains the name of the salesperson, the manufacturer, and the amount of the sale. There is also an indication of whether the spa was purchased or financed, and whether a promotion was in effect.

Your assignment is to read the chapter, open the *Chapter 7 Case Study—The Spa Experts* workbook, and complete the workbook. A criteria range has been established at the top of the worksheet that displays the sales performance for any combination of salesperson, manufacturer, and/or other fields within the sales list. The summary statistics appear immediately below the criteria range, but you will have to enter the appropriate data management functions to compute the indicated statistics.

Use the Edit command to substitute your name for Jessica Benjamin throughout the worksheet. You can then enter your name in cell B5 (within the criteria range) to view your sales statistics for the month. Create a pivot table and associated pivot chart (each in its own worksheet) that displays summary information by vendor and salesperson.

LIST AND DATA MANAGEMENT

All businesses maintain data in the form of lists. Companies have lists of their employees. Magazines and newspapers keep lists of their subscribers. Political candidates monitor voter lists, and so on. This chapter presents the fundamentals of list management as it is implemented in Excel. It begins with the definition of basic terms, such as field and record, then covers the commands to create a list, to add a new record, and to modify or delete an existing record.

The second half of the chapter distinguishes between data and information and describes how one is converted to the other. We introduce the AutoFilter and Advanced Filter commands that display selected records in a list. We use the Sort command to rearrange the list. We discuss database functions and the associated criteria range. We also review date functions and date arithmetic. The chapter ends with a discussion of subtotals, pivot tables, and pivot charts—three powerful capabilities associated with lists.

Imagine that you are the personnel director of a medium-sized company with offices in several cities, and that you manually maintain employee data for the company. Accordingly, you have recorded the specifics of every individual's employment (name, salary, location, title, and so on) in a manila folder, and you have stored the entire set of folders in a file cabinet. You have written the name of each employee on the label of his or her folder and have arranged the folders alphabetically in the filing cabinet.

The manual system just described illustrates the basics of data management terminology. The set of manila folders corresponds to a ***file***. Each individual folder is known as a ***record***. Each data item (fact) within a folder is called a ***field***. The folders are arranged alphabetically in the file cabinet (according to the employee name on the label) to simplify the retrieval of any given folder. Likewise, the records in a computer-based system are also in sequence according to a specific field known as a ***key***.

Excel maintains data in the form of a list. A ***list*** is an area in the worksheet that contains rows of similar data. A list can be used as a simple ***database***, where the rows in a worksheet correspond to records and the columns correspond to fields. The first row contains the column labels or ***field names***, which identify the data that will be entered in that column (field). Each additional row in the list contains a record. Each column represents a field. Each cell in the list area (other than the field names) contains a value for a specific field in a specific record. Every record (row) contains the same fields (columns) in the same order as every other record.

Figure 7.1 contains an employee list with 13 records. There are four fields in every record—name, location, title, and salary. The field names should be meaningful and must be unique. (A field name may contain up to 255 characters, but you should keep them as short as possible so that a column does not become too wide and thus difficult to work with.) The arrangement of the fields within a record is consistent from record to record. The employee name was chosen as the key, and thus the records are in alphabetical order.

Normal business operations require that you make repeated trips to the filing cabinet to maintain the accuracy of the data. You will have to add a folder whenever a new employee is hired. In similar fashion, you will have to remove the folder of any employee who leaves the company, or modify the data in the folder of any employee who receives a raise, changes location, and so on.

Changes of this nature (additions, deletions, and modifications) are known as file maintenance and constitute a critical activity within any system. Indeed, without adequate file maintenance, the data in a system quickly becomes obsolete and the information useless. Imagine the consequences of producing a payroll based on data that is six months old.

	A	B	C	D
1	**Name**	**Location**	**Title**	**Salary**
2	Adams	Atlanta	Trainee	$29,500
3	Adamson	Chicago	Manager	$52,000
4	Brown	Atlanta	Trainee	$28,500
5	Charles	Boston	Account Rep	$40,000
6	Coulter	Atlanta	Manager	$100,000
7	Frank	Miami	Manager	$75,000
8	James	Chicago	Account Rep	$42,500
9	Johnson	Chicag	Account Rep	$47,500
10	Manin	Boston	Accout Rep	$49,500
11	Marder	Chicago	Account Rep	$38,500
12	Milgrom	Boston	Manager	$57,500
13	Rubin	Boston	Account Rep	$45,000
14	Smith	Atlanta	Account Rep	$65,000

- Row 1 contains the field names
- Each row represents a record
- Chicago is misspelled
- Account Rep is misspelled

FIGURE 7.1 The Employee List

Nor is it sufficient simply to add (edit or delete) a record without adequate checks on the validity of the data. Look carefully at the entries in Figure 7.1 and ask yourself whether a computer-generated report that is intended to show the employees in the Chicago office will include Johnson. Will a report listing account reps include Manin? The answer to both questions is *no* because the data for these employees was entered incorrectly.

Chicago is misspelled in Johnson's record (the "o" was omitted). Account rep is misspelled in Manin's title. *You* know that Johnson works in Chicago, but the computer does not, because it searches for the correct spelling. It also will omit Manin from a listing of account reps because of the misspelled title. Remember, a computer does what you tell it to do, not necessarily what you want it to do. There is a significant difference.

GARBAGE IN, GARBAGE OUT (GIGO)

The information produced by a system is only as good as the data on which it is based. It is absolutely critical, therefore, that you validate the data that goes into a system, or else the associated information will not be correct. No system, no matter how sophisticated, can produce valid output from invalid input. In other words, garbage in—garbage out.

IMPLEMENTATION IN EXCEL

Creating a list is easy because there is little to do other than enter the data. You choose the area in the worksheet that will contain the list, then you enter the field names in the first row of the designated area. Each field name should be a unique text entry. The data for the individual records should be entered in the rows immediately below the row of field names.

Once a list has been created, you can edit any field, in any record, just as you would change the entries in an ordinary worksheet. The ***Insert Rows command*** lets you add new rows (records) to the list. The ***Insert Columns command*** lets you add additional columns (fields). The ***Delete command*** in the Edit menu enables you to delete a row or column. You can also use shortcut menus to execute commands more quickly. And finally, you can also format the entries within a list, just as you format the entries in any other worksheet.

Data Form Command

A ***data form*** provides an easy way to add, edit, and delete records in a list. The ***Form command*** in the Data menu displays a dialog box based on the fields in the list and contains the command buttons shown in Figure 7.2. Every record in the list contains the same fields in the same order (e.g., Name, Location, Title, and Salary in Figure 7.2), and the fields are displayed in this order within the dialog box. You do not have to enter a value for every field; that is, you may leave a field blank if the data is unknown.

Next to each field name is a text box into which data can be entered for a new record, or edited for an existing record. The scroll bar to the right of the data is used to scroll through the records in the list. As indicated, the Data Form command provides an easy way to add, edit, and delete records in a list. It is not required, however, and you can use the Insert and Delete commands within the Edit menu as an alternate means of data entry.

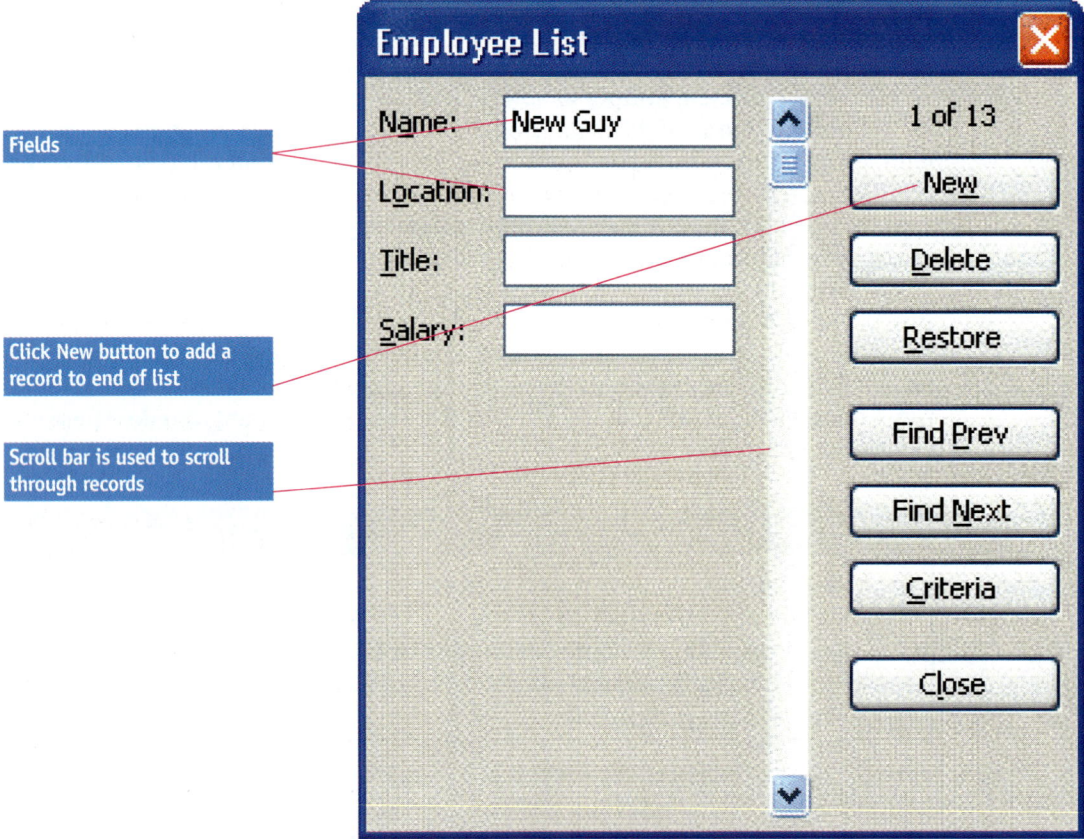

FIGURE 7.2 The Data Form Command

LIST SIZE AND LOCATION

A list can appear anywhere within a worksheet and can theoretically be as large as an entire worksheet (65,536 rows by 256 columns). Practically, the list will be much smaller, giving rise to the following guideline for its placement: Leave at least one blank column and one blank row between the list and the other entries in the worksheet. Excel will then be able to find the boundaries of the list automatically whenever a cell within the list is selected. It simply searches for the first blank row above and below the selected cell, and for the first blank column to the left and right of the selected cell.

The functions of the various command buttons are explained briefly:

New—Adds a record to the end of a list, then lets you enter data into that record. The formulas for computed fields, if any, are automatically copied to the new record.

Delete—Permanently removes the currently displayed record. The remaining records move up one row.

Restore—Cancels any changes made to the current record. (You must press the Restore button before pressing the Enter key or scrolling to a new record.)

Find Prev—Displays the previous record (or the previous record that matches the existing criteria when criteria are defined).

Find Next—Displays the next record (or the next record that matches the existing criteria when criteria are defined).

Criteria—Displays a dialog box in which you specify the criteria for the Find Prev and/or Find Next command buttons to limit the displayed records to those that match the criteria.

Close—Closes the data form and returns to the worksheet.

Sort Command

Data is easier to understand if it is displayed in a meaningful sequence. The ***Sort command*** arranges the records in a list according to the value of one or more fields within that list. You can sort the list in ***ascending*** (low-to-high) or ***descending*** (high-to-low) ***sequence***. (Putting a list in alphabetical order is considered an ascending sort.) You can also sort on more than one field at a time—for example, by location and then alphabetically by last name within each location. The field(s) on which you sort the list is (are) known as the key(s).

Each worksheet in Figure 7.3 displays the same set of employee records, but in a different order. The records in Figure 7.3a are listed alphabetically (in ascending sequence) according to the employees' last names. Adams comes before Adamson, who comes before Brown, and so on. Figure 7.3b displays the identical records but in descending sequence by employee salary. The employee with the highest salary is listed first, and the employee with the lowest salary is last.

Figure 7.3c sorts the employees on two keys—by location, and by descending salary within location. Location is the more important, or primary key. Salary is the less important, or secondary key. The Sort command groups employees according to like values of the primary key (location) in ascending (alphabetical) sequence, then within the like values of the primary key arranges them in descending sequence (ascending could have been chosen just as easily) according to the secondary key (salary). Excel provides a maximum of three keys—primary, secondary, and tertiary.

CHOOSE A CUSTOM SORT SEQUENCE

Alphabetic fields are normally arranged in strict alphabetical order. You can, however, choose a custom sort sequence such as the days of the week or the months of the year. Pull down the Data menu, click Sort, click the Options command button, then click the arrow on the drop-down list box to choose a sequence other than the alphabetic. You can also create your own sequence. Pull down the Tools menu, click Options, click the Custom Lists tab, select NewList, then enter the items in desired sequence in the List Entries Box. Click Add to create the sequence, then close the dialog box.

Records are in ascending sequence by employee name

	A	B	C	D
1	**Name**	**Location**	**Title**	**Salary**
2	Adams	Atlanta	Trainee	$29,500
3	Adamson	Chicago	Manager	$52,000
4	Brown	Atlanta	Trainee	$28,500
5	Charles	Boston	Account Rep	$40,000
6	Coulter	Atlanta	Manager	$100,000
7	Frank	Miami	Manager	$75,000
8	James	Chicago	Account Rep	$42,500
9	Johnson	Chicago	Account Rep	$47,500
10	Manin	Boston	Account Rep	$49,500
11	Marder	Chicago	Account Rep	$38,500
12	Milgrom	Boston	Manager	$57,500
13	Rubin	Boston	Account Rep	$45,000
14	Smith	Atlanta	Account Rep	$65,000

(a) Ascending Sequence (by name)

Records are in descending sequence by salary

	A	B	C	D
1	**Name**	**Location**	**Title**	**Salary**
2	Coulter	Atlanta	Manager	$100,000
3	Frank	Miami	Manager	$75,000
4	Smith	Atlanta	Account Rep	$65,000
5	Milgrom	Boston	Manager	$57,500
6	Adamson	Chicago	Manager	$52,000
7	Manin	Boston	Account Rep	$49,500
8	Johnson	Chicago	Account Rep	$47,500
9	Rubin	Boston	Account Rep	$45,000
10	James	Chicago	Account Rep	$42,500
11	Charles	Boston	Account Rep	$40,000
12	Marder	Chicago	Account Rep	$38,500
13	Adams	Atlanta	Trainee	$29,500
14	Brown	Atlanta	Trainee	$28,500

(b) Descending Sequence (by salary)

Location is the primary key (in ascending sequence)

Salary is the secondary key (in descending sequence)

	A	B	C	D
1	**Name**	**Location**	**Title**	**Salary**
2	Coulter	Atlanta	Manager	$100,000
3	Smith	Atlanta	Account Rep	$65,000
4	Adams	Atlanta	Trainee	$29,500
5	Brown	Atlanta	Trainee	$28,500
6	Milgrom	Boston	Manager	$57,500
7	Manin	Boston	Account Rep	$49,500
8	Rubin	Boston	Account Rep	$45,000
9	Charles	Boston	Account Rep	$40,000
10	Adamson	Chicago	Manager	$52,000
11	Johnson	Chicago	Account Rep	$47,500
12	James	Chicago	Account Rep	$42,500
13	Marder	Chicago	Account Rep	$38,500
14	Frank	Miami	Manager	$75,000

(c) Multiple Keys

FIGURE 7.3 The Sort Command

THE TEXT IMPORT WIZARD

It's easy to create a list in Excel and/or to modify data in that list. What if, however, the data already exists, but it is not in the form of a workbook? This is very common, especially in organizations that collect data on a mainframe, but analyze it on a PC. It can also occur when data is collected by one application, then analyzed in another. Excel provides a convenient solution in the form of the ***Text Import Wizard*** that converts a text (ASCII) file to an Excel workbook as shown in Figure 7.4. (Conversely, you can export an Excel workbook to another application by using the Save As command and specifying a text file.)

Figures 7.4a and 7.4b each contain the 13 records from the employee list shown, but in different formats. Both figures contain text files. The data in Figure 7.4a is in ***fixed width format***, where each field requires the same number of positions in an input record. The data in Figure 7.4b is in ***delimited format***, where the fields are separated from one another by a specific character.

You can access either file via the Open command in Excel, which in turn displays step 1 of the Text Import Wizard in Figure 7.4c. The Wizard prompts you for information about the external data, then it converts that data into an Excel workbook as shown in Figure 7.4d.

```
Name         Location    Title          Salary
Adams        Atlanta     Trainee        29500
Adamson      Chicago     Manager        52000
Brown        Atlanta     Trainee        28500
Charles      Boston      Account Rep    40000
Coulter      Atlanta     Manager        100000
Frank        Miami       Manager        75000
James        Chicago     Account Rep    42500
Johnson      Chicago     Account Rep    47500
Manin        Boston      Account Rep    49500
Marder       Chicago     Account Rep    38500
Milgrom      Boston      Manager        57500
Rubin        Boston      Account Rep    45000
Smith        Atlanta     Account Rep    65000
```

(a) Fixed Width

```
Name,Location,Title,Salary
Adams,Atlanta,Trainee,29500
Adamson,Chicago,Manager,52000
Brown,Atlanta,Trainee,28500
Charles,Boston,Account Rep,40000
Coulter,Atlanta,Manager,100000
Frank,Miami,Manager,75000
James,Chicago,Account Rep,42500
Johnson,Chicago,Account Rep,47500
Manin,Boston,Account Rep,49500
Marder,Chicago,Account Rep,38500
Milgrom,Boston,Manager,57500
Rubin,Boston,Account Rep,45000
Smith,Atlanta,Account Rep,65000
```

(b) Delimited

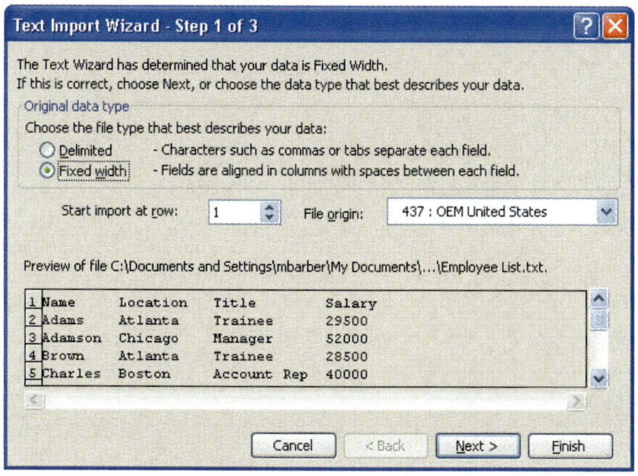

(c) Text Import Wizard

	A	B	C	D
1	Name	Location	Title	Salary
2	Adams	Atlanta	Trainee	$29,500
3	Adamson	Chicago	Manager	$52,000
4	Brown	Atlanta	Trainee	$28,500
5	Charles	Boston	Account Rep	$40,000
6	Coulter	Atlanta	Manager	$100,000
7	Frank	Miami	Manager	$75,000
8	James	Chicago	Account Rep	$42,500
9	Johnson	Chicag	Account Rep	$47,500
10	Manin	Boston	Account Rep	$49,500
11	Marder	Chicago	Accout Rep	$38,500
12	Milgrom	Boston	Manager	$57,500
13	Rubin	Boston	Account Rep	$45,000
14	Smith	Atlanta	Account Rep	$65,000

(d) Workbook

FIGURE 7.4 Importing Data from Other Applications

Excel and XML

A text file is a universal file format, in that it can be read by virtually any application. **XML (Extensible Markup Language)** goes one step further by enabling a developer to create customized tags to define and interpret the data within the file. (XML is an industry standard for structuring data and not a Microsoft product.) XML is not to be confused with **HTML (Hypertext Markup Language)**, nor is it intended as a replacement for HTML.

HTML is intended to display data and it has only a finite set of tags; e.g., <B> or <UL>, for bold and underlining, respectively. XML, however, describes the data and it has an infinite number of tags. XML tags are not defined in any XML standard, however, but are created by the author of the XML document. Consider:

HTML:	XML:
<B>John Doe</B>	<name>
	<first>John</first>
	<last>Doe</last>
	</name>

The HTML code tells us that "John Doe" will appear in boldface, but it does not tell us anything more. We don't know that "John" is the first name or that "Doe" is the last name. XML, on the other hand, is "data about data". You can see at a glance that it is conveying information about a name, and that there is a first name and a last name, within the name. The real advantage of XML, however, is that it is easily expanded (extensible) to include additional information about a person's name such as a prefix or middle initial. We just extend the definition of the elements within the name to include the additional data, and then we mark up the data accordingly by including additional tags.

Microsoft Excel 2003 provides full XML support that enables you to exchange information between an XML source document and an Excel workbook. You attach the XML definition or **schema** to the workbook and then you map the XML elements in the schema to the cells in your workbook. Once this is accomplished you can import and/or export XML data into or out of the individual cells. Figure 7.5a displays the first three employee records in an XML document, Figure 7.5b shows the XML source task pane in which the mapping takes place, and Figure 7.5c displays the associated list within a worksheet.

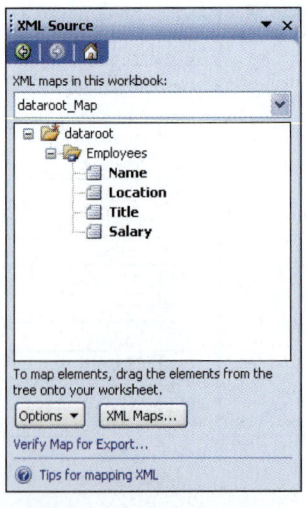

```
<Employees>
    <Name>Adams</Name>
    <Location>Atlanta</Location>
    <Title>Trainee</Title>
    <Salary>29500</Salary>
</Employees>
<Employees>
    <Name>Adamson</Name>
    <Location>Chicago</Location>
    <Title>Manager</Title>
    <Salary>52000</Salary>
</Employees>
<Employees>
    <Name>Brown</Name>
    <Location>Atlanta</Location>
    <Title>Trainee</Title>
    <Salary>28500</Salary>
</Employees>
```

(a) XML Document   (b) XML Source Task Pane   (c) Excel Spreadsheet

FIGURE 7.5 Excel and XML

hands-on exercise

1 Importing, Creating, and Maintaining a List

Objective To use the Text Import Wizard; to add, edit, and delete records in an employee list. Use Figure 7.6 as a guide in the exercise.

Step 1: **The Text Import Wizard**

- Start Excel. Pull down the **File menu** and click the **Open command** (or click the **Open button** on the Standard toolbar) to display the Open dialog box.

- Open the **Exploring Excel folder** that you have used throughout the text. Click the **drop-down arrow** on the Files of Type list box and specify **All Files**, then double click the **Employee List** text document.

- The Text Import Wizard opens automatically as shown in Figure 7.6a. The Wizard recognizes that the file is in Delimited format. Click **Next**.

- Clear the **Tab Delimiter** check box. Check the **Comma Delimiter** check box. Each field is now shown in a separate column. Click **Next**.

- There is no need to change the default format (general) of any of the fields. Click **Finish**. You see the Employee List within an Excel workbook.

- Click and drag to select **cells A1 through D1**, then click the **Bold** and **Center buttons** to distinguish the field names from the data records. Click the **down arrow** for the **Fill Color button** and select **Light Yellow**. Adjust the column widths. Format the Salary field as Currency with zero decimals.

- Save the workbook as **Employee List Solution.** Click the **down arrow** in the Save as type list box and select **Microsoft Excel workbook**. Click **Save**.

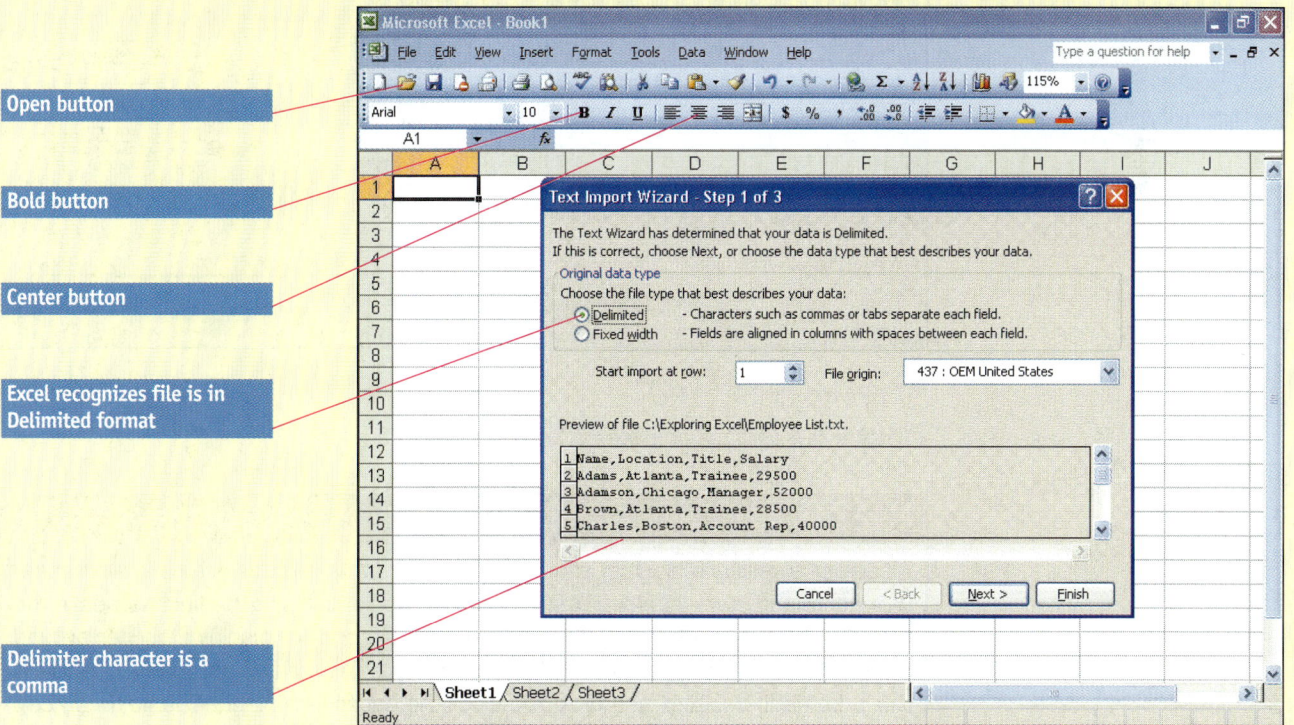

(a) The Text Import Wizard (step 1)

FIGURE 7.6 Hands-on Exercise 1

MICROSOFT OFFICE EXCEL 2003 1307

Step 2: **Add New Records**

- Click a single cell anywhere within the employee list (**cells A1 through D14**). Pull down the **Data menu**. Click **Form** to display a dialog box with data for the first record in the list (Adams).

- Click the **New command button** at the right of the dialog box to clear the text boxes and begin entering a new record.

- Enter the data for **Elofson** as shown in Figure 7.6b, using the **Tab key** to move from field to field within the data form.

- Click the **Close command button** after entering the salary. Elofson has been added to the list and appears in row 15.

- Add a second record for **Gillenson**, who works in **Miami** as an **Account Rep** with a salary of **$55,000**.

- Save the workbook.

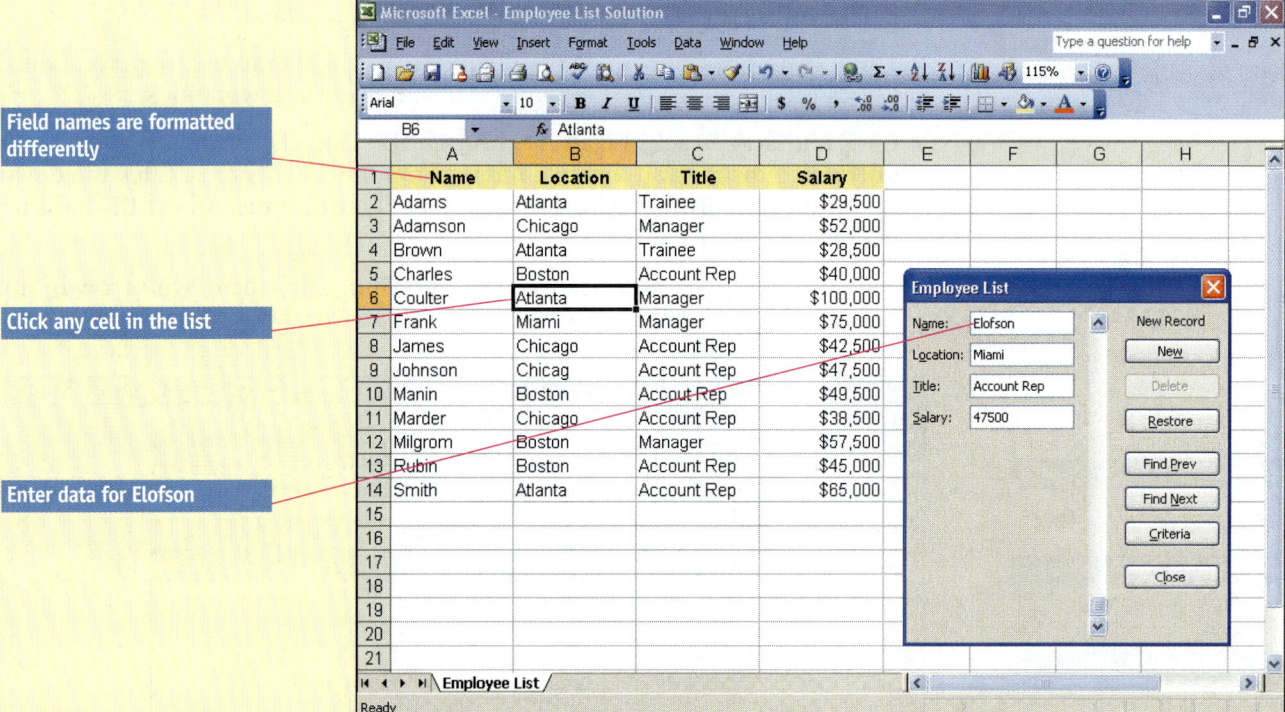

(b) Add New Records (step 2)

FIGURE 7.6 Hands-on Exercise 1 (*continued*)

THE CREATE LIST COMMAND

All previous versions of Excel enabled you to work with a list or area in a worksheet that contained rows of similar data. The user would highlight the field names in the first row, turn the AutoFilter command on and off, and/or display a border around the entire list. Microsoft Excel 2003 introduces a Create List command that does this automatically. Click and drag to select the entire list (include the field names), pull down the Data menu, click the List command, and then click the Create List command. Click anywhere in the list and you will see an asterisk in the last row; enter data in this row and the new record is added to the list automatically.

Step 3: **The Spell Check**

- Select **cells B2:C16** as in Figure 7.6c. Pull down the **Tools menu** and click **Spelling** (or click the **Spelling button** on the Standard toolbar).

- Chicago is misspelled in cell B9 and flagged accordingly. Click the **Change command button** to accept the suggested correction and continue checking the document.

- Account is misspelled in cell C10 and flagged accordingly. Click **Account** in the Suggestions list box, then click the **Change command button** to correct the misspelling.

- Excel will indicate that it has finished checking the selected cells. Click **OK** to return to the worksheet.

- Save the workbook.

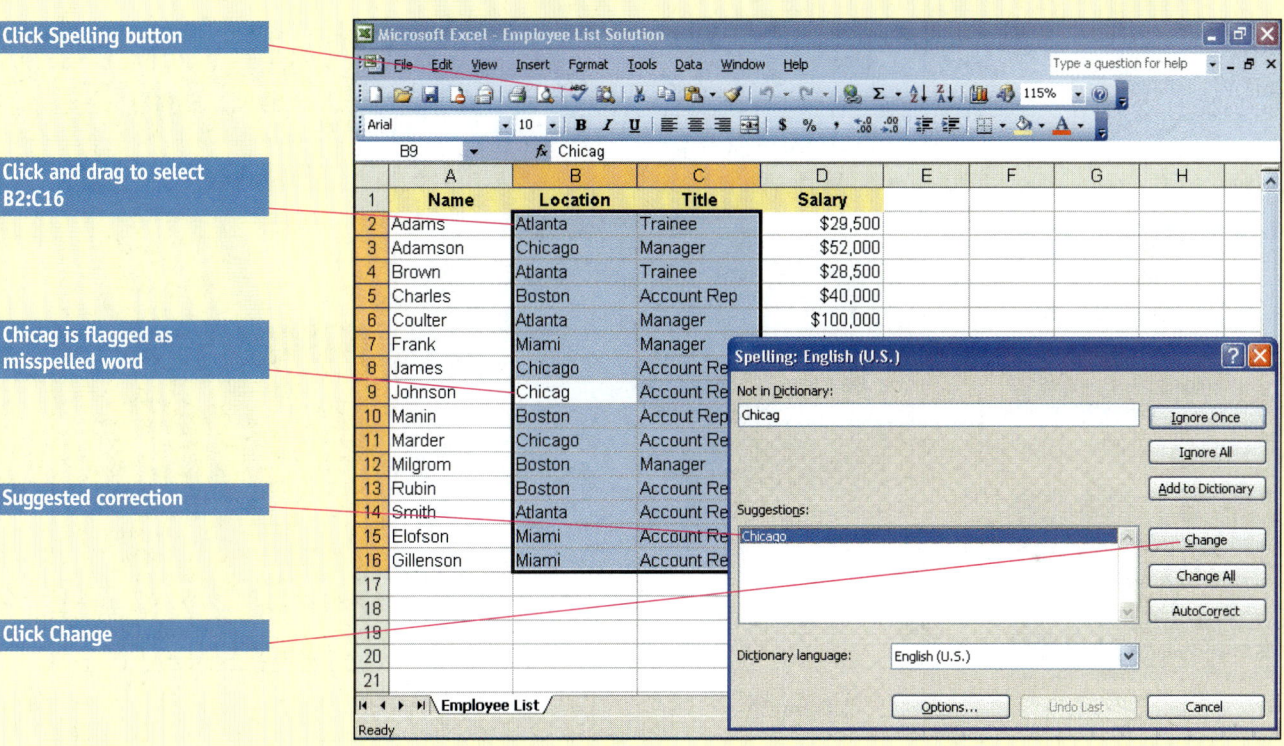

(c) The Spell Check (step 3)

FIGURE 7.6   Hands-on Exercise 1 (*continued*)

CREATE YOUR OWN SHORTHAND

Use the AutoCorrect capability within Microsoft Office to create your own shorthand by having it expand abbreviations such as *cis* for *Computer Information Systems*. Pull down the Tools menu, click AutoCorrect Options to display the associated dialog box, then click the AutoCorrect tab. Type the abbreviation in the Replace text box and the expanded entry in the With text box. Click the Add command button, then click OK to exit the dialog box. The next time you type *cis* in a spreadsheet, it will automatically be expanded to *Computer Information Systems*.

Step 4: **Sort the Employee List**

- Click a single cell anywhere in the employee list (**cells A1 through D16**). Pull down the **Data menu.** Click **Sort** to display the dialog box in Figure 7.6d.
- Click the **drop-down arrow** in the Sort By list box. Select **Location**.
- Click the **drop-down arrow** in the first Then By list box. Select **Name**.
- Be sure the **Header Row option button** is selected (so that the field names are not sorted with the records in the list).
- Check that the **Ascending option button** is selected for both the primary and secondary keys. Click **OK**.
- The employees are listed by location and alphabetically within location.
- Save the workbook.

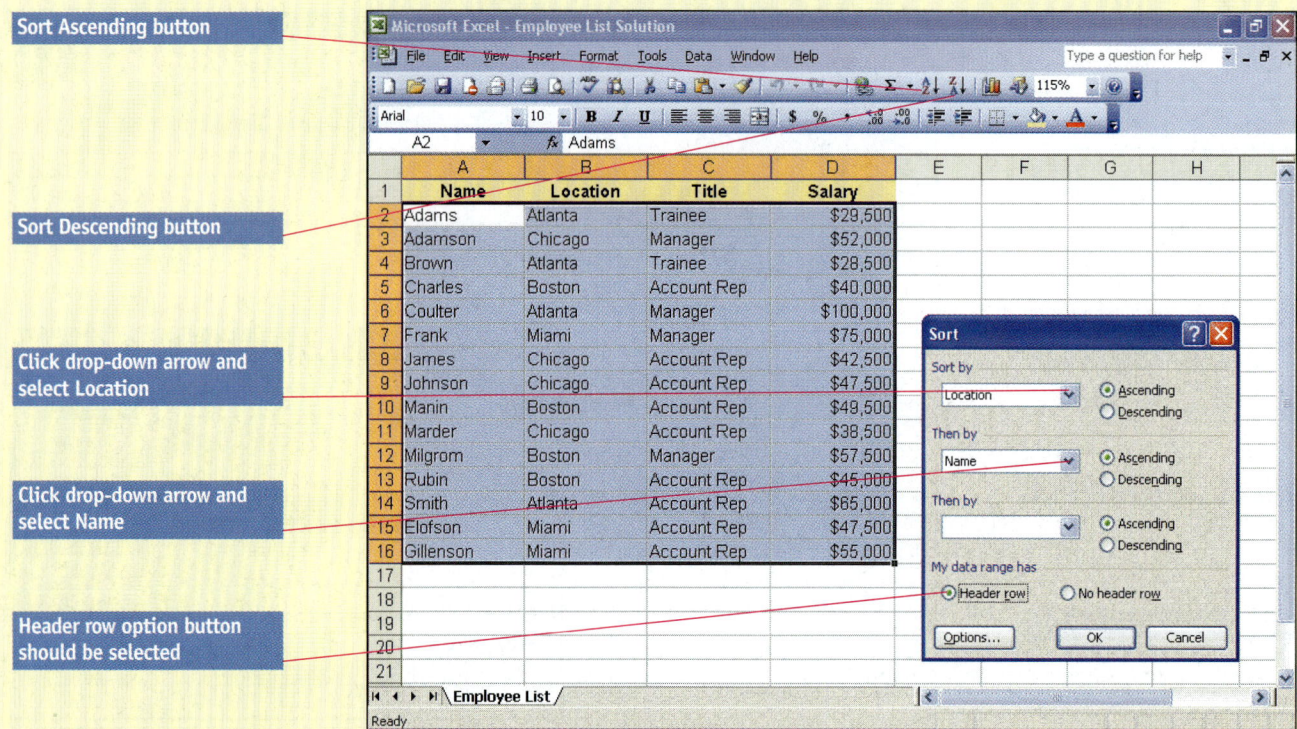

(d) Sort the Employee List (step 4)

FIGURE 7.6 Hands-on Exercise 1 (*continued*)

USE THE SORT BUTTONS

Use the Sort Ascending or Sort Descending button on the Standard toolbar to sort on one or more keys. To sort on a single key, click any cell in the column containing the key, then click the appropriate button, depending on whether you want an ascending or a descending sort. You can also sort on multiple keys, by clicking either button multiple times, but the trick is to do it in the right sequence. Sort on the least significant field first, then work your way up to the most significant. For example, to sort a list by location, and name within location, sort by name first (the secondary key), then sort by location (the primary key).

Step 5: **Delete a Record**

- A record may be deleted by using the Edit Delete command or the Data Form command. To delete a record by using the Edit Delete command:
  - Click the **row heading** in **row 15** (containing the record for Frank, which is slated for deletion).
  - Pull down the **Edit menu**. Click **Delete**. Frank has been deleted.

- Click the **Undo button** on the Standard toolbar. The record for Frank has been restored.

- To delete a record by using the Data Form command:
  - Click a single cell within the employee list. Pull down the **Data menu**. Click **Form** to display the data form. Click the **Criteria button**. Enter **Frank** in the Name text box, then click the **Find Next button** to locate Frank's record.
  - Click the **Delete command button**. Click **OK** in response to the warning message shown in Figure 7.6e. (The record cannot be undeleted as it could with the Edit Delete command.) Click **Close** to close the Data Form.

- Save the workbook.

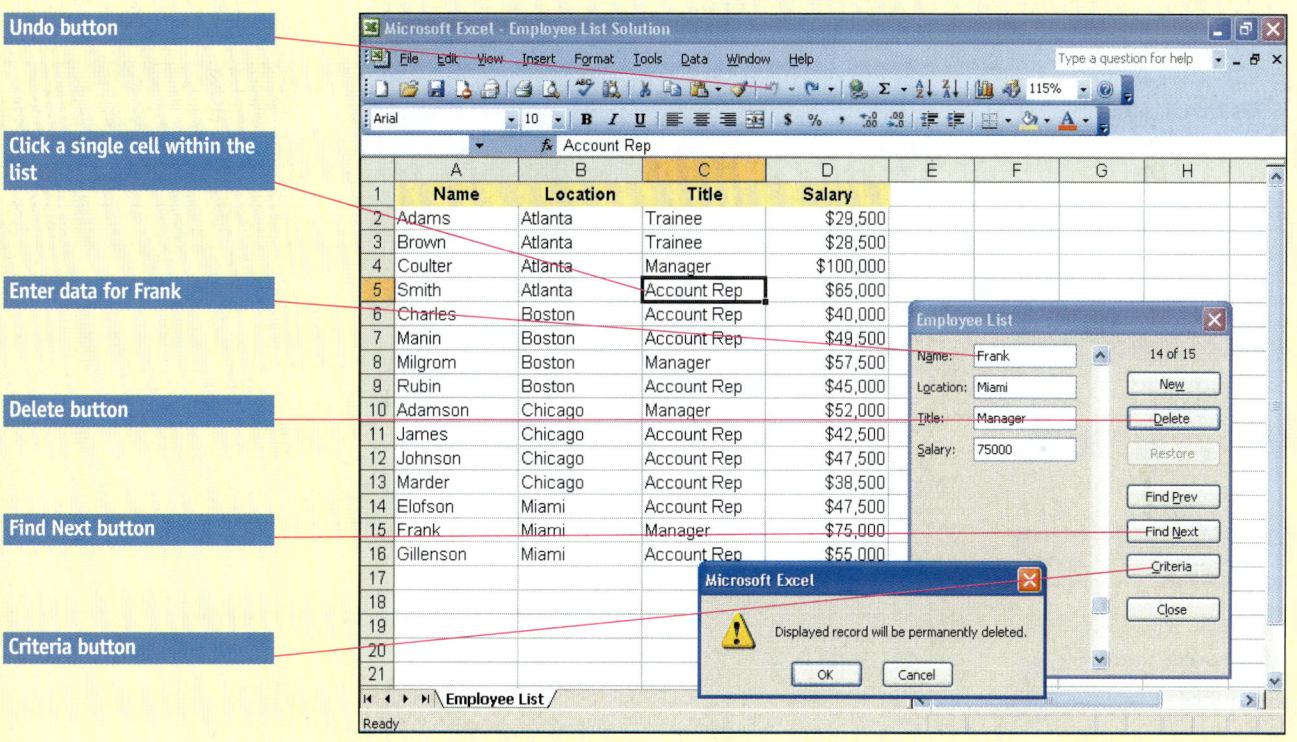

(e) Delete a Record (step 5)

FIGURE 7.6 Hands-on Exercise 1 (*continued*)

EDIT CLEAR VERSUS EDIT DELETE

The Edit Delete command deletes the selected cell, row, or column from the worksheet, and thus its execution will adjust cell references throughout the worksheet. It is very different from the Edit Clear command, which erases the contents (and/or formatting) of the selected cells, but does not delete the cells from the worksheet and hence has no effect on the cell references in formulas that reference those cells. Pressing the Del key erases the contents of a cell and thus corresponds to the Edit Clear command.

Step 6: **Enter the Hire Date**

- Click the **column heading** in column D. Point to the selection, then click the **right mouse button** to display a shortcut menu. Click **Insert**. The employee salaries have been moved to column E, as shown in Figure 7.6f.

- Click **cell D1**. Type **Hire Date** and press **Enter**. Adjust the column width if necessary. Dates may be entered in several different formats.
  - Type **11/24/98** in cell D2. Press the **down arrow key**.
  - Type **11/24/1998** in cell D3. Press the **down arrow key**.
  - Type **Nov 24, 1998** in cell D4. Type a **comma** after the day but do not type a period after the month. Press the **down arrow key** to move to cell D5.
  - Type **11-24-98** in cell D5. Press **Enter**.

- For ease of data entry, assume that the next several employees were hired on the same day, 3/16/99. Click in **cell D6**. Type **3/16/99**. Press **enter**. Click in **cell D6**. Click the **Copy button** on the Standard toolbar.

- Drag the mouse over cells **D7 through D10**. Click the **Paste button**. Press **Esc** to remove the moving border around cell D6.

- Save the workbook.

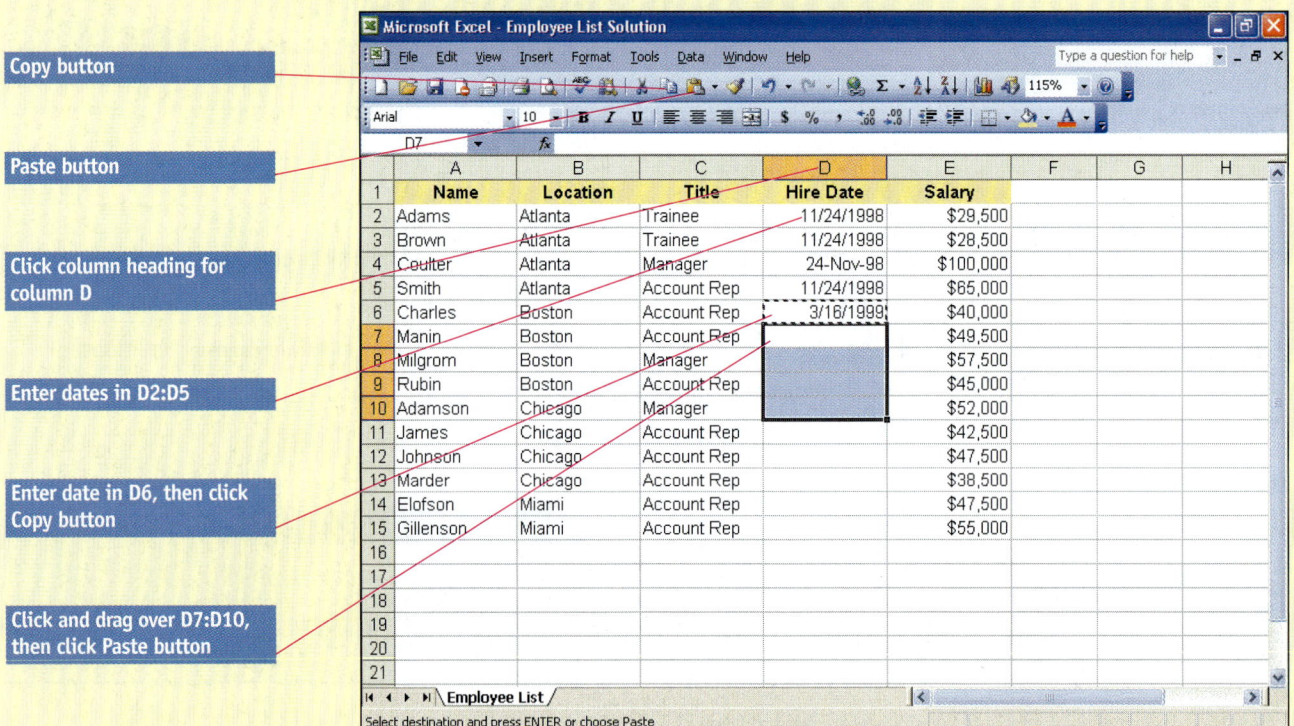

(f) Enter the Hire Date (step 6)

FIGURE 7.6 Hands-on Exercise 1 (*continued*)

TWO-DIGIT DATES AND THE YEAR 2000

Excel assumes that any two-digit year up to and including 29 is in the 21st century; that is, 12/31/29 will be stored as December 31, 2029. (The year 2029 is arbitrary.) Any year after 29, however, is assumed to be in the 20th century; for example, 1/1/30 will be stored as January 1, 1930. When in doubt, however, enter a four-digit year to be sure.

Step 7: **Format the Hire Dates**

- The next five employees were hired one year apart beginning October 31, 1998.
  - Click in cell **D11** and type **10/31/98**. Click in cell **D12** and type **10/31/99**.
  - Select cells **D11 and D12**.
  - Drag the **fill handle** at the bottom of cell D12 over cells **D13**, **D14**, and **D15**. Release the mouse to complete the AutoFill operation.

- Click in the column heading for **column D** to select the column of dates.

- Point to the selected cells and click the **right mouse button** to display a shortcut menu. Click **Format Cells**.

- Click the **Number tab** in the Format Cells dialog box. Click **Date** in the Category list box. Select (click) the date format shown in Figure 7.6g. Click **OK**.

- Click elsewhere in the workbook to deselect the dates. Reduce the width of column D as appropriate. Save the workbook.

- Exit Excel if you do not want to complete the next exercise at this time.

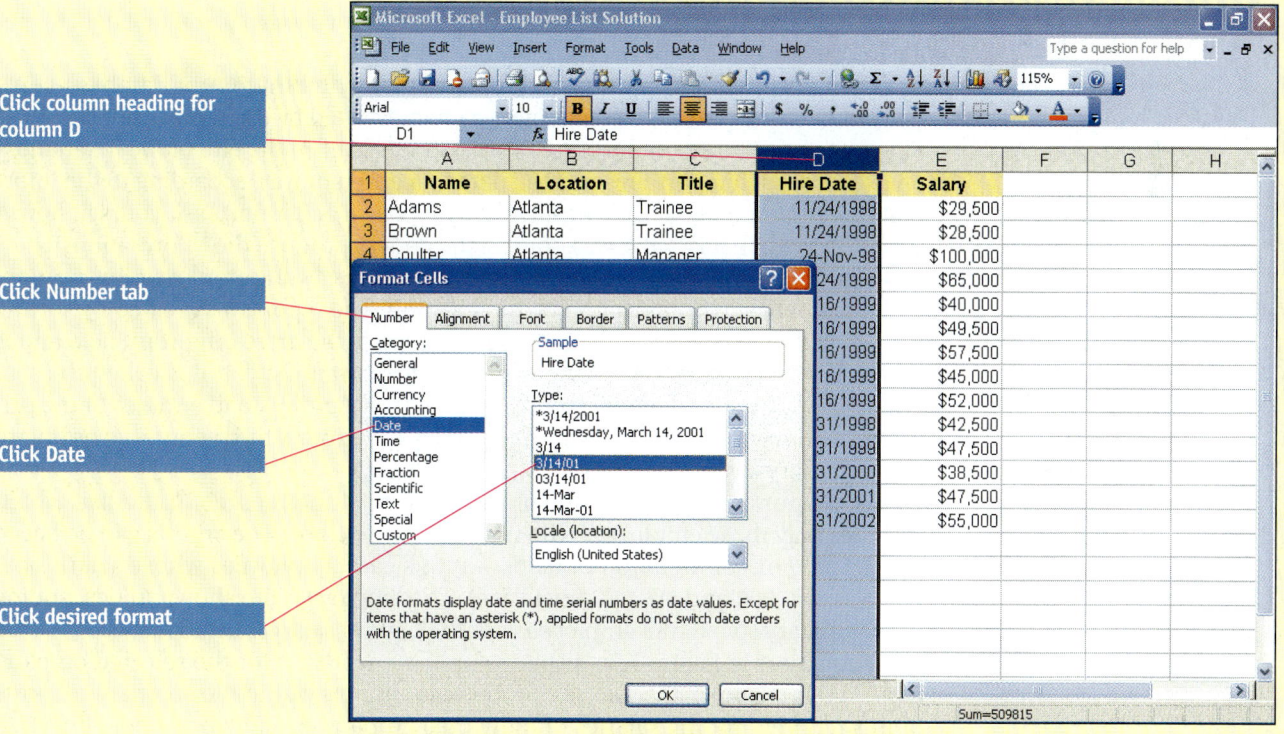

(g) Format the Hire Dates (step 7)

FIGURE 7.6 Hands-on Exercise 1 (*continued*)

EXPORTING DATA FROM EXCEL

We began the exercise by importing data from a text file into an Excel workbook. You can also go in the opposite direction; i.e., you can export the data in an Excel worksheet into a CSV (comma-separated value) or text file, an XML document, or an Access database. Pull down the File menu, click the Save As command, then specify the file type; e.g., a text file. Exporting an Excel worksheet to an Access table is done differently, however, in that you have to import the Excel table from within Access. See the Excel and Access mini case at the end of the chapter.

DATA VERSUS INFORMATION

Data and information are not synonymous. **Data** refers to a fact or facts about a specific record, such as an employee's name, title, or salary. **Information**, on the other hand, is data that has been rearranged into a form perceived as useful by the recipient. A list of employees earning more than $35,000 or a total of all employee salaries are examples of information produced from data about individual employees. Put another way, data is the raw material, and information is the finished product.

Decisions in an organization are based on information rather than raw data; for example, in assessing the effects of a proposed across-the-board salary increase, management needs to know the total payroll rather than individual salary amounts. In similar fashion, decisions about next year's hiring will be influenced, at least in part, by knowing how many individuals are currently employed in each job category.

Organizations maintain data to produce information. Data maintenance entails three basic operations—adding new records, modifying (editing or updating) existing records, and deleting existing records. The exercise just completed showed you how to maintain the data. This section focuses on using that data to create information.

Data is converted to information through a combination of database commands and functions whose capabilities are illustrated by the reports in Figure 7.7. The reports are based on the employee list as it existed at the end of the first hands-on exercise. Each report presents the data in a different way, according to the information requirements of the end-user. As you view each report, ask yourself how it was produced; that is, what was done to the data to produce the information?

Figure 7.7a contains a master list of all employees, listing employees by location, and alphabetically by last name within location. The report was created by sorting the list on two keys, location and name. Location is the more important field and is known as the primary key. Name is the less important field and is called the secondary key. The sorted report groups employees according to like values of the primary key (location), then within the primary key groups the records according to the secondary key (name).

The report in Figure 7.7b displays a subset of the records in the list, which includes only those employees who meet specific criteria. The criteria can be based on any field or combination of fields—in this case, employees whose salaries are between $40,000 and $60,000 (inclusive). The employees are shown in descending order of salary so that the employee with the highest salary is listed first.

The report in Figure 7.7c displays summary statistics for the selected employees—in this example, the salaries for the account reps within the company. Reports of this nature omit the salaries of individual employees (known as detail lines), to present an aggregate view of the organization. Remember, too, that the information produced by any system is only as good as the data on which it is based. Thus, it is very important that organizations take steps to ensure the validity of the data as it is entered into a system.

BIRTH DATE VERSUS AGE

An individual's age and birth date provide equivalent information, as one is calculated from the other. It might seem easier, therefore, to enter the age directly into the list and avoid the calculation, but this would be a mistake. A person's age changes continually, whereas the birth date remains constant. Thus, the date, not the age, should be stored, so that the data in the list remains current. Similar reasoning applies to an employee's hire date and length of service.

Location Report

Name	Location	Title	Service	Hire Date	Salary
Adams	Atlanta	Trainee	4.6	11/24/98	$29,500
Brown	Atlanta	Trainee	4.6	11/24/98	$28,500
Coulter	Atlanta	Manager	4.6	11/24/98	$100,000
Smith	Atlanta	Account Rep	4.6	11/24/98	$65,000
Charles	Boston	Account Rep	4.3	3/16/99	$40,000
Manin	Boston	Account Rep	4.3	3/16/99	$49,500
Milgrom	Boston	Manager	4.3	3/16/99	$57,500
Rubin	Boston	Account Rep	4.3	3/16/99	$45,000
Adamson	Chicago	Manager	4.3	3/16/99	$52,000
James	Chicago	Account Rep	4.7	10/31/98	$42,500
Johnson	Chicago	Account Rep	3.7	10/31/99	$47,500
Marder	Chicago	Account Rep	2.7	10/31/00	$38,500
Elofson	Miami	Account Rep	1.7	10/31/01	$47,500
Gillenson	Miami	Account Rep	0.7	10/31/02	$55,000

(a) Employees by Location and Name within Location

Earnings Between $40,000 and $60,000

Name	Location	Title	Service	Hire Date	Salary
Milgrom	Boston	Manager	4.3	3/16/99	$57,500
Gillenson	Miami	Account Rep	0.7	10/31/02	$55,000
Adamson	Chicago	Manager	4.3	3/16/99	$52,000
Manin	Boston	Account Rep	4.3	3/16/99	$49,500
Johnson	Chicago	Account Rep	3.7	10/31/99	$47,500
Elofson	Miami	Account Rep	1.7	10/31/01	$47,500
Rubin	Boston	Account Rep	4.3	3/16/99	$45,000
James	Chicago	Account Rep	4.7	10/31/98	$42,500
Charles	Boston	Account Rep	4.3	3/16/99	$40,000

(b) Employees Earning Between $40,000 and $60,000, Inclusive

Summary Statistics

Total Salary for Account Reps	$430,500
Average Salary for Account Reps	$47,833
Maximum Salary for Account Reps	$65,000
Minimum Salary for Account Reps	$38,500
Number of Account Reps	9

(c) Account Rep Summary Data

FIGURE 7.7 Data versus Information

AutoFilter Command

A *filtered list* displays a subset of records that meet a specific criterion or set of criteria. It is created by the **AutoFilter command** (or the Advanced Filter command discussed in the next section). Both commands temporarily hide those records (rows) that do not meet the criteria. The hidden records are *not* deleted; they are simply not displayed.

Figure 7.8a displays the employee list in alphabetical order. Figure 7.8b displays a filtered version of the list in which only the Atlanta employees (in rows 2, 4, 6, and 15) are visible. The remaining employees are still in the worksheet but are not shown as their rows are hidden.

	A	B	C	D	E
1	Name	Location	Title	Hire Date	Salary
2	Adams	Atlanta	Trainee	11/24/98	$29,500
3	Adamson		Manager	3/16/99	$52,000
4	Brown	(All)	Trainee	11/24/98	$28,500
5	Charles	(Top 10...)	Account Rep	3/16/99	$40,000
6	Coulter	(Custom...)	Manager	11/24/98	$100,000
7	Elofson	Atlanta	Account Rep	10/31/01	$47,500
8	Gillenson	Boston	Account Rep	10/31/02	$55,000
9	James	Chicago	Account Rep	10/31/98	$42,500
10	Johnson	Miami	Account Rep	10/31/99	$47,500
11	Manin	Boston	Account Rep	3/16/99	$49,500
12	Marder	Chicago	Account Rep	10/31/00	$38,500
13	Milgrom	Boston	Manager	3/16/99	$57,500
14	Rubin	Boston	Account Rep	3/16/99	$45,000
15	Smith	Atlanta	Account Rep	11/24/98	$65,000

- AutoFilter command places drop-down arrow next to field name
- Click to display Atlanta employees only

(a) Unfiltered List

	A	B	C	D	E
1	Name	Location	Title	Hire Date	Salary
2	Adams	Atlanta	Trainee	11/24/98	$29,500
4	Brown	Atlanta	Trainee	11/24/98	$28,500
6	Coulter	Atlanta	Manager	11/24/98	$100,000
15	Smith	Atlanta	Account Rep	11/24/98	$65,000

- Only rows 2, 4, 6, and 15 are visible
- Only Atlanta employees are displayed

(b) Filtered List (Atlanta employees)

	A	B	C	D	E
1	Name	Location	Title	Hire Date	Salary
2	Adams	Atlanta	Sort Ascending	11/24/98	$29,500
4	Brown	Atlanta	Sort Descending	11/24/98	$28,500
6	Coulter	Atlanta	(All)	11/24/98	$100,000
15	Smith	Atlanta	(Top 10...)	11/24/98	$65,000
16			(Custom...)		
17			Account Rep		
18			Manager		
			Trainee		

- Click drop-down arrow to further filter list by Title

(c) Imposing a Second Condition

	A	B	C	D	E
1	Name	Location	Title	Hire Date	Salary
6	Coulter	Atlanta	Manager	11/24/98	$100,000

- Blue drop-down arrows indicate filter condition is in effect for those fields

(d) Filtered List (Atlanta managers)

FIGURE 7.8 Filter Command

Execution of the AutoFilter command places drop-down arrows next to each column label (field name). Clicking a drop-down arrow produces a list of the unique values for that field, enabling you to establish the criteria for the filtered list. Thus, to display the Atlanta employees, click the drop-down arrow for Location, then click Atlanta.

A filter condition can be imposed on multiple columns as shown in Figure 7.8c. The filtered list in Figure 7.8c contains just the Atlanta employees. Clicking the arrow next to Title, then clicking Manager, will filter the list further to display the employees who both work in Atlanta *and* have Manager as a title. Only one employee meets both conditions, as shown in Figure 7.8d. The drop-down arrows next to Location and Title are displayed in blue to indicate that a filter is in effect for these columns.

The AutoFilter command has additional options as can be seen from the drop-down list box in Figure 7.8c. (All) removes existing criteria in that column. (Custom . . .) enables you to use the relational operators (=, >, <, >=, <=, or <>) within a criterion. (Top 10 . . .) displays the records with the top (or bottom) values in the field, and makes most sense if you sort the list to see the entries in sequence.

Advanced Filter Command

The ***Advanced Filter command*** extends the capabilities of the AutoFilter command in two important ways. It enables you to develop more complex criteria than are possible with the AutoFilter Command. It also enables you to filter the list in place and/or to copy (extract) the selected records to a separate area in the worksheet. The Advanced Filter command is illustrated in detail in the hands-on exercise that follows shortly.

Criteria Range

A ***criteria range*** is used with both the Advanced Filter command and the database functions that are discussed in the next section. It is defined independently of the list on which it operates and exists as a separate area in the worksheet. A criteria range must be at least two rows deep and one column wide as illustrated in Figure 7.9.

The simplest criteria range consists of two rows and as many columns as there are fields in the list. The first row contains the field names as they appear in the list. The second row holds the value(s) you are looking for. The criteria range in Figure 7.9a selects the employees who work in Atlanta; that is, it selects those records where the value of the Location Field is equal to Atlanta.

Multiple values in the same row are connected by an AND and require that the selected records meet *all* of the specified criteria. The criteria range in Figure 7.9b identifies the account reps in Atlanta; that is, it selects any record in which the Location field is Atlanta *and* the Title field is Account Rep. (Both fields must be spelled exactly; e.g., specifying Account Rep*s* instead of Account Rep will not return any employees.)

Values entered in multiple rows are connected by an OR in which the selected records satisfy *any* of the indicated criteria. The criteria range in Figure 7.9c will identify employees who work in Atlanta *or* whose title is Account Rep.

Relational operators may be used with date or numeric fields to return records within a designated range. The criteria range in Figure 7.9d selects the employees hired before January 1, 1993. The criteria range in Figure 7.9e returns employees whose salary is more than $40,000.

An upper and lower boundary may be established for the same field by repeating the field within the criteria range. This was done in Figure 7.9f, which returns all records in which the salary is more than $40,000 but less than $60,000.

First row contains field names

Second row contains filter condition

Name	Location	Title	Hire Date	Salary
	Atlanta			

(a) Employees Who Work in Atlanta

Multiple criteria in same row indicate both must be met

Name	Location	Title	Hire Date	Salary
	Atlanta	Account Rep		

(b) Account Reps Who Work in Atlanta (AND condition)

Multiple criteria in different rows indicate either may be met

Name	Location	Title	Hire Date	Salary
	Atlanta			
		Account Rep		

(c) Employees Who Work in Atlanta or Who Are Account Reps (OR condition)

Relational operators may be used with dates and numerical data

Name	Location	Title	Hire Date	Salary
			<1/1/93	

(d) Employees Hired before January 1, 1993

Name	Location	Title	Hire Date	Salary
				>$40,000

(e) Employees Who Earn More Than $40,000

Lower boundary

Upper boundary

Name	Location	Title	Hire Date	Salary	Salary
				>$40,000	≤$60,000

(f) Employees Who Earn More Than $40,000 But Less Than $60,000

Selects records with no entry in Location field

Name	Location	Title	Hire Date	Salary
	=			

(g) Employees without a Location

Empty criteria row returns every record

Name	Location	Title	Hire Date	Salary

(h) All Employees (blank row)

FIGURE 7.9 The Criteria Range

The equal and unequal signs select records with empty and nonempty fields, respectively. An equal sign with nothing after it will return all records without an entry in the designated field; for example, the criteria range in Figure 7.9g selects any record that is missing a value for the Location field. An unequal sign (<>) with nothing after it will select all records with an entry in the field.

An empty row in the criteria range returns *every* record in the list, as shown in Figure 7.9h. All criteria are *case-insensitive* and return records with any combination of upper- and lowercase letters that match the entry. Remember, too, that all text entries must be spelled correctly in order to return the intended records.

THE IMPLIED WILD CARD

Any text entry within a criteria range is treated as though it were followed by the asterisk wild card; that is, *New* is the same as *New**. Both entries will return New York and New Jersey. To match a text entry exactly, begin with an equal sign, enter a quotation mark followed by another equal sign, the entry you are looking for, and the closing quotation mark—for example, = " =New" to return only the entries that say New.

Database Functions

The ***database functions*** DSUM, DAVERAGE, DMAX, DMIN, and DCOUNT operate on *selected* records in a list. These functions parallel the statistical functions (SUM, AVERAGE, MAX, MIN, and COUNT) except that they affect only records that satisfy the established criteria.

The summary statistics in Figure 7.10 are based on the salaries of the managers in the list, rather than the salaries of all employees. Each database function includes the criteria range in cells A17:E18 as one of its arguments, and thus limits the employees that are included to managers. The ***DAVERAGE function*** returns the average salary for just the managers. The ***DMAX*** and ***DMIN functions*** display the maximum and minimum salaries for the managers. The ***DSUM function*** computes the total salary for all the managers. The ***DCOUNT function*** indicates the number of managers.

Each database function has three arguments: the range for the list on which it is to operate, the field to be processed, and the criteria range. Consider, for example, the DAVERAGE function as shown below:

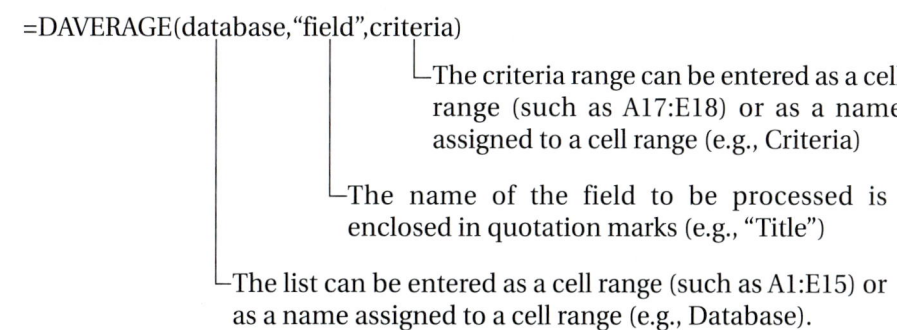

The entries in the criteria range may be changed at any time, in which case the values of the database functions are automatically recalculated. The other database functions have arguments identical to those used in the DAVERAGE function. The functions will adjust automatically if rows or columns are inserted or deleted within the specified range.

	A	B	C	D	E
1	Name	Location	Title	Hire Date	Salary
2	Adams	Atlanta	Trainee	11/24/98	$29,500
3	Adamson	Chicago	Manager	3/16/99	$52,000
4	Brown	Atlanta	Trainee	11/24/98	$28,500
5	Charles	Boston	Account Rep	3/16/99	$40,000
6	Coulter	Atlanta	Manager	11/24/98	$100,000
7	Elofson	Miami	Account Rep	10/31/01	$47,500
8	Gillenson	Miami	Account Rep	10/31/02	$55,000
9	James	Chicago	Account Rep	10/31/98	$42,500
10	Johnson	Chicago	Account Rep	10/31/99	$47,500
11	Manin	Boston	Account Rep	3/16/99	$49,500
12	Marder	Chicago	Account Rep	10/31/00	$38,500
13	Milgrom	Boston	Manager	3/16/99	$57,500
14	Rubin	Boston	Account Rep	3/16/99	$45,000
15	Smith	Atlanta	Account Rep	11/24/98	$65,000
16					
17	Name	Location	Title	Hire Date	Salary
18			Manager		
19					
20					
21			Summary Statistics		
22	Average Salary				$69,833
23	Maximum Salary				$100,000
24	Minimum Salary				$52,000
25	Total Salary				$209,500
26	Number of Employees				3

- Criteria range is A17:E18
- Criteria is Manager
- Summary statistics for Managers

FIGURE 7.10 Database Functions

Insert Name Command

The **Name command** in the Insert menu equates a mnemonic name such as *EmployeeList* to a cell or cell range such as *A1:E15*, then enables you to use that name to reference the cell(s) in all subsequent commands. A name can be up to 255 characters in length, but must begin with a letter or an underscore. It can include upper- or lowercase letters, numbers, periods, and underscore characters but no blank spaces.

Once defined, range names will adjust automatically for insertions and/or deletions within the range. If, in the previous example, you were to delete row 4, the definition of *EmployeeList* would change to A1:E14. And, in similar fashion, if you were to insert a new column between columns B and C, the range would change to A1:F14.

A name can be used in any formula or function instead of a cell address; for example, =SALES–EXPENSES instead of =C1–C10, where Sales and Expenses have been defined as the names for cells C1 and C10, respectively. A name can also be entered into any dialog box where a cell range is required.

> ### THE GO TO COMMAND
> Names are frequently used in conjunction with the Go To command. Pull down the Edit menu and click Go To (or click the F5 key) to display a dialog box containing the names that have been defined within the workbook. Double click a name to move directly to the first cell in the associated range and simultaneously select the entire range.

SUBTOTALS

The **Subtotals command** uses a summary function (such as SUM, AVERAGE, or COUNT) to compute subtotals for groups of records within a list. The records are grouped according to the value in a specific field, such as location, as shown in Figure 7.11. The Subtotals command inserts a subtotal row into the list whenever the value of the designated field (location in this example) changes from one record to the next.

The subtotal for the Atlanta employees is inserted into the list as we go from the last employee in Atlanta to the first employee in Boston. In similar fashion, the subtotal for Boston is inserted into the list as we go from the last employee in Boston to the first employee in Chicago. A grand total is displayed after the last record. The list must be in sequence, according to the field on which the subtotals will be grouped, prior to executing the Subtotals command.

The summary information can be displayed with different levels of detail. Figure 7.11a displays the salary data for each employee (known as the detail lines), the subtotals for each location, and the grand total. Figure 7.11b suppresses the detail lines but shows both the subtotals and grand total. Figure 7.11c shows only the grand total. The worksheet in all three figures is said to be in outline format, as seen by the **outline symbols** at the extreme left of the application window.

The records within the list are grouped to compute the summary information. A plus sign indicates that the group has been collapsed, and that the detail information is suppressed. A minus sign indicates the opposite, namely that the group has been expanded and that the detail information is visible. You can click any plus or minus sign to expand or collapse that portion of the outline. You can also click the symbols (1, 2, or 3) above the plus or minus signs to collapse or expand the rows within the worksheet. Level one shows the least amount of detail and displays only the grand total. Level two includes the subtotals as well as the grand total. Level three includes the detail records, the subtotals, and the grand total.

	A	B	C	D
1	Name	Location	Title	Salary
2	Adams	Atlanta	Trainee	$29,500
3	Brown	Atlanta	Trainee	$28,500
4	Coulter	Atlanta	Manager	$100,000
5	Smith	Atlanta	Account Rep	$65,000
6		**Atlanta Total**		$223,000
7	Charles	Boston	Account Rep	$40,000
8	Manin	Boston	Account Rep	$49,500
9	Milgrom	Boston	Manager	$57,500
10	Rubin	Boston	Account Rep	$45,000
11		**Boston Total**		$192,000
12	Adamson	Chicago	Manager	$52,000
13	James	Chicago	Account Rep	$42,500
14	Johnson	Chicago	Account Rep	$47,500
15	Marder	Chicago	Account Rep	$38,500
16		**Chicago Total**		$180,500
17	Elofson	Miami	Account Rep	$47,500
18	Gillenson	Miami	Account Rep	$55,000
19		**Miami Total**		$102,500
20		**Grand Total**		$698,000

(a) Detail Lines (level 3)

	A	B	C	D
1	Name	Location	Title	Salary
6		Atlanta Total		$223,000
11		Boston Total		$192,000
16		Chicago Total		$180,500
19		Miami Total		$102,500
20		**Grand Total**		$698,000

(b) Location Totals (level 2)

	A	B	C	D
1	Name	Location	Title	Salary
20		Grand Total		$698,000

(c) Grand Total (level 1)

FIGURE 7.11 Subtotals and Outlining

hands-on exercise
2 Data versus Information

Objective To sort a list on multiple keys; to use the AutoFilter and Advanced Filter commands; to define a named range; to use date arithmetic; to use the DSUM, DAVERAGE, DMAX, DMIN, and DCOUNT functions.

Step 1: **Calculate the Years of Service**

- Open the **Employee List Solution workbook** created in the previous exercise.

- Right click the **column heading** in **column D** to display a shortcut menu. Click **Insert**. The column of hire dates has been moved to column E. Click in **cell D1**. Type **Service** and press **Enter**.

- Click in **cell D2** and enter **=(Today()-E2)/365** as shown in Figure 7.12a. Press **Enter**; the years of service for the first employee are displayed in cell D2.

- Click in **cell D2**, then click the **Decrease Decimal button** on the Formatting toolbar several times to display the length of service with only one decimal.

- Drag the **fill handle** in cell D2 to the remaining cells in that column (**cells D3 through D15**) to compute the length of service for the remaining employees.

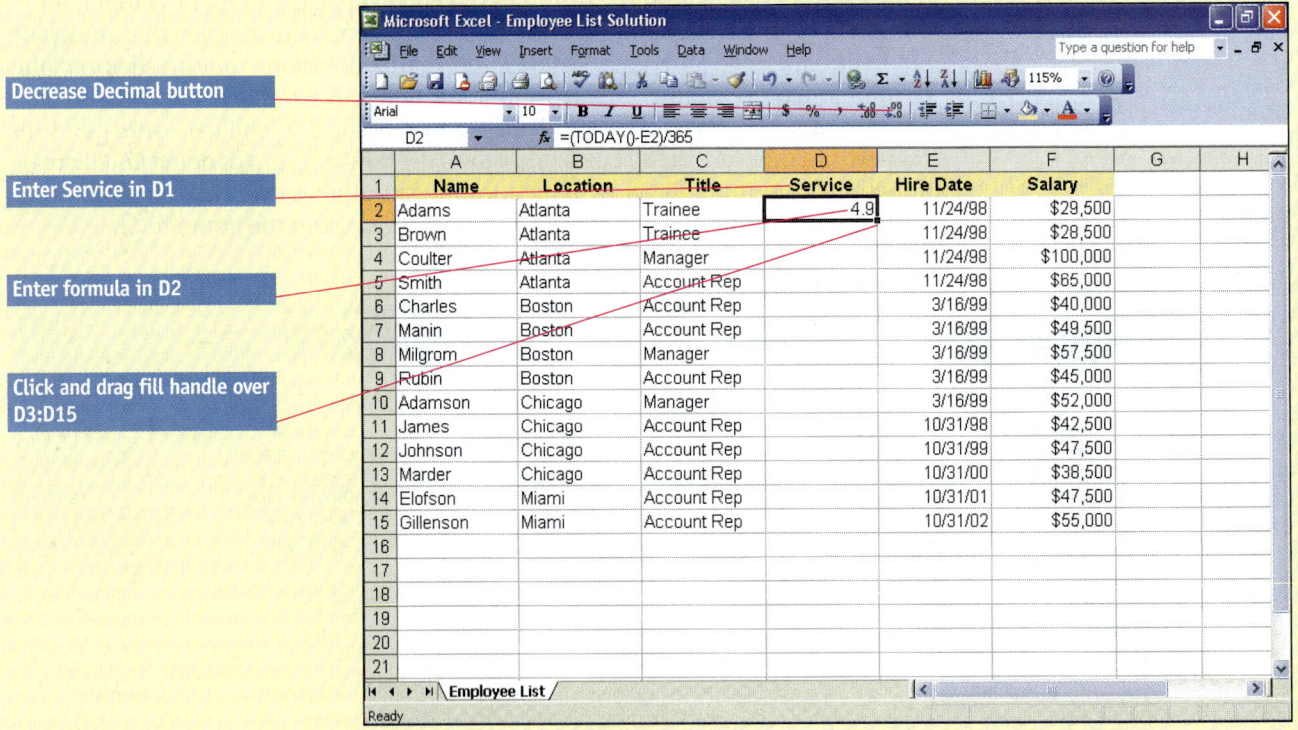

(a) Calculate the Years of Service (step 1)

FIGURE 7.12 Hands-on Exercise 2

DATE ARITHMETIC

Microsoft Excel stores a date as an integer (serial number) equivalent to the elapsed number of days since December 31, 1899; e.g., January 1, 1900 is stored as the number 1, January 2, 1900 as the number 2, and so on. This enables you to use dates in an arithmetic computation. An employee's service, for example, is computed by subtracting the hire date from the Today() function and dividing the result by 365.

Step 2: **The AutoFilter Command**

- Click a single cell anywhere within the list. Pull down the **Data menu**. Click the **Filter command**.
- Click **AutoFilter** from the resulting cascade menu to display the drop-down arrows to the right of each field name.
- Click the **drop-down arrow** next to **Title** to display the list of titles in Figure 7.12b. Click **Account Rep**.
- The display changes to show only those employees who meet the filter. The row numbers for the visible records are blue. The drop-down arrow for Title is also blue, indicating that it is part of the filter condition.
- Click the **drop-down arrow** next to **Location**. Click **Boston** to display only the employees in this city. The combination of the two filter conditions shows only the account reps in Boston.
- Click the **drop-down arrow** next to **Location** a second time. Click **(All)** to remove the filter condition on location. Only the account reps are displayed since the filter on Title is still in effect.
- Save the workbook.

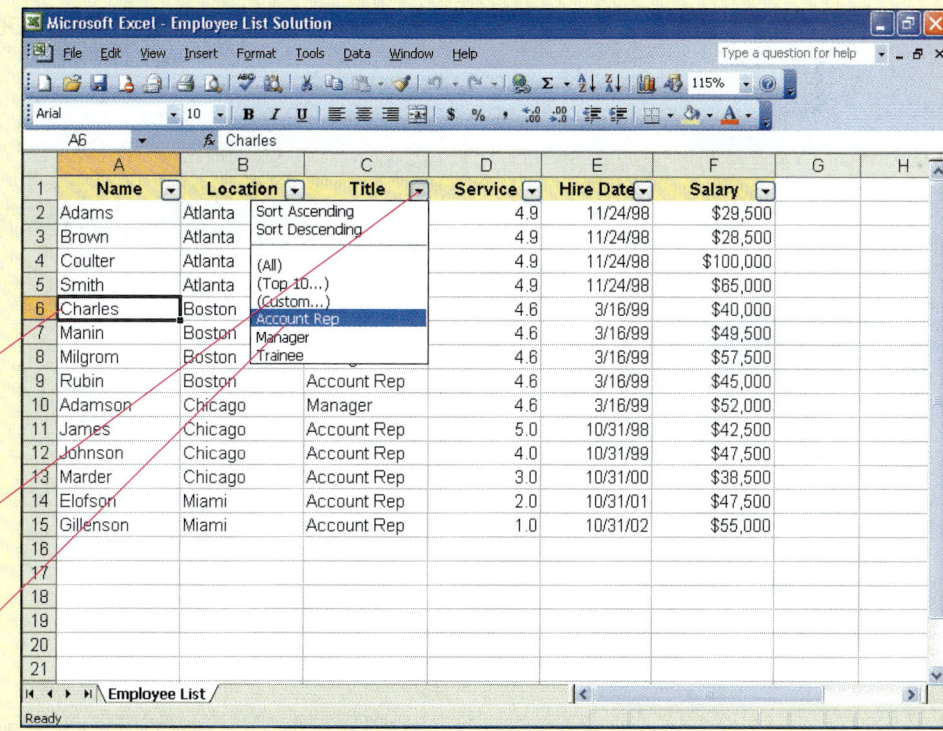

(b) The AutoFilter Command (step 2)

FIGURE 7.12 Hands-on Exercise 2 (*continued*)

THE TOP 10 AUTOFILTER

Use the Top 10 AutoFilter option to see the top (or bottom) 10, or for that matter any number of records in a list. Just turn the AutoFilter condition on, click the down arrow in the designated field, then click Top 10 to display the associated dialog box, where you specify the records you want to view. You can also specify a percentage, as opposed to a number—for example, the top 10% of the records in a list. See exercise 7 at the end of the chapter.

Step 3: **The Custom AutoFilter Command**

- Click the **drop-down arrow** next to **Salary** to display the list of salaries. Click **Custom** to display the dialog box in Figure 7.12c.

- Click the **arrow** in the leftmost drop-down list box for **Salary**, then click the **is greater than** as the relational operator.

- Click in the text box for the salary amount. Type **45000**. Click **OK**.

- The list changes to display only those employees whose title is account rep *and* who earn more than $45,000.

- Pull down the **Data menu**. Click **Filter**. Click **AutoFilter** to toggle the AutoFilter command off, which removes the arrows next to the field names and cancels all filter conditions. All of the records in the list are visible.

- Save the workbook.

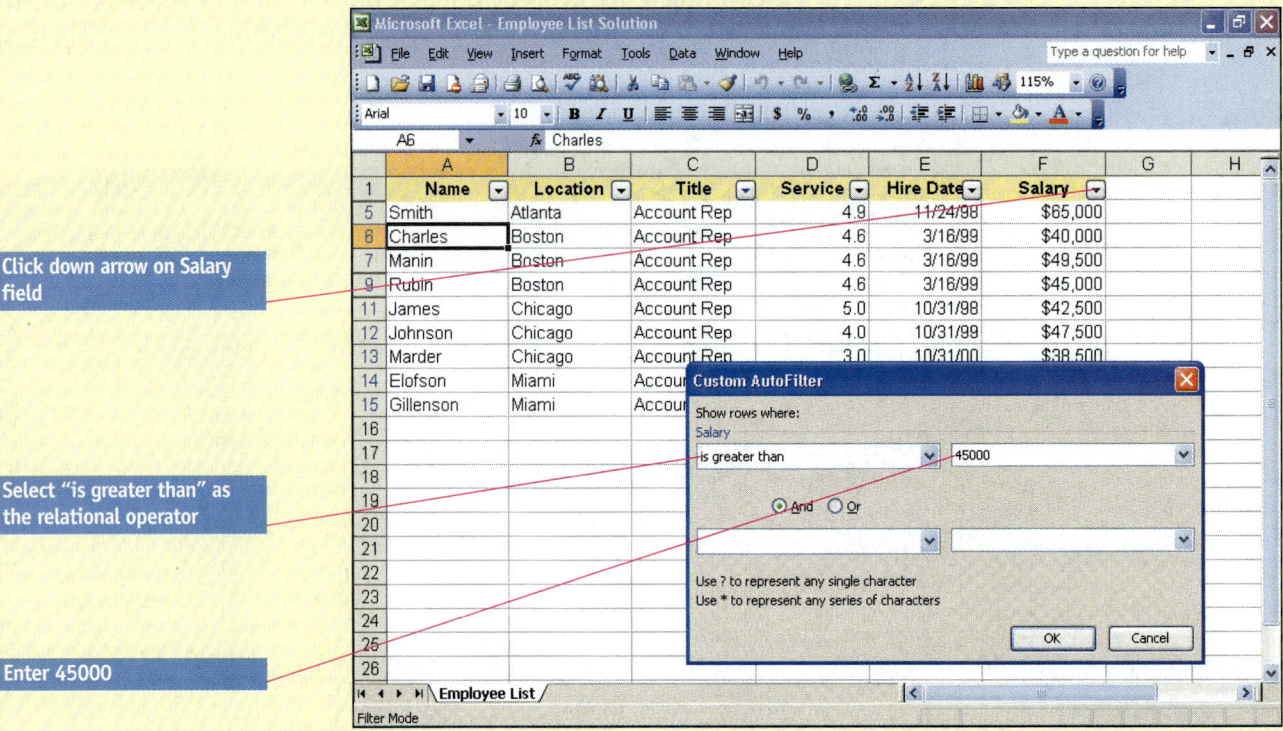

(c) The Custom AutoFilter Command (step 3)

FIGURE 7.12 Hands-on Exercise 2 (*continued*)

THE ANALYSIS TOOLPAK

Do you need to perform a statistical analysis on data within a worksheet? If so, you will want to use the Analysis ToolPak, one of several supplemental programs (or add-ins) that is included with Microsoft Excel. Pull down the Tools menu, click the Add-Ins command to display the associated dialog box, check the box for the Analysis ToolPak, then click OK to load the program. Pull down the Tools menu a second time, and then click the newly added Data Analysis command to access the tool pack, which provides access to a set of statistical functions to provide sophisticated analyses. See practice exercise 9 at the end of the chapter.

Step 4: **The Advanced Filter Command**

- The field names in the criteria range must be spelled exactly the same way as in the associated list. The best way to ensure that the names are identical is to copy the entries from the list to the criteria range.
- Click and drag to select **cells A1 through F1**. Click the **Copy button** on the Standard toolbar. A moving border appears around the selected cells. Click in **cell A17**. Click the **Paste button** on the Standard toolbar to complete the copy operation. Press **Esc** to cancel the moving border.
- Click in **cell C18**. Enter **Manager**. (Be sure you spell it correctly.)
- Click a single cell anywhere within the employee list. Pull down the **Data menu**. Click **Filter**. Click **Advanced Filter** from the resulting cascade menu to display the dialog box in Figure 7.12d. (The list range is already entered because you had selected a cell in the list prior to executing the command.)
- Click in the **Criteria Range** text box. Click in **cell A17** in the worksheet and drag the mouse to cell F18. Release the mouse. A moving border appears around these cells in the worksheet, and the corresponding cell reference is entered in the dialog box.
- Check that the **option button** to Filter the list, in-place is selected. Click **OK**. The display changes to show just the managers; that is, only rows 4, 8, and 10 are visible.
- Click in **cell B18**. Type **Atlanta**. Press **Enter**.
- Pull down the **Data menu**. Click **Filter**. Click **Advanced Filter**. The Advanced Filter dialog box already has the cell references for the list and criteria ranges.
- Click **OK**. The display changes to show just the manager in Atlanta; that is, only row 4 is visible.
- Pull down the **Data menu**. Click **Filter**. Click **Show All** to remove the filter condition. The entire list is visible.

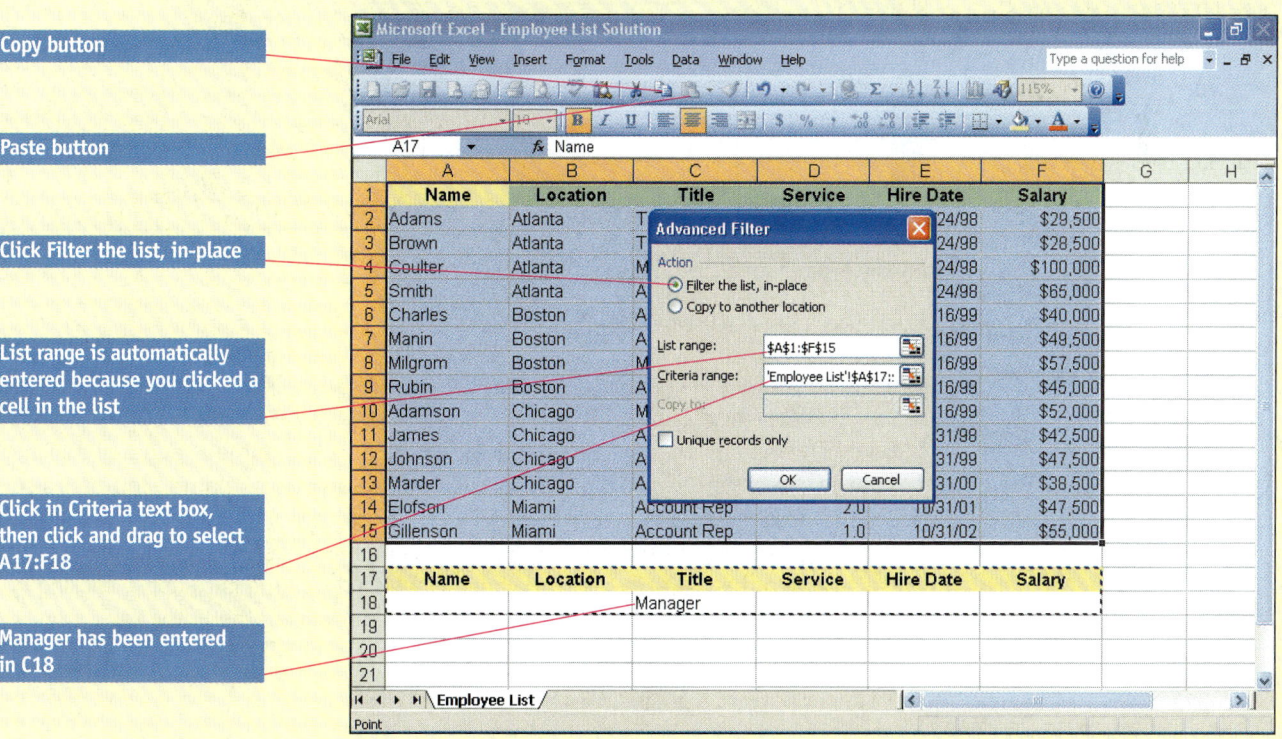

(d) The Advanced Filter Command (step 4)

FIGURE 7.12   Hands-on Exercise 2 (*continued*)

Step 5: **The Insert Name Command**

- Click and drag to select **cells A1 through F15** as shown in Figure 7.12e.

- Pull down the **Insert menu**. Click **Name**. Click **Define**. Type **Database** in the Names in workbook text box. Click **OK**.

- Pull down the **Edit menu** and click **Go To** (or press the **F5 key**) to display the Go To dialog box. There are two names in the box: **Database**, which you just defined, and **Criteria**, which was defined automatically when you specified the criteria range in step 4.

- Double click **Criteria** to select the criteria range **(cells A17 through F18)**. Click elsewhere in the worksheet to deselect the cells.

- Save the workbook.

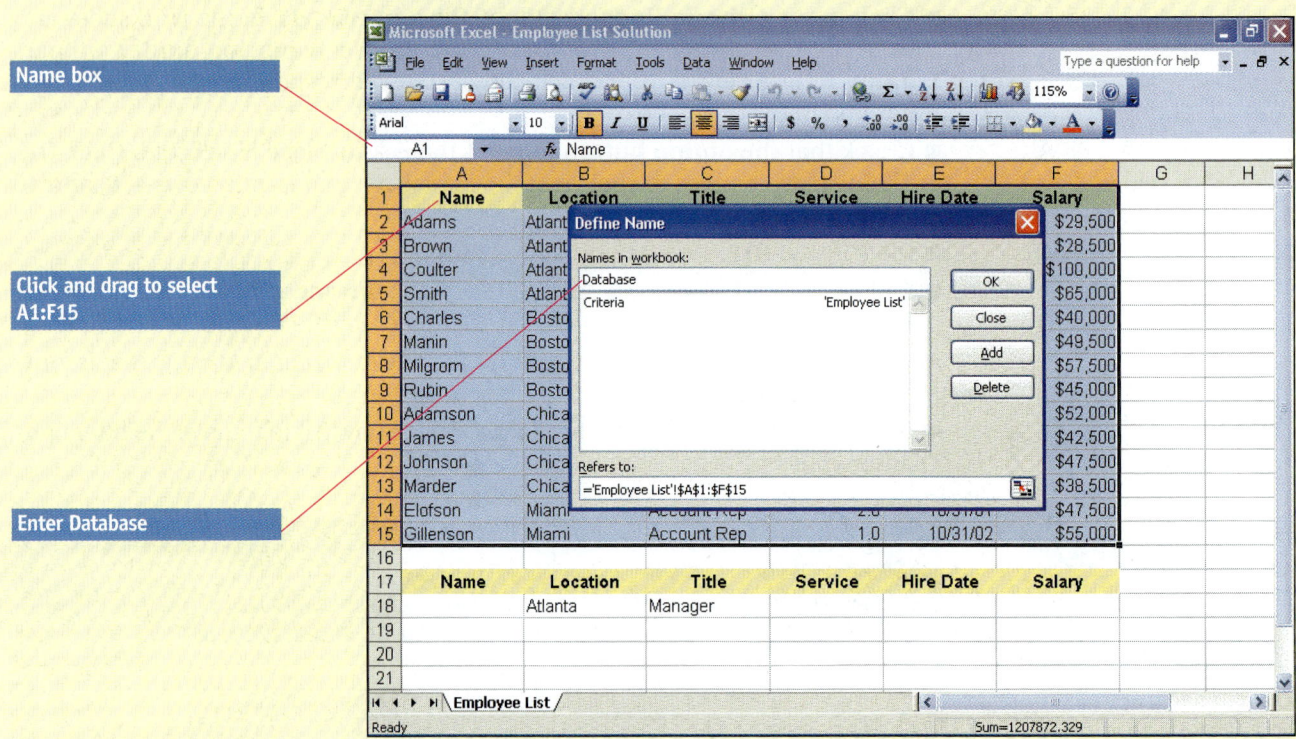

(e) The Insert Name Command (step 5)

FIGURE 7.12 Hands-on Exercise 2 (*continued*)

THE NAME BOX

Use the Name box on the formula bar to select a cell or named range by clicking in the box and then typing the appropriate cell reference or name. You can also click the drop-down arrow next to the Name box to select a named range from a drop-down list. And, finally, you can use the Name box to define a named range, by first selecting the cell(s) in the worksheet to which the name is to apply, clicking in the Name box to enter the range name, and then pressing the Enter key.

Step 6: **Database Functions**

- Click in **cell A21**, type **Summary Statistics**, press the **Enter key**, then click and drag to select cells **A21 through F21**.

- Pull down the **Format menu**, click **Cells**, click the **Alignment tab**, then select **Center Across Selection** as the horizontal alignment. Click **OK**. Change the fill color for this range to **light yellow**.

- Enter the labels for **cells A22 through A26** as shown in Figure 7.12f.

- Click in **cell B18**. Press the **Del key**. The criteria range is now set to select only managers.

- Click in **cell F22**. Click the **Insert Function button** on the formula bar to display the dialog box in Figure 7.12f.

- Select **Database** from the Category list box, select **DAVERAGE** as the function name, then click **OK**.

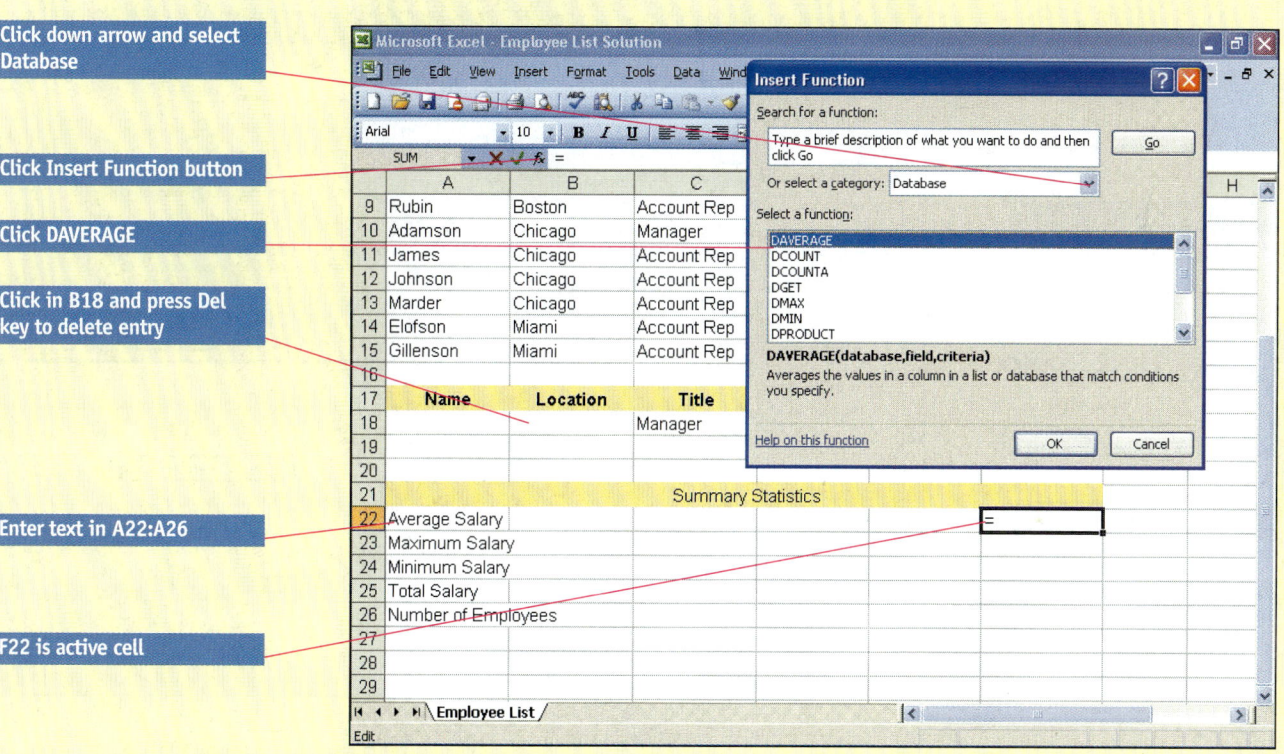

(f) Database Functions (step 6)

FIGURE 7.12 Hands-on Exercise 2 (*continued*)

HIDE A COLUMN

An individual's hire date and length of service convey essentially the same information, and thus there is no need to display both columns. Point to the column heading of the field you wish to hide, then click the right mouse button to select the column and display a shortcut menu. Click the Hide command, and the column is no longer visible (although it remains in the worksheet). To display (unhide) a column, click and drag the adjacent column headings on both sides, click the right mouse button to display a shortcut menu, then click the Unhide command.

Step 7: **The DAVERAGE Function**

- Click the **Database** text box in the dialog box as shown in Figure 7.12g. Type **Database** (the range name defined in step 5), which references the employee list.

- Click the **Field** text box. Type **"Salary"** (you must include the quotation marks), which is the name of the field (column name) within the list that you want to average.

- Click the **Criteria** text box. Type **Criteria** (the range name automatically assigned to the criteria range during the Advanced Filter operation). The dialog box displays the computed value of 69833.33333.

- Click **OK** to enter the DAVERAGE function into the worksheet.

- Save the workbook.

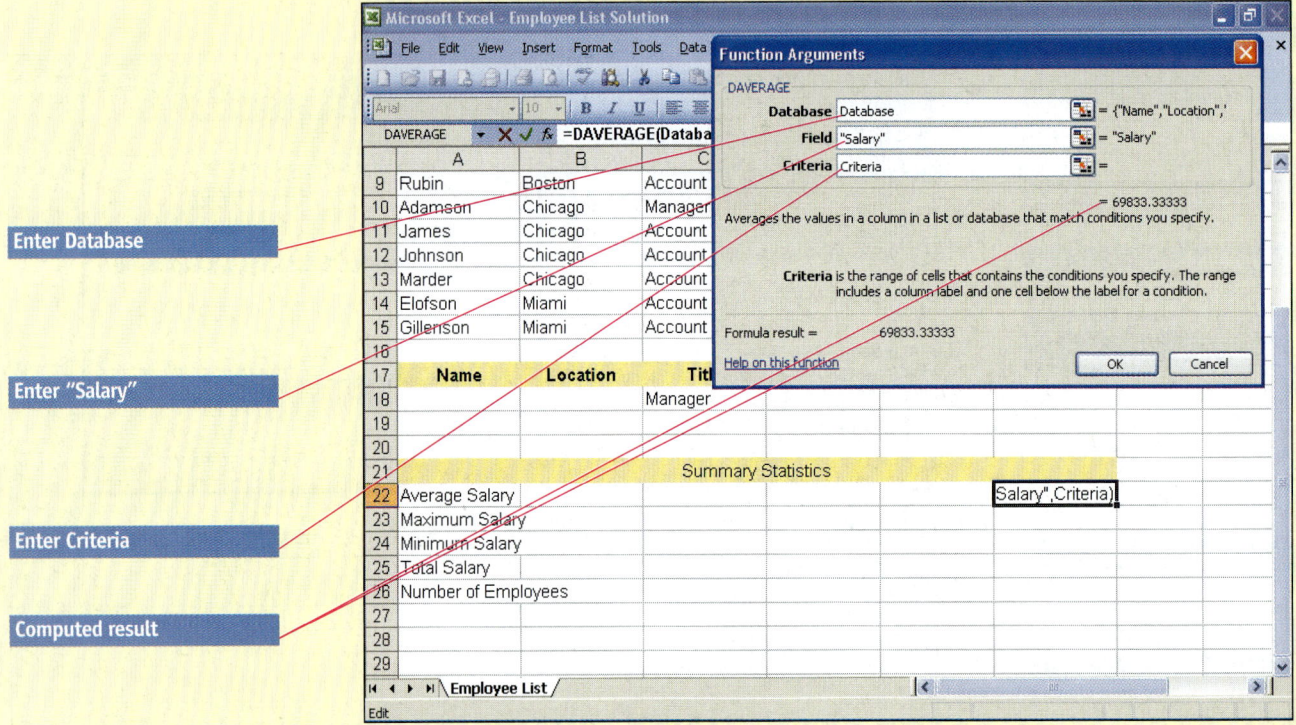

(g) The DAVERAGE Function (step 7)

FIGURE 7.12 Hands-on Exercise 2 (*continued*)

DIVISION BY ZERO—#DIV/0—AND HOW TO AVOID IT

The DAVERAGE function displays a division by zero error message if there are no records that meet the specified criteria. You can hide the error message, however, by using conditional formatting to display the message in white, which renders it invisible. Click in the cell containing the DAVERAGE function, pull down the Format menu, click Conditional formatting, and then click the drop-down arrow in the left list box to select Formula Is. Click in the box to the right and type = ISERROR(F22), where F22 is the cell containing the DAVERAGE function. Click the Format button, click Font, and change the color to white. The message is in the cell but you cannot see it.

Step 8: **The DMAX, DMIN, DSUM, and DCOUNT Functions**

- Enter the DMAX, DMIN, DSUM, and DCOUNT functions in cells F23 through F26, respectively. You can use the **Insert Function button** to enter each function individually, *or* you can copy the DAVERAGE function and edit appropriately:
  - Click in **cell F22**. Drag the **fill handle** to **cells F23 through F26** to copy the DAVERAGE function to these cells.
  - Double click in **cell F23** to edit the contents of this cell, then click within the displayed formula to substitute **DMAX** for DAVERAGE. Press **Enter**.
  - Double click in the remaining cells and edit them appropriately.

- The computed values (except for the DCOUNT function, which has a computed value of 3) are shown in Figure 7.12h.

- Format **cells F22 through F25**, to currency with no decimals.

- Click and drag the border between columns F and G to widen column F as necessary. Save the workbook.

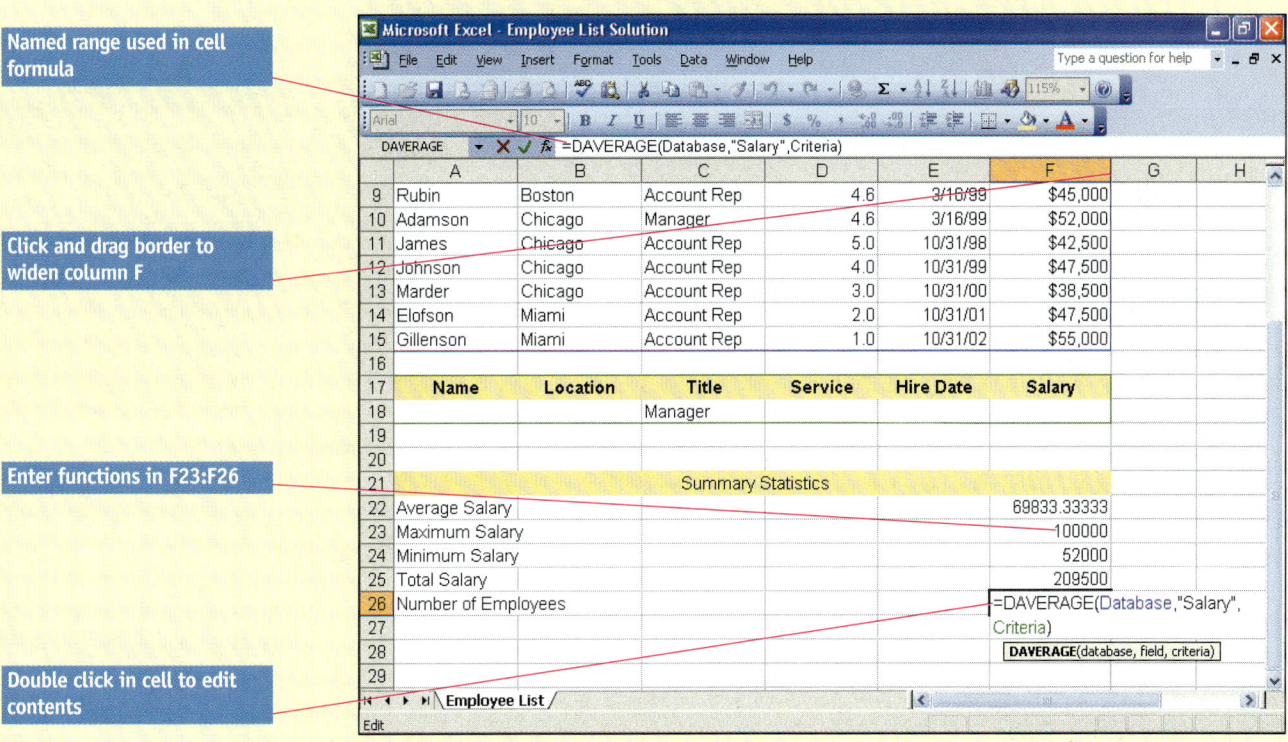

(h) The DMAX, DMIN, DSUM, DCOUNT Functions (step 8)

FIGURE 7.12 Hands-on Exercise 2 (*continued*)

IMPORT DATA FROM ACCESS

The data in a worksheet can be imported from an Access database. Pull down the Data menu, click the Import External Data command, then click Import Data to display the Select Data Source dialog box. Use the Look In list box to locate the folder containing the database and choose Access Databases as the file type. Select the database, then click the Open command to bring the Access table(s) into an Excel workbook. (See Excel and Access mini case at the end of the chapter.)

MICROSOFT OFFICE EXCEL 2003 **1329**

Step 9: **Change the Criteria**

- Click in the **Name box**. Type **B18** and press **Enter** to make cell B18 the active cell. Type **Chicago** to change the criteria to Chicago managers. Press **Enter**.
- The values displayed by the DAVERAGE, DMIN, DMAX, and DSUM functions change to $52,000, reflecting the one employee (Adamson) who meets the current criteria (a manager in Chicago). The value displayed by the DCOUNT function changes to 1 to indicate one employee as shown in Figure 7.12i.
- Click in **cell C18**. Press the **Del key**.
- The average salary changes to $45,125, reflecting all employees in Chicago.
- Click in **cell B18**. Press the **Del key**.
- The criteria range is now empty. The DAVERAGE function displays $49,857, which is the average salary of all employees in the database.
- Click in **cell C18**. Type **Manager** and press the **Enter key**. The average salary is $69,833, the average salary for all managers.
- Save the workbook.

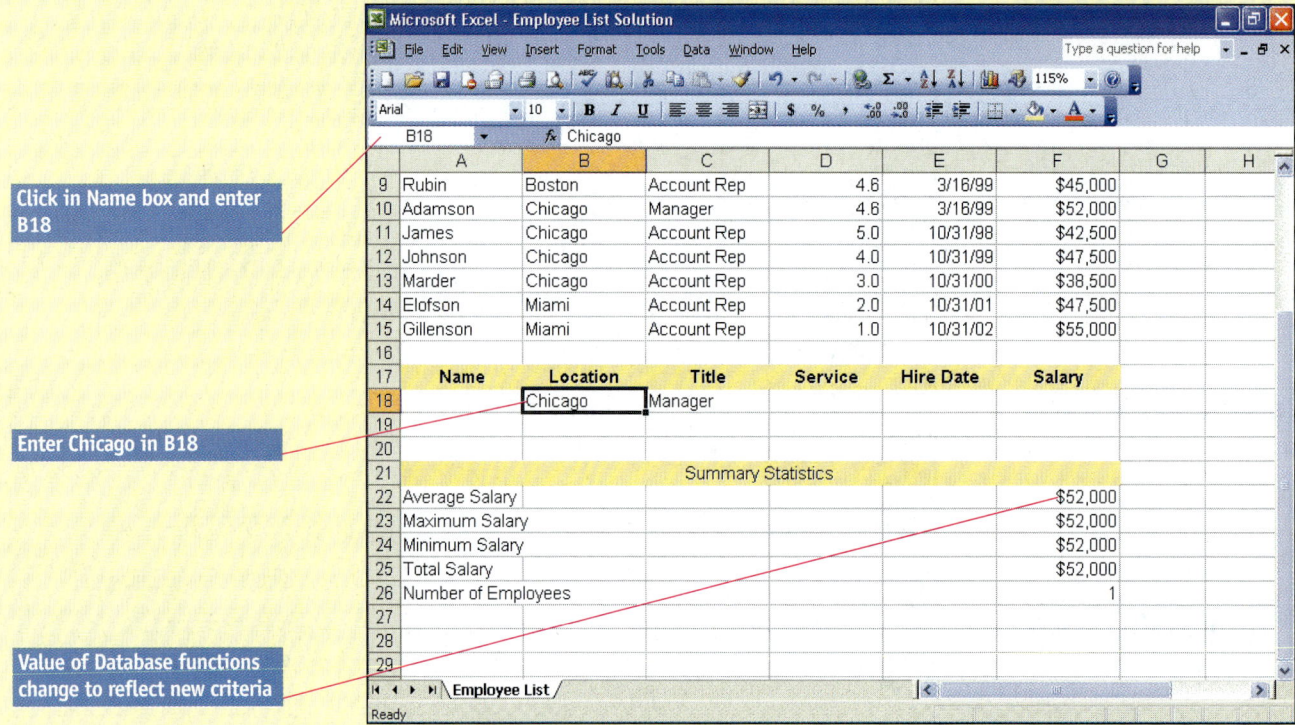

(i) Change the Criteria (step 9)

FIGURE 7.12 Hands-on Exercise 2 (*continued*)

FILTER THE LIST IN PLACE

Use the Advanced Filter command to filter the list in place and display the records that meet the current criteria. Click anywhere in the list, pull down the Data menu, click the Filter command, then choose Advanced Filter to display the Advanced Filter dialog box. Click the option button to filter the list in place, then click OK to display the selected records. You have to execute this command each time the criteria change.

Step 10: **Create the Subtotals**

- A list must be in sequence prior to computing the subtotals. Click any cell in the list in **Column C**, the column containing the employee titles, then click the **Sort Ascending button** on the Standard toolbar. The employees should be sequenced according to title as shown in Figure 7.12j.

- Click in any cell in column F, the column containing the field for which you want subtotals. Pull down the **Data menu** and click the **Subtotals command**. Click the **drop-down arrow** in the **At each change in** list box. Click **Title** to create a subtotal whenever there is a change in title. Set the other options to match the dialog box in Figure 7.12j. Click **OK** to create the subtotals.

- You should see the three subtotals, one for each title, followed by the grand total for the company. The total for the Account Reps should appear first, and it is equal to $430,500.

- The total for managers is $209,500 and matches the value obtained by the DSUM command.

- Save the workbook.

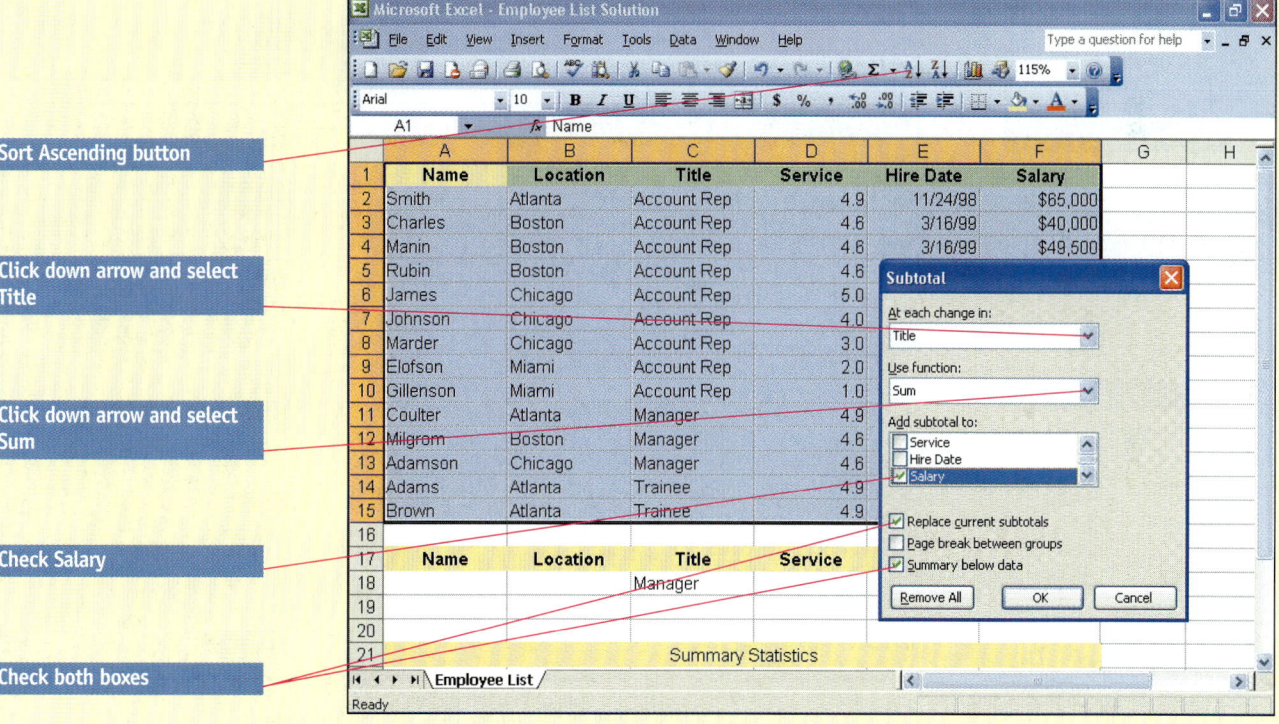

(j) Create the Subtotals (step 10)

FIGURE 7.12 Hands-on Exercise 2 (*continued*)

TWO SETS OF SUBTOTALS

You can obtain multiple sets of subtotals in the same list, provided you do the operations in the correct sequence. First, sort the list according to the sequence you want, for example, by title within location. Click in the list, and compute the subtotals based on the primary key (location in this example). Click on the list a second time and compute the subtotals based on the secondary key (title in this example), but clear the check box to replace the current subtotals. You will see the subtotal for each title in the first location, followed by the subtotal for that location, and so on.

Step 11: **Collapse and Expand the Subtotals**

- The vertical lines at the left of the worksheet indicate how the data is aggregated within the list. Click the **minus sign** corresponding to the total for the Account Reps.

- The minus sign changes to a plus sign, and the detail lines (the names of the Account Reps) disappear from the worksheet as shown in Figure 7.12k. Click the **plus sign** next to the Account Rep total, and you see the detailed information for each Account Rep.

- Click the **level 2 button** (under the Name box) to suppress the detail lines for all employees. The list collapses to display the subtotals and grand total.

- Click the **level 1 button** to suppress the subtotals. The list collapses further to display only the grand total. Click the **level 3 button** to restore the detail lines and subtotals.

- Click the **Print button** to print the list with the subtotals. Close the workbook. Exit Excel if you do not want to continue with the next exercise at this time.

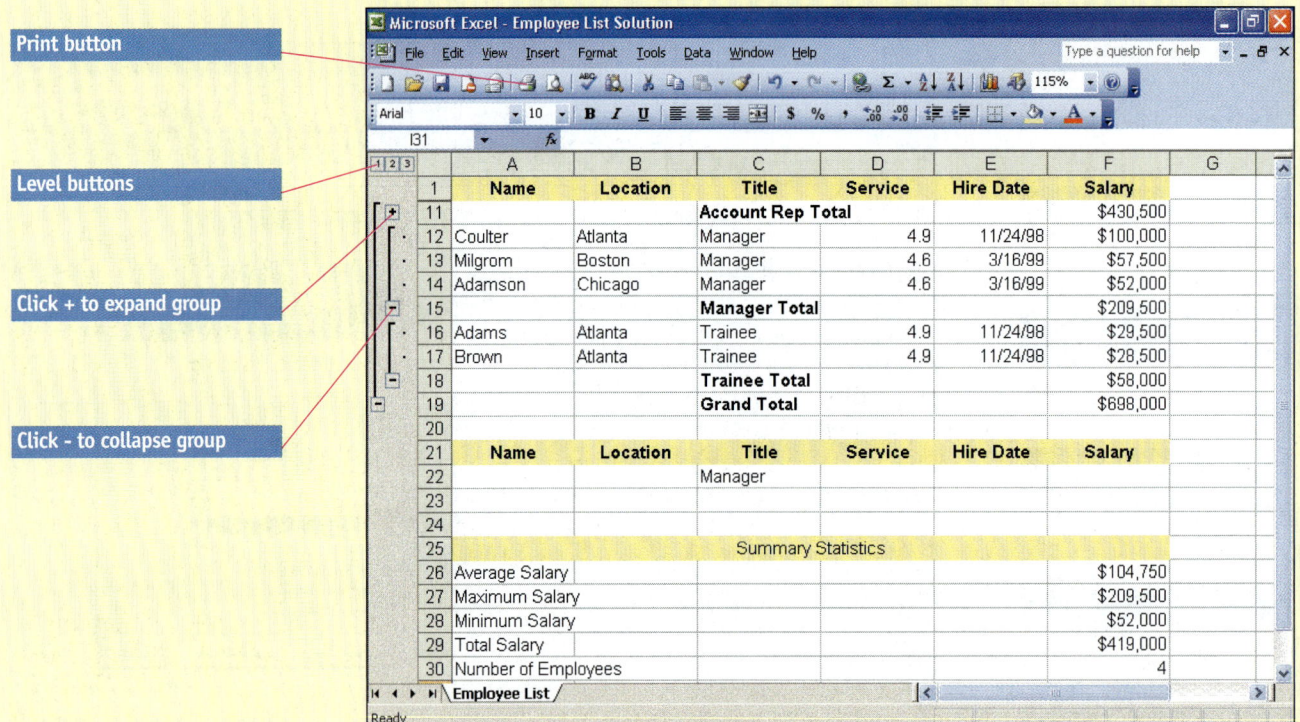

(k) Collapse and Expand the Subtotals (step 11)

FIGURE 7.12 Hands-on Exercise 2 (*continued*)

INCOMPATIBLE FUNCTIONS AND SUBTOTALS

The Subtotals command introduces additional rows within a list, which are then double counted in the computations of the database functions. In this example the total salary for all managers (as computed by the DSUM function in cell F29) is $419,000, when it should be $209,500. This is due to the insertion of row 15, which contains 'Manager Total' in cell C15, which falsely counts this row as a Manager. One way to 'correct' the problem is to move the text entries in cells C11, C15, C18, and C19 to the corresponding cells in column D.

PIVOT TABLES AND PIVOT CHARTS

A *pivot table* provides the ultimate flexibility in data analysis. It divides the records in a list into categories, then computes summary statistics for those categories. Pivot tables are illustrated in conjunction with the data in Figure 7.13 that displays sales information for a hypothetical advertising agency. Each record in the list in Figure 7.13a displays the name of the sales representative, the quarter in which the sale was recorded, the type of media, and the amount of the sale.

The pivot table in Figure 7.13b shows the total sales for each Media–Sales Rep combination. Look closely and you will see four shaded buttons, each of which corresponds to a different area in the table. The Media and Sales Rep buttons are in the row and column areas, respectively. Thus, each row in the pivot table displays the data for a different media type (magazine, radio, or TV), whereas each column displays data for a different sales representative. The Quarter button in the page area provides a third dimension. The value in the drop-down list box indicates that all of the records in the underlying worksheet are used to compute the totals in the body of the table. You can, however, display different pages corresponding to the totals in the first, second, third, or fourth quarters. You can also click the arrows next to the other buttons to suppress selected values for the media type or sales representative.

The best feature about a pivot table is its flexibility because you can change the orientation to provide a different analysis of the associated data. Figure 7.13c, for example, displays an alternate version of the pivot table in which the fields have been rearranged to show the total for each combination of quarter and sales representative. You go from one pivot table to another simply by clicking and dragging the buttons corresponding to the field names to different positions.

You can also change the means of computation within the data area. Both of the pivot tables in Figure 7.13 use the Sum function, but you can choose other functions such as Average, Minimum, Maximum, or Count. You can also change the formatting of any element in the table. More importantly, pivot tables are dynamic in that they reflect changes to the underlying worksheet. Thus, you can add, edit, or delete records in the associated list and see the results in the pivot table, provided you execute the *Refresh command* to update the pivot table.

The *Pivot Table Wizard* is used to create the initial pivot table in conjunction with an optional pivot chart. The *pivot chart* in Figure 7.14, for example, corresponds to the pivot table in Figure 7.13b, and at first glance, it resembles any other Excel chart. Look closely, however, and you will see shaded buttons similar to those in the pivot table, enabling you to change the chart by dragging the buttons to different areas. Reverse the position of the Media and Sales Rep buttons, for example, and you have a completely different chart. Any changes to the chart are reflected in the underlying pivot table and vice versa.

Drop-down arrows next to each button on the pivot chart let you display selected values. Click either arrow to display a drop-down list in which you select the values you want to appear in the chart. You could, for example, click the drop-down arrow next to the Sales Rep field and clear the name of any sales rep to remove his/her data from the chart.

Pivot tables may also be saved as Web pages with full interactivity as shown in Figure 7.15. The Address bar indicates that you are viewing a Web document (note the mht extension), as opposed to an Excel workbook. As with an ordinary pivot table, you can pivot the table within the Web page by repositioning the buttons for the row, column, and page fields. The plus and minus next to the various categories enable you to show or hide the detailed information. (The interactivity extends to Netscape as well as Internet Explorer, provided that you install the Office Web components.)

Pivot tables are one of the best-kept secrets in Excel, even though they have been available in the last several releases of Excel. (Pivot charts were introduced in Excel 2000.) Be sure to share this capability with your friends and colleagues.

	A	B	C	D
1	**Sales Rep**	**Quarter**	**Media**	**Amount**
2	Alice	1st quarter	TV	$15,000
3	Alice	1st quarter	Radio	$4,000
4	Alice	2nd quarter	Magazine	$2,000
5	Alice	2nd quarter	Radio	$4,000
6	Alice	3rd quarter	Radio	$2,000
7	Alice	4th quarter	Radio	$4,000
8	Alice	4th quarter	Radio	$1,000
9	Bob	1st quarter	Magazine	$2,000
10	Bob	1st quarter	Radio	$1,000
11	Bob	2nd quarter	Radio	$4,000
12	Bob	3rd quarter	TV	$10,000
13	Bob	4th quarter	Magazine	$10,000
14	Bob	4th quarter	Magazine	$12,000
15	Bob	4th quarter	Radio	$1,000
16	Bob	4th quarter	Magazine	$7,000
17	Carol	1st quarter	Radio	$4,000
18	Carol	2nd quarter	Magazine	$2,000
19	Carol	2nd quarter	Magazine	$7,000
20	Carol	2nd quarter	TV	$10,000
21	Carol	3rd quarter	TV	$8,000
22	Carol	3rd quarter	TV	$18,000
23	Carol	4th quarter	TV	$13,000
24	Ted	1st quarter	Radio	$2,000
25	Ted	2nd quarter	TV	$6,000
26	Ted	2nd quarter	TV	$6,000
27	Ted	3rd quarter	TV	$20,000
28	Ted	3rd quarter	Magazine	$15,000
29	Ted	3rd quarter	Magazine	$2,000
30	Ted	4th quarter	TV	$13,000
31	Ted	4th quarter	TV	$15,000

(a) Sales Data (Excel list)

	A	B	C	D	E	F
1						
2	Quarter	(All)				
3						
4	Sum of Amount	Sales Rep				
5	Media	Alice	Bob	Carol	Ted	Grand Total
6	Magazine	$2,000	$31,000	$9,000	$17,000	$59,000
7	Radio	$15,000	$6,000	$4,000	$2,000	$27,000
8	TV	$15,000	$10,000	$49,000	$60,000	$134,000
9	Grand Total	$32,000	$47,000	$62,000	$79,000	$220,000

- Quarter is in page area
- Computation is Sum of Amount
- Media is in row area
- Click down arrow to show data for all quarters or to select a specific quarter
- Sales Rep is in column area

(b) Analysis by Media Type and Sales Representative

	A	B	C	D	E	F
1						
2	Media	(All)				
3						
4	Sum of Amount	Quarter				
5	Sales Rep	1st quarter	2nd quarter	3rd quarter	4th quarter	Grand Total
6	Alice	$19,000	$6,000	$2,000	$5,000	$32,000
7	Bob	$3,000	$4,000	$10,000	$30,000	$47,000
8	Carol	$4,000	$19,000	$26,000	$13,000	$62,000
9	Ted	$2,000	$12,000	$37,000	$28,000	$79,000
10	Grand Total	$28,000	$41,000	$75,000	$76,000	$220,000

- Media is in page area
- Sales Rep is in row area
- Quarter is in column area

(c) Analysis by Sales Representative and Quarter

FIGURE 7.13 Pivot Tables

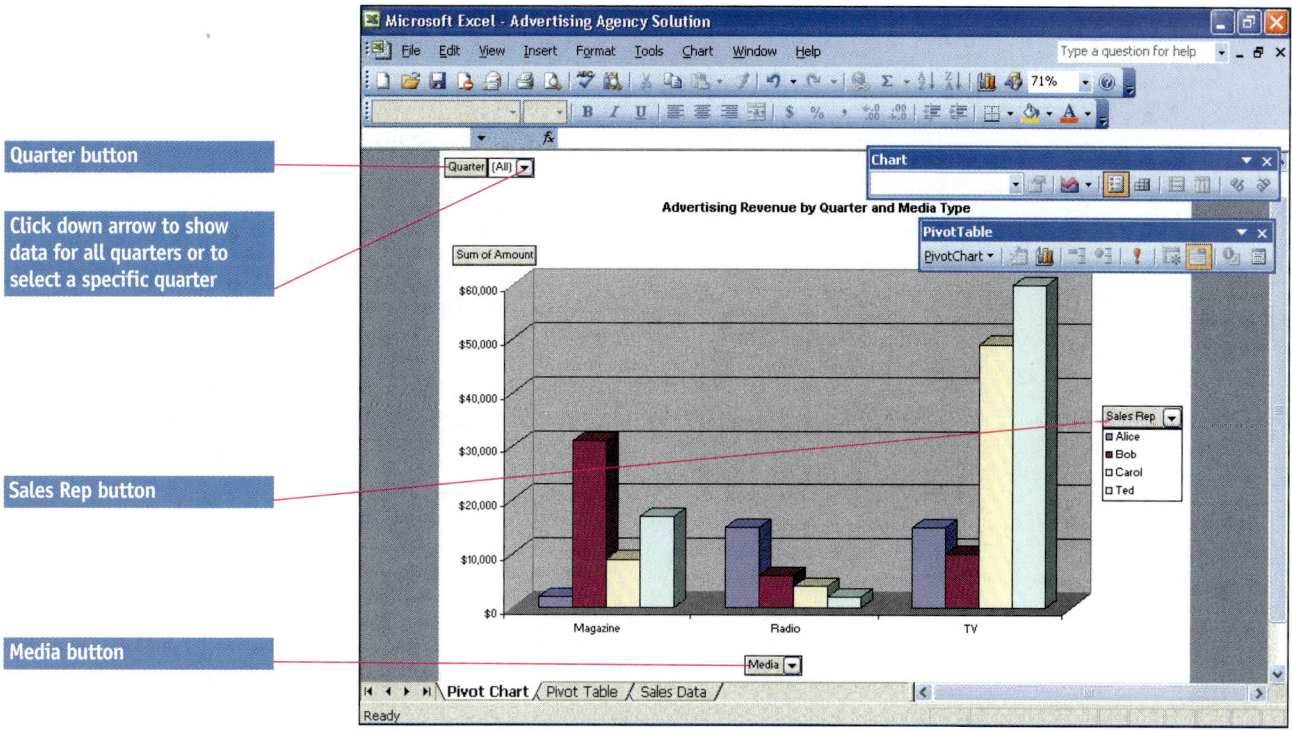

FIGURE 7.14 A Pivot Chart

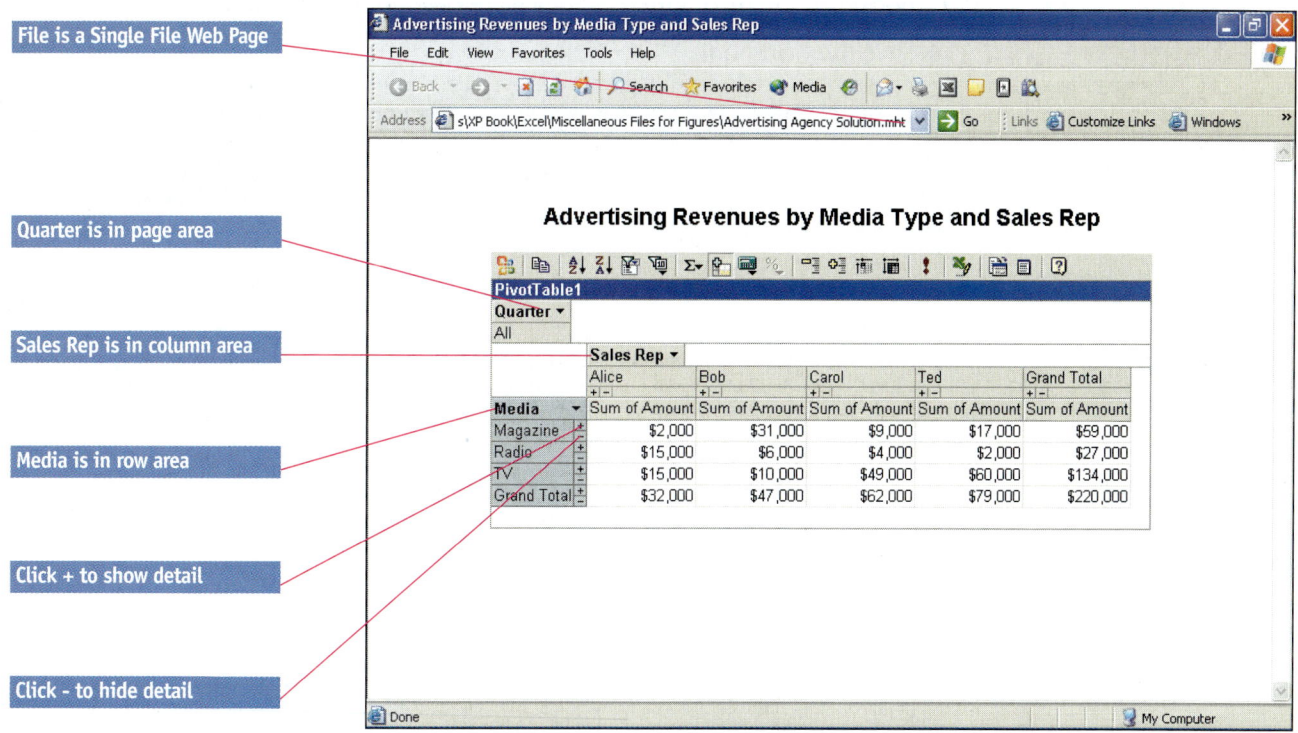

FIGURE 7.15 Pivot Tables on the Web

hands-on exercise

3 Pivot Tables and Pivot Charts

Objective To create a pivot table and pivot chart; to create a Web page based on the pivot table. Use Figure 7.16 as a guide in the exercise.

Step 1: **Start the Pivot Table Wizard**

- Start Excel. Open the **Advertising Agency workbook** in the **Exploring Excel folder**. Save the workbook as **Advertising Agency Solution** so that you will be able to return to the original workbook.

- The workbook contains a list of sales records for the advertising agency. Each record displays the name of the sales representative, the quarter in which the sale was recorded, the media type, and the amount of the sale.

- Click anywhere in the list of sales data. Pull down the **Data menu**. Click **PivotTable and PivotChart Report** to start the Pivot Table Wizard as shown in Figure 7.16a. Close the Office Assistant if necessary.

- Select the same options as in our figure. The pivot table will be created from data in a Microsoft Excel List or Database. In addition, you want to create a Pivot Chart report (that includes the Pivot Table). Click **Next**.

- Cells A1 through D31 have been selected automatically as the basis of the pivot table. Click **Next**.

- The option button to put the pivot table into a new worksheet is already selected. Click **Finish**. Two additional sheets have been added to the workbook, but the pivot table and chart area are not yet complete.

- Save the workbook.

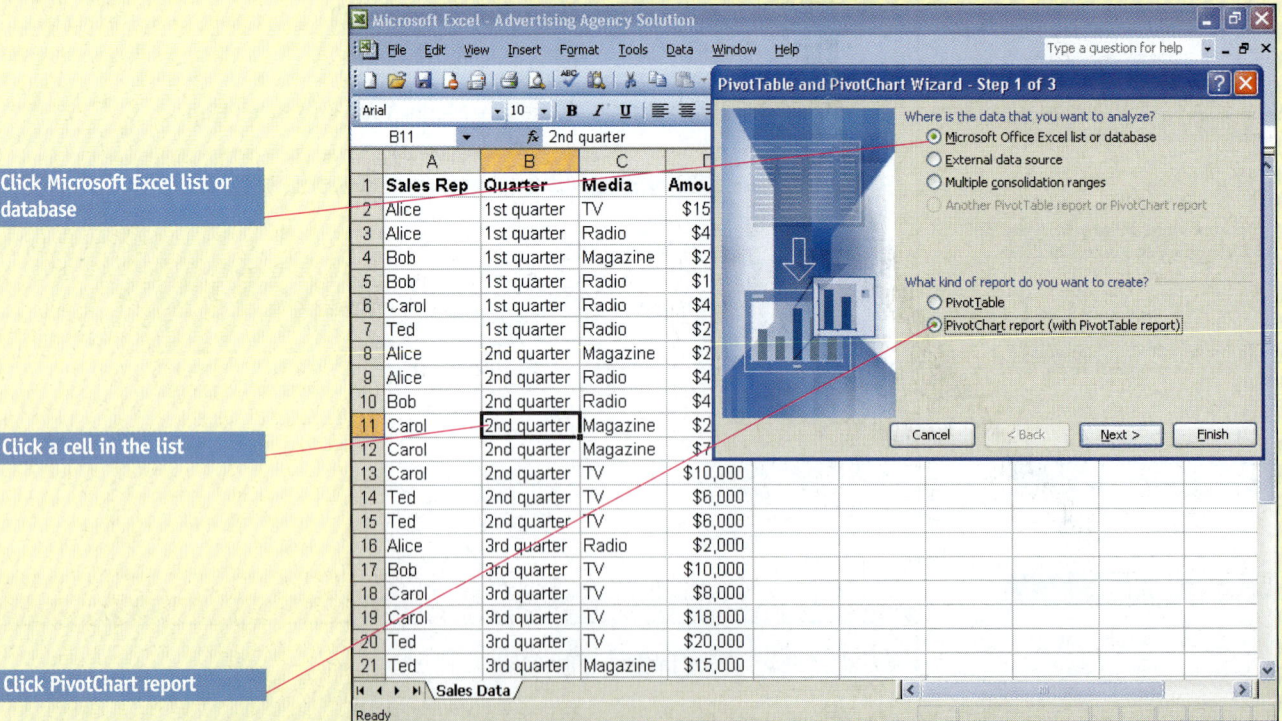

(a) Start the Pivot Table Wizard (step 1)

FIGURE 7.16 Hands-on Exercise 3

1336 CHAPTER 7: LIST AND DATA MANAGEMENT

Step 2: **Complete the Pivot Table**

- Click the tab that takes you to the new worksheet (Sheet1 in our workbook). Your screen should be similar to Figure 7.16b. Complete the pivot table as follows:
  - ❏ Click the **Media field button** and drag it to the row area.
  - ❏ Click the **Sales Rep button** and drag it to the column area.
  - ❏ Click the **Quarter field button** and drag it to the page area.
  - ❏ Click the **Amount field button** and drag it to the data area.

- You should see the total sales for each sales representative for each type of media within a pivot table.

- Rename the worksheets so that they are more descriptive of their contents. Double click the **Sheet1 tab** (the worksheet that contains the pivot table) to select the name of the sheet. Type **Pivot Table** as the new name, and press **enter**.

- Double click the tab for the **Chart1** worksheet and change its name to **Pivot Chart** in similar fashion.

- Save the workbook.

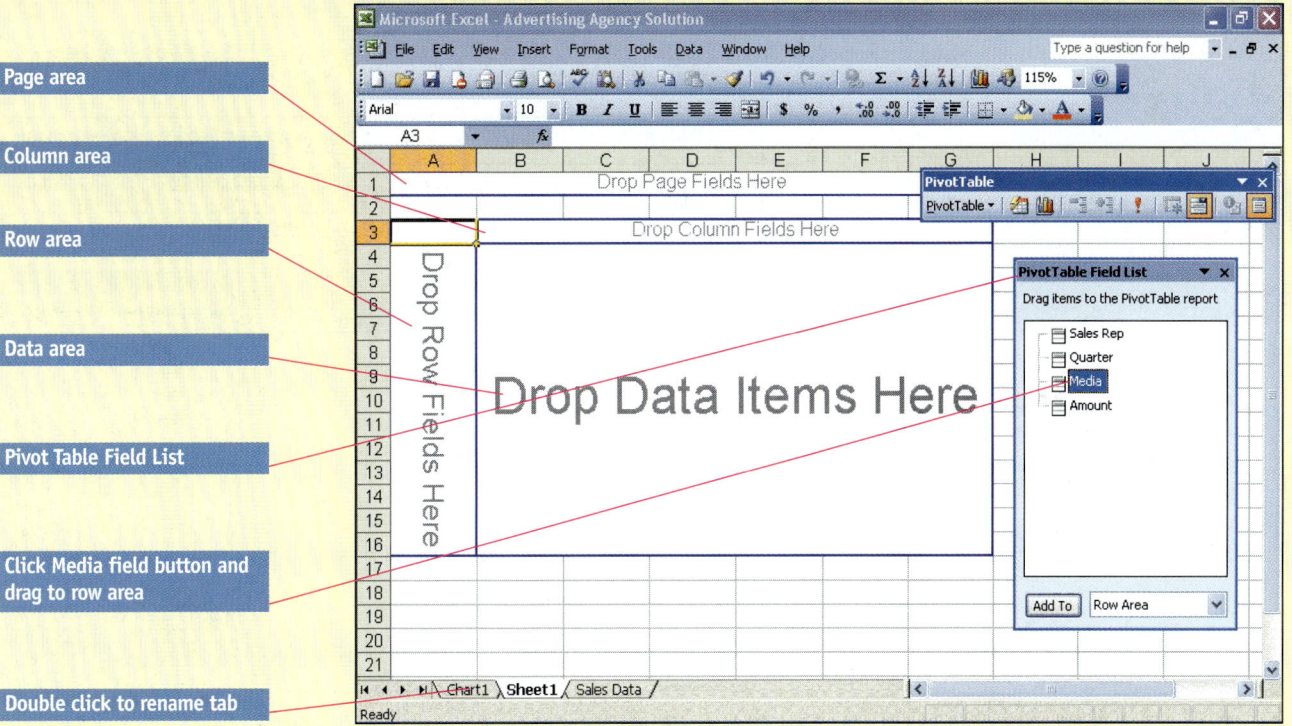

(b) Complete the Pivot Table (step 2)

FIGURE 7.16 Hands-on Exercise 3 (continued)

THE PAGE FIELD

A page field adds a third dimension to a pivot table. Unlike items in the row and column fields, however, the items in a page field are displayed one at a time. Creating a page field on Quarter, for example, lets you view the data for each quarter separately, by clicking the drop-down arrow on the page field list box, then clicking the appropriate quarter.

Step 3: **Modify the Sales Data**

- You will replace Bob's name within the list of transactions with your own name. Click the **Sales Data tab** to return to the underlying worksheet. Pull down the **Edit menu** and click the **Replace command** to display the Find and Replace dialog box.

- Enter **Bob** in the Find What dialog box, type **Your Name** (first and last) in the Replace With dialog box, then click the **Replace All button**. Click **OK** after the replacements have been made. Close the Find and Replace dialog box.

- Click the **Pivot Table tab** to return to the pivot table as shown in Figure 7.16c. The name change is not yet reflected in the pivot table because the table must be manually refreshed whenever the underlying data changes.

- Click anywhere in the pivot table, then click the **Refresh Data button** on the Pivot Table toolbar to update the pivot table. (You must click the Refresh button to update the pivot table whenever the underlying data changes.) You should see your name as one of the sales representatives.

- Save the workbook.

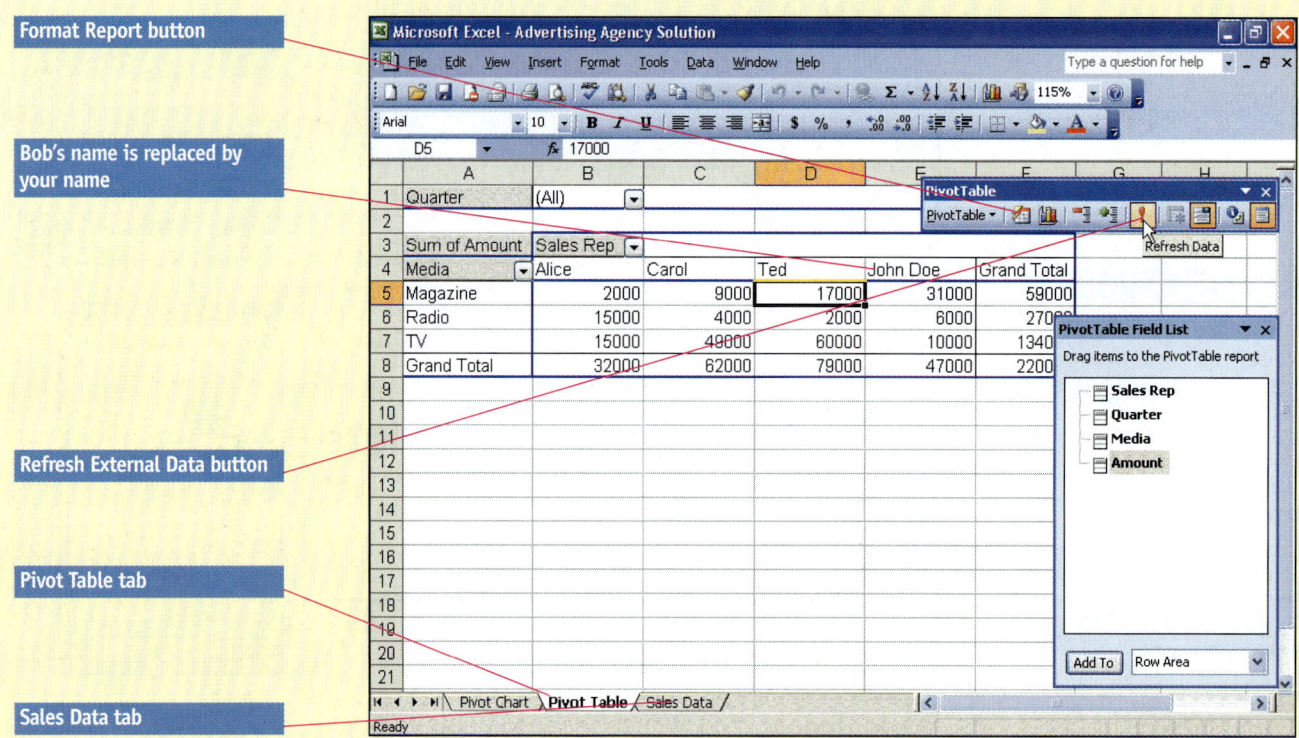

(c) Modify the Sales Data (step 3)

FIGURE 7.16 Hands-on Exercise 3 (continued)

THE FORMAT REPORT BUTTON

Why settle for a traditional report in black and white or shades of gray when you can choose from preformatted reports in a variety of styles and colors? Click the Format Report button on the Pivot Table toolbar to display the AutoFormat dialog box, where you select the style of your report. (To return to the default formatting, scroll to the end of the AutoFormat dialog box and select PivotTable Classic.) Use the Undo command if the result is not what you intended.

Step 4: **Pivot the Table**

- You can change the arrangement of a pivot table simply by dragging fields from one area to another. Click and drag the **Quarter field** to the row area. The page field is now empty, and you can see the breakdown of sales by quarter and media type.

- Click and drag the **Media field** to the column area, then drag the **Sales Rep field** to the page area. Your pivot table should match the one in Figure 7.16d.

- Click anywhere in the pivot table, then click the **Field Settings button** on the Pivot Table toolbar to display the PivotTable Field dialog box.

- Click the **Number button**, choose **Currency format** (with zero decimals). Click **OK** to close the Format Cells dialog box. Click **OK** a second time to close the Pivot Table Field dialog box.

- Save the workbook.

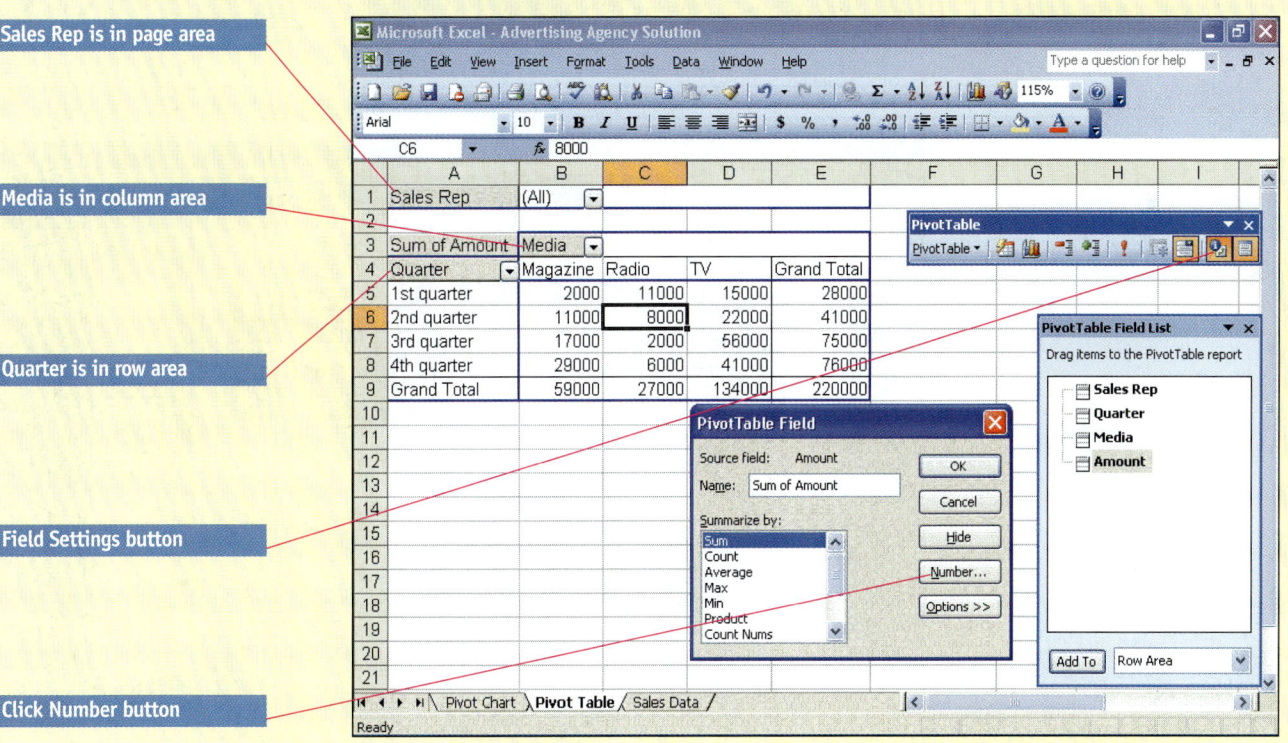

(d) Pivot the Table (step 4)

FIGURE 7.16 Hands-on Exercise 3 (*continued*)

CUSTOMIZE THE PIVOT TABLE

Right click anywhere within a pivot table to display a context-sensitive menu, then click the Table Options command to display the PivotTable Options dialog box. The default settings work well for most tables, but you can customize the table in a variety of ways. You can, for example, suppress the row or column totals or display a specific value in a blank cell. You can also change the formatting for any field within the table by right clicking the field and selecting the Format Cells button from the resulting menu.

MICROSOFT OFFICE EXCEL 2003

Step 5: **Change the Chart Type**

- Click the **Pivot Chart tab** to view the default pivot chart as shown in Figure 7.16e. If necessary, close the field list to give yourself more room in which to work.

- Pull down the **Chart menu** and click the **Chart Type command** to display the dialog box in Figure 7.16e.

- Select the **Clustered column with a 3-D visual effect**. (Take a minute to appreciate the different types of charts that are available.)

- Check the box for **Default formatting**. This is a very important option, because without it, the chart is rotated in an awkward fashion. Click **OK**.

- The chart changes to display a three-dimensional column for each of the media in each quarter.

- Save the workbook.

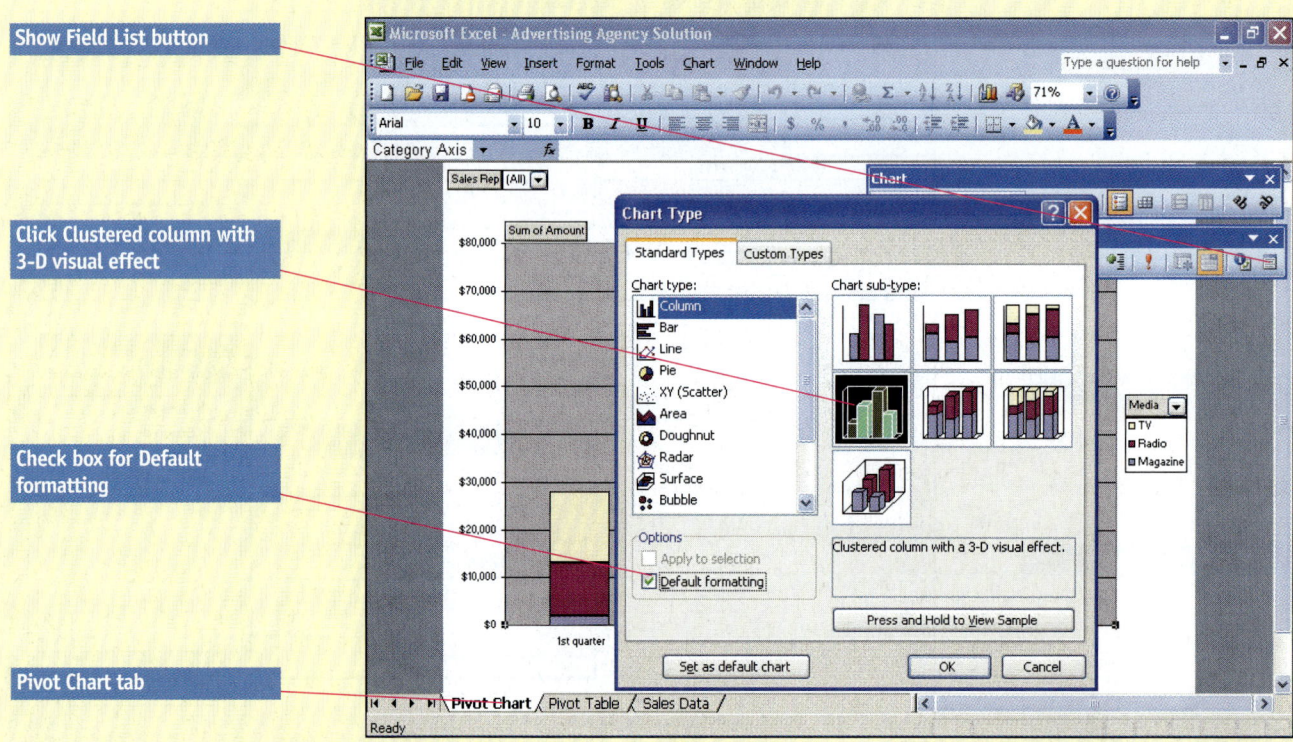

(e) Change the Chart Type (step 5)

FIGURE 7.16 Hands-on Exercise 3 (continued)

IT'S A PIVOT CHART

The shaded buttons for Sales Rep, Quarter, and Media that appear on the chart are similar in appearance and function to their counterparts in the underlying pivot table. Thus you can click and drag any of the buttons to a different position on the chart to change the underlying structure. You can also click and drag a field button from the PivotTable Field List to a new position on the chart. (Click the Show Field List button on the Pivot Table toolbar to show or hide the field list.) Any changes to the pivot chart affect the pivot table and vice versa.

Step 6: **Complete the Chart**

- Pull down the **Chart menu**, click **Chart Options** to display the Chart Options dialog box, then click the **Titles tab**. Enter **Advertising Revenue by Quarter and Media Type** as the chart title. Click **OK** to complete the chart as shown in Figure 7.16f.

- Click the **Sales Data tab** to select this worksheet. Press and hold the **Ctrl key** as you select the **Pivot Table tab** to select the worksheet containing the pivot table. Both worksheets are selected and hence both will be affected by the next command.

- Pull down the **File menu**, click the **Page Setup command**, and click the **Sheet tab**. Check the boxes to print **Gridlines** and **Row and Column headings**.

- Click the **Margins tab** and check the box to center the worksheet **horizontally**. Click **OK**.

- Pull down the **File menu** and click the **Print command** to display the Print dialog box. Click the option button to print the entire workbook. Click **OK**.

- Save the workbook.

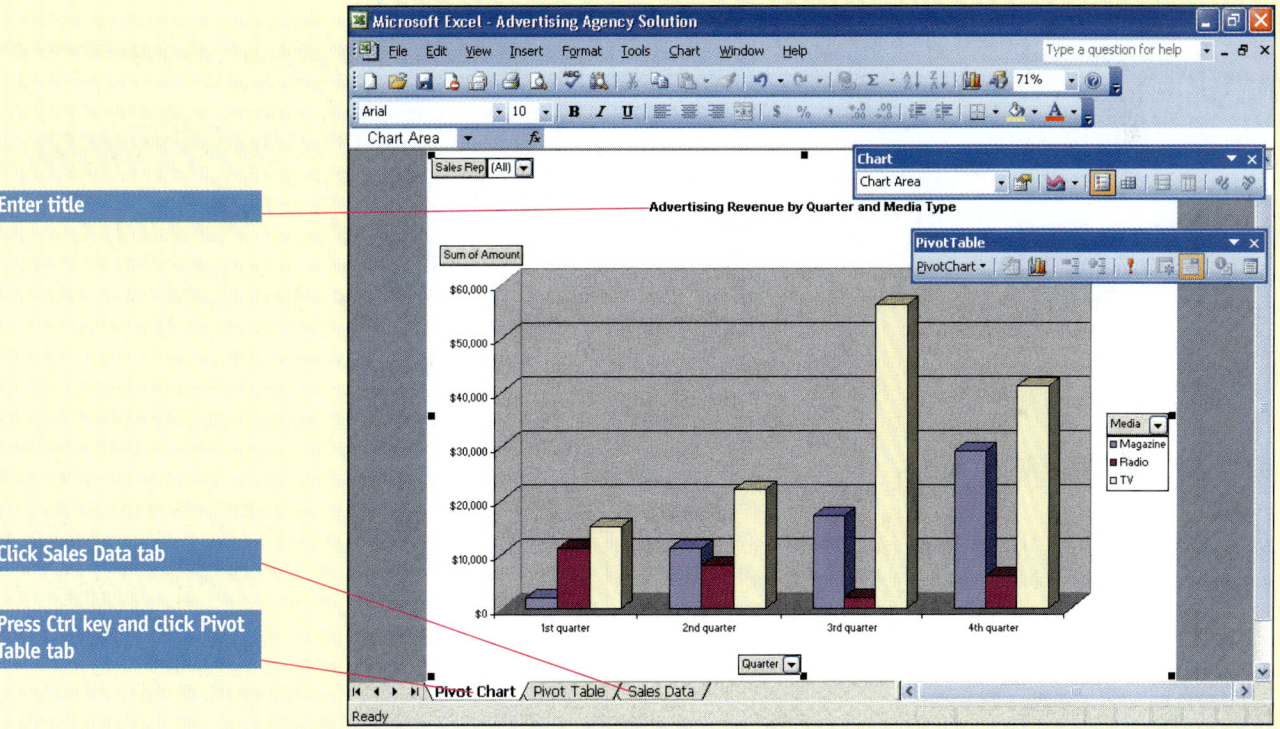

(f) Complete the Chart (step 6)

FIGURE 7.16   Hands-on Exercise 3 (*continued*)

FORMAT THE DATA SERIES

Why settle for a traditional bar chart when you can change the color, pattern, or shape of its components? Right click any column to select a data series to display a shortcut menu, then choose the Format Data Series command to display a dialog box in which you can customize the appearance of the vertical columns. We warn you that it is addictive, and that you can spend much more time than you intended initially. Set a time limit, and stop when you reach it.

Step 7: **Save the Pivot Table as a Web Page**

- Click the **Pivot Chart tab** to deselect the two tabs, then click the **Pivot Table tab**. Click and drag to select the entire pivot table. (If you have difficulty selecting the table, click and drag from the bottom-right cell to the top-left cell.)

- Pull down the **File menu**, click the **Save As Web Page command** to display the Save As dialog box, then click the **Publish button** (within the Save As dialog box) to display the Publish as Web Page dialog box in Figure 7.16g. Click **No** if the Office Assistant offers help.

- Change the name of the web page to **Advertising Agency Solution**. Save it in the **Exploring Excel folder**.

- Check the box to **Add interactivity** and select **Pivot Table functionality**. Check the boxes to **AutoRepublish every time this workbook is saved** and to **Open published web page in browser**.

- Click the **Change button** and enter an appropriate title that includes your name. Click **OK** to close the Set Title dialog box.

- Check that your settings match those in Figure 7.16g. Click the **Publish button** to publish the pivot table.

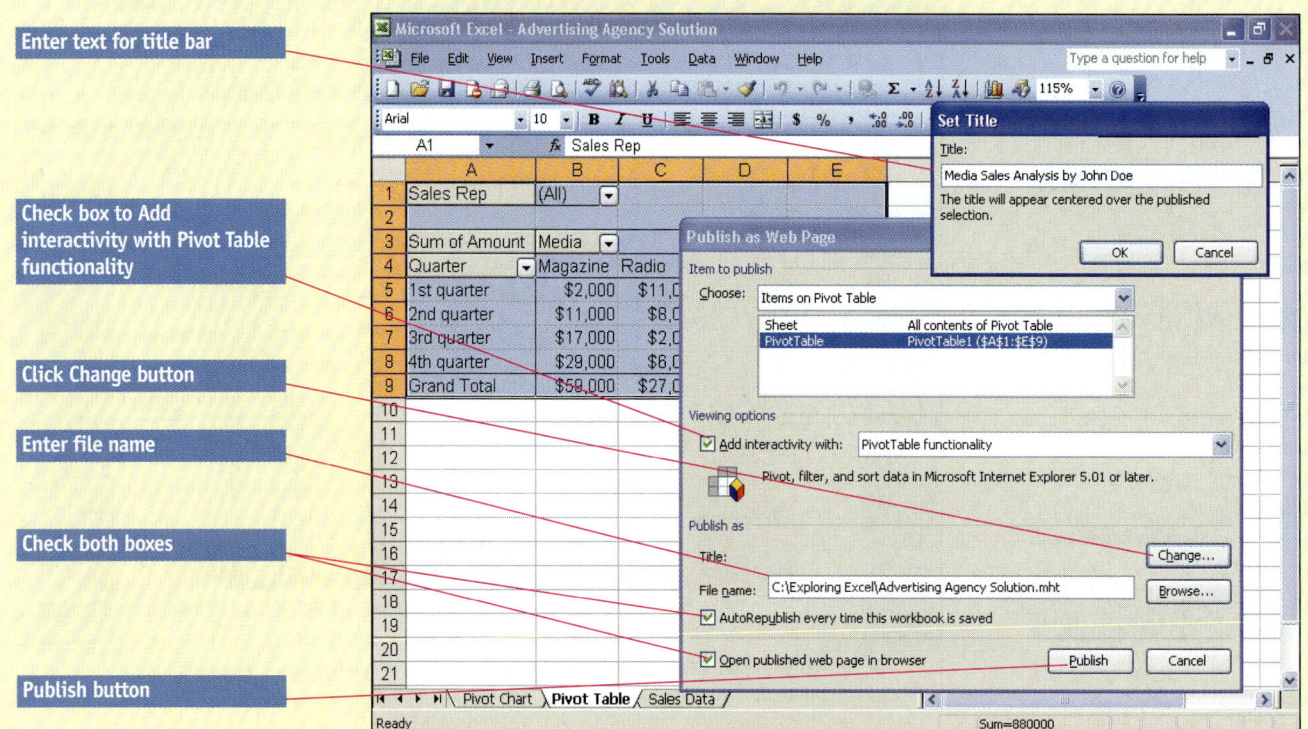

(g) Save the Pivot Table as a Web Page (step 7)

FIGURE 7.16 Hands-on Exercise 3 (*continued*)

SINGLE FILE WEB PAGE

Microsoft Office 2003 introduces the Single File Web Page (MHTML) format that saves all of the elements of a Web page, including text and graphics, in a single file. (A supporting folder to hold the extra elements was created previously.) The new format enables you to upload a single file to a Web server, as opposed to sending multiple files and folders. It also lets you send the entire page as a single e-mail attachment. The new file format is supported by Internet Explorer 4.0 and higher.

Step 8: **Pivot the Web Page**

- The pivot table will open automatically in your browser because of the option you selected in the previous step. If Internet Explorer is your default browser, you will see the pivot table in Figure 7.16h.

- If Netscape Navigator is your default browser, you will be prompted to install the Microsoft Web components, after which you should see the pivot table.

- Pivot the table so that its appearance matches Figure 7.16h. Thus, you need to drag the **Sales Rep button** to the column area and the **Media button** to the row area to the right of the Quarter field. (You can click the **Fields List button** on the Pivot Table toolbar to display/hide the fields in the table, should you lose a field button.)

- Click the **Plus sign** next to each quarter to display the detailed information. Click the **Print button** on the Internet Explorer toolbar to print the pivot table for your instructor.

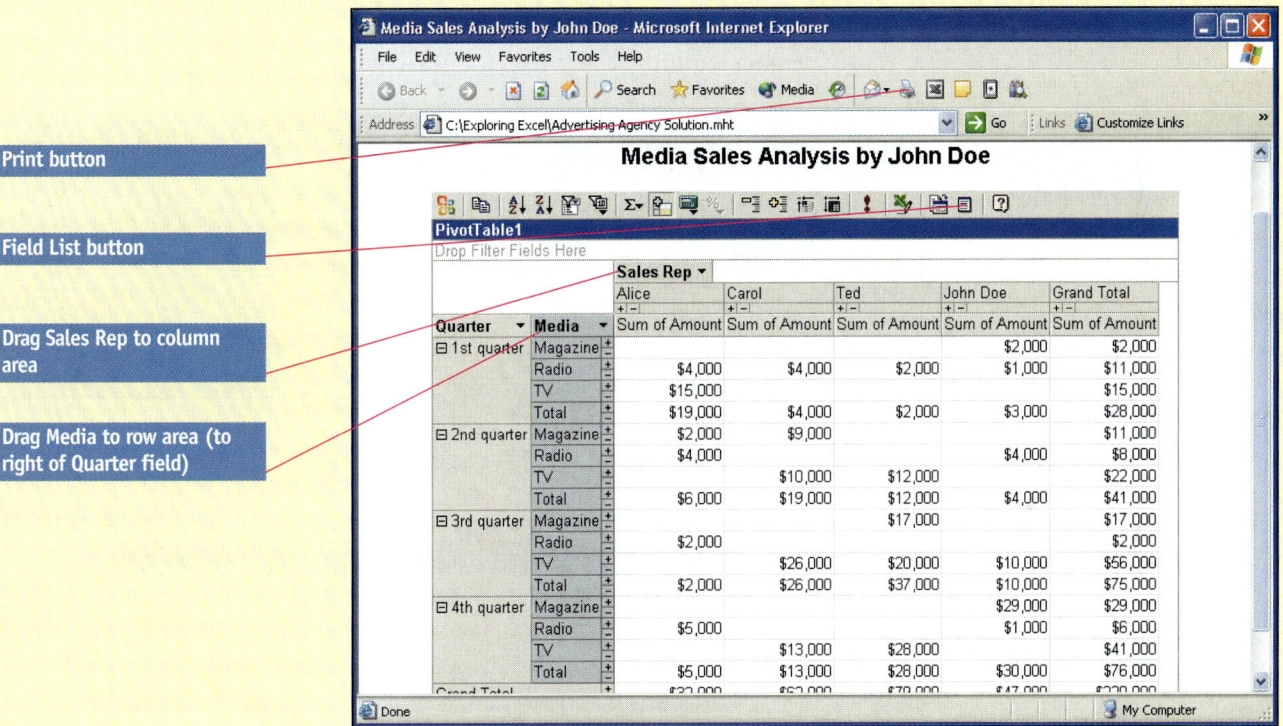

(h) Pivot the Web Page (step 8)

FIGURE 7.16 Hands-on Exercise 3 (*continued*)

XML IS NOT HTML

Extensible Markup Language, or XML for short, is an industry standard for structuring data. It is very different from HTML and it is not intended as a replacement. HTML describes how a document should look; e.g., <B>John Doe</B> indicates that John Doe should appear in boldface, but it does not tell us anything more. You don't know that "John" is the first name or that "Doe" is the last name. XML, on the other hand, is data about data, and it lets you define your own tags; e.g., <name><first>John</first><last>Doe</last></name>. The XML codes can be read by any XML-compliant application and processed accordingly. Formatting can also be implemented in XML through style sheets.

Step 9: **Change the Underlying Data**

- Click the **Excel button** on the Windows taskbar to return to Excel. Click the **Sales Data worksheet** and change the data for John Doe's (your name) magazine sales in the first quarter from $2000 to $22000.

- Click the **Worksheet tab** for the pivot table. Click anywhere in the pivot table and click the **Refresh External Data button** on the Pivot Table toolbar. The magazine sales in the 1st quarter increase to $22,000 and the grand total changes to $240,000.

- Click the **Save button** to save the changes to the worksheet. You will see the dialog box in Figure 7.16i. Click the option button to **Enable the Autopublish feature**. Click **OK**.

- Return to Internet Explorer. Click the **Refresh button** on the Pivot Table toolbar to update the Web page. The numbers within the Web pivot table change to reflect the change in magazine sales. If the numbers do not refresh, close Internet Explorer, reopen it, and then reopen the Web page from the Exploring Excel folder.

- Close Internet Explorer. Close Excel. Click **Yes** if prompted to save the changes.

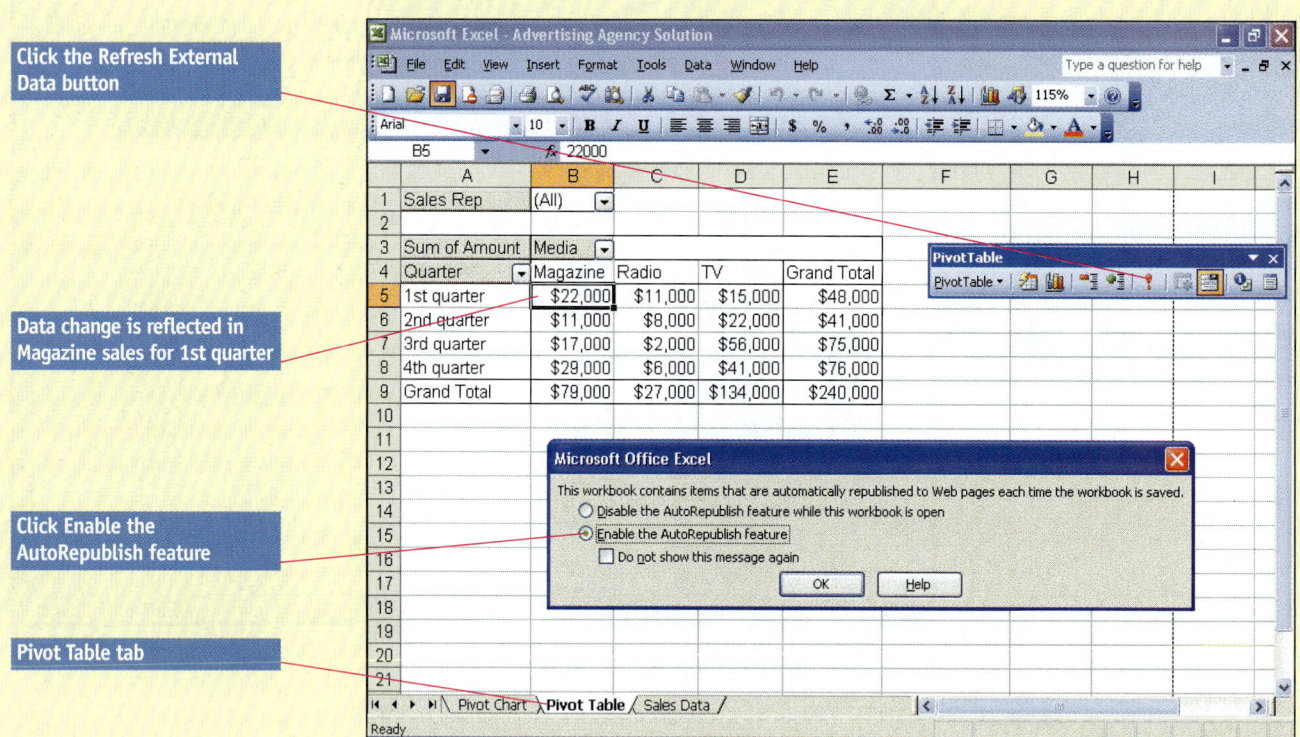

(i) Change the Underlying Data (step 9)

FIGURE 7.16 Hands-on Exercise 3 (*continued*)

THE NEED TO REFRESH

A pivot table and/or a Web page based on a pivot table do not automatically reflect changes in the underlying data. You must first refresh the pivot table as it exists within the workbook, by clicking in the pivot table, then clicking the refresh button on the Pivot Table toolbar. Next, you must save the workbook and enable the AutoPublish feature. And finally, the Single File Web page format requires you to close Internet Explorer, reopen it, and then reopen the Web page.

SUMMARY

A list is an area in a worksheet that contains rows of similar data. The first row in the list contains the column labels (field names). Each additional row contains data for a specific record. A data form provides an easy way to add, edit, and delete records in a list.

The Text Import Wizard converts data in either fixed width or delimited format to an Excel workbook. The Wizard is displayed automatically if you attempt to open a text file. Data can also be imported into an Excel workbook from other applications such as Microsoft Access.

XML (Extensible Markup Language) enables a developer to create customized tags to define data within a file. It is an industry standard for structuring data and not a Microsoft product. XML is not to be confused with HTML (Hypertext Markup Language), nor is it intended as a replacement for HTML. Microsoft Excel 2003 provides full XML support to exchange information between an XML source document and an Excel workbook. You attach the XML definition or schema to the workbook and then you map the XML elements in the schema to the cells in your workbook.

A date is stored internally as an integer number corresponding to the number of days since 1900. (January 1, 1900 is stored as the number 1.) The number of elapsed days between two dates can be determined by simple subtraction. The TODAY function always returns the current date (the date on which a worksheet is created or retrieved).

A filtered list displays only those records that meet specific criteria. Filtering is implemented through AutoFilter or the Advanced Filter command. The latter enables you to specify a criteria range and to copy the selected records elsewhere in the worksheet.

The Sort command arranges a list according to the value of one or more keys (known as the primary, secondary, and tertiary keys). Each key may be in ascending or descending sequence.

The database functions (DSUM, DAVERAGE, DMAX, DMIN, and DCOUNT) have three arguments: the associated list, the field name, and the criteria range. The simplest criteria range consists of two rows and as many fields as there are in the list.

The Subtotals command uses a summary function (such as SUM, AVERAGE, or COUNT) to compute subtotals for data groups within a list. The data is displayed in outline view, where outline symbols can be used to suppress or expand the detail records.

A pivot table extends the capability of individual database functions by presenting the data in summary form. It divides the records in a list into categories, then computes summary statistics for those categories. Pivot tables provide the utmost flexibility in that you can vary the row or column categories and/or the way that the statistics are computed. A pivot chart extends the capability of a pivot table to a chart.

KEY TERMS

Advanced Filter command 1317	DMAX function 1319	Insert Rows command 1301
Analysis ToolPak 1324	DMIN function 1319	ISERROR function 1328
Ascending sequence 1303	DSUM function 1319	Key 1300
AutoFilter command 1316	Extensible Markup	List 1300
Criteria range 1317	Language (XML) 1306	Outline symbols 1321
Data 1314	Field 1300	Pivot chart 1333
Data form 1302	Field name 1300	Pivot table 1333
Database 1300	File 1300	Pivot Table Wizard 1333
Database functions 1319	Filtered list 1316	Record 1300
Date arithmetic 1322	Fixed width format 1305	Refresh command 1333
DAVERAGE function 1319	Form command 1302	Schema 1306
DCOUNT function 1319	Hypertext Markup	Single File Web Page 1342
Delete command 1301	Language (HTML) 1306	Sort command 1303
Delimited format 1305	Information 1314	Subtotals command 1321
Descending sequence 1303	Insert Columns command 1301	Text Import Wizard 1305
Division by zero 1328	Insert Name command 1320	TODAY () function 1322

MULTIPLE CHOICE

1. Which of the following best describes data management in Excel?
   (a) The rows in a list correspond to records in a file
   (b) The columns in a list correspond to fields in a record
   (c) Both (a) and (b)
   (d) Neither (a) nor (b)

2. How should a list be placed within a worksheet?
   (a) There should be at least one blank row between the list and the other entries in the worksheet
   (b) There should be at least one blank column between the list and the other entries in the worksheet
   (c) Both (a) and (b)
   (d) Neither (a) nor (b)

3. Which of the following is suggested for the placement of database functions within a worksheet?
   (a) Above or below the list with at least one blank row separating the database functions from the list to which they refer
   (b) To the left or right of the list with at least one blank column separating the database functions from the list to which they refer
   (c) Both (a) and (b)
   (d) Neither (a) nor (b)

4. Cells A21:B22 have been defined as the criteria range, cells A21 and B21 contain the field names City and Title, respectively, and cells A22 and B22 contain New York and Manager. The selected records will consist of:
   (a) All employees in New York, regardless of title
   (b) All managers, regardless of the city
   (c) Only the managers in New York
   (d) All employees in New York (regardless of title) or all managers

5. Cells A21:B23 have been defined as the criteria range, cells A21 and B21 contain the field names City and Title, respectively, and cells A22 and B23 contain New York and Manager, respectively. The selected records will consist of:
   (a) All employees in New York regardless of title
   (b) All managers regardless of the city
   (c) Only the managers in New York
   (d) All employees in New York and all managers

6. If employees are to be listed so that all employees in the same city appear together in alphabetical order by the employee's last name:
   (a) City and last name are both considered to be the primary key
   (b) City and last name are both considered to be the secondary key
   (c) City is the primary key and last name is the secondary key
   (d) Last name is the primary key and city is the secondary key

7. Which of the following can be used to delete a record from a database?
   (a) The Edit Delete command
   (b) The Data Form command
   (c) Both (a) and (b)
   (d) Neither (a) nor (b)

8. Which of the following is true about the DAVERAGE function?
   (a) It has a single argument
   (b) It can be entered into a worksheet using the Function Wizard
   (c) Both (a) and (b)
   (d) Neither (a) nor (b)

9. Which of the following can be converted to an Excel workbook?
   (a) A text file in delimited format
   (b) A text file in fixed width format
   (c) Both (a) and (b)
   (d) Neither (a) nor (b)

10. Which of the following is recommended to distinguish the first row in a list (the field names) from the remaining entries (the data)?
    (a) Insert a blank row between the first row and the remaining rows
    (b) Insert a row of dashes between the first row and the remaining rows
    (c) Either (a) or (b)
    (d) Neither (a) nor (b)

... continued

multiple choice

11. The AutoFilter command:
    (a) Permanently deletes records from the associated list
    (b) Requires the specification of a criteria range elsewhere in the worksheet
    (c) Either (a) or (b)
    (d) Neither (a) nor (b)

12. Which of the following is true of the Sort command?
    (a) The primary key must be in ascending sequence
    (b) The secondary key must be in descending sequence
    (c) Both (a) and (b)
    (d) Neither (a) nor (b)

13. What is the best way to enter January 21, 2004 into a worksheet, given that you create the worksheet on that date, and further, that you always want to display that specific date?
    (a) =TODAY()
    (b) 1/21/2004
    (c) Both (a) and (b) are equally acceptable
    (d) Neither (a) nor (b)

14. Which of the following best describes the relationship between the Sort and Subtotals commands?
    (a) The Sort command should be executed before the Subtotals command
    (b) The Subtotals command should be executed before the Sort command
    (c) The commands can be executed in either sequence
    (d) There is no relationship because the commands have nothing to do with one another

15. Which of the following may be implemented in an existing pivot table?
    (a) A row field may be added or deleted
    (b) A column field may be added or deleted
    (c) Both (a) and (b)
    (d) Neither (a) nor (b)

16. How many rows (including the header row) are necessary in a criteria range that selects employees in the New York Office who earn more than $100,000 annually?
    (a) 1
    (b) 2
    (c) 3
    (d) 4

17. You have applied the Advanced Filter command to filter a customer list in place, expecting to see a subset of the entire customer list. All of the customers were displayed, however. What is the most likely reason?
    (a) There is a blank row in the criteria range
    (b) There is a blank row in the list (database)
    (c) Both (a) and (b)
    (d) Neither (a) nor (b)

18. You want to use the Subtotals command to show total salaries for each location with the locations appearing in alphabetical order. What should you do before executing the Subtotals command?
    (a) Sort the list by salary in ascending order
    (b) Sort the list by salary in descending order
    (c) Sort the list by location in ascending order
    (d) Sort the list by location in descending order

ANSWERS

1. c	7. c	13. b
2. c	8. b	14. a
3. a	9. c	15. c
4. c	10. d	16. b
5. d	11. d	17. a
6. c	12. d	18. c

PRACTICE WITH EXCEL

1. **Election 2000:** Election 2000 has been decided, but it will always be remembered for its closeness and controversy. Your assignment is to open a partially completed version of the workbook in *Chapter 7 Practice 1*, then complete the workbook so that it matches Figure 7.17. Proceed as follows:

   a. Enter the appropriate IF function in cell C8 to determine the winner of the state's electoral votes. Use conditional formatting to display the indicated colors for Bush and Gore. Develop the formula in such a way that it can be copied to the remaining rows in this column.

   b. Enter the appropriate formulas in cells F8 and G8 to compute the difference in the number of votes and the associated percentages. (Use the absolute value function for the formula in cell F8 so that the difference in the number of votes is always shown as a positive number.) Copy the formulas to the remaining rows in the worksheet.

   c. Use an ordinary SUM function to determine the popular vote for each candidate as shown in cells B4 and C4. Use the DSUM function to determine the number of electoral votes for each candidate. (You will need to establish separate criteria ranges for each candidate.)

   d. Add your name somewhere in the worksheet, then print the completed worksheet to show both displayed values and cell formulas. Be sure the worksheet fits on a single page.

   e. Print the worksheet in at least one other sequence—for example, in order by the vote differential.

   f. What do you remember about the 2000 election? Was the election settled immediately? Do you understand how the Electoral College works? Explain how a candidate can lose the popular vote, yet still win an election. Has this happened prior to the 2000 election?

   g. Add a cover sheet, then submit the completed assignment to your instructor. Be sure to vote in the next election. Your vote makes a difference!

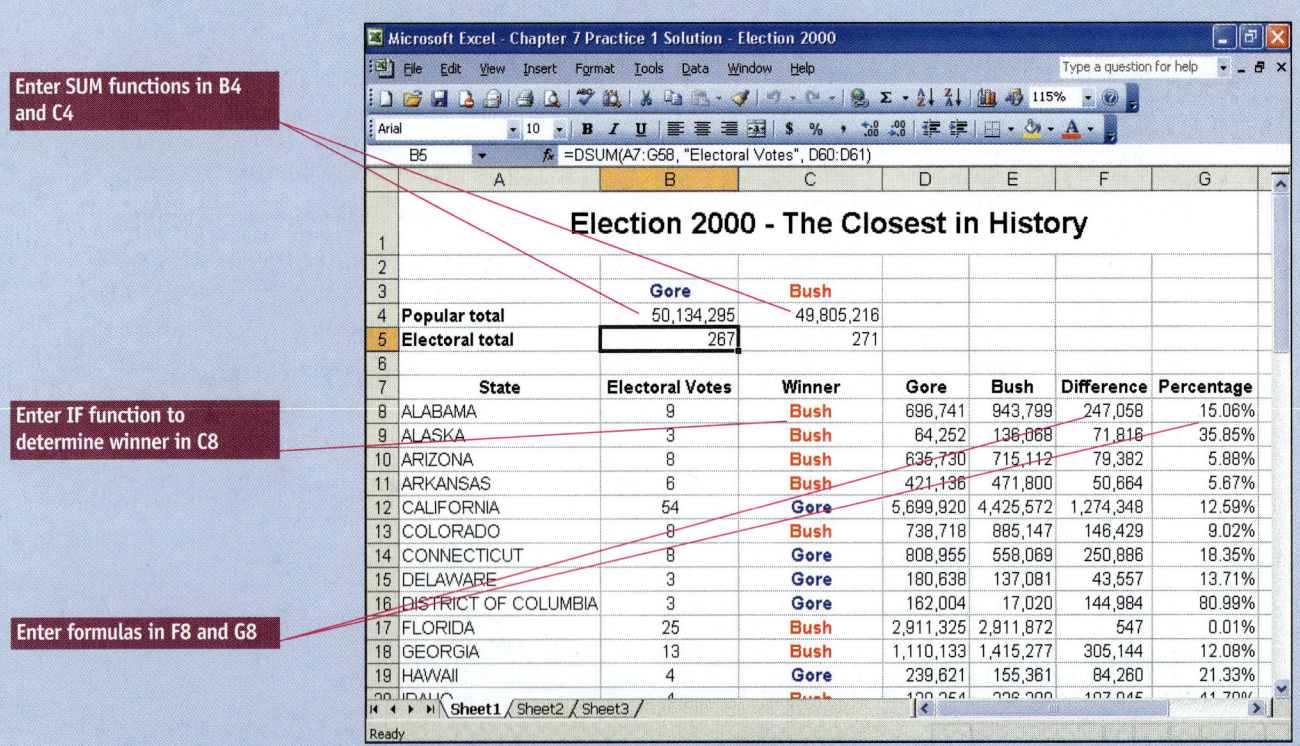

FIGURE 7.17 Election 2000 (exercise 1)

practice exercises

2. **The Dean's List:** The *Chapter 7 Practice 2* workbook contains a partially completed version of the workbook in Figure 7.18. Your assignment is to open the workbook, then implement the following changes:

   a. Add a transfer student, Jeff Borow, majoring in Engineering. Jeff has completed 14 credits and has 45 quality points. (Jeff's record can be seen in Figure 7.18, but it is not in the workbook that you will retrieve from the Exploring Excel folder.) Do not, however, enter Jeff's GPA or year in school, as both will be computed from formulas in the next two steps.

   b. Enter the appropriate formula in F4 to compute the GPA for the first student (the quality points divided by the number of credits). Copy the formula to the other cells in this column.

   c. Enter the appropriate formula in cell G4 to determine the year in school for the first student. (Use the HLOOKUP function based on the table in cells B24 through E25. The entries in cells A24 and A25 contain labels and are not part of the table per se.) Copy the formula to the other cells in this column.

   d. Format the worksheet attractively. You can use our formatting or develop your own. Sort the list so that the students are listed alphabetically.

   e. Use the Advanced Filter command to filter the list in place so that the only visible students are those on the Dean's List (with a GPA greater than 3.2) as shown in Figure 7.18.

   f. Add your name as the academic advisor in cell A28. Print the worksheet two ways, with displayed values and cell formulas. Use the Page Setup command to specify landscape printing and display gridlines and row and column headings. Be sure that each printout fits on a single sheet of paper.

   g. Remove the filter condition, then print the worksheet in a different sequence—for example, by ascending or descending GPA.

   h. Add a cover sheet, then submit the complete assignment to your instructor.

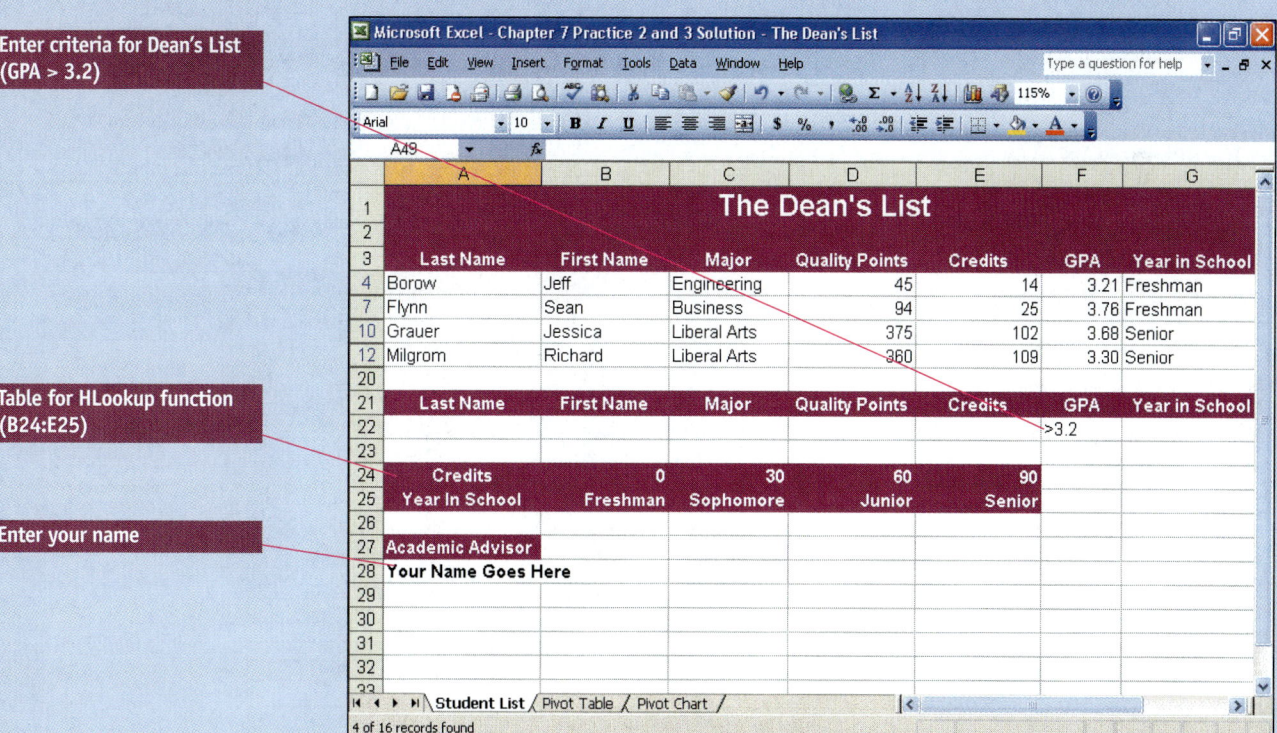

FIGURE 7.18 The Dean's List (exercise 2)

practice exercises

3. **The Pivot Chart:** Complete the previous exercise, then add a pivot table and pivot chart as shown in Figure 7.19. Start the Pivot Table Wizard. In step 1, select the option to create a PivotChart report (with PivotTable report). Specify the range of the pivot table in step 2, then in step 3 select the option to put the pivot table on a new worksheet. Rename the resulting worksheets, Sheet1 and Chart1, to Pivot Table and Pivot Chart as shown in Figure 7.19.

   a. Modify the pivot table so that major and year in school are the row and column fields, respectively. Use GPA as the data field, but be sure to specify the average GPA rather than the sum. Format the GPA to two decimal places.
   b. Change the format of the pivot chart to a 3-D clustered column chart with default formatting. Right click any column within the chart, select the Format Data Series command, then select the Series Order tab. Change the order of the columns to Freshman, Sophomore, Junior, and Senior, as opposed to the default alphabetical order.
   c. Pull down the Chart menu, click the Chart Options command to display the associated dialog box, then select the Data Table tab. Check the box to display the data table. Save the workbook.
   d. Use the Page Setup command to create a custom footer containing your name, the name of the worksheet, and today's date. Check the boxes to include gridlines and row and column headings.
   e. Print the pivot chart as shown in Figure 7.19. You do not need to print the pivot table since the equivalent information is shown in the data table that appears below the pivot chart.
   f. Pivot tables are one of the best-kept secrets in Excel, even though they have been available in the last several releases of Excel. (Pivot charts, however, were first introduced in Excel 2000.) Write a short note to a fellow student that describes how this feature facilitates data analysis.
   g. Add a cover sheet, then submit the complete assignment to your instructor.

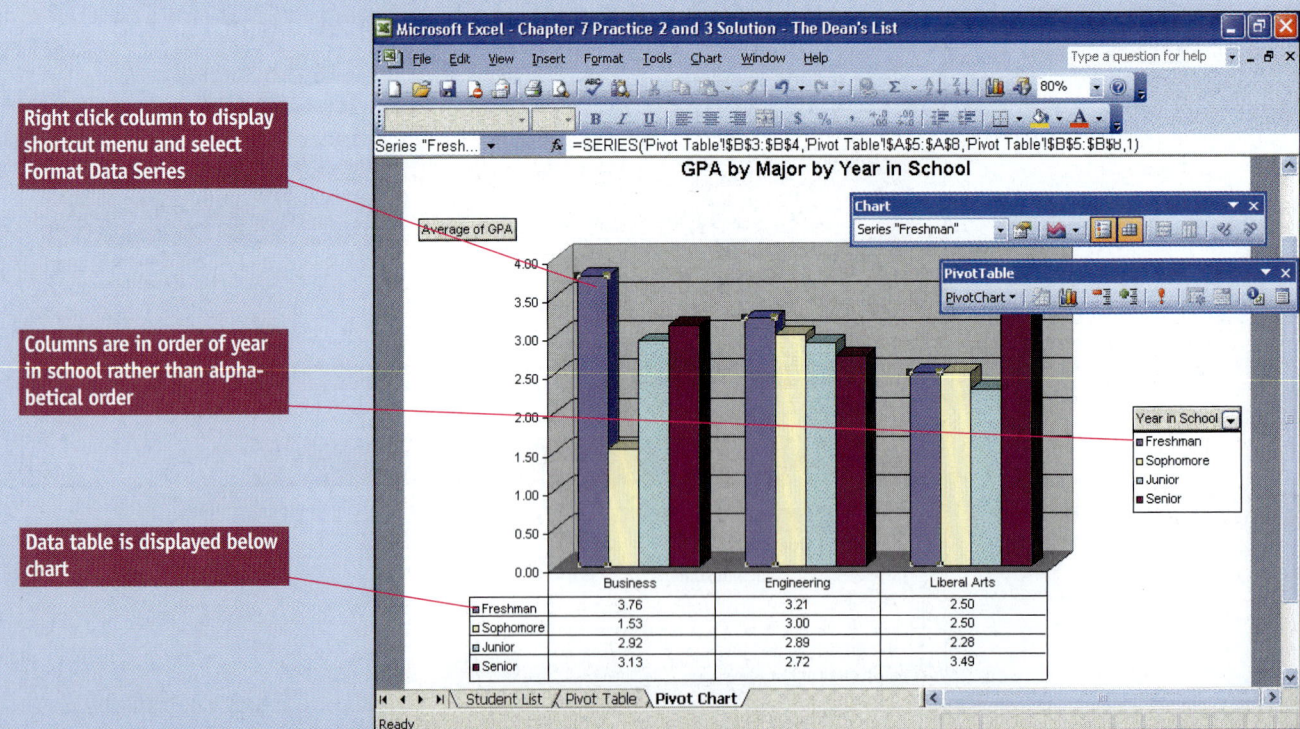

FIGURE 7.19 The Pivot Chart (exercise 3)

practice exercises

4. **Compensation Analysis:** The workbook in Figure 7.20 is used to analyze employee compensation with respect to the dollar amount and percentage of their latest salary increase. Your assignment is to open the partially completed workbook in *Chapter 7 Practice 4* and complete the workbook to match our figure.

   a. Open the workbook, then enter the formula to compute the dollar increase for the first employee in cell G4. Note, however, that not every employee has a previous salary, and thus the formula requires an IF function. Copy this formula to the remaining rows in column G.
   b. Enter the formula to compute the percentage increase for the first employee in cell H4. The percentage increase is found by dividing the amount of the increase by the previous salary. Again, not every employee has a previous salary, and hence the formula requires an IF function to avoid dividing by zero when there is no previous salary. Copy this formula to the remaining rows in column H.
   c. Enter the indicated database functions in rows 21 and 22 to reflect only those employees who have received a raise. Thus, be sure to include the greater than zero entry under Previous Salary in the criteria row.
   d. Format the worksheet in attractive fashion. You can copy our formatting or use your own design. Note, too, that you should suppress the display of zero values. (If necessary, pull down the Tools menu, click the Options command, then click the View tab and clear the box to display zero values.)
   e. Add your name as a financial analyst, then print the worksheet with both displayed values and cell formulas. Use landscape printing as necessary to be sure that the worksheet fits on a single sheet of paper.
   f. Print the worksheet in at least one other sequence—for example, by the smallest (or largest) percentage increase.
   g. Add a cover sheet, then submit the complete assignment to your instructor.

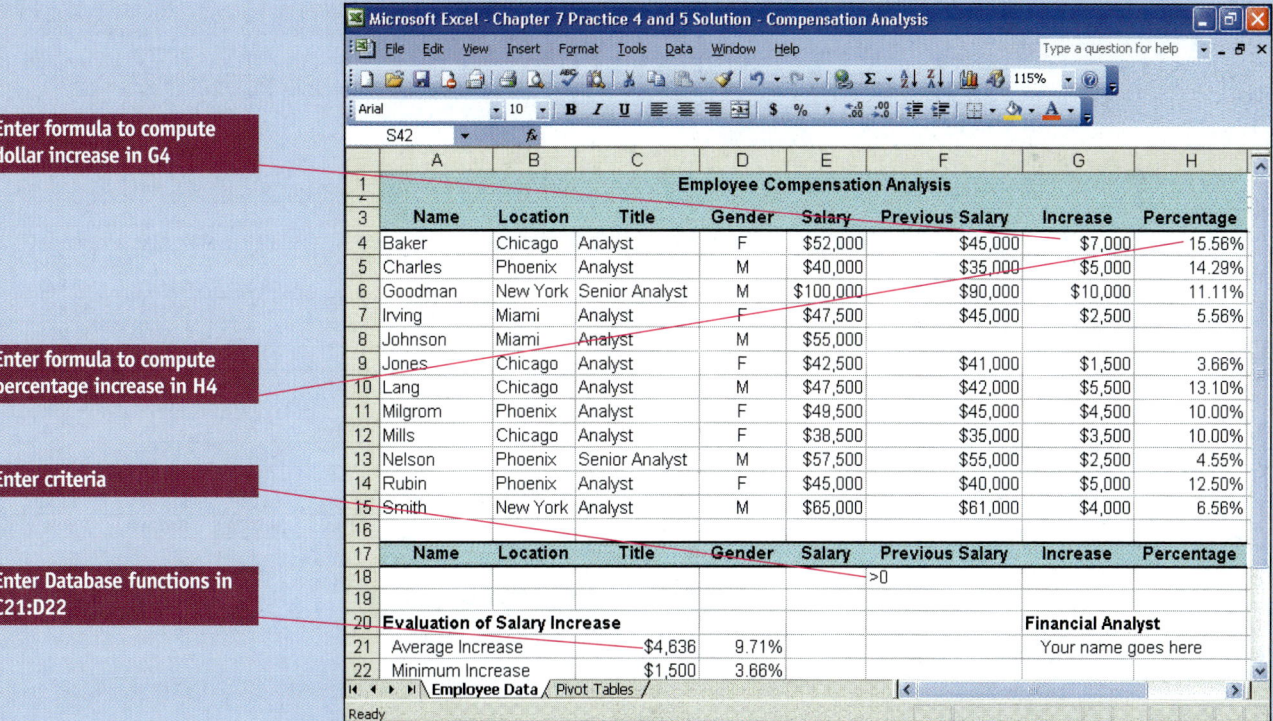

FIGURE 7.20 Compensation Analysis (exercise 4)

practice exercises

5. **Pivot Tables:** The pivot table in Figure 7.21 is based on the compensation analysis in the worksheet from the previous exercise. Open the completed *Chapter 7 Practice 4* workbook (or complete the exercise at this time), then create the associated pivot table. Proceed as follows:

   a. Click anywhere within the Employee table, pull down the Data menu, and create the pivot chart in Figure 7.21. You will need to specify two data fields (the salary increase and the percent of salary increase), and choose the average function for each.

   b. Format the pivot table in an attractive fashion. You do not have to duplicate our formatting exactly, but you are to use the currency and percent symbols as appropriate, as well as a reasonable number of decimal places.

   c. Use the same style of formatting for the text (e.g., 10 point Arial) in your pivot table as in the previous exercise, so that your workbook has a uniform look. Use the Options command as described in the previous exercise to suppress the display of zero values.

   d. Use the Page Setup command to create a custom footer containing your name, the name of the worksheet, and today's date. Check the boxes to print the gridlines and row and column headings.

   e. Print the completed workbook for your instructor to show the displayed values for each worksheet. Print the Employee Data worksheet a second time to show the cell formulas.

   f. Save the worksheet, then experiment with pivoting the table by changing the row, column, and/or page fields and/or the function associated with the data fields. Pivot tables are one of the best-kept secrets in Excel even though they have been available in the last several releases of Excel. Write a short note to your instructor that describes how this feature facilitates data analysis.

   g. Add a cover sheet, then submit the complete assignment to your instructor.

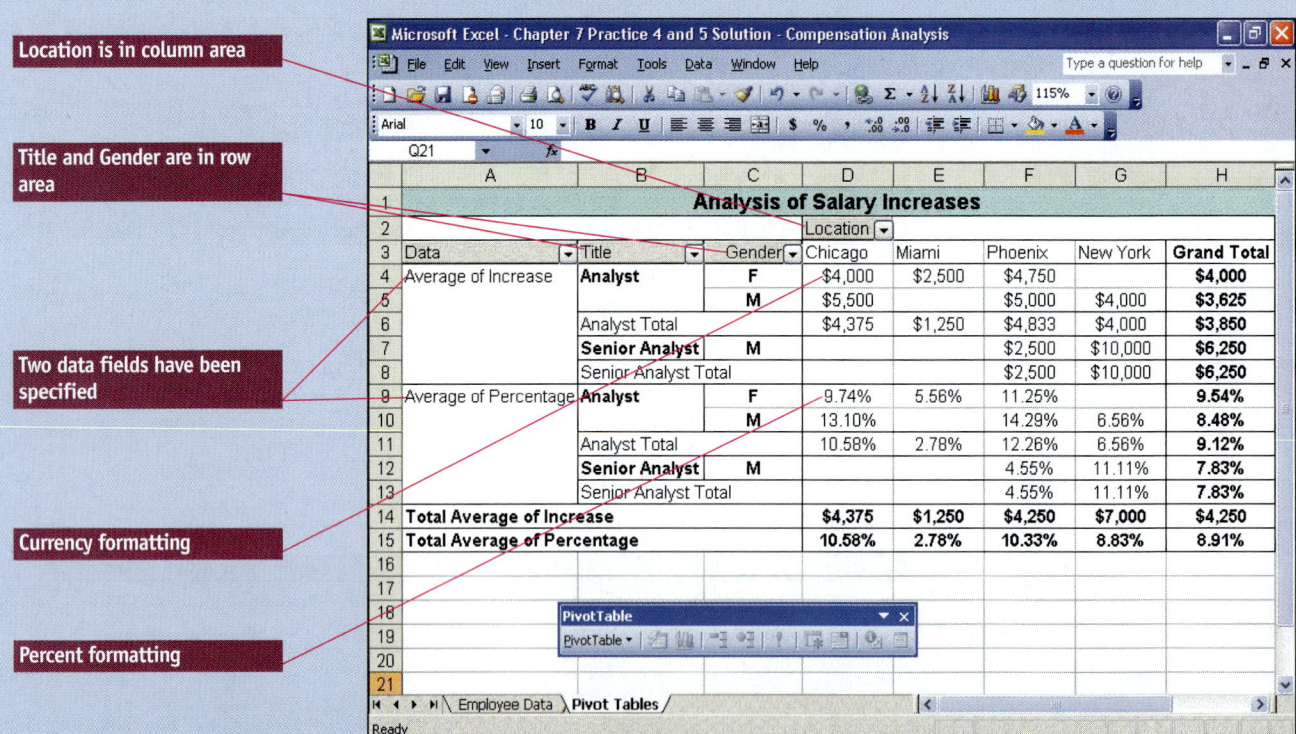

FIGURE 7.21 Pivot Tables (exercise 5)

practice exercises

6. **Consumer Loans:** The worksheet in Figure 7.22 displays selected loans (those with a loan type of "A") from a comprehensive set of loan records. Your assignment is to open the partially completed *Chapter 7 Practice 6* workbook in the Exploring Excel folder to create the worksheet in our figure.

   a. Open the workbook, then go to cell H4, the cell containing the ending date for the first loan. Enter the formula to compute the ending date, based on the starting date and the term of the loan. For the sake of simplicity, you do not have to account for leap year. Thus, to compute the ending date, multiply the term of the loan by 365 and add that result to the starting date. Be sure to format the starting and ending dates to show a date format.

   b. Go to cell I4 and enter the PMT function to compute the monthly payment for the first loan. Copy the formulas in cells H4 and I4 to the remaining rows in the worksheet.

   c. Enter the indicated criteria in cell D29, then enter the indicated database functions toward the bottom of the worksheet.

   d. Use the Advanced Filter command to filter the list in place to display only those loans that satisfy the indicated criteria as shown in Figure 7.22.

   e. Format the list in attractive fashion. Add your name as the loan officer.

   f. Look closely at the bottom of Figure 7.22 and note the presence of a Pivot Table worksheet. You are to create a pivot table that has the loan type and branch location in the row and column fields, respectively. Your pivot table is to contain two data fields, the total amount of the loans, and the average interest rate.

   g. Print the entire workbook for your instructor. Print both the displayed values and cell formulas for the loans worksheet, but only the displayed values for the pivot table. Use the Page Setup command to create a custom footer containing your name, the name of the worksheet, and today's date. Be sure to print the gridlines and row and column headings.

   h. Add a cover sheet, then submit the complete assignment to your instructor.

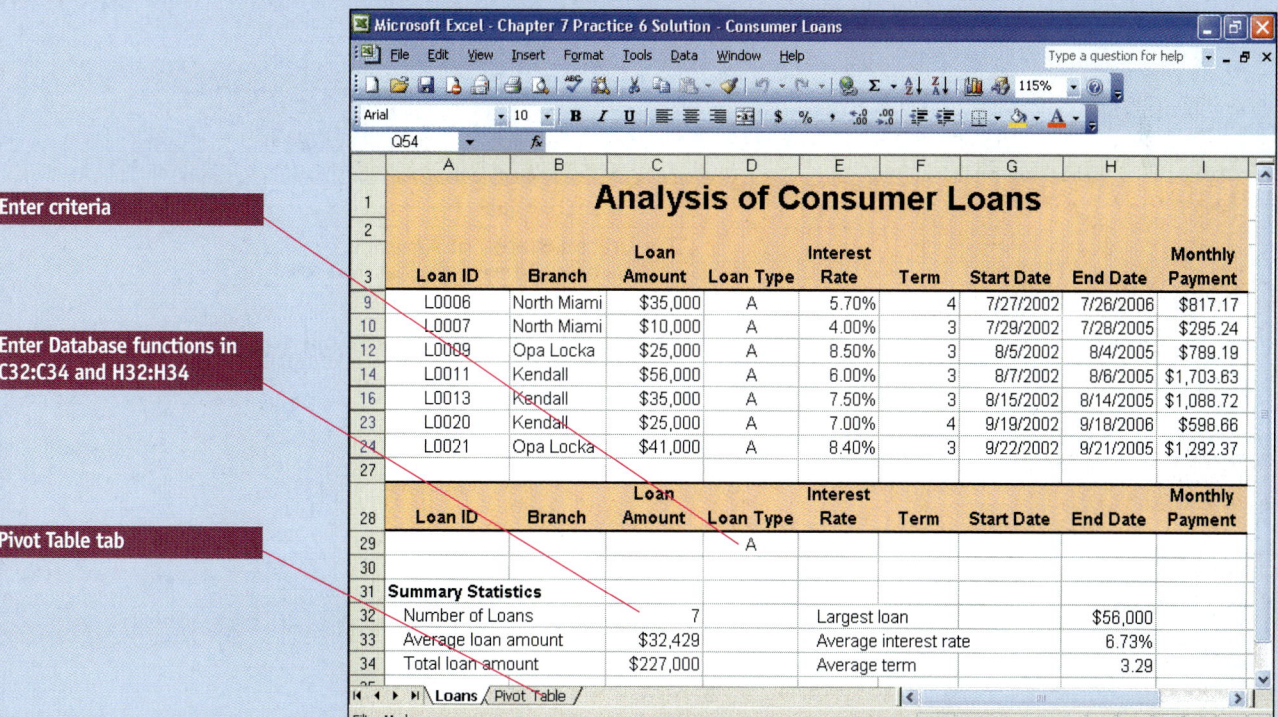

FIGURE 7.22 Consumer Loans (exercise 6)

practice exercises

7. **The Top Ten Filter:** Figure 7.23 displays a workbook containing three worksheets, each with a different view of the same data about the United States. Open the *Chapter 7 Practice 7* workbook in the Exploring Excel folder, which contains just the original data worksheet. Proceed as follows:

   a. Click in cell F5 and enter the formula to compute the population density for the first state in the list. Format the cell to display the value to zero decimal places. Copy the formula to the remaining rows in the list.

   b. Format the worksheet appropriately. You do not have to match our formatting exactly.

   c. Right click the worksheet tab, select the command to Move or Copy the worksheet, check the box to create a copy, click OK, and then rename the copied worksheet to Population Density. Copy the worksheet a second time, renaming this worksheet to 13 Original States as shown in our figure. You will now apply the AutoFilter command to each of the new worksheets.

   d. Click the tab for the Population Density worksheet. Turn on the AutoFilter command. Click the down arrow next to the Population Density field, click Top 10 to display the Top 10 AutoFilter dialog box. Be sure that you have the appropriate entries in each of the three list boxes—that is, Top rather than Bottom, 10 for the number of entries, and items rather than percentages. Click OK to display the filtered list, which displays the filtered records in the same order as in the original list. Click in column F, then click the Sort Descending button on the Standard toolbar to display the population densities in descending sequence. Add the appropriate subtitle to this worksheet.

   e. Click the tab for the 13 Original States worksheet and create a filtered list to display the first 13 states admitted to the Union. Sort the list in ascending sequence by year admitted.

   f. Press and hold the Ctrl key as you select all three worksheets to enter the group mode for editing. Create a custom footer that contains your name, the worksheet tab, and today's date. Check the boxes to show gridlines and row and column headings. Force each worksheet to fit on one page.

   g. Print the entire workbook for your instructor. Add a cover sheet to complete the assignment.

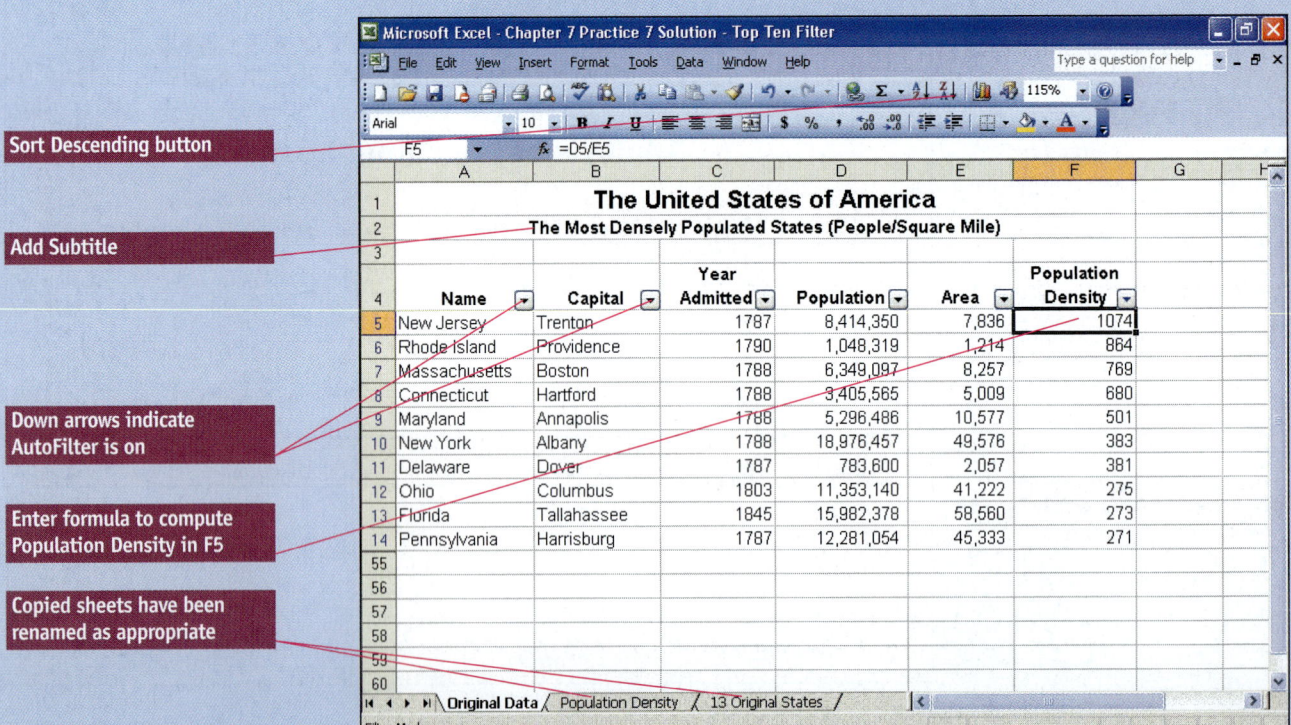

FIGURE 7.23 The Top Ten Filter (exercise 7)

1354 CHAPTER 7: LIST AND DATA MANAGEMENT

practice exercises

8. **Compensation Report:** The document in Figure 7.24 consists of a memo created in Microsoft Word that is linked to a pivot table from exercise 5. The document was created in such a way that any change in the pivot table within the Excel workbook will be automatically reflected in the memo.

   a. Complete practice exercises 4 and 5 in this chapter to create the pivot table that will be used in the memo.
   b. Start Word, create a simple letterhead (we used the Drop Cap command in the Format menu to create our letterhead), then enter the text of the memo in Figure 7.24. You can use our text, or modify the wording as you see fit. Be sure to include your name in the signature area.
   c. Use the Windows taskbar to switch to Excel, copy either pivot table to the clipboard, then use the Paste Link command within Word to bring the pivot table into the Word document as a worksheet object.
   d. Move and/or size the table as necessary. Note, too, that you may have to insert or delete hard returns within the memo to space it properly. *Print this version of the memo for your instructor.*
   e. Prove to yourself that the linking really works by returning to Excel to modify the pivot table to show the total (as opposed to average) salary increase. Change the title of the pivot table as well.
   f. Use the Windows taskbar to return to the Word memo, which should show an updated copy of the pivot table. If you did the exercise correctly, you should see $51,000 as the total amount for all salary increases. Modify the text of the memo to say "revised" salary analysis, as opposed to "preliminary," then print this version of the memo for your instructor.
   g. Add a cover sheet, then submit the complete assignment, consisting of both versions of the memo, to your instructor.
   h. Save the Word document. Exit Word. Save the workbook. Exit Excel.

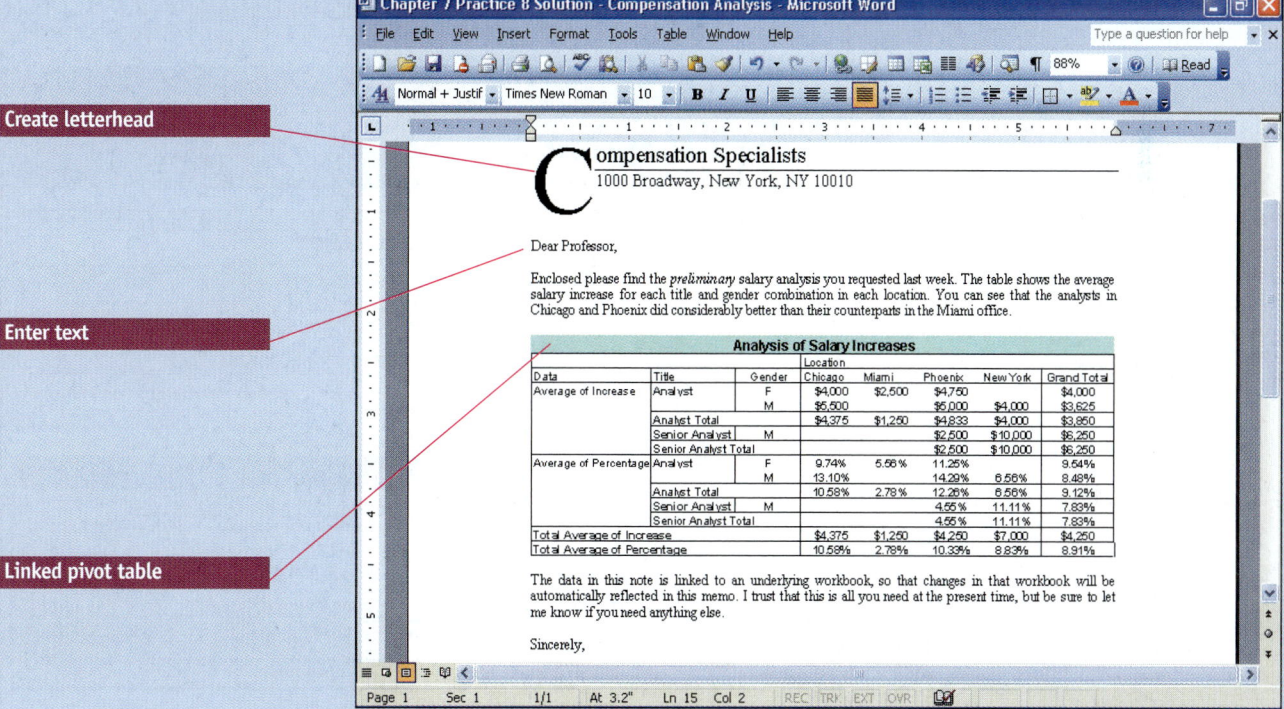

FIGURE 7.24 Compensation Report (exercise 8)

practice exercises

9. **The Analysis ToolPak:** The degree to which you will benefit from the analysis tools in Excel depends in part on your proficiency in statistics. Even if you are not a statistician, however, you can use a few basic techniques as shown in Figure 7.25. This worksheet uses three tools to perform some basic analysis. Start Excel, open a new workbook, and proceed as follows:

   a. Pull down the Tools menu and click the Add-Ins command to display the associated dialog box. Check the box for the Analysis TookPak. Click OK.

   b. Pull down the Tools menu a second time and click the Data Analysis command that has been added to the Tools menu. Scroll down the list of analysis tools until you can select random number generation. Click OK to display the Random Number Generation dialog box where you specify the type of random numbers that you want to generate.

   c. Enter 1 as the number of variables and 200 as the number of random numbers. Choose Normal as the distribution and enter 0 and 1 as the mean and standard deviation, respectively. Specify cell A2 as the output range and click OK. You should see 200 random numbers in cells A2 through A201. (Your values will be different from ours.) Click in cell A1 and enter Random Number as the column heading.

   d. Pull down the Tools menu, click the Data Analysis command, and then scroll down the list of analysis tools until you can select Descriptive Statistics. Enter A1:A201 as the input range, check the box that indicates there are labels in the first row, specify C1 as the output range, and check the box for summary statistics. Click OK. The descriptive statistics for the 200 random numbers will appear in columns C and D. The mean and standard deviation will differ from the theoretical values of 0 and 1, but they should be close.

   e. Enter the lower bounds for the histogram you are about to create in cells F1 through F13 as shown in Figure 7.25. Execute the Data Analysis command one final time and specify Histogram as the analysis tool. Enter A2:A201 as the input range and F2:F12 as the Bin range. Specify C17 as the output range. Click OK to create the histogram. Note how the values are clustered around the middle, which is what you'd expect from a normal distribution.

   f. Format the worksheet as appropriate and then print the completed worksheet for your instructor. Are you less intimated by statistics than previously?

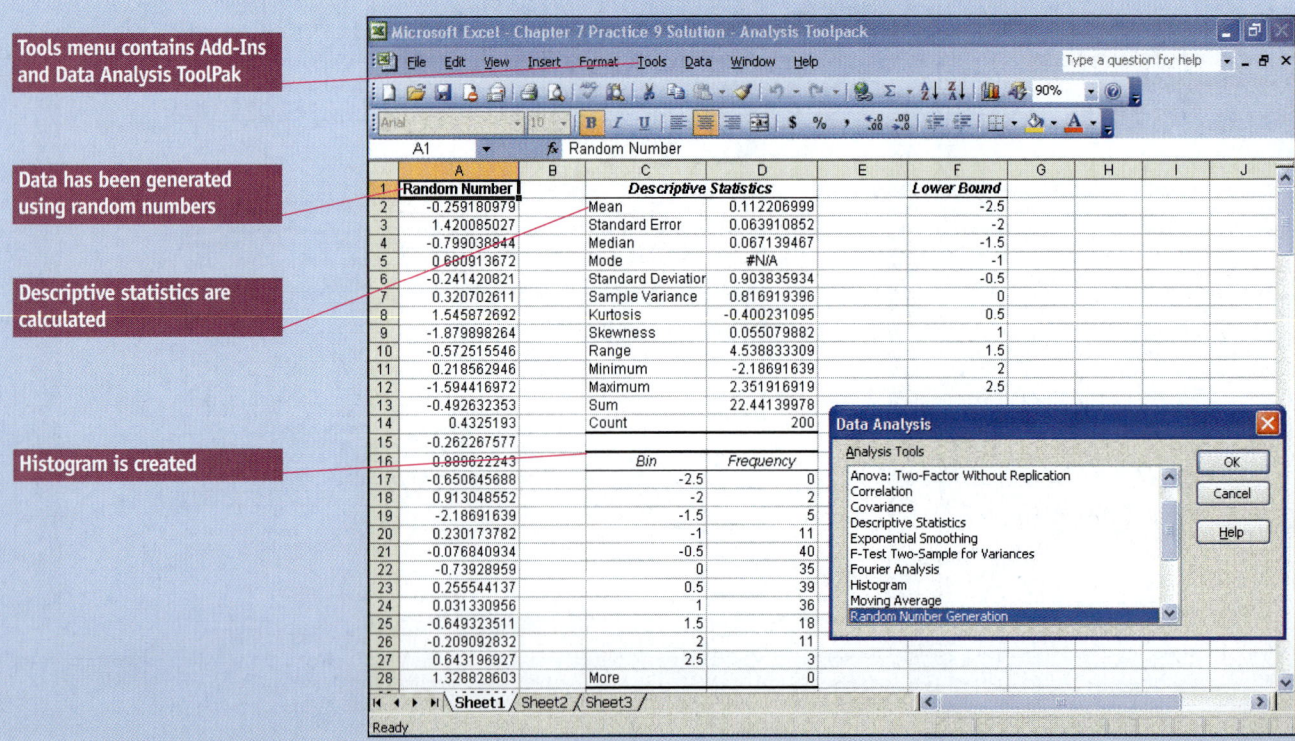

FIGURE 7.25 The Analysis ToolPak (exercise 9)

practice exercises

10. **XML and the Super Bowl:** The workbook in Figure 7.26 was created by importing data from an XML document into an Excel workbook, adding two new fields within the data (Winner and Victory Margin), and inserting two database functions to determine the number of times that each conference has won the big game. Proceed as follows:

   a. Start Excel. Pull down the Data menu, click the Import External Data command, and then click Import Data to display the Select Data Source dialog box. Change to the Exploring Excel folder and specify the file type as XML files. Select the *Chapter 7 Practice 10* XML document and click the Open button. Click OK when you see the message indicating that Excel will create a schema based on the XML source data.

   b. You should see the Import Data dialog box. The option button to put the data as an XML list in an existing worksheet is already selected, with cell A1 specified by default. Change the location of the list to cell A5. Click OK. The XML data is imported into the workbook.

   c. Pull down the View menu and open the XML Source task pane as shown in Figure 7.26. Click the Options button within the task pane to see the available options for an XML list. Press Esc to suppress the option list. Click the XML Maps button to explore a dialog box that allows you to add, delete, or rename an XML map. Close the XML Maps dialog box.

   d. Click in cell F5, type Winner, press the right arrow key to move to cell G5, type Victory Margin, and press enter. These fields have been added to the list (they appear within the blue border), but they do not appear within the XML map in the task pane.

   e. Click in cell F6 and enter an If function to determine the winner for that year. Click in cell G6. Enter the appropriate formula to display the victory margin. (Use the absolute value function to display the result as a positive number.) Copy both formulas to remaining rows in the worksheet.

   f. Complete the worksheet by developing the appropriate database functions to determine the number of times each conference has won the Super Bowl. You will need to create two criteria ranges elsewhere in the worksheet.

   g. Format the worksheet in an attractive fashion. Print the complete workbook for your instructor to show both displayed values and cell formulas.

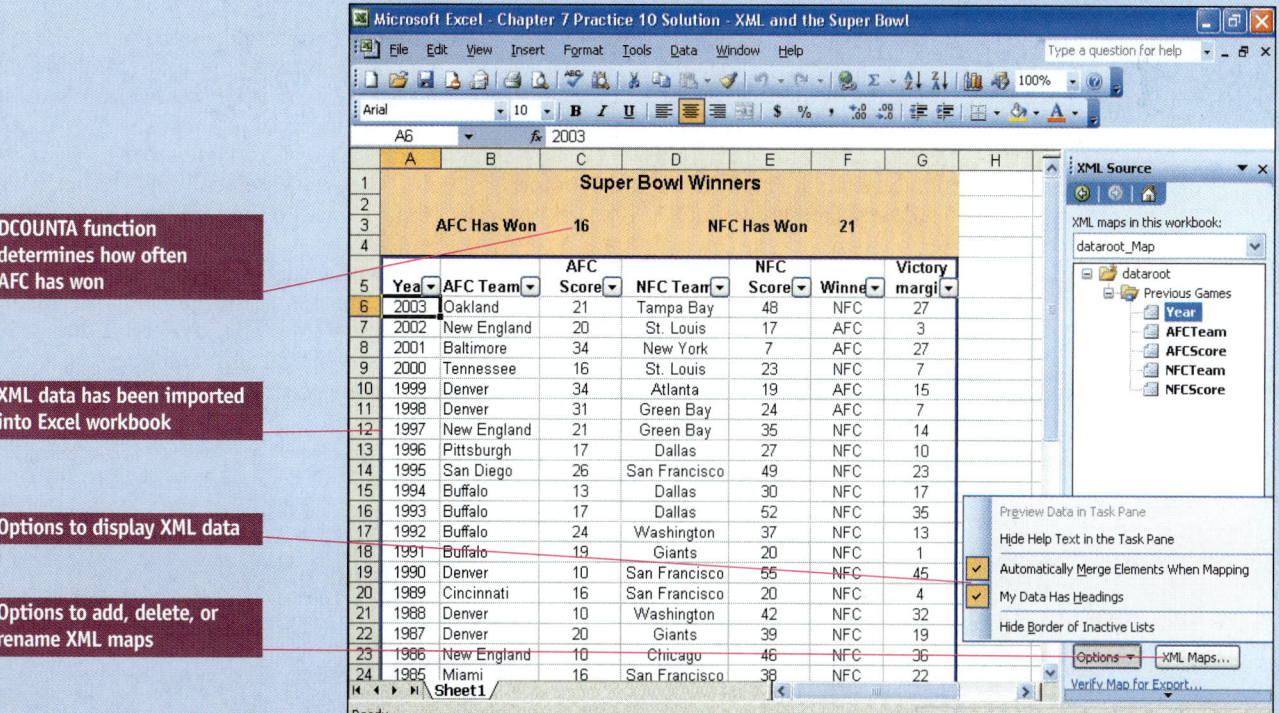

FIGURE 7.26   XML and the Super Bowl (exercise 10)

MINI CASES

Excel and Access

You can import data into Excel from Access. You can also export data from Excel to Access, except there is no Export wizard. Instead, you start Access as a separate application, open an existing database, then import the data from Excel; i.e., exporting data from Excel is equivalent to importing the data within Access.

Start Access and open the *Chapter 7 Mini Case—Excel and Access* database in the Exploring Excel folder. The Tables button should be selected within the Database window. Pull down the File menu, click the Get External Data command, and click Import to display the associated dialog box. Use the Look In box to change to the Exploring Excel folder, specify Microsoft Excel as the file type, and import the *Chapter 7 Mini Case—Excel and Access* workbook, which contains statistical data on countries around the world. You will be taken through the Import Spreadsheet wizard. Import the data into a new table and specify the Country field as the primary key (a unique field in every record). The wizard will end by indicating that it has imported the data. Click the Reports button in the Database window and print one or more of the existing reports that are based on the data that you just imported.

Asset Allocation

It's several years in the future and you find yourself happily married and financially prosperous. You and your spouse have accumulated substantial assets in a variety of accounts. Some of the money is in a regular account for use today, whereas other funds are in retirement accounts for later use. Much of the money, both regular and retirement, is invested in equities (i.e., the stock market), but a portion of your funds is also in nonequity funds such as money-market checking accounts and bank certificates of deposit. Your accounts are also in different places such as banks and brokerage houses. A summary of your accounts can be found in the *Asset Allocation* workbook. Your assignment is to open the workbook and develop a pivot table that will enable you and your spouse to keep track of your investments.

Fly by Night Airways

Fly by Night Airways is an independent airline offering charters and special tours. The airline has several independent agents, each of whom books trips for the airline. The data for all trips is maintained in the *Chapter 7 Mini Case—Fly by Night Airlines* Access database that is stored in the Exploring Excel folder. Your assignment is to start a new Excel workbook and import the data from the Access database into the Excel workbook to create a pivot table for data analysis. (Pull down the File menu, click the Open command, specify an Access database in the File Type list box, select the database in the Exploring Excel folder, and then click the Open button.)

Your pivot table should show the amount of contracts by marketing representative and contract status (whether the trip is still in the proposal stage or whether it has already been signed). The table should also have the flexibility to show all trips or trips that do or do not require passage through customs. Use the Page Setup command to create a custom footer that contains your name and the name of the worksheet. Print the completed workbook for your instructor.

CHAPTER 8

Automating Repetitive Tasks: Macros and Visual Basic for Applications

OBJECTIVES

After reading this chapter you will:

1. Define a macro; describe the relationship between Excel macros and VBA procedures.
2. Record a macro; use the Visual Basic Editor to modify a macro.
3. Use the VBA MsgBox and InputBox statements to enhance a macro.
4. Execute a macro via a keyboard shortcut or button.
5. Describe the Personal Macro workbook.
6. Use the Step Into command to debug a macro.
7. Use the VBA If and Do statements to implement decision making.

hands-on exercises

1. INTRODUCTION TO MACROS
   Input: None
   Output: My Macros

2. THE PERSONAL MACRO WORKBOOK
   Input: None
   Output: Personal Macro workbook

3. DATA MANAGEMENT MACROS
   Input: Employee List Solution (from Chapter 7)
   Output: Employee List Solution (additional changes)

4. ADDITIONAL MACROS
   Input: Employee List Solution (from exercise 3)
   Output: Employee List Solution (additional changes)

5. LOOPS AND DECISION MAKING
   Input: Loops and Decision Making
   Output: Loops and Decision Making Solution

CASE STUDY
THE SLEEPY SHOWROOM

Simon Key opened the Sleepy Showroom 30 years ago with a limited selection of twin and full-sized mattresses from one vendor. Today he offers a complete product line (twin, full, queen, and king-sized mattresses) in a variety of styles and prices from four different vendors. Simon prides himself on his huge selection; for example, he offers 20 different mattresses from just the Heavenly Sleep Company. The business is very profitable, yet Simon believes he has too many vendors and too many choices from each vendor. He has come to you for advice.

Simon has given you complete access to the financial information for his business in the form of an Excel workbook, which contains detailed information for every item in the showroom. The workbook also contains a criteria range and two database functions that display the units sold and corresponding profit for indicated criteria. The Sleep Wonderfully product line, for example, accounted for only 38% of the units sold, yet it generated 69% of the total profit. You can change the criteria to see similar statistics for other vendors and/or other parameters (e.g., mattress size). ■

Your assignment is to read the chapter, open the *Chapter 8 Case Study— The Sleepy Showroom* workbook, and create a series of four macros that will enable Simon to change the criteria to see the results for any vendor and/or any size mattress. The first macro should prompt Simon for the vendor and mattress, enter these values within the criteria range, and then filter the list to display only those items that match the indicated criteria. The second macro should clear the criteria range and display the entire list. The third and fourth macros should display the top ten items according to the percent of the total profit and the number of units sold, respectively. All of your macros should use range names, as opposed to specific cell references. (The range names are already defined in the workbook.) Simon has promised you the king-sized bed of your choice and a sizeable bonus if you can improve his bottom line.

INTRODUCTION TO MACROS

Have you ever pulled down the same menus and clicked the same sequence of commands over and over? Easy as the commands may be to execute, it is still burdensome to have to continually repeat the same mouse clicks or keystrokes. If you can think of any task that you do repeatedly, whether in one workbook or in a series of workbooks, you are a perfect candidate to use macros.

A ***macro*** is a set of instructions that tells Excel which commands to execute. It is in essence a program, and its instructions are written in Visual Basic, a programming language. Fortunately, however, you don't have to be a programmer to write macros. Instead, you use the macro recorder within Excel to record your commands, and let Excel write the macros for you.

The ***macro recorder*** stores Excel commands, in the form of ***Visual Basic*** instructions, within a workbook. (***Visual Basic for Applications***, or ***VBA***, is a subset of Visual Basic that is built into Microsoft Office.) To use the recorder, you pull down the Tools menu and click the Record New Macro command. From that point on (until you stop recording), every command you execute will be stored by the recorder. It doesn't matter whether you execute commands from pull-down menus via the mouse, or whether you use the toolbar or ***keyboard shortcuts***. The macro recorder captures every action you take and stores the equivalent Visual Basic statements as a macro within the workbook.

Figure 8.1 illustrates a simple macro to enter your name and class in cells A1 and A2 of the active worksheet. The macro is displayed in the ***Visual Basic Editor (VBE)***, which is used to create, edit, execute, and debug Excel macros. The Visual Basic Editor is a separate application (as can be determined from its button on the taskbar in Figure 8.1), and it is accessible from any application in Microsoft Office.

The left side of the VBE window in Figure 8.1 contains the ***Project Explorer***, which is similar in concept and appearance to the Windows Explorer, except that it displays only open workbooks and/or other Visual Basic projects. The Visual Basic statements for the selected module (Module1 in Figure 8.1) appear in the ***Code window*** in the right pane. As you shall see, a Visual Basic module consists of one or more procedures, each of which corresponds to an Excel macro. Thus, in this example, Module1 contains the NameAndCourse procedure corresponding to the Excel macro of the same name. Module1 itself is stored in the My Macros.XLS workbook.

As indicated, a macro consists of Visual Basic statements that were created through the macro recorder. We don't expect you to be able to write the Visual Basic procedure yourself, and you don't have to. You just invoke the recorder and let it capture the Excel commands for you. We do think it is important, however, to understand the macro, and so we proceed to explain its statements. As you read our discussion, do not be concerned with the precise syntax of every statement, but try to get an overall appreciation for what the statements do.

A macro always begins and ends with the Sub and End Sub statements, respectively. The ***Sub statement*** contains the name of the macro—for example, NameAndCourse in Figure 8.1. (Spaces are not allowed in a macro name.) The ***End Sub statement*** is physically the last statement and indicates the end of the macro. Sub and End Sub are Visual Basic keywords and appear in blue.

The next several statements begin with an apostrophe, appear in green, and are known as ***comments***. They provide information about the macro, but do not affect its execution. In other words, the results of a macro are the same, whether or not the comments are included. Comments are inserted automatically by the recorder to document the macro name, its author, and ***shortcut key*** (if any). You can add comments (a comment line must begin with an apostrophe), or delete or modify existing comments, as you see fit. Comments may also be added at the end of a statement by typing an apostrophe, then adding the explanatory text; i.e., anything after the apostrophe is considered a comment.

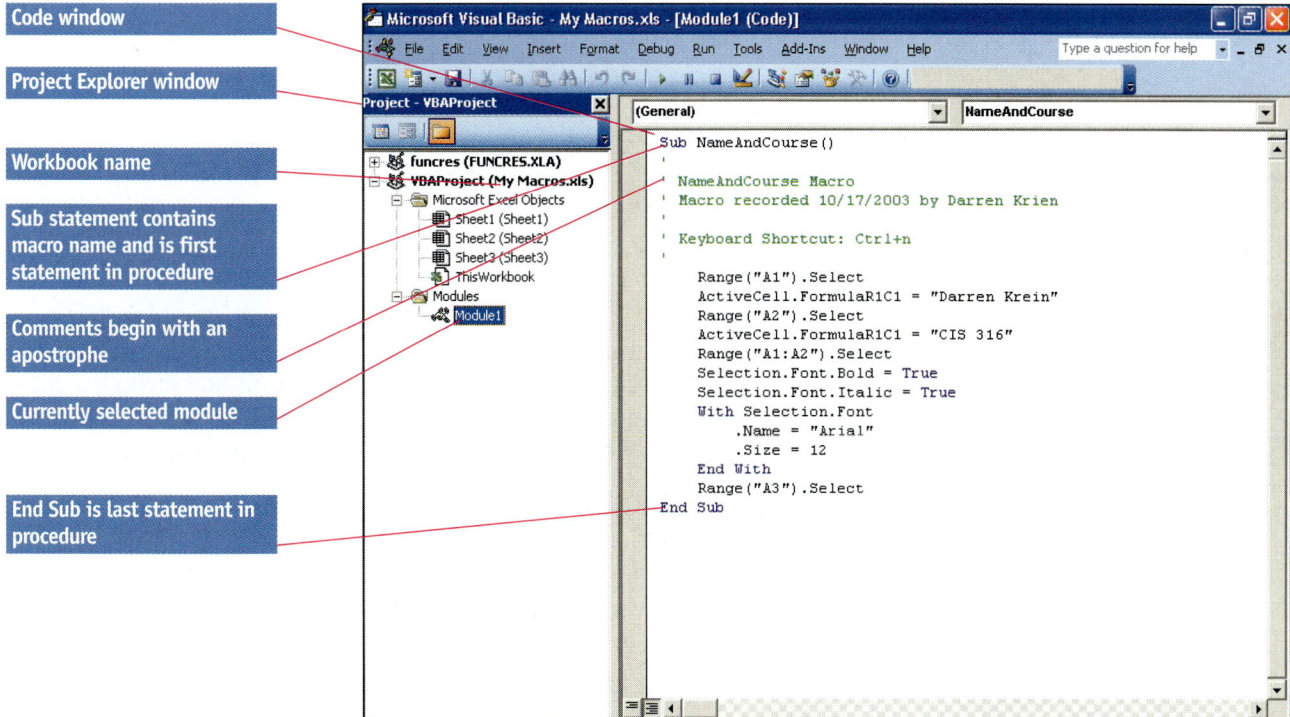

FIGURE 8.1 A Simple Macro

Every other statement is a Visual Basic instruction that was created as a result of an action taken in Excel. For example, the statements

   Range ("A1").Select
and ActiveCell.FormulaR1C1 = "Darren Krien"

select cell A1 as the active cell, then enter the text "Darren Krien" into the active cell. These statements are equivalent to clicking in cell A1 of a worksheet, typing the indicated entry into the active cell, then pressing the Enter key (or an arrow key) to complete the entry. In similar fashion, the statements

   Range ("A2").Select
and ActiveCell.FormulaR1C1 = "CIS 316"

select cell A2 as the active cell, then enter the text entry "CIS 316" into that cell. The concept of select-then-do applies equally well to statements within a macro. Thus, the statements

 Range ("A1:A2").Select
 Selection.Font.Bold = True
 Selection.Font.Italic = True

select cells A1 through A2, then change the font for the selected cells to bold italic. The ***With statement*** enables you to perform multiple actions on the same object. All commands between the With and corresponding ***End With statement*** are executed collectively; for example, the statements

 With Selection.Font
  .Name = "Arial"
  .Size = 12
 End With

change the formatting of the selected cells (A1:A2) to 12 point Arial. The last statement in the macro, Range ("A3").Select, selects cell A3, thus deselecting all other cells, a practice we use throughout the chapter.

hands-on exercise

1 Introduction to Macros

Objective   To record, run, view, and edit a simple macro; to establish a keyboard shortcut to run a macro. Use Figure 8.2 as a guide in doing the exercise.

Step 1:   **Create a Macro**

- Start Excel. Open a new workbook if one is not already open. Save the workbook as **My Macros** in the **Exploring Excel folder**.

- Pull down the **Tools menu**, click (or point to) the **Macro command**, then click **Record New Macro** to display the Record Macro dialog box in Figure 8.2a. (If you don't see the Macro command, click the double arrow at the bottom of the menu to see more commands.)

- Enter **NameAndCourse** as the name of the macro. (Spaces are not allowed in the macro name.)

- The description is entered automatically and contains today's date and the name of the person in whose name this copy of Excel is registered. If necessary, change the description to include your name.

- Click in the **Shortcut Key** check box and enter a **lowercase n**. Ctrl+n should appear as the shortcut as shown in Figure 8.2a. (If you see Ctrl+Shift+N it means you typed an uppercase N rather than a lowercase letter. Correct the entry to a lowercase n.)

- Check that the option to Store macro in **This Workbook** is selected. Click **OK** to record the macro, which displays the Stop Recording toolbar.

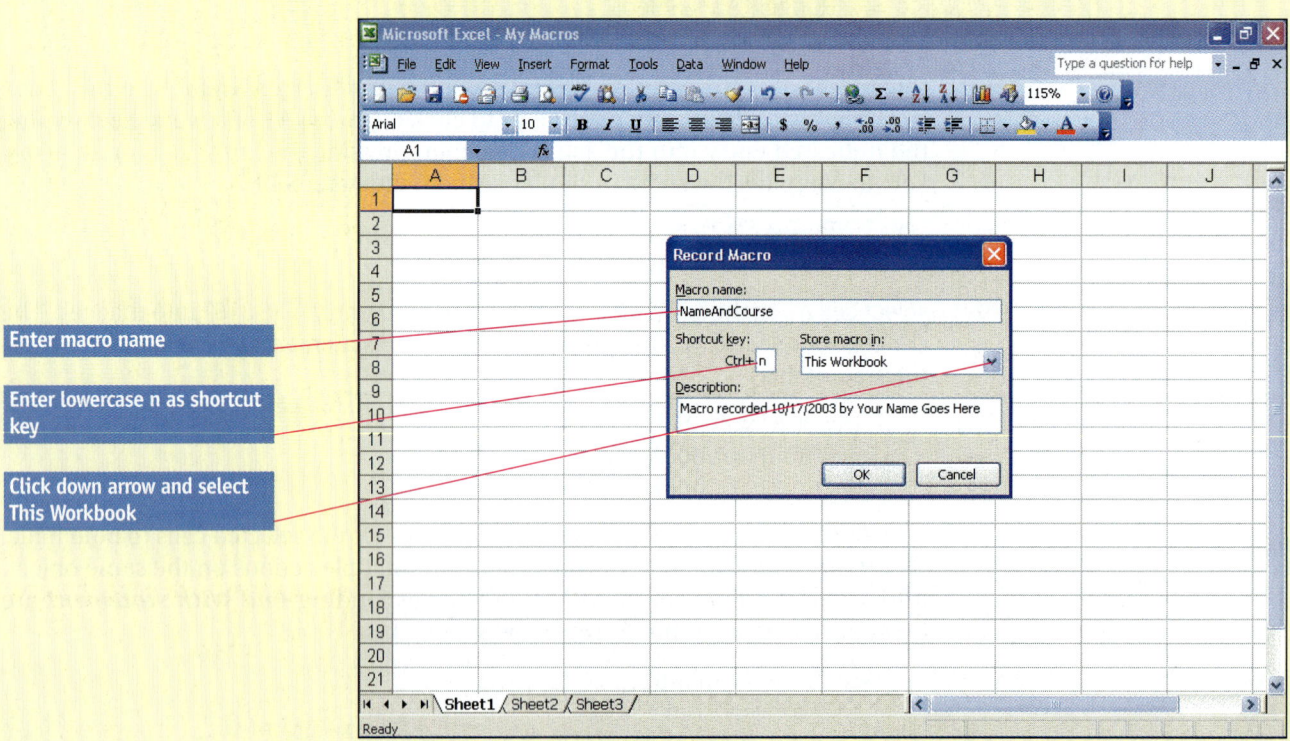

(a) Create a Macro (step 1)

FIGURE 8.2   Hands-on Exercise 1

Step 2: **Record the Macro**

- Look carefully at the Relative References button on the Stop Recording button to be sure it is flush with the other buttons; that is, the button should *not* be pushed in. (See boxed tip on "Is the Button In or Out?")

- You should be in Sheet1, ready to record the macro, as shown in Figure 8.2b. The status bar indicates that you are in the Recording mode:
  - ❏ Click in **cell A1** even if it is already selected. Enter your name.
  - ❏ Click in **cell A2**. Enter the course you are taking.
  - ❏ Click and drag to select **cells A1 through A2**.
  - ❏ Click the **Bold button**. Click the **Italic button**.
  - ❏ Click the arrow on the **Font Size list box**. Click **12** to change the point size.
  - ❏ Click in **cell A3** to deselect all other cells prior to ending the macro.

- Click the **Stop Recording button**. (If you do not see the Stop Recording toolbar, pull down the **Tools button**, click **Macro**, then click the **Stop Recording command**.)

- Save the workbook.

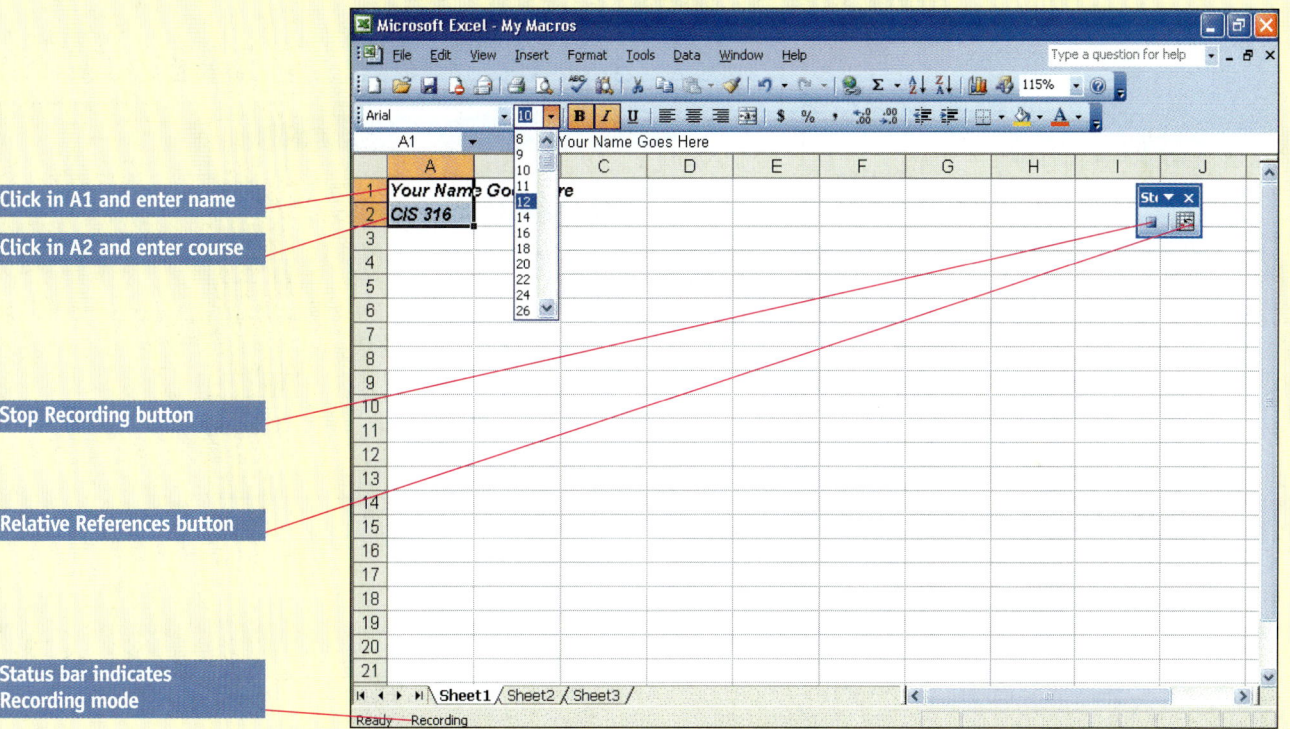

(b) Record the Macro (step 2)

FIGURE 8.2 Hands-on Exercise 1 (*continued*)

IS THE BUTTON IN OR OUT?

The distinction between relative and absolute references within a macro is critical and is described in detail at the end of this exercise. The Relative References button on the Stop Recording toolbar toggles between the two—absolute references when the button is out, relative references when the button is in. The ScreenTip, however, displays Relative References regardless of whether the button is in or out. We wish that Microsoft had made it easier to tell which type of reference you are recording, but they didn't.

MICROSOFT OFFICE EXCEL 2003

Step 3: **Test the Macro**

- To run (test) the macro, you have to remove the contents and formatting from cells A1 and A2. Click and drag to select **cells A1 through A2**.

- Pull down the **Edit menu**. Click **Clear**. Click **All** from the cascaded menu to erase both the contents and formatting from the selected cells. Cells A1 through A2 are empty as shown in Figure 8.2c.

- Pull down the **Tools menu**. Click **Macro**, then click the **Macros . . . command** to display the dialog box in Figure 8.2c.

- Click **NameAndCourse**, which is the macro you just recorded. Click **Run**. Your name and class are entered in cells A1 and A2, then formatted according to the instructions in the macro.

- Clear the contents and formatting in cells A1 and A2. Press **Ctrl+n** (the keyboard shortcut) to rerun the NameAndCourse macro. Your name and class should reappear in cells A1 and A2.

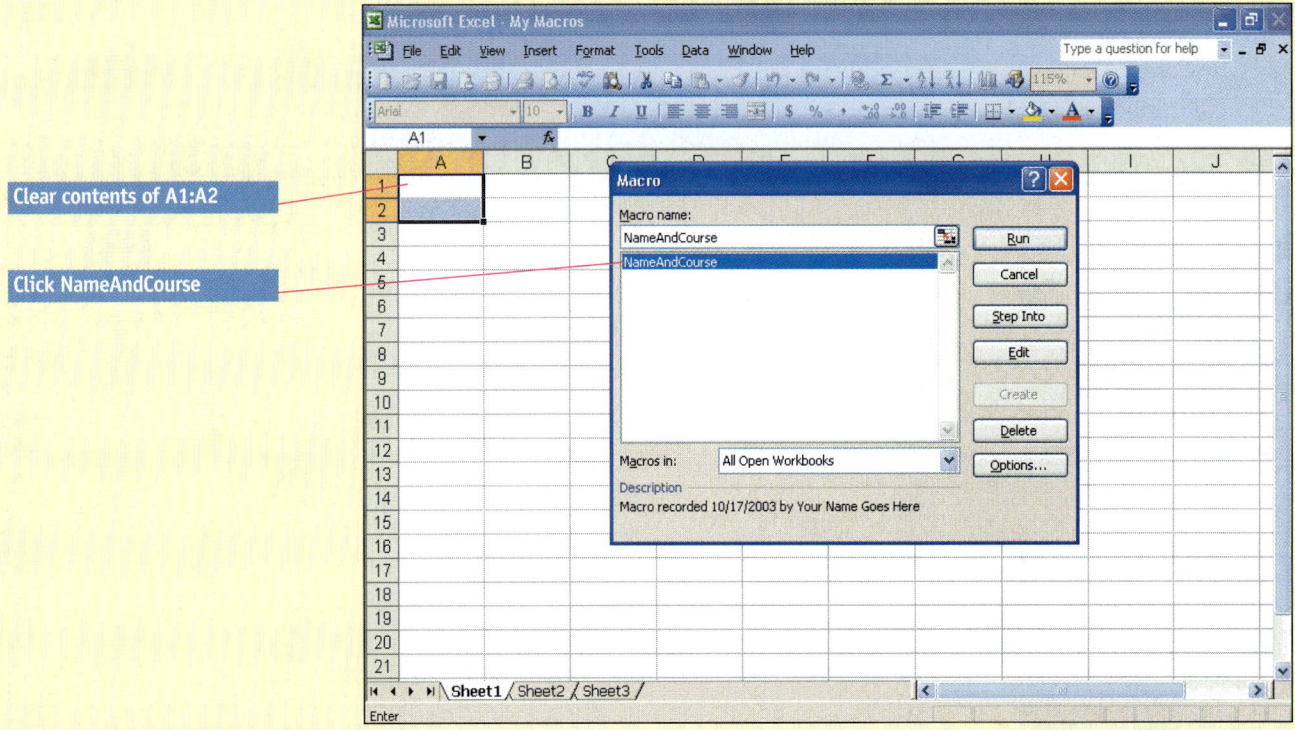

(c) Test the Macro (step 3)

FIGURE 8.2 Hands-on Exercise 1 (*continued*)

THE EDIT CLEAR COMMAND

The Edit Clear command erases the contents of a cell, its formatting, and/or its comments. Select the cell or cells to erase, pull down the Edit menu, click the Clear command, then click All, Formats, Contents, or Comments from the cascaded menu. Pressing the Del key is equivalent to executing the Edit Clear Contents command as it clears the contents of a cell, but retains the formatting and comments.

Step 4: **Start the Visual Basic Editor**

- Pull down the **Tools menu**, click the **Macro command**, then click **Visual Basic Editor** (or press **Alt+F11**) to open the Visual Basic Editor. Maximize the VBE window.
- If necessary, pull down the **View menu**. Click **Project Explorer** to open the Project Explorer window in the left pane. There is currently one open VBA project, My Macros.xls, which is the name of the open workbook in Excel.
- If necessary, click the **plus sign** next to the Modules folder to expand that folder, click (select) **Module1**, pull down the **View menu**, and click **Code** to open the Code window in the right pane. Click the **Maximize button** in the Code window.
- Your screen should match the one in Figure 8.2d. The first statement below the comments should be *Range("A1").Select*, which indicates that the macro was correctly recorded with absolute references.
- If you see a very different statement, *ActiveCell.FormulaR1C1*, it means that you incorrectly recorded the macro with relative references. Right click **Module1** in the Project Explorer window, select the **Remove Module1 command** (respond **No** when asked if you want to export it), then return to step 1 and rerecord the macro.

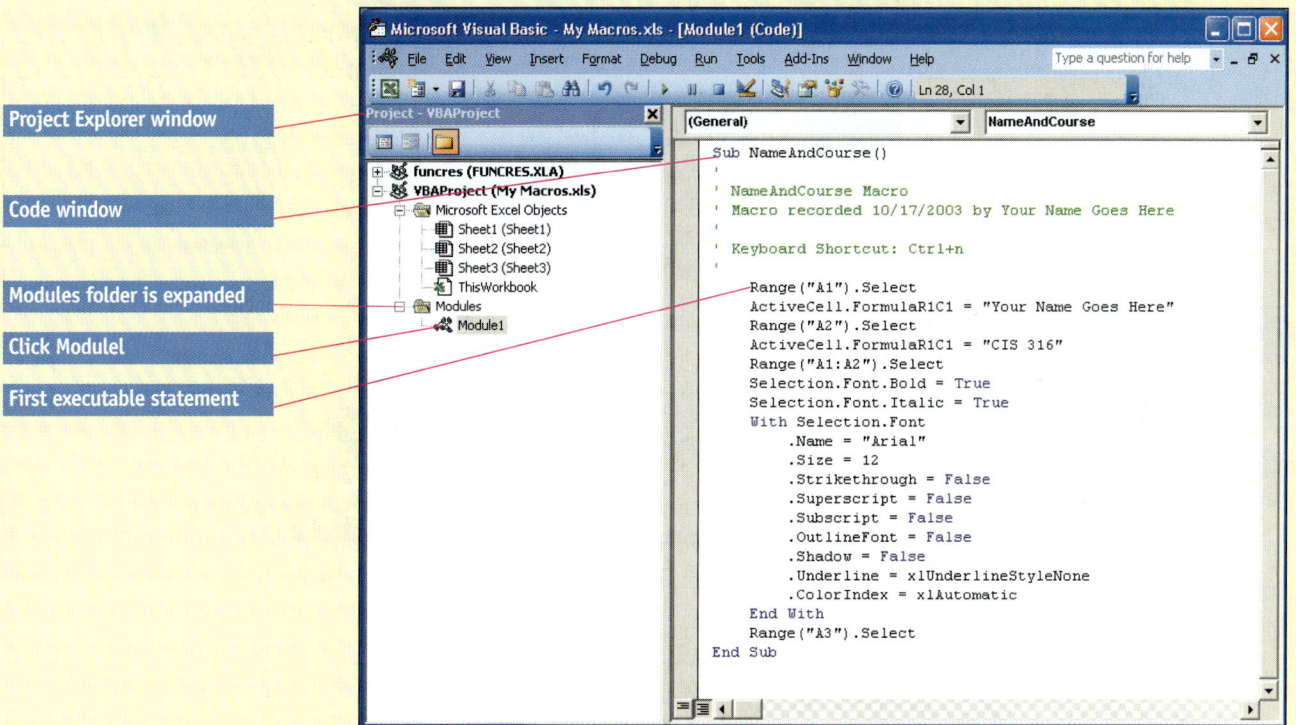

(d) Start the Visual Basic Editor (step 4)

FIGURE 8.2 Hands-on Exercise 1 (*continued*)

THE END RESULT

Excel provides multiple ways to accomplish the same task; for example, you can click the Bold button on the Formatting toolbar, or you can use the Ctrl+B shortcut. The macro recorder records only the end result, with no indication of which technique was used. Thus, you will see Selection.Font.Bold = True (or False) regardless of whether you used the toolbar or the mouse.

Step 5: **Edit the Macro**

- Edit the NameAndCourse macro by changing the font name and size to **"Times New Roman"** and **24**, respectively, as shown in Figure 8.2e.

- Click and drag to select the next seven statements as shown in Figure 8.2e.

- Press the **Del key** to delete these statements from the macro. (These statements contain default values and are unnecessary.) Delete any blank lines as well.

- Press **Alt+F11** to toggle back to the Excel workbook (or click the **Excel button** on the Windows taskbar).

- Clear the entries and formatting in cells A1 and A2 as you did earlier, then rerun the NameAndCourse macro.

- Your name and class should once again be entered in cells A1 and A2 but in a different and larger font. (If the macro does not execute correctly, press **Alt+F11** to toggle back to the Visual Basic Editor to correct your macro.)

- Save the workbook.

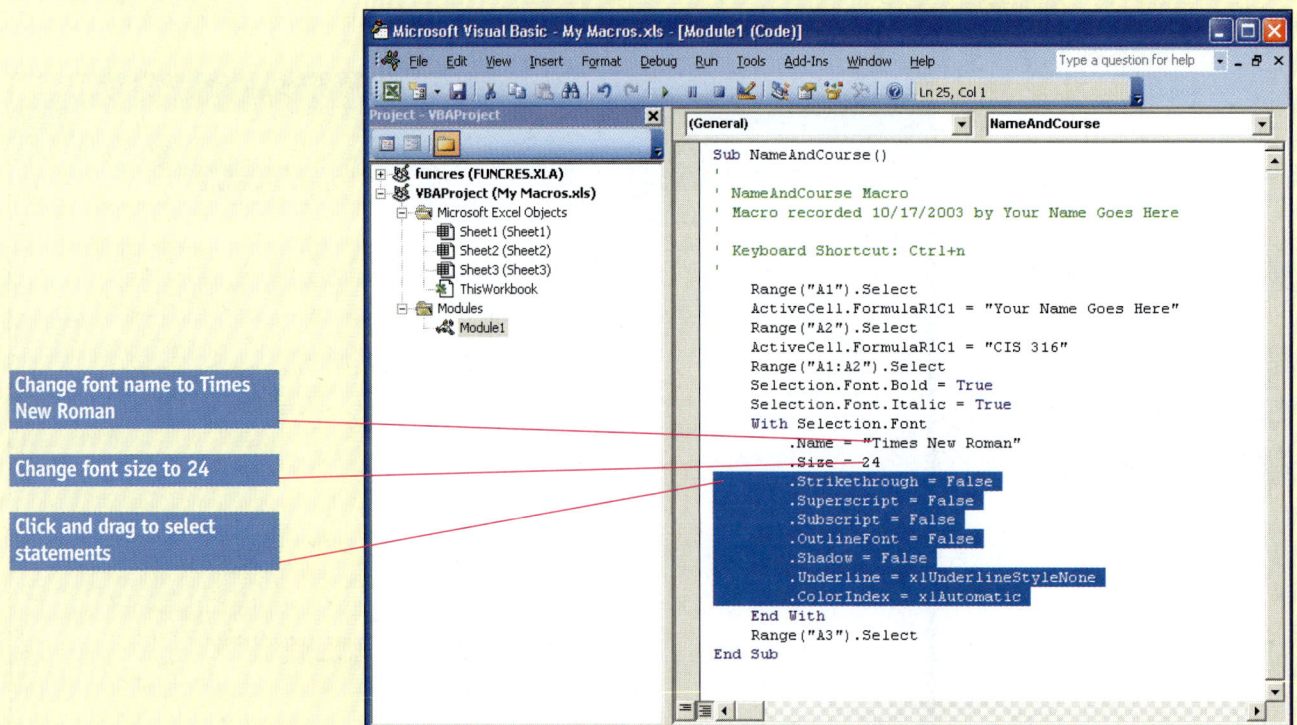

(e) Edit the Macro (step 5)

FIGURE 8.2 Hands-on Exercise 1 (*continued*)

SIMPLIFY THE MACRO

The macro recorder usually sets all possible options for an Excel command or dialog box even if you do not change those options. We suggest, therefore, that you make a macro easier to read by deleting the unnecessary statements. Take a minute, however, to review the statements prior to removing them, so that you can see the additional options. (You can click the Undo button to restore the deleted statements if you make a mistake.)

Step 6: **Create the Erase Macro**

- Pull down the **Tools menu**. Click the **Macro command**, then click **Record New Macro** from the cascaded menu. You will see the Record Macro dialog box.

- Enter **EraseNameAndCourse** as the name of the macro. Do not leave any spaces in the macro name. If necessary, change the description to include your name.

- Click in the **Shortcut Key** check box and enter a **lowercase e**. (Ctrl+e should appear as the shortcut.) Check that the option to Store macro in **This Workbook** is selected.

- Click **OK** to begin recording the macro, which displays the Stop Recording toolbar. Be sure you are recording absolute references (i.e., the Relative References button should be flush on the toolbar).
  - Click and drag to select **cells A1 through A2** as shown in Figure 8.2f, even if they are already selected.
  - Pull down the **Edit menu**. Click **Clear**. Click **All** from the cascaded menu. Cells A1 through A2 should now be empty.
  - Click in **cell A3** to deselect all other cells prior to ending the macro.

- Click the **Stop Recording button** to end the macro.

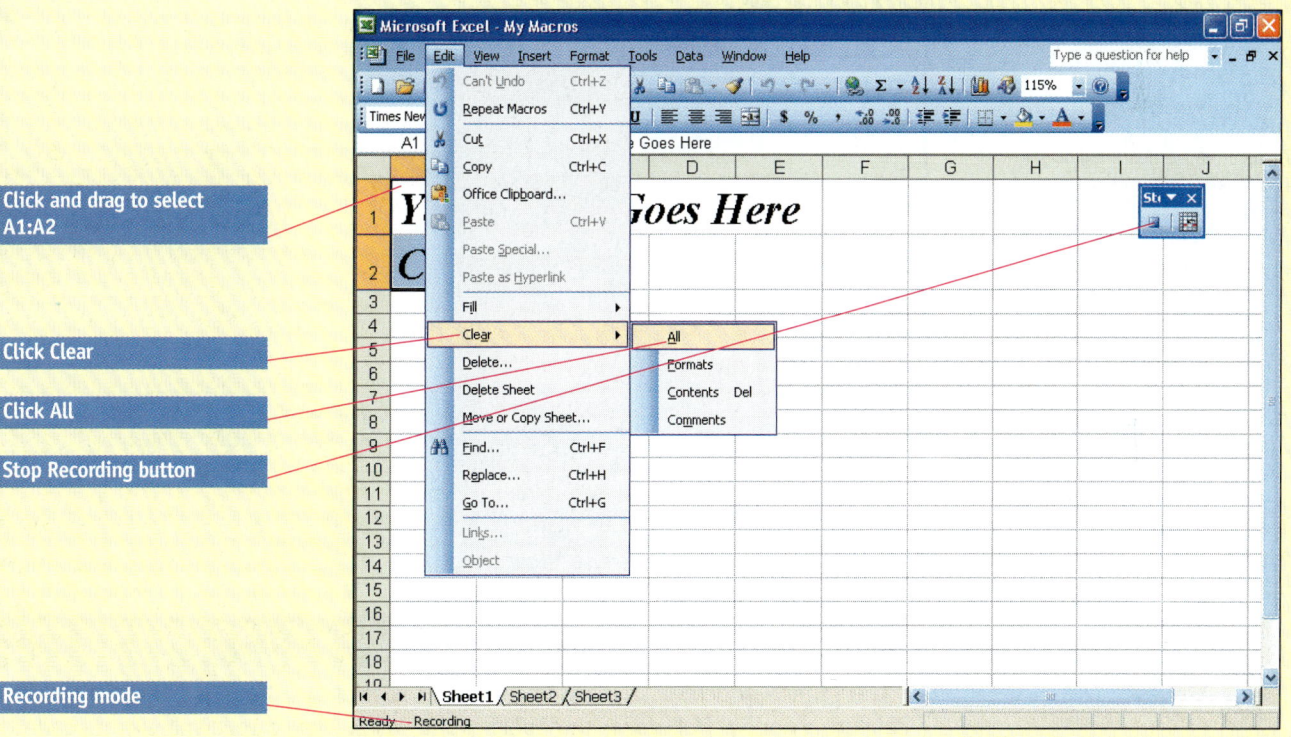

(f) Create the Erase Macro (step 6)

FIGURE 8.2 Hands-on Exercise 1 (*continued*)

TO SELECT OR NOT SELECT

If you start recording, then select a cell(s) within the macro, the selection becomes part of the macro, and the macro will always operate on the same cell. If, however, you select the cell(s) prior to recording, the macro is more general and operates on the selected cells, which may differ every time the macro is executed. Both techniques are valid, and the decision depends on what you want the macro to do.

Step 7: **Shortcut Keys**

- Press **Ctrl+n** to execute the NameAndCourse macro. (You need to reenter your name and course to test the newly created EraseNameAndCourse macro.)
- Your name and course should again appear in cells A1 and A2 as shown in Figure 8.2g.
- Press **Ctrl+e** to execute the EraseNameAndCourse macro. Cells A1 and A2 should again be empty.
- You can press **Ctrl+n** and **Ctrl+e** repeatedly, to enter and then erase your name and course. End this step after having erased the data.
- Save the workbook.

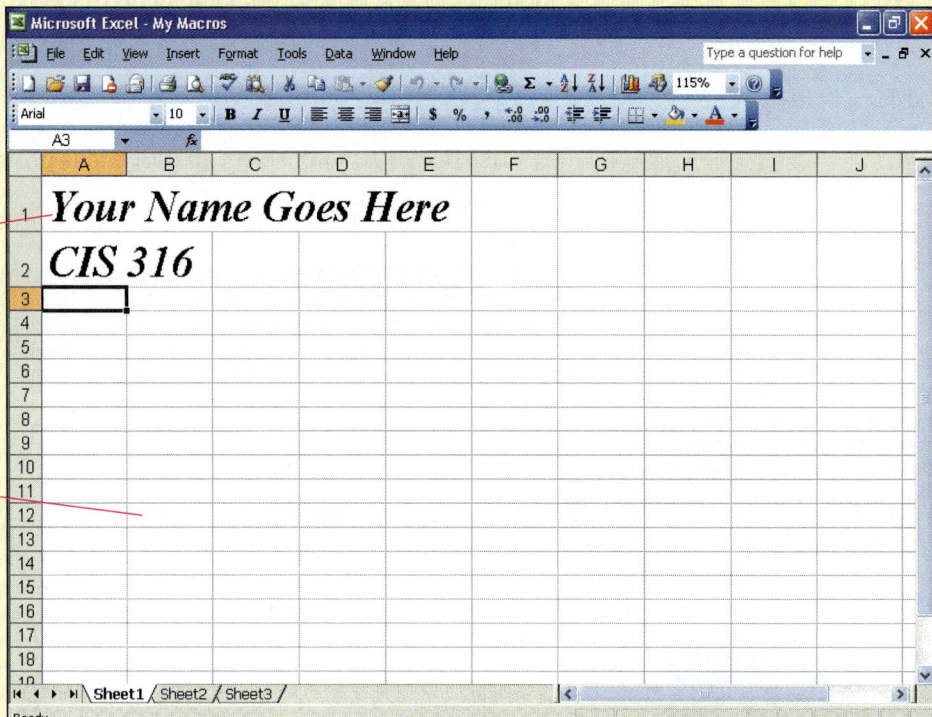

(g) Shortcut Keys (step 7)

FIGURE 8.2 Hands-on Exercise 1 (*continued*)

TROUBLESHOOTING

If the macro shortcut keys do not work, it is probably because they were not defined properly. Pull down the Tools menu, click Macro to display a cascaded menu, click the Macros . . . command, then select the desired macro in the Macro Name list box. Click the Options button, then check the entry in the Shortcut Key text box. A lowercase letter creates a shortcut with just the Ctrl key, whereas an uppercase letter uses Ctrl+Shift with the shortcut. Thus, "n" and "N" will establish shortcuts of Ctrl+n and Ctrl+Shift+N, respectively.

Step 8: **Step through the Macro**

- Press **Alt+F11** to switch back to the VBE window. Click the **Close button** to close the **Project window** within the Visual Basic Editor. The Code window expands to take the entire Visual Basic Editor window.

- Point to an empty area on the Windows taskbar, then click the **right mouse button** to display a shortcut menu. Click **Tile Windows Vertically**.

- Your desktop should be similar to Figure 8.2h. It doesn't matter if the workbook is in the left or right window.

- Click in the **Visual Basic Editor window**, then click anywhere within the NameAndCourse macro. Pull down the **Debug menu** and click the **Step Into command** (or press the **F8 key**). The Sub statement is highlighted.

- Press the **F8 key** to move to the first executable statement (the comments are skipped). The statement is highlighted, but it has not yet been executed.

- Press the **F8 key** again to execute this statement (which selects cell A1 and moves to the next statement). Continue to press the **F8 key** to execute the statements one at a time. You see the effect of each statement in the Excel window.

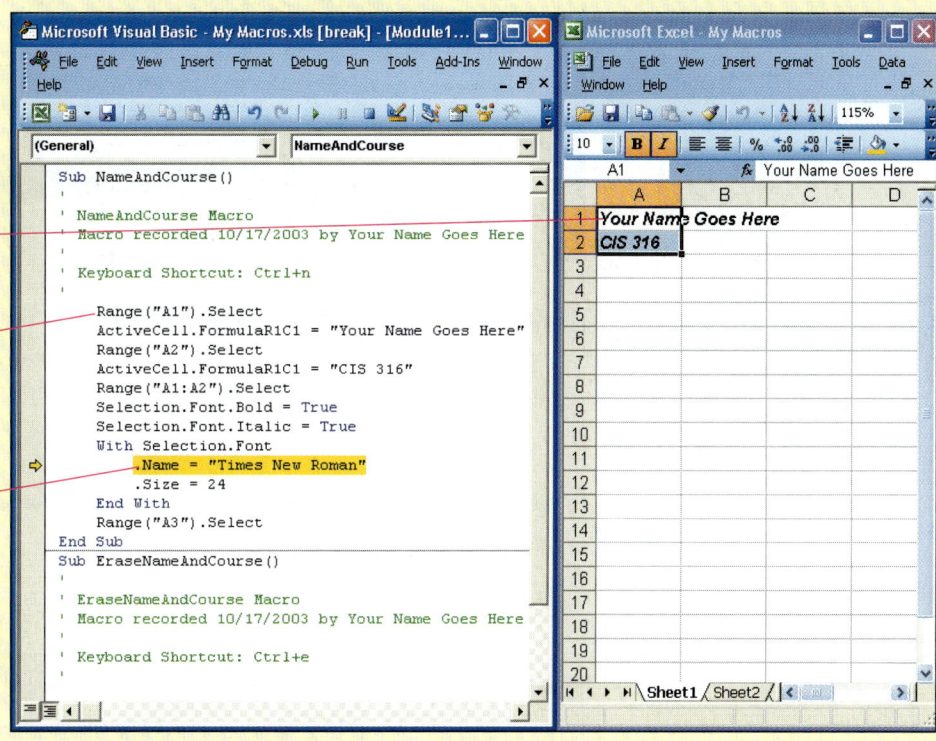

(h) Step through the Macro (step 8)

FIGURE 8.2   Hands-on Exercise 1 (*continued*)

THE STEP INTO COMMAND

The Step Into command is useful to slow down the execution of a macro in the event the macro does not perform as intended. In essence, you execute the macro one statement at a time, while viewing the results of each statement in the associated worksheet. If a statement does not do what you want it to do, just change the statement in the Visual Basic window, then continue to press the F8 key to step through the procedure.

Step 9: **Print the Module**

- Click in the **Visual Basic window**. Pull down the **File menu**. Click **Print** to display the Print - VBAProject dialog box in Figure 8.2i.

- Click the option button to print the current module. Click **OK**. Submit the listing of the current module, which contains the procedures for both macros, to your instructor as proof you did this exercise.

- Close the My Macros workbook. Click **Yes** if asked to save the workbook. The macros are stored within the workbook.

- Exit Excel if you do not wish to continue with the next hands-on exercise at this time.

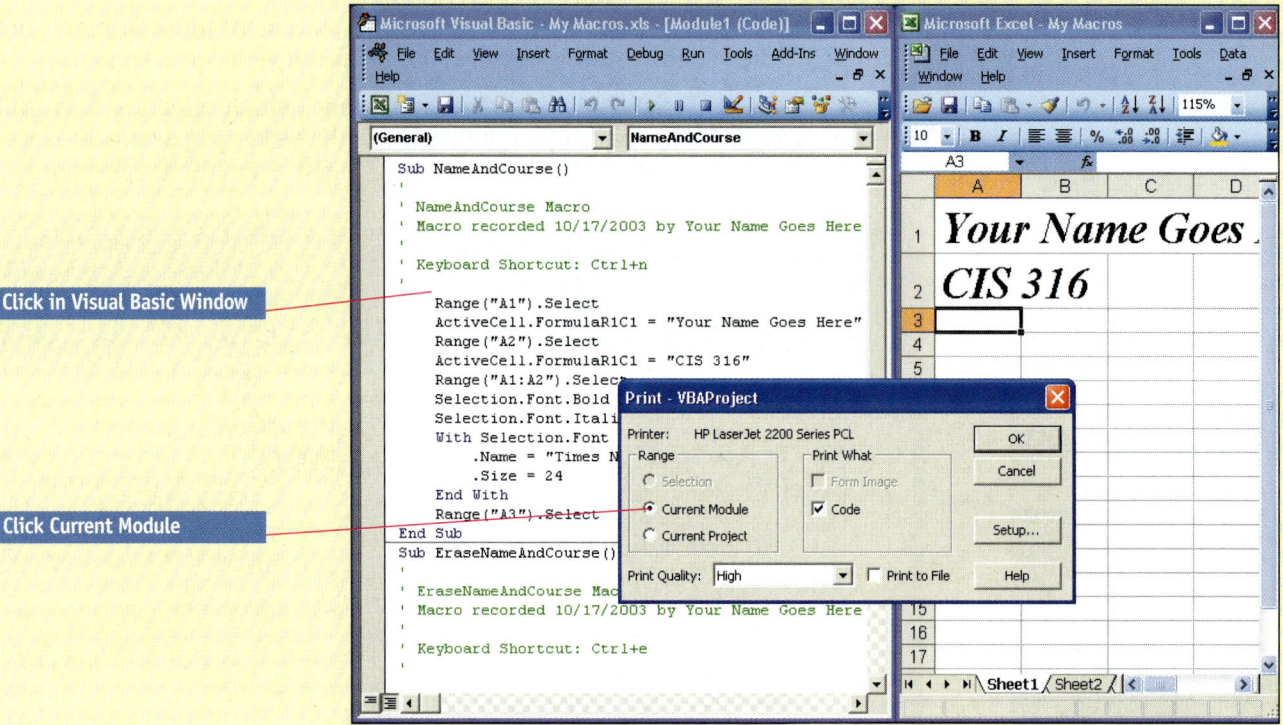

(i) Print the Module (step 9)

FIGURE 8.2 Hands-on Exercise 1 (*continued*)

PROCEDURE VIEW VERSUS FULL MODULE VIEW

The procedures within a module can be displayed individually, or alternatively, multiple procedures can be viewed simultaneously. To go from one view to the other, click the Procedure View button at the bottom of the window to display just the procedure you are working on, or click the Full Module View button to display multiple procedures. You can press Ctrl+PgDn and Ctrl+PgUp to move between procedures in either view. Use the vertical scroll bar to move up and down within the VBA window.

RELATIVE VERSUS ABSOLUTE REFERENCES

One of the most important options to specify when recording a macro is whether the references are to be relative or absolute. A reference is a cell address. An **absolute reference** is a constant address that always refers to the same cell. A **relative reference** is variable in that the reference will change from one execution of the macro to the next, depending on the location of the active cell when the macro is executed.

To appreciate the difference, consider Figure 8.3, which displays two versions of the NameAndCourse macro from the previous exercise, one with absolute and one with relative references. Figure 8.3a uses absolute references to place your name, course, and date in cells A1, A2, and A3. The data will always be entered in these cells regardless of which cell is selected when you execute the macro.

Figure 8.3b enters the same data, but with relative references, so that the cells in which the data are entered depend on which cell is selected when the macro is executed. If cell A1 is selected, your name, course, and date will be entered in cells A1, A2, and A3. If, however, cell E4 is the active cell when you execute the macro, then your name, course, and date will be entered in cells E4, E5, and E6.

A relative reference is specified by an **offset** that indicates the number of rows and columns from the active cell. An offset of (1,0) indicates a cell one row below the active cell. An offset of (0,1) indicates a cell one column to the right of the active cell. In similar fashion, an offset of (1,1) indicates a cell one row below and one column to the right of the active cell. Negative offsets are used for cells above or to the left of the current selection.

Absolute References to cells A1, A2, and A3

```
Range("A1").Select
ActiveCell.FormulaR1C1 = "Darren Krein"
Range("A2").Select
ActiveCell.FormulaR1C1 = "CIS 316"
Range("A3").Select
ActiveCell.FormulaR1C1 = "=TODAY()"
Range("A1:A3").Select
Selection.Font.Italic = True
With Selection.Font
    .Name = "Arial"
    .Size = 12
End With
Range("A4").Select
```

(a) Absolute References

Relative references to cell one row below the active cell

Indicates a column of 3 cells is to be selected

```
ActiveCell.FormulaR1C1 = "Darren Krein"
ActiveCell.Offset(1, 0).Range("A1").Select
ActiveCell.FormulaR1C1 = "CIS 316"
ActiveCell.Offset(1, 0).Range("A1").Select
ActiveCell.FormulaR1C1 = "=TODAY()"
ActiveCell.Offset(-2, 0).Range("A1:A3").Select
Selection.Font.Italic = True
With Selection.Font
    .Name = "Arial"
    .Size = 12
End With
ActiveCell.Offset(3, 0).Range("A1").Select
```

(b) Relative References

FIGURE 8.3 Absolute versus Relative References

Relative references may appear confusing at first, but they extend the power of a macro by making it more general. You will appreciate this capability as you learn more about macros. Let us begin by recognizing that the statement

ActiveCell.Offset (1,0).Range ("A1").Select

means select the cell one row below the active cell. It has nothing to do with cell A1, and you might wonder why the entry Range ("A1") is included. The answer is that the offset specifies the location of the new range (one row below the current cell), and the A1 indicates that the size of that range is a single cell (A1). In similar fashion, the statement

ActiveCell.Offset (–2,0).Range ("A1:A3").Select

selects a range, starting two rows above the current cell, that is one column by three rows in size. Again, it has nothing to do with cells A1 through A3. The offset specifies the location of a new range (two rows above the current cell) and the shape of that range (a column of three cells). If you are in cell D11 when the statement is executed, the selected range will be cells D9 through D11. The selection starts with the cell (cell D9) two rows above the active cell, then it continues from that point to select a range consisting of one column by three rows (cells D9:D11).

RELATIVE VERSUS ABSOLUTE REFERENCES

Relative references appear confusing at first, but they extend the power of a macro by making it more general. Macro statements that have been recorded with relative references include an offset to indicate the number of rows and columns the selection is to be from the active cell. An offset of (–1,0) indicates a cell one row above the active cell, whereas an offset of (0,–1) indicates a cell one column to the left of the active cell. Positive offsets are used for cells below or to the right of the current selection.

THE PERSONAL MACRO WORKBOOK

The hands-on exercise at the beginning of the chapter created the NameAndCourse macro in the My Macros workbook, where it is available to that workbook or to any other workbook that is in memory when the My Macros workbook is open. What if, however, you want the macro to be available at all times, not just when the My Macros workbook is open? This is easily accomplished by storing the macro in the Personal Macro workbook when it is first recorded.

The ***Personal Macro workbook*** opens automatically whenever Excel is loaded. This is because the Personal Macro workbook is stored in the XLStart folder, a folder that Excel checks each time it is loaded into memory. Once open, the macros in the Personal workbook are available to any other open workbook. The following hands-on exercise creates the NameAndCourse macro with relative references, then stores that macro in the Personal Macro workbook.

The exercise also expands the macro to enter the date of execution, and further generalizes the macro to accept the name of the course as input. The latter is accomplished through the Visual Basic ***InputBox function*** that prompts the user for a specific response, then stores that response within the macro. In other words, the Excel macro is enhanced through the inclusion of a VBA statement that adds functionality to the original macro. You start with the macro recorder to translate Excel commands into a VBA procedure, then you modify the procedure by adding the necessary VBA statements. (The InputBox function must be entered manually into the procedure since there is no corresponding Excel command, and hence the macro recorder would not work.)

hands-on exercise
2   The Personal Macro Workbook

Objective To create and store a macro in the Personal Macro workbook; to assign a toolbar button to a macro; to use the Visual Basic InputBox function. Use Figure 8.4 as a guide in the exercise.

Step 1: The Personal Macro Workbook

- Start Excel. Be sure to close the My Macros workbook from the previous exercise to avoid any conflict with an existing macro.

- Open a new workbook if one is not already open. Pull down the **Tools menu**, click (or point to) the **Macro command**, then click **Record New Macro** to display the Record Macro dialog box.

- Enter **NameAndCourse** as the name of the macro. Do not leave any spaces in the macro name. Click in the **Shortcut Key** check box and enter a **lowercase n**. Ctrl+n should appear as the shortcut.

- Click the **drop-down arrow** in the Store macro in list box and select the Personal Macro workbook as shown in Figure 8.4a. (If you are working on a network, as opposed to a standalone machine, you may not be able to access the **Personal Macro workbook**, in which case you can save the macro in This Workbook.)

- Click **OK** to begin recording the macro, which in turn displays the Stop Recording toolbar.

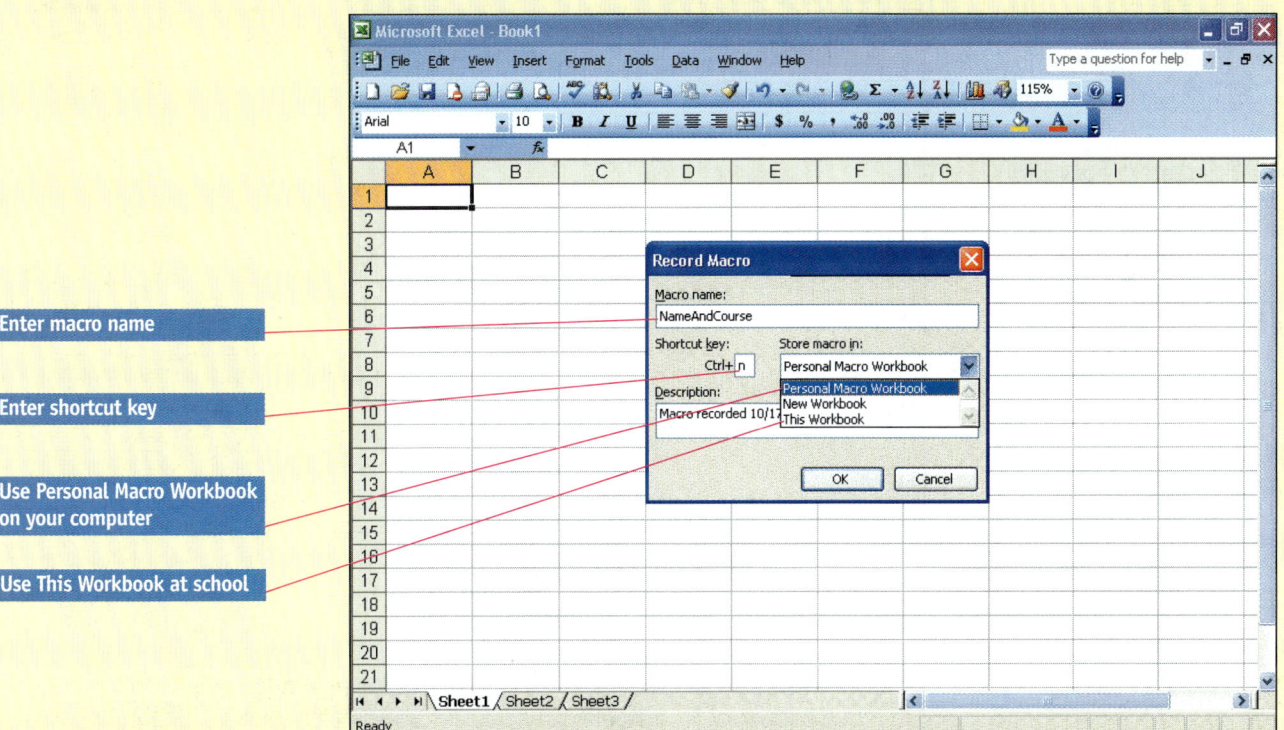

(a) The Personal Macro Workbook (step 1)

FIGURE 8.4   Hands-on Exercise 2

Step 2: **Record with Relative References**

- Click the **Relative References button** on the Stop Recording toolbar so that the button is pushed in as shown in Figure 8.4a.
- The Relative References button functions as a toggle switch—click it, and the button is pushed in to record relative references. Click it again, and you record absolute references. Be sure to record relative references.
- Enter your name in the active cell. Do *not* select the cell.
- Press the **down arrow key** to move to the cell immediately underneath the current cell. Enter the course you are taking.
- Press the **down arrow key** to move to the next cell. Enter **=TODAY()**.
- Click and drag to select the three cells containing the data values you just entered (cells A1 through A3 in Figure 8.4b).
  ❏ Click the **Bold button**. Click the **Italic button**.
  ❏ Click the arrow on the **Font Size list box**. Click **12** to change the point size.
  ❏ Click in **cell A4** to deselect all other cells prior to ending the macro.
- Click the **Stop Recording button** to end the macro.

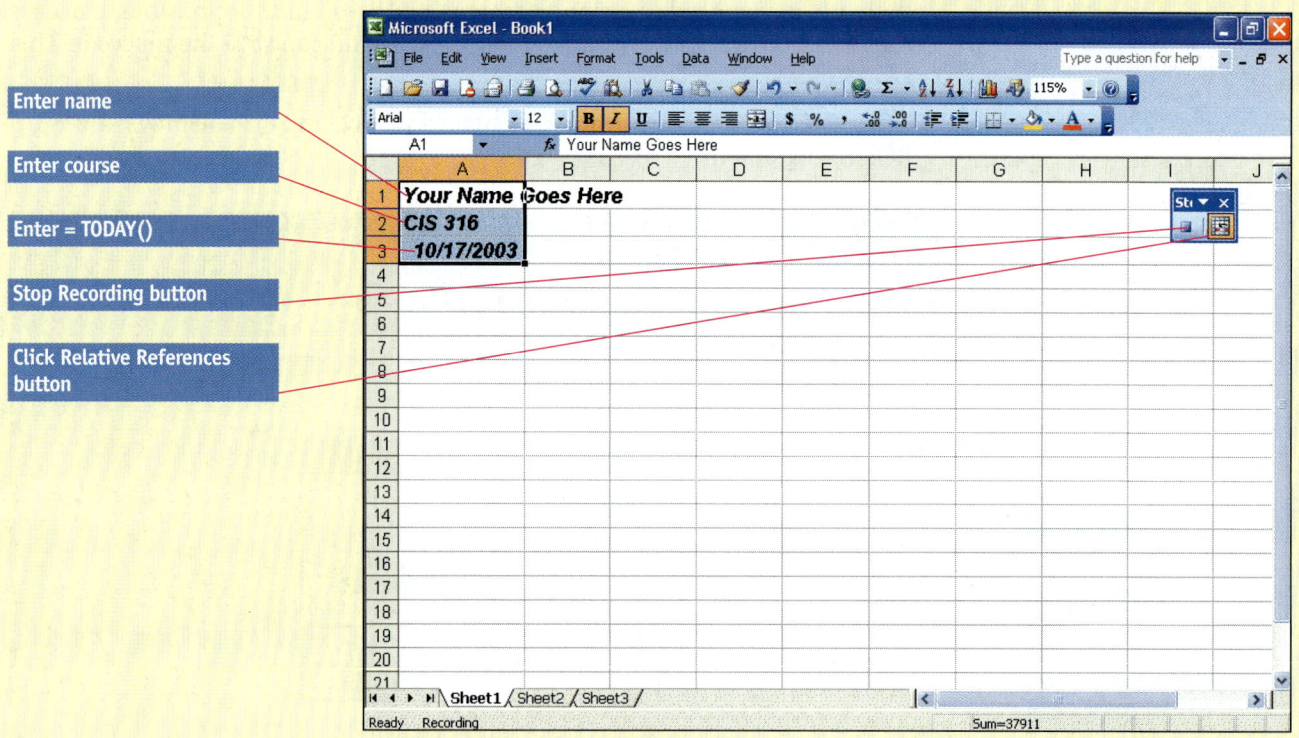

(b) Record with Relative References (step 2)

FIGURE 8.4 Hands-on Exercise 2 (*continued*)

PLAN AHEAD

The macro recorder records everything you do, including entries that are made by mistake or commands that are executed incorrectly. Plan the macro in advance, before you begin recording. Write down what you intend to do, then try out the commands with the recorder off. Be sure you go all the way through the intended sequence of operations prior to turning the macro recorder on.

Step 3: **The Visual Basic Editor**

- Pull down the **Tools menu**, click the **Macro command**, then click **Visual Basic Editor** (or press **Alt+F11**) to open the Visual Basic Editor in Figure 8.4c.

- If necessary, pull down the **View menu**. Click **Project Explorer** to open the Project Explorer window in the left pane.

- There are currently two open VBA projects (Book1, the name of the open workbook, and PERSONAL.XLS, the Personal Macro workbook).

- Click the **plus sign** to expand the Personal Workbook folder, then click the **plus sign** to expand the **Modules** folder within this project.

- Click (select) **Module1**, pull down the **View menu**, and click **Code** to open the Code window in the right pane. Maximize the Code window.

- Close any other open windows within the Visual Basic Editor. The first executable statement should begin with *ActiveCell.FormulaR1C1*.

- If you see a very different statement, *Range("A1").Select*, it means that you incorrectly recorded the macro with absolute references. Right click Module1 in the Project window, select the **Remove Module command** (respond **No** when asked if you want to export it), then return to step 1 and rerecord the macro.

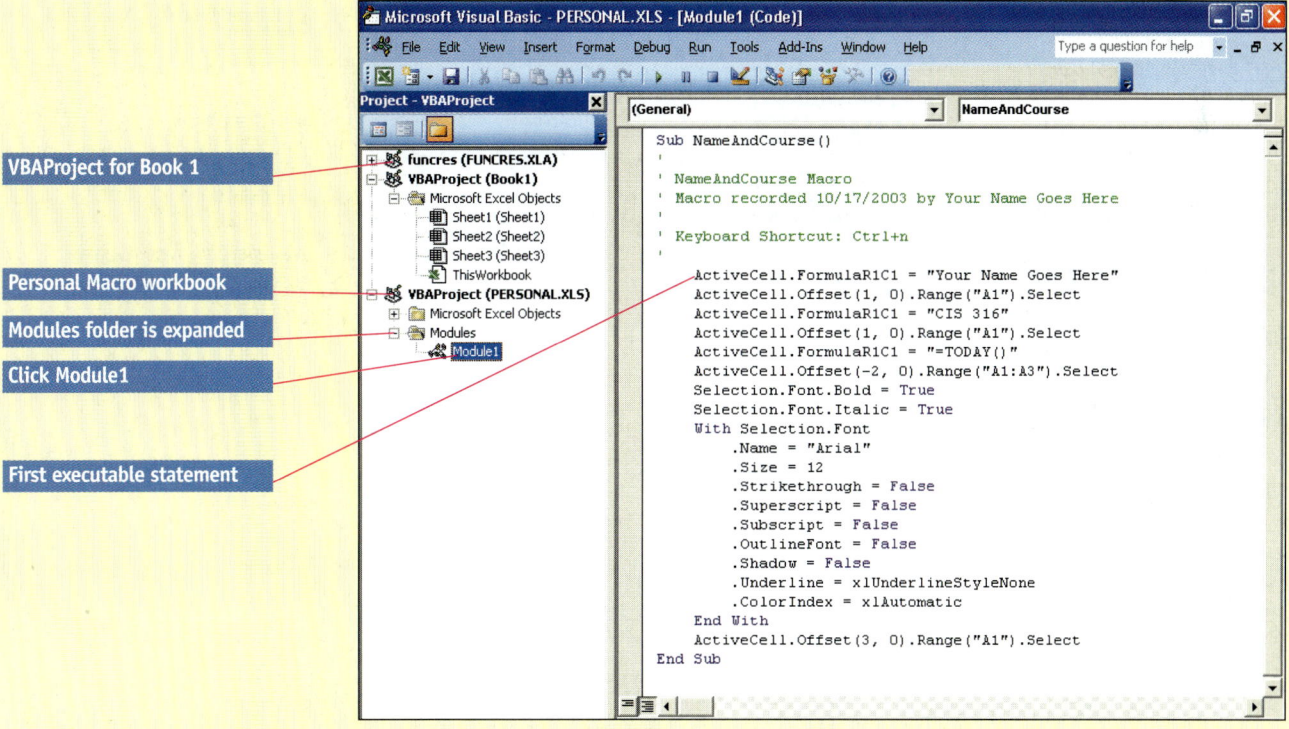

(c) The Visual Basic Editor (step 3)

FIGURE 8.4 Hands-on Exercise 2 (*continued*)

WHAT DOES RANGE ("A1:A3") REALLY MEAN?

The statement ActiveCell.Offset (–2,0).Range ("A1:A3").Select has nothing to do with cells A1 through A3, so why is the entry Range ("A1:A3") included? The effect of the statement is to select three cells (one cell under the other) starting with the cell two rows above the current cell. The offset (–2,0) specifies the starting point of the selected range (two rows above the current cell). The range ("A1:A3") indicates the size and shape of the selected range (a vertical column of three cells).

Step 4: **Edit the Macro**

- Click and drag to select the name of the course, which is found in the third executable statement of the macro. Be sure to include the quotation marks (e.g., "CIS316" in our example) in your selection.

- Enter **InputBox("Enter the Course You Are Taking")** to replace the selected text. Note that as you enter the Visual Basic keyword, *InputBox*, a prompt (containing the correct syntax for this statement) is displayed on the screen as shown in Figure 8.4d.

- Just ignore the prompt and keep typing to complete the entry. Press the **Home key** when you complete the entry to scroll back to the beginning of the line.

- Click immediately after the number **12**, then click and drag to select the next seven statements. Press the **Del key** to delete the highlighted statements from the macro.

- Delete the **Selection.Font.Bold=True** statement. Click the **Save button** to save the modified macro.

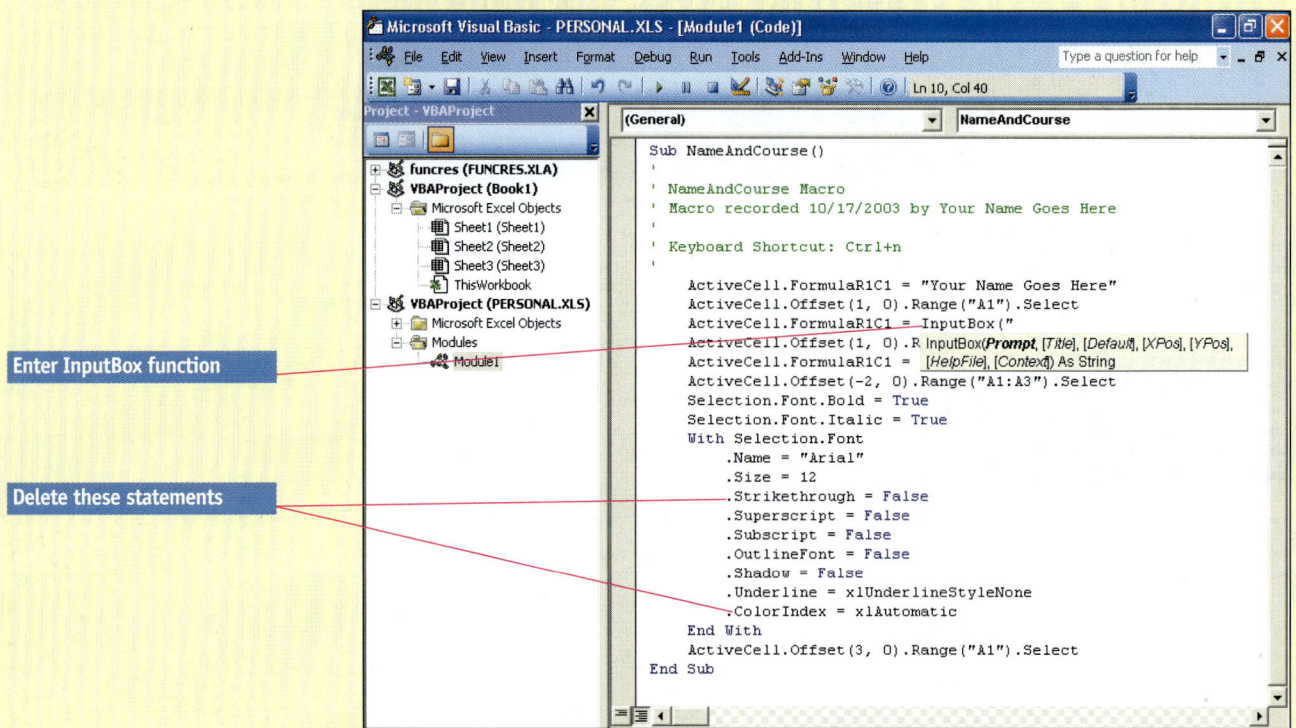

(d) Edit the Macro (step 4)

FIGURE 8.4 Hands-on Exercise 2 (*continued*)

THE INPUTBOX FUNCTION

The InputBox function adds flexibility to a macro by obtaining input from the user when the macro is executed. It is used in this example to generalize the NameAndCourse macro by asking the user for the name of the course, as opposed to storing the name within the macro. The InputBox function, coupled with storing the macro in the Personal Macro workbook, enables the user to personalize any workbook by executing the associated macro.

Step 5: Test the Revised Macro

- Press **Alt+F11** to view the Excel workbook. Click in any cell—for example, **cell C5** as shown in Figure 8.4e.

- Pull down the **Tools menu**. Click **Macro**, click the **Macros . . . command**, select **PERSONAL.XLS!NameAndCourse**, then click the **Run command button** to run the macro. (Alternatively you can use the **Ctrl+n** shortcut.)

- The macro enters your name in cell C5 (the active cell), selects the cell one row below, then displays the input dialog box shown in Figure 8.4e.

- Enter any appropriate course and press the **Enter key**. You should see the course you entered followed by the date. All three entries will be formatted according to the commands you specified in the macro.

- Click in a different cell, then press **Ctrl+n** to rerun the macro. The macro will enter your name, the course you specify, and the date in the selected location because it was recorded with relative references.

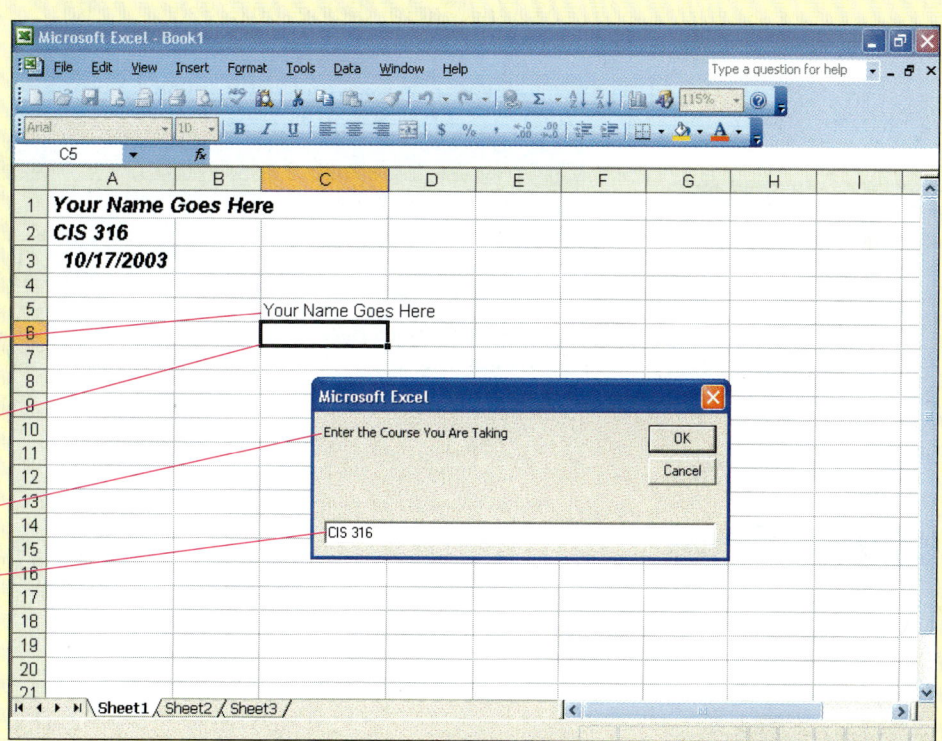

(e) Test the Revised Macro (step 5)

FIGURE 8.4 Hands-on Exercise 2 (*continued*)

RED, GREEN, AND BLUE

Visual Basic automatically assigns different colors to different types of statements (or a portion of those statements). Any statement containing a syntax error appears in red. Comments appear in green. Keywords—such as Sub and End Sub, With and End With, and True and False—appear in blue. The different colors are intended to make the code easier to read. Indentation and/or blank lines can also improve readability.

Step 6: **Add a Custom Button**

- Point to any toolbar, then click the **right mouse button** to display a shortcut menu. Click **Customize** to display the Customize dialog box in Figure 8.4f.

- Click the **Commands tab**. Click the **down arrow** to scroll through the Categories list box until you can select the **Macros category**.

- Click and drag the **Custom (Happy Face) button** to an available space at the right of the Standard toolbar. Release the mouse. (You must drag the button *within* the toolbar.)

- Click the **Modify Selection button** within the Customize dialog box to display the cascaded menu in Figure 8.4f.

- Click and drag to select the name of the button (&Custom Button) and replace it with **NameAndCourse**, to create a ScreenTip for that button. Do not press the Enter key.

- Click the **Assign Macro command** at the bottom of the menu to display the Assign Macro dialog box. Select **PERSONAL.XLS!NameAndCourse** and click **OK**.

- Click **Close** to exit the Custom dialog box.

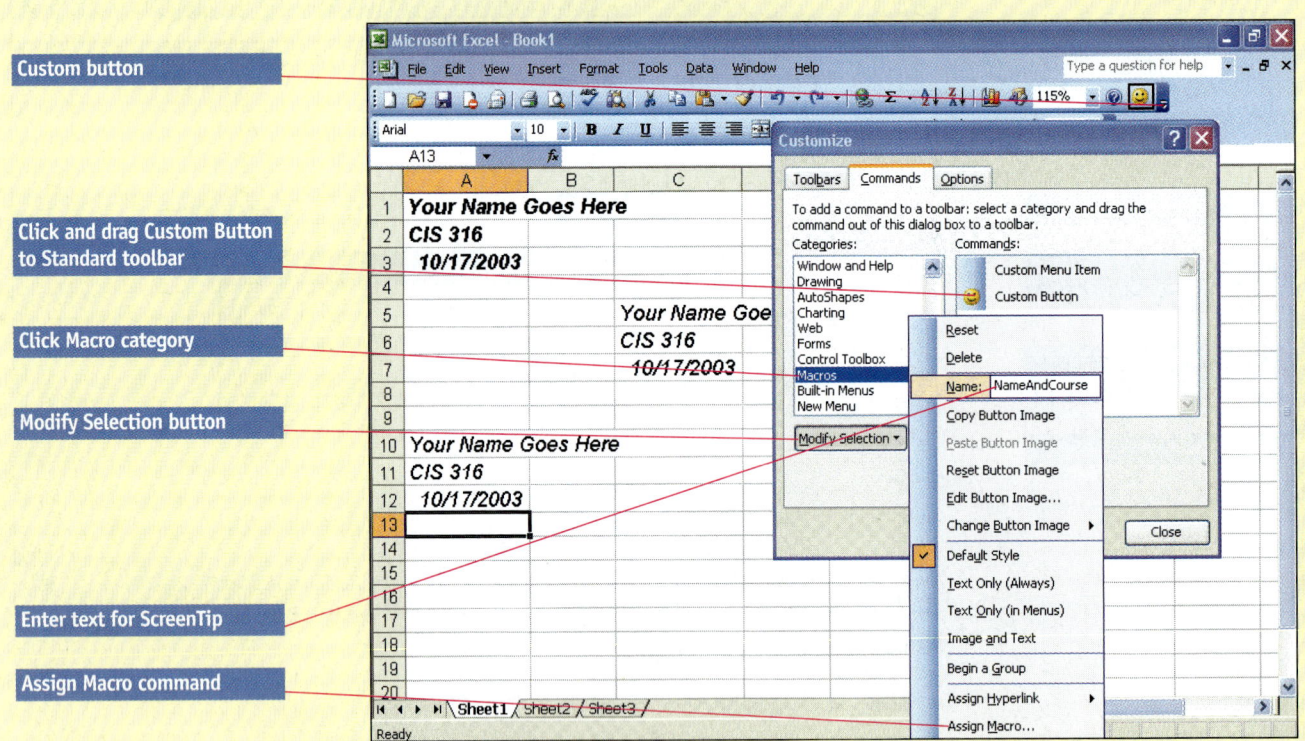

(f) Add a Custom Button (step 6)

FIGURE 8.4 Hands-on Exercise 2 (*continued*)

CUSTOMIZE THE TOOLBAR OR A MENU

You can customize any toolbar or menu to display additional buttons or commands as appropriate. Pull down the View menu, click Toolbars, click Customize to display the Customize dialog box, then click the Commands tab. Choose the category containing the button or command you want, then click and drag that object to an existing toolbar or menu.

Step 7: **Test the Custom Button**

- Click the **New button** on the Standard toolbar to open a new workbook (Book2 in Figure 8.4g; the book number is not important). Click **cell B2** as the active cell from which to execute the macro.

- Point to the **Happy Face button** to display the ScreenTip you just created. The ScreenTip will be useful in future sessions should you forget the function of this button.

- Click the **Happy Face button** to execute the NameAndCourse macro. Enter the name of a course you are taking. The macro inserts your name, course, and today's date in cells B2 through B4.

- Pull down the **File menu** and click the **Exit command** to exit the program.

- Click **No** when prompted to save the changes to Book1 and/or Book2, the workbooks you created in this exercise. Click **Yes** if asked to save the changes to the Personal Workbook.

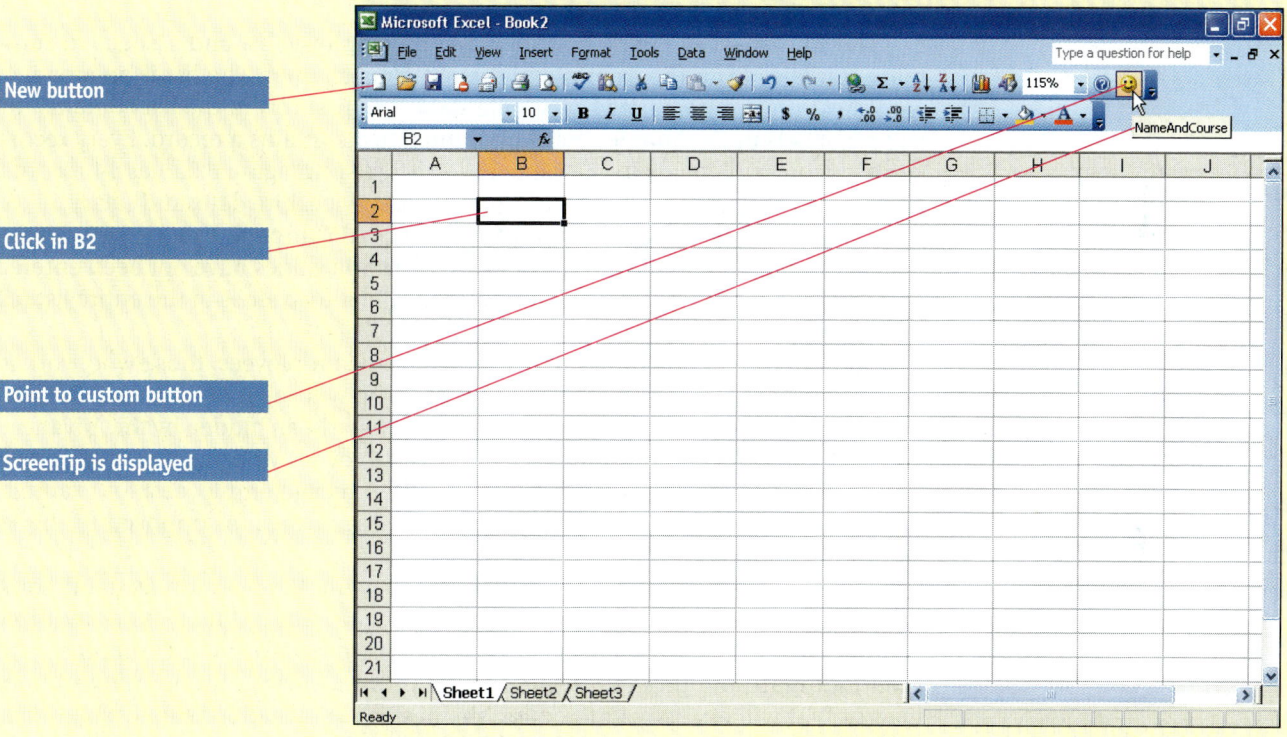

(g) Test the Custom Button (step 7)

FIGURE 8.4 Hands-on Exercise 2 (*continued*)

CHANGE THE CUSTOM BUTTON ICON

The Happy Face icon is automatically associated with the Custom Macro button. You can, however, change the image after the button has been added to a toolbar. Right click the button and click Customize to display the Customize dialog box, which must remain open to change the image. Right click the button a second time to display a different shortcut menu with commands pertaining to the specific button. Click the command to Change Button Image, select a new image, then close the Customize dialog box.

DATA MANAGEMENT MACROS

Thus far we have covered the basics of macros in the context of entering your name, course, and today's date into a worksheet. As you might expect, macros are capable of much more and can be used to automate any repetitive task. The next several pages illustrate the use of macros in conjunction with the list (data) management examples that were presented in an earlier chapter.

Data and information are not synonymous. Data is typically a fact (or facts) about a specific record (or set of records), such as an employee's name or title, or a list of all employees and their titles. Information is something more and refers to data that has been summarized, or otherwise rearranged, into a form perceived as useful by the recipient. A list of all the employees is considered raw data, whereas a subset of that list—such as the employees who worked in Chicago—could be thought of as information derived from that list. Information is also obtained by summarizing the data. Individual salaries are important to the employees who receive those salaries, whereas a manager is more interested in knowing the total of all salaries in order to make decisions. Macros can help in the conversion of data to information.

The worksheet in Figure 8.5a displays the employee list and associated summary statistics from the example in the previous chapter. The list is an area in a worksheet that contains rows of similar data. The first row in the list contains the column labels or field names. Each additional row contains a record. Every record contains the same fields in the same order. The list in Figure 8.5a has 14 records. Each record has six fields: name, location, title, service, hire date, and salary.

A criteria range has been established in cells A17 through F18 for use with the database functions in cells F22 through F26. Criteria values have not been entered in Figure 8.5a, and so the database functions reflect the values of the entire list (all 14 employees).

The worksheet in Figure 8.5b displays selected employees, those who work in Chicago. Look carefully at the worksheet and you will see that only rows 3, 9, 10, and 12 are visible. The other rows within the list have been hidden by the Advanced Filter command, which displays only those employees who satisfy the specified criteria. The summary statistics reflect only the Chicago employees; for example, the DCOUNT function in cell F26 shows four employees (as opposed to the 14 employees in Figure 8.5a).

The previous chapter described how to execute the list management commands to filter the list. The process is not difficult, but it does require multiple commands and keystrokes. Our purpose here is to review those commands and then automate the process through creation of a series of data management macros that will enable you to obtain the desired information with a single click. We begin by reviewing the commands that would be necessary to modify the worksheet in Figure 8.5b to show managers rather than the Chicago employees.

The first step is to clear the existing criterion (Chicago) in cell B18, then enter the new criterion (Manager) in cell C18. You would then execute the Advanced Filter command, which requires the specification of the list (cells A1 through F15), the location of the criteria range (cells A17 through F18), and the option to filter the list in place.

And what if you wanted to see the Chicago employees after you executed the commands to display the managers? You would have to repeat all of the previous commands to change the criterion back to what it was, then filter the list accordingly. Suffice it to say that the entire process can be simplified through creation of the appropriate macros.

The following exercise develops the macro to select the Chicago employees from the worksheet in Figure 8.5a. A subsequent exercise develops two additional macros, one to select the managers and another to select the managers who work in Chicago.

All of the macros use the concept of a ***named range*** to establish a mnemonic name (e.g., database) for a cell range (e.g., A1:F15). The advantage of using a named range in a macro over the associated cell reference is twofold. First, the macro is easier to read. Second, and perhaps more important, a named range adjusts automatically for insertions and/or deletions within the worksheet, whereas a cell reference remains constant. Thus, the use of a named range makes the macro immune to changes in the worksheet in that the macro references a flexible "database," as opposed to a fixed cell range. You can add or delete employee records within the list, and the macro will still work.

Field names are in first row of list →

	A	B	C	D	E	F
1	**Name**	**Location**	**Title**	**Service**	**Hire Date**	**Salary**
2	Adams	Atlanta	Trainee	4.6	11/24/98	$29,500
3	Adamson	Chicago	Manager	4.3	3/16/99	$52,000
4	Brown	Atlanta	Trainee	4.6	11/24/98	$28,500
5	Charles	Boston	Account Rep	4.3	3/16/99	$40,000
6	Coulter	Atlanta	Manager	4.6	11/24/98	$100,000
7	Elofson	Miami	Account Rep	1.7	10/31/01	$47,500
8	Gillenson	Miami	Account Rep	0.7	10/31/02	$55,000
9	James	Chicago	Account Rep	4.7	10/31/98	$42,500
10	Johnson	Chicago	Account Rep	3.7	10/31/99	$47,500
11	Manin	Boston	Account Rep	4.3	3/16/99	$49,500
12	Marder	Chicago	Account Rep	2.7	10/31/00	$38,500
13	Milgrom	Boston	Manager	4.3	3/16/99	$57,500
14	Rubin	Boston	Account Rep	4.3	3/16/99	$45,000
15	Smith	Atlanta	Account Rep	4.6	11/24/98	$65,000
16						
17	**Name**	**Location**	**Title**	**Service**	**Hire Date**	**Salary**
18						
19						
20						
21			**Summary Statistics**			
22	Average Salary					$49,857
23	Maximum Salary					$100,000
24	Minimum Salary					$28,500
25	Total Salary					$698,000
26	Number of Employees					14

Criteria range (A17:F18) → (row 17)

Database functions (F22:F26) → (rows 22–26)

(a) All Employees

Filtered list (Chicago employees) →

	A	B	C	D	E	F
1	**Name**	**Location**	**Title**	**Service**	**Hire Date**	**Salary**
3	Adamson	Chicago	Manager	4.3	3/16/99	$52,000
9	James	Chicago	Account Rep	4.7	10/31/98	$42,500
10	Johnson	Chicago	Account Rep	3.7	10/31/99	$47,500
12	Marder	Chicago	Account Rep	2.7	10/31/00	$38,500
16						
17	**Name**	**Location**	**Title**	**Service**	**Hire Date**	**Salary**
18		Chicago				
19						
20						
21			**Summary Statistics**			
22	Average Salary					$45,125
23	Maximum Salary					$52,000
24	Minimum Salary					$38,500
25	Total Salary					$180,500
26	Number of Employees					4

Criterion is Chicago → (B18)

Database functions reflect data for Chicago employees only → (rows 22–26)

(b) Chicago Employees

FIGURE 8.5 Data Management Macros

hands-on exercise

3 Data Management Macros

Objective To create a data management macro in conjunction with an employee list; to create a custom button to execute a macro. Use Figure 8.6 as a guide in completing the exercise.

Step 1: **Data Management Functions**

- Start Excel. Open the **Employee List Solution workbook** that was created in the previous chapter on data management.

- Click anywhere within the employee list. Pull down the **Data Menu**, click **Subtotals**, and click the **Remove All button**.

- Click any cell between A2 and A15, then click the **Sort Ascending button** on the Standard toolbar. The employees should be listed in alphabetical order as shown in Figure 8.6a.

- Clear all entries in the range **A18 through F18**.

- Click in **cell F22**, which contains the DAVERAGE function, to compute the average salary of all employees who satisfy the specified criteria. No criteria have been entered, however, so the displayed value of $49,857 represents the average salary of all 14 employees.

- Click **cell B18**. Enter **Chicago**. Press **Enter**. The average salary changes to $45,125 to indicate the average salary of the four Chicago employees.

- Click **cell C18**. Enter **Manager**. Press **Enter**. The average salary changes to $52,000 to indicate the average salary of the one Chicago manager.

- Save the workbook.

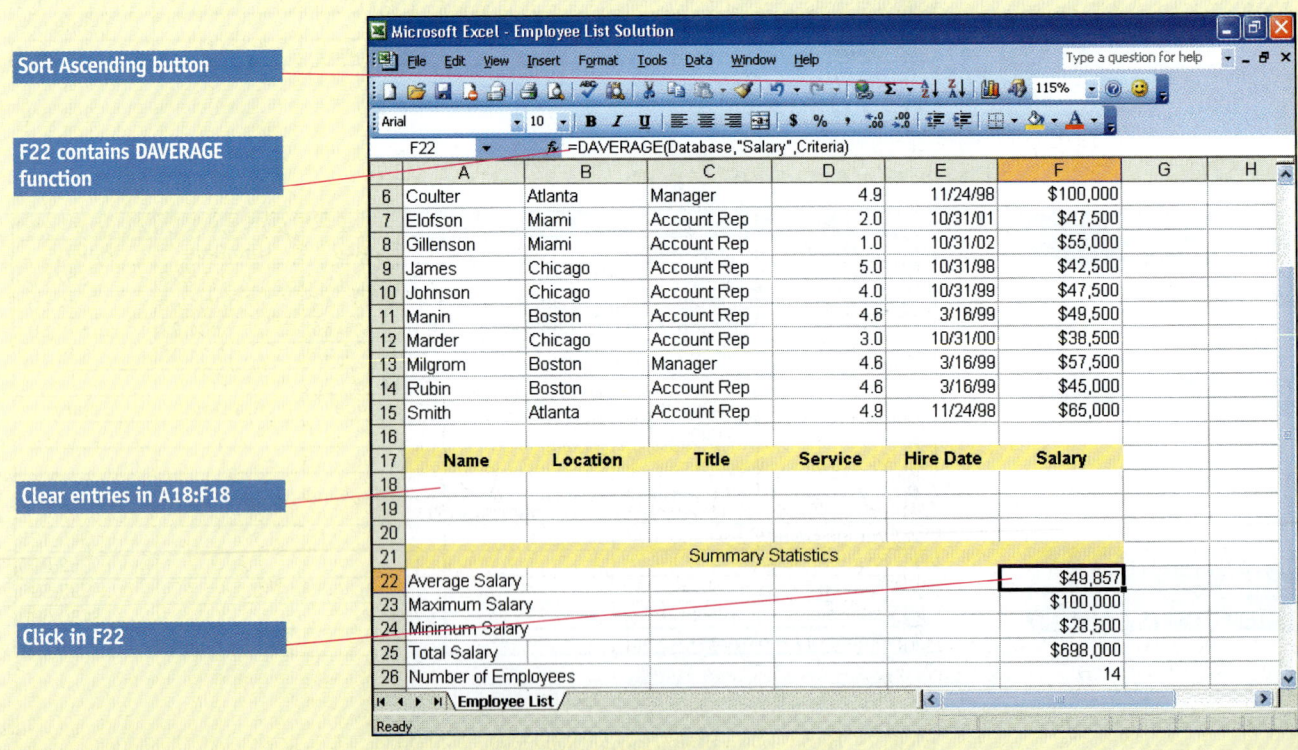

(a) Data Management Functions (step 1)

FIGURE 8.6 Hands-on Exercise 3

1382 CHAPTER 8: AUTOMATING REPETITIVE TASKS

Step 2: **The Create Name Command**

- Click and drag to select **cells A17 through F18** as shown in Figure 8.6b. Pull down the **Insert menu**, click **Name**, then click **Create** to display the Create Names dialog box.

- The box to **Create Names in Top Row is already checked. Click OK**. This command assigns the text in each cell in row 17 to the corresponding cell in row 18; for example, cells B18 and C18 will be assigned the names Location and Title, respectively.

- Click and drag to select only **cells A18 through F18**. (You need to assign a name to these seven cells collectively, as you will have to clear the criteria values in row 18 later in the chapter.)

- Pull down the **Insert menu**. Click **Name**. Click **Define**. Enter **CriteriaValues** in the Define Name dialog box. Click **OK**.

- Save the workbook.

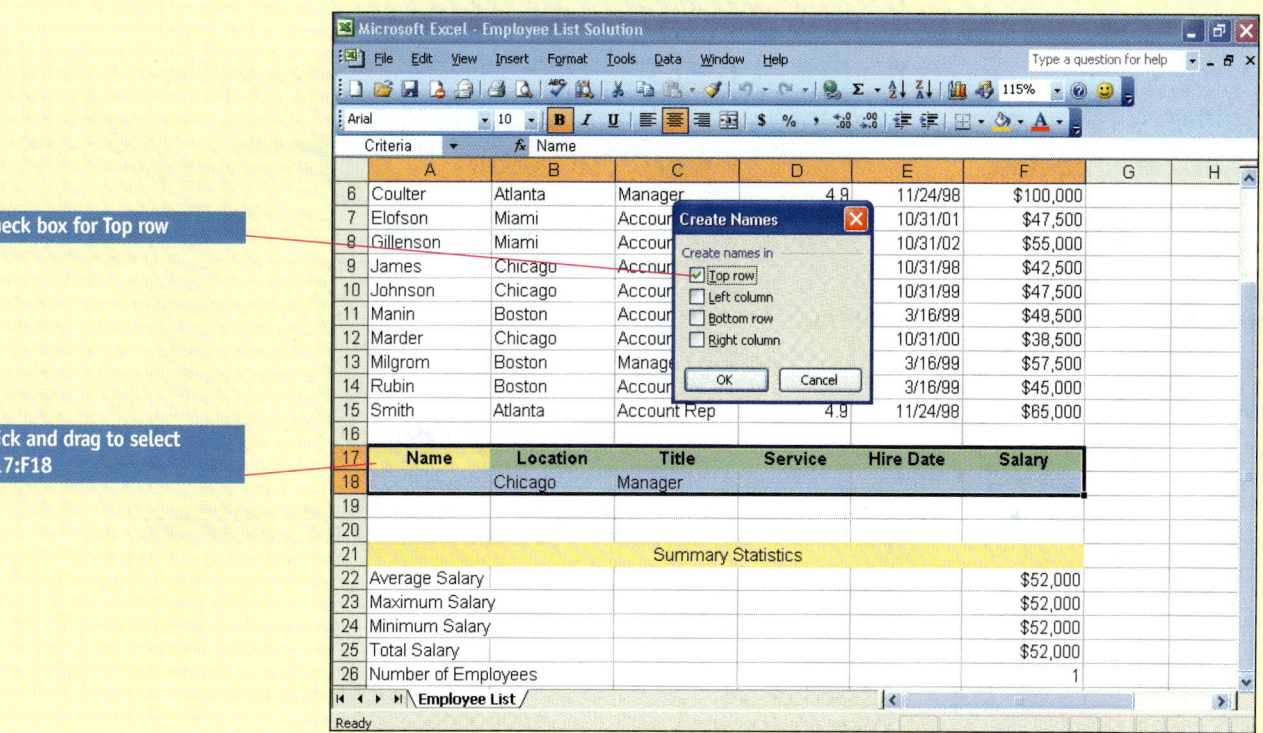

(b) The Create Name Command (step 2)

FIGURE 8.6 Hands-on Exercise 3 (*continued*)

CREATE SEVERAL NAMES AT ONCE

The Insert menu contains two different commands to create named ranges. The Insert Name Define command affects only one cell or range at a time, then has you enter the name into a dialog box. The Insert Name Create command requires you to select adjacent rows or columns, then assigns multiple names from the adjacent row or column in one command. The latter command is very useful in assigning range names within a criteria range.

Step 3: **The Go To Command**

- Pull down the **Edit menu**. Click **Go To** to produce the Go To dialog box in Figure 8.6c. If you do not see the command, click the double arrow to display more commands.

- You should see the names you defined (CriteriaValues, Hire_Date, Location, Name, Salary, Service, and Title) as well as the two names defined previously by the authors (Criteria and Database).

- Click **Database**. Click **OK**. Cells A1 through F15 should be selected, corresponding to cells assigned to the name *Database*.

- Press the **F5 key** (a shortcut for the Edit Go To command), which again produces the Go To dialog box. Click **Criteria**. Click **OK**. Cells A17 through F18 should be selected.

- Click the **drop-down arrow** next to the Name box. Click **Location**. Cell B18 should be selected.

- You are now ready to record the macro.

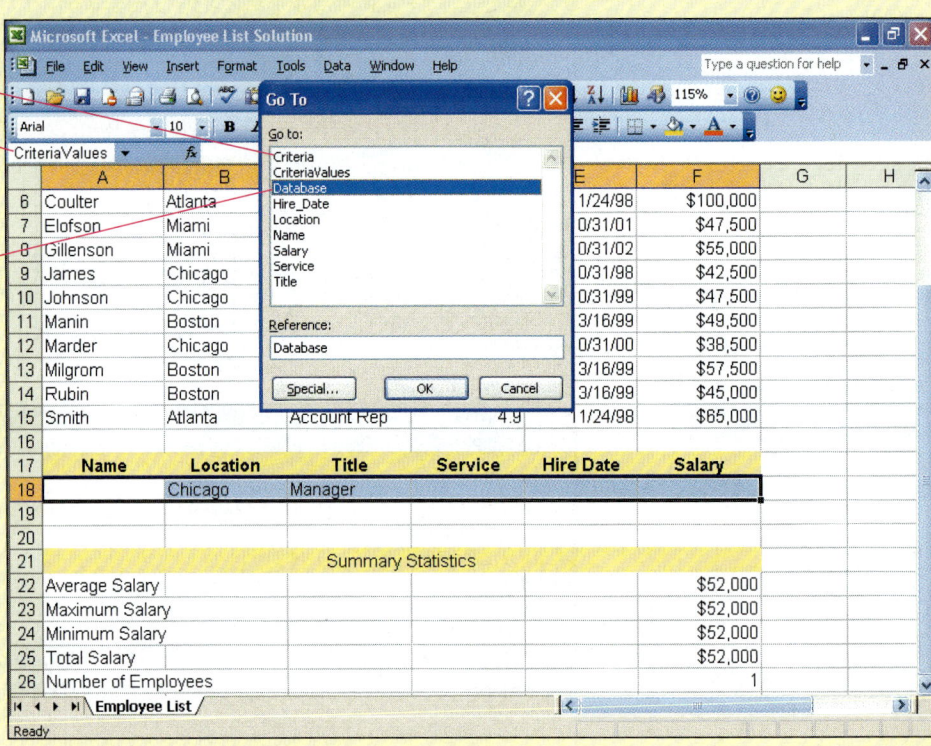

(c) The Go To Command (step 3)

FIGURE 8.6 Hands-on Exercise 3 (*continued*)

THE NAME BOX

Use the Name box (at the left of the Formula bar) to define a range name by selecting the cell(s) in the worksheet to which the name is to apply, clicking the Name box, then entering the name. For example, to assign the name CriteriaValues to cells A18:F18, select the range, click in the Name box, type CriteriaValues, and press Enter. The Name box can also be used to select a previously defined range by clicking the drop-down arrow next to the box and choosing the desired name from the drop-down list.

Step 4: **Record the Macro (Edit Clear command)**

- Pull down the **Tools menu**, click the **Macro command**, then click **Record New Macro** to display the Record Macro dialog box.

- Enter **Chicago** in the Macro Name text box. Verify that the macro will be stored in **This Workbook** and then make sure that the shortcut key text box is empty.

- Click **OK** to begin recording the macro. If necessary, click the **Relative References button** on the Stop Recording toolbar to record Absolute references (the button should be out).

- Pull down the **Edit menu**, click **Go To**, select **CriteriaValues** from the Go To dialog box, and click **OK**. Cells A18 through F18 should be selected as shown in Figure 8.6d. (Alternatively, you can also use the **F5 key** or the **Name box** to select CriteriaValues.)

- Pull down the **Edit menu**. Click **Clear**, then click **All** from the cascaded menu as shown in Figure 8.6d. Cells A18 through F18 (the criteria range) should be empty, and a new criterion can be entered through the macro.

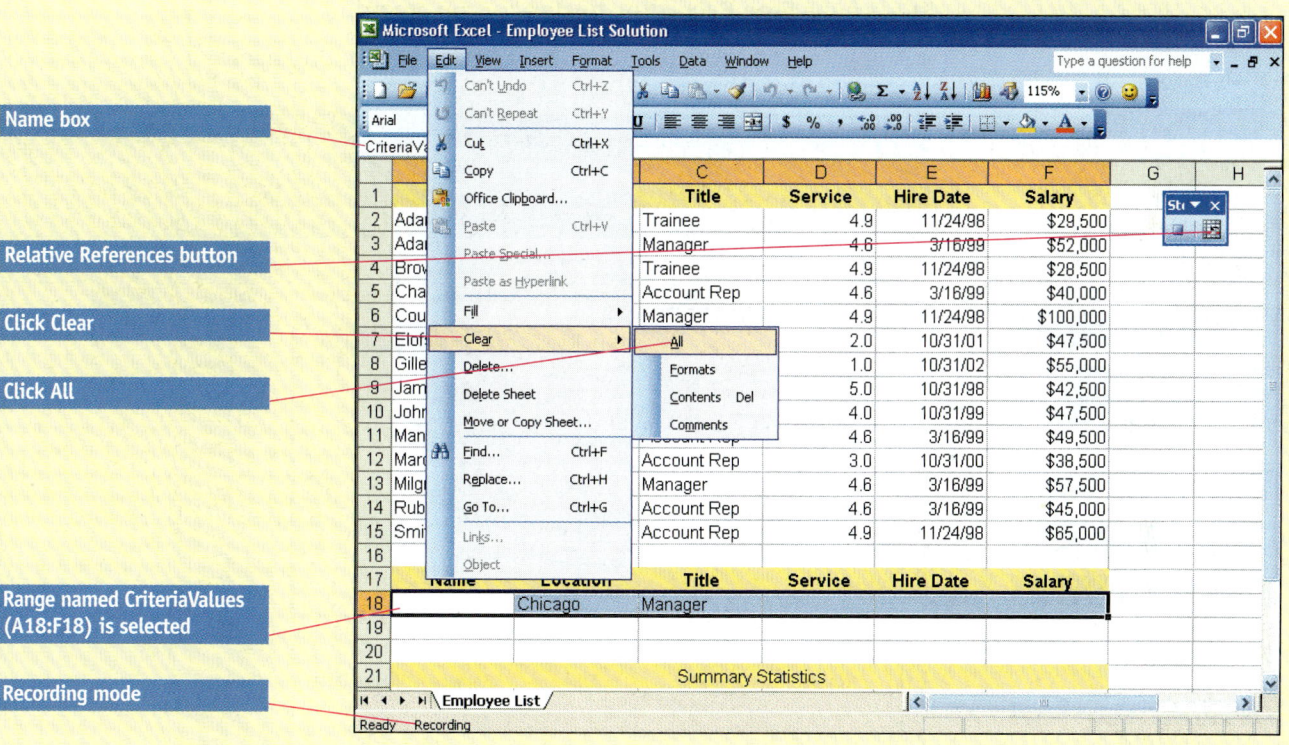

(d) Record the Macro (Edit Clear command) (step 4)

FIGURE 8.6 Hands-on Exercise 3 (*continued*)

GOOD MACROS ARE FLEXIBLE MACROS

The macro to select Chicago employees has to be completely general and work under all circumstances, regardless of what may appear initially in the criteria row. Thus, you have to clear the entire criteria range prior to entering "Chicago" in the Location column. Note, too, the use of range names (e.g., CriteriaValues), as opposed to specific cells (e.g., A18:F18 in this example) to accommodate potential additions or deletions to the employee list. (A macro does not update cell references within its statements to accommodate insertions and/or deletions of rows and columns in the associated worksheet. It is good practice, therefore, to always use range names, as opposed to cell references, within a macro.)

Step 5: **Record the Macro (Advanced Filter command)**

- Pull down the **Edit menu**, click **Go To**, select **Location** from the Go to dialog box, and click **OK**.

- Cell B18 should be selected. Enter **Chicago** to establish the criterion for both the database functions and the Advanced Filter command.

- Click in **cell B2** to position the active cell within the employee list. Pull down the **Data menu**. Click **Filter**, then click **Advanced Filter** from the cascaded menu to display the dialog box in Figure 8.6e.

- Enter **Database** as the List Range. Press the **tab key**. Enter **Criteria** as the Criteria Range.

- Check that the option to **Filter the list, in-place** is checked.

- Click **OK**. You should see only those employees who satisfy the current criteria (i.e., Adamson, James, Johnson, and Marder, who are the employees who work in Chicago).

- Click the **Stop Recording button** to stop recording.

- Click the **Save button** to save the workbook with the macro.

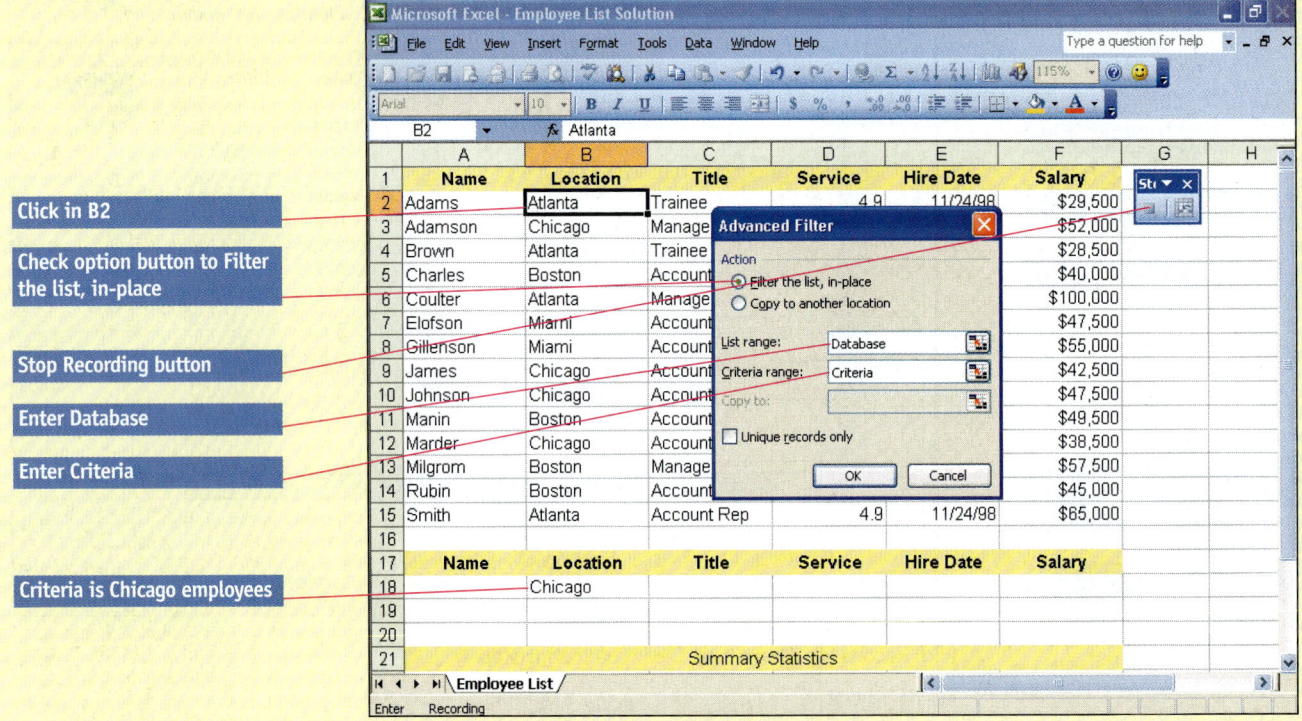

(e) Record the Macro (Advanced Filter command) (step 5)

FIGURE 8.6 Hands-on Exercise 3 (*continued*)

THE FILTER VERSUS THE DATABASE FUNCTIONS

Change the criteria—for example, from Chicago to Chicago Managers—and the values displayed by the database functions (DAVERAGE, DSUM, and so on) change automatically. The filtered records do not change, however, until you reexecute the command to filter the records in place. The advantage of a macro becomes immediately apparent, because the macro is built to change the criteria and filter the records with a single click of the mouse.

Step 6: **View the Macro**

- Press **Alt+F11** to open the Visual Basic editor as shown in Figure 8.6f. If necessary, pull down the **View menu**. Click **Project Explorer** to open the Project window in the left pane.

- If necessary, expand the **Modules folder**, under the VBA project for Employee List Solution. Click (select) **Module1**, pull down the **View menu**, and click **Code** to display the code for the Chicago macro in the right pane. Maximize the Code window.

- Close any other open windows within the Visual Basic Editor. Your screen should match the one in Figure 8.6f. If necessary, correct your macro so that it matches ours.

- If the correction is minor, it is easiest to edit the macro directly; otherwise delete the macro, then return to step 4 and rerecord the macro from the beginning. (To delete a macro, pull down the Tools menu, click **Macro**, click **Macros...**, select the macro you wish to delete, then click the **Delete button**.)

- Click the **View Microsoft Excel button** at the left of the toolbar or press **Alt+F11** to return to the Employee worksheet.

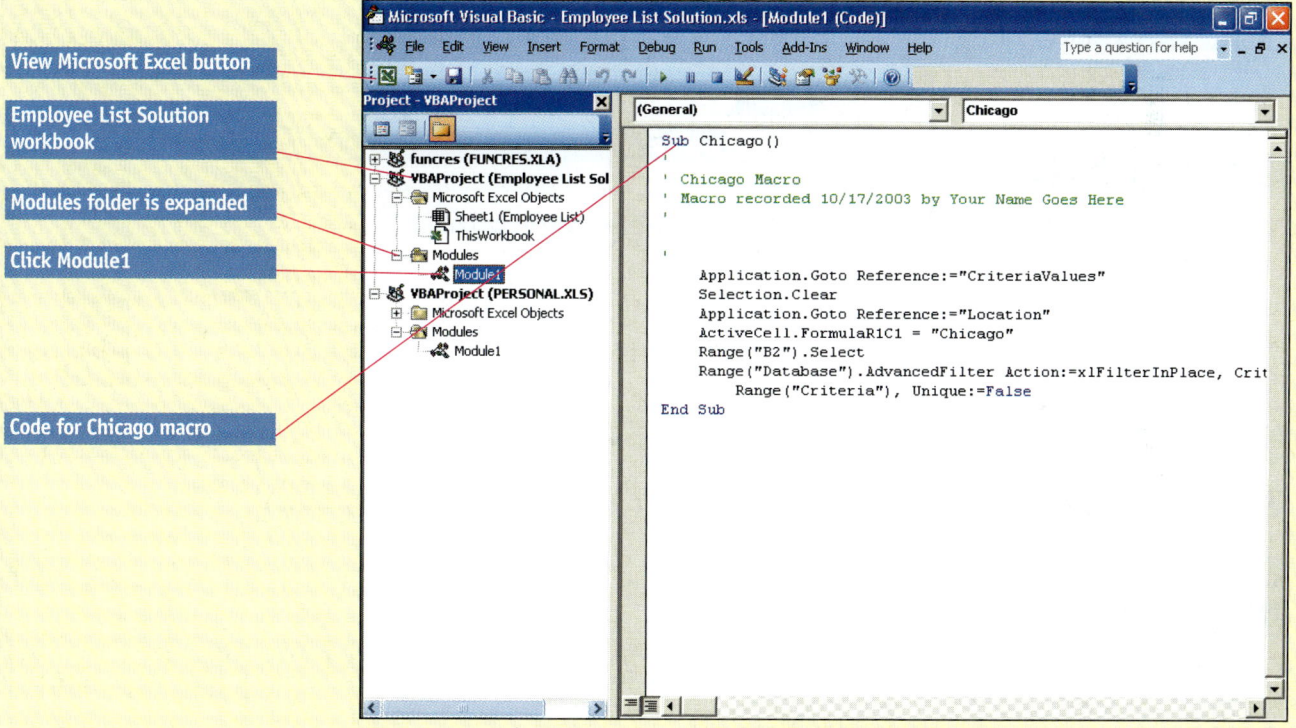

(f) View the Macro (step 6)

FIGURE 8.6 Hands-on Exercise 3 (*continued*)

THE VISUAL BASIC TOOLBAR

The Visual Basic Toolbar consists of seven buttons associated with macros and Visual Basic. You will find a button to run an existing macro, to record (or stop recording) a new macro, and to open (toggle to) the Visual Basic Editor. The toolbar can be displayed (or hidden) by right clicking any visible toolbar, then checking (or clearing) Visual Basic from the list of toolbars.

Step 7: **Assign the Macro**

- Pull down the **View menu**, click **Toolbars**, then click **Forms** to display the Forms toolbar as shown in Figure 8.6g.

- Click the **Button tool** (the mouse pointer changes to a tiny crosshair). Click and drag in the worksheet as shown in Figure 8.6g to draw a command button on the worksheet.

- Be sure to draw the button *below* the employee list, or the button may be hidden when a subsequent Data Filter command is executed.

- Release the mouse, and the Assign Macro dialog box will appear. Choose **Chicago** (the macro you just created) from the list of macro names. Click **OK**.

- The button should still be selected. Click and drag to select the name of the button, **Button 1**.

- Type **Chicago** as the new name. Do *not* press the Enter key. Click outside the button to deselect it.

- Save the workbook.

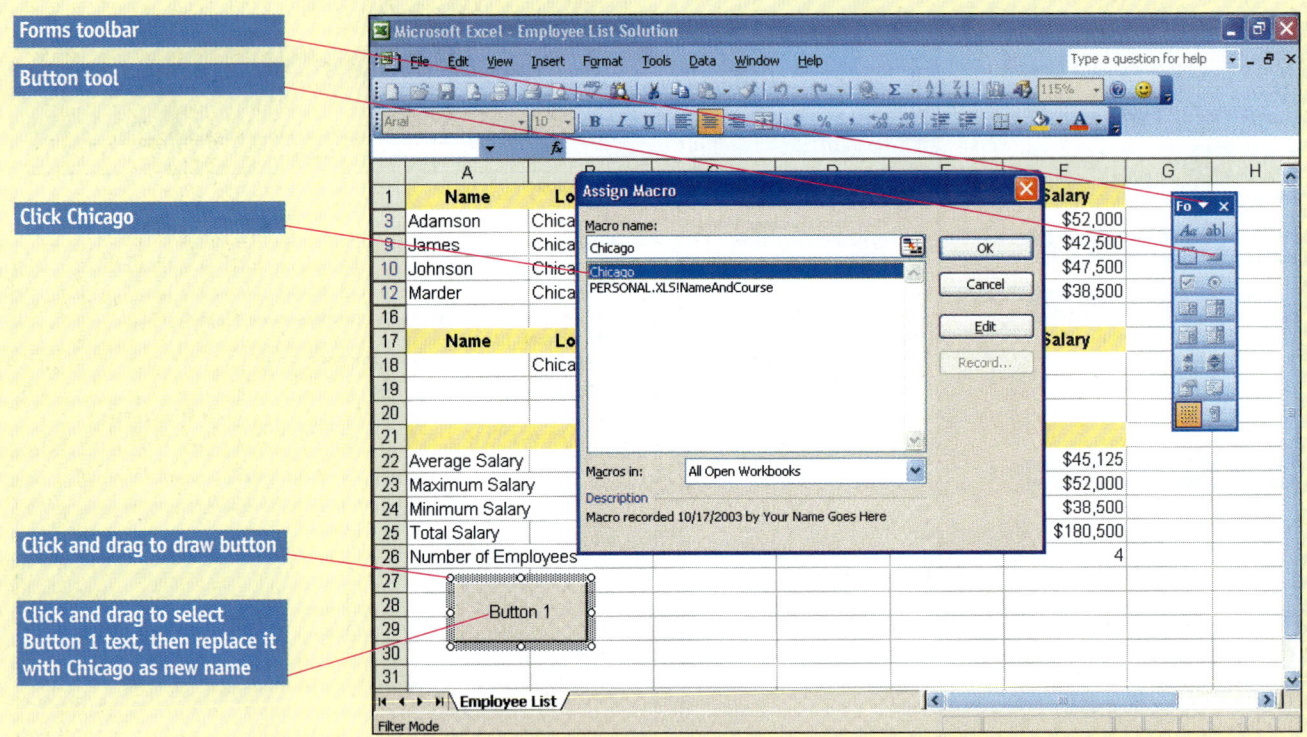

(g) Assign the Macro (step 7)

FIGURE 8.6 Hands-on Exercise 3 (*continued*)

SELECTING A BUTTON

You cannot select a Macro button by clicking it, because that executes the associated macro. Thus, to select a macro button, you must press and hold the Ctrl key as you click the mouse. (You can also select a button by clicking the right mouse button to produce a shortcut menu.) Once the button has been selected, you can edit its name, and/or move or size the button just as you can any other Windows object.

Step 8: **Test the Macro**

- Pull down the **Data menu**, click **Filter**, then click **Show All**.
- Click **cell B12**. Enter **Miami** to change the location for Marder. Press **Enter**. The number of employees in the summary statistics area changes, as do the results of the other summary statistics.
- Click the **Chicago button** as shown in Figure 8.6h to execute the macro. Marder is *not* listed this time because she is no longer in Chicago.
- Pull down the **Data menu**. Click **Filter**. Click **Show All** to display the entire employee list.
- Click **cell B12**. Enter **Chicago** to change the location for this employee back to Chicago. Press **Enter**. Click the **Chicago button** to execute the macro a second time. Marder is once again displayed with the Chicago employees.
- Pull down the **Data menu**. Click **Filter**. Click **Show All**.
- You do not have to print the workbook at this time, since we will print the entire workbook at the end of the next exercise.
- Save the workbook. Exit Excel if you do not want to continue with the next exercise at this time.

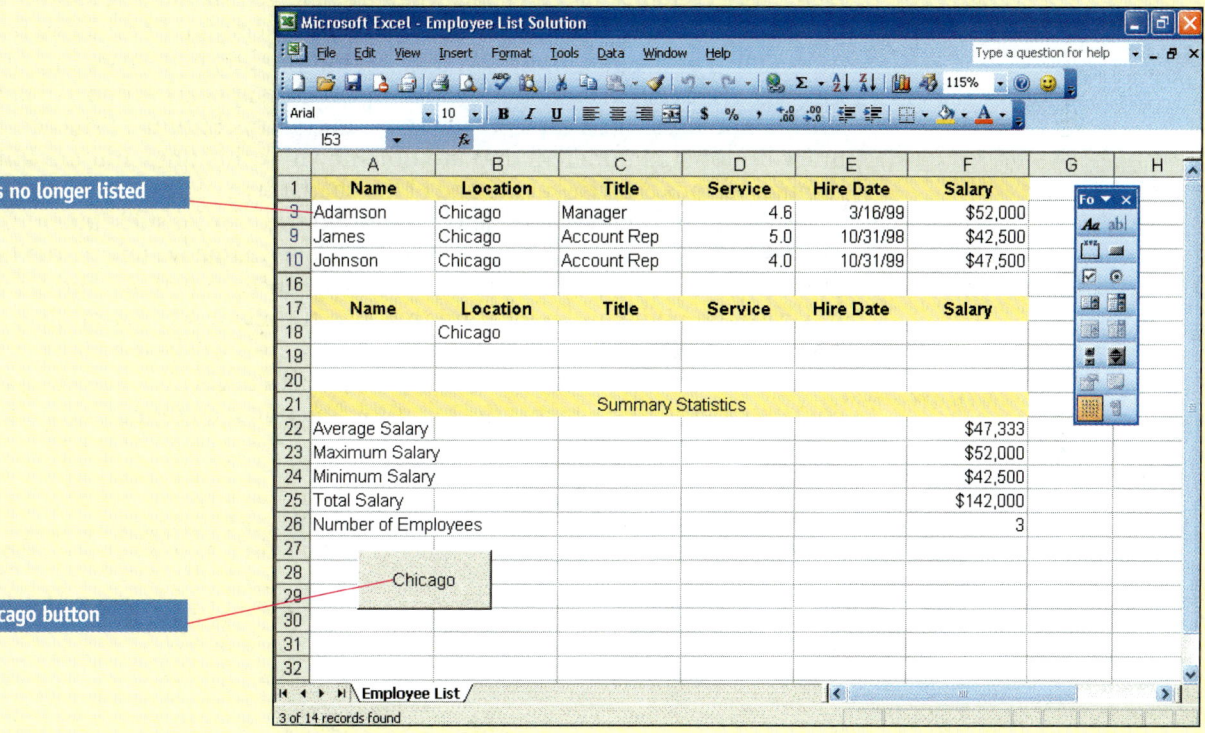

(h) Test the Macro (step 8)

FIGURE 8.6 Hands-on Exercise 3 (*continued*)

EXECUTING A MACRO

There are several different ways to execute a macro. The most basic way is to pull down the Tools menu, click Macro, click Macros . . . to display the Macros dialog box, then double click the desired macro to run it. You can assign a macro to a button within a worksheet or to a custom button on a toolbar, then click the button to run the macro. The fastest way is to use a keyboard shortcut, provided that a shortcut has been defined.

VISUAL BASIC FOR APPLICATIONS

Excel macros were originally nothing more than recorded keystrokes. Earlier versions of Excel had you turn on the macro recorder to capture the associated keystrokes, then "play back" those keystrokes when you ran the macro. Starting with Office 95, however, the recorded keystrokes were translated into Visual Basic commands, which made the macros potentially much more powerful because you could execute Visual Basic programs (known as procedures) from within Excel. (In actuality, Microsoft Office uses a subset of Visual Basic known as *Visual Basic for Applications (VBA)*, and we will use this terminology from now on.)

You can think of the macro recorder as a shortcut to generate the VBA code. Once you have that code, however, you can modify the various statements using techniques common to any programming language. You can move and/or copy statements within a procedure, search for one character string and replace it with another, and so on. And finally, you can insert additional VBA statements that are beyond the scope of ordinary Excel commands. You can, for example, display information to the user in the form of a message box any time during the execution of the macro. You can also accept information from the user into a dialog box for subsequent use in the macro.

Figure 8.7 illustrates the way that these tasks are accomplished in VBA. Figure 8.7a contains the VBA code, whereas Figures 8.7b and 8.7c show the resulting dialog boxes, as they would appear during execution of the associated VBA procedure. The **MsgBox statement** displays information to the user. The text of the message is entered in quotation marks, and the text appears within a dialog box as shown. The user clicks the OK command button to continue. (The MsgBox has other optional parameters that are not shown at this time, but are illustrated through various exercises at the end of the chapter.)

The InputBox function accepts input from the user for subsequent use in the procedure. Note the subtle change in terminology, in that we refer to the InputBox function, but the MsgBox statement. That is because a function returns a value, in this case the name of the location that was supplied by the user. That value is stored in the active cell within the worksheet, where it will be used later in the procedure. There is also a difference in syntax in that the MsgBox statement does not contain parentheses, whereas the InputBox function requires parentheses.

```
MsgBox "The MsgBox statement displays information"
ActiveCell.FormulaR1C1 = InputBox("Enter employee location")
```

(a) Visual Basic Statements

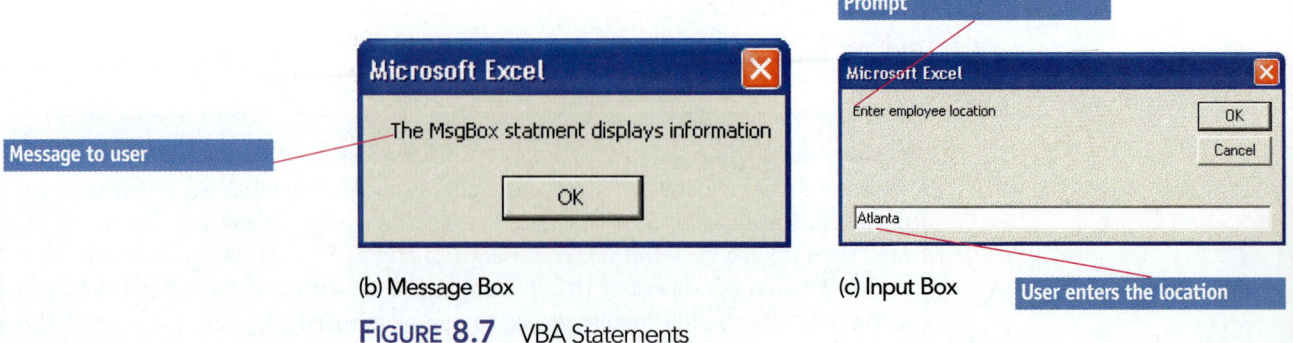

(b) Message Box   (c) Input Box

FIGURE 8.7 VBA Statements

hands-on exercise
4 Creating Additional Macros

Objective To duplicate an existing macro, then modify the copied macro to create an entirely new macro. Use Figure 8.8 as a guide.

Step 1: **Enable Macros**

- Start Excel. Open the **Employee List Solution workbook** from the previous exercise. You should see the warning in Figure 8.8a.
- Click the **More Info button** to display the Help window to learn more about macro virus prevention. (Pull down the **Tools menu**, click **Options**, click the **Security tab**, and click the **Macro Security button** if you do not see the warning message.)
- Click the **Close button** when you are finished reading the information.
- Click the **Enable Macros button** to open the Employee List Solution workbook.

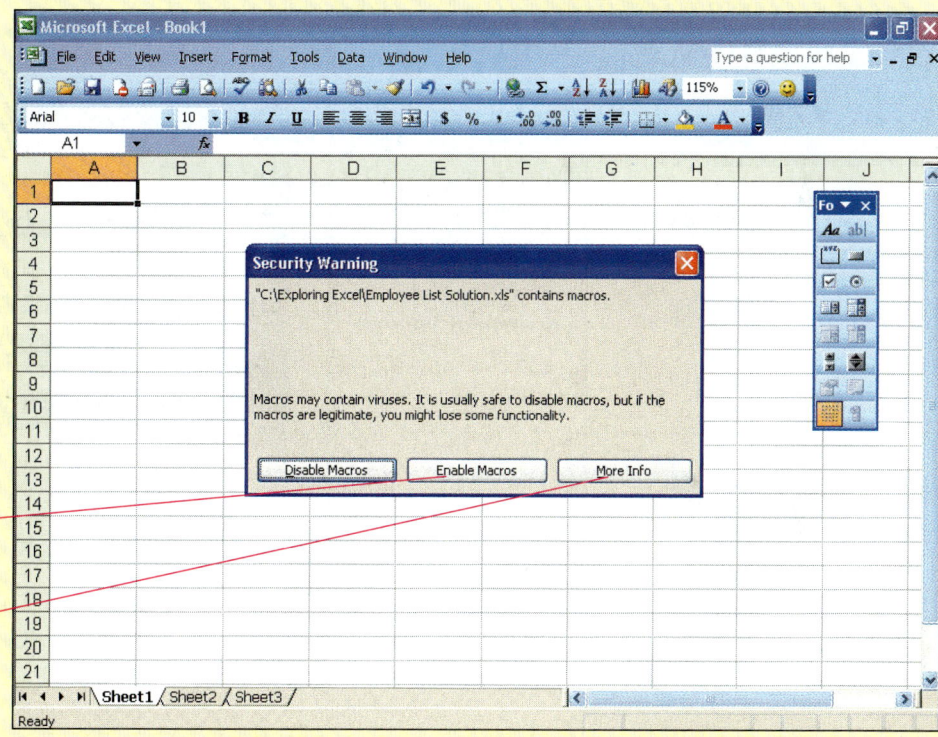

(a) Enable Macros (step 1)

FIGURE 8.8 Hands-on Exercise 4

MACRO SECURITY

A computer virus could take the form of an Excel macro in which case Excel will warn you that a workbook contains a macro, provided the security option is set appropriately. Pull down the Tools menu, click the Options command, click the Security tab, and then set the Macro Security to either High or Medium. High security disables all macros except those from a trusted source. Medium security gives you the option to enable macros. Click the button only if you are sure the macro is from a trusted source.

Step 2: **Copy the Chicago Macro**

- Pull down the **Tools menu**, click the **Macro command**, then click **Visual Basic Editor** (or press **Alt+F11**) to open the Visual Basic Editor.

- Click the **plus sign** on the Modules folder for the Employee List Solution project, select **Module1**, pull down the **View menu**, and click **Code**.

- Click and drag to select the entire Chicago macro as shown in Figure 8.8b.

- Pull down the **Edit menu** and click **Copy**, or press **Ctrl+C**, or click the **Copy button** on the Standard toolbar.

- Click below the End Sub statement to deselect the macro and simultaneously establish the position of the insertion point.

- Pull down the **Edit menu** and click **Paste**, or press **Ctrl+V**, or click the **Paste button** on the Standard toolbar.

- The Chicago macro has been copied and now appears twice in Module1.

- Save the module.

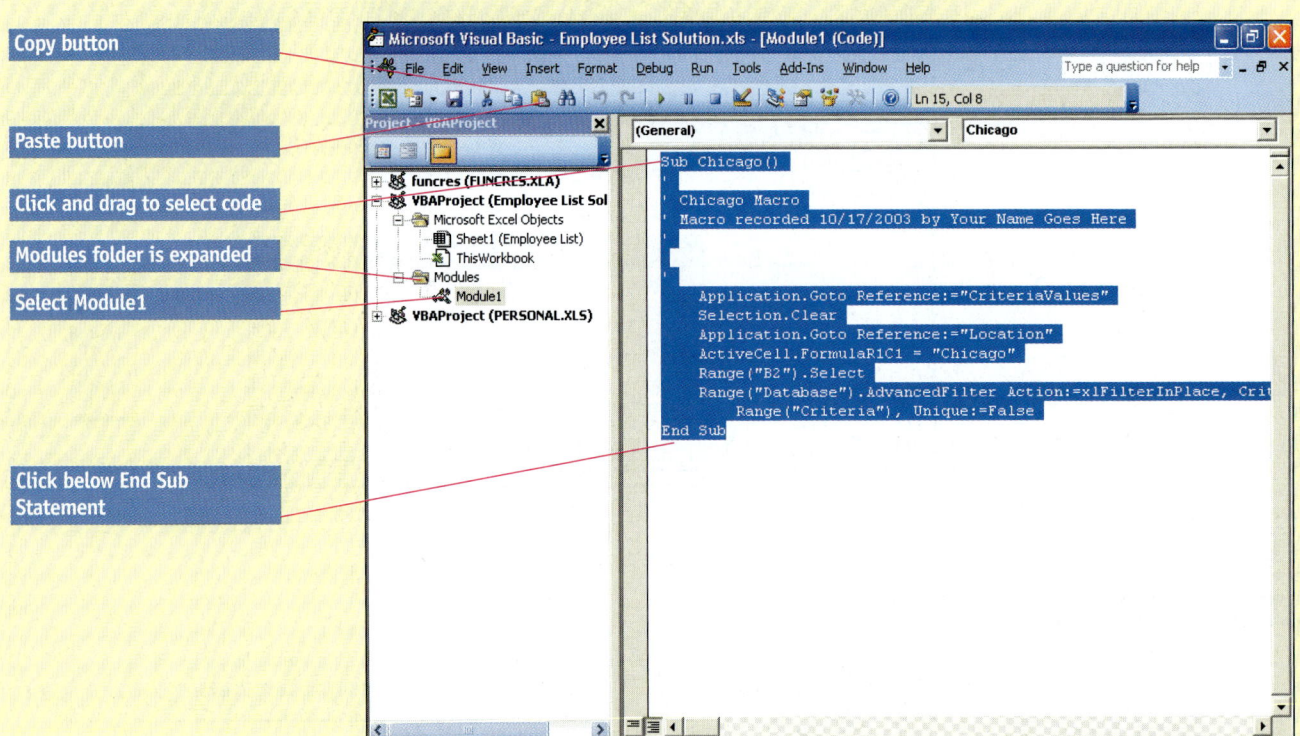

(b) Copy the Chicago Macro (step 2)

FIGURE 8.8 Hands-on Exercise 4 (*continued*)

THE SHIFT KEY

You can select text for editing (or replacement) with the mouse, or alternatively, you can select by using the cursor keys on the keyboard. Set the insertion point where you want the selection to begin, then press and hold the Shift key as you use the cursor keys to move the insertion point to the end of the selection. The selected statements are affected by the next command(s).

Step 3: **Create the Manager Macro**

- Click in front of the second (i.e., the copied) Chicago macro to set the insertion point. Pull down the **Edit menu**. Click **Replace** to display the Replace dialog box as shown in Figure 8.8c.

- Enter **Chicago** in the Find What text box. Press the **tab key**. Enter **Manager** in the Replace With text box. Select the option button to search in the *Current Procedure*. Click the **Find Next command button**.

- Excel searches for the first occurrence of Chicago, which should be in the Sub statement of the copied macro. (If this is not the case, click the **Find Next command button** until your screen matches Figure 8.8c.)

- Click the **Replace command button**. Excel substitutes Manager for Chicago, then looks for the next occurrence of Chicago. Click **Replace**. Click **Replace** a third time to make another substitution. Click **OK** in response to the message that the specified region has been searched. Close the Replace dialog box.

- Click and drag to select **Location** within the Application.Goto.Reference statement in the Manager macro. Enter **Title**. (The criteria within the macro have been changed to employees whose title is Manager.)

- Save the module.

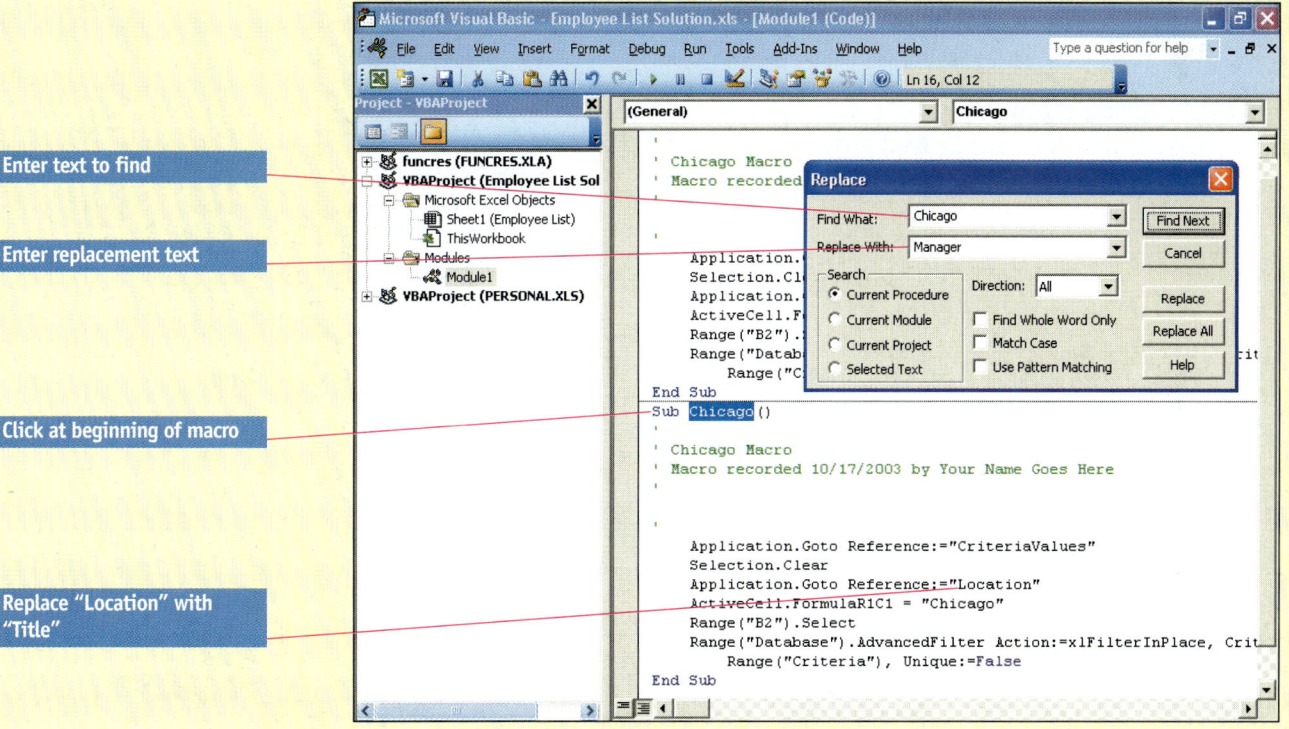

(c) Create the Manager Macro (step 3)

FIGURE 8.8 Hands-on Exercise 4 (*continued*)

THE FIND AND REPLACE COMMANDS

Anyone familiar with a word processor takes the Find and Replace commands for granted, but did you know the same capabilities exist in Excel as well as in the Visual Basic Editor? Pull down the Edit menu and choose either command. You have the same options as in the parallel command in Word, such as a case-sensitive (or insensitive) search or a limitation to a whole-word search.

Step 4: **Run the Manager Macro**

- Click the **Excel button** on the Windows taskbar or press **Alt+F11** to return to the Employee List Solution worksheet.

- Pull down the **Tools menu**. Click **Macro**, then click the **Macros . . . command** to display the Macro dialog box as shown in Figure 8.8d.

- You should see two macros: Chicago, which was created in the previous exercise, and Manager, which you just created. (If the Manager macro does not appear, return to the Visual Basic Editor and correct the appropriate Sub statement to include Manager() as the name of the macro.)

- Select the **Manager macro**, then click **Run** to run the macro, after which you should see three employees (Adamson, Coulter, and Milgrom). If the macro does not execute correctly, return to the Visual Basic Editor to make the necessary corrections, then rerun the macro.

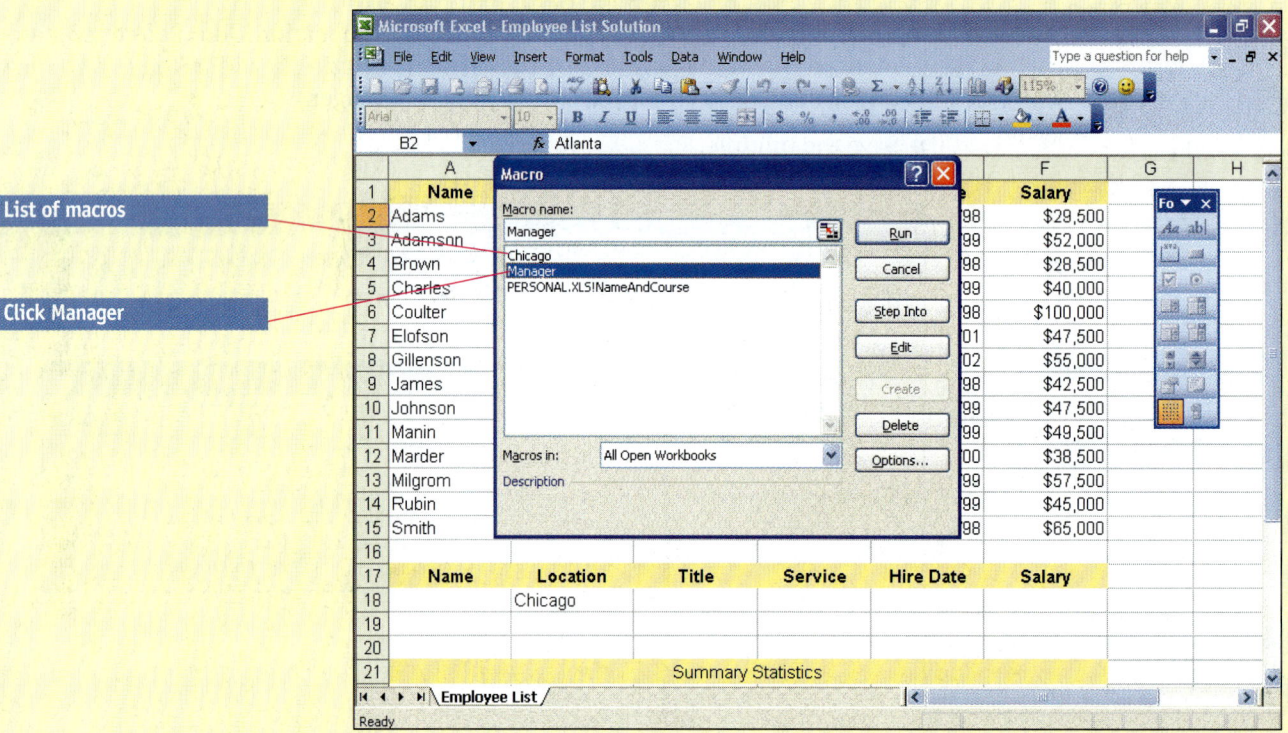

(d) Run the Manager Macro (step 4)

FIGURE 8.8 Hands-on Exercise 4 (*continued*)

THE STEP INTO COMMAND

The Step Into command helps to debug a macro, as it executes the statements one at a time. Pull down the Tools menu, click Macro, click Macros, select the macro to debug, then click the Step Into command button. Move and/or size the Visual Basic Editor window so that you can see both the worksheet and the macro. Pull down the Debug menu and click the Step Into command (or press the F8 function key) to execute the first statement in the macro and view its results. Continue to press the F8 function key to execute the statements one at a time until the macro has completed execution.

Step 5: **Assign a Button**

- Click the **Button tool** on the Forms toolbar (the mouse pointer changes to a tiny crosshair), then click and drag in the worksheet to draw a button on the worksheet. Release the mouse.

- Choose **Manager** (the macro you just created) from the list of macro names as shown in Figure 8.8e. Click **OK** to close the Assign Macro dialog box.

- The button should still be selected. Click and drag to select the name of the button, **Button 2**, then type **Manager** as the new name. Do *not* press the Enter key. Click outside the button to deselect it.

- There should be two buttons on your worksheet, one each for the Chicago and Manager macros.

- Click the **Chicago button** to execute the Chicago macro. You should see four employees with an average salary of $45,125.

- Click the **Manager button** to execute the Manager macro. You should see three employees with an average salary of $69,833.

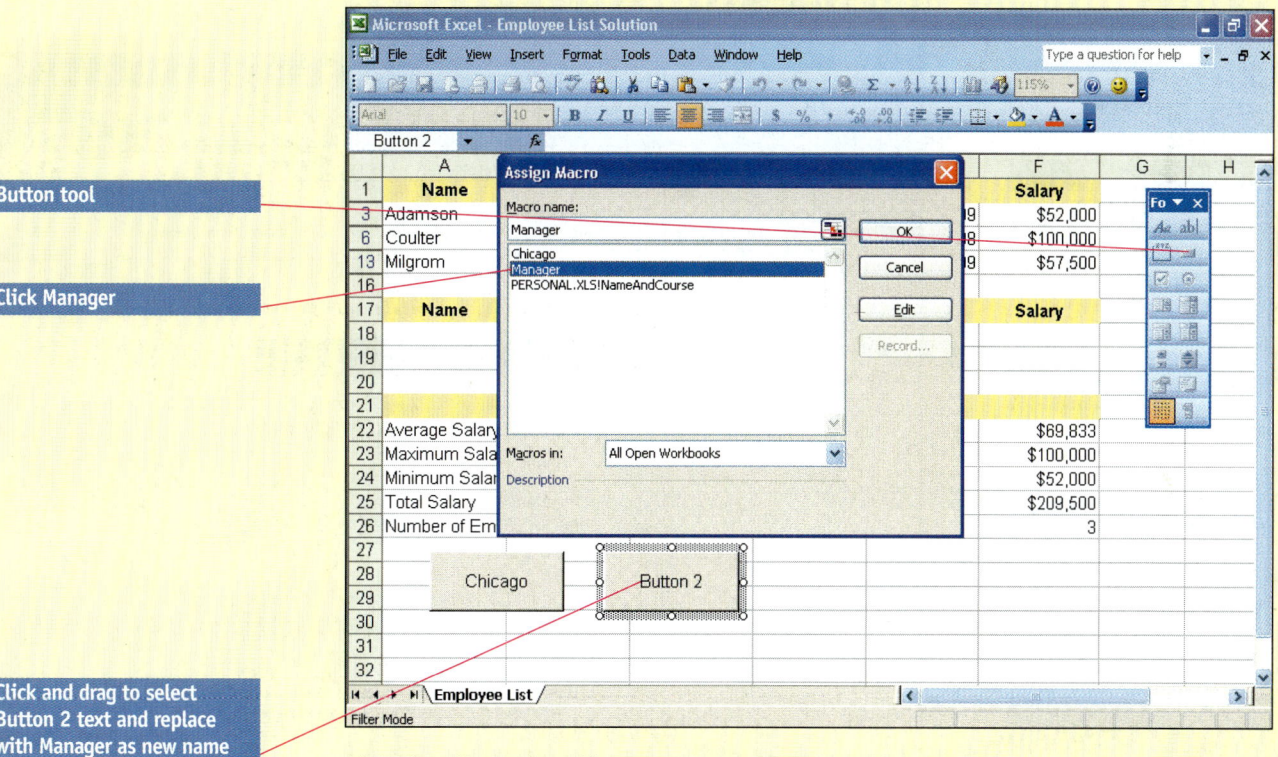

(e) Assign a Button (step 5)

FIGURE 8.8 Hands-on Exercise 4 (*continued*)

CREATE UNIFORM BUTTONS

One way to create buttons of a uniform size is to create the first button, then copy that button to create the others. To copy a button, press the Ctrl key as you select (click) the button, then click the Copy button on the Standard toolbar. Click in the worksheet where you want the new button to appear, then click the Paste button. Click and drag over the name of the button and enter a new name. Right click the border of the new button, then click Assign Macro from the shortcut menu. Select the name of the new macro, then click OK.

Step 6: **Create the ChicagoManager Macro**

- Return to the Visual Basic Editor. Press **Ctrl+Home** to move to the beginning of Module1. Click and drag to select the entire Chicago macro. Be sure to include the End Sub statement in your selection.

- Click the **Copy button** on the Standard toolbar to copy the Chicago macro to the clipboard. Press **Ctrl+End** to move to the end of the module sheet. Click the **Paste button** on the Standard toolbar to complete the copy operation.

- Change **Chicago** to **ChicagoManager** in both the comment statement and the Sub statement as shown in Figure 8.8f.

- Click and drag to select the two statements in the **Manager macro** as shown in Figure 8.8f. Click the **Copy button**.

- Scroll, if necessary, until you can click in the **ChicagoManager macro** at the end of the line, ActiveCell. FormulaR1C1 = "Chicago". Press **Enter** to begin a new line. Click the **Paste button** to complete the copy operation.

- Delete any unnecessary blank lines or spaces that may remain.

- Save the module.

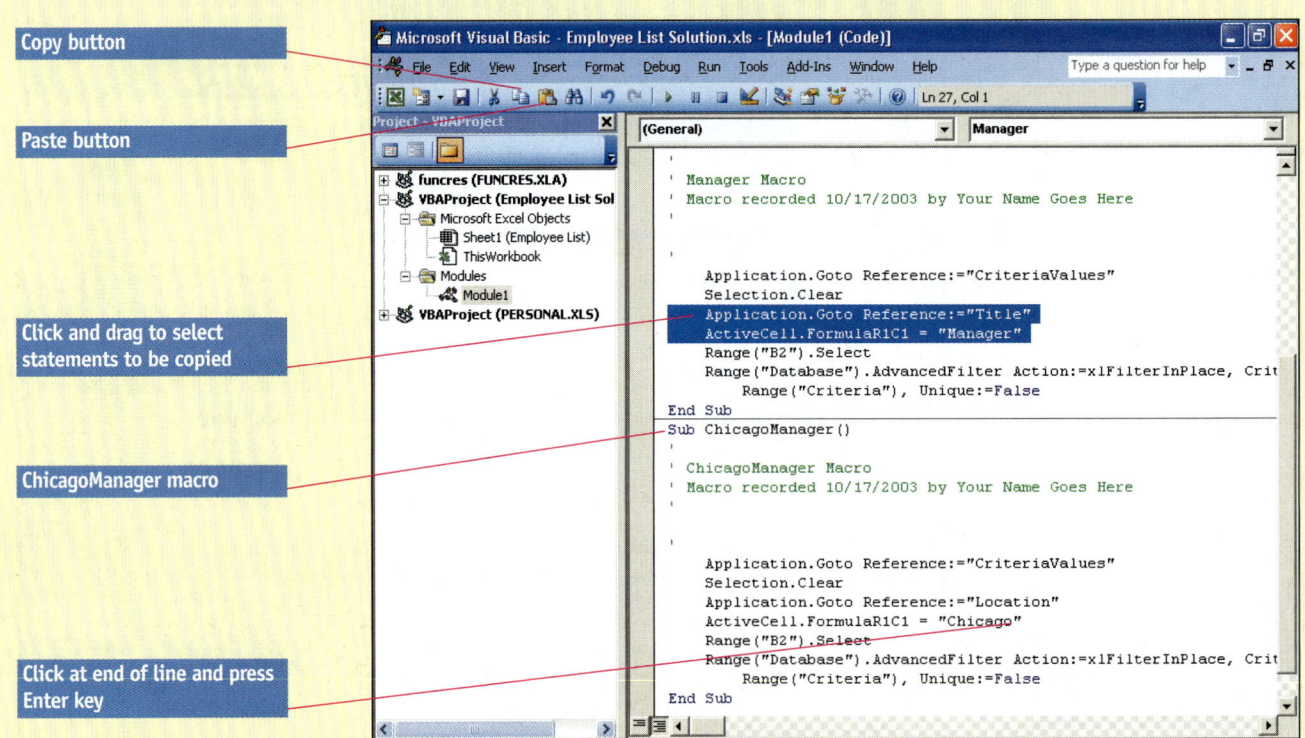

(f) Create the ChicagoManager Macro (step 6)

FIGURE 8.8 Hands-on Exercise 4 (*continued*)

ADD A SHORTCUT

You can add and/or modify the shortcut key associated with a macro at any time. Pull down the Tools menu, click the Macro command, then click Macros to display the Macro dialog box. Select the desired macro and click the Options button to display the Macro Options dialog box, where you assign a shortcut. Type a lowercase letter to create a shortcut with just the Ctrl key, such as Ctrl+m. Enter an uppercase letter to create a shortcut using the Ctrl and Shift keys, such as Ctrl+Shift+M.

Step 7: **The MsgBox Statement**

- Check that the statements in your ChicagoManager macro match those in Figure 8.8g. (The MsgBox statement has not yet been added.)

- Click immediately before the End Sub statement. Press **Enter** to begin a new line, press the **up arrow** to move up one line, then press **Tab** to indent. (Indentation is not a VBA requirement; it is done to enhance the readability of the code.)

- Type the word **MsgBox**, then press the **Space bar**. VBA responds with a Quick Info box that displays the complete syntax of the statement. You can ignore this information at the present time, since we are not entering any additional parameters.

- Enter the rest of the MsgBox statement exactly as it appears in Figure 8.8g. Be sure to include a blank space and the **underscore** at the end of the first line, which indicates that the statement is continued to the next line.

- Save the module, then return to the Excel workbook.

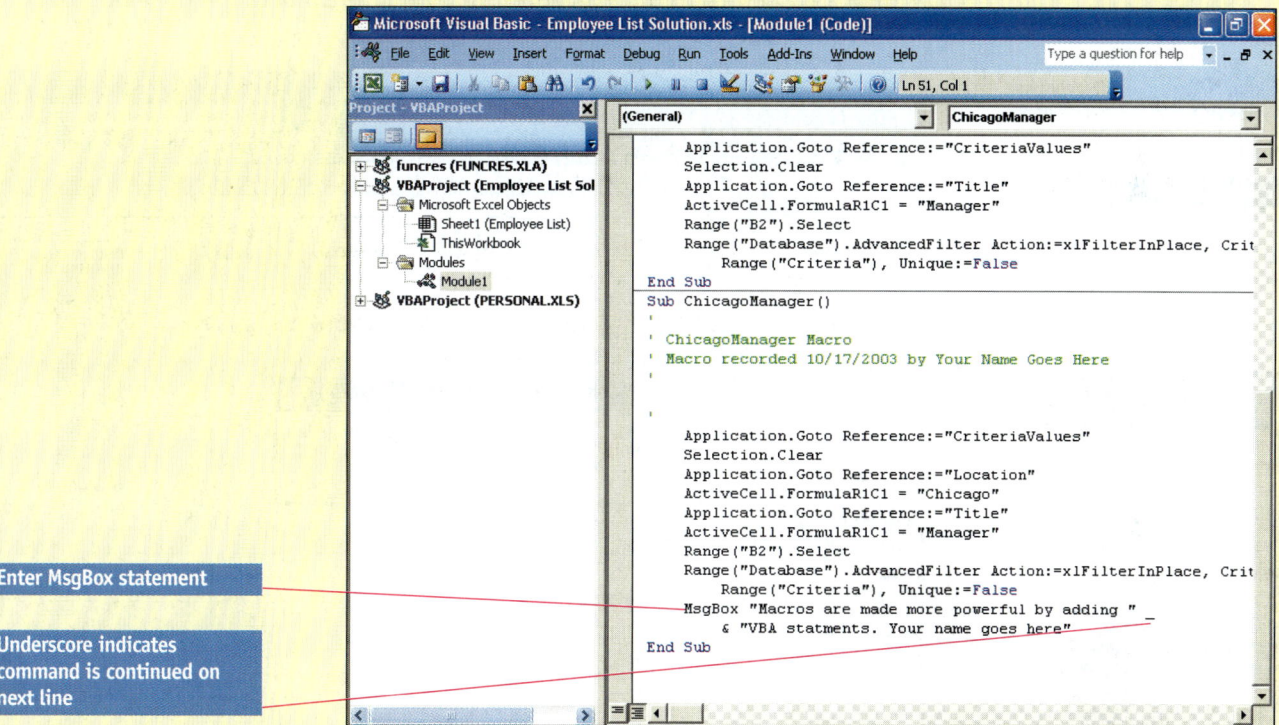

(g) The MsgBox Statement (step 7)

FIGURE 8.8 Hands-on Exercise 4 (*continued*)

THE UNDERSCORE AND AMPERSAND

A VBA statement is continued from one line to the next by typing a blank space followed by an underscore at the end of the line to be continued. You may not, however, break a line in the middle of a literal. Hence, the first line ends with a closing quotation mark, followed by a space and the underscore. The next line starts with an ampersand to indicate continuation of the previous literal, followed by the remainder of the literal in quotation marks.

Step 8: **Test the ChicagoManager Macro**

- You can assign a macro to a command button by copying an existing command button, then changing the name of the button and the associated macro. Right click either of the existing command buttons, click the **Copy command** from the shortcut menu, then click the **Paste button** on the Standard toolbar.

- Click and drag the copied button to the right of the two existing buttons. Click and drag the text of the copied button (which should still be selected) to select the text, then type **Chicago Manager** as the name of the button.

- Click anywhere in the worksheet to deselect the button, then **Right click** the new button, click the **Assign Macro command**, choose the newly created ChicagoManager macro, and click **OK**.

- Click anywhere in the workbook to deselect the button. Save the workbook.

- Click the **Chicago Manager button** to execute the macro. You should see the matching employees as shown in Figure 8.8h, followed by the message box.

- Click **OK**. Return to the VBA editor to correct the macro if it does not execute as intended.

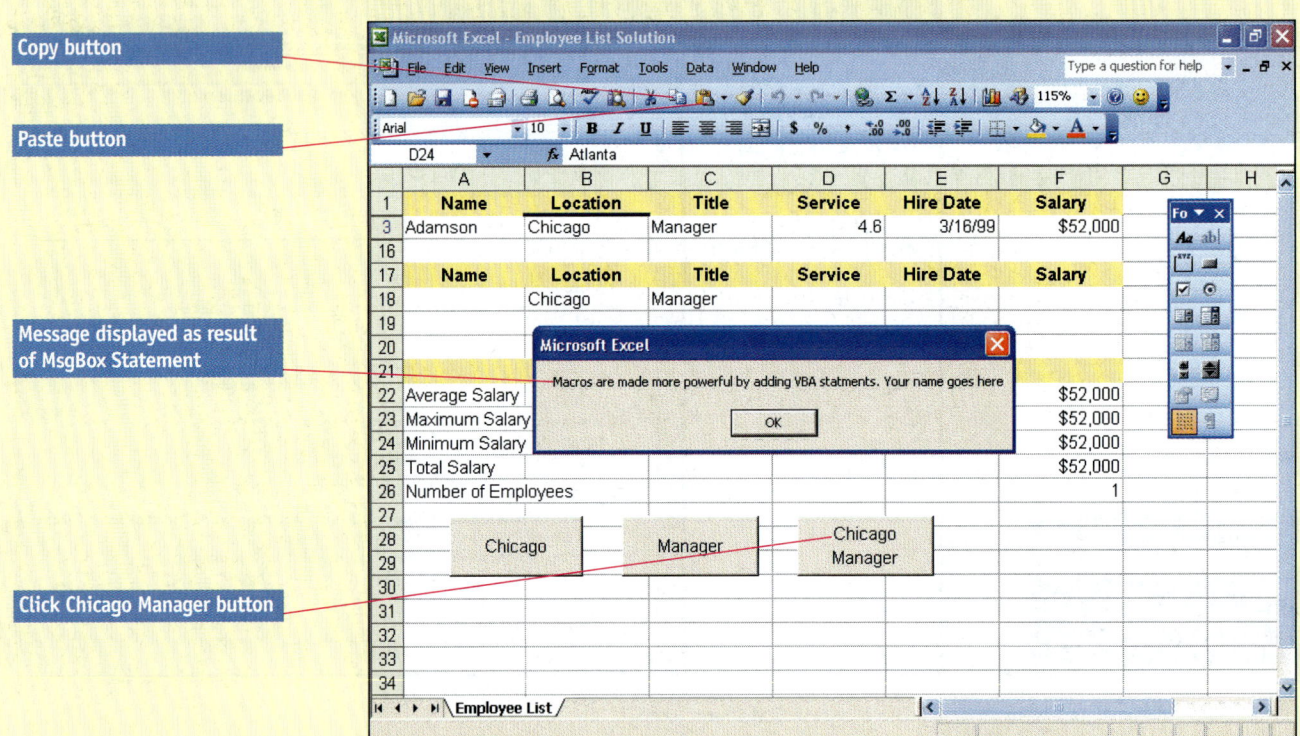

(h) Test the ChicagoManager Macro (step 8)

FIGURE 8.8 Hands-on Exercise 4 (*continued*)

CUSTOMIZE THE MESSAGE BOX

You can add a personal touch to the output of the MsgBox statement by including optional parameters to change the text of the title bar and/or include an icon within the message box. The statement, MsgBox "Hello World", vbinformation, "Your Name on Title Bar" uses both parameters. Be sure to use quotation marks for both the first and last parameter.

Step 9: **Create the AnyCityAnyTitle Macro**

- Press **Alt+F11** to return to the Visual Basic editor. Click and drag to select the entire ChicagoManager macro. Click the **Copy button**, click the blank line below the End Sub statement, then click the **Paste button** to duplicate the module.

- Click and drag the name of the copied macro. Type **AnyCityAnyTitle()** to change the name of the macro. Do not leave any spaces in the macro name. Delete or modify the comments as you see fit.

- Click and drag to select **"Chicago"** as shown in Figure 8.8i. You must include the quotation marks in your selection.

- Type **InputBox("Enter the location")** to replace the specific location with the InputBox function. Be sure to use left and right parentheses and to enclose the literal in quotation marks.

- Click and drag to select **"Manager"**. Type **InputBox("Enter the title")** to replace the specific title with the InputBox function.

- Save the module and return to the Excel workbook.

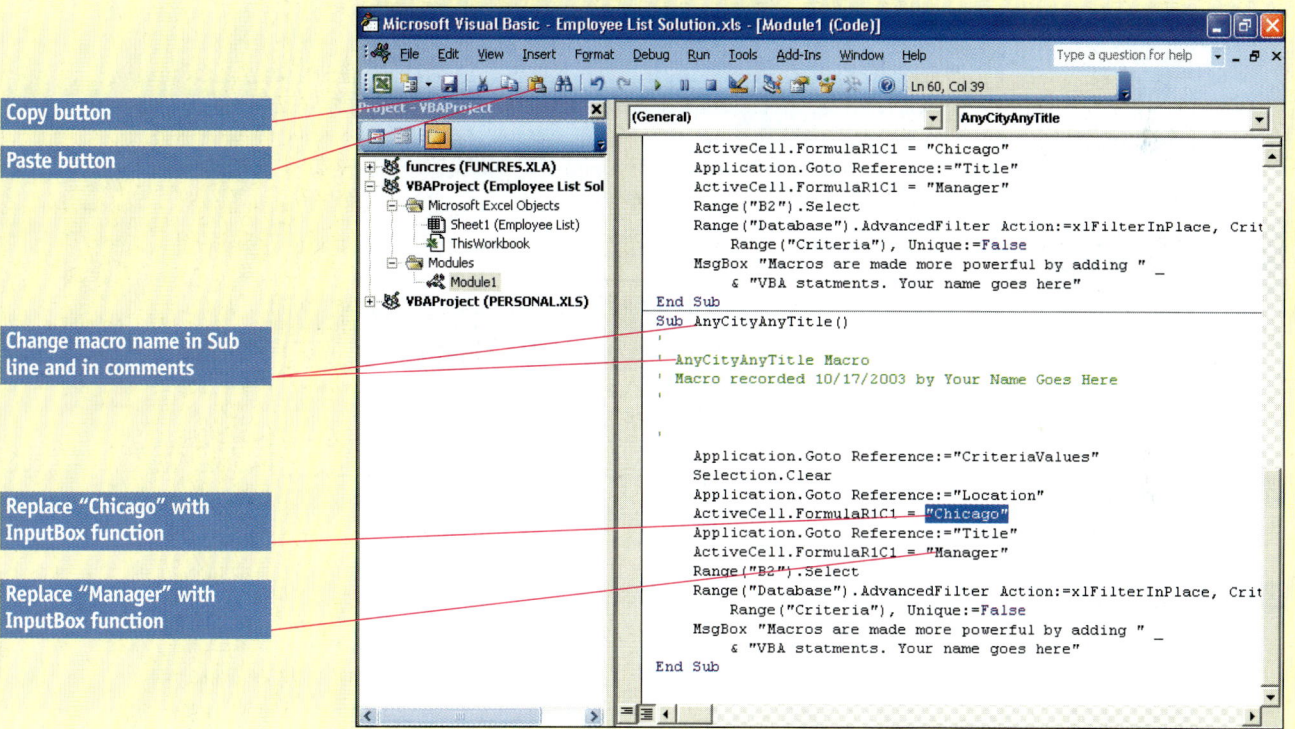

(i) Create the AnyCityAnyTitle Macro (step 9)

FIGURE 8.8 Hands-on Exercise 4 (*continued*)

USE WHAT YOU KNOW

Use the techniques acquired from other applications such as Microsoft Word to facilitate editing within the VBA window. Press the Ins key to toggle between the insert and overtype modes as you modify the statements within a procedure. You can also cut, copy, and paste statements (or parts of statements) within a procedure and from one procedure to another. The Find and Replace commands are also useful.

Step 10: **Test the AnyCityAnyTitle Macro**

- Copy any of the existing command buttons to create a new button for the **AnyCityAnyTitle** macro as shown in Figure 8.8j. Be sure to assign the correct macro to this button.

- Click the **Any City Any Title command button** to run the macro. You will be prompted for the location. Type **Atlanta** and click **OK**. (A second input box will appear in which you will enter the title.)

- At this time Atlanta has been entered into the criteria area, and the summary statistics reflect the Atlanta employees. The filtered list will not change, however, until you have entered the title and completed the Advanced Filter command.

- Enter **Trainee** as the employee title as shown in Figure 8.8j. Click **OK**. The workbook changes to reflect the Atlanta trainees. Click **OK** in response to the message box.

- Return to the VBA editor if the macro does not execute as intended. Save the workbook.

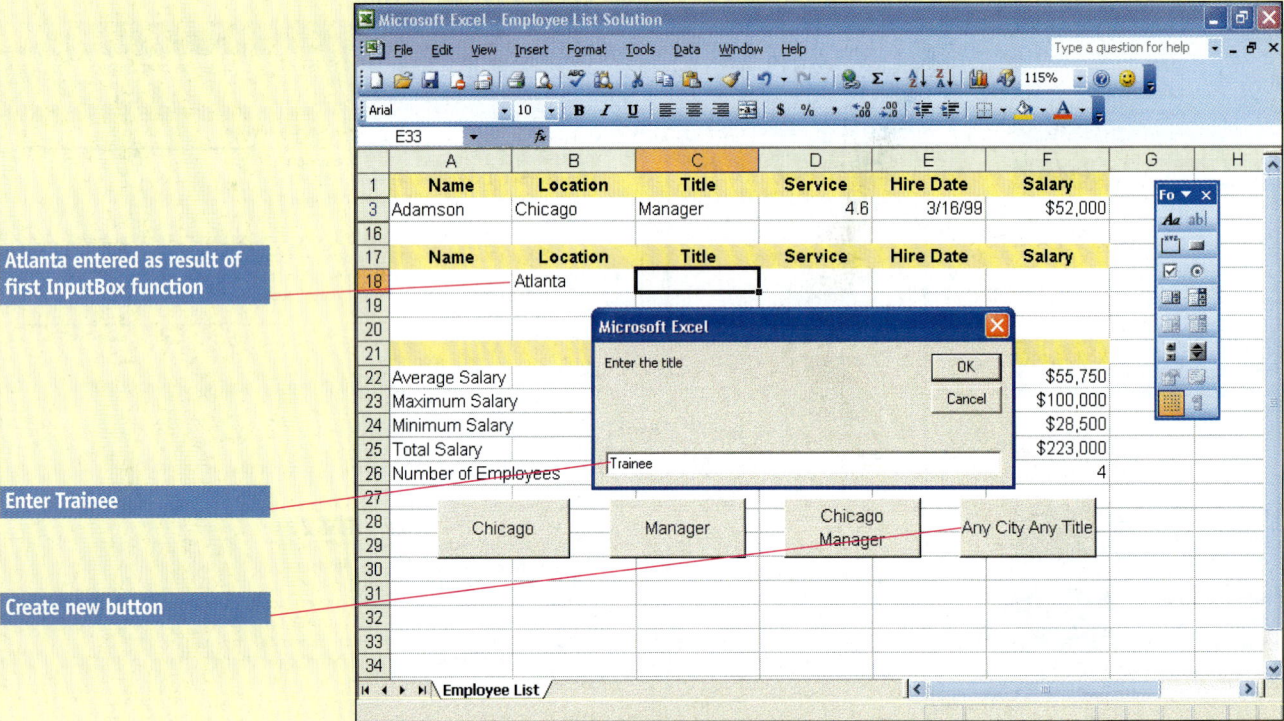

(j) Test the AnyCityAnyTitle Macro (step 10)

FIGURE 8.8 Hands-on Exercise 4 (*continued*)

ONE MACRO DOES IT ALL

The AnyCityAnyTitle macro is the equivalent of the more specific macros that were created earlier; that is, you would enter "Chicago" and "Manager" to replace the Chicago Manager macro. You can also enter "Chicago" as the city and leave the title field blank to select all Chicago employees, or alternatively, leave the city blank and enter "Manager" as the title to select all managers. And finally, you could omit both city and title to select all employees.

Step 11: **Change the Button Properties**

- Press and hold the **Shift** and **Ctrl keys**, then click each of the command buttons to select all four buttons as shown in Figure 8.8k.

- Pull down the **Format menu** and click the **Control command** to display the Format Control dialog box. Click the **Properties tab**, then check the box to **Print object** so that the command buttons will appear on the printed worksheet.

- Click the **Move but don't size with cells option button**. Click **OK** to exit the dialog box and return to the worksheet. Click anywhere in the worksheet to deselect the buttons.

- Click the **Print button** on the Standard toolbar to print the worksheet. Return to the Visual Basic Editor. Pull down the **File menu**, click the **Print command**, select **Current Module**, then click **OK**.

- Save the workbook a final time. Close the workbook. Exit Excel if you don't want to continue with the next exercise at this time.

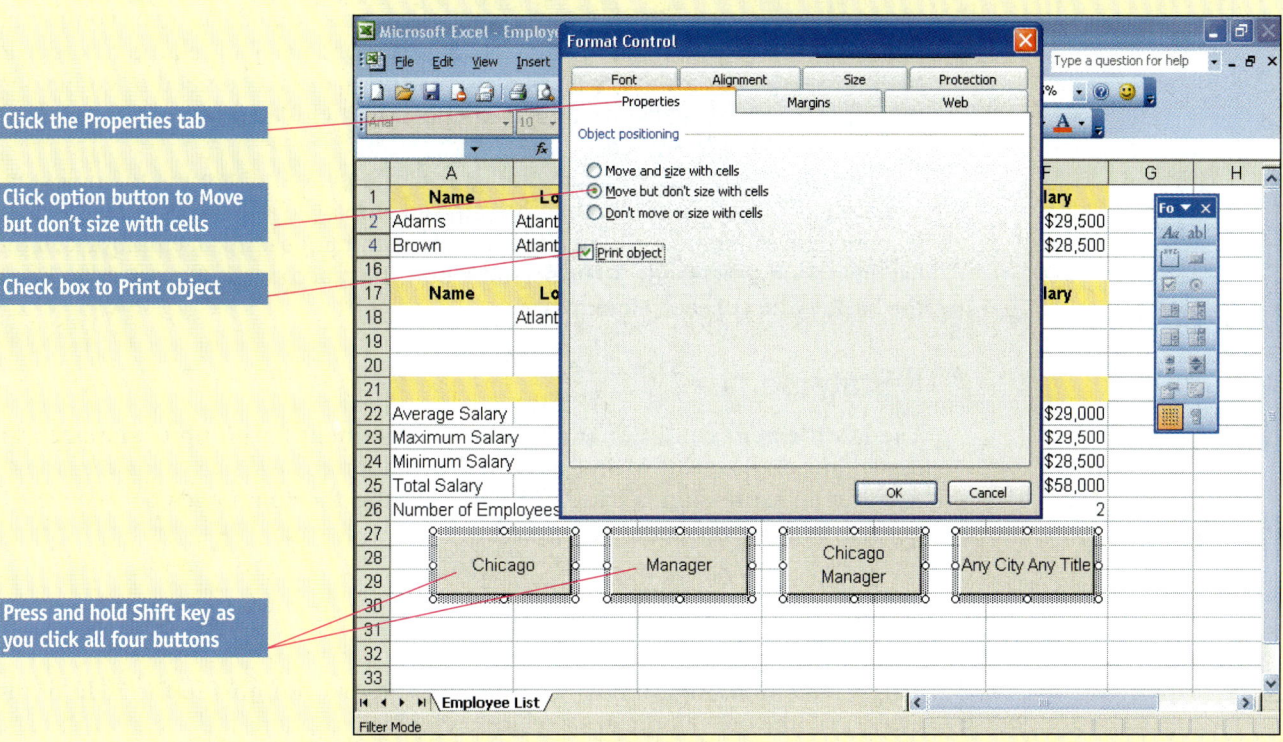

(k) Change the Button Properties (step 11)

FIGURE 8.8   Hands-on Exercise 4 (*continued*)

THE SIZE PROPERTY

Use the Size property to obtain a consistent look for your command buttons. Press and hold the Shift and Ctrl keys as you select the individual buttons. Pull down the Format menu and click the Control command to display the Format Control dialog box. Click the Size tab, enter the width and height for the selected buttons, then click OK. The buttons will be a uniform size, but they may overlap. Click anywhere in the worksheet to deselect the buttons, then right click and drag to reposition a button.

LOOPS AND DECISION MAKING

Excel macros can be made significantly more powerful by incorporating additional Visual Basic statements that enable true programming. These include the If statement for decision making, and the Do statement to implement a *loop* (one or more commands that are executed repeatedly until a condition is met).

Consider, for example, the worksheet and associated macro in Figure 8.9. The worksheet is similar to those used in the preceding exercises, except that the font color of the data for managers is red. Think for a minute how you would do this manually. You would look at the first employee in the list, examine the employee's title to determine if that employee is a manager, and if so, change the font color for that employee. You would then repeat these steps for all of the other employees on the list. It sounds tedious, but that is exactly what you would do if asked to change the font color for the managers.

Now ask yourself whether you could implement the entire process with the macro recorder. You could use the recorder to capture the commands to select a specific row within the list and change the font color. You could not, however, use the recorder to determine whether or not to select a particular row (i.e., whether the employee is a manager) because you have to make that decision by comparing the cell contents to a specific criterion. Nor is there a way to tell the recorder to repeat the process for every employee. In other words, you need to go beyond merely capturing Excel commands. You need to include additional Visual Basic statements within the macro.

The HighlightManager macro in Figure 8.9 uses the If statement to implement a decision (to determine whether the selected employee is a manager) and the Do statement to implement a loop (to repeat the commands until all employees in the list have been processed). To understand how the macro works, you need to know the basic syntax of each statement.

If Statement

The *If statement* conditionally executes a statement (or group of statements), depending on the value of an expression (condition). The If statement determines whether an expression is true, and if so, executes the commands between the If and the *End If statement*. For example:

```
If ActiveCell.Offset(0, 2) = "Manager" Then
    Selection.Font.ColorIndex = 3
End If
```

This If statement determines whether the cell two columns to the right of the active cell (the offset indicates a relative reference) contains the text *Manager,* and if so, changes the font color of the (previously) selected text. The number three corresponds to the color red. No action is taken if the condition is false. Either way, execution continues with the command below the End If.

> ### IF-THEN-ELSE
> The If statement includes an optional Else clause whose statements are executed if the condition is false. Consider:
>
> **If** condition **Then** statements [**Else** statements] **End If**
>
> The condition is evaluated as either true or false. If the condition is true, the statements following Then are executed; otherwise the statements following Else are executed. Either way, execution continues with the statement following End If. Use the Help command for additional information and examples.

Do Statement

The ***Do statement*** repeats a block of statements until a condition becomes true. For example:

```
Do Until ActiveCell = ""
    ActiveCell.Range("A1:F1").Select
    If ActiveCell.Offset(0, 2) = "Manager" Then
        Selection.Font.ColorIndex = 3
    End If
    ActiveCell.Offset(1, 0).Select
Loop
```

The statements within the loop are executed repeatedly until the active cell is empty (i.e., ActiveCell = ""). The first statement in the loop selects the cells in columns A through F of the current row. Relative references are used, and you may want to refer to the earlier discussion that indicated that A1:F1 specifies the shape of a range rather than a specific cell address.

The If statement determines whether the current employee is a manager and, if so, changes the font color for the selected cells. (The offset (0, 2) refers to the entry two columns to the right of the active cell.) The last statement selects the cell one row below the active cell to process the next employee. (Omission of this statement would process the same row indefinitely, creating what is known as an infinite loop.)

The macro in Figure 8.9 is a nontrivial example that illustrates the potential of Visual Basic to enhance a macro. Try to gain a conceptual understanding of how the macro works, but do not be concerned if you are confused initially. Do the hands-on exercise, and you'll be pleased at how much clearer it will be when you have created the macro yourself. The addition of loops and decision-making statements in a VBA procedure enables true programming within an Excel macro.

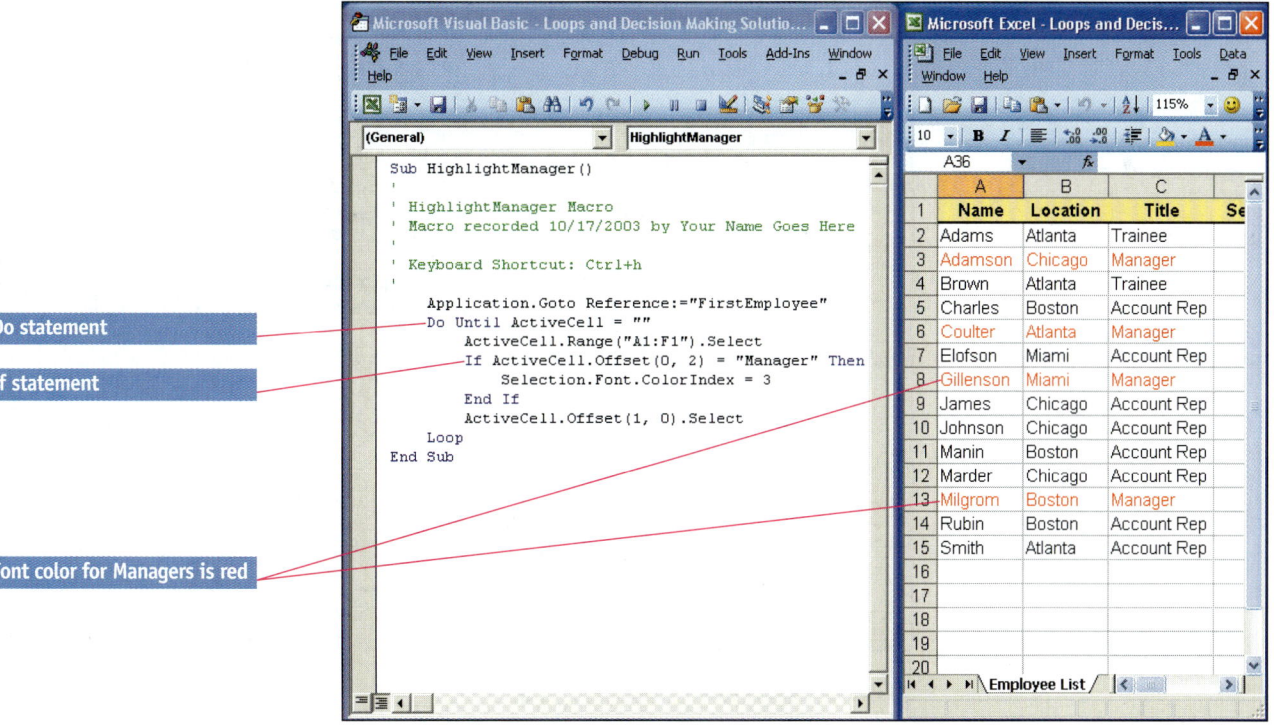

FIGURE 8.9 Loops and Decision Making

hands-on exercise

5 | Loops and Decision Making

Objective To implement loops and decision making in a macro through relative references and the Visual Basic Do Until and If statements. Use Figure 8.10 as a guide in doing the exercise.

Step 1: **The ClearColor Macro**

- Open the **Loops and Decision Making workbook** in the **Exploring Excel folder**. Click the button to **Enable Macros** when prompted by the security warning. Close the Forms toolbar.

- Save the workbook as **Loops and Decision Making Solution workbook**. The data for the employees in rows 3, 6, 8, and 13 appears in red to indicate these employees are managers.

- Pull down the **Tools menu**. Click the **Macro command** and click **Macros** to display the dialog box in Figure 8.10a. (Do not be concerned if you do not see the NameAndCourse macro.)

- Select **ClearColor**, then click **Run** to execute this macro and clear the red color from the managerial employees.

- Use the **Font Color button** on the Standard toolbar to change the color of any entry within the list, then rerun the ClearColor macro. It is important to know that the ClearColor macro works, as you will use it throughout the exercise.

- Save the workbook.

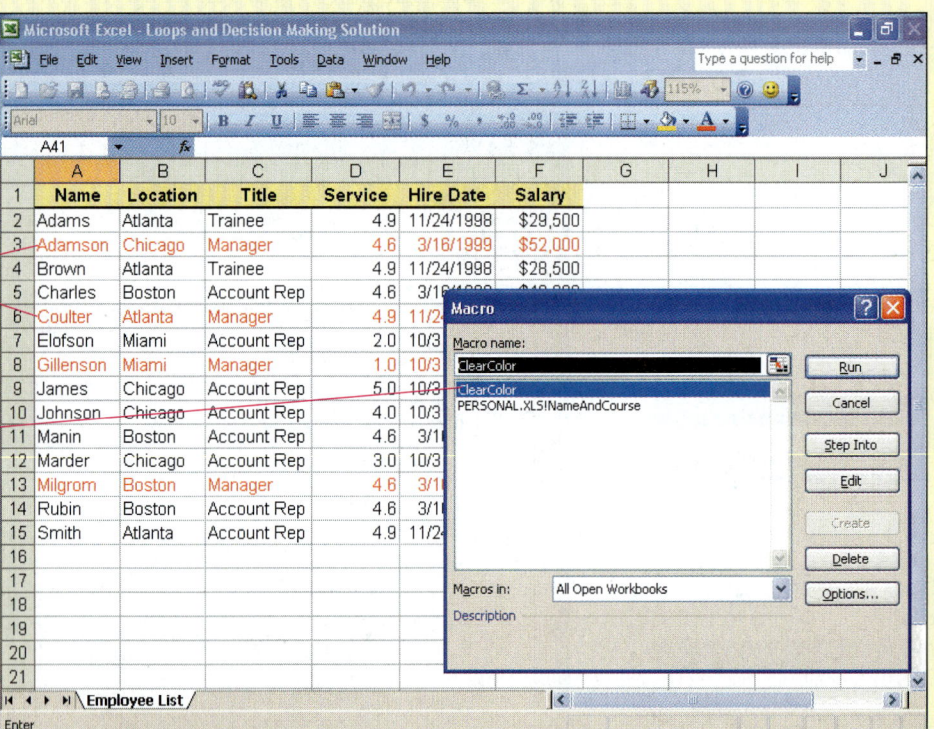

(a) The ClearColor Macro (step 1)

FIGURE 8.10 Hands-on Exercise 5

Step 2: **Record the HighlightManager Macro**

- You must choose the active cell before recording the macro. Click **cell A3**, the cell containing the name of the first manager.

- Pull down the **Tools menu**, click (or point to) the **Macro command**, then click **Record New Macro** (or click the **Record macro button** on the Visual Basic toolbar) to display the Record Macro dialog box.

- Enter **HighlightManager** as the name of the macro. Do not leave any spaces in the macro name. Click in the **Shortcut Key** check box and enter a **lowercase h**. Check that **This Workbook** is selected. Click **OK**.

- The Stop Recording toolbar appears, and the status bar indicates that you are recording the macro as shown in Figure 8.10b. Click the **Relative References button** so that the button is pushed in.

- Click and drag to select **cells A3 through F3** as shown in Figure 8.10b. Click the arrow in the **Font color list box**. Click **Red**. Click the **Stop Recording button**.

- Click anywhere in the worksheet to deselect cells A3 through F3 so you can see the effect of the macro; cells A3 through F3 should be displayed in red.

- Save the workbook.

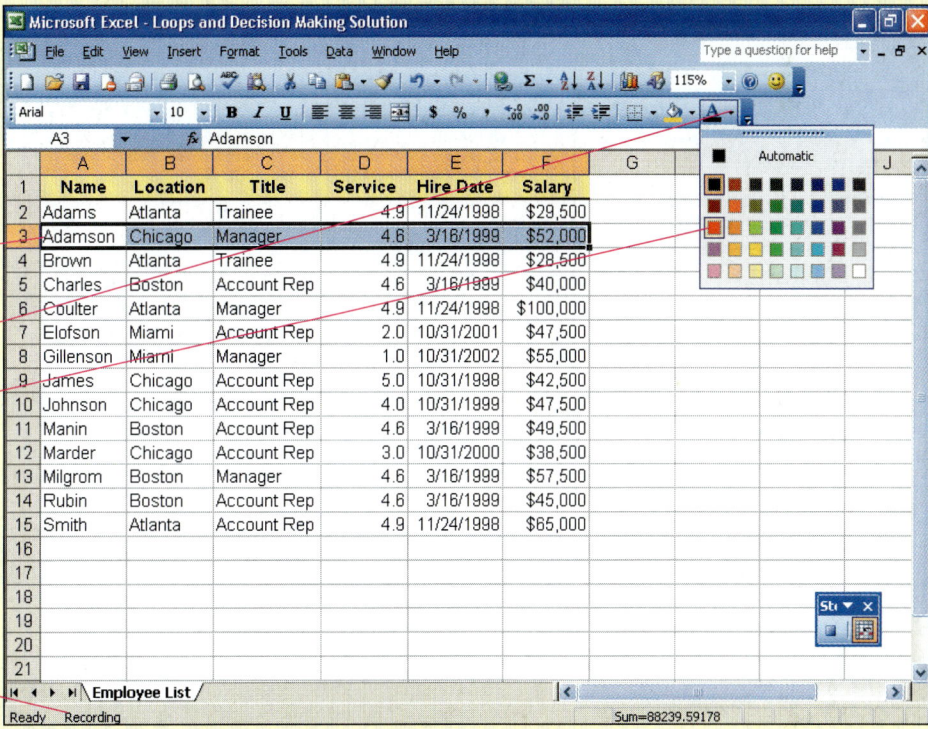

(b) Record the HighlightManager Macro (step 2)

FIGURE 8.10   Hands-on Exercise 5 (*continued*)

A SENSE OF FAMILIARITY

Visual Basic has the basic capabilities found in any other programming language. If you have programmed before, whether in Pascal, C, or even COBOL, you will find all of the familiar logic structures. These include the Do While and Do Until statements, the If-Then-Else statement for decision making, nested If statements, a Case statement, and/or calls to subprograms.

MICROSOFT OFFICE EXCEL 2003   **1405**

Step 3: **View the Macro**

- Press **Alt+F11** to open the Visual Basic Editor. If necessary, double click the **Modules folder** for the Loops and Decision Making Solution Project within the Project Explorer window to display the two modules within the workbook.

- Select (click) **Module2**. Pull down the **View menu** and click **Code** (or press the **F7 key**) to display the Visual Basic code for the HighlightManager macro you just created as shown in Figure 8.10c.

- Be sure that your code is identical to ours (except for the comments). If you see the absolute reference, Range("A3:F3"), rather than the relative reference in our figure, you need to correct your macro to match ours.

- Click the **close button** (the X on the Project Explorer title bar) to close the Project Explorer window. (You can reopen the Project Explorer at any time by pulling down the View menu.) The Code window expands to occupy the entire Visual Basic Editor window.

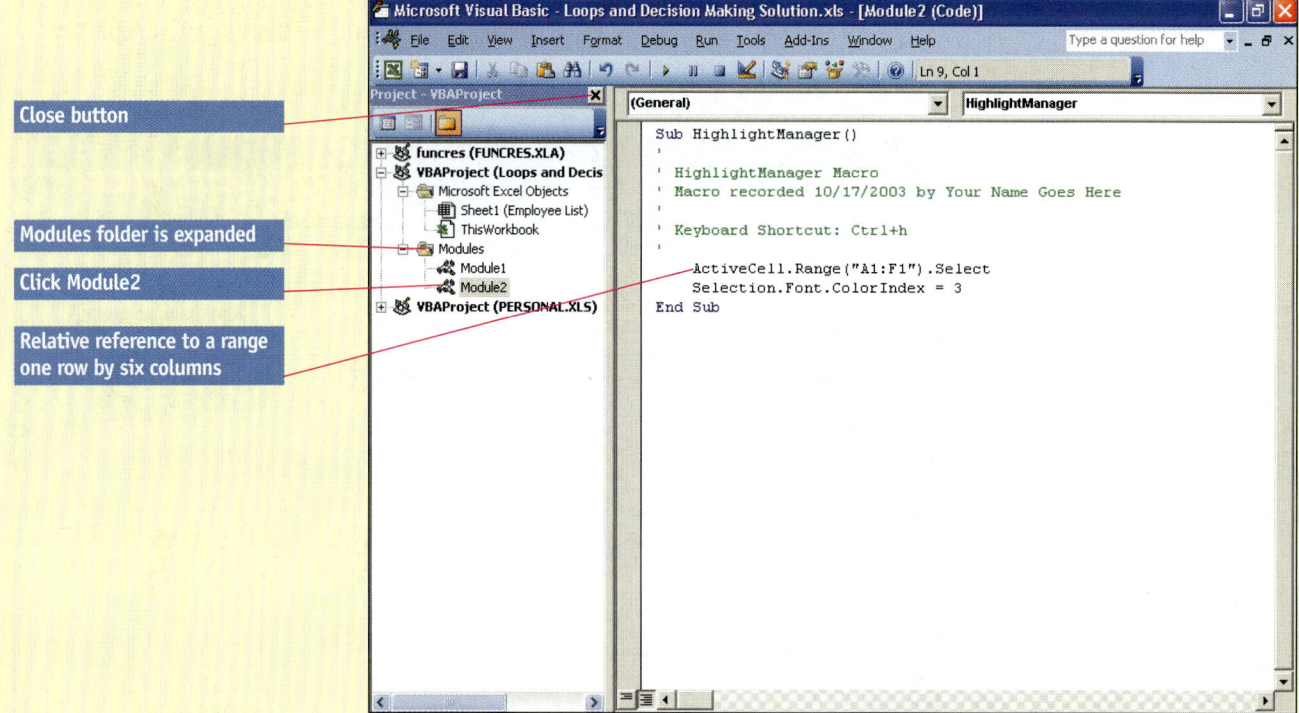

(c) View the Macro (step 3)

FIGURE 8.10 Hands-on Exercise 5 (*continued*)

WHY SO MANY MODULES?

Multiple macros that are recorded within the same Excel session are all stored in the same module. If you close the workbook, then subsequently reopen it, Excel will store subsequent macros in a new module. It really doesn't matter where (in which module) the macros are stored. You can, however, cut and paste macros from one module to another if you prefer to have all of the macros in a single module. Delete the additional (now superfluous) modules after you have copied the procedures.

Step 4: **Test the Macro**

- Point to an empty area on the Windows taskbar, then click the **right mouse button** to display a shortcut menu. Click **Tile Windows Vertically** to tile the open windows (Excel and the Visual Basic Editor).

- Your desktop should be similar to Figure 8.10d except that the additional employees will not yet appear in red. It doesn't matter if the workbook is in the same window as ours. (If additional windows are open on the desktop, minimize each window, then repeat the previous step to tile the open windows.)

- Click the **Excel window**. Click **cell A6** (the cell containing the name of the next manager). Press **Ctrl+h** to execute the HighlightManager macro. The font in cells A6 to F6 changes to red.

- Click **cell A7**. Press **Ctrl+h** to execute the HighlightManager macro. The font for this employee is also in red, although the employee is not a manager.

- Save the workbook.

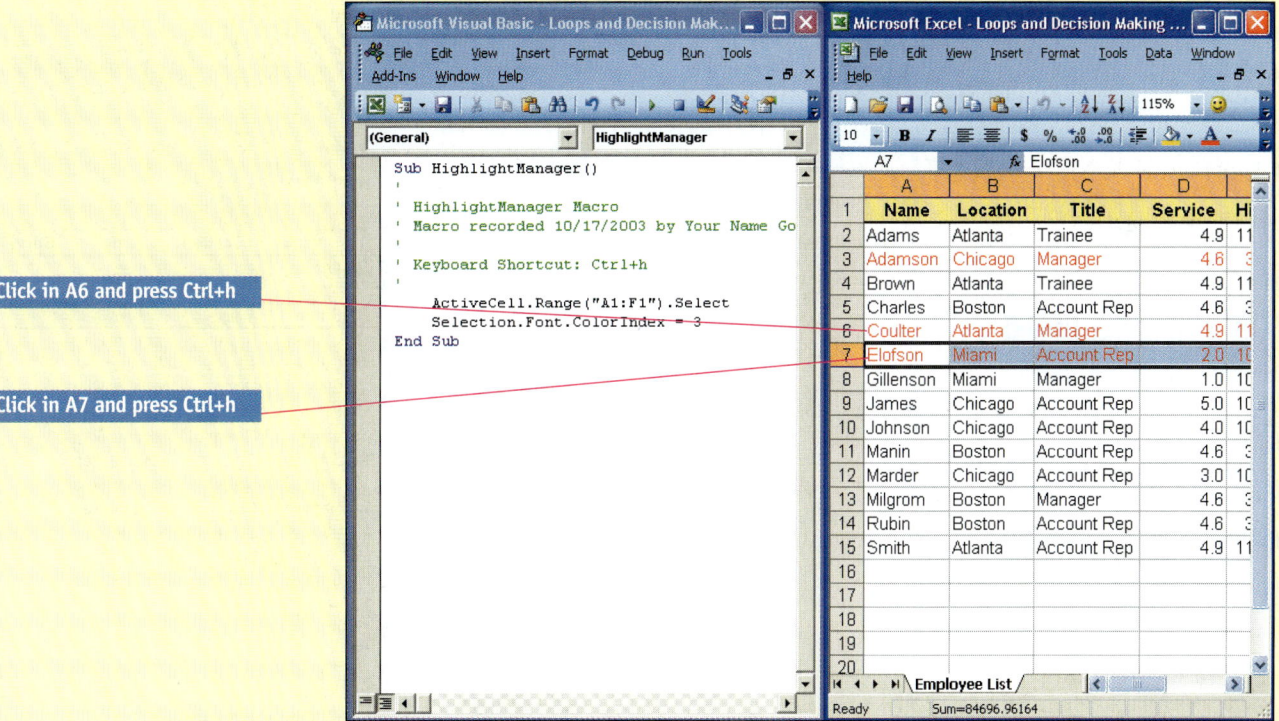

(d) Test the Macro (step 4)

FIGURE 8.10 Hands-on Exercise 5 (*continued*)

THE FIRST BUG

A bug is a mistake in a computer program; hence debugging refers to the process of correcting program errors. According to legend, the first bug was an unlucky moth crushed to death on one of the relays of the electromechanical Mark II computer, bringing the machine's operation to a halt. The cause of the failure was discovered by Grace Hopper, who promptly taped the moth to her logbook, noting, *"First actual case of bug being found."*

Step 5: **Add the If Statement**

- Press **Ctrl+c** to execute the ClearColor macro. The data for all employees is again displayed in black.

- Click in the window containing the **HighlightManager macro**. Add the **If** and **End If** statements exactly as they are shown in Figure 8.10e. Use the **Tab key** (or press the **space bar**) to indent the Selection statement within the If and End If statements.

- Click in the window containing the worksheet, then click **cell A3**. Press **Ctrl+h** to execute the modified HighlightManager macro. The text in cells A3 through F3 is red since this employee is a manager.

- Click **cell A4**. Press **Ctrl+h**. The row is selected, but the color of the font remains unchanged. The If statement prevents these cells from being highlighted because the employee is not a manager. Press **Ctrl+c** to remove all highlighting.

- Save the workbook.

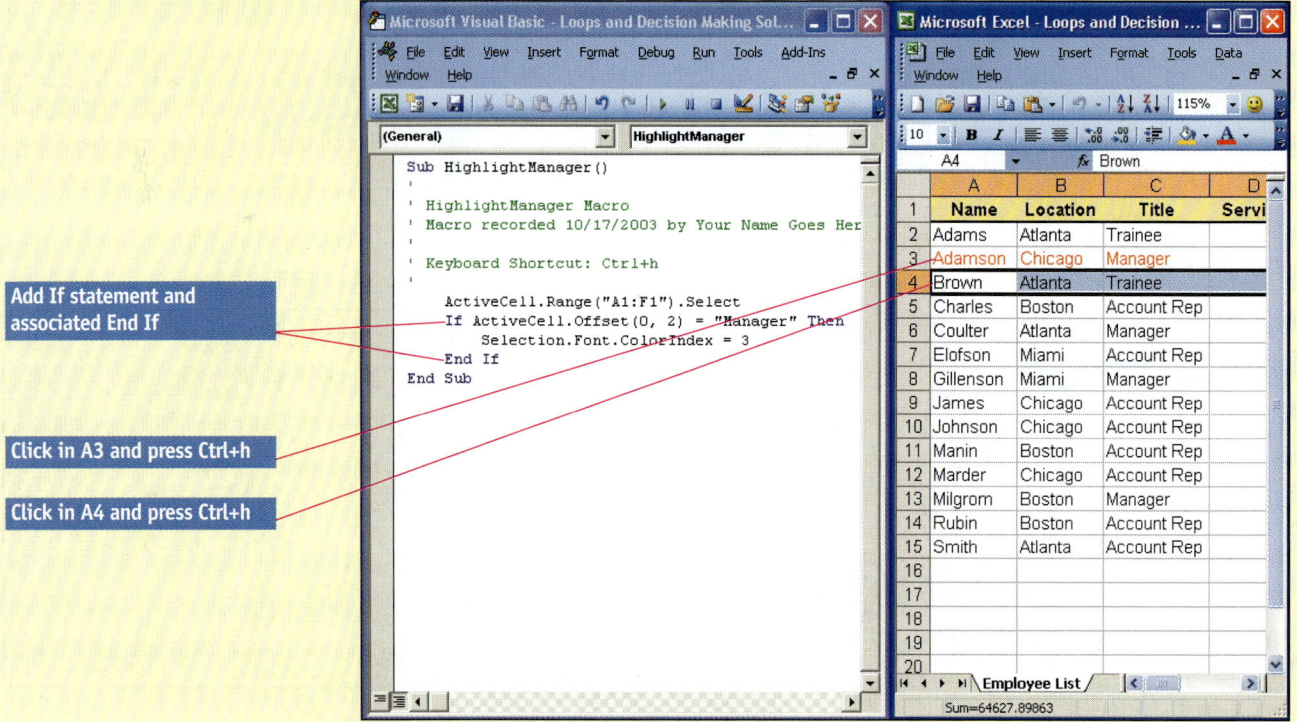

(e) Add the If Statement (step 5)

FIGURE 8.10 Hands-on Exercise 5 (*continued*)

INDENT

Indentation does not affect the execution of a macro. It, does, however, make the macro easier to read, and we suggest you follow common conventions in developing your macros. Indent the conditional statements associated with an If statement by a consistent amount. Place the End If statement on a line by itself, directly under the associated If.

Step 6: **An Endless Loop**

- Click in the window containing the **HighlightManager macro**. Add the **Do Until** and **Loop** statements exactly as they appear in Figure 8.10f. Indent the other statements as shown in the figure.
- Click **cell A3** of the worksheet. Press **Ctrl+h** to execute the macro. Cells A3 through F3 will be displayed in red, but the macro continues to execute indefinitely as it applies color to the same record over and over.
- Press **Ctrl+Break** to cease execution of the macro. You will see the dialog box in Figure 8.10f, indicating that code execution has been interrupted. Click the **End button**.
- Click within the macro code, pull down the **Debug menu**, and click the **Step Into command** (or press the **F8 key**) to enter the macro. The first statement is highlighted in yellow.
- Press the **F8 key** repeatedly to execute the next several steps over and over again. You will see that the macro is stuck in a loop as the If statement is executed indefinitely.
- Click the **Reset button** in the Visual Basic window to end the debugging.

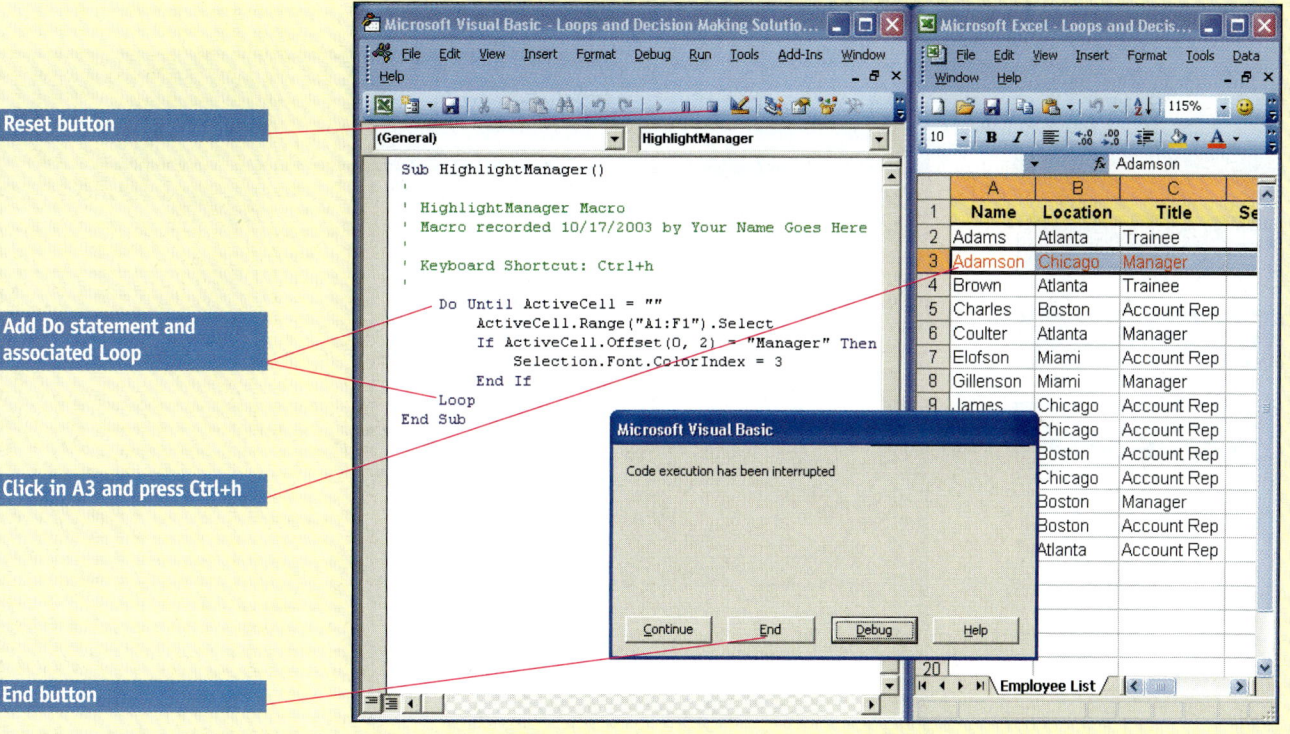

(f) An Endless Loop (step 6)

FIGURE 8.10 Hands-on Exercise 5 (*continued*)

AN ENDLESS LOOP

The glossary in the Programmer's Guide for a popular database contains the following definitions "Endless loop"—See loop, endless and "Loop, endless"—See endless loop.

We don't know whether these entries were deliberate or not, but the point is made either way. Endless loops are a common and frustrating bug. Press Ctrl+Break to halt execution, then click the Debug command button to step through the macro and locate the source of the error.

Step 7: **The Completed Macro**

- Click in **cell A2** of the worksheet. Click in the **Name Box**. Enter **FirstEmployee** to name this cell. Press **Enter**.

- Click in the window containing the macro. Click after the last comment line and press **Enter** to insert a blank line.

- Add the statement to select the cell named FirstEmployee as shown in Figure 8.10g. This ensures that the macro always begins in row two by selecting the cell named FirstEmployee.

- Click immediately after the End If statement. Press **Enter**. Add the statement containing the offset (1,0) as shown in Figure 8.10g, which selects the cell one row below the current row.

- Click anywhere in the worksheet. Press **Ctrl+c** to clear the color. Press **Ctrl+h** to execute the HighlightManager macro.

- The macro begins by selecting cell A2, then proceeds to highlight all managers in red. Save the workbook a final time.

- Print the workbook and its macro for your instructor. Exit Excel. Congratulations on a job well done.

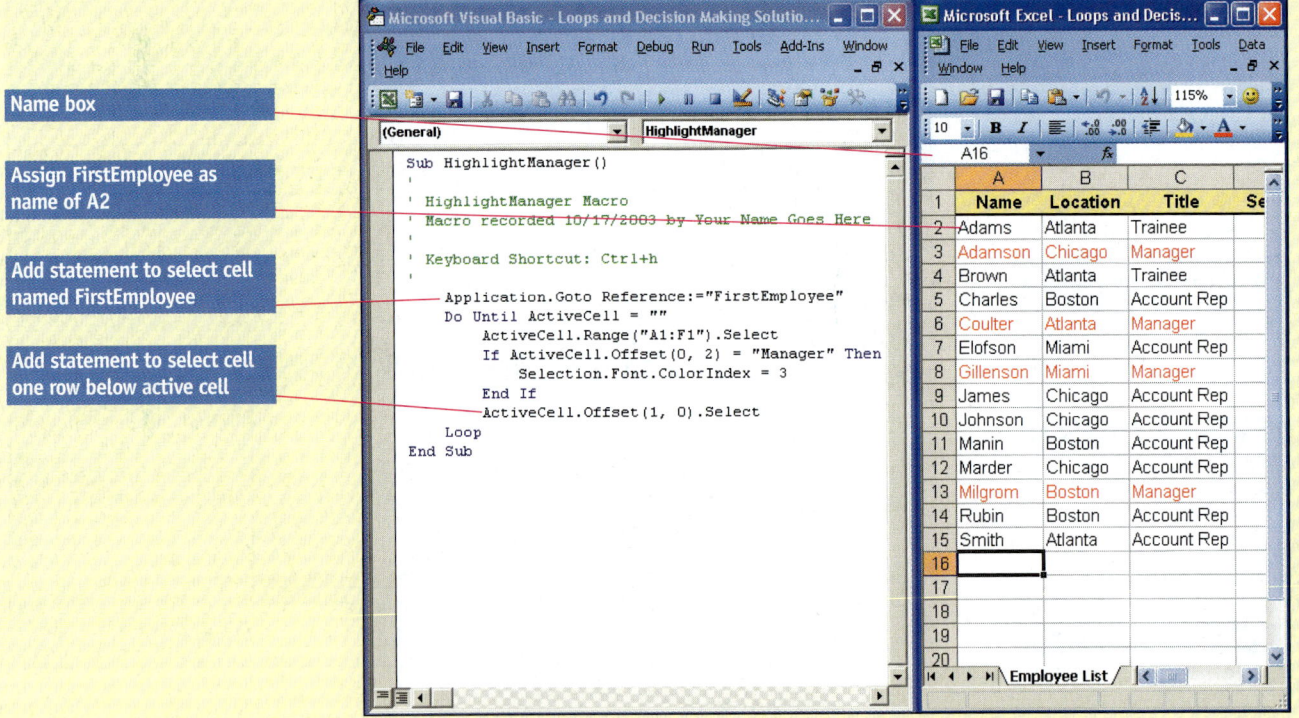

(g) The Completed Macro (step 7)

FIGURE 8.10 Hands-on Exercise 5 (*continued*)

HELP FOR VISUAL BASIC

Click within any Visual Basic keyword, then press the F1 key for context-sensitive help. You will see a help screen containing a description of the statement, its syntax, key elements, and several examples. You can print the help screen by clicking the Printer icon. (If you do not see the help screens, ask your instructor to install Visual Basic Help.)

SUMMARY

A macro is a set of instructions that automates a repetitive task. It is, in essence, a program, and its instructions are written in Visual Basic, a programming language. The macro recorder in Excel records your commands and writes the macro for you. Once a macro has been created, it can be modified in the Visual Basic Editor by manually inserting, deleting, or changing its statements.

Macros are stored in one of two places, either in the current workbook or in a Personal Macro workbook. Macros that are specific to a particular workbook should be stored in that workbook. Generic macros that can be used with any workbook should be stored in the Personal Macro workbook.

A computer virus may be contained in an Excel macro. Thus, Excel will warn you if a workbook you are about to open contains a macro, provided the security option is set appropriately. High security disables all macros except from a previously designated trusted source. Medium security gives you the option to enable macros.

A macro is run (executed) by pulling down the Tools menu and selecting the Run Macro command. A macro can also be executed through a keyboard shortcut, by placing a command button on the worksheet, or by customizing a toolbar to include an additional button to run the macro.

A comment is a nonexecutable statement that begins with an apostrophe. Comments are inserted automatically at the beginning of a macro by the macro recorder to remind you of what the macro does. Comments may be added, deleted, or modified, just as any other statement. A VBA statement is continued from one line to the next by typing a blank space followed by an underscore at the end of the line to be continued. An ampersand concatenates (joins together) two adjacent text strings if a literal has to be continued to a second line.

A macro begins and ends with the Sub and End Sub statements, respectively. The Sub statement contains the name of the macro or VBA procedure. The With statement enables you to perform multiple actions on the same object. All commands between the With and corresponding End With statements are executed collectively.

A macro contains either absolute or relative references. An absolute reference is constant; that is, Excel keeps track of the exact cell address and selects that specific cell. A relative reference depends on the previously selected cell, and is entered as an offset, or number of rows and columns from the current cell. The Relative Reference button on the Stop Recording toolbar toggles between the two.

A good macro is completely general and immune to changes in the underlying workbook. VBA does not, however, update cell references to accommodate insertions or deletions of rows and columns in the associated worksheet. It is good practice, therefore, to always use range names, as opposed to absolute cell references, within a macro.

An Excel macro can be made more powerful through inclusion of Visual Basic statements that enable true programming. These include the MsgBox statement to display information, the InputBox function to obtain user input, the If statement to implement decision making, and the Do statement to implement a loop. The macro recorder creates the initial macro by translating Excel commands to Visual Basic statements. The additional VBA statements are added to the resulting code using the Visual Basic Editor.

A bug is a mistake in a computer program and debugging is the process of finding and correcting program errors. The Step Into command is useful in debugging as it executes a macro (VBA procedure) one statement at a time to see the effects of each statement.

KEY TERMS

Absolute reference 1371	Insert Name command 1383	Relative reference 1371
Code window 1360	Keyboard shortcut 1360	Shortcut key 1360
Comment 1360	Loop 1402	Step Into command 1369
Debugging 1407	Macro 1360	Sub statement 1360
Do statement 1403	Macro recorder 1360	Visual Basic 1360
End If statement 1402	MsgBox statement 1390	Visual Basic Editor (VBE) 1360
End Sub statement 1360	Named range 1381	Visual Basic for
End With statement 1361	Offset 1371	Applications (VBA) 1360
If statement 1402	Personal Macro workbook 1372	With statement 1361
InputBox function 1372	Project Explorer 1360	

MULTIPLE CHOICE

1. Which of the following best describes recording and executing a macro?
   (a) A macro is recorded once and executed once
   (b) A macro is recorded once and executed many times
   (c) A macro is recorded many times and executed once
   (d) A macro is recorded many times and executed many times

2. Which of the following can be used to execute a macro?
   (a) A keyboard shortcut
   (b) A customized toolbar button
   (c) A button on the worksheet
   (d) All of the above

3. A macro can be stored:
   (a) In any Excel workbook
   (b) In the Personal Macro workbook
   (c) Both (a) and (b)
   (d) Neither (a) nor (b)

4. Which of the following is true regarding comments in Visual Basic?
   (a) A comment is executable; that is, its inclusion or omission affects the outcome of a macro
   (b) A comment begins with an apostrophe
   (c) Both (a) and (b)
   (d) Neither (a) nor (b)

5. Which statement must contain the name of the macro?
   (a) The Sub statement at the beginning of the macro
   (b) The first comment statement
   (c) Both (a) and (b)
   (d) Neither (a) nor (b)

6. Which of the following indicates an absolute reference within a macro?
   (a) ActiveCell.Offset(1,1).Range("A1")
   (b) $A$1
   (c) Range("A1")
   (d) All of the above

7. Selection.Offset (1,0).Range ("A1").Select will select the cell that is:
   (a) In the same column as the active cell but one row below
   (b) In the same row as the active cell but one column to the right
   (c) In the same column as the active cell but one row above
   (d) In the same row as the active cell but one column to the left

8. Selection.Offset (1,1).Range ("A1").Select will select the cell that is:
   (a) One cell below and one cell to the left of the active cell
   (b) One cell below and one cell to the right of the active cell
   (c) One cell above and one cell to the right of the active cell
   (d) One cell above and one cell to the left of the active cell

9. Selection.Offset (1,1).Range ("A1:A2").Select will select:
   (a) Cell A1
   (b) Cell A2
   (c) Both (a) and (b)
   (d) Neither (a) nor (b)

10. Which commands are used to duplicate an existing macro so that it can become the basis of a new macro?
    (a) Copy command
    (b) Paste command
    (c) Both (a) and (b)
    (d) Neither (a) nor (b)

11. Which of the following is used to protect a macro from the subsequent insertion or deletion of rows or columns in the associated worksheet?
    (a) Range names
    (b) Absolute references
    (c) Both (a) and (b)
    (d) Neither (a) nor (b)

... continued

multiple choice

12. Which of the following is true regarding a customized button that has been inserted as an object onto a worksheet and assigned to an Excel macro?
    (a) Point to the customized button, then click the left mouse button to execute the associated macro
    (b) Point to the customized button, then click the right mouse button to select the macro button and simultaneously display a shortcut menu
    (c) Point to the customized button, then press and hold the Ctrl key as you click the left mouse to select the button
    (d) All of the above

13. The InputBox function:
    (a) Displays a message (prompt) requesting input from the user
    (b) Stores the user's response in a designated cell
    (c) Both (a) and (b)
    (d) Neither (a) nor (b)

14. You want to create a macro to enter your name into a specific cell. The best way to do this is to:
    (a) Select the cell for your name, turn on the macro recorder with absolute references, then type your name
    (b) Turn on the macro recorder with absolute references, select the cell for your name, then type your name
    (c) Either (a) or (b)
    (d) Neither (a) nor (b)

15. Which of the following is true about indented text in a VBA procedure?
    (a) The indented text is always executed first
    (b) The indented text is always executed last
    (c) The indented text is rendered a comment and is never executed
    (d) None of the above

16. You want to create a macro to enter your name in the active cell (which will vary whenever the macro is used) and the course you are taking in the cell immediately below. The best way to do this is to:
    (a) Select the cell for your name, turn on the macro recorder with absolute references, type your name, press the down arrow, and type the course
    (b) Turn on the macro recorder with absolute references, select the cell for your name, type your name, press the down arrow, and type the course
    (c) Select the cell for your name, turn on the macro recorder with relative references, type your name, press the down arrow, and type the course
    (d) Turn on the macro recorder with relative references, select the cell for your name, type your name, press the down arrow, and type the course

17. A VBA statement contains the reference, ActiveCell.Offset(1,0).Range("A1:A3"). Which cells are selected if cell B3 is the active cell when the command is executed?
    (a) The range B1:B3
    (b) The range B4:B6
    (c) The range A1:A3
    (d) The range A2:A4

18. You have created a named range called AllEmployees which is assigned to cells A2:H100 in the worksheet. Which of the following actions will change the cells that are included in the named range?
    (a) Inserting or deleting an employee in the middle of the list
    (b) Inserting or deleting a field in the middle of the list
    (c) Both (a) and (b)
    (d) Neither (a) nor (b)

ANSWERS

1. b	7. a	13. c
2. d	8. b	14. b
3. c	9. d	15. d
4. b	10. c	16. c
5. a	11. a	17. b
6. c	12. d	18. c

PRACTICE WITH EXCEL

1. **Data Management Macros:** Figure 8.11 displays an alternate version of the Employee List Solution workbook that was used in the third and fourth hands-on exercises. The existing macros have been deleted and replaced by the five macros represented by the command buttons in the figure. Your assignment is to create the indicated macros and assign the macros to the command buttons. The purpose of each macro should be apparent from the name of the command button.

   a. You can "cut and paste" macros from the Employee List Solution workbook as it existed at the end of the fourth hands-on exercise, or you can create the macros from scratch using the *Chapter 8 Practice 1* workbook (which contains the equivalent workbook used in Hands-on Exercise 3). Choose whichever technique you think is easier. You will need to use the Insert Name Create command to assign names to various cells in the worksheet for use in your macros.

   b. The AllEmployees macro should clear the criteria row, then display all employees within the list (the summary statistics will reflect all employees as well). The other four macros prompt the user for the specific criteria. Note that the user can include relational operators for service or salary, such as >60000 to display employees with salaries greater than $60,000. All of the macros should include a MsgBox statement that displays the indicated message in Figure 8.11.

   c. Run the AnySalary macro, then print the workbook as it appears in Figure 8.11. Print the worksheet with row and column headings and be sure that it fits on a single sheet of paper. Be sure to change the properties of the command buttons so that the buttons appear on the printed worksheet.

   d. Run the All Employees macro and then print the worksheet after the macro is complete. Print the worksheet a second time to show the cell formulas.

   e. Change to the Visual Basic Editor, pull down the File menu, click the Print command, then print the current project to print all of the modules (macros) within your workbook.

   f. Add a cover sheet and submit the entire assignment to your instructor.

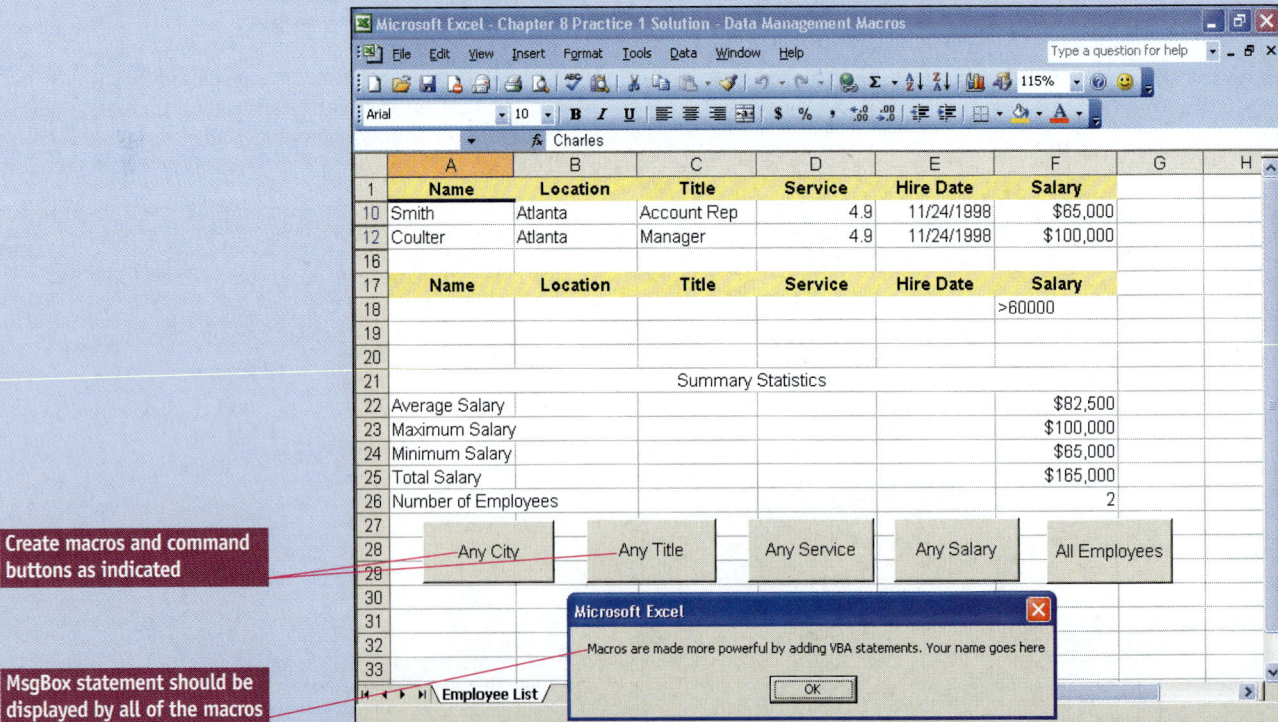

FIGURE 8.11 Data Management Macros (exercise 1)

1414   CHAPTER 8: AUTOMATING REPETITIVE TASKS

practice exercises

2. **Employee Selection:** Figure 8.12 extends the previous problem to include one additional macro that prompts the user for city, title, service, and salary. The user enters all four parameters, then the macro displays the selected records within the list together with the summary statistics. It is quite possible, however, that no employee will meet all the criteria, in which case the macro should display a message to that effect as shown.
   a. Your assignment is to complete the previous problem, then add the additional macro to prompt for the multiple criteria. The macro will always ask the user for all four parameters, but you need not enter every parameter. If, for example, you do not specify a city, the macro will return matching employees regardless of the city.
   b. You can include relational operators in the service and/or salary fields as shown in Figure 8.12. The figure is searching for Chicago Account reps with less than eight years of service, earning more than $60,000.
   c. The DAVERAGE function displays a division by zero error message if there is no record that meets the specified criteria. You can hide the error message, however, by using conditional formatting to display the message in white, which renders it invisible. Click in the cell containing the DAVERAGE function. Pull down the Format menu, click Conditional formatting, and then click the drop-down arrow in the left list box to select Formula Is. Click in the box to the right and type =ISERROR(F22) where F22 is the cell containing the function that caused the error. Now click the Format button, click Font, and change the color to white. The message is in the cell, but you cannot see it.
   d. You need to include an If statement in your macro that tests whether the number of qualified employees is equal to zero, and if so, it should display the associated message box. It's easy to do. Use the Insert Name command within the Excel workbook to assign the name "QualifiedEmployees" to cell F26. Then insert a statement in the macro to go to this cell, which makes it the active cell. The If statement can then compare the value of the active cell to zero, and if it is zero, use the MsgBox statement to display the indicated message.
   e. Print the worksheet in Figure 8.12 for your instructor. (The dialog box will not appear on your printout.) Print the module containing the macro.

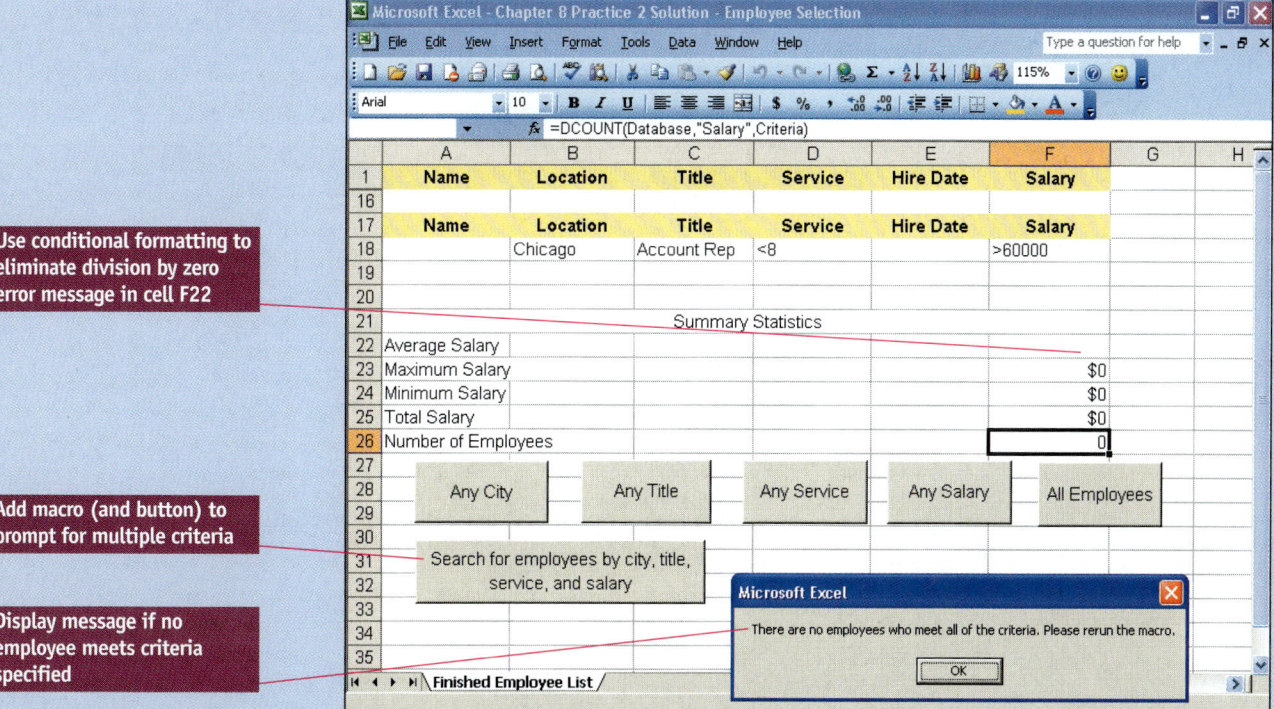

FIGURE 8.12 Employee Selection (exercise 2)

practice exercises

3. **Highlighting Employees:** Figure 8.13 extends the Loops and Decision Making workbook from the fifth hands-on exercise to include command buttons and an additional macro. The new macro highlights the Atlanta and Chicago employees in red and blue, respectively.

   a. Open the Loops and Decision Making Solution workbook from the fifth hands-on exercise. Start the Visual Basic Editor, then copy the existing HighlightManager macro so that you can use it as the basis of the new macro, which will highlight the employees in two locations. Change the name of the copied macro. Then change the offset in the If statement to (0, 1) to reference the location column within the list, and further to compare that value to "Atlanta," as opposed to "Manager."

   b. Switch to the Excel workbook, pull down the Tools menu, select the Macro command, click Macros, select the new macro, click Options, then assign a keyboard shortcut. (We used Ctrl+a). Press Ctrl+c to execute the ClearColor macro, then press Ctrl+a to test the newly created macro. The Atlanta employees should be highlighted in red.

   c. Return to the VBA editor and insert the ElseIf clause immediately above the existing End If clause. The ElseIf should compare the value of the cell with the appropriate offset to "Chicago," and if that condition is true, highlight the selection in blue (color 5). Test the modified macro.

   d. Add command buttons to the worksheet as shown in Figure 8.13, then test the buttons to be sure that they work properly. You will discover that the macros require one subtle adjustment; that is, if you run the Chicago and Atlanta macro, followed immediately by the Manager macro (or vice versa), employees from both macros will be highlighted. In other words, you need to clear any existing highlighting prior to running either of the other two. *You can make this happen automatically by including ClearColor (the name of the macro you want to run) as the first statement in the other two macros.*

   e. Print the completed worksheet for your instructor. Be sure to change the properties of the command buttons so that they print with the worksheet.

   f. Print the module containing the code for all three macros. Add a cover sheet to complete the assignment.

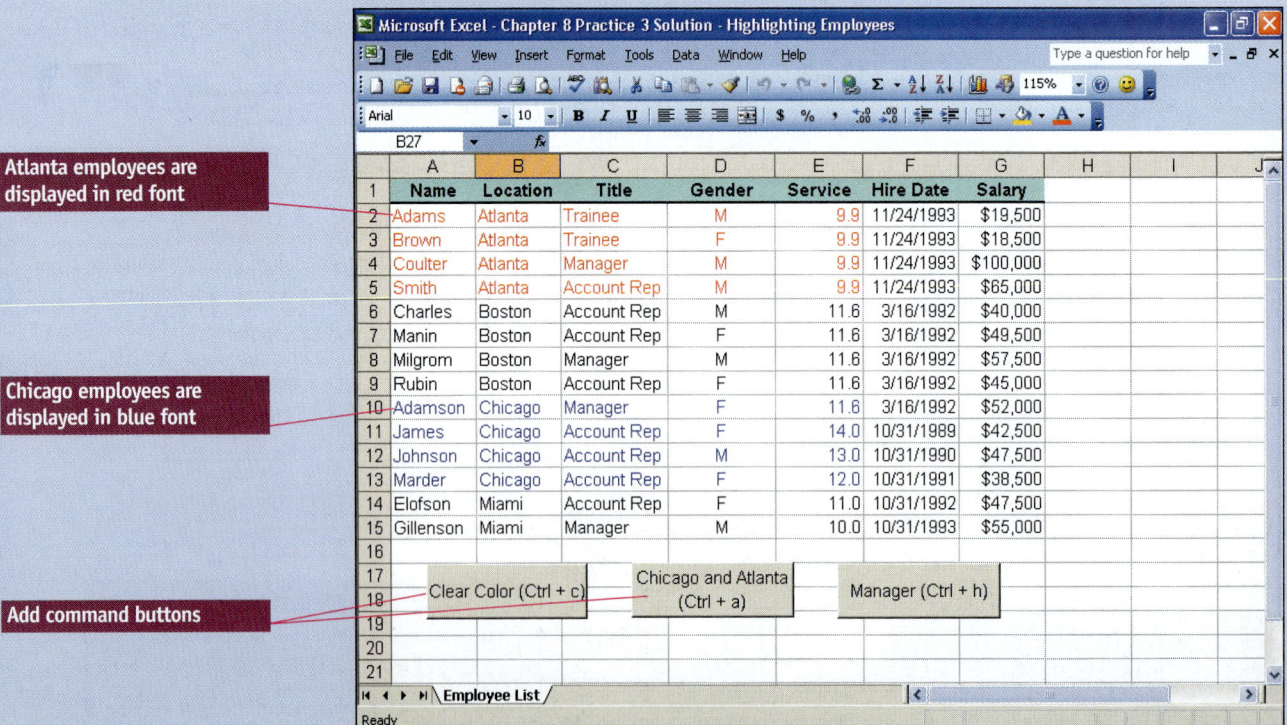

FIGURE 8.13 Highlighting Employees (exercise 3)

practice exercises

4. **Student List:** The worksheet in Figure 8.14 is shown after execution of the macro, Any Year Any Major, which prompts the user for these values, then displays the selected students and summary statistics. All of the macros in the worksheet are flexible and use range names, as opposed to specific cell references. We have created three range names for you: Criteria (A19:G20), CriteriaValues (A20:G20), and StudentList (A1:G17), but you will have to create the remaining names as necessary. Proceed as follows:

   a. Open the *Chapter 8 Practice 4* workbook. Click and drag to select cells A19 through G20, then use the Insert Name Create command (using the entries in the top row) to create the additional range names.

   b. Create the macro to show all students. This requires you to clear the range name CriteriaValues, then use the Advanced Filter command (with the range names StudentList and Criteria) to display all of the students.

   c. Display the Forms toolbar. Click the Button tool, draw a button on the worksheet, and assign the AllStudents macro that you just created to the button. Right click the button, click Format Control, click the Properties tab, then check the box to print the object.

   d. Use the macro recorder to create a macro for a specific major, and then edit the macro to substitute the InputBox function for the name of the major. The macro should begin by clearing the criteria area and end by displaying the message box in Figure 8.14.

   e. Return to the Excel workbook. Right click the All Students command button, click the Copy button, click the Paste button, and drag the duplicate button to the right. Right click the new button and assign the AnyMajor macro to the new button. Change the text of the button as well. Test both buttons to be sure that the associated macros work correctly.

   f. The easiest way to create the remaining macros is to duplicate the AnyMajor macro and then make changes in the VBA editor. Copy an existing macro button, and then assign each new macro to a new button.

   g. Execute the macro to display students in any year and any major (use any values you like). Print the completed worksheet and the module(s) containing the macros for your instructor.

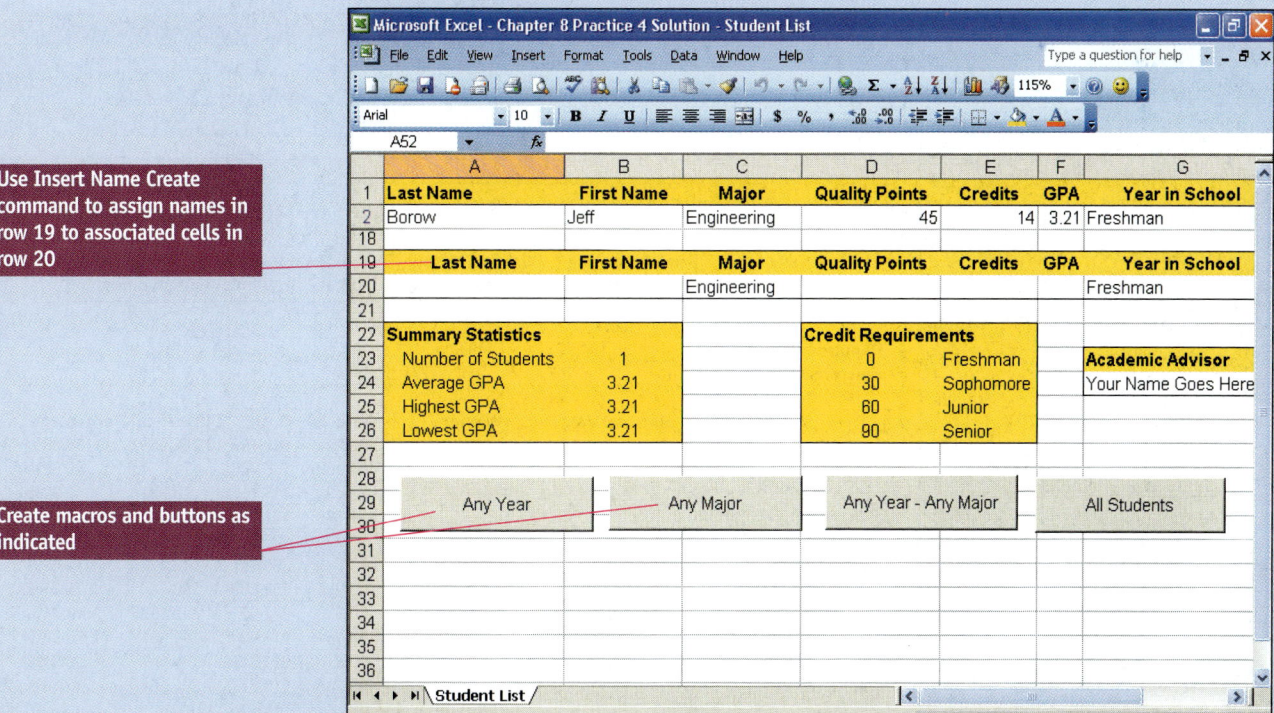

FIGURE 8.14 Student List (exercise 4)

practice exercises

5. **Election Macros:** Open the completed *Chapter 7 Practice 1* workbook from the previous chapter and then add the macros shown in Figure 8.15. The easiest way to complete this exercise is to create the first macro, copy it, make the necessary changes within the VBA editor to create the next macro, and so on. Proceed as follows:

   a. All macros should use range names, as opposed to specific cell references so that they are immune to subsequent insertions or deletions of rows or columns in a worksheet. Assign the range names "State", "Difference", and "Percentage", to cells A7, F7, and G7, respectively.

   b. Start the macro recorder. Specify Alphabetical as the macro name. Click the down arrow in the Name box and select "State" (to go to cell A7), then click the Ascending Sort button. Click the Stop Recording button.

   c. Display the Forms toolbar. Click the Button tool, draw a button on the worksheet, and assign the Alphabetical macro that you just created to the button. Right click the button, click Format Control, click the Properties tab, then check the box to print the object.

   d. Press Alt+F11 to display the Visual Basic editor. Click and drag to select the complete Alphabetical macro (including the Sub and End Sub statements). Press Ctrl+C then Ctrl+V to duplicate the macro. Change the name of the duplicate macro to SmallestPercentage (spaces are not allowed in the name). Change *all* occurrences of the reference to "State" to "Percentage", effectively changing the sort from column A to column F.

   e. Return to Excel. Right click the Alphabetical command button, click the Copy command, click the Paste button, and drag the duplicate button to the right. Right click the new button and assign the SmallestPercentage macro to the new button. Change the text of the button as well.

   f. Create the remaining macros and associated command buttons in similar fashion. Note, however, that you will also have to change the sort order in the macros that specify a descending sequence.

   g. Print the completed worksheet in at least two different sequences. Use the Page Setup command to be sure the entire worksheet fits on one page.

   h. Print the VBA module that contains all five procedures.

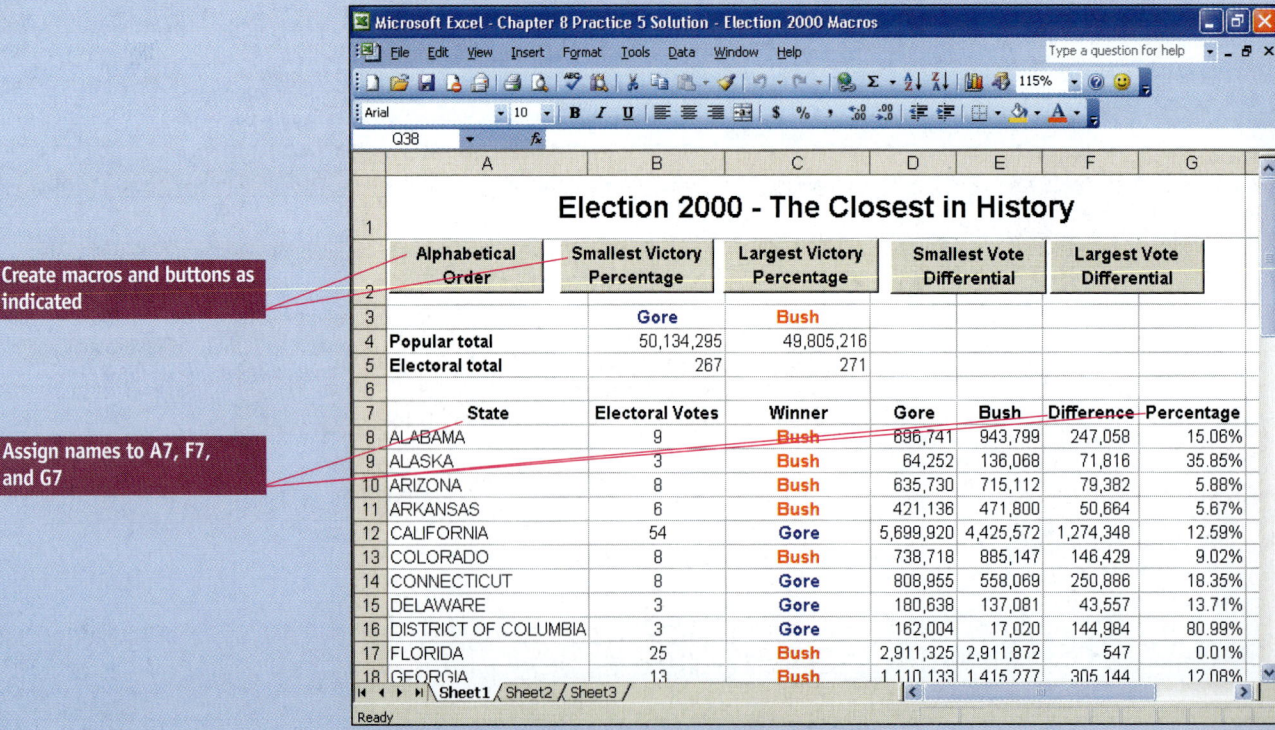

FIGURE 8.15 Election Macros (exercise 5)

practice exercises

6. **Stock Portfolio:** Figure 8.16 displays a worksheet that uses macros in conjunction with Web queries to update a stock portfolio. You have seen this worksheet before, most recently in Chapter 5 when we studied worksheet references within a workbook. Now we complete the example through the introduction of macros.

   a. Open the partially completed *Chapter 8 Practice 6* workbook and click the worksheet tab that contains your portfolio. The macros are already in the worksheet, and all you have to do is click the appropriate command buttons. The macro to enter your investments will prompt you for three investments for which you need to enter the company symbol, number of shares, and purchase price. This macro will also copy the stock symbols you have entered to the end of the stock symbol table in the Stock Prices worksheet.

   b. Click the command button to Update Your Portfolio, which in turn will execute the Web query to retrieve the current price of your investments and automatically calculate the value of your portfolio. The worksheet is password protected to prevent you from accidentally changing any of the formulas that have been entered. (The password is "password", in lowercase letters so you can remove the protection if you like using the Tools menu.)

   c. After you have updated your portfolio, click the button to View Summary to take you to the summary worksheet. The macros for that worksheet have not been created, however, so it is up to you to create the macros and assign them to the indicated command buttons as shown in Figure 8.16. The UpdatePrices macro refreshes the Web query in the Stock Prices worksheet. (It is the same as the UpdateYourPortfolio macro except that it returns to the Summary worksheet.) The Best Investors and Worst Investors list the portfolios in descending and ascending order according to the percentage gain or loss.

   d. Print the Summary worksheet for your instructor as well as the worksheet that contains your portfolio. Print the module(s) containing all of the macros within the worksheet. Add a short note explaining the purpose of the various modules that were originally in the workbook.

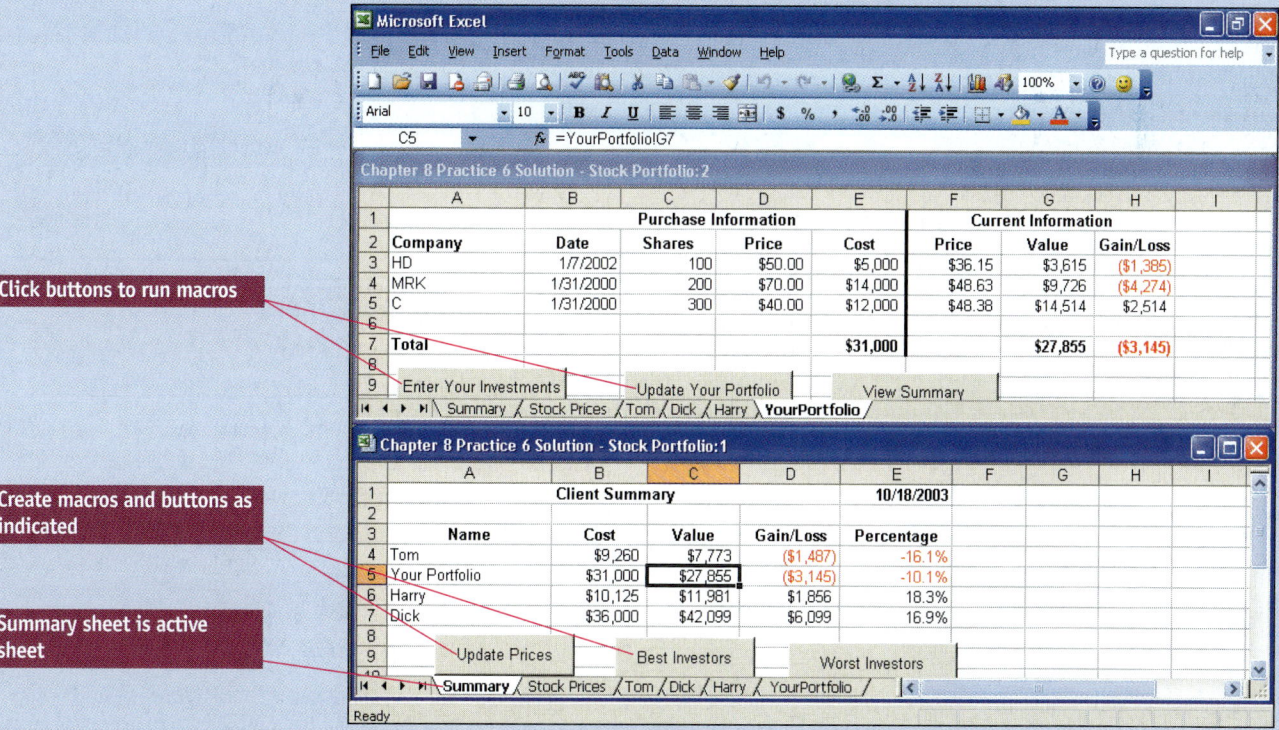

FIGURE 8.16 Stock Portfolio (exercise 6)

practice exercises

7. **Consumer Loans:** Figure 8.17 displays a worksheet containing hypothetical data for a series of consumer loans. The associated workbook also contains four macros: to select loans by type, date, and amount; to clear the associated criteria range and display all loans; to highlight the mortgages in red within the complete list of loans and show the summary statistics for mortgages only; and finally to remove the highlighting and reset the summary statistics to include all records. We have already created the ShowAllLoans and ClearColor macros for you. Your assignment is to create the remaining two macros. Proceed as follows:

   a. Open the *Chapter 8 Practice 7* workbook in the Exploring Excel folder. Use the concepts from the third and fourth hands-on exercises to create the macro to display loans by type, date, and amount. The user is to be prompted for each parameter. The macro should be written to use the range names that have been defined within the workbook rather than specific cell references. End the macro by selecting cell A1 and displaying the message in Figure 8.17. Assign the macro to a command button.

   b. Use the concepts from the fifth hands-on exercise to create the macro to highlight the mortgages within the complete list of loans, and further to set the criteria range so that the summary statistics for only the mortgages are displayed. (*Hint:* The first statement of this macro should be ShowAllLoans, which will execute the existing macro of that name.) Assign the macro to a command button.

   c. Click the button to run the HighlightMortgages macro. You should see all of the mortgage loans in red. Now click the button to run the LoansByTypeDateandAmount macro. Do not enter a loan type in response to the first prompt (to display loans of all types). Specify a start date after 9/20/2002 and a loan amount less than $100,000. You should see the loans in Figure 8.17.

   d. Print the completed worksheet for your instructor. Use the Page Setup command to be sure the entire worksheet fits on one page. Print the worksheet a second time to show the cell formulas.

   e. Print the VBA module that contains all four procedures. Add a cover sheet to complete the assignment.

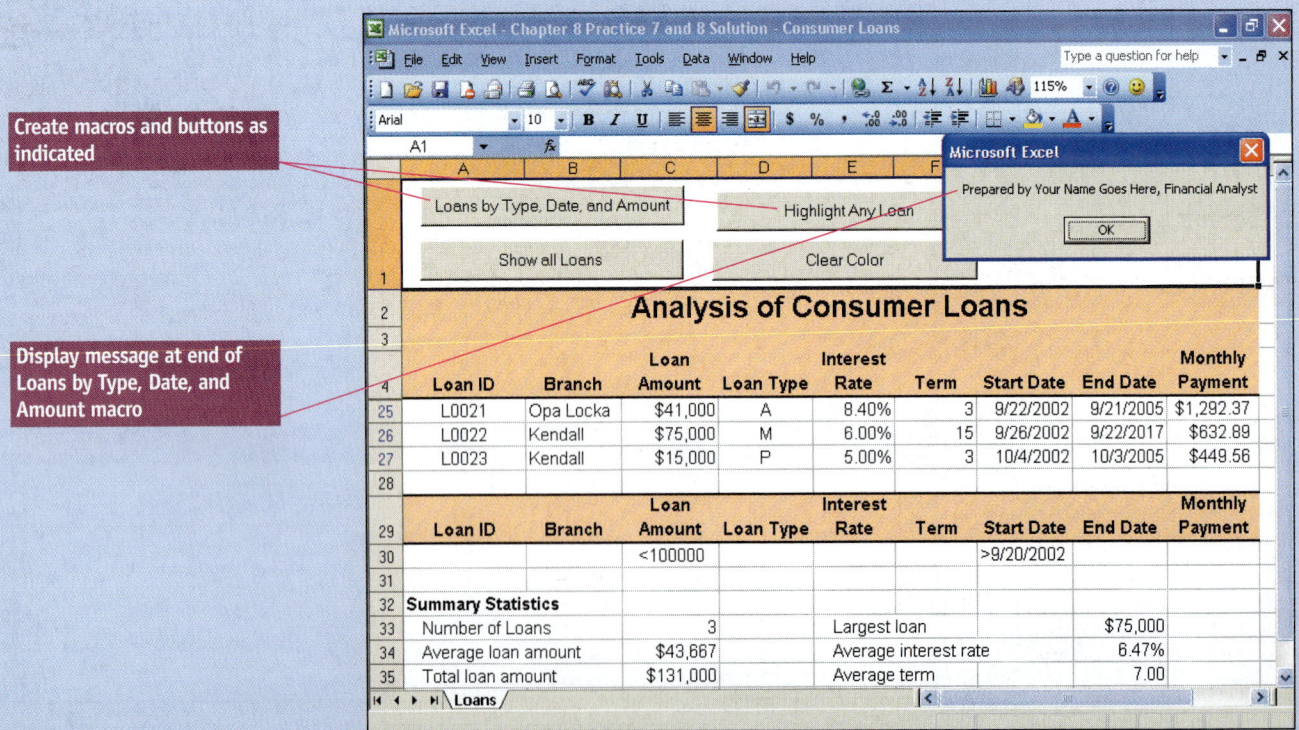

FIGURE 8.17 Consumer Loans (exercise 7)

practice exercises

8. **A Look Ahead:** Figure 8.18 extends the previous exercise to include a procedure to highlight any loan, as opposed to highlighting only mortgages. The VBA code for that procedure is shown in the figure. Your job is to complete the previous hands-on exercise, delete the macro (and associated command button) for the HighlightMortgages macro, then substitute the new macro in its place. The VBA statements within the new procedure parallel those of its predecessor, but introduce some new material in Visual Basic. There are several comments within the macro to explain these statements, with additional explanation added below. Use the VBA primer that appears at the end of the Excel chapters in this text as a reference.

   a. The most important concept is that of a variable to store information received from the user. The Dim statement near the beginning of the procedure assigns a name to the variable (strLoanType) and indicates that it will hold text (i.e., the variable is declared to be a character string). The subsequent Input Box statement prompts the user for the loan type, then stores that value in the strLoanType variable. The procedure will highlight all loans of that type.

   b. The If statement within the loop to highlight the selected records compares the loan type to the uppercase value of the strLoanType variable. This is important because if the user inadvertently enters a lowercase letter, the comparison would fail.

   c. The MsgBox statement at the end of the procedure includes two additional parameters. The vbInformation variable indicates the type of icon that is supposed to appear within the message box. The underscore is there to show that the statement is continued to the next line, which in turn contains the text that will appear in the title bar of the message box.

   d. Enter the procedure as it appears in Figure 8.18. Assign a command button to the macro within the worksheet, then test the macro. Run the procedure two times to show two different loan types. Print each worksheet for your instructor.

   e. Print the VBA module containing all of the procedures. Add a cover sheet to complete the assignment.

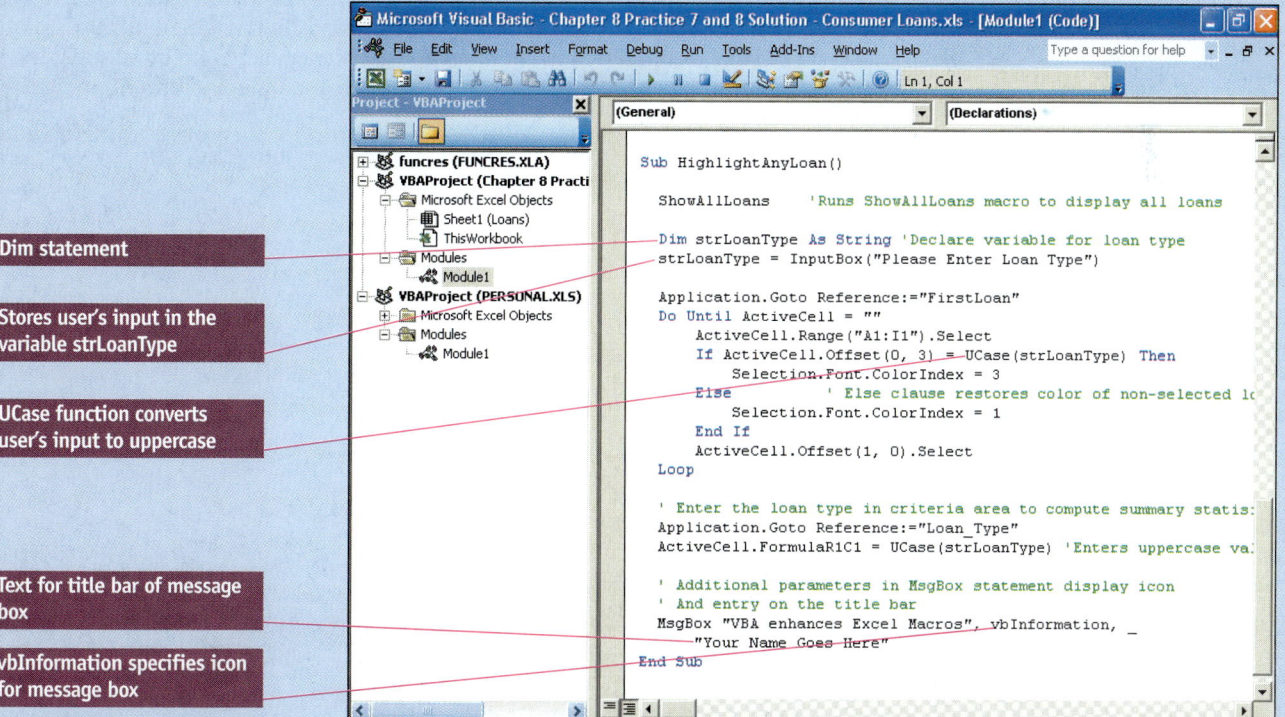

FIGURE 8.18 A Look Ahead (exercise 8)

MINI CASES

Microsoft Word

Do you use Microsoft Word on a regular basis? Are there certain tasks that you do repeatedly, whether in the same document or in a series of different documents? If so, you would do well to explore the macro capabilities within Microsoft Word. How are these capabilities similar to Excel's? How do they differ?

Starting Up

Your instructor is very impressed with the various Excel workbooks and associated macros that you have created. He would like you to take the automation process one step further and simplify the way in which Excel is started and the workbook is loaded. The problem is open ended, and there are many different approaches. You might, for example, create a shortcut on the desktop to open the workbook. You might also explore the use of the Startup folder in Microsoft Excel.

Antivirus Programs

What is an antivirus program and how do you get one? How do these programs supplement the macro virus protection that is built into Microsoft Excel? Use your favorite search engine to find two such programs, then summarize their capability and cost in a short note to your instructor. You can also visit the National Computer Security Association (www.ncsa.com) and the Computer Emergency Response Team (www.cert.org) to learn more about computer security.

Extending Excel Macros through VBA

You do not have to know VBA to create Excel macros, but knowledge of VBA will help you to create better macros. VBA is accessible from all major applications in Microsoft Office, so that anything you learn in one application is also applicable to other applications. The VBA syntax is identical. Locate the VBA primer that appears at the end of this text, study the basic statements it contains, and complete the associated hands-on exercises. Write a short note to your instructor that describes similarities and differences from one Office application to the next.

CHAPTER 9

A Professional Application: VBA and Date Functions

OBJECTIVES

After reading this chapter you will:

1. Explain the importance of data validation in a spreadsheet.
2. Describe the YEAR, MONTH, DAY, and DATE FUNCTIONS.
3. Describe the PMT, IPMT, and PPMT functions.
4. Describe the logical functions AND and OR.
5. Describe the Excel object model.
6. Use the macro recorder to "jump-start" a VBA procedure.
7. Distinguish between event and general procedures.
8. Develop a custom toolbar and attach it to a workbook.
9. Set the print area in a worksheet.
10. Create a user form.
11. Explain how pseudocode is used to develop procedures.

hands-on exercises

1. **AMORTIZATION WORKBOOK**
   Input: Amortization Schedule
   Output: Amortization Schedule Solution

2. **EXPLORING VBA SYNTAX**
   Input: Amortization Schedule Solution (from exercise 1)
   Output: Amortization Schedule Solution (additional modifications)

3. **EVENT PROCEDURES**
   Input: Amortization Schedule Solution (from exercise 2)
   Output: Amortization Schedule Solution (additional modifications)

4. **OPTIONAL PAYMENTS**
   Input: Amortization Schedule Solution (from exercise 3)
   Output: Amortization Schedule Solution (additional modifications)

CASE STUDY
REFINANCE NOW

You purchased your first home three years ago. It's in a great neighborhood, your neighbors are friendly, you have a large yard for your dog, and you are truly at home. You took out a 30-year mortgage for $100,000 at 7.5%, which resulted in a monthly payment of just under $700. You have paid approximately $25,000 to the bank (principal and interest) during the three years you have lived in the house, but are shocked to learn that you still owe approximately $97,000 on the mortgage. In other words, you have paid approximately $22,000 in interest and only $3,000 in principal.

The good news is that interest rates are at or near their lowest level in 40 years. You have been approached by multiple mortgage brokers about the benefits of refinancing, yet you still have doubts about whether you should refinance. You know that your monthly payment will go down, but you will incur additional closing costs of 4% to obtain the new loan on the remaining principal of $97,000; thus, you plan to roll the closing costs into the new mortgage to avoid an out-of-pocket expense. You can obtain either a 15- or 30-year mortgage and you want to explore the advantages of each. Is it possible that the lower interest rates on a new 15-year loan could keep your payments at the same level as your existing 30-year mortgage?

Your assignment is to create a simple workbook that will compare your existing mortgage to a new 15-year mortgage at 5%. It should show the monthly payment, the savings per month, and the total interest over the life of each loan. It should also determine the number of months to break even on the new 30-year mortgage. This is a simple workbook that does not require macros or VBA.

You are then to read the chapter and create the loan amortization workbook that is described within the chapter. The end result is a sophisticated workbook that includes macros and a custom toolbar that allows you to make extra payments. Use the completed workbook to enter one additional payment a year; that is, how long will it take you to pay off a 30-year mortgage if you make 13 payments a year (one every month as scheduled, plus an extra payment once a year)?

APPLICATION DEVELOPMENT

Any application originates with the client or end user. He or she has a need and is willing to pay a developer to fulfill that need. The developer in turn goes through an iterative process that presents the client with multiple versions of the application, until the finished application is delivered. The key to a successful application is a systematic approach that includes continual testing and interaction between the client and the developer. We suggest these basic steps, which provide a broad outline of the chapter:

1. Determine what the application is to accomplish
2. Design the user interface (the worksheet)
3. Develop the spreadsheet
4. Test and debug the spreadsheet
5. Add automation (macros and VBA procedures) as necessary
6. Test and debug the completed application

The first (and perhaps most important) step is to determine precisely what the application is to accomplish. The client has an idea of his or her requirements, and the developer can make suggestions as to the additional functionality that can be included. The example in this chapter is that of a payment *(amortization)* schedule for a loan, based on parameters supplied by the end user. The client has further specified that he wants to see the scheduled date of each payment, how much of each payment goes toward interest, and how much goes toward principal. He also wants the ability to include optional (extra) payments of principal that will shorten the time required to pay off the loan.

Data validation is an implied requirement of any application, something the developer should bring to the attention of the client if the client does not request it independently. Every input parameter should be checked so that the end results will make sense. The end user should be prevented, for example, from entering a term (more than 30 years) that exceeds the maximum number of possible payments. The user might also be cautioned against (but not prevented from) entering an inappropriate (exorbitant) interest rate. A good worksheet will anticipate errors the user may make during data entry and prevent those errors from occurring.

The application should be flexible, visually appealing, easy to use, and bulletproof. A flexible worksheet enables the user to enter parameters in a clearly defined input area, then bases all of its formulas on those parameters, so that any change in the input automatically changes the body of the worksheet. A worksheet should also be visually appealing and include any logo or other formatting requirements of the client.

The completed application should be easy to use and enable the end user to accomplish tasks that he or she would not otherwise be able to do. The specifications may call for macros or VBA procedures to automate command sequences that are executed from custom toolbars or menus. A bulletproof application will work correctly with any set of input parameters and will prevent the display of zero values when they are not appropriate. The application should also insulate itself from the nontechnical user by protecting the formulas in the worksheet so that they cannot be accidentally (or otherwise) altered or deleted.

Continual testing and debugging is essential. The developer has to ensure that the formulas within the worksheet are correct, and further that any and all VBA procedures are also correct. This is an iterative process that occurs throughout the development cycle. All of these requirements should be clearly specified in advance, after which both client and developer should sign a written statement of the intended specifications and schedule. The end result is a polished application that is suitable for general distribution.

The Amortization Workbook

Figure 9.1a displays the application that will be developed throughout this chapter. The worksheet does not appear unduly complex, but it is more sophisticated than any worksheet we have studied thus far. One significant item is what you do *not* see—the payments in the body of the worksheet will not appear until all of the loan parameters have been entered, and further the worksheet will display and print only as many rows (payments) as are necessary. A 30-year loan, for example, requires 360 payments, whereas a 15-year loan takes only 180. Data validation is also built into the worksheet. For example, the worksheet will reject any loans greater than 30 years or any loans with artificially high interest rates.

Figure 9.1b displays the worksheet after the last required parameter has been entered. Only the first several payments are visible, but the information in these rows is indicative of the underlying function. The date of each payment, for example, occurs on the 16th of each month, which is consistent with the specified date of the first payment within the input area. This calculation is accomplished through various date functions and is discussed later in the chapter.

The worksheet also divides the monthly payment of $665.30 into two components, interest and principal. The outstanding balance on the loan is reduced each month by the amount of the payment that went toward principal. Thus, the amount of the next payment that goes toward interest decreases (if only by pennies initially), while the amount that goes toward principal increases.

The summary information in the upper-right portion of the worksheet indicates a total of 360 scheduled payments, which is what you would expect for a 30-year loan. The worksheet also displays the normal payoff date of 2/16/2033, which occurs after the 360th payment has been made. Note, too, that the total interest on the loan is more than $139,000, which is more than the amount of the actual loan.

The client also requested the ability to include additional payments toward principal, which is reflected in Figure 9.1c. Here we see that a constant (optional) payment of $100 a month will reduce the total interest over the life of the loan to just over $89,000 (a savings of more than $50,000). The loan is paid off after 247 payments on September 16, 2023, almost 10 years earlier than the original loan. The borrower has paid $24,700 (247 payments of $100 each) in early payments, but this is not truly "additional" money. It is principal that would have been paid eventually during the original 30-year schedule. The borrower has simply elected to make these payments earlier than necessary in order to reduce the total interest.

All of the calculations within the worksheet are accomplished through various functions, without macros of any kind. Figure 9.1d displays some of the underlying formulas and may appear unduly complicated. We prefer to say, however, that these formulas add functionality, as opposed to complexity. Consider, for example, the ***AND function***, =AND(C4>0,C5>0,C6>0,C7>0), that appears in cell D6.

The AND function returns one of two values, true or false. It is considered true if all of its arguments are true, and false otherwise. In this example the AND function is checking the values in cells C4 through C7, and it requires that each of these entries be greater than zero if the function is to be true. In other words, we can check the value in cell D6 (which has been assigned the name DataEntered) to determine if all of the required parameters have been supplied, and if so, we can display these values in the body of the worksheet. (The ***OR function*** is not used in this worksheet, but it is also very useful. The OR function requires only one argument to be true for the function to be true.)

Cell A14 contains the formula =IF(DataEntered, 1,0). Recall that the IF function has three arguments—a condition that is evaluated as true or false, the value if the condition is true, and the value if the condition is false. Thus, the number of the first payment will be 1 if all parameters have been entered and zero otherwise. (The Options command has been set to hide zero values in the spreadsheet.) All of the other formulas in the worksheet are based on the value in cell A14, which in turn allows us to display only as many rows (payments) as are necessary.

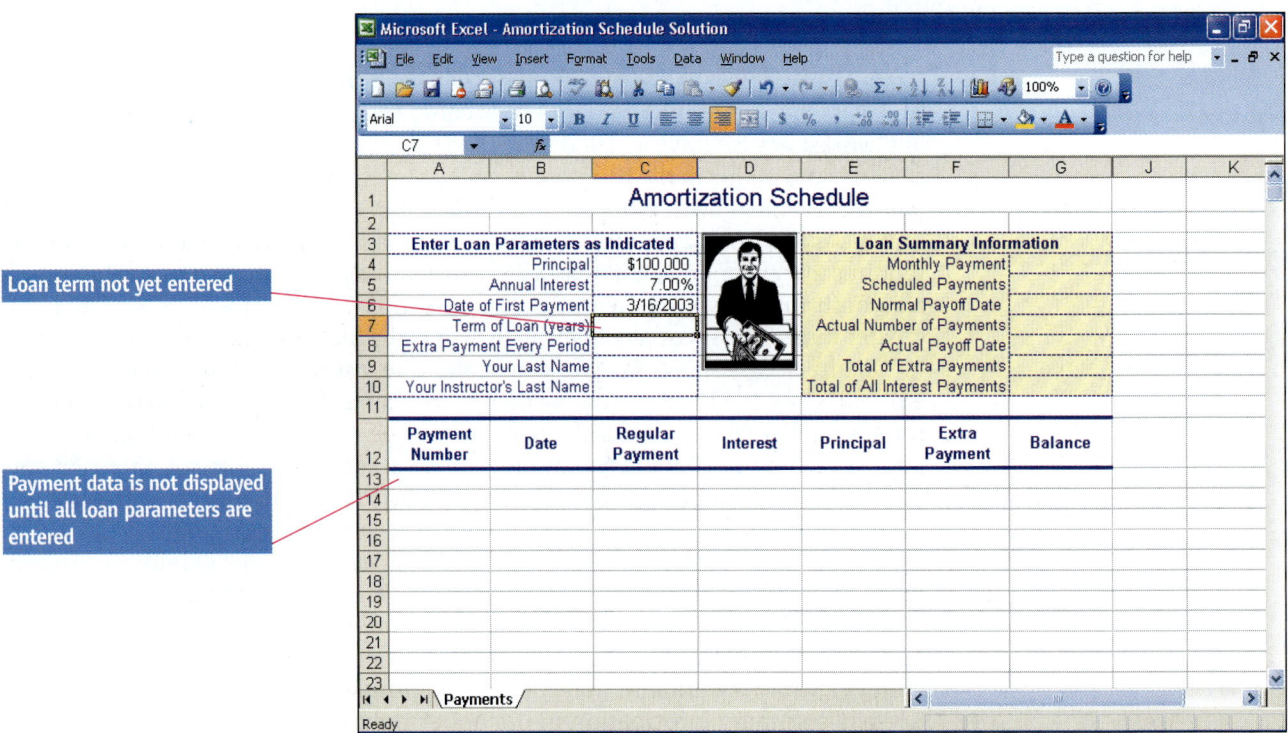

(a) Data Entry

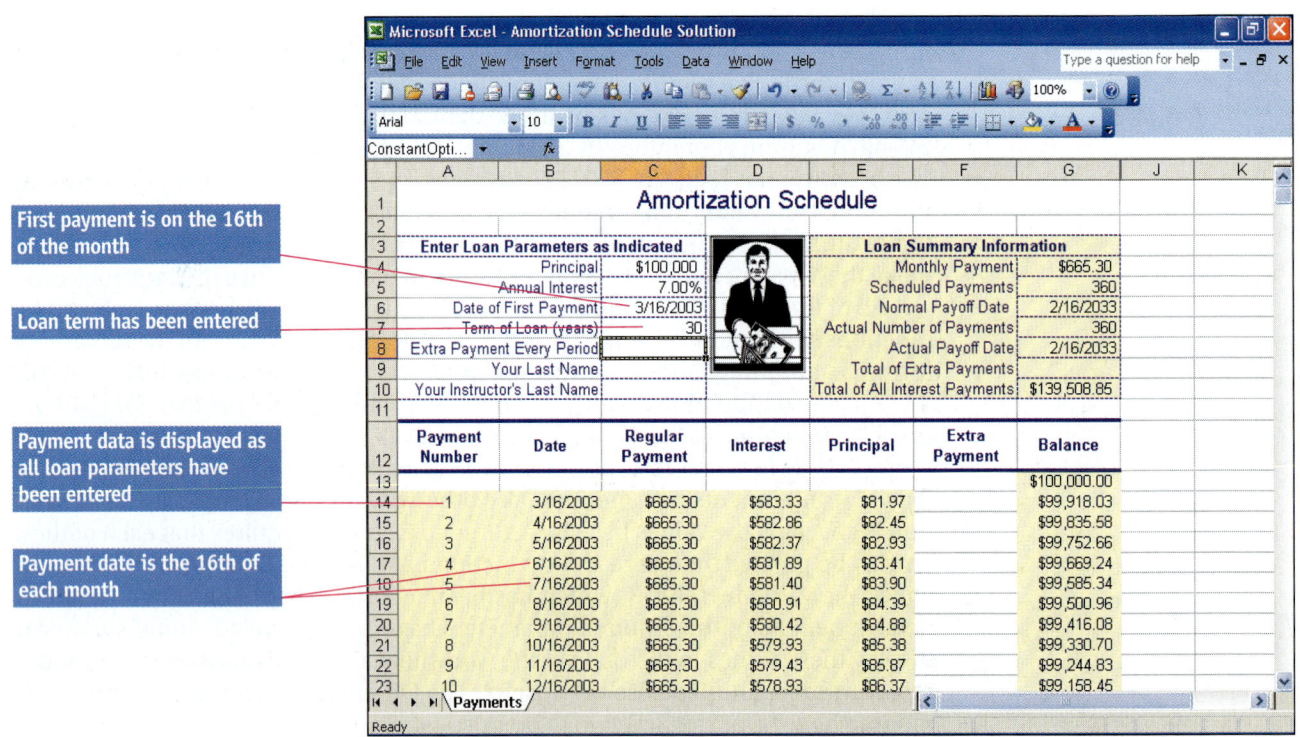

(b) 30-year Mortgage

FIGURE 9.1   The Amortization Schedule Workbook

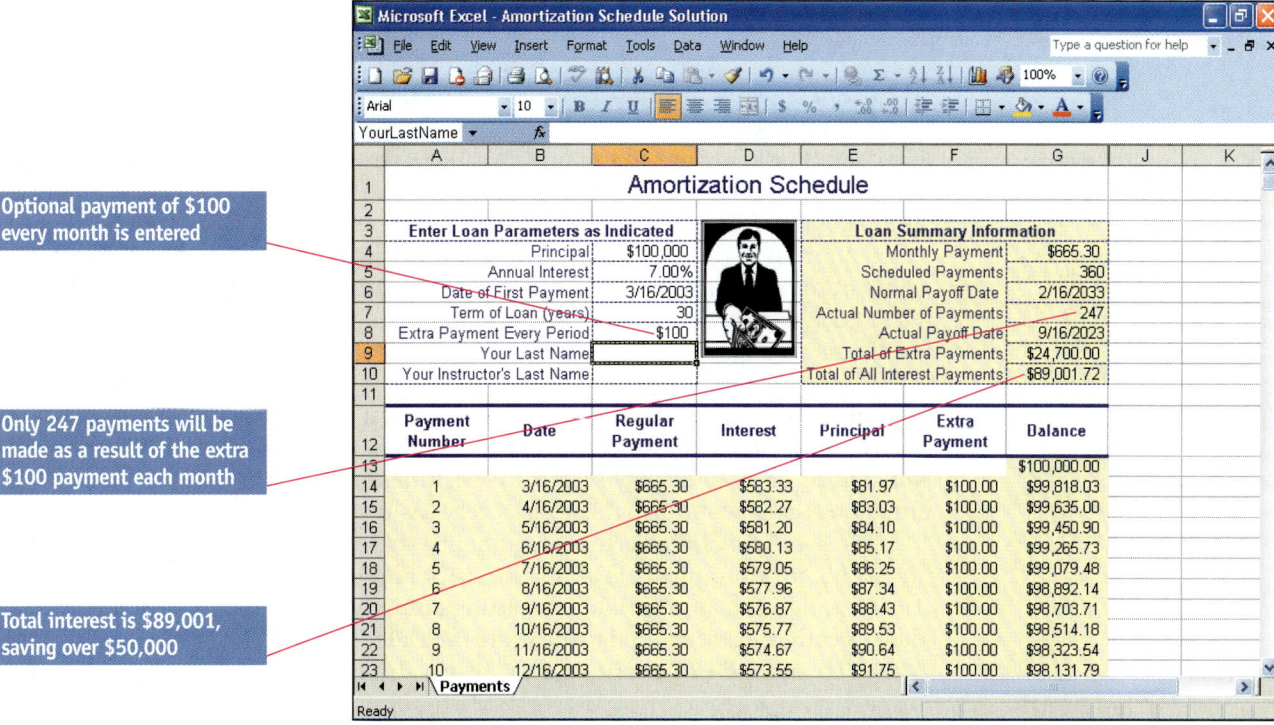

(c) Optional Extra Payment

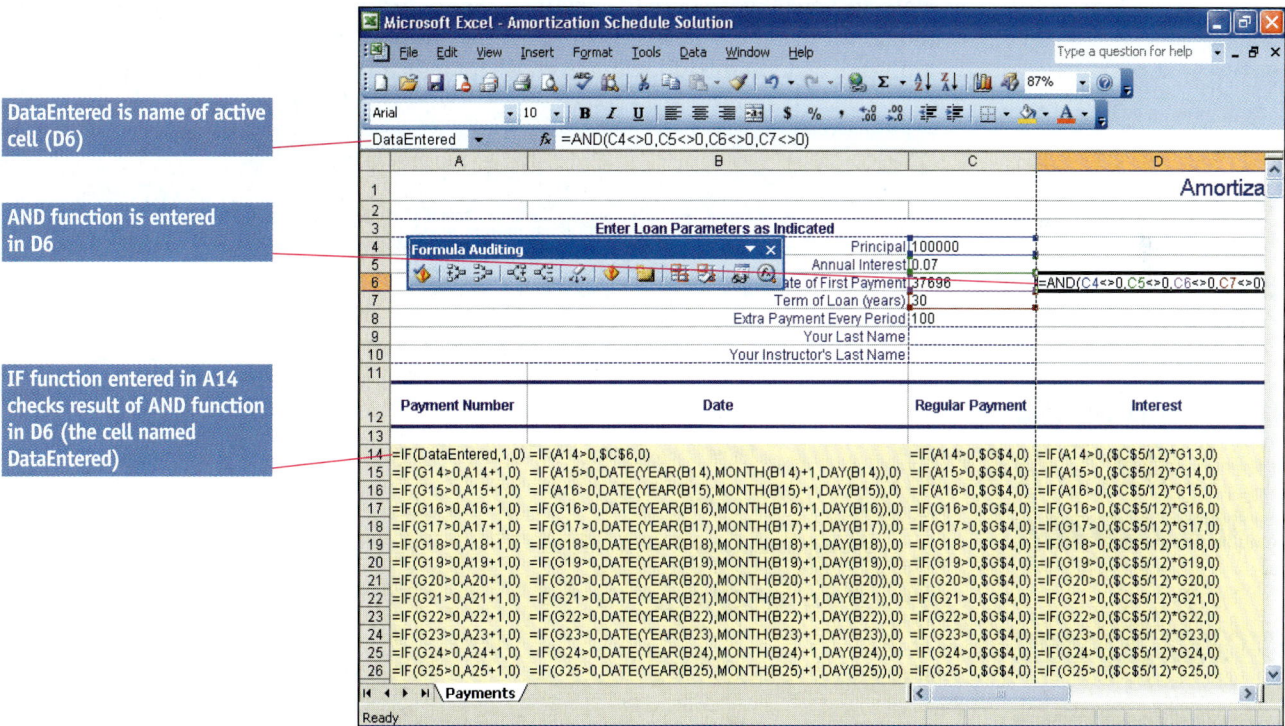

(d) Partial Cell Formulas

FIGURE 9.1 The Amortization Schedule Workbook (*continued*)

DATE FUNCTIONS

The use of dates within a worksheet has been discussed at various points in the text. Recall that Excel stores a date as an integer (serial number) equivalent to the elapsed number of days since January 1, 1900. Thus, January 1, 1900 is stored as the number 1, January 2, 1900 as the number 2, and so on. The fact that dates are stored as integer numbers enables you to perform date arithmetic as illustrated in the age calculation in Figure 9.2. To determine an individual's age, we take the (integer) value of today's date, subtract the birth date, and then divide the result by 365. (The **TODAY function** always returns today's date and is updated automatically each time you open the workbook.)

It's easy enough to determine tomorrow's date because all you have to do is add one to the integer value of today's date. What if, however, you want to determine next month's date? Do you add 30 or 31? And what if today's date is February 15? Do you add 28 or 29 to display March 15? Fortunately, Excel includes additional date functions that accomplish these tasks very easily.

The **DATE function** has three arguments: year, month, and day. The cell formula in cell B5, for example, is =DATE(1982,3,16) and it displays the date as March 16, 1982 through the appropriate formatting command. (We could have entered the date directly, but we wanted to illustrate the Date function.) Excel also has the **DAY, MONTH,** and **YEAR functions** that return the numeric day, month, and year, respectively. The function, =MONTH(B3), for example, returns the numeric month of the date in cell B3. In similar fashion, =MONTH(B3)+1 adds one to the numeric month. Excel is smart enough to know that if today's date is sometime in December, next month will occur in January.

Look now at the cell formulas for cells B11 and B13 that display next month's date and next year's date, respectively. These formulas may have seemed complex initially, but on closer inspection are easy to understand. The various date functions are used in the following exercise to determine the payment schedule.

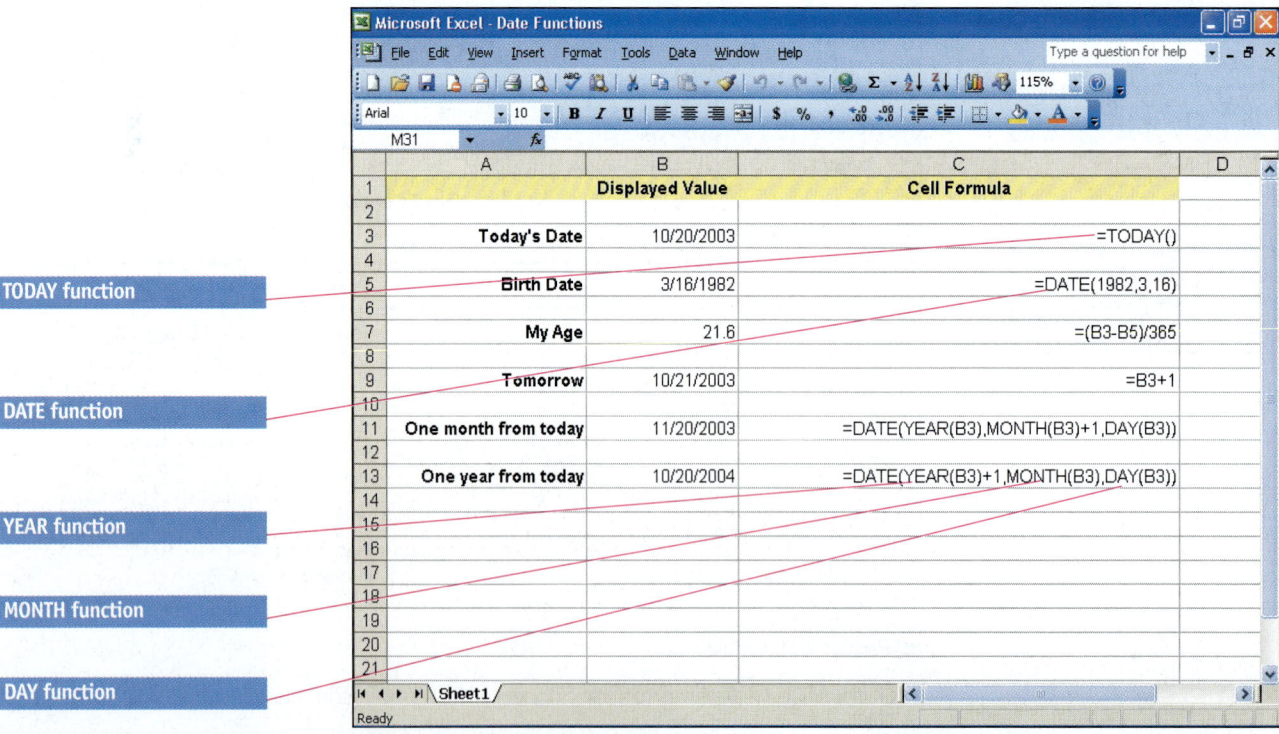

FIGURE 9.2 Date Functions

1428 CHAPTER 9: A PROFESSIONAL APPLICATION

hands-on exercise

1 The Amortization Workbook

Objective Explore the amortization workbook with respect to data validation, cell protection, optional extra payments, and a variable print area.

Step 1: **Data Entry and Validation**

- Start Excel. Open the **Amortization Schedule** workbook in the Exploring Excel folder. Click the button to **Enable macros**. (This exercise, however, accomplishes all of its tasks without the use of macros.)

- Save the workbook as **Amortization Schedule Solution** so that you can return to the original workbook if necessary. Click in **cell C4**. Enter **$100,000** and press **Enter**.

- Enter **.09** as the interest rate, which in turn displays the message box in Figure 9.3a. Click **No**, then enter **.07** as the interest rate. This time the value is accepted, and you see 7.00% in cell B5.

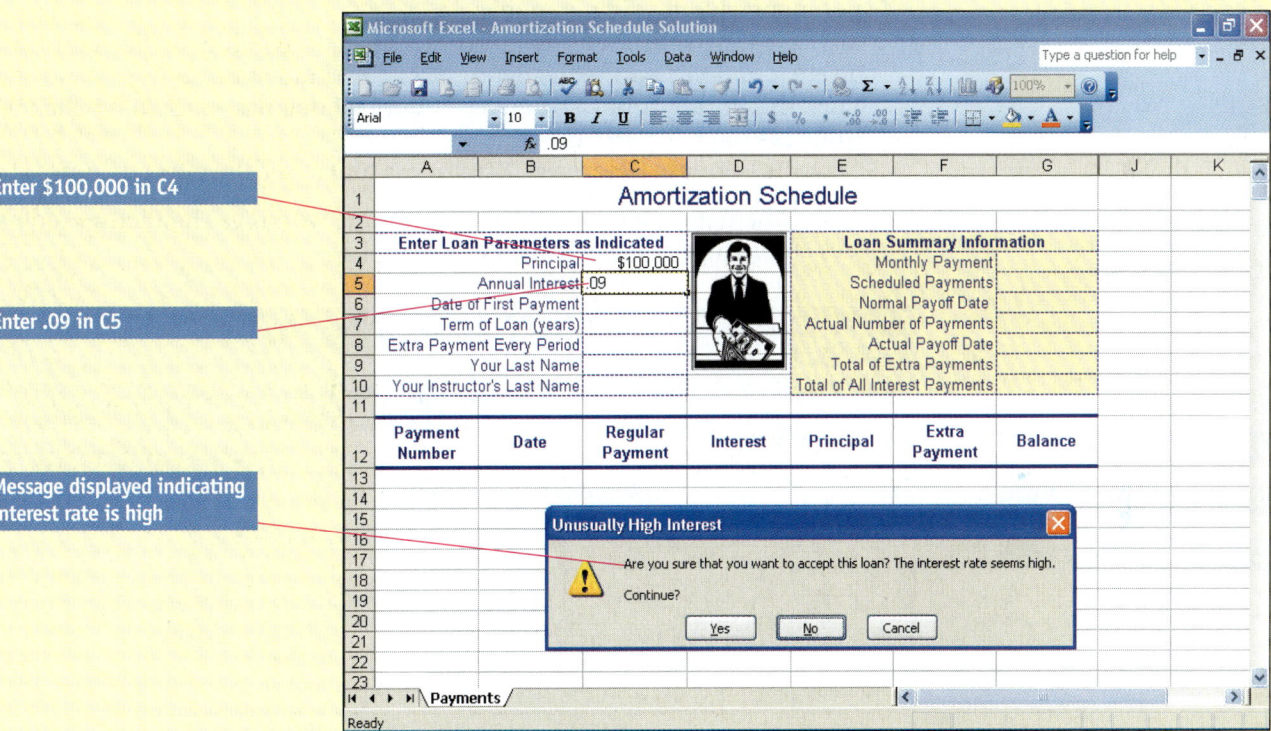

(a) Data Entry and Validation (step 1)

FIGURE 9.3 Hands-on Exercise 1

DATA VALIDATION

The Data Validation command enables you to restrict the values that can be entered into a specific cell. Click in the cell where you want to impose validation, then pull down the Data menu and click the Validation command to display the Data Validation dialog box. (The command is disabled if the worksheet is protected.)

Step 2: **A Protected Worksheet**

- Complete the entries in cells **C6 and C7** as shown in Figure 9.3b. Enter the date of the first payment so as to reflect the 15th of next month. The monthly payments and summary information appear as soon as you complete the last required entry (the term of the loan).

- Click in **cell A1** and attempt to enter a new title for the worksheet. You will see a message box indicating that the cell is protected and that you cannot change its value. Click **OK** after you have read the message.

- Pull down the **Tools menu**, click the **Protection command**, and click the **Unprotect Sheet command** to unprotect the worksheet. (You are not prompted for a password, because we protected the worksheet without a password.) The worksheet is now unprotected and you have full access to all of its cells.

- Click the clip art to select the image and display the sizing handles. Click and drag any of the four corners to increase (decrease) the size of the clip art.

- The Picture toolbar should be displayed automatically. If not, right click the clip art and click the command to **Show Picture toolbar** as shown in Figure 9.3b. Experiment with the different tools:
  - Click the **Crop tool**, then click and drag the bottom border of the figure up to delete (crop) this part of the figure. Click the Undo button.
  - Click the **Rotate tool** to rotate the figure 90 degrees to the left. Click the **Undo button** to reverse the command.
  - Click the **Increase (Decrease) Brightness tool** to see the effect (if any).

- Click off the figure to deselect it and continue working. The Picture toolbar closes automatically. Save the workbook.

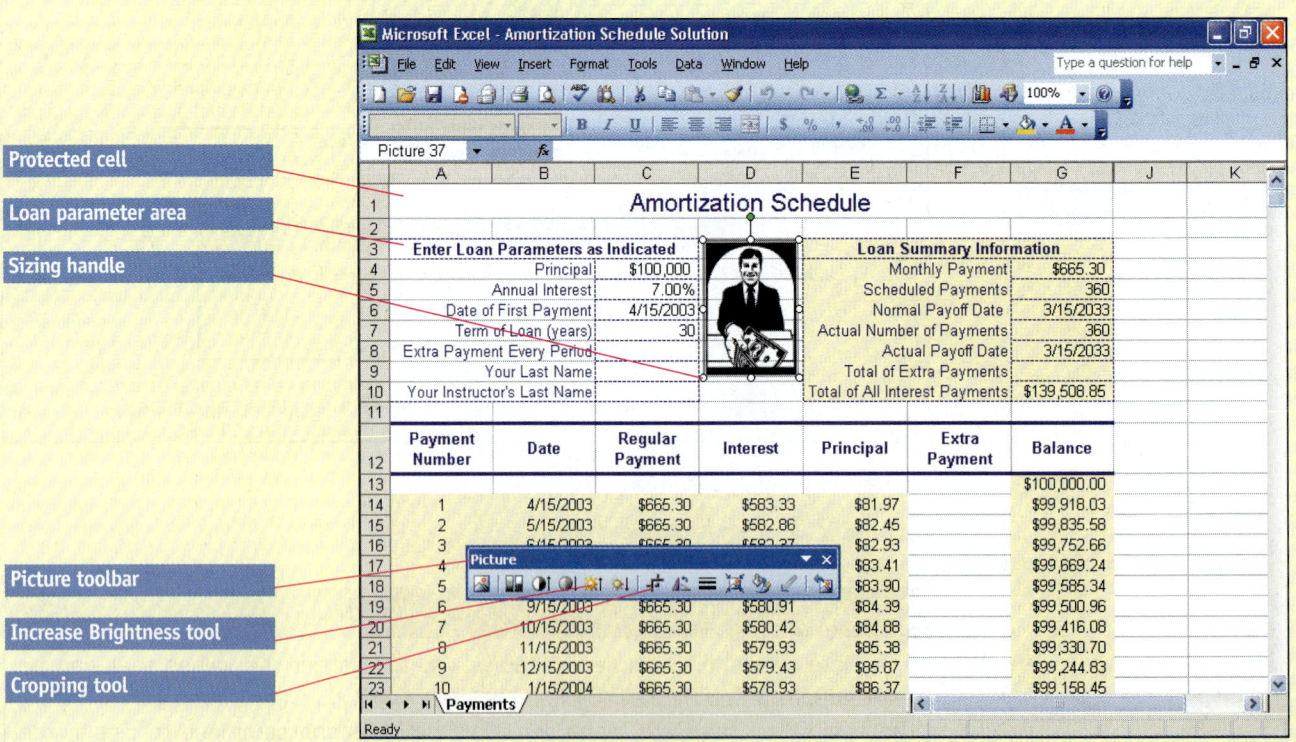

(b) A Protected Worksheet (step 2)

FIGURE 9.3 Hands-on Exercise 1 (*continued*)

Step 3: **The Logical AND Function**

- Click and drag the clip art image to the right as shown in Figure 9.3c. The displayed value in cell D6 is "TRUE", and the monthly payments and summary information are displayed in G4:G10.
- Click in **cell C7** and delete the term of the loan. The value in cell D6 changes to "FALSE", and the payments and summary information are no longer visible.
- Click the **Undo button** to restore the 30 in cell C7. The loan parameters are now complete and the value of cell D6 returns to "TRUE".
- Click in **cell D6** and note the following:
  ❑ The formula bar contains a logical AND function with four arguments, all of which have to be true for the function to be true. In other words, data has to be entered in cells C4, C5, C6, and C7 for the value in cell D6 to be true.
  ❑ The Name box displays "DataEntered" to indicate that cell D6 is associated with this range name, which can be used in any worksheet formula.
- Click in **cell A14**, the cell containing the formula for the first payment. The IF function checks the value of the range name "DataEntered", and if that value is true, enters the number 1 for the payment number. If the value is false, however, zero is entered for the payment number. (Zero values are not displayed.)
- Click and drag the clip art image back to its original place in the worksheet.

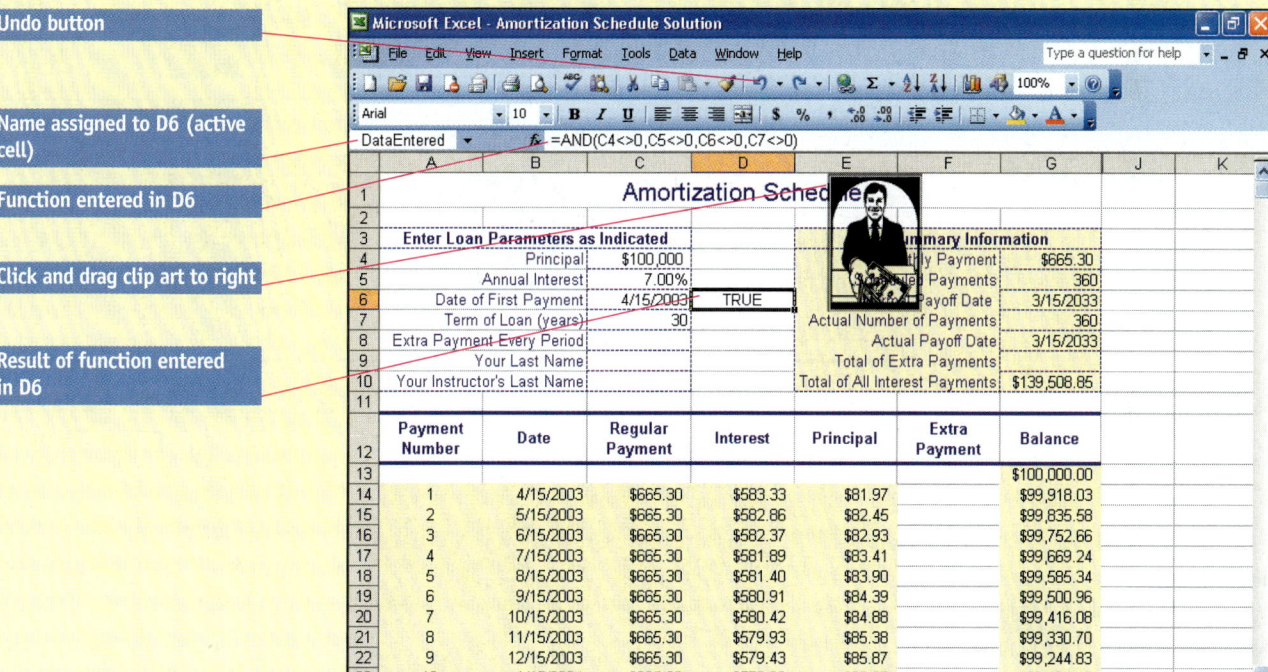

(c) The Logical AND Function (step 3)

FIGURE 9.3 Hands-on Exercise 1 (*continued*)

SUPPRESS ZERO VALUES

Many spreadsheets are visually enhanced by suppressing the display of zero values. The amortization worksheet, for example, contains formulas to compute 360 monthly loan payments, but it displays the entries for only those cells with nonzero values. Pull down the Tools menu, click the Options command, click the View tab, and clear the box for Zero values. Click OK.

Step 4: **Check the Calculations**

- The formulas in columns D and E to compute the portion of each payment towards interest and principal, respectively, are not trivial. It is important, therefore, to verify the results through alternate calculations.

- Click and drag to select **columns G and J**. (Columns H and I are not visible because they are currently hidden.) Pull down the **Format menu**, click the **Column command**, then click **Unhide** to display columns H and I, as shown in Figure 9.3d.

- Click in **cell H14** to examine the amount of the first payment that goes toward interest. The displayed value of $583.33 is obtained through the IPMT function and matches the amount in cell D14.

- Click in **cell I14** to examine the amount of the first payment that goes toward principal. The displayed value of $81.97 is obtained through the PPMT function and matches the amount in cell E14.

- Click and drag the column headings to select **columns H and I**. Pull down the **Format menu**, click the **Column command**, then click **Hide** to suppress these columns. Save the workbook.

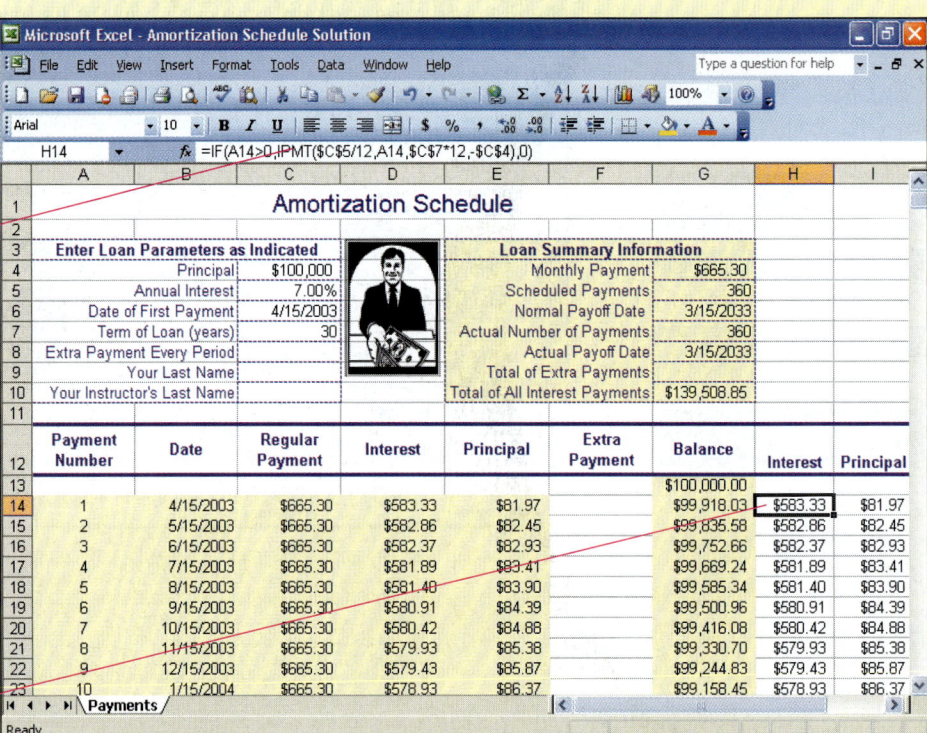

(d) Check the Calculations (step 4)

FIGURE 9.3 Hands-on Exercise 1 (*continued*)

THE IPMT AND PPMT FUNCTIONS

The IPMT and PPMT functions compute the portion of a monthly payment that goes toward interest and principal, respectively. These functions refer to the original principal and cannot accommodate extra payments toward principal. Hence, they could not be used in the body of the worksheet, but serve only to validate that the formulas in columns D and E are correct. These formulas are for the developer to check his or her work, not the user.

Step 5: **What If?**

- Examine the information in the summary area of the worksheet. The total interest for the 30-year loan is found in cell G10 and is equal to $139,508.
- Change the term of the loan to **15 years**, and the interest decreases to $61,789, a savings of almost $80,000. Note, too, that the payoff date is now 15 years (less one month, but 180 payments) from the initial payment.
- Change the starting date of the loan to the first of next month as shown in Figure 9.3e. The payoff date changes, as do the dates for the individual payments.
- Click in **cell C8** and enter **$100** as an optional extra payment you hope to make each month toward principal. The payoff date, actual number of payments, and total interest decrease further.
- Enter **your last name** and **your instructor's last name** in **cells C9 and C10**.
- Pull down the **Tools menu**, click the **Protection command**, and click the **Protect Sheet command** to protect the worksheet. Leave the password blank. Click **OK**.
- Save the workbook.

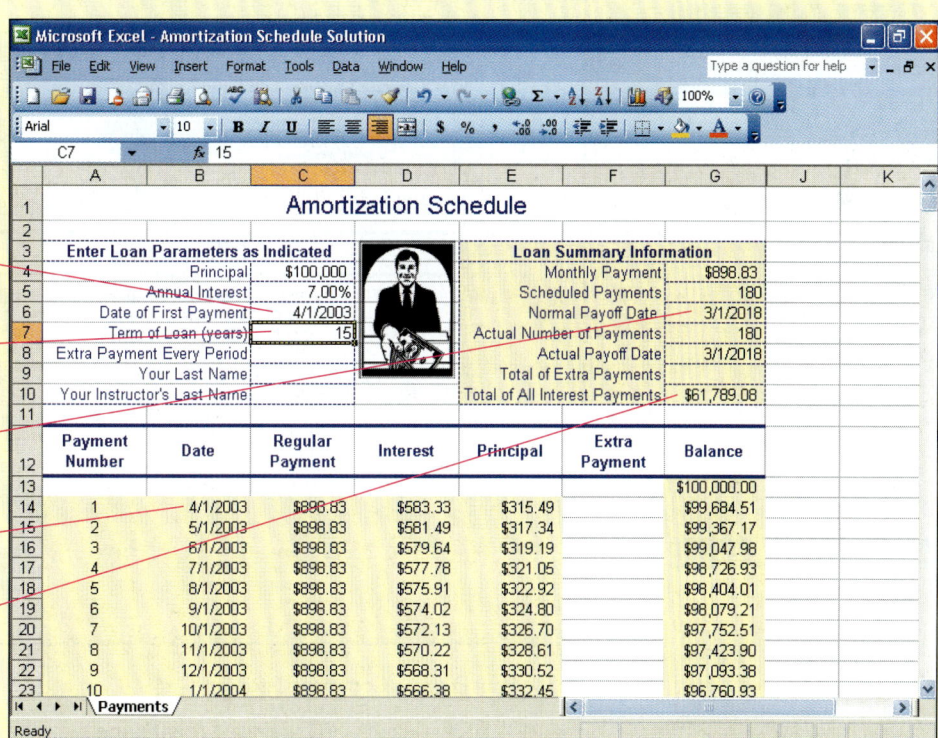

(e) What If? (step 5)

FIGURE 9.3 Hands-on Exercise 1 (*continued*)

PROTECTING A WORKSHEET

Protecting a worksheet is a two-step process. First, you unlock all of the cells that are subject to change, then you protect the worksheet. Select the cell(s) you want to unlock, pull down the Format menu, click the Cells command, then select the Protection tab in the Format Cells dialog box. Clear the Locked check box. To protect the worksheet, pull down the Tools menu, click Protection, then click the Protect Sheet command to display the Protect Sheet dialog box where you can enter a password. *Be careful, because once you password-protect a worksheet, you cannot unprotect it without the password.*

Step 6: **The Print Preview Command**

- Click the **Print Preview button** to see how your worksheet will appear when it is printed, as shown in Figure 9.3f. Click the **Zoom button**, if necessary, so that you see the worksheet more easily.

- Look at the status bar and note that the entire worksheet requires three pages. Click the **Next button** on the Print Preview toolbar to view page two of the printout, which repeats the column headings, then begins with payment number 46. (You may see a different payment number, depending on your printer.)

- Click the **Next button** to move to page 3, which again repeats the payment headings and starts with payment 103 and continues to the last payment.

- Click the **Print button** to print the worksheet for your instructor. Click **OK** when you see the Print dialog box.

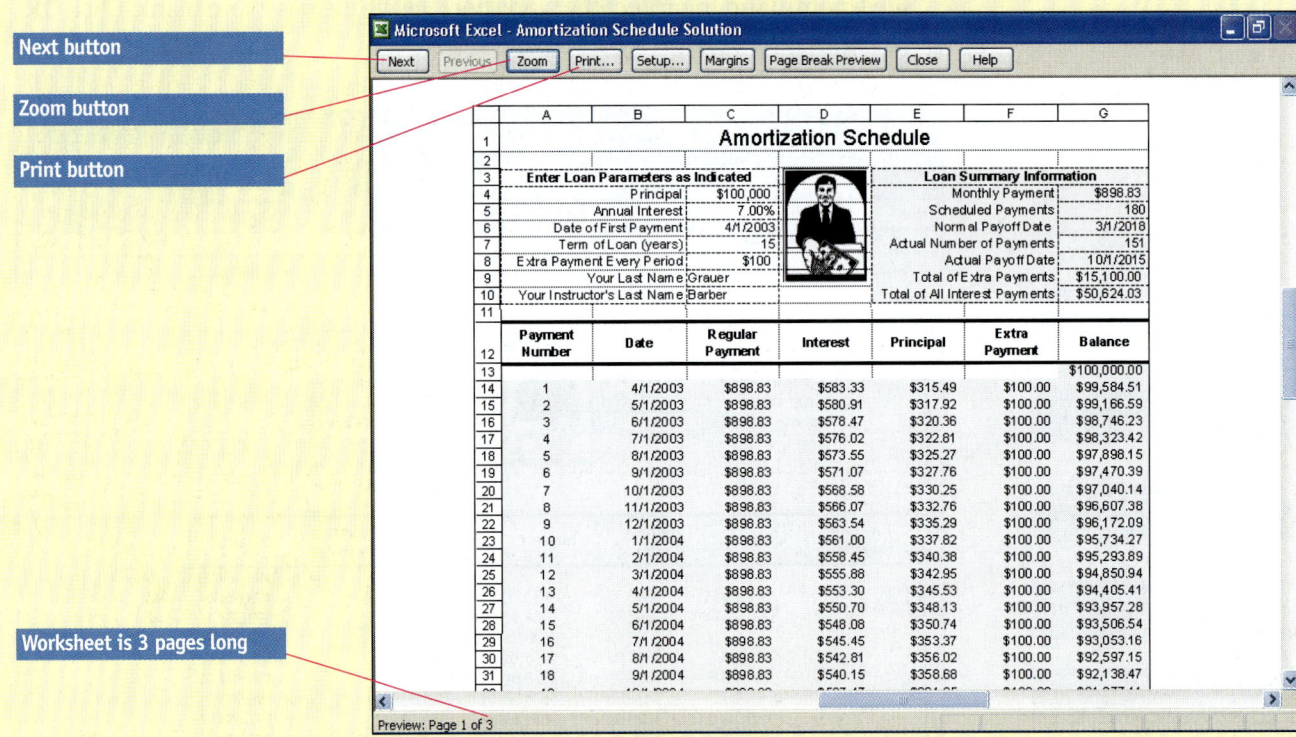

(f) The Print Preview Command (step 6)

FIGURE 9.3 Hands-on Exercise 1 (continued)

THE MULTIPLE-PAGE PRINTOUT—REPEATING ROWS AND COLUMNS

It is very helpful to repeat one or more rows and/or columns of a worksheet if the worksheet extends to several printed pages. Pull down the File menu and click the Page Setup command to display the Page Setup dialog box. Click the Sheet tab. Click in the Rows to repeat at top text box, then click and drag in the worksheet to select the row(s) you want to repeat. Click in the Columns to repeat at left text box, click and drag in the worksheet to select the columns, then click OK to accept the settings and close the dialog box. Use the Print Preview command to see the effect of these changes.

Step 7: **Print the Cell Formulas**

- We want you to print the cell formulas so that you will be able to study the worksheet in detail. We are going to change the term of the loan, however, so that the worksheet will take fewer pages.

- Click in **cell C7** and change the term of the loan to **1 year**. The displayed values will change, but the formulas remain constant. Press **Ctrl+~** (the ~ character appears immediately below the Esc key) to display cell formulas.

- Unprotect the worksheet. Click and drag the column borders to see the entire formula within a cell as shown in Figure 9.3g.

- Click the **Print Preview button**. The worksheet should require three pages. All of the rows fit on one page, but the wider columns spill over to pages two and three. Click **Print**. Click **OK**.

- Close the workbook. Click **No** if asked whether to save the changes. Exit Excel if you do not want to continue with the next exercise at this time.

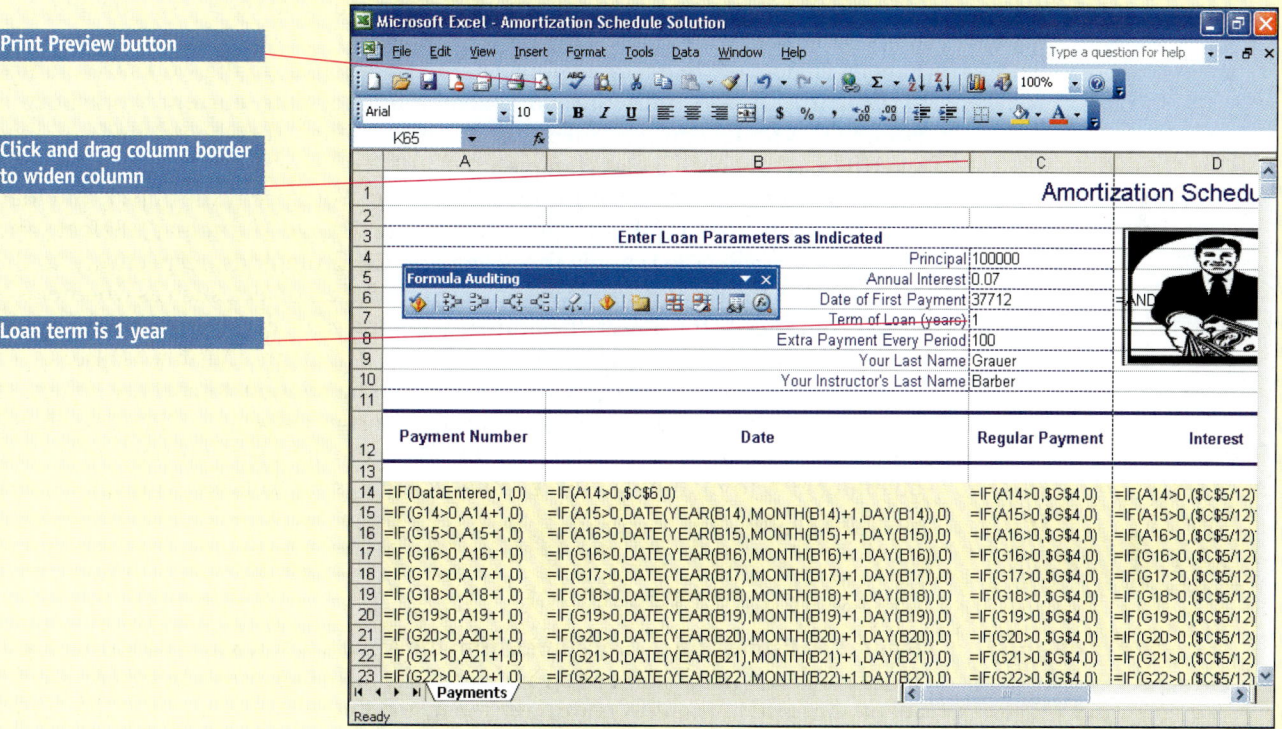

(g) Print the Cell Formulas (step 7)

FIGURE 9.3 Hands-on Exercise 1 (*continued*)

CHANGING THE PRINT AREA

It's easy to set a print area manually. You select the range that is to print, pull down the File menu, click Print Area, and then click Set Print Area. (You can clear the print area by choosing the Clear Print Area command.) The problem with this technique is that the desired print area changes according to the number of required payments, each of which adds a row to the worksheet. We have, however, found a way to set the print area dynamically, according to the number of rows in a worksheet. If this does not happen in your worksheet, press Ctrl+r to execute a macro to reset the dynamic print area. See exercises 3 and 4 at the end of the chapter.

EXPLORING VBA SYNTAX

You could study VBA for weeks on end prior to coding a simple procedure. We prefer to plunge right in, use the ***macro recorder*** to capture Excel commands, and then learn about VBA through inference and observation. Nevertheless, you need a grasp of basic terminology as presented in this section.

VBA accomplishes its tasks by manipulating ***objects***. The objects within Excel include workbooks, worksheets, ranges, charts, pivot tables, and individual cells. The ***object model*** describes the hierarchical way in which different objects are related to one another. The workbook object, for example, contains the worksheet object, which in turn contains the range object, and so on.

A ***collection*** is a group of similar objects within the object model. The worksheet collection is a group of individual worksheets. A specific object within a collection is referenced by the collection name followed by the object name enclosed in quotation marks within parentheses. Worksheets("Documentation"), for example, refers to the worksheet named "Documentation" within the Worksheets collection. In similar fashion, Range("Principal") refers to the range object named "Principal" within the Range collection. A reference to an object may be qualified (joined together with periods) over several objects. Thus, Worksheets("Payments"). Range("Principal") refers to the range named "Principal" in the worksheet named "Payments". If you omit the worksheet reference, the current worksheet is assumed. (VBA recognizes "Sheets" as a synonym for "Worksheets", and you may see either reference in a VBA statement.)

A ***method*** is an action performed by an object. You specify the object, and then you indicate the method. The statements Range("Principal").Select and Range("Principal").Clear apply the Select and Clear methods, respectively, to the indicated range object. A ***property*** is an attribute of an object, such as whether it is visible. You specify the object, the property, and the value of the property; for example, Sheets("Payments").Visible = True or Sheets("Payments").Visible = False.

That's all there is. The object model defines the relationships of the objects to one another and defines the methods and properties associated with each object. The object model also provides a link between the user interface and VBA, enabling VBA to manipulate Excel objects such as workbooks, worksheets, and specific cell ranges.

Three Simple Procedures

Figure 9.4 displays three procedures from the Amortization Schedule workbook to illustrate VBA syntax. A procedure is created in one of two ways—by entering statements directly in the VBA editor and/or by using the macro recorder to capture Excel commands and convert them to their VBA equivalents. You can also combine the two techniques by starting with the recorder to capture basic statements, then view the resulting syntax and embellish those statements with additional VBA statements.

The procedure in Figure 9.4a is used by the developer to verify his or her calculations. The procedure displays two hidden columns that contain the ***IPMT*** and ***PPMT functions***, to compute the amount of each payment for interest and principal, respectively. (See step 4 in the previous hands-on exercise.) The procedure was created entirely through the macro recorder. The resulting VBA statements are easily understood within the context of our basic definitions. The Unprotect method is applied to the active worksheet object so that its contents may be modified. The named range called ValidationColumns is selected, and its hidden property is set to False. The Protect method is then applied to the worksheet so that it cannot be modified further. You might not be able to write the procedure from scratch, but you can understand its statements once they have been created for you. All of a sudden, VBA does not seem so intimidating.

VBA statements were generated by macro recorder

```
Sub DisplayValidationColumns()
    ActiveSheet.Unprotect
    Application.Goto Reference:="ValidationColumns"
    Selection.EntireColumn.Hidden = False
    ActiveSheet.Protect
End Sub
```

(a) Display Validation Columns (Macro Recorder)

If statement tests to see if data has been entered in cell named DataEntered

Else clause

MsgBox statement

```
Sub DisplayValidationColumns()
    ActiveSheet.Unprotect
    If Range("DataEntered").Value = True Then
        Application.Goto Reference:="ValidationColumns"
        Selection.EntireColumn.Hidden = False
        MsgBox "This macro displays additional columns for validation " _
            & "of the spreadsheet formulas using the IPMT and PPMT " _
            & "functions, respectively. The values should match the " _
            & "corresponding columns in the body of the spreadsheet " _
            & "provided that no extra payments are made.", _
                vbInformation, ApplicationTitle
    Else
        MsgBox "Validation meaningless - Loan parameters not entered", _
                vbInformation, ApplicationTitle
    End If
    ActiveSheet.Protect
End Sub
```

(b) Display Validation Columns (Additional VBA Statements)

User is prompted for a Yes or No response, and response is tested against vbYes

```
Public Sub EnableSinglePayments()
    If MsgBox("This procedure unprotects the extra payments " _
        & "columns enabling you to enter individual payments. " _
        & "Do you want to unprotect the spreadsheet?", _
        vbYesNo + vbQuestion, ApplicationTitle) = vbYes _
    Then
        ActiveSheet.Unprotect
    Else
        ActiveSheet.Protect
    End If
End Sub
```

(c) Enable Single Payments

FIGURE 9.4 VBA Procedures

The real power of VBA, however, lies in the ability to add VBA statements that do not have an Excel equivalent to procedures that were created by the macro recorder. The procedure in Figure 9.4b expands the procedure to display the hidden columns by first testing to see that data has been entered in the main body of the worksheet, because it does not make sense to display the validation columns if the data is incomplete. Thus, we took the procedure in Figure 9.4a and added the If . . . Else . . . End If construct to see if data has been entered.

Figure 9.4c displays a procedure that expands the functionality of the worksheet by enabling the user to enter individual payments within the optional payments column. The new procedure uses the *MsgBox function*, as opposed to a simple *MsgBox statement*. The MsgBox function displays a prompt to the user, then returns a value such as which button was clicked.

hands-on exercise

2 Exploring VBA Syntax

Objective To use the Excel macro recorder to jump-start the creation of VBA procedures; to add VBA statements to create more powerful procedures. Use Figure 9.5 as a guide in the exercise.

Step 1: **Open the VBA Editor**

- Start Excel. Open the **Amortization Schedule Solution** from the previous exercise. Click the button to **Enable macros**.

- Pull down the **Tools menu**, click the **Macro command**, then click the **Visual Basic Editor command** (or use the **Alt+F11** keyboard shortcut) to open the editor. You should see a window similar to Figure 9.5a.

- If necessary, pull down the **View menu**, and click **Project Explorer** to display the Project Explorer pane at the left of the window.

- Click the **plus sign** next to the Modules folder to list the existing modules, then double click **Module1** to display its contents in the code window.

- Click and drag to select the public constant, **Your Name Goes Here**. (Do not select the quotation marks.)

- Type your name, and it will replace the selected text. Click the **Save button** to save the changes to Module1.

- Click the **View Microsoft Excel button** to return to the workbook.

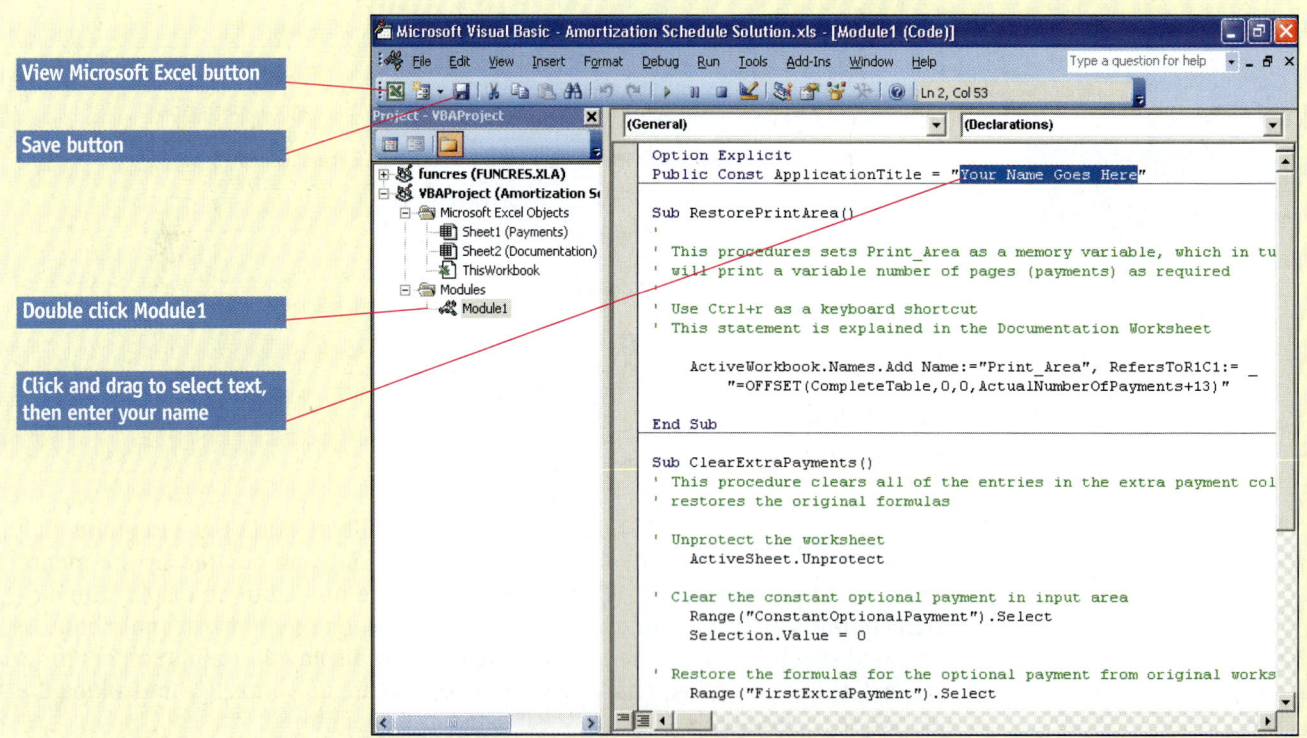

(a) Open the VBA Editor (step 1)

FIGURE 9.5 Hands-on Exercise 2

1438 CHAPTER 9: A PROFESSIONAL APPLICATION

Step 2: **Record the Display Validation Columns Macro**

- Pull down the **Tools menu** and click the **Macro command**, then click **Record New Macro** to display the Record Macro dialog box. Enter **DisplayValidationColumns** (spaces are not allowed) as the name of the macro.

- Click in the **Shortcut Key** text box and enter a **lowercase d**. Ctrl+d should appear as the shortcut. Be sure that the macro is stored in This Workbook. Click **OK** to begin recording and display the Stop Recording toolbar in Figure 9.5b.

- Pull down the **Tools menu**, click **Protection**, and click the **Unprotect Sheet command**. (A password is not required.)

- Click the **down arrow** in the Name box and click **ValidationColumns** to select columns H and I. You see only a thick vertical line between columns G and J because the columns are still hidden.

- Pull down the **Format menu**, click the **Column command** and click **Unhide**. You should see the validation columns. Pull down the **Tools menu**, click **Protection**, and click the **Protect Sheet command**. Click **OK**. (A password is not required.)

- Click the **Stop Recording button**. (If you do not see the Stop Recording toolbar, pull down the **Tools menu**, click **Macro**, and then click **Stop Recording**.)

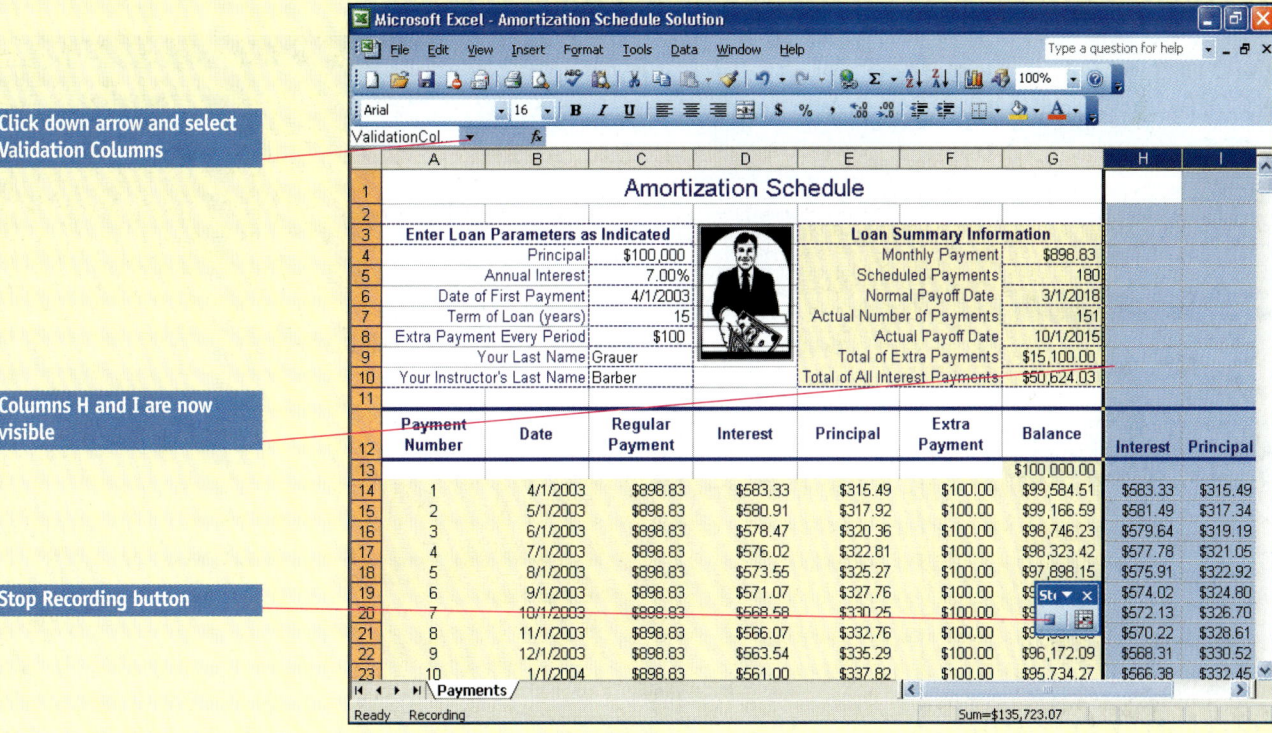

(b) Record the Display Validation Columns Macro (step 2)

FIGURE 9.5 Hands-on Exercise 2 (*continued*)

INSULATE YOUR MACROS AND PROCEDURES

Excel formulas adjust automatically for the insertion or deletion of rows and columns. This is not true of macros and VBA procedures; that is, if you record a macro to go to a specific column, such as column H, then you subsequently add or remove a column, the macro will no longer work. You can prevent this from happening by defining range names within the worksheet, and referring to those range names within a macro.

MICROSOFT OFFICE EXCEL 2003 1439

Step 3: **Create the Hide Validation Columns Macro**

- Press **Alt+F11** to open the VBA editor. Double click **Module2**.
- You should see the DisplayValidationColumns procedure in Figure 9.5c. Modify your procedure to match our code. (The second procedure is not yet there.)
- Return to Excel. Pull down the **Tools menu**, click the **Macro command**, then click **Record New Macro** to display the Record Macro dialog box.
- Enter **HideValidationColumns** as the name of the macro. Click in the **Shortcut Key** text box and enter a **lowercase h**. Click **OK** to begin recording.
- Pull down the **Tools menu**, click **Protection**, and click **Unprotect Sheet**. Click the **down arrow** in the Name box and click **ValidationColumns** to select columns H and I. Do this even if the columns are still selected.
- Pull down the **Format menu**, click the **Column command** and click the **Hide command**. The validation columns should no longer be visible.
- Pull down the **Tools menu**, click **Protection**, click **Protect Sheet**, then click **OK**. Click the **Stop Recording button** to complete the macro. Save the workbook.
- Now test the two macros by using the keyboard shortcuts. Press **Ctrl+d** to display the columns. Press **Ctrl+h** to hide the columns.

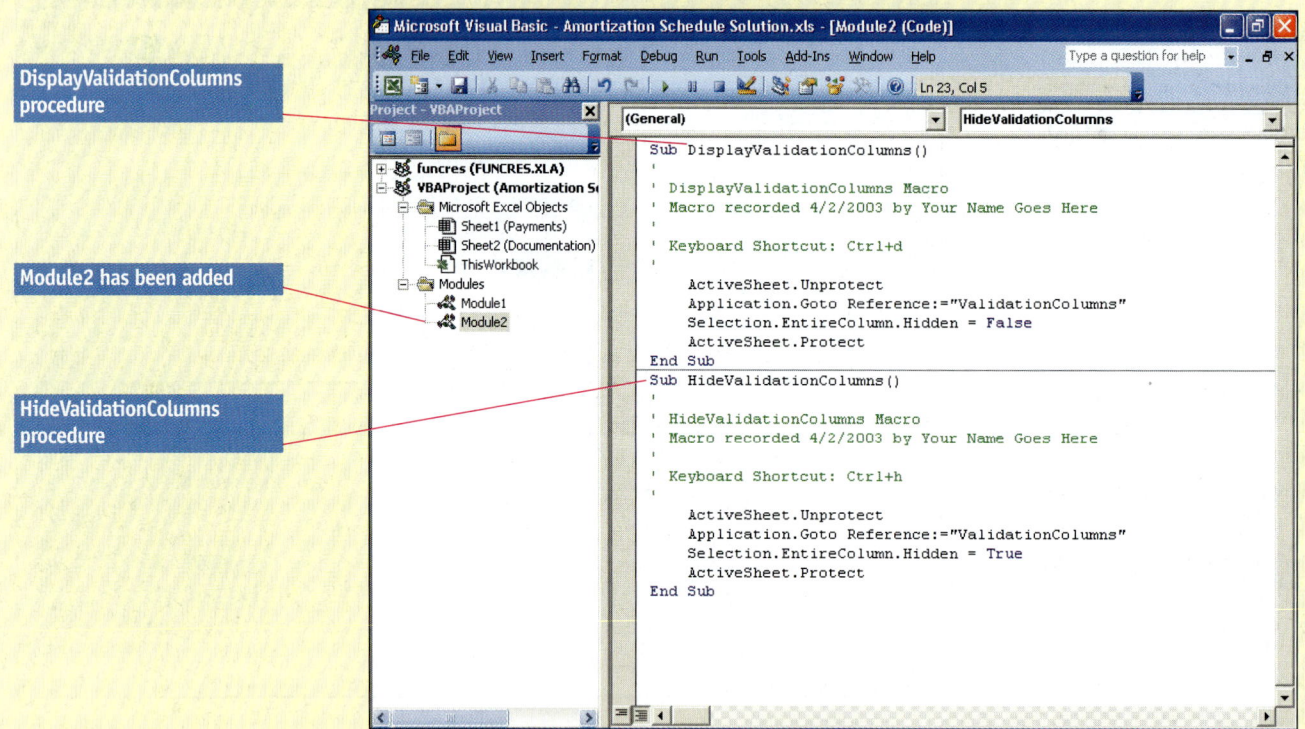

(c) Create the Hide Validation Columns Macro (step 3)

FIGURE 9.5 Hands-on Exercise 2 (*continued*)

WHICH MODULE IS IT IN?

All macros that are recorded within the same Excel session will be stored in the same module. If you close the workbook, however, then subsequently reopen it, Excel will store subsequent macros in a new module. It really doesn't matter where (in which module) the macros are stored. You can, however, move a macro from one module to another for organizational purposes.

Step 4: **Complete the Display Validation Columns Procedure**

- Press **Alt+F11** to return to the VBA editor as shown in Figure 9.5d.
- Think for a minute about what you are doing. You know that the basic macro works, but you want to enhance the macro to include error checking and meaningful messages to the user.
- Click at the end of the first statement, ActiveSheet.Unprotect, in the first procedure, and press the **Enter key**. Add the first line of the **If statement**, indent the next two existing lines, then click after the keyword False and press **Enter** twice.
- Enter the first **MsgBox statement**, continuing from one line to the next as shown in Figure 9.5d. Type **Else**, press **Enter**, then complete the second **MsgBox statement**. Complete the If statement by adding the **End If** delimiter.
- Check that your code matches Figure 9.5d. Click the **Save button**.
- Return to the Excel worksheet to test the procedure. Delete one input parameter, then press **Ctrl+d** to (attempt) to display the validation columns.
- You should see the message box indicating that the validation is meaningless because the loan parameters are not entered. If the procedure does not work as intended, press **Alt+F11** to return to the VBA editor and make corrections.

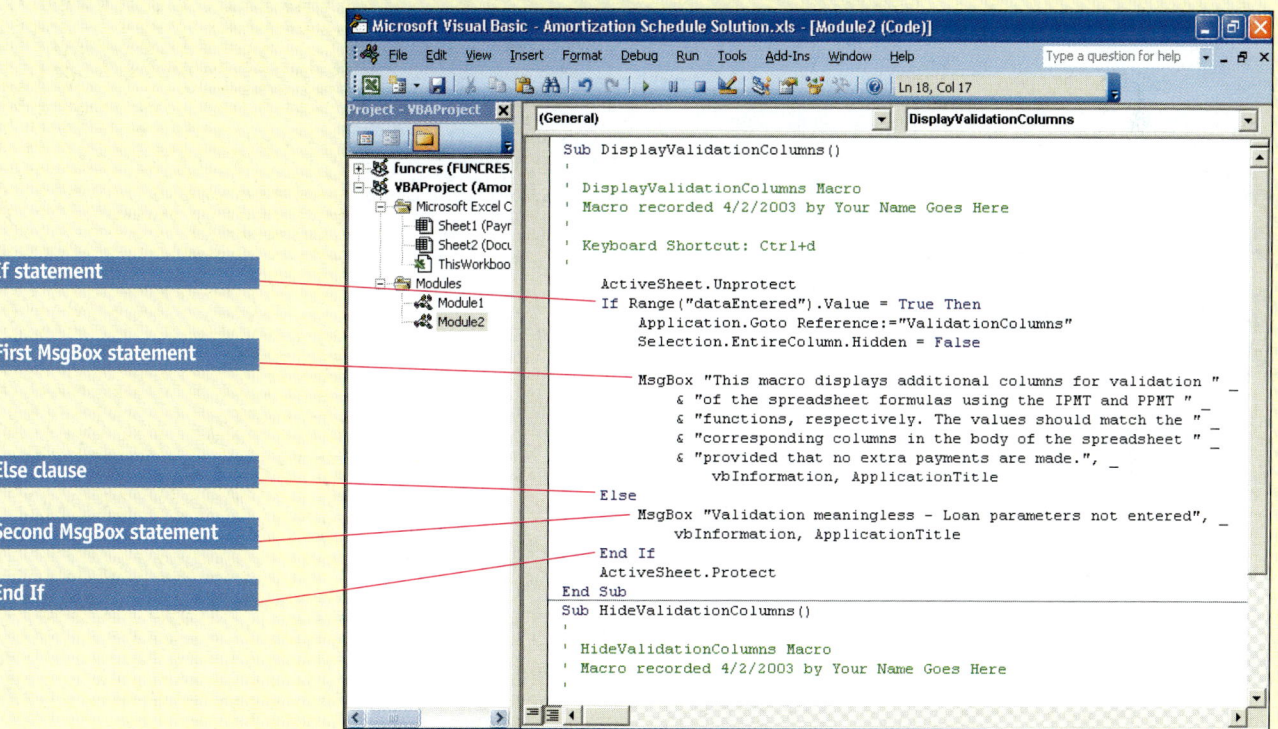

(d) Complete the Display Validation Columns Procedure (step 4)

FIGURE 9.5 Hands-on Exercise 2 (*continued*)

THE UNDERSCORE AND THE AMPERSAND

A VBA Statement is continued from one line to the next by typing an underscore at the end of the line to be continued. You may not, however, break a line in the middle of a literal. Hence, several lines within the MsgBox statement end with a closing quotation mark, followed by a space and the underscore. Each continued line starts with an ampersand to indicated continuation (concatenation) of the previous literal, followed by the remainder of the literal in quotation marks.

Step 5: **Create the Enable Single Payments Procedure**

- The procedure we are about to create enables the user to enter single payments within the extra payments columns. Return to the VBA editor. Press **Ctrl+End** to move to the end of the current module.

- Pull down the **Insert menu** and click the **Procedure command** to display the Add Procedure dialog box. Enter **EnableSinglePayments** (spaces are not allowed) as the procedure name. Select option buttons for **Sub** and **Public**. Click **OK**.

- The Sub and End Sub statements are created automatically. Click the **Procedure View button** to view only this procedure. Complete the procedure as shown in Figure 9.5e. You are using the **MsgBox function**, which means that:
    - The parameters of the MsgBox function are enclosed in parentheses. (Parentheses are not used when MsgBox is used as a statement.)
    - The MsgBox function returns a value, in this case an indication of which button the user clicked, Yes or No.
    - The value returned by the MsgBox function is compared to the VBA intrinsic constant vbYes.

- Click the **Save button**. Click the **Excel button** to test the procedure.

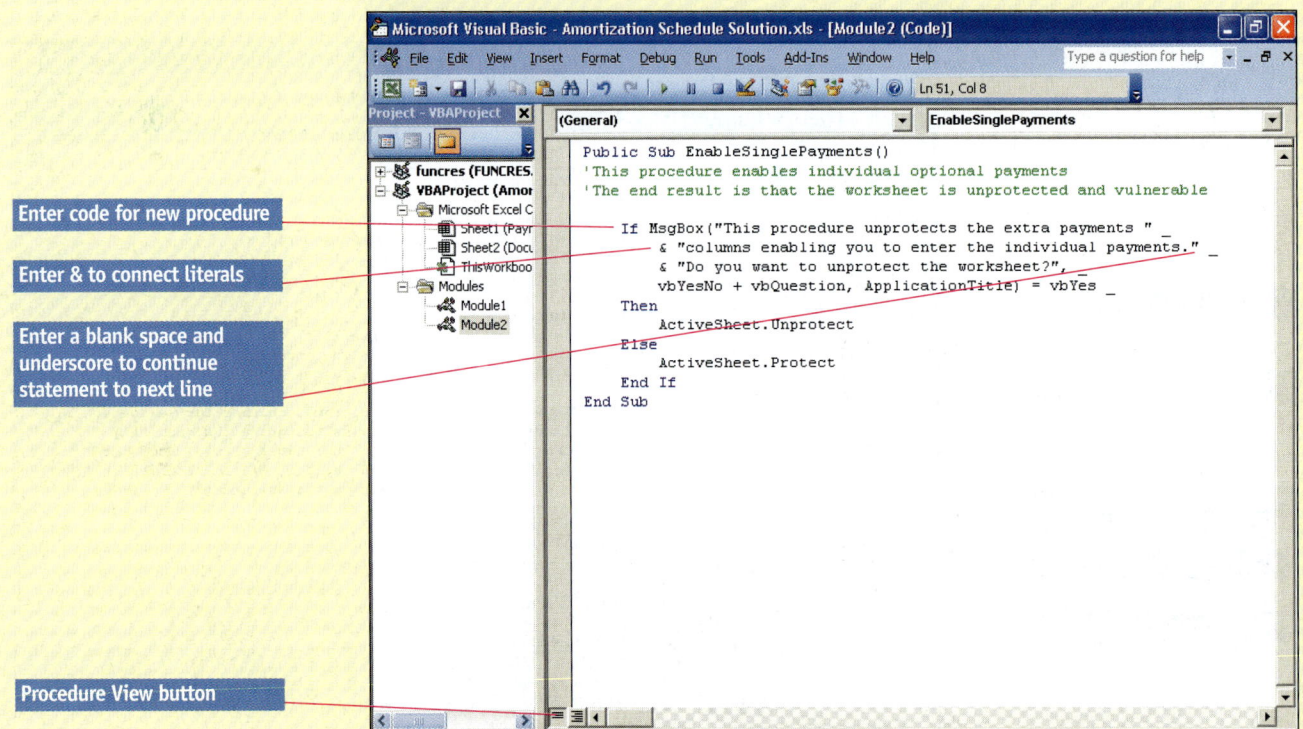

(e) Create the Enable Single Payments Procedure (step 5)

FIGURE 9.5 Hands-on Exercise 2 (*continued*)

> ### USE WHAT YOU KNOW
>
> Use the techniques acquired from other Office applications to facilitate editing within the VBA window. Press the Ins key to toggle between the insert and overtype modes as you modify the statements within a VBA procedure. You can also cut, copy, and paste statements (or parts of statements) within a procedure and from one procedure to another. You can access these commands via buttons on the Standard toolbar, as commands in the Edit menu, or by using the appropriate keyboard shortcuts.

Step 6: **Test the Procedure**

- You should be back in Excel. Delete the entry in **cell C8**. Pull down the **Tools menu**, click **Macro**, then click **Macros** to display the Macro dialog box.

- Double click the **EnableSinglePayments macro** that was just created. You should see the message box in Figure 9.5f. Click **No**.

- Click anywhere in **column F**, the column that contains the optional extra payments, and try to enter a value. You should see a message indicating that the cell is protected and that you cannot alter its contents. Click **OK** when you have read this message.

- Rerun the **EnableSinglePayments macro**, but this time click **Yes**, indicating that you want to enter extra payments. This will unprotect the worksheet.

- Return to any cell in column F and enter **$1000** as an optional payment for that month. This time Excel accepts the payment. Click the **Undo button** to cancel the extra payment.

- If the procedure does not function as intended, return to the Visual Basic editor and correct it. Save the workbook.

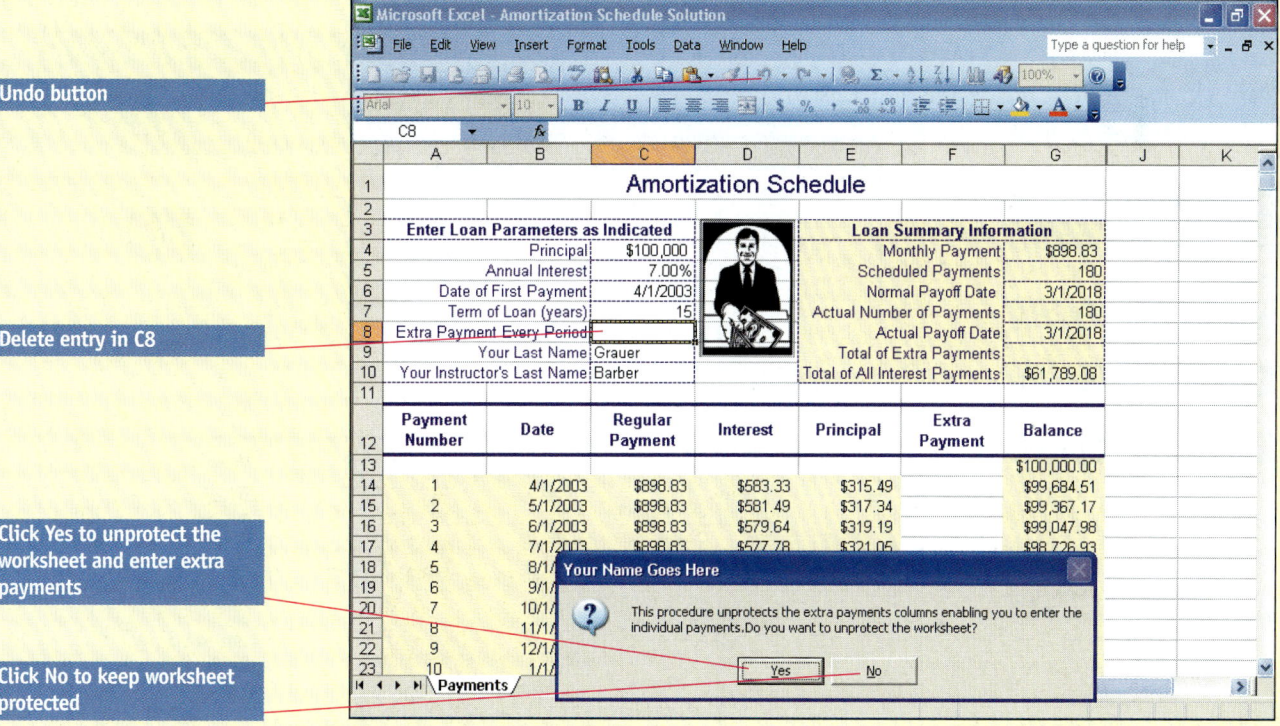

(f) Test the Procedure (step 6)

FIGURE 9.5 Hands-on Exercise 2 (*continued*)

ADD A MACRO SHORTCUT

You can add and/or modify the shortcut key associated with a macro at any time. Pull down the Tools menu, click the Macro command, then click Macros to display the Macro dialog box. Select the desired macro and click the Options button to display the Macro Options dialog box where you assign a shortcut. Type a lowercase letter to create a shortcut with just the Ctrl key such as Ctrl+e. Enter an uppercase letter to create a shortcut using the Ctrl and Shift keys such as Ctrl+Shift+E.

Step 7: **Create a Custom Toolbar**

- Pull down the **View menu**, click the **Toolbars command**, then click **Customize** to display the Customize dialog box. Click the **Toolbars tab**, then click the **New button** to create a new toolbar.

- Type **Amortization Schedule** as the toolbar name and click **OK**. You will see a floating toolbar as shown in Figure 9.5g. Click the **Commands tab** within the Custom dialog box, then scroll until you can select the **Macros category**.

- Click and drag the **Custom button** (with the smiley face image) to the newly created toolbar. Release the mouse. The smiley face appears on the toolbar. Click (select) the **smiley face button**, then click the **Modify Selection button** in the Customize dialog box.

- Click the **Name command** within the menu options, select the existing text, and type **Display Validation Columns** as the name of the button.

- Click the **Change Button Image command**. Choose an icon. We selected the **eye**.

- Click the **Modify Selection button**, click **Assign macro** and choose the **DisplayValidationColumns macro**. Click **OK**. Close the dialog box. Save the workbook.

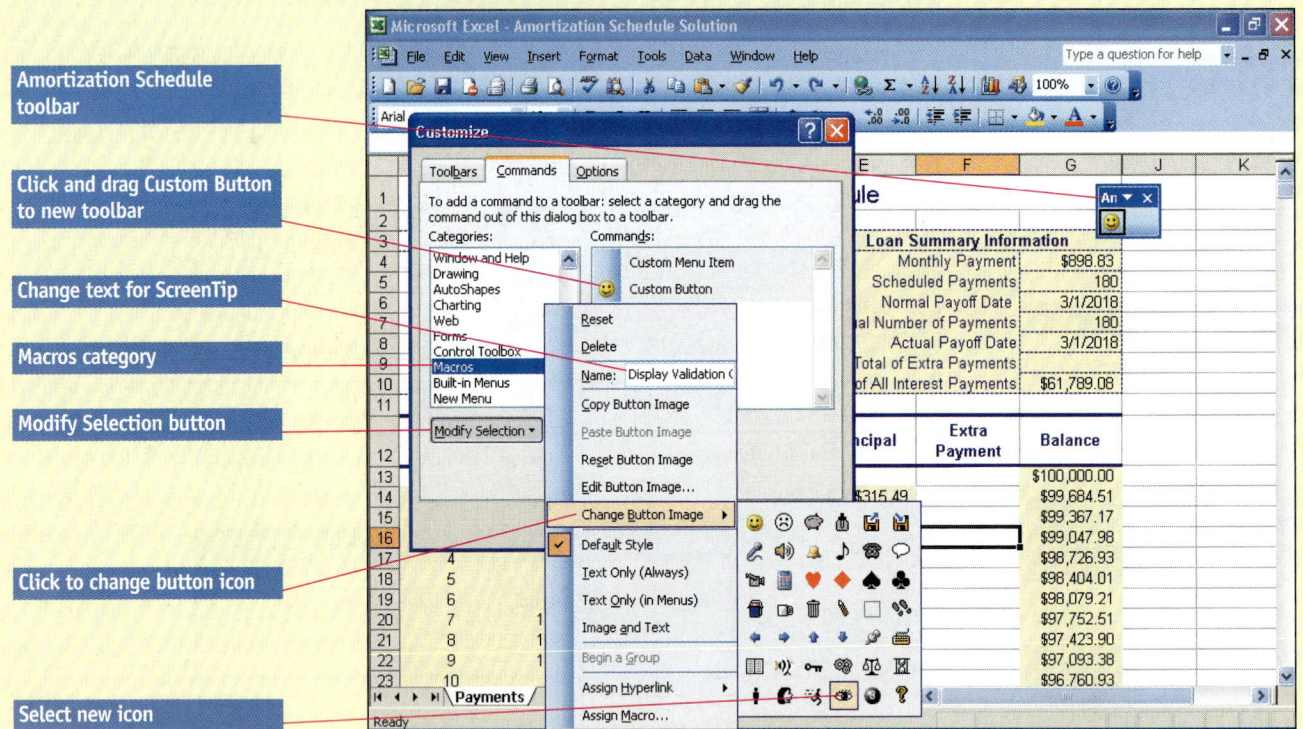

(g) Create a Custom Toolbar (step 7)

FIGURE 9.5 Hands-on Exercise 2 (*continued*)

MOVING AND/OR REMOVING A BUTTON

You can change the position of any button on a custom toolbar and/or remove the button altogether. Pull down the View menu, click Toolbars, then click the Customize command to display the Customize dialog box. To change the position of a button, select the button, then drag it to its new position. To remove the button, just drag the button off the toolbar. The same techniques apply to any standard toolbar within Microsoft Office.

Step 8: Test the Toolbar Button

- Point to the newly created toolbar button. You should see the name (ScreenTip) you entered, just as you would with any other toolbar button.
- Click the button to display the validation columns. Click **OK** after you have read the message.
- If necessary, pull down the **View menu**, click **Toolbars**, and click the **Customize command** to correct any element (the description, image, or macro) that did not work correctly.
- Add buttons for the **HideValidationColumns** and **EnableSinglePayments** macros. We used the runner and piggy bank icons, respectively.
- Test these buttons as shown in Figure 9.5h after they have been created. Make corrections as necessary.
- Save the workbook.

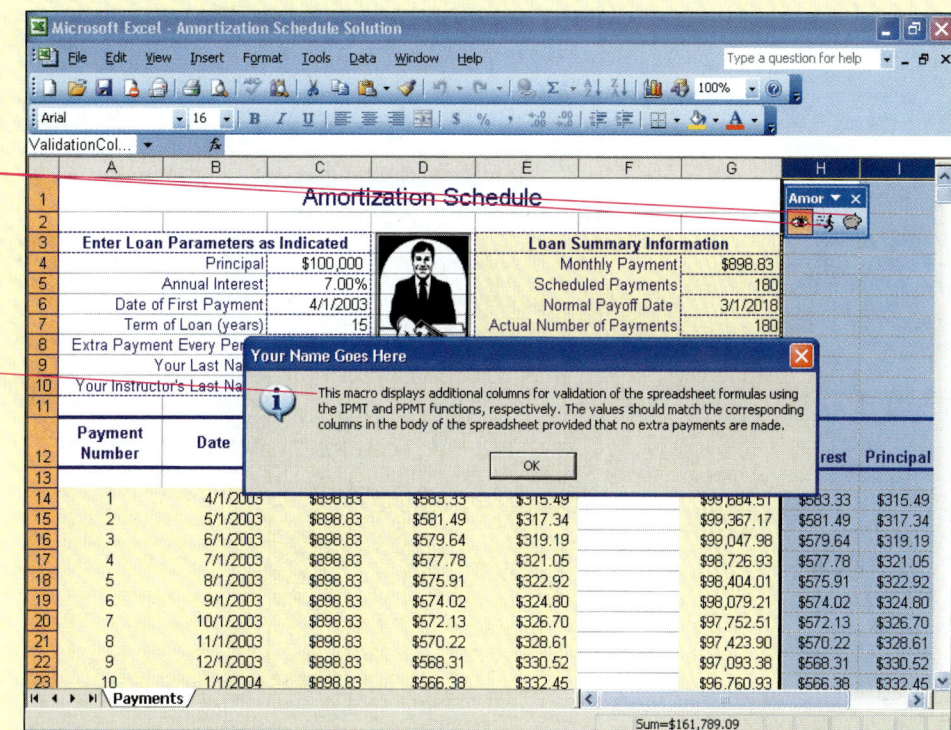

(h) Test the Toolbar Button (step 8)

FIGURE 9.5 Hands-on Exercise 2 (*continued*)

MODIFY THE BUTTON'S IMAGE

Excel provides only a limited number of images from which to choose, so it is convenient to be able to modify the images that are provided. Pull down the View menu, click Toolbars, click Customize to display the Customize dialog box, and click the Commands tab. Select the toolbar button, click Modify Selection, then click the Edit Button Image command to display the Button editor. Each button consists of 256 squares in a 16 by 16 grid. You can change the color of any square by selecting a new color, then clicking the appropriate square within the grid. You can also erase any square by double clicking the square. Click OK.

Step 9: **Attach the Toolbar**

- *This step is very important.* You must attach the custom toolbar to your workbook, so that it (the toolbar) will travel with the workbook if you copy the file and try to use it on a different computer.

- Pull down the **View menu**, click **Toolbars**, and click the **Customize command** to display the Customize dialog box. Click the **Toolbars tab**, then click the **Attach button** to display the Attach Toolbars dialog box in Figure 9.5i.

- Select the Amortization Schedule toolbar in the left pane, then click the **Copy button** to copy the custom toolbar to this workbook. (The custom toolbar resides in a special Excel folder that is stored on your computer and not in the workbook. Only after you attach the toolbar will it travel with the workbook.) Click **OK**. Click **Close**.

- Close the Amortization Schedule toolbar. Save the workbook. Exit Excel if you do not want to continue with the next exercise at this time.

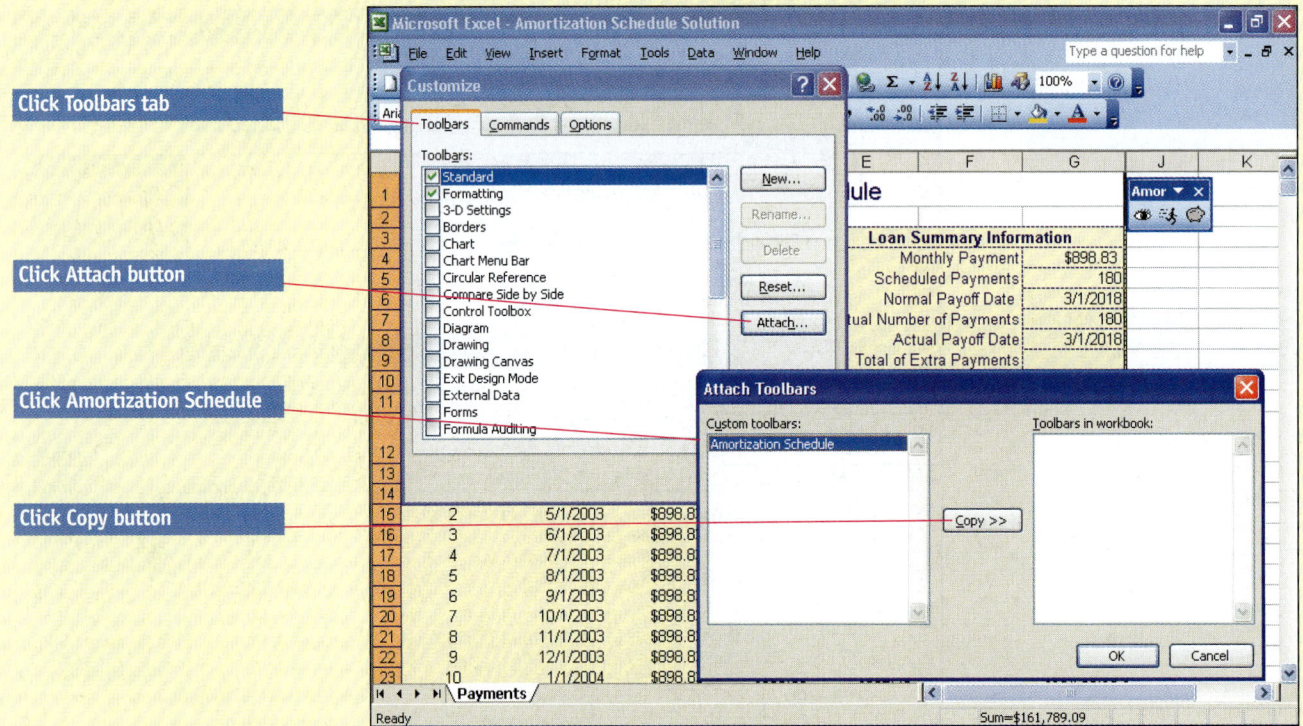

(i) Attach the Toolbar (step 9)

FIGURE 9.5 Hands-on Exercise 2 (*continued*)

ATTACHING TOOLBARS

The copy of the toolbar that is stored in a workbook reflects its contents at the time you attach the toolbar. Thus, if you subsequently modify a toolbar after attaching it, the changes are not automatically stored within the workbook. Pull down the View menu, click Toolbars, click Customize, click the Toolbars tab, then click the Attach button. Select the old toolbar in the Toolbars in workbook area at the right of the Attach Toolbar dialog box. Click the Delete button to delete the old toolbar. Select the new toolbar at the left of the dialog box, then click the Copy command to attach the new version. Click OK and save the workbook.

1446　CHAPTER 9: A PROFESSIONAL APPLICATION

EVENT PROCEDURES

VBA has two types of procedures. There are **general procedures** such as those in the preceding exercise that are executed explicitly by the user whenever the user chooses. VBA also recognizes **event procedures** that are executed automatically when a specified event occurs. An **event** is defined as any action that is recognized by an application. Opening, closing, or printing a workbook is an event, as is clicking a button on a **custom toolbar**. (The Excel object model describes the specific events that are recognized by VBA.)

You can enhance an Excel application by deciding which events are significant, and what is to happen when those events occur. Then you develop the appropriate event procedures to execute automatically in conjunction with those events. This is in contrast to a traditional program that is executed sequentially, beginning with the first line of code and continuing in order through the remainder of the program. It is the program, not the user, that determines the order in which the statements are executed. VBA, on the other hand, is event-driven, meaning that the order in which the procedures are executed depends on the events that occur. It is the user, rather than the program, that determines which events occur, and consequently which procedures are executed.

The **Open workbook event procedure** is common to many applications. It accomplishes a variety of tasks such as the display of a custom toolbar or splash screen, checking for special conditions to alert the user, and/or performing other tasks for the developer. The **Before Close event procedure** is also common and typically hides the custom toolbar and displays a closing message to the user, such as a reminder to back up the system. It may also check for special conditions and/or perform one or more tasks for the developer.

Figures 9.6a and 9.6b display the results of these two event procedures for the Amortization Schedule workbook. The Open workbook event procedure in Figure 9.6a displays the custom toolbar and a splash screen. A **splash screen** is a simple form that appears for a brief period of time to identify an application, and then it disappears from view. (The form itself is created in the VBA editor as described in the next section.) The Open workbook event procedure may also include additional code to accomplish other tasks, but you may not be aware of the additional actions by merely looking at the worksheet.

Figure 9.6b displays the results of the Before Close event procedure. The custom toolbar has been hidden from view and a message is displayed to the user. The message box is different from the splash screen and requires the user to click OK to close the dialog box. Again, there may be additional code within the Before Close event procedure, the effects of which are not visible from this figure.

Remember too that an event procedure is executed regardless of how the event is triggered. Think about the various ways in which you close a workbook. You may pull down the File menu and click the Close command, or you can click the Close button in the application window, or you can use the Ctrl+F4 keyboard shortcut. All of these commands close the active workbook and in turn will trigger the Before Close event procedure.

SIGN YOUR DOCUMENTS

Excel displays a security warning prior to opening any Excel workbook that contains a VBA procedure. You can, however, display a different dialog box that identifies the publisher of the workbook and that the workbook is to be trusted as a safe source. This is accomplished by applying a digital signature, an electronic, encryption-based stamp of authentication, which confirms the origin of a document, and further that the document has not been altered since it was last saved by the signer. (See step 9 in Hands-on Exercise 3.)

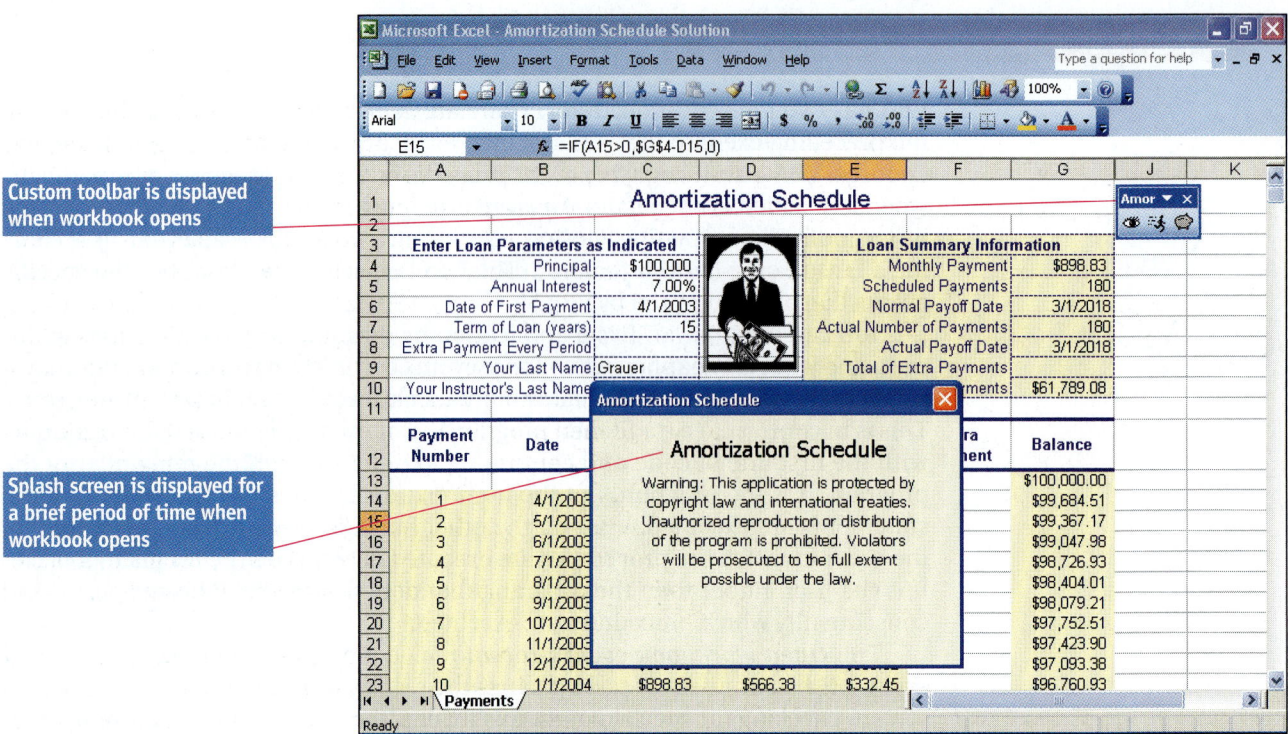

(a) The Open Workbook Event Procedure

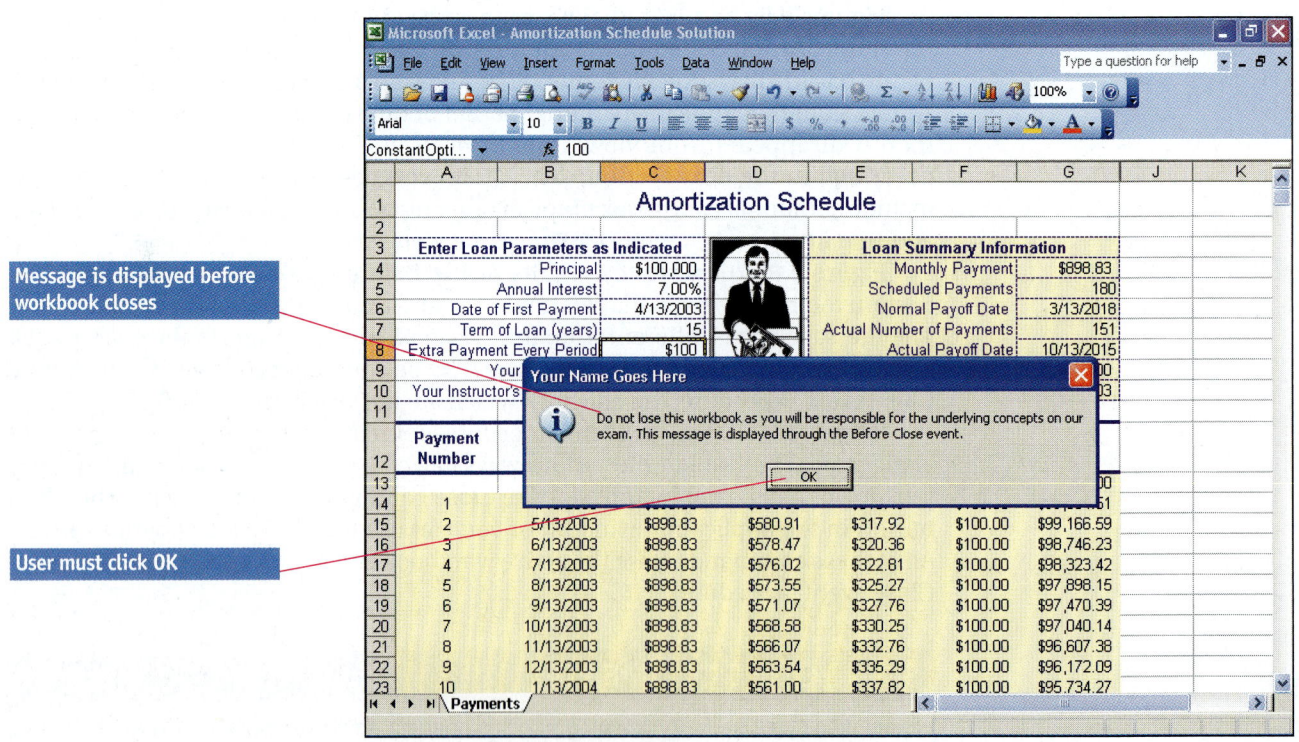

(b) The Before Close Event Procedure

FIGURE 9.6 Event Procedures

USER FORMS

A ***user form*** is typically created to facilitate data entry and is most commonly associated with Microsoft Access. A user form can also be created in Excel to enter data in a worksheet and/or to display a splash screen, which in turn requires several steps. First, you create the user form. Next, you develop the procedure(s) to load (display) the form. And finally, you create the procedure to unload (hide) the form.

Figure 9.7 depicts the creation of a splash screen for the Amortization Schedule workbook. The Project Explorer window in the upper-left pane contains a Forms folder, which contains a single object, UserForm1. The form itself appears in Design view in the upper-right pane. You start with a blank form, then use the controls on the Toolbox to create the form. Click the appropriate tool (e.g., the "A" or label tool), then click and drag on the form to create the corresponding control. Once the label has been created, you click within the control and enter the desired text.

Every object (control) on a form as well as the form itself has a distinct set of properties (attributes) that are displayed and modified in the ***Properties window*** in the lower-left portion of the screen. You select the object on the form, and then you change the desired property, such as the font style, color, or size.

Once the form has been created, you have to develop the procedure to display the form, and another procedure to hide the form after it has been on the screen for the specified amount of time. The form is displayed by a single line of code, UserForm1.Show, which appears in the Open workbook event procedure. (The event procedure is not visible in Figure 9.7.)

The ***UserForm Activate event procedure*** in the lower-right portion of Figure 9.7 executes automatically when the form is opened. The ***OnTime method*** sets the amount of time the form is visible by adding five seconds to the Now function that contains the current time. The OnTime method then calls a third procedure, CloseScreen, which contains a single statement to unload (hide) the form. It's easier than it sounds as you will see in our next hands-on exercise.

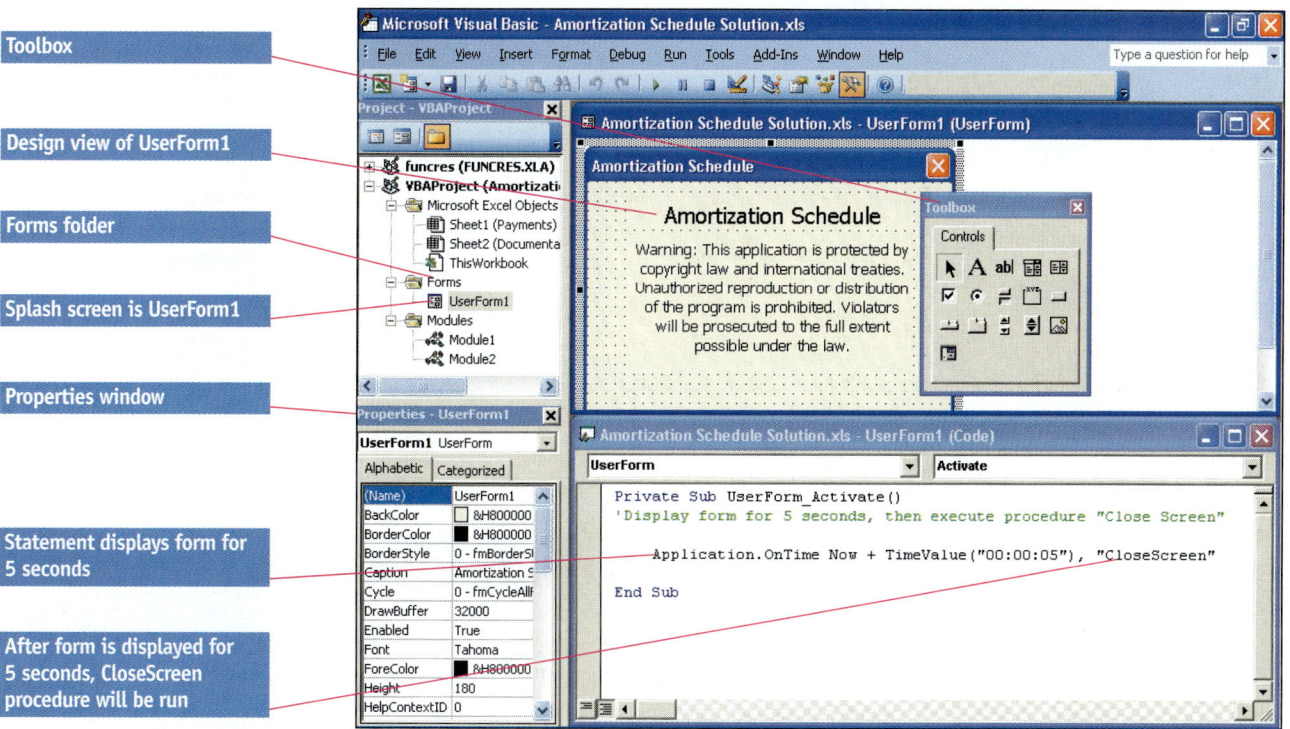

FIGURE 9.7 Creating a User Form

hands-on exercise 3

Event Procedures

Objective To create an Open workbook event procedure that displays a splash screen and custom toolbar; to create a Before Close event procedure to close the custom toolbar and display a message to the user. Use Figure 9.8 as a guide.

Step 1: **Start the Macro Recorder**

- Start Excel. Open the **Amortization Schedule Solution** workbook from the previous exercise. Click the button to **Enable macros**.
- Pull down the **Tools menu**, click the **Macro command**, then click **Record New Macro** to display the Record Macro dialog box. You can accept the default name (such as Macro1), since we are just using the recorder to obtain the correct VBA syntax. Click **OK** to begin recording the macro.
- Pull down the **View menu**, click the **Toolbars command**, then click the **Amortization Schedule toolbar** as shown in Figure 9.8a.
- Click the **Stop Recording button**. (If you do not see the button, pull down the **Tools menu**, click the **Macro command**, and then click **Stop Recording**.)

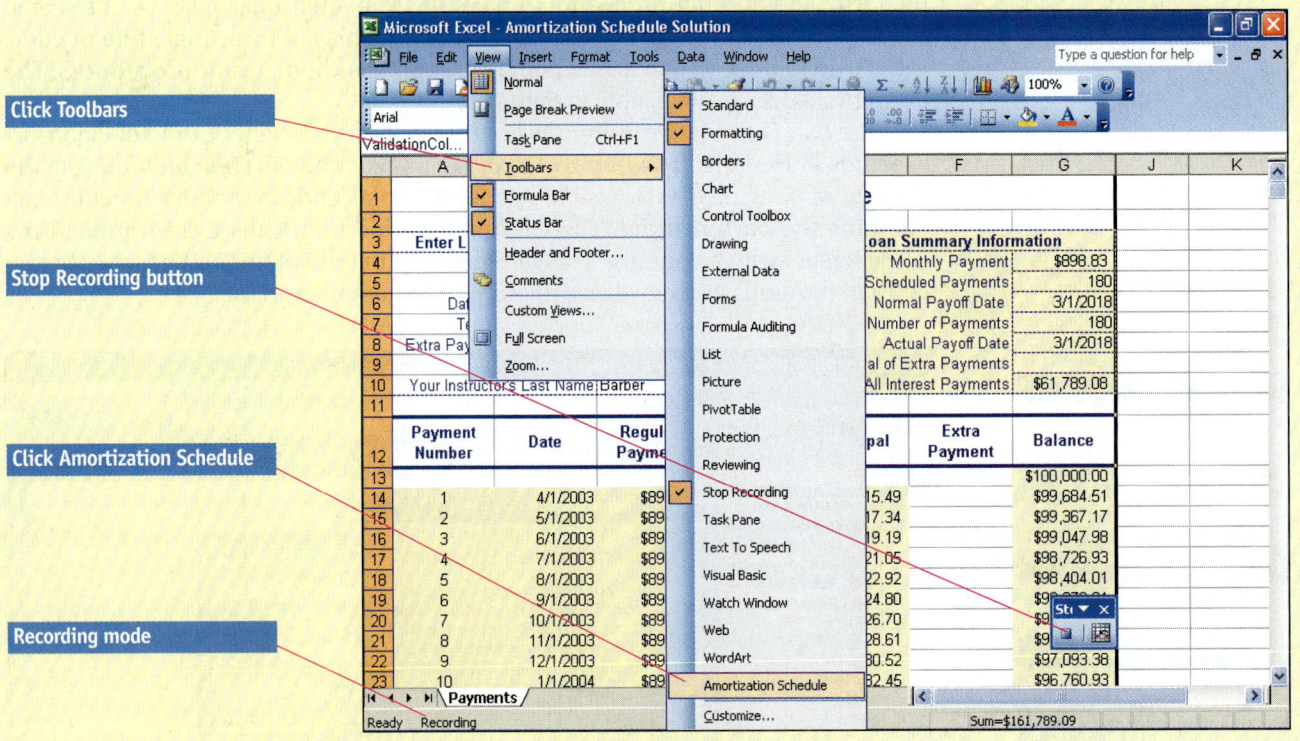

(a) Start the Macro Recorder (step 1)

FIGURE 9.8 Hands-on Exercise 3

WRITE VBA THE EASY WAY

The statement, Application.CommandBars("Amortization Schedule").Visible = True, displays the Amortization Schedule toolbar. It's easy to understand the statement, but it is not so easy to write it. The good news is you do not have to. Start the macro recorder and create a macro to display the toolbar. Stop the recorder, open the VBA editor, then use the generated code as the basis of a more sophisticated VBA procedure.

Step 2: **Create the Open Workbook Event Procedure**

- Press **Alt+F11** to open the VBA editor. Open the **Modules folder**, then select the newest module that contains the macro you just recorded.

- You should see a procedure called Macro1 that contains a single statement to display the Amortization Schedule toolbar. Select that statement, then click the **Copy button** on the Standard toolbar.

- Double click **ThisWorkbook** within the Project Explorer to display the code for the event procedures within the workbook. (There are none so far.)

- Click the **down arrow** in the Object list box (the leftmost list box) to select **Workbook**. The **Open workbook event procedure** is created automatically. The insertion point appears below the procedure header.

- Press the **Tab key** or **space bar** to indent the code, then click the **Paste button** (or use the **Ctrl+V** keyboard shortcut) to paste the VBA statement to display the Amortization schedule toolbar.

- Add the additional statements and comments as shown in Figure 9.8b. Click the **Save button** to save the event procedures within the workbook.

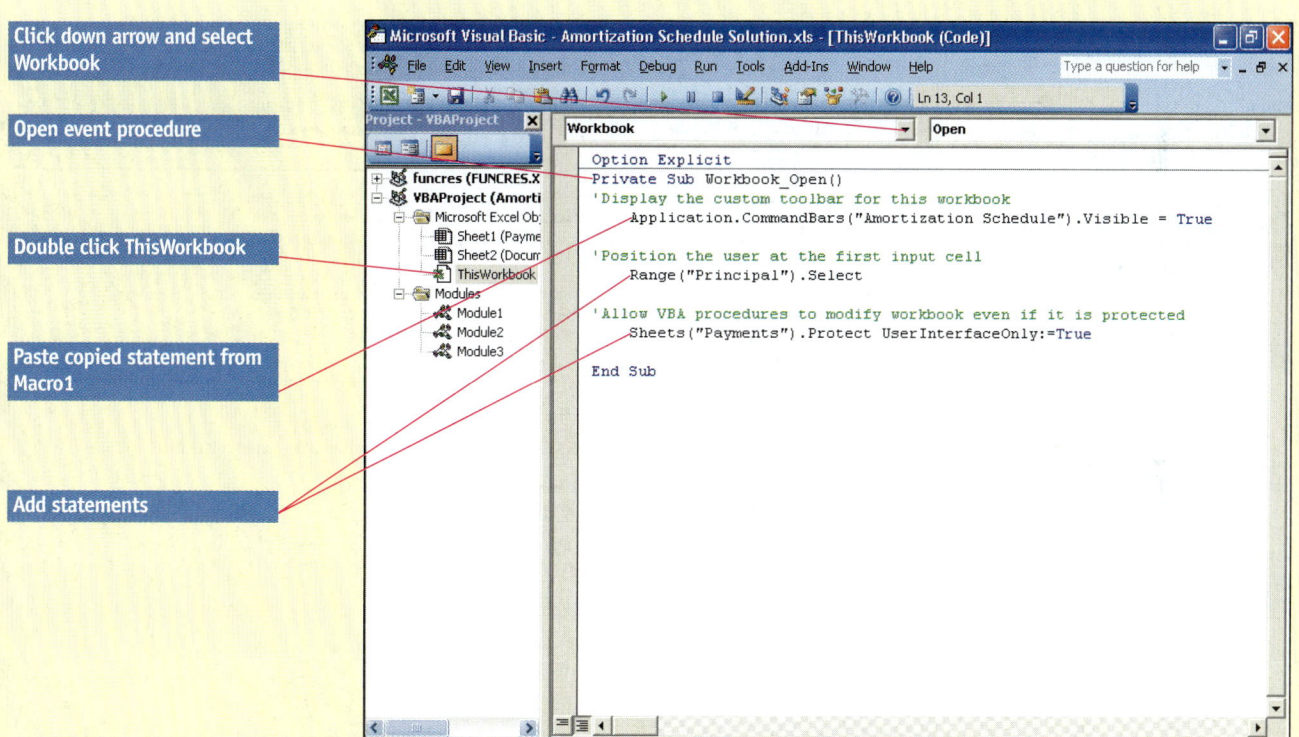

(b) Create the Open Workbook Event Procedure (step 2)

FIGURE 9.8 Hands-on Exercise 3 (*continued*)

PROTECT USER INTERFACE ONLY

A worksheet is protected to prevent the end user from accidentally (or otherwise) altering or deleting the formulas in the worksheet. The developer, however, should be able to modify the worksheet without having to protect and unprotect the worksheet within individual procedures. This is accomplished by setting the UserInterfaceOnly property. All VBA procedures will be able to modify the worksheet. The user, however, will be prevented from doing so when protection is in effect.

Step 3: **Create the Before Close Event Procedure**

- Click the **down arrow** in the Procedure list box (at the top of the right side of the Code window), then scroll until you can select the **Before Close event**. The Before Close event procedure is created automatically as shown in Figure 9.8c.

- Enter the statement and associated comment to hide the Amortization Schedule toolbar. You can type the statement directly, or you can copy the existing statement from the Open workbook event procedure and change the **Visible property** to **False**.

- Create the **MsgBox statement** that will be displayed prior to the workbook closing. The VBA syntax requires the underscore character when the MsgBox statement is continued from one line to the next. The ampersand is used to concatenate (join together) the various literals within the statement.

- Click the **Save button**. (You can remove the module that contains the Macro1 "dummy" procedure. Right click the module, click **Remove Module3**, then click **No** when asked to export the module. This macro was created only to obtain the basic VBA syntax for the event procedures and has no further purpose.)

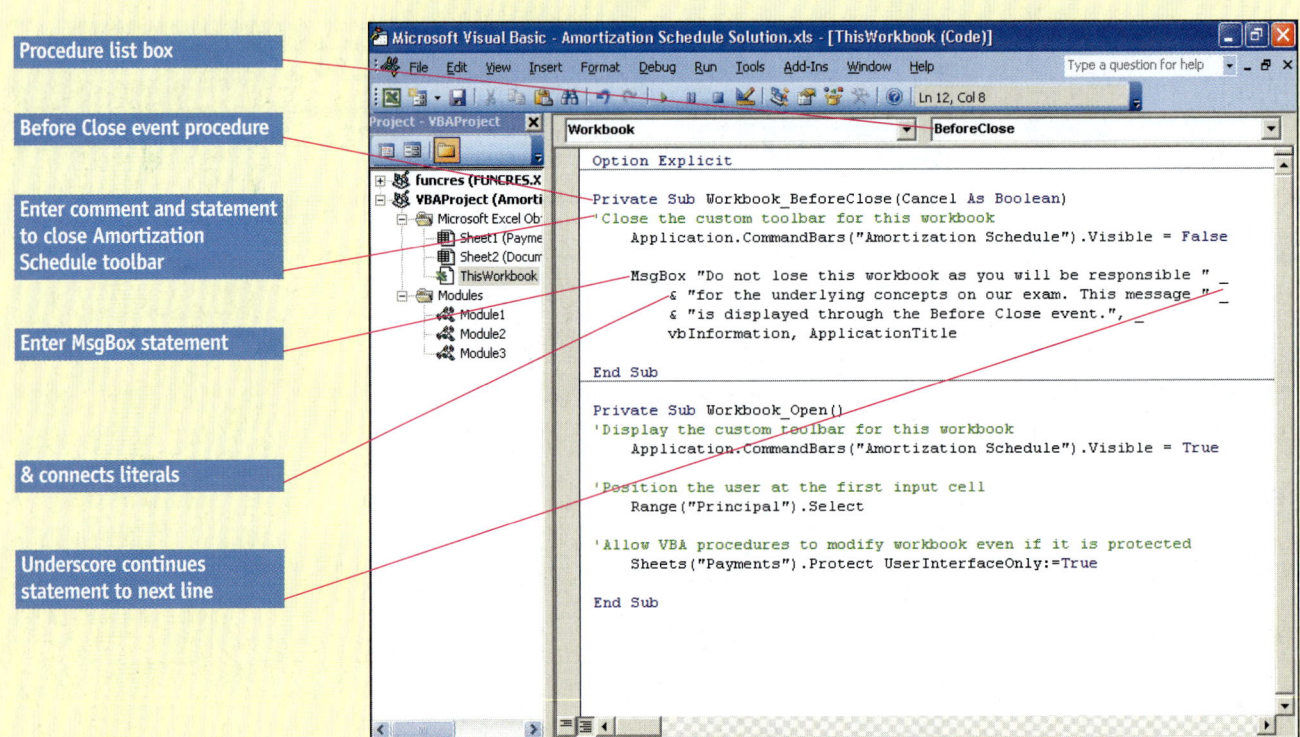

(c) Create the Before Close Event Procedure (step 3)

FIGURE 9.8 Hands-on Exercise 3 (*continued*)

EVENT PROCEDURES VERSUS GENERAL PROCEDURES

Event procedures such as opening and closing a workbook execute only when the designated event occurs. General procedures can be executed at any time. The macro recorder cannot be used with event procedures. Thus, we create a "dummy" macro to obtain the VBA statement to display a toolbar, we copy that statement to the event procedure, and then we delete the "dummy" procedure since it is no longer necessary.

Step 4: **Test the Procedures**

- Return to the Excel worksheet. The Amortization Schedule toolbar should still be visible on your screen (but not in our figure). If you do not see the toolbar, pull down the **View menu**, click **Toolbars** to display the list of available toolbars, then click the **Amortization Schedule toolbar**.
- Pull down the **File menu** and click the **Close command** to close the workbook but leave the Excel application open.
- The Amortization Schedule toolbar disappears, after which you should see the message box in Figure 9.8d, which is displayed by the Before Close event procedure that you just created.
- Read the statement carefully, and make a note of any potential corrections. Click **OK** after you have read the message. Click **Yes** if you are prompted to save the changes to the workbook.
- Excel should still be open. Pull down the **File menu**, click the **Open command**, then double click the **Amortization Schedule Solution** workbook.
- Click the button to **Enable macros**. The workbook opens and you should see the Amortization Schedule toolbar. Make corrections as necessary to the event procedures. Save the workbook.

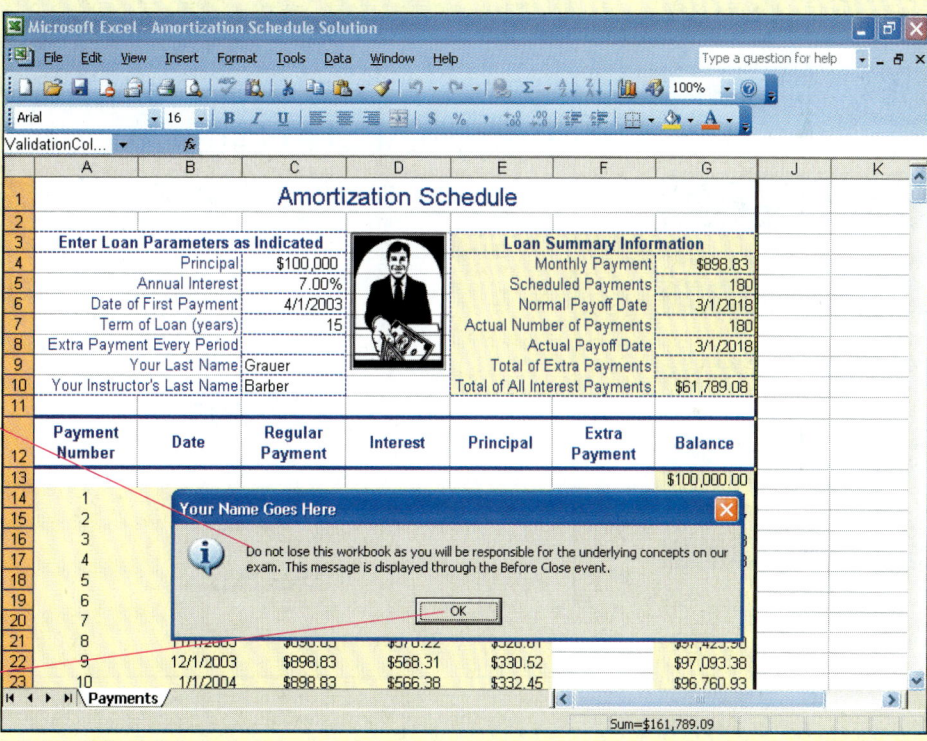

(d) Test the Procedures (step 4)

FIGURE 9.8 Hands-on Exercise 3 (*continued*)

THE WEEKDAY FUNCTION TEST FOR SPECIAL CONDITIONS

Use the WEEKDAY function within the Open and Before Close event procedures to test for special conditions. You can, for example, use the Open event to test for Monday, the first day of the business week, then display a message to check for new interest rates. In similar fashion, you can use the Before Close event to display a message on Friday, reminding the user to perform a weekly backup. See Exercise 5 at the end of the chapter.

Step 5: **Create the User Form**

- Press **Alt+F11** to return to the Visual Basic Editor. Pull down the **Insert menu** and click **UserForm** to create a new user form as shown in Figure 9.8e. The form is stored within the Forms folder that appears automatically within the Project Explorer.

- The toolbox should appear automatically. If not, you can click the **Toolbox button** on the Standard toolbar to toggle the toolbox on and off. Do not be concerned if the size and or position of the window for the form is different from ours.

- Click the **Label tool** (the large letter "A"), then click and drag in the form to create the first label, containing the title of the form. Click and drag within the newly created label to select the default text, **Label1**, then type **Amortization Schedule** to replace the existing text.

- Click the **Label tool** a second time. Click and drag in the form to create the second label, then enter the text shown in the figure.

- Click the **Save button** to save the form.

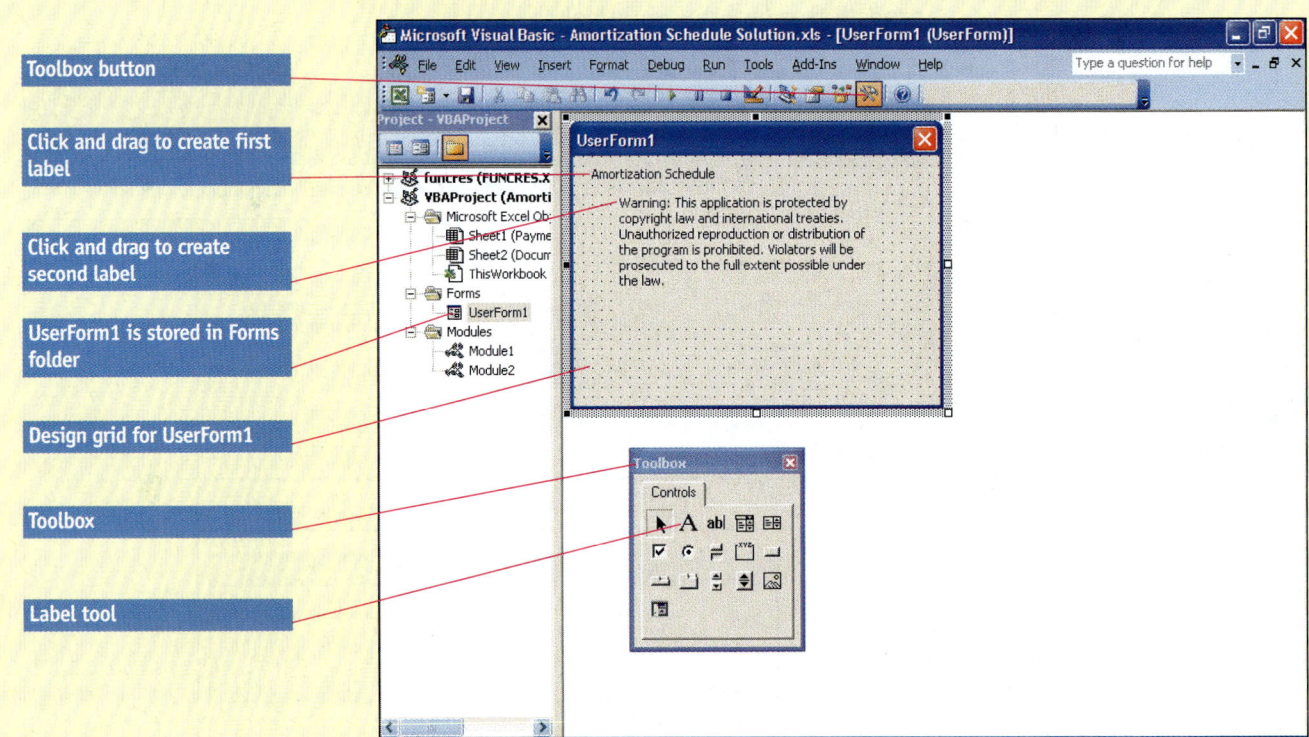

(e) Create the User Form (step 5)

FIGURE 9.8 Hands-on Exercise 3 (*continued*)

MANAGE THE OPEN WINDOWS

Multiple windows are open simultaneously within the VBA editor. Every module and form has its own window. The Project Explorer and Properties sheet are also open in separate windows. It may be helpful, therefore, to close the windows that you do not need. You can also move and size windows within the VBA editor. And finally, you can use the Window menu to tile or cascade the open windows.

Step 6: **Modify the Form Properties**

- Pull down the **View menu** and click the **Properties Window command** (or press the **F4 keyboard shortcut**) to open the Properties window in Figure 9.8f. Click the **Alphabetic tab** so that the properties are displayed alphabetically.

- Click the **second label** (the copyright notice), and you see its properties as shown in Figure 9.8f. Change the **Name property** to **CopyrightNotice**.

- Click in the **Back Color text box** to display a down arrow, then click the **down arrow** to display the available colors. Click the **System tab**, then choose the ToolTip color.

- Change the name and back color of the other label in similar fashion. Change the back color and caption property **(to Amortization Schedule)** of the form itself. Experiment further with the available properties (we changed the font size and alignment). Set a time limit. Five minutes is enough. Close the Properties window.

- Check that the user form is still selected in the Project Explorer. Click the background area on the form. Click the **View Code** and **View Object buttons** to switch between the code and the form, respectively. It doesn't matter if you see both windows simultaneously, or if one window overlays the other. The Code window contains only a Sub and End Sub. Save the form.

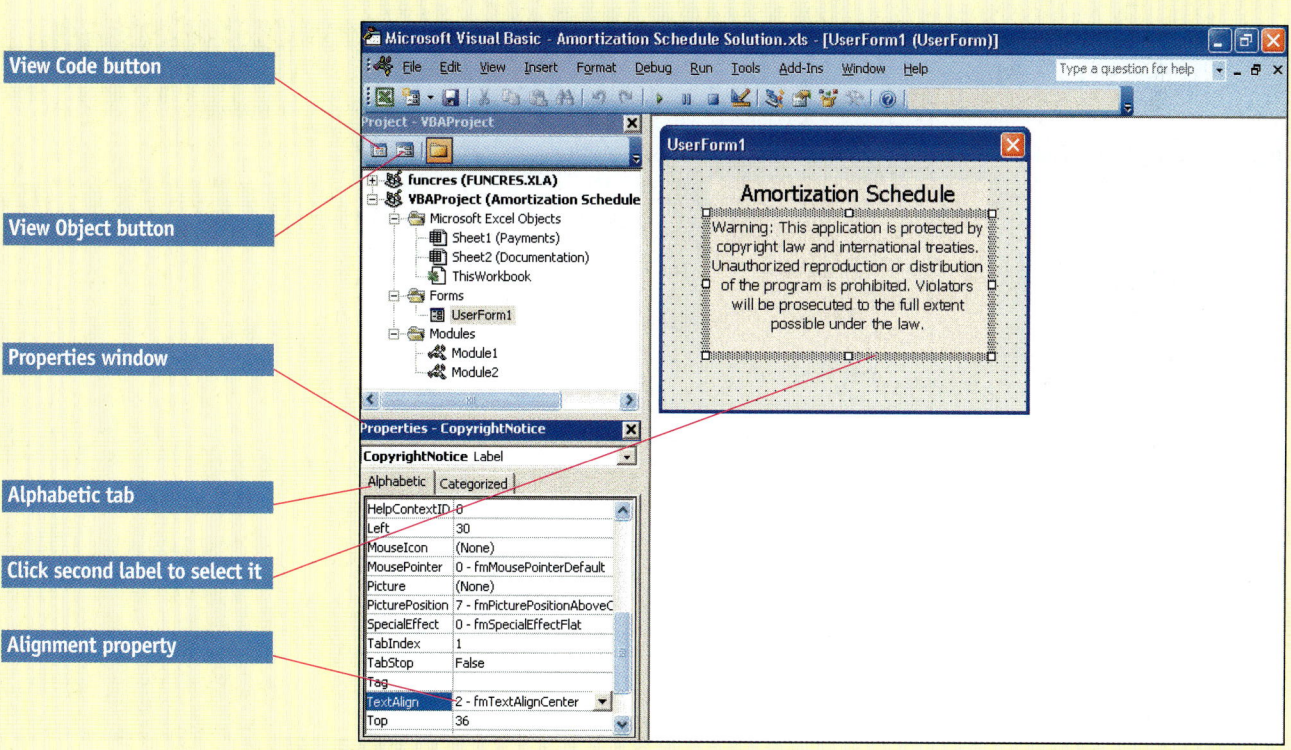

(f) Modify the Form Properties (step 6)

FIGURE 9.8 Hands-on Exercise 3 (*continued*)

THE SPLASH SCREEN

There are four distinct steps to creating a splash screen. First, you create the screen as a user form. Next, you create the Activate event procedure to display the form for a specified time. You then modify the Open workbook event procedure to load the user form when the workbook opens. And finally, you have to create a public procedure to unload the form after it has been displayed for the specified amount of time.

MICROSOFT OFFICE EXCEL 2003 1455

Step 7: **Create the Code for the User Form**

- Display the Code window for the user form. Click the **down arrow** in the Procedure list box (near the top of the VBA window) and select the **Activate event**. Delete the UserForm_Click procedure that is created by default.

- Enter the code for the **ActivateForm** event procedure as shown in Figure 9.8g. This procedure will display the form for five seconds once the form is activated, then it calls a second procedure to unload the form.

- It is still necessary to load the form initially within the Open workbook event procedure. Double click **ThisWorkbook** within the Project Explorer to return to the events associated with the workbook.

- Locate the **Open workbook procedure**. Add the statement **UserForm1.Show** on a separate line, after the statement to display the Amortization Schedule toolbar.

- You're almost finished but not quite. You still have to create the procedure to unload the form after the five seconds are up.

- Double click **Module1** within the Project Explorer window and create the **CloseScreen procedure**, which consists of three statements: **Public Sub CloseScreen()**, **Unload UserForm1**, and **End Sub**. Save the project.

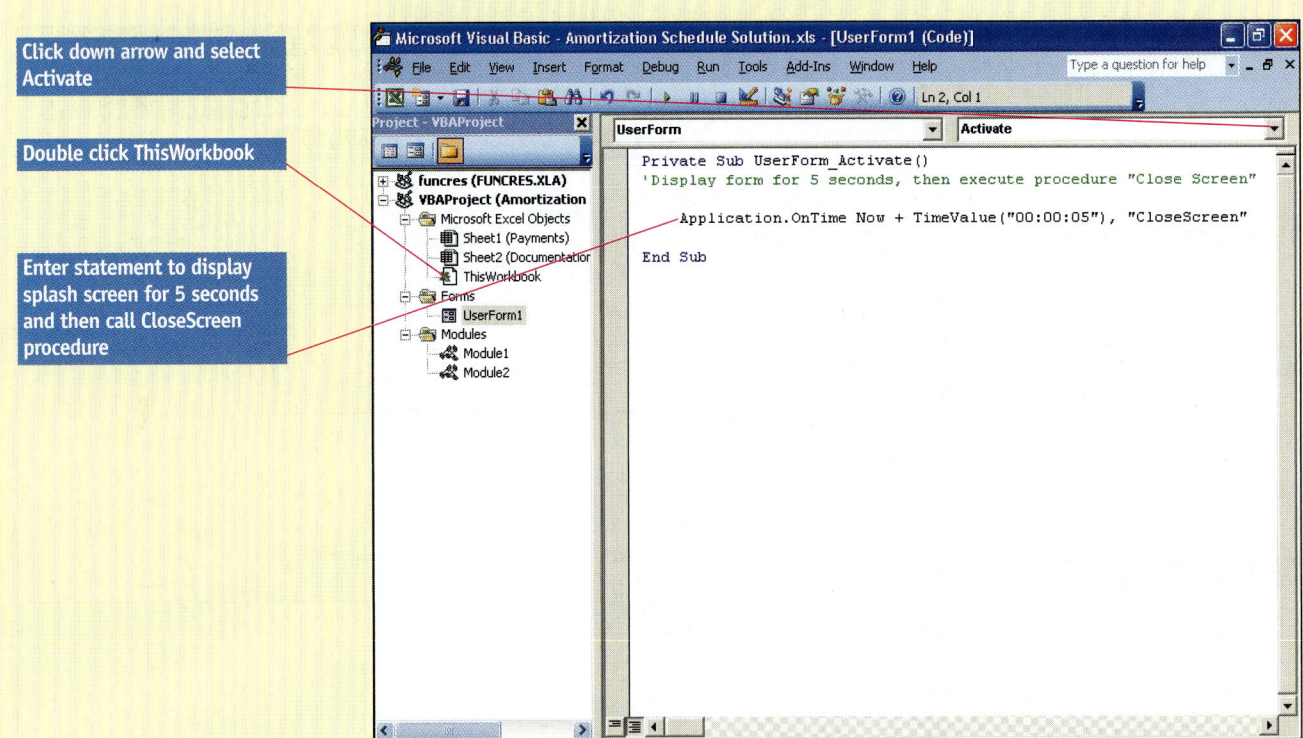

(g) Create the Code for the User Form (step 7)

FIGURE 9.8 Hands-on Exercise 3 (*continued*)

PUBLIC VERSUS PRIVATE PROCEDURES

The Amortization Schedule workbook is a VBA project. Each module in the project contains one or more procedures. Each procedure is either public or private. The scope of a procedure determines how the procedure can be accessed. A public procedure can be called from any module within the VBA project. A private procedure, however, can be accessed only from within the module in which it is stored.

Step 8: **Test the Splash Screen**

- Return to the Excel window. Close the workbook, but remain in Excel. Click **Yes** if asked whether to save the changes.

- Reopen the **Amortization Schedule Solution** workbook that appears at the top of the list of recently opened workbooks. Click the button to **Enable macros** when you see the security warning.

- The workbook opens and the Amortization Schedule toolbar is displayed, followed by the splash screen as shown in Figure 9.8h. The splash screen should remain for approximately five seconds, then it closes automatically.

- Enter any set of loan parameters, then test each of the toolbar buttons to be sure that they work properly. If the buttons do not function as intended, it could be because you forgot to attach the custom toolbar at the end of the previous exercise. Return to that exercise and repeat the steps correctly.

- Save the workbook. Exit Excel if you do not want to apply a digital signature to the workbook.

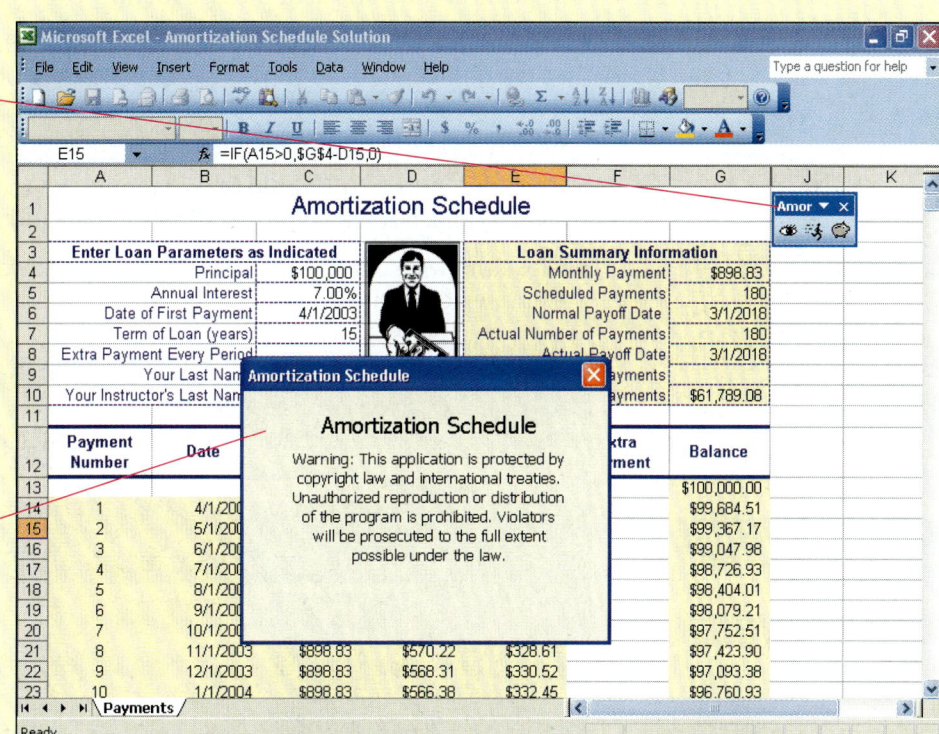

(h) Test the Splash Screen (step 8)

FIGURE 9.8 Hands-on Exercise 3 (*continued*)

SCREEN CAPTURE

The ability to capture a screen, then print the captured screen as part of a document, is very useful. The process is quite simple. Press the PrintScreen key any time you want to capture a screen to copy the screen to the Windows clipboard, an area of memory that is accessible to any Windows application. Next, start (or switch to) a Word document, and then execute the Paste command in the Edit menu to paste the contents of the clipboard into the current document. The screen is now part of the Word document, where it can be moved and sized like any other Windows object. See exercise 10 at the end of the chapter.

Step 9: **Authenticate the Workbook**

- You cannot digitally sign a workbook unless you have a digital signature. Click the **Start button**, click **All Programs**, click **Microsoft Office**, click **Microsoft Office Tools**, and then click **Digital Certificate for VBA Projects**.

- Type **Your Name** in the Create Digital Certificate dialog box. Click **OK** to create your signature and close the dialog box.

- The Amortization Schedule Solution workbook should still be open. Press **Alt+F11** to switch to the VBA editor. Pull down the **Tools menu** and click the **Digital Signature command** to display the associated dialog box.

- Click the **Choose button** to display the Select Certificate dialog box, click the signature you just created, click **OK** to close the Select Certificate dialog box, then click **OK** a second time to close the Digital Signature dialog box. Close the VBA editor.

- Save the workbook. Close the workbook, but leave Excel open. Pull down the **File menu** and click the **Amortization Schedule Solution workbook** that appears at the bottom of the File menu.

- You should see the Security Warning in Figure 9.8i. Your name should appear as the publisher of the workbook. Look closely, however, and note the message that indicates your credentials cannot be trusted. This is because your certificate has not been authenticated by a formal certification agency.

- Click the button to **Enable Macros** to return to the Excel workbook. You will see the splash screen, amortization toolbar, and so on.

- Close the workbook. Exit Excel if you do not want to continue with the next exercise at this time.

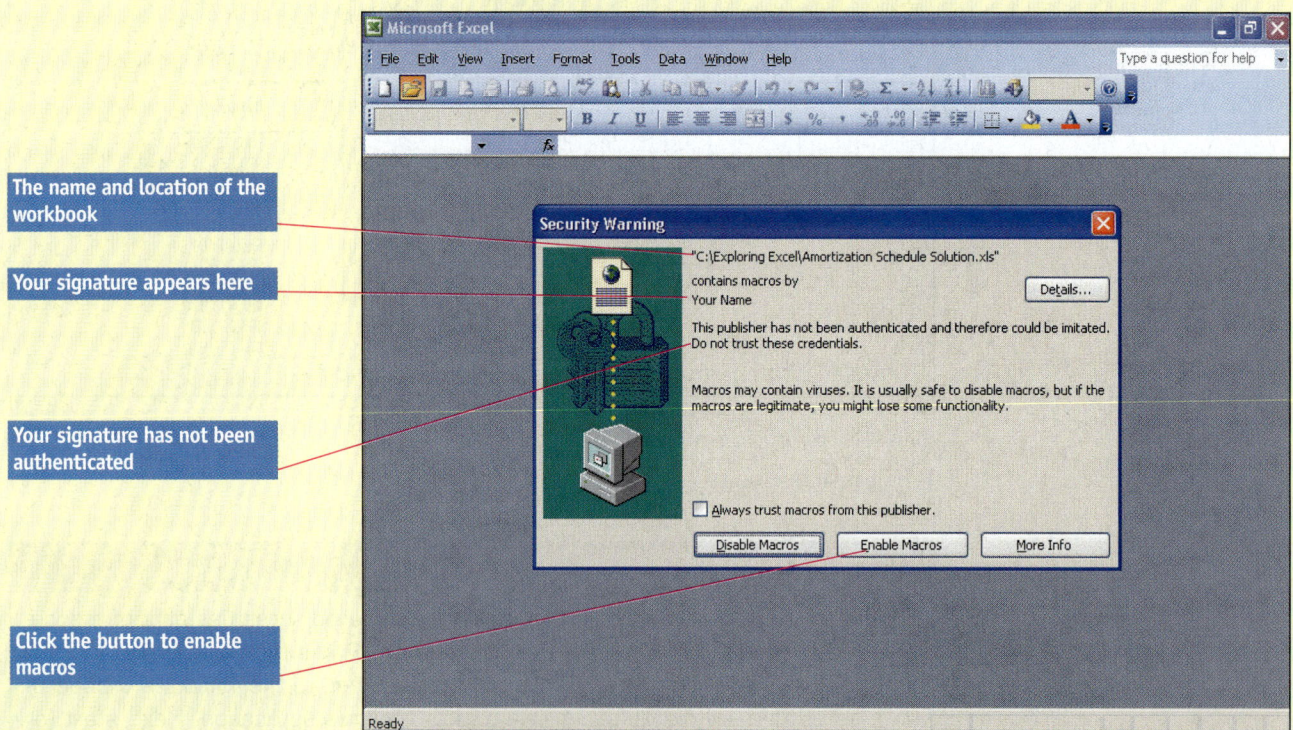

(i) Authenticate the Workbook (step 9)

FIGURE 9.8 Hands-on Exercise 3 (*continued*)

MORE COMPLEX PROCEDURES

A good application lets a user accomplish tasks that he or she could not (easily) do through ordinary Excel commands. The original amortization worksheet gave the user the capability to apply an optional extra payment *every month*. What if, however, the user wanted to see the effect of an *annual* optional payment (that is, an extra payment once a year)? This is best accomplished through a VBA procedure that prompts the user for the amount of the annual payment and the date it is to begin, after which the procedure applies that payment annually until the loan is paid off. Such a procedure entails more complex logic than what we have shown so far.

The difficulty (if any) is not the VBA per se, but rather the underlying logic. Think carefully about the implication of the preceding sentence. VBA is a powerful tool, and because it is powerful, developers use it to implement sophisticated procedures that entail nontrivial logic.

Pseudocode or "neat notes to oneself" is the most common way of expressing logic. Pseudocode does not have any precise syntax and is intended only to convey the logic within a program. One develops pseudocode by thinking in very general terms about the steps required to solve the problem. Our problem, simply stated, is to write a VBA procedure that will apply an annual extra payment to the existing payments table until the loan is paid off. This requires that we

1. Ask the user for the amount of the extra payment.

2. Ask the user when the extra payments are to begin.

3. Determine where in the table the payments are to begin.

4. Apply the extra payments annually until the loan is paid off.

This version of the pseudocode is almost trivial, but it does get you started thinking about the problem. You prompt the user for the amount and date of the periodic payment, go to the first date in the table where the payments are to begin, and then apply the periodic payment annually until the loan is paid off. The logic is accurate and complete, but it is not sufficiently detailed to provide a real help in writing the procedure.

It is necessary, therefore, to further develop the steps that determine when the payments are to begin, and how to apply the payments within the table. The expanded pseudocode is shown in Figure 9.9a and includes decision making and loops. To determine the first extra payment, you go to the first date within the payments table, then look at each successive date within the table until you reach a date greater than or equal to the date the payments are to begin. You then move the active cell to the payments column within this row.

Once you have the position of the first extra payment, you create a second loop in which you apply a payment once a year until the loan is paid off. This is accomplished through a ***switch***, a programming term for a variable that assumes one of two values. We set the switch (PayoffMade in this example) to "No" outside of the loop, then we go through the loop until the loan has been paid off. The first statement in the loop applies the extra payment to the active cell, after which the If statement compares the balance at the end of that year to zero. If the loan has been paid off, the switch is set to "Yes" and the loop is terminated. If the loan has not been paid, we move one year down in the table and return to the top of the loop.

Only when you are comfortable with this logic should you begin to write the VBA procedure, starting with the macro recorder to provide basic syntax. We used the macro recorder to capture the statement to select a specific cell (FirstTableDate in this example). We also used it to get the syntax for the relative references to various cells within the table. Once we had these basic statements, we added the additional VBA control structures to complete the procedure. The indentation within the procedure and the blank lines between statements are there only to enhance the readability.

User supplies amount and start date for extra payments

```
Input amount of extra payment and date payments are to begin

Set active date to first table date
Do Until active cell >= Date that payments are to begin
    Check next date
Loop
Move active cell to the extra payment column in this row

PayoffMade = "No"
Do Until PayoffMade = "Yes"
    Apply extra payment here
    If Ending Balance at end of year <=0
        PayoffMade = "Yes"
    Else
        Drop active cell 12 rows (1 year)
    End if
Loop

Display summary area
```

Determines where in table payments begin

Applies extra payments until loan is paid off

(a) Pseudocode

```
Sub PeriodicExtraPayments()
    Dim DateExtraPaymentsBegin As Date
    Dim AmountofExtraPayment As Currency
    Dim PayoffMade As String
    AmountofExtraPayment = InputBox("Enter amount of extra payment")
    DateExtraPaymentsBegin = InputBox("Enter date when payments begin")

    Application.Goto Reference:="FirstTableDate"

    Do Until ActiveCell >= DateExtraPaymentsBegin
        ActiveCell.Offset(1, 0).Range("A1").Select
    Loop

    ActiveCell.Offset(0, 4).Range("A1").Select

    PayoffMade = "No"
    Do Until PayoffMade = "Yes"
        ActiveCell = AmountofExtraPayment
        If ActiveCell.Offset(11, 1) <= 0 Then  'Check one year later
            PayoffMade = "Yes"
        Else
            ActiveCell.Offset(12, 0).Select     'New Payment necessary
        End If
    Loop

    Range("TotalOfExtraPayments").Select

End Sub
```

User supplies amount and start date for extra payment

Determines where in table payments begin

Applies extra payments until loan is paid off

(b) The VBA Procedure

FIGURE 9.9 Periodic Extra Payments

hands-on exercise

4 Periodic Optional Payments

Objective Develop a procedure to apply periodic extra payments to a loan until the loan is paid off. Use Figure 9.10 as a guide in the exercise.

Step 1: **Start the Macro Recorder**

- Open the **Amortization Schedule Solution** and click the button to **Enable macros**. Pull down the **Tools menu** to start recording a new macro. Enter **PeriodicExtraPayment** as the name of the macro. Click **OK** to begin recording.

- The Relative Reference button on the Stop Recording toolbar should be out, so that you are recording absolute references. Click the **down arrow** in the Name box at the upper left of the window, then select **FirstTableDate**, which positions you in cell B14.

- Click the **Relative Reference button** to record relative references from now on. Click in **cell B15** as shown in Figure 9.10a to move down one row.

- Click the **Stop Recording button**. Save the workbook.

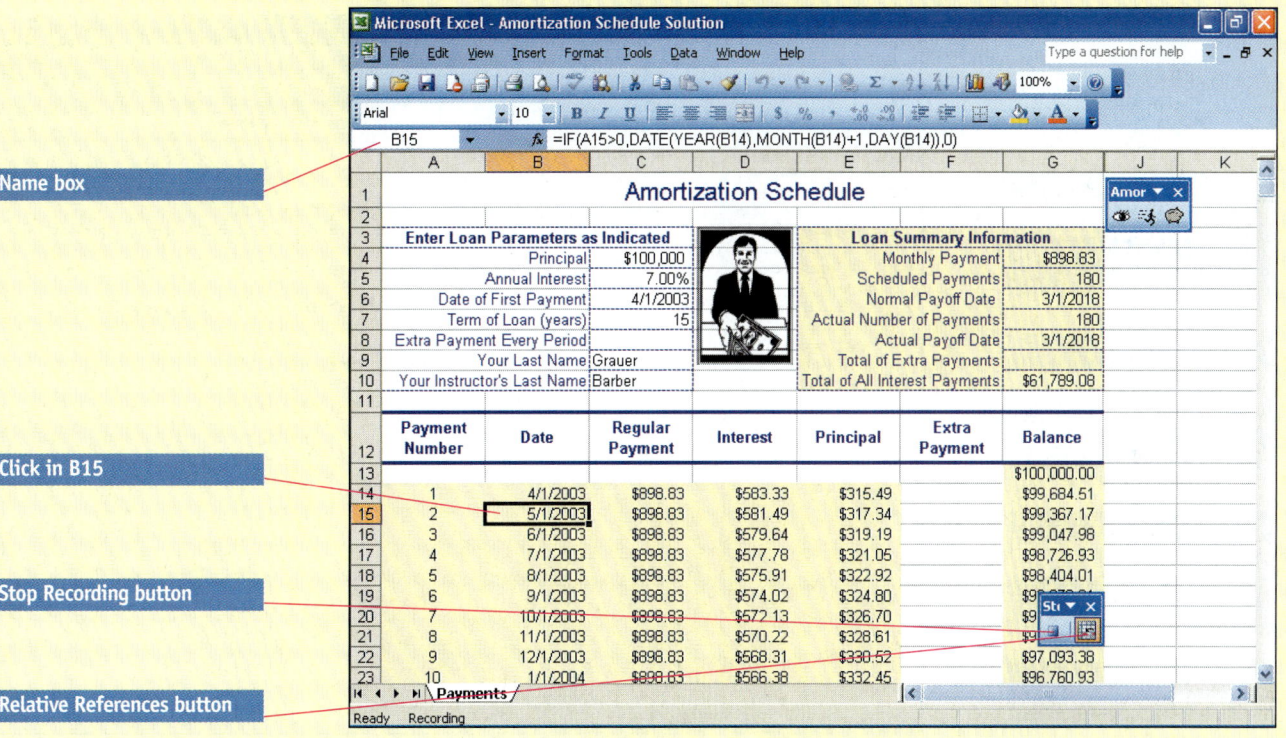

(a) Start the Macro Recorder (step 1)

FIGURE 9.10 Hands-on Exercise 4

IS THE BUTTON IN OR OUT?

The Relative Reference button on the Stop Recording toolbar toggles between relative (the button is in) and absolute (the button is out) references. The ScreenTip, however, displays "Relative References" regardless of whether the button is in or out. We wish that Microsoft had made it easier to tell which type of reference you are recording, but it didn't.

MICROSOFT OFFICE EXCEL 2003 **1461**

Step 2: **View and Add Code**

- Press **Alt+F11** to open the VBA editor. Open the **Modules folder**. Double click the module that contains the current macro (Module3 in our figure).

- You should see two statements within the procedure. The first statement, **Application.Goto Reference: ="FirstTableDate"** goes to the first date within the table (cell B14).

- The second statement, **ActiveCell.Offset(1,0).Range("A1").Select** moves the active cell down one row, but remains in column B. (The Range property can be deleted—see the boxed tip below.)

- Add the remaining statements as shown in Figure 9.10b.
  - The **Dim statement** defines a variable
  - The **InputBox function** prompts the user for the value of this variable.
  - The **Do** and **Loop statements** go down the column of dates until the starting date is reached.
  - The **Offset property** selects the cell four columns to the right of the active cell (the Extra Payment column).

- Save the procedure.

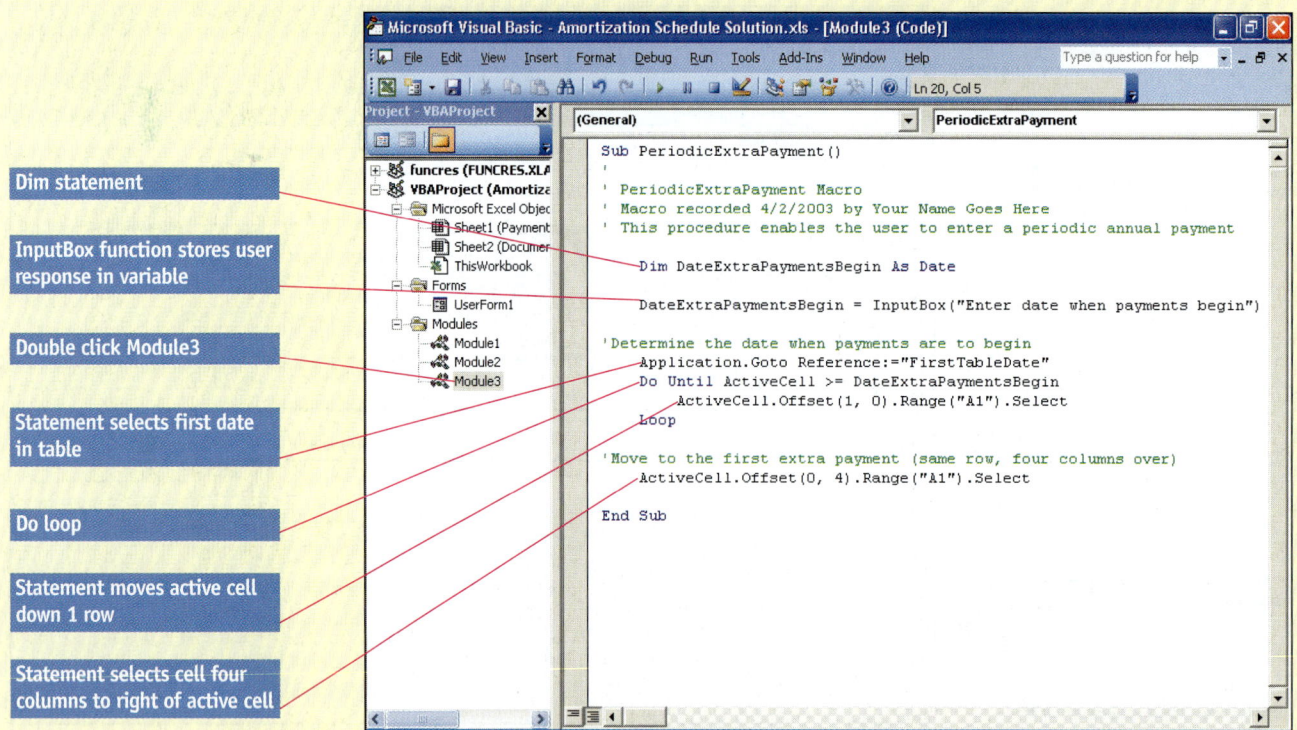

(b) View and Add Code (step 2)

FIGURE 9.10 Hands-on Exercise 4 (*continued*)

WHAT DOES RANGE("A1") REALLY MEAN?

The statement ActiveCell.Offset(1,0).Range("A1").Select has nothing to do with cell A1, so why is the entry (Range"A1") included? The Range property describes the number and shape of the selected cells—Range("A1") refers to a single cell. The default, however, is to select a single cell and so the Range property can be deleted, which results in the simpler statement ActiveCell.Offset(1,0).Select. If, however, you were selecting multiple cells, the Range property would be necessary.

Step 3: **Step through the Procedure**

- Point to a blank area at the right of the Windows taskbar, and then click the **right mouse button**. Click the command to **Show the Desktop**.
- Click the **VBA** and **Excel buttons** on the taskbar. Right click a blank area of the taskbar a second time, then click the command to **Tile Windows Vertically**.
- Your desktop should be similar to Figure 9.10c. It does not matter if the Excel window is on the left or right. Click in the Excel zoom box and lower the zoom percentage to **75%** to view more entries within the payments table.
- Click in the window containing the VBA editor. Close the Project Explorer. Click after the Sub statement within the PeriodicExtraPayment procedure.
- Press the **F8 key** or click the **Step Into button** on the Debug toolbar. The procedure header is highlighted. Press the **F8 key** a second time.
- The InputBox statement is highlighted, indicating that it will be executed next. Press the **F8 key** again to display the input box in the figure. Type any date that occurs two or three months after the first payment, then press **Enter.**
- Press the **F8 key** continually until you reach the date at which payments are to begin. At that point, the cell four columns to the right is selected.
- Press the **F8 key** one last time to move below the End Sub statement.

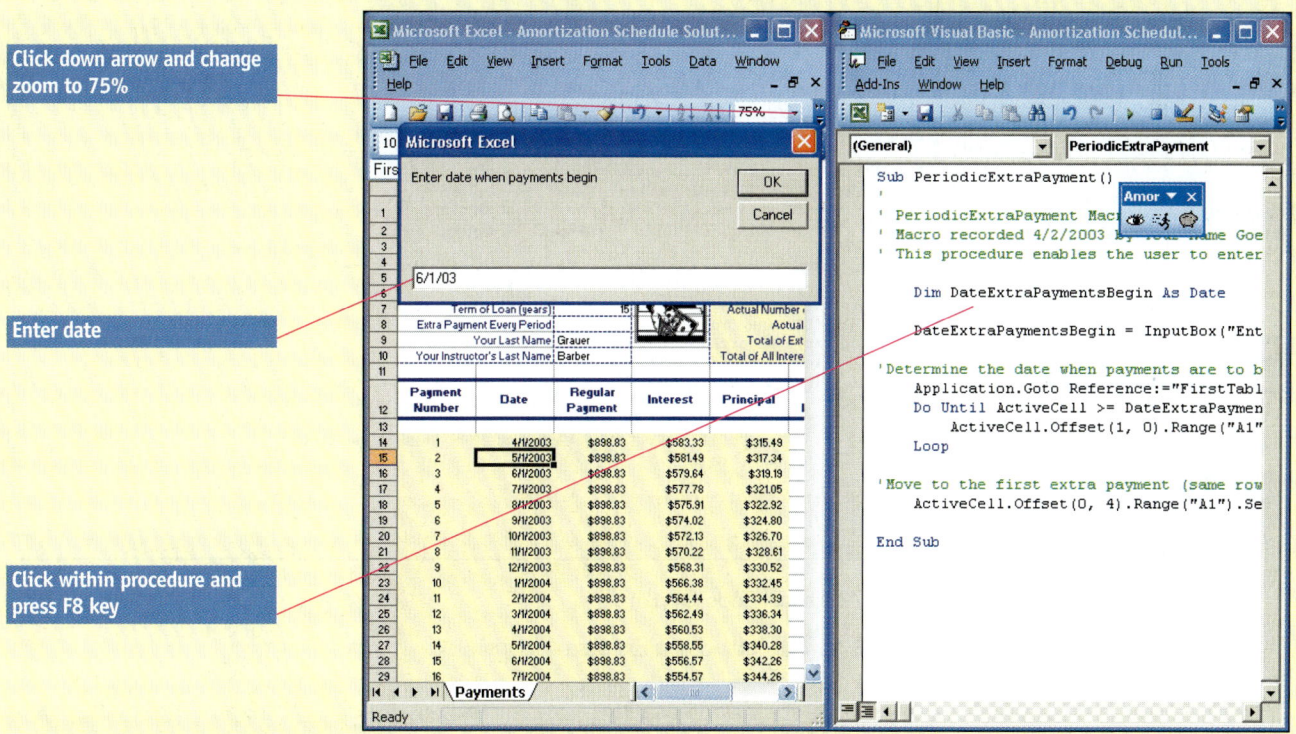

(c) Step through the Procedure (step 3)

FIGURE 9.10 Hands-on Exercise 4 (*continued*)

DIVIDE AND CONQUER

The logic to apply periodic payments is nontrivial and consists of three basic building blocks—obtain input from the user, determine the cell for the first extra payment, and apply periodic payments until the loan is paid off. The best way to develop the procedure is to code and test each block in sequence. Once you are sure of one step, move on to the next.

Step 4: **Add Additional Code**

- Maximize the VBA window. Add the additional statements to complete the procedure as shown in Figure 9.10d. Note the following:
  - The additional Dim statements define the amount of the extra payment and the switch to control the loop to apply the payments.
  - The additional InputBox function obtains the amount of the extra payment.
  - The additional loop applies the first extra payment, then continues to apply an annual payment until the loan is paid off.
  - The last statement selects a cell in the summary portion of the worksheet so that the user sees the relevant information about the loan in a single place.
- Add indentation, blank lines, and comments as you see fit to enhance the readability of the code. (These elements will make the procedure easier to follow and are not required by VBA.)
- Save the procedure.

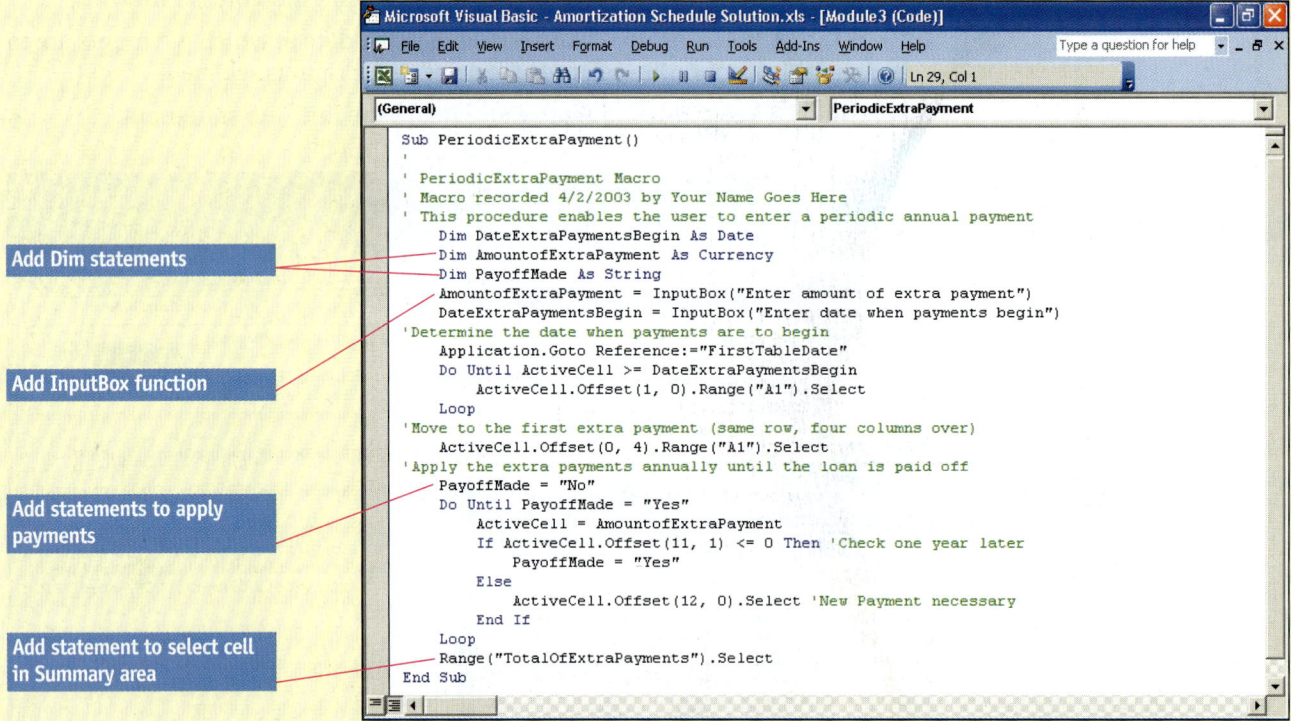

(d) Add Additional Code (step 4)

FIGURE 9.10 Hands-on Exercise 4 (*continued*)

SETTING A SWITCH

The use of a switch to control an action within a procedure is a common programming technique. The PayoffMade switch in this example is initially set to "no", prior to applying the first optional payment. The procedure then steps through the table to apply additional payments, testing after each optional payment to see if the loan is paid off, and if so, resetting the switch to "yes". At that point the loop is terminated and control passes to the next sequential statement.

Step 5: **Test the Procedure**

- Return to Excel. Maximize the Excel window and increase the magnification to **100%**. Check that your loan parameters match those in Figure 9.10e.

- Pull down the **Tools menu**, click **Macro**, click **Macros . . .**, then run the **PeriodicExtraPayment** procedure that you completed in the previous step. Enter **$1,500** and a date two months after the first payment as the amount of the extra payment and the date the payments are to begin.

- The macro executes, and if all goes well, you will see the summary information in our figure. The actual number of payments has been reduced to 145 (from 180). The total of the extra payments was $18,000.

- If you did not get these results, check that your loan parameters match ours and try again. If you still do not get these results, return to the previous step and check your code. If you cannot find an obvious error, tile the Excel and VBA windows as described in step 3 and step through the procedure.

- Pull down the **Tools menu**, click **Macro**, then click **Macros . . .** and run the **ClearExtraPayments** macro that we provided with the workbook. The extra payments disappear, and the loan requires the full 180 payments.

- Delete the term of the loan so that the loan parameters are incomplete. The individual payments disappear from the body of the worksheet. Rerun the **PeriodicExtraPayment** procedure.

- You are prompted for the amount of the extra payment and the starting date. This time the procedure is stuck in a loop because it cannot find the starting date. Press **Ctrl+Break** to stop the execution of the macro.

- Click the **Debug button** in the dialog box that appears. This takes you to the Visual Basic editor, where you can correct the code.

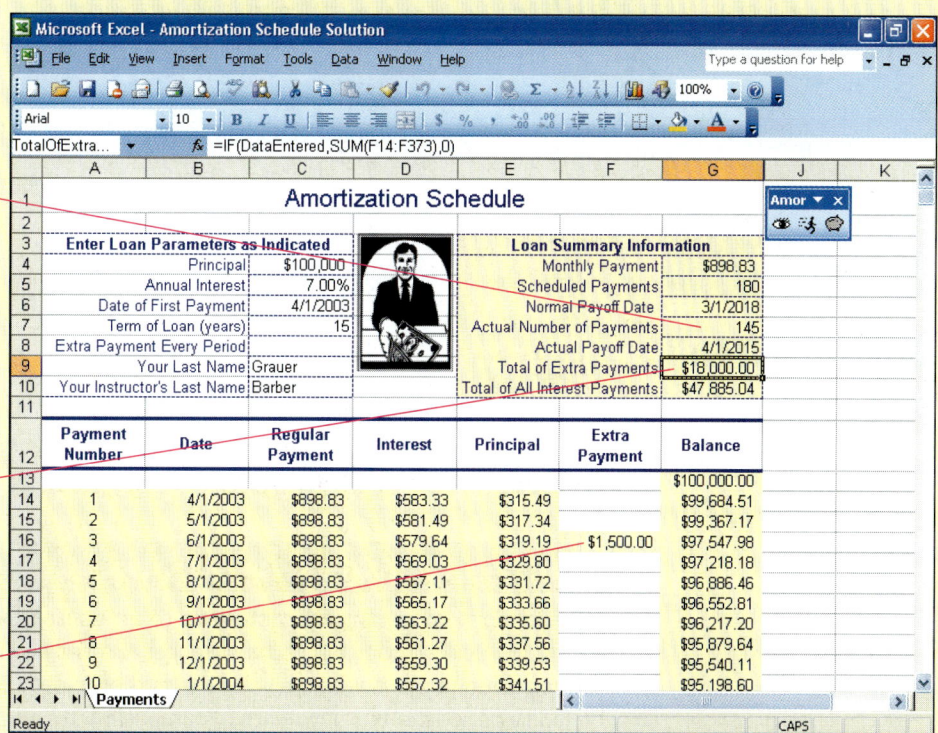

(e) Test the Procedure (step 5)

FIGURE 9.10 Hands-on Exercise 4 (*continued*)

Step 6: **Revise the Procedure**

- You are back in the Visual Basic editor within the PeriodicExtraPayment procedure. One line within the procedure is highlighted, indicating where the procedure stopped executing.

- Click the **Reset button** (the tiny square) on the Standard toolbar. The highlighting disappears. You can now add the additional VBA statements to complete the procedure.

- The procedure executes correctly as long as the loan parameters were entered. It does not work, however, if the information is missing. Hence you need to test for the parameters within an If statement.

- Modify the procedure as shown in Figure 9.10f to include the **If statement**, the associated **Else clause**, and the concluding **End If**.
  - The If statement toward the top of the procedure tests to see if the loan parameters are present in the worksheet.
  - The Else clause displays an error message if the loan parameters are missing.

- Save the revised procedure.

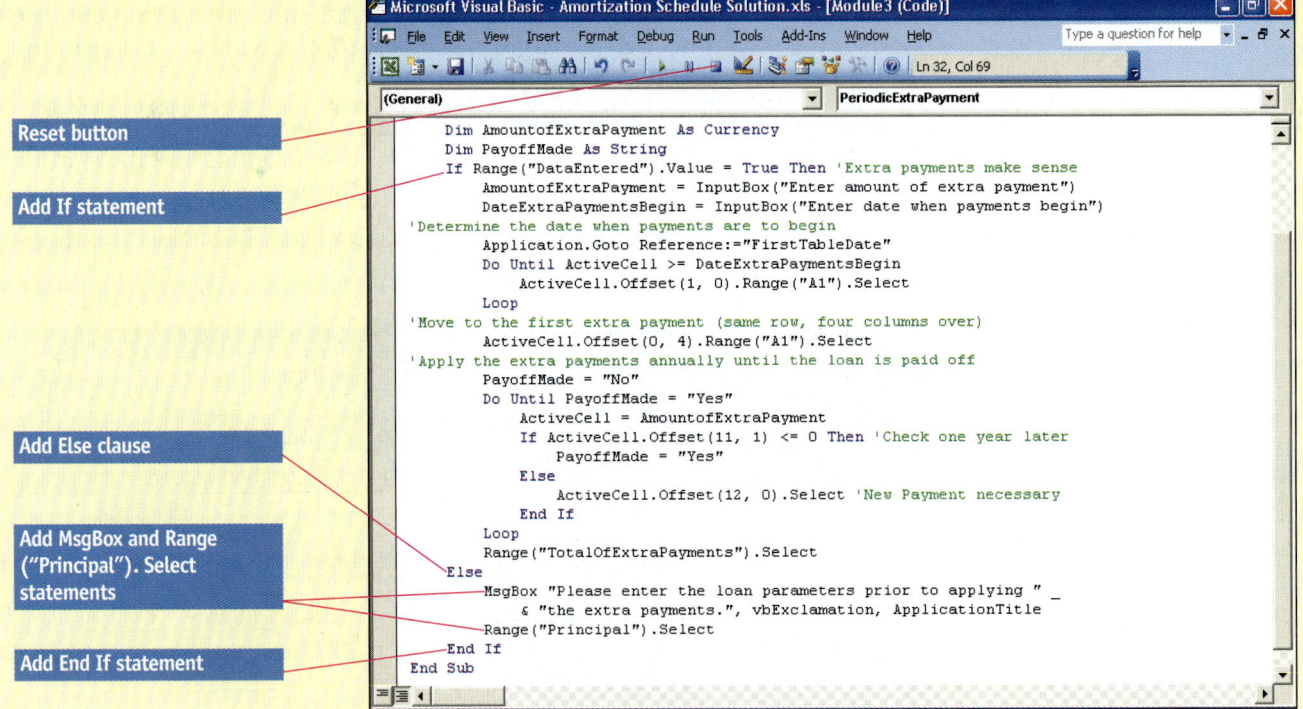

(f) Revise the Procedure (step 6)

FIGURE 9.10 Hands-on Exercise 4 (*continued*)

TEST UNDER ALL CONDITIONS

The most important characteristic of an application is that it works, and further that it works under all circumstances. It must be "bulletproof," and thus it should be tested under any and all conditions that might occur. The user should not try to apply periodic extra payments if loan parameters have not been entered, but what if that happens? The developer should have anticipated the possibility and built in the additional code to prevent the application from crashing.

Step 7: **Retest the Procedure**

- Click the **Excel button** on the Windows taskbar to return to Excel. Check that the loan information is still incomplete, then pull down the **Tools menu** and retest the **PeriodicExtraPayment procedure**.

- You should see the message box in Figure 9.10g that indicates the missing data. Click **OK** to close the dialog box.

- Pull down the **View menu**, click the **Toolbars command**, click **Customize**, and then modify the custom toolbar from the earlier exercise to include buttons for the additional procedures you developed. Use the **smiley face** and **sad face** for the **PeriodicExtraPayment** and **ClearExtraPayments procedures**, respectively.

- You must also attach the modified toolbar to your workbook. Pull down the **View menu**, click **Toolbars**, and click the **Customize command** to display the Customize dialog box. Click the **Toolbars tab**, then click the **Attach button** to display the Attach Toolbars dialog box.

- Select the Amortization Schedule toolbar in the right pane and click the **Delete button** to remove the old version. Select the **Amortization Schedule toolbar** in the left pane and click the **Copy button**. Click **OK**. Click **Close**.

- Save the workbook. The application is complete, but we provide additional practice through end-of-chapter exercises. Exit Excel.

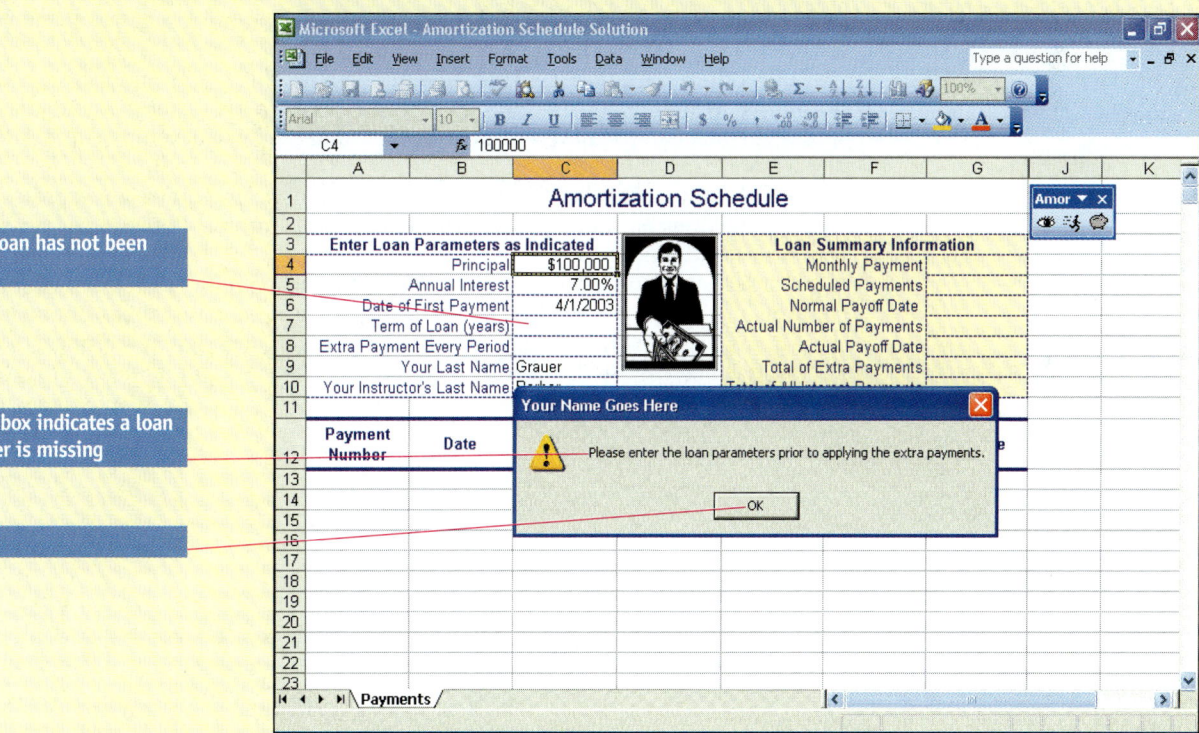

(g) Retest the Procedure (step 7)

FIGURE 9.10 Hands-on Exercise 4 (*continued*)

PRINT THE VBA CODE

It is good practice to obtain hard copy of the modules you have created for future study. Press Alt+F11 to return to the VBA editor. Select Module1. Pull down the File menu and click the Print command to display the Print dialog box. Select the option to print the current module, then click OK. Print any other modules in similar fashion.

SUMMARY

This chapter focused on the development of the Amortization Schedule workbook, a professional application that is suitable for distribution to individuals who need not be proficient in Excel. The workbook is visually appealing. It includes data validation to ensure sensible results and automation to facilitate ease of use. The workbook also enables the end user to do things that he or she could not do without benefit of VBA.

Excel contains various date functions to facilitate date arithmetic and/or to isolate the individual components of a date. The TODAY function returns the current date. The DATE function creates a date from three individual arguments (year, month, and day). The DAY, MONTH, and YEAR functions each have a single argument (a numeric date) and return the numeric day, month, and year, respectively.

VBA accomplishes its tasks by manipulating objects. Each object (such as a workbook, worksheet, a single cell, or chart) has a well-defined set of characteristics called properties, and each object can perform a set of actions called methods. The object model describes the hierarchical way the different objects are related to one another. Each application in Microsoft Office has its own object model. A collection is a group of similar objects within the object model.

An event is any action that is recognized by an application. An event procedure is a procedure that is activated in response to a specific event. To use VBA effectively, you decide which events are significant, and what is to happen when those events occur. Then you develop the appropriate event procedures. Event procedures are distinguished from general procedures that can be executed any time at the discretion of the user.

A custom toolbar can be created as a convenient way to run the procedures for any application. The toolbar must be attached to the workbook to distribute the toolbar with the workbook. The custom toolbar can be displayed and hidden automatically through the Open workbook and Before Close event procedures.

A user form is a convenient way to enter data within an application. A splash screen is a simple form that consists entirely of text. There are two essential tasks to display a splash screen. First, you have to create the form and then you develop the procedure(s) to display (and hide) the form.

Pseudocode or "neat notes to oneself" is the most common way of expressing logic. Pseudocode does not have any precise syntax and is intended only to convey the logic within a procedure.

A digital signature is an electronic, encryption-based stamp of authentication, which confirms the origin of a document, and further that the document has not been altered since it was last saved by the signer. You can create your own signature using a tool within Microsoft Office. Any certificate that you create yourself is unauthenticated, however, and generates a warning in the Security Warning box if the security level is set to High or Medium. You can also obtain an authenticated digital certificate from an internal security administrator and/or a variety of commercial sources.

KEY TERMS

Amortization 1424	Macro recorder 1436	Properties window 1449
AND function 1425	Method 1436	Property 1436
Before Close event procedure . . . 1447	MONTH function 1428	Pseudocode 1459
Collection 1436	MsgBox function 1437	Splash screen 1447
Custom toolbar 1447	MsgBox statement 1437	Switch 1459
Data validation 1424	Object 1436	TODAY function 1428
DATE function 1428	Object model 1436	User form 1449
DAY function 1428	OnTime method 1449	UserForm Activate event
Digital signature 1447	Open workbook event	procedure 1449
Event 1447	procedure 1447	WEEKDAY function 1453
Event procedure 1447	OR function 1425	YEAR function 1428
General procedure 1447	PPMT function 1436	Zero suppression 1431
IPMT function 1436	Print area 1435	

MULTIPLE CHOICE

1. Which of the following will display the date November 16, 2002?
   (a) =DATE(11,16,2002)
   (b) =DATE(2002, 11, 16)
   (c) =DATE(2002, 16, 11)
   (d) =11/16/2002

2. Given that cell A4 contains the date 1/21/2002, what date will be displayed as a result of the function =DATE(YEAR(A4)+1,MONTH(A4)+2,DAY(A4)+3)?
   (a) 2/23/2005
   (b) 1/24/2005
   (c) 3/24/2003
   (d) 2/22/2003

3. What values will be returned by the logical functions =AND(10>5, 6<3) and =OR (10>5, 6<3)?
   (a) Both functions will return True
   (b) Both functions will return False
   (c) True and False, respectively
   (d) False and True, respectively

4. Which of the following is true about the PPMT function?
   (a) It determines the periodic payment for a loan
   (b) It determines the amount of a periodic payment that goes toward principal
   (c) It will adjust automatically if an additional payment toward principal was made during the preceding period
   (d) All of the above

5. What is a program switch?
   (a) A setting to start or stop the macro recorder
   (b) A variable that assumes one of two values, typically "yes" or "no"
   (c) An indication of whether the macro recorder is relative or absolute
   (d) All of the above

6. A single workbook, worksheet, chart, or range is called a(n):
   (a) Object
   (b) Property
   (c) Method
   (d) Collection

7. Which of the following is true, given the VBA statements Selection.Copy and Selection.Value=0?
   (a) Selection is a VBA object
   (b) Copy is a method of the Selection object
   (c) Value is a property of the Selection object
   (d) All of the above

8. Given the statement If MsgBox("Are you George?", vbyesno) = vbNo Then . .
   (a) MsgBox is used as a function rather than a statement
   (b) The question mark icon will be displayed within the message box
   (c) The Then portion of the If statement will address anyone named George
   (d) All of the above

9. Which of the following is typically *not* done in conjunction with adding a button to a custom toolbar?
   (a) An image is selected for the button
   (b) A description is written for the button
   (c) A macro is assigned to the button
   (d) A sound is assigned to the button

10. Which of the following is true regarding a VBA procedure that attempts to modify one or more cells in a protected worksheet?
    (a) The procedure *must* include an Unprotect worksheet statement at the beginning of the procedure
    (b) The procedure *must* include an Unprotect worksheet statement at the beginning and a Protect worksheet statement at the end
    (c) The procedure need not include Protect or Unprotect statements provided the Open workbook event procedure enables changes to the user interface
    (d) The procedure need not include Protect or Unprotect statements provided the Close workbook event procedure enables changes to the user interface

... continued

multiple choice

11. Which of the following is *not* necessary to create a splash screen?
    (a) Create a user form as the basis of the splash screen, then modify the Open workbook event procedure to show the user form
    (b) Create the Activate Form event procedure to set the timer
    (c) Create an Open Form event procedure
    (d) Create a public procedure to unload the form

12. Which of the following is least appropriate in the Open workbook event procedure?
    (a) A statement to display a custom toolbar
    (b) A message to the user to back up the system at the end of the session
    (c) A statement to display a splash screen
    (d) A statement to protect the user interface only

13. Which of the following will trigger the Before Close event procedure?
    (a) Pulling down the File menu and clicking the Close command
    (b) Pulling down the File menu and clicking the Exit command
    (c) Clicking either Close button at the upper right of the Excel window
    (d) All of the above

14. Which of the following best describes how to protect a worksheet but still enable the user to change the value of selected cells within the worksheet?
    (a) Unprotect the cells that are to change, then protect the entire sheet
    (b) Unlock the cells that are to change, then protect the entire worksheet
    (c) Protect the entire worksheet, then unlock the cells that are to change
    (d) Protect the entire worksheet, then unprotect the cells that are to change

15. Which of the following is a true statement about pseudocode?
    (a) It is defined as neat notes to oneself
    (b) It is required by the VBA editor for all procedures that include loops and decision making
    (c) It has a precise set of syntactical rules
    (d) It is displayed automatically within the VBA editor as the associated procedure is executing

16. A group of similar objects within the object model is called a(n):
    (a) Module
    (b) Procedure
    (c) Attribute
    (d) Collection

17. An action performed by an object is called a:
    (a) Command
    (b) Property
    (c) Method
    (d) Procedure

18. Worksheets("Forecast").Range("NextYear") refers to:
    (a) The range "NextYear" in the current worksheet
    (b) The range "NextYear" in the current worksheet in the current workbook
    (c) The range "NextYear" in the worksheet named "Forecast" in the current workbook
    (d) The range "NextYear" in the workbook named "Forecast"

ANSWERS

1. b	7. d	13. d
2. c	8. a	14. b
3. d	9. d	15. a
4. b	10. c	16. d
5. b	11. c	17. c
6. a	12. b	18. c

PRACTICE WITH EXCEL AND VBA

1. **Practice with Dates:** Open the partially completed version of the workbook in Figure 9.1 in *Chapter 9 Practice 1* in the Exploring Excel folder. (Click the button to Enable Macros.) The workbook will open, and you will see the message box that is displayed in the figure indicating that the dates in the workbook are reset automatically. Click OK after you have read the message.

    a. The invoice dates in your worksheet will differ from those in our figure, but the values in the Days Elapsed column should be identical to ours after you complete the worksheet. Enter the appropriate formula in cell B4 and change the formatting as necessary. Copy the formula in cell B4 to the remaining rows in the column.

    b. Enter the appropriate formulas for the first invoice to compute current amount due, as well as the amounts that are 30, 60, and 90 days late. Two of these formulas are simple If statements (the current amount due, and the amount over 90 days). The other two formulas require nested If statements (an If function within an If function). We suggest you do the 60-day formula first, since that is the easier one. Then once you have that formula, you will be able to extend it to the 30-day formula.

    c. Copy the formulas for the first invoice to the remaining rows in the column. Add the formulas to compute the totals in each category, then compare your values to ours. The dollar amounts in each column should match Figure 9.11 even though the individual invoice dates are different.

    d. Open the Visual Basic editor and look at the Open workbook event procedure. What is the significance of the "UpdateDates" statement that is found in this event procedure?

    e. Add your name and birth date in the indicated cells, then add the formula to compute your age as shown in the worksheet. Format the worksheet appropriately, then print it two ways, once to show the displayed values, and once to show the cell formulas.

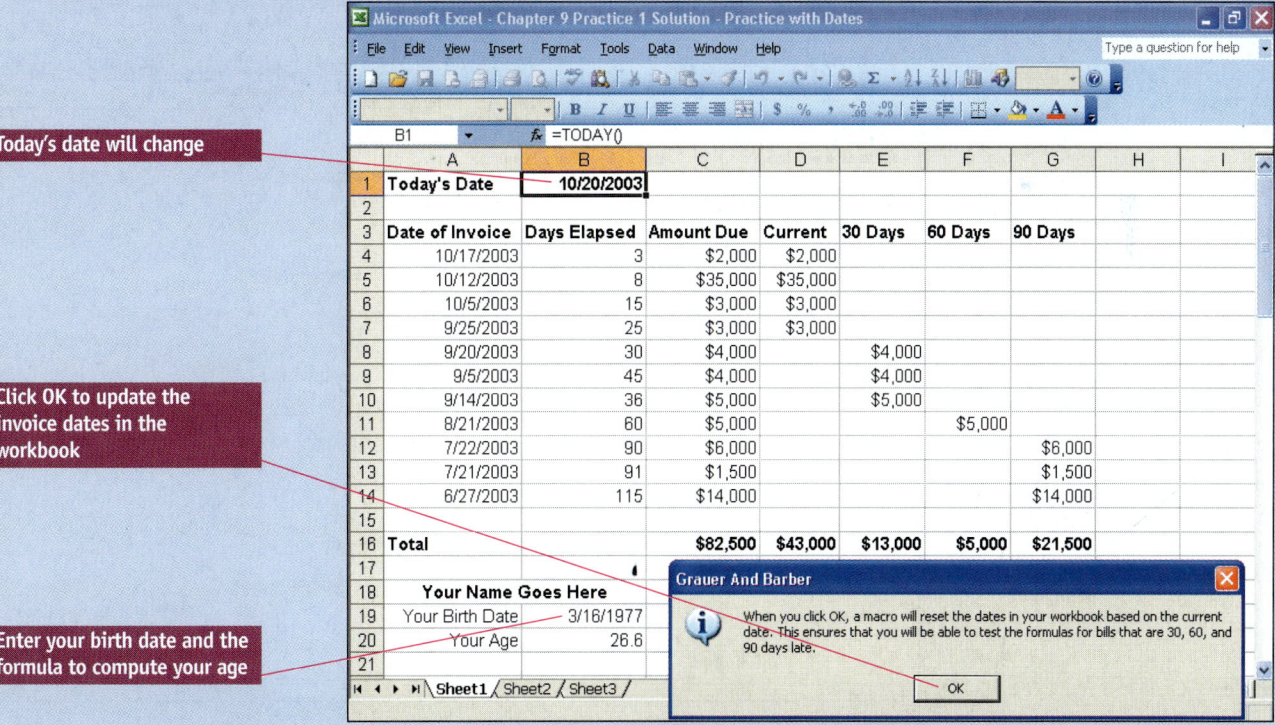

FIGURE 9.11   Practice with Dates (exercise 1)

practice exercises

2. **Change the Magnification:** The screen in Figure 9.12 displays a pair of procedures that increase and decrease the magnification percentage within the Excel window. These procedures do not do anything that the user could not accomplish manually. They are, however, more convenient ways to change the magnification incrementally and are truly useful in that regard. They also serve to illustrate how simple Excel macros are enhanced through the inclusion of VBA statements.

   a. Open the Amortization Schedule Solution workbook and start the macro recorder. Click in the Zoom box and change the magnification to 110. Stop the recorder. Press Alt+F11 to open the Visual Basic Editor.
   b. Locate the module that contains the macro you just created, which contains the single statement ActiveWindow.Zoom =110. That changes the zoom property of the active window to 110. The single statement, plus a little imagination, is all you need to create the procedures in Figure 9.12.
   c. Add a Dim statement to define the variable intMagnification as an integer. The second statement sets this variable 10% higher than the current magnification. It does not change the magnification, however, because you have to check that you do not exceed the maximum magnification (400%) that is permitted—hence the If statement prior to changing the actual magnification, which is controlled by the Zoom property of the ActiveWindow object.
   d. Use the completed procedure to increase the magnification as the basis for the procedure to decrease the magnification. (You can enter the entire procedure manually, or you can copy the existing procedure, then make the necessary modifications.)
   e. Add two additional buttons (an up and a down arrow, respectively) to the custom toolbar to execute these procedures. Be sure to attach the modified toolbar to the completed workbook. Save the workbook.

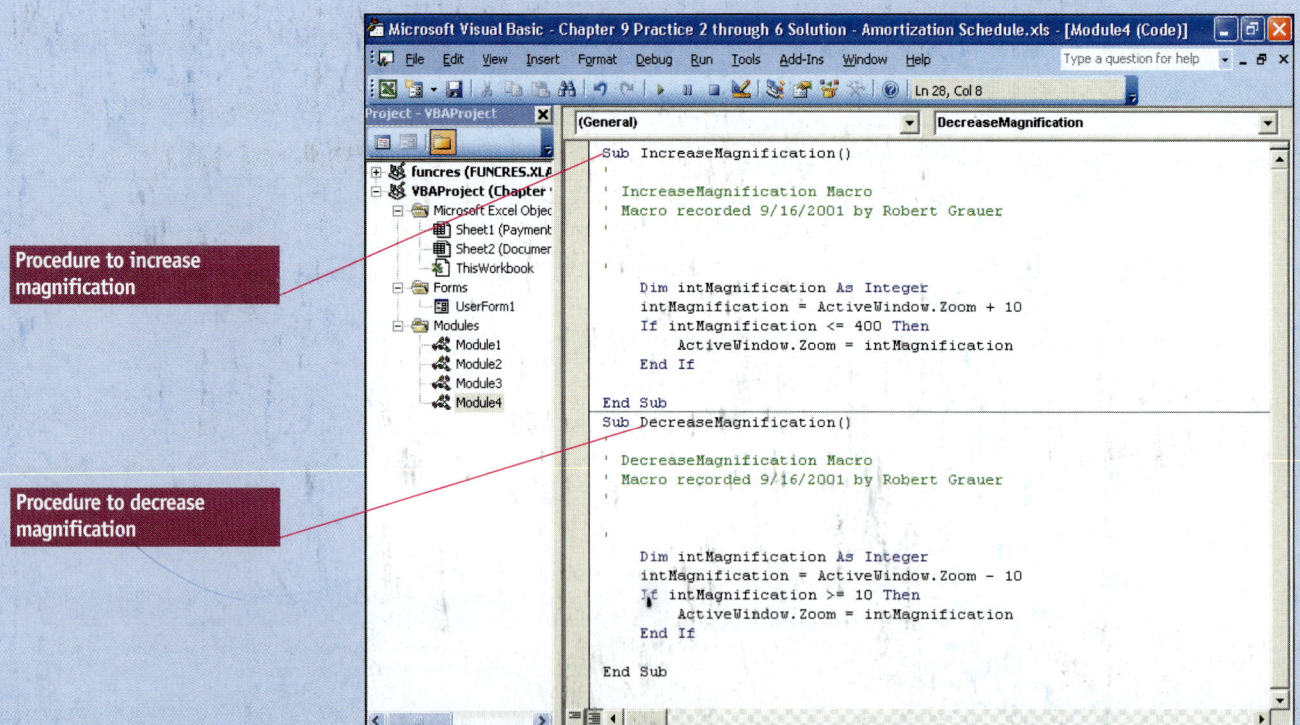

FIGURE 9.12 Change the Magnification (exercise 2)

practice exercises

3. **Toggle the Documentation Worksheet:** Figure 9.13 displays the Documentation worksheet that is included in the Amortization Schedule Solution workbook. This worksheet explains how the OFFSET function is used in conjunction with a memory variable to set a variable print area to print only as many rows as there are payments. This is not an easy concept, and so we include the complete explanation within the workbook so that you can apply this technique to other workbooks that you might create.

   The purpose of this exercise, however, is to create a VBA procedure that will toggle the Documentation worksheet on and off. Thus, if the worksheet is hidden, the procedure will display it; if the worksheet is visible, the procedure will hide it. The logic is simple, but you need to obtain the VBA statement to display or hide the worksheet. Proceed as follows:

   a. Open the Amortization Schedule Solution workbook that you have been working on throughout the chapter. Start the macro recorder. Pull down the Format menu, click Sheet, click the Unhide command, select the worksheet, then click OK. (The Documentation worksheet is hidden initially, and so the Unhide command is active. If the worksheet is already visible, however, click the Hide command instead of Unhide.) Stop the recorder.

   b. Start the Visual Basic editor to view the code in the macro you just created. You will see a single VBA statement that sets the Visible property for the Documentation worksheet to True. Use this statement as the basis of the procedure that will toggle the worksheet on or off. You have to add an If/Else statement that hides a visible worksheet and displays a hidden worksheet.

   c. Assign a button (use the book image) to add the procedure to the custom toolbar. Test the button to be sure that it works properly.

   d. Add your name to cell A2 in the documentation worksheet, then print the documentation worksheet for your instructor.

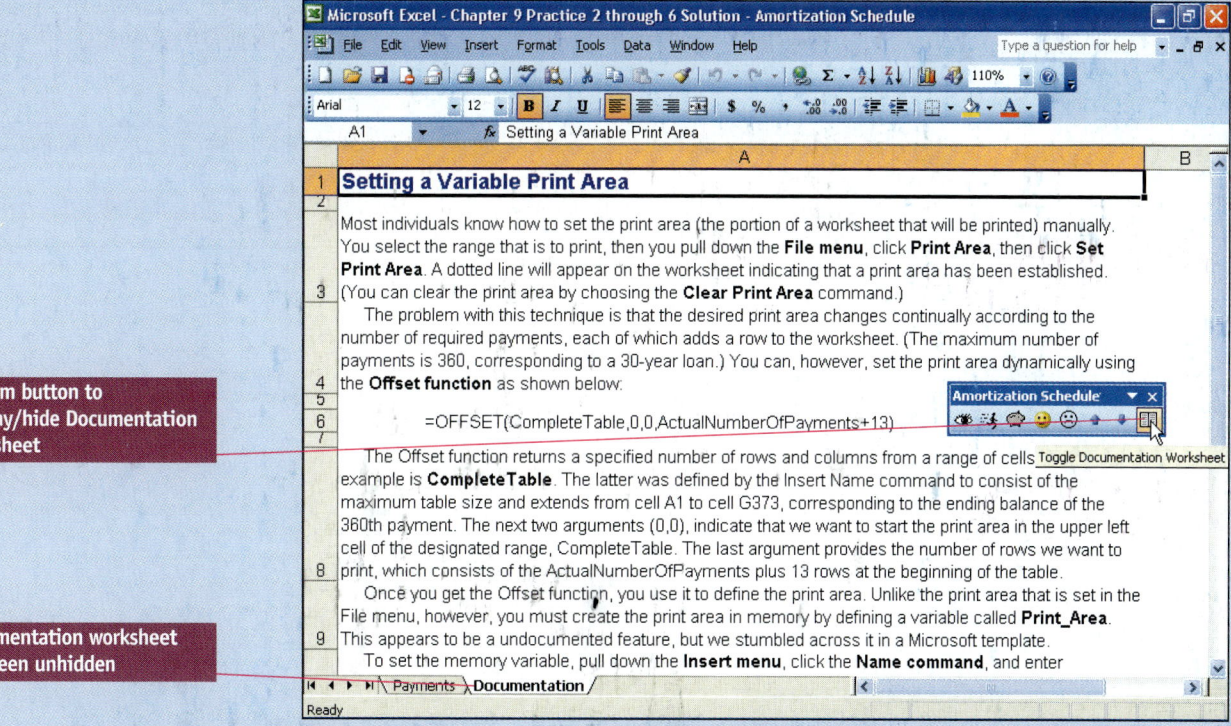

FIGURE 9.13 Toggle the Documentation Worksheet (exercise 3)

practice exercises

4. **Print the Summary Area:** Figure 9.14 displays two VBA procedures, one to print the summary area of the worksheet and a second to reset the print area. The PrintSummaryOnly procedure has not yet been created and is the subject of this exercise. The RestorePrintArea procedure was included in the original workbook; it incorporates the information that was contained in the Documentation worksheet from the previous exercise.

   a. Open the Amortization Schedule Solution workbook. Enter the parameters for any loan, but specify the term as two years. Click the Print Preview button and notice that the printout fits on one page. Change the term of the loan to 10 years, click Print Preview a second time, and the printout requires 3 pages.

   b. Pull down the File menu, click Print Area, then click the Clear Print Area command. Click the Print Preview button. The printout requires 7 pages even though many of the pages are blank. This is because the previous step had you clear the print area which had been set to print only as many rows as contained nonzero values. Close the Print Preview window, and press Ctrl+r, which is the keyboard shortcut for the RestorePrintArea procedure in the workbook. The printout once again takes three pages.

   c. You will set the print area to print just the summary portion of the worksheet. Start the macro recorder. Name the macro PrintSummaryOnly. Click the down arrow in the Name box, select the SummaryArea range name, then pull down the File menu, click Print Area, then click the command to Set the print area. Click the Print button. Stop the macro recorder.

   d. Open the VBA editor to examine the statements you just created. They are similar to, but different from, the code in Figure 9.14. Look closely at the recorded statements, however, and see how they can be simplified to create the code in Figure 9.14. The last statement runs the RestorePrintArea procedure, so that the print area will be automatically reset.

   e. Add a button (use the calculator button) to the custom toolbar to run the Print Summary Area procedure. Add a second button (the pencil) to restore the print area. Attach the toolbar to the workbook.

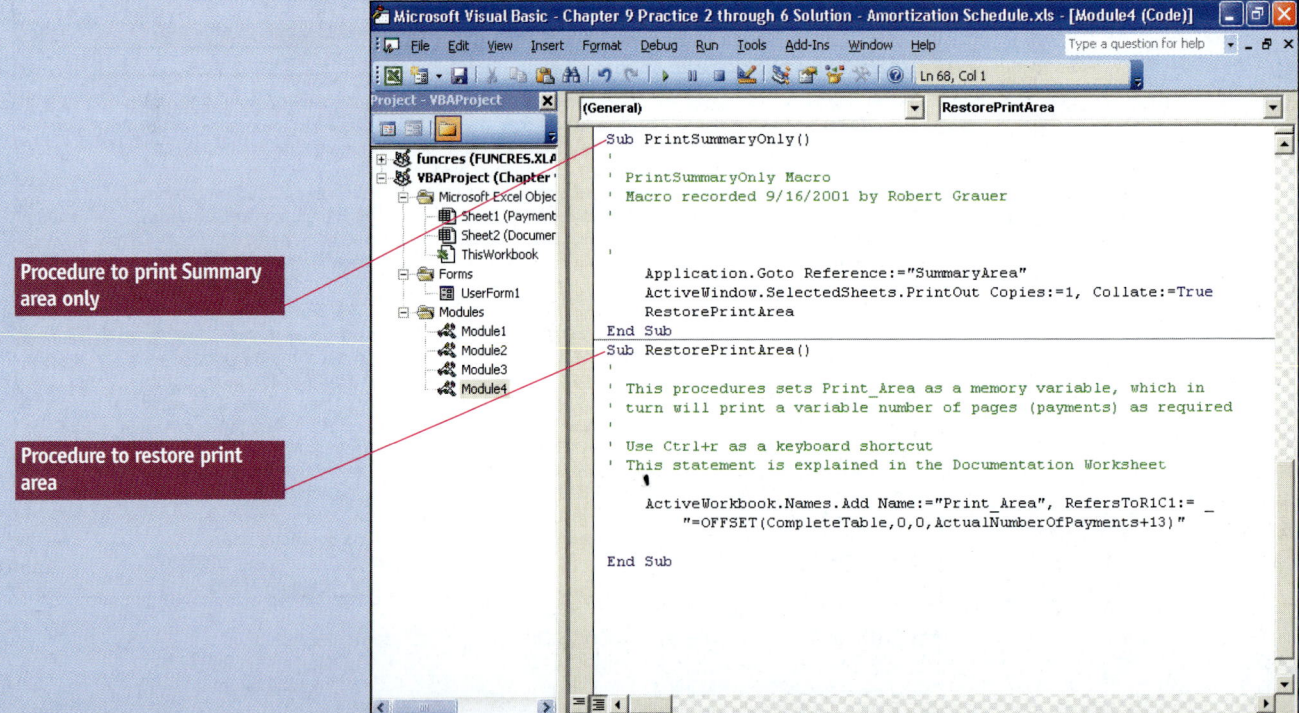

FIGURE 9.14   Print the Summary Area (exercise 4)

practice exercises

5. **Nested Ifs and Other Logic:** A nested If statement (or "an If within an If") is a common logic structure in every programming language. It tests an initial condition, then it tests a second condition if the first condition is true. Open the Amortization Schedule Solution workbook and expand the Before Close event procedure as shown in Figure 9.15. The original procedure has been modified to accomplish several additional tasks.

   a. The procedure checks to see whether your name or your instructor's last name has been omitted from the worksheet, and if so, it gives the user the option to cancel the Close command. First, the procedure sets the active cell to the range name "YourLastName". It then checks that cell and the cell one row below for null values. If either cell is blank, the second If statement is executed.

   b. The MsgBox function within the nested If displays a message to the user and displays Yes and No buttons within the resulting message box. The user's response is compared to the VBA intrinsic constant, vbNo. If the user clicked the No button, then the comparison is true, the close operation is canceled, and the switch to close the workbook is set to No.

   c. The second nested If statement tests to see if the workbook is to be closed, and if so, it hides the custom toolbar, and also displays a message to the user. The custom toolbar is then deleted from the collection of custom toolbars (but not from this workbook). This ensures that the toolbar will work correctly if the workbook is subsequently opened in a different folder.

   d. A second If statement tests for the day of the week (Friday in this example) and displays an appropriate message.

   e. There is a lot of logic here, and hence you might want to close the workbook two or three times (with different responses) to better appreciate the underlying logic. Print this procedure for your professor.

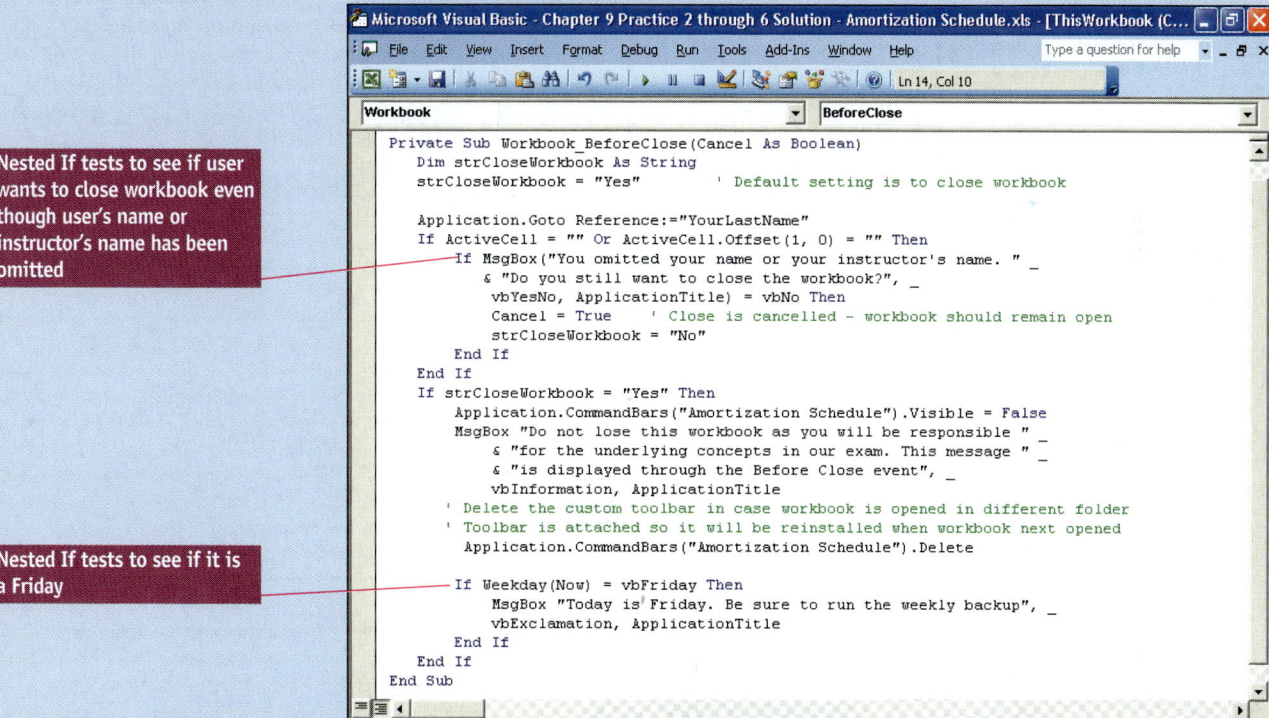

FIGURE 9.15 Nested Ifs and Other Logic (exercise 5)

practice exercises

6. **Custom Menus and Toolbars:** Figure 9.16 displays the completed Amortization Schedule Solution workbook immediately prior to closing the workbook. The custom toolbar (and corresponding menu) contains a total of 10 buttons that were created during the various hands-on exercises and end-of-chapter problems. Compare your toolbar to ours to be sure that you have completed the entire application.

   a. The eye and runner correspond to the procedures to display and hide the validation columns, respectively, and were developed in the second hands-on exercise.
   b. The piggy bank icon runs the procedure to enable individual optional payments of principal and was created in the second hands-on exercise.
   c. The smiley and sad faces contain the procedures to apply an optional payment and clear the optional payments column, respectively. The procedures were developed in the fourth hands-on exercise.
   d. The up and down arrows increase and decrease the magnification within the Excel window. These procedures were developed in problem 2 at the end of the chapter.
   e. The book toggles the documentation worksheet on or off and was developed in problem 3 at the end of the chapter.
   f. The calculator and pencil print the summary area and restore the print area, respectively. These procedures were created in problem 4 at the end of the chapter.
   g. You can also create a custom menu with the same commands. Pull down the View menu, click Tools, click Customize to display the Customize dialog box, then click the Commands tab and scroll until you can select New Menu. Click and drag the New Menu command to the right of the menu bar, then release the mouse to create a menu called "New Menu". Select the new menu on the menu bar, click the Modify Selection button in the Customize dialog box, then change the name of the menu to Amortization.
   h. You are now ready to add commands to the menu. Select the Macros category in the Category area, then drag a Custom button to the Amortization menu. Pull down the menu, select the Custom Button command and assign a macro. Repeat this process to add additional commands.
   i. Complete the Amortization menu. Press the Print Screen key to capture this screen, start Word, then paste the screen into a Word document to submit to your instructor.

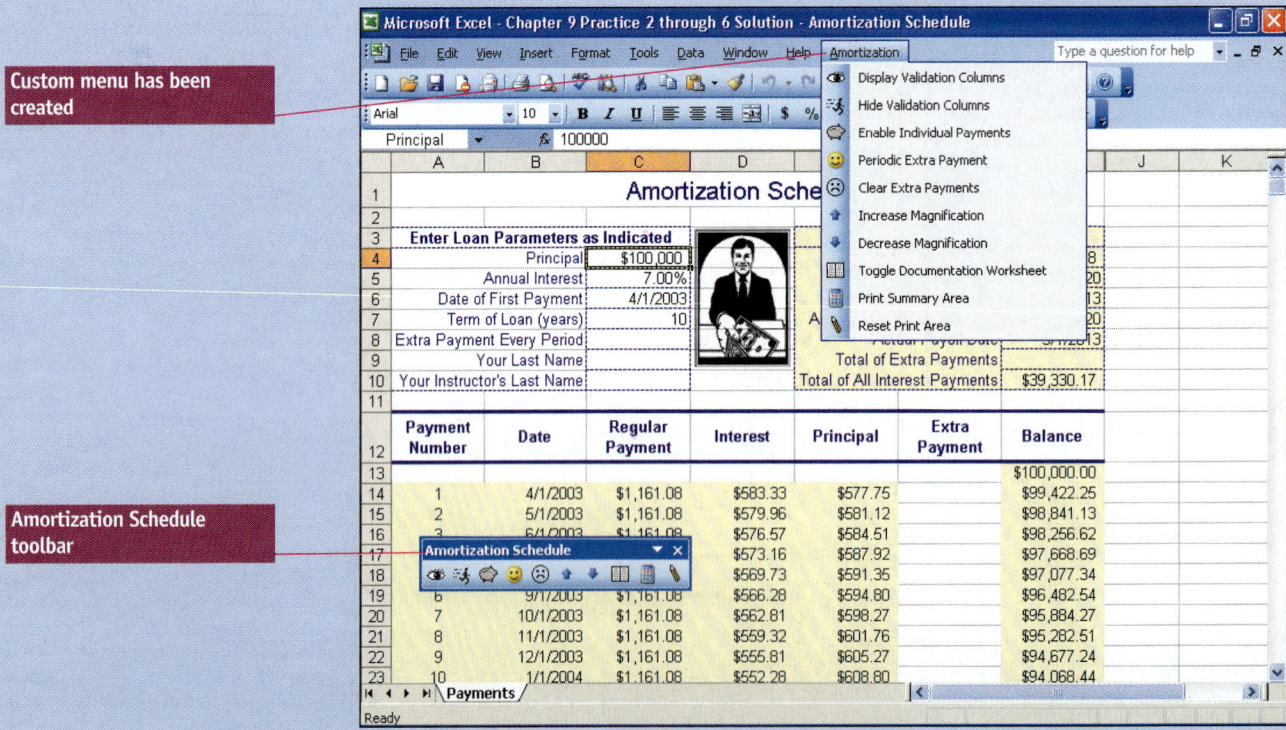

FIGURE 9.16 Custom Menus and Toolbars (exercise 6)

practice exercises

7. **The Get Out of Debt Worksheet:** The Get Out of Debt workbook in Figure 9.17 is similar to the Amortization Schedule Solution application that was developed in the chapter. The new workbook is designed to let you practice all of the skills in the chapter within the context of a different application. It is also intended as a gentle reminder to think twice about using your credit card, because once you acquire this type of debt, it is very difficult to get out from under.

   a. Open the partially completed version of this workbook in *Chapter 9 Practice 7* and complete the basic worksheet. Unprotect the worksheet (a password is not required) so that you can make the necessary modifications.

   b. Implement a validation requirement in cell C7, the cell that contains the projected monthly payment, to ensure that the payment is greater than the interest due in the first month. Use the Insert Name command to assign the range name FirstMonthInterest to cell D13, then use this name as needed throughout the worksheet.

   c. Enter the appropriate If functions in cells E8 and G8 to display the indicated error message and remaining balance (if, in fact, there is a remaining balance after 30 years). These functions check the value in the cell G372, which has been assigned the range name, BalanceAfter30Years. Display these values in red, bold, and italics. Test the functions by entering appropriate values in the spreadsheet; for example, if you make the minimum monthly payment (the amount the credit card company requires), you will still owe $4,800 after 30 years, after paying out more than $25,000 in interest. Press the Print Screen key to capture this screen, start Word, then paste the screen into a Word document to submit to your instructor.

   d. Click the Retry button and drop your monthly payment by $1.00. Not only are you still in debt, but the debt has almost quadrupled to more than $18,000. This is *not* a spreadsheet error, but rather an indication of the power of compound interest. It is wonderful when it works for you, as in a retirement account, but a disaster when it works against you with debt.

   e. Change the monthly payment to $100. You are finally out of debt, but it took more than seven years. Add your name and your instructor's name in the appropriate cells, then print this worksheet for your instructor.

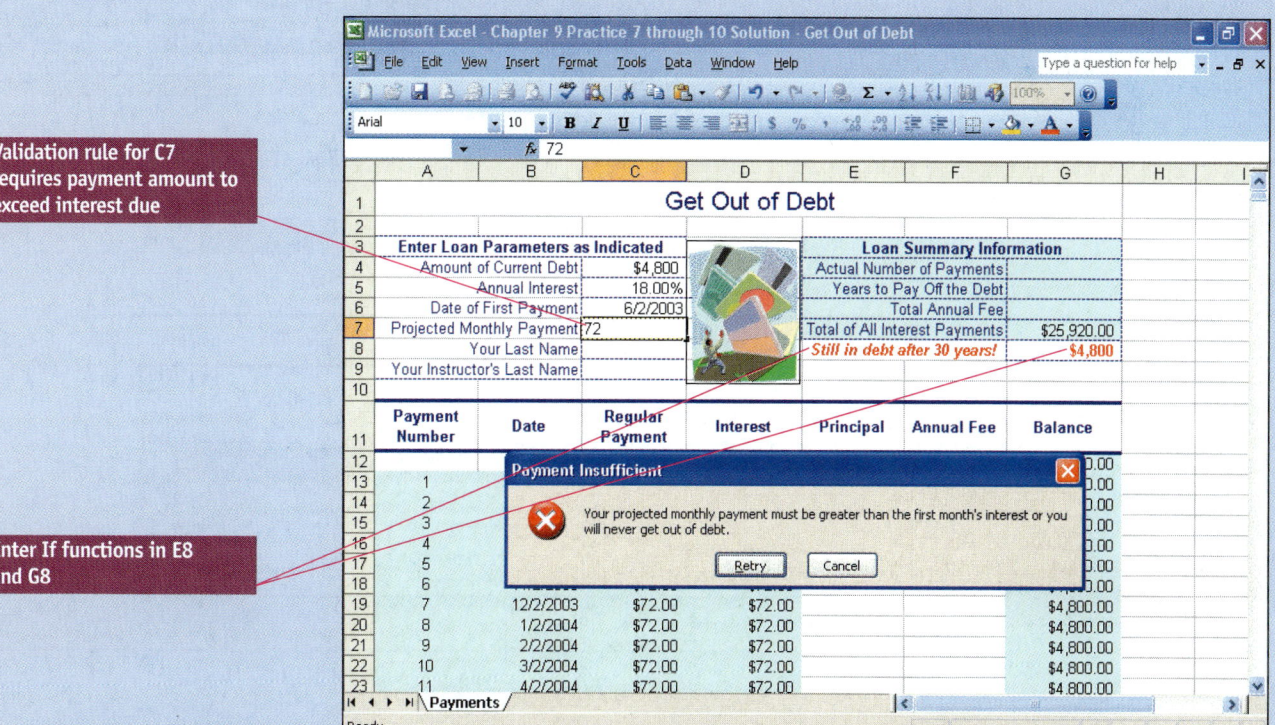

FIGURE 9.17   The Get Out of Debt Worksheet (exercise 7)

practice exercises

8. **Expand the Application:** Create a custom toolbar (and/or a custom menu) to execute the procedures that are already in the workbook to print the summary area and to reset the print area. Use the same icons (the calculator and the pencil) that were used in the Amortization Schedule Solution workbook. Include additional procedures as described below:

   a. Create a general procedure that imposes an annual fee once a year within the body of the worksheet. The procedure should prompt the user for the amount of the fee and the first date that it takes effect. The logic parallels that of the periodic extra payments module in the other workbook. Add a button for this procedure to the custom toolbar using the sad face image.

   b. Use the procedure you just created to enter an annual fee of $50 that takes effect the first month. Compare the results of this calculation with those of the previous exercise; that is, an annual fee of $50 extends the time required to pay off your loan by another seven months. Click the toolbar button to print the summary area for these parameters.

   c. Create a second general procedure to clear the annual fee. Add this procedure to the custom toolbar using the smiley face button.

   d. Create an Open workbook event procedure to display the custom toolbar and to enable VBA procedures to modify a protected worksheet. This logic parallels that in the Amortization workbook. You do not need a splash screen at this time.

   e. Create a Before Close event procedure to hide the custom toolbar and display a meaningful message (choose your own text) as shown in Figure 9.18. The procedure should also check for the presence of your name and your instructor's name prior to closing. You can copy the code from the Amortization Schedule Solution workbook as appropriate.

   f. Add your name and your instructor's name to the worksheet in the indicated cells. Print the summary portion of this worksheet for your instructor.

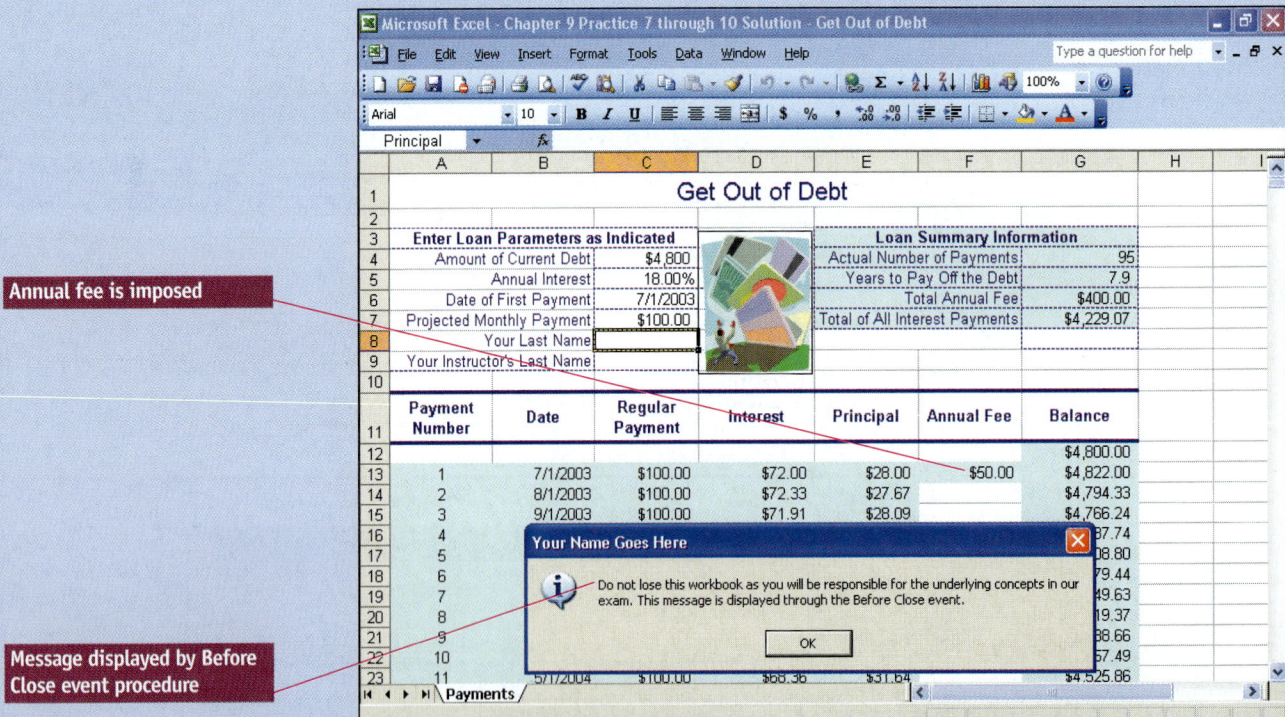

FIGURE 9.18   Expand the Application (exercise 8)

practice exercises

9. **The Get Out of Debt Procedure:** The procedure in Figure 9.19 uses the PMT function to calculate the required monthly payment to pay off the debt within a specified amount of time. The procedure uses existing values within the worksheet for the principal and annual interest rate. It displays an Input Box that prompts the user for the desired number of monthly payments, and then places the result of the calculation (vbPayment) into cell C7 (that has been associated with the range name ProjectedMonthlyPayment).

   a. Open the Get Out of Debt workbook and create the procedure in Figure 9.19. Our procedure includes the statement ClearAnnualFee, which runs the procedure we created in the previous exercise to erase any annual fee that may have been entered into the worksheet. Explain why this is necessary for the Get Out of Debt procedure to work correctly.

   b. Add the completed procedure to the custom toolbar using the image of a heart for the button image.

   c. Test the procedure using the existing loan parameters of $4,800 at 18% interest. Specify that you want to pay off the loan in 36 months. If you do the work correctly, the projected monthly payment should be $173.53. Be sure that your name and your instructor's name have both been entered into the worksheet, then print the payment schedule for your instructor.

   d. Look closely at your worksheet. The value in cell G4 (the cell that contains the actual number of payments) is also 36, which corresponds to the number of months you specified. This is significant because the computation associated with cell G4 is independent of the Get Out of Debt procedure, and thus serves to validate the calculations in the worksheet.

   e. What is the value in cell G48 of the worksheet? How does this serve to further validate the worksheet?

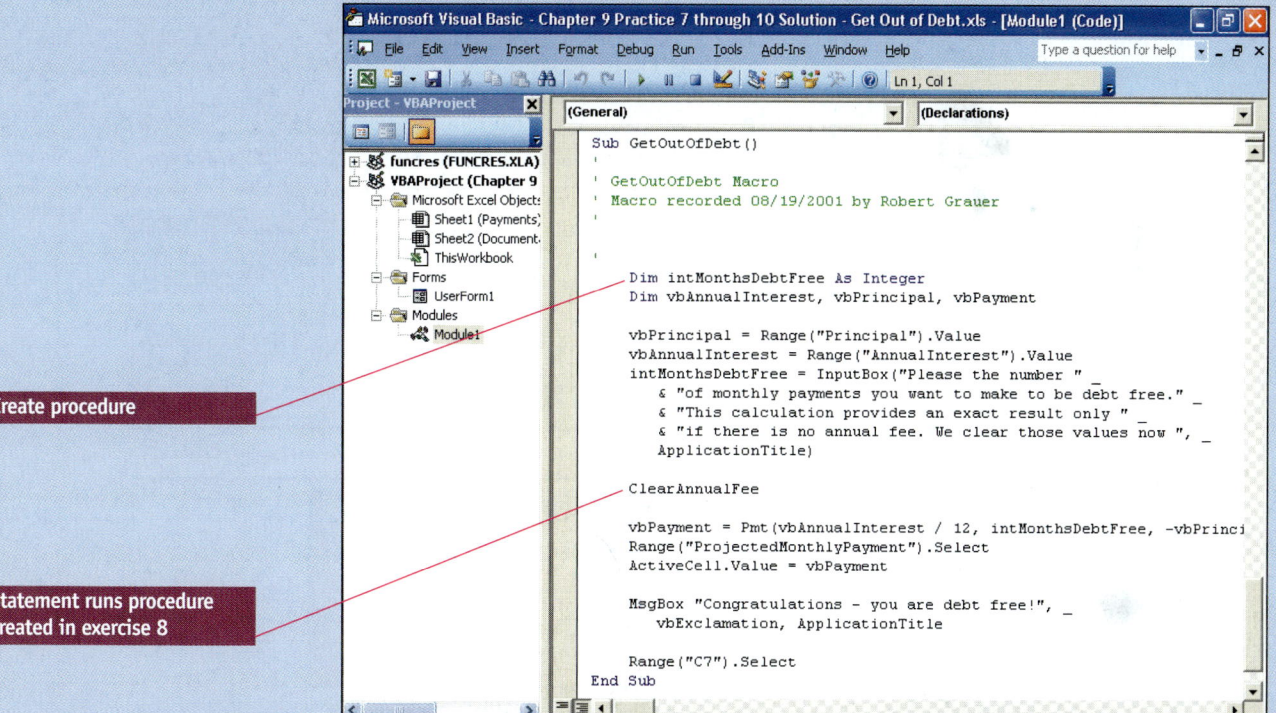

FIGURE 9.19 The Get Out of Debt Procedure (exercise 9)

practice exercises

10. **The Completed Application:** Complete the Get Out of Debt application by adding all of the functionality implied by Figure 9.20. This step is actually quite easy in that you can copy code from the Amortization Schedule Solution workbook as necessary.

   a. Add the procedures and corresponding buttons to toggle the documentation worksheet on and off, and to increase or decrease the magnification in the Excel window.

   b. Add a splash screen that is displayed for 5 seconds when the workbook is opened initially. Press the PrintScreen key to capture the splash screen when it appears, then paste the screen into a Word document. Print the Word document for your instructor to show that you created the splash screen successfully.

   c. Print the procedures within the workbook for your instructor. You can print the VBA procedures from within the VBA editor, but the procedures are printed without any formatting. You get a better result by printing from within Microsoft Word. Open the VBA editor, select the procedures you want to print, then click the Copy button (or use the Ctrl+C keyboard shortcut) to copy these procedures to the Windows clipboard.

   d. Start Microsoft Word and open a new document. Click the Paste button (or use the Ctrl+V keyboard shortcut) to paste the contents of the clipboard (the VBA procedures) into the Word document.

   e. Return to the VBA editor to copy the contents of the other modules to the Word document in similar fashion.

   f. Format the procedures in the Word document as you see fit. We suggest you use a monospaced font such as Courier New so that the indentation and alignment are easier to see. We also suggest that you boldface the Sub and End Sub statements of each procedure, and that you insert a horizontal border to separate the procedures from one another.

   g. Add a title page, then submit the completed assignment to your instructor.

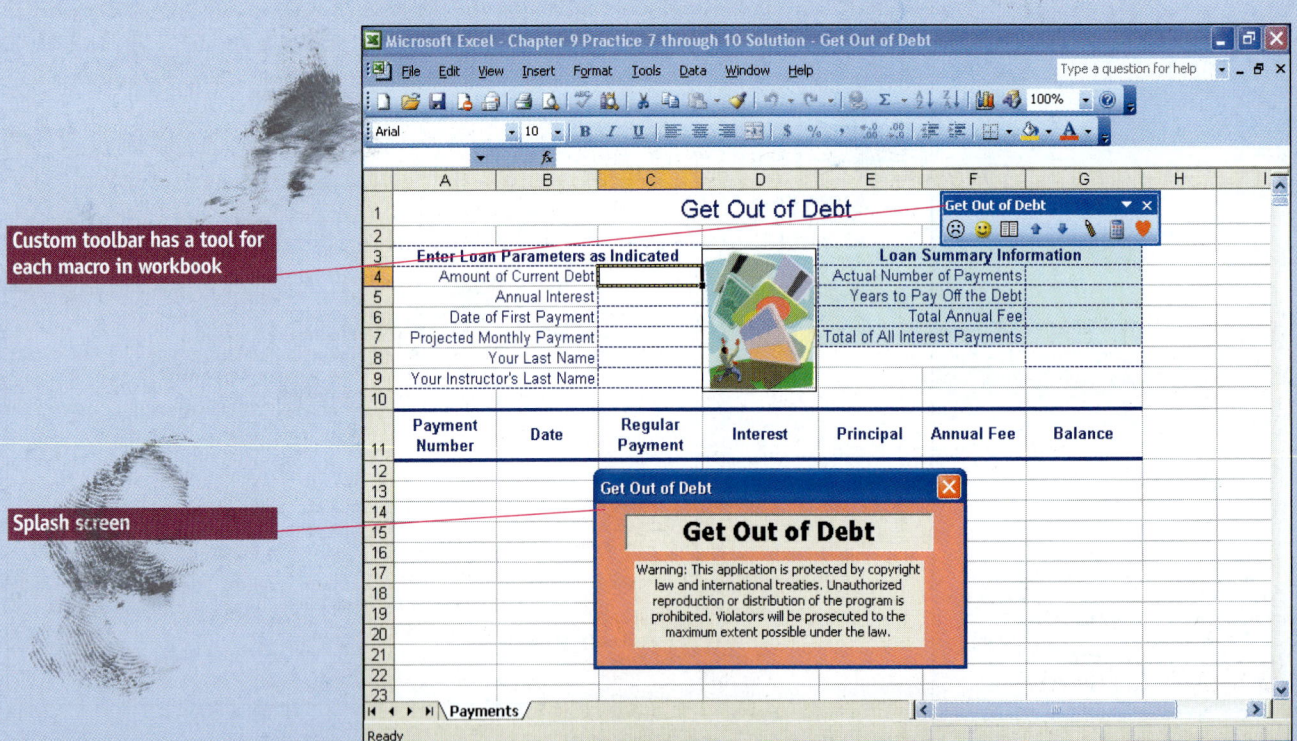

FIGURE 9.20 The Completed Application (exercise 10)

practice exercises

11. **The Mind Reader:** The puzzle in Figure 9.21 was created for the Web by Andy Naughton (www.cyberglass.co.uk) and converted to an Excel workbook by the authors. We thank Andy for permission to use his very clever puzzle. Open the *Chapter 9 Practice 11* workbook, enable the macros, and follow the directions. Choose any two-digit number; add the digits, then subtract the sum from the original number. If you choose 75, for example, the sum is 12, and you wind up with 63 (75 – 12). Look for the number in the table, notice the symbol next to the number, then click the Show Me button. The puzzle will read your mind and display the symbol that is next to your number.

    Click the button to play again. Choose a different number, do the math, and more than likely you will get a different symbol. But no matter how many times you play the game, the puzzle will always be able to guess the symbol. Are you intrigued? We were. Now let's see if we can determine how the puzzle works.

    a. Open the VBA editor and look at Module 1. There are four procedures. Run each procedure to determine what each procedure does. (You may want to tile the Excel and VBA windows to step through each procedure to see the effect of each statement.)

    b. You now know the function of each procedure, but that does not explain how the puzzle works. Return to the Excel window and click the button to Play Again to reset the puzzle. Pull down the Format menu, click the Sheet command, click Unhide, and then unhide the Symbols worksheet. Look at the formula in cell C2. What is the purpose of the RAND function? Press the F9 (Calculate) key. How does the worksheet change?

    c. Click in cell C3 of the Symbols worksheet and examine the formula. How does that formula relate to the value in cell C2 and the table of symbols in column A? Press the F9 key. What happens to the worksheet?

    d. Click the tab for the ReadYourMind worksheet. It would be very helpful to see the cell formulas in this worksheet except that we have protected the worksheet to hide the formulas. We'll give you one more hint. Pull down the Tools menu, click the Protection command, and click the Unprotect Sheet command. A password is not required. Now look at the formulas in the table of symbols to see if you can find the pattern.

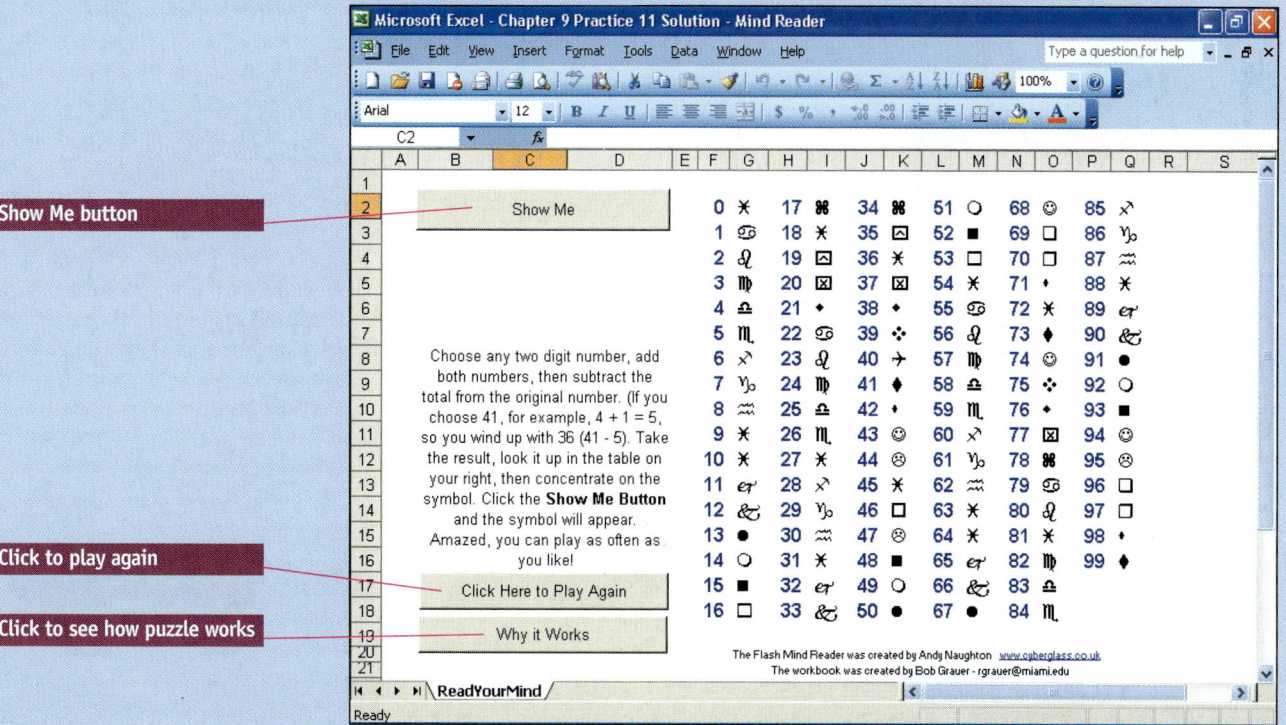

FIGURE 9.21 The Mind Reader (exercise 11)

MINI CASES

The Robot and the Wall

This problem is an exercise in logic and has nothing to do with VBA per se. A robot is sitting on a chair facing a wall a short distance away. Your assignment is to provide the necessary instructions to the robot to stand up, walk to the wall, then turn around, walk back, and sit down in the chair. The robot understands a set of very basic commands—Stand, Sit, Turn (90 degrees to the right), and Step.

The robot can also raise its arms and sense the wall with its fingertips. It cannot, however, sense the chair on its return trip, since the chair is below arm level. Accordingly, the robot must count the number of steps to the wall or chair by using another set of commands—Add (increment a counter by 1), Subtract (decrement the counter by 1), Initialize Counter to zero, Arms Up, and Arms Down. The wall is an integer number of steps away.

Open the partially completed PowerPoint presentation, *Chapter 9 Mini Case—The Robot and the Wall*, which describes this assignment. Enter the completed pseudocode on a new slide, and then present your solution to the class. Ask for a volunteer to play the part of the robot.

The Object Browser

The Object Browser is a useful tool to explore the objects within the Excel object model. Open any Excel workbook, start the VBA editor, pull down the View menu, and choose Object Browser. Specify the Excel object library and then scroll through the various classes that appear within the class list. A class is the formal definition of an object; it describes the properties, methods, and events that are available for that object.

The list is overwhelming at first. We suggest you focus initially on the Range object that was used in multiple procedures throughout the chapter. Once you choose the object (class) in the left pane, you will see the members of that class (its properties, methods, and events) in the right pane. Each type of member has a different symbol. Locate the Select method and Value property for the Range object and try to relate this information to the procedures in the chapter.

Experiment further with the worksheets collection and the worksheet object. (A collection is a group of similar objects.) Summarize your thoughts about the Object Browser in a short note to your instructor.

Your Own Application

Develop a VBA application of comparable function and complexity to the Amortization Schedule or Get Out of Debt applications from the chapter or end-of-chapter exercises. The application should be flexible, visually appealing, easy to use, and bulletproof. Choose any scenario that is of interest to you. The only restriction is that you *cannot* develop an application based on the PMT function.

The completed application should include event procedures for opening and closing the workbook, a splash screen, and a custom toolbar. It should also contain one or two nontrivial procedures that include loops and decision making. You can copy the generic macros to increase or decrease the zoom percentage or toggle a documentation worksheet on or off that were creatd in the chapter. Present the completed application to the class.

CHAPTER 10

Extending VBA: Processing Worksheets and Workbooks

OBJECTIVES

After reading this chapter you will:

1. Use the Dir function to open all workbooks in a specific folder.
2. Explain how the Len function indicates an "empty" folder.
3. Use the On Error and Exit Sub statements for error trapping.
4. Use the Forms toolbar to add a command button to a worksheet.
5. Use the For/Next statement to process all worksheets in a workbook.
6. Change the color of a worksheet tab based on a value in the worksheet.
7. Explain how to "divide and conquer" to create an application.
8. Call one VBA procedure from another procedure.

hands-on exercises

1. CREATE SUMMARY WORKBOOK
   Input: Expense Statement; Expense Summary
   Output: Expense Statement (modified to include your name); Expense Summary Solution

2. ERROR TRAPPING
   Input: Expense Summary Solution
   Output: Expense Summary Solution (additional modifications)

3. CREATE SUMMARY WORKSHEET
   Input: Expense Summary Solution (from exercise 2)
   Output: Expense Summary Solution (additional modifications)

4. BETTER SUMMARY WORKBOOK
   Input: Better Summary
   Output: Better Summary Solution

CASE STUDY
END OF THE MONTH

It happens at the end of every month—you want to leave the office at a reasonable hour, but are inundated with a set of employee expense statements, each in a separate workbook. You cannot leave until you have extracted the data from each individual workbook into a summary workbook, retaining each employee's data on a separate worksheet in the summary workbook. You then have to evaluate each employee's expenses individually to see whether the total is under the allocated amount.

It's time consuming, tedious, and rather boring. Were it not for this monthly "nuisance," your job would be much easier and you would be much happier. If only there were a way to make it happen with the push of a button or two, then you could be spending that extra time making plans for the weekend. Just when you were feeling down about your work, a colleague suggested that you automate the entire process using Excel macros and VBA. ∎

Your assignment is to read the chapter and complete all four hands-on exercises, which have you create the Better Summary Solution workbook. The completed workbook will contain all of the macros to consolidate the expense statements as applied to a specific set of employee worksheets. Prove to yourself how easy the automation procedure is by using the completed workbook to process a different set of expense statements.

Open the *Better Summary Solution* workbook. Pull down the Tools menu, click Macro, run the macro to Reset the Summary Worksheet, then manually delete all of the existing employee worksheets from the Better Summary Solution workbook. Now click the button to Create Summary workbook and enter "*C:\Exploring Excel\Chapter 10 Case Study*" as the name of the folder containing the new set of employee expense statements. You will be prompted to save each workbook in this folder, after which you will be prompted for the maximum allowable expense. Enter $1,000, and then sit back as the new summary workbook is created for you. Print the new summary worksheet for your instructor.

THE EXPENSE SUMMARY APPLICATION

A good application enables an end user to accomplish tasks that he or she could not (easily) do through ordinary Excel commands. Consider, for example, the Expense Summary workbook that appears in Figure 10.1. Each employee submits an expense statement at the beginning of each month with his or her expenses for the previous month. The expense statements are submitted as separate Excel workbooks such as the one in Figure 10.1a. Your task is to consolidate the individual workbooks to create a summary workbook, as shown in Figure 10.1b.

Each individual workbook contains a single worksheet listing the expenses for that employee. The summary workbook, on the other hand, contains multiple worksheets with one worksheet for each employee. The summary workbook also contains a summary worksheet that lists the expenses for all employees, as well as an indication of whether the expenses are approved or require further review.

You could build the summary workbook manually using specific Excel commands to open each employee workbook, and copy the associated worksheet to the summary workbook. You then have to review the employee expenses on each worksheet and copy the relevant information to the summary worksheet. This is tedious, to say the least, and it is also prone to error. And what if there were 100 employees, as opposed to five? Clearly, you need to automate the process.

You should not, however, attempt to write a single VBA procedure to build the summary workbook because it is too complicated. It is better to divide the overall task into a series of smaller, more manageable tasks, each of which requires its own procedure. The procedures are developed and tested individually, then executed collectively to create the summary workbook. This is the methodology that we follow throughout the chapter. The end result will be an "empty" workbook that contains multiple procedures to obtain the individual employee data and produce the summary information. You will be able to click a single command button and build the entire workbook.

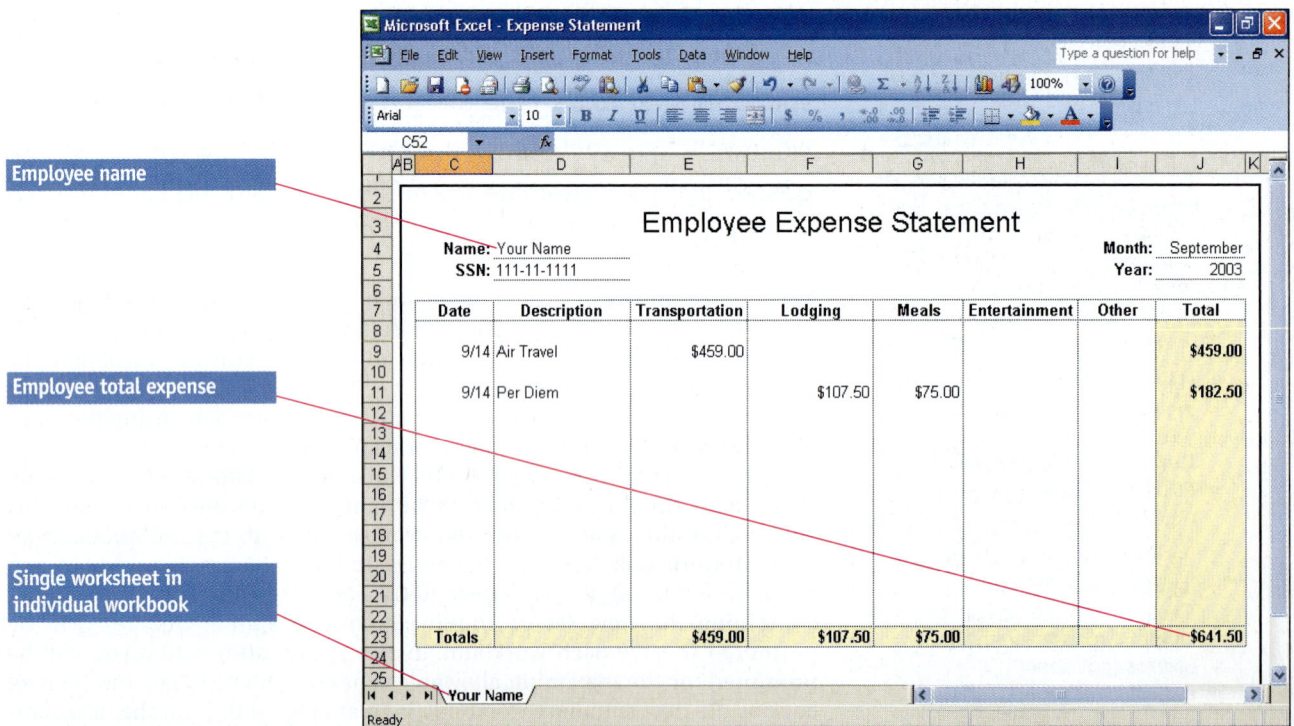

(a) Individual Expense Statement

FIGURE 10.1 The Expense Summary Application

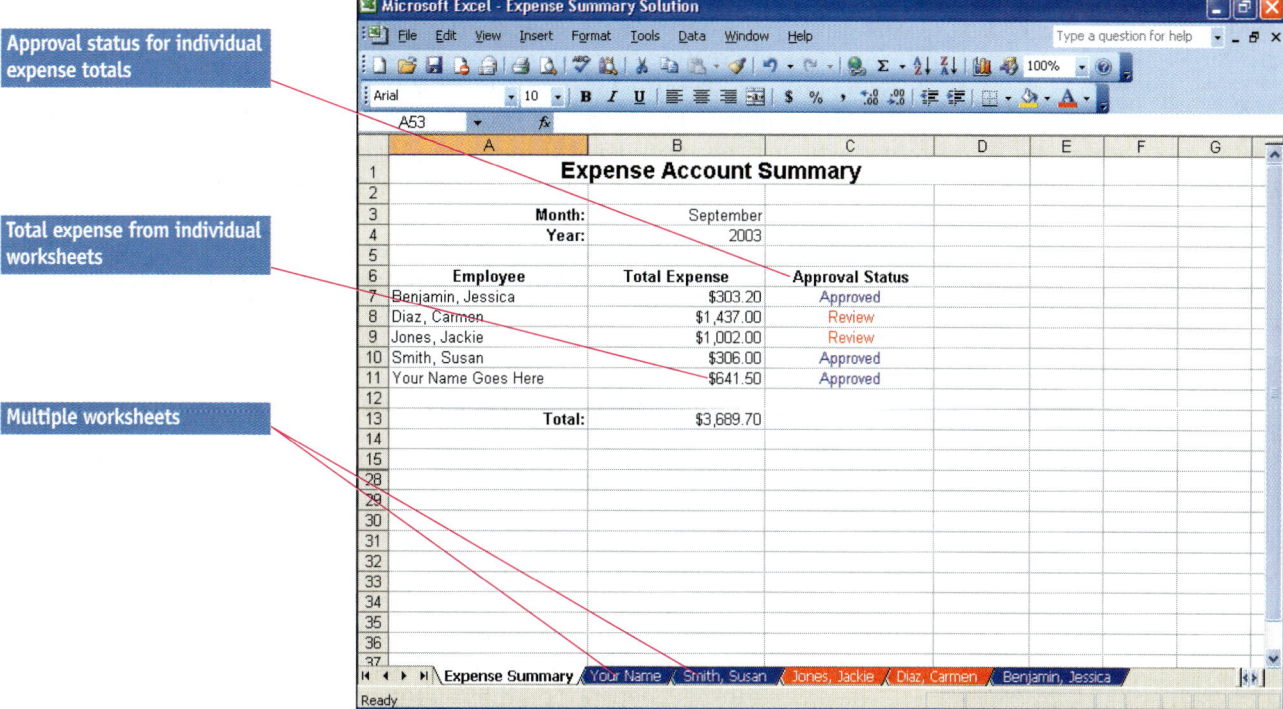

(b) Summary Workbook

FIGURE 10.1 The Expense Summary Application (*continued*)

A QUICK REVIEW

The VBA procedures to create the summary workbook use many VBA statements that do not have equivalent Excel commands. These statements are presented collectively in the VBA primer at the end of this text, and it is important that you are comfortable with their use and syntax. A quick summary is shown below.

The ***MsgBox statement*** displays information to the user. It has one required argument, which is the message (or prompt) that is displayed to the user. The other two arguments, the icon that is to be displayed in the message box, and the text of the title bar, are optional. The ***InputBox function*** displays a prompt for information, and then it stores that information for later use.

Every variable must be declared (defined) before it can be used. This is accomplished through the ***Dim*** (short for Dimension) ***statement*** that appears at the beginning of a procedure. The Dim statement indicates the name of the variable and its type (for example, whether it will hold a character string or an integer number), which in turn reserves the appropriate amount of memory for that variable.

The ability to make decisions within a procedure and then branch to alternative sets of statements is implemented through the ***If...Then...Else statement***. The Else clause is optional, but may be repeated multiple times within an If statement.

The ***For...Next statement*** (or For...Next loop as it is also called) executes all statements between the words For and Next a specified number of times, using a counter to keep track of the number of times the loop is executed. The ***Do Until*** and/or the ***Do While statements*** are used when the number of iterations is not known in advance.

Remember, too, that a VBA procedure is created in one of two ways—by entering statements directly into the VBA editor and/or by using the macro recorder to capture Excel commands and convert them to their VBA equivalents. You can also combine the two techniques by starting with the macro recorder to capture basic statements, view the resulting syntax, and then embellish the original statements.

The Dir Function

The first task in creating the summary workbook is to open the individual workbooks in order to copy the information for each employee to the summary workbook. This requires a procedure to process all of the workbooks in a specified folder, which is accomplished through the Visual Basic Dir function. The **Dir function** returns the name of the first file that matches a specified character string. For example, *Dir(C:\Expense Statements*.xls)* returns the name of the first Excel workbook in the Expense Statements folder on drive C. The file name of the workbook that was found can be stored in a variable for subsequent processing by the following statement:

>   strWorkbookName = Dir("C:\Expense Statements*.xls")

The next workbook in the folder is obtained by calling the Dir function without any arguments as shown below:

>   strWorkbookName = Dir

The two Dir statements are used in conjunction with one another to process all of the workbooks in a folder, as shown in Figure 10.2. The initial Dir statement is executed once to be sure that the specified folder exists, and further, to obtain the name of the first workbook in that folder. The second Dir statement is placed in a loop to access every other workbook in that folder.

The procedure also depends on the Len function to determine when all of the workbooks have been processed. The **Len function** returns the number of characters in the specified variable. (A length of zero indicates an empty character string, which implies that no more workbooks were found.) The Len function appears in an If statement immediately following the initial Dir statement to ensure that the folder contains at least one workbook. The function is also used to terminate the Do While loop after the last employee workbook has been processed; i.e., the loop ends when the length of the file name is zero to indicate there are no more workbooks in the folder.

The procedure in Figure 10.2 contains statements that were inserted by the macro recorder as well as VBA statements that were entered directly. The recorder was used to capture the keystrokes to open a specified workbook, to select a worksheet in the workbook, to copy the selected sheet to the Expense Summary workbook, and finally to close the workbook. The remaining statements were entered explicitly by the developer.

```
Public Sub OpenAllWorkbooks()
    Dim strWorkbookName

    strWorkbookName = Dir("C:\Exploring Excel\Expense Statements\*.xls")
    If Len(strWorkbookName) > 0 Then
        Do While Len(strWorkbookName) > 0
            Workbooks.Open Filename:= _
                "C:\Exploring Excel\Expense Statements\" & strWorkbookName
            Sheets(1).Select
            Sheets(1).Copy After:=Workbooks("Expense Summary Solution.xls").Sheets(1)
            Workbooks(strWorkbookName).Close
            strWorkbookName = Dir
        Loop
    Else
        MsgBox "Error - The folder C:\Exploring Excel\Expense Statements " _
            & "does not exist and/or there are no workbooks in the folder. " _
            & "Please check the folder name and then rerun the macro.", _
            vbCritical, ApplicationTitle
    End If
End Sub
```

Initial Dir function
Len function
Dir Statement within loop

FIGURE 10.2   The Open All Workbooks Procedure

hands-on exercise

1 Create the Summary Workbook

Objective Run a VBA procedure to combine worksheets from multiple workbooks into a single workbook. Use Figure 10.3 as a guide in the exercise.

Step 1: **Open the Expense Statement Workbook**

- Open the **Expense Statement workbook** in the Exploring Excel Folder. Click the button to **Enable Macros** to display the worksheet in Figure 10.3a.

- Enter your name into **cell D4** in the indicated format. Type your **last name, a comma and a space**, then **your first name**.

- Press the **Tab key** to move to **cell J4**, where you will enter the **previous month** (the month for which you are submitting expenses). You can type the month yourself, or you can select the month by clicking the **down arrow** in the list box.

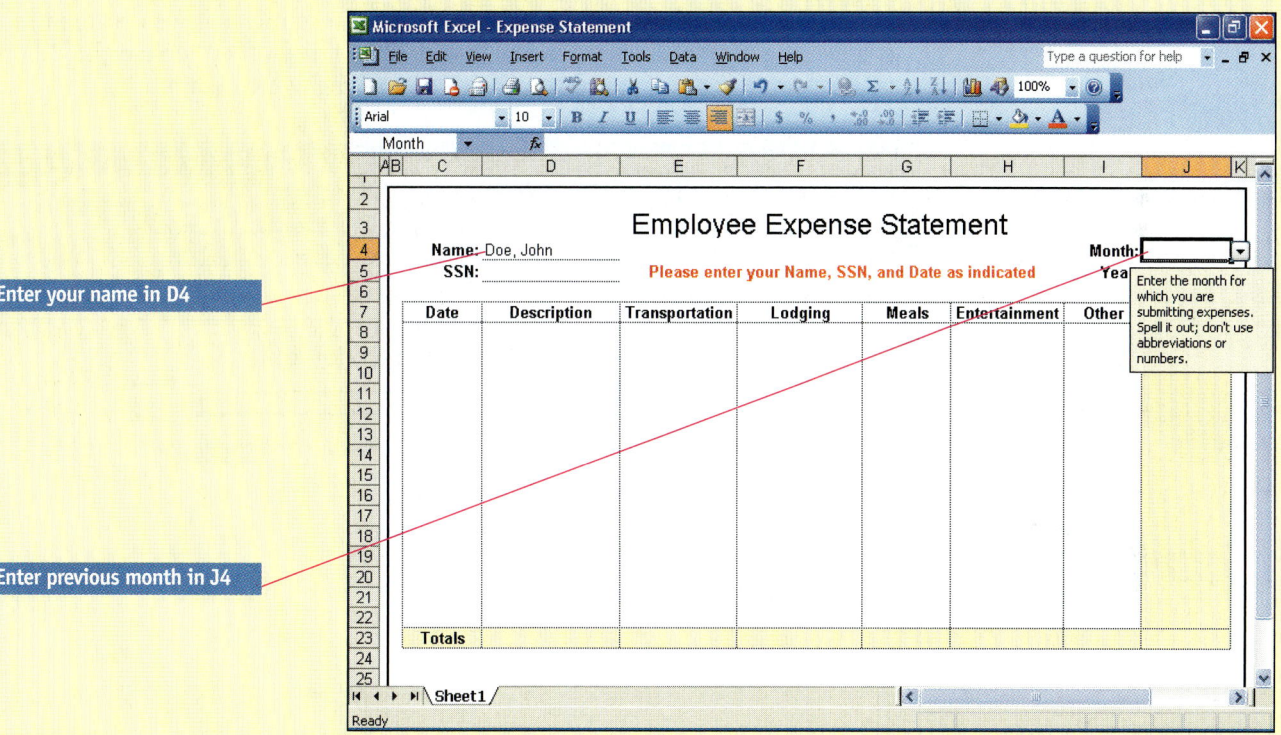

(a) Open the Expense Statement Workbook (step 1)

FIGURE 10.3 Hands-on Exercise 1

DATA VALIDATION

The Expense Statement worksheet uses the Data Validation command to ensure that the user enters a valid month. Pull down the Tools menu, click Protection, then click the Unprotect Sheet command. Scroll down in the worksheet until you can click and drag to select rows 27 to 40, pull down the Format menu, click Row, then click Unhide. Now click in cell J4, pull down the Data menu, and click the Validation command to see how the input for this cell is restricted to the list in cells C28 to C39. Click the Undo command twice to reverse the last commands and hide these rows. Reprotect the worksheet.

Step 2: Understanding the Workbook

- Click in **cell D5** and enter your **student ID number** in place of the Social Security number. The text in cell E5 is no longer visible. Delete your student ID number, and the text reappears.

- Click in **cell E5** as shown in Figure 10.3b. The formula in this cell uses the OR function within an IF function to determine if any of four cells is blank, and if so, it displays the text requesting you to enter the appropriate information.

- Click in **cell D5** and reenter your **Social Security number**.

- The year is entered automatically into the worksheet. Click in **cell J5** to see how this is accomplished. (The worksheet assumes that you are always entering expenses for the previous month.)

- The Expense Statement workbook contains a single worksheet that is named Sheet1. Close the workbook. Click **Yes** when prompted to save the changes.

- Reopen the **Expense Statement workbook**, enable macros, and notice that the worksheet tab has been renamed to match your name as it was entered into cell D4. Press **Alt+F11** to open the Visual Basic Editor, then look at the Before Close event procedure to see how we changed the worksheet tab.

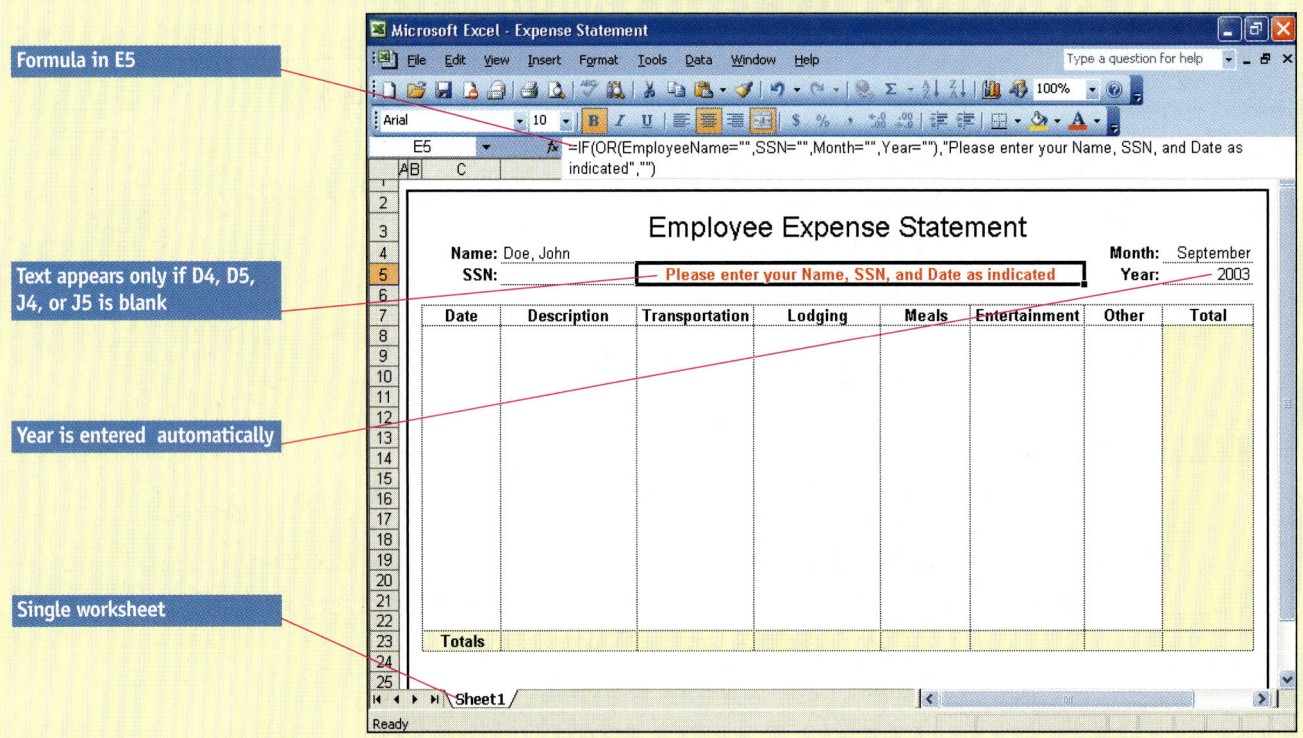

(b) Understanding the Workbook (step 2)

FIGURE 10.3 Hands-on Exercise 1 (*continued*)

EVENT-DRIVEN PROGRAMMING

The Open Workbook and Before Close event procedures may contain VBA code to accomplish certain "housekeeping" at the beginning and end of an application, respectively. The Before Close event procedure in this application confirms that the employee name has been entered, and if so, it changes the worksheet tab to reflect the employee name. This becomes important in subsequent steps, when the individual worksheets are combined into a summary workbook.

Step 3: **The Expense Statements Folder**

- Return to the Excel workbook. Click in **cell C9**. Enter an appropriate date—that is, a date in which the month matches the value in cell J4. You can enter the date with or without the year—for example, as 9/14 or as 9/14/03. (The year will not be displayed.)

- Enter the indicated description and expense for this date as shown in Figure 10.3c. Use the **Tab key** to move from one column to the next within the row. The total is computed automatically.

- Enter the second set of expenses into row 11. You can choose any date (within the month), but use the Description and the dollar amounts that are shown in the figure.

- Pull down the **File menu** and click the **Save As command** to display the Save As dialog box in Figure 10.3c. Double click the **Expense Statements folder** that exists within the Exploring Excel folder.

- Click in the **File name** text box and save the workbook in Expense Statements folder as **Your Last Name - Expense Statement**.

- Pull down the **File menu** and click the **Close command** (or click the **Close button** in the document window) to close your workbook. Click **Yes** if prompted to save the changes.

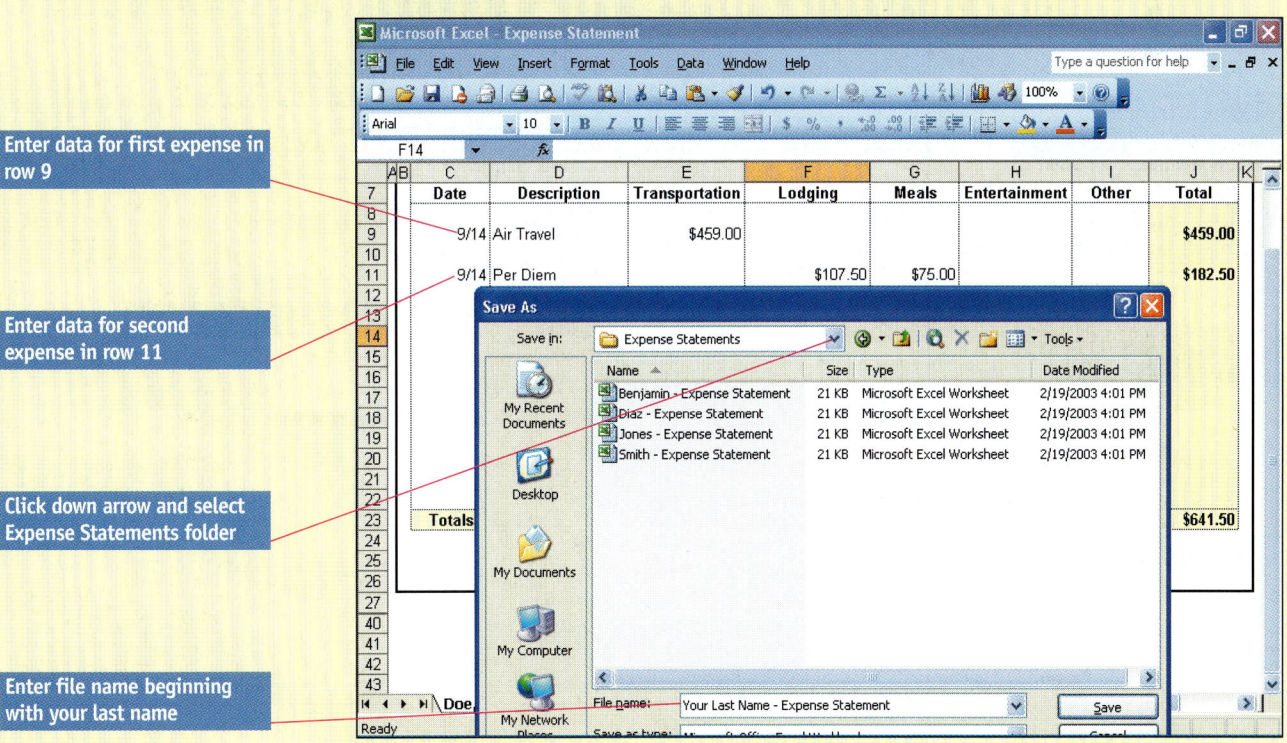

(c) The Expense Statements Folder (step 3)

FIGURE 10.3 Hands-on Exercise 1 (*continued*)

THE EXPENSE STATEMENTS FOLDER

The Expense Statements folder has been created for you. It contains four existing workbooks, each of which represents the expenses of a different employee. You have just added your workbook to this folder. The next step in this exercise will copy the expense worksheet from each of these workbooks into a summary workbook.

Step 4: **Run the Open All Workbooks Procedure**

- Open the **Expense Summary workbook** in the Exploring Excel folder. Click the button to **Enable macros**. Save the workbook as **Expense Summary Solution** so that you can return to the original workbook if necessary.

- The workbook consists of a single worksheet. The month and year are entered automatically and should reflect last month (the month for which the expenses are being submitted).

- Pull down the **Tools menu**, click **Macro**, then click **Macros...** to display the Macro dialog box as shown in Figure 10.3d. Select the **OpenAllWorkbooks macro**, then click the **Run button** to execute the VBA procedure.

- The procedure opens the first employee workbook in the Expense Statements folder, then it displays a message asking whether you want to save the changes to this workbook. Click **No**. (If this does not occur, skip the remainder of this step, and go to step 5.)

- The procedure continues to open each employee workbook in the folder, prompting you to save each workbook. Click **No** and continue in this fashion until all five workbooks have been opened.

- Save the Expense Summary Solution workbook.

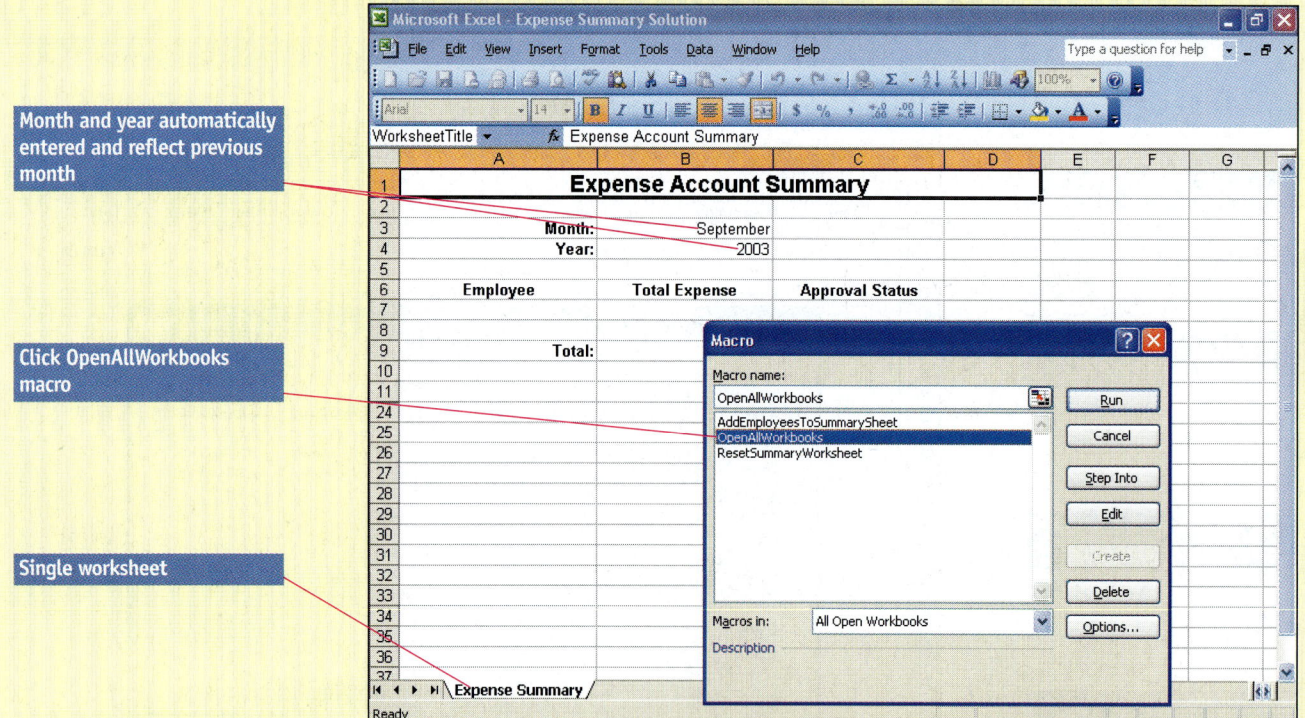

(d) Run the Open All Workbooks Procedure (step 4)

FIGURE 10.3 Hands-on Exercise 1 (*continued*)

SAVING THE INDIVIDUAL WORKBOOKS

Our application takes "poetic license" in that the individual employee workbooks are modified each time they are opened through date functions. This was done to keep the workbooks current; that is, the employee workbooks will reference the same month for which you are submitting your expense report. The contents (dates) in the workbooks change, however, and thus Excel prompts you to save the changes.

Step 5: **Debugging**

- Your actions in this step depend on the success of the previous step:
  - If the procedure executed successfully, press **Alt+F11** to open the editor.
  - If the procedure did not execute correctly, Click **OK** in response to the error message in Figure 10.3e, then press **Alt+F11** to open the VBA editor.

- Double click **Module1** within Project Explorer to display the procedures within this module. Locate the OpenAllWorkbooks procedure that was shown earlier in Figure 10.2. Note the following:
  - The Dir function obtains the names of the Excel workbooks in the **Expense Statements folder**, which is located in the Exploring Excel folder on drive C.
  - If your procedure did not execute correctly, it is most likely because the folder does not exist on your system and/or it is on a different drive. Make the necessary changes, either by changing the folder name and/or location using Windows Explorer or by modifying the procedure. Return to the previous step and reexecute the procedure.

- Close the VBA window to return to Excel.

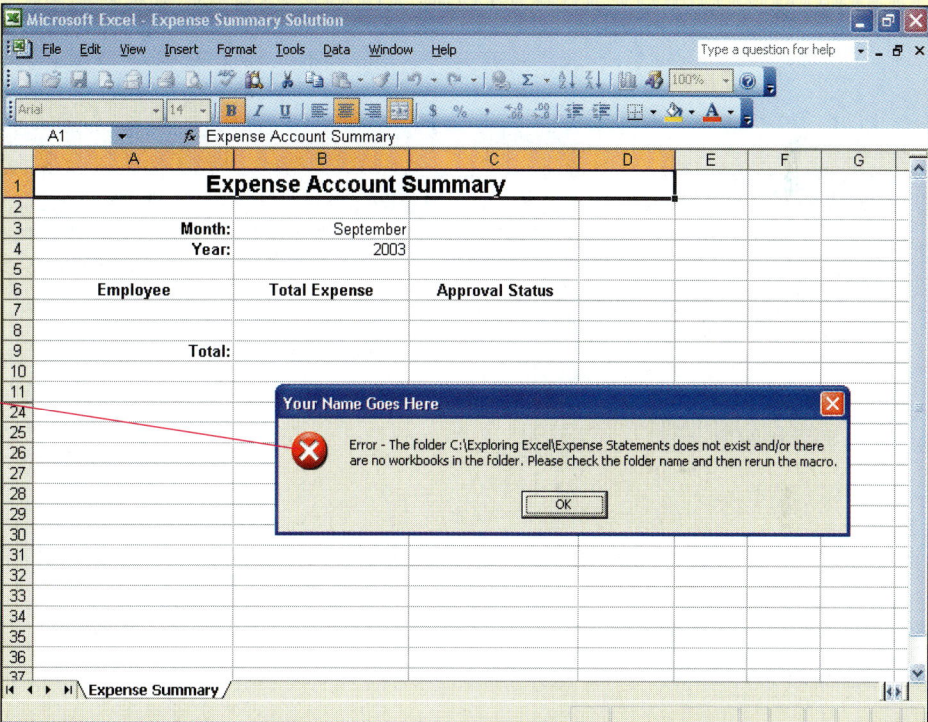

Error message indicates that designated folder was not found

(e) Debugging (step 5)

FIGURE 10.3 Hands-on Exercise 1 (*continued*)

ANTICIPATE USER ERRORS

The developer will understand why a procedure fails to execute properly and/or the meaning of the associated error message. The end user will not, however, and thus a good application anticipates mistakes that a user may make and displays meaningful messages to correct the problem. The OpenAllWorkbooks procedure checks the value returned by the initial Dir function, then displays the appropriate message if the function does not locate an Excel workbook.

Step 6: **The Expense Summary Workbook**

- You should see the Expense Summary Solution workbook as shown in Figure 10.3f. There are a total of six worksheets:
  - The Expense Summary worksheet that existed at the start of the exercise. This worksheet does not yet contain any employee information.
  - A worksheet with your name that contains the expenses you entered earlier.
  - Four additional worksheets that contain the expenses of other employees.

- Select the worksheet containing your expenses. Recall that you entered the month manually into cell J4, and further that you were instructed to enter the previous month. (Expenses are submitted in the current month for the previous month.)

- Select any other employee worksheet. The month and year in this worksheet should match the values in your worksheet. This was accomplished through the use of Date functions and a VLOOKUP function to provide consistency among the worksheets. (See boxed tip.)

- Save the Expense Summary Solution workbook. Exit Excel if you do not want to continue with the next exercise at this time.

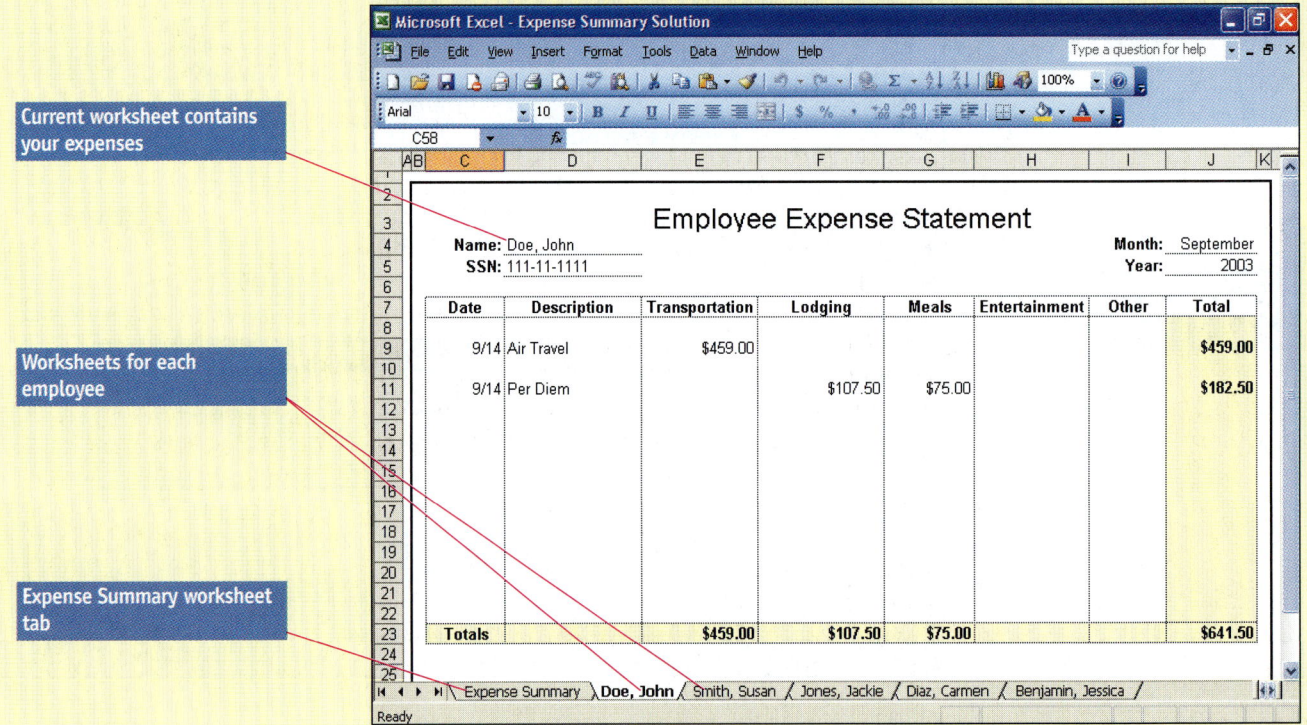

(f) The Expense Summary Workbook (step 6)

FIGURE 10.3 Hands-on Exercise 1 (*continued*)

THE VLOOKUP FUNCTION

Cell D28 in each employee worksheet contains the Excel formula =Month(Today())-1 to determine the previous month. This is a numeric value, however, and it is converted to text through a VLOOKUP function. Click in cell J4 of any employee worksheet to display the formula =VLOOKUP(D28,B28:C39,2). The VLOOKUP function takes the numeric month in cell D28 and applies it to a table of the month names in cells B28 through C39. Unprotect the worksheet, then unhide the indicated rows to see these functions.

DISPLAYING A SPECIFIC WORKSHEET

The summary workbook that has been created contains a worksheet for each employee who submitted an expense report. Our next task is to display the expenses for a specific employee on demand, perhaps when speaking to that employee to obtain additional documentation for his or her expenses. This could be done within the Excel interface, without benefit of a VBA procedure, simply by clicking the worksheet tab for that employee. It's easy to find the worksheet in a workbook with only a few employees, but much more tedious in a large workbook. Excel does not have a command to sort the worksheets within a workbook. Accordingly, we will develop a procedure to display a specific worksheet.

The user is prompted to enter the name of a specific employee as shown in Figure 10.4a, after which the procedure selects (displays) the associated worksheet. It sounds easy, and it is, provided the user enters the employee name *exactly* as it appears on a worksheet tab within the summary workbook. If the user makes a mistake, even one as insignificant as omitting the comma or space, an error results and the worksheet will not be displayed. You may know that "Smith John" and "Smith, John" are one and the same, but VBA does not. If it cannot find the worksheet, it will display a rather intimidating error message, "Run Time Error 9—Subscript Out of Range", and the user is left to decipher the meaning of this message.

Error Trapping

The preceding error is a ***run-time error*** that occurs during the execution of a procedure. (A ***syntax error*** occurs prior to execution and must be corrected to execute the procedure.) A run-time error terminates a procedure immediately, then it displays an explanation in a message box. The developer may know the meaning of the message, but the typical user does not. Thus, a good application will anticipate (trap) errors that are likely to occur and take appropriate action when they do occur. This is accomplished through the ***On Error statement*** that transfers control to a special error-handling section at the end of the procedure. The latter contains additional processing statements and/or simply displays a more meaningful error message.

Consider now the procedure in Figure 10.4b. The Dim statement at the beginning of the procedure defines the variable strEmployeeName. The user is asked to enter the employee's name, and the result is stored in strEmployeeName. The next statement selects the appropriate worksheet, which in turn displays the worksheet in the Excel window. Syntactically, the statement is specifying a ***worksheet object*** and applying the Select method to the object. The generic format for that statement is Sheets("SheetName").Select. Instead of the worksheet name, however, we use the variable strEmployeeName, which contains the name of the desired worksheet. (Quotation marks are not used, or else VBA would attempt to display a worksheet called "strEmployeeName".)

The ***Exit Sub statement*** follows, and it terminates the procedure. The Exit Statement is essential because, without it, the procedure would continue to execute and process the statements in the error-handling routine.

Now consider what happens in the event of an error. The On Error statement takes effect any time a run-time error occurs. The procedure ceases its normal processing and jumps to the section called ErrorHandler. (ErrorHandler is a user-defined name, as opposed to a VBA reserved word.) The ErrorHandler section (note the colon to indicate that ErrorHandler is a label and not an executable statement) appears at the end of the procedure. It consists of a single MsgBox statement to display a more helpful error message. Additional statements could be added to this section to take further action. The End Sub statement is reached, and the procedure terminates. The procedure in Figure 10.4b is a simple, but solid, example of ***error trapping***.

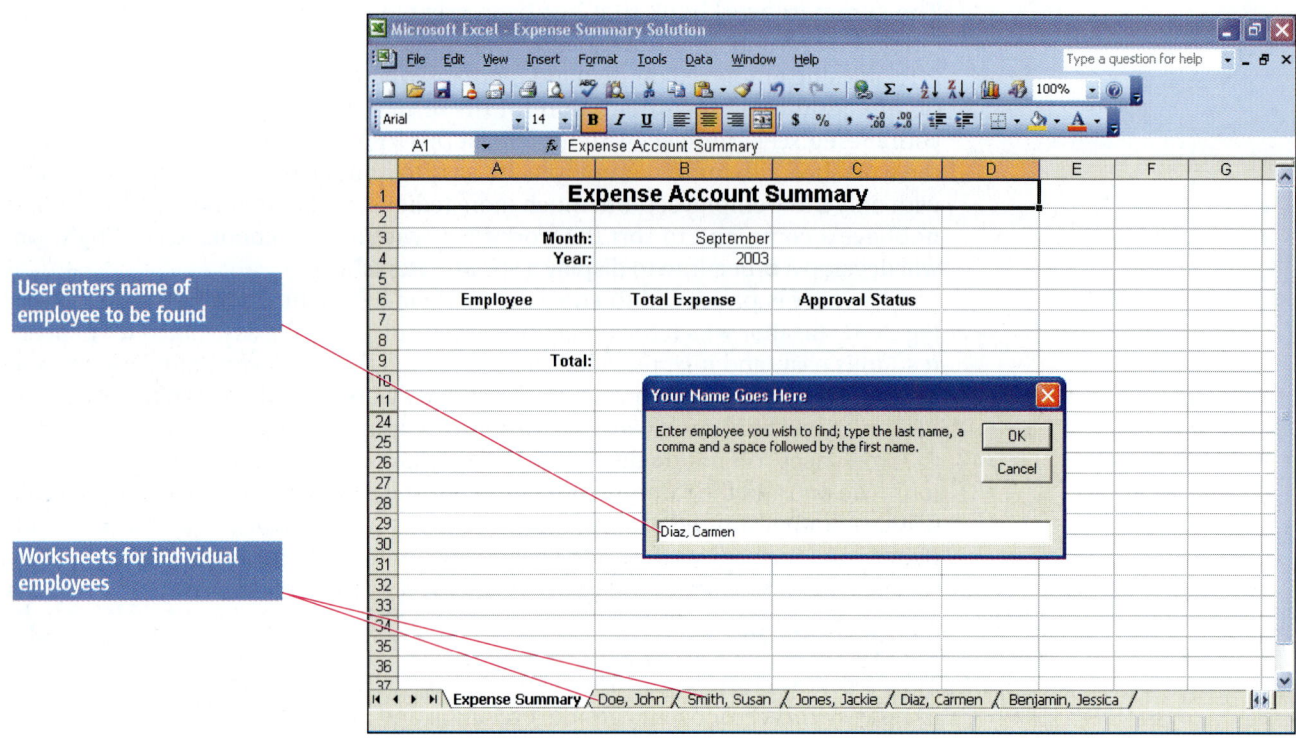

(a) Excel Workbook

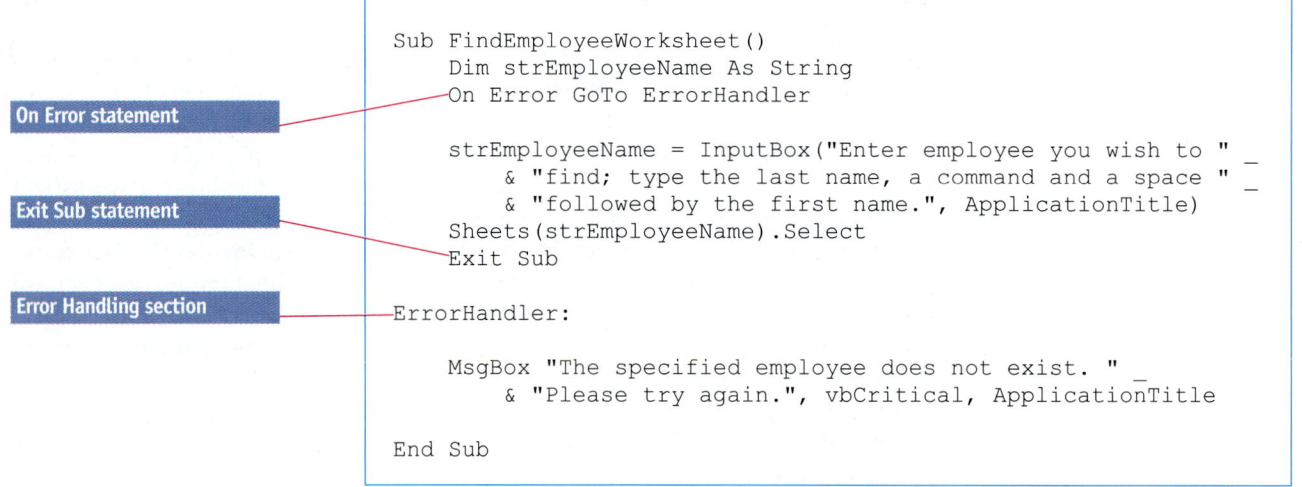

(b) VBA Procedure

FIGURE 10.4 Finding an Employee Worksheet

hands-on exercise
2 Error Trapping

Objective Develop a VBA procedure to display a specific worksheet within a workbook; include the appropriate error-trapping statements.

Step 1: **Start the Macro Recorder**

- Open the **Expense Summary Solution workbook** from the last exercise. Click the button to **Enable Macros**. Click the **Expense Summary worksheet tab**.

- Pull down the **Tools menu**, click the **Macro command**, then click **Record New Macro** to display the Record Macro dialog box in Figure 10.5a.

- Enter **FindEmployeeWorksheet** as the name of the procedure. Click the **Shortcut Key** check box and enter a **lowercase f**. **Ctrl+f** should appear as the keyboard shortcut. Click **OK** to begin recording.

- Click the worksheet tab for **Susan Smith**. Click the **Stop Recording button**. (If you do not see the Stop Recording toolbar, pull down the **Tools menu**, click **Macro**, and click the **Stop Recording command**.)

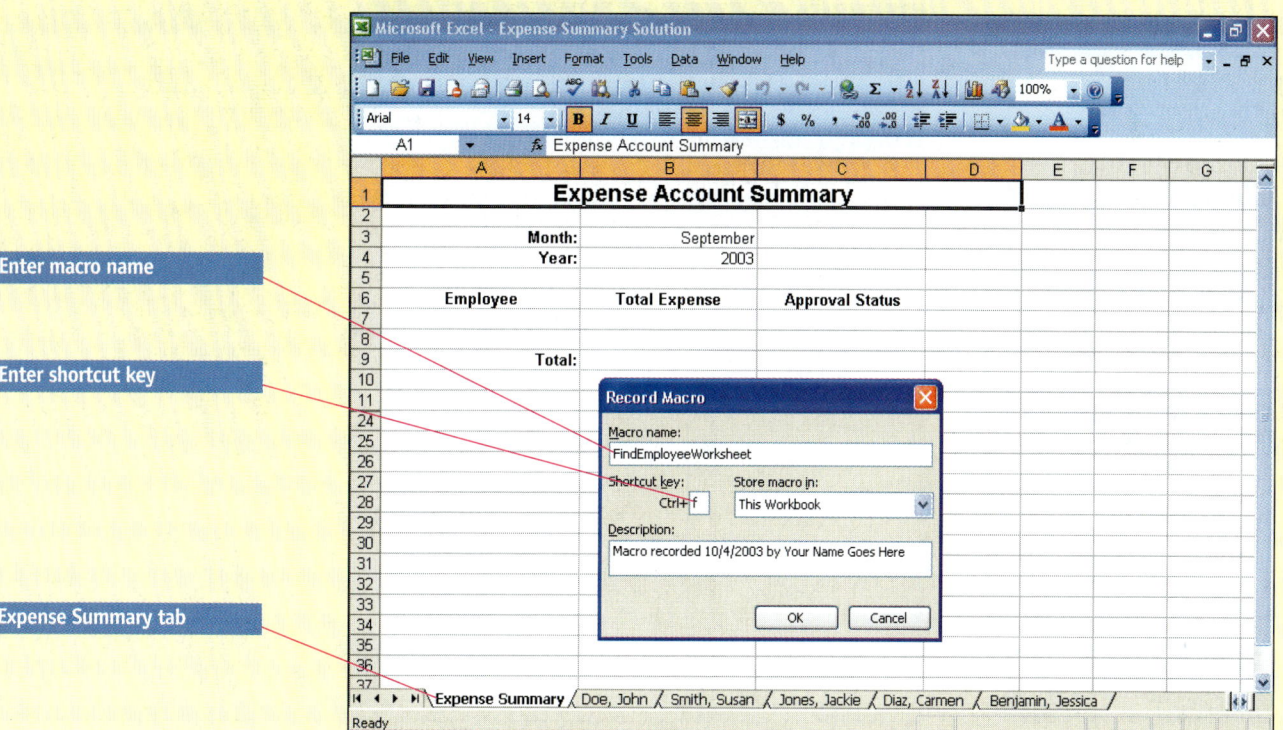

(a) Start the Macro Recorder (step 1)

FIGURE 10.5 Hands-on Exercise 2

KEYBOARD SHORTCUTS

You can add and/or modify the shortcut key associated with a macro at any time. Pull down the Tools menu, click the Macro command, then click Macros. . . to display the Macro dialog box. Select the desired macro and click the Options button to display the Macro Options dialog box, where you assign a shortcut.

Step 2: **Modify the Procedure**

- Press **Alt+F11** to display the VBA editor. Open Project Explorer if it is not visible. You will see that Module2 has been added to the Modules folder. Double click **Module2** to display its contents.

- The procedure at this point consists of a single executable statement, Sheets("Smith, Susan").Select. The other statements include the procedure header and End Sub statement and various comments. Enter the additional code as shown in Figure 10.5b:
  - Add the **Comment statements** as indicated.
  - The **Dim statement** defines the variable strEmployeeName that will contain the name of the employee whose worksheet you want to display.
  - The **InputBox function** prompts the user for the employee name, then stores the result in the strEmployeeName variable.

- Click and drag to select **"Smith, Susan"** (include the quotation marks) as shown in Figure 10.5b. Type **strEmployeeName**. The statement now reads **Sheets(strEmployeeName).Select**.

- Save the procedure.

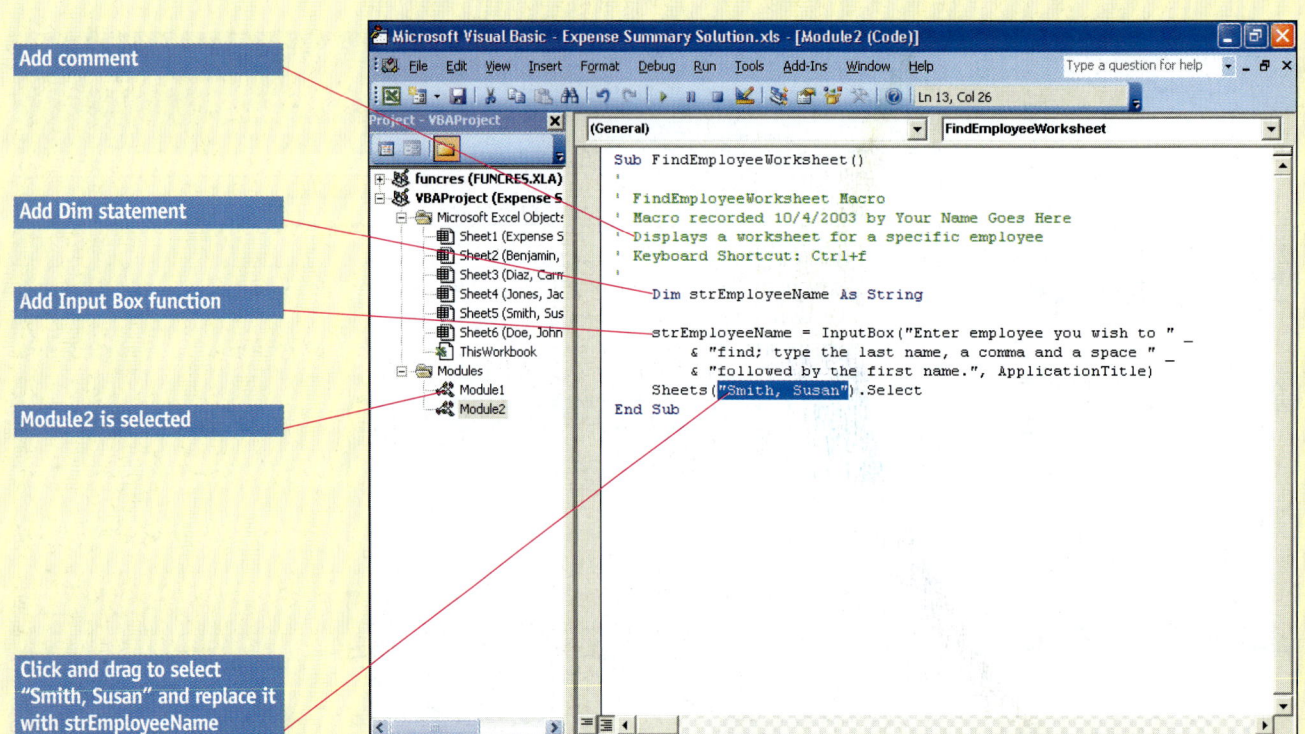

(b) Modify the Procedure (step 2)

FIGURE 10.5 Hands-on Exercise 2 (*continued*)

UNDERSTANDING THE VBA SYNTAX

The syntax of any VBA statement is easy to follow if you go back to the basics. VBA accomplishes its tasks by manipulating objects such as workbooks and worksheets. A collection is a group of similar objects. A method is an action that is performed on an object. Given this information, it is easy to understand the statement, *Sheets("Susan Smith").Select*. VBA is applying the Select method to a specific worksheet within the worksheets collection.

Step 3: **Test the Procedure**

- Return to the Excel window and select the **Expense Summary worksheet**. **Press Ctrl+f** to test the procedure you just created. You should see the message box in Figure 10.5c that asks you to enter an employee name.

- Enter the name that appears on any worksheet tab, but be sure to enter the name correctly. Click **OK** and you should see the worksheet for that employee.

- Press **Ctrl+f** to rerun the procedure, but this time, misspell the name of the employee you wish to find. You will see an error message, "Run-time error 9: Subscript out of range".

- Click the **Debug button**. You are back in the VBA editor, and the statement that caused the problem—Sheets(strEmployeeName).Select—is highlighted.

- Click the **Reset (square) button** on the Standard toolbar to reset the procedure to modify its code, as described in the next step.

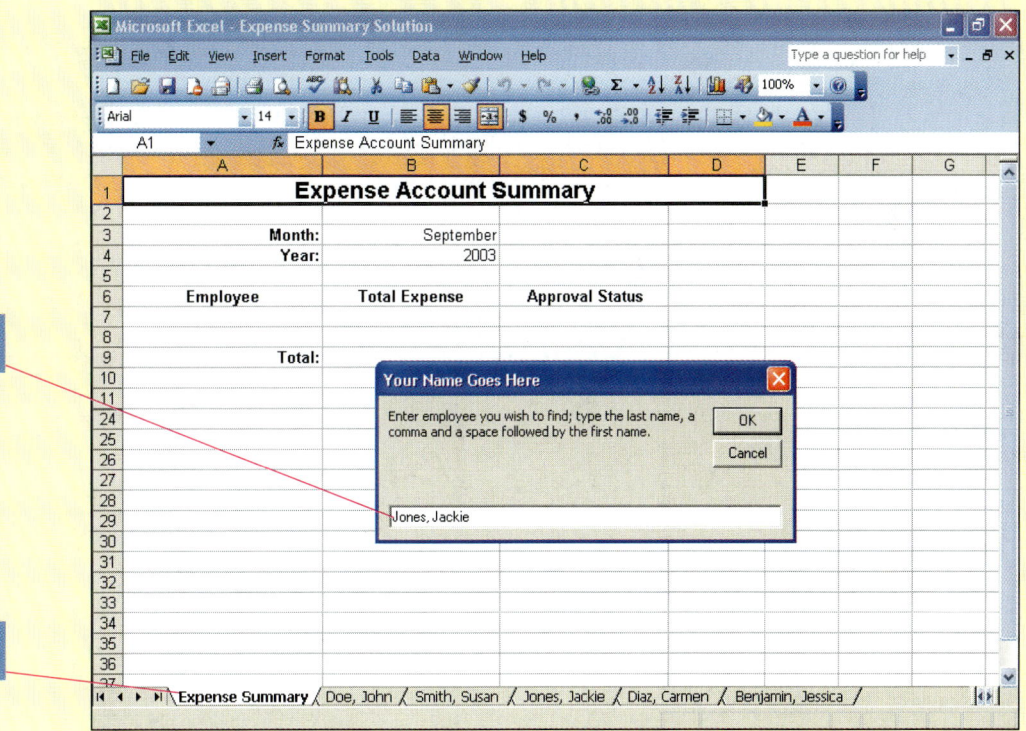

(c) Test the Procedure (step 3)

FIGURE 10.5 Hands-on Exercise 2 (*continued*)

RUN-TIME ERRORS

A run-time (execution) error results when VBA is unable to perform a specific task. VBA displays an explanation for the error, which typically does not make sense to the end user. The error in this example occurs because VBA was unable to reference a specific worksheet because it (the worksheet) does not exist. The internal subscript used by VBA to reference the worksheet within the workbook is out of range and hence the error message. A good application will anticipate (trap) the errors a user is apt to make and provide more meaningful explanations than the standard error messages.

Step 4: **Add the Error Handling**

- You can insulate a procedure against runtime errors by including the appropriate code. Add the additional statements as shown in Figure 10.5d:
  - The **On Error statement** suppresses the normal error message and transfers control to the user-defined location ErrorHandler, which appears elsewhere in the procedure. This statement is executed automatically whenever an error occurs during the procedure.
  - The **Exit Sub statement** exits the procedure immediately, effectively bypassing the statements within the ErrorHandler routine.
  - The **MsgBox statement** within the ErrorHandler routine displays a meaningful message to the user that describes the nature of the error.
- Save the procedure. Return to the Excel window, then press **Ctrl+f** to rerun the procedure to locate a specific employee. **Misspell the employee's name** to test the modified procedure. You should see the message box indicating that the employee worksheet cannot be found. Click **OK**.

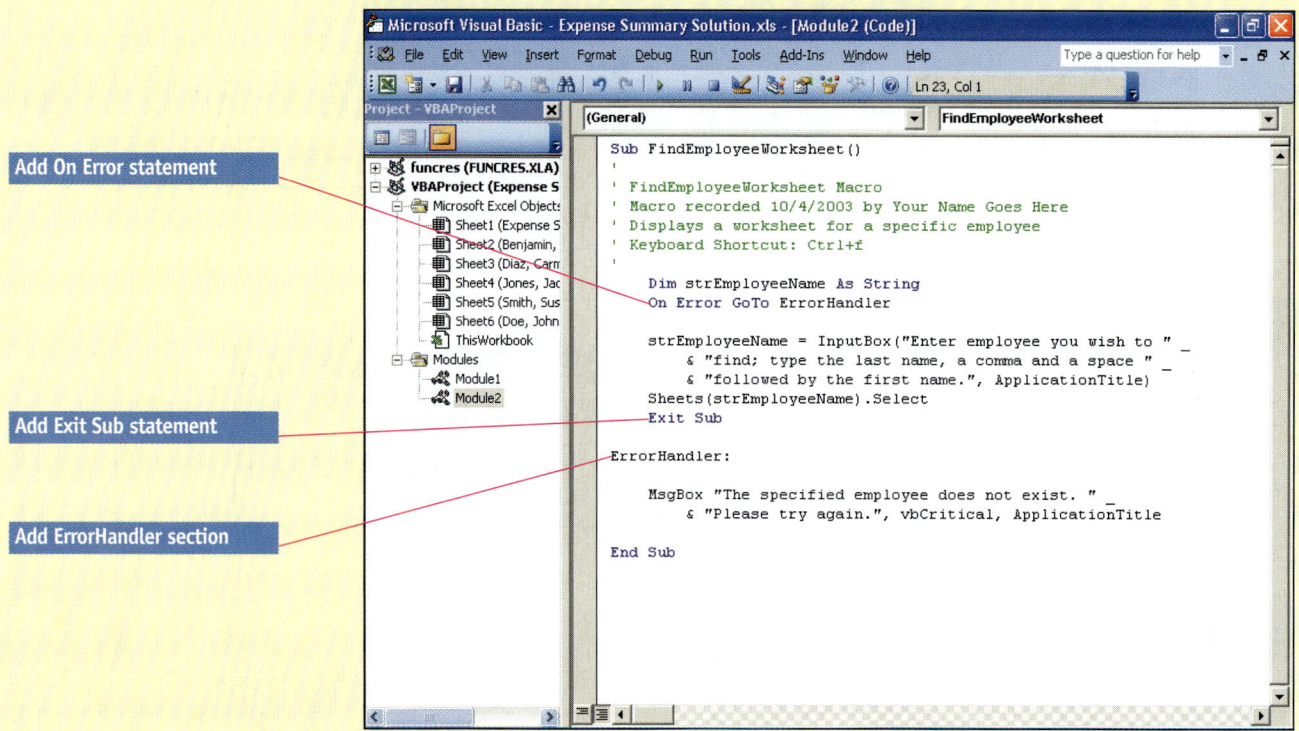

(d) Add the Error Handling (step 4)

FIGURE 10.5 Hands-on Exercise 2 (*continued*)

TOGGLE COMMENTS ON AND OFF

A comment is used primarily to explain the logic within a VBA procedure, but it can also render a statement nonexecutable (as opposed to deleting it altogether). Click at the beginning of the On Error statement within the procedure, type an apostrophe, and then press the down arrow. The statement turns green, indicating that it has been converted to a comment, and thus will not affect the outcome of the procedure. Now reexecute the procedure, misspell the employee name, and you once again see the VBA error message. Remove the apostrophe, try the procedure again, and you see the meaningful error message.

Step 5: **Create a Command Button**

- Select the **Expense Summary worksheet**. Pull down the **View menu**, click **Toolbars**, then click **Forms** to display the Forms toolbar. Click the **Button tool** (the mouse pointer changes to a tiny crosshair).
- Click and drag in the worksheet to draw a command button. Release the mouse. The Assign Macro dialog box will appear as shown in Figure 10.5e. Select **FindEmployeeWorksheet** (the procedure you just created). Click **OK**.
- The button should still be selected. Click and drag to select the name of the button, **Button 1**. Type **Find Employee Worksheet** as the new name. Do not press the Enter key.
- Click outside of the button to deselect it. Right click the button you just created to display a context-sensitive menu, click the **Format Control** to display the associated dialog box, then click the **Properties tab**. Click the Option button that says **Don't move or size with cells**. Click **OK**.
- Add a second command button to run the **OpenAllWorkbooks procedure**.
- Close the Forms toolbar. Save the workbook.

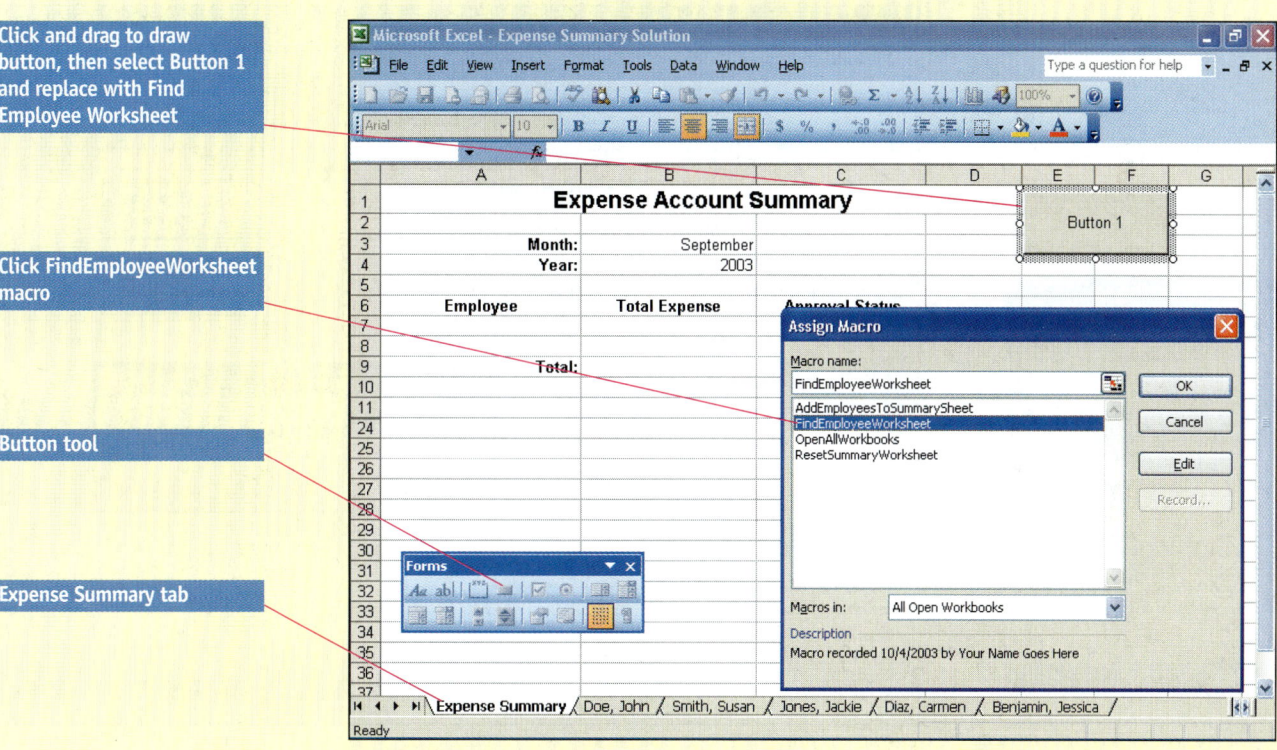

(e) Create a Command Button (step 5)

FIGURE 10.5 Hands-on Exercise 2 (*continued*)

COMMAND BUTTON PROPERTIES

A command button is not physically in a cell, but it will (by default) move and/or resize itself in conjunction with the cells on which it is placed. This is a potential problem if you insert and/or delete rows or columns within a worksheet. Hence we find it convenient to fix the button properties so that the button is unaffected by subsequent changes in the worksheet. Note, too, that you cannot select a command button by clicking it, because that would execute the associated VBA procedure. You can, however, right click the button to display a context-sensitive menu, which in turn selects the button.

Step 6: **Test the Command Buttons**

- You should see two command buttons as shown in Figure 10.5f. Select (click) the worksheet tab for the first employee.
- Press and hold the **Shift key** as you click the name of the last worksheet to select all of the employee worksheets.
- Point to any tab and click the **right mouse button**, then click the **Delete command**. Click the **Delete button** to confirm that you want to delete the employee worksheets.
- Click the command button to **Open All Workbooks**, which in turn runs the procedure from the first exercise. Click **No** when prompted to save the contents of each workbook.
- Select the **Expense Summary** worksheet. Click the button to **Find Employee Worksheet**. Misspell the employee name to test the error handing. Click **OK** when you see the message box in Figure 10.5f.
- Save the workbook. Exit Excel if you do not want to continue with the next exercise at this time.

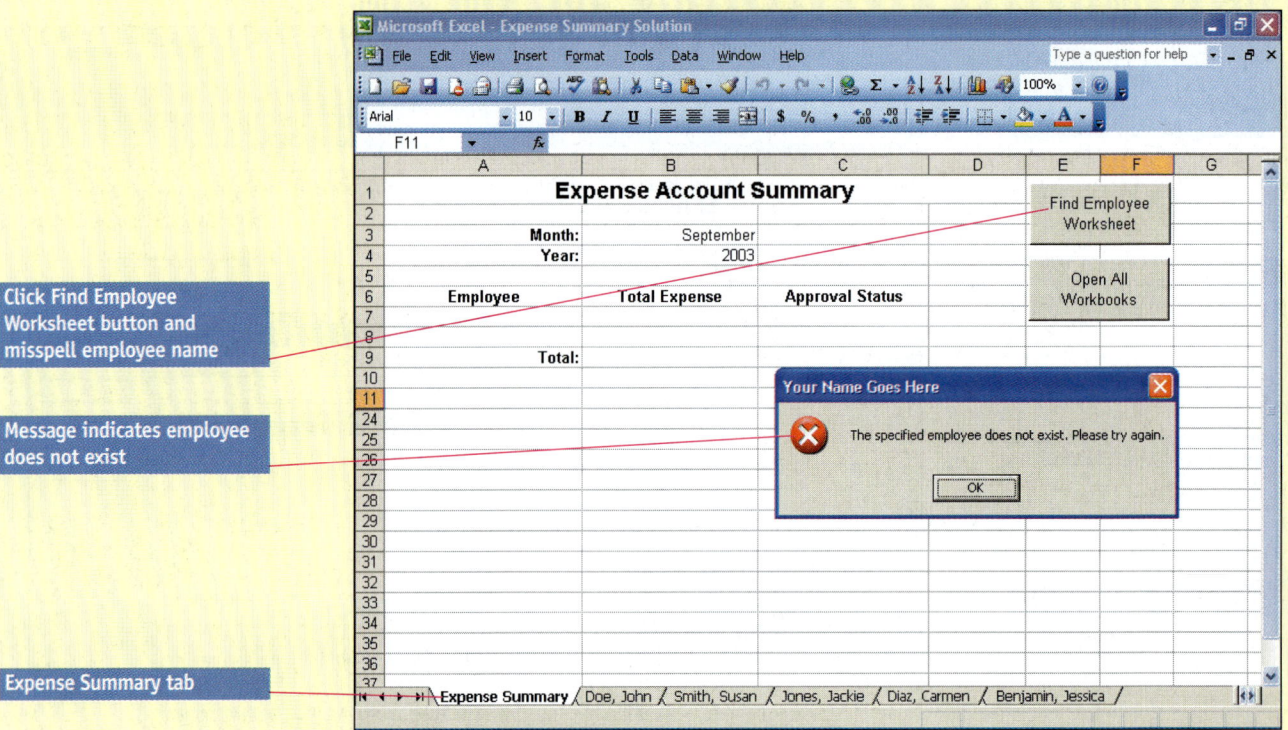

(f) Test the Command Buttons (step 6)

FIGURE 10.5 Hands-on Exercise 2 (continued)

DUPLICATE WORKSHEETS

Excel will not allow you to create multiple worksheets with the same name within a workbook. It is important, therefore, to delete the employee worksheets before running the procedure to add the employee information to the summary workbook. If you inadvertently run the procedure twice in a row, Excel will insert the second worksheet, but will append a subscript to its name within the worksheet tab, such as Your Name(2). Select the first sheet to be deleted, then press and hold the Ctrl key to select the remaining worksheets, click the right mouse button, then click the Delete command to remove the duplicate sheets.

PROCESSING WORKSHEETS IN A WORKBOOK

The Expense Summary workbook contains a single summary worksheet as well as a detailed worksheet for each employee who submitted an expense workbook. Our next task is to process all of the worksheets within the summary workbook. We will develop two separate procedures:

- A procedure to examine the individual worksheets in order to approve the indicated expenses or send the expense worksheet for further review. (The approval criterion is simple. The individual preparing the summary worksheet is asked to enter the threshold amount for the total expense for one employee, below which the expenses are approved automatically.)

- A second procedure to copy the total expense from each employee worksheet, as well as an indication of whether that amount was approved, to a row on the summary worksheet.

Figure 10.6a displays the detailed worksheet for one employee in conjunction with the first procedure. The individual preparing the summary workbook is prompted initially for the threshold amount ($1,000 in this example—the Input Box is not visible in this figure), that value is compared to the employee's total expense in cell J23 ($641.50 on this worksheet), and the approval status is entered into cell D25. Conditional formatting is used in the cell to display "Approved" or "Review" in blue or red, respectively. The procedure also modifies the worksheet tab so that you can see at a glance the status of individual employees. (The ability to change the color of a worksheet tab was introduced in Office XP.)

Figure 10.6b contains the associated VBA procedure, which includes a For . . . Next statement to process all of the worksheets within the workbook. (Technically speaking, it is processing each worksheet object within the worksheets collection.) The logic is not difficult, but it helps to examine the logic in pseudocode prior to looking at the actual VBA statements. Consider this:

> **Loop to process every worksheet**

> **Determines whether expenses are approved**

```
Input threshold amount for automatic approval
For each worksheet in the workbook
   If this is an employee worksheet
      Unprotect this worksheet
      If the expenses are less than or equal to threshold amount
         Approve these expenses and set worksheet tab to blue
      Else
         Review these expenses and set worksheet tab to red
      End if
      Protect this worksheet
   End If
Next worksheet
```

The For. . .Next loop automatically processes all of the worksheets within the workbook. Realize, however, that the first worksheet is a summary (rather than an employee) worksheet and thus the If statement to process only employee worksheets is required. The second If statement compares the total expense on the employee worksheet to the threshold amount and takes the appropriate action.

Figure 10.6b displays the associated VBA procedure. The Dim statement defines the variable mysheet as a worksheet object, which controls the For. . .Next statement that drives the procedure. The loop looks at every worksheet within the workbook, checks to see that each worksheet is an employee worksheet, and if so, compares the total expense on that worksheet to the threshold amount. (WorksheetTitle, TotalExpense, and ApprovedRejected are range names on the Excel worksheet.) The ColorIndex property is set to 5 (blue) or 3 (red), respectively, to indicate whether the expenses are approved or subject to further review.

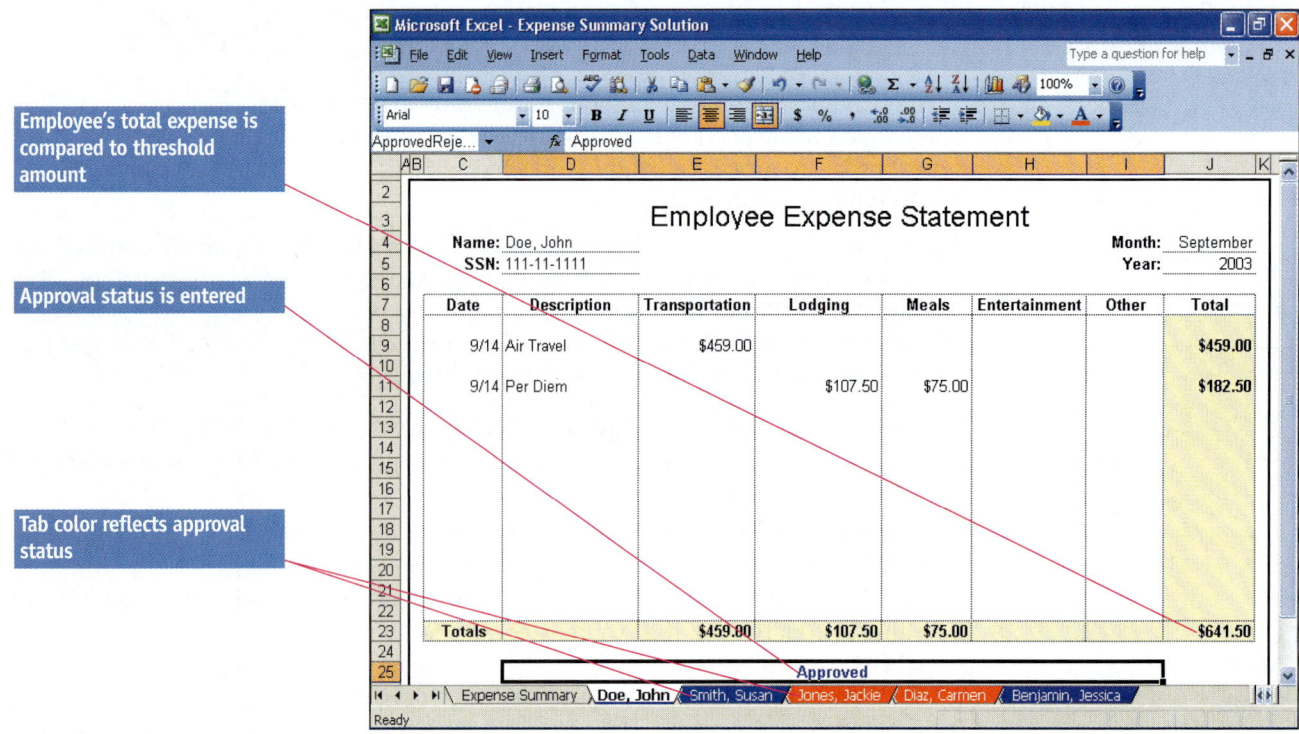

(a) Employee Worksheet

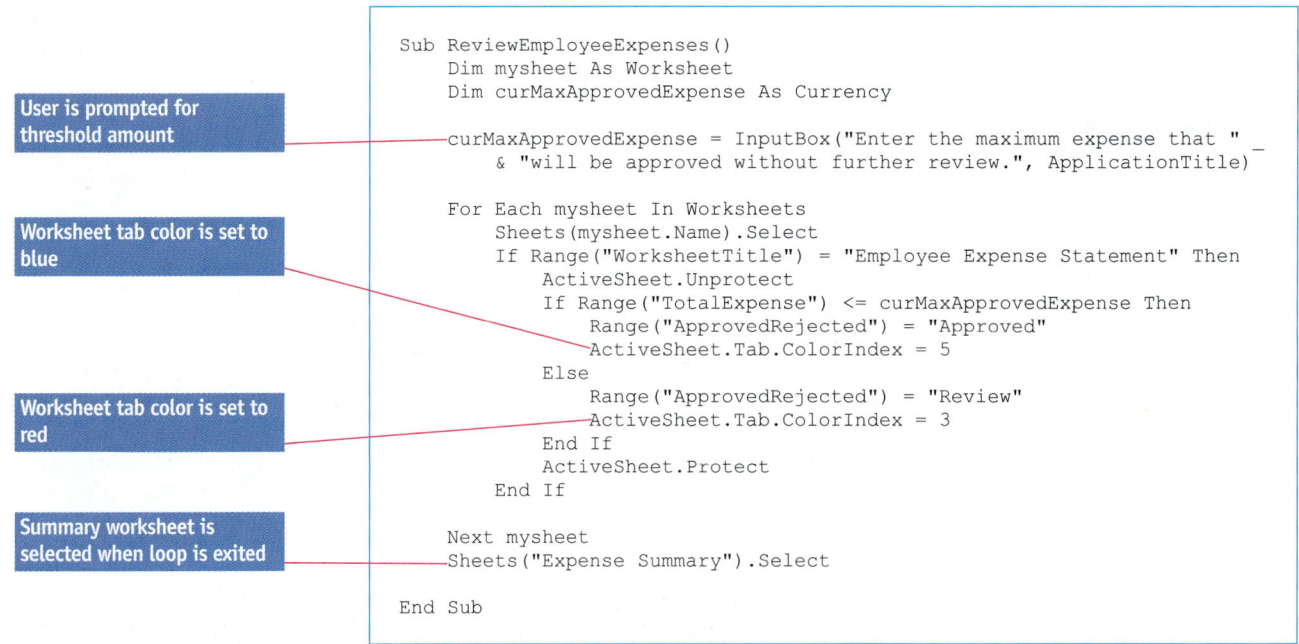

(b) VBA Procedure

FIGURE 10.6   Review Employee Expenses

Adding Employees to the Summary Worksheet

Our next task is to copy the information from the individual employee worksheets (within the summary workbook) to a summary worksheet as shown in Figure 10.7. The summary worksheet contains a single line for each employee with his or her name, the total expense for that employee, and an indication of the approval status. (***Conditional Formatting*** is used to display the status in red or blue for "review" or "approved", respectively.) Row 7, for example, contains the data for Jessica Benjamin, and it reflects the data in the associated worksheet. The color of the worksheet tab also indicates the approval status.

Each of the entries in this row contains a formula that references the appropriate cell from Jessica's worksheet. Cell B7 displays Jessica's total expenses ($303.20) according to the formula ='Benjamin,Jessica'!TotalExpense. The name of the worksheet is enclosed in apostrophes and corresponds to a worksheet tab at the bottom of the window. The exclamation point indicates a worksheet reference. TotalExpense is a range name on that worksheet.

Figure 10.7b displays the procedure to process all of the employee worksheets in the summary workbook and build the appropriate formulas on the summary worksheet. The procedure is easier to understand if we look first at the underlying logic as expressed in pseudocode. Consider the following:

> *Sets insertion point on Summary worksheet* — Select the cell for the first employee on the summary worksheet
>
> For each worksheet in the workbook
>   *Tests for employee worksheet* — If this is an employee worksheet
>   Store the name of this worksheet for use in a cell formula
>   Select the active cell in the summary worksheet
>   Enter the formula to reference cell D4 in the employee worksheet
>   Move one column to the right (on the summary worksheet)
>   Enter the formula for the total expenses in the employee worksheet
>   Move one column to the right (on the summary worksheet)
>   Enter the formula for the approval status in the employee worksheet
>   *Adjusts insertion point for next employee* — Move down one row and two columns to the left (for the next employee)
>   Insert a blank row to update the Sum function for the new employee
>   End If
> Next worksheet
>
> Delete extra blank row after all employees have been processed
> *Sorts Summary worksheet after all employees were added* — Sort the employees in alphabetical order

The procedure begins by selecting the cell that will contain the first employee on the summary worksheet, then it enters a loop to process all of the worksheets in the workbook. The first statement within the loop is an If statement to check that the worksheet is an employee worksheet; we do not want to copy information from the summary worksheet itself. We then build three formulas on the current row of the summary worksheet. The offset property is used to create a relative reference to various cells on this row; for example, Offset (0,1) refers to the cell on the same row, but one column to the right.

Each formula begins with a reference to the current worksheet name, which is then concatenated (joined) to the other parts of the formula. The ampersand indicates concatenation in the formula and joins one character string to another. After the third formula has been created, we drop down one row and move two columns to the left for the next employee. A blank row is inserted to accommodate this employee, and the loop continues.

After all of the employee data has been copied to the summary worksheet, we exit the loop and delete a superfluous blank line after the last employee. The employees are then displayed in alphabetical order by last name. The summary worksheet is complete.

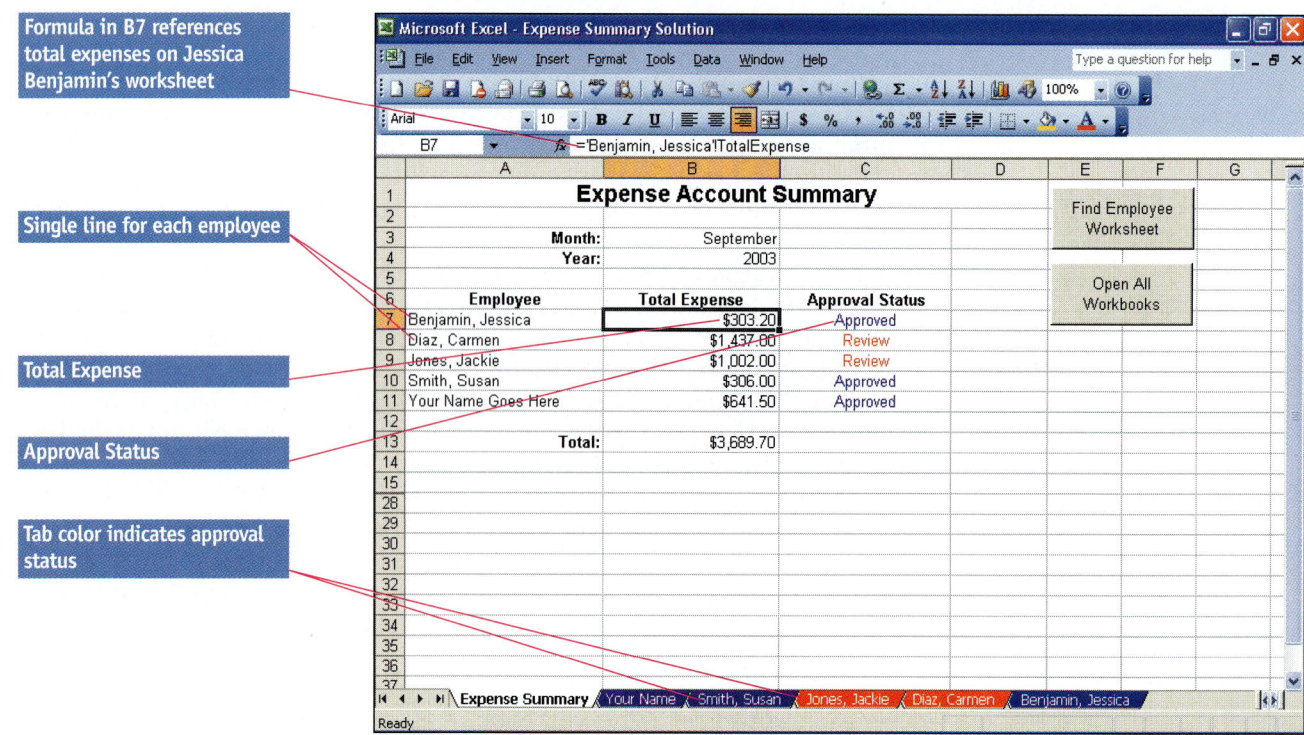

(a) The Summary Worksheet

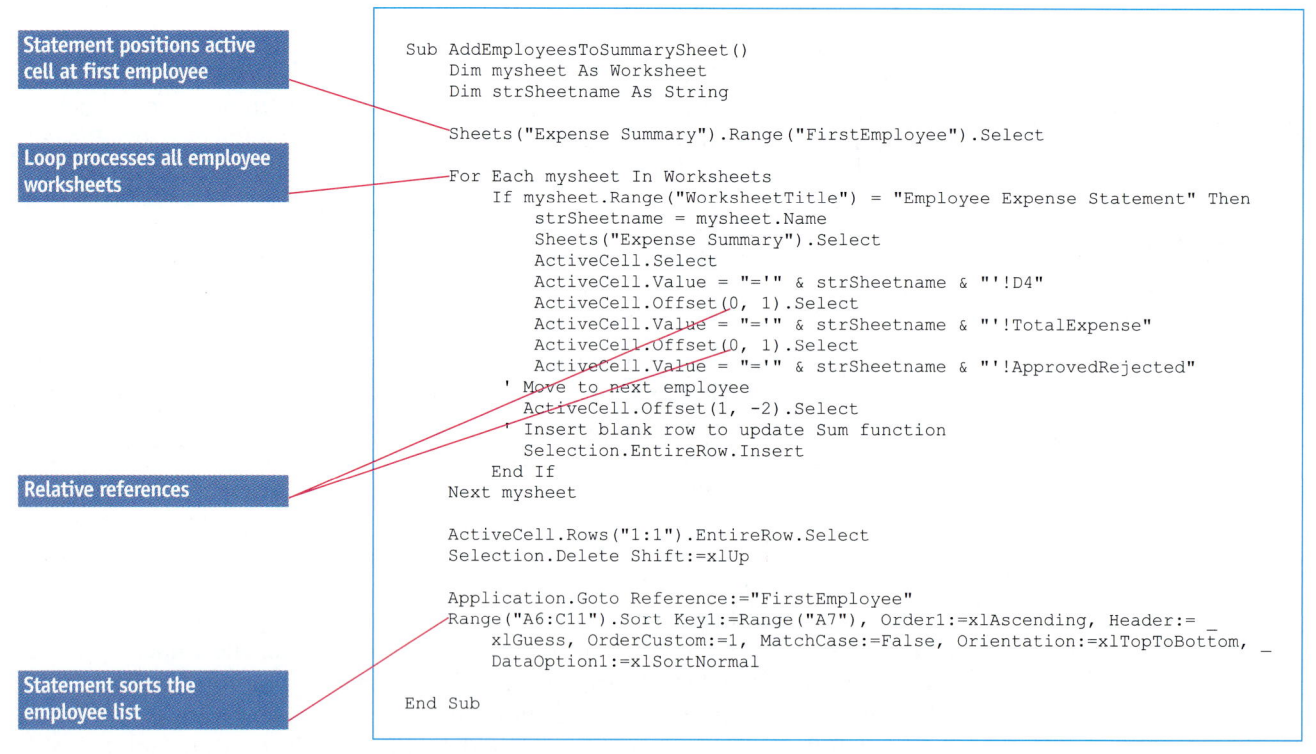

(b) VBA Procedure

FIGURE 10.7 Create the Summary Worksheet

hands-on exercise

3 Create the Summary Worksheet

Objective Create two procedures to process the worksheets in a workbook. Use Figure 10.8 as a guide in the exercise.

Step 1: **Start the Macro Recorder**

- Open the **Expense Summary Solution workbook** from the previous exercise. Enable the macros. Click the worksheet tab that contains your expenses.

- Click the **down arrow** in the Name box to see the range names that have been previously defined in this worksheet. Note the following:
  - The range name WorksheetTitle refers to cell C3, which contains the title of this worksheet, "Employee Expense Statement".
  - The range name ApprovedRejected refers to cell D25. This cell is presently blank, but it will contain an indication of whether the expenses are approved.
  - The range name TotalExpense refers to cell J23, which contains the total expenses for this employee.

- Pull down the **Tools menu**, click the **Macro command**, then click **Record New Macro** to display the Record Macro dialog box in Figure 10.8a.

- Enter **ReviewEmployeeExpenses** as the name of the procedure, enter the description shown, and then click **OK** to begin recording.

- Pull down the **Tools menu**, click **Protection**, then click **Unprotect Sheet**.

- If you are using Excel 2002 or a later release, right click the worksheet tab to display a context-sensitive menu, click **Tab Color** to display the Format Tab Color dialog box, click a **Blue square** from the palette, then click **OK**.

- Click the **Expense Summary worksheet tab**. Click the **Stop Recording button**.

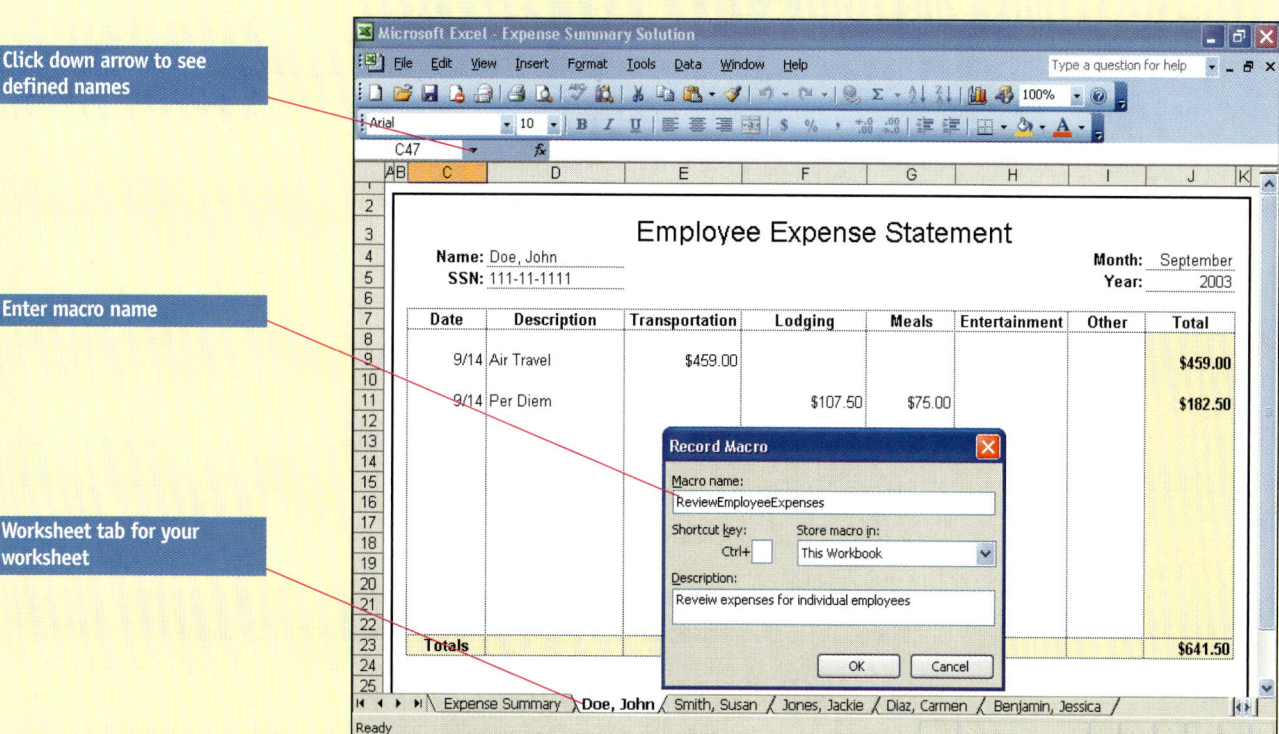

(a) Start the Macro Recorder (step 1)

FIGURE 10.8 Hands-on Exercise 3

Step 2: **Loops and Decision Making**

- Press **Alt+F11** to display the VBA editor. If necessary, pull down the **View menu** and click **Project Explorer** (or use the **Ctrl+r** keyboard shortcut) to display the Project Explorer window.
- Open the modules folder, then double click the last module that appears to display the procedures in that module. Locate the **ReviewEmployeeExpenses procedure** that you just created.
- Close Project Explorer. Your procedure contains only a few of the statements in Figure 10.8b. Proceed as follows:
  - Add the **Dim statement** at the beginning of the procedure to define the variable **mysheet**. Add the **For** and **Next statements** as shown in the figure.
  - Change Sheets("Your Name").Select, to **Sheets(mysheet.Name).Select**.
  - Add the **If** and **End If** statements to test for an employee worksheet.
  - Change the statement for tab color to **ActiveSheet.Tab.ColorIndex = 5**. (This statement will not appear in Office 2000.)
  - Add the statement to protect the worksheet. Check that your procedure matches Figure 10.8b. Save the procedure.
- Click in the procedure, then click the **RunSub button** to run the procedure, then click the **Excel button** to see the results. All of the worksheet tabs (except the summary tab) should be blue. Save the workbook.

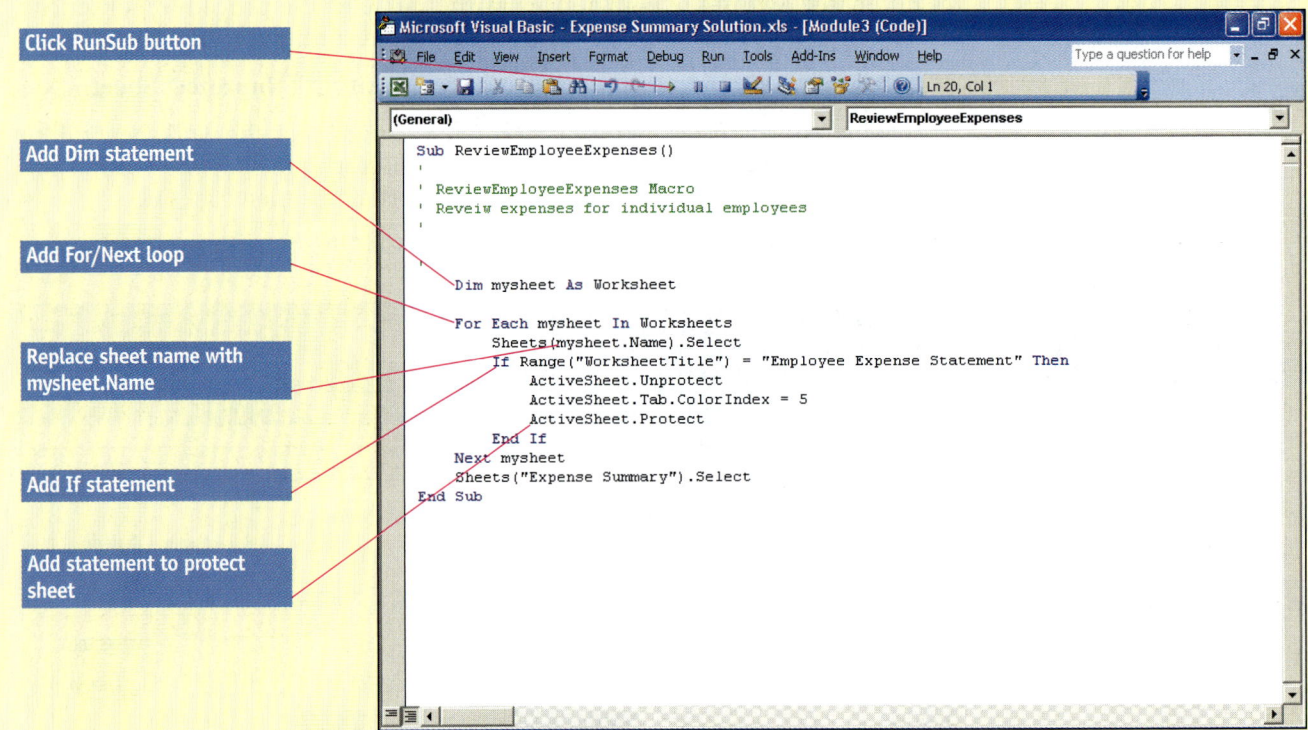

(b) Loops and Decision Making (step 2)

FIGURE 10.8 Hands-on Exercise 3 (*continued*)

CHANGE THE COLOR OF A WORKSHEET TAB

The ability to change the color of a worksheet tab was introduced in Excel 2002. The tab color can be changed in two ways—in VBA by setting the Tab.ColorIndex property and/or from the Excel interface. (Right click the tab, click the Tab Color command to display the associated dialog box, select a color, and click OK.) The feature does not exist in Excel 2000.

Step 3: **Complete the Procedure**

- Return to the VBA editor to complete the procedure as shown in Figure 10.8c. Add a second **Dim statement** to define the **curMaxApprovedExpense** variable. Add **the Input Box function** to prompt the user for the value of this variable.

- Add the second (nested) **If statement** to compare the value in the range named "TotalExpenses" to the maximum approved expense, then take the appropriate action. Enter **"Approved"** in the range named "ApprovedRejected" if the expenses are less than or equal to the maximum amount.

- Add the **Else clause**, which enters "Review" in the range named "ApprovedRejected" and changes the tab color to red if the expenses are greater than the threshold amount. (A color index of 3 changes the worksheet tab to red.)

- Add the **End If** delimiter to complete the statement. Save the procedure. Run the procedure. Enter **$1,000** when prompted for the maximum expense.

- Click the **View Microsoft Excel button** to view the workbook, which should contain a combination of red and blue worksheet tabs. Click any blue tab (e.g., Susan Smith) and you should see an approved message at the bottom of the worksheet. Click any red tab (e.g., Jackie Jones) and you should see the review message.

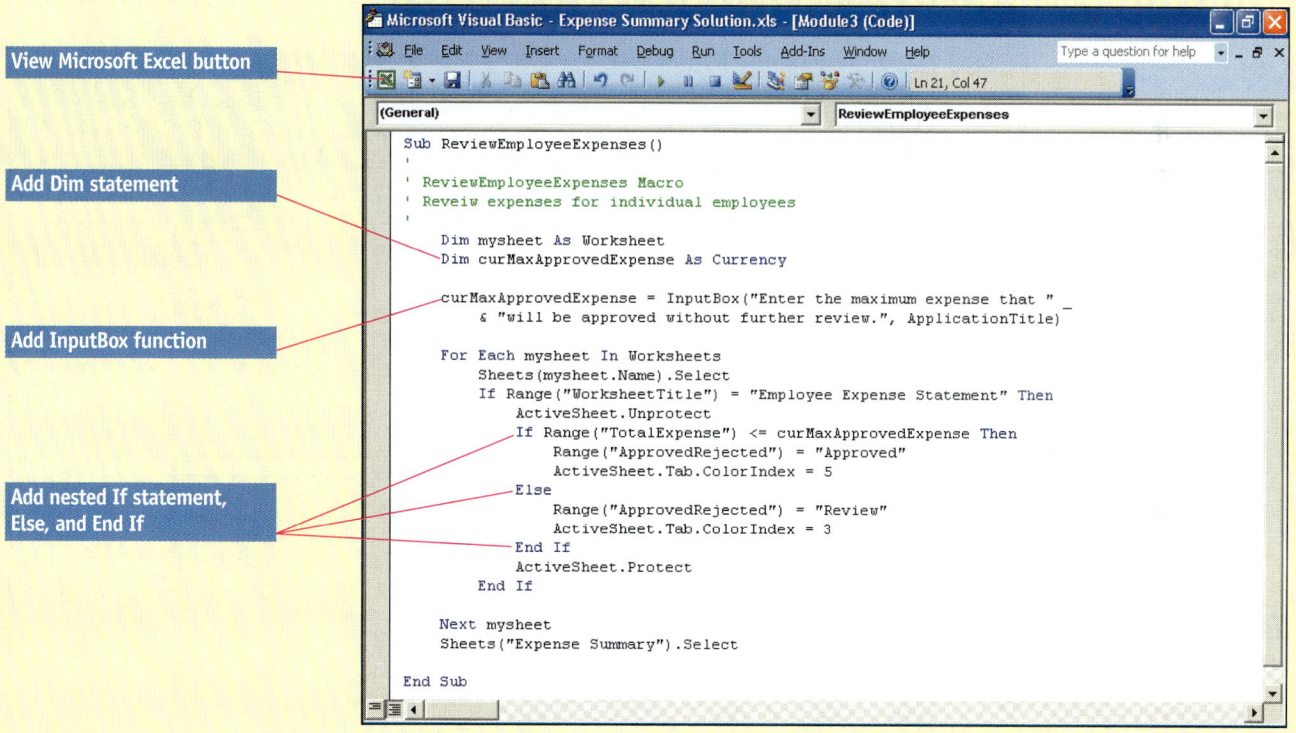

(c) Complete the Procedure (step 3)

FIGURE 10.8 Hands-on Exercise 3 (*continued*)

NESTED IF STATEMENTS

A nested If statement (or an If within an If) is easy to understand if you indent properly and follow basic syntax. Recall that an ordinary If statement tests a condition, then follows one of two paths, depending on whether the condition is true or false. The If statement must end with the End If delimiter, but the Else clause is optional. A nested If simply adds another If statement to either path. Each If (within the nested If) has its own End If delimiter. Indentation is used to make the statement easier to read.

Step 4: **Step through a Procedure**

- Return to the VBA editor. Pull down the **View menu** to display the Project Explorer window, then double click **Module1** to open its code window. Locate the **AddEmployeesToSummarySheet** procedure. Close Project Explorer.

- Point to a blank area at the right of the Windows taskbar and then click the **right mouse button**. Click the command to **Show the Desktop**.

- Click the **VBA** and **Excel buttons** on the taskbar to reopen these windows. Right click a blank area of the taskbar a second time, then click the command to **Tile Windows Vertically**.

- Your desktop should be similar to Figure 10.8d. Click in the Excel window, then click on the **Expense Summary tab** to select that worksheet. Click in the window containing the VBA editor. Click after the **Sub statement**.

- Press the **F8 key**. The procedure header is highlighted. Press the **F8 key** a second time. The Sheets("Expense Summary").Range("FirstEmployee").Select statement is highlighted.

- Continue to press the **F8 key** to view the progress of the procedure as it is executed one statement at a time. Each employee worksheet is selected in succession, and the appropriate information is moved to the summary worksheet.

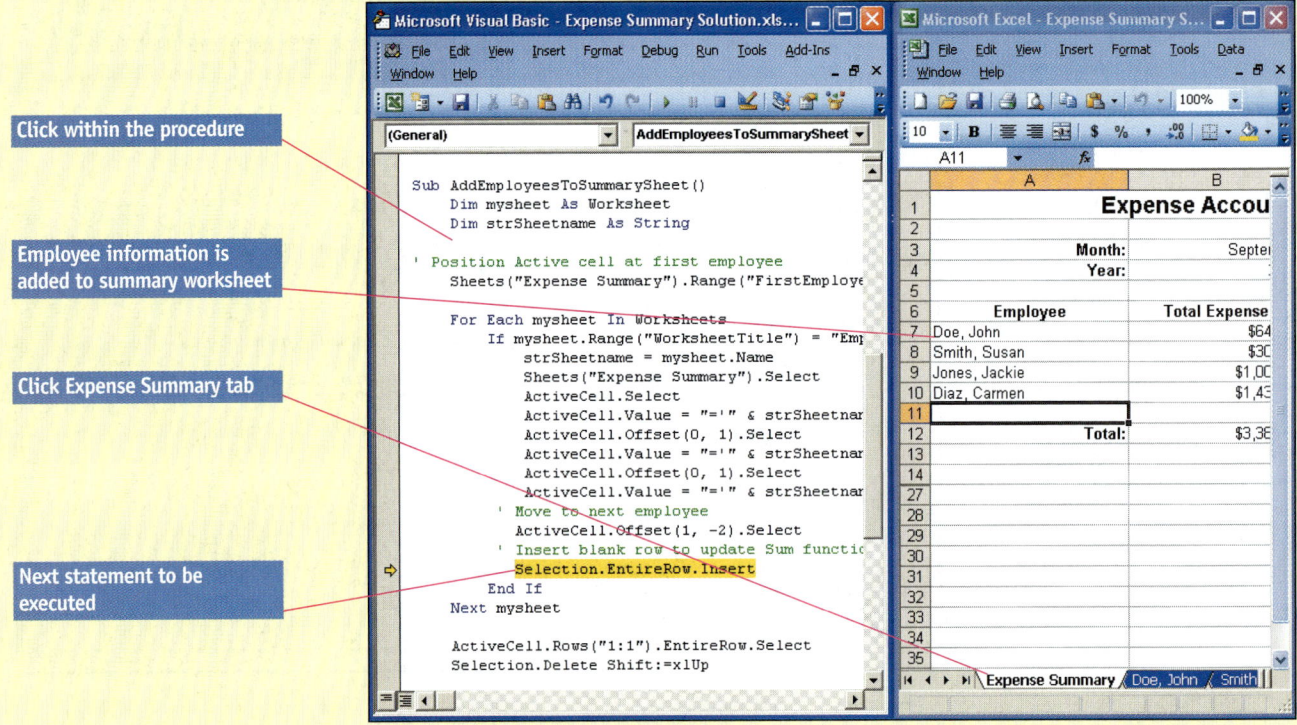

(d) Step through a Procedure (step 4)

FIGURE 10.8 Hands-on Exercise 3 (*continued*)

RELATIVE REFERENCES—THE OFFSET PROPERTY

The Offset property returns a range of cells that is offset (displaced) from the active cell by a designated number of rows and columns; for example, ActiveCell.Offset(0,1).Range("A1").Select selects the cell in the same row and one column to the right of the active cell. The Range object may be omitted if you are selecting only a single cell.

Step 5: **Check Your Progress**

- Maximize the Excel window to check your progress as shown in Figure 10.8e. The total expense for each employee as well as the approval status has been copied to the summary worksheet. The color of the worksheet tabs corresponds to the approval status for each employee.

- Click in any cell in the body of the worksheet—for example, **cell B8**, which contains the total expenses for Susan Smith on our worksheet. Look at the formula bar to see the contents of this cell, ='Smith, Susan'!TotalExpense.

- The employees are not yet in alphabetical order. We could sort the employees at this point, without modifying the existing procedure. We want the procedure to include this function, however, and so we will use the macro recorder to obtain these commands.

- Pull down the **Tools menu**, click the **Macro command**, then click **Record New Macro** to display the Record Macro dialog box. Enter **Dummy** as the name of the procedure. The keyboard shortcut and description are optional. Click **OK**.

- Click the **down arrow** in the Name box and select **FirstEmployee**. Click the **Sort Ascending button**. Click the **Stop Recording button**.

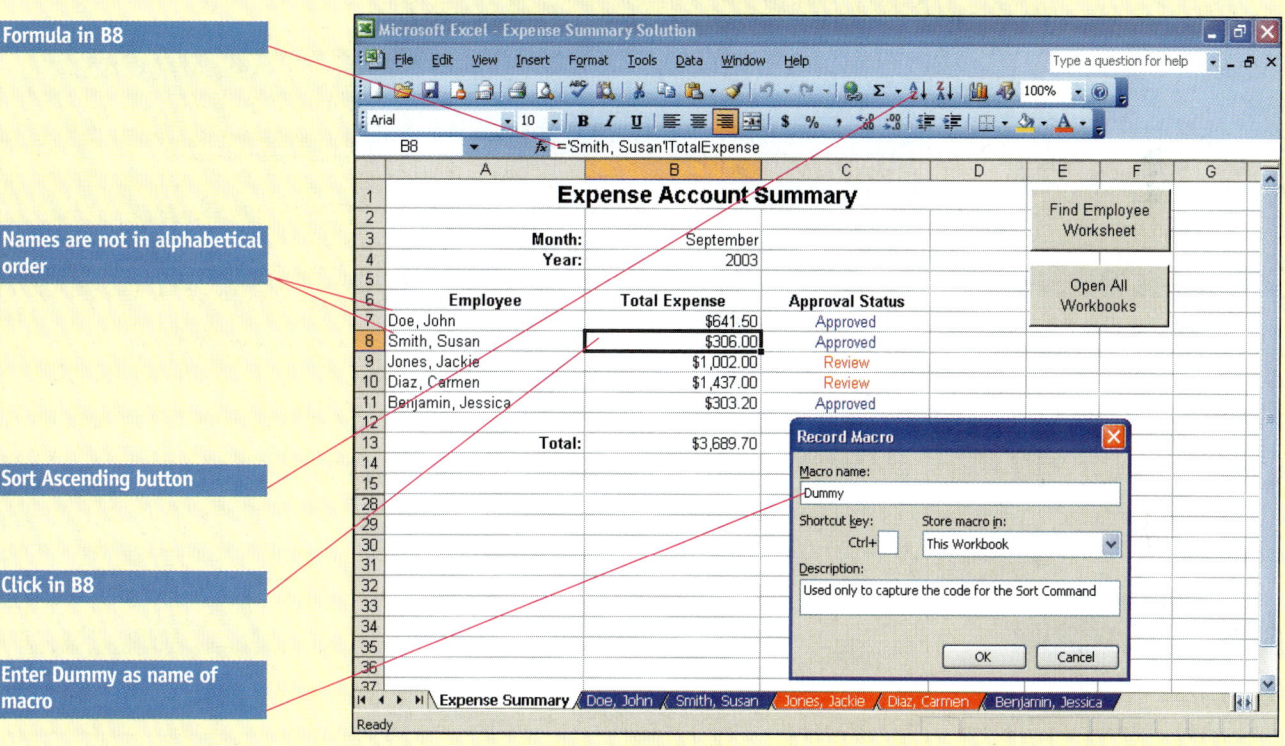

(e) Check Your Progress (step 5)

FIGURE 10.8 Hands-on Exercise 3 (*continued*)

WORKSHEET REFERENCES—THE EXCLAMATION MARK

An Excel formula may reference cells in other worksheets, in which case you need to include the name of the worksheet with the cell address; for example, =Sheet4!A1, references cell A1 in the worksheet called Sheet4. The name of the worksheet is always followed by an exclamation point. The cell reference, A1, may be replaced by a named range such as TotalExpense. The name of the worksheet is enclosed in apostrophes if it (the worksheet name) contains a space, as in 'Smith, Susan'!TotalExpense.

MICROSOFT OFFICE EXCEL 2003   1509

Step 6: **Complete the Procedure**

- Press **Alt+F11** to return to the VBA editor. Maximize the window. Open Project Explorer and double click the module that contains the newly recorded Dummy procedure.

- Click and drag to select the four lines of code in that procedure. You will see a statement to select the cell called "FirstEmployee", followed by a Sort statement that is continued over several lines. Select all four lines.

- Click the **Copy button** on the Standard toolbar or use the **Ctrl+C** keyboard shortcut to copy these statements to the clipboard.

- Switch to the **AddEmployeesToSummarySheet** procedure on Module1 that you were working on earlier. Click to the left of the **End Sub** statement and press the **Enter key** to insert a blank line, then click the **up arrow key** to move to the blank line.

- Click the **Paste button** or use the **Ctrl+V** keyboard shortcut. Close Project Explorer. The statements from the Dummy procedure should appear as shown in Figure 10.8f.

- Save the procedure.

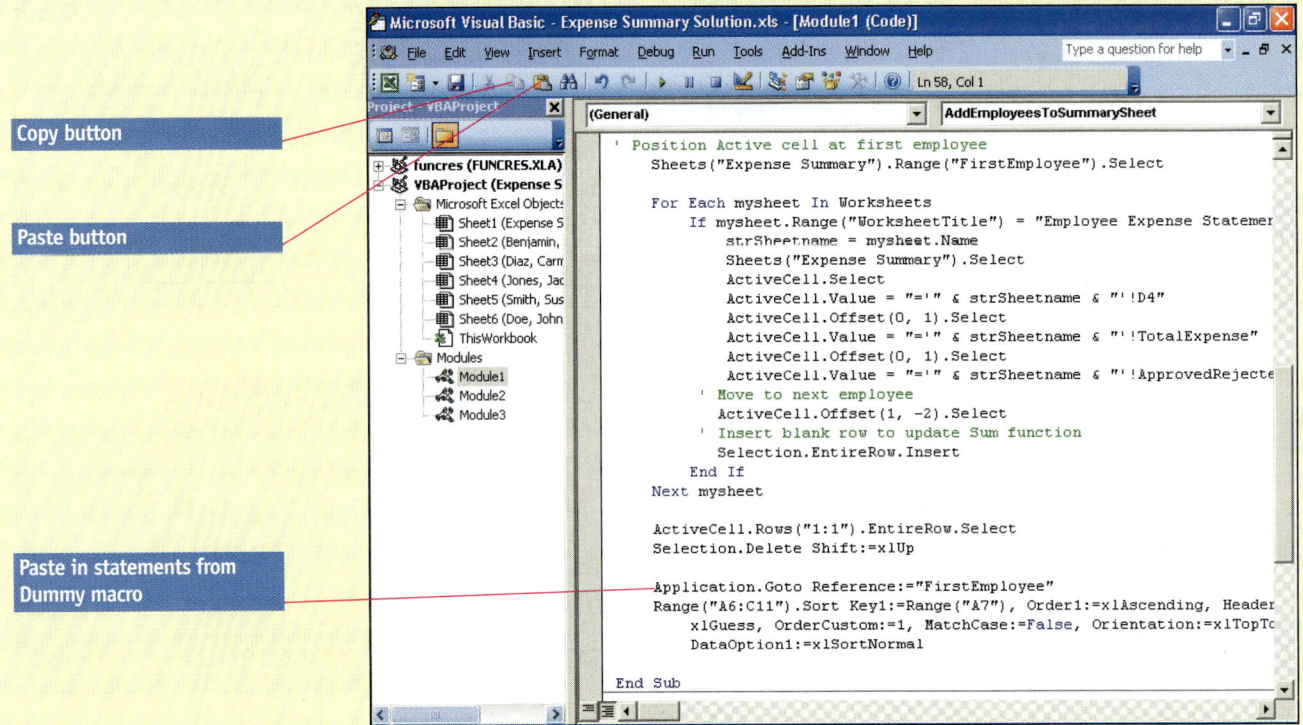

(f) Complete the Procedure (step 6)

FIGURE 10.8 Hands-on Exercise 3 (*continued*)

> **BE FLEXIBLE AND USE WHAT YOU KNOW**
>
> There is no single way to create a VBA procedure. You can use the Excel macro recorder to "jump-start" the process to obtain the syntax for lesser-known VBA statements. You can also create a procedure by entering code directly into the VBA editor. Once you have the procedure, you can return to the macro recorder to capture additional statements you may not have thought of initially. Be flexible and use the editing techniques that you learned in other applications.

Step 7: **Test the Completed Procedure**

- Click the **Excel button** to return to the Excel worksheet, where you can test the completed procedure. First, however, you need to delete and/or clear the rows containing the employee information. Thus:
  - Click and drag to select **rows 8 through 11** (do not select row 7) as shown in Figure 10.8g. Right click the selected rows to display the context-sensitive menu, then click the **Delete command** to remove these rows.
  - Click and drag to select the entries in **row 7**. Press the **Del key** to erase the contents of these cells—the cells, however, remain in the workbook.
  - Click in **cell A7**. Be sure that the Name box contains the reference FirstEmployee (since this reference is used in a VBA procedure).
  - Click in **cell B9**. Be sure that this cell contains the formula =Sum(B7:B8).
- Pull down the **Tools menu** and rerun the **AddEmployeesToSummarySheet** procedure. The employee data is added to the worksheet, but this time the employees should be in alphabetical order.
- Save the workbook.

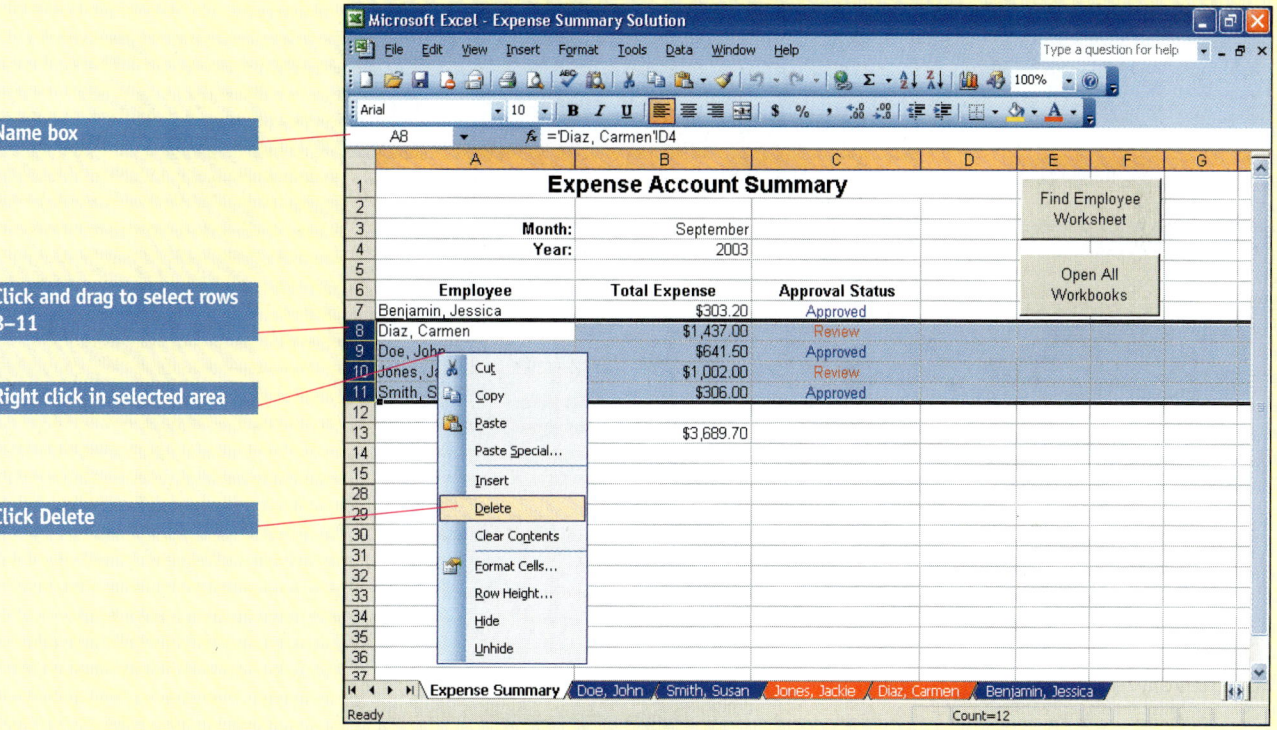

(g) Test the Completed Procedure (step 7)

FIGURE 10.8 Hands-on Exercise 3 (*continued*)

KEYBOARD SHORTCUTS

We have created a procedure to reset (clear) the Summary worksheet and have assigned the keyboard shortcut Ctrl+r to that procedure. You can test this procedure in conjunction with the procedure to add the employee data to the summary worksheet. Thus, press Ctrl+a to add the employee data, then press Ctrl+r to clear the summary data. You can execute the latter procedure several times in succession. The first procedure should be executed only once; that is, if you add the employee data twice in a row, you will wind up with duplicate rows for each employee.

Step 8: **Print the Cell Formulas**

- Press **Ctrl+~** to display the cell formulas as shown in Figure 10.8h. (Press **Ctrl+~** a second time to return to the displayed values.)

- Click and drag to select the row headers for **rows 15 through 28** (rows 16 through 27 are currently hidden). Right click the selected rows, then click the **Unhide command** to display these cells.

- Click in **cell B3**, the cell containing the month for which the expenses were submitted. Note how the VLOOKUP function uses the data in rows 16 to 27 to display the current month.

- Click and drag to adjust the column widths. Pull down the **File menu**, select the **Page Setup command** and switch to **Landscape printing**. Select the **scaling option** to force the output onto one page. Print the formulas for the summary worksheet.

- Close the workbook. Do not save the workbook when the cell formulas are displayed. Exit Excel if you do not want to continue with the next hands-on exercise at this time.

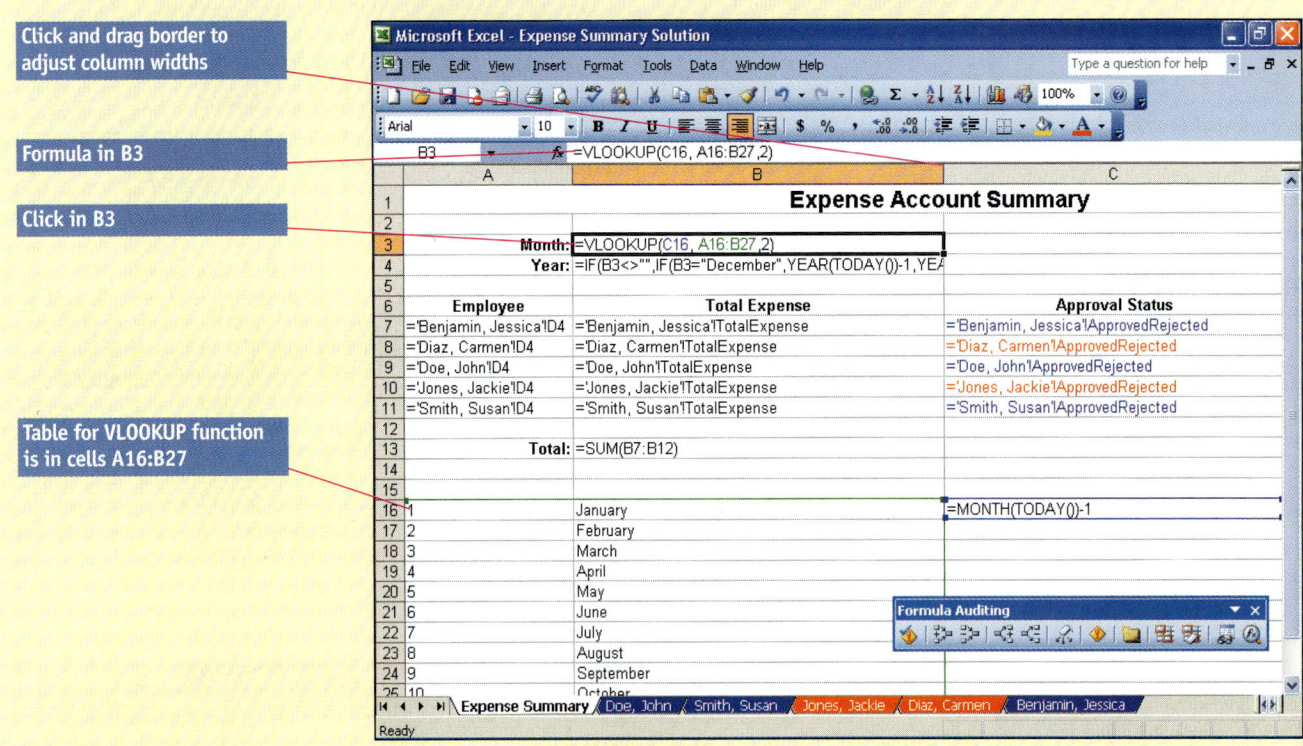

(h) Print the Cell Formulas (step 8)

FIGURE 10.8 Hands-on Exercise 3 (continued)

PRINT THE CELL FORMULAS—THE PAGE SETUP COMMAND

A worksheet should always be printed twice—once to show the displayed values and once to show the underlying cell formulas. Use the keyboard shortcut, Ctrl+~ to toggle between the two. Pull down the File menu and click the Page Setup command to change settings as necessary, when printing the cell formulas. You may want to change the orientation, column width, and/or margins.

A BETTER SUMMARY WORKBOOK

The summary workbook is finished, but you had to complete three hands-on exercises to accomplish that task. First, you had to open each individual workbook to copy the information for that employee to a new worksheet in the summary workbook. Next, you had to review the expenses on each worksheet within the summary workbook, and finally, you had to add the individual employee data to the summary worksheet. It would be much easier if you could execute a single procedure and with one click of the mouse, create the entire workbook. This is accomplished by creating a simple procedure that calls the three procedures (you ran individually) as shown below:

> *Three procedures are executed in succession*

```
Public Sub CreateSummaryWorkbook()
    OpenAllWorkbooks
    ReviewEmployeeExpenses
    AddEmployeesToSummarySheet
End Sub
```

The CreateSummaryWorkbook procedure calls three procedures in succession, resulting in the completed summary workbook. The subordinate procedures may reside in the same module or in different modules provided that they have been defined as public procedures. The ***scope*** of a procedure refers to its availability or use by another procedure. ***Public procedures*** are available to any procedure in any module. ***Private procedures*** are available only to other procedures in the same module.

What if, however, the OpenAllWorkbooks procedure was unable to locate the folder containing the individual employee workbooks? It would be pointless to run the subsequent procedures because the summary worksheet would not contain any employee data. Accordingly, we modified the CreateSummaryWorkbook procedure to include an If statement to check that the number of worksheets in the summary workbook is greater than one (i.e., that the summary workbook contains the individual employee worksheets), and if so, it executes the next two procedures. (There is no need to include an error message since the OpenAllWorkbooks procedure contains its own error message if it is unsuccessful.) The modified procedure becomes:

> *These procedures are executed provided there is at least one employee worksheet*

```
Public Sub CreateSummaryWorkbook()
    OpenAllWorkbooks
    If Worksheets.Count > 1
        ReviewEmployeeExpenses
        AddEmployeesToSummarySheet
    End If
End Sub
```

The workbook in Figure 10.9a displays the "empty" summary workbook prior to adding the employee information. The user clicks the Create Summary Workbook command button to execute the associated procedure, which runs the three individual procedures, one after the other.

Look closely at the input box in Figure 10.9a, which is displayed by a modified OpenAllWorkbooks procedure in Figure 10.9b. The user is prompted to enter the path of the folder that contains the employee workbooks. This is a more general approach than was used in the first hands-on exercise in which the name of the folder was coded directly into the macro. The user's response (the name of the folder) is stored in the variable strPathName, which becomes an argument in the subsequent Dir statements. The end result is a flexible procedure that lets the user specify where the individual expense statements are stored.

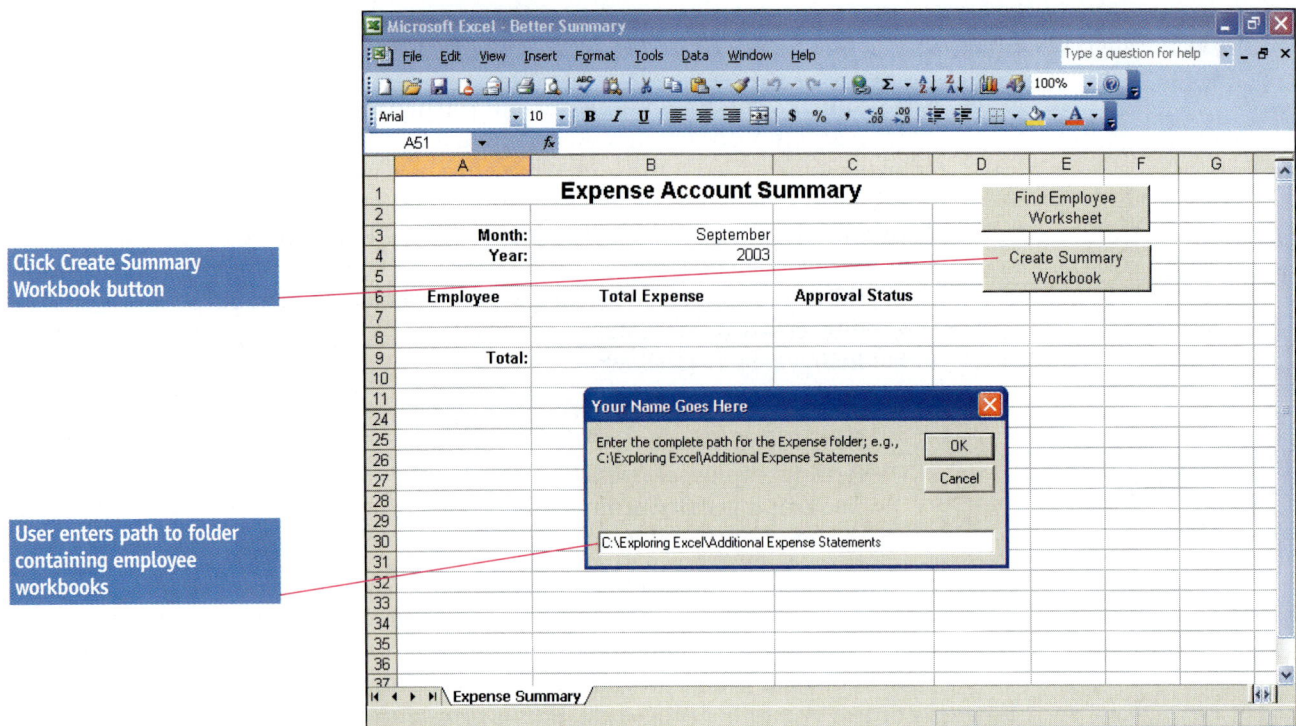

(a) Variable Input Folder

```
Public Sub ModifiedOpenWorkbooks()
    Dim strWorkbookName As String
    Dim strThisWorkbookName As String
    Dim strPathName As String

    strThisWorkbookName = ActiveWorkbook.Name
    strPathName = InputBox("Enter the complete path for the Expense folder; " _
        & "e.g., C:\Exploring Excel\Additional Expense Statements", _
            ApplicationTitle)

    strWorkbookName = Dir(strPathName & "\*.xls")
    If Len(strWorkbookName) > 0 Then
        Do While Len(strWorkbookName) > 0
            Workbooks.Open Filename:= _
                strPathName & "\" & strWorkbookName
            Sheets(1).Select
            Sheets(1).Copy After:=Workbooks(strThisWorkbookName).Sheets(1)
            Workbooks(strWorkbookName).Close
            strWorkbookName = Dir
        Loop
    Else
        MsgBox "Error - The folder " & strPathName & " does not exist. " _
            & "Please check the folder name and then rerun the macro.", _
                vbCritical, ApplicationTitle
    End If

End Sub
```

(b) The VBA Procedure

FIGURE 10.9 An Improved Summary Worksheet

hands-on exercise
4   A Better Summary Workbook

Objective Use a modified version of the Expense Summary workbook with additional flexibility and automation. Use Figure 10.10 as a guide in the exercise.

Step 1: **Open the Better Workbook**

- Open the **Better Summary workbook** in the Exploring Excel folder. Click the button to **Enable Macros** in response to the security warning.
- You will see the message box in Figure 10.10a. Click **No**. You will see a second message indicating that you can run the procedure at a later time. Click **OK**.
- Save the workbook as **Better Summary Solution** so that you can return to the original workbook if necessary.
- The Better Summary workbook contains a single (empty) summary worksheet and parallels the Expense Summary workbook you were using earlier. The command buttons correspond to the command buttons that you added in a previous hands-on exercise.
- The previous month (the month for which expenses are submitted) is determined automatically using Date functions. The year is also entered automatically.

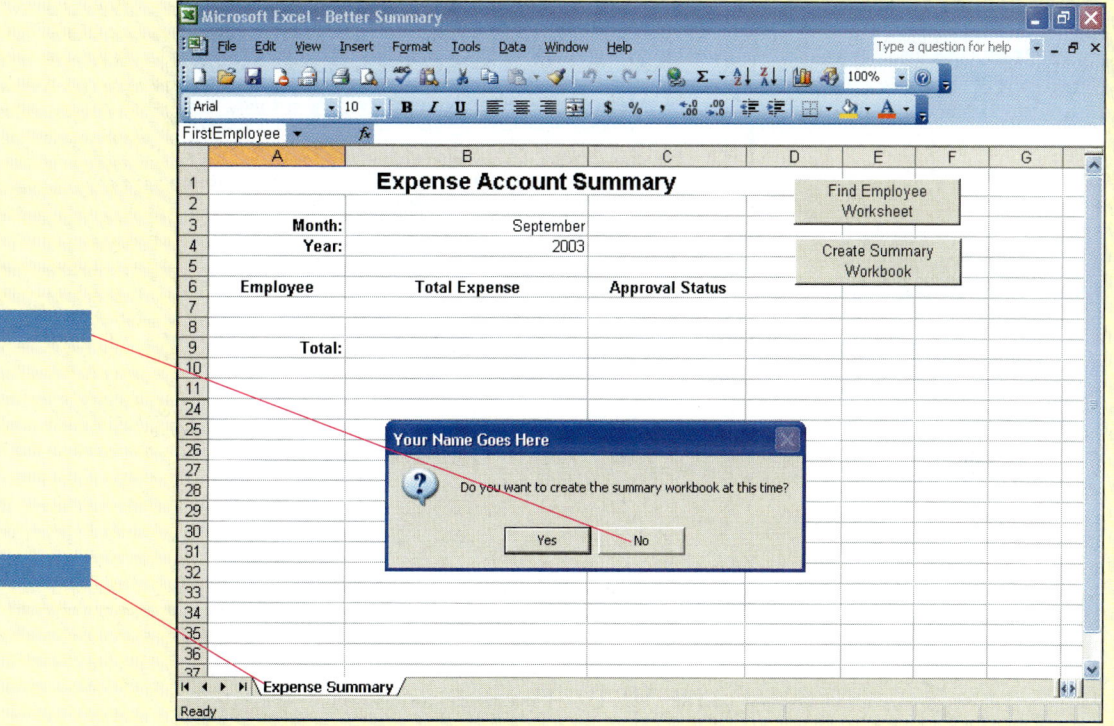

(a) Open the Better Workbook (step 1)

FIGURE 10.10   Hands-on Exercise 4

A BETTER SUMMARY WORKBOOK

The workbook in this exercise improves on its predecessor in two important ways. It is more general because it enables the user to enter the folder containing the employee workbooks, verifies that the folder exists, and displays an error message if it doesn't. It is also easier to use because the summary workbook is created with a single mouse click, as opposed to executing multiple procedures.

Step 2: **Event Procedures**

- Press **Alt+F11** to open the VBA Editor. Maximize this window. If necessary, pull down the **View menu** to display the Project Explorer window.
- Double click **ThisWorkbook** within the list of Excel objects to display the event procedures for this workbook as shown in Figure 10.10b. (The BeforeClose event procedure has not yet been created.) Close Project Explorer.
- Look at the Open Workbook event procedure. The MsgBox function asks the user whether to create the summary workbook, and if so, runs a general procedure called CreateSummaryWorkbook. (We examine this procedure in step 3.)
- If necessary, click the **down arrow** on the Object list box and select **Workbook**. Click the **down arrow** on the Procedure list box and select the **BeforeClose** event to create this event procedure.
- Enter the statements in the BeforeClose event procedure as shown in Figure 10.10b. Save the workbook. Click the **Close button** to close the window containing the event procedures.

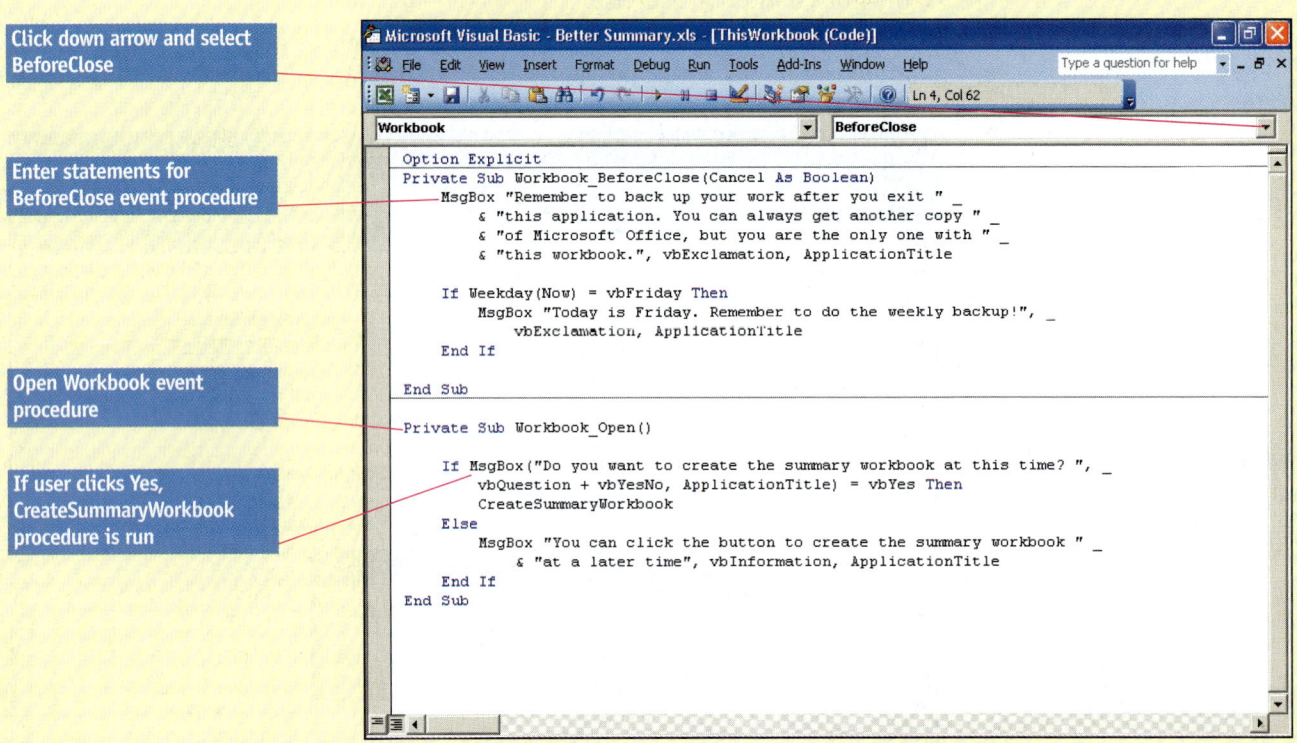

(b) Event Procedures (step 2)

FIGURE 10.10 Hands-on Exercise 4 (*continued*)

DAYS OF THE WEEK—INTRINSIC CONSTANTS

You can test for a specific day of the week using a combination of the Weekday and Now functions in conjunction with VBA intrinsic (predefined) constants. The Now function returns today's date. Thus, the expression Weekday(Now) returns today's day, which is then compared to a specific day of the week such as vbFriday. In other words, the condition in the If statement will be considered true if today is Friday. Use the Help function in VBA to search for other sets of intrinsic constants.

Step 3: **Test the CreateSummaryWorkbook Procedure**

- Open Project Explorer. Double click **Module1** to display the code for this module. Maximize the code window. Close Project Explorer.

- Click within the **CreateSummaryWorkbook procedure**, then click the **Procedure View button** at the bottom of the window to display one procedure at a time. (Use the **PgUp** and **PgDn keys** to move between procedures.)

- Right click an empty area of the taskbar, then click the **Show the Desktop command**. Click the Excel and VBA buttons to reopen these windows.

- Right click the taskbar a second time and click the **Tile Windows Vertically command** to display the windows as shown in Figure 10.10c. Close Project Explorer.

- Click the **Run button** on the VBA standard toolbar. Enter an **invalid folder** when prompted for the name of the folder that contains the expense statements. Click **OK**. You will see the error message in Figure 10.10c. Click **OK**.

- Rerun the **CreateSummaryWorkbook** procedure, but this time, enter the correct folder, **C:\Exploring Excel\Additional Expense Statements**. Click **Yes** when prompted to save each employee workbook.

- You will be asked for the maximum expense. Enter **$1,000**. Click **OK**. The summary workbook is created for you.

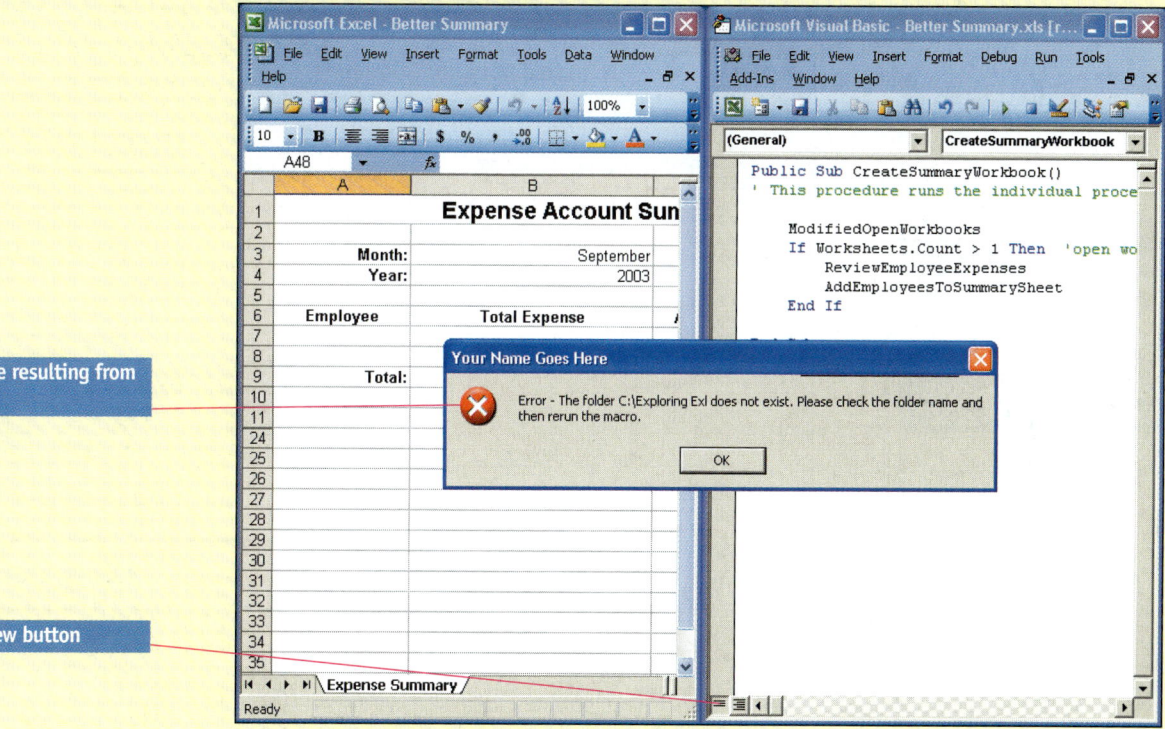

(c) Test the CreateSummaryWorkbook Procedure (step 3)

FIGURE 10.10 Hands-on Exercise 4 (*continued*)

OBJECTS, COLLECTIONS, AND PROPERTIES

A collection is a set of similar objects. For example, the worksheets collection is the set of worksheets in a workbook. Collections, like objects, have properties that can be tested. The statement If Worksheets.Count > 1 in our procedure is testing the Count property of the Worksheets collection to ensure that there are multiple worksheets within the workbook before executing the next two commands.

Step 4: **Find an Employee's Worksheet**

- Maximize the Excel window. You should see the summary worksheet with the employees listed in alphabetical order as shown in Figure 10.10d. (The input box is not yet visible.)

- The names in the worksheet are different from those in the earlier exercise because we used a different folder to obtain the employee workbooks.

- Save the workbook. Print the summary worksheet for your instructor as proof you completed the exercise.

- Click the button to **Find Employee Worksheet**. Disregard the message in the box and enter only the employee's last name; for example, enter **Beesaw**, then click **OK**. You will see an error message indicating that the specified employee does not exist.

- Click **OK** in response to the error message. Click the **Find Employee Worksheet button** a second time, and enter the name correctly as shown in Figure 10.10d. Click **OK**.

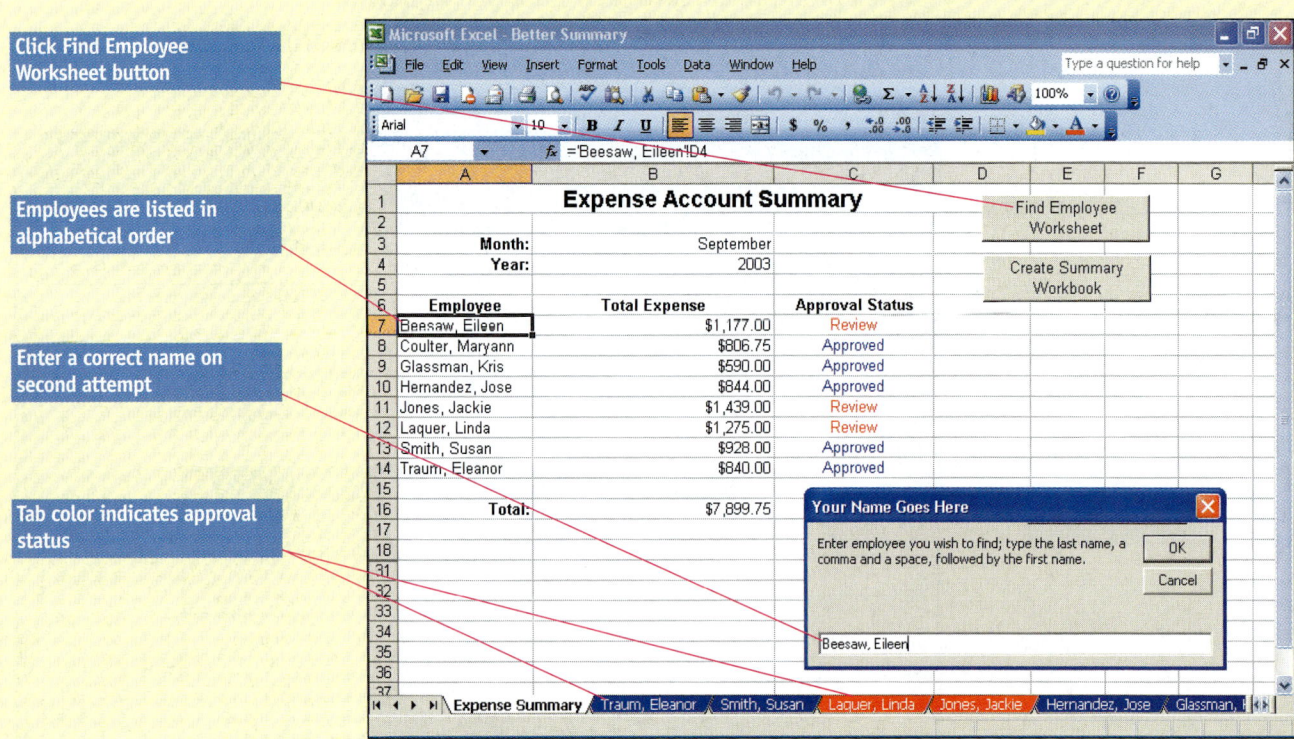

(d) Find an Employee's Worksheet (step 4)

FIGURE 10.10 Hands-on Exercise 4 (*continued*)

ENTER THE EMPLOYEE'S LAST NAME

The existing procedure requires you to enter the employee's complete name in a precise syntax. What if, however, you know only the last name? You can develop an alternate procedure to prompt the user for the employee's last name, then search through the workbook to see if any worksheet tab contains that name. The resulting procedure will be driven by a For...Next statement to process all of the worksheets within the workbook. It also requires elementary string processing to search for the last name within the combination of first and last name that appears on the worksheet tab. See exercise 3 at the end of the chapter.

Step 5: **Exit the Application**

- You should see the worksheet for Eileen Beesaw as shown in Figure 10.10e. Note the indication to review Eileen's expenses at the bottom of the worksheet is consistent with the red color of the worksheet tab.

- Take a minute to review all that was accomplished in this exercise.
  - You opened the Better Summary workbook and were asked if you wanted to create the summary workbook. If you answered yes, you were asked to enter the name of the folder that contained the employee workbooks.
  - Each employee workbook was opened automatically, the worksheets were copied to the summary workbook, the expenses on the individual worksheets were evaluated, and the associated information was copied to the summary worksheet.
  - You were able to display an employee worksheet that needed review.
  - The BeforeClose event procedure reminds the user to back up the workbook.

- Press **Alt+F11** to switch to the VBA editor. Print the event procedures as well as the procedures in Module1 for your instructor. Close the VBA window.

- Exit Excel. Congratulations on a job well done.

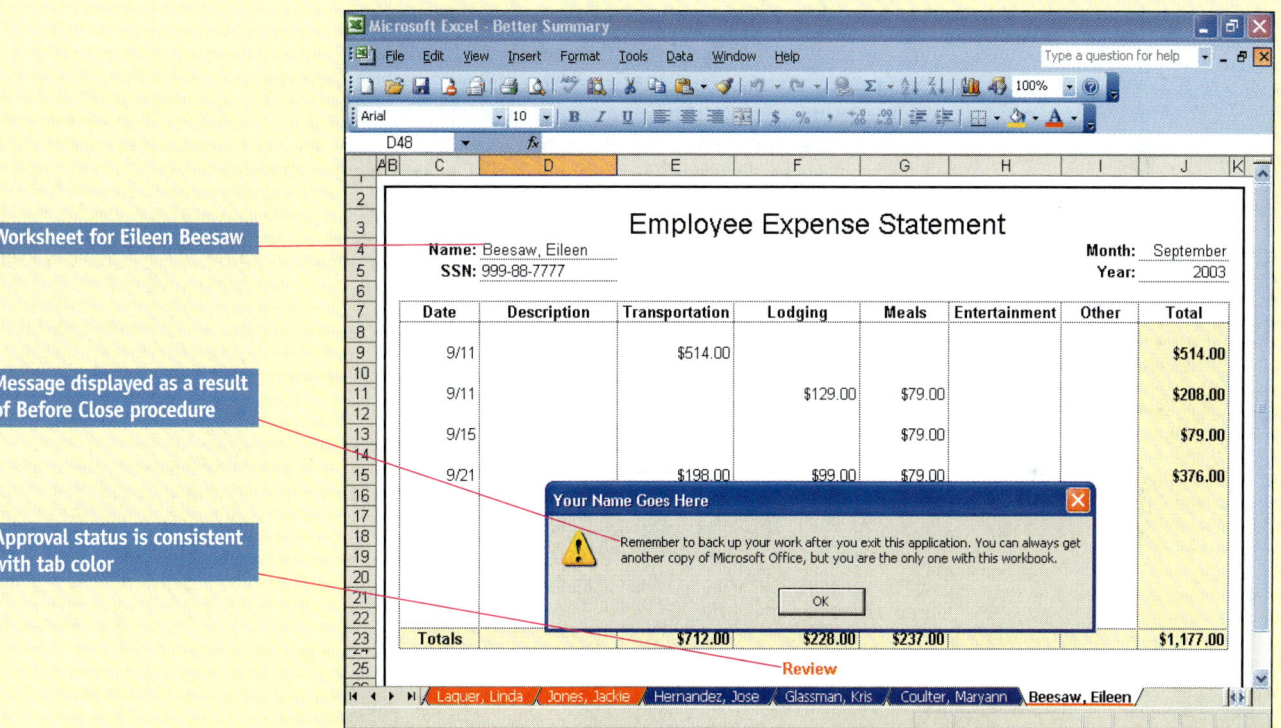

(e) Exit the Application (step 5)

FIGURE 10.10   Hands-on Exercise 4 (*continued*)

PRINT THE PROCEDURES FROM MICROSOFT WORD

The Print command within the VBA editor will print all of the procedures in the current module or in the entire project. The command is limited, however, in that it prints the procedures without formatting of any kind, and thus we find it helpful to print the final version of our procedures using Microsoft Word. The end result is a more polished document from which to study. See exercise 6 at the end of the chapter.

MICROSOFT OFFICE EXCEL 2003   1519

SUMMARY

The chapter developed an Excel application to process employee expenses that exist initially in individual workbooks. The overall objective is to automate the process of consolidating data from different sources. A "divide and conquer" approach is used to divide a complex task into smaller, more manageable tasks. The end result is an "empty" summary workbook that contains multiple VBA procedures to accomplish the objective. These procedures include several VBA statements that do not have equivalent Excel menu commands such as MsgBox, InputBox, If…Else, For…Next, Do Until, and Do While. (The VBA primer at the end of the text contains detailed information on these statements.)

The reader is presented with an expense statement workbook at the beginning of the chapter and asked to enter a set of hypothetical expenses to gain familiarity with the application. The completed workbook is then saved in an Expense Statement folder that contains additional workbooks from other employees, which in turn will be incorporated into the summary workbook.

The Visual Basic Dir function is used to process all of the workbooks in the Expense Statement folder. The first time this function is called, it returns the name of the first file in the folder, then each subsequent time the function is called, it returns the next file (if any) in the same folder. Eventually no additional files are found and the function returns a null value. The Dir function is incorporated into a loop that opens each individual workbook, then copies the information from that workbook onto a worksheet in the summary workbook.

Two additional procedures are developed to process the employee worksheets once they have been added to the summary workbook. The first procedure evaluates the expenses on each worksheet to indicate immediate approval or further review. Conditional formatting is used to display the approved or rejected expenses in blue or red, respectively. The color of the worksheet tab is also changed to reflect the approval status. A second procedure then copies information from the individual worksheets to a summary worksheet.

Both procedures use the For…Next statement to process all of the worksheets within the worksheets collection (i.e., with a specified workbook). The three procedures to create the summary workbook may be executed individually (as was done in the first three hands-on exercises). The procedures may also be executed collectively from a single procedure as illustrated in the fourth hands-on exercise.

The scope of a procedure or variable refers to its availability or use by another procedure. Public procedures are available to any procedure in any module. Private procedures are available only to other procedures in the same module.

A procedure was also developed to display a specific worksheet. The user is prompted for the employee's first and last name, after which the worksheet is displayed, provided the information was entered correctly. The procedure also introduces error processing in the event that the worksheet cannot be found. This is accomplished through the On Error statement that transfers control to a special error-handling section at the end of the procedure.

KEY TERMS

Conditional Formatting 1503	Exit Sub statement 1493	On Error statement 1493
Debugging 1491	For…Next statement 1485	Private procedure 1513
Dim statement 1485	If…Then…Else statement 1485	Public procedure 1513
Dir function 1486	InputBox function 1485	Run-time error 1493
Do Until statement 1485	Intrinsic constant 1516	Scope 1513
Do While statement 1485	Len function 1486	Syntax error 1493
Error Trapping 1493	MsgBox statement 1485	Worksheet object 1493

MULTIPLE CHOICE

1. The statement strWorkbookName = Dir("C:\My Assignments*.xls") will
   (a) Open the My Assignments workbook on drive C
   (b) Return the names of all workbooks in the My Assignments folder
   (c) Return the name of the first workbook in the My Assignments folder
   (d) Display the message "File Does Not Exist" if there are no workbooks in the My Assignments folder

2. What happens if the Dir function cannot find the specified file?
   (a) The function returns an empty (zero length) character string
   (b) The associated procedure displays an error message
   (c) The associated procedure ceases execution
   (d) All of the above

3. The statement strWorkbookName = Dir(strFolderName & "*.xls") will
   (a) Open the workbook called strFolderName
   (b) Return the name of the first workbook in the folder called strFolderName
   (c) Return the name of the first workbook in the folder where the folder name is stored in the variable strFolderName
   (d) Display the message "File Does Not Exist" if there are no workbooks in the strFolderName folder

4. Which of the following is a true statement?
   (a) A run-time error occurs because the user violated a syntactical requirement of VBA
   (b) The statement that produced a run-time error is indicated in red within the VBA procedure
   (c) A run-time error is accompanied by a standard VBA error message unless the procedure includes an error-handling procedure
   (d) All of the above

5. How do you implement an error-handling procedure?
   (a) Include an On Error statement that transfers control elsewhere in the procedure if a run-time error occurs
   (b) Develop an error-handling section that is referenced by the On Error statement
   (c) Include an Exit Sub statement to bypass the error-handling code if the error does not occur
   (d) All of the above

6. Which of the following statements is true regarding VBA syntax?
   (a) An underscore at the end of a line indicates continuation
   (b) An ampersand indicates concatenation of a character string
   (c) An apostrophe at the beginning of a line indicates a comment
   (d) All of the above

7. Where does the macro recorder store the macros (procedures) it creates?
   (a) In a hidden worksheet called Module1
   (b) In a hidden worksheet, but not necessarily Module1
   (c) In Module1 of the current project
   (d) In a module of the current project, but not necessarily Module1

8. The statement ActiveCell.Offset(1, -2).Select moves to the cell that is:
   (a) One row down and two columns to the left of the current cell
   (b) One row down and two columns to the right of the current cell
   (c) One row up and two columns to the left of the current cell
   (d) One row up and two columns to the right of the current cell

9. The Excel formula ='Smith'!TotalExpense is
   (a) Syntactically incorrect because a worksheet tab must include the employee's first and last name
   (b) Syntactically incorrect because a cell formula must contain a relative or absolute cell reference
   (c) Referencing the range name TotalExpense on the current worksheet
   (d) Referencing the range name TotalExpense on the worksheet called Smith

10. What value will be returned by the function Len(strName), given that the variable strName was previously initialized to "Your Name"?
    (a) Seven
    (b) Nine
    (c) Eleven
    (d) Impossible to determine

... continued

multiple choice

11. Which of the following statements is true, given the VBA statement ActiveWorkbook.Sheets("Jessica Benjamin").Tab.ColorIndex = 3?

    (a) ActiveWorkbook is used as a qualifier to indicate the specific workbook that contains the indicated worksheets collection
    (b) "JessicaBenjamin" is a worksheet within the worksheets collection of the active workbook
    (c) ColorIndex is a property of the Tab object
    (d) All of the above

12. Which of the following is a true statement?

    (a) Every If statement must include an Else clause
    (b) Every If statement must include an End If delimiter
    (c) An If statement must be precisely indented if it is to compile correctly
    (d) All of the above

13. Given that the variable strName contains the value "George", what will be displayed by the statement, msgbox "Hello", & strName & ". How are you?"?

    (a) HelloGeorge. How are you?
    (b) HelloGeorge.How are you?
    (c) Hello George.How are you?
    (d) Hello George. How are you?

14. The statement If Worksheets.Count > 1 is:

    (a) Applying the Count method to a worksheet object
    (b) Testing the Count property of a worksheet object
    (c) Applying the Count method to the worksheets collection
    (d) Testing the Count property of the worksheets collection

15. Given the partial statement MsgBox ("Do you want to continue?", vbYesNo), which of the following is true?

    (a) The user will see the indicated prompt and Yes and No command buttons
    (b) A question mark icon will appear in the resulting message box
    (c) "Your Name Goes Here" will appear on the title bar of the message box
    (d) All of the above

16. Which statement will prompt the user to enter his or her name and store the result in a variable called strUserName?

    (a) InputBox.strUserName
    (b) strUserName = MsgBox("Please enter your name.")
    (c) strUserName = InputBox("Please enter your name.")
    (d) InputBox("Please enter strUserName.")

17. Given the statement Sheets("Sheet1").Select

    (a) Sheets is the collection, Select is the method
    (b) Sheets is the object, Select is the method
    (c) Sheets is the collection, Select is the property
    (d) Sheets is the object, Select is the property

18. If the variable strName is set to "George", the expression "Good morning, strName" will return:

    (a) Good morning, George
    (b) Good morning, strName
    (c) Good morning George
    (d) Good morning strName

ANSWERS

1. c	7. d	13. a
2. a	8. a	14. d
3. c	9. d	15. a
4. c	10. b	16. c
5. d	11. d	17. a
6. d	12. b	18. b

PRACTICE WITH EXCEL AND VBA

1. **Finding the Month and Day:** The workbook in Figure 10.11 illustrates table lookup functions in conjunction with date functions. Proceed as follows:
   a. Create a new workbook. Enter the title of the worksheet into cell A1, then merge cells A1 through D1 to center the title at the top of the worksheet. Enter the indicated labels in cells A3, A4, and C4. Enter the tables for the day of the week and month of the year into cells A9 through B15 and C9 through D20, respectively. Widen columns as necessary.
   b. Enter any date into cell B3. Use the Weekday and Month functions in cells B8 and D8, respectively, to obtain the numerical value for the day of the week and month of the year, respectively. Cell B8, for example, will contain the function =Weekday(B3).
   c. Enter a VLOOKUP function into cell B4 to display the day of the week based on the numeric value in cell B8 and the associated table. Enter a second VLOOKUP function into cell D4 to display the month of the year based on the numeric value in cell D8 and the associated table.
   d. Modify the formulas in cells B4 and D4 to include an IF statement that displays a blank value if cell B3 is empty. Modify the formulas in cells B8 and D8 to include similar If statements. Delete the date in cell B3 to test the revised formulas.
   e. Create an Open Workbook event procedure to prompt the user for his or her birth date to enter the response into cell B3.
   f. Turn on the macro recorder to create a "dummy" macro to hide rows 8 through 20 in the worksheet. Modify the Open Workbook event procedure to prompt the user as shown in Figure 10.11. Use the VBA statements that were captured in part e to hide the indicated rows.
   g. Print the cell formulas for the completed worksheet. Print the Open Workbook event procedure. Capture the screen in Figure 10.11 and use that as a cover sheet when you submit the completed assignment.

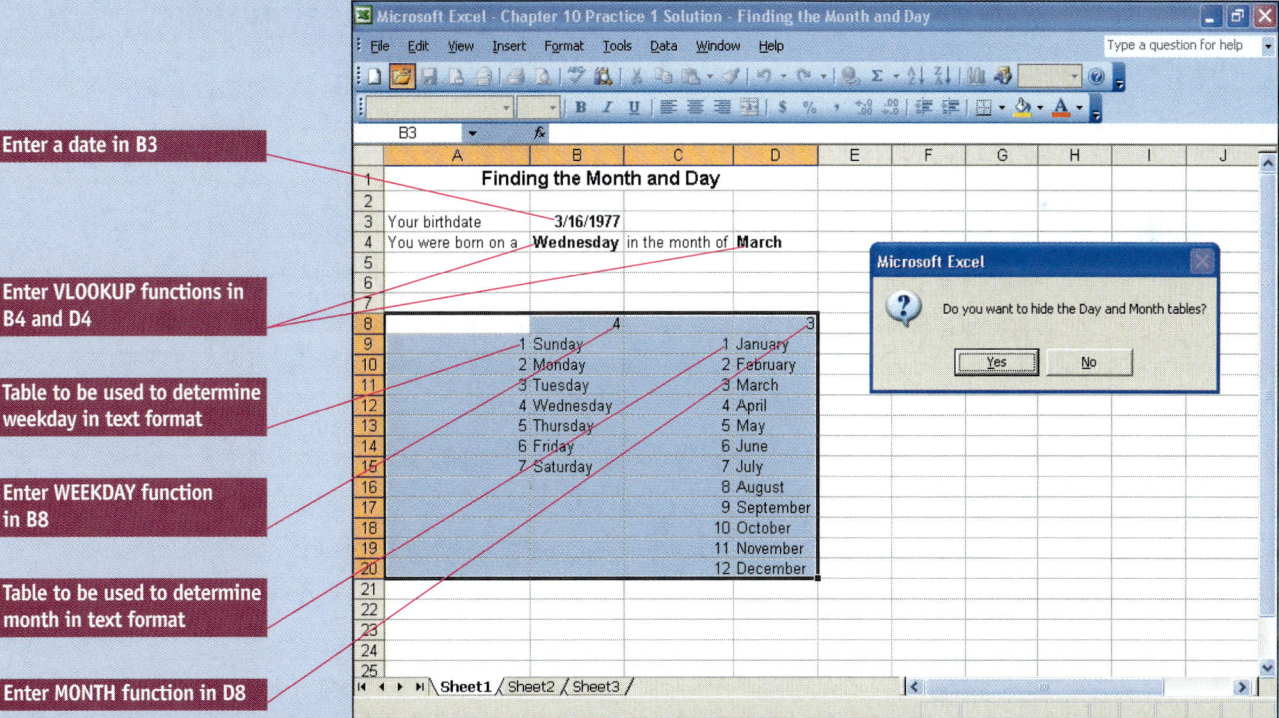

FIGURE 10.11   Finding the Month and Day (exercise 1)

practice exercises

2. **A Puzzle for You:** The workbook in Figure 10.12 contains a traditional puzzle that you may have seen before. Even so, you may not be able to solve every entry. We don't want you to be unduly frustrated, and so we have included the answers in the workbook, but you have to find the hidden password to see the solution. The intent of the exercise, however, is not to solve the puzzle per se, but to use your knowledge of Excel and VBA to display the password. Proceed as follows:

   a. Open the *Chapter 10 Practice 2* workbook in the Exploring Excel folder. Click the button to Enable Macros to see the worksheet in Figure 10.12. Try to solve as many of the entries as possible, without resorting to the answers. There are 26 questions. A good score is 20 or better.

   b. You can begin your quest for the solution without knowing the password. Use the appropriate Excel command to display the gridlines and the row and column headings.

   c. Look for a hidden worksheet. Does this worksheet contain any hints to help you find the password?

   d. Locate the VBA procedure that will display the cell formulas, provided you make the necessary change. Once you run the modified procedure, the password will become obvious to you.

   e. Use the password to unhide the columns containing the solution to complete the workbook.

   f. Print the workbook two ways, once to show the displayed values and once to show the cell formulas. (You will not be able to print the cell formulas until you complete part d correctly.) Print all of the VBA procedures within the workbook.

   g. Add a cover sheet, then submit the completed assignment to your instructor. Include a brief discussion of how you found the hidden password. Can you create an Excel workbook with another puzzle that contains the solution and a hidden password?

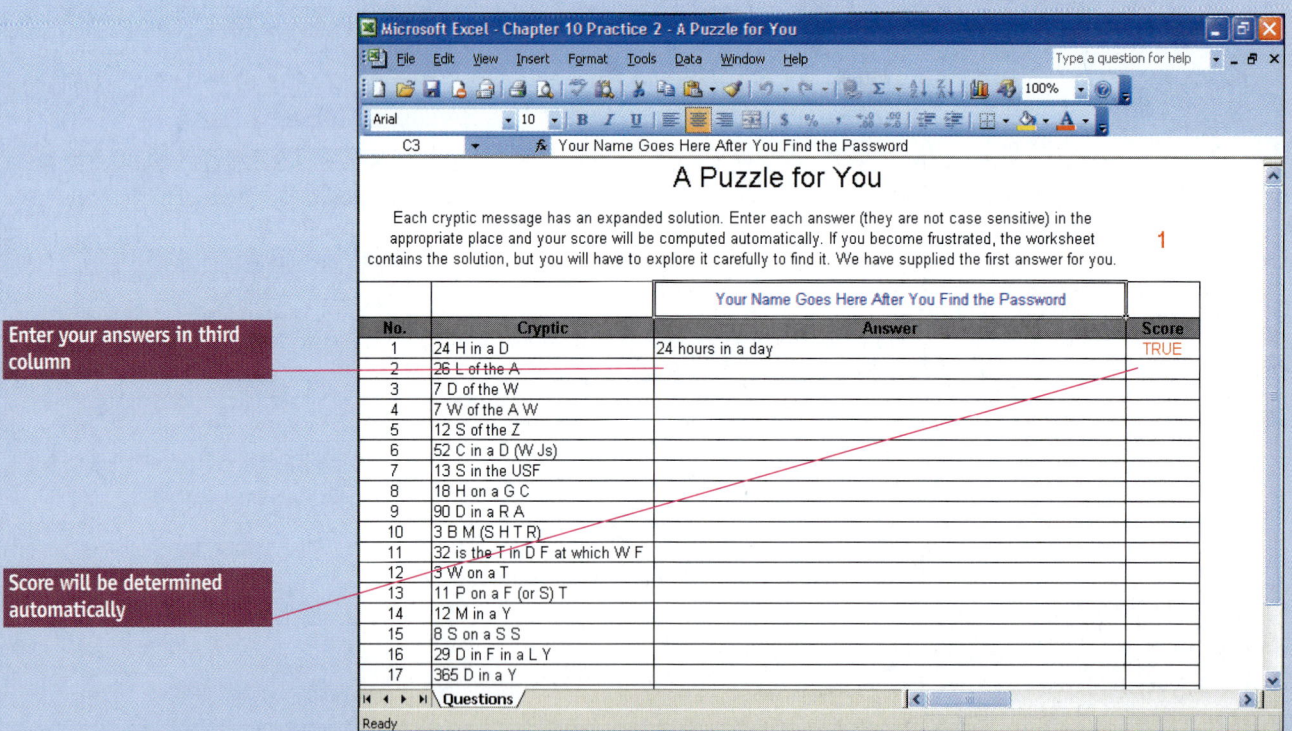

FIGURE 10.12 A Puzzle for You (exercise 2)

practice exercises

3. **Search for an Employee's Last Name:** Figure 10.13 displays a procedure to search for an employee's last name, and then to display the associated worksheet. It achieves the same result as the procedure in the second hands-on exercise, but it allows the user to enter only the last name, as opposed to the combination of last name and first name. It also introduces additional programming techniques. Open the *Chapter 10 Practice 3* workbook and click "Yes" when asked whether to create the summary workbook. (Use the expense statements in the Additional Expense Statements folder and specify $1,000 as the amount required for review.) You now have the same workbook as at the end of the fourth hands-on exercise. You will improve this workbook by adding additional procedures, beginning with the procedure in Figure 10.13, which can be added to any existing module.

   a. Use the VBA Help function to determine the meaning of the Visual Basic Like function. What is the statement Like strEmployeeName & "*" searching for?
   b. The variable strFoundWorksheet is an example of a programming switch. It is set to "No" prior to looking at the first worksheet, then set to "Yes" if the last name entered by the user matches the last name in any worksheet tab within the workbook. What action will the procedure take if the designated name cannot be found?
   c. What happens if the procedure locates a worksheet that contains the designated last name? Is it possible to locate more than one worksheet for the same last name?
   d. What is the significance of the intrinsic constant vbQuestion? How is it used in this procedure?
   e. Test the completed procedure to be sure that it works correctly. Print the completed procedure for your instructor.
   f. Modify the error-handling section in the FindEmployeeWorksheet procedure to execute this procedure if the combination of the employee's first and last name is not found. Is this a meaningful enhancement to the earlier procedure?
   g. Submit your answers to the various questions in this exercise to your instructor. Be sure to include the printed procedure with your submission. Add a cover sheet to complete the assignment.

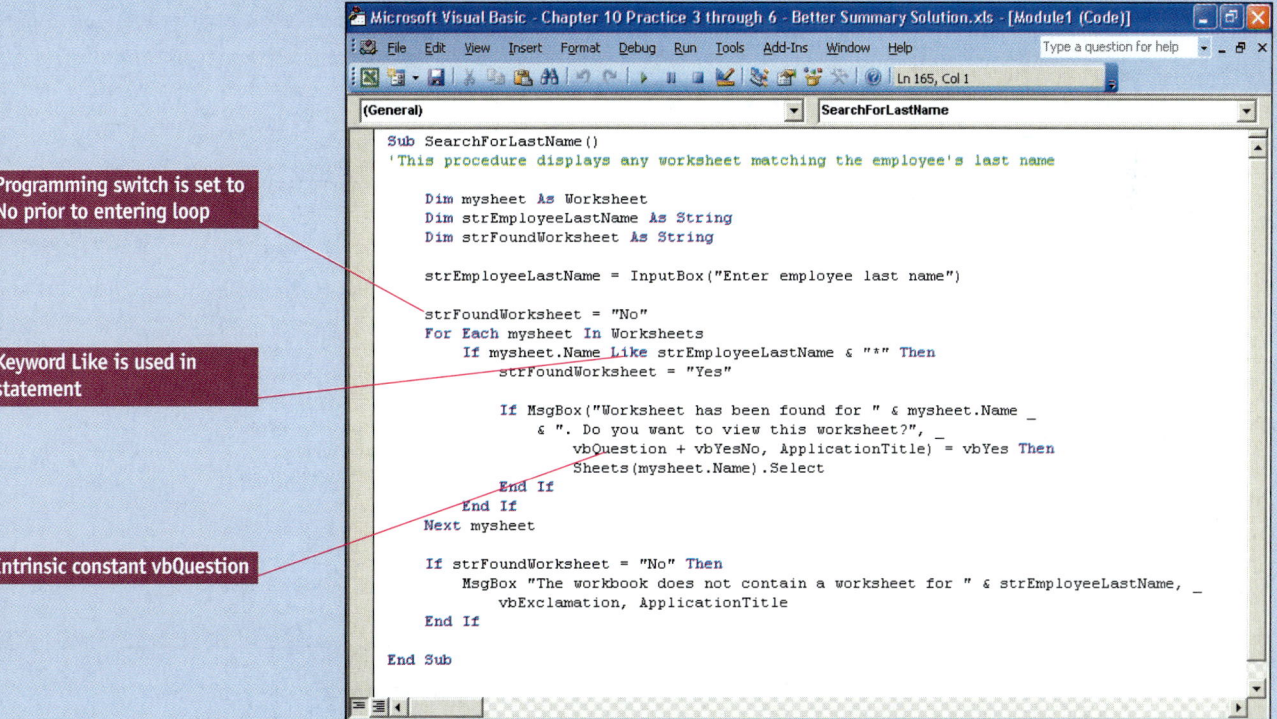

FIGURE 10.13 Search for an Employee's Last Name (exercise 3)

practice exercises

4. **Print Selected Worksheets:** The completed summary workbook has evaluated the expenses for each employee and colored the corresponding worksheet tabs to blue or red, respectively, indicating expenses that are approved or expenses subject to further review. Either (or both) sets of worksheets may be printed at different times by manually selecting the worksheets. It's better to do it automatically.

   The SelectSheetsForPrinting procedure in Figure 10.14 prompts the user to determine which set of worksheets to print, then it calls one of three other procedures to comply with the request. Your assignment is to complete the four required procedures using Figure 10.14 as a guide.

   a. Use the macro recorder to capture the Excel key strokes to print the selected worksheet. Once you have the Print statement, use it as the basis for three separate procedures—to print the approved expense worksheets, to print the worksheets for further review, and to print every employee worksheet. Look closely at Figure 10.14 to see the beginning of the PrintApprovedExpenses procedure.

   b. Create the SelectSheetsForPrinting procedure as shown in Figure 10.14. The Msgbox statement within this procedure inserts line feeds within the message box to force a break from one line to the next. (You can see this message box by looking at Figure 10.15 in the next exercise.) The procedure also uses a Case statement to test the user's response to ensure that it is valid. Note, too, the use of the Visual Basic UCase function to make the user's response case insensitive.

   c. Return to Excel and execute the SelectSheetsForPrinting procedure. Capture the screen that displays the input box asking for the user's response and use that image as the cover sheet for this assignment.

   d. Print all four procedures for your instructor as proof you completed this exercise. Include a short note describing how to call one procedure from another. Add a cover sheet with your name and date.

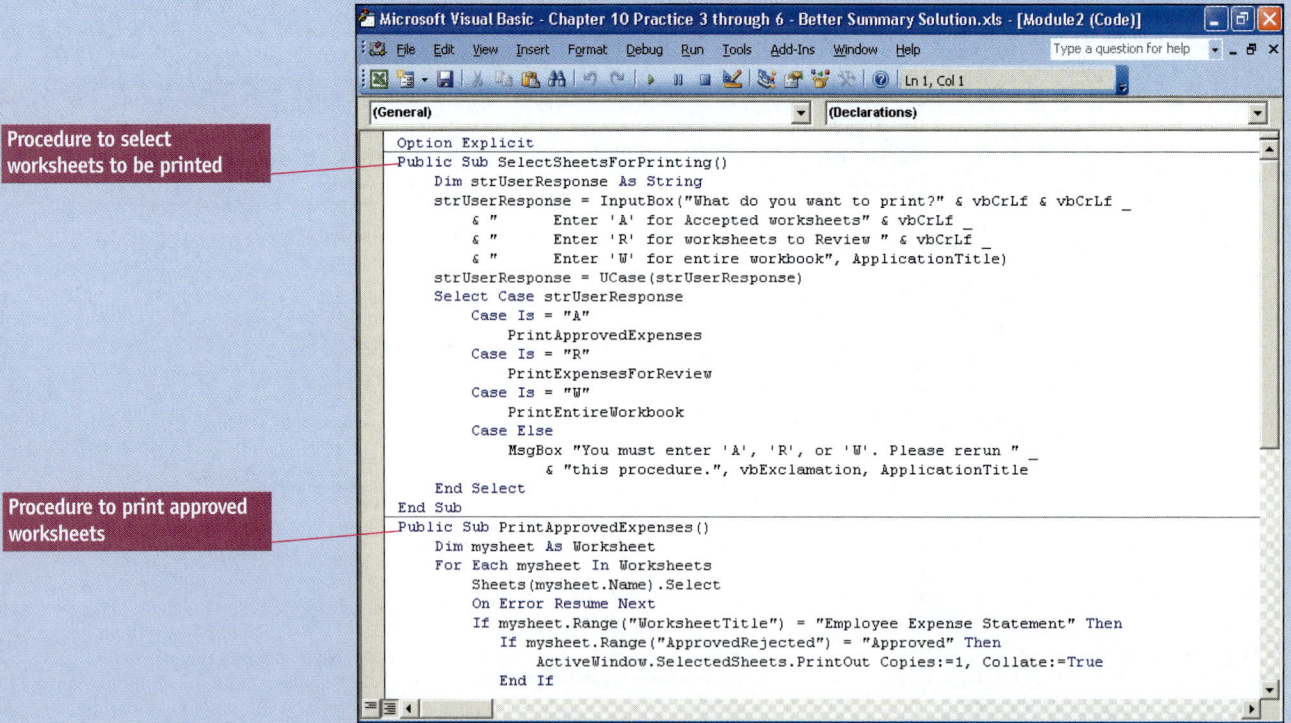

FIGURE 10.14 Print Selected Worksheets (exercise 4)

practice exercises

5. **Add Command Buttons:** The workbook in Figure 10.15 contains a total of five command buttons that collectively execute all of the procedures associated with the Better Summary workbook that has been developed throughout the chapter.
   a. Complete the fourth hands-on exercise in the chapter, which creates the basic version of the Better Summary Solution workbook. There are two command buttons on the summary worksheet at this point.
   b. Complete practice exercise 3 to develop the procedure to search for an employee using only the last name. Add the command button corresponding to this procedure to the worksheet.
   c. Add the fourth command button to change the approval criterion, which runs the ReviewEmployeeExpenses procedure from the third hands-on exercise. Click the button and change the approval criterion to $500 (rather than $1,000 used earlier).
   d. Complete the previous problem to print selected worksheets, then add the fifth command button to run this procedure. Enter "A" to print just the approved worksheet(s).
   e. You can improve the appearance of the worksheet by creating command buttons of uniform size. Choose any command button and size it appropriately. Now right click that button, click the Format Control command, and click the Size tab to see the size of your button. Click the Properties tab and check the box to Print Object. Change the properties of the other command buttons in similar fashion.
   f. Print the summary worksheet (with the command buttons) for your instructor as proof you did this exercise. Use landscape printing if necessary to print the worksheet on a single page.
   g. Create a custom menu that contains five commands that are equivalent to the command buttons in the worksheet. Which technique do you prefer—command buttons on the worksheet or a custom menu? Summarize your thoughts in a short note to your instructor.
   h. Capture the screen in Figure 10.15 (or a different screen that displays the custom menu) to use as a cover sheet for your completed assignment.

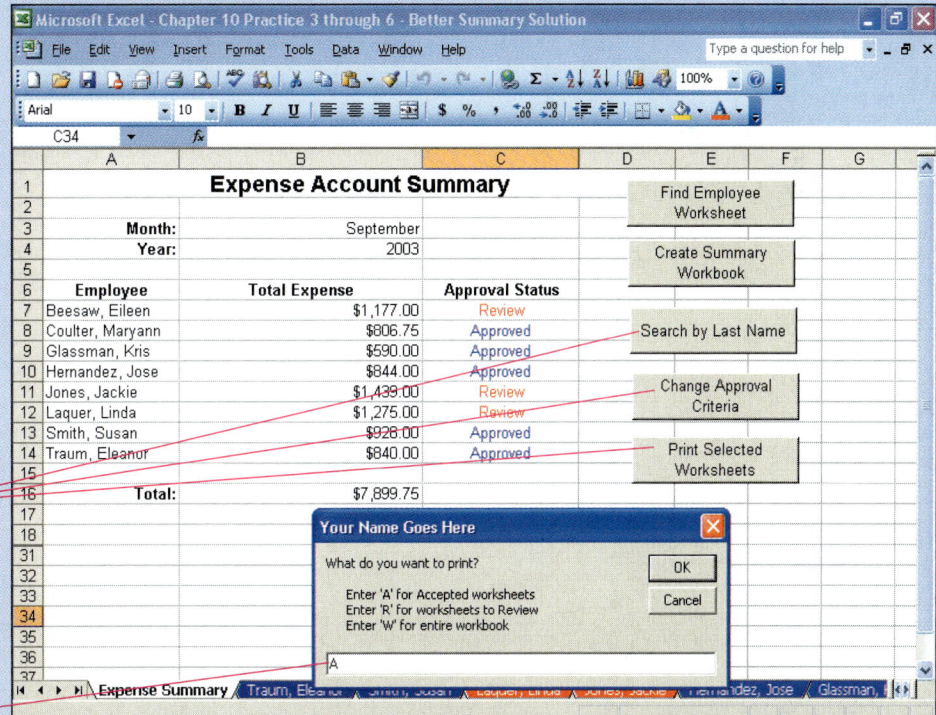

FIGURE 10.15 Add Command Buttons (exercise 5)

practice exercises

6. **Print the VBA Procedures in Microsoft Word:** You can print VBA procedures from within the VBA editor, but the procedures are printed without any formatting. You get a better result by printing from within Microsoft Word as shown in Figure 10.16. Complete the previous exercise to create all of the VBA procedures, and then print the procedures as described below.

   a. Open the VBA editor, select ThisWorkbook within Project Explorer, and click and drag to select all of the statements in both event procedures. Click the Copy button (or use the Ctrl+C keyboard shortcut) to copy these procedures to the Windows clipboard.

   b. Start Microsoft Word and open a new document. Click the Paste button (or use the Ctrl+V keyboard shortcut) to paste the contents of the clipboard (the VBA procedures) into the Word document.

   c. Use the Windows taskbar to return to the VBA editor to copy the contents of the other modules to the Word document in similar fashion. Be sure to copy all of the procedures in all of the modules.

   d. Format the procedures in the Word document as you see fit. We suggest you use a monospaced font such as Courier New so that the indentation and alignment are easier to see. We also suggest that you boldface the Sub and End Sub statements of each procedure, and that you insert a horizontal border to separate the procedures from one another.

   e. Experiment with styles and a table of contents. Format each procedure in a heading style, then use the Reference command in the Insert menu to create the table of contents automatically.

   f. Add a title page, then submit the completed assignment to your instructor. Do you think the additional formatting is worth the trouble? What happens if a procedure changes in the Excel workbook?

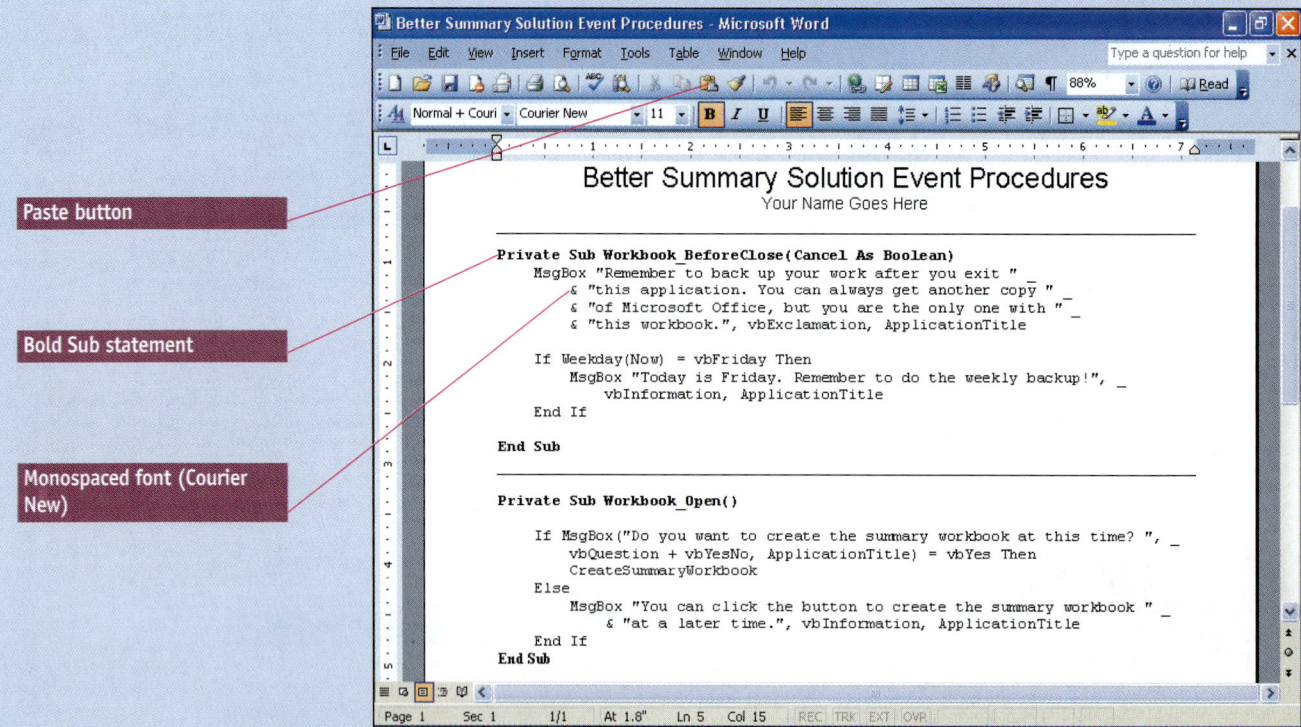

FIGURE 10.16 Print the VBA Procedures in Microsoft Word (exercise 6)

practice exercises

7. **Random Numbers as Test Data:** Open the partially completed version of the workbook in Figure 10.17, which can be found in the *Chapter 10 Practice 7* workbook in the Exploring Excel folder. You will not be able to duplicate the figure exactly, however, because the random number function is used to generate test data for the workbook. Proceed as follows:

   a. Click in cell C4 and note that the formula contains the expression 70+20*Rand( ). The random number function returns a value between 0 and 1, so that the expression returns a value between 70 and 90. (The Round function is used in the actual cell formula to eliminate the decimal portion.)

   b. Pull down the Tools menu, click the Options command, click the Calculation tab, then click the Calculate now button. The test grade changes. Press the F9 (shortcut) key. The value changes again. Click in Cell G1, enter your name, and press the Enter key. The random numbers change again because the spreadsheet is automatically recalculated each time you change the contents of a cell.

   c. Copy the formulas in cells C4 to G4 to rows 5 through 21 to generate the grades for the remaining students. Press the F9 key once or twice to see how the grades change.

   d. The worksheet you just created will be used in a subsequent problem where it will be combined with other grade books. Pull down the File menu and click the Save As command to display the Save As dialog box in Figure 10.17. Change the folder to VBA Grade Books (within the Exploring Excel folder). This folder was created automatically when you installed the practice files. Change the file name to Section R. Click the Save button.

   e. The last step is to convert the formulas (containing the random numbers) in the workbook to fixed values so that they remain constant. Click and drag to select cells C4 through G21. Click the Copy button. Pull down the Edit menu, click the Paste Special command to display the Paste Special dialog box, click the option button for Values, then click OK.

   f. Press the F9 key to recalculate the spreadsheet. The displayed values do not change because the formulas have been converted to a constant value.

   g. Save the spreadsheet a final time.

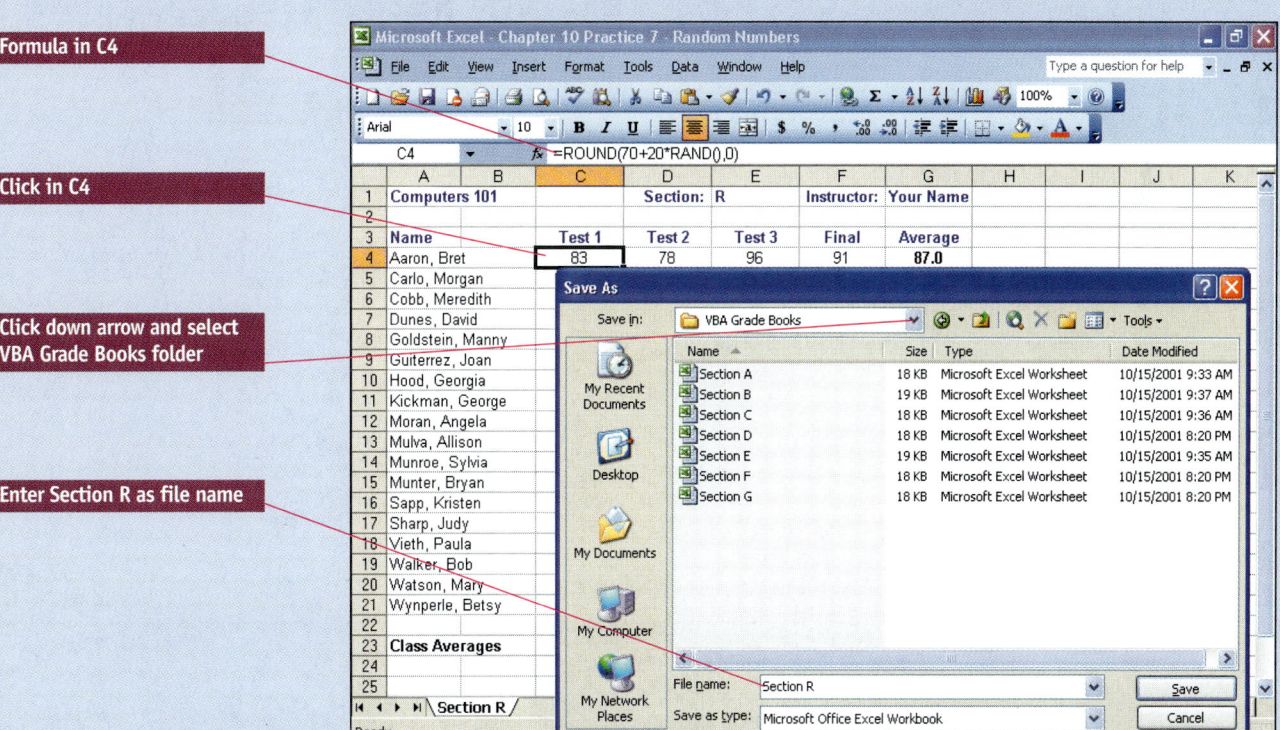

FIGURE 10.17 Random Numbers as Test Data (exercise 7)

MICROSOFT OFFICE EXCEL 2003 1529

practice exercises

8. **The Composite Grade Book:** The workbook in Figure 10.18 is similar in concept to the expense summary workbook that was developed in the chapter. We started with an empty summary workbook and developed the necessary procedures to create the composite grade book by inserting data from individual workbooks. Proceed as follows:

   a. Open the partially completed workbook in *Chapter 10 Practice 8* to display a partially completed workbook. Click Yes when asked whether to create the Summary Grade Book.

   b. You will be prompted for the path to the individual grade books. Type C:\Exploring Excel\VBA Grade Books (assuming that you used the default location when you installed the practice files).

   c. Sit back and relax. The individual grade books will be brought into the summary workbook, after which the summary worksheet will be created. You will not be prompted to save the changes to the individual workbooks because there are no calculations associated with opening and closing these workbooks.

   d. The appearance of Section R in the workbook and on the summary worksheet depends on whether you did the previous exercise, and further, whether you saved this workbook in the VBA Grade Books folder as instructed.

   e. Print the All Sections worksheet two ways—once to show the displayed values, and once to show the cell contents.

   f. Open the VBA editor and print the event procedures that exist within this workbook. What differences (if any) are there in the procedures in this workbook compared to those in the Better Summary that you developed earlier? What differences (if any) are there in the procedures in Module1 compared to the comparable procedures in the Better Summary workbook?

   g. Add a cover sheet and submit the assignment to your instructor.

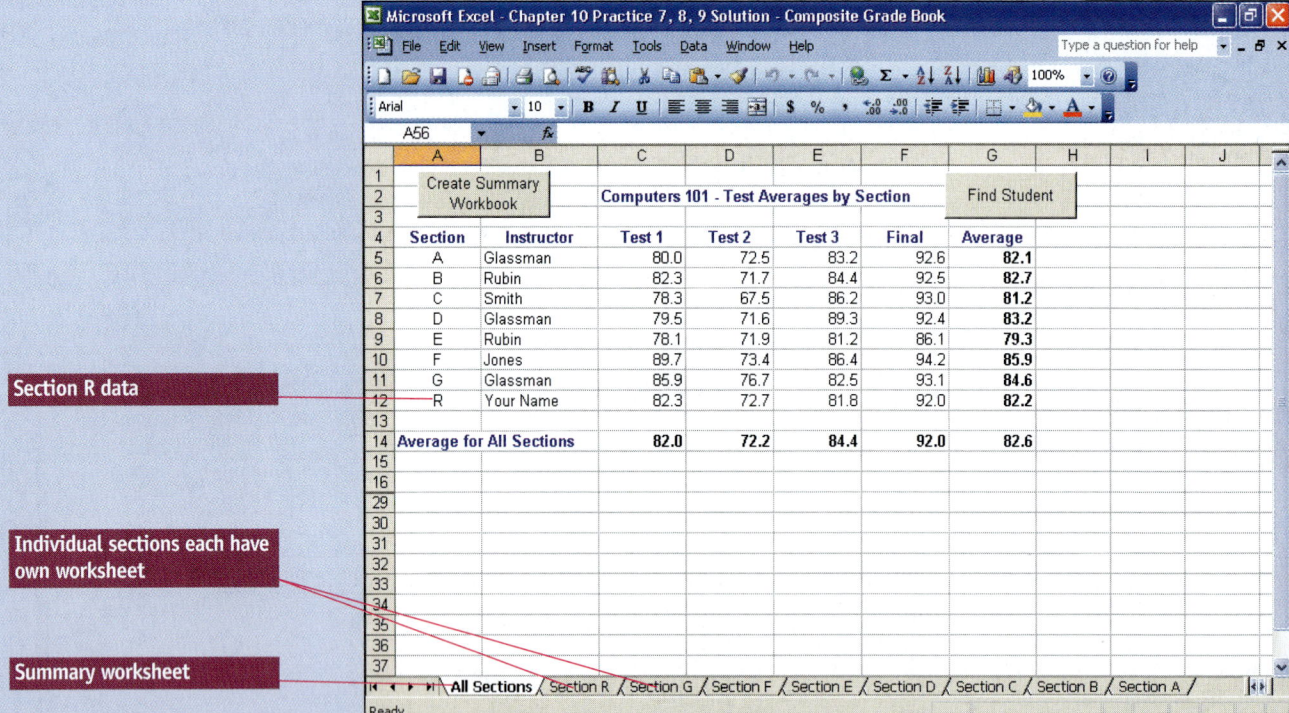

FIGURE 10.18 The Composite Grade Book (exercise 8)

practice exercises

9. **Locate a Student:** This exercise continues the development of the Composite Grade Book by developing a procedure to locate a specific student. It is similar to the Expense Summary workbook from the chapter, except that you are searching for student names within a worksheet, as opposed to an employee name on a worksheet tab.

   a. Open the *Chapter 10 Practice 8* workbook from the previous exercise. What happens if you click the Find Student command button? Is this a reasonable action for the original workbook?

   b. You will replace the original procedure with the VBA code in Figure 10.19, but first we want you to see how the procedure was created. Start the macro recorder. Pull down the Edit menu, click the Find command, then search for a student, "Smith, Doe". Click the Stop Recording button. Which part of the procedure in Figure 10.19 was adopted from the macro you just recorded?

   c. Replace the existing FindStudent procedure in the *Chapter 10 Practice 8* workbook with the VBA code in Figure 10.19. Test the procedure by looking for two students, one who is somewhere in the workbook, and one who is not in the workbook at all. Does the procedure work correctly in both instances?

   d. Place an apostrophe in front of the On Error statement to convert the statement to a comment. Rerun the procedure, specifying the name of a student who is not in the workbook. Does the procedure run successfully? What is the purpose of the On Error statement?

   e. Summarize your answers in a short note to your instructor. Add a cover sheet to complete the assignment.

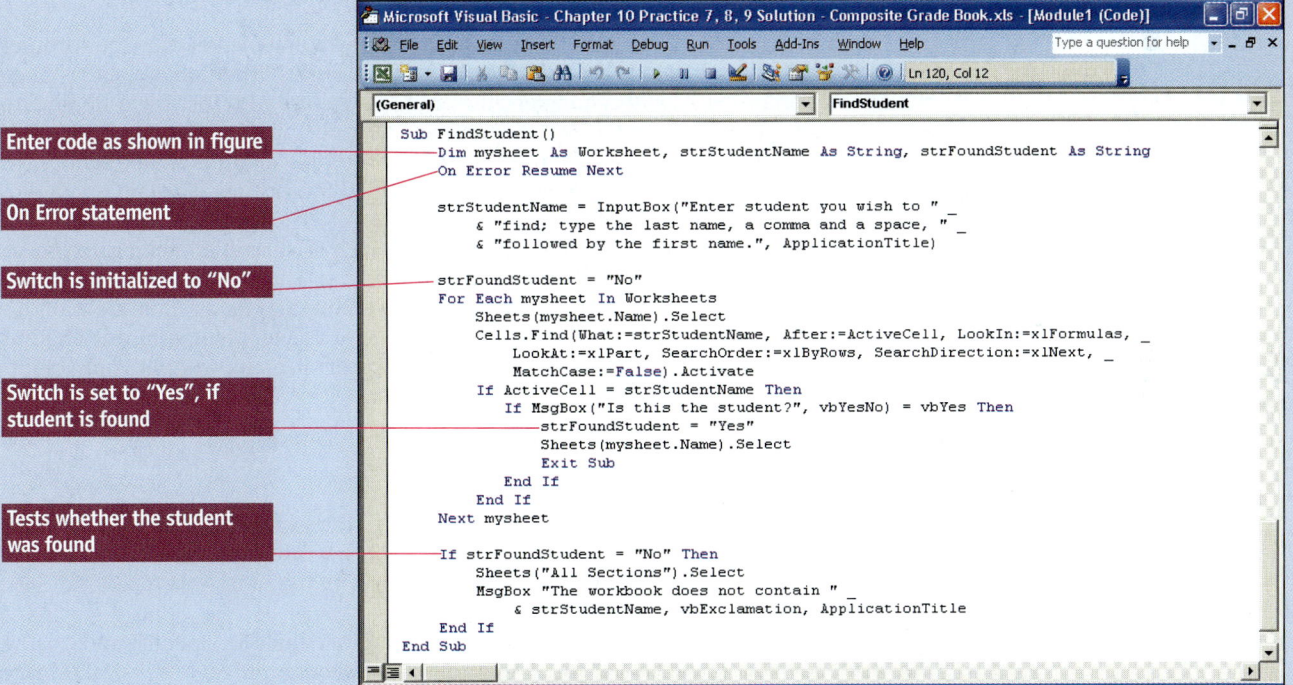

FIGURE 10.19 Locate a Student (exercise 9)

MINI CASES

VBA Review

You should be very familiar with the syntax of Visual Basic. You should also be comfortable with the definition of key terms such as object model, collection, method, and property. Nevertheless, we have created a Word document to review this material. Open the *Chapter 9 Mini Case—VBA Review* document in the Exploring Excel folder, fill in the blanks, add a cover page, and submit the completed document to your instructor.

Your Own Help Manual

Detailed help is available on any VBA topic if only you will take the trouble to look. Start the VBA editor, pull down the Help menu, and select Visual Basic Help (or press the F1 key) to display the Visual Basic Help window. You will see the same type of Help screen that is common to all Office applications. Click the Contents tab, select at least five topics of interest to you, and print the associated Help pages. Add a cover sheet and submit the information to your instructor.

Cleaning Up VBA Code

The macro recorder jump-starts the process of creating a VBA procedure by capturing Excel commands and converting them to their VBA equivalents. The result, however, can be cluttered (inefficient) code that can be simplified by going to the VBA editor and deleting the superfluous entries. For example, turn on the macro recorder, pull down the File menu, click the Page Setup command, and change to Landscape orientation. Turn off the recorder, then look at the resulting procedure.

You may be somewhat surprised at the number of statements because the recorder set every property associated with printing a worksheet. If your intention is just to change the orientation property, you can replace the entire procedure with the single statement, ActiveSheet.PageSetup.Orientation = xlLandscape. Not only is this easier to read, but it runs much more efficiently. You can find similar examples if you use the recorder to change the font or style. A different example is obtained by selecting a cell on a different worksheet.

Turn on the macro recorder, click the tab for Sheet2, select cell A5, then turn off the recorder. The macro recorder produces two statements, Sheets("Sheet2").Select and Range("A5").Select, but you can combine the statements using qualification to Sheets("Sheet2").Range("A5").Select. Study the procedures you created in this chapter and the previous chapter for other examples. Add a cover sheet and submit your assignment to your instructor.

Your Own Application

Develop a VBA application of comparable function to the Expense Summary workbook from the chapter or the Composite Grade Book from the end-of-chapter exercises. The application should be flexible, visually appealing, easy to use, and bulletproof. Choose any scenario that is of interest to you.

The completed application should include event procedures for opening and closing the workbook, for copying a worksheet from other workbooks into an "empty" summary workbook, and for copying information from worksheets within a workbook to a summary worksheet. Present the completed application to the class.

APPENDIX A

Toolbars for Microsoft® Office Excel 2003

TOOLBARS

- 3-D Settings
- Borders
- Chart
- Circular Reference
- Compare Side by Side
- Control Toolbox
- Diagram
- Drawing
- Drawing Canvas
- Exit Design Mode
- External Data
- Formatting
- Forms
- Formula Auditing
- Full Screen
- List and XML
- Organization Chart
- Picture
- Pivot Table
- Protection
- Reviewing
- Shadow Settings
- Standard
- Stop Recording
- Text to Speech
- Visual Basic
- Watch Window
- Web
- WordArt

OVERVIEW

Microsoft Excel has 29 predefined toolbars that provide access to commonly used commands. The toolbars are displayed in Figure A.1 and are listed here for convenience. They are: the Standard, Formatting, 3-D Settings, Borders, Chart, Circular Reference, Compare Side by Side, Control Toolbox, Diagram, Drawing, Drawing Canvas, Exit Design Mode, External Data, Forms, Formula Auditing, Full Screen, List, Organization Chart, Picture, Pivot Table, Protection, Reviewing, Shadow Settings, Stop Recording, Text to Speech, Visual Basic, Watch Window, Web, and WordArt. The Standard and Formatting toolbars are displayed by default and appear on the same row immediately below the menu bar. The other predefined toolbars are displayed (hidden) at the discretion of the user, and in some cases, are displayed automatically when their corresponding features are in use (e.g., the Chart toolbar and the Pivot Table toolbar).

The buttons on the toolbars are intended to be indicative of their function. Clicking the Printer button (the sixth button from the left on the Standard toolbar), for example, executes the Print command. If you are unsure of the purpose of any toolbar button, point to it, and a ScreenTip will appear that displays its name.

You can display multiple toolbars at one time, move them to new locations on the screen, customize their appearance, or suppress their display.

- To separate the Standard and Formatting toolbars and simultaneously display all of the buttons for each toolbar, pull down the Tools menu, click the Customize command, click the Options tab, then check the box to show the toolbars on two rows. Alternatively, the toolbars appear on the same row, so that only a limited number of buttons are visible on each toolbar; hence you may need to click the double arrow at the end of the toolbar to view additional buttons. Additional buttons will be added to either toolbar as you use the associated feature, and conversely, buttons will be removed from the toolbar if the feature is not used.

- To display or hide a toolbar, pull down the View menu and click the Toolbars command. Select (deselect) the toolbar that you want to display (hide). The selected toolbar will be displayed in the same position as when last displayed. You may also point to any toolbar and click with the right mouse button to bring up a shortcut menu, after which you can select the toolbar to be displayed (hidden). If the toolbar to be displayed is not listed, click the Customize command, click the Toolbars tab, check the box for the toolbar to be displayed, and then click the Close button.

1533

- To change the size of the buttons, suppress the display of the ScreenTips, or display the associated shortcut key (if available), pull down the View menu, click Toolbars, and click Customize to display the Customize dialog box. If necessary, click the Options tab, then select (deselect) the appropriate check box. Alternatively, you can right click on any toolbar, click the Customize command from the context-sensitive menu, then select (deselect) the appropriate check box from within the Options tab in the Customize dialog box.

- Toolbars are either docked (along the edge of the window) or floating (in their own window). A toolbar moved to the edge of the window will dock along that edge. A toolbar moved anywhere else in the window will float in its own window. Docked toolbars are one tool wide (high), whereas floating toolbars can be resized by clicking and dragging a border or corner as you would with any window.
    - To move a docked toolbar, click anywhere in the background area and drag the toolbar to its new location. You can also click and drag the move handle (the single vertical line) at the left of the toolbar.
    - To move a floating toolbar, drag its title bar to its new location.

- To customize one or more toolbars, display the toolbar on the screen. Then pull down the View menu, click Toolbars, and click Customize to display the Customize dialog box. Alternatively, you can click on any toolbar with the right mouse button and select Customize from the shortcut menu.
    - To move a button, drag the button to its new location on that toolbar or any other displayed toolbar.
    - To copy a button, press the Ctrl key as you drag the button to its new location on that toolbar or any other displayed toolbar.
    - To delete a button, drag the button off the toolbar and release the mouse button.
    - To add a button, click the Commands tab in the Customize dialog box, select the category (from the Categories list box) that contains the button you want to add, then drag the button to the desired location on the toolbar.
    - To restore a predefined toolbar to its default appearance, pull down the View menu, click Toolbars, click Customize, click the Toolbars tab, select (highlight) the desired toolbar, and click the Reset command button.

- Buttons can also be moved, copied, or deleted without displaying the Customize dialog box.
    - To move a button, press the Alt key as you drag the button to the new location.
    - To copy a button, press the Alt and Ctrl keys as you drag the button to the new location.
    - To delete a button, press the Alt key as you drag the button off the toolbar.

- To create your own toolbar, pull down the View menu, click Toolbars, click Customize, click the Toolbars tab, then click the New command button. Alternatively, you can click on any toolbar with the right mouse button, select Customize from the shortcut menu, click the Toolbars tab, and then click the New command button.
    - Enter a name for the toolbar in the dialog box that follows. The name can be any length and can contain spaces.
    - The new toolbar will appear on the screen. Initially it will be big enough to hold only one button. Add, move, and delete buttons following the same procedures as outlined above. The toolbar will automatically size itself as new buttons are added and deleted.
    - To delete a custom toolbar, pull down the View menu, click Toolbars, click Customize, and click the Toolbars tab. *Verify that the custom toolbar to be deleted is the only one selected (highlighted).* Click the Delete command button. Click Yes to confirm the deletion. (Note that a predefined toolbar cannot be deleted.)

MICROSOFT OFFICE EXCEL 2003 TOOLBARS

Standard

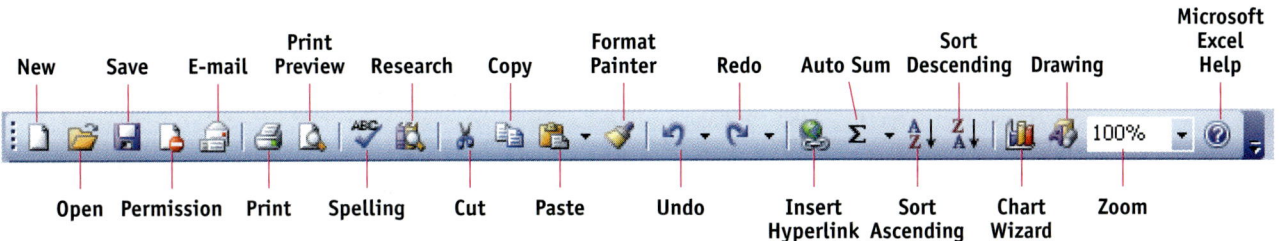

Formatting

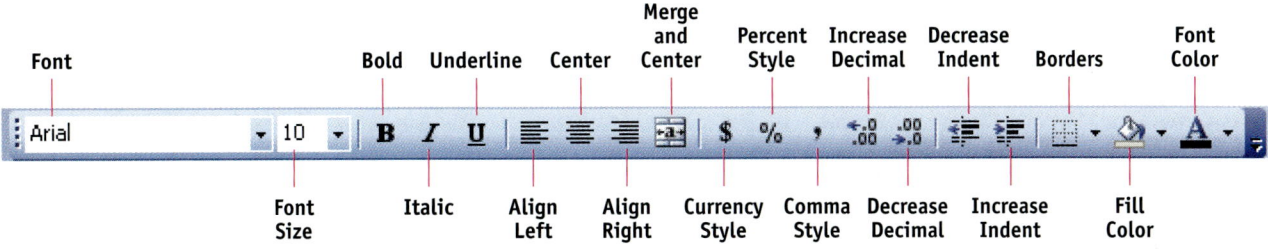

3-D Settings

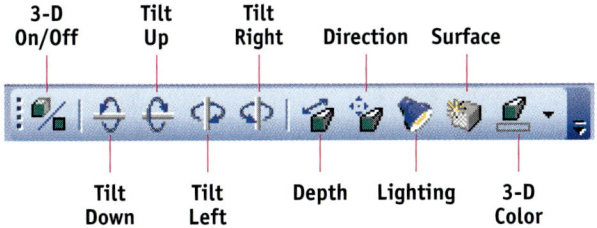

Borders

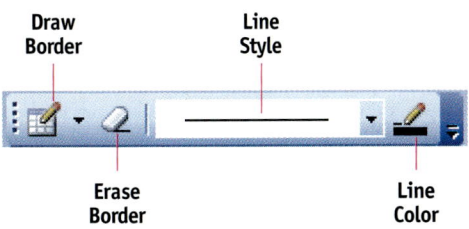

FIGURE A.1 Toolbars

Chart

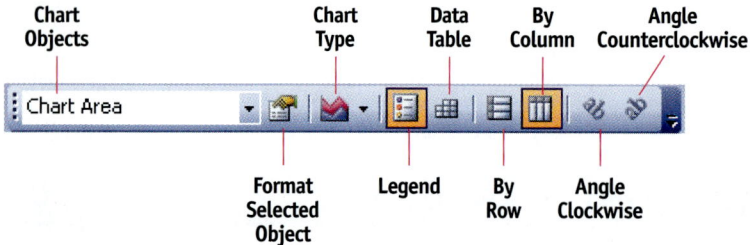

Circular Reference

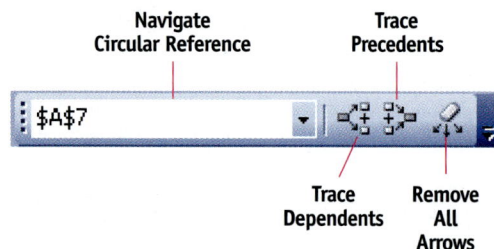

Compare Side by Side

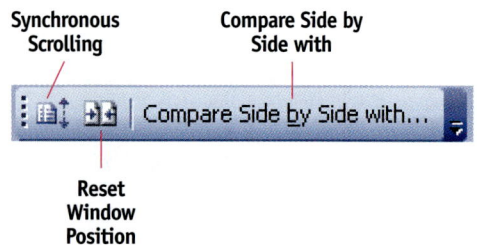

Control Toolbox

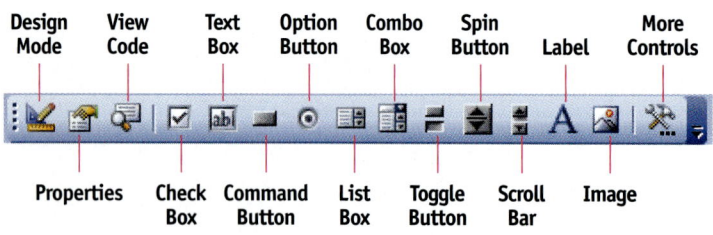

FIGURE A.1 Toolbars (*continued*)

Diagram

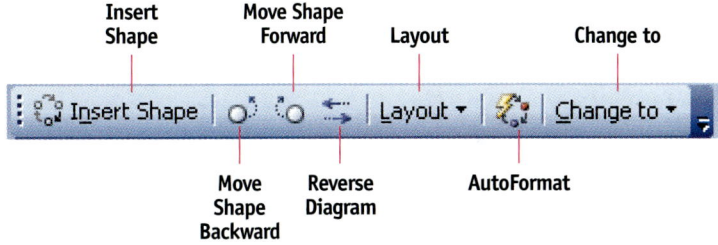

Drawing

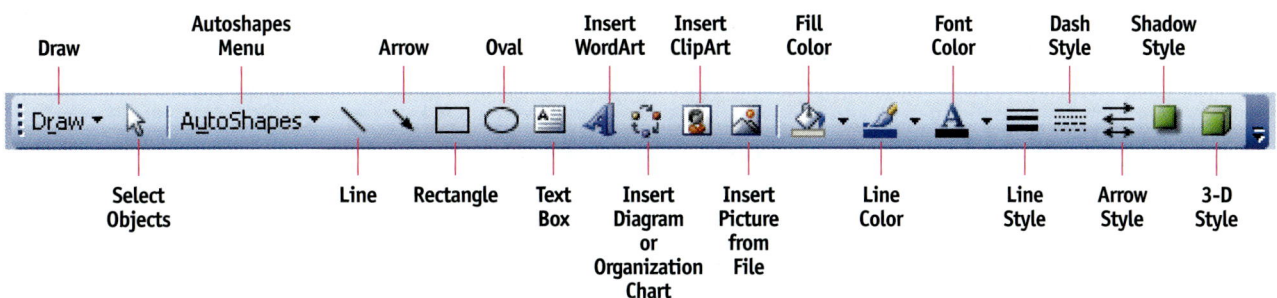

Drawing Canvas

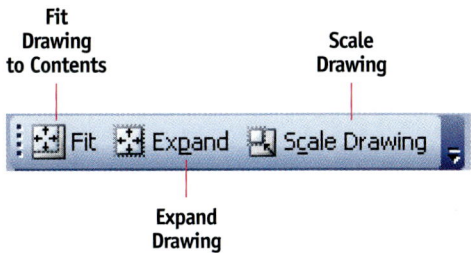

Exit Design Mode

Design Mode

FIGURE A.1 Toolbars (*continued*)

External Data

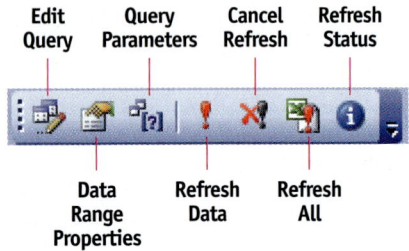

Forms

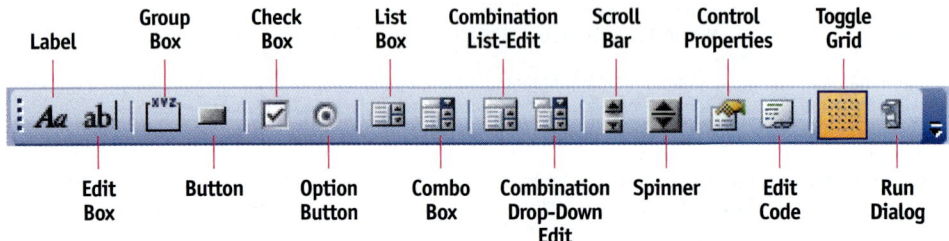

Formula Auditing

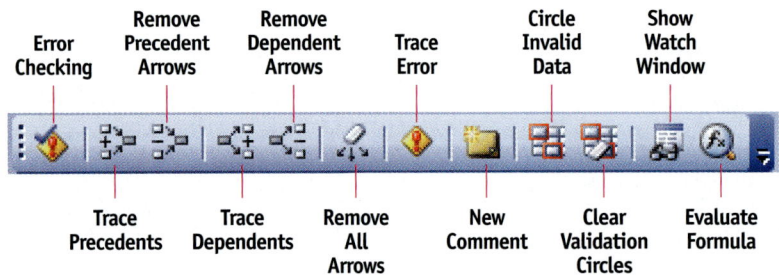

Full Screen

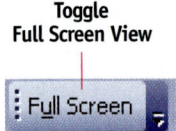

FIGURE A.1 Toolbars (*continued*)

List

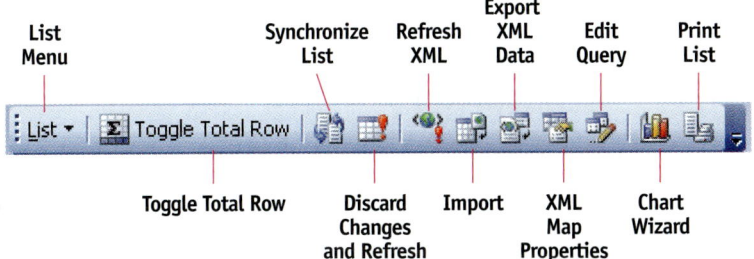

Organization Chart

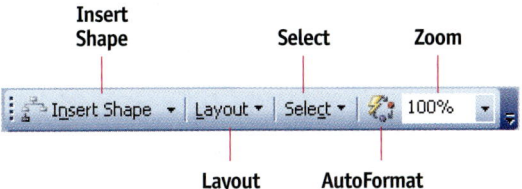

Picture

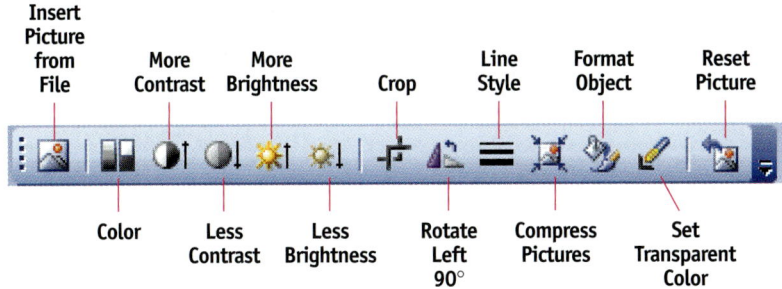

Pivot Table

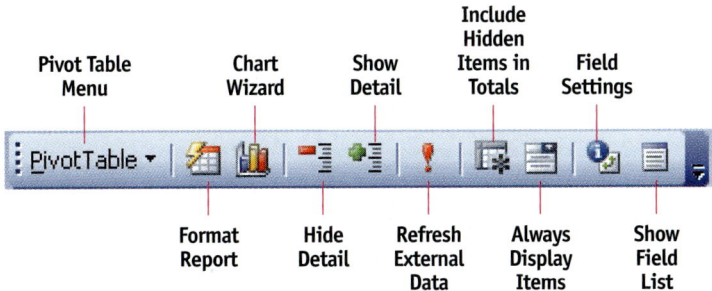

FIGURE A.1 Toolbars (*continued*)

Protection

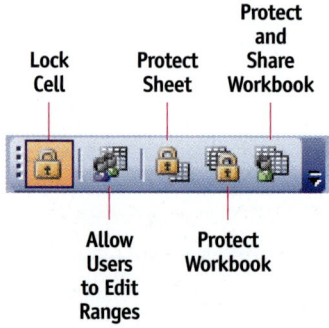

Reviewing

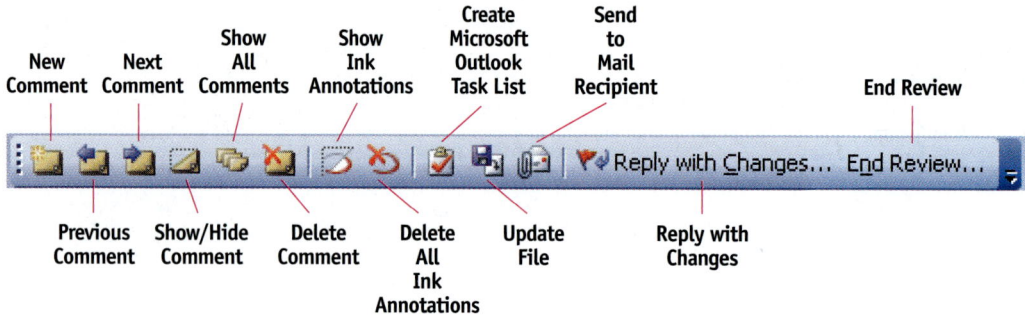

Shadow Settings

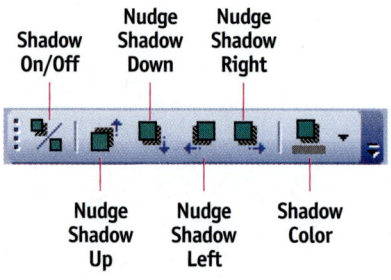

FIGURE A.1 Toolbars (*continued*)

Stop Recording

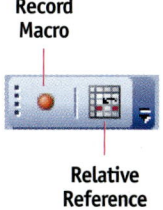

Text to Speech

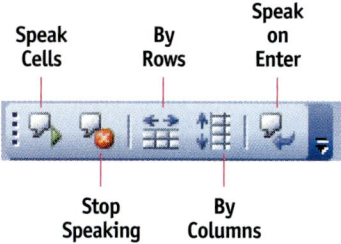

Visual Basic

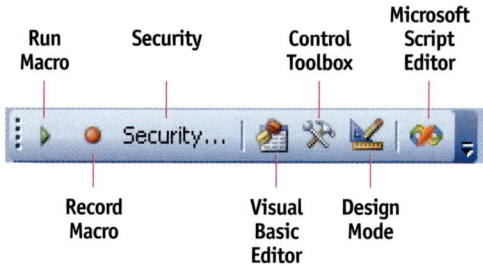

Watch Window

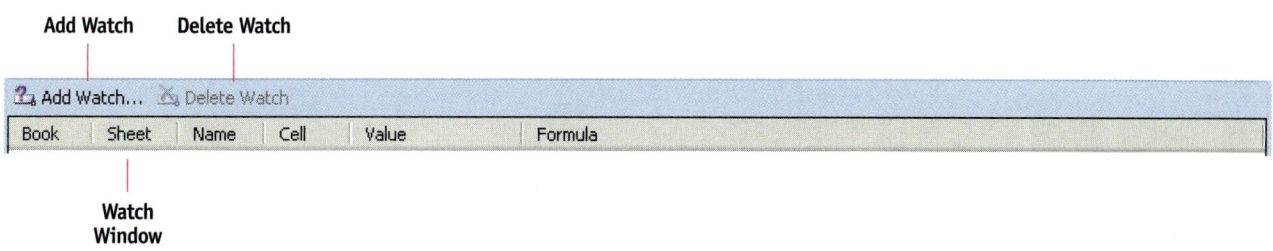

FIGURE A.1 Toolbars (*continued*)

Web

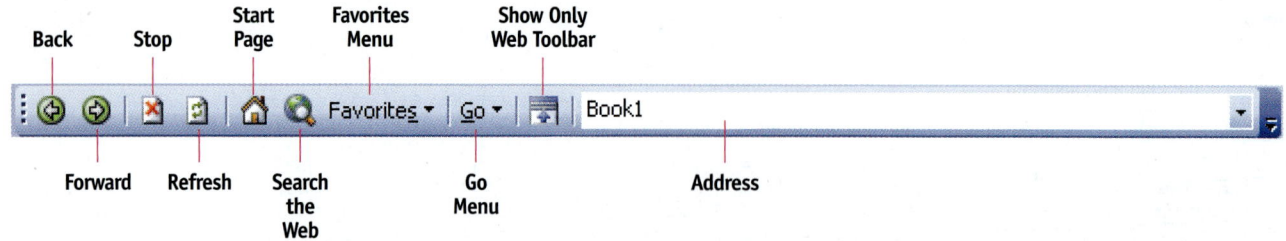

WordArt

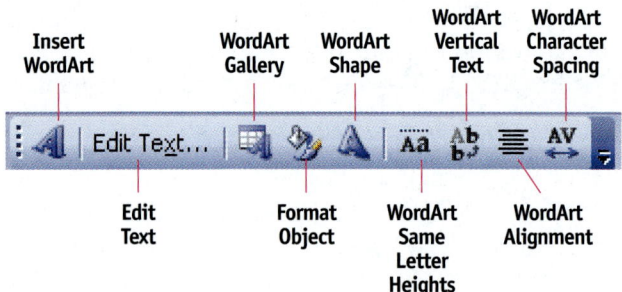

FIGURE A.1 Toolbars (*continued*)

Solver: A Tool for Optimization

CASE STUDY
MAXIMIZE PROFIT

Assume that you are the production manager for a company that manufactures computers. Your company divides its product line into two basic categories—desktop computers and laptops. Each product is sold under two labels, a discount line and a premium line. As production manager you are to determine how many computers of each type, and of each product line, to make each week.

Your decision is subject to various constraints that must be satisfied during the production process. Each computer requires a specified number of hours for assembly. Discount and premium-brand desktops require two and three hours, respectively. Discount and premium-brand laptops use three and five hours, respectively. The factory is working at full capacity, and you have only 4,500 hours of labor to allocate among the various products.

Your production decision is also constrained by demand. The marketing department has determined that you cannot sell more than 800 desktop units, nor more than 900 laptops, per week. The total demand for the discount and premium lines is 700 and 1,000 computers, respectively, per week.

Your goal (objective) is to maximize the total profit, which is based on a different profit margin for each type of computer. A desktop and a laptop computer from the discount line have unit profits of $600 and $800, respectively. The premium desktop and laptop computers have unit profits of $1,000 and $1,300, respectively. How many computers of each type do you manufacture each week to maximize the total profit?

This is a complex problem, but one that can be easily solved provided you can design a spreadsheet that is equivalent to Figure B.1. The top half of the spreadsheet contains the information about the individual products. There are three numbers associated with each product—the quantity that will be produced, the number of hours required, and the unit profit. The bottom half of the spreadsheet contains the information about the available resources, such as the total number of labor hours that are available. The spreadsheet also contains various formulas that relate the resources to the quantities that are produced. Cell E8, for example, will contain a formula that computes the total number of hours used, based on the quantity of each computer and the associated hourly requirements.

The problem is to determine the values of cells B2 through B5, which represent the quantity of each computer to produce. You might be able to solve the problem manually through trial and error, by substituting different values and seeing the impact on profit. That is exactly what Solver will do for you, only it will do it much more quickly. (Solver uses various optimization techniques that are beyond the scope of this discussion.)

Once Solver arrives at a solution, assuming that it can find one, it creates a report such as the one shown in Figure B.2. The solution shows the value of the target cell (the profit in this example), based on the values of the adjustable cells (the quantity of each type of computer). The solution that will maximize profit is to manufacture 700 discount laptops and 800 premium desktops for a profit of $1,270,000.

The report in Figure B.2 also examines each constraint and determines whether it is binding or not binding. A *binding constraint* is one in which the resource is fully utilized (i.e., the slack is zero). The number of available hours, for example, is a binding constraint because every available hour is used, and hence the value of the target cell (profit) is limited by the amount of this resource (the number of hours). Or stated another way, any increase in the number of available hours (above 4,500) will also increase the profit.

A *nonbinding constraint* is just the opposite. It has a nonzero slack (i.e., the resource is not fully utilized), and hence it does not limit the value of the target cell. The laptop demand, for example, is not binding because a total of only 700 laptops were produced, yet the allowable demand was 900 (the value in cell E13). In other words, there is a slack value of 200 for this constraint, and increasing the allowable demand will have no effect on the profit. (The demand could actually be decreased by up to 200 units with no effect on profit.)

1543

Problem is to determine values of cells B2:B5, given the constraints

	A	B	C	D	E
1		Quantity	Hours	Unit Profit	
2	**Discount desktop**		2	$600	
3	**Discount laptop**		3	$800	
4	**Premium desktop**		3	$1,000	
5	**Premium laptop**		5	$1,300	
6					
7		Constraints			
8	Total number of hours used				
9	Labor hours available				4,500
10	Number of desktops produced				
11	Total demand for desktop computers				800
12	Number of laptops produced				
13	Total demand for laptop computers				900
14	Number of discount computers produced				
15	Total demand for discount computers				700
16	Number of premium computers produced				
17	Total demand for premium computers				1,000
18	Hourly cost of labor				$20
19	**Profit**				

E8 will contain formula to compute total hours used

Formula to calculate total profit will be entered in E19

FIGURE B.1 The Initial Worksheet

Target Cell (Max)

Cell	Name	Original Value	Final Value
$E$19	Profit	$0	$1,270,000

Value of target cell (E19)

Adjustable Cells

Cell	Name	Original Value	Final Value
$B$2	Discount desktop Quantity	0	0
$B$3	Discount laptop Quantity	0	700
$B$4	Premium desktop Quantity	0	800
$B$5	Premium laptop Quantity	0	0

Quantities to be produced (B2:B5)

Constraints

Cell	Name	Cell Value	Formula	Status	Slack
$E$8	Total number of hours used	4500	$E$8<=$E$9	Binding	0
$E$10	Number of desktops produced	800	$E$10<=$E$11	Binding	0
$E$12	Number of laptops produced	700	$E$12<=$E$13	Not Binding	200
$E$14	Number of discount computers produced	700	$E$14<=$E$15	Binding	0
$E$16	Number of premium computers produced	800	$E$16<=$E$17	Not Binding	200
$B$2	Discount desktop Quantity	0	$B$2>=0	Binding	0
$B$3	Discount laptop Quantity	700	$B$3>=0	Not Binding	700
$B$4	Premium desktop Quantity	800	$B$4>=0	Not Binding	800
$B$5	Premium laptop Quantity	0	$B$5>=0	Binding	0

Constraints

Status indicates whether constraint is binding or not binding

FIGURE B.2 The Solution

SOLVER

The information required by Solver is entered through the **Solver Parameters dialog box** as shown in Figure B.3. The dialog box is divided into three sections: the target cell, the adjustable cells, and the constraints. The dialog box in Figure B.3 corresponds to the spreadsheet shown earlier in Figure B.1.

The *target cell* identifies the goal (or objective function)—that is, the cell whose value you want to maximize, minimize, or set to a specific value. Our problem seeks to maximize profit, the formula for which is found in cell E19 (the target cell) of the underlying spreadsheet.

The *adjustable cells* (or decision variables) are the cells whose values are adjusted until the constraints are satisfied and the target cell reaches its optimum value. The changing cells in this example contain the quantity of each computer to be produced and are found in cells B2 through B5.

The *constraints* specify the restrictions. Each constraint consists of a cell or cell range on the left, a relational operator, and a numeric value or cell reference on the right. (The constraints can be entered in any order, but they always appear in alphabetical order.) The first constraint references a cell range, cells B2 through B5, and indicates that each of these cells must be greater than or equal to zero. The remaining constraints reference a single cell rather than a cell range.

The functions of the various command buttons are apparent from their names. The Add, Change, and Delete buttons are used to add, change, or delete a constraint. The Options button enables you to set various parameters that determine how Solver attempts to find a solution. The Reset All button clears all settings and resets all options to their defaults. The Solve button begins the search for a solution.

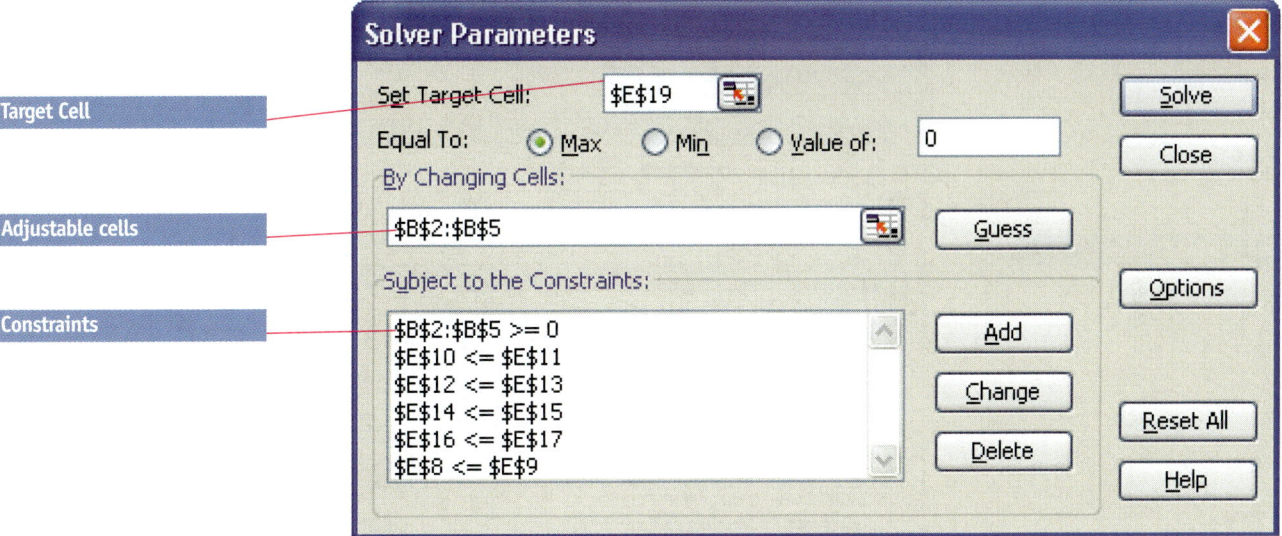

FIGURE B.3 Solver Parameters Dialog Box

THE GREATER-THAN-ZERO CONSTRAINT

One constraint that is often overlooked is the requirement that the value of each adjustable cell be greater than or equal to zero. Physically, it makes no sense to produce a negative number of computers in any category. Mathematically, however, a negative value in an adjustable cell may produce a higher value for the target cell. Hence the nonnegativity (greater than or equal to zero) constraint should always be included for the adjustable cells.

hands-on exercise

1 Maximize Profit

Objective To use Solver to maximize profit; to create a report containing binding and nonbinding constraints. Use Figure B.4 as a guide in the exercise.

Step 1: **Enter the Cell Formulas**

- Start Excel. Open the **Optimization workbook** in the Exploring Excel folder. Save the workbook as **Optimization Solution** so that you can return to the original workbook if necessary.

- If necessary, click the tab for the **Production Mix worksheet**, then click **cell E8** as shown in Figure B.4a.

- Enter the formula shown in Figure B.4a to compute the total number of hours used in production.

- Enter the remaining cell formulas as shown below:
  - Cell E10 (Number of desktops produced) =**B2+B4**
  - Cell E12 (Number of laptops produced) =**B3+B5**
  - Cell E14 (Number of discount computers produced) =**B2+B3**
  - Cell E16 (Number of premium computers produced) =**B4+B5**
  - Cell E19 (Profit) =**B2*D2+B3*D3+B4*D4+B5*D5−E18*E8**

- Save the workbook.

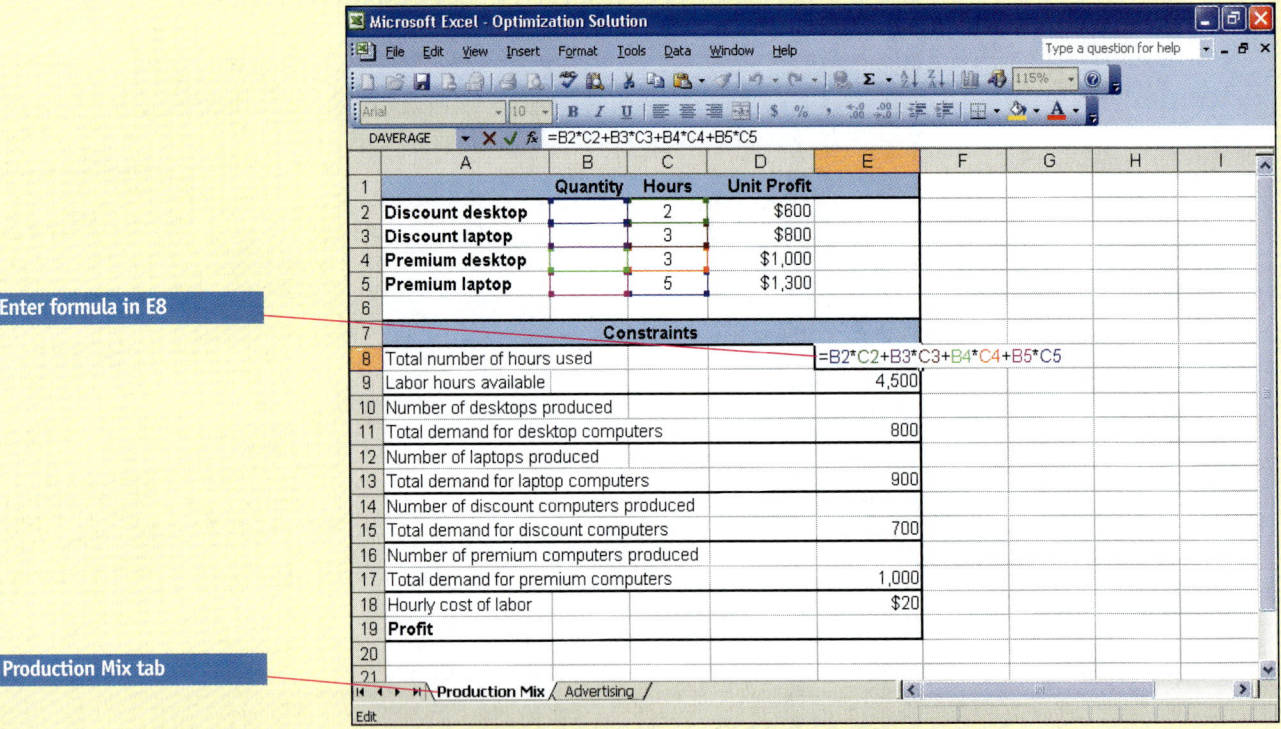

(a) Enter the Cell Formulas (step 1)

FIGURE B.4 Hands-on Exercise 1

1546 APPENDIX B: SOLVER

Step 2: **Set the Target and Adjustable Cells**

- Check that the formula in cell E19 is entered correctly as shown in Figure B.4b. Pull down the **Tools menu**. Click **Solver** to display the Solver Parameters dialog box shown in Figure B.4b.

- If necessary, click in the text box for **Set Target Cell**. Click in **cell E19** to set the target cell. The Max option button is selected by default.

- Click in the **By Changing Cells** text box. Click and drag **cells B2 through B5** in the worksheet to select these cells.

- Click the **Add command button** to add the first constraint as described in step 3.

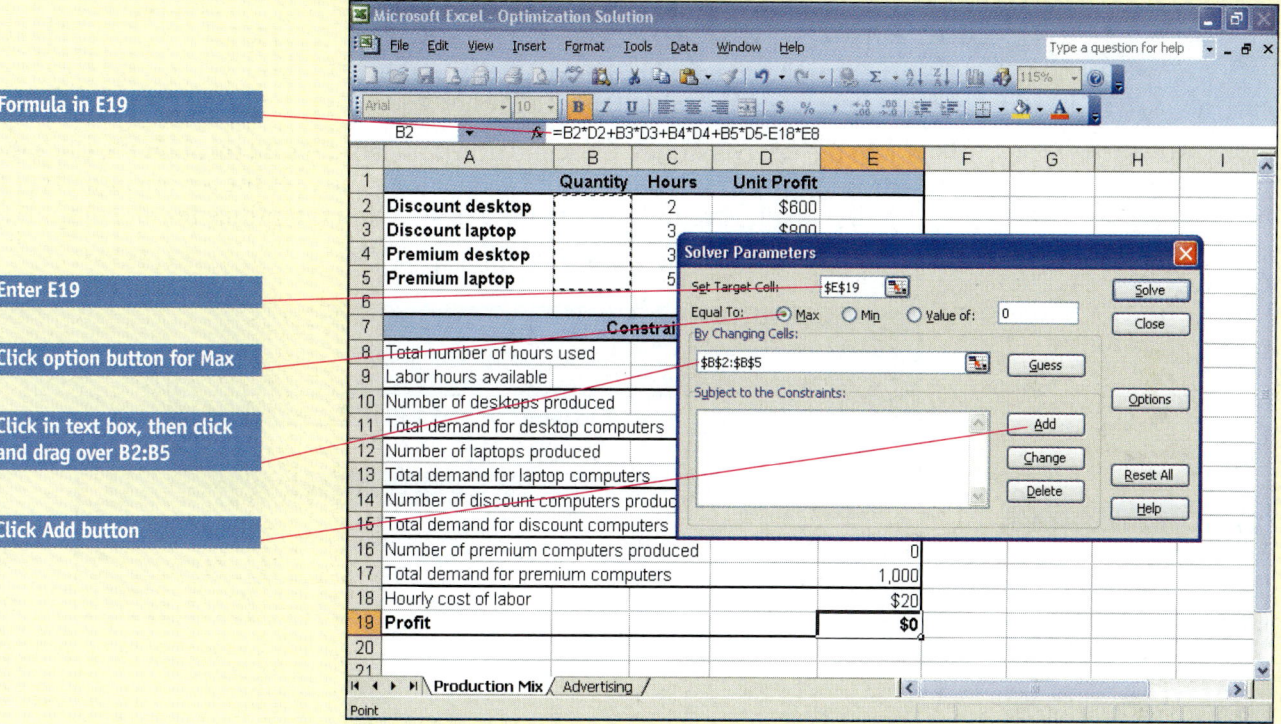

(b) Set the Target and Adjustable Cells (step 2)

FIGURE B.4 Hands-on Exercise 1 (*continued*)

MISSING SOLVER

Solver is an optional component of Microsoft Excel, and hence it may not be installed on your system. If you are working on a computer at school, your instructor should be able to notify the network administrator to correct the problem. If you are working on your own machine, pull down the Tools menu, click the Add-Ins command, check the box for Solver, then click OK to close the Add-Ins dialog box. Click Yes when asked to install Solver. You will need the Microsoft Office CD.

Step 3: **Enter the Constraints**

- You should see the Add Constraint dialog box in Figure B.4c with the insertion point (a flashing vertical line) in the Cell Reference text box.
    - Click in **cell E8** (the cell containing the formula to compute the total number of hours used). The <= constraint is selected by default.
    - Click in the **Constraint** text box, which will contain the value of the constraint, then click **cell E9** in the worksheet to enter the cell reference.
    - Click **Add** to complete this constraint and add another.

- You will see a new (empty) Add Constraint dialog box, which enables you to enter additional constraints. Use pointing to enter each of the constraints shown below. (Solver automatically enters each reference as an absolute reference.)
    - Enter the constraint **E10<=E11**. Click **Add**.
    - Enter the constraint **E12<=E13**. Click **Add**.
    - Enter the constraint **E14<=E15**. Click **Add**.
    - Enter the constraint **E16<=E17**. Click **Add**.

- Add the last constraint. Click and drag to select **cells B2 through B5**. Click the drop-down arrow for the relational operators and click the **>=** operator. Type **0** in the text box to indicate that the production quantities for all computers must be greater than or equal to zero. Click **OK**.

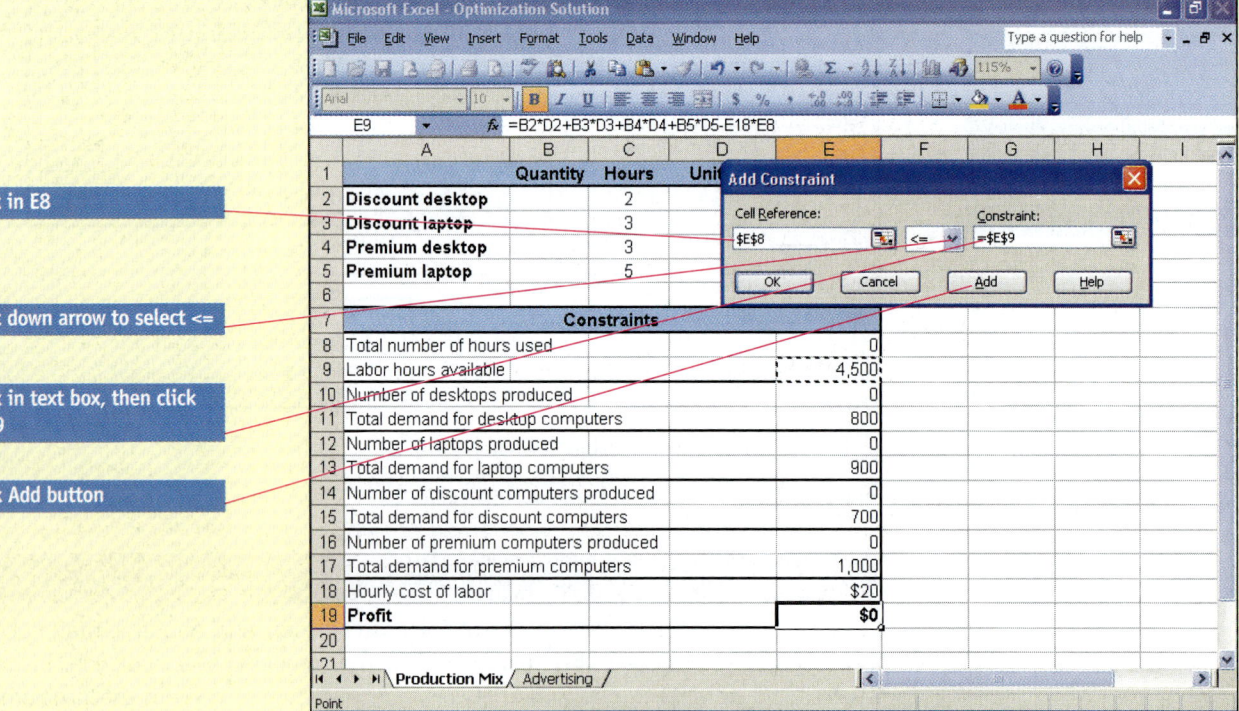

(c) Enter the Constraints (step 3)

FIGURE B.4 Hands-on Exercise 1 (*continued*)

ADD VERSUS OK

Click the Add button to complete the current constraint and display an empty dialog box to enter another constraint. Click OK only when you have completed the last constraint and want to return to the Solver Parameters dialog box to solve the problem.

Step 4: Solve the Problem

- Check that the contents of the Solver Parameters dialog box match those of Figure B.4d. (The constraints appear in alphabetical order rather than the order in which they were entered.)
  - To change the Target cell, click the **Set Target Cell** text box, then click the appropriate target cell in the worksheet.
  - To change (edit) a constraint, select the constraint, then click the **Change button**.
  - To delete a constraint, select the constraint and click the **Delete button**.

- Click the **Solve button** to solve the problem.

- You should see the Solver Results dialog box, indicating that Solver has found a solution. The maximum profit is $1,270,000. The option button to Keep Solver Solution is selected by default.

- Click **Answer** in the Reports list box, then click **OK** to generate the report. You will see the report being generated, after which the Solver Results dialog box closes automatically.

- Save the workbook.

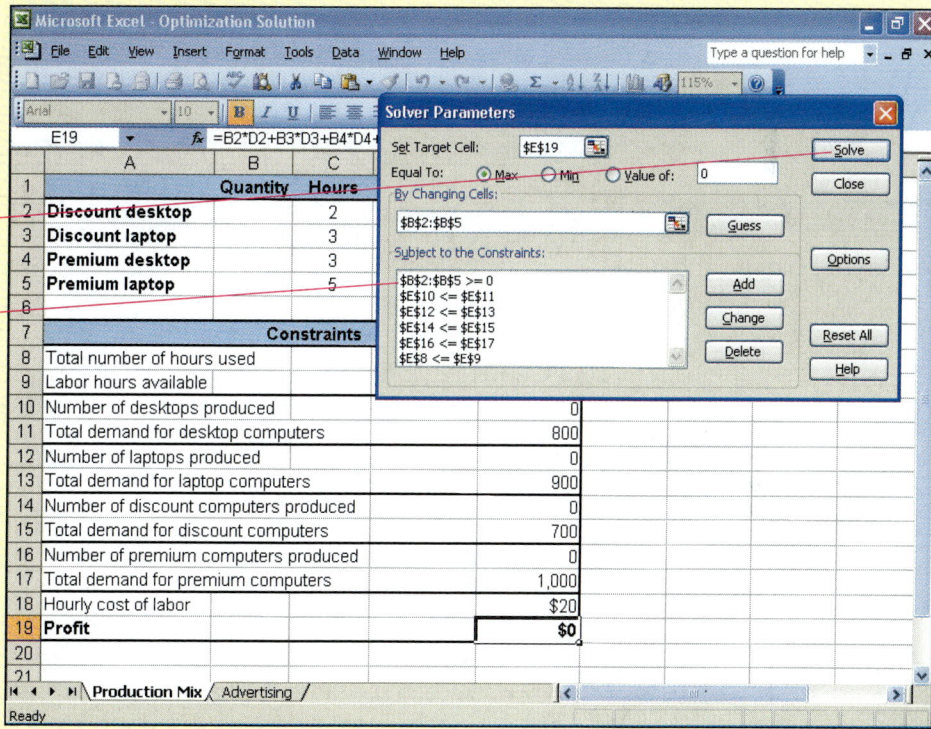

(d) Solve the Problem (step 4)

FIGURE B.4   Hands-on Exercise 1 (*continued*)

MICROSOFT OFFICE EXCEL 2003   1549

Step 5: View the Report

- Click the **Answer Report 1 worksheet tab** to view the report as shown in Figure B.4e. Click in **cell A4**, the cell immediately under the entry showing the date and time the report was created. (The gridlines and row and column headings are suppressed by default for this worksheet.)

- Enter your name in boldface as shown in the figure, then press **Enter** to complete the entry. Print the answer sheet and submit it to your instructor as proof you did the exercise.

- Save the workbook. Exit Excel if you do not wish to continue with the next exercise at this time.

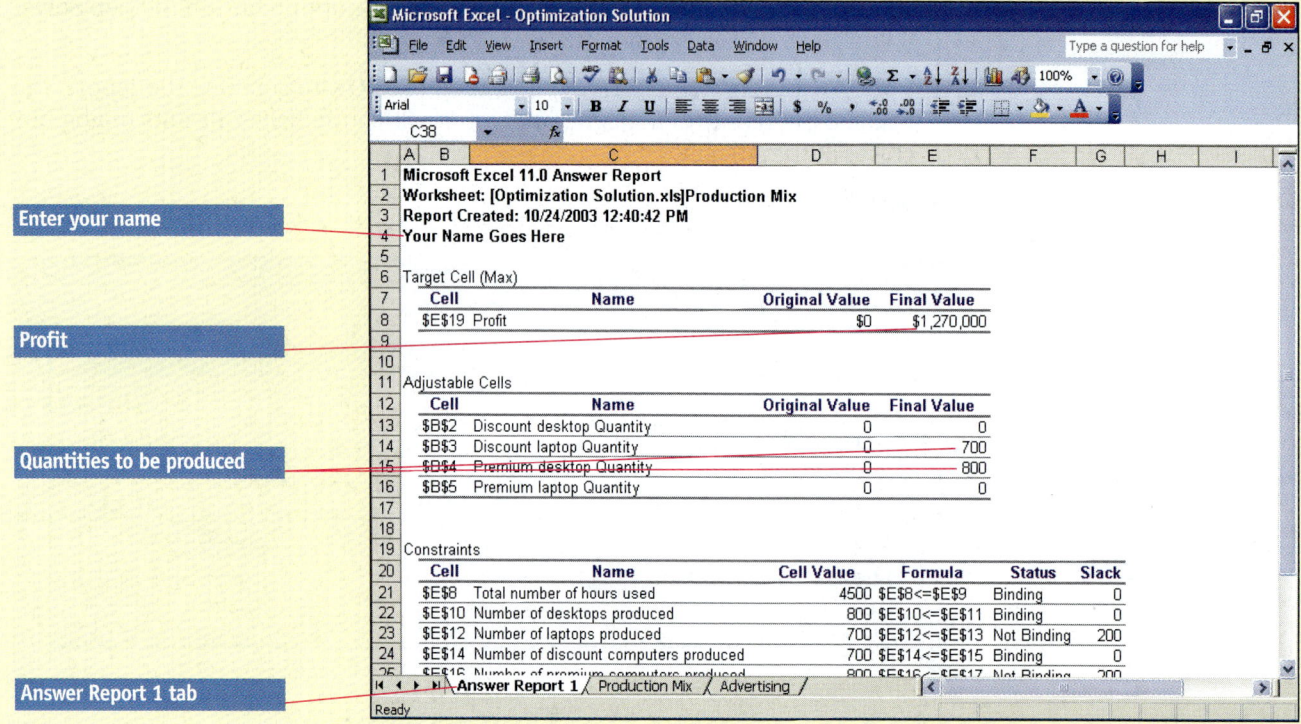

(e) View the Report (step 5)

FIGURE B.4 Hands-on Exercise 1 (*continued*)

VIEW OPTIONS

Any worksheet used to create a spreadsheet model will display gridlines and row and column headers by default. Worksheets containing reports, however, especially reports generated by Excel, often suppress these elements to make the reports easier and more appealing to read. To suppress (display) these elements, pull down the Tools menu, click Options, click the View tab, then clear (check) the appropriate check boxes under Window options.

EXAMPLE 2—MINIMIZE COST

The example just concluded introduced you to the basics of Solver. We continue now with a second hands-on exercise, to provide additional practice, and to discuss various subtleties that can occur. This time we present a minimization problem in which we seek to minimize cost subject to a series of constraints. The problem will focus on the advertising campaign that will be conducted to sell the computers you have produced.

The director of marketing has allocated a total of $125,000 in his weekly advertising budget. He wants to establish a presence in both magazines and radio, and requires a minimum of four magazine ads and ten radio ads each week. Each magazine ad costs $10,000 and is seen by one million readers. Each radio commercial costs $5,000 and is heard by 250,000 listeners. How many ads of each type should be placed to reach at least 10 million customers at minimum cost?

All of the necessary information is contained within the previous paragraph. You must, however, display that information in a worksheet before you can ask Solver to find a solution. Accordingly, reread the previous paragraph, then try to set up a worksheet from which you can call Solver. (Our worksheet appears in step 1 of the following hands-on exercise. Try, however, to set up your own worksheet before you look at ours.)

FINER POINTS OF SOLVER

Figure B.5 displays the **Solver Options dialog box** that enables you to specify how Solver will approach the solution. The Max Time and Iterations entries determine how long Solver will work on finding the solution. If either limit is reached before a solution is found, Solver will ask whether you want to continue. The default settings of 100 seconds and 100 *iterations* are sufficient for simpler problems, but may fall short for complex problems with multiple constraints.

The Precision setting determines how close the computed values in the constraint cells come to the specified value of the resource. The smaller the precision, the longer Solver will take in arriving at a solution. The default setting of .0000001 is adequate for most problems and should not be decreased. The remaining options are beyond the scope of our discussion.

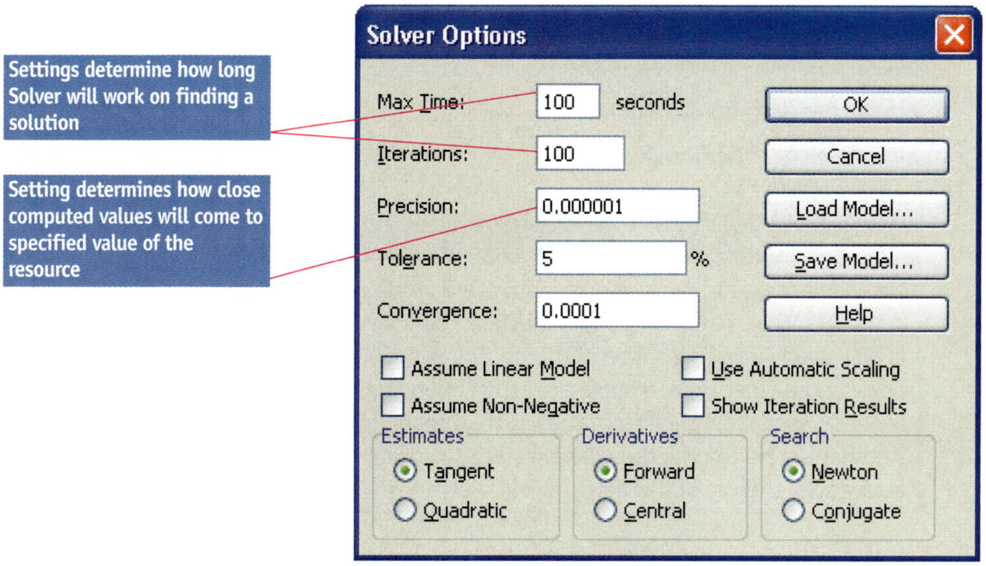

FIGURE B.5 Options Dialog Box

hands-on exercise 2 | Minimize Cost

Objective To use Solver to minimize cost; to impose an integer constraint and examine its effect on the optimal solution; to relax a constraint in order to find a feasible solution. Use Figure B.6 as a guide in the exercise.

Step 1: **Enter the Cell Formulas**

- Open the **Optimization Solution workbook** from the previous exercise.

- Click the tab for the **Advertising worksheet**, then click in **cell E6**. Enter the formula =B2*C2+B3*C3 as shown in Figure B.6a.

- Click in **cell E10**. Enter the formula =B2*D2+B3*D3 to compute the size of the audience. Save the workbook.

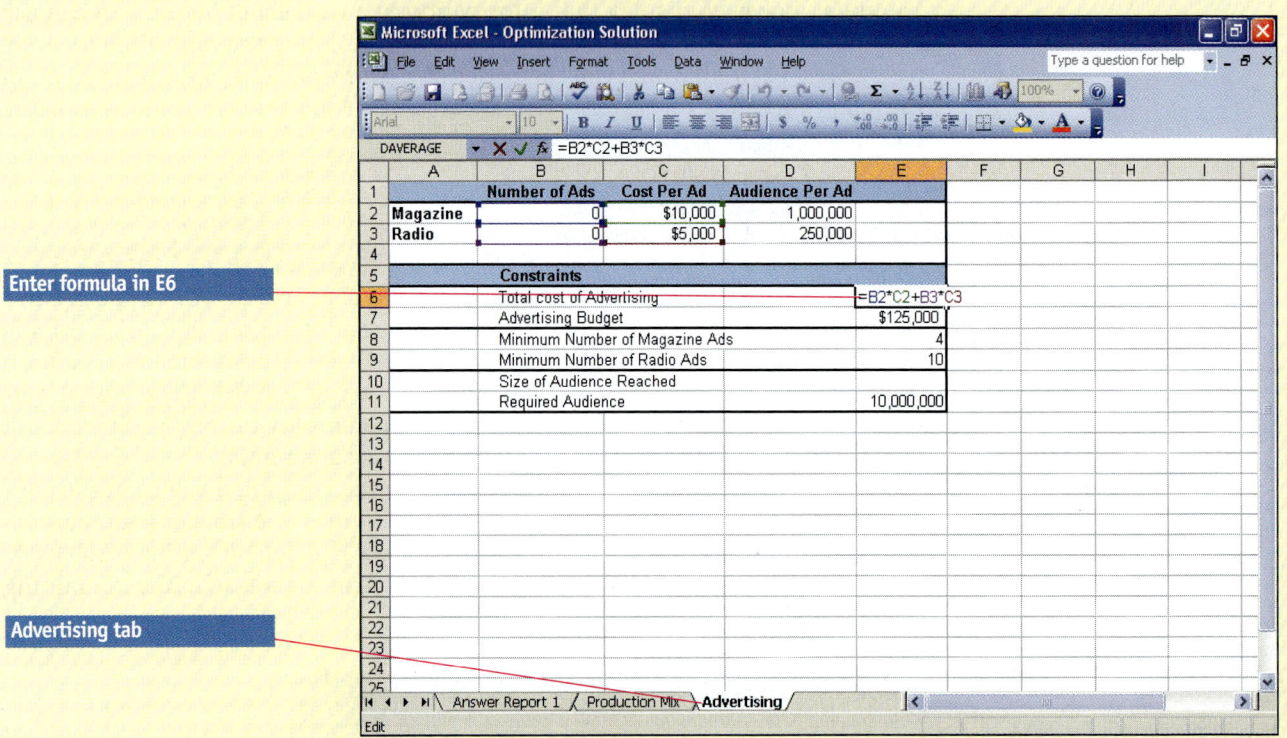

(a) Enter the Cell Formulas (step 1)

FIGURE B.6 Hands-on Exercise 2

USE THE TASK PANE

The easiest way to reopen a recently used workbook is to use the task pane. Pull down the View menu and toggle the Task Pane command on so that the task pane is displayed in the right side of the application window. Click the name of the workbook in the Open a workbook area to reopen the workbook. You can also open a recently used workbook from the list that appears at the bottom of the File menu. Another way is to click the Windows Start button, click the My Recent Documents command, then click the name of the workbook when it appears in the submenu.

Step 2: **Set the Target and Adjustable Cells**

- Pull down the **Tools menu**. Click **Solver** to display the Solver Parameters dialog box shown in Figure B.6b.

- Set the target cell to **cell E6**. Click the **Min (Minimize) option button**. Click in the **By Changing Cells** text box.

- Click and drag **cells B2 and B3** in the worksheet to select these cells as shown in Figure B.6b.

- Click the **Add command button** to add the first constraint as described in step 3.

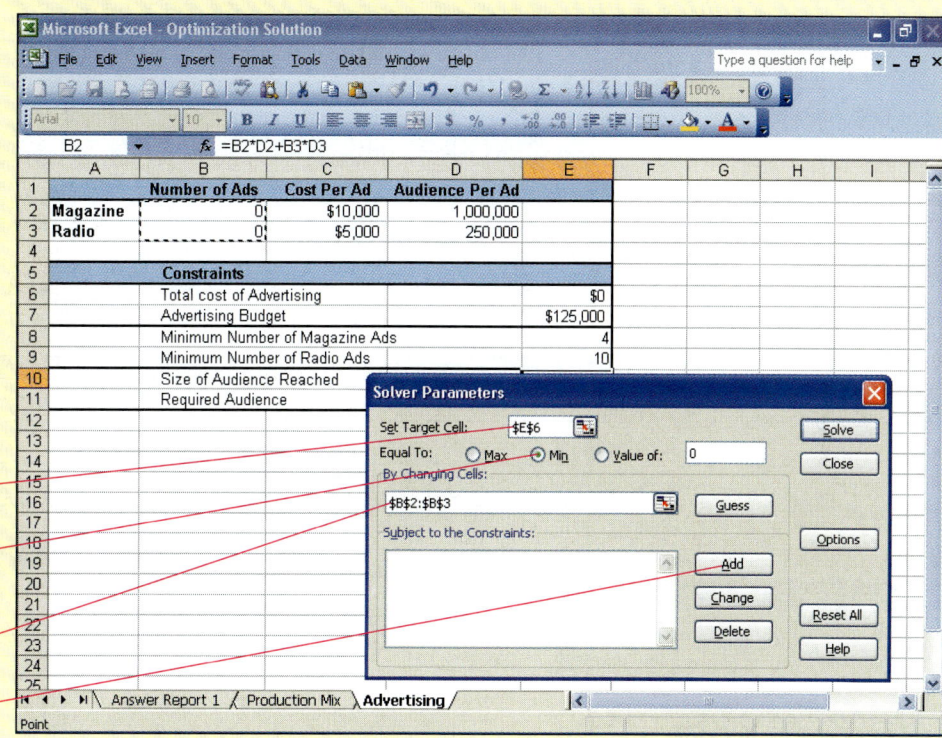

(b) Set the Target and Adjustable Cells (step 2)

FIGURE B.6 Hands-on Exercise 2 (*continued*)

REVIEW THE TERMINOLOGY

Solver is an optimization technique that allows you to maximize or minimize the value of an objective function, such as profit or cost, respectively. The formula to compute the objective function is stored in the target cell within the worksheet. Other cells in the worksheet contain the variables or adjustable cells. Another set of cells contains the value of the available resources or constraints. This type of optimization problem is referred to as linear programming.

Step 3: **Enter the Constraints**

- You should see the Add Constraint dialog box in Figure B.6c with the insertion point (a flashing vertical line) in the Cell Reference text box.
  - Click in **cell E6** (the cell containing the total cost of advertising).
  - The <= constraint is selected by default.
  - Click in the text box to contain the value of the constraint, then click **cell E7** to enter the cell reference in the Add Constraint dialog box. Click **Add**.

- You will see a new (empty) Add Constraint dialog box, which enables you to enter additional constraints. Use pointing to enter each of the constraints shown below. (Solver converts each reference to an absolute reference.)
  - Enter the constraint **E10>=E11**. Click **Add**.
  - Enter the constraint **B2>=E8**. Click **Add**.
  - Enter the constraint **B3>=E9**. Click **OK** since this is the last constraint.

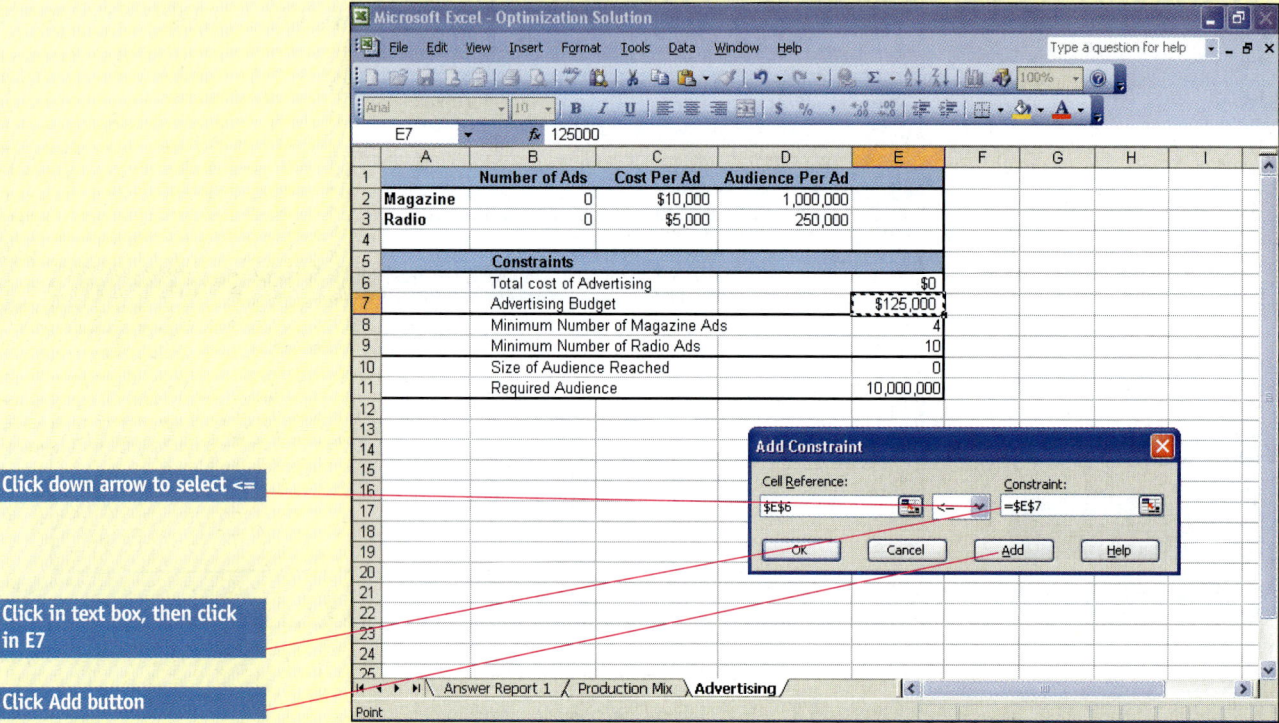

(c) Enter the Constraints (step 3)

FIGURE B.6 Hands-on Exercise 2 (*continued*)

SHOW ITERATION RESULTS

Solver uses an iterative (repetitive) approach in which each iteration (trial solution) is one step closer to the optimal solution. It may be interesting, therefore, to examine the intermediate solutions, especially if you have a knowledge of optimization techniques, such as linear programming. Click the Options command button in the Solver Parameters dialog box, check the Show Iterations Results box, click OK to close the Solver Options dialog box, then click the Solve command button in the usual fashion. A Show Trial Solutions dialog box will appear as each intermediate solution is displayed in the worksheet. Click Continue to move from one iteration to the next until the optimal solution is reached.

Step 4: **Solve the Problem**

- Check that the contents of the Solver Parameters dialog box match those in Figure B.6d. (The constraints appear in alphabetical order rather than the order in which they were entered.)

- Click the **Solve button** to solve the problem. The Solver Results dialog box appears and indicates that Solver has arrived at a solution.

- The option button to Keep Solver Solution is selected by default. Click **OK** to close the Solver Results dialog box and display the solution.

- Save the workbook.

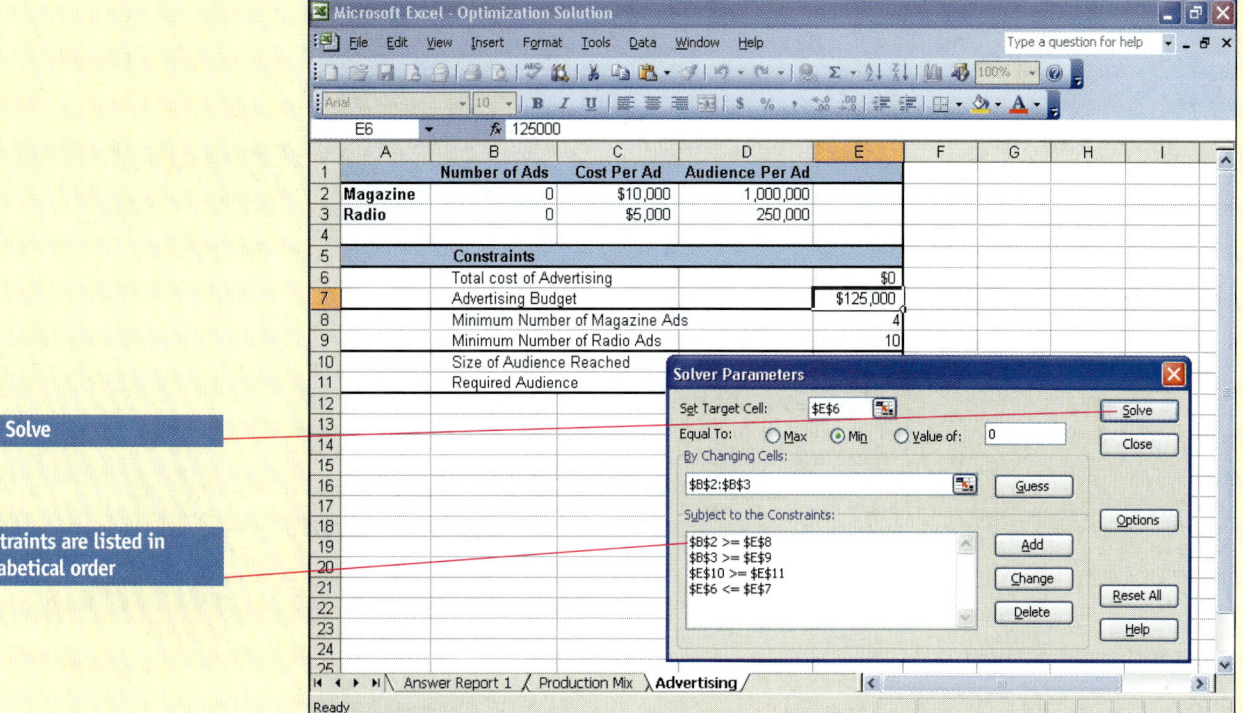

(d) Solve the Problem (step 4)

FIGURE B.6 Hands-on Exercise 2 (continued)

USE POINTING TO ENTER CELL FORMULAS

A cell reference can be typed directly into a formula, or it can be entered more easily through pointing. To use pointing, select (click) the cell to contain the formula, type an equal sign to begin entering the formula, then click (or move to) the cell containing the value to be used. Type any arithmetic operator to place the cell reference into the formula, then continue pointing to additional cells. Press the Enter key (instead of typing an arithmetic operator) to complete the formula.

Step 5: **Impose an Integer Constraint**

- The number of magazine ads in the solution is 7.5 as shown in Figure B.6e. This is a noninteger number, which is reasonable in the context of Solver but not in the "real world" as one cannot place half an ad.

- Pull down the **Tools menu**. Click **Solver** to once again display the Solver Parameters dialog box. Click the **Add button** to display the Add Constraint dialog box in Figure B.6e.

- The insertion point is already positioned in the Cell Reference text box. Click and drag to select **cells B2 through B3**. Click the **drop-down arrow** in the Constraint list box and click **int** (for integer).

- Click **OK** to accept the constraint and close the Add Constraint dialog box.

- The Solver Parameters dialog box appears on your monitor with the integer constraint added. Click **Solve** to solve the problem.

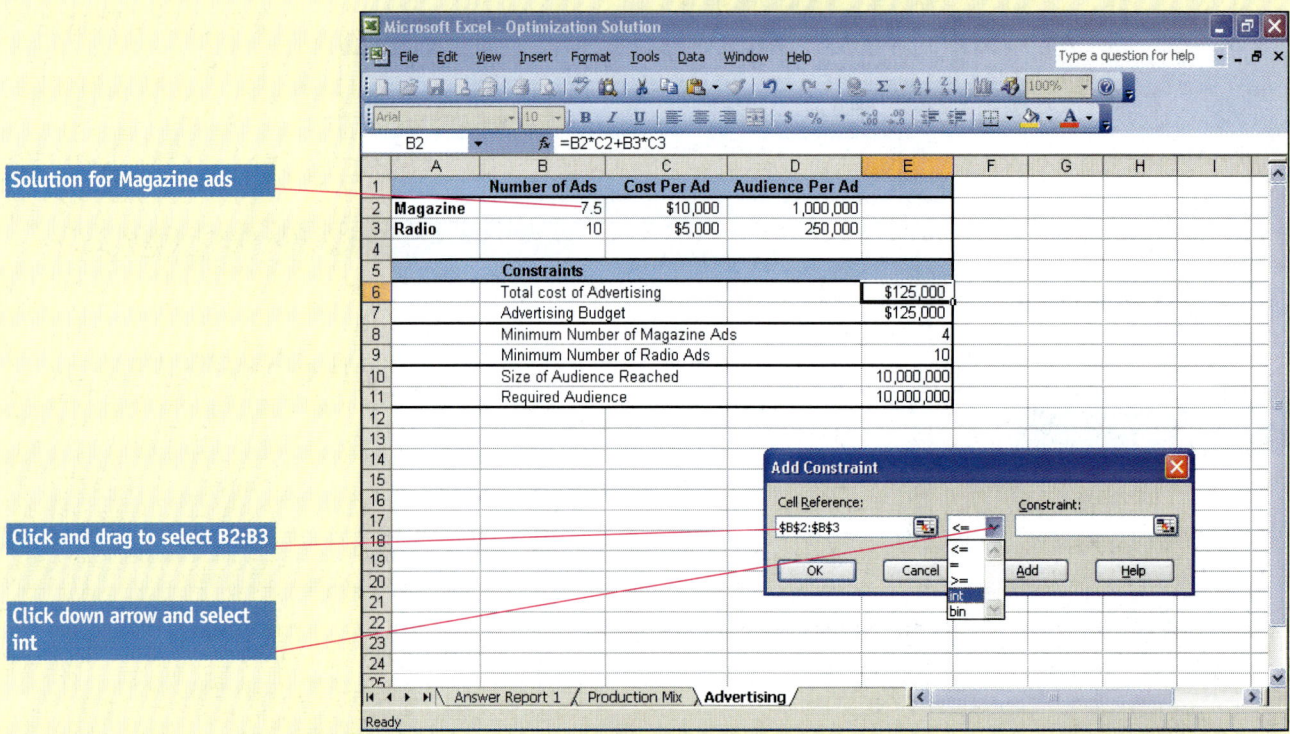

(e) Impose an Integer Constraint (step 5)

FIGURE B.6 Hands-on Exercise 2 (*continued*)

DO YOU REALLY NEED AN INTEGER SOLUTION?

It seems like such a small change, but specifying an integer constraint can significantly increase the amount of time required for Solver to reach a solution. The examples in this chapter are relatively simple and did not take an inordinate amount of time to solve. Imposing an integer constraint on a more complex problem, however, may challenge your patience as Solver struggles to reach a solution.

Step 6: **The Infeasible Solution**

- You should see the dialog box in Figure B.6f, indicating that Solver could *not* find a solution that satisfied the existing constraints. This is because the imposition of the integer constraint would raise the number of magazine ads from 7.5 to 8, which would increase the total cost of advertising to $130,000, exceeding the budget of $125,000.

- The desired audience can still be reached but only by relaxing one of the binding constraints. You can, for example, retain the requisite number of magazine and radio ads by increasing the budget. Alternatively, the budget can be held at $125,000, while still reaching the audience by decreasing the required number of radio ads.

- Click **Cancel** to exit the dialog box and return to the worksheet.

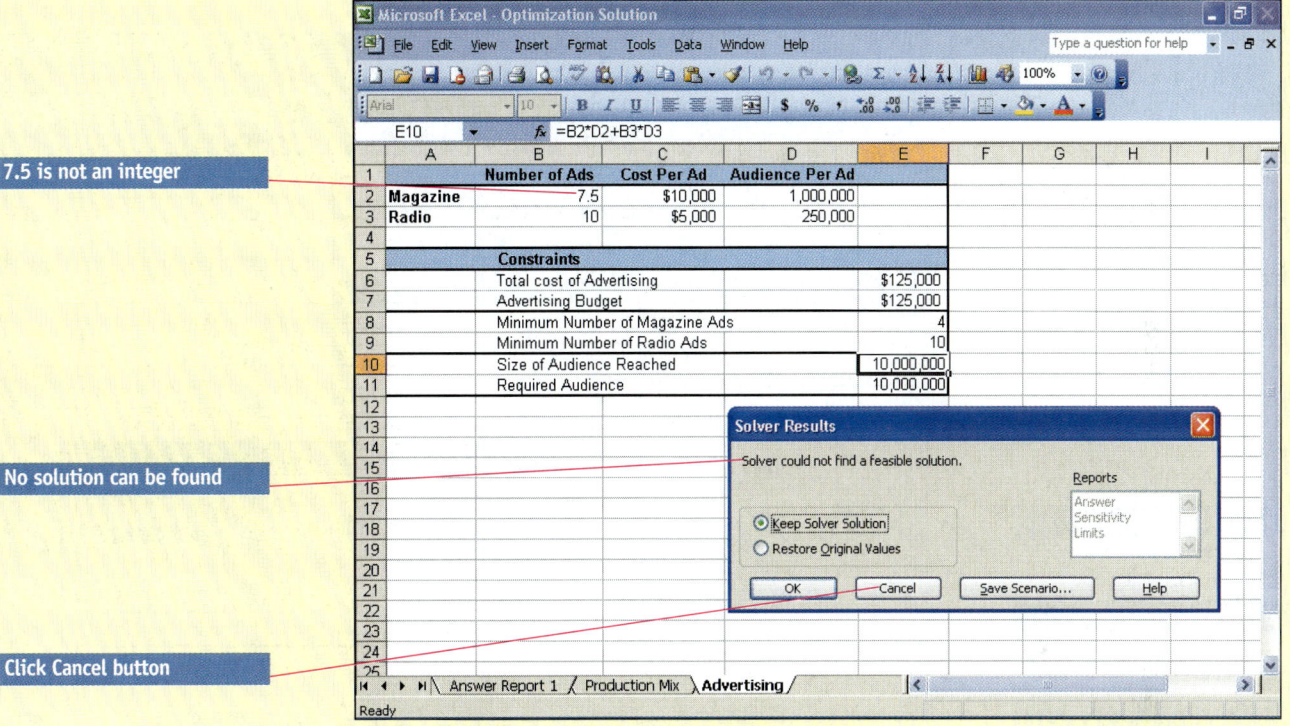

(f) The Infeasible Solution (step 6)

FIGURE B.6 Hands-on Exercise 2 (*continued*)

UNABLE TO FIND A SOLUTION

Solver is a powerful tool, but it cannot do the impossible. Some problems simply do not have a solution because the constraints may conflict with one another, and/or because the constraints exceed the available resources. Should this occur, and it will, check your constraints to make sure they were entered correctly. If Solver is still unable to reach a solution, it will be necessary to relax one or more of the constraints.

Step 7: **Relax a Constraint**

- Click in **cell E9** (the cell containing the minimum number of radio ads). Enter **9** and press **Enter**.

- Pull down the **Tools menu**. Click **Solver** to display the Solver Parameters dialog box. Click **Solve**. This time Solver finds a solution as shown in Figure B.6g.

- Click **Answer** in the Reports list box, then click **OK** to generate the report. You will see the report being generated, after which the Solver Results dialog box closes automatically.

- Click the **Answer Report 2 worksheet tab** to view the report. Add your name to the report, boldface your name, print the answer report, and submit it to your instructor.

- Save the workbook.

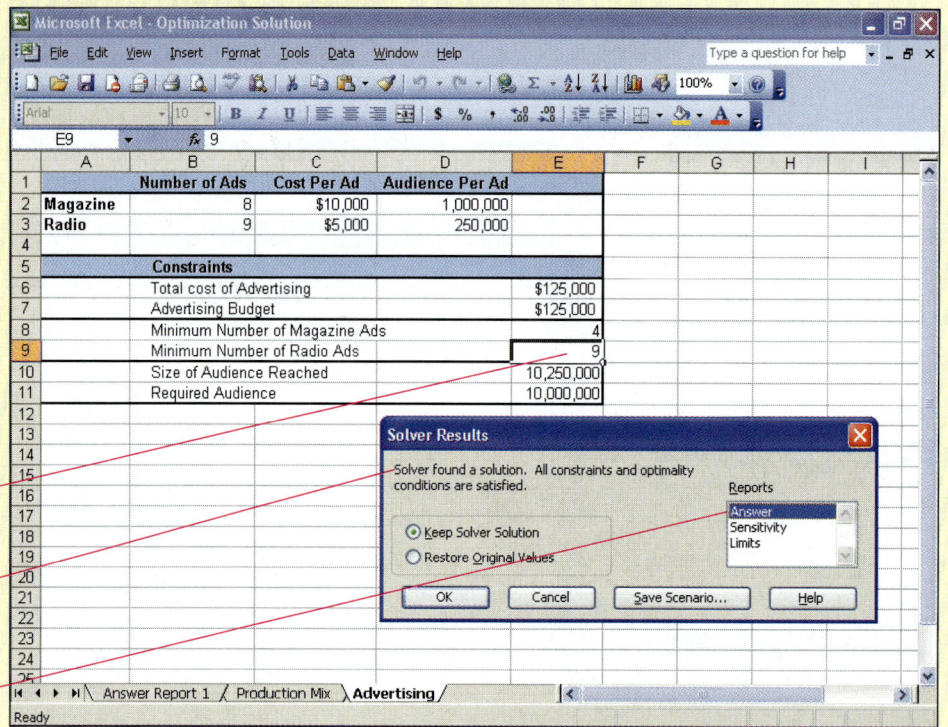

(g) Relax a Constraint (step 7)

FIGURE B.6 Hands-on Exercise 2 (*continued*)

SENSITIVITY, BINDING, AND NONBINDING CONSTRAINTS

A sensitivity report shows the effect of increasing resources associated with the binding and nonbinding constraints within the optimization problem. A binding constraint has a limiting effect on the objective value; that is, relaxing a binding constraint by increasing the associated resource will improve the value of the objective function. Conversely, a nonbinding constraint does not have a limiting effect, and increasing its resource has no effect on the value of the objective function.

Step 8: **Add the Documentation Worksheet**

- This step creates a documentation worksheet similar to the one in Chapter 6. Pull down the **Insert menu** and click the **Worksheet command**.

- Double click the **tab** of the newly inserted worksheet. Enter **Documentation** as the new name and press **Enter**. If necessary, click and drag the worksheet tab to move it to the beginning of the workbook.

- Enter the descriptive entries in **cells A3**, **A4**, **and A6** as shown in Figure B.6h. Use boldface as shown. Increase the width of column A.

- Enter your name in **cell B3**. Enter **=Today( )** in **cell B4**. Press **Enter**. Click the **Left Align button** to align the date as shown in the figure.

- Increase the width of column B, then click in **cell B6** and enter the indicated text. Do not press the Enter key until you have completed the entry.

- Click in **cell B6**, then pull down the **Format menu** and click the **Cells command** to display the Format Cells dialog box. Click the **Alignment tab**, click the box to **Wrap Text**, then click **OK**.

- Point to **cell A6**, then click the **right mouse button** to display a shortcut menu. Click **Format Cells** to display the Format Cells dialog box. If necessary, click the **Alignment tab**, click the **drop-down arrow** in the Vertical list box, and select **Top**. Click **OK**.

- Click in **cell A1**. Enter **Solver—An Optimization Technique**. Change the font size to **18**. Click and drag to select **cells A1** and **B1**. Click the **Merge and Center button** to center the title across cells A1 and B1.

- Complete the entries in the remainder of the worksheet. Check the worksheet for spelling. Save the workbook. Print the documentation worksheet.

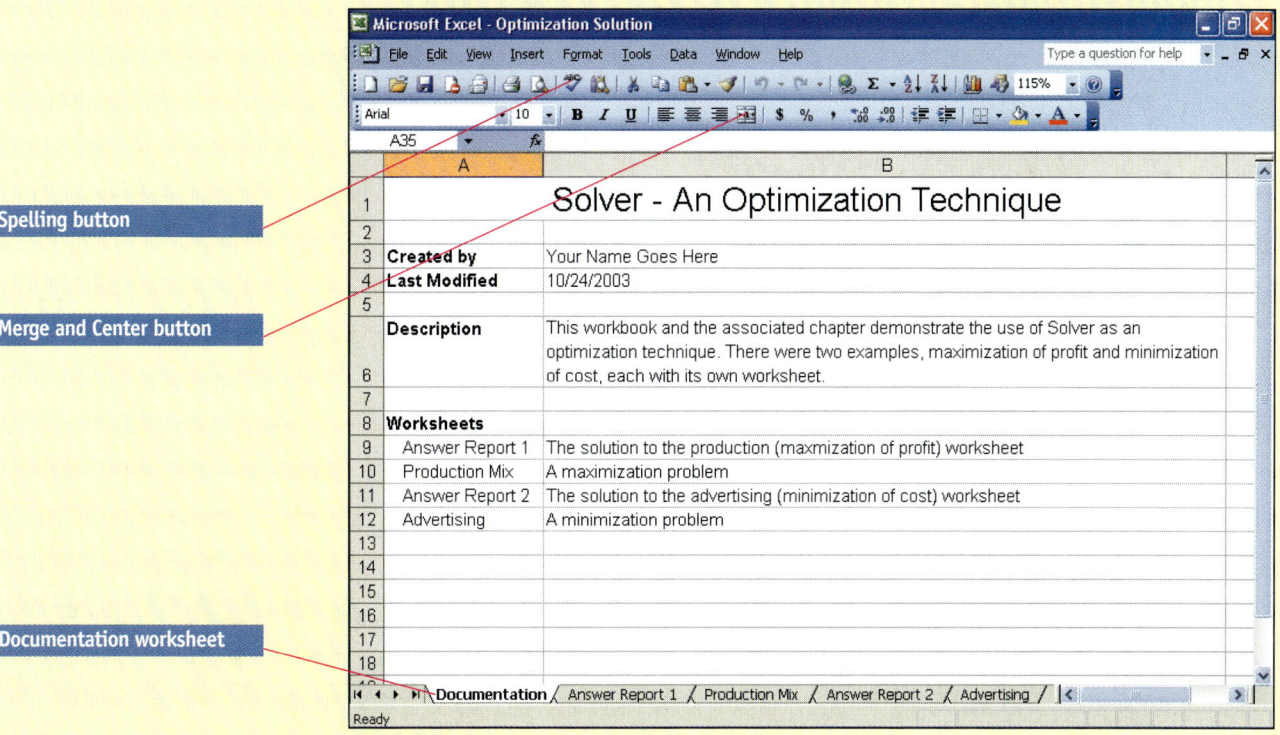

(h) Add the Documentation Worksheet (step 8)

FIGURE B.6   Hands-on Exercise 2 (*continued*)

SUMMARY

Solver is an optimization and resource allocation tool that helps you achieve a desired goal, such as maximizing profit or minimizing cost. The information required by Solver is entered through the Solver Parameters dialog box, which is divided into three sections: the target cell, the adjustable cells, and the constraints.

The target cell identifies the goal (or objective function), which is the cell whose value you want to maximize, minimize, or set to a specific value. The adjustable cells are the cells whose values are changed until the constraints are satisfied and the target cell reaches its optimum value. The constraints specify the restrictions. Each constraint consists of a comparison containing a cell or cell range on the left, a relational operator, and a numeric value or cell reference on the right.

The Solver Options dialog box lets you specify how Solver will attempt to find a solution. The Max Time and Iterations entries determine how long Solver will work on finding a solution. If either limit is reached before a solution is found, Solver will ask whether you want to continue. The default settings of 100 seconds and 100 iterations are sufficient for simpler problems, but may not be enough for complex problems with multiple constraints.

KEY TERMS

Adjustable cells 1545	Nonbinding constraint 1543	Solver Parameters dialog
Binding constraint 1543	Solver 1545	box 1545
Constraint 1545	Solver Options dialog box 1551	Target cell 1545
Iteration 1551		

CHAPTER 5

One-to-many Relationships: Subforms and Multiple-table Queries

OBJECTIVES

After reading this chapter you will:

1. Distinguish between a primary key and a foreign key.
2. Define referential integrity.
3. Use the Relationships window to create a one-to-many relationship.
4. Explain how the AutoNumber field type simplifies data entry.
5. Distinguish between a main form and a subform.
6. Create a multiple-table query, then use the query to create a report.
7. Create a main form with linked subforms.

hands-on exercises

1. ONE-TO-MANY RELATIONSHIPS
   Input: National Bank
   Output: National Bank (modified)

2. CREATING A SUBFORM
   Input: National Bank (from exercise 1)
   Output: National Bank (modified)

3. QUERIES AND REPORTS
   Input: National Bank (from exercise 2)
   Output: National Bank (modified)

4. LINKED SUBFORMS
   Input: National Bank (from exercise 3)
   Output: National Bank (modified)

CASE STUDY
EVERGREEN FLYING CLUB

The Evergreen Flying Club is a 45-year-old, nonprofit flying club whose members fly and maintain antique airplanes. The airplanes are delicate and require hangar storage, as opposed to being left out in the open air. The club has affiliations with several private airports in the tri-state area in order to provide timely information to its members as new hangar space becomes available. Each airport has multiple hangars, but a specific hangar is associated with only one airport. Most club members lease space in more than one airport; they may own more than one airplane, and/or they may lease a hangar at different airports so that they will be able to store their plane overnight when they take trips.

Frank Barber, the president of Evergreen, maintains all information about the club on paper, but this is no longer practical. The membership has grown, as has the number of affiliated airports as well as the number of hangars in individual airports. Frank needs an Access database and has come to you for help in return for flying lessons. This is an exciting project and you cannot wait to get started. ■

Your assignment is to read the chapter, paying special attention on how to create a one-to-many relationship and enforce referential integrity. You will then create a new database with the required tables for the Evergreen Flying Club. You do not have to enter data into any of the tables, but you are to include all necessary fields and set the properties appropriately. Frank suggests three tables for airports, members, and hangars.

The Hangars table is especially important and should include the HangarID, AirportID, CustomerID, length, width, height, the date the lease begins, the date the lease ends, and the monthly rental. The design of the Airports and Customers tables is left to you. Your database should also include a basic switchboard, an About form, and a relationships diagram. Use a common clip art image and consistent design elements for each object in the database. Print the switchboard form, the table of switchboard items, the relationships diagram, and the About form for your instructor.

A DATABASE FOR CONSUMER LOANS

The real power of Access stems from its use as a relational database that contains multiple tables and the objects associated with those tables. We introduced this concept at the end of Chapter 1 when we looked briefly at a database that had three tables. We revisited the concept in the previous chapter when we looked at a second relational database. This chapter presents an entirely new case study that focuses on a relational database.

Let us assume that you are in the Information Systems department of a commercial bank and are assigned the task of implementing a system for consumer loans. The bank needs complete data about every loan (the amount, interest rate, term, and so on). It also needs data about the customers holding those loans (name, address, telephone, etc.). The problem is how to structure the data so that the bank will be able to obtain all of the information it needs from its database. The system must be able to supply the name and address of the person associated with a loan. The system must also be able to retrieve all of the loans for a specific individual. We present two alternative solutions.

The first solution is based on an expanded loans table as shown in Figure 5.1. At first glance this solution appears to be satisfactory. You can, for example, search for a specific loan (e.g., L0006) and determine that Lori Sangastiano is the customer associated with that loan. You can also search for a particular customer (e.g., Michelle Zacco) and find all of her loans (L0007, L0008, L0009, and L0021).

LoanID	Loan Data	Customer Data
L0001	Loan data for loan L0001	Customer data for Wendy Solomon
L0002	Loan data for loan L0002	Customer data for Wendy Solomon
L0003	Loan data for loan L0003	Customer data for Alex Rey
L0004	Loan data for loan L0004	Customer data for Wendy Solomon
L0005	Loan data for loan L0005	Customer data for Ted Myerson
L0006	Loan data for loan L0006	Customer data for Lori Sangastiano
L0007	Loan data for loan L0007	Customer data for Michelle Zacco
L0008	Loan data for loan L0008	Customer data for Michelle Zacco
L0009	Loan data for loan L0009	Customer data for Michelle Zacco
L0010	Loan data for loan L0010	Customer data for Eileen Faulkner
L0011	Loan data for loan L0011	Customer data for Scott Wit
L0012	Loan data for loan L0012	Customer data for Alex Rey
L0013	Loan data for loan L0013	Customer data for David Powell
L0014	Loan data for loan L0014	Customer data for Matt Hirsch
L0015	Loan data for loan L0015	Customer data for Benjamin Grauer
L0016	Loan data for loan L0016	Customer data for Eileen Faulkner
L0017	Loan data for loan L0017	Customer data for Eileen Faulkner
L0018	Loan data for loan L0018	Customer data for Benjamin Grauer
L0019	Loan data for loan L0019	Customer data for Scott Wit
L0020	Loan data for loan L0020	Customer data for Benjamin Grauer
L0021	Loan data for loan L0021	Customer data for Michelle Zacco
L0022	Loan data for loan L0022	Customer data for Matt Hirsch
L0023	Loan data for loan L0023	Customer data for Benjamin Grauer
L0024	Loan data for loan L0024	Customer data for Wendy Solomon
L0025	Loan data for loan L0025	Customer data for Lori Sangastiano

FIGURE 5.1 Single-table Solution

There is a problem, however, in that the table duplicates customer data throughout the database. Thus, when one customer has multiple loans, the customer's name, address, and other data are stored multiple times. Maintaining the data in this form is a time-consuming and error-prone procedure, because any change to the customer's data has to be made in many places.

A second problem arises if you were to enter data for a new customer before a loan has been approved. The bank receives the customer's application data prior to granting a loan, and it wants to retain the customer data even if a loan is turned down. Adding a customer to the database in Figure 5.1 is awkward, however, because it requires the creation of a "dummy" loan record to hold the customer data.

The deletion (payoff) of a loan creates a third type of problem. What happens, for example, when Ted Myerson pays off loan L0005? The loan record would be deleted, but so too would Ted's data as he has no other outstanding loans. The bank might want to contact Mr. Myerson about another loan in the future, but it would lose his data with the deletion of the existing loan.

The database in Figure 5.2 represents a much better design because it eliminates all three problems. It uses two different tables, a Loans table and a Customers table. Each record in the Loans table has data about a specific loan (LoanID, Date, Amount, Interest Rate, Term, Type, and CustomerID). Each record in the Customers table has data about a specific customer (CustomerID, First Name, Last Name, Address, City, State, Zip Code, and Phone Number). Each record in the Loans table is associated with a matching record in the Customers table through the CustomerID field common to both tables. This solution may seem complicated, but it is really quite simple and elegant.

Consider, for example, how easy it is to change a customer's address. If Michelle Zacco were to move, you would go into the Customers table, find her record (Customer C0008), and make the necessary change. You would not have to change any of the records in the Loans table, because they do not contain customer data, but only a CustomerID that indicates who the customer is. In other words, you would change Michelle's address in only one place, and the change would be automatically reflected for every associated loan.

The addition of a new customer is done directly in the Customers table. This is much easier than the approach of Figure 5.1, which required an existing loan in order to add a new customer. And finally, the deletion of an existing loan is also easier than with the single-table organization. A loan can be deleted from the Loans table without losing the corresponding customer data.

The database in Figure 5.2 is composed of two tables in which there is a ***one-to-many relationship*** between customers and loans. One customer (Michelle Zacco) can have many loans (Loan numbers L0007, L0008, L0009, and L0021), but a specific loan (e.g., L0007) is associated with only one customer (Michelle Zacco). The tables are related to one another by a common field (CustomerID) that is present in both the Customers and the Loans table.

Access enables you to create the one-to-many relationship between the tables, then uses that relationship to answer questions about the database. It can retrieve information about a specific loan, such as the name and address of the customer holding that loan. It can also find all loans for a particular customer.

Use the tables in Figure 5.2 to answer the queries below and gain an appreciation for the power of a relational database.

Query: What are the name, address, and phone number of the customer associated with loan number L0003?

Answer: Alex Rey, at 3456 Main Highway is the customer associated with loan L0003. His phone number is (303) 555-6666.

To determine the answer, Access searches the Loans table for loan L0003 to obtain the CustomerID (C0005 in this example). It then searches the Customers table for the customer with the matching CustomerID and retrieves the name, address, and phone number. Consider a second example.

LoanID	Date	Amount	Interest Rate	Term	Type	CustomerID
L0001	1/15/2003	$475,000	6.90%	15	M	C0004
L0002	1/23/2003	$35,000	7.20%	5	C	C0004
L0003	1/25/2003	$10,000	5.50%	3	C	C0005
L0004	1/31/2003	$12,000	9.50%	10	O	C0004
L0005	2/8/2003	$525,000	6.50%	30	M	C0006
L0006	2/12/2003	$10,500	7.50%	5	O	C0007
L0007	2/15/2003	$35,000	6.50%	5	O	C0008
L0008	2/20/2003	$250,000	8.80%	30	M	C0008
L0009	2/21/2003	$5,000	10.00%	3	O	C0008
L0010	2/28/2003	$200,000	7.00%	15	M	C0001
L0011	3/1/2003	$25,000	10.00%	3	C	C0002
L0012	3/1/2003	$20,000	9.50%	5	O	C0005
L0013	3/3/2003	$56,000	7.50%	5	C	C0009
L0014	3/10/2003	$129,000	8.50%	15	M	C0010
L0015	3/11/2003	$200,000	7.25%	15	M	C0003
L0016	3/21/2003	$150,000	7.50%	15	M	C0001
L0017	3/22/2003	$100,000	7.00%	30	M	C0001
L0018	3/31/2003	$15,000	6.50%	3	O	C0003
L0019	4/1/2003	$10,000	8.00%	5	C	C0002
L0020	4/15/2003	$25,000	8.50%	4	C	C0003
L0021	4/18/2003	$41,000	9.90%	4	C	C0008
L0022	4/22/2003	$350,000	7.50%	15	M	C0010
L0023	5/1/2003	$150,000	6.00%	15	M	C0003
L0024	5/3/2003	$350,000	8.20%	30	M	C0004
L0025	5/8/2003	$275,000	9.20%	15	M	C0007

(a) Loans Table

CustomerID	First Name	Last Name	Address	City	State	Zip Code	Phone Number
C0001	Eileen	Faulkner	7245 NW 8 Street	Minneapolis	MN	55346	(612) 894-1511
C0002	Scott	Wit	5660 NW 175 Terrace	Baltimore	MD	21224	(410) 753-0345
C0003	Benjamin	Grauer	10000 Sample Road	Coral Springs	FL	33073	(305) 444-5555
C0004	Wendy	Solomon	7500 Reno Road	Houston	TX	77090	(713) 427-3104
C0005	Alex	Rey	3456 Main Highway	Denver	CO	80228	(303) 555-6666
C0006	Ted	Myerson	6545 Stone Street	Chapel Hill	NC	27515	(919) 942-7654
C0007	Lori	Sangastiano	4533 Aero Drive	Santa Rosa	CA	95403	(707) 542-3411
C0008	Michelle	Zacco	488 Gold Street	Gainesville	FL	32601	(904) 374-5660
C0009	David	Powell	5070 Battle Road	Decatur	GA	30034	(301) 345-6556
C0010	Matt	Hirsch	777 NW 67 Avenue	Fort Lee	NJ	07624	(201) 664-3211

(b) Customers Table

FIGURE 5.2 Multiple-table Solution

Query: Which loans are associated with Wendy Solomon?
Answer: Wendy Solomon has four loans: loan L0001 for $475,000, loan L0002 for $35,000, loan L0004 for $12,000, and loan L0024 for $350,000.

This time Access begins in the Customers table and searches for Wendy Solomon to determine the CustomerID (C0004). It then searches the Loans table for all records with a matching CustomerID.

The AutoNumber Field Type

Every table requires a *primary key*, a field (or combination of fields) that makes every record in the table unique. The selection of the primary key in certain applications may be obvious, such as a Social Security Number in an employee database. Even so, it is always possible, and often convenient, to create a new field and assign that field the *AutoNumber field* type to generate the primary key for you. In other words, the AutoNumber specification will automatically assign the next sequential number to the primary key of a new record.

The records in both the Customer and Loans tables of Figure 5.2 are numbered consecutively: C0001, C0002, or L0001, L0002, and so on. The C (or L) and the associated leading zeros that appear are *not* part of the fields themselves, but are displayed through the *Format property* associated with the field.

Referential Integrity

Microsoft Access automatically implements certain types of data validation during data entry to ensure that the database will produce accurate information. Access always lets you enter a record in the "one" table, the Customers table in this example, provided that all existing rules for data validation are met. You cannot, however, enter a record in the "many" table (the Loans table in this example) if that record contains an invalid (nonexistent) value for the CustomerID. This type of data validation is known as *referential integrity* and it guarantees that the tables within a database are consistent with one another. Consider:

Query: Can you add a loan to the Loans table (as it presently exists) for Customer C0001? Can you add a loan for Customer C0020?

Answer: Yes, you can add a loan for Customer C0001, provided that the other rules for data validation are met. You cannot add a loan for Customer C0020 because that customer is not in the table.

Implementation in Access

Figure 5.3a displays the *Relationships window* that is used to create the one-to-many relationship between customers and loans. Each table stores data about a specific subject, such as customers or loans. CustomerID is the primary key in the Customers table. LoanID is the primary key in the Loans table.

The one-to-many relationship between the tables is based on the fact that the same field (CustomerID) appears in both tables. The CustomerID is the primary key in the Customers table, where its values are unique, but it is a *foreign key* in the Loans table, where its values are not unique. (A foreign key is simply the primary key of another table.) In other words, multiple records in the Loans table can have the same CustomerID to implement the one-to-many relationship between customers and loans.

To create a one-to-many relationship, you open the Relationships window in Figure 5.3a and add the necessary tables. You then drag the field on which the relationship is built from the field list of the "one" table (Customers) to the matching field in the related table (Loans). Once the relationship has been established, you will see a *relationship line* connecting the tables that indicates the one and many sides of the relationship.

Figure 5.3b displays the Customers table after the one-to-many relationship has been created. A plus (or minus) sign appears to the left of the CustomerID to indicate that there are corresponding records in a related table. You can click the plus sign next to any customer record to display the related records (called a *subdatasheet*) for that customer. Conversely, you can click the minus sign (after the related records have been displayed) and the records are hidden. Look carefully at the related records for customer C0004 (Wendy Solomon) and you will see the answer to one of our earlier queries.

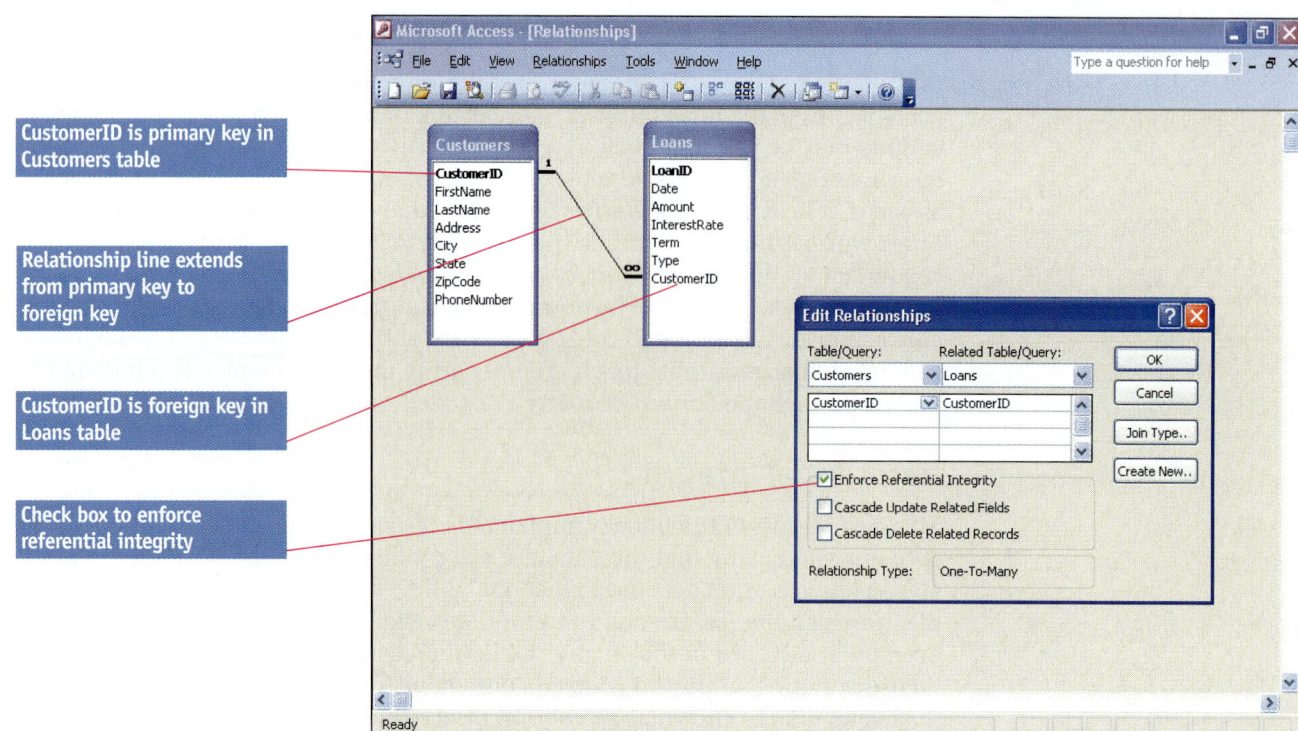

(a) The Relationships Window

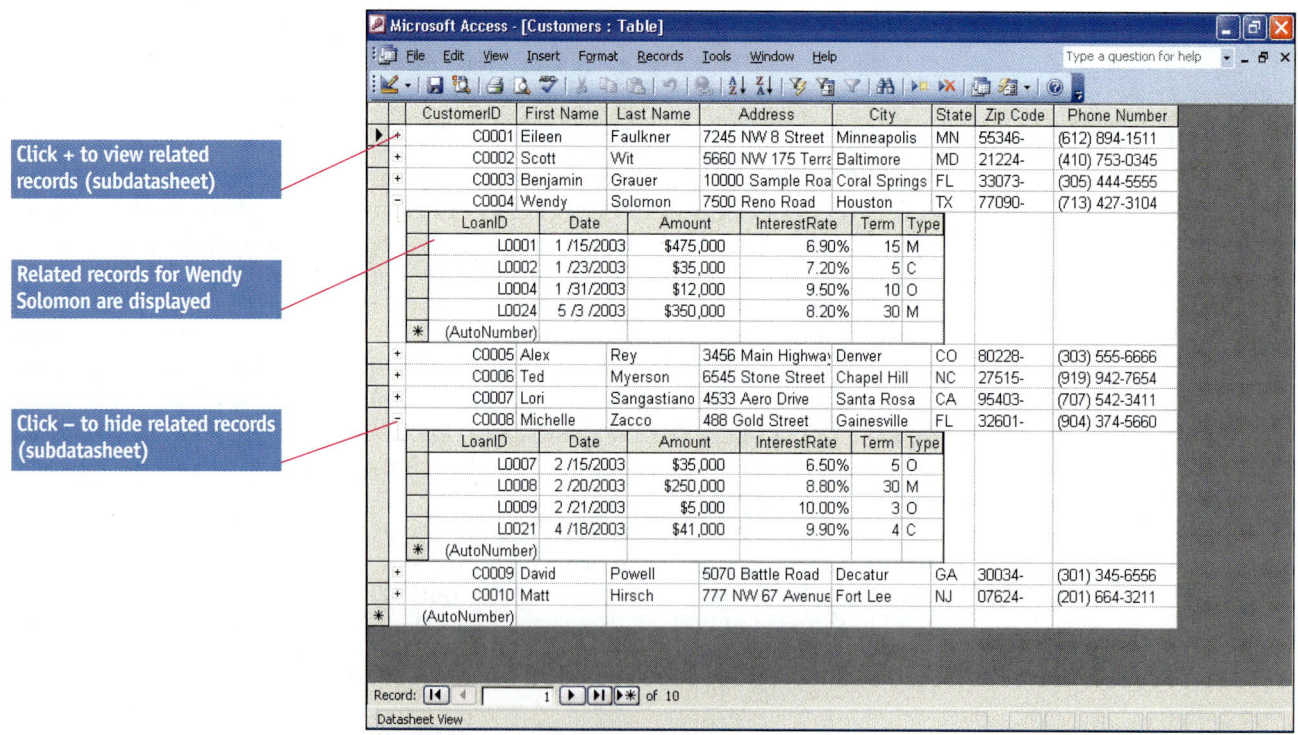

(b) The Customers Table with Related Records

FIGURE 5.3 One-to-many Relationship

1566   CHAPTER 5: ONE-TO-MANY RELATIONSHIPS

hands-on exercise

1 One-to-many Relationships

Objective To create a one-to-many relationship between existing tables in a database; to demonstrate referential integrity between the tables in a one-to-many relationship. Use Figure 5.4 as a guide in the exercise.

Step 1: **The Relationships Window**

- Start Access. Open the **National Bank database** in the **Exploring Access folder**. The database contains three tables: for Customers, Loans, and Payments. (The Payments table will be used later in the chapter.)

- Pull down the **Tools menu** and click **Relationships** to open the Relationships window as shown in Figure 5.4a. (The Customers and Loans tables are not yet visible.) If you do not see the Show Table dialog box, pull down the **Relationships menu** and click the **Show Table command**.

- The **Tables tab** is selected within the Show Table dialog box. Click (select) the **Customers table**, then click the **Add Command button**.

- Click the **Loans table**, then click the **Add Command button** (or simply double click the **Loans table**) to add this table to the Relationships window. Do *not* add the Payments table at this time. Close the Show Table dialog box.

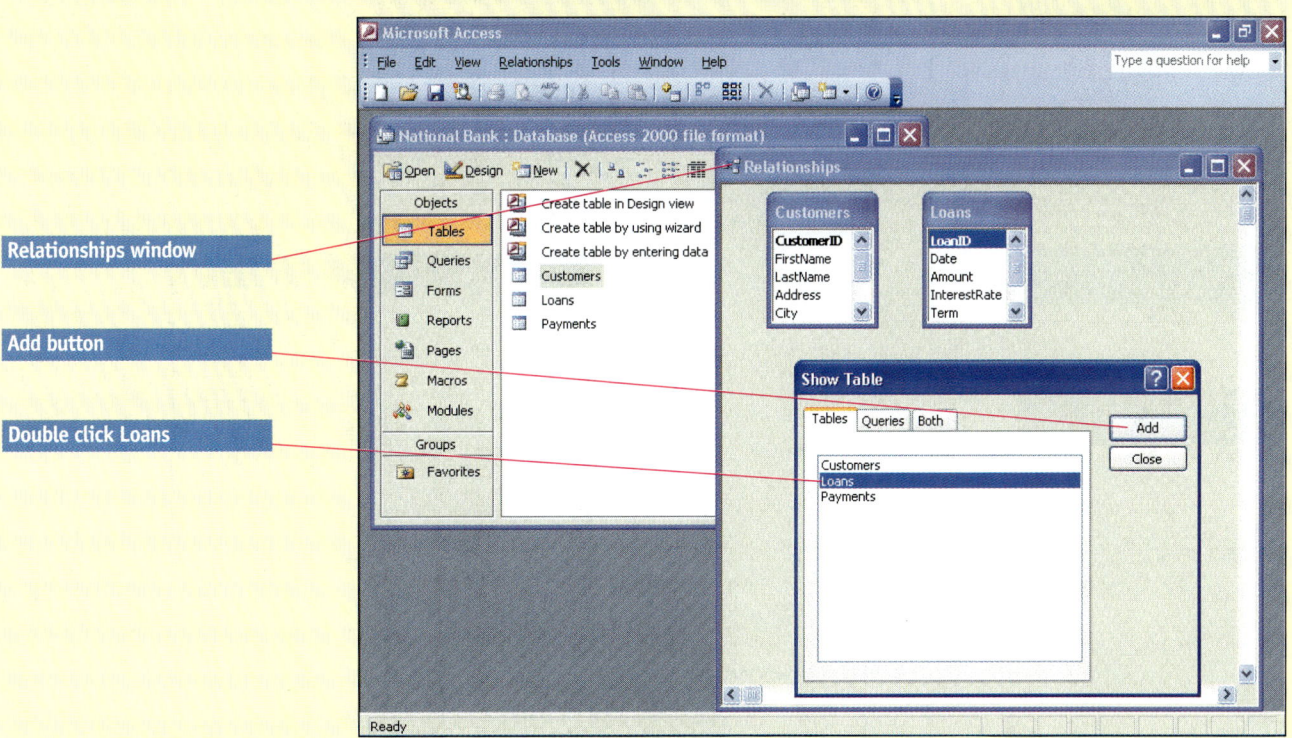

(a) The Relationships Window (step 1)

FIGURE 5.4 Hands-on Exercise 1

DATABASE DESIGN

Each entity in a relational database requires its own table. Each table in turn requires a primary key to ensure that the records in the table are unique. The physical order of the rows (records) and columns (fields) in the table is immaterial. See Appendix B for additional examples of database design.

Step 2: **Create the Relationship**

- Maximize the Relationships window. Point to the bottom border of the **Customers field list** (the mouse pointer changes to a double arrow), then click and drag the border until all of the fields are visible.

- Click and drag the bottom border of the **Loans field list** until all of the fields are visible. Click and drag the title bar of the **Loans field list** so that it is approximately one inch away from the Customers field list.

- Click and drag the **CustomerID field** in the Customers field list to the **CustomerID field** in the Loans field list. You will see the Relationships dialog box in Figure 5.4b.

- Check the **Enforce Referential Integrity** check box. (If necessary, clear the check boxes to Cascade Update Related Fields and Cascade Delete Related Records.)

- Click the **Create command button** to establish the relationship and close the Relationships dialog box. You should see a line indicating a one-to-many relationship between the Customers and Loans tables.

- Close the Relationships window. Click **Yes** to save the layout changes.

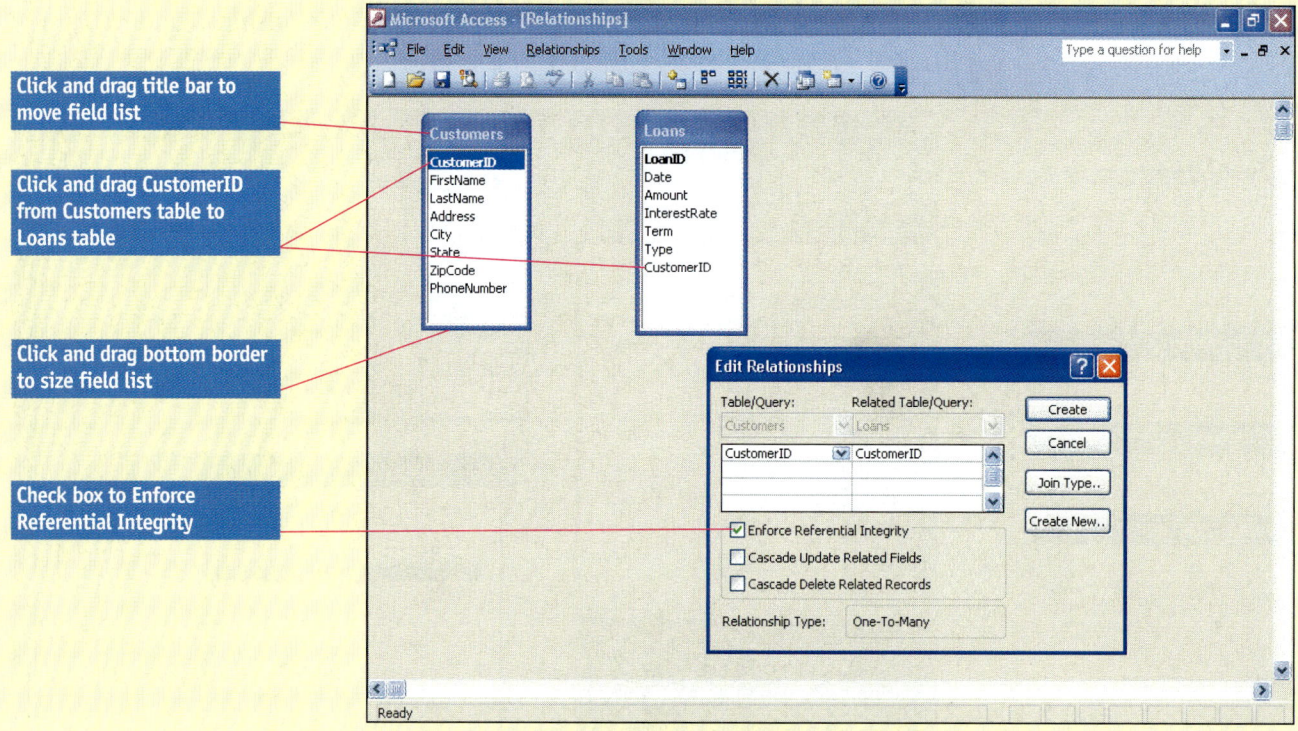

(b) Create the Relationship (step 2)

FIGURE 5.4 Hands-on Exercise 1 (*continued*)

RELATED FIELDS AND DATA TYPES

The fields on both sides of a relationship must have the same data type; for example, both fields should be text fields or both fields should be number fields. In addition, Number fields must also have the same field size. The exception is an AutoNumber field in the primary table, which is joined to a Number field with a field size of Long Integer in the related table.

Step 3: **Add a Customer Record**

- The Database window is again visible with the Tables button selected. Open the **Customers table**. If necessary, click the **Maximize button** to give yourself additional room when adding a record. Widen the fields as necessary.

- Click the **New Record button** on the toolbar, which moves the record selector to the last record (record 11). You are positioned in the CustomerID field.

- You do not enter the field, however, because the value of an AutoNumber field is entered automatically. Press **Tab** to move to the First Name field. You should see C0011 appear automatically in the CustomerID field as soon as you begin to enter the name as shown in Figure 5.4c.

- Enter data for yourself as the new customer. Data validation has been built into the Customers table, so you must enter the data correctly.

- Press **Enter** when you have completed your record.

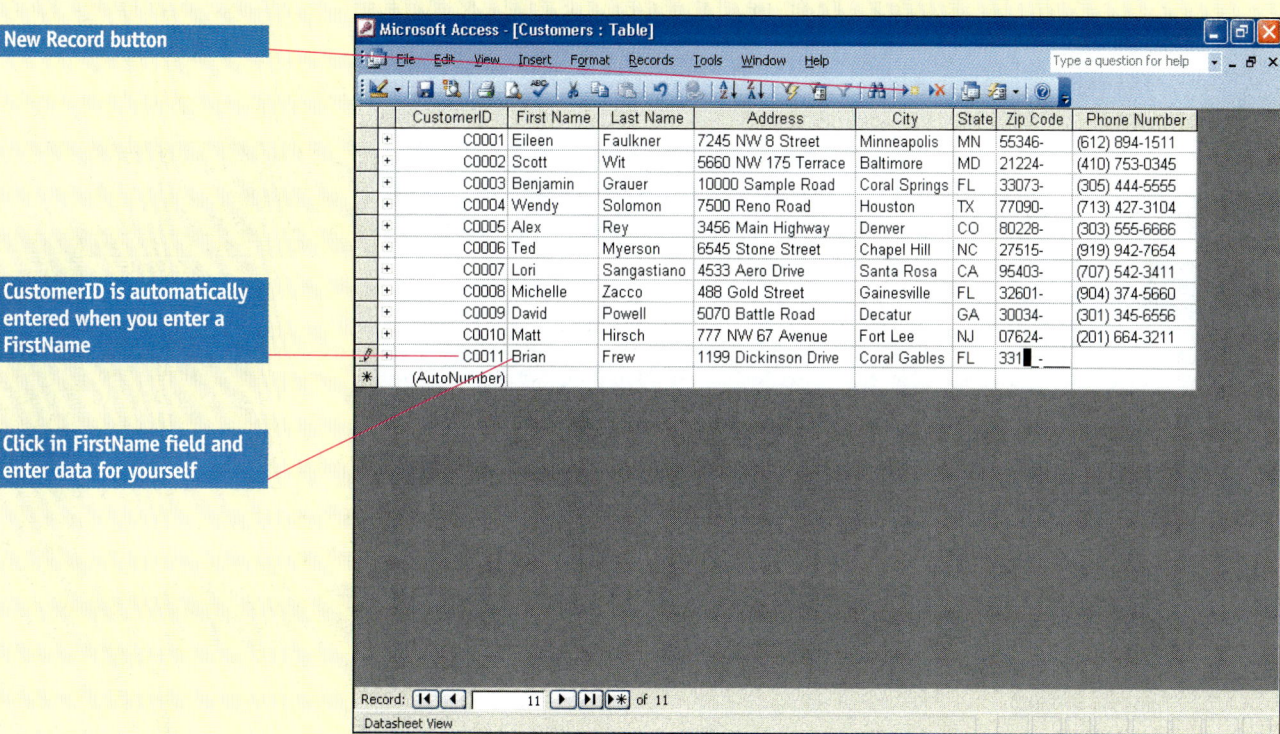

(c) Add a Customer Record (step 3)

FIGURE 5.4 Hands-on Exercise 1 (*continued*)

THE AUTONUMBER VALUES REMAIN CONSTANT

The values in an AutoNumber field type are permanent and are not affected by deletions to the table. If, for example, there are 10 records initially, with AutoNumber values of 1 to 10 inclusive, and you delete record 6, the remaining records retain the AutoNumber values of 7 to 10. The next record will be given an AutoNumber of 11. Note, too, that if you attempt to add a new record and are unsuccessful for any reason, the value (the next sequential number) will not appear in the table. Regardless of whether the actual numbers are consecutive or not, however, the inclusion of an AutoNumber field ensures a set of unique values for the primary key.

Step 4: **Add a Loan Record**

- Click the **plus sign** next to the record selector for customer C0003 (Benjamin Grauer). The plus sign changes to a minus sign and you see the related records. Click the **minus sign** and it changes back to a plus sign. The related records for this customer are no longer visible.

- Click the **plus sign** next to your customer record (record C0011 in our figure). The plus sign changes to a minus sign but there are no loans as yet. Enter data for a new loan record as shown in Figure 5.4d.

- The LoanID will be entered automatically since it is an AutoNumber field. Thus, click in the Date field for the first loan and enter today's date. The next available loan number (L0026) is entered automatically as you begin to enter the date.

- Data validation has been built into the Loans table. The term of the loan, for example, cannot exceed 30 years. The interest rate must be entered as a decimal. The type of the loan must be C, M, or O for Car, Mortgage, or Other. Enter **C** for a car loan.

- Press **Enter** when you have completed the loan record.

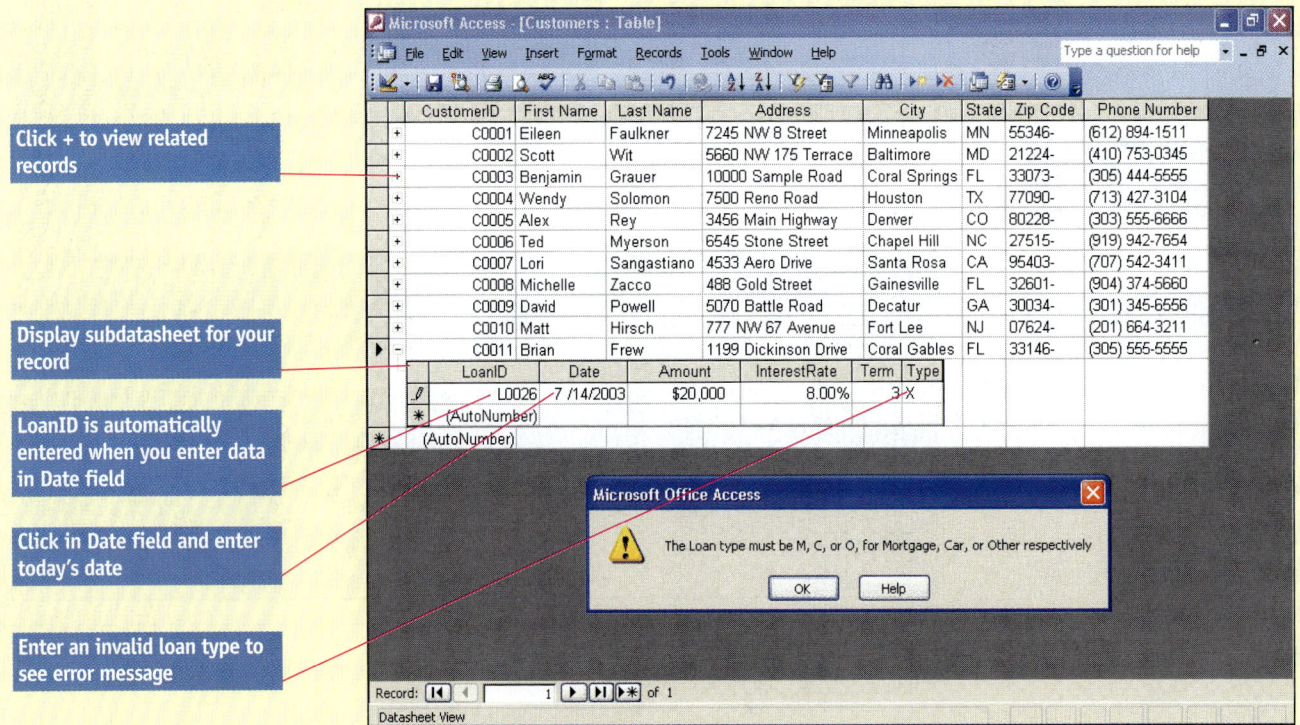

(d) Add a Loan Record (step 4)

FIGURE 5.4 Hands-on Exercise 1 (*continued*)

ADD AND DELETE RELATED RECORDS

Take advantage of the one-to-many relationship that exists between Customers and Loans to add or delete records in the Loans table from within the Customers table. Open the Customers table, then click the plus sign next to the Customer for whom you want to add or delete a loan record. To add a Loan, click in the blank row marked by the asterisk, then enter the new data. To delete a loan, select the Loan record, then click the Delete Record button on the Standard toolbar.

Step 5: **Referential Integrity**

- Click the **plus sign** next to the record selector for Customer C0009 (David Powell). Click in the **CustomerID field** for this customer, then click the **Delete Record button** to (attempt to) delete this customer.

- You will see the error message in Figure 5.4e indicating that you cannot delete the customer record because there are related loan records. Click **OK**.

- Click in the **LoanID field** for L0013 (the loan for this customer). Click the **Delete Record button**. Click **Yes** when warned that you will not be able to undo this operation. The loan is deleted.

- Click in the **CustomerID field**, click the **Delete Record button**, then click **Yes** to delete the record. The deletion was permitted because there were no longer any related records in the Loans table.

- Close the Customers table. Close the National Bank database. Exit Access if you do not want to continue with the next exercise at this time.

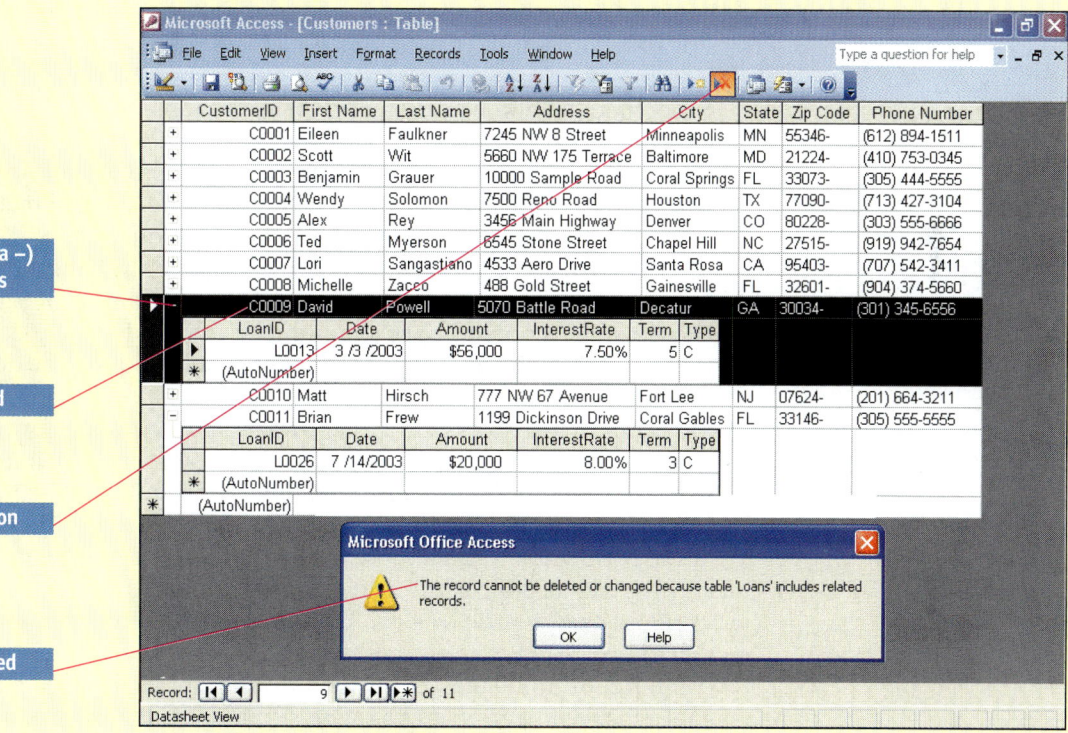

(e) Referential Integrity (step 5)

FIGURE 5.4   Hands-on Exercise 1 (*continued*)

CASCADE DELETED RECORDS

The enforcement of referential integrity prevents the deletion of a record in the primary (Customers) table if there is a corresponding record in the related (Loans) table. In other words, in order to delete a customer, you first have to delete all of the loans for that customer. This restriction can be relaxed if you modify the relationship by checking the Cascade Delete Related Records option in the Relationships dialog box. The Cascade Delete option may make sense in some applications, but not here since the bank wants the loan to remain on the books.

SUBFORMS

A **subform** is a form within a form. It appears inside a main form to display records from a related table. A main form and its associated subform, to display the loans for one customer, are shown in Figure 5.5. The **main form** (also known as the primary form) is based on the primary table (the Customers table). The subform is based on the related table (the Loans table).

The main form and the subform are linked to one another so that the subform displays only the records related to the record currently displayed in the main form. The main form shows the "one" side of the relationship (the customer). The subform shows the "many" side of the relationship (the loans). The main form displays the customer data for one record (Eileen Faulkner with CustomerID C0001). The subform shows the loans for that customer. The main form is displayed in the ***Form view***, whereas the subform is displayed in the ***Datasheet view***. (A subform can also be displayed in the Form view, in which case it would show one loan at a time.)

Each form in Figure 5.5a has its own status bar and associated navigation buttons. The status bar for the main form indicates that the active record is record 1 of 10 records in the Customers table. The status bar for the subform indicates record 1 of 3 records. (The latter shows the number of loans for this customer rather than the number of loans in the Loans table.) Click the navigation button to move to the next customer record, and you will automatically see the loans associated with that customer. If, for example, you were to move to the last customer record (C0011, which contains the data you entered in the first hands-on exercise), you would see your customer and loan information.

The Loans form also contains a calculated control, the payment due, which is based on the loan parameters. Loan L0010, for example (a $200,000 mortgage at 7% with a 15-year term), has a monthly payment of $1,797.66. The amount of the payment is calculated using a predefined function, as will be described in the next hands-on exercise.

Figure 5.5b displays the Design view of the Customers form in Figure 5.5a. The Loans subform control is an object on the Customers form and can be moved and sized (or deleted) just like any other object. It should also be noted that the Loans subform is a form in and of itself, and can be opened in either the Datasheet view or the Form view. It can also be opened in the Design view (to modify its appearance) as will be done in the next hands-on exercise.

Note, too, that reports can be linked to one another in exactly the same way that forms are linked to each other. Thus, you could create a main report/subreport combination to display the same information as the forms in Figure 5.5a. The choice between a form and a report depends on the information requirements of the system. Access, however, gives you the capability to create both. There is a learning curve, but everything that you learn about creating a subform also pertains to creating a subreport.

> ### THE PMT FUNCTION
> The PMT function is one of several predefined functions built into Access. It calculates the payment due on a loan based on the principal, interest rate, and term and is similar to the PMT function in Excel. The PMT function is reached most easily through the Expression Builder and can be entered onto any form, query, or report. (The periodic payment is a calculated field and thus it is used in a query rather than a table.)

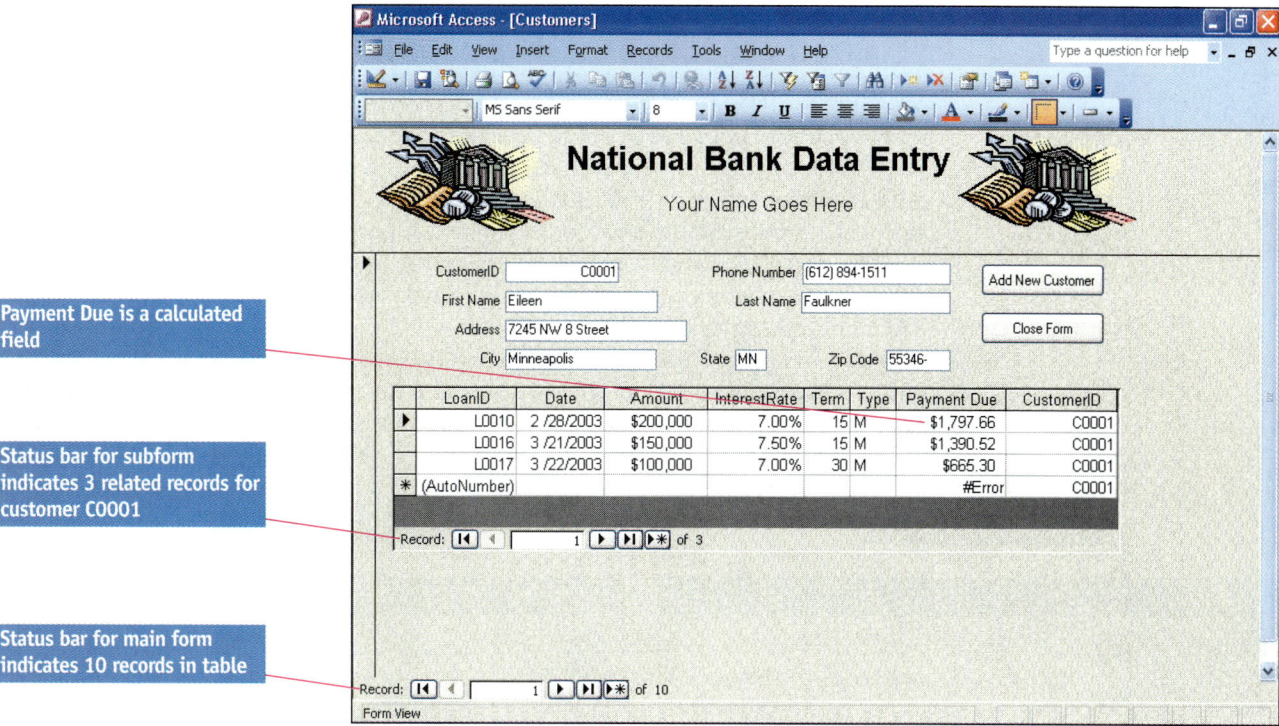

(a) Form View

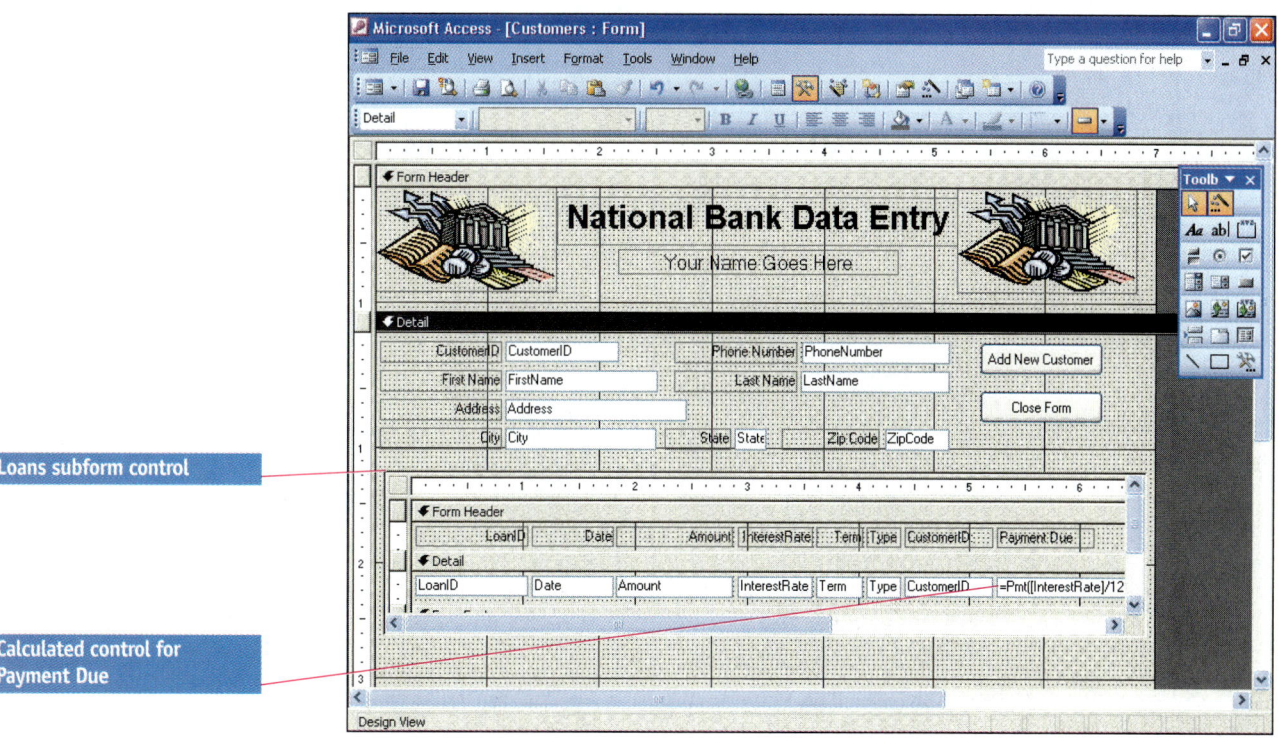

(b) Design View

FIGURE 5.5 A Main Form and a Subform

The Form Wizard

A subform is created in different ways depending on whether or not the main form already exists. The easiest way is to create the two forms at the same time by using the Form Wizard as depicted in Figure 5.6. The wizard starts by asking you which fields you want to include in your form. You will need to select fields from the Customers table, as shown in Figure 5.6a, as well as from the Loans table as shown in Figure 5.6b, since these tables are the basis for the main form and subform, respectively.

The wizard will do the rest. It gives you the opportunity to view the records by customer, as shown in Figure 5.6c. (Additional screens, not shown in Figure 5.6, let you choose the style of the forms.) Finally, you save each form as a separate object as shown in Figure 5.6d. You will find that the wizard provides an excellent starting point, but you usually have to customize the forms after they have been created. This is done in the Form Design view using the identical techniques that were presented earlier to move and size controls and/or modify their properties.

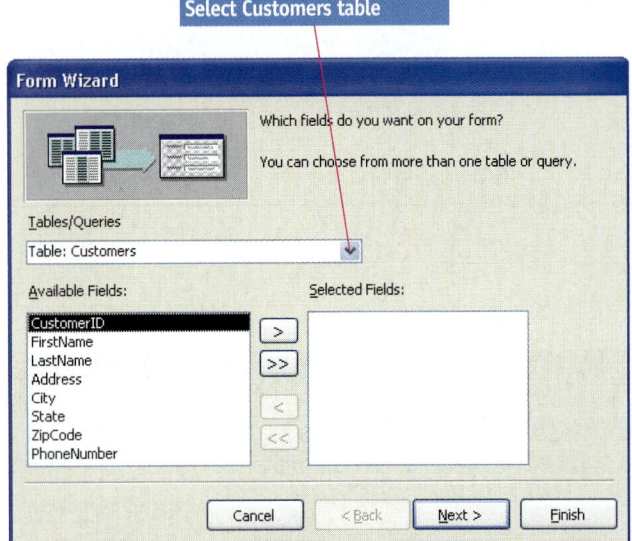

(a) The Customers Table   (b) The Loans Table

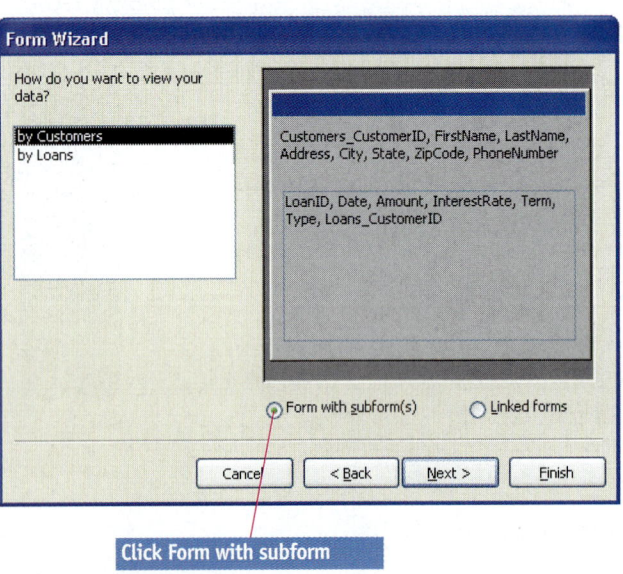 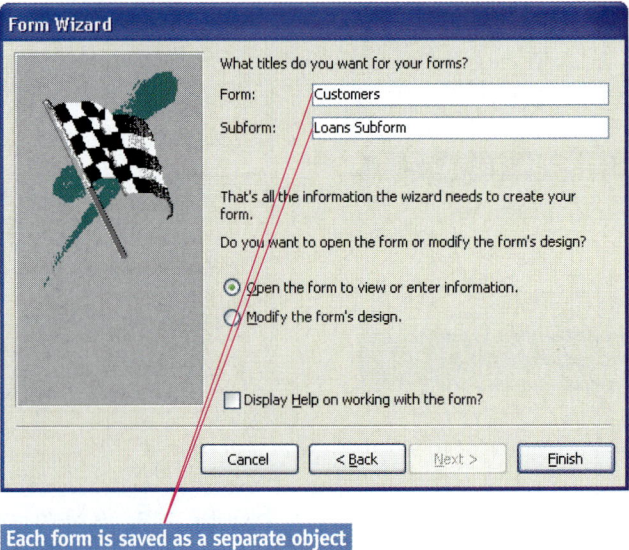

(c) View Data by Customers   (d) Save the Form

FIGURE 5.6 The Form Wizard

hands-on exercise
2   Creating a Subform

Objective   To create a subform that displays the many records in a one-to-many relationship; to move and size controls in an existing form; to enter data in a subform. Use Figure 5.7 as a guide in doing the exercise.

Step 1:   **Start the Form Wizard**

- Open the **National Bank database** from the previous exercise. Click the **Forms button** in the Database window, then double click the **Create form by using wizard button** to start the Form Wizard.

- You should see the Form Wizard dialog box in Figure 5.7a, except that no fields have been selected.

- The Customers table is selected by default. Click the **>> button** to enter all of the fields in the Customers table on the form.

- Click the **drop-down arrow** in the Tables/Queries list box to display the tables and queries in the database.

- Click **Loans** to select the Loans table as shown in Figure 5.7a. Click the **>> button** to enter all of the fields in the Loans table on the form.

- Be sure that the Selected Fields area contains the fields from both the Loans form and the Customers form.

- Click **Next** to continue with the Form Wizard.

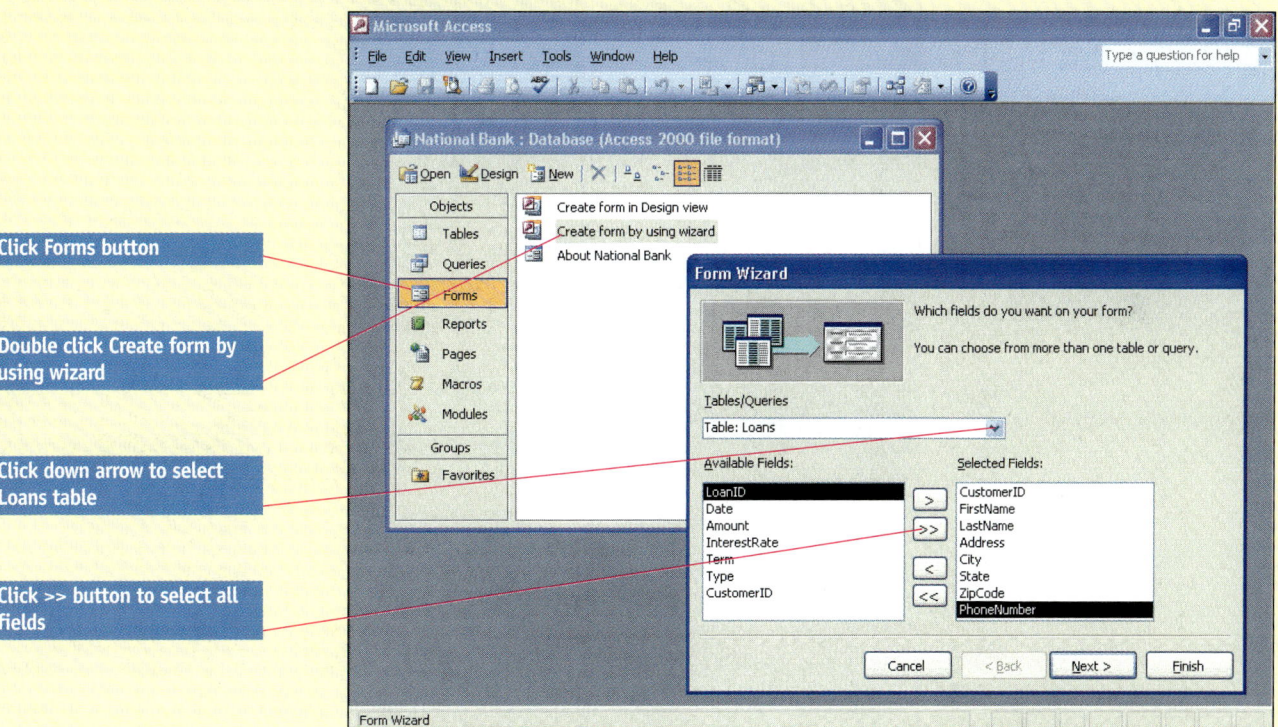

(a) Start the Form Wizard (step 1)

FIGURE 5.7   Hands-on Exercise 2

Step 2: **Complete the Form**

- The wizard will prompt you for the additional information it needs to create the Customers form and the associated Loans subform. The next screen suggests that you view the data by customers and that you are going to create a form with subforms. Click **Next**.

- The Datasheet option button is selected as the default layout for the subform. Click **Tabular**. Click **Next**.

- Click **Standard** as the style for your form. Click **Next**.

- You should see the screen in Figure 5.7b, in which the Form Wizard suggests **Customers** as the title of the form and **Loans Subform** as the title for the subform.

- Click the option button to **Modify the form's design**, then click the **Finish command button** to create the form and exit the Form Wizard.

- You should be in the Design view of the Customer form you just created. Click the **Save button** to save the form and continue working.

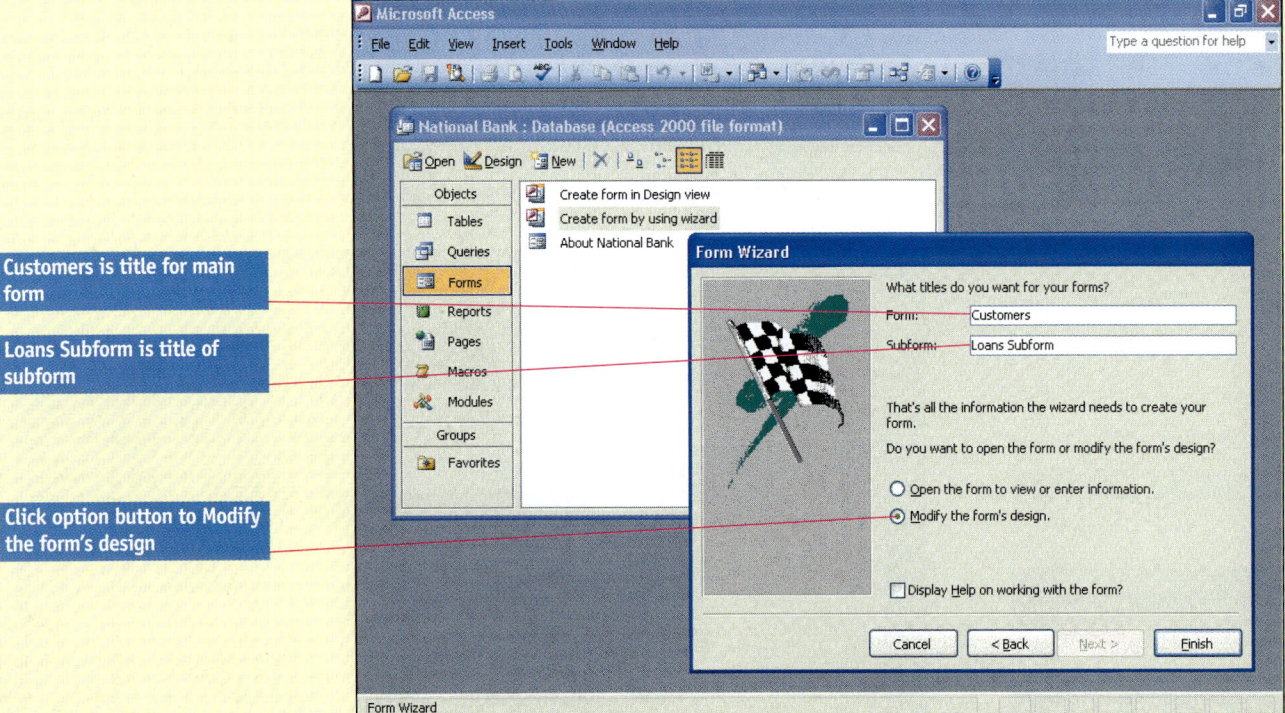

(b) Complete the Form (step 2)

FIGURE 5.7 Hands-on Exercise 2 (*continued*)

THE NAME'S THE SAME

The Form Wizard automatically assigns the name of the underlying table (or query) to each form (subform) it creates. The Report Wizard works in similar fashion. The intent of the similar naming convention is to help you select the proper object from the Database window when you want to subsequently open the object. This becomes increasingly important in databases that contain a large number of objects.

Step 3: **Modify the Customers Form**

- You should see the Customers form in Figure 5.7c. The appearance of your form will be different from our figure, however, as you need to rearrange the position of the fields on the form. Maximize the form window.

- Click and drag the bottom of the Detail section down to give yourself additional room in which to work.

- It takes time (and a little practice) to move and size the controls within a form. Try the indicated command, then click the **Undo button** if you are not satisfied with the result.
  - Move the **State, ZipCode, and PhoneNumber** to the bottom of the detail section. (This is only temporary, but we need room to work.)
  - Increase the width of the form to **seven inches**. Click the **LastName control** to select the control and display the sizing handles, then drag the **LastName control** and its attached label so that it is next to the FirstName control. Align the tops of the LastName and FirstName controls.
  - Move the **Address control** up. Place the controls for **City, State**, and **ZipCode** on the same line, then move these controls under the Address control. You may need to size some of the other labels to fit everything on one line. Align the tops of these controls as well.
  - Click and drag the control for **PhoneNumber** to the right of the CustomerID field. Align the tops of the controls.
  - Right align all of the labels so that they appear close to the bound control they identify. Size and move controls as needed.

- Your form should now match Figure 5.7c. Click the label attached to the subform control and press the **Del key**. Be sure you delete only the label and not the control for the subform.

- Save the form.

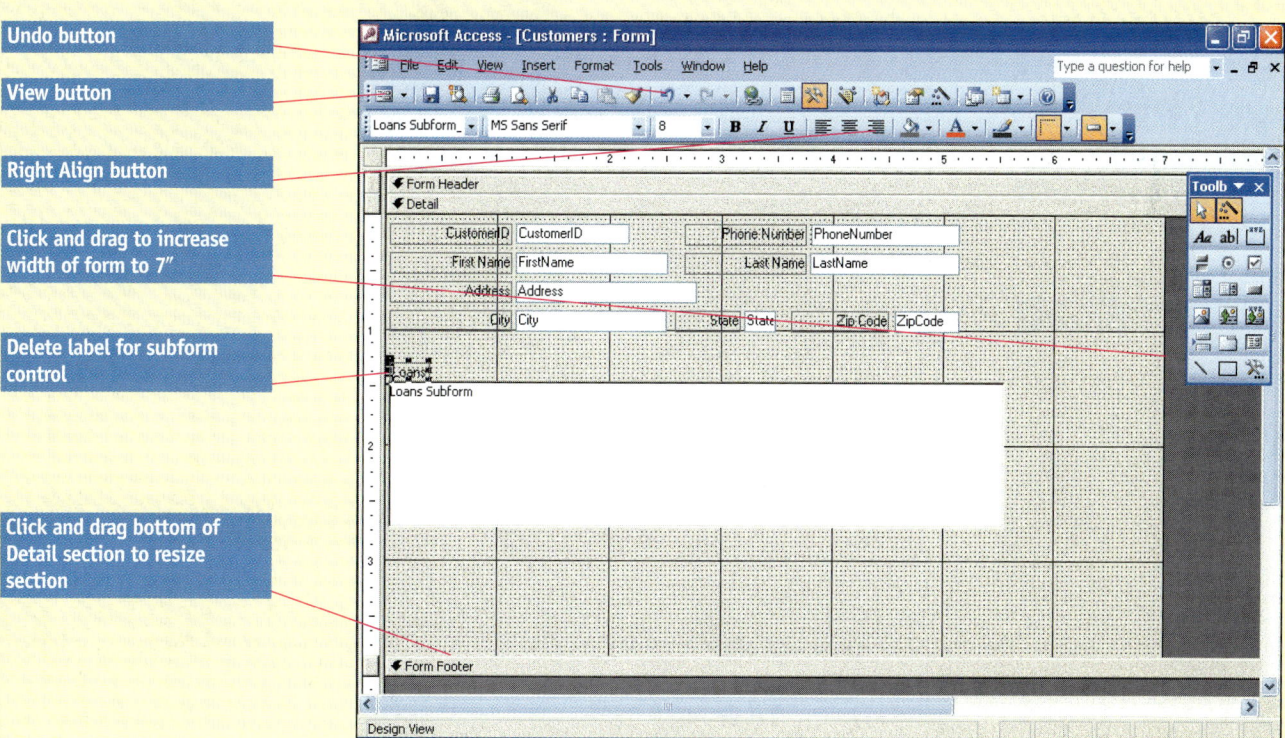

(c) Modify the Customers Form (step 3)

FIGURE 5.7 Hands-on Exercise 2 (*continued*)

Step 4: **View the Customers Form**

- Click the **View button**. You should see the Customers form in the Form view as in Figure 5.7d. Do not be concerned about the column widths in the subform or the fact that you may not see all of the fields at this time. Our objective is simply to show the relationship between the main form and the subform.
  - The customer information for the first customer (C0001) is displayed in the main portion of the form. The loans for that customer are in the subform.
  - The status bar at the bottom of the window (corresponding to the main form) displays record 1 of 10 records (you are looking at the first record in the Customers table).
  - The status bar for the subform displays record 1 of 3 records (you are on the first of three loan records for this customer).

- Click the ▶ **button** on the status bar for the main form to move to the next customer record. The subform is updated automatically to display the two loans belonging to this customer.

- Close the Customers form. Click **Yes** if asked to save the changes.

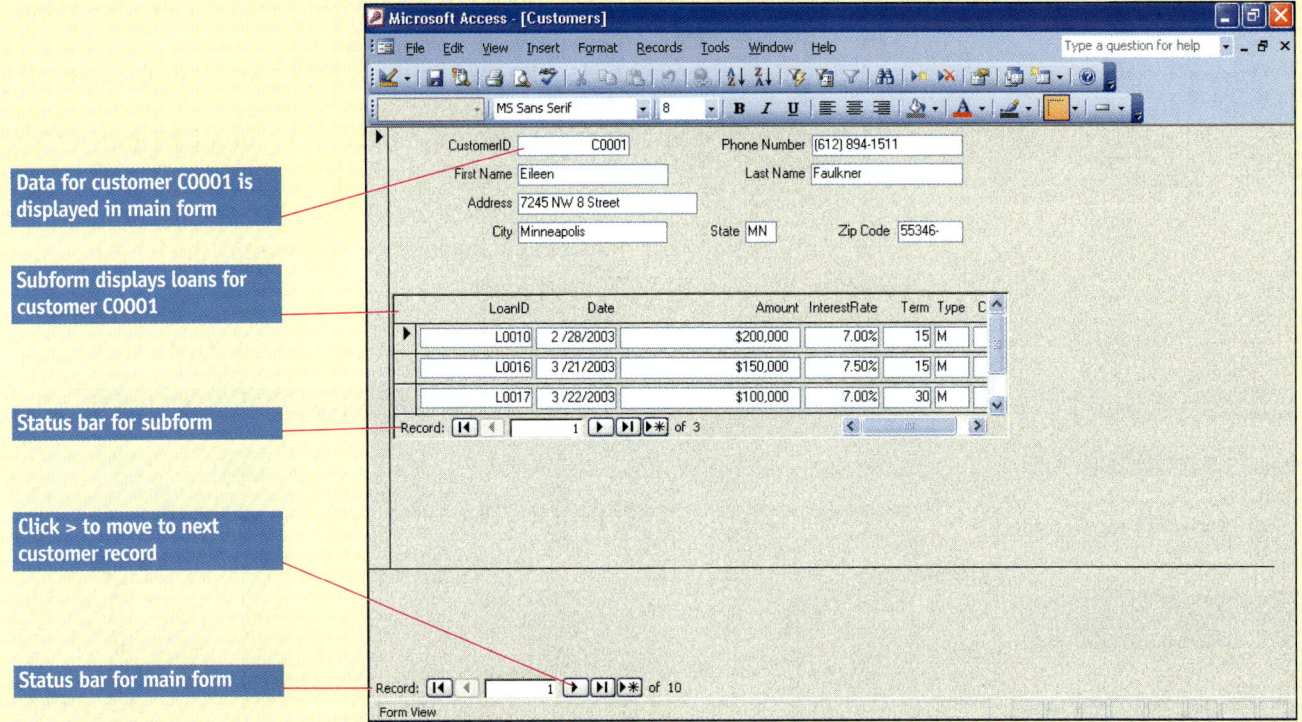

(d) View the Customers Form (step 4)

FIGURE 5.7 Hands-on Exercise 2 (*continued*)

WHY IT WORKS

The main form (Customers) and subform (Loans) work in conjunction with one another so that you always see all of the loans for a given customer. To see how the link is actually implemented, change to the Design view of the Customers form and point anywhere on the border of the Loans subform. Click the right mouse button to display a shortcut menu, click Properties to display the Subform/Subreport properties dialog box, and, if necessary, click the All tab within the dialog box. You should see CustomerID next to two properties (Link Child Fields and Link Master Fields).

Step 5: **Add the Payment Amount**

- Click the **Forms button** in the Database window. Open the **Loans subform** in Design view. Click and drag the right edge of the form to **7 inches**.
- Right click the **Form Selector button** to display a context-sensitive menu, then click **Properties** to display the Properties sheet for the form. Click the **All Tab**, click in the **Default View** text box, then select **Datasheet**. Close the Property sheet.
- Click the **Label button** on the Toolbox toolbar, then click and drag in the **Form Header** to create an unbound control. Enter **Payment Due** as the text for the label as shown in Figure 5.7e. Size and align the label.
- Click the **Text Box button**, then click and drag in the **Detail section** to create an unbound control that will contain the amount of the monthly payment. Click the label for the control (e.g., Text 15), then press the **Del key**.
- Point to the unbound control, click the **right mouse button**, then click **Properties** to open the Properties dialog box. Click the **All tab**. Click the **Name property**. Enter **Payment Due** in place of the existing label.
- Click the **Control Source property**, then click the **Build (...) button**.
  - Double click **Functions** (if there is a plus sign in its icon), then click **Built-In Functions**. Click **Financial** in the second column, then double click **Pmt**.
  - You need to replace each of the arguments in the Pmt function with the appropriate field names from the Loans table. Select the arguments one at a time and enter the replacement as shown in Figure 5.7e. Click **OK**.
- Click the **Format property**, click the **down arrow**, and specify **Currency**. Click the **Decimal Places property**, click the **down arrow**, and select **2**.
- Close the Properties dialog box. Change to the **Datasheet view**, and check the column widths, making adjustments as necessary. Close the Loans subform. Click **Yes** to save the changes.

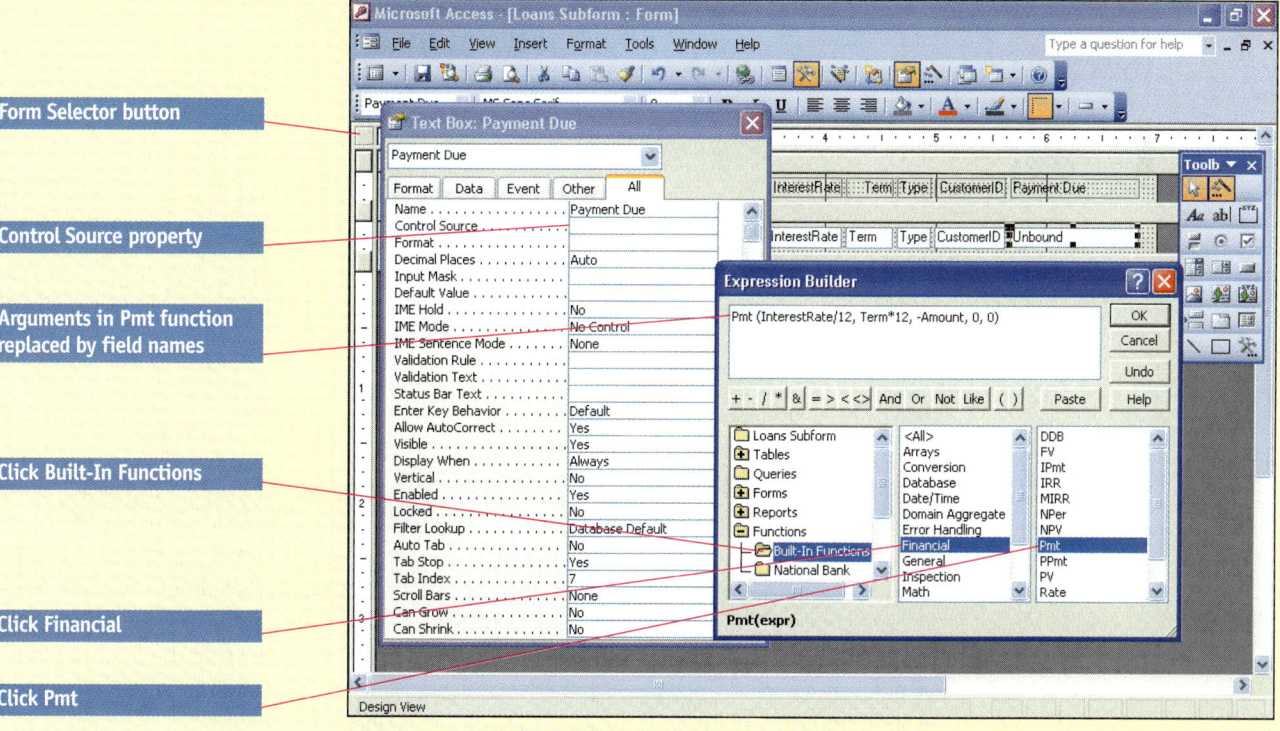

(e) Add the Payment Amount (step 5)

FIGURE 5.7 Hands-on Exercise 2 (*continued*)

Step 6: **Check Your Progress**

- Open the **Customers form**. You should see the first customer in the database, together with the associated loan information as shown in Figure 5.7f. As before, you are on customer 1 of 10, and loan 1 of 3 for that customer. (The CustomerID appears in the Loans subform to check that the forms are linking correctly. We will delete the control from the subform in the next step.)

- The payment for each loan has been added to the subform, but you may have to adjust the column widths. You can drag the border between column headings, just as you would adjust the columns in an Excel worksheet.

- You may also have to adjust the size or position of the subform within the main form. Change to **Design view**.
  - Click the **subform control** to select it, then click and drag a sizing handle to change the size of the subform within the main form.
  - Click and drag a border of the control to change its position.

- You may have to switch back and forth between the Form and Design views to get the correct size and position. Save the completed form.

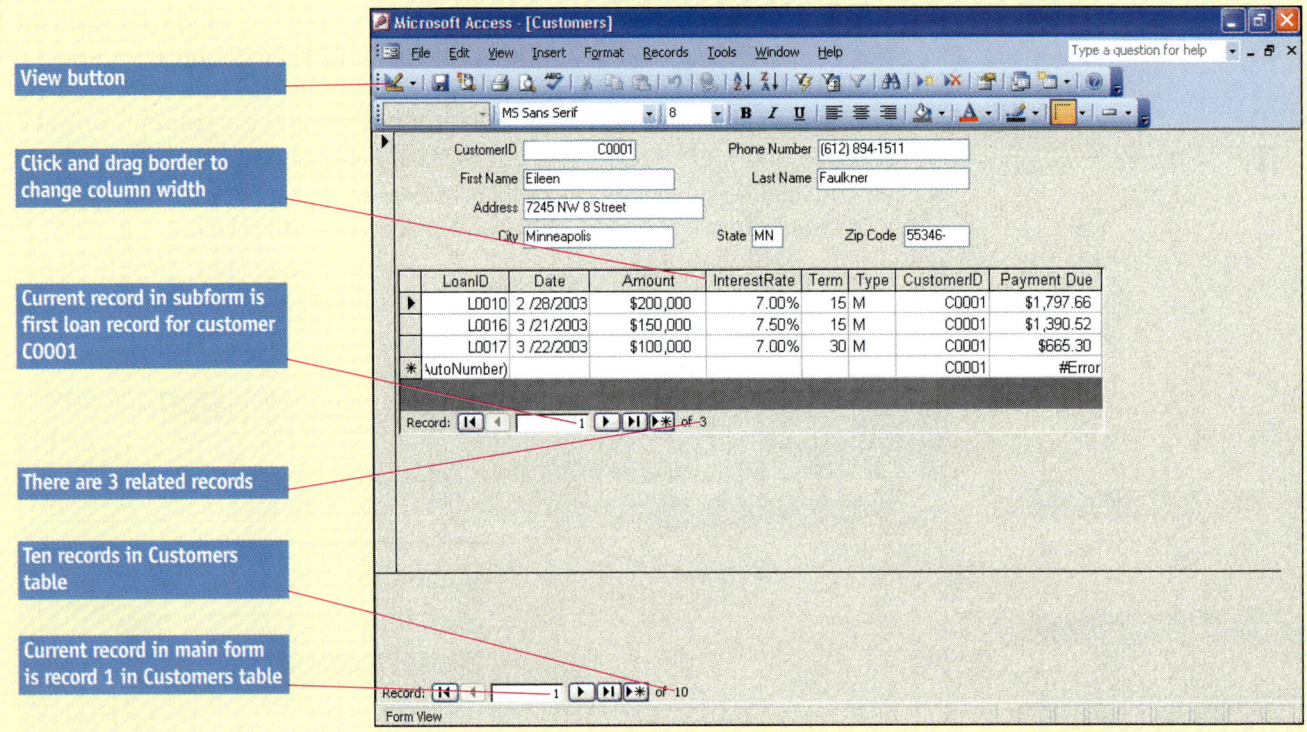

(f) Check Your Progress (step 6)

FIGURE 5.7 Hands-on Exercise 2 (*continued*)

ERROR AND HOW TO AVOID IT

A # Error message will be displayed in the Form view if the PMT function is unable to compute a payment for a new loan prior to entering the terms of the loan. You can, however, suppress the display of the message using the IIF (Immediate If) function to test for a null argument. In other words, if the term of the loan has not been entered, do not display anything; otherwise compute the payment. Use the IIF function, =IIF(Term Is Null," ",PMT(InterestRate/12, Term*12, -Amount)) as the control source for the payment amount.

Step 7: Complete the Customers Form

- Return to **Design view**. Click and drag the bottom of the **Form Header** down in the form to create room in which to work. Click in the Form Header.
- Pull down the **Insert menu**, click **Picture**, select the **Exploring Access folder** in the Look in box, select the **National Bank clip art** image, and click **OK**.
- Move and size the clip art as shown. Right click the clip art, click **Properties**, click **Size Mode**, click the **down arrow**, then choose **Stretch**, so that the clip art fills the placeholder. Close the Properties sheet.
- Select the clip art, click the **Copy button**, then click the **Paste button** to duplicate the image. Drag the copied image to the right side of the form.
- Use the **Label tool** to create unbound controls for the title of the form and your name. Move, size, and format the labels. Size the form header appropriately.
- Use the **Command Button Wizard** to create command buttons to **Add New Customer** and **Close the Form** as shown in Figure 5.7g.
- Press and hold the **Shift key** to select both command buttons. Use the **Format command** to size and align the buttons. Right click either button, click Properties, then set the **Tab Stop property** to **No** so that the Tab key skips both buttons in Form view. Close the Properties sheet.
- Pull down the **View menu**, click the **Tab Order command**, click the **AutoOrder button** to set the order in which the controls are selected (top to bottom, left to right), then click **OK** to accept the settings and close the dialog box.
- You're almost finished. Click the **CustomerID control** in the Loans subform and press the **Del key**. Delete the label for the control as well. The CustomerID field is still in the Loans table, but it need not appear in the Loans form, since its value corresponds to the CustomerID in the main form.
- Move the payment control and its label to the left. Size and move the subform control as necessary. Save the completed form.

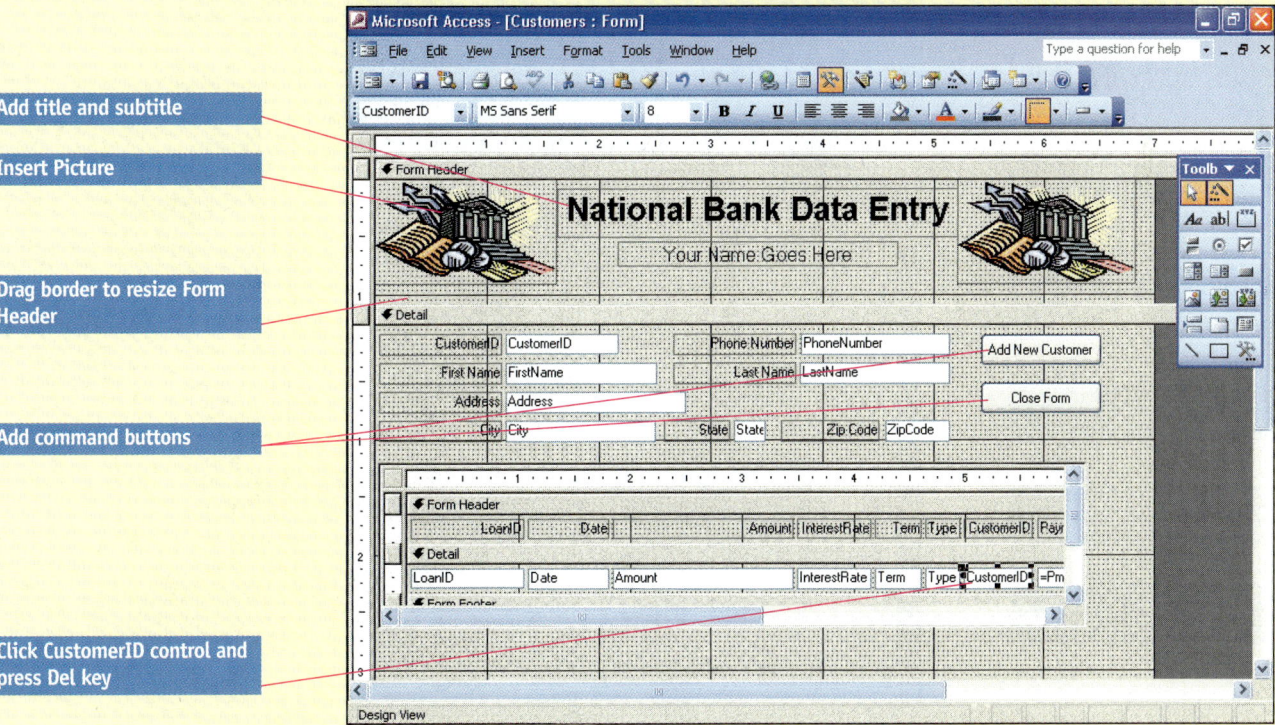

(g) Complete the Customers Form (step 7)

FIGURE 5.7 Hands-on Exercise 2 (*continued*)

Step 8: **Enter a New Loan**

- Click the **View button** to switch to the Form view as shown in Figure 5.7h. You should see the form Header. The CustomerID has also disappeared from the subform.

- Click the ▶| on the status bar of the main form to move to the last record (customer C0011), which is the record you entered in the previous exercise. (Click the **PgUp key** if you are on a blank record.)

- Click in the **Date field** for the blank record in the subform. Enter data for the new loan as shown in Figure 5.7h.

- The LoadID is entered automatically because it is an AutoNumber field. (It should be L0027 if you have followed the exercise exactly.) The payment due will be computed automatically as soon as you complete the Term field.

- Press the **down arrow** when you have entered the last field (Type), which saves the data in the current record. (The record selector symbol changes from a pencil to a triangle.)

- Check that you are still on the record for customer 11 (the record containing your data), then click the **selection area** at the left of the form.

- Pull down the **File menu** and click **Print** (or click the **Print button**) to display the Print dialog box. Click the **Selected Record(s) option button**. Click **OK**. (It may be necessary to use the **Page Setup command** to change the margins so that the form fits on one page.)

- Close the Customers form. Click **Yes** if asked to save the changes to the form or subform. Close the National Bank database.

- Exit Access if you do not want to continue with the next hands-on exercise at this time.

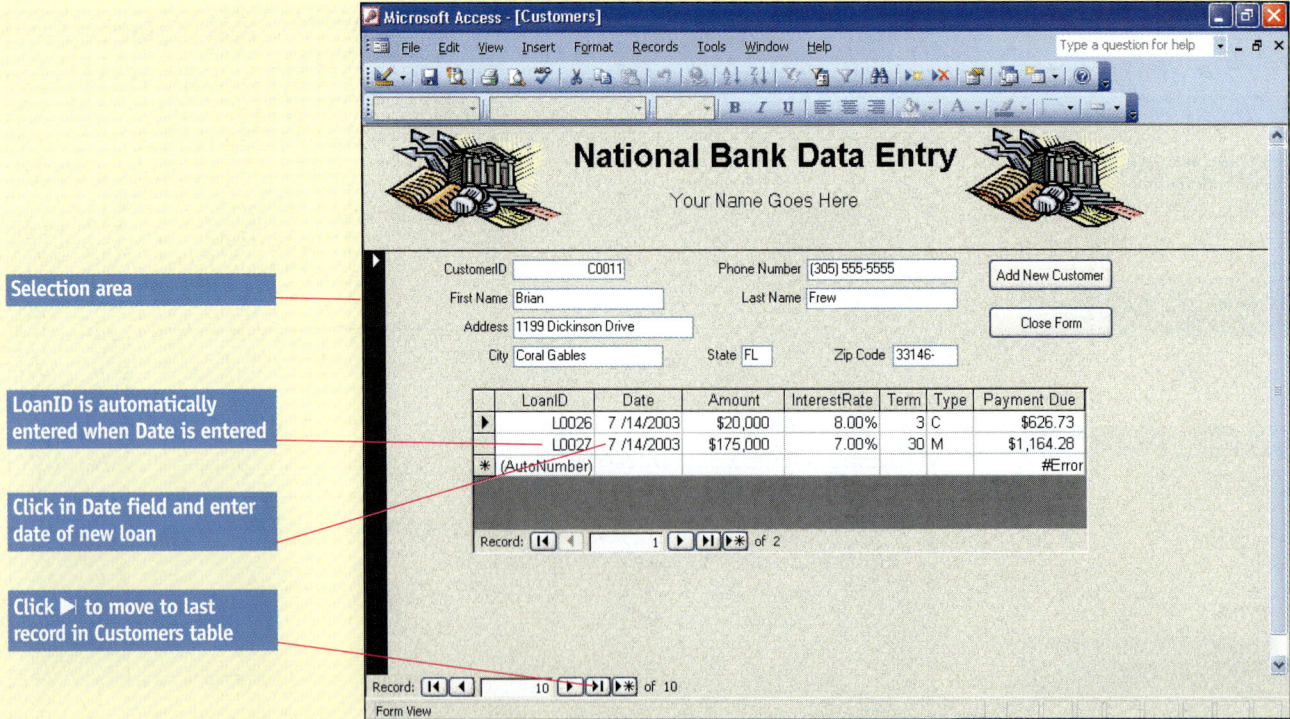

(h) Enter a New Loan (step 8)

FIGURE 5.7 Hands-on Exercise 2 (*continued*)

MULTIPLE-TABLE QUERIES

The chapter began with a conceptual view of the National Bank database, in which we described the need for separate tables to store data for customers and loans. We created a database with sample data, asked several questions about various customers and their loans, then intuitively drew on both tables to derive the answers. Access simply automates the process through creation of a ***multiple-table query***. This type of query was introduced in the previous chapter, but it is reviewed in this section because of its importance.

Let's assume that you wanted to know the name of every customer who held a 15-year mortgage that was issued after April 1, 2003. To answer that question, you would need data from both the Customers table and the Loans table, as shown in Figure 5.8. You would create the query using the same grid as for a simple select query, but you would have to add fields from both tables to the query. The Design view of the query is shown in Figure 5.8a. The resulting dynaset is displayed in Figure 5.8b.

The Query window contains the Field, Sort, Show, and Criteria rows that appear in simple select queries. The ***Table row*** is necessary only in multiple-table queries and indicates the table where the field originates. The customer's last name and first name are taken from the Customers table. All of the other fields are from the Loans table. The one-to-many relationship between the Customers table and the Loans table is shown graphically within the Query window. The tables are related through the CustomerID field, which is the primary key in the Customers table and a foreign key in the Loans table. The line between the two field lists is called a ***join line***, and its properties determine how the tables will be accessed within the query.

Figure 5.8 extends the earlier discussion on multiple-table queries to include the SQL statement in Figure 5.8c and the Join Properties dialog box in Figure 5.8d. This information is intended primarily for the reader who is interested in the theoretical concepts of a relational database. ***Structured Query Language*** (**SQL**) is the universal way to access a relational database, meaning that the information provided by any database is obtained through SQL queries. Access simplifies the creation of an SQL query, however, by providing the Design grid, then converting the entries in the grid to the equivalent SQL statements. You can view the SQL statements from within Access as we did in Figure 5.8c, by changing to the SQL view, and in so doing you can gain a better appreciation for how a relational database works. (You can also ignore the SQL view and work exclusively from the Design grid.)

The concept of a "join" is also crucial to a relational database. In essence, Access, or any other relational database, combines (joins) all of the records in the Customers table with all of the records in the Loans table to create a temporary working table. The result is a very large table in which each record contains all of the fields from both the Customers table and the Loans table. The number of records in this table is equal to the product of the number of Customer records times the number of Loans records; for example, if there were 10 records in the Customers table, and 30 records in the Loans table, there would be 300 records in the combined table. However, Access displays only those records wherein the value of the joined field (CustomerID) is the same in both tables. It sounds complicated (it is), but Access does the work for you. And as we said earlier, you need only to master the Design grid in Figure 5.8a and let Access do the rest.

The power of a relational database is its ability to process multiple-table queries, such as the example in Figure 5.8. The forms and reports within a database also become more interesting when they contain information based on multiple-table queries. Our next exercise has you create a query similar to the one in Figure 5.8, then create a report based on that query.

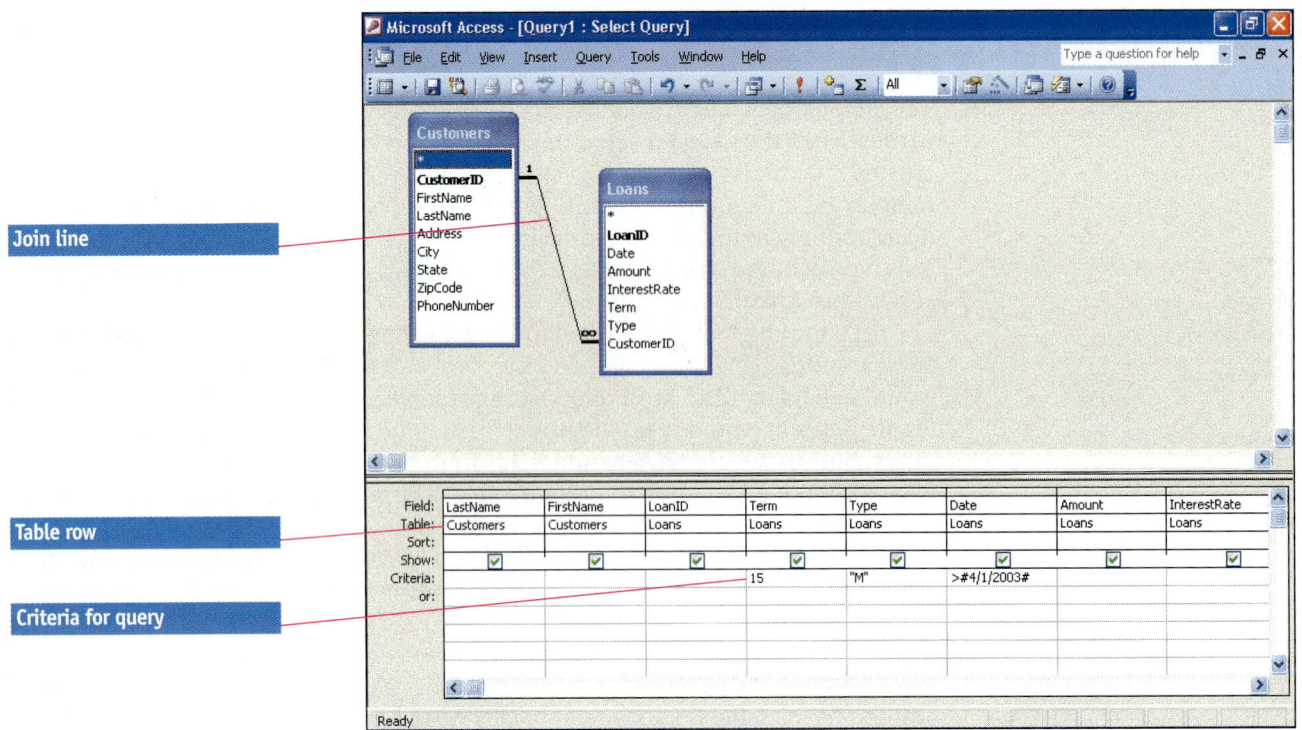

(a) Query Window

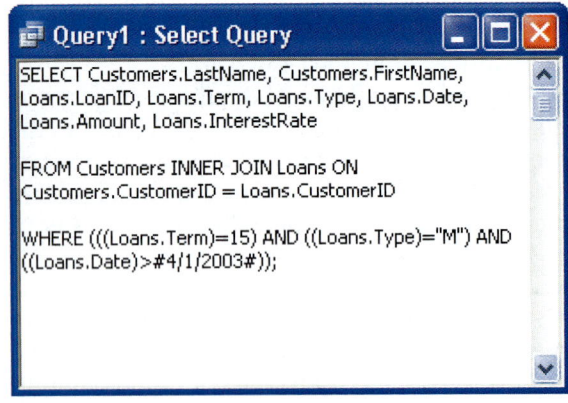

(b) Dynaset

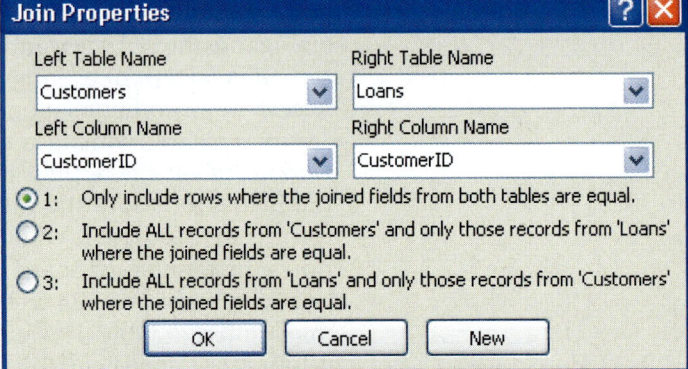

(c) SQL View

(d) Join Properties

FIGURE 5.8   A Multiple-table Query

hands-on exercise

3 Queries and Reports

Objective To create a query that relates two tables to one another, then create a report based on that query; to use the query to update the records in the underlying tables. Use Figure 5.9 as a guide in the exercise.

Step 1: **Add the Tables**

- Open the **National Bank database** from the previous exercise.
- Click the **Queries button** in the Database window. Double click **Create query in Design view**.
- The Show Table dialog box appears as shown in Figure 5.9a, with the Tables tab already selected.
- Click the **Customers table**, then click the **Add button** (or double click the **Customers table**) to add the Customers table to the query.
- Double click the **Loans table** to add the Loans table to the query.
- Click **Close** to close the Show Table dialog box.

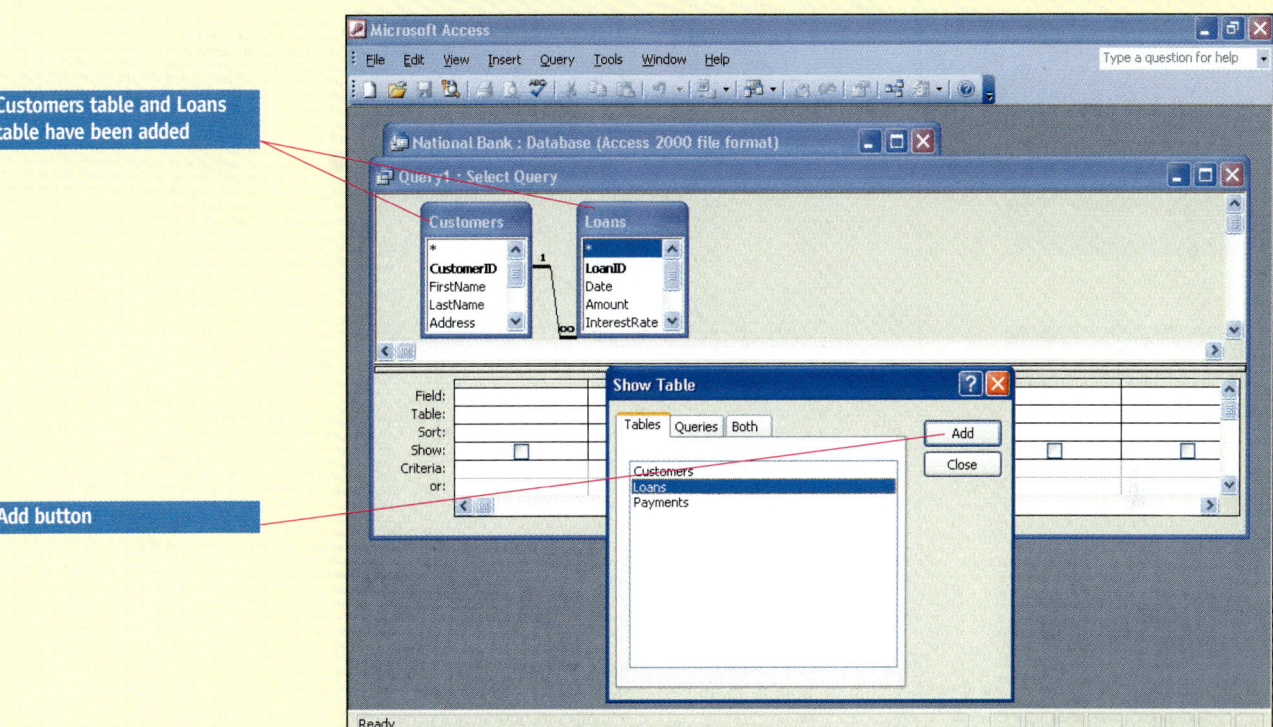

Customers table and Loans table have been added

Add button

(a) Add the Tables (step 1)

FIGURE 5.9 Hands-on Exercise 3

ADDING AND DELETING TABLES

To add a table to an existing query, pull down the Query menu, click Show Table, then double click the name of the table from the Table/Query list. To delete a table, click anywhere in its field list and press the Del key, or pull down the Query menu and click Remove Table.

MICROSOFT OFFICE ACCESS 2003   1585

Step 2: **Move and Size the Field Lists**

- Click the **Maximize button** so that the Query Design window takes the entire desktop.

- Point to the line separating the field lists from the design grid (the mouse pointer changes to a cross), then click and drag in a downward direction. This gives you more space to display the field lists for the tables in the query as shown in Figure 5.9b.

- Click and drag the bottom of the **Customers table field list** until you can see all of the fields in the Customers table.

- Click and drag the bottom of the **Loans table field list** until you can see all of the fields in the Loans table.

- Click and drag the title bar of the **Loans table** to the right until you are satisfied with the appearance of the line connecting the tables.

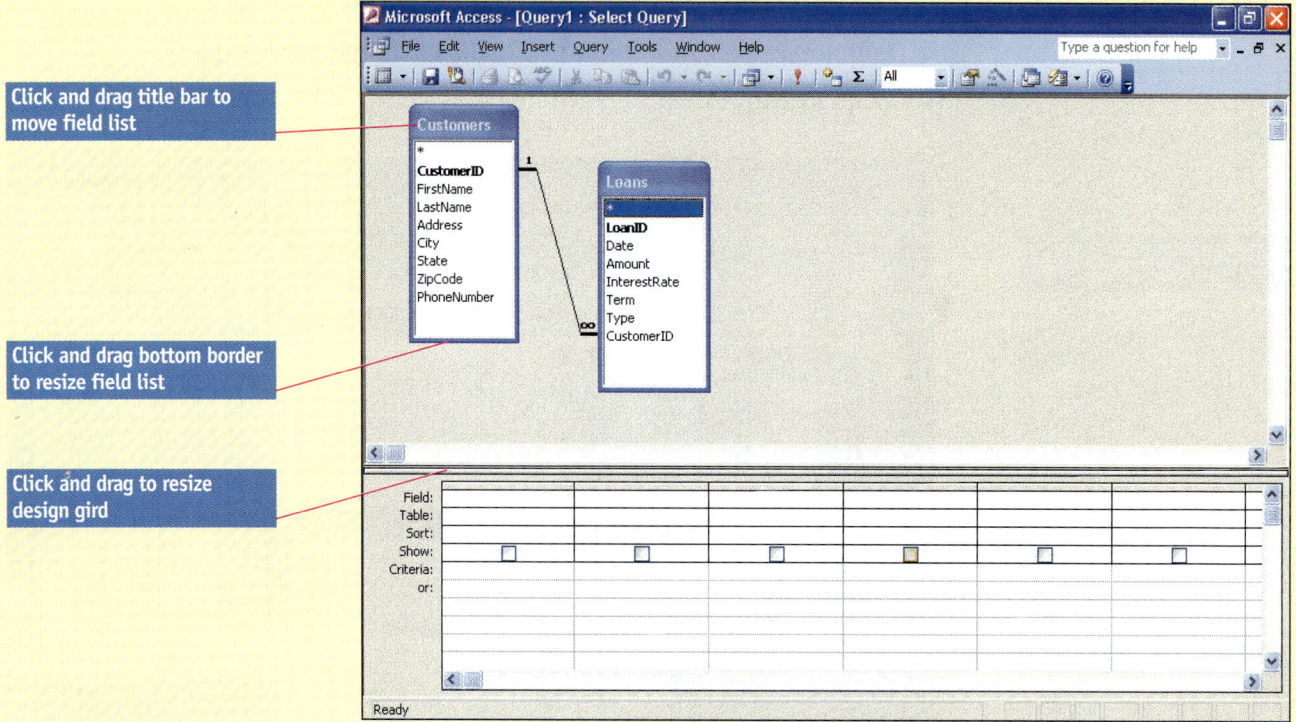

(b) Move and Size the Field Lists (step 2)

FIGURE 5.9 Hands-on Exercise 3 (*continued*)

CONVERSION TO STANDARD FORMAT

Access is flexible in accepting text and date expressions in the Criteria row of a select query. A text entry can be entered with or without quotation marks (e.g., M or "M"). A date entry can be entered with or without pound signs (you can enter 1/1/03 or #1/1/03#). Access does, however, convert your entries to standard format as soon you move to the next cell in the design grid. Thus, text entries are always displayed in quotation marks, and dates are always enclosed in pound signs.

Step 3: **Create the Query**

- The Table row should be visible within the design grid. If not, pull down the **View menu** and click **Table Names** to display the Table row in the design grid as shown in Figure 5.9c.

- Double click the **LastName** and **FirstName fields**, in that order, from the Customers table to add these fields to the design grid.

- Double click the **title bar** of the Loans table to select all of the fields, then drag the selected group of fields to the design grid.

- Enter the selection criteria (scrolling if necessary) as follows:
  ❑ Click the **Criteria row** under the **Date field**. Type **Between 1/1/03 and 3/31/03**. (You do not have to type the pound signs.)
  ❑ Click the **Criteria row** for the **Amount field**. Type **>200000**.
  ❑ Type **M** in the Criteria row for the **Type field**. (You do not have to type the quotation marks.)

- Select all of the columns in the design grid by clicking the column selector in the first column, then pressing and holding the **Shift key** as you scroll to the last column and click its column selector.

- Double click the right edge of any column selector to adjust the column width of all the columns simultaneously.

- Click the **Sort row** under the LastName field, then click the **down arrow** to open the drop-down list box. Click **Ascending**.

- Click the **Save button** on the Query Design toolbar. Save the query as **First Quarter 2003 Jumbo Loans**.

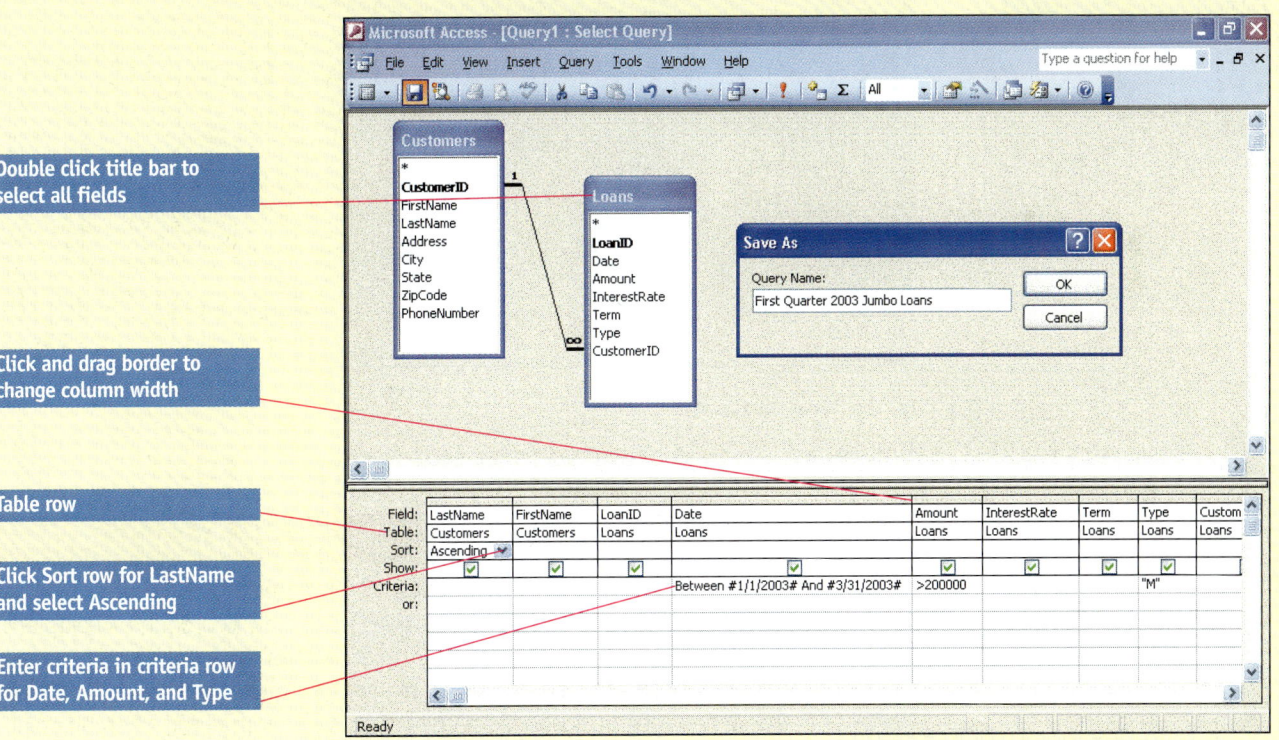

(c) Create the Query (step 3)

FIGURE 5.9 Hands-on Exercise 3 (*continued*)

Step 4: **The Dynaset**

- Click the **Run button** (the exclamation point) to run the query and create the dynaset in Figure 5.9d. Three jumbo loans are listed. The loans appear in alphabetical order according to the customer's last name.

- Click the **Amount field** for loan L0008. Enter **100000** as the corrected amount and press **Enter**. (This will reduce the number of jumbo loans in subsequent reports to two.)

- Click the **View button** to return to the Design view in order to rerun the query.

- This time, only two loans are listed, because loan L0008 is no longer a jumbo loan. Changing a value in a dynaset automatically changes the underlying table.

- Click the **Close button** to close the query. Click **Yes** if asked whether to save the changes to the query.

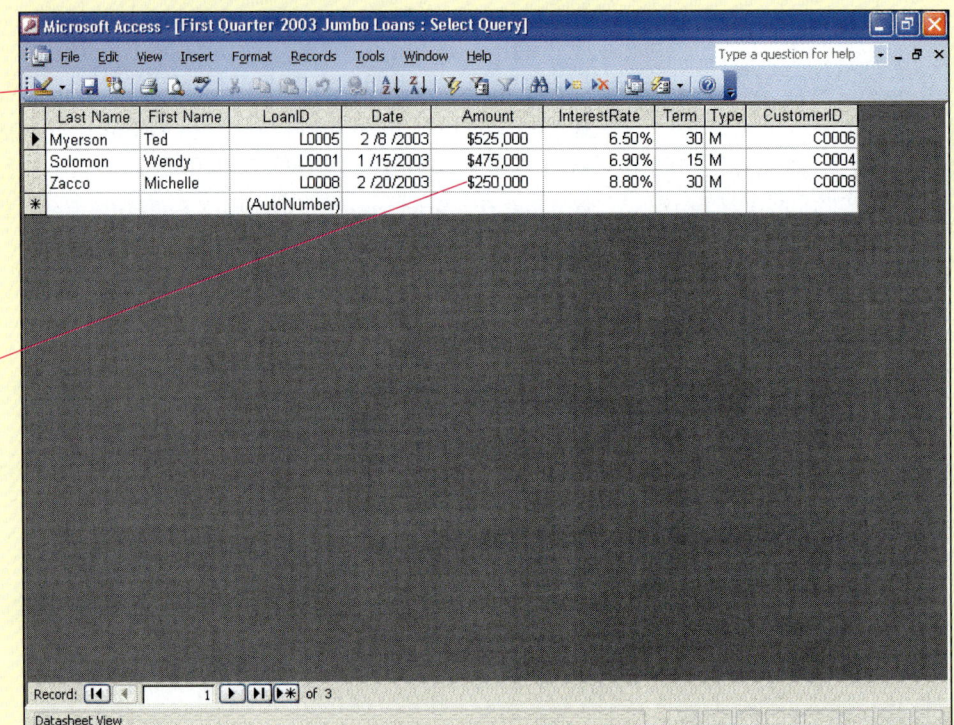

(d) The Dynaset (step 4)

FIGURE 5.9   Hands-on Exercise 3 (*continued*)

DATA TYPE MISMATCH

The data type determines the way in which criteria appear in the design grid. A text field is enclosed in quotation marks. Number, currency, and counter fields are shown as digits with or without a decimal point. Dates are enclosed in pound signs. A Yes/No field is entered as Yes or No without quotation marks. Entering criteria in the wrong format produces a Data Type Mismatch error when attempting to run the query.

Step 5: **Create a Report**

- The National Bank database should still be open (although the size of your window may be different from the one in the figure).

- Click the **Reports button** in the Database window. Double click **Create report by using wizard**.

- Click the **drop-down arrow** to display the tables and queries in the database to select the one on which the report will be based.

- Select **First Quarter 2003 Jumbo Loans** (the query you just created) as the basis of your report as shown in Figure 5.9e.

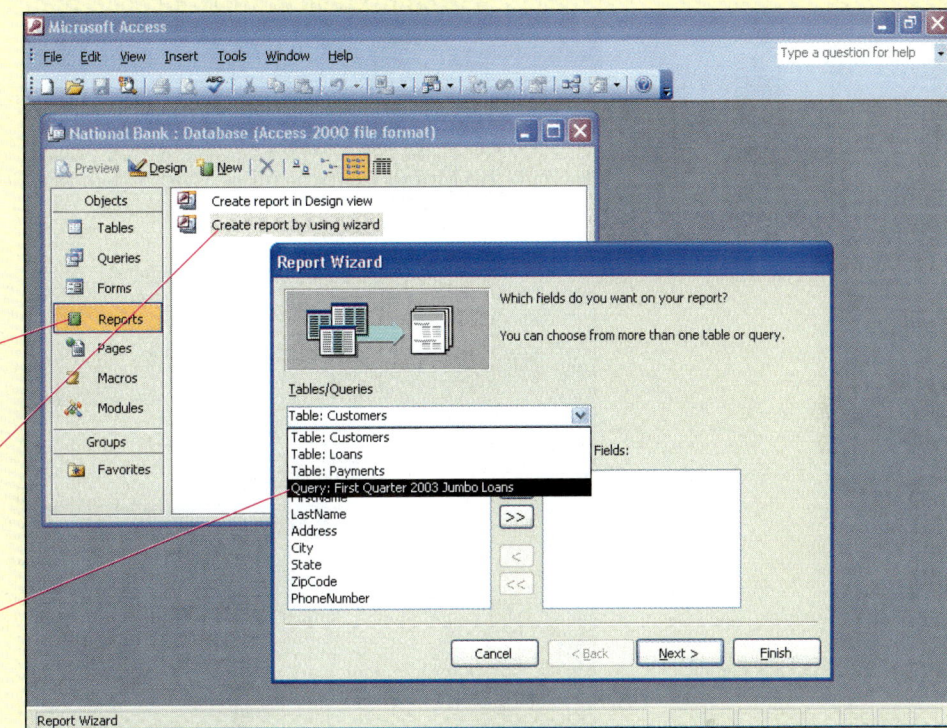

(e) Create a Report (step 5)

FIGURE 5.9 Hands-on Exercise 3 (*continued*)

CHANGE THE REPORT PROPERTIES

Do you want the Page Header or Page Footer to appear on every page of a report, or would you prefer to suppress the information on pages where there is a Report Header or Footer? You can customize a report to accommodate this and other subtleties by changing the report properties. Open the report in Design view, right click the Report Selector button (the solid square in the upper-left corner), then click the Properties command to display the property sheet for the report. Click the All tab, locate the Page Header or Page Footer property, and make the appropriate change.

Step 6: **The Report Wizard**

- Double click **LoanID** from the Available Fields list box to add this field to the report. Add the **LastName, FirstName, Date**, and **Amount fields** as shown in Figure 5.9f. Click **Next**.

- You will be asked how you want to view your data, by Customers or by Loans. Select **Loans**. Click **Next**.

- There is no need to group the records. Click **Next**.

- There is no need to sort the records. Click **Next**.

- The **Tabular layout** is selected, as is **Portrait orientation**. Be sure the box is checked to **Adjust field width so all fields fit on a page**. Click **Next**.

- Choose **Soft Gray** as the style. Click **Next**.

- Enter **First Quarter 2003 Jumbo Loans** as the title for your report. The option button to **Preview the Report** is already selected.

- Click the **Finish Command button** to exit the Report Wizard and preview the report.

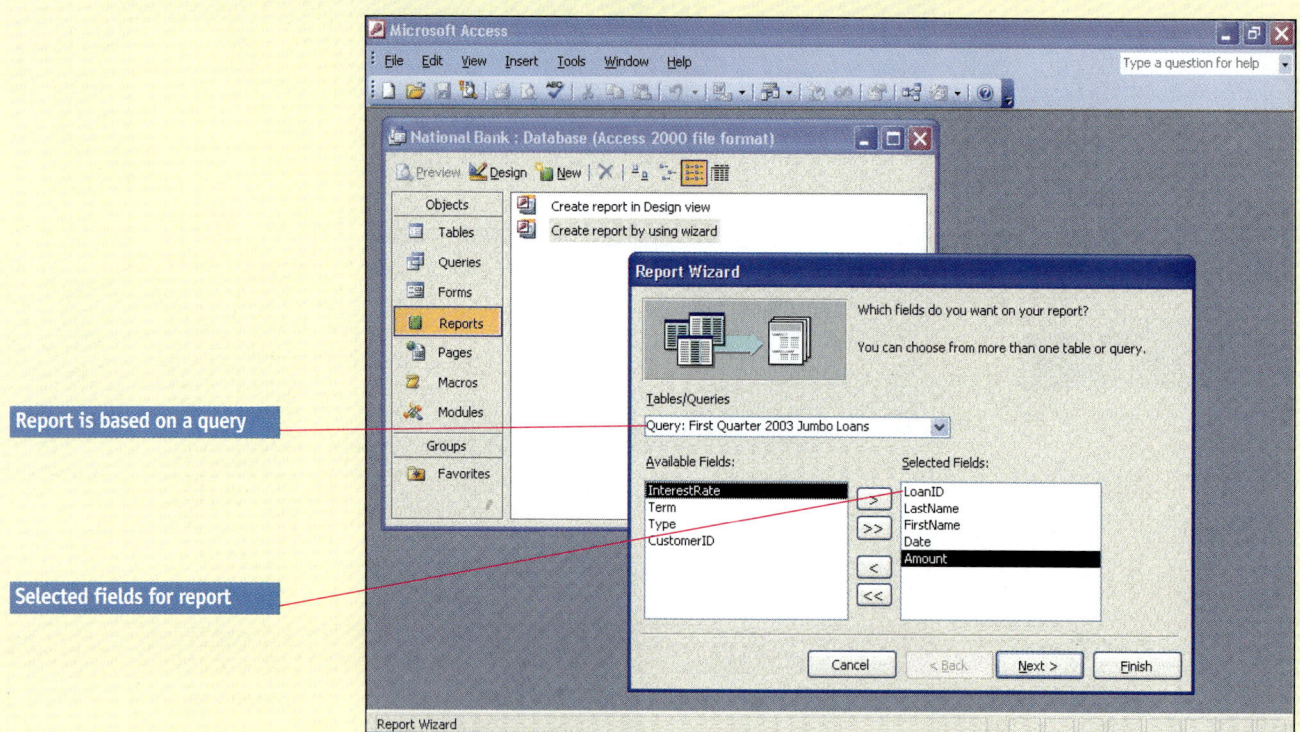

(f) The Report Wizard (step 6)

FIGURE 5.9 Hands-on Exercise 3 (*continued*)

GROUPING RECORDS WITHIN A REPORT

What if you wanted a report that showed all of the customers in a database, and for each customer, all of the loans for that customer? Start the Report Wizard, select fields from the Customers table (name, telephone, and so on), then select additional fields from the Loans table. Access will ask you how to view the report (specify by customer) and how to sort the records (specify LoanID). Go to Design view when the wizard is finished to add a logo and/or modify the formatting. See practice exercise 4 at the end of the chapter.

Step 7: **Print the Completed Report**

- Change to Design view. Modify the Form Header so that it is similar to the report in Figure 5.9g. (Use the same clip art image as in the Customers form for consistency within the application.)

- Move, size, and align the controls in the Detail section as necessary. Save the modified report.

- Click the **Print Preview button** to view the report and see the customers with jumbo loans. (Return to Design view to make additional changes if necessary.)

- The report in Figure 5.9g is based on the query created earlier. Michelle Zacco is *not* in the report because the amount of her loan was updated in the query's dynaset in step 4.

- Click the **Print button** to print the report. Close the Preview window, then close the Report window. Click **Yes** if asked to save the changes.

- Close the National Bank database and exit Access if you do not want to continue with the next exercise at this time.

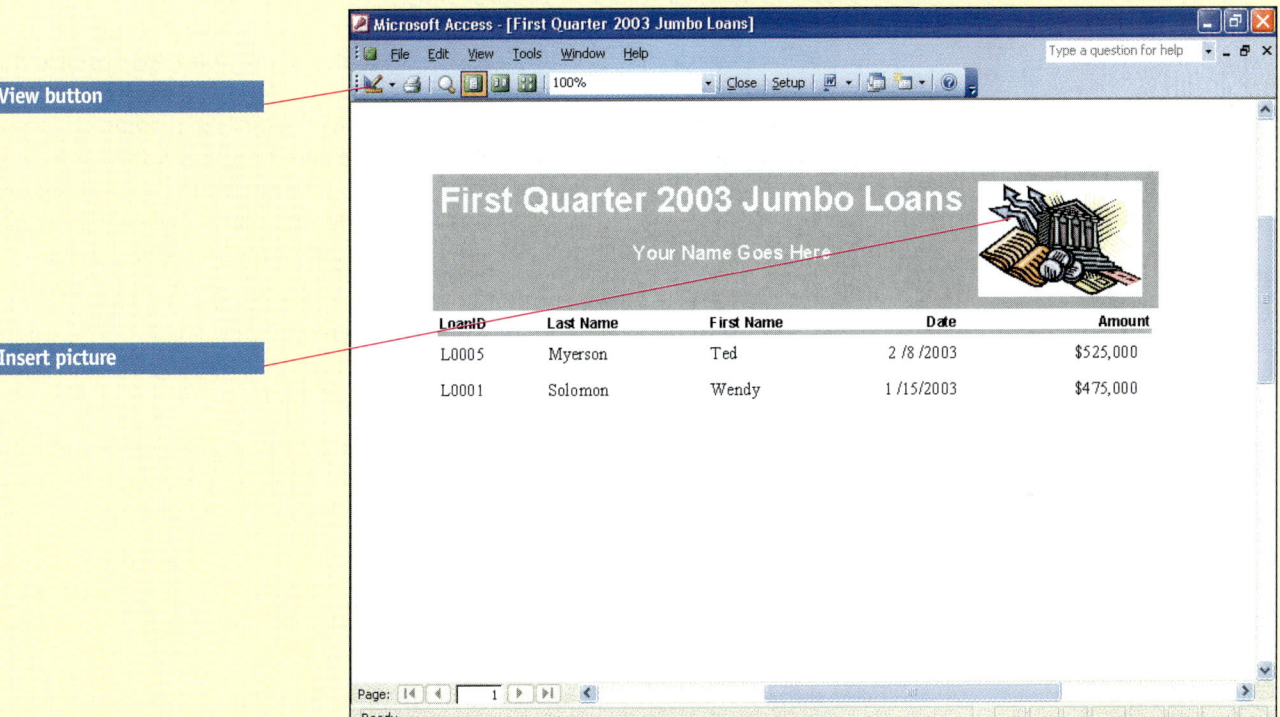

(g) Print the Completed Report (step 7)

FIGURE 5.9 Hands-on Exercise 3 (*continued*)

COMPACT AND REPAIR THE DATABASE

Access databases tend to grow very quickly, especially as you create and edit new forms and reports, and thus you should always compact a database before you exit. Pull down the Tools menu; click Database Utilities, then click Compact and Repair Database. The database will close and then reopen, after the compacting process has eliminated the fragmentation that occurs as you work on a database. Compacting is different from compressing; that is, you can use WinZip (or a similar utility) to further reduce the file size of a compacted database.

EXPANDING THE DATABASE

The database we have used throughout the chapter contained only two tables; a Customers table and a Loans table. A relational database can be easily expanded, however, to include additional data without disturbing the existing tables. Thus, we expand the National Bank database to include a Payments table as shown in Figure 5.10. Recall that the original database had a one-to-many relationship between customers and loans. The expanded database will contain a second one-to-many relationship between loans and payments. One loan has many payments, but a specific payment is associated with only one loan. The primary key of the Loans table (LoanID) will appear as a foreign key in the Payments table.

The Payments table in Figure 5.10c contains four fields for each record: PaymentID, LoanID, PaymentDate (the date the payment was received), and the AmountReceived. The PaymentID is the primary key, and it has been designated as an AutoNumber field. Thus, the payments are numbered sequentially according to the order they were received by the bank. (An alternate design would be to eliminate the PaymentID in favor of a primary key consisting of both the LoanID and PaymentDate. Although there are multiple records in the Payments table with the same loan number, as well as multiple records with the same payment date, the *combination* of LoanID and PaymentDate is unique, assuming that multiple payments for the same loan are not received on the same date. We prefer the PaymentID with the AutoNumber field type.)

We began the chapter by showing you hypothetical records in the database and asking you to answer queries based on that data. We end the chapter the same way, by asking you to consider several queries in conjunction with the data in Figure 5.10. Realize, too, that while you go through the tables manually, Access will obtain the information automatically for you when you create a multiple-table query.

Query: How many payments have been received for loan L0002? What was the date of the most recent payment?
Answer: Three payments have been received for loan L0002. The most recent payment was received on 4/15/2003.

This query is answered with reference to just the Payments table. You search the Payments table for all records containing the designated LoanID, sort these records in ascending order (earliest date first), and then select the last record.

Query: How many payments have been received from Matt Hirsch?
Answer: Only one payment has been received from Matt Hirsch. The payment was for $1,270.31 and was received on April 10, 2003 for LoanID L0014.

This requires data from all three tables. First you look in the Customers table to determine the CustomerID for Matt Hirsch (C0010), then you search the Loans table for all loans for this customer (L0014 and L0022), and finally you go to the Payments table to retrieve the payments for the indicated loans. Note that loan L0022 was granted on April 22 and thus no payments have been made.

Query: Can you add a payment to the Payments table for LoanID L0100? Can you add a payment to the Payments table without specifying the LoanID?
Answer: The answer to the first question is always no because the loan does not exist. The answer to the second question is also no, provided LoanID is a *required field* in the Payments table. Referential integrity prevents you from adding a payment record with an *invalid* LoanID, but lets you omit the LoanID. Since this does not make sense in the physical environment, the LoanID should be specified as a required field in the Payments table.

LoanID	Date	Amount	Interest Rate	Term	Type	CustomerID
L0001	1/15/2003	$475,000	6.90%	15	M	C0004
L0002	1/23/2003	$35,000	7.20%	5	C	C0004
L0003	1/25/2003	$10,000	5.50%	3	C	C0005
L0004	1/31/2003	$12,000	9.50%	10	O	C0004
L0005	2/8/2003	$525,000	6.50%	30	M	C0006
L0006	2/12/2003	$10,500	7.50%	5	O	C0007
L0007	2/15/2003	$35,000	6.50%	5	O	C0008
L0008	2/20/2003	$250,000	8.80%	30	M	C0008
L0009	2/21/2003	$5,000	10.00%	3	O	C0008
L0010	2/28/2003	$200,000	7.00%	15	M	C0001
L0011	3/1/2003	$25,000	10.00%	3	C	C0002
L0012	3/1/2003	$20,000	9.50%	5	O	C0005
L0013	3/3/2003	$56,000	7.50%	5	C	C0009
L0014	3/10/2003	$129,000	8.50%	15	M	C0010
L0015	3/11/2003	$200,000	7.25%	15	M	C0003
L0016	3/21/2003	$150,000	7.50%	15	M	C0001
L0017	3/22/2003	$100,000	7.00%	30	M	C0001
L0018	3/31/2003	$15,000	6.50%	3	O	C0003
L0019	4/1/2003	$10,000	8.00%	5	C	C0002
L0020	4/15/2003	$25,000	8.50%	4	C	C0003
L0021	4/18/2003	$41,000	9.90%	4	C	C0008
L0022	4/22/2003	$350,000	7.50%	15	M	C0010
L0023	5/1/2003	$150,000	6.00%	15	M	C0003
L0024	5/3/2003	$350,000	8.20%	30	M	C0004
L0025	5/8/2003	$275,000	9.20%	15	M	C0007

(a) Loans Table

CustomerID	First Name	Last Name	Address	City	State	Zip Code	Phone Number
C0001	Eileen	Faulkner	7245 NW 8 Street	Minneapolis	MN	55346	(612) 894-1511
C0002	Scott	Wit	5660 NW 175 Terrace	Baltimore	MD	21224	(410) 753-0345
C0003	Benjamin	Grauer	10000 Sample Road	Coral Springs	FL	33073	(305) 444-5555
C0004	Wendy	Solomon	7500 Reno Road	Houston	TX	77090	(713) 427-3104
C0005	Alex	Rey	3456 Main Highway	Denver	CO	80228	(303) 555-6666
C0006	Ted	Myerson	6545 Stone Street	Chapel Hill	NC	27515	(919) 942-7654
C0007	Lori	Sangastiano	4533 Aero Drive	Santa Rosa	CA	95403	(707) 542-3411
C0008	Michelle	Zacco	488 Gold Street	Gainesville	FL	32601	(904) 374-5660
C0009	David	Powell	5070 Battle Road	Decatur	GA	30034	(301) 345-6556
C0010	Matt	Hirsch	777 NW 67 Avenue	Fort Lee	NJ	07624	(201) 664-3211

(b) Customers Table

PaymentID	LoanID	Payment Date	Amount Received
P0001	L0001	2/15/2003	$4,242.92
P0002	L0002	2/15/2003	$696.35
P0003	L0003	2/25/2003	$301.96
P0004	L0004	2/28/2003	$155.28
P0005	L0005	3/8/2003	$3,318.36
P0006	L0006	3/12/2003	$210.40
P0007	L0001	3/15/2003	$4,242.92
P0008	L0002	3/15/2003	$696.35
P0009	L0007	3/15/2003	$684.82
P0010	L0008	3/20/2003	$1,975.69
P0011	L0009	3/21/2003	$161.34
P0012	L0003	3/25/2003	$301.96
P0013	L0010	3/28/2003	$1,797.66
P0014	L0004	3/31/2003	$155.28
P0015	L0011	4/1/2003	$806.68
P00016	L0012	4/1/2003	$420.04
P00017	L0005	4/8/2003	$3,318.36
P00018	L0014	4/10/2003	$1,270.31
P00019	L0015	4/11/2003	$1,825.73
P00020	L0006	4/12/2003	$210.40
P00021	L0001	4/15/2003	$4,242.92
P00022	L0002	4/15/2003	$696.35
P00023	L0007	4/15/2003	$684.82
P00024	L0008	4/20/2003	$1,975.69
P00025	L0009	4/21/2003	$161.34
P00026	L0016	4/21/2003	$1,390.52
P00027	L0017	4/22/2003	$665.30
P00028	L0003	4/25/2003	$301.96
P00029	L0010	4/28/2003	$1,797.66
P00030	L0004	4/30/2003	$155.28

(c) Partial Payments Table

FIGURE 5.10 Expanding the Database

Multiple Subforms

Subforms were introduced earlier in the chapter as a means of displaying data from related tables. Figure 5.11 continues the discussion by showing a main form with two levels of subforms. The main (Customers) form has a one-to-many relationship with the first (Loans) subform. The Loans subform in turn has a one-to-many relationship with the second (Payments) subform. The Customers form and the Loans subform are the forms that you created in the second hands-on exercise. (The Loans subform is displayed in the Form view, as opposed to the Datasheet view.) The Payments subform is new and will be developed in our next hands-on exercise.

The records displayed in the three forms are linked to one another according to the relationships within the database. There is a one-to-many relationship between customers and loans so that the first subform displays all of the loans for one customer. There is also a one-to-many relationship between loans and payments so that the second subform (Payments) displays all of the payments for the selected loan. Click on a different loan (for the same customer), and the Payments subform is updated automatically to show all of the payments for that loan.

The status bar for the main form indicates record 5 of 10, meaning that you are viewing the fifth of 10 Customer records. The status bar for the Loans subform indicates record 1 of 2, corresponding to the first of two loan records for the fifth customer. The status bar for the Payments subform indicates record 1 of 5, corresponding to the first of five payment records for this loan for this customer.

The three sets of navigation buttons enable you to advance to the next record(s) in any of the forms. The records move in conjunction with one another. Thus, if you advance to the next record in the Customers form, you will automatically display a different set of records in the Loans subform, as well as a different set of Payment records in the Payments subform. Note, too, the command buttons that appear in the upper-right portion of the form to add a new customer and to close the Customers form.

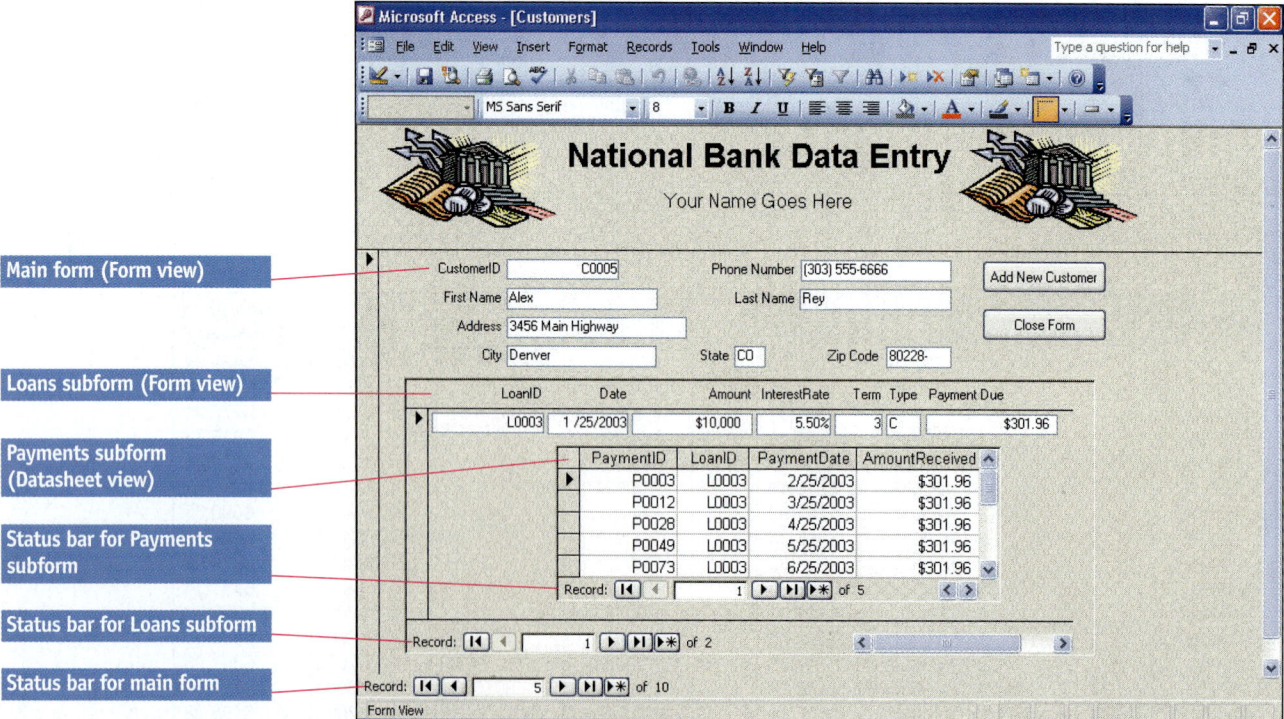

FIGURE 5.11 Multiple Subforms

hands-on exercise

4 Linked Subforms

Objective To create a main form with two levels of subforms; to display a subform in Form view or Datasheet view. Use Figure 5.12 as a guide.

Step 1: **Add a Relationship**

- Open the **National Bank database**. Pull down the **Tools menu**. Click **Relationships** to open the Relationships window as shown in Figure 5.12a.
- Maximize the Relationships window. Pull down the **Relationships menu**. Click **Show Table** to display the Show Table dialog box.
- The **Tables tab** is selected within the Show Table dialog box. Double click the **Payments table** to add the table to the Relationships window. Close the Show Table dialog box.
- Click and drag the title bar of the **Payments Field list** so that it is positioned approximately one inch from the Loans table.
- Click and drag the **LoanID field** in the Loans field list to the **LoanID field** in the Payments field list. You will see the Relationships dialog box.
- Check the **Enforce Referential Integrity** check box. (If necessary, clear the check boxes to Cascade Update Related Fields and Cascade Delete Related Records.)
- Click the **Create button** to establish the relationship. You should see a line indicating a one-to-many relationship between the Loans and Payments tables.
- Click the **Save button**, then close the Relationships window.

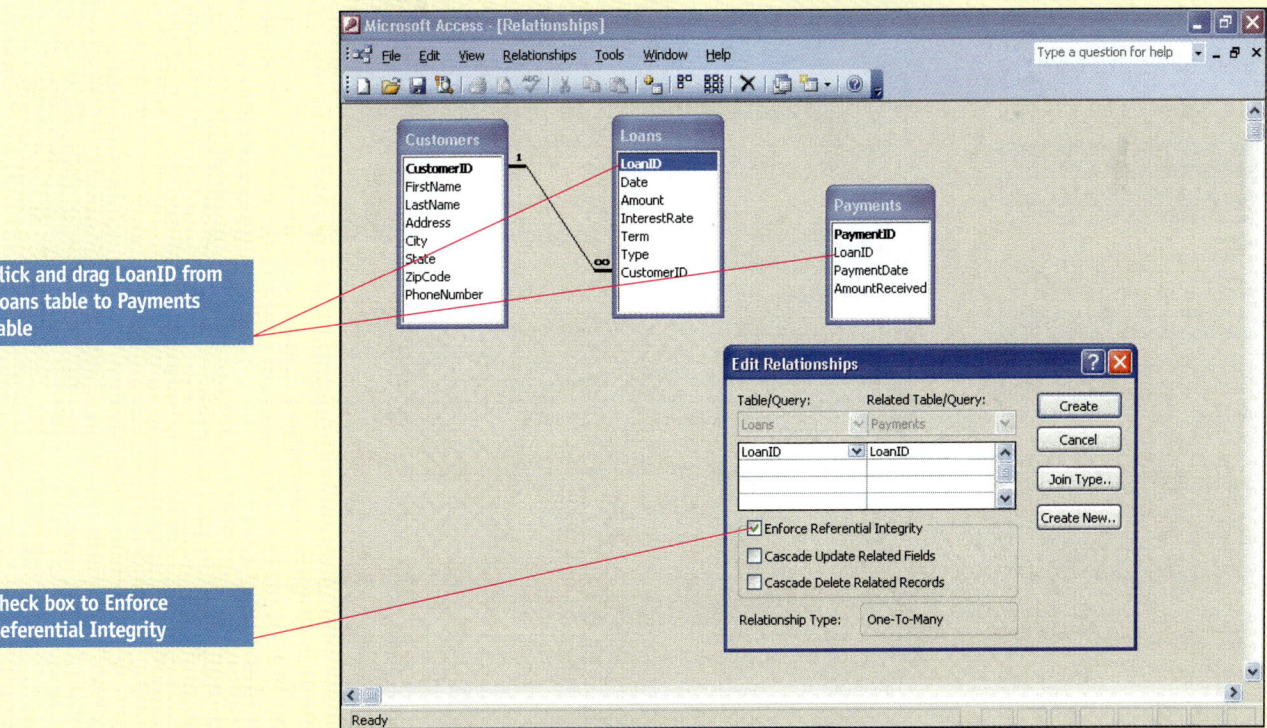

(a) Add a Relationship (step 1)

FIGURE 5.12 Hands-on Exercise 4

Step 2: **Create the Payments Subform**

- You should be back in the Database window. Click the **Forms button**, then open the **Loans subform** in Design view as shown in Figure 5.12b.

- Click and drag the bottom edge of the **Details section** so that you have approximately 2 to 2½ inches of blank space in the Detail section.

- Click the **Subform/Subreport button** on the Toolbox toolbar, then click and drag in the **Loans form** to create the Payments subform. Release the mouse.

- The **Use Existing Tables and Queries option button** is selected, indicating that we will build the subform from a table or query. Click **Next**. You should see the Subform/Subreport dialog box in Figure 5.12b.

- Click the **drop-down arrow** on the Tables and Queries list box to select the **Payments table**. Click the **>> button** to add all of the fields in the Payments table to the subform. Click **Next**.

- The Subform Wizard asks you to define the fields that link the main form to the subform. The option button to **Choose from a list** is selected, as is **Show Payments for each record in Loans using LoanID**. Click **Next**.

- **Payments subform** is entered as the name of the subform. Click **Finish**.

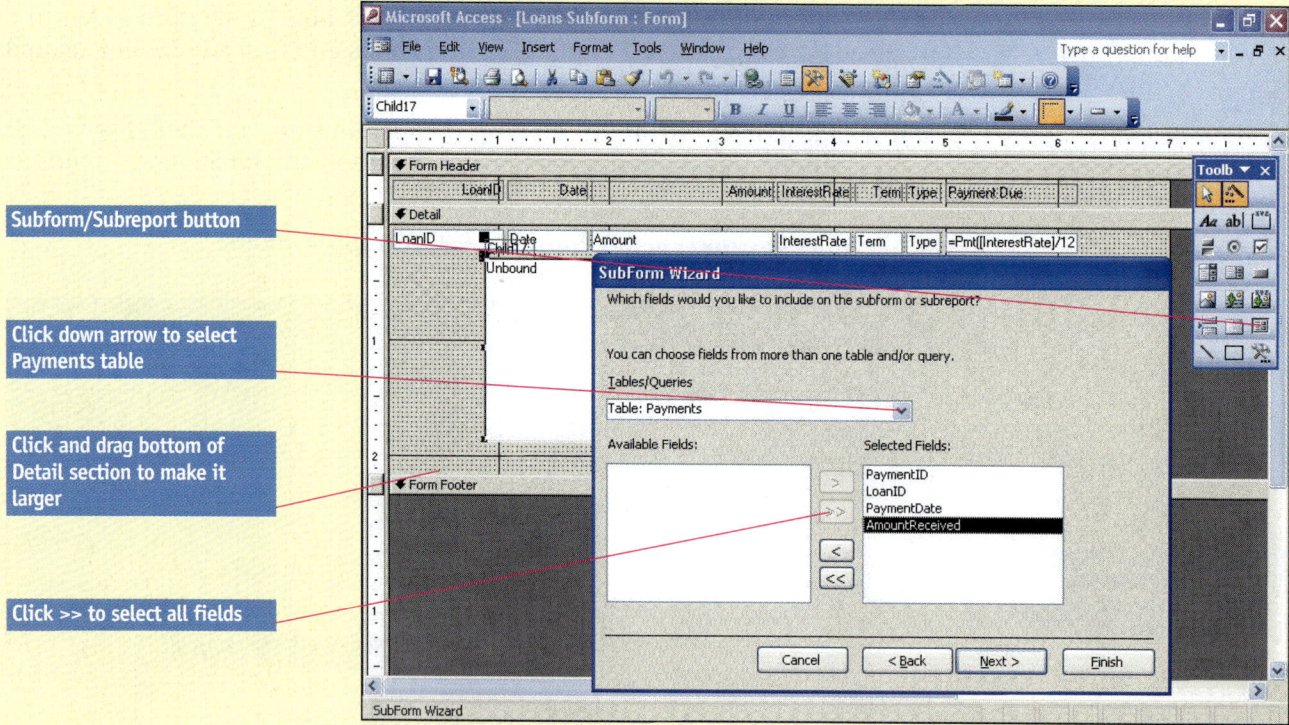

(b) Create the Payments Subform (step 2)

FIGURE 5.12 Hands-on Exercise 4 (*continued*)

LINKING FIELDS, FORMS, AND SUBFORMS

Linking fields do not have to appear in the main form and subform but must be included in the underlying table or query. The LoanID, for example, links the Loans form and the Payments form and need not appear in either form. We have, however, chosen to display the LoanID in both forms to emphasize the relationship between the corresponding tables.

Step 3: **Change the Loans Subform**

- Maximize the window. Point to the **Form Selector box** for the Loans subform in the upper-left corner of the Design window and click the **right mouse button** to display a shortcut menu.
- Click **Properties** to display the Form Properties dialog box in Figure 5.12c.
- The property sheet pertains to the form as a whole, as can be seen from the title bar. Click in the **Default View box**, click the **drop-down arrow** to display the views, then click **Single Form**. Close the Properties dialog box.
- Select the label for the Payments subform control, then press the **Del key** to delete the label.
- Save the form.

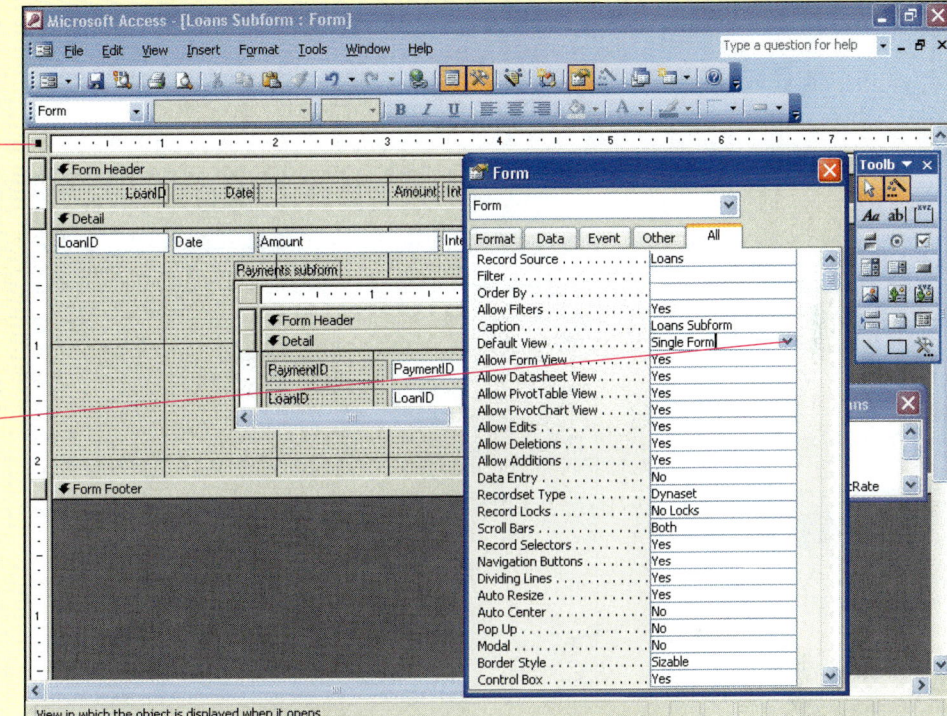

(c) Change the Loans Subform (step 3)

FIGURE 5.12 Hands-on Exercise 4 (*continued*)

THE DEFAULT VIEW PROPERTY

The Default View property determines how a form is dislayed initially and is especially important when working with multiple forms. In general, the highest level form(s) is (are) displayed in the Single Form view and the lowest level in the Datasheet view. In this example, the Customers and Loans forms are both set to the Single Form view, whereas the Payment form is set to the Datasheet view. To change the default view, right click the Form Selector box to display the property sheet for the form as a whole, click the All tab, then change the entry in the Default View property.

MICROSOFT OFFICE ACCESS 2003 **1597**

Step 4: **The Loans Subform in Form View**

- Click the **drop-down arrow** next to the **View button** to switch to the Form view for the Loans subform as shown in Figure 5.12d.

- Do not be concerned if the size and/or position of your Payments subform is different from ours as you can return to the Design view to make the necessary changes.
  - The status bar of the Loans subform indicates record 1 of 26, meaning that you are positioned on the first of 26 records in the Loans table.
  - The status bar for the Payments subform indicates record 1 of 5, corresponding to the first of five payment records for this loan.

- Pull down the **View menu**, click **Datasheet** to change to the Datasheet view of the Loans subform. Click the **plus sign** next to the first loan record to expand the record and see its associated payments.

- Change the column widths in the Payments datasheet as necessary.

- Change to the **Design view** to size and/or move the Payments subform control within the Loans subform. Save, then close, the Loans subform.

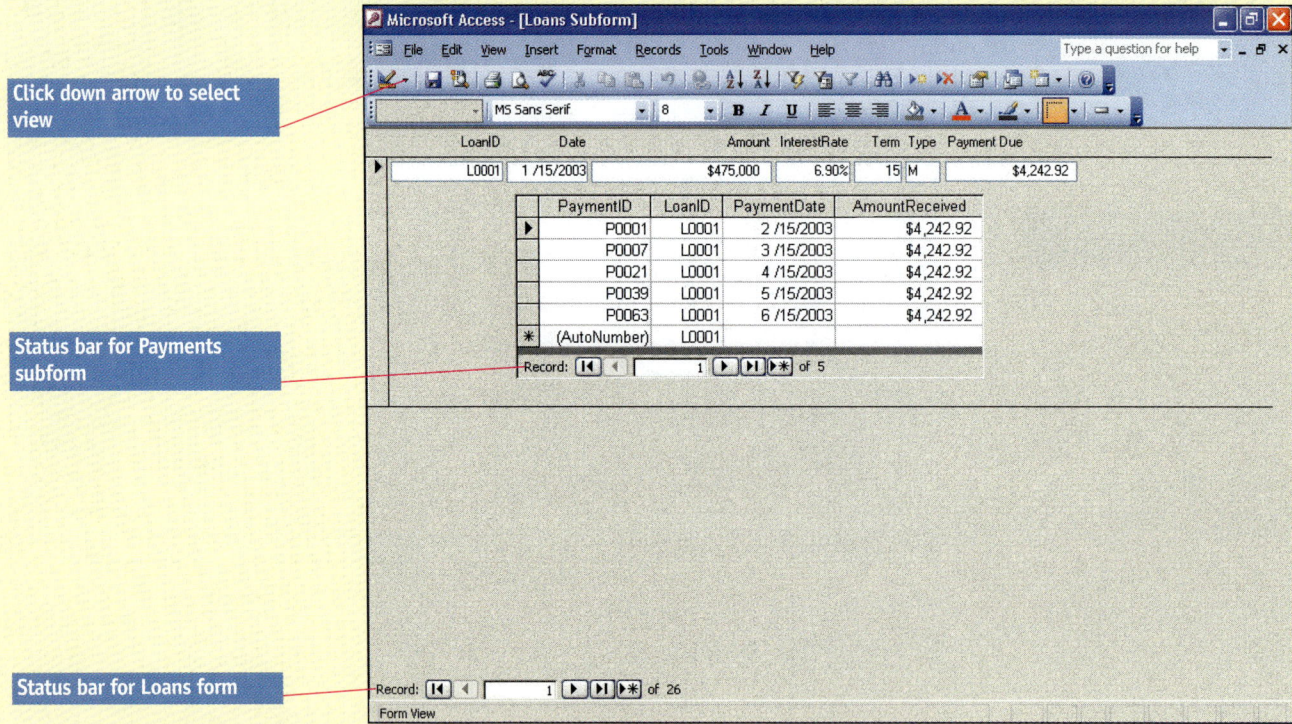

(d) The Loans Subform in Form View (step 4)

FIGURE 5.12 Hands-on Exercise 4 (*continued*)

USER-FRIENDLY FORMS

The phrase "user-friendly" appears so frequently that we tend to take it for granted. The intention is clear, however, and you should strive to make your forms as clear as possible so that the user is provided with all the information he or she may need. It may be obvious to the designer that one has to click the navigation buttons to move to a new loan, but a novice unfamiliar with Access may not know that. Adding a descriptive label to the form goes a long way toward making a system successful.

Step 5: **The Customers Form**

- You should be back in the Database window. Click the **Forms button** (if necessary), then open the **Customers form** as shown in Figure 5.12e.

- Do not be concerned if the sizes of the subforms are different from ours as you can return to the Design view to make the necessary changes.

- The status bar of the Customers form indicates record 1 of 10, meaning that you are positioned on the first of 10 records in the Customers table.

- The status bar for the Loans subform indicates record 1 of 3, corresponding to the first of three records for this customer.

- The status bar for the Payments subform indicates record 1 of 4, corresponding to the first of four payments for this loan.

- Change to the **Design view** to move and/or size the control for the Loans subform as described in step 6.

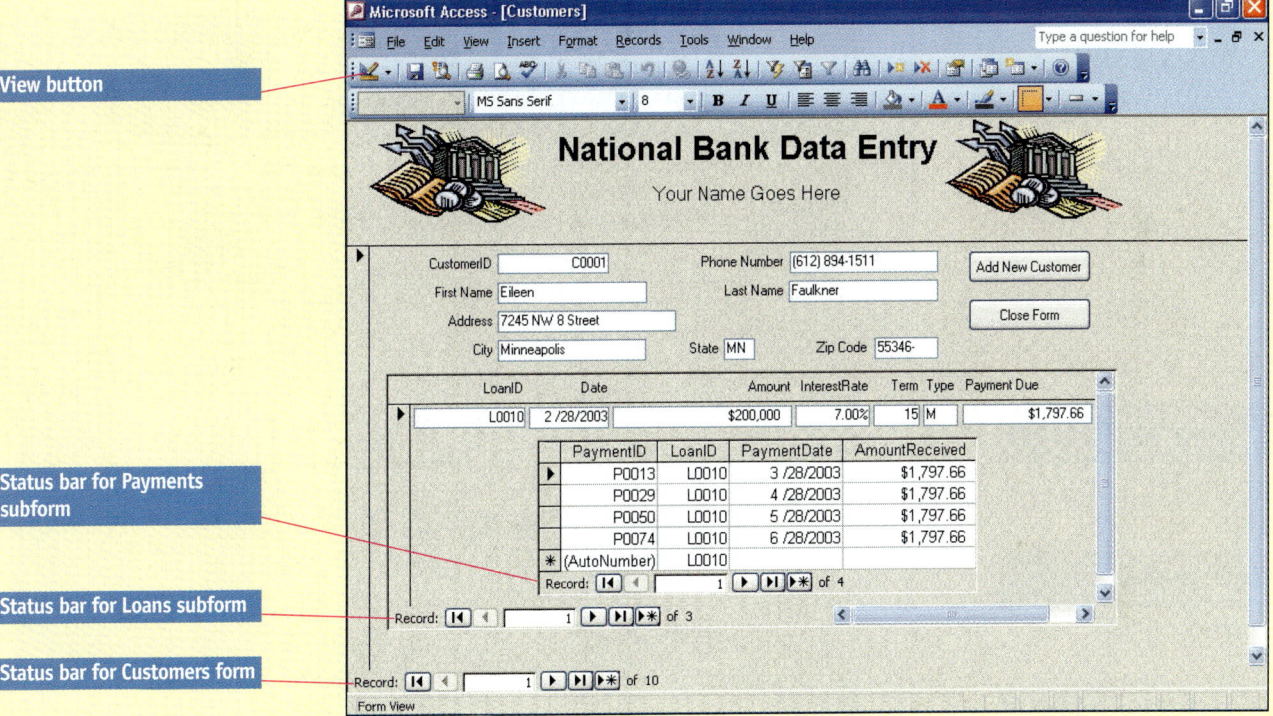

(e) The Customers Form (step 5)

FIGURE 5.12   Hands-on Exercise 4 (*continued*)

THE STARTUP PROPERTY

The Startup property determines how a database will appear when it is opened. One very common option is to open a form automatically so that the user is presented with the form without having to navigate through the Database window. Pull down the Tools menu, click Startup to display the Startup dialog box, then click the drop-down arrow in the Display Form/Page list box. Select the desired form, such as the Customers form created in this exercise, then click OK. The next time you open the database the designated form will be opened automatically.

Step 6: **The Finishing Touches**

- You may need to increase the size of the Loans subform control. Click and drag the bottom edge of the **Detail section** in Figure 5.12f to make the section larger. You may also have to click and drag the **Loans subform** to the left, then click and drag its right border to make it wider.

- We also found it necessary to decrease the size of the Amount field within the Loans subform. Click the label for the **Amount field** in the Form Header.

- Press and hold the **Shift key** as you select the bound control for the Amount field in the Detail section, then click and drag the right border to make both controls narrower.

- Click the **Interest Rate label**. Press and hold the **Shift key** as you select the remaining controls to the left of the Amount field, then click and drag these fields to the left.

- Move and size the subform control as necessary. Save the changes.

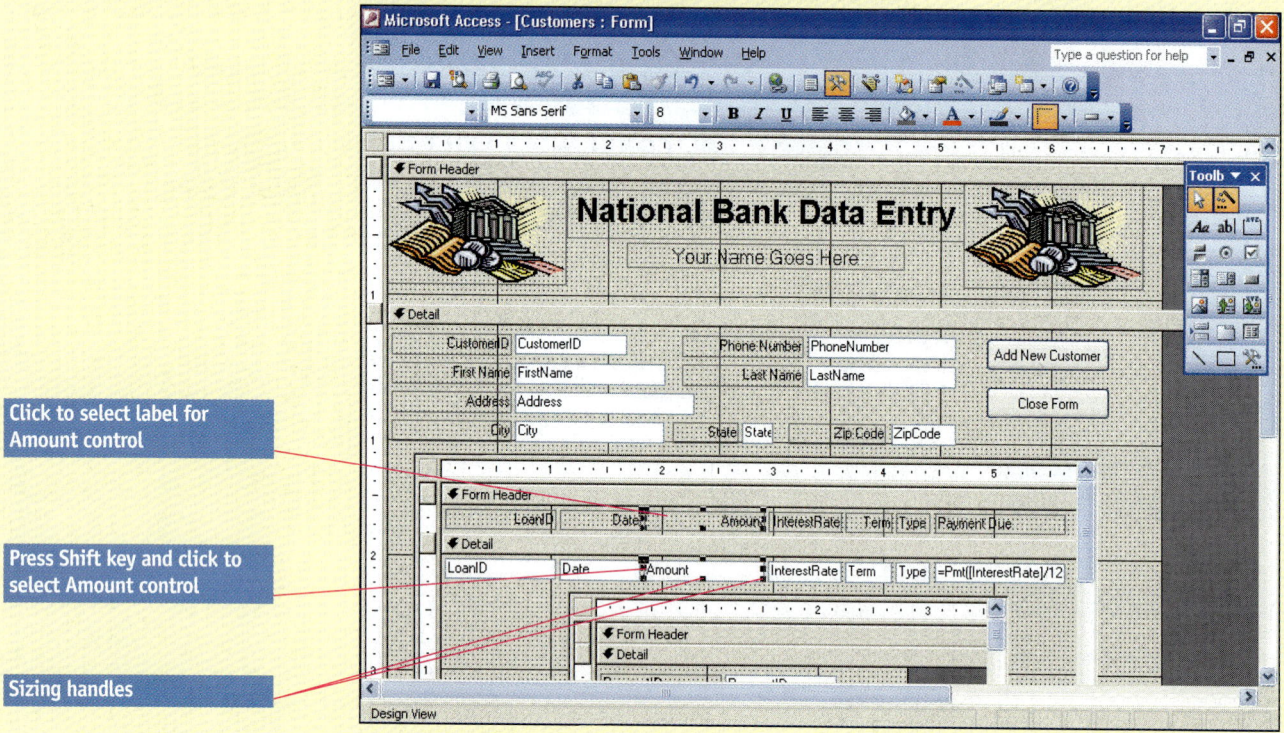

(f) The Finishing Touches (step 6)

FIGURE 5.12 Hands-on Exercise 4 (*continued*)

MULTIPLE CONTROLS AND PROPERTIES

Press and hold the Shift key as you click one control after another to select multiple controls. To view or change the properties for the selected controls, click the right mouse button to display a shortcut menu, then click Properties to display a property sheet. If the value of a property is the same for all selected controls, that value will appear in the property sheet; otherwise the box for that property will be blank. Changing a property when multiple controls are selected changes the property for all selected controls.

Step 7: Make Your Payments

- Change to the **Form view**. Click the ▶ on the status bar for the Customers form to move to the last record as shown in Figure 5.12g. This should be Customer C0011 (your record) that you entered in the earlier exercises in this chapter. You currently have two loans, L0026 and L0027, the first of which is displayed.

- Click in the **PaymentDate field** of **Payments subform**. Enter the date of your first payment, press **Tab,** then enter the amount paid. (The PaymentID and LoanID are entered automatically.)

- Press **Enter** to move to the next payment record and enter this payment as well. Press **Enter** and enter a third payment.

- Click the **selection area** at the left of the form to select this record. Pull down the **File menu** and click **Print** to display the Print dialog box. Click the **Selected Records option button**. Click **OK** to print the selected form.

- Close the Customers form. Click **Yes** if asked to save the changes to the form.

- Close the National Bank database. Exit Access.

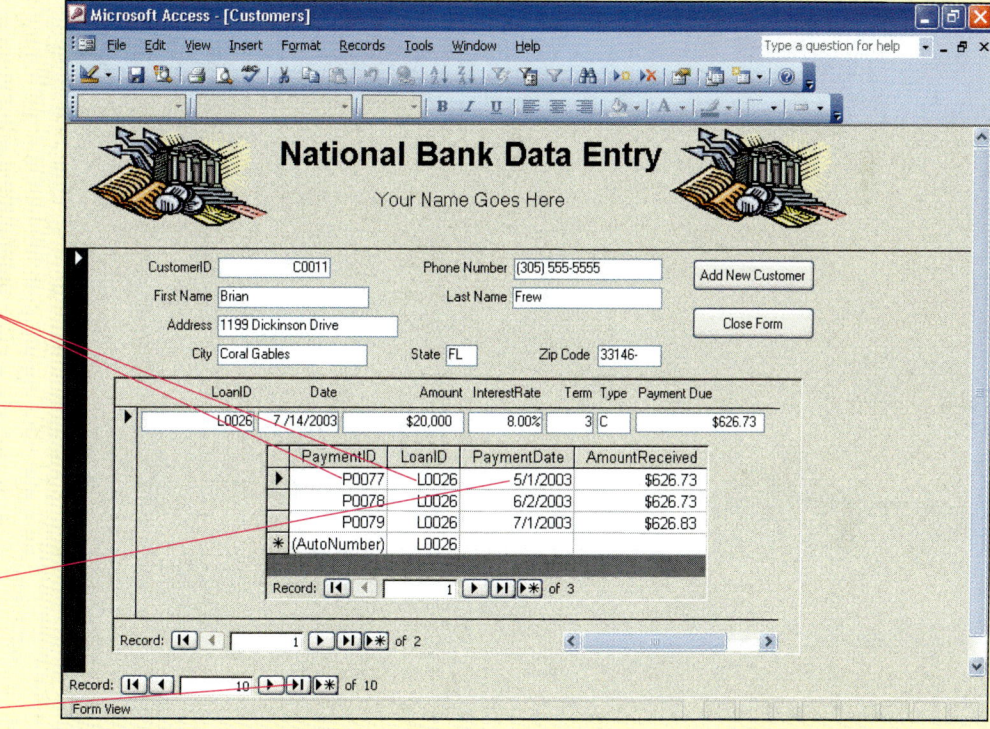

(g) Make Your Payments (step 7)

FIGURE 5.12 Hands-on Exercise 4 (*continued*)

THREE SETS OF NAVIGATION BUTTONS

Each form or subform has its own set of navigation buttons. Thus, in this example you are looking at record 10 of 10 in the Customers form, loan 1 of 2 in the Loans form for this customer, and payment 3 of 3 in the Payments form for this loan. Click the next or previous button in the Customers form and you will be taken to the next or previous customer record, respectively. Click the next button in the Loans form, however, and you are taken to the next loan for the current customer. In similar fashion, clicking the next button in the Payments form takes you to the next payment for the current loan for the current customer.

SUMMARY

An Access database may contain multiple tables. Each table stores data about a specific subject. Each table has a primary key, which is a field (or combination of fields) that uniquely identifies each record. A one-to-many relationship uses the primary key of the "one" table as a foreign key in the "many" table. (A foreign key is simply the primary key of the related table.) The Relationships window enables you to graphically create a one-to-many relationship by dragging the join field from one table to the other.

The AutoNumber field type automatically assigns the next sequential number to the primary key of a new record. The values in an AutoNumber field type are permanent and are not affected by deletions to the table. The Format property can be used to display an AutoNumber field with high-order zeros and/or a letter; e.g. a format of \C0000 will display customer numbers as C0001, C0002, and so on.

Referential integrity ensures that the tables in a one-to-many relationship (such as the Customers and Loans tables used throughout the chapter) are consistent with one another. Thus, it prevents you from adding a record to the "many" table if that record contains an invalid reference to the "one" table; for example, you cannot add a record to the Loans table that contains a value of CustomerID that does not exist in the Customers table. Referential integrity will also prevent you from deleting a record in the "one" table if there are corresponding records in the "many" table; for example, you cannot delete a record from the Customers table if there are loan records for that customer.

Referential integrity does not prevent you from adding a record to the "many" table that omits the reference to the primary table; for example, it would allow you to add a record to the Loans table without specifying a customer. Since this does not make sense in the physical system, the CustomerID should be specified as a required field in the Loans table.

A subform is a form within a form and is used to display data from a related table. It is created most easily with the Form Wizard, then modified in the Form Design view just as any other form. A main form can have any number of subforms. Subforms can extend to two levels, enabling a subform to be created within a subform.

The power of a select query lies in its ability to include fields from several tables. The Design view of a query shows the relationships that exist between the tables by drawing a join line that indicates how to relate the data. The Tables row displays the name of the table containing the corresponding field. Once created, a multiple table query can be the basis for a form or report.

The results of a query are displayed in a dynaset, a dynamic subset of the underlying tables that contains the records that satisfy the criteria within the query. Any changes to the dynaset are automatically reflected in the underlying table(s).

Tables can be added to a relational database without disturbing the data in existing tables. A database can have several one-to-many relationships. All relationships are created in the Relationships window.

KEY TERMS

AutoNumber field 1565	Main form 1572	Relationships window 1565
Datasheet view 1572	Multiple-table query 1583	Startup property 1599
Foreign key 1565	One-to-many relationship 1563	Structured Query
Form view 1572	PMT function 1572	Language (SQL) 1583
Form Wizard 1574	Primary key 1565	Subdatasheet 1565
Format property 1565	Referential integrity 1565	Subform 1572
Join line 1583	Relationship line 1565	Table row 1583

MULTIPLE CHOICE

1. Which of the following will cause a problem of referential integrity?
   (a) The deletion of a customer record that has corresponding loan records
   (b) The deletion of a customer record that has no corresponding loan records
   (c) The deletion of a loan record with a corresponding customer record
   (d) All of the above

2. Which of the following will cause a problem of referential integrity?
   (a) The addition of a new customer prior to entering loans for that customer
   (b) The addition of a new loan that references an invalid customer
   (c) Both (a) and (b)
   (d) Neither (a) nor (b)

3. Which of the following is true about a database that monitors players and the teams to which those players are assigned?
   (a) The PlayerID will be defined as a primary key within the Teams table
   (b) The TeamID will be defined as a primary key within the Players table
   (c) The PlayerID will appear as a foreign key within the Teams table
   (d) The TeamID will appear as a foreign key within the Players table

4. Which of the following relationships exist in the expanded *National Bank* database?
   (a) A one-to-many relationship between customers and loans
   (b) A one-to-many relationship between loans and payments
   (c) Both (a) and (b)
   (d) Neither (a) nor (b)

5. Which of the following is true about a query?
   (a) It may reference fields in one or more tables
   (b) It may have one or more Criteria rows
   (c) It may sort on one or more fields
   (d) All of the above

6. A database has a one-to-many relationship between branches and employees (one branch can have many employees). Which of the following is a true statement about that database?
   (a) The EmployeeID is the primary key within the Branches table
   (b) The BranchID will be defined as a primary key within the Employees table
   (c) The EmployeeID will appear as a foreign key within the Branches table
   (d) The BranchID will appear as a foreign key within the Employees table

7. Every table in an Access database:
   (a) Must be related to every other table
   (b) Must have one or more foreign keys
   (c) Both (a) and (b)
   (d) Neither (a) nor (b)

8. Which of the following is true of a main form and subform that are created in conjunction with the one-to-many relationship between customers and loans?
   (a) The main form should be based on the Customers table
   (b) The subform should be based on the Loans table
   (c) Both (a) and (b)
   (d) Neither (a) nor (b)

9. Which of the following is true regarding the navigation buttons for a main form and its associated subform?
   (a) The navigation buttons pertain to just the main form
   (b) The navigation buttons pertain to just the subform
   (c) There are separate navigation buttons for each form
   (d) There are no navigation buttons at all

10. Which of the following is true?
    (a) A main form may contain multiple subforms
    (b) A subform may contain another subform
    (c) Both (a) and (b)
    (d) Neither (a) nor (b)

... continued

multiple choice

11. The status bar of the main form shows record 1 of 10 while the status bar of the subform displays record 2 of 3. What happens if you click the next record button on the status bar for the main form?
    (a) The status bar for the main form will show record 2 of 10
    (b) The status bar for the subform will show record 3 of 3
    (c) The status bar for the main form will show record 2 of 10 and the status bar for the subform will show record 3 of 3
    (d) None of the above

12. The status bar of the main form shows record 1 of 10 while the status bar of the subform displays record 2 of 3. What happens if you click the next record button on the status bar for the subform?
    (a) The status bar for the main form will show record 2 of 10
    (b) The status bar for the subform will show record 3 of 3
    (c) The status bar for the main form will show record 2 of 10 and the status bar for the subform will show record 3 of 3
    (d) None of the above

13. Which of the following describes how to move and size a field list within the Relationships window?
    (a) Click and drag the title bar to size the field list
    (b) Click and drag a border or corner to move the field list
    (c) Both (a) and (b)
    (d) Neither (a) nor (b)

14. Which of the following is true regarding the Criteria row of a query?
    (a) A text field may be entered with or without quotation marks
    (b) A date may be entered with or without surrounding number (pound) signs
    (c) Both (a) and (b)
    (d) Neither (a) nor (b)

15. A report may be based on:
    (a) A table
    (b) A query
    (c) Both (a) and (b)
    (d) Neither (a) nor (b)

16. You are working with an investment database. The Brokers and Clients tables are joined in a one-to-many relationship. If referential integrity is enforced, which records can you delete?
    (a) A client, regardless of the records in the Brokers table
    (b) A client, only if there are no corresponding records in the Brokers table
    (c) A broker, regardless of the records in the Clients table
    (d) A broker, only if there are corresponding records in the Clients table

17. You are working with an investment database. The Brokers and Clients tables are joined in a one-to-many relationship. The BrokerID is a required field in the Clients table. If referential integrity is enforced, which of the following actions can you take?
    (a) Add a client without specifying the broker
    (b) Delete a broker, regardless of the records in the Clients table
    (c) Add a broker, regardless of the records in the Clients table
    (d) None of the above

18. Which combination of views would you select to see all clients for a specific broker, given that you were looking at a main and subform based on the Brokers and Clients tables, respectively?
    (a) The main form in Form view and the subform in Datasheet view
    (b) The main form in Datasheet view and the subform in Form view
    (c) Both the main and subform in Datasheet view
    (d) Both the main and subform in Form view

ANSWERS

1. a	7. d	13. d
2. b	8. c	14. c
3. d	9. c	15. c
4. c	10. c	16. a
5. d	11. a	17. c
6. d	12. b	18. a

PRACTICE WITH ACCESS

1. **Understanding Database Design:** The presentation in Figure 5.13 represents a *hypothetical* assignment for a group project in which the group is asked to present the design for their project to the class as a whole. We have created a similar presentation for you to illustrate what we mean; your only task is to view our presentation, which in turn will help you to review the *National Bank* database that was developed in the chapter. Your instructor may want to extend the assignment and ask you to create a parallel presentation for a different database, which he or she may assign as an actual group project. Proceed as follows:

   a. Open the *Chapter 5 Practice 1* presentation in the Exploring Access folder. This is a PowerPoint presentation, but you do not have to know PowerPoint to complete this exercise. Pull down the View menu and change to the Normal view. If necessary, click the Slide tab to see the miniature slides instead of the outline.

   b. There are nine slides in the complete presentation. The left pane shows the slide miniatures. The right pane shows a larger view of the selected slide (slide one in this example). The slide describes the hypothetical assignment, which is to create a 10-minute presentation to the class describing the physical problem and the associated database design.

   c. Select (click) the first slide. Pull down the View menu and click the Slide Show command (or click the Slide Show button above the status bar). Click the mouse continually to move through the slide show. You will see a recap of the *National Bank* database, its design, and several suggested queries.

   d. Press the Esc button at the end of the show. Pull down the File menu, and click the Print command. Select the All option button in the Print Range area. Click the down arrow in the Print What area, and select handouts. Choose 6 slides per page. Be sure to check the box to frame the slides. Click OK to print the presentation. Print the presentation a second time, but this time print only the title slide (as a full slide) to use as a cover sheet for your assignment.

   e. Review the printed presentation. Do you see how the discipline provided by this assignment can help to ensure the accuracy of the design?

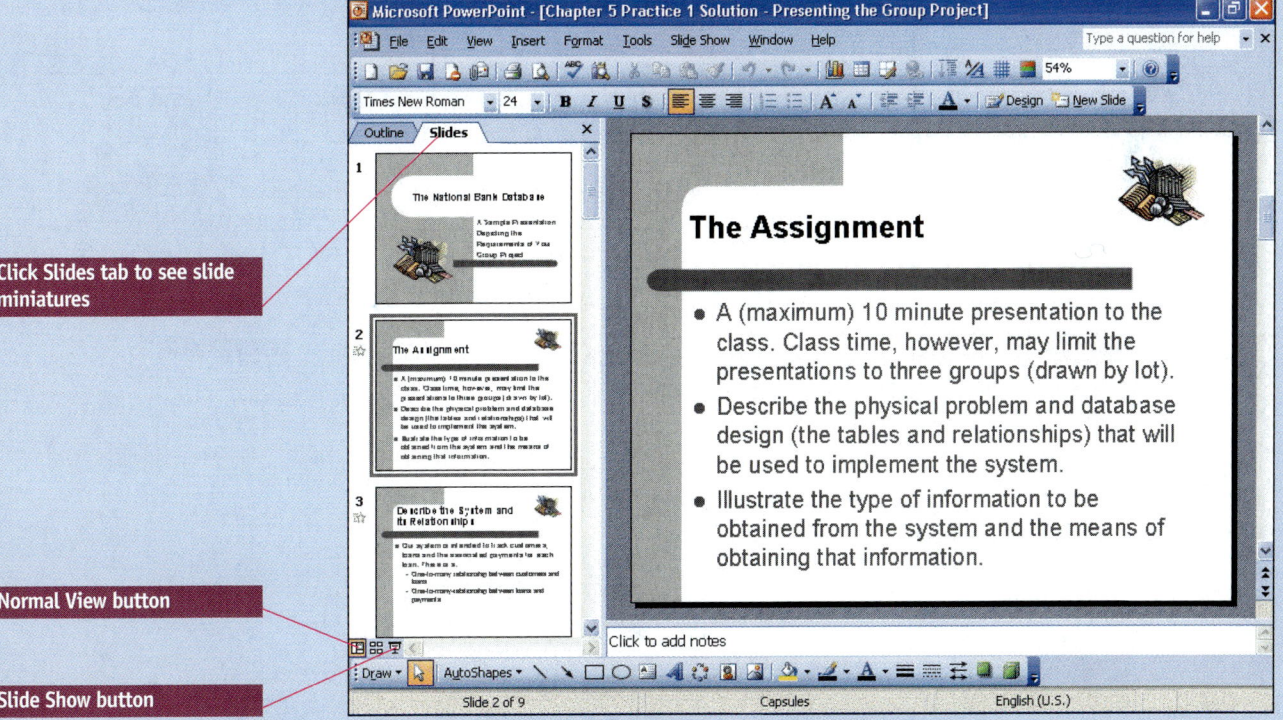

FIGURE 5.13   Understanding Database Design (exercise 1)

practice exercises

2. **Widgets of America (database design):** Figure 5.14 displays the relationships diagram in the *Widgets of America* database that tracks the orders generated by the company's sales staff. Your task is to implement the design in Figure 5.14 by creating the indicated tables and establishing the necessary relationships. Proceed as follows:

   a. Start Access and create a new database. You do not have to enter data into any of the tables, but you have to create the tables and set all of the field properties in each table. Pay particular attention to the required property as it pertains to the related fields in the various tables. Note that a customer must have an assigned sales representative in order to place an order. In addition, the company will not accept an order unless it (the order) is associated with a specific customer.

   b. Pull down the Tools menu and click the Relationships command to establish the relationships in Figure 5.14. Stay in the Relationships window, pull down the File menu, and then click the Print Relationships command to preview the report containing the relationships diagram. Change to the Design view to modify the Report Header to include a title, today's date, your name, and an appropriate clip art image. (The clip art can be used as a logo for the other objects in the database.)

   c. Create a simple About Widgets of America form that is similar to the other forms that were presented in the previous chapter. Use the same clip art as in the relationships diagram.

   d. Create a simple switchboard with three menu options—a button to display the About Widgets of America, a button to print the relationships diagram, and a button to exit the application. The switchboard should contain the same clip art, color scheme, and fonts as the relationships diagram.

   e. Test the switchboard thoroughly to be sure it works correctly. Use the Startup property in the Tools menu to display the switchboard automatically when the database is opened initially.

   f. Print the relationships diagram, the switchboard form, and the Switchboard Items table for your instructor. Add a cover sheet to complete the assignment.

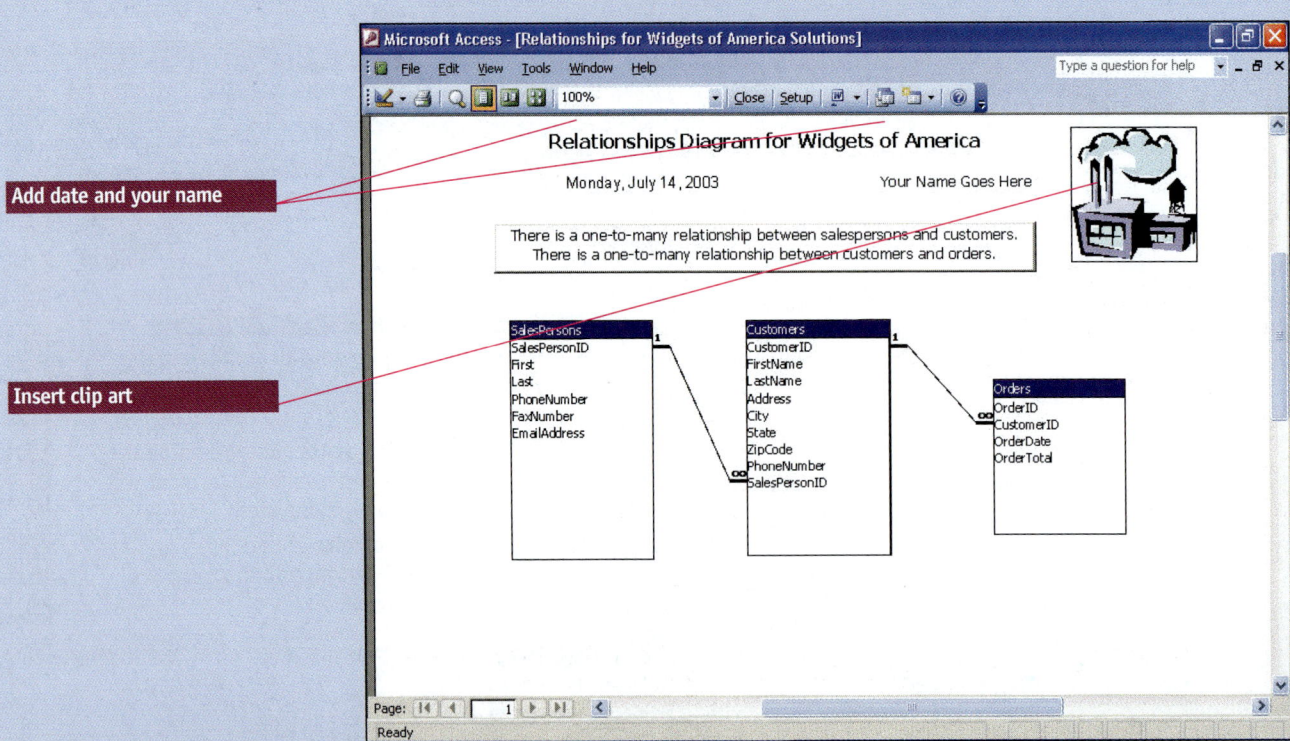

FIGURE 5.14 Widgets of America (database design) (exercise 2)

practice exercises

3. **Expanding National Bank:** Expand the *National Bank* database to include a table for Loan Officers, the bank employees who approve each loan before it is granted. One officer is assigned to many loans, but a specific loan is approved by only one officer, and the loan cannot be granted until the officer approves. Complete the four hands-on exercises in the chapter, then proceed as follows:

a. Open the *National Bank* database after completing the fourth hands-on exercise. Go to the Database window, click the Tables button, and create the Loan Officers table. The table contains only four fields—LoanOfficerID, LastName, FirstName, and DateHired. The LoanOfficerID should be an AutoNumber field. Set the Format property to \O0000 to be consistent with the other tables in the database. Add two records, Robert Grauer and Maryann Barber, as loan officers one and two, respectively.

b. Modify the Loans table to include a field for the LoanOfficerID. Set the Format property to \O0000. Switch to the Datasheet view, display the loans by LoanID (if they are not yet in this sequence), then assign each loan to an officer by typing 1 or 2 in the LoanOfficerID field. Assign all loans with a LoanID of 10 or less to Bob. Assign the other loans to Maryann.

c. Change to the Design view of the Loans table and make the LoanOfficerID a required field. This ensures that all subsequent loans will be approved by a loan officer.

d. Open the Relationships window and create the one-to-many relationship between loan officers and loans. Enforce referential integrity.

e. Open the existing Loans subform in Design view and insert a control for the Loan Officer as shown in Figure 5.15. The control should be created as a combo box so that a user can select the loan officer by name, as opposed to having to enter the LoanOfficerID. Pull down the View menu and use the Tab Order command to adjust the order in which the data is entered.

f. Open the Customer form. Click the navigation button to go to the last customer record (it should be Customer C0011 with the data you entered for yourself during the hands-on exercises). Click the record selector, pull down the File menu, click the Print command, select the option to print the selected record, and print this form for your instructor.

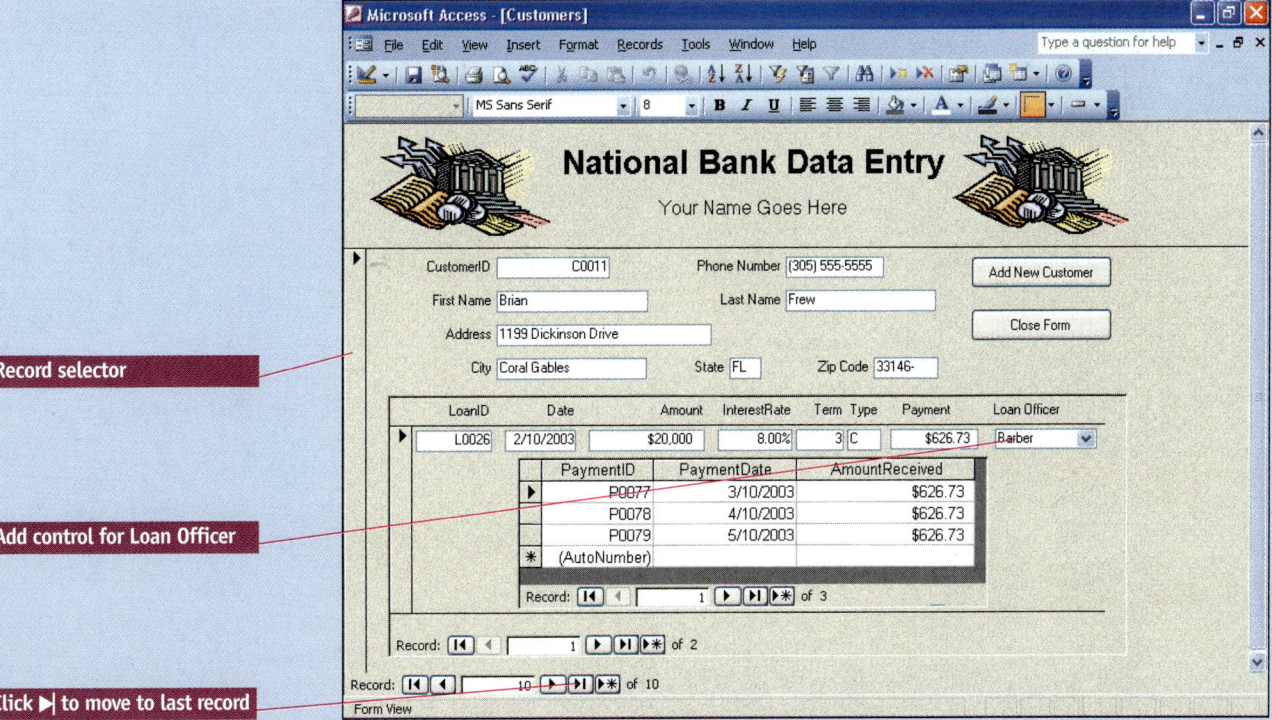

FIGURE 5.15 Expanding National Bank (exercise 3)

practice exercises

4. **National Bank Customer List:** The report in Figure 5.16 reflects the newly entered information about loan officers from the previous exercise. The Report Wizard does a good job creating the basic report, but it is up to you to format the report in an attractive fashion. You do not have to match our design exactly, but your report is to contain all of the indicated data. Proceed as follows:

   a. Open the *National Bank* database from the previous exercise. Click the Reports button and double click the icon to Create report by using wizard. Select the Customers table in the Tables/Query list box and choose all of the fields for inclusion in the report. Select the Loans table and choose all of the fields *except* the CustomerID and the LoanOfficerID. Now choose the LoanOfficers table and choose the officer's last name. Click Next.

   b. Group the report by customers. Click Next. There are no additional grouping requirements. Click Next. Sort the report by LoanID. Click Next.

   c. Choose the Align Left 1 layout. Be sure to choose this layout, or else the data for one customer will not fit on one page. Choose portrait orientation. Check the box to force the fields to fit on one page. Click Next.

   d. Choose Soft Gray for the style. Click Next. Enter Customer List as the name of the report. Click Finish to preview the report. You should see the same data as in Figure 5.16, but the formatting needs improvement. Go to Design view. The easiest modification is the Report Header. Use the Insert Picture command to insert the National Bank logo in the Report Header. Change the title of the report and add your name.

   e. We suggest that you eliminate the borders that appear around all of the controls in the customer information. Press and hold the Shift key to select multiple controls, right click any of the selected controls, click Properties, then change the Border Style property to transparent. Close the property sheet. Click anywhere in the report to deselect the controls.

   f. We also removed the double lines above and below the loan information for each customer and added a line immediately above the Customer data. Change the label for Loan Officer Last Name to Loan Officer. Experiment with formatting, sizing, and alignment as you see fit. Print the completed report for your instructor.

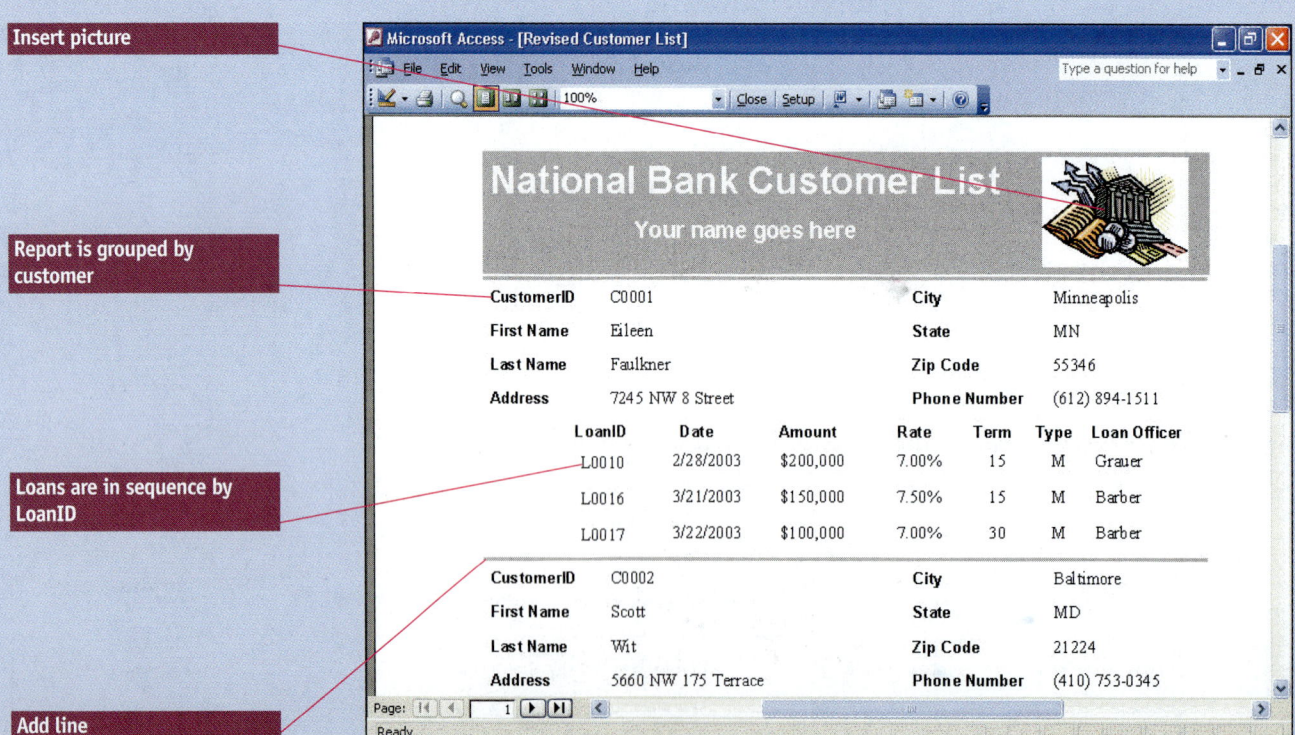

FIGURE 5.16 National Bank Customer List (exercise 4)

practice exercises

5. **National Bank Switchboard:** Figure 5.17 displays a switchboard for the *National Bank* database that encompasses all of the hands-on exercises in the chapter as well as the two previous exercises. Your present assignment is to create the main switchboard, a subsidiary switchboard with buttons to display the various reports that already exist, as well as a new report that will be created in this exercise. You also have to create the relationships diagram. Proceed as follows:

   a. The About National Bank form is included with the original database. All you have to do is modify the text on this form to include your name instead of Bob and Maryann's. Close the form.

   b. Open the Relationships window, pull down the File menu, click the Print Relationships command, and then view the completed report in Design view. Modify the report to include a title, date, your name and the National Bank logo that has been used for other objects in the database.

   c. Use the Report Wizard to create a new report that displays the existing automobile loans. The report should contain the customer's first and last name, address, telephone number, and amount of the loan. The customers should be listed alphabetically by last name. The address should appear on two lines; i.e., the street address on one line, and the city, state, and zip code on a second line. (Create the associated query before creating the report.)

   d. Use the Switchboard Manager to create the main switchboard and the subsidiary report switchboard as shown in Figure 5.18. The latter should contain three reports (the First Quarter Jumbo Loans report from Hands-on Exercise 3, the Customer List from the previous exercise, and the Report on Car Loans that you just created). The report switchboard should also have a button to return to the main menu.

   e. Use the StartUp property to display the switchboard automatically when the database is opened. Test both switchboards completely to be sure that they work correctly. Print the Switchboard Items table, the switchboard form, the relationships diagram, and the Report on Car Loans. Add a cover sheet and submit the completed assignment.

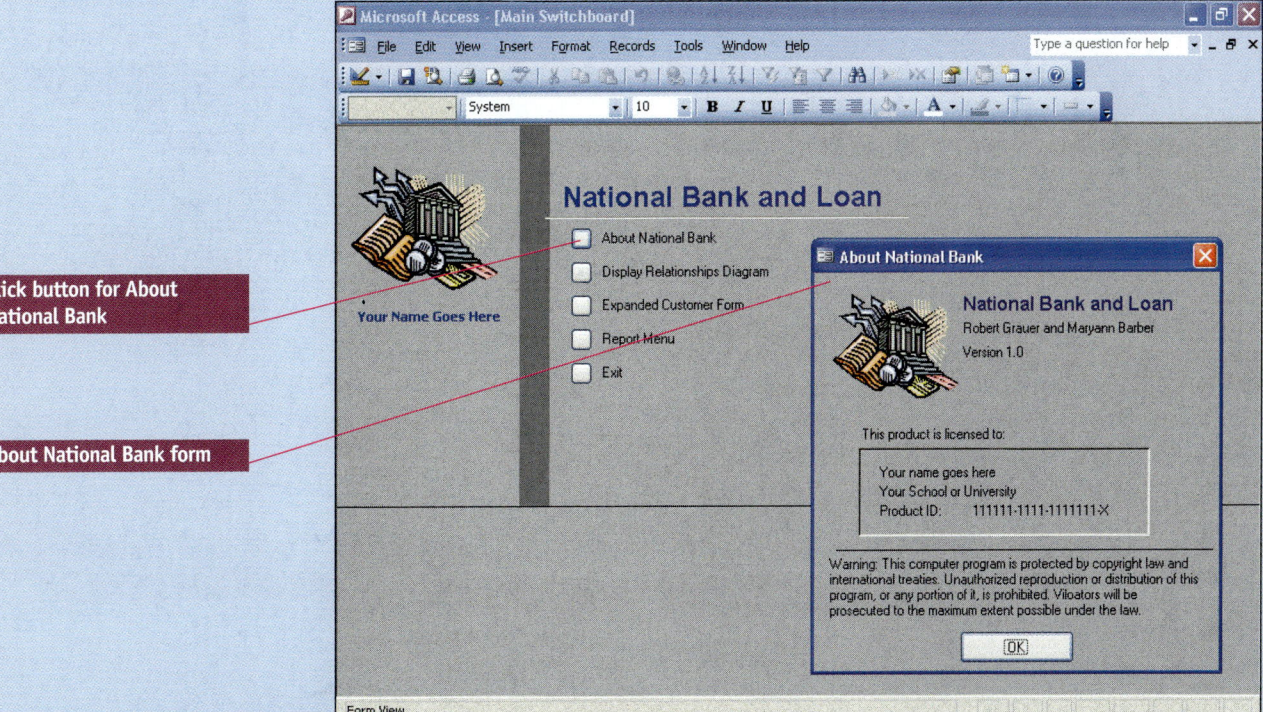

FIGURE 5.17 National Bank Switchboard (exercise 5)

practice exercises

6. **Turkeys To Go Restaurants:** Turkeys To Go Restaurants is a small regional company that builds restaurants to order for individuals seeking a turn-key franchise operation. The company encourages its franchisees to own many restaurants, but a specific restaurant is associated with only one person. Your predecessor at the company has started a database to keep track of restaurants and franchisees, but left unexpectedly, so it is up to you to complete the work. Proceed as follows:

   a. Open the *Chapter 5 Practice 6* database in the Exploring Access folder. The Restaurants and Franchisees tables have already been created, and data has been entered into both tables. The RestaurantID and FranchiseeID have been set as AutoNumber fields in their respective tables. Note that the FranchiseeID is a required field in the Restaurants table because the company will not build a restaurant unless a franchisee has already been approved for that restaurant.

   b. Open the Relationships window and create the one-to-many relationship between franchisees and restaurants. Enforce referential integrity.

   c. Your first task is to create a main form/subform combination that is similar to Figure 5.18. The forms contain all of the fields in both the Franchisees and Restaurants tables, and thus all data entry can be accomplished from this screen. Start the Form Wizard. Select the Franchisee table and include all of the fields in this table. Now select the Restaurants table and include all of the fields except the FranchiseeID; this field need not appear in the subform because it is already in the main form. View the data by Franchisees, choose datasheet as the layout for the subform, select a style (we chose standard), then modify the completed form in Design view.

   d. You do not have to match our design exactly, but you are to include all of the indicated controls. Your name should appear in the Form Header. Add the commands buttons to the main form as shown in Figure 5.18.

   e. Use the completed form to enter data for yourself. You will automatically be assigned a Franchisee number (F0008). Add two restaurants once you have completed your personal data. The restaurant numbers will be assigned automatically as well. You can use any address and restaurant information that you deem appropriate. The annual sales of each restaurant should exceed $500,000. Print the completed form for your instructor.

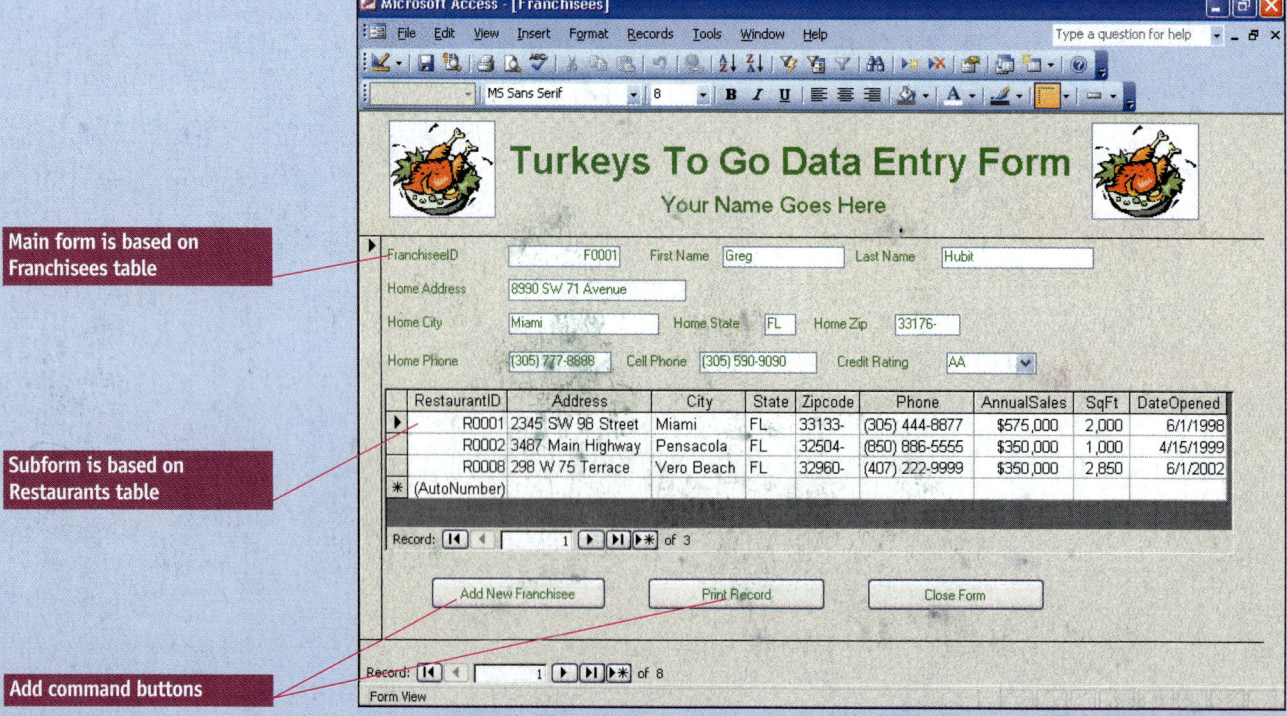

FIGURE 5.18 Turkeys To Go Restaurants (exercise 6)

practice exercises

7. **Turkeys To Go Switchboard:** This assignment asks you to continue the development of the *Turkeys To Go* database by creating the switchboard in Figure 5.19. The Data Entry form referenced in the switchboard is the form you created in the previous exercise. The About form is included in the original database, but you have to modify the text on this form to include your name instead of Bob and Maryann's. All of the other objects that are referenced on the switchboard have to be created, however, before you can create the switchboard. Proceed as follows:

   a. Open the Relationships window, pull down the File menu, click the Print Relationships command, and then view the completed report in Design view. Modify the report to include your name and the turkey logo.

   b. Three additional reports are required as can be seen by looking at the switchboard. We leave the design and exact content of each report to you, but try to achieve a uniform look (design) for all of your reports. Use the company logo on all reports. (You can copy the clip art from the About form that is already in the database.)

   c. Use the Switchboard Manager to create the switchboard in Figure 5.19. You do not have to match our design exactly, but you are required to have all of the menu options; further, the design of the switchboard should be consistent with the About form that is in the database.

   d. Set the Startup property to display the switchboard automatically when the database is opened. Pull down the Tools menu, click the Database Utilities command, and then compact and repair the database. This does two things—first, it compacts the database, which is always a good idea. Second, it tests the Startup property; that is, the database should open immediately after compacting and display the switchboard.

   e. Test the switchboard completely to be sure that it works correctly. Print the Switchboard Items table, the switchboard form, the relationships diagram, and each of the indicated reports. Add a cover sheet and submit the completed assignment to your instructor.

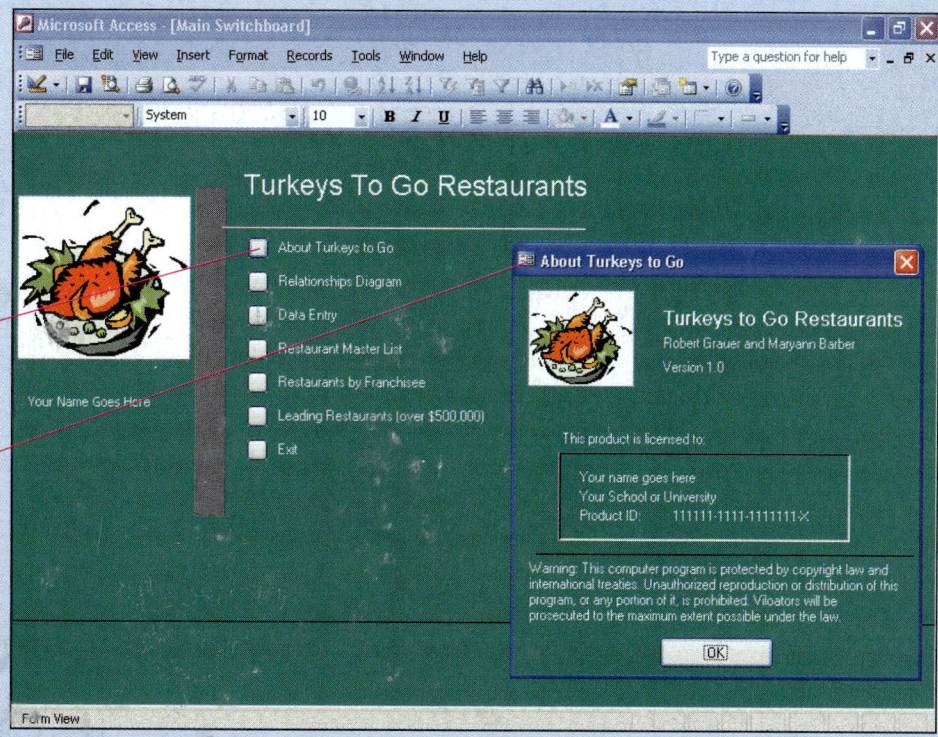

FIGURE 5.19 Turkeys To Go Switchboard (exercise 7)

practice exercises

8. **The Richards Company:** The Richards Company maintains a relational database that tracks its employees, the locations in which they work, and the various positions to which they have been assigned. There is a one-to-many relationship between locations and employees (one location can have many employees, but a specific employee is assigned to only one location). There is a second one-to-many relationship between titles and employees (one title can have many employees, but a specific employee is assigned only one title). Your assignment is to open the partially completed *Chapter 5 Practice 8* database and develop the necessary forms for data entry. The tables have been created for you, and sample data has been entered into each table. Proceed as follows:

   a. Open the Relationships window, display all three tables, and then implement the one-to-many relationships that exist in the system.

   b. Create a main form/subform combination that is similar to the form in Figure 5.20. The easiest way to create the form is to use the Form Wizard. Select all of the fields from the Locations table, as well as all fields from the Employees table except the LocationID. View the data by locations, choose datasheet as the layout for the subform, select a style (we chose Blueprint), then modify the completed form in Design view.

   c. You do not have to match our design exactly, but you are to include all of the indicated controls. Your name should appear in the Form Header. Add the commands buttons to the main form as shown in Figure 5.18. Close the Locations form, then open the Employees subform in Design view. Substitute a combo box for the TitleID, so that you can enter an employee's title by selecting its description.

   d. Open the Locations form and use it to add a new location for New York City. The address is 580 5th Avenue, New York, NY, 10036. The phone number is (212) 333-4444. Add an employee record for yourself (EmployeeID 88888) as a new account rep. Add a second record for your instructor as a manager (EmployeeID 99999). Print the form for New York with both employees.

   e. Create a parallel main form/subform combination for the Title and Employee tables. The title information will appear in the main form and the employee information in the subform. Go to the first record in the Titles table (Account Reps) and print the associated form for your instructor.

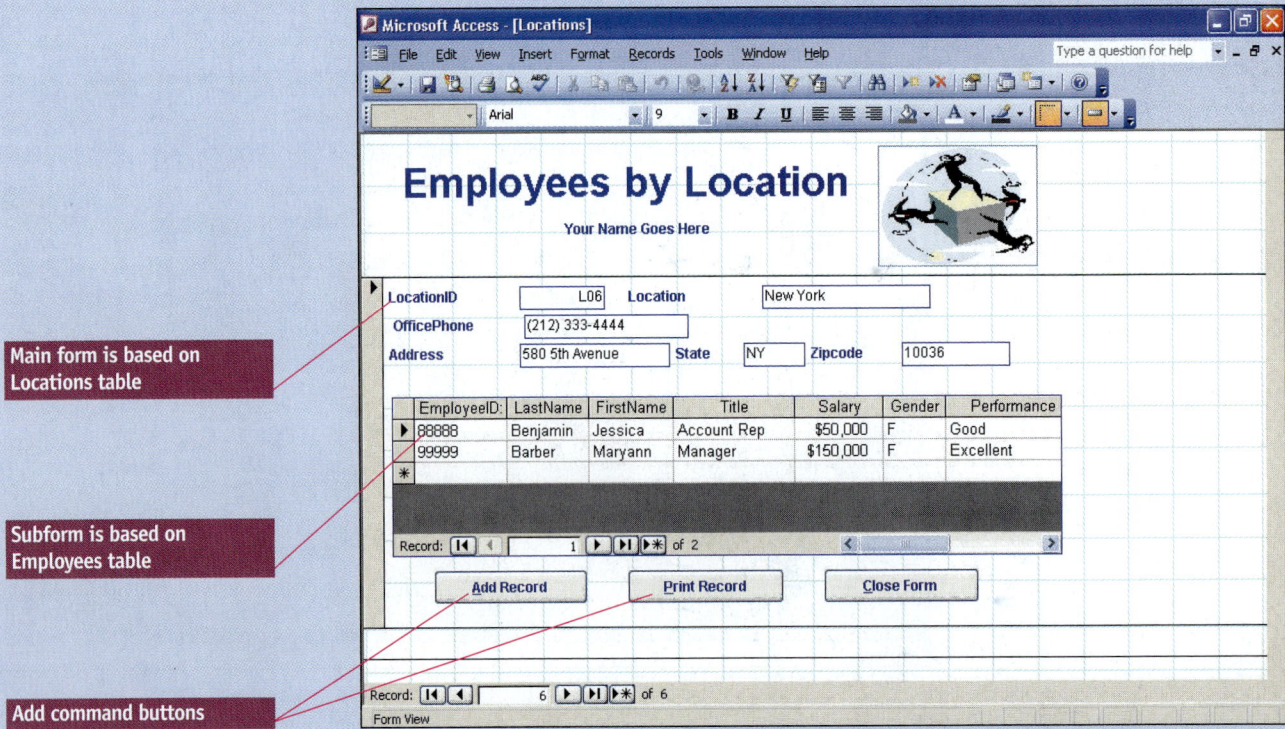

FIGURE 5.20 The Richards Company (exercise 8)

practice exercises

9. **The Richards Company Switchboard:** This assignment asks you to continue the development of the *Richards Company* database by creating the switchboard in Figure 5.21. The Employees by Location and Employees by Title forms that are referenced in the switchboard are the forms you created in the previous exercise. The About form is included in the original database, but you have to modify the text on this form to include your name instead of Bob and Maryann's. All of the other objects have to be created, however, before you can create the switchboard. Proceed as follows:

   a. Open the Relationships window, pull down the File menu, click the Print Relationships command, and then view the completed report in Design view. Modify the report to include a title, your name, and the company logo.

   b. Three additional reports are required as can be seen by looking at the switchboard. We leave the design and exact content of each report to you, but try to achieve a uniform look (design) for all of your reports. (You may also have to create a query for one or more of the reports.) Include the clip art from the About form in the Report Header to create a sense of continuity in the application.

   c. Start the switchboard manager and use it to create the switchboard. You do not have to match our design exactly, but you are required to have all of the menu options.

   d. Set the Startup property to display the switchboard automatically when the database is opened. Pull down the Tools menu, click the Database Utilities command, and then compact and repair the database. This does two things—first, it compacts the database, which is always a good idea. Second, it tests the startup property; that is, the database should open immediately after compacting and display the switchboard.

   e. Test the switchboard completely to be sure that it works correctly. Print the Switchboard Items table, the switchboard form, the relationships diagram, and each of the indicated reports. Add a cover sheet and submit the completed assignment to your instructor.

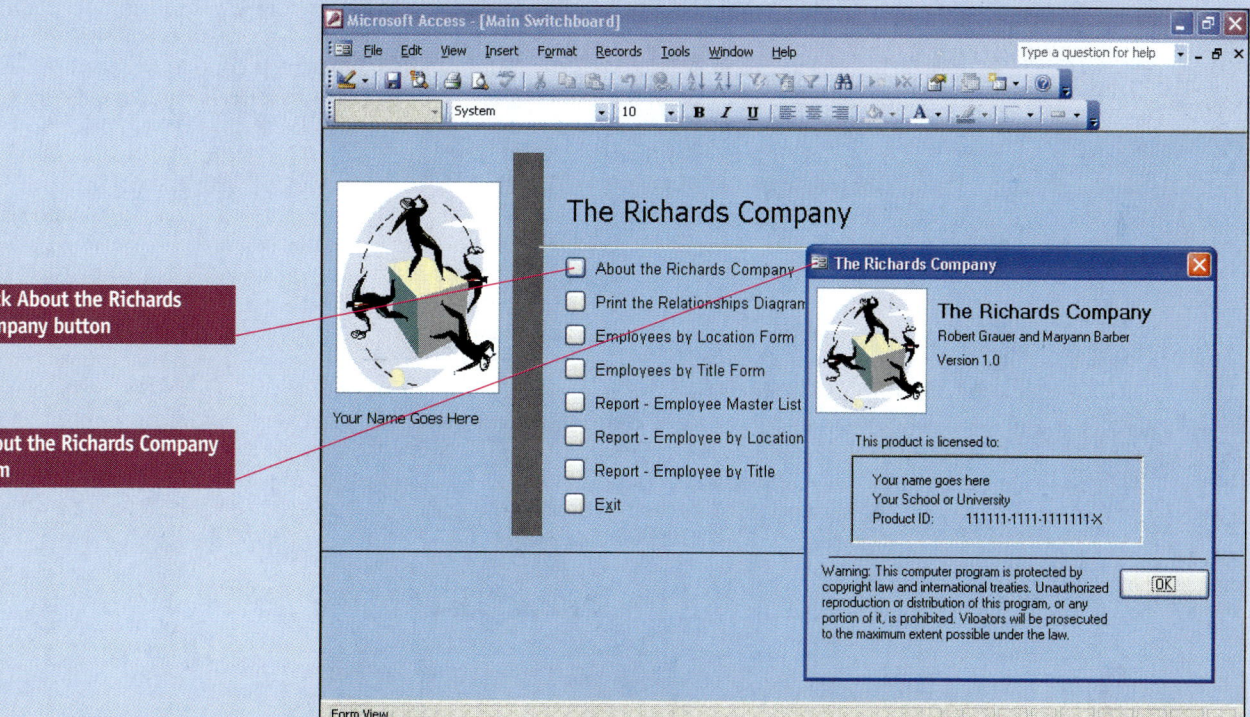

FIGURE 5.21 The Richards Company Switchboard (exercise 9)

MINI CASES

University Apartments

You have just signed your lease for next year at University Apartments, where you have the opportunity to design a database for the complex and thereby save on your rent. The complex has 500 apartments, which are divided into various categories as determined by the number of bedrooms, and additional amenities such as a washer/dryer, patio, and so on. There are many apartments in each category, but a given apartment has only one category.

Your database is to track all apartments in the complex and the students who live in those apartments. Each apartment is leased to one or more students, who sign the identical lease with the same rent and the same starting date for the lease. The lease information is stored within the Apartment record. Each student pays his or her rent individually each month. Your database should produce a report showing the total rent received for each apartment and another report showing the total rent paid by each student.

Design a database that will satisfy the information requirements. You do not have to enter data into the tables, but you do have to create the tables in order to create the relationships diagram, which you will submit to your instructor. Create a simple switchboard with three menu options—a button to display an "About the Apartments" form describing the database, a button to print the relationships diagram, and a button to exit the application. The switchboard should contain the same clip art as the relationships diagram. Use the Startup property to display the switchboard when the database is opened.

The Automobile Dealership

You have been retained as a database consultant for a local automobile dealership. The dealership has been in the community for fifty years, and it places a premium on customer loyalty, as the typical customer has made repeated purchases over time. The dealership maintains the usual data about its customers—name, address, phone number, credit rating, and so on. It also maintains the usual data about its sales staff. The dealership is large and has several sales managers, each of whom is responsible for multiple salespersons.

The key to the database is the Automobiles table, which contains a record for every car that passes through the dealership. The table contains fields to indicate the date the car was received and the dealer price. It also contains fields for the sale price and sale date, information that is entered when the car is sold. The Automobiles table also contains fields that describe the vehicle such as the make, model, year, and color.

Only one salesperson gets credit for each sale, and that is the individual who closes the deal. The salesperson receives a commission based on the difference between the sale price and dealer cost. Managers receive an override on all sales generated by their sales staff.

Design a database that will enable the dealership to track its sales by customer, salesperson, and manager. You do not have to enter data into the tables, but you do have to create the tables in order to create the relationships diagram, which you will submit to your instructor. Create a simple switchboard with three menu options—a button to display an "About the Dealership" form describing the database, a button to print the relationships diagram, and a button to exit the application. The switchboard should contain the same clip art as the relationships diagram. Use the Startup property to display the switchboard when the database is opened.

CHAPTER 6

Many-to-many Relationships: A More Complex System

CASE STUDY
UNIVERSITY CAREER PLACEMENT CENTER

The director of the University Career Placement Center has asked you to design a database that will keep track of the interviews that are being conducted in the Career Center. The director has to track which companies are conducting on-campus interviews at the Center, which students are being interviewed, and by which company. In designing the database, keep in mind that a company can interview many students and that a student has the option of interviewing with as many companies as he/she wishes. In addition, each student is assigned to one of the Center's three advisors, and that advisor will work with that student until he/she graduates.

The system you design must be able to generate reports on the advisors (name, office, phone number, fax number), students (name, campus address, campus phone number, major, GPA, graduation date), and companies (name, interviewer, address, phone number, industry). It should also be able to create reports that list the students interviewed by a given company, the companies that a given student has interviewed with, and the students assigned to a given advisor.

Your assignment is to read the chapter, paying special attention to the discussion of many-to-many relationships and referential integrity. You will then create a new database with the required tables for the Placement Center. You do not have to enter data into any of the tables, but you are to include all necessary fields and set the properties appropriately. You are also to implement the relationships within the system.

Your database should include a basic switchboard, an About form, and a relationships diagram. You should also use a common clip art image and consistent design elements for each object in the database. Print the switchboard form, the table of switchboard items, the relationships diagram, and the About form for your instructor.

OBJECTIVES

After reading this chapter you will:

1. Use the AutoNumber field type as the primary key for a new record.
2. Explain the field types required when an AutoNumber field is in a relationship.
3. Implement a many-to-many relationship in Access.
4. Use the Cascade Update and Cascade Delete options in a relationship.
5. Create a main form and subform based on a query.
6. Create a parameter query.
7. Use aggregate functions in a select query to perform calculations on groups of records.
8. Use the Get External Data command to add tables from another database.

hands-on exercises

1. RELATIONSHIPS AND REFERENTIAL INTEGRITY
   Input: Computer Store
   Output: Computer Store (modified)

2. SUBFORMS AND MULTIPLE-TABLE QUERIES
   Input: Computer Store (from exercise 1)
   Output: Computer Store (modified)

3. ADVANCED QUERIES
   Input: Computer Store (from exercise 2)
   Output: Computer Store (modified)

4. EXPANDING THE DATABASE
   Input: Salespersons database; Computer Store (from exercise 2)
   Output: Computer Store (modified)

THE COMPUTER SUPER STORE

This chapter introduces a new case study to give you additional practice in database design. The system extends the concept of a relational database to include both a one-to-many and a many-to-many relationship. The case solution reviews earlier material on establishing relationships in Access and the importance of referential integrity. Another point of particular interest is the use of an AutoNumber field to facilitate the addition of new records.

The chapter extends what you already know about subforms and queries, and uses both to present information from related tables. The forms created in this chapter are based on multiple-table queries rather than tables. The queries themselves are of a more advanced nature. We show you how to create a parameter query, where the user is prompted to enter the criteria when the query is run. We also review queries that use the aggregate functions built into Access to perform calculations on groups of records.

The case study in this chapter is set within the context of a computer store that requires a database for its customers, products, and orders. The store maintains the usual customer data (name, address, phone, etc.). It also keeps data about the products it sells, storing for each product a ProductID, description, quantity on hand, quantity on order, and unit price. And finally, the store has to track its orders. It needs to know the date an order was received, the customer who placed it, the products that were ordered, and the quantity of each product.

Think, for a moment, about the tables that are necessary and the relationships among those tables, then compare your thoughts to our solution in Figure 6.1. You probably have no trouble recognizing the need for the Customers, Products, and Orders tables. Initially, you may be puzzled by the Order Details table, but you will soon appreciate why it is there and how powerful it is.

You can use the Customers, Products, and Orders tables individually to obtain information about a specific customer, product, or order, respectively. For example:

Query: What is Jeffrey Muddell's phone number?
Answer: Jeffrey Muddell's phone is (305) 253-3909.

Query: What is the price of a Pentium IV notebook? How many are in stock?
Answer: A Pentium IV notebook sells for $2,599. Fifteen systems are in stock.

Query: When was order O0003 placed?
Answer: Order O0003 was placed on April 18, 2003.

Other queries require you to relate the tables to one another. There is, for example, a **one-to-many relationship** between customers and orders. One customer can place many orders, but a specific order can be associated with only one customer. The tables are related through the CustomerID, which appears as the **primary key** in the Customers table and as a foreign key in the Orders table. Consider:

Query: What is the name of the customer who placed order number O0003?
Answer: Order O0003 was placed by Jeffrey Muddell.

Query: How many orders were placed by Jeffrey Muddell?
Answer: Jeffrey Muddell placed five orders: O0003, O0014, O0016, O0024, and C0025.

These queries require you to use two tables. To answer the first query, you would search the Orders table to find order O0003 and obtain the CustomerID (C0006 in this example). You would then search the Customers table for the customer with this CustomerID and retrieve the customer's name. To answer the

(a) Customers Table

Customer ID	First Name	Last Name	Address	City	State	Zip Code	Phone Number
C0001	Benjamin	Lee	1000 Call Street	Tallahassee	FL	33340	(904) 327-4124
C0002	Eleanor	Milgrom	7245 NW 8 Street	Margate	FL	33065	(305) 974-1234
C0003	Neil	Goodman	4215 South 81 Street	Margate	FL	33065	(305) 444-5555
C0004	Nicholas	Colon	9020 N.W. 75 Street	Coral Springs	FL	33065	(305) 753-9887
C0005	Michael	Ware	276 Brickell Avenue	Miami	FL	33131	(305) 444-3980
C0006	Jeffrey	Muddell	9522 S.W. 142 Street	Miami	FL	33176	(305) 253-3909
C0007	Ashley	Geoghegan	7500 Center Lane	Coral Springs	FL	33070	(305) 753-7830
C0008	Serena	Sherard	5000 Jefferson Lane	Gainesville	FL	32601	(904) 375-6442
C0009	Luis	Couto	455 Bargello Avenue	Coral Gables	FL	33146	(305) 666-4801
C0010	Derek	Anderson	6000 Tigertail Avenue	Coconut Grove	FL	33120	(305) 446-8900
C0011	Lauren	Center	12380 S.W. 137 Avenue	Miami	FL	33186	(305) 385-4432
C0012	Robert	Slane	4508 N.W. 7 Street	Miami	FL	33131	(305) 635-3454

(b) Products Table

Product ID	Product Name	Units In Stock	Units On Order	UnitPrice
P0001	Celeron® at 2.0GHz	50	0	$899.00
P0002	Pentium® IV at 2.6GHz	25	5	$1,099.00
P0003	Pentium® IV at 3.0GHz	125	15	$1,399.00
P0004	Pentium® III Notebook at 800 MHz	25	50	$1,599.00
P0005	Pentium® IV Notebook at 2.0GHz	15	25	$2,599.00
P0006	17" CRT Monitor	50	0	$499.00
P0007	19" CRT Monitor	25	10	$899.00
P0008	21" CRT Monitor	50	20	$1,599.00
P0009	2 Years On Site Service	15	20	$299.00
P0010	4 Years On Site Service	25	15	$399.00
P0011	Multi Media Projector	10	0	$1,245.00
P0012	Digital Camera - 2.0 megapixels	40	0	$249.00
P0013	Digital Camera - 4.0 megapixels	50	15	$449.95
P0014	HD Floppy Disks (50 pack)	500	200	$9.99
P0015	CD-R (25 pack spindle)	100	50	$14.79
P0016	Digital Scanner	15	3	$179.95
P0017	Serial Mouse	150	50	$69.95
P0018	Trackball	55	0	$59.95
P0019	Joystick	250	100	$39.95
P0020	Wireless broadband router	35	10	$189.95
P0021	Fax/Modem 56 Kbps	20	0	$65.95
P0022	Digital Photography Package	100	15	$1,395.00
P0023	Ink Jet Printer	50	50	$249.95
P0024	Laser Printer (personal)	125	25	$569.95
P0025	Windows® XP Home Edition	400	200	$95.95
P0026	Antivirus/Firewall Upgrade	150	50	$75.95
P0027	Tax Preparaton Software	150	50	$115.95
P0028	Typing Tutor	75	25	$29.95
P0029	Microsoft Office Home Edition	250	100	$129.95
P0030	Learning Adventure	25	10	$59.95
P0031	Surge Protector	15	0	$45.95

(c) Orders Table

OrderID	CustomerID	Order Date
O001	C0004	4/15/2003
O002	C0003	4/18/2003
O003	C0006	4/18/2003
O004	C0007	4/18/2003
O005	C0001	4/20/2003
O006	C0001	4/21/2003
O007	C0002	4/21/2003
O008	C0002	4/22/2003
O009	C0001	4/22/2003
O010	C0002	4/22/2003
O011	C0001	4/24/2003
O012	C0007	4/24/2003
O013	C0004	4/24/2003
O014	C0006	4/25/2003
O015	C0009	4/25/2003
O016	C0006	4/26/2003
O017	C0011	4/26/2003
O018	C0011	4/26/2003
O019	C0012	4/27/2003
O020	C0012	4/28/2003
O021	C0010	4/29/2003
O022	C0010	4/29/2003
O023	C0008	4/30/2003
O024	C0006	5/1/2003
O025	C0006	5/1/2003

(d) Order Details Table

OrderID	ProductID	Quantity
O0001	P0013	1
O0001	P0014	4
O0001	P0027	1
O0002	P0001	1
O0002	P0006	1
O0002	P0020	1
O0002	P0022	1
O0003	P0005	1
O0003	P0020	1
O0003	P0022	1
O0004	P0003	1
O0004	P0010	1
O0004	P0022	2
O0005	P0003	2
O0005	P0012	2
O0005	P0016	2
O0006	P0007	1
O0006	P0014	10
O0007	P0028	1
O0007	P0030	3
O0008	P0001	1
O0008	P0004	3
O0008	P0008	4
O0008	P0011	2
O0008	P0012	1
O0009	P0006	1
O0010	P0002	2
O0010	P0022	1
O0010	P0023	1
O0011	P0016	2
O0011	P0020	2
O0012	P0021	10
O0012	P0029	10
O0012	P0030	10
O0013	P0009	4
O0013	P0016	10
O0013	P0024	2
O0014	P0019	2
O0014	P0028	1
O0015	P0018	1
O0015	P0020	1
O0016	P0029	2
O0017	P0019	2
O0018	P0009	1
O0018	P0025	2
O0018	P0026	2
O0019	P0014	25
O0020	P0024	1
O0021	P0004	1
O0022	P0027	1
O0023	P0021	1
O0023	P0028	1
O0023	P0029	1
O0024	P0007	1
O0024	P0013	5
O0024	P0014	3
O0024	P0016	1
O0025	P0012	2
O0025	P0029	2

FIGURE 6.1 Super Store Database

second query, you would begin in the Customers table and search for Jeffrey Muddell to determine the CustomerID (C0006), then search the Orders table for all records with this CustomerID.

The system is more complicated than earlier examples in that there is a ***many-to-many relationship*** between orders and products. One order can include many products, and at the same time a specific product can appear in many orders. The implementation of a many-to-many relationship requires an additional table, the Order Details table, containing (at a minimum) the primary keys of the individual tables.

The Order Details table will contain many records with the same OrderID because there is a separate record for each product in a given order. It will also contain many records with the same ProductID because there is a separate record for every order containing that product. However, the *combination* of OrderID and ProductID is unique, and this ***combined key*** becomes the primary key in the Order Details table. The Order Details table also contains an additional field (Quantity), whose value depends on the primary key (the *combination* of OrderID and ProductID). Thus:

Query: How many units of product P0014 are in order O0001?
Answer: Order O0001 included four units of product P0014. (The order also included one unit of Product P0013 and one unit of P0027.)

The Order Details table has four records with a ProductID of P0014. It also has three records with an OrderID of O0001. There is, however, only one record with a ProductID P0014 *and* an OrderID O0001, which is for four units.

The Order Details table makes it possible to determine all products in a given order or all orders for a given product. You can also use the Products table in conjunction with the Order Details table to determine the names of those products. Consider:

Query: Which orders include a Celeron 2.0GHz desktop system?
Answer: A Celeron 2.0GHz system is found in orders O0002 and O0008.

Query: Which products were included in Order O0003?
Answer: Order O0003 consisted of products P0005 (a Pentium IV notebook), P0020 (a wireless router), and P0022 (a digital photography package).

To answer the first query, you would begin in the Products table to find the ProductID for the Celeron system (P0001). You would then search the Order Details table for records containing a ProductID of P0001, which in turn identifies orders O0002 and O0008. The second query is processed in similar fashion except that you would search the Order Details table for an OrderID of O0003. This time you would find three records with ProductIDs P0005, P0020, and P0022, respectively. You would then go to the Products table to look up the ProductIDs to return the name of each product.

We've emphasized that the power of a relational database comes from the inclusion of multiple tables and the relationships between those tables. As you already know, you can use data from several tables to compute the answer to more complex queries. For example:

Query: What is the total cost of order O0006? Which products are in the order and how many units of each product?
Answer: The total cost of order O0006 is $998.90. The order consists of one 19-inch monitor at $899 and ten boxes of HD floppy disks at $9.99 each.

To determine the cost of an order, you must first identify all of the products associated with that order, the quantity of each product, and the price of each product. The previous queries have shown how you would find the products in an order and the associated quantities. The price of a specific product is obtained from the Products table, which enables you to compute the invoice by multiplying the price of each product by the quantity. Thus, the total cost of order O0006 is $998.90. (One unit of P0007 at $899.00 and ten units of product P0014 at $9.99.)

The AutoNumber Field Type

Look carefully at the Customer, Order, and Product numbers in their respective tables and note that each set of numbers is consecutive. This is accomplished by specifying the *AutoNumber field* type for each of these fields in the design of the individual tables. The AutoNumber specification automatically assigns the next sequential number to the primary key of a new record. If, for example, you were to add a new customer to the existing Customers table, that customer would be assigned the number 13. In similar fashion, the next order will be order number 26, and the next product will be product number 32. (Deleting a record does not, however, renumber the remaining records in the table; that is, once a value is assigned to a primary key, the primary key will always retain that value.)

The C, O, and P that appear as the initial character of each field, as well as the high-order zeros, are *not* part of the fields themselves, but are displayed through the *Format property* associated with each field. Our Customers table, for example, uses the format \C0000, which displays a "C" in front of the field and pads it with high-order zeros. The Format property determines how a value is displayed, but does not affect how it is stored in the table. Thus, the CustomerID of the first customer is stored as the number 1, rather than C0001. The zeros provide a uniform appearance for that field throughout the table.

The Relationships Window

The *Relationships window* in Figure 6.2 shows the Computer Store database as it will be implemented in Access. The database contains the Customers, Orders, Products, and Order Details tables as per the previous discussion. The field lists display the fields within each table, with the primary key shown in bold. The OrderID and ProductID are both shown in bold in the Order Details table, to indicate that the primary key consists of the combination of these fields.

The many-to-many relationship between Orders and Products is implemented by a *pair* of one-to-many relationships. There is a one-to-many relationship between the Orders table and the Order Details table. There is a second one-to-many relationship between the Products table and the Order Details table. In other words, the Orders and Products tables are related to each other through the pair of one-to-many relationships with the Order Details table.

The *relationship lines* show the relationships among the tables. The number 1 appears next to the Products table on the relationship line connecting the Products table and the Order Details table. The infinity symbol appears at the end of the relationship line next to the Order Details table. The one-to-many relationship between these tables means that each record in the Products table can be associated with many records in the Order Details table. Each record in the Order Details table, however, is associated with only one record in the Products table.

In similar fashion, there is a second one-to-many relationship between the Orders table and the Order Details table. The number 1 appears on the relationship line next to the Orders table. The infinity symbol appears at the end of the line next to the Order Details table. Thus, each record in the Orders table can be associated with many records in the Order Details table, but each record in the Order Details table is associated with only one order.

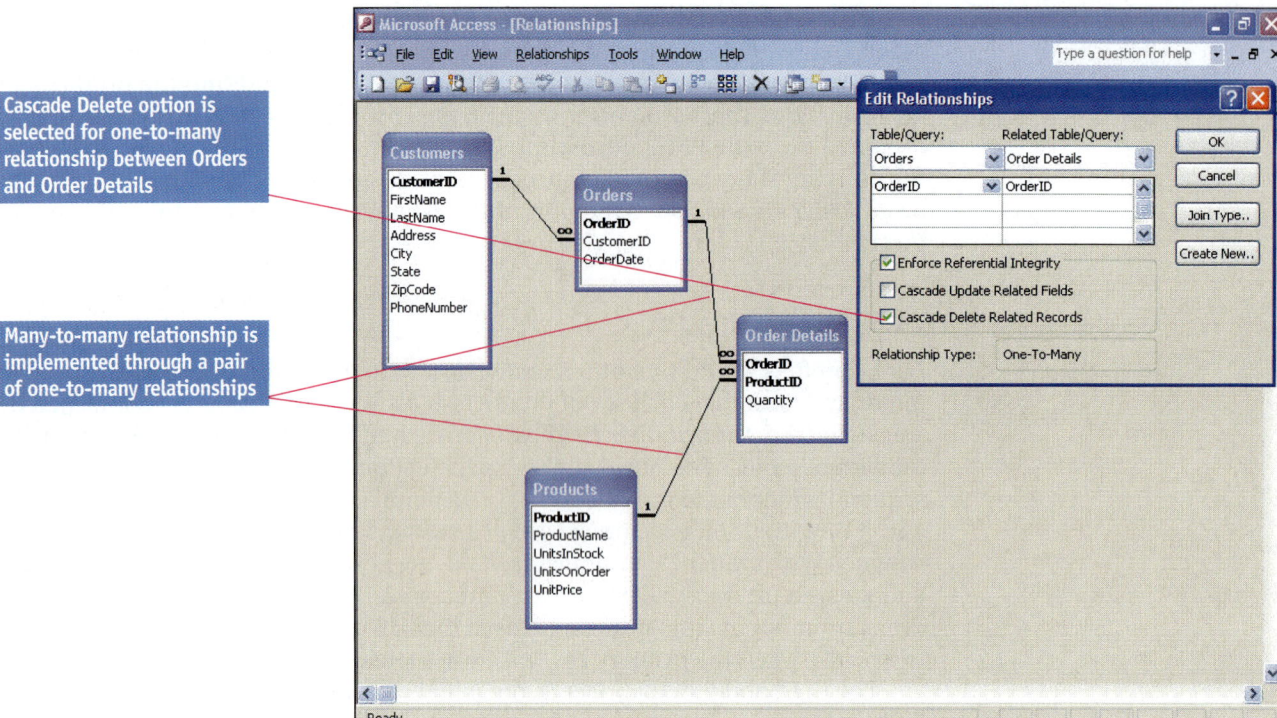

FIGURE 6.2 The Relationships Window

Referential integrity ensures that the records in related tables are consistent with one another by preventing you from adding a record to a related table with an invalid foreign key. You could not, for example, add a record to the Order Details table that referenced a nonexistent order in the Orders table. The enforcement of referential integrity will also prevent you from deleting a record in the primary (Orders) table when there are corresponding records in the related (Order Details) table.

There may be times, however, when you want to delete an order and simultaneously delete the corresponding records in the Order Details table. This is accomplished by enabling the ***cascaded deletion*** of related records (as shown in Figure 6.2), so that when you delete a record in the Orders table, Access automatically deletes the associated records in the Order Details table. If, for example, you were to delete order number O0006 from the Orders table, any records with this OrderID in the Order Details table would be deleted automatically.

You might also want to enable the ***cascaded updating*** of related fields to correct the value of an OrderID. Enforcement of referential integrity would ordinarily prevent you from changing the value of the OrderID field in the Orders table when there are corresponding records in the Order Details table. You could, however, specify the cascaded updating of related fields so that if you were to change the OrderID in the Orders table, the corresponding fields in the Order Details table would also change.

PRACTICE WITH DATABASE DESIGN

An Access database contains multiple tables, each of which stores data about a specific entity. To use Access effectively, you must be able to relate the tables to one another, which in turn requires knowledge of database design. Appendix B provides additional examples that enable you to master the principles of a relational database.

hands-on exercise
1 Relationships and Referential Integrity

Objective   To create relationships between existing tables in order to demonstrate referential integrity; to edit an existing relationship to allow the cascaded deletion of related records. Use Figure 6.3 as a guide in the exercise.

Step 1:   **Add a Customer Record**

- Start Access as you have throughout the text. Open the **Computer Store database** in the **Exploring Access folder**.

- Click the **Tables button** in the Database window. Open the **Customers table**, then click the **Maximize button** (if necessary) so that the table takes the entire screen as shown in Figure 6.3a.

- Click the **New Record button**, then click in the **FirstName field**. Enter the first letter of your first name (e.g., "J" as shown in the figure):
  - The record selector changes to a pencil to indicate that you are in the process of entering a record.
  - The CustomerID is assigned automatically as soon as you begin to enter data. *Remember your customer number as you will use it throughout the chapter.* (Your CustomerID is 13, not C0013. The prefix and high-order zeros are displayed through the Format property.)

- Complete your customer record, pressing the **Tab key** to move from one field to the next. Press **Tab** after you have entered the last field (phone number) to complete the record.

- Close the Customers table.

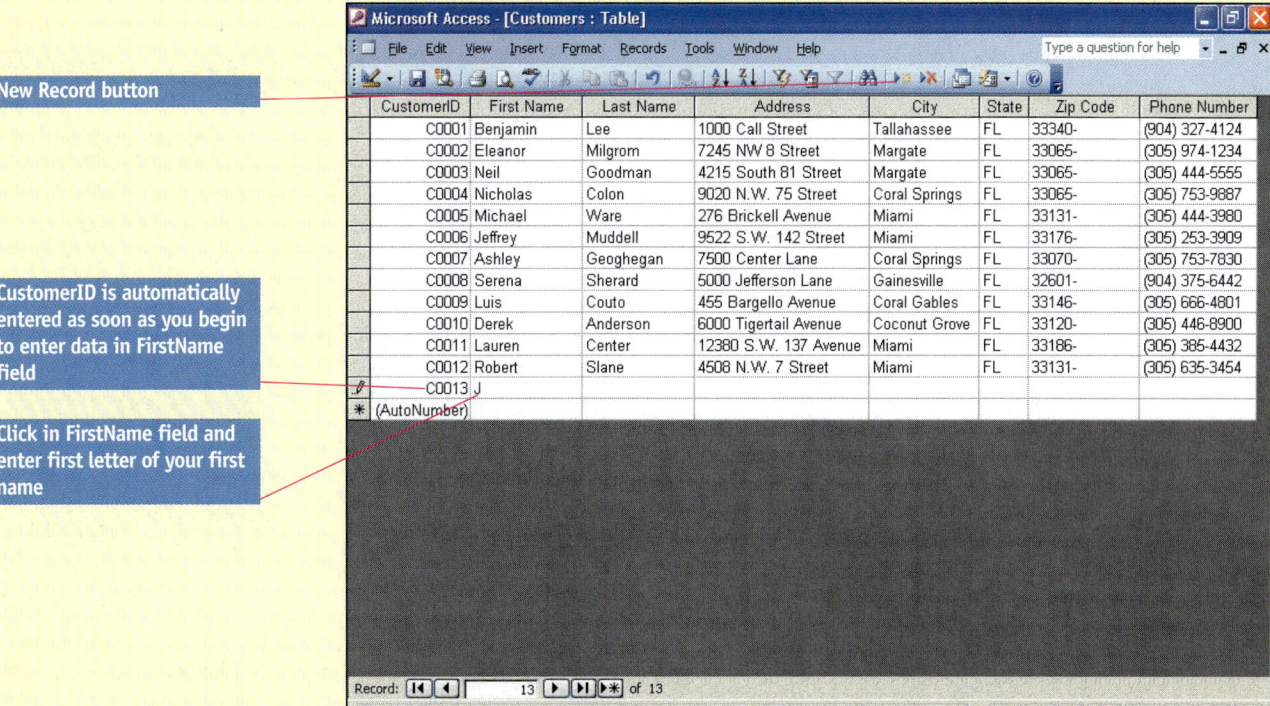

(a) Add a Customer Record (step 1)

FIGURE 6.3   Hands-on Exercise 1

Step 2: **Create the Relationships**

- Pull down the **Tools menu** and click **Relationships** to open the Relationships window as shown in Figure 6.3b. Maximize the Relationships window.
- Pull down the **Relationships menu** and click **Show Table** (or click the **Show Table button**) to display the Show Table dialog box.
- The **Tables tab** is selected within the Show Table dialog box, and the **Customers table** is selected. Click the **Add Command button**.
- Add the **Order Details**, **Orders**, and **Products** tables in similar fashion. Close the Show Table dialog box.
- Point to the bottom border of the **Customers field list**, then click and drag the border until all of the fields are visible.
- If necessary, click and drag the bottom border of the other tables until all of their fields are visible. Click and drag the title bars to move the field lists.
- Click and drag the **CustomerID field** in the Customers field list to the **CustomerID field** in the Orders field list. You will see the Relationships dialog box in Figure 6.3b when you release the mouse.
- Click the **Enforce Referential Integrity** check box. Click the **Create Command button** to establish the relationship.
- Click and drag the **OrderID field** in the Orders field list to the **OrderID field** in the Order Details field list. Click the **Enforce Referential Integrity** check box, then click the **Create Command button**.
- Click and drag the **ProductID field** in the Products field list to the **ProductID field** in the Order Details field list. Click the **Enforce Referential Integrity** check box, then click the **Create Command button**.
- Click the **Save button**. Close the Relationships window.

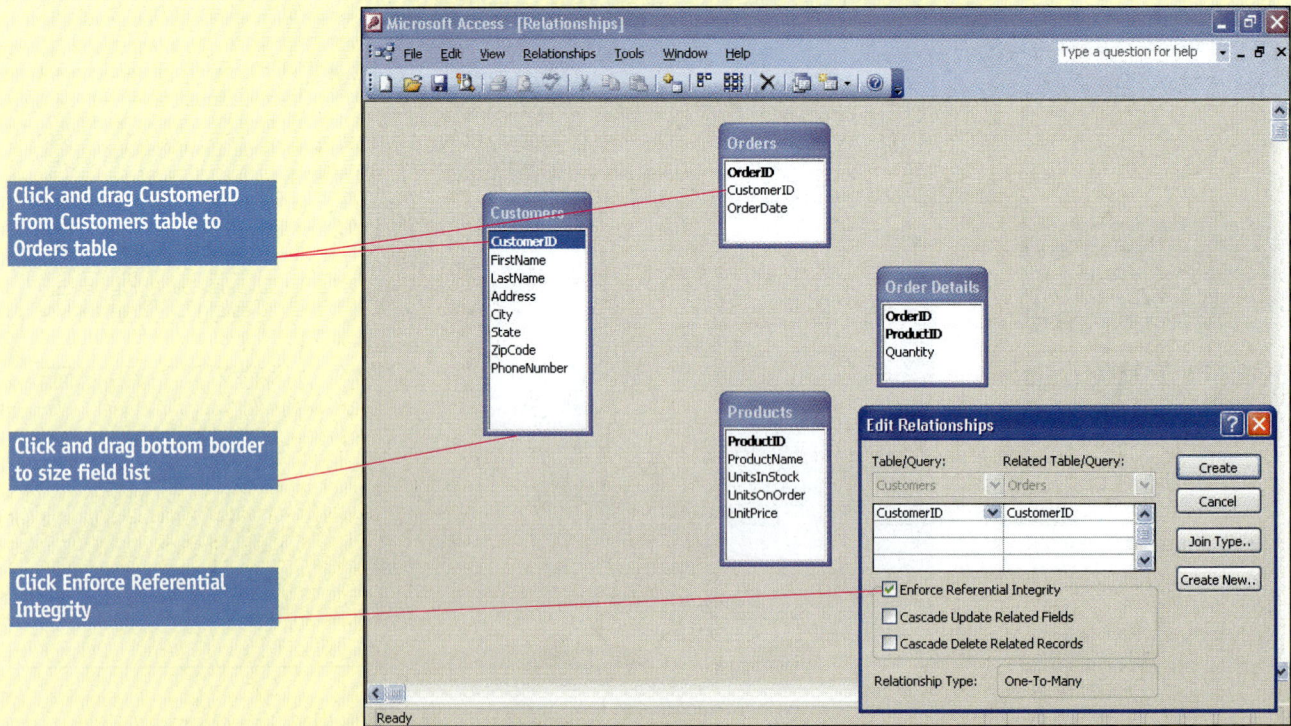

(b) Create the Relationships (step 2)

FIGURE 6.3 Hands-on Exercise 1 (*continued*)

1622 CHAPTER 6: MANY-TO-MANY RELATIONSHIPS

Step 3: **Delete an Order Details Record**

- You should be in the Database window. If necessary, click the **Tables button**, then open the **Orders table** as shown in Figure 6.3c.

- Click the **plus sign** next to order O0005. The plus sign changes to a minus sign, and you see the order details for this record. Click the **row selector column** to select the Order Details record for product **P0016** in order **O0005**.

- Press the **Del key**. You will see a message indicating that you are about to delete one record. Click **Yes**. The Delete command works because you are deleting a "many" record in a one-to-many relationship.

- Click the **minus sign** next to **Order O0005**. The minus sign changes to a plus sign, and you no longer see the order details. Click the **row selector column** to select the record, then press the **Del key** to (attempt to) delete the record.

- You will see a message indicating that you cannot delete the record. The Delete command does not work because you are attempting to delete the "one record" in a one-to-many relationship. Click **OK** to close the dialog box. The record for order O0005 is not deleted.

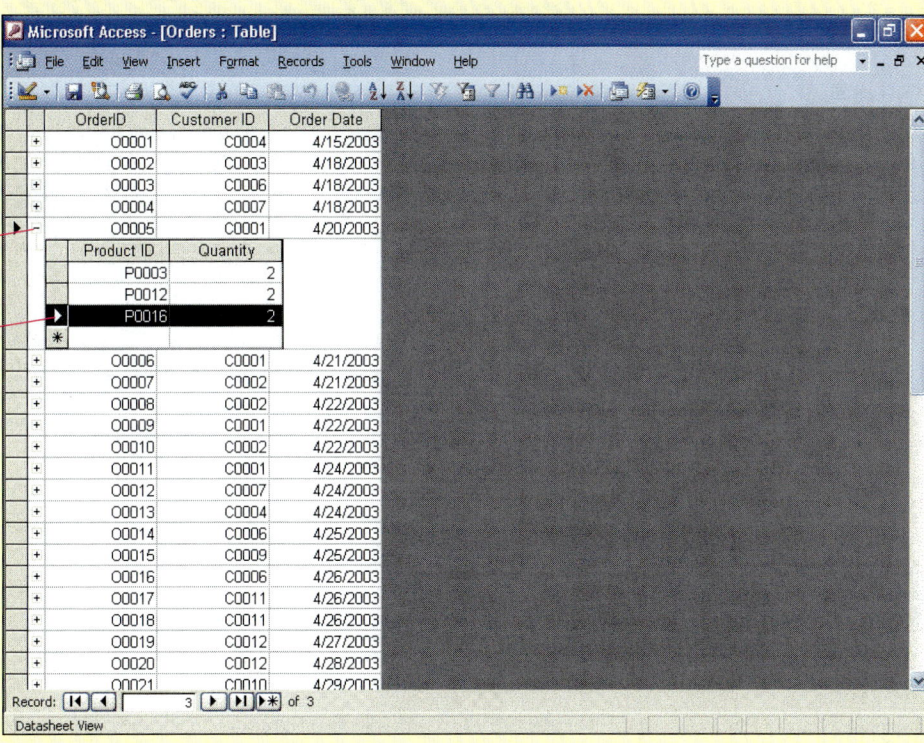

Click + (which becomes a −) to display related records

Click record selector column and press Del key

(c) Delete an Order Details Record (Step 3)

FIGURE 6.3 Hands-on Exercise 1 (*continued*)

WHAT YOU CAN AND CANNOT DELETE

You can always delete a record from the "many" table, such as the Order Details table in this example. The enforcement of referential integrity, however, will prevent you from deleting a record in the "one" table (i.e., the Orders table) when there are related records in the "many" table (i.e., the Order Details table). Thus, you may want to modify the relationship to permit the cascaded deletion of related records, in which case deleting a record from the "one" table will automatically delete the related records.

Step 4: **Edit a Relationship**

- Close the Orders table. (The tables in a relationship must be closed before the relationship can be edited.)
- Pull down the **Tools menu** and click **Relationships** to reopen the Relationships window (or click the **Relationships button** on the toolbar). Maximize the window.
- Point to the line connecting the Orders and Order Details tables, then click the **right mouse button** to display a shortcut menu. Click **Edit Relationship** to display the Relationships dialog box in Figure 6.3d.
- Check the box to **Cascade Delete Related Records**, then click **OK** to accept the change and close the dialog box. Click the **Save button** on the Relationships toolbar to save the edited relationship.
- Close the Relationships window.

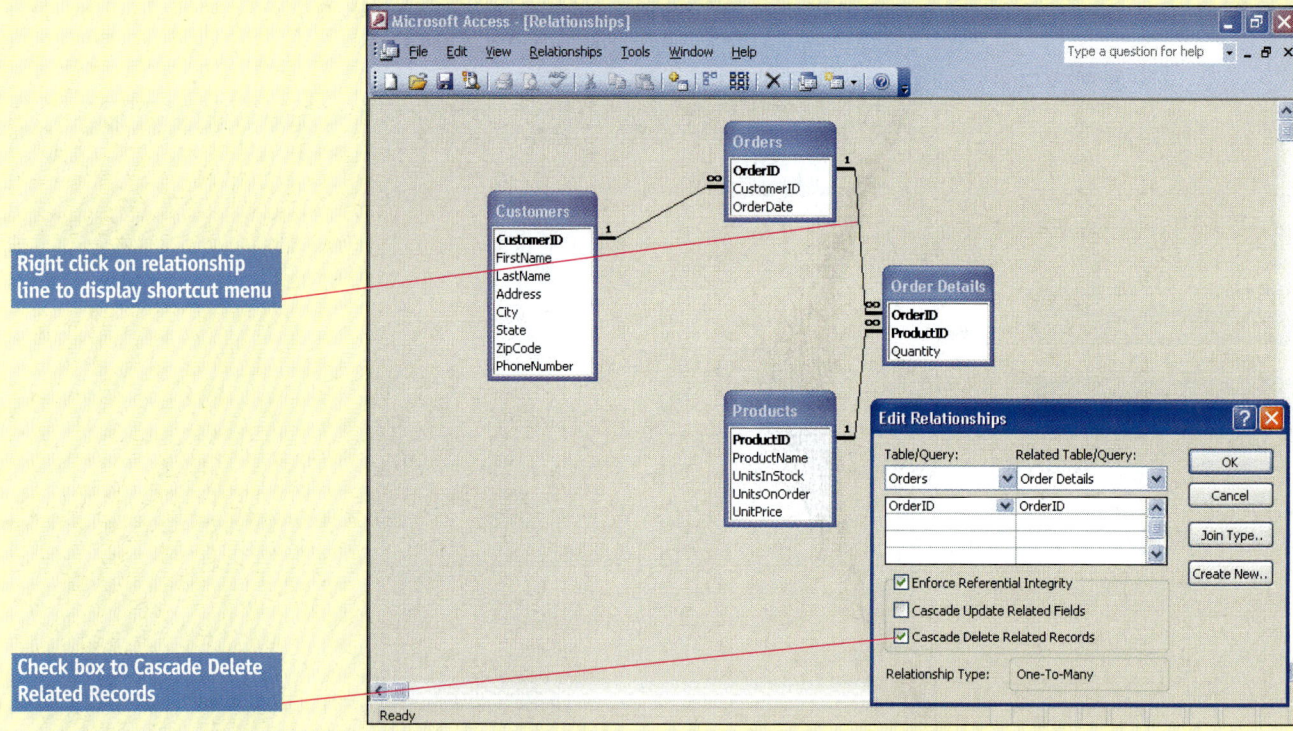

(d) Edit a Relationship (step 4)

FIGURE 6.3 Hands-on Exercise 1 (*continued*)

RELATED FIELDS AND DATA TYPE

The related fields on both sides of a relationship must be the same data type—for example, both number fields or both text fields. (Number fields must also have the same field size setting.) You cannot, however, specify an AutoNumber field on both sides of a relationship. Accordingly, if the related field in the primary table is an AutoNumber field, the related field in the related table must be specified as a number field, with the Field Size property set to Long Integer.

1624 CHAPTER 6: MANY-TO-MANY RELATIONSHIPS

Step 5: **Delete a Record in the Orders Table**

- You should be back in the Database window. Open the **Orders table**. Click the **record selector column** for **Order O0005**. Press the **Del key**.

- Record O0005 is deleted from the table (although you can cancel the deletion by clicking No in response to the message that is displayed on your screen). We want you to delete the record, however. Thus, click **Yes** in response to the message in Figure 6.3e.

- Order O0005 is permanently deleted from the Orders table as are the related records in the Order Details table. The Delete command works this time (unlike the previous attempt in step 3) because the relationship was changed to permit the deletion of related records.

- Close the Orders table. Close the database. Click **Yes** if prompted to save the tables or relationships.

- Exit Access if you do not want to continue with the next exercise at this time.

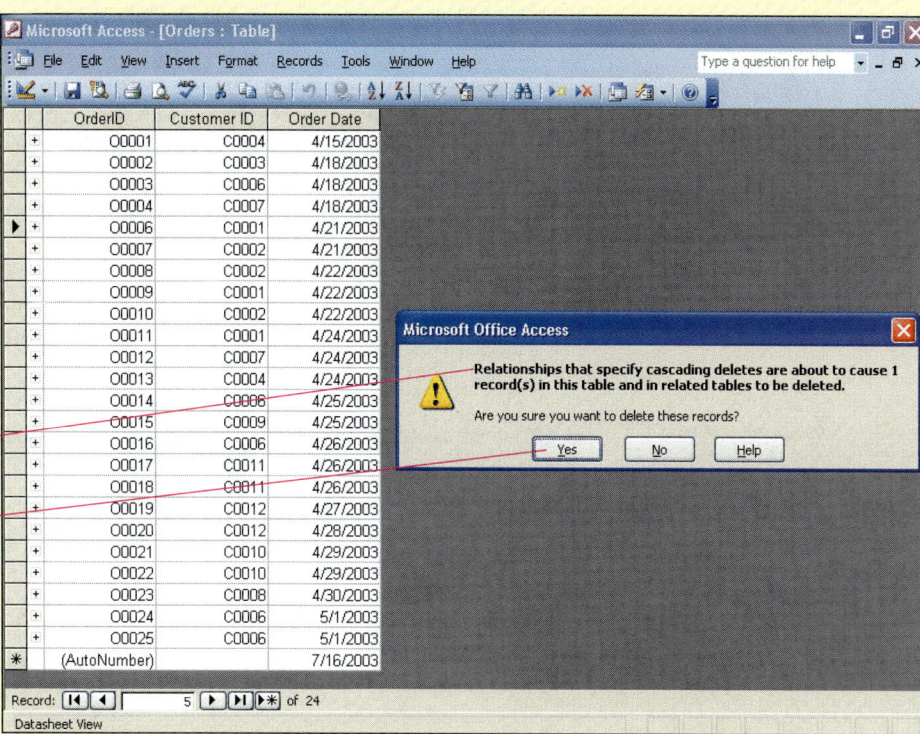

(e) Delete a Record in the Orders Table (step 5)

FIGURE 6.3 Hands-on Exercise 1 (*continued*)

USE WITH CAUTION

The cascaded deletion of related records relaxes referential integrity and eliminates errors that would otherwise occur during data entry. That does not mean, however, that the option should always be selected, and in fact, most of the time it is disabled. What would happen, for example, in an employee database with a one-to-many relationship between branch offices and employees, if cascade deleted records was in effect and a branch office was deleted?

SUBFORMS, QUERIES, AND AUTOLOOKUP

The main and subform combination in Figure 6.4 is used by the store to enter a new order for an existing customer. The forms are based on queries (rather than tables) for several reasons. A query enables you to display data from multiple tables, to display a calculated field, and to take advantage of AutoLookup, a feature that is explained shortly. A query also lets you display records in a sequence other than by primary key.

The *main form* contains fields from both the Orders table and the Customers table. The OrderID, OrderDate, and CustomerID (the join field) are taken from the Orders table. The other fields are taken from the Customers table. The query is designed so that you do not have to enter any customer information other than the CustomerID; that is, you enter the CustomerID, and Access will automatically look up *(AutoLookup)* the corresponding customer data.

The *subform* is based on a second query containing fields from the Order Details table and the Products table. The OrderID, Quantity, and ProductID (the join field) are taken from the Order Details table. The ProductName and UnitPrice fields are from the Products table. AutoLookup works here as well so that when you enter the ProductID, Access automatically displays the Product Name and Unit Price. You then enter the quantity, and the amount (a calculated field) is determined automatically.

The queries for the main form and subform are shown in Figures 6.5a and 6.5b, respectively. The upper half of the Query window displays the field list for each table and the relationship between the tables. The lower half of the Query window contains the design grid.

The following exercise has you create the main and subform in Figure 6.4. We supply the query for the main form (Figure 6.5a), but we ask you to create the query for the subform (Figure 6.5b). Once both queries are available, you can proceed to create the Super Store Order form.

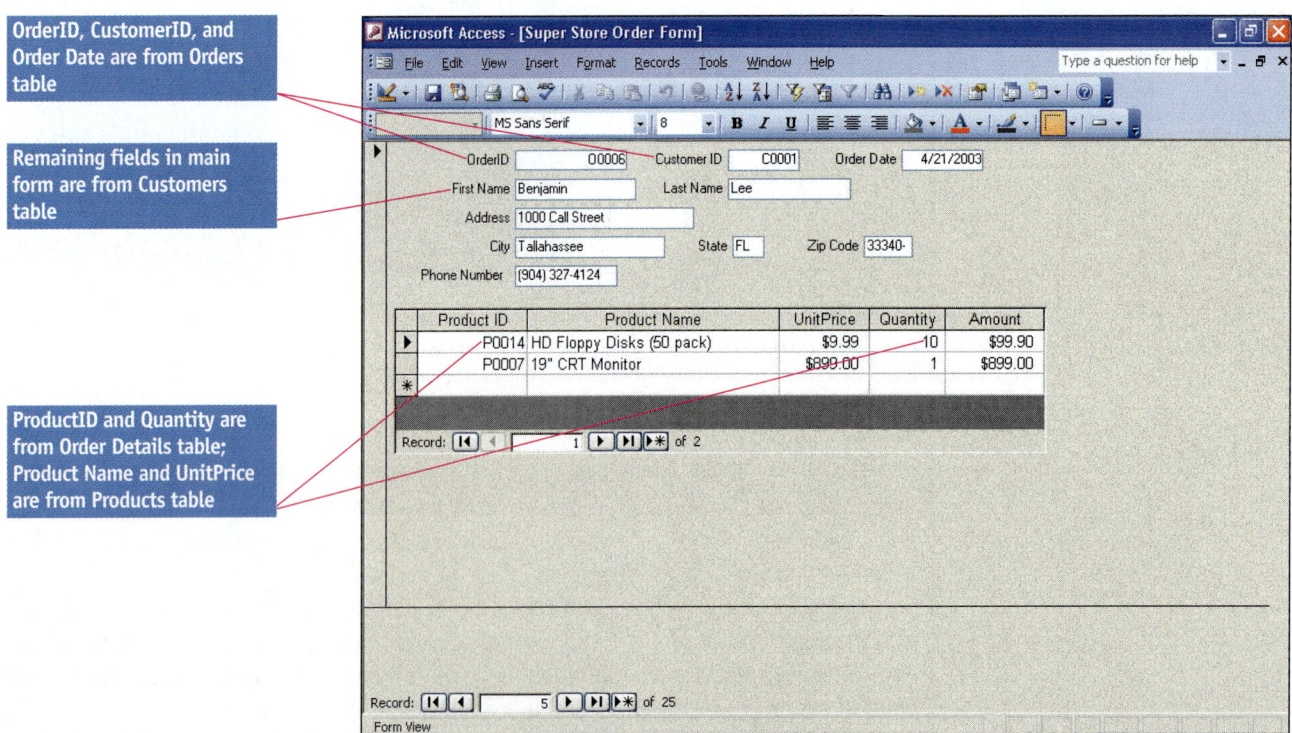

FIGURE 6.4 The Super Store Order Form

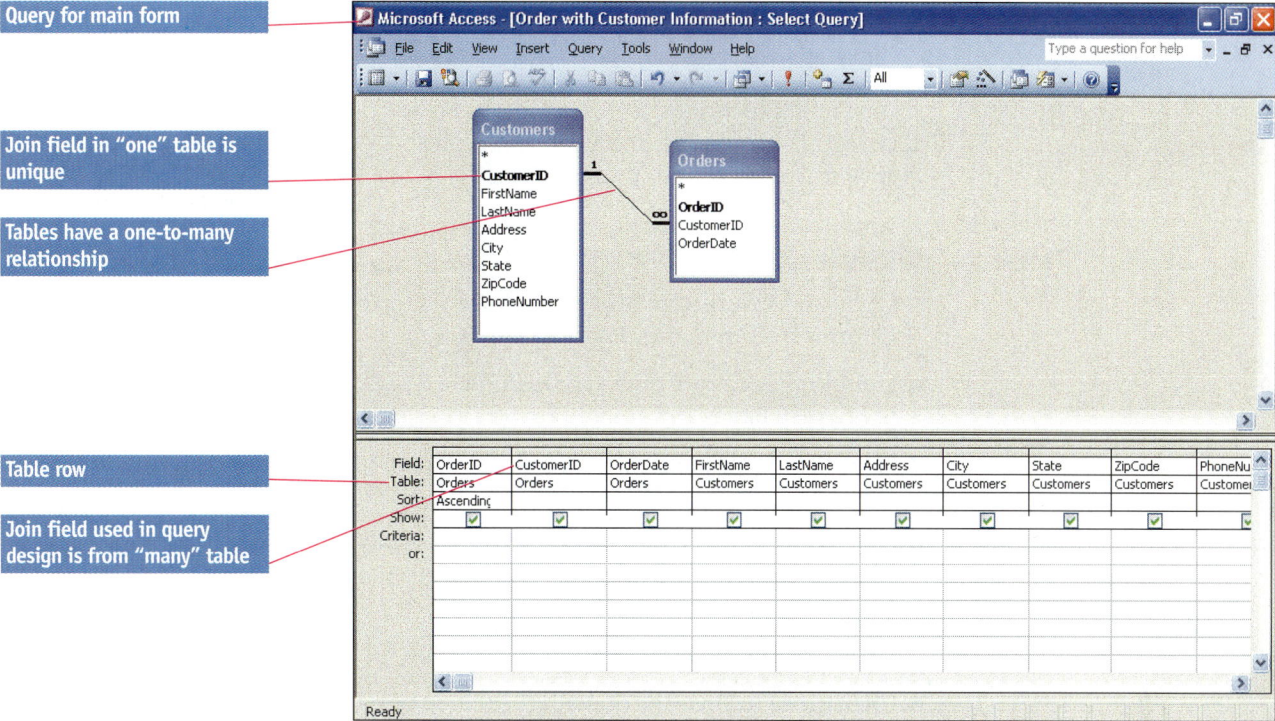

(a) Order with Customer Information Query (used for the main form)

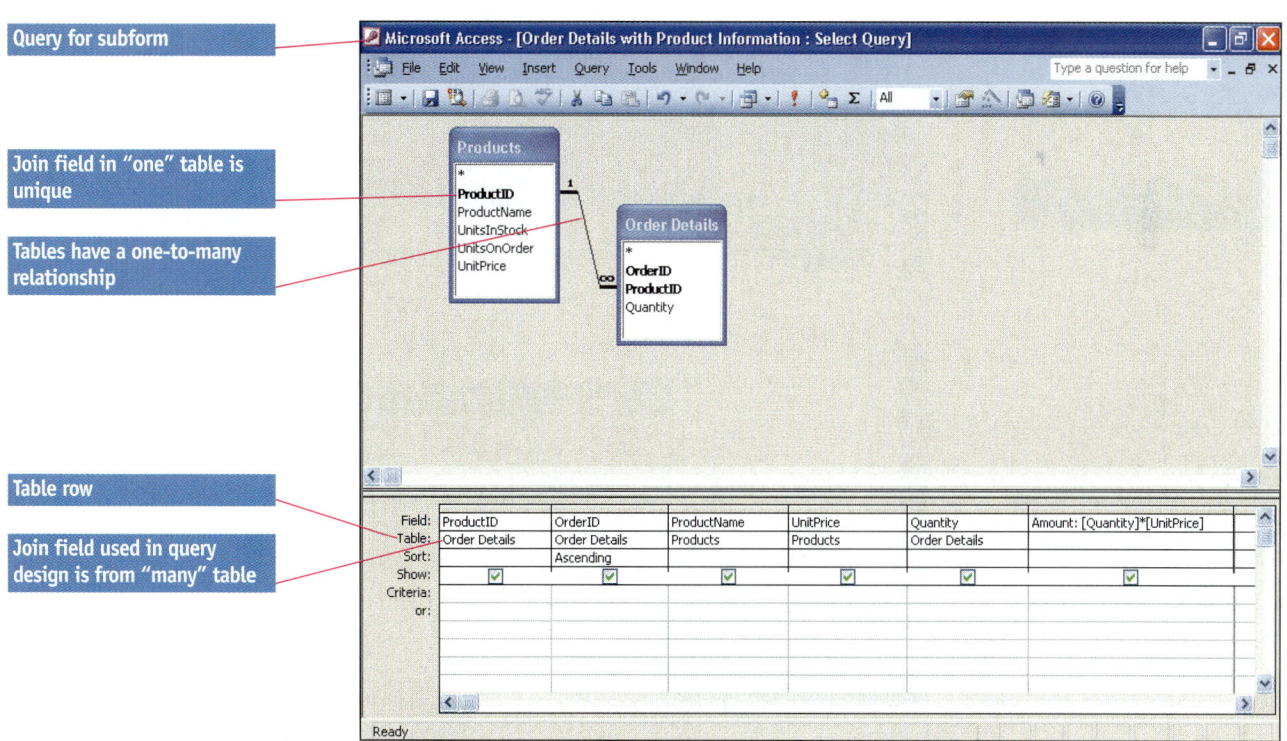

(b) Order Details with Product Information Query (used for subform)

FIGURE 6.5 Multiple-table Queries

hands-on exercise 2

Subforms and Multiple-table Queries

Objective To use multiple-table queries as the basis for a main form and its associated subform; to create the link between a main form and subform manually. Use Figure 6.6 as a guide in the exercise.

Step 1: Create the Subform Query

- Open the **Computer Store database** from the previous exercise. Click the **Queries button** in the Database window.

- Double click **Create query in Design view** to display the Query Design window in Figure 6.6c.

- The Show Table dialog box appears as shown in Figure 6.6a with the Tables tab already selected.

- Double click the **Products table** to add this table to the query. Double click the **Order Details table** to add this table to the query.

- A join line showing the one-to-many relationship between the Products and Order Details tables appears automatically.

- Click **Close** to close the Show Table dialog box. If necessary, click the **Maximize button**. Resize the field lists as necessary.

- Click and drag the border separating the two parts of the query window to better display the field list. You are ready to create the query.

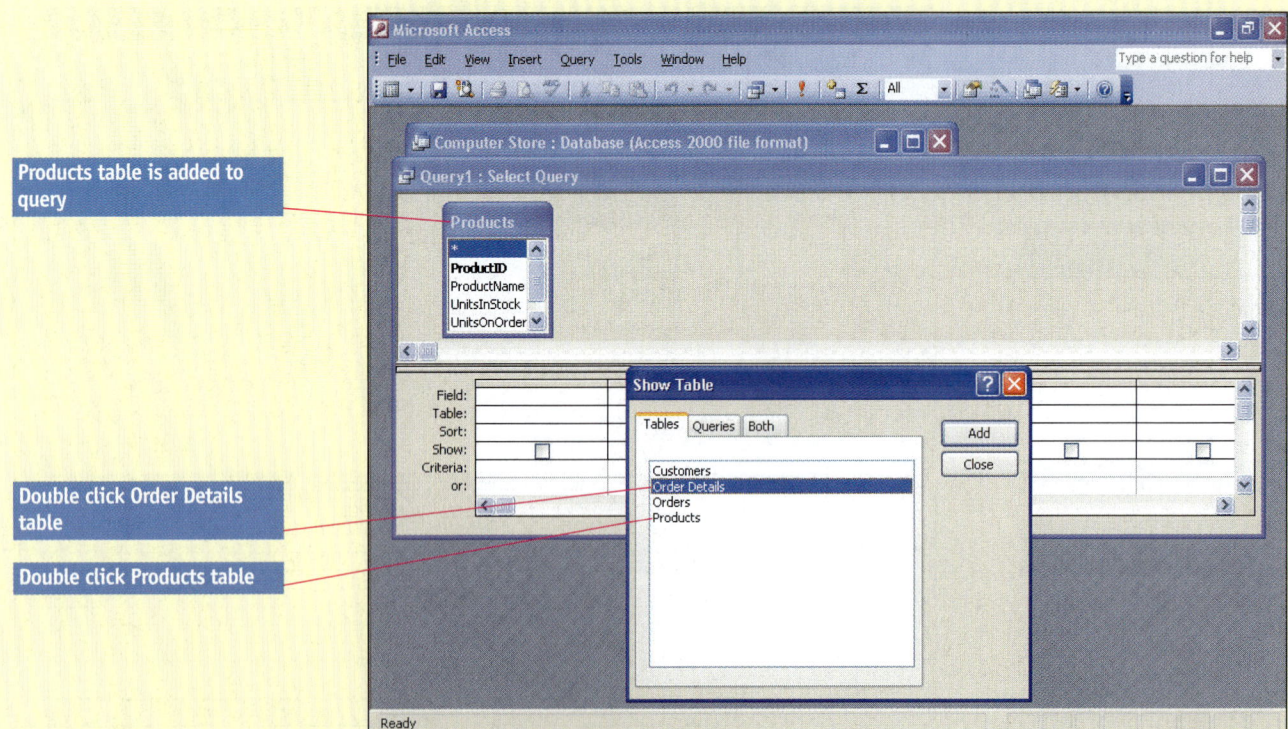

(a) Create the Subform Query (step 1)

FIGURE 6.6 Hands-on Exercise 2

1628 CHAPTER 6: MANY-TO-MANY RELATIONSHIPS

Step 2: **Create the Subform Query (continued)**

- Add the fields to the query as follows:
  - Double click the **ProductID** and **OrderID fields** in that order from the Order Details table.
  - Double click the **ProductName** and **UnitPrice fields** in that order from the Products table.
  - Double click the **Quantity field** from the Order Details table.

- Click the **Sort row** under the **OrderID field**. Click the **drop-down arrow**, then specify an **ascending** sequence.

- Click the first available cell in the Field row. Type =[Quantity]*[UnitPrice]. Do not be concerned if you cannot see the entire expression.

- Press **Enter**. Access has substituted Expr1: for the equal sign you typed. Drag the column boundary so that the entire expression is visible as in Figure 6.6b. (You may need to make the other columns narrower to see all of the fields in the design grid.)

- Click and drag to select **Expr1**. (Do not select the colon.) Type **Amount** to substitute a more meaningful field name.

- Point to the expression and click the **right mouse button** to display a shortcut menu. Click **Properties** to display the Field Properties dialog box in Figure 6.6b.

- Click the box for the **Format property**. Click the **drop-down arrow**, then scroll until you can click **Currency**. Close the Properties dialog box.

- Save the query as **Order Details with Product Information**. Click the **Run button** to test the query so that you know the query works prior to using it as the basis of a form.

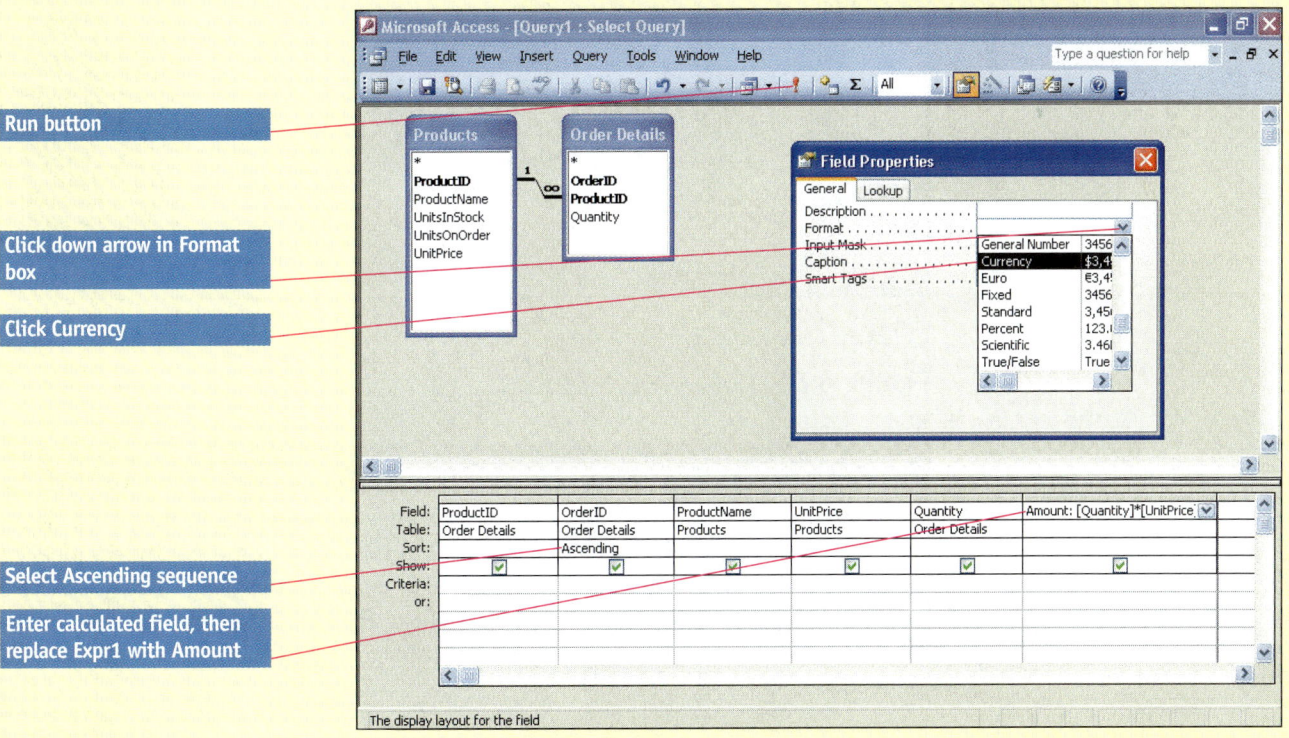

(b) Create the Subform Query (continued) (step 2)

FIGURE 6.6 Hands-on Exercise 2 (*continued*)

Step 3: **Test the Query**

- You should see the dynaset shown in Figure 6.6c. (See the boxed tip if the dynaset does not appear.)
- Enter **1** (not P0001) to change the ProductID to 1 (from 14) in the very first record. (The Format property automatically displays the letter P and the high-order zeros.)
- Press **Enter**. The Product Name changes to a Celeron® at 2.0GHz system as you hit the Enter key. The unit price also changes, as does the computed amount.
- Click the **Undo button** to cancel the change. The ProductID returns to P0014, and the Product Name changes back to HD Floppy Disks (50 pack). The unit price also changes, as does the computed amount.
- Close the query. Save the changes to the query design if prompted to do so.

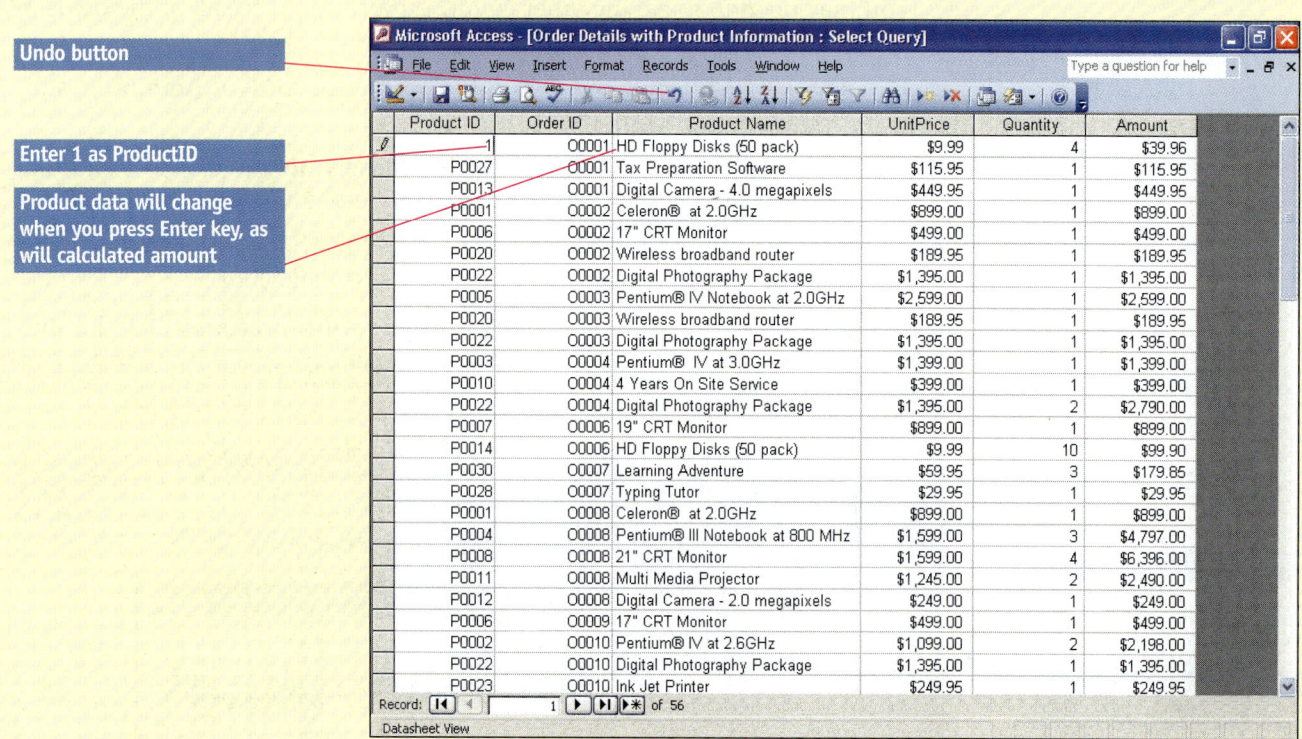

(c) Test the Query (step 3)

FIGURE 6.6 Hands-on Exercise 2 (*continued*)

A PUZZLING ERROR

If you are unable to run a query, it is most likely because you misspelled a field name in the design grid. Access interpets the misspelling as a parameter query (discussed later in the chapter) and asks you to enter a parameter value (the erroneous field name is displayed in the dialog box). Press the Esc key and return to the Design view. Click the field row for the problem field and make the necessary correction.

Step 4: **Create the Orders Form**

- Click the **Forms button** in the Database window, then double click the **Create form by using wizard icon** to start the Form Wizard. You should see the dialog box in Figure 6.6d except that no tables have been selected at this time.

- Click the **drop-down arrow** on the Tables/Queries list box to display the tables and queries in the database. Select **Order with Customer Information** (the query we provided), then click the **>> button** to enter all of the fields from the query onto the form.

- Click the **drop-down arrow** to redisplay the tables and queries in the database. Click **Order Details with Product Information** to select this query as shown in Figure 6.6d. Select every field *except* OrderID.

- Be sure that the Selected Fields area contains the selected fields from both queries. Click **Next**. The wizard will prompt you for the additional information it needs to create the form and its associated subform:
  - The next screen suggests that you view the data by **Order with Customer Information** and that you create a form with subforms. Click **Next**.
  - The **Datasheet option button** is selected as the default layout for the subform. Click **Next**.
  - Click **Standard** as the style for your form. Click **Next**.
  - Enter **Super Store Order form** as the title of the form, but accept the wizard's suggestion for the name of the subform (**Order Details with Product Information subform**).
  - Click the option button to **Modify the form's design**, then click the **Finish command button** to create the form and exit the Form Wizard.

- You should be in the Design view of the Super Store Order form you just created. Click the **Save button** to save the form and continue working.

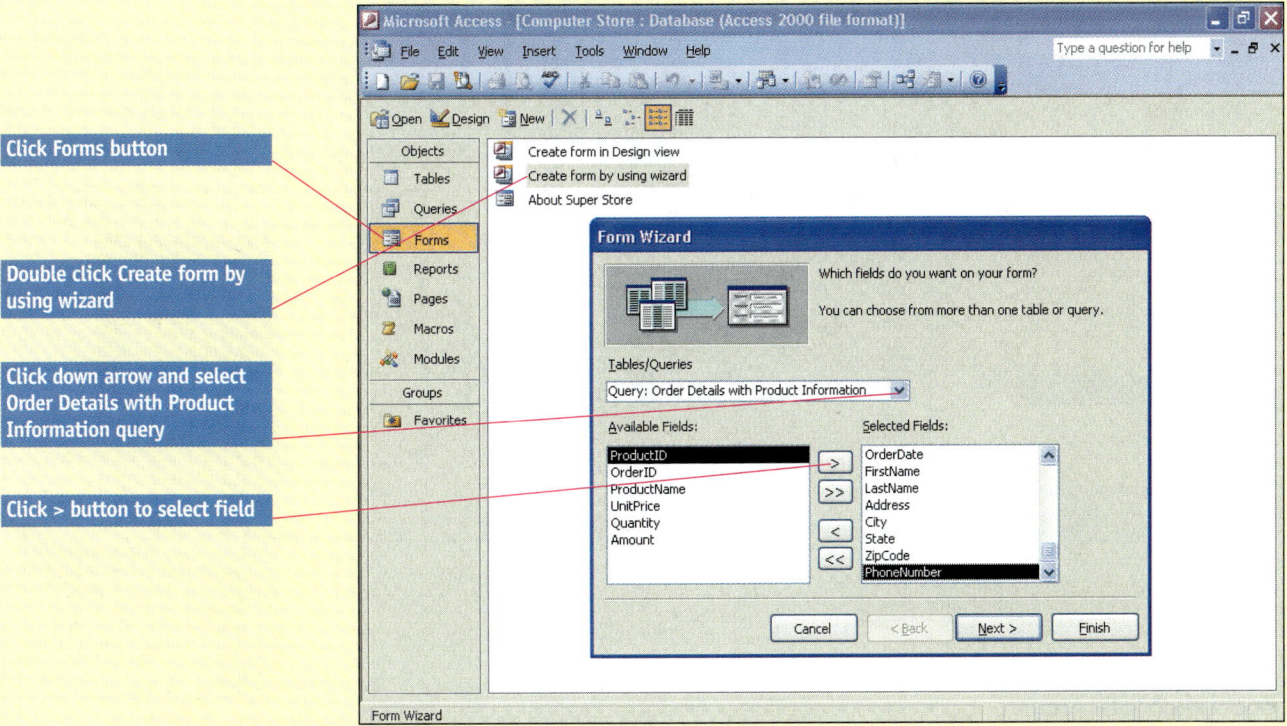

(d) Create the Orders Form (step 4)

FIGURE 6.6 Hands-on Exercise 2 (*continued*)

Step 5: **Modify the Orders Form**

- You are in the Design view. Maximize the window (if necessary), then **click and drag the bottom of the Details section** down to give yourself additional room in which to work.
- It takes time (and a little practice) to move and size the controls within a form. Try the indicated command, then click the **Undo button** if you are not satisfied with the result.
- Click and drag the control for the subform and its label toward the Form Footer. Select the label of the subform control, then press the **Del key** to delete the label as shown in Figure 6.6e. Click and drag the left border of the subform control toward the left to make the subform wider.
- Click the **PhoneNumber control** to select the control and display the sizing handles, then drag the control above the subform control.
- Click and drag the controls for **City**, **State**, and **ZipCode** (one at a time) on the line above the PhoneNumber control.
- Click and drag the **LastName control** so that it is next to the FirstName control. Click and drag the **Address control** under the control for FirstName.
- Move the **CustomerID control** to the right of the OrderID control. Click and drag the **OrderDate control** so that it is next to the CustomerID. The width of the form will change automatically if the form is not wide enough. You may, however, need to extend the width a little further when you release the mouse.
- Select the **Page Break tool**, then click below the subform control to insert a page break on the form. The page break will print one order per page.
- Adjust the size, spacing, and alignment of the labels and bound controls as necessary, switching back and forth between Form view and Design view.
- Save the form.

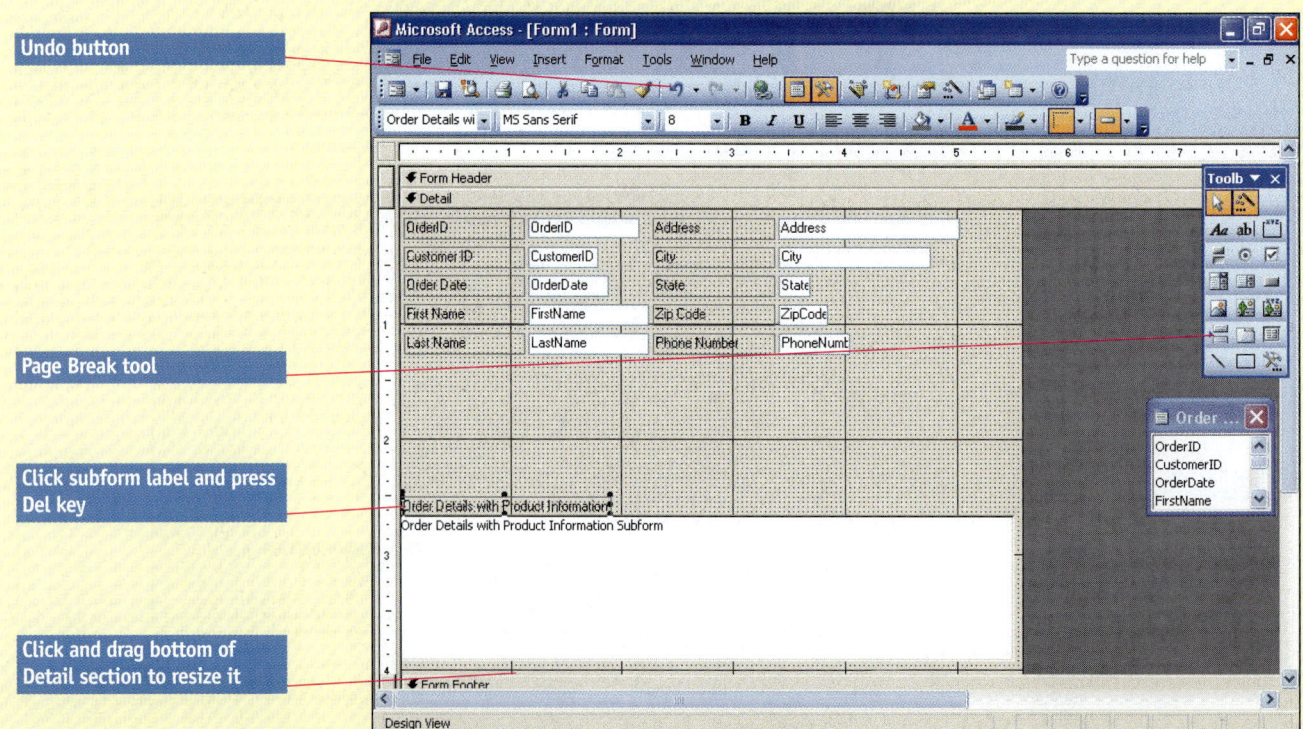

(e) Modify the Orders Form (step 5)

FIGURE 6.6 Hands-on Exercise 2 (*continued*)

Step 6: **Change the Column Widths**

- Click the **View button** to change to the Form view. You should see the first order in the database together with the associated product information. You may, however, have to adjust the width of the columns within the subform and/or change the size and position of the subform within the main form.

- To change the width of the columns within the subform:
  - Click the **down arrow** on the **View button** and change to the **Datasheet view**. Click the **plus sign** next to the OrderID column for the first order to display the related records as shown in Figure 6.6f.
  - Click and drag the border of the various column headings until you can read all of the information. Click the **Save button** to save the new layout, then close the form. You must close the main form, then reopen the form for the changes in the subform to be visible.
  - You should be back in the Database window. Double click the **Super Store Order form** to reopen the form and check the width of the columns in the subform. If necessary, click the **down arrow** on the **View button** to return to the Datasheet view to further adjust the columns.

- It may also be necessary to change the size or position of the subform within the main form. Click the **View button** and change to the **Design view**.

- Click and drag a sizing handle to change the size of the subform control. Click and drag the subform control to change its position. If necessary, extend the width of the form.

- The process is one of trial and error, but it should take only a few minutes to size the subform properly.

- Save the completed form.

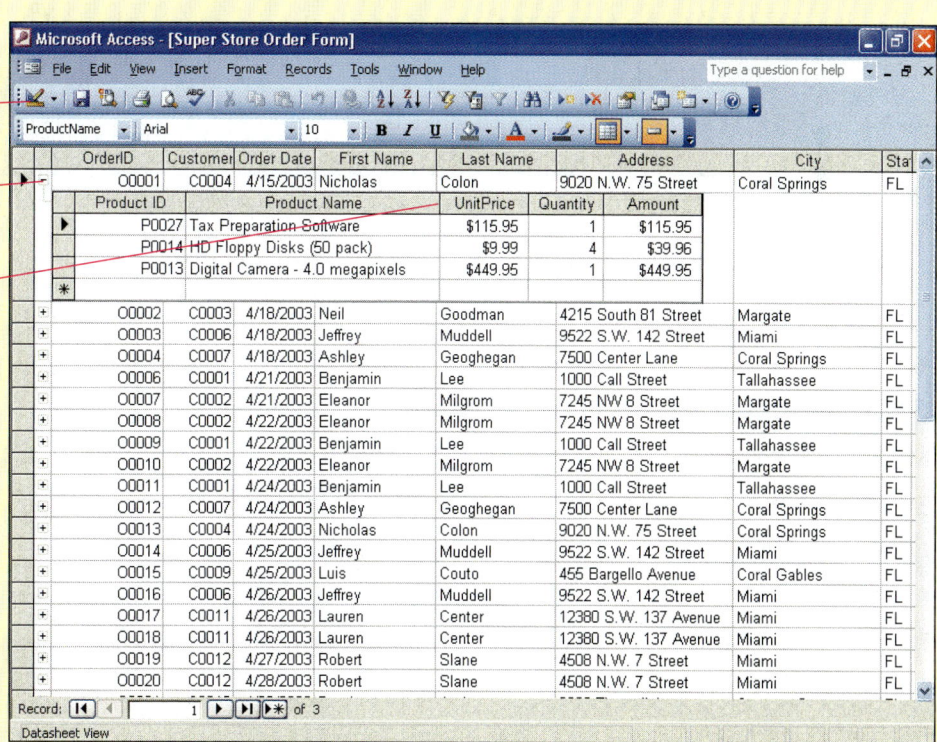

(f) Change the Column Widths (step 6)

FIGURE 6.6 Hands-on Exercise 2 (*continued*)

Step 7: **Enter a New Order**

- Change to the **Form view** of the Super Store Order form as shown in Figure 6.6g. The navigation buttons on the main form move from one order to the next. The navigation buttons on the subform move between products in an order.

- Click the **New Record button** on the main form to display a blank form so that you can place an order. Click in the **CustomerID** text box. Enter **13** (your customer number from exercise 1), then press the **Tab** or **Enter key** to move to the next field.
  - ❏ The OrderID is entered automatically since it is an AutoNumber field.
  - ❏ All of your customer information (your name, address, and phone number) is entered automatically because of the AutoLookup feature that is built into the underlying query.
  - ❏ Today's date is entered automatically as the default value.

- Click the **ProductID** text box in the subform. Enter **1** (not P0001) and press the **Enter key**. The Product Name and Unit Price are entered automatically.

- Press the **Tab key** twice to move to the Quantity field, enter **1**, and press the **Tab key** twice more to move to the ProductID field for the next item. (The amount is calculated automatically.)

- Complete your order as shown in Figure 6.6g. The navigation buttons in the figure show that you are currently working in the third (of three) order detail records, in the 25th (of twenty-five) orders.

- Click the **Selection Area** to select the current record (the order entered).

- Pull down the **File menu**, click **Print** to display the Print dialog box, then click the option button to specify **Selected Record(s)** as the print range. Click **OK** to print the form. Close the form.

- Exit Access if you do not want to continue with the next exercise at this time.

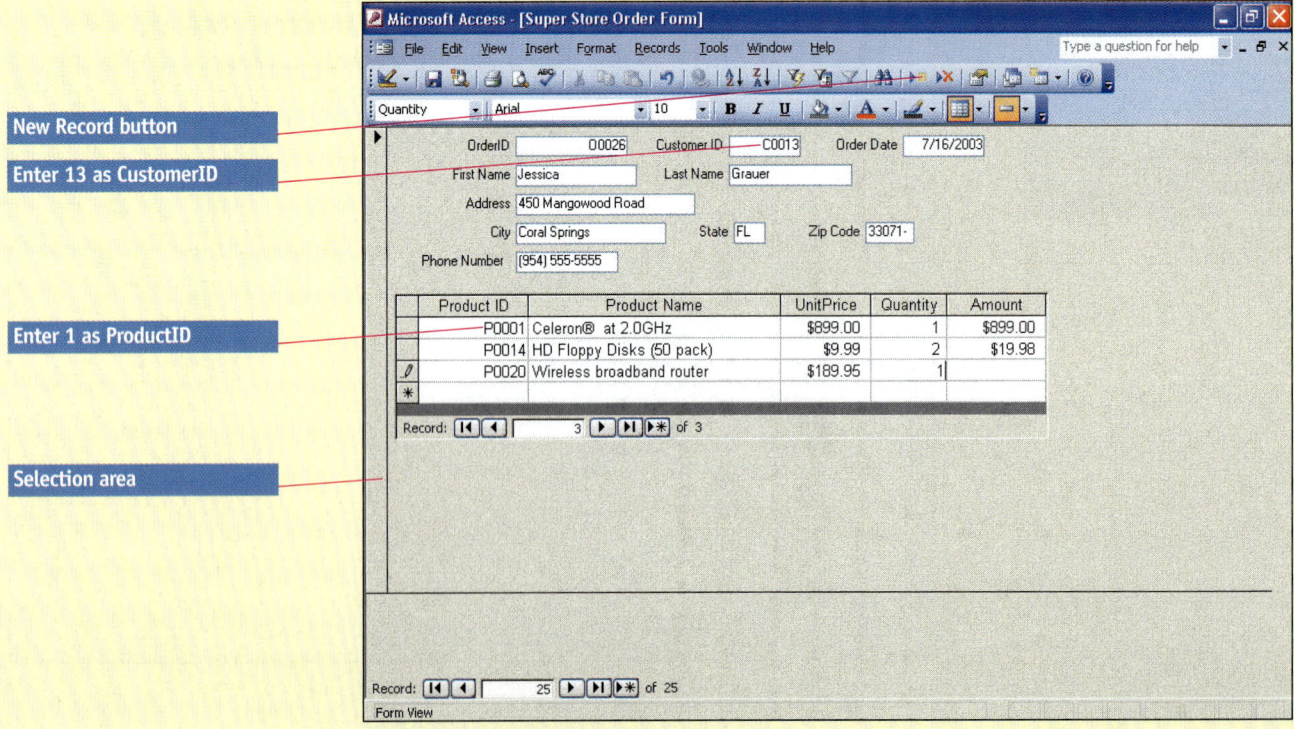

(g) Enter a New Order (step 7)

FIGURE 6.6 Hands-on Exercise 2 (*continued*)

PARAMETER QUERIES

A select query, powerful as it is, has its limitations. It requires you to enter the criteria directly into the query, which means you have to change the query every time you vary the criteria. What if you wanted to use a different set of criteria (e.g., a different customer's name) every time you ran the "same" query?

A *parameter query* prompts you for the criteria each time you execute the query. It is created in similar fashion to a select query and is illustrated in Figure 6.7. The difference between a parameter query and an ordinary select query is the way in which the criteria are specified. A select query contains the actual criteria. A parameter query, however, contains a *prompt* (message) that will request the criteria when the query is executed.

The design grid in Figure 6.7a creates a parameter query that will display the orders for a particular customer. The query does not contain the customer's name, but a prompt for that name. The prompt is enclosed in square brackets and is displayed in a dialog box in which the user enters the requested data when the query is executed. Thus, the user supplies the customer's name in Figure 6.7b, and the query displays the resulting dynaset in Figure 6.7c. This enables you to run the same query with different criteria; that is, you can enter a different customer name every time you execute the query. (You can also omit the customer name by pressing Enter immediately, in which case you will see every record in the underlying table.)

A parameter query may prompt for any number of variables (parameters), which are entered in successive dialog boxes. The parameters are requested in order from left to right, according to the way in which they appear in the design grid.

TOTAL QUERIES

A *total query* performs calculations on a *group* of records using one of several summary (aggregate) functions available within Access. These include the Sum, Count, Avg, Max, and Min functions to determine the total, number of, average, maximum, and minimum values, respectively. Figure 6.8 illustrates the use of a total query to compute the total amount for each order.

Figure 6.8a displays the dynaset from a select query with fields from both the Products and Order Details tables. (The dynaset contains one record for each product in each order and enables us to verify the results of the total query in Figure 6.8c.) Each record in Figure 6.8a contains the price of the product, the quantity ordered, and the amount for that product. There are, for example, three products in order O0001. The first product costs $449.95, the second product costs $39.96 (four units at $9.99 each), and the third product costs $115.95). The total for the order comes to $605.86, which is obtained by (manually) adding the amount field in each of the records for this order.

Figure 6.8b shows the Design view of the total query to calculate the cost of each order. The query contains only two fields, OrderID and Amount. The QBE grid also displays a *Total row* in which each field in the query has either a Group By or aggregate entry. The *Group By* entry under OrderID indicates that the records in the dynaset are to be grouped (aggregated) according to the like values of OrderID; that is, there will be one record in the total query for each distinct value of OrderID. The *Sum function* specifies the arithmetic operation to be performed on that field for each group of records.

The dynaset in Figure 6.8c displays the result of the total query and contains *aggregate* records, as opposed to *individual* records. There are three records for order O0001 in Figure 6.8a, but only one record in Figure 6.8c. This is because each record in a total query contains a calculated result for a group of records. In similar fashion, there are four detail records for order O0002 but only one summary record.

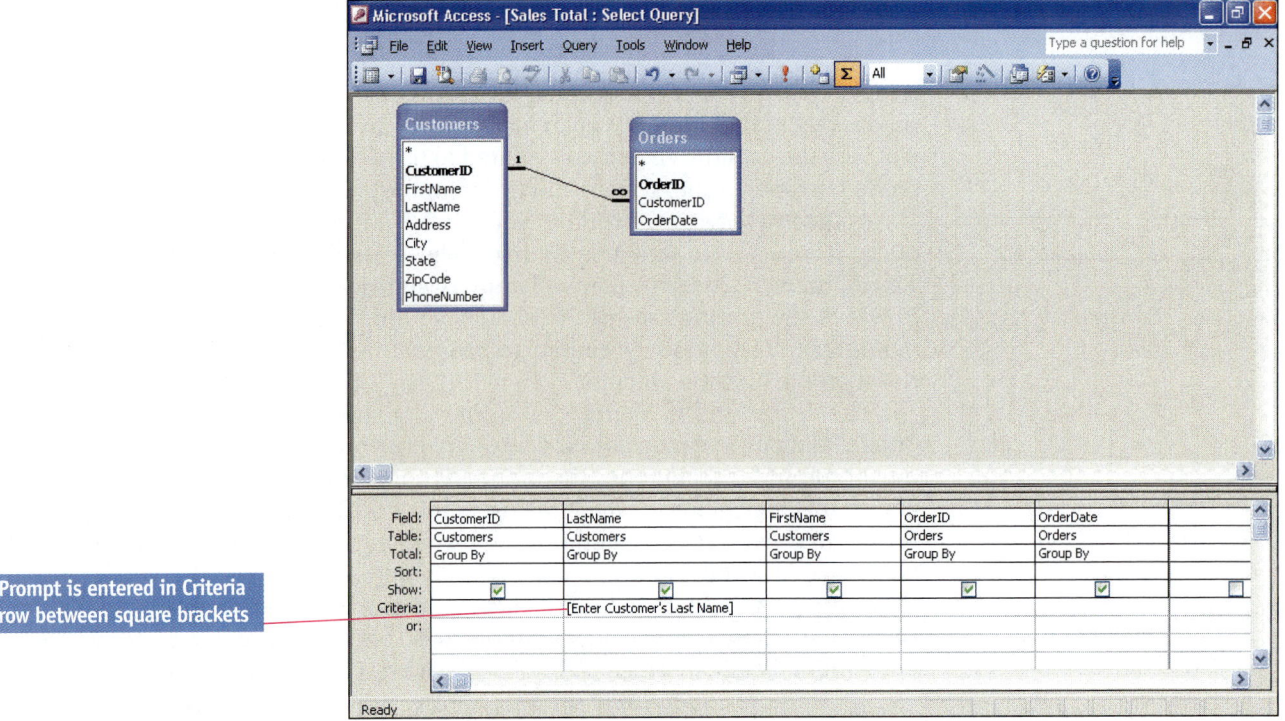

(a) Design grid

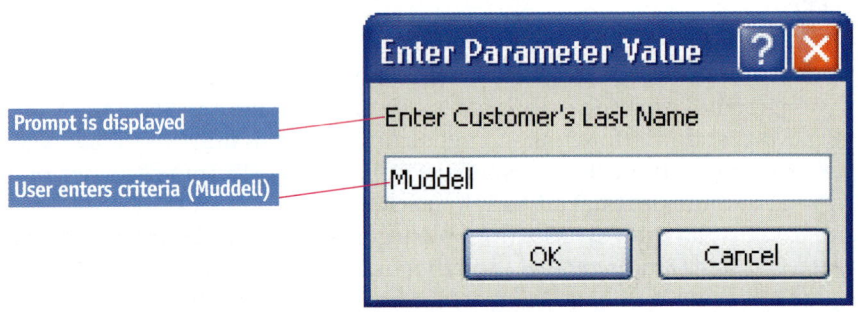

(b) Dialog Box

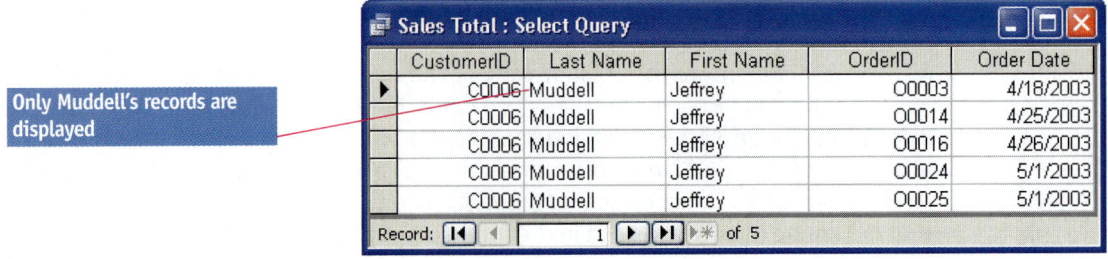

(c) Dynaset

FIGURE 6.7 Parameter Query

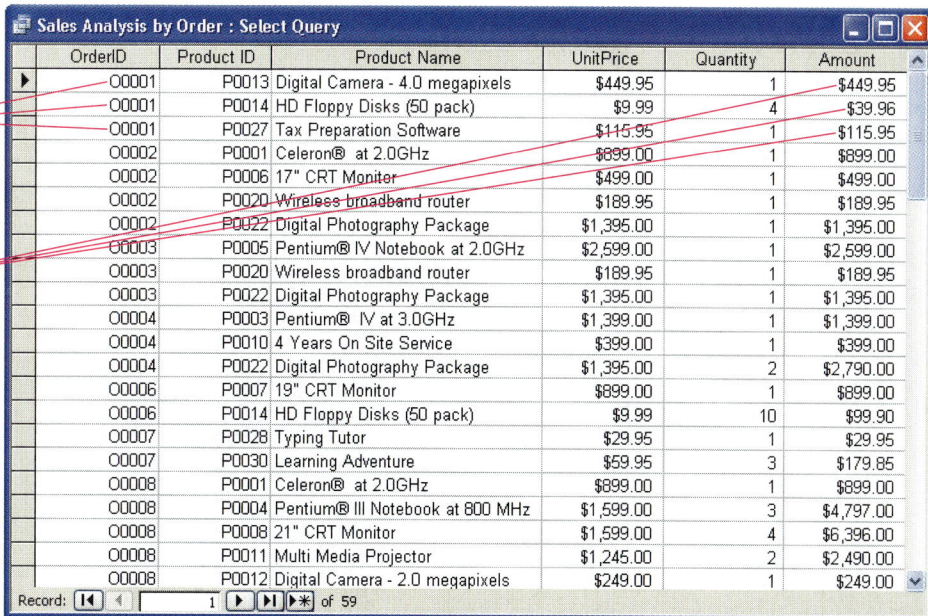

(a) Order Details with Product Information Dynaset

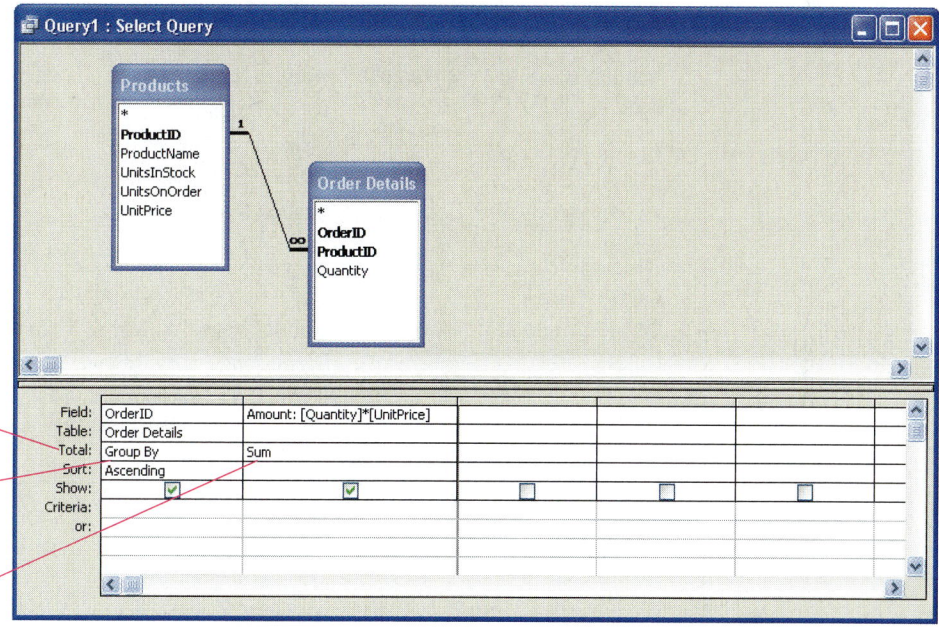

(b) Design grid

(c) Dynaset

FIGURE 6.8 Total Query

MICROSOFT OFFICE ACCESS 2003 1637

LEARNING BY DOING

The exercise that follows begins by having you create the report in Figure 6.9. The report is a detailed analysis of all orders, listing every product in every order. The report is based on a query containing fields from the Orders, Customers, Products, and Order Details tables. The exercise also provides practice in creating parameter queries and total queries. Note, too, the attractive formatting throughout the report in addition to the clip art in the report header.

Sales Analysis by Order
Prepared by: Your Name Goes Here

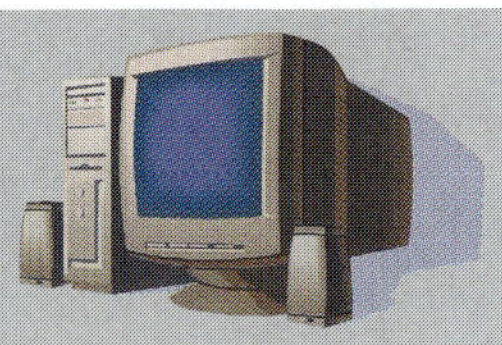

Order	Customer	Date	Product Name	Quantity	Unit Price	Amount
O0001	Colon	4/15/2003	Digital Camera - 4.0 megapixels	1	$449.95	$449.95
			HD Floppy Disks (50 pack)	4	$9.99	$39.96
			Tax Preparation Software	1	$115.95	$115.95
					Sum	$605.86
O0002	Goodman	4/18/2003	17" CRT Monitor	1	$499.00	$499.00
			Celeron® at 2.0GHz	1	$899.00	$899.00
			Digital Photography Package	1	$1,395.00	$1,395.00
			Wireless broadband router	1	$189.95	$189.95
					Sum	$2,982.95
O0003	Muddell	4/18/2003	Digital Photography Package	1	$1,395.00	$1,395.00
			Pentium® IV Notebook at 2.0GHz	1	$2,599.00	$2,599.00
			Wireless broadband router	1	$189.95	$189.95
					Sum	$4,183.95
O0004	Geoghegan	4/18/2003	4 Years On Site Service	1	$399.00	$399.00
			Digital Photography Package	2	$1,395.00	$2,790.00
			Pentium® IV at 3.0GHz	1	$1,399.00	$1,399.00
					Sum	$4,588.00
O0006	Lee	4/21/2003	19" CRT Monitor	1	$899.00	$899.00
			HD Floppy Disks (50 pack)	10	$9.99	$99.90
					Sum	$998.90

Wednesday, July 16, 2003   Page 1 of 5

FIGURE 6.9 Sales Analysis by Order

hands-on exercise

3 Advanced Queries

Objective To copy an existing query; to create a parameter query; to create a total query using the Aggregate Sum function. Use Figure 6.10 as a guide.

Step 1: **Create the Query**

- Open the **Computer Store database** from the previous exercise. Click the **Queries button** in the Database window. Double click **Create query in Design view** to display the Query Design window.

- By now you have had sufficient practice creating a query, so we will just outline the steps:
  - Add the **Customers**, **Orders**, **Products**, and **Order Details** tables. Move and size the field lists within the Query window to match Figure 6.10a. Maximize the window.
  - Add the **OrderID** field from the Orders table. Add the additional fields to the design grid as shown in Figure 6.10a. Be sure to take each field from the appropriate table.
  - Add the calculated field to compute the amount by multiplying the quantity by the unit price. Point to the expression, click the **right mouse button** to display a shortcut menu, then change the Format property to **Currency**.
  - Check that your query matches Figure 6.10a. Save the query as **Sales Analysis by Order**.

- Click the **Run button** (the exclamation point) to run the query. The dynaset contains one record for every item in every order.

- Close the query.

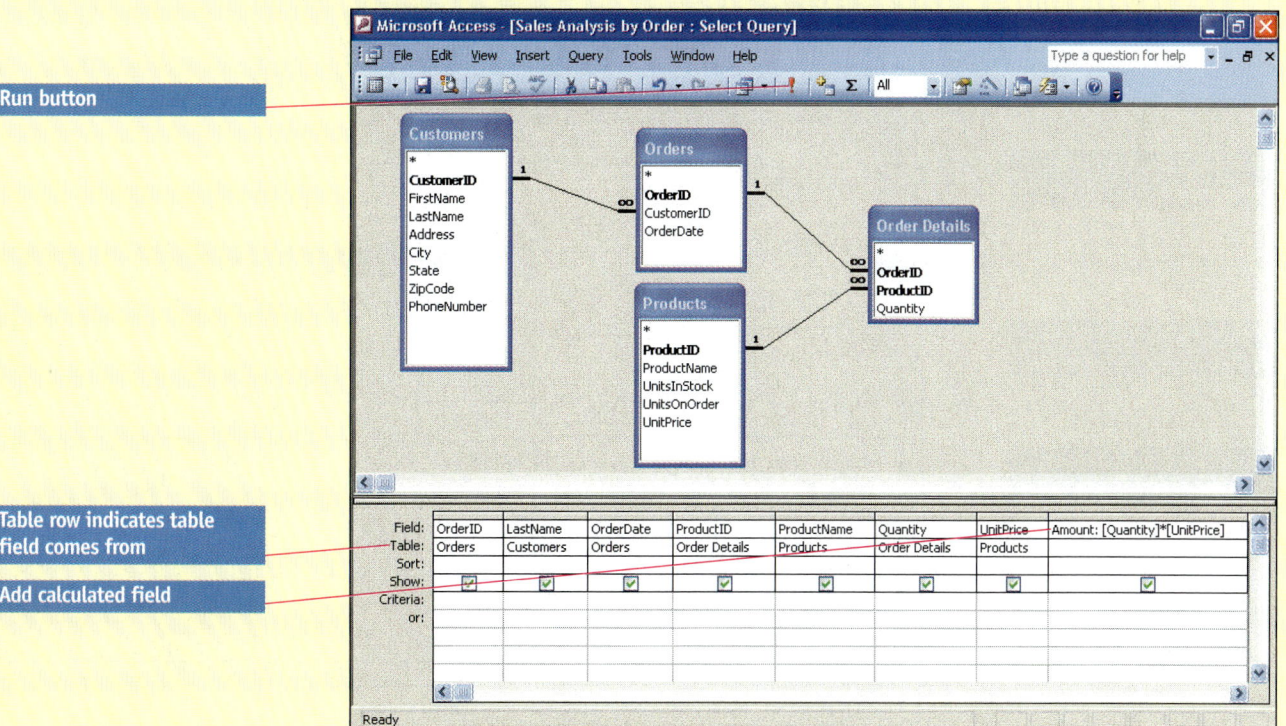

(a) Create the Query (step 1)

FIGURE 6.10 Hands-on Exercise 3

Step 2: **The Report Wizard**

- Click the **Reports button** in the Database window. Double click the **Create report by using wizard** icon to start the Report Wizard.

- Click the **drop-down arrow** to display the tables and queries in the database, then select **Sales Analysis by Order** (the query you just created).

- By now you have had sufficient practice using the Report Wizard, so we will just outline the steps:
  - Select all of the fields in the query *except* the ProductID. Click the **>> button** to move every field in the Available Fields list box to the Selected Fields list.
  - Select the **ProductID field** in the Selected Fields list and click the **< button** to remove this field. Click **Next**.
  - Group the report by **OrderID**. Click **Next**.
  - Sort the report by **ProductName**. Click the **Summary Options button** to display the Summary Options dialog box in Figure 6.10b. Check **Sum** under the Amount field. The option button to **Show Detail and Summary** is selected. Click **OK** to close the Summary Options dialog box. Click **Next**.
  - The **Stepped Layout** is selected, as is **Portrait orientation**. Be sure the box is checked to **Adjust field width so all fields fit on a page**. Click **Next**.
  - Choose **Soft Gray** as the style. Click **Next**.
  - **Sales Analysis by Order** is entered as the title of the report. The option button to **Preview the Report** is selected. Click **Finish**.

- The report you see approximates the finished report, but requires several modifications to improve the formatting. The OrderDate and LastName, for example, are repeated for every product in an order, when they should appear only once in the Group (OrderID) Header.

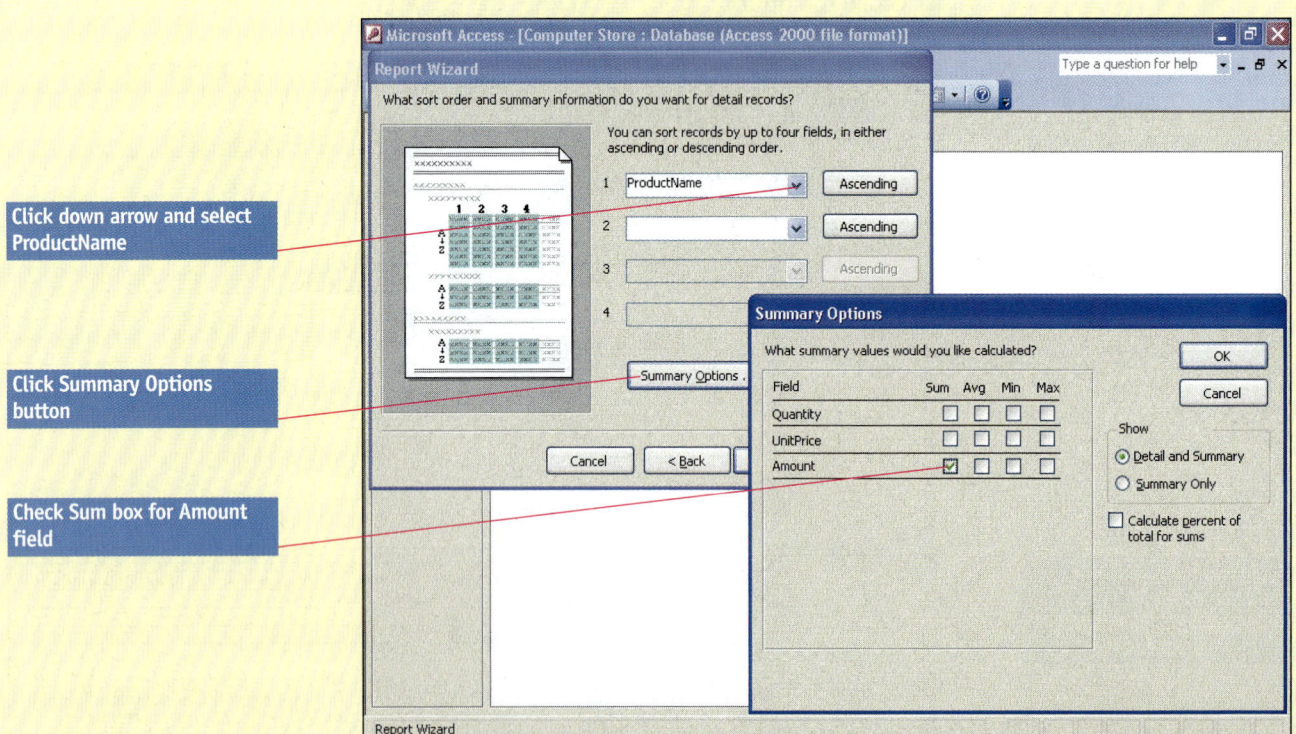

(b) The Report Wizard (step 2)

FIGURE 6.10 Hands-on Exercise 3 (*continued*)

CHAPTER 6: MANY-TO-MANY RELATIONSHIPS

Step 3: **Modify the Report Design**

- Change to **Design view**. Pull down the **View menu** and click the **Sorting and Grouping command** to display the dialog box in Figure 6.10c.

- Click in the **OrderID** box under Field/Expression. Click the **down arrow** in the **Keep Together property** and choose **Whole Group**. Close the dialog box.

- Press and hold the **Shift key** as you click the **LastName** and **OrderDate controls** in the Detail Area, then drag the controls to the Group Header next to the OrderID. Click anywhere to deselect the controls.

- Press and hold the **Shift key** to select the **OrderID**, **LastName**, and **OrderDate** labels in the Page Header. Press the **Del key** to delete the labels.

- Click and drag the **Product Name label** from the Page Header to the OrderID header. Press and hold the **Shift key** to select the remaining labels (**Quantity**, **UnitPrice**, and **Amount**) in the Page Header and drag them to the OrderID header. Move, size, and align the labels as necessary.

- Click the **OrderID control** in the Group Header. Click the **right mouse button**, click **Properties**, and change the Border Style to **Transparent**. Close the Properties dialog box. Move, size, and align the controls as necessary.

- Select (click) the first control in the OrderID footer (which begins with the literal ="Summary for). Press the **Del key**.

- Click and drag the unbound control containing the word **Sum** to the right of the Group Footer so that the label is next to the computed total for each order. (Change the contents of the label from "Sum" to **"Total"**.) Change the font size for the label and calculated control to **10 points**. Do the same for the **Grand Total** label in the Report Footer.

- Save the report, then click the **Report View button** to preview the report.

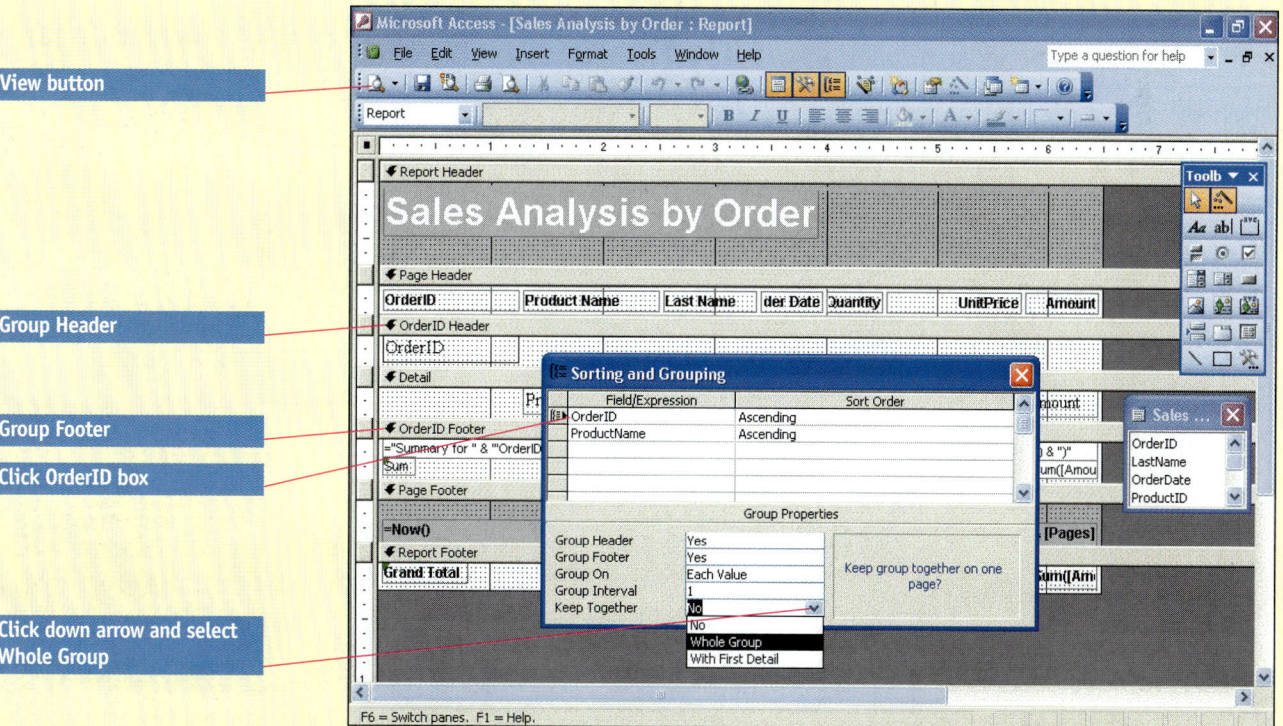

(c) Modify the Report Design (step 3)

FIGURE 6.10 Hands-on Exercise 3 (*continued*)

Step 4: **Complete the Report Design**

- Return to **Design view** as shown in Figure 6.10d. This is our goal, but do not be concerned if you do not duplicate our report exactly.
- Press and hold the **Shift key** to select the **OrderID**, **LastName**, and **OrderDate controls** in the OrderID header. These are controls and not labels. Change to **9 point bold Arial** to match the formatting of the labels in this header.
- Move and size the **ProductName**, **Quantity**, **UnitPrice**, and **Amount controls** in the Detail area so they are under their respective labels in the OrderID header. Change back and forth between Design view and Print Preview to check your work.
- Click the **Line tool**. Click at the bottom of the OrderID footer, then press and hold the **Shift key** as you drag the mouse to draw a line of approximately one inch. Right click the line, click the **Properties command**, then change the **width** to **6.5 inches**. Close the Properties sheet.
- Look closely and you will see a gray line in the Page Header. Select the line and click the **Del key**. Close the Page Header.
- Click in the Report Header. Use the **Label tool** to enter your name. Pull down the **Insert menu** and click the **Picture command** to display the Insert Picture dialog box. Change to the **Exploring Access folder**.
- Select the **Computer picture**, then click **OK** to insert the picture into the report. Be sure you insert the picture in the Report Header.
- **Right click** the picture to display a context-sensitive menu, then click **Properties** to display the Property dialog box. Click the **Size Mode property**, click the **down arrow**, and click **Stretch**. Close the Properties sheet.
- Click and drag to size the picture. Resize the Report Header as appropriate. View the report. Make additional corrections as necessary.

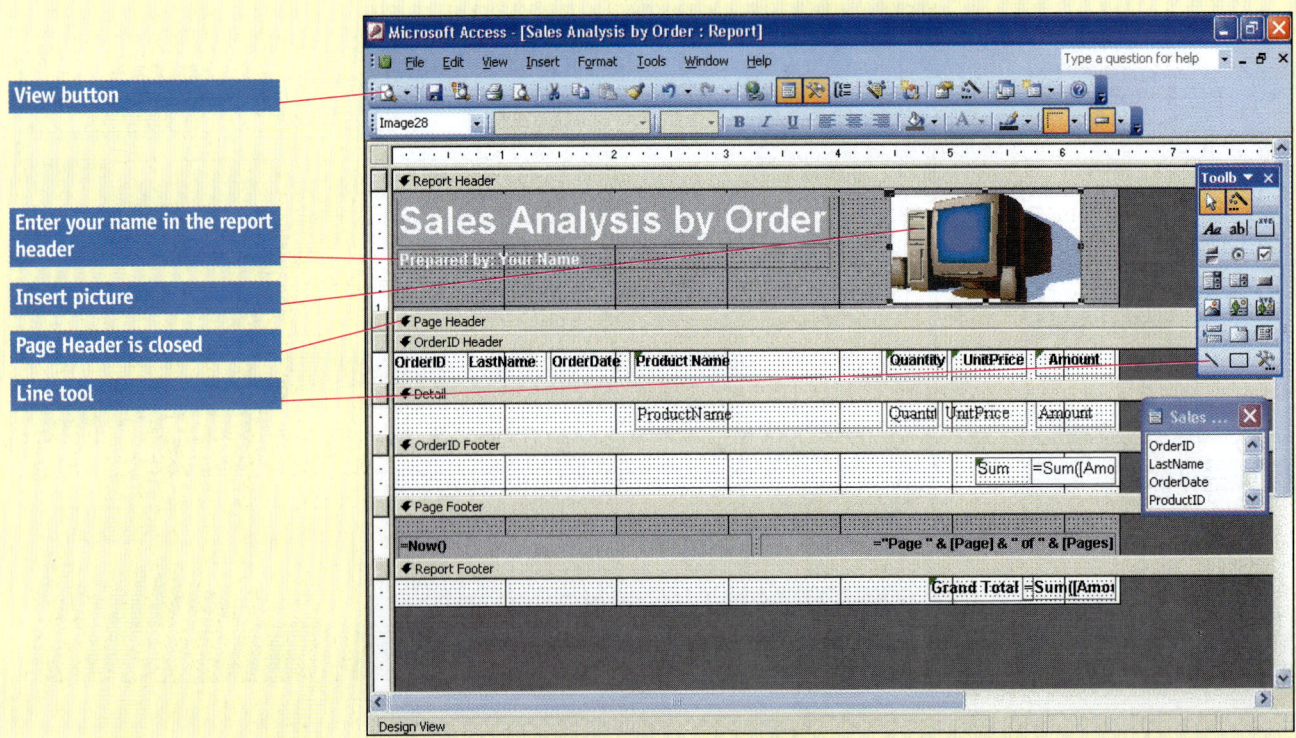

(d) Complete the Report Design (step 4)

FIGURE 6.10 Hands-on Exercise 3 (*continued*)

CHAPTER 6: MANY-TO-MANY RELATIONSHIPS

Step 5: **Print the Report**

- You should see the report in Figure 6.10e, which groups the reports by OrderID. The products are in alphabetical order within each order.

- Click the **Zoom button** to see the entire page. Click the **Zoom button** a second time to return to the higher magnification.

- Use the navigation buttons at the bottom of the window to see other pages in the report.

- Click the **Printer button** if you are satisfied with the appearance of the report, or return to the Design view to make any needed changes.

- Pull down the **File menu** and click **Close** to close the report. Click **Yes** if asked whether to save the changes.

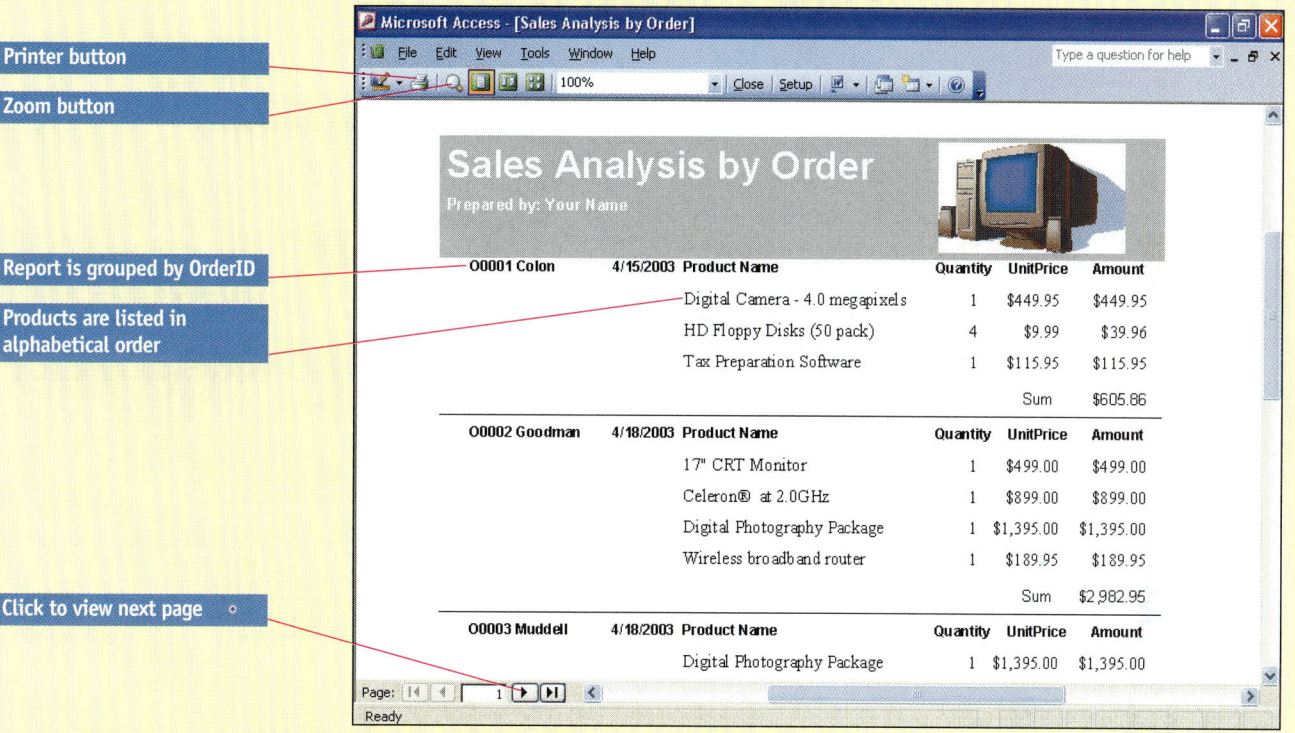

(e) Print the Report (step 5)

FIGURE 6.10 Hands-on Exercise 3 (*continued*)

THE UNMATCHED QUERY WIZARD

The cost of inventory is a significant expense for every business. It is one thing to maintain inventory of products that are selling well, and quite another to stock products that have never been ordered. The Unmatched Query Wizard identifies records in one table (such as the Products table) that do not have matching records in another table (such as the Order Details table). In other words, it will tell you which products (if any) have never been ordered. See exercise 2 at the end of the chapter.

Step 6: **Create a Total Query**

- Open the **Sales Analysis by Order** query in Design view as shown in Figure 6.10f. (The Save As dialog box is not yet visible.)

- Click the **column selector** for the **OrderDate field** to select the column. Press the **Del key** to delete the field from the query. Delete the **ProductID**, **ProductName**, **Quantity**, and **UnitPrice fields** in similar fashion.

- Pull down the **View menu** and click **Totals** to display the Total row (or click the **Totals button** on the toolbar).

- Click the **Total row** under the Amount field, then click the **drop-down arrow** to display the summary functions. Click **Sum** as shown in the figure.

- Pull down the **File menu** and click the **Save As command** to display the associated dialog box. Enter **Sales Total** as the name of the query. Click **OK**.

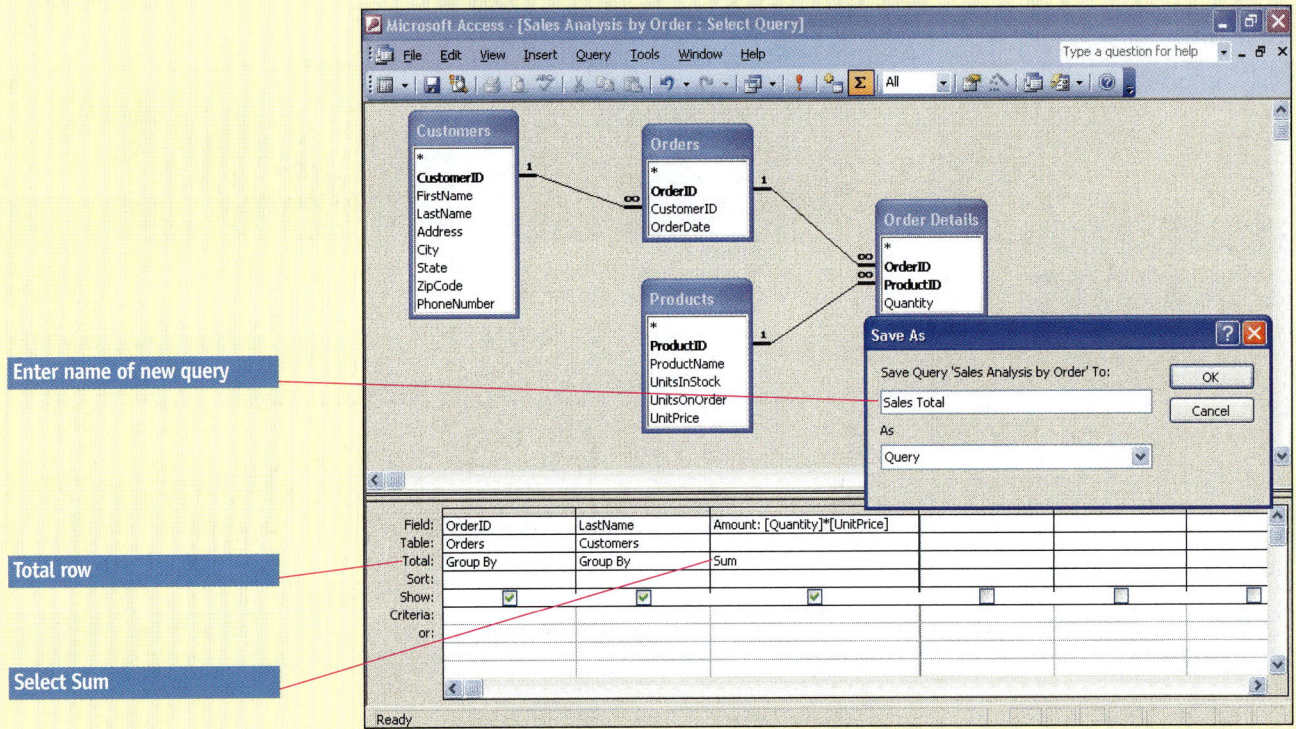

(f) Create a Total Query (step 6)

FIGURE 6.10 Hands-on Exercise 3 (*continued*)

THE DESCRIPTION PROPERTY

A working database will contain many different objects of the same type, making it all too easy to forget the purpose of the individual objects. The Description property helps you to remember. Point to any object within the Database window, click the right mouse button to display a shortcut menu, click Properties to display the Properties dialog box, enter an appropriate description, then click OK to close the Properties sheet. Once a description has been created, you can right click any object in the Database window, then click the Properties command from the shortcut menu to display the information.

Step 7: **Run the Query**

- Pull down the **Query menu** and click **Run** (or click the **Run button**) to run the query. You should see the datasheet in Figure 6.10g, which contains one record for each order with the total amount of that order.

- Click any field and attempt to change its value. You will be unable to do so as indicated by the beep.

- Print the dynaset for your instructor to show that you have successfully created the totals query.

- Click the **View button** to return to the Query Design view.

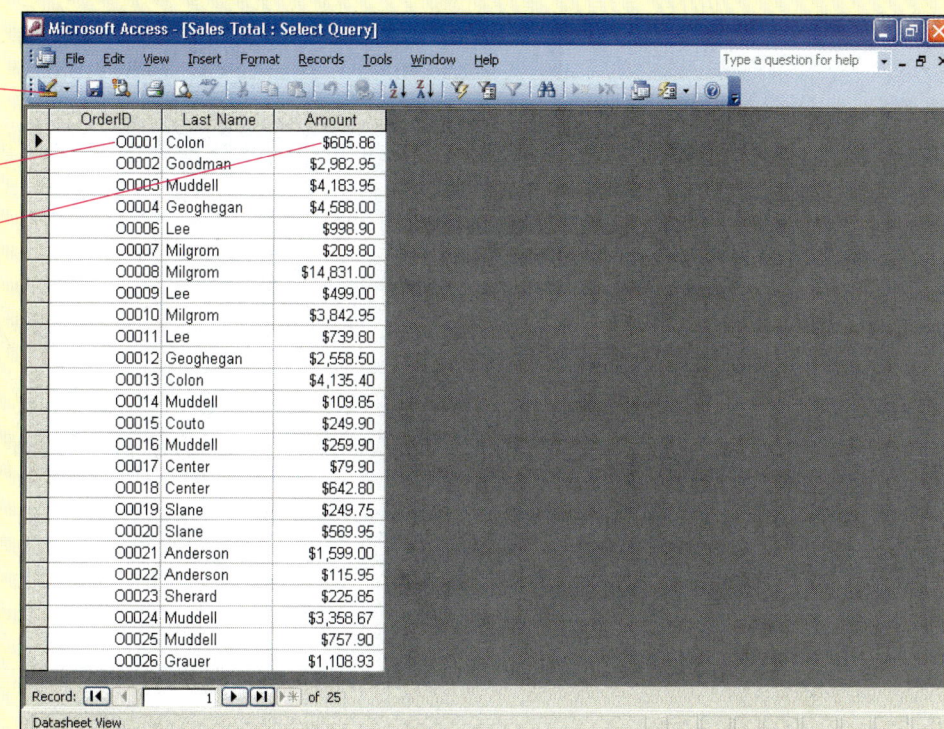

(g) Run the Query (step 7)

FIGURE 6.10   Hands-on Exercise 3 (*continued*)

UPDATING THE QUERY

The changes made to a query's dynaset are automatically made in the underlying table(s). Not every field in a query is updatable, however, and the easiest way to determine if you can change a value is to run the query, view the dynaset, and attempt to edit the field. Access will prevent you from updating a calculated field, a field based on an aggregate function (such as Sum or Count), or the join field on the "one side" of a one-to-many relationship. If you attempt to update a field you cannot change, the system will beep.

Step 8: **Create a Parameter Query**

- Click the **Criteria row** under **LastName**. Type **[Enter Customer's Last Name]**. Be sure to enclose the entry in square brackets.

- Pull down the **file menu**. Click **Save As**. Enter **Customer Parameter Query** in the Save Query "Sales Total" To box. Click **OK**.

- Run the query. Access will display the dialog box in Figure 6.10h, asking for the Customer's last name. Type **Muddell** and press **Enter**.

- Access displays the five orders for Jeffrey Muddell. (This is the same information that you retrieved manually when the database was presented at the beginning of the chapter.)

- Print the dynaset for your instructor. Close the query. Exit Access if you do not want to continue with the next exercise at this time.

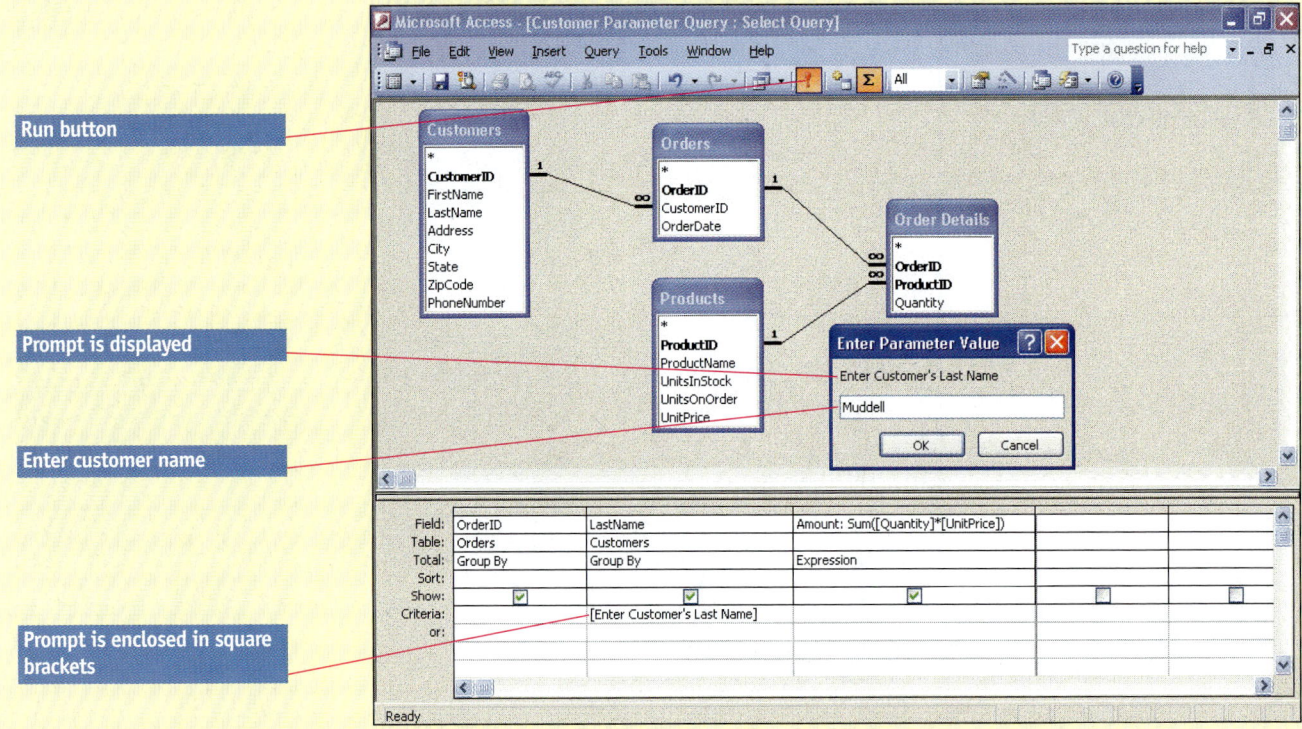

(h) Create a Parameter Query (step 8)

FIGURE 6.10 Hands-on Exercise 3 (*continued*)

THE TOPVALUES PROPERTY

The TopValues property returns a designated number of records rather than the entire dynaset. Open the query in Design view, then click the right mouse button *outside* the design grid to display a shortcut menu. Click Properties, click the box for TopValues, and enter the desired value as either a number or a percent; for example, 5 to list the top five records, or 5% to display the records that make up the top five percent. The dynaset must be in sequence according to the desired field for the TopValues property to work properly.

EXPANDING THE DATABASE

One of the advantages of an Access database is that it can be easily expanded to include additional data without disturbing the existing tables. The database used throughout the chapter consisted of four tables: a Customers table, a Products table, an Orders table, and an Order Details table. Figure 6.11 extends the Computer Super Store database to include a Sales Persons table with data about each member of the sales staff.

The salesperson helps the customer as he or she comes into the store, then receives a commission based on the order. There is a one-to-many relationship between the salesperson and orders. One salesperson can generate many orders, but an order can have only one salesperson. (One customer can work with a different salesperson each time he or she enters the store; i.e., there is no direct relationship between customers and the sales staff.) The Sales Persons and Orders tables are joined by the SalesPersonID field, which is common to both tables.

Figure 6.11 is similar to Figure 6.1 at the beginning of the chapter except that the Sales Persons table has been added and the Orders table has been expanded to include a SalesPersonID. This enables management to monitor the performance of the sales staff. Consider:

Query: How many orders has Cori Rice taken?
Answer: Cori has taken five orders.

The query is straightforward and easily answered. You would search the Sales Persons table for Cori Rice to determine her SalesPerson ID (S03). You would then search the Orders table and count the records containing S03 in the SalesPersonID field.

The Sales Persons table is also used to generate a report listing the commissions due to each salesperson. The store pays a 5% commission on every sale. It's easy to determine the salesperson for each order. It's more complicated to compute the commission. Consider:

Query: Which salesperson is associated with order O0003? When was this person hired?
Answer: Cori Rice is the salesperson for order O0003. Ms. Rice was hired on March 15, 1999.

The determination of the salesperson is straightforward, as all you have to do is search the Orders table to locate the order and obtain the SalesPerson ID (S03). You then search the Sales Persons table for this value (S03) and find the corresponding name (Cori Rice) and hire date (3/15/99).

Query: What is the commission on order O0003?
Answer: The commission on order O0003 is $209.20.

The calculation of the commission requires a fair amount of arithmetic. First, you need to compute the total amount of the order. Thus, you would begin in the Order Details table, find each product in order O0003, and multiply the quantity of that product by its unit price. The total cost of order O0003 is $4,183.95, based on one unit of product P0005 at $2,599, one unit of product P0020 at $189.95, and one unit of product P0022 at $1,395. (You can also refer to the sales report in Figure 6.9 that was developed in the previous exercise to check these calculations.)

Now that you know the total cost of the order, you can compute the commission, which is 5% of the total order, or $209.20 (.05 × $4,183.95). The complete calculation is lengthy, but Access does it automatically, and therein lies the beauty of a relational database.

(a) Customers Table

Customer ID	First Name	Last Name	Address	City	State	Zip Code	Phone Number
C0001	Benjamin	Lee	1000 Call Street	Tallahassee	FL	33340	(904) 327-4124
C0002	Eleanor	Milgrom	7245 NW 8 Street	Margate	FL	33065	(305) 974-1234
C0003	Neil	Goodman	4215 South 81 Street	Margate	FL	33065	(305) 444-5555
C0004	Nicholas	Colon	9020 N.W. 75 Street	Coral Springs	FL	33065	(305) 753-9887
C0005	Michael	Ware	276 Brickell Avenue	Miami	FL	33131	(305) 444-3980
C0006	Jeffrey	Muddell	9522 S.W. 142 Street	Miami	FL	33176	(305) 253-3909
C0007	Ashley	Geoghegan	7500 Center Lane	Coral Springs	FL	33070	(305) 753-7830
C0008	Serena	Sherard	5000 Jefferson Lane	Gainesville	FL	32601	(904) 375-6442
C0009	Luis	Couto	455 Bargello Avenue	Coral Gables	FL	33146	(305) 666-4801
C0010	Derek	Anderson	6000 Tigertail Avenue	Coconut Grove	FL	33120	(305) 446-8900
C0011	Lauren	Center	12380 S.W. 137 Avenue	Miami	FL	33186	(305) 385-4432
C0012	Robert	Slane	4508 N.W. 7 Street	Miami	FL	33131	(305) 635-3454

(b) Products Table

Product ID	Product Name	Units In Stock	Units On Order	UnitPrice
P0001	Celeron® at 2.0GHz	50	0	$899.00
P0002	Pentium® IV at 2.6GHz	25	5	$1,099.00
P0003	Pentium® IV at 3.0GHz	125	15	$1,399.00
P0004	Pentium® III Notebook at 800 MHz	25	50	$1,599.00
P0005	Pentium® IV Notebook at 2.0GHz	15	25	$2,599.00
P0006	17" CRT Monitor	50	0	$499.00
P0007	19" CRT Monitor	25	10	$899.00
P0008	21" CRT Monitor	50	20	$1,599.00
P0009	2 Years On Site Service	15	20	$299.00
P0010	4 Years On Site Service	25	15	$399.00
P0011	Multi Media Projector	10	0	$1,245.00
P0012	Digital Camera - 2.0 megapixels	40	0	$249.00
P0013	Digital Camera - 4.0 megapixels	50	15	$449.95
P0014	HD Floppy Disks (50 pack)	500	200	$9.99
P0015	CD-R (25 pack spindle)	100	50	$14.79
P0016	Digital Scanner	15	3	$179.95
P0017	Serial Mouse	150	50	$69.95
P0018	Trackball	55	0	$59.95
P0019	Joystick	250	100	$39.95
P0020	Wireless broadband router	35	10	$189.95
P0021	Fax/Modem 56 Kbps	20	0	$65.95
P0022	Digital Photography Package	100	15	$1,395.00
P0023	Ink Jet Printer	50	50	$249.95
P0024	Laser Printer (personal)	125	25	$569.95
P0025	Windows® XP Home Edition	400	200	$95.95
P0026	Antivirus/Firewall Upgrade	150	50	$75.95
P0027	Tax Preparaton Software	150	50	$115.95
P0028	Typing Tutor	75	25	$29.95
P0029	Microsoft Office Home Edition	250	100	$129.95
P0030	Learning Adventure	25	10	$59.95
P0031	Surge Protector	15	0	$45.95

(c) Orders Table

OrderID	CustomerID	Order Date	SalesPersonID
O001	C0004	4/15/2003	S01
O002	C0003	4/18/2003	S02
O003	C0006	4/18/2003	S03
O004	C0007	4/18/2003	S04
O006	C0001	4/21/2003	S05
O007	C0002	4/21/2003	S01
O008	C0002	4/22/2003	S02
O009	C0001	4/22/2003	S03
O010	C0002	4/22/2003	S04
O011	C0001	4/24/2003	S05
O012	C0007	4/24/2003	S01
O013	C0004	4/24/2003	S02
O014	C0006	4/25/2003	S03
O015	C0009	4/25/2003	S04
O016	C0006	4/26/2003	S05
O017	C0011	4/26/2003	S01
O018	C0011	4/26/2003	S02
O019	C0012	4/27/2003	S03
O020	C0012	4/28/2003	S04
O021	C0010	4/29/2003	S05
O022	C0010	4/29/2003	S01
O023	C0008	4/30/2003	S02
O024	C0006	5/1/2003	S03
O025	C0006	5/1/2003	S04

(d) Order Details Table

OrderID	ProductID	Quantity
O0001	P0013	1
O0001	P0014	4
O0001	P0027	1
O0002	P0001	1
O0002	P0006	1
O0002	P0020	1
O0002	P0022	1
O0003	P0005	1
O0003	P0020	1
O0003	P0022	1
O0004	P0003	1
O0004	P0010	1
O0004	P0022	2
O0006	P0007	1
O0006	P0014	10
O0007	P0028	1
O0007	P0030	3
O0008	P0001	1
O0008	P0004	3
O0008	P0008	4
O0008	P0011	2
O0008	P0012	1
O0009	P0006	1
O0010	P0002	2
O0010	P0022	1
O0010	P0023	1
O0011	P0016	2
O0011	P0020	2
O0012	P0021	10
O0012	P0029	10
O0012	P0030	10
O0013	P0009	4
O0013	P0016	10
O0013	P0024	2
O0014	P0019	2
O0014	P0028	1
O0015	P0018	1
O0015	P0020	1
O0016	P0029	2
O0017	P0019	2
O0018	P0009	1
O0018	P0025	2
O0018	P0026	2
O0019	P0014	25
O0020	P0024	1
O0021	P0004	1
O0022	P0027	1
O0023	P0021	1
O0023	P0028	1
O0023	P0029	1
O0024	P0007	1
O0024	P0013	5
O0024	P0014	3
O0024	P0016	1
O0025	P0012	2
O0025	P0029	2

(e) Sales Persons Table

SalesPersonID	First Name	Last Name	Work Phone	Hire Date
S01	Linda	Black	(305) 284-6105	2/3/2000
S02	Michael	Vaughn	(305) 284-3993	2/10/2001
S03	Cori	Rice	(305) 284-2557	3/15/1999
S04	Karen	Ruenheck	(305) 284-4641	11/24/2002
S05	Richard	Linger	(305) 284-4662	1/21/2003

FIGURE 6.11 Super Store Database

The Sales Commission Query

Figure 6.12a displays the design view of a parameter query to calculate the commissions for a specific sales person. (This query determines the commissions for Cori Rice, which you computed manually in the previous discussion.) Enter the last name of the sales associate, Rice, and the query returns the dynaset in Figure 6.12b, showing all of her commissions. Note, too, that the commission returned for order O0003 is $209.20, which corresponds to the amount we arrived at earlier.

The query in Figure 6.12a includes fields from all five tables in the database. The relationships are shown graphically in the top half of the query window and reflect the earlier discussion—for example, the one-to-many relationship between salespersons and orders. These tables are joined through the SalesPersonID field, which is the primary key in the Sales Persons table but a foreign key in the Orders table. (The Orders table has been modified to include this field.)

The query can easily be modified to show the sales commission on every order by removing the criteria under the salesperson's last name. The resulting query will then compute the commissions for every salesperson and can be used as the basis of the sales commission report in Figure 6.12c.

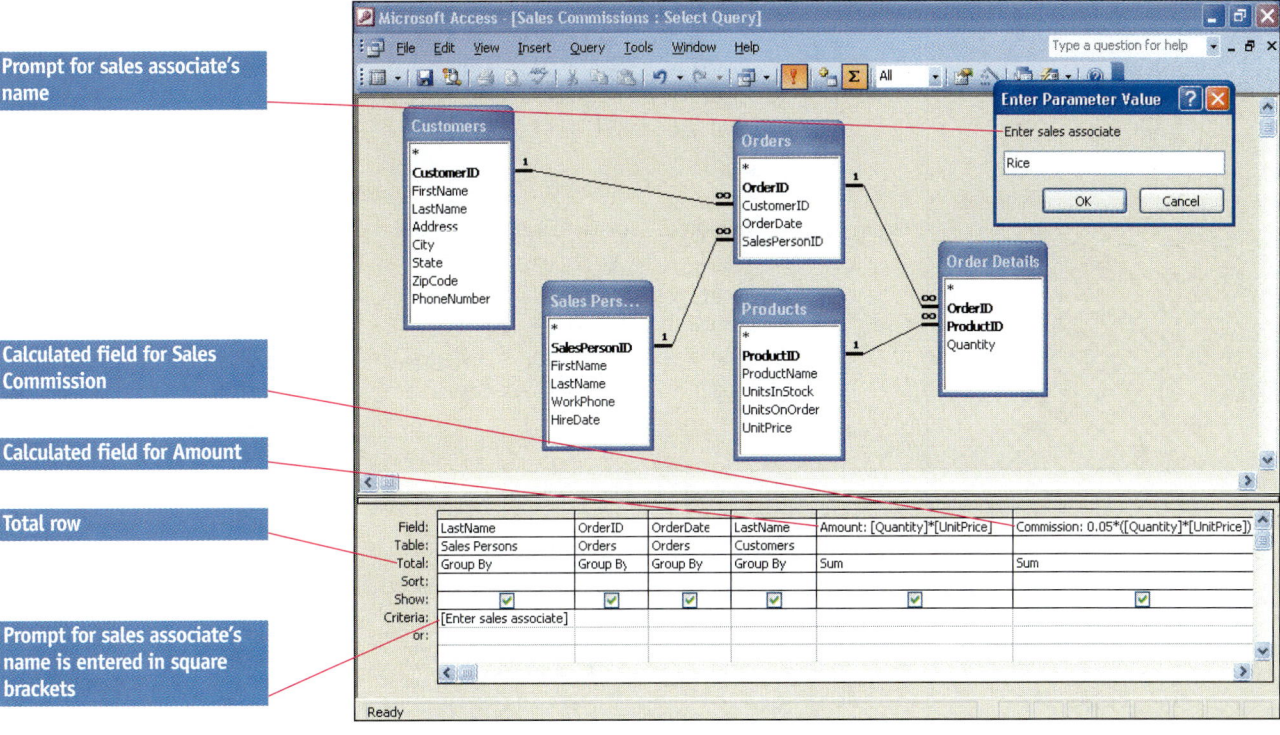

(a) Design View

(b) Dynaset

FIGURE 6.12 Sales Commissions

The report in Figure 6.12c parallels the sales analysis report of Figure 6.9 that was developed in the previous hands-on exercise. This time, however, the entries in the report are grouped by salesperson and sorted by OrderID for each salesperson. The total sales and commission for each salesperson are also calculated.

The exercise that follows has you import the Sales Persons table from another database. It then directs you to modify the existing Orders table to include a SalesPersonID, which references the records in the Sales Persons table, and finally to modify the Computer Store Order form to include the salesperson data. The sales commission report is left to you as an end-of-chapter exercise.

Sales Commission Report
Prepared by: Your Name Goes Here

Black	OrderID	Order Date	Last Name	Amount	Commission
	O0001	4/15/2003	Colon	$605.86	$30.29
	O0007	4/21/2003	Milgrom	$209.80	$10.49
	O0012	4/24/2003	Geoghegan	$2,558.50	$127.93
	O0017	4/26/2003	Center	$79.90	$4.00
	O0022	4/29/2003	Anderson	$115.95	$5.80
	O0027	7/17/2003	Grauer	$2,698.00	$134.90
			Total:	$6,268.01	$313.40
Linger	OrderID	Order Date	Last Name	Amount	Commission
	O0006	4/21/2003	Lee	$998.90	$49.95
	O0011	4/24/2003	Lee	$739.80	$36.99
	O0016	4/26/2003	Muddell	$259.90	$13.00
	O0021	4/29/2003	Anderson	$1,599.00	$79.95
	O0026	7/16/2003	Grauer	$1,108.93	$55.45
			Total:	$4,706.53	$235.33
Rice	OrderID	Order Date	Last Name	Amount	Commission
	O0003	4/18/2003	Muddell	$4,183.95	$209.20
	O0009	4/22/2003	Lee	$499.00	$24.95
	O0014	4/25/2003	Muddell	$109.85	$5.49
	O0019	4/27/2003	Slane	$249.75	$12.49
	O0024	5/1/2003	Muddell	$3,358.67	$167.93
			Total:	$8,401.22	$420.06
Ruenheck	OrderID	Order Date	Last Name	Amount	Commission
	O0004	4/18/2003	Geoghegan	$4,588.00	$229.40
	O0010	4/22/2003	Milgrom	$3,842.95	$192.15
	O0015	4/25/2003	Couto	$249.90	$12.50
	O0020	4/28/2003	Slane	$569.95	$28.50
	O0025	5/1/2003	Muddell	$757.90	$37.90
			Total:	$10,008.70	$500.44

Thursday, July 17, 2003   Page 1 of 2

(c) Sales Commission Report

FIGURE 6.12 Sales Commissions (*continued*)

hands-on exercise

4 Expanding the Database

Objective To import a table from another database; to modify the design of an existing table. Use Figure 6.13 as a guide in the exercise.

Step 1: **Import the Sales Persons Table**

- Open the **Computer Store database**. Click the **Tables button**. Pull down the **File menu**. Click **Get External Data**, then click the **Import command**.

- Click (select) the **Sales Persons database** from the **Exploring Access folder**, then click **Import** to display the Import Objects dialog box in Figure 6.13a.

- If necessary, click the **Tables button**, click **SalesPersons** (the only table in this database), then click **OK**.

- A dialog box will appear briefly on your screen as the Sales Persons table is imported into the Computer Store database.

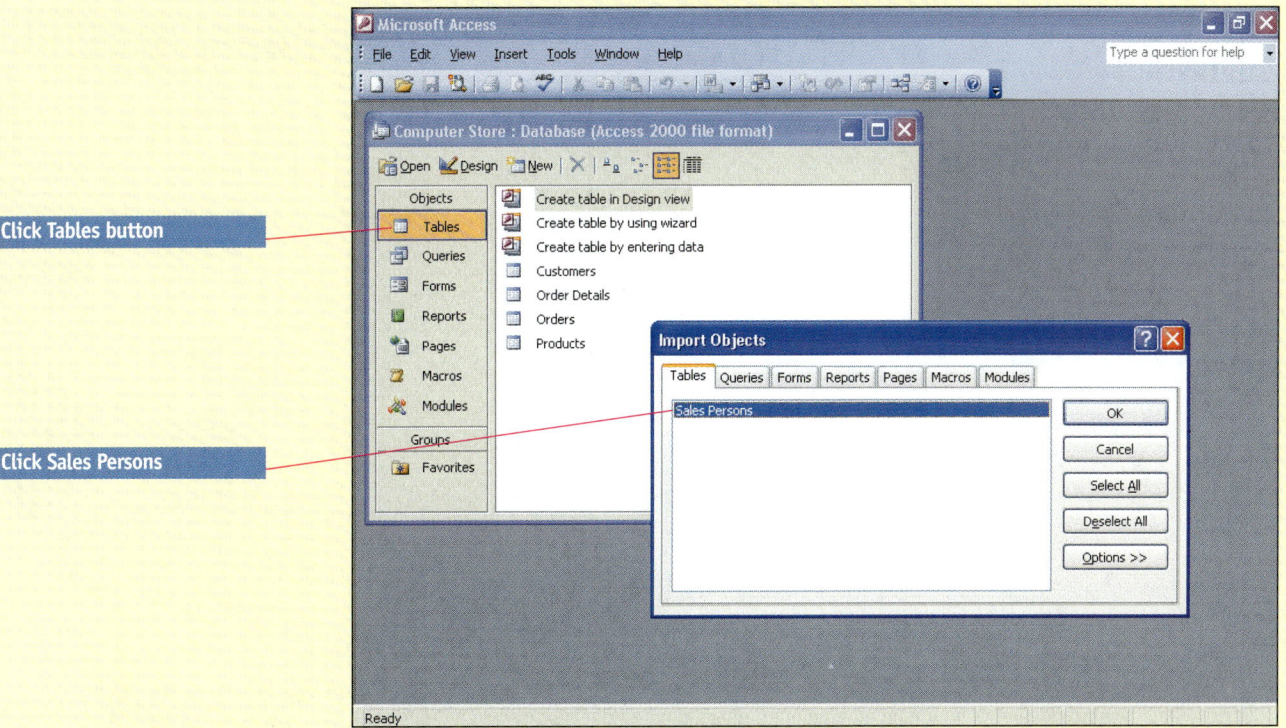

(a) Import the Sales Persons Table (step 1)

FIGURE 6.13 Hands-on Exercise 4

THE DOCUMENTS SUBMENU

The My Recent Documents menu in Windows XP contains shortcuts to the last 15 files that were opened. Click the Start button, click (or point to) the My Recent Documents menu, then click the document you wish to open (e.g., Computer Store), assuming that it appears on the menu. Windows will start the application, then open the indicated document.

Step 2: **Modify the Orders Table Design**

- Select the **Orders table** from the Database window as shown in Figure 6.13b. Click the **Design button**.

- Click in the first available row in the **Field Name** column. Enter **SalesPersonID** as shown in Figure 6.13b. Choose **Number** as the data type. The Field Size property changes to Long Integer by default.
  - Click the **Format** property. Enter **\S00**.
  - Click the **Default Value** property and delete the **0**.

- Click the **Save button** to save the modified design of the Orders table. You will enter data for the new field in the next step.

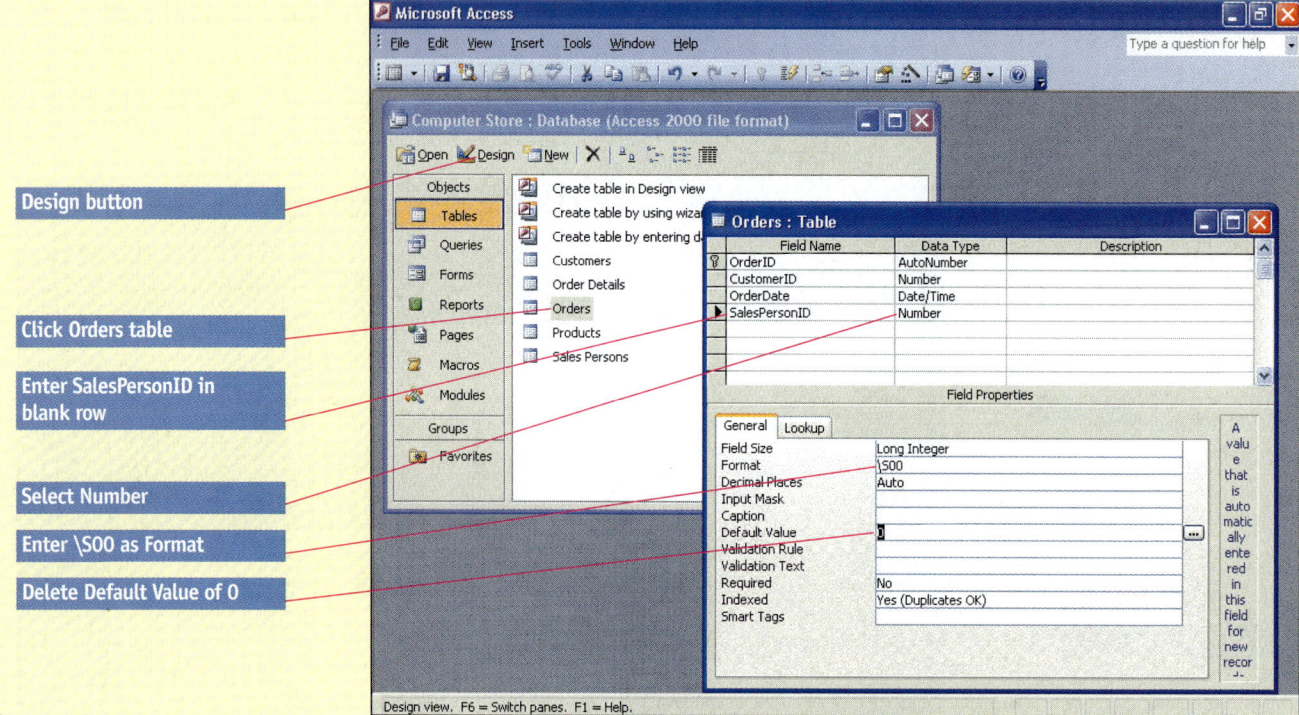

(b) Modify the Orders Table Design (step 2)

FIGURE 6.13 Hands-on Exercise 4 (*continued*)

RELATIONSHIPS AND THE AUTONUMBER FIELD TYPE

The join fields on both sides of a relationship must be the same data type—for example, both number fields or both text fields. The AutoNumber field type, however, cannot be specified on both sides of a relationship. Thus, if the join field (SalesPersonID) in the primary table (Sales Persons) is an AutoNumber field, the join field in the related table (Orders) must be specified as a Number field, with the Field Size property set to Long Integer.

Step 3: **Add the Sales Person to Existing Orders**

- Click the **Datasheet View button** to change to the Datasheet view as shown in Figure 6.13c. Maximize the window.
- Enter the **SalesPersonID** for each existing order as shown in Figure 6.13c.
- Enter only the number (e.g., 1, rather than S0001) as the S and leading zeros are displayed automatically through the Format property. We are adding the data in random fashion so that we will be able to generate meaningful reports later on in the exercise.
- You should now set the Required property for the SalesPersonID in the Orders table to **Yes** to make this a required field for new orders.
- Close the Orders table. Click **Yes** if prompted to save the table. Click **Yes** to retain the changes to the data integrity rules.

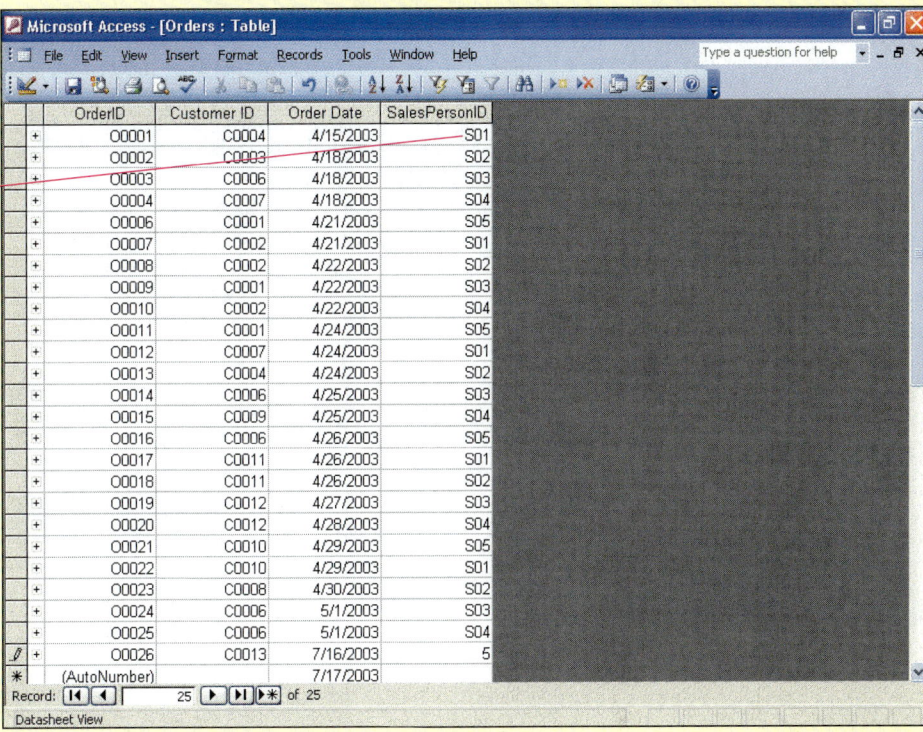

Enter SalesPersonID for each order (enter 1,2,3,4, or 5 only)

(c) Add the Sales Person to Existing Orders (step 3)

FIGURE 6.13 Hands-on Exercise 4 (*continued*)

HIDE THE WINDOWS TASKBAR

The Windows taskbar is great for novices because it makes task switching as easy as changing channels on a TV. It also takes up valuable real estate on the desktop, and hence you may want to hide the taskbar when you don't need it. Point to an empty area on the taskbar, click the right mouse button to display a shortcut menu, and click Properties to display the Taskbar Properties dialog box. Click the Taskbar tab (if necessary), check the box to Autohide the taskbar, and click OK. The taskbar should disappear. Now point to the bottom of the screen (or the edge where the taskbar was last displayed), and it will reappear.

Step 4: **Create the Relationship**

- Pull down the **Tools menu**. Click **Relationships** to open the Relationships window as shown in Figure 6.13d. (The Sales Persons table is not yet visible.) Click the **Maximize button**.
- If necessary, drag the bottom border of the **Orders table** until you see the SalesPersonID (the field you added in step 2).
- Pull down the **Relationships menu**. Click **Show Table**. Click the **Tables button** if necessary, select the **Sales Persons table**, then click the **Add button**. Close the Show Table dialog box.
- Drag the title bar of the **Sales Persons table** to position the table as shown in Figure 6.13d. Drag the **SalesPersonID field** from the Sales Persons table to the SalesPersonID in the Orders table.
- Check the box to **Enforce Referential Integrity**. Click the **Create button** to create the relationship. Click the **Save button** to save the Relationships window.
- Close the Relationships window.

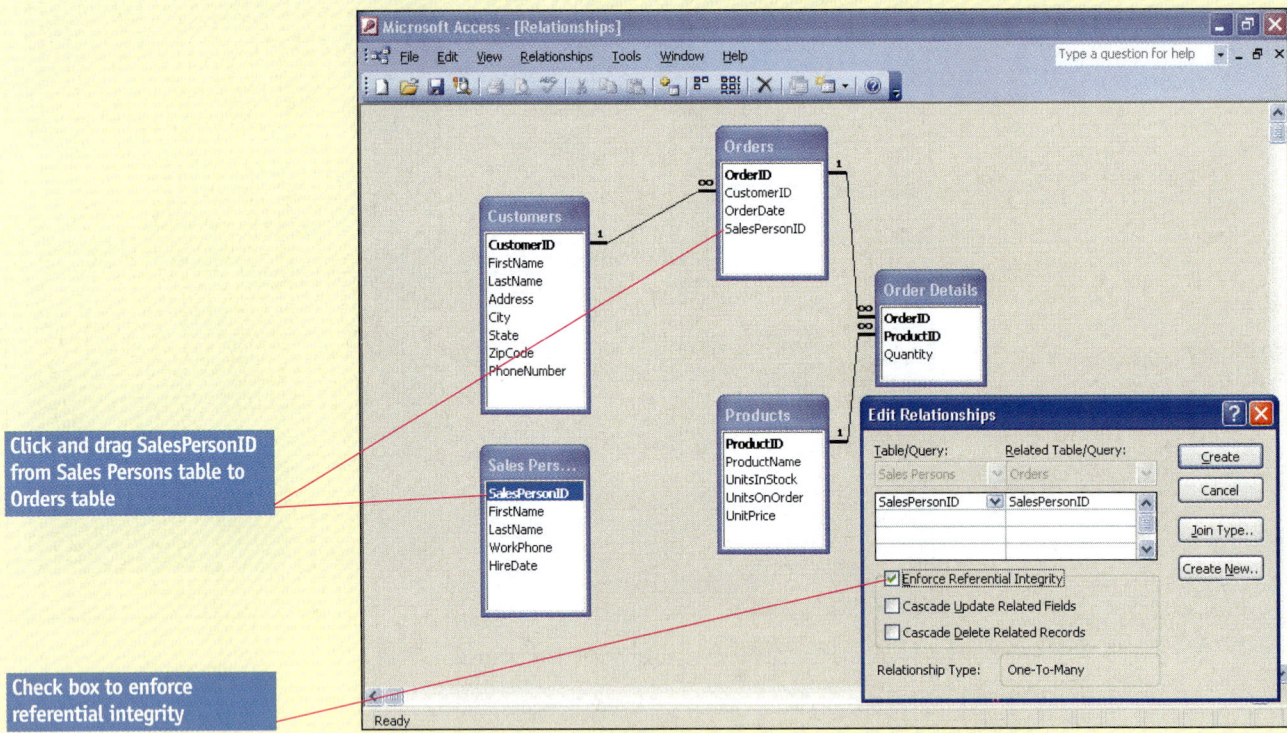

(d) Create the Relationship (step 4)

FIGURE 6.13 Hands-on Exercise 4 (*continued*)

PRINT THE RELATIONSHIPS

Pull down the Tools menu and click the Relationships command to open the Relationships window, then pull down the File menu and click the Print Relationships command. You will see the Print Preview screen of a report that displays the contents of the Relationships window. Click the Print button to print the report, or change to the Design view to modify the report, perhaps by adding your name. Save the report after printing so that it will be available at a later time.

Step 5: Modify the Order with Customer Information Query

- You should be back in the Database window. Click the **Queries button**, select the **Order with Customer Information query**, then click the **Design button** to open the query in the Design view as shown in Figure 6.13e.

- If necessary, click and drag the border of the **Orders table** so that the newly added SalesPersonID field is displayed. Click the **horizontal scroll arrow** until a blank column in the design grid is visible.

- Click and drag the **SalesPersonID** from the Orders table to the first blank column in the design grid.

- Save the query. Close the query.

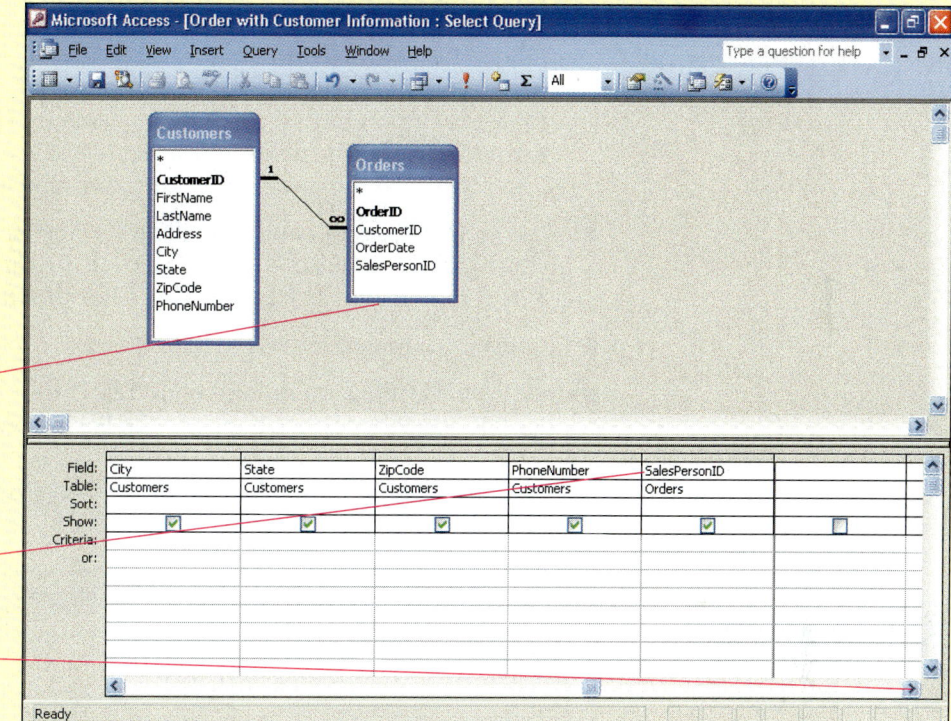

(e) Modify the Order with Customer Information Query (step 5)

FIGURE 6.13 Hands-on Exercise 4 (*continued*)

OPTIMIZE QUERIES USING INDEXES

The performance of a database becomes important as you progress from a "student" database with a limited number of records to a real database with large tables. Thus, it becomes advantageous to optimize the performance of individual queries by creating indexes in the underlying tables. Indexes should be specified for any criteria field in a query, as well as for any field that is used in a relationship to join two tables. To create an index, open the table in Design view and set the indexed property to Yes.

Step 6: **Modify the Order Form**

- You should be back in the Database window. Click the **Forms button**, select the **Super Store Order Form**, then click the **Design button**.

- Move and size the controls on the first line to make room for the SalesPersonID as shown in Figure 6.13f.

- Click the **Combo Box tool**, then click and drag in the form where you want the combo box to go. Release the mouse to start the Combo Box Wizard.
  - Check the option button that indicates you want the combo box to look up values in a table or query. Click **Next**.
  - Choose the **Sales Persons table** in the next screen. Click **Next**.
  - Select the **SalesPersonID** and **LastName**. Click **Next**.
  - Click the **down arrrow** in the first text box and click **Last Name** to sort the list alphabetically by last name. Click **Next**.
  - Adjust the column width if necessary. Be sure the box to hide the key column is checked. Click **Next**.
  - Click the option button to store the value in the field. Click the **drop-down arrow** to display the fields and select the **SalesPersonID field**. Click **Next**.
  - Enter **Sales Person** as the label for the combo box. Click **Finish**.

- Move and/or size the combo box and its label so that it is spaced attractively on the form. Point to the combo box, click the **right mouse button** to display a shortcut menu, and click **Properties**. Click the **Other tab**.

- Change the name of the box to **Sales Person**. Close the dialog box.

- Pull down the **View menu** and click **Tab Order**. Click the **AutoOrder button**. Click **OK**. Save the form. Change to the **Form view**.

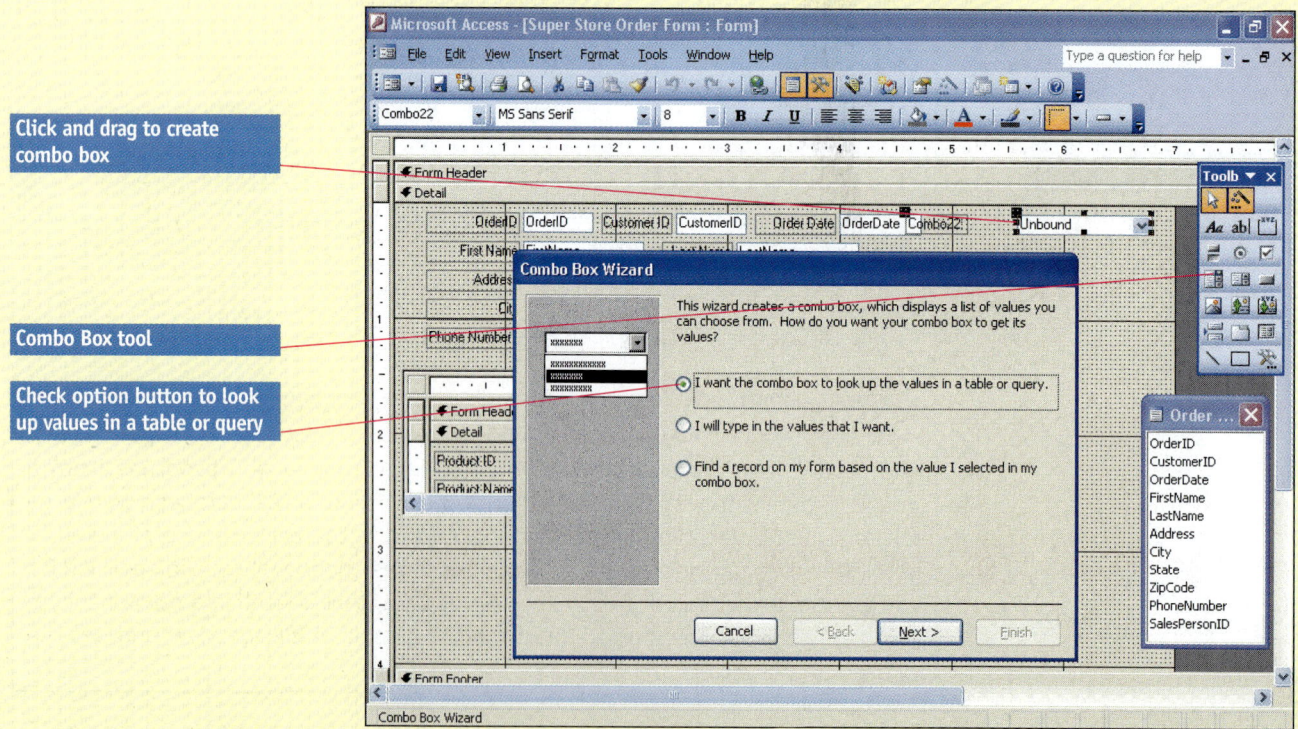

(f) Modify the Order Form (step 6)

FIGURE 6.13 Hands-on Exercise 4 (*continued*)

Step 7: **The Completed Order Form**

- You should see the completed form as shown in Figure 6.13g. Click the **New Record button** on the Form View toolbar to display a blank form.

- Click in the **Customer ID text box**. Enter **13** (your customer number from the first exercise), then press the **Tab key** to move to the next field.

- The OrderID is entered automatically as it is an AutoNumber field. Your customer information is entered automatically because of the AutoLookup feature. Today's date is entered automatically as the order date.

- Click the **drop-down arrow** on the Sales Person combo box. Select **Black** (or click in the box and type **B**), and the complete name is entered automatically.

- Click the **ProductID text box** in the subform. Enter **2** (not P0002) and press **Enter**. The Product Name and Unit Price are entered automatically.

- Press the **Tab key** twice to move to the Quantity field. Enter **1**. The amount is computed automatically. Close the Order form.

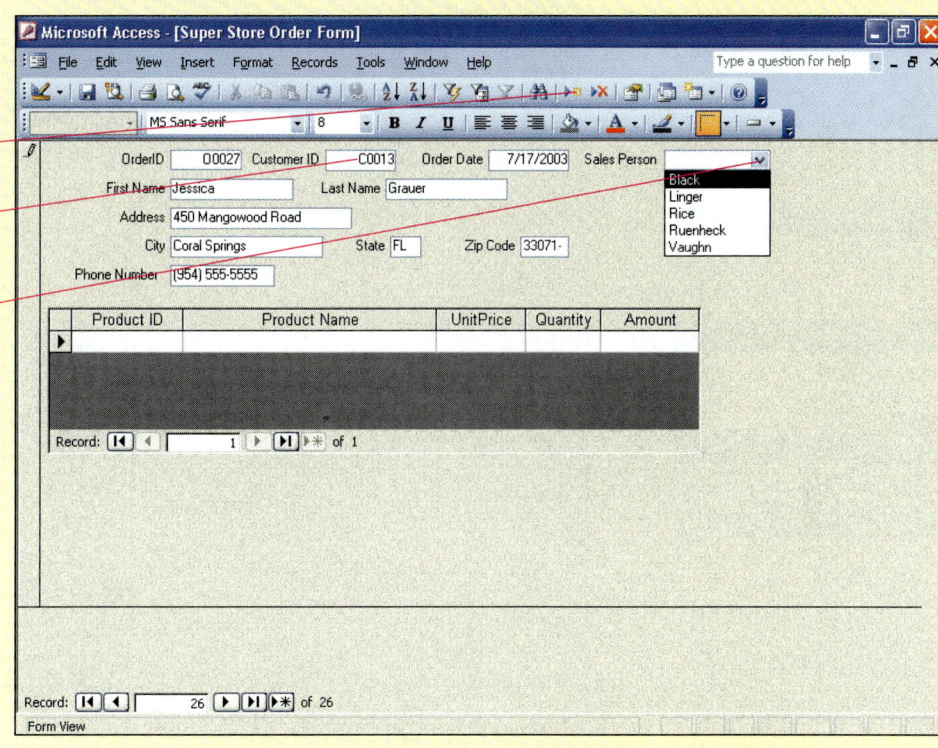

(g) The Completed Order Form (step 7)

FIGURE 6.13 Hands-on Exercise 4 (*continued*)

ENTER A NEW CUSTOMER

The Order form is based on a query that contains required fields from both the Customers table and the Orders table, enabling you to add a new customer at the same time you enter his or her order. Click the New Record button to add a new order. Skip the OrderID, CustomerID, and Order Date fields, and then select the Sales Person. Click in the First Name text box, enter a value, press Tab, and notice that a value has been entered into the CustomerID field for the new customer. Continue to add the customer information, and then complete the order in the usual fashion. See exercise 3 at the end of the chapter.

Step 8: **Database Properties**

- You should be back in the Database window. Pull down the **File menu** and click **Database Properties** to display the dialog box in Figure 6.13h.

- Click the **Contents tab** to display the contents of the Computer Store database.
  - There are five tables (Customers, Order Details, Orders, Products, and Sales Persons).
  - There are five queries, which include the Total and Parameter queries you created in Hands-on Exercise 3.
  - There are three forms—the main form, which you have completed in this exercise, the associated subform, and an About Super Store form for use in an end-of-chapter exercise.
  - There is one report, the report you created in exercise 3.

- Click **OK** to close the dialog box. Close the Computer Store database. Exit Access. Congratulations on a job well done.

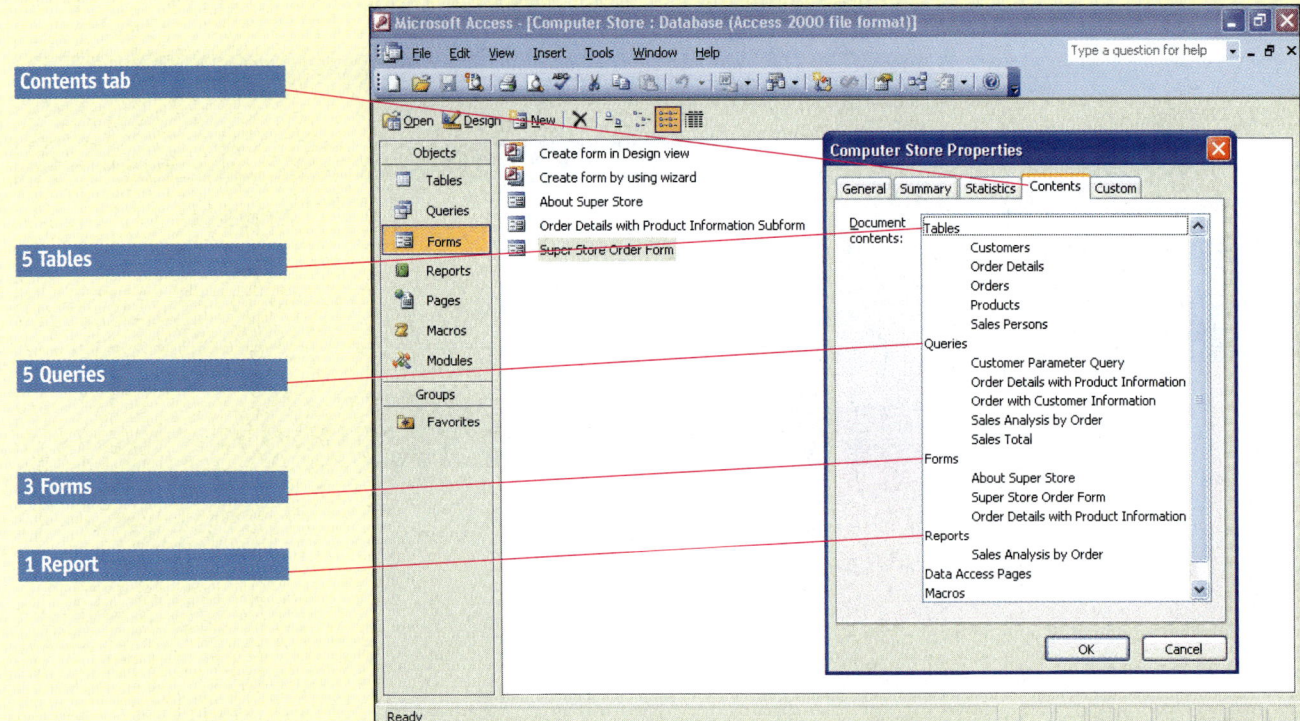

(h) Database Properties (step 8)

FIGURE 6.13   Hands-on Exercise 4 (*continued*)

OBJECT DEPENDENCIES

The objects in an Access database depend on one another; for example, a report is created from a query, which in turn is created from a table. Over time, the report may become obsolete, so you delete the report and the underlying query; but if the same query were the basis of another report, the latter object would no longer function. The ability to view object dependencies can prevent this type of error from occurring. Select the object in the Database window, pull down the View menu, and click Object Dependencies. Click OK if prompted to turn the feature on. The task pane will open, and you will see the objects that depend on the selected object.

SUMMARY

The implementation of a many-to-many relationship requires an additional table whose primary key consists of (at least) the primary keys of the individual tables. The many-to-many table may also contain additional fields whose values are dependent on the combined key. All relationships are created in the Relationships window by dragging the join field from the primary table to the related table. A many-to-many relationship in the physical system is implemented by a pair of one-to-many relationships in an Access database.

Enforcement of referential integrity prevents you from adding a record to the related table if that record contains an invalid value of the foreign key. (You cannot, for example, add a record to the Orders table that contains an invalid value for CustomerID.) Referential integrity also prevents the deletion and/or updating of records on the "one" side of a one-to-many relationship when there are matching records in the related table. The deletion (updating) can take place, however, if the relationship is modified to allow the cascaded deletion (updating) of related records (fields).

Referential integrity does not prevent you from adding a record to the "many" table that omits a value for the field from the "one" table. You could, for example, add a record to the Orders table that omitted CustomerID. If this does not make sense in the physical situation, then you have to make the CustomerID a required field in the Orders table.

There are several reasons to base a form (or subform) on a query rather than a table. A query can contain a calculated field; a table cannot. A query can contain fields from more than one table and take advantage of AutoLookup. A query can also contain selected records from a table and/or display those records in a different sequence from that of the table on which it is based.

A parameter query prompts you for the criteria each time you execute the query. The prompt is enclosed in square brackets and is entered in the Criteria row within the Query Design view. Multiple parameters may be specified within the same query.

Aggregate functions (Avg, Min, Max, Sum, and Count) perform calculations on groups of records. Execution of the query displays an aggregate record for each group, and individual records do not appear. Updating of individual records is not possible in this type of query.

Tables may be added to an Access database without disturbing the data in existing tables. The Get External Data command enables you to import an object(s) from another database.

KEY TERMS

AutoLookup 1626	Main form 1626	Relationships window 1619
AutoNumber field 1619	Many-to-many relationship . . . 1618	Subform 1626
Cascaded deletion 1620	Object Dependencies 1658	Sum function 1635
Cascaded updating 1620	One-to-many relationship 1616	TopValues property 1646
Combined key 1618	Parameter query 1635	Total query 1635
Description property 1644	Primary key 1616	Total row 1635
Format property 1619	Prompt 1635	Unmatched Query Wizard 1643
Group By 1635	Referential integrity 1620	
Keep Together property 1641	Relationship lines 1619	

MULTIPLE CHOICE

1. Which table(s) is(are) necessary to implement a many-to-many relationship between students and the courses they take?
   (a) A Students table
   (b) A Courses table
   (c) A Students–Courses table
   (d) All of the above

2. Which of the following would be suitable as the primary key in a Students–Courses table, where there is a many-to-many relationship between Students and Courses, and further, when a student is allowed to repeat a course?
   (a) The combination of StudentID and CourseID
   (b) The combination of StudentID, CourseID, and semester
   (c) The combination of StudentID, CourseID, semester, and grade
   (d) All of the above are equally appropriate

3. Which of the following is necessary to add a record to the "one" side in a one-to-many relationship in which referential integrity is enforced?
   (a) A unique primary key for the new record
   (b) One or more matching records in the many table
   (c) Both (a) and (b)
   (d) Neither (a) nor (b)

4. Which of the following is necessary to add a record to the "many" side in a one-to-many relationship in which the join field is a required field in the "many" table?
   (a) A unique primary key for the new record
   (b) A matching record in the primary table
   (c) Both (a) and (b)
   (d) Neither (a) nor (b)

5. Under which circumstances can you delete a "many" record in a one-to-many relationship?
   (a) Under all circumstances
   (b) Under no circumstances
   (c) By enforcing referential integrity
   (d) By enforcing referential integrity with the cascaded deletion of related records

6. Under which circumstances can you delete the "one" record in a one-to-many relationship?
   (a) Under all circumstances
   (b) Under no circumstances
   (c) By enforcing referential integrity
   (d) By enforcing referential integrity with the cascaded deletion of related records

7. Which of the following would be suitable as the primary key in a Patients–Doctors table, where there is a many-to-many relationship between patients and doctors, and where the same patient can see the same doctor on different visits?
   (a) The combination of PatientID and DoctorID
   (b) The combination of PatientID, DoctorID, and the date of the visit
   (c) Either (a) or (b)
   (d) Neither (a) nor (b)

8. How do you implement the many-to-many relationship between patients and doctors described in the previous question?
   (a) Through a one-to-many relationship between the Patients table and the Patients–Doctors table
   (b) Through a one-to-many relationship between the Doctors table and the Patients–Doctors table
   (c) Both (a) and (b)
   (d) Neither (a) nor (b)

9. A database has a one-to-many relationship between teams and players. Which data type and field size should be assigned to the TeamID field in the Players table, if TeamID is defined as an AutoNumber field in the Teams table?
   (a) AutoNumber and Long Integer
   (b) Number and Long Integer
   (c) Text and Long Integer
   (d) Lookup Wizard and Long Integer

10. Which of the following is true about a main form and an associated subform?
    (a) The main form can be based on a query
    (b) The subform can be based on a query
    (c) Both (a) and (b)
    (d) Neither (a) nor (b)

...continued

multiple choice

11. A parameter query:
    (a) Displays a prompt within brackets in the Criteria row of the query
    (b) Is limited to a single parameter
    (c) Both (a) and (b)
    (d) Neither (a) nor (b)

12. Which of the following is available as an aggregate function within a select query?
    (a) Sum and Avg
    (b) Min and Max
    (c) Both (a) and (b)
    (d) Neither (a) nor (b)

13. The Relationships window is displayed, and you notice that one of the tables has two fields shown in bold. What does this mean?
    (a) The primary key for the table consists of both fields
    (b) The table is joined to two others in two many-to-many relationships
    (c) The table has both primary and foreign keys
    (d) Those two fields allow cascaded updating and deleting

14. Which of the following can be imported from another Access database?
    (a) Tables and forms
    (b) Queries and reports
    (c) Both (a) and (b)
    (d) Neither (a) nor (b)

15. Which of the following is true of the TopValues query property?
    (a) It can be used to display the top 10 records in a dynaset
    (b) It can be used to display the top 10 percent of the records in a dynaset
    (c) Both (a) and (b)
    (d) Neither (a) nor (b)

16. You are working with a bookstore database. The Publishers and Books tables are joined in a one-to-many relationship. If referential integrity is enforced, which records can you delete?
    (a) A book, regardless of the records in the Publishers table
    (b) A book, only if there are no corresponding records in the Publishers table
    (c) A publisher, regardless of the records in the Books table
    (d) A publisher, only if there are corresponding records in the Books table

17. You are working with a bookstore database. The Publishers and Books tables are joined in a one-to-many relationship. The PublisherID is a required field in the Books table. If referential integrity is enforced, which of the following actions can you take?
    (a) Add a book without specifying the publisher
    (b) Delete a publisher, regardless of the records in the Books table
    (c) Add a publisher, regardless of the records in the Books table
    (d) None of the above

18. You are working with a bookstore database. The Publishers and Books tables are joined in a one-to-many relationship. The options to cascade updated or deleted records are both in effect. Which of the following actions is *prevented*?
    (a) Adding a book that references a publisher not found in the Publishers table
    (b) Changing the primary key of a record in the Publishers table if there are matching records in the Books table
    (c) Both (a) and (b)
    (d) Neither (a) nor (b)

ANSWERS

1. d
2. b
3. a
4. c
5. a
6. d
7. b
8. c
9. b
10. c
11. a
12. c
13. a
14. c
15. c
16. a
17. c
18. a

PRACTICE WITH ACCESS

1. **Understanding Database Design:** The presentation in Figure 6.14 represents a *hypothetical* assignment for a group project in which the group is asked to present the design for their project to the class as a whole. We have created a similar presentation for you to illustrate what we mean; your only task is to view our presentation, which in turn will help you to review the *Computer Store* database that was developed in the chapter. (Your instructor may want to extend the assignment and ask you to create a parallel presentation for a different database, which he or she may assign as an actual group project.) Proceed as follows:

   a. Open the *Chapter 6 Practice 1* presentation in the Exploring Access folder. This is a PowerPoint presentation, but you do not have to know PowerPoint to complete this exercise. Pull down the View menu and change to the Normal view. If necessary, click the Slide tab to see the miniature slides instead of the outline.

   b. There are nine slides in the complete presentation. The left pane shows the slide miniatures. The right pane shows a larger view of the selected slide (slide one in this example). The slide describes the hypothetical assignment, which is to create a 10-minute presentation to the class describing the physical problem and the associated database design.

   c. Select (click) the first slide. Pull down the View menu and click the Slide Show command (or click the Slide Show button above the status bar). Click the mouse continually to move through the slide show. You will see a recap of the *Computer Store* database, its design, and several suggested queries.

   d. Press the Esc button at the end of the show. Pull down the File menu, and click the Print command. Select the All option button in the Print Range area. Click the down arrow in the Print What area and select handouts. Choose 6 slides per page. Be sure to check the box to frame the slides. Click OK to print the presentation. Print the presentation a second time, but this time print only the title slide (as a full slide) to use as a cover sheet for your assignment.

   e. Review the printed presentation. Do you see how the discipline provided by this assignment can help to ensure the accuracy of the design?

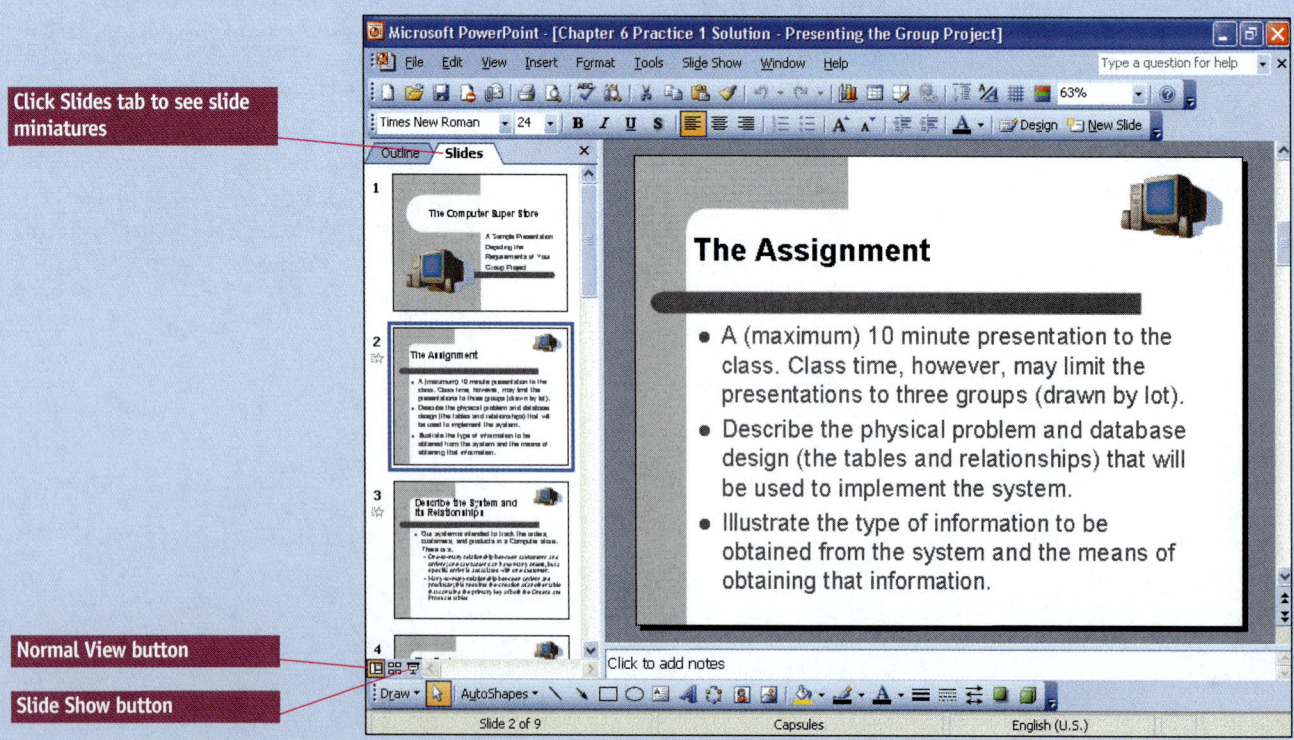

FIGURE 6.14 Understanding Database Design (exercise 1)

practice exercises

2. **Unmatched Query Wizard:** The report in Figure 6.15 is based on a query that was created by the Unmatched Query Wizard, and indicates the products that have never been purchased. This type of information is very valuable to management, which can realize significant cost savings by eliminating these products from inventory. In essence, the query takes each record in the Products table and searches for a matching entry in the Order Details table. Any products that do not appear in the latter table are "unmatched entries" and correspond to a product that has never been ordered. Proceed as follows:

   a. Open the *Computer Store* database that you have used throughout the chapter. Click the Queries button in the Database window. Click the New button, select the Find Unmatched Query Wizard and click OK. Choose Products as the table whose records you want to see in the query results. Click Next. Choose Order Details as the table that contains the related records.

   b. Product ID is selected automatically as the matching field. Click Next. Select every field from the Available Fields list. Click Next. The Wizard enters Products without Matching Order Details as the name of the query.

   c. Click Finish to display a list of the products (if any) that have never been purchased. You should see the same data as in Figure 6.15. Close the query.

   d. Use the Report Wizard to create a report based on the query you just created. Grouping is not required but the report should be sorted by ProductID. Choose the tabular layout and the Soft Gray style.

   e. Modify the report in Design view. You will (most likely) have to modify the column headings and associated controls so that they are spaced more attractively. (You may find it useful to press and hold the Shift key to select both the column heading and associated control in order to move and/or size both objects simultaneously. The Format Align command is also useful.)

   f. Modify the report header to include your name and clip art as shown in Figure 6.15. You do not have to match our design exactly.

   g. Print the completed report for your instructor. What advice would you give to management regarding the inventory of these items?

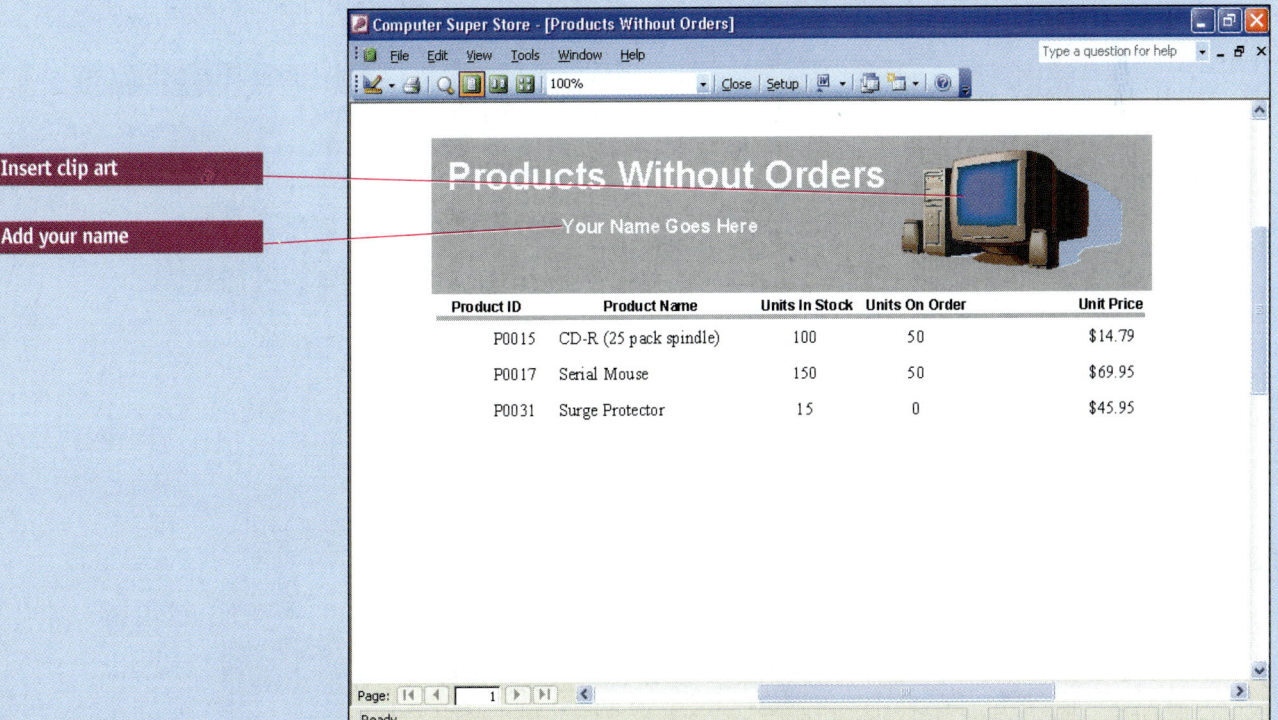

FIGURE 6.15 Unmatched Query Wizard (exercise 2)

practice exercises

3. **An Improved Order Form:** The order form in Figure 6.16 builds on the form that was developed in the fourth hands-on exercise in the chapter. A header has been added that includes clip art and a label for your name and three command buttons have also been added. The most significant change, however, is the inclusion of a Product Name combo box on the subform in place of the ProductID.

   a. Open the *Computer Store* database. Click the Forms button in the Database window and open the Order Details with Product Information subform in Design view. Delete the controls and associated labels for ProductID and Product Name. Click the Combo Box Wizard tool, then click and drag in the Detail area of the subform to create a combo box.

   b. Click the option button to indicate that you want the Combo box to look up values in a table or query. Click Next. Specify the Products table. Click Next. Select the ProductID and ProductName fields. Click Next. Click the down arrow in the text box and select Product Name to sort the list alphabetically. Adjust the column width of the ProductName field. Click Next. Click the option button to store the value in a field and specify ProductID. Click Finish.

   c. Right click the combo box, click Properties, and change the name of the combo box to ProductName. Pull down the View menu, click the Tab Order command and specify AutoOrder. Click OK. Save the subform. Close the subform.

   d. Open the Computer Store Order form in Design view. Add command buttons to add a new order, close the form, and print a record. Press and hold the Shift key to select all three buttons. Use the Format Size and Format Align commands to size and align the buttons as shown. Pull down the View menu, click the Tab Order command and specify AutoOrder.

   e. Add a form header. You do not have to match our design exactly, but you are to include your name and a clip art image. Save the form. Go to Form view.

   f. Click the button to add a new order, but skip the OrderID, CustomerID, and date fields. Click in the list box for the salesperson and choose anyone. The OrderID is created and today's date appears as the order date. Click in the First Name text box, enter your instructor's first name, and press Tab to create a new CustomerID. Complete the address and other information for your instructor, then click in the subform to create the actual order. Print the record for your instructor. Close the form.

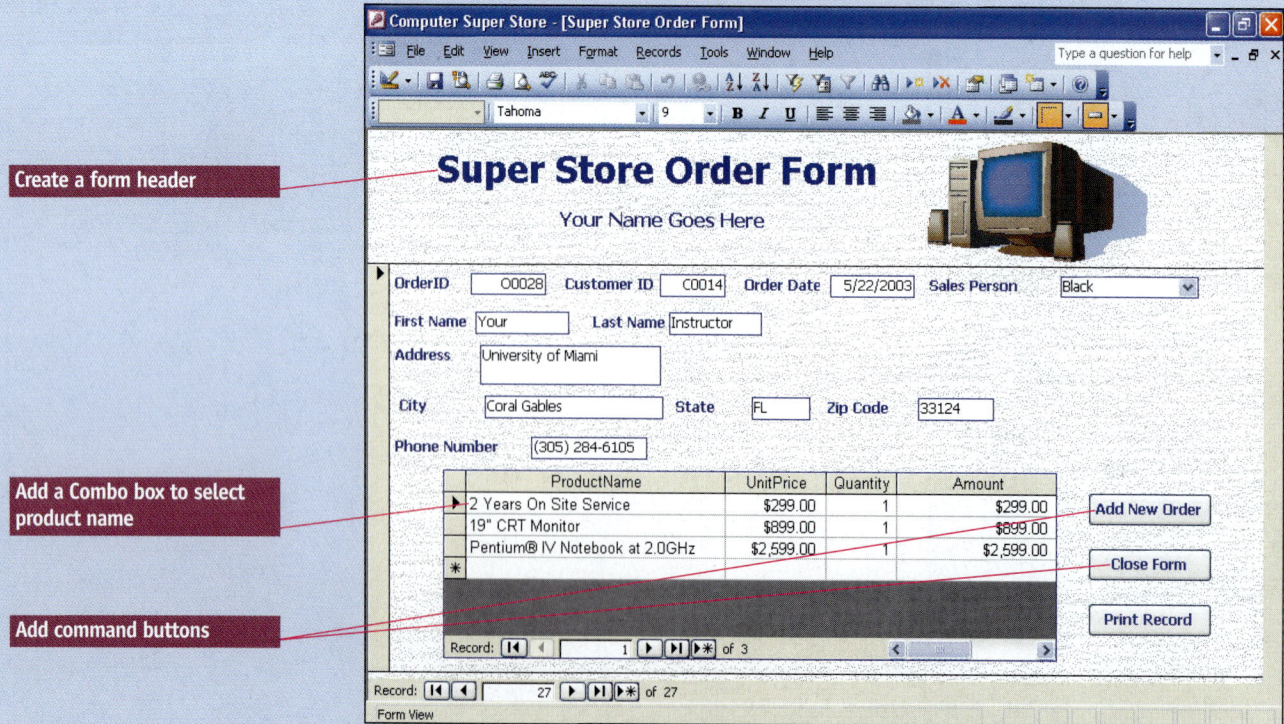

FIGURE 6.16 An Improved Order Form (exercise 3)

practice exercises

4. **Computer Store Switchboard:** Implementation of the switchboard in Figure 6.17 completes the *Computer Store* database that you have worked on throughout the chapter. All of the objects referenced in the switchboard have already been created with the exception of the Sales Commission report that was described on page 298 in the chapter (see Figure 6.12c to see the completed report). Your first task is to create that report, after which you can complete the switchboard. Proceed as follows:

   a. Open the *Computer Store* database from the previous exercise. Click the Queries button in the Database window to create the Sales Commission query, which computes the total amount for each order and the commission on that order (5% of the total). The query is identical to the query in Figure 6.12a except that it omits the prompt under salesman's last name, so as to show commissions for every sales person, as opposed to a specific sales person.

   b. Use the Report Wizard to create the initial version of the Sales Commission report (Figure 6.12c), based on the query that you just created, and then modify the report in Design view. You need not match our design exactly, but you have to display equivalent information. (Use steps 3 and 4 in Hands-on Exercise 3 as a guide in modifying the report design.)

   c. The About Computer Store form is already in the database. Open the form in Design view and substitute your name in place of ours.

   d. Use the Switchboard Manager to create the switchboard in Figure 6.17. All of the objects were created in the hands-on exercises and/or the previous end-of-chapter problems. You do not have to match our design exactly, but you have to include all of the command buttons as well as a logo.

   e. Change the Startup property to display the switchboard automatically when the database is opened. Pull down the Tools menu, click the Database and Utilities command, then choose the Compact and Repair command. The database should close, and then reopen with the switchboard visible.

   f. Print the completed switchboard for your instructor as well as the table of switchboard items. Include a printed version of each object referenced in the switchboard. Add a cover sheet, then submit all of the printed information to your instructor.

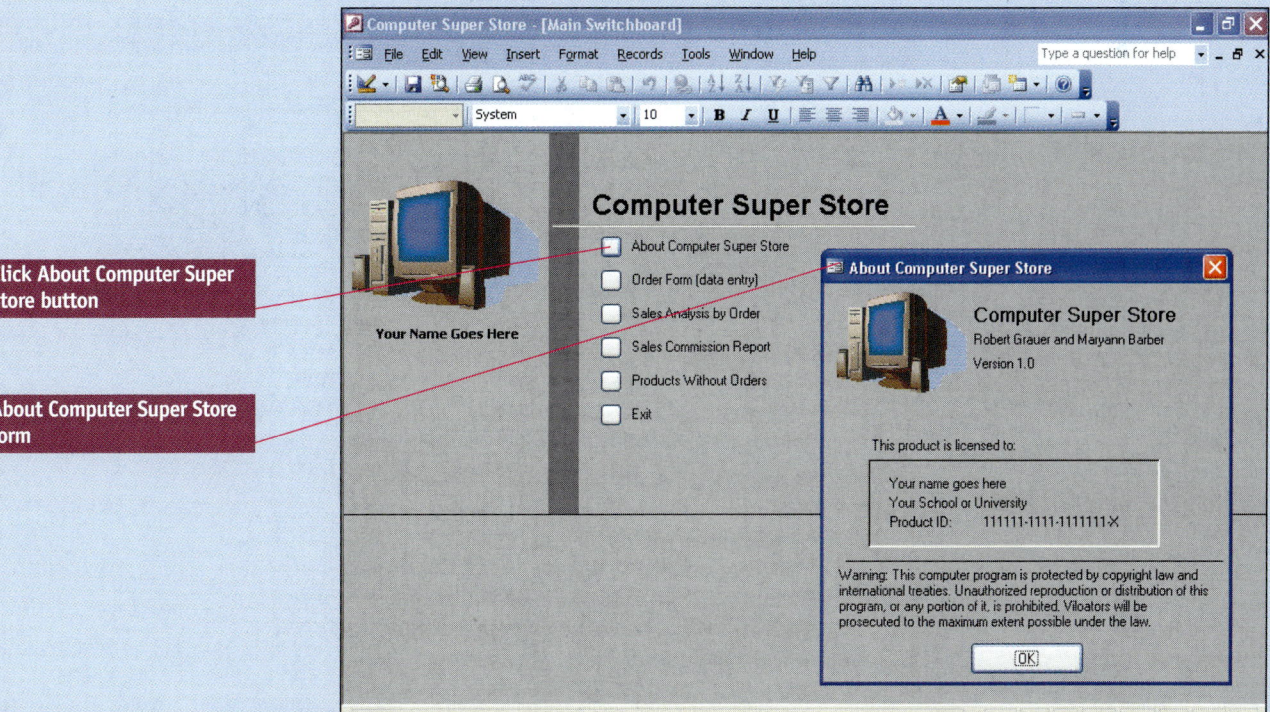

FIGURE 6.17 Computer Store Switchboard (exercise 4)

MICROSOFT OFFICE ACCESS 2003 **1665**

practice exercises

5. **Return to National Bank:** The report in Figure 6.18 lists all of the payments that were received from a specific customer in the order in which the payments were received. The report is based on a parameter query that requests the customer's first and last name, after which the payments are displayed. Open the *National Bank* database from Chapter 5 and proceed as follows:

   a. Click the Queries tab in the Database window, then double click the icon to Create query in Design view. Add the Customers, Loans, and Payments tables to the query. Recall that there is a one-to-many relationship between customers and loans, and a second one-to-many relationship between loans and payments.

   b. Add the LastName and FirstName fields from the Customers table, the LoanID field from the Loans table, and the PaymentDate and AmountReceived fields from the Payments table.

   c. Click in the Criteria row under the LastName field and added the bracketed entry, [Enter Customer's Last Name]. Add a similar entry under the FirstName field as well. Click in the Sort row of the Payment Date field and specify an ascending sequence. Save the query as Customer Payment Query.

   d. Run the query. Enter the customer's first and last name when prompted. You should see the same data as in Figure 6.18. Close the query.

   e. Click the Reports button in the Database window, then use the Report Wizard to create a report based on the query you just created. Select the option to view the report by Customers.

   f. Grouping is not required, but the report should be in ascending sequence by Payment date. Select the stepped layout and the Soft Gray style.

   g. Enter the customer's first and last name when prompted. You should see the same information as in Figure 6.18, but the report requires some modification.

   h. Press and hold the Shift key to select the FirstName and LastName controls from the group header, then drag these fields to the Report Header. Right click either control, click Properties, then change the border property to transparent. Delete the corresponding labels from the Page Header. Move and align the remaining controls and their labels. Add clip art to the Report Header, then print the completed report.

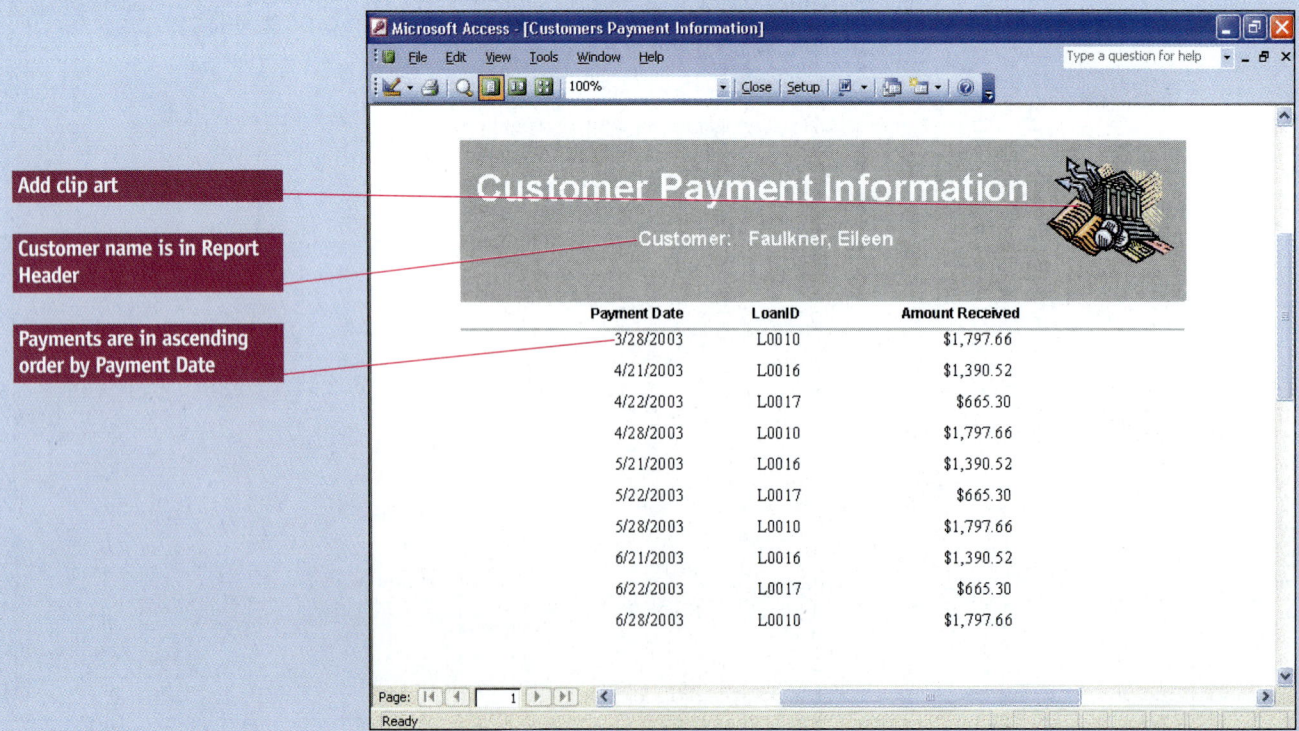

FIGURE 6.18 Return to National Bank (exercise 5)

practice exercises

6. **Medical Research Database Design:** Your first assignment as an intern in the School of Medicine is to design a database that will track research studies, the physicians who work on those studies, and the volunteers (subjects) who participate. The system is required to produce multiple reports, such as the volunteers and physicians assigned to a specific study, as well as a list of physicians who are not assigned to a research study. Additional specifications are provided below:

   a. There is a one-to-many relationship between studies and volunteers; that is, one study requires several subjects, but a specific subject may participate in only one study. Physicians, however, can work on multiple studies, and one study will have multiple physicians assigned to it. Each physician is designated as either a primary or a secondary investigator. (The same physician may be a primary investigator in one study and a secondary investigator in a different study.)

   b. The Volunteers table stores all data about a specific volunteer (subject) such as name, birth date, gender, height, weight, blood pressure, cholesterol level, and so on. The Physicians table holds basic data about each physician. The Studies table contains all characteristics associated with a particular study such as the title, beginning date, ending date, and so on.

   c. A preliminary database design is shown in Figure 6.19. Your assignment is to open the partially completed *Chapter 6 Practice 6* database and create the relationships diagram that is shown in the figure. The tables have been created for you, and data has been entered into those tables to enable you to create various forms and reports as described in the next exercise. The relationships diagram should contain an appropriate logo or clip art image that will be used throughout the database.

   d. You are also to create a simple switchboard with three menu options—a button to display an "About Medical Research" form describing the database, a button to print the relationships diagram, and a button to exit the application. The switchboard should contain the same clip art as the relationships diagram. (You can copy the clip art from the About form that is already in the database.) Use the Startup property to display the switchboard when the database is opened. Print the relationships diagram for your instructor.

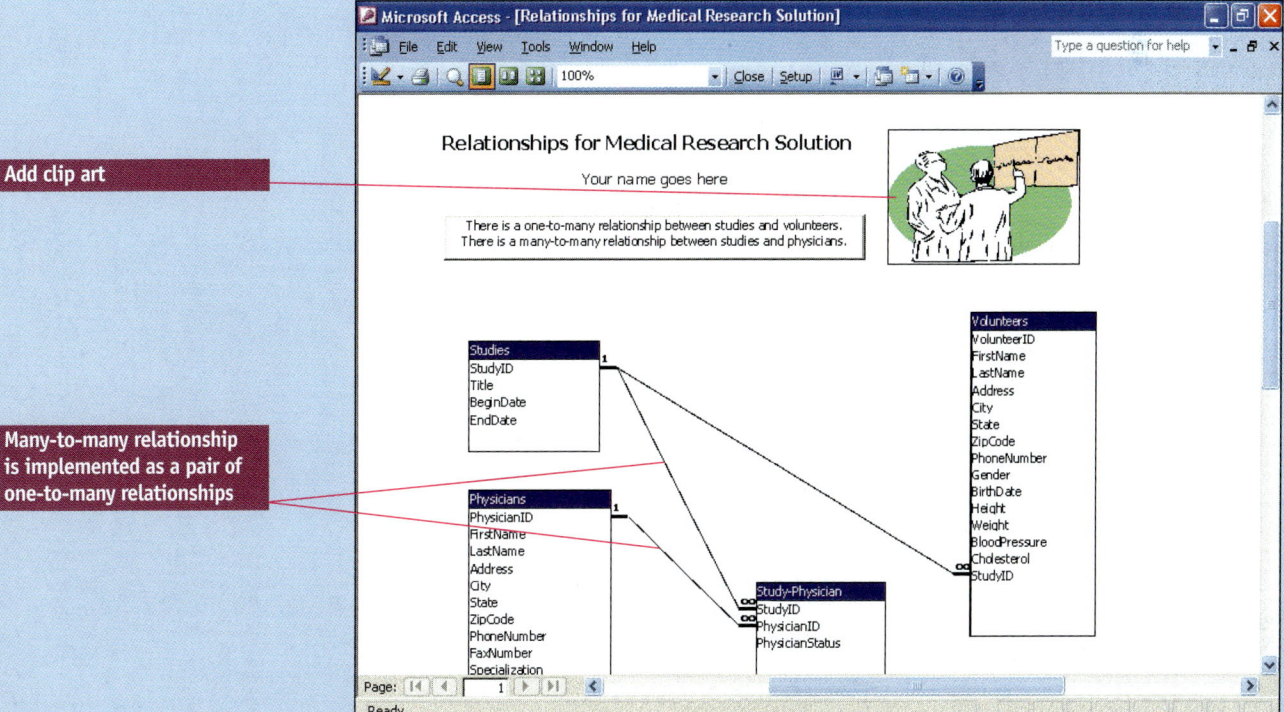

FIGURE 6.19 Medical Research Database Design (exercise 6)

practice exercises

7. **Medical Research Switchboard:** Implementation of the switchboard in Figure 6.20 completes the *Medical Research* database that was introduced in the previous exercise. The main switchboard provides access to various forms that enable you to add, edit, and/or delete records in every table within the database. The Report menu provides buttons to print the relationships diagram as well as each of the reports in parts (c), (d), and (e) below. Proceed as follows:

   a. Use the Form Wizard to create a simple form to enter or modify data in the Studies table. Use the Form Wizard to create a second form for the Volunteers table. Open the Volunteers form in Design view, remove the StudyID, and replace it with a combo box that lets the user select the Study title (but store the StudyID).

   b. Use the Form Wizard to create a main form/subform combination that enables data entry for the physicians and the studies in which they will participate. The main form should contain every field in the Physicians table so that a physician can be added using this form. The subform should be based on a query that uses the StudyID from the StudyPhysicians table so that you can assign a physician to a study. (Delete the StudyID and replace it with a combo box that lets the user select the Study title but store the StudyID.) Print the form for Dr. Holly Davis.

   c. Use the Unmatched Query Wizard to create a query that lists physicians that have not been assigned to a study. Use the Report Wizard to create a report based on that query. Print the completed report.

   d. Create a parameter query that requests the number of a specific study, then lists all of the volunteers for that study. Use the Report Wizard to create a report based on that query. Print the completed report.

   e. Create a master list that displays all studies (in sequence by StudyID) and the associated volunteers in each study. The report should be grouped by StudyID and should display the name of the study and the start and end dates. The volunteers for each study should be listed in alphabetical order together with their telephone and address. Print the completed report.

   f. Print the switchboard form and table of switchboard items for your instructor. Add a cover sheet, then submit all of the printed information to your instructor.

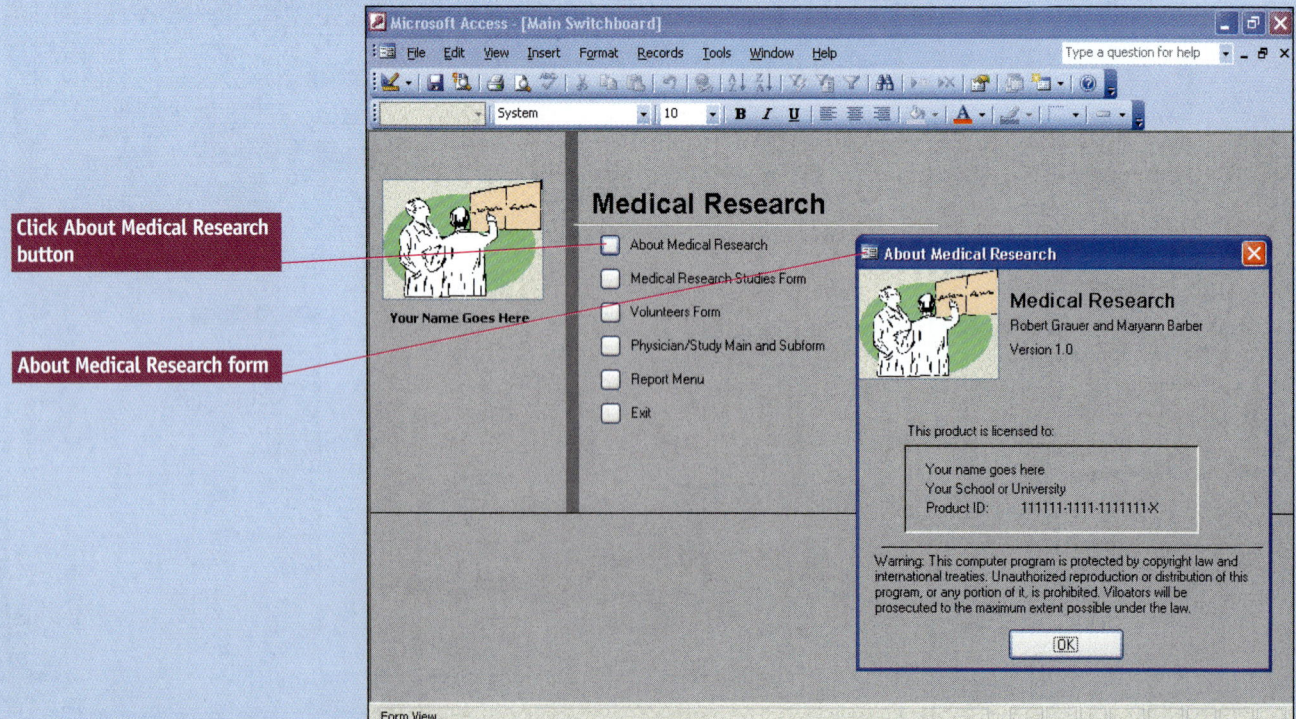

FIGURE 6.20 Medical Research Switchboard (exercise 7)

practice exercises

8. **National Conference Database Design:** You have been retained as a consultant to design a database for the national conference for a professional organization. This is an annual event, and the planning is extensive. The database is to track the speakers that come to the conference, the sessions at which they speak, and the rooms in which the sessions are held. The most important report produced by the system is the conference program, which is a master list of sessions and speakers. Additional specifications are provided below:

   a. There is a many-to-many relationship between sessions and speakers; that is, one speaker can participate in many sessions, and one session can have many speakers. The Speakers table stores data for every speaker (name, address, telephone, e-mail, and so on). The Sessions table stores data for every session (the title, a more detailed synopsis of up to 500 words, the date, starting time, duration, and the room).

   b. The database also tracks the rooms within the hotel to facilitate the session assignments. One room will host many sessions during the conference, but a particular session will be held in only one room. The Rooms table stores the capacity of each room as well as the special facilities within the room (e.g., large screens, the ability to serve refreshments, and so on).

   c. A preliminary database design is shown in Figure 6.21. Your assignment is to open the partially completed *Chapter 6 Practice 8* database and create the relationships diagram that is shown in the figure. The tables have been created for you, and data has been entered into those tables to enable you to create various forms and reports as described in the next exercise. The relationships diagram should contain an appropriate logo or clip art image that will be used throughout the database.

   d. You are also to create a simple switchboard with three menu options—a button to display an "About the Conference" form describing the database, a button to print the relationships diagram, and a button to exit the application. The switchboard should contain the same clip art as the relationships diagram. (You can copy the clip art from the About form that is already in the database.) Use the Startup property to display the switchboard when the database is opened. Print the relationships diagram for your instructor.

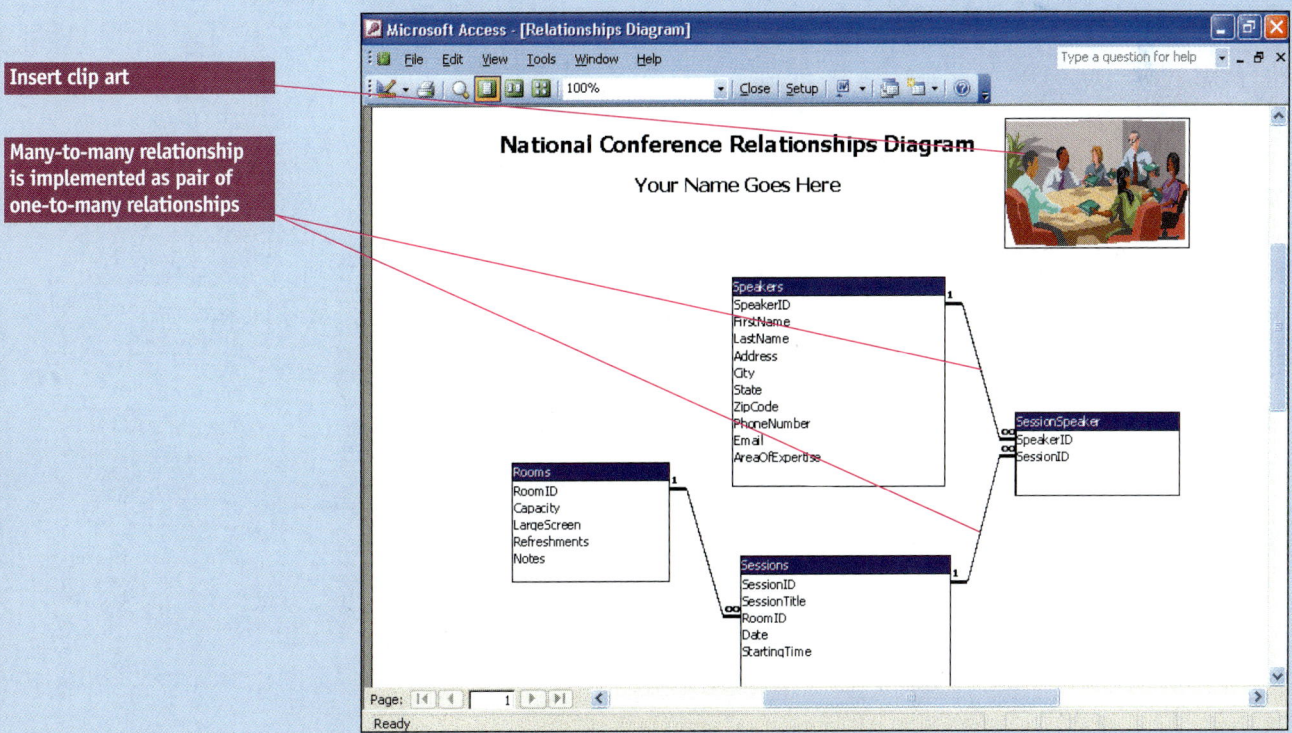

FIGURE 6.21 National Conference Database Design (exercise 8)

practice exercises

9. **National Conference Switchboard:** Implementation of the switchboard in Figure 6.22 completes the *National Conference* database that was introduced in the previous exercise. The main switchboard provides access to various forms that enable you to add, edit, and/or delete records in every table within the database. The Report menu provides buttons to print the relationships diagram as well as each of the reports in parts (c), (d), and (e) below. Proceed as follows:

   a. Use the Form Wizard to create a simple form to add or modify data to the Rooms table. Use the wizard a second time to create a form for the Sessions table. (Replace the RoomID field with a combo box that enables the user to select the room for the session from the existing Rooms table.)

   b. Use the Form Wizard to create a main form/subform combination that enables data entry for the speakers and the sessions they will participate in. The main form should contain every field in the Speakers table so that speakers can be added using this form. The subform should be based on a query that uses the SpeakerID from the SessionSpeaker table so that you can assign a speaker to a session. (Delete the SessionID and replace it with a combo box that lets the user select the Session title but store the SessionID.) Print the completed form to show the sessions for Cheryl Ashley.

   c. Use the Unmatched Query Wizard to create a query that lists rooms that do not have sessions scheduled. Use the Report Wizard to create a report based on that query. Print the completed report.

   d. Create a parameter query that requests a speaker's last name, then lists all of the sessions for that speaker. Use the Report Wizard to create a report based on that query. Print the completed report.

   e. Create a report that shows the master schedule for the conference. The report contains data from both the Sessions and Speakers tables. It should group the report by session and display the name, time, and room of every session in sequence by session number, together with the speakers for that session, their phone number, and their e-mail address. Print the completed report.

   f. Print the switchboard form and table of switchboard items for your instructor. Add a cover sheet, then submit all of the printed information to your instructor.

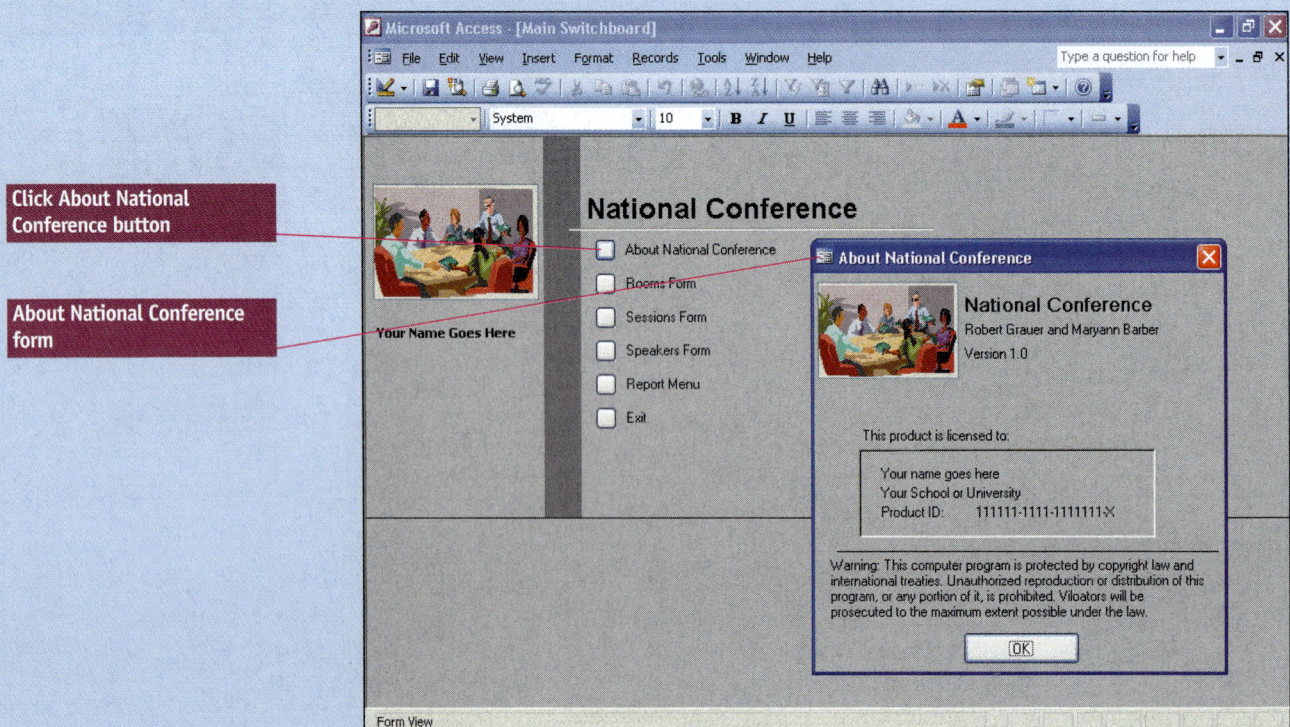

FIGURE 6.22 National Conference Switchboard (exercise 9)

MINI CASES

Health Clubs

Your interest in physical fitness has led to a part-time job at a local health club, where you have been asked to design a database for its members and trainers. The health club runs promotions periodically, and so individuals join under different membership plans. Each plan specifies the initial fee (if any), monthly payment (if any), and duration (in months). One plan can have many members, but a specific member has only one plan.

The health club needs to track the number of hours that each employee works, which is accomplished through time cards that record the date, time in, and time out. The health club also wants to know how often members work out, and which trainer they use—thus, all members complete a simple workout form each time they are at the club that contains the member's identification number, the date, the time in and the time out of the workout, and the trainer seen. The workout form also indicates the specific facilities that were used in that session. One member can work out with different trainers, and one trainer will work out with many different members.

The database should be capable of computing the total revenue that is received by the health club. One report should show the sum of all initial fees that have been paid by all members. A second report should show the projected revenue each month, based on the monthly payment due from each member.

Print the report containing the relationships diagram for your instructor as proof that you completed this exercise. Create a simple switchboard with three menu options—a button to display an "About the Health Clubs" form describing the database, a button to print the relationships diagram, and a button to exit the application. The switchboard should contain the same clip art as the relationships diagram. Use the Startup property to display the switchboard when the database is opened.

The Morning Paper

We take the delivery of our morning paper for granted, but there is a lot of planning to ensure that we receive it each day. You are to design a database for a large metropolitan newspaper that is printed at a central location within the area. Once printed, the papers are delivered to multiple warehouses. Each warehouse services multiple carriers, each of whom goes to the assigned warehouse to pick up the requisite number of papers for his or her customers. One carrier has many customers, but a particular customer has only one carrier.

The database is further complicated by the fact that the newspaper has several editions such as a Spanish edition, a daily (Monday through Saturday) edition, and a Sunday edition. One edition can go to many customers, and one customer can order many editions. There is a specific price associated with each edition. You are to design a database that will enable the paper to determine how many of each edition is to be sent to each warehouse. The database should also be capable of producing a report that shows the total amount of business that each carrier brings in.

Print the report containing the relationships diagram for your instructor as proof that you completed this exercise. Create a simple switchboard with three menu options—a button to display an "About the Morning Paper" form describing the database, a button to print the relationships diagram, and a button to exit the application. The switchboard should contain the same clip art as the relationships diagram. Use the Startup property to display the switchboard when the database is opened.

The College Bookstore

The manager of a college bookstore has asked for your help in improving its database. The bookstore needs to know which books are used in which courses. One course may require several books, and the same book can be used in different courses. A book may be required in one course and merely recommended in another. The only course information that is required by the bookstore is the course number, the name of the course, and the faculty coordinator.

mini cases

The design of this database begins with the creation of a Books table that contains the ISBN for each book, its title and author, year of publication, price, and publisher. Books are ordered directly from the publisher, so it is necessary to know the address and telephone for each publisher. One publisher has many books, but a specific book has only one publisher.

The bookstore places multiple orders with each publisher. One order can specify many books, and the same book can appear in multiple orders. The manager must know the date that each order was placed and the total cost of each order. The manager must also be able to create a report showing the books that are used in each course and its status for that course (i.e., whether the book is required or suggested). Your assignment is to design a database that will fulfill all of the requirements of the bookstore manager.

Print the report containing the relationships diagram for your instructor as proof that you completed this exercise. Create a simple switchboard with three menu options—a button to display an "About the Bookstore" form describing the database, a button to print the relationships diagram, and a button to exit the application. The switchboard should contain the same clip art as the relationships diagram. Use the Startup property to display the switchboard when the database is opened.

Bob's Burgers

The corporate office of Bob's Burgers has asked you to design a database to track its restaurants and managers. The database is to produce reports that show the sales of each restaurant and the performance of each manager, as measured by the total sale of all restaurants for that manager. Each restaurant has one manager, but a manager is responsible for multiple restaurants. The company stores the typical personnel data (name, salary, and so on.) for each manager as well as basic data for each restaurant such as the telephone and address of each restaurant, its size in square feet, and annual sales for last year. The company would like objective ways to measure the performance of a manager such as the total revenue for which he or she is responsible, the average revenue per restaurant, the average revenue per square foot, and so on.

The database also tracks the orders that are placed by the individual restaurants to the corporate office for various food supplies. Each order is associated with a specific restaurant, and of course, one restaurant will place multiple orders during the course of the year. The company uses a standard set of product numbers, product descriptions, and associated prices that applies to every restaurant. Each order can specify multiple products, and one product may appear in several orders. The database should be capable of computing the total cost of each order.

Print the report containing the relationships diagram for your instructor as proof that you completed this exercise. Create a simple switchboard with three menu options—a button to display an "About Bob's Burgers" form describing the database, a button to print the relationships diagram, and a button to exit the application. The switchboard should contain the same clip art as the relationships diagram. Use the Startup property to display the switchboard when the database is opened.

CHAPTER 7

Building Applications: Macros and a Multilevel Switchboard

OBJECTIVES

After reading this chapter you will:

1. Use the Switchboard Manager to create a multiple-level switchboard.
2. Use the Link Tables command to associate tables in one database with objects in a second database.
3. Describe how macros automate an application.
4. Explain the special role of the AutoExec macro.
5. Explain how prototyping facilitates the development of an application.
6. Use the Unmatched Query Wizard and explain its significance.
7. Create a macro group.

hands-on exercises

1. THE SWITCHBOARD MANAGER
   Input: Sports Objects database; Sports Tables database
   Output: Sports Objects (modified); Sports Tables (modified)

2. MACROS AND PROTOTYPING
   Input: Sports Objects (from exercise 1); Sports Tables (from exercise 1)
   Output: Sports Objects (modified); Sports Tables (modified)

3. THE PLAYER DRAFT
   Input: Sports Objects (from exercise 2); Sports Tables (from exercise 2)
   Output: Sports Objects (modified); Sports Tables (modified)

CASE STUDY
THE ECOADVENTURES CRUISE LINE

The EcoAdventures Cruise Line, based in Victoria, British Columbia, is known for its exploration cruises on smaller ships that carry approximately 100 passengers. These specialty cruises appeal to the traveler who is seeking an expedition rather than a traditional cruise vacation, and who wants to go to the many places around the world where larger ships cannot venture. This ambition is reflected in the company's mission statement: *"EcoAdventures Cruise Lines—our job to make your cruise an adventure!"*

The cruise line is seeking more efficient ways of doing business and has hired you to complete the Access database that was started by your predecessor. The company needs to track its ships, the cruises for each ship, and the ports of call for each cruise. There is a one-to-many relationship between ships and cruises; that is, one ship will go on many cruises, but a specific cruise, such as Cruise Number 8012—Exploration Down Under, is assigned to only one ship. There is also a many-to-many relationship between cruises and ports; that is, a specific cruise will stop at many ports, whereas the same port will be a destination for many different cruises. ■

Your assignment is to read the chapter, complete the hands-on exercises, then open the partially completed *Chapter 7 Case Study—The EcoAdventures Cruise Line*, and review the existing table design and relationships diagram. Your main task, however, is to develop an application prototype in the form of a two-level switchboard that will provide the "look and feel" of the completed application. The main switchboard should include an About form, a relationships diagram, a form template, a button to display the report switchboard, and an option to exit. The second level (report) switchboard should contain the report template and various hypothetical reports. The visual design is very important, and you should include common clip art and design elements throughout. Use macros where appropriate (e.g., AutoExec, Prototype, and CloseDatabase) that are similar to those contained in this chapter.

A RECREATIONAL SPORTS LEAGUE

This chapter revisits the concept of a user interface (or switchboard) that ties the objects in a database together, so that the database is easy to use. The switchboard displays a menu, often a series of menus, which enables a nontechnical person to move easily from one Access object to another. Any database containing a switchboard is known as an application and, unlike an ordinary Access database, it does not require knowledge of Microsoft Access on the part of the user.

The development of an application may also entail the splitting of a database into two files—one containing the tables and the other containing the remaining objects (the forms, reports, queries, and macros). The tables are then linked to the other objects through the Link Tables command. It sounds complicated, but this approach has several advantages, as you will see.

The chapter also covers macros and prototypes, two techniques that are used by developers in creating applications. A macro automates common command sequences and further simplifies the system for the end user. Prototypes are used in conjunction with developing the various switchboards to demonstrate the "look and feel" of an application, even before the application is complete.

You have probably played in a sports league at one time or another, whether in Little League as a child or in an intramural league at school or work. Whatever the league, it had teams, players, and coaches. The typical league registers the players and coaches individually, then holds a draft among the coaches to divide the players into teams according to ability. The league may have been organized informally, with manual procedures for registering the participants and creating the teams. Now we automate the process.

Let's think for a moment about the tables and associated relationships that will be necessary to create the database. There are three tables, one each for players, coaches, and teams. There is a one-to-many relationship between teams and players (one team has many players, but a player is assigned to only one team). There is also a one-to-many relationship between teams and coaches (one team has many coaches, but a coach is assigned to only one team).

In addition to the tables, the database will contain multiple forms, queries, and reports based on these tables. A Players form is necessary in order to add a new player, or edit or delete the record of an existing player. A similar form should exist for Coaches. There might also be a sophisticated main and subform combination for the Teams table that displays the players and coaches on each team, and through which data for any table (Team, Player, or Coach) can be added, edited, or deleted. And, of course, there will be a variety of reports and queries.

Let's assume that this database has been created. It would not be difficult for a person knowledgeable in Access to open the database and select the various objects as the need arose. He or she would know how to display the Database window and how to select the various buttons to open the appropriate objects. But what if the system is to be used by someone who does not know Access, which is typically the case? You can see that the user interface becomes the most important part of the system, at least from the viewpoint of the end user. An interface that is intuitive and easy to use will be successful. Conversely, a system that is difficult to use or visually unappealing is sure to fail.

Figure 7.1a displays the *switchboard* that will be created for this application. We have added a soccer ball as a logo, but the application applies to any type of recreational sports league. The interface is intuitive and easy to use. Click the About Sports button, the first button on our menu, and the system displays the informational screen we like to include in all of our applications. Click any other button, and you display the indicated form. Click the Teams button, for example, and you see the form in Figure 7.1b, where you can add a new team, view, edit, or print the data for any existing team, then click the Close Form button to return to the main menu.

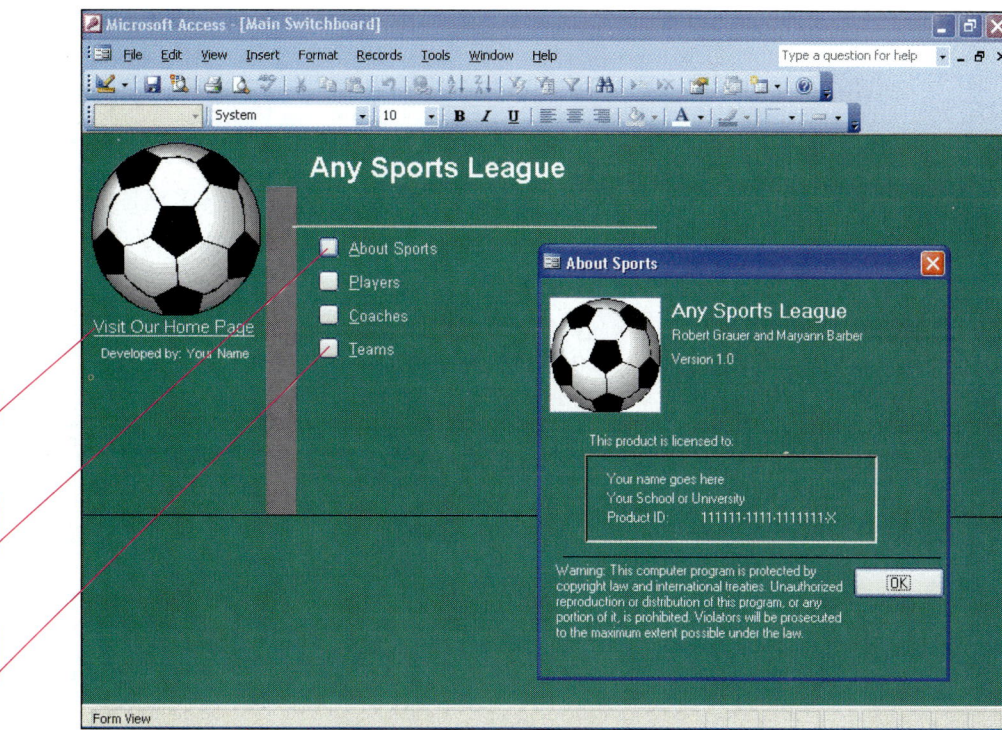

(a) The Main Menu

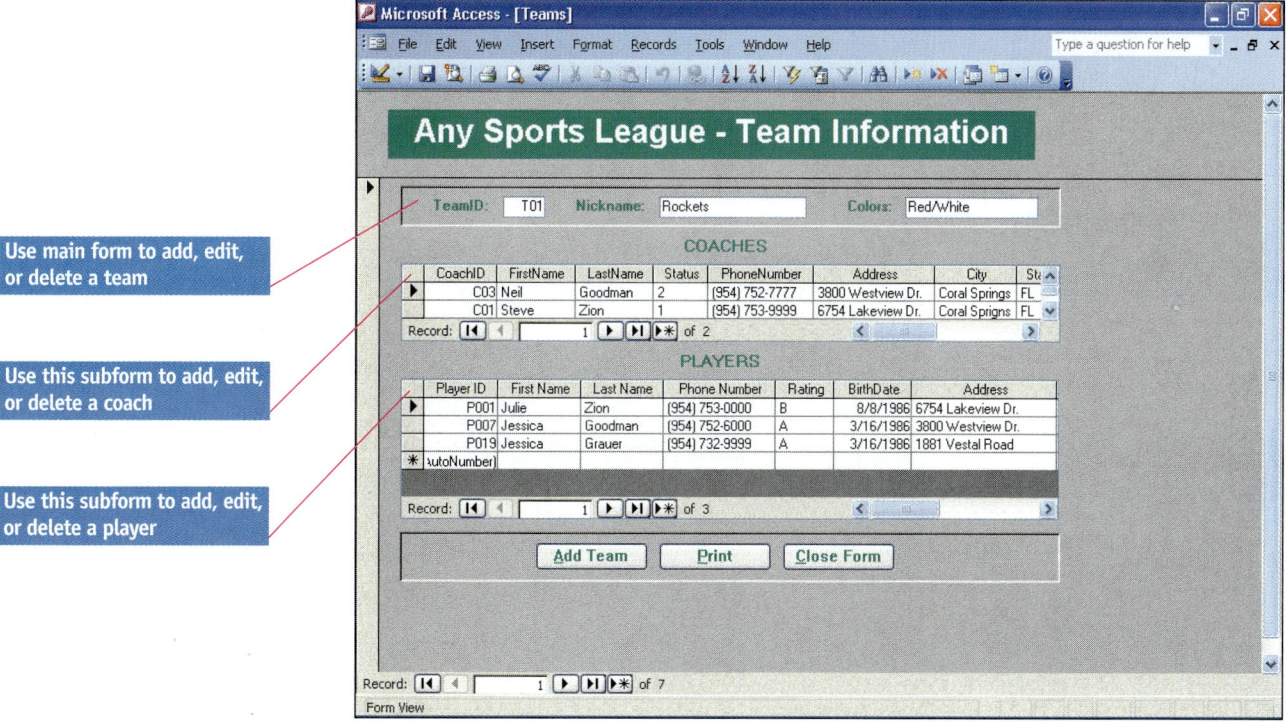

(b) The Teams Form

FIGURE 7.1 Building a User Interface

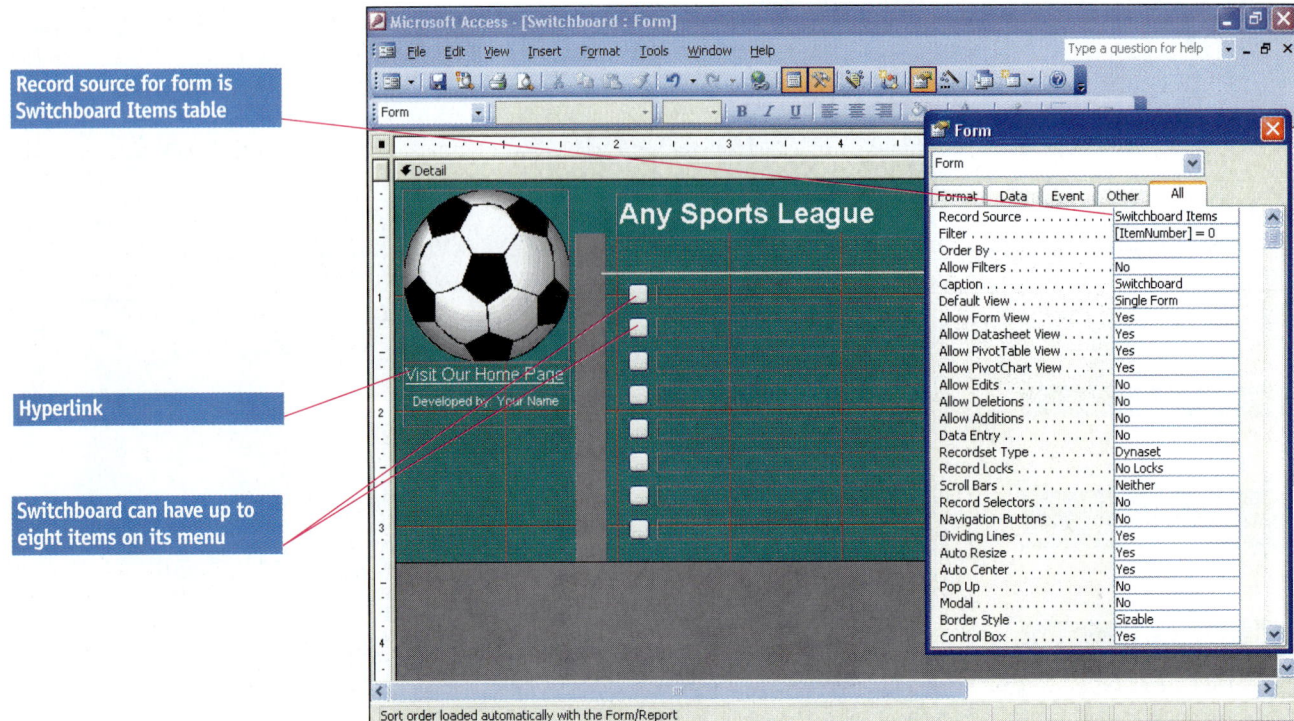

(c) Design View

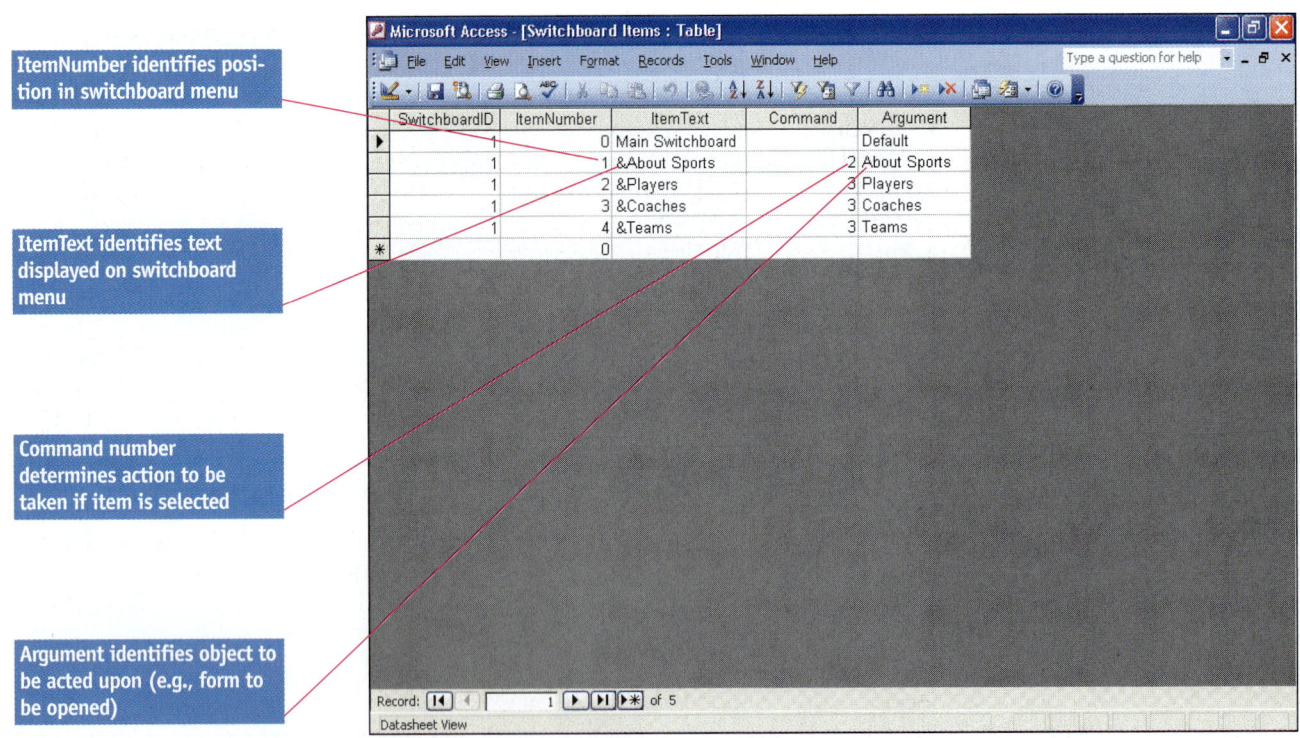

(d) Switchboard Items

FIGURE 7.1 Building a User Interface (*continued*)

The switchboard in Figure 7.1a exists as a form within the database. Look closely, however, and you will see it is subtly different from the forms you have developed in previous chapters. The record selector and navigation buttons, for example, have been suppressed because they are not needed. In other words, this form is not used for data entry, but as the basis of a menu for the user. You can even visit the league's Web site by clicking the indicated hyperlink.

The essence of the form, however, lies in the command buttons that enable the user to open the other objects in the database. Thus, when a user clicks a button, Access interprets that action as an *event* and responds with an action that has been assigned to that event. Clicking the Teams button, for example, causes Access to open the Teams form. Clicking the Players button is a different event, and causes Access to open the Players form.

The Switchboard Manager

The ***Switchboard Manager*** creates a switchboard automatically by prompting you for information about each menu item. You supply the text of the item as it is to appear on the switchboard, together with the underlying command. Access does the rest. It creates a ***switchboard form*** that is displayed to the user and a ***Switchboard Items table*** that stores information about each command.

The switchboard form is shown in both the Form view and the Design view, in Figures 7.1a and 7.1c, respectively. At first, the views do not appear to correspond to one another, in that text appears next to each button in the Form view, but it is absent in the Design view. This, however, is the nature of a switchboard, because the text for each button is taken from the Switchboard Items table in Figure 7.1d, which is the record source for the form, as can be inferred from the Form property sheet. In other words, each record in the Switchboard Items table has a corresponding menu item in the switchboard form. Note, too, that you can modify the switchboard form after it has been created, perhaps by inserting a picture or a hyperlink as was done in Figure 7.1.

As indicated, the Switchboard Items table is created automatically and can be modified through the Switchboard Manager or by directly opening the table. It helps, therefore, to have an appreciation for each field in the table. The SwitchboardID field identifies the number of the switchboard, which becomes important in applications with more than one switchboard. Access limits each switchboard to eight items, but you can create as many switchboards as you like, each with a different value for the SwitchboardID. Every application has a main switchboard by default, which can in turn display other switchboards as necessary.

The ItemNumber and ItemText fields identify the position and text of the item, respectively, as it appears on the switchboard form. (The & that appears within the ItemText field will appear as an underlined letter on the switchboard to enable a keyboard shortcut; for example, &Teams is displayed as T̲eams and recognizes the Alt+T keyboard shortcut in lieu of clicking the button.) The Command and Argument fields determine the action that will be taken when the corresponding button is clicked. Command number 3, for example, opens a form.

The Linked Tables Manager

Every application consists of tables *and* objects (forms, queries, reports, macros, and modules) based on those tables. The tables and objects may be stored in the same database (as has been done throughout the text), or they may be stored in separate databases, as will be done for the soccer application. Look closely at the Database window in Figure 7.2a. The title bar displays "Sports Objects" and indicates the name of the database that is currently open. Note, however, the arrows that appear next to the icons for the Players, Teams, and Coaches tables to indicate that the tables are stored in a different database. The name of the second database, "Sports Tables," is seen in the Linked Table Manager dialog box in Figure 7.2b.

The tables and objects are associated with one another through the **Link Tables command** and/or through the **Linked Table Manager**. Once the linking has been established, however, it is as though the Players, Coaches, and Teams tables were in the Sports Objects database with respect to maintaining the data. In other words, you can add, edit, and delete a record in any of the three tables as if the tables were physically in the Sports Objects database.

The advantage to storing the tables and objects in separate databases is that you can enhance an application by creating a new version of the Sports Objects database, without affecting the underlying tables. The new version has the improved features, such as a new form or report, but attaches to the original data, and thus retains all of the transactions that have been processed.

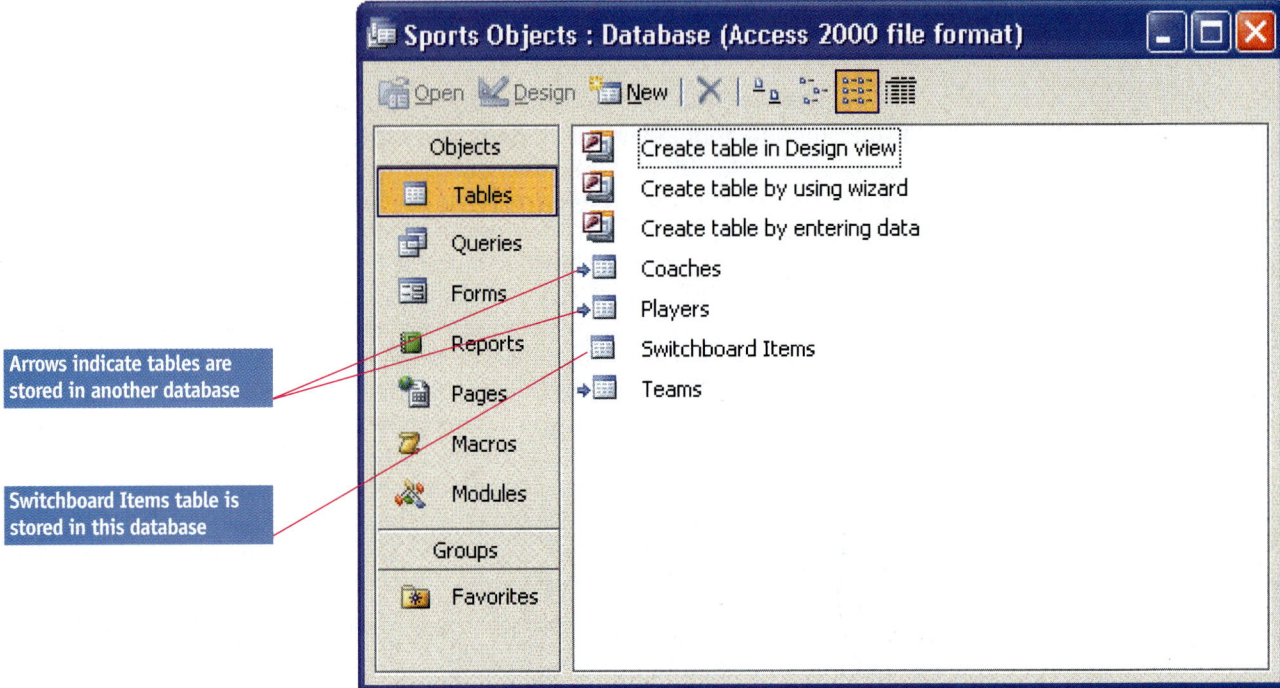

(a) The Database Window

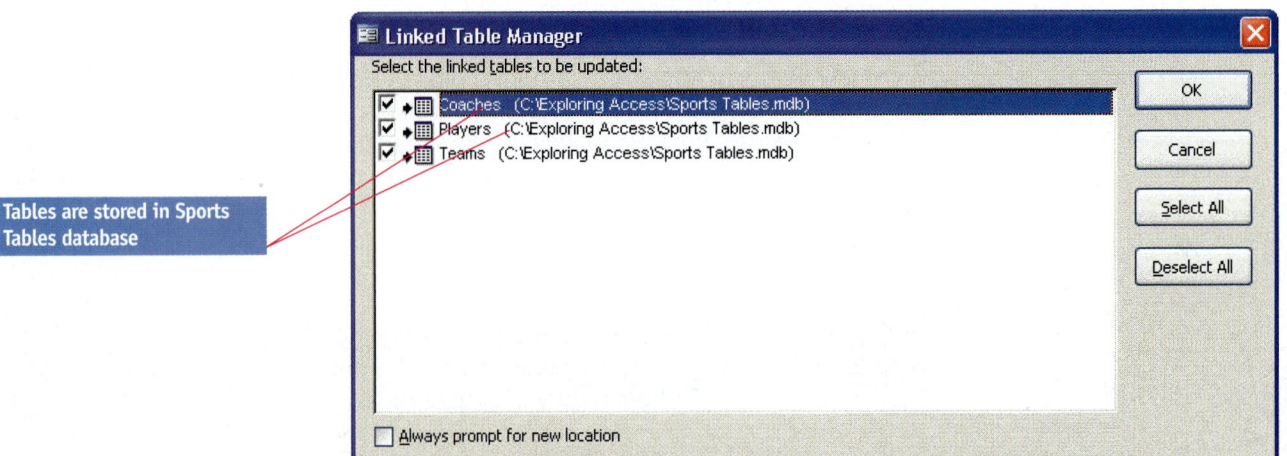

(b) The Linked Table Manager

FIGURE 7.2 Linking Tables

hands-on exercise

1 The Switchboard Manager

Objective   To create a switchboard; to use the Link Tables command to associate tables in one database with the objects in a different database. Use Figure 7.3 as a guide in the exercise.

Step 1:   **The Sports Objects Database**

- Start Access. Change to the **Exploring Access folder** as you have been doing throughout the text.

- Open the **Sports Objects database** as shown in Figure 7.3a, then click the various buttons in the Database window to view the contents of this database. This database contains the various objects (forms, queries, and reports) in the soccer application, but not the tables.
  - Click the **Tables button**. There are currently no tables in the database.
  - Click the **Queries button**. There is one query in the database.
  - Click the **Forms button**. There are seven forms in the database.
  - Click the **Reports button**. There is one report in the database.

- Pull down the **File menu**, click **Database Properties**, then click the **Contents tab** to see the contents of the database as shown in Figure 7.3a. The Database Properties command enables you to see all of the objects on one screen.

- Click the other tabs in the Properties dialog box to see the other information that is available.

- Close the Properties dialog box.

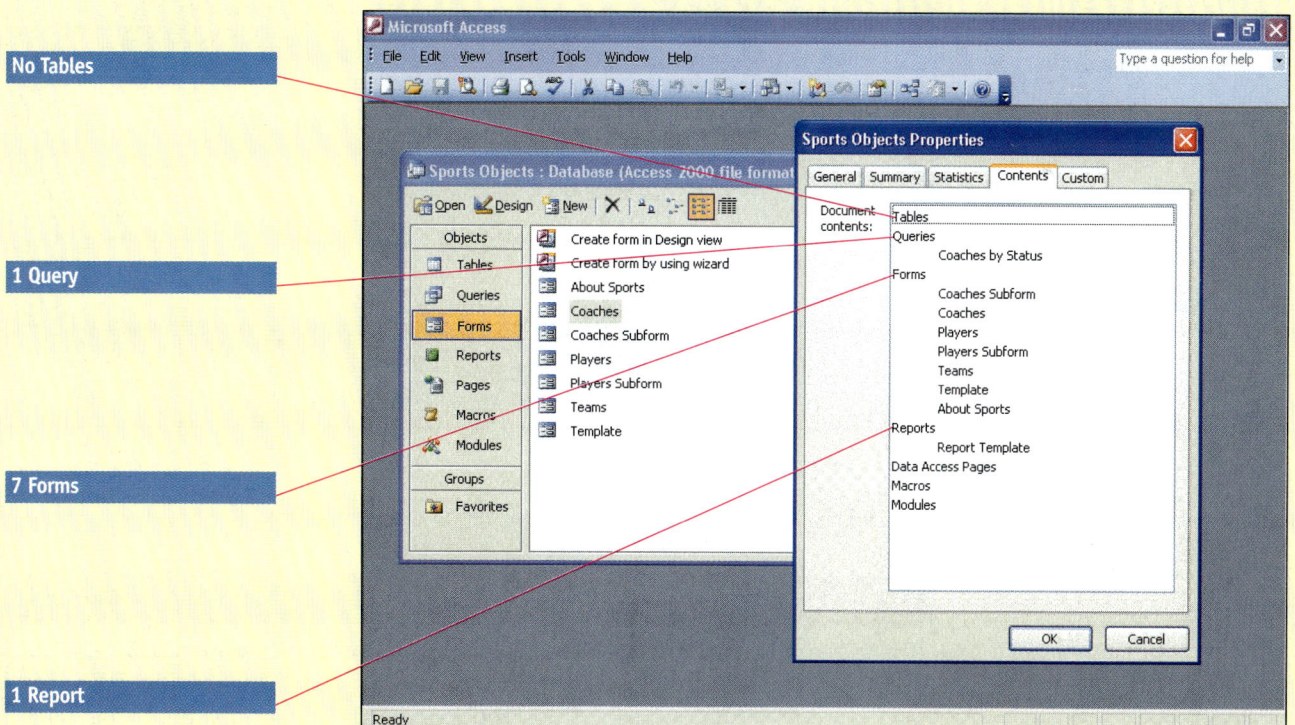

(a) The Sports Objects Database (step 1)

FIGURE 7.3   Hands-on Exercise 1

Step 2: **The Link Tables Command**

- Pull down the **File menu**. Click **Get External Data**, then click **Link Tables** from the cascaded menu. You should see the Link dialog box (which is similar in appearance to the Open dialog box).

- Select the **Exploring Access folder**, the folder you have been using throughout the text. Scroll (if necessary) until you can select the **Sports Tables database**, then click the **Link command button**.

- You should see the Link Tables dialog box in Figure 7.3b. Click the **Select All command button** to select all three tables, then click **OK**.

- The system (briefly) displays a message indicating that it is linking the tables, after which the tables should appear in the Database window.

- Click the **Tables button** in the Database window. The arrow next to each table indicates that the table physically resides in another database. (You may have to relink the tables if you move the database to another computer and/or to a different folder on this computer.)

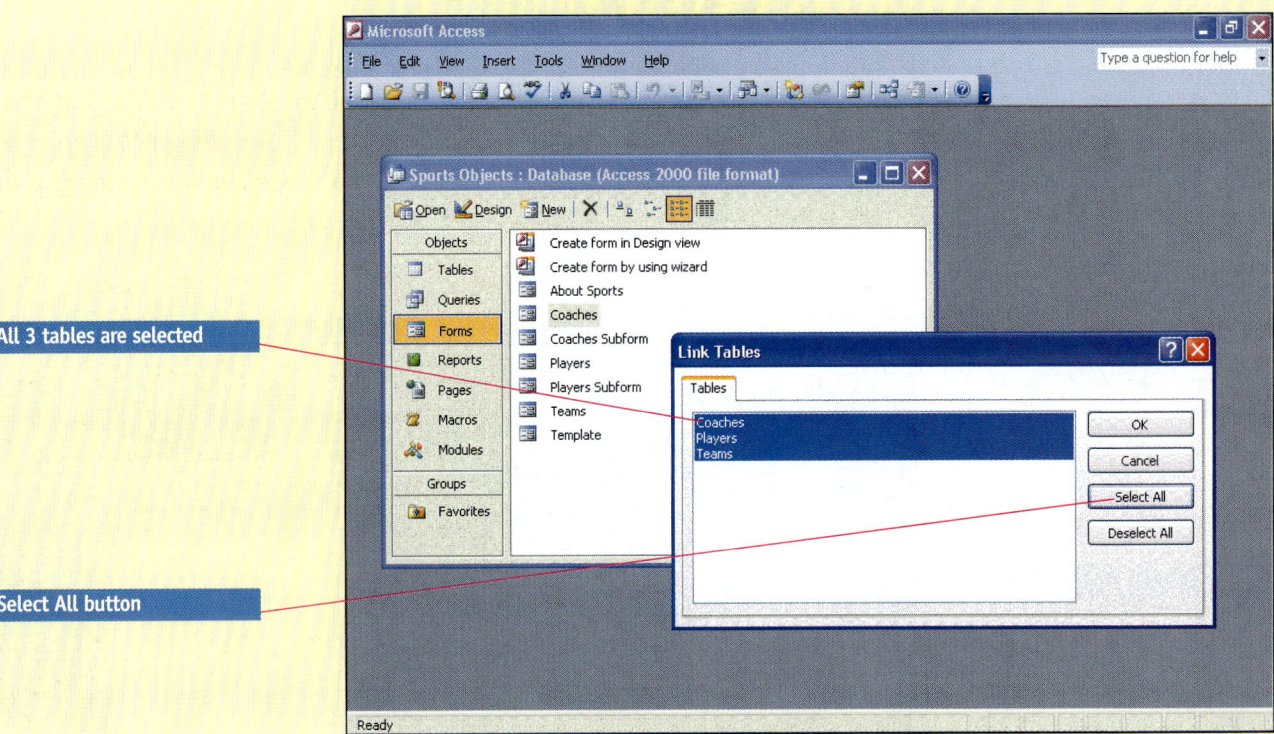

(b) The Link Tables Command (step 2)

FIGURE 7.3 Hands-on Exercise 1 (*continued*)

THE DATABASE SPLITTER

The tables and associated objects are typically stored in separate databases. But what if you created the application prior to learning about the ability to link tables and objects to one another? Open the existing database, pull down the Tools menu, click (or point to) the Database Utilities, select the Database Splitter command, and follow the onscreen instructions. You will wind up with two separate databases, a back end that contains the tables, and a front end that contains the other objects.

Step 3: **Start the Switchboard Manager**

- Minimize the Database window. Pull down the **Tools menu**, click the **Database Utilities command**, and choose **Switchboard Manager**.
- Click **Yes** if you see a message indicating that there is no valid switchboard. You should see the Switchboard Manager dialog box in Figure 7.3c.
- Click the **Edit command button** to display the Edit Switchboard Page dialog box. Click the **New command button** to add an item to this page, which in turn displays the Edit Switchboard Item dialog box.
- Click in the **Text** list box and type **&About Sports**, which is the name of the command as it will appear in the switchboard.
- Click the **drop-down arrow** on the Command list box. Choose the command to open the form in either Add or Edit mode (it doesn't matter for this form).
- Click the **drop-down arrow** in the Form list box and choose **About Sports**.
- Click **OK** to create the switchboard item. The Edit Switchboard Item dialog box closes and the About Sports item appears in the Main Switchboard.

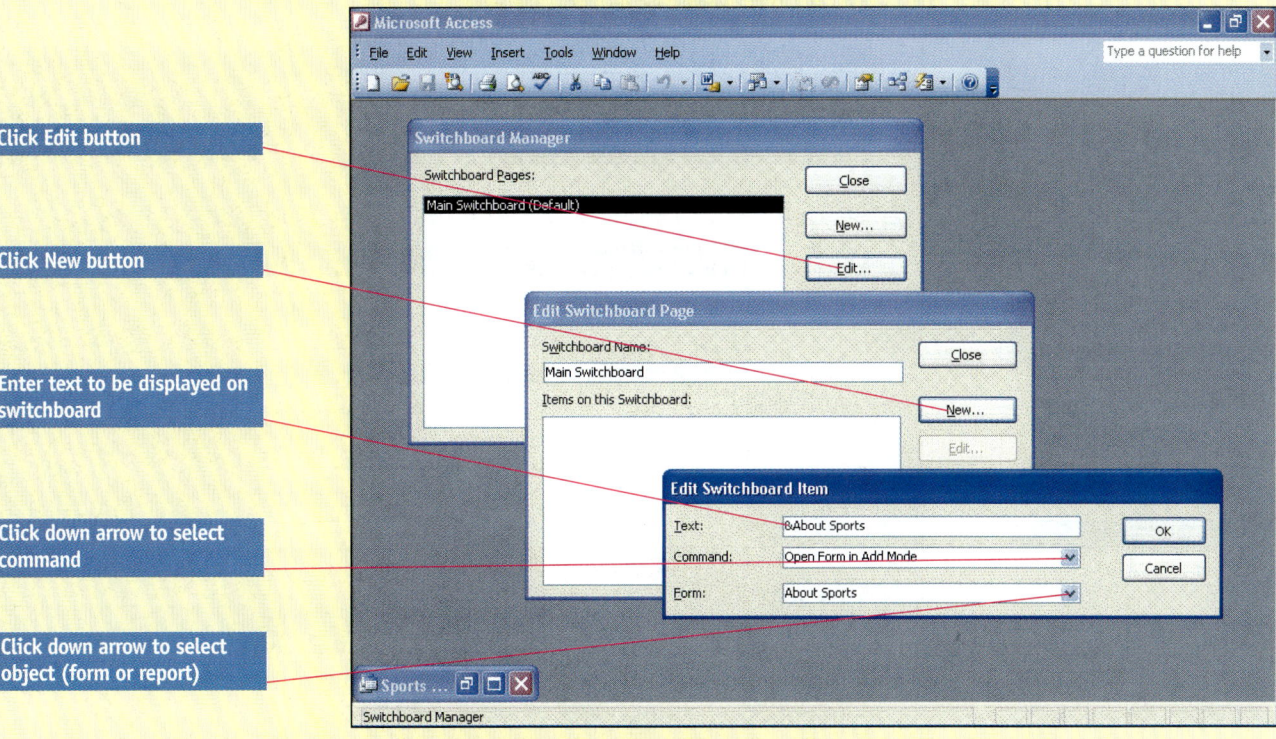

(c) Start the Switchboard Manager (step 3)

FIGURE 7.3 Hands-on Exercise 1 (*continued*)

CREATE A KEYBOARD SHORTCUT

The & has special significance when used within the name of an Access object because it creates a keyboard shortcut to that object. Enter "&About Sports", for example, and the letter A (the letter immediately after the ampersand) will be underlined and appear as "About Sports" on the switchboard. From there, you can execute the item by clicking its button, or you can use the Alt+A keyboard shortcut. Be sure to select a different shortcut (letter) for each menu item.

Step 4: **Complete the Switchboard**

- Click the **New command button** in the Edit Switchboard Page dialog box to add a second item to the switchboard. Once again, you see the Edit Switchboard dialog box.

- Click in the **Text** list box and type **&Players**. Click the **drop-down arrow** on the Command list box and choose **Open Form in Edit Mode** (see boxed tip).

- Click the **drop-down arrow** in the Form list box and choose **Players** as the form.

- Click **OK** to close the Edit Switchboard Item dialog box. The &Players command appears as an item on the switchboard.

- Create two additional switchboard items for **&Coaches** and **&Teams** in similar fashion. Your switchboard should contain four items as shown in Figure 7.3d.

- Click **Close** to close the Edit Switchboard Page dialog box. Click **Close** to close the Switchboard Manager dialog box.

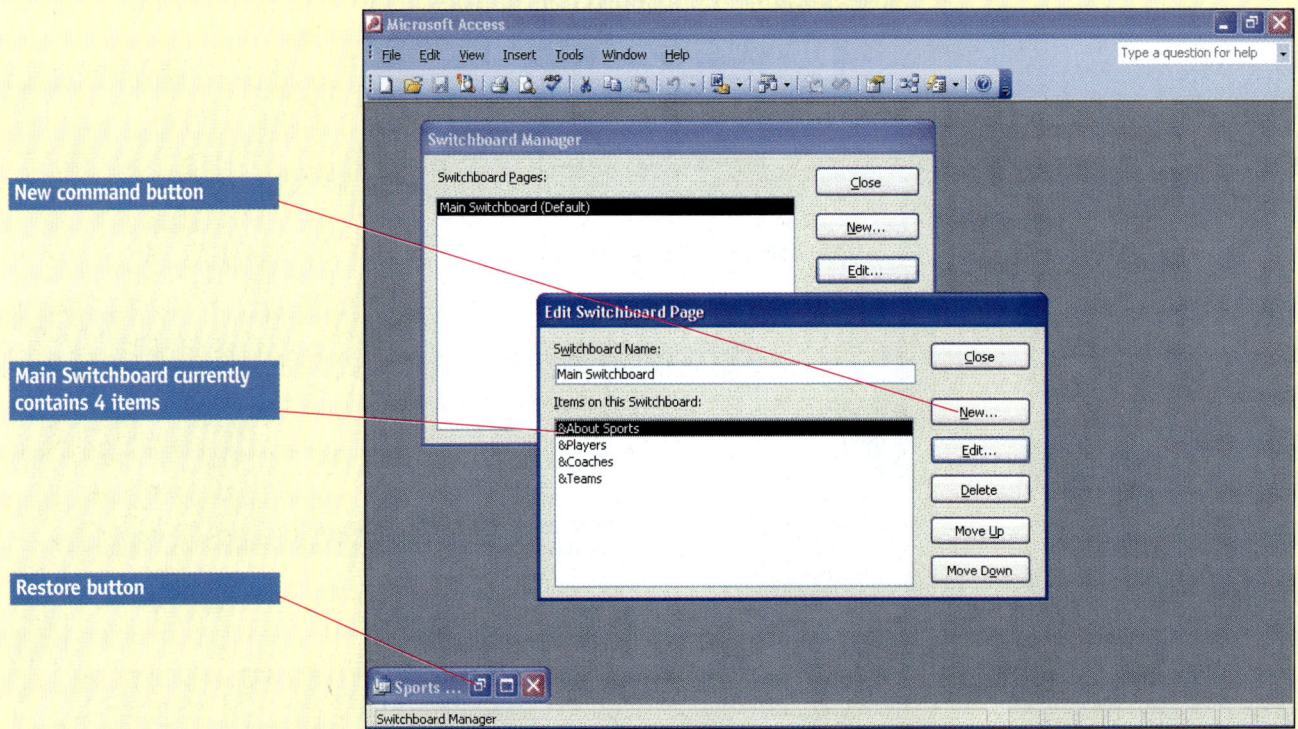

(d) Complete the Switchboard (step 4)

FIGURE 7.3 Hands-on Exercise 1 (*continued*)

ADD MODE VERSUS EDIT MODE

It's easy to miss the difference between opening a form in the Add mode versus the Edit mode. The Add mode lets you add new records to a table, but it precludes you from viewing records that are already in the table. The Edit mode is more general and lets you add new records and/or edit existing records. Select the Add mode if you want to prevent a user from modifying existing data. Choose the Edit mode to give the user unrestricted access to the table.

Step 5: **Test the Switchboard**

- Click the **Restore button** in the Database window to view the objects in the database. Click the **Tables button**. The Switchboard Items table has been created for you (see boxed tip).

- Click the **Forms tab**. The Switchboard form has been created automatically by the Switchboard Manager. Double click the **Switchboard form** to open the Main Switchboard.

- Do not be concerned about the design of the switchboard at this time, as your immediate objective is to make sure that the buttons work. (We modify the design of the switchboard at the end of the exercise.) Maximize the window.

- Click the **About Sports button** (or use the **Alt+A** shortcut) to display the About Sports form as shown in Figure 7.3e. Click the **OK button** to close the form.

- Click the **Players button** (or use the **Alt+P** shortcut) to open the Players form. Click the **Maximize button** so that the Players form takes the entire window.

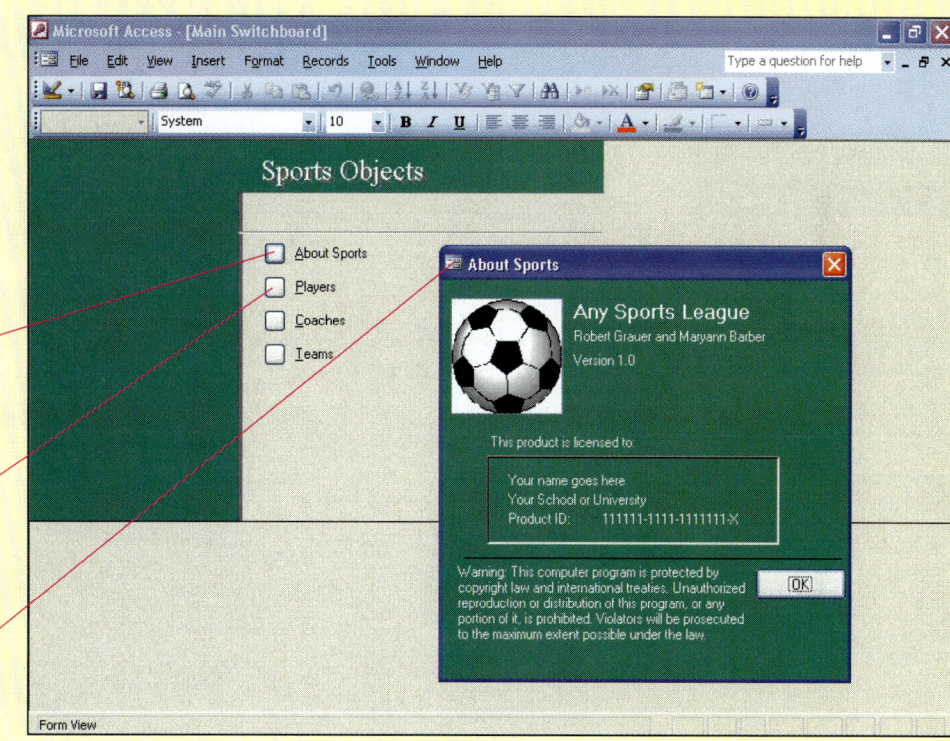

(e) Test the Switchboard (step 5)

FIGURE 7.3   Hands-on Exercise 1 (*continued*)

THE SWITCHBOARD ITEMS TABLE

You can modify an existing switchboard in one of two ways—by using the Switchboard Manager or by making changes directly in the underlying table of switchboard items. Press the F11 key to display the Database window, click the Tables button, then open the Switchboard Items table, where you can make changes to the various entries on the switchboard. We encourage you to experiment, but start by changing one entry at a time. The ItemText field is a good place to begin.

Step 6: **Add Your Record**

- Click the **Add Player button** on the bottom of the form (or use the **Alt+A** shortcut) to display a blank record where you will enter data for yourself as shown in Figure 7.3f.

- Click the **text box** to enter your first name. (The PlayerID is an AutoNumber field that is updated automatically.) Enter your name, then press the **Tab key** to move to the next field.

- Continue to enter the appropriate data for yourself, but please assign yourself to the **Comets team**. The team is entered via a drop-down list. Type **C** (the first letter in Comets) and Comets is entered automatically from the drop-down list for teams.

- The player rating is a required field (all players are evaluated for ability in order to balance the teams) and must be A, B, C, or D.

- Click the **Close Form button** to return to the switchboard.

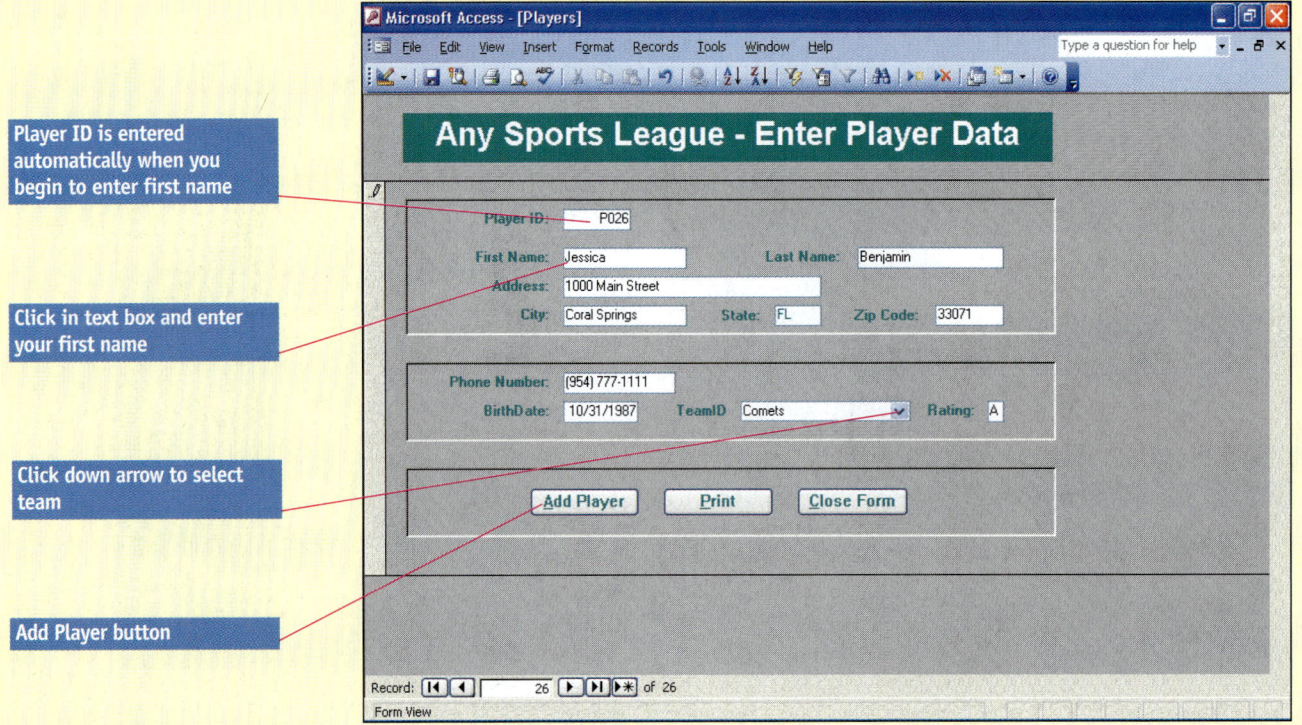

(f) Add Your Record (step 6)

FIGURE 7.3 Hands-on Exercise 1 (*continued*)

A LOOK AHEAD

The Add Record button in the Players form was created through the Command Button Wizard. The Wizard in turn creates a VBA *event procedure* that selects the blank record at the end of the underlying table and enables you to add a new player. The procedure does not, however, position you at a specific control within the Players form; that is, you still have to click in the First Name text box to start entering the data. You can, however, modify the event procedure by adding a VBA statement that automatically moves to the First Name control. See exercise 5 at the end of the chapter.

Step 7: **Complete the Data Entry**

- You should once again see the switchboard. Click the **Coaches button** (or use the **Alt+C** shortcut) to open the Coaches form.

- Click the **Add Coach button** at the bottom of the form. Click the **text box** to enter the coach's first name. (The CoachID is entered automatically since it is an AutoNumber field.)

- Enter data for your instructor as the coach. Click the appropriate **option button** to make your instructor a **Head Coach**. Assign your instructor to the Comets. Click the **Close Form button** to return to the switchboard.

- Click the **Teams command button** on the switchboard to open the Teams form and move to Team T02 (the Comets). You should see your instructor as the head coach and yourself as a player as shown in Figure 7.3g.

- Pull down the **Edit menu** and click **Select Record** (or click the selection area), then click the **Print button** to print the roster for your team.

- Click the **Close Form button** to return to the switchboard.

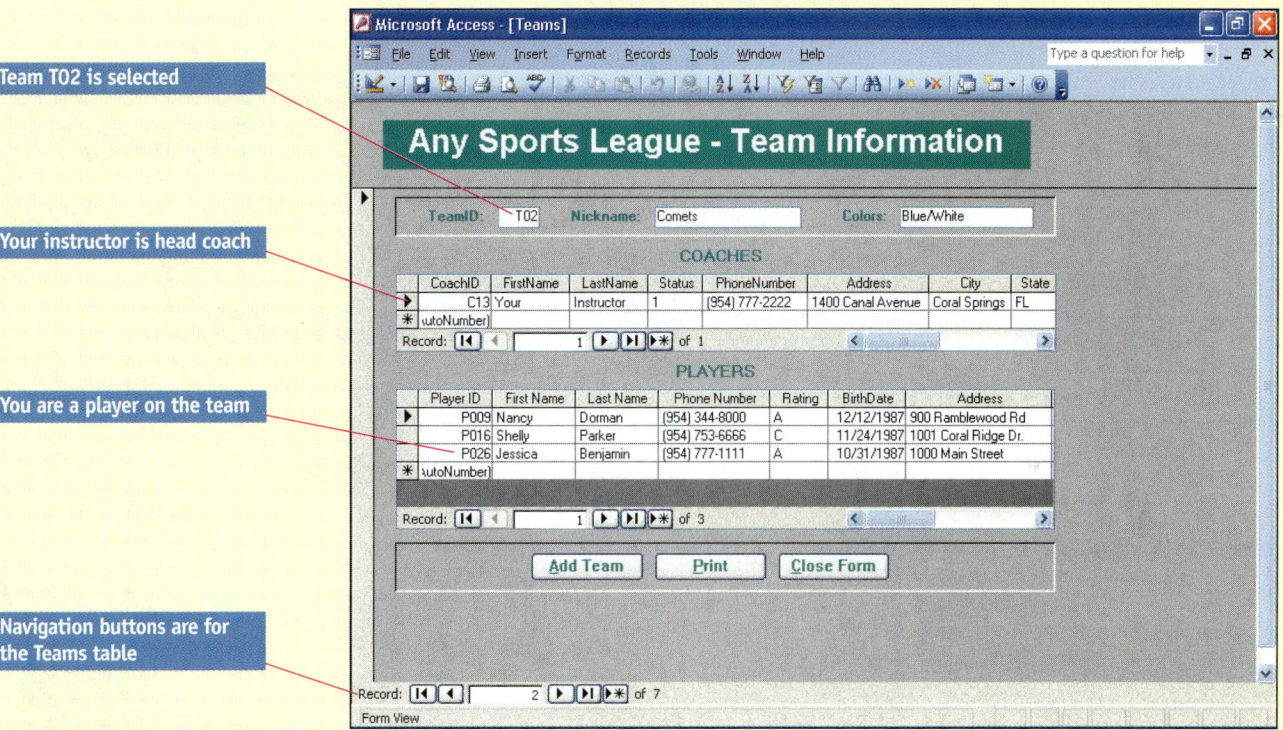

(g) Complete the Data Entry (step 7)

FIGURE 7.3 Hands-on Exercise 1 (*continued*)

THE DISPLAY WHEN PROPERTY

The Add, Print, and Close Form command buttons appear on the various forms (Team, Player, or Coach) when the forms are displayed on the screen, but not necessarily when the forms are printed. Open a form in Design view, point to an existing command button, then click the right mouse button to display a shortcut menu. Click the Properties command, click on the line for the Display When property, and choose when you want the button to appear—that is, when the form is displayed, printed, or both.

Step 8: **Insert the Clip Art**

- Change to the **Design view**. **Right click** in the Picture area of the form to display a context-sensitive menu, then click the **Properties command** to display the Properties sheet. Click the **All tab**.

- The Picture property is currently set to "none" because the default switchboard does not contain a picture. Click in the **Picture box**, then click the **Build button** to display the Insert Picture dialog box.

- Click the **down arrow** in the Look In box to change to the **Exploring Access folder**, then select the **SoccerBall** as shown in Figure 7.3h. Click **OK**.

- Size the picture as appropriate. The dimensions of the soccer ball should be changed to a square—for example, 1.5 inches × 1.5 inches. Close the property sheet.

- **Right click** below the picture in the Detail area of the form. Point to the **Fill/Back Color command** from the context-sensitive menu to display a color palette. Choose the same shade as appears on the rest of the form. (It is the fifth square from the left in the second row.)

- Click the **Undo button** if the color does not match. Save the form.

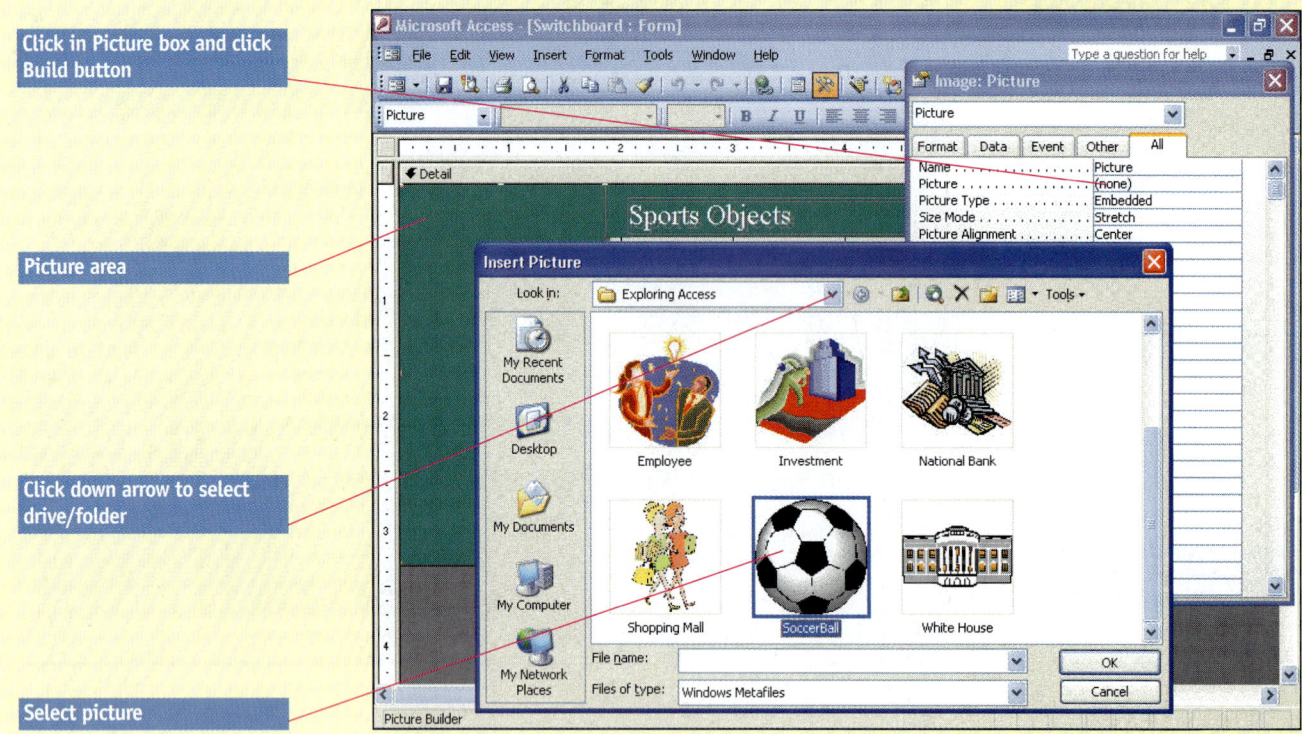

(h) Insert the Clip Art (step 8)

FIGURE 7.3 Hands-on Exercise 1 (*continued*)

THE OBJECT BOX

The easiest way to familiarize yourself with the design of the switchboard is to click the down arrow on the Object box on the Formatting toolbar, scrolling as necessary to see the various objects. Select (click) any object in the Object box and it is selected automatically in the form. Right click the selected object to display its property sheet.

Step 9: **Complete the Design**

- Delete the label that contains the title of the switchboard, "Sports Objects". (You will have to delete two labels, because the switchboard manager automatically creates a shadow.)

- Click and drag the **Label tool** to create a new unbound control for the title of the switchboard. Enter **Any Sports League** as the title. Use **18 point Arial bold, in white** for the formatting.

- Click the **Label tool**, then click and drag to create a label under the picture. Enter your name in an appropriate font, point size, and color. Move and/or size the label containing your name as appropriate.

- Press and hold the **Shift key** as you click each text box in succession. The boxes appear to be empty, but the text will be drawn from the Switchboard Items table.

- Be sure that you selected all text boxes. Click the **drop-down arrow** on the Font/Fore Color button and change the color to white as shown in Figure 7.3i. Change the font and point size to **Arial** and **10pt**, respectively. Save the form.

- Change to the **Form view** to see the result of your changes. Exit Access if you do not want to continue with the next exercise at this time.

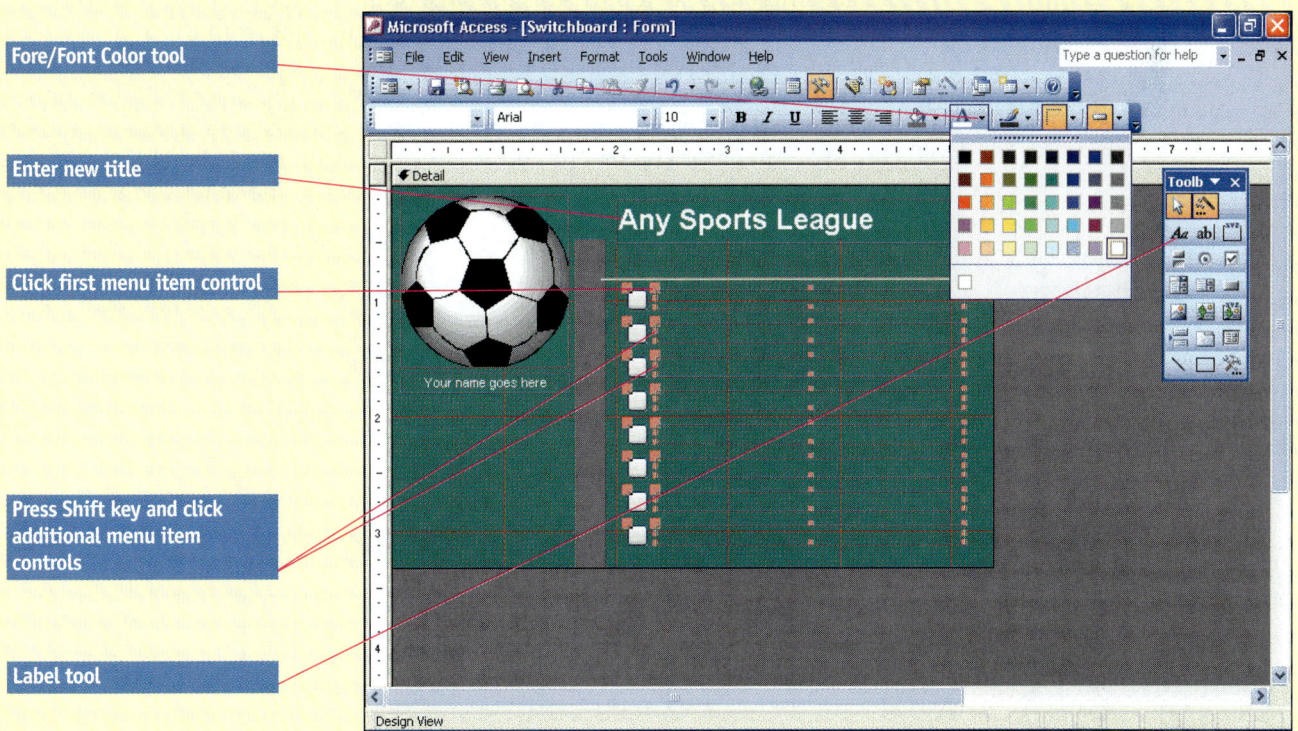

(i) Complete the Design (step 9)

FIGURE 7.3 Hands-on Exercise 1 (*continued*)

SET A TIME LIMIT

It's easy to spend an hour or more on the design of the switchboard, but that is counterproductive. The objective of this exercise was to develop a user interface that provides the "look and feel" of a system by selecting various menu options. That has been accomplished. Yes, it is important to fine-tune the interface, but within reason. Set a time limit for your design, then move on to the next exercise.

MICROSOFT OFFICE ACCESS 2003 1687

INTRODUCTION TO MACROS

The exercise just completed created a switchboard that enabled a nontechnical user to access the various tables within the database. It did not, however, automate the application completely in that the user still has to open the form containing the switchboard to get started, and further may have to maximize the switchboard once it is open. You can make the application even easier to use by including macros that perform these tasks automatically.

A *macro* automates a command sequence. Thus, instead of using the mouse or keyboard to execute a series of commands, you store the commands (actions) in a macro and execute the macro. You can create a macro to open a table, query, form, or report. You can create a macro to display an informational message, then beep to call attention to that message. You can create a macro to move or size a window, or to minimize, maximize, or restore a window. In short, you can create a macro to execute any command (or combination of commands) in any Access menu and thus make an application easier to use.

The Macro Window

A macro is created in the *Macro window*, as shown in Figure 7.4. The Macro window is divided into two sections. The *actions* (commands) that comprise the macro are entered at the top. The *arguments*, or information for those actions, are entered in the lower section. Access macros are different from those in Word or Excel, in that Access lacks the macro recorder that is common to those applications. Hence, you have to enter the actions explicitly in the Macro window rather than have the recorder do it for you. In any event, macros are stored as separate objects in a database. The macro name can contain up to 64 characters (letters, numbers, and spaces), and it appears in the title bar of the Macro window (e.g., Back up Your System in Figure 7.4).

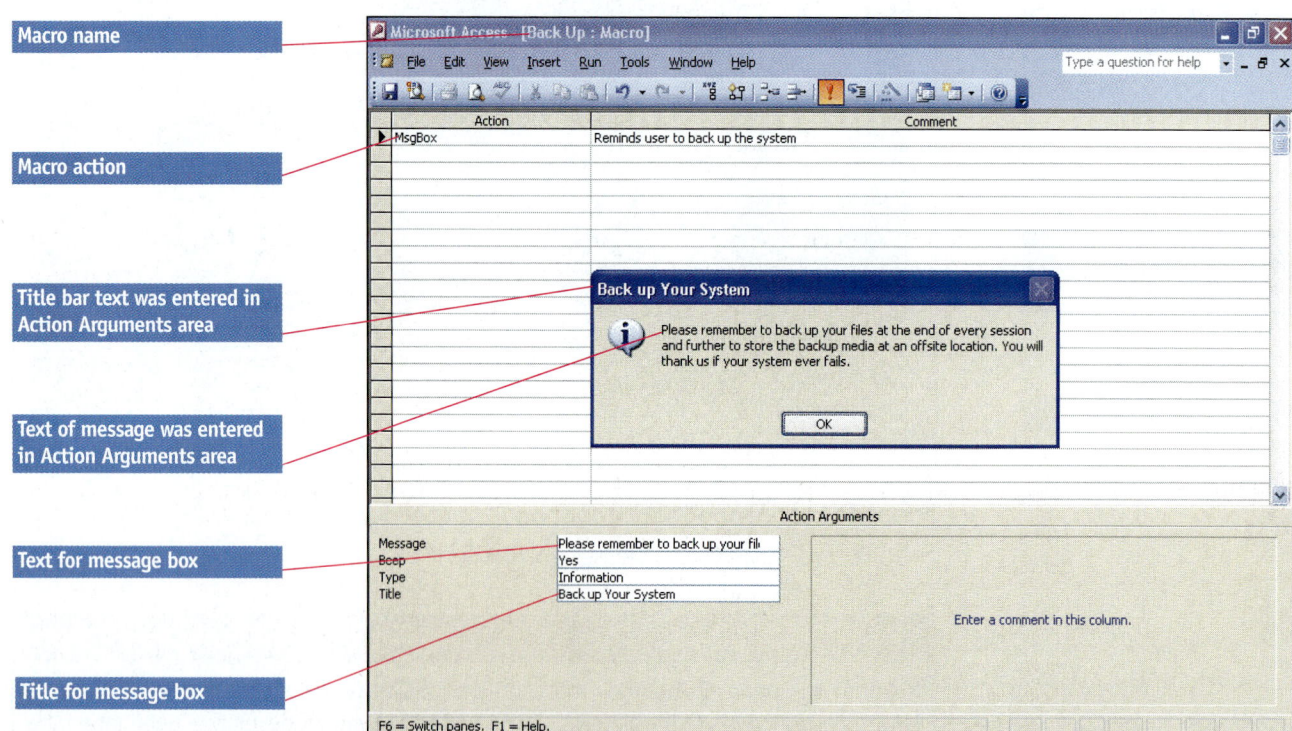

FIGURE 7.4 The Macro Window

1688 CHAPTER 7: BUILDING APPLICATIONS

To create a macro, select the Macros button in the Database window, then click the New button to display the Macro window. You add actions to a macro by clicking in the Action area, then choosing the action from a drop-down list, or by typing the name of the action. The arguments for an action are entered in similar fashion—that is, by choosing from a drop-down list (when available) or by typing the argument directly. The macro in Figure 7.4 consists of a single action with four arguments. As indicated, you specify the action, *MsgBox* in this example, in the top portion of the window, then you enter the values for the various arguments (Message, Beep, Type, and Title) in the bottom half of the window.

After the macro is created, you can execute it whenever the application is open. Execution of the macro in Figure 7.4, for example, will display the dialog box shown in the figure, to remind the user to back up his or her data. The contents of the dialog box are determined by the value of the arguments. The text of the dialog box is specified in the Message argument, only a portion of which is visible in the Macro window. The value of the Type argument determines the icon that is displayed within the dialog box (Information in this example). The Title argument contains the text that appears in the title bar of the dialog box.

The *macro toolbar* is displayed at the top of the Macro window and contains buttons that help create and test a macro. Many of the buttons (e.g., the Database window, Save, and Help buttons) are common to other toolbars you have used in conjunction with other objects. Other buttons are specific to the Macro window and are referenced in the hands-on exercises. As with other toolbars, you can point to a button to display its ScreenTip and determine its purpose.

The AutoExec Macro

The *AutoExec macro* is unique in that it is executed automatically whenever the database in which it is stored is opened. The macro is used to automate a system for the end user. It typically contains an OpenForm action to open the form containing the main switchboard. It may also perform other housekeeping chores, such as maximizing the current window.

Every database can have its own AutoExec macro, but there is no requirement for the AutoExec macro to be present. We recommend, however, that you include an AutoExec macro in every application to help the user get started.

Debugging

Writing a macro is similar to writing a program, in that errors occur if the actions and/or the associated arguments are specified incorrectly. Should Access encounter an error during the execution of a macro, it displays as much information as it can to help you determine the reason for the error.

Figure 7.5 contains an erroneous version of the AutoExec macro that attempts to open the Switchboard form. The macro contains two actions, Maximize and OpenForm. The Maximize action maximizes the Database window and affects all subsequent screens that will be displayed in the application. The OpenForm macro is intended to open the switchboard from the previous exercise. The name of the form is deliberately misspelled.

When the AutoExec macro is executed, Access attempts to open a form called "Switchboards", but is unable to do so, and hence it displays the informational message in the figure. Click OK, and you are presented with another dialog box, which attempts to step you through the macro and discover the cause of the error. As indicated, the error is due to the fact that the name of the form should have been "Switchboard" rather than "Switchboard*s*". The errors will not always be this easy to find, and hopefully, you will not make any. Should a bug occur, however, you will know where to begin the *debugging* process.

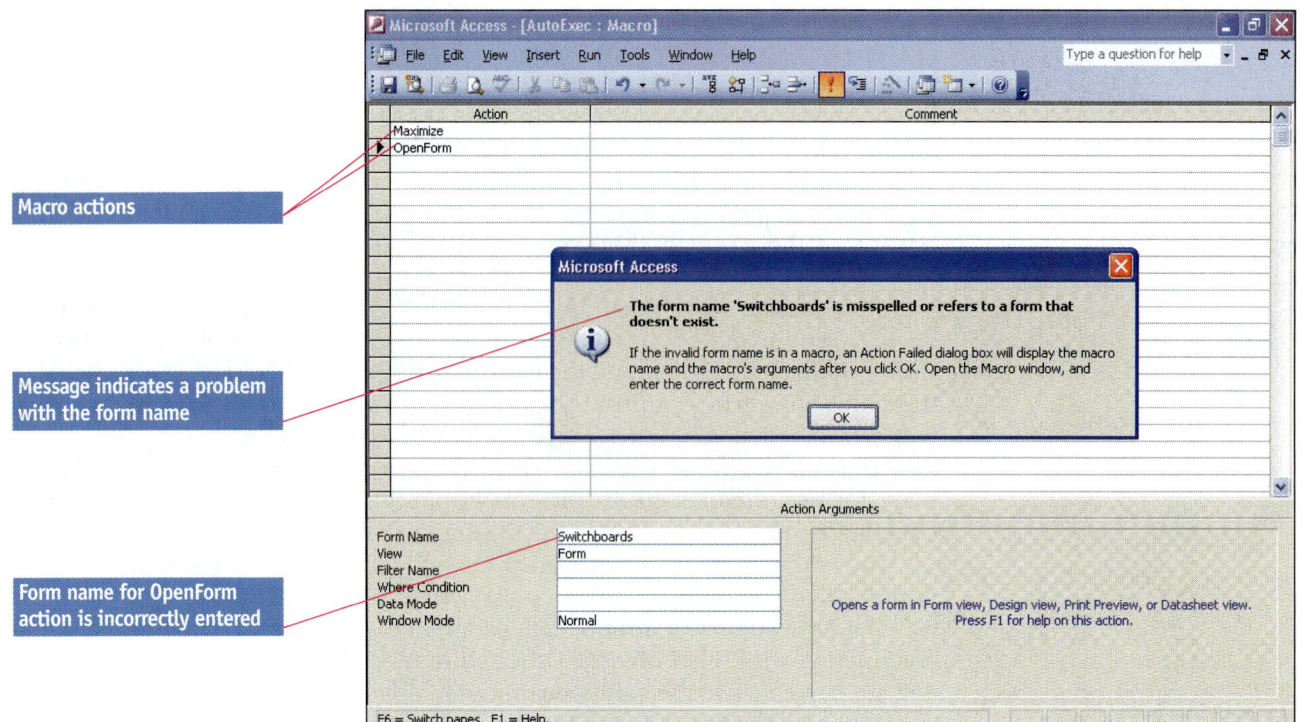

FIGURE 7.5 Debugging

APPLICATION DEVELOPMENT

Application development is an iterative process that entails continual dialog between the end user (client) and the developer. In essence, the developer presents the client with multiple versions of the application, with each successive version containing additional functionality. The user tests and evaluates each version and provides comments to the developer, who incorporates the feedback and delivers a new version (release) of the application. The process continues with each successive release containing increased functionality until the system is complete.

The user is presented with a working system (or ***prototype***) at every stage of testing that captures the "look and feel" of the finished application. The switchboard in Figure 7.6a, for example, is an updated version of the main switchboard from the first hands-on exercise. Two menu options have been added—a report menu that displays the report switchboard in Figure 7.6b and a player draft. (The latter is a form that is used to assign players to teams and is developed later in the chapter.) The Switchboard Manager creates both switchboards.

The reports, however, have not yet been created, nor do they need to be, because the user can click any of the buttons on the report switchboard and see the indicated message, which was created by a simple macro. The application is "complete" in the sense that every button on the switchboard works, but it is incomplete in that the reports have not been fully developed. Nevertheless, the prototype lets the user see a working system and enables the user to provide immediate feedback. He or she sees immediately all of the planned reports and can comment on whether any additional reports are required.

The Report switchboard also provides access to the report template. The purpose of the ***template*** is to provide additional feedback to the user with respect to the appearance of the eventual reports. It is just as easy to create an attractive report as an ugly one, and a uniform Report Header adds to the professional look of an application. The sooner the user communicates the requested changes to the developer, the easier (and less costly) it is for the developer to incorporate those changes.

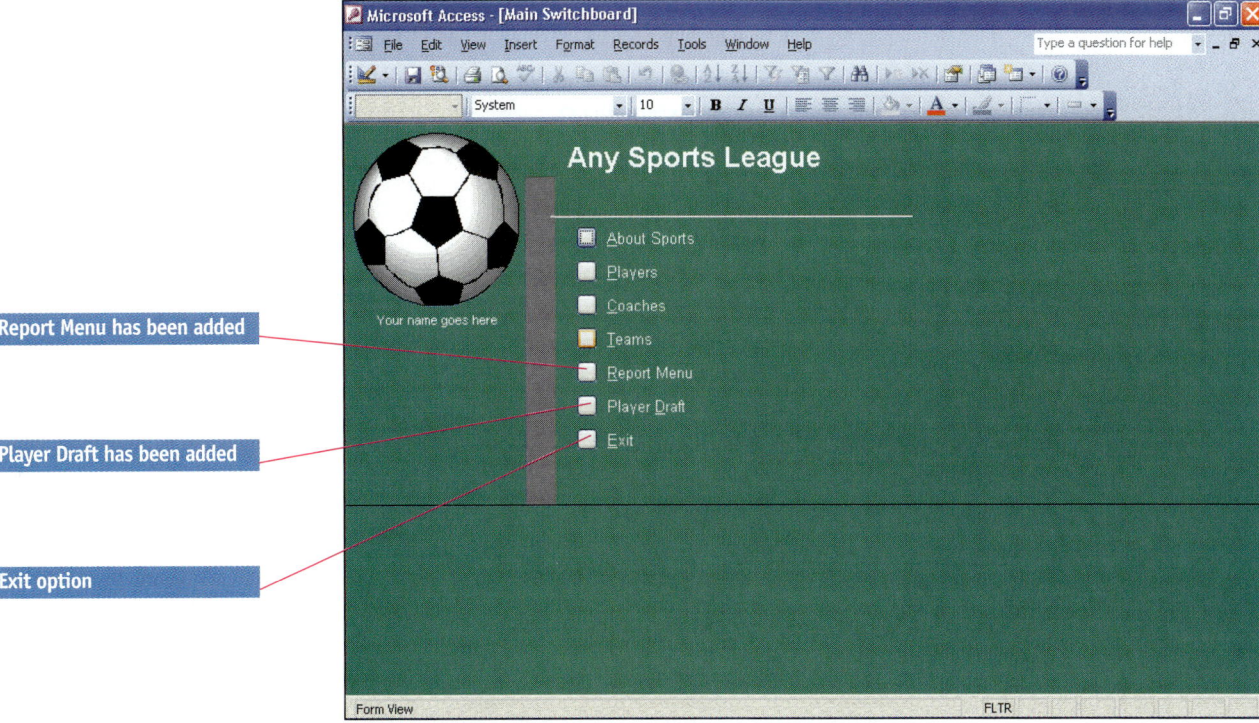

(a) Main Switchboard

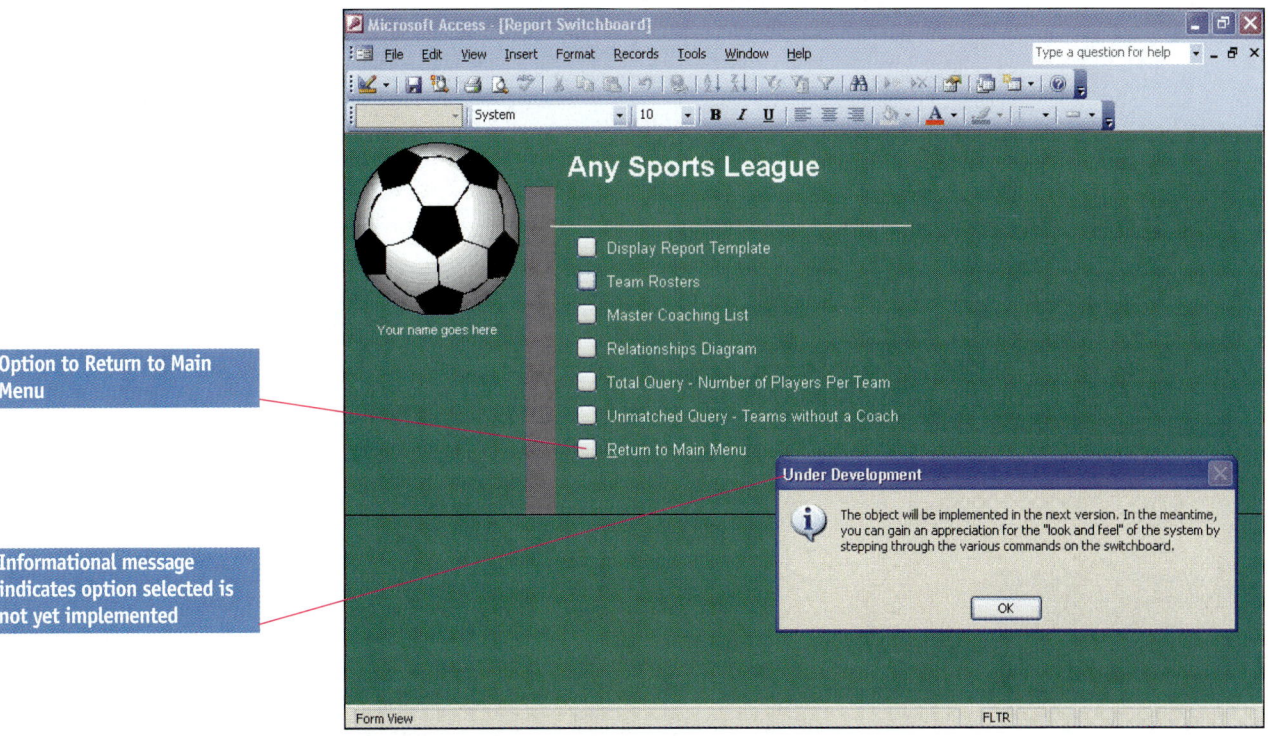

(b) Report Switchboard

FIGURE 7.6 Application Development

hands-on exercise 2

Macros and Prototyping

Objective To create an AutoExec and a Close Database macro; to create a subsidiary switchboard. Use Figure 7.7 as a guide in the exercise.

Step 1: **Create the AutoExec Macro**

- Start Access. Open the **Sports Objects database** from the previous exercise. Click the **Macros button** in the Database window.

- Click the **New button** to create a new macro. If necessary, click the **Maximize button** so that the Macro window takes the entire screen as in Figure 7.7a.

- Click the **drop-down arrow** in the Action box to display the available macro actions. Scroll until you can select the **Maximize** action. (There are no arguments for this action.)

- Click the **Action box** on the second line, click the **drop-down arrow** to display the macro actions, then scroll until you can click the **OpenForm action**. Click the text box for the **Form Name** argument in the lower section of the Macro window.

- Click the **drop-down arrow** to display the list of existing forms and select **Switchboard** (the form you created in the previous exercise).

- Click the **Save button** to display the Save As dialog box in Figure 7.7a. Type **AutoExec** as the macro name and click **OK**.

- Click the **Run button** to run the macro and open the switchboard.

- Close the switchboard. Close the AutoExec macro.

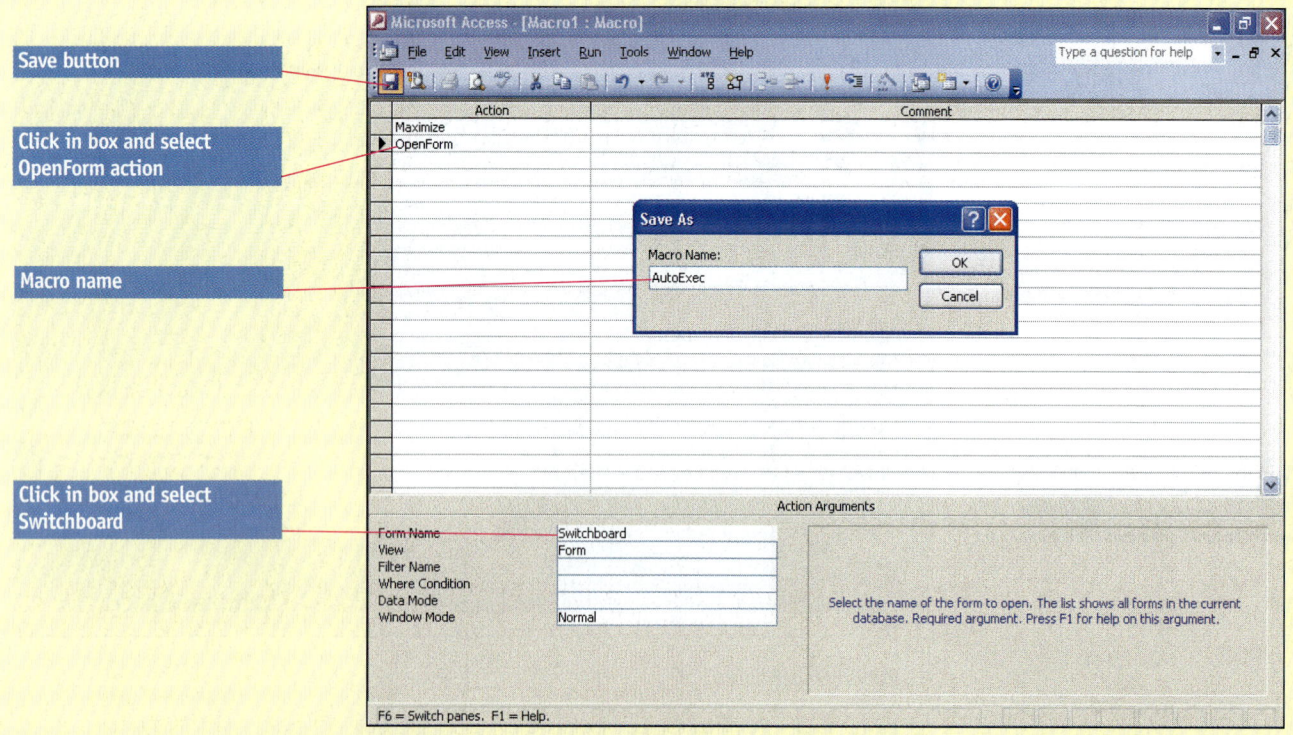

(a) Create the AutoExec Macro (step 1)

FIGURE 7.7 Hands-on Exercise 2

1692 CHAPTER 7: BUILDING APPLICATIONS

Step 2: **Create the Prototype Macro**

- You should be back in the Database window, which should display the name of the AutoExec macro. Click the **New button** to create a second macro.

- Type **Ms** (the first two letters in the MsgBox action), then press **Enter** to accept this action. Enter the comment shown in Figure 7.7b.

- Click the text box for the **Message** argument, then press **Shift+F2** to display the zoom box so that you can see the contents of your entire message. Enter the message in Figure 7.7b. Click **OK**.

- Click the text box for the **Type** argument, click the **drop-down arrow** to display the list of message types, and select **Information**.

- Click in the text box for the **Title** argument, and enter **Under Development**.

- Click the **Run button** to test the macro. You will see a message indicating that you have to save the macro. Click **Yes** to save the macro, type **Prototype** as the name of the macro, and click **OK**.

- You will see a dialog box containing the message you just created. Click **OK**. Close the macro.

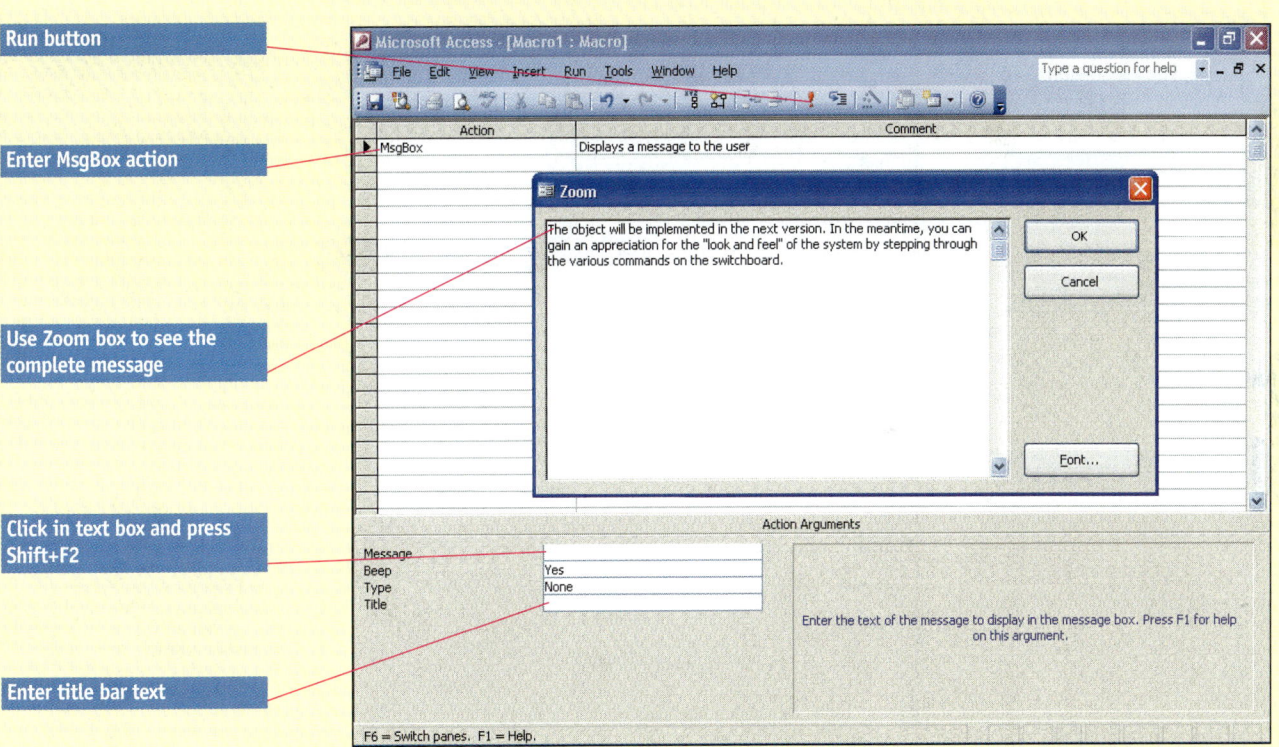

(b) Create the Prototype Macro (step 2)

FIGURE 7.7 Hands-on Exercise 2 (*continued*)

TYPE ONLY THE FIRST LETTER(S)

Click the Action box, then type the first letter of a macro action to move immediately to the first macro action beginning with that letter. Type an M, for example, and Access automatically enters the Maximize action. If necessary, type the second letter of the desired action; for example, type the letter i (after typing an M), and Access selects the Minimize action.

Step 3: **Create the Close Database Macro**

- Click the **New button** once again to create the third (and last) macro for this exercise. Specify the **MsgBox** action as the first command in the macro. Enter the comment shown in Figure 7.7c.

- Enter an appropriate message that stresses the importance of backup. Select Warning as the message type. Enter an appropriate title for the message box.

- Click the **Action box** on the second line. Type **Cl** (the first two letters in Close) and press **Enter**. Enter the indicated comment as shown in Figure 7.7c.

- Click the text box for the **Object Type** argument. Click the **drop-down arrow** and choose **Form** as the Object type. Click the **Object Name** argument, click the **drop-down arrow**, and choose **Switchboard** as the Object (form) name.

- Click the **Action box** on the third line. Type **Cl** (the first two letters in Close) and press **Enter**. Click the **comments line** for this macro action and enter the comment shown in the figure. No arguments are necessary.

- Save the macro as **Close Database**, then close the macro. If necessary, press the **F11 key** to return to the Database window, where you should see three macros: AutoExec, Close Database, and Prototype.

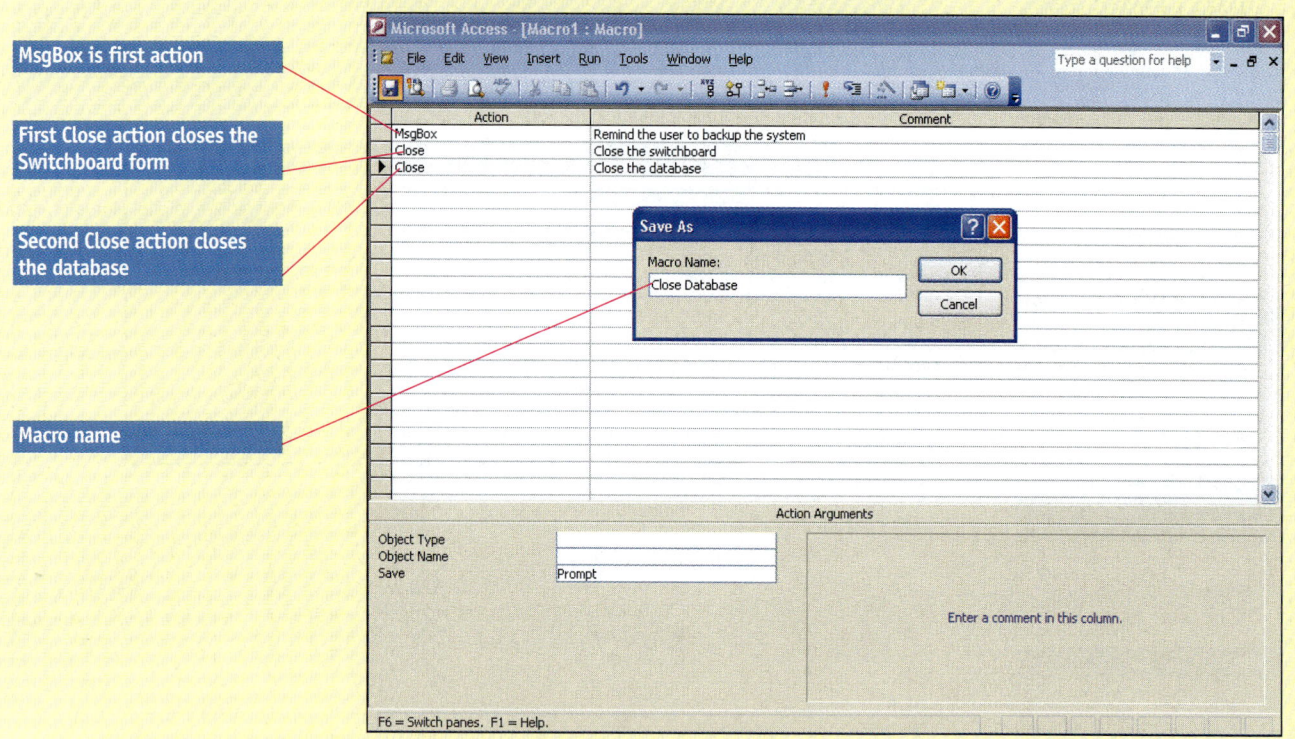

(c) Create the Close Database macro (step 3)

FIGURE 7.7 Hands-on Exercise 2 (*continued*)

USE KEYBOARD SHORTCUTS—F6, F11, AND SHIFT+F2

Use the F6 key to move back and forth between the top and bottom halves of the Macro window. Press Shift+F2 to display a zoom box that enables you to view long arguments in their entirety. Use the F11 key at any time to display the Database window.

Step 4: **Create the Report Switchboard**

- Minimize the Database window to give yourself more room in which to work. Pull down the **Tools menu**, click the **Database Utilities command**, and choose **Switchboard Manager** to display the Switchboard Manager dialog box.

- Click **New**. Enter **Report Switchboard** as the name of the switchboard page. Click **OK**. The Create New dialog box closes and the Report Switchboard page appears in the Switchboard Manager dialog box.

- Select the **Report Switchboard**, click **Edit** to open the Edit Switchboard Page dialog box. Click **New** to open the Edit Switchboard Item dialog box.

- Add the first switchboard item. Click in the **Text** list box and type **Display Report Template** as shown in Figure 7.7d.

- Press the **Tab key** to move to the Command list box and type **Open R** (the first several letters in Open Report). Press **Tab** to move to the Report list box and type **R** (the first letter in the report name, "Report Template").

- Click **OK** to create the switchboard item. The Edit Switchboard Item dialog box closes and Display Report Template appears on the Report Switchboard page.

- Add **Team Rosters** as the next switchboard item. Specify the **Run macro command** and choose **Prototype** as the macro. Add additional buttons for the **Master Coaching List** and **Relationships Diagram**, both of which run the Prototype macro.

- Add an additional item that will return the user to the main switchboard. Click **New** to open the Edit Switchboard Item dialog box. Click in the **Text** list box and type "**&Return to Main Menu...**"

- Press the **Tab key** to move to the Command list box, where the Go to Switchboard command is entered by default. Press the **Tab key** to move to the Switchboard list box, and type **M** (the first letter in the "Main Switchboard"). Click **OK** to create the switchboard item. Close the Edit Switchboard Page.

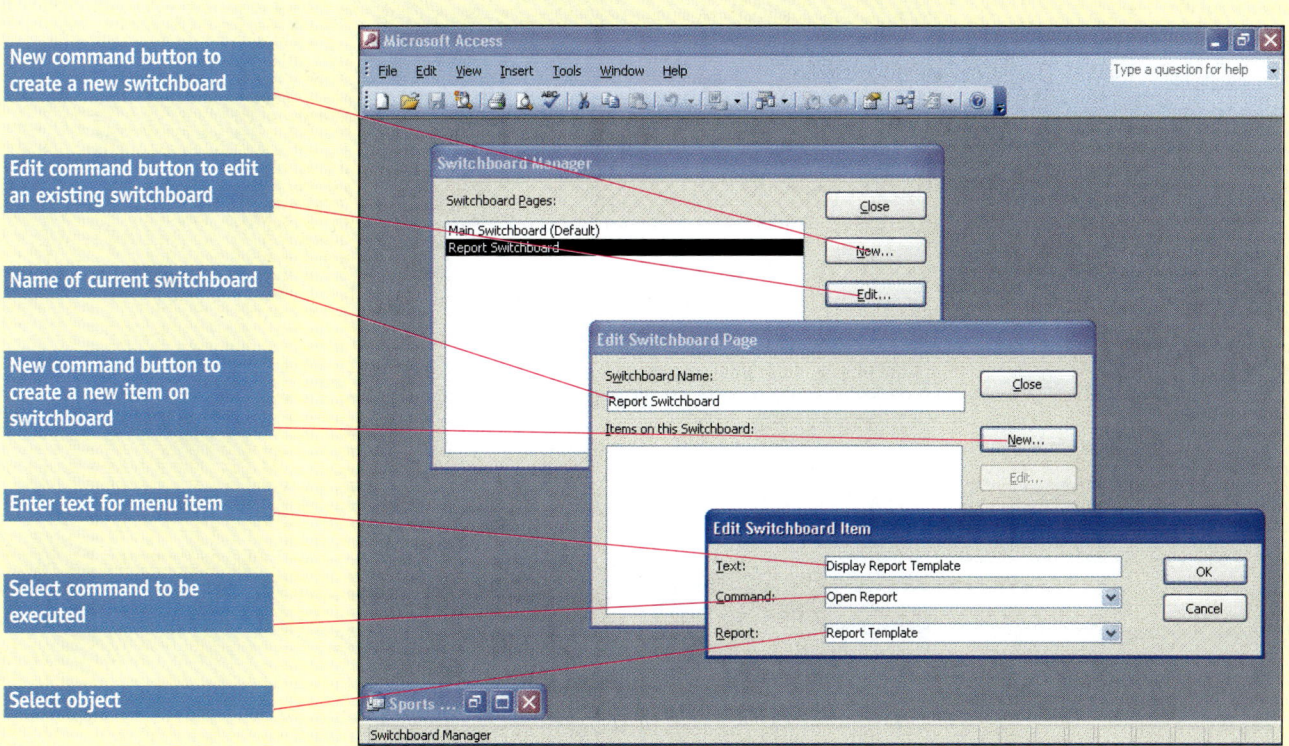

(d) Create the Report Switchboard (step 4)

FIGURE 7.7 Hands-on Exercise 2 (*continued*)

Step 5: Modify the Main Switchboard

- Select the **Main Switchboard** in the Switchboard Manager dialog box, click the **Edit button** to open the Edit Switchboard Page dialog box, then click **New** to open the Edit Switchboard Item dialog box as shown in Figure 7.7e.

- Add a new switchboard item to open the Report Switchboard. Click in the **Text** list box and type **"&Report Menu . . ."**, the name of the command as it will appear in the switchboard.

- Press the **Tab key** to move to the Command list box, where "Go to Switchboard" is already entered, then press the **Tab key** a second time to move to the Switchboard list box. Type **R** (the first letter in the "Report Switchboard"). Click **OK** to create the switchboard item.

- The Edit Switchboard Item dialog box closes and "&Report Menu" appears on the main switchboard.

- The main switchboard needs one last command to close the database. Thus, click **New** to open the Edit Switchboard Item dialog box. Type **&Exit** as the name of the command.

- Press the **Tab key** to move to the Command list box and type **R** (the first letter in "Run Macro"). Press the **Tab key** a second time to move to the Macro list box, and type **C** (the first letter in the "Close Database" macro). Click **OK** to create the switchboard item.

- The main switchboard should contain six items—&About Sports, &Players, &Coaches, and &Teams from the first exercise, and &Report Menu and &Exit from this exercise.

- Close the Edit Switchboard Page dialog box. Close the Switchboard Manager.

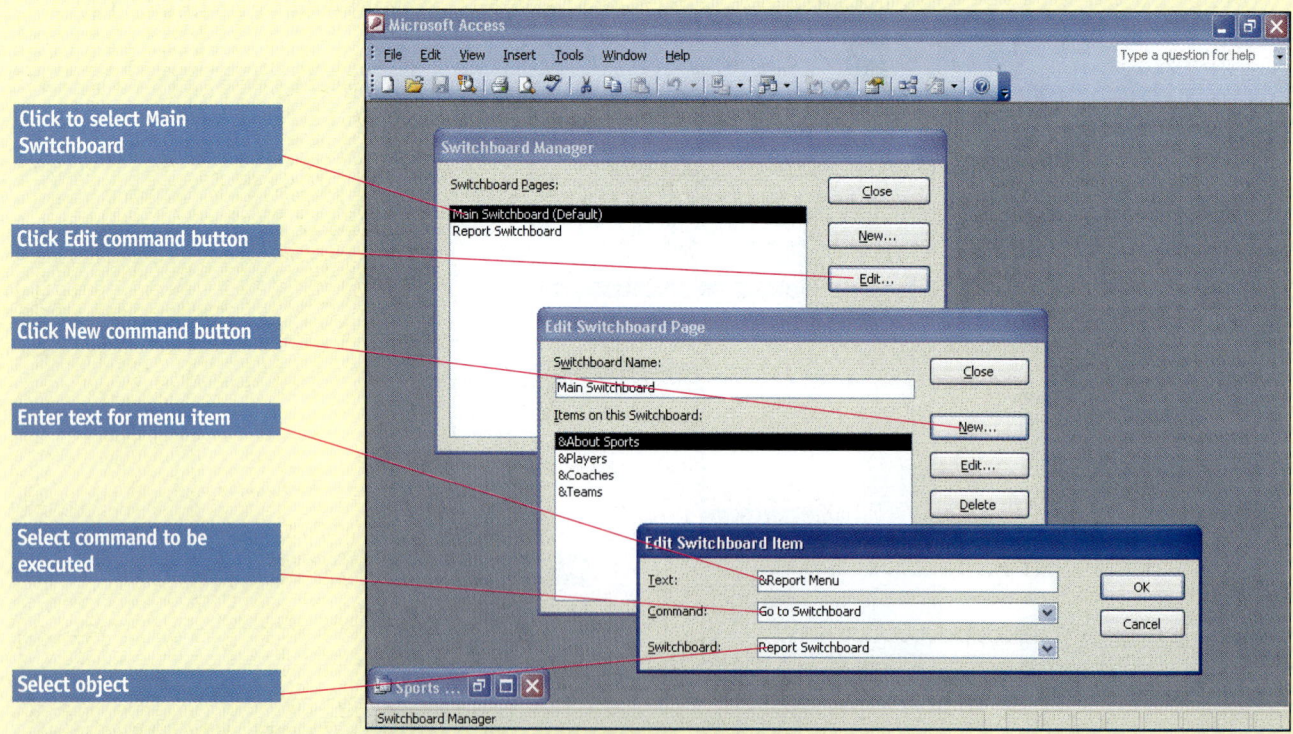

(e) Modify the Main Switchboard (step 5)

FIGURE 7.7 Hands-on Exercise 2 (*continued*)

Step 6: **Test the Main Switchboard**

- Click the **Restore button** in the Database window to view the objects in the database, click the **Forms button**, then double click the **Switchboard form** to open the main switchboard.

- Click the **Exit button** (or use the **Alt+E** shortcut):
  - You should see an informational message similar to the one shown in Figure 7.7f. (The message is displayed by the MsgBox action in the Close Database macro.)
  - Click **OK** to accept the message. The Close Database macro then closes the database.

- Pull down the **File menu**, then click **Sports Objects** from the list of recently opened databases. Click **Open** in response to the security warning.

- The AutoExec macro executes automatically, maximizes the current window, and displays the main switchboard.

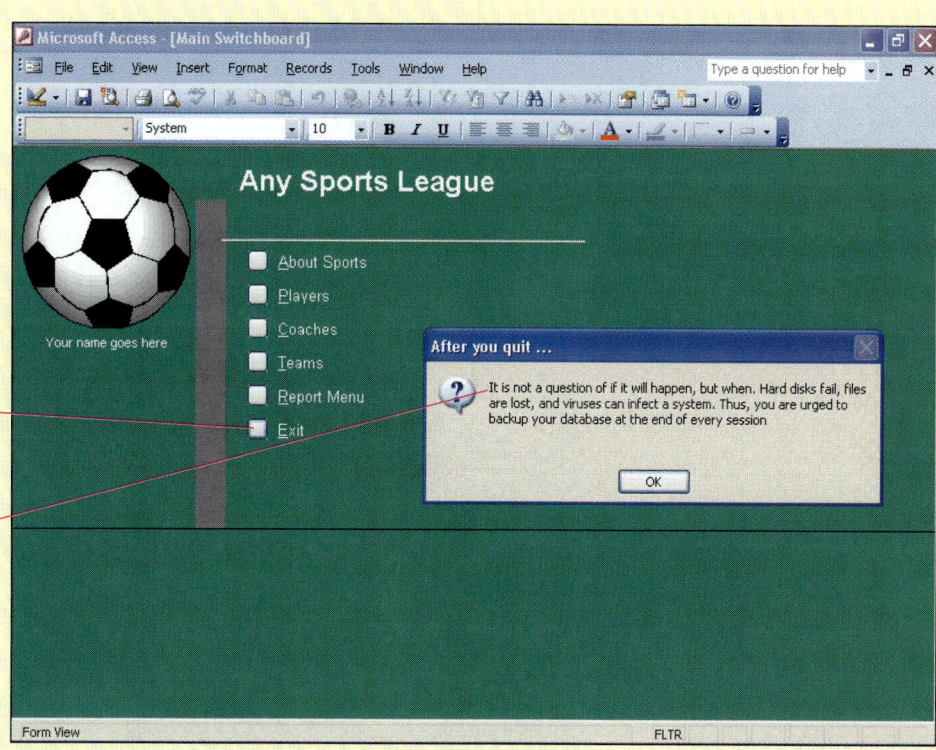

(f) Test the Main Switchboard (step 6)

FIGURE 7.7 Hands-on Exercise 2 (*continued*)

ADD A HYPERLINK

You can enhance the appeal of your switchboard through inclusion of a hyperlink. Open the switchboard form in Design view, then click the Insert Hyperlink button to display the Insert Hyperlink dialog box. Enter the text to be displayed and the Web address, then click OK to close the dialog box and return to the Design view. Right click the hyperlink to display a shortcut menu, click the Properties command to display the Properties dialog box, then change the font and/or point size as appropriate.

Step 7: **Test the Report Switchboard**

- Click the **Report Menu button** (or use the **Alt+R** keyboard shortcut) on the main switchboard to display the Report switchboard in Figure 7.7g.
- Click the button to **Display the Report Template**. Click the **Print button** to print a copy of this report for your instructor. Close the Report Preview window to return to the Report switchboard.
- Click the buttons for the other reports which should display the message in Figure 7.7g.
- Click the **Return to Main Menu button** to exit the Report Menu and return to the main switchboard.
  - To continue working, click the **Close button** on the title bar (or pull down the **File menu** and click the **Close command**) to close the form and continue working on this database. (You should not click the Exit command button as that would close the database.) You should be back in the Database window, where you can continue with the next hands-on exercise.
  - To close the database, click the **Exit button** (or use the **Alt+E** shortcut).
- Either way, you have demonstrated the "look and feel" of the system to the extent that you can step through the various menus. Good work.

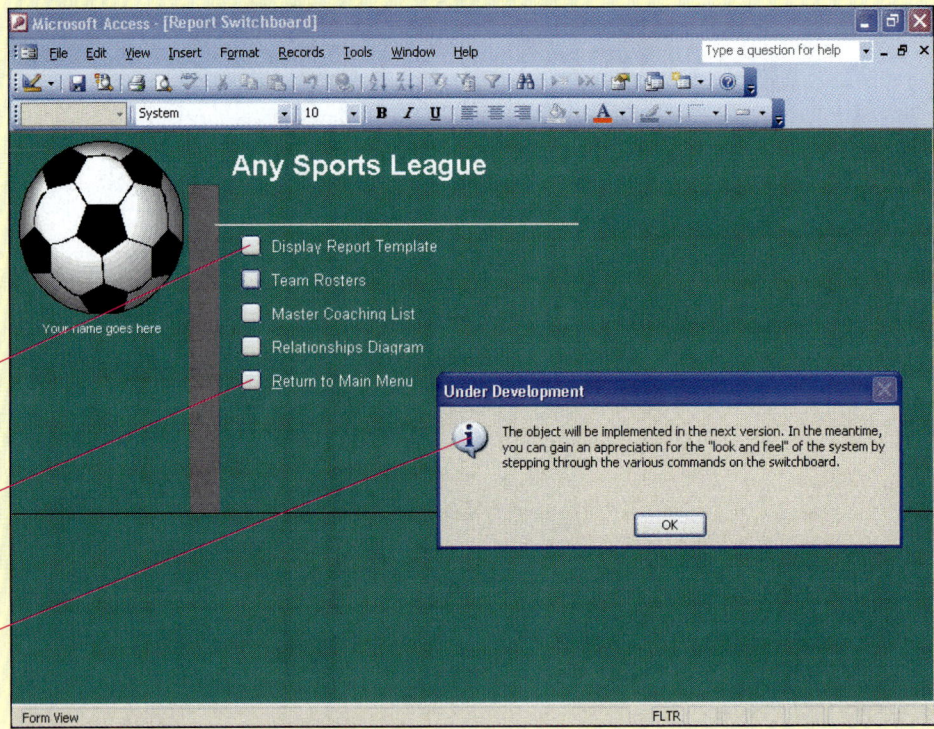

(g) Test the Report Switchboard (step 7)

FIGURE 7.7 Hands-on Exercise 2 (*continued*)

BE CONSISTENT

Consistency within an application is essential to its success. Similar functions should be done in similar ways to facilitate learning and build confidence in the application. The sports application, for example, has similar screens for the Players, Coaches, and Teams forms, each of which contains the identical buttons to add or print a record and close the form.

THE PLAYER DRAFT

A player draft is essential to the operation of the league. Players sign up for the coming season at registration, after which the coaches meet to select players for their teams. All players are rated as to ability, and the league strives to maintain a competitive balance among teams. This is accomplished through a draft in which the coaches take turns selecting players from the pool of unassigned players.

The player draft is implemented through the form in Figure 7.8, which is based on a query that identifies players who have not yet been assigned to a team. The easiest way to create the underlying query is through the ***Unmatched Query Wizard*** that identifies records in one table (the Players table) that do not have matching records in another table (the Teams table). The wizard prompts you for the necessary information, then it creates the required query.

The query is displayed within a form as shown in Figure 7.8. The coaches will view the list of unassigned players during the actual draft and make the team assignments. A ***combo box*** within the query simplifies data entry in that a coach is able to click the drop-down list box to display the list of teams, rather than having to remember the TeamID.

In addition to displaying the list of unassigned players, the form in Figure 7.8 also contains three command buttons that are used during the player draft. The Find Player button moves directly to a specific player, and enables a coach to see whether a specific player has been assigned to a team, and if so, to which team. The Update List button refreshes the underlying query on which the list of unassigned players is based. It is used periodically during the draft as players are assigned to teams, to remove those players from the list of unassigned players. The End Draft button closes the form and returns to the switchboard. Note, too, that the appearance of the form matches the other forms in the application. This type of consistency is important to give your application a professional look.

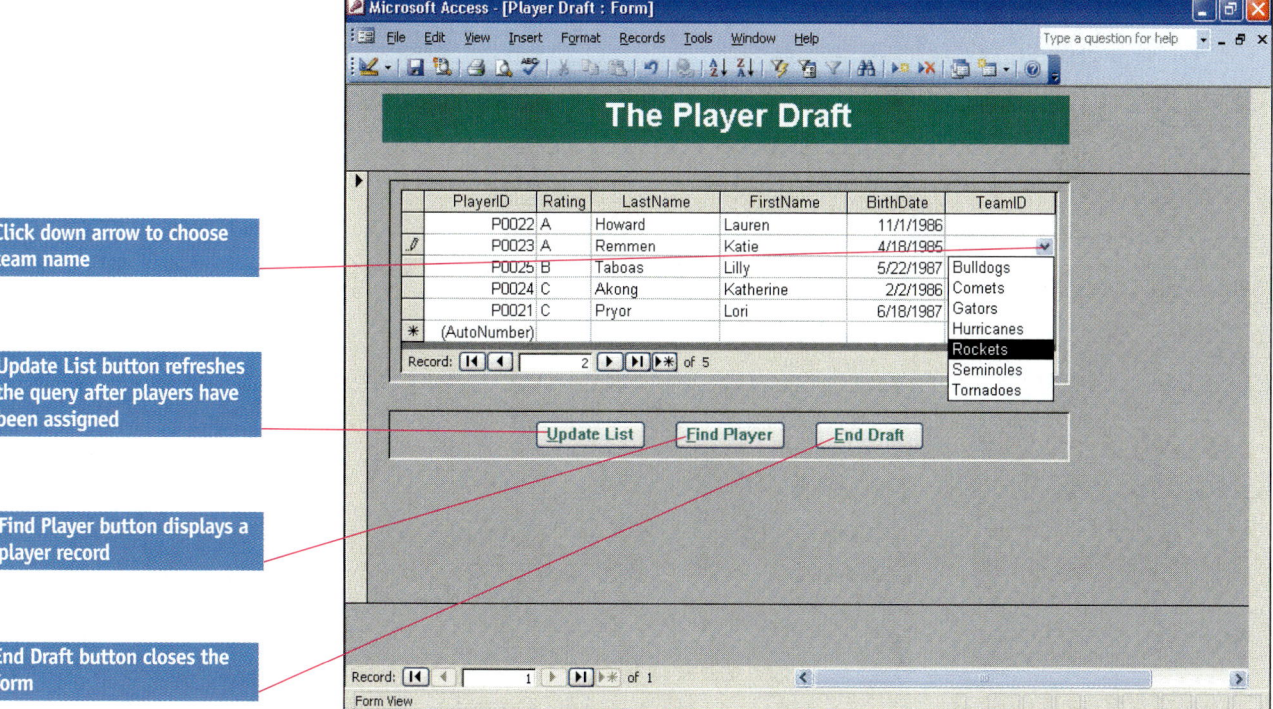

FIGURE 7.8 The Player Draft

Macro Groups

Implementation of the player draft requires three macros, one for each command button. Although you could create a separate macro for each button, it is convenient to create a *macro group* that contains the individual macros. The macro group has a name, as does each macro in the group. Only the name of the macro group appears in the Database window.

Figure 7.9 displays a Player Draft macro group containing three individual macros (Update List, Find Player, and End Draft), which run independently of one another. The name of each macro appears in the Macro Name column (which is displayed by clicking the Macro Names button on the Macro toolbar). The actions and comments for each macro are shown in the corresponding columns to the right of the macro name.

The advantage of storing related macros in a macro group, as opposed to storing them individually, is purely organizational. Large systems often contain many macros, which can overwhelm the developer as he or she tries to locate a specific macro. Storing related macros in macro groups limits the entries in the Database window, since only the (name of the) macro group is displayed. Thus, the Database window would contain a single entry (Player Draft, which is the name of the macro group), as opposed to three individual entries (Update List, Find Player, and End Draft, which correspond to the macros in the group).

Access must still be able to identify the individual macros so that each macro can be executed at the appropriate time. If, for example, a macro is to be executed when the user clicks a command button, the **On Click property** of that command button must specify both the individual macro and the macro group. The two names are separated by a period; for example, Player Draft.Update List to indicate the Update List macro in the Player Draft macro group.

As indicated, each macro in Figure 7.9 corresponds to a command button in the Player Draft form. The macros are created in the following hands-on exercise that implements the player draft.

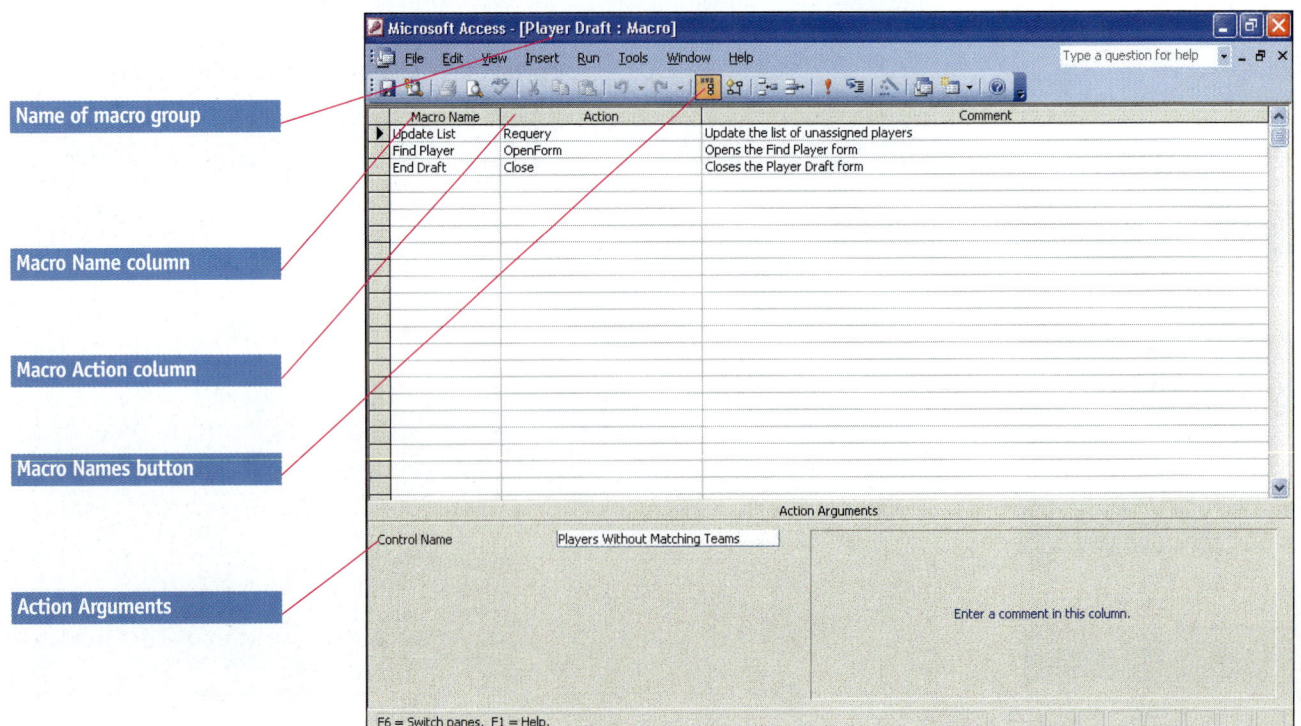

FIGURE 7.9 Macro Group

hands-on exercise

3 The Player Draft

Objective Use the Unmatched Query Wizard, then create a form based on the resulting query. Create a macro group containing three macros to implement a player draft. Use Figure 7.10 as a guide in the exercise.

Step 1: **The Unmatched Query Wizard**

- Start Access and open the **Sports Objects database**. Pull down the **File menu** and click **Close** (or click the **Close button**) to close the Main Menu form but leave the database open.

- Click the **Queries button** in the Database window. Click **New**, select the **Find Unmatched Query Wizard**, then click **OK** to start the wizard:
  - Select **Players** as the table whose records you want to see in the query results. Click **Next**.
  - Select **Teams** as the table that contains the related records. Click **Next**.
  - **TeamID** is automatically selected as the matching field. Click **Next**.
  - Select the following fields from the Available Fields list: **PlayerID, Rating, LastName, FirstName, BirthDate**, and **TeamID**. Click **Next**.
  - **Players Without Matching Teams** is entered as the name of the query. Check that the option button to **View the results** is selected, then click **Finish** to exit the wizard and see the results of the query.

- You should see a dynaset containing five players (Pryor, Howard, Remmen, Akong, and Taboas) as shown in Figure 7.10a.

- The TeamID field for each of these players is blank, indicating that these players have not yet been assigned.

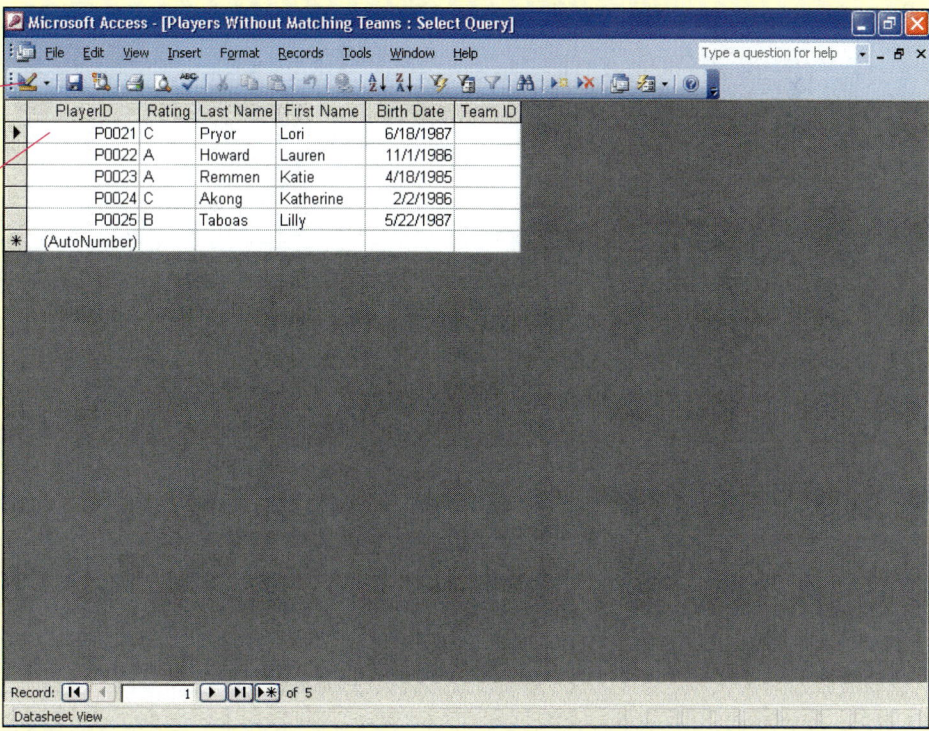

(a) The Unmatched Query Wizard (step 1)

FIGURE 7.10 Hands-on Exercise 3

Step 2: **Modify the Query**

- Change to **Design view** to see the underlying query as displayed in Figure 7.10b.

- Click and drag the line separating the upper and lower portions of the window. If necessary, click and drag the field lists to match the figure.

- Click in the **Sort row** for **Rating**, then click **Ascending** from the drop-down list. Click in the **Sort row** for **LastName**, then click **Ascending** from the drop-down list.

- Click the **Run button** to view the revised query, which lists players according to their player rating and alphabetically within rating.

- Close the query. Click **Yes** if asked whether to save the changes to the Players Without Matching Teams query.

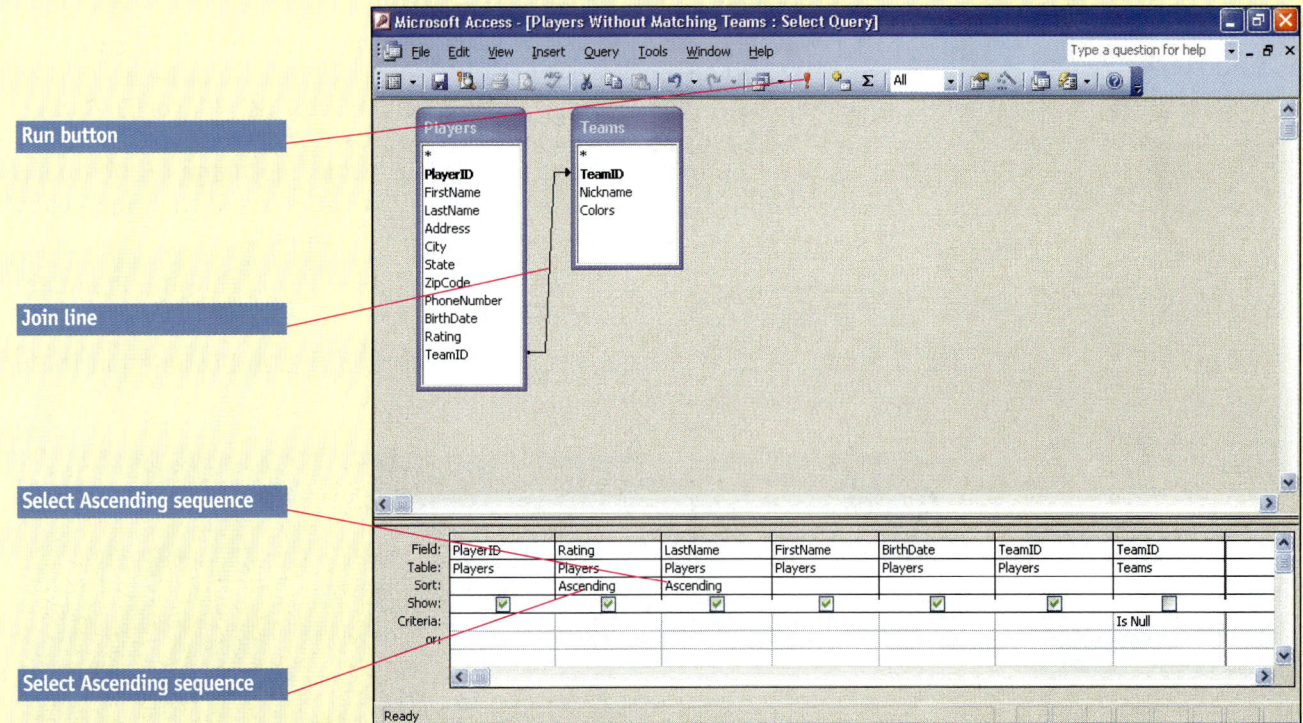

(b) Modify the Query (step 2)

FIGURE 7.10 Hands-on Exercise 3 (*continued*)

THE IS NULL CRITERION

The Is Null criterion selects those records that do not have a value in the designated field. It is the essence of the Unmatched Query Wizard, which uses the criterion to identify the records in one table that do not have a matching record in another table. The NOT operator can be combined with the Is Null criterion to produce the opposite effect; that is, the criterion Is Not Null will select records with any type of entry (including spaces) in the specified field.

Step 3: **Create the Unmatched Players Form**

- Click the **Forms button** in the Database window, click **New**, and select **AutoForm:Tabular**. Click the **drop-down arrow** to choose a table or query. Select the **Players Without Matching Teams** query. Click **OK**.

- Maximize the window if necessary, then change to the **Design view**. Select the **TeamID control** in the Detail section, then press the **Del key**.

- Click the **Combo Box tool**. Click and drag in the **Detail section**, then release the mouse to start the Combo Box Wizard:
  - Check the option button that indicates you want the combo box to **look up values in a table or query**. Click **Next**.
  - Choose the **Teams table** in the next screen. Click **Next**.
  - Select the **TeamID** and **Nickname fields**. Click **Next**.
  - Select **Nickname** as the field on which to sort. Click **Next**.
  - Adjust the column width if necessary. Be sure the box to **Hide the key column** is checked. Click **Next**.
  - Click the option button to store the value in the field. Click the **drop-down arrow** to display the fields and select the **TeamID field**. Click **Next**.
  - Enter **Team** as the label for the combo box. Click **Finish**.

- Click (select) the label next to the control you just created. Press the **Del key**. Point to the combo box, click the **right mouse button** to display a shortcut menu, and click **Properties**. Change the name of the control to **TeamID**.

- Click the **Form Selector box**. Click the **Default View** text box, click the **drop-down arrow**, and select **Datasheet**. Close the Properties sheet.

- Click the **Save button** to display the Save As dialog box in Figure 7.10c. Click **OK** to save the form, then close the form.

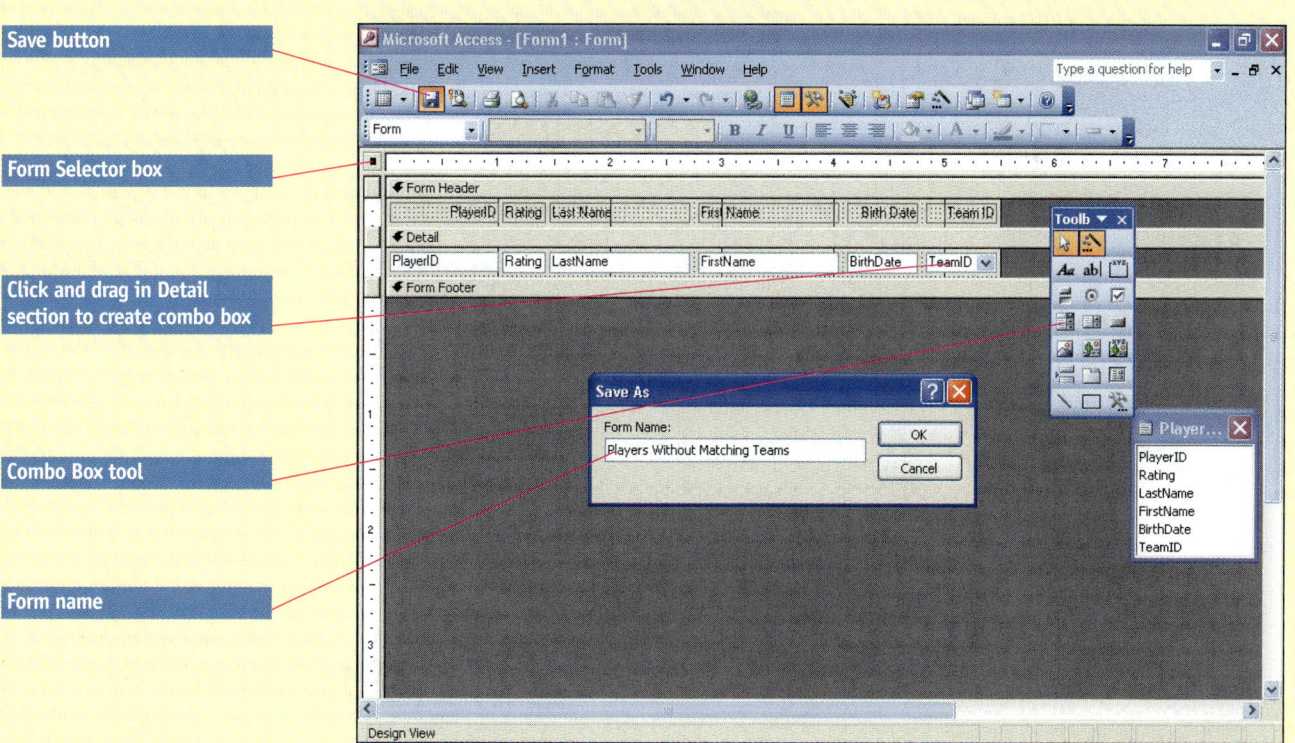

(c) Create the Unmatched Players Form (step 3)

FIGURE 7.10 Hands-on Exercise 3 (*continued*)

Step 4: **Create the Find Player Query**

- Click the **Queries button** in the Database window. Double click the icon to **Create Query in Design view**. Add the **Players table**. Close the Show Table dialog box.

- Click and drag all of the fields from the Players table to the Design grid. Click the **Criteria row** of the LastName field and type **[Enter Player's Last Name]** as shown in Figure 7.10d. Save the query as **Find Player**. Close the query.

- Click the **Forms button** in the Database window. Select the **Players form**, press **Ctrl+C** to copy the form, then press **Ctrl+V** to display the Paste As dialog box. Enter **Find Player** as the name of the form and click **OK**.

- Open the **Find Player** form in Design view. Right click the **Form Selector box** in the upper-left corner, click **Properties** to display the property sheet for the form as a whole, and click the **All tab**.

- Click the **down arrow** in the Record Source box and select the **Find Player query** that you just created. Close the property sheet. Save the form.

- Go to **Form view**, enter your last name when prompted, then click **OK**. You should see a form that displays your record. Close the form.

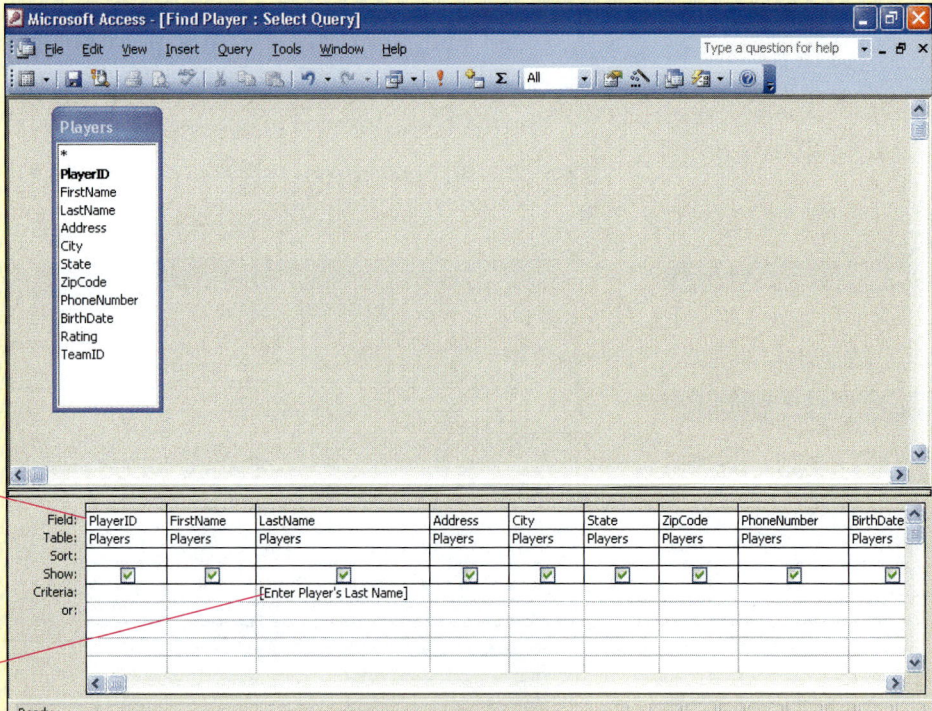

(d) Create the Find Player Query (step 4)

FIGURE 7.10 Hands-on Exercise 3 (*continued*)

BE FLEXIBLE—CREATE A PARAMETER QUERY

A parameter query prompts you for the criteria each time you execute the query, enabling you to change the criteria whenever the query is run. Any number of prompts may be specified; the prompts are read from left to right when the query is run. A form and/or a report can be based on a parameter query, in which case the user is asked for the criteria prior to generating the form or report.

Step 5: **Create the Player Draft Macro Group**

- Click the **Macros button** in the Database window. Click **New** to create a new macro. Click the **Maximize button** to maximize the Macro window.
- If you do not see the Macro Names column, pull down the **View menu** and click **Macro Names** to display the column.
- Enter the macro names, comments, and actions, as shown in Figure 7.10e.
  - The Requery action (in the UpdateList macro) has a single argument in which you specify the control name (the name of the query). Type **Players Without Matching Teams**, which is the query you created in step 1.
  - The FindPlayer macro requires you to open the **Find Player** form that was created earlier.
  - The arguments for the End Draft macro are visible in Figure 7.10d. The Player Draft form will be created in the next step. (You must enter the name manually since the form has not yet been created.)
- Save the Macro group as **Player Draft**. Close the Macro window.

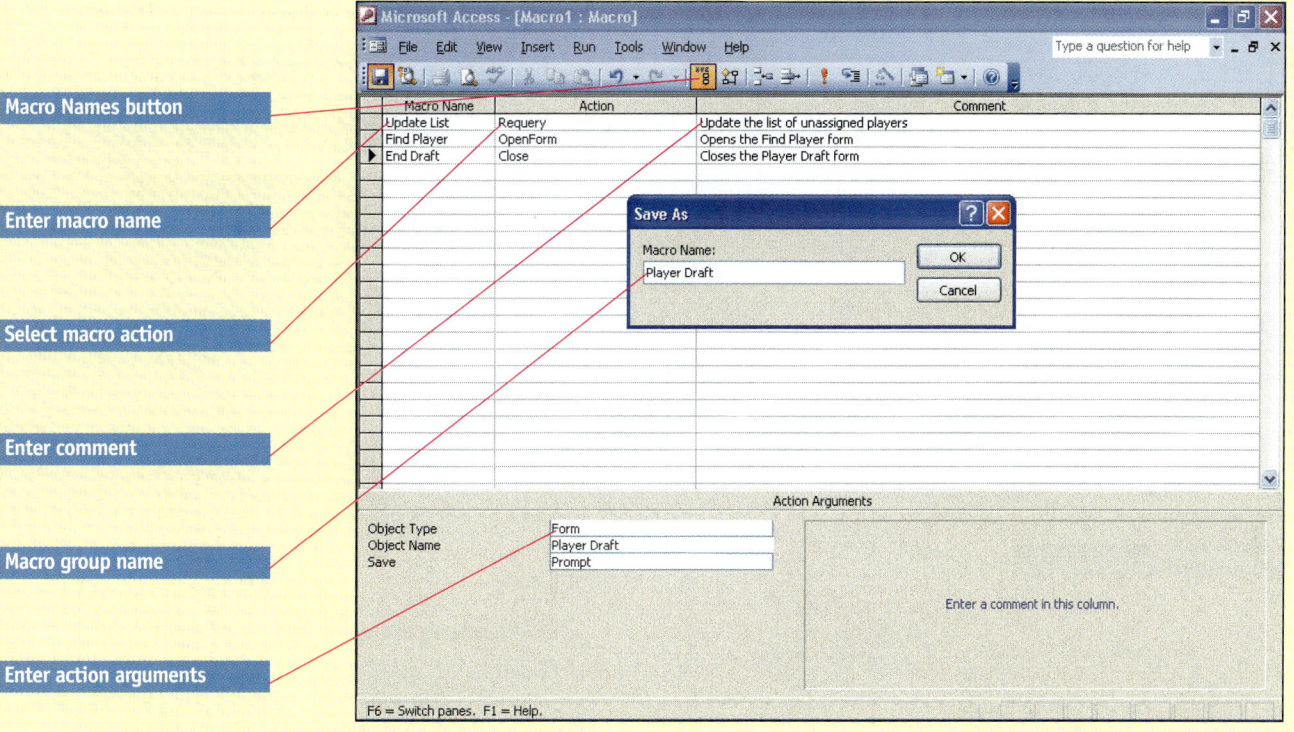

(e) Create the Player Draft Macro Group (step 5)

FIGURE 7.10 Hands-on Exercise 3 (*continued*)

REQUERY COMMAND NOT AVAILABLE

The macros in the Player Draft group are designed to run only when the Player Draft form is open. Do not be concerned, therefore, if you attempt to test the macros at this time and the Action Failed dialog box appears. The macros will work correctly at the end of the exercise, when all of the objects for the player draft have been created.

Step 6: **Create the Player Draft Form**

- Click the **Forms button** in the Database window. Select the **Template form** and click the **Copy button** to copy the form to the clipboard.

- Click the **Paste button** to complete the copy operation. Type **Player Draft** as the name of the copied form. Click **OK**.

- Open the **Player Draft** form in Design view. Pull down the **Window menu** and click **Tile Horizontally** to arrange the windows as shown in Figure 7.10f. (If necessary, close any open windows besides the two in our figure, then retile the windows.)

- Click in the **Player Draft** form. Delete the labels and text boxes for fields 1 and 2.

- Click in the **Database window**. Click and drag the **Players Without Matching Teams** form into the Detail section of the Player Draft form as shown in Figure 7.10f. Maximize the Player Draft window.

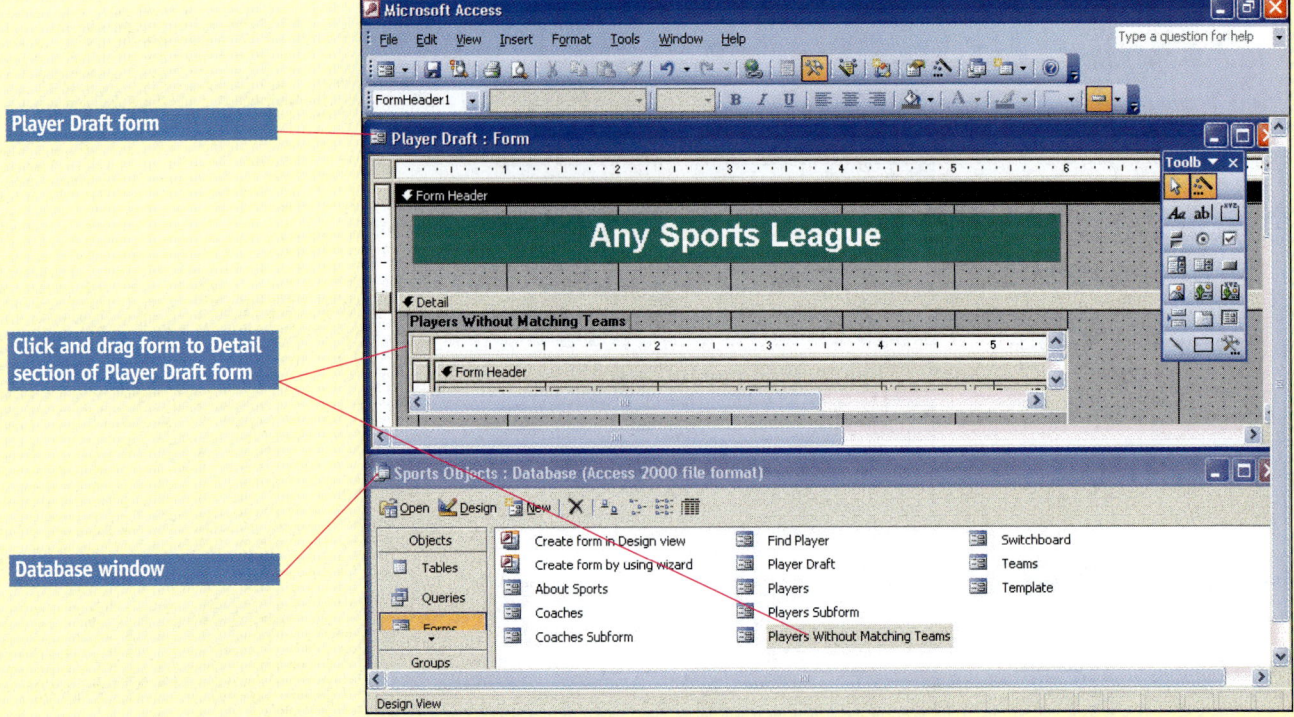

(f) Create the Player Draft Form (step 6)

FIGURE 7.10 Hands-on Exercise 3 (*continued*)

USE A TEMPLATE

Avoid the routine and repetitive work of creating a new form by basing all forms for a given application on the same template. A template is a partially completed form or report that contains graphic elements and other formatting specifications. A template does not, however, have an underlying table or query. We suggest that you create a template for your application and store it within the database, then use that template whenever you need to create a new form. It saves you time and trouble. It also promotes a consistent look that is critical to the application's overall success.

Step 7: **Modify the Player Draft Form**

- Click and drag the decorative box so that it is larger than the Players Without Matching Forms control. Move the control within the decorative box.
- Select the control for the form, then click and drag the **sizing handles** in the Players Without Matching Team form so that its size approximates the form in Figure 7.10g.
- Select (click) the label, **Players Without Matching Teams**, as shown in Figure 7.10g, then press the **Del key** to remove the label. Change the text in the Form Header to say **The Player Draft**.
- Change to the **Form view**. You should see the Form view of the subform, which displays the players who have not yet been assigned to a team. Change the column widths if necessary.
- Return to the **Form Design view** to change the width of the subform. Continue to switch back and forth between the Form view and the Design view until you are satisfied.
- Save the form.

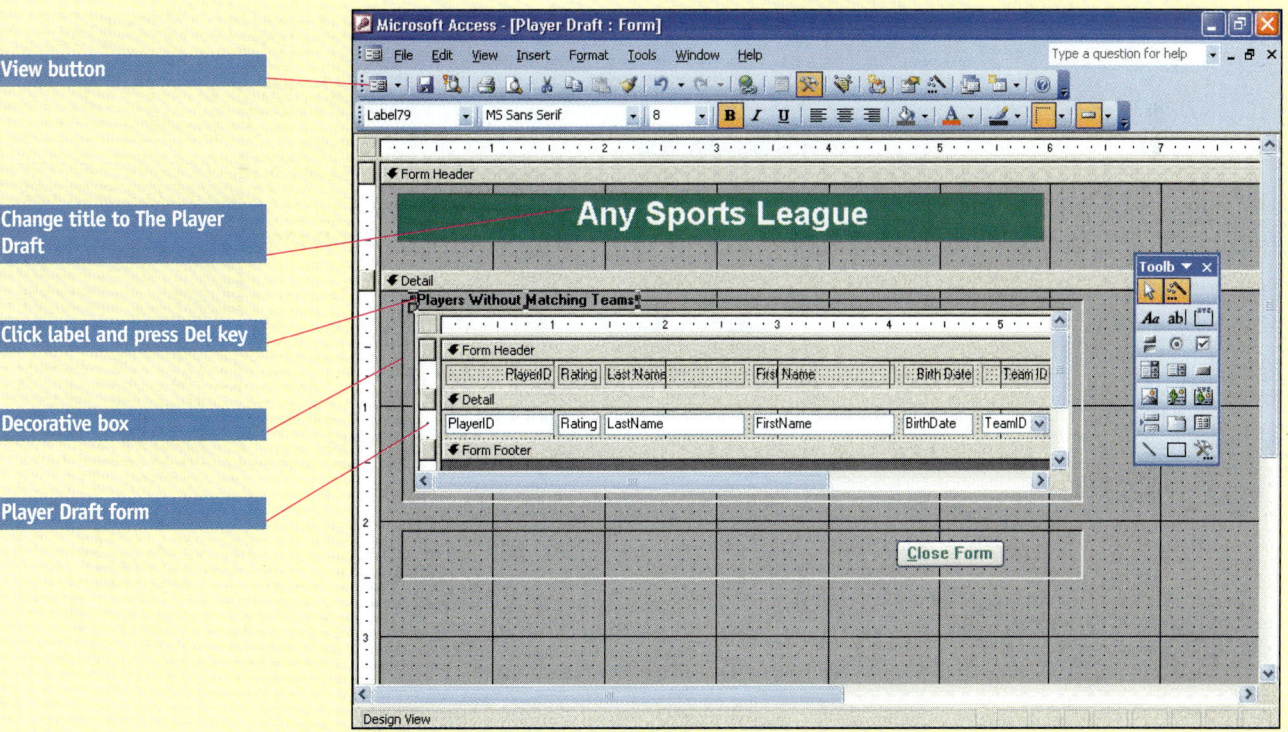

(g) Modify the Player Draft Form (step 7)

FIGURE 7.10 Hands-on Exercise 3 (*continued*)

SUPPRESS THE RECORD SELECTOR AND NAVIGATION BUTTONS

On the Player Draft form you can suppress the Record Selector and navigation buttons, which have no active function and only confuse the user. Change to the Design view, right click the Form Selector box to the left of the ruler, then click the Properties command to display the Properties dialog box. Click the Record Selectors text box and click No to disable it. Click the Navigation Buttons text box and click No to disable it. Close the Properties dialog box, then return to the Form view to see the effect of these changes, which are subtle but worthwhile.

Step 8: **Add the Command Buttons**

- Click and drag the **Command Button tool** to create a command button, as shown in Figure 7.10h. Click **Miscellaneous** in the Categories list box. Select **Run Macro** from the list of actions. Click **Next**.

- Select **Player Draft. Update List** from the list of existing macros. Click **Next**.

- Click the **Text option button**. Click and drag to select the default text (Run Macro), then type **&Update List** as the text to display. Click **Next**.

- Enter **Update List** (in place of the button number). Click **Finish**.

- Create a second command button to find a player. The caption of the button should be **&Find Player** and it should run the FindPlayer macro.

- Change the caption property of the existing button on the template that closes the form to **&End Draft**.

- Size, align, space, and color the command buttons. Use the **Format Painter button** so that all of the buttons have the same appearance. Save the form.

- Change to the **Form view**. Click the **End Draft button** to close the form.

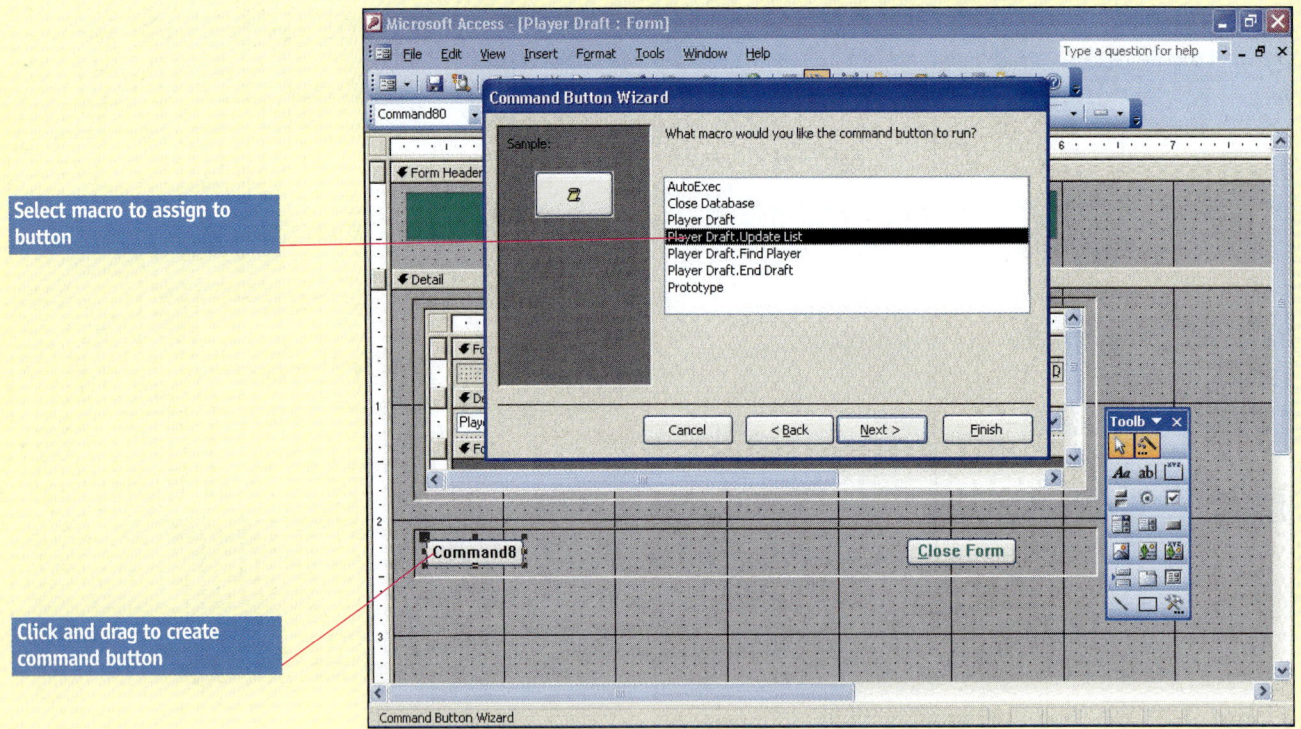

(h) Add the Command Buttons (step 8)

FIGURE 7.10 Hands-on Exercise 3 (*continued*)

ASSIGN MACROS TO CONTROLS AND COMMAND BUTTONS

Right click any command button or control to display a context-sensitive menu in which you click the Properties command, then click the Event tab in the resulting property sheet. Click in the text box of the desired event, then click the down arrow to assign an existing macro to the control or command button. Note, too, that you can click the Build button, instead of the down arrow, to select the Macro Builder and create a macro if it does not yet exist.

Step 9: **Modify the Main Switchboard**

- Pull down the **Tools menu**, click the **Database Utilities command**, and choose **Switchboard Manager**. Select the **Main Switchboard** in the Switchboard Manager dialog box, then click the **Edit button**.

- Click **New** to open the Edit Switchboard Item dialog box. Click in the **Text** list box and type **Player &Draft**. (The ampersand in front of the letter "D" establishes Alt+D as a shortcut for this button.)

- Press the **Tab key** to move to the Command list box. Select the command to open the form in the **Edit mode**. Press the **Tab key** to move to the Form list box and select the **Player Draft form** as shown in Figure 7.10i.

- Click **OK** to create the switchboard item. The Edit Switchboard Item dialog box closes and Player &Draft appears on the Main Switchboard. Select the **Player &Draft** entry, then click the **Move Up button** to move this command above the &Exit command.

- Close the Edit Switchboard page, then close the Switchboard Manager.

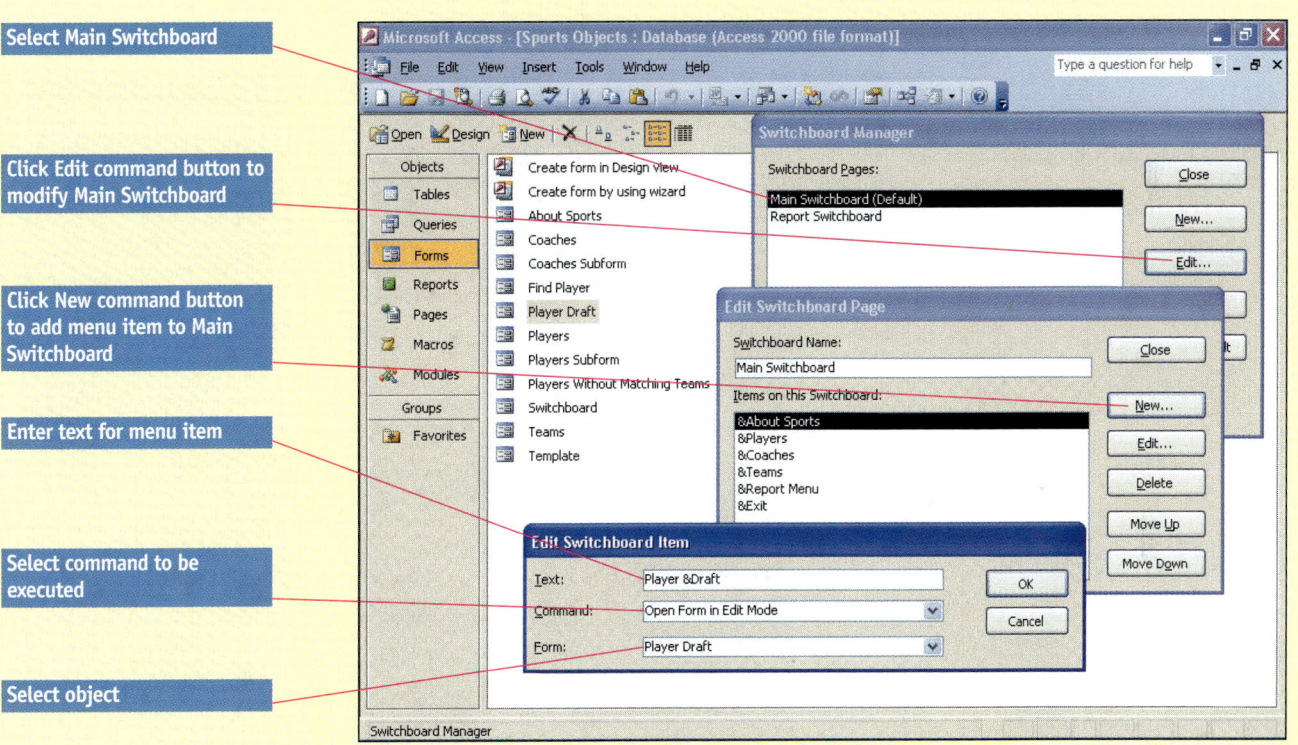

(i) Modify the Main Switchboard (step 9)

FIGURE 7.10 Hands-on Exercise 3 (*continued*)

COMPACT AND REPAIR THE DATABASE

Access databases tend to grow very quickly, especially as you create and edit new forms and reports, and thus you should always compact a database before you exit. Pull down the Tools menu, click Database Utilities, then click Compact and Repair database. The database will close, then reopen, after the compacting process has eliminated the fragmentation that occurs as you work on a database. Compacting is different from compressing; that is, you can use WinZip (or a similar utility) to further reduce the file size of a compacted database.

Step 10: **Test the Completed Switchboard**

- Click the **Macros button** in the Database window. Double click the **AutoExec macro** to execute this macro, as though you just opened the database.
- Click the **Player Draft button** on the Main Switchboard to display the form you just created, as shown in Figure 7.10j.
- Click the **TeamID field** for Katie Remmen. Type **R** (the first letter in Rockets) and Katie is assigned automatically to this team. Click the **Update List command button**. Katie disappears from the list of unassigned players.
- Click the **Find Player button**. Enter **Remmen** when prompted for the player's last name, and click **OK**. You will see a player form for Katie Remmen, indicating that she has been assigned to the Rockets. Click the **Close Form button**. Click the **End Draft button**.
- Click the **Teams command button** to view the team rosters. Team T01 (Rockets) is the first team you see, and Katie Remmen is on the roster. Click the **Close Form button** to return to the switchboard.
- Click the **Exit button**. Click **OK** in response to the message for backup. Congratulations on a job well done.

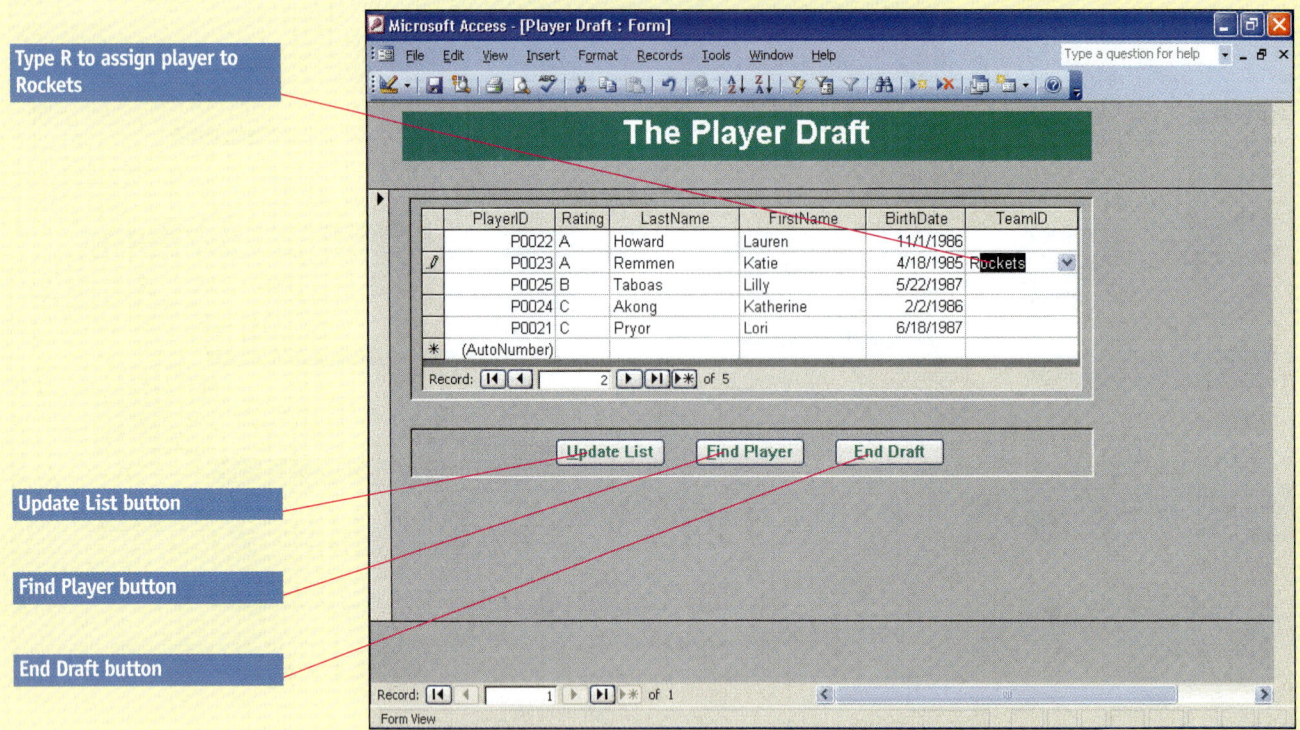

(j) Test the Completed Switchboard (step 10)

FIGURE 7.10 Hands-on Exercise 3 (*continued*)

PASSWORD PROTECT A DATABASE

Protect your database from unauthorized access through imposition of a password. It's a two-step process. First, close the database, then pull down the File menu, click the Open command to display the Open dialog box, select the database, then click the drop-down Open button and choose Open Exclusive. Click Open in response to the security warning. Next, pull down the Tools menu, click Security, click Set Database password, and follow the onscreen prompts. Be careful, however, because you cannot open the database if you forget the password.

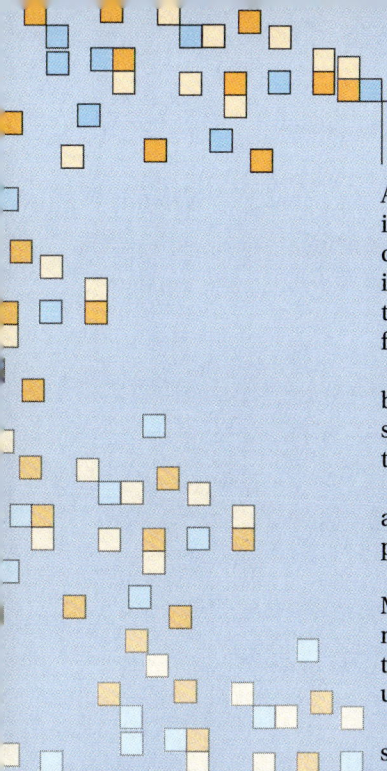

SUMMARY

An Access application is different from an ordinary database in that it contains an intuitive user interface known as a switchboard. The switchboard can be created automatically using the Switchboard Manager, a tool that prompts you for each item you want to include. You supply the text of the menu item, as it is to appear on the switchboard, together with the underlying command. Access does the rest and creates the switchboard form and associated table of switchboard items.

The tables in a database can be separated from the other objects to enable the distribution of updated versions of the application without disturbing the data. The tables are stored in one database and the objects in another. The Link Tables command associates the tables with the objects.

A template is a partially completed report or form that contains graphical elements and other formatting specifications. It is used as the basis for other objects and helps to promote a consistent look throughout an application.

A macro automates a command sequence and consists of one or more actions. The Macro window has two sections. The upper section contains the name (if any) of the macro and the actions (commands) that make up the macro. The lower section specifies the arguments for the various actions. A macro group consists of multiple macros and is used for organizational purposes.

The AutoExec macro is executed automatically whenever the database in which it is stored is opened. Each database can have its own AutoExec macro, but there is no requirement for an AutoExec macro to be present.

The Unmatched Query Wizard identifies the records in one table (e.g., the Players table) that do not have matching records in another table (e.g., the Teams table).

A prototype is a model (mockup) of a completed application that demonstrates the "look and feel" of the application. Prototypes can be developed quickly and easily through the use of simple macros containing the MsgBox action. Continual testing through prototyping is essential to the success of a system.

A database can be protected from unauthorized use through imposition of a password. Once a password has been implemented, the database cannot be opened without it.

KEY TERMS

- Action 1688
- Argument 1688
- AutoExec macro 1689
- Combo box 1699
- Database properties 1679
- Database splitter 1680
- Debugging 1689
- Display When property 1685
- Event 1677
- Event procedure 1684
- Get External Data command . . 1680
- Is Null criterion 1702
- Linked Table Manager 1678
- Link Tables command 1678
- Macro 1688
- Macro group 1700
- Macro toolbar 1689
- Macro window 1688
- MsgBox action 1689
- On Click property 1700
- Password protection 1710
- Prototype 1690
- Requery command 1705
- Switchboard 1674
- Switchboard form 1677
- Switchboard Items table 1677
- Switchboard Manager 1677
- Template 1690
- Unmatched Query Wizard 1699

MULTIPLE CHOICE

1. Which of the following is created by the Switchboard Manager?
   (a) A form to hold the switchboard
   (b) A table containing the commands associated with the switchboard
   (c) Both (a) and (b)
   (d) Neither (a) nor (b)

2. Which of the following describes the storage of the tables and objects for the application developed in the chapter?
   (a) Each table is stored in its own database
   (b) Each object is stored in its own database
   (c) The tables are stored in one database and the objects in another
   (d) The tables and objects are stored in the same database

3. Which of the following is true regarding the Link Tables command as it was used in the chapter?
   (a) It was executed from the Sports Objects database
   (b) It was executed from the Sports Tables database
   (c) Both (a) and (b)
   (d) Neither (a) nor (b)

4. What happens when an Access database is opened initially?
   (a) Access executes the AutoExec macro if the macro exists
   (b) Access opens the AutoExec form if the form exists
   (c) Both (a) and (b)
   (d) Neither (a) nor (b)

5. Which statement is true regarding the AutoExec macro?
   (a) Every database must have an AutoExec macro
   (b) A database may have more than one AutoExec macro
   (c) Both (a) and (b)
   (d) Neither (a) nor (b)

6. Which of the following are examples of arguments?
   (a) MsgBox and OpenForm
   (b) Message type (e.g., critical) and Form name
   (c) Both (a) and (b)
   (d) Neither (a) nor (b)

7. Which of the following can be imported from another Access database?
   (a) Tables and forms
   (b) Queries and reports
   (c) Both (a) and (b)
   (d) Neither (a) nor (b)

8. How do you change the properties of a command button on a form?
   (a) Open the form in Form view, then click the left mouse button to display a shortcut menu
   (b) Open the form in Form view, then click the right mouse button to display a shortcut menu
   (c) Open the form in Form Design view, then click the left mouse button to display a shortcut menu
   (d) Open the form in Form Design view, then click the right mouse button to display a shortcut menu

9. Which of the following is true regarding the Unmatched Query Wizard with respect to the Sports league database?
   (a) It can be used to identify teams without players
   (b) It can be used to identify players without teams
   (c) Both (a) and (b)
   (d) Neither (a) nor (b)

10. Which of the following can be associated with the On Click property of a command button?
    (a) An event procedure created by the Command Button Wizard
    (b) A macro created by the user
    (c) Either (a) or (b)
    (d) Neither (a) nor (b)

...continued

multiple choice

11. Which of the following was suggested as essential to a backup strategy?
    (a) Backing up files at the end of every session
    (b) Storing the backup file(s) at another location
    (c) Both (a) and (b)
    (d) Neither (a) nor (b)

12. Which of the following is true if the On Click property of a command button contains the entry, *Player Draft.Update List*?
    (a) Update List is an event procedure
    (b) Player Draft is an event procedure
    (c) Player Draft is a macro in the Update List macro group
    (d) Update List is a macro in the Player Draft macro group

13. Which of the following is true?
    (a) An existing database may be split into two separate databases, one containing the tables, and one containing the other objects
    (b) Once the objects in a database have been linked to the tables in another database, the name and/or location of the latter database can never be changed
    (c) Both (a) and (b)
    (d) Neither (a) nor (b)

14. The F6 and F11 function keys were introduced as shortcuts. Which of the following is true about these keys?
    (a) The F6 key switches between the top and bottom sections of the Macro window
    (b) The F11 key makes the Database window the active window
    (c) Both (a) and (b)
    (d) Neither (a) nor (b)

15. Which of the following was suggested as a way to organize macros and thus limit the number of macros that are displayed in the Database window?
    (a) Avoid macro actions that have only a single argument
    (b) Avoid macros that contain only a single action
    (c) Create a macro group
    (d) All of the above

16. You are developing an Access application, which you expect to upgrade periodically. Which of the following statements is true?
    (a) It will be easier to upgrade if the objects and tables are in the same database.
    (b) It will be easier to upgrade if the objects are in one database and the tables in another.
    (c) Every table should be in its own database.
    (d) Every object should be in its own database.

17. Which macro is executed automatically when the database in which it is stored is opened?
    (a) Switchboard
    (b) AutoExec
    (c) StartDatabase
    (d) Startup

18. Which command is used to associate tables in one database with objects in another database?
    (a) The Join Tables command
    (b) The Link Tables command
    (c) The Import Tables command
    (d) The Get External Data command

ANSWERS

1. c	7. c	13. a
2. c	8. d	14. c
3. a	9. c	15. c
4. a	10. c	16. b
5. d	11. c	17. b
6. b	12. d	18. b

PRACTICE WITH ACCESS

1. **Understanding Database Design:** The presentation in Figure 7.11 represents a *hypothetical* assignment for a group project in which the group is asked to present the design for their project to the class as a whole. We have created a similar presentation for you to illustrate what we mean; your only task is to view our presentation, which in turn will help you to review the *Sports* database that was developed in the chapter. (Your instructor may want to extend the assignment and ask you to create a parallel presentation for a different database, which he or she may assign as an actual group project.) Proceed as follows:

   a. Open the *Chapter 7 Practice 1* presentation in the Exploring Access folder. This is a PowerPoint presentation, but you do not have to know PowerPoint to complete this exercise. Pull down the View menu and change to the Normal view. If necessary, click the Slide tab to see the miniature slides instead of the outline.

   b. There are nine slides in the complete presentation. The left pane shows the slide miniatures. The right pane shows a larger view of the selected slide (slide one in this example). The slide describes the hypothetical assignment, which is to create a 10-minute presentation to the class describing the physical problem and the associated database design.

   c. Select (click) the first slide. Pull down the View menu and click the Slide Show command (or click the Slide Show button above the status bar). Click the mouse continually to move through the slide show. You will see a recap of the Sports database, its design, and several suggested queries.

   d. Press the Esc button at the end of the show. Pull down the File menu and click the Print command. Select the All option button in the Print Range area. Click the down arrow in the Print What area and select handouts. Choose six slides per page. Be sure to check the box to frame the slides. Click OK to print the presentation. Print the presentation a second time, but this time print only the title slide (as a full slide) to use as a cover sheet for your assignment.

   e. Review the printed presentation. Do you see how the discipline provided by this assignment can help to ensure the accuracy of the design?

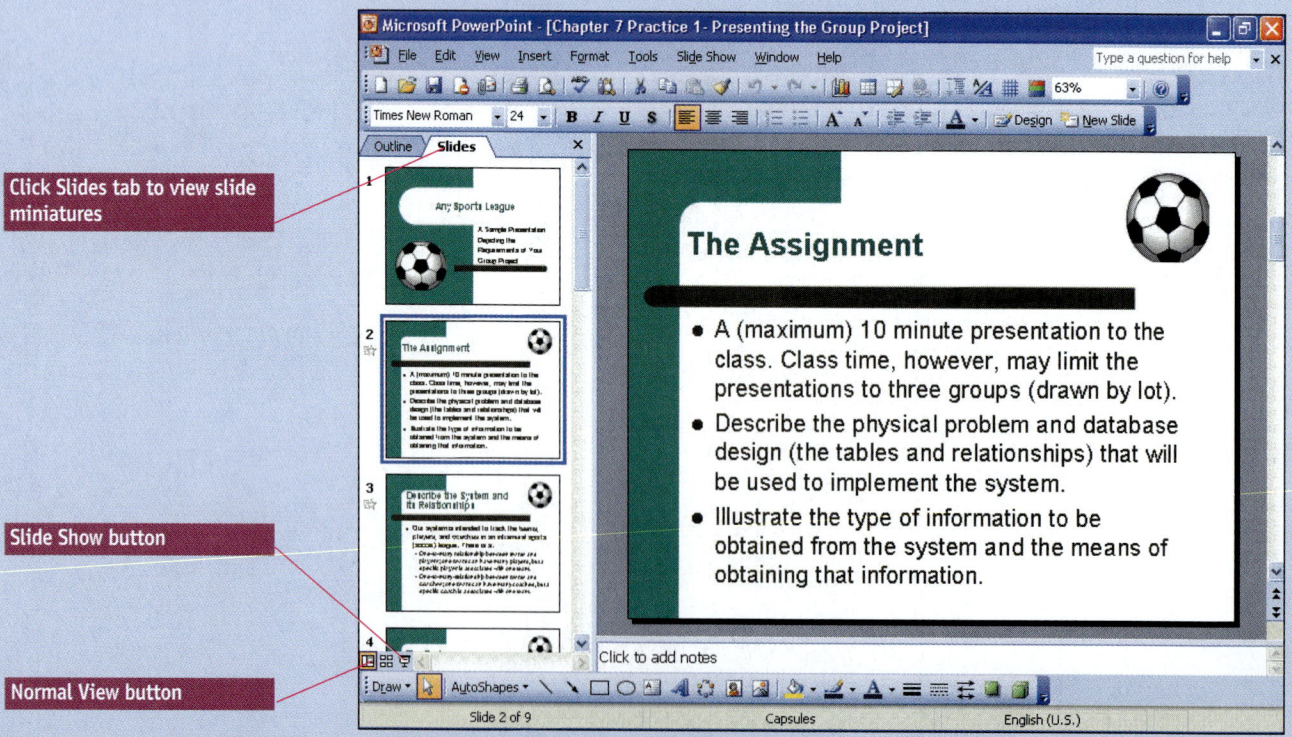

FIGURE 7.11 Understanding Database Design (exercise 1)

practice exercises

2. **Report Design:** Figure 7.12 displays the Design view of a report that prints the team rosters, showing all the players on each team, with their birth date and telephone number. The teams are listed alphabetically by team nickname, and by last name within each team. The report was created using a report template, as opposed to the Report Wizard, in order to maintain a consistent design throughout the application. Open the *Sports Objects* database and proceed as follows:

   a. Create the Team Rosters query containing fields from the Teams table and the Players table. The query requires a concatenated field with the player's first and last name as follows, = LastName & ", " & FirstName. Assign "Player" as the name of this field, as opposed to the default name Expr1.

   b. Click the Reports button. Select the Report Template, press Ctrl+C to copy the report, then press Ctrl+V to display the Paste As dialog box. Enter Team Rosters as the name of the report. Open the report in Design view. Right click the Report Selector box in the upper-left corner, click Properties to display the property sheet for the report as a whole, and click the All tab. Click the down arrow in the Record Source box and select the Team Rosters query that you just created. The field list should open automatically. Close the property sheet.

   c. Pull down the View menu and click the Sorting and Grouping command to insert a Group Header for each team nickname as shown in Figure 7.12. Note the specification to keep the whole group together, which prevents a page break within a team; that is, all players on a given team are printed on the same page. Close the Sorting and Grouping dialog box.

   d. Click and drag the Nickname field from the field list to the header you just created. Delete the attached label. Click and drag the remaining fields to the Detail area. Delete the attached labels because the template already contains formatted labels in the Page Header. You will have to change the text of each label to match the column headings in Figure 7.12. (The Page Header contains labels, as opposed to bound controls.) Move, size, and align the controls as needed.

   e. Save the report. Print the completed report for your instructor.

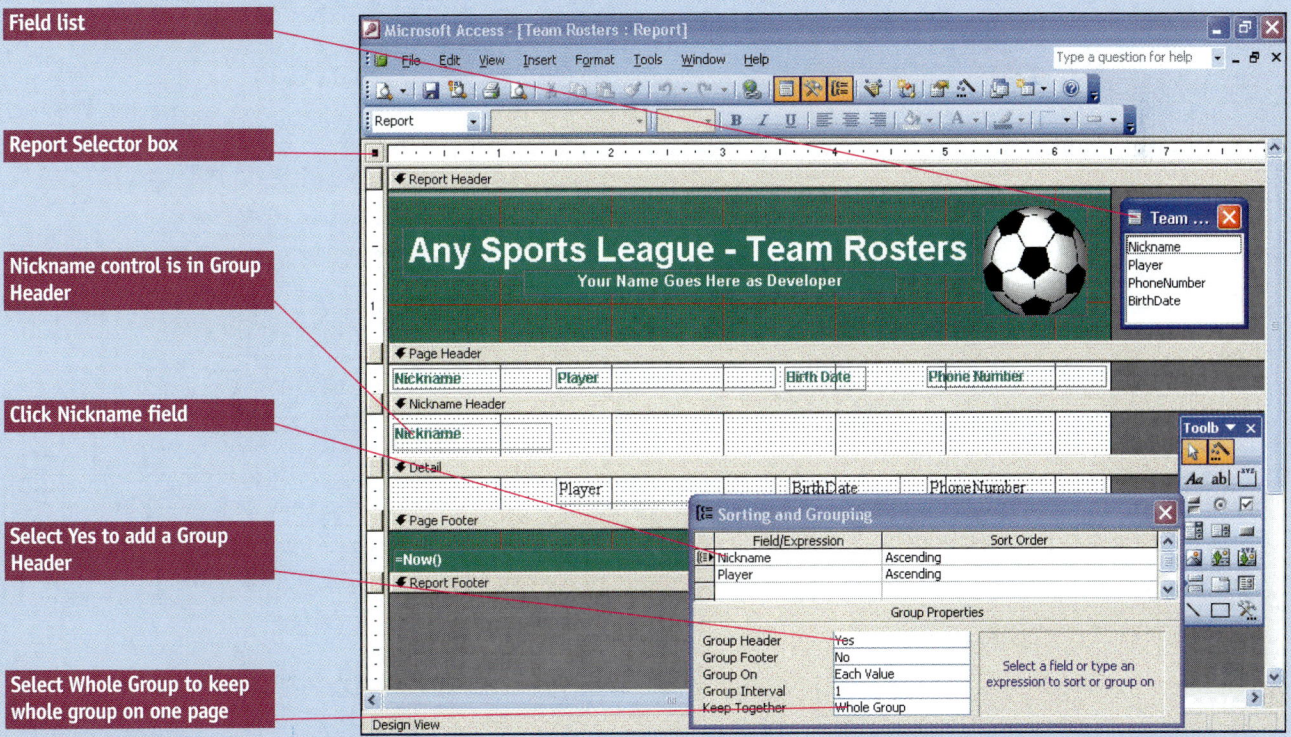

FIGURE 7.12 Report Design (exercise 2)

practice exercises

3. **Master Coaching List:** The query in Figure 7.13 is the basis of the Master Coaching List report. Your task is to create the query, and then create the associated report. The latter is based on the report template that is already in the database to ensure a consistent design throughout the application. Proceed as follows:

   a. Click the Queries button. Double click the icon to Create query in Design view. Add the Teams and Coaches table to the query. The join line should appear automatically as shown in Figure 7.13. Right click the join line, click Join Properties, and choose option 3, which will list every coach, regardless of whether the coach is assigned to a team.

   b. Click in the Field row of the leftmost column. Type LastName & ", " & FirstName and press Enter. Double click Expr1 (which is created automatically) and type Name in its place as the name of the expression. Click the Run button to verify that the expression works as intended.

   c. Complete the query as shown in Figure 7.13. The IIF (Immediate IF function) in the third field displays "Head Coach" or "Assistant" according to the value of the Status field in the Coaches table. Save the query as Master Coaching List.

   d. Click the Reports button. Select the Report Template, press Ctrl+C to copy the report, then press Ctrl+V to display the Paste As dialog box. Enter Master Coaching List as the name of the report. Open the report in Design view. Right click the Report Selector box in the upper-left corner, click Properties to display the property sheet for the report as a whole, and click the All tab. Click the down arrow in the Record Source box and select the Master Coaching List query. The field list should open automatically. Close the property sheet.

   e. Click and drag the first field (Name) from the field list to the Detail area. Click the label next to the control and press the Del key, then change the label in the Page Header from "Field Name" to "Name". Click and drag the remaining three fields (Nickname, Title, and PhoneNumber) to the Detail area, delete the attached label, and then change the label for each field in the Page Header.

   f. Move and/or size the controls so that they are aligned properly under their associated label in the Page Header. Save the report. Print the report.

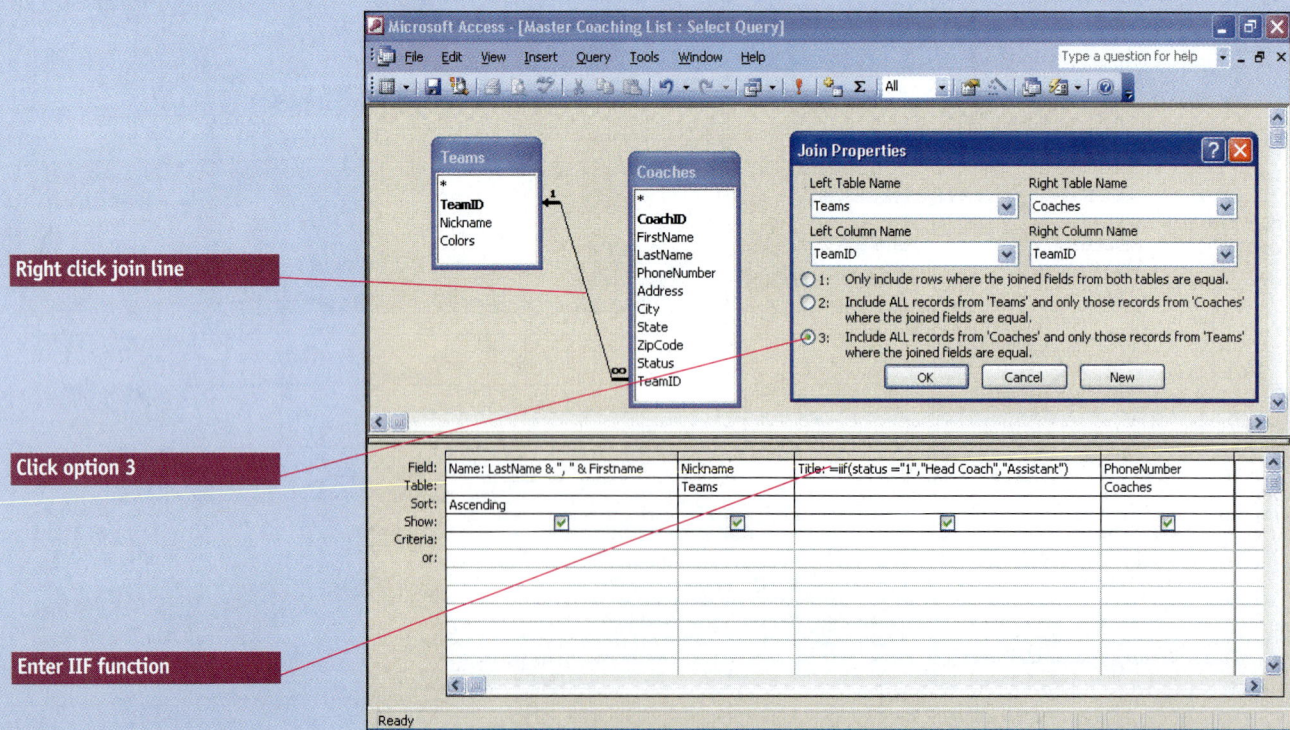

FIGURE 7.13 Master Coaching List (exercise 3)

1716 CHAPTER 7: BUILDING APPLICATIONS

practice exercises

4. **The Report Switchboard:** The switchboard in Figure 7.14 is an expanded version of the switchboard that was created in the third hands-on exercise. Your assignment is to create the indicated reports and queries, then modify the existing switchboard so that it matches Figure 7.14. (The Report Template, Team Rosters, and Master Coaches List have already been created in previous exercises.) Proceed as follows:

   a. The Relationship Diagram is created from the Relationships window. Pull down the Tools menu, click the Relationships command, pull down the File menu, and then click the Print Relationships command. The report is created automatically for you. Change to Design view, and then modify the Report Header to contain your name and the clip art image of the soccer ball.

   b. The totals query displays the number of players per team. It contains only two fields: the team nickname from the Teams table and the player's last name from the Players Table. The Count function is used in the Total row of the player's last name field to display the number of players on each team. Note, however, that you cannot run a query directly through the switchboard. Thus, you have to create a macro to open the query, and then run the macro from the switchboard.

   c. Use the Unmatched Query Wizard to create a query that will list the teams that do not have a coach. Create a macro to open the query, then run the macro from the switchboard as described in part (b). (The master coaching list that was created in the previous exercise lists all coaches, including those that are not currently assigned to a team. You can use this report to find a coach for any team that does not have one.)

   d. Once you have created the required objects, you can use the Switchboard Manager to modify the existing Report Switchboard from the hands-on exercises in the chapter to duplicate the switchboard in Figure 7.14.

   e. Use the completed switchboard to print each report if you have not done so previously. Print the switchboard form itself as well as the table of switchboard items. Add a cover sheet and submit the completed assignment to your instructor. The Sports League application is complete.

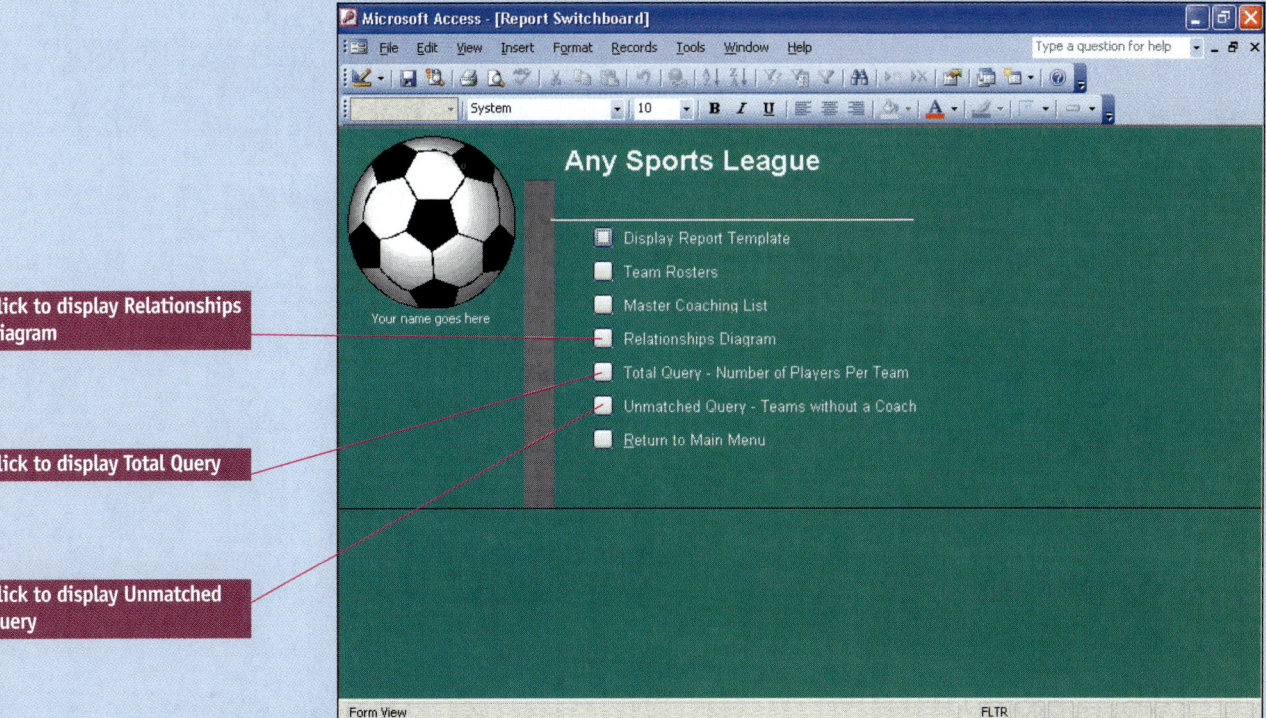

FIGURE 7.14 The Report Switchboard (exercise 4)

practice exercises

5. **A Look Ahead:** The Add Record button that appears on the Players form was created through the Command Button Wizard. Test the button to see how it works; i.e., open the Players form, click the button to add a player, then note that in order to add a player you must first click the First Name text box. You can automate the process by adding a statement to the event procedure that will position the user in the First Name text box automatically. Proceed as follows:

   a. Open the Players form in Design view. Point to the Add Player command button, then click the right mouse button to display a shortcut menu. Click Properties to display the Properties dialog box. Click the down arrow on the vertical scroll bar until you can see the On Click property, which contains the entry [Event Procedure]. Click this entry, then click the Build Button (the three dots to the right of the box) to display the associated VBA code. Maximize the window. Click the Procedure View button at the bottom of the screen.

   b. Click under the DoCmd statement and add the line FirstName.SetFocus as shown in Figure 7.15. This tells Access to go to the control called FirstName after inserting a new record. Click the Save button, then close the VBA window.

   c. Click the Form View button to switch to Form view and test the Add Player macro. Click the Add Player command button. You should be positioned in the First Name box, where you can start typing immediately.

   d. Click the Close Form command button when you have completed the record. Click Yes if prompted to save the changes to the Players form.

   e. Open the Coaches form in Design view and make a similar modification to the Add Coach command button. This may seem like a lot of trouble, but the end user appreciates this type of convenience.

   f. The programming statements that you have been working with are written in VBA (Visual Basic for Applications). VBA is a powerful programming language and is covered in the next chapter, where you will learn how to further enhance an Access application through VBA. Additional information on VBA is found in the "Getting Started with VBA" module at the end of the text.

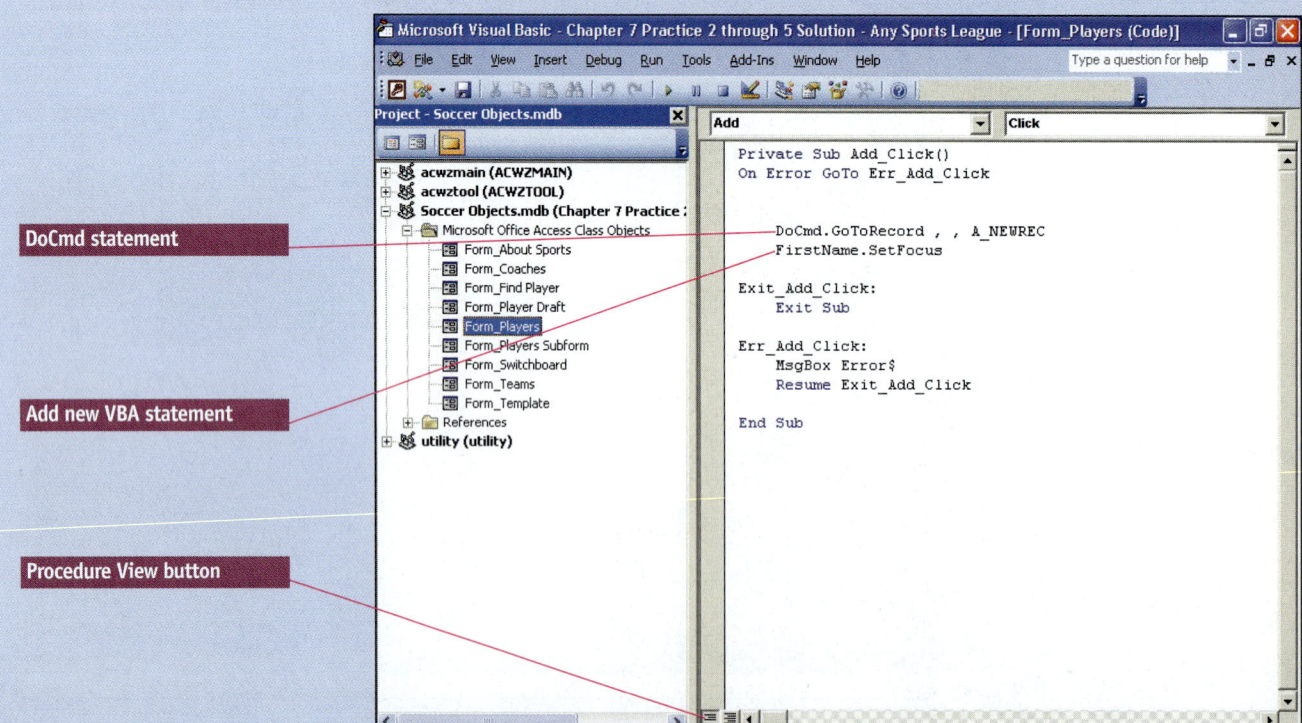

FIGURE 7.15 A Look Ahead (exercise 5)

1718 CHAPTER 7: BUILDING APPLICATIONS

practice exercises

6. **Class Scheduling:** The database design in Figure 7.16 is intended to implement a class scheduling application at a typical college or university. The scheduling process entails the coordination of course offerings as published in a registration schedule together with faculty assignments. The university may offer multiple sections of any given course at different times. The information about when a class meets is stored within the one-letter section designation; for example, section A meets from 9:00 to 9:50 on Mondays, Wednesdays, and Fridays. Note the following:

   a. The database contains separate tables for courses, sections, and faculty as can be seen in Figure 7.16. There are many-to-many relationships between courses and sections, between courses and faculty, and between faculty and sections.

   b. The key to the design is the creation of an additional Offerings table that includes the CourseID, SectionID, and FacultyID. The combination of these three fields could serve as the primary key of the Offerings table, but it is easier to add an additional field, the OfferingID with the AutoNumber field type. The additional fields in the Offerings table, Building and Room, provide information as to where the specific course will meet.

   c. We have designed the database for you. Your task is to implement our design by creating a database that contains the indicated tables and associated relationships. You do not have to enter data into any of the tables, but you will need to create the tables in order to create a Relationships Diagram.

   d. We have embellished the report containing the Relationships Diagram to include a Report Header, with modified font and clip art. (Use any appropriate image.) Print the completed report for your instructor. The clip art will also be used in the next two practice exercises that develop the switchboard and templates for the forms and reports in the database. The visual design of a system is an important consideration that should be given careful attention.

   e. Would this design be applicable to the comparable database at your school or university? Summarize your thoughts in a short note to your instructor.

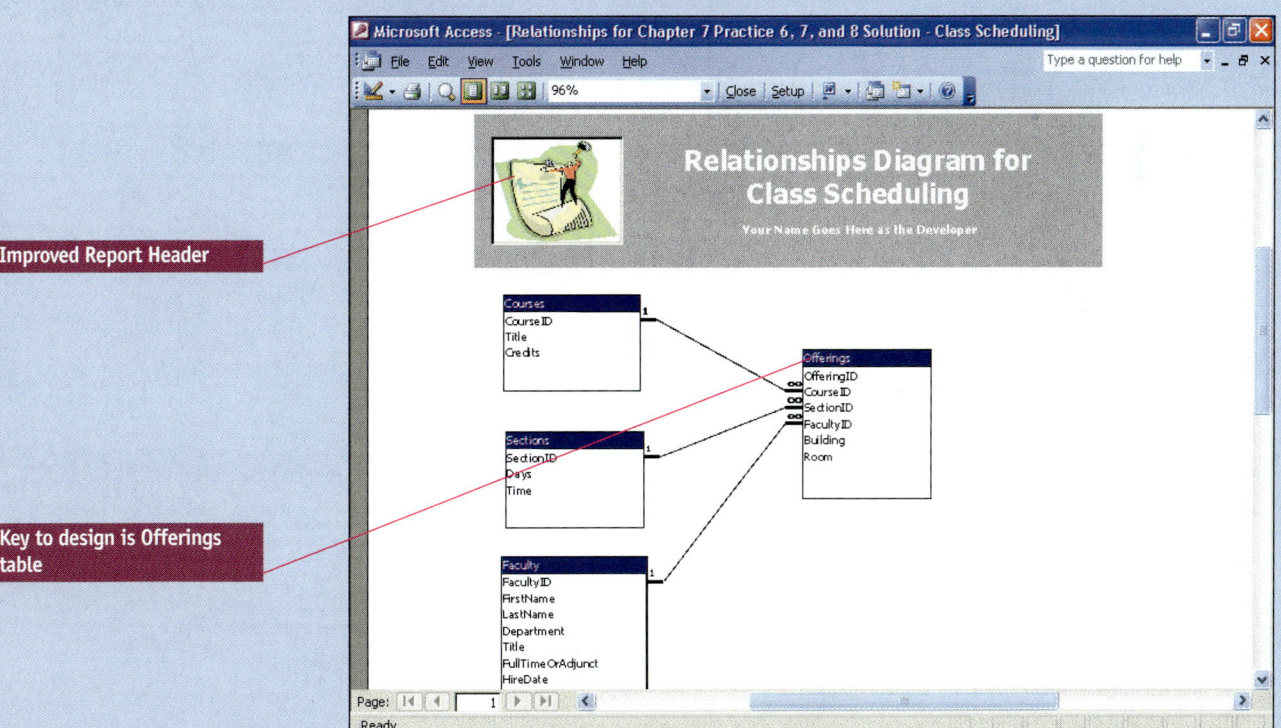

FIGURE 7.16 Class Scheduling (exercise 6)

practice exercises

7. **Class Scheduling Switchboard:** The switchboard in Figure 7.17 continues the development of the *Class Scheduling* database from the previous exercise and represents Version 1.0 of the completed system. You do not have to follow our design exactly, but you are required to include the indicated functionality. It is important, however, that you use a consistent design so that all of the objects in your database have a uniform look. This attention to detail enhances the visual appeal of a database and gives it a more professional appearance. Note the following:

   a. The switchboard should open automatically whenever the database is opened. This can be accomplished through the Startup property or through the creation of an AutoExec macro.

   b. The About Class Scheduling form contains the same logo that appears on the switchboard and is similar to the other About forms that have appeared throughout the text. The form should also contain your name and any other information required by your instructor.

   c. The second menu option should print the report containing the Relationships Diagram from the previous exercise.

   d. Create a prototype macro to indicate items under development as shown in Figure 7.17. The associated message box will appear upon clicking any of the next four items, which are not yet developed.

   e. The Report Switchboard button should display a secondary switchboard that contains buttons for several reports that will be available in the completed system. Clicking any of the report buttons should also display the message from the prototype macro. The Report Switchboard must contain a button to return to the main switchboard.

   f. The Exit button should run a macro that displays a message to the user to back up the system, then exits Access.

   g. Print the switchboard and the table of switchboard items for your instructor. Add a cover sheet to complete the assignment. Does the switchboard in its present form provide the user with a meaningful understanding of the finished application?

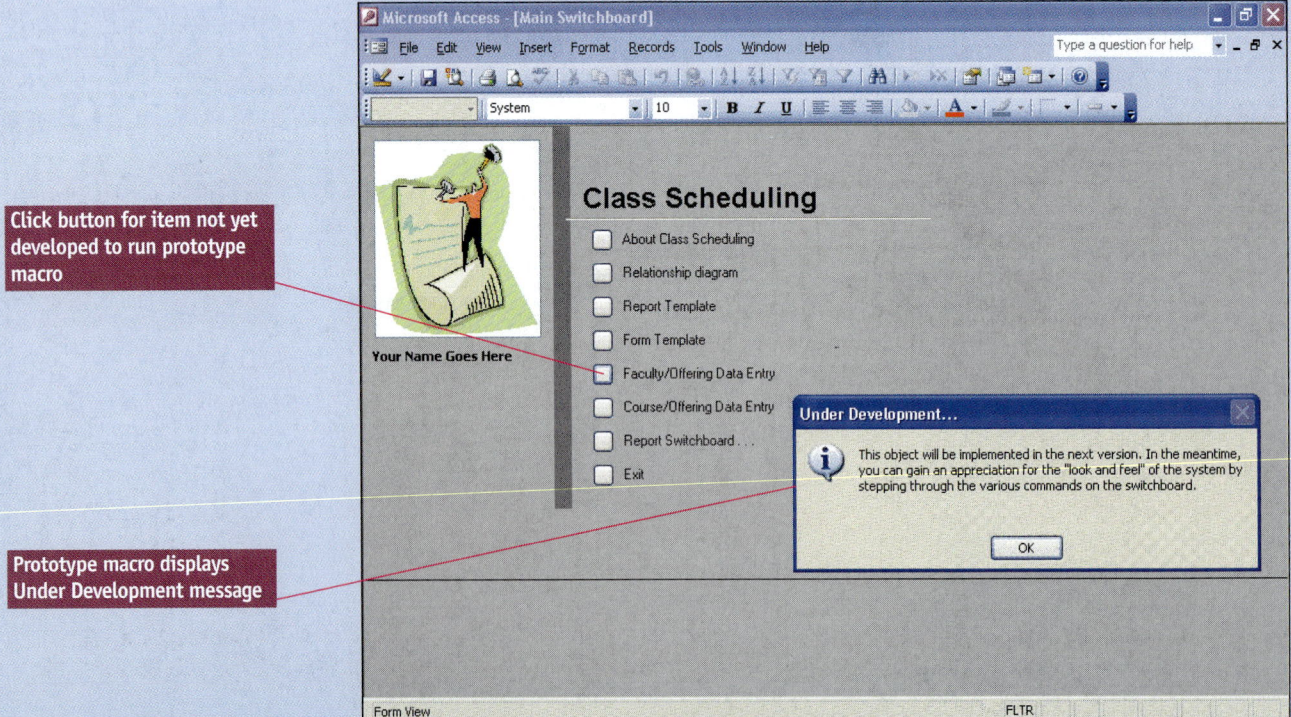

FIGURE 7.17 Class Scheduling Switchboard (exercise 7)

practice exercises

8. **Class Scheduling Templates:** The forms and reports within an application should have a consistent look that is also visually appealing. This exercise asks you to create the templates on which those objects will be based. The templates are created early in the development process so that the user has the opportunity to provide feedback as soon as possible in the event that changes are required. Proceed as follows:

   a. Click the Forms button in the Database window and then double click the icon to Create form in Design view. Enter a title for the form in the Form Header. Change the font, font size, and/or the color as you see fit. The formatting is important because it will appear in every subsequent form. Insert the same clip art that you used in the previous exercise for the switchboard and Relationships Diagram.

   b. Go to the Detail area and create two or three labels to identify the controls that will appear in the form. The text per se is not important; the formatting is. Use the Command Button Wizard to create a button to close the form. Add final changes as you see fit. Save the form as Form Template as shown in Figure 7.18. Print the completed template for your instructor.

   c. Click the Reports button in the Database window and then double click the icon to Create report in Design view. Enter a title for the report in the Report Header. Change the font, font size, and/or the color as you see fit. The formatting is important because it will appear in every subsequent report. Insert the same clip art that you used for the other objects.

   d. Click in the Page Header and enter the text for three or four labels (column headings). The text per se is not important; the formatting is. Create the Page Footer as a combination of text and fields. Our footer will print today's date, the page number, and the total number of pages in the report. Save the report as Report Template. Print the completed template for your instructor.

   e. Modify the main switchboard to display each template, as opposed to running the prototype macro. You have now completed Version 2.0 of the Class Scheduling application. The user has the opportunity to review both the technical design (the Relationships Diagram) and the visual design (the two templates you just created) within the context of a fully functional switchboard.

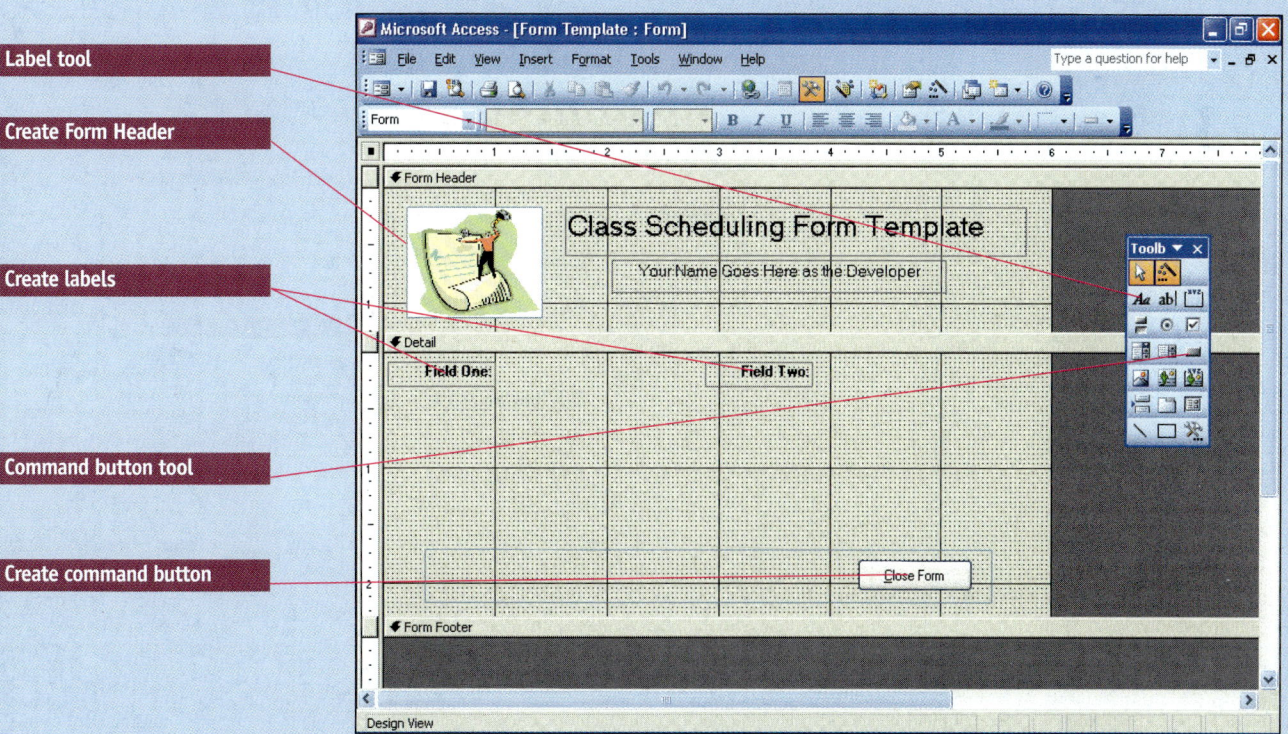

FIGURE 7.18 Class Scheduling Templates (exercise 8)

MICROSOFT OFFICE ACCESS 2003   1721

practice exercises

9. **The Video Store:** You have an internship at the local video store, which rents and/or sells tapes or DVDs to its customers. The store maintains the usual information about every customer (name, address, phone number, and so on.) It also has detailed information about every movie such as its duration, rating, rental price, and purchase price. There is a subtlety in the design because the video store stocks multiple copies (tapes and/or DVDs) of the same movie. Thus, a customer can rent a copy of the movie (from the Copies table), as opposed to renting a movie from the Movies table.

   a. The Movies table contains the detailed information about each movie. There is a one-to-many relationship between movies and copies; that is, one movie can have many copies, but a specific copy is associated with only one movie.

   b. There is a many-to-many relationship between customers and copies; that is, one customer can rent several copies, and the same copy will (over time) be rented to many customers. This in turn gives rise to the Rentals table as shown in Figure 7.19, which contains the additional fields as indicated.

   c. We have created the database design for you. Your task is to implement our design by creating a database that contains the indicated tables and associated relationships. You do not have to enter data into any of the tables, but you will need to create the tables in order to create a Relationships Diagram for your instructor.

   d. We have embellished the report containing the Relationships Diagram to include a Report Header, with a modified font and clip art (use any appropriate image). The elements will also be used in the next two practice exercises that develop the switchboard and templates for forms and reports. The visual design of a system is an important consideration that should be given careful attention. Print the completed report for your instructor.

   e. Would this design be applicable for the system in place at your local video store? Summarize your thoughts in a brief note to your instructor. Add a cover sheet to complete the assignment.

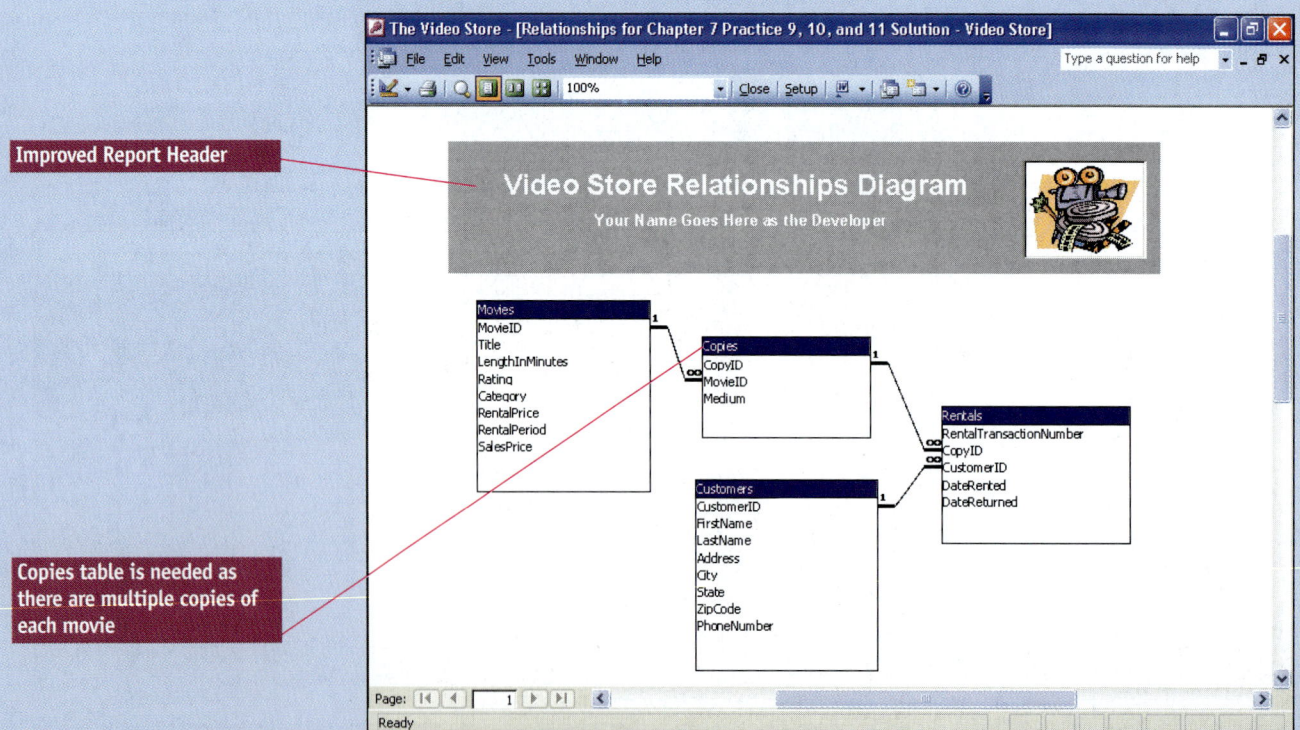

FIGURE 7.19 The Video Store (exercise 9)

1722 CHAPTER 7: BUILDING APPLICATIONS

practice exercises

10. **Video Store Switchboard:** The switchboard in Figure 7.20 continues the development of the *Video Store* database from the previous exercise and represents Version 1.0 of the completed system. You do not have to follow our design exactly, but you are required to include the indicated functionality. It is important, however, that you use a consistent design so that all of the objects in your database have a uniform look. This attention to detail enhances the visual appeal of a database and gives it a more professional appearance. Note the following:

   a. The switchboard should open automatically whenever the database is opened. This can be accomplished through the Startup property or through the creation of an AutoExec macro.

   b. The About Video Store form contains the same logo that appears on the switchboard and is similar to the other About forms that have appeared throughout the text.

   c. The second menu option should print the report containing the relationships diagram from the previous exercise.

   d. Create a prototype macro to indicate items under development as shown in Figure 7.20. The associated message box will appear upon clicking any of the next four items, which are not yet developed.

   e. The Report Switchboard button should display a secondary switchboard that contains buttons for several reports that will be available in the completed system. Clicking any of the report buttons should also display the message from the prototype macro. The Report Switchboard must contain a button to return to the main switchboard.

   f. The Exit button should run a macro that displays a message to the user to back up the system, then exits Access.

   g. Print the switchboard and the table of switchboard items for your instructor. Add a cover sheet to complete the assignment. Does the switchboard in its present form provide a meaningful understanding of the finished application?

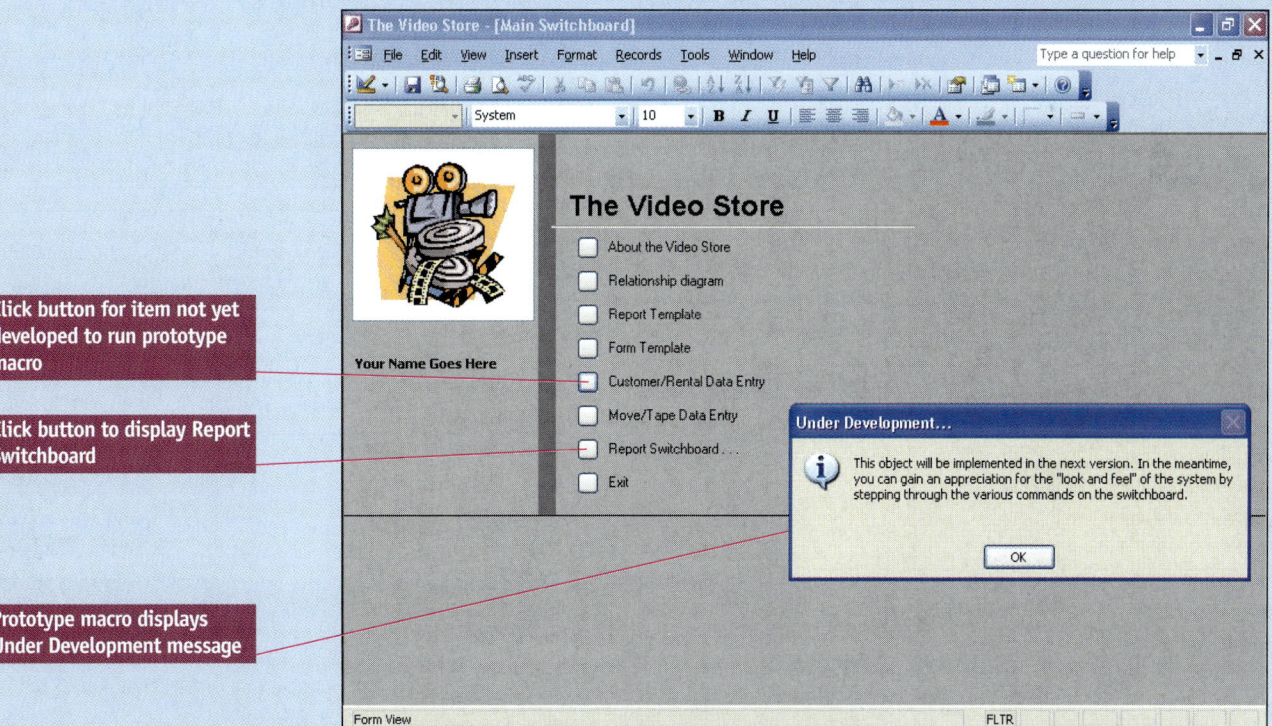

FIGURE 7.20   Video Store Switchboard (exercise 10)

MICROSOFT OFFICE ACCESS 2003   1723

practice exercises

11. **Video Store Templates:** The forms and reports within an application should have a consistent look that is also visually appealing. This exercise asks you to create the templates on which those objects will be based. The templates are created early in the development process so that the user has the opportunity to provide feedback as soon as possible in the event that changes are required. Proceed as follows:

   a. Click the Reports button in the Database window and then double click the icon to Create report in Design view. Enter a title for the report in the Report Header. Change the font, font size, and/or the color as you see fit. The formatting is important because it will appear in every subsequent report. Insert the same clip art that you used for the switchboard and Relationships Diagram.

   b. Click in the Page Header and enter the text for three or four labels (column headings). The text per se is not important; the formatting is. Create the Page Footer as a combination of text and fields. Our footer will print today's date, the page number, and the total number of pages in the report. Save the report as Report Template as shown in Figure 7.21. Print the completed template for your instructor.

   c. Click the Forms button in the Database window and then double click the icon to Create form in Design view. Enter a title for the form in the Form Header. Change the font, font size, and/or the color as you see fit. The formatting is important because it will appear in every subsequent form. Insert the same clip art that you used for the other objects.

   d. Go to the Detail area and create two or three labels to identify the controls that will appear in the form. The text per se is not important; the formatting is. Use the Command Button Wizard to create a button to close the form. Add final changes as you see fit. Save the form as Form Template. Print the completed template for your instructor.

   e. Modify the main switchboard to display each template, as opposed to running the prototype macro. You have now completed Version 2.0 of the Video Store application. The user has the opportunity to review both the technical design (the Relationships Diagram) and the visual design (the two templates you just created) within the context of a fully functional switchboard.

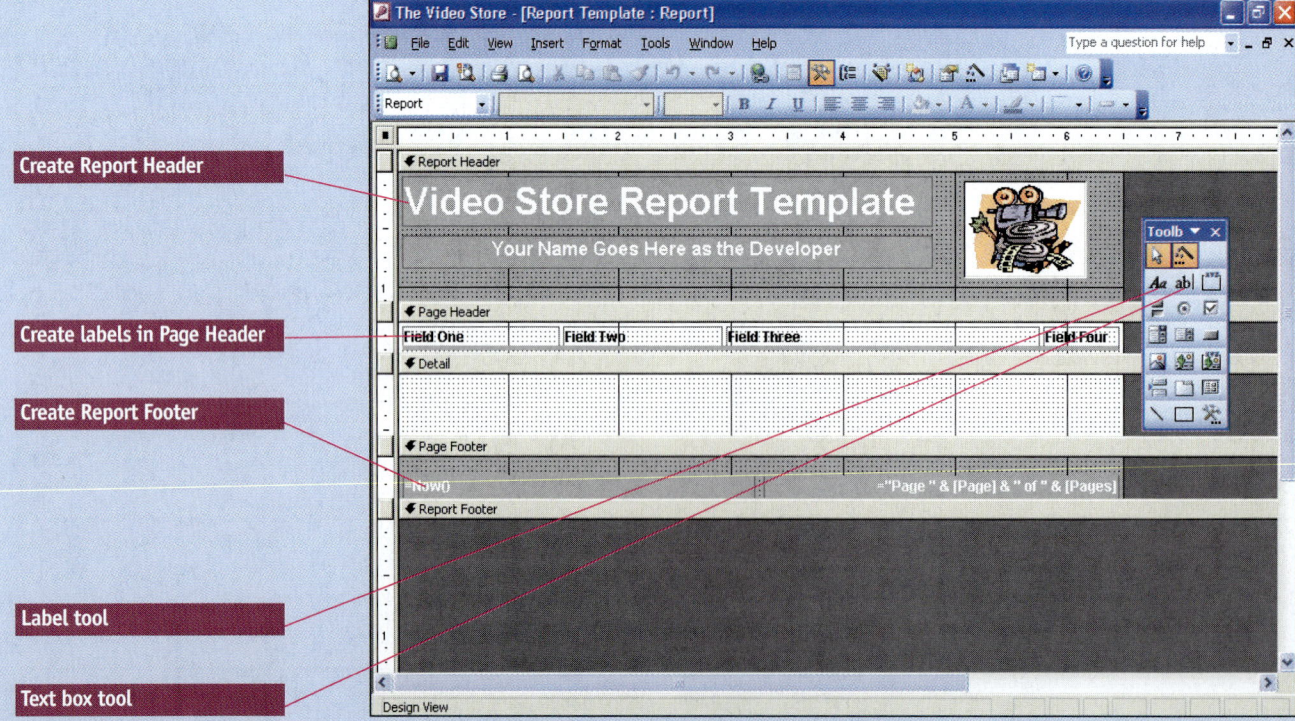

FIGURE 7.21 Video Store Templates (exercise 11)

MINI CASES

Computer Repair

The Director of Administrative Services has come to you for assistance in implementing a system to track the repairs associated with the computers on campus. The data about each computer, such as the make and model, operating system, location on campus, and so on, is stored in a Computers table within an Access database. The faculty or staff member assigned to that computer is also indicated. The data about the faculty/staff is stored in a separate table. One individual (a faculty or staff member) can be assigned to many computers, but a given computer is assigned to only one person.

Problems inevitably occur, and when they do, the faculty or staff member responsible for that computer calls the Director's office to report the problem. The nature of the problem is recorded, and a technician is assigned to fix it. (Technicians are employed as independent contractors and do not appear in the Faculty/Staff table.) One technician can work on many computers, and a specific computer may be worked on by different technicians. Your assignment is to design a database that will maintain this data and produce the associated reports. The database should be able to list all computers that are currently under repair. It should also provide a report that shows all completed repairs. Other reports might include all problems assigned to a specific technician, or all problems reported by a particular faculty or staff member.

A previous consultant has suggested four tables in all. You are to create each table, then create the Relationships Diagram, but you do not have to enter data into any of the tables. You have also been asked to create a simple switchboard with three menu options—a button to display an "About the Repair Service" form describing the database, a button to print the Relationships Diagram, and a button to exit the application. The switchboard should contain the same clip art as the Relationships Diagram and the About form. Use the Startup property to display the switchboard when the database is opened. Print the switchboard form, the table of switchboard items, the relationships diagram, and the About form.

Find a Mate Dating Service

The Find a Mate Dating Service employs dating counselors to match its clients to one another. Each counselor works with many clients, but a specific client always works with the same counselor. Each client completes an extensive questionnaire that describes themselves and the qualities they wish to find in a mate. The counselors evaluate this information and pair the agency's clients with one another to create a date. One client can have many dates, and a date has many (actually two) clients. Feedback is important, and each client is asked for his or her reaction to the date by rating it from one (a bad night) to five (outstanding).

Your assignment is to design a database that will track counselors, clients, and their dates. It should be able to list all dates for a specific client as well as all dates arranged by a specific counselor. A previous consultant has suggested four tables in all. You are to create each table and then create the Relationships Diagram, but you do not have to enter data into any of the tables. You have also been asked to create a simple switchboard with three menu options—a button to display an "About the Dating Service" form describing the database, a button to print the Relationships Diagram, and a button to exit the application. The switchboard should contain the same clip art as the Relationships Diagram and About form. Use the Startup property to display the switchboard when the database is opened. Print the switchboard form, the table of switchboard items, the Relationships Diagram, and the About form.

The Medical Practice

You have been asked to design a database for a small medical practice. Any patient may see any physician, and over time, one patient will see many physicians. This many-to-many relationship between physicians and patients is best expressed in a separate appointments table within the database that contains the PhysicianID, the PatientID, and the date and

mini cases

time of the appointment. A Procedures table has also been created for insurance and billing purposes; each record in this table contains the ProcedureID, a description of the procedure, and the associated fee.

A patient calls the office to make an appointment. (The patient sees only one physician per appointment.) The patient is billed for one or more procedures during that appointment—for example, a blood test and a chest x-ray. There is a many-to-many relationship between procedures and appointments; one appointment will reference multiple procedures, and the same procedure can be administered in multiple appointments.

You have been asked to design a database for the practice. A previous consultant has suggested five tables in all. You are to create each table and then create the Relationships Diagram, but you do not have to enter data into any of the tables. You have also been asked to create a simple switchboard with three menu options—a button to display an "About the Practice" form describing the database, a button to print the Relationships Diagram, and a button to exit the application. The switchboard should contain the same clip art as the Relationships Diagram and About form. Use the Startup property to display the switchboard when the database is opened. Print the switchboard form, the table of switchboard items, the Relationships Diagram, and the About form.

CHAPTER 8

Creating More Powerful Applications:
Introduction to VBA

OBJECTIVES

After reading this chapter you will:

1. Describe the relationship of VBA to Microsoft Office.
2. Create an event procedure.
3. Describe the VBA editor.
4. Distinguish between the Procedure view and the Full Module view.
5. Create a combo box to locate a record on a form.
6. Describe the parameters associated with the MsgBox function.
7. Create a procedure to facilitate data entry through keyboard shortcuts.
8. Create a procedure to display application-specific error messages.
9. Describe several types of data validation and various ways of implementation.

hands-on exercises

1. **CREATING A COMBO BOX AND ASSOCIATED VBA PROCEDURES**
   Input: Introduction to VBA
   Output: Introduction to VBA (modified)

2. **FACILITATING DATA ENTRY**
   Input: Introduction to VBA (from exercise 1)
   Output: Introduction to VBA (modified)

3. **ERROR TRAPPING**
   Input: Introduction to VBA (from exercise 2)
   Output: Introduction to VBA (modified)

4. **DATA VALIDATION**
   Input: Introduction to VBA (from exercise 3)
   Output: Introduction to VBA (modified)

CASE STUDY
BACK TO NATALIE'S

You have been working at Natalie's Cuppa Joe, the locally famous coffee shop that was introduced in Chapter 1, for almost two years. It has been a rewarding experience, and business has grown steadily during your employment. With so many new customers the data entry has become quite time-consuming, and Natalie has asked you to improve the database. She is leaving the specific changes to your discretion, but Natalie would like you to focus on facilitating data entry. She would also like the reports in the database to be easier to read, and suggests that you shade the alternate lines in the "Cuppa Card" report that is generated daily.

You have become quite proficient in Access, but you will need to take it to the next level and develop VBA code to make the necessary improvements to the database. Thankfully, you are enrolled in a more advanced computer applications course and will soon have the skill required to comply with Natalie's request. This ability will increase your value as an employee and it may even help you earn a promotion! ■

Your assignment is to read the chapter, paying special attention to the many ways to enhance a database through VBA. You will then open *Chapter 8 Case Study—Back to Natalie's* Access database and add procedures to the existing Customers form, basing your enhancements on the code that was developed in the chapter. Start by modifying the existing Add Record procedure to move directly to the appropriate field on the form, as opposed to having the user click in the text box. You should also include a Find Record combo box to the form to locate a specific customer, as well as shortcuts to enter the city, state, and zip code with a single keystroke combination. And finally, be sure to display a message that reminds the user to back up the system upon closing the database.

INTRODUCTION TO VBA

You can accomplish a great deal in Access without using Visual Basic. You can create an Access database consisting of tables, forms, queries, and reports, by executing commands from pull-down menus. You can use macros to create menus that tie those objects together so that the database is easier to use. Nevertheless, there comes a point where you need the power of a programming language to develop a truly useful application. Hence, this introduction to **Visual Basic for Applications** (or **VBA**), a subset of Visual Basic that is accessible from every application in Microsoft Office.

VBA is different from traditional programming languages in that it is event-driven. An **event** is any action that is recognized by Access. Opening or closing a form is an event. So is clicking a button in a form or entering data in a text box or other control on the form. The essence of VBA is the creation of **procedures** (or sets of VBA statements) that respond to specific events.

To enhance an application through VBA, you decide which events are significant and what is to happen when those events occur. Then you develop the appropriate event procedures. You can, for example, create an event procedure that displays a splash (introductory) screen for the application every time a user opens the database. You can write an event procedure that creates a keyboard shortcut for data entry that executes when the user presses a particular keystroke combination. You can create an event procedure to display a specific message in place of the standard error message supplied by Access. In all instances, the execution of your procedures depends entirely on the user, because he or she triggers the underlying events through an appropriate action.

You can also use VBA to modify the event procedures that Access has created for you. If, for example, you used the Command Button Wizard to create a button to close a form, Access created the event procedure for you. The user clicks the button, and the event procedure closes the form. You can, however, use VBA to improve the procedure created by Access by adding a statement that reminds the user to back up the database after closing the form.

This chapter provides a general introduction to VBA through four hands-on exercises that enhance an application in different ways. Our approach is very different from that of other texts that run several hundred pages and cover the subject in extended detail. Our objective is to provide you with an appreciation for what can be accomplished, rather than to cover VBA in detail. We will show you how to create and modify simple procedures. We will also provide you with the conceptual framework to explore the subject in greater detail on your own.

One last point before we begin is that VBA is common to every application in Microsoft Office, and thus anything that you learn about VBA from within Access is applicable to the other applications as well. If, for example, you create a macro in Word or Excel, the macro recorder captures the keystrokes and then generates a VBA procedure that is accessible through the Word document or Excel workbook, respectively. You can modify the procedure by changing existing statements and/or by adding additional statements using the techniques in this chapter.

GETTING STARTED WITH VBA

There are two ways to learn the rudiments of VBA. You can begin your study with this chapter, which has you look at typical VBA procedures within an Access form, then proceed to the VBA primer at the end of the text to study the syntax more precisely. Alternatively, you may want to start with the primer, then return to this chapter to see the application of the various VBA statements within Access. Either way, the two chapters reinforce each other and provide a solid foundation in this important programming language.

A BETTER STUDENT FORM

The form in Figure 8.1 will be used throughout the chapter as the basis of our VBA examples. The form itself is unremarkable and parallels many of the forms that were developed throughout the text. It was created initially through the Form Wizard, then modified by moving and sizing controls as appropriate. What then is so special about the form, and how does it utilize VBA?

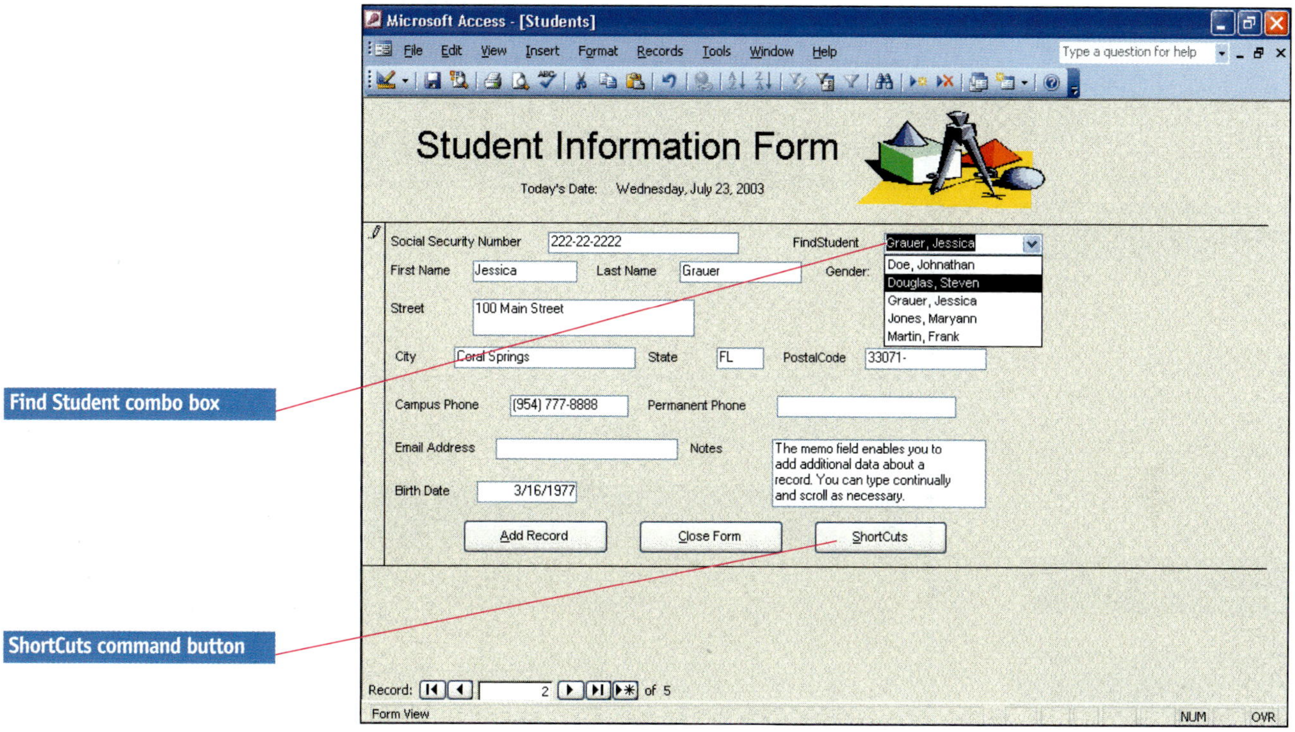

FIGURE 8.1 A Better Student Form

The answer lies beneath the surface and is best explained in conjunction with the dialog boxes in Figure 8.2. At first glance the dialog boxes look like typical messages displayed by Microsoft Access. Look closely at the title bar of any message, however, and note that it has been changed to reflect the student or author's name. This is a subtle change that is easily implemented through VBA, and it gives your application a personal touch. Note, too, the different icons that are displayed in the various messages. This, too, is a subtle touch that further customizes the application and its messages.

Look closely at the content of each dialog box to learn more about the underlying VBA capability. The message in Figure 8.2a indicates that the user has omitted the e-mail address, then asks if the record should be saved anyway. This is an improvement over the built-in routines for data validation, which use the Required property to reject any record that omits the e-mail address. Should this occur, the user is notified that the field is required, but he or she cannot save the record unless a value is specified. Through VBA, however, the user has a choice and can opt to save the record even when there is no e-mail address.

The dialog box in Figure 8.2b is displayed as a result of clicking the ShortCuts command button on the form. The message implies that the user can use keyboard shortcuts to enter the city, state, and zip code for Miami or Coral Springs. True, the user could enter the data manually, but think how much time can be saved when there is extensive data entry.

FIGURE 8.2   Dialog Boxes

Figure 8.2c displays a message indicating that one is attempting to add a student whose Social Security number is already in the file. The text is very straightforward and that is exactly the point. The default Access error message would not be as clear, and would have indicated that changes to the table were not successful because they would have created a duplicate value of the primary key. In other words, we used VBA to first detect the error, and then substituted a more explicit message. Finally, the message in Figure 8.2d simply reminds the user to back up the database upon exiting Access.

Modules and Procedures

There are, in essence, two different ways to learn VBA. The first is to immerse yourself in the theory and syntax before you attempt to develop any applications on your own. The second, and the one we follow, is to start with an overall appreciation of what it can do, then plunge right in. You need some basic vocabulary, but after that you can model your procedures on ours and create some very powerful applications in the process. (You can also review the "Getting Started with VBA" module at the end of this text.)

Visual Basic code is developed in units called procedures. There are two types of procedures, general procedures and event procedures. ***Event procedures*** are the essence of an Access application and run automatically in response to an event such as clicking a button or opening a form. ***General procedures*** do not run automatically, but are called explicitly from within another procedure. We focus exclusively on event procedures.

All (general and event) procedures are stored in modules; that is, one module contains one or more procedures. Every form in an Access database has its own module (known as a ***class module***), which contains the procedures for that form. A procedure is either public or private. A ***private procedure*** is accessible only from within the module in which it is contained. A ***public procedure*** is accessible from anywhere.

The procedures in a module are displayed and edited through the ***Module window*** within the Visual Basic editor. Figure 8.3, for example, displays the Module window for the student form shown earlier in Figure 8.1. Four different procedures are visible, each of which is associated with a different event. Each procedure begins with a procedure header that names the procedure. This is followed by the executable statements within the procedure, followed by the End Sub statement to mark the end of the procedure. Do not be concerned if you do not understand the precise syntax of every statement. Try, instead, to gain an overall appreciation for what the procedures do.

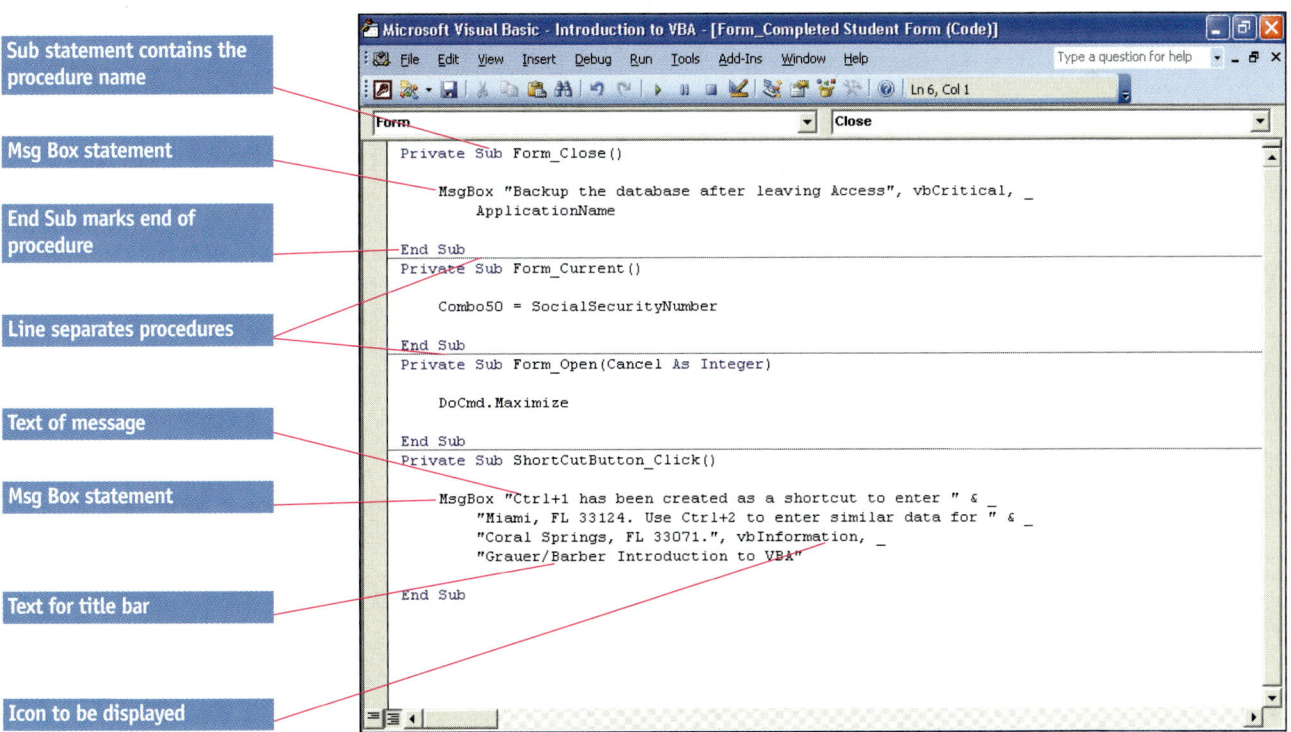

FIGURE 8.3 The Module Window

The first event procedure is for the ***Close Form event***. The procedure header contains the keyword Sub, followed by the procedure name (Form_Close). The ***MsgBox statement*** within the procedure displays the message box (shown earlier in Figure 8.2d) when the event occurs. Thus, whenever the user closes the form, either by clicking the Close button on the form or by clicking the Close button in the document window, the event procedure is triggered and one is reminded to back up the database. (See boxed tip.)

The syntax of the MsgBox statement is typical of many VBA statements and is best understood if you view the statement as it might appear in a Help screen: *MsgBox (prompt, buttons, title)*. The various entries are known as ***arguments*** (or ***parameters***) and determine the contents of the message box. The first argument is contained in quotation marks, and it specifies the prompt (or message text) that appears within the message box. The second argument indicates the type of command buttons (if any) and the associated icon that appear within the dialog box. This argument is specified as an ***intrinsic*** (or previously defined) ***constant*** (vbCritical in this example), and it determines the icon that is to appear in the message box. The third argument contains the text that appears in the title bar of the message box. It, too, appears in quotation marks.

The second event procedure is associated with the ***Current event*** of the form and is the focus of our first hands-on exercise. The nature of this procedure is much less intuitive than the previous example, yet this event procedure is critical to the success of the form. Return to the Student Form shown in Figure 8.1 and note the presence of a combo box to find a specific student. The user clicks the drop-down arrow on the combo box and selects a student from the displayed list, after which the data for that student is displayed in the form.

The combo box was created through the Combo Box Wizard, and it works well, but it does have one limitation. If the user elects to move from one record to the next by clicking a navigation button at the bottom of the form, the combo box is out of sync in that it does not reflect the name of the new student. Hence the need to write a VBA procedure for the Current event to change the value in the combo box to match the current record. In other words, the VBA procedure will move the SocialSecurityNumber of the current record to the combo box control whenever the record changes.

The third event procedure is associated with the Open Form event, and it needs almost no explanation. The single executable statement will maximize the form when it is opened. Again, do not be concerned if you do not understand the precise syntax of every statement in our initial examples as we add further explanation in the chapter. The fourth and final procedure is associated with the Click event of the ShortCut command button, and it contains another example of the MsgBox function. Note, too, that for this procedure to make sense, other event procedures have to be created to implement the shortcuts as described.

We would be misleading you if we said that VBA is easy. It's not, but neither is it as complicated as you might think. And more importantly, VBA is extremely powerful. We think you will be pleased with what you can accomplish by the end of this chapter. Once again, it is time for a hands-on exercise.

A SIMPLE STRATEGY FOR BACKUP

We cannot overemphasize the importance of adequate backup. Backup procedures are personal and vary from individual to individual as well as from installation to installation. Our suggested strategy is very simple, namely that you back up whatever you cannot afford to lose and that you do so at the end of every session. Be sure to store the backup at a different location from the original file. Develop a consistent strategy and follow it faithfully!

hands-on exercise

1 Creating a Combo Box and Associated VBA Procedure

Objective To create a combo box to locate a record; to create a VBA procedure to synchronize the combo box with the current record. Use Figure 8.4.

Step 1: **Open the Introduction to VBA Database**

- Start Access. Open the **Introduction to VBA database** in the **Exploring Access folder** as shown in Figure 8.4a.

- If necessary, click the **Forms button**. Select (click) the **Original Student Form**. Pull down the **Edit menu** and click the **Copy command** (or press **Ctrl+C** or click the **Copy button** on the Database toolbar). The form is copied to the clipboard.

- Pull down the **Edit menu** a second time and click the **Paste command** (or press **Ctrl+V** or click the **Paste button** on the Database toolbar) to display the Paste As dialog box. Type **Completed Student Form** and press **Enter**.

- The Database window contains two forms—the Original Student form and the Completed Student form you just created.

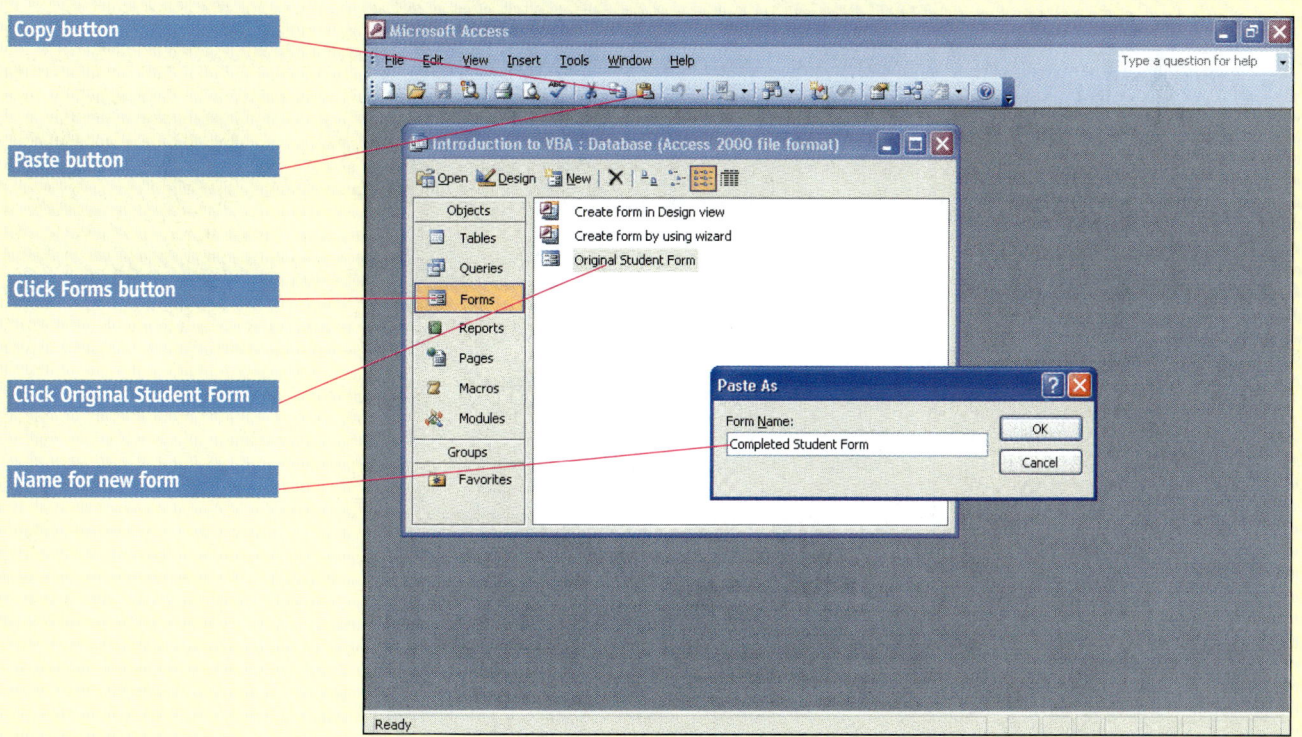

(a) Open the Introduction to VBA Database (step 1)

FIGURE 8.4 Hands-on Exercise 1

KEYBOARD SHORTCUTS—CUT, COPY, AND PASTE

Ctrl+X, Ctrl+C, and Ctrl+V are shortcuts to cut, copy, and paste, respectively, and apply to Windows applications in general. The shortcuts are easier to remember when you realize that the operative letters X, C, and V are next to each other at the bottom-left side of the keyboard.

Step 2: **The Combo Box Wizard**

- Open the newly created **Completed Student Form** in Design view. Maximize the window.

- Click the **Combo Box tool** on the Toolbox toolbar, then click and drag on the form next to the SSN control to create a combo box and start the wizard.

- Select the option button to **Find a record on my form based on the value I selected in my combo box** as shown in Figure 8.4b. Click **Next**.

- Double click the **SocialSecurityNumber field** to move it from the list box of available fields (on the left of the Combo Box Wizard) to the list of selected fields. Double click the **LastName field** to move this field as well. Click **Next**.

- You should see the columns in the combo box as they will appear in the form. Be sure the Check box to Hide key column is checked. Click **Next**.

- Change the label of the combo box to **FindStudent** (do not use a space in the label). Click **Finish** to exit the Combo Box Wizard. The combo box should appear on the form.

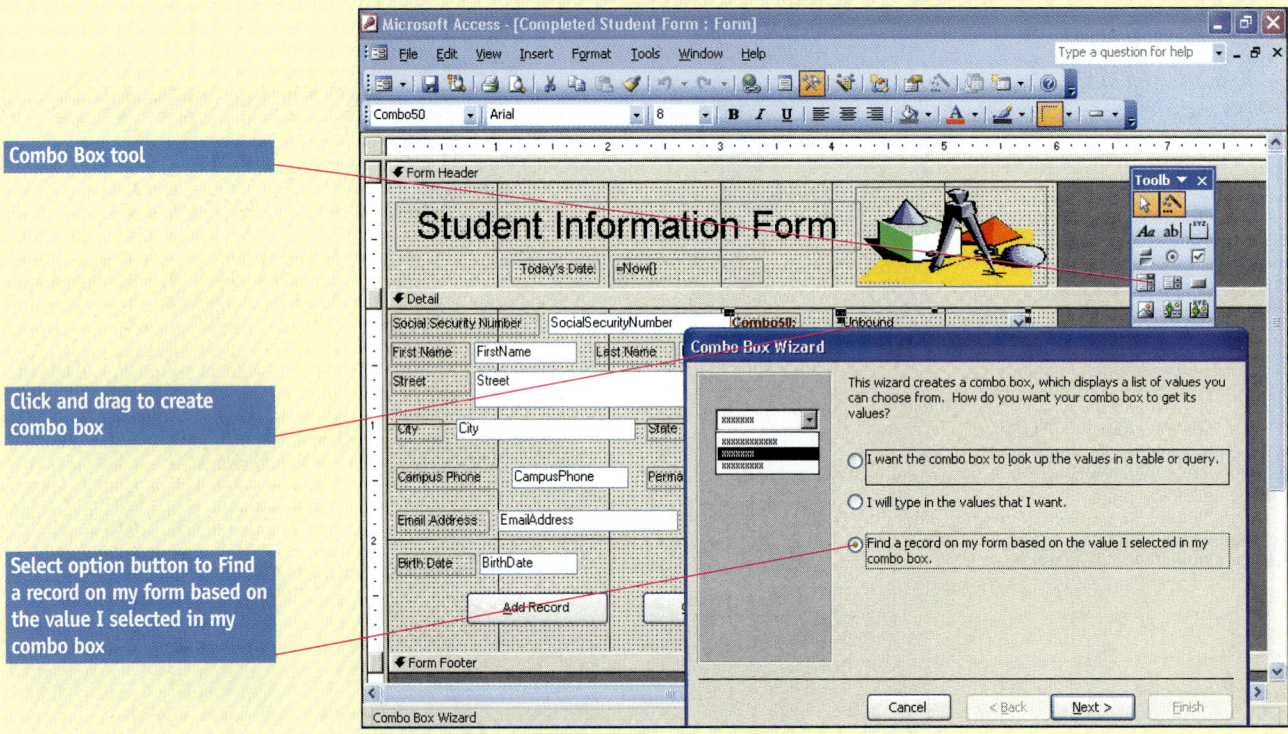

(b) The Combo Box Wizard (step 2)

FIGURE 8.4 Hands-on Exercise 1 (*continued*)

SIZING AND MOVING A COMBO BOX AND ITS LABEL

A combo box is always created with an attached label. Select (click) the combo box, and it will have sizing handles and a move handle, but the label has only a move handle. Select the label (instead of the combo box) and the opposite occurs. To move a combo box and its label, click and drag the border of either object. To move either the combo box or its label, click and drag the move handle (a tiny square in the upper-left corner) of the appropriate object. Use the Undo command if the results are not what you expect.

Step 3: **Move and Size the Combo Box**

- Move and size the newly created combo box to match the layout in Figure 8.4c. The Properties sheet is not yet visible. You will most likely have to decrease the size of the combo box and/or increase the size of the label.

- Change the format of the label to match the other labels on the form. (Use **Arial 8 point black** for the font.)

- To align the combo box and/or its label with the other controls on the same row of the form, press and hold the **Shift key** to select the controls you want to align. Pull down the **Format menu**, click **Align**, then click **Top** to align the top of all selected elements.

- Point to the combo box, click the **right mouse button** to display a shortcut menu, then click **Properties** to display the Properties dialog box in Figure 8.4c. If necessary, click the **All tab**.

- Write down the name of the combo box (Combo50 in our figure) as you will need it in step 7. The name of your control may be different from ours.

- Click the **Row Source property** to select it, then click the **Build button** (the button with three dots) that appears when the row is selected.

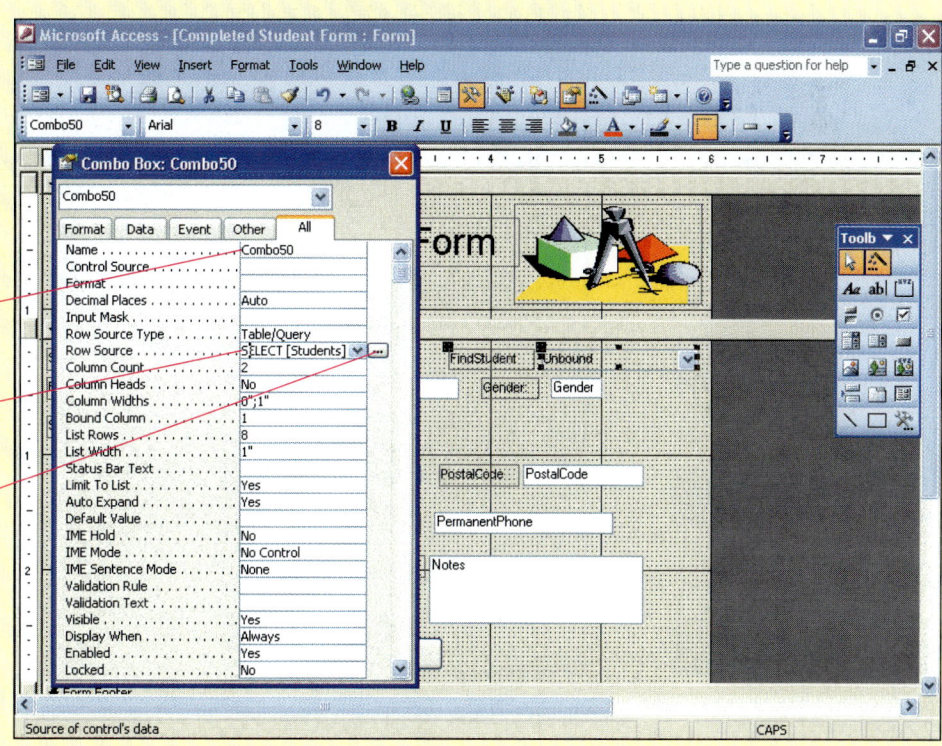

(c) Move and Size the Combo Box (step 3)

FIGURE 8.4 Hands-on Exercise 1 (*continued*)

THE PROPERTY DIALOG BOX

You can change the appearance or behavior of a control in two ways—by changing the actual control on the form itself or by changing the underlying properties. Anything you do to the control automatically changes the associated property, and conversely, any change to the property sheet is reflected in the appearance or behavior of the control. We find ourselves continually switching back and forth between the two techniques.

Step 4: **Update the Row Source**

- You should see the query in Figure 8.4d, except that your query has not yet been completed. Click in the second column of the Field row, immediately after the LastName control.

- Press the **space bar**, then type **&","& FirstName**. Leave a space after the comma within the quotation marks. Press **Enter**.

- Double click the border between this cell and the next to increase the column width so that you can see the entire expression. Note that Expr1: has been entered automatically in front of the expression.

- Click in the **Sort row** of the same column, click the **down arrow** if necessary, then click **Ascending** to display the records in alphabetical order by last name. Close the Properties sheet.

- Close the query. Click **Yes** when asked whether to save the changes that were made to the SQL statement.

- Click the **View button** to return to Form view.

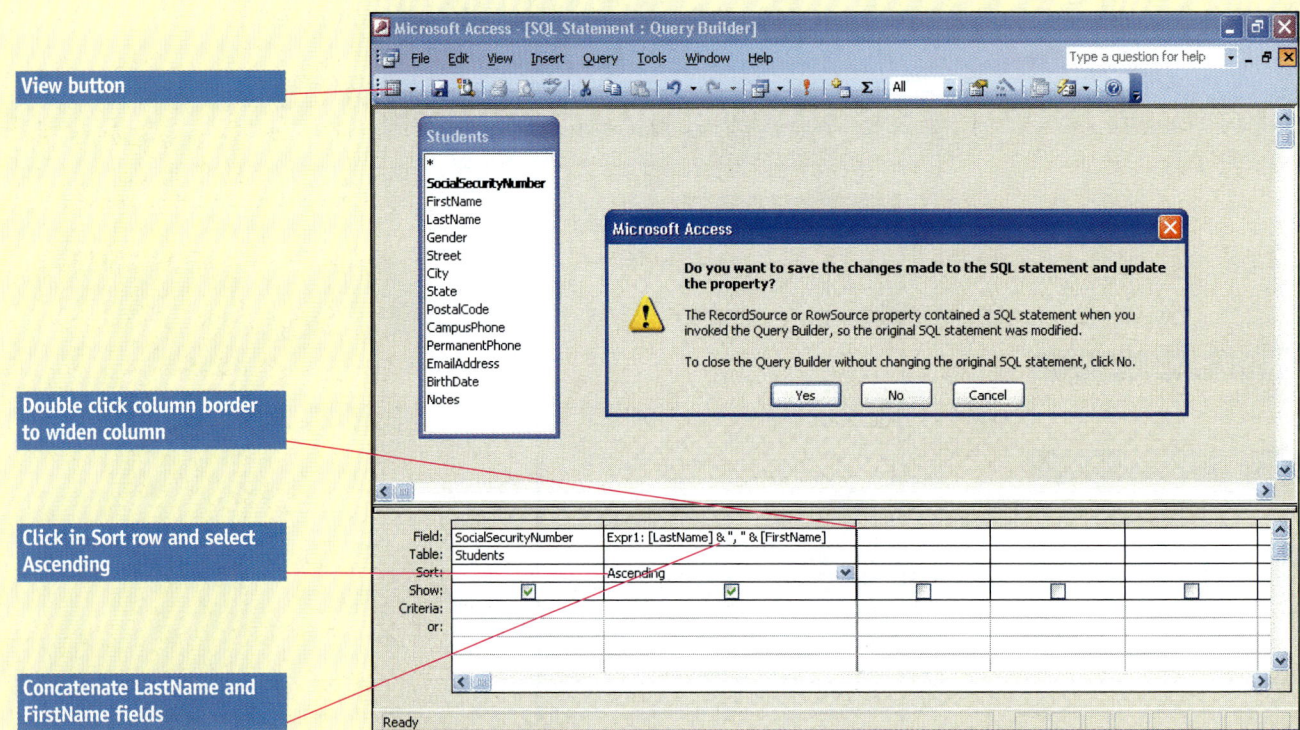

(d) Update the Row Source (step 4)

FIGURE 8.4 Hands-on Exercise 1 (*continued*)

CONCATENATING A STRING

The ampersand (&), or concatenation operator, indicates that the elements on either side of an expression are to appear adjacent to one another when the expression is displayed. You can also concatenate a literal and a field name such as "The employee's last name is " & LastName to display "The employee's last name is Smith," assuming that Smith is the current value in the LastName field. (Note the blank space that appears after the word "is" within the literal.)

Step 5: **Test the Find Student Combo Box**

- If necessary, click the **navigation button** above the status bar to return to the first record in the table, Maryann Jones, as shown in Figure 8.4e.

- Click the **drop-down arrow** on the combo box you just created to display a list of students in alphabetical order. (If you do not see the list of students, press **Esc** to cancel whatever operation is in effect, then return to Design view to repeat the instructions in the previous steps.)

- Select (click) **Grauer, Jessica** from the list of names in the combo box. The form is updated to display the information for this student.

- Click the **drop-down arrow** a second time and select **Douglas, Steven** from the combo box. Again the form is updated.

- Click the **navigation button** to return to the first student. The form displays the record for Maryann Jones, but the combo box is *not* updated; it still displays Douglas, Steven.

- Click the **View button** to return to Design view to create the required event procedure.

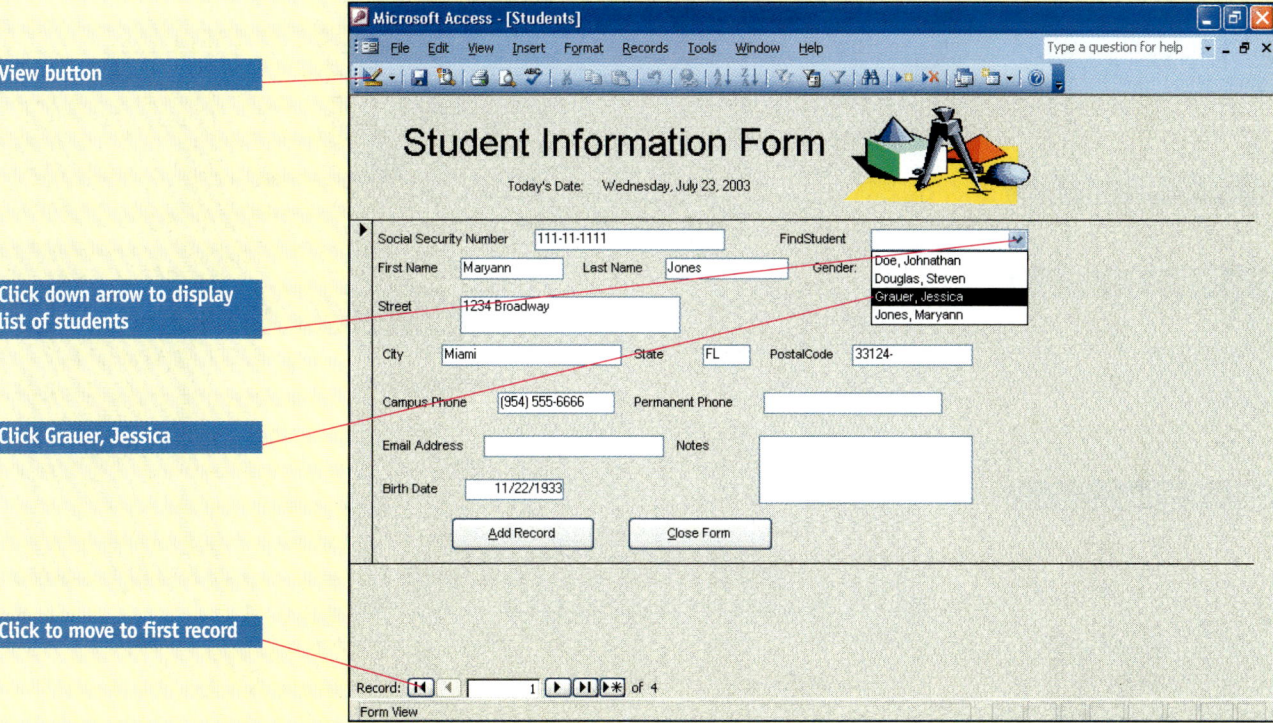

(e) Test the Find Student Combo Box (step 5)

FIGURE 8.4 Hands-on Exercise 1 (*continued*)

WHY USE VBA?

The combo box enables you to select a name from an alphabetical list, then updates the form to display the data for the corresponding record. All of this has been accomplished without the use of VBA. The problem is that the combo box is not updated automatically when records are selected via the navigation buttons. The only way to correct this problem is by writing a VBA procedure.

Step 6: **Create an Event Procedure**

- Point to the **Form Selector box** (the tiny square at the upper left of the form), click the **right mouse button** to display a shortcut menu, then click **Properties** to display the Form property sheet.

- Click the **Event tab**. Click the **On Current** event, then click the **Build button** to display the Choose Builder dialog box as shown in Figure 8.4f.

- Click (select) **Code Builder**, then click **OK**. A VBA window will open containing the module for the Completed Student Form.

- If necessary, maximize the VBA window and/or click the **Procedure View button** above the status bar. The insertion point is positioned automatically within a newly created event procedure.

- You should see a statement beginning Private Sub Form_Current( ) corresponding to the On Current event. You should also see the line ending End Sub, but no code appears between the Sub and End Sub statements.

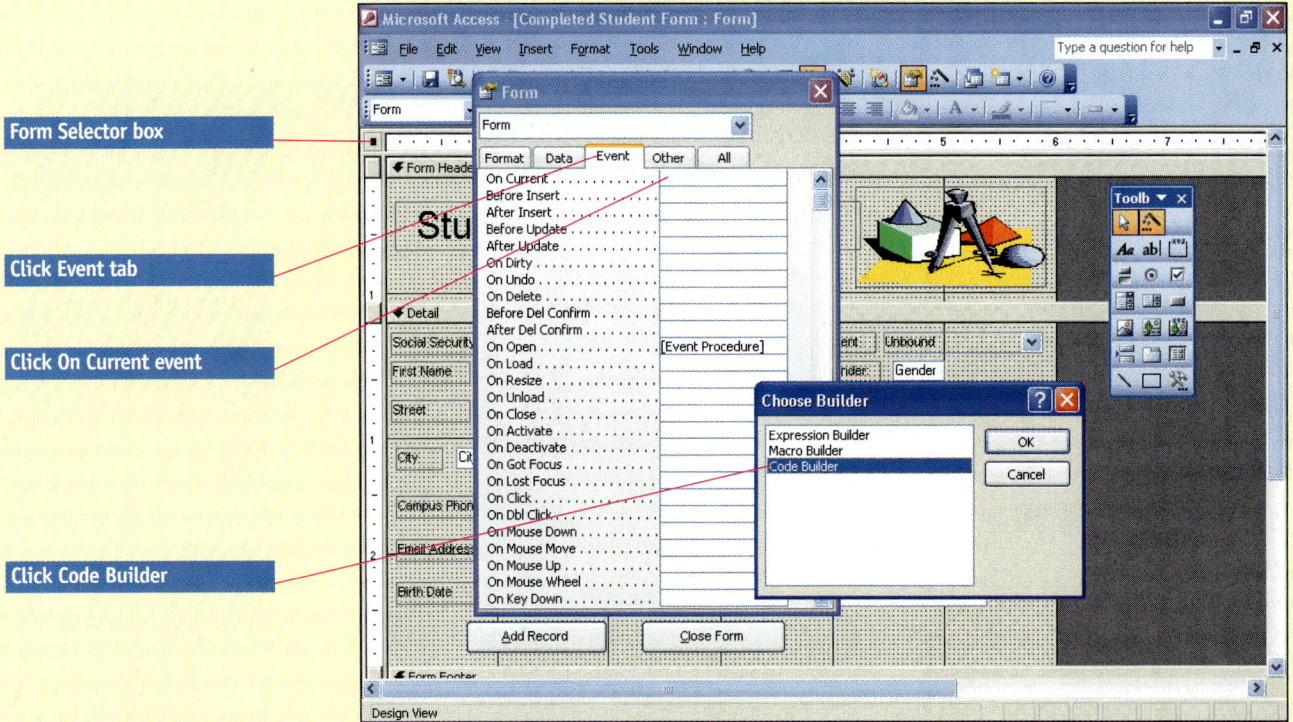

(f) Create an Event Procedure (step 6)

FIGURE 8.4   Hands-on Exercise 1 (*continued*)

CREATING AN EVENT PROCEDURE

There is only one correct way to create an event procedure, and that is the technique used in this exercise. Thus, you right click the Form Selector box to display the form properties, click the Event tab to select the desired event, click the Build button, and click the Code Builder. This in turn takes you to the VBA editor, where you enter the procedure. Do *not* create the event directly in the module window (without first clicking the Event tab). The latter technique appears reasonable, but it will not create the necessary association between the event and the code.

Step 7: **Complete the On Current Event Procedure**

- The insertion point should be on a blank line, between the Sub and End Sub statements. If not, click on the blank line. Press the **Tab key** to indent the statements within the procedure. Indentation makes your code easier to read, but is not a syntactical requirement.

- Type **Combo50** (use the number of your combo box as determined in step 3).

- If you do not remember the name of the combo box, click the button on the taskbar to return to the Form window, click in the combo box and click the **All tab**. Look at the entry in the **Name property**.

- Press the **space bar** after you have entered the name of your combo box, type an **equal sign**, and press the **space bar** a second time. Type **Social** (the first several letters in the name of the SocialSecurityNumber control).

- Pull down the **Edit menu** and click **Complete Word** (or press **Ctrl+Space**) to display all of the objects, properties, and methods that start with these letters.

- SocialSecurityNumber is already selected as shown in Figure 8.4g. Press the **space bar** to copy the selected item and complete the statement.

- Click the **Save button** on the Visual Basic toolbar. Close the VBA window.

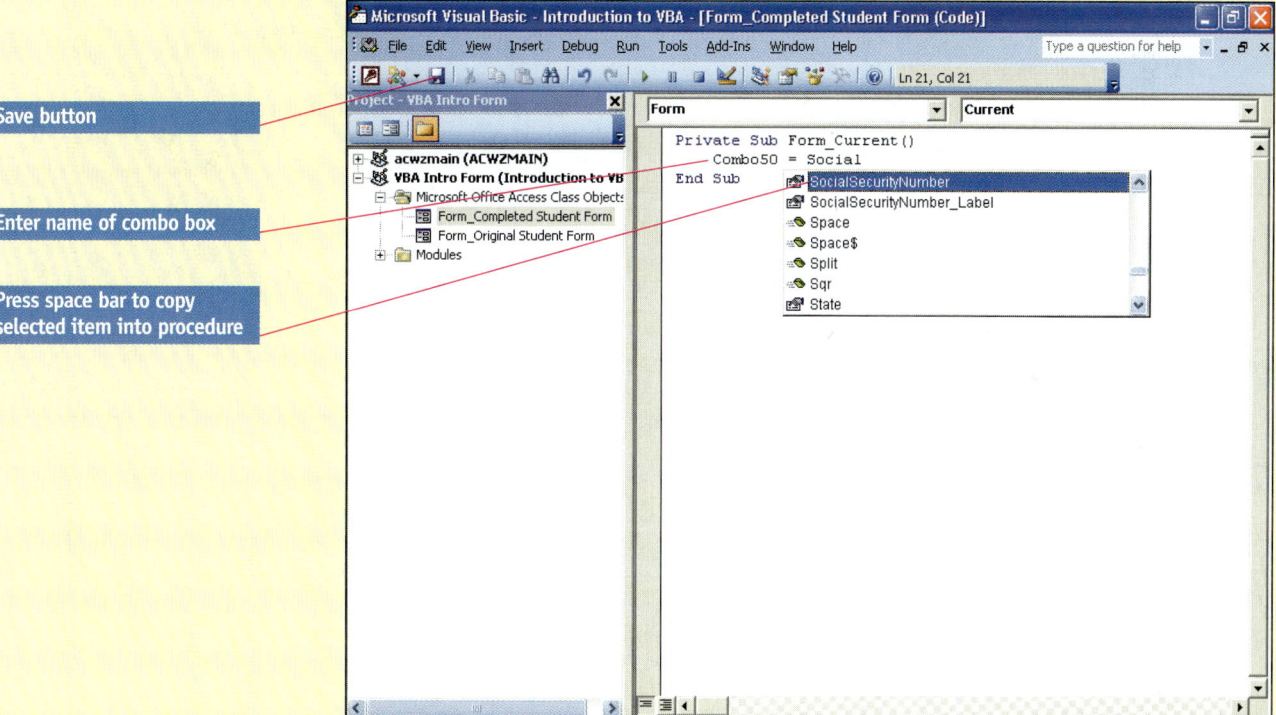

(g) Complete the On Current Event Procedure (step 7)

FIGURE 8.4 Hands-on Exercise 1 (*continued*)

USE THE RIGHT MOUSE BUTTON

The Quick Info and AutoList features are activated automatically as you create a VBA statement. The features can also be activated at any time by pulling down the Edit menu and selecting the Quick Info or List Properties/Methods commands, respectively. You can also point to any portion of a VBA statement and click the right mouse button to display a shortcut menu with options to display this information.

Step 8: **Add Your Record**

- If necessary, click the button for the Access form on the task bar. Close the Properties sheet. Click the **View button** to return to Form view.

- You should see the Student Information form. Click the **navigation button** to move to the next record. The data in the form and combo box is updated.

- Click the **navigation button** to return to the first record. Once again the data in the form is updated, as is the name in the combo box.

- Click the form's **Add Record command button**. You should see a blank form as shown in Figure 8.4h.

- Click in the **SocialSecurityNumber** text box and enter your Social Security number. Continue to enter your personal data.

- Close the form when you have finished entering data. Exit Access if you do not want to continue with the next exercise at this time.

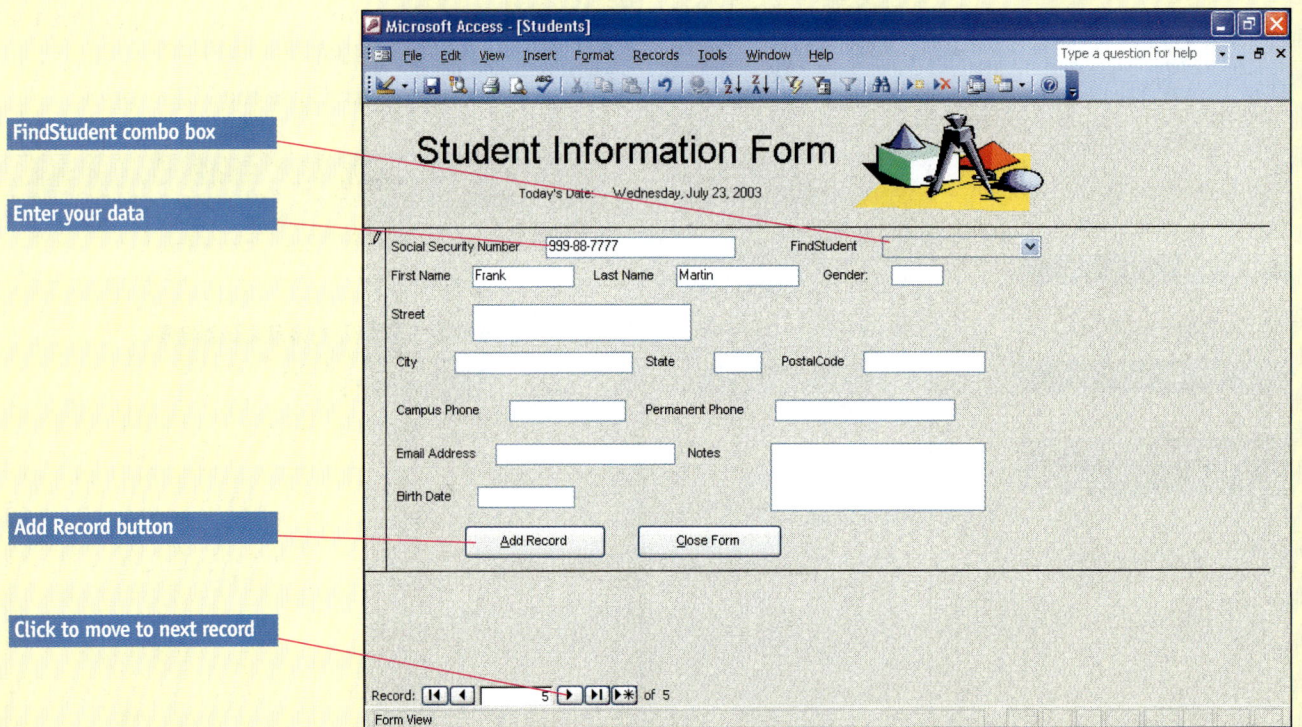

(h) Add Your Record (step 8)

FIGURE 8.4 Hands-on Exercise 1 (*continued*)

THE SET FOCUS METHOD

Ideally, clicking the Add Record button on the Student form should position you in the SocialSecurityNumber field, without your having to click in the field to begin entering data. Open the Student form in Design view, right click the Add Record button and display the Properties dialog box. Click the Event tab, click the On Click property, then click the Build button. Insert the statement SocialSecurityNumber.SetFocus immediately after the DoCmd statement. Go to Form view, then click the Add button. You should be positioned in the SocialSecurityNumber field.

FACILITATING DATA ENTRY

One of the most useful things you can accomplish through VBA is to provide the user with shortcuts for data entry. Many forms, for example, require the user to enter the city, state, and zip code for incoming records. In certain systems, such as a local store or company, this information is likely to be repeated from one record to the next. One common approach is to use the ***Default property*** in the table definition to specify default values for these fields, so that the values are automatically entered into a record.

What if, however, there are several sets of common values? Our local store, for example, may draw customers from two or three different cities, and we need to constantly switch among the different cities. The Default property is no longer effective because it is restricted to a single value. A better solution is to use VBA to provide a set of keyboard shortcuts such as Ctrl+1 for the first city, state, and zip code, Ctrl+2 for the next set of values, and so on. The user selects the appropriate shortcut, and the city, state, and zip code are entered automatically. The VBA code is shown in Figure 8.5.

Figure 8.5a displays the ***KeyDown event*** procedure to implement two shortcuts, Ctrl+1 and Ctrl+2, corresponding to Miami and Coral Springs, respectively. Figure 8.5b displays the ***Click event*** procedure for the shortcut button on the data entry form (which was shown in Figure 8.1). The user clicks the button, and a message is displayed that describes the shortcuts. The latter is very important because the system must communicate the availability of the shortcuts to the user, else how is he or she to know that they exist?

```
Private Sub Form_KeyDown(KeyCode As Integer, Shift As Integer)
'The Key Preview Property of the form must be set to Yes
    If KeyCode = vbKey1 And Shift = acCtrlMask Then 'Ctrl+1 was pressed
        City = "Miami"
        State = "FL"
        PostalCode = "33124"
        CampusPhone.SetFocus
    End If
    If KeyCode = vbKey2 And Shift = acCtrlMask Then 'Ctrl+2 was pressed
        City = "Coral Springs"
        State = "FL"
        PostalCode = "33071"
        CampusPhone.SetFocus
    End If
End Sub
```

- KeyCode argument
- SetFocus method

(a) Form KeyDown Event Procedure

```
Private Sub ShortCutButton_Click()
    MsgBox "Ctrl+1 has been created as a shortcut to enter " & _
        "Miami, FL 33124. Use Ctrl+2 to enter similar data for " & _
        "Coral Springs, FL 33071.", vbInformation, _
        "Grauer/Barber Introduction to VBA"
End Sub
```

- MsgBox statement
- Click event procedure

(b) ShortCutButton Click Event Procedure

FIGURE 8.5 Procedure for Exercise 2

Consider now the event procedure in Figure 8.5a and think about what it takes to implement a keyboard shortcut. In essence, the procedure must determine whether the user has used any of the existing shortcuts, and if so, enter the appropriate values in the form. There are different ways to accomplish this, the easiest being through a series of If statements, each of which checks for a specific shortcut. In other words, check to see if the user pressed Ctrl+1, and if so, enter the appropriate data. Then check to see if the user pressed Ctrl+2, etc. (If you have a previous background in programming, you may recognize alternate ways to implement this logic, either through the Else clause in the If statement, or through a Case statement. We explore these alternate structures later in the chapter, but for the time being, we want to keep our statements as simple as possible.)

Once again, we ask that you try to gain an overall appreciation for the procedure, as opposed to concerning yourself with every detail in every statement. You should recognize, for example, that the KeyDown event procedure requires two arguments, KeyCode and Shift, as can be seen from the parenthetical information in the ***procedure header***. (The procedure header is created automatically as you shall see in the following hands-on exercise.)

The ***KeyCode argument*** tests for a specific number or letter; for example, KeyCode = vbKey1 determines whether the number 1 has been pressed by the user. (VBA defines several intrinsic constants such as vbKey1 or vbKeyA corresponding to the number 1 and letter A, respectively.) In similar fashion, the Shift argument tests for the Ctrl, Shift, or Alt key by checking for the intrinsic constants acCtrlMask, acShiftMask, and acAltMask, respectively. The And operator ensures that both keys (Ctrl and the number 1) have been pressed simultaneously.

Once a determination has been made as to whether a shortcut has been used, the corresponding values are moved to the indicated controls (City, State, and PostalCode) on the form. The ***SetFocus method*** then moves the insertion point to the CampusPhone control, where the user can continue to enter data into the form.

The Click event procedure in Figure 8.5b contains a single MsgBox statement, which displays information about the shortcuts to the user when he or she clicks the Shortcuts button. The MsgBox statement has three parameters—a literal that is continued over two lines containing the text of the message, an intrinsic constant (vbInformation) indicating the icon that is to be displayed with the message, and a second literal indicating the text that is to appear in the title bar of the message dialog box.

The statement is straightforward, but it does illustrate the rules for continuing a VBA statement from one line to the next. To continue a statement, leave a space at the end of the line to be continued, type the underscore character, then continue the statement on the next line. You may not, however, break a line in the middle of a character string. Thus, you need to complete the character string with a closing quotation mark, add an ampersand (as the concatenation operator to display this string with the character string on the next line), then leave a space followed by the underscore to indicate continuation.

BUILD CODE BY OBSERVATION AND INFERENCE

VBA is a powerful language with a subtle syntax and an almost endless variety of intrinsic constants. The expertise required to build the procedures for the keyboard shortcuts is beyond the novice, but once you are given the basic code, it is relatively easy to extend or modify the code to accommodate a specific application. Look at the code in Figure 8.5, for example, and decide how you would change the existing Ctrl+1 keyboard shortcut to reflect a different city. Can you add a third If statement to create a Ctrl+3 shortcut for a new city?

hands-on exercise
2 Facilitating Data Entry

Objective Create keyboard shortcuts to facilitate data entry. Use Figure 8.6 as a guide in the exercise.

Step 1: Create the KeyDown Event Procedure

- Open the **Introduction to VBA database** from the previous exercise. Click the **Forms button**, then open the **Completed Student Form** in Design view.

- Pull down the **View menu** and click **Code** (or click the **Code button** on the Database toolbar).

- If necessary, pull down the **View menu** and click **Project Explorer** to display the Project Explorer pane at the left of the window. If you are in Full Module view, click within any procedure, then click the **Procedure View button**.

- Click the **down arrow** in the Object list box and select **Form**.

- Click the **down arrow** in the Procedure list box to display the list of events for the form. Click **KeyDown** to create a procedure for this event.

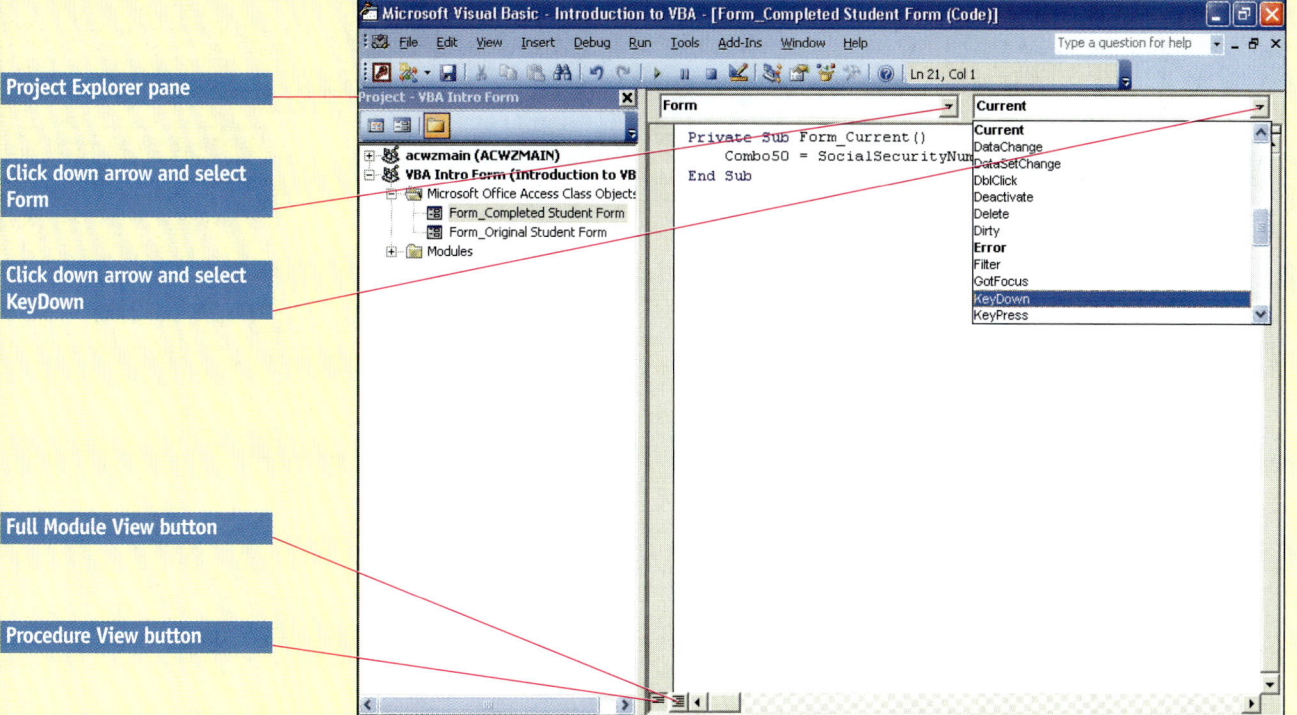

(a) Create the KeyDown Event Procedure (step 1)

FIGURE 8.6 Hands-on Exercise 2

PROCEDURE VIEW VERSUS FULL MODULE VIEW

Procedures can be displayed individually, or multiple procedures can be viewed simultaneously. Click the Procedure View button to display one procedure, or click the Full Module View button to show multiple procedures. Either way, you can press Ctrl+PgDn and Ctrl+PgUp to move between procedures in the Module window.

Step 2: **Correct the Compile Error**

- The Procedure header and End Sub statements for the KeyDown event procedure are created automatically as shown in Figure 8.6b. The insertion point is positioned on the blank line between these two statements.

- Type an **apostrophe** (to indicate a comment), then enter the text of the comment as shown in the figure. Press **Enter** when you have completed the comment. The line turns green to indicate it is a comment.

- Press the **Tab key** to indent the first line of code, then enter the statement exactly as it appears in the figure. Press **Enter**.

- You should see the error message in Figure 8.6b because we made a (deliberate) error in the If statement to illustrate what happens when you make an error.

- Click **OK** if you know the reason for the error, or click **Help** to display a screen describing the error, then close the Help window.

- Now return to the VBA statement, type a **space** at the end of the line, and add the key word **Then** to correct the error. Press **Enter** to move to the next line in order to complete the statement.

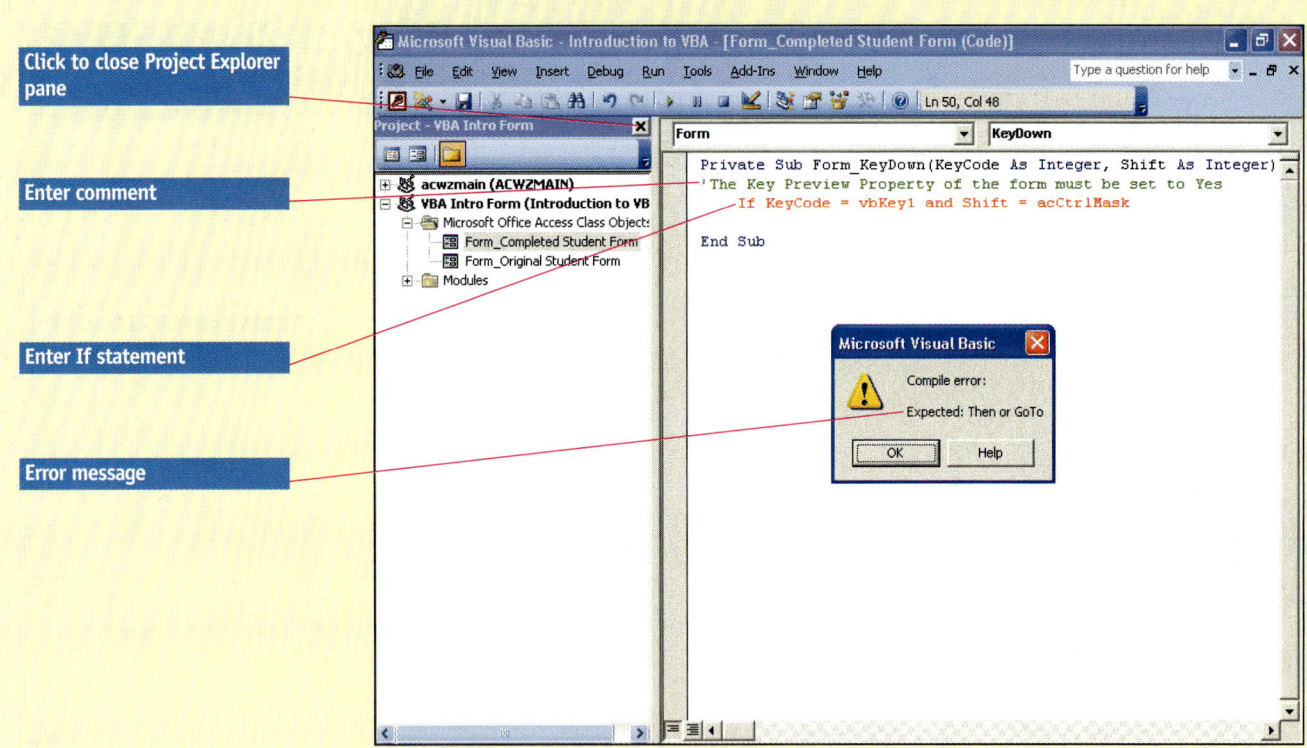

(b) Correct the Compile Error (step 2)

FIGURE 8.6 Hands-on Exercise 2 (*continued*)

RED, GREEN, AND BLUE

Visual Basic for Applications uses different colors for different types of statements (or a portion of those statements). Any statement containing a syntax error appears in red. Comments appear in green. Keywords, such as Sub and End Sub, appear in blue.

Step 3: **Complete the KeyDown Event Procedure**

- Close the Project Explorer window and complete the KeyDown procedure as shown in Figure 8.6c. Use what you know about the Cut, Copy, and Paste commands to facilitate entering the code.
- You could, for example, copy the first If statement, then modify the code as appropriate, rather then typing it from scratch. Select the statements to cut or copy to the clipboard, then paste them elsewhere in the module.
- If the results are different from what you expected or intended, click the Undo command immediately to reverse the effects of the previous command.
- Be sure that your code matches the code in Figure 8.6c. The indentation is not a syntactical requirement of VBA, per se, but is used to make the statements easier to read.
- Click the **Save button** to save the module.

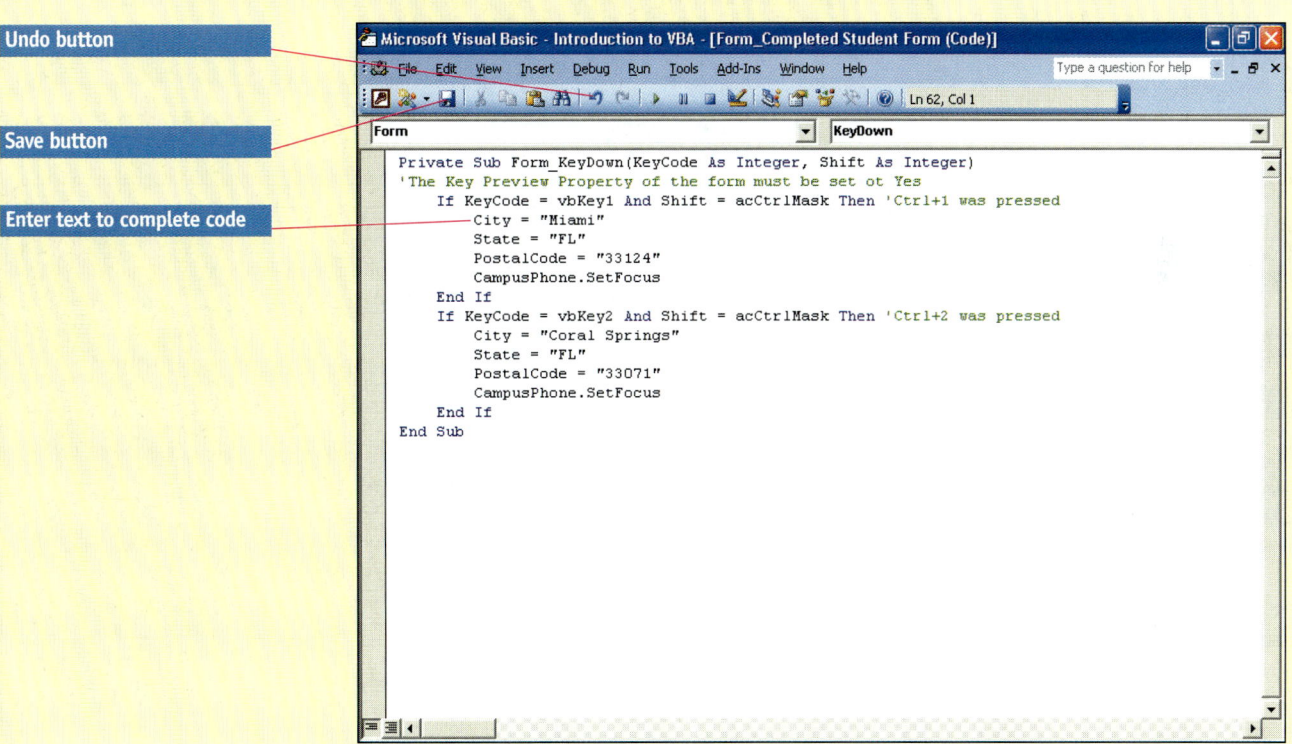

(c) Complete the KeyDown Event Procedure (step 3)

FIGURE 8.6 Hands-on Exercise 2 (*continued*)

THE COMPLETE WORD TOOL

You know that your form contains a control to reference the postal code, but you are not quite sure of the spelling. The Complete Word tool can help. Enter the first several characters, then press Ctrl+Space (or pull down the Edit menu and click Complete Word). VBA will complete the term for you if you have entered a sufficient number of letters, or it will display all of the objects, properties, and methods that begin with the letters you have entered. Use the down arrow to scroll through the list until you find the item, then press the space bar to complete the entry.

MICROSOFT OFFICE ACCESS 2003   1745

Step 4: **Set the Key Preview Property**

- The Key Preview property of the form must be set to **Yes** to complete the keyboard shortcut. Click the taskbar button to return to the **Completed Student Form**.

- Point to the **Form Selector box** (the tiny square at the upper left of the form). Click the **right mouse button** to display a context-sensitive menu with commands for the entire form.

- Click **Properties** to display the Form Properties dialog box. Click the **Event tab** and scroll until you can click the **Key Preview property**. If necessary, change the property to **Yes** as shown in Figure 8.6d.

- Close the Form Property dialog box. Save the form, which now contains the new procedure for the keyboard shortcut. The procedure should be tested as soon as it is completed.

- Click the **View button** on the Form Design toolbar to return to Form view.

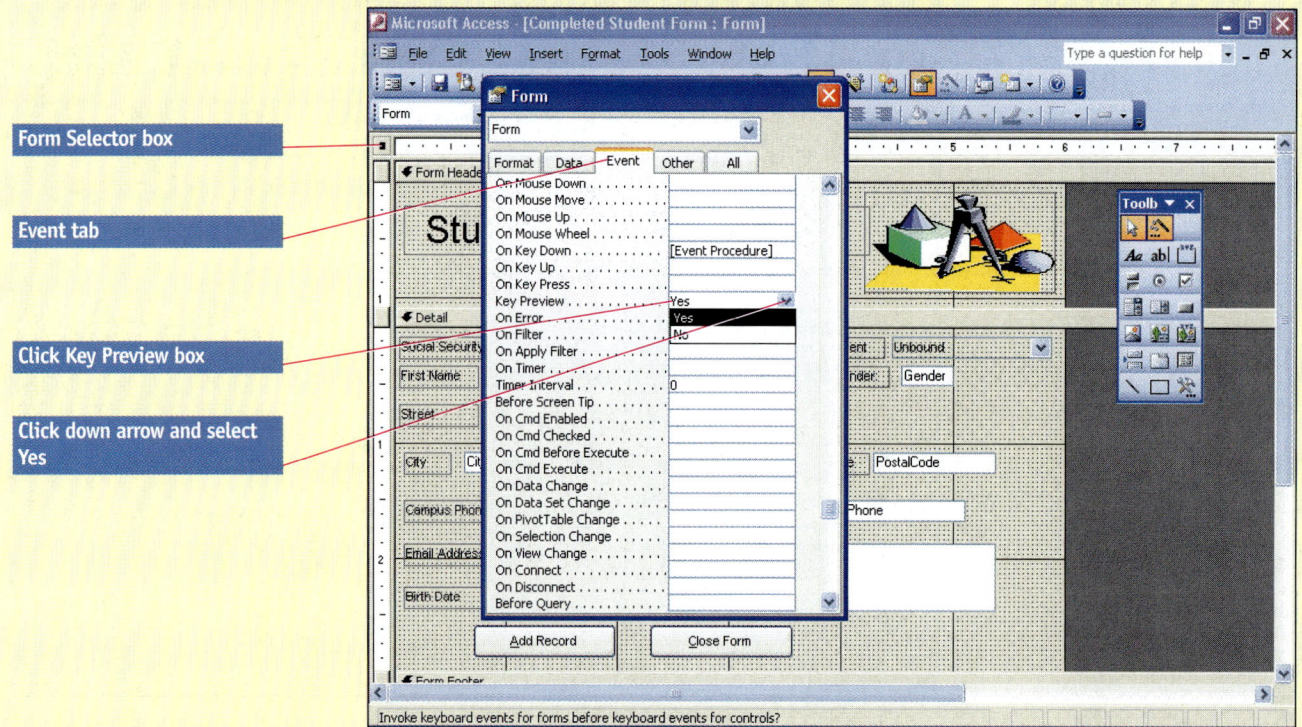

(d) Set the Key Preview Property (step 4)

FIGURE 8.6 Hands-on Exercise 2 (*continued*)

USE THE PROPERTY SHEET

Every object on a form has its own property sheet. This enables you to change the appearance or behavior of a control in two ways—by changing the control through application of a menu command or toolbar button, or by changing the underlying property sheet. Anything you do to the control changes the associated property, and conversely, any change to the property sheet is reflected in the appearance or behavior of the control.

1746 CHAPTER 8: CREATING MORE POWERFUL APPLICATIONS

Step 5: **Test the Procedure**

- Click the **navigation button** to move to the first record in the table as shown in Figure 8.6e. Press **Ctrl+2** to change the City, State, and Postal Code to reflect Coral Springs, as per the shortcut you just created.

- The data changes automatically, and you are automatically positioned on the CampusPhone field. The record selector changes to a pencil to indicate that the data has been edited, but not yet saved.

- If the shortcut does not work, return to step 4 and check that the Key Preview property has been set to Yes. If the shortcut still does not work, return to the module for the form and check the VBA statements.

- Press **Ctrl+1** to change the city to Miami. The data should change automatically, after which you are positioned in the CampusPhone field.

- Click the **View button** to return to the Design view of the form.

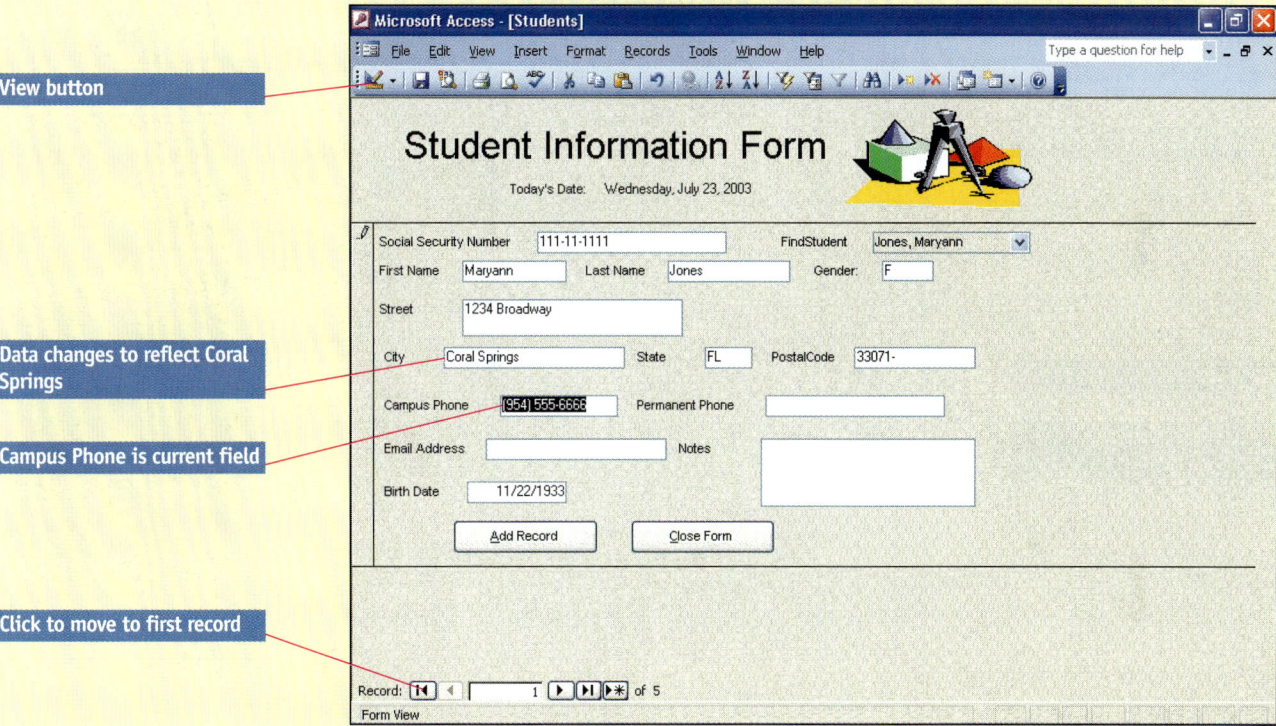

(e) Test the Procedure (step 5)

FIGURE 8.6 Hands-on Exercise 2 (*continued*)

CHANGE THE TAB ORDER

The Tab key provides a shortcut in the finished form to move from one field to the next; that is, you press Tab to move forward to the next field and Shift+Tab to return to the previous field. The order in which fields are selected corresponds to the sequence in which the controls were entered onto the form, and need not correspond to the physical appearance of the actual form. To restore a left-to-right, top-to-bottom sequence, pull down the View menu, click Tab Order, then select AutoOrder.

Step 6: **Create the ShortCut Command Button**

- Click and drag the **Command Button tool** on the Toolbox toolbar to create a new command button as shown in Figure 8.6f.

- The Command Button Wizard starts automatically. This time, however, you want to create the Click event procedure for this button yourself.

- Click the **Cancel button** as soon as you see the wizard. Right click the newly created command button and display its property sheet. Click the **All tab**.

- Change the Name property to **ShortCutButton**. Change the Caption property to **&ShortCuts**.

- Click the **Event tab**. Click the **On Click property**, click the **Build button**, click **Code Builder**, then click **OK** to display the Module window.

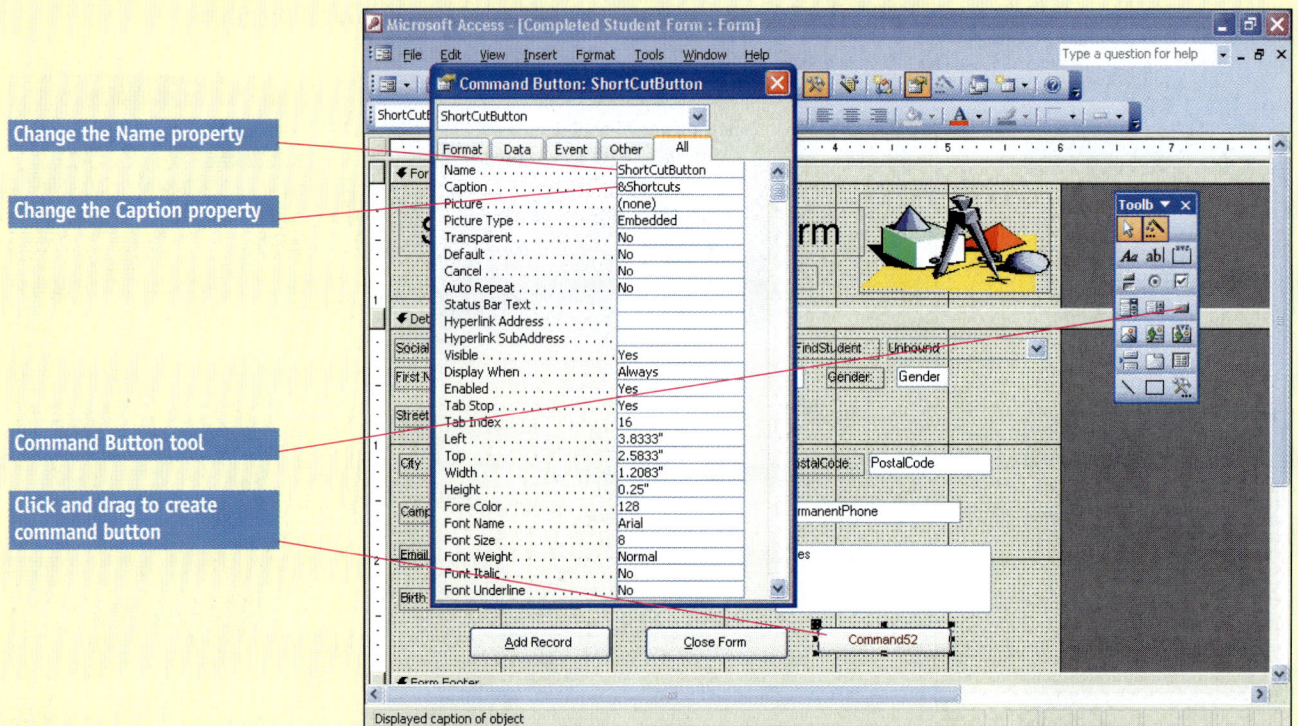

(f) Create the ShortCut Command Button (step 6)

FIGURE 8.6   Hands-on Exercise 2 (continued)

ACCELERATOR KEYS AND THE CAPTION PROPERTY

The Caption property enables you to create a keyboard shortcut for a command button. Right click the button in the Form Design view to display the Properties dialog box for the command button. Click the All tab, then modify the Caption property to include an ampersand immediately in front of the letter that will be used in the shortcut (e.g., &Help if you have a Help button). Close the dialog box, then go to Form view. The command button will contain an underlined letter (e.g., Help) that can be activated in conjunction with the Alt key (e.g., Alt+H) as a shortcut or accelerator key.

Step 7: **Create the OnClick Procedure**

- You should be positioned in the ShortCutButton_Click procedure, as shown in Figure 8.6g. Press the **Tab key** to indent, then enter the VBA statement exactly as it is shown in the figure. Note the following:
  - A tip (known as "Quick Info") appears as soon as you type the space after the MsgBox keyword. The tip displays the syntax of the statement and lists its arguments.
  - Indentation is not a requirement of VBA per se, but is done to make the VBA code easier to read. Continuation is also optional and is done to make the code easier to read.
- Complete the statement exactly as shown in the figure, except substitute your name for Grauer/Barber. Click the **Save button**. Close the Module window.
- Return to the **Form Design view**. Close the property sheet. Size and align the new button. Change the text on the button to **8 point Arial**. Save the form.
- Click the **View button** to change to Form view.

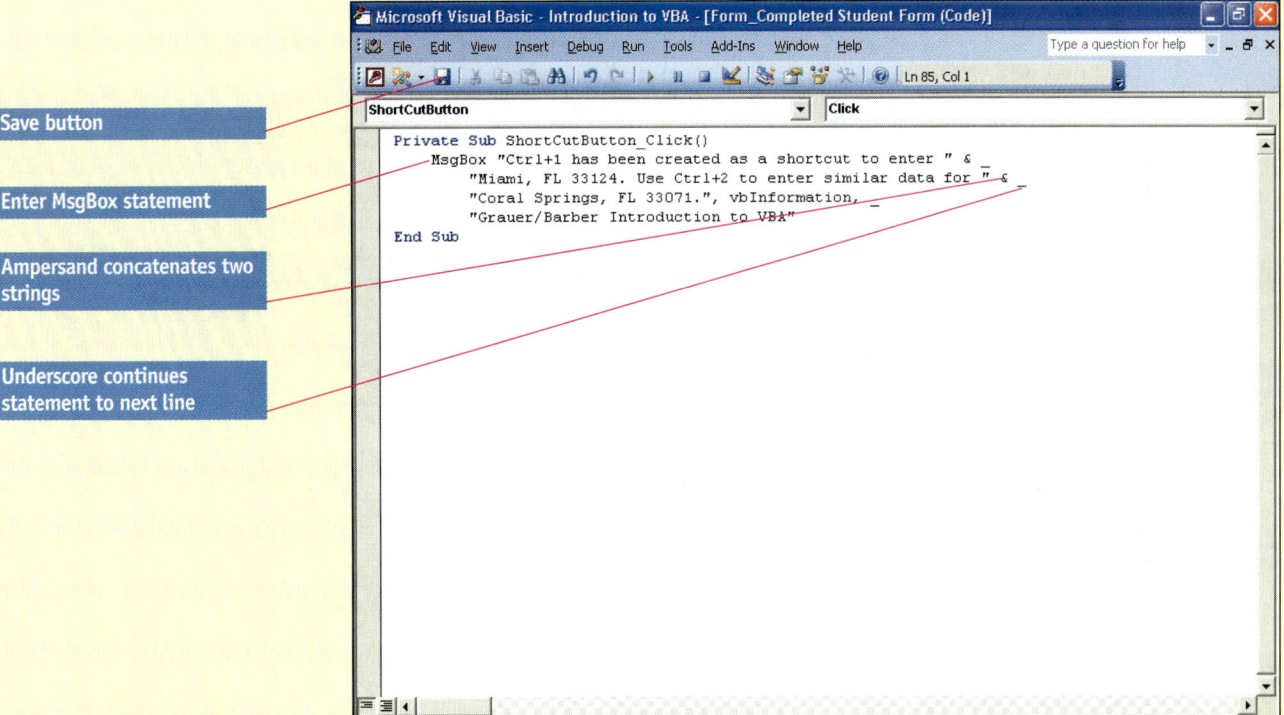

(g) Create the OnClick Procedure (step 7)

FIGURE 8.6   Hands-on Exercise 2 (continued)

THE MSGBOX STATEMENT

The MsgBox statement has three parameters—the text of the message to be displayed, an icon identifying the message type, and the text that appears on the title bar. The message itself is divided into multiple character strings, which continue from one line to the next. The ampersand concatenates the two character strings to display a single message. The underscore character indicates that the statement is continued to the next line.

Step 8: **Test the ShortCuts Button**

- Click the **ShortCuts button**. You can also use the keyboard shortcut, **Alt+S**, as indicated by the underlined letter on the button name that was established through the Caption property for the button.

- You should see the message box that is displayed in Figure 8.6h. Your name should appear in the title bar of the dialog box rather than ours. Click **OK** to close the dialog box.

- Try the other shortcuts that have been built into the form. Press **Ctrl+1** and **Ctrl+2** to switch back and forth between addresses in Miami and Coral Springs, respectively.

- Press **Alt+C** to close the form. Not everyone prefers the keyboard to the mouse, but you have nonetheless created a powerful set of shortcuts.

- Exit Access if you do not want to continue with the next exercise at this time.

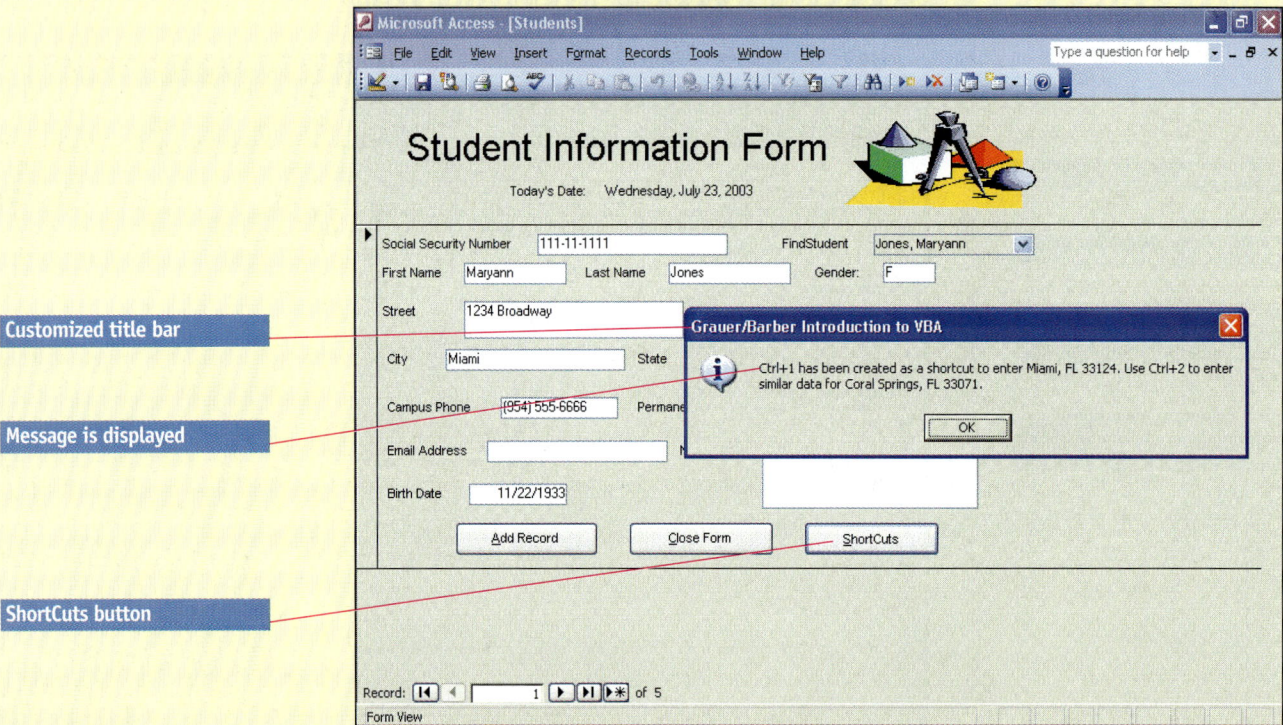

(h) Test the ShortCuts Button (step 8)

FIGURE 8.6 Hands-on Exercise 2 (*continued*)

CREATE UNIFORM COMMAND BUTTONS

A form is made more appealing if all of its command buttons have similar properties. Change to Design view, then press and hold the Shift key as you select each of the command buttons. Pull down the Format menu, click Size, then choose the desired parameter for all of the buttons such as widest and tallest. (You have to execute the command once for each parameter.) Leave the buttons selected, pull down the Format menu, select the Align command, then choose the desired alignment. Pull down the Format menu a final time, select the Horizontal Spacing command, then implement the desired (e.g., uniform) spacing for the buttons.

ERROR TRAPPING

It is not a question of whether errors in data entry will occur, but rather how quickly a user will understand the nature of those errors in order to take the appropriate corrective action. If, for example, a user attempts to add a duplicate record for an existing customer, Access will display an error message of the form, "changes to the table were not successful because they would create duplicate values of the primary key." The issue is whether this message is clear to the nontechnical individual who is doing the data entry.

An experienced Access programmer will realize immediately that Access is preventing the addition of the duplicate record because another record with the same primary key (e.g., a Social Security or account number) is already in the file. A nontechnical user, however, may not understand the message because he or she does not know the meaning of "primary key." Wouldn't it be easier if the system displayed a message indicating that a customer with that Social Security or account number is already in the file? In other words, errors invariably occur, and it is important that the user sees a message which clearly indicates the problem so that it may be corrected promptly.

Figure 8.7 displays the event procedure that is developed in the next hands-on exercise to display application-specific error messages in place of the standard messages provided by Access. The procedure is triggered any time there is an error in data entry. Realize, however, that there are literally hundreds of errors, and it is necessary to test for each error for which we want a substitute message. Each error has a unique error number, and thus the first task is to determine the number associated with the error you want to detect. This is accomplished by forcing the error to occur, then printing the error number in the *Immediate window* (a special window within the VBA editor that enables you to display results of a procedure as it is executing). It's easier than it sounds, as you will see in the hands-on exercise.

Once you know the error numbers, you can complete the procedure by checking for the errors that you wish to trap, then displaying the appropriate error messages. One way to implement this logic is through a series of individual If statements, with one *If statement* for each error. It is more efficient, however, to use a Case statement as shown in Figure 8.7.

The *Case statement* tests the value of an incoming variable (DataErr in our example, which contains the error number), then goes to the appropriate set of statements, depending on the value of that variable. Our procedure tests for two errors, but it could be easily expanded to check for additional errors. Error 2237 occurs if the user attempts to find a record that is not in the table. Error 3022 results when the user attempts to add a duplicate record. Once an error is detected, the MsgBox statement is used to display the custom error message that we created, after which Access will continue normal processing without displaying the default error message.

Note, too, the last case (Else), which is executed when Access detects an error other than 2237 or 3022. This time we do not display our own message because we do not know the nature of the error. Instead we set the Response variable to the intrinsic constant acDataErrContinue, which causes Access to display the default error message for the error that occurred.

Figure 8.7b displays the *General Declarations section*, which contains statements that apply to every procedure in the form. The section defines the constant ApplicationName as a string and sets it to the literal value "John Doe did his homework." Note, too, how the two MsgBox statements in Figure 8.7a reference this constant as the third argument, and recall that this argument contains the text that is displayed on the title bar of the message box. In other words, we can change the value of the ApplicationName constant in one place, and have that change reflected automatically in every MsgBox statement.

```
Private Sub Form_Error(DataErr As Integer, Response As Integer)
' You need to determine the specific error number
'   1. Create the error in Access to determine the error number
'   2. Use the Print method of the Debug object to display the error
'   3. Press Ctrl+G to open the Immediate window where the error will be displayed

    Debug.Print "Error Number = ", DataErr

    Select Case DataErr
        Case 2237
            MsgBox "The student is not in our file. Please " & _
                "check the spelling and reenter correctly, or click the " & _
                "Add button to enter a new record.", vbInformation, _
                ApplicationName
            Response = acDataErrContinue
        Case 3022
            MsgBox "You are trying to add a student whose " & _
                "social security number is already in the file. Please " & _
                "correct the social security number or cancel this " & _
                "record and move to the original record.", vbExclamation, _
                ApplicationName
            Response = acDataErrContinue
        Case Else
            Response = acDataErrDisplay
    End Select
End Sub
```

- **Error number**
- **Improved error message will be displayed**
- **Default error message displayed for all other errors**

(a) Form Error Event Procedure

```
Option Compare Database
Option Explicit

Const ApplicationName As String = "John Doe has done his homework"
```

- **Statement defines ApplicationName constant**

(b) General Declarations Section

FIGURE 8.7 Procedures for Exercise 3

THE CASE STATEMENT

The Case statement tests the value of a variable, then branches to one of several sets of statements, depending on the value of that variable. You may not be able to write a Case statement intially, but once you see the statement, you can extend the code to accommodate any application. Look at the code in Figure 8.7, for example, and decide the required modifications to reflect employees rather than students. How would you extend the existing Case statement to include an additional error message?

hands-on exercise

3 Error Trapping

Objective To create an event procedure that substitutes application-specific messages for the standard Access error messages. Use Figure 8.8 as a guide.

Step 1: **Force the Error Message**

- Open the **Introduction to VBA database**. If necessary, click the **Forms button**, then open the **Completed Student Form** in Form view.

- Click and drag to select the name in the **Find Student** combo box. Type **XXXX** (an obviously invalid name). Press **Enter**. You should see the error message in Figure 8.8a, which may be confusing to a nontechnical user.

- Click **OK** to close the message box. Press the **Esc key** and erase the XXXX, since we are not interested in finding this student.

- Click the **View button** to change to **Design view**.

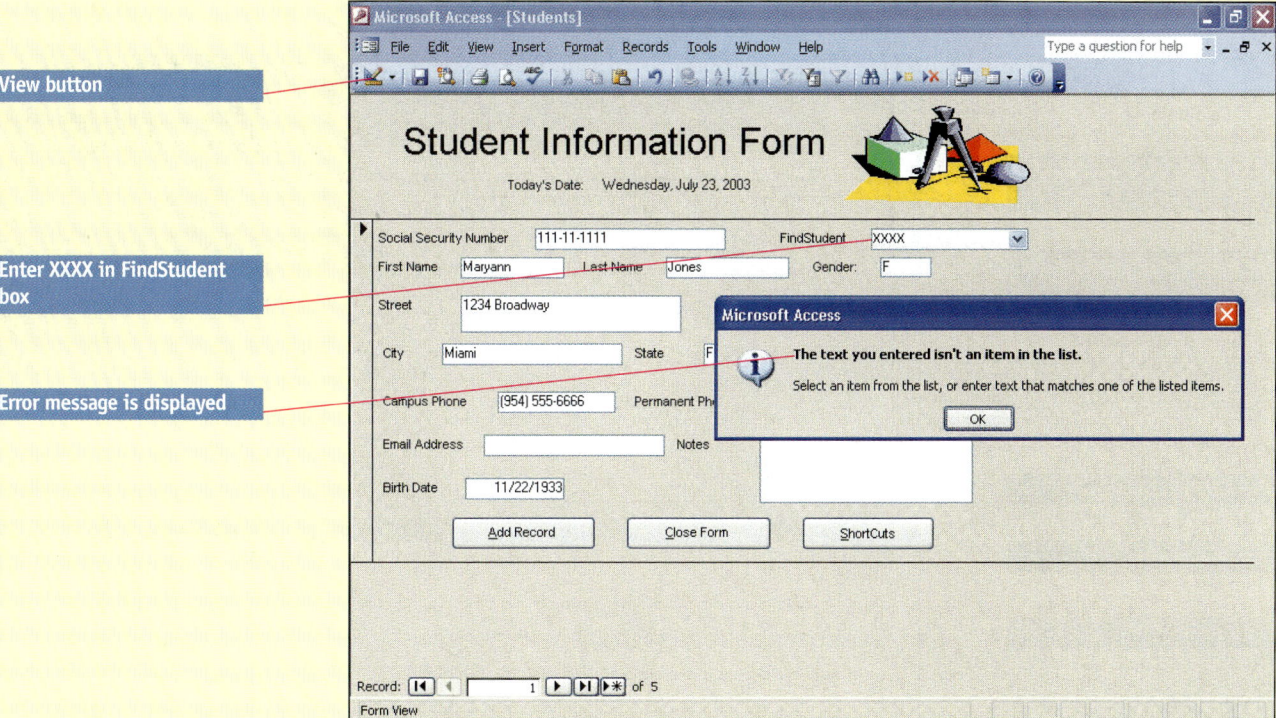

(a) Force the Error Message (step 1)

FIGURE 8.8 Hands-on Exercise 3 (*continued*)

EVENT-DRIVEN VERSUS TRADITIONAL PROGRAMMING

A traditional program is executed sequentially, beginning with the first line of code and continuing in order through the remainder of the program. VBA, however, is event-driven, meaning that its procedures are executed when designated events occur. Thus, it is the user, and not the program, who determines which procedures are executed and when. This exercise creates a procedure that will run if specified errors occur during data entry.

Step 2: **Determine the Error Number**

- Pull down the **View menu** and click **Code** (or click the **Code button** on the Form Design toolbar) to display the Module window. If necessary, click the **down arrow** for the Object box and select the **Form object**.

- Click the **down arrow** in the Procedure box and click **Error** to display the event procedure that will execute when an error occurs in the form. Click the **Procedure View button** as shown in Figure 8.8b.

- We created this procedure for you. It consists of a single executable statement, to print a literal, followed by the number of the error. The comments explain how to use the procedure.

- Pull down the **View menu** and click **Immediate Window** (or press **Ctrl+G**) to open the Immediate window. You should see number 2237.

- This is the error number reserved by Access to indicate that the value that was entered in the text portion of a combo box does not match any of the entries in the associated list.

- Close the Immediate window.

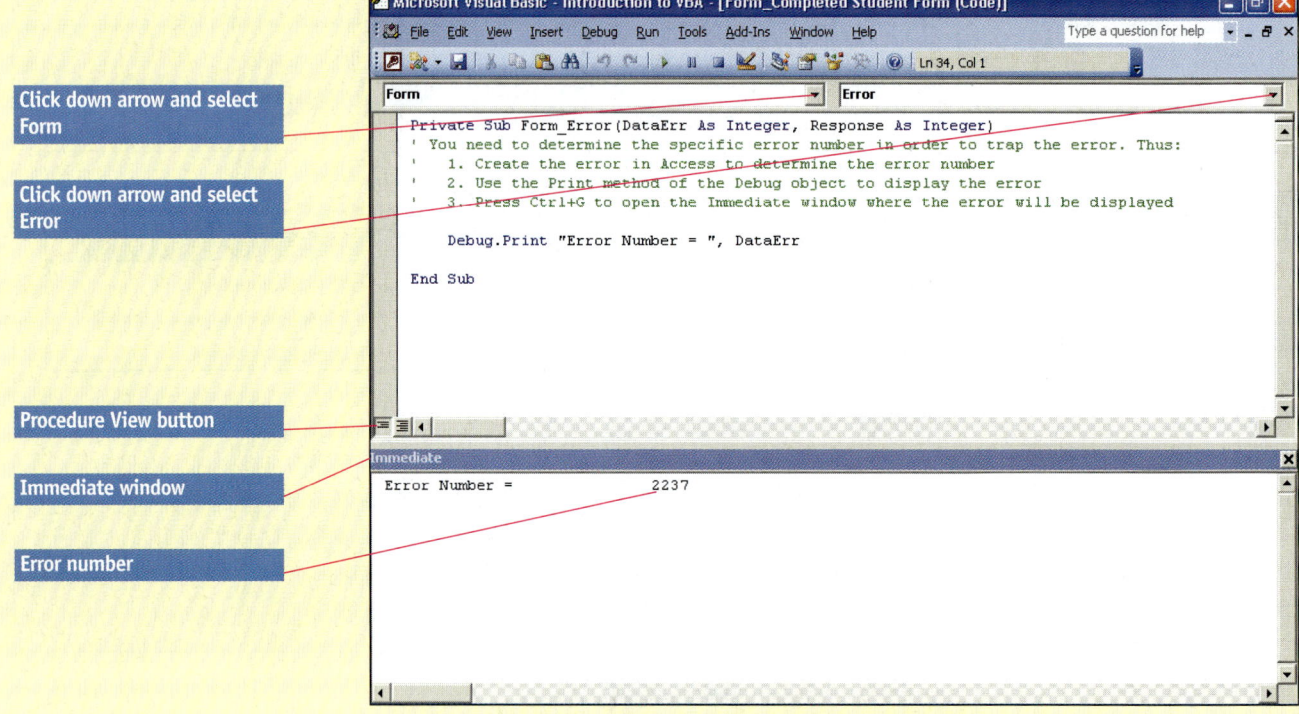

(b) Determine the Error Number (step 2)

FIGURE 8.8 Hands-on Exercise 3 (*continued*)

INSTANT CALCULATOR

Use the Print method (action) in the Immediate window to use VBA as a calculator. Press Ctrl+G at any time to display the Immediate window. Type the statement Debug.Print, followed by your calculation, for example, Debug.Print 2+2, then press Enter. The answer is displayed on the next line in the Immediate window.

Step 3: **Trap the First Error**

- Click in the event procedure at the end of the Debug statement, press the **Enter key** twice, then enter the VBA statements in Figure 8.8c. Note the following:
  - Comments appear at the beginning of the procedure.
  - The Case statement tests the value of an incoming variable (DataErr), then goes to the appropriate set of statements, depending on the value of that variable. The procedure currently tests for only one error, but it will be expanded later in the exercise to check for additional errors.
  - The indentation and blank lines within the procedure are not requirements of VBA per se, but are used to make the code easier to read.
  - A "Quick Info" tip appears as soon as you type the space after MsgBox. The tip displays the syntax of the statement.

- Complete the procedure exactly as shown in Figure 8.8c. Click the **Save button** to save the procedure.

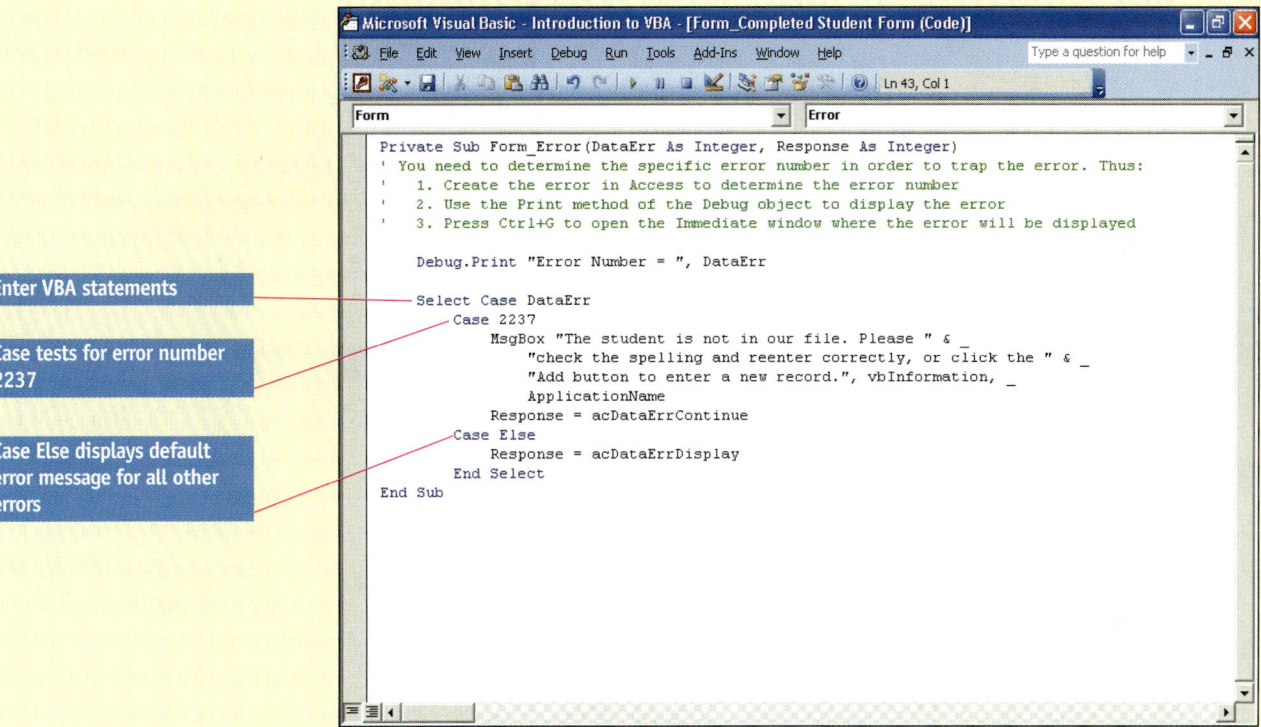

(c) Trap the First Error (step 3)

FIGURE 8.8 Hands-on Exercise 3 (*continued*)

CONTINUING A VBA STATEMENT—THE & AND THE UNDERSCORE

A VBA statement can be continued from one line to the next by leaving a space at the end of the line to be continued, typing the underscore character, then continuing on the next line. You may not, however, break a line in the middle of a literal (character string). Thus, you need to complete the character string with a closing quotation mark, add an ampersand (as the concatenation operator to display this string with the character string on the next line), then leave a space followed by the underscore to indicate continuation.

Step 4: **Test the Error Event Procedure**

- Click the taskbar button to return to the **Completed Student Form**. Change to the **Form view** as shown in Figure 8.8d.

- Click and drag to select the name in the FindStudent combo box. Type **XXXX** (an obviously invalid name). Press **Enter**.

- This time you should see the error message in Figure 8.8d corresponding to the text you entered in the previous step. (Note the title bar on the dialog box indicating that your name goes here. We tell you how to modify the title bar later in the exercise.)

- Click **OK** to close the message box. Press the **Esc key** and erase the XXXX. Return to **Design view**.

- Pull down the **View menu** and click **Code** (or click the **Code button** on the Form Design toolbar) to display the Module window.

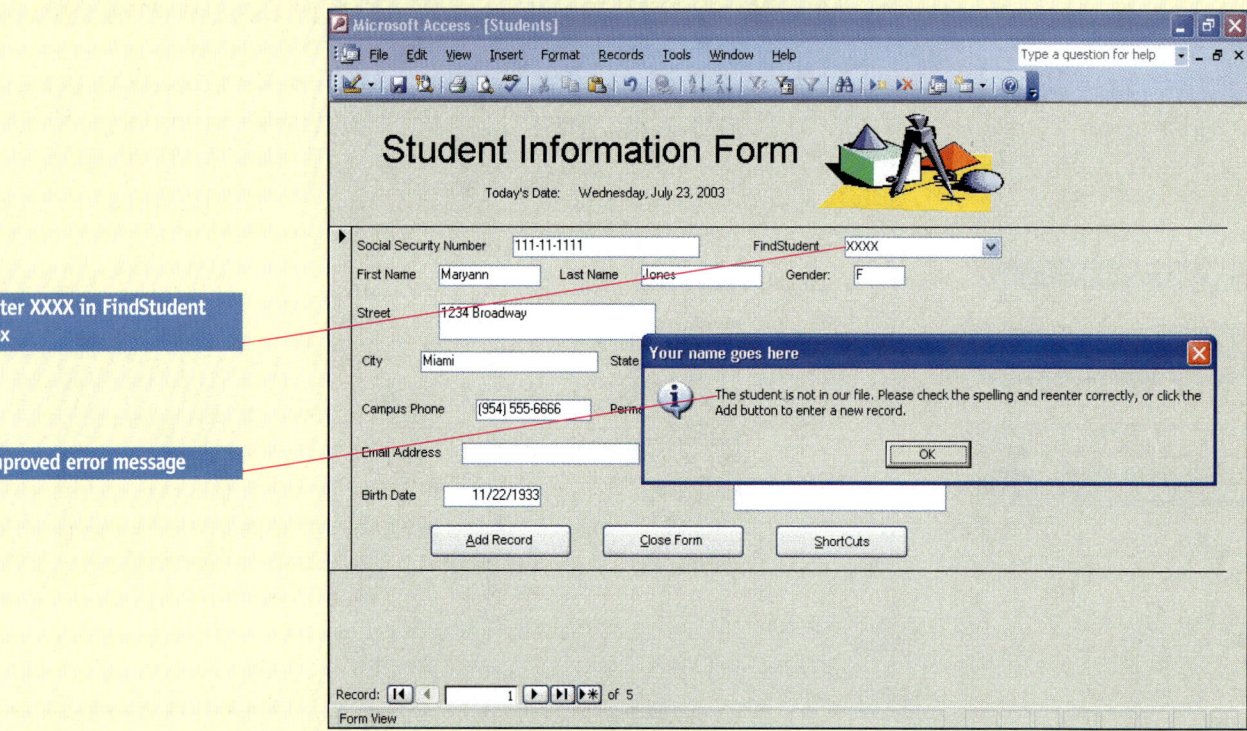

(d) Test the Error Event Procedure (step 4)

FIGURE 8.8 Hands-on Exercise 3 (*continued*)

THE FIRST BUG

A bug is a mistake in a computer program; hence debugging refers to the process of finding and correcting program errors. According to legend, the first bug was an unlucky moth crushed to death on one of the relays of the electromechanical Mark II computer, bringing the machine's operation to a halt. The cause of the failure was discovered by Grace Hopper (at one point the oldest officer on active duty in the United States Navy), who promptly taped the moth to her logbook, noting, "First actual case of bug being found."

Step 5: **Change the Application Name**

- Click the **down arrow** for the Object box and select **(General)** at the beginning of the list of objects.

- We have defined the Visual Basic constant **ApplicationName**, and initialized it to "Your name goes here." This was the text that appeared in the title bar of the dialog box in the previous step.

- Click and drag to select **Your name goes here**. Enter **John Doe has done his homework**, substituting your name for John Doe.

- Pull down the **Edit menu**, click the **Find command** to display the Find dialog box. Enter **ApplicationName** in the Find What text box. Specify the option to search the **Current module** and specify **All** as the direction.

- Use the **Find Next command button** to locate all occurrences of the ApplicationName constant. Can you appreciate the significance of this technique to customize your application?

- Save the procedure.

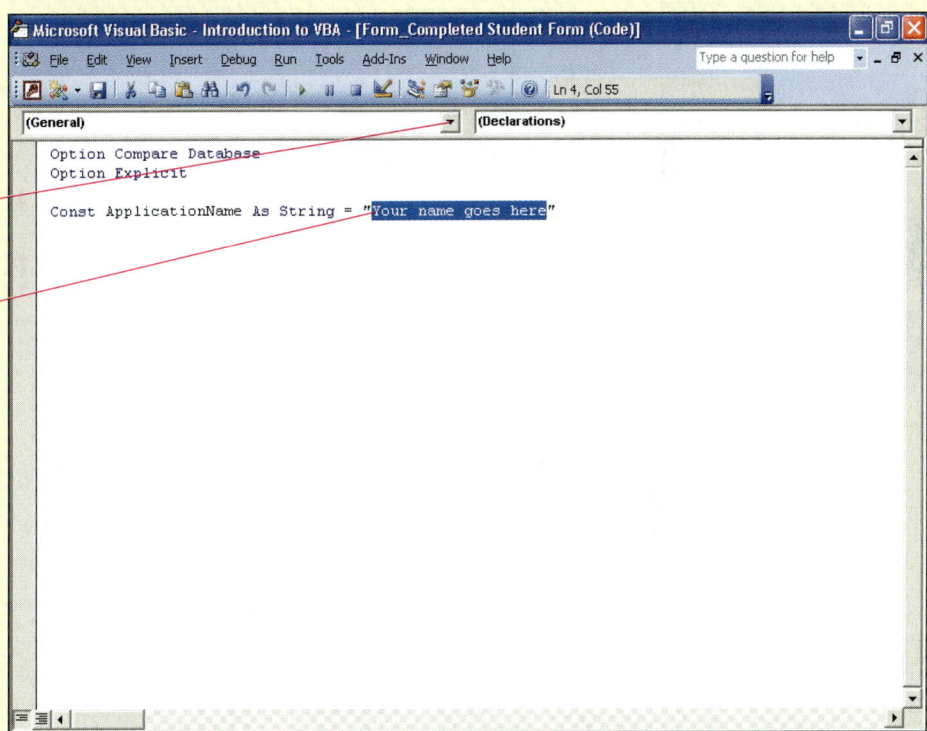

(e) Change the Application Name (step 5)

FIGURE 8.8 Hands-on Exercise 3 (*continued*)

THE MSGBOX STATEMENT—CONSTANTS VERSUS LITERALS

The third parameter in the MsgBox statement can be entered as a literal such as "John Doe's Application." It's preferable, however, to specify the argument as a constant such as ApplicationName, then define that constant in the Declarations section. That way, you can change the name of the application in one place, and have the change automatically reflected in every MsgBox statement that references the constant.

Step 6: Complete the Error Event Procedure

- Click the **down arrow** for the Object box and select the **Form object**. Click the **down arrow** for the Procedure box and click the **Error procedure**.

- Click immediately before the Case Else statement, then enter the additional code shown in Figure 8.8f. Use the Copy and Paste commands to enter the second Case statement. Thus:
  - Click and drag to select the first Case statement, click the **Copy button**, click above the Case Else statement, and click the **Paste button**.
  - Modify the copied statements as necessary, rather than typing the statements from scratch. Use the **Ins key** to toggle between insertion and replacement. Be sure that your code matches ours.

- Click the **Save button** to save the procedure. Click the taskbar button to return to the **Completed Student Form**.

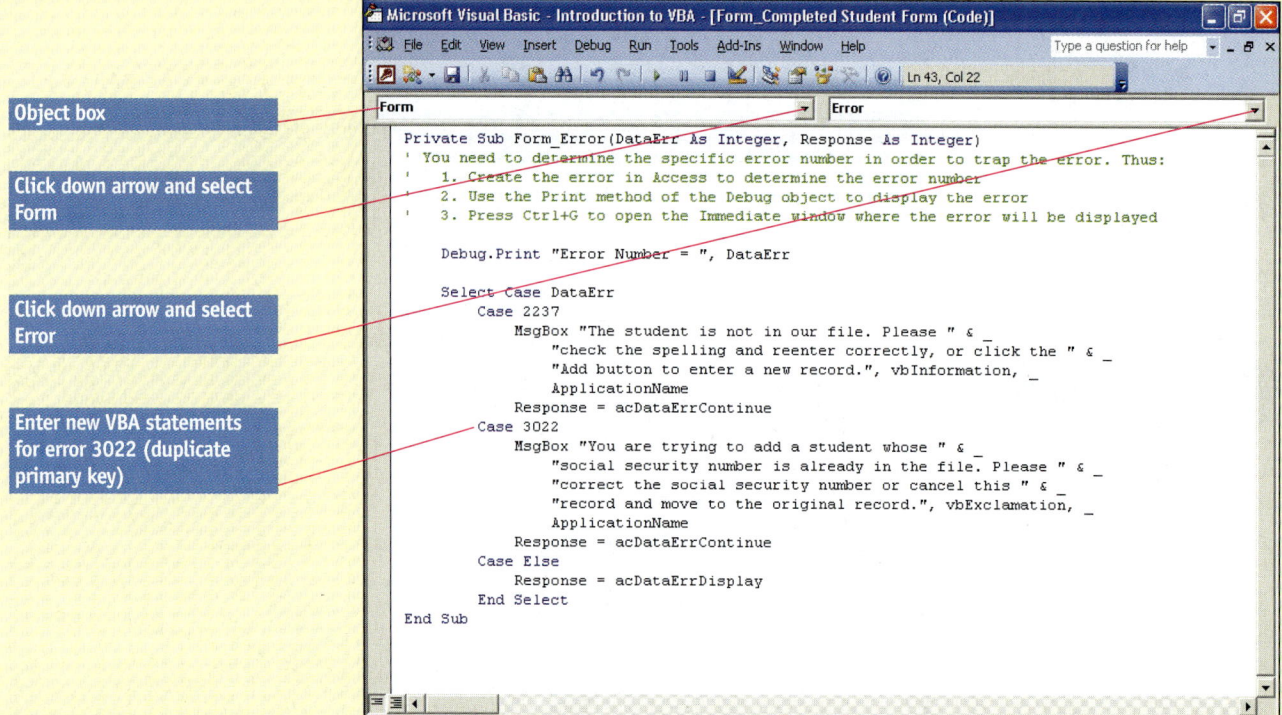

(f) Complete the Error Event Procedure (step 6)

FIGURE 8.8 Hands-on Exercise 3 (*continued*)

THE OBJECT AND PROCEDURE BOXES

The Object box at the top left of the Module window displays the current object, such as a form or a control on the form. The Procedure box displays the name of the current procedure for the selected object. To create or navigate between events for a form, click the down arrow on the Object box to select the Form object, then click the down arrow on the Procedure box to display the list of events. Events that already have procedures appear in bold. Clicking an event that is not bold creates the procedure header and End Sub statements for that event.

Step 7: **Complete the Testing**

- You should be back in Design view of the Completed Student Form. Pull down the **View menu** and change to the **Datasheet view** as shown in Figure 8.8g. (You can also click the **down arrow** next to the View button on the Form Design view and select Datasheet view.)

- Enter **222-22-2222** as a duplicate Social Security number for the first record. Press the **down arrow** (or click the appropriate **navigation button**) to attempt to move to the next record.

- You should see the error message in Figure 8.8g which clearly explains the nature of the error. The title bar displays the value of the ApplicationName constant that was entered earlier in the exercise.

- Click **OK** (or press **Esc**) to close the dialog box. Press **Esc** to restore the original value of the Social Security number. Close the window.

- Exit Access if you do not want to continue with the next exercise at this time.

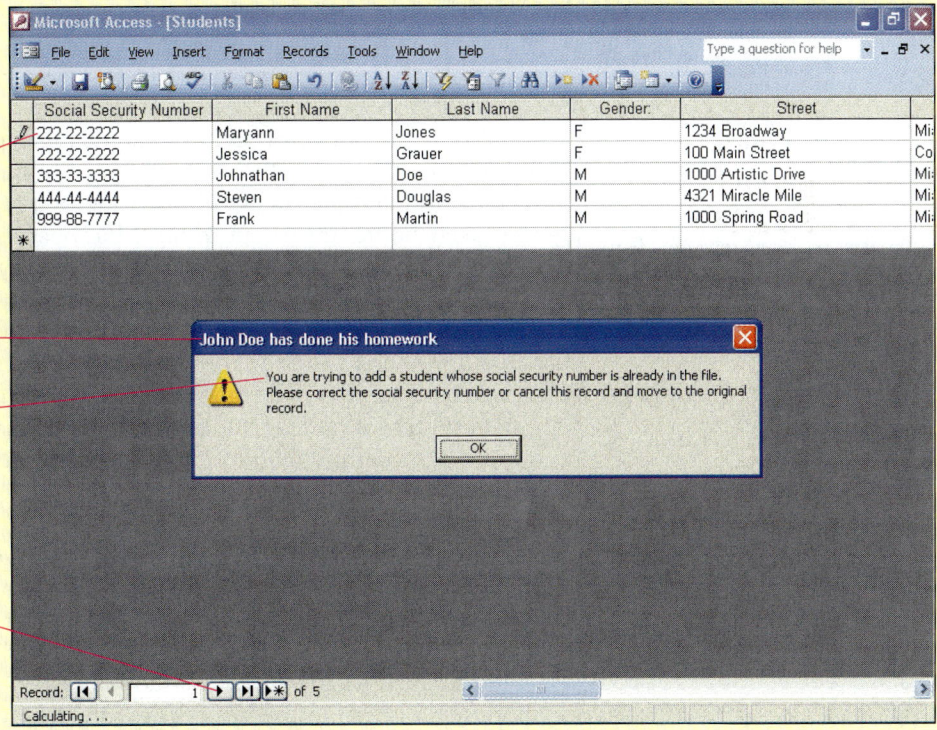

(g) Complete the Testing (step 7)

FIGURE 8.8 Hands-on Exercise 3 (*continued*)

LISTEN TO YOUR USER

One source of continual frustration to the end user are the default error messages which are steeped in technical jargon. What's obvious to you as a developer or student is often beyond the unsophisticated end user. Thus, anything that you can do to simplify a system will increase its chances for success. Listen to your users. Find out where they are having trouble and what they don't understand, then act accordingly.

DATA VALIDATION

Data validation is a crucial component of any system. The most basic type of validation is implemented automatically, without any additional effort on the part of the developer. A user cannot, for example, enter data that does not conform to the designated field type. The user cannot enter text into a numeric field, nor can one enter an invalid date—such as February 30—into a date field. Access also prevents you from entering a duplicate record (i.e., a record with the same primary key as another record).

Other validation checks are implemented by the developer for the specific application, at either the field or record level. The former performs the validation as soon as you move from one field to the next within a table or form. The latter waits until all of the fields have been completed, then checks the entire record prior to updating the record. Both types of validation are essential to prevent invalid data from corrupting the system.

The developer can also use VBA to extend the data validation capabilities within Access. You can, for example, write an event procedure to remind the user that a field is empty and ask whether the record should be saved anyway. The field is not required and hence the Required property is not appropriate. However, you do not want to ignore the omitted field completely, and thus you need to create a VBA procedure.

The VBA code in Figure 8.9 implements this type of check through a **nested If statement** in which one If statement is contained inside another. The second (inner) If statement is executed only if the first statement is true. Thus, we first check to see whether the e-mail address has been omitted, and if it has, we ask the user whether he or she wants to save the record anyway.

The outer If statement in Figure 8.9, *If IsNull (EmailAddress),* checks to see if the e-mail address is blank, and if it is, it executes the second If statement that contains a MsgBox function, as opposed to a simple MsgBox statement. The difference between the two is that the MsgBox function displays a prompt to the user, then returns a value (such as which button a user clicked). A MsgBox statement, however, simply displays a message. MsgBox, when used as a function, requires parentheses around the arguments. MsgBox, as a statement, does not use parentheses.

Look carefully at the second argument, *vbYesNo + vbQuestion* within Figure 8.9. The intrinsic constant vbYesNo displays two command buttons (Yes and No) within the message box. The If in front of the message box function enables VBA to test the user's response and branch accordingly. Thus, if the user clicks the No button, the save operation is cancelled and the focus moves to the EmailAddress control in the form, where the user enters the address. If, however, the user clicks the Yes button, the If statement is false, and the record is saved without the e-mail address.

```
Private Sub Form_BeforeUpdate(Cancel As Integer)
    If IsNull(EmailAddress) Then
        If MsgBox("You did not enter an e-mail address. Save anyway?", _
            vbYesNo + vbQuestion, ApplicationName) = vbNo Then
            Cancel = True
            EmailAddress.SetFocus
        End If
    End If
End Sub
```

- Nested If statement
- MsgBox function
- vbYesNo displays Yes and No command buttons in dialog box

FIGURE 8.9 Procedure for Exercise 4

hands-on exercise
4 Data Validation

Objective To use Field and Table properties to implement different types of data validation. Use Figure 8.10 as a guide in the exercise.

Step 1: **Set the Field Properties**

- Open the **Introduction to VBA database**. Click the **Tables button**, then open the **Students table** in Design view as shown in Figure 8.10a.

- Click the field selector column for the **Gender**. Click the **Validation Rule box**. Type **="M" or "F"** to accept only these values on data entry.

- Click the **Validation Text box**. Type **Please enter either M or F as the gender**.

- Click the **Required property** and change its value to **Yes**.

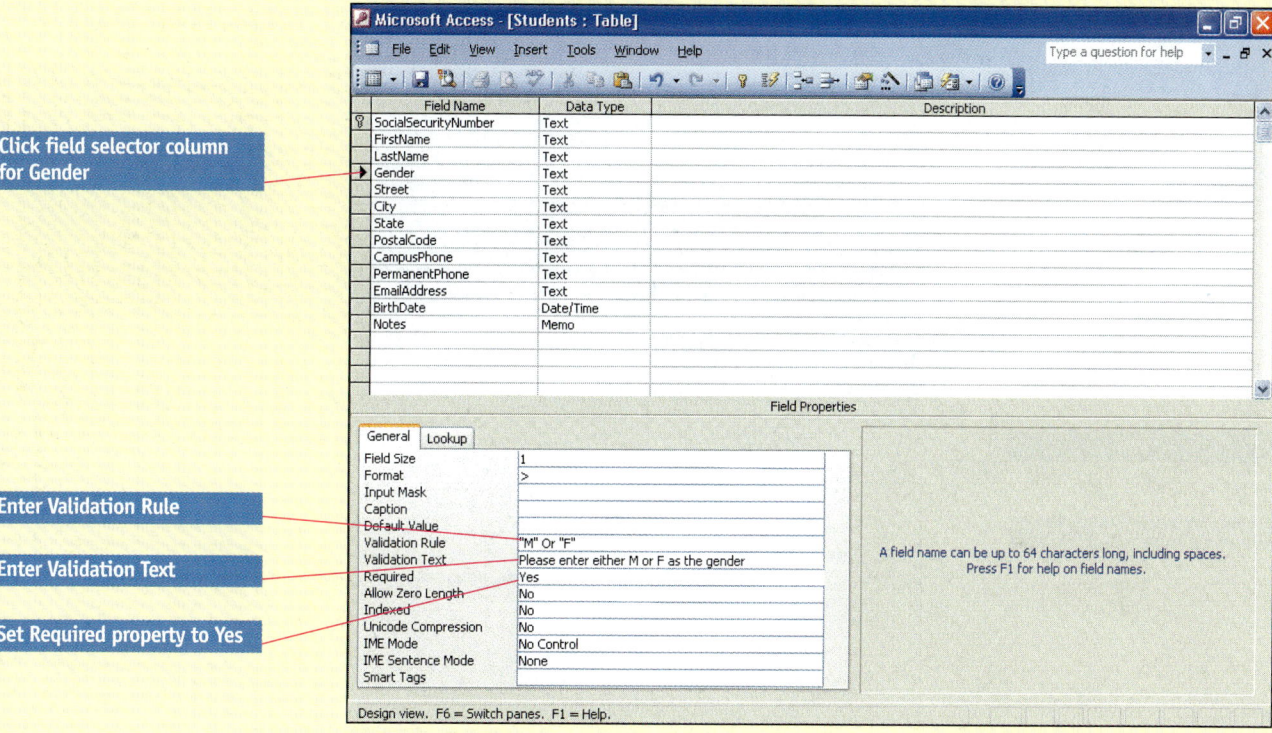

(a) Set the Field Properties (step 1)

FIGURE 8.10   Hands-on Exercise 4

OPTIMIZE DATA TYPES AND FIELD SIZES

The data type property determines the data that can be accepted into a field and the operations that can be performed on that data. Any field that is intended for use in a calculation should be given the numeric data type. You can, however, increase the efficiency of an Access database by specifying the appropriate value for the Field Size property of a numeric field. The Byte, Integer, and Long Integer field sizes hold values up to 256; 32,767; and 2,147,483,648, respectively. Use the appropriate field size for your application.

Step 2: **Set the Table Properties**

- Point to the **selector box** in the upper-left corner, then click the **right mouse button** and display the Table Properties dialog box as shown in Figure 8.10b. You are viewing the properties of the entire table, rather than the properties of a specific field.

- Click in the **Validation Rule box** and enter **[CampusPhone] Is Not Null Or [PermanentPhone] Is Not Null** to ensure that the user enters one phone number or the other. (The field names should not contain any spaces and are enclosed in square brackets.)

- Press **Enter**, then type, **You must enter either a campus or permanent phone number** (which is the validation text that will be displayed in the event of an error).

- Click the **Save button** to save the table. Click **No** when you see the message asking whether existing data should be tested against the new rules.

- Close the Table Properties dialog box. Close the Students table.

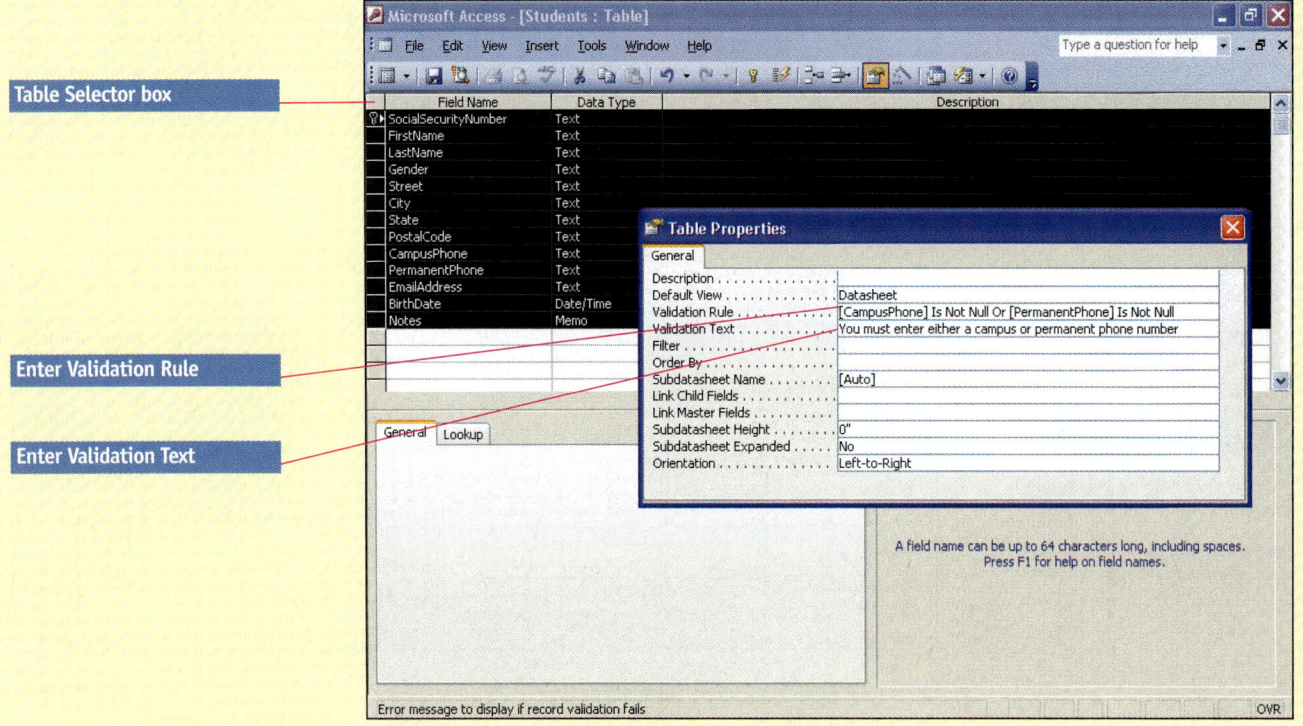

(b) Set the Table Properties (step 2)

FIGURE 8.10 Hands-on Exercise 4 (*continued*)

DAY PHONE OR PERMANENT PHONE

You can set the Required property of a field to force the user to enter data for that field. But what if you wanted the user to enter one of two fields and were indifferent to which field was chosen? Setting the Required property of either or both fields would not accomplish your goal. You can, however, implement this type of validation at the record (rather than the field) level by setting the properties of the table as a whole, rather than the properties of the individual fields. This example forces the user to enter a phone number, but it does not matter which number (campus or permanent) is entered.

Step 3: Test the Validation Rules

- Open the **Completed Student Form** in Form view. If necessary, move to Maryann Jones, the first record in the table.
- Click and drag to select the gender field, then type **X** to replace the gender. Press **Enter**. You will see an error message pertaining to the gender field.
- Press **Esc** (or click **OK**) to close the dialog box. Press **Esc** a second time to restore the original value.
- Click and drag to select the existing CampusPhone number, then press the **Del key** to erase the phone number. Press the **Tab key** to move to the PermanentPhone field. Both phone numbers should be blank.
- Click the ▶ **button** to move to the next record. You should see the error message in Figure 8.10c pertaining to the table properties.
- Press **Esc** (or click **OK**) to close the dialog box. Press **Esc** a second time to restore the original value.

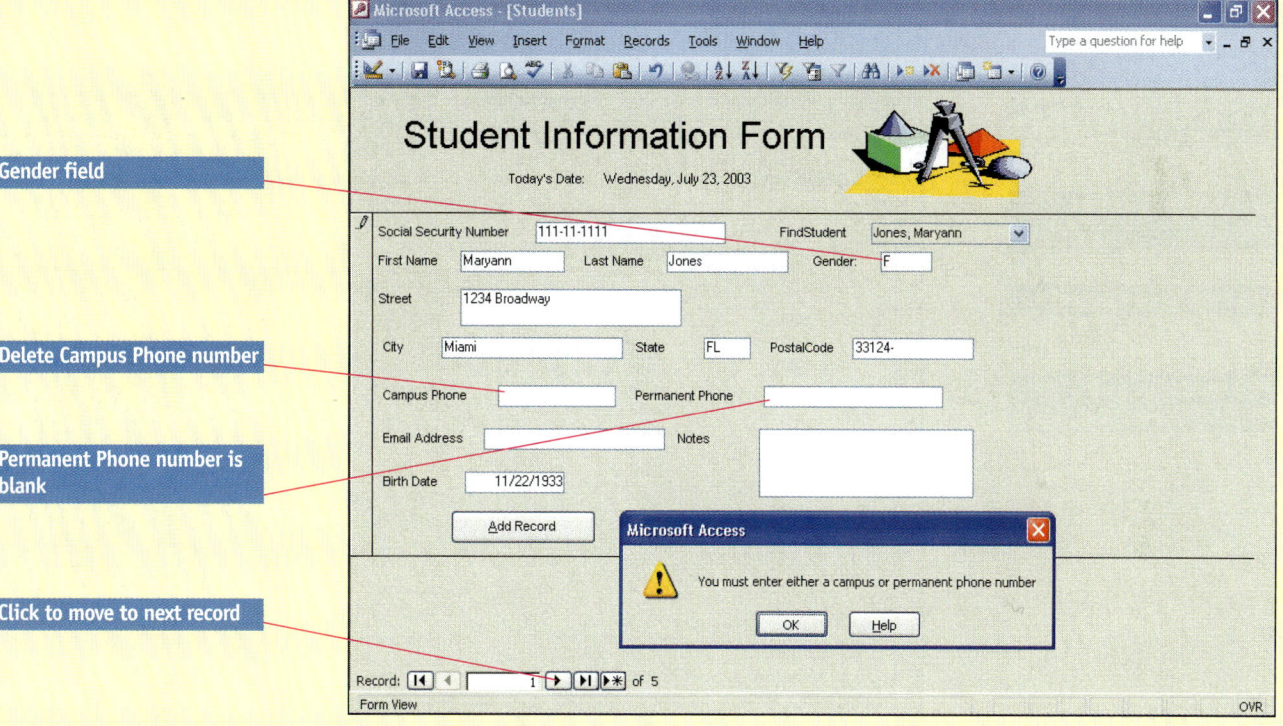

(c) Test the Validation Rules (step 3)

FIGURE 8.10 Hands-on Exercise 4 (*continued*)

VALIDATING AT THE FIELD VERSUS THE RECORD LEVEL

Data validation is performed at the field or record level. If it is done at the field level (e.g., by specifying the Required and Validation Rule properties for a specific field), Access checks the entry immediately as soon as you exit the field. If it is done at the record level, however (e.g., by checking that one of two fields has been entered), Access has to wait until it has processed every field in the record. Thus, it is only on attempting to move to the next record that Access informs you of the error.

Step 4: **Create the BeforeUpdate Event Procedure**

- Change to the **Form Design view**. Pull down the **View menu** and click **Code** (or click the **Code button**) on the Form Design toolbar. If necessary, click the **Procedure view button** to view one procedure at a time.

- Click the **down arrow** on the Object list box and click **Form**. Click the **down arrow** on the Procedure list box to display the list of events for the form. Click **BeforeUpdate** to create a procedure for this event.

- Press the **Tab key** to indent, then enter the statements exactly as shown in Figure 8.10d. Note that as soon as you enter the period after "EmailAddress," Access displays the methods and properties for the EmailAddress control.

- Type **set** (the first three letters in the SetFocus method), watching the screen as you enter each letter. Access moves through the displayed list automatically, until it arrives at the **SetFocus method**. Press **Enter**.

- Add an **End If** statement to complete the If statement testing the MsgBox function. Press **Enter**, then enter a second **End If** statement to complete the If statement testing the IsNull condition.

- Save the procedure.

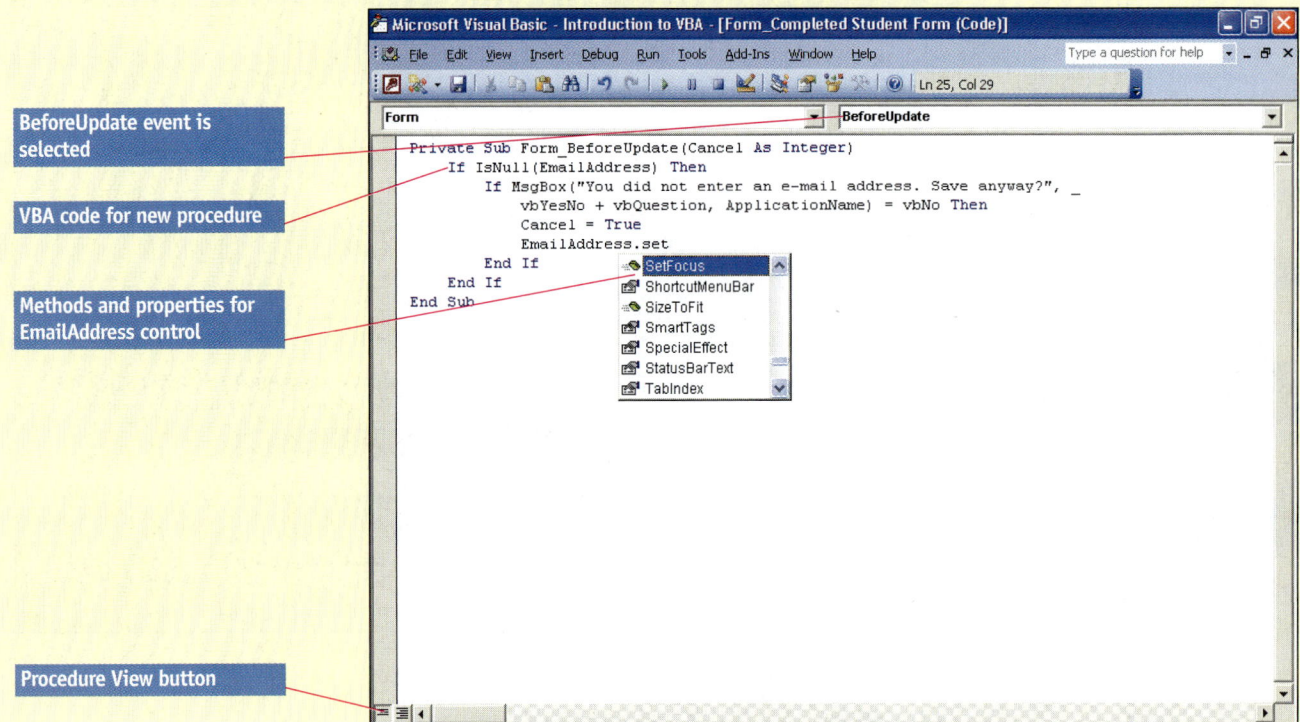

(d) Create the BeforeUpdate Event Procedure (step 4)

FIGURE 8.10 Hands-on Exercise 4 (*continued*)

AUTOLIST MEMBERS—HELP IN WRITING CODE

Access displays the methods and properties for a control as soon as you enter the period after the control name. Type the first several letters to select the method or property. Press the space bar to accept the selected item and remain on the same line, or press the Enter key to accept the item and begin a new line.

Step 5: **Test the BeforeUpdate Event Procedure**

- Click the taskbar button for the Access form. Change to the **Form view**. Click in the **memo field** and enter the text shown in Figure 8.10e.

- Check the remaining fields, but be sure to leave the Email Address blank. Click the navigation button to (attempt to) move to the next record.

- You should see the error message in Figure 8.10e. Note the entry in the title bar that corresponds to the value of the ApplicationName constant you entered earlier.

- Click **No** to cancel the operation, close the dialog box, and automatically position the insertion point within the text box for the Email Address.

- Enter an e-mail address such as **mjones@anyschool.edu**, then click the navigation button to move to the next record. This time Access does not display the error message and saves the record.

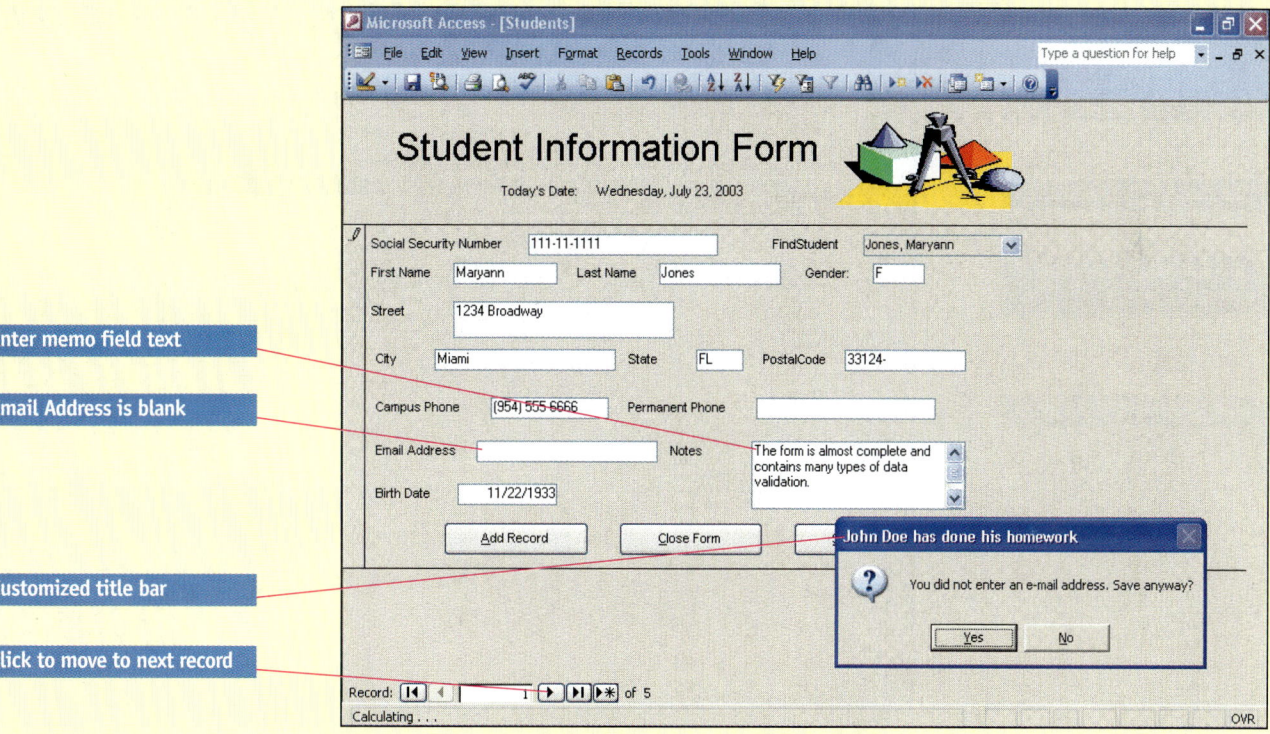

(e) Test the BeforeUpdate Event Procedure (step 5)

FIGURE 8.10 Hands-on Exercise 4 (*continued*)

MEMO FIELDS VERSUS TEXT FIELDS

A text field can store up to 255 characters. A memo field, however, can store up to 64,000 characters and is used to hold descriptive data that runs for several sentences, paragraphs, or even pages. A vertical scroll bar appears in the Form view when the memo field contains more data than is visible at one time. Note, too, that both text and memo fields store only the characters that have been entered; that is, there is no wasted space if the data does not extend to the maximum field size.

Step 6: **Create the CloseForm Event Procedure**

- Change to the **Form Design view**, then click the **Code button** on the Form Design toolbar to display the Module window. If necessary, click the **Object box** to select **Form**, then click the **Procedure box** to select the **Close event**.

- You should see the event procedure in Figure 8.10f. Press **Tab** to indent the statement, then enter **MsgBox** followed by a blank space. The Quick Info feature displays the syntax of this statement.

- Complete the message, ending with the closing quotation mark and comma. The AutoList feature displays the list of appropriate arguments. Type **vbc**, at which point you can select the **vbCritical** parameter by typing a **comma**.

- Type a **space** followed by an **underscore** to continue the statement to the next line. Press **Enter** and type **ApplicationName** as the last parameter.

- Save the module.

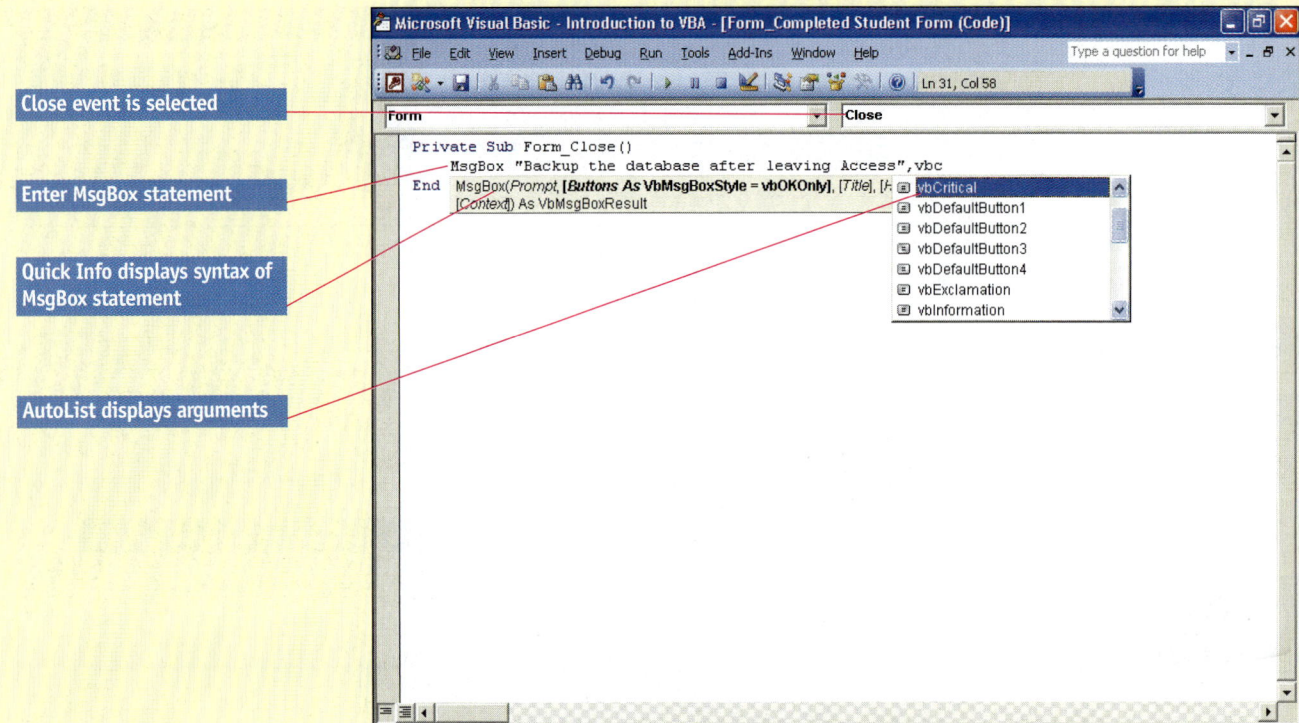

(f) Create the CloseForm Event Procedure (step 6)

FIGURE 8.10 Hands-on Exercise 4 (*continued*)

CHOOSE THE RIGHT EVENT

We associated the message prompting the user to back up the database with the Close event for the form. Would it work equally well if the message were associated with the Click event of the Close Form command button? The answer is no, because the user could bypass the command button and close the form by pulling down the File menu and choosing the Close command, and thus never see the message. Choosing the right object and associated event is one of the subtleties in VBA.

Step 7: **Close the Form**

- Click the **Access form button** on the taskbar. Return to **Form view**. The form looks very similar to the form with which we began, but it has been enhanced in subtle ways:
  - The drop-down list box has been added to locate a specific student.
  - Accelerator keys have been created for the command buttons (e.g., Alt+A to add a record and Alt+C to close the form).
  - The Ctrl+1 and Ctrl+2 keyboard shortcuts have been created. (Click the **ShortCuts button** to display the associated action.)
  - The data validation has been enhanced through custom error messages.
  - The application has been customized through the entry on the title bar.
- Click the **Close Form button** to display the dialog box in Figure 8.10g. Click **OK** to close the dialog box, which in turn closes the form.
- Close the database. Exit Access. Congratulations on a job well done.

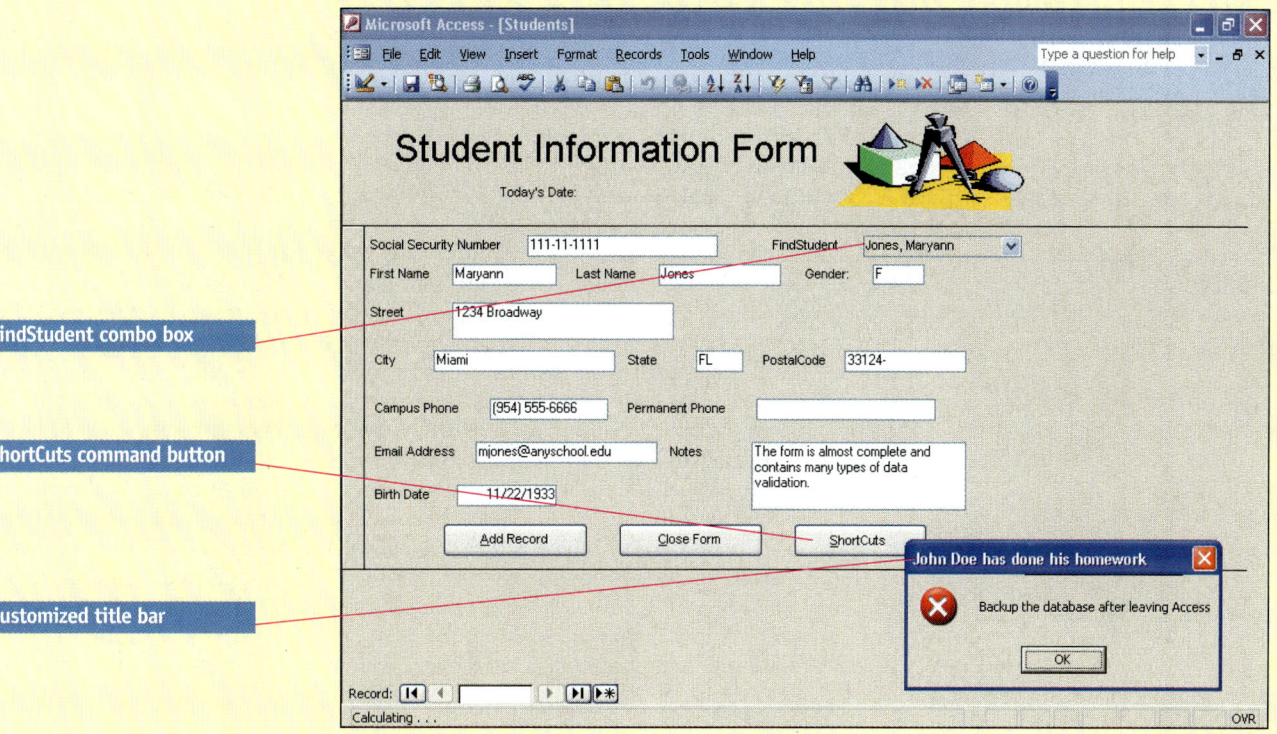

(g) Close the Form (step 7)

FIGURE 8.10 Hands-on Exercise 4 (*continued*)

BACK UP IMPORTANT FILES

It's not a question of *if* it will happen, but *when*—hard disks die, files are lost, or viruses may infect a system. It has happened to us, and it will happen to you, but you can prepare for the inevitable by creating adequate backup before the problem occurs. Decide which files to back up (your data), how often to do the backup (whenever it changes), and where to keep the backup (away from the computer). Do it! One day you will thank us.

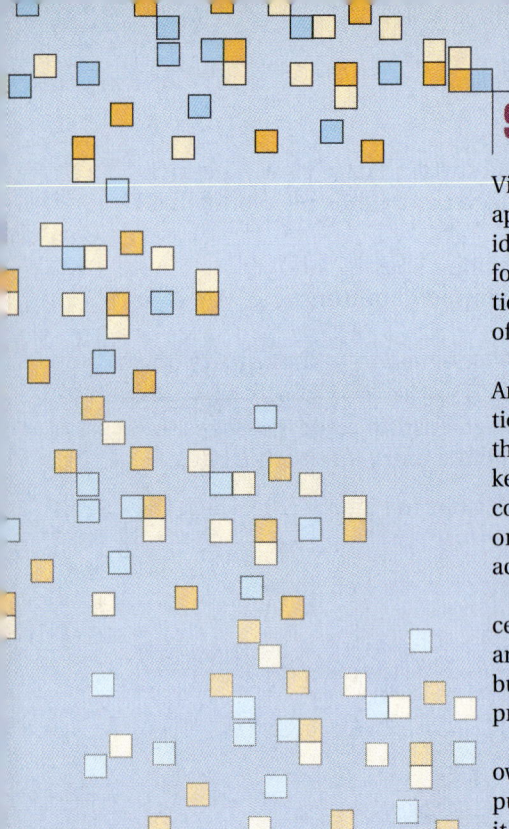

SUMMARY

Visual Basic for Applications (VBA) is a subset of Visual Basic that is accessible from every application in Microsoft Office. The programming statements (such as If and MsgBox) are identical for every application. The objects on which those statements operate (such as forms and reports in Access) differ from one application to the next. A general introduction to VBA is presented in the "Getting Started with VBA" module that appears at the end of this text.

VBA is different from traditional programming languages in that it is event-driven. An event is any action that is recognized by the application. Thus, to enhance an application through VBA, you decide which events are significant and what is to happen when those events occur. Then you develop the appropriate event procedures—for example, a keyboard shortcut for data entry that occurs when the user presses a particular keystroke combination in filling out a form. The execution of the event procedure depends entirely on the user, because he or she triggers the underlying events through an appropriate action.

Visual Basic code is developed in units called procedures. There are two types of procedures—general procedures and event procedures. Event procedures are the essence of an Access application and run automatically in response to an event such as clicking a button or opening a form. General procedures are called explicitly from within another procedure.

All VBA procedures are stored in modules. Every form in an Access database has its own module that contains the event procedures for that form. All procedures are either public or private. A private procedure is accessible only from within the module in which it is contained. A public procedure is accessible from anywhere. All procedures are displayed and edited in the Module window within Access.

Several event procedures were created in this chapter to illustrate how VBA can be used to enhance an Access application. Hands-on exercise 1 focused on the Current event to synchronize the displayed record in a form with a combo box used to locate a record by last name. Exercise 2 developed a KeyDown event procedure to facilitate data entry. Exercise 3 developed the Error event to substitute application-specific error messages for the default messages provided by Access. Exercise 4 created a BeforeUpdate event procedure to enhance the data validation for the form. Additional procedures can be developed by expanding the existing code through inference and observation.

The MsgBox statement has three arguments—the prompt (or message to the user), a VBA intrinsic constant that specifies the icon to be displayed within the box, and the text that is to appear on the title bar of the box. MsgBox may be used as a statement or a function. The difference between the two is that the MsgBox function displays a prompt to the user, then returns a value (such as which button a user clicked). A MsgBox statement, however, simply displays a message. MsgBox, when used as a function, requires parentheses around the arguments. MsgBox, as a statement, does not use parentheses.

KEY TERMS

Argument 1732	Error trapping 1751	MsgBox statement 1732
BeforeUpdate event 1764	Event 1728	Nested If statement 1760
Case statement 1751	Event procedure 1731	Object box 1758
Class module 1731	Full Module view 1743	Parameter 1732
Click event 1741	General Declarations section .. 1751	Private procedure 1731
Close Form Event 1732	General procedure 1731	Procedure 1728
Compile error 1744	If statement 1751	Procedure box 1758
Complete Word tool 1745	Immediate window 1751	Procedure header 1742
Concatenation 1736	Intrinsic constant 1732	Procedure view 1743
Continuation 1755	KeyDown event 1741	Public procedure 1731
Current event 1732	Key Preview property 1746	SetFocus method 1742
Data validation 1760	KeyCode argument 1742	Visual Basic for
Default property 1741	Module window 1731	Applications (VBA) 1728

MULTIPLE CHOICE

1. Which of the following applications can be enhanced through VBA?
   (a) Word and Excel
   (b) Access and PowerPoint
   (c) Outlook
   (d) All of the above

2. Which application enhancements are accomplished using VBA event procedures?
   (a) Improved data validation
   (b) Creation of keyboard shortcuts for data entry
   (c) Substitution of customized error messages for the standard messages provided by Access
   (d) All of the above

3. Which of the following is necessary in order to establish a keyboard shortcut to facilitate data entry on a form?
   (a) Create a procedure for the KeyUp event of the form and set the Key Preview property to No
   (b) Create a procedure for the KeyUp event of the form and set the Key Preview property to Yes
   (c) Create a procedure for the KeyDown event of the form and set the Key Preview property to No
   (d) Create a procedure for the KeyDown event of the form and set the Key Preview property to Yes

4. Which of the following characters continues a VBA statement?
   (a) A hyphen
   (b) An underscore
   (c) A hyphen and an ampersand
   (d) An underscore and an ampersand

5. Which of the following types of data validation requires an event procedure?
   (a) Checking that a required field has been entered
   (b) Checking that one of two fields has been entered
   (c) Prompting the user with a message indicating that an optional field has been omitted, and asking for further instruction
   (d) All of the above

6. Which of the following is *not* used to implement a validation check that requires the user to enter a value of Atlanta or Boston for the City field?
   (a) Set the Required property for the City field to Yes
   (b) Set the Validation Rule property for the City field to either "Atlanta" or "Boston"
   (c) Set the Default property for the City field to either "Atlanta" or "Boston"
   (d) Set the Validation Text property for the City field to display an appropriate error message if the user does not enter either Atlanta or Boston

7. Which of the following would you use to require the user to enter either a home or a business phone?
   (a) Set the Required property of each field to Yes
   (b) Set the Validation Rule property for each field to true
   (c) Set the Validation Rule for the table to [HomePhone] or [BusinessPhone]
   (d) All of the above are equally acceptable

8. Which is a true statement about the Procedure box in the Module window?
   (a) Events that have procedures appear in bold
   (b) Clicking an event that appears in boldface displays the event procedure
   (c) Clicking an event that is not in bold creates a procedure for that event
   (d) All of the above

9. Which event procedure was created in conjunction with the combo box to locate a record on the form?
   (a) An On Current event procedure for the combo box control
   (b) An On Current event procedure for the form
   (c) A KeyDown event procedure for the combo box
   (d) A KeyDown event procedure for the form

10. Which event procedure was created to warn the user that the e-mail address was omitted and asking whether the record is to be saved anyway?
    (a) An On Error event procedure for the e-mail control
    (b) An On Error event procedure for the form
    (c) A BeforeUpdate event procedure for the e-mail control
    (d) A BeforeUpdate event procedure for the form

...continued

multiple choice

11. Which of the following does *not* create an event procedure for a form?
    (a) Display the Properties box for the form in Design View, click the Event tab, select the event, then click the Build button
    (b) Select the form in the Object box of the Module window, then click the event (displayed in regular, as opposed to boldface) in the Procedure box
    (c) Pull down the View menu in the Database window and click the code command or click the Code button on the Database toolbar
    (d) All of the above create an event procedure

12. You want to display a message in conjunction with closing a form. Which of the following is the best way to accomplish this?
    (a) Write a VBA procedure for the Close Form event
    (b) Create a Close command button for the form, then write a VBA procedure for the On Click event of the command button to display the message
    (c) Either (a) or (b)
    (d) Neither (a) nor (b)

13. Which of the following is not an Access-intrinsic constant?
    (a) ApplicationName
    (b) vbCritical
    (c) acCtrlMask
    (d) vbKey1

14. Which of the following would display "Hello" in a message box?
    (a) MsgBox "Hello", vbCritical, "Your Name"
    (b) MsgBox "Your Name", "Hello", vbCritical
    (c) MsgBox vbCritical, "Hello", "Your Name"
    (d) MsgBox "Your Name", vbCritical, "Hello"

15. Which of the following statements was used to display the Error Number associated with an error in data entry?
    (a) Debug.Print "Error Number = "
    (b) Debug.Print "Error Number = ", DataErr
    (c) Print "Error Number = "
    (d) Print "Error Number = ", DataErr

16. Which of the following is true about indented text in a VBA procedure?
    (a) The indented text is always executed first
    (b) The indented text is always executed last
    (c) The indented text is rendered a comment and is never executed
    (d) None of the above

17. Which of the following is likely to be used within an Add Record procedure to position the insertion point?
    (a) The SetFocus method
    (b) The SetFocus property
    (c) The SetFocus event
    (d) The SetFocus procedure

18. What advantage, if any, is gained by using VBA to create a keyboard shortcut to enter the city, state, and zip code in an incoming record, as opposed to using the Default Value property in the table definition?
    (a) It's easier to use VBA than to specify the Default Value property
    (b) The Default Value property cannot be applied to multiple fields for the same record, and thus VBA is the only way to accomplish this task
    (c) VBA can be used to create different shortcuts for different sets of values, whereas the Default Value property is restricted to a single value
    (d) All of the above

ANSWERS

1. d
2. d
3. d
4. b
5. c
6. c
7. c
8. d
9. b
10. d
11. c
12. a
13. a
14. a
15. b
16. d
17. a
18. c

PRACTICE WITH ACCESS AND VBA

1. **MsgBox Examples:** VBA is different from Visual Basic in that its procedures must exist within an Office document. Thus, you have to create a new database to contain the procedures in Figure 8.11. (The database need not contain any tables.) Start Access, create a new database, and then click the Modules button from within the Database window. Click the New button to create a general module (called Module1 by default). This opens the VBA editor as shown in Figure 8.11.

    a. Define a constant to hold your name. The constant will be available to all of the procedures within the module and should be referenced as the third parameter in all three MsgBox statements. This will display your name in the title bar of the associated dialog boxes.

    b. Create the first procedure, consisting of three simple MsgBox statements, with one, two, and three parameters, respectively. Click the procedure header, then click the Run button on the VBA toolbar to test the procedure. Do you see the effect of each procedure on the associated dialog boxes?

    c. Create the second procedure that uses the MsgBox function to test the value of the user's response by comparing it to the vbYes intrinsic constant. Change the second argument to vbYesNo+vbQuestion and note the effect in the resulting dialog box.

    d. Add the third procedure, which closes the database and exits Access. The MsgBox statement should remind the user to back up the database.

    e. Pull down the File menu and click the Print command to print the entire module for your instructor.

    f. Use the Switchboard Manager to create a simple switchboard with three buttons—to run MsgBoxStatement procedure, to run the MsgBoxFunction procedure, and to exit the database.

    g. Use the Startup property to display the switchboard automatically when the database is opened. Test the switchboard completely to be sure that it works properly.

    h. Print the Switchboard form and table of Switchboard Items for your instructor. Add a cover sheet to complete the assignment.

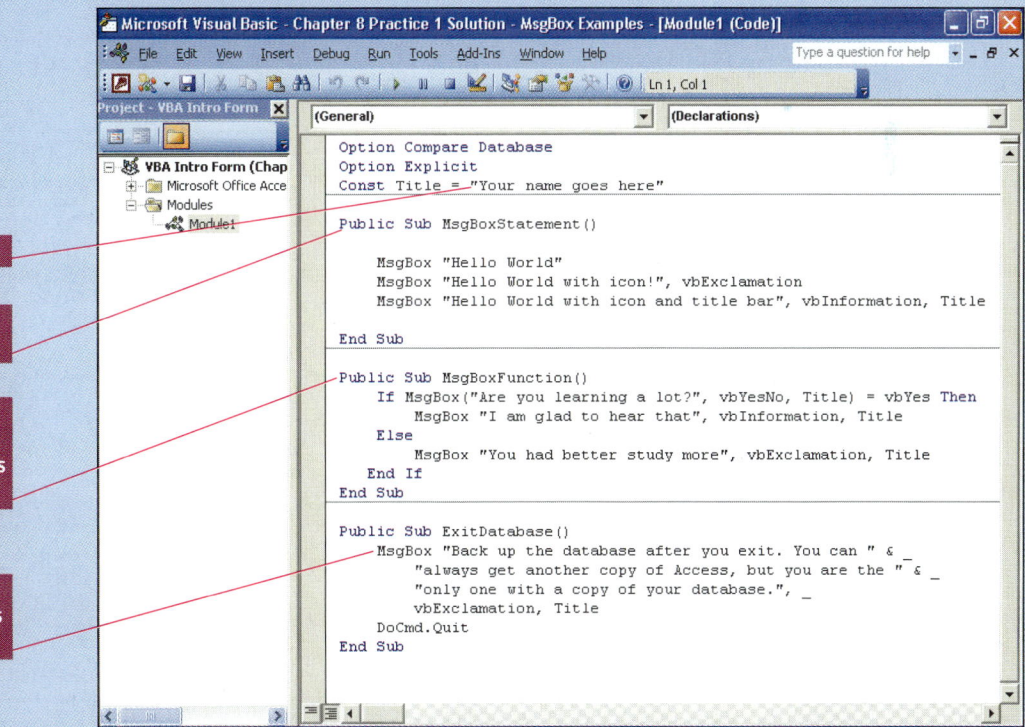

FIGURE 8.11 MsgBox Examples (exercise 1)

practice exercises

2. **Expanded Student Form:** VBA includes a variety of string processing functions that enable you to test the individual characters within a character string. Two of these functions are illustrated in conjunction with the procedure to validate an e-mail address as shown in Figure 8.12. (Use the VBA Help command to learn more about the Len and InStr functions.) Complete the four hands-on exercises in the chapter, then proceed as follows to modify the Student form:

   a. Open the completed Student form in Design view. Right click the Email Address control, click the Properties command to display the property sheet, click the Event tab, then click the Build button for the Before Update property. Click Code Builder and click OK.
   b. Click the Procedure View button. Create the procedure in Figure 8.12, which consists of three simple If statements. The first statement uses the Len function to ensure that there are at least ten characters in the e-mail address. The next two statements use the InStr function to start at the first character in the EmailAddress control and search for the @ and period, respectively. Omission of either character will result in an error message during data entry.
   c. Modify the BeforeUpdate procedure for the form to test for the student's birth date, and then if the birth date is omitted, to warn the user and give the option to save the record anyway.
   d. Add a new keyboard shortcut, Ctrl+3, to the existing KeyDown procedure that will enter New York, NY, and 10010 in the city, state, and postal code controls, respectively.
   e. Modify the VBA procedure associated with the Add Record button, so that the insertion point moves automatically to the SocialSecurityNumber control. (See the tip at the end of step 8 in Hands-on Exercise 1 in the chapter for help.)
   f. Print the completed VBA module for the Student form for your instructor.
   g. Can you think of any other procedures that would further enhance the form? Summarize your thoughts in a short note to your instructor.

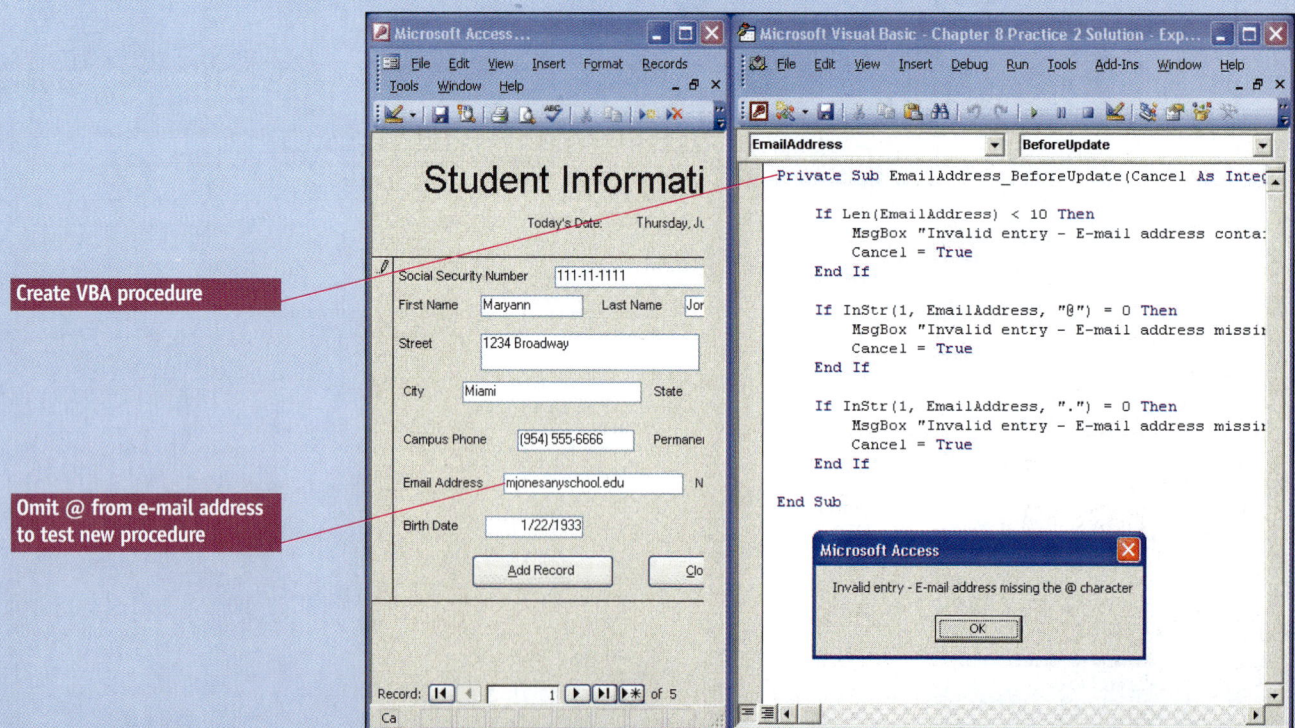

FIGURE 8.12 Expanded Student Form (exercise 2)

practice exercises

3. **Return to Soccer:** Figure 8.13 contains a modified version of the Players form for the *Any Sports League* database. The form does not appear very different from the original form in Chapter 7, but it has been enhanced with several underlying VBA procedures to facilitate data entry. Open your latest version of the *Sports Objects* database from Chapter 7 and proceed as follows:

   a. Add a combo box to the form to locate a player within the Players table. Create the necessary VBA procedure to update the contents of the combo box when the navigation buttons are used to move to a different record.

   b. Add a VBA statement to the On Click event procedure, which is associated with the Add Player button, to position the user in the First Name text box after clicking the Add button. (See the boxed tip at the end of step 8 in Hands-on Exercise 1 in the chapter for help.)

   c. Create a procedure for the BeforeUpdate event for the form that tests if the player's birth date was entered, warns the user if the birth date is omitted, and then gives the user the option to save the record anyway. Display a message in the same procedure that asks the user to try out for an all-city team if a player rating of A (upper- or lowercase) is entered.

   d. Create two shortcuts to simplify data entry. The Ctrl+1 shortcut should enter Miami, FL, and 33124 in the city, state, and zip code fields, respectively. Create a similar shortcut for Ctrl+2 to enter Coral Springs, FL, and 33071. Create a Shortcuts button that will display this information for the user. (Remember to set the Key Preview property to "Yes" so that the shortcuts are operational.)

   e. Print the completed Player's form and associated VBA module for your instructor.

   f. Modify the Coaches form so that it parallels the Players form with respect to the procedures in parts (a), (b), (c), and (d). You may find it convenient to copy procedures, such as those that create and display keyboard shortcuts, from one form to another, as opposed to reentering the code.

   g. Print the completed Coach's form and associated VBA module for your instructor. Do you see how VBA procedures can enhance an application?

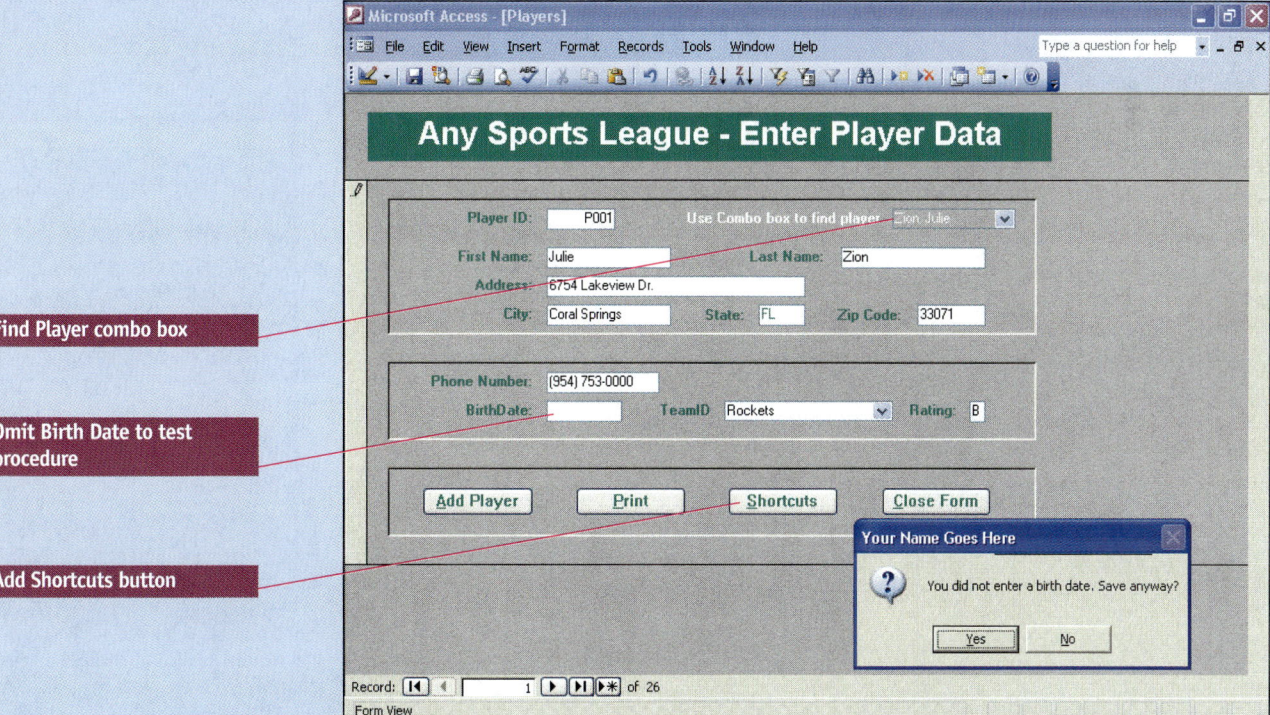

FIGURE 8.13   Return to Soccer (exercise 3)

practice exercises

4. **Enhancing a Report.** The screen in Figure 8.14 is divided in two so that you can view the VBA code and the associated report at the same time. The left portion of the screen displays the VBA editor whereas the right side shows the associated report. Look closely, and you will see that alternating lines in the report are displayed in gray, so that the names on the report are easier to read. This is accomplished by adding the appropriate code to the Print Detail event of the report. Open your latest version of the *Sports Object* database and proceed as follows:

   a. Open the Master Coaching List report in Design view. (See *Chapter 7 Practice Exercise 3*). Right click the Detail section, click the Properties command, click the Event tab, and click the On Print event. Click the Build button, select Code Builder, then click OK to open the VBA editor and create the Detail Print event procedure shown in Figure 8.14. Note the following:

      i. VBA defines a series of intrinsic constants such as vbRed, vbWhite, and vbBlue, but additional colors must be defined by the user. This is accomplished most easily in a Const statement within the procedure as shown in Figure 8.14. Thus, conGray is associated with the indicated numeric value, which corresponds to a shade of gray.

      ii. The If statement in Figure 8.14 tests the background color of the current detail line. If the color is gray, then the color is changed to white. If the color is not gray, the Else clause sets it to gray. The effect of the statement is to print every other line in the report in gray.

      iii. Comments are added within the procedure to explain the code.

   b. Click the save button to save the procedure. Print the completed procedure for your instructor. Close the VBA window.

   c. Return to Access to preview the report, and then print the completed report for your instructor. Experiment with different colors and/or highlighting a different set of records; for example, you could highlight only those coaches who have not been assigned to a team.

   d. Add a cover sheet to complete the assignment.

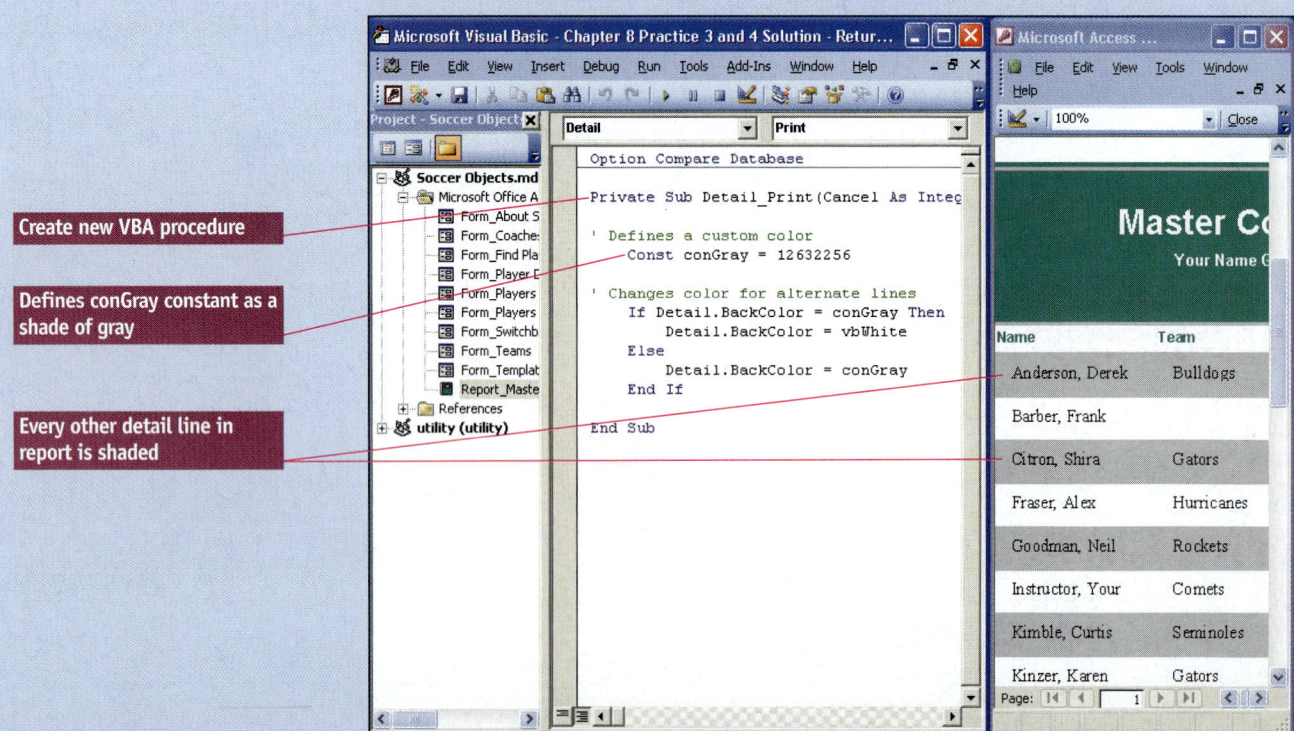

FIGURE 8.14 Enhancing a Report (exercise 4)

practice exercises

5. **Acme Computers:** The *Acme Computers* database in Figure 8.16 provides additional practice with forms and basic VBA procedures. The form itself is unremarkable and similar to virtually all of the forms that have been presented throughout the text. The differences are "under the hood" within the various VBA procedures that you will create in this exercise. Open the *Chapter 8 Practice 5* database in the Exploring Access folder and proceed as follows:

   a. Change the properties of the Customers table so that the user must enter either a home or a business phone. (You have to set the required property at the record level rather than the field level.) Close the Customers table.

   b. Open the Customers form in Design view. Use the Command Button Wizard to create a button to add a new customer. Add a VBA statement to the procedure to position the user in the FirstName field after clicking the button.

   c. Create a BeforeUpdate event procedure that asks the user if the record should be saved if zip code is omitted.

   d. Add a combo box to find a customer record. Be sure to change the On Current event so that the value shown in the Find Customer control matches the customer information currently displayed on the form.

   e. Create a KeyDown procedure so that Ctrl+1 enters a credit rating of A and a credit limit of $10,000, Ctrl+2 enters a credit rating of B and a credit limit of $5,000, and Ctrl+3 enters a credit rating of C and a credit limit of $1,000. Create a command button to display the shortcuts for the user. Remember to set the KeyPreview property to "Yes" for the shortcuts to be operational.

   f. Create a procedure to validate the e-mail address by checking for the presence of the @ sign and a period, and further that the length of the field is at least ten characters (see practice exercise 2).

   g. Use the completed form to add a record for yourself as a customer, then print that form for your instructor. Print the VBA module as well.

   h. Create a simple switchboard with three menu items—a button to display an About form, a button to display the Customers form, and a button to exit the database. Use the Startup property to display the switchboard automatically when the database is opened.

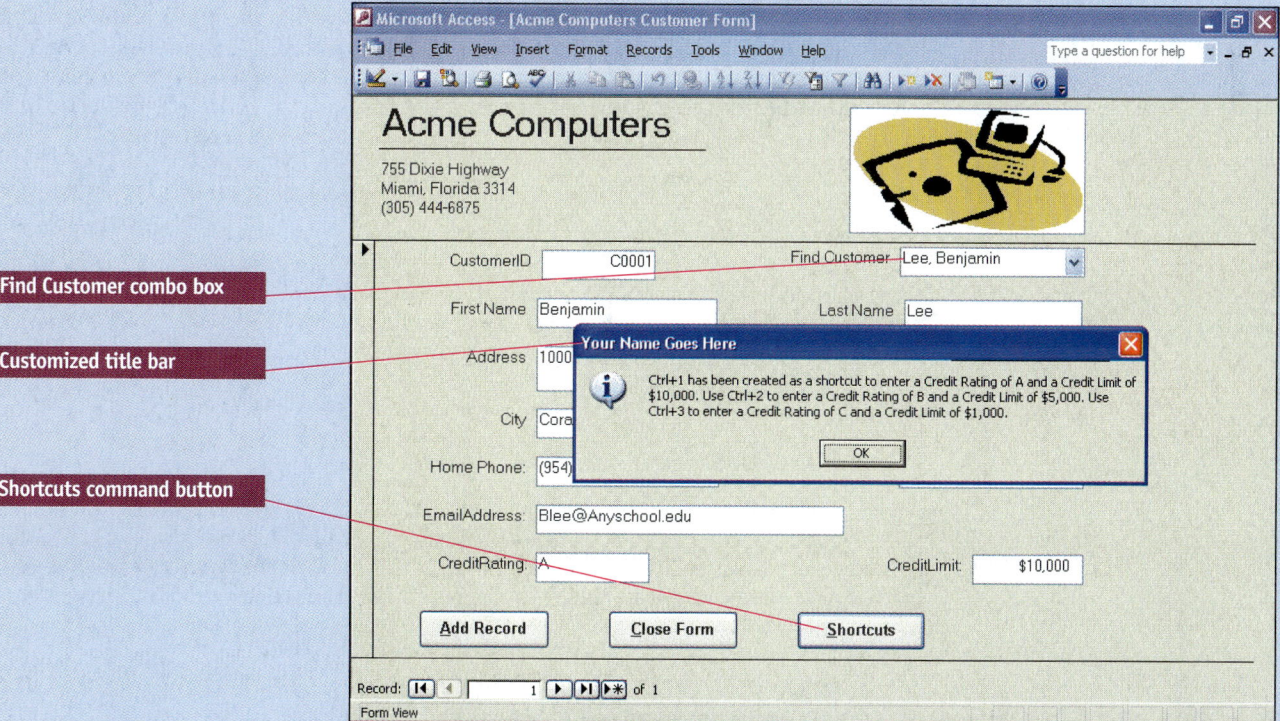

FIGURE 8.15   Acme Computers (exercise 5)

MINI CASES

Expanding Soccer

The Sports Objects (Soccer) database that was used throughout Chapter 7 contained three tables: a Teams table, a Players table, and a Coaches table. This exercise extends the database to include a Sponsors table that has been created for you in another database. Thus, your first task is to import the Sponsors table and associated form into the Sports Objects database that you have been working on. Open the *Sports Objects* database from Chapter 7. Close the switchboard and return to the Database window. Click the Tables button, pull down the File menu, click the Get External Data command, and then import the Sponsors table from the *Chapter 8 Mini Case—Expanding Soccer* database. Import the Sponsors form from the same database.

For the sake of simplicity, we will import the other tables, as opposed to maintaining the external links. Thus, delete the existing links to the Players, Teams, and Coaches tables, and then import these tables into the database. Your next task is to modify the existing tables to accommodate the one-to-many relationship that exists between sponsors and teams. One sponsor can support many teams, but a specific team has only one sponsor. Open the Teams table in Design view, add the SponsorID as a foreign key, and set the Format property to \S00. Go to Datasheet view and assign sponsor number 1 to teams 1, 3, and 5. Assign sponsor number 2 to teams 2, 4, and 6.

Pull down the Tools menu, click the Relationships command, then modify the Relationships window to include the one-to-many relationship between sponsors and teams. Delete the existing Relationships report, then create a new report that includes the Sponsors table. Modify the Team form to contain the name of the team's sponsor and the associated contact person and phone number. The user should be able to select the sponsor from a drop-down list box; the name of the contact person and the phone number will appear automatically. Modify the main switchboard to include an option to display the Sponsors form. Print the new and/or modified objects for your instructor as proof that you completed this exercise.

The VBA Primer

VBA is a powerful programming language that can be accessed from any application within Microsoft Office. Each application uses the same basic statements such as MsgBox or If/Else to create procedures that are executed from within the application. It helps, therefore, to examine basic VBA statements in depth, which is the purpose of the VBA primer at the end of this text. This is an appropriate time for you to study the primer and to complete the first three hands-on exercises. Use Access as the Office application to host the resulting VBA procedures. Print the completed module for your instructor.

Debugging

The Debug toolbar contains several tools to help you debug a procedure if it does not work as intended. The Step Into command is especially useful as it executes the procedure one statement at a time. Choose any of the procedures you created in this chapter, then investigate the procedure in detail using the Debug toolbar. Summarize your results in a short note to your instructor.

Help for VBA

Review the hands-on exercises in the chapter to review the various ways to obtain help in VBA. In addition, you can click on any Visual Basic key word, then press the F1 key to display a context-sensitive help screen. Summarize this information in a short note to your instructor. It will be an invaluable reference as you continue to explore VBA in Access as well as other applications in Microsoft Office.

APPENDIX A

Toolbars for Microsoft® Office Access 2003

TOOLBARS

Alignment and Sizing

Database

Filter/Sort

Form Design

Form View

Formatting (Datasheet)

Formatting (Form/Report)

Formatting (Page)

Formatting (PivotTable/PivotChart)

Macro Design

Page Design

Page View

PivotChart

PivotTable

Print Preview

Query Datasheet

Query Design

Relationship

Report Design

Shortcut Menus

Source Code Control

Table Datasheet

Table Design

Toolbox

Utility 1

Utility 2

Web

OVERVIEW

Microsoft Access has 27 predefined toolbars that provide access to commonly used commands. The toolbars are displayed in Figure A.1 and are listed here for convenience: Alignment and Sizing, Database, Filter/Sort, Form Design, Form View, Formatting (Datasheet), Formatting (Form/Report), Formatting (Page), Formatting (PivotTable/PivotChart), Macro Design, Page Design, Page View, PivotChart, PivotTable, Print Preview, Query Datasheet, Query Design, Relationship, Report Design, Shortcut Menus, Source Code Control, Table Datasheet, Table Design, Toolbox, Utility 1, Utility 2, and Web.

The buttons on the toolbars are intended to be indicative of their function. Clicking the Printer button, for example (the fifth button from the left on the Database toolbar), executes the Print command. If you are unsure of the purpose of any toolbar button, point to it, and a ScreenTip will appear that displays its name.

You can display multiple toolbars at one time, move them to new locations on the screen, customize their appearance, or suppress their display.

- To display or hide a toolbar, pull down the View menu and click the Toolbars command. Select (deselect) the toolbar that you want to display (hide). The selected toolbar will be displayed in the same position as when last displayed. You may also point to any toolbar and click with the right mouse button to bring up a shortcut menu, after which you can select the toolbar to be displayed (hidden). If the toolbar to be displayed is not listed, click the Customize command, click the Toolbars tab, check the box for the toolbar to be displayed, and then click the Close button.

- To change the size of the buttons, suppress the display of the ScreenTips, or display the associated shortcut key (if available), pull down the View menu, click Toolbars, and click Customize to display the Customize dialog box. If necessary, click the Options tab, then select (deselect) the appropriate check box. Alternatively, you can right click on any toolbar, click the Customize command from the context-sensitive menu, then select (deselect) the appropriate check box from within the Options tab in the Customize dialog box.

- Toolbars are either docked (along the edge of the window) or floating (in their own window). A toolbar moved to the edge of the window will dock along that edge. A toolbar moved anywhere else in the

window will float in its own window. Docked toolbars are one tool wide (high), whereas floating toolbars can be resized by clicking and dragging a border or corner as you would with any other window.
- To move a docked toolbar, click anywhere in the background area and drag the toolbar to its new location. You can also click and drag the move handle (the single vertical line) at the left of the toolbar.
- To move a floating toolbar, drag its title bar to its new location.

- To customize one or more toolbars, display the toolbar on the screen. Then pull down the View menu, click Toolbars, and click Customize to display the Customize dialog box. Alternatively, you can click on any toolbar with the right mouse button and select Customize from the shortcut menu.
  - To move a button, drag the button to its new location on that toolbar or any other displayed toolbar.
  - To copy a button, press the Ctrl key as you drag the button to its new location on that toolbar or any other displayed toolbar.
  - To delete a button, drag the button off the toolbar and release the mouse button.
  - To add a button, click the Commands tab in the Customize dialog box, select the category (from the Categories list box) that contains the button you want to add, then drag the button to the desired location on the toolbar.
  - To restore a predefined toolbar to its default appearance, pull down the View menu, click Toolbars, click Customize, click the Toolbars tab, select (highlight) the desired toolbar, and click the Reset command button.

- Buttons can also be moved, copied, or deleted without displaying the Customize dialog box.
  - To move a button, press the Alt key as you drag the button to the new location.
  - To copy a button, press the Alt and Ctrl keys as you drag the button to the new location.
  - To delete a button, press the Alt key as you drag the button off the toolbar.

- To create your own toolbar, pull down the View menu, click Toolbars, click Customize, click the Toolbars tab, then click the New command button. Alternatively, you can click on any toolbar with the right mouse button, select Customize from the shortcut menu, click the Toolbars tab, and then click the New command button.
  - Enter a name for the toolbar in the dialog box that follows. The name can be any length and can contain spaces.
  - The new toolbar will appear on the screen. Initially it will be big enough to hold only one button. Add, move, and delete buttons following the same procedures as outlined above. The toolbar will automatically size itself as new buttons are added and deleted.
  - To delete a custom toolbar, pull down the View menu, click Toolbars, click Customize, and click the Toolbars tab. *Verify that the custom toolbar to be deleted is the only one selected (highlighted)*. Click the Delete command button. Click Yes to confirm the deletion. (Note that a predefined toolbar cannot be deleted.)

Alignment and Sizing

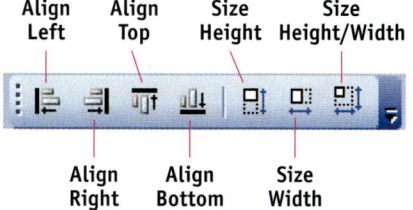

Database

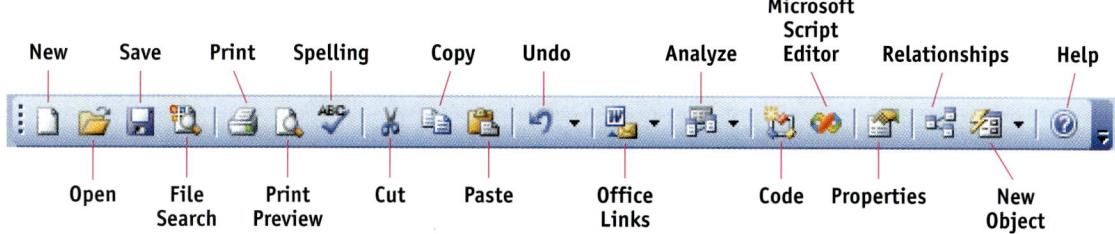

Filter/Sort

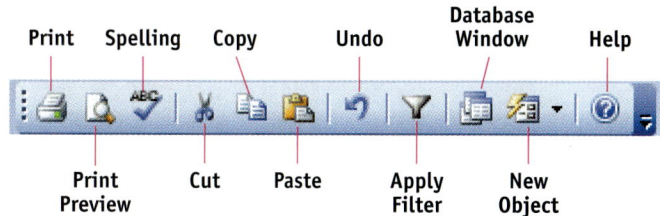

Form Design

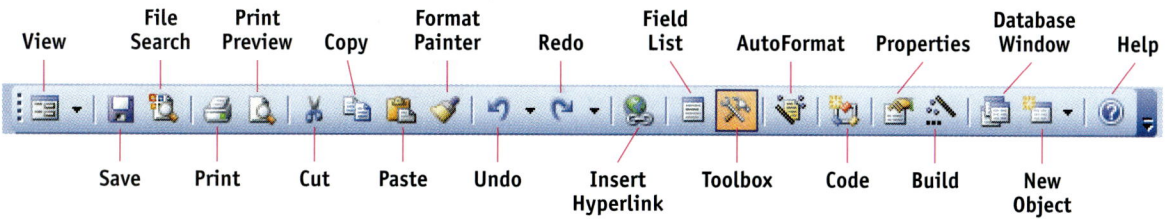

FIGURE A.1 Access Toolbars

Form View

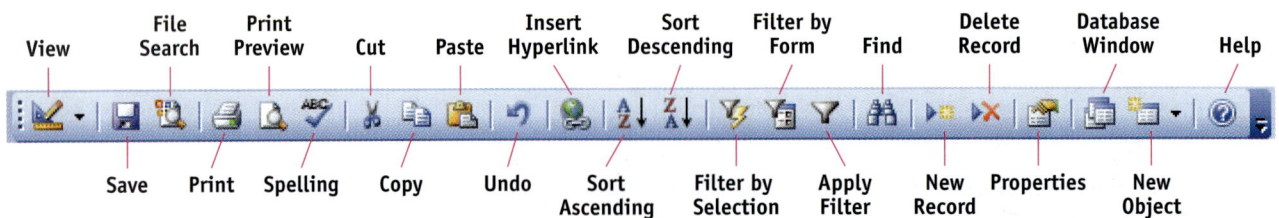

Formatting (Datasheet)

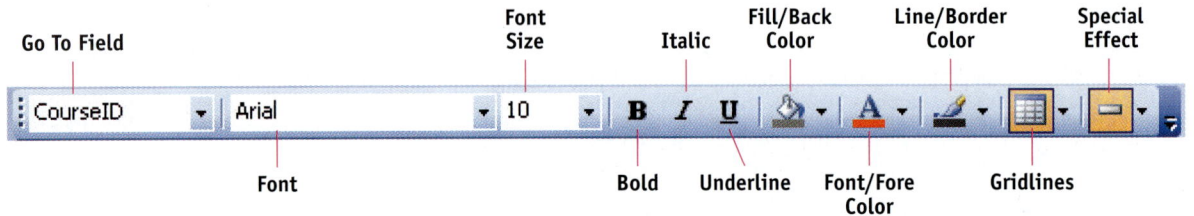

Formatting (Form/Report)

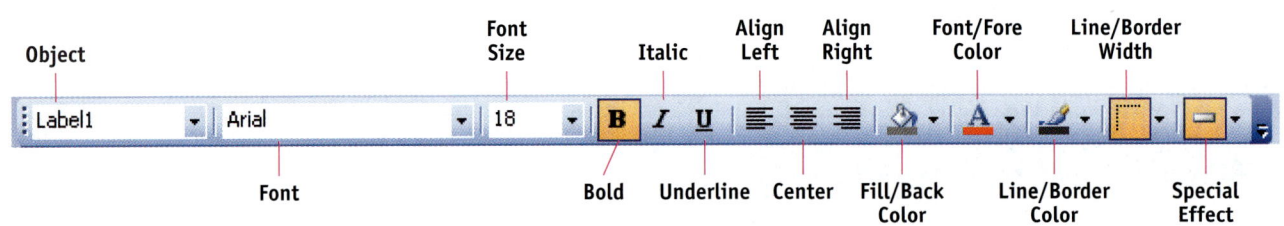

Formatting (Page)

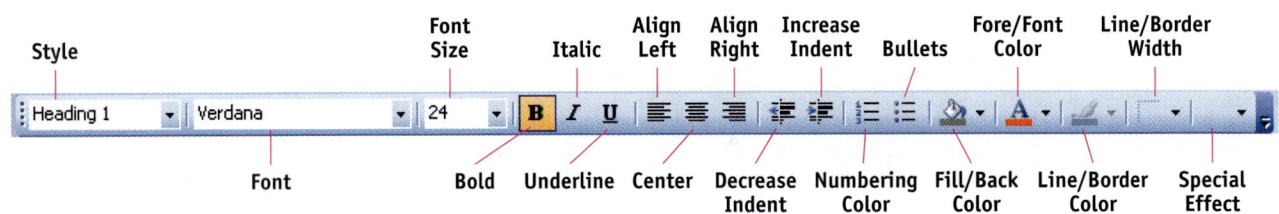

Formatting (PivotTable/PivotChart)

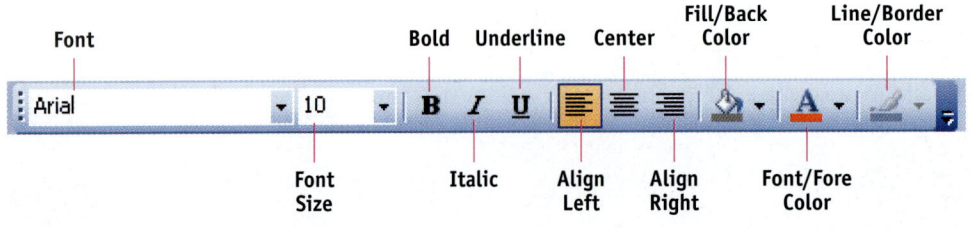

FIGURE A.1   Access Toolbars (*continued*)

Macro Design

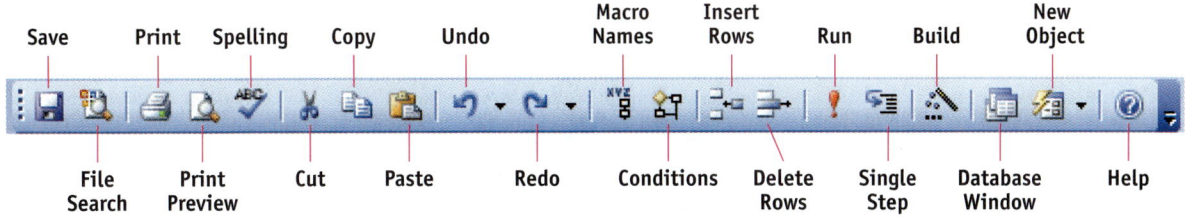

Page Design

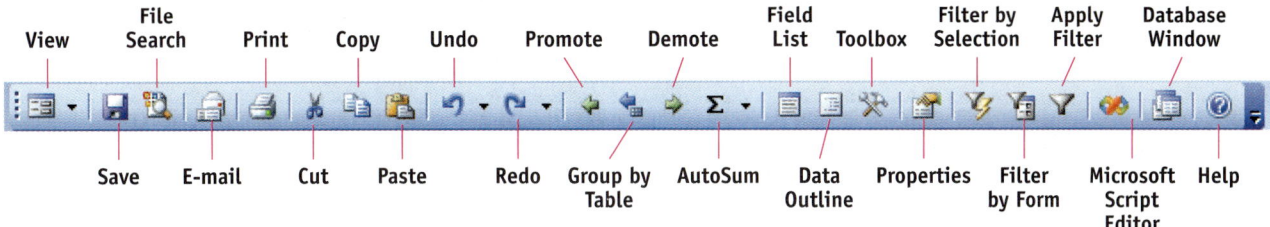

Page View

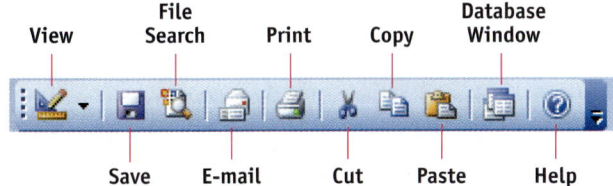

PivotChart

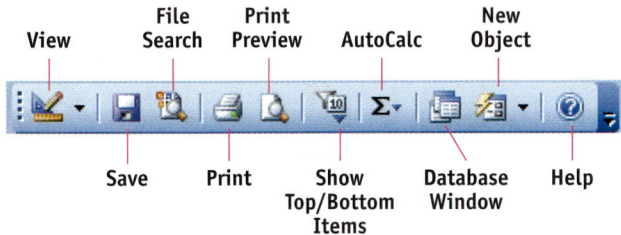

FIGURE A.1 Access Toolbars (*continued*)

PivotTable

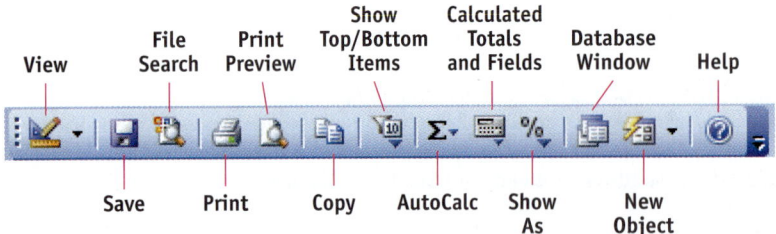

Print Preview

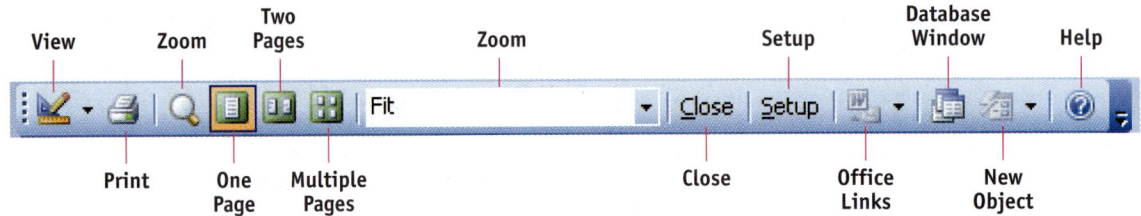

Query Datasheet

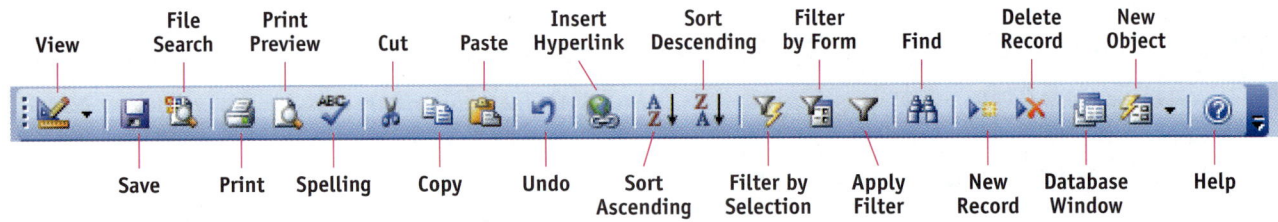

Query Design

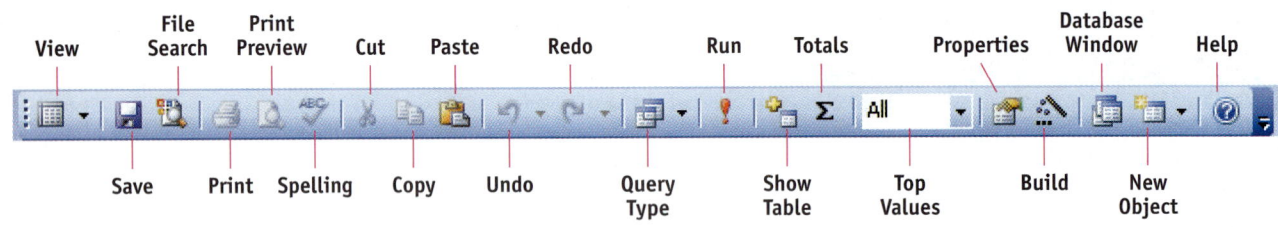

FIGURE A.1   Access Toolbars (*continued*)

Relationship

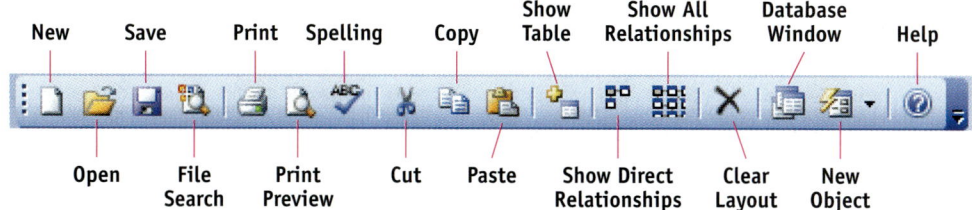

Report Design

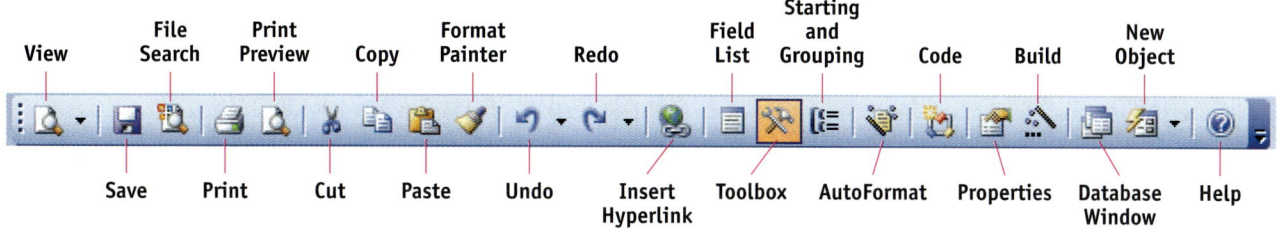

Shortcut Menus

Source Code Control

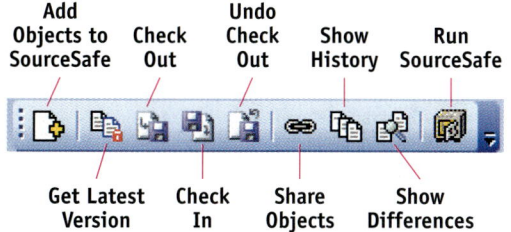

Table Datasheet

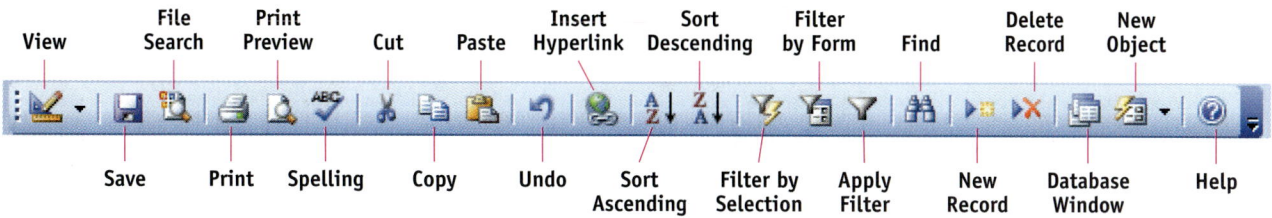

FIGURE A.1 Access Toolbars (*continued*)

Table Design

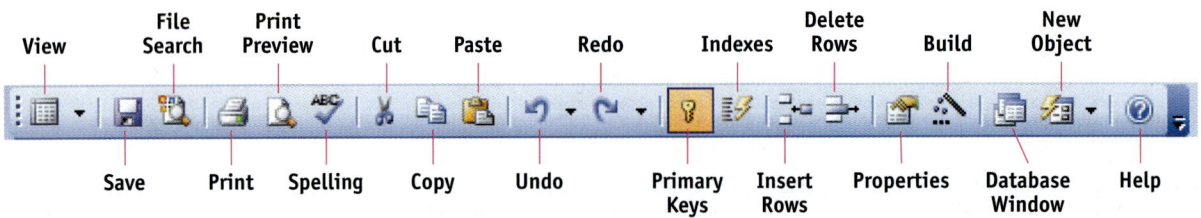

Toolbox

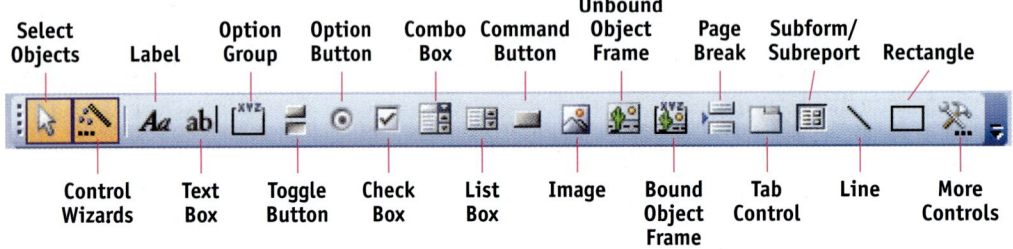

Utility 1

Add or Remove Buttons

Utility 2

Add or Remove Buttons

Web

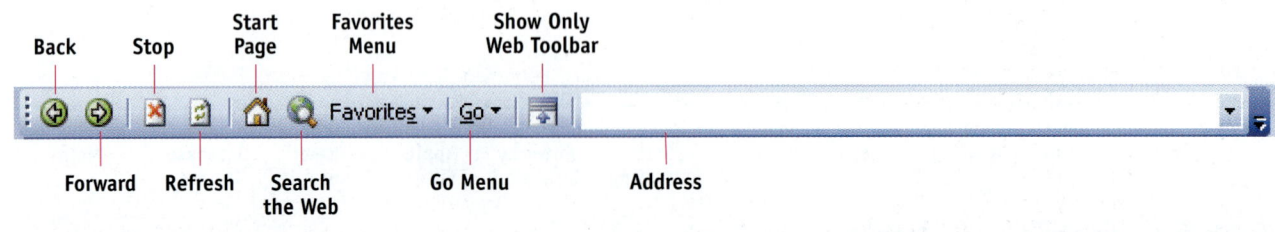

FIGURE A.1 Access Toolbars (*continued*)

APPENDIX B: Designing a Relational Database

OVERVIEW

An Access database consists of multiple tables, each of which stores data about a specific subject. To use Access effectively, you must relate the tables to one another. This in turn requires a knowledge of database design and an understanding of the principles of a relational database under which Access operates.

Our approach to teaching database design is to present two case studies, each of which covers a common application. The first case centers on franchises for fast food restaurants and incorporates the concept of a one-to-many relationship. One person can own many restaurants, but a given restaurant is owned by only one person. The second case is based on a system for student transcripts and incorporates a many-to-many relationship. One student takes many courses, and one course is taken by many students. The intent in both cases is to design a database capable of producing the desired information.

CASE STUDY: FAST FOOD FRANCHISES

The case you are about to read is set within the context of a national corporation offering franchises for fast food restaurants. The concept of a franchise operation is a familiar one and exists within many industries. The parent organization develops a model operation, then franchises that concept to qualified individuals (franchisees) seeking to operate their own businesses. The national company teaches the franchisee to run the business, aids the person in site selection and staffing, coordinates national advertising, and so on. The franchisee pays an initial fee to open the business followed by subsequent royalties and marketing fees to the parent corporation.

The essence of the case is how to relate the data for the various entities (the restaurants, franchisees, and contracts) to one another. One approach is to develop a single-restaurant table, with each restaurant record containing data about the owner and contract arrangement. As we shall see, that design leads to problems of redundancy whenever the same person owns more than one restaurant or when several restaurants have the same contract type. A better approach is to develop separate tables, one for each of the objects (restaurants, franchisees, and contracts).

The entities in the case have a definite relationship to one another, which must be reflected in the database design. The corporation encourages individuals to own multiple restaurants, creating a ***one-to-many relationship*** between franchisees and restaurants. One person can own many restaurants, but a given restaurant is owned by only one person. There is also a one-to-many relationship between contracts and restaurants because the corporation offers a choice of contracts to each restaurant.

The company wants a database that can retrieve all data for a given restaurant, such as the annual sales, type of contract in effect (contract types are described below), and/or detailed information about the restaurant owner. The company also needs reports that reflect the location of each restaurant, all restaurants in a given state, and all restaurants managed by a particular contract type. The various contract arrangements are described below:

Contract 1: 99-year term, requiring a one-time fee of $250,000 payable at the time the franchise is awarded. In addition, the franchisee must pay a royalty of 2 percent of the restaurant's gross sales to the parent corporation, and contribute an additional 2 percent of sales to the parent corporation for advertising.

Contract 2: 5-year term (renewable at franchisee's option), requiring an initial payment of $50,000. In addition, the franchisee must pay a royalty of 4 percent of the restaurant's gross sales to the parent corporation, and contribute an additional 3 percent of sales to the parent corporation for advertising.

1785

Contract 3: 10-year term (renewable at franchisee's option), requiring an initial payment of $75,000. In addition, the franchisee must pay a royalty of 3 percent of the restaurant's gross sales to the parent corporation, and contribute an additional 3 percent of sales to the parent corporation for advertising.

Other contract types may be offered in the future. The company currently has 500 restaurants, of which 200 are company owned. Expansion plans call for opening an additional 200 restaurants each year for the next three years, all of which are to be franchised. There is no limit on the number of restaurants an individual may own.

Single-table Solution

The initial concern in this, or any other, system is how best to structure the data so that the solution satisfies the information requirements of the client. We present two solutions. The first is based on a single-restaurant table and will be shown to have several limitations. The second introduces the concept of a relational database and consists of three tables (for the restaurants, franchisees, and contracts).

The single-table solution is shown in Figure B.1a. Each record within the table contains data about a particular restaurant, its franchisee (owner), and contract type. There are five restaurants in our example, each with a *unique* restaurant number. At first glance, Figure B.1a appears satisfactory; yet there are three specific types of problems associated with this solution. These are:

1. Difficulties in the modification of data for an existing franchisee or contract type, in that the same change may be made in multiple places.

2. Difficulties in the addition of a new franchisee or contract type, in that these entities must first be associated with a particular restaurant.

3. Difficulties in the deletion of a restaurant, in that data for a particular franchisee or contract type may be deleted as well.

The first problem, modification of data about an existing franchisee or contract type, stems from **redundancy**, which in turn requires that any change to duplicated data be made in several places. In other words, any modification to a duplicated entry, such as a change in data for a franchisee with multiple restaurants (e.g., Grauer, who owns restaurants in Miami and Fort Lauderdale), requires a search through the entire table to find all instances of that data so that the identical modification can be made to each of the records. A similar procedure would have to be followed should data change about a duplicated contract (e.g., a change in the royalty percentage for contract Type 1, which applies to restaurants R1, R2, and R4). This is, to say the least, a time-consuming and error-prone procedure.

The addition of a new franchisee or contract type poses a different type of problem. It is quite logical, for example, that potential franchisees must apply to the corporation and qualify for ownership before having a restaurant assigned to them. It is also likely that the corporation would develop a new contract type prior to offering that contract to an existing restaurant. Neither of these events is easily accommodated in the table structure of Figure B.1a, which would require the creation of a dummy restaurant record to accommodate the new franchisee or contract type.

The deletion of a restaurant creates yet another type of difficulty. What happens, for example, if the company decides to close restaurant R5 because of insufficient sales? The record for this restaurant would disappear as expected, but so too would the data for the franchisee (Coulter) and the contract type (C3), which is not intended. The corporation might want to award Coulter another restaurant in the future and/or offer this contract type to other restaurants. Neither situation would be possible as the relevant data would be lost with the deletion of the restaurant record.

Restaurant Number	Restaurant Data (Address, annual sales . . .)	Franchisee Data (Name, telephone, address . . .)	Contract Data (Type, term, initial fee . . .)
R1	Restaurant data for Miami . . .	Franchisee data (Grauer . . .)	Contract data (Type 1 . . .)
R2	Restaurant data for Coral Gables . . .	Franchisee data (Moldof . . .)	Contract data (Type 1 . . .)
R3	Restaurant data for Fort Lauderdale. . .	Franchisee data (Grauer . . .)	Contract data (Type 2 . . .)
R4	Restaurant data for New York . . .	Franchisee data (Glassman . . .)	Contract data (Type 1 . . .)
R5	Restaurant data for Coral Springs . . .	Franchisee data (Coulter . . .)	Contract data (Type 3 . . .)

(a) Single-table Solution

This "intuitive" solution is based on a single table, but it is shown to have several deficiencies

Restaurant Number	Restaurant Data	Franchisee Number	Contract Type
R1	Restaurant data for Miami . . .	F1	C1
R2	Restaurant data for Coral Gables . . .	F2	C1
R3	Restaurant data for Fort Lauderdale. . .	F1	C2
R4	Restaurant data for New York . . .	F3	C1
R5	Restaurant data for Coral Springs . . .	F4	C3

The correct design requires three tables that are related to one another

Contract Type	Contract Data
C1	Contract data. . .
C2	Contract data. . .
C3	Contract data. . .

Franchisee Number	Franchisee Data (Name, telephone, address, . . .)
F1	Grauer. . .
F2	Moldof. . .
F3	Glassman. . .
F4	Coulter. . .

(b) Multiple-table Solution

FIGURE B.1 Single- versus Multiple-table Solution

Multiple-table Solution

A much better solution appears in Figure B.1b, which uses a different table for each of the entities (restaurants, franchisees, and contracts) that exist in the system. Every record in the restaurant table is assigned a unique restaurant number (e.g., R1 or R2), just as every record in the franchisee table is given a unique franchisee number (e.g., F1 or F2), and every contract record a unique contract number (e.g., C1 or C2).

The tables are linked to one another through the franchisee and/or contract numbers, which also appear in the restaurant table. Every record in the restaurant table is associated with its appropriate record in the franchisee table through the franchisee number common to both tables. In similar fashion, every restaurant is tied to its appropriate contract through the contract number, which appears in the restaurant record. This solution may seem complicated, but it is really quite simple and elegant.

Assume, for example, that we want the name of the franchisee for restaurant R5, and further, that we need the details of the contract type for this restaurant. We retrieve the appropriate restaurant record, which contains franchisee and contract numbers of F4 and C3, respectively. We then search through the franchisee table for franchisee F4 (obtaining all necessary information about Coulter) and search again through the contract table for contract C3 (obtaining the data for this contract type). The process is depicted graphically in Figure B.1b.

The multiple-table solution may require slightly more effort to retrieve information, but this is more than offset by the advantages of table maintenance. Consider, for example, a change in data for contract C1, which currently governs restaurants R1, R2, and R4. All that is necessary is to go into the contract table, find record C1, and make the changes. The records in the restaurant table are *not* affected because the restaurant records do not contain contract data per se, only the number of the corresponding contract record. In other words, the change in data for contract C1 is made in one place (the contract table), yet that change would be reflected for all affected restaurants. This is in contrast to the single-table solution of Figure B.1a, which would require the identical modification in three places.

The addition of new records for franchisees or contracts is done immediately in the appropriate tables of Figure B.1b. The corporation simply adds a franchisee or contract record as these events occur, without the necessity of a corresponding restaurant record. This is much easier than the approach of Figure B.1a, which required an existing restaurant in order to add one of the other entities.

The deletion of a restaurant is also easier than with the single-table organization. You could, for example, delete restaurant R5 without losing the associated franchisee and contract data as these records exist in different tables.

Queries to the Database

By now you should be convinced of the need for multiple tables within a database and that this type of design facilitates all types of table maintenance. However, the ultimate objective of any system is to produce information, and it is in this area that the design excels. Consider now Figure B.2, which expands upon the multiple-table solution to include additional data for the respective tables.

As indicated, there are three tables—for restaurants, franchisees, and contracts, respectively. The tables are linked to one another through the franchisee and/or contract numbers that also appear in the restaurant table. These fields are color-coded so that you can see the relationships more clearly.

To be absolutely sure you understand the multiple-table solution of Figure B.2, use it to answer the questions at the bottom of the next page. Check your answers with those provided.

(a) Restaurant Table

Restaurant Number	Street Address	City	State	Zip Code	Annual Sales	Franchisee Number	Contract Type
R1	1001 Ponce de Leon Blvd	Miami	FL	33361	$600,000	F1	C1
R2	31 West Rivo Alto Road	Coral Gables	FL	33139	$450,000	F2	C1
R3	333 Las Olas Blvd	Fort Lauderdale	FL	33033	$250,000	F1	C2
R4	1700 Broadway	New York	NY	10010	$1,750,000	F3	C1
R5	1300 Sample Road	Coral Springs	FL	33071	$50,000	F4	C3

(b) Franchisee Table

Franchisee Number	Franchisee Name	Telephone	Street Address	City	State	Zip Code
F1	Grauer	(305) 755-1000	2133 NW 102 Terrace	Coral Springs	FL	33071
F2	Moldof	(305) 753-4614	1400 Lejeune Blvd	Miami	FL	33365
F3	Glassman	(212) 458-5054	555 Fifth Avenue	New York	NY	10024
F4	Coulter	(305) 755-0910	1000 Federal Highway	Fort Lauderdale	FL	33033

(c) Contract Table

Contract Type	Term (years)	Initial Fee	Royalty Pct	Advertising Pct
C1	99	$250,000	2%	2%
C2	5	$50,000	4%	3%
C3	10	$75,000	3%	3%

FIGURE B.2   Fast Food Franchises (database queries)

Questions

1. Who owns restaurant R2? What contract type is in effect for this restaurant?
2. What is the address of restaurant R4?
3. Which restaurant(s) are owned by Mr. Grauer?
4. List all restaurants with a contract type of C1.
5. Which restaurants in Florida have gross sales over $300,000?
6. List all contract types.
7. Which contract type has the lowest initial fee? How much is the initial fee? Which restaurant(s) is (are) governed by this contract?
8. How many franchisees are there? What are their names?
9. What are the royalty and advertising percentages for restaurant R3?

Answers

1. Restaurant R2 is owned by Moldof and governed by contract C1.
2. Restaurant R4 is located at 1700 Broadway, New York, NY 10010.
3. Mr. Grauer owns restaurants R1 and R3.
4. R1, R2, and R4 are governed by contract C1.
5. The restaurants in Florida with gross sales over $300,000 are R1 ($600,000) and R2 ($450,000).
6. The existing contract types are C1, C2, and C3.
7. Contract C2 has the lowest initial fee ($50,000); restaurant R3 is governed by this contract type.
8. There are four franchisees: Grauer, Moldof, Glassman, and Coulter.
9. Restaurant R3 is governed by contract C2 with royalty and advertising percentages of 4% and 3%, respectively.

THE RELATIONAL MODEL

The restaurant case study illustrates a **relational database**, which requires a separate table for every entity in the physical system (restaurants, franchisees, and contracts). Each occurrence of an **entity** (a specific restaurant, franchisee, or contract type) appears as a row within a table. The properties of an entity (a restaurant's address, owner, or sales) appear as columns within a table.

Every row in every table of a relational database must be distinct. This is accomplished by including a column (or combination of columns) to uniquely identify the row. The unique identifier is known as the **primary key**. The restaurant number, for example, is different for every restaurant in the restaurant table. The franchisee number is unique in the franchisee table. The contract type is unique in the contract table.

The same column can, however, appear in multiple tables. The franchisee number, for example, appears in both the franchisee table, where its values are unique, and in the restaurant table, where they are not. The franchisee number is the primary key in the franchisee table, but it is a **foreign key** in the restaurant table. (A foreign key is simply the primary key of a related table.)

The inclusion of a foreign key in the restaurant table enables us to implement the one-to-many relationship between franchisees and restaurants. We enter the franchisee number (the primary key in the franchisee table) as a column in the restaurant table, where it (the franchisee number) is a foreign key. In similar fashion, contract type (the primary key in the contract table) appears as a foreign key in the restaurant table to implement the one-to-many relationship between contracts and restaurants.

It is helpful perhaps to restate these observations about a relational database in general terms:

1. Every entity in a physical system requires its own table in a database.
2. Each row in a table is different from every other row because of a unique column (or combination of columns) known as a primary key.
3. The primary key of one table can appear as a foreign key in another table.
4. The order of rows in a table is immaterial.
5. The order of columns in a table is immaterial, although the primary key is generally listed first.
6. The number of columns is the same in every row of the table.

> **THE KEY, THE WHOLE KEY, AND NOTHING BUT THE KEY**
>
> The theory of a relational database was developed by Dr. Edgar Codd, giving rise to the phrase, "*The key, the whole key, and nothing but the key . . . so help me Codd.*" The sentence effectively summarizes the concepts behind a relational database and helps to ensure the validity of a design. Simply stated, the value of every column other than the primary key depends on the key in that row, on the entire key, and on nothing but that key.

Referential Integrity

The concept of **referential integrity** requires that the tables in a database be consistent with one another. Consider once again the first row in the restaurant table of Figure B.2a, which indicates that the restaurant is owned by franchisee F1 and governed by contract type C1. Recall also how these values are used to obtain additional information about the franchisee or contract type from the appropriate tables in Figures B.2b and B.2c, respectively.

What if, however, the restaurant table referred to franchisee number F1000 or contract C9, neither of which exists in the database of Figure B.2? There would be a problem because the tables would be inconsistent with one another; that is, the restaurant table would refer to rows in the franchisee and contract tables that do not exist. It is important, therefore, that referential integrity be strictly enforced and that such inconsistencies be prevented from occurring. Suffice it to say that data validation is critical when establishing or maintaining a database, and that no system, relational or otherwise, can compensate for inaccurate or incomplete data.

CASE STUDY: STUDENT TRANSCRIPTS

Our second case is set within the context of student transcripts and expands the concept of a relational database to implement a **many-to-many relationship**. The system is intended to track students and the courses they take. The many-to-many relationship occurs because one student takes many courses, while at the same time, one course is taken by many students. The objective of this case is to relate the student and course tables to one another to produce the desired information.

The system should be able to display information about a particular student as well as information about a particular course. It should also display information about a student–course combination, such as *when* a student took the course and *what grade* he or she received.

Solution

The (intuitive and incorrect) solution of Figure B.3 consists of two tables, one for courses and one for students, corresponding to the two entities in the physical system. The student table contains the student's name, address, major, date of entry into the school, cumulative credits, and cumulative quality points. The course table contains the unique six-character course identifier, the course title, and the number of credits.

There are no problems of redundancy. The data for a particular course (its description and number of credits) appears only once in the course table, just as the data for a particular student appears only once in the student table. New courses will be added directly to the course table, just as new students will be added to the student table.

The design of the student table makes it easy to list all courses for one student. It is more difficult, however, to list all students in one course. Even if this were not

Course Number	Course Description	Credits
ACC101	Introduction to Accounting	3
CHM100	Survey of Chemistry	3
CHM101	Chemistry Lab	1
CIS120	Microcomputer Applications	3
ENG100	Freshman English	3
MTH100	Calculus with Analytic Geometry	4
MUS110	Music Appreciation	2
SPN100	Spanish I	3

(a) Course Table

Student Number	Student Data	Courses Taken with Grade and Semester													
S1	Student data (Adams. . .)	ACC101	SP03	A	CIS120	FA02	A	MU100	FA02	B					
S2	Student data (Fox. . .)	ENG100	SP03	B	MTH100	SP03	B	SPN100	SP03	B	CIS120	FA02	A		
S3	Student data (Baker. . .)	ACC101	SP03	C	ENG100	SP03	B	MTH100	FA02	C	CIS120	FA02	B		
S4	Student data (Jones. . .)	ENG100	SP03	A	MTH100	SP03	A								
S5	Student data (Smith. . .)	CIS120	SP03	C	ENG100	SP03	B	CIS120	FA02	F					

(b) Student Table

FIGURE B.3 Student Transcripts (repeating groups)

the case, the solution is complicated by the irregular shape of the student table. The rows in the table are of variable length, according to the number of courses taken by each student. Not only is this design awkward, but how do we know in advance how much space to allocate for each student?

The problems inherent in Figure B.3 stem from the many-to-many relationship that exists between students and courses. The solution is to eliminate the *repeating groups* (course number, semester, and grade), which occur in each row of the student table in Figure B.3, in favor of the additional table shown in Figure B.4. Each row in the new table is unique because the *combination* of student number, course number, and semester is unique. Semester must be included since students are allowed to repeat a course. Smith (student number S5), for example, took CIS120 a second time after failing it initially.

The implementation of a many-to-many relationship requires an additional table, with a *combined key* consisting of (at least) the keys of the individual entities. The many-to-many table may also contain additional columns, which exist as a result of the combination (intersection) of the individual keys. The combination of student S5, course CIS120, and semester SP03 is unique and results in a grade of C.

Note, too, how the design in Figure B.4 facilitates table maintenance as discussed in the previous case. A change in student data is made in only one place (the student table), regardless of how many courses the student has taken. A new student may be added to the student table prior to taking any courses. In similar fashion, a new course can be added to the course table before any students have taken the course.

Review once more the properties of a relational database, then verify that the solution in Figure B.4 adheres to these requirements. To be absolutely sure that you understand the solution, and to illustrate once again the power of the relational model, use Figure B.4 to answer the following questions about the student database.

Course Number	Course Description	Credits
ACC101	Introduction to Accounting	3
CHM100	Survey of Chemistry	3
CHM101	Chemistry Lab	1
CIS120	Microcomputer Applications	3
ENG100	Freshman English	3
MTH100	Calculus with Analytic Geometry	4
MUS110	Music Appreciation	2
SPN100	Spanish I	3

(a) Course Table

Student Number	Student Data
S1	Student data (Adams. . .)
S2	Student data (Fox. . .)
S3	Student data (Baker. . .)
S4	Student data (Jones. . .)
S5	Student data (Smith. . .)

(b) Student Table

Student Number	Course Number	Semester	Grade
S1	ACC101	SP03	A
S1	CIS120	FA02	A
S1	MU100	FA02	B
S2	ENG100	SP03	B
S2	MTH100	SP03	B
S2	SPN100	SP03	B
S2	CIS120	FA02	A
S3	ACC101	SP03	C
S3	ENG100	SP03	B
S3	MTH100	FA02	C
S3	CIS120	FA02	B
S4	ENG100	SP03	A
S4	MTH100	SP03	A
S5	CIS120	SP03	C
S5	ENG100	SP03	B
S5	CIS120	FA02	F

(c) Student–Course Table

FIGURE B.4 Student Transcripts (improved design)

Questions

1. How many courses are currently offered?
2. List all three-credit courses.
3. Which courses has Smith taken during his stay at the university?
4. Which students have taken MTH100?
5. Which courses did Adams take during the Fall 2002 semester?
6. Which students took Microcomputer Applications in the Fall 2002 semester?
7. Which students received an A in Freshman English during the Spring 2003 semester?

Answers

1. Eight courses are offered.
2. The three-credit courses are ACC101, CHM100, CIS120, ENG100, and SPN100.
3. Smith has taken CIS120 (twice) and ENG100.
4. Fox, Baker, and Jones have taken MTH100.
5. Adams took CIS120 and MU100 during the Fall 2002 semester.
6. Adams, Fox, Baker, and Smith took Microcomputer Applications in the Fall 2002 semester.
7. Jones was the only student to receive an A in Freshman English during the Spring 2003 semester.

SUMMARY

The design of a database is crucial if one is to use Access successfully. This appendix consisted of two case studies to illustrate database design. The first example was set in the context of a franchise operation and illustrated one-to-many relationships. The second example developed a simple database for a university and focused on many-to-many relationships.

Our approach to database design is intuitive and focused on several key concepts that were illustrated in both case studies. A relational database consists of multiple two-dimensional tables. Each entity in a physical system requires its own table in the database. Every row in a table is unique due to the existence of a primary key. The order of the rows and columns in a table is immaterial. Every row in a table contains the same columns in the same order as every other row.

A one-to-many relationship is implemented by including the primary key of one table as a foreign key in the other table. Implementation of a many-to-many relationship requires an additional table whose primary key combines (at a minimum) the primary keys of the individual tables. Referential integrity ensures that the information in a database is internally consistent.

KEY TERMS

Codd, Edgar 1791	Many-to-many relationship ... 1791	Referential integrity 1791
Combined key 1792	One-to-many relationship 1785	Relational database 1790
Entity 1790	Primary key 1790	Repeating group 1792
Foreign key 1790	Redundancy 1786	

APPENDIX C

Mail Merge:
An Access Database and a Word Form Letter

OVERVIEW

One of the greatest benefits of using the Microsoft Office suite is the ability to combine data from one application with another. An excellent example is a **mail merge**, in which data from an Access table or query is input into a Word document to produce a set of individualized form letters. You create the **form letter** using Microsoft Word, then you merge the letter with the **records** in the Access table or query. The merge process creates the individual letters, changing the name, address, and other information as appropriate from letter to letter. The concept is illustrated in Figure C.1, in which John Smith uses a mail merge to seek a job upon graduation. John writes the letter describing his qualifications, then merges that letter with a set of names and addresses to produce the individual letters.

The mail merge process uses two input files (a main document and a data source) and produces a third file as output (the set of form letters). The **main document** (e.g., the cover letter in Figure C.1a) contains standardized text together with one or more **merge fields** that indicate where the variable information is to be inserted in the individual letters. The **data source** (the set of names and addresses in Figure C.1b) contains the data that varies from letter to letter and is a table (or query) within an Access database. (The data source may also be taken from an Excel list, or alternatively, it can be created as a table in Microsoft Word.)

The main document and the data source work in conjunction with one another, with the merge fields in the main document referencing the corresponding fields in the data source. The first line in the address of Figure C.1a, for example, contains three merge fields, each of which is enclosed in angle brackets, *<<Title>> <<FirstName>> <<LastName>>*. (These entries are not typed explicitly but are entered through special commands as described in the hands-on exercise that follows shortly.) The merge process examines each record in the data source and substitutes the appropriate field values for the corresponding merge fields as it creates the individual form letters. For example, the first three fields in the first record will produce *Mr. Jason Frasher;* the same fields in the second record will produce, *Ms. Lauren Howard,* and so on.

In similar fashion, the second line in the address of the main document contains the *<<Job Title>>* field. The third line contains the *<<Company>>* field. The fourth line references the *<<Address1>>* field, and the last line contains the *<<City>>, <<State>>,* and *<<Postalcode>>* fields. The salutation repeats the *<<Title>>* and *<<LastName>>* fields. The first sentence in the letter uses the *<<Company>>* field a second time.

The mail merge prepares the letters one at a time, with one letter created for every record in the data source until the file of names and addresses is exhausted. The individual form letters are shown in Figure C.1c. Each letter begins automatically on a new page.

The same data source can be used to create additional form letters, mailing labels, or envelopes. You could, for example, use a mail merge in a marketing campaign in which you send an initial letter to the entire list, and then send follow-up letters at periodic intervals to the same mailing list. Alternatively, you could filter the original mailing list to include only a subset of names, such as the individuals who responded to the initial letter. You can also sort the data source prior to printing the mailing labels or envelopes to print the documents in zip-code order to take advantage of bulk mail.

A mail merge can be started from either Microsoft Word or Microsoft Access. Either way, two input files are required—the form letter (main document) and the data source. The order in which these files are created depends on how the merge is initiated. When starting in Microsoft Word, you begin with the form letter, then create the data source. The process is reversed in Access—you start with a table or query, then exit to Word to create the form letter. The merge itself, however, is always performed from within Microsoft Word.

John H. Smith

426 Jenny Lake Drive   **Coral Gables, FL 33146**   **(305) 555-5555**

August 8, 2003

«Title» «FirstName» «LastName»
«JobTitle»
«Company»
«Address1»
«City», «State» «PostalCode»

Dear «Title» «LastName»:

I would like to inquire about a position with «Company» as an entry-level programmer. I have just graduated from the University of Miami with a Bachelor's Degree in Computer Information Systems (May 2001) and I am very interested in working for you. I am proficient in all applications in Microsoft Office and also have experience with Visual Basic, C++, and Java. I have had the opportunity to design and implement a few Web applications, both as a part of my educational program, and during my internship with Personalized Computer Designs, Inc.

I am eager to put my skills to work and would like to talk with you at your earliest convenience. I have enclosed a copy of my résumé and will be happy to furnish the names and addresses of my references. You may reach me at the above address and phone number. I look forward to hearing from you.

Sincerely,

John H. Smith

(a) The Form Letter (a Word document)

FIGURE C.1   The Mail Merge

Title	First Name	Last Name	JobTitle	Company	Address1	City	State	Postal Code
Mr.	Jason	Frasher	President	Frasher Systems	100 S. Miami Avenue	Miami	FL	33103-
Ms.	Lauren	Howard	Director of Human Resources	Unique Systems	475 LeJeune Road	Coral Gables	FL	33146-
Ms.	Elizabeth	Scherry	Director of Personnel	Custom Computing	8180 Kendall Drive	Miami	FL	33156-

(b) The Data Source (an Access table or query)

John H. Smith
426 Jenny Lake Drive   Coral Gables, FL 33146   (305) 555-5555

August 8, 2003

Mr. Jason Frasher
Frasher Systems
100 S. Miami Avenue
Miami, FL 33103

Dear Mr. Frasher:

I would like to inquire about a position with Frasher Systems as an entry-level programmer. I have just graduated from the University of Miami with a Bachelor's Degree in Computer Information Systems (May 2001) and I am very interested in working for you. I am proficient in all applications in Microsoft Office and also have experience with Visual Basic, C++, and Java. I have had the opportunity to design and implement a few Web applications, both as a part of my educational program, and during my internship with Personalized Computer Designs, Inc.

I am eager to put my skills to work and would like to talk with you at your earliest convenience. I have enclosed a copy of my résumé and will be happy to furnish the names and addresses of my references. You may reach me at the above address and phone number. I look forward to hearing from you.

Sincerely,

John H. Smith

John H. Smith
426 Jenny Lake Drive   Coral Gables, FL 33146   (305) 555-5555

August 8, 2003

Ms. Lauren Howard
Unique Systems
475 LeJeune Road
Coral Gables, FL 33146

Dear Ms. Howard:

I would like to inquire about a position with Unique Systems as an entry-level programmer. I have just graduated from the University of Miami with a Bachelor's Degree in Computer Information Systems (May 2001) and I am very interested in working for you. I am proficient in all applications in Microsoft Office and also have experience with Visual Basic, C++, and Java. I have had the opportunity to design and implement a few Web applications, both as a part of my educational program, and during my internship with Personalized Computer Designs, Inc.

I am eager to put my skills to work and would like to talk with you at your earliest convenience. I have enclosed a copy of my résumé and will be happy to furnish the names and addresses of my references. You may reach me at the above address and phone number. I look forward to hearing from you.

Sincerely,

John H. Smith

John H. Smith
426 Jenny Lake Drive   Coral Gables, FL 33146   (305) 555-5555

August 8, 2003

Ms. Elizabeth Scherry
Custom Computing
8180 Kendall Drive
Miami, FL 33156

Dear Ms. Scherry:

I would like to inquire about a position with Custom Computing as an entry-level programmer. I have just graduated from the University of Miami with a Bachelor's Degree in Computer Information Systems (May 2001) and I am very interested in working for you. I am proficient in all applications in Microsoft Office and also have experience with Visual Basic, C++, and Java. I have had the opportunity to design and implement a few Web applications, both as a part of my educational program, and during my internship with Personalized Computer Designs, Inc.

I am eager to put my skills to work and would like to talk with you at your earliest convenience. I have enclosed a copy of my résumé and will be happy to furnish the names and addresses of my references. You may reach me at the above address and phone number. I look forward to hearing from you.

Sincerely,

John H. Smith

(c) The Printed Letters

FIGURE C.1 The Mail Merge (*continued*)

hands-on exercise

1 Mail Merge

Objective To merge data from an Access database with a Word document to create a set of individual form letters. Use Figure C.2 as a guide.

Step 1: **Open the Names and Addresses Database**

- Start Access. Open the **Names and Addresses database** in the Exploring Access folder. The Tables button is selected. The Contacts table is the only table in the database.

- Click the **down arrow** on the **Office Links button** on the Database toolbar, then click **Merge It with Microsoft Office Word** to display the dialog box in Figure C.2a.

- The form letter has already been created for you. Thus, you can select the option to **Link your data to an existing Word document**. Click **OK**.

Click down arrow on Office Links button

Click option button to Link your data to an existing Microsoft Word document

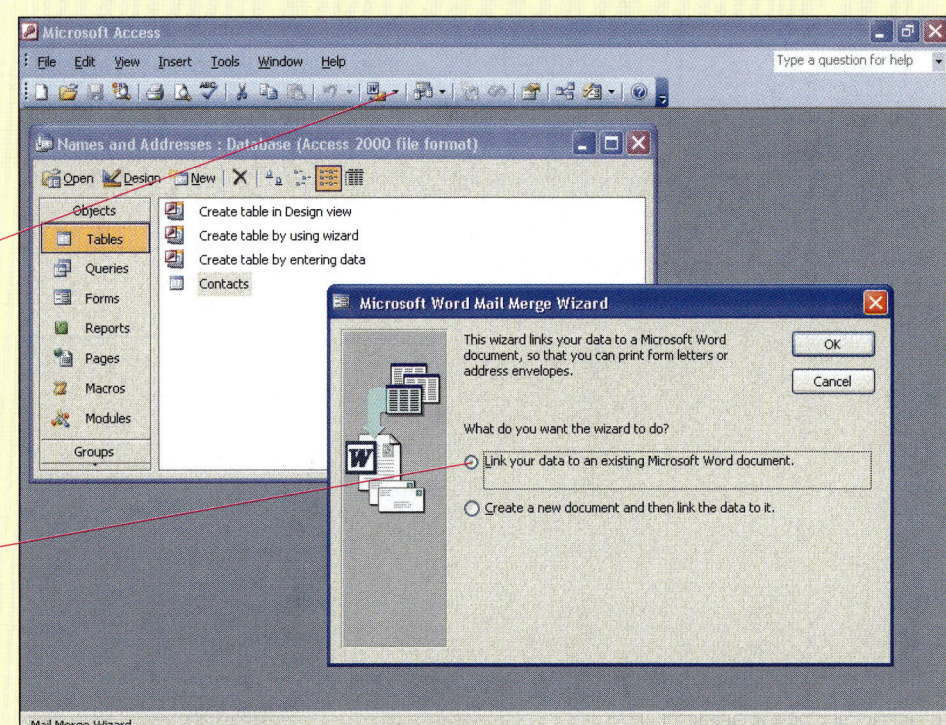

(a) Open the Names and Addresses Database (step 1)

FIGURE C.2 Hands-on Exercise 1

START ANYWHERE

A mail merge can be started from Microsoft Word or Microsoft Access. Either way, two input files are required, a form letter and a data source. The order in which these files are created is unimportant, and you can switch back and forth between the two. Eventually, however, the data source will be merged with the form letter to create the individual set of form letters.

Step 2: **Open the Form Letter**

- You should see the Select Microsoft Word Document dialog box as shown in Figure C.2b. Click the **down arrow** in the Look in box and select the **Exploring Access folder**.

- Select the **Form Letter** document and click the **Open button**. This starts Microsoft Word and opens the Form Letter document.

- Click anywhere within the date to select it, then press **Shift+F9** to toggle between the displayed value and the date code, which is set to always display today's date (see boxed tip below).

- The task pane also opens automatically. If necessary, maximize the application window for Word so that you have more room in which to work.

- Pull down the **File menu**, click the **Save As command** to display the Save As dialog box, and enter **Form Letter Solution** as the name of the document. Click **Save**.

- You are ready to begin the mail merge process.

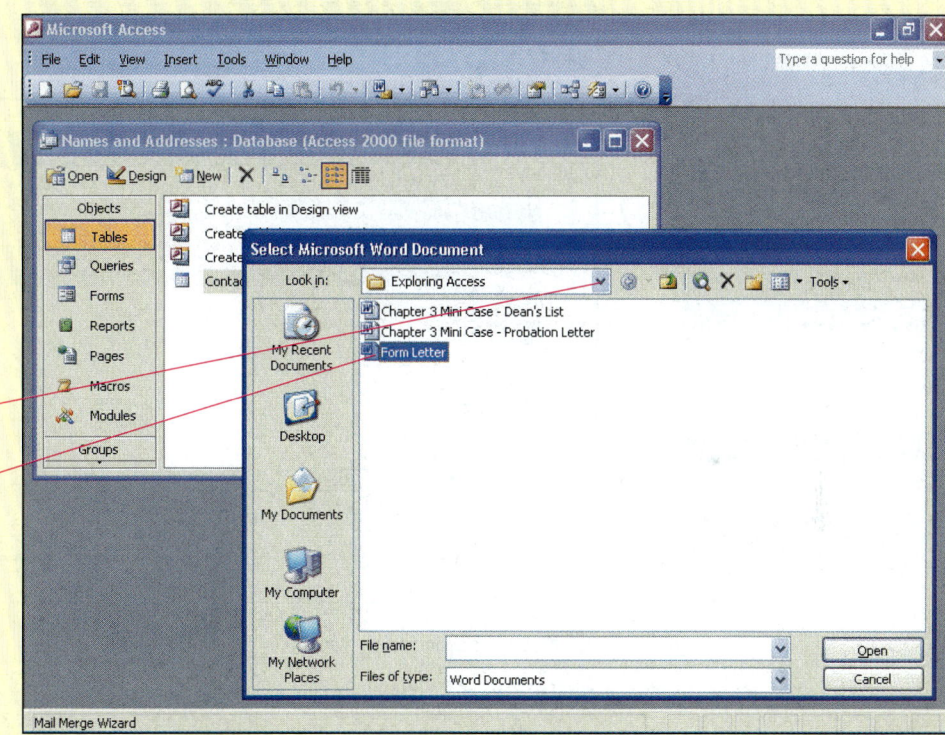

(b) Open the Form Letter (step 2)

FIGURE C.2 Hands-on Exercise 1 (*continued*)

THE INSERT DATE COMMAND

Pull down the Insert menu and click the Date and Time command to display the associated dialog box, where you choose the desired format for the date and/or time information. You can insert today's date as a fixed date (by clearing the box to Update automatically). Alternatively, you can check the box, in which case the current date will appear whenever the document is opened.

Step 3: Edit the Recipient List

- Click the link to **Edit recipient list** to display the Mail Merge Recipients dialog box, as shown in Figure C.2c. Three names appear, corresponding to the records within the Names and Addresses database that you opened to begin the exercise.

- Clear the check box for Elizabeth Scherry. Click **OK**. The form letter will be sent to the two remaining recipients, Jason Frasher and Lauren Howard.

- Modify the letterhead to reflect your name and address. Select **"Your Name Goes Here"**, then type a new entry to replace the selected text. Enter your address on the second line.

- Save the document. Click the link to **Next: Write your letter** at the bottom of the task pane to continue with the mail merge.

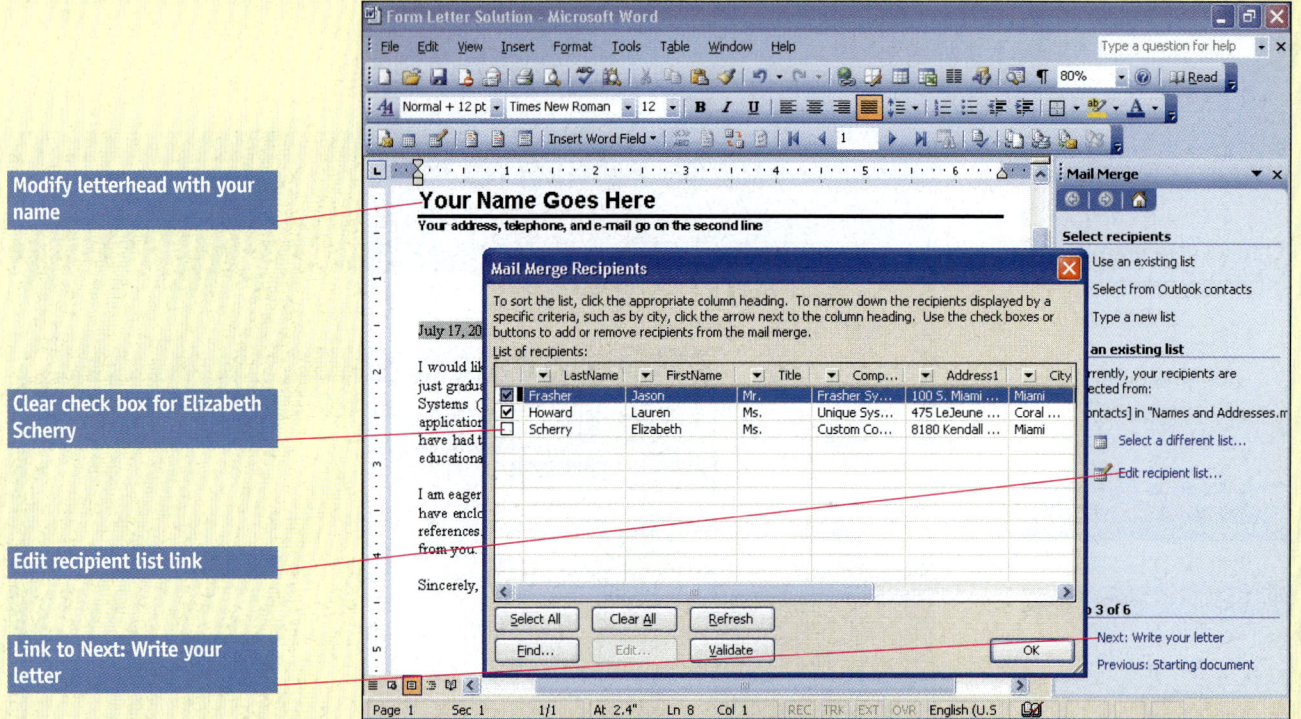

(c) Edit the Recipient List (step 3)

FIGURE C.2 Hands-on Exercise 1 (*continued*)

THE MAIL MERGE WIZARD

The Mail Merge Wizard simplifies the process of creating form letters and other types of merge documents through step-by-step directions that appear automatically in the task pane. The options for the current step appear in the top portion of the task pane and are self-explanatory. Click the link to the next step at the bottom of the pane to move forward in the process, or click the link to the previous step to return to a previous step to correct any mistakes you might have made.

Step 4: **Insert the Fields**

- The task pane indicates that you are in step 4 of the merge process. Click immediately after the date. Press the **Enter key** twice to insert a blank line. Click the link to the **Address block** in the task pane to display the dialog box in Figure C.2d.

- Verify that the four check boxes have been selected as shown in Figure C.2d. Click **OK** to insert the AddressBlock field into the document.

- Press the **Enter key** twice to leave a blank line after the address block. Click the link to the **Greeting line** to display the Greeting Line dialog box. Choose the type of greeting you want.

- Change the comma that appears after the greeting to a colon since this is a business letter. Click **OK**. The GreetingLine field is inserted into the document and enclosed in angled brackets.

- Save the document. Click **Next: Preview your letters** to continue.

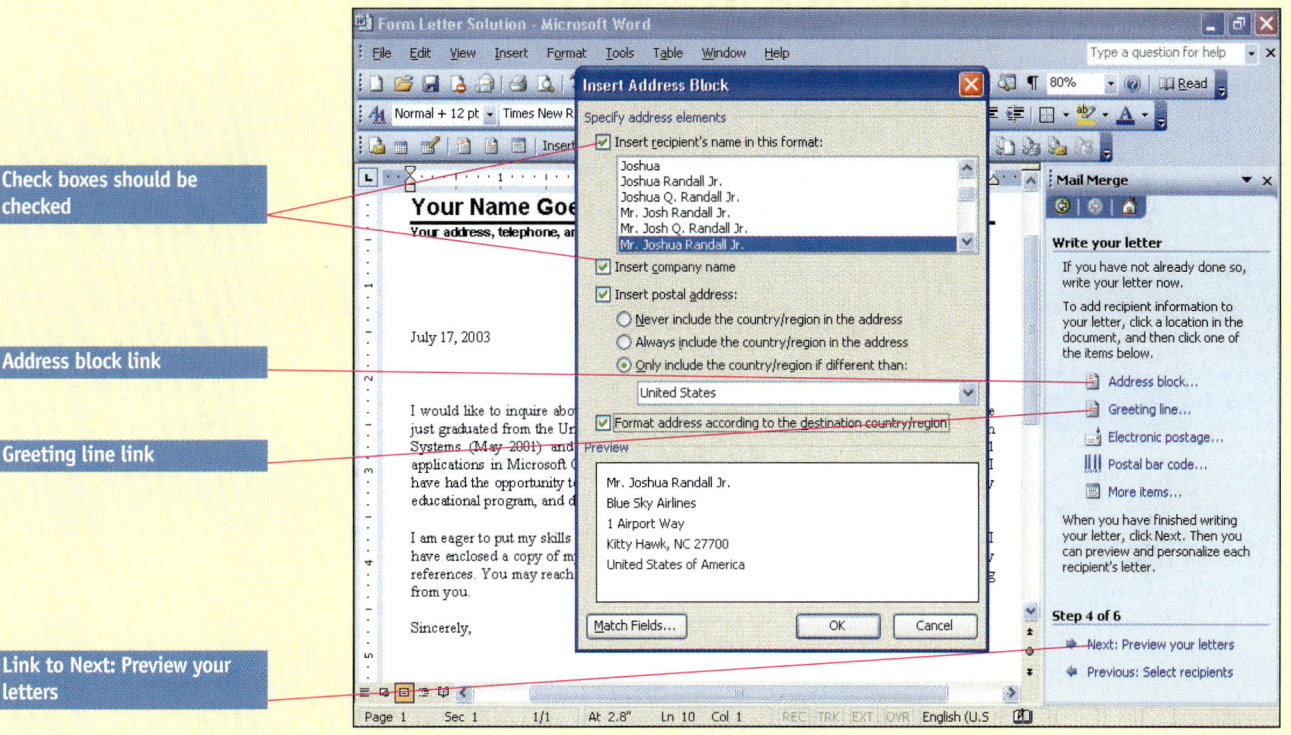

(d) Insert the Fields (step 4)

FIGURE C.2   Hands-on Exercise 1 (*continued*)

BLOCKS VERSUS INDIVIDUAL FIELDS

The Mail Merge Wizard simplifies the process of entering field names into a form letter by supplying two predefined entries, AddressBlock and GreetingLine, which contain multiple fields that are typical of the ways in which an address and salutation appear in a conventional letter. You can still insert individual fields, by clicking in the document where you want the field to go, then clicking the Insert Merge Fields button on the Mail Merge toolbar. The blocks are easier.

Step 5: **Preview the Letters**

- You should be in step 5 of the mail merge, where you see the first form letter, as shown in Figure C.2e. (If you see a date code, rather than an actual date, pull down the **Tools menu** and click the **Options command** to display the Options dialog box. Click the **View tab** and clear the check box next to Field Codes.)

- View the records individually to be sure that the form letter is correct and that the data has been entered correctly. Use the link to the previous step(s) at the bottom of the task pane to make corrections if necessary.

- Save the letter. Click the link to **Next: Complete the merge** to continue.

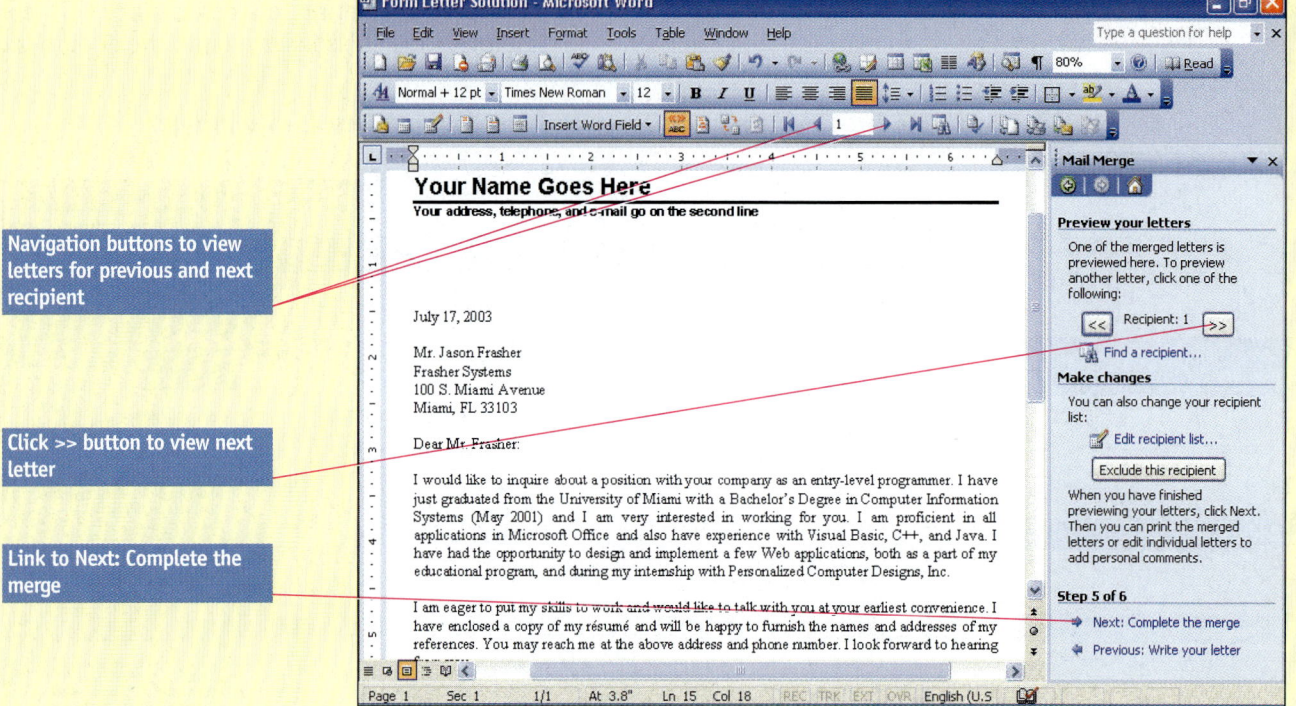

(e) Preview the Letters (step 5)

FIGURE C.2 Hands-on Exercise 1 (*continued*)

THE MAIL MERGE TOOLBAR

The Mail Merge toolbar appears throughout the mail merge process and contains various buttons that apply to different steps within the process. Click the <<abc>> button to display field values rather than field codes. Click the button a second time, and you switch back to field codes from field values. Click the <<abc>> button to display the field values, then use the navigation buttons to view the different letters. Click the ▶ button, for example, and you move to the next letter. Click the ▶| button to display the form letter for the last record.

Step 6: **Edit and Print the Individual Letters**

- You should be in step 6 of the mail merge. Click the link to **Edit individual letters** in the task pane, which displays the Merge to New Document dialog box. The All option is selected. Click **OK** to create a third document (Letters1), consisting of the individual form letters as shown in Figure C.2f.

- Click the **Next (Previous) Page button** to move forward (backward) within the set of individual letters. (You have the option to personalize any of the individual letters.)

- Pull down the **File menu** and click the **Print command** to display the Print dialog box. Check the option to print all of the letters. Click **OK**.

- Close the Letters1 document. Click **No** if prompted to save changes to this document because you can always re-create the individual letters from the form letter and Access database.

- Close the Form Letter Solution document. Click **Yes** when asked to save changes to this document.

- Exit Word. Exit Access.

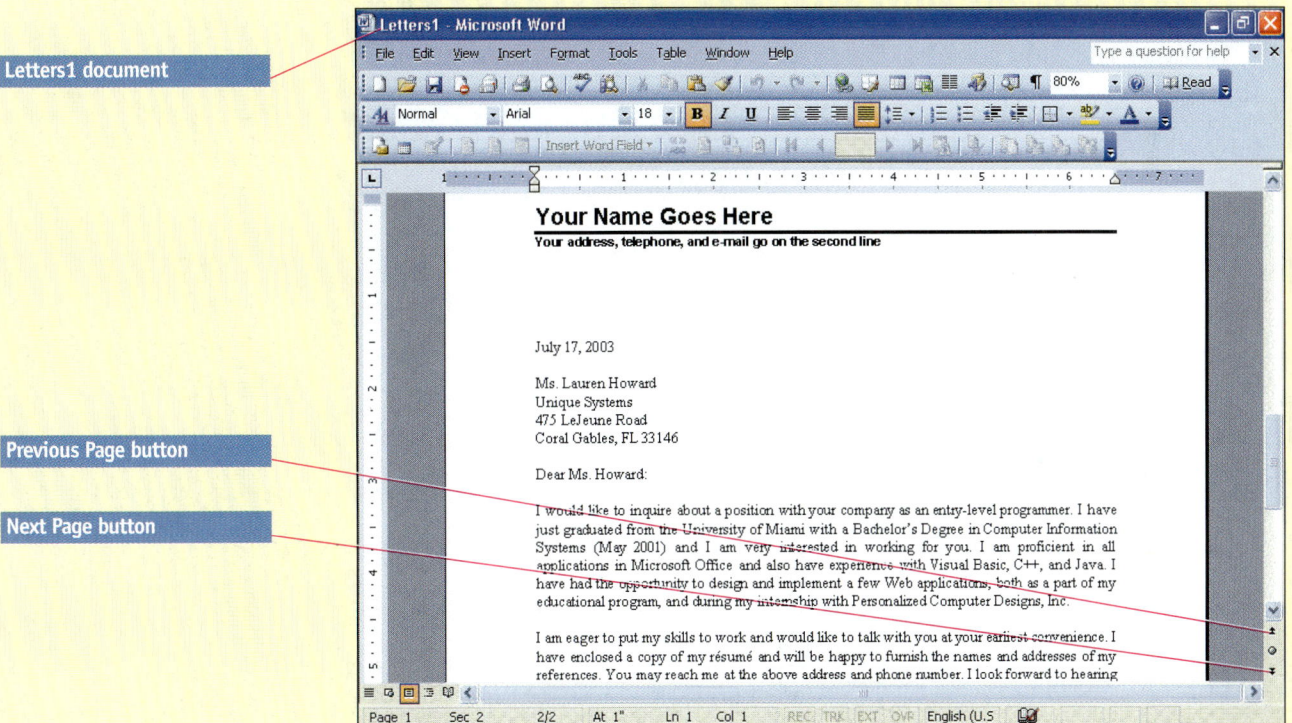

(f) Edit and Print the Individual Letters (step 6)

FIGURE C.2   Hands-on Exercise 1 (*continued*)

THREE DIFFERENT FILES

A mail merge works with a minimum of two files. The main document and data source are input to the mail merge, which creates a set of merged letters as output. The latter can be saved as a separate file, but typically that is not done. You can use the same data source (e.g., a set of names and addresses) with different main documents (a form letter and an envelope) and/or use the same main document with multiple data sources. You typically save, but do not print, the main document(s) and the data source(s). As indicated earlier, you print the set of merged letters, but typically do not save them.

SUMMARY

One of the greatest benefits of the Microsoft Office suite is the ability to combine data from one application with that from another. A mail merge is an excellent example, as it combines data from an Access table or query with a Word document. The mail merge creates the same letter many times, changing only the variable data, such as the addressee's name and address, from letter to letter. The merge fields within the main document indicate where the variable information is to be inserted in the individual letters. The same data source can be used with different documents (e.g., to create form letters, envelopes, and/or mailing labels) for a single set of names and addresses. Conversely, the same document (such as a form letter) can be used with different data sources as additional data is obtained.

A mail merge can be started from either Microsoft Word or Microsoft Access, but either way, two input files are required—the form letter and the data source. The order in which the files are created is not important. The main document and data source are saved but typically not printed. The merged file (e.g., the set of form letters) is usually printed, but not saved because you can always recreate the form letters by rerunning the mail merge. The Mail Merge Wizard provides step-by-step instructions.

KEY TERMS

Data source 1795	Mail Merge toolbar 1802	Merge fields 1795
Form letter 1795	Mail Merge Wizard 1800	Recipient list 1800
Insert Date command 1799	Main document 1795	Records 1795
Mail Merge 1795		

A Project for the Semester:
Applying What You Have Learned

OVERVIEW

This appendix describes the student project we require in our course in Microsoft Access at the University of Miami. It is intended for both student and instructor, as it describes the various milestones in the administration of a class project. Our experience has been uniformly positive. Students work hard, but they are proud of the end result, and we are continually impressed at the diversity and quality of student projects. The project is what students remember most about our course, and it truly enhances the learning experience.

The Groups

The class is divided into groups of three or four students each, and students work together to submit a collective project. It is critical that the groups are balanced with respect to student abilities, and hence our groups are always formed after the first exam, when we have additional information with which to create the groups. We distribute a questionnaire in which we ask students whom they want to work with (and conversely, if there is anyone they would be uncomfortable working with). We try to honor the former requests, but will always honor the latter, so that the groups work as smoothly as possible.

Once the groups have been formed, we establish a series of milestones that are described in the remainder of the appendix. There is absolutely no requirement for you or your class to follow our milestones exactly. We have found, however, that providing detailed feedback through a series of continual assignments is the most effective way to move each group toward its final goal.

One other suggestion is to have the groups engage in a continuing presentation to the class as a whole. We allocate the beginning of each class period to group presentations of 10 to 15 minutes each on the current class assignment. The group presentations accomplish two goals—they enable students to learn from each other, and they provide valuable practice in presenting one's work to an audience.

Phase I—Preliminary Design

Describe, in a one- or two-page narrative, the relational database that your group will design and implement. You can select any of the case studies at the end of the chapters on one-to-many or many-to-many relationships, or alternatively, you can choose an entirely different system. Regardless of which system you choose, the preliminary design is one of the most important aspects of the entire project since it is the foundation for the project. A good design will enable you to implement the project successfully, and hence you should give considerable thought to the document you prepare. Your project need not be unduly complex, but it must include at least three tables. The relationships between the tables can be one-to-many or many-to-many. The information can be contained in a written document to your instructor and/or a PowerPoint presentation for the class. Either way, it must do all of the following:

1. Describe the physical system for which you will create the database.

2. Develop a "wish list" describing in general terms the information the system is to produce.

3. Design a database capable of producing the required information. List the tables in the database, the fields in each table, and the relationships among the tables.

4. Describe in general terms how the database will be able to produce at least three of the reports on the wish list by describing the underlying queries, each of which references fields from multiple tables in the database.

Phase II—Detailed Design

Implement the refinements (if any) to the preliminary design from Phase I, then expand that design to include all of the necessary fields in each table. You are also asked to develop the properties for each field at this time. Be sure to include adequate data validation and to use input masks as appropriate. One additional requirement is that the primary key of at least one table is an AutoNumber field.

After you have completed the design, create an Access database containing the necessary tables, with all fields in each table, but no other objects. You do not have to enter any data at this time, but you are required to document your work. Use the Print Relationships command in the File menu to create a one-page document that gives you a visual overview of your database. Submit this document to your instructor.

You are also asked to provide detailed documentation for each table. Pull down the Tools menu, click Analyze, click Documentor. Select Tables in the Object Type drop-down list box, then select all of the tables. Click the Options button, then include for each table the Properties and Relationships but not the Permissions by User and Group. Include for each field Names, Data types, Sizes, and Properties. Do not include any information on indexes. Print the information for each table in the database and submit it to your instructor for review.

Phase III—The User Interface

Phase III focuses on the design of the switchboard and associated templates that will be replicated throughout the system. The switchboard, or user interface, is critical to the success of any system as a user spends his or her day in front of the screen. It should be functional and visually compelling. We have found that the best way to arrive at an attractive design is for each member to submit a design independently.

Thus, each member of the group creates a simple Help form for the group project, which is similar to the form that has appeared in the end-of-chapter exercises throughout the text. The form should include the names of all group members, a logo (clip art or other object), and an appropriate color scheme. All of the forms for each group are then imported into a single database (use the Get External Data command) that will be shown in class. The best design for each group can be picked by consensus, at which point the design is frozen, and development begins with the initial switchboard.

The switchboard should contain a logo for the project and establish a color scheme. The initial version need contain only two buttons—one to display the "Help About" form and one button to exit from the application. Use clip art as appropriate, but clip art for the sake of clip art is often juvenile. You may want to use different fonts and/or simple graphics (e.g., horizontal or vertical lines are often quite effective). A simple design is generally the best design.

Each group then creates a form template and a report template based on the design of the Help form and switchboard. The templates are created in Design view, without benefit of a wizard, and neither object is based on a table or query. All subsequent forms and reports are based on the templates, at which point the data source is specified. The result is a uniform look throughout the system that adds to its visual appeal. The switchboard is then expanded to include five items—the Help form and exit buttons as before, new buttons to show the form and report templates, and a fifth button to print the Relationships Diagram from Phase II.

Phase IV—Create the Forms and Enter Test Data

Phase IV has you create the forms in which to enter test data, based on the template of Phase III. You need a form (or subform) for every table that will enable you to add, edit, and delete records in that table. You are also required to have at least one subform, and you must structure your forms to facilitate data entry in a logical way. All forms should have a consistent look (via a common template).

The forms should be user friendly and display command buttons so that there is no requirement on the part of the end user to know Access. Each form is to include buttons to add, delete, find, and print a record, and to close the form. A Help button is a nice touch. Include drop-down list boxes to facilitate data entry in at least two places. The forms should be designed so that they fit on one screen and do not require the user to scroll.

Use the forms after they have been created to enter test data for each table. (Each table should contain 10 to 15 records.) Be sure that the data will adequately test all of the queries and reports that will be in your final system. Submit a printout of the data in each table to your instructor. (You can print the Datasheet view of each table.) In addition, submit a printed copy of each form to your instructor.

Phase V—Prototyping

Phase V has you develop a "complete" system using a switchboard and prototyping as described in Chapter 7. The main menu should be displayed automatically (via an AutoExec macro) when the database is opened, and the user should be able to step through the entire system. The final reports and queries need not be implemented at this time (a "not yet implemented" message is fine at this stage). The user should, however, be able to go from one form to the next without leaving Access or encountering an error message.

Phase VI—The Finishing Touches

The system should be "up and running" as you continue to build the various objects during the testing phase. (The reports should be based on the report template to promote a uniform look.) It is at this point that you can add the finishing touches through VBA as described in Chapter 8, if in fact you are able to cover that material during the semester. Another finishing touch to consider is the creation of a Web page for the group. The page can be simple and contain descriptive information about the project and the members in the group. Load the page onto your school server, then include a hyperlink on the main switchboard to display the page.

Phase VII—The Completed System

Submit the completed Access database that should contain all of the reports and/or queries needed to satisfy the initial wish list. To obtain a grade of A, you will need to satisfy the following requirements (many of which have been completed) in the earlier phases:

1. An approved design of sufficient complexity similar to the completed soccer database in Chapter 7.
2. Separation of the objects and tables into separate databases that are subsequently linked to one another.
3. Use of the Data Validation and Input Mask properties to validate and facilitate data entry. In addition, at least one table is to contain an AutoNumber field as its primary key.
4. Existing data in all tables with 10 to 15 records in each table.
5. An AutoExec macro to load the main menu and maximize the document window.
6. A Help button on one or more screens that displays the name of the group and an appropriate help message (e.g., a phone number). An "About" button

on the opening switchboard that opens a form with introductory information about the project.

7. A working form (or subform) for each table in the database so that you can maintain each table. You must have at least one subform in your system. The forms should have a consistent look (via a common template). The system and especially the forms are to make sense; that is, just because you have all of the forms does not mean you satisfy the requirements of the project. Your forms should be designed to facilitate data entry in a logical way.

8. The forms should be user friendly and display command buttons so that there is no requirement on the part of the end user to know Access. Each form is to include buttons to add, delete, find, and print a record, and to close the form. Include drop-down list boxes to facilitate data entry in at least two places.

9. Three working reports, at least one of which is a group/total report.

10. Inclusion of a parameter query to drive a form or report.

11. At least one unmatched query. A top-value query is a nice touch, but depends on the system.

12. Various VBA modules on one or more forms that parallel the examples from Chapter 8. We suggest a combo box to locate a specific record, shortcuts for data entry (with a command button to display the shortcuts), and an error-trapping procedure for a duplicate record. Additional procedures can include a prompt to the user if a recommended field is omitted and a modified Add Record procedure to position the insertion point in the first control within the form.

13. The completed system should be as visually compelling as possible. Clip art for the sake of clip art tends to be juvenile without effect. In general, a consistent logo (one image) is much better from slide to slide than multiple images. No clip art is better than poor clip art or too much clip art.

14. You will be judged on whether your system actually works; that is, the instructor will enter and/or modify data at random. The effects of the new data should be manifest in the various reports and queries.

The Written Document

In addition to demonstrating a working system, you are to submit a written document as described below. The submission of the written project will be an impressive (lengthy) document but easily generated, as much of the material is created directly from Access. The objective is for you to have a project of which you will be proud and something that you can demonstrate in the future. Include the following:

1. Title page plus table (list) of the contents; pages need not be numbered, but please include "loose-leaf" dividers for each section.

2. A one- or two-page description of the system taken from the earlier presentation to the class.

3. Technical documentation that includes the relationships diagram and table properties, as prepared in the detailed design phase.

4. Hard copy of each form (one per page).

5. Hard copy of each report (one per page).

6. A working disk.

CHAPTER 3

Animating a Presentation: Diagrams and Charts

OBJECTIVES

After reading this chapter you will:

1. Describe the diagrams that are available in the Diagram Gallery
2. Create a pyramid, a target diagram, and an organization chart
3. Use custom formatting to change the appearance of various diagrams
4. Use Microsoft Graph to create and edit a chart
5. Distinguish between charts with data series in rows versus columns.
6. Add custom animation to individual objects on a slide
7. Animate an organization chart so objects appear by level or branch.
8. Animate a chart so that data appears by category or series.

hands-on exercises

1. DIAGRAMS AND ORGANIZATION CHARTS
   Input: None
   Output: Diagrams and Organization Charts

2. MICROSOFT GRAPH
   Input: None
   Output: Introduction to Charts

3. CUSTOM ANIMATION
   Input: Super Zoo; Diagrams and Organization Charts (from exercise 1); Introduction to Charts (from exercise 2)
   Output: Super Zoo Solution

CASE STUDY
THE KELSO PERFORMING ARTS CENTER

An appreciation for the arts is essential to the quality of life in any society, but the recent budget shortfall at every level of government has put cultural programs in jeopardy throughout the country. The city of Kelso is no exception as its residents have tried unsuccessfully for several years to persuade the city council to build a Performing Arts Center. This year there is a renewed sense of optimism because the political climate has changed, and there is a strong focus on revitalizing the downtown area. In addition, the Kelso family, for whom the city is named, has agreed to donate a prime five-acre site if the council will approve a $30 million bond issue to fund construction.

You are civic minded and a patron of the arts. Kenneth Kelso is also a close personal friend, and he has asked you to spearhead the effort to secure the funding. You and two colleagues from the Chamber of Commerce Leadership Committee are to go before the council on Monday evening to present your case. The Kelso family has worked for several hours to prepare the contents of the presentation, but it is not yet finished. Ken is counting on you to add the finishing touches. He is seeking an eye-catching, attention-grabbing, interest-keeping presentation, which you will also submit to your instructor for his or her entertainment.

Your assignment is to read the chapter, taking note of the many ways a presentation can be enhanced through the use of animation, charts, diagrams, and sound. You will then open the partially completed *Chapter 3 Case Study—Kelso Performing Arts Center* presentation and add the objects indicated below, together with the associated animations. Start by modifying the opening slide to include your name and the sound of a drum roll.

Add animation to the existing chart for revenue projection, as well as to the slide that shows the project's time table. Copy the existing pyramid on the fifth slide, modify the copy to create a target diagram on the same slide, and then animate both the pyramid and the target diagram. Create an organization chart on the penultimate (next-to-last) slide, and then animate the chart so that the blocks appear one at a time. You have done a good job, so be sure to include the sound of applause on the last slide. Print the completed presentation as audience handouts for your records.

ANIMATING A PRESENTATION

Figure 3.1 displays a six-slide presentation for a hypothetical "Super Zoo." The presentation is interesting in and of itself; what you cannot see, however, is the animation that is associated with every slide. The giraffe in slide 1, for example, is made to walk across the slide, and then disappear. The boxes in the organization chart on slide 2 appear one branch at a time, as do the columns in the chart on slide 3. There are "exploding fireworks" on the last slide.

The presentation also includes additional objects that we have not seen previously. The organization chart in slide 2 is created through the Diagram Gallery (as described below). The chart in slide 3 is created through Microsoft Graph, a charting program that is built into Microsoft Office. (Charts can also be imported from Microsoft Excel.)

The timeline in slide 4 is developed from a table. Look closely, and you should see the structure of an underlying 2×12 table (two rows and 12 columns, the latter corresponding to the months of the year). Clip art and block arrows were placed on top of the table to create the timeline. Animation was added at the end, so that the arrows (milestones in the project) appear sequentially.

The drawing in slide 5 was created using various tools on the Drawing toolbar. Clip art was placed on top of the various shapes, after which animation was applied to the individual objects. Slide 6 uses the AutoShapes tool to create an exploding slide in conjunction with sound and animation.

As indicated, animation is the common element in every slide and the driving concept throughout this chapter. Before we can apply the animation, however, we must first describe how to create the various objects on the slides. We begin with the organization chart on slide 2.

The Diagram Gallery

An organization chart is one of six types of diagrams that can be created using the **Diagram Gallery** in Microsoft Office. Each diagram is intended to convey a different type of relationship that may exist within an organization. We focus on the organization chart, but it is useful to mention all six diagram types. Thus, we use

- ***Organization chart*** to show hierarchical relationships
- ***Cycle diagram*** to show a process with a continuous cycle
- ***Radial diagram*** to show elements revolving around a core
- ***Pyramid diagram*** to show foundation relationships
- ***Venn diagram*** to show overlap between elements
- ***Target diagram*** to show steps toward a goal

All diagrams are developed within the ***drawing canvas*** (an area enclosed within hashed lines) that appears when you first create the diagram. Every diagram has a default format, which contains a limited number of entries (shapes). You can insert additional shapes, such as subordinate or coworker boxes on an organization chart. You can also delete existing shapes (e.g., a specific box on an organization chart) by selecting the box and pressing the Del key.

You can change the appearance of a diagram as well as its structure. All diagrams provide access to the ***AutoFormat tool*** that displays a Style Gallery, which formats the diagram as a whole. Alternatively, you can select individual (and/or multiple) shapes within a diagram and format them independently. You can change the style of the connecting lines in an organization chart as well as their color. You can also change the font and/or alignment of the text within the individual shapes. It's easy, it's fun, and as you might have guessed, it is time for our next hands-on exercise.

(a) Title Slide

(b) Organization Chart

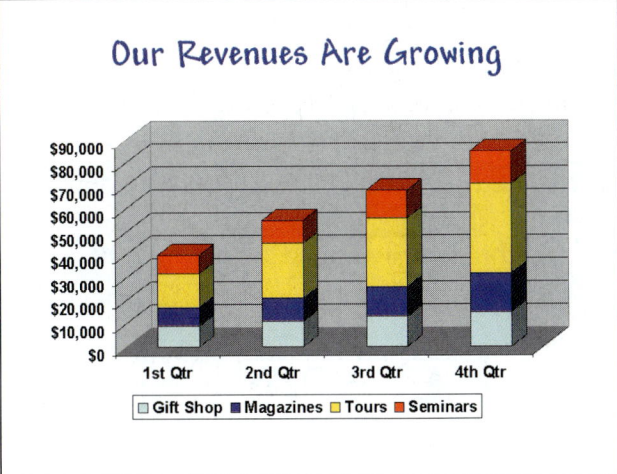

(c) Chart

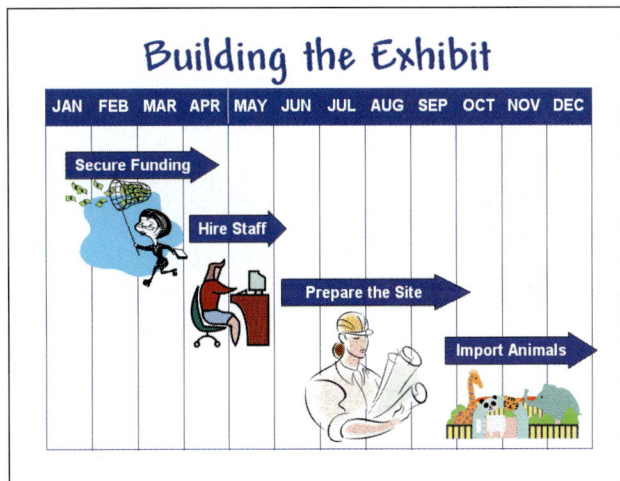

(d) Timeline (table)

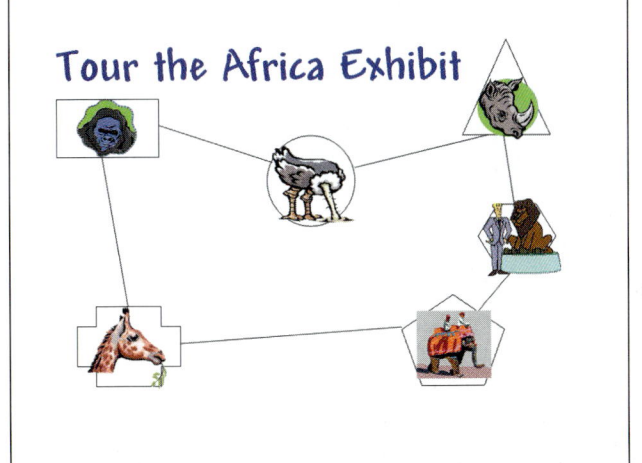

(e) Drawing

(f) AutoShape

FIGURE 3.1 The Super Zoo Presentation

hands-on exercise

1 Diagrams and Organization Charts

Objective To create and format an organization chart; to create a pyramid and target using the Diagram Gallery. Use Figure 3.2 as a guide in the exercise.

Step 1: **Insert a Diagram**

- Start PowerPoint. Click the **New button** to begin a new presentation. Enter the title **Diagrams and Organization Charts** and your name on the title slide.

- Save the presentation as **Diagrams and Organization Charts** in the **Exploring PowerPoint folder**.

- Click the **New Slide button** to insert a new slide. If necessary, click the **down arrow** at the top of the task pane and select **Slide Layout**. Scroll in the task pane until you can select (click) the **Title and Diagram or Organization Chart layout**.

- Double click the icon to **add diagram or organization chart** to display the Diagram Gallery as shown in Figure 3.2a. Select **Organization Chart**. Click **OK**.

- Your slide should contain the default organization chart surrounded by a nonprinting hashed line to indicate the drawing area. Close the task pane.

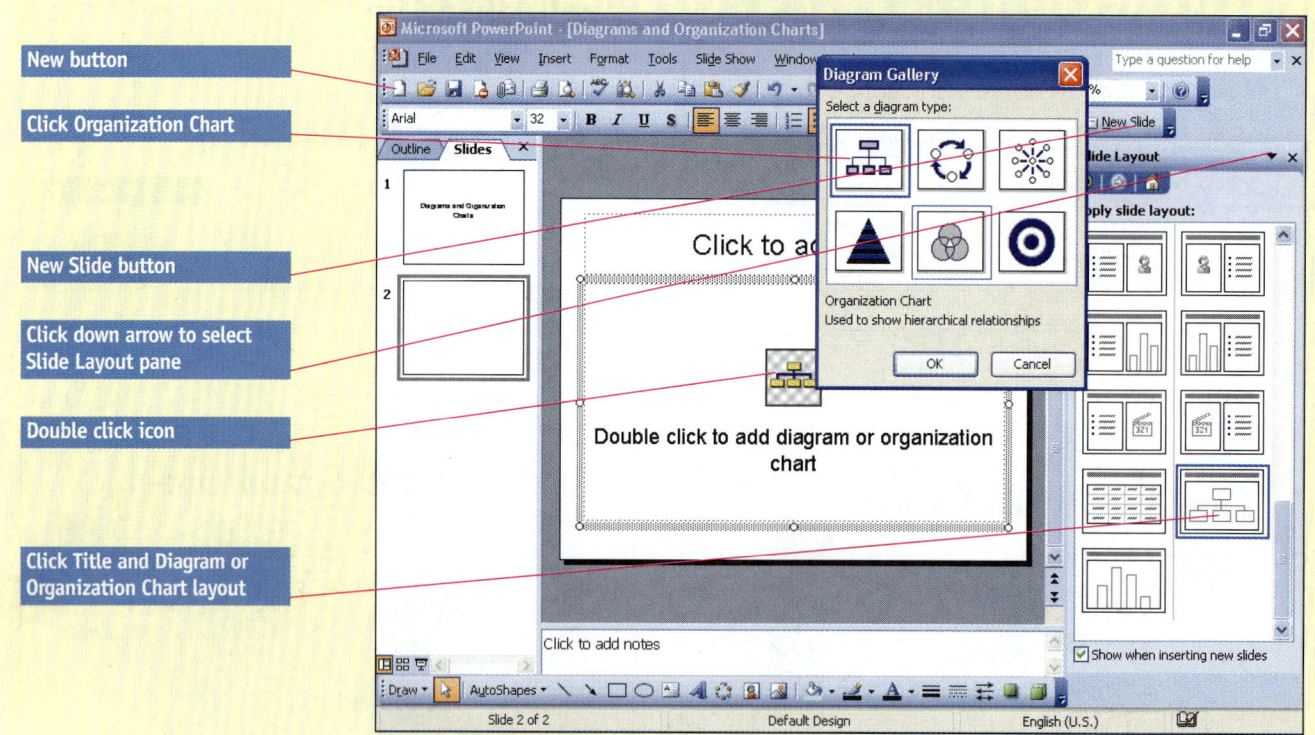

(a) Insert a Diagram (step 1)

FIGURE 3.2 Hands-on Exercise 1

USE THE TOOLBAR BUTTONS

You don't have to change the slide layout to insert a diagram onto an existing slide. Just select the slide, and then click the Insert Diagram or Organization Chart button on the Drawing toolbar. The Drawing toolbar also contains buttons to insert WordArt or clip art.

1812   CHAPTER 3: ANIMATING A PRESENTATION

Step 2: **Create the Organization Chart**

- Click the **title place holder** and enter the title of this slide, **The Organization of Our Zoo**, as shown in Figure 3.2b.

- Click in the top box of the organization chart and type **Super Zoo**. (Do not press the Enter key or you will create an extra line and unnecessarily increase the depth of the box.)

- Click in the **leftmost box** on the second line and type **Asian Exhibit**. Stay in the box after you have entered the text, click the **down arrow** on the **Insert Shape tool** in the Organization Chart toolbar, and click **Subordinate**.

- Click in the newly created box (which appears under the Asian Exhibit) and type **Bengal Tigers** as shown in Figure 3.2b.

- Add **Komodo Dragons** as a second subordinate for **Asian Exhibit**. Enter the text for the remaining boxes as shown in Figure 3.2b. (The remaining boxes in the second row are **Aviary** and **Australian Exhibit**. **Kangaroos** and **Koala Bears** are subordinates for the **Australian Exhibit**.)

- Save the presentation.

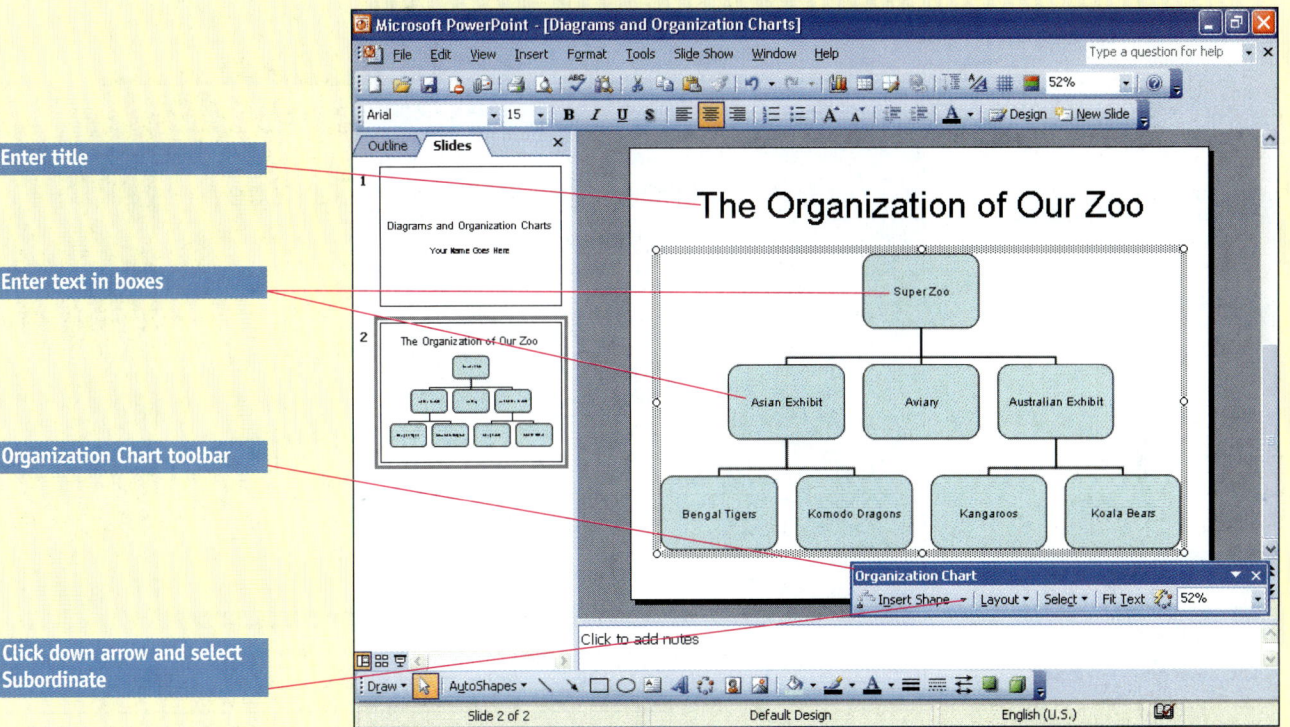

(b) Create the Organization Chart (step 2)

FIGURE 3.2 Hands-on Exercise 1 (*continued*)

IF YOU MAKE A MISTAKE

You can delete any box in the organization chart by selecting the box and pressing the Del key. If necessary, you can delete the entire chart (and start over) by clicking the hashed line surrounding the drawing area and pressing the Del key. You can also cancel (reverse) the last command(s) by clicking the Undo button or using the Ctrl+Z keyboard shortcut.

Step 3: **Add the African Exhibit**

- Close the left pane to give yourself additional room in which to work. (You can reopen the left pane at any time by clicking the **Normal View button** above the status bar.)

- Add the **African Exhibit** in one of two ways:
  ❏ Click at the top of the organization chart and insert a **subordinate**, *or*
  ❏ Click in the rightmost box on the second level and insert a **coworker**.

- Type **African Exhibit** in the box that appears at the end of the second line. Enter **Giraffes** and **Elephants** as subordinates for this box. Do not be concerned that the organization chart is becoming awkward due to its increased width.

- Click the **African Exhibit box**, click **Layout** on the Organization Chart toolbar to display the available layouts as shown in Figure 3.2c, and select **Right Hanging**. The subordinate boxes appear one under the other, as opposed to horizontally.

- Add **Lions** and **Tigers** as additional subordinates to the African Exhibit. Save the presentation.

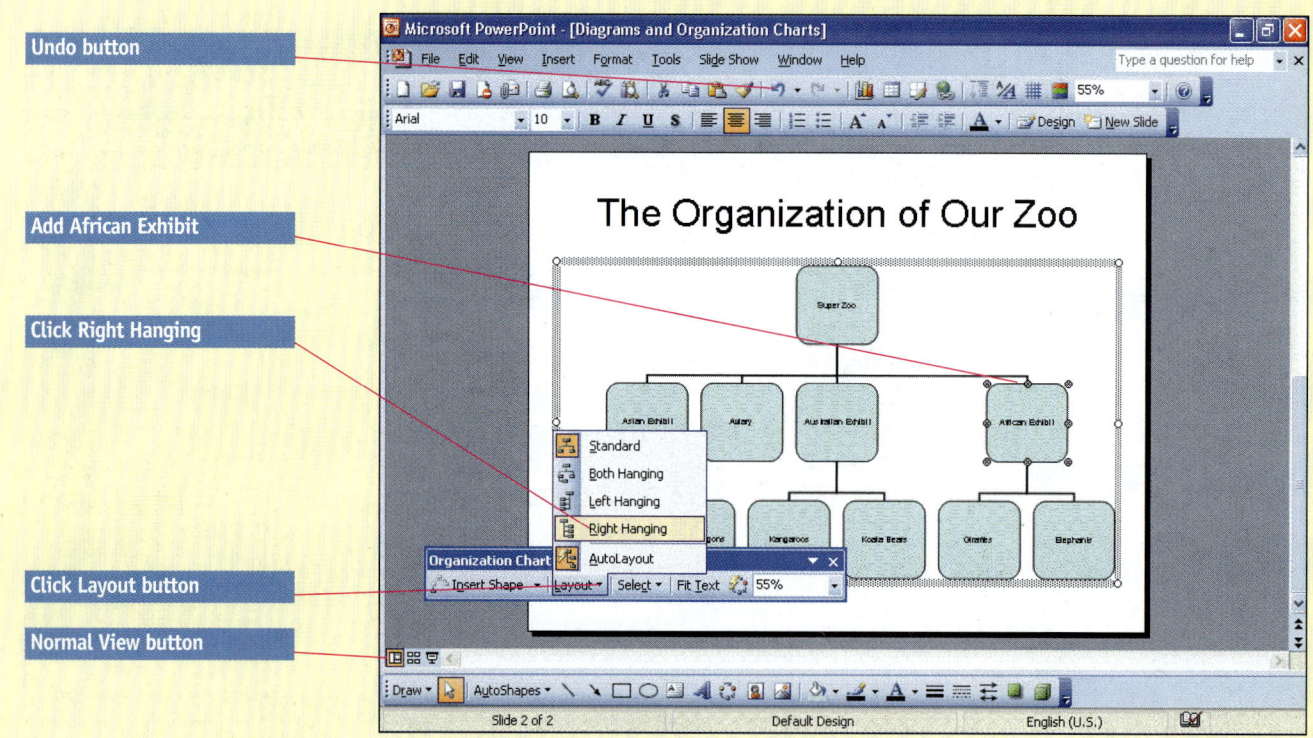

(c) Add the African Exhibit (step 3)

FIGURE 3.2 Hands-on Exercise 1 (*continued*)

THE ORGANIZATION CHART TOOLBAR

The Organization Chart toolbar appears automatically when the chart is selected and disappears when the chart is no longer active. The Insert Shape tool adds a subordinate (a box on the level below the selected box), a coworker (a box on the same level as the selected box), or an assistant (a staff position). The Layout tool changes the design of the chart, the size of the drawing area, or the size of chart within the drawing area. Experiment with the different options. Use the Undo command if the results are unexpected or different from what you intended.

Step 4: **Format the Chart**

- Right click in the background area of the organization chart to display a context-sensitive menu, and, if necessary, toggle the **Use AutoFormat command** off (the check should disappear).

- Click the **Super Zoo box** at the top of the organization chart. Click the **down arrow** next to the **Select tool** in the Organization Chart toolbar and click **Branch** to select the entire organization chart as shown in Figure 3.2d.

- Pull down the **Format menu**. Click **AutoShape** to display the associated dialog box. Click the **Colors and Lines tab**, then click the **down arrow** next to the **color box** (in the fill area) and select **red**. Click **OK**.

- Click off the chart, click the **African Exhibit box**, click the **down arrow** next to the **Select tool** and click **Branch**. Use the **Format AutoShape command** to change the color of this branch to blue.

- Reselect all of the boxes in the organization chart. Click the **Font Size list box** on the Formatting toolbar and enter **11 point** type. Click the **Bold button** to change the font to bold. Click the **down arrow** next to the **Font color box** on the Formatting toolbar. Click **White**. Save the presentation.

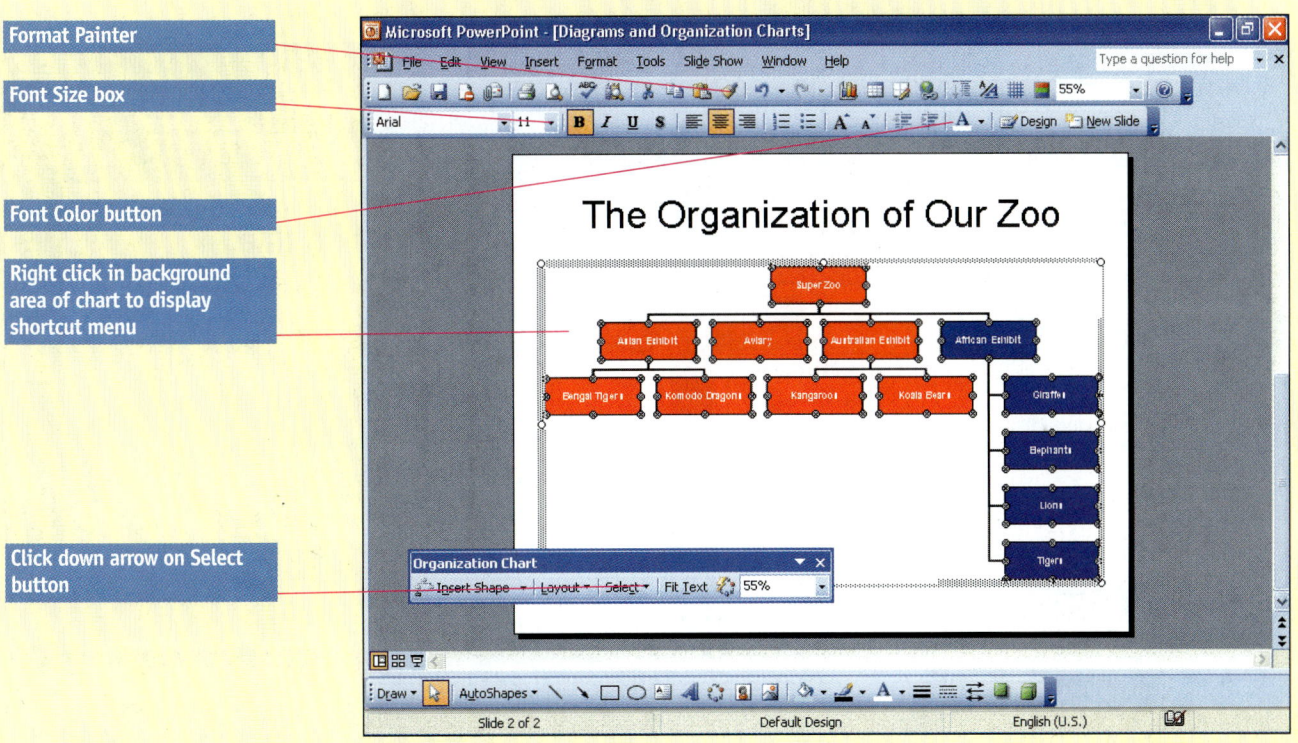

(d) Format the Chart (step 4)

FIGURE 3.2   Hands-on Exercise 1 (*continued*)

THE FORMAT PAINTER

The Format Painter copies the formatting of the selected text to other places in a presentation. Select the text with the formatting you want to copy, then click or double click the Format Painter. Clicking the button will paint only one selection. Double clicking the button will paint multiple selections until the feature is turned off by again clicking the button. Either way, the mouse pointer changes to a paintbrush, which you can drag over text to give it the formatting characteristics of the original selection.

Step 5: **Create a Pyramid Diagram**

- Click the **Normal View button** above the status bar and then click the **Slides tab** to check your progress. You should see the newly created organization chart as the second slide in your presentation.
- Click the **New Slide button**, then scroll in the Slide Layout task pane until you can select (click) the **Title and Diagram or Organization Chart layout**. Close the task pane.
- Double click the icon to **add diagram or organization chart** to display the Diagram Gallery. Click the **Pyramid Diagram icon**. Click **OK**. The default pyramid is created with three components.
- Click (select) the top triangle. Click the **Insert Shape button** on the Diagram toolbar twice in a row so that the pyramid has five components. Enter the text of each component as shown in Figure 3.2e.
- Click the **AutoFormat button** on the Diagram toolbar to display the Diagram Style Gallery. Select (click) the **Primary Colors** design, then click the **Apply button** to implement this design. Each block on the pyramid is now a different color.
- Click in the title placeholder and enter **Sponsorship Levels** as the title of the slide. Save the presentation.

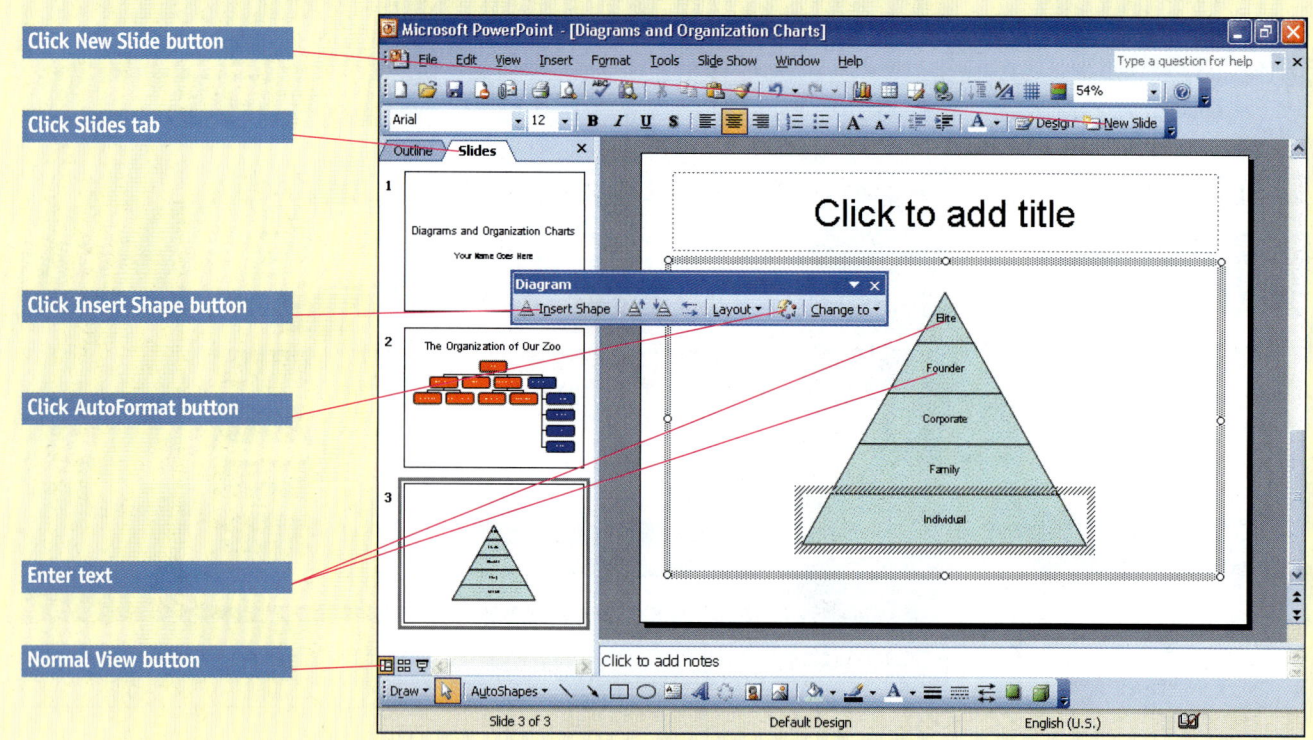

(e) Create a Pyramid Diagram (step 5)

FIGURE 3.2   Hands-on Exercise 1 (*continued*)

AUTOFORMAT ON AND OFF

You can format individual elements within a diagram, provided that auto formatting is not in effect. Right click any element (e.g., a shape in a pyramid or a box in a hierarchy chart), toggle the Use AutoFormat command off (the check should disappear), then use the Format AutoShape command to display the associated dialog box. Click the Colors and Lines tab, change the fill color, line color, and/or thickness as desired, then click OK.

Step 6: **Create a Target Diagram**

- Select (click) any element on the pyramid. Click the **Layout button** on the Diagram toolbar, then click **Fit Diagram to Contents**.

- The size of the drawing canvas shrinks to more closely surround the pyramid. Click and drag the canvas to the left side of the slide.

- Click the **Copy button** on the Standard toolbar (or use the **Ctrl+C** keyboard shortcut). Click the **Paste button** (or press **Ctrl+V**). You should now have two pyramids side by side as shown in Figure 3.2f.

- Select the second pyramid, click the **Change to button** on the Diagram toolbar, and select **Target** to change the second pyramid to a target.

- Move and size the two diagrams as necessary, so that they both fit comfortably on the slide.

- Save the presentation.

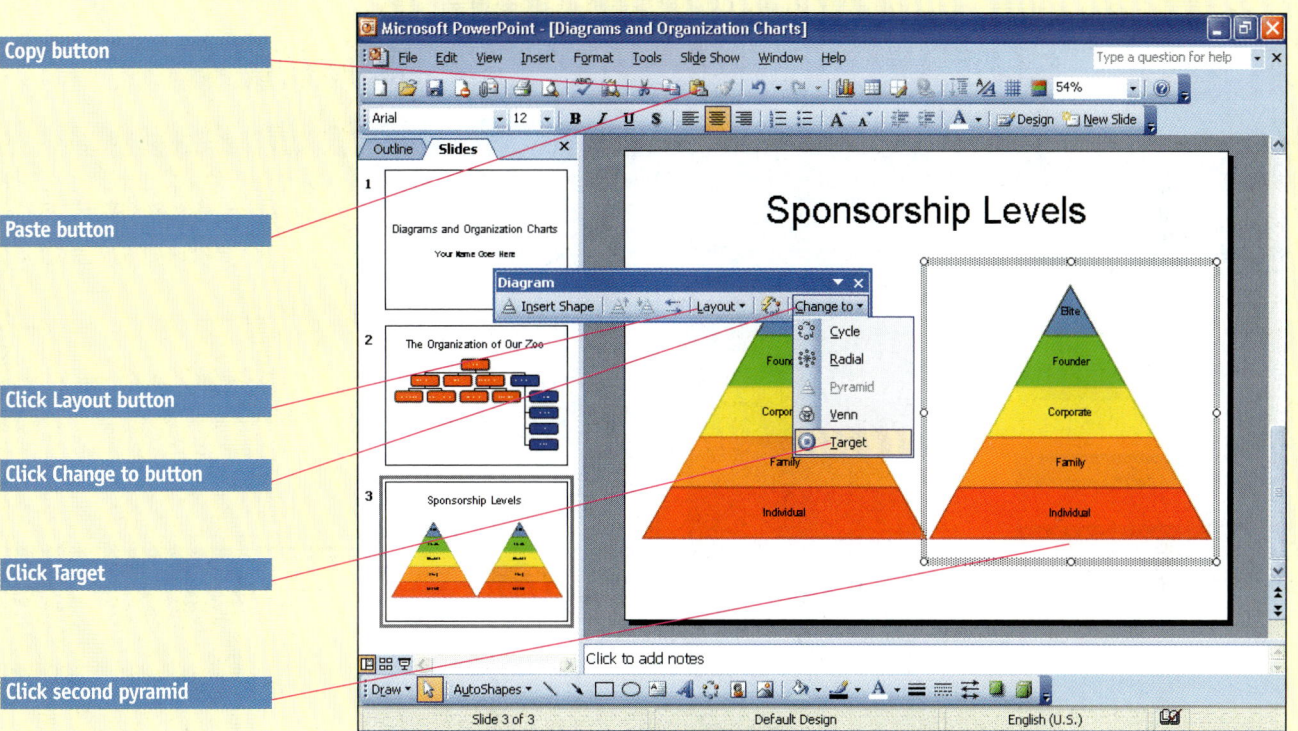

(f) Create a Target Diagram (step 6)

FIGURE 3.2 Hands-on Exercise 1 (*continued*)

THE DIAGRAM TOOLBAR

Start with one of five diagram types (radial, cycle, pyramid, Venn, or target), then click the Change to button to convert to a different type, while retaining all of your text and formatting information. Each diagram type has a unique strength, and you can experiment to find the best diagram type to deliver your message. (Organization charts have their own toolbar and are not convertible to another diagram type.) Use the Insert Shape button to add the appropriate shape to any diagram. You can also use the AutoFormat button to display the Diagram Style Gallery to format the diagram as a whole.

Step 7: **Print the Audience Handouts**

- Pull down the **File menu** and click the **Print command** to display the Print dialog box. Click the **down arrow** in the **Print What** area and select **Handouts**. Specify **three slides** per page. Check the box to **Frame slides**.

- Click the **Preview button** to display a screen similar to Figure 3.2g. The complete presentation consists of three slides. The target diagram is on the last slide. A series of ruled lines appears next to each slide.

- Click the **Options button**, then click the **Header and Footer command** to display the associated dialog box. Check the box to include **Date and time**, then choose the option to **Update automatically**.

- Enter **your name and class** as the header. Uncheck the boxes for page number and footer. Click the **Apply to All button**, then click the **Print button** and click **OK** to print the audience handouts for your instructor. Close the Preview window.

- Save the presentation a final time. Exit PowerPoint if you do not want to continue with the next exercise at this time.

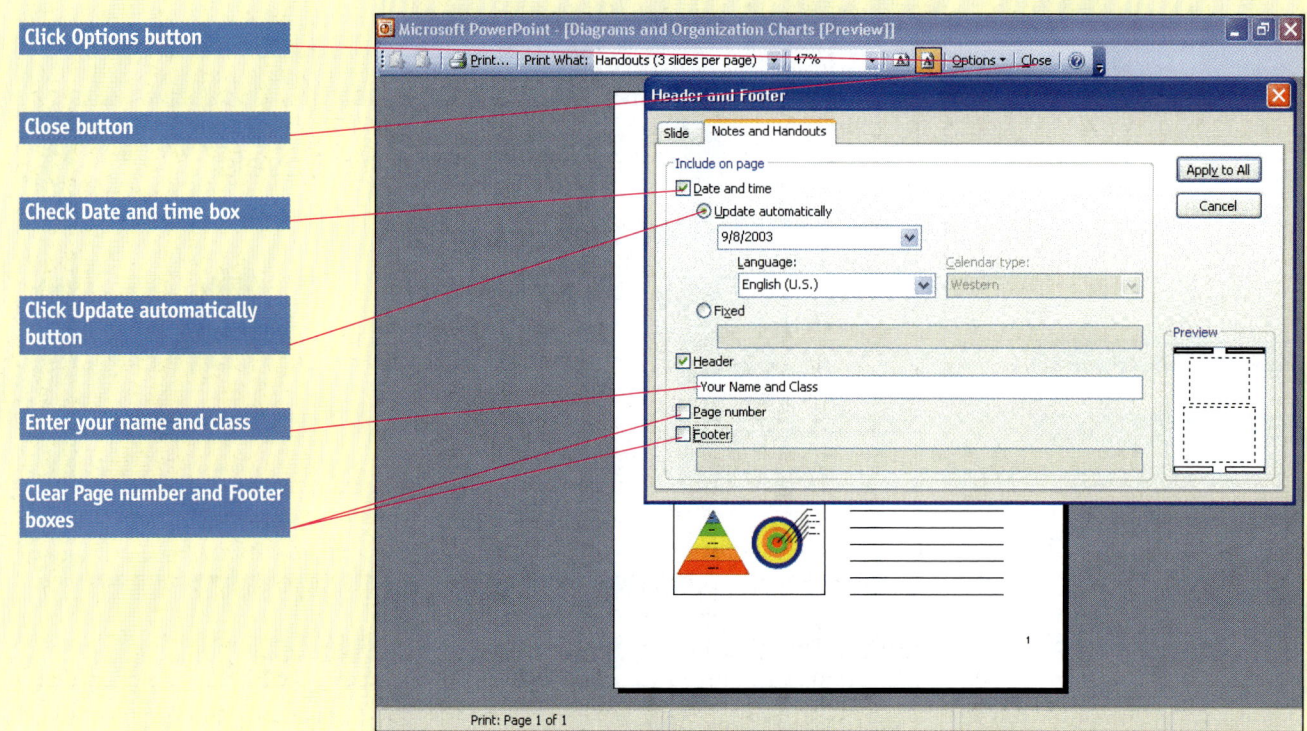

(g) Print the Audience Handouts (step 7)

FIGURE 3.2   Hands-on Exercise 1 (*continued*)

PRINT IN A VARIETY OF FORMATS

Use the flexibility inherent in the Print command to print a presentation in a variety of formats. Pull down the File menu, click the Print command to display the Print dialog box, and then select the desired output. Print handouts for your audience that contain the slide miniatures, or give your audience an outline containing the text of the entire presentation. Print the Notes Pages for yourself as a guide in preparing for the presentation. And finally, you can print the slides themselves, one per page, on overhead transparency masters as backup in case the computer is not available.

MICROSOFT GRAPH

A ***chart*** (or graph) is a graphic representation of data. You can import an Excel chart into a PowerPoint presentation, and/or you can create a chart from scratch. The latter is accomplished through ***Microsoft Graph***, the default charting program for Microsoft Office that is installed automatically with PowerPoint. The program has many of the same capabilities as the charting component of Microsoft Excel.

All charts are based on numeric values called ***data points*** and descriptive entries called ***category labels***. The data points are grouped into one or more ***data series*** that appear in rows or columns on the worksheet. This terminology is illustrated in Figure 3.3. The ***datasheet*** in Figure 3.3a contains 16 data points that are divided into four data series. The data represents revenue that has been raised through various funding sources in each of four quarters. Figure 3.3b displays the associated side-by-side column chart when the data series are plotted in rows. Figure 3.3c displays a comparable chart except that the data series are in columns.

Both charts plot a total of 16 data points (four revenue categories over four quarters), but they group the data differently. Figure 3.3b displays the data by quarter whereas Figure 3.3c displays the data by funding source. The choice between the two charts depends on your message and whether you want to emphasize revenue by quarter or by funding source. It sounds complicated, but it's not, and Microsoft Graph will create either chart for you according to your specifications.

- If you specify that the data series are in rows (Figure 3.3b), Microsoft Graph will
  - Use the first row in the datasheet for the category labels on the X axis.
  - Use the remaining rows for the four data series (each funding source represents a different series).
  - Use the first column for the legend text (the legend appears below the chart).

- If you specify that the data series are in columns (Figure 3.3c) the wizard will
  - Use the first column in the datasheet for the category labels on the X axis.
  - Use the remaining columns for the four data series (each quarter represents a different series).
  - Use the first row for the legend text (the legend appears below the chart).

Stacked Column Charts

Multiple data series are typically plotted as one of two chart types—***side-by-side column charts*** or ***stacked column charts***. Once again, the choice depends on the intended message. If, for example, you want to emphasize the individual revenue amounts in each quarter or revenue category, then the side-by-side columns in Figures 3.3b and 3.3c are more appropriate. If, on the other hand, you want to emphasize the total revenue for each quarter or category, the stacked columns in Figures 3.3d and 3.3e are preferable. The advantage of the stacked column is that the totals are clearly shown and can be easily compared. The disadvantage is that the segments within each column do not start at the same point, making it difficult to determine the actual sales for the individual categories.

Note, too, that the scale on the Y axis in the charts is different for charts with side-by-side columns versus charts with stacked columns. The side-by-side columns in Figure 3.3 show the revenue of each category or quarter, and so the Y axis goes only to $40,000. The stacked columns, however, reflect the total revenue in each quarter or category, and thus the scale goes to $90,000 or $120,000, respectively. Realize, too, that for a stacked column chart to make sense, its numbers must be additive; you shouldn't automatically convert a side-by-side column chart to its stacked column equivalent. It would not make sense, for example, to convert a column chart that plots unit sales and dollar sales side by side, to a stacked column chart that adds the two, because units and dollars represent different physical concepts, and do not make sense when added together.

(a) Datasheet

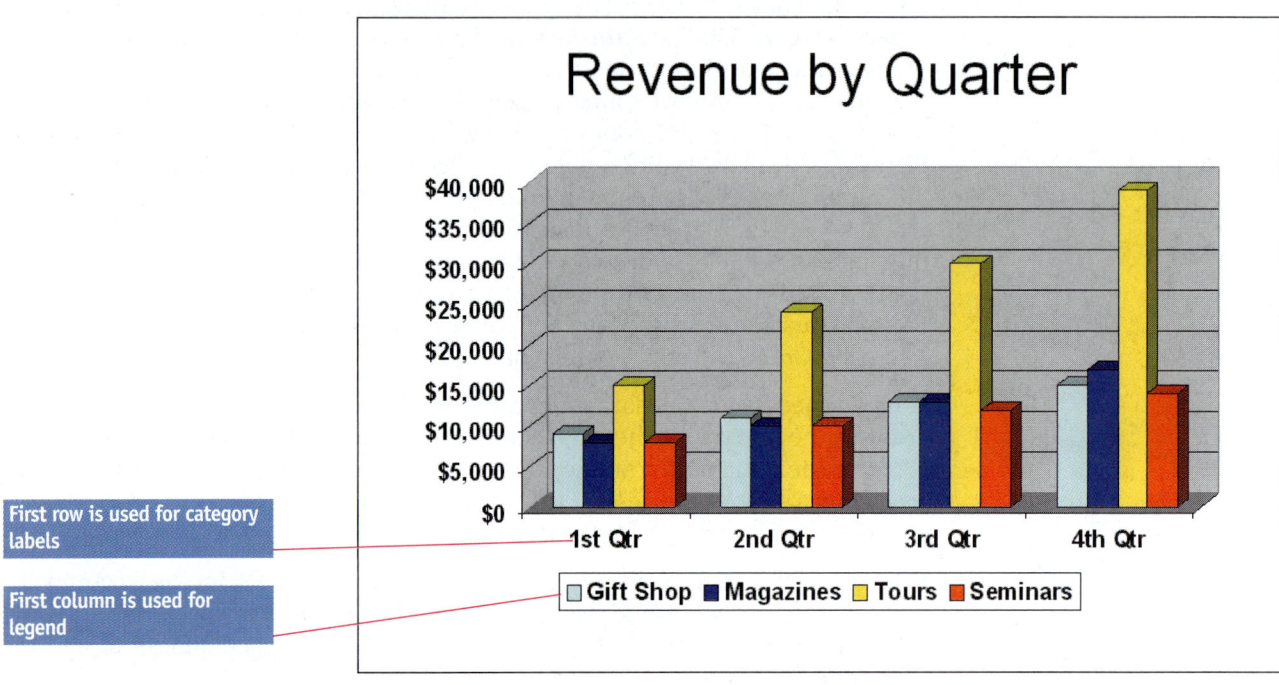

(b) Side-by-side Column Chart (data in rows)

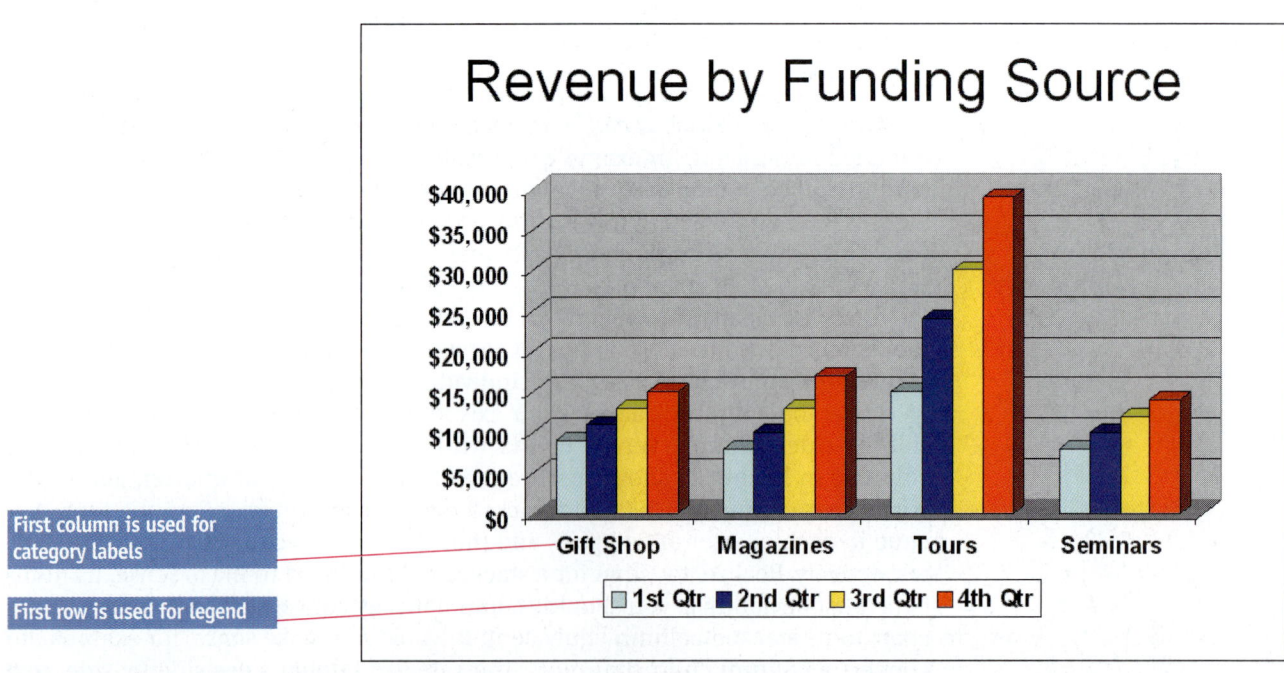

(c) Side-by-side Column Chart (data in columns)

FIGURE 3.3 Microsoft Graph

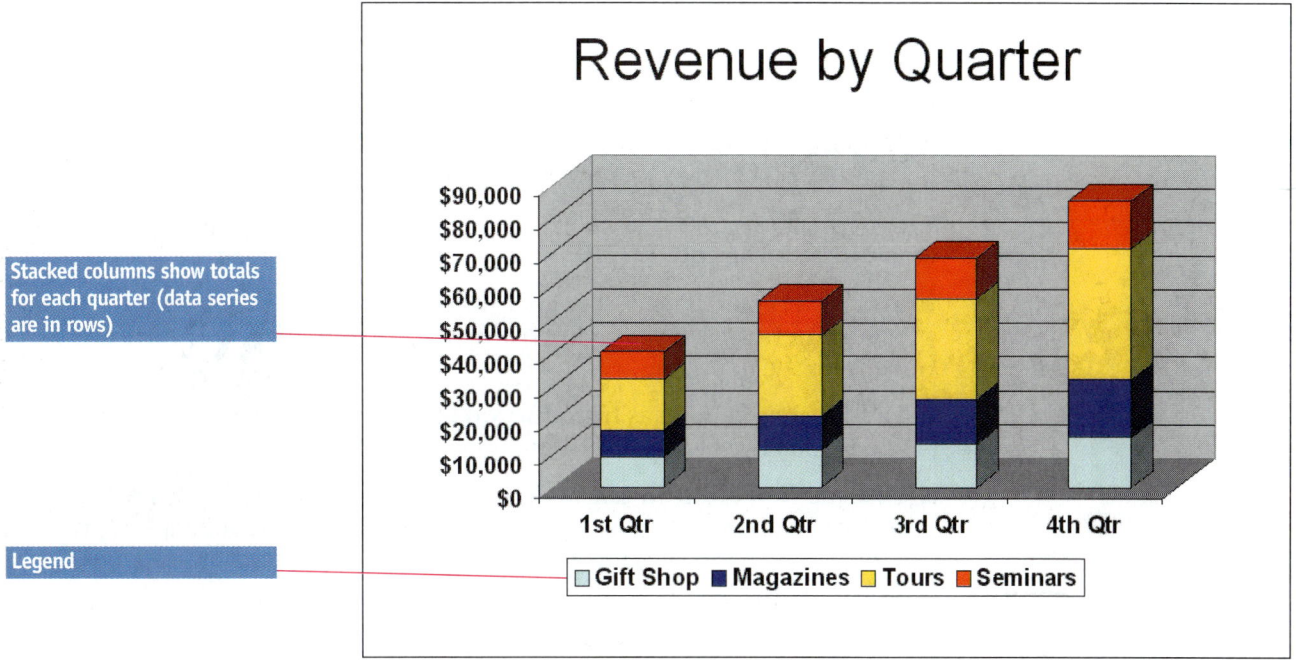

(d) Stacked Column Chart (data in rows)

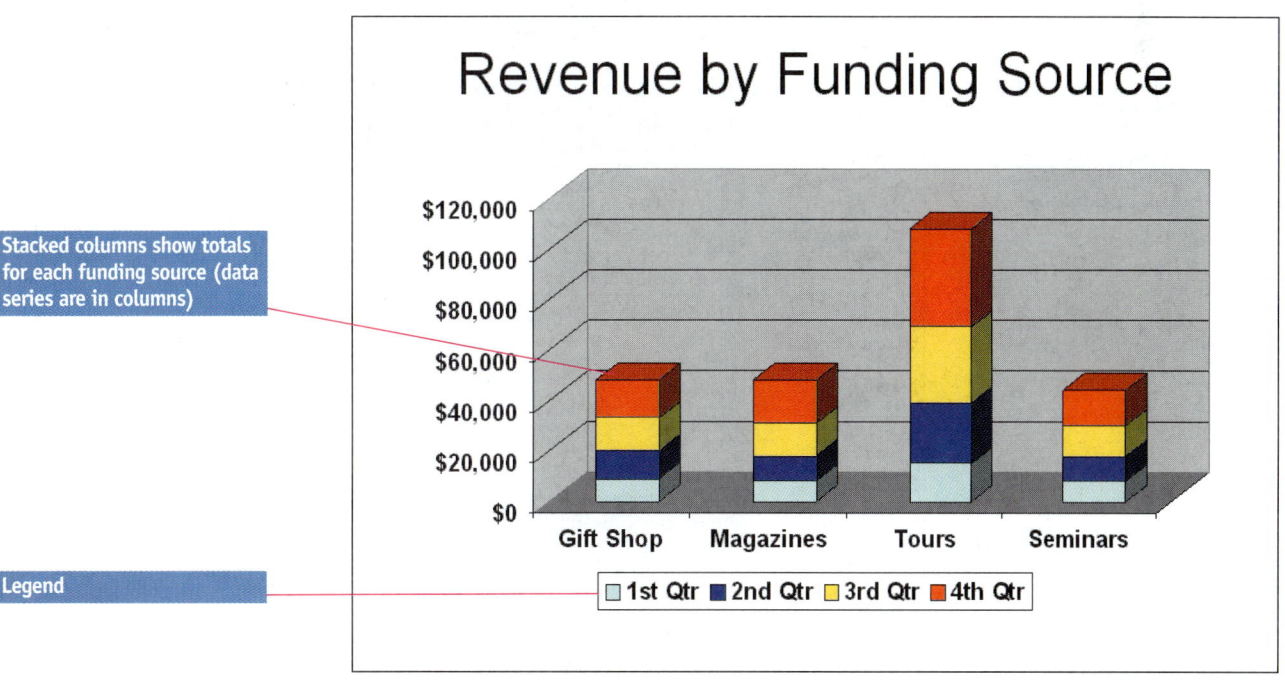

(e) Stacked Column Chart (data in columns)

FIGURE 3.3 Microsoft Graph (continued)

EMPHASIZE YOUR MESSAGE

A chart exists to deliver a message, and you want that message to be as clear as possible. One way to help put your point across is to choose a title that leads the audience. A neutral title such as *Revenue by Quarter* does nothing and requires the audience to reach its own conclusion. A better title might be *Our Revenues Are Growing*, which conveys an optimistic sense of a growing business.

hands-on exercise

2 Microsoft Graph

Objective Use Microsoft Graph to insert a graph into a presentation; modify the graph to display the data in rows or columns; change the graph format and underlying data. Use Figure 3.4 as a guide in the exercise.

Step 1: **Start Microsoft Graph**

- Start PowerPoint. If necessary, click the **New button** on the Standard toolbar to begin a new presentation. Enter the title **Introduction to Charts** and your name on the title slide.

- Save the presentation as **Introduction to Charts** in the **Exploring PowerPoint folder** you have been using throughout the text.

- Click the **New Slide button** to insert a new slide. If necessary, click the **down arrow** at the top of the task pane and select **Slide Layout**. Scroll in the task pane until you can select (click) the **Title and Chart layout** as shown in Figure 3.4a. Close the task pane.

- Double click the icon to **add chart** to start Microsoft Graph.

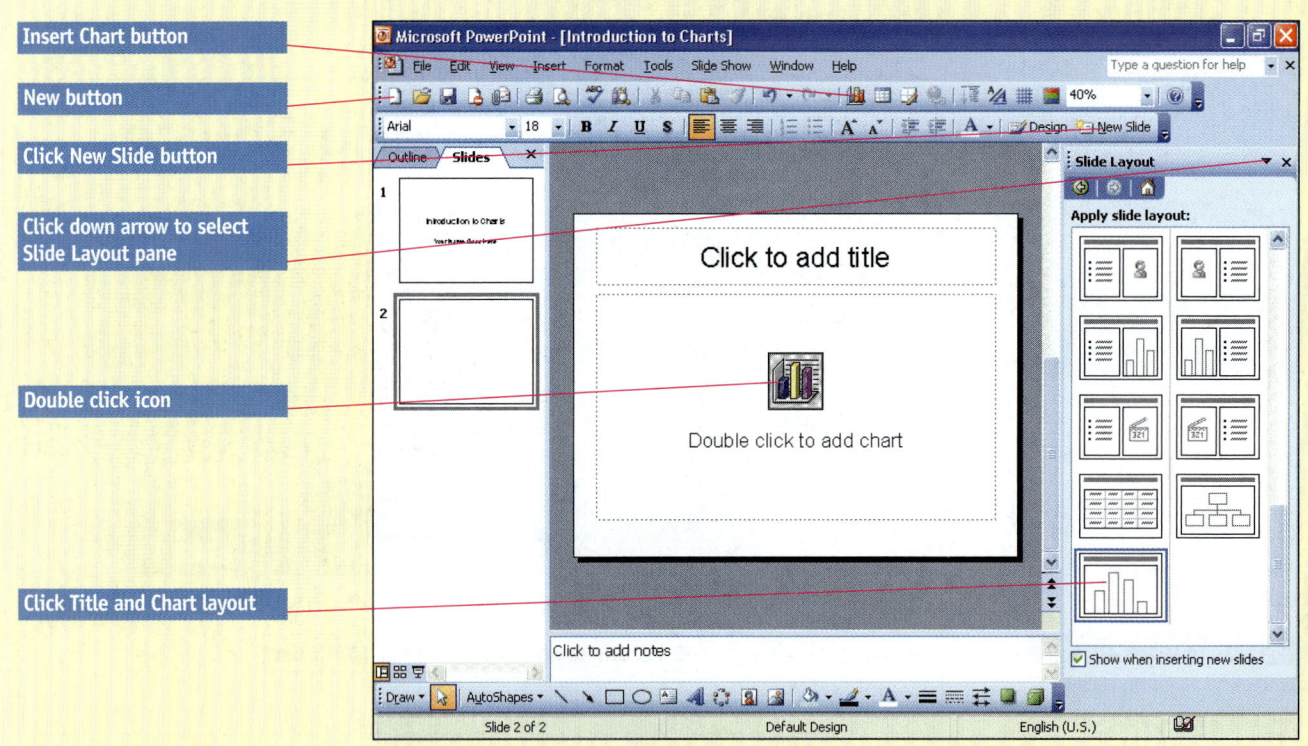

(a) Start Microsoft Graph (step 1)

FIGURE 3.4 Hands-on Exercise 2

INSERTING A CHART

There are several different ways to insert a chart into a presentation. You can insert a new slide and choose one of several slide layouts that contain a placeholder for a chart. You can pull down the Insert menu and select the Chart command, or you can click the Insert Chart button on the Standard toolbar. You can also link or embed a chart from an Excel workbook.

Step 2: **The Default Chart**

- The default datasheet and chart should be displayed on your monitor. The menus and toolbar have changed to reflect the Microsoft Graph application.

- Click and drag the **title bar** to move the datasheet so that you can see more of the chart, as shown in Figure 3.4b. Click and drag the borders of the datasheet to enlarge (shrink) the datasheet as appropriate. Do not be concerned if the values in your datasheet are different from those in the figure.

- Click in the cell containing "East". Type **Gift Shop** and press **Enter**. The legend changes to reflect the new entry. (We complete the data entry in the next step.)

- Click the **View Datasheet button** on the (Microsoft Graph) Standard toolbar to close the datasheet. Click the **View Datasheet button** a second time to open the datasheet.

- Click the **Legend button** on the Standard toolbar to suppress the legend on the graph. Click the **Legend button** a second time to display the legend.

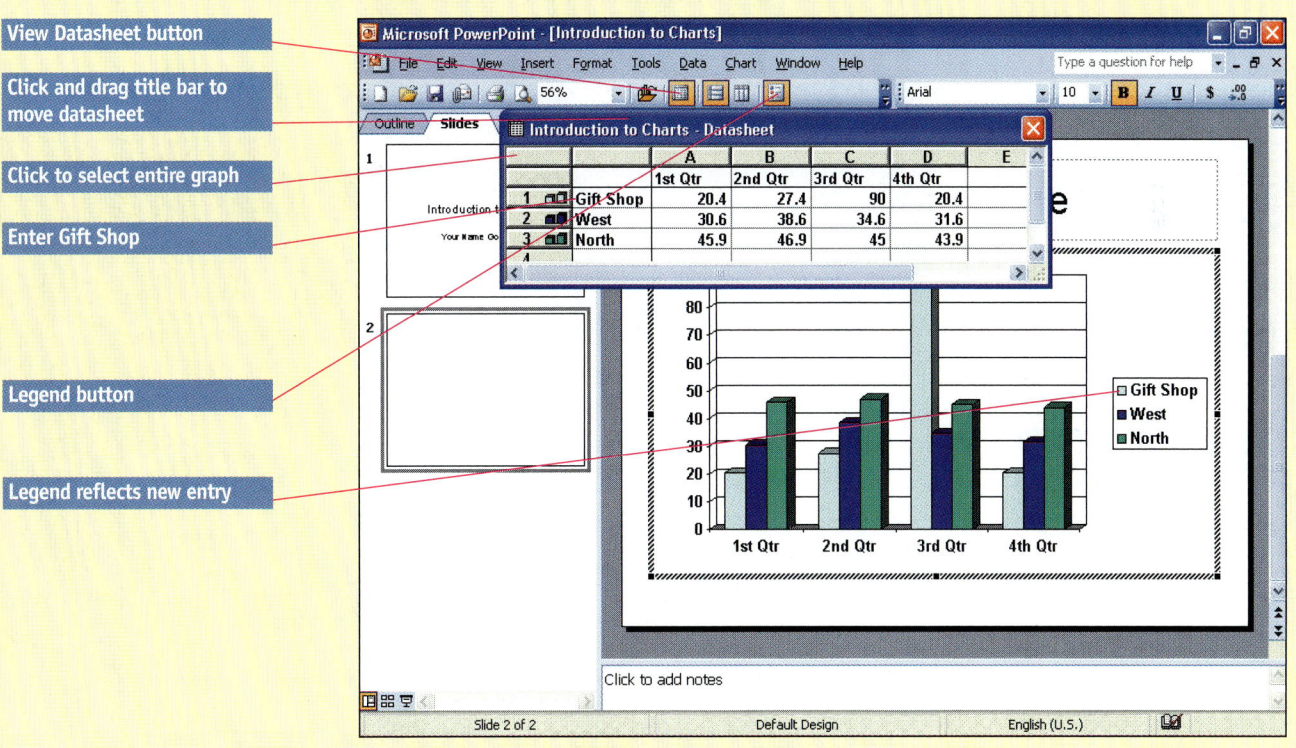

(b) The Default Chart (step 2)

FIGURE 3.4 Hands-on Exercise 2 (*continued*)

IMPORT THE DATA

Microsoft Graph enables you to import data from Microsoft Excel and use that data as the basis for the chart. (You should know the name of the workbook, the appropriate worksheet in that workbook, and the cell range in that worksheet prior to importing the data.) Start Microsoft Graph, click in the upper left square (the area above row 1 and to the left of column A) to select the entire datasheet, then click the Import File button on the Microsoft Graph toolbar to display the Import File dialog box. Select the appropriate drive and folder containing the workbook you want to import, select the file, specify the worksheet and associated range, then click OK. (See practice exercise 6 at the end of the chapter.)

Step 3: **Change the Data**

- Close the left pane and give yourself more room in which to work. (You can reopen the left pane at any time by clicking the **Normal View button** above the status bar.)

- Click in **cell A1**, the cell containing the gift shop data for the first quarter. Type **9000** and press the **Tab** or **right arrow key** to move to cell B1. The chart changes automatically to reflect the new data.

- Complete the data for the first data series (**Gift Shop**). Enter data for the next two series, (**Magazines** and **Tours**) as shown in Figure 3.4c. Enter data for the fourth series (**Seminars**) to complete the datasheet. Size the datasheet as necessary.

- Click and drag to select all of the numeric data as shown in Figure 3.4c. Click the **Currency Style button** to display a dollar sign next to each value, then click the **Decrease Decimal button** twice to eliminate the cents. Adjust the column width as necessary.

- Check that all of the values in your datasheet match those in Figure 3.4c. Close the datasheet. Save the presentation.

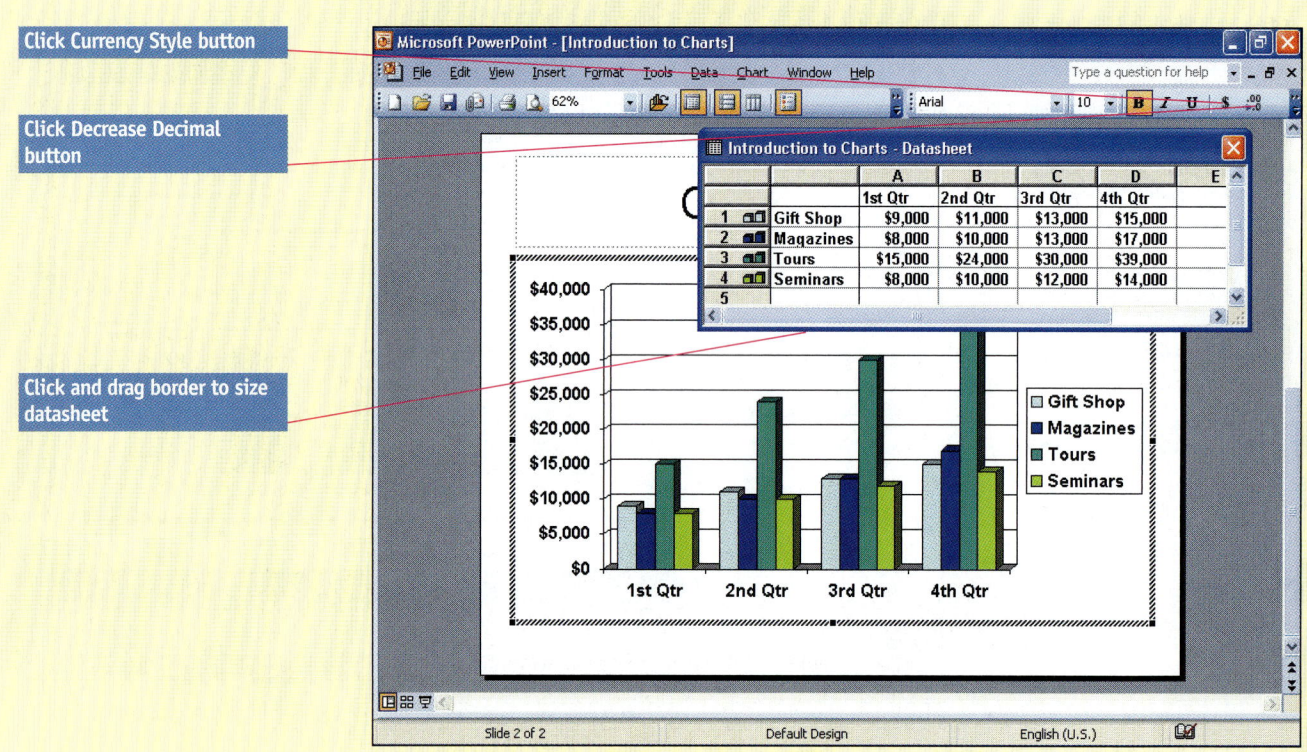

(c) Change the Data (step 3)

FIGURE 3.4   Hands-on Exercise 2 (*continued*)

REMOVING (HIDING) A DATA SERIES

Open the datasheet, right click the row number or column header of the data series you want to delete, and click the Delete command. The series disappears from both the datasheet and the associated chart. Alternatively, you can leave the data series in the datasheet, but can exclude (hide) it from the chart. Click the row number or column header to select the data series, pull down the Data menu, and select the Exclude Row/Column command. To restore the data series in the graph, select the series, pull down the Data menu, and select the Include Row/Column command.

Step 4: **Change the Orientation and Chart Type**

- Click the **By Column button** on the Standard toolbar to change the data series from rows to columns as shown in Figure 3.4d. The X axis changes to display the funding sources. The legend indicates the quarter.

- Click the **By Row button** on the Standard toolbar to change the data series back to rows. Click the **By Column button** a second time to match the orientation in Figure 3.4d.

- Pull down the **Chart menu** and click **Chart Type** to display the associated dialog box. Click the **Standard Types tab**, click **Column**, then select **Stacked column with a 3-D visual effect**.

- Check the box to preserve the **Default formatting**. Click **OK** to accept the settings and close the dialog box.

- The chart changes to a stacked column chart, which more clearly shows the total revenue from each funding source.

- Save the presentation.

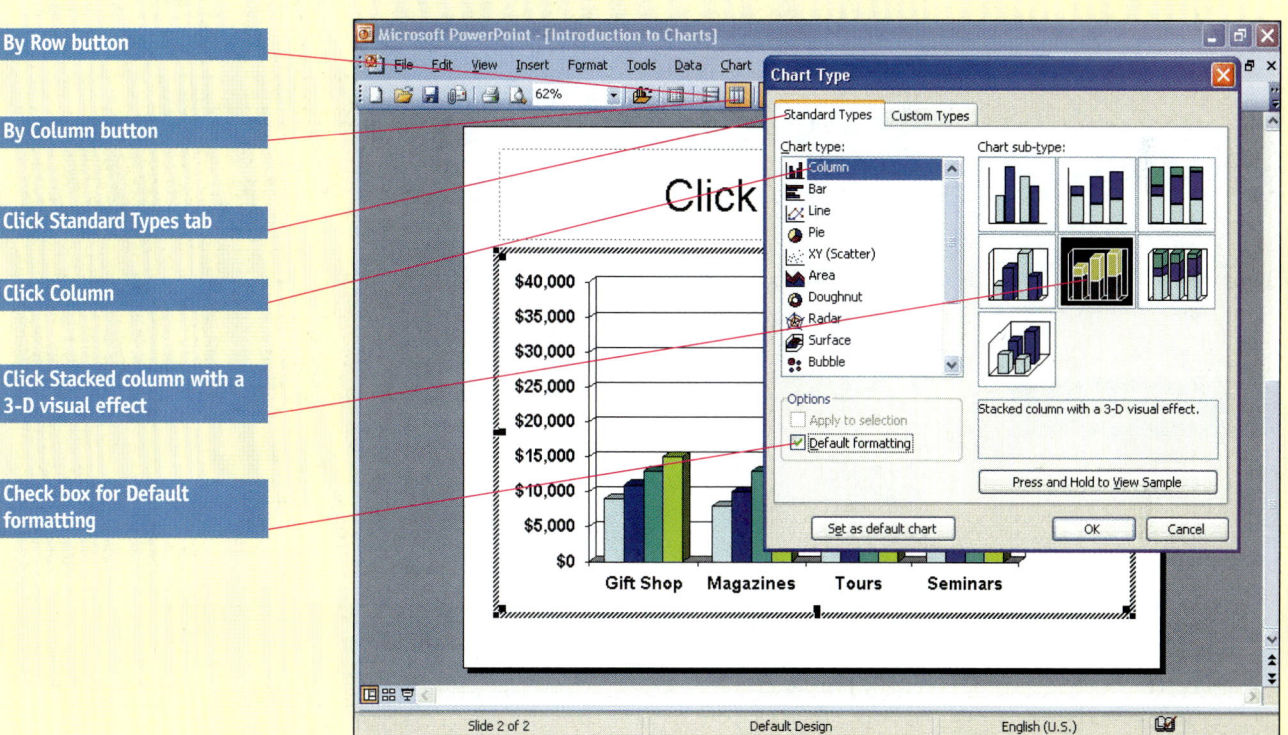

(d) Change the Orientation and Chart Type (step 4)

FIGURE 3.4 Hands-on Exercise 2 (*continued*)

TO CLICK OR DOUBLE CLICK

Once created, a chart becomes an object in a presentation that retains its connection to Microsoft Graph for easy editing. Click any object on the slide other than the chart to deselect the chart. Now click the chart once to select the chart and display the conventional sizing handles to move or size the chart just as you would any other Windows object. Double click the chart (it will be surrounded with a hashed border) to restart Microsoft Graph to edit the chart.

Step 5: **Complete the Chart**

- The chart should still be selected. Pull down the **Chart menu**, click the **Chart Options command** to display the associated dialog box, then click the **Legend tab**.
- Click the option to display the legend on the **Bottom**, then click **OK**.
- **Right click** the top section on any stacked column to display a context-sensitive menu and click the command to **Format Data Series** to display the associated dialog box.
- Click the **Patterns tab**, click **Red**, then click **OK** to change the color of this data series (the amounts for the fourth quarter) to **red**. Change the color of the next data series (the 3rd quarter) to **yellow**.
- Click outside the hashed area, then click in the title placeholder to enter the title of the slide, **Revenue by Funding Source**, as shown in Figure 3.4e.
- Save the presentation.

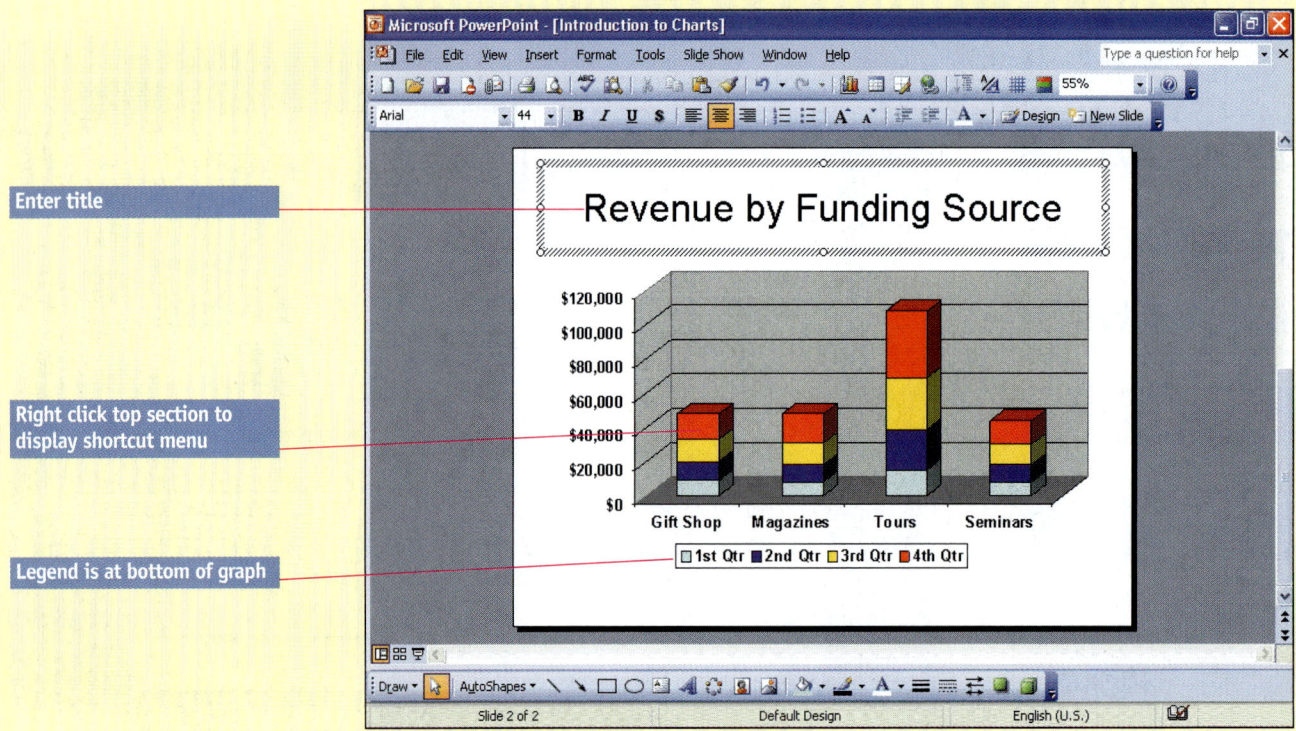

(e) Complete the Chart (step 5)

FIGURE 3.4   Hands-on Exercise 2 (*continued*)

SET A TIME LIMIT

Microsoft Graph gives you (almost too much) control over the appearance of a chart. Save the presentation before you begin, then use the Format Data Series command to change the color, shape, and pattern and/or add labels to columns within a chart. Use the Undo command if the results are different from what you expected. (If the Undo command is inoperative, you can always use the Chart Type command to return to the default formatting.) It is fun to experiment, but set a time limit and stick to it! Remember, too, that the type of chart is more important than the formatting.

Step 6: **Copy the Chart**

- Click the **Normal View button** to restore the left pane in Figure 3.4f. Click (select) the slide containing the chart. Click the **Copy button** (or press **Ctrl+C**) to copy the slide to the clipboard.

- Click the **Paste button** (or press **Ctrl+V**) to complete the copy operation. The presentation should contain two identical charts. We will now modify the copied chart by changing its orientation.

- Select (click) the third slide if necessary. Double click the chart to start Microsoft Graph, then click the **By Row button** to display the data series by rows. The name of each quarter appears on the X axis, and the funding sources appear in the legend as shown in Figure 3.4f.

- Click outside the chart area, then click in the placeholder for the title. Change the title to **Our Revenues Are Growing**.

- Print the completed presentation for your instructor (print the slides as handouts, with three slides per page).

- Save the presentation. Exit PowerPoint if you do not want to continue with the next exercise at this time.

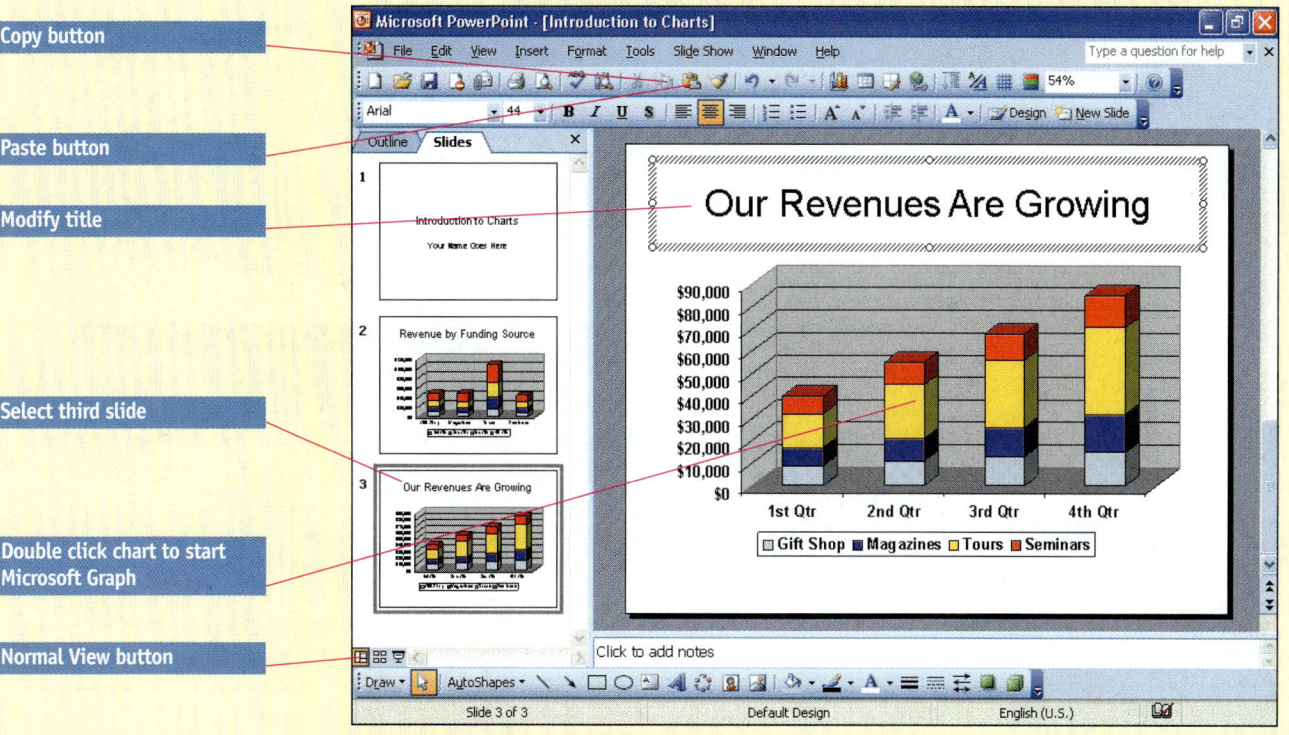

(f) Copy the Chart (step 6)

FIGURE 3.4 Hands-on Exercise 2 (*continued*)

DON'T FORGET HELP

Microsoft Graph includes its own Help system, which functions identically to the Help system in any other application. Pull down the Help menu, click Microsoft Graph Help, and search on any topic for which you want additional information. Remember, too, that you can print the contents of a help screen by clicking the Printer icon at the top of the Help window.

CUSTOM ANIMATION

Custom animation determines when and how objects appear on a slide, what they do after they appear on the screen, and how the objects are to exit. It's difficult to describe animation on a static page, but we do our best in Figure 3.5. The sequence begins in Figure 3.5a with the appearance of the title and giraffe, who walks across the screen in Figure 3.5b, after which the author's name appears on the slide. The giraffe makes his exit in Figure 3.5c, and the author's name increases in size.

The ***animation*** is accomplished through the effects specified in the task pane of Figure 3.5d. The icons are color coded—green, red, and yellow to indicate an ***entrance effect***, an ***exit effect***, and an ***emphasis effect***, respectively. The custom animation for the title is selected. The effect is "fly in," which starts on a mouse click. The object enters from the top at medium speed. Look closely and you will see a Mouse icon next to the selected animation within the task pane. Look further and you see a Clock icon next to all subsequent animations to indicate that the animations take place automatically one after another. The ***advanced timeline*** shows the sequence and duration of each effect.

(a) Giraffe Entering

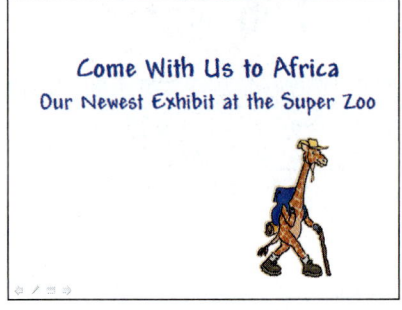

(b) Giraffe Walking

(c) Ending Slide

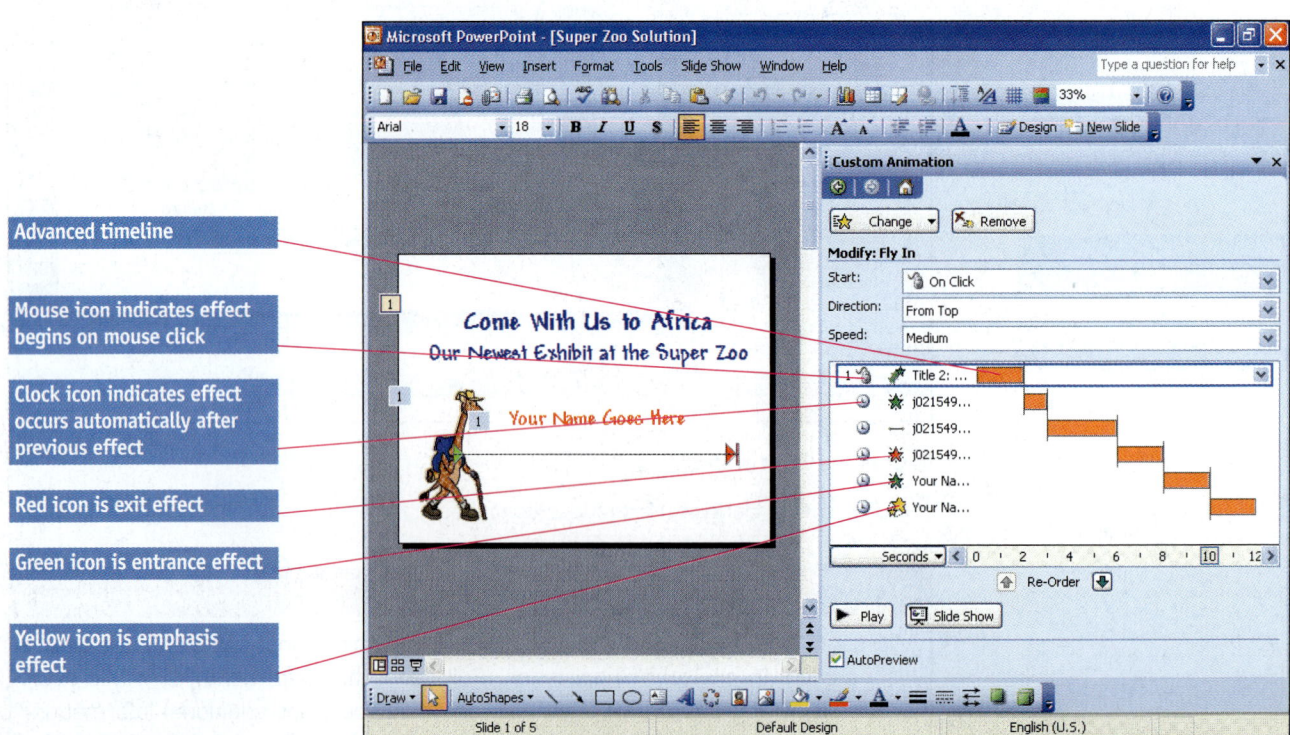

(d) Custom Animation Task Pane

FIGURE 3.5 Custom Animation (title slide)

Animating a Chart

Figure 3.6 displays an animation series in conjunction with a chart. The various categories (the stacked columns) appear sequentially upon a series of mouse clicks, after which the title increases in size. Figure 3.6a shows the slide with just the title, Figure 3.6b shows the slide after two columns have appeared, and Figure 3.6c shows the completed slide, with an enlarged title. The corresponding animation task pane is shown in Figure 3.6d. The green and yellow icons indicate entrance and emphasis effects, respectively.

The Mouse icons within the task pane indicate that the entrance of each column (category) takes place in conjunction with a mouse click. The Clock icon next to the title object, however, indicates that this effect follows automatically after the previous effect—i.e., the title appears automatically after the last column is displayed. The title animation is selected in the task pane and the details for the animation appear toward the top of the task pane. The title will grow to 150% of its size at a medium speed. Note, too, that you can select any effect, then use the up and down arrows to reorder the sequence in which the objects appear.

(a) Title Only

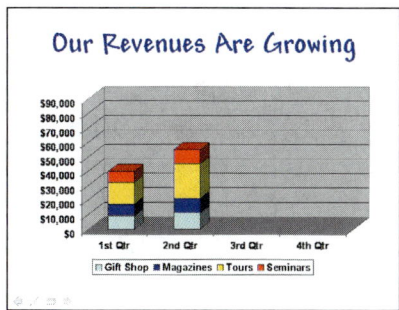

(b) After Two Categories

(c) Ending Slide

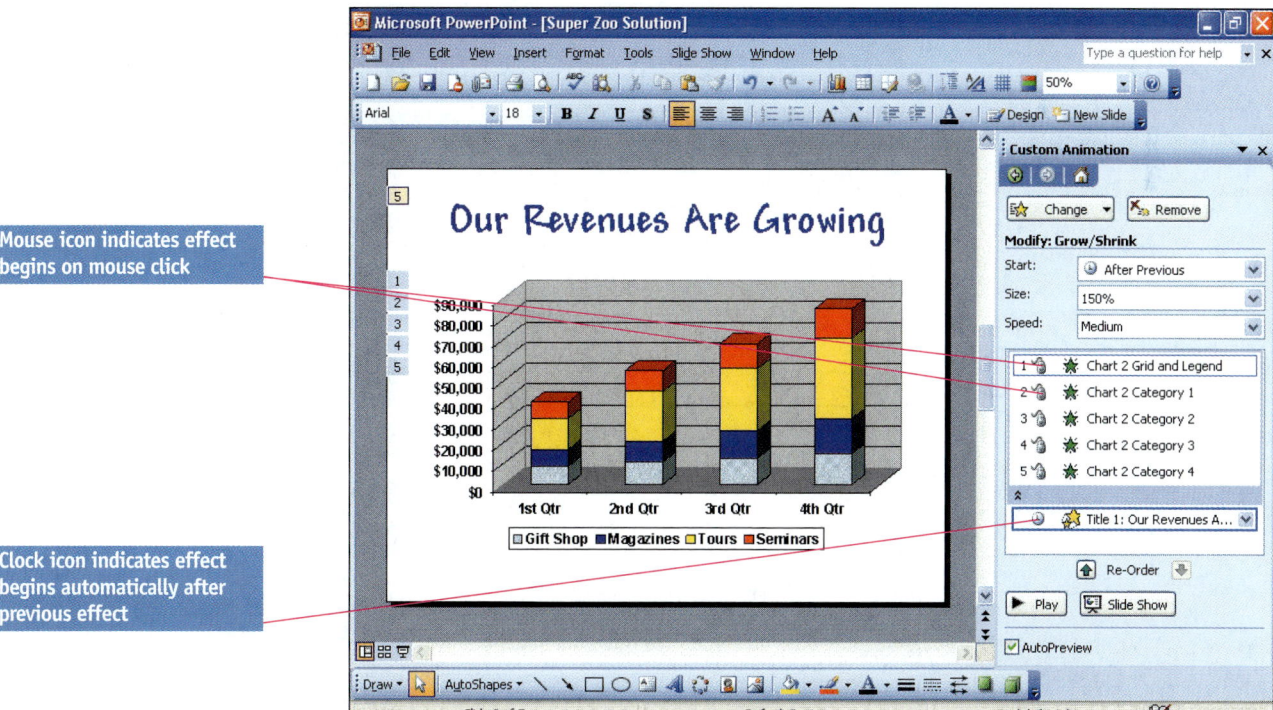

(d) Custom Animation Task Pane

FIGURE 3.6 Custom Animation (the chart)

MICROSOFT OFFICE POWERPOINT 2003

Animating an Organization Chart

Figure 3.7 displays an animation sequence in conjunction with an organization chart for the Super Zoo. (The chart contains the same boxes as previously, but the coloring is different to illustrate the variation that is possible within a specific chart.) The intent of this example is to show the organization of the zoo, one level at a time. Figure 3.7a displays the title of the chart with a single box to represent the zoo as a whole. Figure 3.7b introduces the second level, with the African exhibit shown in a different color. Figure 3.7c displays the third (and last) level of the organization chart.

The task pane to create this animation is shown in Figure 3.7d. The Mouse icon indicates that each level enters on a mouse click. Thus, the mouse is clicked once to display the highest-level box (Super Zoo). The mouse is clicked a second time to bring in the boxes at the second level (Asian Exhibit, Aviary, Australian Exhibit, and African Exhibit). The mouse is clicked a third and last time to bring in the third (lowest) level. Note, too, that each branch of the organization chart is shown in a different color to emphasize the different exhibits within the zoo.

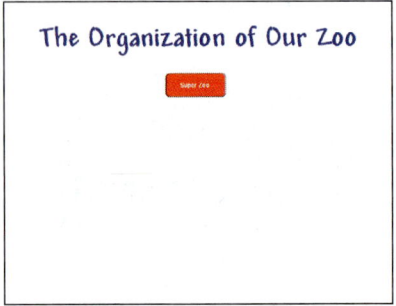

(a) Level 1

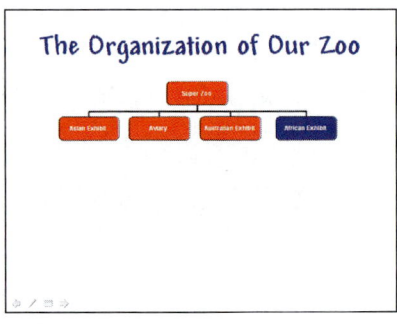

(b) Level 2

(c) Level 3

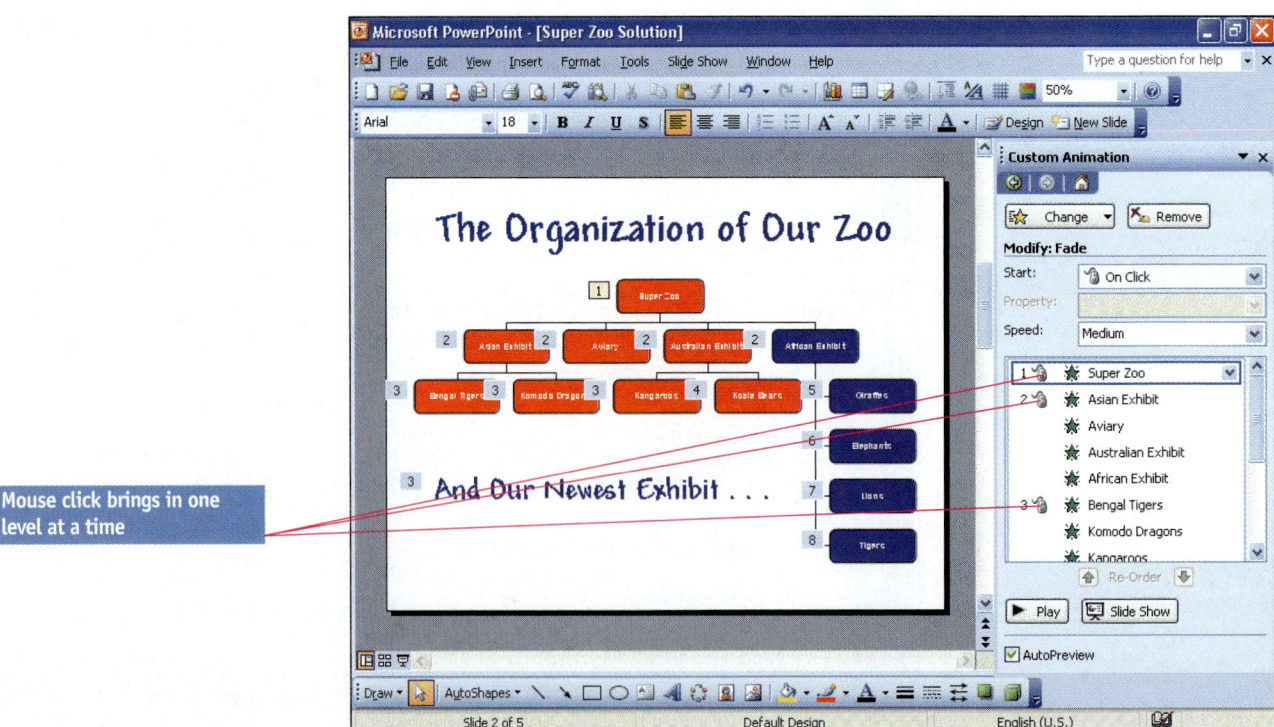

(d) Custom Animation Task Pane

FIGURE 3.7 Custom Animation (organization chart)

1830 CHAPTER 3: ANIMATING A PRESENTATION

hands-on exercise

3 Custom Animation

Objective Add custom animation to individual objects on a slide; use custom animation to animate an organization chart and a graphical chart.

Step 1: **Insert a Slide**

- Start PowerPoint. Open the **Super Zoo presentation** in the **Exploring PowerPoint folder**. Add your name to the title slide.

- Pull down the **Insert menu**, click the **Slides from Files command** to display the Slide Finder dialog box in Figure 3.8a.

- Click the **Browse button** and open the **Diagrams and Organization Charts presentation** from the first hands-on exercise. Select the **organization chart**, then click the **Insert button** to insert this slide into the presentation.

- Click the **Browse button** a second time, but this time select the **Introduction to Charts presentation** from the second exercise. Insert the chart that plots **revenue by quarter** (the second chart). Close the Slide Finder dialog box.

- Save the presentation as **Super Zoo Solution** in the **Exploring PowerPoint folder**.

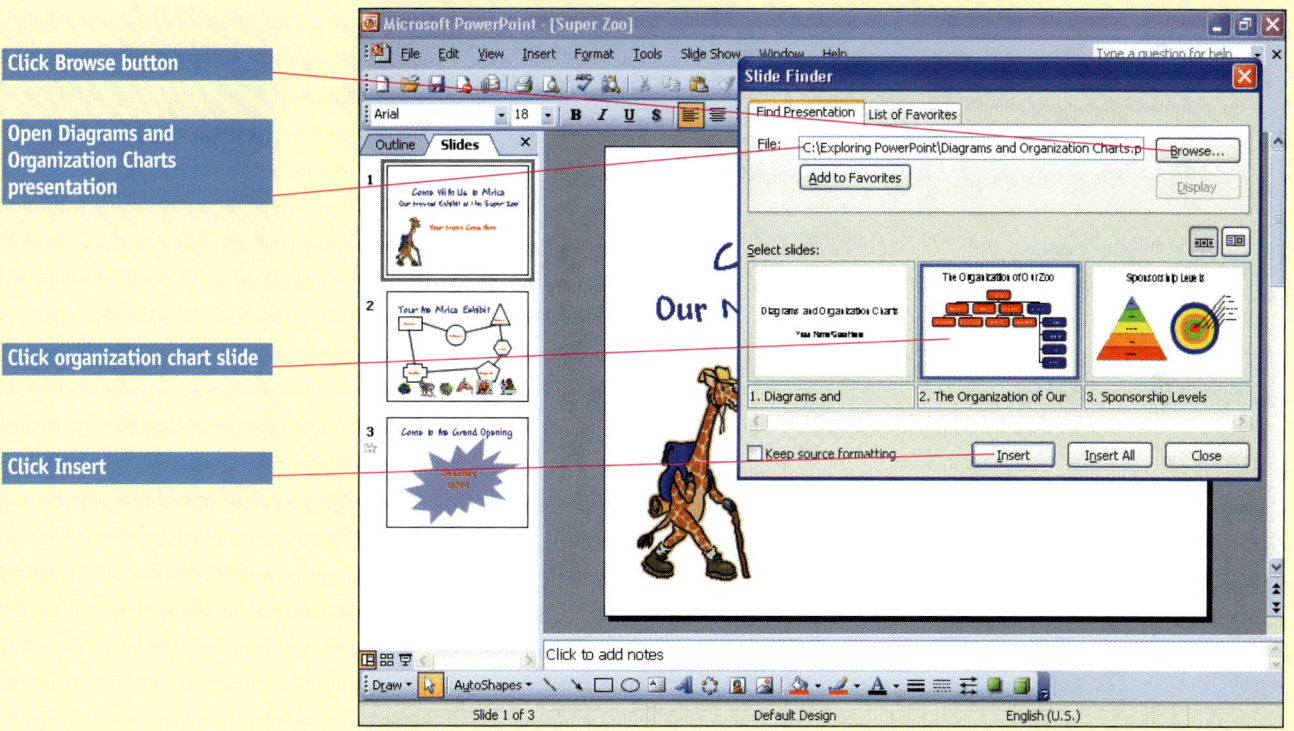

(a) Insert a Slide (step 1)

FIGURE 3.8 Hands-on Exercise 3

CREATE A NEW FOLDER

Pull down the File menu, click the Open or Save As command as appropriate, then click the Create New Folder button to display the New Folder dialog box. Enter the name of the new folder, then click OK. Use the Look In box to change to the new folder the next time you open a document.

Step 2: **Animate the Title Slide**

- The font for the slide titles of the newly inserted slides does not match the font on the title slide. Use the **Format Painter** to copy the font (**Andy**, **54-point**, **blue**) from the title slide to the inserted slides.

- Select the title slide. Pull down the **Slide Show menu** and click the **Custom Animation command** to open the task pane as shown in Figure 3.8b.

- Click anywhere in the title to select the title. Click the **Add Effect button** in the task pane, click **Entrance**, and click the **Fly In** effect. The title flies in from the bottom of the slide (the default position).

- Modify the parameters for the Fly In effect by clicking the **down arrows** in the appropriate list boxes. Set the direction to **From Top** and the speed to **Medium**. Click the **Play button** to see how these parameters modify the animation.

- Select the **giraffe**. Click the **Add Effect button**, choose the **Dissolve In** entrance effect, change the start to **After Previous**, and set the speed to **Fast**. A second effect appears in the task pane.

- Save the presentation.

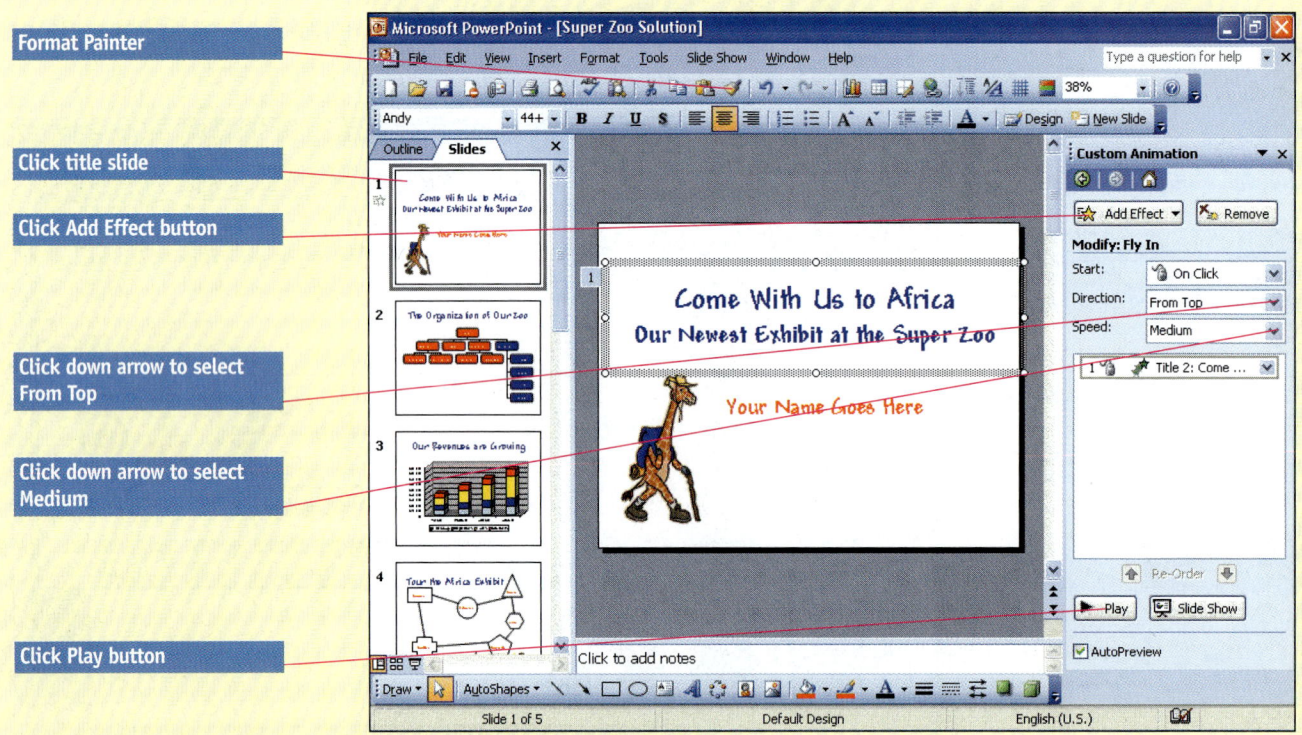

(b) Animate the Title Slide (step 2)

FIGURE 3.8   Hands-on Exercise 3 (*continued*)

YOU'RE THE DIRECTOR

No one ever said that animating a presentation was quick or easy. It takes time, more time than you might expect initially, as each slide has to be choreographed in detail. Think of yourself as the director who must tell the actors (the objects on a slide) when to come on stage and how to make their entrance. Try to think of the overall performance, and then develop one object at a time. Save the presentation continually as you add new effects. Click the Undo command anytime the result is not what you intended it to be.

Step 3: **Complete the Animation**

- Close the left pane to give yourself more room in which to work as shown in Figure 3.8c. Add the animation effects in the order below. Set each effect to start **After Previous effect**:
  - A **motion path to the right** for the giraffe at **slow speed**. (Increase the length of the motion path by dragging the line on the red arrow to the right.)
  - The giraffe should **dissolve out** (exit effect) at a **medium speed**.
  - Your name should dissolve in at **medium speed**.
  - Your name should **grow 150 percent** (emphasis effect) at **medium speed**.

- Click the **down arrow** on the last effect in the task pane. Set the option to **Show Advanced timeline**, then click the **left arrow** below the timeline so that you see the entire sequence. Increase the width of the task pane to see the timeline for all animations.

- Select the first effect, then click the **Play button** to view the animation for the entire slide. (You can modify any existing effect by selecting the effect in the task pane, and clicking the **Change button**.)

- Save the presentation.

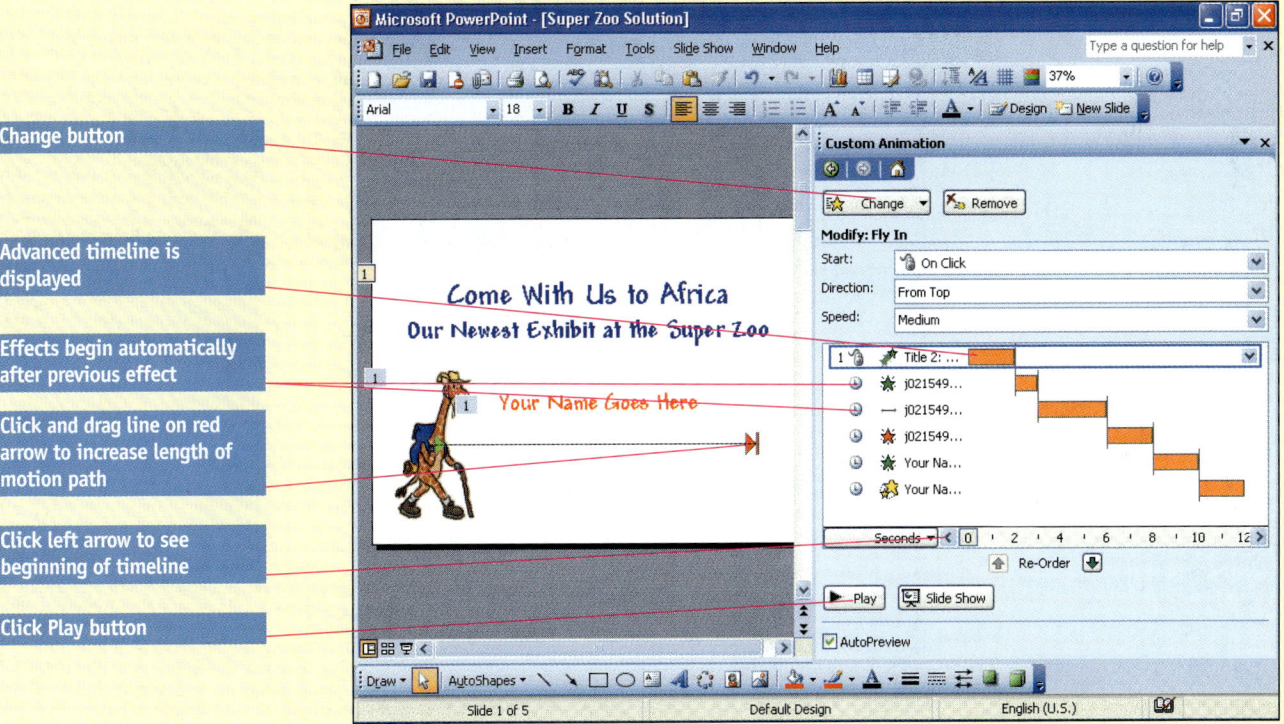

(c) Complete the Animation (step 3)

FIGURE 3.8   Hands-on Exercise 3 (*continued*)

THE CUSTOM ANIMATION TASK PANE

The icon next to each effect in the custom animation task pane indicates when the effect is to appear within the animation sequence. A Mouse icon indicates that the effect begins with a mouse click, whereas the Clock icon shows that the effect will appear automatically after the previous effect. The absence of an icon means that the effect will start simultaneously with the previous effect. Note, too, that the various effects are color coded, where green, red, and yellow denote an entrance, exit, and emphasis effect, respectively.

Step 4: **Animate the Organization Chart**

- Press the **PgDn key** to move to the second slide (the slide with the organization chart). Click the **Text Box tool** on the Drawing toolbar, then click and drag to create a text box at the bottom of the slide.

- Enter the text of the box "**And Our Newest Exhibit . . .**" as shown in Figure 3.8d. Change the font to match the font on the title of the slide, albeit in a smaller point size.

- If necessary, open the Custom Animation task pane. Select the text box, and then add the **Fade entrance effect**, at **Medium speed**, to begin **After Previous effect**. Now click anywhere in the organization chart to make it the active object, and add the **Fade entrance effect**.

- Click the **down arrow** next to the Organization Chart animation in the task pane. Click **Effect Options** to display the Fade dialog box as shown in Figure 3.8d, then click the **Diagram Animation tab**. Click the **down arrow** in the Group diagram list box, select **Each branch, shape by shape**, and click **OK**.

- The Organization Chart animation should be selected. Change the start of the animation to **After Previous**. Click the **Play button** to see the animation thus far.

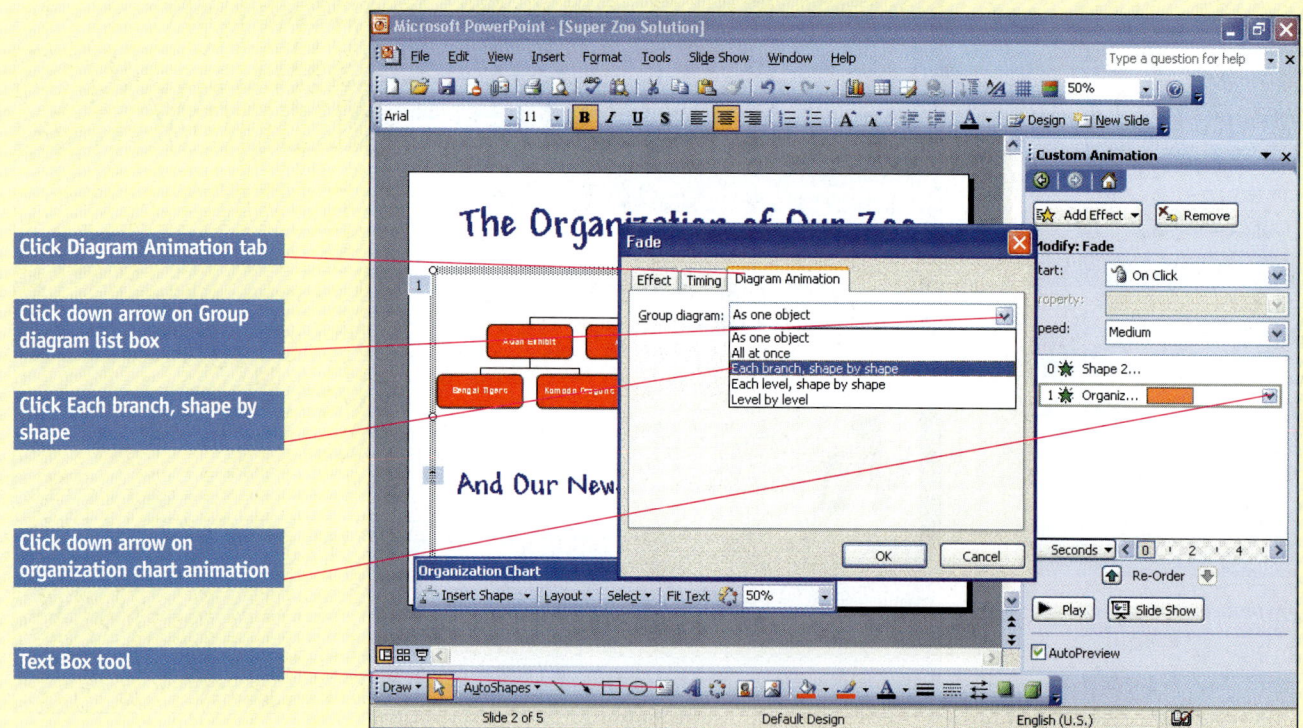

(d) Animate the Organization Chart (step 4)

FIGURE 3.8 Hands-on Exercise 3 (*continued*)

ANIMATING DIAGRAMS

Each shape in an organization chart requires its own animation effect if the shapes are to appear individually. You do not, however, have to apply the effects individually. Select the entire chart and apply an entrance effect, then go to the Custom Animation task pane, click the arrow on the effect, click the Effect Options command, click the Diagram Animation tab, and choose the type of animation. You can animate each branch shape by shape or each level shape by shape.

Step 5: **Change the Animation Sequence**

- We will change the animation sequence so that the text announcing the new exhibit appears prior to the entrance of the associated branch in the organization chart.
- Click the **double arrow (chevron)** in the animation pane. The single effect for the chart expands to display the animation of the individual boxes as shown in Figure 3.8e.
- Select the animation effect for **Shape 29** (the number on your text box may be different from ours).
- Click the **Reorder down arrow** repeatedly until this effect is immediately above the **African Exhibit**. Click the **Play button** to test the presentation.
- The blocks in the organization chart should come in sequentially (top to bottom, one branch at a time), until you see the box for **Koala Bears**.
- You should then see the text for the newest exhibit, after which you will see the branch for the **African exhibit**.
- Save the presentation.

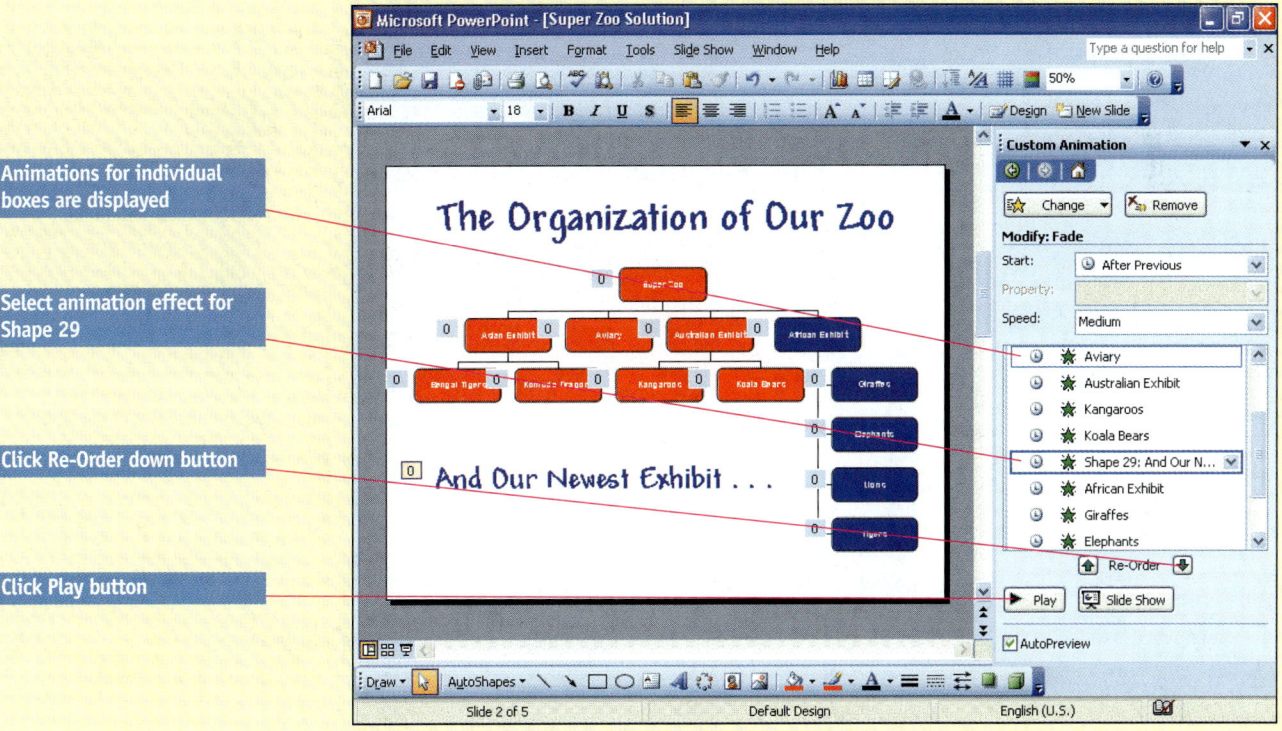

(e) Change the Animation Sequence (step 5)

FIGURE 3.8 Hands-on Exercise 3 (continued)

DELETE THE EFFECT NOT THE OBJECT

Click any object on a slide to select the object and display the associated sizing handles. This action also selects the associated animation effect (if any) in the Custom Animation task pane by surrounding the descriptive text with a rectangle. Be careful, however, about pressing the Del key; pressing the Del key when the object is selected deletes both the object and the animation affect. To delete the animation, but retain the object, click off (deselect) the object, click (select) the animation effect, then press the Del key. Use the Undo command if you make a mistake and try again.

Step 6: Animate the Chart

- Press the **PgDn key** to move to the slide containing the chart. Select the chart.
- Click the **Add Effect button** in the task pane and choose the **Fade entrance effect** at **Medium speed**.
- Click the **down arrow** next to the chart animation in the task pane, click **Effect Options** to display the Fade dialog box, and click the **Chart Animation tab**. Click the **down arrow** in the Group chart list box and select **By Category**.
- Clear the box to **animate the grid and legend**. Click **OK**. You should see the columns appear one at a time as the effect is previewed automatically. Click the **chevron** in the animation task pane to see the individual animations.
- Select the title of the slide. Click the **Add effect button**, select **Emphasis**, and then choose the **Grow/Shrink effect** as shown in Figure 3.8f. The default setting is to increase the font size 150%.
- Save the presentation.

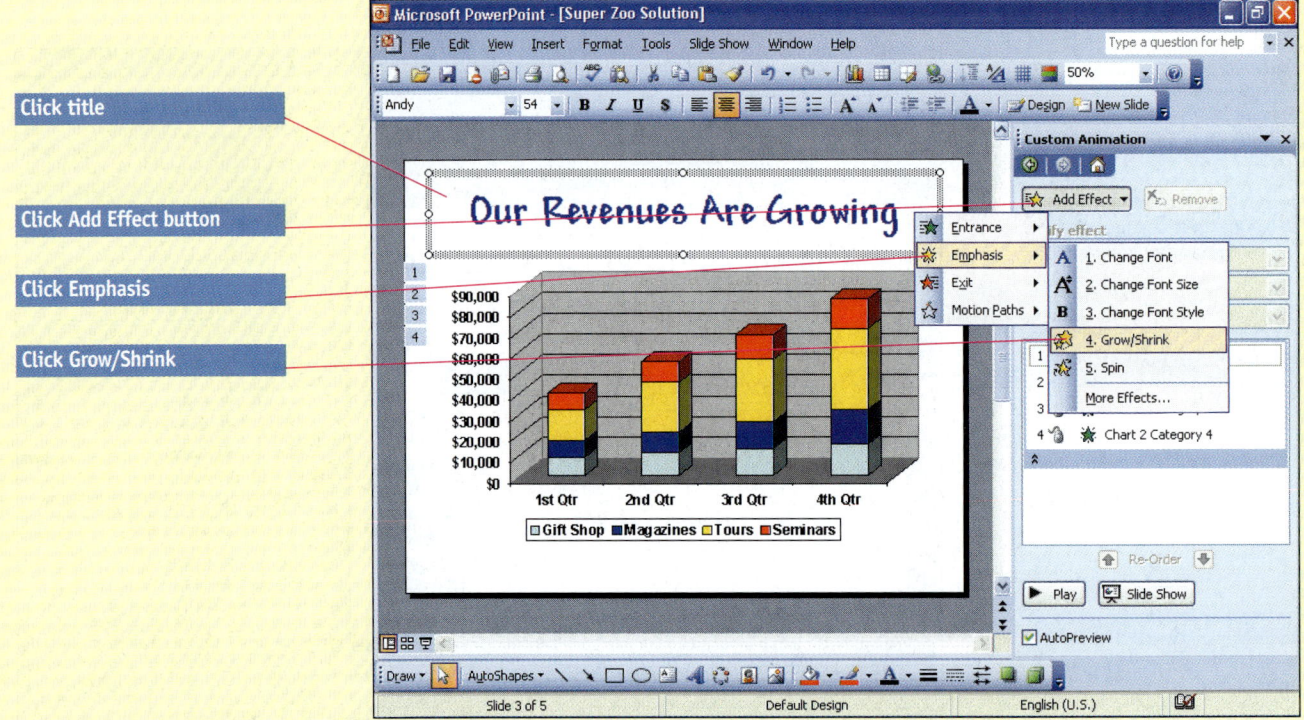

(f) Animate the Chart (step 6)

FIGURE 3.8 Hands-on Exercise 3 (*continued*)

CATEGORY VERSUS SERIES

Choose the effect that will best convey your intended message. Animating by category displays the stacked columns one column at a time, focusing on the difference between columns. Animating by series displays one element at a time from every column, emphasizing the growth of each column. Note, too, that the ability to animate a chart by its components exists only for charts created by Microsoft Graph; you cannot animate a chart that was dynamically linked to an Excel workbook.

Step 7: **Animate Multiple Objects**

- Press the **PgDn key** to move to the next slide. Press and hold the **Shift** (or **Ctrl**) **key** as you click the multiple clip art images that are on the slide.

- Click the **Add Effect button**, click **Entrance**, then click **Random Effects** to apply a different effect to each of the selected objects. The effects have been created, but you still have to set the timing.

- The first effect is set to begin on a mouse click. Press and hold the **Ctrl key** to deselect the first effect. Click the **down arrow** next to the Start list box in the animation task pane. Choose **After Previous** as shown in Figure 3.8g.

- Click and drag each animal to its appropriate place on the slide. Click the **Play button** to test the animation.

- Click the **Slide Show button**, then click the mouse to begin the animation. Note the movement within the elephant and lion after these (animated GIF) objects appear on the screen. Press **Esc** to cancel the show and continue working.

- Save the presentation.

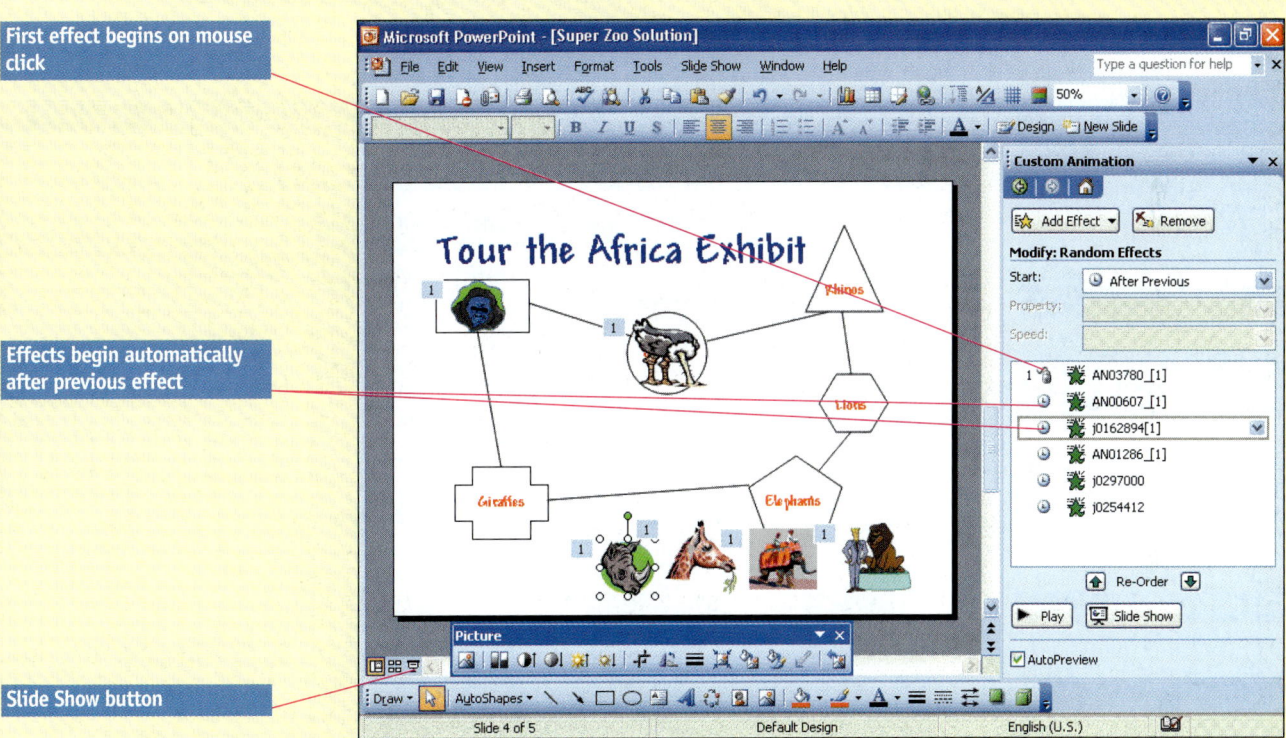

(g) Animate Multiple Objects (step 7)

FIGURE 3.8 Hands-on Exercise 3 (*continued*)

USE ANIMATED GIFS

An animated GIF file, as its name implies, adds motion to the associated clip art. Click the Insert Clip Art button on the Drawing toolbar to open the task pane. Click the down arrow in the Results Should be list box, then clear the check boxes next to all four major categories: clip art, photographs, movies, and sound. Expand the Movie category and check the box for an animated GIF file. Click in the Search text box, type "animal", then click the Go button to look for animated GIF files related to animals. Remember to reset the search criteria (i.e., check the high-level box for all media types) the next time you insert clip art.

Step 8: **Create the Explosion**

- Press the **PgDn key** to move to the last slide. Click in the left pane, click the down arrow in the **Zoom box**, and change the magnification to **33%**. You may be surprised to see that there is an AutoShape above the actual slide as shown in Figure 3.8h.

- The animation effects for this object have been set. The object will zoom in from the screen center, at a very fast speed, to the sound of an explosion, automatically after the previous effect.

- Select the **AutoShape**, click the **Copy button**, then click the **Paste button** to duplicate the shape. The animation effects are copied with the object.

- Click and drag the copied shape away from the original, then click and drag a sizing handle to change its size. Click the **down arrow** on the **Fill Color button** on the Drawing toolbar and change its color. Repeat this process to create 10 to 20 similar AutoShapes around the slide.

- Click the **Play button** to see the completed animation. Experiment with a different sound and/or a different timing for some of the shapes.

- Save the presentation.

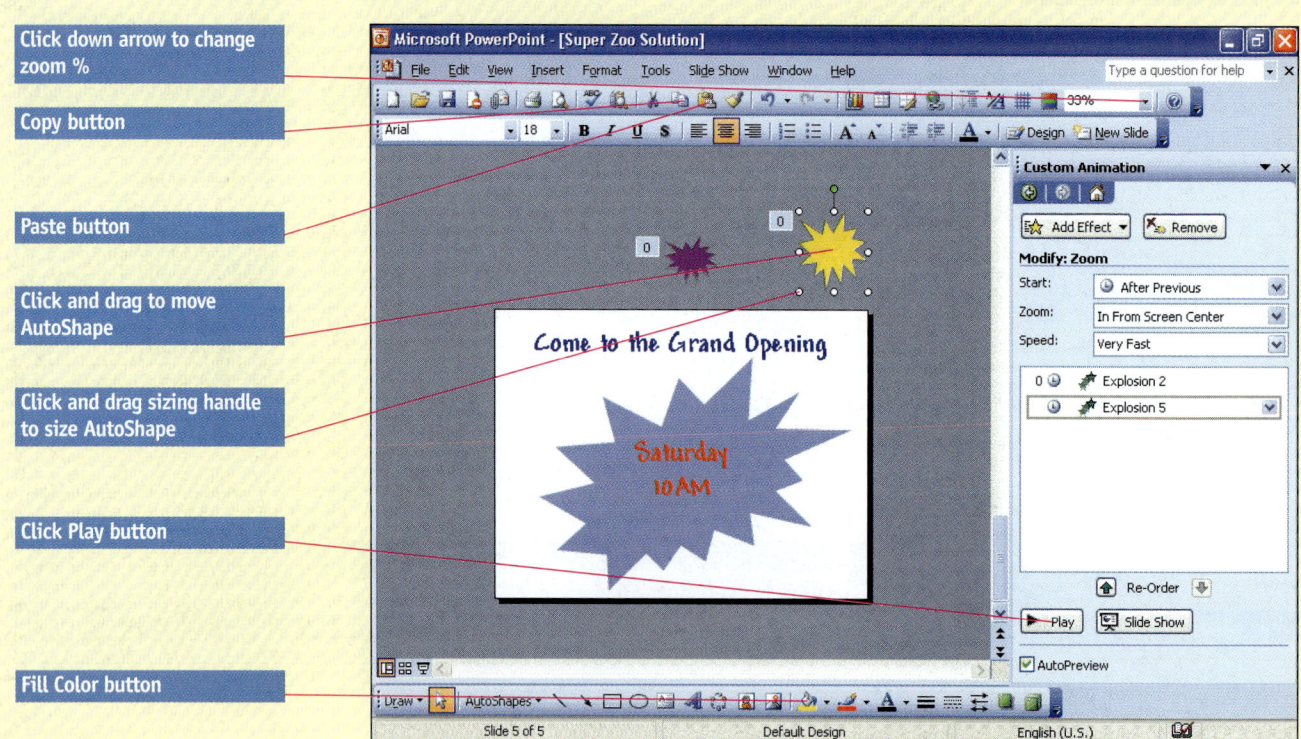

(h) Create the Explosion (step 8)

FIGURE 3.8 Hands-on Exercise 3 (*continued*)

COPY EFFICIENTLY

You start with one object and need a total of 15. You can copy and paste the individual object multiple times, or you can duplicate groups of objects. Copy the first object, then press and hold the Ctrl key to select both objects. Press Ctrl+C to copy, then Ctrl+V to paste. You now have four objects. Click and drag the copied objects to position them on the screen (you may want to select the objects individually). Now select and copy all four objects to get eight, then copy the eight, and so on.

Step 9: **Show Time**

- Close the Animation task pane. Change to the **Slide Sorter view**, where you should see five slides in the completed presentation. (The AutoShapes in the ending slide do not appear in this view, because they are off the slide.)

- Select the first slide, and click the **Slide Show button**. The screen is blank.
  - Click the mouse, the title appears, the giraffe walks across the screen in Figure 3.8i, and then your name appears.
  - Click the mouse to move to the next slide and see the animation for the organization chart. Click the mouse to move to the next slide.
  - You should see an empty chart because we opted not to animate the grid or legend. Click the mouse repeatedly to display the stacked columns for each series, then click the mouse a final time to enlarge the title. Click the mouse to move to the next slide.
  - Click the mouse to display the animals as you tour the **Africa exhibit**. Click the mouse when you are ready to move to the last slide.
  - The fireworks begin immediately. Press **Esc** when the presentation ends.

- Exit PowerPoint. Congratulations on a job well done.

Giraffe walks across screen and disappears

(i) Show Time (step 9)

FIGURE 3.8   Hands-on Exercise 3 (*continued*)

ANNOTATING A SLIDE AND OTHER KEYBOARD SHORTCUTS

Press Ctrl+P to change the mouse pointer to a point, then click and drag on the slide during the presentation to annotate the slide. Press the letter E to erase the annotations or press Ctrl+A to change the mouse pointer back to an arrow. Press Ctrl+S to display a list of the slides in a presentation, and then double click the slide you want to view. (You can also type the number of a slide followed by the Enter key to go to that slide.) If you can't remember these shortcuts, press the F1 key to see the entire list.

SUMMARY

The Diagram Gallery provides six figure types to describe different types of relationships within an organization. The diagrams include an organization chart (hierarchical relationships), a cycle diagram (continuous cycle), a radial diagram (elements around a core), a pyramid diagram (foundation relationships), a target diagram (steps toward a goal), and a Venn diagram (overlap between elements).

All diagrams are developed within the drawing canvas (an area enclosed within hashed lines) that appears automatically as you create a diagram. Additional (e.g., subordinate) shapes can be inserted, and/or existing shapes can be deleted. The appearance of the diagram as a whole can be changed through the AutoFormat command, and/or individual shapes can be formatted independently.

A chart (or graph) is a graphic representation of data that is based on numeric values called data points and descriptive entries called category labels. The data points are grouped into one or more data series that appear in rows or columns of a spreadsheet. Multiple data series are typically plotted as one of two chart types—side-by-side column charts or stacked column charts.

The choice between plotting data in rows or columns, as well as the decision on the type of chart, depends on the intended message. If the data series are in rows, Microsoft Graph will use the first row in the datasheet for the category labels on the X axis and the first column for the legend. If the data series are in columns, then Microsoft Graph will use the first column in the datasheet for the category labels on the X axis and the first row for the legend. An Excel chart can be imported into a PowerPoint presentation, and/or it can be created within the presentation. The latter is accomplished through Microsoft Graph, the default charting program for Microsoft Office that is installed automatically with PowerPoint.

Custom animation determines when and how objects appear on a slide, what they do after they appear on the screen, and how the objects are to exit. The animation is accomplished in the Custom Animation task pane. The effects in the task pane are color coded—green, red, and yellow to indicate an entrance effect, an exit effect, and an emphasis effect, respectively.

The icon next to each effect indicates when the effect is to appear within the animation sequence. A Mouse icon indicates that the effect begins with a mouse click, whereas the Clock icon shows that the effect will appear automatically after the previous effect. The absence of an icon means that the effect will start simultaneously with the previous effect. The advanced timeline shows the sequence and duration of each effect. Custom animation may be applied to charts and/or organization charts to display the series, branches, or levels individually, as opposed to displaying the entire object at one time.

KEY TERMS

Advanced timeline 1828	Data series 1819	Organization chart 1810
Animation 1828	Datasheet 1819	Pyramid diagram 1810
AutoFormat tool 1810	Diagram Gallery 1810	Radial diagram 1810
Category labels 1819	Drawing canvas 1810	Side-by-side column charts 1819
Chart 1819	Emphasis effect 1828	Stacked column charts 1819
Custom animation 1828	Entrance effect 1828	Target diagram 1810
Cycle diagram 1810	Exit effect 1828	Venn diagram 1810
Data points 1819	Microsoft Graph 1819	

MULTIPLE CHOICE

1. Which diagram type is recommended to show hierarchical relationships?
   (a) Organization chart
   (b) Pyramid diagram
   (c) Venn diagram
   (d) Radial diagram

2. You have created an organization chart with two levels. The president is at the top and there are three vice presidents. How do you add a fourth vice president?
   (a) Click in the President box and add an assistant
   (b) Click in the rightmost vice president's box and add a coworker
   (c) Both (a) and (b)
   (d) Neither (a) nor (b)

3. Which of the following best describes the formatting options for a diagram?
   (a) The entire diagram can be formatted as a single object using AutoFormat
   (b) Individual shapes can be selected and formatted independently
   (c) Both (a) and (b)
   (d) Neither (a) nor (b)

4. Which of the following *cannot* be accomplished using the Change to button on the Diagram toolbar?
   (a) Change an organization chart to a cycle diagram
   (b) Change a cycle diagram to a radial diagram
   (c) Change a radial diagram to a pyramid diagram
   (d) Change a pyramid diagram to a Venn diagram

5. Which of the following is true regarding custom animation?
   (a) An object may have an entrance effect but not an exit effect
   (b) An object may have an exit effect but not an entrance effect
   (c) An object may have both an entrance effect and an exit effect
   (d) An object may have neither an entrance effect nor an exit effect

6. Which of the following best describes the colors associated with custom animation effects?
   (a) Red, green, and yellow for entrance, exit, and emphasis, respectively
   (b) Red, yellow, and green for entrance, exit, and emphasis, respectively
   (c) Green, red, and yellow for entrance, exit, and emphasis, respectively
   (d) Green, yellow, and red for entrance, exit, and emphasis, respectively

7. Which of the following parameters is *not* specified in conjunction with the "Fly in" entrance effect?
   (a) The direction (e.g., top or bottom)
   (b) The speed (e.g., fast or slow)
   (c) The starting time (e.g., on a mouse click or after the previous animation)
   (d) The exit path

8. Which of the following animations is available for an organization chart?
   (a) A branch at a time and shape by shape within the branch
   (b) A level at a time and shape by shape within the level
   (c) As a single object (the entire chart comes in at once)
   (d) All of the above

9. What happens if you click the View Datasheet button on the Microsoft Graph toolbar twice in a row?
   (a) The datasheet is closed (hidden)
   (b) The datasheet is opened (displayed)
   (c) The datasheet is in the same status as it was before it was clicked
   (d) Impossible to determine

10. Which of the following is true of data series that are plotted in rows?
    (a) The first row in the datasheet contains the category names for the X axis
    (b) The first column in the datasheet contains the legend
    (c) Both (a) and (b)
    (d) Neither (a) nor (b)

... continued

multiple choice

11. Which of the following is true of data series that are plotted in columns?
    (a) The first column in the datasheet contains the category names for the X axis
    (b) The first row in the datasheet contains the legend
    (c) Both (a) and (b)
    (d) Neither (a) nor (b)

12. How do you create a new slide containing a chart?
    (a) Add a blank slide, pull down the Insert menu, and click the Chart command
    (b) Add a blank slide, then click the Insert Chart button on the Standard toolbar
    (c) Add a blank slide, select a slide layout that contains a chart, then double click the placeholder for the chart in the Slide view
    (d) All of the above

13. Which effect will display the columns in a stacked column chart one at a time?
    (a) Animation by series
    (b) Animation by category
    (c) Animation by elements in a series
    (d) Animation by elements in a category

14. Custom Animation enables you to:
    (a) Specify a different animation effect for each object on a slide
    (b) Change the order in which the objects appear on a slide
    (c) Both (a) and (b)
    (d) Neither (a) nor (b)

15. You are working on an organization chart. The hashed border surrounds the drawing canvas, but none of the objects in the chart is selected. What happens if you press the Del key?
    (a) The entire organization chart is deleted
    (b) The slide itself is deleted
    (c) The last box selected is deleted
    (d) Nothing, since no objects are selected within the drawing area

16. Which type of diagram is *not available* in the Diagram Gallery?
    (a) Pyramid diagram
    (b) Cycle diagram
    (c) Target diagram
    (d) Periodic table

17. What happens if you click a chart that is not currently selected?
    (a) The chart is selected
    (b) The chart is deleted
    (c) The chart is animated
    (d) The application that created the chart (e.g., Microsoft Graph) is started

18. What happens if you double click a chart that is not currently selected?
    (a) The chart is selected
    (b) The chart is deleted
    (c) The chart is animated
    (d) The application that created the chart (e.g., Microsoft Graph) is started

ANSWERS

1. a	7. d	13. b
2. b	8. d	14. c
3. c	9. c	15. a
4. a	10. c	16. d
5. c	11. c	17. a
6. c	12. d	18. d

PRACTICE WITH POWERPOINT

1. **Animation 101:** You will find a partially completed version of the presentation in Figure 3.9 in the file *Chapter 3 Practice 1* in the Exploring PowerPoint folder. Open the presentation and add the indicated animation effects on each slide. Be sure to include a sound effect where indicated. Use any trigger that you deem appropriate; that is, you can specify that the effect begins on a mouse click or after the previous effect as you see fit. Proceed as follows:

   a. Add your name on the title slide. The slide title should fly in from the top to the accompaniment of a drum roll.

   b. Slide 2 illustrates different entrance effects, each of which is denoted by a green icon in the custom animation task pane. Add sound where indicated, such as the whoosh for the last bullet.

   c. Slide 3 shows different ways to add emphasis to text. Note the specification of a typewriter sound for the last effect, which displays the letters one at a time

   d. Slide 4 contains various effects for emphasis. Once again, you have a sound effect, this time a gentle breeze.

   e. Slide 5 describes how to create motion paths.

   f. Slide 6 contains exit strategies, each of which is indicated by a red icon in the custom animation task pane.

   g. Save the completed presentation. Print the title slide as a full slide to use as a cover sheet for the assignment. Print the audience handouts of the revised presentation (six slides in all) for your instructor.

   h. View the completed presentation. Do you have a better appreciation for custom animation? Summarize your thoughts in a brief note to your instructor. Be sure to mention the different colors that are associated with entrance and exit effects in the custom animation task pane. Describe the timeline and the associated icons that show when an object appears.

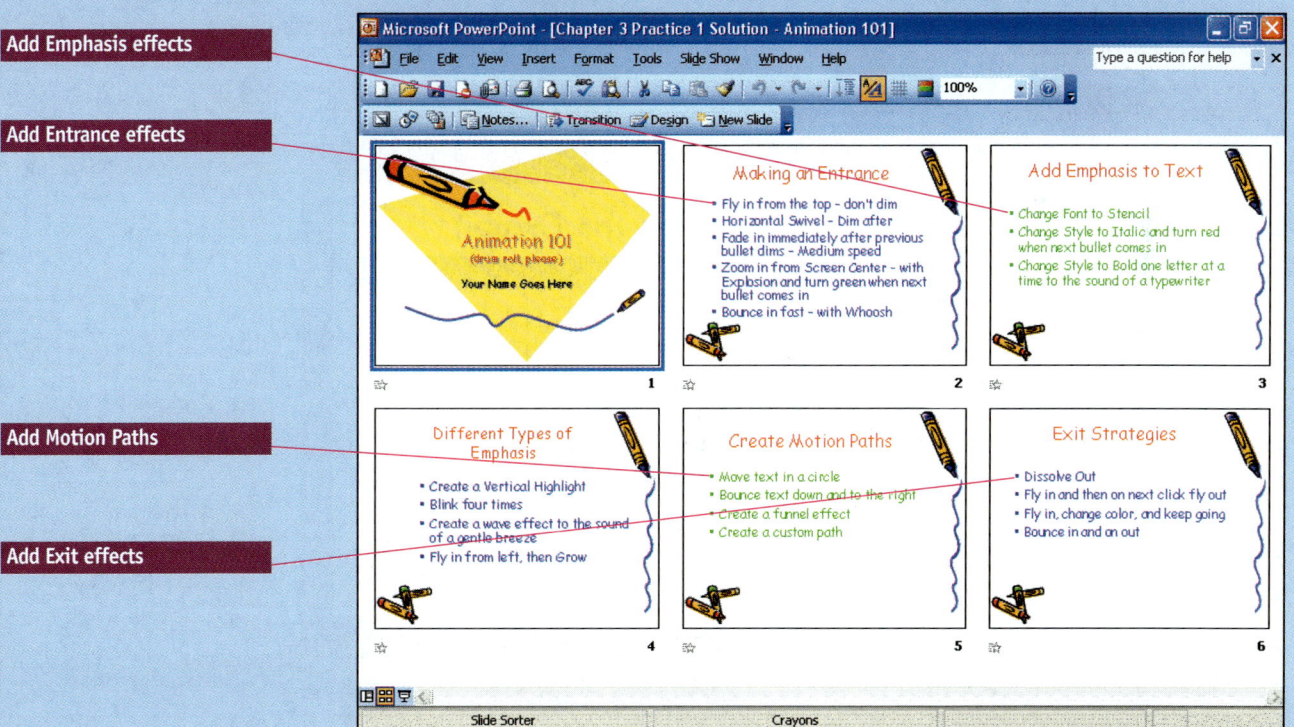

FIGURE 3.9 Animation 101 (exercise 1)

practice exercises

2. **Adding a Timeline:** Create a new slide containing the timeline in Figure 3.10 for the existing Super Zoo presentation from the third hands-on exercise. You do not have to duplicate our slide exactly, but you are required to include the equivalent functionality which includes a table, clip art, and custom animation. Proceed as follows:

   a. Open the Super Zoo presentation from the last hands-on exercise. Insert a new (title only) slide as the fourth slide in the presentation (i.e., insert the new slide after the stacked column chart). Add the title of the slide as shown in the figure.

   b. Click the Insert Table tool on the Standard toolbar to create a 2 × 12 (2 rows and 12 columns) table as shown in Figure 3.10. Click and drag the line separating the two rows in the table so that the top row is much narrower than the bottom. Click in the second row, then press Enter two or three times to increase row size.

   c. Enter the months of the year in the top row. Format the text for January, as you see fit, then use the Format Painter to copy the formatting to the remaining months.

   d. Click the AutoShapes tool on the Drawing toolbar, choose Block Arrows, and create the first arrow. Right click the arrow and click the command to add text, then enter the appropriate text as shown in the figure.

   e. Copy this arrow (or create additional arrows) so that you have four milestones on the slide. Edit the text in each arrow as necessary. Use the same formatting for all four arrows.

   f. Insert an appropriate clip art image under each arrow.

   g. Animate the completed slide so that the individual milestones appear on successive mouse clicks. Use any effects that you deem appropriate. Experiment with different speeds for each animation.

   h. Save the completed presentation. Print the title slide as a full slide to use as a cover sheet for the assignment. Print the audience handouts of the revised presentation (six slides in all) for your instructor.

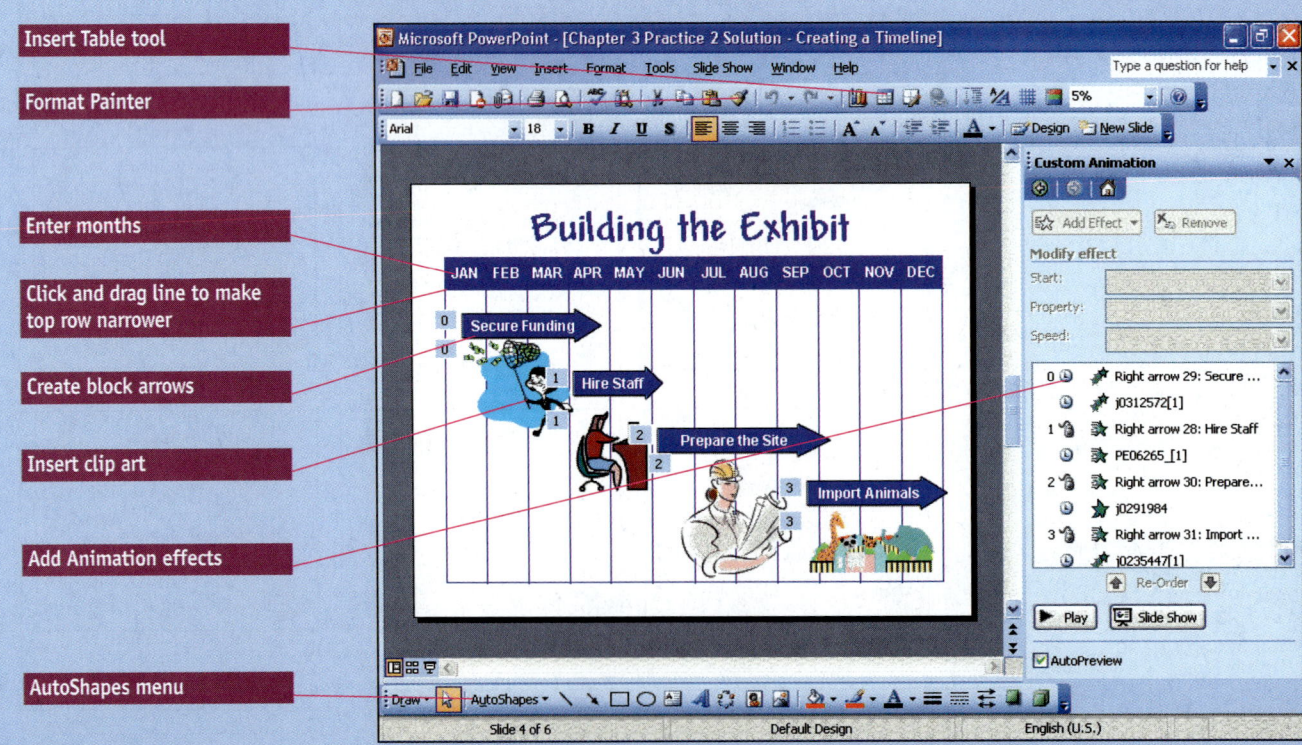

FIGURE 3.10 Adding a Timeline (exercise 2)

practice exercises

3. **Working with Photographs:** The presentation in Figure 3.11 displays a collection of photographs. All of the photographs were obtained by searching the Clip Organizer within Microsoft Office. Click the button to Insert Clip Art to open the task pane, enter "Animals" as the text for your search, then restrict the results to photographs. The command works best with an active Internet connection that extends the search to the Microsoft Web site. Proceed as follows:

   a. Start a new presentation. Create a title slide, and then insert a blank slide. Use the Insert Clip Art command as just described to locate multiple photographs for insertion on the slide. Arrange the pictures in an attractive overlapping fashion.

   b. Select all of the photographs, then use the Format Picture command to apply a black 4-point border around every picture.

   c. Check that all of the photographs are still selected. Click the Compress Photographs tool on the Picture toolbar to compress the pictures and reduce the file sizes.

   d. Click on any picture to deselect all of the pictures. Pull down the Slide Show menu, click Custom Animation, and apply individual entrance effects to each of the photographs. Set each entrance so that it begins automatically after the previous animation effect has ended.

   e. Insert a second blank slide. Create six separate WordArt objects, each of which is a single letter, (S, A, F, A, R, and I), and each of which uses a different photograph for fill. (You have to save each picture as a separate file in order to use it as background fill for a WordArt object.)

   f. Use custom animation so that the objects appear in sequence, one after the other. Include the sound of applause in conjunction with the letter i when "Safari" is spelled out completely.

   g. Print the title slide as a full slide to use as a cover sheet for the assignment. Print the presentation as an audience handout (two slides per page) for your instructor. Add a footer at the bottom of the page that includes your name.

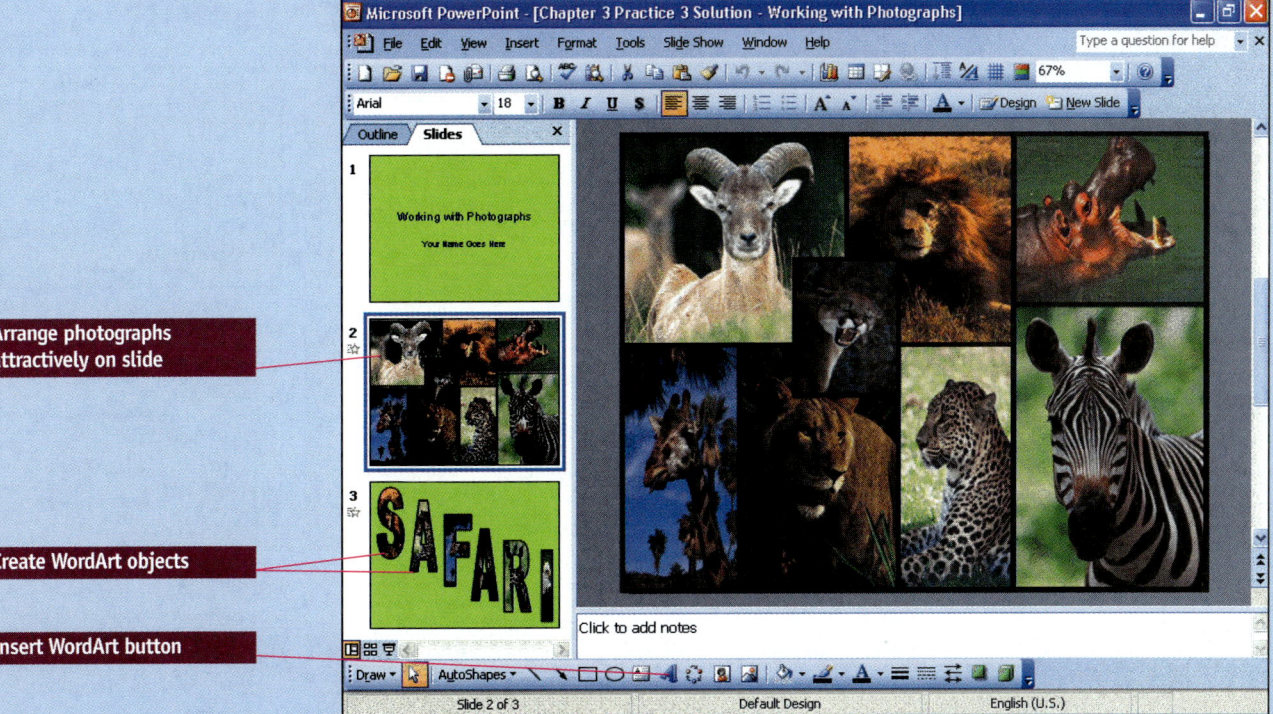

FIGURE 3.11   Working with Photographs (exercise 3)

practice exercises

4. **Organization Charts:** The presentation in Figure 3.12 illustrates various ways in which to format and/or animate an organization chart. Open the partially completed presentation in *Chapter 3 Practice 4* in the Exploring PowerPoint folder and proceed as follows.

   a. Add your name to the title slide, then choose any appropriate animation for the two text objects.

   b. Go to the second slide and create an organization chart of at least four levels. Each box in the chart should contain a title and the name of an individual. Your instructor should appear at the top of the chart as the president. You should appear at the left of the second level as the first vice president. Use the default formatting that is provided for an organization chart.

   c. Copy the chart you just created to the remaining slides in the presentation (slides 3 to 6). Set the formatting for each of these charts to the formatting depicted in Figure 3.12. Note, too, that in addition to changing the color and/or shape of the boxes, you are also to change the style. Slide 3, for example, has left hanging subordinates. Slide 4, however, has right hanging subordinates.

   d. Animate each chart according to the instructions that appear at the bottom of the slide. Slides 2 and 3 bring the chart in as a single object. Slides 4 and 5, however, bring in the shapes individually, by branch and level, respectively. Slide 6 brings in one level at a time.

   e. Save the completed presentation. Print the title slide as a full slide to use as a cover sheet for the assignment. Print the completed presentation as audience handouts (six per page) for your instructor.

   f. Do you have a better understanding of how to create and modify organization charts? Which type of animation is the most effective? Summarize your thoughts in a brief note to your instructor.

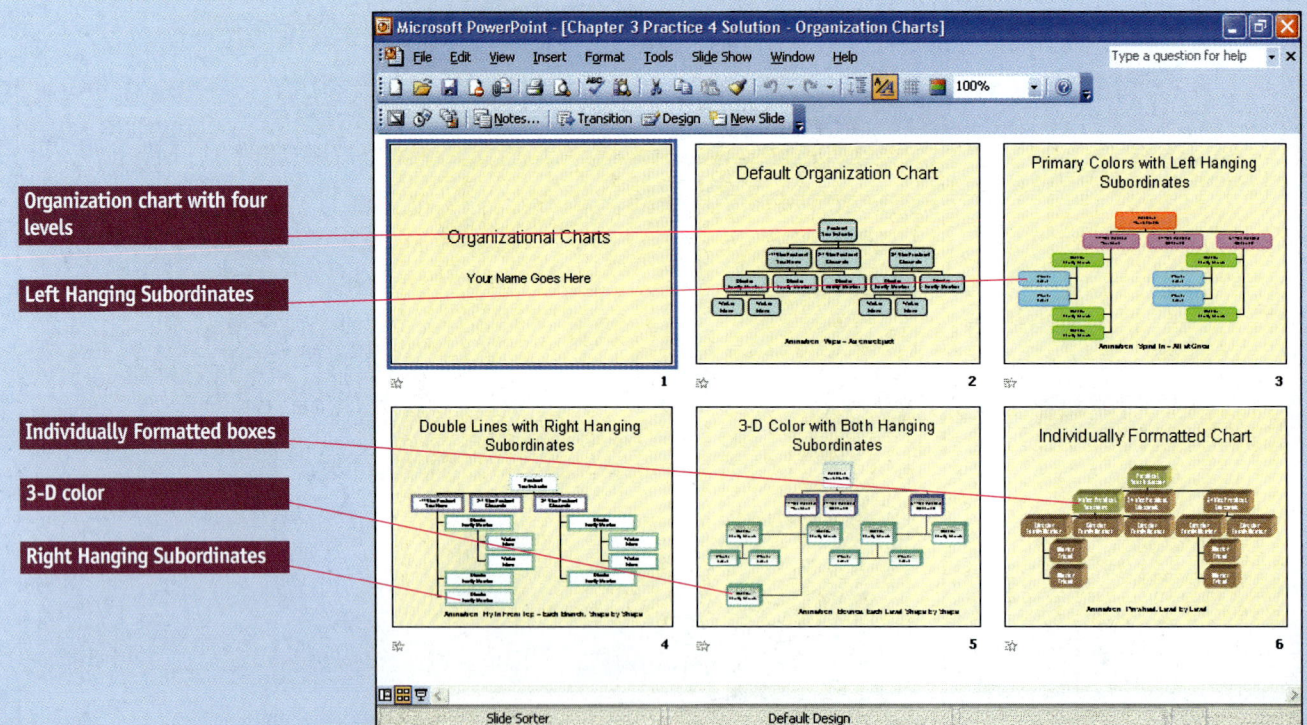

FIGURE 3.12 Organization Charts (exercise 4)

practice exercises

5. **The Diagram Gallery:** Create a six-slide presentation that is similar to the one in Figure 3.13. You do not have to match our presentation exactly, but you are required to include all of the indicated shapes. (The presentation includes all diagram types except for the organization chart.) Proceed as follows:

   a. Start a new presentation. The title slide includes the title, "The Diagram Gallery", and your name.
   b. The cycle diagram in slide 2 depicts the relationship between faculty, residential assistants (RAs), and administration. The goals of all three groups are to build community, promote personal growth, and support academic success.
   c. The target diagram illustrates fund-raising goals and associated milestones. The outer circle has a goal of $250,000 by February 1st. Each successive (smaller) circle has a higher goal in a subsequent month.
   d. The pyramid diagram illustrates Maslow's hierarchy of needs. Use your favorite search engine to locate the five levels of the hierarchy if you are unable to read the text in our figure.
   e. The Venn diagram illustrates a probability calculation.
   f. The radial diagram depicts a simple computer network. Clip art has been placed on top of each circle in the diagram.
   g. Use auto formatting and/or custom formatting to make your presentation more attractive. Add animation to each diagram as you see fit.
   h. Copy the completed diagrams to the title slide, then move and size each diagram as shown in our figure.
   i. Save the completed presentation. Print the title slide as a full slide to use as a cover sheet for the assignment. Print the completed presentation as audience handouts (six per page) for your instructor.
   j. Do you have a better understanding of the Diagram Gallery? Which type of diagram(s) will be most useful to you? Summarize your thoughts in a brief note to your instructor.

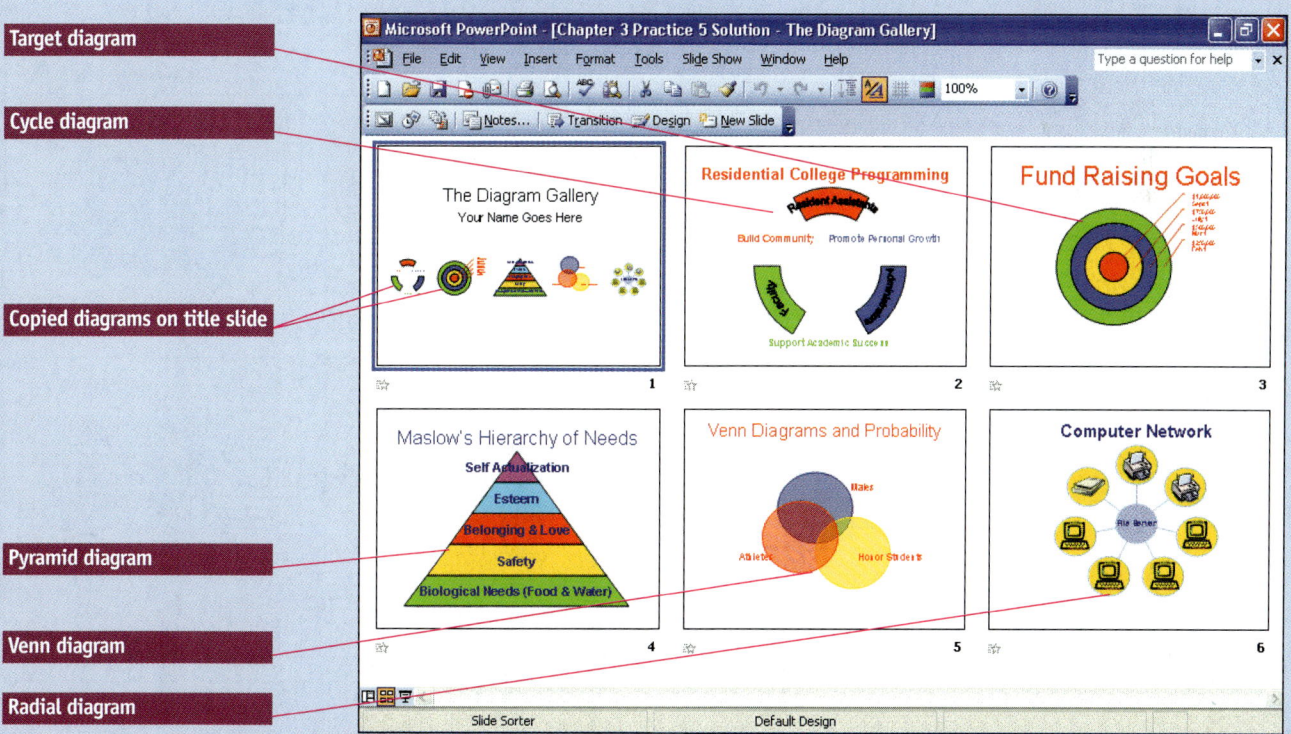

FIGURE 3.13 The Diagram Gallery (exercise 5)

practice exercises

6. **Charts and Animation Effects:** The charts in Figure 3.14 are based on the data in an Excel worksheet. We want to animate the charts by individual series and category, however, and thus you have to create the charts in Microsoft Graph, as opposed to importing charts from Excel. You can, however, import the worksheet on which the charts are based. Open the partially completed presentation in *Chapter 3 Practice 6* in the Exploring PowerPoint folder and proceed as follows:

   a. Add your name to the title slide. The font color for both the title and your name is black. Animate both objects to change to red automatically at the beginning of the slide show. (Use the Change Font Color effect.)

   b. Select the second slide. Use the Insert Object command to insert the worksheet from the *Chapter 3 Practice 6 Excel workbook* that is found in the Exploring PowerPoint folder. Increase the size of the worksheet as shown in Figure 3.14. Use the Pinwheel animation effect for both the title and the worksheet.

   c. Select the third slide and start Microsoft Graph to create the chart. Click in the upper-left area of the datasheet (the cell above row 1 and to the left of column A) to select the entire datasheet, then click the Import Data button on the Microsoft Graph toolbar to display the Import Data dialog box. Select the *Chapter 3 Practice 6 Excel workbook*. (There is only one worksheet in the workbook, and you should import the entire worksheet.)

   d. Move and size the chart so that it approximates the slide in Figure 3.14. Change the color of the Appetizers and Beverage series to red and yellow, respectively.

   e. Copy the chart that you just created to slides 4, 5, and 6. Modify each chart individually to match those in Figure 3.16. Add animation effects to the individual charts as you see fit.

   f. Save the completed presentation. Print the title slide as a full slide to use as a cover sheet for the assignment. Print the completed presentation as audience handouts (six per page) for your instructor.

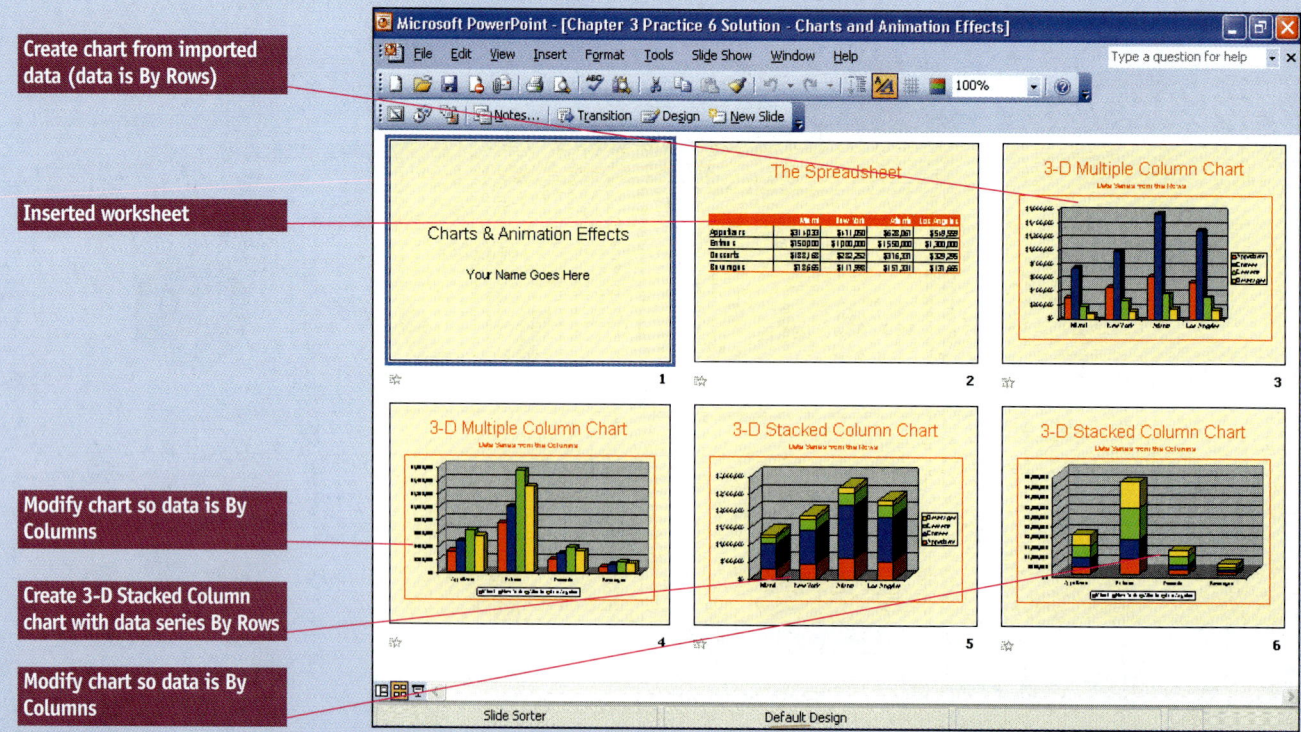

FIGURE 3.14 Charts and Animation Effects (exercise 6)

practice exercises

7. **Left Brain/Right Brain Conflict:** The presentation in Figure 3.15 describes the different modes of thinking in the left and right sides of the brain. The left brain is the logical part and controls speech, language, and mathematical reasoning. The right brain is the creative part and thinks in images and colors, and remembers music and complex pictures. Open the partially completed presentation in *Chapter 3 Practice 7* and proceed as follows:
   a. Add your name to the title slide, then animate the slide as you see fit.
   b. The three yellow rectangles on slide 2 are intended to emphasize the text behind each rectangle during the presentation. Select all three rectangles and add the Dissolve In entrance effect at slow speed. The first rectangle should start on a mouse click; the next two rectangles should dissolve after the previous animation.
   c. Animate slide 3 so that the left and right sides of the brain fly in at medium speed, from the appropriate sides of the slide, on successive mouse clicks. Each column of bulleted text should appear one item at a time as the brain appears on the slide.
   d. There is no animation for slide 4. Read the text of this slide carefully, however, because it represents the essence of the presentation. The slide does not contain a typo; that is, the word "blue" appears in red letters. Your right brain tries to say the color (red), but your left brain insists on reading the word (blue).
   e. Animate the words on the fifth slide so that they appear automatically, without having to click the mouse. Vary the speed at which the words appear; the first word can appear slowly, the next few at medium speed, then fast, then very fast. Test yourself to see if you can say the written color.
   f. Save the completed presentation. Print the title slide to use as a cover sheet for the assignment. Print the completed presentation as audience handouts (six per page).
   g. View the presentation. The last slide contains two hyperlinks to Web sites that provide additional information on the brain. Visit both sites and print a page from each site for your instructor. Submit these pages with the printout of your presentation.

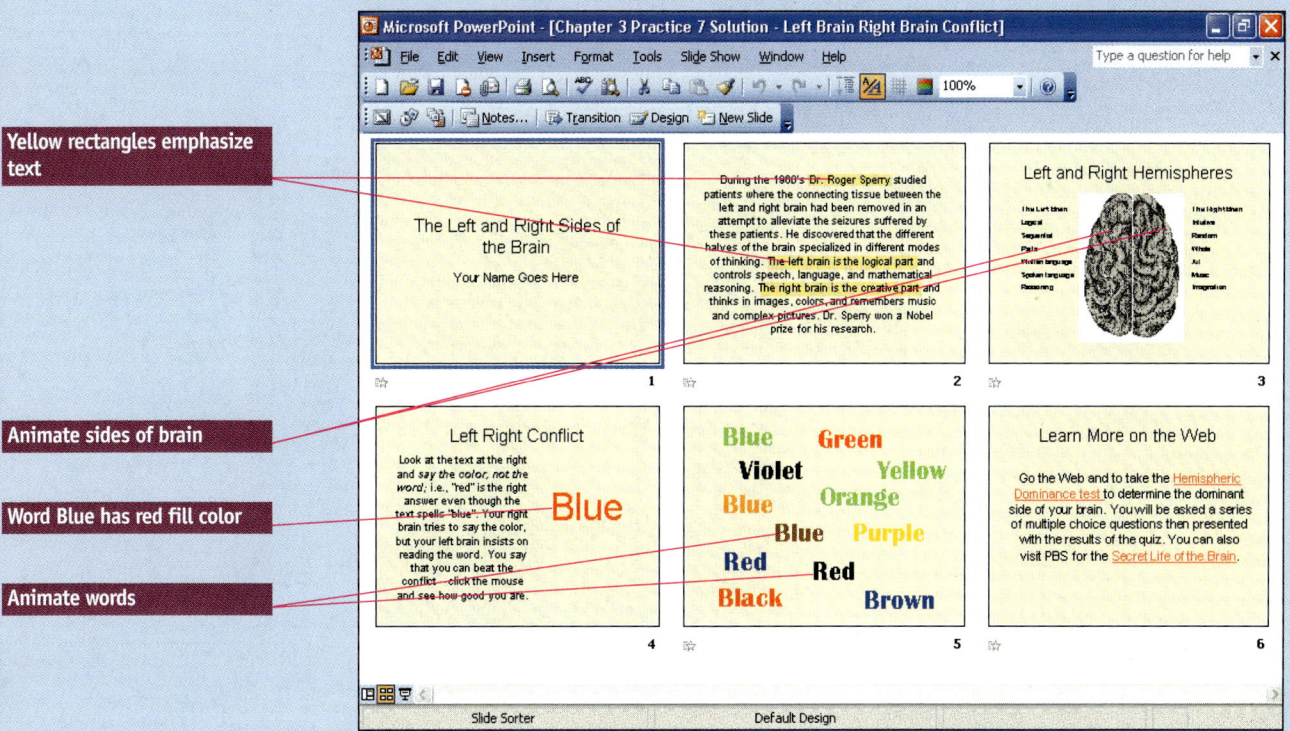

FIGURE 3.15 Left Brain/Right Brain Conflict (exercise 7)

practice exercises

8. **The Grand Finale:** The presentation in Figure 3.16 shows you how to end a presentation with flair. You do not have to duplicate our fireworks exactly, but you are to retain the equivalent functionality. Start a new presentation and enter "The Grand Finale" as its title. Add your name to the title slide. (The title slide is there only to identify the presentation to your instructor when you submit the assignment.)

   a. Add a blank slide after the title and proceed as follows to create the fireworks. Draw and animate a curved (freeform) line to start the show. Sound and motion are important. We used Wipe from bottom as the entrance effect, at a very fast speed, to the sound of a laser. The intent is to represent a flare as it might appear during an actual fireworks display.

   b. Use the AutoShape button to create a series of large 24-point stars that appear one after another to the sound of an explosion. These large bursts are followed by a series of five-point stars that appear to the sound of a chime. The speed of these smaller stars has been manually adjusted to one tenth of a second to create a more realistic effect. (Very fast is only five tenths of a second.)

   c. Use WordArt to create the text. (You may want to use a font color other than white initially, to make it easier to see the object on the slide.) The WordArt should appear automatically when the slide is first displayed. We chose the Dissolve In entrance effect at medium speed. Now add a second effect to increase the size of the WordArt by 25% to the sound of applause, and then add a faded zoom as an exit effect. All three effects should execute automatically, one after another at medium speed.

   d. The entire presentation should then fade to black. We found the easiest way to do this was to create a black rectangle that extended beyond the slide (use the Order command to move the rectangle to the back of the slide, so that you can see the other objects). The rectangle should simply appear after the previous effect.

   e. Print the title slide as a full slide to use as a cover sheet for the assignment. Save the completed presentation. Print the audience handouts of the revised presentation (two slides in all) for your instructor.

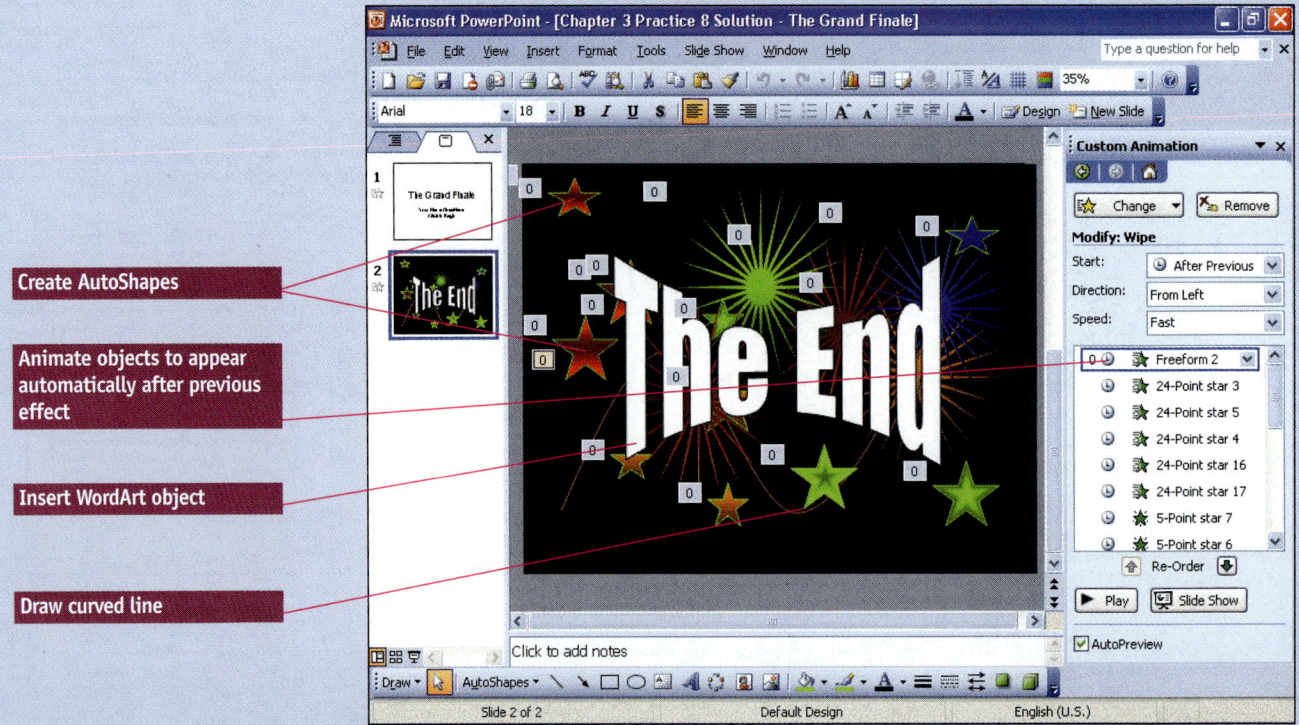

FIGURE 3.16 The Grand Finale (exercise 8)

MINI CASES

Digital Cameras

As with all technology, the price of a digital camera has come down significantly while performance has gone up dramatically. What are the most significant capabilities in a digital camera? What is the least amount of money you have to spend to purchase (what you consider) a worthwhile camera? What are the parameters and cost of your ideal camera? Be sure to consider the size and weight of the camera—the more functionality, the larger the camera. The worst picture is the one you do not take because the camera is too big to take with you.

Microsoft Producer

An "add-on" is a supplemental program that extends the capabilities of Microsoft Office by adding custom commands and specialized features. Microsoft Producer is a PowerPoint add-on that makes it easy to capture, synchronize, and publish audio, video, slides, and images. Where do you obtain the Microsoft Producer add-on and how much does it cost? How is it installed? How easy is it to use? Try to obtain a copy in order to experiment with the program, then summarize your findings in a short note to your instructor.

Microsoft Excel versus Microsoft Graph

An Excel chart can be imported into a PowerPoint presentation, and/or a chart can be created from scratch within the presentation using Microsoft Graph. Which technique is easier? Can either type of chart be linked or embedded into the presentation? What capabilities (if any) are present in Microsoft Graph, but not in the charting component of Microsoft Excel?

Movies and Video

Use the Search command on your computer to locate any movie or video files that may exist. It's easiest in Windows XP because you can specify "video," as opposed to a specific file type. How large are these files compared to documents created by other programs? Which program is required to play the video files you find? What is the Windows Movie Maker program? What features does it have, and how does it compare to similar offerings by other vendors? Summarize your findings in a short note to your instructor for class discussion.

CHAPTER 4

Advanced Techniques:
Slide Masters, Narration, and Web Pages

OBJECTIVES

After reading this chapter you will:

1. Distinguish between a template and a color scheme.
2. Explain the role of the slide master in formatting a presentation.
3. Add action buttons to each slide for easy navigation.
4. Use the Sound Recorder to create an original sound, then insert that sound on a slide.
5. Insert hyperlinks into a presentation.
6. Save a presentation as a Web document using the Single File Web Page format in Office 2003.
7. Use the Record Narration command to add sound to a presentation.
8. Create a custom slide show; explain the advantage of having multiple shows in one presentation.

hands-on exercises

1. COLOR SCHEMES, SOUND, AND THE SLIDE MASTER
   Input: PowerPoint Quiz
   Output: PowerPoint Quiz Solution

2. PRESENTATIONS ON THE WEB
   Input: Create a Quiz
   Output: Constitution Quiz (Single File Web Page)

3. NARRATING A PRESENTATION
   Input: Welcome to Computers 101
   Output: Welcome to Computers 101 Solution

CASE STUDY
GET UP AND GO

The alarm rings and you struggle to get out of bed. If you are typical of your generation, you may begin your day with some type of hot drink, such as coffee, hot chocolate, or tea, none of which offers significant nutritional value. There should be a better product, and the food products company where you are interning this summer is planning to introduce an alternative beverage. The product is named *Get Up and Go*, and it is slated for introduction into the college market next fall. The company believes that there is a large potential demand for a beverage that contains a significant portion of the daily recommended nutritional requirement as recommended by the FDA (Food and Drug Administration).

The marketing department has conducted a series of focus groups to determine consumer preferences for the precise formulation of the new drink. The study also sought to determine whether consumers would be inclined to give up their morning coffee in favor of the new drink. These sessions are over, and it is your task to complete a PowerPoint presentation that shows the results. The presentation is to be posted to the company's internal Web site for others to view. This is an ideal assignment. You are health conscious, an avid coffee drinker, and you enjoy hot chocolate. It is also a paid internship, and you will get college credit upon completing the presentation. ■

Your assignment is to read the chapter and complete the *Chapter 4 Case Study—Get Up and Go* presentation in the Exploring PowerPoint folder. You are to apply a design template to the existing presentation and add action buttons to the master slide for easy navigation. The presentation is confidential, and this should be indicated at the bottom of every slide. Animate the presentation as you see fit and include limited sound effects. Use the Sound Recorder, if possible, to create an original sound file for added interest. Save the presentation as a Web page, but you are not required to post the presentation to a Web server. Print the completed presentation for your instructor.

A POWERPOINT QUIZ

Figure 4.1 displays a six-slide presentation in the form of a quiz. Sound is used throughout the presentation although you cannot hear anything by merely looking at our figure. Look closely, however, and you will see a Sound icon next to each potential answer in slides 4 and 5. Click any of these icons and you will hear whether or not you are correct. A sound file is also embedded on the third slide in the form of a reminder to test the speakers and adjust the volume. Custom animation has been added to this slide, so that clicking the clip art (the icon is hidden behind the image of the speakers) will play an appropriate sound.

The use of sound requires additional hardware, namely a sound card, speakers, and a microphone if you want to record your own sound files. Multiple sound files are supplied, however, within Microsoft Windows as well as Microsoft Office. Additional sounds may be imported from the Web and/or created through the ***Sound Recorder***, a Windows accessory, which creates a digitized recording of an actual sound.

The Sound Recorder uses a chip in the sound card on your computer to convert the recorded sound into a file, and then stores the file on disk. You can record any type of sound, such as your voice to narrate a presentation, and/or special effects such as the sound of applause. Sound files are stored just like any other type of file and can be moved and copied from one folder to another. The size of a sound file is directly proportional to its duration.

The Crayons template in Figure 4.1 may look familiar, but we have changed the underlying color scheme. A ***template*** controls every aspect of a presentation's design such as the background, fonts and formatting, and the size and placement of bullets and other elements. Each template has a default ***color scheme***, consisting of eight balanced colors that are used for the background, text, slide title, shadows, and other accents. Change the template and you change every aspect of a presentation. Change the color scheme within a template (every template has several alternate color schemes from which to choose) and you retain the overall look, but effect a subtle change in the appearance.

Most presentations are designed for sequential viewing, starting with the first slide and ending with the last. You can also build flexibility into a presentation by including ***action buttons*** that will take you through the slides in a different sequence. Thus, each slide in Figure 4.1, except the title slide, contains a uniform set of four buttons to move to the first, previous, next, and last slides, respectively. You are under no obligation to use the action buttons, and indeed, you can still move through the presentation sequentially by clicking the left mouse button (or pressing the PgDn key) to move to the next sequential slide. Nevertheless, action buttons (or navigation buttons as they are sometimes called) provide a convenient way to return to the previous slide and/or jump to the last slide, which in this example contains the answer key.

The answer key on the last slide contains three ***hyperlinks***, two of which return to earlier slides that contain questions one and two, and a third branches to an external link (www.prenhall.com/grauer). All three hyperlinks are created through the ***Insert Hyperlink command***. Hyperlinks, like action buttons, provide flexibility for the speaker; for example, in reviewing the answers, you can click the hyperlink to return to the associated question. You do not have to use the hyperlinks during the presentation, but the more effective public speakers are sensitive to their audience, anticipate potential questions, and take advantage of this flexibility.

Hidden slides provide additional flexibility during delivery in that they do not appear during a regular slide show. The answer key, for example, is hidden, which means that the presenter has to take explicit action to display that slide, such as clicking the appropriate action button. The hidden slide can be displayed during a slide show by right clicking the slide, clicking the Go to Slide command, and then choosing the hidden slide from the list of slides.

(a) Title Slide

(b) Test Your Speakers

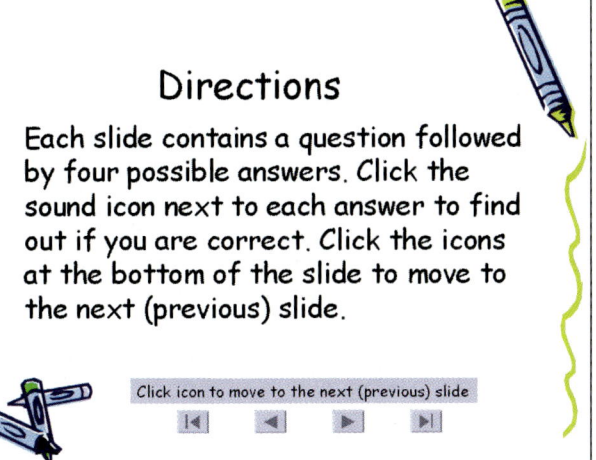
(c) Directions

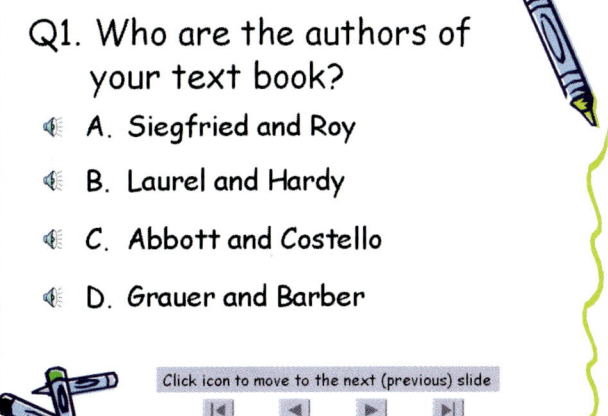
(d) Question 1

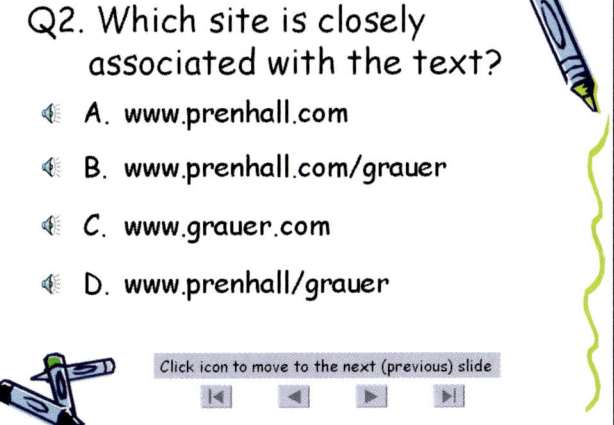
(e) Question 2

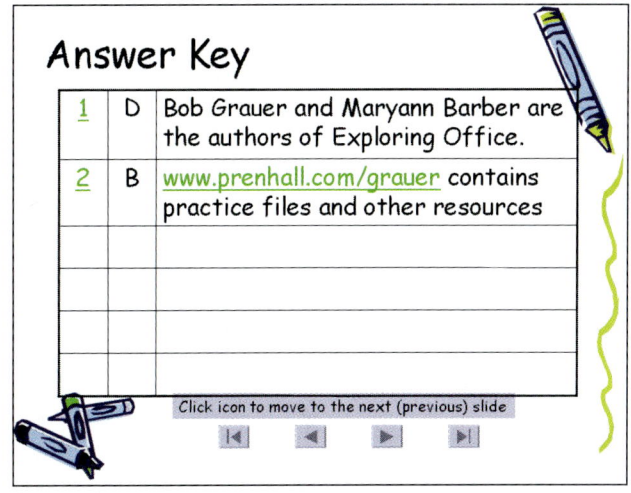
(f) Answer Key with Hyperlinks

FIGURE 4.1 An Online Quiz

The Slide Master

The action buttons in our presentation can be added individually to every slide, but that would be unnecessarily tedious. It is much more efficient to add the buttons to the ***slide master***, as opposed to the individual slides shown in Figure 4.2. The slide master stores information about the template, including font styles, placeholder sizes and positions, background design, additional clip art or other elements, and color schemes.

The slide master is the easiest way to make global changes to a presentation. Any change to any element on the slide master is automatically reflected in every existing slide (except the title slide) as well as any new slides that are subsequently added. The title slide has its own master (as seen in Figure 4.2), although it is just as easy to make changes to the title slide itself. Additional masters are available for handouts and speaker notes.

The slide master provided by PowerPoint contains a placeholder for the title of the slide, a second placeholder for the bulleted text, additional placeholders at the bottom of the slide for the date, footer, and slide number, and two clip art images. We also modified the master to include the additional text box and associated action buttons. Change the position of any of these elements on the slide master, and the corresponding element will be changed throughout the presentation. In similar fashion, any change to the font, point size, or alignment within a placeholder also carries through to all of the individual slides.

The slide master is modified by using commands from the appropriate menu or from a toolbar. The action buttons, for example, were created through the Action Buttons command in the Slide Show menu. Clip art, such as a corporate logo, can also be added. Once the objects have been created, they can be moved and sized like any other Windows object. And, as indicated, every slide in the presentation will contain the objects that appear on the slide master. It's easy and powerful, and as you might have guessed, it is time for our first hands-on exercise.

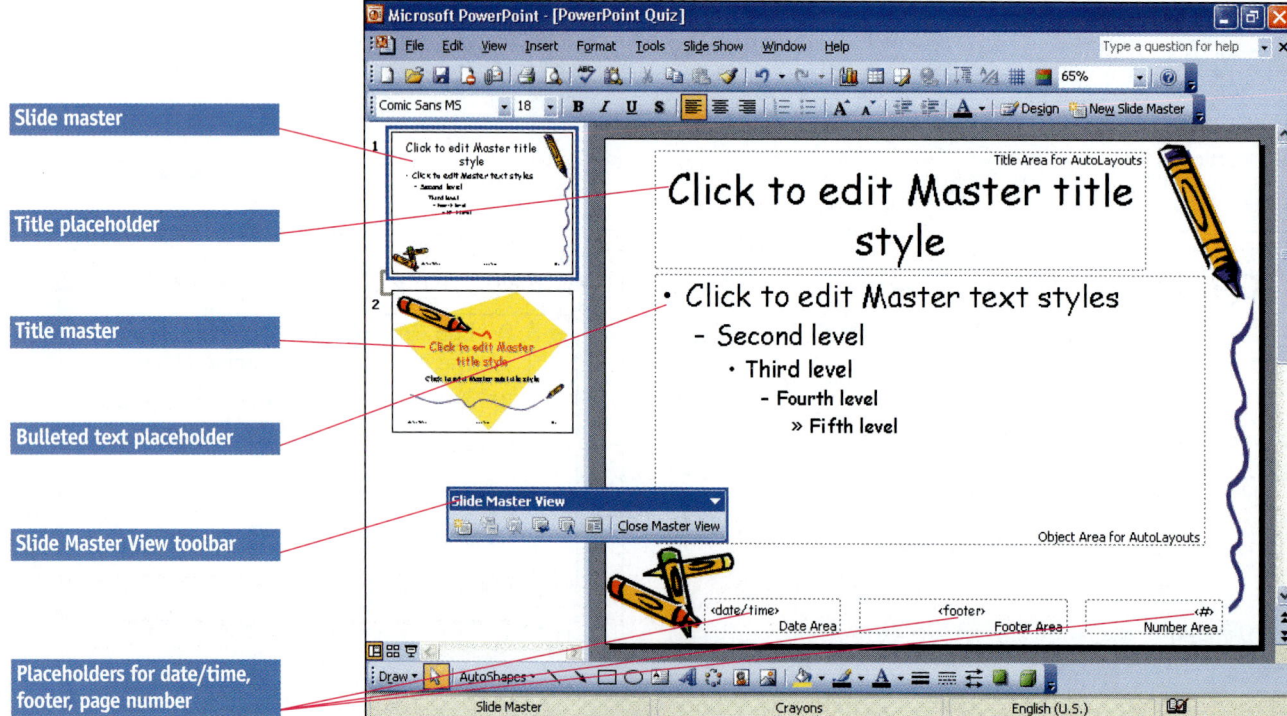

FIGURE 4.2 The Slide Master

hands-on exercise

1 Color Schemes, Sound, and the Slide Master

Objective To change a color scheme; to record a sound, then insert the sound onto a slide; to use the slide master to add action buttons to every slide.

Step 1: **Change the Color Scheme**

- Open the **PowerPoint Quiz presentation** in the Exploring PowerPoint folder. Add **your name** to the title slide.
- Save the presentation as **PowerPoint Quiz Solution** so that you can return to the original presentation if necessary.
- Click the **Design button** to open the task pane, then click the link to **Color Schemes** to display the color schemes for the selected design.
- Click the **down arrow** next to the second color scheme, then click the **Apply to All Slides** as shown in Figure 4.3a. The accent color on the title slide changes to light purple (the background remains white).
- Close the task pane.

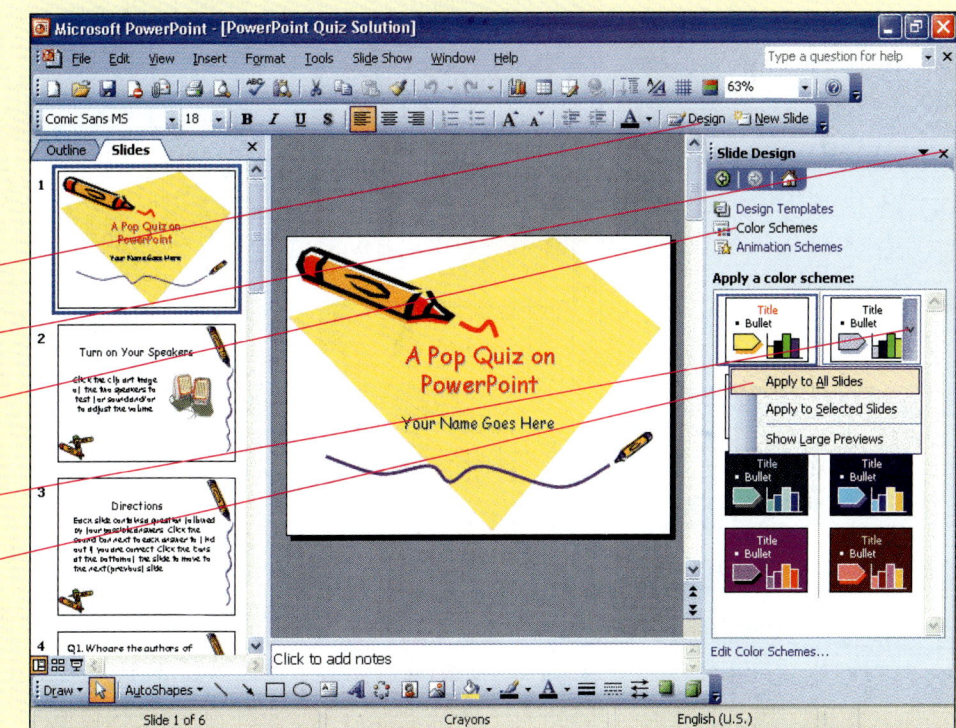

(a) Change the Color Scheme (step 1)

FIGURE 4.3 Hands-on Exercise 1

ADD A FAVORITE

Select the desired folder in the Open or Save As dialog boxes, click the down arrow next to the Tools button, and click the Add to "My Places" command. The next time you open either dialog box, you will be able to click the Folder icon at the left of the dialog box to go directly to the folder, as opposed to having to select the folder from the Look in list box.

Step 2: **Record the Sound(s)**

- Skip this step if you do not have a microphone to record your own sounds.
- Click the **Start button** on the Windows taskbar. Click **All Programs**, click **Accessories**, click **Entertainment**, then click **Sound Recorder** to display the associated dialog box in Figure 4.3b.
- Click the **red dot** to begin recording, be sure you speak directly into the microphone, and say the word "Incorrect". Click the **Stop button**.
- Click the **Rewind button**, then click the **Play button** to listen to the sound. If you are not satisfied, pull down the **File menu**, click **New**, then click **No** when asked whether to save the file, and start a new recording.
- Pull down the **File menu** (in the Sound Recorder window) and save the file as **Incorrect** in the **Exploring PowerPoint folder**. You should see a message that the file already exists (we created a default file) and asking if you want to replace it. Click **Yes**.
- Record two additional files, **Sorry** and **Try Again**, in similar fashion. Close the Sound Recorder.

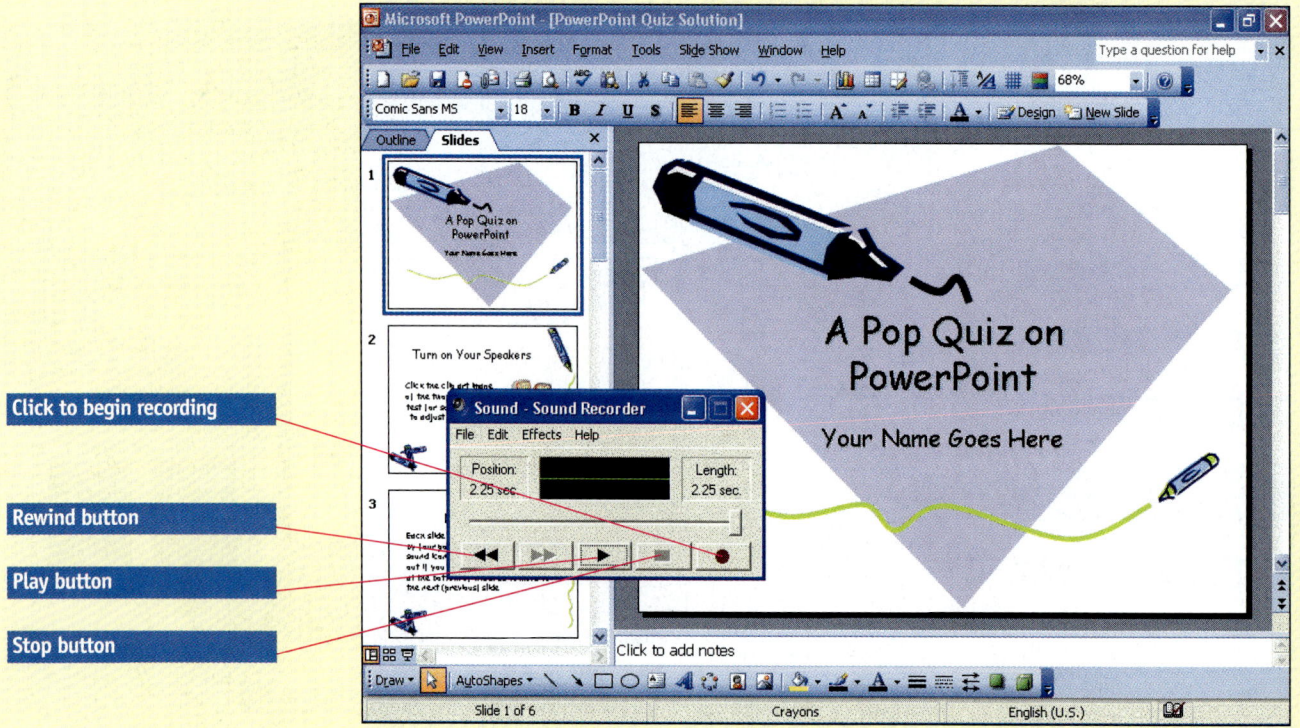

(b) Record the Sound(s) (step 2)

FIGURE 4.3 Hands-on Exercise 1 (*continued*)

YOU DON'T NEED STEREO

A voice can generally be converted to a lesser-quality (smaller) file, without an appreciable difference in quality. Open the Sound Recorder, pull down the File menu and click the Properties command to view the existing parameters. Click the down arrow in the Choose From list box, choose All Formats, and click the Convert Now button. Select 11kHz, 8 bit, Mono, which requires 10K bytes per second. Other settings can require as much as 180K bytes per second.

Step 3: **Insert the Sound**

- Select the fourth slide (the slide containing the first question in our quiz). The Sound icon does not yet appear next to the answer, "Siegfried and Roy". Pull down the **Insert menu**, click **Movies and Sounds**, then click **Sound from File** to display the Insert Sound dialog box.

- Change to the **Exploring PowerPoint folder**, then select the **Incorrect** sound you recorded earlier.

- Click the **OK button** (not visible in the figure) to insert the sound. Click the **When Clicked button** when asked how you want the sound to start. A Sound icon should appear in the middle of the slide. Click and drag the **Sound icon** to the left of the first answer as shown in Figure 4.3c.

- Insert the **Try Again**, **Sorry**, and **Applause** sound files in similar fashion so that the associated Sound icons appear next to answers (b), (c), and (d), respectively. Click the **When Clicked button** when asked how you want the sound to start.

- Press and hold the **Ctrl key** as you select all four **Sound icons**. Pull down the **Format menu**, click **Picture** to display the Format Picture dialog box, then click the **Position tab**. Enter **.75"** in the Horizontal list box. Click **OK**.

- Save the presentation.

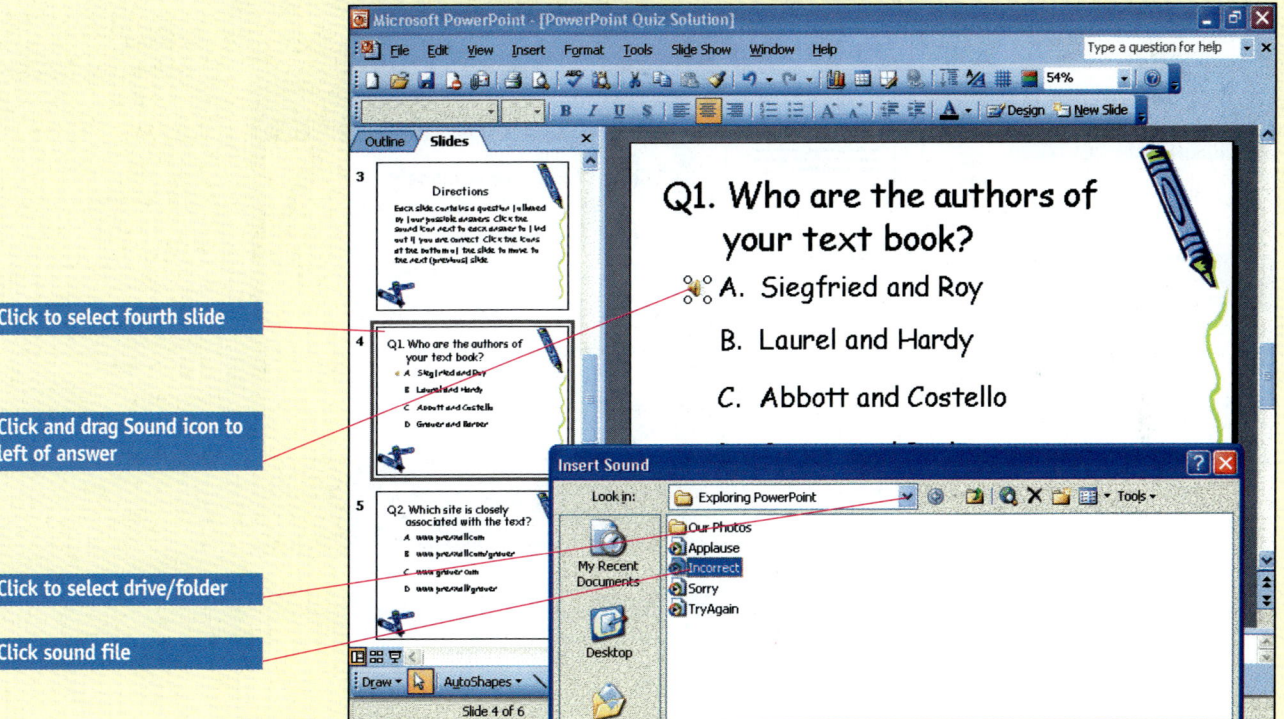

(c) Insert the Sound (step 3)

FIGURE 4.3 Hands-on Exercise 1 (*continued*)

DISCONNECT YOUR MICROPHONE

The speech recognition capabilities in Microsoft Office are quite impressive. There is a downside, however, in that a microphone will often mistake ambient noise for Office commands. You can tell this is happening if menus appear for no reason and/or random characters are continually inserted into a document. Turn the microphone off and the problem should disappear.

Step 4: **Check the Answers**

- Select the fifth slide (the slide containing the second question in our quiz) and insert an appropriate sound file next to each answer. (The correct answer is (B), **www.prenhall.com/grauer**.) All of the sound files should be in the Exploring PowerPoint folder.

- Position the icons .75″ from the left border as in the previous step.

- Pull down the **Slide Show menu** and click the **Custom Animation command** to open the animation task pane as shown in Figure 4.3d. You should see a trigger next to each animation effect, although the number next to each sound object may be different from ours.

- Click the **Slide Show button** to test the slide. Click the **Sound icon** next to each answer to test the presentation. You can click each icon as often as you like. (You advance to the next slide when you click a blank space on the slide, as opposed to clicking a Sound icon.)

- Press **Esc** when you are satisfied the slide is correct. Close the task pane. Save the presentation.

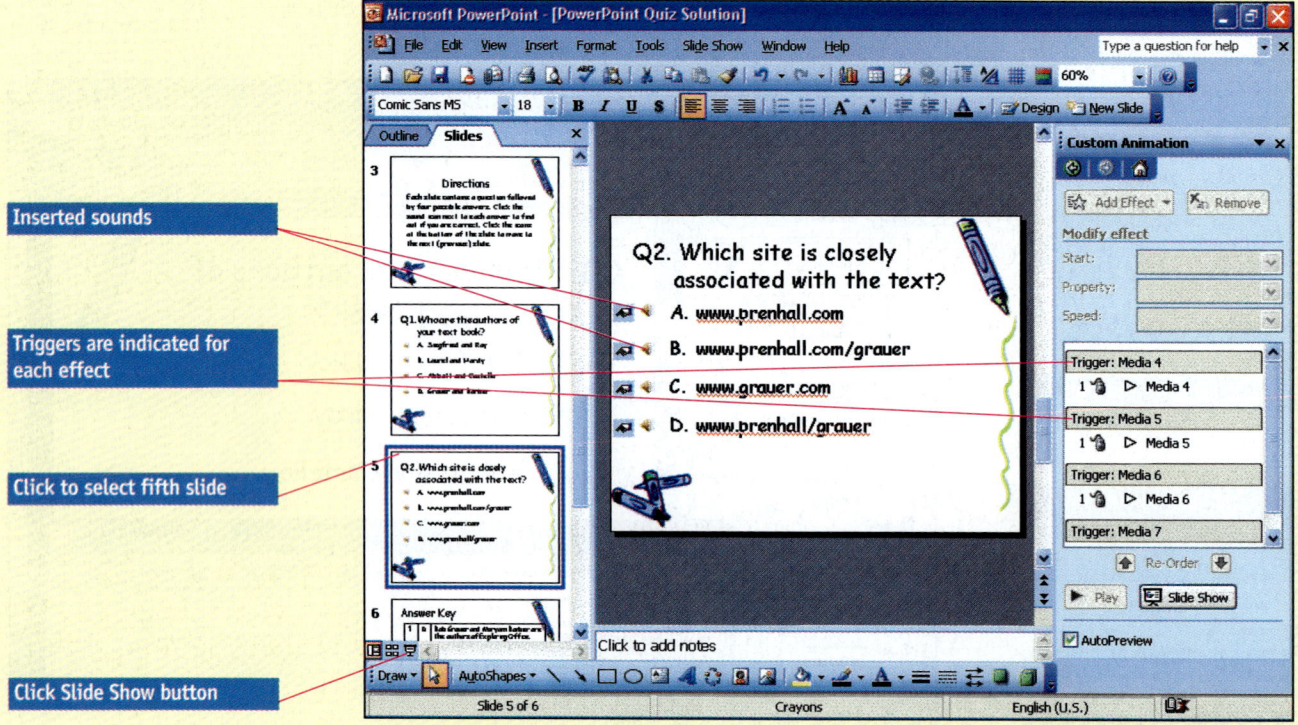

(d) Check the Answers (step 4)

FIGURE 4.3 Hands-on Exercise 1 (*continued*)

TRIGGERING A SOUND EFFECT

An animation or sound effect can be "triggered" to play in conjunction with clicking a specific object; for example, clicking the clip art image of the microphone plays the associated sound. This differs from simply starting the effect on a mouse click, because you can click the trigger object repeatedly to play the sound as many times as you like. This technique is used on slide 2, where the sound is triggered by clicking the clip art image of the speakers.

1860 CHAPTER 4: ADVANCED TECHNIQUES

Step 5: **Add the Action Buttons**

- Pull down the **View menu**, click the **Master command**, then select the **Slide Master** to display the view in Figure 4.3e. Be sure the bulleted slide is selected, as opposed to the title slide.

- Pull down the **Slide Show menu**, click the **Action buttons command**, and select (click) the beginning ◀ **button** that indicates the first slide. The mouse pointer changes to a tiny crosshair.

- Click in the footer area at the bottom of the slide, then drag the mouse to create an action button. Release the mouse. The Action Settings dialog box is displayed automatically.

- The **Hyperlink to Option button** is selected and the First Slide is specified in the associated list box. Click **OK** to accept the default settings and close the Action Settings dialog box.

- Repeat this process three additional times to create action buttons for the previous, next, and ending slides in that sequence. Do not be concerned about the precise size or location of the buttons at this time. Save the presentation.

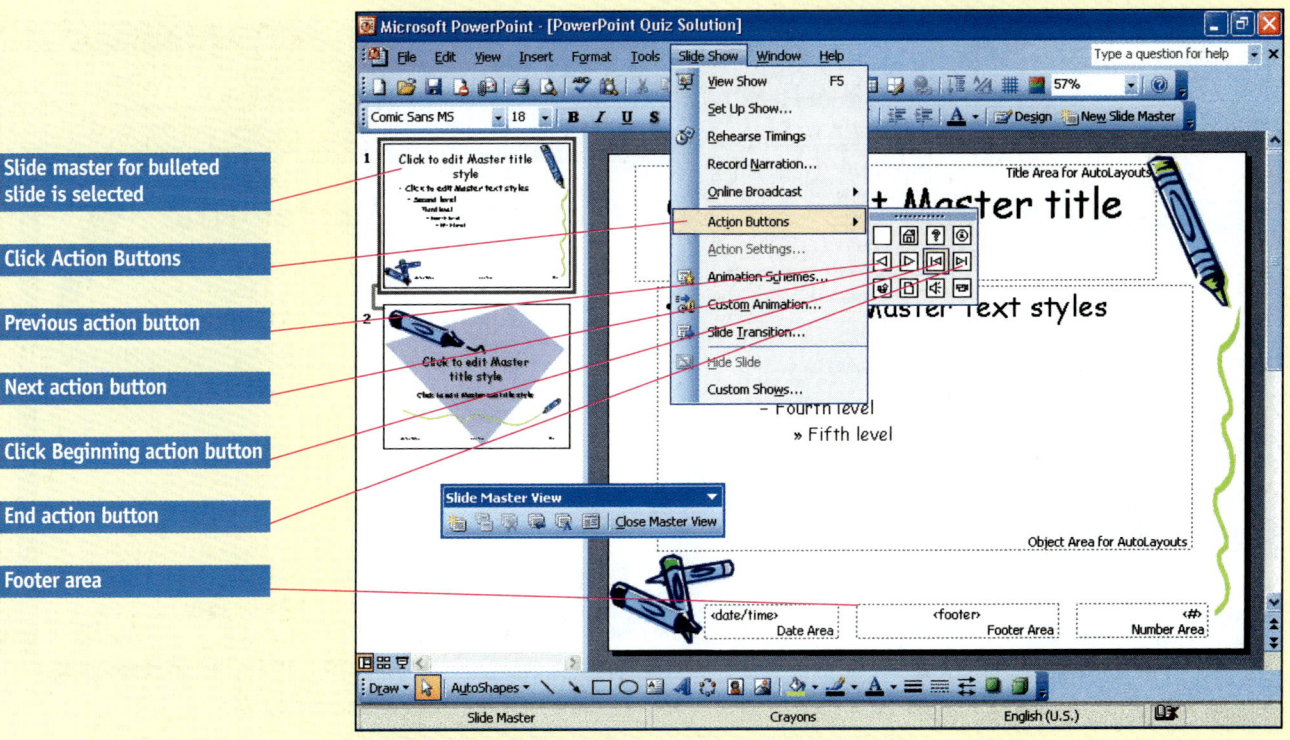

(e) Add the Action Buttons (step 5)

FIGURE 4.3 Hands-on Exercise 1 (*continued*)

THE HEADER AND FOOTER COMMAND

The Header and Footer command provides another way to display information on every slide. Pull down the View menu, click the Header and Footer command, then enter the date of the presentation, a descriptive footer, and/or the slide number in the associated dialog box. Click the Apply to All button to display these fields on every slide (or check the box to suppress the information on the title slide). The contents of these fields do not show on the slide master, but are hidden within the <date/time>, <footer>, <#> fields that appear in the footer area.

Step 6: **Size and Align the Action Buttons**

- Click and drag the individual action buttons so that there is sufficient space between the buttons to increase their size to ½ inch each. Press and hold the **Shift key** as you click each action button to select all four buttons.
- Point to any button, click the **right mouse button** to display a context-sensitive menu, then click **Format AutoShape** to display the Format AutoShape dialog box.
- Click the **Size tab**, then enter **.35** and **.5** as the height and width of each button. Click **OK** to accept the settings and close the dialog box.
- Click the **Draw button** on the Drawing toolbar, select the **Align or Distribute command**, then click **Align Top** to align the buttons.
- Click the **Draw button** a second time, select the **Align or Distribute command**, then click **Distribute Horizontally** to allocate a uniform amount of space between each button.
- Add a **text box** above the action buttons as shown in Figure 4.3f. Change the fill color to match the color of the buttons.
- Click the **Close Master View button** on the Slide Master View toolbar. Save the presentation.

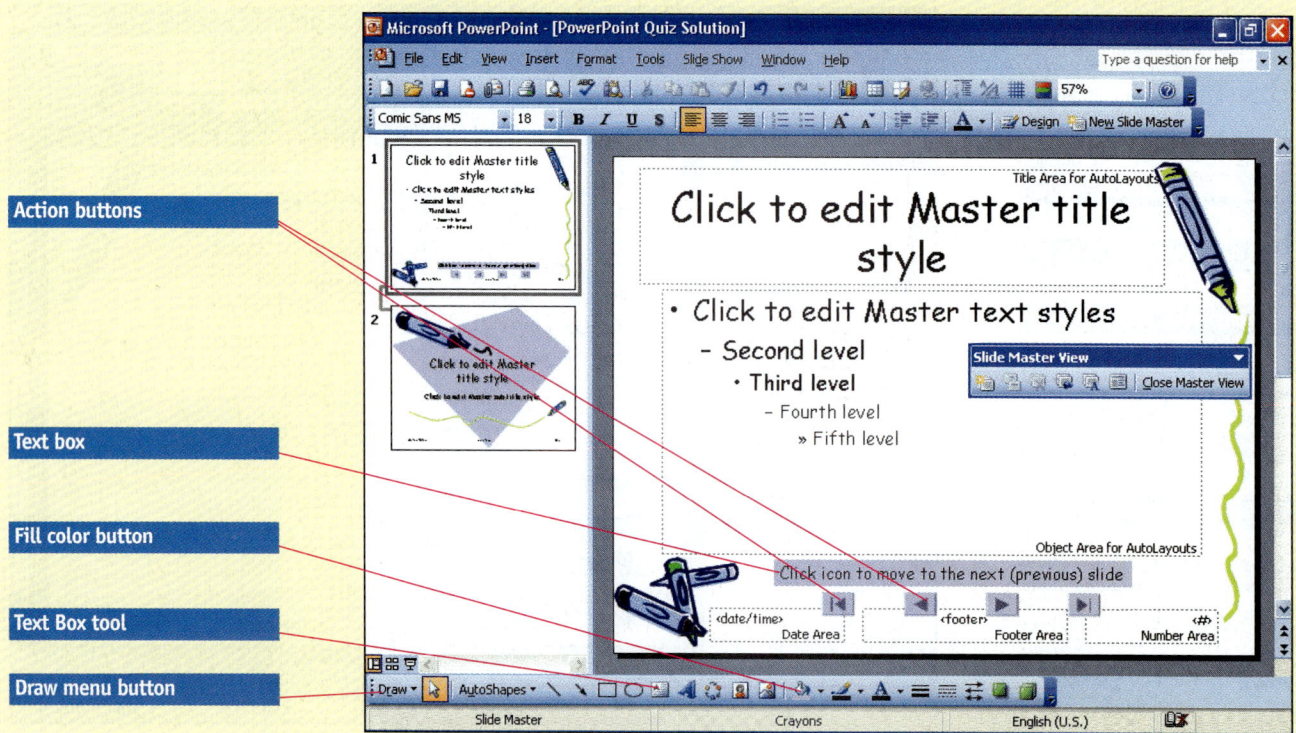

(f) Size and Align the Action Buttons (step 6)

FIGURE 4.3 Hands-on Exercise 1 (*continued*)

MULTIPLE SLIDE MASTERS ARE POSSIBLE

Most presentations use only a single template, but there are occasions when you want to include multiple designs in the same presentation. Change to the Slide Sorter view, then press and hold the Ctrl key to select the slides that will reflect the alternate template. Click the Slide Design button on the Slide Sorter toolbar to open the task pane, click the down arrow next to the desired design, then apply the design to the selected slide(s). Repeat the process to include another design. See problem 4 at the end of the chapter.

Step 7: **Create the Hyperlinks**

- Press **Ctrl+End** to move to the last slide in the presentation. The action buttons appear at the bottom of the slide because you modified the master slide layout in the previous step.

- Click and drag to select the number **1** in the first cell of the table, then click the **Insert Hyperlink button** on the Standard toolbar to display the associated dialog box. Click the **Place in This Document icon** and select the slide containing the first question as shown in Figure 4.3g. Click **OK**.

- The number 1 has been converted to a hyperlink. Create a hyperlink to the second question in similar fashion.

- Click and drag to select the text **www.prenhall.com/grauer** (which appears as a partial explanation for the second question). Press **Ctrl+C** to copy this link to the Windows clipboard.

- Click the **Insert Hyperlink button**, click the icon for **Existing file or Web page**, click in the **Address text box**, then press **Ctrl+V** to enter the actual address. Click **OK** to create the hyperlink. Save the presentation.

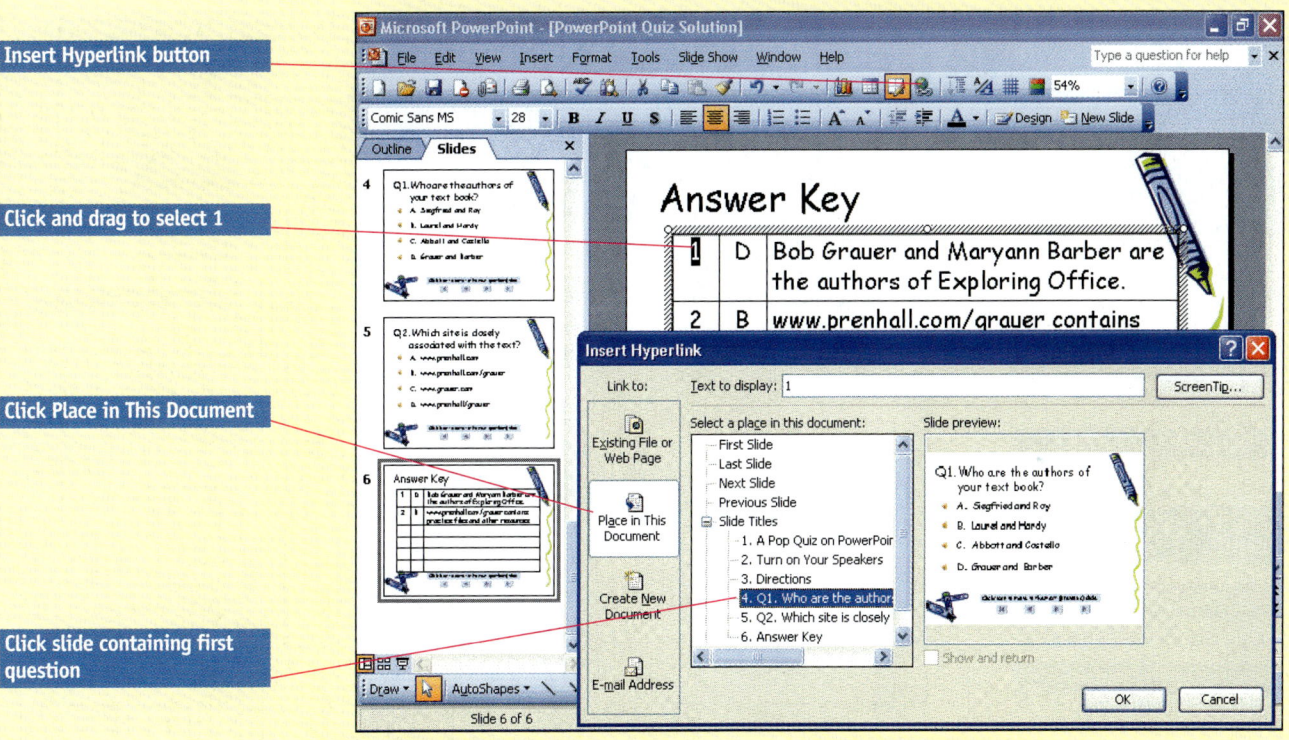

(g) Create the Hyperlinks (step 7)

FIGURE 4.3 Hands-on Exercise 1 (*continued*)

THE TABLES AND BORDERS TOOLBAR

Pull down the View menu, click the Toolbars command, and then display the Tables and Borders toolbar. (Point to any button to display a ToolTip that is indicative of the underlying function.) You can change the line style or thickness, distribute rows and columns evenly within a table, merge or split cells, or add a fill color. Click the down arrow next to the Table command for additional commands to insert or delete rows and columns. The tools and conventions are identical to those in Microsoft Word.

Step 8: **Hide the Answer Key**

- Change to the **Slide Sorter view**. You should see three hyperlinks on the last slide, one link to each question within the presentation and one link to the Grauer Web site at www.prenhall.com/grauer.

- Select the last slide. Click the **Hide Slide button** on the Slide Sorter toolbar. The slide will be hidden during the slide show as can be seen from the Hidden Slide icon over the slide number below the slide.

- The **Hide Slide command** functions as a toggle switch. Click the button, and the slide is marked to be hidden during the presentation. Click the button a second time, and the slide is marked as visible. Set the button to hide the last slide.

- Check that the last slide is still selected, then click the **Transition button** on the Slide Sorter toolbar to open the task pane. Select a transition effect, a transition speed, and optionally a sound. A Transition icon appears below the slide.

- Save the presentation.

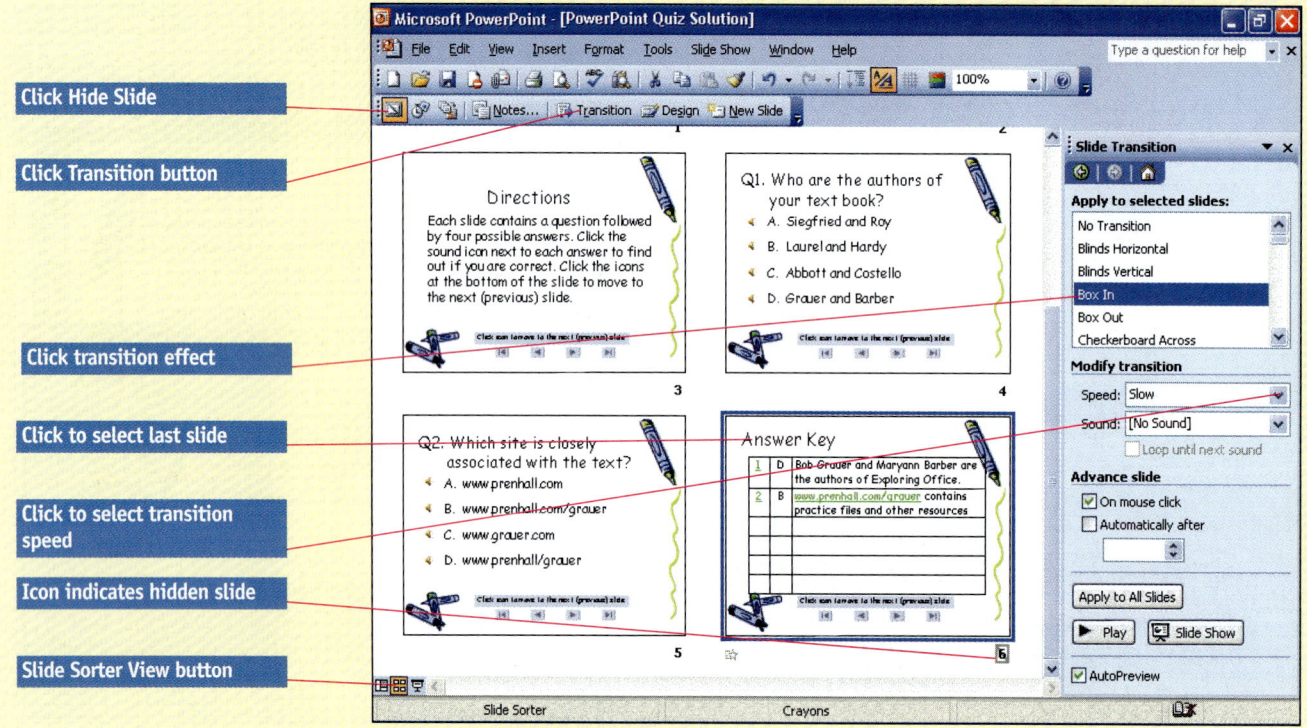

(h) Hide the Answer Key (step 8)

FIGURE 4.3 Hands-on Exercise 1 (*continued*)

DISPLAY THE HIDDEN SLIDE

A hidden slide does not appear during a regular slide show, but it can be displayed at any time using the Go to Slide command. Right click any slide during a presentation and click the Go to Slide command to display a list of every slide. Click any slide (parentheses appear around the number of a hidden slide) to display that slide, and then continue with the presentation from that point.

Step 9: **Take the Quiz**

- Press **Ctrl+Home** to move to the first slide in the presentation. Pull down the **Slide Show menu** and click the **View Show command**.
- You should see the title slide. Click the mouse or press the **PgDn key** to move to the second slide.
- Click the **icon** to test the speakers. Move to the next slide.
- Read the directions. Click the **action button** to move to the next slide.
- You should see the first question as shown in Figure 4.3i. Click the **Sound icon** next to each answer. Move to the next slide.
- Click the **Sound icon** next to each answer. Click a blank area to move to the next slide. You do not see the answer key because the slide is hidden.
- Press **Esc** to return to PowerPoint. Print audience handouts (six per page) for your instructor. Exit PowerPoint if you do not want to continue with the next exercise at this time.

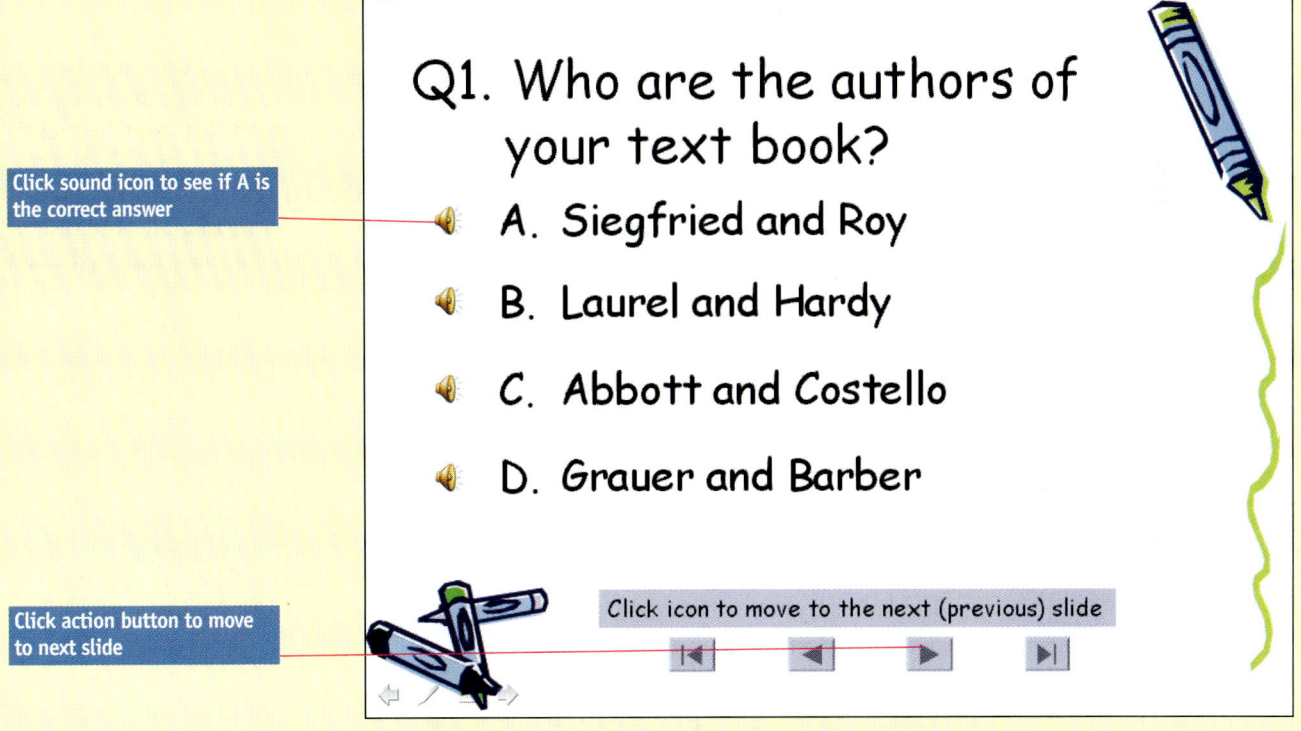

(i) Take the Quiz (step 9)

FIGURE 4.3 Hands-on Exercise 1 (*continued*)

KEYBOARD SHORTCUTS DURING THE SLIDE SHOW

Use the keyboard to gain additional flexibility during a slide show. Press the letter B to toggle between a black screen and the slide show (or the letter W to toggle between a White screen and the slide show). Type a number plus the Enter key to go to a specific slide. Use Ctrl+P to change the mouse pointer to a pen to annotate the slide, then press E to erase the annotations. Press Ctrl+A to change the mouse pointer back to an arrow. And if you can't remember these shortcuts, press the F1 key to see the entire list of shortcuts.

PRESENTATIONS ON THE WEB

All Web pages are written in a language called *HTML (HyperText Markup Language)*. Initially, the only way to create a *Web page* was to learn HTML. Microsoft Office simplifies the process as it lets you create the document in any Office application, then simply save it as a Web page. In other words, you start PowerPoint in the usual fashion and enter the text of the presentation with basic formatting. However, instead of saving the document in the default format (as a PowerPoint presentation), you use the *Save As Web Page command* to convert the presentation to a Web document. (PowerPoint 2003 introduces the *Single File Web Page* format to store all of the elements of a presentation in a single file.) PowerPoint does the rest and generates the HTML statements for you. You do not have to place the resulting document on the Web, but can view it locally using an Internet browser.

Figure 4.4 displays two different views of the title slide of our next presentation. Figure 4.4a shows the expanded outline and the associated speaker notes (if any) with the selected slide. Figure 4.4b shows only the title of each slide and suppresses the details in the outline. The most significant difference, however, is the location of the presentation. Figure 4.4a displays the presentation from a local drive, whereas Figure 4.4b displays the presentation from a Web server. Viewing a Web page locally is useful for two reasons. First, it lets you test the page before uploading to the Web. Second, you can restrict access to a local area network, which is useful in a corporate setting to view documents on an "Intranet," which is limited to those within the organization.

In any event, the Internet Explorer window is divided into two vertical frames and is similar to the Normal view in PowerPoint. The left frame displays the title of each slide, and these titles function as links; that is, you can click any title in the left frame, and the corresponding slide is displayed in the right pane. You can also click and drag the border separating the panes to change the size of the panes.

The buttons above the status bar provide additional options for viewing the presentation. (The buttons were created automatically in conjunction with the Save As Web Page command when the presentation was saved initially.) The Show/Hide Outline button toggles the left (outline) pane on and off. The Expand/Collapse Outline button appears to the right of the outline when the outline is visible and lets you vary the detail of the outline. The Show/Hide Notes button toggles a notes pane on and off at the bottom of the slide. The left and right arrows move to the previous and next slide, respectively. The Slide Show button at the lower right creates a slide show on the Internet that is identical to the slide show viewed within PowerPoint.

Uploading a Presentation

Creating a Web document is only the beginning in that you may want to place the page on the Web, so that other people will be able to access it. This in turn requires you to obtain an account on a Web server, which is a computer with Internet access and adequate disk space to hold the various pages you create. You need to check with your system administrator at school or work, or with your local Internet provider, to determine how to submit your Web page when it is complete.

As indicated earlier, you can still view a Web page locally, even if you do not place it on a Web server. This is the approach we follow in the next hands-on exercise, which has you create a Web document. Your document is stored on a local drive (e.g., on drive A or drive C) rather than on a Web server, but it can still be viewed through Internet Explorer (or any other browser). After you have completed the exercise, you (and/or your instructor) can determine if it is worthwhile to place your page on your school or university's server, where it can be accessed by anyone.

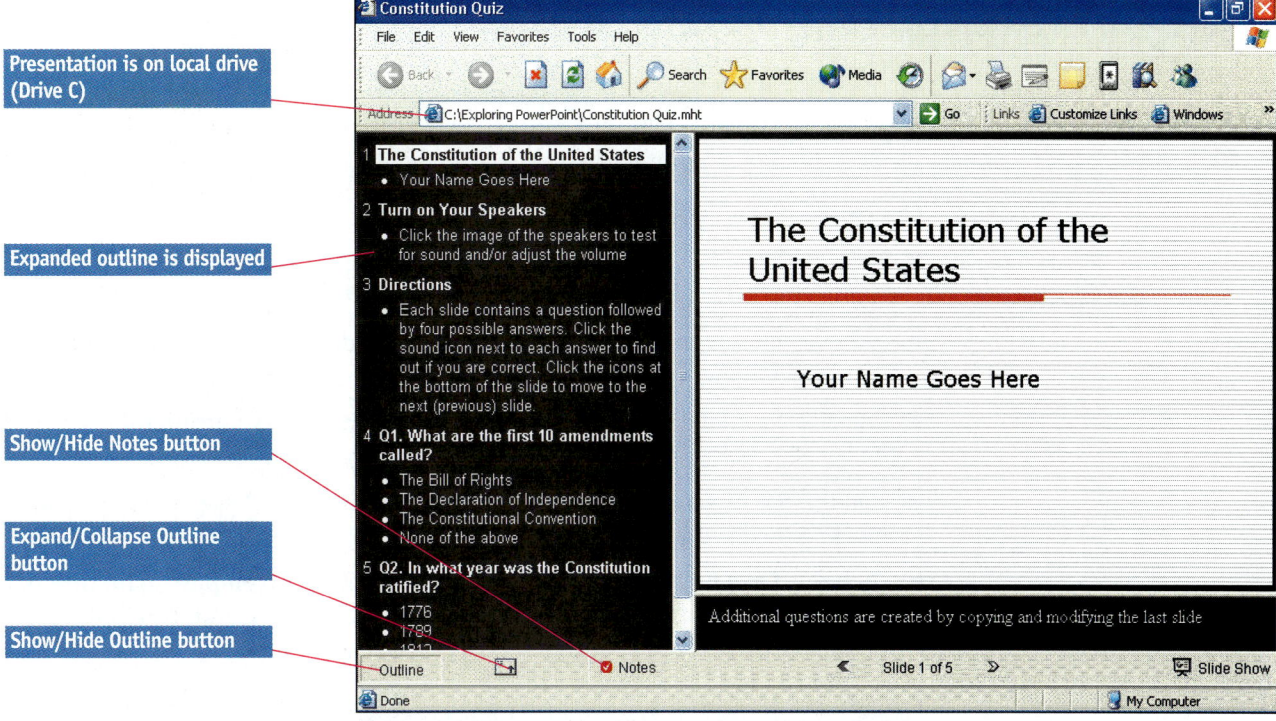

(a) Viewed Locally

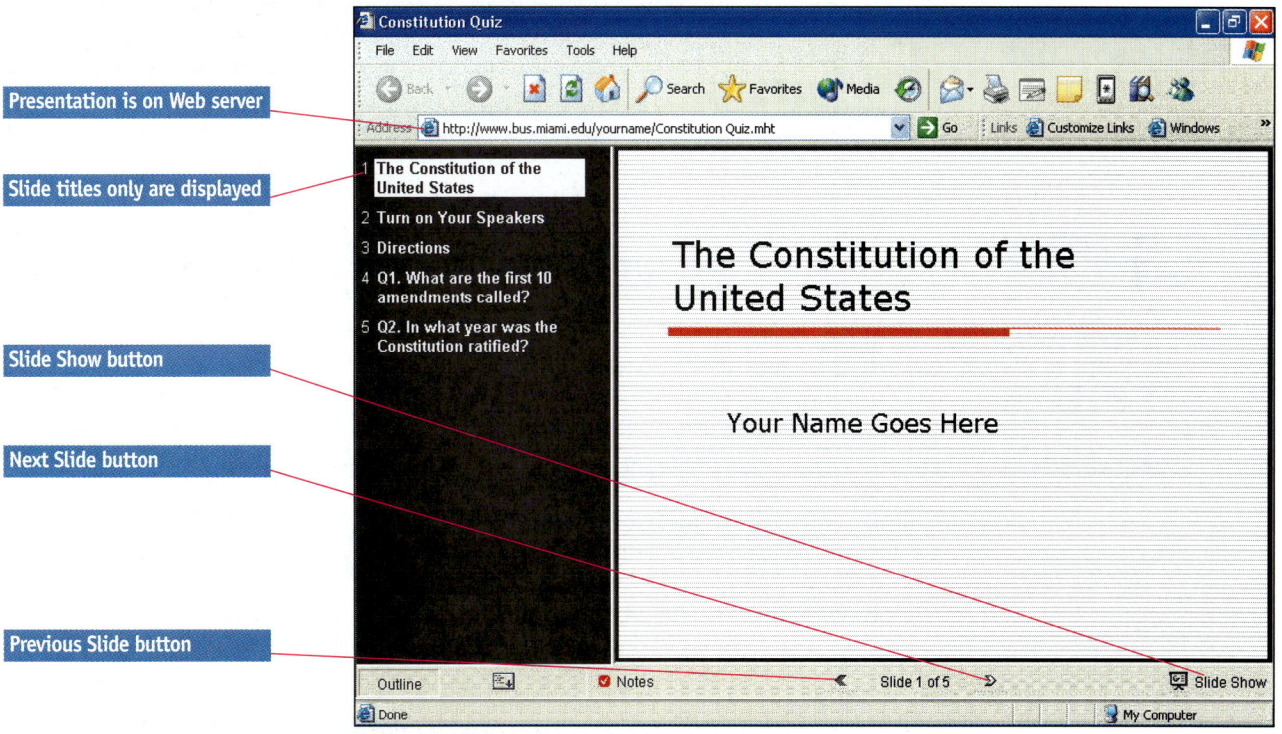

(b) On a Web Server

FIGURE 4.4 PowerPoint Web Pages

hands-on exercise

2 Presentations on the Web

Objective To save a presentation as a Web page, then view the result in Internet Explorer; to modify the newly created Web document in PowerPoint.

Step 1: **Create the Web Page**

- Open the **Create a Quiz presentation** in the **Exploring PowerPoint folder**. Change the title to **The Constitution of the United States**.
- Add your name to the title slide. Click in the **Speaker Notes** area and enter the text shown in Figure 4.5a.
- Pull down the **File menu** and click the **Save As Web Page command** to display the Save as dialog box. Select the **Exploring PowerPoint folder**.
- Save the file as **Constitution Quiz**. The file type should be specified as **Single File Web Page**, which was introduced in Office 2003.
- Click the **Save button** to save the presentation as a Web page. The title bar changes to the name of the Web page (Constitution Quiz), but the display does not change in any other way.

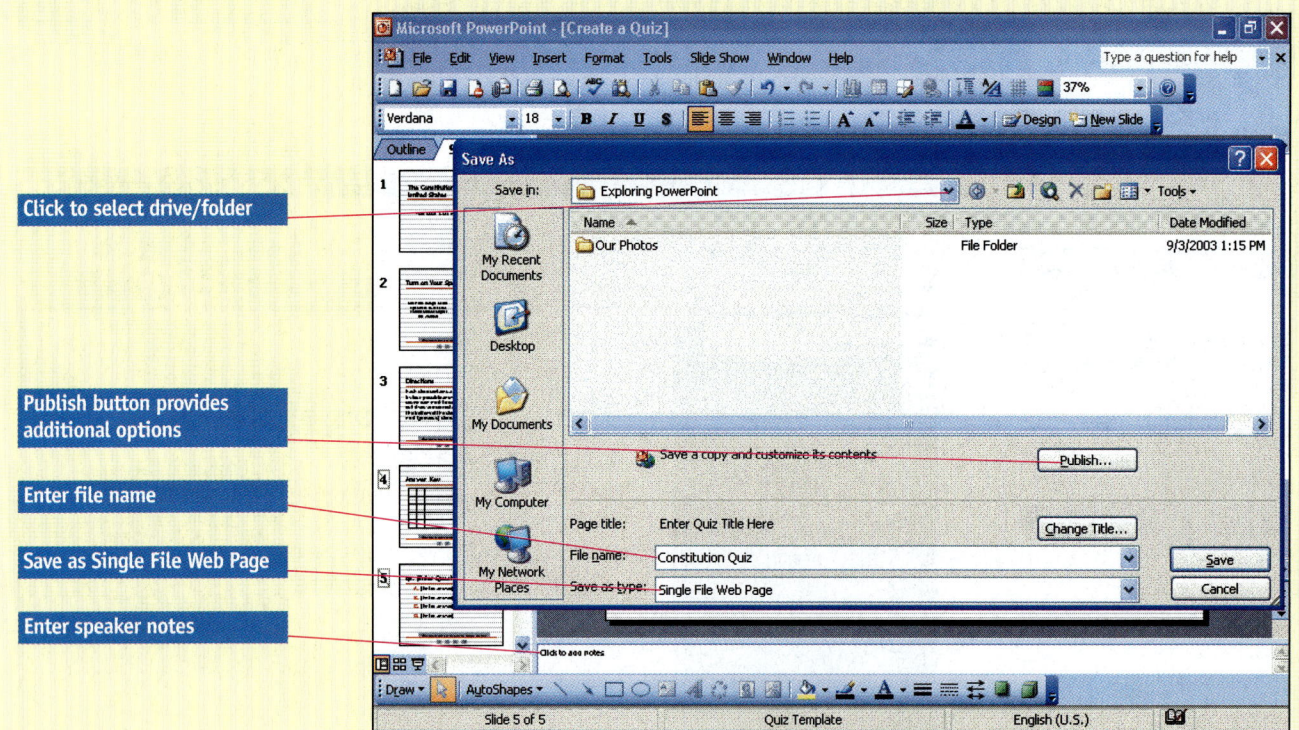

(a) Create the Web Page (step 1)

FIGURE 4.5 Hands-on Exercise 2

PUBLISHING OPTIONS

Click the Publish button in the Save as dialog box to display the Publish as Web page dialog box, where you view and/or modify the various options associated with an HTML document. The default publishing options work well, and you have total control over your Web pages.

1868 CHAPTER 4: ADVANCED TECHNIQUES

Step 2: **Add the Additional Slides**

- The Create a Quiz Presentation, with which we began the exercise, is generic, and thus specific questions have to be added. This will be accomplished by copying the last (empty question) slide multiple times, and modifying each slide accordingly.

- Change to the **Slide Sorter view**. Press **Ctrl+End** to move to the last slide. Press and hold the **Ctrl key** as you drag the last slide to the left of the answer key. Release the mouse to duplicate the slide.

- The newly copied slide should still be selected. Click the **Hide Slide button** on the Slide Sorter toolbar to unhide this slide as shown in Figure 4.5b.

- Click the **Copy button** or press **Ctrl+C** to copy the new (and unhidden) slide to the clipboard. Click the **Paste button** or press **Ctrl+V** to paste the copied slide into the presentation.

- The presentation should now contain a total of seven slides (the original five slides plus the two you just added).

- Save the presentation.

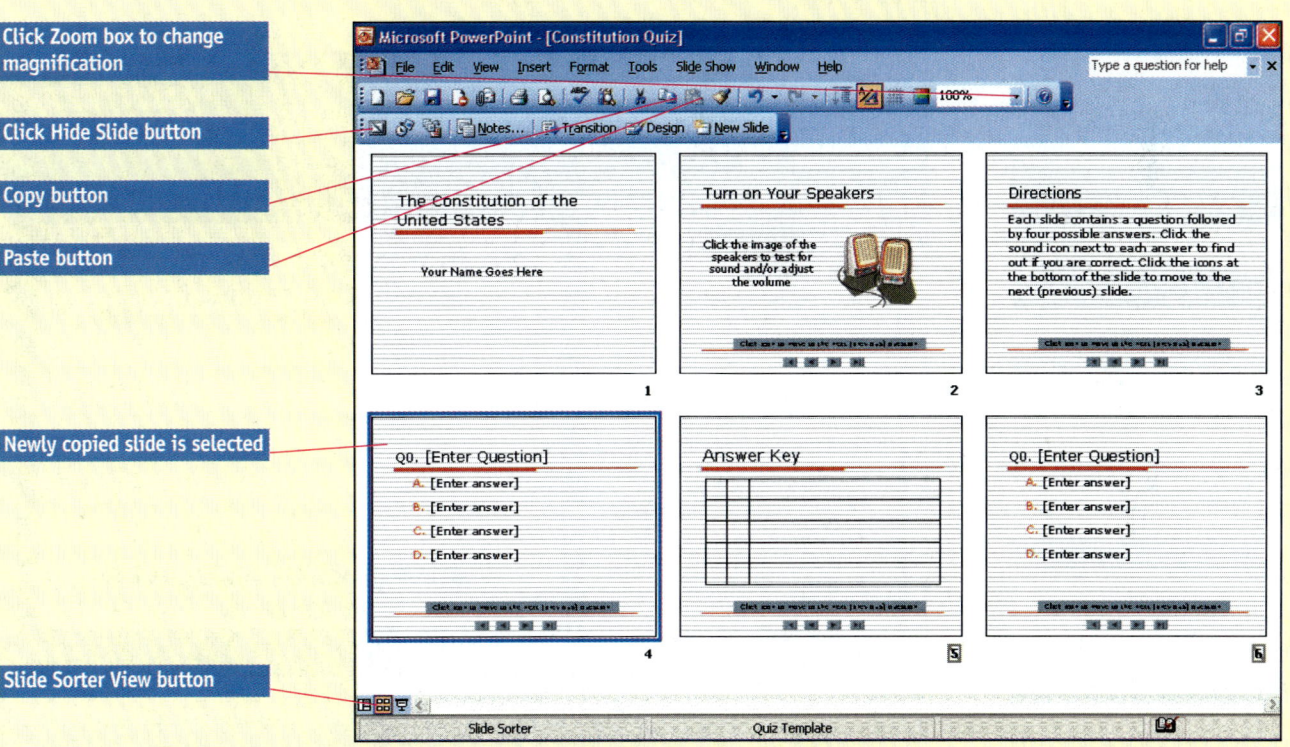

(b) Add the Additional Slides (step 2)

FIGURE 4.5 Hands-on Exercise 2 (*continued*)

CHANGE THE MAGNIFICATION

Click the down arrow on the Zoom box to change the display magnification, which in turn determines the size of individual slides. The higher the magnification, the easier it is to read the text of an individual slide, but the fewer slides you see at one time. Conversely, changing to lower magnification decreases the size of the individual slides, but enables you to see more of the presentation. You can also change the size of either pane in the Normal view in similar fashion.

Step 3: **Create the Questions**

- Change to the **Normal view** and select the fourth slide. Change Q0 to **Q1**. Replace the default text with the question and answers on the first 10 amendments to the Constitution as shown in Figure 4.5c.

- Pull down the **Insert menu**, click **Movies and Sounds**, then click **Sound from File** to display the Insert Sound dialog box. Select the **Applause** sound and click **OK**. Click the **When Clicked button** when asked how you want the sound to start. A Sound icon should appear in the middle of the slide.

- Click and drag the **Sound icon** to the left of the first answer, **The Bill of Rights**, which is the correct answer. Insert the other sounds to signify an erroneous answer next to the remaining choices.

- Press and hold the **Ctrl key** as you select all four **Sound icons**. Pull down the **Format menu**, click **Picture** to display the Format Picture dialog box, then click the **Position tab**. Enter **.75″** in the Horizontal list box. Click **OK**.

- Create the second question as shown in Figure 4.5c. Insert the appropriate sound files next to each answer, placing the Applause file next to part (b). Align the sound icons **.75 inch** from the left edge of the slide.

- Save the presentation.

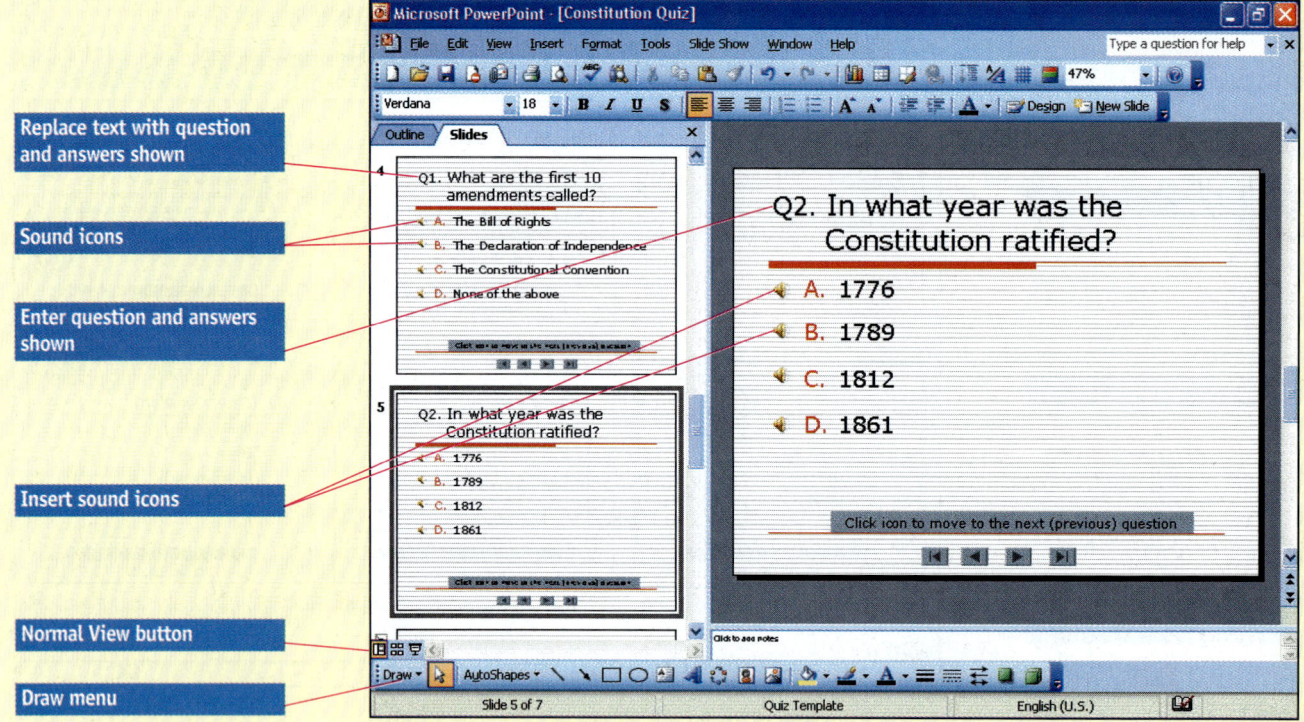

(c) Create the Questions (step 3)

FIGURE 4.5 Hands-on Exercise 2 (*continued*)

ALIGN, DISTRIBUTE, AND NUDGE

You can align objects left, center, or right (vertical stack), or top, middle, or bottom (horizontal row). Press and hold the Ctrl key as you select multiple objects on a slide, then click the down arrow on the Draw button within the Drawing toolbar to align the selected objects. You can also create uniform space between the objects by distributing horizontally or vertically. You can even nudge the objects by moving them slightly in the desired direction.

Step 4: **Open the Web Page**

- You can view the Web page you just created even if it has not been saved on a Web server. Start **Internet Explorer** if it is not already open, or click its button on the Windows taskbar.

- Pull down the **File menu** and click the **Open command** to display the Open dialog box in Figure 4.5d.

- Click the **Browse button**, then select the folder and drive (e.g., **Exploring PowerPoint** on drive C) where you saved the Web page.

- Select **Constitution Quiz** and click **Open**, which closes the dialog box. The selected file name has been inserted into the original Open dialog box. Click **OK** to open the presentation.

- You should see the presentation that was created earlier, except that you are viewing it in Internet Explorer rather than PowerPoint. The Address bar reflects the local address (the Exploring PowerPoint folder) of the presentation.

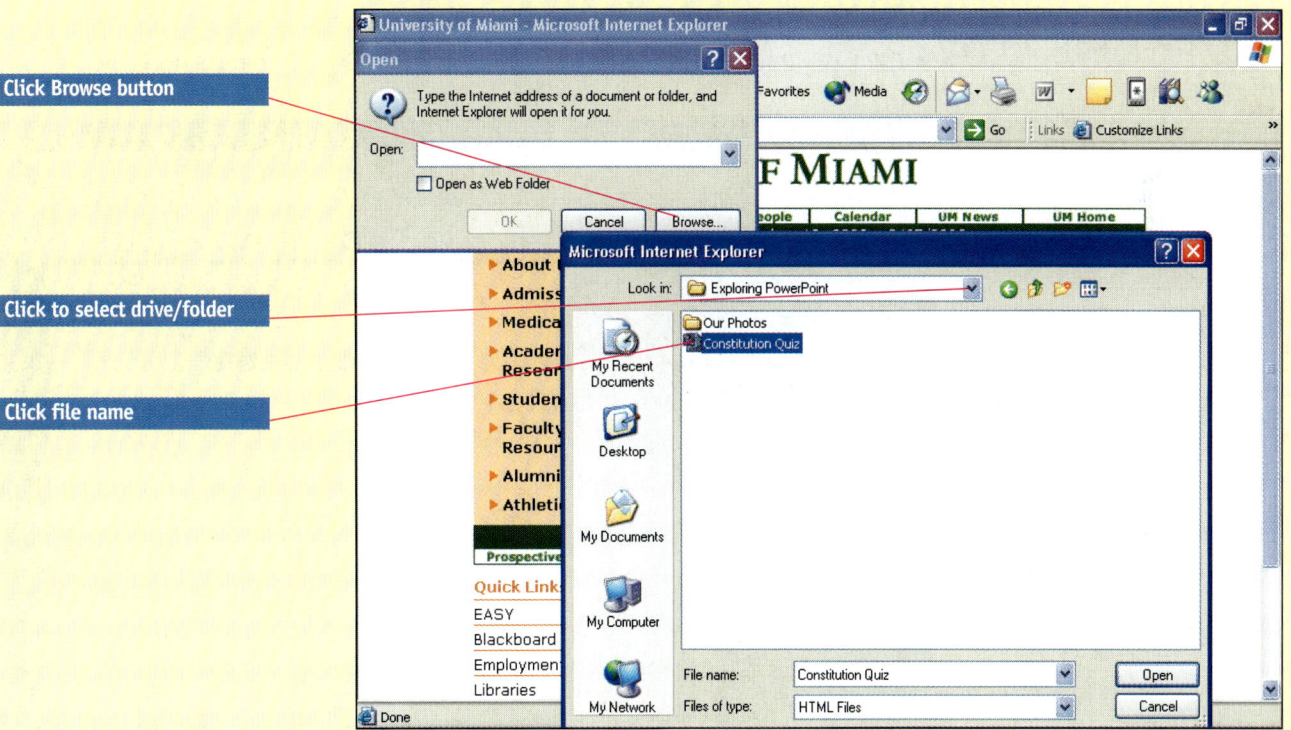

(d) Open the Web Page (step 4)

FIGURE 4.5 Hands-on Exercise 2 (*continued*)

SINGLE FILE WEB PAGE

Microsoft Office 2003 introduces a Single File Web Page format that saves all of the elements of a Web page, including text and graphics, in a single file. The new MHTML format lets you upload your page to a Web server as a single file, as opposed to sending multiple files and folders. It also lets you send the entire page as a single e-mail attachment. The new file format is supported by Internet Explorer 4.0 and higher.

Step 5: **View the Presentation**

- Explore the navigation controls that appear at the bottom of the Internet Explorer window as shown in Figure 4.5e. (If you do not see these controls, return to step 3 and save the presentation with these controls. Click the **Publish button** in the Save as dialog box, click the **Web Options command button**, click **General**, then check the appropriate box.)

- Click the **Show/Hide Outline button** at the bottom left to show or hide the outline. Click the **Expand/Collapse Outline button** (when the outline is visible) to vary the detail of the outline.

- Click the **Notes button** to show/hide the Notes pane at the bottom of the window. The title page is the only slide that contains a note.

- Click the **Slide Show button** at the lower right of the Internet Explorer window to start the slide show.

- This is the identical slide show that you would see if you were viewing the presentation from within PowerPoint. Stop the show at any time by pressing the **Esc key** to return to the view in Figure 4.5e.

- Click the **PowerPoint button** on the Windows taskbar to return to PowerPoint.

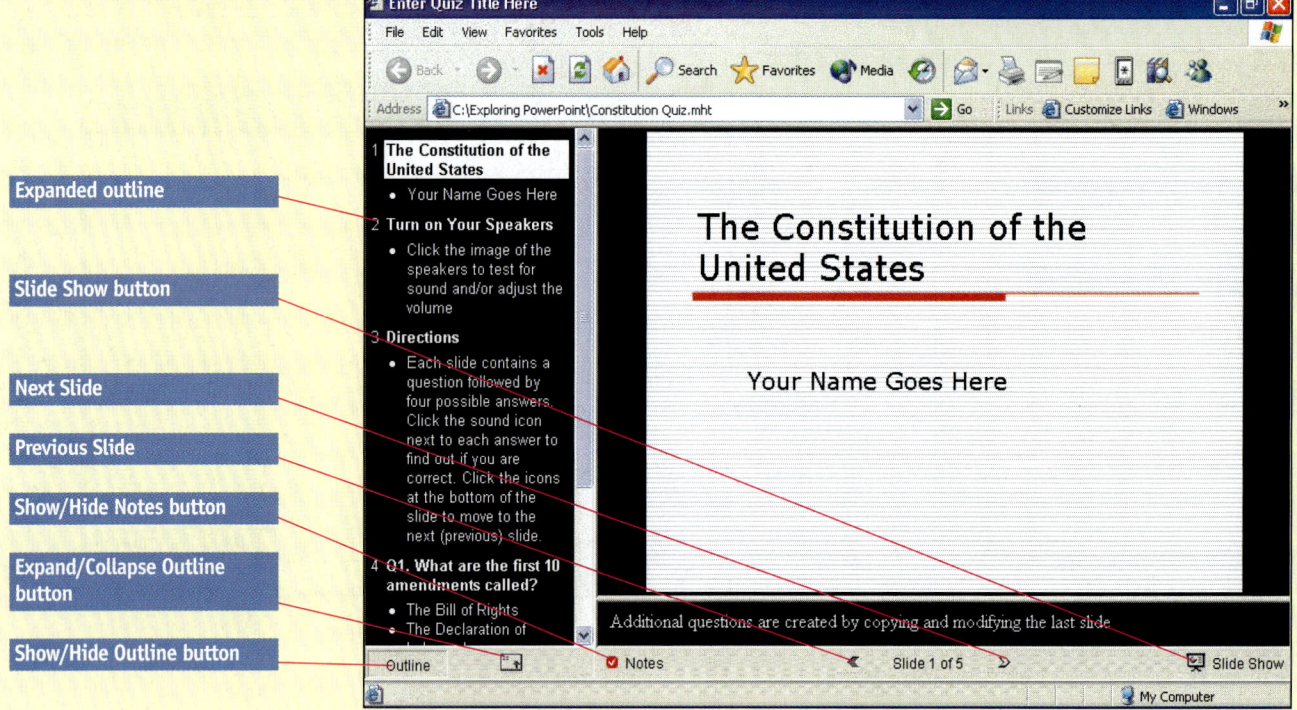

(e) View the Presentation (step 5)

FIGURE 4.5 Hands-on Exercise 2 (*continued*)

TWO WAYS TO NAVIGATE

The Previous and Next Slide buttons within the Internet Explorer window may appear redundant with the corresponding action buttons that were added explicitly to the PowerPoint slides. Note, however, that you can click the Slide Show button within Internet Explorer to show a presentation on the Web, which in turn (temporally) closes Internet Explorer and reverts to a true PowerPoint presentation in which the action buttons are useful.

Step 6: **Modify the Presentation**

- You should be back in PowerPoint. If necessary, change to the **Normal view**, and then select the sixth slide (the slide containing the answer key). Enter the answers to the first two questions as shown in Figure 4.5f.

- Click and drag to select the number of the first question, click the **Insert Hyperlink button** on the Standard toolbar, click **Places in this Document**, and set the link to slide 4 (the slide containing the first question). Create a hyperlink for the second question in similar fashion.

- Click the **Slides tab** in the left pane. Right click the slide containing the answer key to display a context-sensitive menu as shown in Figure 4.5f, then click the **Hide Slide command** to display the slide during a slide show. The icon next to the slide will change to show that the slide is no longer hidden.

- **Save the presentation.** This is very important, because if you do not save the presentation, these changes will not be visible when you return to Internet Explorer.

- Click the **Internet Explorer button** on the Windows taskbar to return to the Web presentation.

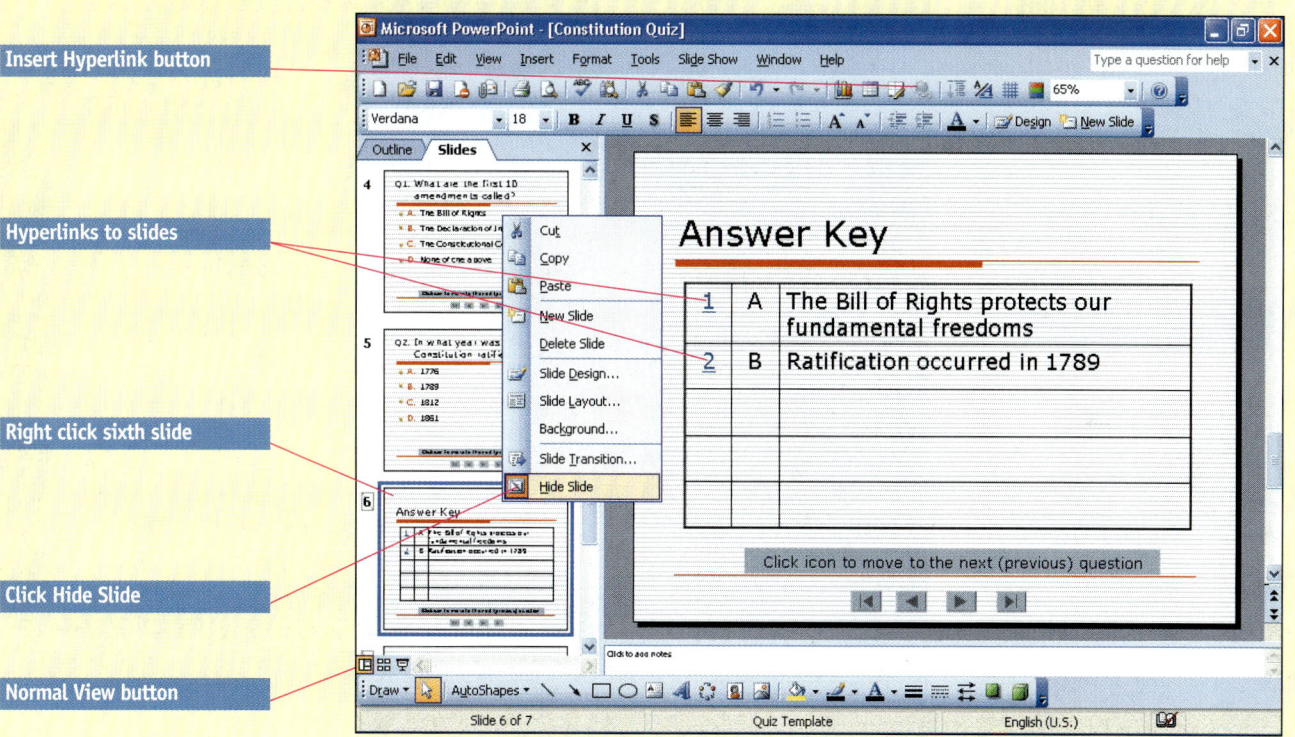

(f) Modify the Presentation (step 6)

FIGURE 4.5 Hands-on Exercise 2 (*continued*)

ROUND TRIP HTML

All applications in Microsoft Office enable you to open an HTML or MHTML document in the Office application that created it. In other words, you can start with a PowerPoint presentation, use the Save as Web page command to convert the presentation to a Web document, then view that document in a Web browser. You can then reopen the Web document in PowerPoint (the original Office application) and have full access to all PowerPoint commands in order to edit the presentation.

Step 7: **View the Corrected Presentation**

- Close Internet Explorer, then reopen Internet Explorer and reload the **Constitution Quiz** presentation.

- Select the **Answer Key slide** in the left pane to display the associated slide in the right pane. Click the **hyperlink** to the first question to test the link. Return to the slide containing the answer key. Test the hyperlink to the second question in similar fashion.

- You can improve the presentation further by changing the text of the title bar (which currently says, "Enter Quiz Title Here"). Return to PowerPoint.

- Pull down the **File menu** and click the **Save As Web Page command** to display the associated dialog box. Click the **Change Title button** to display the Set Page Title dialog box, enter **Constitution Quiz**, and click **OK**. Click **Save** to save the page. Click **Yes** if asked whether to replace the existing presentation.

- Close Internet Explorer, then reopen Internet Explorer and reload the **Constitution Quiz** presentation. The title bar should reflect the new title as shown in Figure 4.7g.

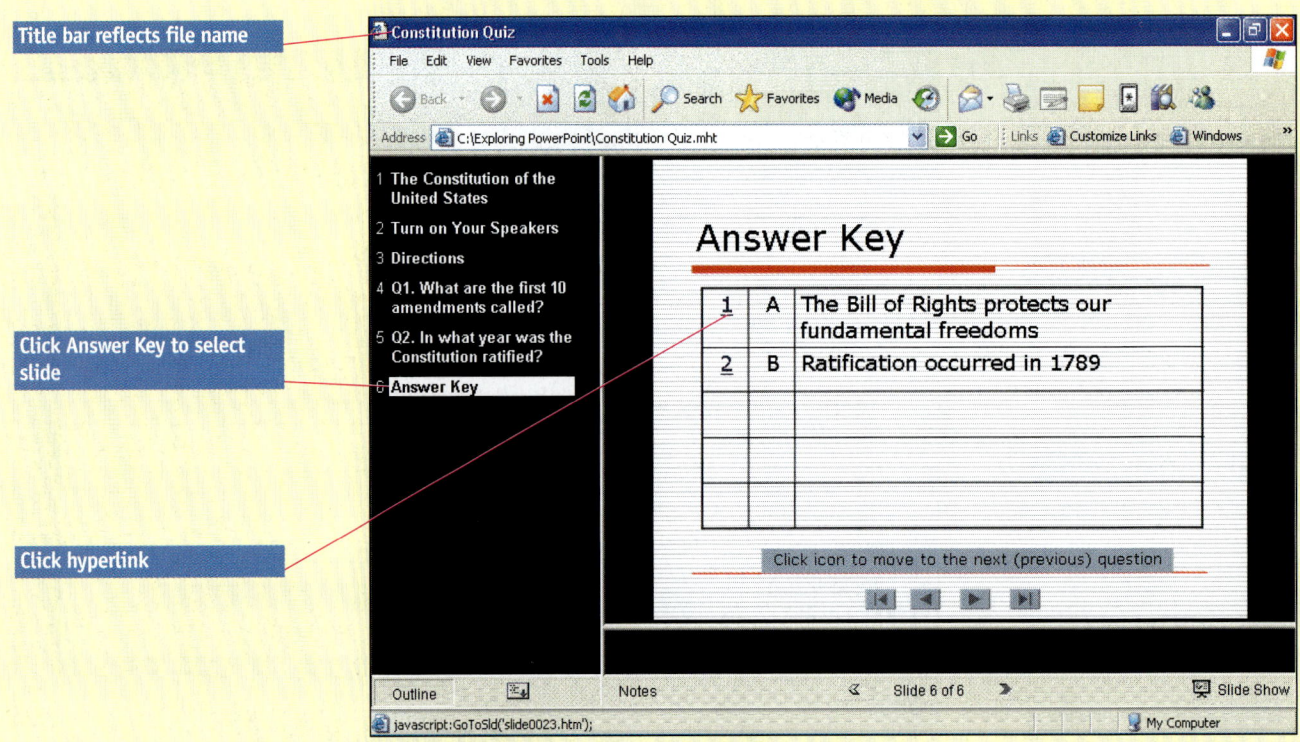

(g) View the Corrected Presentation (step 7)

FIGURE 4.5 Hands-on Exercise 2 (*continued*)

WHY REFRESH DOESN'T WORK

A Web browser cannot display an MHTML document directly, but must expand it to one or more temporary HTML documents. Thus, if you update a presentation that is saved in MHTML format and then click the Refresh button in Internet Explorer, the browser simply reloads the previous HTML documents. You have to close Internet Explorer, reopen Internet Explorer, and then open the updated MHTML file. The file then expands to display an updated set of HTML documents that show the modified presentation.

Step 8: **Print the Web Page**

- Select the first slide. Pull down the **File menu** (in Internet Explorer) and click the **Print Preview command** to display the screen in Figure 4.5h. If necessary, click the **down arrow** on the zoom box to adjust the magnification so that you can read the page header.

- Click the **Page Setup button** on the Print Preview toolbar to display the associated dialog box.

- Click the **question mark** (Help button) in the Page Setup dialog box, then point to the header list box to see an explanation of the associated codes, then compare these codes to the appearance of the printed page. The default settings display the title and the number of pages at the top of the page.

- Close the Page Setup dialog box. Print the title page of the presentation for your instructor to show that you have created the Web page.

- Close Internet Explorer and return to PowerPoint. Print the audience handouts, six per page, to show the completed presentation.

- Save the presentation. Exit PowerPoint if you do not want to continue with the next exercise at this time.

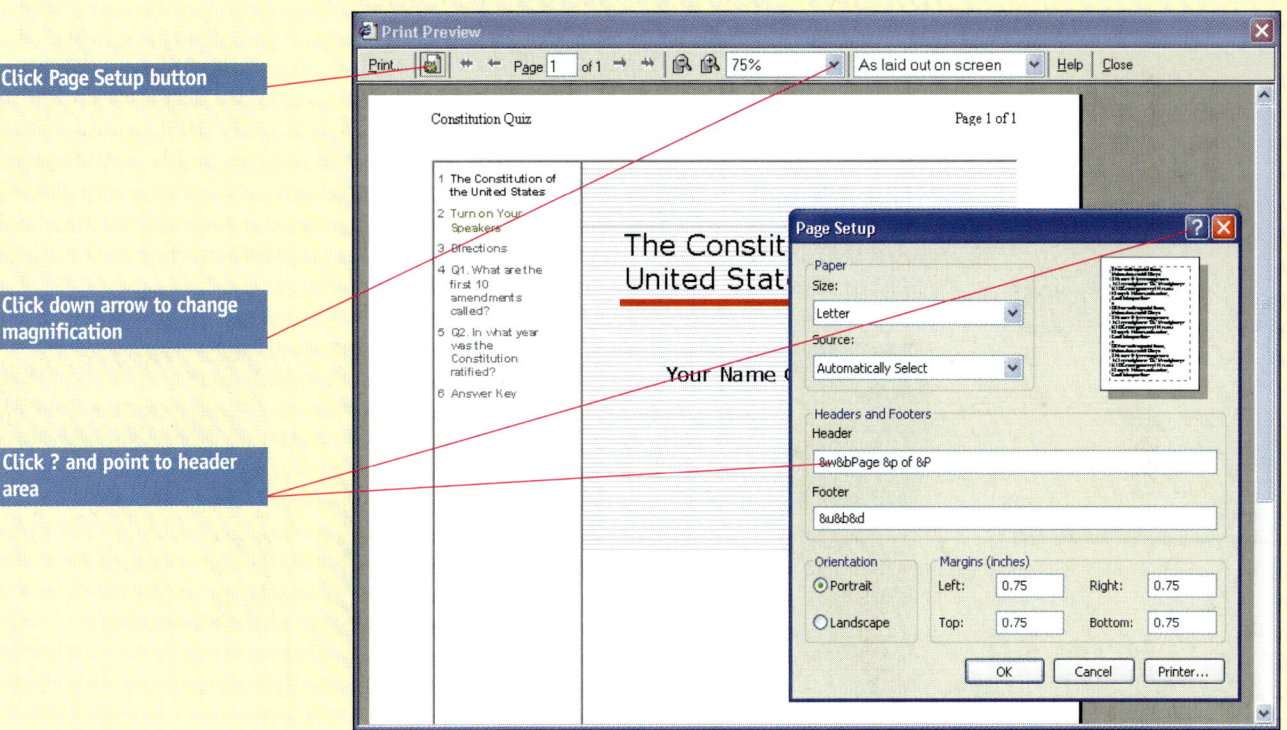

(h) Print the Web Page (step 8)

FIGURE 4.5 Hands-on Exercise 2 (*continued*)

PRINT FROM POWERPOINT

Internet Explorer is great for viewing Web pages, but less than ideal for printing them. PowerPoint provides far more flexibility. Click the PowerPoint button on the Windows taskbar to return to PowerPoint, then pull down the File menu and click the Print command. You can print individual slides, audience handouts, a presentation outline, and/or speaker notes.

NARRATING A PRESENTATION

The presentations thus far have used limited sound, which was played on demand by the viewer. This section describes how to add narration (or voiceover) that plays automatically when a presentation is delivered. Narration is very useful to create a self-running presentation for a trade show or kiosk and/or to embellish a Web-based presentation.

Figure 4.6 displays a six-slide presentation in the Slide Sorter view that represents a hypothetical introduction to this course as it might be delivered by your professor. The **Record Narration command** creates a specific narrative (sound file) for each slide and also records the required time for that narrative. Look closely, and you will see a sound icon on each slide as well as the associated time. Once the narrative has been created, you can set the presentation to play automatically, advancing from one slide to the next, in conjunction with your voice.

We recommend that you create a script and rehearse the presentation prior to recording it, so that the narrative flows smoothly, but if necessary you can rerecord the entire presentation as often as you like. You can also delete the sound file on an individual slide, use the Windows Sound Recorder to create a new file for just that slide, and then use the Custom Animation command to substitute the new recording.

Sound files can grow very large as the duration increases, and thus you are given the choice to link or embed the narration at the time of recording. Linking creates individual sound files for each slide, which in turn decreases the size of the presentation itself. Linking makes it more difficult, however, to copy the presentation to another computer (or upload it to the Web) because you must remember to take all of the files (the presentation as well as the individual sound files). Embedding creates a larger presentation, but results in a single file. Either technique is acceptable, however, and the choice is up to you.

Our next exercise also describes how to create a *custom show*, consisting of a subset of slides within the presentation, to play for a specific audience. Multiple custom shows can be created within one presentation.

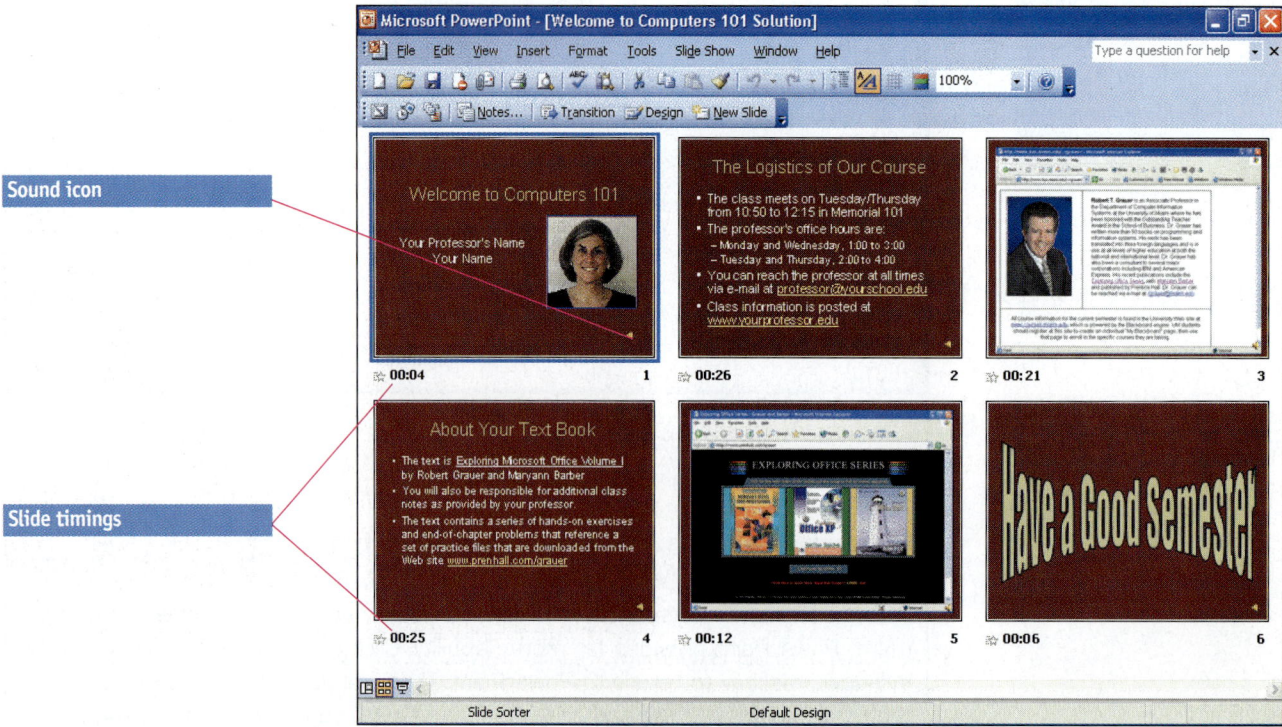

FIGURE 4.6 Narrating a Presentation

BROADCASTS AND ONLINE MEETINGS

Any presentation, including video and audio, can be delivered as a **Web broadcast**. The **broadcast** can be live or recorded. A live broadcast is scheduled at a precise time, and invitations are sent to a designated list of attendees. A recorded broadcast is uploaded to a Web server and configured for on-demand viewing. Either type of broadcast is ideal for reaching large and/or geographically dispersed audiences. PowerPoint alone is sufficient to deliver a broadcast to groups of 10 or fewer individuals. Additional software, such as Microsoft Windows Media Server, is required to reach larger audiences.

PowerPoint also supports ***online meetings*** in addition to Web broadcasts. A broadcast is a one-way connection in which you speak, and the audience listens. An online meeting is a two-way connection in which everyone can communicate with everyone else. Online meetings are limited to 10 or fewer attendees and require the Microsoft NetMeeting software.

Figure 4.7 displays the opening slide in a hypothetical Web broadcast. A Web broadcast is viewed in Internet Explorer and is similar in appearance to a presentation that is saved as a Web page. The controls for the presentation appear in the left pane. You can start and stop the presentation at will and/or adjust the volume of the narration. The links at the top of the right pane let you return to previous slides and/or e-mail the author of the presentation. The broadcast is stored on a Web server, where it is accessed by the invited audience. (Our presentation is stored locally, however, because it has not yet been uploaded to the Web.)

A live broadcast, like any other presentation, should be rehearsed several times prior to the actual delivery. This is accomplished entirely on a stand-alone computer without having to upload the broadcast pages to the Web. Note, however, that a broadcast contains its own audio, which means that the associated PowerPoint presentation should not contain its own sound files.

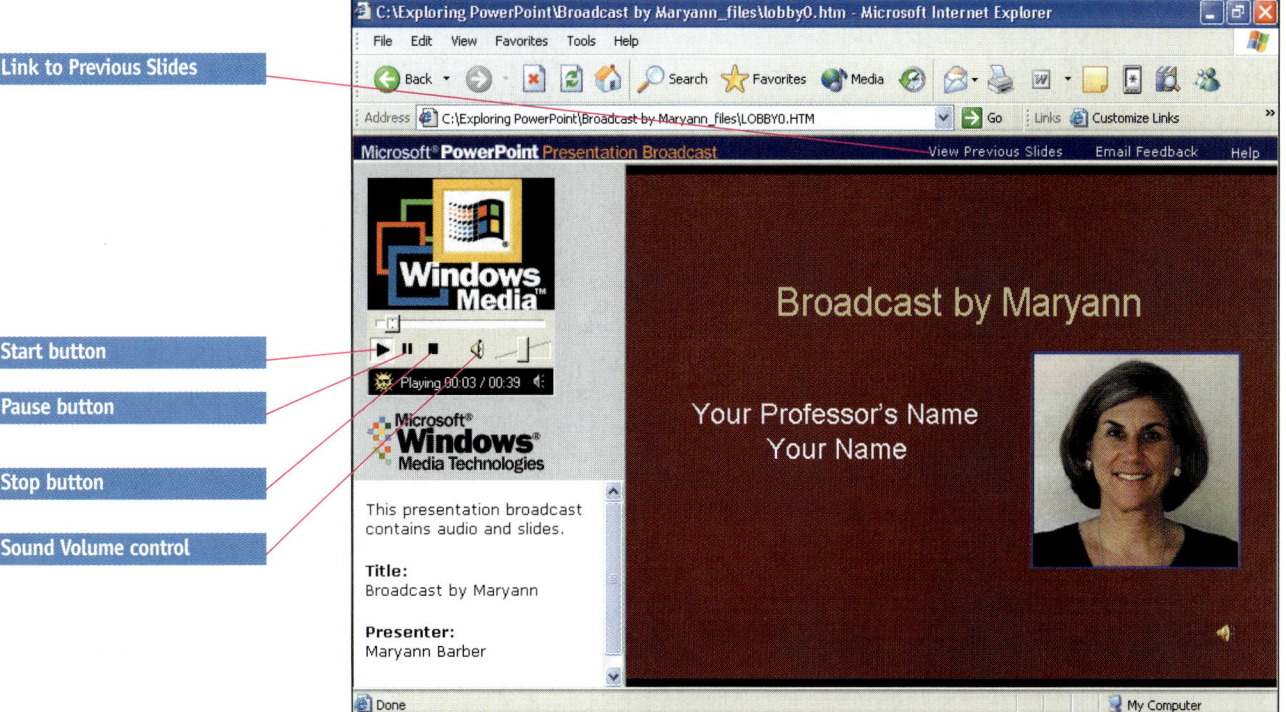

FIGURE 4.7   Broadcasting a Presentation

hands-on exercise

3 Narrating a Presentation

Objective Add narration to a presentation; create a custom show within an existing presentation. Use Figure 4.8 as a guide in doing the exercise.

Step 1: **Open the Presentation**

- Open the **Welcome to Computers 101** presentation in the **Exploring PowerPoint folder** as shown in Figure 4.8a. The presentation consists of six slides that describe an introductory computer course.
- Add **your name** and **your professor's name** to the title slide. Replace Maryann's picture with your own or with that of an instructor if a photo is available.
- Change the text of the second slide so that the information corresponds to the logistics of your specific course. The remaining slides can be used without any modification.
- Save the presentation as **Welcome to Computers 101 Solution**.

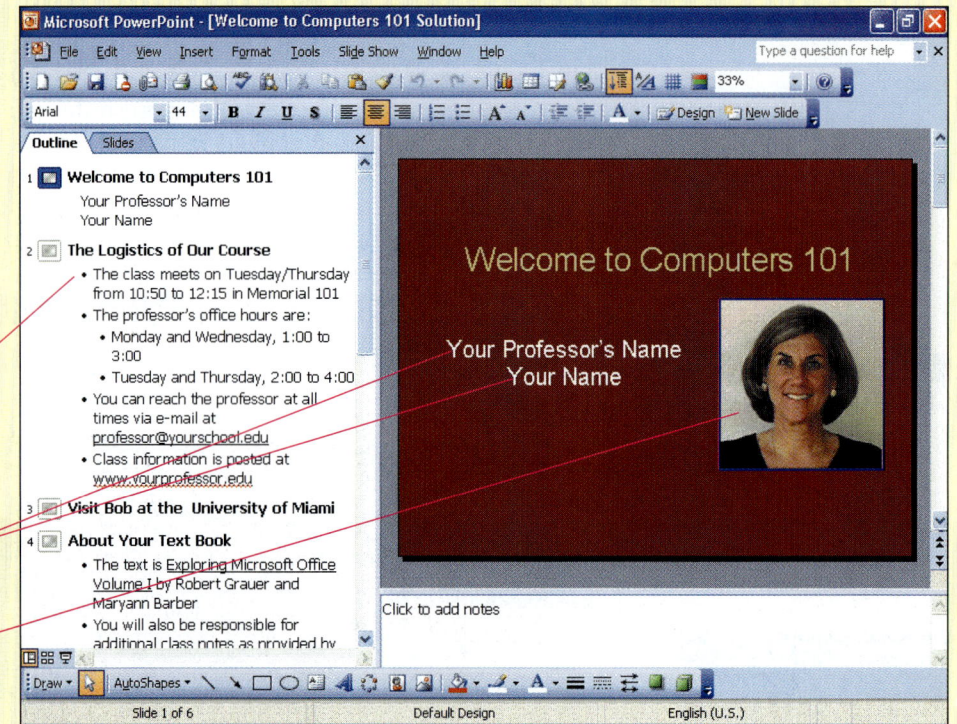

(a) Open the Presentation (step 1)

FIGURE 4.8 Hands-on Exercise 3

REHEARSE THE PRESENTATION

You should create a script and rehearse your presentation before recording so that the narrative flows smoothly. Even if you are well rehearsed, you can still make a mistake, in which case you can simply rerecord the entire presentation. You can also delete the sound file on an individual slide, then use the Windows Sound Recorder to create a new file for just that slide.

Step 2: **Record the Narration**

- Press **Ctrl+Home** to move to the first slide. Pull down the **Slide Show menu** and click the **Record Narration command** to display the Record Narration dialog box.
- Click the **Change Quality command button** to display the Sound Selection dialog box in Figure 4.8b.
- Click the **down arrow** in the Name box and select **Telephone Quality**. Click **OK.** You do not need CD quality if you are recording a speaking voice.
- It's easier to embed the sound files into the presentation, as opposed to linking to individual files. Thus, the box to link narration should be clear.
- Click the **Set Microphone Level command button** to test the microphone. Read the text into the mike. You should see a set of green squares to indicate that the microphone is working properly. Click **OK** to close the Microphone Check dialog box.
- Click **OK** to begin recording your presentation. You should see the first slide in your presentation. Speak naturally and introduce yourself as the instructor.
- Pause briefly when you have finished recording the first slide, then click the mouse to move to the next slide. Continue speaking into the microphone as you move from one slide to the next. Press **Esc** when finished.

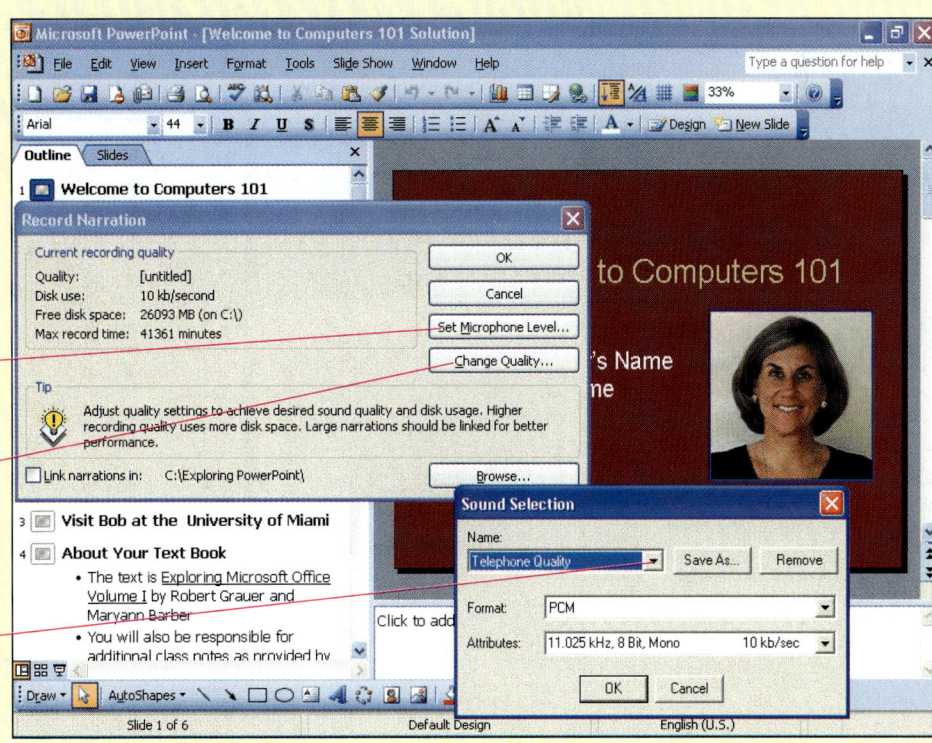

(b) Record the Narration (step 2)

FIGURE 4.8 Hands-on Exercise 3 (*continued*)

CHOOSE THE APPROPRIATE OPTIONS

A two-minute voice recording will require approximately 1,200 kilobytes or 1.2 megabytes of storage, given a recording rate of 10kb per second. At CD quality, however, the same recording requires almost 20 megabytes, given a recording rate of 172 kb/second, and you will be hard pressed to hear the difference. Be sure to select telephone quality prior to recording.

Step 3: **Set Up the Presentation**

- You will see a message indicating that the narrations have been saved with each slide and asking whether you want to save the slide timings as well. Click the **Save button**.

- You should see a screen similar to Figure 4.8c. The time required for each slide appears under the slide within the Slide Sorter view.

- Pull down the **Slide Show menu** and click the **Set Up Show command** to display the associated dialog box. The check boxes in the Show options area should be clear. Be sure the option to Advance slides Using timings is selected.

- Click **OK**. Select the first slide, then click the **Slide Show button** above the status bar to begin the presentation. The slides should advance automatically, and you should hear the associated narration as each slide appears on the screen.

- You can replace the narration for the entire presentation by repeating step 2 on the previous page. Alternatively, you can replace the narration (sound file) for an individual slide as described in step 4.

- Save the presentation.

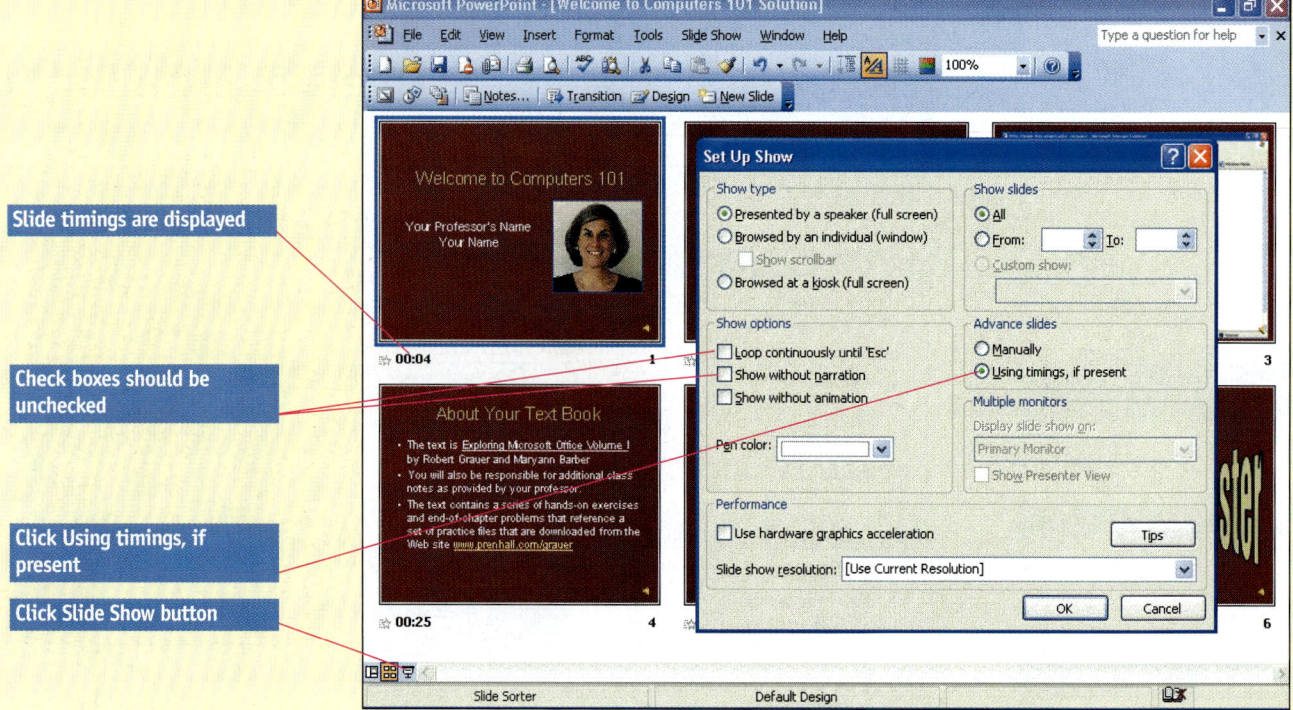

(c) Set Up the Presentation (step 3)

FIGURE 4.8 Hands-on Exercise 3 (*continued*)

THE REHEARSE TIMINGS COMMAND

The Record Narration command is similar in concept to the Rehearse Timings command, except that the latter does not include recorded sound. The Rehearse Timings command does, however, display a Rehearsal toolbar that lets you pause and catch your breath as you practice your speech for each slide. The Rehearsal toolbar also displays the amount of time spent on each slide as well as the total time for the presentation. Unfortunately, the toolbar is not available in conjunction with the Record Narration command.

Step 4: **Modify the Narration**

- Skip this step if you are satisfied with the narration for the entire presentation. Otherwise, return to the **Normal view** and select the slide where you want to replace the narration. Select the **Sound icon**.

- Pull down the **Slide Show menu** and open the Custom Animation task pane as shown in Figure 4.8d. Click the **Play button** to hear the narration to be sure you want to replace it. The Sound icon should still be selected. Press the **Del key**.

- Start the Sound Recorder (see boxed tip), click the **red dot** to begin recording, and click the **Stop button** when you are finished. Click the **Rewind button**, then click the **Play button** to listen to the sound. Save this file in the same folder as the other sounds for this presentation. Close the Sound Recorder.

- Pull down the **Insert menu**, click **Movies and Sounds**, then click **Sound from File** to display the Insert Sound dialog box. Locate the new narration, click **OK**, then click **Automatically** when asked how you want the sound to start. Move the Sound icon to the lower-right corner of the slide.

- The Animation task pane should show that the sound object (Welcome Message on our slide) will play automatically after the previous effect; in other words, the narration plays automatically when the slide is displayed. Close the task pane.

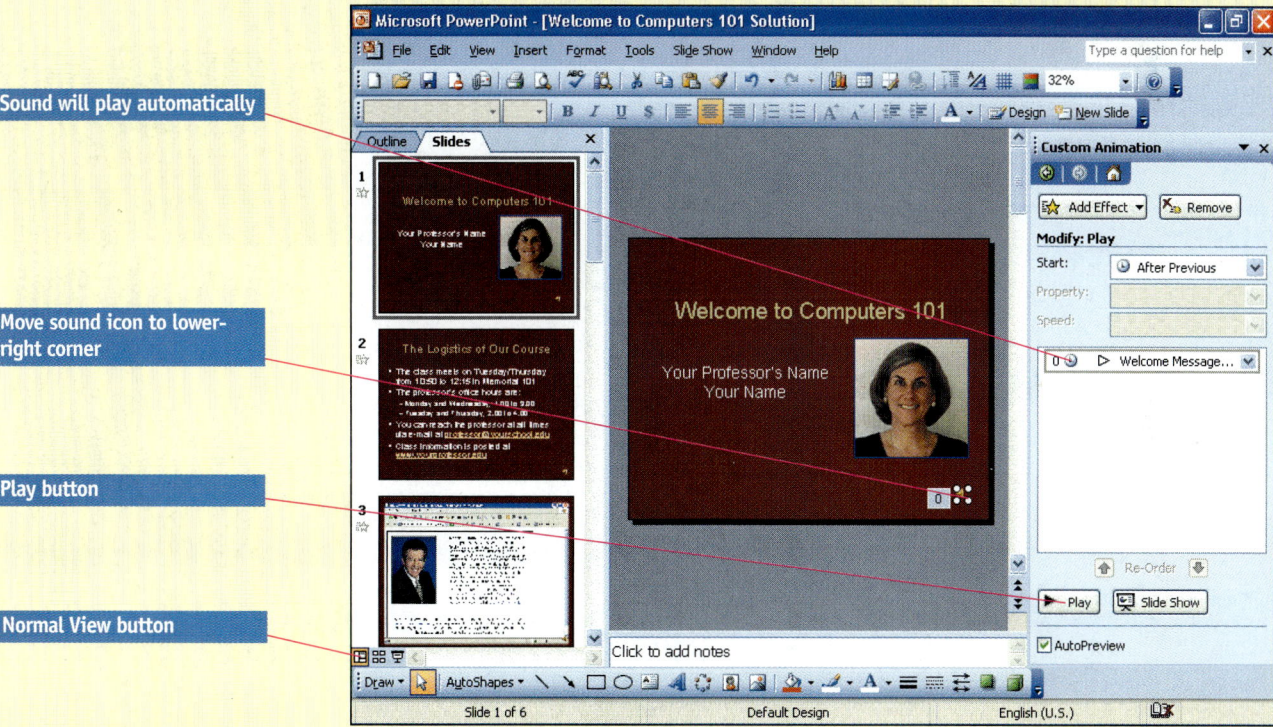

(d) Modify the Narration (step 4)

FIGURE 4.8   Hands-on Exercise 3 (continued)

THE SOUND RECORDER

Click the Start button, click All Programs, click Accessories, click Entertainment, then click Sound Recorder to display the associated dialog box. Pull down the File menu, click the Properties command and select All Formats in the Choose From list box. Click the Convert Now button. Select telephone quality as both the recording and playback format. Be sure to save the recorded file in the appropriate folder.

Step 5: **Create the Custom Shows**

- Pull down the **Slide Show menu** and click the **Custom Shows command** to display the Custom Shows dialog box. Click the **New button** to display the Define Custom Show dialog box in Figure 4.8e.

- Enter **Grauer on the Web** as the name of the new show. Select (click) **slide 3**, **Visit Bob Grauer at the University of Miami**, then click the **Add button**. The selected slide appears in the left column as the first slide in the custom show.

- Double click **slide 5**, **The Grauer Web Site**, to add this slide as well. Both slides should now appear in the left column. Click **OK** to close this dialog box. The newly created show, Grauer on the Web, should appear in the Custom Shows dialog box.

- Click the **New button** to create a second custom show. Enter **Logistics and Text** as the name of the second custom show. Double click **slides 2 and 4** to add these slides to this show. Click **OK** to create the show.

- Click the **Close button** to close the Custom Shows dialog box. Save the presentation.

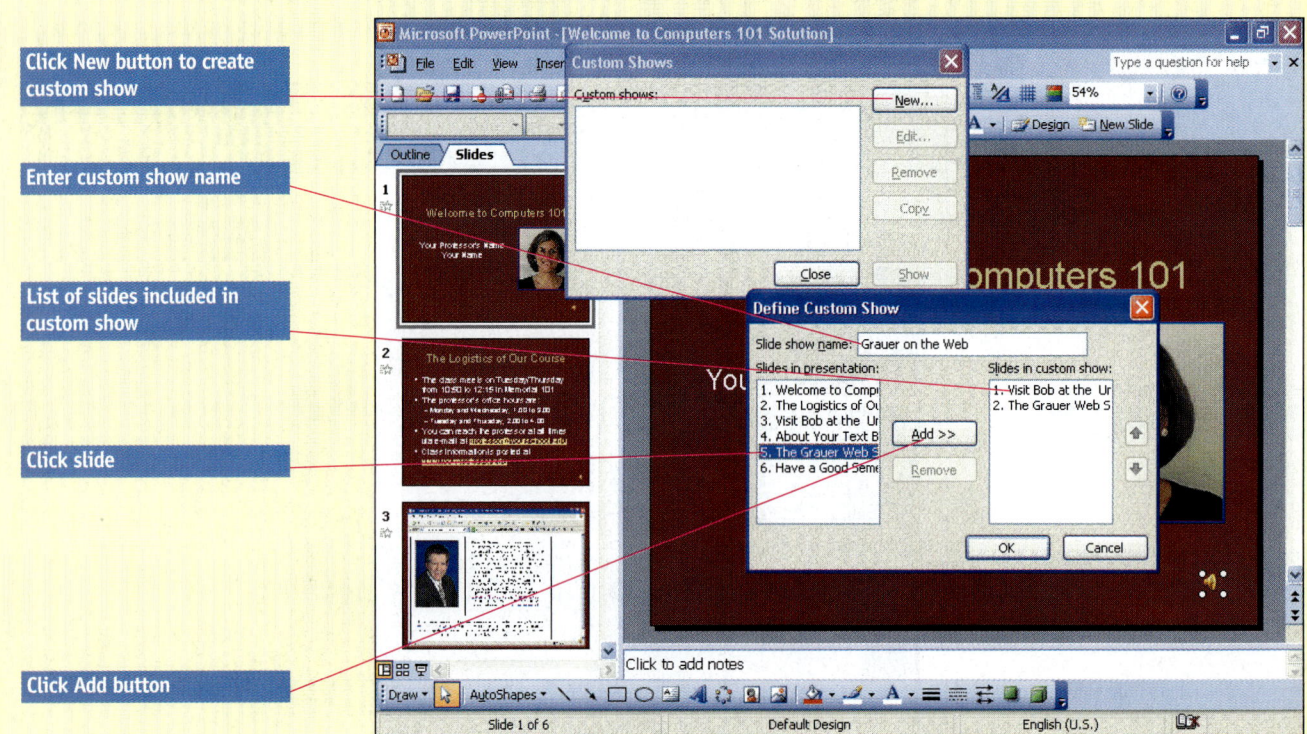

(e) Create the Custom Shows (step 5)

FIGURE 4.8 Hands-on Exercise 3 (*continued*)

DIFFERENT SHOWS FOR DIFFERENT AUDIENCES

Many presenters are faced with the task of creating nearly identical shows for different audiences. There is a "basic show" common to every audience, followed by a few special slides for each audience. You could create multiple presentations and store each presentation in its own file. It is much more efficient, however, to create custom shows within a single presentation. This saves time and effort, especially if you have to update information on a basic slide, in that you would make the change only once.

1882 CHAPTER 4: ADVANCED TECHNIQUES

Step 6: **Show Time**

- Pull down the **Slide Show menu** and click the **Custom Shows command**. Select the first custom show, **Grauer on the Web**. Click the **Show button**.

- You should see the slide containing Bob's home page at the University of Miami as shown in Figure 4.8f. You should also hear the accompanying narration.

- The next slide in the custom show, **The Grauer Web site**, should appear automatically with its narration, after which the presentation ends. Press **Esc** to return to PowerPoint.

- Pull down the **Slide Show menu** and click **Custom Shows** to view the second custom show, **Logistics and Text**, which also contains two slides. Press the **Esc key** at the end of the show to return to PowerPoint.

- Exit PowerPoint if you do not want to continue with the next exercise at this time.

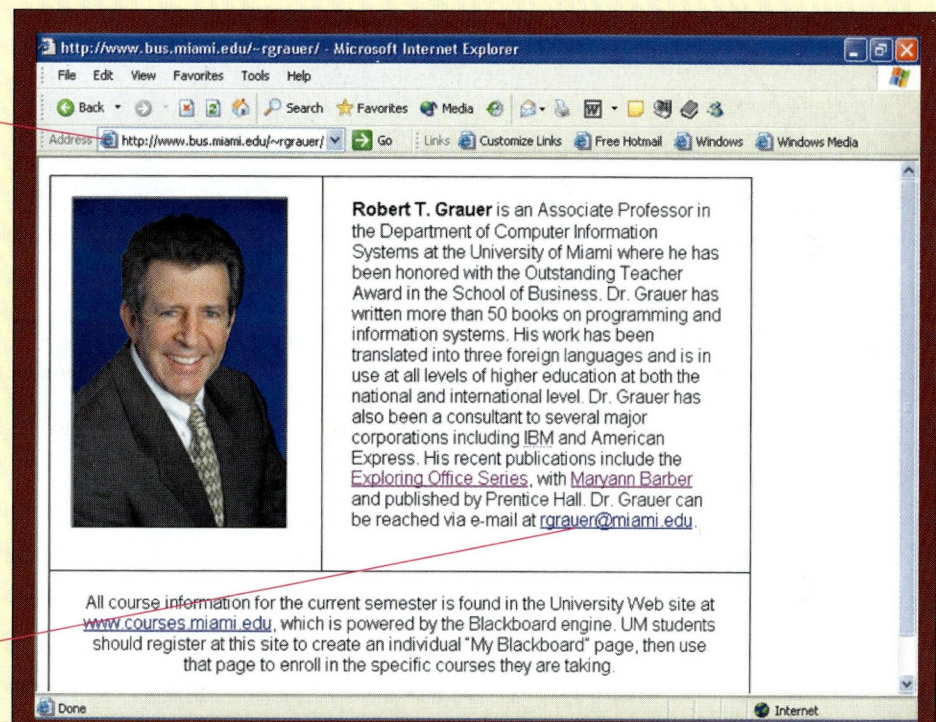

Bob's home page

Bob's e-mail address

(f) Show Time (step 6)

FIGURE 4.8   Hands-on Exercise 3 (*continued*)

ADD HYPERLINKS TO YOUR CUSTOM SHOWS

Create a table of contents in the form of hyperlinks to the various custom shows in your presentation. Press Ctrl+Home to move to the title slide, insert a text box, then enter the name of each custom show on a separate line. Click and drag to select the name of the first custom show, click the Insert Hyperlink button to display the associated text box, and click the Place in this Document icon at the left. Scroll, if necessary, until you can select the appropriate custom show. Check the box to show and return, and click OK. Do this for each custom show. Click the Slide Show button, then view your custom shows from the title slide.

SUMMARY

The use of sound requires additional hardware, namely, a sound card and speakers. A microphone is necessary to record a sound file, although multiple sounds are supplied within Microsoft Windows as well as Microsoft Office. All sounds are created through the Sound Recorder (a Windows accessory), which creates a WAV file or digitized recording of an actual sound. Sound files are stored just like any other type of file and can be moved and copied from one folder to another.

A template controls every aspect of a presentation's design, such as the background, the fonts and formatting of the text, and the size and placement of bullets and other elements. Each template has a default color scheme, consisting of eight balanced colors that are used for the background, text, slide title, shadows, and other accents. Change the template, and you change every aspect of a presentation. Change the color scheme within a template (each template has several alternate color schemes from which to choose), and you retain the overall look, but effect a subtle change in the appearance.

Action buttons build flexibility into a presentation by enabling easy access to the first, previous, next, and/or last slide in a presentation. Hyperlinks to specific slides provide another means of alternate navigation. Hidden slides provide additional flexibility during delivery in that they do not appear during a regular slide show without deliberate action by the presenter.

The slide master enables you to modify the design of a presentation. Select the slide master from the View menu, then change any element on the slide master, and you automatically change that element on every slide in the presentation. The slide master is frequently used to add a unifying element such as a corporate logo and/or action buttons to facilitate navigation during the slide show. You can also fine-tune a presentation by changing its color scheme.

The Save As Web page command converts a PowerPoint presentation to a Web document, after which it can be uploaded to a Web server, where it can be accessed through an Internet Browser such as Internet Explorer or Netscape Navigator.

The Record Narration command creates a narrative (sound file) for each slide and simultaneously records the time required for that narrative. The narration can be made to play automatically to create a self-running presentation for a trade show or kiosk and/or to embellish a Web-based presentation.

Any presentation, including video and audio, can be delivered as a Web broadcast. The broadcast can be live or recorded. A live broadcast is scheduled at a precise time, and invitations are sent to a designated list of attendees. A recorded broadcast is uploaded to a Web server and configured for on-demand viewing. Either type of broadcast is ideal for reaching large and/or geographically dispersed audiences.

PowerPoint also supports online meetings in addition to Web broadcasts. A broadcast is a one-way connection in which you speak, and the audience listens. An online meeting is a two-way connection in which everyone can communicate with everyone else.

KEY TERMS

Action buttons 1854	Insert Hyperlink command 1854	Set Up Show command 1880
Broadcast 1877	MHTML document 1871	Single File Web Page 1866
Color scheme 1854	Online meeting 1877	Slide master 1856
Custom show 1876	Record Narration command . . . 1876	Sound Recorder 1854
Hidden slide 1854	Rehearse Timings command . . 1880	Template 1854
HTML 1866	Round trip HTML 1873	Web broadcast 1877
Hyperlink 1854	Save As Web Page command . . . 1866	Web page 1866

MULTIPLE CHOICE

1. How do you insert a corporate logo or other identifying information on every slide in a presentation?
   (a) Select the object, change to the Slide Sorter view, then paste the object on every slide
   (b) Insert the object on the title slide, then pull down the View menu and specify every slide
   (c) Insert the object on the title and slide masters
   (d) Insert the object on the title and handouts masters

2. Which of the following is true?
   (a) PowerPoint supplies many different templates, but each template has only one color scheme
   (b) PowerPoint supplies many different templates, and each template in turn has multiple color schemes
   (c) You cannot change the template of a presentation once it has been selected
   (d) You cannot change the color scheme of a presentation

3. Which of the following is true?
   (a) A color scheme specifies eight different colors, one color for each element in a presentation
   (b) You can change any color within a color scheme
   (c) A given template may have many different color schemes
   (d) All of the above

4. What happens if you click the Hide Slide button twice in a row?
   (a) The slide is hidden
   (b) The slide is visible
   (c) The slide has the same status as before the button was clicked initially
   (d) The slide has the opposite status as before the button was clicked initially

5. What is the best way to switch between PowerPoint and Internet Explorer if both are open?
   (a) Click the appropriate button on the taskbar
   (b) Click the Start button, click Programs, then choose the appropriate program from the displayed list
   (c) Minimize all applications to display the Windows desktop, then double click the icon for the appropriate application
   (d) All of the above are equally convenient

6. Internet Explorer can display a Web page stored on:
   (a) A local area network
   (b) A Web server
   (c) Drive A or drive C of a stand-alone PC
   (d) All of the above

7. How do you save a presentation as a Web page?
   (a) Click the Save button on the Standard toolbar
   (b) Pull down the File menu and click the Save As Web Page command
   (c) Both (a) and (b)
   (d) Neither (a) nor (b)

8. Which of the following requires an Internet connection?
   (a) Using Internet Explorer to view the Microsoft home page
   (b) Using Internet Explorer to view a Web page that is stored locally
   (c) Both (a) and (b)
   (d) Neither (a) nor (b)

9. A Record Narration command that checks the box to link narrations will:
   (a) Create a separate sound file for each slide
   (b) Record the time required to narrate each slide
   (c) Both (a) and (b)
   (d) Neither (a) nor (b)

... continued

multiple choice

10. You are using Internet Explorer to view a presentation saved as a Single File Web Page when you notice an error. You return to PowerPoint and fix the presentation. Which of the following must you do in order to see the changes in Internet Explorer?
    - (a) Save the PowerPoint presentation after the changes have been made
    - (b) Close Internet Explorer, then reload the MHTML document
    - (c) Both (a) and (b)
    - (d) Nothing at all; the changes will be visible as soon as you return to Internet Explorer

11. What sound quality and approximate storage requirement was recommended for recording a voice to narrate a presentation?
    - (a) CD quality at 172 kb/sec
    - (b) Telephone quality at 172 kb/sec
    - (c) CD quality at 10 kb/sec
    - (d) Telephone quality at 10 kb/sec

12. Which of the following is true?
    - (a) You can replace the narration for the entire presentation by executing the Record Narration command a second time
    - (b) You delete the narration associated with a specific slide, then use the Sound Recorder to replace the narration for just that slide
    - (c) Both (a) and (b)
    - (d) Neither (a) nor (b)

13. Which of the following is true about a custom slide show?
    - (a) It contains a subset of the slides in a presentation
    - (b) There can be only one custom show within a specific presentation
    - (c) It must contain narration
    - (d) All of the above

14. Which of the following was introduced in Office 2003?
    - (a) The Save As Web Page command
    - (b) The Single File Web Page format
    - (c) Both (a) and (b)
    - (d) Neither (a) nor (b)

15. Which vehicle is best to deliver a live presentation to 100 people in different locations?
    - (a) A broadcast
    - (b) An online meeting
    - (c) A Web discussion
    - (d) All of the above are equally suitable

16. Which technique should you use to minimize the file size of a presentation that contains multiple sound files?
    - (a) Embed each sound file directly into the presentation
    - (b) Link each sound file to the presentation
    - (c) Display a sound icon on every slide
    - (d) All of the above

17. Which of the following can be easily accomplished with action buttons?
    - (a) Jumping to the first or last slide
    - (b) Advancing to the next slide
    - (c) Returning to the previous slide
    - (d) All of the above

18. In which view is a hidden slide truly hidden (i.e., you do not see it unless you take special action)?
    - (a) Slide Sorter
    - (b) Normal
    - (c) Slide Show
    - (d) All of the above

ANSWERS

1. c	7. b	13. a
2. b	8. a	14. b
3. d	9. c	15. a
4. c	10. c	16. b
5. a	11. d	17. d
6. d	12. c	18. c

PRACTICE WITH POWERPOINT

1. **A Modified Quiz:** The presentation in Figure 4.9 is based on the completed PowerPoint quiz from the first hands-on exercise. The modified presentation contains three additional questions and a slightly modified design. Your assignment is to open the *PowerPoint Quiz Solution* presentation as it existed at the end of the first hands-on exercise and proceed as follows:

   a. Insert three additional slides, each containing a multiple choice question, so that the completed presentation contains a total of nine slides, as opposed to the six slides in the original presentation. You can select questions from the list of multiple choice questions for this chapter and/or you can make up your own. Be sure, however, that the text for the question fits on two lines and that each answer takes only a single line.

   b. Add the appropriate Sound icon next to each choice. Position the icons uniformly from the left edge of the slide.

   c. Modify the slide containing the answer key to reflect the new questions. Include hyperlinks next to each answer to return you to the slide with the corresponding question.

   d. Use the slide master to add a second small crayon at the bottom right of each slide. In addition, delete the large crayon that appears at the upper right of each slide. (You will have to press the Del key multiple times since the crayon comprises multiple ungrouped objects.)

   e. Change the font on the master slide to Arial. In addition, create a shadow effect for the title of each slide.

   f. Restore the color scheme of the presentation to the default color scheme for the Crayons template.

   g. Print the completed presentation for your instructor as follows. Print the title slide as a slide to use as a cover page, then print the entire presentation as audience handouts (six per page).

   h. Exchange your presentation with at least one other classmate. Are you able to answer his or her questions? Is this exercise a good way to review the conceptual material in the chapter?

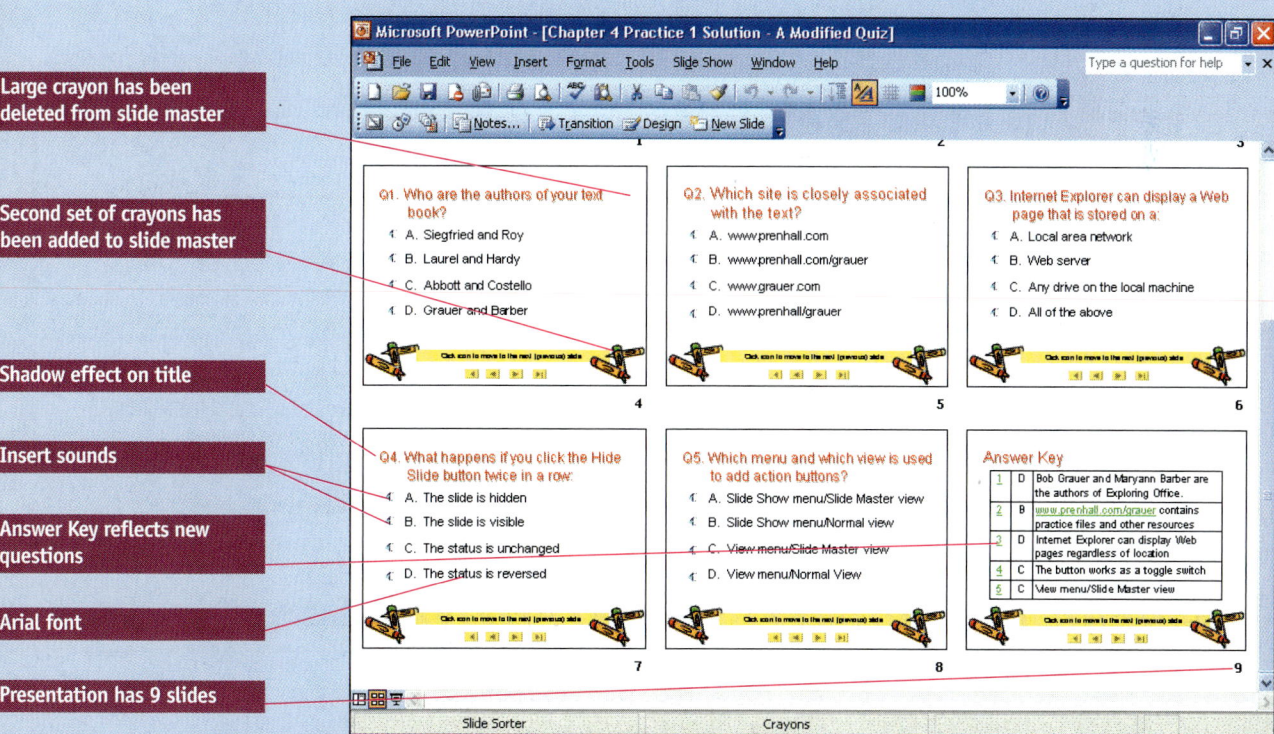

FIGURE 4.9 A Modified Quiz (exercise 1)

practice exercises

2. **Expanded Constitution Quiz:** Open the Constitution Quiz solution from the second hands-on exercise. (This is a Web document, so you will need to click the PowerPoint button on the taskbar to return to PowerPoint.) Proceed as follows:

   a. Create three additional multiple choice questions (slides 6, 7, and 8) as shown in Figure 4.10. Add the appropriate Sound icon next to each answer to indicate whether the answer is correct or not. Position the icons uniformly from the left edge of the slide.

   b. Modify the answer key to reflect the new questions. Include hyperlinks next to each answer to return you to the slide with the corresponding question.

   c. Print the completed presentation from PowerPoint for your instructor. Print the title slide as a slide to use as a cover page, then print the entire presentation as audience handouts (six per page).

   d. Exchange your presentation with at least one other classmate. Are you able to answer his or her questions? Did you learn anything about the United States Constitution?

   e. Open the presentation from Internet Explorer, then print the slide containing the answer key to show that you have successfully created a Web document. Is printing from a browser limited compared to printing from PowerPoint?

   f. The Web pages corresponding to this presentation can be viewed locally as was done in the hands-on exercise. What additional steps have to be taken to upload the presentation to a Web server? What additional software (if any) is required for uploading? Summarize the procedure to upload your presentation in a short note to your instructor.

   g. Explain how to convert the Web page to a recorded broadcast. How do you schedule the broadcast so that it runs at a designated time? Would the sound files and action buttons continue to work in a Web broadcast? Do you need additional software to broadcast the presentation?

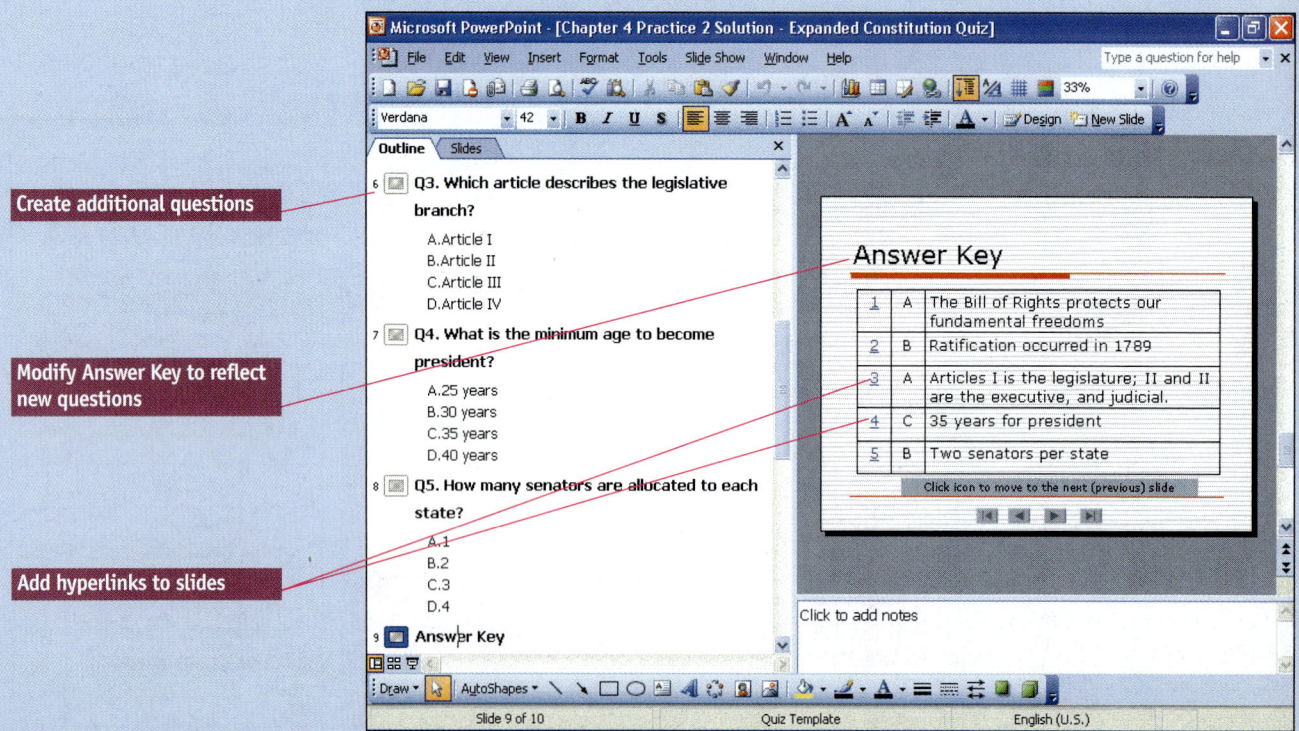

FIGURE 4.10 Expanded Constitution Quiz (exercise 2)

practice exercises

3. **Nutrition Quiz:** Create a PowerPoint presentation, consisting of at least five multiple choice questions, on any desired topic. Our quiz is on nutrition, and the end result is shown in Figure 4.11. (Slides 7 and 8 contain two additional questions. Slide 9 contains the answer key.) Proceed as follows:

   a. Open the *Create a Quiz* presentation in the Exploring PowerPoint folder that was used in the second hands-on exercise. Save the presentation as *Chapter 4 Practice 3 Solution*.

   b. Copy the last slide in the presentation (containing the sample question) several times, moving the copied slides to their appropriate places in the presentation. Add the text and suggested answers for each question. Try to keep the questions and answers brief so that they fit attractively on the slide.

   c. Add the appropriate sound file next to each answer. Align the icons uniformly from the left edge of the slide.

   d. Create the answer key for your quiz with hyperlinks to the corresponding question next to each answer. At least one of your answers should contain a hyperlink to an external Web site.

   e. Insert clip art as appropriate next to the individual questions.

   f. Change the template and/or the associated color scheme as you see fit. Set a time limit, or else you will spend too much time with your selection.

   g. Print the completed presentation for your instructor as follows. Print the title slide as a slide to use as a cover page, then print the entire presentation as audience handouts (six per page).

   h. Save the completed presentation as a Web page. You do not have to upload the presentation to the Web. Print the first slide in the presentation from Internet Explorer to show that you have successfully created a Web document.

   i. Exchange your presentation with at least one other classmate. Are you able to answer his or her questions? Was the quiz interesting? Did you learn anything?

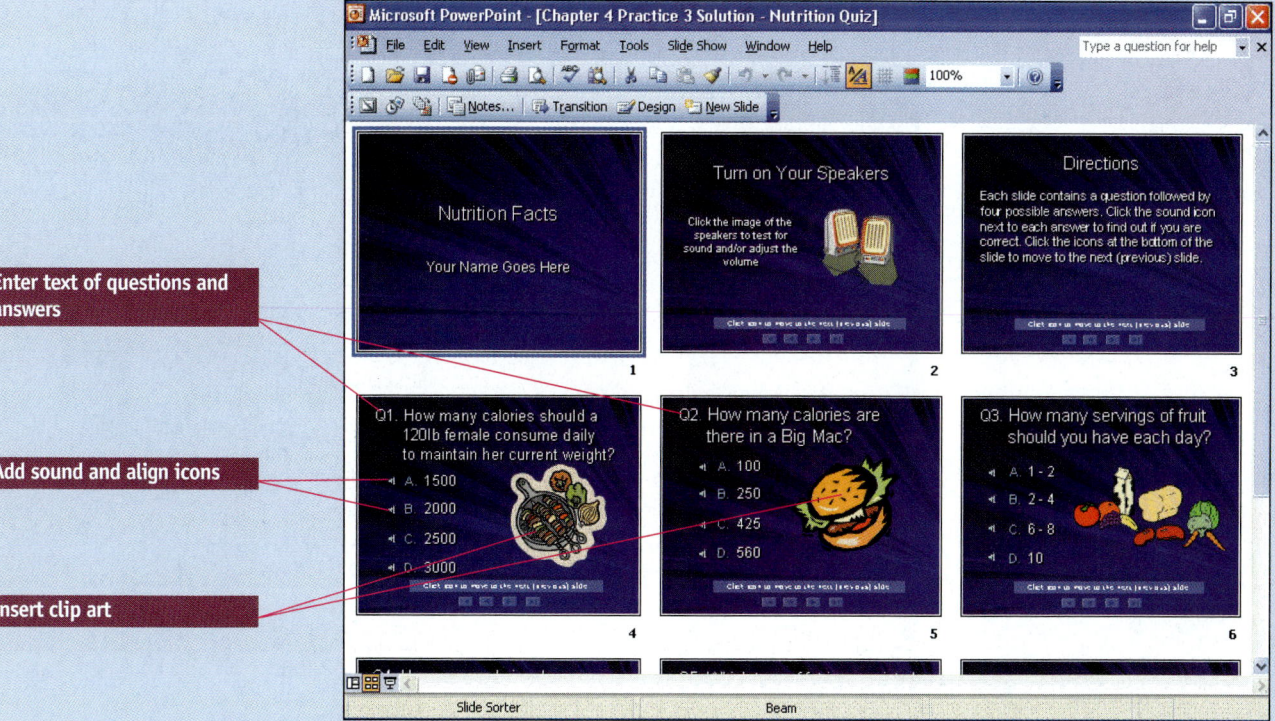

FIGURE 4.11   Nutrition Quiz (exercise 3)

practice exercises

4. **A Business Plan:** The presentation in Figure 4.12 was created from the AutoContent Wizard and saved as a Web page. The presentation can be viewed locally as in Figure 4.12, or it can be uploaded to the Web. Either way, it is a sophisticated presentation that can be created in a matter of minutes.

   a. Use the AutoContent Wizard to create a presentation for a business plan. Change the title slide to include a specific name for the business, such as Widgets of America. Add your name to the title page. On every slide (except the title slide) include a footer that contains the date, your school, and the slide number.
   b. The default presentation contains 12 slides as can be seen from Figure 4.12. Modify the text on three or four slides to make the business plan your own.
   c. Print the completed presentation as audience handouts (six per page). Be sure to frame the slides.
   d. Save the completed presentation as a Single File Web page. (This file format was not available in previous versions of Microsoft Office.)
   e. Close PowerPoint. Start Internet Explorer and open the presentation as shown in Figure 4.12. Experiment with the various controls at the bottom of the Internet Explorer window to view the presentation. How do you go to a specific slide? What happens if you click the Outline button? What happens if you click the Slide Show button in Internet Explorer?
   f. Print the title slide from Internet Explorer to prove to your instructor that you have created the Web page. How does this page differ from the same page printed within PowerPoint? What additional steps are necessary if you want to place your presentation on the Web so that it can be viewed by others?
   g. Attach the audience handouts that you printed in part (c) and submit the completed assignment to your instructor.

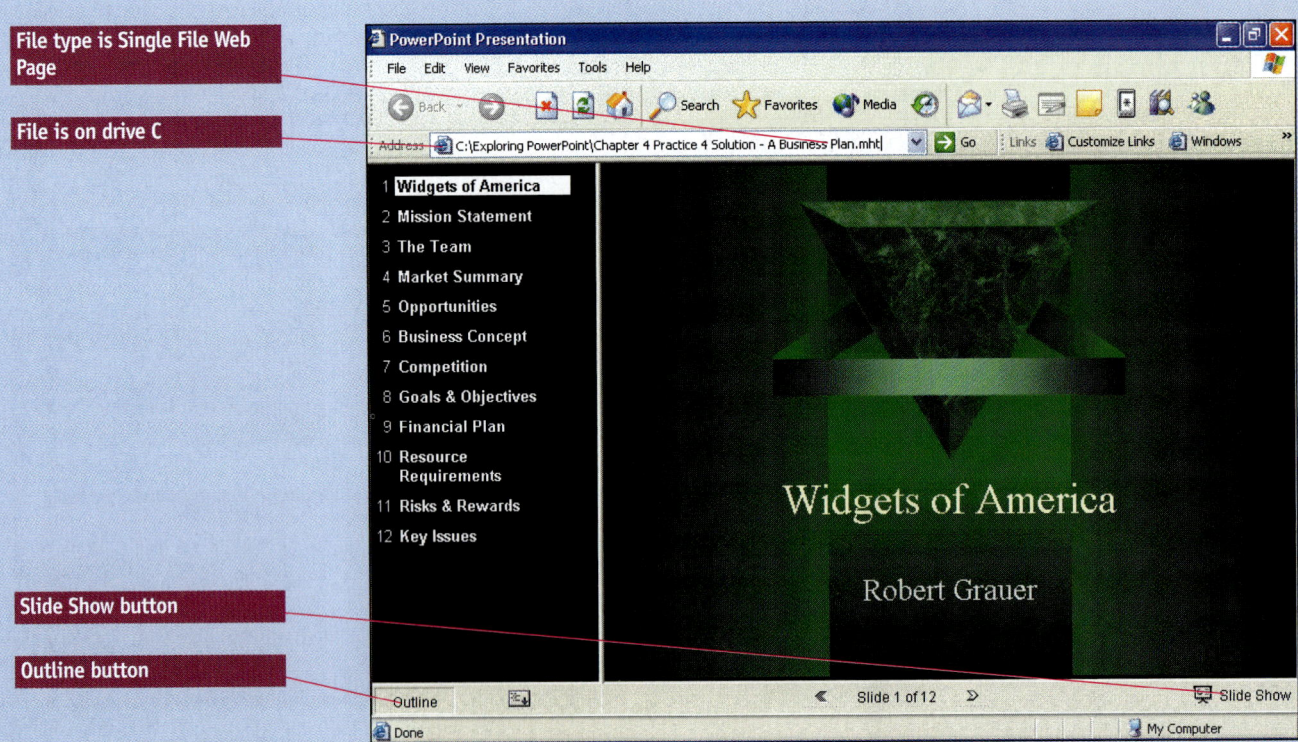

FIGURE 4.12 A Business Plan (exercise 4)

practice exercises

5. **Photographs on the Web:** Choose any collection of photographs to create a Web-based presentation similar to the one in Figure 4.13. You can select your own pictures, download photographs from the Microsoft Design Gallery, and/or use the photographs we supply in the Exploring PowerPoint folder. Each photograph must be saved as a separate file. (The photographs can be stored in different folders.)

   a. Start a new presentation. Create a title slide containing your name. Insert five or six new slides (choose the title only layout) for the photographs.
   b. Select the second slide in your presentation (the slide that will contain the first photograph). Pull down the Format menu, click Background to display the Background dialog box, click the down arrow in the background fill list box, and choose Fill Effects. Click the Picture tab, click the Select Picture button, insert the desired picture, and apply it to this slide. The photograph should fill the entire slide, a technique that adds interest to any presentation.
   c. Enter an appropriate title for the picture in the title placeholder, changing the font color and/or the position of the placeholder as necessary in order to read the title.
   d. Repeat steps b and c to insert additional photographs and the associated titles on the remaining slides.
   e. Change to the Slide Sorter view after all of the pictures have been inserted into the presentation. Press and hold the Shift key to select multiple slides, pull down the Slide Show menu, and click the Transition command. Add a transition effect for each slide, which includes the camera sound.
   f. Print the audience handouts (six per page) for your instructor. You must specify color (even if you do not have a color printer) within the Color/Grayscale list box within the Print dialog box in order to see the slide backgrounds.
   g. Save the completed presentation as a Single File Web Page as shown in Figure 4.13. You do not have to upload the presentation to the Web. Print the first slide in the presentation from Internet Explorer to show that you have successfully created a Web document.

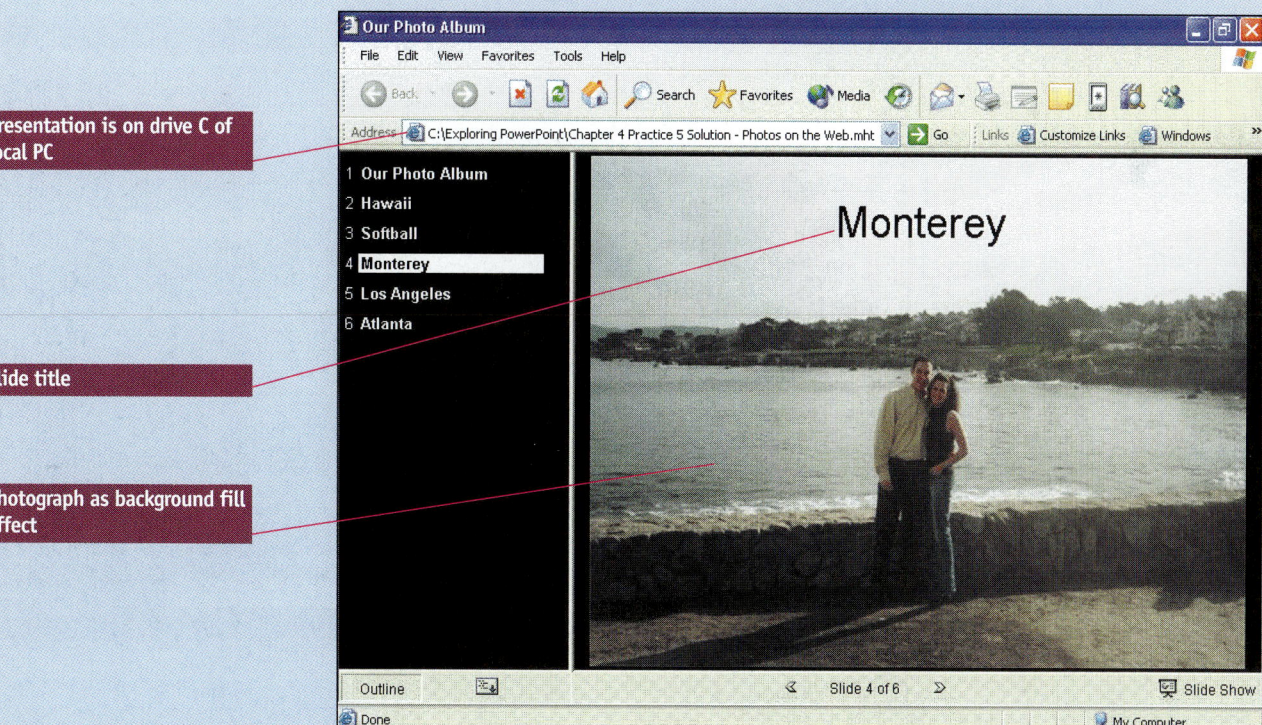

FIGURE 4.13 Photographs on the Web (exercise 5)

practice exercises

6. **Brainstorming Session:** The presentation in Figure 4.14 was created using the AutoContent Wizard, which provided the design as well as the content. The wizard "jump starts" the creative process by asking you a series of leading questions, then it creates the presentation for you. Proceed as follows:

   a. Start PowerPoint, close any open presentations, then pull down the File menu and click the New command. The task pane opens automatically. Select the link to the AutoContent Wizard. Click the Next button when you see the first screen.

   b. Select the Brainstorming Session presentation. Click Next. Select the onscreen presentation. Click Next. Enter Brainstorming Session as the title of the presentation. Clear the check boxes that include specific information on each slide. Click Next. Click Finish.

   c. The wizard pauses a second, then it creates a very general presentation similar to Figure 4.14. This is a good start, but you have to modify the presentation.

   d. Delete the third slide (overview) because the information on this slide is redundant with the agenda slide that is displayed in the figure. Delete the overview bullet on the agenda slide as well.

   e. Open the slide master. Use the Text Box tool on the Drawing toolbar to create the text box for the first action button. Create five additional buttons, each of which contains the title of another slide in the presentation.

   f. Add the appropriate hyperlink to each of the action buttons you just created. Move and size the action buttons as appropriate. All of the buttons should be the same size and should be a uniform distance from the bottom of the slide.

   g. Add your name to the title slide. Print the completed presentation for your instructor as follows. Print the first slide as a slide to use as a cover page. Print the entire presentation as audience handouts (six per page).

   h. How many additional presentations are available from the AutoContent Wizard? Do you see the value of the wizard in jump-starting the creative process? How much time did you save by using the wizard?

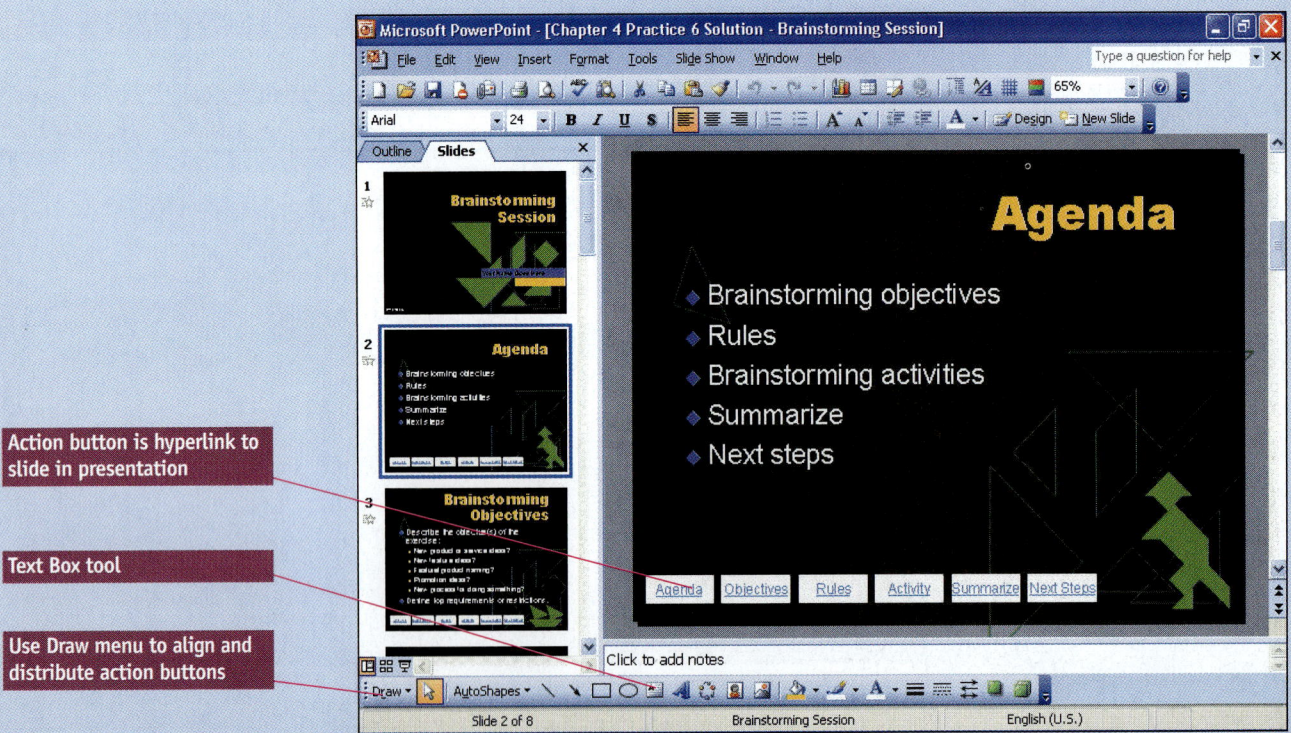

FIGURE 4.14   Brainstorming Session (exercise 6)

practice exercises

7. **Copyright and the Law:** The 10-slide presentation in Figure 4.15 contains useful information about copyrights and software piracy. Open the partially completed presentation in *Chapter 4 Practice* 7. Add your name to the title slide, then proceed as follows to complete the presentation:
   a. Select an appropriate template and a color scheme within that template. (We used default color scheme for the Network template.) Limit the time that you spend searching for a template.
   b. Add action buttons to the slide master that go to the first, previous, next, and last slides, respectively. Copy the copyright symbol that appears on the title slide and add it to the slide master as well.
   c. Insert the hyperlinks on the last slide so that the displayed text for each link is the Web address of that link. Visit at least one of the Web sites. Did you learn anything about copyright law?
   d. Create three custom shows as follows:
      (i) The Basics of Copyright Law (slides 2, 3, and 4)
      (ii) Infringement and Piracy (slides 5, 6, and 9)
      (iii) Using Copyright Material (slides 7 and 8)
   e. View each custom show. Press the Esc key at the end of each show to return to PowerPoint. Do the action buttons function differently within a custom show, as opposed to the entire presentation?
   f. Print each custom show separately as audience handouts (three slides per page).
   g. Save the completed presentation as a Web page. You do not have to upload the presentation to the Web.
   h. Print the first slide in the presentation from Internet Explorer to show that you have successfully created a Web document.
   i. Print the title slide as a slide to use as a cover page. Submit all of the printed pages to your instructor.

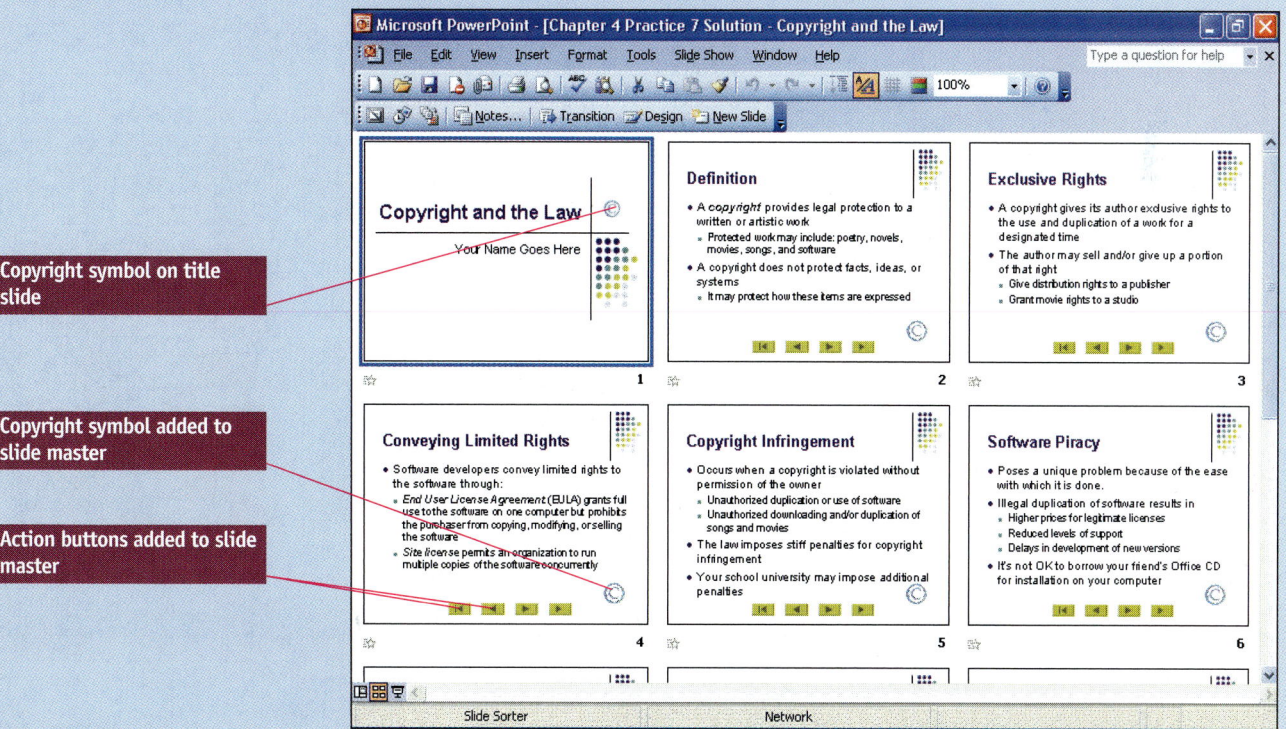

FIGURE 4.15 Copyright and the Law (exercise 7)

MICROSOFT OFFICE POWERPOINT 2003

practice exercises

8. **Navigating within a Presentation:** The presentation in Figure 4.16 depicts a different way to navigate through a presentation in which hyperlinks to other slides appear in a menu on the title slide. The hyperlinks are the equivalent of a table of contents as they provide immediate access to every other slide. Open the partially completed presentation in *Chapter 4 Practice 8*, click Update Links, and proceed as follows.

   a. Switch to the Normal view. Move the placeholders containing the title of the presentation and your name to the top of the title slide. Add a new text box and enter the titles of the other slides in the presentation. The slide titles should appear in two columns within the text box, which was achieved simply by pressing the Tab key as appropriate.

   b. Select the title of each slide as it appears on the title slide, pull down the Insert menu, and select the Hyperlink command. Click the icon for a Place in This Document and select the appropriate slide to complete the hyperlink.

   c. The navigation (action) buttons that appear at the bottom of every slide (except the title slide) were created on the slide master. Pull down the View menu, change to the Slide Master, click the Slide Show menu, click Action Buttons, then select the button you want. Click and drag to create the button on the slide master, then supply the necessary link (such as the next or previous slide). Select all four action buttons and size them uniformly. Place the buttons a uniform distance from the bottom of the slide.

   d. Every slide except the title also contains today's date as well as the number of the slide within the presentation. Pull down the View menu, click the Header and Footer command, then complete the associated dialog box to display this information.

   e. Go to the Slide Show view and test the navigation. Print the audience handouts (six per page) of the completed presentation for your instructor. Print the title slide as a full slide to use as a cover page for this assignment.

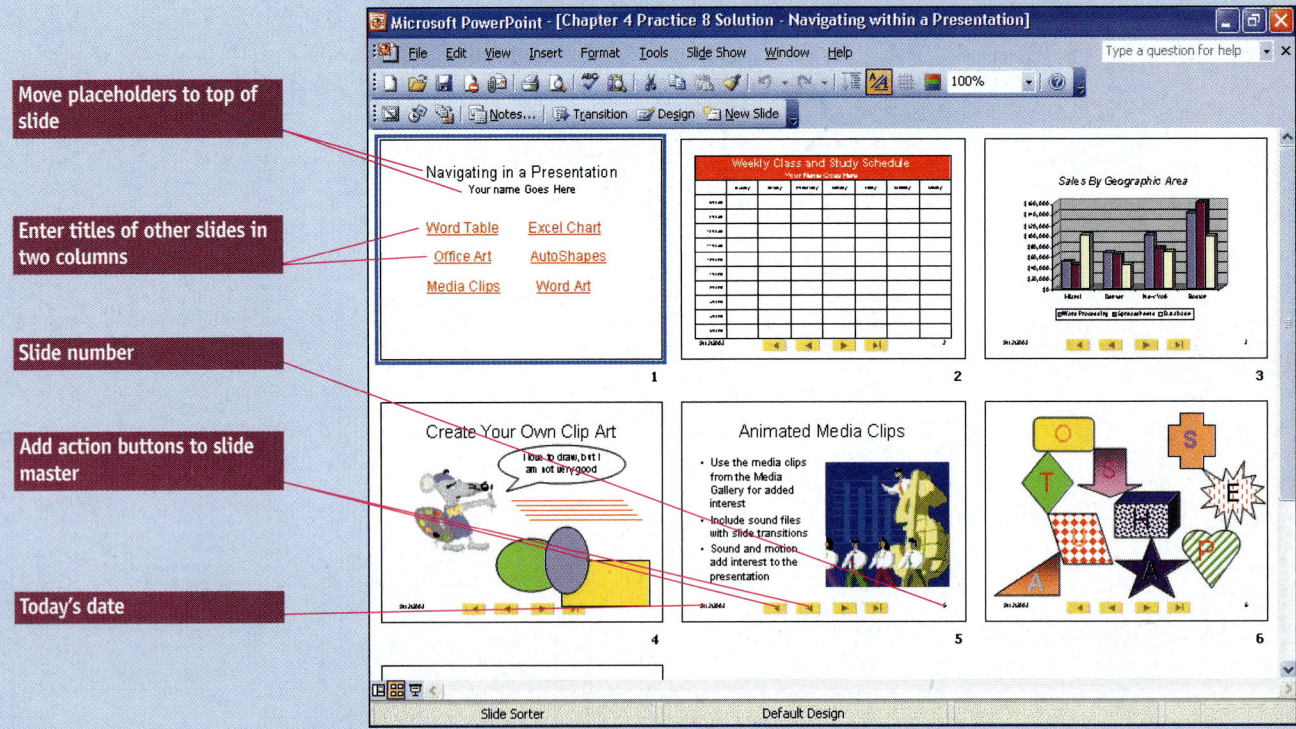

FIGURE 4.16   Navigating within a Presentation (exercise 8)

MINI CASES

FTP for Windows

Microsoft Office simplifies the process of uploading a page to a Web server by including a basic FTP (File Transfer Protocol) capability. That is the good news. The bad news is that the capability is limited when compared to stand-alone FTP programs. One advantage of the latter is the ability to display the progress of a file transfer. In PowerPoint you click the Save button to upload your presentation, then you wait several seconds (or longer) before the system displays any additional information. An FTP program, however, will display the progress of the file transfer as it takes place.

Use your favorite search engine to locate an FTP program. There are many such programs available, and many permit a free trial period. Locate a specific program, then compare its capabilities to the FTP capability in Office NET. Summarize your findings in a short note to your instructor.

Speech Recognition

Explore the speech recognition capability that is built into Microsoft Office. Use the Help command to distinguish between the Voice Command mode and the Dictation mode. What is the language bar? How do you display or hide this toolbar? How long does it take to train your computer to recognize your voice? What drawbacks, if any, are there to using this feature? Summarize your findings in a short note to your instructor.

Windows Media Player

The Windows Media Player combines the functions of a radio, a CD or DVD player, and an information database into a single program. You can copy selections from a CD to your computer, organize your music by artist and album, and then create a customized playlist to play the music in a specified order. The playlist may include as many songs from as many albums as you like and is limited only by the size of your storage device. The Media Player will also search the Web for audio or video files and play clips from a favorite movie. Is the Media Player (or an equivalent program) installed on your computer? If not, how do you obtain the Media Player and how much does it cost? Experiment with the software, then summarize your findings in a short note to your instructor.

Searching for Sound

Click the Start button on the Windows taskbar to access the Search command, then search for the sound files that have been installed on your machine. (The installation of Microsoft Windows automatically includes several sound files.) Go to the Web (e.g., the Microsoft Design Gallery) to search for and download at least two additional sound files. Describe your experience in a short note to your instructor.

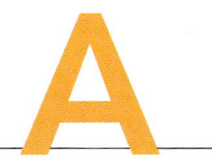

Toolbars for Microsoft® Office PowerPoint® 2003

TOOLBARS

- Standard
- Formatting
- 3-D settings
- Control Toolbox
- Diagram
- Drawing
- Drawing Canvas
- Formatting
- Organization Chart
- Outlining
- Picture
- Reviewing
- Shadow Settings
- Shortcut Menus
- Slide Show
- Standard
- Tables and Borders
- Visual Basic
- Web
- WordArt

OVERVIEW

Microsoft PowerPoint has 18 predefined toolbars that provide access to commonly used commands. The toolbars are displayed in Figure A.1 and are listed here for convenience. They are the Standard, Formatting, 3-D Settings, Control Toolbox, Diagram, Drawing, Drawing Canvas, Organization Chart, Outlining, Picture, Reviewing, Shadow Settings, Shortcut Menus, Slide Show, Tables and Borders, Visual Basic, Web, and WordArt. The Standard and Formatting toolbars are displayed by default and appear on the same row immediately below the menu bar. The other predefined toolbars are automatically displayed with various views (e.g., the Slide Sorter View) or are displayed (hidden) at the discretion of the user.

The buttons on the toolbars are intended to be indicative of their function. Clicking the Printer button, for example (the sixth button from the left on the Standard toolbar), executes the Print command. If you are unsure of the purpose of any toolbar button, point to it, and a ScreenTip will appear that displays its name.

You can display multiple toolbars at one time, move them to new locations on the screen, customize their appearance, or suppress their display.

- To separate the Standard and Formatting toolbars and simultaneously display all of the buttons for each toolbar, pull down the Tools menu, click the Customize command, click the Options tab, then check the box to show the toolbars on two rows. Alternatively, the toolbars appear on the same row so that only a limited number of buttons are visible on each toolbar and hence you may need to click the double arrow at the end of the toolbar to view additional buttons. Additional buttons will be added to either toolbar as you use the associated feature, and conversely, buttons will be removed from the toolbar if the feature is not used.

- To display (or hide) a toolbar, pull down the View menu and click the Toolbars command. Select (deselect) the toolbar that you want to display (hide). The selected toolbar will be displayed in the same position as when last displayed. You may also point to any toolbar and click with the right mouse button to bring up a shortcut menu, after which you can select the toolbar to be displayed (hidden). If the toolbar to be displayed is not listed, click the Customize command, click the Toolbars tab, check the box for the toolbar to be displayed, and then click the Close button.

- To change the size of the buttons, suppress the display of the ScreenTips, or display the associated shortcut key (if available), pull down the View menu, click Toolbars, and click Customize to display the Customize dialog box. If necessary, click the Options tab, then select (deselect) the appropriate check box. Alternatively, you can right click on any toolbar, click the Customize command from the context-sensitive menu, then select (deselect) the appropriate check box from within the Options tab in the Customize dialog box.

- Toolbars are either docked (along the edge of the window) or floating (in their own window). A toolbar moved to the edge of the window will dock along that edge. A toolbar moved anywhere else in the window will float in its own window. Docked toolbars are one tool wide (high), whereas floating toolbars can be resized by clicking and dragging a border or corner as you would with any window.
    - To move a docked toolbar, click anywhere in the background area and drag the toolbar to its new location. You can also click and drag the move handle (the single vertical line) at the left of the toolbar.
    - To move a floating toolbar, drag its title bar to its new location.

- To customize one or more toolbars, display the toolbar on the screen. Then pull down the View menu, click Toolbars, and click Customize to display the Customize dialog box. Alternatively, you can click on any toolbar with the right mouse button and select Customize from the shortcut menu.
    - To move a button, drag the button to its new location on that toolbar or any other displayed toolbar.
    - To copy a button, press the Ctrl key as you drag the button to its new location on that toolbar or any other displayed toolbar.
    - To delete a button, drag the button off the toolbar and release the mouse button.
    - To add a button, click the Commands tab in the Customize dialog box, select the category (from the Categories list box) that contains the button you want to add, then drag the button to the desired location on the toolbar.
    - To restore a predefined toolbar to its default appearance, pull down the View menu, click Toolbars, click Customize, click the Toolbars tab, select (highlight) the desired toolbar, and click the Reset command button.

- Buttons can also be moved, copied, or deleted without displaying the Customize dialog box.
    - To move a button, press the Alt key as you drag the button to the new location.
    - To copy a button, press the Alt and Ctrl keys as you drag the button to the new location.
    - To delete a button, press the Alt key as you drag the button off the toolbar.

- To create your own toolbar, pull down the View menu, click Toolbars, click Customize, click the Toolbars tab, then click the New command button. Alternatively, you can click on any toolbar with the right mouse button, select Customize from the shortcut menu, click the Toolbars tab, and then click the New command button.
    - Enter a name for the toolbar in the dialog box that follows. The name can be any length and can contain spaces.
    - The new toolbar will appear on the screen. Initially it will be big enough to hold only one button. Add, move, and delete buttons following the same procedures as outlined above. The toolbar will automatically size itself as new buttons are added and deleted.
    - To delete a custom toolbar, pull down the View menu, click Toolbars, click Customize, and click the Toolbars tab. *Verify that the custom toolbar to be deleted is the only one selected (highlighted)*. Click the Delete command button. Click Yes to confirm the deletion. (Note that a predefined toolbar cannot be deleted.)

MICROSOFT OFFICE POWERPOINT 2003 TOOLBARS

Standard

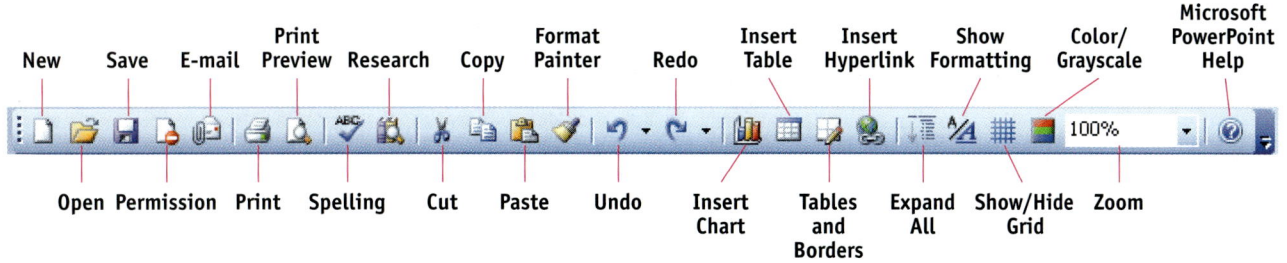

Formatting

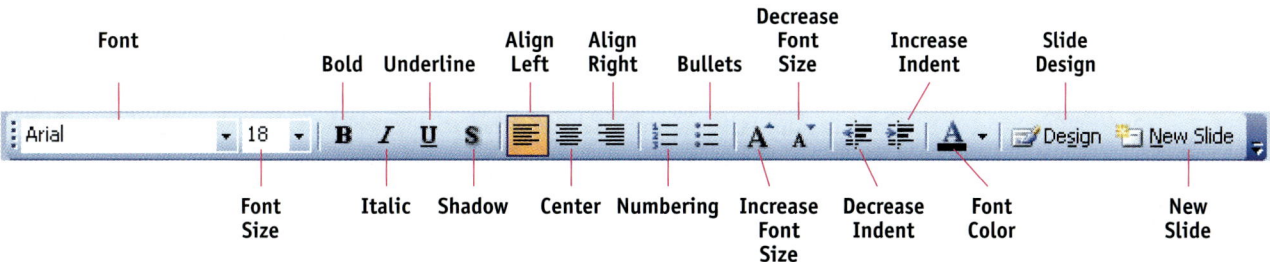

3-D Settings

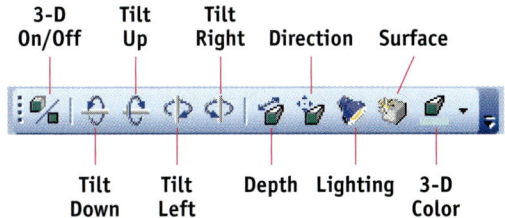

Control Toolbox

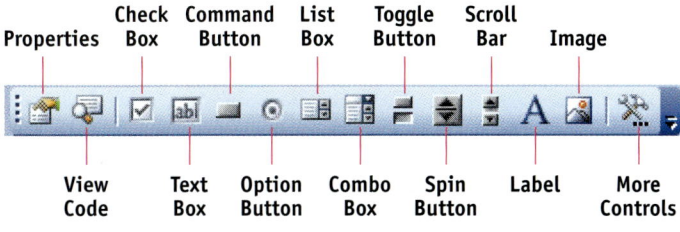

FIGURE A.1 Toolbars

Diagram

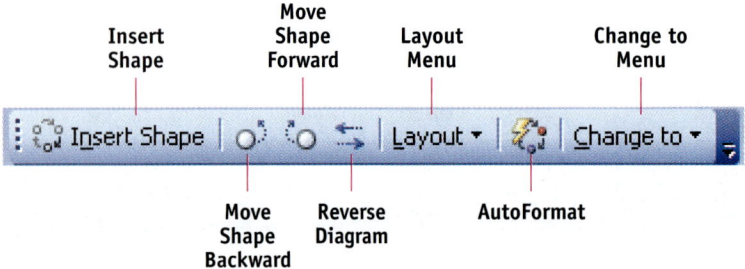

Drawing

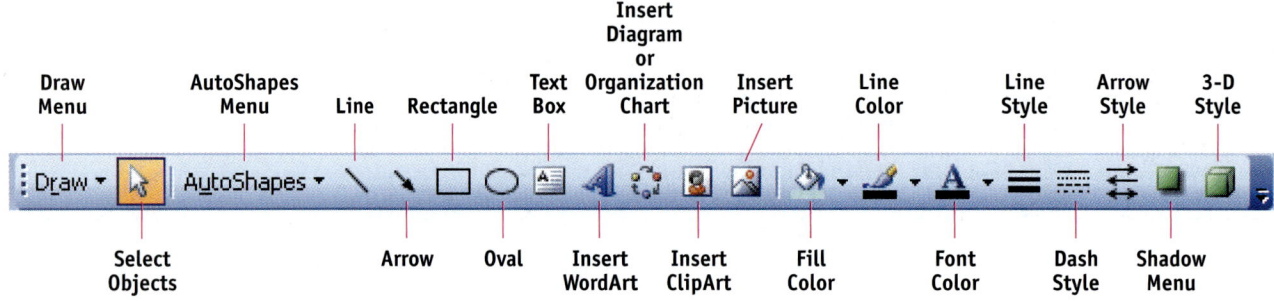

Drawing Canvas

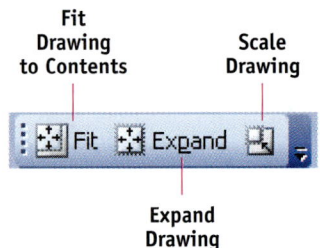

Organization Chart

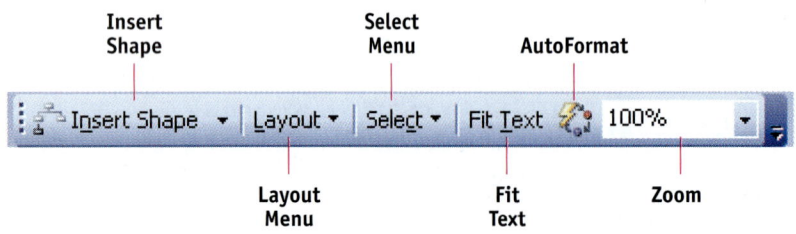

FIGURE A.1   Toolbars (*continued*)

Outlining

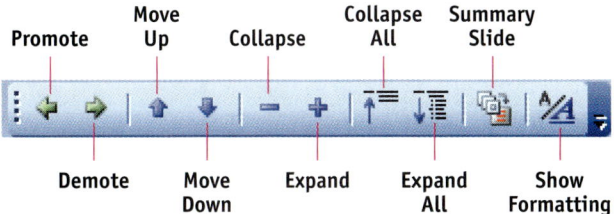

Picture

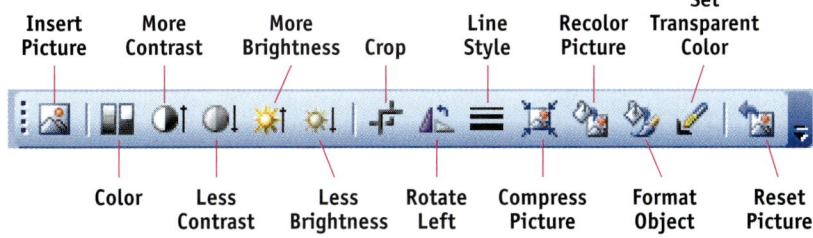

Reviewing

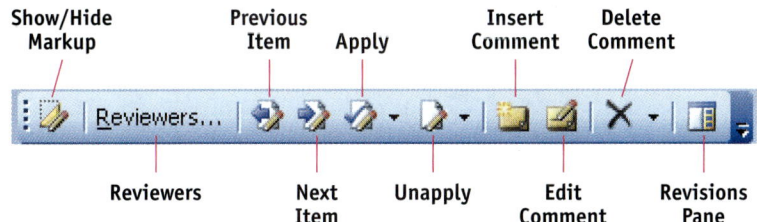

Shadow Settings

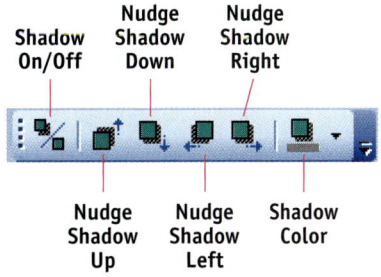

FIGURE A.1 Toolbars (*continued*)

Shortcut Menus

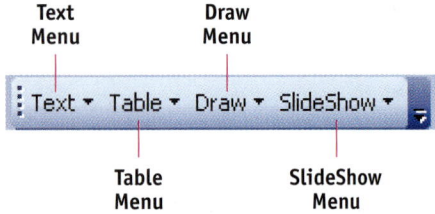

Slide Sorter

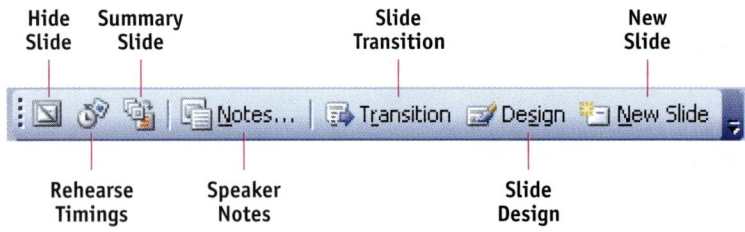

Tables and Borders

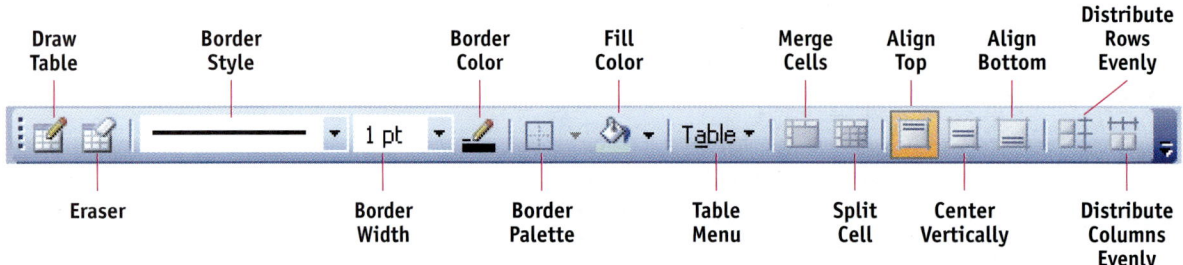

Visual Basic

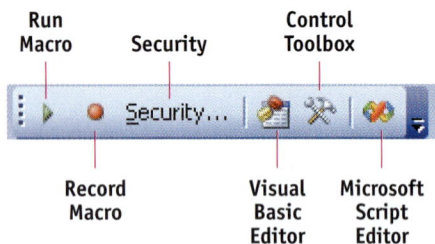

FIGURE A.1 Toolbars (*continued*)

Web

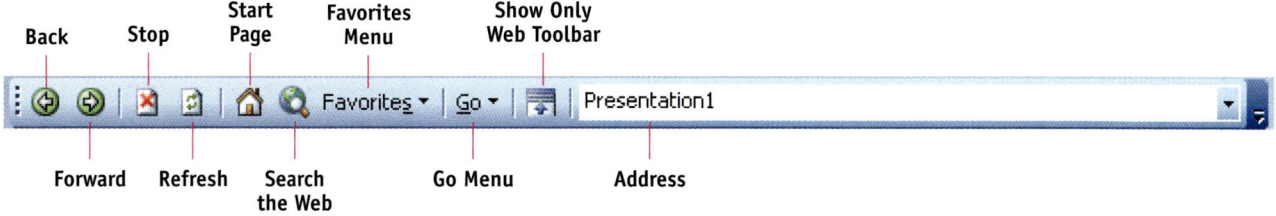

WordArt

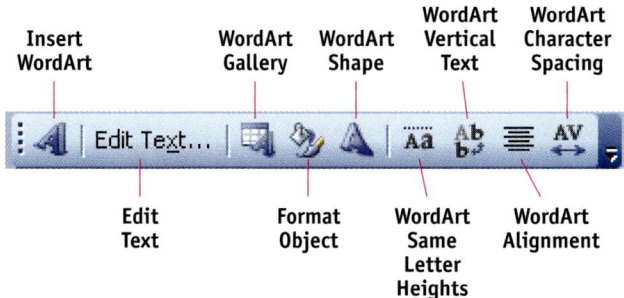

FIGURE A.1 Toolbars (*continued*)

CHAPTER 1

Getting Started with VBA:
Extending Microsoft Office 2003

OBJECTIVES

After reading this chapter you will:

1. Describe the relationship of VBA to Microsoft Office 2003.
2. Explain how to create, edit, and run a VBA procedure.
3. Use the MsgBox statement and InputBox function.
4. Explain how to debug a procedure by stepping through its statements.
5. Use the If. . . Then. . .Else statement to implement a decision.
6. Explain the Case statement.
7. Create a custom toolbar.
8. Describe several statements used to implement a loop.
9. Describe event-driven programming.

hands-on exercises

1. INTRODUCTION TO VBA
   Input: None
   Output: VBA workbook

2. DECISION MAKING
   Input: VBA workbook
   Output: VBA workbook

3. LOOPS AND DEBUGGING
   Input: VBA workbook
   Output: VBA workbook

4. EVENT-DRIVEN PROGRAMMING
   Input: VBA workbook; Financial Consultant workbook
   Output: VBA workbook; Financial Consultant workbook

5. EVENT-DRIVEN PROGRAMMING
   Input: VBA Switchboard and Security database
   Output: VBA Switchboard and Security database

CASE STUDY
ON-THE-JOB TRAINING

Your first job is going exceedingly well. The work is very challenging and your new manager, Phyllis Simon, is impressed with the Excel workbooks that you have developed thus far. Phyllis has asked you to take it to the next level by incorporating VBA procedures into future projects. You have some knowledge of Excel macros and have already used the macro recorder to record basic macros. You are able to make inferences about the resulting code, but you will need additional proficiency in VBA to become a true expert in Excel.

The good news is that you work for a company that believes in continuing education and promotes from within. Phyllis has assigned you to a new interdepartmental team responsible for creating high-level Excel applications that will be enhanced through VBA. Moreover, you have been selected to attend a week-long seminar to learn VBA so that you can become a valued member of the team. The seminar will be held in San Diego, California, where there is a strong temptation to study sand and surf rather than VBA. Thus, Phyllis expects you to complete a series of VBA procedures upon your return—just to be sure that you were not tempted to skip class and dip your toes in the water.

Your assignment is to read the VBA primer at the end of the text and focus on the first three hands-on exercises that develop the syntax for basic VBA statements—MsgBox, InputBox, decision making through If/Else and Case statements, and iteration through the For . . . Next and Do Until statements. You will then open the partially completed *VBA Case Study—On-the-Job Training*, start the VBA editor, and then complete the tasks presented in the procedures in Module1. (The requirements for each procedure appear as comments within the procedure.) Add a command button for each macro to the Excel workbook, and then print the worksheet and a copy of the completed module for your instructor. Last, but not least, create a suitable event procedure for closing the workbook.

INTRODUCTION TO VBA

Visual Basic for Applications (VBA) is a powerful programming language that is accessible from all major applications in Microsoft Office XP. You do not have to know VBA to use Office effectively, but even a basic understanding will help you to create more powerful documents. Indeed, you may already have been exposed to VBA through the creation of simple macros in Word or Excel. A ***macro*** is a set of instructions (i.e., a program) that simplifies the execution of repetitive tasks. It is created through the ***macro recorder*** that captures commands as they are executed, then converts those commands into a VBA program. (The macro recorder is present in Word, Excel, and PowerPoint, but not in Access.) You can create and execute macros without ever looking at the underlying VBA, but you gain an appreciation for the language when you do.

The macro recorder is limited, however, in that it captures only commands, mouse clicks, and/or keystrokes. As you will see, VBA is much more than just recorded keystrokes. It is a language unto itself, and thus, it contains all of the statements you would expect to find in any programming language. This lets you enhance the functionality of any macro by adding extra statements as necessary—for example, an InputBox function to accept data from the user, followed by an If . . . Then . . . Else statement to take different actions based on the information supplied by the user.

This supplement presents the rudiments of VBA and is suitable for use with any Office application. We begin by describing the VBA editor and how to create, edit, and run simple procedures. The examples are completely general and demonstrate the basic capabilities of VBA that are found in any programming language. We illustrate the MsgBox statement to display output to the user and the InputBox function to accept input from the user. We describe the For . . . Next statement to implement a loop and the If . . . Then . . . Else and Case statements for decision making. We also describe several debugging techniques to help you correct the errors that invariably occur. The last two exercises introduce the concept of event-driven programming, in which a procedure is executed in response to an action taken by the user. The material here is application-specific in conjunction with Excel and Access, but it can be easily extended to Word or PowerPoint.

One last point before we begin is that this supplement assumes no previous knowledge on the part of the reader. It is suitable for someone who has never been exposed to a programming language or written an Office macro. If, on the other hand, you have a background in programming or macros, you will readily appreciate the power inherent in VBA. VBA is an incredibly rich language that can be daunting to the novice. Stick with us, however, and we will show you that it is a flexible and powerful tool with consistent rules that can be easily understood and applied. You will be pleased at what you will be able to accomplish.

VBA is a programming language, and like any other programming language its programs (or procedures, as they are called) are made up of individual statements. Each ***statement*** accomplishes a specific task such as displaying a message to the user or accepting input from the user. Statements are grouped into ***procedures***, and procedures, in turn, are grouped into ***modules***. Every VBA procedure is classified as either public or private. A ***private procedure*** is accessible only from within the module in which it is contained. A ***public procedure***, on the other hand, can be accessed from any module.

The statement, however, is the basic unit of the language. Our approach throughout this supplement will be to present individual statements, then to develop simple procedures using those statements in a hands-on exercise. As you read the discussion, you will see that every statement has a precise ***syntax*** that describes how the statement is to be used. The syntax also determines the ***arguments*** (or parameters) associated with that statement, and whether those arguments are required or optional.

THE MSGBOX STATEMENT

The ***MsgBox statement*** displays information to the user. It is one of the most basic statements in VBA, but we use it to illustrate several concepts in VBA programming. Figure 1a contains a simple procedure called MsgBoxExamples, consisting of four individual MsgBox statements. All procedures begin with a ***procedure header*** and end with the ***End Sub statement***.

The MsgBox statement has one required argument, which is the message (or prompt) that is displayed to the user. All other arguments are optional, but if they are used, they must be entered in a specified sequence. The simplest form of the MsgBox statement is shown in example 1, which specifies a single argument that contains the text (or prompt) to be displayed. The resulting message box is shown in Figure 1b. The message is displayed to the user, who responds accordingly, in this case by clicking the OK button.

Example 2 extends the MsgBox statement to include a second parameter that displays an icon within the resulting dialog box as shown in Figure 1c. The type of icon is determined by a VBA ***intrinsic*** (or predefined) ***constant*** such as vbExclamation, which displays an exclamation point in a yellow triangle. VBA has many such constants that enable you to simplify your code, while at the same time achieving some impressive results.

Example 3 uses a different intrinsic constant, vbInformation, to display a different icon. It also extends the MsgBox statement to include a third parameter that is displayed on the title bar of the resulting dialog box. Look closely, for example, at Figures 1c and 1d, whose title bars contain "Microsoft Excel" and "Grauer/Barber", respectively. The first is the default entry (given that we are executing the procedure from within Microsoft Excel). You can, however, give your procedures a customized look by displaying your own text in the title bar.

```
Public Sub MsgBoxExamples()
'This procedure was written by John Doe on 6/10/2003

    MsgBox "Example 1 - VBA is not difficult"
    MsgBox "Example 2 - VBA is not difficult", vbExclamation
    MsgBox "Example 3 - VBA is not difficult", vbInformation, "Grauer/Barber"
    MsgBox "Example 4 - VBA is not difficult", , "Your name goes here"
End Sub
```

Procedure header → Public Sub MsgBoxExamples()
End Sub statement → End Sub

(a) VBA Code

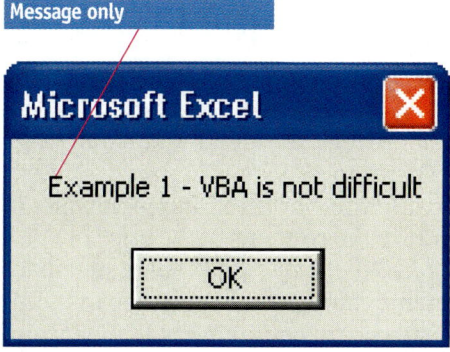

(b) Example 1—One Argument

(c) Example 2—Two Arguments

FIGURE 1 The MsgBox Statement

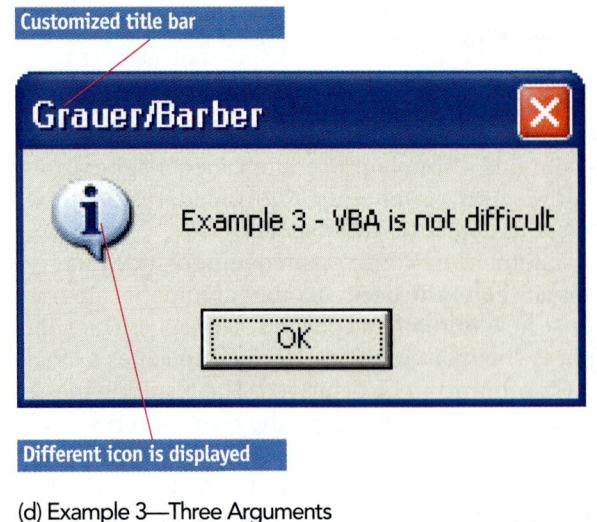
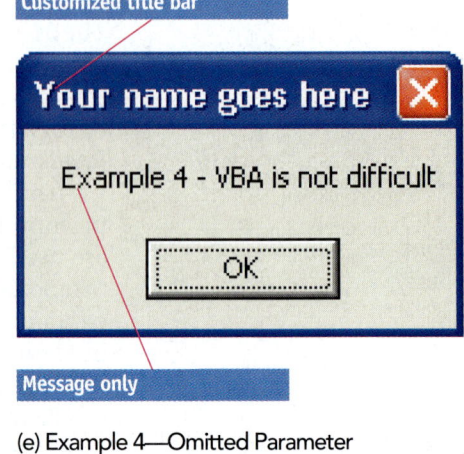

(d) Example 3—Three Arguments (e) Example 4—Omitted Parameter

FIGURE 1 The MsgBox Statement (*continued*)

Example 4 omits the second parameter (the icon), but includes the third parameter (the entry for the title bar). The parameters are positional, however, and thus the MsgBox statement contains two commas after the message to indicate that the second parameter has been omitted.

THE INPUTBOX FUNCTION

The MsgBox statement displays a prompt to the user, but what if you want the user to respond to the prompt by entering a value such as his or her name? This is accomplished using the **InputBox function**. Note the subtle change in terminology in that we refer to the InputBox *function*, but the MsgBox *statement*. That is because a function returns a value, in this case the user's name, which is subsequently used in the procedure. In other words, the InputBox function asks the user for information, then it stores that information (the value returned by the user) for use in the procedure.

Figure 2 displays a procedure that prompts the user for a first and last name, after which it displays the information using the MsgBox statement. (The Dim statement at the beginning of the procedure is explained shortly.) Let's look at the first InputBox function, and the associated dialog box in Figure 2b. The InputBox function displays a prompt on the screen, the user enters a value ("Bob" in this example), and that value is stored in the variable that appears to the left of the equal sign (strFirstName). The concept of a variable is critical to every programming language. Simply stated, a **variable** is a named storage location that contains data that can be modified during program execution.

The MsgBox statement then uses the value of strFirstName to greet the user by name as shown in Figure 2c. This statement also introduces the ampersand to **concatenate** (join together) two different character strings, the literal "Good morning", followed by the value within the variable strFirstName.

The second InputBox function prompts the user for his or her last name. In addition, it uses a second argument to customize the contents of the title bar (VBA Primer in this example) as can be seen in Figure 2d. Finally, the MsgBox statement in Figure 2e displays both the first and last name through concatenation of multiple strings. This statement also uses the **underscore** to continue a statement from one line to the next.

VBA is not difficult, and you can use the MsgBox statement and InputBox function in conjunction with one another as the basis for several meaningful procedures. You will get a chance to practice in the hands-on exercise that follows shortly.

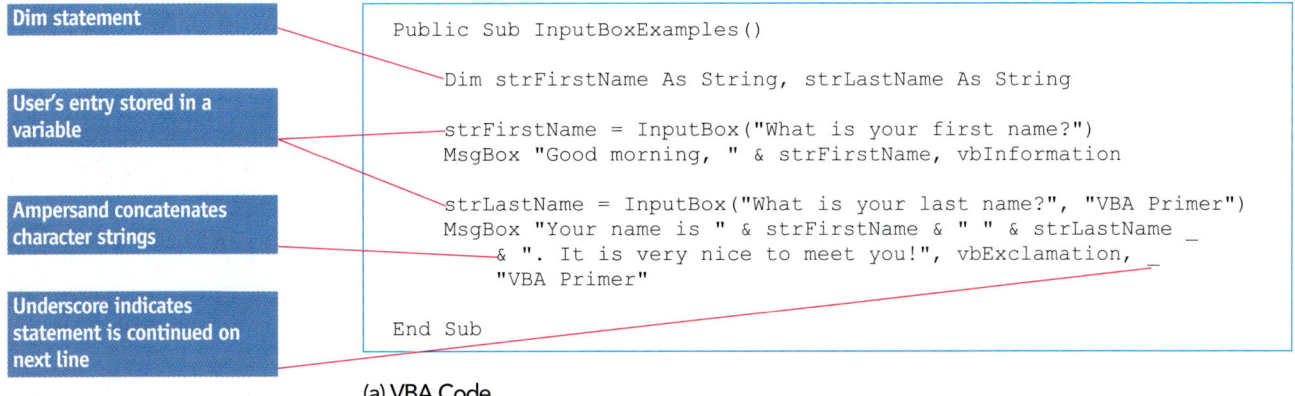

- **Dim statement**
- **User's entry stored in a variable**
- **Ampersand concatenates character strings**
- **Underscore indicates statement is continued on next line**

(a) VBA Code

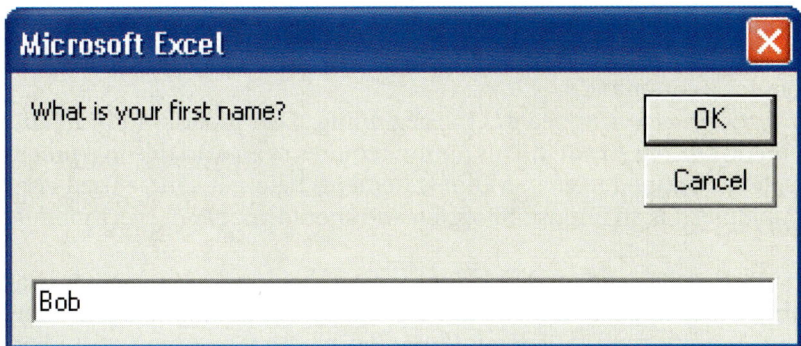

(b) InputBox

(c) Concatenation

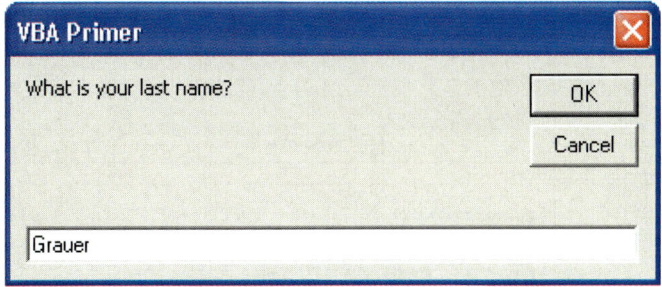

(d) Input Box Includes Argument for Title Bar

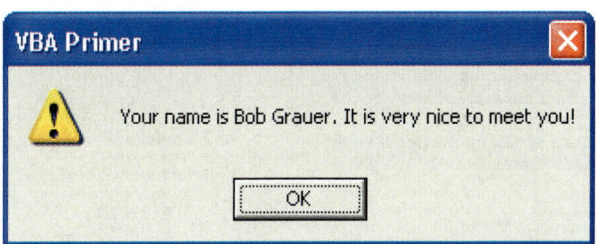

(e) Concatenation and Continuation

FIGURE 2 The InputBox Function

Declaring Variables

Every variable must be declared (defined) before it can be used. This is accomplished through the ***Dim*** (short for Dimension) ***statement*** that appears at the beginning of a procedure. The Dim statement indicates the name of the variable and its type (for example, whether it will hold characters or numbers), which in turn reserves the appropriate amount of memory for that variable.

A variable name must begin with a letter and cannot exceed 255 characters. It can contain letters, numbers, and various special characters such as an underscore, but it cannot contain a space or the special symbols !, @, &, $, or #. Variable names typically begin with a prefix to indicate the type of data that is stored within the variable such as "str" for a character string or "int" for integers. The use of a prefix is optional with respect to the rules of VBA, but it is followed almost universally.

THE VBA EDITOR

All VBA procedures are created using the *Visual Basic editor* as shown in Figure 3. You may already be familiar with the editor, perhaps in conjunction with creating and/or editing macros in Word or Excel, or event procedures in Microsoft Access. Let's take a moment, however, to review its essential components.

The left side of the editor displays the *Project Explorer*, which is similar in concept and appearance to the Windows Explorer, except that it displays the objects associated with the open document. If, for example, you are working in Excel, you will see the various sheets in a workbook, whereas in an Access database you will see forms and reports.

The VBA statements for the selected module (Module1 in Figure 3) appear in the code window in the right pane. The module, in turn, contains declarations and procedures that are separated by horizontal lines. There are two procedures, MsgBoxExamples and InputBoxExamples, each of which was explained previously. A *comment* (nonexecutable) statement has been added to each procedure and appears in green. It is the apostrophe at the beginning of the line, rather than the color, that denotes a comment.

The *Declarations section* appears at the beginning of the module and contains a single statement, *Option Explicit*. This option requires every variable in a procedure to be explicitly defined (e.g., in a Dim statement) before it can be used elsewhere in the module. It is an important option and should appear in every module you write.

The remainder of the window should look reasonably familiar in that it is similar to any other Office application. The title bar appears at the top of the window and identifies the application (Microsoft Visual Basic) and the current document (VBA Examples.xls). The right side of the title bar contains the Minimize, Restore, and Close buttons. A menu bar appears under the title bar. Toolbars are displayed under the menu bar. Commands are executed by pulling down the appropriate menu, via buttons on the toolbar, or by keyboard shortcuts.

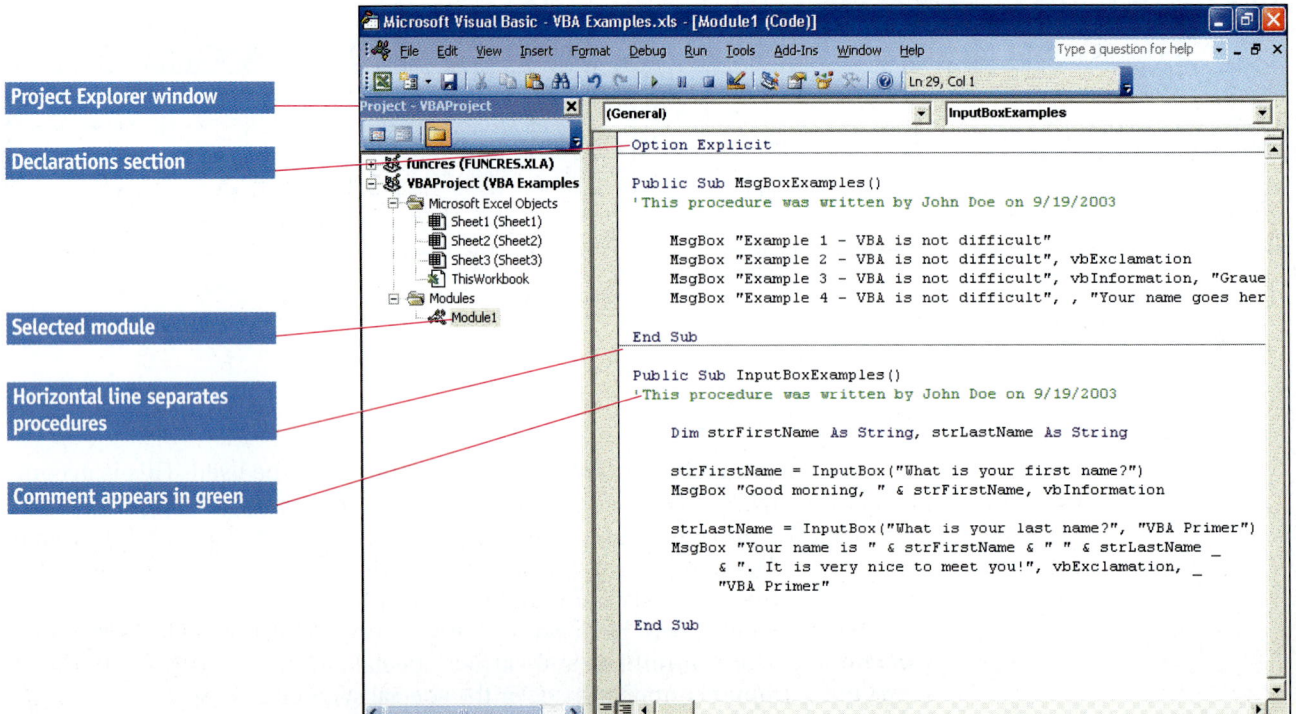

FIGURE 3 The VBA Editor

hands-on exercise

1 Introduction to VBA

Objective To create and test VBA procedures using the MsgBox and InputBox statements. Use Figure 4 as a guide in the exercise. You can do the exercise in any Office application.

Step 1a: **Start Microsoft Excel**

- We suggest you do the exercise in either Excel or Access (although you could use Word or PowerPoint just as easily). Go to step 1b for Access.

- Start **Microsoft Excel** and open a new workbook. Pull down the **File menu** and click the **Save command** (or click the **Save button** on the Standard toolbar) to display the Save As dialog box. Choose an appropriate drive and folder, then save the workbook as **VBA Examples**.

- Pull down the **Tools menu**, click the **Macro command**, then click the **Visual Basic Editor command** as shown in Figure 4a. Go to step 2.

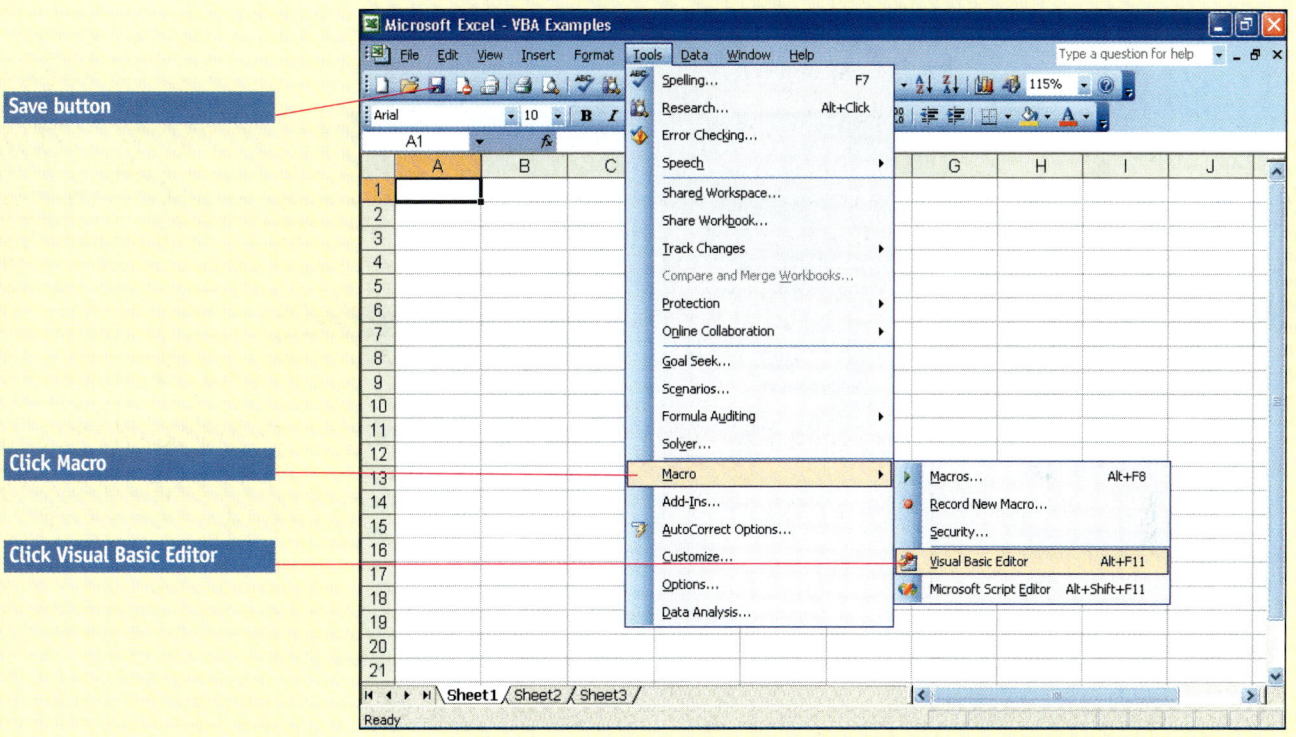

(a) Start Microsoft Excel (step 1a)

FIGURE 4 Hands-on Exercise 1

Step 1b: **Start Microsoft Access**

- Start **Microsoft Access** and choose the option to create a **Blank Access database**. Save the database as **VBA Examples**.

- Pull down the **Tools menu**, click the **Macro command**, then click the **Visual Basic Editor command**. (You can also use the **Alt+F11** keyboard shortcut to open the VBA editor without going through the Tools menu.)

EXTENDING MICROSOFT OFFICE 2003   **1911**

Step 2: **Insert a Module**

- You should see a window similar to Figure 4b, but Module1 is not yet visible. Close the Properties window if it appears.

- If necessary, pull down the **View menu** and click **Project Explorer** to display the Project Explorer pane at the left of the window. Our figure shows Excel objects, but you will see the "same" window in Microsoft Access.

- Pull down the **Insert menu** and click **Module** to insert Module1 into the current project. The name of the module, Module1 in this example, appears in the Project Explorer pane.

- The Option Explicit statement may be entered automatically, but if not, click in the code window and type the statement **Option Explicit**.

- Pull down the **Insert menu** a second time, but this time select **Procedure** to display the Add Procedure dialog box in Figure 4b. Click in the **Name** text box and enter **MsgBoxExamples** as the name of the procedure. (Spaces are not allowed in a procedure name.)

- Click the option buttons for a **Sub procedure** and for **Public scope**. Click **OK**. The sub procedure should appear within the module and consist of the Sub and End Sub statements.

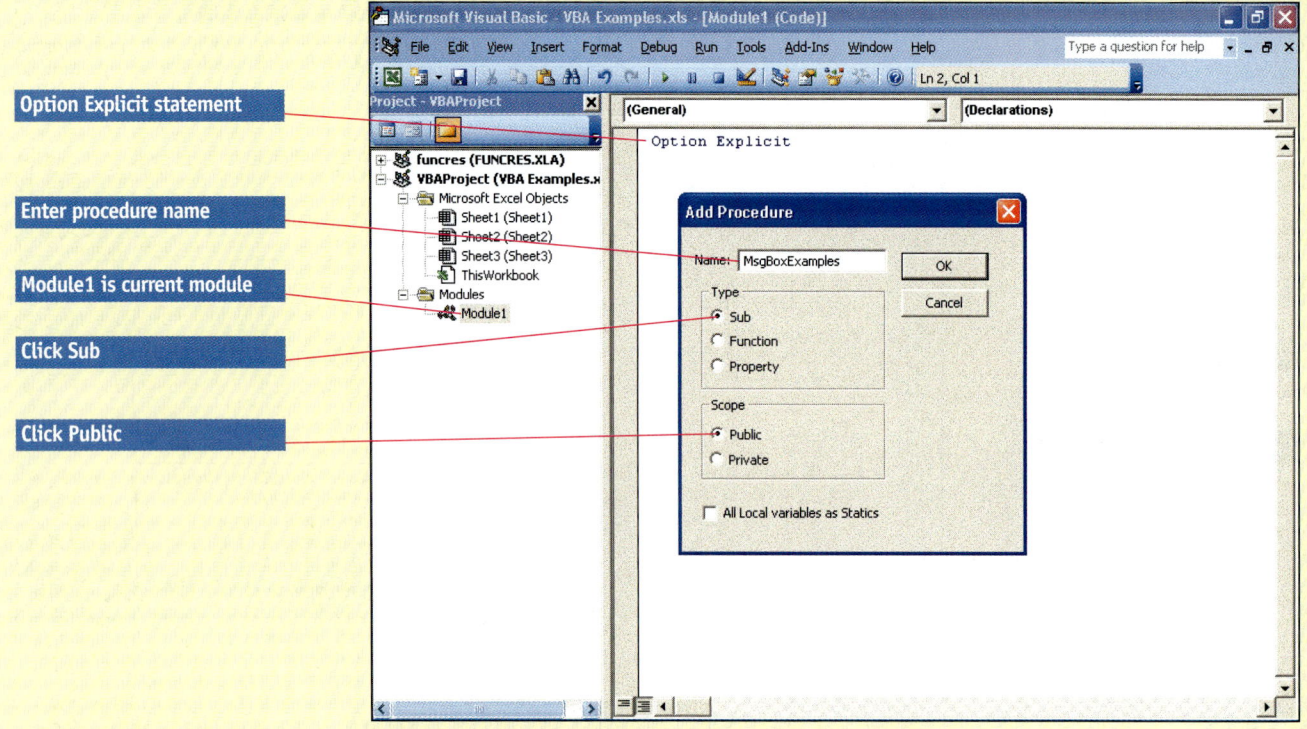

(b) Insert a Module (step 2)

FIGURE 4 Hands-on Exercise 1 (*continued*)

THE OPTION EXPLICIT STATEMENT

The Option Explicit statement is optional, but if it is used it must appear in a module before any procedures. The statement requires that all variables in the module be declared explicitly by the programmer (typically with a Dim, Public, or Private statement), as opposed to VBA making an implicit assumption about the variable. It is good programming practice and it should be used every time.

Step 3: **The MsgBox Statement**

- The insertion point (the flashing cursor) appears below the first statement. Press the **Tab key** to indent the next statement. (Indentation is not a VBA requirement, but is used to increase the readability of the statement.)
- Type the keyword **MsgBox**, then press the **space bar**. VBA responds with Quick Info that displays the syntax of the statement as shown in Figure 4c.
- Type a **quotation mark** to begin the literal, enter the text of your message, **This is my first VBA procedure**, then type the closing **quotation mark**.
- Click the **Run Sub button** on the Standard toolbar (or pull down the **Run menu** and click the **Run Sub command**) to execute the procedure.
- You should see a dialog box, containing the text you entered, within the Excel workbook (or other Office document) on which you are working.
- After you have read the message, click **OK** to return to the VBA editor.

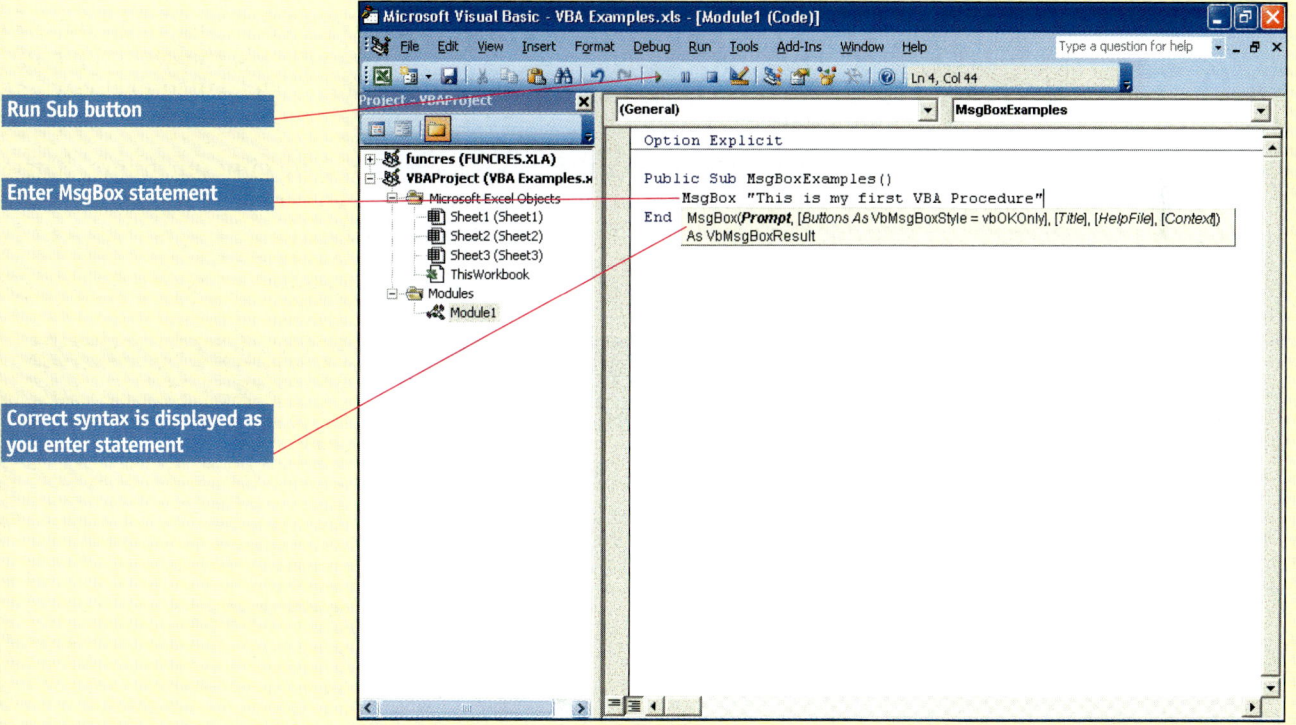

Run Sub button

Enter MsgBox statement

Correct syntax is displayed as you enter statement

(c) The MsgBox Statement (step 3)

FIGURE 4 Hands-on Exercise 1 (*continued*)

QUICK INFO—HELP WITH VBA SYNTAX

Press the space bar after entering the name of a statement (e.g., MsgBox), and VBA responds with a Quick Info box that displays the syntax of the statement. You see the arguments in the statement and the order in which those arguments appear. Any argument in brackets is optional. If you do not see this information, pull down the Tools menu, click the Options command, then click the Editor tab. Check the box for Auto Quick Info and click OK.

Step 4: **Complete the Procedure**

- You should be back within the MsgBoxExamples procedure. If necessary, click at the end of the MsgBox statement, then press **Enter** to begin a new line. Type **MsgBox** and press the **space bar** to begin entering the statement.

- The syntax of the MsgBox statement will appear on the screen. Type a **quotation mark** to begin the message, type **Add an icon** as the text of this message, then type the closing **quotation mark**. Type a **comma**, then press the **space bar** to enter the next parameter.

- VBA automatically displays a list of appropriate parameters, in this case a series of intrinsic constants that define the icon or command button that is to appear in the statement.

- You can type the first several letters (e.g., **vbi**, for vbInformation), then press the **space bar**, or you can use the **down arrow** to select **vbInformation** and then press the **space bar**. Either way you should complete the second MsgBox statement as shown in Figure 4d. Press **Enter**.

- Enter the third MsgBox statement as shown in Figure 4d. Note the presence of the two consecutive commas to indicate that we omitted the second parameter within the MsgBox statement. Enter your name instead of John Doe where appropriate. Press **Enter**.

- Enter the fourth (and last) MsgBox statement following our figure. Select **vbExclamation** as the second parameter, type a **comma**, then enter the text of the title bar, as you did for the previous statement.

- Click the **Save button** to save the changes to the module.

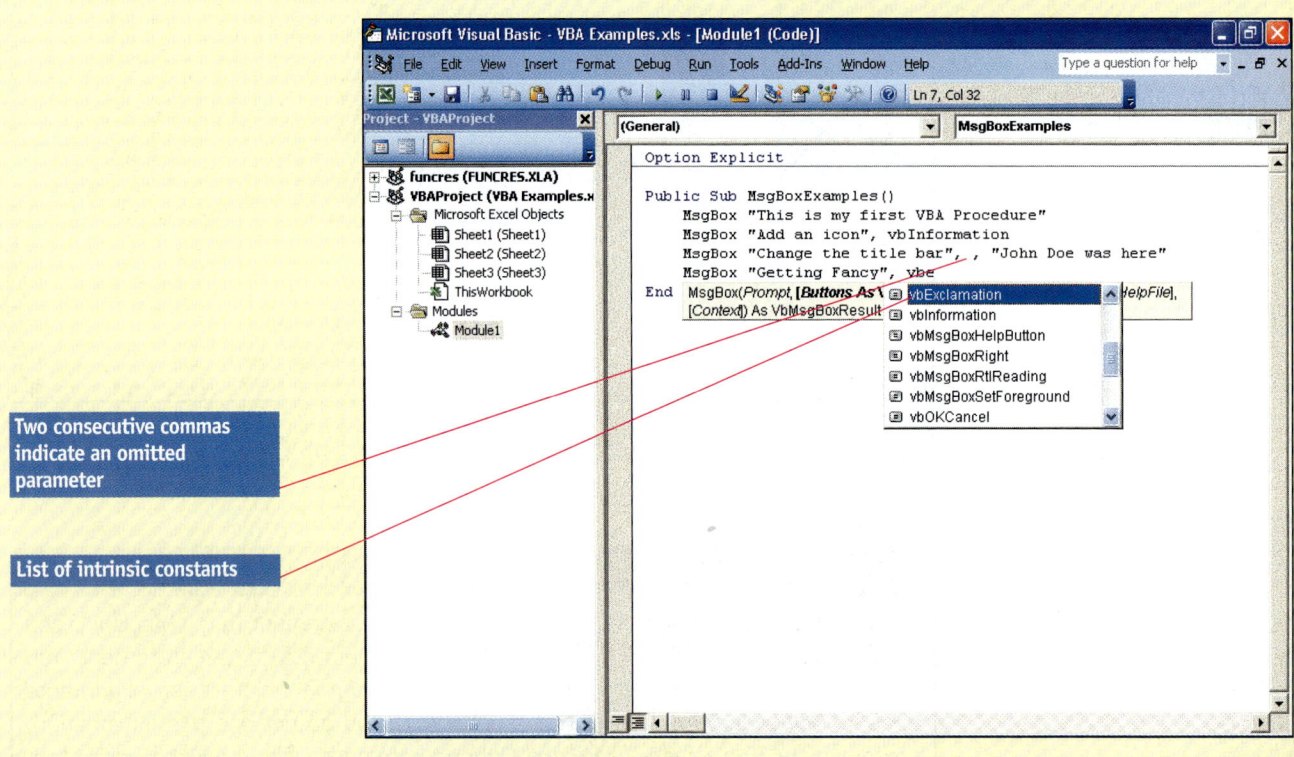

Two consecutive commas indicate an omitted parameter

List of intrinsic constants

(d) Complete the Procedure (step 4)

FIGURE 4   Hands-on Exercise 1 (*continued*)

Step 5: **Test the Procedure**

- It's convenient if you can see the statements in the VBA procedure at the same time you see the output of those statements. Thus we suggest that you tile the VBA editor and the associated Office application.

- Minimize all applications except the VBA editor and the Office application (e.g., Excel).

- Right click the taskbar and click **Tile Windows Horizontally** to tile the windows as shown in Figure 4e. (It does not matter which window is on top. (If you see more than these two windows, minimize the other open window, then right click the taskbar and retile the windows.)

- Click anywhere in the VBA procedure, then click the **Run Sub button** on the Standard toolbar.

- The four messages will be displayed one after the other. Click **OK** after each message.

- Maximize the VBA window to continue working.

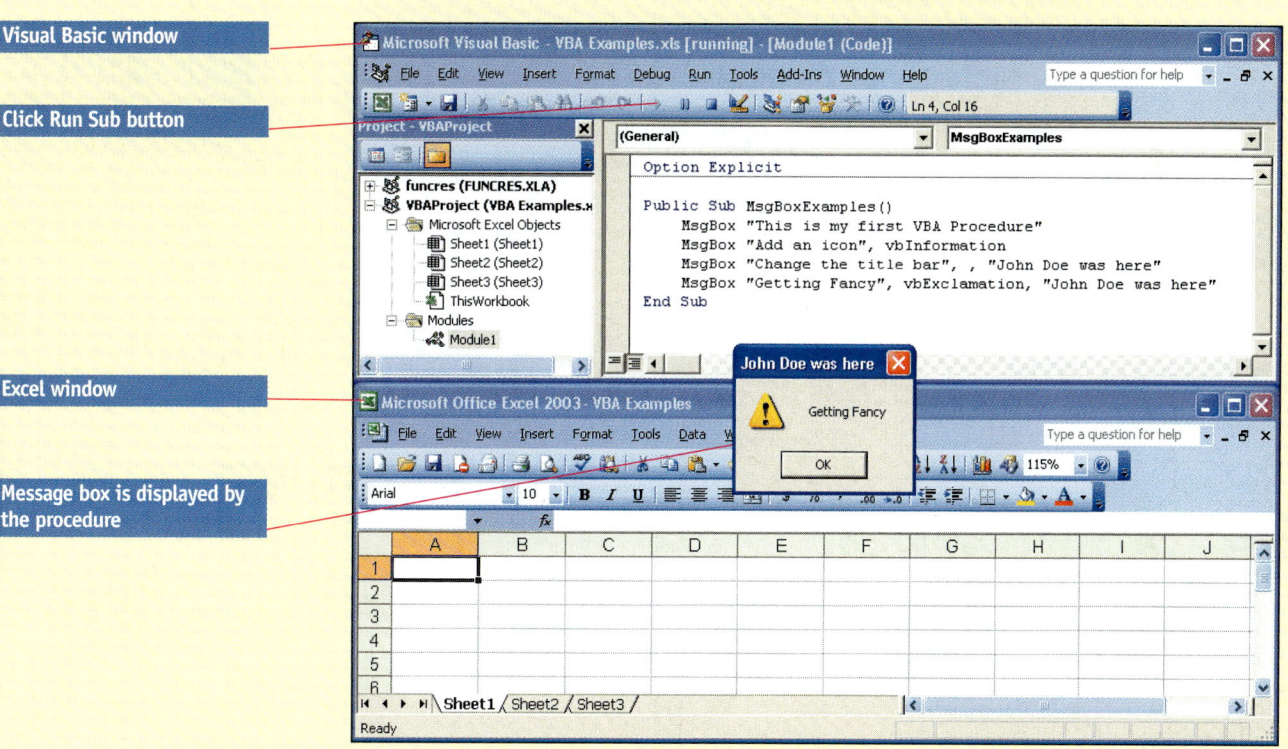

(e) Test the Procedure (step 5)

FIGURE 4 Hands-on Exercise 1 (*continued*)

HIDE THE WINDOWS TASKBAR

You can hide the Windows taskbar to gain additional space on the desktop. Right click any empty area of the taskbar to display a context-sensitive menu, click Properties to display the Taskbar properties dialog box, and if necessary click the Taskbar tab. Check the box to Auto Hide the taskbar, then click OK. The taskbar disappears from the screen but will reappear as you point to the bottom edge of the desktop.

Step 6: **Comments and Corrections**

- All VBA procedures should be documented with the author's name, date, and other comments as necessary to explain the procedure. Click after the procedure header. Press the **Enter key** to leave a blank line.

- Press **Enter** a second time. Type an **apostrophe** to begin the comment, then enter a descriptive statement similar to Figure 4f. Press **Enter** when you have completed the comment. The line turns green to indicate it is a comment.

- The best time to experiment with debugging is when you know your procedure is correct. Go to the last MsgBox statement and delete the quotation mark in front of your name. Move to the end of the line and press **Enter**.

- You should see the error message in Figure 4f. Unfortunately, the message is not as explicit as it could be; VBA cannot tell that you left out a quotation mark, but it does detect an error in syntax.

- Click **OK** in response to the error. Click the **Undo button** twice, to restore the quotation mark, which in turn corrects the statement.

- Click the **Save button** to save the changes to the module.

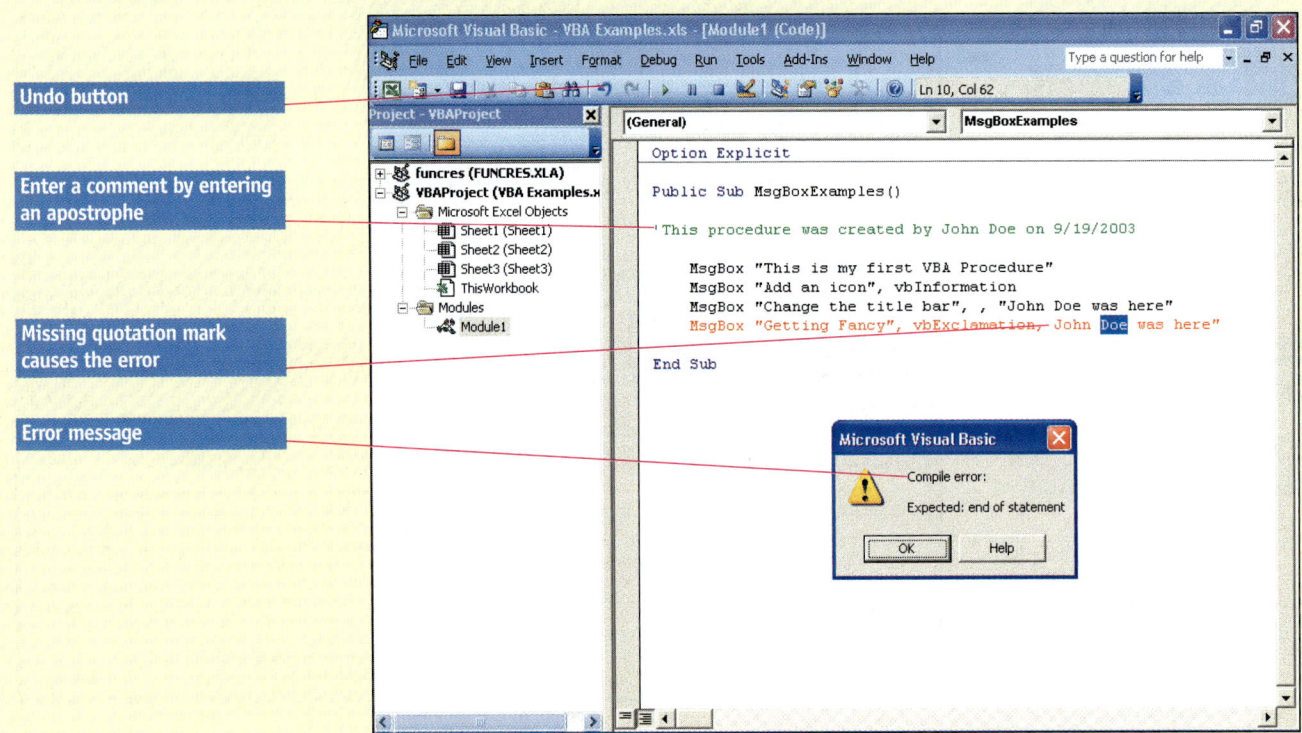

(f) Comments and Corrections (step 6)

FIGURE 4 Hands-on Exercise 1 (*continued*)

RED, GREEN, AND BLUE

Visual Basic for Applications uses different colors for different types of statements (or a portion of those statements). Any statement containing a syntax error appears in red. Comments appear in green. Keywords, such as Sub and End Sub, appear in blue.

Step 7: **Create a Second Procedure**

- Pull down the **Insert menu** and click **Procedure** to display the Add Procedure dialog box. Enter **InputBoxExamples** as the name of the procedure. (Spaces are not allowed in a procedure name.)

- Click the option buttons for a **Sub procedure** and for **Public scope**. Click **OK**. The new sub procedure will appear within the existing module below the existing MsgBoxExamples procedure.

- Enter the statements in the procedure as they appear in Figure 4g. Be sure to type a space between the ampersand and the underscore in the second MsgBox statement. Click the **Save button** to save the procedure before testing it.

- You can display the output of the procedure directly in the VBA window if you minimize the Excel window. Thus, **right click** the Excel button on the taskbar to display a context-sensitive menu, then click the **Minimize command**. There is no visible change on your monitor.

- Click the **Run Sub button** to test the procedure. This time you see the Input box displayed on top of the VBA window because the Excel window has been minimized.

- Enter your first name in response to the initial prompt, then click **OK**. Click **OK** when you see the message box that says "Hello".

- Enter your last name in response to the second prompt and click **OK**. You should see a message box similar to the one in Figure 4g. Click **OK**.

- Return to the VBA procedure to correct any mistakes that might occur. Save the module.

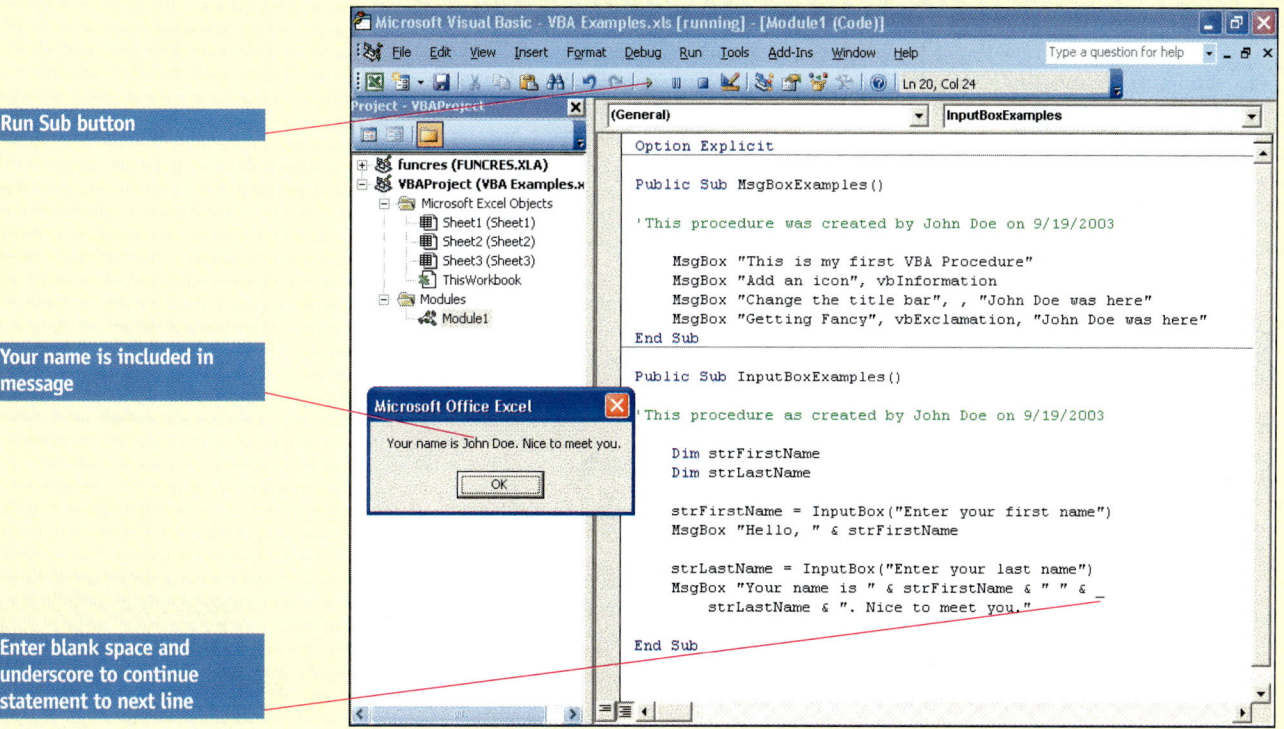

(g) Create a Second Procedure (step 7)

FIGURE 4   Hands-on Exercise 1 (*continued*)

Step 8: **Create a Public Constant**

- Click after the Options Explicit statement and press **Enter** to move to a new line. Type the statement to define the constant, **ApplicationTitle**, as shown in Figure 4h, and press **Enter**.

- Click anywhere in the MsgBoxExamples procedure, then change the third argument in the last MsgBox statement to ApplicationTitle. Make the four modifications in the InputBoxExamples procedure as shown in Figure 4h.

- Click anywhere in the InputBoxExamples procedure, then click the **Run Sub button** to test the procedure. The title bar of each dialog box will contain a descriptive title corresponding to the value of the ApplicationTitle constant.

- Change the value of the ApplicationTitle constant in the General Declarations section, then rerun the InputBoxExamples procedure. The title of every dialog box changes to reflect the new value.

- Save the procedure. Do you see the advantage of defining a title in the General Declarations section?

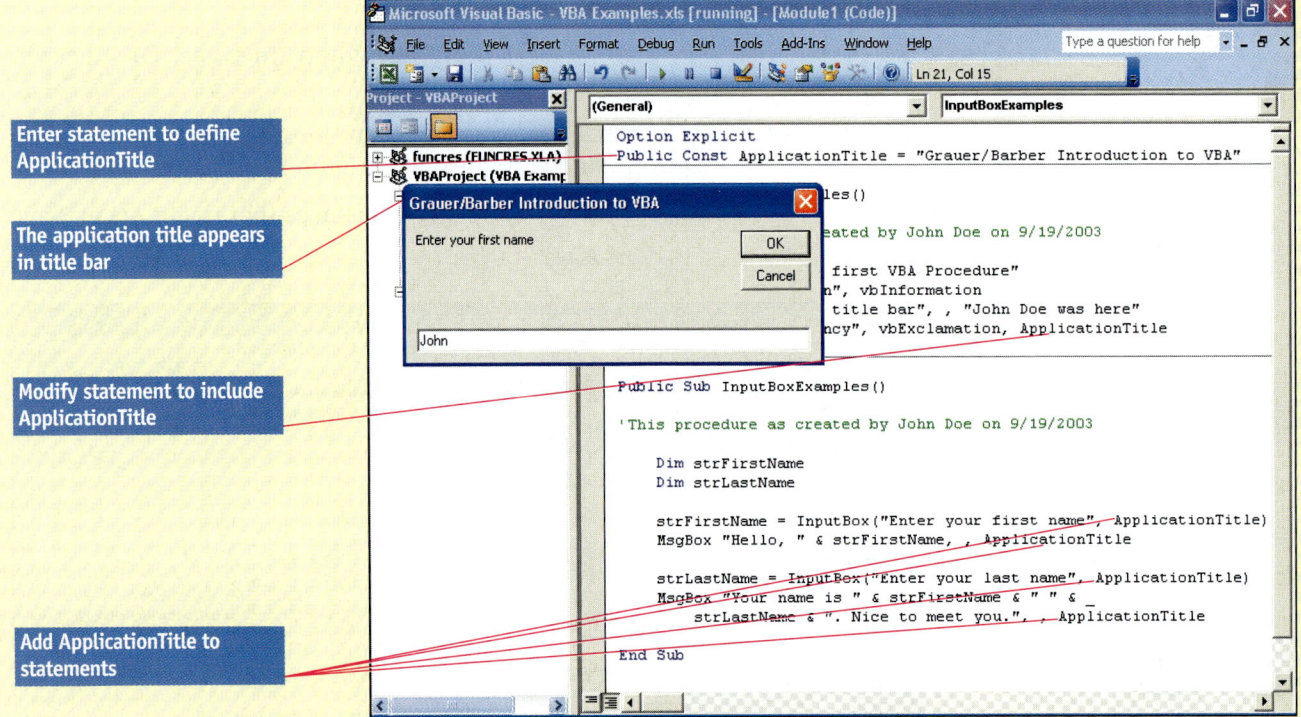

(h) Create a Public Constant (step 8)

FIGURE 4   Hands-on Exercise 1 (*continued*)

CONTINUING A VBA STATEMENT—THE & AND THE UNDERSCORE

A VBA statement can be continued from one line to the next by typing a space at the end of the line to be continued, typing the underscore character, then continuing on the next line. You may not, however, break a line in the middle of a literal (character string). Thus, you need to complete the character string with a closing quotation mark, add an ampersand (as the concatenation operator to display this string with the character string on the next line), then leave a space followed by the underscore to indicate continuation.

Step 9: **Help with VBA**

- You should be in the VBA editor. Pull down the **Help menu** and click the **Microsoft Visual Basic Help command** to open the Help pane.

- Type **Input Box function** in the Search box, then click the arrow to initiate the search. The results should include a hyperlink to InputBox function. Click the **hyperlink** to display the Help screen in Figure 4i.

- Maximize the Help window, then explore the information on the InputBox function to reinforce your knowledge of this statement.
  - Click the **Print button** to print this page for your instructor.
  - Click the link to **Example** within the Help window to see actual code.
  - Click the link to **See Also**, which displays information about the MsgBox statement.

- Close the Help window, but leave the task pane open. Click the **green** (back) **arrow** within the task pane to display the Table of Contents for Visual Basic Help, then explore the table of contents.
  - Click any closed book to open the book and "drill down" within the list of topics. The book remains open until you click the icon a second time to close it.
  - Click any question mark icon to display the associated help topic.

- Close the task pane. Pull down the **File menu** and click the **Close and Return to Microsoft Excel command** (or click the **Close button** on the VBA title bar) to close the VBA window and return to the application. Click **Yes** if asked whether to save the changes to Module1.

- You should be back in the Excel (or Access) application window. Close the application if you do not want to continue with the next exercise at this time.

- Congratulations. You have just completed your first VBA procedure. Remember to use Help any time you have a question.

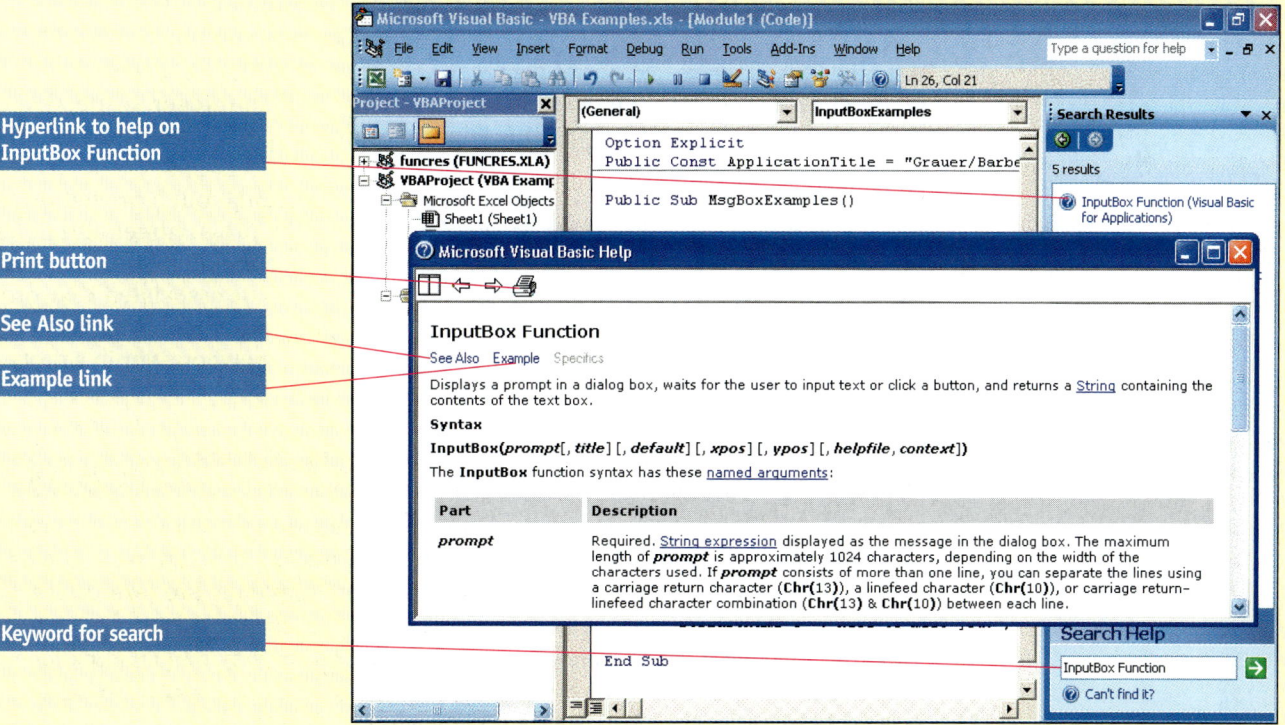

(i) Help with VBA (step 9)

FIGURE 4 Hands-on Exercise 1 (*continued*)

IF...THEN...ELSE STATEMENT

The ability to make decisions within a program, and then execute alternative sets of statements based on the results of those decisions, is crucial to any programming language. This is typically accomplished through an *If statement*, which evaluates a condition as either true or false, then branches accordingly. The If statement is not used in isolation, however, but is incorporated into a procedure to accomplish a specific task as shown in Figure 5a. This procedure contains two separate If statements, and the results are displayed in the message boxes shown in the remainder of the figure.

The InputBox statement associated with Figure 5b prompts the user for the name of his or her instructor, then it stores the answer in the variable strInstructorName. The subsequent If statement then compares the user's answer to the literal "Grauer". If the condition is true (i.e., Grauer was entered into the input box), then the message in Figure 5c is displayed. If, however, the user entered any other value, then the condition is evaluated as false, the MsgBox is not displayed, and processing continues with the next statement in the procedure.

The second If statement includes an optional *Else clause*. Again, the user is asked for a value, and the response is compared to the number 50. If the condition is true (i.e., the value of intUserStates equals 50), the message in Figure 5d is displayed to indicate that the response is correct. If, however, the condition is false (i.e., the user entered a number other than 50), the user sees the message in Figure 5e. Either way, true or false, processing continues with the next statement in the procedure. That's it—it's simple and it's powerful, and we will use the statement in the next hands-on exercise.

You can learn a good deal about VBA by looking at existing code and making inferences. Consider, for example, the difference between literals and numbers. *Literals* (also known as *character strings*) are stored differently from numbers, and this is manifested in the way that comparisons are entered into a VBA statement. Look closely at the condition that references a literal (strInstructorName = "Grauer") compared to the condition that includes a number (intUserStates = 50). The literal ("Grauer") is enclosed in quotation marks, whereas the number (50) is not. (The prefix used in front of each variable, "str" and "int", is a common VBA convention to indicate the variable type—a string and an integer, respectively. Both variables are declared in the Dim statements at the beginning of the procedure.)

Note, too, that indentation and spacing are used throughout a procedure to make it easier to read. This is for the convenience of the programmer and not a requirement for VBA. The If, Else, and End If keywords are aligned under one another, with the subsequent statements indented under the associated keyword. We also indent a continued statement, such as a MsgBox statement, which is typically coded over multiple lines. Blank lines can be added anywhere within a procedure to separate blocks of statements from one another.

THE MSGBOX FUNCTION—YES OR NO

A simple MsgBox statement merely displays information to the user. MsgBox can also be used as a function, however, to accept information from the user such as clicking a Yes or No button, then combined with an If statement to take different actions based on the user's input. In essence, you enclose the arguments of the MsgBox function in parentheses (similar to what is done with the InputBox function), then test for the user response using the intrinsic constants vbYes and vbNo. The statement, If MsgBox("Are you having fun?", vbYesNo)=vbYes asks the user a question, displays Yes and No command buttons, then tests to see if the user clicked the Yes button.

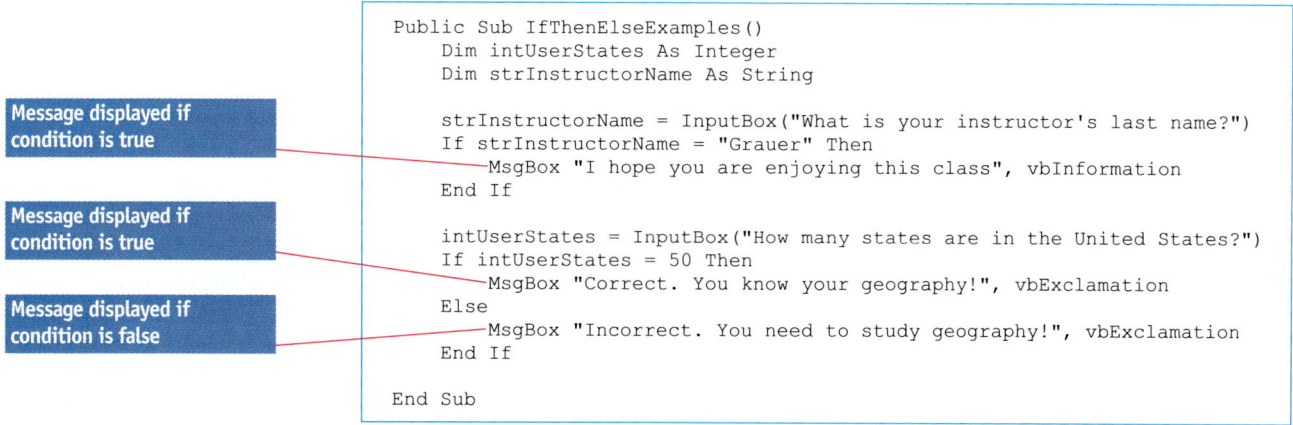

(a) VBA Code

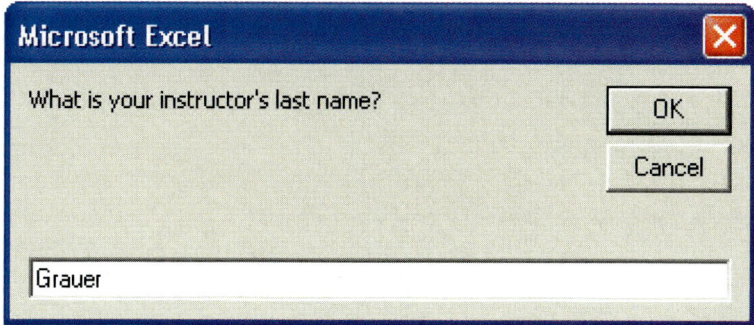

(b) InputBox Prompts for User Response

(c) Condition Is True

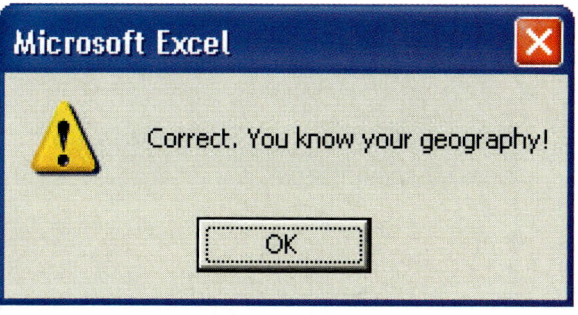

(d) Answer Is Correct (condition is true)

(e) Answer Is Wrong (condition is false)

FIGURE 5 The If Statement

CASE STATEMENT

The If statement is ideal for testing simple conditions and taking one of two actions. Although it can be extended to include additional actions by including one or more ElseIf clauses (If . . . Then . . . ElseIf . . . ElseIf . . .), this type of construction is often difficult to follow. Hence the **Case statement** is used when multiple branches are possible.

The procedure in Figure 6a accepts a student's GPA, then displays one of several messages, depending on the value of the GPA. The individual cases are evaluated in sequence. (The GPAs must be evaluated in descending order if the statement is to work correctly.) Thus, we check first to see if the GPA is greater than or equal to 3.9, then 3.75, then 3.5, and so on. If none of the cases is true, the statement following the Else clause is executed.

Note, too, the format of the comparison in that numbers (such as 3.9 or 3.75) are not enclosed in quotation marks because the associated variable (sngUserGPA) was declared as numeric. If, however, we had been evaluating a string variable (such as, strUserMajor), quotation marks would have been required around the literal values (e.g., Case Is = "Business", Case Is = "Liberal Arts", and so on.) The distinction between numeric and character (string) variables is important.

```
Public Sub CaseExample()

    Dim sngUserGPA As Single

    sngUserGPA = InputBox("What is your GPA?")
    Select Case sngUserGPA
        Case Is >= 3.9
            MsgBox "Congratulations! You are graduating Summa Cum Laude!"
        Case Is >= 3.75
            MsgBox "Well Done! You are graduating Magna Cum Laude!"
        Case Is >= 3.5
            MsgBox "Congratulations! You are graduating Cum Laude!"
        Case Is >= 1.8
            MsgBox "You made it"
        Case Else
            MsgBox "Check your schedule for Summer School!"
    End Select
```

- Variable is declared as numeric
- Numbers are not enclosed in quotes
- Message is displayed if no case is true

(a) VBA Code

(b) Enter the GPA

(c) Third Option Is Selected

FIGURE 6 The Case Statement

CUSTOM TOOLBARS

A VBA procedure can be executed in several different ways. It can be run from the Visual Basic editor by pulling down the Run menu and clicking the Run Sub button on the Standard toolbar, or using the F5 function key. It can also be run from within the Office application (Word, Excel, or PowerPoint, but not Access), by pulling down the Tools menu, clicking the Macro command, then choosing the name of the macro that corresponds to the name of the procedure.

Perhaps the best way, however, is to create a ***custom toolbar*** that is displayed within the application as shown in Figure 7. (A custom menu can also be created that contains the same commands as the custom toolbar.) The toolbar has its own name (Bob's Toolbar), yet it functions identically to any other Office toolbar. You have your choice of displaying buttons only, text only, or both buttons and text. Our toolbar provides access to four commands, each corresponding to a procedure that was discussed earlier. Click the Case Example button, for example, and the associated procedure is executed, starting with the InputBox statement asking for the user's GPA.

A custom toolbar is created via the Toolbars command within the View menu. The new toolbar is initially big enough to hold only a single button, but you can add, move, and delete buttons following the same procedure as for any other Office toolbar. You can add any command at all to the toolbar; that is, you can add existing commands from within the Office application, or you can add commands that correspond to VBA procedures that you have created. Remember, too, that you can add more buttons to existing office toolbars.

Once the toolbar has been created, it is displayed or hidden just like any other Office toolbar. It can also be docked along any edge of the application window or left floating as shown in Figure 7. It's fun, it's easy, and as you may have guessed, it's time for the next hands-on exercise.

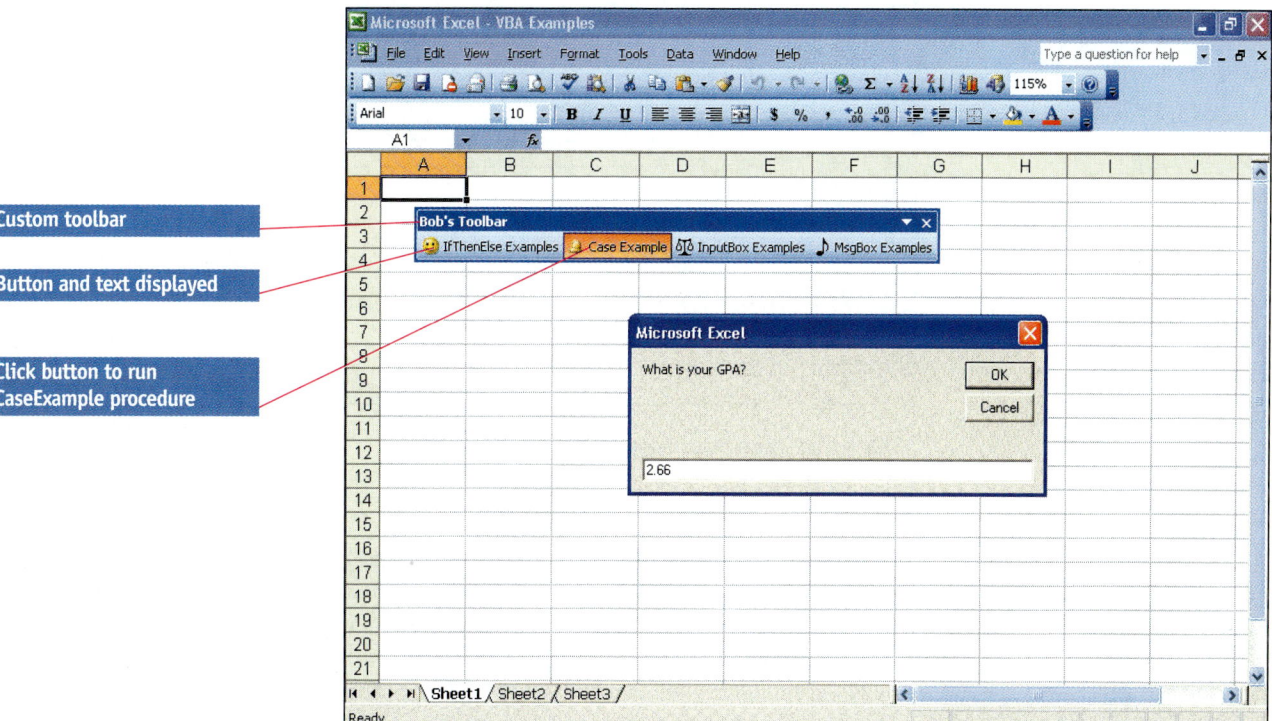

FIGURE 7 Custom Toolbars

hands-on exercise 2

Decision Making

Objective To create procedures with If . . . Then . . . Else and Case statements, then create a custom toolbar to execute those procedures. Use Figure 8 as a guide in the exercise.

Step 1: **Open the Office Document**

- Open the **VBA Examples workbook** or Access database from the previous exercise. The procedure differs slightly, depending on whether you are using Access or Excel.
  - In Access, you simply open the database.
  - In Excel you will be warned that the workbook contains a macro as shown in Figure 8a. Click the button to **Enable Macros**.

- Pull down the **Tools menu**, click the **Macro command**, then click the **Visual Basic Editor command**. You can also use the **Alt+F11** keyboard shortcut to open the VBA editor without going through the Tools menu.

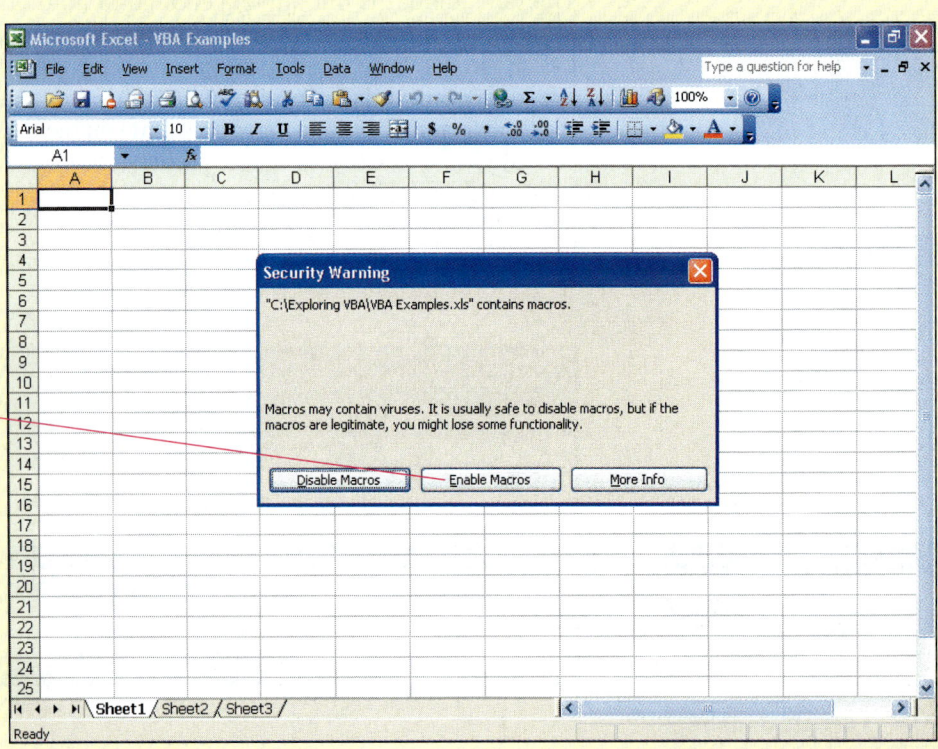

Click Enable Macros

(a) Open the Office Document (step 1)

FIGURE 8 Hands-on Exercise 2

MACRO SECURITY

A computer virus could take the form of an Excel macro; thus, Excel will warn you that a workbook contains a macro, provided the security option is set appropriately. Pull down the Tools menu, click the Options command, click the Security tab, and then set the Macro Security to either High or Medium. High security disables all macros except those from a trusted source. Medium security gives you the option to enable macros. Click the button only if you are sure the macro is from a trusted source.

Step 2: **Insert a New Procedure**

- You should be in the Visual Basic editor as shown in Figure 8b. If necessary, double click **Module1** in the Explorer Window to open this module. Pull down the **Insert menu** and click the **Procedure command** to display the Add Procedure dialog box.

- Click in the **Name** text box and enter **IfThenElseExamples** as the name of the procedure. Click the option buttons for a **Sub procedure** and for **Public scope**. Click **OK** to create the procedure.

- The Sub procedure should appear within the module and consist of the Sub and End Sub statements as shown in Figure 8b.

- Click within the newly created procedure, then click the **Procedure View button** at the bottom of the window. The display changes to show just the current procedure.

- Click the **Save button** to save the module with the new procedure.

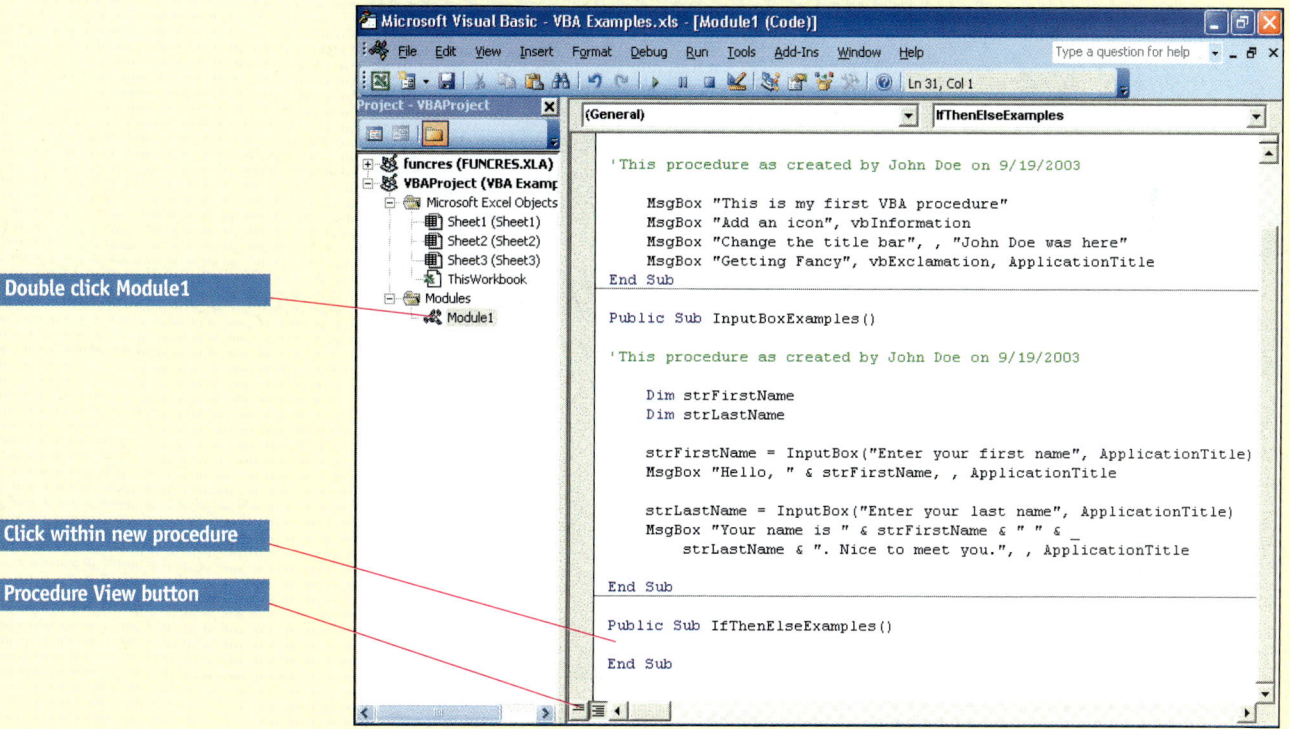

(b) Insert a New Procedure (step 2)

FIGURE 8 Hands-on Exercise 2 (*continued*)

PROCEDURE VIEW VERSUS FULL MODULE VIEW

The procedures within a module can be displayed individually, or alternatively, multiple procedures can be viewed simultaneously. To go from one view to the other, click the Procedure View button at the bottom of the window to display just the procedure you are working on, or click the Full Module View button to display multiple procedures. You can press Ctrl+PgDn and Ctrl+PgUp to move between procedures in either view.

EXTENDING MICROSOFT OFFICE 2003   1925

Step 3: **Create the If . . . Then . . . Else Procedure**

- Enter the IfThenElseExamples procedure as it appears in Figure 8c, but use your instructor's name instead of Bob's. Note the following:
  - The Dim statements at the beginning of the procedure are required to define the two variables that are used elsewhere in the procedure.
  - The syntax of the comparison is different for string variables versus numeric variables. String variables require quotation marks around the comparison value (e.g., strInstructorName = "Grauer"). Numeric variables (e.g., intUserStates = 50) do not.
  - Indentation and blank lines are used within a procedure to make the code easier to read, as distinct from a VBA requirement. Press the **Tab key** to indent one level to the right.
  - Comments can be added to a procedure at any time.
- Save the procedure.

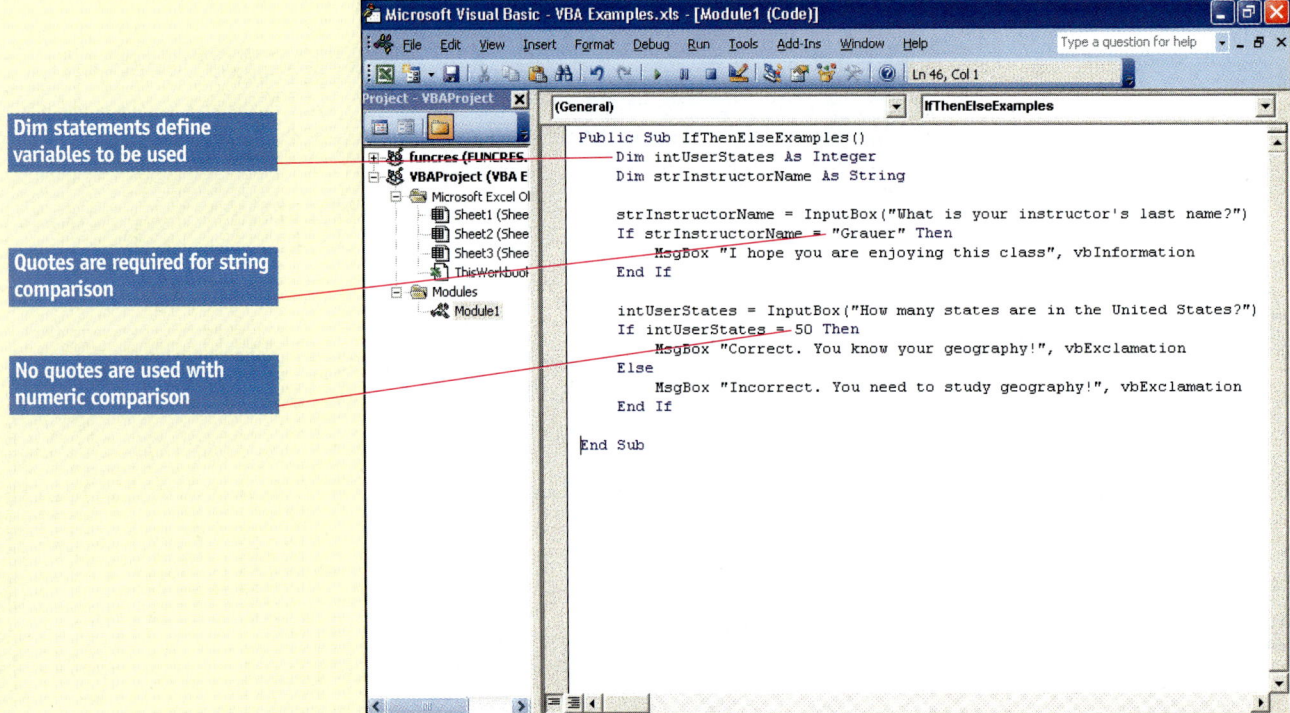

(c) Create the If . . . Then . . . Else Procedure (step 3)

FIGURE 8 Hands-on Exercise 2 (*continued*)

THE COMPLETE WORD TOOL

It's easy to misspell a variable name within a procedure, which is why the Complete Word tool is so useful. Type the first several characters in a variable name (such as "intU" or "strI" in the current procedure), then press Ctrl+Space. VBA will complete the variable name for you, provided that you have already entered a sufficient number of letters for a unique reference. Alternatively, it will display all of the elements that begin with the letters you have entered. Use the down arrow to scroll through the list until you find the item, then press the space bar to complete the entry.

Step 4: **Test the Procedure**

- The best way to test a procedure is to display its output directly in the VBA window (without having to switch back and forth between that and the application window). Thus, right click the Excel button on the taskbar to display a context-sensitive menu, then click the **Minimize command**.

- There is no visible change on your monitor. Click anywhere within the procedure, then click the **Run Sub button**. You should see the dialog box in Figure 8d.

- Enter your instructor's name, exactly as it was spelled within the VBA procedure. Click **OK**.

- You should see a second message box that hopes you are enjoying the class. This box will be displayed only if you spell the instructor's name correctly. Click **OK**.

- You should see a second input box that asks how many states are in the United States. Enter **50** and click **OK**. You should see a message indicating that you know your geography. Click **OK** to close the dialog box.

- Click the **Run Sub button** a second time, but enter a different set of values in response to the prompts. Misspell your instructor's name, and you will not see the associated message box.

- Enter any number other than 50, and you will be told to study geography.

- Continue to test the procedure until you are satisfied it works under all conditions. We cannot overemphasize the importance of thorough testing!

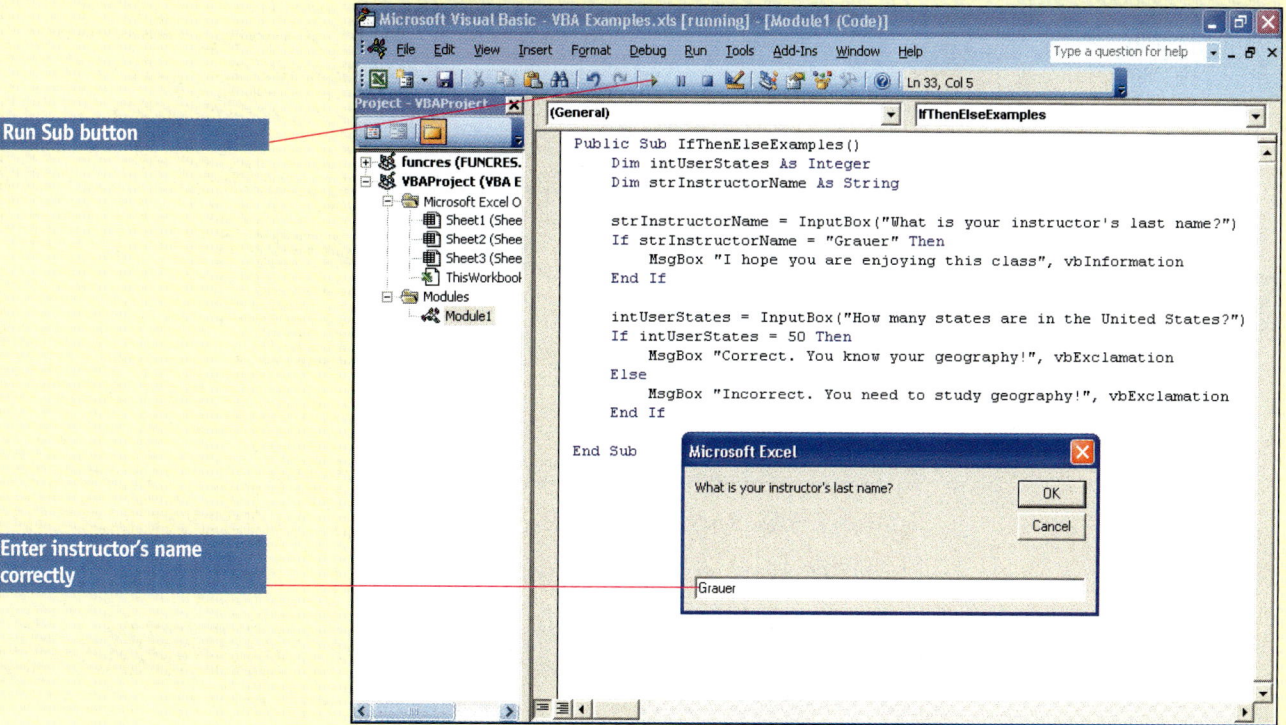

(d) Test the Procedure (step 4)

FIGURE 8 Hands-on Exercise 2 (*continued*)

EXTENDING MICROSOFT OFFICE 2003 **1927**

Step 5: **Create and Test the CaseExample Procedure**

- Pull down the **Insert menu** and create a new procedure called **CaseExample**, then enter the statements exactly as they appear in Figure 8e. Note:
    - The variable sngUserGPA is declared to be a single-precision floating-point number (as distinct from the integer type that was used previously). A floating-point number is required in order to maintain a decimal point.
    - The GPA must be tested in descending order if the statement is to work correctly.
    - You may use any editing technique with which you are comfortable. You could, for example, enter the first case, copy it four times in the procedure, then modify the copied text as necessary.
    - The use of indentation and blank lines is for the convenience of the programmer and not a requirement of VBA.

- Click the **Run Sub button**, then test the procedure. Be sure to test it under all conditions; that is, you need to run it several times and enter a different GPA each time to be sure that all of the cases are working correctly.

- Save the procedure.

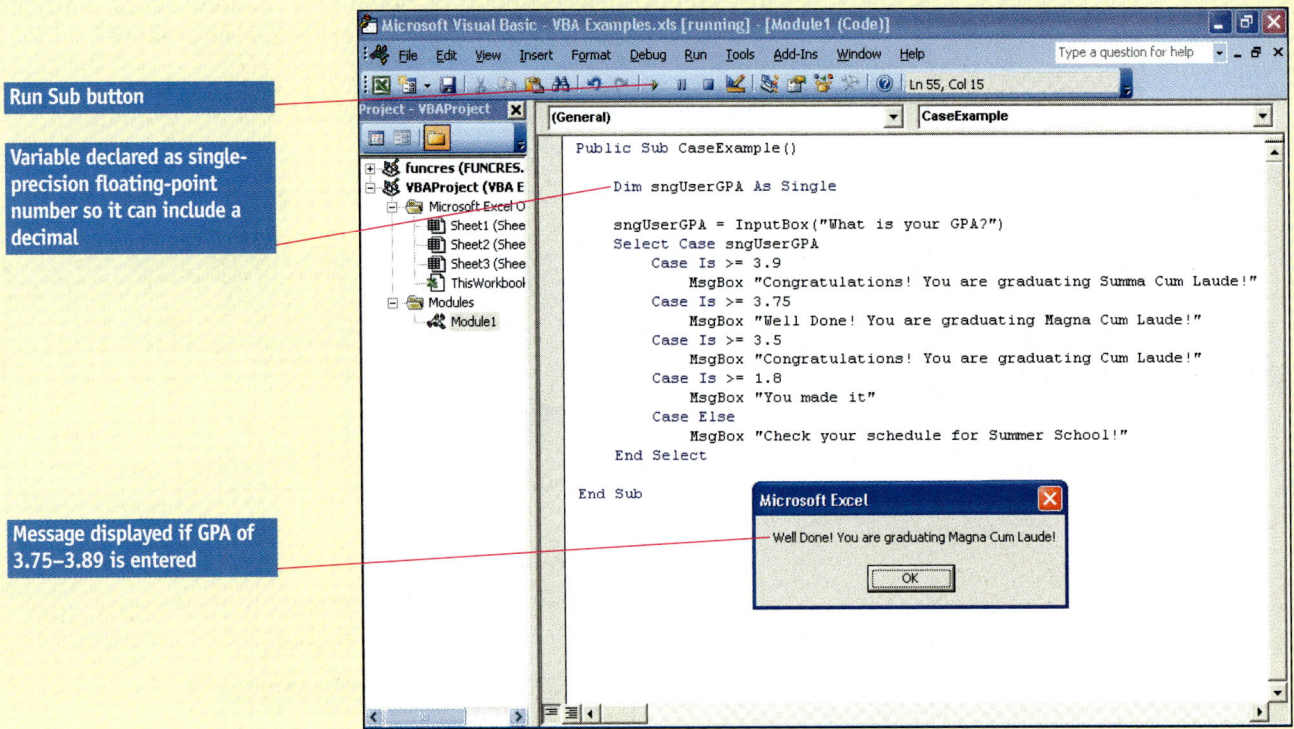

(e) Create and Test the CaseExample Procedure (step 5)

FIGURE 8 Hands-on Exercise 2 (*continued*)

RELATIONAL OPERATORS

The condition portion of an If or Case statement uses one of several relational operators. These include =, <, and > for equal to, less than, or greater than, respectively. You can also use >=, <=, or <> for greater than or equal to, less than or equal to, or not equal. This is basic, but very important, information if you are to code these statements correctly.

Step 6: **Create a Custom Toolbar**

- Click the **View Microsoft Excel** (or **Access**) **button** to display the associated application window. Pull down the **View menu**, click (or point to) the **Toolbars command**, then click **Customize** to display the Customize dialog box in Figure 8f. (Bob's toolbar is not yet visible.) Click the **Toolbars tab**.

- Click the **New button** to display the New Toolbar dialog box. Enter the name of your toolbar—e.g., **Bob's toolbar**—then click **OK** to create the toolbar and close the New Toolbar dialog box.

- Your toolbar should appear on the screen, but it does not yet contain any buttons. If necessary, click and drag the title bar of your toolbar to move the toolbar within the application window.

- Toggle the check box that appears next to your toolbar within the Customize dialog box on and off to display or hide your toolbar. Leave the box checked to display the toolbar and continue with this exercise.

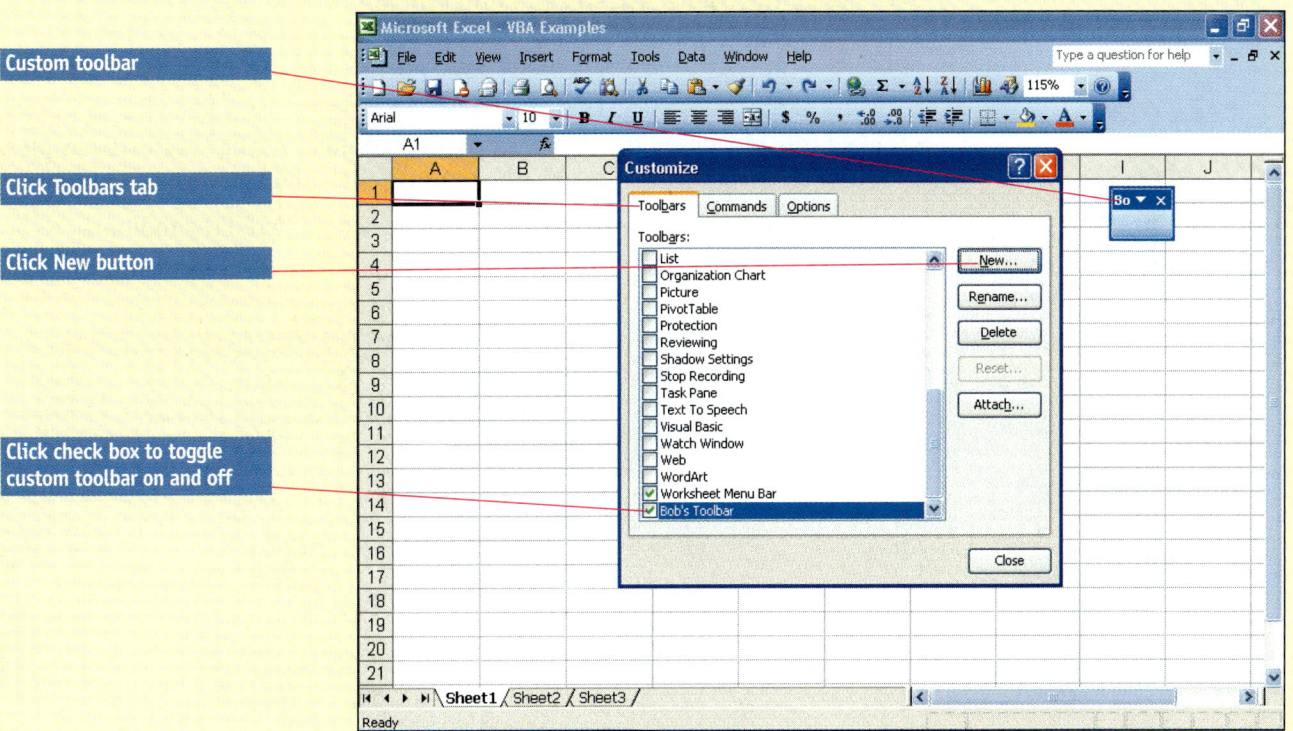

(f) Create a Custom Toolbar (step 6)

FIGURE 8 Hands-on Exercise 2 (*continued*)

FIXED VERSUS FLOATING TOOLBARS

A toolbar may be docked (fixed) along the edge of the application window, or it can be displayed as a floating toolbar anywhere within the window. You can switch back and forth by dragging the move handle of a docked toolbar to move the toolbar away from the edge. Conversely, you can drag the title bar of a floating toolbar to the edge of the window to dock the toolbar. You can also click and drag the border of a floating toolbar to change its size.

Step 7: **Add Buttons to the Toolbar**

- Click the **Commands tab** in the Customize dialog box, click the **down arrow** in the Categories list box, then scroll until you can select the **Macros category**. (If you are using Access and not Excel, you need to select the **File category**, then follow the steps as described in the boxed tip on the next page.)

- Click and drag the **Custom button** to your toolbar and release the mouse. A "happy face" button appears on the toolbar you just created. (You can remove a button from a toolbar by simply dragging the button from the toolbar.)

- Select the newly created button, then click the **Modify Selection command button** (or right click the button to display the context-sensitive menu) in Figure 8g. Change the button's properties as follows:
  - Click the **Assign Macro command** at the bottom of the menu to display the Assign Macro dialog box, then select the **IfThenElseExamples macro** (procedure) to assign it to the button. Click **OK**.
  - Click the **Modify Selection button** a second time.
  - Click in the **Name Textbox** and enter an appropriate name for the button, such as **IfThenElseExamples**.
  - Click the **Modify Selection button** a third time, then click **Text Only (Always)** to display text rather than an image.

- Repeat this procedure to add buttons to the toolbar for the MsgBoxExamples, InputBoxExamples, and CaseExample procedures that you created earlier.

- Close the Customize dialog box when you have completed the toolbar.

- Save the workbook.

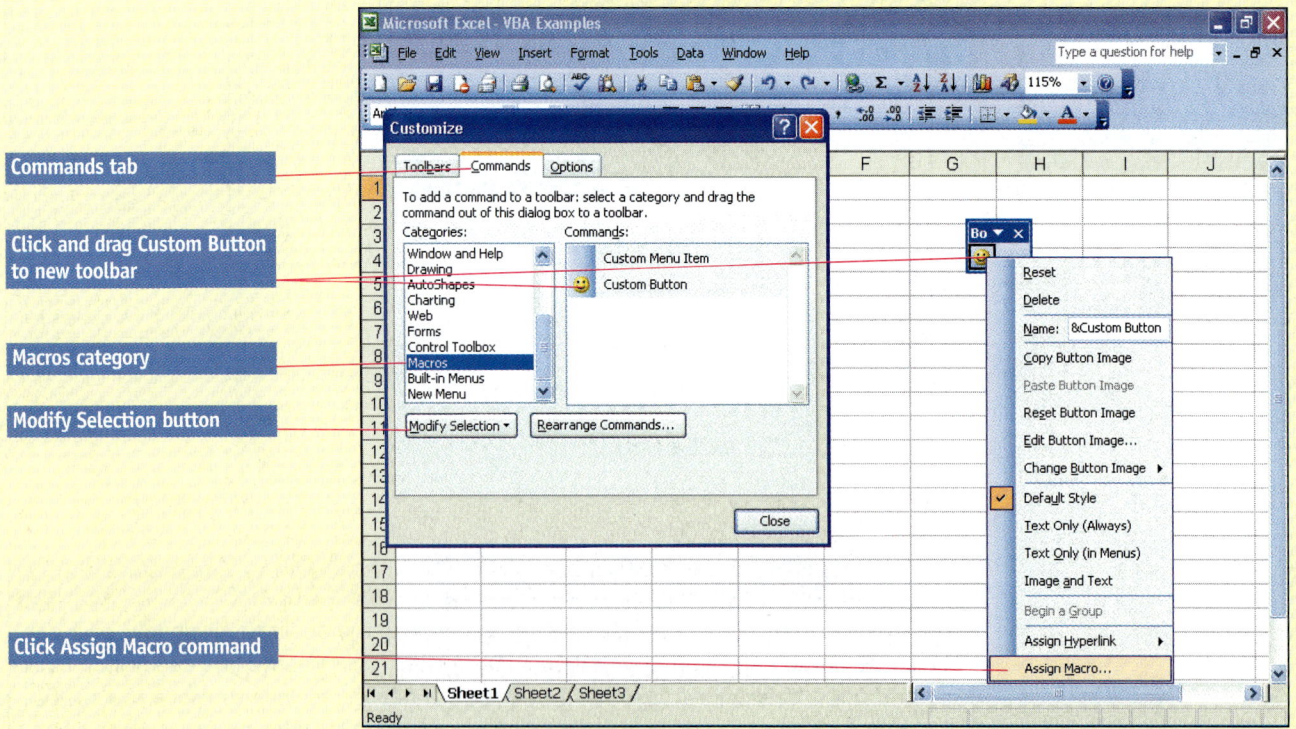

(g) Add Buttons to the Toolbar (step 7)

FIGURE 8 Hands-on Exercise 2 (*continued*)

1930 GETTING STARTED WITH VBA

Step 8: **Test the Custom Toolbar**

- Click any command on your toolbar as shown in Figure 8h. We clicked the **InputBoxExamples button**, which in turn executed the InputBoxExamples procedure that was created in the first exercise.

- Enter the appropriate information in any input boxes that are displayed. Click **OK**. Close your toolbar when you have completed testing it.

- If this is not your own machine, you should delete your toolbar as a courtesy to the next student. Pull down the **View menu**, click the **Toolbars command**, click **Customize** to display the Customize dialog box, then click the **Toolbars tab**. Select (highlight) the toolbar, then click the **Delete button** in the Customize dialog box. Click **OK** to delete the button. Close the dialog box.

- Exit Office if you do not want to continue with the next exercise.

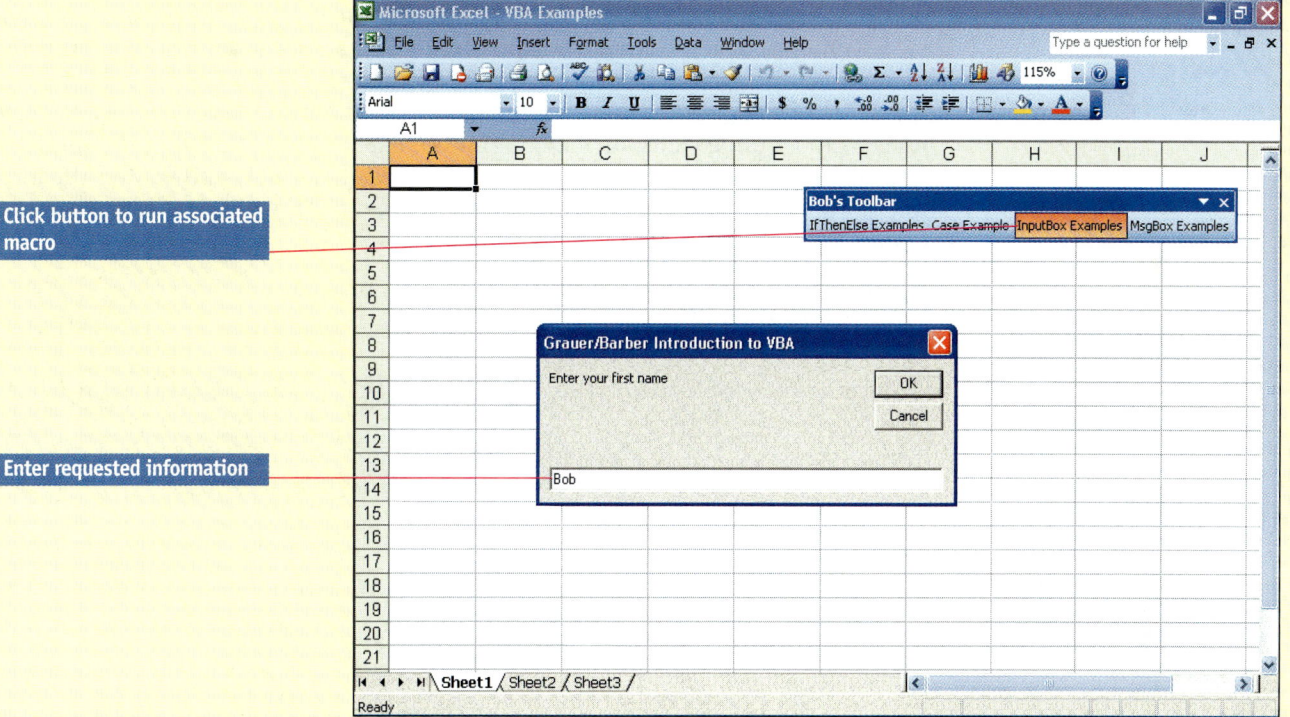

(h) Test the Custom Toolbar (step 8)

FIGURE 8   Hands-on Exercise 2 (*continued*)

ACCESS IS DIFFERENT

The procedure to add buttons to a custom toolbar in Access is different from the procedure in Excel. Pull down the View menu, click the Toolbars command, then click the Customize command. Select the File category within the Customize dialog box, then click and drag the Custom command to the newly created toolbar. Select the command on the toolbar, then click the Modify Selection command button in the dialog box. Click Properties, click the On Action text box, then type the name of the procedure you want to run in the format, =procedurename(). Close the dialog boxes, then press Alt+F11 to return to the VBA editor. Change the keyword "Sub" that identifies the procedure to "Function". Return to the database window, then test the newly created toolbar.

EXTENDING MICROSOFT OFFICE 2003   1931

FOR...NEXT STATEMENT

The **For...Next statement** executes all statements between the words For and Next a specified number of times, using a counter to keep track of the number of times the statements are executed. The statement, For intCounter = 1 to N, executes the statements within the loop N times.

The procedure in Figure 9 contains two For...Next statements that sum the numbers from 1 to 10, counting by 1 and 2, respectively. The Dim statements at the beginning of the procedure declare two variables, intSumofNumbers to hold the sum and intCounter to hold the value of the counter. The sum is initialized to zero immediately before the first loop. The statements in the loop are then executed 10 times, each time incrementing the sum by the value of the counter. The result (the sum of the numbers from 1 to 10) is displayed after the loop in Figure 9b.

The second For...Next statement increments the counter by 2 rather than by 1. (The increment or step is assumed to be 1 unless a different value is specified.) The sum of the numbers is reset to zero prior to entering the second loop, the loop is entered, and the counter is initialized to the starting value of 1. Each subsequent time through the loop, however, the counter is incremented by 2. Each time the value of the counter is compared to the ending value, until it (the counter) exceeds the ending value, at which point the For...Next statement is complete. Thus the second loop will be executed for values of 1, 3, 5, 7, and 9. After the fifth time through the loop, the counter is incremented to 11, which is greater than the ending value of 10, and the loop is terminated.

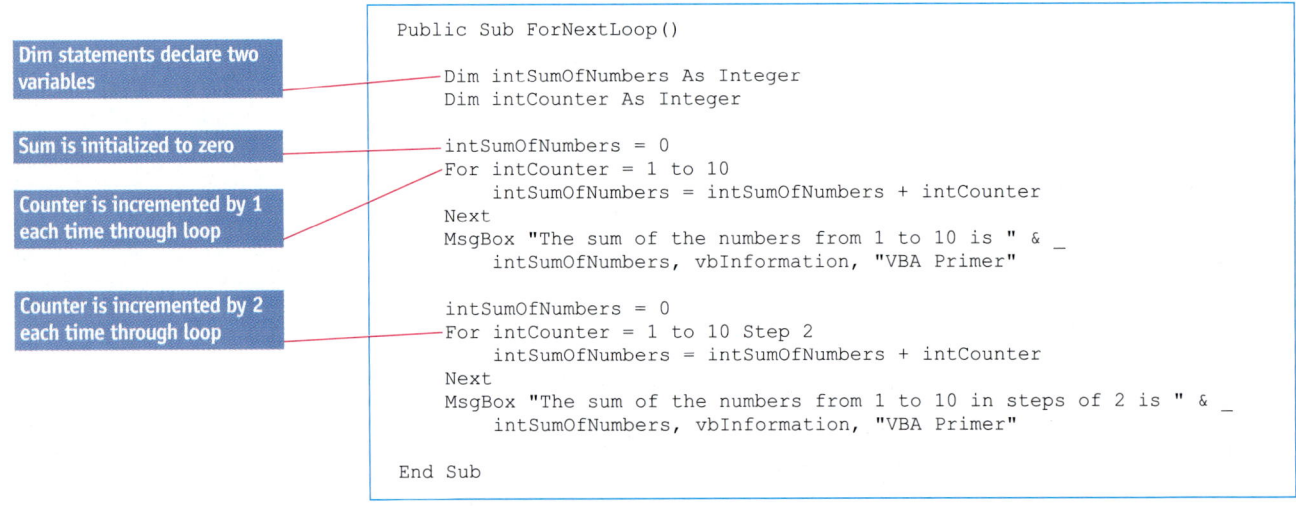

(a) VBA Code

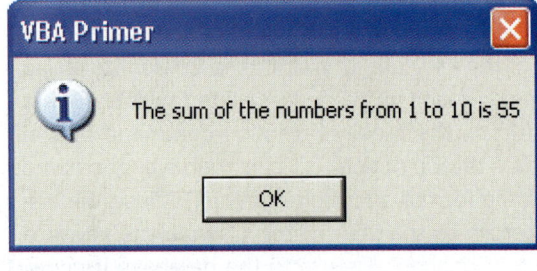

(b) In Increments of 1

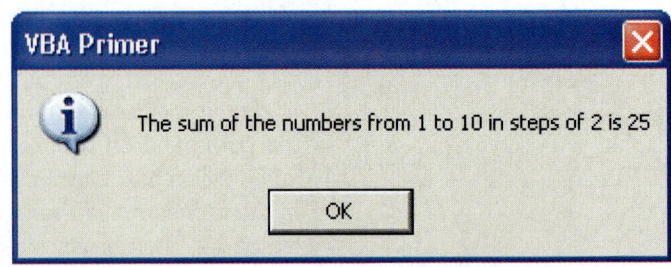

(c) In Increments of 2

FIGURE 9 For...Next Loops

DO LOOPS

The For . . . Next statement is ideal when you know in advance how many times you want to go through a loop. There are many instances, however, when the number of times through the loop is indeterminate. You could, for example, give a user multiple chances to enter a password or answer a question. This type of logic is implemented through a Do loop. You can repeat the loop as long as a condition is true (Do While), or until a condition becomes true (Do Until). The choice depends on how you want to state the condition.

Regardless of which keyword you choose, Do While or Do Until, two formats are available. The difference is subtle and depends on whether the keyword (While or Until) appears at the beginning or end of the loop. Our discussion will use the Do Until statement, but the Do While statement works in similar fashion.

Look closely at the procedure in Figure 10a, which contains two different loops. In the first example the Until condition appears at the end of the loop, which means the statements in the loop are executed, and then the condition is tested. This ensures that the statements in the loop will be executed at least once. The second loop, however, places the Until condition at the beginning of the loop, so that it (the condition) is tested prior to the loop being executed. Thus, if the condition is satisfied initially, the second loop will never be executed. In other words, there are two distinct statements ***Do . . . Loop Until*** and ***Do Until . . . Loop***. The first statement executes the loop, then tests the condition. The second statement tests the condition, then enters the loop.

```
Public Sub DoUntilLoop()

    Dim strCorrectAnswer As String, strUserAnswer As String

    strCorrectAnswer = "Earth"

    Do
        strUserAnswer = InputBox("What is the third planet from the sun?")
    Loop Until strUserAnswer = strCorrectAnswer
    MsgBox "You are correct, earthling!", vbExclamation

    strUserAnswer = InputBox("What is the third planet from the sun?")
    Do Until strUserAnswer = strCorrectAnswer
        strUserAnswer = InputBox("Your answer is incorrect. Try again.")
    Loop
    MsgBox "You are correct, earthling!", vbExclamation

End Sub
```

Until appears at end of loop

Until appears at beginning of loop

(a) (VBA Code)

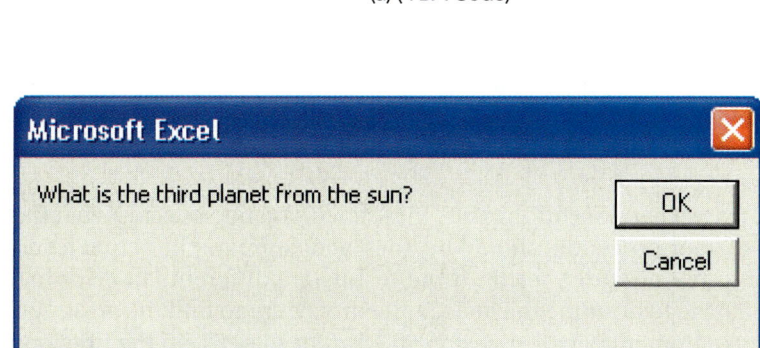

(b) Input the Answer

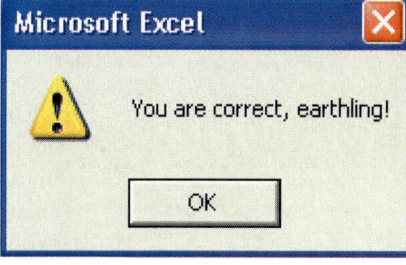

(c) Correct Response

FIGURE 10 Do Until Loops

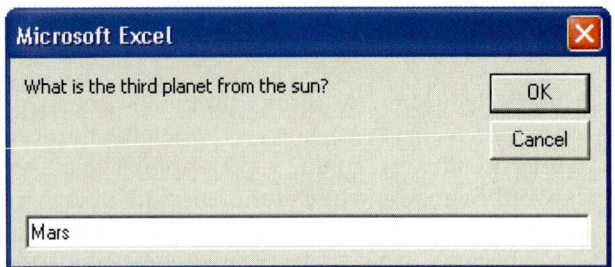
(d) Wrong Answer Initially

(e) Second Chance

FIGURE 10 Do Until Loops (*continued*)

It's tricky, but stay with us. In the first example the user is asked the question within the loop, and the loop is executed repeatedly until the user gives the correct answer. In the second example the user is asked the question outside of the loop, and the loop is bypassed if the user answers it correctly. The latter is the preferred logic because it enables us to phrase the question differently, before and during the loop. Look carefully at the difference between the InputBox statements and see how the question changes within the second loop.

DEBUGGING

As you learn more about VBA and develop more powerful procedures, you are more likely to make mistakes. The process of finding and correcting errors within a procedure is known as ***debugging*** and it is an integral part of programming. Do not be discouraged if you make mistakes. Everyone does. The important thing is how quickly you are able to find and correct the errors that invariably occur. We begin our discussion of debugging by describing two types of errors, ***compilation errors*** and ***execution*** (or ***run-time***) ***errors***.

A compilation error is simply an error in VBA syntax. (Compilation is the process of translating a VBA procedure into machine language, and thus a compilation error occurs when the VBA editor is unable to convert a statement to machine language.) Compilation errors occur for many reasons, such as misspelling a keyword, omitting a comma, and so on. VBA recognizes the error before the procedure is run and displays the invalid statement in red together with an associated error message. The programmer corrects the error and then reruns the procedure.

Execution errors are caused by errors in logic and are more difficult to detect because they occur without any error message. VBA, or for that matter any other programming language, does what you tell it to do, which is not necessarily what you want it to do. If, for example, you were to compute the sales tax of an item by multiplying the price by 60% rather than 6%, VBA will perform the calculation and simply display the wrong answer. It is up to you to realize that the results of the procedure are incorrect, and you will need to examine its statements and correct the mistake.

So how do you detect an execution error? In essence, you must decide what the expected output of your procedure should be, then you compare the actual result of the procedure to the intended result. If the results are different, an error has occurred, and you have to examine the logic in the procedure to find the error. You may see the mistake immediately (e.g., using 60% rather than 6% in the previous example), or you may have to examine the code more closely. And as you might expect, VBA has a variety of tools to help you in the debugging process. These tools are accessed from the ***Debug toolbar*** or the ***Debug menu*** as shown in Figure 11 on the next page.

The procedure in Figure 11 is a simple For ... Next loop to sum the integers from 1 to 10. The procedure is correct as written, but we have introduced several debugging techniques into the figure. The most basic technique is to step through the statements in the procedure one at a time to see the sequence in which the statements are executed. Click the **Step Into button** on the Debug toolbar to enter (step into) the procedure, then continue to click the button to move through the procedure. Each time you click the button, the statement that is about to be executed is highlighted.

Another useful technique is to display the values of selected variables as they change during execution. This is accomplished through the ***Debug.Print statement*** that displays the values in the ***Immediate window***. The Debug.Print statement is placed within the For ... Next loop so that you can see how the counter and the associated sum change during execution.

As the figure now stands, we have gone through the loop nine times, and the sum of the numbers from 1 to 9 is 45. The Step Into button is in effect so that the statement to be executed next is highlighted. You can see that we are back at the top of the loop, where the counter has been incremented to 10, and further, that we are about to increment the sum.

The ***Locals window*** is similar in concept except that it displays only the current values of all the variables within the procedure. Unlike the Immediate window, which requires the insertion of Debug.Print statements into a procedure to have meaning, the Locals window displays its values automatically, without any effort on the part of the programmer, other than opening the window. All three techniques can be used individually, or in conjunction with one another, as the situation demands.

We believe that the best time to practice debugging is when you know there are no errors in your procedure. As you may have guessed, it's time for the next hands-on exercise.

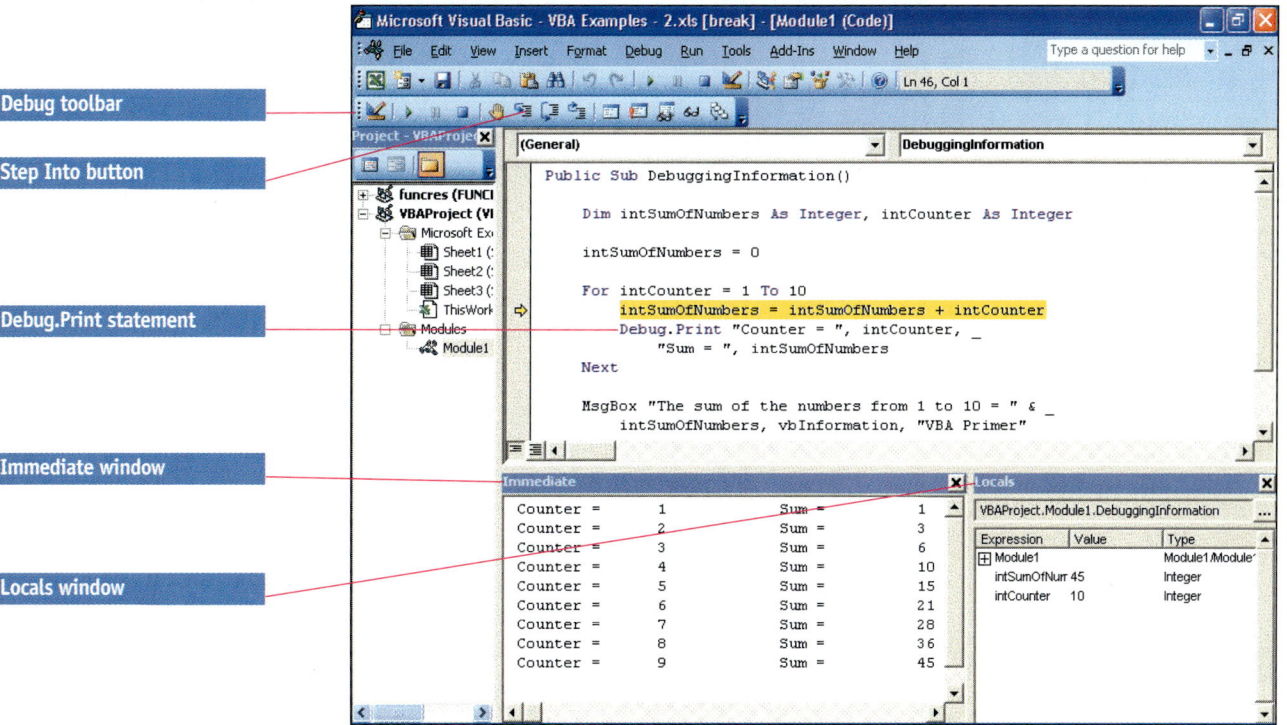

FIGURE 11 Debugging

hands-on exercise

3 Loops and Debugging

Objective To create a loop using the For . . . Next and Do Until statements; to open the Locals and Immediate windows and illustrate different techniques for debugging. Use Figure 12 as a guide in the exercise.

Step 1: **Insert a New Procedure**

- Open the **VBA Examples workbook** or the Access database from the previous exercise. Either way, pull down the **Tools menu**, click the **Macro command**, then click **Visual Basic editor** (or use the **Alt+F11** keyboard shortcut) to start the VBA editor.

- If necessary, double click **Module1** within the Project Explorer window to open this module. Pull down the **Insert menu** and click the **Procedure command** to display the Add Procedure dialog box.

- Click in the **Name** text box and enter **ForNextLoop** as the name of the procedure. Click the option buttons for a **Sub procedure** and for **Public scope**. Click **OK** to create the procedure.

- The Sub procedure should appear within the module and consist of the Sub and End Sub statements as shown in Figure 12a.

- Click the **Procedure View button** at the bottom of the window as shown in Figure 12a. The display changes to show just the current procedure, giving you more room in which to work.

- Save the module.

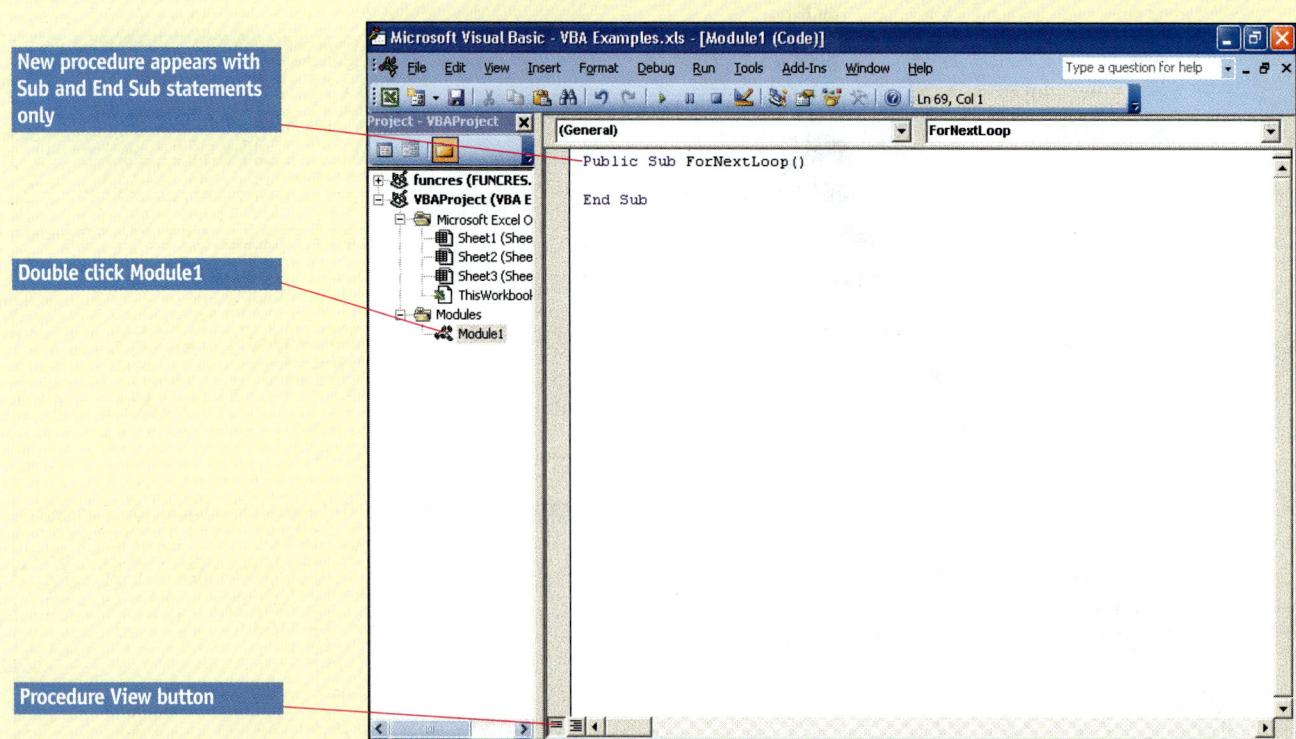

(a) Insert a New Procedure (step 1)

FIGURE 12 Hands-on Exercise 3

Step 2: **Test the For ... Next Procedure**

- Enter the procedure exactly as it appears in Figure 12b. Note the following:
  - A comment is added at the beginning of the procedure to identify the author and the date.
  - Two variables are declared at the beginning of the procedure, one to hold the sum of the numbers and the other to serve as a counter.
  - The sum of the numbers is initialized to zero. The For ... Next loop varies the counter from 1 to 10.
  - The statement within the For ... Next loop increments the sum of the numbers by the current value of the counter. The equal sign is really a replacement operator; that is, replace the variable on the left (the sum of the numbers) by the expression on the right (the sum of the numbers plus the value of the counter.
  - Indentation and spacing within a procedure are for the convenience of the programmer and not a requirement of VBA. We align the For and Next statements at the beginning and end of a loop, then indent all statements within a loop.
  - The MsgBox statement displays the result and is continued over two lines as per the underscore at the end of the first line.
  - The ampersand concatenates (joins together) the text and the number within the message box.

- Click the **Save button** to save the module. Right click the **Excel button** on the Windows taskbar to display a context-sensitive menu, then click the **Minimize command**.

- Click the **Run Sub button** to test the procedure, which should display the MsgBox statement in Figure 12b. Correct any errors that may occur.

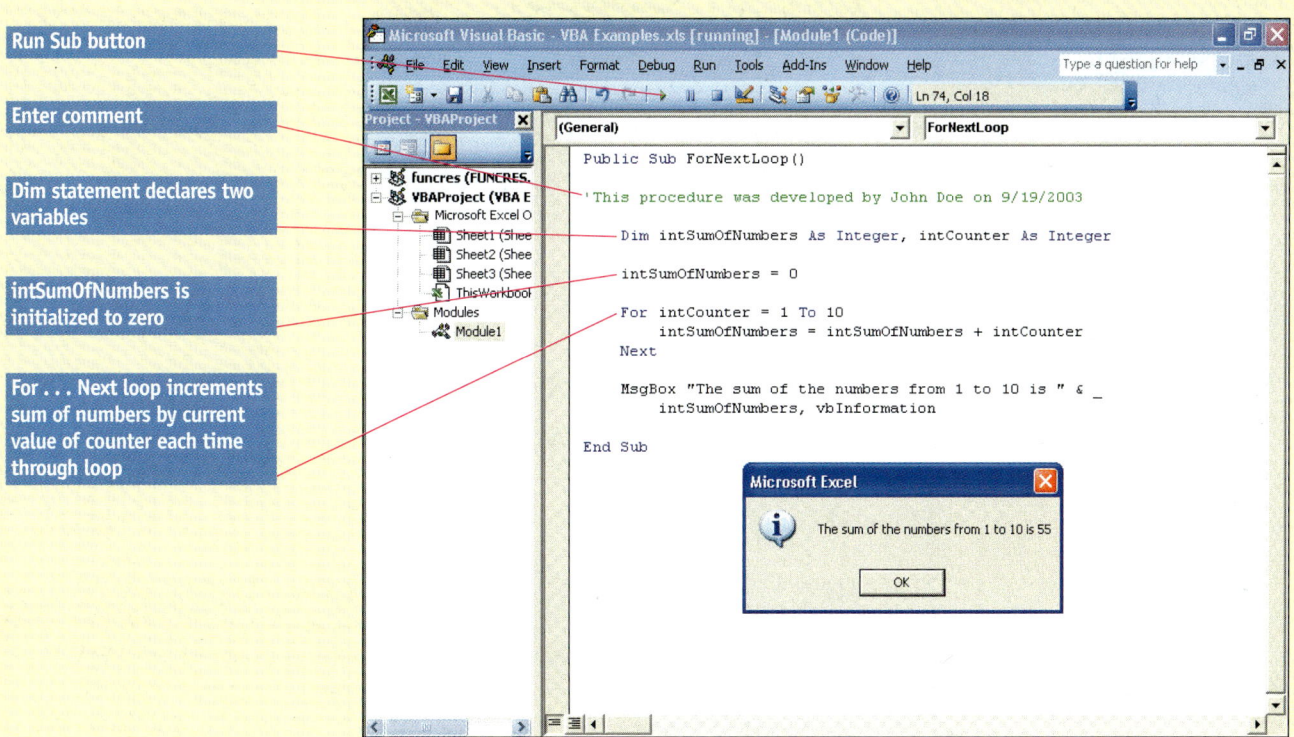

(b) Test the For ... Next Procedure (step 2)

FIGURE 12 Hands-on Exercise 3 (*continued*)

Step 3: **Compilation Errors**

- The best time to practice debugging is when you know that the procedure is working properly. Accordingly, we will make some deliberate errors in our procedure to illustrate different debugging techniques.

- Pull down the **View menu**, click the **Toolbars command**, and (if necessary) toggle the Debug toolbar on, then dock it under the Standard toolbar.

- Click on the statement that initializes intSumOfNumbers to zero and delete the "s" at the end of the variable name. Click the **Run Sub button**.

- You will see the message in Figure 12c. Click **OK** to acknowledge the error, then click the **Undo button** to correct the error.

- The procedure header is highlighted, indicating that execution is temporarily suspended and that additional action is required from you to continue testing. Click the **Run Sub button** to retest the procedure.

- This time the procedure executes correctly and you see the MsgBox statement indicating that the sum of the numbers from 1 to 10 is 55. Click **OK**.

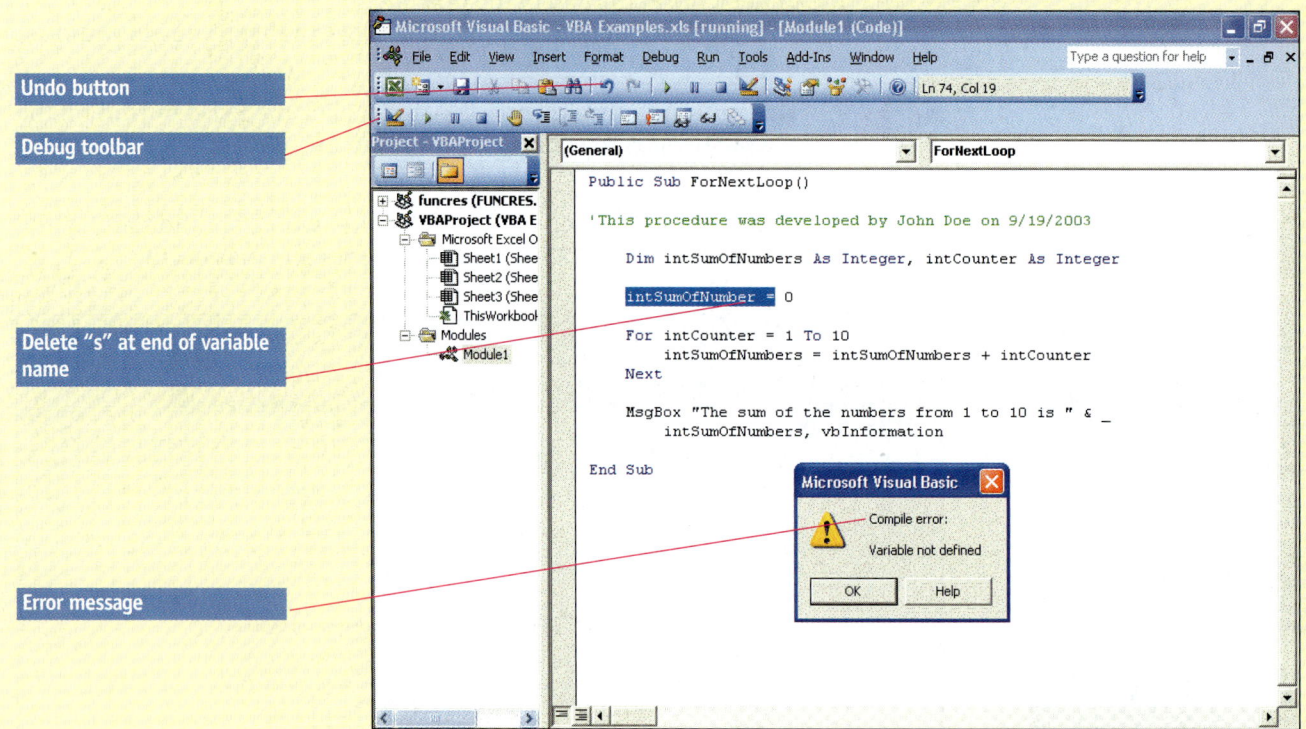

(c) Compilation Error (step 3)

FIGURE 12   Hands-on Exercise 3 (*continued*)

USE HELP AS NECESSARY

Pull down the Help menu at any time (or press the F1 key) to access the VBA Help facility to explore at your leisure. Use the Print command to create hard copy. (You can also copy the help text into a Word document to create your own reference manual.) The answers to virtually all of your questions are readily available if only you take the time to look.

Step 4: **Step through a Procedure**

- Pull down the **View menu** a second time and click the **Locals Window command** (or click the **Locals Window button** on the Debug toolbar).
- If necessary, click and drag the top border of the Locals window to size the window appropriately as shown in Figure 12d.
- Click anywhere within the procedure. Pull down the **Debug menu** and click the **Step Into command** (or click the **Step Into button** on the Debug toolbar). The first statement (the procedure header) is highlighted, indicating that you are about to enter the procedure.
- Click the **Step Into button** (or use the **F8** keyboard shortcut) to step into the procedure and advance to the next executable statement. The statement that initializes intSumOfNumbers to zero is highlighted, indicating that this statement is about to be executed.
- Continue to press the **F8 key** to step through the procedure. Each time you execute a statement, you can see the values of intSumOfNumbers and intCounter change within the Locals window. (You can click the **Step Out button** at any time to end the procedure.)
- Correct errors as they occur. Click the **Reset button** on the Standard or Debug toolbars at any time to begin executing the procedure from the beginning.
- Eventually you exit from the loop, and the sum of the numbers (from 1 to 10) is displayed within a message box.
- Click **OK** to close the message box. Press the **F8 key** a final time, then close the Locals window.
- Do you see how stepping through a procedure helps you to understand how it works?

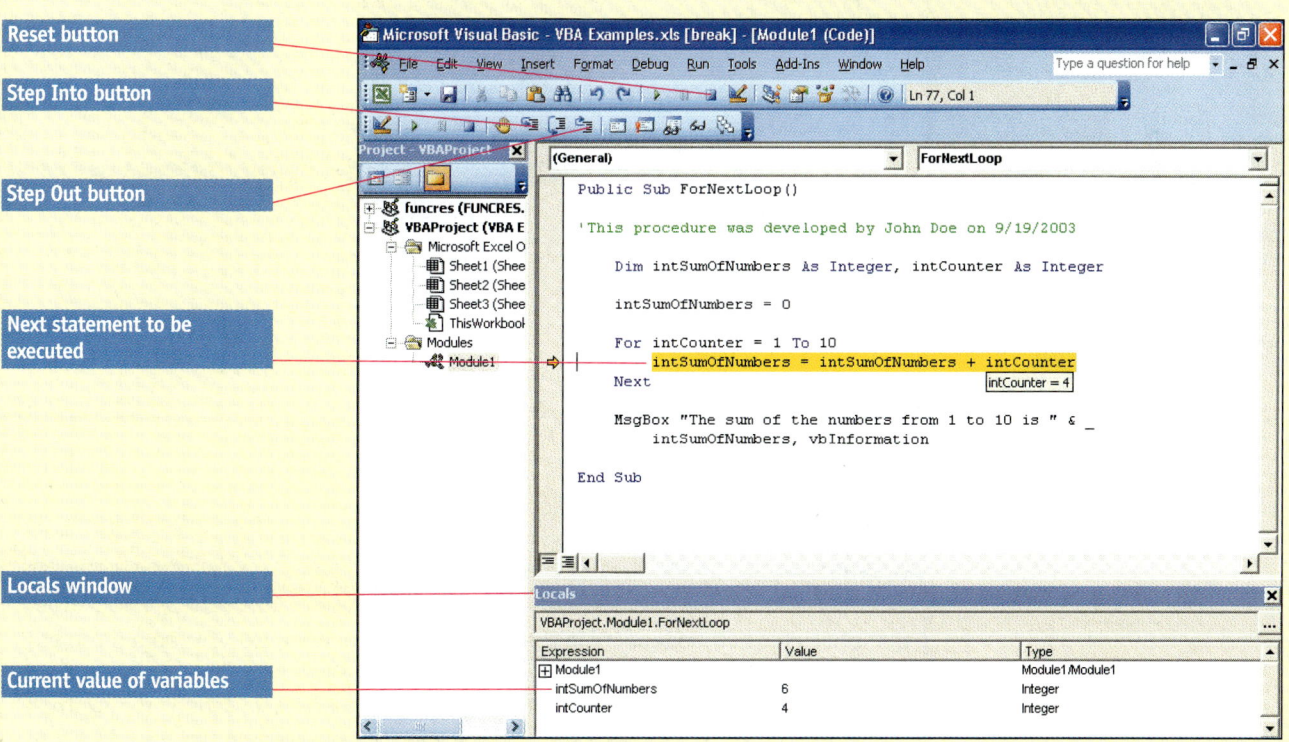

(d) Step through a Procedure (step 4)

FIGURE 12 Hands-on Exercise 3 (*continued*)

Step 5: **The Immediate Window**

- You should be back in the VBA window. Click immediately to the left of the Next statement and press **Enter** to insert a blank line. Type the **Debug.Print** statement exactly as shown in Figure 12e. (Click **OK** if you see a message indicating that the procedure will be reset.)

- Pull down the **View menu** and click the **Immediate Window command** (or click the **Immediate Window button** on the Debug toolbar). The Immediate window should be empty, but if not, you can click and drag to select the contents, then press the **Del key** to clear the window.

- Click anywhere within the For . . . Next procedure, then click the **Run Sub button** to execute the procedure. You will see the familiar message box indicating that the sum of the numbers is 55. Click **OK**.

- You should see 10 lines within the Immediate window as shown in Figure 12e, corresponding to the values displayed by the Debug.Print statement as it was executed within the loop.

- Close the Immediate window. Do you see how displaying the intermediate results of a procedure helps you to understand how it works?

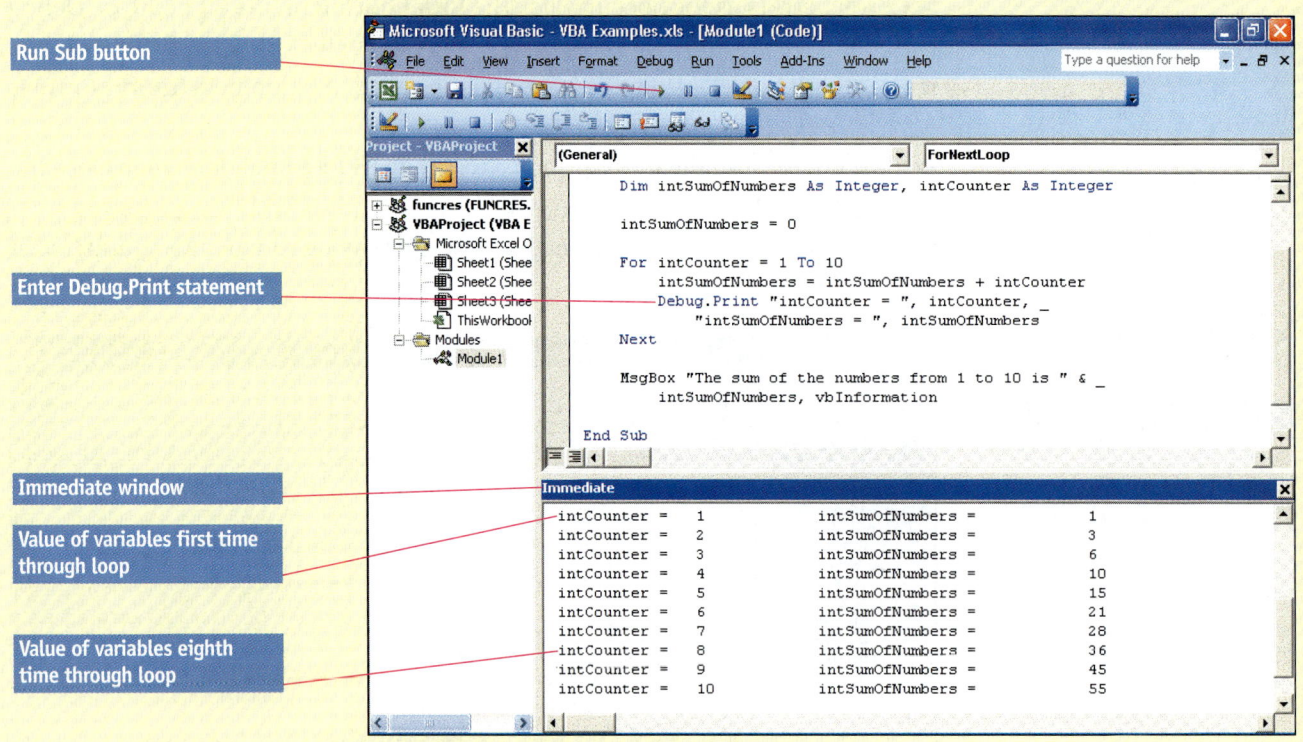

(e) The Immediate Window (step 5)

FIGURE 12 Hands-on Exercise 3 (*continued*)

INSTANT CALCULATOR

Use the Print method (action) in the Immediate window to use VBA as a calculator. Press Ctrl+G at any time to display the Immediate window. Click in the window, then type the statement Debug.Print, followed by your calculation, for example, Debug.Print 2+2, and press Enter. The answer is displayed on the next line in the Immediate window.

Step 6: **A More General Procedure**

- Modify the existing procedure to make it more general—for example, to sum the values from any starting value to any ending value:
  - Click at the end of the existing Dim statement to position the insertion point, press **Enter** to create a new line, then add the second **Dim statement** as shown in Figure 12f.
  - Click before the For statement, press **Enter** to create a blank line, press **Enter** a second time, then enter the two **InputBox statements** to ask the user for the beginning and ending values.
  - Modify the For statement to execute from **intStart** to **intEnd** rather than from 1 to 10.
  - Change the MsgBox statement to reflect the values of intStart and intEnd, and a customized title bar. Note the use of the ampersand and the underscore, to indicate concatenation and continuation, respectively.
- Click the **Save button** to save the module.

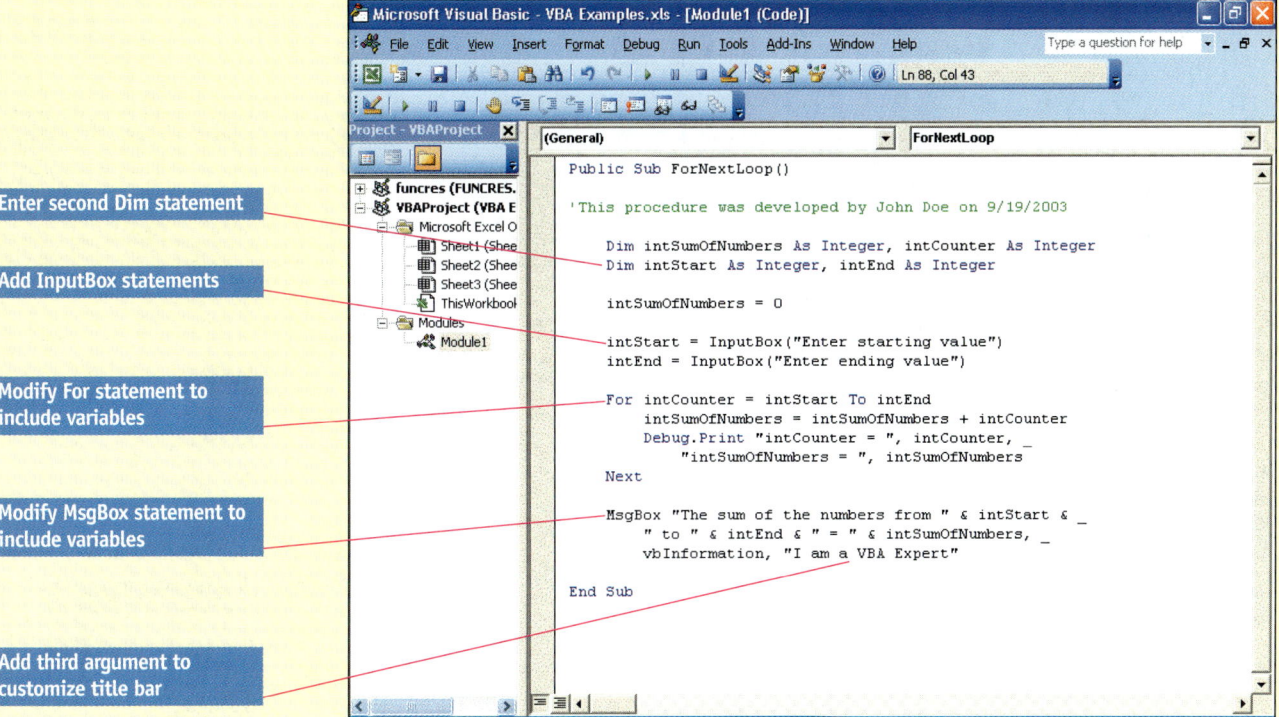

(f) A More General Procedure (step 6)

FIGURE 12 Hands-on Exercise 3 (*continued*)

USE WHAT YOU KNOW

Use the techniques acquired from other applications such as Microsoft Word to facilitate editing within the VBA window. Press the Ins key to toggle between the insert and overtype modes as you modify the statements within a VBA procedure. You can also cut, copy, and paste statements (or parts of statements) within a procedure and from one procedure to another. The Find and Replace commands are also useful.

Step 7: **Test the Procedure**

- Click the **Run Sub button** to test the procedure. You should be prompted for a beginning and an ending value. Enter any numbers you like, such as 10 and 20, respectively, to match the result in Figure 12g.

- The value displayed in the MsgBox statement should reflect the numbers you entered. For example, you will see a sum of 165 if you entered 10 and 20 as the starting and ending values.

- Look carefully at the message box that is displayed in Figure 12g. Its title bar displays the literal "I am a VBA expert", corresponding to the last argument in the MsgBox statement.

- Note, too, the spacing that appears within the message box, which includes spaces before and after each number. Look at your results and, if necessary, modify the MsgBox statement so that you have the same output. Click **OK**.

- Save the procedure.

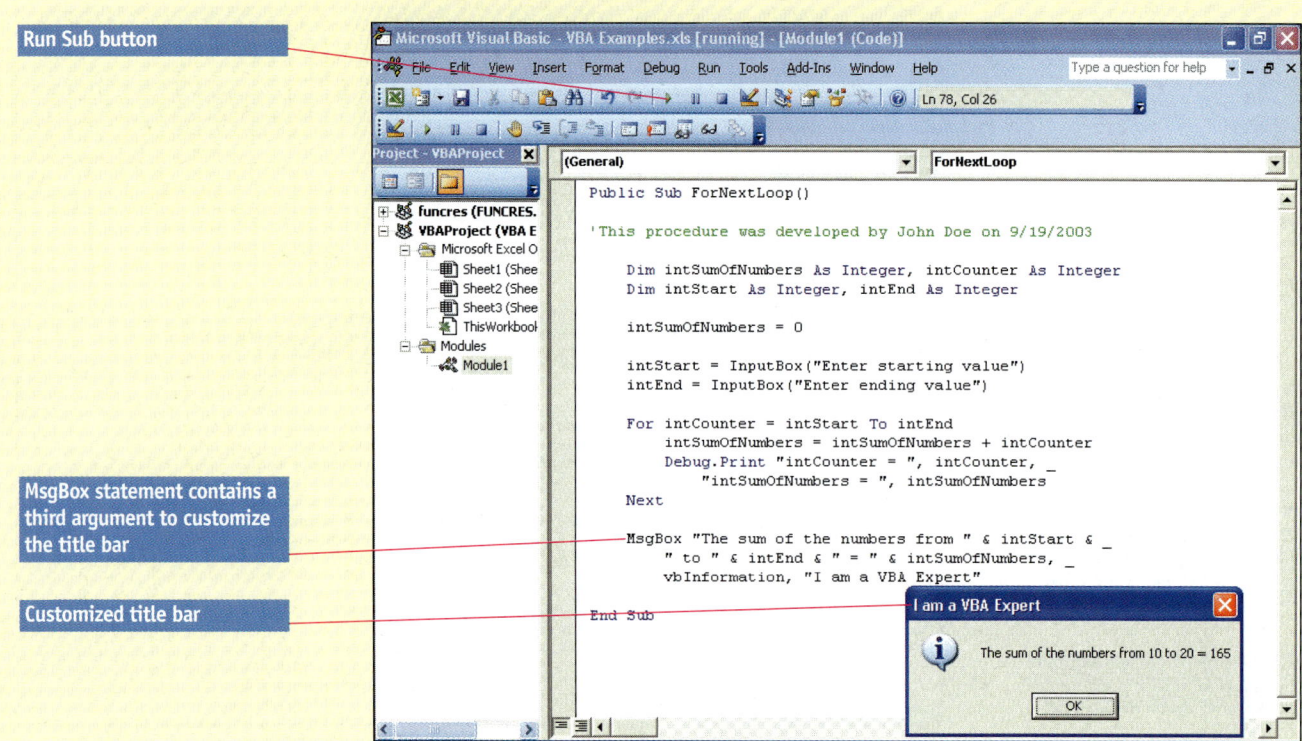

(g) Test the Procedure (step 7)

FIGURE 12 Hands-on Exercise 3 (*continued*)

CHANGE THE INCREMENT

The For . . . Next statement can be made more general by supplying an increment within the For statement. Try For intCount = 1 To 10 Step 2, or more generally, For intCount = intStart to intEnd Step intStepValue. "Step" is a Visual Basic keyword and must be entered that way. intCount, intEnd, and intStepValue are user-defined variables. The variables must be defined at the beginning of a procedure and can be initialized by requesting values from the user through the InputBox statement.

Step 8: **Create a Do Until Loop**

- Pull down the **Insert menu** and click the **Procedure command** to insert a new procedure called **DoUntilLoop**. Enter the procedure as it appears in Figure 12h. Note the following:
  - Two string variables are declared to hold the correct answer and the user's response, respectively.
  - The variable strCorrectAnswer is set to "Earth", which is the correct answer for our question.
  - The initial InputBox function prompts the user to enter his/her response to the question. A second InputBox function appears in the loop that is executed if and only if the user enters the wrong answer.
  - The Until condition appears at the beginning of the loop, so that the loop is entered only if the user answers incorrectly. The loop executes repeatedly until the correct answer is supplied.
  - A message to the user is displayed at the end of the procedure after the correct answer has been entered.

- Click the **Run Sub button** to test the procedure. Enter the correct answer on your first attempt, and you will see that the loop is never entered.

- Rerun the procedure, answer incorrectly, then note that a second input box appears, telling you that your answer was incorrect. Click **OK**.

- Once again you are prompted for the answer. Enter **Earth**. Click **OK**. The procedure ends.

- Save the procedure.

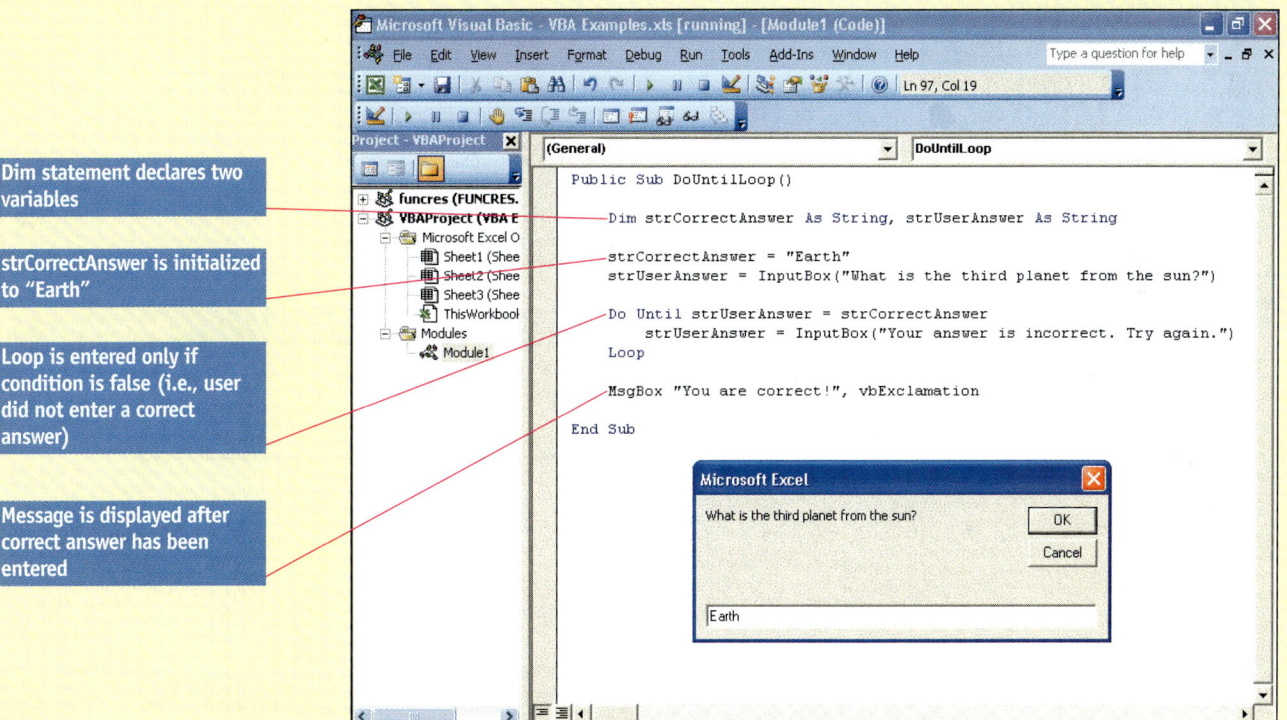

(h) Create a Do Until Loop (step 8)

FIGURE 12 Hands-on Exercise 3 (*continued*)

Step 9: **A More Powerful Procedure**

- Modify the procedure as shown in Figure 12i to include the statements to count and print the number of times the user takes to get the correct answer.
  - The variable intNumberOfAttempts is declared as an integer and is initialized to 1 after the user inputs his/her initial answer.
  - The Do loop is expanded to increment intNumberOfAttempts by 1 each time the loop is executed.
  - The MsgBox statement after the loop is expanded prints the number of attempts the user took to answer the question.
- Save the module, then click the **Run Sub button** to test the module. You should see a dialog box similar to the one in Figure 12i. Click **OK**. Do you see how this procedure improves on its predecessor?
- Pull down the **File menu** and click the **Print command** to display the Print dialog box. Click the option button to print the current module for your instructor. Click **OK**.
- Close the Debug toolbar. Exit Office if you do not want to continue with the next hands-on exercise at this time.

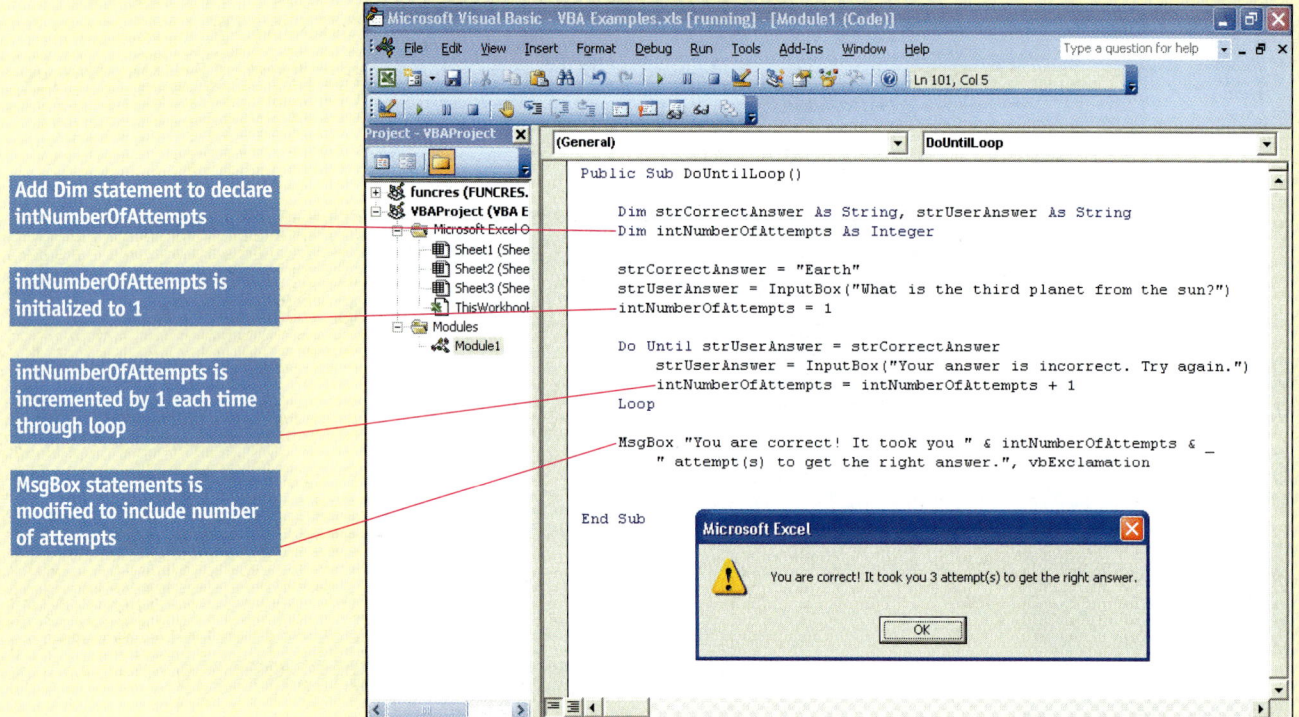

(i) A More Powerful Procedure (step 9)

FIGURE 12 Hands-on Exercise 3 (*continued*)

IT'S NOT EQUAL, BUT REPLACE

All programming languages use statements of the form N = N + 1, in which the equal sign does not mean equal in the literal sense; that is, N cannot equal N + 1. The equal sign is really a replacement operator. Thus, the expression on the right of the equal sign is evaluated, and that result replaces the value of the variable on the left. In other words, the statement N = N + 1 increments the value of N by 1.

PUTTING VBA TO WORK (MICROSOFT EXCEL)

Our approach thus far has focused on VBA as an independent entity that can be run without specific reference to the applications in Microsoft Office. We have covered several individual statements, explained how to use the VBA editor to create and run procedures, and how to debug those procedures, if necessary. We hope you have found the material to be interesting, but you may be asking yourself, "What does this have to do with Microsoft Office?" In other words, how can you use your knowledge of VBA to enhance your ability in Microsoft Excel or Access? The answer is to create ***event procedures*** that run automatically in response to events within an Office application.

VBA is different from traditional programming languages in that it is event-driven. An ***event*** is defined as any action that is recognized by an application such as Excel or Access. Opening or closing an Excel workbook or an Access database is an event. Selecting a worksheet within a workbook is also an event, as is clicking on a command button on an Access form. To use VBA within Microsoft Office, you decide which events are significant, and what is to happen when those events occur. Then you develop the appropriate event procedures.

Consider, for example, Figure 13, which displays the results of two event procedures in conjunction with opening and closing an Excel workbook. (If you are using Microsoft Access instead of Excel, you can skip this discussion and the associated exercise, and move to the parallel material for Access that appears after the next hands-on exercise.) The procedure associated with Figure 13a displays a message that appears automatically after the user executes the command to close the associated workbook. The procedure is almost trivial to write, and consists of a single MsgBox statement. The effect of the procedure is quite significant, however, as it reminds the user to back up his or her work after closing the workbook. Nor does it matter how the user closes the workbook—whether by pulling down the menu or using a keyboard shortcut—because the procedure runs automatically in response to the Close Workbook event, regardless of how that event occurs.

The dialog box in Figure 13b prompts the user for a password and appears automatically when the user opens the workbook. The logic here is more sophisticated in that the underlying procedure contains an InputBox statement to request the password, a Do Until loop that is executed until the user enters the correct password or exceeds the allotted number of attempts, then additional logic to display the worksheet or terminate the application if the user fails to enter the proper password. The procedure is not difficult, however, and it builds on the VBA statements that were covered earlier.

The next hands-on exercise has you create the two event procedures that are associated with Figure 13. As you do the exercise, you will gain additional experience with VBA and an appreciation for the potential event procedures within Microsoft Office.

HIDING AND UNHIDING A WORKSHEET

Look carefully at the workbooks in Figures 13a and 13b. Both figures reference the identical workbook, Financial Consultant, as can be seen from the title bar. Look at the worksheet tabs, however, and note that two worksheets are visible in Figure 13a, whereas the Calculations worksheet is hidden in Figure 13b. This was accomplished in the Open workbook procedure and was implemented to hide the calculations from the user until the correct password was entered.

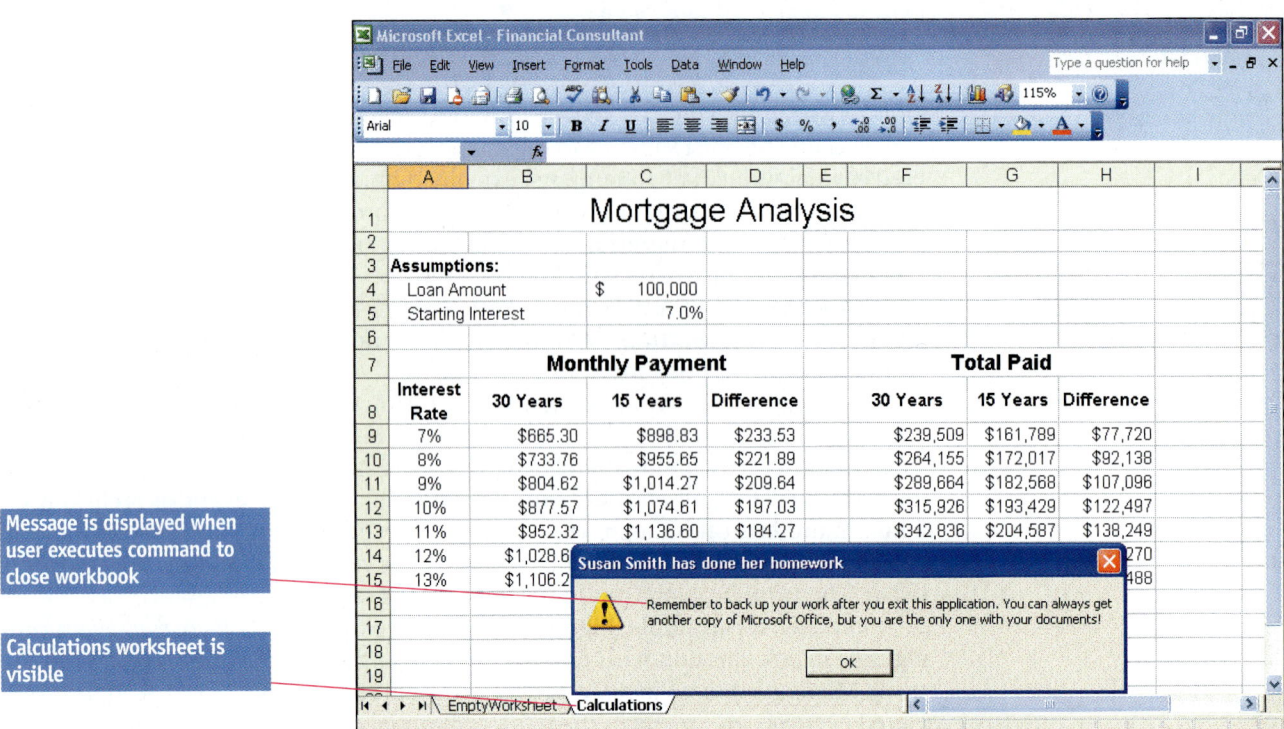

(a) Message to the User (Close Workbook event)

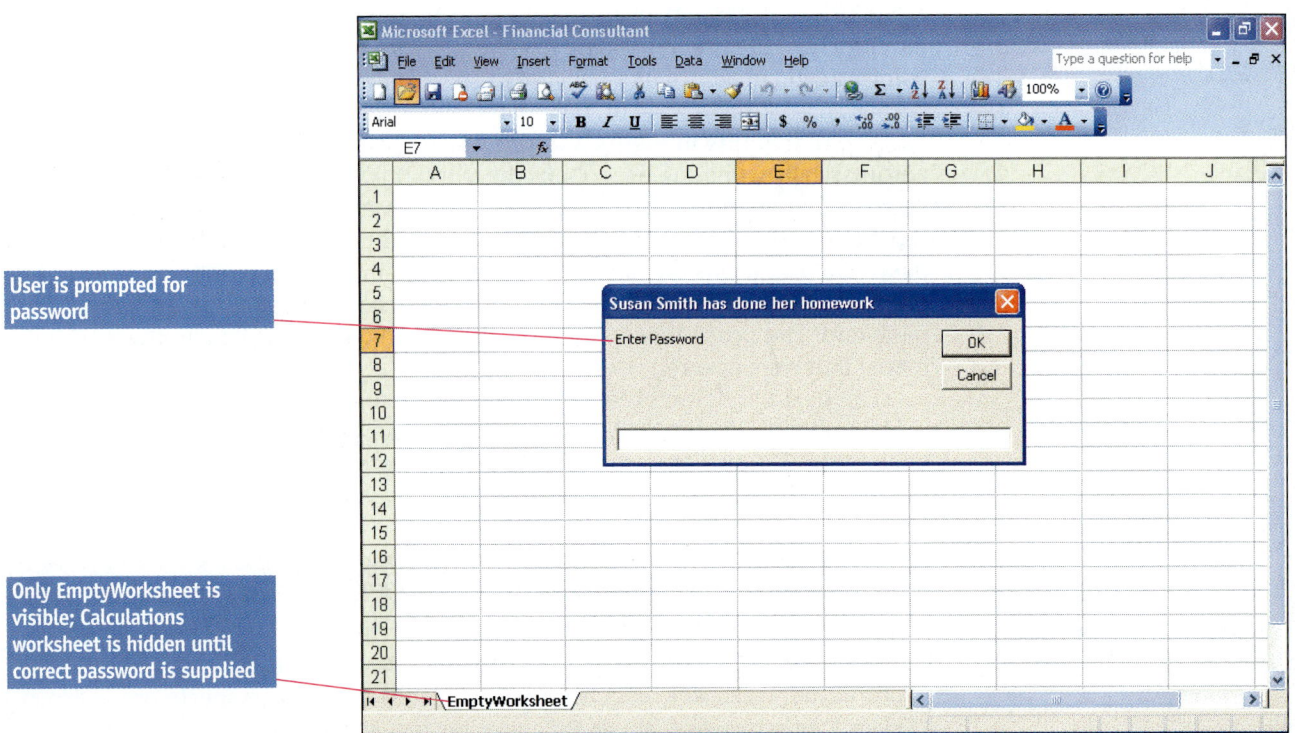

(b) Password Protection (Open Workbook event)

FIGURE 13 Event-Driven Programming

hands-on exercise

4 Event-Driven Programming (Microsoft Excel)

Objective To create an event procedure to implement password protection that is associated with opening an Excel workbook; to create a second event procedure that displays a message to the user upon closing the workbook. Use Figure 14 as a guide in the exercise.

Step 1: **Create the Close Workbook Procedure**

- Open the **VBA Examples workbook** you have used for the previous exercises and enable the macros. If you have been using Access rather than Excel, start Excel, open a new workbook, then save the workbook as **VBA Examples**.

- Pull down the **Tools menu**, click the **Macro command**, then click the **Visual Basic Editor command** (or use the **Alt+F11** keyboard shortcut).

- You should see the Project Explorer pane as shown in Figure 14a, but if not, pull down the **View menu** and click the **Project Explorer**. Double click **ThisWorkbook** to create a module for the workbook as a whole.

- Enter the **Option Explicit statement** if it is not there already, then press **Enter** to create a new line. Type the statement to declare the variable, **ApplicationTitle**, using your name instead of Susan Smith.

- Click the **down arrow** in the Object list box and select **Workbook**, then click the **down arrow** in the Procedure list box and select the **BeforeClose event** to create the associated procedure. (If you choose a different event by mistake, click and drag to select the associated statements, then press the **Del key** to delete the procedure.)

- Enter the comment and MsgBox statement as it appears in Figure 14a.

- Save the procedure.

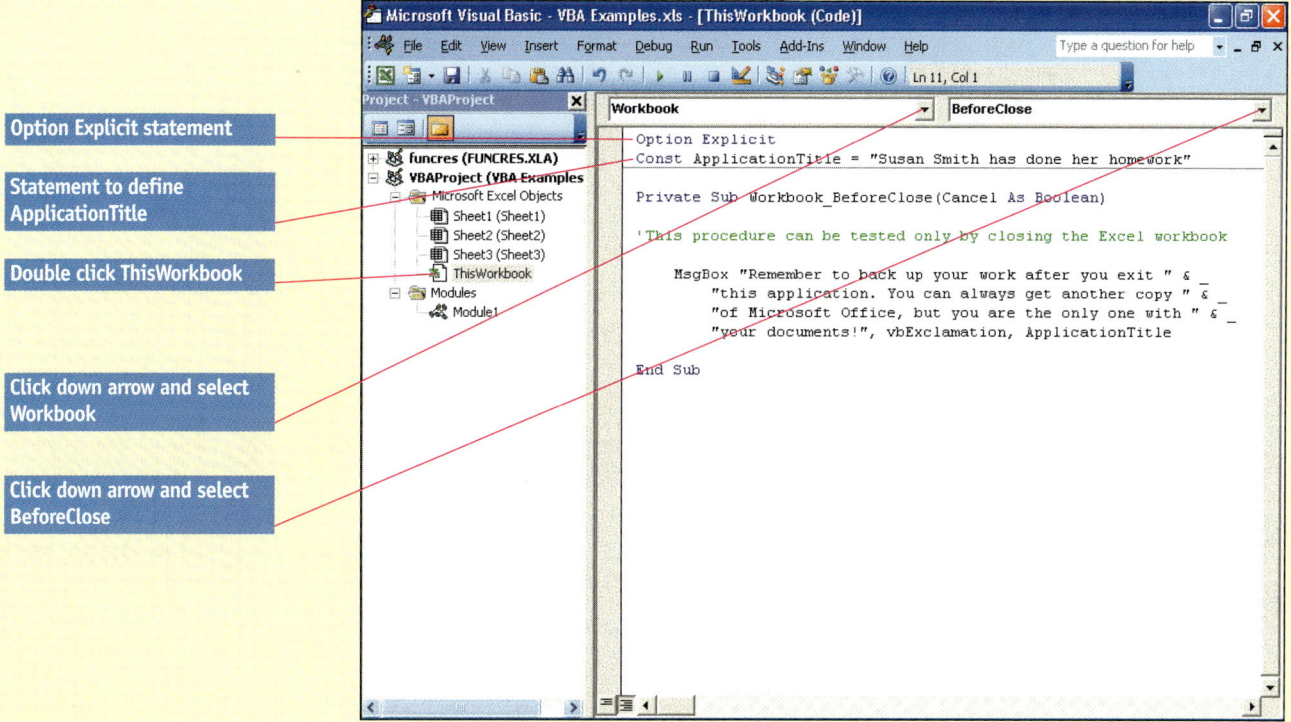

(a) Create the Close Workbook Procedure (step 1)

FIGURE 14 Hands-on Exercise 4

EXTENDING MICROSOFT OFFICE 2003 **1947**

Step 2: **Test the Close Workbook Procedure**

- Click the **View Microsoft Excel button** on the Standard toolbar or on the Windows taskbar to view the Excel workbook. The workbook is not empty; that is, it does not contain any cell entries, but it does contain multiple VBA procedures.

- Pull down the **File menu** and click the **Close command**, which runs the procedure you just created and displays the dialog box in Figure 14b. Click **OK** after you have read the message, then click **Yes** if asked to save the workbook.

- Pull down the **File menu** and reopen the **VBA Examples workbook**, enabling the macros. Press **Alt+F11** to return to the VBA window to create an additional procedure.

- Double click **ThisWorkbook** from within the Project Explorer pane to return to the BeforeClose procedure and make the necessary corrections, if any.

- Save the procedure.

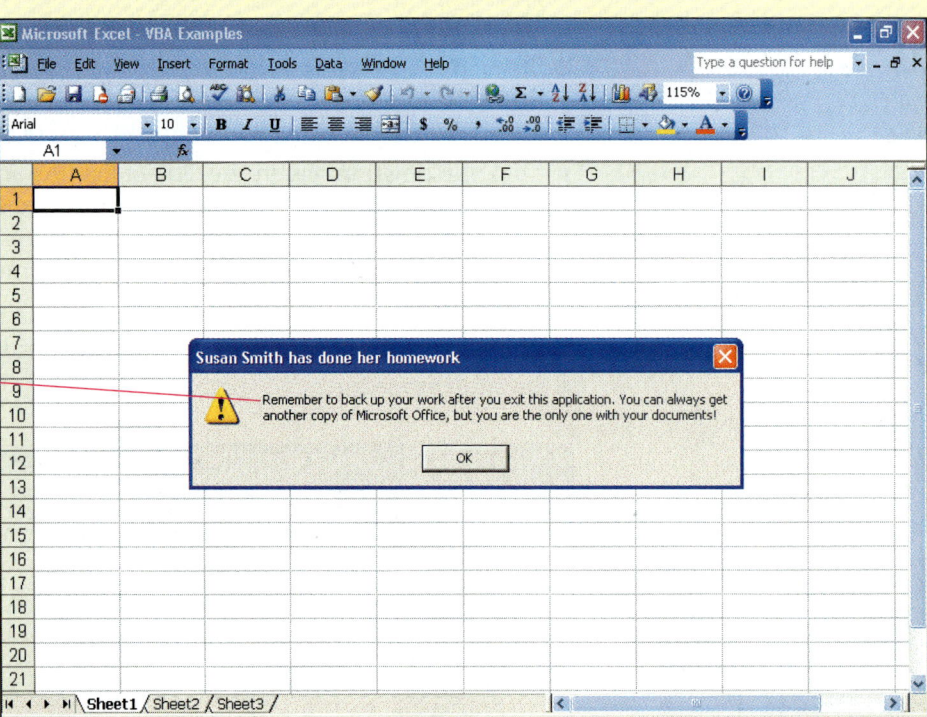

Message is displayed when you execute the Close command

(b) Test the Close Workbook Procedure (step 2)

FIGURE 14   Hands-on Exercise 4 (*continued*)

THE MOST RECENTLY OPENED FILE LIST

One way to open a recently used workbook is to select the workbook directly from the File menu. Pull down the File menu, but instead of clicking the Open command, check to see if the workbook appears on the list of the most recently opened workbooks located at the bottom of the menu. If so, just click the workbook name, rather than having to make the appropriate selections through the Open dialog box.

Step 3: **Start the Open Workbook Event Procedure**

- Click within the Before Close procedure, then click the **Procedure View button** at the bottom of the Code window. Click the **down arrow** in the Procedure list box and select the **Open event** to create an event procedure.

- Enter the VBA statements as shown in Figure 14c. Note the following:
  - Three variables are required for this procedure—the correct password, the password entered by the user, and the number of attempts.
  - The user is prompted for the password, and the number of attempts is set to 1. The user is given two additional attempts, if necessary, to get the password correct. The loop is bypassed, however, if the user supplies the correct password on the first attempt.

- Minimize Excel. Save the procedure, then click the **Run Sub button** to test it. Try different combinations in your testing; that is, enter the correct password on the first, second, and third attempts. The password is case-sensitive.

- Correct errors as they occur. Click the **Reset button** at any time to begin executing the procedure from the beginning. Save the procedure.

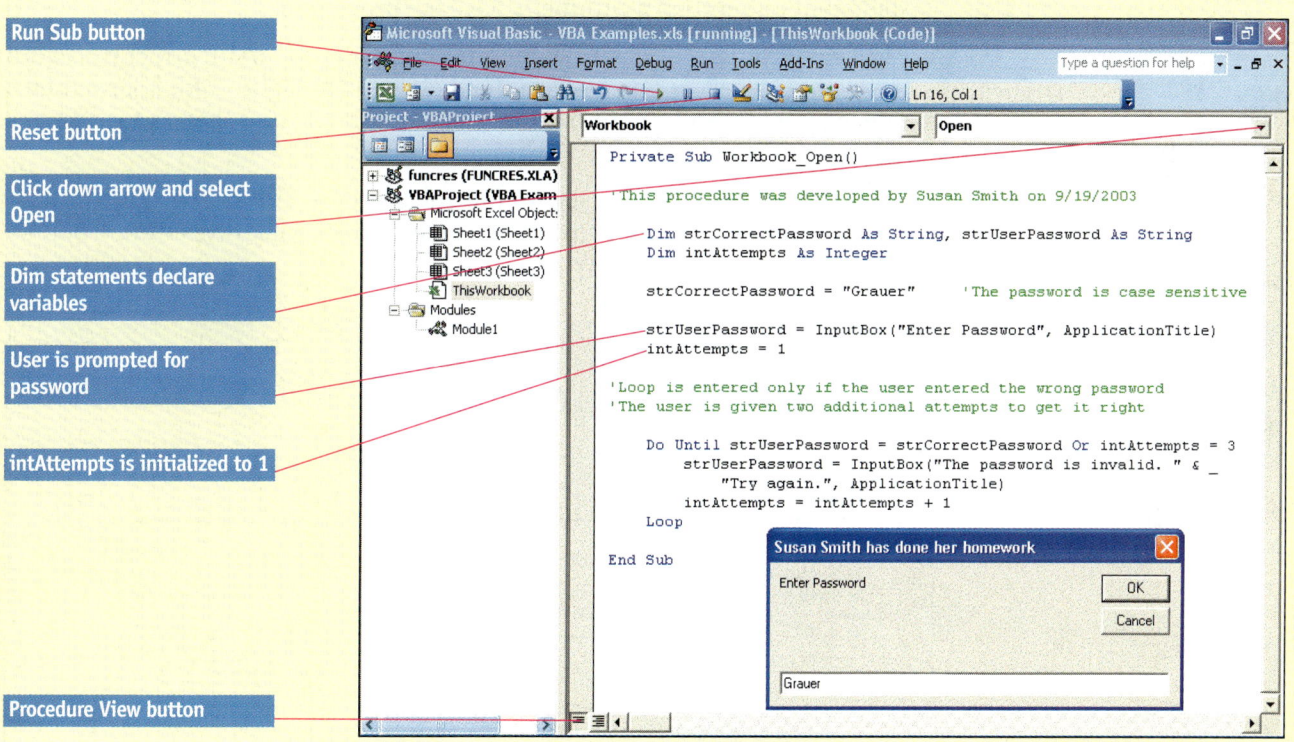

(c) Start the Open Workbook Event Procedure (step 3)

FIGURE 14   Hands-on Exercise 4 (*continued*)

THE OBJECT AND PROCEDURE BOXES

The Object box at the top of the code window displays the selected object such as an Excel workbook, whereas the Procedure box displays the name of the events appropriate to that object. Events that already have procedures appear in bold. Clicking an event that is not bold creates the procedure header and End Sub statements for that event.

Step 4: **Complete the Open Workbook Event Procedure**

- Enter the remaining statements in the procedure as shown in Figure 14d. Note the following:
  - The If statement determines whether the user has entered the correct password and, if so, displays the appropriate message.
  - If, however, the user fails to supply the correct password, a different message is displayed, and the workbook will close due to the **Workbooks.Close statement** within the procedure.
  - As a precaution, put an apostrophe in front of the Workbooks.Close statement so that it is a comment, and thus it is not executed. Once you are sure that you can enter the correct password, you can remove the apostrophe and implement the password protection.

- Save the procedure, then click the **Run Sub button** to test it. Be sure that you can enter the correct password (**Grauer**), and that you realize the password is case-sensitive.

- Delete the apostrophe in front of the Workbooks.Close statement. The text of the statement changes from green to black to indicate that it is an executable statement rather than a comment. Save the procedure.

- Click the **Run Sub button** a second time, then enter an incorrect password three times in a row. You will see the dialog box in Figure 14d, followed by a message reminding you to back up your workbook, and then the workbook will close.

- The first message makes sense, the second does not make sense in this context. Thus, we need to modify the Close Workbook procedure when an incorrect password is entered.

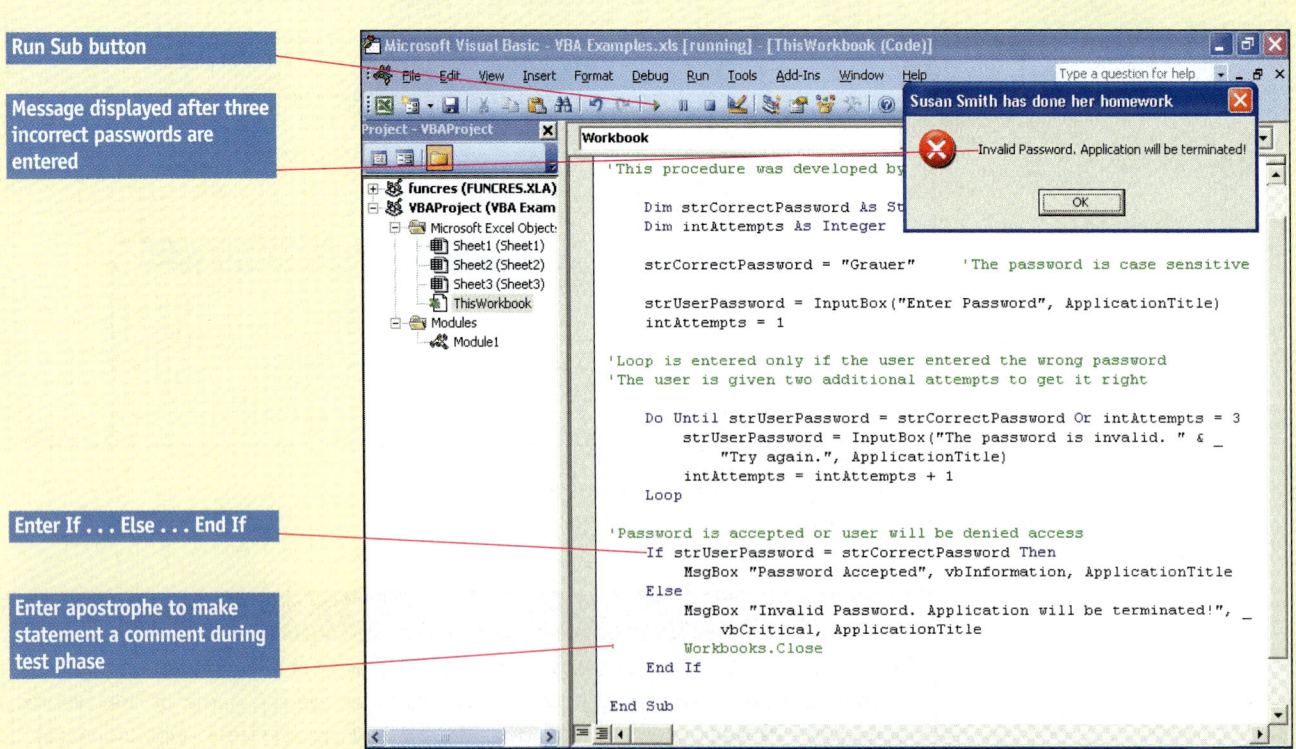

(d) Complete the Open Workbook Event Procedure (step 4)

FIGURE 14 Hands-on Exercise 4 (*continued*)

Step 5: Modify the Before Close Event Procedure

- Reopen the **VBA Examples workbook**. Click the button to **Enable Macros**.
- Enter the password, **Grauer** (the password is case-sensitive), press **Enter**, then click **OK** when the password has been accepted.
- Press **Alt+F11** to reopen the VBA editor, and (if necessary) double click **ThisWorkbook** within the list of Microsoft Excel objects.
- Click at the end of the line defining the ApplicationTitle constant, press **Enter**, then enter the statement to define the **binNormalExit** variable as shown in Figure 14e. (The statement appears initially below the line ending the General Declarations section, but moves above the line when you press Enter.)
- Modify the BeforeClose event procedure to include an If statement that tests the value of the binNormalExit variable as shown in Figure 14e. You must, however, set the value of this variable in the Open Workbook event procedure as described in step 6.
- Save the procedure.

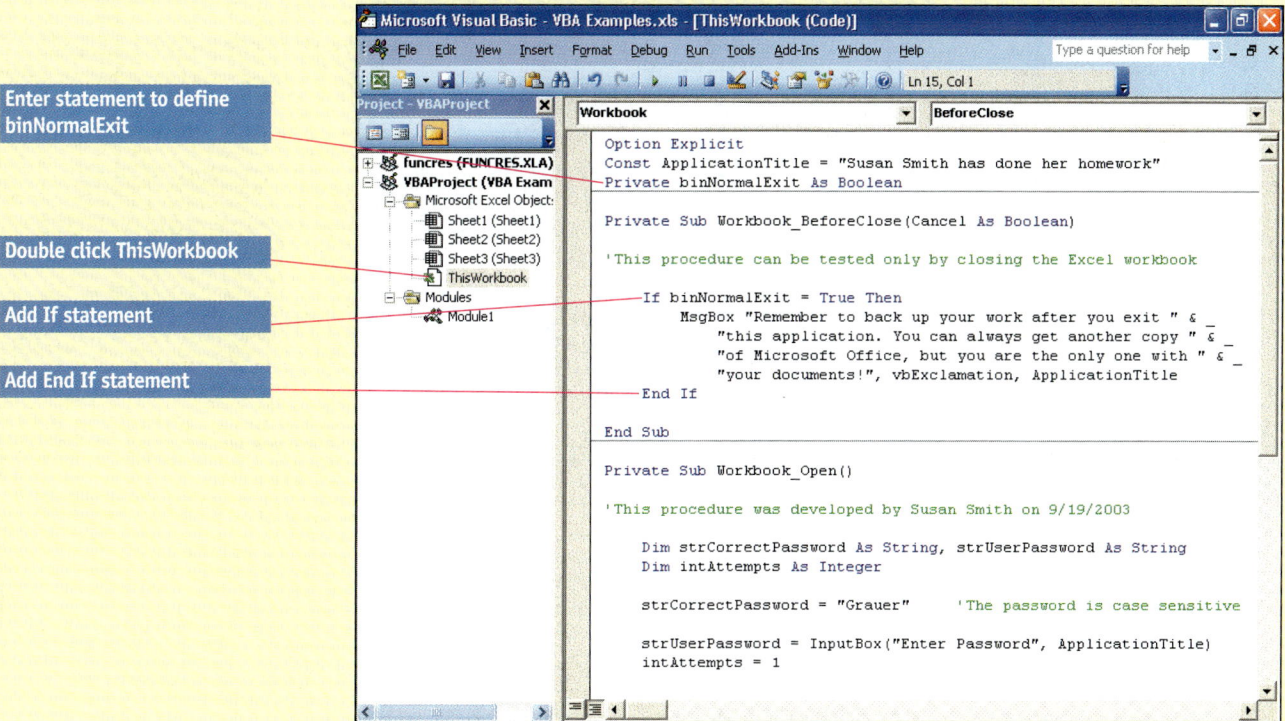

(e) Modify the Before Close Event Procedure (step 5)

FIGURE 14 Hands-on Exercise 4 (*continued*)

SETTING A SWITCH

The use of a switch (binNormalExit, in this example) to control an action within a procedure is a common programming technique. The switch is set to one of two values according to events that occur within the system, then the switch is subsequently tested and the appropriate action is taken. Here, the switch is set when the workbook is opened to indicate either a valid or invalid user. The switch is then tested prior to closing the workbook to determine whether to print the closing message.

Step 6: **Modify the Open Workbook Event Procedure**

- Scroll down to the Open Workbook event procedure, then modify the If statement to set the value of binNormalExit as shown in Figure 14f:
  - Take advantage of the Complete Word tool to enter the variable name. Type the first few letters, "**binN**", then press **Ctrl+Space**, and VBA will complete the variable name.
  - The indentation within the statement is not a requirement of VBA per se, but is used to make the code easier to read. Blank lines are also added for this purpose.
  - Comments appear throughout the procedure to explain its logic.
  - Save the modified procedure.

- Click the **Run Sub button**, then enter an incorrect password three times in a row. Once again, you will see the dialog box indicating an invalid password.

- Click **OK**. This time you will not see the message reminding you to back up your workbook. The workbook closes as before.

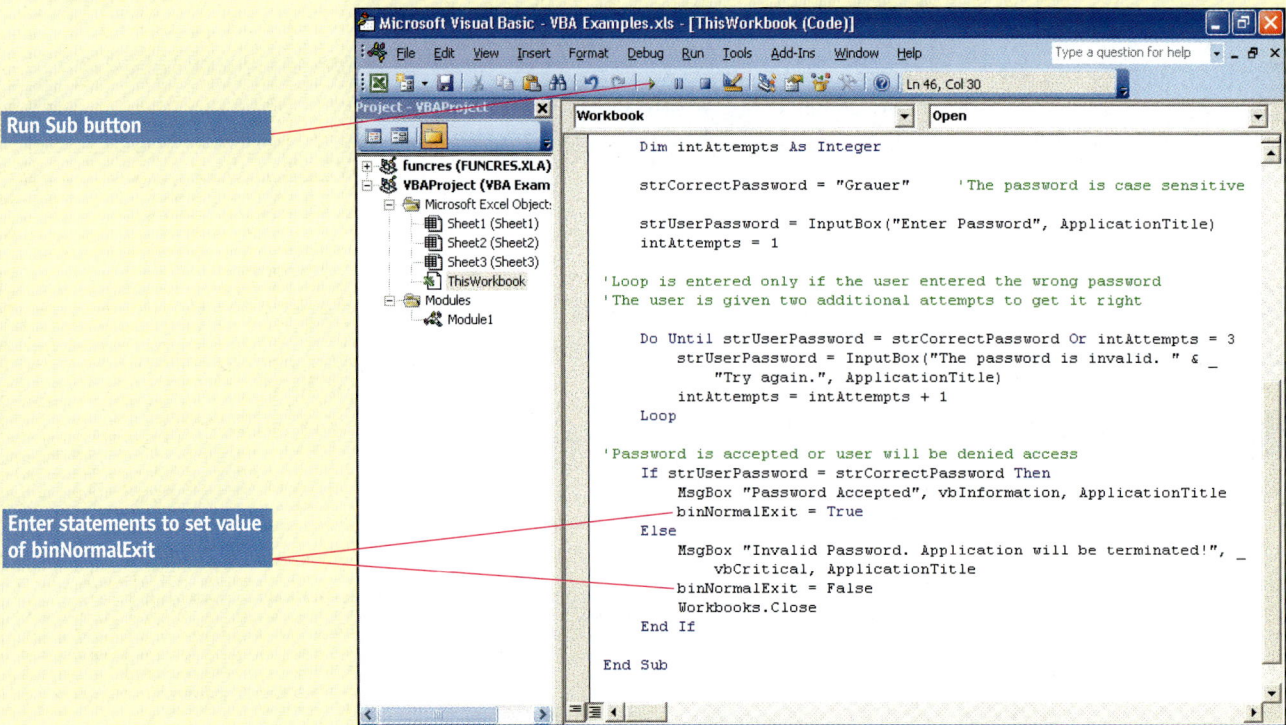

(f) Modify the Open Workbook Event Procedure (step 6)

FIGURE 14 Hands-on Exercise 4 (*continued*)

TEST UNDER ALL CONDITIONS

We cannot overemphasize the importance of thoroughly testing a procedure, and further, testing it under all conditions. VBA statements are powerful, but they are also complex, and a misplaced or omitted character can have dramatic consequences. Test every procedure completely at the time it is created, while the logic of the procedure is fresh in your mind.

Step 7: **Open a Second Workbook**

- Reopen the **VBA Examples workbook**. Click the button to **Enable Macros**.
- Enter the password, **Grauer**, then press **Enter**. Click **OK** when you see the second dialog box telling you that the password has been accepted.
- Pull down the **File menu** and click the **Open command** (or click the **Open button** on the Standard toolbar) and open a second workbook. We opened a workbook called **Financial Consultant**, but it does not matter which workbook you open.
- Pull down the **Window menu**, click the **Arrange command**, click the **Horizontal option button**, and click **OK** to tile the workbooks as shown in Figure 14g. The title bars show the names of the open workbooks.
- Pull down the **Tools menu**, click **Macro**, then click **Visual Basic editor**.

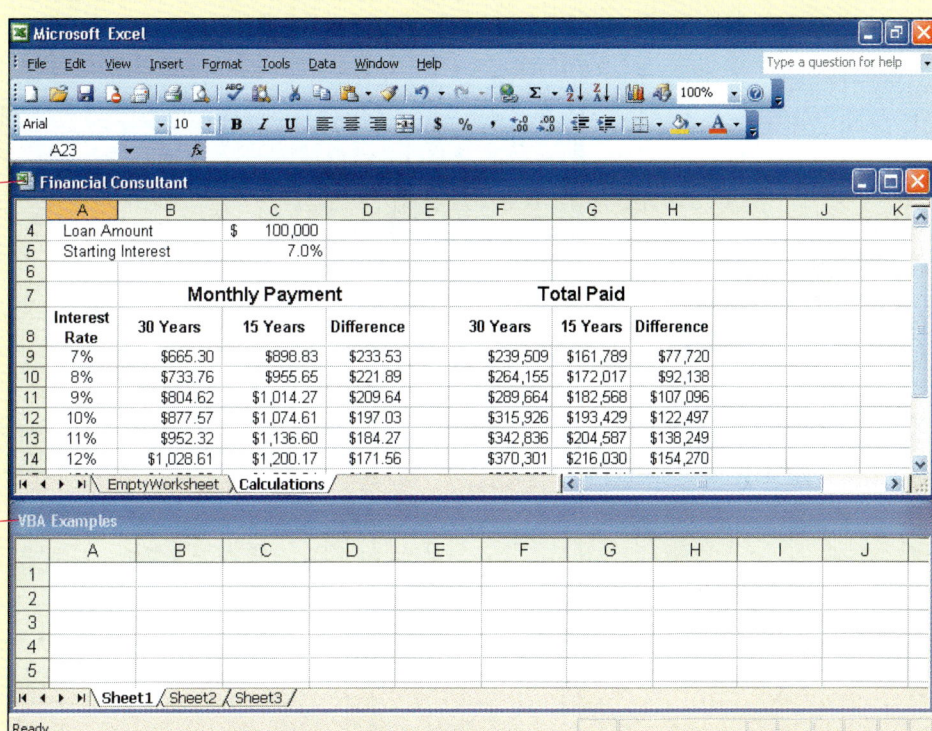

(g) Open a Second Workbook (step 7)

FIGURE 14 Hands-on Exercise 4 (*continued*)

THE COMPARISON IS CASE-SENSITIVE

Any literal comparison (e.g., strInstructorName = "Grauer") is case-sensitive, so that the user has to enter the correct name and case for the condition to be true. A response of "GRAUER" or "grauer", while containing the correct name, will be evaluated as false because the case does not match. You can, however, use the UCase (uppercase) function to convert the user's response to uppercase, and test accordingly. In other words, UCase(strInstructorName) = "GRAUER" will be evaluated as true if the user enters "Grauer" in any combination of upper- or lowercase letters.

EXTENDING MICROSOFT OFFICE 2003   **1953**

Step 8: **Copy the Procedure**

- You should be back in the Visual Basic editor as shown in Figure 14h. Copy the procedures associated with the Open and Close Workbook events from the VBA Examples workbook to the other workbook, Financial Consultant.
    - Double click **ThisWorkbook** within the list of Microsoft Excel objects under the VBA Examples workbook.
    - Click and drag to select the definition of the ApplicationTitle constant in the General Declarations section, the binNormalExit definition, plus the two procedures (to open and close the workbook) in their entirety.
    - Click the **Copy button** on the Standard toolbar.
    - If necessary, expand the Financial Consultant VBA Project, then double click **ThisWorkbook** with the list of Excel objects under the Financial Consultant workbook. Click underneath the **Option Explicit command**.
    - Click the **Paste button** on the Standard toolbar. The VBA code should be copied into this module as shown in Figure 14h.
- Click the **Save button** to save the module.

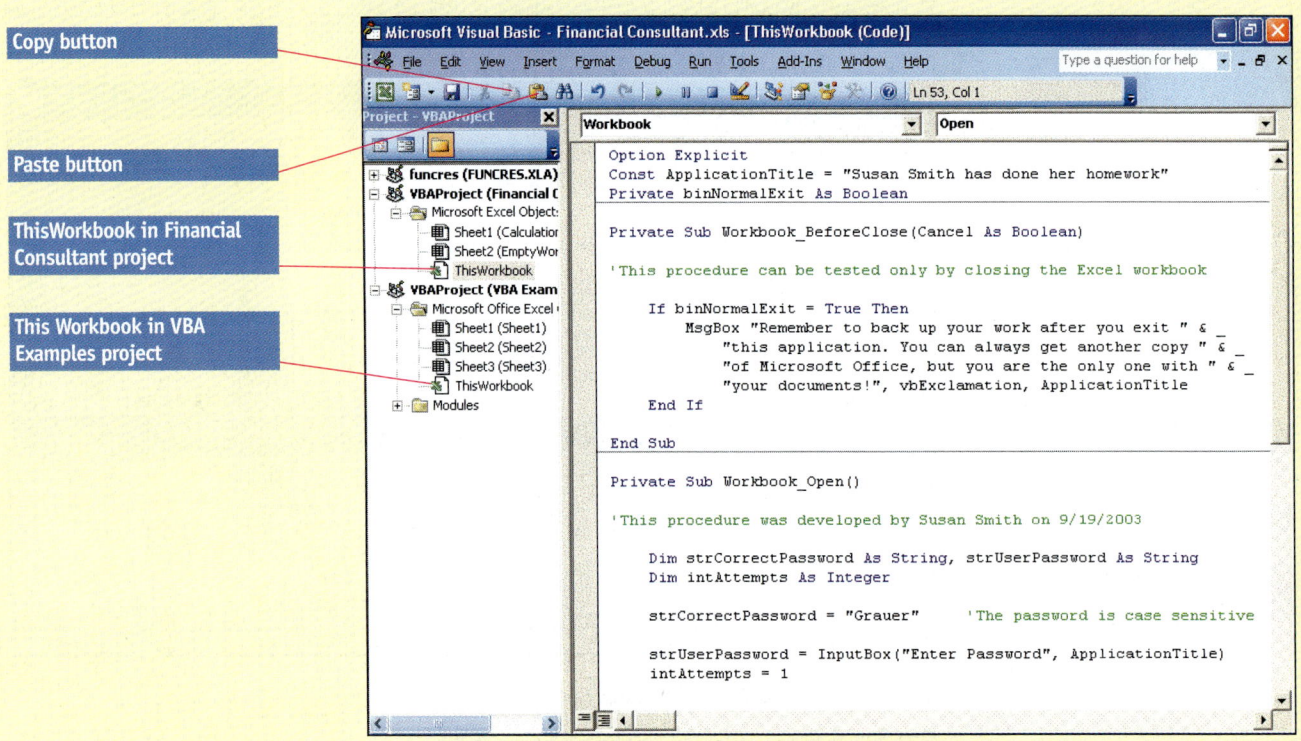

(h) Copy the Procedure (step 8)

FIGURE 14 Hands-on Exercise 4 (*continued*)

THE VISIBLE PROPERTY

The Calculations worksheet sheet should be hidden until the user enters the correct password. This is accomplished by setting the Visible property of the worksheet to false at the beginning of the Open Workbook event procedure, then setting it to true after the correct password has been entered. Click in the Open Workbook event procedure after the last Dim statement, press Enter, then enter the statement Sheet1.Visible = False to hide the Calculations worksheet. Scroll down in the procedure (below the MsgBox statement within the If statement that tests for the correct password), then enter the statement Sheet1.Visible = True followed by the statement Sheet1.Activate to select the worksheet.

Step 9: **Test the Procedure**

- Click the **View Microsoft Excel button** on the Standard toolbar within the VBA window (or click the **Excel button** on the Windows taskbar) to view the Excel workbook. Click in the window containing the Financial Consultant workbook (or whichever workbook you are using), then click the **Maximize button**.

- Pull down the **File menu** and click the **Close command**. (The dialog box in Figure 14i does not appear initially because the value of binNormalExit is not yet set; you have to open the workbook to set the switch.) Click **Yes** if asked whether to save the changes to the workbook.

- Pull down the **File menu** and reopen the workbook. Click the button to **Enable Macros**, then enter **Grauer** when prompted for the password. Click **OK** when the password has been accepted.

- Close this workbook, close the **VBA Examples workbook**, then pull down the **File menu** and click the **Exit command** to quit Excel.

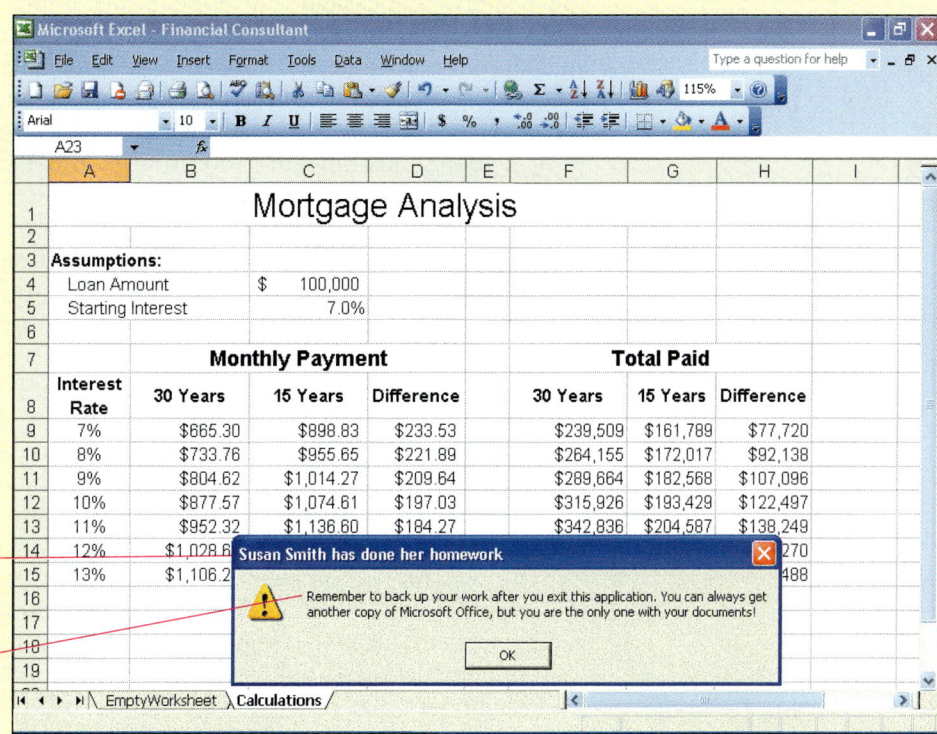

(i) Test the Procedure (step 9)

FIGURE 14 Hands-on Exercise 4 (*continued*)

SCREEN CAPTURE

Prove to your instructor that you have completed the hands-on exercise correctly by capturing a screen, then pasting the screen into a Word document. Do the exercise until you come to the screen that you want to capture, then press the PrintScreen key at the top of the keyboard. Click the Start button, start Word, and open a Word document, then pull down the Edit menu and click the Paste command to bring the captured screen into the Word document. Right click the screen within the Word document, click the Format Picture command, click the Layout tab, and select the Square layout. Click OK to close the dialog box. You can now move and size the screen within the document.

PUTTING VBA TO WORK (MICROSOFT ACCESS)

The same VBA procedure can be run from multiple applications in Microsoft Office, despite the fact that the applications are very different. The real power of VBA, however, is its ability to detect events that are unique to a specific application and to respond accordingly. An event is defined as any action that is recognized by an application. Opening or closing an Excel workbook or an Access database is an event. Selecting a worksheet within a workbook is also an event, as is clicking on a command button on an Access form. To use VBA within Microsoft Office, you decide which events are significant, and what is to happen when those events occur. Then you develop the appropriate *event procedures* that execute automatically when the event occurs.

Consider, for example, Figure 15, which displays the results of two event procedures in conjunction with opening and closing an Access database. (These are procedures similar to those we created in the preceding pages in conjunction with opening and closing an Excel workbook.) The procedure associated with Figure 15a displays a message that appears automatically after the user clicks the Switchboard button to exit the database. The procedure is almost trivial to write, and consists of a single MsgBox statement. The effect of the procedure is quite significant, however, as it reminds the user to back up his or her work. Indeed, you can never overemphasize the importance of adequate backup.

The dialog box in Figure 15b prompts the user for a password and appears automatically when the user opens the database. The logic here is more sophisticated in that the underlying procedure contains an InputBox statement to request the password, a Do Until loop that is executed until the user enters the correct password or exceeds the allotted number of attempts, then additional logic to display the switchboard or terminate the application if the user fails to enter the proper password. The procedure is not difficult, however, and it builds on the VBA statements that were covered earlier.

The next hands-on exercise has you create the event procedures that are associated with the database in Figure 15. The exercise references a switchboard, or user interface, that is created as a form within the database. The switchboard displays a menu that enables a nontechnical person to move easily from one object in the database (e.g., a form or report) to another.

The switchboard is created through a utility called the Switchboard Manager that prompts you for each item you want to add to the switchboard, and which action you want taken in conjunction with that menu item. You could do the exercise with any database, but we suggest you use the database we provide to access the switchboard that we created for you. The exercise begins, therefore, by having you download a data disk from our Web site.

EVENT-DRIVEN VERSUS TRADITIONAL PROGRAMMING

A traditional program is executed sequentially, beginning with the first line of code and continuing in order through the remainder of the program. It is the program, not the user, that determines the order in which the statements are executed. VBA, on the other hand, is event-driven, meaning that the order in which the procedures are executed depends on the events that occur. It is the user, rather than the program, that determines which events occur, and consequently which procedures are executed. Each application in Microsoft Office has a different set of objects and associated events that comprise the application's object model.

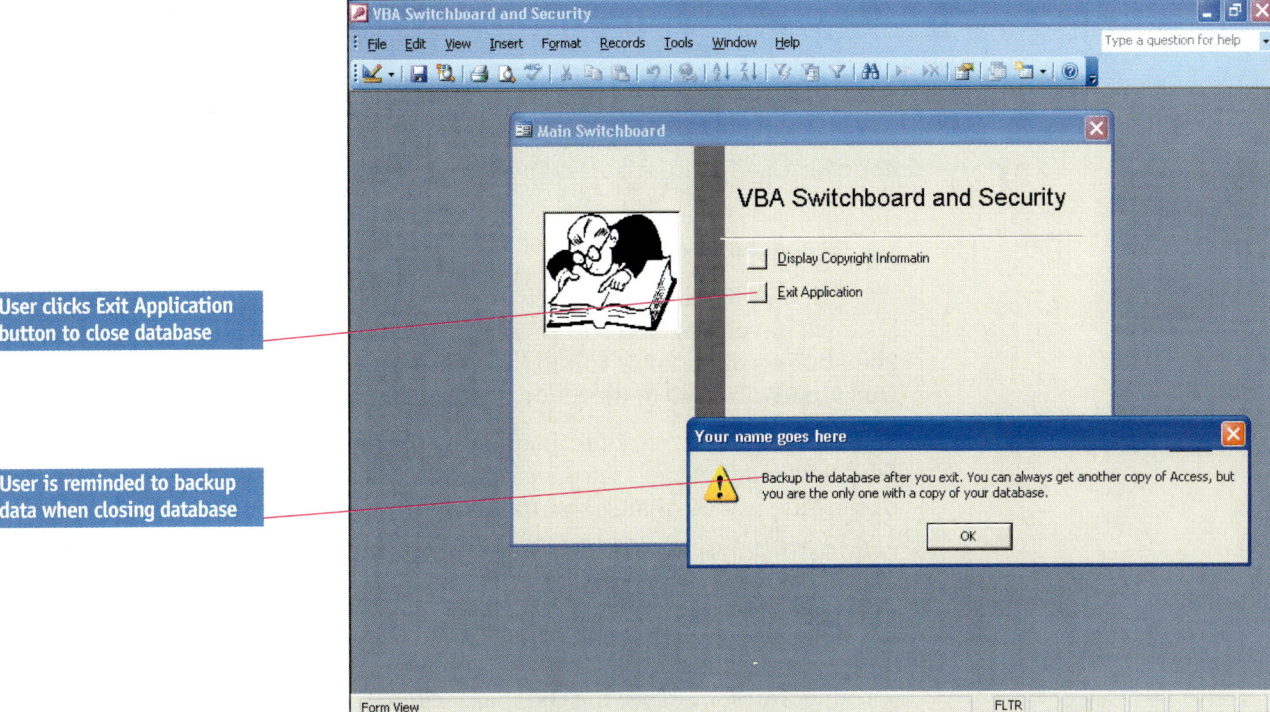

(a) Reminder to the User (Exit Application event)

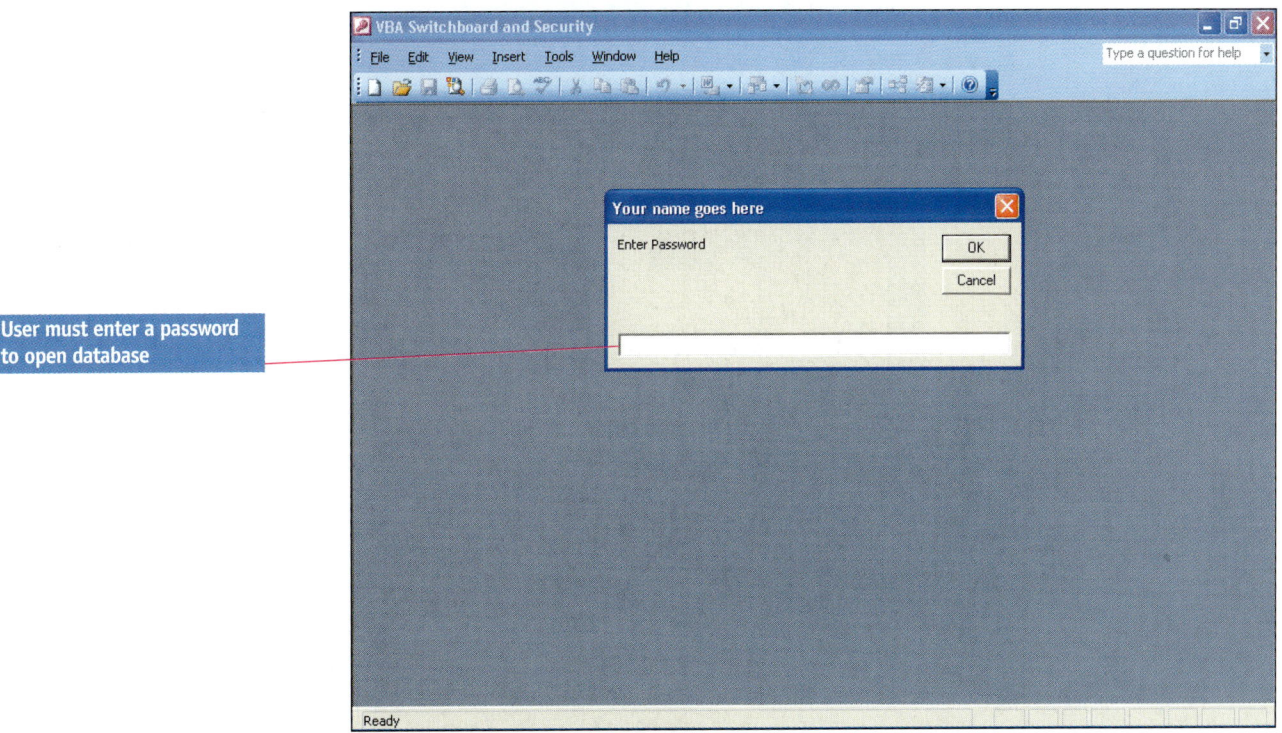

(b) Password Protection (Open Form event)

FIGURE 15   Event-Driven Programming (Microsoft Access)

hands-on exercise

5 Event-Driven Programming (Microsoft Access)

Objective To implement password protection for an Access database; to create a second event procedure that displays a message to the user upon closing the database. Use Figure 16 as a guide in the exercise.

Step 1: **Open the Access Database**

- You can do this exercise with any database, but we suggest you use the database we have provided. Go to **www.prenhall.com/grauer**, click the **Office 2003 book**, which takes you to the Office 2003 home page. Click the **Student Download tab** to go to the Student Download page.

- Scroll until you can click the link for **Getting Started with VBA**. You will see the File Download dialog box asking what you want to do. Click the **Save button** to display the Save As dialog box, then save the file on your desktop.

- Double click the file after it has been downloaded and follow the onscreen instructions to expand the self-extracting file that contains the database.

- Go to the newly created **Exploring VBA folder** and open the **VBA Switchboard and Security database**. Click the **Open button** when you see the security warning. You should see the Database window in Figure 16a.

- Pull down the **Tools menu**, click the **Macro command**, then click the **Visual Basic Editor command**. Maximize the VBA editor window.

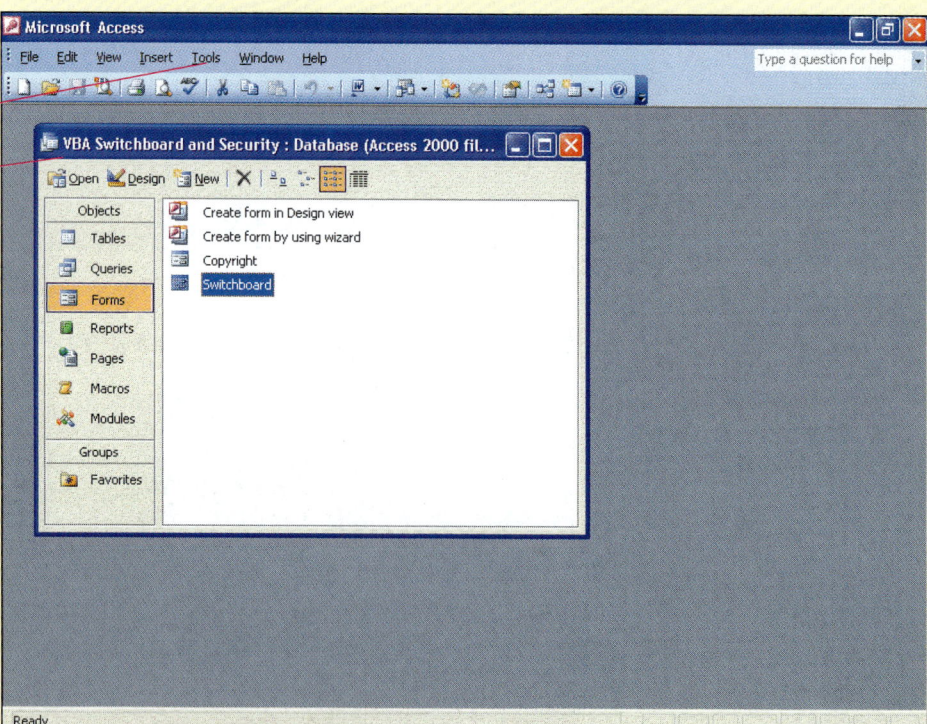

(a) Open the Access Database (step 1)

FIGURE 16 Hands-on Exercise 5

1958 GETTING STARTED WITH VBA

Step 2: **Create the ExitDatabase Procedure**

- Pull down the **Insert menu** and click **Module** to insert Module1. Complete the **General Declarations section** by adding the Option Explicit statement (if necessary) and the definition of the ApplicationTitle constant as shown in Figure 16b.

- Pull down the **Insert menu** and click **Procedure** to insert a new procedure called **ExitDatabase**. Click the option buttons for a **Sub procedure** and for **Public scope**. Click **OK**.

- Complete the ExitDatabase procedure by entering the **MsgBox** and **DoCmd.Quit** statements. The DoCmd.Quit statement will close Access, but it is entered initially as a comment by beginning the line with an apostrophe.

- Click anywhere in the procedure, then click the **Run Sub button** to test the procedure. Correct any errors that occur, then when the MsgBox displays correctly, **delete the apostrophe** in front of the DoCmd.Quit statement.

- Save the module. The next time you execute the procedure, you should see the message box you just created, and then Access will be terminated.

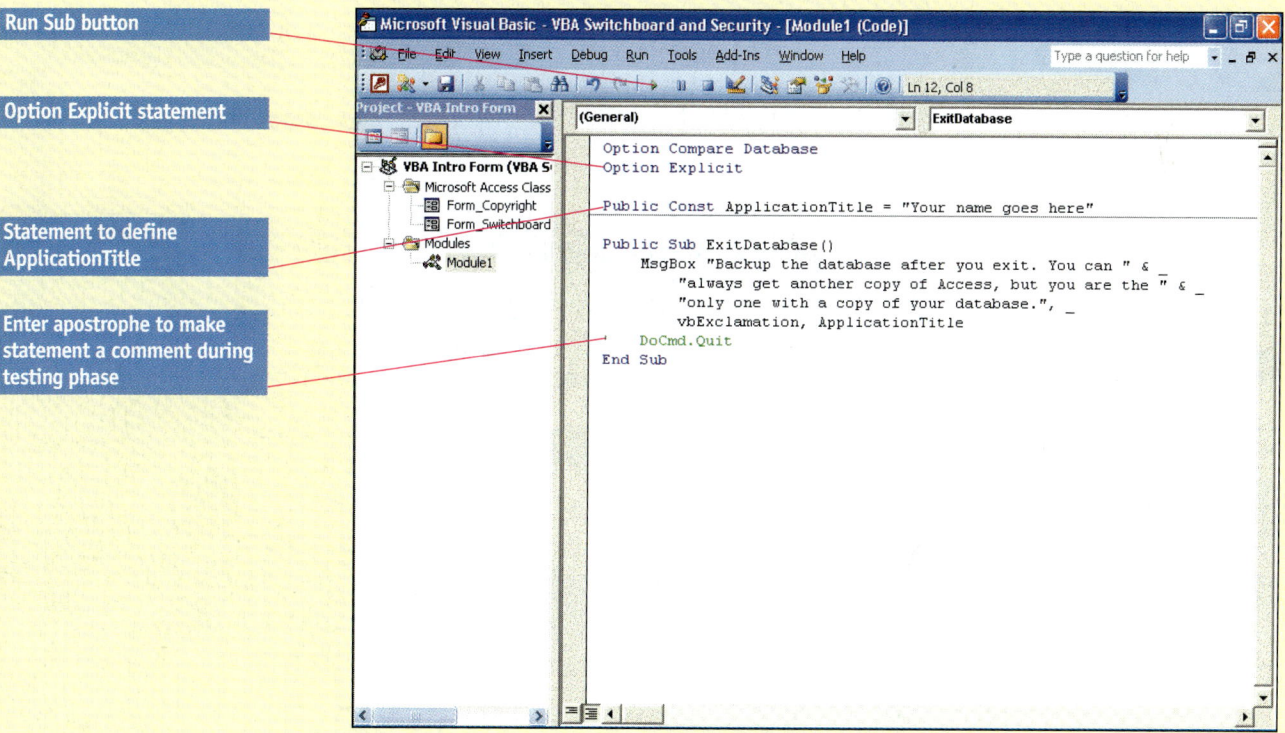

(b) Create the ExitDatabase Procedure (step 2)

FIGURE 16 Hands-on Exercise 5 (*continued*)

CREATE A PUBLIC CONSTANT

Give your application a customized look by adding your name or other identifying message to the title bar of the message and/or input boxes that you use. You can add the information individually to each statement, but it is easier to declare a public constant from within a general module. That way, you can change the value of the constant in one place and have the change reflected automatically throughout your application.

Step 3: **Modify the Switchboard**

- Click the **View Microsoft Access button** on the Standard toolbar within the VBA window to switch to the Database window (or use the **F11** keyboard shortcut).

- Pull down the **Tools menu**, click the **Database Utilities command**, then choose **Switchboard Manager** to display the Switchboard Manager dialog box in Figure 16c.

- Click the **Edit button** to edit the Main Switchboard and display the Edit Switchboard Page dialog box. Select the **&Exit Application command** and click its **Edit button** to display the Edit Switchboard Item dialog box.

- Change the command to **Run Code**. Enter **ExitDatabase** in the Function Name text box. Click **OK**, then close the two other dialog boxes.

- The switchboard has been modified so that clicking the Exit button will run the VBA procedure you just created.

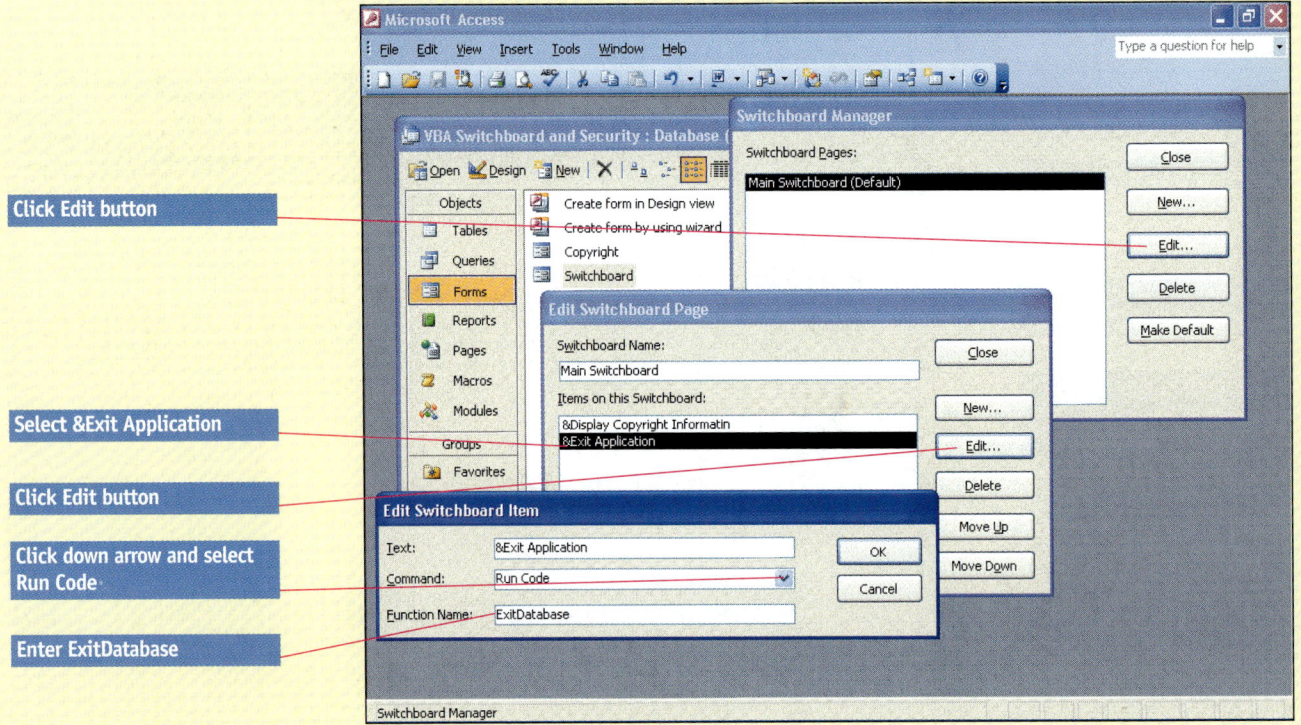

(c) Modify the Switchboard (step 3)

FIGURE 16   Hands-on Exercise 5 (*continued*)

CREATE A KEYBOARD SHORTCUT

The & has special significance when used within the name of an Access object because it creates a keyboard shortcut to that object. Enter "&Exit Application", for example, and the letter E (the letter immediately after the ampersand) will be underlined and appear as "Exit Application" on the switchboard. From there, you can execute the item by clicking its button, or you can use the Alt+E keyboard shortcut (where "E" is the underlined letter in the menu option).

1960   GETTING STARTED WITH VBA

Step 4: **Test the Switchboard**

- If necessary, click the **Forms button** in the Database window. Double click the **Switchboard form** to open the switchboard as shown in Figure 16d. The switchboard contains two commands.

- Click the **Display Copyright Information command** to display a form that we use with all our databases. (You can open this form in Design view and modify the text to include your name, rather than ours. If you do, be sure to save the modified form, then close it.)

- Click the **Exit Application command** (or use the **Alt+E** keyboard shortcut). You should see the dialog box in Figure 16d, corresponding to the MsgBox statement you created earlier. Click **OK** to close the dialog box.

- Access itself will terminate because of the DoCmd.Quit statement within the ExitDatabase procedure. (If this does not happen, return to the VBA editor and remove the apostrophe in front of the DoCmd statement.)

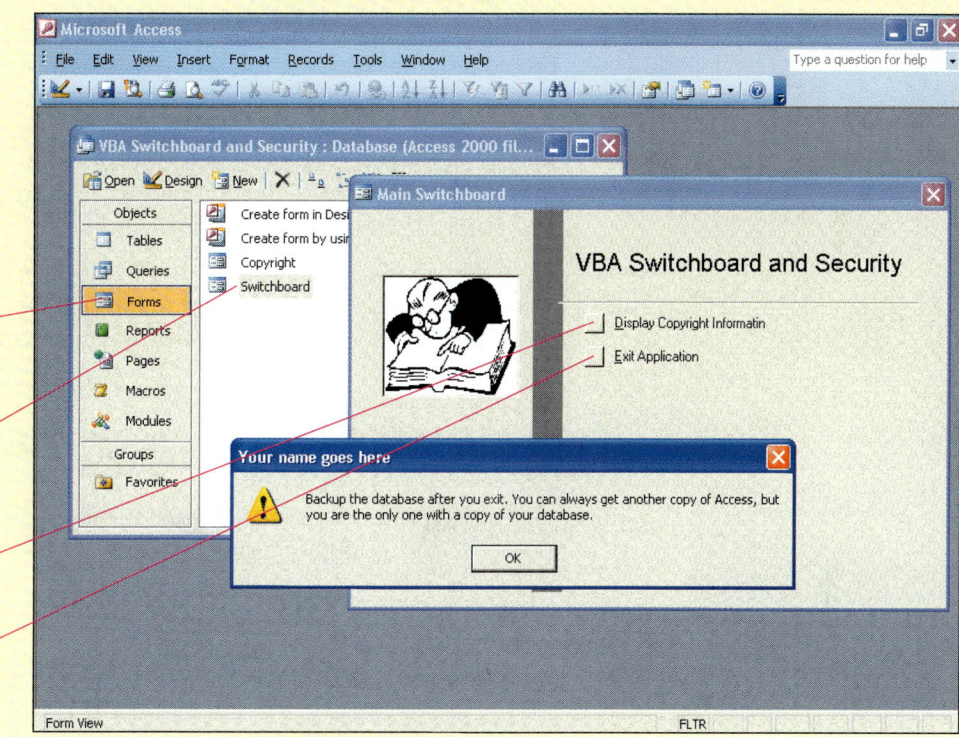

(d) Test the Switchboard (step 4)

FIGURE 16 Hands-on Exercise 5 (*continued*)

BACK UP IMPORTANT FILES

It's not a question of *if* it will happen, but *when*—hard disks die, files are lost, or viruses may infect a system. It has happened to us, and it will happen to you, but you can prepare for the inevitable by creating adequate backup before the problem occurs. The essence of a backup strategy is to decide which files to back up (your data), how often to do the backup (whenever it changes), and where to keep the backup (away from your computer). Do it!

Step 5: **Complete the Open Form Event Procedure**

- Start Access and reopen the **VBA Switchboard and Security database**. Press **Alt+F11** to start the VBA editor.

- Click the **plus sign** next to Microsoft Office Access Class objects, double click the module called **Form_Switchboard**, then look for the partially completed **Form_Open procedure** as shown in Figure 16e.

- The procedure was created automatically by the Switchboard Manager. You must, however, expand this procedure to include password protection. Note the following:
  - Three variables are required—the correct password, the password entered by the user, and the number of attempts.
  - The user is prompted for the password, and the number of attempts is set to 1. The user is given two additional attempts, if necessary, to get the correct password.
  - The If statement at the end of the loop determines whether the user has entered the correct password, and if so, it executes the original commands that are associated with the switchboard. If, however, the user fails to supply the correct password, an invalid password message is displayed and the **DoCmd.Quit** statement terminates the application.
  - We suggest you place an **apostrophe** in front of the statement initially so that it becomes a comment, and thus it is not executed. Once you are sure that you can enter the correct password, you can remove the apostrophe and implement the password protection.

- Save the procedure. You cannot test this procedure from within the VBA window; you must cause the event to happen (i.e., open the form) for the procedure to execute. Click the **View Microsoft Access button** on the Standard toolbar to return to the Database window.

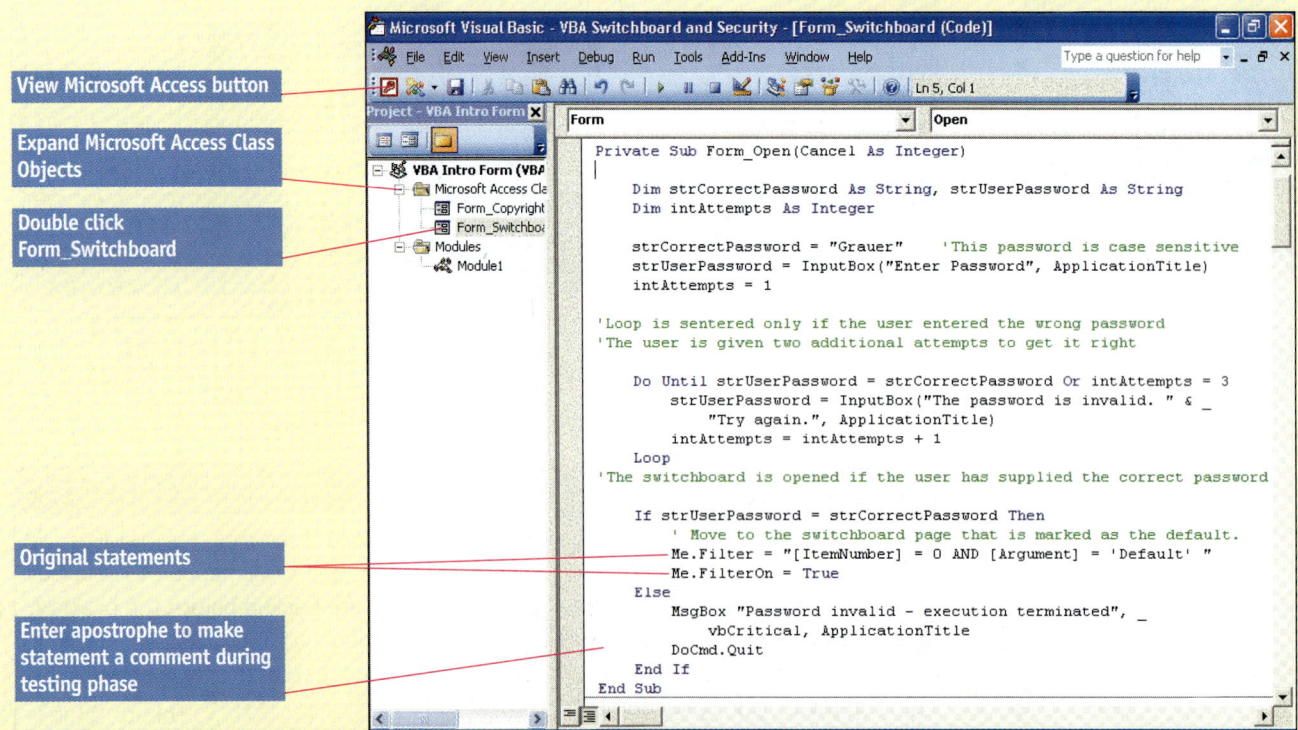

(e) Complete the Open Form Event Procedure (step 5)

FIGURE 16 Hands-on Exercise 5 (*continued*)

Step 6: **Test the Procedure**

- Close all open windows within the Access database except for the Database window. Click the **Forms button**, then double click the **Switchboard form**.

- You should be prompted for the password as shown in Figure 16f. The password (in our procedure) is **Grauer**.

- Test the procedure repeatedly to include all possibilities. Enter the correct password on the first, second, and third attempts to be sure that the procedure works as intended. Each time you enter the correct password, you will have to close the switchboard, then reopen it.

- Test the procedure one final time, by failing to enter the correct password. You will see a message box indicating that the password is invalid and that execution will be terminated. Termination will not take place, however, because the DoCmd.Quit statement is currently entered as a comment.

- Press **Alt+F11** to reopen the VBA editor. Open the **Microsoft Access Class Objects folder** and double click on **Form_Switchboard**. Delete the apostrophe in front of the DoCmd.Quit statement. The text of the statement changes from green to black to indicate that it is an executable statement. Save the procedure.

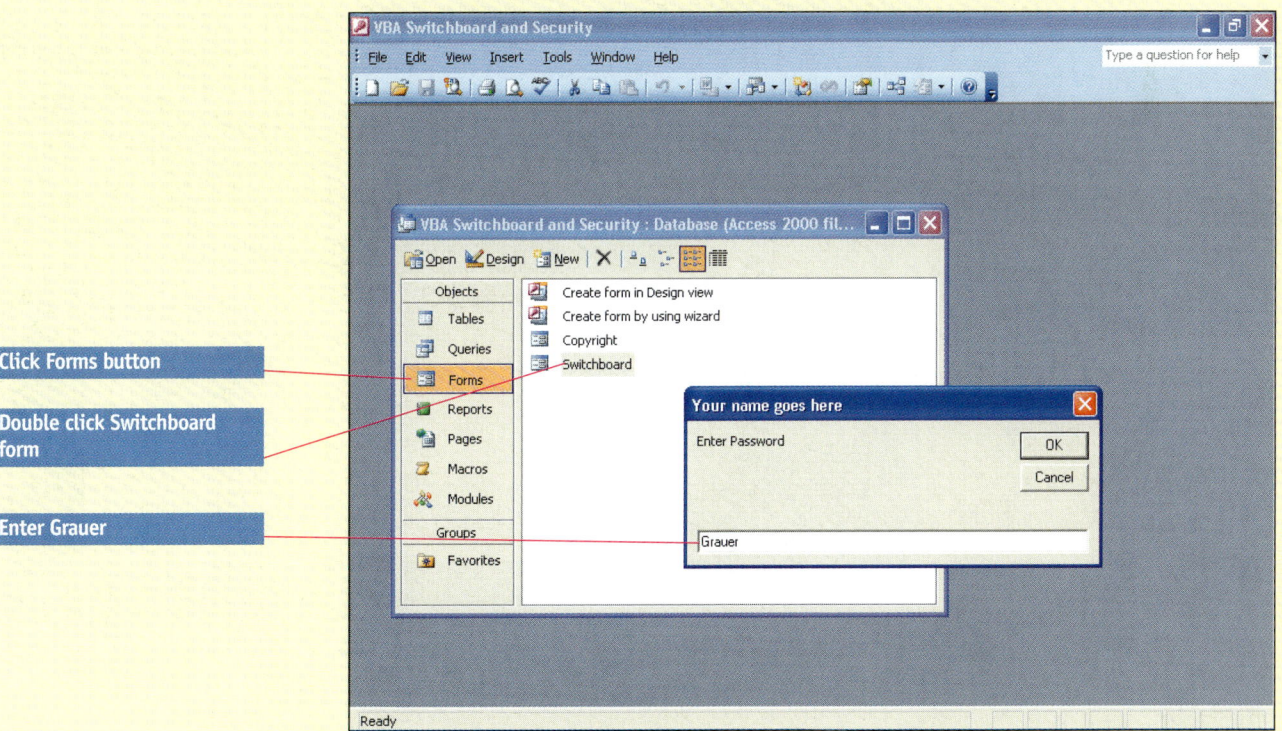

(f) Test the Procedure (step 6)

FIGURE 16 Hands-on Exercise 5 (*continued*)

TOGGLE COMMENTS ON AND OFF

Comments are used primarily to explain the purpose of VBA statements, but they can also be used to "comment out" code as distinct from deleting the statement altogether. Thus, you can add or remove the apostrophe in front of the statement, to toggle the comment on or off.

EXTENDING MICROSOFT OFFICE 2003   1963

Step 7: **Change the Startup Properties**

- Click the **View Microsoft Access button** on the VBA Standard toolbar to return to the Database window.
- Close all open windows except the Database window. Pull down the **Tools menu** and click **Startup** to display the Startup dialog box as shown in Figure 16g.
- Click in the **Application Title** text box and enter the title of the application, **VBA Switchboard and Security** in this example.
- Click the **drop-down arrow** in the Display Form/Page list box and select the **Switchboard form** as the form that will open automatically in conjunction with opening the database.
- Clear the check box to display the Database window. Click **OK** to accept the settings and close the dialog box.
- The next time you open the database, the switchboard should open automatically, which in turn triggers the Open Form event procedure that will prompt the user to enter a password.

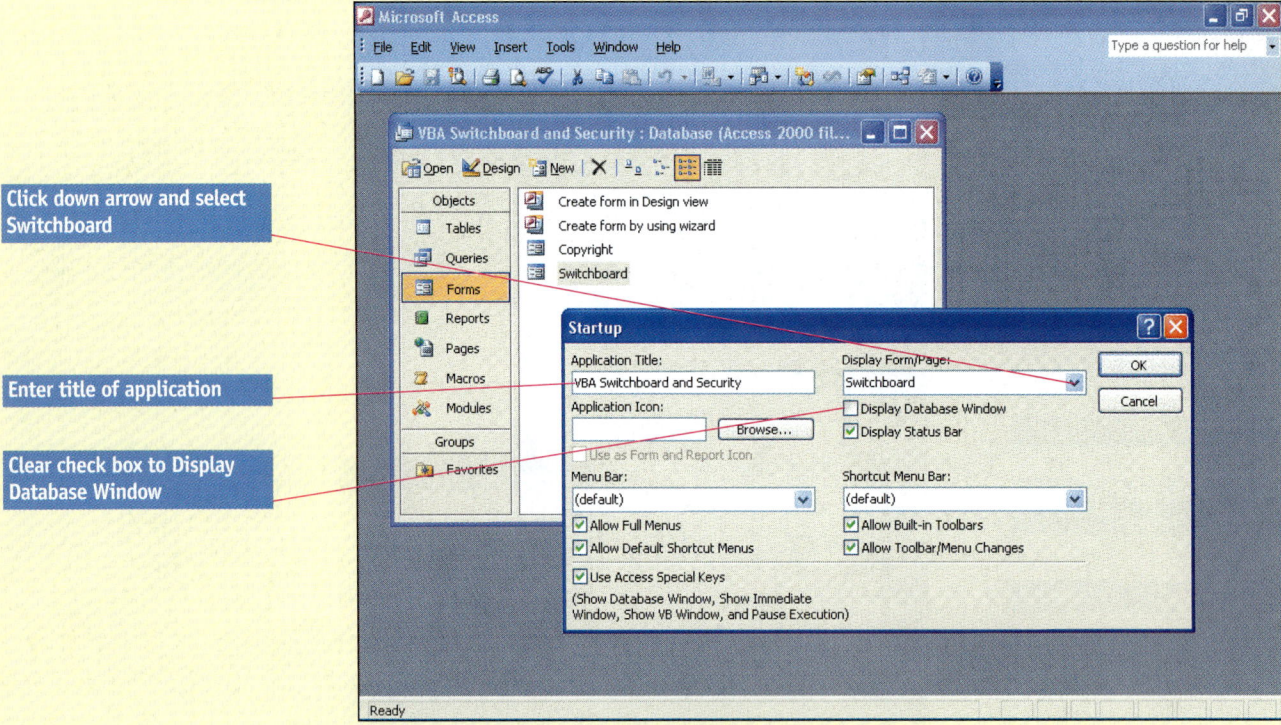

(g) Change the Startup Properties (step 7)

FIGURE 16 Hands-on Exercise 5 (*continued*)

HIDE THE DATABASE WINDOW

Use the Startup property to hide the Database window from the novice user. You avoid confusion and you may prevent the novice from accidentally deleting objects in the database. Of course, anyone with some knowledge of Access can restore the Database window by pulling down the Window menu, clicking the Unhide command, then selecting the Database window from the associated dialog box. Nevertheless, hiding the Database window is a good beginning.

Step 8: **Test the Database**

- Close the database, then reopen the database to test the procedures we have created in this exercise. The sequence of events is as follows:
  - The database is loaded and the switchboard is opened but is not yet visible. The Open Form procedure for the switchboard is executed, and you are prompted for the password as shown in Figure 16h.
  - The password is entered correctly and the switchboard is displayed. The Database window is hidden, however, because the Startup Properties have been modified.

- Click the **Exit Application command** (or use the **Alt+E** keyboard shortcut). You will see the message box reminding you to back up the system, after which the database is closed and Access is terminated.

- Reopen the database. This time, however, you are to enter the wrong password three times in a row. You should see a message indicating that the execution was terminated due to an invalid password.

- Testing is complete and you can go on to add the other objects to your Access database. Congratulations on a job well done.

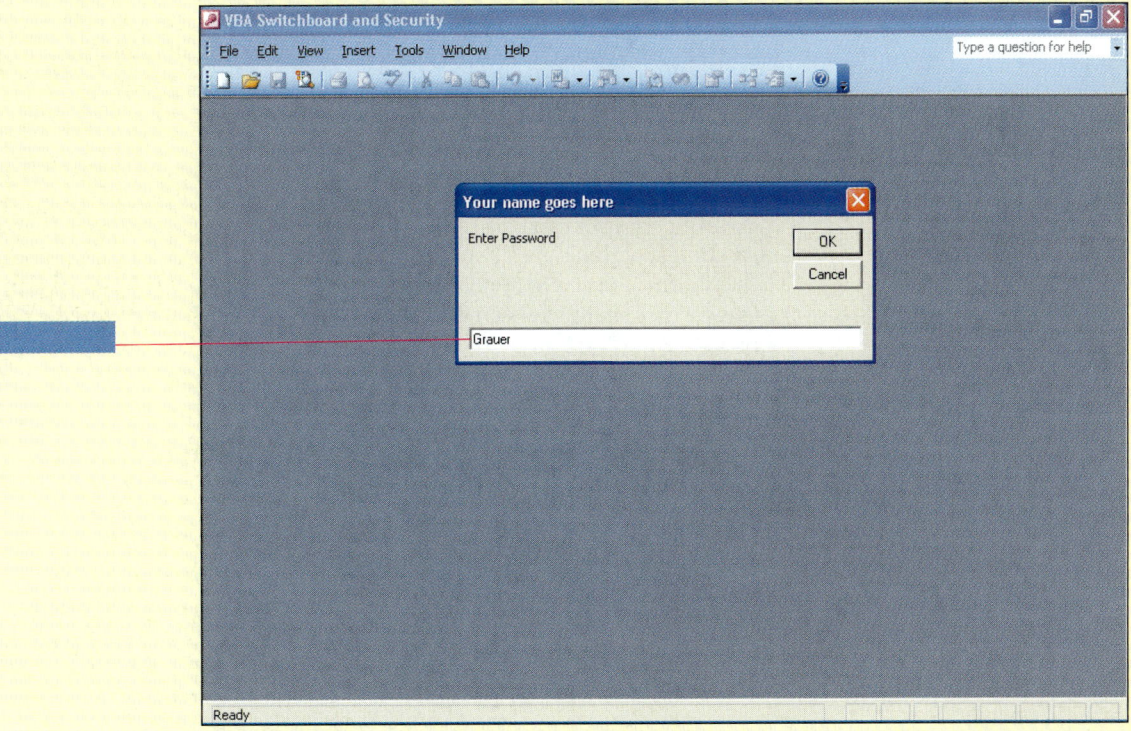

(h) Test the Database (step 8)

FIGURE 16   Hands-on Exercise 5 (*continued*)

RESTORING HIDDEN MENUS AND TOOLBARS

You can use the Startup property to hide menus and/or toolbars from the user by clearing the respective check boxes. A word of caution, however—once the menus are hidden, it is difficult to get them back. Start Access, pull down the File menu, and click Open to display the Open dialog box, select the database to open, then press and hold the Shift key when you click the Open button. This powerful technique is not widely known.

SUMMARY

Visual Basic for Applications (VBA) is a powerful programming language that is accessible from all major applications in Microsoft Office XP. A VBA statement accomplishes a specific task such as displaying a message to the user or accepting input from the user. Statements are grouped into procedures, and procedures in turn are grouped into modules. Every procedure is classified as either private or public.

The MsgBox statement displays information to the user. It has one required argument, which is the message (or prompt) that is displayed to the user. The other two arguments—the icon that is to be displayed in the dialog box and the text of the title bar—are optional. The InputBox function displays a prompt to the user requesting information, then it stores that information (the value returned by the user) for use later in the procedure.

Every variable must be declared (defined) before it can be used. This is accomplished through the Dim (short for Dimension) statement that appears at the beginning of a procedure. The Dim statement indicates the name of the variable and its type (for example, whether it will hold a character string or an integer number), which in turn reserves the appropriate amount of memory for that variable.

The ability to make decisions within a procedure, then branch to alternative sets of statements is implemented through the If . . . Then . . . Else or Case statements. The Else clause is optional, but may be repeated multiple times within an If statement. The Case statement is preferable to an If statement with multiple Else clauses.

The For . . . Next statement (or For . . . Next loop as it is also called) executes all statements between the words For and Next a specified number of times, using a counter to keep track of the number of times the loop is executed. The Do . . . Loop Until and/or Do Until . . . Loop statements are used when the number of times through the loop is not known in advance.

VBA is different from traditional programming languages in that it is event-driven. An event is defined as any action that is recognized by an application, such as Excel or Access. Opening or closing an Excel workbook or an Access database is an event. Selecting a worksheet within a workbook is also an event, as is clicking on a command button on an Access form. To use VBA within Microsoft Office, you decide which events are significant, and what is to happen when those events occur. Then you develop the appropriate event procedures.

KEY TERMS

Term	Page	Term	Page	Term	Page
Argument	1906	Event	1945	Private procedure	1906
Case statement	1922	Event procedure (Access)	1956	Procedure	1906
Character string	1920	Event procedure (Excel)	1945	Procedure header	1907
Comment	1910	Execution error	1934	Project Explorer	1910
Compilation error	1934	For . . . Next Statement	1932	Public procedure	1906
Complete Word tool	1926	Full Module view	1925	Run-time error	1934
Concatenate	1908	If statement	1920	Statement	1906
Custom toolbar	1923	Immediate window	1935	Step Into button	1935
Debug menu	1934	InputBox function	1908	Syntax	1906
Debug toolbar	1934	Intrinsic constant	1907	Underscore	1908
Debug.Print statement	1935	Literal	1920	Variable	1908
Debugging	1934	Locals window	1935	VBA	1906
Declarations section	1910	Macro	1906	Visible property	1954
Dim statement	1909	Macro recorder	1906	Visual Basic editor	1910
Do Loops	1933	Module	1906	Visual Basic for Applications	1906
Else clause	1920	MsgBox statement	1907		
End Sub statement	1907	Option Explicit	1910		

MULTIPLE CHOICE

1. Which of the following applications in Office XP has access to VBA?
   (a) Word
   (b) Excel
   (c) Access
   (d) All of the above

2. Which of the following is a valid name for a VBA variable?
   (a) Public
   (b) Private
   (c) strUserFirstName
   (d) int Count Of Attempts

3. Which of the following is true about an If statement?
   (a) It evaluates a condition as either true or false, then executes the statement(s) following the keyword "Then" if the condition is true
   (b) It must contain the keyword Else
   (c) It must contain one or more ElseIf statements
   (d) All of the above

4. Which of the following lists the items from smallest to largest?
   (a) Module, procedure, statement
   (b) Statement, module, procedure
   (c) Statement, procedure, module
   (d) Procedure, module, statement

5. Given the statement, MsgBox "Welcome to VBA", "Bob was here", which of the following is true?
   (a) "Welcome to VBA" will be displayed within the resulting message box
   (b) "Welcome to VBA" will appear on the title bar of the displayed dialog box
   (c) The two adjacent commas will cause a compilation error
   (d) An informational icon will be displayed with the message

6. Where are the VBA procedures associated with an Office document stored?
   (a) In the same folder, but in a separate file
   (b) In the Office document itself
   (c) In a special VBA folder on drive C
   (d) In a special VBA folder on the local area network

7. The Debug.Print statement is associated with the:
   (a) Locals window
   (b) Immediate window
   (c) Project Explorer
   (d) Debug toolbar

8. Which of the following is the proper sequence of arguments for the MsgBox statement?
   (a) Text for the title bar, prompt, button
   (b) Prompt, button, text for the title bar
   (c) Prompt, text for the title bar, button
   (d) Button, prompt, text for the title bar

9. Which of the following is a true statement about Do loops?
   (a) Placing the Until clause at the beginning of the loop tests the condition prior to executing any statements in the loop
   (b) Placing the Until clause at the end of the loop executes the statements in the loop, then it tests the condition
   (c) Both (a) and (b)
   (d) Neither (a) nor (b)

10. Given the statement, For intCount = 1 to 10 Step 3, how many times will the statements in the loop be executed (assuming that there are no statements in the loop to terminate the execution)?
    (a) 10
    (b) 4
    (c) 3
    (d) Impossible to determine

...continued

multiple choice

11. Which of the following is a *false* statement?
    (a) A dash at the end of a line indicates continuation
    (b) An ampersand indicates concatenation
    (c) An apostrophe at the beginning of a line signifies a comment
    (d) A pair of quotation marks denotes a character string

12. What is the effect of deleting the apostrophe that appears at the beginning of a VBA statement?
    (a) A compilation error will occur
    (b) The statement is converted to a comment
    (c) The color of the statement will change from black to green
    (d) The statement is made executable

13. Which of the following If statements will display the indicated message if the user enters a response other than "Grauer" (assuming that "Grauer" is the correct password)?
    (a) If strUserResponse <> "Grauer" Then MsgBox "Wrong password"
    (b) If strUserResponse = "Grauer" Then MsgBox "Wrong password"
    (c) If strUserResponse > "Grauer" Then MsgBox "Wrong password"
    (d) If strUserResponse < "Grauer" Then MsgBox "Wrong password"

14. Which of the following will execute the statements in the loop at least once?
    (a) Do . . . Loop Until
    (b) Do Until ….. Loop
    (c) Both (a) and (b)
    (d) Neither (a) nor (b)

15. The copy and paste commands can be used to:
    (a) Copy statements within a procedure
    (b) Copy statements from a procedure in one module to a procedure in another module within the same document
    (c) Copy statements from a module in an Excel workbook to a module in an Access database
    (d) All of the above

16. Which of the following is true about indented text in a VBA procedure?
    (a) The indented text is always executed first
    (b) The indented text is always executed last
    (c) The indented text is rendered a comment and is never executed
    (d) None of the above

17. Which statement will prompt the user to enter his or her name and store the result in a variable called strUser?
    (a) InputBox.strUser
    (b) strUser = MsgBox("Enter your name")
    (c) strUser = InputBox("Enter your name")
    (d) InputBox("Enter strUser")

18. Given that strUser is currently set to "George", the expression "Good morning, strName" will return:
    (a) Good morning, George
    (b) Good morning, strName
    (c) Good morning George
    (d) Good morning strName

ANSWERS

1. d	7. b	13. a
2. c	8. b	14. a
3. a	9. c	15. d
4. c	10. b	16. d
5. a	11. a	17. c
6. b	12. d	18. b

Index

Page References for Individual Modules

- Word, 1065–1208
- Excel, 1209–1560
- Access, 1561–1808
- PowerPoint, 1809–1904
- VBA, 1905–1968

DIV/0 error, 1328
Error, 1580
3-D reference, 1220

A

Absolute reference (in a macro), 1371–1372
Accept Change button, 1152, 1157
Accept or reject changes, 1276
Action, 1688
Action buttons, 1854, 1861, 1894
Add button (modification of), 1740
Add mode, 1682
Adjustable cells, 1545
Advanced Filter command, 1317, 1325
Advanced timeline, 1828
Aligning objects, 1870
Amortization, 1424
Ampersand (as concatenation operator), 1397, 1441, 1736, 1918
Analysis ToolPak, 1324, 1356
AND function, 1425, 1431
Animated GIF, 1837
Animation, 1828
Annotating a slide, 1839
Argument, 1688, 1732, 1906
Arial, 1068
Arrange command, 1212, 1224
Ascending sequence, 1303
Assumptions, 1254, 1266
Audience handouts, 1818
AutoContent Wizard, 1892
AutoCorrect command, 1309
AutoExec macro, 1689, 1692
AutoFill command, 1237
AutoFilter command, 1316, 1323
AutoFit column width, 1228
AutoFormat command, 1221, 1227
  with a diagram, 1816
AutoFormat tool, 1810
AutoLookup, 1626
AutoNumber field, 1565, 1569, 1619, 1624, 1652
  in relationship, 1568
AutoShape, 1090
  animation of, 1850
  toolbar, 1090
AutoSum, 1226

B

Back up, 1732, 1961
BeforeClose event procedure, 1447, 1947–1948
BeforeUpdate event, 1764
Binding constraint, 1543
Block fields (in mail merge), 1801
Bookmark, 1123, 1126
Borders and Shading, 1066, 1087
Broadcast, 1877
Bulleted list, 1066, 1084

C

Caption property, 1748
Cascade deleted records, 1571, 1620, 1624–1625
Cascade updated records, 1620
Case statement, 1751–1752, 1922, 1928
Category labels, 1819
Cell formulas (printing of), 1234, 1435
Cells, 1163
Centimeters (as measurement unit), 1070
Changing cells, 1257
Character string, 1920
Chart, 1819
  animation of, 1829, 1836, 1848
Check box, 1154, 1158
Circle invalid data, 1270, 1290
Circular reference, 1276, 1296
Class module, 1731
Click event, 1741, 1749
Clip art, 1066, 1085–1086, 1119, 1686
Close Form Event, 1732
Codd, Edgar, 1791
Code builder, 1738
Code window, 1181, 1360
Collection, 1436, 1517
Color scheme, 1854
Columns, 1069
  balance of, 1073
  changing of, 1072, 1083
  column break, 1072
Combined key, 1618, 1792
Combo box, 1699
Combo Box Wizard, 1656, 1734

Command button
  assigning to a macro, 1388, 1395
  properties of, 1401, 1499
Comment, 1180, 1277, 1360, 1910, 1916
  toggle on or off, 1498, 1963
  in VBA, 1360
Common user interface, 1096
Compact and Repair Database, 1591, 1709
Compare and merge workbooks, 1297
Compilation error, 1744, 1934, 1938
Complete Word tool, 1745, 1926
Concatenation, 1736, 1908, 1918
Conditional formatting, 1256, 1263, 1503
Consolidating data, 1210–1213
Constraint, 1545
Context-sensitive menu, 1225
Continuation (of VBA statement), 1397, 1755, 1918
Copy command (shortcut for), 1733
Copyright, 1893
Create Name command, 1383
Create New Folder command, 1172
Create Subdocument command, 1172, 1175
Criteria range, 1317–1318, 1330
Crop tool, 1430
Current event, 1732, 1739
Custom animation, 1828–1839
  task pane, 1833
Custom format, 1256
Custom menu, 1476
Custom series, 1237
Custom show, 1876, 1882
Custom sort sequence, 1303
Custom toolbar, 1444–1447, 1923, 1929–1931
  in Access, 1931
Custom view, 1234, 1264
Cut command (shortcut for), 1733
Cycle diagram, 1810

D

Data, 1314
Data entry (facilitation of), 1741–1750
Data form, 1302

Page References for Individual Modules

■ Word, 1065–1208
■ Excel, 1209–1560
■ Access, 1561–1808
■ PowerPoint, 1809–1904
■ VBA, 1905–1968

Data management macros, 1380–1401
Data points, 1093, 1819
Data series, 1093
   formatting of, 1341
   removal of, 1824
Data source, 1795
Data type mismatch, 1588
Data validation, 1424, 1429, 1487, 1760–1767
   field versus record level, 1763
Data Validation command, 1270–1271, 1278
Database, 1300
   expansion of, 1592–1593, 1647–1648
Database design, 1567, 1785–1794
   expansion of, 1592–1593
   PowerPoint presentation for, 1605, 1662, 1714
Database functions, 1319, 1327–1330
Database properties, 1658, 1679
Database splitter, 1680
Database window (hiding of), 1964
Datasheet, 1819
Datasheet view, 1572
Date (entering of), 1312
Date arithmetic, 1322
DATE function, 1428
DAVERAGE function, 1319, 1328
DAY function, 1428
DCOUNT function, 1319, 1329
Debug menu, 1934
Debug toolbar, 1934
Debug.Print statement, 1935
Debugging, 1407, 1491, 1689, 1756, 1934
Declarations section, 1910
Decrease Brightness tool, 1430
Default folder (changing of), 1165
Default frame, 1136
Default property, 1741
Default View property, 1597
Define Name command, 1257
Delete command, 1301
Delimited format, 1305
Dependent cells, 1270, 1274
Dependent workbook, 1235
Descending sequence, 1163, 1303
Description property, 1644
Desktop publishing, 1066–1103
Diagram Gallery, 1810, 1847
Diagram toolbar, 1817
Digital signature, 1162, 1447, 1458

Dim statement, 1485, 1909
Dir function, 1486
Display for Review list box, 1156
Display When property, 1685
Division by zero, 1328
DMAX function, 1319, 1329
DMIN function, 1319, 1329
Do loops, 1933, 1943–1944
Do statement, 1403
Do Until statement, 1485
Do While statement, 1485
Document map, 1179
Document properties, 1171
Documentation worksheet, 1229
Documents submenu, 1651
Drawing canvas, 1810
Drawing toolbar, 1066, 1082, 1101
Drop-down list box, 1154
Dropped-capital letter, 1066, 1089
DSUM function, 1319, 1329

E

Edit Clear command, 1311, 1364
Edit Delete command, 1311
Edit mode, 1682
Else clause, 1920, 1926
Embedded object, 1093
Emphasis, 1080
Emphasis effect, 1828, 1843
End If statement, 1402
End Sub statement, 1180, 1360, 1907
End With statement, 1361
Entity, 1790
Entrance effect, 1828, 1843
Error checking, 1328
Error trapping, 1493, 1498, 1751–1759
Evaluate formula tool, 1295
Event, 1447, 1677, 1728, 1945
Event procedure, 1447, 1452, 1684, 1731
   Access, 1956
   Excel, 1945
Event-driven programming, 1753
Execution error, 1934
Exit effect, 1828, 1843
Exit Sub statement, 1493
Exporting data, 1313, 1358
Expression Builder, 1579
Extensible Markup Language (*See* XML)
External reference, 1235, 1239

F

Favorite (adding of), 1857
Field, 1154, 1300
Field codes, 1159, 1163
Field name, 1300
File, 1300
File name (rules for), 1118
File Transfer Protocol (FTP), 1123
Fill handle, 1260
Filtered list, 1316
Final Showing Markup, 1152–1153
Find and Replace command, 1393
Fixed toolbar, 1135, 1929
Fixed width format, 1305
Floating toolbar, 1135, 1929
Folder (creation of), 1124, 1174, 1831
Font, 1068
Footer, 1861
For…Next statement, 1485, 1932, 1937, 1941–1942
Foreign key, 1565, 1790
Form, 1154–1162
   protection of, 1161
Form command, 1302
Form letter, 1795
Form view, 1572
Form Wizard (with subforms), 1574–1576, 1631
Format Object command, 1098
Format Painter, 1815
Format Picture command, 1080
Format property, 1565, 1619
FormOpen event procedure, 1962
Forms toolbar, 1154
Formula Auditing toolbar, 1270, 1272
Frame, 1130
Frames toolbar, 1130
Full Module view, 1743, 1925

G

Garbage in, garbage out (GIGO), 1301
General Declarations section, 1751
General procedure, 1447, 1452, 1731
Get External Data command, 1651, 1680
Go To command, 1320
Grammar check, 1071
   foreign language, 1117
Graphic design, 1078–1081

Grid, 1078
Group By command, 1635
Grouping records, 1590
Grouping worksheets, 1221, 1226, 1246

H

Header, 1861
Header and Footer command, 1095
Header row, 1168
Heading style, 1076
Help, 1919
Hidden slide, 1854, 1864
Home page, 1116
Hopper, Grace, 1407, 1756
HTML, 1114–1115, 1306, 1343, 1866
Hyperlink, 1116, 1854, 1883, 1894
   automatic creation of, 1126
   color of, 1128
HyperText Markup Language (*See* HTML)

I

If statement, 1402, 1408, 1751, 1920, 1926
If...Then...Else statement, 1402, 1485
IIF function, 1580
Immediate window, 1751, 1754, 1935, 1940
Inches (as measurement unit), 1070
Increase Brightness tool, 1430
Indent text, 1256, 1262
Index.html (as a file name), 1118
Information, 1314
Initial conditions, 1254
InputBox function, 1372, 1376, 1485, 1908, 1917
Insert Columns command, 1301
Insert Comment command, 1157, 1277
Insert Date command, 1184, 1799
Insert Hyperlink command, 1116, 1120, 1697, 1854
Insert Name command, 1265, 1320, 1326, 1383
Insert Rows command, 1301
Insert Slides command, 1831
Insert Sound command, 1859, 1870
Insert Table command, 1844
Internet Explorer, 1123
Intrinsic constant, 1516, 1732, 1907
Invalid data (circling of), 1270, 1290
IPMT function, 1432, 1436
Is Null criterion, 1702
ISERROR function, 1328
Iteration, 1551

J

Join line, 1583
Join properties, 1716

K

Keep Together property, 1641
Key, 1300
Key Preview property, 1746
Keyboard shortcut, 1360
   within Access, 1694
   creation of, 1681
   in slide show, 1865
KeyCode argument, 1742
KeyDown event, 1741, 1743–1745

L

Len function, 1486
Line break, 1072
Link Tables command, 1678, 1680
Linked object, 1093
Linked subforms, 1595–1601
Linked Table Manager, 1677–1678
Linking, 1235, 1238, 1245
List, 1300–1301
Literal, 1920
Locals window, 1935
Loop, 1402

M

Macro, 1180–1192, 1360, 1688–1690, 1906
   assign to command button, 1708
   execution of, 1389
Macro group, 1700, 1705
Macro recorder, 1180, 1360, 1436, 1906
Macro security, 1391, 1924
Macro toolbar, 1689
Macro window, 1688
Mail Merge, 1795–1804
Mail Merge toolbar, 1802
Mail Merge Wizard, 1800
Main document, 1795
Main form, 1572, 1626
Many-to-many relationship, 1618, 1791
Margin (changing of), 1070
Master document, 1172–1179
Masthead, 1066, 1074
Measurement unit (changing of), 1070
Memo field, 1765
Menu (customization of), 1378
Merge fields, 1795

Method, 1436
MHTML document, 1871
Microsoft Access
   exporting data to, 1313, 1358
   importing data from, 1329
Microsoft Excel, 1093, 1096, 1099
Microsoft FrontPage, 1124
Microsoft Graph, 1819–1827
   importing data, 1823
Module, 1181, 1906
Module view, 1370
Module window, 1731
Monospaced typeface, 1068
MONTH function, 1428
Motion path, 1833, 1843
MsgBox action, 1689
MsgBox function, 1437, 1920
MsgBox statement, 1390, 1398, 1437, 1485, 1732, 1749, 1757, 1907, 1913–1915
Multiple-table query, 1583–1584, 1626–1630, 1639

N

Name box, 1265, 1326, 1384
Named range, 1381
   use in a macro, 1385
Navigation buttons
   with subform, 1594, 1601
   suppression of, 1707
Nested If, 1475, 1507, 1760
New Window command, 1212
Newsletter, 1066–1067
Nonbinding constraint, 1543
Numbered list, 1066, 1084
Numeric field (size of), 1761

O

Object, 1436
Object box, 1758
Object dependencies, 1658
Object linking and embedding (OLE), 1093, 1095–1102, 1247
Object model, 1436
Office Links button, 1798
Offset, 1371
Offset property, 1508
On Click property, 1700
On Error statement, 1493
One-to-many relationship, 1563–1564, 1616, 1785
Online meeting, 1877
OnTime method, 1449
Open workbook event procedure, 1447
Option Explicit, 1910, 1912
Options menu, 1282

> **Page References for Individual Modules**
> - Word, 1065–1208
> - Excel, 1209–1560
> - Access, 1561–1808
> - PowerPoint, 1809–1904
> - VBA, 1905–1968

OR function, 1425
Organization chart, 1810, 1812–1815
   animation of, 1830, 1834–1835, 1846
Organization Chart toolbar, 1814
Original Showing Markup, 1152–1153
Outline symbols, 1321
Outline view, 1177
Outlining toolbar, 1172

P

Page Border command, 1190
Page break, 1072
Page Setup command, 1070, 1233
Parameter, 1732
Parameter query, 1635–1636, 1704
Password protection, 1152, 1710
Paste command (shortcut for), 1733
Personal Macro workbook, 1372–1373
Photographs (animation of), 1845
Pica, 1070
Picture toolbar, 1430
Pivot chart, 1333, 1336–1341
Pivot Table Wizard, 1333
Pivot table, 1333, 1336–1341
   formatting of, 1338
   from multiple ranges, 1251
   refreshing of, 1344
PMT function, 1572–1573, 1579
PPMT function, 1432, 1436
Practice files (downloading of), 1215
Precedent cells, 1270, 1275
Primary key, 1565, 1616, 1790
Print area, 1435, 1473
Print Preview command, 1077, 1233
Print Preview toolbar, 1077
Private procedure, 1456, 1513, 1731, 1906
Procedure, 1180, 1728, 1906
   printing of, 1467
   stepping through, 1508
Procedure box, 1758
Procedure header, 1742, 1907
Procedure view, 1370, 1743, 1925
Project Explorer, 1181, 1360, 1910
Prompt, 1635
Properties window, 1449
Property, 1436
Proportional typeface, 1068
Protected workbook, 1284
Protected worksheet, 1279, 1433

Prototype, 1690, 1693
Prototyping, 1137
Pseudocode, 1459
Public constant, 1918, 1959
Public procedure, 1456, 1513, 1731, 1906
Publishing options, 1868
Pull quote, 1066, 1088
Pyramid diagram, 1810, 1816–1817, 1847

Q

Query
   multiple table, 1626–1630, 1639
   updating of, 1645

R

Radial diagram, 1810, 1847
Record, 1300
Record Narration command, 1876, 1879
Record New Macro command, 1362
Record selector (suppression of), 1707
Redundancy, 1786
Referential integrity, 1565, 1568, 1571, 1620, 1622, 1791
Refresh command, 1129, 1333
   problems with, 1874
Rehearse Timings command, 1880
Reject Change button, 1152
Relational database, 1790
Relational operator, 1928
Relationship
   editing of, 1624
   printing of, 1654
Relationship line, 1565, 1619
Relationships window, 1565, 1567–1568, 1595, 1619, 1622, 1654
Relative reference (in a macro), 1371–1372, 1374
Relative reference button, 1363, 1461
Repeat columns, 1434
Repeat rows, 1434
Repeating group, 1792
Report properties, 1589
Report switchboard, 1695, 1717
Report Wizard, 1590, 1640
Requery command, 1705
Result cells, 1257

Reverse, 1066, 1075
Reviewing toolbar, 1152, 1155, 1269, 1272
Revision mark, 1152
Right mouse button, 1214
Rotate text, 1256, 1262
Rotate tool, 1430
Roth IRA, 1290
Round trip HTML, 1116, 1873
Ruler, 1073
Run-time error, 1493, 1497, 1934

S

Sans serif typeface, 1068
Save As Web Page command, 1116, 1118, 1124, 1866, 1868, 1871
Scenario, 1257, 1266
Scenario list box, 1267, 1294
Scenario Manager, 1257
Scenario summary, 1257, 1268, 1291
Schema, 1306
Scope (of a procedure), 1513
Screen capture, 1457, 1955
Section break, 1069
Semester project, 1805–1808
Serif typeface, 1068
Set Focus method, 1740, 1742
Set Up Show command, 1880
Shared workbook, 1269
Shortcut key (with macros), 1360, 1362, 1368, 1396
Side-by-side column chart, 1093, 1819–1820
Single File Web Page, 1118, 1122, 1133, 1342, 1866
Slide master, 1856
   multiple masters, 1862
Solver, 1543–1559
Solver Options dialog box, 1551
Solver Parameters dialog box, 1545
Sort, 1163
Sort ascending button, 1310
Sort command, 1303–1304, 1310
Sort descending button, 1310
Sorting and Grouping command, 1641
Sound effect (triggering of), 1860
Sound Recorder, 1854, 1858, 1881
Source workbook, 1235
Spell check, 1071, 1232, 1309
   foreign language, 1117
Splash screen, 1447, 1455–1457
Stacked column chart, 1093, 1819, 1821

Standard format, 1586
Startup property, 1599
Statement, 1906
Step Into button, 1935, 1939
Step Into command, 1369, 1394
Stop Recording button, 1363
Structured Query Language (SQL), 1583–1584
Student project, 1805–1808
Style, 1256
Sub statement, 1180, 1360
Subdatasheet, 1565–1566, 1570
Subdocument, 1172, 1175–1178
Subform, 1572, 1575–1582, 1594–1601, 1626
Subtotals command, 1321, 1331–1332
Sum function, 1635
Switch, 1459, 1464, 1951
Switchboard, 1674–1677, 1679–1683
    modification of, 1960
Switchboard form, 1677
Switchboard Items table, 1677, 1683
Switchboard Manager, 1677, 1681–1682
Syntax, 1906
Syntax error, 1493

T

Tab color property, 1506
Tab key (with a table), 1167
Tab order, 1747
Table (properties of), 1762
Table math, 1163–1170
Table menu, 1125, 1163
Table row, 1583
Tables and Borders toolbar, 1125, 1163, 1863
Target cell, 1545
Target diagram, 1810, 1847
Target frame, 1130
Taskbar, 1097
Template, 1279, 1690, 1706, 1715, 1721, 1724, 1854
Templates folder, 1279
Text box, 1091
Text field, 1154, 1158
Text Import Wizard, 1305, 1307
Theme, 1116, 1121, 1133
Times New Roman, 1068
Title page (creation of), 1095
TODAY() function, 1322, 1428

Toolbar
    attachment of, 1446
    creation of, 1444, 1476
    customization of, 1378, 1777–1778
    listing of, 1535–1540
    working with, 1533–1534
Toolbar button (modification of), 1445
Top 10 AutoFilter, 1323
Top Values property, 1646
Top-of-document book mark, 1127
Total query, 1635, 1637
Total row, 1635
Tracers, 1270
Track Changes command, 1152, 1156, 1269
Trend line, 1285
TRK indicator, 1156
Type size, 1068
Typeface, 1068
Typography, 1068

U

Ucase function, 1953
Under Construction Web page, 1133
Underscore (as continuation), 1397, 1441, 1908, 1918
Unlock cells, 1279
Unmatched Query Wizard, 1643, 1663, 1699, 1701
Unprotect sheet command, 1505
Uploading a presentation, 1866
User form, 1449, 1454–1455
UserForm Activate procedure, 1449

V

Variable, 1908
VBA, 1906
VBA statement (continuation of), 1755
VBA syntax, 1913
Venn diagram, 1810, 1847
Versions command, 1152, 1160
Visual Basic, 1360
Visual Basic Editor (VBE), 1181, 1360, 1365, 1375, 1910
Visual Basic for Applications (VBA), 1180, 1360, 1728, 1906
Visual Basic toolbar, 1387
Visible property, 1954
VLOOKUP function, 1492

W

Watch window, 1296
Web broadcast, 1877
Web Layout command, 1117
Web page, 1866
    printing of, 1875
Web queries, 1249
Web site, 1130
    creation of, 1133–1138
    expansion of, 1138
Web toolbar, 1137
WEEKDAY function, 1453, 1516
Wild card, 1319
Windows taskbar
    hiding of, 1915
With statement, 1361
WordArt, 1091
Workgroup, 1152, 1269
    authentication of, 1458
    protection of, 1284
Workbook properties, 1230, 1281
Workbook reference, 1235
WorkbookOpen event procedure, 1949–1950, 1952
Worksheet
    copying, 1216–1218
    inserting, 1222
    moving, 1218
    protection of, 1433
    selecting multiple, 1227
    summing, 1223
Worksheet (hiding of), 1945
Worksheet object, 1493
Worksheet reference, 1219–1220, 1509
Worksheet tab (color of), 1506
Workspace, 1240
Wrap text command, 1231

X

XML, 1114, 1306, 1343, 1357

Y

YEAR function, 1428

Z

Zero suppression, 1431
Zoom (changing of), 1216, 1869